CONFERENCE PROCEEDINGS

AF849626

CHI 2012

it's the experience!

The 30th ACM Conference on Human Factors In Computing Systems (CHI)

AUSTIN • TEXAS • USA

MAY 5-10, 2012

acm Association for Computing Machinery

chi2012.acm.org

SIGCHI special interest group computer human interaction

Association for
Computing Machinery

Advancing Computing as a Science & Profession

The Association for Computing Machinery
2 Penn Plaza, Suite 701
New York, New York 10121-0701

Copyright © 2012 by the Association for Computing Machinery, Inc. (ACM). Permission to make digital or hard copies of portions of this work for personal or classroom use is granted without fee provided that copies are not made or distributed for profit or commercial advantage and that copies bear this notice and the full citation on the first page. Copyright for components of this work owned by others than ACM must be honored. Abstracting with credit is permitted. To copy otherwise, to republish, to post on servers or to redistribute to lists, requires prior specific permission and/or a fee. Request permission to republish from: permissions@acm.org or Fax +1 (212) 869-0481.

For other copying of articles that carry a code at the bottom of the first or last page, copying is permitted provided that the per-copy fee indicated in the code is paid through www.copyright.com.

Notice to Past Authors of ACM-Published Articles
ACM intends to create a complete electronic archive of all articles and/or other material previously published by ACM. If you have written a work that has been previously published by ACM in any journal or conference proceedings prior to 1978, or any SIG Newsletter at any time, and you do NOT want this work to appear in the ACM Digital Library, please inform permissions@acm.org, stating the title of the work, the author(s), and where and when published.

ISBN: 978-1-4503-1015-4 (Digital)

ISBN: 978-1-4503-1939-3 (Print Vol 2)

Additional copies may be ordered prepaid from:

ACM Order Department
PO Box 30777
New York, NY 10087-0777, USA

Phone: 1-800-342-6626 (USA and Canada)
+1-212-626-0500 (Global)
Fax: +1-212-944-1318
E-mail: acmhelp@acm.org
Hours of Operation: 8:30 am – 4:30 pm ET

ACM Order Number: 609121

Printed in the USA

Welcome to CHI 2012!

After nearly two years of preparation, we are thrilled to welcome you to CHI 2012 in Austin, Texas. Austin is justifiably proud of being the Live Music Capital of the World (R), and it is home to a world-class university, innovative technology and design firms, superb restaurants, exciting culture and nightlife, and genuinely friendly people--what a perfect fit for our CHI conference. We encourage you to get out and explore the city.

But we also are working hard to lure you back indoors with a phenomenal technical program. At the core of the program are over a hundred technical sessions with research papers and notes, case studies, and other exciting presentations that bring you the best new work on human-computer interaction.

We give thanks to our hundreds of review committee members and our more than one thousand reviewers--they invested thousands of hours to help make sure that we've picked the best content. All of the technical content can be found in the ACM Digital Library.

At the same time, we hope to lure you into our useful courses, engaging panels, and thoughtful invited talks. We're very excited to have Margaret Gould Stewart and Hugh Herr as our keynote speakers. In spanning from Margaret's talk on connecting the world through video to Hugh's talk on designing intelligent orthotics and prosthetics we span the scope of this conference--from social interaction with each other through computing to the very personal and intimate interaction of a human with computerized limbs or other assistive devices. We're also excited to have two special invited talks: Stu Card, SIGCHI's 2000 Lifetime Achievement Award winner, will talk about what interaction science means in today's environment; and Richard Shusterman will bridge HCI and the humanities as he introduces us to Somaesthetics and how it can improve our understanding and experience. We are also honored to have Dan Olsen, Joy Mountford, and Batya Friedman--SIGCHI's Lifetime Research, Lifetime Practice, and Social Impact awardees--each giving talks at CHI 2012. Each of the three of them has made an indelible impact on our field.

The theme of this year's CHI conference is "It's the Experience!" and from the beginning it has been our goal to ensure that CHI 2012 attendees don't only hear about HCI, but experience it with all of their senses. We are therefore delighted to have more than 60 interactivity demonstrations and installations--opportunities for you to see, feel, hear, and interact with exciting new technologies and also to reflect on technologies of the past, thanks to Roger Ibars' HWD collection--a hands-on installation of historic hard-wired input devices. We'll be featuring the full set of interactivity on Tuesday afternoon and Wednesday lunchtime; selected installations will be available at other times--check the Interactivity tab for more details. Our video program will provide another way to experience innovative forms of HCI.

CHI 2012 has new depth in Computer Games (including a new student games competition), digital arts, and the humanities. We have an unusually rich collection of Digital Arts installations--we invite you to take some time to interact with the artists and learn about how art--like science, engineering, and design--has its own ways of posing and exploring challenging questions.

And there's so much more. We will also have over 250 posters representing exciting works-in-progress and much more. Student venues at CHI 2012 include our doctoral consortium--an intimate opportunity for extensive mentoring and peer support; student research and design competitions, and the games competition. Come see the competition finalists! And let's not forget CHI Madness--a frenetic but highly efficient whirlwind tour through each days technical papers.

Even before we "formally" open the conference Monday morning, we will have had an intensive weekend of workshops where CHI attendees gather to address emerging fields, tackle challenging questions, and simply support each other in areas of common interest. The mutual support continues both in formal SIG gatherings and in informal gatherings in the convention center halls and at tables in our exhibit hall. We particularly invite you to gather together in affinity groups built around our nine communities--these communities not only shape our program, they also can help enrich your experience as an attendee.

In the end, though, it is been quite an Experience! for us. We are grateful to all the dedicated volunteers and staff that have made this conference possible. We appreciate the support of our sponsors and participation of our exhibitors. And most of all, we thank you for joining us here at the conference. We hope you find things some things that are useful, some things that are inspiring, and some things that are just plain fun. We hope you have an incredible CHI 2012 Experience!

Joseph A. Konstan
University of Minnesota
CHI 2012
General Conference Chair

Ed H. Chi
Google
CHI 2012
Technical Program Chairs

Kristina Höök
Mobile Life at KTH
CHI 2012
Technical Program Chairs

From ACM SIGCHI's President and Vice President for Conferences

SIGCHI is proud to sponsor the premier annual conference in the field of human-computer interaction. We are extremely grateful to the CHI 2012 Conference Chair Joseph Konstan, to Technical Program Chairs Ed Chi and Kristina Höök, and to their wonderful crew, who succeeded to build an impressive program and experience.

CHI 2012 marks the 30th anniversary of our society. The first conference, on Human Factors in Computer Systems, took place in Gaithersburg, MD, on March 15-17, 1982.

The second and third conferences were a year and a half apart, and from then on CHI, as the conference has been called since 1983, has been an annual event with the official name: "ACM Conference on Human Factors in Computing Systems".

The first conference drew over 900 attendees, and since then CHI has continued to grow and broaden its range of topics and contributing disciplines: the founding psychologists and software engineers began to meet new visions from ethnography, sociology, communication sciences and arts, among others. Relevant industries, as well as research institutes and academia, showed an increasing-and often long-lasting-interest and involvement (through volunteers and through sponsorship for conference expenses).

CHI is an ideal forum for people to meet formally as well as informally, to exchange knowledge and views, to share experiences, and to learn. The CHI conference brings together professionals from research and practice; people from industry, academia, and from government; long-term veterans of HCI, young professionals and students; all in an environment designed to encourage interaction. We invite you to actively participate in that interaction: introduce yourself to people, interact with presenters and speakers, renew old friendships and make new ones.

CHI is organized on behalf of ACM's Special Interest Group on Computer-Human Interaction (SIGCHI), an international community of professionals who share an interest in the many diverse facets of HCI. SIGCHI is committed both to advancing the field of HCI, to facilitate exchange of information within the SIGCHI community, and to support students to enter the domain.

The CHI conference is arguably the single most visible activity of SIGCHI, but we also sponsor and support a wide range of specialized conferences in areas ranging from interactive systems design to user interface technology to computer-supported cooperative work to "intelligent" user interfaces. Visit the SIGCHI website at http://www.sigchi.org to find our conference schedule, listing upcoming as well as past conferences.

SIGCHI and ACM produce some of the most respected publications in the field. All members receive interactions, a highly-acclaimed magazine covering the broad field of HCI and user interface design. ACM Transactions on Computer-Human Interactions (ToCHI), now in its 18th year, is our flagship journal - a quarterly publication with the top-quality archival research aimed at researchers and those translating research into practice.

SIGCHI is truly an international organization, with over 30 local chapters and 3 student chapters in 19 countries on 5 continents. We encourage all SIGCHI members to join their local chapter - or if there isn't one in your area, we would love to help you create one. And don't forget virtual communities! SIGCHI hosts dozens of electronic mailing lists on topics ranging from HCI and the Web, to HCI educations, to public policy and beyond. Those lists range from dozens of subscribers to thousands, and are an excellent way to keep up with the field and with friends and colleagues.

Finally, on behalf of ACM SGICHI, we again want to thank the conference committee and all of the hundreds of volunteers who make this conference possible. Their work makes this a rewarding experience for all of us.

Gerrit C. van der Veer
SIGCHI President

John "Scooter" Morris
SIGCHI Vice-President for Conferences

ABOUT SIGCHI

CHI 2012 is sponsored by ACM's Special Interest Group on Computer-Human Interaction (ACM SIGCHI). ACM, the Association for Computing Machinery, is an educational and scientific society uniting the world's computing educators, researchers, and professionals to inspire dialogue, share resources, and address the field's challenges. ACM strengthens the profession's collective voice through strong leadership, promotion of the highest standards, and recognition of technical excellence. ACM supports the professional growth of its members by providing opportunities for life-long learning, career development, and professional networking. ACM offers its more than 100,000 worldwide members cutting edge technical information through world class journals and magazines, dynamic special interest groups, and globally recognized conferences.

Visit www.acm.org for more information about the ACM.

SIGCHI is the premier international society for professionals, academics, and students who are interested in human-computer interaction (HCI). We provide a forum for the discussion of all aspects of HCI through our conferences, including our flagship CHI conference, publications, web sites, email discussion groups, and other services. We advance education in HCI through courses, workshops, and outreach, and we promote informal access to a wide range of individuals and organizations involved in HCI. Members can be involved in HCI-related activities with others in their region through local SIGCHI chapters. Come to the SIGCHI Town Hall meeting on Wednesday at 12:50 in Meeting Room 16AB, 4th Floor or visit www.sigchi.org to learn more about SIGCHI.

ACM, the Association for Computing Machinery http://www.acm.org/, is an educational and scientific society uniting the world's computing educators, researchers and professionals to inspire dialogue, share resources and address the field's challenges. ACM strengthens the profession's collective voice through strong leadership, promotion of the highest standards, and recognition of technical excellence.ACM supports the professional growth of its members by providing opportunities for life-long learning, career development, and professional networking. ACM offers its 87,000 global members cutting-edge technical information through world class journals and magazines, dynamic specia linterest groups and globally recognized conferences.

Table of Contents

Getting Around: Menus, Scrolling, & Advanced Navigation

Session Chair: Emmanuel Pietriga *(INRIA)*

Spectators

Session Chair: Barry Brown *(University of California, San Diego)*

Immateriality as a Design Feature

Session Chair: Joonhwan Lee *(Seoul National University)*

Privacy + Self Disclosure

Session Chair: Manfred Tscheligi *(University of Salzburg)*

Supporting Visually Impaired Users

Session Chair: Vicki Hanson *(University of Dundee)*

Text Visualization

Session Chair: Jean-Daniel Fekete *(INRIA)*

Brain & Body

Session Chair: Eve Hoggan *(University of Helsinki)*

Games: Community + Communication

Critical Perspectives on Design

I Am How I Touch: Authenticating Users

Visionary Models + Tools

It's a Big Web!

Tools & Stats in Evaluation Studies

Values in Research Practice

Interfaces for Health & Well Being

Session Chair: Ian Li *(Carnegie Mellon University)*

Needle in the Haystack

Session Chair: Mark Dunlop *(University of Strathclyde)*

Understanding Online Communication

Session Chair: Sharoda Paul *(GE Global Research)*

Performative Emergency Simulation

Session Chair: Olav W. Bertelsen *(Aarhus University)*

Crowdsourcing & Peer Production I

Session Chair: Mira Dontcheva *(Adobe Advanced Technology Labs)*

Pasts + Futures

Session Chair: Siân Lindley *(Microsoft Research Cambridge)*

Mobile Computing & Interaction

Session Chair: Daniel Fallman *(Umea University)*

Future Design

Session Chair: Orit Shaer *(Wellesley College)*

Visualization + Visual Analysis

Session Chair: Luciano Gamberini *(University of Padova)*

Outside the Box

Sensing + Sensible Interaction

Time + Task: Managing Work Life

Search Interfaces

Session Chair: Remco Chang *(Tufts University)*

Music

Session Chair: Karyn Moffatt *(McGill University)*

ICT4D

Session Chair: Brygg Ullmer *(Louisiana State University)*

Movement-Based Gameplay

Session Chair: Shaun Kane *(University of Maryland, Baltimore County)*

Beyond Paper

Session Chair: Mikael B. Skov *(Aalborg University)*

Dimensions of Sensory Interaction

Session Chair: Shwetak Patel *(University of Washington)*

Phone Fun: Extending Mobile Interaction

Session Chair: Ken Hinckley *(Microsoft Research)*

Check This Out: Recommender Systems

Session Chair: James Fogarty *(University of Washington)*

See Hear Speak: Redesigning I/O for Effectiveness

Session Chair: Eytan Adar *(University of Michigan)*

Triple T: Touch, Tables, Tablets

Session Chair: Bjoern Hartmann *(University of California, Berkeley)*

Defying Environmental Behavior Changes

Session Chair: Alan Borning *(University of Washington)*

Health & Children

Comfortable Aging

Touch Text Entry

Understanding Gamers

Session Chair: Peter Tolmie *(University of Nottingham)*

Better Together

Session Chair: Gary Hsieh *(Michigan State University)*

Bigger is Better: Large & Multiple Display Environments

Session Chair: David Dearman *(Nokia Research Center)*

What a Lovely Gesture

Session Chair: Hrvoje Benko *(Microsoft Research)*

Crowdsourcing & Peer Production II

Session Chair: Erika Poole *(Penn State)*

Usability & User Research

Session Chair: Anna Cox *(University College London)*

Do You See What Eye See

Session Chair: Andrew Duchowski *(Clemson University)*

Home & Family

Session Chair: Andrea Grimes Parker *(Georgia Institute of Technology)*

Designing for Learners' Complex Needs

Session Chair: Hilary Hutchinson *(Google)*

Groups @ Work

Session Chair: Eric Gilbert *(Georgia Institute of Technology)*

Use the Force

Session Chair: Mike Horn *(Northwestern University)*

Human Performance Gives Us Fitts'

Session Chair: Olivier Chapuis *(Univ Paris-Sud)*

With a Little Help from My Friends

Session Chair: Amy Hurst *(Carnegie Mellon University)*

Conference Committee

CHI 2012 ORGANIZING COMMITTEE

Conference Chair
Joseph A. Konstan, *University of Minnesota*

TECHNICAL PROGRAM

Chairs
Ed H. Chi, *Google Research*
Kristina Höök, *Mobile Life @ KTH*

Papers
Susanne Bødker, *Aarhus University*
Dan R. Olsen Jr., *Brigham Young University*

alt.chi
Amanda Williams, *Wyld Collective Ltd.*
Erica Robles, *New York University*

Case Studies
Daniela Busse, *Samsung Research*
Elizabeth Buie, *Luminanze Consulting LLC*

Courses
Nancy Frishberg, *MSB Associates*
Gregorio Convertino, *Palo Alto Research Center (PARC)*

Doctoral Consortium
Steve Brewster, *University of Glasgow*
Erik Stolterman, *Indiana University Bloomington*

Interactivity
Patrick Baudisch, *Hasso Plattner Institut*
Florian 'Floyd' Mueller, *Exertion Games Lab*
Eva Hornecker, *University of Strathclyde*
Danielle Wilde, *daniellewilde.com*

Panels
Allison Druin, *University of Maryland*
Joseph 'Jofish' Kaye, *Nokia Research Center*

Special Interest Groups (SIGS)
Daphne Raban, *University of Haifa*
Kaisa Väänänen-Vainio-Mattila, *Tampere University of Technology*

Student Design Competition
Gilbert Cockton, *Northumbria University*
Thecla Schiphorst, *Simon Fraser University*

Student Research Competition
Anne Aula, *Google*
Shaowen Bardzell, *Indiana University Bloomington*

Student Game Competition
Seth Cooper, *University of Washington*
Winslow Burleson, *Arizona State University*

Video
Michael Bernstein, *MIT CSAIL*
Jeffrey Bardzell, *Indiana University, Bloomington*

Work-in-Progress (WIPs)
Lichan Hong, *Google*
Henriette Cramer, *Mobile Life @ SICS*

Workshops
Helena Mentis, *Microsoft Research Cambridge*
Ido Guy, *IBM Research Haifa*

CHI 2012 COMMUNITIES

Chairs
Arnie Lund, *Microsoft*
Bo Begole, *Samsung's User Experience Center*

Core Communities

Design
Ellen Yi-Luen Do, *Georgia Tech*
Patrick Olivier, *Newcastle University*

User Experience
Jhilmil Jain, *Microsoft*
Kath Straub, *Usability.org*

Engineering
Ruven Brooks, *Independent Consultant*
Fabio Paternò, *CNR-ISTI*

Management
Janice Rohn, *Experian*
Dennis Wixon, *Microsoft*

Featured Communities

Child Computer Interaction
Janet C Read, *University of Central Lancashire*
Panos Markopoulos, *Eindhoven University of Technology*
Allison Druin, *University of Maryland*

Digital Arts
David England, *Liverpool John Moores University*
Jill Fantauzzacoffin, *Georgia Tech*

Games and Entertainment
Regina Bernhaupt, *IRIT*
Katherine Isbister, *NYU-Poly*

Health
Karen Cheng, *University of California, Irvine*
Julie Kientz, *University of Washington*

Sustainability
Eli Blevis, *Indiana University at Bloomington*
Samuel Mann, *Otago Polytechnic*

PARTICIPATION AND VOLUNTEERING

Student Volunteer Coordinators
Vicky McArthur, *York University*
Bobby Beaton, *Virginia Tech*

Madness
Paul André, *University of Southampton*
Petra Sundström, *Salzburg University*

Social Media
Cliff Lampe, *Michigan State University*
Sean McNee, *FTI Consulting*

Publicity
Rosemary Stevens, *Ace Public Relations*
Eelco Herder, *L3S Research Center*

Local Experience
Annette Priest, *Revel Insight*

MAKING THINGS HAPPEN

Design Directors
Apala Lahiri Chavan, *Human Factors International*
Srikanth Vellore, *Human Factors International*

Webmaster
William Hudson, *Syntagm Ltd. and Hult International Business School*

Posters
Oleg Komogortsev, *Texas State University-San Marcos*

Proceedings
Max Van Kleek, *University of Southampton*
Nirmal Patel, *Georgia Tech*
Alireza Sahami Shirazi, *University of Stuttgart*
Michael Ekstrand, *University of Minnesota*

Mobile Apps
Stephen Oney, *Carnegie Mellon University*
Jason Wiese, *Carnegie Mellon University*
Eiji Hayashi, *Carnegie Mellon University*

Communications Director
Garett Dworman, Tec-Ed Inc

Program Production
Joan Johnson, *Joan Johnson Design*
Max Van Kleek, *University of Southampton*

Mailing Lists
Adam Sporka, *Czech Technical University*

ACM Staff Liaison
Ashley Cozzi, *ACM*

Sponsors and Exhibits
Carol Klyver, *Foundations of Excellence*

Conference Logistics
Janeé Pelletier, *CLC*
Allison Perrelli, *CLC*

Technology Liaison
Scooter Morris, *University of California, San Francisco*
Sara Drenner, *BI Worldwide*

CMC Liaison
Scooter Morris, *University of California, San Francisco*

Registration
Yvonne Lopez, *Executive Events*

Special thanks for the financial support provided by the following sponsors:

CHI Champion Sponsors

Autodesk®

Bloomberg

Google

ebay® | PayPal™

Microsoft®

NSF

SAP®

CHI Contributing Sponsors

facebook

NOKIA

Friends of CHI

Adobe Systems, Inc. **Disney Research** **University of Michigan School of Information**

Printed on Rolland Enviro 100
100% post-consumer fiber
Certified EcoLogo
Processed chlorine free
Manufactured using biogas energy
Printed using soy-based inks

Natural Use Profiles for the Pen: An Empirical Exploration of Pressure, Tilt, and Azimuth

Yizhong Xin[1,2], Xiaojun Bi[3], Xiangshi Ren[1]

[1]School of Information
Kochi University of Technology, Japan
ren.xiangshi@kochi-tech.ac.jp

[2]School of Information
Shenyang University of Technology, China
xyz@sut.edu.cn

[3]Department of Computer Science, University of Toronto, Canada
xiaojun@dgp.toronto.edu

ABSTRACT

Inherent pen input modalities such as tip pressure, tilt and azimuth (PTA) have been extensively used as additional input channels in pen-based interactions. We conducted a study to investigate the *natural use profiles* of PTA, which describes the features of PTA in the course of normal pen use such as writing and drawing. First, the study reveals the ranges of PTA in normal pen use, which can distinguish pen events accidently occurring in normal drawing and writing from those used for mode switch. The *natural use profiles* also show that azimuth is least likely to cause false pen mode switching while tip pressure is most likely to cause false pen mode switching. Second, the study reveals correlations among various modalities, indicating that pressure plus azimuth is superior to other pairs for dual-modality control.

Author Keywords

Pen input; tip pressure; tilt; azimuth; natural use profiles.

ACM Classification Keywords

H.5.2 [Information Interfaces and Presentation]: User Interfaces - Interaction styles; I.3.6 [Methodology and Techniques] - Interaction techniques.

General Terms

Design; Experimentation; Human Factors.

INTRODUCTION

Pen input has been widely adopted as a major interaction modality for slate computers, handheld devices, and large format electronic whiteboards, due to its portability, outdoor availability, short learning curve, and ease of manipulation. Despite these advantages, pen input suffers from its low communication bandwidth: typically, only a single point, the x-y position of the pen tip, is used for interaction. To expand the communication bandwidth and offer users more interaction flexibility, researchers have explored using additional pen characteristics, including tilting, tip pressure, rolling, and azimuth, as auxiliary interaction modalities [2, 6, 10, 11, 13, 14].

One big benefit of adding extra interaction modalities is that a user can select different pen modes by simply adjusting the added modality, without moving the pen tip away from the interaction focus. For example, Ramos el al. [7] proposed applying pen tip pressure beyond 60% of the maximum value to invoke a magnified lens; Bi et al. [2] and Xin el al. [12] utilized different rolling or tilt angles to select different pen modes.

To effectively switch pen modes via extra modalities, the designers need to choose appropriate thresholds for triggering the mode switch process. Otherwise, the mode switch might be falsely activated because normal pen use, such as drawing or writing, also affects the values of these modalities.

Using values that are unlikely to occur in normal pen use would help prevent false activations. For example, research [2] shows that the rolling angles of a pen range from -10° to +10° in normal pen use. Therefore, the ±10° was used as the threshold for triggering a rolling menu to avoid accidental activation. The *natural use profiles* of a pen, which describe the features of various modalities during the course of normal pen use, provide hints for the thresholds of other modalities.

Besides suggesting thresholds for mode switching, *natural use profiles* reveal the correlations among various modalities. A loose correlation pair means that the two modalities are unlikely to interfere with each other, indicating that a user can independently control each modality. These modalities are highly recommended for multi-degree-of-freedom control tasks, e.g., curve manipulation [2], or 3D objects manipulations [5, 12].

Overall, an understanding of *natural use profiles* will provide pen-based interface design with a proven foundation. However, prior work (e.g., [8] on pressure and [2] on rolling) mostly addressed the use of a particular dimension for enriching pen-based interaction. The profiles about tip pressure, tilt and azimuth (PTA) still remain unknown. In this paper, we, conduct a study to fill this gap.

Permission to make digital or hard copies of all or part of this work for personal or classroom use is granted without fee provided that copies are not made or distributed for profit or commercial advantage and that copies bear this notice and the full citation on the first page. To copy otherwise, or republish, to post on servers or to redistribute to lists, requires prior specific permission and/or a fee.
CHI'12, May 5–10, 2012, Austin, Texas, USA.
Copyright 2012 ACM 978-1-4503-1015-4/12/05...$10.00.

EXPERIMENT

Participants and Apparatus

Twenty volunteers (3 females, 17 males), age from 21 to 33, participated in the experiment. All of them were right-handed. The experiment was conducted on a Wacom Cintiq 21UX interactive LCD display (resolution 1280 x 1024, 96 dpi) with a digital stylus. The hardware can detect the tip pressure range [0, 1023], corresponding to the force range [0, 4] (Newton), tilt angle range [22°, 90°] (90° means that the pen is perpendicular to the tablet display), and azimuth angle range [0°, 359°] (0° is the north direction). The experimental program was developed in Java and ran on a 2.13 GHz Intel Core2 CPU PC with Windows XP.

Design

Our basic objective is to investigate the *natural use profiles* of PTA, which describe the features of PTA and correlations among them in normal drawing and writing. Therefore, besides the common symbols and English letters, we also included Chinese characters in the experiment, which contain most basic strokes in daily drawing and writing such as points, lines, turns, crosses, and arcs. In particular, the following characters are involved in the experiment:

- Symbols (@, ☆, &, ×),
- Letters (S, E, M, B),
- Chinese characters which were classified by structure and complexity (see Table 1).

Structure / Complexity	Left-to-right	Mixed	Top-to-bottom
Simple (1~5 strokes)	人 (2 strokes)	中 (4 strokes)	之 (3 strokes)
Medium (6~10 strokes)	如 (6 strokes)	我 (7 strokes)	宜 (8 strokes)
Complex (beyond 10 strokes)	橋 (16 strokes)	幾 (12 strokes)	蜜 (14 strokes)

Table 1. Chinese characters classified by structure and complexity.

Task and Procedure

Subjects were seated in front of the display tablet which was placed on the horizontal plane [1]. Subjects were instructed to write and draw three types of characters in seven sizes (50, 100, 200, 400, 600, 800, and 1000 pixels in length, which equates to 1.67, 3.33, 6.67, 13.34, 20, 26.67, 33.34 cm respectively). At the beginning of each trial, a character appeared on the upper left corner of the display in the font size 36. In the meantime, a translucent green square was displayed at the center of the display, the length of which was one of the seven tested sizes. Subjects were instructed to write/draw characters as large as the square size. By pressing the spacebar on the keyboard the user proceeded to the next trial. Each character appeared twice in total. All characters were mixed and counterbalanced in random order. In summary, the experiment consisted of:

20 participants ×
17 characters ×
7 sizes ×
2 repetitions
= 4760 trials.

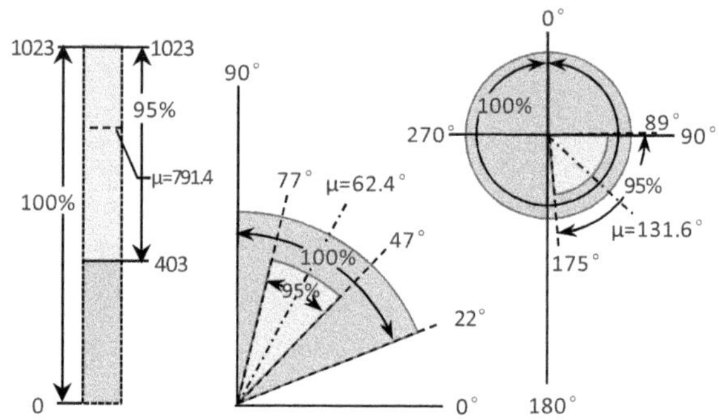

Figure 1. Means and 95% ranges of tip pressure (left), tilt (middle), and azimuth (right).

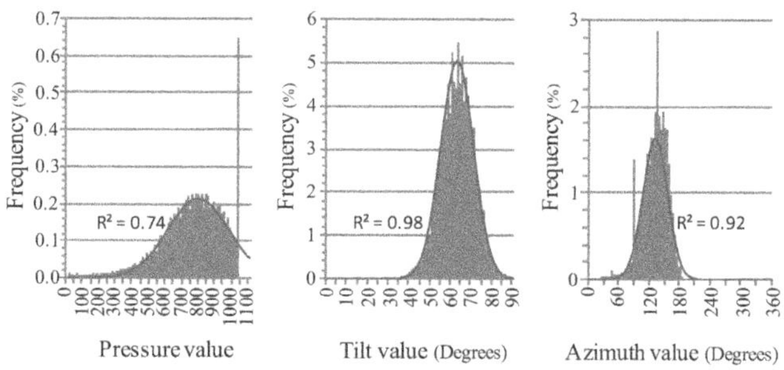

Figure 2. PTA Distributions and Gaussian regressions.

Results

PTA Distributions. Means (SD) across all the trials are 791.4 (194.1), 62.4° (7.52°), and 131.64° (21.53°) for tip pressure, tilt and azimuth, respectively (Figure 1). Figure 2 shows the distribution for each of them. R-squares of Gaussian distribution regression were 0.74 (pressure), 0.98 (tilt), and 0.92 (azimuth), indicating that the tilt and azimuth data well fit Gaussian distributions. The frequency of pressure value 1023 was extraordinarily high, probably because pressures above 1023 were also recorded as 1023. Excluding it (level 1023), the R-square of Gaussian distribution regression is 0.98, also showing a strong fit of Gaussian distribution.

Size Condition. Figure 3 illustrates how character size affects PTA modalities. A repeated measure ANOVA revealed significant main effects for character size on pressure ($F_{6, 114}$ = 308.75), tilt ($F_{6, 114}$ = 5.75) and azimuth ($F_{6, 114}$ = 4.393), all $p < .001$. *Post hoc* pair-wise comparisons showed significant differences for all pairs in pressure, and 50 vs. other sizes in tilt, and 100 vs. other sizes in azimuth.

[1] Our pilot studies indicated that the preferred display-table angle varied for different users. Thus, we decided to place the tablet horizontally to eliminate potential effects caused by different display-table angles. The horizontal plane is also a common tablet usage, e.g., where a user flattens a tablet laptop and places it on the lap or on a desk.

Figure 3 also shows that pressure is susceptible while tilt and azimuth are robust to the change of character size. Along with the increase of character size, pressure increased rapidly and remained stable at around 763 when character size reaches 800 pixels. However, tilt and azimuth did not undergo drastic changes: the gaps between the lowest and highest values were 2.77° for tilt and 3.23° for azimuth.

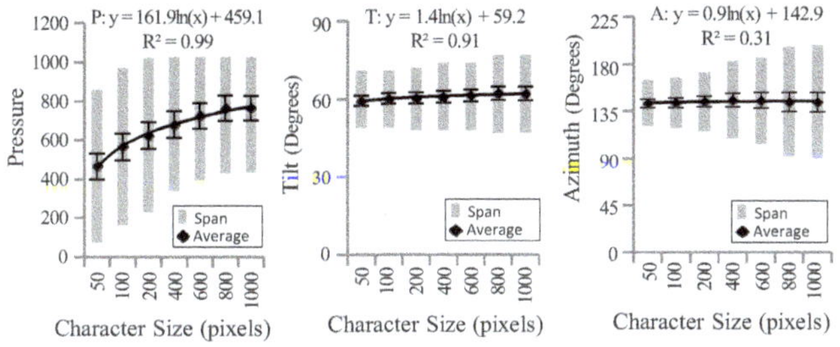

Figure 3. Mean (Std. Error) of PTA per character size. The green spans represent 2 × Std. Dev intervals.

The susceptibleness of pressure is probably due to the following two reasons. First, users tend to control a pen mainly by the muscle groups of fingers and palm when drawing/writing small-sized characters, while muscle groups of the arm are involved for large-sized characters. Using different muscle groups to control the pen probably leads to the large variation in pressure. This finding also concurs with the literature [1, 3, 4]. Second, research literature [9] shows that human mechanoreceptors in a person's fingers (responsible from sensing isometric force/pressure) adapt after a few milliseconds. In other words, users become less aware of the absolute amount of pressure they are applying with a pen. This is one of the reasons why the user's grip gets tighter as time goes by, and also a possible explanation as to why pressure is greater while drawing larger characters, which require more drawing/writing time.

Combination Distribution between PTA. The combined distributions for each pair of PTA as well as the correlations among them were also investigated (Figure 4). Two-tailed Pearson Correlation Analyses revealed small correlations between pressure and tilt (r = 0.24), tilt and azimuth (r = -0.37), and a very minor correlation between pressure and azimuth (r = -0.09), all $p < .001$.

DISCUSSION

Mode Switch

During the course of normal pen use, 95% of pen events fall within the ranges of [403, 1023] (pressure), [47°, 77°] (tilt), and [89°, 175°] (azimuth). We suggest using the PTA values outside these ranges to trigger pen mode switching in order to prevent false activation.

Our study also shows that the azimuth is least likely to cause accidental pen mode switching while tip pressure is most likely to cause accidental pen mode switching. The range of azimuth in normal pen use takes only 24% of the full range [0°, 359°]. The remaining 76% of full range, [0°, 88°] and [176°, 359°] is available for activating different modes. Moreover, the azimuth value remains relatively consistent regardless of the change of character size. In contrast, the pressure modality is the opposite: the range of tip pressure in normal pen use [403, 1023] takes 61% of the full range [0, 1023] and it is susceptible to the change of character size. Also, as the pen pressure always starts from the level 0 when the pen tip lands on the tablet, the values outside the normal use range, which are [0, 402], still occasionally occur in normal drawing and writing, especially when the pen tip just lands on the tablet. Therefore, tip pressure is not recommended for triggering pen mode switch.

Our experiment shows that plenty of pen events exceeded the maximum tip pressure, 1023 (see Figure 2), suggesting that the manufactures should enlarge the detectable range to accurately capture tip pressures.

Controlling Dual Degrees of Freedom

If a user needs to control two PTA modalities to manipulate multiple degrees of freedom (e.g., control the scale of an object by tip pressure and adjust its rotation angle by azimuth), the best option is pressure & azimuth. The combined distribution of PTA shows that pressure & azimuth is the most loosely correlated pair, with the correlation coefficient of -0.09, which is substantially lower than pressure & tilt (r = 0.24), and tilt & azimuth (r = -0.37). This loose correlation is probably caused by different muscle groups controlling pressure and azimuth: a user usually adjusts the pen tip pressure by changing the

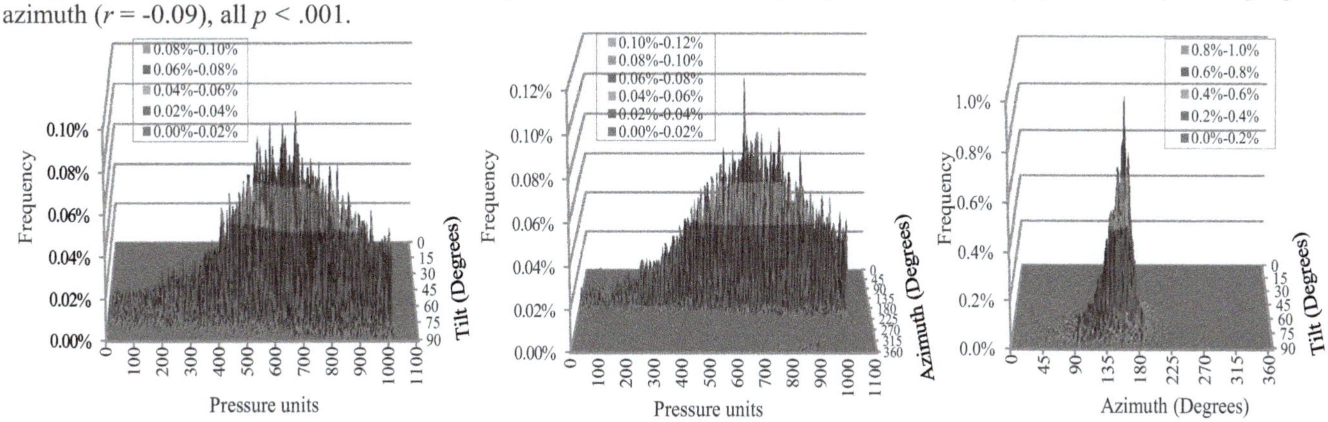

Figure 4. Distributions of pressure & tilt (left), pressure & azimuth (middle), and azimuth & tilt (right).

downward force of the fingers gripping the pen; the user alters the azimuth angle by rotating the wrist.

The minor correlation shows that pressure and azimuth almost never interfere with each other in normal pen use, in which a user does not even consciously avoid interference between different modalities. This suggests that pressure and azimuth are promising candidates for dual-modality control: they can be independently controlled without causing interference.

Our study focuses on natural pen use, which means the results revealed the correlations among PTA in a natural usage scenario. Correlations among PTA in intentional control applications (e.g., deliberately control variables using PTA modalities) are also worthy of exploration. We will investigate these in future work.

Other Applications

Besides providing specific ranges for trigging pen mode switching and for dual-modality control, understanding PTA profiles can also benefit the following applications:

(1) *Adaptive mode switching based on personal PTA use profiles.* As PTA profiles vary across different users, thresholds for mode switching may be designed for different users.
(2) *Signature verification.* Personal PTA profiles can serve to distinguish different users.
(3) *Reducing the dependence between PTA.* Understanding the correlations among PTA allows designers to better leverage these modalities used in tandem.

CONCLUSIONS

We have conducted a study systematically investigating the natural use profiles of pressure, tilt and azimuth (PTA). Our study reveals that the ranges of PTA during the course of normal pen use are [403, 1023] (pressure), [47°, 77°] (tilt), and [89°, 175°] (azimuth). Detailed analysis shows that using azimuth is least likely to cause accidental activation while tip pressure is most likely to cause false activation for pen mode switching, and that pressure plus azimuth is the best option for dual-modality control due to their loose correlation.

This study is the first one that investigates the natural profiles of pen pressure, pen tilt, and pen azimuth simultaneously and their mutual relationships as well. It might open up a promising new field of research on multiple pen modalities. Furthermore, comparing prior studies on pen input modalities which mainly focused on the human ability to control pen input modalities, this work focuses on *natural pen use* and thus reflects the spirit of human computer interaction. The results of our study provide guidelines on how to use multiple degrees of freedom which are intrinsic to a pen in realistic pen usage situations.

ACKNOWLEDGEMENTS

This study has been partially supported by Grant-in-Aid for Scientific Research (No.20500118), National Natural Science Foundation of China (No. 61100091), Microsoft Research Asia Mobile Computing in Education Theme and Exploratory Software Project of IPA (information technology promotion agency in Japan).

REFERENCES

1. Balakrishnan, R. and MacKenzie, S. (1997). Performance differences in the fingers, wrist, and forearm in computer input control. *ACM CHI*, 303-310.
2. Bi, X., Moscovich, T., Ramos, G., Balakrishnan, R. and Hinckley, K. (2008). An exploration of pen rolling for pen-based interaction. *ACM UIST*, 191-200.
3. Hammerton, M. and Tickner, A. H. (1966). An investigation into the comparative suitability of forearm, hand and thumb controls in acquisition tasks. *Ergonomics,* 9(2), 125-130.
4. Napier, J. R. (1956). The prehensile movements of the human hand. *Bone and Joint Surgery.* 38B(4), 902-913.
5. Oshita, M. (2004). Pen-to-mime: pen based interface for interactive control of a human figure. *Eurographics Workshop on Sketch-Based Interfaces and Modeling*, 43-52.
6. Ramos, G. and Balakrishnan. R. (2007). Pressure marks. *ACM CHI*, 1375-1384.
7. Ramos, G., Cockburn, A., Balakrishnan, R. and Beaudouin-Lafon, M. (2007). Pointing lenses: facilitating stylus input through visual-and motor-space magnification. *ACM CHI*, 757-766.
8. Ren, X., Yin, J., Zhao, S. and Li, Y. (2007). The adaptive hybrid cursor: A pressure-based target selection technique for pen-based user interfaces. *INTERACT*, 310-323.
9. Stevens, S.S. (1986). Psychophysics: introduction to its perceptual, neural, and social prospects. *Transaction Publishers.*
10. Tian, F., Ao, X., Wang, H., Setlur, V. and Dai, G. (2007). The tilt cursor: enhancing stimulus-response compatibility by providing 3D orientation cue of pen. *ACM CHI*, 303-306.
11. Tian, F., Xu, L., Wang, H., Zhang, X., Liu, Y., Setlur, V. and Dai, G. (2008). Tilt menu: using the 3D orientation information of pen devices to extend the selection capability of pen-based user interfaces. *ACM CHI*, 1371-1380.
12. Xin, Y., Bi, X., and Ren, X. (2011). Acquiring and pointing: an empirical study of pen-tilt-based interaction. *ACM CHI*, 849-858.
13. Xin, Y. and Ren, X. (2010). An investigation of adaptive pen pressure discretization method based on personal pen pressure use profile, *IEICE Transactions on Information and Systems*, E93-D(5), 1205-1213.
14. Xin, Y. and Ren, X. (2009). A study of inherent pen input modalities for precision parameter, *IEICE Transactions on Information and Systems*, E92-D(12), 2454-2461.

A-Coord Input: Coordinating Auxiliary Input Streams for Augmenting Contextual Pen-Based Interactions

Khalad Hasan[1], Xing-Dong Yang[2], Andrea Bunt[1], Pourang Irani[1]

[1]Department of Computer Science,
University of Manitoba,
Winnipeg, Manitoba, Canada
{khalad, bunt, irani}@cs.umanitoba.ca

[2]Department of Computing Science
University of Alberta,
Edmonton, Alberta, Canada
xingdong@cs.ualberta.ca

ABSTRACT
The human hand can naturally coordinate multiple finger joints, and simultaneously tilt, press and roll a pen to write or draw. For this reason, digital pens are now embedded with *auxiliary input* sensors to capture these actions. Prior research on auxiliary input channels has mainly investigated them in isolation of one another. In this work, we explore the coordinated use of two auxiliary channels, a class of interaction techniques we refer to as *a-coord input*. Through two separate experiments, we explore the design space of *a-coord input*. In the first study we identify if users can successfully coordinate two auxiliary channels. We found a strong degree of coordination between channels. In a second experiment, we evaluate the effectiveness of *a-coord input* in a task with multiple steps, such as multi-parameter selection and manipulation. We find that *a-coord input* facilitates coordination even with a complex, aforethought sequential task. Overall our results indicate that users can control at least two auxiliary input channels in conjunction which can facilitate a number of common tasks can on the pen.

Author Keywords
Pen-based interaction; pen roll; pen pressure; pen tilt; dual-channel input.

ACM Classification Keywords
H.5.2 [Information Interfaces And Presentation]: User Interfaces - Interaction styles.

INTRODUCTION
The digital pen has evolved into a sophisticated input device, with the ability to capture a large range of natural manipulations such as finger roll, pressure and tilt, through *auxiliary input channels*. Given these capabilities in comparison to the mouse, it is not surprising that some visionaries tout the pen as becoming a highly relied upon device for the next two decades [2]. Prior research has demonstrated the merits in using the pen's auxiliary channels. These include rapid access to contextual commands [22], fine-grained parameter manipulation [15], and improved stimulus-response compatibility [21].

Permission to make digital or hard copies of all or part of this work for personal or classroom use is granted without fee provided that copies are not made or distributed for profit or commercial advantage and that copies bear this notice and the full citation on the first page. To copy otherwise, or republish, to post on servers or to redistribute to lists, requires prior specific permission and/or a fee.
CHI'12, May 5–10, 2012, Austin, Texas, USA.
Copyright 2012 ACM 978-1-4503-1015-4/12/05...$10.00.

Naturally, prior work has investigated the design space for each of these pen input channels in isolation of one another, or when merged with pen-tip movement [3, 15-17, 21, 22]. Such research has been instrumental in identifying the fundamental properties and limitations of these auxiliary pen input streams [3, 16, 22]. However, a new collection of results is necessary to explore whether users can control such channels simultaneously, beyond our abilities to do so with highly familiar and well-practiced tasks, such as writing and drawing. If such coordination is possible, this would expand the pen's interactive space.

We build on these earlier results and investigate *a-coord input*, the ***[coord]***ination of at least two different ***[a]***uxiliary channels, such as roll and pressure, or tilt and roll, on the pen (Figure 1). The *a-coord input* style raises many human performance questions that warrant long-term research. At this early stage we focus on the most basic questions: 1) can users coordinate two auxiliary channels simultaneously?; 2) can multi-channel coordination extend the bandwidth (number of controllable items) that is available with single auxiliary channels?; 3) how does coordination differ between different auxiliary channels?; and, 4) how can *a-coord* be applied to tasks involving continuous manipulation, such as multi-parameter selection and manipulation?

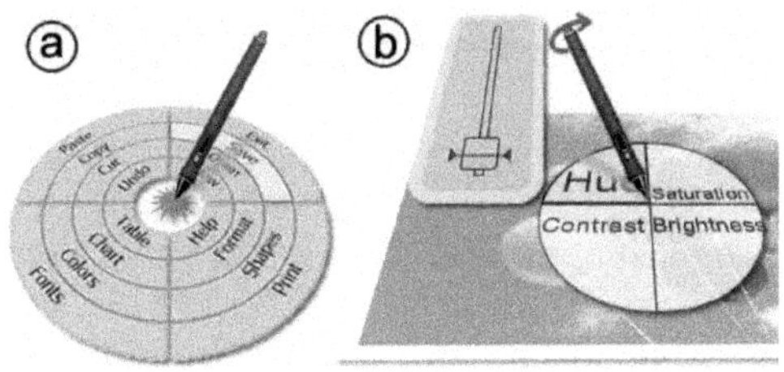

Figure 1 – An illustration of (a) contextual 2D menu interaction with *a-coord* Tilt+Pressure; and (b) multi-parameter selection and manipulation.

We restrict this initial investigation to contextual input, i.e., to tasks for which pen tip movement is not required. Based on the primary features of the pen's auxiliary channels, we designed two experiments to respond to the above listed questions. Our findings show that *a-coord input* successfully extends the control of auxiliary input from 1D to 2D. We observe a high degree of coordination with 2D contextual tasks, with certain *a-coord input* styles exhibiting more parallelism than others. Our findings also show that we can apply *a-coord input* to multi-parameter selection and manipulation, a task that involves continuous manipulation. This latter task also has a clearer two-step delineation than the 2D contextual menus, allowing us to test *a-coord input* in a situation where one channel is designated as the leading channel and must be held steady while the user operates the second channel. We follow these experiments with an illustration of how carefully composing the pen's auxiliary inputs can provide a diverse set of interactive techniques.

Our contributions include: (1) an examination of the coordinated control of the pen's auxiliary channels, which we term *a-coord* input; (2) an extension of such input for 2D contextual tasks; (3) evidence of good coordination with some *a-coord input* styles; (4) a demonstration of *a-coord input's* effectiveness for complex tasks, such as multi-parameter selection and manipulation; (5) a demonstration of a varied sample of interactive tasks possible with the pen's auxiliary input channels.

RELATED WORK

Our research builds on the benefits and limitations of the pen's auxiliary input channels, which we review first. We then briefly cover work in the area of parallel input control and conclude this section with a presentation of techniques for multi-parameter selection and manipulation, a task to which we apply our designs of *a-coord* input.

Auxiliary Pen Input Channels

Numerous studies have explored the benefits and limitations of each of the pen's auxiliary input channels [3, 13, 6, 1]. Existing findings with pen pressure, tilt-azimuth (angle around the interaction plane), tilt-altitude (angle between pen and plane) and roll serve as a reference for our design of a-coord input.

Pen pressure has received considerable attention in recent years. Ramos and Balakrishnan [14-17], as well as Ren *et al.* [18] demonstrated that pen pressure is suited for numerous tasks, including menu selection and single parameter manipulation. Studies confirm that users can comfortably control no more than 7±1 discrete pressure levels [13, 16], which can further be improved with proper pressure space discretization techniques [18,16]. Additionally, users can control a limited number of pressure levels with simultaneous pen movement, as in PressureMarks [17], or for fine parameter manipulation, such as with Zliding [15].

The pen's tilt has an azimuth and an altitude component [22, 23]. Tilt Cursor [21] and the TiltMenu [22], two early systems, respectively showed improved stimulus-response compatibility [21] and strong compatibility with command selection and direct manipulation [22]. The TiltMenu worked well for fewer than 8 discrete items, and some orientations were better than others [22]. A recent study revealed a decreasing power relationship between angular width and pointing performance when using the tilt's altitude for selection [23].

Pen roll was shown to be useful for mode switching, document navigation, or for fluid parameter manipulation [3, 20]. Bi *et al.* [3] have shown that targets should be at least 10° in width and within a range of ±80°, to roll with reasonable speed and accuracy.

Prior results focusing on each channel in isolation serve as a foundation for the work we present here. We investigate how these channels interact when used in a coordinated manner on the pen. With this knowledge, designers can leverage *a-coord input* to create improved and fluid interactive pen techniques.

Parallel Input Control

One potential advantage to using *a-coord input* is the ability to coordinate the channels simultaneously. Users' ability to operate multiple degrees-of-freedom of input has been explored in a number of other contexts (e.g., [1, 7, 11]). Jacob *et al.* [7] characterized input devices as either integral or separable based on whether they allowed users to manipulate multiple DOF simultaneously. Their study revealed the importance of matching the perceptual nature of a task to that of the input device. Other work has examined the degree of parallelism exhibited in specific settings, such as a 3D docking task [11] and in bimanual interaction [1]. We use this body of prior work to inform our visual feedback and our methods for assessing coordination.

Parameter Selection and Manipulation Techniques

To demonstrate that *a-coord input* can benefit a range of tasks, we consider its use in multi-parameter selection and manipulation. This task is normally carried out in two distinct steps; to first select a parameter, and then to adjust its value. Numerous techniques have been proposed for fluidly merging multi-parameter selection and manipulation. Flowmenu [6] is a stroke-based interface with a radial layout of regions that define various commands. Selecting a feature takes place by stroking across a wedge-shaped menu item. Adjusting the value of a parameter occurs by tracing radially around the FlowMenu. The FaST sliders interface [12] consists of using marking menus with a typical linear slider. Users first apply a mark, in the marking menu, which then triggers a value adjusting slider. The user then moves the slider in the desired position. An informal user study showed that both FaST sliders and FlowMenus effectively support parameter manipulation, but that FaST sliders were easier for participants to learn [12].

In contrast to the above systems, with *a-coord input* it is possible that experienced users could execute some degree of parallelism, in that they could begin to manipulate the value of a parameter while they are selecting the parameter.

PROPERTIES OF AUXILIARY CHANNELS

Key to our investigation is a comparative analysis of the various auxiliary channels on the pen. We do not explore all of the possible channels, such as hover [5], or capacitance based multi-touch [19] as we leave these for future work. In our analysis we include Tilt, Roll, and Pressure. We leave Tilt-Altitude for future work, as it shares similar properties with Tilt-Azimuth (which we explore). We first compare the various features of these channels and then describe the design choices for our study of *a-coord input*.

Channel Properties

We distinguish each of these channels along five major axes: range of discrete control, bi-directionality, visuo-motor mappings, cyclicality and access method, introduced below and summarized in (Table 1).

Range of discrete control. Researchers have identified the number of discrete levels a channel can control. For pressure this number is 7±1 [13, 16], for Roll it is ±80°/10° (smallest allowable angle) or 16 levels [3] and for Tilt-Azimuth, performance degrades before attaining 8 discrete levels [22]. These ranges place an upper bound on what is possible in terms of item selection.

Bi-directionality. Most channels provide a reasonably good control of the input space in the forward and backward movements. Pressure is a slight exception. Because of how the sensors operate, pressure affords better control when moving forward and less control returning from higher to lower values [8]. Bi-directionality allows for better control if the user were to overshoot a desired target.

Visuo-motor mapping. Visual feedback (i.e., a mapping from motor to display space) is key for operating auxiliary channel input, particularly in the absence of body-based feedback (i.e., Pressure) [16]. Prior work has employed radial controls for Roll and Tilt, but linear for Pressure. Roll and Pressure can also be mapped to a linear or radial control, respectively. On the other hand, mapping tilt-azimuth to a linear control would not be a good match with the corresponding biomechanical operation.

Cyclicality. Channel control can be either cyclical or non-cyclical. For example, Roll affords cyclical control, as the user can return to the starting point (for example, an angle of 0°) in a single stroke without changing movement direction. In contrast, Pressure can only return to its originating value if the pen were to be lifted.

Access method. This feature suggests how quickly a channel can access an item. This can happen sequentially, by going through each value, or by leaping through a number of intermediary values and going directly to an item of interest, as observed in [22]. Only Tilt-Azimuth works this efficiently as one can directly tilt the pen (or leap) to the orientation of interest; all the other channels require sequentially traversing through values in their range.

Design Considerations

Guided by the comparative analysis above, we restricted our implementation of *a-coord input* to the following constraints and scope.

Visual Feedback

In our experiments, visual mappings were congruent with motor movement. We map Tilt to a radial layout, but Pressure and Roll are mapped to either a radial or linear layout, to provide flexibility in our visual feedback methods.

Selection Techniques

Selection is necessary to complete the final step of an action. For Pressure, a quick release or dwell have been preferred over selection with the pen's barrel button [16]. For Tilt, Tian *et al.* [22] proposed using the altitude of tilt for selection. For Roll, Bi *et al.* [3] proposed using quick release. Prior results also show that a button press with the non-dominant hand provides good control and efficiency [10, 16]. We use this latter method in our studies, especially since two channels are being controlled at once.

Discretizing Raw Sensory Input

Raw sensor information does not always provide an ideal mapping of sensor values to interaction [8]. Researchers have proposed discretizing the input for better control. Pressure input has been discretized into distinct levels using linear [15], quadratic [4], a dynamic fisheye-based [8] or a sigmoid [16] discretization function. We used a hysteresis function similar to that found in [16] for pressure. All other channels employed a one-to-one mapping from raw Tilt or Roll motor displacements to visual effecter.

	Roll	Pressure	Tilt Azimuth
Discrete Levels	16	7±1	< 8
Bi-Directionality	Good	Weak	Good
Visuo-Motor Mapping(s)	Radial (P) Linear (S)	Linear (P) Radial (S)	Radial
Cyclicality	Cyclical	Non-cyclical	Cyclical
Access Method	Sequential	Sequential	Leaping

Table 1- A summary of key features of the pen's auxiliary input channels based on the literature. We used these to guide our design choices. P, S refer to primary, secondary.

EXPERIMENT 1 – COORDINATING TWO CHANNELS

The goal of this experiment was to explore whether *a-coord* input (a) allows users to effectively coordinate auxiliary channels conjunctively, and (b) extends the number of controllable items with auxiliary input. Without *a-coord input*, the latter goal could be realized by first applying one channel, a selector, and then the same channel again (i.e. Roll+selector+Roll). The selector would indicate movement into the next dimension. Alternatively one could apply one channel, a selector, and then another channel, but this would resemble *a-coord input* which makes the selector redundant. Furthermore, sequential operation of two channels does not provide the freedom to re-adjust the first channel after it has been 'locked in' (i.e., to proceed to the second channel). Therefore, we used the first design as a baseline.

Participants and Apparatus

Ten right-handed participants (2 females) between the ages of 18 and 35 were recruited for this study. Participants had little or no experience with digital pen input.

We used a Wacom Intuos4 tablet with an Intuos4 Art Pen. The pen can produce pressure, tilt and roll values with a maximum of 2048 levels of pressure, and 360° of roll and tilt. We displayed visual feedback in full-screen mode on a 22-inch monitor with a resolution of 1680×1050 pixels.

Tasks and Procedure

We used a 2D discrete-target selection task. All first level items were arranged in a 360° circular layout (Figure 2). Second level items were placed in concentric rings. We chose this mapping as it would allow us to explore a range of *a-coord* techniques without introducing any confounds related to unintuitive visuo-motor mappings. The size of each target was determined by the number of items in the menu (i.e., fewer items resulted in larger targets).

A target was highlighted in red. The user's cursor was displayed in yellow. Participants were asked to select the target using either a single channel input twice or *a-coord input* as quickly and accurately as possible. In the single channel condition, participants first selected the correct wedge using one channel (e.g. pressure or roll). Once the participants landed on the desired wedge, they could then move up to second dimension in the 2D menu by pressing the CTRL key with the non-dominant hand, and then applying the same channel again. In the *a-coord input* condition, participants selected the wedge using one channel (e.g. roll) and the target item using another channel (e.g. pressure). With *a-coord input*, simultaneous movement across both channels was possible. In both conditions, the final target selection was made by pressing a hardware button (CTRL key) using the non-dominant hand. To undo any action users could simply lift up the pen.

Prior to the experiment, participants were shown the experimental setup, and were given several practice trials in each condition. For the *a-coord input* techniques, participants were shown how channels could be engaged simultaneously (e.g., applying pressure towards the target circle and rolling the pen towards the desired wedge, at the same time). However, participants were not required to engage in parallel action and could complete the task by allocating control to one channel and then the other. Breaks were enforced at the end of each block of trials. The entire experiment lasted approximately 30 minutes.

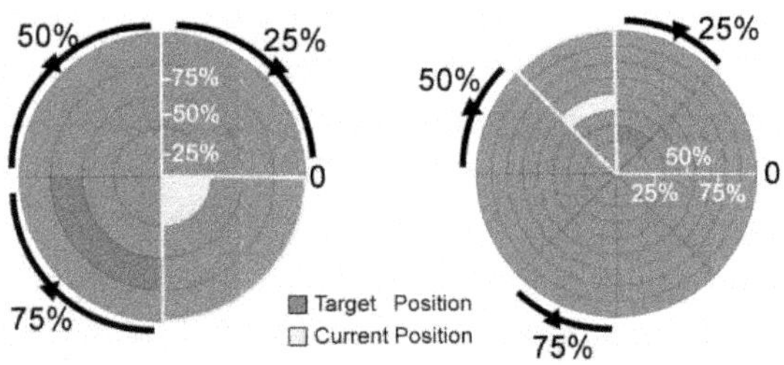

Figure 2 – Visual feedback for 4 × 4 (left) and 8 × 8 (right) levels. The black arrowheads indicate the target wedge.

Design

As indicated above, to avoid a combinatorial explosion of different *a-coord input* styles, we restricted our study to only three input channels: pressure, roll and tilt. We acknowledge that our results may not generalize to all combinations of *a-coord inputs*, but hope to show that at least some combinations provide clear benefits. We used these three channels with the following parameters.

Pressure – We applied a hysteresis function similar to that found in [16]. However, we excluded pressure readings that were simply resulting from the weight of the pen as this could confound our results. The range selected was thus between 819 and 2048 pressure units (where 2048 was approximately 1.5N of force). The initial pressure value was mapped to 0° as indicated in Figure 2.

Roll - For roll input, we defined the initial roll value of 0° as indicated in Figure 2. According to prior work, rolling under 10° was usually incidental and anything beyond ±90° is suboptimal [3]. Participants could roll the pen in either direction. Since our visual feedback consisted of a full circular layout, we employed a 1:2 mapping between the motor and visual space for roll.

Tilt – For the tilt channel, we consider only tilt in the azimuth angles, where 0° was mapped to a tilt to the East as indicated in Figure 2.

Combining these three channels, we get three different *a-coord* techniques: Roll + Pressure (R+P) (Figure 3.a), Tilt + Pressure (T+P) (Figure 3.b) and, Tilt + Roll (T+R) (Figure 3.c), where the first channel moves along the first dimension (radially) and the second channel controls the cursor in the second dimension (linearly). We selected these visuo-motor mappings based on prior work (as described in the section "Properties of Auxiliary Channels").We included two baseline single-channel techniques: Pressure + Pressure (P+P) and Roll + Roll (R+R). Tilt + Tilt requires a different visual mapping, since tilt works best with radial feedback, which we did not want to restrict ourselves to. Therefore, we excluded Tilt + Tilt to avoid introducing potential confounds.

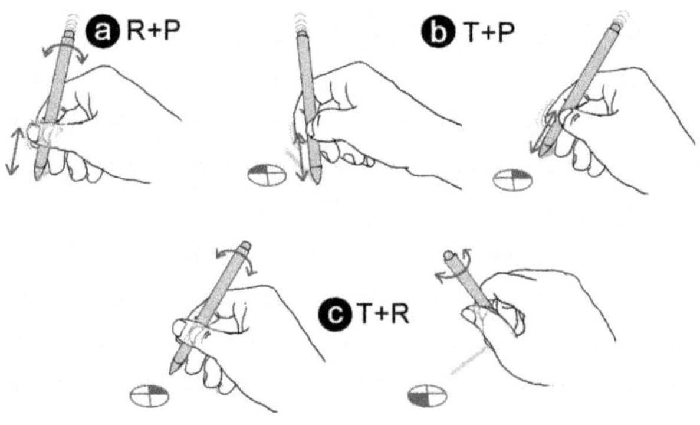

Figure 3 – Three a-coord techniques we evaluated. Roll+Pressure (R+P); Tilt+Pressure (T+P); Tilt+Roll (T+R).

We placed the target at 3 distances: 25%, 50%, and 75%, of the total input range for each channel, for both the first and second dimensions (Figure 2).

Overall, the experiment employed a 5×2×3 within-subjects factorial design. The independent variables were *Technique*: P+P, R+R, R+P, T+P and T+R; *Number of Levels* per dimension (low, high, 4 and 8 levels in both dimensions respectively); and *Target Distance* (25%, 50%, and 75%). *Technique* was counterbalanced across participants using a Latin square, while the other factors were presented in random order. Each trial representing a *Technique* × *Number of Level* × *Target Distance* combination, was repeated 4 times by each participant.

Given that our focus is on the feasibility of *a-coord input* as opposed to developing a novel 2D menu technique, we omit comparisons to techniques such as marking menus [9]. With respect to marking menus, we also wish to focus on contextual tasks, where pen movement is not involved.

Results

The data were analyzed using Repeated-Measures ANOVA and Bonferroni corrections for post-hoc comparisons.

Task Completion Time

Completion time measured the time from the target's appearance to the time participants successfully selected it, including errors.

The RM-ANOVA yielded a significant main effect of *Technique* ($F_{4,36} = 46.33$, $p < 0.001$) on completion time. The means for each technique are displayed in Figure 4. Post-hoc comparisons showed the 3 dual-channel techniques (T+P: 2315 ms, s.e. 1821; T+R: 2830 ms, s.e. 185; R+P: 2841 ms, s.e. 179) were all significantly faster than the 2 single-channel techniques (R+R: 4338 ms, s.e. 127; P+P: 4341 ms, s.e. 231; $p < 0.001$). There was also a non-significant trend indicating that T+P was faster than R+P (p=0.065), but there was no difference between R+P and T+R (p = 1). The difference between the two single-channel techniques was not significant (p = 1).

For the single-channel techniques, completion time can be decomposed into two sequential target acquisition components: the time it takes to make a successful selection on the first level, and the time from the end of the first task to the end of the trial. For P+P, since pressure is unidirectional, there was an additional adjustment cost between the two task components, where participants had to release the pressure after the first task by lifting the pen tip, and to land down the pen again to start the second task (Figure 4.left).

Figure 4 shows the task decomposition for each of the two single-channel combinations. We observe that participants require less time on the second invocation of the channel. This goes contrary to our expectations, in that the second invocation should take longer due to the mechanical re-adjustment of the finger after having invoked that channel once. We believe that this is still likely the case, but that users probably built muscle memory from the first phase, given that the targets were all laid out at the same distance in the second level. In retrospect, we created a condition that unintentionally favoured the single channel input. Despite this, we find that *a-coord* is more efficient than using a single channel alone.

As to be expected, there was a significant effect of Number *of Levels* on completion time ($F_{1,9} = 135.2$, $p < 0.001$), with participants slower at 8 levels (4006 ms, s.e. 181) than at 4 levels (2661 ms, s.e. 104). This effect was generally consistent across techniques.

There was no main effect of Target Distance on completion time ($F_{2,18} = 1.93$, $p = 0.17$), however, the interaction effect between *Technique* and *Target Distance* was significant ($F_{8,72} = 6.15$, $p < 0.001$). The nature of the interaction was difficult to interpret; however, it appears as though the poor performance of techniques involving pressure (P+P, R+P, and T+P) was mainly caused by the poor performance of those techniques when low pressure levels were required (targets at 25%). This is consistent with the findings from the prior work [8], showing that people have difficulty controlling pressure at its lower end.

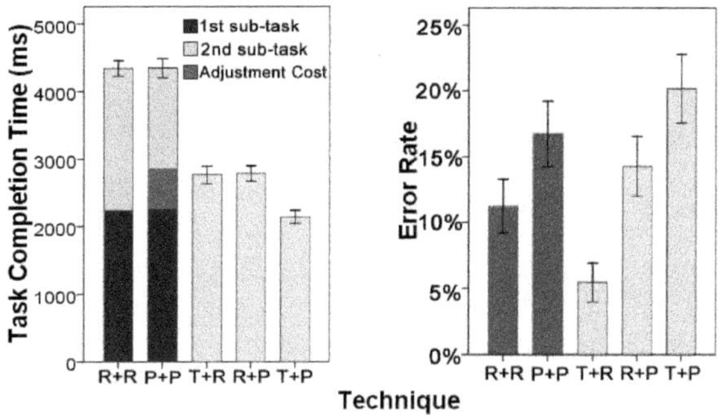

Figure 4 – Left: Task completion time shown by technique. Right: Error Rate shown by technique. (Error Bars represent ±1 s.e.)

Number of Errors

An error occurred if the participant selected the wrong target. For single channels, error was recorded only if the item on the second level was not selected properly. The trial did not stop until the proper target was selected.

The RM-ANOVA yielded a significant main effect of *Technique* ($F_{4,36} = 4.47$, $p = 0.01$) on error rate. Post-hoc analysis showed that T+R (5.4%, s.e. 0.9%) had significantly fewer errors than P+P (17.5%, s.e. 3%) (p=0.034). There were also non-significant trends indicating that T+R might be less error prone than R+R (11.2%, s.e. 1.9%, p=0.067) and T+P (20.6%, s.e. 4.6%, p=0.072). There was no significant difference between T+R and R+P (14.3%, s.e. 3.1%, p=0.220), nor were there significant differences between the remaining techniques (p=1).

There were significant main effects of *Numbers of Levels* ($F_{1,9} = 35$, $p < 0.001$) and *Target Distance* ($F_{2,18} = 1.93$, $p < 0.001$) on error rate. Participants made twice as many errors with 8 levels (18.2% s.e. 1.8%) than they did with 4 levels (9.4% s.e. 1.8%). For target distances, there were significantly more errors with targets at 25% distance (23.1%, s.e. 3.3) than with targets at 50% distance (11.3%, s.e. 1.2%) and 75% (7%, s.e. 1.5%) ($p < 0.05$). Post-hoc analysis showed no significant difference between the 50% and 75% distances ($p = 0.1$).

Finally, there was a significant *Technique* × *Target Distance* interaction effect ($F_{8, 72} = 0.07$, $p < 0.05$). Similar to our results for completion time, the interaction was at least partly due to the techniques involving pressure, where the error rate decreased rapidly as the target distance increased.

Discussion

A-Coord Input Performance

Our results reveal several trends. For all a-coord input styles tested, users were faster than using an auxiliary channel twice. Based on our results across all our measures, Tilt+Roll afforded the best overall result, with completion times below those of the single channels, and error rates in an acceptable range. One primary reason is that Tilt does not require users to traverse a range of item before reaching the target (Table 1). Additionally, Roll can control a larger number of items than pressure, thus disadvantaging this latter channel (Table 1). While Tilt+Pressure showed a trend towards being the fastest technique, it also exhibited a high error rate, making it perhaps the least desirable technique of all three a-coord styles we tested.

Error Rates

Error rates are similar to the ranges found in earlier studies on single channel input (see [3, 16, 22]). These range between 5% and 20%. Such errors can be minimized with better discretization functions [8] and by using fewer number of items [22]. Other improvements can be found when users are trained and improve with learning [8].

Extending the Number of Controllable Items

Our results show that any A-coord technique with 4×4 items has a comparable performance with other single channel techniques. These results show that we can extend the range of discrete items that was previously possible with single auxiliary channels. We see that *a-coord input* facilitates a factor of 2 to 3 times the possible range with single channels. Even with a conservative extension, of up to 4×4 items, error rates across *a-coord input* are within the bounds of what was previously reported with single channels alone.

Coordination

We examine the amount of coordination facilitated by *a-coord* input by breaking down the total completion time by the amount of control exhibited by each individual channel (Figure 6). We observe a few trends. First, we notice that while users still operate both channels in conjunction, they tend to stabilize one channel before completing the task with the other. This result goes contrary to our initial expectation that both channels would always be operated together, instead of one leading the other. Furthermore, stabilizing one channel before the other might explain the improved efficiency and error rates we observed with certain a-coord styles. For example, users stabilize Tilt very quickly, which may explain why combinations with this channel, such as Tilt+Roll, worked better than other techniques.

The fact that Tilt takes considerably less time to stabilize than either roll or pressure is to be expected due to the non-sequential nature of acquiring items through tilt-azimuth. Users take roughly 22% of the total task time to operate and stabilize tilt. This corresponds to a value between 700 and 850 msecs, which matches very closely to tilt performance when operated alone, as shown in earlier work [22]. Input with the second channel, i.e. Roll or Pressure with Tilt, takes approximately 75% of the total task time (i.e. users seem to take the remaining 25% of total task time to select the target with the button using the non-dominant hand). With Roll+Pressure, we see users on average operate Roll at 50%, and Pressure at 72% of total task time. These results indicate that users stabilized the first channel before proceeding to the final goal. They may also suggest that the channel with more controllable input range (Table 1), i.e. in this case Roll or Tilt, gets stabilized before the one with less control.

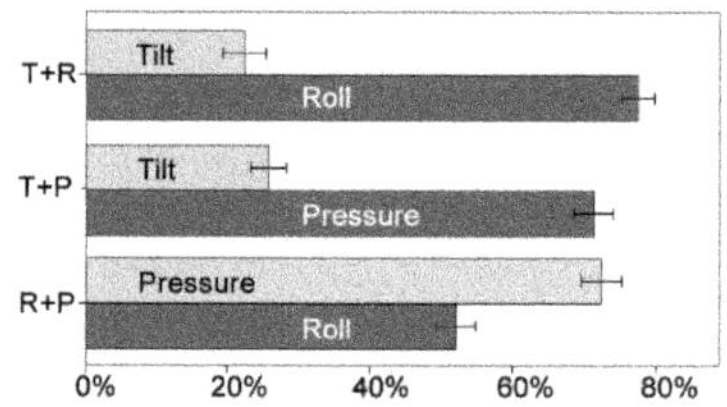

Figure 6 – Average percentage of time consumed by each channel over the length of a trial.

We further examine the performance of the non-leading channel (i.e. the channel which stabilized last) for the period in which both channels operate simultaneously. For example, during the period it takes Tilt to stabilize (22% of the overall task time in Tilt+Roll or roughly 700 msecs, represented by the red vertical bar in Figure 7) we observe several trends. With Tilt+Roll we find that while users are operating Tilt, the values of Roll also grow linearly and this continues even after Tilt gets stabilized. In the case of Tilt+Pressure and Roll+Pressure, the non-leading channel Pressure is controlled in a log manner. This suggests that during the period that both channels are operating, pressure quickly ramps up and then slows down after the leading channel's becomes steady.

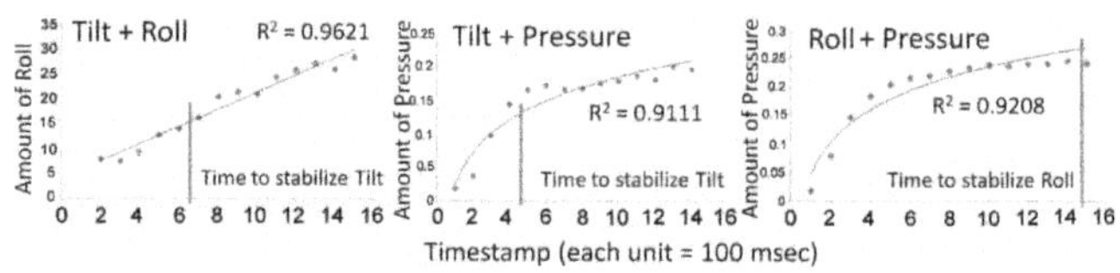

Figure 7 – Degree of control with the non-leading channel until the leading channel stabilizes, i.e. stops changing. The red vertical bar represents the timestamp at which the leading channel stabilizes. Left: with Tilt+Roll, Roll is controlled in a linear fashion; Middle, Right: non-leading channel Pressure, is controlled in a log manner. All R^2 are above 0.9.

Overall, these observations on channel coordination suggest that users tend to operate both channels conjunctively, within the time frame used for operating the leading channel. The conjunctive operation of *a-coord input* has the potential to yield performance gains in tasks other than 2D discrete item selection. We demonstrate how to extend this conjunctive operation to a different task in our next study.

COORDINATING CHANNELS FOR MULTI-PARAMETER SELECTION AND MANIPULATION

Our first study revealed that users can conjunctively coordinate two auxiliary channels. In our next study we explored this *a-coord input* feature through multi-parameter selection and manipulation, a task that involves continuous manipulation and has a more inherent two-step structure:.

The common task of multi-parameter selection and manipulation requires users to first select a desired parameter before they can actually change its value. We adapt *a-coord input* such that users concurrently choose a parameter and manipulate it. This form of interaction would be suitable for users who know a priori the value of the target they wish to set a parameter at. In these situations, *a-coord input* could be used to select and manipulate the value of a parameter through a single and continuous action. We note that the pen's auxiliary channels were designed for continuous and fluid input, such as for drawing. We therefore harness this natural design feature but in a multi-step fashion.

One challenge in adapting a-coord input for a multi-parameter selection and manipulation task is to avoid inadvertently setting values for parameters that were not selected. Figure 8 (left) shows how to adjust the value of multiple parameters, e.g. brightness or contrast of an image, with P+R. A user can move between sliders using pressure. Only the active slider will get highlighted, for which its value can be altered by rolling the pen. Users can press a key to confirm the change. With *a-coord input*, rolling the pen while pressing will unintentionally change the value of all sliders, active or inactive. To address this issue, we introduce a *ghost* wiper on every slider. Ghost wipers are semi-transparent and work the same way as real wipers but without changing the value of the parameters. They only show the potential change of the value. When users press the selection key, the change takes place on the active slide, while all other sliders remain unchanged (Figure 8 left). As an add-on benefit, *a-coord* interfaces allow designers to hide the inactive sliders to save expensive screen real estate. For example the P+R interface could consist of stacked sliders with only the active one being visible. Similarly, the T+R interface only shows the slider associated with the pen's tilt angle (Figure 1).

EXPERIMENT 2 – EXPLOTING A-COORD INPUT FOR A TWO-STEP CONTINUOUS MANIPULATION TASK

This study measures user performance of *a-coord input* in a multi-parameter selection and manipulation task. Unlike 2D discrete item selection, the two sub-tasks in a multi-parameter selection and manipulation task are asymmetric, i.e. each channel plays a different role – one for discrete item selection and the other for continuous variable manipulation. The two-step process requires users to hold the leading channel steady while manipulating the non-leading channel, thus testing the users' ability to exhibit this type of control with *a-coord input*. An additional distinction between this task and the 2D selection is that manipulating a continuous variable requires finer control. We use only Roll for manipulating the continuous variable as our pilot studies showed that Pressure did not afford sufficient bi-directional control for fine-grain input, and Tilt did not map naturally to such a task. We thus mapped parameter selection to Pressure and Tilt. Finally, we were also interested in knowing if *a-coord input* affords a comparable performance to an existing multi-parameter selection and manipulation technique. We included the FaST Slider [12] as a baseline technique in the study. Other techniques exist (as described earlier) but FaST sliders have shown to be easier to learn, than for example, FlowMenus [6].

Participants and Apparatus

Twelve right-handed participants (2 females) between the ages of 20 and 35 were recruited for this study. Participants had little or no experience with pen-based interfaces. We used the same apparatus as in Experiment 1.

Tasks and Procedure

For the a-coord techniques, participants were asked to select a desired slider using Pressure or Tilt, and then use Roll to adjust the position of the wiper to a target value shown by a vertical bar (Figure 8 left). The wiper was initially placed in the middle of the slider of 360 pixels (50.4 mm) high. Rolling the pen 1° in the counter-clockwise moved the wiper up by 1 pixel, and vice versa, providing 360 discrete levels and ensuring sufficient smoothness and continuity. When the wiper reached the target distance, participants pressed the CTRL key using the non-dominant hand to confirm a selection.

With the FaST Slider, participants first selected a desired slider using a marking menu [9]. The slider appeared at the position where the participants lifted the pen (Figure 8 right). They then used the pen tip to drag the wiper to the target value, pressing the CTRL button to confirm selection. The height of the entire slider widget remained the same for all techniques.

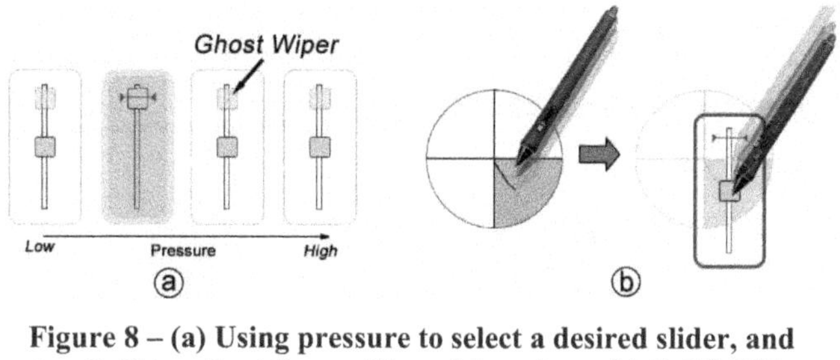

Figure 8 – (a) Using pressure to select a desired slider, and using Roll to adjust the position of the wiper. (b) FaST Slider.

A trial ended when participants successfully changed the desired parameter to the target value. Prior to the study, participants were given practice trials to familiarize themselves with all techniques. Similar to Experiment 1, they were shown how to engage in a-coord input in a coordinated manner, but this was not enforced in the study.

Design

The experiment employed a 3×2×2×3 within-subjects factorial design. The independent variables were *Technique*: P+R, T+R, and FaST Slider; *Number of Parameters*: Low (4) and High (6); *Granularity*: Coarse-grain, Fine-grain; and *Target Distance*: Near, Mid, and Far.

Number of Parameters – High was set to 6 items since results from the first study showed that pressure was hard to control with 8 levels.

Granularity – we used wipers of 2 different sizes to adjust the level of granularity. For the fine-grain setting, we used a wiper of 15 × 30 pixels (4.5 × 8.4 mm), and for the coarse-grain setting, we used a wiper of 30 × 30 pixels (8.4 × 8.4 mm).

Target Distance - we randomly placed the target within 3 intervals: Near (10%-30%), Mid (40%-60%), and Far (70%-90%), of the total input range. For rolling, the direction of roll was randomly chosen for each of the 3 target distances. In other words, distance Near could be randomly interpreted to be between ±(9°-27°).

Technique - was counterbalanced across participants using a Latin square, while the other factors were presented in a random order. The study consisted of four blocks, each consisting of 2 trials. There were 3 *Techniques* × 2 *Numbers of Parameters* × 2 *Granularities* × 3 *Target Distances* × 4 *Blocks* × 2 *Repetitions* × 12 *Participants* = 3456 trials in total.

Results

The data were again analyzed using Repeated-Measures ANOVA and Bonferroni corrections for post-hoc pair-wise comparisons. For the sake of brevity, we concentrate our reporting on our primary factor of interest, *Technique*.

Task Completion Time

RM-ANOVA yielded a significant effect of *Technique* ($F_{2, 22} = 23.86$, $p < 0.001$) on task completion time. The means for each technique are displayed in Figure 9. Post-hoc comparisons showed that T+R (1703 ms, s.e. 91) was significantly faster than FaST Slider (2219 ms, s.e. 88) and P+R (2339 ms, s.e. 106) ($p < 0.001$). The difference between FaST Slider and P+R was not significant ($p = 1$).

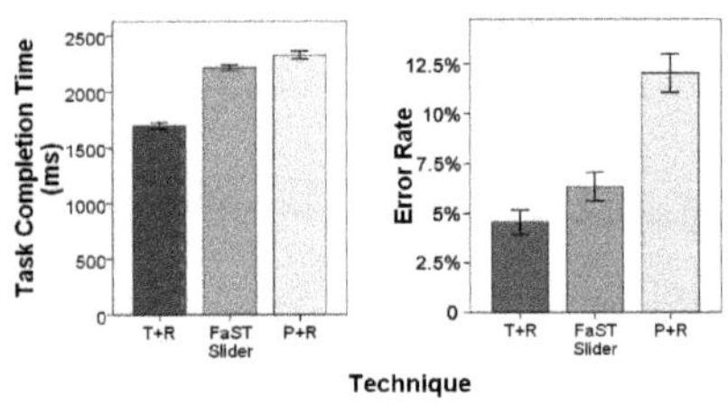

Figure 9 - Left: Task completion times. Right: Error rates.

In addition to the above main effect, there were significant interactions between *Technique* × *Number of Parameters* ($F_{2, 22} = 22.79$, $p < 0.001$), *Technique* × *Granularity* ($F_{2, 22} = 4.89$, $p = 0.01$), and *Technique* × *Target Distance* ($F_{4, 44} = 5.25$, $p = 0.001$) (Figure 10). These effects demonstrate that T+R was always faster than P+R and FaST Sliders, but that differences between the latter two were more nuanced. In some conditions (e.g. coarse-grained and 4 parameters), P+R showed a comparable performance with FaST Slider.

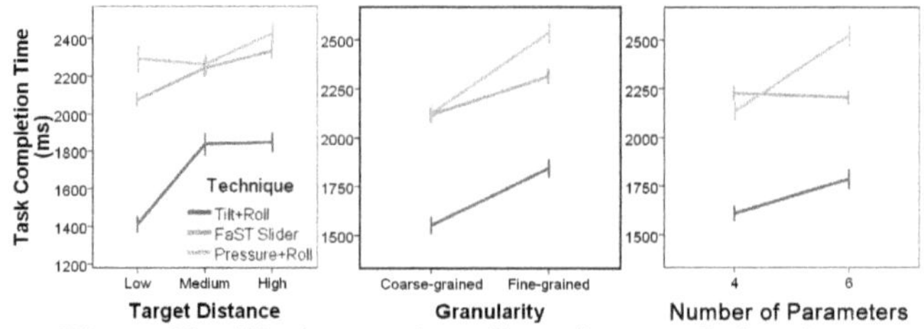

Figure 10 – The interaction effects for completion time.

Number of Errors

The RM-ANOVA yielded a significant main effect of *Technique* ($F_{2, 22} = 12.48$, $p < 0.001$) on the number of errors (Figure 9). Post-hoc analysis showed that P+R (12.1%, s.e. 1.7%) had significantly more errors than T+R (4.5%, s.e. 1%) and FaST Slider (6.3%, s.e. 1.5%) ($p < 0.05$). There was no significant difference on between T+R and FaST Sliders ($p = 0.82$). There was, however, a significant *Technique* × *Target Distance* interaction ($F_{4,44} = 22.03$, $p < 0.001$), indicating that the difference between P+R and the other two techniques occurred mainly at Low target distances, where P+R was more error prone.

DISCUSSION

Experiment 2 Results

Results of experiment 2 show that *a-coord input* can be applied to a task involving continuous manipulation and a more distinct two-step process than the discrete item selection task studied in experiment 1. Of the techniques evaluated, combining Tilt+Roll led to the lowest completion times and was comparable to an existing technique, FaST Sliders, in terms of errors. We also note that holding a Tilt value while rolling was more controllable than holding a certain Pressure value. Although the results showed that combining Tilt and Roll was superior to combining Pressure and Roll for a task of this nature, the latter combination can still have a comparable performance with a careful design, e.g. few discrete items (i.e., number of parameters) for pressure and coarse-grained control for rolling.

Utility of *A-Coord Input*

We summarize the primary findings from our two studies as follows:

- *A-coord* input provides a larger input range than what is available with single channels (up to 64 or 8×8 items vs. 16 items, table 1);
- Some *a-coord* styles are more efficient than combining single channels serially;
- Of the combinations studied, Tilt+Roll affords the best a-coord control for discrete 2D target selection;
- Tilt+Roll *a-coord* input is efficient for parameter selection and manipulation, and is a viable alternative or addition to existing techniques such as FaST sliders.

Expanding on these primary findings, our experiments show that *a-coord input* is a viable input technique across two qualitatively different tasks. Experiment 1 showed that *a-coord input* can extend the bandwidth available through a single auxiliary channel as channels are operated in conjunction. On a conservative side the bandwidth with *a-coord input* easily extends to 16 items (4×4), with much higher levels possible for techniques that don't involve Pressure. Our results also indicate that when combining two channels, users have a tendency to stabilize one channel first - either Tilt, which is stabilized rapidly, or Roll. This tendency fits with other research on parallel control, which found that users will not always allocate control equally when operating a multiple degrees-of-freedom input device, particularly when equal allocation results in a biomechanically awkward motion [11]. However, we also observed that while both channels are in operation, users exhibit a high amount of parallelism. This latter result suggests that coordinating multiple auxiliary channels on the pen is a relatively natural motion.

In experiment 2, we demonstrated that *a-coord input* is applicable to a more continuous task and one with a more distinct division of responsibilities for the channels. This latter task characteristic adds the challenge of having to hold the leading channel steady while operating the second channel. Our results indicated that Tilt and Roll was particularly effective for this multi-parameter selection and manipulation task, with performance either exceeding or comparable to an alternative technique (FaST Sliders).

A loose correlation of our results to the comparative analysis of the techniques summarized in Table 1, may suggest the following. When an auxiliary channel has a rapid access method to discrete items, such as with Tilt, this channel stabilizes quicker in *a-coord* style interaction. However, in the process of stabilization, the channels involved are still being coordinated conjunctively. A second observation is in the amount of control possible and mapping of a task to a channel. For example, Roll was relegated to continuous parameter manipulation. This seems intuitive but also worked well since rolling affords a high degree of control.

Application Scenarios

Single channel input on the pen has been primarily proposed for in-context interactions [22], where the user does not need to move the pen for interaction. We feel that the *a-coord input* enhances interactions in these types of scenarios but further facilitates input with the pen in ways that were not easily captured with single channels alone. We present three application scenarios: 2D menus, improved stimulus-response compatibility, and integral actions.

2D Menus - With a-coord input, contextual menus take on a new dimension. The technique can, increase the range and number of items selectable and allow for 2D organization of menu items. Tilt menus have been shown to work well for menu selection [22], but are limited in range. In our case, using even a conservative technique, (pressure and tilt) we can immediately get 16 items for selection (Figure 1.a), with much larger item sets possible, such as for the color palette (shown in Figure 11.a), with Tilt and Roll.

Beyond simply extending the number of items, *a-coord input* also permits 2D menu organization, with the structure (e.g., number of items per level) tailored to the strengths of the specific dual-channel combination. We don't necessarily need to constrain menus to one level before showing the next - we can show all menu items and then allow the user to simply move to their target in a more parallel manner.

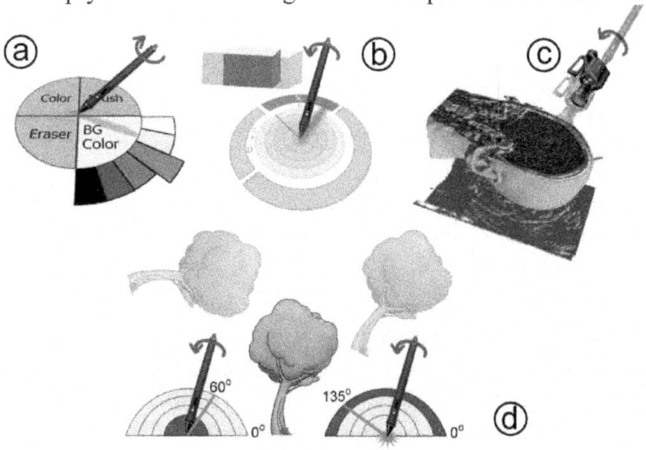

Figure 11 - Sample applications that can benefit from a-coord input, as per our results. (a) Tilt-Roll 2D color palette; (b) Tilt-Roll 3D-manipulation; (c) Tilt-Roll Volumetric data navigation ; (d) Pressure-Roll dynamic CD ratio adjustment.

Extended Stimulus-Response Compatibility – A-coord input can also enhance stimulus-response compatibility. For example, Tilt can easily be used to select a mode (i.e. 2-6 modes) before engaging in a rolling action. Examples of combining channels in this manner include common transformations in 3D applications: we can map Tilt to axis selection, and Roll to manipulation; the latter could rotate or scale an object along the axis selected by Tilt (Figure 11.b). This can replace the use of small handles commonly used for such tasks in graphics applications, which are prone to parallax issues with the pen. Volumetric data navigation often requires users to change the viewing angle of a virtual camera while manipulating the camera's depth. Tilt and Roll can provide a smoother control, for changing the orientation of the clipping plane (Tilt) and simultaneously the depth of the plane (Roll) (Figure 11.c).

Integral Actions - A-coord input can also support integral actions, ones that map well to the perceptual structure of the task [7]. For example to fine-tune rotation of an object, Pressure can be mapped to controlling the CD ratio while Roll rotates the object (Figure 11.d). These sub-actions could be easily carried out simultaneously to enhance fluidity with contextual actions.

CONCLUSION AND FUTURE WORK

In this paper, we investigate the benefits of the design space of *a-coord input* through two experiments, which systematically studied several fundamental questions of such an input style. The results of the first study show that *a-coord input* can effectively improve the bandwidth of the pen's auxiliary channels with high efficiency and accuracy and by operating the channels in parallel for at least some duration of the task. These findings can be applied to a continuous two-step task.

We caution, however, that our understanding of *a-coord input* is still in its infancy. Additional empirical work is required to: (i) identify more precise usable ranges for each channel combination; (ii) determine the generalizability of our results across all other channel combinations; (iii) empirically verify the value *of a-coord input* in some of the application scenarios we have proposed; (iv) explore *a-coord* input for direct settings; (v) investigate the effect of *a-coord* input for different visual mappings; and (vi) determine users' qualitative responses to *a-coord* input in comparison to other alternatives. Answers to some of these pertinent questions along with our findings can make *a-coord input* a reliable, effective and common interaction method for pen-based interfaces.

ACKNOWLEDGEMENTS

We acknowledge NSERC for providing the funds, our study participants and our lab mates, David McCallum and Cary Williams for assisting with the video.

REFERENCES

1. Balakrishnan, R. and Hinckley, K. (2000). Symmetric bimanual interaction. In *CHI'00*. 33-40.
2. Buxton, B., Wired Magazine, 7/26 2011, http://www.wired.com/magazine/2011/07/st_thompson_breakthrough/, accessed January 2012.
3. Bi, X., Moscovich, T., Ramos, G., Balakrishnan, R. and Hinckley, K. (2008). An exploration of pen rolling for pen-based interaction. In *UIST'08*. 191-200.
4. Cechanowicz, J., Irani, P. and Subramanian, S. (2007). Augmenting the mouse with pressure sensitive input. In *CHI'07*. 1385-1394.
5. Grossman, T., Hinckley, K., Baudisch, P., Agrawala, M. and Balakrishnan, R. (2006). Hover widgets: using the tracking state to extend the capabilities of pen-operated devices. In *CHI'06*. 861-870.
6. Guimbretiére, F. and Winograd, T. (2000). FlowMenu: combining command, text, and data entry. In *UIST'00*. 213-216.
7. Jacob, R. J. K., Sibert, L. E., McFarlane, D. C. and Jr, M. P. M. (1994). Integrality and Separability of Input Devices. *TOCHI*, 1 (1), 3-26, 1994.
8. Kang, S., Irani, P., Gustafson, S. and Subramanian, S. (2008). PressureFish: a method to improve control of discrete pressure-based input. In *CHI'08*. 1295-1298.
9. Kurtenbach, G. P., Sellen, A. J. and Buxton, W. A. S. An empirical evaluation of some articulatory and cognitive aspects of "marking menus", *HCI*, 8(1), 1-23 1993.
10. Li, Y., Hinckley, K., Guan, Z. and Landay, J. A. (2005). Experimental analysis of mode switching techniques in pen-based user interfaces. In *CHI'05*. 461-470.
11. Masliah, M. R. and Milgram, P. (2000). Measuring the allocation of control in a 6 degree-of-freedom docking experiment. In *CHI'00*. 25-32.
12. McGuffin, M., Burtnyk, N. and Kurtenbach, G. (2002). FaST Sliders: Integrating Marking Menus and the Adjustment of Continuous Values. In *GI'02*, 35-42.
13. Mizobuchi, S., Terasaki, S., Keski-Jaskari, T., Nousiainen, J., Ryynanen, M. and Silfverberg, M. (2005). Making an impression: force-controlled pen input for handheld devices. In *CHI'05*. 1661-1664.
14. Ramos, G. and Balakrishnan, R. (2003). Fluid interaction techniques for the control and annotation of digital video. In *UIST'03*. 105-114.
15. Ramos, G. and Balakrishnan, R. (2005). Zliding: fluid zooming and sliding for high precision parameter manipulation. In *UIST'05*. 143-152.
16. Ramos, G., Boulos, M. and Balakrishnan, R. (2004). Pressure widgets. In *CHI'04*. 487-494.
17. Ramos, G. A. and Balakrishnan, R. (2007). Pressure marks. In *CHI'07*. 1375-1384.
18. Ren, X., Yin, J., Zhao, S. and Li, Y. (2007). The Adaptive Hybrid Cursor: A Pressure-Based Target Selection Technique for Pen-Based User Interfaces. In *INTERACT'07*. 310-323.
19. Song, H., Benko, H., Guimbretière, F., Izadi, S., Cao, X. and Hinckley, K. (2011). Grips and gestures on a multi-touch pen. In *CHI'11*. 1323-1332.
20. Suzuki, Y., Misue, K. and Tanaka, J. (2007). Stylus Enhancement to Enrich Interaction with Computers. In *HCII'07*. 133-142.
21. Tian, F., Ao, X., Wang, H., Setlur, V. and Dai, G. (2007). The tilt cursor: enhancing stimulus-response compatibility by providing 3d orientation cue of pen. In *CHI'07*. 303-306.
22. Tian, F., Xu, L., Wang, H., Zhang, X., Liu, Y., Setlur, V. and Dai, G. (2008). Tilt menu: using the 3D orientation information of pen devices to extend the selection capability of pen-based user interfaces. In *CHI'08*. 1371-1380.
23. Xin, Y., Bi, X. and Ren, X. (2011). Acquiring and pointing: an empirical study of pen-tilt-based interaction. In *CHI'11*. 849-858.

Personalized Input: Improving Ten-Finger Touchscreen Typing through Automatic Adaptation

Leah Findlater[1,2] and Jacob O. Wobbrock[2]

[1]College of Information Studies
University of Maryland, College Park, MD
leahkf@umd.edu

[2]The Information School | DUB Group
University of Washington, Seattle, WA
wobbrock@uw.edu

ABSTRACT

Although typing on touchscreens is slower than typing on physical keyboards, touchscreens offer a critical potential advantage: they are software-based, and, as such, the keyboard layout and classification models used to interpret key presses can dynamically adapt to suit each user's typing pattern. To explore this potential, we introduce and evaluate two novel personalized keyboard interfaces, both of which adapt their underlying key-press classification models. The first keyboard also visually adapts the location of keys while the second one always maintains a visually stable rectangular layout. A three-session user evaluation showed that the keyboard with the stable rectangular layout significantly improved typing speed compared to a control condition with no personalization. Although no similar benefit was found for the keyboard that also offered visual adaptation, overall subjective response to both new touchscreen keyboards was positive. As personalized keyboards are still an emerging area of research, we also outline a design space that includes dimensions of adaptation and key-press classification features.

Author Keywords

Touchscreen text input, personalization, adaptive interfaces.

ACM Classification Keywords

H5.2 [Information interfaces and presentation]: User interfaces—*input devices and strategies*.

INTRODUCTION

Large touchscreen devices such as tablets and interactive tabletops are being adopted for an increasingly wide range of tasks. While these devices support ten-finger text input and full size QWERTY keyboards, providing rapid text entry remains a challenge [4,14,27]. The reduced tactile and kinesthetic feedback of a touchscreen not only increases the visual attention required to position hands and fingers on the keyboard but also impacts the user's knowledge of whether a key has been depressed [3]. Spurious input may also occur from hands or arms touching the surface [31], further impacting text entry.

Permission to make digital or hard copies of all or part of this work for personal or classroom use is granted without fee provided that copies are not made or distributed for profit or commercial advantage and that copies bear this notice and the full citation on the first page. To copy otherwise, or republish, to post on servers or to redistribute to lists, requires prior specific permission and/or a fee.
CHI'12, May 5–10, 2012, Austin, Texas, USA.
Copyright 2012 ACM 978-1-4503-1015-4/12/05...$10.00.

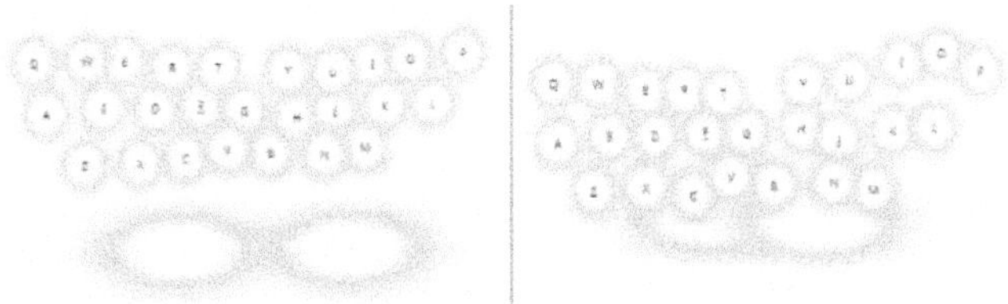

Figure 1. Personalization with a visually adaptive keyboard, showing the adapted layouts for two participants at the end of three study sessions.

Despite these challenges, touchscreens offer a major potential advantage over physical keyboards: they are software-based, and, consequently, the keyboard layout and key-press classification models can dynamically adapt to each user. In previous work, for example, we used simulations of touchscreen typing data to show that a *personalized* input model for ten-finger typing greatly improves key-press classification accuracy over a model aggregated across all users [6]. However, we did not actually build an adaptive keyboard, leaving future work to capitalize on the implications of those findings. Furthermore, other empirical exploration of personalized keyboards for ten-finger typing has been almost nonexistent, with the only user evaluation to our knowledge showing no performance benefit over a static keyboard [7].

To study the effect of keyboard adaptation on touchscreen typing performance, we designed and evaluated two novel adaptive keyboards for ten-finger typing (Figure 1). These prototypes explore two points in the design space of personalized touchscreen keyboards. While both use the same approach to personalize the underlying key-press classification model, one keyboard also *visually adapts* the location of keys while the other maintains a visually stable rectangular layout. We used an iterative approach to design the keyboards, including simulation analyses of ten-finger typing data to select and tune the final underlying key-press classification model, a J48 decision tree classifier trained on finger location and movement features.

We conducted a three-session study with 12 participants to compare performance and subjective reactions with the two adaptive keyboards and a traditional, static QWERTY layout. Our findings show that a personalized keyboard can improve typing speed over the static alternative. The personalized keyboard that did *not* visually adapt improved typing speed by 12.9% across all three sessions, rising to 15.2% for the third session; no discernible difference was found in error rates. In contrast, the personalized keyboard that *did* visually adapt did not provide a performance benefit over the static keyboard. It was, however, considered to be the most comfortable and natural of the three keyboards.

This paper makes the following contributions. First, as keyboard adaptation is still an emerging area of research, we outline a design space for personalized touchscreen keyboards, including major dimensions of adaptation and key-press classification features. This design space provides both a rationale for the design choices that we made and highlights open areas of future work. Second, we provide two novel personalized keyboard interfaces that use more sophisticated classification models than previous work [6,7] and can accommodate a wide range of typing features. Finally, we provide empirical evidence for the benefit of such personalization, both in terms of typing performance and user experience. These findings show that the way in which keyboard adaptation is visualized can significantly impact the efficacy of and reaction to that adaptation. While our focus is on ten-finger touch-typing, our contributions are also relevant to mobile devices, where research has only begun to explore personalized text input [30].

RELATED WORK

We discuss work most relevant to personalized touchscreen keyboards in the context of our design space (next section). Here, we focus on tabletop text input, touchscreen typing, and adaptive interfaces in general.

The lack of efficient methods for entering text on interactive tabletops is well documented (*e.g.*, [4,14,31]) and may potentially detract from long-term sustained use of such devices [27,37]. As one solution, distal tactile feedback, applied not on the surface itself but on the wrist or arm, has been shown to improve typing speed [26]. The use of physical keyboards [12] and physical silicon keyboards overlaid on the surface [36] have also been proposed, highlighting the challenge of text entry on interactive tabletops. Finally, although not for tabletops *per se*, techniques to support ten-finger typing on arbitrary flat surfaces using computer vision [29] or augmented gloves [8] have been explored. The 1Line keyboard [22] has also been proposed to save visual space on smaller touchscreens.

In contrast to ten-finger typing, a large body of work exists on virtual keyboards for a *single point of input*, most often a finger or stylus. These include techniques that utilize the geometric relationship between keys to improve input accuracy [20] or enable typing without a priori determining the position of the keyboard, albeit with a high error rate [28]. Alternatives to tapping a QWERTY keyboard have also been proposed, including alternate key layouts [21,24,40] and methods to stroke between keys [19]. Though highly relevant to our work, one difference between single point of input and multiple-finger typing is highlighted by comparing two past papers on keyboard size ([25] *vs.* [33]). With stylus input, MacKenzie and Zhang [25] showed that a smaller keyboard increased errors but did not reduce speed compared to a larger keyboard. In contrast, with multiple finger input, Sears *et al.* [33] showed that smaller keys reduce speed *and* increase errors.

Regardless of the exact keyboard layout or method used to identify key presses, language modeling is commonly used to improve input accuracy with virtual keyboards. For keyboards where a single key is overloaded with multiple letters, these models can clarify the ambiguity of key presses (*e.g.*, [8]). More generally, language modeling can be used to improve typing accuracy by reducing the chance of improbable key presses (*e.g.*, [1,2,9,10]). These approaches combine the user's key-press location with language model predictions for the next possible letter to more accurately classify which key the user was attempting to hit [9]. As discussed in the next section, work on language modeling is complementary to our research.

Our design space and, particularly, the comparison of visual and nonvisual adaptation in that design space are inspired by previous work on adaptive user interfaces. Adaptive user interfaces can introduce new challenges compared to traditional interfaces (see [5,16,17]). Those most applicable to text input include: lack of user control, unpredictability, lack of transparency of the system's decision making process, and obtrusiveness, or the degree to which the adaptations are distracting. Evaluations are also often more complicated than for non-adaptive user interfaces. For example, not only does the user need time to learn about the system, but the system needs to learn about the user.

DESIGN SPACE OF PERSONALIZED KEYBOARDS

Before describing our specific approach, we first outline a design space for touchscreen keyboard personalization. This design space is useful to introduce and define concepts that our classification models leverage as well as to map out this emerging research area. Since the focus of this paper is on adaptive (automatic) forms of personalization, we use the terms "adaptive" and "personalized" interchangeably. We also rely on a distinction made by Goodman *et al.* [9] between *touch models* and *language models* for touchscreen typing. A touch model describes how the user's finger touch is interpreted as a key press while the language model adds knowledge such as the distribution of words in a given language. These two sources of information are often combined to improve overall typing accuracy (*e.g.*, [9,10]). Our focus is primarily on improving touch models, which has received less attention of the two.

Dimensions of Adaptation

We outline three major dimensions of touch-model adaptation for touchscreen keyboards. No one dimension is entirely independent of the others, but each one may elicit different design considerations.

Dimension 1: Key-Press Classification Model

A key-press classification model classifies finger touches as specific keys, such as A, S, or D. Perhaps the simplest adaptive model is the *closest-centroid* approach, where key centroids are updated as the user types, and touches are assigned to the key with the closest centroid. For ten-finger typing, simulation results have demonstrated the potential of a personalized closest-centroid approach to increase classification accuracy over a model aggregated across all users [6]. However, user evaluations with a ten-finger keyboard [7] and a 9-key numeric keyboard [13] have so far found no performance improvement.

Bivariate Gaussian distributions computed for each key offer a more sophisticated, probabilistic classification approach and have been used for small touchscreen devices [9,10,28] though not, to our knowledge, for ten-finger typing. Most work with bivariate Gaussian distributions has focused on models aggregated across multiple users; however, simulations by Rudchenko *et al.* [30] have demonstrated the benefit of personalized versus aggregate models. Both closest-centroid and bivariate Gaussian models only make use of the (*x*,*y*) location of the finger touch. In this paper, we explore machine learning approaches that can accommodate a larger set of features.

Dimension 2: Visual Key Layout

When the key-press classification model adapts to the user, the visual key layout may also change. Figure 2 shows an example from Go and Endo [7]: a Voronoi tessellation drawn about the adapted centroids of a closest-centroid classification model. *Not* adapting the visual layout when the underlying model changes increases the chance that the classifier's output will not match the visual key the user appears to touch. Thus, *visual adaptation* may increase the predictability of the keyboard. How users react to visual adaptation, however, has so far been inconclusive (see [7] *vs.* [13]). This issue may reflect a broader challenge with adaptive user interfaces: adaptations can demand so much attention from the user that even theoretically beneficial adaptations have a negative effect [5,17].

The issue of visual adaptation can arise with language model predictions as well. Some text input techniques increase the size of probable keys based on a language model's prediction of the next letter [1,2,10]. In this

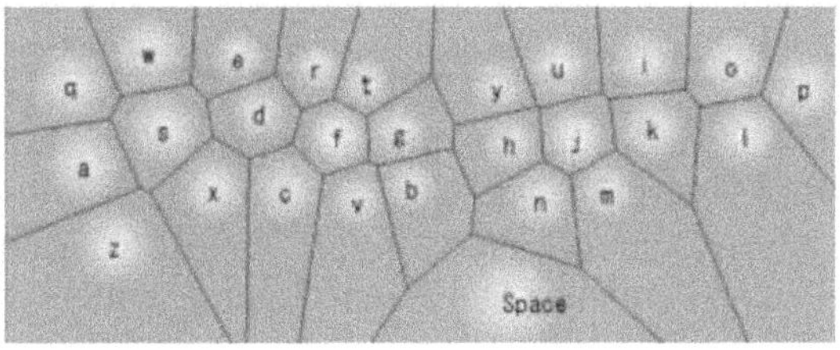

Figure 2. Visual adaptation of CATKey, showing Voronoi tessellation around adapted key centers (from [7]; copyright Springer).

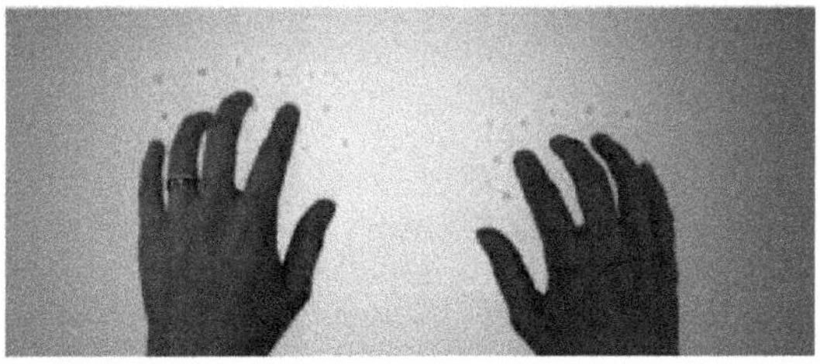

Figure 3. Adapting keyboard halves to hands in our system.

context, Gunawardana *et al.* [10] defined an *anchor* area in the center of each drawn key to improve key-press predictability. This technique, where touch points within an anchor area *always* return the anchored key, may also be useful when combined with adaptive touch models.

Dimension 3: Keyboard Positioning and Orientation

While the previous two dimensions focused on *individual* keys, the keyboard itself can also adapt more holistically to the user's hand and arm placement. This adaptation can occur when the user first places their hands on the surface: for example, the keyboard may be displayed automatically in two halves under the user's hands (see Figure 3). This type of adaptation has been previously proposed [15,32] but not evaluated. The keyboard can also adjust itself more subtly over time to account for drift as the user is typing.

Classification Features for Touchscreen Typing

The above subsections defined three dimensions of adaptation for personalized touchscreen keyboards. Here we focus on *Dimension 1*, key-press classification models, and consider what features may be most useful for classification (Figure 4). Ultimately, the set of possible features will be determined by the input hardware used (*e.g.*, a vision system may provide more features than a capacitive touchscreen). While our focus is on ten-finger typing, many features listed here are also applicable to smaller devices. Our goal is to highlight the breadth of features that exist for personalizing keyboards as well as to introduce the particular features that we later test.

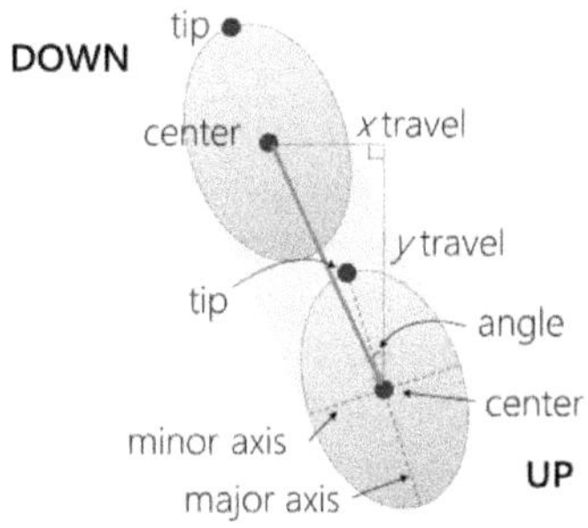

Figure 4. A subset of classification features based on a single key press event. This subset was tested in our simulations.

Touch location features are based on finger-down and finger-up locations. These features can include: (1) *finger center* (*x*,*y*) and (2) *fingertip* (*x*,*y*) locations. On large touchscreens, the keyboard can move, so these coordinates must be relative to some point(s) of reference. For adaptation to the left and right hands, *two* relative center locations can be calculated, *e.g.*, one as an offset from the F key and one as an offset from the J key (the *home* keys). Absolute values can be used for smaller screens.

Touch area features describe the size and angle of the finger on the screen; these features greatly depend on the hardware device. We used a Microsoft Surface, which provides ellipses fitted to the touch area and allows for (3) *major axis*, (4) *minor axis* and (5) *orientation*.

Movement features describe the movement of the finger

during the key-press action. Different keys may result in different movement signatures based on the finger used and how the user reaches for that key. Specific features include (6) *travel* and (7) *elapsed time* between finger down and up. Travel can be calculated as the distance in x and y directions for either the fingertip or the finger center.

Features relative to previous key presses incorporate knowledge about previous key presses. These include (8) *inter-key-press timing*, or the elapsed time between key presses, and (9) *(x,y) distance offset from previous key*. The latter may be useful if, for example, the current key-press location is affected by whether the last key was to its left or right. A simulation study by Rashid and Smith [28] showed low accuracies for a touch model based only on this feature.

Hand or arm features are based on the position of the hand and/or arm. Again, these features are highly dependent on the underlying touchscreen system in that only certain systems can provide this information.

Summary and Discussion

We have defined three dimensions of adaptation and a list of potential classification features for personalized touch models. Of course, the particular touchscreen device used will dictate which subset of features is possible and useful. In addition, any adaptive system needs to account for how the user model is trained: online, as the user types (*e.g.*, [7,13]), or offline, perhaps in an explicit training period (*e.g.*, [30]). Furthermore, if the training occurs online, the *rate* at which the adaptation occurs may impact the effectiveness of a personalized keyboard.

ITERATIVE DESIGN OF AN ADAPTIVE KEYBOARD

We took an iterative approach to design and build two personalized keyboards that were the same in all respects except for their *visual* adaptation. Here, we describe the general personalization method used, a pilot study of our early keyboard designs, and, finally, the designs that we ultimately evaluated in the full user study.

General Personalization Approach

We implemented static (non-adaptive) and personalized (adaptive) keyboard interfaces in C♯ .NET 4.0. The most basic of these interfaces, used as a control condition, was a static rectangular QWERTY layout with keys 0.9" × 0.9" (39 px × 39 px; based on the Surface's native keyboard).

For the personalized keyboards, we used Weka 3.6[1] and IKVM[2] to provide online adaptation in real-time. That is, each personalized keyboard collected training data as the user typed and, at natural break points in the user's input, this training data was used to update the classification model and possibly the visual layout of the keyboard. In our studies, model updating occurred at the end of each phrase. Key presses whose letters were subsequently backspaced were considered errors and removed from the training set.

[1] http://www.cs.waikato.ac.nz/ml/weka/

[2] http://www.ikvm.net/

Additionally, each key was initially seeded from 5 points sampled from a bivariate Gaussian distribution around the key's center, with x and y variance of 40 pixels and no covariance. The keyboards only began adapting after a minimum of 10 training points (key presses) were collected for every key. Based on early user feedback, we required that *all* keys achieve this minimum for consistency so that some keys did not begin adapting sooner than others (*e.g.*, E collects training data more quickly than Q). To accommodate the possibility that the user could adjust his or her typing patterns over time, the training history only stored the last 100 strikes per key.

The frequency of model-updating and the size of the training history used were determined by informal feedback from six early users and input from the research team. This process allowed us to identify a reasonable rate of adaptation for the personalized keyboards. However, determining the *optimal* rate is an open area of research and only one of many design considerations with adaptive user interfaces (see [5][17]).

Pilot Study to Select a Classifier and Feature Set

We conducted a pilot study that informed the final keyboard designs in two important ways: (1) it inspired us to reflect on the role of visual adaptation in personalized keyboards; (2) it provided realistic typing data with which to evaluate and select an appropriate machine learning classifier for the key-press classification models.

Typing Interfaces for Pilot Study

We built and tested three keyboards in the pilot study, two of which were seeded using a dataset we had previously collected on 10-finger typing patterns from 20 participants [6]. In particular, since we hoped to create novel keyboards that would allow for typing with reduced visual attention, we used data from a condition in the previous study that was meant to emulate just that: in the *no visual keyboard* condition in [6], participants typed on a blank surface.

The keyboards used in the pilot study were as follows:

- *Conventional* was a static rectangular QWERTY layout.
- *Static-Centroid* provided a static layout where the locations of keys were adjusted to the aggregate centroids of key presses across all participants from the previously collected dataset (from [6]).
- *Adaptive-Bayes* began with the same aggregate key layout and switched to a Naïve Bayes classifier after 10 training points had been observed for each key (using finger center (x, y) and fingertip (x, y) as the feature set). As with all machine learning classifiers in this paper, we used Weka 3.6. Naïve Bayes was chosen for this early keyboard implementation because it performed well in simulations we ran on the dataset from [6].

The pilot study system provided language model correction trained on an existing corpus [38]. We used a source-channel approach [9,10]: at each key press, we reduced the chance of outputting improbable letters by combining letter probabilities from the touch model with those from the language model. Additionally, at the end of each word, the language model auto-corrected to the most likely full word in its dictionary if the currently displayed word was not recognized (similar to auto-correction in the Apple iOS).

Pilot Participants, Procedure and Performance Data

Four participants each volunteered for three 1.5-hour long study sessions where they used each of the three keyboards. For each session they entered a combination of pangrams and random phrases from the MacKenzie and Soukoreff phrase set [23]. Participants were asked to type quickly and accurately, and corrected errors with a right-to-left horizontal swipe (as in [6]). They typed 5 practice phrases and 40 test phrases with each keyboard during each session. Mean typing speeds and uncorrected error rates were similar across all keyboard conditions, from 27.7 to 28.2 WPM (comparable to [6]) and 0.7% to 0.9% error rate.

Discussion and Simulation Analysis of Pilot Data

Although we had predicted that the personalized keyboard (*Adaptive-Bayes*) would offer a performance benefit over the control condition, typing speeds across all three conditions were similar. We identified two potential areas for improvement. First, the visual adaptation of the keyboard was unsettling to some participants, suggesting that the role of visual adaptation was more complex than we had expected. Second, we had chosen the Naïve Bayes classifier based on simulations with our previous dataset [6], but our current keyboard interface was substantially different; for example, [6] did not provide a visible keyboard or standard typing output. As such, it seemed prudent to reassess the choice of machine learning classifier based on the newly collected pilot study data.

We ran simulations with the data from the *Conventional* keyboard condition to compare the accuracy of several machine learning classifiers on this new dataset. The simulations tested personalized key-press classification models by running 10-fold cross validations on each participant's data. We tested a number of classifiers provided in Weka, including Naïve Bayes, Support Vector Machines, and Decision Trees. J48, Weka's implementation of the C4.5 decision tree algorithm, produced consistently high classification accuracy (with all features in Table 1: 82.3% on average across all participants). In contrast, the Naïve Bayes classifier that we had used for the *Adaptive-Bayes* condition did not perform as well (58.0% for the same setup). In addition, J48 was fast for building/updating the model and classifying key presses, which is obviously critical for a real-time system such as ours. Based on these findings, we chose the J48 classifier for the full study, with a normalization filter and default classifier settings.

Final Implementation

Based on the insights from the pilot study, we implemented two personalized keyboards that were exactly the same in all respects except that one visually adapted the keyboard (*Visual-Adaptive*) while the other did not (*NonVisual-Adaptive*). Both keyboards were initially rendered as rectangular QWERTY layouts (see Figure 6). *Visual-Adaptive* adapted the visual center of each key to be located at the centroid of all fingertip locations in that key's training history. To avoid excessive visual overlap between keys, *Visual-Adaptive* also reshuffled keys to maintain a minimum of 30 pixels (0.7") between key centers (Figure 5). For stability, reshuffling was done by maintaining the F and J "home" keys at a fixed location and translating neighboring keys away from F and J; this effect then cascaded toward outer keys.

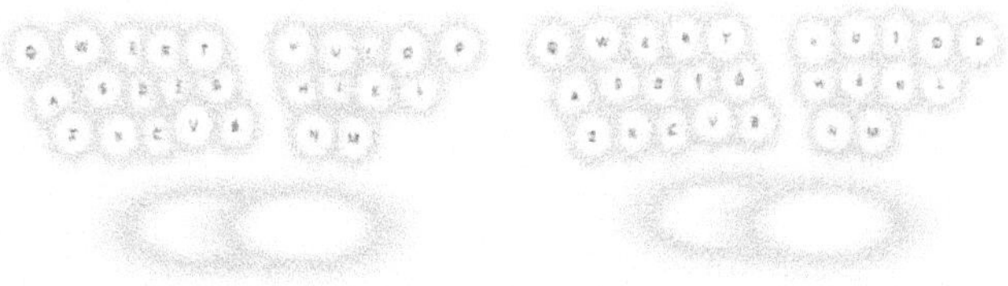

(a) Layout before reshuffling (b) Layout after reshuffling

Figure 5. Removing overlap between neighboring keys.

In contrast, *NonVisual-Adaptive* always retained a visually stable rectangular layout (Figure 6). As discussed earlier, adapting the underlying key-press model without changing the visual layout *increases* the chance that the user will press one visual key but the system will output a different letter. To mitigate this issue, *NonVisual-Adaptive* disabled the J48 classifier for one keystroke after a backspace, or if the user was typing slowly (< 1 key stroke per second). In those situations, the user is more likely to look down at the keys and target carefully, so the system simply checked which visual key boundaries contained the fingertip.

To select which subset of classification features to include in the J48 classification model, we used a wrapper-based feature selection technique [18]. That is, we incrementally added features to the model until no improvement in performance occurred. This process resulted in all features in Table 1 marked with a '*'. Additionally, we included the finger center *y* relative to the F and J keys for continuity, since the finger center *x* was already in the feature set; this inclusion did not reduce classification accuracy. With the

Feature Set	Classification Accuracy
Tip *x* relative to F and J keys*	53.3% (*SD* = 3.3)
Center *x* relative to F and J keys*	43.4% (*SD* = 6.7)
Tip *y* relative to F and J keys*	35.4% (*SD* = 2.0)
Center *y* relative to F and J keys*	29.7% (*SD* = 1.5)
Angle	28.0% (*SD* = 3.9)
Tip travel in *x* and *y* directions*	27.4% (*SD* = 1.9)
Center travel in *x* and *y* directions	24.8% (*SD* = 1.4)
Major axis	22.4% (*SD* = 1.5)
Minor axis	19.0% (*SD* = 1.9)
Elapsed time	14.2% (*SD* = 1.0)
Inter-key-press time	11.7% (*SD* = 2.3)
Majority classifier (right space key)	11.8%

* Used in feature set for final implementation.

Table 1. Explanatory power of classification features based on the pilot study data: mean 10-fold cross-validation results from a J48 classifier trained on individual features or pairs of related features. The majority classifier is the accuracy rate if we always classify as the most frequent key (right space key).

selected set of classification features, the J48 algorithm achieved on average a classification accuracy of 82.6% (*SD* = 3.8) across all participants.

Language model correction was not used in the full study because we observed in the pilot study that the *accuracy* of the language model—in our case perhaps unrealistically accurate—appeared to affect typing patterns. As such, we disabled the language model to control this possible interaction between the language and touch models and to isolate the effects of the touch model personalization.

Finally, to reduce the chance of inadvertent or spurious input, the user had to *activate* the keyboard by briefly placing all 10 fingers on the screen. The keyboards deactivated after 5 seconds of inactivity.

STUDY

We conducted a controlled, three-session study to compare the two personalized keyboards to a conventional static keyboard. We hypothesized that the personalized keyboards would improve typing performance and subjective experience compared to the conventional keyboard. Since previous findings are inconclusive with respect to visual adaptation [7,13], this study also allowed for an exploratory comparison of the two personalized keyboards, one of which adapted visually and one of which did not.

Method

Participants

Twelve participants were recruited through on-campus mailing lists (5 male, 7 female). Participants were volunteers and were compensated for their time. They ranged in age from 21 to 48 (M = 33.8). All were regular computer users and had experience with touch devices, with 10 of the 12 indicating they enter text on mobile touch devices often. In terms of physical keyboard use, one participant regularly used a natural or split keyboard, while the remaining participants used standard rectangular layouts. On a *physical* keyboard typing test administered during the study, participants typed 79.2 WPM (*SD* = 16.6) and had an uncorrected error rate of 0.2% (*SD* = 0.2).

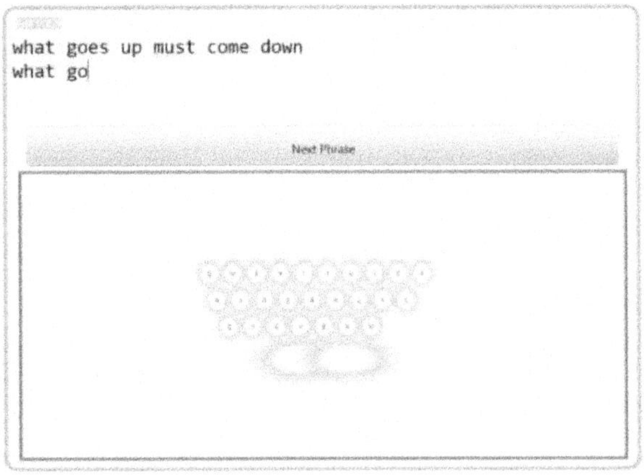

Figure 6. Experimental application showing the Conventional keyboard. Two space bar keys appear because the right and left halves of the space bar (corresponding to each thumb) were modeled separately in all keyboard interfaces.

Apparatus

We used a Microsoft Surface running custom software written in C# .NET 4.0. The system recorded all down and up touch events during the typing tasks. Participants sat at the Surface, which was raised ~5" off the ground with a custom-built platform to about the same height as a standard desk. The task interface, shown in Figure 6, presented phrases to be typed at the top of the screen. After typing a phrase, participants advanced by pressing the "Next Phrase" button. At the end of each condition, the system wrote all information related to the personalized key-press classification model and visual key layout to an XML file. This data was reloaded when the participant used the same keyboard condition in future sessions.

Experiment Design

The study was a 3×3 within-subjects factorial design with the following factors and levels:

- **Session:** Participants completed three sessions each.
- **Keyboard:** *Conventional*, *NonVisual-Adaptive*, and *Visual-Adaptive*. The *Conventional* layout was the same as the initial rectangular layouts for the personalized keyboards. Key presses in *Conventional* were interpreted simply by which key's visual bounds contained the fingertip. The personalized keyboards began adapting as soon as they had obtained 10 training instances for each key in Session 1.

Order of presentation for the keyboard conditions was fully counterbalanced within each session and participants were randomly assigned to orders.

Procedure

Participants completed three 1.5-hour sessions spaced at least 4 hours and at most 48 hours apart. Session 1 began with a brief introduction to the Microsoft Surface and experiment software. From the user's perspective, the adaptive keyboards behaved exactly the same as the *Conventional* keyboard until a minimum number of training examples had been recorded for each key; therefore, all participants began by typing 10 practice phrases and 20 test phrases with the *Conventional* keyboard. This data was used to seed the personalized keyboards. Participants then typed 5 practice phrases and 20 test phrases with each of the three keyboards. In Sessions 2 and 3, participants typed 5 practice phrases and 40 test phrases on each keyboard.

The typing task interspersed two pangrams with randomly selected phrases from the MacKenzie and Soukoreff phrase set [23]. To ensure we collected sufficient training data for each key in Session 1, the ratio of regular phrases to pangrams was 1:1. In Sessions 2 and 3, that ratio increased to 9:1. Subjective questionnaires were given after each keyboard condition and at the end of each session. At the end of Session 3, we interviewed participants about the keyboards. Additionally, participants completed a physical keyboard typing test (20 phrases) at the beginning of Session 1 or end of Session 2.

Analysis

The main quantitative measures were speed and uncorrected error rate. Speed was calculated as WPM [39]:

$$WPM = \frac{|T| - 1}{S} \times 60 \times \frac{1}{5} \quad (1)$$

where T is the final transcribed string and S is the elapsed time in seconds from the first to the last letter in the phrase. Uncorrected error rate was calculated as [35]:

$$uncorrected\ error\ rate = \frac{INF}{(C + INF + IF)} \quad (2)$$

where C is the total number of correct characters, IF is the number of incorrect but fixed (backspaced) characters, and INF is the number of incorrect (but not fixed) characters. Uncorrected error rate measures the errors *remaining* in the transcribed input, as opposed to those fixed "along the way," which take time and are thus subsumed in WPM.

For WPM and uncorrected error rate, we analyzed the 20 test phrases with each keyboard in Session 1 and the 40 phrases from each of Sessions 2 and 3. Since presentation order was counterbalanced within each session, we tested for effects of *Order* on WPM within each session. Two-way ANOVAs with *Order* as a between-subjects factor and *Keyboard* as a within-subjects factor revealed no main or interaction effects of *Order* on WPM. Thus, our counterbalancing seemed effective. We used a two-way repeated measures ANOVA for WPM with both *Session* and *Keyboard* as within-subjects factors for the final analysis. For all *post hoc* pairwise comparisons, Bonferroni adjustments were used.

The main subjective measures were NASA TLX workload scales [11] and rankings of the keyboards based on ease of use, efficiency, preference, comfort, how natural the typing felt, and frustration. We report the final subjective measures collected at the end of Session 3. For workload data, we ran one-way repeated measures ANOVAs with *Keyboard* as a single factor. For the ranking data, we used Chi-square tests to evaluate whether the number of times each keyboard was top-ranked in a category differed from chance. When the expected frequency values were too low for Chi-square (< 5), we used a randomization test of goodness-of-fit, which uses a Monte Carlo simulation to calculate the probability of the observed frequency values occurring by chance; it is robust against low expected values [34].

Quantitative Results

Figure 7 shows sample personalized keyboard layouts.

Speed (WPM)

As hypothesized, the keyboards affected typing speed differently; see Figure 8. A significant main effect of *Keyboard* was found on WPM ($F_{2,22} = 9.086$, $p = .001$, $\eta^2 = .452$). *Post hoc* pairwise comparisons revealed that *NonVisual-Adaptive* was the fastest keyboard. That keyboard offered a 12.9% improvement overall compared to *Conventional* ($p = .003$), a gap which increased to 15.2% by Session 3. *NonVisual-Adaptive* was also significantly faster than *Visual-Adaptive* ($p = .016$), which suggests that

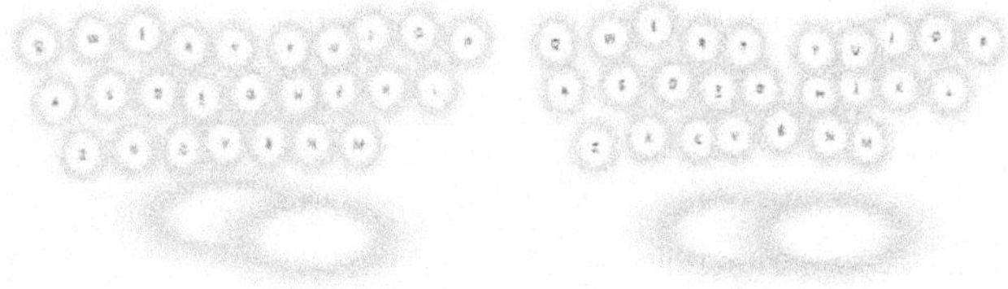

(a) Illustration of *underlying* model for NonVisual-Adaptive (b) Actual Visual-Adaptive layout, as shown to the participant

Figure 7. Sample adaptive keyboard layouts from Participant 10 at the end of Session 3. To the user, the NonVisual-Adaptive keyboard looked exactly like the Conventional keyboard, so (a) is an illustrative visualization of the *x,y* coordinates stored in the *underlying* model. This general pattern of increased adaptation from (a) to (b) is representative of all participants.

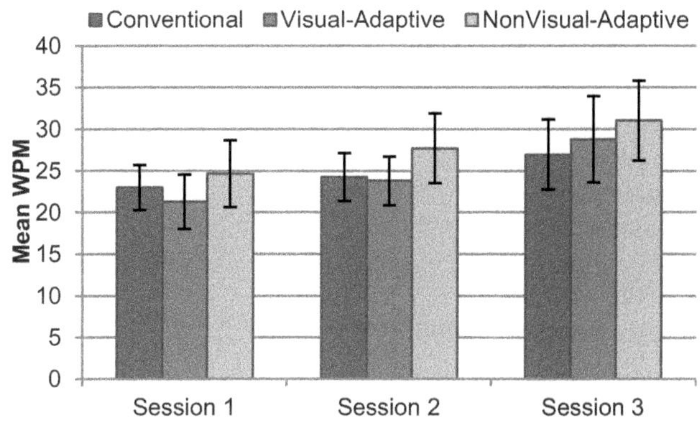

Figure 8. Mean typing speed across sessions . Higher is better. There was a general increase in speed over time, as well as an advantage of NonVisual-Adaptive compared to the other keyboards. Error bars show 95% confidence intervals.

the visual adaptation had a negative effect that counteracted the positive effects of the personalized classification model on its own. No significant difference was found between *Visual-Adaptive* and *Conventional*.

Participants also exhibited a general learning effect as the sessions progressed, shown through a main effect of *Session* on WPM ($F_{2,22} = 13.590$, $p < .001$, $\eta^2 = .553$). Trends shown in Figure 8 suggest that with additional sessions, typing speeds on all conditions would increase further. No significant interaction effect was found between *Session* and *Keyboard* on WPM ($F_{4,44} = 1.450$, $p = .234$, $\eta^2 = .116$), indicating all keyboards improved at about the same rate during the study.

Uncorrected Error Rate

All three keyboard conditions resulted in extremely low uncorrected error rates. The mean error rates were: *Conventional* at 0.30% (*SD* = 0.43%), *NonVisual-Adaptive* at 0.22% (*SD* = 0.26%), and *Visual-Adaptive* at 0.30% (*SD* = 0.49%). Because of the low error rates (29% of conditions had no uncorrected errors at all), we did not perform inferential statistics on this data. Note, however, that the means for both adaptive conditions were the same as or lower than for the Conventional keyboard. This data dispels the notion that *NonVisual-Adaptive* improved speed at the expense of increased errors.

Subjective Measures
Participants were asked to rank the three keyboards based on ease of use, efficiency, frustration, comfort, how natural the typing felt, and overall preference. Since some of these questions appeared to be capturing redundant information, we calculated Cohen's κ (a measure of categorical agreement) to group related questions. The three groups shown in Table 2 emerged, suggesting that the six questions had only captured three underlying themes. Cohen κ values between each pair of characteristics *in a group* ranged from 0.86 to 1.00; κ values between pairs *across different groups* ranged from .48 to .74. Thus, we tallied and analyzed the top keyboard votes within each group.

The majority of the time, *NonVisual-Adaptive* was rated highest in the Efficiency/Ease/Preference group, whereas *Visual-Adaptive* received the most votes in the Comfort/Naturalness group. Regardless, *Conventional* ranked poorly in both groups. Chi-square tests showed that the tally frequencies in these two groups differed significantly from chance (Efficiency/Ease/Preference: $\chi^2_{(2, N=36)} = 7.170$, $p = .028$; Comfort/Naturalness: $\chi^2_{(2,N=24)} = 6.250$, $p = .044$). For Least Frustration, a randomization test of goodness-of-fit using a Monte Carlo simulation with 10,000 random samples was not significant ($p = .423$).

NASA TLX workload ratings at the end of Session 3 were slightly higher for the *Conventional* keyboard ($M = 8.3$, $SD = 3.6$ across all measures) than for *Visual-Adaptive* ($M = 7.6$, $SD = 3.6$) and *NonVisual-Adaptive* ($M = 7.1$, $SD = 3.1$), but no significant differences were found.

Qualitative Findings
To contextualize the quantitative results, we interviewed participants at the end of the study. One potential issue with adaptive interfaces is the degree to which the adaptation requires the users' attention and distracts them from users' primary task; Jameson [17] calls this *obtrusiveness*. Eight participants remarked *negatively* on the visual adaptation in the *Visual-Adaptive* condition. This keyboard appeared to increase cognitive overhead for at least some participants because of the unusual layout; for example, P8 stated, "I felt I was constantly looking at my hands."

Interestingly, however, negative comments about the visual look of *Visual-Adaptive* keyboard were not necessarily reflective of overall preference or perceived efficiency. Four of those same 8 participants either commented that they could type quickly on *Visual-Adaptive* when *not* looking at the keyboard or ranked that condition as their preferred keyboard at the end of the study. P9 expressed this sentiment as: "[*Visual-Adaptive*]...seemed easiest this time – as long as I didn't look and see the odd spacing."

Ranking Characteristics	Conven-tional	NonVisual-Adaptive	Visual-Adaptive
Efficiency/Ease/Preference*	6	19	11
Comfort/Naturalness*	3	8	13
Least Frustration	2	6	4

Table 2. Tallies (higher is better) for top-ranked keyboard in each of three subjective groups. An asterisk (*) denotes a Chi-square test is significant at $p < .05$ on the distribution of tally frequencies.

In contrast, the *NonVisual-Adaptive* keyboard was designed to be much less obtrusive than *Visual-Adaptive*, yet to still provide adaptive benefits. Highlighting this distinction, the majority of participants (7) stated they had trouble defining the difference between *Conventional* and *NonVisual-Adaptive*. For example, P5 said of *NonVisual-Adaptive*, "I felt I just got more into a flow. I didn't notice a big difference between the two. I just felt that I performed better with [*NonVisual-Adaptive*]." Likewise, P7 said she couldn't "tell what the difference is but there's something about [*NonVisual-Adaptive*] that is easier to type with." Since *NonVisual-Adaptive* and *Conventional* looked identical, these comments reflect *NonVisual-Adaptive*'s benefit in terms of the mechanics or "feel" of the typing.

Unprompted, participants also commented on the ability to type without looking frequently at the keyboard. While no one brought this up in the context of *Conventional*, 5 participants commented that either *NonVisual-Adaptive* or *Visual-Adaptive* allowed them to get into more of a "flow" than *Conventional*. P6 also compared the keyboards to the iPad: "With the iPad you see the wrong letters and it corrects in front of you [using language model correction]. But this, I know I'm hitting in the wrong place and the right letter comes up, which is nice. I'm just not used to it."

Finally, a few participants made negative comments about *how* the *Visual-Adaptive* keyboard chose to move the keys, suggesting that there may be room for improvement for this design. For example, P10 commented that although he felt he was most consistent with the *Visual-Adaptive* keyboard, the keys had migrated quite close together, causing him difficulty. Two participants also explicitly commented that *Visual-Adaptive* got easier across the three sessions, which suggests that more training (both for the user and for the system) may further improve that keyboard's usefulness.

Summary
The *NonVisual-Adaptive* keyboard provided a typing speed improvement over *Conventional*, but *Visual-Adaptive* did not. Both personalized keyboards, however, fared well in terms of subjective feedback. *NonVisual-Adaptive* was ranked as most Efficient/Easy-to-use/Preferred, while *Visual-Adaptive* was considered the most Comfortable/Natural. Qualitative feedback suggested participants recognized the performance benefits of *NonVisual-Adaptive* even though they could not necessarily recognize the source of those benefits (because it looked the same as the control condition). Error rates in all three conditions were extremely low.

DISCUSSION
Our results show that a personalized key-press classification model improves ten-finger touchscreen typing performance. Moreover, *how* this personalization is

visualized has a significant impact. We found that the visually adaptive keyboard resulted in lower performance than the non-visually adaptive keyboard, which suggests users incurred a cognitive cost from visual adaptation that counteracted the benefits of personalizing the key-press model. This theory is supported by comments from participants, which confirm previous research by Himberg *et al.* [13] examining visually adaptive 9-key numeric keypads. Despite these issues, however, the visually adaptive keyboard shows promise in that it was considered to be the most comfortable and natural of the keyboards.

While we have focused on improving the underlying touch model for ten-finger keyboards, we envision that these personalized keyboards can be combined with language models. As noted in the implementation section, we disabled language model correction for this study to isolate the impact of the touch model adaptation. However, using a source-channel approach [9,10] to combine probabilities from the personalized key-press classifier with predictions from a language model should further improve typing accuracy. An open question is whether the use of a language model will result in changes to user typing behavior such that the touch models also change—might the two models interact, and if so, how?

In addition to incorporating language models, augmenting the personalized keyboards with audio or tactile feedback is also possible. Indeed, even the distal tactile feedback that has been previously used for tabletop interaction [26] should provide a benefit here.

In creating the two personalized keyboards, we made a number of design decisions that could potentially impact performance and user satisfaction. For example, only the last 100 key presses were stored for each key and the keyboards only began adapting after 10 training points had been recorded for *every* key (our study task included pangrams to expedite this process). Future work should explore how these decisions ultimately impact the effectiveness of the adaptation. One potential area for improvement is to ensure that *over-adaptation* does not occur. Particularly with the visually adaptive keyboards, a cycle of adaptation exists between the user and the system (the system adapts to the user, which, in turn, changes the user's behavior). Identifying points of stability in the input model may reduce the potential negative effects of this adaptation cycle.

With personalized interfaces, evaluations need to be designed not only to account for training time for the user, but also training time for the system. Although we conducted a multi-session study, performance improvements from the second session to the third session indicate that learning had yet to plateau for any condition. This issue may be most pertinent to the visually adaptive condition, since it was the most unfamiliar of the keyboards. Although not statistically significant, typing speed with this keyboard appeared to improve the most from Session 2 to Session 3 (Figure 8). A longer study would be useful for determining where performance stabilizes for all three keyboards, but particularly for the visually adaptive one.

Although we have focused on ten-finger typing, much of the design space for personalized keyboards and the study findings have implications for other modes of touchscreen typing. Two of the three major dimensions of adaptation—the underlying classification model and the visual layout of keys—should be equally applicable to mobile devices. Additionally, we tested a range of machine learning classifiers in the Weka toolkit that yielded reasonably high key-press classification accuracies, but further exploration likely will yield even better models.

CONCLUSION

We have introduced and evaluated two novel personalized keyboard interfaces that adapt their underlying key-press classification models based on an individual user's typing patterns. In addition, these keyboards explore two points in the design space of adaptive keyboards: one visually adapts while the other always maintains a visually stable rectangular layout. Results from a user evaluation showed non-visual personalization can significantly improve typing speed. However, visualizing adapted key layouts can negatively impact speed. Both adaptive keyboards received a positive subjective response and, as such, point to the further promise of this area of research. We have also presented a design space for personalized keyboards to ground our design decisions and to identify areas for future work. Although our focus has been on ten-finger touch-typing, the results and design space should also be applicable to adaptive text input techniques on small mobile devices. We believe this work is one step in a larger trend towards increased personalized interaction with devices.

Acknowledgments

The authors thank Rebecca Fiebrink, Jon Froehlich and Mayank Goel. This work was supported in part by NSERC, Microsoft Research, and the National Science Foundation under grant IIS-0811063. Any opinions, findings, conclusions or recommendations expressed in this work are those of the authors and do not necessarily reflect those of any supporter.

REFERENCES

1. Al Faraj, K., Mojahid, M., Vigouroux, N. 2009. BigKey: A Virtual Keyboard for Mobile Devices. *Proc. HCII*, 3-10.
2. Aulagner, G., François, R., Martin, B., Michel, D., Raynal, M. 2010. Floodkey: increasing software keyboard keys by reducing needless ones without occultation. *Proc. ACS'10*, 412-417.
3. Barrett, J. 1994. Performance effects of reduced proprioceptive feedback on touch typists and casual users in a typing task. *Behaviour & Information Technology 13(6)*, 373-381.
4. Benko, H., Morris, M. R., Brush, A.J.B., Wilson, A.D. 2009. Insights on Interactive Tabletops: A Survey of

Researchers and Developers. *Microsoft Research Technical Report MSR-TR-2009-22*. March, 2009.
5. Findlater, L., Gajos, K. 2010. Design space and evaluation challenges of adaptive graphical user interfaces. *AI Magazine 30(4)*, 68-73.
6. Findlater, L., Wobbrock, O., Wigdor, D. 2011. Typing on flat glass: examining ten-finger expert typing patterns on touch surfaces. *Proc. CHI 2011*, 2453-2462.
7. Go, K., Endo, Y. 2007. CATKEY: Customizable and adaptable touchscreen keyboard with bubble cursor-like visual feedback. *Proc. IFIP Interact*, 493-496.
8. Goldstein, M., Book, R., Alsiö, G., Tessa, S. 1999. Non-keyboard QWERTY touch typing: a portable input interface for the mobile user. *Proc. CHI'99*, 32-39.
9. Goodman, J., Venolia, G., Steury, K., Parker, C. 2002. Language modeling for soft keyboards. *Proc. IUI '02*, 194-195.
10. Gunawardana, A., Paek, T., Meek, C. 2010. Usability guided key-target resizing for soft keyboards. *Proc. IUI '10*, 111-118.
11. Hart, S. G., Staveland, L. E. 1988. Development of Nasa Tlx (Task Load Index): Results of Empirical and Theoretical Research. *Human Mental Workload (1988)*, 139-183.
12. Hartmann, B., Morris, M. R., Benko, H., Wilson, A. D. 2009. Augmenting interactive tables with mice & keyboards. *Proc. UIST '09*, 149-152.
13. Himberg, J., Häkkilä, J., Kangas, P., Mäntyjärvi, J. 2003. On-line personalization of a touch screen based keyboard. *Proc. IUI 2003*, 77-84.
14. Hinrichs, U., Hancock, M., Collins, C., Carpendale, S. 2007. Examination of text-entry methods for tabletop displays. *Proc. Tabletop 2007*, 105-112.
15. Hirche, J., Bomark, P., Bauer, M., Solyga, P. 2008. Adaptive interface for text input on large-scale interactive surfaces. *Proc. IEEE International Workshop on Horizontal Interactive Human Computer System (TABLETOP)*, 153-156.
16. Höök, K. 2000. Steps to take before intelligent user interfaces become real. *Journal of Interacting with Computers 12(4)*, 409–426.
17. Jameson, A. 2008. Adaptive interfaces and agents. In A. Sears & J. Jacko (Eds.), The human-computer interaction handbook: Fundamentals, evolving technologies and emerging applications (2nd ed.), 433-458. CRC Press.
18. Kohavi, R., John, G.H. 1997. Wrappers for feature subset selection. *Artificial Intelligence 97*, 1-2, 273-324.
19. Kristensson, P. & Zhai, S. 2004. SHARK2: a large vocabulary shorthand writing system for pen-based computers. *Proc. UIST '04*, 43-52.
20. Kristensson, P. & Zhai, S. 2005. Relaxing stylus typing precision by geometric pattern matching. *Proc. IUI '05*, 151-158.
21. Langendorf, D.J.: Textware solution's Fitaly keyboard v1.0 easing the burden of keyboard input. *WinCELair Review*, February 1998.
22. Li, F.C.Y, Guy, R.T., Yatani, K., Truong, K.N. 2011. The 1line keyboard: a QWERTY layout in a single line. *Proc. UIST '11*, 461-470.
23. MacKenzie, I.S., Soukoreff, R. W. 2003. Phrase sets for evalua-ting text entry techniques. *Extended Abstracts CHI '03*, 754-755.
24. MacKenzie, I.S., Zhang, S. X. 1999. The design and evaluation of a high-performance soft keyboard. *Proc. CHI '99*, 25-31.
25. MacKenzie, I.S., Zhang, S.X. 2001. An empirical investigation of the novice experience with soft keyboards. *Behaviour & Information Technology 20*, 411-418.
26. McAdam, C., Brewster, S. 2009. Distal tactile feedback for text entry on tabletop computers. *Proc. BCS-HCI'09*, 504-511.
27. Morris, M.R., Lombardo, J., Wigdor, D. 2010. WeSearch: Supporting Collaborative Search and Sensemaking on a Tabletop Display. *Proc. CSCW 2010*, 401-410.
28. Rashid, D.R. and Smith, N.A. 2008. Relative keyboard input system. *Proc. IUI '08*, 397-400.
29. Roeber, H., Bacus, J., Tomasi, C. 2003. Typing in thin air: the Canesta projection keyboard—a new method of interaction with electronic devices. *Proc. CHI '03*, 712-713.
30. Rudchenko, D., Paek, T., Badger, E. 2011. Text Text Revolution: a game that improves text entry on mobile touchscreen keyboards. *Proc. Pervasive 2011*, 206-213.
31. Ryall, K., Forlines, C., Shen, C., Ringel Morris, M., Everitt, K. 2006. Experiences with and Observations of Direct-Touch Tabletops. *Proc. Tabletop 2006*, 89-96.
32. Sax, C., Lau, H., Lawrence, E. 2011. LiquidKeyboard: an ergonomic, adaptive QWERTY keyboard for touchscreens and surfaces. *Proc. ICDS 2011*, 117-122.
33. Sears, A., Revis, D., Swatski, J., Crittenden, R., Shneiderman, B. 1993. Investigating touchscreen typing: the effect of keyboard size on typing speed. *Behavour & Information Technology 12(1)*, 17-22.
34. Sokal, R. R., Rohlf, F. J. 1994. Biometry: The Principles and Practices of Statistics in Biological Research. 3rd ed. New York, NY: W. H. Freeman.
35. Soukoreff , R.W., MacKenzie, I.S. 2003. Metrics for text entry research: an evaluation of MSD and KSPC, and a new unified error metric. *Proc. CHI '03*, 113-120.
36. Weiss, M., Wagner, J., Jansen, Y., Jennings, R., Khoshabeh, R., Hollan, J. D., Borchers, J. 2009. SLAP widgets: bridging the gap between virtual and physical controls on tabletops. *Proc. CHI '09*, 481-490.
37. Wigdor, D., Penn, G., Ryall, K., Esenther, A., Shen, C. 2007. Living with a Tabletop: Analysis and Observations of Long Term Office Use of a Multi-Touch Table. *Proc. Tabletop 2007*, 60-67.
38. Wobbrock, J.O, Myers, B.A. 2006. From letters to words: efficient stroke-based word completion for trackball text entry. *Proc. Assets '06*, 2-9.
39. Wobbrock, J.O. 2007. Measures of text entry performance. In *Text Entry Systems: Mobility, Accessibility, Universality*, I. S. MacKenzie and K. Tanaka-Ishii (eds.). San Francisco: Morgan Kaufmann, 47-74.
40. Zhai, S., Smith, B.A., Hunter, M. 2002. Performance Optimization of Virtual Keyboards. *Human-Computer Interaction 17(2&3)*, 229-269.

Bimanual Marking Menu for Near Surface Interactions

François Guimbretière
Information Science Department
Cornell University
Ithaca, NY 14850
francois@cs.cornell.edu

Chau Nguyen
Computer Science Department
Cornell University
Ithaca, NY 14850
cnguyen@cs.cornell.edu

ABSTRACT

We describe a mouseless, near-surface version of the Bimanual Marking Menu system. To activate the menu system, users create a pinch gesture with either their index or middle finger to initiate a left click or right click. Then they mark in the 3D space near the interactive area. We demonstrate how the system can be implemented using a commodity range camera such as the Microsoft Kinect, and report on several designs of the 3D marking system.

Like the multi-touch marking menu, our system offers a large number of accessible commands. Since it does not rely on contact points to operate, our system leaves the non-dominant hand available for other multi-touch interactions.

Author Keywords

Near surface interactions; Range camera; Bimanual marking menu.

ACM Classification Keywords

H.5.2 [Information Interfaces And Presentation]: User Interfaces - Interaction styles;

INTRODUCTION

With the wide availability of multi-touch surfaces, we have seen a revival of gesture-based interfaces based on this technology [4, 20, 21, 23]. The two prevalent tracking technologies (capacitive and optical tracking) are focusing on contact interactions. Although optical tracking technology can be modified to allow for interactions above the surface [2], interactions in free space may cause fatigue during long periods of use. Following the example of hover interfaces in pen-computing [7], we are exploring near-surface interactions, which take place a couple of inches above the surface. Because these interactions can be performed with the users' arms resting on the surface, they are better adapted to long periods of use. To explore this design space, we built an indirect tracking pad using a Microsoft Kinect, a commodity depth of field camera scanning a hand through a piece of acrylic (Figure 1). Using this system, we implemented a mouseless, near surface version of the Bimanual Marking Menu technique [16].

Permission to make digital or hard copies of all or part of this work for personal or classroom use is granted without fee provided that copies are not made or distributed for profit or commercial advantage and that copies bear this notice and the full citation on the first page. To copy otherwise, or republish, to post on servers or to redistribute to lists, requires prior specific permission and/or a fee.
CHI'12, May 5–10, 2012, Austin, Texas, USA.
Copyright 2012 ACM 978-1-4503-1015-4/12/05...$10.00.

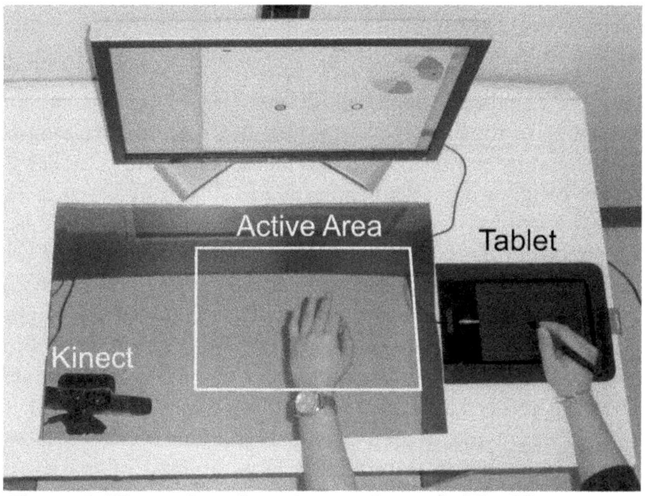

Figure 1: The setting of our interactive pad. The Kinect scans the hand through a hole covered with a piece of acrylic

As an invocation mechanism, we extended Wilson's pinching interaction [22] to take into account depth data and detect which finger is creating the pinch. This lets us simulate multi-button mouse interactions. We then explored the possibility of significantly increasing the number of markings by allowing users to mark in the 3D space just above the interaction surface. In the *layered* setting, users are marking on three different levels that are each parallel to the resting surface. In the *spherical* setting, an approach similar to C^3 [6] and Grossman et al.'s Volumetric display system [8], users are marking directly in 3D, both upward and downward. In the *hemispherical setting*, users are also marking in 3D but markings are flat or directed upward. The 3 designs have a similar number of available markings (24, 26 and 24 respectively) but different pros and cons we report on. Together, these extensions offer access to a very large number commands without introducing any devices or contact points for the non-dominant hand. This leaves this hand free to participate in other gesture-based activities.

PREVIOUS WORKS

Our work draws on prior extensions of the original Marking Menu system [10]. Several systems have demonstrated the use of marking menu in 3D to interact in virtual environments [6], to control devices from a distance [1, 11, 15], and interact with Volumetric displays [8]. While these approaches are considering free space interaction, we are studying near surface interaction for which both arms are resting on the interactive surface. Further with the exception of Lenman et al. [11] and Bally et al. [1] these

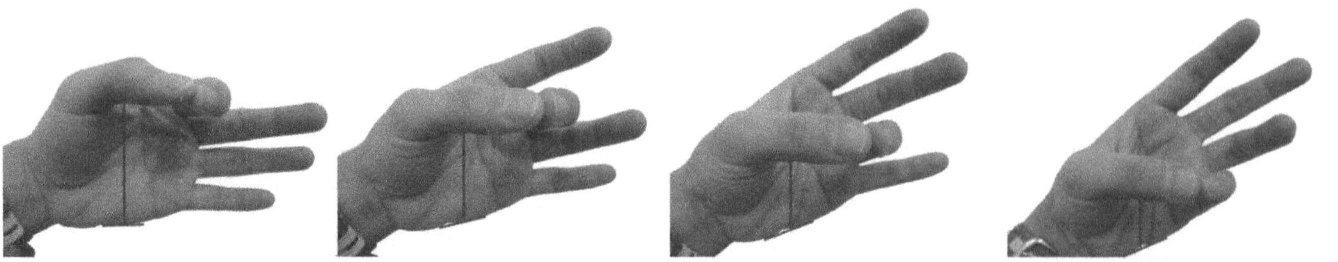

Figure 2: Multi-finger pinching showing the different poses of the hand depending on which finger is pinched

systems require users to wear a hand tracking system while we are focusing on bare-hand interactions using a Kinect.

Odel's bimanual marking menu (BMM) [16] is an extension of the marking menu [10] in which the marking is performed by the non-dominant hand. This setting makes it a very efficient bimanual technique as shown by Chen et al. [3]. The original implementation relies on a simple mouse for marking. This makes BMM somewhat unpractical for table-top surfaces because it forces users to switch between the mouse and bare handed interactions. One solution might be to use the SDMouse proposed by Matejka et al. [14], but our approach offers a larger number of directly accessible marks. Another alternative might be to use Lepinski et al.'s multi-touch marking menu system [12]. Our approach is an alternative solution to provide a large number of marks. It does not conflict with other multi-touch gestures, can be extended to parameter entry in 3D space and relies on a more relaxed posture for the marking hand.

NEAR SURFACE BMM

Our setting, shown in Figure 1, is based on a Kinect placed under a table that tracks the non-dominant hand above the table through a transparent window. To the right of the window is a Wacom tablet used to track pen interactions performed by the dominant hand. While the system described here could be used to mark with the dominant hand, BMM is very well adapted to the capabilities of our Kinect-based prototype. The Kinect is a somewhat low-resolution sensor (about 18dpi on the surface of the table). As such, it seems best to focus on marking interactions performed by the non-dominant hand, while leaving touch or pen interactions for the dominant hand.

We replace the multi-button mouse by combining Wilson's pinching system [22] with depth data provided by the Kinect. Depth data provide two important pieces of information: 1) they let us detect which finger is forming a pinch with the thumb; 2) they let us track the hand in 3D space allowing for marks in 3 dimensions.

A multi-button pinch using the Kinect

To simulate a multi-button mouse, we use the 3D information provided by the Kinect to detect which finger is forming a pinch with the thumb (similar to the PinchWatch [13] design). This is possible because, while the thumb is able to move in front of each finger, each finger has relatively little leeway to move up or down. As a result, the plane defined by each finger pinch is very distinctive (Figure 2).

To activate the menu system, the user performs a pinch gesture with his or her non-dominant hand. The user then moves the hand towards the direction of the desired menu command, and finally releases the pinch to finish marking. Our system includes a dead-zone of about 30mm, and feedback is provided after a 500ms timeout. A typical gesture is 45 mm long.

Implementation

We initially expected that implementing the pinching interaction with the Kinect would be fairly simple since the hand would appear much closer than any other object visible through the window. Unfortunately, the complex shape of a pinching hand creates a set of shadows in the tracking pattern (Figure 3). This in turn creates "holes" in the tracking data returned by the camera which makes simple 3D thresholding unreliable.

Upon receiving the depth data from the Kinect, our system uses PrimeSense NITE library to detect a hand entering the frame. It then limits further processing to a 200 pixel wide bounding box around the hand. Next, we apply Felzenszwalb et al.'s [5] segmentation algorithm on the depth map to identify possible holes and reject holes with skin color [19]. If a hole is detected, we proceed to compute the hole's plane by using a least square plane-fitting on the points at the border of the hole. To normalize the data, we then re-project the point cloud so that the plane's normal becomes the vertical axis. In this coordinate system, we

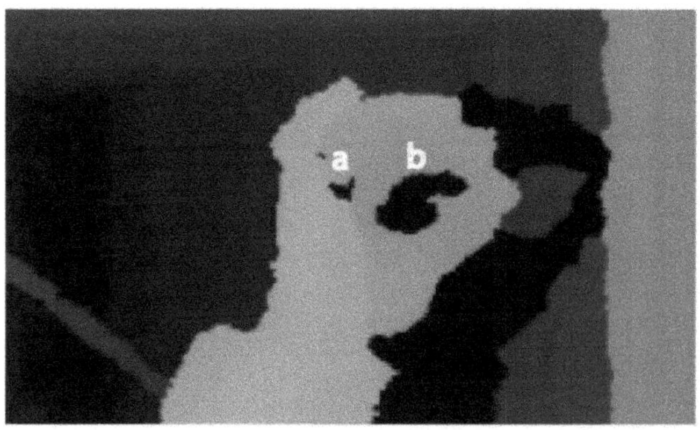

Figure 3: Multiple shadows created by the hand during pinching. a) self shadow within the hand; b) shadow of the hand seen through the pinch

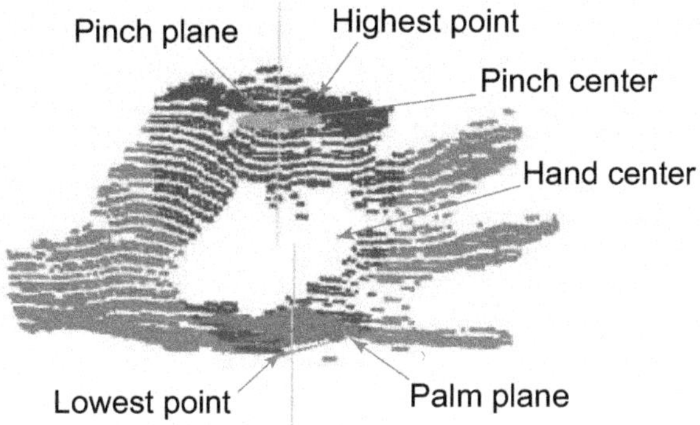

Figure 4: Raw parameters to be used by the Support Vector Machine for an index pinch. Only purple points are considered for computing the highest and lowest point.

compute the plane defined by the bottom of the palm, the points with maximum and minimum height inside a cylindrical bounding box centered on the hole, the middle of the hand, and the middle of the hole (Figure 4). These parameters are used as features to infer which finger is forming the pinch using a Support Vector Machine multiclass classifier [18]. We observed 93% recognition rate for the index pinch and 89% for the middle finger. We also considered pinching with the ring and pinky, but the recognition rate was too low and pinching with the pinky proved uncomfortable.

Near surface 3D marking

Since we receive 3D information from the camera, we can track 3D gestures. We focused on near surface interactions for which the forearms can comfortably rest on the table during marking. Importantly, the hand can still perform small vertical movements in this context. We considered several different approaches for marking in near space. The *layered* design was inspired by hover interactions [7]. In that case, a different set of menus is called depending on the height at which the marking is performed (Figure 5 left column). Three levels (each about one inch apart) offered a good compromise between the size of hand movements and robust detection. Assuming a detection system differentiating between two pinch types (index and middle finger), this allowed us to access 48 commands with a single mark (3 layers * 8 directions * 2 pinch types).

Another approach is to consider marking in 3D instead of 2D [6, 8]. In this *spherical* approach, one can mark in one of 26 directions accessible by combining compass directions with up and down gestures (Figure 5, middle). When differentiating between two pinch types, users can access up to 52 commands in a single marking. Noting that marking downward might be awkward, we considered a *hemi-spherical* scheme, in which marking is performed either flat, at a shallow upward angle (~30°), or at a steeper upward angle (>45°, Figure 5 right column). Assuming two pinch types, this yields 48 commands in a single mark. For all layouts, the number of accessible commands can be significantly increased by considering multi-marks hierarchical menus [24].

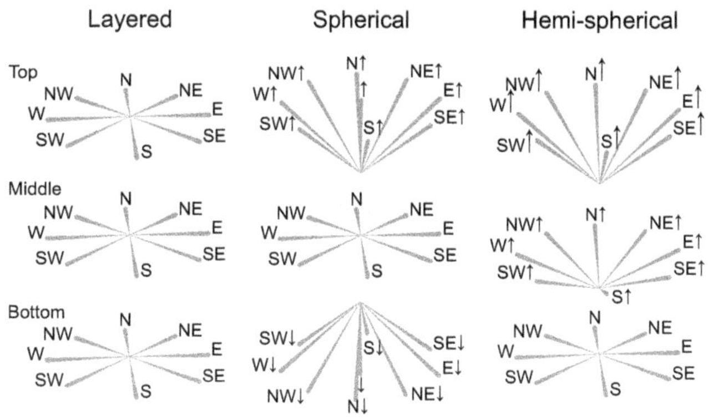

Figure 5: Three different settings for 3D marking in near space. ***Left*****: layered approach;** ***Middle*****: spherical approach similar to C^3 [6] and Grossman et al. system [8];** ***Right*****: 3-level hemispherical approach.**

DISCUSSION

We now report specific observations made in fine-tuning our marking system.

Sensor limitations

While the Kinect served well as an inexpensive prototyping tool, its main limitation is its resolution. This curtails reliability in detecting the pinch gesture. Based on an analysis of video footage, we discovered that the system detects a pinch earlier than perceived by users. This leads to longer stroke marking time, but may not influence total performance time since the extra marking time occurs during the preparation phase.

Another important problem is the default latency introduced by the processing time of the Kinect, which we estimate at about 150ms. At present, this limits the overall response time of our interface, although a more powerful image processing system would address this concern.

The placement of the camera is very important. In our implementation we had to place the Kinect below and to the left of the tracking area to allow for a clear view of the pinch gesture when the hand was in a natural resting position (see Figure 1). This setting also limited glare problems observed when the Kinect was placed below the mid-point of the window in the table. We believe that a custom designed optical system would allow us to address most of the occlusions problem we observed.

3D marking

Among the 3 marking solutions described above, the *layered* approach (Figure 5, left column) was found to be the most reliable in informal testing. As expected, the *spherical* approach was awkward with respect to downward markings, since one has to remember to raise the hand above the surface before marking down. The *hemi-spherical* design was unreliable since it is difficult to gauge the proper angle of a mark. Instead one relies on the height of the hand at the end of the mark. This approach negates the scale invariance which is key to Marking Menu [10] performance. Empirical evaluation will be needed to characterize these problems.

FUTURE WORK AND CONCLUSION

As a next step, we are planning to conduct an empirical evaluation of our system to compare its overall performance with systems such as the Multi-Touch Marking Menu [12]. We are also planning to explore how it can be extended to implement versions of FlowMenu [9] and control menu [17] allowing the non-dominant hand to control one parameter with 6 degrees of freedom after completing command selection.

We presented an extension of the Bimanual Marking Menu in which users mark in 3D using a pinch gesture of their non-dominant hand. We implemented our system using an off-the-shelf Kinect camera and demonstrated that we can reliably detect two different pinch types and up to 52 different markings. Our preliminary findings indicate that assuming a faster camera, the system has the potential to be a viable option for selecting a large number of commands on a multi-touch surface. Given these characteristics, our approach can aid in the implementation of complex applications on multi-touch surfaces.

ACKNOWLEDGMENTS

This work was supported in part by the National Science Foundation under grant IIS-0936105. Shenwei Liu provided the template for the drawing application we used for our prototype. We thank Corinna Löckenhoff for comments on an earlier draft of this paper.

REFERENCES

1. Bailly, G., R. Walter, r. M, ller, T. Ning, and E. Lecolinet. Comparing free hand menu techniques for distant displays using linear, marking and finger-count menus. *Proceedings of INTERACT'11*, pp. 248 - 262.
2. Benko, H. and A.D. Wilson, DepthTouch: Using Depth-Sensing Camera to Enable Freehand Interactions On and Above the Interactive Surface, Microsoft Research, MSR-TR-2009-23, 2009.
3. Chen, N., F. Guimbretière, and C. Loeckenhoff, Relative Role of Merging and Two Handed Operation on Command Selection Speed. *International Journal of Human-Computer Studies*, 2008. **66**(10): p. 729 - 740.
4. Dang, C.T., M. Straub, and E. André. Hand distinction for multi-touch tabletop interaction. *Proceedings of ITS'09*, pp. 101 - 108.
5. Felzenszwalb, P.F. and D.P. Huttenlocher, Efficient Graph-Based Image Segmentation. *International Journal of Computer Vision*, 2004. **59**(2): p. 167 - 181.
6. Grosjean, J., J.-M. Burkhardt, S. Coquillart, and P. Richard. Evaluation of the Command and Control Cube. *Proceedings of ICMI'02*, pp. 473 - 479.
7. Grossman, T., K. Hinckley, P. Baudisch, M. Agrawala, and R. Balakrishnan. Hover widgets: using the tracking state to extend the capabilities of pen-operated devices. *Proceedings of CHI'06*, pp. 861 - 870.
8. Grossman, T. and R. Balakrishnan. Collaborative interaction with volumetric displays. *Proceedings of CHI'08*, pp. 383 - 392.
9. Guimbretière, F. and T. Winograd. FlowMenu: combining command, text, and data entry. *Proceedings of UIST'00*, pp. 213 - 216.
10. Kurtenbach, G., The Design and Evaluation of Marking Menus. *PhD thesis, University of Toronto*, 1993.
11. Lenman, S., L. Bretzner, and B. Thuresson. Using marking menus to develop command sets for computer vision based hand gesture interfaces. *Proceedings of NordiCHI'02*, pp. 239 - 242.
12. Lepinski, G.J., T. Grossman, and G. Fitzmaurice. The design and evaluation of multitouch marking menus. *Proceedings of CHI'10*, pp. 2233 - 2242.
13. Loclair, C., S. Gustafson, and P. Baudisch. PinchWatch: A Wearable Device for One-Handed Microinteractions. *Proceedings of MobileHCI'10, Workshop on Ensembles of On-Body Devices*, pp. 1 - 4.
14. Matejka, J., T. Grossman, J. Lo, and G. Fitzmaurice. The design and evaluation of multi-finger mouse emulation techniques. *Proceedings of CHI'09*, pp. 1073 - 1082.
15. Ni, T., R.P. McMahan, and D.A. Bowman. rapMenu: Remote Menu Selection Using Freehand Gestural Input. *Proceedings of 3DUI'08*, pp. 55 - 58.
16. Odell, D., R. Davis, A. Smith, and P.K. Wright. Toolglasses, Marking Menus, and Hotkeys: A Comparison of One and Two-Handed Command Selection Techniques. *Proceedings of GI'04*, pp. 17 - 24.
17. Pook, S., E. Lecolinet, G. Vaysseix, and E. Barillot. Control menus: excecution and control in a single interactor. *Proceedings of CHI'00 Extended Abstracts*, pp. 263 - 264.
18. Tsochantaridis, I., T. Hofmann, T. Joachims, and Y. Altun. Support vector machine learning for interdependent and structured output spaces. *Proceedings of ICML'04*, pp. 104 - 111.
19. Vijayanandh, R. and G. Balakrishnan. Human face detection using color spaces and region property measures. *Proceedings of ICARCV'10*, pp. 1605 - 1610.
20. Wang, F., X. Cao, X. Ren, and P. Irani. Detecting and leveraging finger orientation for interaction with direct-touch surfaces. *Proceedings of UIST'09*, pp. 23 - 32.
21. Wang, F. and X. Ren. Empirical evaluation for finger input properties in multi-touch interaction. *Proceedings of CHI'09*, pp. 1063 - 1072.
22. Wilson, A.D. Robust computer vision-based detection of pinching for one and two-handed gesture input. *Proceedings of UIST'06*, pp. 255 - 258.
23. Wobbrock, J.O., M.R. Morris, and A.D. Wilson. User-defined gestures for surface computing. *Proceedings of CHI'09*, pp. 1083 - 1092.
24. Zhao, S. and R. Balakrishnan. Simple vs. compound mark hierarchical marking menus. *Proceedings of UIST'04*, pp. 33 - 42.

Group Hedonic Balance and Pair Programming Performance: Affective Interaction Dynamics as Indicators of Performance

Malte F. Jung
Management Science & Engineering
Stanford University
Stanford, CA, 94305, USA
mjung@stanford.edu

Jan Chong
OnLive
181 Lytton Avenue, Palo Alto, CA, 94301, USA
jan.chong@onlive.com

Larry J. Leifer
Mechanical Engineering
Stanford University
Stanford, CA, 94305, USA
leifer@cdr.stanford.edu

ABSTRACT
Inspired by research on the role of affect in marital interactions, the authors examined whether affective interaction dynamics occurring within a 5-minute slice can predict pair programming performance. In a laboratory experiment with professional programmers, Group Hedonic Balance, a measure of the balance between positive and negative expressed affect, accounted for up to 35% of the variance in not only subjective but also objective pair programming performance. Implications include a new set of methods to study pair programming interactions and recommendations to improve pair programming performance.

Author Keywords
Pair programming; affective interaction dynamics; emotion; systematic observation of behavior; thin slicing; team performance

ACM Classification Keywords
H.5.0 [Information Interfaces And Presentation]: General

General Terms
Human Factors, Theory

INTRODUCTION
Pair programming is a method where two people work together shoulder-to-shoulder at a single computer. Studies of pair programming in university programming classes have shown that pair programming yields better design, more compact code, and fewer defects for roughly equivalent person-hours [13, 30, 46, 55, 56]. Studies have also noted that pair programmers exhibit greater confidence in their code and more enjoyment of the programming process [8, 29, 30, 44, 47]. Positive results with pair programming have led to speculation that a collateral benefits of the practice may include improved morale and project knowledge shared efficiently across the development team in a manner that can be expected to improve productivity in subsequent development cycles [8]. In spite of these compelling results, the adoption of pair programming has faced resistance and skepticism from both managers and programmers. While this may simply be a result of either the novelty of the practice or skepticism of the larger methodological context (Extreme Programming/Agile methods) in which pair programming is often introduced, there is some evidence that pair programming may not necessarily be appropriate for everyone [16]. Furthermore there is evidence that demonstrates that pair programming can be less efficient than solo programming [4, 45]. Given these contradictions it is still an open question as to when and why pair programming works.

Permission to make digital or hard copies of all or part of this work for personal or classroom use is granted without fee provided that copies are not made or distributed for profit or commercial advantage and that copies bear this notice and the full citation on the first page. To copy otherwise, or republish, to post on servers or to redistribute to lists, requires prior specific permission and/or a fee.
CHI'12, May 5–10, 2012, Austin, Texas, USA.
Copyright 2012 ACM 978-1-4503-1015-4/12/05...$10.00.

While past research focusing on pair programming interactions has looked at personality type influences [31, 50, 51, 53], and collaborative behavior such a keyboard switching [10], driving and navigating behavior [10, 12], communication [16, 52], and system complexity [4], no research up to date has focused on the quality of pair programming interactions by investigating affective interaction dynamics nor have methods been proposed to measure and study these dynamics.

Group Hedonic Balance: From Marital Interactions to Programming Pairs
In contrast to researchers of pair programmers, researchers of married couples have developed powerful methods to gain insights into relationship between affective interaction dynamics and long term subjective as well as objective outcomes [23]. Especially illustrative is a study in which Gottman and Levenson [27] showed that it is possible to accurately (93%) predict the fate of a marriage based on the affective interaction quality determined from just a 15 minute video sample of a couple's interaction. In another study, divorce could be predicted based on the affective interaction quality during the first 3 minutes of a conflict episode with 80% accuracy [9]. Using the same methods, it was possible to predict subjective marital outcomes such as

satisfaction and objective outcomes such as divorce across a wide range of studies [24, 25, 33, 40-42]. Central to these studies was the idea of a balance theory of marriage which posits that couple's ability to regulate the hedonic balance of positive and negative affect is critical for the quality of their interaction and long-term outcomes [22]. A classification of couples based on their hedonic balance into regulated (more positive than negative) and non-regulated (more negative than positive) couples in the studies cited above was repeatedly shown to be predictive of marital satisfaction and divorce. The notion of hedonic balance as a predictor of individual well being has been established in several studies [17-19, 35, 36], but besides the work of Losada [20, 43], to the authors' knowledge no research has been done to explore the relationship between hedonic balance and outcomes in work groups and programming pairs in particular.

The first aim of the research presented here was therefore to adapt a set of methods that have been successful in predicting satisfaction and divorce in marriages to solve the problem of understanding the relationships between affective interaction dynamics and performance in pair programming teams. Core to this set of methods are two techniques: Thin Slicing and Systematic Observation of Behavior. The second aim was to extend Gottman's balance theory of affect to pair programming groups and explore the role of Group Hedonic Balance as an indicator of pair programming performance. Specifically we hypothesized that Group Hedonic Balance would correlate with performance relevant outcomes:

> *Hypothesis: Pairs with a higher group hedonic balance will outperform those with a lower group hedonic balance.*

Thin Slicing

Thin-slicing refers to the process of making accurate classifications based on small samples, or "thin slices" of expressive behaviors [2]. The thin-slicing research showed powerfully that certain behavioral characteristics are stable over time and that only a small interaction sample is necessary to make meaningful judgments about behavior occurring over longer durations such as hours, or even months. For example, in a frequently cited study, Ambady and Rosenthal [3] showed that end-of-semester teacher evaluations could be accurately classified based on judgments of 30 second silent video clips of the respective teachers. In addition to its more prominent applications in predicting teacher evaluations [3] and marital outcomes [9, 27], the method of thin slicing has been applied successfully across a wide range of other contexts such as doctor-patient interactions, family interactions, interviews, or work related interactions [2]. Particularly relevant is also a study by Curhan and Pentland who used thin slicing to show that the affective interaction patterns occurring in a short time interval are predictive of performance in dyadic negotiation interactions [15].

Systematic Observation of Behavior

Systematic observation refers to a particular approach of quantifying behavior according to which trained observers record occurrences of specific behaviors in correspondence with a preciously defined coding scheme [5]. The goal of this approach is "for properly trained observers to produce identical protocols, given that they observed the same stream of behavior" [5]. Often audio or video recordings are used as a basis for coding. One of two central components of the method of Systematic Observation is the catalog of behavior codes or "Coding Scheme". Two approaches can be distinguished in developing a coding scheme: To (1) derive it from existing theory "top down", or (2) develop it using a more grounded approach "bottom up", deriving it from the close observation of behavior itself [54]. The other central component of Systematic Observation is the demonstration of reliability of coders. Coder reliability refers to the level of agreement between two independent observers of the same stream of behavior. A common measure for the assessment of coder reliability is Cohen's Kappa [14] which determines the level of agreement corrected for chance agreements, in comparison to the often used percent-agreement. To test our hypothesis we employed both methods of Thin Slicing and Systematic Observation of Behavior as described in the following sections.

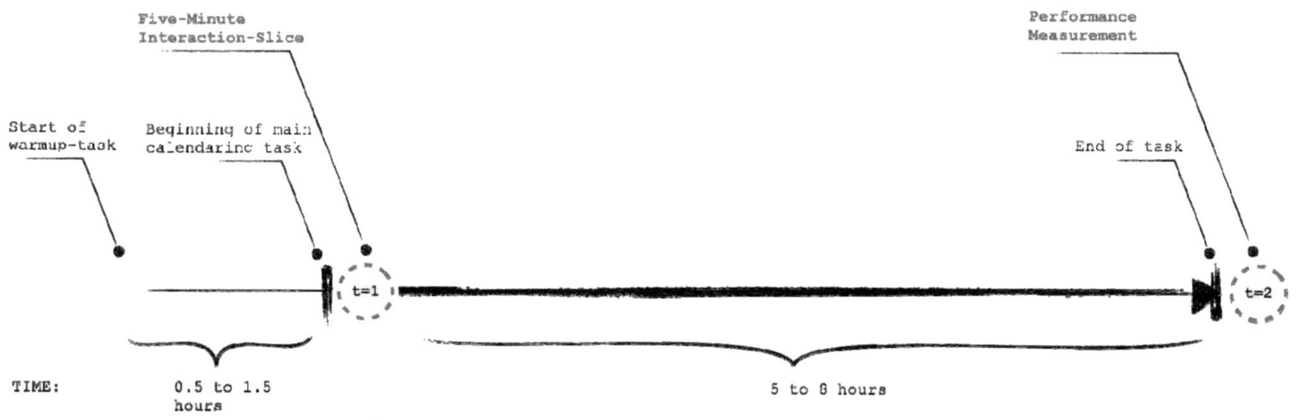

Figure 1. Pair programming study: Procedure overview.

METHOD

For the purpose of our investigation into the emotional dynamics of pair programming interactions we re-investigated a data set that was collected in a previous laboratory study [11, 39]. The original study was designed to explore differences in programming performance between pair programming and solo programming and therefore compared the performance of 19 pair programming groups with that of 19 solo programmers. For this investigation, we were only interested in the pair programming groups and their performance. The previous study had shown that the performance of the various pairs varied considerably but none of the collected metrics could explain the large variance in performance. For example, performance did not improve with similarity of the lab task to work tasks the programmers were familiar with, proficiency in Java, length of acquaintance with partner (possibly zero), or prior experience in pair programming with a specific partner. This made it particularly interesting for a detailed analysis of the differences in the affective quality of their interactions.

Materials and Measures

Video Data: Starting point for our analysis were 16 of the originally 19 hi-8 videotapes that were recorded during the original study. Two video records were missing at the time of our analysis and one additional pair had to be dropped because they misinterpreted the task. A video record always showed one pair programming group engaging in a short (ranging between 30 and 90 minutes) warm-up task followed by a longer calendaring task to develop a java program to find the best meeting times for a group of required and optional participants (see figure 1). Each pair was working on a single computer with two large flat-panel monitors, a single keyboard, and a single mouse.

The videos were recorded in a quad-view format, showing the pair from four different angles, resulting in a very low video resolution per stream. All subjects in the study were professional programmers, who were paid near-industry-standard rates for their time. Some of the programmers had known each other previously and some had not. The average time for a team to finish the calendaring task was 5 hours and 2 minutes ranging from 2 hours and 23 minutes for the fastest pair to 7 hours and 55 minutes for the slowest pair.

	Age	Professional Experience in years	Years to know Partner	Pair-Programming Experience (yrs)
M	27.6	5.05	3.38	0.5
SD	3.5	3.17	3.77	0.72
Minimum	23.5	1.75	0.0	0.0
Maximum	37.0	13.5	10.0	2.5

N = 16

Table 1. Participant statistics.

Performance Measures: We used two subjective and two objective performance measures that had been generated as part of the original study. The two subjective measures were (1) satisfaction with the programming experience, and (2) satisfaction with the developed code. Both measures were operationalized using one Likert scale survey item ranging from 1 (low) to 7 (high). The two objective measures were (3) duration to solve the calendaring task, and (4) code performance. Code performance was operationalized by scoring the developed code. The scoring procedure consisted of running the subjects' code on a comprehensive suite of 19 test cases that exercised all of the features they were meant to implement. Scores were determined by awarding one point for each test passed, resulting in a scale of 0 to 19 points. The average score for all pairs was 11.5, ranging from 0 points for the lowest performing pairs to 19 points for the highest performing pairs.

	(1)	(2)	(3)	(4)
Outcome Variables				
(1) Code Performance [0-19]	–	-.59*	.71**	.68**
(2) Duration [min]		–	-.07	-.60*
(3) Feelings about Code [1-7]			–	.79**
(4) Feelings about Experience [1-7]				–
Descriptives				
M	12.27	289.33	4.3	5.43
SD	7.52	98.96	1.53	0.92
Minimum	0	143	1.5	4
Maximum	19	447	7	7

Note: All correlations are Pearson correlations.
N = 16
*p < .05, **p < .01 (two-tailed)

Table 2. Performance measures: Pearson correlations and descriptive statistics.

Procedure

As an overall procedure for coding the occurrence of affective behavior in the videos, we combined a thin-slices approach with that of systematic observation of behavior.

Sampling of 5-Minute Slices: We extracted five-minute "slices" from each of the 16 video clips inspired by studies on dyadic negotiation interaction [15] and marital interactions [9]. We always selected the first five minutes of each video showing the pairs working on the calendaring task for a detailed affect-interaction analysis (Figure 1).

Five minutes segments were chosen because of what was thought to be a reasonable compromise between accuracy of the analysis and effort to code the videos. Ambady and Rosenthal's study about teacher evaluations showed that a 30-second sample is enough to even assess an interaction that lasts several months thus giving us confidence that a five minute sample is more than enough to assess a pair's interaction style [3]. This choice was also supported by Ambady and Rosenthal's [2] meta-analysis on thin slicing. They found that assessments made based on just 30 seconds did not vary significantly from those made from samples that were 5 minutes long. It is especially encouraging that they could show strong correlations across 38 different interaction contexts.

The first five minutes were chosen for several reasons. (1) When looking at interactions qualitatively from start to finish, we observed, that the general interaction style did not change over time. This notion is also supported by the thin slicing literature that showed that accurate predictions are possible, independent of the time the sample is taken at. (2) In research on marital interactions, it has been shown that particularly the startup phase of an interaction can give valuable insights and higher predictive accuracy. Therefore, even though any five-minute sample would have probably given us sufficient insight of the interaction style of a pair, this research suggests that the first 5 minutes are particularly useful in making accurate assessments.

Coding of the Selected Samples: For systematic observation, we used a slightly adapted version of the Rapid Couples Interaction Scoring System (RCISS) [37]. We chose RCISS for two reasons: First, it is faster than the Specific Affect Coding System (SPAFF), and second, it is more granular in capturing minute differences in listener behavior. The modifications to the original coding scheme were necessary to adapt the coding system so that it would capture the affective differences between the various pairs. Couples interactions such as the ones that were used to develop RCISS, show huge differences in expressive behavior because they were generated in the context of a highly engaging conflict discussion. The pair programming teams, on the other hand, were not set out to be in conflict, and they did not share a long history together and thus affective differences in between them were much more subtle. For example expressions of contemptuous or frustrated behavior are common in marital conflict interactions but could hardly be observed during interactions of programming pairs. The adapted RCISS used for this study consisted of 13 speaker codes and 10 listener codes (see table 3).

	Speaker Codes	Listener Codes
☺	Interest	Backchannels present
	Validation	Facial movement present
	Excitement	Looking at each other
	Humor/Laugh	Positive facial expression
	Empathy	Responsive facial movement
	Other Positive	
☹	Complain	No backchannels
	Criticize	No facial movement
	Constrained Anger	No looking at each other
	Defensive	Negative facial expression
	Yes-but	Stonewalling
	Put down	
	Tension/Tense humor	
	Other negative	

Table 3. Modified RCISS coding scheme.

The coding itself was performed in two steps using VCode, a behavioral coding software [28]. In the first step each video was segmented into speaker-turns (81 speaker turns on average). The second step then consisted of watching one speaker-turn at a time and checking all codes that applied from the list of available RCISS codes. An average 5-minute segment had a total of 146 codes with 22 speaker codes and 124 listener codes. Figure 2 shows a 16-second window of a coded video. The first author initially coded all videos, and 50% of the videos were randomly selected and coded by an additional observer. It took approximately 20 minutes to code speaker turns for each video in a first pass and 30 minutes to do the affect coding using RCISS for each video in the second pass. At the time the videos were coded, both observers were blind to the performance of the pair programming groups. Additional performance related data was only accessed after the coding was completed.

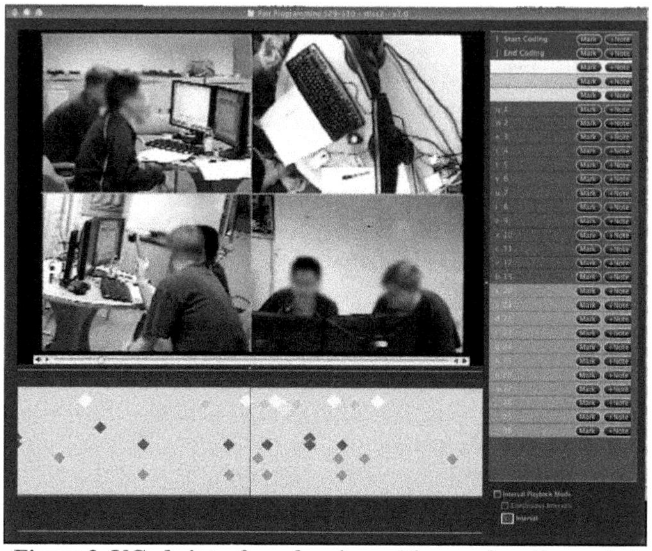

Figure 2. VCode interface showing a 16-second section coded with the modified RCISS. The orange and yellow squares in the upper rows indicate speaker turns. The red and green squares in the lower part mark occurrences of negative and positive behaviors respectively.

RESULTS

The average Kappa [14] for the modified RCISS coding was computed using GSEQ, a software for sequential data analysis [6]. The coder reliability analysis for the eight double-coded videos revealed a Kappa of κ=0.50 for the speaker codes and a Kappa of κ=0.44 for the listener codes. According to Altman [1] and Landis & Koch [38], these are considered moderate levels of agreement. From the videos that were coded twice, we followed established practice and randomly selected one file to be included in the analysis [21].

To analyze the data we compared measures of affective balance of each pair with the respective performance relevant outcomes. Based on the RCISS codes, we classified the programming pairs into five regulated and eleven non-regulated pairs as the main predictor variable. In studies of marital interaction this distinction was highly predictive of subjective (e.g. marital satisfaction) as well as objective (e.g. divorce) marital outcomes [23]. For each conversational turn the total number of positive RCISS codes minus the total number of negative codes was computed for each programmer. Then the cumulative total of the resulting scores were plotted over the number of speaker turns for each programmer.

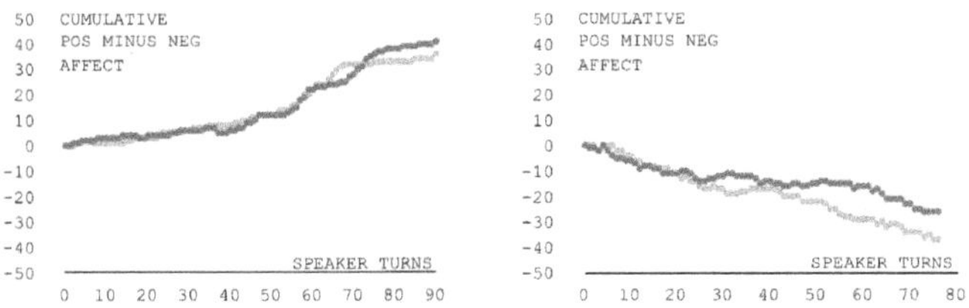

Figure 3. Point graphs of a regulated and a non-regulated programming pair. The graphs always show the emotion trajectories for each programmer separately. The left graph is drawn from a pair that scored amongst the lowest in the sample and the right graph is drawn from a pair that scored amongst the highest of the pairs studied.

We determined the slopes of each point graph using linear regression analysis. The average r-squared for a linear fit to the point graphs was 0.87, indicating a stable trend in each pair's affective style. As described in [26], we then classified a pair as regulated if both slopes were significantly positive and non-regulated if they did not both have significant slopes. Figure 3.3 shows an example of a regulated and a non-regulated programming pair. Additionally we calculated a second continuous predictor variable by taking the mean slope of the two regression lines as a measure of Group Hedonic Balance. As subjective outcome variables we used the satisfaction with the code and the satisfaction with the programming experience. As objective outcome variables we used the Code Performance Score and the Duration. A t-test was performed to test the relationship between the binary (regulated vs. non-regulated) predictor variable and the outcome variables. Pearson correlations were used to test the relationship between group hedonic balance and performance. Because the Code Performance score, $D(17) = 0.25$, $p < .05$, was significantly non-normal, we examined Kendall's tau correlation coefficients to test the relationship between group hedonic balance and Code Performance.

To recall, our hypothesis was that group hedonic balance would be correlated with performance and indeed the hedonic balance based classification into regulated and non-regulated pairs was predictive of several performance relevant outcomes as described in more detail below.

Group Hedonic Balance and Subjective Performance:

On average, regulated pairs ($M = 6.10$, $SE = 0.33$) were significantly more satisfied with the overall programming experience than the non-regulated pairs ($M = 5.10$, $SE = 0.27$), $t(13) = 2.25$, $p < 0.05$ (one-tailed), $r = .53$.

In addition, regulated pairs ($M = 5.60$, $SE = 0.40$) were significantly more satisfied with the developed code than the non-regulated pairs ($M = 3.65$, $SE = 0.43$), $t(13) = 2.85$, $p < 0.01$ (one-tailed), $r = .62$.

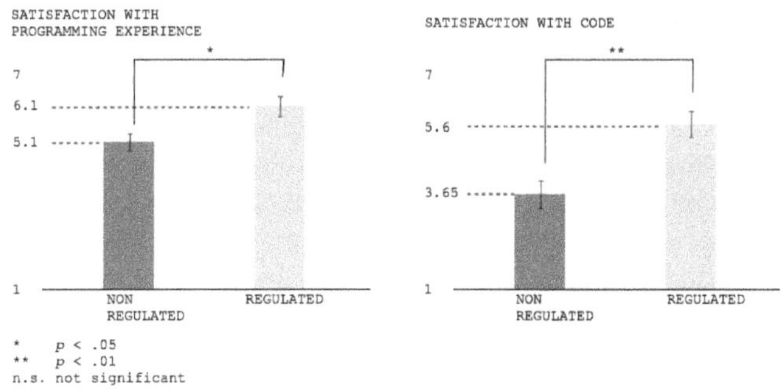

Figure 4. Bar charts comparing subjective performance between regulated and non regulated pairs. The figures above show the differences in subjective performance measures for regulated vs. non-regulated programming pairs. All error bars are +- 1 standard error.

We also noted that the continuous Group Hedonic Balance score was significantly related to the satisfaction with the developed code, $r = .73$, p (one-tailed) $< .01$, and to the satisfaction with the overall programming experience $r = .63$, p (one-tailed) $< .01$.

Group Hedonic Balance and Objective Performance:

In terms of the code performance scores, regulated pairs ($M = 18.20$, $SE = 0.58$) wrote, on average, significantly better code than the non-regulated pairs ($M = 10.18$, $SE = 2.35$), $t(14) = 2.25$, $p < 0.01$ (one-tailed), $r = .66$. In addition, regulated pairs ($M = 235.20$, $SE = 20.01$) took, on average, less time to finish the task than the non-regulated pairs ($M = 317.55$, $SE = 31.23$). This difference was not significant, $t(14) = -1.68$, $p > 0.05$ (one-tailed); however it did represent a medium-sized effect $r = .41$.

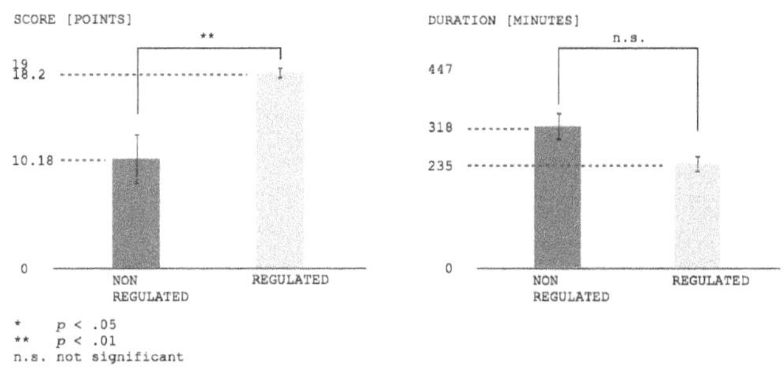

Figure 5. Bar charts comparing objective performance between regulated and non regulated pairs. The figures above show the differences in objective performance measures for regulated vs. non-regulated programming pairs. All error bars are +- 1 standard error.

We also noted that the continuous Group Hedonic Balance score was significantly related to the Code Performance, $\tau = .40$, p (one-tailed) $< .05$. Group Hedonic Balance was not significantly related to the Duration it took a pair to complete the task. However, pairs that scored high in terms of their code performance also took significantly less time to complete the task, $\tau = -.40$, p (one-tailed) $< .05$.

Exploratory Analyses and Results

In addition to testing the correlation between Group Hedonic Balance and performance, we performed an exploratory analysis to generate insights into specific affect behaviors and their relationship with pair programming performance. For each of the speaker and listener code categories, we calculated the average number of codes per turn and compared it with the subjective and objective performance measures (see table below). Additionally we explored correlations between the number of speaker turns and outcomes. Due to the exploratory nature of this analysis, correlations at the 10 percent level are flagged as significant as well.

The number of speaker turns in the five-minute slice was negatively correlated with the time it took for a pair to finish the programming task, $r = -.61$, $p < .05$, (two-tailed). Several positive and negative speaker behaviors were significantly correlated with subjective and objective performance metrics as shown in the table below. The strongest correlate with performance among the listening behaviors was the mere presence or absence of any listening behavior. The presence of back-channeling behavior (BCP) to take one, was significantly correlated with objective code performance ($r = .47$, $p < .05$, two-tailed), programming duration ($r = -.53$, $p < .05$, two-tailed), satisfaction with the code ($r = .69$, $p < .01$, two-tailed), and satisfaction with the overall programming experience ($r = .66$, $p < .01$, two-tailed).

	Objective Performance		Subjective Performance	
	Code □Performance	**Duration**	**Satisfaction with Code**	**Satisfaction with□ Experience**
Interactivity				
Speaker Turns	.26	**-.61***	.14	.24
Positive Speaker Behaviors (Counts per Turn)				
Interest	-.16	.40	-.06	-.03
Validation	.08	.19	.21	.03
Excitement	**.41***	-.31	**.50□**	.43
Humor	**.43***	-.24	.31	.44
Negative Speaker Behaviors				
Defensiveness	-.02	-.04	-.39	-.41
Yes-But	-.12	.10	.05	-.36
Put-Down	**-.40***	.24	-.17	**-.56***
Complaint	-.20	.37	-.39	-.32
Other Negative	.08	-.37	.04	.02
Tension	-.10	-.10	-.04	.02
Constrained Anger	-.27	.38	-.31	-.45□
Positive Listener Behaviors				
BCP	**.47***	**-.53***	**.69****	**.66****
FMP	.13	-.11	.48□	.21
LSP	.10	-.01	.55*	.42
PFE	-.29	.21	-.57*	-.26
RFP	.05	-.12	.18	.28
Negative Listener Behaviors				
NBC	**-.42***	**.50***	**-.71****	**-.64***
NFM	-.05	-.11	.21	-.15
NLS	-.10	-.10	.21	-.15
NFE	-.27	-.10	-.41	-.20
STW	-.20	.00	-.43	-.23
Aggregated Behaviors				
Positive Speaker Behaviors	**.38***	.03	**.46***	.28
Positive Listener Behaviors	**.34□**	-.27	**.58****	**.54****
Positive Behaviors	**.38***	.03	**.46***	.28
Negative Speaker Behaviors	-.15	.03	-.12	-.18
Negative Listener Behaviors	**-.38***	.25	**-.56****	**-.46***
Negative Behaviors	-.15	.03	-.10	-.14

Note: All correlations are Pearson correlations, only correlations with Code Performance (First Column) are Kendall's Tau correlations. The codes "Criticism" and "Empathy" are dropped because no occurrences were observed in the data. Variables are mean counts of behavior occurrences per turn. Negative Listener Codes: NBC = no backchannel behavior, NFM = no facial movement, NLS = no looking at speaker, NFE = no facial expression, STW = stonewalling. Positive Listener Codes: BCP = backchannel behavior present, FMP = facial movement present, LSP = looking at speaker, PFE = positive facial expression, RFP = responsive facial movement. N = 16. □p < .1, *p < .05, **p < .01 (two-tailed)

Table 4. Results of the exploratory analysis for the pair-programming study

DISCUSSION

We introduced the concept of Group Hedonic Balance to describe the affective quality of pair programming interactions. We found Group Hedonic Balance to be a powerful indicator for the performance of pair programming groups. A continuous Group Hedonic Balance measure assessed during the first five minutes of a software engineering interaction significantly correlated not only with subjective performance measures but also with the objective quality of the developed code. Overall the continuous measure was able to account for up to 53% of the variance in subjective performance and up to 20% of the variance in objective performance. In addition, we found that it is possible and meaningful to draw a binary distinction between regulated and non-regulated programming pairs based on differences in their affective interaction dynamics. This classification of programming teams into regulated and non-regulated pairs was predictive of subjective (up to 38% of variance) as well as objective performance measures (up to 44% of variance).

The usefulness of the distinction between regulated and non-regulated pairs was also supported by qualitative observations. What characterized non-regulated pairs were generally low levels of energy, with little interactivity, evidence of non-listening, and a constant presence of friction between the programmers. There was rarely any humor, or curiosity expressed in those pairs. Regulated pairs, on the other hand, exhibited high levels of energy and interactivity, participants often laughed or told jokes, and there were ample signs that the participants were listening to each other and visibly seemed to enjoy working with each other.

These results are especially exciting, given that our measures did not capture any content that was exchanged during the interactions but only their affective quality. We were able to explain large portions of the variance in team performance through affective measures, while measures of professional experience or familiarity with a partner did not correlate at all with performance (see table 5). These findings are consistent with recent discoveries that the performance of a team is not so much dependent on the individual intelligence of its members, but rather on their social sensitivity [57].

	Age	Professional Experience in years	Years to know Partner	Pair-Programming Experience
Code Performance	-.16	-.04	.23	-.11
Duration	.46	.27	-.24	.05
Feelings about Code	-.19	.0	.30	.07
Feelings about Experience	-.49	-.30	.47	.23

Note: All correlations are Pearson correlations.
N = 16, *p < .05, **p < .01 (two-tailed)

Table 5. Correlating team characteristics and performance.

Limitations

A limitation of our study is that the resulting sample size of 16 pairs can be considered low. However, a meta analysis by Hannay and colleagues [32], reviewing 18 empirical studies of pair programming, revealed that 16 pairs is a relatively large sample in comparison with current studies on pair programming: Of 18 investigated studies, twelve studies (67%) used smaller or equal samples sizes than the sample size investigated in our study.

One of the key questions to explore in future studies is the role of task complexity in relating affective interaction dynamics with performance. As can be seen from the error bars, the variance of scores in each group (regulated vs. non-regulated) varied greatly. While the regulated pairs all performed well, the performance of the non-regulated pairs covered a wider range of higher and lower scores. The large variance in scores is in line with the data collected in the original study that compared single programmers with pairs [39]. The study showed that in this task pairs did not show any significant performance advantages over solo programmers. Therefore a possible explanation might be that in the non-regulated pairs, one person might have just developed the solution alone. This is in line with research done by Arisholm and others who showed that pair programming performance depends on expertise and system complexity [4]. In one of the non-regulated pairs for example that still reached the highest possible code performance score, a highly experienced programmer took on most of the work by himself, leaving his partner to just watch most of the time. This explanation would suggest that in more complex and interdependent tasks less of the non-regulated pairs would be able to perform that well and the performance related variance might be lower. Further research on affective dynamics should therefore attempt to create task settings that are complex enough, highly relevant, and engaging. A possibility to accomplish this would be to recruit pair programming groups working on real long-term projects and video-tape them during a standard arousal task such as a conflict interaction [49].

Implications

Our research points to a range of implications. From a practical perspective it is important that affective interaction dynamics are seen as critical to technical design work in teams. It is important for both coaches of pair programming groups and pair programmers themselves to develop skills in monitoring and adapting the hedonic balance of their interactions. Design methodologies such as pair programming should be taught and practiced with a focus on affective interaction dynamics. Practically, this means that one should pay close attention to listening behaviors, subtle signs such as nods and "mhm", that signal that one is being listened to (coded as BCP and NBC). Any signs of condescension, domineering, or contempt (all coded as Put-Down) can also be powerful indicators for a programming pair not performing well. In addition to training coaches and programmers, automated sensing technology such as the sociometer [48] can be used to assess Group Hedonic Balance in order to give automated feedback about the state of a team. Possibilities could be considered to integrate affective sensing technology into software development environments to give feedback that can be acted upon by designers.

CONCLUSION

We showed in this study that methods and findings from studies of marital interactions generalize from those to work-groups such as pair programming teams. Our findings provide evidence that a balance theory of affect can be adapted from marital interactions to work groups. There is initial evidence that our methods and findings apply to design teams with three or four designers in longitudinal project settings [34].

Previous literature on affect and team-performance have focused on several aspects: (1) Trait affect or how people's emotional personality affects outcomes, (2) mood or how team member's internal emotional state affects outcomes, and (3) interpersonal trait attributions or liking, i.e. how the kind of attributions that people have about each other affect outcomes [7]. In contrast, we have focused on measuring specific emotion behaviors and the overall affective quality of team interactions and their dynamics. Rather than examining static affective properties of people, or their surroundings, with the methods introduced here we can unfold the dynamic affective properties of team interactions and how they relate to performance in ways never accessible before.

The quality of technical work in groups is often seen as dependent on the level of expertise, specific skills, or cognitive capabilities. We provided evidence that emotions are more than just ornament. On the contrary, they are critical not only for successful romantic relationships but also for high performance team work.

ACKNOWLEDGMENTS

We want to thank particularly Dan Lopez for coding videos, and for his incredibly valuable support without which this paper would not have been possible. We also want to thank Pamela Hinds, Scott Klemmer, and Robert Plummer for providing generous help in making this paper happen. Finally we would like to acknowledge unrestricted gifts from Microsoft Corporation, and the Kempe Foundation, that were used to support this research.

REFERENCES

1. 1. Altman, D.G., *Practical statistics for medical research*. 1991: Chapman & Hall.

2. 2. Ambady, N. and R. Rosenthal, *Thin slices of expressive behavior as predictors of interpersonal consequences: A meta-analysis*. Psychological Bulletin, 1992. **111**(2): p. 256-274.

3. 3. Ambady, N. and R. Rosenthal, *Half a minute: Predicting teacher evaluations from thin slices of nonverbal behavior and physical attractiveness*. Journal of Personality and Social Psychology, 1993. **64**(3): p. 431-441.

4. 4. Arisholm, E., et al., *Evaluating Pair Programming with Respect to System Complexity and Programmer Expertise*. IEEE Trans. Softw. Eng., 2007. **33**(2): p. 65-86.

5. 5. Bakeman, R. and J. Gottman, *Observing interaction: An introduction to sequential analysis*. 1997, Cambridge, UK: Cambridge University Press.

6. 6. Bakeman, R. and V. Quera, *Analyzing interaction: Sequential analysis with SDIS & GSEQ*. 1995, Cambridge, UK: Cambridge University Press.

7. 7. Barsade, S.G. and D.E. Gibson, *Why Does Affect Matter in Organizations?* The Academy of Management Perspectives (formerly The Academy of Management Executive)(AMP), 2007. **21**(1): p. 36-59.

8. 8. Beck, K. and C. Andres, *Extreme Programming Explained: Embrace Change (2nd Edition)*. 2004: Addison-Wesley Professional.

9. 9. Carrere, S. and J.M. Gottman, *Predicting divorce among newlyweds from the first three minutes of a marital conflict discussion*. Family Process, 1999. **38**(3): p. 293-301.

10. 10. Chong, J. and T. Hurlbutt, *The Social Dynamics of Pair Programming*, in *29th International Conference on Software Engineering (ICSE'07)*. 2007, IEEE Computer Society: Minneapolis, Minnesota. p. 354-363.

11. 11. Chong, J., et al., *Pair programming: When and why it works*, in *17th Workshop of the Psychology of Programming Interest Group PPIG17*. 2005, Citeseer: Brighton, UK.

12. 12. Chong, J., et al. *Pair programming: When and why it works*. in *The 17th Workshop of the Psychology of Programming Interest Group PPIG17*. 2005. Brighton, UK: Citeseer.

13. 13. Cockburn, A. and L. Williams, *The costs and benefits of pair programming*, in *First International Conference on Extreme Programming and Flexible Processes in Software Engineering (XP2000)*. 2000, Citeseer: Cagliari, Sardinia, Italy. p. 223-248.

14. 14. Cohen, J., *A coefficient of agreement for nominal scales*. Educational and Psychological Measurement, 1960. **20**: p. 37-46.

15. 15. Curhan, J.R. and A. Pentland, *Thin slices of negotiation: Predicting outcomes from conversational dynamics within the first 5 minutes*. Journal of Applied Psychology, 2007. **92**(3): p. 802-811.

16. 16. Dick, A. and B. Zarnett. *Paired programming and personality traits*. in *XP2002*. 2002. Sardinia, Italy.

17. 17. Diener, E., *Subjective well-being: The science of happiness and a proposal for a national index.* American Psychologist, 2000. **55**(1): p. 34-43.

18. 18. Diener, E. and C. Diener, *Most people are happy.* Psychological Science, 1996. **7**(3): p. 181-185.

19. 19. Diener, E. and E. Suh, *Measuring quality of life: Economic, social, and subjective indicators.* Social Indicators Research, 1997. **40**(1-2): p. 189-216.

20. 20. Fredrickson, B.L. and M.F. Losada, *Positive Affect and the Complex Dynamics of Human Flourishing.* American Psychologist, 2005. **60**(7): p. 678-686.

21. 21. GIESE-DAVIS, J., et al., *Macrovariables in affective expression in women with breast cancer participating in support groups*, in *The New Handbook of Methods In Nonverbal Behavior Research*, J.A. Harrigan, R. Rosenthal, and K.R. Scherer, Editors. 2005, Oxford University Press: Oxford, UK. p. 397-446.

22. 22. Gottman, J.M., *A theory of marital dissolution and stability.* Journal of Family Psychology, 1993. **7**(1): p. 57-75.

23. 23. Gottman, J.M., *What predicts divorce? The relationship between marital processes and marital outcomes.* 1994: Hillsdale, NJ, England: Lawrence Erlbaum Associates, Inc. xvi, 521.

24. 24. Gottman, J.M., et al., *Predicting marital happiness and stability from newlywed interactions.* Journal of Marriage & the Family, 1998. **60**(1): p. 5-22.

25. 25. Gottman, J.M., L.F. Katz, and C. Hooven, *Parental meta-emotion philosophy and the emotional life of families: Theoretical models and preliminary data.* Journal of Family Psychology, 1996. **10**(3): p. 243-268.

26. 26. Gottman, J.M. and R.W. Levenson, *Marital processes predictive of later dissolution: Behavior, physiology, and health.* Journal of Personality and Social Psychology, 1992. **63**(2): p. 221-233.

27. 27. Gottman, J.M. and R.W. Levenson, *The timing of divorce: Predicting when a couple will divorce over a 14-year period.* Journal of Marriage & the Family, 2000. **62**(3): p. 737-745.

28. 28. Hagedorn, J., J. Hailpern, and K.G. Karahalios, *VCode and VData: illustrating a new framework for supporting the video annotation workflow*, in *Proceedings of the working conference on Advanced visual interfaces*. 2008, ACM: Napoli, Italy. p. 317-321.

29. 29. Hanks, B., et al., *Program quality with pair programming in CS1*, in *Proceedings of the 9th annual SIGCSE conference on Innovation and technology in computer science education.* 2004, ACM: Leeds, United Kingdom. p. 176-180.

30. 30. Hanks, B.F., *Empirical studies of distributed pair programming.* 2005, University of California at Santa Cruz: Santa Cruz. p. 168.

31. 31. Hannay, J., et al., *Effects of personality on pair programming.* Software Engineering, IEEE Transactions on, 2010. **36**(1): p. 61-80.

32. 32. Hannay, J., et al., *The effectiveness of pair programming: A meta-analysis.* Information and Software Technology, 2009. **51**(7): p. 1110-1122.

33. 33. Jacobson, N.S., et al., *Psychological factors in the longitudinal course of battering: When do the couples split up? When does the abuse decrease?* Violence and Victims, 1996. **11**(4): p. 371-392.

34. 34. Jung, M.F., *Engineering Team Performance and Emotion: Affective Interaction Dynamics as Indicators of Design Team Performance*, in *Mechanical Engineering*. 2011, Stanford University: Stanford, CA. p. 109.

35. 35. Kahneman, D., *Objective happiness*, in *Well-being: The foundations of hedonic psychology.*, D. Kahneman, E. Diener, and N. Schwarz, Editors. 1999, New York, NY, US: Russell Sage Foundation. p. 3-25.

36. 36. Kahneman, D. and A.B. Krueger, *Developments in the Measurement of Subjective Well-Being.* The Journal of Economic Perspectives, 2006. **20**(1): p. 3-24.

37. 37. Krokoff, L.J., J.M. Gottman, and S.D. Hass, *Validation of a global rapid couples interaction scoring system.* Behavioral Assessment, 1989. **11**(1): p. 65-79.

38. 38. Landis, J.R. and G. Koch, *The measurement of observer agreement for categorical data.* Biometrics, 1977. **33**(1): p. 159-174.

39. 39. Leifer, L., et al., *Pair Programming: Myths Dispelled by Evidence. Unpublished Paper. Stanford University.* 2008: Stanford, CA.

40. 40. Levenson, R.W., L.L. Carstensen, and J.M. Gottman, *Influence of age and gender on affect, physiology, and their interrelations: A study of long-term marriages.* Journal of Personality and Social Psychology, 1994. **67**(1): p. 56-68.

41. 41. Levenson, R.W. and J.M. Gottman, *Marital interaction: Physiological linkage and affective exchange.* Journal of Personality and Social Psychology, 1983. **45**(3): p. 587-597.

42. 42. Levenson, R.W. and J.M. Gottman, *Physiological and affective predictors of change in relationship satisfaction.* Journal of Personality and Social Psychology, 1985. **49**(1): p. 85-94.

43. 43. Losada, M. and E. Heaphy, *The role of positivity and connectivity in the performance of business*

teams: A nonlinear dynamics model. American Behavioral Scientist, 2004. **47**(6): p. 740-765.

44. 44. McDowell, C., et al., *The impact of pair programming on student performance, perception and persistence*, in *25th International Conference on Software Engineering (ICSE'03)*. 2003, Published by the IEEE Computer Society: Portland, Oregon. p. pp.602.

45. 45. Nawrocki, J. and A. Wojciechowski, *Experimental evaluation of pair programming*, in *European Software Control and Metrics (Escom 2001)*. 2001, Citeseer: London, England. p. 99-101.

46. 46. Nicolescu, R. and R. Plummer, *A pair programming experiment in a large computer course.* Romanian Journal of Information Science and Technology, 2003. **6**(1-2): p. 199-216.

47. 47. Nosek, J.T., *The case for collaborative programming.* Commun. ACM, 1998. **41**(3): p. 105-108.

48. 48. Pentland, A., *Honest Signals: How They Shape Our World.* 2008: MIT Press.

49. 49. Roberts, N.A., J.L. Tsai, and J.A. Coan, *Emotion elicitation using dyadic interaction tasks*, in *Handbook of emotion elicitation and assessment.*, J.A. Coan and J.J.B. Allen, Editors. 2007, New York, NY, US: Oxford University Press. p. 106-123.

50. 50. Salleh, N., et al., *An empirical study of the effects of personality in pair programming using the five-factor model.* 2009.

51. 51. Sfetsos, P., et al., *An experimental investigation of personality types impact on pair effectiveness in pair programming.* Empirical Software Engineering, 2009. **14**(2): p. 187-226.

52. 52. Stapel, K., et al., *Towards Understanding Communication Structure in Pair Programming.* Agile Processes in Software Engineering and Extreme Programming, 2010: p. 117-131.

53. 53. Walle, T. and J. Hannay. *Personality and the nature of collaboration in pair programming*. 2009: IEEE.

54. 54. Weingart, L.R., M. Olekalns, and P.L. Smith, *Quantitative Coding of Negotiation Behavior.* International Negotiation, 2004. **9**(3): p. 441-456.

55. 55. Williams, L. and R. Kessler, *Pair Programming Illuminated.* 2002: Addison-Wesley Longman Publishing Co., Inc. 288.

56. 56. Williams, L., et al., *Strengthening the case for pair programming.* IEEE software, 2000. **17**(4): p. 19-25.

57. 57. Woolley, A.W., et al., *Evidence for a Collective Intelligence Factor in the Performance of Human Groups.* Science, 2010. **330**(6004): p. 686-688.

Learning How to Feel Again: Towards Affective Workplace Presence and Communication Technologies

Anbang Xu [1], Jacob T. Biehl [2], Eleanor Rieffel [2], Thea Turner [2], William van Melle [2]

[1] Department of Computer Science
University of Illinois
Urbana, IL 61801 U.S.A
xu26@illinois.edu

[2] FX Palo Alto Laboratory, Inc.
3174 Porter Drive
Palo Alto, CA 94304 U.S.A
{biehl,rieffel,turner,billvm}@fxpal.com

ABSTRACT

Affect influences workplace collaboration and thereby impacts a workplace's productivity. Participants in face-to-face interactions have many cues to each other's affect, but work is increasingly carried out via computer-mediated channels that lack many of these cues. Current presence systems enable users to estimate the availability of other users, but not their affective states or communication preferences. This work demonstrates the feasibility of estimating affective state and communication preferences from a stream of presence states that are already being shared in a deployed presence system.

Author Keywords

Affect; affect awareness; affect computing; workplace communication; presence; myUnity.

ACM Classification Keywords

H.5.3 [Information Interface and Presentation]: Group and Organization Interfaces – Collaborative computing.

INTRODUCTION

Affect plays a fundamental role in achieving effective communication and collaboration in the workplace [7, 21, 22]. In traditional work environments, where face-to-face interactions predominate, workers can leverage their perception skills to pick up on behaviors and non-verbal feedback to recognize others' affective states [13, 23, 25]. They use these cues to facilitate communication and decide when and how to initiate interactions [11, 18, 19]. Many of these cues are absent from computer-mediated communication channels, such as e-mail and instant messaging. As work becomes increasingly distributed, and reliance on computer-mediated communication increases, many of these cues will be absent. Misinterpreting others' affective state may lead to ineffective communication among workers, possibly forming barriers to the development and maintenance of cooperative relationships.

Permission to make digital or hard copies of all or part of this work for personal or classroom use is granted without fee provided that copies are not made or distributed for profit or commercial advantage and that copies bear this notice and the full citation on the first page. To copy otherwise, or republish, to post on servers or to redistribute to lists, requires prior specific permission and/or a fee.
CHI'12, May 5–10, 2012, Austin, Texas, USA.
Copyright 2012 ACM 978-1-4503-1015-4/12/05...$10.00.

Developing technology that supports communication and coworker awareness has been a focus of much research, including studies of presence systems [4, 12, 17, 41, 44, 45]. These systems fuse software and environmental sensing with communication tools to provide users with insights into physical presence and availability of workers, providing states such as *in office*, *in a meeting*, or *working remotely*. Presence systems have proven valuable in improving workplace communication [4, 41, 45].

Current state-of-the-art presence technologies provide users with little support for assessing others' affective states. Typically presence systems are designed to be passive, running in the background with little user intervention. In contrast, current techniques to measure affect are quite invasive or burdensome to users. Many techniques require users to wear sensors, to accept linguistic analysis of their writing as they type, or to actively input their affective state [5, 14, 26, 32, 36, 38].

In this work, our main goal was to explore the feasibility of modeling users' affective states and communication preferences using non-invasive information already being shared in a particular presence system, myUnity [45]. We used experience sampling methodology [8] to collect ground truth data for this modeling effort, and to assess the existing level of affect awareness in a workplace whose employees are technologically sophisticated and fluent in the use of computer-mediated communication media. Most of the participants in our study had more than one year of experience using the myUnity presence system, used a variety of communication technologies, and many had worked together for several years and knew each other well. Nevertheless, the results of our study confirm prior research that even workers who know each other well need better tools to assess each other's affect and communication preferences when they are not communicating face-to-face.

Using data from a presence stream already being shared within myUnity, we developed a modeling approach that significantly outperforms humans in estimating affective state and current communication channel preferences. Our results show that this modeling approach, using only presence states, compared favorably to results from prior, heavier weight approaches. We also modeled affect using a rich array of keyboard, mouse, and desktop window activity data. The accuracy of our lower bandwidth and less invasive presence-stream approach is comparable to the more comprehensive approach. Combining both approaches provides yet higher overall accuracy.

The major contributions of this paper are:

- Results showing that using less invasive sensing to model affective state and communication preferences can achieve accuracy rates as high as 87%.
- Confirmation that users fluent in the use of computer-mediated technology and experienced with presence systems have poor estimates of each other's moods.

RELATED WORK

Presence systems

Early projects, such as the Active Badge system [44] and the Portholes project [12], provided awareness of people's physical environments via a closed-circuit video feed. Instant message systems often show whether contacts are online or not and generally provide means for users to set their status. More advanced systems, such as MyVine [17], ConNexus [41], and Connecto [4], collect information from a variety of sources, including shared calendars, IM status, and various sensors, to report a user's activity and location.

One such system is myUnity [45]. Our work leverages myUnity's data stream to provide estimates of affect and communication preferences. We chose it because it is one of the only presence systems that has been adopted for daily use in a workplace: myUnity has been in continuous use by more than 30 users for over two years. Like other presence systems, myUnity collects data from cameras, Bluetooth and WiFi devices, mouse and keyboard activity, network connectivity, IM availability, and employee calendars. At regular intervals, each user's data is aggregated and summarized into a presence state. These states include, but are not limited to: *in office, has visitor, in building, active online remotely,* and *connected via mobile client.*

A field study [45] showed that myUnity was well received by its users, who incorporated it into their daily routine to help coordinate with colleagues. It has been effective in improving users' awareness of others' availability. While users have found myUnity to be useful in choosing communication media, it does not provide information on communication preferences or emotional state. In our work, we examine the feasibility of estimating communication preferences and emotional states from presence data.

Affect in Communication and Collaboration

We are interested in estimating affect because it plays such a key role in communication throughout the communication process [11]. According to the Affect Infusion Model (AIM) [19], the extent to which affect influences people's behavior depends on the complexity of a situation. Tasks that require elaborate, substantive processing are more likely to be influenced by affect than simple tasks. Empirical findings show that affect impacts cognitive processes involved in communication, such as decision making [18]. These effects are significantly greater for responses to unexpected than to expected requests. Also, people in negative moods form a more negative impression of the requests.

Affect influences a variety of performance-relevant outcomes, such as judgments, attitudinal responses, creativity, risk taking, and absenteeism [6]. Positive affect enhances creative problem solving and cognitive flexibility [31, 33] and facilitates the generation, selection, and amplification of ideas during collaboration [1]. Positive mood enhances altruistic behavior, including in the workplace [31]. A study involving self-report of positive moods over a week predicted workers' ratings of altruism on the job [21]. Helping others was found to be useful in maintaining a momentary positive mood [15].

Ekman demonstrated that facial expressions for anger, disgust, fear, joy, sadness, and surprise are universally recognized across cultures [13]. While Guillory et al. showed that affect information can be transferred via linguistic cues in computer-mediated channels [23], there are cultural and individual differences in the ability to perceive this information [35]. Affect awareness is an essential component of *emotional intelligence* [35]. Workers with higher emotional intelligence demonstrate higher social competence [7], better strategic decision-making [22], stronger workgroup cohesion, employee performance, and organizational commitment [10]. Our work examines the degree of affect awareness in the modern workplace and proposes techniques to enhance affect awareness among workers.

Systems that estimate affect

Systems can estimate affect from a variety of features, such as facial expressions, gestures, vocal intonation, language, and physiological factors [38]. Signals from wearable sensors, such as pupil dilation, arm movement, skin temperature, and heat flux, can be used to infer users' affective states [32]. Affect can be linguistically inferred in the textual domain via word choice, word count, punctuation, and timing (text-based chat [26], weblog [36], microblog [5]). Epp et al. [14] utilize keystroke dynamics to determine users' affective states. Their method is less invasive and more likely to be accepted than linguistic analysis or wearable sensors. However, the model performs well only when users type predefined text. In this work, we explore the less invasive approach of using a passive awareness system's data stream to estimate emotional state.

Communication medium selection

Our work also examines communication medium selection. Media richness theory suggests that different communication channels have different capacities for resolving equivocality and uncertainty. Rich media, such as face-to-face communication and phone conversation, are suitable for handling equivocality, while lean media such as email

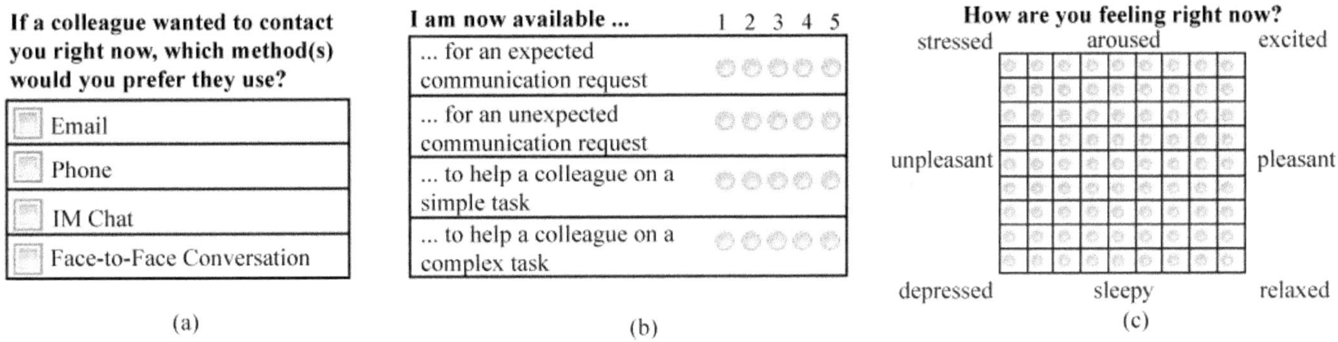

Figure 1. An example of questions in the survey. (a) Communication channel preference; (b) Responses to communication and task requests, using a 5 point scale (1=strongly disagree, 2 = disagree, 3=neutral, 4=agree, 5=strongly agree; and (c) the affect grid.

are more appropriate for reducing uncertainty [9]. Context also influences communication medium selection [27, 42]. People use contextual information, such as availability [40], interruptibility [16], breakpoints [30], and activity content [34], to help decide when to contact their colleagues.

Systems that estimate communication preferences

Horvitz et al. have inferred the cost of interruption based on activity sensing [28]. Their system recognizes office activities [37] and can make automated decisions to defer communication requests such as phone calls according to its users' cost of interruption [29]. ActivitySpotter can estimate the content or topic of a user's activity from accessed documents. This information can influence other users' decisions as to whether and when to contact the user [34]. Our work is complementary to this research. It advances the state of the art by proposing an estimation technique that is less invasive than prior techniques. Our method produces valid predictions even when users are not using their desktop computers, a limitation of many prior approaches.

AFFECT AND GROUND TRUTH

We gathered the ground truth data needed to build and evaluate a predictive model of affect in a field study. While affect is covered well in prior work, this investigation also provides further evidence of the need for and potential value of affect awareness technologies. More importantly, it would show the existence of such need and value *within* the same population that yielded the data from which our predictive models are to be created.

Twenty-three employees from a multi-national corporation were recruited to participate in our study. They were all knowledge workers who were familiar with modern communication technologies. The primary work location was the same for all participants, a single floor of an office building located on the US West Coast. All have been using the myUnity presence system, many for well over a year. Participants consisted of 17 men and 6 women ranging in age from the late twenties to the early sixties. Most participants generally worked in teams on several projects at a time, where the project team members varied by project. Six participants were summer interns who shared a room. Two were administrative assistants who could see each other from their cubicle desks. Others included staff members, executives, IT, and administrators, all of whom had their own offices or cubicles.

Experience Sampling Study

To gather as accurate an assessment as possible from participants, we chose an in-situ experience sampling methodology [8] for data collection. In this method, participants are asked to stop at certain times to make notes of their experience, such as current feelings and preferences. We sent participants a link to a survey form via both text message (SMS) and email five to eight times a day during their working hours over a two-week period. We collected data only during normal work hours of 8 AM to 7 PM. Thus, the number of times the survey was sent varied, as some participants work part time or irregular hours.

At each time period, participants were asked to report their location, current communication media preferences (Figure 1a), preferences with respect to requests from colleagues (Figure 1b), current affective state (Figure 1c), and, optionally, their estimate of another colleague's affective state. They had a 20-minute window to fill out the survey after receiving the alert. Participants knew that their reports were anonymous and available only to the researchers.

They reported their feelings via an *affect grid*, a frequently used in situ measure [39]. This 9×9 grid places pleasantness along the horizontal dimension and arousal along the vertical one. Endpoints are marked with emotion words to facilitate reporting. The middle row and column are neutral. Participants marked the position in the affect grid that best corresponded to how they felt at the sampling moment.

Our instructions provided several examples of each type of communication request and task. For instance, expected communications included scheduled meetings or discussions with colleagues the user works with closely and talks with daily. An example of a complex task was helping a colleague generate ideas for a project. Examples were also provided for the use of the affect grid.

	Distribution	Mean	sd
Pleasure Score		0.44	1.93
Arousal Score		0.55	1.84

Figure 2. Distributions of pleasure and arousal responses with means and standard deviations. The light red bars indicate medians.

Awareness Data

During the two-week study, we also collected two types of empirical awareness data from participants:

- MyUnity usage data. 18 presence states are provided by myUnity (e.g., *in office*, *in building*, *connected via mobile client*). For each transition in presence state, the state was captured with its corresponding timestamps.
- Computer usage data. We logged the state of each user's desktop (e.g., number of maximized, minimized, normal windows, window size, window coordinates) every second. Also, whenever a participant moved the mouse or pressed a key, the action was logged. These data were captured to allow us to compare our new method against those already proposed in the literature.

Post-study Questionnaire

At the end of the study, participants completed a semi-structured questionnaire designed to elicit quantitative responses regarding their subjective experience with perceiving and sharing affect information.

RESULTS FROM THE STUDY

We received 1,445 responses from the participants with an overall response rate of 76%. Responses per participant ranged from 26 to 97, with a median of 58 (mean = 60.2, sd = 24.3). While the main goal of the study was to collect ground truth for our affective state and communication preference modeling, it also provided further data on affect

	Pleasure (n=1184)	Arousal (n=1217)	Location (n=1445)
Email	χ^2 (1) = 4.33 $p < 0.05$	χ^2 (1) = 2.09 *ns*	χ^2 (1) = 34.16 $p < 0.001$
Phone	χ^2 (1) = 65.55 $p < 0.001$	χ^2 (1) = 1.33 *ns*	χ^2 (1) = 0.95 *ns*
IM	χ^2 (1) = 4.29 $p < 0.05$	χ^2 (1) = 11.09 $p < 0.001$	χ2 (1) = 15.08 $p < 0.001$
Face-to-Face	χ^2 (1) = 44.71 $p < 0.001$	χ^2 (1) = 2.47 *ns*	χ^2 (1) = 96.82 $p < 0.001$

Figure 3. Each cell shows the chi-square test with Yates correction for preference differences for a communication channel by pleasure, arousal, or location.

awareness in the workplace. Results confirm and extend the findings of previous studies *within the same population from which our predictive models are created.* We will describe these findings first, then the modeling approach and its results.

Figure 2 shows the distributions of participants' affect for both pleasure and arousal. Both distributions are slightly skewed in the direction of positive pleasure and arousal. Medians for both pleasure and arousal were 1. Consistent with past psychology research [39], pleasure and arousal were uncorrelated (Pearson r = 0.03, p = 0.23). Additionally, responses for most participants ranged across 6 or more of 9 possible values (86% of users for pleasure; 73% for arousal), suggesting no response bias.

Due to the nature of ESM, we cannot control the number of samples in each category. In order to ensure sufficiently high bin counts for statistical analysis, we followed [14] in removing the neutral category, which had many fewer responses than either the positive or negative categories, then collapsed the ground truth data to positive (score > 0) or negative (score < 0) in our analyses. This approach also enables us to compare directly with prior affect research studies that use a similar coarse level [14, 33, 19, 20, 43].

Media Preference

Figure 3 shows chi square tests comparing participants'

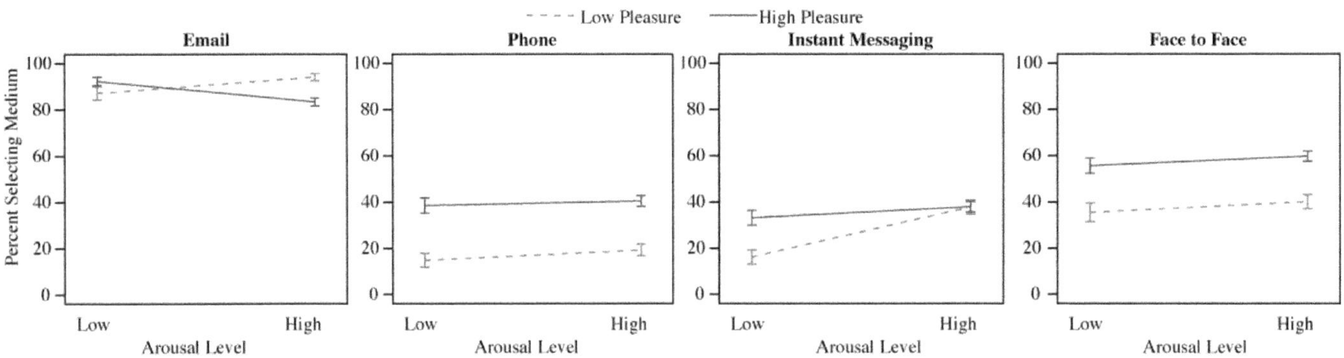

(a) (b) (c) (d)

Figure 4. Comparison of selection for four types of media by arousal and pleasure. A three-way chi-square test on pleasure, arousal, and preference was performed. Results indicate significant interactions between arousal and each communication channel: (a) χ^2 = 16.56, p<0.001; (b) χ^2 = 1.48, p = 0.48; (c) χ^2 =22.68, p <0.001; (d) χ^2 = 1.94, p = 0.38. In each test, df = 2, n = 1095.

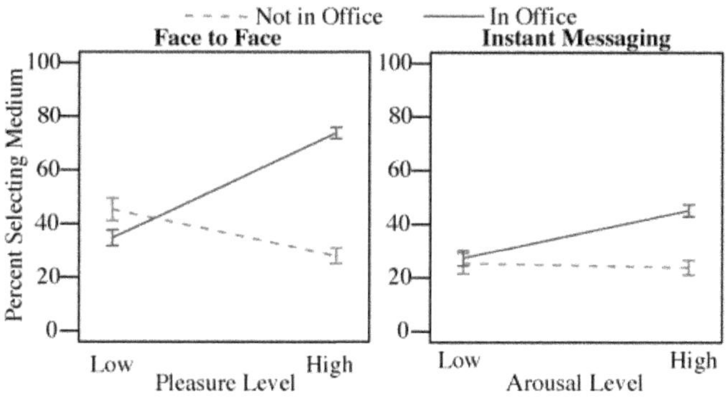

(a) (b)

Figure 5. (a) Comparison of selection of face-to-face by pleasure and location. (b) Comparison of selection of IM by arousal and location. In a chi-square test of pleasure, arousal, and location, significant effects were obtained for pleasure and face-to-face ($\chi^2(2) = 113.56, p < 0.001$) and for arousal and IM (χ^2 (2) = 19.62, $p < 0.001$).

preference for each medium by pleasure, arousal, and location (in or out of office). In general, participants are willing to receive emails most of the time, consistent with the findings of Turner et al [42]. They are more likely to select face-to-face communication when in a positive affective state than when they are in a negative one (34.5% vs. 14.8%). Similarly, preference rates for phone and IM increase from 17.7% to 40.9% and from 30.3% to 36.5%, respectively, as affect changes from negative to positive. In contrast, preference for email decreases from 91.0% to 86.7% as affect changes from negative to positive. AIM theory suggests that when people are in a negative mood, they are more likely to wish to delay responding [35], preferring channels that do not require immediate feedback.

Figure 4 shows the relationship between pleasure and arousal on media selection. Participants were more likely to select IM when both pleasure and arousal were positive. The effect of arousal was stronger when participants were in a negative affective state.

Participants were in their own offices 66.1% of the time. Their locations (in or out of office) did not influence the distributions of pleasure ($\chi^2_{(1)}$ = 1.66) and arousal ($\chi^2_{(1)}$ = 1.22); however, the location influenced participants' preferences for face-to-face, IM, and email communication (Figure 5). Specifically, when out of the office, participants selected face-to-face and IM less frequently (61.5% to 35.5%, 38.3% to 26.5%, respectively), and e-mail more frequently (85.5% to 93.4%). Location had no effect on preference for phone communication.

The effects of pleasure and arousal on the face-to-face and IM communication preferences become more salient when participants were in their offices (Figure 5). One possible explanation is that when participants are not in their offices, it may not be possible to use those communication methods.

Request Preference

Figure 6 provides an overview of the participants' responses to four types of requests from colleagues. They are usually willing to accept expected communication requests from colleagues, but less willing to help colleagues on complex tasks. We performed an analysis to assess the relative independence and possible interactions among pleasure, arousal, and location on willingness to accept each type of request (Figure 7). Positive pleasure increases willingness to have an unexpected communication or help a colleague on a task, particularly a complex one. Thus, pleasure plays a larger role in request preference as the communication uncertainty or task complexity is increased. This result is consistent with AIM theory, which postulates that negative affect negatively impacts peoples' feelings about unexpected or uncertain events and tasks requiring higher levels of cognitive processing more than it does for certain or simple tasks [18].

Figure 7 shows that arousal level impacts all types of requests except for complex tasks. Furthermore, pleasure and arousal interact (Figure 8). When participants had positive affect, their level of arousal made no difference in their willingness to accept any types of request. However, when their affect is negative, their willingness to accept all types of requests was significantly higher when they were aroused than when they were not. Thus, arousal plays a more significant role when participants have a negative affective state than a positive one.

	Distribution	Mean	sd
Expected Comm.	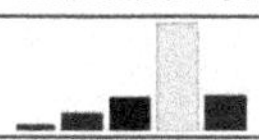	3.76	0.94
Unexpected Comm.		3.12	1.11
Simple Task		3.23	1.07
Complex Task		2.60	1.08

Figure 6. Distributions of willingness to accept each type of request on a five-point scale from strongly disagree (1) to strongly agree (5), with means and standard deviations. The light red bars indicate medians.

	Pleasure	Arousal	Location
Expected Communication	$F = 0.86$ $p = 0.35$	$F = 19.76$ $p < 0.001$	$F = 10.25$ $p = 0.0014$
Unexpected Communication	$F = 32.98$ $p < 0.001$	$F = 26.63$ $p < 0.001$	$F = 0.02$ $p = 0.90$
Simple Task	$F = 4.41$ $p = 0.036$	$F = 25.63$ $p < 0.001$	$F = 5.36$ $p = 0.0179$
Complex Task	$F = 42.82$ $p < 0.001$	$F = 4.94$ $p = 0.0265$	$F = 1.3$ $p = 0.2389$

Figure 7. Analysis of variance results for pleasure, arousal, and location on willingness to accept a certain type of request. All F-ratios have 1 and 1088 degrees of freedom.

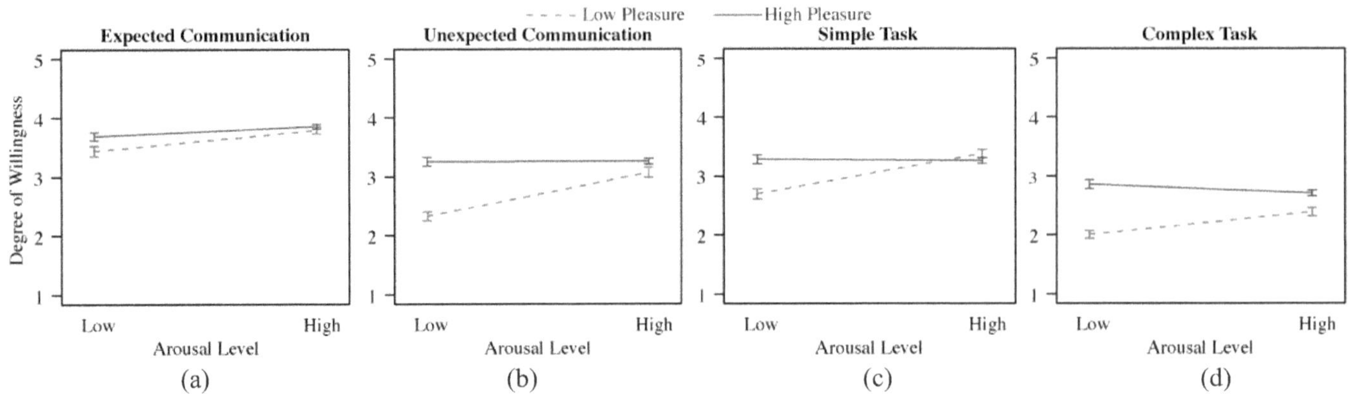

Figure 8. Comparison of willingness to accept four types of request by arousal and pleasure. The three way ANOVA results for the interactions between pleasure and arousal are (a) $F_{(1, 1088)} = 3.11, p = 0.078$; (b) $F_{(1, 1088)} = 26.51, p < 0.001$; (c) $F_{(1, 1088)} = 5.63, p = 0.018$; (d) $F_{(1, 1088)} = 14.23, p < 0.001$.

Additionally, location interacted with pleasure and with arousal for type of request. Similar to the interaction between pleasure and location for selecting communication media, when participants are in their offices, the positive effects of pleasure and arousal on accepting the communication and task requests become more significant.

Awareness of others' affect

Participants were only confident in inferring the affective state of a colleague participating in the study 26.0% of the time. Nevertheless, most participants (82.6%) felt confident enough to infer a co-workers' affect at least once during the study. Since all participants received the survey links at the same time, we can compute the accuracy of participants' inference of another's affective state by comparing with the other person's self-report. Of the samples in which a participant inferred another colleague's affective state, that colleague reported his/her current affect 85.1% of the time. In these samples, participants inferred the valence (positive or negative) of a co-workers' pleasure and arousal correctly only 57.4% and 55.9% of the time, respectively.

Participants can be clustered into three groups based on their inferring behavior (Figure 9). In the first group (two solid nodes and two empty nodes on the left), the four participants work on joint projects, and two of them share a cubicle (solid nodes) while the others have private offices (empty nodes). The six participants of the second group (six solid nodes in the top right) work in a shared room but on separate projects. The third group's participants have private offices and are frequently working on joint projects. Workers in shared offices more frequently inferred each other's affective states than workers in private offices.

Echoing these results, participants' comments in the post-study questionnaire suggest that having face-to-face communication greatly increases their confidence in inferring another's affect, and that sharing an office and working collaboratively increases the chance of face-to-face communication. For example, one participant was confident enough to infer a colleague's affective state "*when I can see my co-worker*", while another was unable to make an inference "*when co-worker is not in sight*". Another commented, "*I am confident to infer a co-worker's mood, when I've just had a face-to-face meeting with them.*" One participant explained that another's affective state could not be inferred "*If I have not had face-to-face contact, but I have had other (e.g., email) contact I was unsure how to interpret.*" These comments underscore how more frequent use of computer-mediated communication channels and less frequent face-to-face communication may hinder affect awareness among workers.

MODELING AFFECT TO IMPROVE AWARENESS

This study provides a corpus of presence and desktop behavior data that is coupled with participants' reports of their affective state. Its results also reinforce the importance affective states have on workers' communication preferences and willingness to interact with colleagues. Thus, they provide a rich data set on which algorithmic

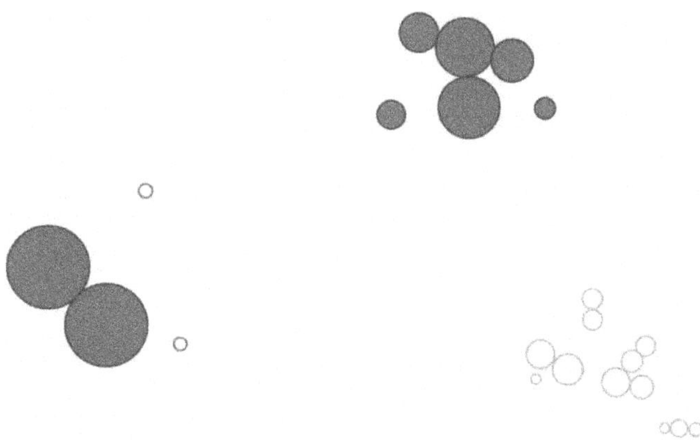

Figure 9. Visualization of inferring activities among participants. Each node denotes one participant. Solid nodes represent participants in shared offices, while empty nodes denotes participants in private offices. Node size represents the total number of inferences made by the participant. The distance between two nodes is proportional to the frequency of inference between two participants.

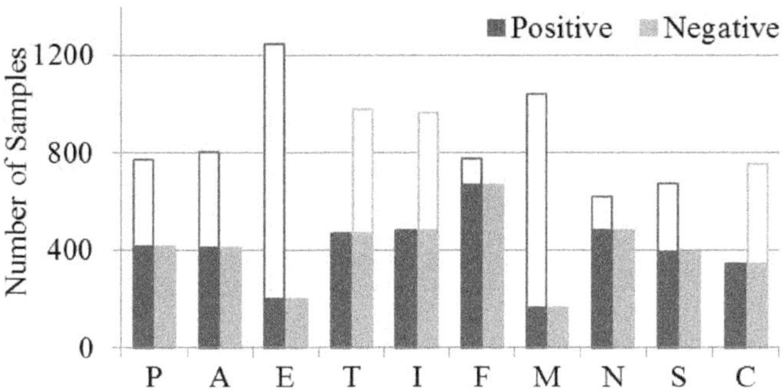

Figure 10. Distribution of responses before (empty bars) and after under-sampling (solid bars). P = Pleasure, A = Arousal, E = Email, T = Telephone, I = Instant Message, F = Face-to-Face, M = Expected Communication, N = Unexpected Communication, S = Simple Task, C = Complex Task.

techniques can be explored to model workers' affective states and evolving communication media preferences using both more traditional data (e.g., desktop behavior) and presence data (e.g., passive sensing data from myUnity).

As explained earlier, we removed neutral samples and clustered both the pleasure and arousal dimensions into two classes (positive and negative) based on affect score in order to obtain high cell counts. Furthermore, following methods used in prior work on affect modeling [14, 43], we performed an under-sampling technique to address class skew. This method is straightforward—it randomly removes samples from the majority class so that it has an equal number of instances as the minority class (Figure 10). It also avoids having to perform algorithm-dependent methods of correction (e.g., increasing the penalty for misclassification of a minority class point).

For each sample in the data, our classification model considers 10 minutes of myUnity usage data and 20 minutes of computer usage data prior to when the corresponding survey link was sent. Keyboard and mouse activity were observed in only 43.6% and 72.4% of the samples, respectively, indicative of the fact that workers do not use their keyboard and mouse all the time. Finally, all features are normalized for each participant using z-scores to account for individual differences [14, 43].

The correlation-based feature subset attribute selection method [24] was applied to select salient features for each estimation model separately. To handle missing values in the features of the dataset, we used Weka's J48 Decision Tree classifier. The decision tree is constructed by selecting the node with the highest information gain as the root, then continuing the calculation recursively. Decision trees were implemented with a 15% confidence threshold for pruning.

To evaluate performance, 10-fold cross validation was employed. Figure 12 shows that the overall accuracy for estimating pleasure is 76.5% (true-positive (TP) rate 76.1%, true-negative (TN) rate 76.9%) and for arousal is 76.4% (TP rate 74.5%, TN rate 78.1%), and that the estimation accuracy exceeds human performance. Our models achieve

Feature	P	A	E	T	I	F	M	N	S	C
Num. of myUnity States			○	●	○	○	●	○	○	●
Duration of a myUnity state	●	●	●	●	○	●	●	●	●	●
STD Interval of myUnity states				○			○			○
Median Interval of myUnity states								○		○
Min Interval of myUnity states			○							
Max motion pixels changed										○
Median motion pixels changed	○									
STD motion pixels changed					○					
Avg. motion pixels changed						○				
Num. of Focused Wins (Windows)		●		○		○		○	○	
Avg. Interval of Win Switch	●	●		●	○		○	●	○	○
Median Interval of Win Switch		○		○						
Max. Interval of Win Switch								○	○	
Min. Interval of Win Switch	○		○			○		○		
states of Focused Win	○	○		○	○	●	○	●	○	○
Min. Height of Focused Win			●		○	○		○		
Max. Width of Focused Win			○							
Min. Width of Focused Win										○
Median. Size of Focused Win				●						
Avg. Size of Focused Win										○
Avg. of X-Coord of Focused Win				○						
Min of Y-Coord of Focused Win			○							
Min. of Max. Sizes of Wins									●	●
Median. Of Max. Sizes of Wins										●
Avg. of Max. Sizes of Wins					●					
S.D. of Max. sizes of Wins							●			○
Max. of Min. Sizes of Wins			○						●	
Min. of Min Sizes of Wins	○			○		●	○			
Median. of Min Sizes of Wins	○		●							
Avg. of Min Sizes of Wins		○		○	●			○	○	○
S.D. of Min Sizes of Wins	●	○		○	○	○				
Max. of Median Sizes of Wins				○		○			○	
Median of Median sizes of Wins	○		○							
S.D. of Median sizes of Wins						○				
Avg. of Avg. sizes of Wins		○								
S.D. of Avg. sizes of Wins								○		
Max. Num. of Maximized Wins					●				○	
Min. Num. of Maximized Wins				○		○		○	○	
Avg. Num. of Maximized Wins				○						
S.D. Num. of Maximized Wins	●									
Max. Num. of Minimized Wins							○			
Median. Num. of Minimized Wins	○			○						
S.D. Num. of Minimized Wins									○	
Min. Num. of Normal Wins								○		
S.D. Num. of Normal Wins	○									
Num. of Backspace				○			○			
Num. of Keystroke						○				
Min. Velocity of Mouse					○	○				
Median Velocity of Mouse	○									
Median. Acceleration of Mouse									○	○
Jerk Index of Mouse	○					●	○		○	

Figure 11. Circles represent features selected for each estimation model. Solid circles indicate a feature located in the upper level (top 3 levels) of nodes in the decision tree. See Figure 10 for column key,

accuracy similar to [43] with less invasive sensing (without analyzing linguistic features of text), and succeeds where [14] fails in the free text model.

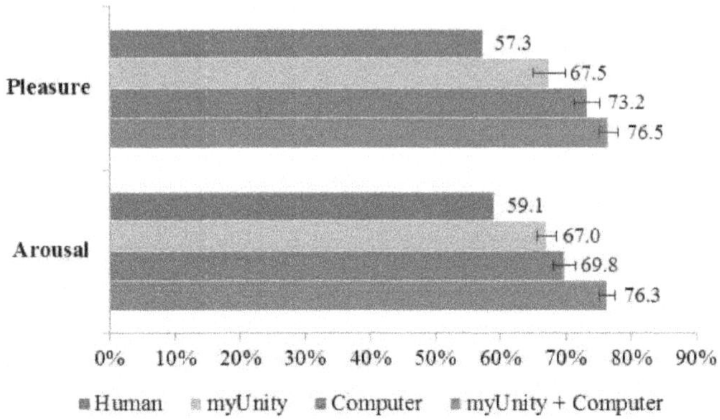

Figure 12. Performance of classifier on affect states of pleasure and arousal. Error bars represent the standard deviation in classification rates after 10 random under-samplings.

Figure 11 shows that features related to myUnity presence states and users' desktop information were frequently selected to construct prediction models and that these features were often located in the top 3 levels of nodes in decision trees for most prediction models. This indicates that the two types of features have higher information gain than other features, such as keyboard and mouse information. For example, the feature "duration of a myUnity state" was used to construct all prediction models and it was located in the top 3 levels of nodes in decision trees. In contrast, the feature "number of keystrokes" was only selected in the models of preference for IM and face-to-face communication. The poor predictive power of keystroke data is likely due to the fact that keyboard use throughout a workday is not persistent in the data set we collected. While previous studies [14, 43] claimed that keystroke information can be a general technique to infer affective state, this result shows that considering keyboard information alone is not sufficient to estimate affective state in real working environments.

Following prior studies on routing phone calls [37] and estimating preference for IM communication [2], the collected awareness data can be used to directly estimate participants' preferences for communication channels (Figure 13). Using myUnity data alone can achieve an accuracy rate higher than 70% for the preference of phone, IM, and face-to-face communication. The accuracy is increased above 80% for IM and phone by considering both myUnity and computer usage data. Prior studies [2, 3] can successfully predict user response time to incoming instant messages, while our method can reliably predict whether a user wants to be engaged in an IM chat in the first place.

More importantly, the awareness data can successfully estimate preference for communication and task requests in workplace communication, going beyond predicting just channel preference. It can help workers decide when to initiate a communication as well as assist in forming communication strategies [20]. Specifically, presence data alone can reach an accuracy of over 70% for preferences for

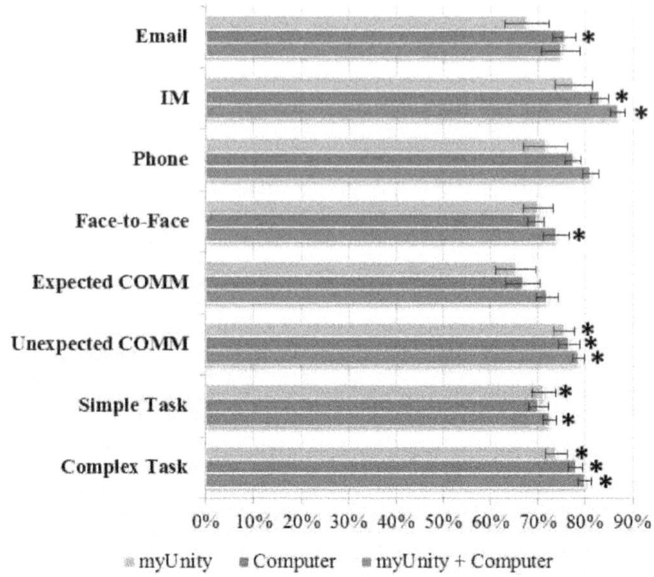

Figure 13. Performance of classifier on media and request preferences. Error bars represent the standard deviation in classification rates after 10 random under-samplings. Asterisk "*" means that TP rate > 70%, TN rate > 70% for each class.

unexpected communication, and requests for simple and complex tasks. The accuracy is improved to over 80% for preference of complex task request when considering both presence and computer usage data (Figure 13).

The prediction model does not perform well on willingness to accept an expected communication request. One possible reason is that our dataset for expected communication request contains few examples of the negative class (see "M" in Figure 10). However, users accept these requests most of the time, reducing the overall utility of such a model. In contrast, the accurate prediction of unexpected communication requests by our approach is much more meaningful to users (see "N" in Figure 10).

DISCUSSION

Our work demonstrates the feasibility of modeling affect and communication preferences from a stream of presence information that is already shared in myUnity, an existing presence system that uses passive sensing. This work represents a significant step forward in the design and evaluation of technologies that can detect affective states and communication preferences in a real world context using automatically collected, non-invasive data. It is the first to explore and demonstrate the effectiveness of using a low-bandwidth signal such as presence states to model affective states. MyUnity is just one of many presence systems that could be leveraged to provide such models. The successful use of myUnity data is particularly meaningful, given that it has achieved strong acceptance by its users and is extensively used by them.

Our study results highlight the need for technologies to aid workers in assessing the affective state of peers, especially in work settings where most communication is computer mediated. Even though our participants knew each other well, and worked in the same building, participants rarely felt confident enough to assess a colleague's affective state (only 26.0% of the time) and, when they did, their accuracy was poor (57.3% and 59.1% correct for pleasure and arousal respectively). A clear trend in the results was that participants had difficulty estimating the affective state of colleagues unless they had frequent face-to-face interactions. This trend may be a preview of the larger communication difficulties office workers will face as they spend less time co-located with colleagues.

Our modeling results suggest that presence streams can be mined to provide salient information about people's affect and communication preferences. However, these models of affect and communication preferences must be presented in a form that is usable and acceptable to users. How to do so is not straightforward. Just because an affective state can be inferred from the data does not mean that users will be comfortable having it shared explicitly. For instance, users may not accept a system that communicates their negative affective states (e.g., stressed or overwhelmed).

Users must be comfortable with the information shared; otherwise they may not accept the system or may learn to game the system. In any system attempting to estimate potentially sensitive information about its users' affective states, some amount of discretion and user control is desirable. However, affect modeling can still be of high value even if the model's results are not presented to end users. For example, predictions of communication media preference can be made without exposing the underlying reasoning. Doing so would also allow users to maintain some level of plausible deniability. A future thrust of our research will be to investigate this tension.

Display of affect information is further complicated by the inevitable errors of estimation due to imperfect models. In addition, there will always be information that cannot be sensed or is not accessible to a reasoning algorithm. A person's affect is impacted by outside experiences, such as a fight with a spouse or concerns about a child's health. These influences are difficult to quantify and detect, making them difficult to model.

We are interested in how well these techniques can be applied to estimating the affect of groups, such as teams or divisions within a company. For example, the overall affective state of call centers or sales offices could be used to route calls and customers to less "stressed" centers.

While we feel our participants are representative of information workers, replication of our approach in other populations is critical. As future work, we plan to deploy the system and collect ground truth data from several different populations, across a variety of work practices and geographic locations. Some of our deployments will be to overseas offices, enabling us to explore cultural differences. Of particular interest is the variation in predictive power of the features in Figure 11 across populations.

This work is an initial step that demonstrated the feasibility of our approach and the predictive power of the features selected. Although we observed significant individual differences, our classifiers were for the entire population. Classifiers customized to each user are likely to yield improved results. Also, we will explore online learning techniques to minimize initial data collection and labeling.

We are interested in understanding how sharing estimates of affective state impacts overall communication and collaboration behaviors. As we develop ways to visualize affective state, we will have the opportunity to study how this information impacts work. We are particularly interested in examining how it impacts the communication structure and feeling of "connectedness" in teams that spend little or no time working face-to-face.

CONCLUSION

Affect awareness is important in achieving effective workplace communication. The increase use of computer-mediated communication tools poses a challenge for affect awareness. We present a new method to model affective state using non-invasive sensing to predict affect and communication preferences with accuracy rates as high as 87%.

ACKNOWLEDGEMENTS

We thank Brian Bailey for the many helpful comments and suggestions in the writing of this paper.

REFERENCE

1. Aragon, C.R., and Williams, A. Collaborative creativity: a complex systems model with distributed affect. In *Proc. CHI 2011*, 1875-1884.
2. Avrahami, D., and Hudson, S.E. Responsiveness in Instant Messaging: Predictive Models Supporting Inter-Personal Communication. In *Proc. CHI 2006*, 731-740.
3. Avrahami, D., Fussell, S.R., and Hudson, S.E. IM Waiting: Timing and Responsiveness in Semi-Synchronous Communication. In *Proc. CSCW 2008*, 285-294.
4. Barkhuus, L., Brown, B., Bell, M., Sherwood, S., Hall, M., and Chalmers, M. From awareness to repartee: sharing location within social groups. In *Proc. CHI 2008*, 497-506.
5. Bermingham, A., and Smeaton, A.F. Classifying sentiment in microblogs: is brevity an advantage? In *Proc. CIKM 2010*, 1833-1836.
6. Brief, A.P., and Weiss, H. M. Current Emotion Research in Organizational Behavior. *Emotion Rev. 3*, 2, (2011), 214–224.
7. Cherniss, C. Emotional intelligence: What it is and why it matters. *Annual Meeting of the Society for Industrial and Organizational Psychology*, (2000).
8. Csikszentmihalyi, M., and Larson, R.W. Validity and reliability of the experience sampling method. *Journal of Nervous and Mental Disease*, 175, (1987), 526-536.

9. Daft, R.L., and Lengel, R.H. Organizational information requirements, media richness, and structural design. *Management Science 32*, 5, (1986), 554-571.
10. Daniels, K., Harris, C., and Briner, R.B. Linking work conditions to unpleasant affect: Cognition, categorization and goals. *Journal of Occupational and Organizational Psychology 77*, 3, (2004), 343–363.
11. Donohew, L., Sypher, H.E., and Higgins, E.T. Communication, social cognition, and affect. Hillsdale, N J: Erlbaum, 1988.
12. Dourish, P. and Bly, S. Portholes: supporting awareness in a distributed work group. In *Proc. CHI 1992*, 541-547.
13. Ekman, P. Universals and cultural differences in facial expressions of emotion. In Cole, J. Ed. *Nebraska Symposium on Motivation*, Lincoln, NE: University of Nebraska Press, 1972, 207-283.
14. Epp, C., Lippold, M., and Mandryk, R.L. Identifying emotional states using keystroke dynamics. In *Proc. CHI 2011*, 715-724.
15. Fisher, C.D. Antecedents and consequences of real-time affective reactions at work. *Motivation and Emotion 26*, 1, (2002), 3-30.
16. Fogarty, J., Hudson, S.E., and Lai, J. Examining the robustness of sensor-based statistical models of human interruptibility. In *Proc. CHI 2004*, 207-214.
17. Fogarty, J., Lai, J., and Christensen, J. Presence versus availability: the design and evaluation of a context-aware communication client. Int. *J. Human Computer Studies 61*, 3, (2003), 299-317.
18. Forgas, J.P. Feeling and doing: Affective influences on interpersonal behavior. *Psych. Inquiry 13*, 1, (2002), 1-28.
19. Forgas, J.P. Mood and judgment: The affect infusion model (AIM). *Psychological Bulletin 117*, 1, (1995), 39-66.
20. Forgas, J.P., and George, J.M. Affective influences on judgments and behavior in organizations: An information processing perspective. *Organizational Behavior and Human Decision Processes 86*, 1, (2001), 3-34.
21. George, J.M., and Brief, A.P. Feeling good-doing good: A conceptual analysis of the mood at work-organizational spontaneity relationship. *Psychological Bulletin 112*, 2, (1992), 310-329.
22. Goleman, D. Emotional intelligence: Why it can matter more than IQ. New York: Bantam Books, 1995.
23. Guillory, J., Spiegel, J., Drislane, M., Weiss, B., Donner, W., and Hancock, J. Upset now?: emotion contagion in distributed groups. In *Proc. CHI 2011*, 745-748.
24. Hall, M.A. Correlation-Based Feature Selection for Discrete and Numeric Class Machine Learning. In *Proc. ICML 2000*, 359-366.
25. Hancock, J.T., Gee, K., Ciaccio, K., and Lin, J.M.-H. I'm sad you're sad: emotional contagion in CMC. In *Proc. CSCW 2008*, 295-298.
26. Hancock, J.T., Landrigan, C., and Silver, C. Expressing emotion in text-based communication. In *Proc. CHI 2007*, 929-932.
27. Hinds, P., and Kiesler, S. Organizational colleagues, media richness, and electronic mail: a test of the social influence model of technology use. *Org. Science 6*, 4, (1995), 373-393.
28. Horvitz, E., and Apacible, J. Learning and reasoning about interruption. In *Proc. ICMI 2003*, 20-27.
29. Horvitz, E., Apacible, J., Subramani, M., Sarin, R., Koch, P., Cadiz, J., Narin, A., & Rui, Y. Experiences with the Design, Fielding, and Evaluation of a Real-Time Communications Agent. Microsoft Research Technical Report MSR-TR-2003.
30. Iqbal, S.T., and Bailey, B.P. Effects of intelligent notification management on users and their tasks. In *Proc. CHI 2008*, 93-102.
31. Isen, A.M., and Baron, R.A. Positive affect as a factor in organizational behavior. In Cummings, L.L. and Staw, B.M. Eds. Research in Organizational Behavior, Greenwich, CT: JAI Press, 1991, 1-53.
32. Krause, A., Smailagic, A., & Siewiorek, D.P. Context-aware mobile computing: learning context-dependent personal preferences from a wearable sensor array. *IEEE Trans. Mobile Computing 5*, 2, (2006), 113-127.
33. Lewis, S., Dontcheva, M., & Gerber, E. Affective computational priming and creativity. In *Proc. CHI 2011*, 735-744.
34. Lim, B.Y., Brdiczka, O., & Bellotti, V. Show me a good time: using content to provide activity awareness to collaborators with ActivitySpotter. In *Proc. GROUP 2010*, 263-272.
35. Mayer, J.D., and Salovey, P. What is emotional intelligence? In Salovey, P. and Sluyter, D. Eds. Emotional Development and Emotional Intelligence: Implications for Educators, New York: Basic Books, 1997, 3-31.
36. Minamikawa, A., and Yokoyama, H. Blog tells what kind of personality you have: egogram estimation from Japanese weblog. In *Proc. CSCW 2011*, 217-220.
37. Oliver, N., and Horvitz, E. Selective perception policies for guiding sensing and computation in multimodal systems: a comparative analysis. *J. Computer Vision and Image Understanding 100*, 1-2, (2005), 198-224.
38. Picard, R.W. Affective Computing. MIT Press, 1997.
39. Russell, J. Affect Grid: A single-item scale of pleasure and arousal. *Journal of Personality and Social Psychology 57*, 3, (1989), 493-502.
40. Salovaara, A., Lindqvist, A., Hasu, T., and Häkkilä, J. The phone rings but the user doesn't answer: unavailability in mobile communication. In *Proc. MobileHCI 2011*, 503-512.
41. Tang, J.C., Yankelovich, N., Begole, J., Kleek, M.V., Li, F., and Bhalodia, J. ConNexus to awarenex: extending awareness to mobile users. In *Proc. CHI 2001*, 221-228.
42. Turner, T., Qvarfordt, P., Biehl, J.T., Golovchinsky, G., and Back, M. Exploring the workplace communication ecology. In *Proc. CHI 2010*, 841-850.
43. Vizer, L.M., Zhou, L., and Sears, A. Automated stress detection using keystroke and linguistic features: An exploratory study. *Int. J. of Human-Computer Studies 67*, 10, (2009), 870-886.
44. Want, R., Hopper, A., Falcão, V., and Gibbons, J. The active badge location system. *ACM Transactions on Information Systems 10*, 1, (1992), 91-102.
45. Wiese, J., Biehl, J., Turner, T., & van Melle, W. Beyond 'yesterday's tomorrow': Towards the design of awareness technologies for the contemporary worker. In *Proc. MobileHCI 2011*, 455-464.

AffectAura: An Intelligent System for Emotional Memory

Daniel McDuff[1,2], Amy Karlson[1], Ashish Kapoor[1], Asta Roseway[1], Mary Czerwinski[1]
[1]Microsoft Research, One Microsoft Way, Redmond, USA
[2]MIT Media Lab, 75 Amherst St, Cambridge, USA
djmcduff@mit.edu, {karlson, akapoor, astar, marycz}@microsoft.com

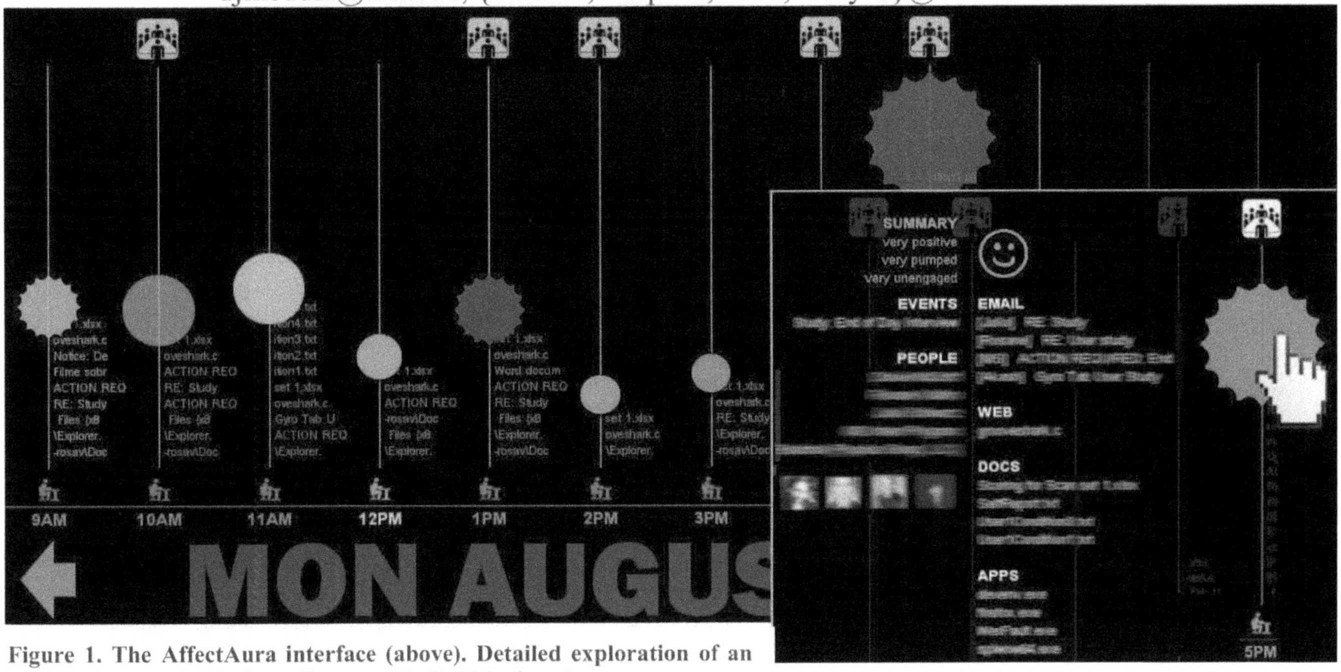

Figure 1. The AffectAura interface (above). Detailed exploration of an hour (5pm) enabled by hovering over the bubble (inset).

ABSTRACT

We present AffectAura, an emotional prosthetic that allows users to reflect on their emotional states over long periods of time. We designed a multimodal sensor set-up for continuous logging of audio, visual, physiological and contextual data, a classification scheme for predicting user affective state and an interface for user reflection. The system continuously predicts a user's valence, arousal and engagement, and correlates this with information on events, communications and data interactions. We evaluate the interface through a user study consisting of six users and over 240 hours of data, and demonstrate the utility of such a reflection tool. We show that users could reason forward and backward in time about their emotional experiences using the interface, and found this useful.

Author Keywords

Affect; Visualization; Machine Learning.

Permission to make digital or hard copies of all or part of this work for personal or classroom use is granted without fee provided that copies are not made or distributed for profit or commercial advantage and that copies bear this notice and the full citation on the first page. To copy otherwise, or republish, to post on servers or to redistribute to lists, requires prior specific permission and/or a fee.
CHI'12, May 5–10, 2012, Austin, Texas, USA.
Copyright 2012 ACM 978-1-4503-1015-4/12/05...$10.00.

ACM Classification Keywords

H.5.2. User Interfaces: Graphical user interfaces (GUI); I.2.6. Artificial Intelligence: Learning

INTRODUCTION

How accurate are we in terms of reflecting on our everyday emotional experiences? While we may expect that we are fairly good at assessing our current emotional state, or on average how we have been feeling over the last day or so, do we really accurately assess the highs and lows over the course of a week or month or longer? And, might it be interesting to correlate the spectrum of emotions we experience with particular activities, people or places? One can imagine that a targeted assessment of one's emotional state could be valuable when considering health issues, mental health issues, eating habits, and socializing habits, to name a few. Even dramatic and stressful life changing events might be handled differently if the apparent or expected toll could be reviewed or estimated from previous experience.

With the availability of an increasing number of ubiquitous sensors it is becoming possible to more accurately document activities and make predictions about a user's future actions, behaviors and internal state. This is reflected in the growing numbers involved in the 'Quantified Self' movement [28], which is characterized by members who collect detailed long-term data about themselves, through a variety of sensors and devices, with the ultimate goal of making optimal health and behavioral choices in their daily lives.

One facet of data we can log and monitor about ourselves is how we experience the world from an emotional perspective. Our so-called *affective state* can have a significant impact on our day to day lives, not the least in the decisions we make [24]. In capturing affect, we need to consider that affect is a general term that encompasses several experiential dimensions. One of the most popular models of affect includes dimensions of valence and arousal [22]. It is widely held that valence (whether it is a positive or a negative state) is important in decision making [18] whereas arousal (the intensity or excitement level) has significant impact on memory [6]. Over long periods of time there is great potential utility in measuring these dimensions of affect, such as for capturing significant events that may affect decision making, but which may not be readily remembered. In addition to valence and arousal, the cognitive state of engagement might help users discover mental and behavioral patterns associated with episodes of high and low productivity. To explore this possibility, we tackle the challenge of tracking states of valence, arousal and engagement and provide an interactive tool for users to reflect upon. The specific contributions of this paper are:

(1) The design of a multimodal system that continuously estimates users' state valence, arousal and engagement using a variety of non-verbal and contextual cues.

(2) The design of a reflective tool, called AffectAura, that combines automatic labels for valence (negative, neutral, positive), arousal (low, high) and engagement (low, high) with contextual information to construct and present a life log tagged with affective states for the user. While prior work has looked primarily at arousal and stress [23,30], valence has received less attention because it has been harder to calculate historically due to a lack of adequate sensing technologies or the ability to track additional variables like context, which as we will see, helps with valence estimation.

(3) The evaluation of AffectAura in a multi-day user study. We demonstrate that affect estimation and presentation are key to the user experience of an emotional life log.

RELATED WORK

Over the past 15 years, there have been significant advances in the domain of affect recognition from multiple modalities [25]. However, many of these research efforts do not evaluate the results of such an affective system from the user's perspective. Kapoor and Picard [21] developed one of the first multimodal affect recognition systems, predicting student interest in a learning environment. One of the most complete multimodal systems [9] was built to predict user activities (instead of affective states) throughout their day. Other examples are: StartleCam [17], designed to detect startle responses automatically from video, and Fogarty et al's [19] system for predicting user interruptibility. None of these examples attempted to evaluate the utility of the information for the user from the perspective of reflection. G.I.R.L.S. is a technology designed to support reflection, specifically reflection on the affective impact of stories [9].

El Kaliouby et al. [14] have discussed the idea of an emotional prosthetic using wearable sensors to aid understanding and interpretation of emotion. We extend the concept of an emotional prosthetic by combining continuous affect recognition using a multimodal sensor system with contextual data drawn from events, communications and data interactions, and conduct a multi-day user study of the results.

As stated, the purpose of our evaluation was to better understand people's reactions to a retrospective memory tool that surfaces automated interpretations of their affective experiences. While this goal shares similarities with the work of Ståhl et al. [29], our approach differs in important ways. Their Affective Diary was a tool that provided semi-automated diary entry creation by incorporating abstract representations of mood and activity (cognitive and physical experiences) together with data streams from the user's phone, and users' own hand-written entries. The tool was designed for the active daily creation of diary entries, and the authors studied how incorporating affect enhanced the creation experience. Our system, in contrast, is designed as a technology probe to explore the potential reflective power that might be offered by pairing affective data with knowledge of workers' information and data interaction artifacts. We specifically designed transparency into the system so that participants could view and reflect upon the relative affective measures predicted by the system, namely; positive vs. negative valence, low vs. high arousal, and low vs. high engagement.

Reflection on one's internal mental and cognitive state has been shown to help us better understand our, and others', responses to stress [23,30]. Visual representations of users' activities have been used to great effect in providing intuitive portraits of a user and their behaviors [12]. We present a solution that allows automatic life logging and encourages reflection on emotional experiences more generally. In our design of AffectAura, our reflective interface was particularly inspired by Themail [31] and lessons learned in prior work [2,29] that demonstrate the power of visual abstraction in encouraging flexible, personal interpretation of affect-based data. Themail represents the changing nature of email correspondence between two parties over time. We use a similar abstraction but rather than representing email communications as bubbles we represent the user's predicted affective state in a somewhat similar way.

When looking through digital material for reminders of events past, triggers—rather than complete details—are frequently sufficient in order to recreate useful details from memory [5]. By combining affective labels with detailed contextual information we investigate this principle from the perspective of emotional events, and show that they can also serve as powerful memory aids.

USER SURVEY

We conducted a survey of 83 (37 females) men and women working at a large IT company around how well they felt they were able to recall their affective state and activity levels over the course of a day, a week, or a month. We also asked them whether they would appreciate a tool that helped them to reflect on their mood and activity levels over time. The purpose of this survey was to verify that users did feel that they had trouble tracking their emotional state and activity levels over time, and whether or not they thought an emotional diary might be useful.

Respondents represented a wide range of professional roles (e.g., designers, researchers, engineers, managers) and ages (18% were in their 20's, 49% in their 30's, 22% in their 40's, and 11% were 50 or older). On average, our survey participants felt fairly confident that they could track their emotional states in the near term, such as within a day, but were much less confident in their ability to do so over the course of a week or month (Figure 2). In addition, it was clear from the survey respondents that they believed there were key triggers to their emotional states. In addition to people, places and activities there were many more important triggers offered to us by participants. For instance, physical exercise and outdoor activities, playing music and sunshine or weather were most frequently cited. The majority of the survey respondents thought an affective life-logging tool might be beneficial for reflective purposes, motivating our efforts.

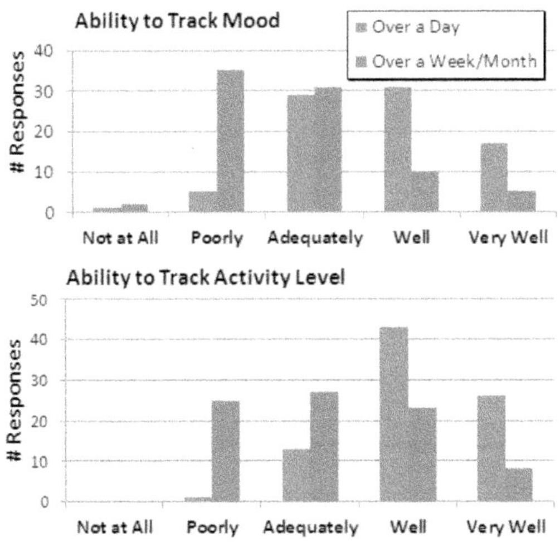

Figure 2. Survey results showing the ability with which people feel they can track their mood (top) and activity levels (bottom) over a day vs. a week/month.

LIFE LOGGING

Given our goal of developing a visualization tool for aiding user reflection on emotional states, our first task was to use Machine Learning (ML) to develop an affect recognition engine based on sensed data. Drawing from past research on appropriate end-user signals for capturing user affect, we developed a suite of desktop-based and body-worn sensors. A multimodal sensor setup using a combination of portable and workstation-based sensors was created to collect data for prospective users. We describe the individual components of the system below:

Webcam: Facial actions and expressions have been studied widely in the context of affect recognition. Facial actions such as smiles, frowns, eyebrow raises, head nods and shakes can be good indicators of valence (positive vs. negative). In order to capture such activity, a webcam was used to analyze facial actions and head motion while the participant was at their desktop. An active appearance model (AAM) [7] was used to track 100 feature points on the face, Euler angles for pitch, jaw and roll of the head and x, y and z displacement of the head within the frame. The webcam was mounted on top of the participants' computer screen. The sampling rate was 5fps.

Kinect: Posture has been found to be a good indicator of interest levels in prior work on affect recognition [21]. For example, a person highly engaged in a task can be expected to maintain still upright posture, when compared to the fidgets and slouched posture of a disengaged person. We hoped to capture such dynamics using a Kinect device. Specifically, a Kinect was used to record posture features from the participant while they were at their desk. The depth information and skeletal tracking [27] was used to determine direction of lean (left-to-right and forward-to-back) of the participant. The sampling rate was 1fps.

Microphone: Speech can be a very rich modality in terms of affect information it contains. For example, the change in prosody, structure of pauses, relative volume of the subject's speech, the exhalation of breaths can be very indicative of the person's internal state and can provide important cues both about arousal as well as valence [15]. A microphone within the Kinect sensor was used to record a raw WAV file of the audio at the workspace.

EDA Sensor: Electro-dermal activity (EDA) is widely considered one of the strongest features that can be used for detecting arousal [3]. Our sensor suite included a wearable wrist sensor [26] to record EDA and three axis acceleration of the wrist of the participant throughout each day. The sampling rate was 8Hz.

GPS: Based on the initial survey, we expected location to be an important variable associated with the affective state of the users. Consequently, a portable GPS device was carried by the participants to record latitude and longitude data. The sampling rate was 0.1Hz.

File Activity: The task that a user is working on can be fairly informative about a user's level of engagement as well as their affective states. This is also supported by the initial survey where more than 60 respondents mentioned that the projects they work on can act as a trigger to put them in a positive mood. A custom logging application was used to record file activity at the user's desktop, including web URLs visited, documents opened, applications used and emails sent and received.

Calendar Scraper: Finally, the people we interact with are one of the most important components of affective states we experience. Our system captures people interactions using calendar information extracted using custom software; in particular, we extract times and attendees of meetings scheduled in users' calendars. An example of the desktop set-up for one of the participants is shown in Figure 3.

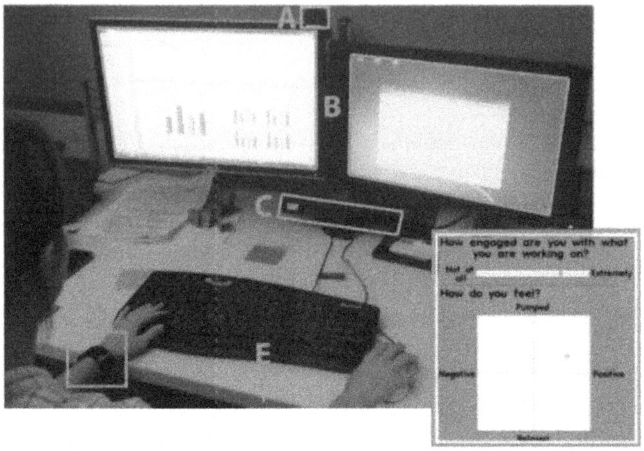

Figure 3. Sensor configuration: A) webcam, B) file activity and calendar monitor, C) Kinect, D) EDA sensor, and E) GPS. F) The self-report interface.

Using Machine Learning for Recognizing Affect

To provide a system for surfacing affective signals to the user, we required a way to take the multiple streams of data we described above and output a prediction across the three dimensions of valence (negative, neutral, positive), arousal (low, high) and engagement (low, high); that is, we needed to develop an affect prediction engine. To develop the predictive models necessary for the affect prediction engine, we gathered data from five participants and used well-known machine learning methods to build models for mapping raw multi-sensor streams to discrete values for valence, arousal and engagement.

Specifically, the sensor streams were each normalized and features were extracted as detailed in Table 1. The data was divided up into 10 minute segments. To train the model to predict the affect labels, we collected training data and self-report labels from five participants over two days each. To obtain affect labels for training, the participants reported their valence, arousal and engagement levels at regular intervals during the day. In this phase, labels consisted of numerical values between -1 and +1 for the three dimensions of valence, arousal, and engagement, collected using the custom tool shown in Figure 3, similar in design to that used by Dietz and Lang [11]. The labels were normalized along each dimension and thresholded to form discrete classes (e.g., positive vs. neutral vs. negative, low vs. high). We collected 110 training examples, each of which corresponds to features extracted from a 10 minute segment.

We chose to use a simple nearest-neighbor classifier in order to make the predictions. In particular, any new incoming 10 minute "test" segment can be classified for valence, arousal and engagement by finding the closest annotated 10 minute segment already present in the training dataset; the test segment thus inherits the affective annotation of the closest match found. For this scheme to work well requires a method for computing distances between the features of the 10 minute episode, which is optimally accomplished using a distance-metric learning technique. In particular, we use Neighborhood Component Analysis (NCA) [16]. Intuitively, the goal behind NCA is to weight different features such that the examples belonging to the same class have a minimal distance, while the ones belonging to different classes are as far apart as they can be. In our system, we learn a separate distance-metric for each of the three different labels (arousal, valence and engagement).

How Good is the Affect Recognition Engine?

In order to make sure that our recognition engine would work, we performed experiments to evaluate its classification performance. Our approach to training and testing the classifier is consistent with accepted practice. In particular, we employed a leave-one-out validation scheme. The idea behind leave-one-out analysis is to select a data point from the training set and then attempt to predict its label using the rest of the examples. This process is then repeated for all the examples present in the training data and the aggregate results therefore reflect the predictive capability of the ML system. Data used for validating the classifier was different from that collected for the user study described later.

We found that such a leave-one-out analysis resulted in an overall accuracy of 68% across all three states and indicates that our scheme does have the ability to predict the affective states. The system was able to predict the state of engagement most accurately (71%). Note that, these affect recognition results are on par with existing systems that operate on natural data, recorded mostly in uncontrolled environments [21] (as opposed to enacted ones recorded in a lab environment). Also note that for our application purposes, we do not require an affect recognition engine that is 100% accurate. AffectAura simply uses the output of the predictor for purposes of guiding the visualization and can thus benefit from a system that has any predictive information.

Finally, it is interesting to analyze our ML model and see what stream of data matters in terms of predicting affect. In particular, we can look at the weights of the input feature space that NCA finds most significant for each class label. High weights correspond to more important features, thus they can provide some insight into the importance of different modalities. Figure 4 shows the total weight each modality was assigned in this mapping after performing NCA. We can observe that EDA sensor (EDA + Acceler.) and posture (Kinect) information are most useful for predicting arousal and engagement respectively. In addition, of the three affect dimensions, head displacements, rotations and facial activity (AAM features) contributed the most weight to the valence prediction. These observations are in line with our intuitive beliefs about the importance of different channels and reinforce the benefit of using a range of sensors to capture diverse information for affect classification.

AFFECTAURA'S INTERFACE

AffectAura is a visualization of the user's estimated affective states over time. It incorporates two components 1) the affect prediction engine for labeling users states and 2) a timeline interface, surrounded by other context, for the user to reflect on these data. Our intention was to create a compelling experience that might engage the user to reflect on their emotional state throughout the day. We were inspired by many timeline visualizations [1] of activities and data.

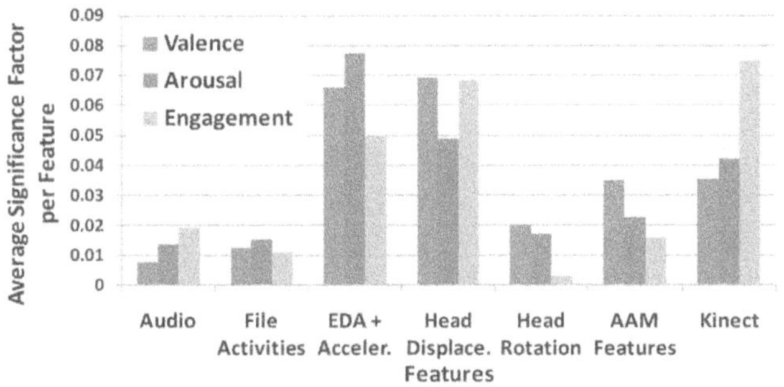

Figure 4. The factors each feature contributed to the final NCA mapping for each of the three classes. EDA sensor features were given the most weight in total.

AffectAura consists of an 'affect timeline' capturing the ebb and flow of affect represented by a series of bubbles. The user can drill down by hovering over a bubble to reveal a detailed breakdown of their activities and interactions associated with that time. We chose to display daily and hourly granularities of data for the user, to simplify the visualization. Each "page" shows one day divided into hour intervals (columns). An example of AffectAura is shown in Figure 1. **Valence** of the affective state is represented by the **color** of the bubble. We used a "hot/cold" metaphor as our starting point, as emotions are often characterized as hot or cold, but ended up with pink, purple and blue representing positive, neutral and negative affect, respectively.

Arousal of the user is represented by the **shape** of the bubble, a circle or a "burst" that were chosen to represent calm and "pumped up" respectively. This type of mapping has been shown to be effective in the SAM (Self-Assessment Manikin) representation [4].

Engagement of the user is represented by **opacity**, with higher opacity corresponding to greater engagement.

Figure 5. Annotated representation of an hour.

We iterated through many visualizations of timeline events, such as "streams", bars and various other shapes but the bubbles provided multiple parameters (size, shape, color and opacity) that could represent different dimensions of the affective states and were most aesthetically pleasing. The representations of engagement and arousal changed significantly from size and motion to opacity and shape for clarity and aesthetic reasons during the iterations.

For each hour, the user's desktop activity (file and application activations) is represented by the size and height of each bubble (radius and height were linear functions of the number of activities), as shown in Figure 5. A subset of the activities themselves are listed as a ghosted column of text to lend a sense of the amount of file and application interaction that occurred. This text list representation was inspired by the Themail visualization of email keywords [31].

If the user had a meeting scheduled in their digital calendar during a particular hour, a meeting icon was displayed at the top of the column. Similarly, the location of the user for

Sensor	Stream	Normalization	Features (calculated for every signal window)
Webcam	AAM Features	Used Procrustes analysis [8] to remove 2D variations due to rotation, displacement and scaling.	Mean smile intensity, Mean eyebrow activity, Mean mouth activity
	Rotations	Remove mean from axes	Pitch, yaw and roll (standard deviation)
	Displacements	Remove mean from axes	X, Y, Z displacement*
Mic	WAV audio file	N/A	Length of conversation, no of turns in conversation, zero-crossing rate*, normalized frame energy*, gradient index*, local kurtosis*, spectral centroid* [20]
Kinect	Depth frame	Remove mean	Gradient of lean (front-to-back)
	Skeletal tracker	Remove mean	Gradient of lean (side-to-side)
EDA Sensor	EDA	Remove mean and low pass filter (cut-off 0.4Hz)	Mean, gradient, different between first value and max, position of max, difference between value and min, position of min, zero crossings, number of peaks.
	3-axis accelerometer	Remove mean and unit std for each axis	Standard deviation.
File Activity	File instances	N/A	No of activities, no of unique activities

Table 1. Table showing the sensors used, data streams recorded, the method of normalizing each data stream and the features calculated from the normalized streams. *Mean and standard deviation was calculated for these values. Calendar events and attendees and GPS latitudes and longitudes were also collected for context but are not used for classification.

a particular hour, based on GPS and file activity, was represented as an icon at the bottom of the column; three icons were used, representing 'home', 'work' and 'elsewhere'. These icons were included to aid recall of events. The user could navigate to different days by clicking on the left and right arrows at the bottom of the screen.

To allow for exploration of the events of each hour, the user could hover over any bubble to reveal details of their activity logged during that hour (Figure 1, inset). The artifacts presented on hover included calendar events, people (names and when available, images), email titles (with sender name), website URLs, document names, and applications used. All artifact data presented was gathered via our custom logging application and calendar scraper utility. Additionally, a text summary of the predicted affective state was displayed at the top of the column for quick perusal. AffectAura was written in Processing, (www.processing.org), an open source environment suitable for rapid prototyping.

USABILITY STUDY

We conducted a study using AffectAura as a probe to understand the reflective opportunities afforded by visualizations that pair event artifacts with predictions of user affect. Inspired by our survey, which suggested that memories of events and emotions drop off rapidly after a day, we targeted the work-week as an interesting multi-day period of time over which to investigate memory and reflection.

Method

Each participant recorded data using the sensor set-up described previously for four consecutive days, Monday to Thursday of a working week. At the end of each day, the participants were asked to complete a short survey reporting the single most positive and negative emotional experience that day (if any) along with the magnitude of the valence of the experience on a 7-point scale (1=Negative, 7=Positive), as well as the people (maximum 5) with whom they had significant interactions that day, again assigning an emotional magnitude to the interaction. On the subsequent Friday, participants completed another short survey about the emotional events and significant interactions they had with people that week, and took part in a semi-structured interview in which they first explored AffectAura using a think-aloud protocol and then answered questions related to aspects of AffectAura that did (and did not) help them recall events of the week and associated affective responses. The evaluation concluded with a survey that gathered participants' subjective reactions to the usability of the AffectAura visualization. Total evaluation time was 60 minutes.

Participants

Six participants (3 females) took part in the evaluation of AffectAura. Their ages ranged from 26 to 33 (Mean: 28.5). Four were graduate students and two were professional researchers. Our only screening requirement was that participants regularly spent at least four hours a day at their desk. On average, participants recorded over 10 hours of sensed data per day, totaling over 240 hours of logged data. Participants were compensated with a $250 gift card.

Results

Emotional memory

To understand how the passage of time impacted participants' memories of emotions and events experienced during the week, we compared survey responses that participants gave on interview day (Fri) to the responses they gave on each day of data collection (Mon-Thurs). We compared participants' memories of the people they interacted with, the most positive and most negative event that happened each day, and the emotional charge associated with each.

Considering first the participants' memories of interactions with people, participants generally recalled more people that they interacted with two days prior to the interview (Wednesday, μ=3.2; Thursday, μ=3) than from the beginning of the week (Monday, μ=2; Tuesday μ=2). Overall, the vast majority of social interactions were considered relatively positive (79%) vs. relatively negative (8%) on the day of the event, and participants were quite good at recalling the relative emotional charge of the interaction; out of the 62 people interactions that participants correctly recalled, the emotional scale value (1-7) of the interaction was correctly recalled 63% of the time. In the 23 cases where participants did not recall the precise emotional value of the interaction, they were off 1 point in all but one case, thus correctly recalling the general tone of the interaction. Participants were twice as likely (15 instances) to misremember the exact tone of interaction slightly more positively than slightly more negatively (8 instances). In the 1 case that a participant did not correctly recall the negative tone of interaction, the participant had had several positive interactions with that person during the week, which we hypothesize overshadowed the one negative interaction. This interpretation agrees with our interview with one participant, who claimed that she generally associates a certain tone of interaction with a person. However, this may suggest that exceptions to the norm are worth noting.

Participants recalled a similar percentage of positive and negative events from the prior four days (55% of the 31 total events) as they did their significant people interactions (56% of 111 people). As with people, on average, participants recalled more events from the previous day (Thursday, μ=1.5 events per participant) than from the beginning of the week (Monday, μ=0.8 events per participant), with a curious dip in recollection on Tuesday (μ= 0.2). Of the events recalled later in the week (Wednesday and Thursday), 81% of those that had a negative tone (<4) were recalled, versus only 40% of the ones with a positive tone (>4). The opposite trend was seen for Monday events, with participants recalling 67% of the positive events versus only 25% of the negative events. This supports evidence that memory of unpleasant events fades faster than that of pleasant events [32], and probably reflects the effects of primacy/recency on long-term memory [13].

We also asked participants to recall the overall emotional tone of each day of the week, and to rate their confidence in their recollection on a 7 point scale (1="not very confident", 7="very confident"). Participants reported that their days were positive (a score of greater than 4) 66% of the time, negative 25% of the time, and neutral otherwise. While participants were more confident in their recollections of the previous 24 hours (Thursday μ=5.2) than from early in the week (Monday μ=4.3), participants' confidence levels did not lead to better recollection. We saw particularly poor performance for recalling details about Tuesday, with 5/6 participants misremembering the exact tone of the day and 3 misremembering the general tone of the day (e.g., recalling a generally positive day as negative and vice versa). Since participants did relatively well in recalling the general positive or negative tone of prior days (83% correct), perhaps the most useful observation from this data is that people can suffer lapses in memory about the emotional tone of a day in as little as 24 hours.

Using AffectAura

Overall, our study participants were successful in reconstructing a "story" of their workday activities by exploring and reasoning over the data artifacts presented in AffectAura (e.g., events, people, emails, web sites, documents and applications). Gaps in the data we collected sometimes made it difficult for participants to determine what they were working on in a given hour; for example, participants could not always discern what document or application they were working with. Even so, participants could often reason forward and backward in time based on information presented earlier or later in the day, which allowed them to piece together the major activities of the day and to reason about whether the affective signals resonated with them. We consider this a novel and impactful contribution to the life logging and 'Quantified Self' movement efforts.

Recalling Forgotten Events with AffectAura

During exploration of the interface, all six recalled at least one event, generally involving a person that they had forgotten about at the time of the interview, and agreed that a system that helped them remember the event and tone of the event at a future date would be useful. However, comments by four participants suggested that not all interactions with people are created equal, and that events worth remembering are those that are out of the ordinary:

> *"If there was a visitor that day and I had a very nice interaction with that visitor, and [months] later, I want to recall what are the important highlights of my week, yes, that would be helpful to recall. But these people I interact with every day, I already know that I like him, or that I like interacting with that person, so it wouldn't really help me that much" –P1.*

In addition, a quote by P5 suggests that what qualifies as "out of the ordinary" may be based on many factors, including the frequency of interaction with a known person, meeting a new person, using a different medium to interact with the person, or even an unusual topic of discussion:

> *"For a person whom I'm interacting very regularly with like my manager or my intern on the project, there would be so many entries I probably wouldn't be so interested. But if it's an outlier, like a visitor, or somebody I met, or an email from a friend which is not a usual email, I would be interested in remembering those [...] The reason it [an IM chat with his father] stands out in memory is because I normally don't talk to my parents a lot on the chat [it] was not the regular kind of talk, so that's why I would be happy if I could remember that." – P5*

We expect that existing life logging tools and systems could readily be instrumented to detect infrequent or new interactions with people, but that the addition of affective sensing technology might be particularly useful for tagging interactions with people that trigger an atypical emotional response. The potential utility of tagging interactions based on emotion is supported by the comments of several participants who provided examples of events that would be useful to remember because of their positive or negative tone, even though it was someone they typically interacted with.

How Participants Used Affective Cues in AffectAura

Two questions we were particularly interested in understanding as we explored AffectAura with our participants was 1) whether participants used the affective information to recall events; and 2) whether the affective information resonated with their own memory of a day.

Affective Cues Aren't Memory Triggers. Through our interviews, we found little evidence to suggest that affective cues alone helped people recall events from earlier in the week. Instead, participants tended to reason about the affective information cues once they had reconstructed what they were doing that hour or day based on other artifacts. All six participants found multiple hours across the week where the activity that the interface suggested that they were doing during an hour (e.g., from events, people, emails, etc) was accurately reflected by the affective information presented, e.g., P5: "*At 11 I was in the talk and it shows me as engaged, calm and neutral, and that was definitely true*". We also saw examples that the visualization accurately reflected the overall mood of the day, again, once the participant had reconstructed the day from specific data artifacts:

> *"I'm seeing the emails I sent out and at this point people are replying to my emails, essentially pointing out things are broken and I'm realizing throughout the day that the problem is bigger than I think it is. But it could have been Wednesday when I really realized...[looking at the emails] no, it was this day....Now that I scan through the emails and remember what the day was, and *now* I look at the interface, it makes total sense that this was what was collected. Mainly because it looks like I was excited at the beginning of the day,*

things are going great, and there was a sudden drop off and all of a sudden I'm very negative, which is exactly what happened on Tuesday." –P4

P4 provided another example for Thursday, where the highs and lows related to a talk he gave were accurately reflected at the day view. P2 had a similar experience: once he had reconstructed the events of Monday he commented "*I like this curve [the varying height of the bubbles indicating "activity"] and that probably feels about like my day*". Whereas the patterns over a specific day resonated strongly with P2 and P4, other participants found that the interface provided some insights about patterns across days, for example that P3 is more pumped in the morning and more positive when interacting with people and that P1 was more positive at lunchtime because of her interactions with friends.

Participants did discover examples where they could not find direct evidence for the affective information that the system was presenting. Interestingly, this often led participants to rationalize the information based on what they remembered about the day that would not have been captured by our system, such as having had morning coffee could have made P1 pumped or having ridden his bike to work could have made P2 calm. The fact that such explanations are only hypotheses suggests there may be some danger of creating false memories. This is especially true given that all participants provided examples for which the affective information contradicted their memory of an hour. A particularly introspective participant commented "*I don't know how much of this [his interpretation] is coming from the data itself or what I'm reading into it—apophenia.*" (P2).

Rationalizing 3 Dimensions of Affect Simultaneously is Hard. Despite the numerous examples that participants provided where they agreed with the positive/negative, pumped up/relaxed, or engaged/unengaged affect reflected in the visualization on a given hour, it was relatively rare that all dimensions of affect made sense simultaneously. While we intentionally surfaced the system's predictions for all three affective aspects to understand what information resonated with participants and what did not, the act of rationalizing all three clearly increased the cognitive demands of using the interface and a simpler design should be explored.

Affective Cues that Aligned with Memory Reinforced the Experience. While AffectAura's affective cues did not always aligned with a participant's memory of an event, participants typically made a simple verbal note of the disconnect and continued their exploration. By contrast, when AffectAura' affective cues did correspond with the participant's memory of the event, participants often declared the fact emphatically (e.g. P2: "*it did exactly what I recall*", P4: "*that's exactly what happened…I'm shocked you were able to collect this data so well*"; P5: "*that was definitely true*"), and took a moment to explain why the prediction was correct. Participants *enjoyed* finding examples that accurately reflected their memories. While this is an early finding, it offers intriguing evidence that capturing and reflecting on affect can create engaging retrospection experiences.

To summarize, the visualization of affect across an entire day often made sense to participants in retrospect, but was not sufficient to reconstruct the events of the day. Even so, participants appreciated the times that the system's affective information matched their memories, which seemed to contribute to a more engaging reflective experience. This helped them discover and reflect on productivity-based and emotion-based patterns in their day.

How Participants Used Data Cues

We were curious to understand whether certain data types were more (or less) useful in reconstructing events of the day, and what important types of data were missing from the interface. Drawing from both our interviews and a post-interview questionnaire that asked participants to rate the utility of each data type in helping them reconstruct their day (1="not very useful" to 7="very useful"), we found no consensus among participants; every data type except for URLs was ranked highest by at least one participant.

URLs, Applications, and Documents Didn't Work. URLS received the lowest median rating (3) across data types, perhaps best explained by P2 who found the URLs "*meaningful but noisy*". Participants also did not consider application information to be very useful (median=3.5) as it was represented in the interface. While documents were one of the highest ranked data type in our survey (median=5), participants never mentioned a document when reconstructing the week's events using the interface; we suspect the discrepancy arises from the fact that AffectAura did not display the complete list of documents for space saving reasons, but that participants *perceived* that document names accurately reflect what they were working on.

Email, Events and People Did Work. All the data types that directly or indirectly referred to people—email, (calendar) events, and people—featured prominently in helping participants reconstruct the events of the week, and all were rated similarly in terms of their utility (median=4). All agreed that email would be more useful if it were prioritized by sender, recipients or time. Even so, in 6 instances, email played a critical role in helping participants recall events from the week. Calendar events were particularly useful in helping participants tell a "story" about a particular day. Calendar events were also strong anchor points in helping participants recall their mood, engagement level and energy level; without exception, when a participant reflected upon a calendar event, they were able to judge whether or not the affective information corresponded to their mood

Given the role that people play in both email and calendar events, it is not surprising that people were by far the most often mentioned data type as participants explored the interface. The power that a person's name can hold in helping users recall past events is described by well by P1:

> *"I recall it now, but three months from now I wouldn't be able to recall [that I interacted with] that person .... it brings back the sequence—there is a story behind that interaction. So seeing that name brings back all the context of that day." – P1*

Participants extracted a surprising amount of value from behavioral information about when they were and were not at work. For four participants, seeing the work pattern (e.g., arrived late, left early) not only triggered a previously forgotten memory of an event, but was sufficient to recollect several other events that happened that day. This provides further evidence that exposing and prioritizing "out of the ordinary" events may be valuable in a retrospective system.

How Participants Used the Visualization Features

Drawing from participant feedback as well as our observations as participants explored the AffectAura interface, we developed insights into the design considerations for future systems that support retrospective memory.

Data Granularity. One tension was the interface providing too much data to make sense of at a glance, but too little data to reconstruct the activities of every hour, or even some of the major events of the day. When participants were successful at reconstructing a "story" of the day, it was mostly because they discovered one or two cues while sifting through the details of the day that they could then use to reason forward and backward in time. Participants cited important streams of data that were not captured by AffectAura, such as face to face interactions, chat/IM/skype history, web-based email, phone calls and text messages.

While future systems can certainly strive to include ever more data streams to offer a more complete picture of people's days, participants' comments suggest that it is equally important to reduce the complexity of the interface. For example, web and email lists included unimportant items that masked the meaningful ones. Consider P3, who on the one hand appreciated AffectAura ("*I think it was great because I usually don't recall details. But looking through here I remembered things. Even if it wasn't data in the UI it helped me remember facts of the week*"), was also overwhelmed by the volume of data presented ("*daily, this is too much*"). This sentiment was echoed by P6, who found that "*going through the day was tedious.*"

Such user comments highlight the need for judicious presentation of the available data. Most participants suggested that they did not want to *give up* the details, but that higher levels of abstraction coupled with drill down would be appropriate. Furthermore, two participants explained why even more detail might be required at the lowest level, since an hour was too coarse a timescale to reason about certain events (e.g., meaningful events can get swamped by less meaningful events), and that the boundaries of an hour were too rigid (e.g., meetings that start halfway through an hour have little to do with the deskwork that was done in the first half of the hour.) It remains an open question as to whether adding more detail would support users in discovering the precise source of an emotional experience. This would require robust, fine-grained prediction coupled with "complete" data streams, neither of which is possible today.

Cue Mappings. The visual cues for arousal and valence made sense to most participants. Size/height related to desktop activity did not resonate with most participants as they preferred out of the ordinary events, which were not always correlated with desktop activity, to be highlighted.

How Participants Anticipated Using Such a System

The interviews highlighted a number of potential uses for a system like AffectAura. Firstly, as a memory aid to record events automatically and help the user recall events upon reflection. In particular, the serendipitous recall of interesting or special events was highlighted by two users. The ability to edit entries was raised as an important feature.

The use of the system as a search tool, not purely for reflection, was raised by two users. This was tied to the ability to better understand patterns within the affective and contextual data on which four of the users commented. Examples given were of the relationship between physical activity and productivity to one's affective state and more generally patterns of stress over time. Most participants said they would be interested in this type of data weekly or monthly, reflecting their desire to use this information retrospectively to aid memory, which drops off quickly after a day or two.

The study highlighted challenges for future iterations of such a design. One user indicated that over longer periods of time it would be important for the system to discern between the highs and lows of a day (which may be relatively insignificant) and the highs and lows of a month or year.

> *"The highs and lows of this day were not even high enough and low enough to be memorable. Although this was a bad moment, and although I may remember it ... that's a blip on the radar." – P2*

FUTURE WORK

In this work most of the sensors and contextual information was limited to data that could be collected at the participant's desktop. Sensors could be utilized in order to capture significant emotional experiences and memory triggers may occur in other contexts. In this work we did not explore additional classification techniques for predicting the users' states. More comprehensive training examples and person-specific training data could improve the classification results. Several users commented that being able to view the data at more granularities may be desirable. A system that detected abnormal patterns of behavior could also be useful. Finally, users could assist the system with prioritization learning.

CONCLUSION

We have presented AffectAura, an emotional prosthetic that allows users to reflect on their emotional states over time. We designed a multimodal sensor set-up for continuous logging of audio, visual, physiological and contextual data, and a classification scheme for predicting affective dimensions, including valence, arousal and engagement. We presented and evaluated an interface for user reflection using the system. We demonstrated that users were able to leverage cues from AffectAura to construct stories about their days, even after they had forgotten these particular incidents or their related emotional tones. Five of the six participants told us that affect would be useful for reflecting on events collected in the user interface. We believe this is the first automatically collected, longitudinally evaluated emotion memory system. We have delineated many benefits to emotion and activity tracking and the particular visualization we chose to expose the information to users.

REFERENCES

1. Aigner, W., Miksch, S., Schumann, H. and Tominski,C. Visualization of Time-Oriented Data. Springer, 2011.
2. Boehner, K., DePaula, R., Dourish, P. and Sengers, P. Affect: from information to interaction. *In Proc. CC '05*, ACM (2005), 59-68.
3. Boucsein, W. *Electrodermal Activity*. Springer-Verlag, New York, 1992.
4. Bradley, M.M. and Lang, P.J. Measuring emotion: the self-assessment manikin and the semantic differential. J *Behav Ther Exp Psy*, 25, 1 (1994), 49-59.
5. Brush, AJ, Meyers, B.R., Tan, D.S. and Czerwinski, M. Understanding memory triggers for task tracking. *In Proc. CHI '07*, ACM (2007), 947-950.
6. Cahill, L. and McGaugh, J.L. A novel demonstration of enhanced memory associated with emotional arousal. *Conscious Cogn*, 4 (1995), 410-421.
7. Cootes, T.F., Edwards, G.J. and Taylor, C.J. Active appearance models. *IEEE Pattern Anal* (2001), 681-685.
8. Cootes, T.F., Taylor, C.J., Cooper, D.H., Graham, J. et al. Active shape models-their training and application. *Comput Viz Image Und* (1995), 38-59.
9. Daily, S. B. and Picard, R. W. Girls Involved in Real Life Sharing: Utilizing Technology to Support the Emotional Development of Teenaged Girls, *J School Counseling,* 5,1(2007), 20.
10. De la Torre, F. and Agell, C. Multimodal Diaries. *In Proc. ICME '07* (2007), IEEE, 839-842.
11. Dietz, R. and Lang, A. Affective agents: Effects of agent affect on arousal, attention, liking and learning. *In Proc. COGNITIVE '11*, (1999).
12. Donath, J., Dragulescu, A., Zinman, A., and Viegas, F. Data portraits. *In Art Gallery ACM SIGGRAPH* (2010).
13. Ebbinghaus, H. (1885). Memory: A Contribution to Experimental Psychology. *Tran.Ruger & Bussenius(1913).*
14. El Kaliouby, R., Teeters, A. and Picard, R.W. Invited Talk: An Exploratory Social-Emotional Prosthetic for Autism Spectrum Disorders. *In BSN '06*, (2006), IEEE.
15. Fernandez, R. A computational model for the automatic recognition of affect in speech. Massachusetts Institute of Technology, 2004.
16. Goldberger, J. and Roweis, S. and Hinton, G. and Salakhutdinov, R. Neighbourhood Components Analysis. *In Proc. NIPS '04*, MIT (2004).
17. Healy, J. and Picard, R. W. StartleCam: A cybernetic Wearable Camera, *In Proc. 2nd International Symposium on Wearable Computers*, 1998.
18. Higgins, E.T. Beyond pleasure and pain. *Am Psychol* (1997), 1280.
19. Fogarty, J., Ko, A.J., Aung, H.H., Golden, E., Tang, K.P. and Hudson, S.E. Examining task engagement in sensor-based statistical models of human interruptibility. *Proc. CHI '05*, ACM (2005), 331-340.
20. Jax, P. and Vary, P. On artificial bandwidth extension of telephone speech. *Signal Processing* (2003), 1707-1719.
21. Kapoor, A. and Picard, R.W. Multimodal affect recognition in learning environments. *In Proc. MULTIMEDIA '05* (2005), ACM, 677-682.
22. Larsen, R.J. and Diener, E. Promises and problems with the circumplex model of emotion. *Pers Soc Psychol Rev* (1992), 25-59.
23. Liu, K.K.L. A personal, mobile system for understanding stress and interruptions. MIT, 2004.
24. Loewenstein, G. and Lerner, J.S. *The role of affect in decision making*. In Handbook of affective science. Oxford University Press, Oxford, 2003.
25. Nicolaou, M.A., Gunes, H. and Pantic, M. Continuous Prediction of Spontaneous Affect from Multiple Cues and Modalities in Valence-Arousal Space. *IEEE T Affect Comput* (2011).
26. Poh, M.Z., Swenson, N.C. and Picard, R.W. A wearable sensor for unobtrusive, long-term assessment of electrodermal activity. IEEE T Bio-med Eng (2010).
27. Shotton, J., Fitzgibbon, A., et al. Real-time human pose recognition in parts from single depth images. In Proc. CVPR '11, IEEE (2011), 1297-1304.
28. Singer, E. The Measured Life. Technology Review (July/August 2011).
29. Ståhl, A., Höök, K., Svensson, M., Taylora, A. and Combetto, M. Experiencing the affective diary. Pers *Ubiquit Comput* (2009), 365-378.
30. Suls, J., Green, P. and Hillis, S. Emotional reactivity to everyday problems, affective inertia, and neuroticism. *Pers Soc Psychol B* (1998), 127.
31. Viégas, F., Golder, S. and Donath J. Visualizing email content: portraying relationships from conversational histories. *In Proc. CHI '06*, ACM (2006), 979-988.
32. Walker, W.R. and Skowronski, J.J. and Thompson, C.P. Life is pleasant-and memory helps to keep it that way! *Rev Gen Psychol* (2003), 203.

Understanding Heart Rate Sharing: Towards Unpacking Physiosocial Space

Petr Slovák[1], Joris H. Janssen[2,3], Geraldine Fitzpatrick[1]
[1]Vienna University of Technology, Argentinierstrasse 8, Vienna, Austria
[2]Philips Research, High Tech Compus 34, Eindhoven, The Netherlands
[3]Eindhoven University of Technology, Den Dolech 2, Eindhoven, The Netherlands
{petr,geraldine.fitzpatrick}@igw.tuwien.ac.at, joris.h.janssen@philips.com

ABSTRACT
Advances in biosensing make it possible to include heart rate monitoring in applications and several studies have suggested that heart rate communication has potential for improving social connectedness. However, it is not known how people understand heart rate feedback, or what issues need to be taken into account when designing technologies including heart rate feedback. To explore this, we created a heart rate communication probe that was used in two qualitative in-lab studies and a two-week field trial in participants' homes. Results show that heart rate feedback is a strong connectedness cue that affects the interaction in various ways, depending on a number of interrelated factors. In particular, we found two distinct categories of effects: heart rate as information and heart rate as connection. We propose two mechanisms that could explain these observations and draw out the implications they have for future use of heartbeat communication to support social connectedness or other aspects of social interaction.

Author Keywords
social connectedness; relationships; physiological signals

ACM Classification Keywords
H.5.3 Information Interfaces and Presentation: Group and Organization Interfaces

INTRODUCTION
Social connectedness is one of the most important predictors of well-being [22, 32], increasing happiness [3] and reducing the risk of depression [8]. Moreover, social connectedness also has strong effects on physical health, influencing, for instance, neuroendocrine and cardiovascular systems [29] and systolic blood pressure. This importance of social connectedness has sparked research on systems and technologies in HCI that can improve our sense of belonging and help reduce our feeling of loneliness, such as awareness systems for families and friends [7, 10, 24, 31] and devices supporting social connectedness for remote couples [12, 34].

Permission to make digital or hard copies of all or part of this work for personal or classroom use is granted without fee provided that copies are not made or distributed for profit or commercial advantage and that copies bear this notice and the full citation on the first page. To copy otherwise, or republish, to post on servers or to redistribute to lists, requires prior specific permission and/or a fee.
CHI'12, May 5–10, 2012, Austin, Texas, USA.
Copyright 2012 ACM 978-1-4503-1015-4/12/05...$10.00.

Recent work has also pointed towards the potential of heartbeat communication for increasing social connectedness. Such studies are building on an increasing maturity of biosensors, which is becoming an area of increasing interest for the CHI community also in other contexts, e.g., [23, 11]. The imPulse system by Lotan and Croft [20] wirelessly transmits heartbeat rhythms to companion units, synchronizing light and vibrations with participants' heartbeats. Similarly, Werner et al [35] proposed the 'united-pulse' system for sharing heartbeats, using pulsing rings to measure and present heartbeats. Interviews suggested that participants from both studies thought that such systems can increase social connectedness. Finally, Janssen et. al. [15] showed that participants rate connectedness higher when led to believe that they hear another's heartbeat. Moreover, participants adapted their nonverbal behavior towards the person they were hearing the heartbeat from in reaction to the felt increases in connectedness. Altogether, these findings suggest that sharing heartbeats could potentially be a powerful mechanism for awareness systems to increase social connectedness.

Although previous work identifies the potential for heartbeat communication, it does not investigate how people make sense of the heartbeat feedback or provide an understanding of why the observed effects take place [15]. It is important to understand such mechanisms to aid design of potential systems for practical situations and to identify potential caveats and pitfalls of using heartbeat communication. Furthermore, only relatively short studies in laboratory environments have been conducted so far and we have little understanding of how people might make sense of heartbeat communication in more authentic social settings and over longer periods of time.

In this paper, we present the results of a qualitative study aimed at understanding the effects of heartbeat communication in various contexts, using a technology probe. We first review HCI literature on social connectedness as well as additional psychology literature supporting the idea that heartbeat feedback might be a viable signal to support social connectedness. Next, we describe the technology probe and its deployment into the homes of couples, as well as the use of the same system in two qualitative in-lab studies. Focusing on data from interviews, we draw out the recurring patterns that appeared over both home deployment and laboratory contexts. In particular, we discuss two core categories of heart rate (HR) sharing effects that have emerged from our data: *HR as information* and *HR as connection*. We then propose a mechanism for each category, giving a plausible explanation for the observed effects, and discuss their implications for future work.

The main contribution of this work is identifying how people themselves make sense of heart rate feedback within the context of different social situations and articulating the possible mechanisms underlying the observed increases in social connectedness during HR sharing. Moreover, our data extends prior work by suggesting how previously described effects of HR sharing, found in the lab, transfer to everyday contexts and to inferences of *other* people's HR. By noting the key differences between two categories emerging from our data, i.e., HR as information and HR as connection, we point to future research directions investigating how HR feedback can be used to support social connectedness.

BACKGROUND

Previous research has used several ways to support social connectedness (or a related concept, intimacy) between people, especially focusing on families and remote couples. Several studies aimed to support the partners or family to get in touch with one another via various kinds of messaging systems. In addition to using generally available technologies such as videoconferencing (e.g., [1]) or exchange of SMS messages, more elaborate concepts were developed. For instance, Strong and Gaver [30] suggested systems that change the physical surrounding (e.g., release scent) when a remote partner interacts with another object. Similarly, Garnaes et al. [12] designed systems to allow the partners to send expressive and emotional messages using a personalised code language. Also, a number of systems have been developed to support tangible communication with the partner, (e.g., Secret Touch in [34]). Other studies aimed at providing awareness of other's everyday activities, for example by linking physical objects (e.g., pillows in [28]). Similarly, technologies such as the Whereabouts Clock [7] increased the feelings of connectedness to other members of a family by providing coarse information about the other's location (e.g., also [10]). People also often use tokens like an object linked to a shared experience, photo in their wallet or picture on their workdesk to reduce the felt distance to people they would like to be close to.

The work referenced above draws on several mechanisms to support social connectedness. For example, some of the work (e.g., [1, 12, 30, 34]) is building on the observation that intentional exchange of messages with a loved one often increases feelings of connectedness [24, Chp. 7], as it implies we are being thought of and cared for. Other work builds on the link between awareness (i.e., making the activities of a remote other more visible in our life), and feelings of connectedness, as argued for example by Dey and Guzman [10]. In this case, it is not the intentionality of the act, but rather the background awareness of the other's activities that matters.

Yet other work, as discussed in the Introduction, makes use of physiological biosensors to communicate heart rate to increase social connectedness, leading to, e.g., higher levels self-reported measures of closeness and adaptation of nonverbal behaviour. For heart rate communication, it is however yet unclear which mechanisms are behind the observed effects [15]. For example, one possible explanation might be that its effects are inherent to heartbeat itself, given that it is a well known bodily signal connected in Western culture to love, life and emotions. Another possible explanation is that the observed effects could stem from heart rate as a signal that provides background awareness of the existence of the other, which would correspond to a similar mechanism as in Dey et al.'s work [10]. There are, however, other plausible explanations. For example, studies suggest that sharing heart rate could be understood as an involuntary self-disclosure, which has been repeatedly linked to increases in social connectedness (e.g., [18, 34]). The underlying rationale comes in several steps. In general, heart rate is strongly related to emotions. In a review of 134 studies, Kreibig [17] shows that HR changes during both negative and positive emotions (also, e.g., [25]). Related literature also suggests that people tend to interpret (their own) heart rate information in terms of emotions. Building on a seminal paper by Valins [33], a number of studies show how providing a false heart rate feedback influences participants' perceptions of the situation (see [26] for a review). For example, when the false heart rate was higher, participants judged themselves as being more aroused. While we know that people make such appraisals based on their own perceived heart rate, we do not know how people interpret heart rate information of another person, although it is plausible to assume that similar effects might arise. Taken together, if people can interpret heart rate as information about the emotional state of another, sharing heart rate can be seen as a form of emotional self-disclosure. Due to the strong relation between increases in self-disclosure and connectedness, this could be another mechanism for the observed effects.

In summary, heart rate can play a role in social connectedness and controlled laboratory studies show that communicating heart rate can make people feel closer together [15]. However, we do not understand the mechanisms underlying the observed increases of closeness and if and how these play out in more authentic social situations. A better understanding of these mechanisms will be useful for designers in deciding which contexts HR sharing might be useful (e.g., synchronous communication or background sharing), who might benefit most (e.g., couples, family, friends, strangers), and what other effects it might bring.

STUDY METHOD

As there is little prior work on HR sharing in everyday contexts, we chose to focus on understanding people's experiences with, and use of, HR sharing technology in their everyday life. To explore these issues we developed a technology probe for sharing heart rate and conducted qualitative studies of its use in two different settings. Such qualitative approaches are often argued as a good method when analyzing a novel technology in HCI (e.g., [14, 16]). In order to tap into the initial reactions of a larger number of people, we set up two social interaction scenarios in the laboratory for 13 pairs of participants. To understand reactions based on longer term use in a home setting, we also conducted 2 week deployments with 5 couples who used the probe at home. We go on to describe the probe, each of the studies and the analysis.

Figure 1. Example of visual feedback mode – random ripples

The technology for HR sharing

Following the suggestions of Hutchinson et. al. [14], we aimed to design a relatively simple technology that would nevertheless give the participants a possibility to interact with it freely, and, hopefully, use it in unexpected ways. A heartbeat belt (Zephyr HxM BT) was paired with a standard laptop (HP EliteBook 8440P), connected to the heartbeat belt using Bluetooth radio. Each pair of participants received two such sets, with the pairing of belts to computers clearly marked. Participants wear the belt on their body around their chest. The system logged the HR and system status (e.g., receiving HR information or not) at 1 Hz. Furthermore, every time a setting was changed this was logged and the latest settings were saved.

The laptop could present the HR information both visually and aurally. The two modes of feedback ran independently, so the participant could choose if (s)he wants to use both at the same time, or select just one. The *aural feedback* was implemented by increasing the volume of a sound linearly with increases in HR. We provided the participants with two preselected sounds of nature (soft rain and crackling of campfire), aiming for sounds that could create a natural, unobtrusive background, as well as blend together well. The system supported three types of *visual feedback* on the display of the laptop. The first type used water ripples displayed over an image, either along the horizon (where the position of the ripple indicated current HR), or at random locations (the number of ripples shown simultaneously corresponded to HR, see Figure 1). The second type consisted of an image that was linearly faded to black with decreases in HR. The last possibility was a white number on a black background, with history over the last minutes on the bottom. Participants in the home study could switch between the feedback modes at will, add and change the visualised pictures and sounds, and also specify ranges in which the feedback will be active. The in-lab participants were provided with a default settings, see below.

Laboratory studies

In the two short-term in-lab studies, we wanted to tap into the initial impressions of participants in two different contexts, specifically: watching a movie together and doing a negotiation task. In both cases, the researcher conducted a 20 to 30 minute interview with the pair of participants about their experiences during the task. Participants got feedback using the same technology probe system as in the home deployment.

In the *first in-lab study* seven pairs of volunteers participated. Participants (6 men and 8 women) knew each other mostly as colleagues and friends, or in the case of one pair, romantic partners. All participants worked at a large electronics company and were over 18 years old. When the participants came into the laboratory, the system was explained to them. They put on the HR belts and were asked to watch two videos together (when sitting on the couch next to each other). Both videos were animated short pictures that have received various awards at recent film festivals. The first was chosen to be slightly scary and the second funny, to lighten the mood. The movie watching took approx 10 minutes. During this time, the participants could perceive each their own and other's HR, first in the form of the aural (5 minutes) and then visual feedback (5 minutes, ripples along the horizon mode).

In the *second in-lab study*, six new pairs of volunteers participated (6 men and 6 women). The participants were recruited from the same population as in the first in-lab study. In this study, the participants first watched an 8 minute long neutral nature movie and were told that they can use the time to observe how their HR reacts. The system presented HR feedback both in the visual (ripples on horizon) as well as aural form. Afterwards, the participants played a classical task, called the desert survival situation (as used, e.g., in [6]), in which they have to negotiate what items are most useful for surviving in the desert. This took about 20 minutes. During this task they could again see and hear their own and other's HR feedback.

Home deployment study

Five couples participated in the home deployment studies. *Household A* consisted of a married couple in their late 20s, both with a post-graduate education and working at a university. *Household B* consisted of a couple in their late 20s, who have been together for 2 years. Both have a PhD degree, John is a physicist and Maddie a medical doctor. *Household C* consisted of a couple in their early 20s, who have been together for 1 year. Both were post-graduate students at a university, on topics of HCI and design. *Household D* was a family of four: the father works as a Senior Manager at a big electronics company, the mother is a kindergarden teacher. They have two sons, aged 14 and 16. *Household E* consisted of a couple in their 20s, who have been together for 5 years. Stacy has just finished her master's degree in design, and Brad has a PhD in Chemical engineering, working at a research department of a medium sized company.

The home deployment started with an hour long session in which the researcher visited the home of the participants and explained the working of the system. Participants were told that they could use it in any way they wanted including changing the feedback, to feel free to explore, and that we were interested in their experiences with it. Apart for asking the participants to try the system out during the first two days, we left the decision whether, when, where, and how long to use the system up to them. We also did not tell them anything about the fact that we were interested in social interaction and the effects of HR on this. Participants then tested the system and the researcher left when everything was clear and setup prop-

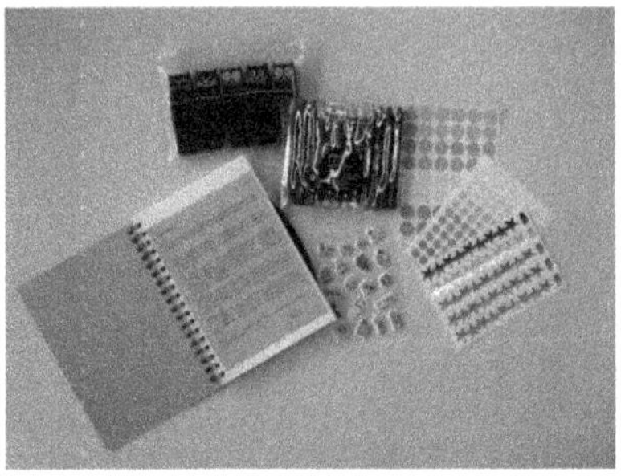

Figure 2. The diary probe package

Figure 3. Set-up for the poker game (photo courtesy of our participants, published with their consent)

erly. Participants also received a probe package with a diary to stimulate them in thinking about possibilities of the system and record experiences they had with it (see Figure 2). The diary contained various stickers and colourful small objects to subtly promote the playful behaviour we were interested in. However, we did not include any catch-phrases or tasks to see what uses of the system the participants come up with by themselves. Participants were encouraged to write something in the diary once a day.

After a week of use, the researcher conducted an interim interview with the participants for about 30 to 40 minutes. We were interested in their initial experiences, asked them to tell us notable stories from the last week and went through their diaries together. We were also interested in any changes to the system the participants would like, and whenever possible, tried to provide them with it (see, e.g., the poker game described in the next section). Finally, after two weeks of use, the researcher conducted a final interview with the participants lasting about one hour on average. We were interested in the situations they used it in and whether it changed their interaction in any way. We tried to explore what the participants found as important during their experience with the system rather then strictly following a prepared interview guide. The issue of social connectedness was often brought up by the participants independently, in which case we probed more deeply into it. In other cases, it was one of the last questions, not to skew participants' responses.

Analysis

We analysed the data by first transcribing the interviews and then conducted thematic analysis of the data. Two of the authors went through all the transcriptions, diaries and recordings of the interviews independently and identified concepts and issues that were present in the data. We used a bottom up approach, with the concepts arising directly from the data, not from a predefined framework. The findings were then compared and clustered. Where there were disagreements, we went back to the audio recordings to check our findings to resolve issues. Finally, clusters of data were structured and related to each other.

USAGE AND REACTIONS TO THE TECH PROBE

This section presents an overview of the observations concerning the design and usage of the system. Due to space constraints and the fact that the main concern of this paper is with the *interpretation* of HR feedback by the participants in social settings, rather than the design of the feedback system, we keep this section brief.

With regards to usage, our short-term in-lab participants were generally interested in the HR feedback, often comparing their HR with their partner's and doing little experiments (e.g., "what happens when I stand up"). They had similar reactions to the design as the home participants did. All of our home participants were initially very excited about the probe and were curious to see how their heart reacted to various situations. This initial curiosity and engagement wore off however after few days and all our couples reported that they soon knew what to expect with their HR in everyday activities and it became boring afterwards. As Annie put it in the final interview, *"... so that's what I learned from that. It's not very exciting to monitor your HR [in everyday situations] because it's you know always between 70-100"*. However, most of our participants still tried various 'experiments' throughout to explore their HR changes – emotionally intense movies (e.g., Clockwork Orange), darts, playing computer games, physical activity etc. One couple in particular (Household A) thought it would be interesting to use the the system playing poker and requested 4 additional laptops for one night when they had friends over for a poker game. They enjoyed the game immensely, and considered it the highlight of the study.

With regards to the offered feedback modalities, participants had often their personal favourite choices, depending on their prefered usage and personal taste. We report some of the more generalisable observations below. Most participants found that HR feedback is not very informative in many everyday moments, and continuous monitoring requires attention that does not provide enough value. In this sense, the continuous *audio feedback* provided enough information, but was often obtrusive at moments "when nothing happened". Instead, many would have preferred notification of sudden changes in HR together with the possibility for more precise readings available if they wanted to pay attention. Similarly, the *visual feedback* gave detailed information, but participants felt that it required too much attention if monitored continuously. Participants suggested notifications based e.g., on a short sound when reaching a given threshold, or changes in lighting in the room (i.e., ambient, peripheral and unobtrusive feedback). Some also suggested various history options, allowing for example a shared reflection of the day with the partner. Participants also noted that the laptop was often too heavy and big to carry around easily if they wanted to move it to a different room, and would prefer tablet-like devices to provide a more fluent movement of the feedback throughout the home.

We saw some differences in extent of usage of the system between households. Households A, B and D used it quite often, with the system running on 9, 8, and 10 days respectively (the average usage in minutes per participant was approximately 2200, 800 and 1200, respectively). The remaining Households C and E used the system less: Household C on 3 days, for approx 200 minutes altogether; Household E then on 5 days, for approximately 600 minutes altogether. The differences in usage between households A, B and D arose from various work related constraints, spending a few nights out of the appartment etc. Participants from households C and E were all quite busy with work related activities during the evenings. This might be one of the reasons why they did not experiment with the system so much, never tried it out in situations different from everyday routine, and did not use it much after the initial curiosity wore off.

EFFECTS OF HEART RATE SHARING

Our particular focus in the analysis was on how people used and interpreted HR data in various social situations. We present data from both the shorter-term in-lab studies and home deployments together as most of the concepts appeared consistently over both contexts. We identified two main categories in our data. The first is about interpreting HR as objective *information* about one's own or someone else's internal state. The second is about HR as a direct *connection* to the other, without the need for it to give any understandable information about the others' state. The next two sections discuss the main results respectively under these two themes.

HR as information

A strong majority of participants from both the short-term in-lab and longer-term in-home studies consistently related HR to emotions (or stress). They tended to interpret both their own and others' HR information accordingly. However, the ways in which participants interpreted HR and the effects it could have on them were influenced by several interrelated factors: availability of context (e.g., non-verbal cues), how relevant emotions were in the situation, and the type of relation they had with the person they perceived the HR from. In the rest of this section, we provide an overview of these recurring patterns in our interviews.

First of all, we found differences among our participants in the extent of interpretations they thought were possible from heart rate. Some participants were optimistic, expecting that HR *"actually shows what you're thinking, what is going on in your mind"* (Erik, Lab 2). Others had lower expectations of HR interpretation. For instance, Abby (Lab 2) thought that *"you can't draw direct conclusions from it, but it is a measure of not being completely settled"*. Even if the participants were unsure of what information they could get out of HR, just the presence of the feedback made them think about possible interpretations. For instance, Debbie (Lab 2) said: *"I think this is a bit distracting, because even if you can't interpret much, you'll start thinking about it, just because you have the information"*. Similarly, many participants thought they would not be able to hold back on interpreting.

Need for context

Although most participants thought HR could be interpreted to a certain extent, they all acknowledged that there is a need for additional cues to guide the interpretation. As Marianne (Lab 1) put it, *"you also have to know what that person is doing because otherwise [you'd think] oh he's nervous but he's just walking up the stairs."*

Similarly, the general understanding among our participants was that while you might try to interpret HR even without sufficient additional cues, you will not get it right. Mary (Lab 1) said: *"without the context you cannot really interpret it, you can only* mis*interpret it"* (emphasis Mary's). Having additional cues to interpret HR remained important, even after two weeks of usage. For example, Annie (Home A) talked about calling her parents on Skype while sharing HR: *"In face-to-face I have the impression that [the HR feedback] is natural and everything [is] clear, but here when I have the video and the HR, then the interpretation might not be correct, they might think something else, they might misunderstand me ... I would expect such kind of effects ... Not that much in face-to-face though."*

Emotional relevance of situation

Having enough context to make the interpretation of HR plausible did not necessarily mean that the participants felt that HR is adding any new or interesting information. Our participants generally expected that interpretation of HR feedback could provide additional information only in situations that are *emotionally relevant* for them or their partner. For example, Abby (Lab 2) says *"[It was ok to show HR to a friend] it's nothing to be embarrassed about, it's just a heart rate"*. Nonetheless, a few minutes later she continues to say that *"but I guess that when you're in the middle of a social interaction that is not completely casual to you, you wouldn't want the other person to see"*.

In particular, participants often mentioned that HR feedback would be most effective in situations where there is something to conceal or, more generally, where one wants to setup an impression. Participants usually added that they would not like to share their HR during such moments; that it feels *"too personal"*. For example, Margit (Lab 2) was thinking about HR feedback during an interaction with her boss: *"[I wouldn't like this] because sometimes, you can look like you're not that stressed and in fact you are ... [with this] you just can't hide anything, you don't have a choice"*. Furthermore, participants remarked that they could not control the HR. For instance, Mary (Lab 1) said *"I think that this is why its weird... because it's your own but you cannot control it."* In contrast, participants were happy to share HR during less emotionally relevant situations. As Margit (Lab 2) talks about the lab session, *"we didn't have any really personal things to do, it was just the movie and this task ... I think it's not enough personal to use this information"*. Similarly, Annie (Home A), said that she probably wouldn't mind having the HR feedback on the door of her office during casual work days, as *"I think it wouldn't be very interesting for other people because it would be somehow constant [. . .] but if it were interesting, then I would mind."*

Effect of relationship type

Besides the emotional relevance of the situation, expectations of how informative HR could be also depended on the *relationship between the interacting individuals*. In particular, participants were often much more concerned about sharing their HR with someone they did not know well. This was common to both in-lab as well as home participants. For example, when we asked John (Home B) during the final interview to tell us with whom he would *not* be comfortable sharing his HR, he said: *"People who you don't want to tell every, all ins and outs immediately ... who you want to keep distance sometimes ... Sometimes you don't want to express everything you have on your heart ... like metaphorically on your heart [laughs]."* Similarly, Annie (Home A), said *"If they are a complete foreigner to me and they are commenting on my physiological state ... I wouldn't like that."*

Sharing of HR was understood as implying a great openness in what you are willing to share. As John (Home B) puts it when asked if it would change anything in his interaction with close family: *" Yeah, not so much ... maybe when my mum is on the telephone and she would hear that, she could get really concerned, then she wants to know everything ... I'm willing to tell her, it's no issue, but it also implies more or less that when you share your HR, you have more to tell. Has implications for the further communication."*

However, interviews from the in-lab studies as well as the home deployment indicate that participants thought that HR often does not bring new information when the other person is well known. In particular, most participants felt that in a long term relationship, HR sharing (while collocated) usually does not add any new information into what you already should be able to understand from other social cues. Stacy (Lab 1) puts it *"Yeah when I'm together with my boyfriend I can see like this if he's relaxed or not so I don't really need the HR visualized I can see it in his movement and his eyes if he really is relaxed and I'm not sure if this tool really adds something to that."* Similarly, Mary (Lab 1) was even more strict: *"Its like sending text messages when you're in the same room ... why not just talk to each other."* In line with this, none of our home participants expressed any problems or issues with sharing their heartbeat with their partner in everyday situations. The only situations suggested by our home participants, where HR might reveal something new in a long-term relationship, were tied to emotionally relevant contexts, in which one would like to conceal his/her internal state, such as a fight or white lies.

All in all, these findings suggest that for many situations in which HR could be used as information, people prefer not to share it. An exception were games or generally fun activities, i.e., emotionally low-risk contexts. An example was the poker game at Annie's and Michael's place, where the HR feedback played a major role in the experience. Michael (Home A) told us: *"People were quite enthusiastic about it. When we were receiving the new cards, everyone was looking there, just to check what's there ... because you know, you have the poker face, but there is everything"* and continued that *"it something new, nice additional thing for the game."*

HR as connection

HR as a connection came up as an aspect of HR communication independently for three of our home deployment couples and two pairs from the in-lab studies. In contrast to findings about HR as information, HR as connection seems to be based on the feeling of being connected to the other just by the fact that the partner's HR is available. Hence, this is independent of the additional information the other's HR could provide.

The three couples felt that the HR can provide a particular form of a *direct connection* to the other person. For instance, Michael (Home A) came up with the idea of a living picture frame, where you would have the photo or another link to the person, together with his/her HR. Relating to this, Michael said: *"I see it moving and it is somehow connected ... you can see that something is happening there ... much more directly connected to the other person. Always a bit different, when you see it, you don't know what the others are doing, but you know that they are doing something."* In response, Annie, his wife, remarked: *"[laughs] ... like that I'm existing, that I'm still alive"*. Similarly, Maddie (Home B) thought that such feedback could help her be closer to her partner. *"I think if you have something very important like an interview or something, then the other can see"* John, her husband agrees and continues *"John: It's like that you can feel what the other person feels .. Maddie: That you sort of together you go through something."* In the same vein, Adrian (Home D) remarked that *"[HR] would help to create a bond with them. That I can imagine would work. If you are far away, and you can hear the other's heartbeat, I can imagine that would work. However, it does not work when someone is sitting next to you already, because you have contact with them anyway. You have much less contact with someone overseas, so there it could be beneficial ... it would create the feeling of being much closer to the other."*

All three couples noted that this HR as connection is most relevant in situations in which they are physically *apart* (although the distance between them does not need to be large). For example, John (Home B) said during the interim interview: *"I like the fireplace sound when Maddie is doing something in the kitchen. . . so then the computer is here [living room] and I hear this firesound ... yeah, it's a little bit like somebody is present, that's nice."* He again mentioned in another interview as one of the highlights of the technology probe experience. *"[And what I liked most was] when I heard Maddie in the kitchen. It's like communicating in a different way [...] there is at least some link ... It would be nice if you had something [at your work] and I would have it [at my work]."* This could be also one of the reasons why this effect was not mentioned often by our in-lab participants, who spend all of the time collocated.

The participants made it clear that for this effect of connection to take place, *less* context is better. They mentioned two types of reasons for this. First, to get context about the current activities of the other, you need to be already connected; either by physically being together, or for example talking on the phone. In such cases, the HR would not add to the feeling of connection that was already existing. Second, less context also reduces privacy concerns as it would be more difficult, if not impossible, to interpret HR without context. Michael (Home A) says: *" [just] HR is less intrusive, in a sense. If you have video its like sort of surveillance ... HR I think is less... in some situations it can be, but you need to have some extra information ... if you just have HR it doesn't tell you anything ... just that someone is moving, or is agitated somehow"*. Nevertheless, Michael still continues to say that *"it's a kind of presence information ... Like someone is living there [...] you might feel more connected to the person."*

In sum, these findings show that although HR might be problematic to use as information in practical applications, most of the couples from the home deployment agree that HR communication could have value by providing a feeling of connection. As suggested by our participants, this could be for instance implemented in a picture frame or other unobtrusive display that can be put in the background and does not take a lot of attention. Especially because the viewers of such displays would not know the context in which the HR is displayed, participants did not express privacy concerns for this way of using HR communication, as long as only close family members can see it.

DISCUSSION

To gain insights into possible mechanisms underlying the effects of sharing HR, we deployed a technology probe for sharing HR in two in-lab studies and in a two week home deployment. Interviews with participants in the in-lab and home deployment studies showed that HR can provide *information* about another and that HR can create a *connection* to another. In this section, we propose two mechanisms that could help in understanding our results. For HR as information, we suggest that the observed effects could be explained in terms of *impression management*. Similarly, we propose that the effects of HR as a connection can be understood based on the idea that people perceive the source of HR feedback as *a representation of a part of their body*, even if it is physically remote. Finally, we discuss the implications these mechanisms would have for future work.

HR as information

Our results show that participants tended to interpret HR in terms of emotional states. In that light, participants often considered HR as an objective signal about one's state that cannot be voluntarily controlled. This corresponds with findings of studies that gave participants false feedback on their own HR [26, 33]. These studies suggest that people tend to reappraise situations when there is a mismatch between their understanding of the situation and a change in HR.

The results showed several interrelated factors that can influence the extent to which HR is informative for the participants: Participants thought that having context (e.g., additional nonverbal cues) could help by guiding the interpretation of the HR. This shows that our participants acknowledged the multi-facetedness of HR, where it's changes can have different meaning depending on the context [11, 17]. HR was also thought to be more informative in situations in which emotions were relevant to the interaction or to one of the interactors. Additionally, the type of relationship between the interactors also influences if HR can be informative. Yet, in most of the cases where people thought the HR could be informative, they were not willing to share it. We think that it can prove useful to explain these findings by the idea that HR sharing undermines *impression management*.

Concept of impression management draws on an idea that social interaction can be viewed as a form of role playing, as postulated in one of the most influential works on impression management by Goffman [13]. In this role play, each individual tries to set up an impression (e.g., that of an eager, hardworking, funny, or serious individual) for those he or she interacts with. Goffman uses a theater-based metaphor to explain the interplay between a presenter as well as his or her audience. The audience is usually expected to play along, helping the individual to maintain the plausibility of the situation (i.e., the role he or she tries to convey). See, e.g., Consolvo et. al. [9] for examples of how impression management has been already utilised in other HCI contexts.

As HR was perceived by our participants as both uncontrollable and related to emotions, it is plausible that participants could feel that their impression management was undermined if others could use their HR to reappraise the impression they try to present. We argue that this would explain why HR sharing felt more informative in situations where (hiding) emotions is relevant, as well as the changes in effects depending on the relationship type: In situations where one wants to appear differently from what one actually feels (e.g., confident during a presentation, while actually feeling nervous), HR sharing might undermine this impression management. Other examples of such situations where we often try to conceal or otherwise manage our real emotions are meeting with a boss, an early date, or an argument with your partner, all of which were specifically mentioned during the interviews as situations where HR could be informative. In contrast, our participants were generally fine with sharing the HR in everyday situations that were not emotionally relevant – recall, for example, Annie's quote about having her HR on her office door. In these situations, emotions are not important for keeping up appearances.

Seeing HR as undermining impression management could also explain the fact that the type of relationship participants had with the person they were sharing HR with could influence how comfortable they felt about sharing HR. For instance, participants tended to feel more comfortable sharing their HR with their romantic partners than with strangers. This can be explained by the observation that when relationships become closer, the amount of self disclosure increases [18, 34], lowering the need to keep up appearances. Furthermore, our interviews suggest that participants feel that sharing HR implies a willingness to disclose emotional information, which might not be congruent with an impression one wants to give when interacting with people one is less close with (e.g., [13]). In general, the described threat to impression management would also explain the consistent uncomfortableness with sharing HR feedback in situations where it could add new information, as HR sharing in this case precludes our ability to manage how others view us.

It is also possible to link the assumed HR effects on impression management to the reported increases in closeness. First, sharing HR can be seen as a form of emotional self-disclosure in situations where emotions are a part of impression management. Emotional self-disclosures have been repeatedly shown to increase feelings of connectedness (e.g., [18, 15]). This is in line with the idea that people believe that HR can reveal emotional information which you would normally choose not to show, and that it therefore undermines impression management. Second, psychological literature on intimacy (i.e., felt connectedness) builds on equilibrium theory, that states that people try to keep a certain intimacy equilibrium with their interaction partners [4]. Whenever the interaction becomes too intimate, people will start to feel uncomfortable and try to reduce the intimacy in the interaction [2]. Altogether, in situations in which sharing HR can be regarded as a form of emotional self-disclosure (i.e., those where emotions play role in impression management), it seems that sharing HR leads to increases in closeness. However, as people cannot control HR, the self-disclosure is not controllable and may lead to interaction that feels too intimate, thence, uncomfortable. Moreover, people keep different equilibria with different people, depending also on their relationship status [4]. This is in line with the observations that HR feedback did not feel uncomfortable for long-term couples as opposed to strangers.

Finally, we found that there were some interactions in which people did not feel uncomfortable sharing HR although it could undermine impression management. These were situations of low personal risk. An example of such a situation is an informal poker game, where part of the fun is in managing a particular impression, a "poker face". Therefore, adding HR to a poker game can give new challenges and interesting dimensions to the impression management in the game. Similar reasoning holds for example also for watching movies in a social setting, also mentioned by our participants.

HR as a connection

Beside the finding that HR can be informative, our findings also suggested that some participants thought HR could be valuable as it provides a direct connection to another. In particular, three out of five couples in the home study remarked that sharing HR is a way of creating a connection to someone in a remote location. It is important to separate this from HR as information, as there are some fundamental differences between them. For example, with HR as information, participants consistently said that there was a need for context in order for the HR to be informative. In contrast, with HR as connection, participants suggested that less context was better. Instead of being able to interpret the HR, participants remarked that it was more important that the HR was available and coming from someone they feel close to. This suggests that the results of HR as information and HR as connection are based on separate mechanisms.

We suggest that the effects of HR as connection could be explained by the idea that participants saw the HR as a part of the other. For example, participants used statements like *"someone is living there"*, *"she is present here with me"*, *"direct connection"* to talk about the HR feedback in this sense. This suggests that having the HR feedback can feel as if a part of the other is (physically) closer. Such a physical connection can be compared to tokens of loved ones that we sometimes keep close to us, like pictures or jewelry. If enhanced with HR, the token might be more potent as it is not just a static representation of the other, but it seems to create a continuous, open connection with the other.

Leveraging HR feedback as a continuous open connection to another could contribute to previous work in HCI on supporting intimacy for remote couples or close family (e.g., [30, 34, 21]). In such projects, feelings of closeness were often created through either explicit actions that express thinking of the other [30], or by facilitating the feeling of awareness [10]. Both processes can lead to presence in absence. In this vein, sharing HR can be also seen as a way of creating presence in absence, as it might facilitate awareness and trigger actions that express thinking of the other. As long there is no context, HR is difficult to interpret and participants are less likely to be concerned with privacy issues of sharing their HR with their close ones.

Implications, caveats and future work

We identified two core categories of effects appearing during HR sharing: 'HR as information' and 'HR as connection'. Previous sections then suggested two possible mechanisms, namely HR as *threat to impression management* and understanding the source of HR as *representation of the body*, that could explain how and why sharing HR leads to the observed effects. We will now discuss implications of these mechanisms and identify opportunities for future work.

Our results suggest that, due to the effects on impression management, HR sharing might not be a viable way to improve closeness in workplace related situations, or everyday encounters of strangers, friends and collocated couples. However, our results do not imply that all HR sharing must be uncomfortable or ineffective. On the contrary, when impression management is not an issue, HR as information could be useful. For instance, in self-reflective situations in which people are learning or training their social skills (e.g., marital therapy), it could be important to understand the differences between impressions one puts up and the underlying feelings one has. Therefore, HR feedback could have useful effects in such situations, helping people to reflect on what is happening "here and now". More generally, results of this study could inform also other contexts currently relevant for HCI, where biometric data are collected and displayed, such as projects related to Ambient Assisted Living, hospital environment etc.

Another possibility is to use HR as information based on *composite signals* (i.e., combining physiological signals from different people together), which was also suggested by some of our participants. For example, composite signal based on synchronization of HRs can, for instance, indicate situational empathy [19]. Using such indicators and reflecting them back to people might improve their social interactions [5]. Moreover, if such feedback methods use composite signals, they might not necessarily affect the impression management in the same way. As such, sharing composite feedback of HR might be a viable alternative to using individual signals that could be explored further.

Additionally, it seems that HR feedback might support feelings of closeness for remote couples. Several of our participants from the longer-term in-home study found that it brought them closer to another, without undermining impression management as it was not interpreted. We suggested that the effect could be based on understanding HR feedback as a representation of the other person, directly connected to him/her. We expect that using haptics to represent the HR might increase closeness even more than visual or aural presentations, as it further reduces physical distance to the feedback source. This suggests that HR sharing could serve as a basis for future systems enhancing feelings of social connectedness for remote couples.

More generally, while many studies in HCI focus on extracting higher-level concepts from physiological signals automatically by machines or researchers (e.g., [11, 23]), this work explores another approach for using physiological signals in HCI, where the focus is on what the people themselves make of the provided feedback, and applying it in a social context. The utility of such approach is also supported by, e.g., recent work of Sanches at al. [27] on personal HR feedback, suggesting its usefulness for self-reflection; as well as social psychological research, e.g., showing that false HR feedback influences one's perception of a social situation [36].

We recognise that this exploratory study is limited in several ways. For instance, we tested only a particular form of feedback design. Other design decisions (e.g., tactile or light-based feedback devices) might yield different effects. This study uses a combination of a longer-term in-home study and short-term in-lab explorations with friends and couples, mainly in everyday situations. Although, our results show that the core observations appeared consistently in both these contexts, further research is desirable to verify and replicate our findings with users interacting in different cultural and situational contexts, as well as with different relationship types (e.g., colleagues or strangers). Finally, this work focused on reaching a qualitative understanding of how users understand and make sense of HR feedback, providing several hypotheses on the processes behind the observed effects of HR sharing. Further work is now needed to test these hypotheses in more quantitatively oriented studies. For HR as information effects, such studies could for example draw on the large body of psychology literature in the social dilemma paradigm.

Future research could also investigate if our findings generalize to other bodily signals. For example, we suggest that the effects in the HR as information category are based on the participant's expectation that HR is interpretable in terms of emotions. Therefore, we would expect that these findings generalize to any bodily stimulus that participants could interpret in term of emotions, e.g., skin conductance.

CONCLUSIONS

This work has explored the possibilities of heart rate (HR) communication, providing a first step towards understanding the mechanisms behind physiosocial interaction. We support the suggestion that HR communication can have strong effects on intimacy, complementing previous quantitative studies by testing outside the lab in an everyday context, and by using HR sharing within a social context (whereas prior studies focused on highly structured tasks in the lab, with a self-feedback scenario without social interaction). Our data suggests that HR effects similar to those found in the lab transfer also to everyday contexts and, more importantly, to inferences of *other* people's HR. Moreover, we extend previous work by drawing out how the perceived value and effect of sharing HR changes in various various social situations and identify two core categories of effects arising from HR sharing in our data: i.e., HR as information and HR as connection. Finally, we propose two mechanisms that could help understanding the interplay between factors influencing the effects of HR sharing and draw out their implication for further work.

This work also connects to the recent interest in CHI community on bio-feedback technologies, suggesting additional opportunities for applications based on physiological signals, applied in social situations. We believe that such physiosocial technologies form a promising possibilities for future communication technologies, and we hope that this work provides a first step towards unpacking the physiosocial design space.

Acknowledgements

We thank our participants for their time and engagment in the studies. Many thanks to Joyce Westerink, Wijnand IJsselsteijn, Aaron Houssian, and our reviewers, for helpful comments. The first author also thanks Philips for their support in conducting this research.

REFERENCES

1. M. G. Ames, J. Go, J. J. Kaye, and M. Spasojevic. Making love in the network closet: the benefits and work of family videochat. In *CSCW '10*, page 145. ACM Press, 2010.
2. P. A. Andersen, L. K. Guerrero, D. B. Buller, and P. F. Jorgensen. An empirical comparison of three theories of nonverbal immediacy exchange. *Human Communication Research*, 24:501–535, 1998.
3. M. Argyle. *The psychology of happiness*. Methuen, London, 1987.
4. M. Argyle and J. Dean. Eye-contact, distance, and affiliation. *Sociometry*, 28:289–304, 1965.
5. M. Balaam, G. Fitzpatrick, J. Good, and E. Harris. Enhancing interactional synchrony with an ambient display. In *CHI '11*, pages 867–876. ACM Press, 2011.
6. E. Bradner and G. Mark. Why distance matters: effects on cooperation, persuasion and deception. In *CSCW '02*, page 226. ACM Press, 2002.
7. B. Brown, A. S. Taylor, S. Izadi, A. Sellen, J. J. Kaye, and R. Eardley. Locating family values: a field trial of the whereabouts clock. In *Ubicomp '07*, pages 354–371. Springer-Verlag, 2007.

8. J. T. Cacioppo, M. E. Hughes, L. J. Waite, L. C. Hawkley, and R. A. Thisted. Loneliness as a specific risk factor for depressive symptoms: Cross-sectional and longtitudinal analyses. *Psychology and Aging*, 21:140–151, 2006.
9. S. Consolvo, D. W. McDonald, and J. A. Landay. Theory-driven design strategies for technologies that support behavior change in everyday life. In *CHI '09*, pages 405–414, New York, USA, 2009. ACM.
10. A. K. Dey and E. de Guzman. From awareness to connectedness: the design and deployment of presence displays. In *CHI '06*, page 899. ACM Press, 2006.
11. S. H. Fairclough. Fundamentals of physiological computing. *Interacting with Computers*, 21(1-2):133–145, 2009.
12. K. Garnaes, O. Grünberger, J. Kjeldskov, and M. B. Skov. Designing technologies for presence-in-absence. *Personal Ubiquitous Computing*, 11:403–408, 2007.
13. E. Goffman. *The presentation of self in everyday life*. Anchor Books, New York, 1959.
14. H. Hutchinson, H. Hansen, N. Roussel, B. Eiderbäck, W. Mackay, B. Westerlund, B. B. Bederson, A. Druin, C. Plaisant, M. Beaudouin-Lafon, S. Conversy, and H. Evans. Technology probes: inspiring design for and with families. In *CHI '03*, pages 17–24. ACM Press.
15. J. H. Janssen, J. N. Bailenson, W. A. IJsselsteijn, and J. H. D. M. Westerink. Intimate heartbeats: Opportunities for affective communication technology. *IEEE Transactions on Affective Computing*, 1:72–80, 2010.
16. P. Klasnja, S. Consolvo, and W. Pratt. How to evaluate technologies for health behavior change in HCI research. In *CHI '11*, pages 3063—-3072. ACM, 2011.
17. S. D. Kreibig. Autonomic nervous system activity in emotion: A review. *Biological Psychology*, 84:394–421, 2010.
18. J. P. Laurenceau, L. M. Rivera, A. R. Schaffer, and P. R. Pietromonaco. Intimacy as an interpersonal process: Current status and future directions. In D. Mashek and A. Aron, editors, *Handbook of closeness and intimacy*, pages 61–78. Lawrence Erlbaum, Mahwah, NJ, 2004.
19. R. W. Levenson and A. M. Ruef. Empathy: A physiological substrate. *Journal of Personality and Social Psychology*, 63(2):234–246, 1992.
20. G. Lotan and C. Croft. imPulse. In *CHI '07 Extended Abstracts CHI '07*, pages 1983–1988. ACM Press.
21. D. Lottridge, N. Masson, and W. Mackay. Sharing empty moments: design for remote couples. In *CHI '09*, page 2329. ACM Press, 2009.
22. J. J. Lynch. *The broken heart: The medical consequences of loneliness*. Basic Books, New York, 1979.
23. R. Mandryk, K. Inkpen, and T. Calvert. Using psychophysiological techniques to measure user experience with entertainment technologies. *Behaviour & Information Technology*, 25(2):141–158, 2006.
24. P. Markopoulos, B. De Ruyter, and W. Mackay. *Awareness systems: Advances in theory, methodology, and design*. Human-Computer Interaction Series. Springer, 2009.
25. H. Murakami and H. Ohira. Influence of attention manipulation on emotion and autonomic responses. *Perceptual and Motor Skills*, 105(1):299–308, 2007.
26. B. Parkinson. Emotional effects of false autonomic feedback. *Psychological Bulletin*, 98:471–494, 1985.
27. P. Sanches, K. Höök, E. Vaara, C. Weymann, M. Bylund, P. Ferreira, N. Peira, and M. Sjölinder. Mind the body!: designing a mobile stress management application encouraging personal reflection. In *DIS '10*, pages 47–56. ACM Press, 2010.
28. T. Scherini, P. Melo, T. van Craenendonck, W. Zou, and M. Kaptein. Enhancing the sleeping quality of partners living apart. In *DIS '10*, page 171. ACM Press, 2010.
29. A. Steptoe, N. Owen, S. R. Kunz-Ebrecht, and L. Brydon. Loneliness and neuroendocrine, cardiovascular, and inflammatory stress response in middle-aged men and women. *Psychoneuroendocrinology*, 29:593–611, 2004.
30. R. Strong and W. Gaver. Feather, Scent & Shaker: Supporting Simple Intimacy in Videos. In *Extended Proceedings of CSCW'96*, pages 29–30, 1996.
31. H. Tsujita, K. Tsukada, and S. Itiro. InPhase: evaluation of a communication system focused on "happy coincidences" of daily behaviors. In *CHI '10*, page 2481. ACM Press, 2010.
32. G. E. Vaillant. *Aging Well: Surprising Guideposts to a Happier Life from the Landmark Harvard Study of Adult Development*. Little, Brown and Company, New York, 2003.
33. S. Valins. Cognitive effects of false heart-rate feedback. *Journal of Personality and Social Psychology*, 4:400–408, 1966.
34. F. Vetere, M. R. Gibbs, J. Kjeldskov, S. Howard, F. F. Mueller, S. Pedell, K. Mecoles, and M. Bunyan. Mediating intimacy: designing technologies to support strong-tie relationships. In *CHI '05*, pages 471–480. ACM Press, 2005.
35. J. Werner, R. Wettach, and E. Hornecker. United-pulse: feeling your partner's pulse. In *MobileHCI '08*, pages 535–538. ACM Press, 2008.
36. J. Wild, D. M. Clark, A. Ehlers, and F. McManus. Perception of arousal in social anxiety: effects of false feedback during a social interaction. *Journal of behavior therapy and experimental psychiatry*, 39(2):102–16, 2008.

Athletes and Street Acrobats: Designing for Play as a Community Value in Parkour

Annika Waern
Mobile Life
Stockholm University, Kista
annikaw@dsv.su.se

Elena Balan
Mobile Life
Interactive Institute, Kista
elena.balan@ymail.com

Kim Nevelsteen
Mobile Life
Interactive Institute, Kista
kim@mobilelifecentre.org

ABSTRACT
Participatory design methods face challenges when designing for a widespread youth community. In such projects, it is not enough to design in collaboration with a few selected individuals; one must also strive to understand the community at a deeper level and incorporate its values and practices into the design solution.

We report on our process of designing with, and for, an identified youth group: the Parkour and Freerunning community. We show how the successful design relied not only on employing methods of participatory observation and participatory design, but also on acquiring an understanding of the practice as a 'fun community', valuing play over achievement and competition.

Author Keywords
Parkour; Freerunning; Youth Culture; Design; Mobile service; Location-based service; fun; sports; community

ACM Classification Keywords
H.5.m [Information Systems]: Information Interfaces and Presentation – Miscellaneous;

General Terms
Design, Human Factors

INTRODUCTION
It is not entirely straightforward to transfer the practices of participatory design to designing for an established but widespread youth community. If the aim is to address the community as a whole, it doesn't suffice to design together with representatives from the community; one must also understand the values shared within the community, so that the design will be acceptable to others than the local representatives participating in the project. Finally, gaining access to a youth community is often an issue; its members must be willing to adopt and appropriate a proposed design.

In this paper, we describe our experiences with applying participatory design methodologies to a community service for the Parkour community, a recent and self-organized youth community that has, after first emerging in France, gone global.

We recount how working with expert Parkour runners created both a path into the community, but also friction related to some of the design intentions. In order to understand and address the issues, we needed to take a step back from our participatory design methods, to also incorporate a cultural and sociological understanding of the community. We analysed the problem as arising from the risk of turning a play practice into a sport, and the crucial importance of solving it as related to the way Parkour enables its practitioners to express an alternative form of masculinity. Through participatory studies of the community activities, participatory design, and our deeper understanding of the sociological structure at stake, we were able to redesign the service to be more readily accepted by the community.

AN INTRODUCTION TO PARKOUR AND FREERUNNING
Parkour is a type of sportive leisure activity, which takes place in urban space. Those who do Parkour will climb on walls, jump over rails and buildings, defying the normal roads and paths offered by the given architecture.

Parkour has received some academic attention. The most widely adopted definition of Parkour is that it is the art of moving through almost any environment as quickly and efficiently as possible [11]. Bavinton sees Parkour as a method of navigation in urban space [1], in which a key concept is the reinterpretation of potentially dangerous objects in the path, as being not obstacles but support for continuing and amplifying the runner's motion. Another core element is efficiency [4]. Practitioners move as fast as they can, while at the same time use as little energy as possible. The efficiency concept also includes avoiding injuries as much as possible.

Active participants, *traceurs*, distinguish between two forms of the activity: Parkour and Freerunning. Where Parkour is more focused on the fluency and efficiency of moves, Freerunning turns the city-space as a training ground for acrobatics. Very often, the moves have a high aesthetic value but no functional purposes. Freerunners tend to stay in one area (such as a city square) for a longer period, to explore its possibilities and affordances.

Permission to make digital or hard copies of all or part of this work for personal or classroom use is granted without fee provided that copies are not made or distributed for profit or commercial advantage and that copies bear this notice and the full citation on the first page. To copy otherwise, or republish, to post on servers or to redistribute to lists, requires prior specific permission and/or a fee.
CHI'12, May 5–10, 2012, Austin, Texas, USA.
Copyright 2012 ACM 978-1-4503-1015-4/12/05...$10.00.

In Sweden, the sport is becoming increasingly organized. It is now possible to find organized training clubs as well as partake in competitions and performances. The community is divided in its appreciation of such phenomena.

Studies of Parkour

Just as skateboarding, Parkour first emerged as a grassroots movement. Daskalaki et al. [6] suggests that Parkour originally was a political transgressive activity, aimed at the inhuman architecture of the Parisian suburbs where the sport was invented:

> "The infamous Parisian suburbs, where *parkour* was invented, are among the most alienating and dehumanising urban clusters in the world." … "It is easy to see *parkour* as a direct response to these spaces, an attempt to 'trick' them, through unconventional use, into yielding creative possibilities and a sense of one's own body and humanity."

An alternative interpretation is that it is more of an escapist than a transgressive movement. Several authors place the primary experience of Parkour as modifying the participants' perception of space, as it takes on new meaning in the context of the sport. Brown [2] notices that urban space is normally defined by the purposes that it is supposed to serve. By finding new uses and new ways of perceiving the urban objects, traceurs redefine the objectives of the shared urban space and eventually develop a different 'eye' for the environment. Saville [16] calls this the 'spatially transformative powers' of Parkour:

> "When the traceur attempts to master some movements through space, such mastery, as it occurs (or not) is always accompanied by an emotional refiguring of spatial possibilities. In this sense, parkour speaks quite forcefully to an enchanted notion of place which, through wonderment, imagination and participation, is in continuous composition."

This reading of Parkour is inspired by the situationist movement [7], their concept of 'derivé', an unplanned journey through the city that changes our perception of it. Saville also congenially identifies the emotion of *fear* as a main challenge and driver in Parkour. This relates to Klausen's analysis of Parkour as a way to 'constantly challenge borders and do what nobody thought possible' [13].

Parkour has spread rapidly, is often referred to in popular culture[1] and now attracts new participants around the globe. Hence, the culture surrounding the activity is also changing. Today, the Parkour community is in many ways similar to that of Skateboarding as described by Karsten and Pel [12].

[1] Such as in the game 'Mirror's Edge', which depicts a female Traceur as its protagonist.

Both cultures maintain a collaborative ideal in which it is the individual's progression that is important. Players will often gather spontaneously (or on very short notice) to train together, and will congratulate each other on succeeding with a new move rather than engage in informal competitions. Although some individuals are known as 'gurus' within the community, there is no formal ranking system and a general resistance to hierarchies exists. For now the majority of the traceurs are male youth; in Sweden they also seem to primarily belong to the middle-class and be of Swedish origin. These traits are shared with the skateboarding community.

The sport is becoming increasingly organized. In Sweden, it is now possible to find organized training clubs as well as partake in competitions and performances.

Parkour as a medialised practice

Klausen goes further to classify Parkour as a body, city and *media* culture [13]. His analysis is grounded in the deeply integrated use of video in Parkour. Klausen recounts how traceurs often will repeatedly watch Internet videos, aiming to bodily incorporate a pattern of movement into their own repertoire, and conversely film and upload their own moves in the landscape. The practice might originally have emerged due to the rapid spread of the Parkour practice and a consequential lack of available tutors, but has today become such an integral part of the movement that Klausen speaks of the traceur body as at the same time physical and mediated. Traceurs will watch films to learn a move, as well as invent new moves as variants of other moves. Just as the film is an integral part of the sport, so is the camera: Klausen notices that when out training, it is common that somebody brings a camera to film moves. In such situation it is common for the group to sometimes pause, and gather around the camera screen to watch and discuss what has been captured. He also recounts how the use of video serves to unite traceurs at a distance, such as when a practitioner gathers video clips from a large number of traceurs around Denmark to create a joint video representing them all.

What is less well documented is the high level of mobile phone usage that the sport already features. Already during our early pre-study, it became clear that the practitioners are deeply dependent on mobile phones, also for organizing the activity. In the Swedish Parkour community, text messaging seems to be the most widely used communication means, a trait shared with Swedish youth culture in general.

PARTICIPATY DESIGN METHODOLOGY IN TRAVEUR

The Traveur project was initiated in collaboration between the Helsingborg-based Parkour and Freerunning group Air-Wipp, our research team, and Street Media 7, a small company developing mobile phone technology. Air-Wipp is one of a very few professional Freerunning performance teams in Sweden.

The project was organized as a fairly standard participatory design project [15], with the performance team filling a central role of stakeholders and informants. Their participation in design workshops and their feedback on prototype helped answer an array of questions and shape the goals of the project. As the application was intended for the wider Parkour community, much time went into explicit discussions of the values and practices of the community. In this sense, our project employed what Cockton [3] calls worth centered design.

The project went through four distinguishable phases. It was initiated by a design brainstorming workshop, in which a host of ideas for community functions, games, and playful technology uses were explored in collaboration within the full team (including all three parties). The second phase focused on 'technology probes', which were very simple one-function applications that Air-Wipp would use in their daily practice and evaluate for their usefulness. Next came the prototype phase, in which the preferred set of functionalities were implemented and tested in practice in two iterations. A semi-functional version was first evaluated by Air-Wipp together with their students in Helsingborg, and then a fully functional prototype was evaluated through a public test in Uppsala with traceurs participating also from both Stockholm Parkour Academy and Uppsala Parkour. It was during these tests that some problems with the design started to surface. This article focuses on the value conflicts uncovered in these tests, and the fourth phase of the project: the subsequent redesign and trial period.

BRAINSTORMING, DESIGN AND PROTOTYPING

Project context and requirements

The goal of our project – to create a mobile community for traceurs – was proposed by Air-Wipp. Creating such a community was also the prime motivation for Street Media 7 to participate, seeing great potential for similar services in other domains. During our subsequent engagement with other practitioners, we could also confirm the desire for such a service within the general Swedish Parkour community. Due to the mobile nature of Parkour training, the most important requirement for the project was to create a community service accessible on fairly ordinary mobile phones.

The performance group also voiced a strong desire for a second function; they wanted to promote the sport by advocating safe training methods. The Parkour practice has spread rapidly, and many traceurs train on their own without any guidance from more experienced practitioners. The video-based online culture induces a risk of newcomers getting hurt by training moves that are too hard, too early, or under unsafe conditions (as many of the online videos show Parkour moves carried out at great height). Incorrect training methods can also lead to strain injuries. Hence, the Freerunner team set the project's second requirement; a training 'Academy' that would guide newcomers into an effective, healthy and safe way to train.

From the research groups' understanding of the Parkour community (gained through literatures studies as well as interviews primarily with the performance team), we identified three more ways we potentially could support the community.

The third proposed functionality stemmed from Klausen's observations on the use of video. The current medialisation of moves focuses on the body, whereas the environment where the move is performed plays a secondary role, and is reduced to its significant shapes, regardless of its actual location. Considering a gymnastics hall full of equipment functioning as obstacles can serve a similar purpose in a video, there exists an increasing amount of instructional videos filmed indoors rather than in the urban landscape. One of our objectives thus became to re-introduce awareness of urban space also in the medialisation of the practice. By using the map and GPS functions available on modern mobile phones, it would be possible to mark suitable spots for training and relate videos shot on location to those spots, creating a medialised correspondent of the Parkour 'eye' for the environment discussed by Brown [2] and Saville [16].

Our fourth proposal pertained to the ad-hoc structure and timing of the Parkour training sessions. We proposed a map-based 'meet-up' functionality, enabling traceurs who want to train together to seek out their friends by inviting them to share their current location in real time.

Finally, our fifth proposal was slightly more speculative. We proposed to explore the possibility of creating playful or gamelike activities around Parkour that also could involve outsiders. This, we saw as a potential means to increase the interaction between the traceurs and bystanders in the city, promoting the sport as well as potentially recruiting new practitioners.

During the brainstorming workshop, it became clear that Air-Wipp did not desire any gamelike aspects to be developed. There were two reasons for this: firstly the fear that the Parkour community would reject any design that had a competitive aspect (due to its strong emphasis on collaboration), and secondly that the incitement to interact with people in public, outside the Parkour community, was perceived as very low. Hence, we decided to focus our development on the first four objectives: creating a mobile community tool, support training, mediate Parkour as a spatial activity, and support the ad-hoc nature of urban training activities.

Initial design of Traveur

The design grew gradually through a number of iterations with feedback from Air-Wipp and field-tests with their students. During the whole process we were careful to not only get their feedback on the functionalities and interfaces,

Figure 1. The community and map functions

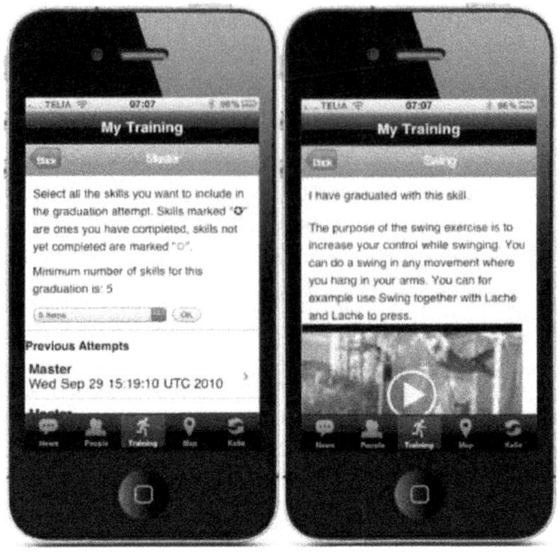

Figure 2. The Academy function

but also to observe their use of phones in general, and in particular our application in their practice.

In this section, we first summarize the functions designed and implemented during this phase of the project, and then discuss how we envisioned these would be used.

The Traveur application was split into three parts: the community function, the map-based marking function (that also supported the meet-up function), and a training function.

The basic community function is shown in Figure 1 (left). It consisted of a list of all members, a page describing each individual member and a community chat function.

Figure 1 (right) shows the map function. This view allowed users to mark points of interest on the map; add comments to such spots, select moves that could be performed in that particular location, and finally upload videos showing how those moves were performed on location. The collection of skills at locations was intended to aid traceurs in 'reading' each location, searching for obstacles that facilitated moves. The video upload function allowed traceurs to invent and spread entirely new moves related to a location.

The map function also supported the meet-up functionality. If a user wanted to meet with a group of friends, he or she could select them from the list of members and send them a 'meet-up' message. The message was sent to each participating mobile phone, giving recipients the option to accept or reject the request. If the request was accepted, the participants were able to monitor each others' location on the map for limited amount of time. The function is similar to that described in Williamson et al. [17], but conceptually simpler, as the exact positions of the meeting participants were shown.

The training function was informally called the 'Academy'. It consisted of a set of acrobatic moves that the community members could train. Each move was described by a short text, a video (filmed outdoors, to maintain the focus on urban space), and a level indicating its difficulty.

There were three levels implemented: the 'basic' level, that just consisted of a few basic moves and safety instructions, the 'intermediate' level which contained most of the singular moves, and an 'advanced' level which focused on more intricate combinations of moves. Each move was also assigned prerequisite moves, so that the system could keep track of the moves one should have mastered before trying it.

In order to generate a true 'academy', the system was designed to let some of the community members act as trainers. Students of the academy would send in videos of themselves performing a sequence of moves, and the trainers would judge whether the student had learned the moves sufficiently well to 'graduate', based on their video. Graduating meant the student would get access to a new set of moves to train.

Traveur was implemented as both a web service and an iPhone application. Basic community and chat functions were implemented in HTML making them accessible on a wide variety of platforms. However, as the web technologies could not support the meet-up and location functionalities, these were prototyped in a native iPhone client. To create a single point of access for iPhone users, web functions were embedded into the native client. This combination was made in order to satisfy the requirement for an accessible mobile community service, while simultaneously allowing us to experiment with more advanced functionalities.

Usage Patterns

Through observing the prototypes in use, we obtained good insights into how the Traveur service might be used in practice.

On one occasion, we observed a group of roughly ten individuals as they were training intensely. The whole group entered into a state of engagement similar to that of "flow" [5] where the phones were not really used. These ended up lying around on the ground or put away. A person who was not quite as active would occasionally use the phone to do bookkeeping or shoot a video of others in the group.

These observations had a direct effect on our design solution. Since an individual would not be documenting her/himself while engaged in training, this demanded a multiple login feature, where one member could upload videos to document the progress of another. A second consequence was that we saw no need, or desire, for immediate video upload from the phones. We had initially envisioned a 'single-step' function, in which a video would be shot, reviewed, and uploaded on location. In practice, there were typically several videos shot of the same person in the same place. These would be reviewed (and potentially even edited) *after* the training session. Hence, we decided to separate the function of marking a location on the map and uploading a video, so that videos could be attached to any previously marked location.

Finally, we also envisioned a special harness to allow traceurs to strap the phones to their body, a solution that could have potentially allowed us to use the sensors in the iPhone to trace movements.

NEW TRACEURS, NEW CONSIDERATIONS

As previously discussed, the public tests with the first prototype had uncovered some vague but distinctly negative feedback. To dig deeper into the issue, we decided to involve a larger group of traceurs in a new feedback and redesign cycle. The first step was to carry out three in-depth interviews with traceurs, who were active in two different Parkour groups. None of them came from the original stakeholder team, Air-Wipp. These interviews consisted of, first, a discussion and rapid prototyping session pertaining to their wishes and needs for support from a mobile service, followed by a presentation of Traveur and a feedback discussion on its design. The interview sessions lasted between 45 and 60 minutes.

All quotes below have been translated from Swedish by the author.

Rapid prototyping session

First, the participants were asked to draw or name at least three functionalities that they would like to have in a mobile application. Participants were encouraged to sketch an interface for such a service. All three subjects sketched, and verbally expressed, a wish for a map function. They unanimously identified the need of marking good training locations and some of them pointed out a need to communicate with other traceurs through a chat function, in order to arrange a training meeting. One subject sketched and described a library with videos of moves to serve as inspiration. His suggestion was to structure videos according to their role in training (warm up, training a particular skill, and actual Parkour moves), but did not suggest any separation into difficulty levels.

Feedback on the existing prototype

Following the "feature imagination" part of the interview, we demonstrated Traveur. This allowed the interviewees to compare their expectations for a mobile service with the implemented prototype. During this session, the app was shown and all functions were explained in detail. Here, we go through the reactions per function.

Community. The three interviewees were much less active in online communities than we anticipated. Rather, they associated community participation with sitting in front of the computer instead of actually practicing the discipline:

> "Some while ago there was le-parkour Sweden. There was information there. But people started discussing, instead of going out and starting training, arguing about what Parkour is. It took a lot of time"
> "people are stuck in an effort to show what they can... it becomes too much talk"

This does not necessarily mean that the mobile community function was undesirable. For example, subject B reacted positively towards the introduction of a mobile community. This, he hoped, would make it difficult to write a lot of 'useless text', and that the result would be a community site with increased quality of content.

Training. All three interviewees immediately reacted against the design of the Academy functionality. The respondents interpreted the grading of moves into three levels as introducing a hierarchy *between participants*, so that the members who have accomplished more complicated tasks also would have a higher status in the community. Even more important for the respondents was the fear that those who achieved less (or failed) would lose self-esteem. It was clear that the hierarchical level system of the training function was in conflict with the philosophy of Parkour as non-competitive, and particularly in conflict with the concept that an individual trains for her/his own development.

> "The only thing I can think of is that people will think that they are not good enough if they do not reach a level. There is little competition and it does not work together with Parkour.
> ...one might think that if you do it you are great and if you do not, you are worthless. You need to do something so that you know that it is not so serious."

It also became clear that it would be very difficult to create a training structure that could be universally agreed upon. It was hard to set difficulty levels, since practitioners have varying predominant skills, such as balance over strength. As noted previously, one of the core features of Parkour is that anyone can invent or change a move. Hence, the merit that a traceur has in the community comes not only from his or her capability to accomplish individual moves, but also from showing creativity and imagination. The respondents seemed to share a fear that the training function could become too normative:

> "People have different ranks, but this concept is far from what Parkour is. You can train at different levels. One might be better at balance and one better at strength. Who can say which one is higher in the classification? You have to be distanced from having a ranking system. It doesn't match with what Parkour is."

Safety concerns were expressed by two of the interviewees, suggesting that people may attempt moves that they would not be ready for, only in order to move faster in the community hierarchy.

The videos supplied through the training function were still seen as a good source of inspiration, indicating new moves to train or new obstacles types to be aware of.

> "Sometimes you don't focus enough and you don't know what to do next. Which is the next step? Where should I go? In [the city] there are not enough places to train. This is too difficult, this is too easy and I stay somewhere in-between."

However, in regard to serving as a source of inspiration, judging and graduation hindered users. The grading feature limited access to videos for moves that were judged as being too difficult. In practice, this meant that, most of the time, the traceur would only have access to videos with moves he or she had already tried.

Map and Meet. In contrast, the utility of the 'map' function was immediately obvious, as the traceurs recognized in it many essential features that they had already named to be useful for a Parkour application. All respondents confirmed that the number of spontaneous trainings is quite high, especially during summer, and believed that the map and meet-up functions would support such activities in a positive way.

ANALYSIS

Before going into our redesign, let's pause for a moment on the values that are at stake in this design project. What we have here is not primarily a clash between the goals of the professional Freerunners and the more 'normal' community members – both groups desire better support for training. The problem emerges due to a clash between values more deeply embedded into the design, and those generally upheld in the community. We can identify three layers to these values.

Firstly, we have the explicitly voiced concern regarding the design forcing an explicit hierarchy on the community. It is important to note that this interpretation was unintended: it was the *moves* that were graded as being beginner, intermediate and advanced level, and not the participants. Air-Wipp supported this design, fully aware of the general dislike for hierarchical structures in the community. Still, the design was read as instilling a hierarchy over participants, as some moves were accessible only when you had mastered a sufficient amount of the moves at lower levels. Even more problematic was the fact that 'trainers', through watching and judging the videos, were in control of graduations. This built-in separation of the participants into groups of trainers and trainees was too large a step away from the equality ideal ingrained in the community.

In noting this, we have to be aware that this ideal is not unchallenged within the community. In practice, advanced traceurs are acknowledged by the community and held in high esteem. (We believe that without the presence of Sweden's top professionals in our project, we would not have gained access to the community at all!) But this valuation of hierarchies is implicit, and cannot be made explicit in a design, or the community will reject it.

The second layer we discuss is the valuation of the personal achievement and progression, rather than the precise performance of a particular move. Parkour is *not* a sport, and our community members resisted making it into a sport. The valuation of creative innovation illustrates this. When a traceur comes up with a new move or invent a new execution of an existing move, it is appreciated as a creative and artistic intervention. This appreciation of change in Parkour is similarly shared with the *New Games* movement. Bernie DeKoven [8] writes in his blog 'deep fun' about 'fun' communities:

> "In the sports community, the rules and officials decide if the players are good enough to play. If not, they change players." …
> "In the fun community, the players decide if the game is good enough to play, if not, they change rules. For them, the rules are always negotiable, the ultimate criteria for success being not so much who won, but much more, how much fun they were able to create for each other."

The Parkour community seems to be torn between these two ideals. It identifies itself mostly with the ideals of a 'fun' community, whereas at the same time the increased emphasis in the community on organised training, performing and even competing, causes parts of the community to drift more towards a 'sports' attitude. Our design of the training function promoted an increased standardization of moves. In this, the design implicitly brought the practice closer to becoming a sport. Giving participants the freedom to design their own graduation video was not sufficient, as the success of a graduation would be supervised by 'trainers', who presumably had been designing the training instructions and recording the training videos.

Why then, it is so important for the community to resist Parkour becoming more of a sport? A possible interpretation can be made from the fact that Parkour is a predominantly adolescent male practice. As with many masculine practices that gain widespread attention more and more women are beginning to practice Parkour, but still, they remain a minority. Hence, it is relevant to describe Parkour as masculine practice.

In analyzing skateboarding, Karsten and Pel [12] marks the sport as carving out a space for an alternative, and in some sense 'softer', form of masculinity. Some significant markers of this are the focus on personal improvement rather than competition, and also the soft, baggy style of clothing that gives the skateboarder a more feminine touch. Parkour shares the first of these traits, albeit the clothing style needs to be more streamlined due to the acrobatic style of the sport.

By contrast, appreciating and practicing sports is an important aspect of a normative masculinity [9]. Through its focus on non-competitiveness and creativity, the Parkour community manages to distance itself from the standard athlete stereotype, and by this, carve out an alternative masculine role that still incorporates physical proficiency. This observation is consistent with the way the practice has established itself primarily as a middle-class practice (in Sweden). Whereas the middle-class can risk experimenting with alternative role models, there is too much at stake for low status men. Compare this with how the athlete is established as one of a few, if not the only, way for lower class Afro-Americans to rise in society [9].

REDESIGN

The redesign was the direct result of the feedback discussed above and our analysis thereof. Our interaction designer also actively trained with a Parkour team. This facilitated her access to them for the final extended trials, and allowed her to some extent 'go native', and partially internalize the values of the community.

As the map and community functions received positive comments, redesign efforts were focused on the training function. Here we were faced with a conflict: although the traceurs had rejected the Academy concept, its structure does reflect the expert knowledge of a professional group who also actively trained newcomers. Hence, we wanted to redesign the function to, at the same time, be more open, but also maintain some of the guidance the original system provided. Since access to videos, as inspirational resources, was considered to be beneficial, the redesign focused on leveraging this existing resource.

The very first decision was to take out the graduation requirement. This change had profound implications for the training system, which as a result could no longer can be seen as an Academy. The entire function thus changed character, to become more of a personal training guide.

Figure 3 shows the main screens of the re-designed training function. The screenshot at the left depicts an overview over the different types of core skills for training.

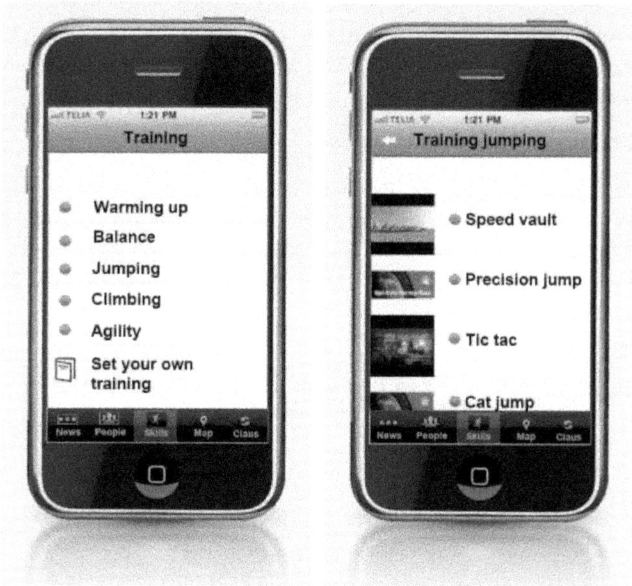

Figure 3. Main screenshots of the re-designed training function. Note in particular the 'Set your own training' option.

Figure 4: Screenshots of the re-designed training video interface.

After selecting one of the training categories, the user can browse through a list of videos as shown on the right. We also added the option "Set your own training", which allows the user to select the moves that they are interested in training.

Figure 4 shows how a move is shown to the Parkour runner. After selecting one of the videos from list, the user is prompted with the prerequisite moves for the selected move and a dialog with the options, "I have this", "Just watch, don't try" and "Don't watch, go back". If "Just watch, don't try" is selected, the video will be presented accompanied by a button "You might like also this", leading to a list of related videos. If they select "I have this", indicating that they have the necessary skills to attempt the move, they will also get access to a "Description of technique" button, leading to a step-by-step guide for executing the move.

Feedback, second iteration

A Flash mockup of the redesigned training function was presented to a total of four practitioners from the same two Parkour groups as before. Again, the respondents were tasked with giving feedback to the design and suggesting improvements.

The redesigned functionality was considered by the subjects to be radically more in line with the Parkour mentality.

> "It is good to easily go in, choose out two or three videos. It used to work to go on YouTube and look at "this is what I want to learn" and then go out and practice it. But now you have the phone and a bit more specific can choose things to train."

Being given a gallery of videos to browse through provided the traceurs with the possibility of creating their personal training program, according to their personal skills and interests.

Having a description for the technique utilized in each video was also perceived as positive.

> "It can be good to be able to see this [description of the technique], when one is beginner, for example."

The warning text, stating the prerequisite skills required for a move, was also appreciated. In general, traceurs saw the videos as a source of information and inspiration. Giving open access to information and enforcing own risk evaluation was thought to be an advantage in the design.

> "It's like this, one must try for oneself. Achieve by oneself. One must try. Even if one knows "I have bad balance". All should try so that one sort of gets better balance when trying new things."

Overall, the traceurs found the design very much inspired by what 'Parkour is', or what it is perceived to be.

> "One should decide by himself if one can or can't accomplish a move. [...] It is really good and spreads a better message about Parkour."

USAGE PATTERNS – LONG-TERM USE

The final, extended, user trial had as its goal to place Traveur in a real-life context. Four traceurs were equipped with the iPhone application during two and a half weeks. They had all been training Parkour for at least two years. (The advantage of recruiting experienced traceurs is that they train regularly on the streets, whereas newcomers tend to train more in gymnastics halls.) Three of them, two men and one woman, were aged between 15 and 17; the fourth was a man of 24 years. Some of their training sessions were observed, and all four traceurs were subject to an elaborate interview after the test period.

The goal was to better understand how the Traveur prototype would correspond to actual training needs, and if using Traveur would in some way change their practice. We selected to focus entirely on the map function, leaving the training function for a later and more large-scale public test. The major reason for this was that the training function was being re-implemented at the time, but also because the training function was intended for less experienced traceurs.

Community This study again confirmed that the mobile community function was appreciated. In the limited context of the study the participants only had access to each other, but they expressed a strong wish to increase their number of contacts.

Map The map function provided several new opportunities for the participants. During the testing period, the traceurs set new spots on the map, added skills and commented on the additions of others. The videos that they did upload came from YouTube and were previously edited, confirming our expectations that video production is done separately from training.

The map marking feature received positive reactions from all subjects and was thought to have large potential for positively influencing trainings. One person reported finding new training locations that he was unaware of. The feature was considered to be especially useful when visiting a new city.

> "I remember when we were in Malmö, X and I we would meet some of those who were training Parkour in Malmö. If we had Parkour spots as there are in Traveur, it would have been easier to find places to train. We used a website for Parkour spots. It was really complicated to find."

Before using Traveur, there was no other entirely reliable source of information on good training locations, information desired by most subjects.

> "It was just to go around and look [for a good place to train Parkour]. If you want a new place that's just to go around and see what works well for one. "
> "Actually, it would be like this. If I'm on my way home from school and see a new place that I think it is good [for training Parkour], I would try to train there." ... "Then I would definitely train more. I would explore more as well. I would take more time for practicing new things."

As searching for new places is time-consuming, the sharing of knowledge about training spots was thought to have high potential for adding novelty and diversity to the current training habits.

Meet-up The meet-up functionality was highly appreciated. The participants reported that they currently used multiple communication modes for arranging meetings, such as phoning, sending sms/texting, or the posting of messages to their Parkour group on Facebook. The meet-up function was thought to be among those capable of bringing the highest amount of change in training habits. In particular, it was seen to provide good support for spontaneous trainings, as it allows interaction in real time.

> "Then [previously to using Traveur] you would just text or call someone, but now you can send a meet-up message."

Integrating the meet-up function with the mobile community function was also seen as promising, as it did not require them to know the phone numbers of all others in order to initiate a joint training session.

> "It is easier to find someone else who is training [Parkour] if you have an iPhone with Traveur on."

> "I would have just sent to everybody" [regarding meet-up messages]

Another advantage of the meet-up function over traditional technology used was noticed and explained by one of our subjects:

> "What happens is that you can only turn on the mobile and leave it aside. You normally don't hear if someone is calling. But if you can just start Traveur, initiate a meet-up with everyone, then people can accept [the invitation for training] at their own pace."

The meet-up function also became incorporated into the training activity. During one participatory observation session, the traceurs used the meet-up function to invent a new training game. One of the group members would run away from the others, who were given the objective to catch him. The rest of the traceurs split into three groups, each with one person carrying one of the iPhones with Traveur. They gave a head start to the traceur being chased, and then started chasing. The group member having Traveur on the mobile would keep the iPhone in their hand most of the time, and in a couple of situations, when needing both hands, would quickly put it in a pocket.

From time to time, the chasing group would stop to look together at the map, in order to identify the position of the runner on the map. They would discuss how to best catch the runner with everyone contributing suggestions for shortcuts in the urban space in order for their team to be first. The area where the training was taking place was extended over a large area familiar to the Parkour group.

The invention of this game shows how much the Parkour community still identifies itself as a 'fun community' [8] rather than a sport. One of our trial participants comments on this occasion indicating the same:

> "Quite Parkour-inspired is to go away from the person that follows after. It was really fun when we tried it. It's fun to play with it."

The subject considered including this in the actual training as a new "thing".

DISCUSSION

As discussed in the initial methods section, our design project was deeply rooted in participatory design. Through the close collaboration with a group of stakeholders from start, the identified problem with online video material, and the articulated purpose to contribute to a safe way of training Parkour, its original approach lies close to participatory action research [15]. It should also be noted that the community's general reluctance towards competition was brought up several times during the initial design phase and was used to rule out more game-like design suggestions. Hence, our design approach also explicitly discussed community values from start, as advocated by Cockton [3] and Le Dantec et al [14]. In this section, we wish to highlight what we believe were the main reasons why we still met with problems in applying such well-established methods, and point towards some keys to why we (eventually) succeeded.

A dispersed and changing community

As emphasised by Ozanne and Saatcioglu [15], participatory design is typically done in close interaction with a local and identified community. The Parkour community is dispersed and heterogeneous. Hence, a major issue for the project related to grasping the values and practices of the community *as a community*. Here, ethnographic work on Parkour runners and similar communities was instrumental in shaping our understanding of the practice, as well as grasp why the valuation of play was so important for the traceurs. By engaging with several Parkour groups, we could also see that 'the theory matched the reality'. The local groups had a slightly different way of practicing Parkour than previous studies have shown, but still largely upheld the same values. Even Air-Wipp did, but due to its near-professional status they have compromised them further in their daily practice than our latter informants had.

Designing for play as a community value

Although design for experience is a well established research subject [10], designing for play remains underexplored. It differs from designing for a game or a sport, in that the goals and rules of the activity are subordinate to the act of having fun together, and may change. *Designing for play requires open design solutions.* By introducing technology into an existing play activity, we run the risk of constraining it through rigid structures and instructions - as our initial design did through its fixed training sequence and rigid instructions on how to perform moves. At the same time, technology can support a play community in inventing new forms of play - as our testers did by using the meet-up functionality for a chase game. We were particularly pleased to see that our original goal of designing a street game around Parkour was, in fact, realised. However, rather than us implementing it in code, it was created by the users, enabled by an open design.

Designing for conflicting values

Within the Parkour community, the play value was contested by a tendency towards more sport-like characteristics. While our participants expressed a strong resistance to hierarchies, gradings, and competitions, the community still upheld informal hierarchies and desired structured training functions for beginners.

In our design, we needed to strike a balance between the requirement on openness, so as to support a variety of play practices, and the need for supporting safe training. Although this may not be desirable for an ethnographer, *a designer can benefit by 'going native'*. By training and socialising with traceurs, our interaction designer internalized the complexity of this value conflict, allowing her to find a design solution that struck a balance between the two requirements.

CONCLUSIONS

In designing for the (Swedish) Parkour community, we ran into issues related to employing user-participatory design, arising from the fact that our access route to the community was through a near-professional Parkour team. In order to understand and address the issues, we needed to take a step back from our participatory design methods, to also incorporate a cultural and sociological understanding of the community. The problems arose from an internal conflict within the community, that at the same time embodies values that mark it out as a 'community of fun', and the desire for more structure pushing the activity towards becoming more sport-like.

Our project illustrates the importance of simultaneously understanding a community 'from the outside' through ethnographic studies and social theory, and internalize its value system in all its conflicting complexity in design. Our final design is a compromise, made acceptable through its focus on openness and support for appropriation.

ACKNOWLEDGMENTS

This project was funded by Vinnova under the 'Vardags-IT' program. Traveur is currently under consideration for commercial launch by Street Media 7. We thank Stockholm Parkour Academy and Uppsala Parkour for their unwavering support for the project.

REFERENCES

1. Bavinton, N. From obstacle to opportunity: Parkour, leisure, and the reinterpretation of constraints, *Annals of leisure research*, 10(3-4), (2010) 391-412.
2. Brown, N. The art of displacement. Parkour as a challenge to social perceptions of body and space. Parkour Generations, blog post (2007). http://www.parkourgenerations.com/articles.php?id_cat=2&idart=21
3. Cockton, G. Designing worth is worth designing. *Nordic CHI* (2006) 165–174
4. Colting, F. and Gadd, C-J.*Extremsport*, Nicotext (2008).
5. Csikszentmihalyi, M. *Flow: The psychology of optimal experience*, Harper Perennial reprint 2008 (1991).
6. Daskalaki, M., Starab, A. and Imasa, M. The 'Parkour organisation': inhabitation of corporate spaces. *Culture and Organization* 14(1) (2008) 49–64
7. DeBord, G. Theory of the Dérive, *Les Lèvres Nues* #9 (1956) reprint in *Internationale Situationniste* #2 (1958)
8. DeKoven, B. Coliberation continued. Deep fun, blog post (2011) http://www.deepfun.com/coliberation-continued/
9. Harrison, L., Harr*ison C.K, and Moore, L.N.* African American racial identity and sport. *Sport, education and leisure* 7(2) (2002) 121–133.
10. Hassenzahl, M. and Tractinsky, N. User experience - a research agenda. *Behaviour and information technology*, 25(2) (2006) 91–97.
11. Jonasson, K. Parkour – en posthumanistisk idrott?, *Proc. of Kultur~Natur: Konferens för kulturstudier i Sverige*, Norrköping, Sweden. (2009)
12. Karsten, L., and Pel, E. Skateboarders exploring urban public space: Ollies, obstacles and conflicts. *Journal of housing and the built environment* 15, (2000) 327–340.
13. Klausen, M. Parkour og den mobile teknologi: En etnografisk undersøgelse af fænomenet parkour i dimensionerne krop, by og medialisering. *Qualitative Studies* 1(1), (2010) 33-47.
14. Le Dantec, C., Shehan Poole, E., and Wyche, S.P., Values as lived experience: Evolving value sensitive design in support of value discovery. Proc. CHI'09, ACM (2009) 1141-1150
15. Ozanne, J.L, and Saatcioglu, B. Participatory action research. *Journal of consumer research* 35 (2008) 423–439.
16. Saville, S.J. Playing with fear: Parkour and the mobility of emotion. *Social & cultural geography* 9(8) (2008) 891-914
17. Williamson, J., Robinson, S., Stewart, C., Murray-Smith, R., Jones, M., and Brewster, S. Social Gravity: A virtual elastic tether for casual, privacy-preserving pedestrian rendezvous, CHI'10 ACM (2010). 1485–1494.

Communication and Commitment in an Online Game Team

Laura Dabbish[12], Robert Kraut[1], and Jordan Patton[1]
[1]Human-Computer Interaction Institute and [2]H. John Heinz III College
Carnegie Mellon University
5000 Forbes Ave., Pittsburgh, PA 15213
{dabbish, robert.kraut}@cs.cmu.edu, jordanpatton@gmail.com

ABSTRACT

Theories about commitment in online settings and empirical evidence from offline environments suggest that greater communication in online groups should lead members to become more committed and participate longer. However, experimental evidence is sparse, in part because of difficulties inducing communication online. Moreover, previous work has not identified the route by which communication leads to increased commitment. In this paper, we investigated whether task versus social communication modeled by a leader versus a peer influenced the amount that group members talked and their willingness to continue participating in the group. We conducted an experiment within ad hoc groups in the online game World of Warcraft. Results suggest that communication early in a group's history causes members to talk more later on and that the early communication increases their commitment through its influence on group atmosphere rather than through increased member participation. Social communication by a peer is especially valuable in increasing commitment.

Author Keywords
Virtual teams; commitment; conversation; communication; status; online games.

ACM Classification Keywords
H5.3. Group and Organizational Interfaces.

General Terms
Human Factors

INTRODUCTION

An online group is more likely to be successful if it is composed of members who are committed to it. Commitment is "a force that binds an individual to an organization and thereby reduces the likelihood of turnover" (p. 993, [30]). By commitment, we mean members' affective connection to and caring for the group in which they become involved [1]. Members who are committed to an online group are crucial to its success. These are the members most likely to provide the content that others value—answers to others' questions in technical and health support groups (e.g., [43]), or code in open source projects (e.g., [32]). Committed members also help enforce norms of appropriate behavior [47], police the community and sanction deviant behaviors [8], and perform behind the scenes work to help maintain the community [6].

Permission to make digital or hard copies of all or part of this work for personal or classroom use is granted without fee provided that copies are not made or distributed for profit or commercial advantage and that copies bear this notice and the full citation on the first page. To copy otherwise, or republish, to post on servers or to redistribute to lists, requires prior specific permission and/or a fee.
CHI'12, May 5–10, 2012, Austin, Texas, USA.
Copyright 2012 ACM 978-1-4503-1015-4/12/05...$10.00.

Extensive research in social psychology and organizational behavior suggests that there are two distinct routes to commitment to a group. People can identify with the group as an entity (common identity) or they can feel close to individual members of the group (common bonds; [40]). These processes also seem to apply in online groups [45].

CSCW researchers have proposed design interventions to increase identity-based commitment to online groups by emphasizing the group as an entity and bond-based commitment by emphasizing individuals and supporting communication among them [42]. Experimental research shows that it is possible to substantially increase identity-based commitment by, for example, partitioning a larger group into subgroups and exposing subgroup members to its logo, slogan or accomplishments. However, it is much more difficult to increase bond-based commitment [13, 41], in large part because of the difficulty inducing a sufficient number of group members to communicate with each other. For example, only two percent of 12,000 unique members who had visited a money recommender site in the year after it launched discussion forums ever posted a message [18].

Failures in communication are more general, even when communication is essential to the success of the online group. For example, only approximately 14% of Wikipedia editor discuss the articles they work on in the article's talk page [23]. A large percent of subscribers to email-based discussion groups are lurkers, never participating in discussions, with a majority of lists having no communication over a three-month period [6]. One of the goals of the current research is to investigate ways of increasing communication in online groups where little otherwise occurs.

> *Research Question 1: How can we increase communication in online groups?*

There is good reason to believe that conversation among members is important to generating bond-based commitment in an online group. Communication is the basis for interpersonal relationships, on which bond-based commitment depends. Interpersonal communication drives the development of interpersonal attraction [14]. As people's interactions increase in frequency, their liking for one another also increases [34]. In online communities, especially, frequency of interpersonal communication is a major determinant of the extent to which people can build relationships with one another [28]. Interpersonal relationships are especially likely to arise from exchanges of personal information and self-disclosure [10, 38].

Meta-analyses of the research on commitment suggest that communication among members of a group or organization is strongly related to the level of commitment to that social entity [26, 38]. However, much of this work simply correlates self-reports about the frequency of various kinds of communication with feelings of commitment. These cross-sectional, correlational analyses do not demonstrate that communication among group members actually increases commitment.

If interpersonal communication in online groups actually increases commitment, the mechanisms involved remain unclear. That is, there is still an open question about what that communication should look like. Specifically, does communication lead to commitment as a function of production of communication (i.e., group members feel involved when they talk to others) or receipt of communication (i.e., they feel wanted when others talk to them)? Does the content of the communication matter? For example, if members exchange personal information through task-oriented oriented talk or if they bond through task-oriented talk? Finally, does the conversational partner matter (i.e., is communication from peers versus leaders equally as important to commitment)? A second aim of this research is to better understand whether communication in online groups increases commitment and the causal pathways that might produce this effect.

> *Research Question 2: Does communication in online groups influence commitment?*

In order to investigate these research questions, we conducted the research described here in the context of ad hoc groups that form to accomplish difficult goals within World of Warcraft, a popular multiplayer, online game. These massively multiplayer games are important businesses in their right. For example, over 11 million players pay about $15 per month to subscribe to the game. Moreover, the ad hoc groups in these game share many features of virtual teams used both online (e.g., the editors creating a Wikipedia article) or in the business world (e.g., a task force designing new product). They consistent of multiple people, often strangers, coming together for a defined time to perform a meaningful (at least to the participants) interdependent task.

Virtual teams are increasingly present in the business world as well. In 2002 Gartner Group suggested that more than 60 percent of professional employees work in teams with some level of virtuality and this number has only increased since then [16, 22]. Developing commitment is particularly a challenge for a virtual team [39]. Members of these teams have difficulty forming a shared identity [46], are more likely to make negative attributions about their fellow members' behavior [11] and feel they are not committed to the team [12], resulting in less willingness to help teammates and higher turnover [19, 52].

We were interested in whether we could induce communication in ad hoc virtual teams and whether this communication would influence team members' subsequent commitment to the team. In an experiment, we manipulated the presence and type of communication an experimental confederate in a leadership or non-leadership role produced early in the team's history. We examined how this influenced how much the other team members talked amongst themselves and their subsequent commitment (measured by whether they wanted to stay with the team or not). Our results suggest that injecting communication early in the team's history significantly increased the amount of talk overall and commitment to the team. Talk by non-leaders was especially effective when it was socially oriented, not task oriented. In addition we find evidence that being talked to leads to commitment irrespective of the amount an individual talks, suggesting commitment is a more a function of the social environment rather than direct engagement with the group.

BACKGROUND AND HYPOTHESES

Modeling and Communication

As discussed previously, communication within an online team is not automatic. How can one foster conversation within an online group? Research on communication structure and conversation in online settings suggests a series of factors that could influence the amount of talking with a group, including the effort required to produce an utterance [18], requests and other linguistic obligations [27, 44], and behavioral mimicry or modeling [37]. In this research we focus on modeling, because it is under a manager or group leader's control to some degree. They can serve as role models by performing the behavior they desire from their team or by recruiting a subset of team members with appropriate qualities (e.g., extraversion).

Previous work suggests that in both social and nonsocial situations the behavior of others is a powerful cue for one's own behavior [9], and is effective in influencing both private actions (e.g., towel recycling in hotel rooms, where information about the behavior of previous occupants seems to encourage individuals to conserve and reuse towels; [17]) and communication. In the domain of communication, response to models seems to occur subconsciously, for example, when individuals seem to automatically mimic a conversational partner's nonverbal gestures, body language or speech [2, 37].

Modeling done early in a group's history may set norms for appropriate behavior that have long lasting effects. In groups and teams the appropriate or accepted ways of behaving (or norms) serve as a model for how other members should act. Theory about group development suggests that these norms are set very early in a group's history together and established by observable patterns of interaction [33]. These models of group development suggest that communication in the early stage of a group's history should set the tone for the group and suggest the nature of their behavior or interaction during later stages. These considerations motivate our first hypothesis:

Hypothesis 1: When a role model communicates early in a group's history, this will cause more communication by other members later in its history.

Participant roles may also influence the effectiveness of communication made early in a group's history on subsequent communication within the group. Research on conformity and influence in groups and teams suggests that leaders, because of their high status, may have greater influence on group norms [24]. Similarly, in teams, leaders can often have more influence on a group's conversation and decisions [48]. Social identity theory suggests this is because leaders serve as the prototypical member of the group, in that they embody the values of the team, and represent how an 'ideal' group member should behave [20]. Social identity theory, then, suggests that conversation by leaders should more strongly influence the behavior of other members than conversation by peers.

Hypothesis 2: Conversation delivered early in a group's history by an individual in a leadership role should have a stronger influence on subsequent group communication than conversation delivered by an individual in a peer role.

Communication and Commitment

As discussed above, research on organizational commitment suggests that more communication between members should strengthen commitment to a group [26, 29, 38]. However, previous work on this relationship has been predominantly correlational in nature showing, for example, that long time members of an online community are more talkative and vice versa [36]. This makes it difficult to ascertain the route by which conversation increases commitment to the community. We suggest that there are two possible routes by which conversation increases commitment to a group: (1) by creating a friendly atmosphere or tone, or (2) through participants own communication and investment in the group.

Conversational Environment

The mere presence of conversation may create an inviting atmosphere, resulting in increased feelings of commitment to a group. Theories of commitment suggest that socialization and value congruence are important antecedents of commitment to a group [30, 31]. A communicative environment is inviting and could suggest a norm of openness in a group. For groups that have recently formed, this environment could lead to feelings of cohesion and connection among members, even if they themselves do not talk. If this were the case, the presence of higher levels of communication among some members of a group would be sufficient to increase commitment, regardless of whether an individual themselves is talking. The large number of repeat lurkers on many sites suggests that it is possible to be committed to a site without directly interacting with other members [35].

Hypothesis 3: Role model communication in the early period of a group's history should foster higher levels of commitment to the group.

Talking Increases Commitment

Simply seeding a group with communication may not be sufficient to foster commitment to that group. It may be that one must actively participate in the conversation to feel a higher level of commitment. Theories of commitment also suggest that involvement with a team is an important antecedent to commitment [30]. This corresponds with research on communication in interpersonal relationship development which suggests that sharing information with someone can foster bonds and make you feel closer to that person. For example, research on disclosure and liking suggests that sharing personal information about yourself with another person increases liking for that person [4]. In groups, being highly engaged with the group and involved may lead you to feel closer to the other members and increase your desire to stay with the group. Parks & Floyd's research on membership in online text-based discussion forums showed a relationship between the amount of posts an individual had made in an online forum and their tenure in the group [36]. If communication leads to commitment through a feeling of involvement, then directly interacting with other members should increase feelings of commitment to that group. This perspective suggests that the effectiveness of a communication intervention will be dependent on the participant's own amount of communication in response to initial seeded comments:

Hypothesis 4: The influence of a role model's communication on member's commitment to the group will be mediated by the amount they communicate.

Member role and conversation type

The relationship between communication and commitment may depend largely on who does the talking and what they say. The previous work on communication and commitment has suggested that leader communication is an important influence on commitment [50]. Research on leader communication has often focused on task-related communication in the form of feedback. However, the research on leader-member exchange has suggested that fostering a close relationship with subordinates through socio-emotional (socially-oriented) communication can increase subordinate motivation, commitment and satisfaction [15]. Other work on communication and commitment has suggested that leaders should instead focus on task-related communication, which leads to higher organizational commitment. In a series of surveys within two organizations, Postmes et al. [38] found that leader communication about task-related topics was more strongly associated with organizational commitment than peer communication about socio-emotional topics. At the same time, peer communication about socio-emotional topics was an important determinant of commitment to the immediate group (versus the larger organization).

Unfortunately, the previous work on communication and commitment has largely conflated communicator role and conversation topic. It is unclear whether socio-emotional communication from leaders would be equally effective as socio-emotional communication from peers in generating commitment to the team. Similarly, we do not know whether task-related communication from peers would increase or decrease commitment relative to socio-emotional communication. The relationship between communication topic and role could further illuminate the mechanism by which communication leads to commitment.

Postmes et al.'s [38] results suggest that when the leader is talking, communication should lead to commitment when that communication is related to the group's task. This is because the communication will serve to reinforce the identity of the group as an entity [20].

> *Hypothesis 5a: The relationship between communication and commitment will be strongest when that communication is focused on the group's task (rather than socio-emotional) and delivered by an individual in a leadership role (rather than a peer).*

However, if commitment is ultimately more a function of interpersonal relationships among members of the team [29], socially-oriented social communication delivered by peers should result in the strongest connection to the group.

> *Hypothesis 5b: The relationship between communication and commitment will be strongest when that communication is socio-emotional (rather than focused on the group's task) and delivered by a peer (rather than an individual in a leadership role).*

Summary

In summary, based on the previous research on commitment, communication, and group development, we expected that injecting communication early in a team's history would lead to more communication among the rest of the team in a subsequent time period and ultimately higher commitment to the team. We also expected that the communicator's role would interact with the nature of the communication. We evaluated our stated hypotheses in an experiment within real groups in an online game. The setting allowed us to manipulate the communicator's role, the content of their communication, and measure the group's response in terms of subsequent communication and commitment.

METHOD

Setting and Task

We conducted our experiment in the World of Warcraft massively multiplayer online role-playing game, which is accessed by players over the Internet using personal computers. Over 11.1 million people have a monthly subscription to World of Warcraft [51].

We applied our experimental manipulations within groups completing dungeon raids. "Raiding" is a common activity in World of Warcraft, in which groups of players work together to accomplish a common goal which none of them could accomplish on their own. When players participate in a raid, they form a group using in-game tools and journey into an area of the game known as a "dungeon." Players almost never venture into dungeons on their own, as their characters would quickly die without help. In a raid, however, a very well coordinated group may successfully defeat all of monsters in a dungeon. When these monsters are defeated, they release special weapons, armor, and other "loot" that players desire. To increase the generalizability of the research, we selected three dungeons that span a range of difficulties, time requirements, and participant motivations: Pit of Saron, Forge of Souls, and the Culling of Stratholme.

In organizing for a dungeon raid, players can select to work with an existing team or can be randomly assigned to a team using an in-game tool called the Dungeon Finder. After each raid, they have the option to continue as a team beyond the immediate task. During the raid players have available text-based channels of communication seen by all participants (called the party chat). Players can also chat privately with selected other players. Any player can record in game activity and all chat visible to them using game tools and add-ons. Figure 1 shows a player's screen during a dungeon raid, with chat in the lower left corner.

Figure 1. World of Warcraft Dungeon Image, players cooperate to defeat a dungeon monster.

Participants

Participants in the study were World of Warcraft players who used the Random Dungeon Finder tool to enter the three dungeons of interest. This tool allows players to sign up for random dungeons that require five participants. The Random Dungeon Finder matches players into teams so that all the necessary roles are filled. Additionally, it limits access only to players with characters that have attained an appropriate level, armor, and weapons to complete the dungeon. We conducted trials with 108 different groups (5 person groups made up of 3-4 naïve participants per group plus one confederate) for a total of 457 participants.

Experimental Manipulations

In order to examine our hypotheses of interest, we modified the role and behavior of a confederate embedded in dungeon raid groups. Our experiment had two main manipulations: the type of chat the confederate used early in the groups existence (silent, socially-oriented, and task-oriented), and the role of the confederate within the group (leader vs. peer). These variables were manipulated across dungeon raid groups, for a 3 (chat type) by 2 (role) between subjects design. We examined the influence of these interventions on the amount of communication by other group members and their commitment to the team, measured by their willingness to stay in the group following the immediate task. We describe our independent and dependent variables in more detail below.

Conversant role

We were interested in whether the relationship between conversation and commitment would vary depending upon whether the role model was a leader of the group or just a peer member. We manipulated leadership by having the same confederate play different functional roles in the five-man dungeon raid groups as they battled monsters using two different level 80 characters.

Three unique roles must be fulfilled in a five-man dungeon. The first role, called "Tank," is a character with great defensive capabilities who will soak up damage from attacks by dungeon monsters. The Tank is commonly viewed as the natural leader of the group, as his actions determine a course through the dungeon and when and where fights will take place. The second role is called "Healer." A Healer keeps all group members alive (and resurrects the dead) by repairing damage to the other group members as it occurs. The third and final role is called "Damage Dealer," and may also be referred to as the "DPS" or "Damage Per Second (DPS)." Damage Dealers attack designated targets to quickly kill them in the order prescribed by the Tank. A five-man dungeon group includes one Tank, one Healer, and three Damage Dealers.

During the course of this study, the same research assistant played either the Tank role for the "leader" condition or the Damage Dealer role for the "peer" condition. Members of a group can vary in status as a function of their instrumentality to the group's task, i.e. the skills and resources they posses that directly impact successful task performance [7]. Leadership in random dungeon groups in WoW play out differently than in other small, task-oriented groups because they are based on character's in-game functions rather than any special leadership ability. In the dungeon raid task, the Tank role was highly instrumental because participants with Tank characters are less common in the game than Healer or Damage Dealer characters, and so more difficult to replace. The Damage Dealer role, on the other hand, was less instrumental because each team contained three Damage Dealer players that were easy to replace. Our hypotheses suggest that role modeling performed by different characters (Tank vs. DPS) should have different effects because the characters are differentially important in the game.

Communication type

The five-man dungeon raids in this experiment took between 15 and 30 minutes to complete. In order to manipulate the presence and nature of conversation and view its effects on the group's own conversation, we segmented the dungeon runs into three time periods. The confederate administered the conversation intervention during the first time period, which was approximately one third of the dungeon run (e.g. the first 5 minutes during a 15 minute run) and observed with minimal communication during the next two-thirds of the dungeon run (e.g. 10 minutes during a fifteen minute run).

The confederate manipulated the presence of conversation in the first time period by initiating chat based on a script or remaining silent unless spoken to. When conversation was present, the confederate varied the type of the conversation by selecting conversational turns from a task-oriented or socially-oriented script. The scripts were created from utterances observed in use by WoW players during pilot dungeon raids. Thus we had three levels in our manipulation of communication type: silent, task-oriented, and socially-oriented.

During the silent condition, the confederate did not initiate any conversation and did not respond to general questions asked to the group as a whole, but offered short, polite replies if asked a direct question. During the task-oriented and socially-oriented conditions, the confederate made utterances in the group text chat at three points during the first five minutes of the dungeon raid: (a) at the very beginning of the dungeon run, (b) after the second monster in the dungeon was killed, (c) after the fourth group of monsters were defeated. These points were selected because they are effectively subtask breakpoints within the dungeon raid task and group members would be more likely to attend to and have time to respond to the communication.

At each of these time points, the confederate selected randomly among conversational prompts. In the task-oriented condition, conversational prompts were questions directly related to the current dungeon raid task. Questions were utilized because the prior literature shows that questions are more effective at initiating conversation than statements [44]. In the socially-oriented condition, the conversational prompts were questions related to aspects of the game outside of the immediate task or related to the players' real lives outside of the game. Table 1 shows examples of task and socially-oriented prompts.

Conversational prompt	Task-oriented	Socially-oriented
(a) At the beginning of the dungeon	"Is everybody ready?"	"What did you do today?"
(b) After second monster	"What rotation do you use?"	"I'm thinking of creating a new alt, any recommendations?"
(c) After fourth monster	"Does anyone need specific loot from here?"	"Any of you working on hard modes in icc?"

Table 1. Examples of task and socially-oriented prompts

After the confederate manipulated his communication, in the remaining two-thirds of the dungeon run, he was silent, responding only to direct questions.

Outcome Measures

We collected two dependent variables: the amount of talk by team members following the conversation intervention and commitment to the team.

Conversation generated

In order to measure the effectiveness of conversational modeling on subsequent conversation among group members, we measured the amount of talk in the second period of the dungeon run. We did this by logging the chat from all group members using an in-game feature that captured all text communication and recorded it to a file on the confederate's computer. Chat logging appended timestamps to all text messages. We calculated the amount of talk generated by each member of the group during the second time period of play in terms of lines of communication, with each line representing an utterance, after eliminating the confederate's communication. It is important to note that this measure includes only chat messages sent using the party chat (hence visible to all members of the group) while private messages between pairs of players were not captured in the logs.

Commitment

We were interested in whether the initial conversation directly or indirectly influenced commitment to the team. Here we defined commitment as a desire to stay with team beyond the original team goal of completing the dungeon raid for which they formed [5]. In order to measure this, near the end of the dungeon raid but before participants left the dungeon, our confederate queried the group to ask whether they wanted to continue together on an additional dungeon raid. Before the final monster (the boss) in the dungeon was killed, the confederate posted a message to the group chat asking if they want to queue for another dungeon. After the boss was killed, he/she immediately activated the Random Dungeon Finder and recorded which (if any) team members queued for another dungeon. Thus our measure of individual commitment was behavioral -- a binary variable set to one if a team member re-queued for the next dungeon, and zero if not.

Control variables

In addition to our outcome measures of interest (communication volume and behavioral commitment), we also identified control variables measured to account for other factors that may influence the dependent variables. These included the specific dungeon name, the participant's potential performance (character level, armor quality) based on data retrieved from a public database that publishes information on characters from World of Warcraft, the participant's actual performance during the dungeon raid task (damage or heals per second), and their role (Tank, Healer, or Damage Dealer).

RESULTS

We conducted 108 trials within the dungeons in World of Warcraft, with approximately 4 participants per trial for a total of 457 participants. Data from participants across all three roles are included in our analysis. Twenty-two team members dropped out of the raid before completion and were replaced by the Random Dungeon Finder. The results reported below do not change whether or not the 22 replacements were included in the analysis.

We were interested in whether our communication manipulation generated communication by the other members of the team (Hypothesis 1), whether communication role modeling was more effective when done by a group leader or peer (Hypothesis 2) whether the presence of communication increased team member commitment directly (Hypothesis 3) or in a mediated fashion (Hypothesis 4) and whether these possible effects varied by member role (Hypothesis 5a and 5b).

We first examined the influence of our communication manipulation in the first period of play on the amount of talk generated by members of the group in the second period. We conducted a negative binomial regression of the number of lines of talk generated by each member in the second time period of the session to account for the skewed distribution of the count data, with individual nested within group to account for the non-independence of observations across members of the same group. We included member role, conversation type, and their interaction as independent variables in our model, along with the dungeon and player performance potential as control variables. Statistical tests are reported as Incident Report Ratios (IRR), the ratio of the amount of lines of talk as an independent variable changed from a baseline condition (e.g., the peer role model) to another (e.g., the leader role model). Figure 2 shows the pattern of results for amount of communication.

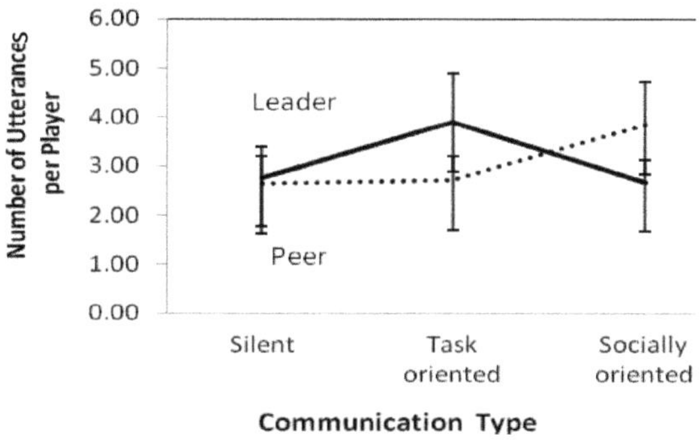

Figure 2: Effects of confederate role and communication type on players' communication

H1 predicts that group members would talk more when a role model talked early in the groups history than when the role model was silent. This hypothesis was confirmed. We created a nominal variable to contrast talk versus silent conditions (effectively collapsing the task-oriented and socially-oriented talk manipulations). When the role model talked in the first third of a group's life, the other members talked more in the remaining two-thirds (IRR=1.61; p=.05).

We conducted exploratory analyses to determine whether the type of talk mattered, including a nominal variable representing the three levels of talk in our experiment (silent, task- and socially-oriented). Both types of talk had an influence on the amount of participant talk, with early socially-oriented talk by our confederate having the strongest influence on the lines of talk (IRR=1.75; p=.04) and task-oriented talk only marginally increasing the amount of talk among the other members of the group (IRR=1.49; p=.15).

H2 predicted that the effects of role model talk would increase when the role model was a group leader. However, this hypothesis was not confirmed. The effects of role modeling were not different when the model was a leader or peer (for the Role by Talk interaction, IRR=0.79; p=.47). In addition, the leadership role did not influence the power of role modeling when we separately examine their task-oriented communication (for the Role by task-oriented communication interaction, IRR=0.82; p=.61) and their socially-oriented communication (for the Role by Socially-oriented communication interaction, IRR= 0.76; p=.48).

Conversant role, communication type, and commitment

Because the outcome measure of commitment is binary (whether a group member signed up to play with the group again or nor), we conducted a random-effects logistic regression on the decision to continue. Results are reported in odds ratios (OR), the ratio of the odds of staying in the group when an independent variable increases by a unit compared to a baseline condition. Because decisions within a single group are not independent of each other, the analysis nested members within groups with participant id included as a random effect in the model, to account for this non-independence of observations. Players were substantially more likely to want to continue playing in groups where the confederate was a leader than when it was a peer (OR=4.94; p=.001).

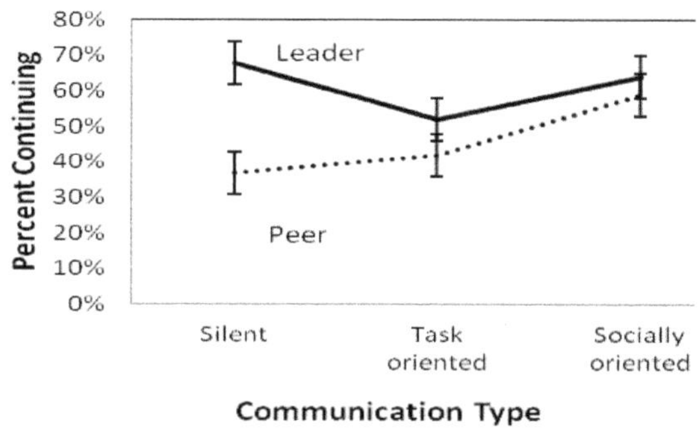

Figure 3: Effects of confederate role and communication type on players' commitment

H3, which predicted that more communication early in a group's life cycle would increase group members' commitment, was confirmed. Figure 3 shows the pattern of results for commitment across conditions.

The presence of conversation doubled the odds of staying with the group (OR=2.10; p=.01). The effect of the leadership role was large. However, the communication had different effects when the confederate performed different roles in the group (for the role by communication interaction, OR=.28, p=.04). In particular, communication increased players' commitment when the role model was a peer (OR=2.75, p=.12), but depressed it when they were leaders (OR=.61, p=.10).

Distinguishing among the types of communication shows that socially-oriented chat tripled the odds of staying with the group (IRR=3.10; p=.02), while task-oriented communication did not reliably increase the odds of staying (OR=1.35, p=.54). However, as Figure 2 shows, the effects of different types of communication varied with the confederate's role. Socially oriented communication increased the probability of players' staying when the confederate was a peer (OR=4.65, p=.04), but had no effect when the confederate was a leader (OR=.79, p=.50; for role by socially-oriented communication interaction, p=.03). In contrast, task-oriented communication depressed a player's probability of staying when the confederate was a leader (OR=.48, p=.03), but had no effect when the confederate was a peer (OR=1.64, p=.49; for the role by task-oriented communication interaction, p=.08).

These results suggest that players wanted to continue in groups when the confederate was a leader. He made the group attractive by dint of his status and irreplaceability. Communication didn't enhance his position in the group, and even hurt it when he engaged in task-based communication. In contrast, players were less likely to want to continue playing in groups when the confederate was their peer. His position, gameplay and replaceability made the group less attractive than if he had been a leader. However, he could compensate for these problems of status and performance through social communication. We suspect that other players grew to like the group more because of his social rather than task competence.

Finally we examined whether the influence of early communication on commitment occurred as a function of communication environment, or was mediated by member communication, suggesting involvement as a pathway. Having established the direct influence of chat presence and type on the amount of member communication, and the influence of communication type on commitment, we next added member communication to our model of commitment (as lines of talk). We found that the presence of chat continued to have a positive influence on commitment (likelihood of staying with the group), even with the amount of member communication included in the model (OR=2.05; p=.11), particularly for the peer conversant's (role by talk interaction: OR=1.75; p=.03). This result suggests that member talk does not mediate the influence of leader or peer communication on member commitment to the group. We examined this pathway using a binomial regression in order to compare the coefficients for the direct effect of commitment with and without member communication in the model using mediation tests. We found the mediation was not significant according to this test [3]. Thus, we find support for Hypothesis 3, that conversation influences commitment by creating a positive climate in the group. Support for our hypotheses is summarized in table 2.

DISCUSSION

The results from our study indicate that it is possible to induce communication in a temporary online team through the use of a role model. We found that communication early in a group's history led to increased levels of communication by group members. In addition, the role model's communication was effective in increasing commitment to the group in the form of member retention.

Our results also illuminate the causal pathway between communication and commitment to a group. We found that communication influences commitment to a group by creating a supportive environment within which members choose to remain. This is evidenced by the fact that early communication by either a peer or a leader led to higher levels of member communication (which could be construed as evidence of affective or behavioral commitment), but this member communication did not explain the increase in likelihood to stay with a group (continuance commitment). Thus it is through an environmental effect, rather than direct involvement, that communication can increase commitment to a group. Additionally, our results showed this occurred regardless of the type of communication (task or socially-oriented talk).

Hypothesis	**Supported?**
1: *When a role model communicates early in a group's history, this will cause more communication by other members later in its history.*	**Yes.** Presence of chat increased the amount of member chat across all role conditions.
2: *Conversation delivered early in a group's history by an individual in a leadership role should have a stronger influence on subsequent group communication than conversation delivered by an individual in a peer role.*	**No.** Early conversation by both peers and leaders increased member conversation volume.
3: *Role model communication in the early period of a group's history should foster higher levels of commitment to the group.*	**Yes.** Chat manipulation significantly increased likelihood of staying in the group.
4: *The influence of a role model's communication on member's commitment to the group will be mediated by the amount they communicate.*	**No.** Early conversation had a direct influence on the likelihood of staying with a group. In particular, socially-oriented communication had the strongest influence on retention.
5a: *The relationship between communication and commitment will be strongest when that communication is delivered by an individual in a leadership role (rather than a peer) focused on the group's task (rather than socio-emotional).*	**No.** Communication type did not influence commitment when delivered by an individual in a leadership role.
5b: *The relationship between communication and commitment will be strongest when that communication is socio-emotional and delivered by a peer.*	**Yes.** Significant interaction between role and conversation type, with talk type having the strongest influence on commitment to peer conversant (and no influence of talk type for leaders).

Table 2 – Summary of Hypotheses and Experimental Support

This suggests that the nature of the communicative environment may matter less than the fact that members are interacting with one another.

Future work is needed to ascertain exactly how and why the communicative environment leads to commitment to a group. Previous work has suggested that social support is particularly important antecedent to commitment to a social group, and it may be that presence of communication induces a feeling of this type of support. It may also be that communication changes member perceptions of the group as an entity. For example, communication may increase the general attractiveness of a group, by suggesting members are more involved or committed to the task. Particularly in a distributed environment, this evidence of commitment may reduce uncertainty about whether or not members are engaged and committed to the group.

We also found that the communicator role had a significant influence on the effect of communication content, with socially-oriented communication substantially increasing commitment only when the communicator was a peer (rather than the leader of the group). This relates to work on liking and relationship formation in work groups, where personality can increase attractiveness of less skilled members but may not influence the perceived utility of clearly instrumental members [7]. It may be that communication is attended to more when it is delivered by members whose utility is uncertain to the group.

Limitations

It is important to note the potential limitations of our study, which was conducted in a virtual environment primarily used for entertainment by its players, with small groups. It is unclear to what extent these results would generalize to a traditional organizational setting where members are being paid for task completion, and rewards depend on successful task completion. World of Warcraft is a setting where individuals engaged in game tasks like dungeon raids typically converse only when needed to support task performance. The way communication is viewed and used in this environment, and the level of communication typically experienced in these types of groups, may have influenced our results. In addition, groups used in this study were small in size. Thus it will be important to examine whether these results hold in other settings with different communication norms and with larger group sizes.

CONCLUSION

Overall our results suggest that online community and virtual team managers and social media system designers may have the ability to influence member commitment by introducing communication early in a group's history. This communication seems to influence commitment by creating a supportive or friendly environment within a group (versus by inducing member involvement).

REFERENCES

1. Allen, N. J., and Meyer, J. P. The measurement and antecedents of affective, continuance, and normative commitment to the organization. *J. of Occupational and Organizational Psychology 63* (1990), 1-8.
2. Bargh, J., and Williams, E. The automaticity of social life. *Current Directions in Psychological Science 15*, 1 (2006), 1-4.
3. Baron, R.M., and Kenny, D.A. The moderator-mediator variable distinction in social psychological research. *J. of Personality and Social Psychology 51*, 6 (1986), 1173-1182.
4. Berg, J.H., and Archer, R.L. The disclosure-liking relationship: Effects of self-perception, order of disclosure, and topical similarity. *Human Communication Research 10*, 2 (1983), 269-281.
5. Bettenhausen, K. L. Five years of groups research: What we've learned and what needs to be addressed. *J. of Management 17* (1991), 345-381.
6. Butler, B. Membership size, communication activity, and sustainability: A resource-based model of online social structures. *Information Systems Research 12*, 4 (2001), 346–362.
7. Casciaro, T., and Lobo, M.S. When task competence is irrelevant: The role of positive and negative interpersonal affect in instrumental ties, *Administrative Science Quarterly 53* (2008), 655-684.
8. Chua, C., Wareham, J., and Robey, D. The role of online trading communities in managing internet auction fraud, *MIS Quarterly 31*, 4 (2004), 759-781.
9. Cialdini, R.B., and Goldstein N.J. Social Influence: Conformity and Compliance. *Annual Review of Psychology 55* (2004), 591–621.
10. Collins, M., and Miller, L.C. Self-disclosure and liking: A meta-analytic review. *Psychological Bulletin 116*, 3(1994), 457-475.
11. Cramton, C.D., Orvis, K.L., and Wilson, J.M. Situation invisibility and attribution in distributed collaborations. *J. of Management 33*, 4 (2007), 525-546.
12. Crossman, A., and Lee-Kelly, L. Trust, commitment, and team working: The paradox of virtual organizations. *Global Networks 4* (2004), 375-390.
13. Farzan, R., Dabbish, L., Kraut, R. E., and Postmes, T. (2011). Increasing Commitment in Online Communities via Building Social Attachment, In *Proc. CSCW 2011,* ACM Press (2011), 321-330.
14. Festinger, L. Informal social communication. *Psychological Review 57* (1950), 271-282.
15. Gerstner, C.R., and Day, D.V. Meta-analytic review of leader-member exchange theory: Correlates and construct issues. *J. of Applied Psychology 82*, 6 (1997), 827-844.
16. Gibson, C., and Gibbs, J.L. Unpacking the concept of virtuality. *Administrative Science Quarterly 51* (2006), 451-495.
17. Goldstein, N. J., Cialdini, R. B., and Griskevicius, V. A room with a viewpoint: Using social norms to motivate environmental conservation in hotels. *J. of Consumer Research 35*(2008).
18. Harper, F., Frankowski, D., Drenner, S., Yuqing Ren, Kiesler, S., Terveen, L., et al. Talk Amongst Yourselves. In *Proc. IUI 2007*, ACM Press (2007), 62-71.
19. Herbsleb, J. D., and Mockus, A. An empirical study of speed and communication in globally-distributed software development. *IEEE Transactions on Software Engineering 29*, 3 (2003), 1-14.

20. Hogg, M.A. A social identity theory of leadership. *Personality and Social Psychology Review 5* (2001), 184-200.
21. Johnson, S.K., Bettenhausen, K., and Gibbons, E. Realities of working in virtual teams. *Small Group Research 40*, 6 (2009), 623-649.
22. Kanawattanachai, P., and Yoo, Y. Dynamic nature of trust in virtual teams. Case Western Reserve University, USA . *Sprouts: Working Papers on Information Systems*, *2*, 10 (2002). http://sprouts.aisnet.org/2-10.
23. Kittur, A., and Kraut, R. E. Harnessing the wisdom of crowds in Wikipedia: Quality through coordination. In *Proc. CSCW 2008,* ACM Press (2008), 37-46.
24. Levine, J., and Moreland, D. Small Groups. *Handbook of Social Psychology* (2998), 415-469.
25. Luthans, F., Wahl, L.V.K., and Steinhaus, C.S. The importance of social support for employee commitment. *Org. Dev. J., Winter (*1992), 1-10.
26. Mathieu, J. E., and Zajac, D. M. A review and meta-analysis of the antecedents, correlates, and consequences of organizational commitment. *Psychological Bulletin 108*, 2 (1990), 171-194.
27. Markey, P. M. Bystander intervention in computer-mediated communication. *Computers in Human Beh. 16*, 2 (2000), 183-188.
28. McKenna, K.Y.A., Green, A.S., and Gleason, M.E.J. Relationship formation on the Internet: What's the big attraction? *J. of Social Issues 58*,1 (2002), 9-31.
29. Meyer, J.P., and Allen, N.J. A three-component conceptualization of organizational commitment. *Human Resource Management Rev. 1*, (1991), 61-89.
30. Meyer, J.P., Becker, T.E., and Vandenberghe, C. Employee commitment and motivation: A Conceptual analysis and integrative model. *J. of Applied Psychology 89,* 6(2004), 991-1007.
31. Meyer, J.P., and Herscovitch, L. Commitment in the workplace: Toward a general model. *Human Resource Management Review 11* (2001), 299-326.
32. Mockus, A., Fielding, R., and Herbsleb, J.D. Two case studies of open source software development: Apache and Mozilla. *ACM Transactions on Software Engineering and Methodology 11*, 3 (2002), 309-346.
33. Moreland, R. L., and Levine, J. M. Socialization in organizations and work groups. In M. E. Turner (Ed.), *Groups at Work: Theory and Research* (pp. 69-112). Erlbaum: Mahwah, NJ, 2001.
34. Newcomb, T. *The Acquaintance Process.* Holt, Rinehart & Winston: New York, 1961.
35. Nonnecke, B., and Preece, J. Lurker demographics: Counting the silent. *ACM CHI Conference, CHI Letters 4*, 1(2000), 73-80.
36. Parks, M.R., and Floyd, K. Making friends in cyberspace. *J. of Communication 46* (1995), 80-97.
37. Pickering, M. J., and Garrod, S. Toward a mechanistic psychology of dialogue. *Behavioral and Brain Sciences 27* (2004), 169-226.
38. Postmes, T., Tanis, M., and de Wit, B. Communication and committment in organizations: A social identity approach. *Group Processes and Intergroup Relations 4*, 3 (2001), 227-426.
39. Powell, A., Piccoli, G., and Ives, B. Virtual teams: A review of current literature and directions for future research. *ACM SIGMIS Database 35*, 1 (2004), 6-36.
40. Prentice, D. A., Miller, D. T., and Lightdale, J. R. Asymmetries in attachments to groups and to their members, *Personality and Social Psychology Bulletin 20*, 5 (1994), 484-493.
41. Ren, Y., Harper, F. M., Drenner, S., Terveen, L., Kiesler, S., Riedl, J., et al. Increasing attachment to online communities. *MIS Quarterly* (under review).
42. Ren, Y., Kraut, R. E., and Kiesler, S. Applying common identity and bond theory to design of online communities," *Org. Studies 28*,3 (2007), 377-408.
43. Rodgers, R., and Chen, Q. Internet community group participation: Psychosocial benefits for women with breast cancer. *JCMC 10*, 4(2005) np.
44. Sacks, H., andJefferson, G. *Lectures on conversation*: Wiley-Blackwell: New York, 1995.
45. Sassenberg, K. Common bond and common identity groups on the internet: Attachment and normative behavior in on-topic and off-topic chats, *Group Dynamics 6*,1(2002), 27-37.
46. Shapiro, D. L., Furst, S. A., Spreitzer, G. M., and Von Glinow, M. A. Transnational teams in the electronic age: Are team identity and high performance at risk? *J. of Org. Behavior 23* (2002), 455-467.
47. Smith, C.B., McLaughlin, M.L., and Osborne, K.K. Conduct control on usenet. *JCMC 2*, 4(1997), np.
48. Strodbeck, F.L., James, R.M., and Hawkins, C. Social status in jury deliberations. *American Sociological Review 22* (1957), 713-719.
49. Tangirala, S., and Alge, B. J. Reactions to unfair events in computer-mediated groups: A test of uncertainty management theory. *OBHDP 100* (2004), 1-20.
50. Vandenberghe, C., Bentein, K., and Stinglhamber, F. Affective commitment to the organization, supervisor, and work group. *J. of Vocational Beh. 64* (2004), 47-71.
51. Wikipedia. (2011). World of Warcarft Retrieved Sep 9, 2011, from http://en.wikipedia.org/wiki/World_of_Warcraft
52. Workman, M., Kahnweiler, W., and Bommer, W. The effects of cognitive style and media richness in commitment to telework and virtual teams. *J. of Vocational Beh. 63* (2003), 199-219.

Twiage: A Game for Finding Good Advice on Twitter

Max Van Kleek, Daniel Alexander Smith, Ruben Stranders, mc schraefel
School of Electronics and Computer Science, University of Southampton
{emax, ds, rs06r, mc}@ecs.soton.ac.uk

ABSTRACT
Millions of recommendations, opinions and experiences are shared across popular microblogging platforms and services each day. Yet much of this content becomes quickly lost in the stream shortly after being posted. This paper looks at the feasibility of identifying useful content in microblog streams so that it might be archived to facilitate wider access and reference. Towards this goal, we present an experiment with a game-with-a-purpose called *Twiage* that we designed to determine how well the deluge of content in "raw" microblog streams could be turned into filtered and ranked collections using ratings from players. Experiments with Twiage validate the feasibility of applying human-computation to this problem, finding strong agreement about what constitutes the "most useful" content in our test dataset. Second, we compare the effectiveness of various methods of eliciting such ratings, finding that a "choose-best" interface and Elo rating ranking scheme yield the greatest agreement in the fewest rounds. External validation of resulting top-rated twitter content with a domain expert found that while the top Twiage-ranked "tweets" were among the best of the set, there was a tendency for players to also select what we term "weak spam" – e.g., promotional content disguised as articles or reviews, indicating a need for more stringent content filtering.

Author Keywords
Microblogs; Social Information Filtering; Games with a purpose; Crowdsourcing; Human-computation

ACM Classification Keywords
H.5.m. Information Interfaces and Presentation: Miscellaneous

General Terms
Human Factors; Design; Measurement.

INTRODUCTION
Microblogging is a significant data-generating enterprise: more than 100 million users create over 200 million posts — roughly the textual volume of a 10 million page book — each day on Twitter alone[1]. Studies of this flood of user-created content have derived assorted classifications for the material in the stream [8, 6, 17, 2, 13, 14], identifying common categories such as the expression of "random thoughts", conversational posts, acts of "social maintenance" (e.g., to express interest, attention, or care for others), and the "passing along" of various kinds of information, opinions or content for others' potential benefit.

Among these categories, the last is particularly interesting in that it is created with the intent of being useful to others — yet little of it is kept, and, as a result, it is quickly lost in the deluge of content. How much of this "passed along" content might be worth keeping beyond the ephemeral tweeted moment? In particular, how much of this information represents good, potentially useful and well-informed advice that might help someone make a critical decision or achieve a goal? In this paper, we examine the problem of whether and how useful content in microblog streams might be, so that it might be archived and turned into re-usable knowledge resources for all.

While factual questions are served well by today's document search engines and knowledge engines such as Wolfram Alpha[2], these services are less appropriate when, instead of facts, advice is needed. Advice is most often sought when a single factual answer is unknown or cannot be derived, or where multiple, subjective viewpoints are needed for insight on a difficult or complicated issue. Therefore, there is considerable opportunity for social information services, such as microblogs, Q&A sites and newsgroup forums, to address this unmet need. Unfortunately, it is extremely difficult to find advice on current microblog platforms. If, for instance, one searches Twitter for "How should I lose weight in a month?" one would likely end up with zero results because Twitter's search facility matches on exact phrases only. Meanwhile, shorter substrings, such as "lose weight" or "weight loss", typically yield an overwhelming quantity of irrelevant hits. These poor results are due to the fact that microblog search engines, unlike those for Web pages, lack relevance measures with which content can be ranked for particular queries. As a result, they typically return matches ordered by recency instead of relevance. Other factors detracting from discovery of relevant content are: the high volume of spam and the conversational content flooding microblog platforms. The quantity of these types of tweets mean that sample queries into the microblog stream yield spam and noise instead of content people want.

Permission to make digital or hard copies of all or part of this work for personal or classroom use is granted without fee provided that copies are not made or distributed for profit or commercial advantage and that copies bear this notice and the full citation on the first page. To copy otherwise, or republish, to post on servers or to redistribute to lists, requires prior specific permission and/or a fee.
CHI'12, May 5–10, 2012, Austin, Texas, USA.
Copyright 2012 ACM 978-1-4503-1015-4/12/05...$10.00.

[1] http://blog.twitter.com/2011/06/200-million-tweets-per-day.html
[2] Wolfram Alpha — `http://www.wolframalpha.com`

In this paper, we investigate whether a metric like 'usefulness' can be derived for microblog content, so that useful content might be identified and archived for others that might later seek it. Such a process would allow microblogs like Twitter to act as information sources for standing knowledge archives such as Q&A sites (e.g., Yahoo! Answers[3] or Quora[4]). Such popular services currently serve answers to hundreds of millions of general questions worldwide [12].

A challenge towards assessing the 'usefulness' of microblog content is establishing the context of usefulness – e.g., 'useful *to what end*?' In this experiment, we chose examples of questions from Quora from the domain of *health and well-being advice*, including the "how might I lose weight?" example already mentioned.

The domain of health and well-being advice was chosen because questions in this domain commonly occur in online forums and Q&A sites, yet remain relatively poorly served using existing social information systems. First, domains such as health, fitness and nutrition, perhaps due to their potentially lucrative nature, remain favourite targets for scammers and spammers who flood sites with fake products and offers. In such an environment, determining whether a particular offer, drug or treatment represents a legitimate offer (and whether it further represents sound medical advice) is difficult for those outside the medical profession even in off-line contexts [10]. Furthermore, unlike in friend-based social networks, where personally knowing the source of a piece of information can be used to to assess its trustworthiness, in many social information services such as microblogging platforms, such background information might be minimal, absent, or even faked. Therefore, trustworthiness must be able to be evaluated without such context.

A second challenge pertaining to assessing the usefulness of content are people's differing perceptions about it. For example, the relevance, and therefore utility, of particular health or well-being advice to an individual is likely to be dependent on their physical condition, preferences, environment, medical history and so on. Since such person-specific factors may influence people's perceptions of other kinds of microblog content as well, we wished to understand whether, and in which situations, identifying useful content was still feasible.

The approach we have taken towards these goals is to leverage a human-computation process — specifically a Game with a Purpose (GWAP) [23], designed to elicit ratings about the usefulness of microblog content as players compete towards achieving a high score. Since GWAPs have been previously successfully applied to subjective evaluation problems such as identifying preference for images (e.g. Matchin [11]), we were encouraged to pursue *Twiage* as an experimental vehicle for collecting microblog usefulness labels so that analysis, including measuring agreement and consistency, could be made possible. Furthermore, like previous GWAPs such as the ESP Game[22], this data could further be used to create corpora for direct use in information retrieval contexts, or, as we wish to pursue in follow-up work, as training data for machine learning/natural language classification approaches for predicting usefulness.

In the following sections, we begin with a discussion of the background motivation behind this approach, continue with a description of our methodology, present our results, analysis, and plans for future work.

MOTIVATION AND BACKGROUND

Our interest in mining microblogs for advice-oriented information was derived from the following five observations pertaining to the potential for microblog content to take a more significant role in serving social information needs:

1. *People often seek information from social sources* — Evans and Chi found that people often sought information from other people — e.g., friends, coworkers, people nearby — in the course of primary and routine information-seeking activities [9].
2. *People commonly seek advice on Q&A sites* — Adamic et al. found that advice was one of three major categories of questions asked on Yahoo! Answers [1], while Harper et al. found that advice-oriented questions received the highest-quality answers, signifying their importance [12].
3. *Q&A sites have shortcomings: questions get stale, get uneven coverage* — Mamykina et al. found that while questions were often very rapidly answered on Q&A sites, old questions were less frequently revisited, corrected, or kept updated [16]. Moreover, Harper et al. found that questions received an average of 0.5–4.0 answers each (depending on site) and may not represent adequate diversity to satisfy particular individuals' advice-seeking needs.
4. *Extracting advice from microblogs remains hard* — While Twitter may be overflowing with advice — by previous accounts 22% comprising opinions and 25% recommendations [17] — getting to good advice remains hard. In addition to the aforementioned problems of searching Twitter with its keyword-search facilities, the alternative strategy of direct information solicitation (i.e., asking one's followers for advice) also yields mixed results. Paul et al. showed that, while sometimes successful, results varied significantly on topic, phrasing, and the individual. Furthermore, they demonstrated that a mere 18.7% of questions asked by Twitter users got responses [18] — with certain topics gaining a disproportionate share while others went unanswered. Moreover, questions in that study received an average 2.9 responses, significantly less than Q&A sites [12].
5. *Human Computation yields insight on subjective domains and computationally hard problems* - "Games with a purpose" systems such as the ESP Game [22], TagATune [4], and Matchin [11] have demonstrated the ability to elicit preferences in subjective domains, and to generate rankings over such sets.

Observations 1 and 2 suggest that social information sources are often very important, and Q&A sites are currently the

[3] Yahoo! Answers — http://answers.yahoo.com/
[4] Quora — `http://quora.com`

popular go-to for social, advice-oriented questions. Observation 3 lists two shortcomings of the use of Q&A sites for advice-oriented questions, while Question 4 reveals the potential and difficulties with using microblogs to try to satisfy advice-oriented information needs today. Finally, Observation 5 points at a potential mechanism for coping with the subjectivity of assessing "goodness" of advice-oriented information. Together, these observations inspired us to investigate how a human-powered game might identify "good" advice freshly shared on microblog services, and used to build automatically renewed knowledge archives.

METHODOLOGY

The main goal of this investigation is to determine the feasibility of deriving a quality metric for advice-oriented microblog content using a game-with-a-purpose (GWAP). More explicitly, this asks whether a suitably-designed GWAP could efficiently yield ratings that can used to reliably identify "high quality" advice in these streams. To answer this question, however, we must also determine how to design such a game. Therefore, we end up with two sets of questions as follows:

1. *Feasibility*
    (a) *How consistent are the resulting rankings?*
    (b) *How well do rankings agree with an expert? / How 'good' is the best-ranked content?*
    (c) *How efficiently can it process content?*
2. *Game design*
    (a) *What interface mechanisms should be used to elicit ratings?*
    (b) *How should raw ratings be transformed into a quality metric for identifying useful content?*

These questions essentially depend on one another — assessing the feasibility of the approach first requires a game so that this performance may be evaluated; designing an appropriate game, on the other hand, relies on an understanding of how particular game mechanics influence results.

We approached this chicken-and-egg problem through an iterative approach, starting by generating and testing game designs with a small number of players until we arrived at several simple and playable designs; then, three best interface designs were combined into a single game as different kinds of rounds so that they may be comparatively evaluated, as described next.

Designing Twiage: a game for finding advice

As described by von Ahn [23], the design space of games is very large, and achieving the two goals of being engaging and effective at serving its intended purpose can be challenging. We pursued an iterative design process [19] in which several designs were proposed, tested with a few people each in our laboratory, and used to generate new designs, aimed at being playable, effective, and efficient. In so doing, we considered such game dimensions as: "should play be co-operative or competitive?"; "should matches be synchronous (e.g., where two people pair off with one another at the same time)?"; "how should ratings be computed?"; and "how can we maintain player interest and motivation?".

Four games were mocked up in HTML and JavaScript and loaded with 40 hand-chosen tweets from our laboratory: Twiage, which we describe in detail next, Tweetfolio, a stock-market inspired game where players get to choose a fixed-size "portfolio" of "best tweets" per question, Flashtweet — a rapid serial visual presentation of tweets to be rated, and Tweetris — a Tetris clone that requires the player to manoeuvre tweets into categories as they fall from the sky. Based upon initial user testing, we chose Twiage as it presented a balance between "fun" (Flashtweet was deemed "too boring") and yet remained simple enough that it did not introduce too many factors that might influence player performance. For example, although more fun, tweetris emphasized speed and dexterity over thinking about the content and value of the tweets themselves.

Twiage walk-through

Keeping the game mechanics as simple as possible, we designed Twiage to be a one-versus-all game, where players compete to have the top score in each tournament. The player is invited to play in an open tournament, where each corresponds to a single topic, in the form of an advice-oriented question inspired by popular questions on 43things[5] and Quora. In this paper, we describe our experiments with the initial two tournaments we ran: "How should I lose weight?" and "How can I sleep better?".

Figure 1 illustrates the complete game flow. As can be seen, the game is extremely simple and consists of 4 main states: log-in, scoreboard/tournament selection, round, and the round result/bonus screen. When the user logs in, Twiage presents the Scoreboard/Leaderboard, and is invited to select a tournament. Each tournament corresponds to a question, such as "How should I lose weight?"; when a question is selected, Twiage delivers one of 3 round types: "Pick-best", "Likert", or "Ordering" corresponding to different elicitation interfaces.

In the Pick-best condition, 6 tweets are shown and the player is invited to choose one. In the likert condition, the player must supply a 1–7 rating for each tweet to proceed. In the ordering condition, the player must drag and drop tweets into slots labeled "best" to "worst". Due to the greater effort required to complete a Likert or Ordering round, these were presented 1/8th as frequently as "Bonus rounds" as Pick-best rounds. Rounds are timed, and time elapsed is displayed in the upper right corner during each round. In case all 6 tweets in a round were useless, "no good advice here — pass" option was provided at no score penalty to players.

As described in Tweet Candidate Selection below, since our selection process only included tweets containing a URL string, we included a thumbnail image of the page linked to in the URL of each tweet. This was done so that players could glimpse at the contents and visual features of the target page, which has been shown in previous studies to help identify spam, and to assist in judging site helpfulness [3]. Hovering

[5] 43 Things — `http://www.43things.com`

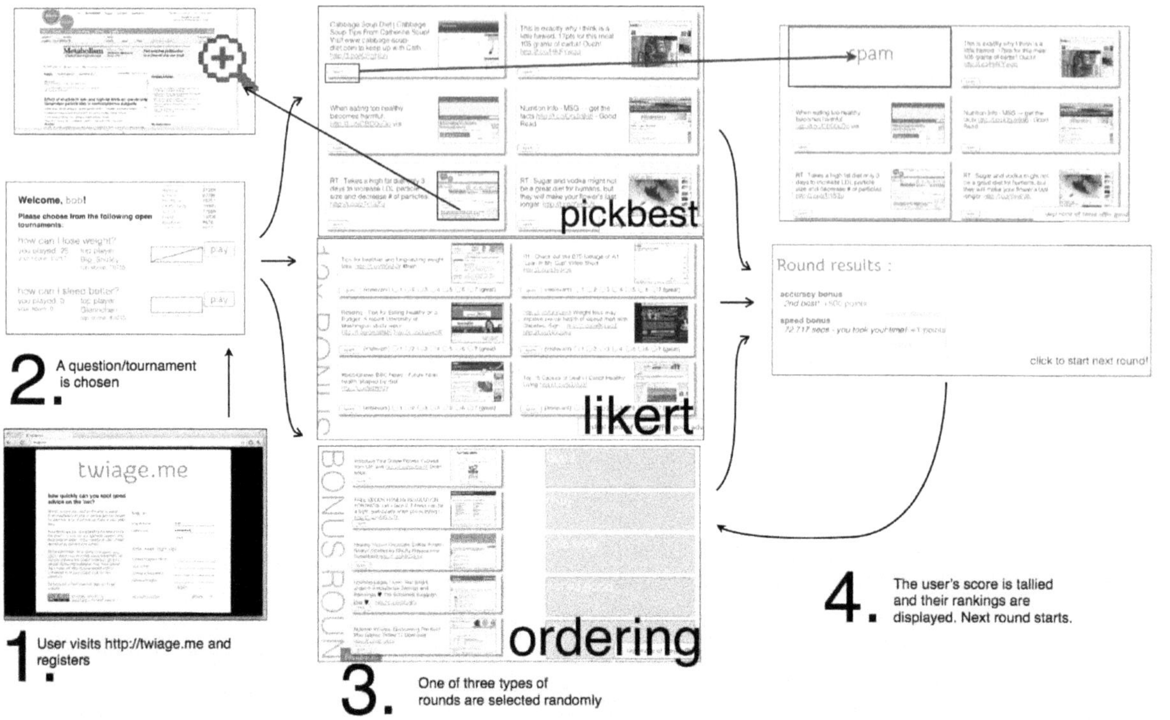

Figure 1. Flow of the Twiage game. When a player logs in (1) the leader board and tournament selection screen (2) is presented. From here, a tournament is selected and Twiage randomly selects one of three round (interface) types: Pick-best, Likert, and Ordering (3). Tweets are presented with a thumbnail image of the web page linked to by them. This thumbnail may be enlarged by clicking on it. A tweet may be flagged as Spam by clicking on the spam button. At the conclusion of the round, scores are computed and presented (4). The game proceeds to the next round (3) until the user chooses to quit.

on a thumbnail shows a full-resolution rendering of the target page so that content can be read. If users wish to actually navigate to the site, clicking on the link pops open a new tab containing the target page.

In the initial game design, our plan for spam handling was as follows: filter automatically upfront, and avoid being concerned about the remaining false negatives (e.g., spam leaking into the system), as they will likely not be selected anyway. However, after the first day of deployment, 3 of 5 test players reported they were annoyed or bored by having to see the same spam repeatedly. In response to this, we added a "SPAM" button on each tweet to allow players to signal that they wished to never see a particular tweet again. When pressed, this button "flips" the relevant tweet over, and the tweet is added to a personal blacklist consulted during round creation.

Although initially created merely to enhance game playability and reduce boredom, these votes proved useful in an effort to further cut down spam. We used these votes as seeds in a second-stage spam removal technique, as described in Spam Reduction, below. Although points were not directly awarded for marking spam, marking spam increased likelihood of scoring more points on rounds by reducing the total candidates in the round, thereby making each tweet individually worth more points.

At the completion of each round, points are computed by assessing agreement between the person's choices and the global ranking. While scores were important for providing motivation and allowing players to gauge their progress and standings, they were not used in generating final rankings.

Game mechanics

In this section, we describe how tweets are handled from input to selection, ranking and output.

Tweet Candidate Selection - Spam Reduction

One of the biggest concerns about using the "raw" Twitter stream as a source for Twiage is the abundance of spam. In an initial test-run, users complained that nearly all tweets they saw were spam, making the game too boring to play. Thus, to keep the game challenging and engaging, we deduced that it would be critical to eliminate as much mechanically-detectable spam as possible.

A number of previous studies have looked at the problem of identifying Twitter spam. Such studies examined the characteristics of this "micro-spam", including content features, features from spam authors' profiles, and the follower-followee networks of these spam authors. In particular, Benevenuto et al.'s method [5] of identifying spam achieved 87% accuracy on their hand-coded test dataset, but this was achieved by amassing a large data set, including crawling the entire Twitter history of each user who posted a tweet in their data set, as well as the entire histories of all of these users' followers and followees. This process required them to use 54 servers, which were specially white-listed by Twitter.

Thus, when special access to Twitter is available, this work demonstrates that a high accuracy of spam detection can be achieved. However, the general public only have rate-limited access to Twitter, and therefore we restricted ourselves to similarly use the public "spritzer" API [20], which provides real-time access of 1–2% of all tweets. In order to remove spam from this stream, we devised a simple two-step method informed by the aforementioned work done by others, and validated our approach using test data. This method employs features of the link target page, a unique feature which greatly assisted in identifying phishing links.

Our method first removes tweets that are replies to a single person (i.e., those which start with the "@" character), as this is a common technique spammers use to direct attention at particular individuals. Second, we found hundreds of duplicate tweets that vary only the target URL and reply-to (@) references when posting. Thus, in evaluating a particular tweet, we checked to see if it matched others, when both stripped of URL and reply-to (@) references, and removed all such duplicated tweets.

This first step reduced inflow, (see Table 1), however after seeing an unacceptable amount of phishing remaining, we added a second stage. We observed that many of the spam target pages looked nearly identical; in particular, many of the links yielded "do not go here" blocking transition pages offered by URL shorteners. To use this information to filter out all tweets to known phishing sites, we manually selected 15 of the most common blocker pages and spam sites, creating a collection thumbnails for each. Then, a simple image comparison algorithm was devised using image subtraction to identify images that matched each of these spam seed images; keeping the images low-resolution ensured that small details would be ignored. Spam assertions submitted by players in-game were then added for tips that were marked as spam by 3 or more players. As described in Table 1 below, running this "visual" spam detection algorithm cut an additional 4551 tweets from the initial spam reduction process, resulting in the removal of 7999 (or 31.25%) tweets total from the initially collected corpus of 25688. We visually verified the filtered tweets to minimize the number of false positives. A more detailed description and evaluation of this filtering approach is available [21].

Tweet Candidate Selection - Process

To collect tweets from the spritzer stream relevant to the specific advice questions we were seeking, we first filtered the stream based upon keywords related to the topics. Although we chose the filter terms manually for our initial experiment, for future questions, Twiage will be made to automatically select key noun-phrase terms using a part-of-speech tagger [7] and perform term expansion using WordNet [15].

For our "how should I lose weight?" question, we used the following keywords: "weight loss", "lose weight", "fitness", "healthy" and "in shape". For the "how can I sleep better?" question, we used the keywords "insomnia", "insomniac", "no sleep", and "can't sleep". These keywords were chosen to give us a large number of tweets for the specific domain of the question. We then limited the results to those which

question	keyword and geo filter	dictionary, URL and duplicate filter	image spam filter
"weight loss"	1.70 TPS in spritzer (estimated 255 TPS in full stream)	0.048 TPS (estimated 7.2 TPS in full stream)	0.033 TPS (estimated 4.95 TPS in full stream)
"sleep"	0.92 TPS in spritzer (estimated 138 TPS in full stream)	0.0015 TPS (estimated 0.225 TPS in full stream)	0.0010 TPS (estimated 0.15 TPS in full stream)

Table 1. The number of tweets per second (TPS) after each successive filtering stage, for both questions.

contained URLs, and rendered screenshots of the sites to use as thumbnails in the game.

Since currently approximately 50% of all Twitter posts are in English [6] and since we wished to run our initial experiment in English, we combined geographic and dictionary-based filtering to eliminate non-English posts, first restricting tweets to those tagged as being posted within the continental United States, and filtered to those containing at least 3 words from a standard English dictionary.

Finally, we applied our spam reduction methods described above. The statistics in Table 1 show that the sequence of filtering steps significantly reduced the throughput of domain-related tweets. Specifically, we retained only 1.94% of "weight-loss" tweets, and 0.1% of "sleep" tweets, after spam filtering. The overall volume estimates of posted tweets are computed assuming the spritzer API provides a sampling of 1.5% of total tweets [20] (the documentation claims between 1% and 2% are typically supplied).

Rounds and tweet selection

Each tournament consists of a series of rounds. Invisibly to the user, rounds are grouped into sets, which constitute a collection of candidate tweets sampled from the entire incoming candidate tweet pool. Since the candidate pool is potentially huge, these round sets act as a sparsity control to ensure that once admitted into a round set, each tweet receives sufficient exposure before newer tweets are considered:

1. A round set is randomly sampled with probability mass inversely proportional to the average number of times the player has seen the tweets in the pool. A new round-set is created with fixed (small) probability mass.

2. Once a round set is chosen, a round is constructed from the round set by sampling tips with probability inversely proportional to the number of times the player has seen them.

The round selection strategy served merely as a simplest possible point — simple in both the sense that it had only 1 parameter to set, and because it was naive, e.g., did not take into consideration any notion of "certainty" around the status of any particular tweet. Yet, it ensured that all tweets

[6] Semiocast Press Release: "Half of messages on Twitter are not in English" (2010) — `http://semiocast.com/downloads/Semiocast_Half_of_messages_on_Twitter_are_not_in_English_20100224.pdf`

received play while not exhausting the user with too many of the same ones. Sampling from the round set with every round also ensured consecutive rounds would not feature the same tweets, further avoiding boring the user with repetition. We are currently considering more efficient strategies for performing this sampling in our ongoing work.

Computing round scores

The purpose of having scores in Twiage is merely to motivate repeated play by adding a competitive element to the game, and allowing for the creation of a leaderboard and top scorer of each category. As described in results, this seems to have been fairly effective (as several users played more than 50 rounds), although additional competitive elements would likely improve this.

At the conclusion of each round, points are awarded to users based upon a combination of agreement (with the crowd) and speed. To compute agreement, all tips shown in the round were ranked by all users' previous plays using the (EWR) strategy described in Results. Then, rank agreement was assessed between the player's submission and the global ranking. Possible levels of agreement were discretized into 6 levels and awarded an extra 100 points per level (i.e., 0, 100, 600 points). Speed was discretized into bonuses of: 50, 25, 10, 5 points for taking less than 15 seconds, 30 seconds, 1 minute, and 2 minutes, respectively. These times were chosen based upon a pilot study with users in our lab.

In initial trials, we tried omitting the speed bonus and timer, since we feared users would be motivated to go too quickly and fail to take careful attention to the tweets. However, adding the timer had the perceived advantage of giving players "momentum" and according to initial self-report from our lab subjects, a desire to play more rounds. Therefore, we opted to keep the timer and speed bonuses, but reduce their score weight so that players would realize they could gain the more points for agreement than speed.

Ranking

To rank the tips, we applied the Empirical Winning Rate (EWR) and Elo-rating based ranking algorithms (ELO) which were previously used in a similar setting to rank images in the Matchin' game [11]. The former algorithm uses the ratio between wins and presentations as a metric for a tip's quality. The advantage of this algorithm is its simplicity; one need only keep track of the number of wins and losses. However, its main drawback is that it ignores the relative strength of the tip's opponents. Thus, its score increases by the same amount regardless of whether it beat a good or a spam tip. While the former victory is an indication of high quality, the latter yields little information about the relative ranking of the tip.

This weakness is addressed by the ELO ranking algorithm, which was originally devised to calculate relative skill levels of chess players. In brief, the score gain resulting from a win is adjusted to reflect the relative strength of the opponent; winning against a strong opponent yields a higher increase than winning against a weak one. For more details of this algorithm, we refer to [11].

An important difference with the Matchin game is that Twiage uses 6-way comparative ranking instead of two-way comparative ranking. The implication of this on the application of the aforementioned ranking algorithms is that the concepts of "winner" and "loser" have to be carefully redefined. Therefore, we transformed each Twiage round into a set of two-way competitions, each with a winner and loser. This transformation is different for each type of round:

Pick-best The winner of a Pick-best round is considered to have won in individual competitions against the losers. Thus, this results in 5 two-way competitions.

Likert For each pair of tips presented in a Likert round, there is a two-way competition if the one scored higher than the other. For a Likert round with 6 distinct scores, this yields 15 two-way competitions ($n/2 * (n-1) = 6 \times 5/2$).

Ordering Similar to Likert, there are 15 two-way competitions in a Ordering round, one for each pair. Moreover, for each pair, the higher ranked tip is considered the winner.

It is important to note under this transformation, Likert rounds are considered to order the tips within a round, rather than treating the scores as comparable across users and tips. Put differently, a score of "6" means that a tip was preferred over other tips in that same round with a lower score, but is not considered to be comparable with tips from other rounds. As an alternative ranking method for Likert rounds, we also included the Likert Ranking (LR) algorithm, which simply takes the average score of a tip across all Likert rounds as measure of its quality. This algorithm assumes the commensurability of Likert scores across users and rounds.

In Analysis we benchmark the EWR, ELO and LR algorithms by measuring their ability to predict user preferences.

RESULTS

Player participation

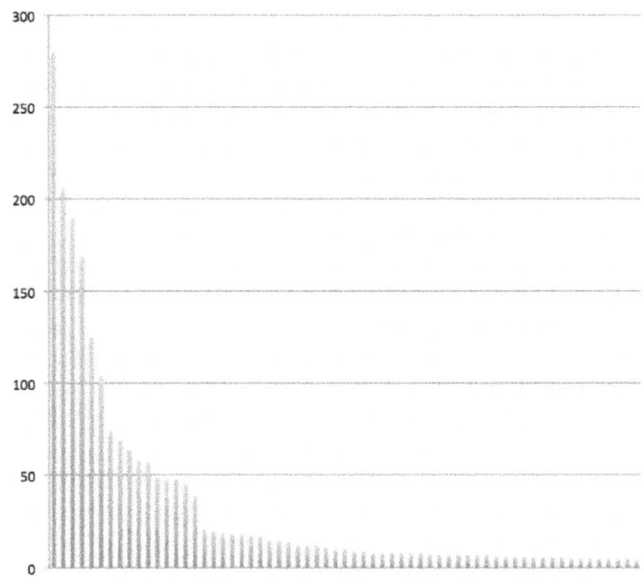

Figure 2. Number of microrounds played per player, 1 week into deployment, out of 100 users who signed up in 7 days.

	non-pass	total	% non pass
pick-best	1162	1549	75.02
likert	209	291	71.8213058
ordering	188	306	61.4379085

Table 2. The number of rounds played (not-passed) per round type.

	pick-best	likert	ordering
Avg time per round (stdd)	16.276s (54.3s)	25.89s (33.9s)	40.35s (38.32s)
Thumbnail views per round (6 tweets each)	0.41 (1.00)	1.09 (1.91)	0.80 (2.01)
Links clicked per round (6 tweets each)	0.05 (0.32)	0.17 (0.99)	0.08 (0.71)

Table 3. Average time, number of thumbnails views and links clicked, per round, per game type.

After 10 days of deployment 101 participants had signed up to play. As can be seen in Figure 2, the number of rounds played varied from 0 to 280, with $M = 22$ (median:6) rounds per person. Thirty-five people who signed up played fewer than 4 rounds, clearly skewing the median to the right. The 68 remaining players played an average M=34 rounds (median:10 rounds) each.

Roughly 14% of the rounds were the "likert" type, and 14% were the "ordering" type, while the remaining 72% were the "Pick-best" game type. A chi-squared test reveals that the percentage of rounds that were passed were different in the 3 conditions ($\chi^2 = 23.8232; df = 2; p < 0.0001$). Since round selection procedure was identical for all round types, we believe that the differences in pass rate arose not from the tips themselves but because of playability factors — specifically, likert and ordering rounds take significantly more time and effort to complete and thus people are more likely to "give up" on them.

Speed and use of thumbnails/link following

Looking at each of the rounds separately, Pick-best appears to take the shortest amount of time, while ordering took the longest. To test the significance of these differences, we ran an ANOVA comparing these times, which rejected the null hypothesis ($F(2, 1439) = 18.77, p \ll 0.001$). Examining for significance with Tukey correction revealed the Pick-best vs Likert difference, and Pick-best vs Ordering differences to both be significant ($p < 0.0001$). Thus, players were significantly faster than on the Likert or Ordering rounds, whose difference was insignificant.

With respect to image thumbnail viewing, we were surprised at how little thumbnails were viewed in general — ranging from 0.41 views per round (corresponding to $0.41/6 = .06$ per tweet) to 1.09 per round (0.18 per tweet) in the Likert rounds . Pick-best appeared to have the least while likert had the most use. Testing this difference rejected the null hypothesis ($F(2, 1656) = 29.638, p \ll 0.001$), and Tukey-corrected differences in thumbnail viewing use were all significant ($p \ll 0.001$, except ordering vs likert, $p < 0.05$). Thus while seldom used, the data suggests that players actually looked at significantly more thumbnails in both likert and ordering conditions, and the most in the Likert condition.

Players even less frequently followed links. Like time and thumbnail use, an ANOVA test examining differences in link-following among round types demonstrated differences ($F(2, 1656) = 13.12$); but only the difference between Pick-best vs Likert was significant.

ANALYSIS

In this section we analyze the quality of the output of the game and analyze inter-player variation in performance on the task.

Quality of output

We used two complimentary measures to evaluate the quality of the resulting tweets selected by the system: consistency and expert evaluation. In the first, we determine how consistently players agree with one another when selecting tweets, compared to random chance. The second evaluation assesses the value of information conveyed by the best selected tweets in the eyes of a nutrition expert, who has specialized knowledge about both question domains.

Self agreement

The first measure of quality we used was the self agreement of the rankings obtained from applying the ranking algorithms from Rankings, above. Self agreement simultaneously measures the consistency of the players choices and the quality of the ranking algorithms. We computed two types of self agreement: ranking agreement and classification agreement. The former measures how consistently user rank tips, while the latter determines how consistently users classify tips into categories of best 5% and worst 95%. Ranking agreement has been previously used by Hacker et al. [11] to measure the performance of ranking algorithms. Classification agreement is a new metric, which is more appropriate in the context of Twiage, where the goal is not to rank tips, but rather to identify the top tips. This distinction might seem subtle, but is nonetheless significant in choosing a proper ranking algorithm; while it is necessary to rank the entire dataset accurately to do well in terms of ranking agreement, the ranking of low-quality tips is completely irrelevant as long as the tips are ranked correctly around the top 5% threshold.

To compute ranking agreement, we first created a training set consisting of a randomly selected 66% of rounds in the dataset, and a test set with the remaining 33%. The tips in the training set were then ranked using EWR, ELO and LR. Finally, we used this ranking to predict the winner of each round in the training set (which were first converted to two-way competitions according to the method described in Results, above.) The ranking agreement is then defined as the percentage of correct predictions.

Classification agreement is computed in a similar fashion as ranking agreement. First, tips in the training and test sets are ranked. Classification agreement is then computed as the percentage of the top 5% tips in the test set that appear in the top 5% of the training set. To understand this metric, assume the ranking of the training set is ground truth; in that case, classification agreement is the percentage of top 5% tips in the training set that comes from the true top 5% percent of tips.

	Ranking Algorithm		
Type of Round	ELO	EWR	LR
All	72.8 (0.9)	69.7 (0.9)	n/a
Pick-Best Only	75.5 (0.8)	71.2 (3.0)	n/a
Likert Only	71.4 (1.6)	67.7 (1.6)	64.8 (2.0)
Ordering Only	62.4 (2.2)	63.3 (1.9)	n/a

Table 4. Ranking agreement results. Numbers in parentheses indicate standard deviation.

	Ranking Algorithm		
Type of Round	ELO	EWR	LR
All	49.3 (5.0)	25.6 (5.0)	n/a
Pick-Best Only	62.2 (5.6)	21.0 (5.6)	n/a
Likert Only	34.6 (9.3)	14.5 (8.2)	21.3 (6.3)
Ordering Only	28.3 (14.6)	8.1 (4.5)	n/a

Table 5. Classification agreement results for the top 5% tips. Numbers in parentheses indicate standard deviation.

Tables 4 and 5 show the performance of the ranking algorithms in terms of ranking agreement and classification agreement respectively. We tested ELO, EWR and LR on four datasets: the full dataset, and datasets with Pick-Best, Likert and Ordering rounds only. Each combination of dataset and ranking algorithm was performed 100 times to control for the random selection of training and test sets.

Two clear patterns emerge from these results. First, ELO achieves a higher level of agreement than EWR and LR. This is more pronounced for classification than ranking, making ELO the preferred ranking algorithm for Twiage (within the set of algorithms used). This agrees with the findings of Hacker et al.[7] Second, Pick-Best rounds score much higher in terms of self agreement than the other types of rounds. This suggests, thus, that humans are most consistent when selecting the best tip (as performed in Pick-Best rounds) than objectively judging them (Likert) or ordering them (Ordering rounds).

Expert Evaluation

To obtain an external measure of quality of top-ranking tweets, we asked a certified nutritionist to examine and rate the top 10% as yielded by the ELO rankings described above.

Out of these 63 (55%) she ranked with a Likert value of 1 (worst). When asked why these were were given a low rating, she commented that these entries were either "entirely marketing", "fake blogs" or product-slanted advertisements "clearly written to try to get an individual to try a product" — instead of being a genuine product review. For the remaining, the average pairwise agreement between the expert and derived rankings was 77% (as displayed in Figure 3), with an average Likert rating of 3.52. The fact that so many of such articles made it into the top 10% is clearly a problem, demonstrating that the spam problem is even more difficult than initially thought. We discuss potential approaches to mitigate this issue in under Discussion.

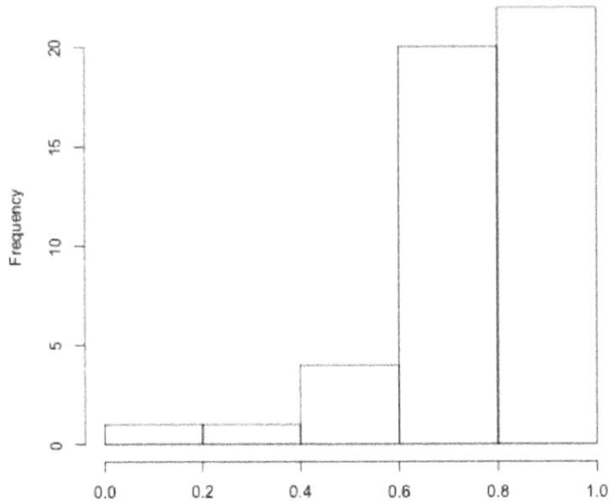

Figure 3. ***Agreement of expert ratings with ELO rankings*** **— This histogram represents the percentage agreement of the nutritionist expert's ratings (df=49;M=77%) with the ELO rankings, when her identified "marketing spam" was removed. Before such removal, agreement was 58%.**

Efficiency

Next, we studied the efficiency of Twiage by performing a cost-benefit analysis of the human effort per tip vs. performance. To do this, we varied the minimum number of presentations of each tip and determined the classification agreement of the top 5% tips (see Section Self Agreement).

Since Twiage was configured to present each tip a minimum of 14 times, we artificially created datasets with lower minimum number of presentations by selectively discarding rounds. Specifically, these were obtained by greedily discarding rounds with the highest minimum number of presentations. This yielded datasets with a very homogeneous number of presentations per round.

Results are shown in Figure 4. Clearly, there is an intuitive relation between the number of presentations per tip and the classification agreement: an increase in the former yields a roughly proportional increase in the latter. The results also show suggest that the classification agreement has not converged at 14 presentations, and might further improve as the number of presentations is increased beyond 14. Further analysis on larger sets of data is required in future work.

Factors influencing player performance

To identify the factors that most influenced a player's performance on each round, we performed ANOVA tests to determine whether player identity, time spent on a round, number of rounds played total, and whether or not the round significantly impacted performance. For this analysis, the accuracy was computed using pairwise rank-correspondence against the global ranking output by the better-performing ELO strategy described in Ranking, above.

[7]They also used a Collaborative filtering method called Relative Singular Value Decomposition (Relative SVD), which was found to perform well, particularly on large datasets. Perhaps because of this, Relative SVD performed very poorly on our datasets, which are quite small (about 2,000) compared to theirs (> 2, 000, 000). More data is needed to study the application of this method.

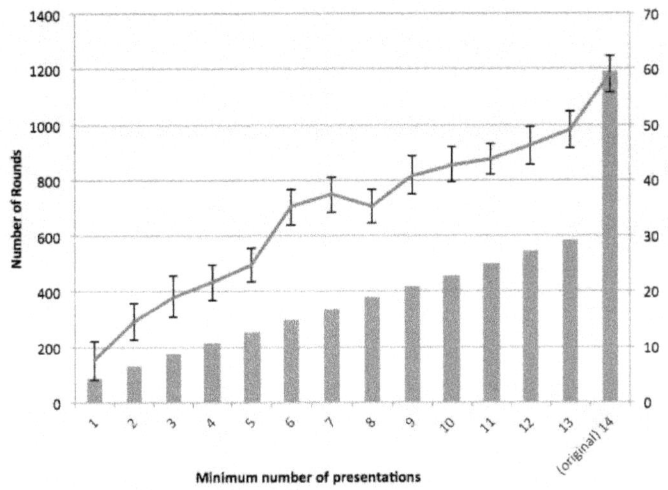

Figure 4. Classification agreement as a function of the minimum number of presentations per tip. The blue bar chart shows the number of rounds contained in each dataset, the red line the classification agreement percentage.

Player identity carried a significant effect on accuracy, meaning some players performed significantly better or worse than the average ($F(75, 1148) = 2.21; p \ll 0.001$). Starting with predicting time to completion, player identity carried a significant predictive effect ($F(1, 2289) = 4.404, p < 0.001$), and question 2 ("How can I sleep better?") rounds took significantly shorter time ($F(1, 2289) = 4.404; p < 0.05$) than rounds in the "How can I lose weight?" tournament. Other than this, other factors carried no significant effect.

DISCUSSION

In this section we return to the original question: is devising a game to filter for "good advice" feasible? In other words, is there consistency in the notion of "usefulness" among different individuals, and, if so, can such "useful" microblog content be reliably identified with ratings provided by players? The high agreement rates resulting from Twiage suggest that, indeed, reliably predicting which tweets would be chosen (given others' ratings) was possible (RQ.1a). Moreover, comparison among elicitation interfaces (round types) and ranking methods demonstrated that the Pick-best round format for the former (addressing RQ.2a), and ELO ranking scheme for the latter (RQ2.b) were most effective.

The expert evaluation agreed strongly (RQ.1b) with the relative goodness of the top tips, but also revealed a significant problem – the abundance of "weak spam" such as promotional articles and advertisements disguised as reviews for products or services, as well as sponsored "testimonials" for the use of these products. These spam types eluded both our spam filters, as well as, seemingly, the players who selected them, as this content resembled legitimate content, in particular, product reviews. Yet, other factors pertaining to game mechanics and micro-round selection may have also contributed to the promotion of weak spam. Based upon the expert's evaluation, tweets containing high quality advice were exceedingly rare in the sample obtained. This "underflow" of good advice caused microrounds to be sometimes saturated with mediocre content, consisting entirely of irrelevant or promotional content. In such rounds, some promotional content may have been perceived as "not as bad" as the rest, and therefore selected. The expert, meanwhile, having access to the complete data set at once (and not being forced to select the best-of-six at a time) quickly and uniformly labeled anything she could identify as marketing/promotional as untrustworthy.

We are evaluating several ways to address these problems. The first is simply more stringent upfront filtering, for which machine-classification approaches will undoubtedly outperform our initial simple filter. The second is to improve the way tweets are selected when micro-rounds are assembled; in particular, to avoid the 'mediocre saturation' problem, an adaptive selection strategy centered around the notion of "tournaments" has been devised; tweets that are selected are gathered into sets by the number of rounds they have "won" and battled one another until one fails to dominate the others, or against new winning tweets. This tournament design is intended to more rapidly focus player effort on the best tweets rather than across the entire collection. Furthermore, a slight change in game mechanics is being tested, where, instead of displaying a fixed number (in this case, 6) per microround, the number is dynamically adjusted based upon the estimated quality of the tweets in the microround. For example, for newly obtained tweets (which are mostly likely of low-quality), the number shown is increased to make it more likely that a good tweet will be among them; conversely, for tweets that have been previously selected, this window could be reduced to allow finer discrimination. These changes are being evaluated and will be discussed in follow-up work.

The efficiency analysis addressing question RQ.1c revealed that 14 showings were adequate to achieve a strong agreement, but that more showings per tweet would likely improve agreement. Looking at our participation numbers, while the game motivated 7 people to play the game extensively (ie, for more than 100 rounds), most played fewer (median of 10 rounds — corresponding to 60 showings of tweets). Our measurements of tweet inflow rates suggest the need for a constant stream of players (2-70 depending on the question) in order to derive rankings for all tweets being posted without modification. To achieve such sustained participation, we would need to motivate players to play the game longer and more often, which we believe will be possible by adding competitive elements and rewards.

CONCLUSION

The work in this paper examines the feasibility of crowdsourcing the identification of "good advice" in online micro-blog streams. The contributions consist of proof that it is feasible and practical to transform ratings from a Game with a Purpose (GWAP) into reliable ratings of "usefulness", and a set of design guidelines for designing such a GWAP. A number of outstanding challenges remain, however. In particular, there is the need to reduce the amount of "weak spam" introduced, and to make the game more engaging so that players will be compelled to return to play the game again, thereby powering the system's ability to continually filter and distill advice from the vast quantity of content being posted each day.

ACKNOWLEDGEMENTS
This work has been supported by the Engineering and Physical Sciences Research Council grants EnAKTing (EP/G008493/1) and Orchid (EP/I011587/1), UK. We thank the volunteers who played Twiage and provided feedback to improve its design, and our testing team Chris Clarke and Glen Martin.

REFERENCES
1. Adamic, L. A., Zhang, J., Bakshy, E., and Ackerman, M. S. Knowledge sharing and yahoo answers: everyone knows something. In *Proceeding of the 17th international conference on World Wide Web*, WWW '08, ACM (New York, NY, USA, 2008), 665–674.
2. Andre, P., Bernstein, M., and Luther, K. Who gives a tweet: Evaluating microblog content value. In *ACM Conference on Computer-Supported Cooperative Work* (2012).
3. Aula, A., Khan, R. M., Guan, Z., Fontes, P., and Hong, P. A comparison of visual and textual page previews in judging the helpfulness of web pages. In *Proceedings of the 19th international conference on World wide web*, WWW '10, ACM (New York, NY, USA, 2010), 51–60.
4. Barrington, L., O'Malley, D., Turnbull, D., and Lanckriet, G. User-centered design of a social game to tag music. In *Proceedings of the ACM SIGKDD Workshop on Human Computation*, HCOMP '09, ACM (New York, NY, USA, 2009), 7–10.
5. Benevenuto, F., Magno, G., Rodrigues, T., and Almeida, V. Detecting spammers on twitter. In *Collaboration, Electronic messaging, Anti-Abuse and Spam Conference (CEAS)* (2010).
6. Boyd, D., Golder, S., and Lotan, G. Tweet, Tweet, Retweet: Conversational Aspects of Retweeting on Twitter. vol. 0, IEEE Computer Society (Los Alamitos, CA, USA, Jan. 2010), 1–10.
7. Brill, E. A simple rule-based part of speech tagger. In *Proceedings of the third conference on Applied natural language processing*, ANLC '92, Association for Computational Linguistics (Stroudsburg, PA, USA, 1992), 152–155.
8. Dann, S. Twitter content classification. *First Monday 15*, 12 (2010), 1–11.
9. Evans, B. M., and Chi, E. H. Towards a model of understanding social search. In *Proceedings of the 2008 ACM conference on Computer supported cooperative work*, CSCW '08, ACM (New York, NY, USA, 2008), 485–494.
10. Gernburd, P., and Jadad, A. R. Will spam overwhelm our defenses? evaluating offerings for drugs and natural health products. *PLoS Med 4*, 9 (09 2007), e274.
11. Hacker, S., and von Ahn, L. Matchin: eliciting user preferences with an online game. In *Proceedings of the 27th international conference on Human factors in computing systems*, CHI '09, ACM (New York, NY, USA, 2009), 1207–1216.
12. Harper, F. M., Raban, D., Rafaeli, S., and Konstan, J. A. Predictors of answer quality in online q&a sites. In *Proceeding of the twenty-sixth annual SIGCHI conference on Human factors in computing systems*, CHI '08, ACM (New York, NY, USA, 2008), 865–874.
13. Jansen, B. J., Zhang, M., Sobel, K., and Chowdury, A. Twitter power: Tweets as electronic word of mouth. *J. Am. Soc. Inf. Sci. 60*, 11 (2009), 2169–2188.
14. Java, A., Song, X., Finin, T., and Tseng, B. Why we twitter: understanding microblogging usage and communities. In *Proceedings of the 9th WebKDD and 1st SNA-KDD 2007 workshop on Web mining and social network analysis*, WebKDD/SNA-KDD '07, ACM (New York, NY, USA, 2007), 56–65.
15. Liu, S., Liu, F., Yu, C., and Meng, W. An effective approach to document retrieval via utilizing wordnet and recognizing phrases. In *Proceedings of the 27th annual international ACM SIGIR conference on Research and development in information retrieval*, SIGIR '04, ACM (New York, NY, USA, 2004), 266–272.
16. Mamykina, L., Manoim, B., Mittal, M., Hripcsak, G., and Hartmann, B. Design lessons from the fastest q&a site in the west. In *Proceedings of the 2011 annual conference on Human factors in computing systems*, CHI '11, ACM (New York, NY, USA, 2011), 2857–2866.
17. Naaman, M., Boase, J., and Lai, C.-H. Is it really about me?: message content in social awareness streams. In *Proceedings of the 2010 ACM conference on Computer supported cooperative work*, CSCW '10, ACM (New York, NY, USA, 2010), 189–192.
18. Paul, S., Hong, L., and Chi, E. Is twitter a good place for asking questions? a characterization study, 2011.
19. Savage, P. *User interface evaluation in an iterative design process: a comparison of three techniques.* ACM, New York, NY, United States, 1996, 307–308.
20. Twitter, I. Streaming api methods. `https://dev.twitter.com/docs/streaming-api/methods` (2011).
21. Van Kleek, M., Smith, D. A., Stranders, R., and schraefel, m. Spam filtering on twitter: a web thumbnail image comparison technique. In *Technical Report, ECS* (2011).
22. von Ahn, L., and Dabbish, L. Labeling images with a computer game. In *Proceedings of the SIGCHI conference on Human factors in computing systems*, CHI '04, ACM (New York, NY, USA, 2004), 319–326.
23. von Ahn, L., and Dabbish, L. Designing games with a purpose. *Commun. ACM 51* (August 2008), 58–67.

Findings of e-ESAS: A Mobile Based Symptom Monitoring System for Breast Cancer Patients in Rural Bangladesh

Munirul M. Haque[1], Ferdaus Kawsar[1], Md. Adibuzzaman[1], Sheikh I. Ahamed[1], Richard Love[2], Rumana Dowla[3], David Roe[2], Syed Mozammel Hossain[3], Reza Selim[3]

[1]Marquette University
Ubicomp Lab, WI, USA
{mhaque, fkawsar, madibuz, iq}@mscs.mu.edu

[2]International Breast Cancer Research Foundation
Madison, WI, USA
{richard, davidroe}@ibcrf.org

[3]AGBC Center
Khulna, Bangladesh
{rumanadowla, rezasalim02, s_m_hossain}@yahoo.com

ABSTRACT

Breast cancer (BC) patients need traditional treatment as well as long term monitoring through an adaptive feedback-oriented treatment mechanism. Here, we present the findings of our 31-week long field study and deployment of e-ESAS – the first mobile-based remote symptom monitoring system (RSMS) developed for rural BC patients where patients are the prime users rather than just the source of data collection at some point of time. We have also shown how '*motivation*' and '*automation*' have been integrated in e-ESAS and creating a unique *motivation-persuasion-motivation* cycle where the motivated patients become proactive change agents by persuading others. Though in its early deployment stages (2 months), e-ESAS demonstrates the potential to positively impact the cancer care by (1) helping the doctors with graphical charts of long symptom history (automation), (2) facilitating timely interventions through alert generation (automation) and (3) improving three way communications (doctor-patient-attendant) for a better decision making process (motivation) and thereby improving the quality of life of BC patients.

Author Keywords

Breast cancer; mobile computing; symptom monitoring;

ACM Classification Keywords

H.5.m [Information Interfaces and presentation (e.g., HCI)]: Miscellaneous -

INTRODUCTION

According to Bangladesh Bureau of Statistics, cancer is the sixth leading cause of morbidity and mortality in Bangladesh [1]. BC is the 2nd most common type of female cancer in Bangladesh. The Government of Bangladesh devised the 'National Non Communicable Diseases Strategy and Plan of Action' with technical support from WHO in 2007. Even in this scenario, more than 22,000 new BC patients being added each year and 70% of them die due to lack of treatment [5] though it is possible to prevent at least one-third of the cancers based on early detection, availability of resources, and effective treatment [2].

Permission to make digital or hard copies of all or part of this work for personal or classroom use is granted without fee provided that copies are not made or distributed for profit or commercial advantage and that copies bear this notice and the full citation on the first page. To copy otherwise, or republish, to post on servers or to redistribute to lists, requires prior specific permission and/or a fee.
CHI'12, May 5–10, 2012, Austin, Texas, USA.
Copyright 2012 ACM 978-1-4503-1015-4/12/05...$10.00.

Many women in Bangladesh either never seek treatment or arrive at hospitals with late-stage cancer. Our field study shows numerous social, economic, traditional and health-system related issues factor into these circumstances. In this scenario, women need motivation to overcome the barriers to reach the door of medication. Patients are also reluctant to visit the health centers regularly due to factors including financial, poor transportation, and physical status. Key issues of BC like early detection and long term monitoring are rare events here. Lack of patient information and scarcity of doctors complicate an already challenging situation. In this regard a mobile based RSMS can play a potentially revolutionary role. Fortunately mobile phones penetrated the masses of Bangladesh with 76.4 million users by 2011 [3]. Our field study found 43 out of 45 rural BC patients have access to cell phones.

Therefore, we have developed a mobile based RSMS named e-ESAS based on Edmonton Symptom Assessment System (ESAS) [6], which is used by the doctors for the assessment of symptoms of cancer patients. e-ESAS has been developed considering the literacy level, familiarity with mobile technology and capability of the rural patients. This system has been deployed in Bangladesh as a pilot project for data collection. Patients can submit values for different symptoms from their home and doctors can view the graphical representation of that data using a cell phone.

The contribution of the work can be documented in broad scale as: *(1) the first mobile based RSMS for rural patients suffering from chronic disease like BC, (2) the first system where patients have become the sole user from home, (3) improvement on awareness of primary and secondary symptoms of BC, which is crucial for early detection, (4) creation of a positive environment through motivating videos, and (5) improvement of quality of life of rural BC patients.*

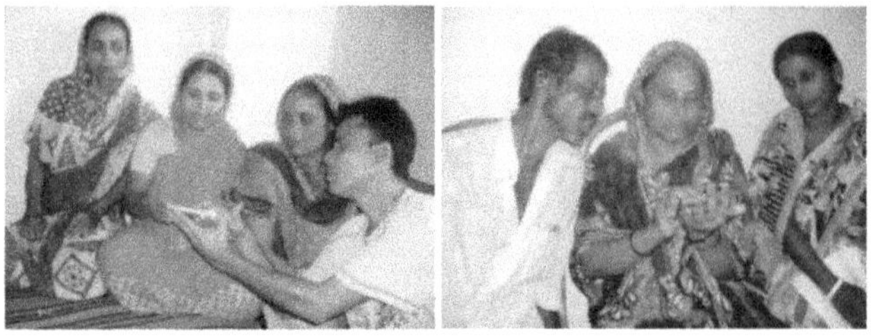

Figure 1. a) Patient and family members enjoying the video. b) Patient showing e-ESAS to others in AGBCC.

We begin with the background information. Next we describe the need assessment. Then we describe the design protocol of e-ESAS followed by the findings of final deployment of e-ESAS. Then we describe the related work. Based on the experience of the field studies, we have discussed some design implications. Finally we conclude with a couple of pitfalls and directions to our future work.

SYSTEM BACKGROUND

Amader Gram (literally 'Our Village') is one of the pioneer NGOs who are working for the betterment of BC patients since 2006 through Amader Gram Breast Care Center (AGBCC). The mission for AGBCC is to reduce morbidity and mortality from BC and other breast diseases in women. The breast problem clinic is held three days per week. A trained female doctor and medical assistant attend each clinic. Patients need to pay a onetime registration fee of BDT 100 ($1.5). Furthermore, 1,405 patients have been registered with BC and 239 of them have been referred for further care from 2006 to 2010. Since then 21 patients have died. Amader Gram also works for the rural ICT (Information, Communication and Technology) efforts which make the NGO an ideal choice for our pilot study.

NEED ASSESSMENT

To get a better understanding of the real scenario we made 2 field trips for 7 weeks in 2010.

Methodology

As part of our need assessment, we interviewed 39 BC patients whom are registered with AGBCC. They were interviewed for 60 to 90 minutes in different settings: hospitals (9), patients' homes (5), and in AGBCC centers of Khulna, Bagerhat and Rampal (25). One researcher and one HW took part in the interview. The interview covered the problems faced by patients in achieving treatment and their familiarity with cell phones. Patients' ages ranged from 21 to 45 and education varied from illiterate (34.9%) to high school level. 87.1% of the patients came from a family with monthly income less than 84.5 dollars. Twenty nine patients had breast cancer for the first time and 10 had it for the second time. Finally, it is interesting to note that almost 96% of the patients said that they have access to cell phones that belong to themselves or to some member of the family.

We had 2 group sessions with 12 doctors. All the researchers participated in the session in Khulna with 8 doctors. The 2nd session was conducted in Dhaka Medical College Hospital with 3 doctors and 2 researchers. The sessions focused on finding the barriers from doctors' point of view. Two members of the research team also talked with 6 HWs in AGBCC of Khulna and Bagerhat.

Problem Identification

The problems identified are classified as follows.

Lack of Motivation

The biggest problem for BC patients is the lack of knowledge and motivation for treatment. Due to lack of familiarity, most women identify BC really late. They are very shy and sometimes are afraid to talk with anyone regarding breast problems. Most of the time they think this will be automatically cured as time goes by. Long standing superstitions and social and religious beliefs also stand against visiting and receiving treatment. In many rural families, the husband and mother-in-law believe spending money on women is a complete waste, whereas the male members of the family are treated differently. Long traffic jams, poor road conditions and long distances to health centers complicate the already challenging situation. Due to the lengthy nature of treatment, BC patients become habituated with the disease and start neglecting treatment (fading out issue). Patients also mentioned the problems of finding a companion who will accompany them to health centers. Typically, patients visit doctors with long delay between appointments and miss appointments on a regular basis. Based on the results of our field study, we have generated the following barrier tree shown in figure 2.

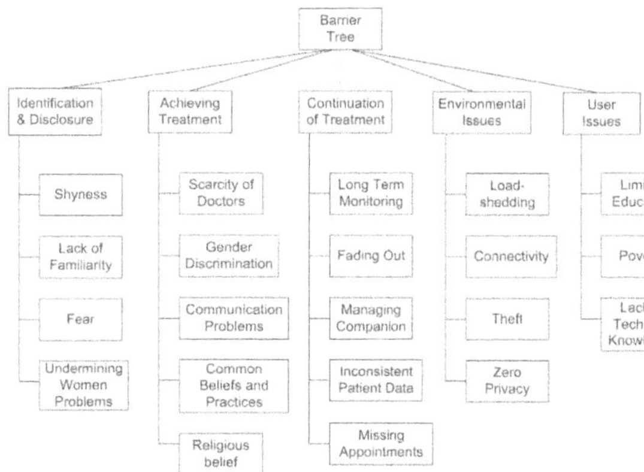

Figure 2. Barrier tree for rural BC patients.

Lack of Automation

Manual paper-based medication process forms this problem domain. Based on our clinic observation, we found that doctors use a paper-based symptom monitoring system named ESAS. This form mentions 10 symptoms, namely pain, tiredness, nausea, depression, anxiety, drowsiness, appetite, well-being, shortness of breath and others. Each of them has an associated scale from 0 to 10. Doctors talk with the patients and ask the value they want to assign against each symptom. Though the form is supposed to be filled out by patients, it was always filled out by the doctors. Later the values given by the patients are put in paper-based ESAS graph for visual representation. Completing the paper- based ESAS takes quite a long time (on an average 8 minutes based on 35 observations). This leaves the doctors with very short time to talk with patients about other issues they might want to discuss. Along with that, we have found several incomplete paper-based ESAS graphs that, according to doctors, resulted due to time limitation.

Patients visit the doctors with frequently irregular and long intervals between visits. Since patients' symptom levels are recorded only when they come, doctors have very little data about the patients' history. In addition, loss of previous prescriptions is also quite common. We have found 7 patients during our clinic observation who have either forgot or lost their previous prescriptions.

e-ESAS DESIGN

Based on the findings of the need assessment, we have decided to approach the overall solution from two different perspectives – motivation and automation.

Motivation

Motivation is needed to overcome most of the barriers faced by patients. We have developed 2 different videos named 'Motivating Video for Women (MVW)' and 'Motivating Video for Society (MVS)' for this issue. One patient took part in the MVW and local influential persons took part in the MVS. The statements of the MVW and MVS were carefully chosen to cover different areas of motivation. In MVW, the patient talks about her experience, symptoms of BC, and motivates other women to visit doctors. At the end of the MVW, doctors made some important comments. The MVS video is directed towards the family heads (husbands) and addresses the social and cultural challenges to create a better environment for BC patients. At the same time, both the videos convey important information regarding BC. At the end of the 1st month of deployment, we replaced the MVW with a new patient statement to continue the viewers' interest. Below are the excerpts of a patient and doctor from the MVW:

"*When I first found a* ***lump*** *in my breast I took homeopathy treatment... It was also* ***paining, irritating*** *and I found* ***discharge from the nipple****... then I visited AGBCC and visited a* ***foreign doctor****...Later I went through an operation. I'm going there* ***every month*** *and taking medicines regularly. Now I am better than earlier. Whoever has this problem, don't feel* ***shy*** *or* ***don't get afraid*** *and get treatment* ***as soon as possible****.*" (patient)

"*We should give importance to all the* ***lumps*** *whether it is a cancer or not. We should check it* ***regularly*** *by expert doctor at least* ***once a year****... We the doctor and health workers of AGBCC are always beside you.*" (doctor)

The statement of MVS is as follows:

"*Breast cancer is a* ***curable disease****. It is* ***not infectious*** *and it is also not true that if someone has breast cancer then other members of the family will also have it. Mothers and sisters please be conscious...I will request the male members of the house not to neglect the health issues of the women...We are lucky that AGBCC is located close by where doctors are ready to give you all necessary treatments.*"

Automation

From the clinic observation, it was obvious that it is not feasible for doctors to complete the paper-based ESAS considering the timing restriction due to high patient load. Also, a better tool is needed to obtain patient data on a regular basis. Therefore, we developed a mobile based ESAS named e-ESAS for Nokia X6. On the server side, we have used Tomcat 6.0 as the server and MySQL as database. The client in turn has two modules. We call these modules as patients' module and doctors' module.

Patients' Module

This consists of 2 questions from the original paper-based ESAS on each page, and at the end, we have added 3 extra questions according to doctors' suggestions. These 3 questions are: the minimum, maximum, and average pain in the last 24 hours. We have put a button with the Bengali label for each symptom and a sliding bar following each button which can be set for any values between 0 and 10. If the button is pressed, it will play a voice instruction in local Bengali dialect. When the user presses the 'submit' button located at the bottom, it will send all the sliding bar values set by the patient to the database server as a string. Patients can also view their prescriptions. Sample screenshots of e-ESAS system have been shown in figure 3.

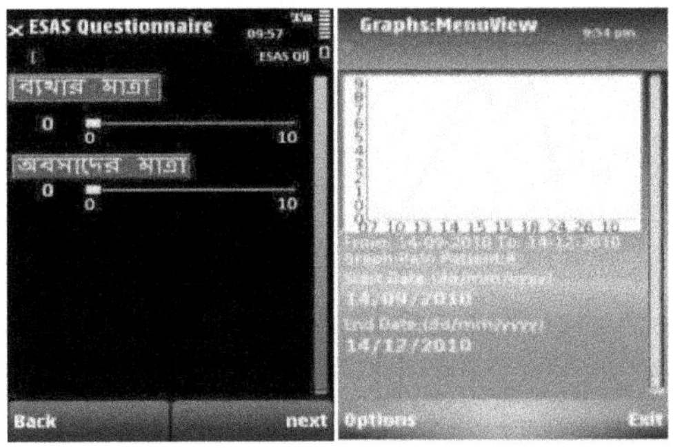

Figure 3. a) e-ESAS for patients. b) Longitudinal pain graph for doctors.

Doctors' Module

The doctors' module has the following features:

1. *Longitudinal graph*: Doctors can choose a patient and one or more symptoms to see the values of that symptom represented across a selected period of time.
2. *Prescription*: Doctors can check their previous prescriptions or add new prescriptions.
3. *Alert Generation*: An alert will be generated for doctors based on predefined conditions. For example, an alert might be generated if 'the pain level is more than 6 for 3 consecutive days'.

Methodology

We conducted our 3rd field trip in June '11 for deploying the final version of e-ESAS and collecting data. But due to delayed BMRC (Bangladesh Medical Research Council) approval we have been prohibited to use the data collected in the 3rd field trip. So we conducted the 4th field trip to collect and analysis the data after receiving the approval. The following figure 4 shows the timeline of deployment.

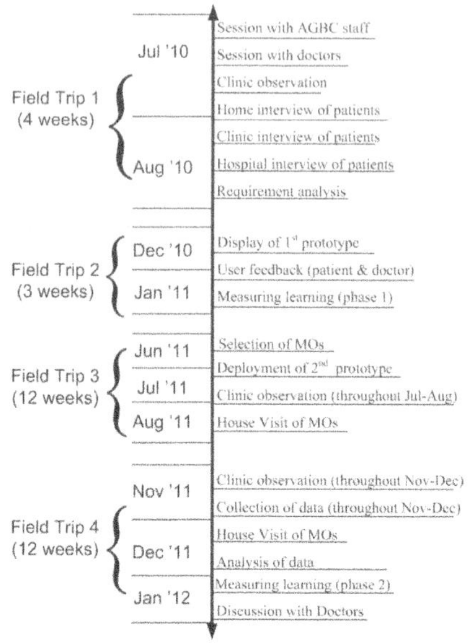

Figure 4. Timeline of design and deployment of e-ESAS.

We have deployed e-ESAS in 12 Nokia X6 phones. Two of them will be used by doctors in different AGBCCs. The rest will be used by 10 BC patients for six months.

Selection of e-ESAS User

Patients were selected based on the following criteria.

- Chronic pain score, usual level, on ESAS 0-10 scale reported to be less than or equal to 5.
- Life expectancy, greater than 6 months.
- Normal mental status.
- Performance status 0, 1, or 2 based on ECOG scale [4].
- Able to understand and cooperate with study protocol.
- Patient has two people living with her (attendant).
- Patient lives less than one hour commuting distance from either AGBCC or DMCH.

We refer to these 10 patients as Mobile Owners (MOs) in the rest of the paper. MOs have been provided with the cell phone and a prepaid internet card worth BDT 100 ($1.30) to send the e-ESAS data once daily to the server.

Training of MOs

We arranged a small ceremony where all MOs were present with at least one attendant and received the phone. One researcher showed each of the MOs and attendants how to use e-ESAS. Then both MOs and attendants used e-ESAS for 15 minutes under the supervision of the researcher. Later MOs and attendants were handed a piece of paper with 13 random values and asked to set these values sequentially using e-ESAS. We followed this procedure 3 times with each of them.

House Visit

A team of one researcher and one HW visited the houses of the MOs after 1 month of deployment. The purpose was twofold. We first replaced the old MVW with the new one. We then had open discussion with the MOs and attendants regarding their experience with using e-ESAS.

Group Session with Doctors

We arranged a group discussion with all doctors (8) and researchers in AGBCC Khulna in Jan '12. Doctors shared their experience with patient interaction using e-ESAS. We also discussed future plans regarding e-ESAS.

Clinic Observation

In order to assess the quality of the patient visits, we observed 77 patient-doctor interactions. A research team member acted as passive observer during these interviews.

FINDINGS

Though we first deployed e-ESAS in mid June '11, here we publish result starting from Nov '11 due to delayed BMRC clearance.

Usability Findings

At the end of Dec '11, one of the research team members conducted the following steps for all 10 MOs and 10 attendants.

- Each patient is given 13 random numbers from 0 to 10 and asked to set these values using the sliding bars of e-ESAS sequentially.
- Record the time required by the patient to set the values.
- Count the number of errors (the values set by the patient that are different than the given values are considered errors).

The following figure 5 shows the timing requirement for MOs and attendants.

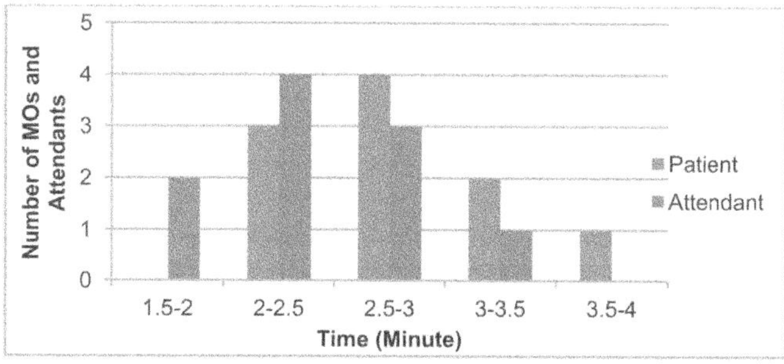

Figure 5. Timing requirement histogram

The average time required by attendants is 2.4 minutes which is slightly less than that of the patients (2.8 minutes). This is expected since, in most cases, attendants were younger than the patients and more familiar with mobile phones. One of the patients made 1 error and none of the attendants made any errors. This indicates the simplicity and easy-to-use nature of e-ESAS.

Measurement of Learning

One of the major goals of e-ESAS was to increase the knowledge and awareness of women regarding BC. During our 2nd visit (Dec '10) in Bangladesh we asked 39 BC patients and 15 other patients the following questions separately.

Q1. Have you heard about Breast cancer before?
Q2. What is the most common sign of breast cancer?
Q3. What are the other signs of breast cancer?
Q4. If someone has breast cancer do you believe her daughter will must have breast cancer?
Q5. Do you think it is infectious?
Q6. Have you heard of mammogram or Breast Self-Exam?

All 39 BC patients were registered with AGBCC and the others came to AGBCC with different breast-related problems. The former class of patients will be termed as BC1 and the later as OP1. Three teams (each consisting of one researcher and one HW) were formed to conduct the interviews. On the first day of interviews, we noted a problem. Every time the patients asked to explain the questions, the HWs were eager to give long explanations that contain partial or full answers. We then stopped the procedure and arranged a focus group session with all 3 teams to ensure congruency in explaining each of the questions to patients in a non-leading way. We followed the same procedure in Jan '12 on 45 BC patients (BC2) and 21 other patients (OP2). In both phases the interview ranged over 3 weeks and took place in different AGBCCs. All the interviews were audio recorded and later transcribed in English. The BC patients, being already diagnosed, naturally have better knowledge than the other patients. This was the reason for making two separate groups while analyzing the data. The measurement of learning has been summarized in the following figure 6.

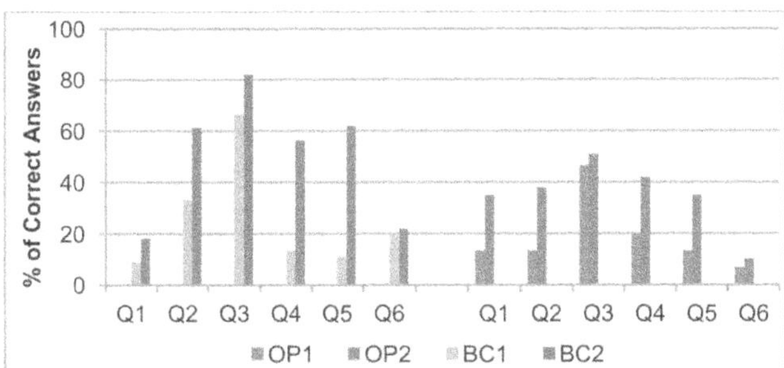

Figure 6. Comparison of percentage of correct answers for BC and other patients before and after e-ESAS deployment.

In most cases patients provided overlapping answers for questions 2 and 3. The correct answer for question 2 is 'breast lump', while that of question 3 is swelling, pain, discharge from nipple, etc. If a patient mentions a lump and at least one of the other symptoms, we have included their responses as correct answers for questions 2 and 3. The percentage of correct answers for question 3 is significantly higher than that of question 2 since it is easier to mention at least one of the common symptoms.

The graphs show a large increase of correct answers for questions 1, 2, 4 and 5. We have identified 2 sources that contributed to the improvement of learning. First, a big fair was held in Jan '11 where AGBCC had a stall for breast screening and distributed booklets containing important information regarding BC. Second, the motivating videos and e-ESAS created an interest among women. Thirty patients said they have seen the e-ESAS and the motivating videos at least once when they met the MOs in either AGBCC or their houses. We found that when patients wait for their turn to meet the doctors, they flock around the MOs to see the e-ESAS and motivating videos. It should be noted that the MVW contains the answers for questions 2 and 3, where as MVS contains the answers for questions 4 and 5. Question number 6 was covered neither in our pilot study nor in the booklets of AGBCC, and the percentage of correct answers is pretty much the same in both phases. This also indicates that the motivating videos and booklets are the main contributors in the increased learning for other questions.

Improvement of Motivation

The deployment of e-ESAS and its advertisement (through MVW, MVS and posters in AGBCC) made a positive impact in encouraging women to come out of the shell and be proactive about their health issues. According to one of the doctors (D2), "*In the last 2 weeks I have received 3 patients with minor furuncle in their breasts. It is not usual for patients coming to the center with such minor breast problems. Normally I always see patients coming to the center only when major complications occur. Otherwise either they just do nothing or go to local herbalists at best.*" Another notable change supports this fact. Doctors reported 6 incidents of non-scheduled visits by current BC patients. This is unusual in a setting where AGBCC patients miss roughly half of their scheduled appointments. Moreover, all of these 6 patients had a history of missed appointments, with 3 of them missing appointments at least 3 times. One of these motivated patients explained to the doctor saying, "*I have reported my pain level more than 7 for the last 5 days. So I thought I should come and talk to the doctor.*"

Improvement on Self-reporting

During our clinic observation in the first field trip, we found that several times doctors get irritated due to the inability of patients in answering their questions. It was very difficult for doctors to get a clear idea about the symptom levels of the patients due to their indefinite and sometimes inappropriate answers. When the doctors ask about the level of nausea during the last week, patients answered the following way:

"I think I vomited sometimes but I cannot recall exactly."

"When I was returning to my house from here last month I vomited in the bus."

"I feel like vomiting whenever I go to the restroom."

But during the clinic observation in the 3rd visit, we found that the answers of the MOs are overall accurate and concise. Since they were submitting about these symptom levels each day, they became knowledgeable and up to date about their current health conditions. We found the MOs making additional useful comments when doctors were observing their symptom curves. One of the MOs (MO2) said to the doctor, "*I vomited 2/3 times for 3 days last week. That is why I have put 10 in the sliding bar of nausea for those 3 days.*" Though we have not seen a notable improvement in the answers of other BC patients (who did not receive the mobile phone), we expect to see improvements in the long run. This is because the other patients always talk with the MOs about the videos, how they fill e-ESAS and why they have put a specific value in different symptoms. As a result they are expected to become familiar with how to answer the common questions.

Change in Social Dynamics

As a result of receiving such mobile the MOs became an object of attraction. The research team went to visit the MOs. Other women having higher status also started coming to their houses. All these issues created a symbol of higher status for the patient in that family. The result is similar to that of 'Avaaj Otalo' [9]. MO1 described this change: "*Since the starting of the disease, my mother-in-law was very rude on me. She always used to say to my husband that he should not spend money for my treatment. I have missed several appointments because either she did not permit me or she assigned me some other task. But now when she saw that people are coming to see me and the mobile, she has become pleased with me. Even she said that she wants to go with me to AGBCC next time.*"

Reduction in Missed Appointments

The most common complaint we heard from doctors was missed appointment schedules. We were interested to see the effect of the deployment of e-ESAS on this issue. We analyzed the data in two time frames; Dec '10- May '11 (before the deployment of e-ESAS) and Nov '11-Dec '11. We will call these periods time frame 1 (TF1) and time frame 2 (TF2) respectively. We also divided the cancer patients into 2 groups: MOs and the rest. This is because the MOs, having received the mobiles, are naturally expected to be more punctual in their appointments. We show the missing appointments statistics of each of the MOs for TF1 in figure 7. These 10 MOs were scheduled for a total of 107 appointments over the six month period, making an average of 1.78 appointments per patient per month. They missed a total of 40 appointments, thus the average percentage of missed appointments became 37.4. According to the records of AGBCC, only 2 MOs missed one of their appointments each in TF2.

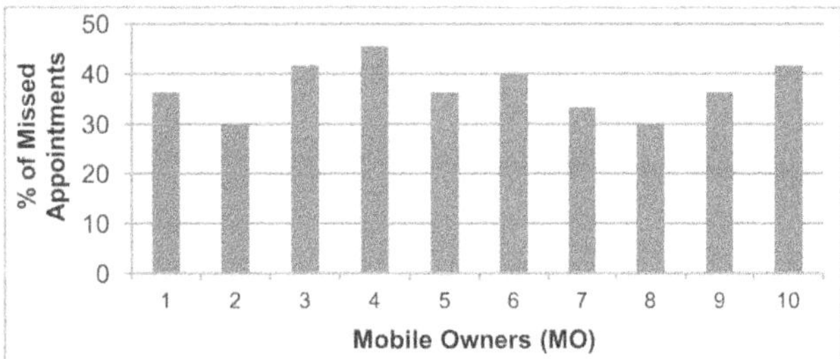

Figure 7. Missing appointments data for MOs in TF1.

Then, we focused on the appointment history of the other BC patients for TF1 and TF2. The average percentage of missed appointments are 48.8 in TF1 and 39.8 in TF2 as shown by yellow and red solid lines in figure 8.

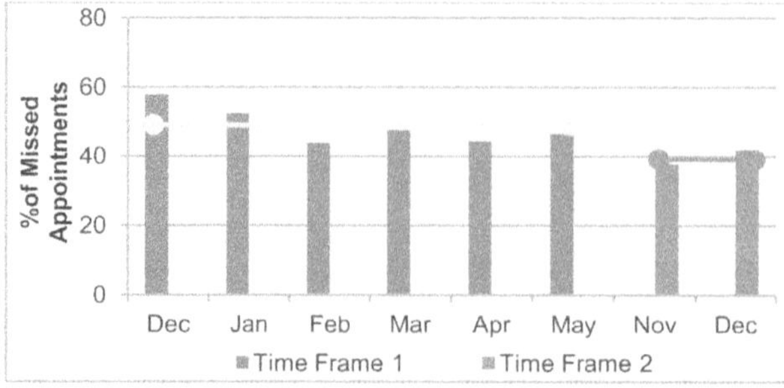

Figure 8. Comparison of percentage of missed appointments for BC patients in TF1 and TF2.

We can clearly see an average drop of 9%. We identified two possible reasons for this fact.

- Deployment of e-ESAS created an environment where women are more encouraged to participate.
- Some of the patients said that they think the MOs are selected based on appointment history and are also getting better treatment. They want to reach that level so doctors give more attention to them. However we need more time to make any conclusive remarks on this issue.

It is to be noted that the local doctors have been operating since 2nd week of August when the foreign doctors left. Also November to January is the winter season in Bangladesh and the percentage of missed appointments is much less in Dec '11 (42%) compared to that of Dec '10 (58%). This indicates that the drop in percentage of missed appointments is not just due to external factors like foreign doctors or weather.

Reduction in Number of Appointments

Normally, doctors ask the BC patients to meet weekly or biweekly based on their current health status. But in case of MOs doctors asked them to come monthly. They were also encouraged to come if they feel any problems in between. As a result of this, the number of appointments assigned for MOs has been reduced automatically. According to figure 9, the average number of appointments for each patient per month has been reduced to 1.25 in TF2 compared to that of 1.78 in TF1.

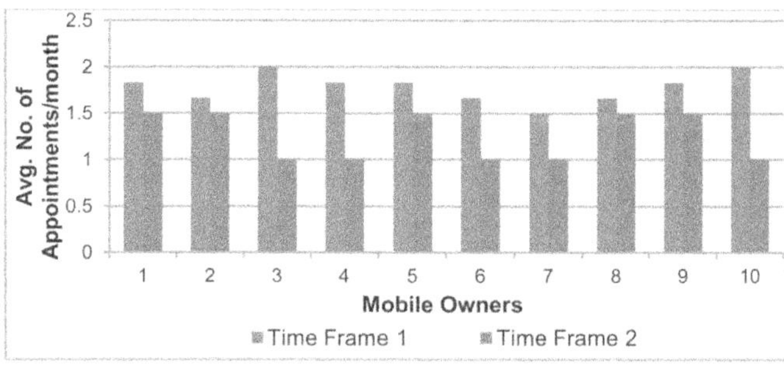

Figure 9. Comparison graph of required number of appointments in TF1 and TF2.

Along with normal monthly visit, MO1 and MO2 received 1 extra appointment each from doctors due to their unusual pain curves. MO5, MO8 and MO9 made one nonscheduled visit each to discuss their health conditions. Reduction in number of appointments is in turn reducing the cost and transportation hazards of patients.

Timing Requirement

The effectiveness of doctors can be increased by reducing the visit time required by each patient without compromising the level of care. During TF2 we recorded the duration of clinic visits of MOs and other BC patients through clinic observation. MOs made 12 and 13 appointments in Nov '11 and Dec '11 respectively and that of the other BC patients are 51 and 48. Along with all MO visits we recorded the timing of 23 and 29 visits of other BC patients in Nov '11 and Dec '11 respectively. The average timing requirement of MOs and other BC patients in TF2 is shown in figure 10. The figures are based on averaging the time recorded during those visits. To avoid biasness, doctors were not notified about the timing issue.

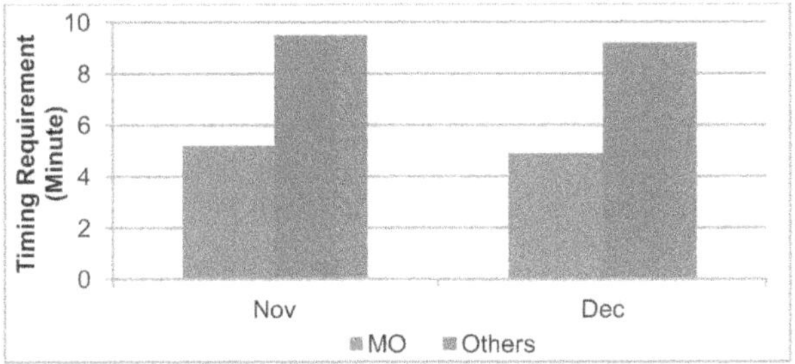

Figure 10. Average timing requirements of MOs and others during TF2.

The reduced timing requirement by MOs is pretty much anticipated since the doctors do not need to ask them about their symptom values and fill the paper-based ESAS graph.

Video Download

In order to analyze how many times the motivating videos have been played from each of the specific mobiles we added a log counter in the server. On an average the MVW video has been played for 3 times per day from each mobile where as that of MVS is 2.3. The following figure 11 shows the total number of times (considering all 10 mobiles) the MVW and MVS videos have been played over TF2. As expected the curve has been gradually decreased with an exception in week 5. At the end of Nov '11 we replaced the old MVW with new one. This is the possible reason for sudden increase in the otherwise declining video played graph shown in figure 11.

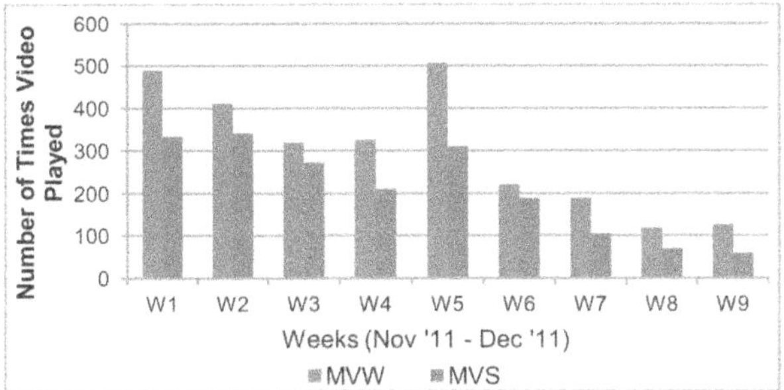

Figure 11. Week wise download statistics of MVW and MVS videos (Nov '11-Dec '11).

When analyzed the data patient wise, as shown in figure 12, we found notable discrepancy with 3 MOs.

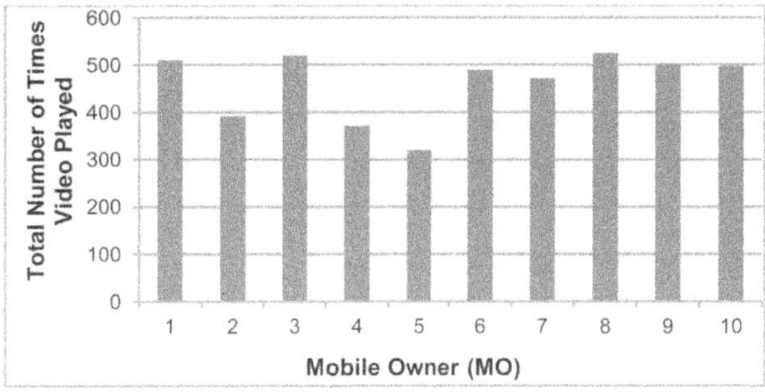

Figure 12. Device wise total video played statistics (Nov '11-Dec '11).

While the total number of times videos played of the other MOs ranged from 351 to 391 averaging 372, that of MO2, MO4, and MO5 records 245, 259, and 236 respectively. When we asked the other patients living in the neighborhood of these MOs one patient said, "*Husband of MO4 is a powerful person in our village. So She has a very high status and we do not feel that comfortable going to her house and asking her mobile.*" We found that MO2 also has a significant higher status compared to other MOs. But MO5 has a social status just like the rest 7 MOs. Then we discovered that she is the only women in the MO list who has neither husband nor any children. This is the most likely cause for less number of downloads from MO5 since all other MOs said that their children play with the mobile and also watch videos. We also found children taking the mobiles to their friends to show them the videos.

Along with that the log records of MO4 and MO5 indicate that they are the only two who have played MVS more than MVW. When we asked them they said that their husbands have good terms with the local community representatives and several times they take the mobiles to show the MVS video to them.

We also found that women are more interested to watch the MVW video where the participant is a woman where as their counterparts are more interested in the MVS video where the participant is a male. One of the women who was watching the MVW video during our house visit said, "*I have watched the MVS video once but I like to see the MVW since I want to hear breast related things from a woman.*" On the other hand the husband of MO2 said, "*I took the mobile with me yesterday night when we all had a meeting with the community members. There many people saw the MVS video because they wanted to see what our chairman is saying about this issue.*"

Multiple Entry of e-ESAS

The MOs were instructed to submit e-ESAS once every day. But interestingly we have received multiple submissions from all of the MOs within the very first week of deployment. When we delved through the matter we found that excited neighbors, husbands, and in some cases the children also submitted the form without noticing the

MOs. Then we requested the MOs to be present while others are playing with the video or e-ESAS. We also modified the server setup to make sure that it will take only one submission from each mobile every day (the 1st one) and discard the multiple entries. At the same time we also added a counter to keep track of the number of entries being submitted from each mobile every day. By the end of 1st month of deployment this issue became a rare event.

Improvement of Quality of Life

Inauguration of the pilot study by the health advisor of Bangladesh (equivalent to minister), presence of foreign doctors, visits of the research team to the houses of the patients, receiving of new mobile all these contributed to create a positive atmosphere for the rural BC patients. Interaction of the MOs with other patients in the AGBCC and with other women in their village area started to make women more knowledgeable and caring about their health. The motivating videos are also playing their part to change the social customs in patients' favor. Doctors are getting regular data of patients which help them to make better diagnosis. By addressing the following three barriers e-ESAS is encouraging BC patients for a better life.

Enhanced Clinic Visit Experience

e-ESAS helps the doctors to better prepared for the patients in 2 ways. First, they can see the longitudinal symptom curves for a selected period of time which was not possible before. Secondly, since they do not need to fill the ESAS chart anymore during the patient visit, they get more time to listen to the problems and questions of the patients. One doctor (D3) shared her experience during open discussion session as, "*I feel much relax now because I have visual representation of the data I need and I feel I have enough time compared to my previous experience.*"

Facilitating Earlier Intervention

In cancer care early intervention might help to avert a potentially critical situation. From our experience we have seen that patients normally visit the AGBCC once a month. So if there is any change in their pain level or other symptoms meantime, it goes unreported and unattended. Since there is no other way to contact with the doctors other than visiting them personally, in most cases the patients just continue with the same medication given in the previous visit. But now doctors can make timely intervention since e-ESAS automatically generates alert for doctors when any symptom value exceeds its predefined threshold. We have seen 6 cases where the doctors have changed the medication and in 4 cases they asked the MOs to visit them. When the doctors change the prescription a notification is sent to the mobile of the MO. They can simply take the mobile to the pharmacy and get medicine accordingly.

Enhanced 3 Way Communication

e-ESAS helps to bridge the communication gaps among patients, attendants, and doctors by endowing them to actively participate in the process of cancer care. Previously patients/attendants used to think themselves as passive participants of the medication process but now when they are submitting data each day they feel more responsible and part of the decision making process. This issue helps all to be more co-operative in information sharing thus bridging the communication gap. Similar results are found in [18, 20] in urban settings.

RELATED WORK

Several projects work based on implementing a guideline set by WHO or other standard organizations in computer or handheld devices [7,12,13]. Early Diagnosis and Prevention System [12], a computer based healthcare management software, registers patient history for screening. e-IMCI [7] describes a PDA based system for administering the Integrated Management of Childhood Illness (IMCI) protocol. The feasibility of mobile applications for collecting health data or survey information has been proven in many developing countries including India [11], Tanzania [10], Ghana [14], and Uganda [15]. Our project has three fundamental differences with these projects. Here instead of trained professionals (HWs or doctors), patients or attendants are filling the symptom information by themselves. Secondly, patients are doing this from home and sending data by using the data network of mobile carriers. In all the aforementioned projects, either patient has to come to the health center or HWs need to go to remote houses of the patients to collect such information. Finally, our project handles the issue of '*motivation*' as part of the implementation.

The effectiveness of electronic symptom monitoring has been proven in chronic diseases like asthma [16], diabetes [17], and cancer [18]. CHESS [19] is another well known patient archival system. But all these projects have been deployed in high class urban settings and they use web based online monitoring system which is not feasible for illiterate women of rural settings. Current literature review concludes that mobile applications intended to help long term monitoring of patients suffering from chronic diseases like BC of developing world is yet to be implemented.

DISCUSSION

Here we discuss the key lessons derived from our study.

Motivation-Persuasion-Motivation Loop

As mentioned in [8] motivation and persuasion go hand by hand for successful ICT projects in developing countries. But they have shown this to be applied on 2 different classes of people- the target audience (persuasion) and those who work for the project termed as change agent (motivation). In our case we have generated an end user scenario where motivation and persuasion have been merged to a single point. The patients get the initial motivation when they see a new approach (automation of ESAS) has been developed for them and feel pride that others are watching their videos. They automatically become very active in persuading others since they are getting respect and a different status in the village. These issues of motivation transform an ordinary village woman from mere patient to change agent. Overall we got better result by creating a cycle where motivated patients are persuading others and the end result of persuasion (praise, higher status, and feeling of being different) giving motivation again to the patients. **Try to create a never ending cycle of motivation and persuasion.**

Concept 'Part of the Team'

In current rural settings doctors are single handedly in the position of decision making. As a result patients do not feel themselves as important as it should be. This is a barrier in the effective communication between patients and doctors though several studies have proved the necessity and importance of information sharing [21, 22]. In our experience as a result of using e-ESAS patients became more active in information sharing. Instead of being passive patients they felt that they are providing the necessary information that doctors are using for medication. This gave the patients and attendants (who are filing e-ESAS on behalf of the patients) a sense of 'part of the team' for decision making. The lesson here is that a successful health care based IT project should **facilitate active participation of individuals' (patients, attendants, and doctors) in care and decision-making**.

Bottom up Approach

Current literature does not show any project where the patients, being the end user, use the system by themselves. We find ICT projects for doctors, nurses, or HWs being the user of the desktop or mobile applications. Though the symptom levels stated or inputted by the patients for any disease are considered as 'gold standard', we have not found any health care project for rural village people where the real patients have been given the priority to use the IT application by themselves. At least 2 symptom monitoring systems being studied in USA [20, 21] have concluded that active user participation approach resulted in better care. **The patients should be the primary user of any symptom monitoring system and the system should be developed based on analyzing their needs, capabilities, and drawbacks.**

Entertainment and Attention

Any application for patients should have something that serves as their entertainment. By doing a specific task on regular basis patients may feel obligated and loose interest in doing that. At the same time the application might need to have new look and feel which will help to regain the attention of the patients. In our case the videos serve the purpose of entertainment. But as time goes by the number of downloads decreased sharply. Then we changed the subjects of the video with similar type of statement. This increased the number of video downloads again. The lesson is that the **application should be entertaining to patients and changes might be necessary to keep the attention of the target audience**.

PITFALLS

We are concerned about the 2 following issues.

Financial Issues and Sustainability

We wanted to study the sustainability of our study when the project ends. We prepared the following table 1 to show the cost analysis of e-ESAS.

	Avg. no. of appointments	Avg. transportation cost/appointment	Avg. time in transportation	Total cost/month	Total time/ month in transportation
Without e-ESAS	1.84	380.45	5.19	700.03	9.55
With e-ESAS	1.25	380.45	5.19	475.5	6.5

Table 1. Summary of patient information

Then we classified the patients in 3 groups: a) patients with high end mobile where e-ESAS application can be deployed, b) patients with Java enabled mobiles, and c) patients with non Java enabled mobiles. On an average BDT 1.02 is needed to submit e-ESAS information each time. So each patient of the 1st group needs only 31 taka ($0.41) each month to submit e-ESAS once a day. The patients of 2nd and 3rd group can use our proposed SMS based system. For 30 SMSs patients need around BDT 5 ($0.07). Those who do not have Java enabled mobile needs a onetime purchase cost of around BDT 3500 ($48). We detailed this information to the patients and ask them whether they will be willing to bear this cost by themselves at the end of the study. The answers have been summarized in table 2.

Patient Groups	Yes	No	Not Sure
1st group (2)	100%	0%	0%
2nd group (14)	100%	0%	0%
3rd group (16)	43%	24%	33%

Table 2. Summary of patient information

Though the statistics seem promising we have to wait to see the actual results.

Misconception in Motivation

Distribution of the mobiles and visiting the MOs houses created some misconceptions in the mind of other BC patients that contributed in their motivation and increased participation. Six patients asked the doctors during their visits in TF2 whether they will get the mobile next time if they maintain their appointment schedules properly. Two of them added that they also thought if they follow the medications properly and come to the center regularly foreign doctors would visit their houses in future and they would receive better treatment.

NEXT STEPS

As we walked through the time line of the project we got exciting ideas that we decided to add in future. We plan to develop the following extensions.

SMS based ESAS

In order to make this project a real success we need to reach the mass poor people of the villages. We are working on developing a SMS based e-ESAS system for low end mobiles. For this system client software will be developed and deployed in patients' mobile. The software will ask questions, collect answers, and then send the data as SMS. There will be a SMS server (Server and mobile connected with server) to receive the patients' SMS and parse the SMS to collect necessary data. At least java supported mobile will be required to run this software. We have decided to build the SMS based system in java enabled phone due to extreme penetration of Nokia phones in rural Bangladesh. 32 out of 43 patients who have access to mobile possess a Nokia phone and 46.7% of these phones were java enabled.

Forum for BC Patients

People always like to find them as part of a homogeneous community. BC patients, be in rural or urban settings, always find it difficult to mix with other members of the society. Rather they prefer to interact with other BC patients whom they think are in the same boat. Especially patients do not prefer to talk about psychosocial issues with doctors but which is a very important issue to be discussed and shared for terminally ill patients [18]. Based on this finding we plan to develop a forum among MOs where they can submit audio based questions and answers. We prefer the audio version since most of the MOs do not know how to write. At the same time it will have a FAQ section with answers from experienced doctors. We believe such a platform is highly needed by the BC patients to express their closed thoughts and to increase their social interaction.

Long Term Data Analysis

Currently we are getting 10 symptom values and 3 pain related values from each BC patient each day. This is going to build an enormous database which can be used by medical researchers for analysis. We also plan to analyze these data for finding behavioral patterns of terminally ill patients. At the same time we would like to compare the life expectancy of the MOs with that of other BC patients of similar status (same physical, mental, and disease state).

ACKNOWLEDGMENTS

We thank Mridul Chowdhury for creating the videos. This work has been supported by grant from IBCRF.

REFERENCES

1. Bangladesh Bureau of Statistics. (2008).Ministry of Planning. Statistical Yearbook of Bangladesh, 2007.
2. http://www.whoban.org/LinkFiles/Publication_Cancer_Strategy.pdf.pdf
3. http://www.btrc.gov.bd/newsandevents/mobile_phone_subscribers/mobile_phone_subscribers_june_2011.php
4. http://ecog.dfci.harvard.edu/general/perf_stat.html
5. http://english.peopledaily.com.cn/90001/90782/6521649.html
6. http://www.empainline.org/linked_site_content/pdf/Edmonton%20Functionl%20Assess%20System.pdf
7. DeRenzi, B., Lesh, N., Parikh, T., Sims, C., Mitchell, M., Maokola, W., Chemba, M., Hamisi, Y., Schellenbe, D., Borriello,G. e-IMCI: Improving Pediatric Health Care in Low-Income Countries. In *Proc. CHI '08*,(2008)
8. Divya Ramachandran, John Canny, Prabhu Dutta Das, and Edward Cutrell. 2010. Mobile-izing health workers in rural India. In *Proc. CHI '10*, 1889-1898, (2010).
9. Neil Patel, Deepti Chittamuru, Anupam Jain, Paresh Dave, and Tapan S. Parikh. 2010. Avaaj Otalo: a field study of an interactive voice forum for small farmers in rural India. In *Proc. CHI '10*, 733-742, (2010).
10. Shimira, K., Mukasa, O., Schellenberg,A. J., Manzi, F., John, D., Mushi, A., Mrisho, M., Tanner, M., Mshinda, H., Schellenberg, D. The use of personal digital assistants for data entry at the point of collection in a large household survey in southern Tanzania. *Emerging Themes in Epidemiology* (2007), 4:5.
11. Luk R., Ho M., and Aoki M. P. Asynchronous remote medical consultation for Ghana. In *Proc. CHI '08*, 743-752, (2008).
12. Peters, D., Kohli, M., Mascarenhas, M. Can computers improve patient care by primary health care workers in India? *International Journal for Quality Health Care*. 2005 18 (6): 435-445.
13. Mitchell, M., Lesh, N., Crammer, H., Fraser, H., Haivas, I. Wolf, K. Improving Care – Improving Access: The Use of Electronic Decision Support with AIDS patients in South Africa. *International Journal of Healthcare Technology and Management*. In process.
14. http://www.bridges.org/case_studies/351
15. http://www.healthnet.org/hnuganda.php
16. Adams WG, Fuhlbrigge AL, Miller CW, et al. TLC-Asthma: an integrated information system for patient-centered monitoring, case management, and point-of-care decision support. Proceedings of the AMIA Annual Symposium 2003 Nov 8–12; Washington DC.
17. Cherry JC, Moffatt TP, Rodriguez C, Dryden K. Diabetes disease management program for an indigent population empowered by telemedicine technology. *Diabetes Technol & Ther* 2002;4(6):783-791.
18. Dubenske LL Chih MY Dinauer S Gustafson DH Cleary JF . Development and implementation of a clinician reporting system for advanced stage cancer: initial lessons learned. J Am Med Inform Assoc. 2008 Sep-Oct;15(5):679-86
19. Gustafson DH, McTavish FM, Stengle W, et al. Use and impact of eHealth system by low-income women with breast cancer J Health Commun 2005;10:195-218.
20. Bielli E, Carminati F, La Capra S, Lina M, Brunelli C, Tamburini M. A wireless health outcomes monitoring system (WHOMS): development and field testing with cancer patients using mobile phones *BMC Med Inform Dec Making* 2004;4(7)Jun 15.
21. DuBenske LL Gustafson DH Shaw BR Cleary JF . Web-based cancer communication and decision making systems: connecting patients, caregivers, and clinicians for improved health outcomes. Med Decis Making. 2010 Nov-Dec;30(6):732-44
22. Celler BG, Lovell NH, Basilakis J. Using information technology to improve the management of chronic disease *MJA* 2003;179:242-246.

Problems of Data Mobility and Reuse in the Provision of Computer-based Training for Screening Mammography

Mark Hartswood
Rob Procter
University of Manchester
Manchester eResearch Centre,
Oxford Road,
Manchester, M13 9PL
rob.procter@manchester.ac.uk
mjh@inf.ed.ac.uk

Paul Taylor
UCL, Centre for Health Informatics and Multiprofessional Education,
p.taylor@ucl.ac.uk
Lilian Blot
University of York
lilian.blot@york.ac.uk

Stuart Anderson
University of Edinburgh
soa@inf.ed.ac.uk
Mark Rouncefield
Lancaster University
m.rouncefield@lancaster.ac.uk
Roger Slack
University of Bangor
r.slack@bangor.ac.uk

ABSTRACT
This paper explores some of the problems encountered in using a data archive to build tools for training radiologists to interpret breast screening images. We detail our experiences of taking images and case notes created as part of the work of breast cancer screening and using them as resources for training. Four instances of the use of the archive in training are described in detail and the problems they reveal are discussed. We formulate some general lessons for the mobility and re-use of rich ensembles of data and artefacts drawn from complex professional settings. We argue for a richer representation of the context from which the data was taken than can be achieved through making selected relations explicit in metadata. We also conclude that facilities for correcting and elaborating data should be available at the point of use, and not separated out as distinct activities.

Author Keywords
Data curation; data re-use; data sharing; data mobility; metadata; breast cancer screening; eLearning.

ACM Classification Keywords
H.5.3 Group and Organization Interfaces: Computer-supported cooperative work;

INTRODUCTION
Data collections are increasingly viewed as resources to be exploited in different research contexts. The e-Research vision sees collaboration, interdisciplinary work and 'reduced time to discovery' being facilitated by increased data re-use and sharing as key to future scientific advances [11, 12, 13]. This paper explores some issues raised by data re-use and sharing. It draws on our experiences in two related projects involving the creation and curation of an archive of digital mammograms and its use in training.

Permission to make digital or hard copies of all or part of this work for personal or classroom use is granted without fee provided that copies are not made or distributed for profit or commercial advantage and that copies bear this notice and the full citation on the first page. To copy otherwise, or republish, to post on servers or to redistribute to lists, requires prior specific permission and/or a fee.
CHI'12, May 5–10, 2012, Austin, Texas, USA.
Copyright 2012 ACM 978-1-4503-1015-4/12/05...$10.00.

eDiaMoND was a UK e-Science programme project to create a shared national archive of digital mammograms from the UK breast screening programme, and use it to support a range of activities, including training. A follow-on project (LEMI) developed a training tool in collaboration with clinicians - its aim was to draw upon archive materials and use them in 'live' training situations [10]. It quickly became apparent, however, that the data were not fit for purpose and that there was a persistent requirement for additional data curation activities, including capture, cleaning, annotating, repairing, structuring and restructuring. Taken at face value, the two projects seem to comprise complementary 'upstream' and 'downstream' aspects of data reuse, their different emphases implying a clear separation between production and use, with the data flowing in an unproblematic and linear way between them. In practice we found the opposite: that the production and use of data were hard to separate either as conceptually or practically distinct activities, and that data flows were problematic, complex and non-linear.

This paper describes our experience of using the eDiaMoND archive to prepare and deliver training materials. This revealed problems with the data that demanded costly investigations and repairs, typically in ways that were poorly supported by existing tools and resources. It became clear that the processes involved in creating the eDiaMoND archive (case selection, digitization, data entry) had shaped the data in various ways, often acting as a series of haphazard filters that sometimes preserved data and data relations, and at other times erased them. It was only at the point of use that the various effects of data capture processes became apparent and emerged as troublesome. We found also that the data were rarely 'self-contained' – users interpreted the data in light of their understandings of the broader context of its production and the procedures associated with its capture. Crucially, users' ability to identify problems (e.g. omissions, inaccuracies, etc) relied on these understandings, and their ability to subsequently effect repairs depended on access to originating documents where richer traces of the screening episode were preserved.

We suggest that tools for effective data reuse should support users in making sense of, repairing and renewing the data. In this paper we explore problems encountered in incorporating screening data into the training tool, tracing how they emerged and were managed. We detail experiences of taking materials (images, case notes) created as part of the work of breast cancer screening and using them as resources for training, and formulate some more general lessons concerning data curation, sharing and reuse.

COLLABORATION, DATA SHARING AND DATA MOBILITY

The eDiaMoND project aimed to demonstrate the benefits of collaboration between distributed groups of radiologists through the enhanced 'mobility of data' afforded by advanced digital infrastructures. Such data-sharing initiatives are increasingly sought after by research funding. However, several barriers tend to limit collaboration in research [3]. Despite (or perhaps because of) these barriers, Bos et al. note the existence of a growing number of 'computer-supported scientific collaboration environments', or 'collaboratories'. One form of these – *Community Data Systems: "an information resource that is created, maintained, or improved by a geographically-distributed community"* – [op cit., p. 660] – provided a template for the eDiaMoND project.

Our experiences suggest that trust, ownership, and ethics are important challenges for the creation of Community Data Systems [12]. However, making it possible for members to contribute data and share data contributed by others is also an exercise in making data *mobile*. Part of this is about establishing standards [3]. However, it is also necessary to look beyond the standardising of data formats if we are to understand under what conditions data may be disentangled from the context of its production, become commoditised and truly mobile. It is to these wider and more challenging issues of data curation that we now turn.

As many have observed, data curation is an issue of critical importance [2, 4]. A key element is capturing of metadata. As Day [6, p. 19] suggests: *"This 'preservation metadata' is understood to be all of the various types of data that allows the re-creation and interpretation of the structure and content of digital data over time... Understood in this way, it is clear that such metadata needs to support an extremely wide range of different functions, including discovery, the technical rendering of objects, the recording of contexts and provenance, to the documentation of repository actions and policies."*

The mobility of data depends upon recording context and provenance. Coopmans' [5] study of digital mammograms as 'mobile data' challenges the assumption that mobility follows straightforwardly as a consequence of digitisation. For Coopmans, what mobility consists in is tied to the social-technical configuration through which it is achieved. Thus, mammograms *as films* demand a certain sort of infrastructure, and mammograms *as digital images* another. *"An understanding of mobility in terms of the creation of passages does not only emphasize that transit is an active achievement but also draws attention to the craft like nature of that achievement: the artful connecting of time, space, material and immaterial elements into a 'mobility effect'"* [op cit, p. 7]. Coopmans draws attention to Berg and Goorman's 'law of medical information': *"the further information has to be able to circulate (i.e. the more different contexts it has to be usable in) the more work is required to disentangle the information from the context of its production"* [1, p. 52]. Berg and Goorman identify three ways in which medical data are entangled with the context of its production. (1) That they are produced for a reason; (2) That they gain sense from other items of data around them, so the meaning of any given data item is not necessarily fixed; (3) That clinicians assess the quality or adequacy of medical data with reference to their source. They argue that data do not straightforwardly become a commodity and thus mobile simply by being made available digitally.

In the following sections we introduce the domain of breast cancer screening and the LEMI project that provided our case study. We then examine record keeping practices in breast screening and explain how the original eDiaMoND archive was compiled from clinical sources. This leads us to explore a series of the data quality issues that arose when we attempted to use the eDiaMonD data to support training in LEMI. Finally we draw conclusions for data reuse practices and tool design to better support reuse.

BREAST CANCER SCREENING AND TRAINING DELIVERY

Breast cancer is the second leading cause of cancer death among women in the US and Europe. A screening programme has been in operation in the UK for more than 20 years. Initial screening is by mammography, where X-ray films (mammograms) are taken of each breast. Each mammogram is examined for evidence of abnormality by at least one trained reader. Abnormalities can be very subtle and interpretation is often difficult. The practice of breast screening calls for readers to exercise a combination of perceptual skills, to find what may be faint and small features in a complex visual environment, and interpretative skills to classify them appropriately as benign or suspicious. Where suspicious lesions are found at screening, the woman is recalled to an 'assessment' clinic where additional imaging tests (X-Rays and ultrasound) and biopsies are undertaken to confirm or rule out cancer.

Training in mammography follows an apprenticeship model whereby an experienced mentor 'guides' a trainee's interpretation of actual screening cases during the course of a year's rotation. While this provides a rich and supportive environment for the trainee to hone their skills, it is also limiting in a number of respects: the trainee is exposed to relative few abnormal cases; progress is monitored only informally; and the trainee often does not receive feedback on the outcome of their decisions. The LEMI project aimed to address these shortcomings by providing trainees with access to a large archive of cases with known outcomes in a simulated screening environment to augment 'on the job' training. In this way, trainees would gain access to presentations that they might not otherwise encounter, they would receive feedback based upon known case outcomes, and a score that would allow them to measure their progress. In time, differentiated training sets would allow trainees to focus on particular aspects of their performance.

Figure 1: Example of a typical patient record. Anonymous (i.e. blank) films and forms are shown.

PATIENT RECORDS AND COMPUTER DATA STRUCTURES

In this section we explore the relationship between the patient records and the data structure representation of those records within the eDiaMoND database. In the introduction we saw how Coopmans focused on the *mammogram* as a focal entity that eDiaMoND attempts to make mobile. Here, and throughout the paper, we are interested in the *'case record'* as a focal entity. Figure 1 shows the contents of a typical case record, comprising of a labelled film bag, various forms and the X-Rays themselves.

In contrast, the eDiaMoND database contained a schema populated with data extracted from the case record, such as the screening decision, biopsy and pathology findings, and so on. This database was created during specially convened sessions using two dedicated pieces of software developed as part of the eDiaMoND project. The first of these (dubbed EDAS) supported entry of basic details by the project radiographer. The second (the 'Annotation Tool') provided drawing tools that an expert radiologist used to mark-up lesions. Although the eDiaMoND data structure contains a significant amount of detail about each screening episode, it is not nearly as rich as the patient record documents shown in Figure 1. The patient record comprises a number of forms and letters that document various parts of the screening process. Most straightforwardly (for women screened for the first time with a normal mammogram) the record would contain a blue screening form, four films, a copy of the letter sent to the patient confirming attendance, and indicating a 'normal' outcome. Where a patient is recalled for assessment, which happens if suspicious features are found at screening, then further films would be taken and tests conducted and these would be included with associated documentation.

Different parts of the documentation are assembled in different ways. Some documents are completed as clinical staff undertake screening and review clinics. Some documents follow tissue samples to the labs, where results of tests are added, before returning to the record. Fields on some forms are completed by administrative staff via an Electronic Medical Record (EMR). For example, the pink surgery form details the treatment received, including whether this included radiotherapy or use of various chemotherapy agents. Decisions about treatment occur downstream of screening and assessment clinics, but are available to centre staff via the EMR. Other fields (such as the tumour size) can be retrieved from earlier documentation (e.g. the surgery pathology form). In this way the final pink form 'closes the patient's account' as it is the final piece of documentation created until the next screening, and constitutes a summary view of findings and treatment (if any). Thus the documents associated with a screening episode serve a number of different purposes in both guiding and documenting practice, tying together aspects of diagnostic work conducted at different times in different places and by different personnel, with some serving to provide an overview of downstream decisions and feeding into other records systems.

This bears a striking similarity to Gorman et al.'s characterisation of medical documents as information 'bundles' [9]. Although screening record components are generally less ad hoc and improvised in character, they nonetheless also exhibit redundancy, flexibility, overlapping content, a specificity to particular activities or procedures, a single physical representation and so on. Returning to our discussion of the paper record and the original eDiaMoND data structure, and in light of this brief sketch of the record's content, a series of contrasts can be drawn between the original documents and their digital counterparts.

Completeness: Inevitably decisions had to be made about which parts of the screening record to include in the eDiaMoND database. Ultrasound films were not included in the eDiaMoND database, largely for pragmatic reasons, despite requests for their inclusion. These requests arrived 'late in the day' and required significant work. Via various rounds of consultation, argument and lobbying a *dataset* for the project was established that aimed to support adequately each of the different use scenarios (including training), and which inevitably comprised only a *subset* of the data, leaving the record far less *complete* than the originating documentation.

Orderliness and Structure: The documents comprising the patient record exhibit far less explicit 'structure' than its digital counterpart. It is instructive to watch a clinician interpreting the contents of a record, as this typically involves organising and (re)ordering the documents and films to establish a context (e.g. that the patient was recalled), and to reconstruct 'what happened' (working out the reason a test was done, which tests were done, what the final outcome was). Fresh visits to a record involve re-establishing the various relations between the documents and the activities they describe, usually by constructing plausible narratives that account for the record contents. Often the process is a little messy, as candidate narratives carry implications about what sorts of documents one should find in the film bag that then need to be hunted out for confirmation. If additional or unexpected documents are found, then these need to be accounted for, or an alternative narrative found that better explains them.

This interpretation work turns upon the clinician's understanding of the different ways that a screening episode might unfold – the sorts of things that are usually done, in what order, how, by who, what further activities certain outcomes imply, possible exceptions, typical workarounds, allowable shortcuts and so on. This contrasts with the digital version of the record where many of the relations are necessarily explicitly drawn to support automated handling of the data.

Richness and redundancy: Because of selection, it is clear that there is less information available in the eDiaMoND database than in the documents from which it was derived. The act of selection, however, is not only way information is lost. Cherry-picking information from the different screening forms and aggregating it into a single digital 'report' inevitably means that report no longer has the interpretable contextures of those originating documents, which are specific to particular screening activities, procedures or outcomes. A general point can be made that the eDiaMoND dataset is far less rich, and contains far less redundant information than the paper record. Losing the very richness and redundancy that makes it possible to re-establish the case narrative is compensated for by making various sorts of relations explicit in the electronic data model, thus reducing (but not eliminating) the amount of work needed to establish what the case is about, and rendering reconstruction and presentation of the record amenable to automation.

The eDiaMoND database is significantly different from the patient records from which it is derived, since the processes involved in its creation impact on its final constitution. First, since all cases cannot be included, one has to decide on selection criteria that determine the overall makeup of the database. Second, there is the work of drawing out cases and checking their suitability, which is subject to various sorts of contingency. Third, there is the work of selecting relevant data and films from the patient record to include in the database. Finally, there are the modes of data capture themselves; typing, scanning and annotating that each add to the shape of the data in one way or another. All of these activities were undertaken in a way that oriented to the potential future uses of the data. It was only using the data that laid bare fully the shortcomings in its capture and representation, which we explore in the examples below. As we shall see, it was also through understanding these processes that problems were diagnosed, and often only by referencing the original patient record that they were eventually remedied.

EXAMPLE 1: USING THE EDIAMOND LEGACY DATA

The eDiaMoND project finished in December 2004 and the LEMI project started 30 months later. Returning to the eDiaMoND data after this interval reminded the project team that there were a number of 'problems' with the data from the perspective of delivering training. The most significant of these were errors in image descriptions (e.g. mammograms were sometime incorrectly labelled), and issues with data organisation (e.g. images taken at assessment clinic were 'lumped together' with images taken at screening). Describing images accurately is important if they are to be correctly displayed. For training it is also essential to be able to distinguish between mammograms taken at screening and those taken at assessment clinics – it would be inappropriate to test a trainee's understanding of screening using a kind of film (say a magnification view[1]) that is only taken if the women is referred from screening following the detection of an abnormality.

It quickly became apparent that it would be difficult to devise an automated means of correcting the data because the various ways this might be achieved were themselves affected by data quality issues. There was enough information embedded in the images, however, that someone with experience would be able to make the necessary corrections. This meant that we could undertake data correction without having to retrieve the patient record from which the data was derived. This is an important consideration, since this incurs a significant cost. The LEMI project was fortunate in that a member of staff employed in the clinic (and who had been involved in the original eDiaMoND data entry process) was willing to undertake the data repair work. This was our first encounter with the eDiaMoND data, but one that led to lengthy, complex and costly data correction work. The following three sections deal with further encounters with the data in different contexts: expert film readers selecting cases for training sets, using cases for delivering training and for mentoring trainees.

EXAMPLE 2: TRAINING SET SELECTION

We had been working up the training tool through a series of design meetings with clinicians. As the tool matured our attention turned towards authoring appropriate training content. A session was set up with two expert film readers (Mary and Jane), and the radiographer who had helped with the data cleaning (Ann). We worked through the archive, selecting cases either for Mary's training set (taking trainees through the entire process of screening and

[1] An image taken at assessment to show part of the breast in greater detail.

assessment) or Jane's training set (simulating screening conditions and assisting trainees to make a screening decision) or both.

To begin with, Mary, Jane and the tool developer (Jim) worked through the cases sequentially, deciding if they were suitable for each of the training sets. During this process we happened upon a number of data quality issues that are illustrated below.

Uncovering omissions

Here Mary and Jane are trying to make sense of the first case in the dataset:

Mary: Right, we've got erm no pathology done and no associated findings.

Jim: Mmm

Mary: And we've got ah - R3 - now, if we were calling it R3 we would be obliged to biopsy. [Ann: that's right] So...

Jane: This is a funny one, this

Mary: Which is always... that's 'cus it's the first one. The first one's never straightforward... [Jim: laughs] ...erm, did it have ultrasound, I thought I saw an ultrasound lurking somewhere. Now, wait a minute - biopsy assessment 4.

Jim: Oh, ok.

Mary: Ultrasound three

Jim: So we didn't - [Mary: So, Hang on, hang on, wait a minute] we're missing the pathology - sorry.

Jane: Hmmm.

Mary: Erm. Pathology - no pathology done, but we've got biopsy (…) Four. And no pathology done, so…

In this transcript Mary draws attention to the report that states there is "no pathology done" and then says "if we are calling it R3 we would be obliged to biopsy". 'R3' is a grade indicating how suspicious the radiologists regard the lesion, on the basis of all the X-Rays taken during the course of both the screening and assessment clinics. A five point scale is used, with 5 indicating definite malignancy, and 1 indicating normal breast tissue. 'R3', then, sits at the midpoint of the scale and is used when, from the films alone, it is hard to be sure if the lesion is malignant or normal. Mary is pointing out that the data in the electronic report are inconsistent given her knowledge of screening practice – if the radiology score is 3, then she would expect a biopsy outcome as a matter of course. Mary then tries to make sense of this by examining other items in the report, looking to find the ultrasound result, and then finding there actually is a biopsy assessment score (4), but apparently no pathology description available from the biopsy (the 'no pathology done'). So, on the face of, it there is a data quality problem – a data item is missing. Building the training set created the circumstances whereby experts closely scrutinised the data in a mode where this type of inconsistency suddenly stands out. Both spotting the omission and working out how it might have come about, depend upon Mary, Jane and Ann's understandings of the clinical context of screening work, the process of data entry and its intersection with the normal timings and routines associated with obtaining completed test results.

Aging cases

The following transcript illustrates a different sort of data quality issue in the training set selection process:

Jim: Radial scar

Jane: I like it

Ann: I like that one too.

Jane: Yeah, we'll have that one.

Mary: Now, does that one have an ultrasound, can you show us the sort of text that goes with that case?

Jane: Ultrasound not done. Couldn't, they didn't do it.

Ann: It's a long time ago

Mary: Well, it'll be a long [Jane: yes] time ago

Ann: That's right. I mean ultrasounds...

Jane: What did it have? Let's see... don't tell me it had cytology - it did.

Jane: Unfortunate because our practice has changed so much since (... ...?)

At the outset Jane and Ann are enthusiastic about the "Radial scar" that Jim announces. Mary asks for the ultrasound and the text associated with the case. They quickly establish that an ultrasound image is not available and ascribe its absence to subsequent changes in assessment clinic practice. Where Jane says "What did it have? Let's see... don't tell me it had cytology – it did" we find her again looking at the report data for items that confirm or contradict her opinion, and finding a cytology result is consistent with the narrative that this case represents outmoded practice. Initially this case is a desirable one for the training set, but Jane finds that it has not aged well.

Making an assessment of data quality depends upon linking understandings of the demands of training (the use context) with an understanding of the sorts of practice predominating at the time the patient was screened (the production context). It is noteworthy that training as the relevant use context actually creates a data quality issue out of the noted changes in practice. This is because a good visual example is not by itself sufficient (as it might be for a picture in a text book); for the modes of training envisaged, it is also necessary to demonstrate appropriate work-up. Here we can see how data quality is not necessarily an inherent function of the data, but instead dependent upon the relation between the data and the purpose to which it is to be put. For these types of cases the data are often resistant to correction – it is not possible to revisit the context of production and carry out the tests in ways that conform to current practice. It is possible, however, to repair the data, to provide an explanation of the differences between practices now and then, that will do for the purposes at hand. These annotations however represent further 'mark up' of the data, requiring they be given a place in the data structure, tools to support their creation, and thought given as to how they would be presented to the trainees.

EXAMPLE 3: USING THE CASES FOR TRAINING

In this section we describe what happened when the trainee began reading the case training set. This was the point where a number of our efforts came together: data capture, set selection, additional annotation, data cleaning, tool development, rounds of evaluation, re-design and re-configuration. The trainee was a radiographer who was training to be a film reader, near the end of her year of formal training. The tool simulates the context in which readers make a screening decision. The trainee is presented with mammograms that they have to examine. She has to decide if the breasts contain a lesion and mark and describe it. Finally, the trainee has to record an overall decision - whether to recall the patient for further tests. The current mammograms are compared with any previous screening mammograms ('priors') that are available, as changes over time can be highly significant. The current mammograms are presented on the bottom half of the computer monitors, and priors appear in the top half of the monitor when selected (see Figure 2). As one might expect, the session uncovered a number of problems with the tool, as well as indicating which of the known problems were more troublesome than others. Here we focus on one particular issue related to data capture, handling and presentation.

When reading Case 5, the trainee selected to view the prior round films (The trainee is Tina, the consultant radiologist is Mary and the tool developer is Jim):

Tina: And the previous. (priors, including craniocaudal view mammograms appear on the display[2]) So do I assume those are ... current CCs?

Jim: Good question [Tina: How would I know?], because they are done by somebody else, aren't they?

When the trainee loads the priors she sees the selection and arrangement of mammograms shown in Figure 2, which is consistent with screening practice. But the trainee questions whether the CCs are really priors, or whether they actually belong to the current screening round. Jim notices that they have been taken by a different radiographer than the one that had taken the prior MLOs, "they are done by somebody else", which is not consistent with the CCs and MLOs being taken at the same visit.

Jim: But yeah. ... Is that just because they have got a different number on them, because (...?) they were probably taken by someone else?

[2] At screening it is usual to image each breast at two different angles. These are the mediolateral-oblique (MLO) and craniocaudal (CC) views.

Tina: Well the that's - yeah that is the case but, they (pointing) actually look like the old ones and they (pointing) look like the new ones, you know what I mean, because of the contrast [Jim: ahhhhhh] so I'm not sure [Jim: Oh ok] actually [Jim: which one's which] which ones are which.

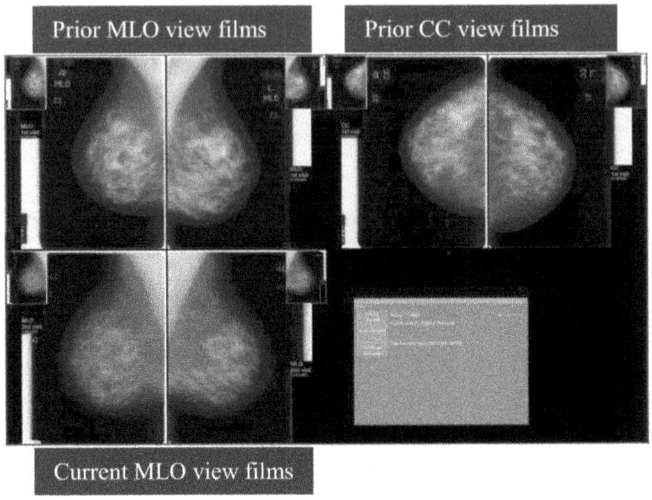

Figure 2: This shows Case 5. Films taken during the most recent screening round are displayed on the bottom row. These are displayed first and the top row is initially blank. The trainee can request to see films from a prior screening round (if there are any), which then appear on the top row as shown.

The ambiguity in this case stems from a confluence of misleading signs that together point to a non-straightforward reading: the change in contrast, that different radiographers took films in the same round, and (as we later learned) a residual chinagraph mark visible on the prior films. The best narrative the trainee could assemble to account for the anomalous signs was that the prior and current round films had somehow being presented in an incorrect order. Although some residual contextual detail was available in the image (the radiographer's number, the chinagraph mark) this was confusing rather than helpful. Other contextual details available to users of the hardcopy film bag had not been similarly preserved, making it hard to judge confirm the trainee's candidate narrative one way or another.

Investigating the data

The debrief following the session provided additional clues as to why the trainee had become suspicious; talking to the radiographer who selected the mammograms uncovered various aspects of case selection that not been apparent; and examining the unmediated artefacts helped resolve which actually was the prior and which was the current one. The trainee had not mentioned initially that she had spotted a residual chinagraph pencil mark on the prior film, but did so in the post session debrief. Suspicious lesions are marked with a chinagraph pencil during reading and although the films were cleaned prior to scanning, an indentation remained that was visible on the scanned image. She also pointed out that prior CCs are not usually displayed unless there are current round CCs to compare them with. This might also signal that the case had been assessed.

Further investigation focussed on the selection process. Great pains had been taken to select cases that would not 'stand out' when mixed in with abnormal cases. For example, they had been selected only if taken during the same sessions as the abnormal cases, and balanced so that there was not an excessive number from a particular source, so that the marks on the mammogram identifying the X-ray set (for example) would not give away that this case might be a normal one. To minimise the risk of including missed cancers as 'normal' cases, one criterion used in selection was to obtain *time proven normal cases,* that is, cases for which a subsequent mammogram had been judged to be normal. We found, however, that some patients in the archive had an apparent abnormality which was detected at screening and subsequently found to be normal at assessment. Case 5 followed this pattern. As a consequence of the recall decision it had a chinagraph mark around the suspect tissue. As a consequence of the assessment clinic visit, one set of films was taken on a different day by a different radiographer. Simply providing details of prior assessments and outcomes would be sufficient to account for the chinagraph marks and prevent them from posing awkward and ambiguous interpretive possibilities for future trainees.

EXAMPLE 4: MENTORING THE TRAINEE

Each of the different encounters with the eDiaMoND dataset, from initial appraisal, case selection to training revealed different sorts of problems with the data and instigated different sorts of repair activities. Often problems could not be resolved by reference to the eDiaMoND dataset alone, and it was necessary to return to the originating patient record to repair the data, or resolve an ambiguity. Further data correction work was undertaken prior to the trainees reading subsequent cases and this seemed to eliminate most sources of confusion, particularly improvements to the clarity of the labelling and advising that some women in the set may have been previously recalled with a normal outcome. Thus we were much more confident in the quality of the data in the training set we had assembled. However, further issues relating to data quality arose during the 'mentoring sessions' where the trainee and mentor examined the trainee's work together. Here Jane (the mentor) and Tina (the trainee) discuss a case Tina read using our training tool:

Jane: I can see what you mean on the CC erm, and it does seem to be slightly outside the breast (tissue?) disk though?) I don't think that you are making it up. I think it is genuine. But, er I don't know, I think it's quite possible that I... You see, I don't, I don't think that I've even looked at these normals.

Tina: Have you not, no?

Jane: No, so erm I don't know - is it possible that some of them were arbitrated ... out.

In the first line Jane is talking about a 'lesion' that the trainee has marked on the image that in fact is benign. This should therefore be viewed as an incorrect decision. But from what Jane says it is clear that the trainee's decision should not be judged harshly – Jane can see the merit in at least giving the lesion some attention even though the case is a 'time proven normal'. Jane says that she "can see what you mean", that the lesion is "genuine", and not the result of the trainee "making it up", suggesting she is happy that the trainee is not erroneously construing something out of the confluence of normal breast tissue and structures. This then led Jane to consider whether she had "even looked at these" indicating that the normal cases had been included in the training roller without her scrutinising them first and speculating if some of them had been "arbitrated out". Screening cases are normally are read by two film readers. If their opinions differ (one says recall, one says not) then the case is referred to a third reader for 'arbitration'. The normal set could contain cases that an experienced reader had recalled, but that the 'third reader' had decided were normal. Such cases are likely to be tricky (but quite possibly instructive) for the novice, since, by definition, they contain a lesion whose significance is disputed by experienced film readers. In common with many of the previously discussed data quality issues, one way of fixing this problem would be to go back to the original record and see if the case was arbitrated. Instead, the mentor insisted on a further annotation session during which she examined each normal case for features that might be construed as lesions and added explanations as to why they should be read as normal. The explanation would be made available to the trainee after they made their own decision.

This example adds to an emerging pattern of how each use occasion creates an opportunity for participants to learn something new about the data, as when the mentor, in examining the trainee's responses, discovers the 'normal' cases to be trickier than she had anticipated. (Similarly, in example 2, during case selection the participants developed an appreciation for the archive's coverage of different abnormality types.) Such learning has typically been hard to capitalise on, despite the opportunities it affords for adding value to the training archive. In the discussion below we explore how rethinking the relationships between production and use contexts, and the processes by which we move between the two, could help us to more effectively mobilise complex ensembles of data like mammography case records.

DISCUSSION: DATA AND ITS CONTEXTS

At the outset of the paper we explored how literatures on data mobility focus on the relation between data and the context of its production, and the need for work to 'disentangle' or 'decontextualise' data so that they can circulate and be useful in remote use contexts. We show that making interpretation and use of the data less dependent on the originating context is only a part contributor to effective mobility, and (seemingly paradoxically) that maintaining an understanding of, or link to, the data's originating context is also highly significant. This is partly because there are so many ways that the originating context can potentially intrude upon our use of the data that we can never be entirely happy that our data has been disentangled in the right sorts of ways, and will always find new ways in which it hasn't. One point to note here is that the figure-ground relation between data and its interpretative context is not a fixed thing. From one perspective an item of data maybe our principal focus, from another it might provide part of the contextual background for the interpretation of a different data item [8]. While it is valid to think of a data item in the training record in relation to the context of its production in the screening clinic, at the same time, we need to recognise there are many other interpretative contexts in which it might also figure. It is also important to appreciate that for complex artefacts, like screening cases, we are not liberating single data items, but 'bundles' of interrelated data (patient record contents) and data rich artefacts (mammograms), any one part of which might be foregrounded and interpreted in the light of other elements of the record.

Numerous examples of this are evident in the fieldwork. The training record is not comprised of carefully lifted individual data items, but rather whole 'chunks of context' carved out of screening practice, and then selectively embedded within computer data structures. While it is highly desirable to preserve certain contextually relevant relations between data elements (so that the trainee can see, for example, what a lesion's appearance amounted to in terms of pathology outcomes), it is also evident that others can be unwanted and troublesome (the hard to erase chinagraph pencil marks on the mammograms that give away a lesion's location). Thus, the processes of selection and data capture preserve some data relations and erase others, often in a somewhat haphazard way, so that for an observer with certain sort of expertise it is entirely possible for the training record to have both anticipated and unanticipated content. This clarifies the claim in the introduction, that for complex ensembles of data, mobility and reuse is more about carefully managing relations with its originating context, than about disentangling or decontextualising individual data items.

Similar points follow from our description of the patient record and the practices associated with its creation. Here we show that the patient record is not a 'product', not something assembled for consumption by a third party. It never represents a complete or definitive account of screening or its outcomes (until the patient is discharged, or dies) but rather is forever a work in progress; it is provisional, and continuously updated, amended and elaborated as the work of screening unfolds. Its use and sense depend upon the ongoing work practices in which it is embedded. This has two important consequences. The first is that the record no longer continues to be elaborated in line with practice and so may omit important details that only later come to light (as in the example of the missing pathology data in example 2). The second is that while we carve out a 'chunk of context', we also throw away significant detail when we transfer the record to a computer data structure, and no longer have easy access to the full range of situated resources that we would usually depend upon for making sense of its contents. Abstracting case materials in this way is powerful, because of all the other things that we can now use it for, but fraught with danger too because of the assumptions we make when we depend upon the fidelity and stability of meaning of our abstracted representation, and because of the 'unwanted content' that might reveal itself in a particular use context.

Moving on from the eDiaMoND data curation model

During the course of each of the activities explored in this paper (Correction, Selection, Training and Mentoring) new and distinctive sorts of 'problems' with the data came to light that demanded attention. Users' detailed understanding of screening practice enabled them to identify problems with the data, to see it as deficient, incomplete or inaccurate. Typically, though, those understandings did not extend to the detailed aspects of each case in question, and additional investigations were needed to establish the reason for the problem and effect a repair. Sometimes it was necessary to re-examine data selection and entry practices, and often to return to the originating documents to resolve ambiguities and supply missing detail, which had, over the course of the two projects, become increasingly difficult to access due to their relocation off-site. This leads us to articulate a tacit assumption underpinning the eDiaMoND model of data curation, namely, that data abstracted from a working context can be treated as self-sufficient and self-contained, whereby any new demand on the data can be discharged solely by the existing contents or structure of the set. This model is embedded in the software and data management practices developed for eDiaMoND, where a linear data collection process produced a fixed data archive which was then exploited in different use contexts by virtue of entirely separate suites of tools from those used for data capture.

It is fair to say that the eDiaMoND project focussed primarily on *data production* by developing and populating a supporting infrastructure with mammography cases. In contrast, the LEMI project focused on *data use*; it aimed to exploit the eDiaMoND archive for training. In doing so the LEMI perspective on the requirements for data management tools and practices differs radically from that of eDiaMoND. In the LEMI project data production and data use were intimately related activities, to the extent that it would be a mistake to try to uncouple them functionally or conceptually. Data use frequently has consequences for data collection practices, driving the need for additional elaboration of the existing data set, often by referring to originating documents. Users' interpretation of the data's consistency and correctness depended upon their understanding of and access to the data's originating context and the process of its production. This suggests a variety of ways that data mobility can be enhanced by supporting (a) better access to originating practices and contexts and (b) ease of correcting and amending the data in-situ.

Better access to originating practices and contexts

While our training record can be thought of as a 'chunk of context' whereby important relations present in the originating context are preserved, there are many occasions when this is not sufficient to resolve an ambiguity or effect a repair. An obvious way of easing access to a richer representation of the record's originating context would be to make the film bag contents available alongside the abstracted record, by scanning in the patient documentation and storing in the database as a browsable set of documents. It is not important for them to have an orderly, structured machine-readable instantiation, since their purpose is different from the explicitly represented training record. Their aim would be to provide a rich context for human interpretation of the abstract computer based record, supporting the sorts of disambiguation and repair activities documented in this paper. While the patient record contents usefully fulfil this role in the domain of mammography and in the context of training, in other domains and contexts other approaches might be more appropriate. For example, our users of the data also have considerable expertise in its production, whereas other potential users of the data (e.g. computer scientists, epidemiologists) might not. The requirements in 'poor domain expertise' use contexts might be for means of accessing or acquiring that expertise. The main point is to consider how the interpretative practices attendant on data use which inevitably involve linking the originating and use context by some channel *other than that provided by the data or metadata* can be effectively supported.

Ease of correcting and amending the data in-situ

The computer-based representation of the training record only partially replicates the detail available in the screening record from which it was derived. Access to richer native representations of context would mean that we would not be so reliant on accurately judging *a priori* what the precise composition of the training record should be. There would be less need to anticipate (and inevitably misdiagnose) the relations that are necessary in the data, and the degree of their fidelity. But this does not give us a significant advantage unless we are in a position to appropriately amend the data when we discover a problem, implying that facilities for data correction and elaboration need to be available at the point of use, and not separated out into different processes and activities.

From our fieldwork data, there were a number of occasions where even simple requests to add annotations to cases were deferred to specially convened sessions when, given the right tooling, it would have been a simple matter to deal with them as they became apparent. A number of omissions might have been speedily repaired with access to the original case materials, coupled with a facility to edit or annotate the basic data at the point of use. This would also enable users to capitalise on the learning observed during occasions of use. There are undoubtedly more complex issues here, where a requirement is discovered that implies a change to the underlying data structure, or its presentation in the application, particularly where older versions may need to maintained to ensure the coherence of prior use of the case data by trainees. But even on occasions with complex implications, a simple, integrated means of tagging troublesome or offending cases would have assisted data correction. Whatever the concrete solution, the general rubric is to avoid thinking about data use and data production as conceptually and practically distinct activities, and orient to tool design accordingly.

CONCLUSIONS

In charting data production and use in our projects, we effectively chart the process of mammograms becoming a commodity. For complex artefacts like mammograms achieving this commodity status is less about making them independent of the context of their production, and more about appropriately maintaining and carefully managing links to their originating context. We find that use and interpretation of the record as a training resource depends on a rich mix of diverse practices, understandings and activities. Some of these are practices aimed at stabilising meaning in a context independent way (following Berg and Goorman), while others concern the production of an appropriate enabling 'transport' infrastructure supportive of mobility (following Coopmans).

When we focus on how the newly created training data are put to use, we find that users continually (re)appraise the data based on their understandings of the practices associated with its production and abstraction. This also is powerfully shown in Zimmerman's study of data reuse by ecologists, whereby the appropriateness (and perils) of using third party datasets are gauged according to what ecologists know and understand about the specific phenomena, data collection practices and the original researcher's status [15]. In this way, work done to decontexutalise data never provides an entirely isolated 'frame' for its interpretation, but becomes itself a topic for sense-making as part of data users' interpretative practices.

Latour uses the metaphor of a 'black box' for aggregated or abstracted data that conceals the controversies associated with its production, enabling it to be presented as a 'fact' [14]. Similarly, Goodwin point out that assigning a phenomenon to a professionally relevant category erases the detail of the deliberation that went into making the assignment [7]. However, we suggest that both of these characterisations provide us with an incomplete picture. While abstracted or coded data are never entirely transparent, neither are they completely opaque. Instead, abstracted data are 'translucent' to a degree that depends upon our familiarity with the process by which they were abstracted, the context in which they originated and the phenomena that they represent.

We note that Zimmerman's study [15] and our own revealed similar findings, despite the evident differences in professional domains, the sorts of data and the purposes of their reuse. This is significant because it confirms that we are uncovering phenomena that are common to data reuse practices across disparate contexts.

In addition to providing confirmation, our study also advances Zimmerman's work in a number of important respects. First, Zimmerman asked ecologists to report retrospectively how they *selected* data for reuse whereas, in our study, we examined actual *occasions* of data reuse. This enabled us to draw a number of additional lessons, including: how to capitalize on learning processes that occur with reuse and how to appropriately support data curation in ways which avoid embedding a strong distinction between data use and data production. Second, while agreeing with Zimmerman that greater detail of data collection practices should be made available to facilitate reuse, we take the more radical step of recommending capture of richer representations of the originating context (perhaps by taking video or scanning documents) rather than further elaboration of metadata.

The problems with data content and structure observed in this study might recede, as repeated use gradually uncovers each discrepancy until they are eliminated, with the need for repair or elaboration confined to the early days of the data's exploitation. We believe, however, that requirements to amend data are likely to emerge continuously as demands on the data change, circumstances of use change, and use leads to learning. That is not to say that the sorts of changes or modifications required would always be of the same sort. In training, for example, we would expect demands on the data to change in line with the evolving character of clinical practice and training delivery.

In many ways it is quite surprising that, in only ten years since the start of eDiaMoND, the data (considered by many to be the project's most valuable assets) are rapidly acquiring a 'use by' date. These reflections move us away from ideas of linear processes and static data sets towards thinking of data as more organic, 'living' artefacts in need of periodic amendment, repair, renewal and retirement. If we shift our focus to accommodate non-linear aspects of data collection and the dynamic character of 'live' data, then this opens various opportunities for a radical reconfiguration of a variety of data management practices. This reconfiguration of data management needs to be taken seriously if the benefits of increased data re-use and sharing envisaged by e-Research are going to be realised fully.

ACKNOWLEDGMENTS

We thank the UK EPSRC Engineering and Physical Sciences Research Council for funding this work under grant number EP/E03165X/1 and the radiologists who gave so generously of their time.

REFERENCES

1. Berg, M., Goorman, E. (1999). The Contextual Nature of Medical Information. *J. of Med Inf.* 56(1-3): 51–60.
2. Borgman C., Wallis J., Enyedy, N. (2007). Little science confronts the data deluge: habitat ecology, embedded sensor networks, and digital libraries. *Int. J. on Digital Libraries*, 7(1-2): 17-30.
3. Bos, N. et al. (2007). From Shared Databases to Communities of Practice: A Taxonomy of Collaboratories. *J. of Computer-Mediated Communication*, 12(2): 652-672.
4. Carlson S., Anderson, B. (2007). What Are Data? The Many Kinds of Data and Their Implications for Data Re-Use. *J. of Computer-Mediated Comm* 12(2): 635-651.
5. Coopmans, C. (2006). Making mammograms mobile: Suggestions for a sociology of data mobility. *Information, Communication & Society* 9(1): 1–19.
6. Day, M. (2005). Metadata: Digital Data Curation Manual. http://www.dcc.ac.uk/sites/default/files/documents/resource/curation-manual/chapters/metadata/metadata.pdf
7. Goodwin, C. (1994). Professional vision. *American Anthropologist* 96(3): 606–633.
8. Goodwin, C., Duranti, A. (1992). *Rethinking Context: an introduction*, pp. 1–42. Cambridge University Press, University Press, Cambridge, UK.
9. Gorman, P. et al. (2000). Bundles in the Wild: Managing Information to Solve Problems and Maintain Situation Awareness. *Library Trends* 46(2): 266–289.
10. Hartswood, M., Procter, R., Taylor, P., Blot, L, Anderson, S. (2012). Computer-Supported Cooperative Learning in the Workplace: A Case Study in Radiology. In Goggins, S., Janke, I. (Eds.) *Computer-Supported Cooperative Learning at Work*. Springer.
11. Hey, T., Tansley, S., Tolle, K. (Eds.) (2009). *The Fourth Paradigm: Data-Intensive Scientific Discovery*. Microsoft Research.
12. Jirotka, M, Procter R, Hartswood M, Slack R, Simpson A, Coopmans C, Hinds C, Voss A. (2005). Collaboration and trust in healthcare innovation: The eDiaMoND case study. *JCSCW* 14(4): 369-398.
13. Karasti, H., Baker, K., Halkola, E. (2006). Enriching the Notion of Data Curation. *JCSCW*, 15(4): 321-358.
14. Latour, B. (1988). *Science in Action: How to Follow Scientists and Engineers Through Society*. Harvard UPUP.
15. Zimmerman, A. (2008). New Knowledge from Old Data: The Role of Standards in the Sharing and Reuse of Ecological Data. *Science Technology & Human Values* 33(5): 631-652.

Supporting Visual Assessment of Food and Nutrient Intake in a Clinical Care Setting

Rob Comber[1], Jack Weeden[1], Jennifer Hoare[2], Stephen Lindsay[1], Gemma Teal[3], Alastair Macdonald[3], Lisa Methven[4], Paula Moynihan[2] and Patrick Olivier[1]

[1]Culture Lab, School of Computing Science, Newcastle University, UK {robert.comber/ p.l.olivier}@ncl.ac.uk

[2]Institute for Ageing and Health, Newcastle University, UK paula.moynihan@ncl.ac.uk

[3]School of Design, Glasgow School of Art, Glasgow, Scotland {g.teal/a.macdonald}@gsa.ac.uk

[4] Department of Food and Nutritional Sciences, University of Reading, UK l.methven@reading.ac.uk

ABSTRACT

Monitoring nutritional intake is an important aspect of the care of older people, particularly for those at risk of malnutrition. Current practice for monitoring food intake relies on hand written food charts that have several inadequacies. We describe the design and validation of a tool for computer-assisted visual assessment of patient food and nutrient intake. To estimate food consumption, the application compares the pixels the user rubbed out against predefined graphical masks. Weight of food consumed is calculated as a percentage of pixels rubbed out against pixels in the mask. Results suggest that the application may be a useful tool for the conservative assessment of nutritional intake in hospitals.

Author Keywords

Nutrition; dietary assessment; portion estimation;

ACM Classification Keywords

H.5.m [Information interfaces and presentation (e.g., HCI)]: Miscellaneous;

INTRODUCTION

Monitoring food and nutrient intake is particularly important for those at risk of malnutrition, such as older people in hospitals or care homes. According to the British Association for Parenteral and Enteral Nutrition [10] as many as 33% of adults are at medium or high risk of malnutrition on admission to hospitals or care homes, and 60% of older people are at risk [1]. Malnutrition on admission indicates a need for the development of integrated multi-disciplinary strategies to identify, prevent and treat malnutrition across all health care settings. However, hospitalization can lead to further deterioration [e.g. 7] even when additional nutritional supplementation is provided [4]. Therefore, accurate monitoring of regular dietary intake is a key part of patient care.

Permission to make digital or hard copies of all or part of this work for personal or classroom use is granted without fee provided that copies are not made or distributed for profit or commercial advantage and that copies bear this notice and the full citation on the first page. To copy otherwise, or republish, to post on servers or to redistribute to lists, requires prior specific permission and/or a fee.
CHI'12, May 5–10, 2012, Austin, Texas, USA.
Copyright 2012 ACM 978-1-4503-1015-4/12/05...$10.00.

Dietary assessment methodologies

In the UK the accurate measurement of the food and nutrient intake of individuals in hospitals is not a routine practice. Some patients may have their dietary intake assessed by a dietician but resources limit this to a few highly selected individuals. Nursing staff typically record subjective written assessments of the amount of food consumed as either "none, half or all" on patient food charts. This information is not accurate enough to be useful, as it does not inform on the intake of calories or nutrients. Assessing the amount of food (and subsequently nutrients) consumed from a partially consumed meal constitutes a significant interaction design challenge given the manpower, skill and time required to assess food and nutrient intake in the large number of patients that are at risk of malnutrition. Current methods, which are most suited to the assessment of average intakes by populations include: 1) weighed food intakes where the participant weighs and records foods pre- and post-consumption in a food diary; 2) estimated food diaries, where the participant self-reports estimated amounts of foods consumed in a food diary and 3) food frequency questionnaires [8]. These methods require a trained dietician to translate the information reported into actual intake of nutrients. However, the availability of a trained dietician for this purpose is beyond the capacity of hospital dietetic departments [9]. Consequently, evaluation can occur much after the fact, removing the ability to make timely adjustments for the next meal. There is a clear need for a system to accurately and timeously assess food and nutrient intake that can be used by non-specialist staff.

Related work

A number of digital tools for portion size and plate waste estimation have been developed. These typically replicate existing methods such as 24 hour recall interviews, using digital food atlases (sequences of images showing varying portion sizes for typical foods), and food models. Such photographic measures have been shown to have high accuracy across a number of age groups and populations for estimation of portion size [3, 5] but exhibit large variances at the level of the individual and depending on how the images are presented. Difficulties with photographic measures include representing 3D foods, the differences in perception, conceptualization and memory across individuals and demographics of individuals [11].

Examining these effects in low literacy populations, [2] describe the development of a prototype mobile digital portion size estimation tool. The prototype tool uses digital images of various objects (e.g. deck of cards, light bulb) and representations of familiar measures (e.g. weights, hand measures) to assist in the estimation of food portion size and plate waste. Overall, when objects or measures are familiar to the evaluator and match certain food characteristics (i.e. solid, liquid, amorphous), they produce accurate assessments. Although such a tool may increase the availability of a dietary monitoring, particularly self-monitoring, they remain time consuming, as the patient must identify the portion size and plate waste for each food item in a meal and nutritional intake must be calculated by a trained dietician.

THE MAPPMAL BEDSIDE ASSESSMENT TOOL

The measurement tool works under the assumption of some constraints established through a number of workshops involving clinicians, dieticians and care staff [6]. Firstly, the environment provides a digital information system at the patient's bedside through which the patient can order food, call for assistance, view menus and so on. The mappmal tool would be integrated with this system. Secondly, food images, food weights and nutritional composition can be determined prior to assessment since hospital meals are of a consistent, standardized size and content. Given that hospital meals are standardized, the mappmal assessment tool assumes set portion sizes at the start of a meal and is used to assess plate waste at the end of the meal, that is the amount of food left after consumption. Third, as trained staff are not always available in hospitals to continuously monitor nutritional intake for all patients, the assessment tool is designed to replace the broad estimates of current methods of food consumption in hospital settings and to give timely feedback for patient care. Given the constraints on trained staff for full assessment of food consumption, the mappmal application must be reliable, fast, accurate and sufficiently easy to use for any member of staff.

To assess portions consumed the user replicates a direct visual assessment of the remaining portion size on a touch-enabled device by rubbing away the parts of the meal that have been consumed (See Figure 1). To measure food consumption, the application compares the pixels the user rubbed out from the food image against a series of predefined graphical masks. A mask defines the area and position of individual food items in the original image, identifying each with a unique color. Weight of food consumed is calculated as a percentage of pixels rubbed out against pixels in the mask. Nutritional intake is subsequently derived by reference to food composition tables according to the weight of the rubbed out food. As the assessment utilizes direct observation, no intermediary metaphors, objects or measures, which may be culturally exclusive, are required. By using the tool at time of consumption recall bias may be avoided. The software allows the user to add food to the image, should they rub out too much, by redrawing pixels from the original food image.

Figure 1: The application prior to and in use. Meals are presented in a top down view. The user rubs out food items based on a visual assessment.

EVALUATION

A preliminary evaluation of the efficacy of the design was conducted. In this study, we examined: a) how consistent a single user could be, b) how consistent the ratings were between individuals and c) if the system was accurate for novice users. The following describes a typical trial: a meal was prepared and each component weighed using electronic scales. The portion size provided was controlled across trials to reflect those appropriate for hospital patients aged 70 years and over. A volunteer then consumed a portion of each food item from the meal. To ensure that all components could be assessed in the application, part of each component was left uneaten in all trials. The portions of food consumed in each meal were independently rated using the mappmal tool by two primary raters, a system expert and a dietician, and by each of the participants. Participants received no training and were instructed to erase the image to represent the plate in front of them. For each meal a total of 16 evaluations were made (5 x primary rater A, 6 x primary rater B, and 1 x five secondary raters - difference in total number of ratings for primary raters due to faster estimations by dietician). Two participants were female, and all had completed a university degree or above. A total of six trials were carried out, representing six different meals with various food types. The primary raters were used to assess intra-rater reliability. When testing inter-rater reliability the primary raters were represented by the average of each of their ratings to avoid being swayed by the number of ratings. Outlying ratings made by participants were excluded. In order to validate the data generated by the application the meal components remaining after consumption were manually weighed after the trial.

RESULTS

Average weights for each food item were calculated and compared with actual weight (See Table 1). On average a subject's use of the application underestimates food consumed by approximately 5.12 grams (-15.3% of actual consumed food or -9.8% of portion size). Novice secondary raters performed only moderately worse than primary raters (7g average error as opposed to 5g), though some were more accurate). Ratings of individual meals typically took less than 1 minute.

Meal	Food item	Actual	$\bar{x}$	σ
Beef (with gravy)	Beef	37	23.11	5.10
	Yorkshire	20	20.13	2.82
	Potato	18	13.11	1.99
	Carrots	25	17.15	3.41
	Peas	27	24.57	2.22
Beef (without gravy)	Beef	38	29.65	3.04
	Yorkshire	20	19.26	0.61
	Potato	19	14.84	1.15
	Carrots	25	17.95	2.47
	Peas	28	25.43	0.71
Porridge	Porridge	25	23.68	4.86
Scram. egg & toast	Scram. egg	34	24.89	8.29
	Toast	21	18.17	1.51
Jam sponge & custard	Custard	100	100.36	2.01
	Jam sponge	77	64.69	7.03
Fish pie	Carrots	22	16.46	3.34
	Fish Pie	59	46.41	5.74

Table 1: Actual, mean and standard deviation scores (grams) for each food item.

Certain food items presented higher levels of error (E) and standard deviation (σ) and were not limited to one food type (i.e. solid, liquid, or amorphous). These include beef (E: -13.89g, σ: 5.10g), scrambled egg (E: -9.11g, σ: 8.29g), Jam sponge (E: -12.31g, σ: 7.03g) and fish pie (E: -12.59g, σ: 5.74g).

Intra-rater reliability was high for primary raters with reliability coefficient of .916 (5 ratings) and .954 (6 ratings). In both cases, reliability could be increased slightly by excluding the first trial (α = .926 and .964 respectively), suggesting a low learning curve. Inter-rater reliability, including naïve raters, was moderately high, with a reliability coefficient of .856. Reliability between raters could be increased by the exclusion of the second primary rater (α = .882). This appears to be due to a different rating style used for porridge. Further investigations are required to examine this effect.

DISCUSSION

The preliminary results suggest that: (1) rating of food consumed was consistent between raters with few exceptions; (2) there was a consistent under-estimation of amount of food consumption for the majority of items; and (3) certain food items, such as fish pie, beef and scrambled egg, were problematic for estimation with higher standard deviations than most. These are discussed in relation to the intended use case.

The consistent rating suggests that both the specific application and the generic visual assessment technique may be reliable tools for estimating food and nutrient intake. The intra-rater reliability shows that a consistent rating is achieved after just one use of the system. This low learning curve will increase the perceived ease of use, which will be important in settings where technology acceptance can be low, such as hospitals. The high inter-rater reliability may also be important in hospital settings where a number of staff may attend to a patient. Given that the ratings are consistent across raters it would be conceivable that the evaluation of nutritional intake could be carried out by any member of a patient care team. This could contribute to more efficient, effective and timely monitoring of nutrition intake for patients at risk of malnutrition.

However, the assessment appears to be a conservative measure, with most ratings being below the actual weight. [3] report that use of visual estimates typically results in overestimation of portion size. This may remain to be true, as users of the mappmal tool may overestimate food remaining on the plate, thus underestimating food consumed. While this is not ideal for all settings, in a clinical setting underestimation is preferred to overestimation, as the assumption should be made that patients below a target intake are at risk of malnourishment.Difficulties were presented by the nature of consumption of particular food items. In later iterations of the mappmal assessment tool, a variety of measures may be necessary to reflection different food types (i.e. solid, liquid, amorphous). As per [2], known measures such as handfuls, may be more appropriate for amorphous foods, such as fish pie and scrambled egg. The tool may allow individuals to remove known portions, such as a spoon of scrambled egg at a time. In the case of beef, it is likely that the error occurred due to different thickness in beef presented in the image (and therefore assumed in the application) and that on the plate. Therefore, it would be necessary to make secondary assessments using other measures, such as angled images [11] or cross-sectional side views.

Discussions with raters after the measuring exercise suggested that different strategies for estimation were employed in the cases of ambiguous foods items. This was most notable for the assessment of porridge where one participant's estimates averaged around 2g compared with the 23g average for the remainder of the group. The extreme under-estimation appeared to be due to the direct mapping of the visual representation to the bowl. That is, the individual erased only the edges of the porridge that equated to the decrease in height of the porridge. The more accurate raters transformed the approximated consumption and carried out a representative assessment, erasing a continuous block of the porridge corresponding to estimated consumption. This suggests that when appropriate input is ambiguous mental transformations may allow for an accurate estimate. However, this is not ideal since transformations may not be consistent between individuals. Guideline for transformations could be established and relayed at time of use. As with other liquids, a cross-sectional side view may also be effective.

The application could be used to assist in the measurement of food where standardized meals are prepared and where a conservative estimation of nutritional intake might be of benefit. As such, it is ideally situated for use in hospitals where it could provide benefits on a number of levels. The application could prove beneficial for patients, in terms of improved monitoring and timely care, for staff, in terms of decreased effort required to monitor nutrition without decreased accuracy, and for hospital management in the reduction of costs associated with nutritional monitoring. While it is unsuitable to be used by the patients themselves (for reasons of accountability), the simplistic nature of the interface, coupled with the richness of the data it provides, allows a much broader range of staff to assist with the nutritional intake assessments. The general applicability of the approach is limited by the fact that the application requires images of standardized meals to be entered into the system prior to use. Therefore, the application is most suited to environments where meals are planned ahead of time and portion size, quality and composition are relatively standardized, such as the intended use in hospitals where standardized meals are the norm. Further investigation of the tool in a typical use setting is required.

CONCLUSION

The application provides a reliable but conservative measure of nutritional intake from partially consumed meals. The findings suggest that the application may be suitable for use in a hospital setting where technology acceptance may be low, the demand for efficiency and effectiveness are high, but where the need for accurate monitoring is paramount. The application provides an interaction design that meets these requirements and can contribute to the timely, effective care of patients at risk of malnutrition.

ACKNOWLEDGMENTS

This research was part of the mappmal project, funded by the New Dynamics of Ageing Programme administrated by the ESRC. We would also like to thank reviewers for their input.

REFERENCES

1. Age Concern. Hungry to be Heard: The scandal of malnourished older people in hospital. Age Concern England, London, UK, 2006.
2. Chaudry, B., Connelly, K., Siek, K.A., and Welch, J.L. The design of a mobile portion size estimation interface for a low literacy population. In 5th International Conference on Pervasive Computing Technologies for Healthcare, (2011), 160-167.
3. Hernandez, T., Wilder, L., Kuehan, D., Rubotzky, K., Moser-Veillon, P., Godwin, S., et al., Portion size estimation and expectation of accuracy. J. Food Comp. Anal., 19, (2006), 814-821.
4. Larsson, J., Unosson, M., Ek, A.-C., Nilsson, L., Thorslund, S., and Bjurulf, P. Effect of dietary supplement on nutritional status and clinical outcome in 501 geriatric patients--a randomised study. Clinical Nutrition 9, 4 (1990), 179-184. DOI: 10.1016/0261-5614(90)90017-M.
5. Lucas, F., Niravong, M., Villeminot, S., Kaaks, R. and Clavel-Chapelon, F. Estimation of food portion size using photographs: validity, strengths, weaknesses and recommendations. Journal of Human Nutrition and Dietetics 8, (1995), 65–74.
6. Macdonald A.S., Teal G., and Moynihan P. A smarter food service for nutritionally vulnerable older adult hospital patients. In Proc. of CWUAAT 10, (2010), 169-177.
7. McWhirter, J. P. and Pennington, C. R. Incidence and recognition of malnutrition in hospital. British Medical Journal 308, (1994), 945-948.
8. Moynihan, P., Thomason, J. M., Walls, A. W. G., Gray-Donald, K., Morais, J. A., Ghanem, H., Wollin, S., Ellis, J. S., Steele, J., Lund, J., and Feine, J. Researching the impact of oral health on diet and nutritional status: methodological issues. Journal of Dentistry 37, 4 (2009), 237-249.
9. Reilly, H. M. Screening for nutritional risk. Proceedings of the Nutrition Society 55, (1996), 841-853. http://dx.doi.org/10.1017/S0029665196000286
10. Russell, C. and Elia, M. Nutrition Screening Survey in the UK and Republic of Ireland in 2010. A report by the British Association for Parenteral and Enteral Nutrition (BAPEN). BAPEN, Redditch, 2011.
11. Subar, A.F., Crafts, J., Zimmerman, T.P., Wilson, M., Mittl, B., Islam, N.G., et al. Assessment of the accuracy of portion size reports using computer-based food photographs aids in the development of an automated self-administered 24-hour recall. J. Am. Diet. Assoc., 110, (2010), 55-64.

Tackling Dilemmas in Supporting "The Whole Person" in Online Patient Communities

Jina Huh, Rupa Patel, Wanda Pratt
Division of Biomedical and Health Informatics
University of Washington

{jinahuh,rupatel,wpratt}@uw.edu

ABSTRACT
Online health communities that engage the patient as a *whole person* attend to personal and medical needs in a holistic manner. Whether current communities structure interaction between health professionals and patients to address the whole person is an open question. To gain insights into this question, we examined a sample of online patient communities to understand health professionals' involvement in bringing in medical advice into peer-patient conversations. We found the communities fall short in supporting the whole person, because (1) patient expertise and clinical expertise generated by health professionals are shared separately, and (2) patients' quantified data are separate from narrative experiences. Such separation in the design of these systems can lead to limitations in addressing patients' interwoven medical and personal concerns. We discuss dilemmas and design implications for supporting the whole person in online patient communities.

Author Keywords
Health; online patient communities; the whole person; collaborative help

ACM Classification Keywords
H.5.2 User Interfaces; J.3 Life and Medical Sciences: Medical information systems.

INTRODUCTION
Consider a scenario about a breast cancer patient whose information needs are not fulfilled by online communities:

Sally started hormone therapy for breast cancer a few weeks ago and is now experiencing sexual dysfunction. She is wondering whether it could be a side effect of the hormone therapy that her doctor did not mention. Sally turned to an online breast cancer community, but there was not a convenient way to share her symptom-tracking logs along with the post. Patients shared their similar experiences, strategies for communicating with their partners about the issue, and treatments they found helpful. However, patients began having conflicting opinions about the suggestions. Sally turned to an expert Q&A section to ask about her situation. The health expert suggested asking her doctor about vaginal estrogen therapy. Sally did not feel comfortable about the vaginal treatment. She wished the patients who were participating in her post were part of the conversation with the health expert so that the expert and patients can comment on one another's posts.

Permission to make digital or hard copies of all or part of this work for personal or classroom use is granted without fee provided that copies are not made or distributed for profit or commercial advantage and that copies bear this notice and the full citation on the first page. To copy otherwise, or republish, to post on servers or to redistribute to lists, requires prior specific permission and/or a fee.
CHI 2012, May 5-10, 2012, Austin, TX, USA.
Copyright 2012 ACM 978-1-4503-1015-4/12/05...$10.00.

Sally's scenario illustrates limitations in current online patient communities. Sally ended up getting conflicting experiences from other patients and medical advice that she was not satisfied with. Sally wished she had a better way of conveying her experience in her posts using symptom logs. Sally's case portrays how online patient communities fall short in addressing patient's experience of a disease as a closely interwoven matter of both the medical and personal side of an individual, as suggested by the "whole person model" [8].

To examine how online patient communities currently engage the whole person model, we studied 27 online patient communities. We found two limitations: (1) patient and clinical expertise are not interwoven and (2) quantified and narrative experiences are disconnected during patients' experience sharing. With the findings, we discuss implications and challenges in improving online patient communities.

BACKGROUND
Patient-centered medicine promotes exploring both the disease and the personal experience of that disease [8]. The field further suggests the importance of understanding not only medical issues but also *the whole person*—including details about the world in which he or she lives, such as family, friendship, employment, religion, and culture [2, 14]. Health professionals who respond to the whole person's needs provide care that integrates knowledge of patients' values and life circumstances, rather than only medical facts [14].

As designers of consumer health technologies, we also should consider what it means to support the whole person through design. Online health communities are an example of a technology that could potentially support whole person needs. On the personal side, online patient communities have been shown as great resources for providing patient expertise and empowering patients to learn from one another [5]. Furthermore, researchers examined online patient communities as a way for patients to give and receive emotional support [12] while also enhancing self-efficacy and self-management [10].

Although the main benefit of patient communities comes from peer-patient interaction, studies have also shown the importance of health professionals' roles in online support groups for behavioral changes [3,9]. A growing number of health organizations offer online patient communities together with medical information (connect.diabetes.org, www.juvenation.org) to address medical issues. However, users' interaction with medical information is independent from patient forums, making it difficult to weave together both peer and professional advice.

Another emerging area in patient communities is capturing aspects of illness experiences through personal informatics tools [16]. These tools enable patients to share quantifiable information that they can use to reflect and monitor their health. Websites such as PatientsLikeMe and CureTogether (www.patientslikeme.com, www.curetogether.com) support such a notion from patients' perspectives. However, such exclusively quantifiable information lacks context for appropriate interpretation [4]. Researchers explored ways to combine quantifiable experiences with contextual information, such as adding photography with glucose measurements [13] and capturing patient histories of both physiological data and events [11] for individual reflection. However, close integration of quantifiable information within patient conversations in community settings is still under-supported.

The whole person model provides a framework for examining how online patient communities can support delivering clinical and patient expertise to patients and what form this should take.

METHODS

We analyzed 27 publicly accessible online patient communities for patients with cancer or diabetes, reported as U.S.'s leading causes of death and disability (http://www.cdc.gov/chronicdisease). We gathered lists of patient community websites from U.S. based representative organizations and medical help portals (e.g., National Cancer Institute). We excluded listservs and chose the top 9 community websites that had the most posting activities in the preceding week of data collection for cancer (cancerconnect.com, breastcancer.org, cancer-forums.org, mylifeline.org, forums.networkofstrength.org, mycrcconnections.ning.com, cancerforums.net, cancer-forums.net, rare-cancer.org), diabetes (dlife.com, diabeticconnect.com, diabeticgourmet.com, childrenwithdiabetes.com, tudiabetes.org, juvenation.org, connect.diabetes.com, diabetesforum.com, diabetesdaily.com), and multi-disease communities (patientslikeme.com, webMD.com, inspire.com, healingwell.com, healthcentral.com, medhelp.com, dailystrength.com, curetogether.com, ehealthforum.com). Among the 19 communities that explicitly showed the total number of registered members, the number ranged from 583 to over 600,000 members (average 54,866). There were 15 communities that were run by for-profit companies and 11 by non-profit organizations.

We used iterative coding [14] to understand features of these communities that could be important for our analysis. The codes included the presence of: *administrative moderators* including patient advocates who regulate discussion content; *health professional moderators* that participate in patient forums to give medical advice; *expert Q&A feature* where patients can directly ask questions to health professionals; *medical advisory board,* an official board of members from business and medical field that shape the community; *a discussion place for health professionals only,* a place for health professionals to share information; and *quantified experience sharing*, features that patients can share quantifiable health experiences. We used these codes to analyze communities' "About Us" sections, disclaimers, and introductions.

FINDINGS

We report three main findings. First, health professionals' engagement was largely separate from peer-patients interaction. Second, whether a community is non-profit or for-profit shaped the level of health professionals' involvement. Lastly, none of the communities that allowed patients to share their quantified experience supported linking that quantitative data with illness narratives.

Separation of Medical Advice from Patient Expertise

As Table 1 shows, although 81% of the online communities had administrative moderators, only 19% had moderators that were health professionals. Rather than directly engaging in patient conversations, most of these communities claimed that health professionals regularly monitor patients' conversations. The other 81% of the communities claimed no responsibility for the credibility of the content and suggested that patients should consult their primary care doctors for medical advice.

In one community that enabled health professionals' direct engagement in the patient forums, the posts showed that the patient forum became similar to expert Q&A sessions, where patients and health professionals conversed and patients rarely interacted with one another.

Although 48% of the communities had advisory boards with medical professionals, only 30% had expert Q&A features where patients can directly ask questions of health professionals.

For-Profit Versus Non-Profit Online Communities

When we broke down findings into subcategories (Table 2), interesting findings emerged about the link between being a for- or non-profit online community and health professionals' engagement. Among the codes shown in Table 2, how much health professional moderators and expert Q&A features were offered showed a significant difference between for-profit and non-profit online communities at a 5% significance level using a two-tailed proportion test. None of the non-profit sites offered health

Whether the online community had:	For-profit communities (15 total)			Non-profit communities (12 total)			All (27 communities)
	Cancer 11% (1)	Diabetes 67% (6)	Multi- 89%(8)	Cancer 89% (8)	Diabetes 33% (3)	Multi- 11% (1)	
Administrative moderators	73% (11 out of 15)			92% (11 out of 12)			81% (22)
Health professional moderators*	33% (5 out of 15)			0% (0 out of 12)			19% (5)
Expert Q&A feature*	47% (7 out of 15)			8% (1 out of 12)			30% (8)
Advisory board	53% (8 out of 15)			42% (5 out of 12)			48% (13)
Health professionals only	13% (2 out of 15)			8% (1 out of 12)			11% (3)

Table 2: Breakdown of how non-profit and for-profit online communities support engagement of health professionals. (Multi-: multiple-disease) *: There were significant differences between for-profit and non-profit communities at a 5% significance

professional moderators and fewer non-profit communities supported some forms of health professionals' engagement in all categories than for-profit online communities.

Quantified Experiences and Narrative Experiences

Five online communities (19%) offered patients' sharing of quantified experiences. Meanwhile, 26 communities (96%) offered free-form discussions among patients. However, none offered explicit ways of connecting quantified experiences with narrative experiences in forums. Given that all but one of the communities supporting quantified experience sharing were for-profit, a possible assumption is that a community needs resources to develop tools for sharing quantified experiences. In addition, these for-profit sites often sell anonymized versions of that quantified data.

DISCUSSION AND DESIGN IMPLICATIONS

Below, we discuss two points for considering the whole person model in designing online patient communities..

Point 1: Dualistic View Towards Patient and Clinical Expertise

Only a small number of online communities supported health professionals' involvement with the communities. Even when supported, communities separated out where patients ask for medical questions and where patients share experiences. The health professional moderators' engagement was minimal. In one case where health professionals' engagement was bigger than other forums, it seemed to discourage peer-patient interaction. This result is congruent with a previous study; In patient support groups, unless the leader of the group actively promotes discussion among patients, it becomes a Q&A session between health professionals and patients [6].

This finding brings out an interesting social challenge. A study [5] found that 56% of the patients' posted content in a sample of online patient communities were medical in nature, 31% were personal, and 13% were for both medical and personal. This finding, along with literature in patient-centered medicine, points to the importance of weaving together clinical and patient expertise in online communities. However, involving health professionals could take away value that patients provide to one another. Also, depending on supporting organizations' resources to pay for health professionals' participation, the quality and amount of engaging clinical expertise can vary greatly.

Then the key becomes how we can bring in clinical expertise without hindering patient-to-patient interaction, and how we can minimize the effort of health professionals who usually have limited resources to spend. Below we discuss potential automated and crowd-based solutions for this problem.

Design Implication: Linking Medical Advice with Patient Experiences

Collaboratively elevate medical problems to health professionals. We propose that online forums add a feature that allows patients to collectively vote on discussions that focus on the medical side. This thread could then be forwarded to health professionals' attention. In addition, long threads could indicate conflicting stories that could be flagged for health professionals to participate.

Help patients become critical part of building clinical and patient expertise. Once a patient receives advice from health professionals, the members can challenge, confirm, or augment health professionals' responses with their personal experiences. Patients could take an active role in sharing their illness narratives and collaboratively making sense of clinical and patient expertise [1].

Outsource clinical expertise. Not all communities have resources to hire health professionals to provide medical expertise. Currently, patients work around this problem by sharing related materials from health professionals who they have communicated with. Alternatively, an automated aggregator could bring in publicly available resources from other communities, websites, blogs, and medical articles for the threads that patients have voted for.

Point 2: Quantified Experiences as a Reduced View of Illness

Quantified experiences have advantages in scalability and efficiency in sharing patient experiences. However, our findings show quantified experiences are shared separately from patients' illness narratives. Quantified experiences fall short in capturing patients' holistic illness experience [4], and with narrative data the information can gain richness in context [7]. Below we explore ways to link quantified experiences with narrative experiences.

Design Implication: Integrating Quantified Information with Illness Narratives

Link quantified data to forum posts. Patients can link back to their tracking history during forum posts. The tracking history can also show links to forum posts. Linking tracking history with forum posts can help contextualize patients' medical and personal experiences.

Allow easy sharing of narratives on tracking histories. Similar to Willett et al's [15] work, patients can point to one's tracking history to discuss various interpretations. Furthermore, parts of tracking history can be pulled back into forum conversations. Such intertwined sharing of tracking histories within conversations can trigger rich stories to be constructed through peer-patient interaction.

LIMITATIONS

In discussing the whole person model, we examined intertwining medical and personal expertise and quantifiable and narrative patient experiences. Further work should explore other aspects of the whole person model, such as cultural and institutional constraints around patients' illness trajectories. Our work analyzes content from the information pages of the community websites, rather than patient exchanges. Future work will be necessary to understand patients' perspectives and evaluate design suggestions.

CONCLUSION

In this paper, we discussed design implications for better supporting the whole person in online patient communities. Given the improved design, our hope is to help Sally's case turn into a scenario as shown in the following:

Sally turned to an online breast cancer community to share her log of this potential side effect. Patients shared their similar experiences using logs, strategies for communicating with their partner about the issue, and treatments they found helpful. After patients voted this issue as a top concern, an oncologist participating in the community replied that such natural remedies are good ways to begin treating side effects before diving into more serious treatments. Other patients began discussing their experiences of going through the treatments the oncologist mentioned, giving Sally an idea of what to consult with her doctor.

ACKNOWLEDGEMENTS

This work has been in part funded by NLM training fellowship and NSF grant #1117187.

REFERENCES

1. Anderson, R.M., Funnell, M.M., Butler, P.M., Arnold, M.S., Fitzgerald, J.T., and Feste, C.C. Patient empowerment. Results of a randomized controlled trial. *Diabetes Care 18*, 7 (1995), 943.
2. Brown, J., Weston, W., and Stewart, M. The first component: exploring both the disease and the illness experience. *Patient-centered Medicine. Transforming the Clinical Method 2*, 3–52.
3. Cuijpers, P., Donker, T., van Straten, A., Li, J., and Andersson, G. Is guided self-help as effective as face-to-face psychotherapy for depression and anxiety disorders? A systematic review and meta-analysis of comparative outcome studies. *Psychological medicine 40*, 12 (2010), 1943-57.
4. Frost, J.H. and Massagli, M.P. Social uses of personal health information within PatientsLikeMe, an online patient community: What can happen when patients have access to one another's data. . *Journal of Medical Internet Research 10*, 3 (2008), e15.
5. Hartzler, A. and Pratt, W. Managing the Personal Side of Health: How Patient Expertise Differs from the Expertise of Clinicians. *JMIR 13*, 3 (2011), e62.
6. Huh, J. Collaborative Help for Individualized Problems: Learning from the MythTV User Community and Diabetes Patient Support Groups. PhD Thesis. University of Michigan. 2011.
7. Kleinman, A., Eisenberg, L., and Good, B. Culture, Illness, and Care: Clinical Lessons from Anthropologic and Cross-Cultural Research. *Ann Intern Med 88*, 2 (1978), 251-258.
8. Levenstein, J.H., McCracken, E.C., McWhinney, I.R., Stewart, M.A., and Brown, J.B. The Patient-Centred Clinical Method. 1. A Model for the Doctor-Patient Interaction in Family Medicine. *Family Practice 3*, 1 (1986), 24-30.
9. Lindsay, S. and Smith, S. The health impact of an online heart disease support group: a comparison of moderated versus unmoderated support. *Health Education Research 24*, 4 (2009), 646-654.
10. Lorig, K., Ritter, P.L., Laurent, D.D., et al. Online diabetes self-management program: a randomized study. *Diabetes care 33*, 6 (2010), 1275-81.
11. Plaisant, C., Mushlin, R., Snyder, A., Li, J., Heller, D., and Shneiderman, B. LifeLines: using visualization to enhance navigation and analysis of patient records. *AMIA*, (1998), 76.
12. Preece, J. Empathic communities: Reaching out across the web. *Interactions 5*, 2 (1998), 32-43.
13. Smith, B.K., Frost, J., Albayrak, M., and Sudhakar, R. Integrating glucometers and digital photography as experience capture tools to enhance patient understanding and communication of diabetes self-management practices. *Personal and Ubiquitous Computing 11*, 4 (2006), 273-286.
14. Strauss, A.L. and Corbin, J. *Basics of qualitative research: Grounded theory procedures and techniques.* Sage Newbury Park, CA, 1990.
15. Willett, W., Heer, J., Hellerstein, J., and Agrawala, M. CommentSpace. *CHI '11*, ACM Press (2011), 3131.
16. Wolf, G. Know Thyself: Tracking Every Facet of Life, from Sleep to Mood to Pain, 24/7/365. *Wired Magazine*, 2009.

Interaction Proxemics and Image Use in Neurosurgery

Helena M. Mentis[1], Kenton O'Hara[1], Abigail Sellen[1], and Rikin Trivedi[2]

[1]Microsoft Research
Cambridge, UK
{hementis, v-keohar, asellen}@microsoft.com

[2]Addenbrookes Hospital
Cambridge, UK
riki.trivedi@addenbrookes.nhs.uk

ABSTRACT
Within medical settings there is a growing interest in exploring touchless interaction technologies. The primary motivation here is to avoid contact during interaction with data so as to maintain asepsis. However, there is another important property of touchless interaction that has significant implications for their use within such settings – namely that interaction behaviour is spatially distal from the device being interacted with. To further understand these implications we present fieldwork observations of work practice in neurosurgery theatres. Drawing on the notion of *interaction proxemics* and the theory of *F-formations*, our analysis articulates the spatial organization of collaborative work practices and interaction in these settings. From this understanding of spatial practices, we discuss opportunities and difficulties relating to the design of touchless interaction technologies for in surgical settings.

Author Keywords
Gestural; touchless interaction; space; proxemics; health; surgery; imaging.

ACM Classification Keywords
H.5.m [Information Interfaces and Presentation (e.g. HCI)]: Miscellaneous;

General Terms
Design; Human Factors; Performance.

INTRODUCTION
For several decades now, advances in medical imaging technologies have impacted widely on medical procedures from diagnosis to treatment. Surgery, in particular, is increasingly dependent on medical imaging to visualize and interpret anatomical structures and processes with minimal invasiveness. Capturing, browsing, and manipulating images are a substantial component of many contemporary operating procedures. In recent years, interaction with images during surgery has drawn attention from a variety of stakeholders and researchers. One focus in particular has been the requirement of surgical settings to maintain boundaries between sterile and non-sterile practices. This has led to concerns with the transfer of matter arising through traditional touch-based interaction mechanisms. In response, we have seen interaction mechanisms designed to remove the consequences of touch (e.g. wipeable surfaces) or to mitigate contact (e.g. keyboard covers). With recent advances in computer vision, there has also been growing interest in systems that avoid touch altogether through the use of cameras to capture gestural interaction [11, 30, 19].

In this paper, we also wish to explore the potential of touchless interaction systems in surgical contexts. However, rather than being motivated by the need for asepsis, it is clear that other properties of touchlessness warrant consideration in these settings [11, 19, 2]. The particular property that we focus on in this paper is that which deals with touch and touchlessness as a spatial concern. That is, touch-based interaction entails a proximal relationship with the interaction mechanism, whereas touchless interaction supports a more distal relationship with the device (depending on the sensors concerned). The different *interaction proxemics* [27] of these technologies enable and require different spatial relationships between interactors and the technologies with which they are interacting. The broader significance of this is that the spatial configurations of a setting (its architecture, furniture and artefacts) profoundly affect the social, informational, and collaborative practices that take place within them [e.g. 13, 22, 23, 27, 15, 24]. The introduction of touchless imaging systems, with their distal interaction properties, potentially transforms the spatial configurations of a medical setting and thereby how social, informational, and collaborative practices are organized.

With this in mind, our concerns in this paper are with the spatial organization of collaborative work practices involving medical imaging systems in surgical theatres. The findings we present are drawn from fieldwork of neurosurgery procedures. We describe how surgical theatre personnel interact with the current imaging technologies where the interaction is currently mouse- or stylus-based. Through these findings, we articulate the shifting spatial relationships between surgeons and imaging technologies during procedures and the factors shaping these relationships. Our aim is to use an understanding of current practices in surgical settings viewed through a lens of proxemics [cf. 19] to uncover implications for the design of touchless interaction systems.

Understanding current practice helps to explain the motivations, factors and constraints that lead to the organization of work. It helps to identify issues where

Permission to make digital or hard copies of all or part of this work for personal or classroom use is granted without fee provided that copies are not made or distributed for profit or commercial advantage and that copies bear this notice and the full citation on the first page. To copy otherwise, or republish, to post on servers or to redistribute to lists, requires prior specific permission and/or a fee.
CHI'12, May 5–10, 2012, Austin, Texas, USA.
Copyright 2012 ACM 978-1-4503-1015-4/12/05...$10.00.

practices may have to adapt and accommodate to new modes of interaction. Some aspects of the work are so fundamental that we would not expect or want these to be altered with the introduction of new technologies. This includes, for example, the importance of organising spatial practices around the patient; the fact that images often need to be referred to next to the body; the need to rearrange equipment, personnel and patient for particular procedures which in turn creates a shifting spatial relationship between surgeon and imaging systems; and the need for close proximity of other members of the medical team. It is these kinds of features highlighted in the following study that remain stable and are useful to consider in the design and deployment of particular touchless systems.

RELATED WORK

There is a long tradition of work articulating how social action and behaviour are influenced by the spatial configuration of actors with respect to other people and objects in the physical environment. A number of these have found particular influence with the CHI and CSCW communities [e.g. 3, 7, 5, 14, 1, 12, 27, 24]. It is beyond both the scope and purposes of this paper to offer complete coverage of this work. Rather, our intent here is to highlight some of the key theoretical works and conceptual apparatus that particularly influence, motivate and inform our analytic contributions in this paper. Of particular significance here is Ed Hall's notion of *Proxemics* [13], which explores one's use of space as a specialized elaboration of culture. For Hall, human interaction is fundamentally spatially organized with factors such as interpersonal distances, orientations, architectural arrangements, or configurations of furniture impacting how communication and social interaction unfold in particular settings. Of significance is that one's sense of space and distance is "dynamic because it is related to action – what can be done in a given space – rather than what is seen by passive viewing" (p.108). The significance of this for us is that new interaction mechanisms create different possibilities for action at different spatial distances. The notion of proxemics has been particularly influential within CSCW and HCI [e.g. 20, 12, 27, 6]. For example, Greenberg et al [12], introduce the notion of *proxemic interactions* – that is, interactive behaviours based upon the proxemic relationships (e.g. distance, orientation, movement, identity, and location) between people, digital devices, and non-digital things. A number of authors (e.g. [28], [24]) have discussed concepts such as *zones of interaction* around interactive devices and displays where different kinds of human behaviour occur at different distances from the displays with different interactive possibilities and information granularity

Another way to think about the spatially significant interactions around devices is put forth by O'Hara et al [27] who raise the notion of *interaction proxemics* - how properties of interactive devices configure people in spatial ways with respect to technology, content, and each other. For example, touch screens require groups of people to be lined up in front of the screen while large screens allow for shared information to be viewed from greater distances. Along related lines, Hornecker and Buur [18] discuss notions of *embodied constraints* in which configurations of space and objects (size, form, or location) and *interaction access points* (options to observe, access, and interact with objects in a space) shape emerging social configurations and behaviours. A more descriptive treatment of different spaces is given in [6], categorising different types of conceptual spaces around interactive displays including: *interaction spaces, potential interaction spaces, gap spaces, social interaction spaces, comfort space, and activation space.* These concepts help explain why viewing distance differs from interaction distance – an issue that is significant in our later discussions of touchless interaction.

Similarly influential theoretical contributions to our understanding of spatial configuration of social action can be found in the work of Kendon [22, 23]. Of significance is his articulation of the *F-formation* – the "system of spatial and orientational behavior" of participants [22] (p. 212) – from which we can draw several important concepts for our concerns. One such concept concerns *transactional segments* (the area in front of each body to which attention and action are directed in the context of a particular activity). An F-formation (Face Address or Facing formations) is created when the transactional segments of two or more actors overlap in the context of social interaction forming a shared interactional space to which the participants have mutual access – the *o-space*. In the context of interaction, people continually arrange themselves to sustain the *o-space* – in other words, people arrange themselves in a circle, ellipse, or horseshoe pattern in order to have easy access to one another and excluding the outside world. Of note is that transactional segments are organized not just between actors but also between artefacts and features in the spatial environment towards which action is directed. When we watch television or look at a computer monitor, a transaction segment is defined between us and the display [23]. Several authors in HCI and CSCW have used Kendon's theory to understand technological impact on social action. This includes video conferencing [27], social interaction around interactive tabletops in tourist information centres [24], and the impact of electronic patient records in hospital wards on communication and collaboration [25].

These notions can be applied to imaging technologies within a surgical setting. Our argument is that the interaction proxemics, properties of space, and interaction access points shape and define the transactional segments of the F-formation and o-space in coordinated work. Through our analyses of these qualities we can define the opportunities for touchless interaction in supporting the social action as well as potential pitfalls for successful introduction of touchless technologies.

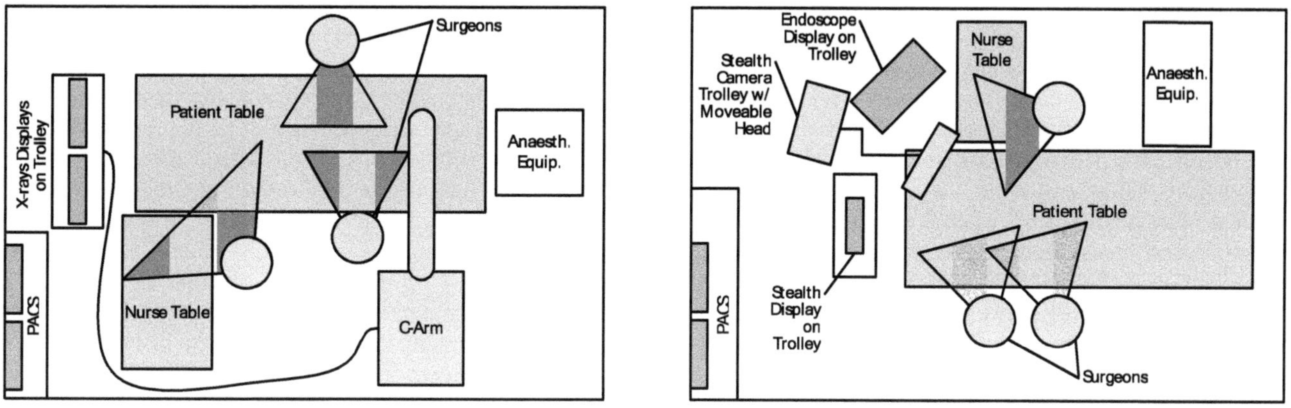

Figure 1. Typical Configurations of Theatres. Theatre 1 is on the left and Theatre 2 on the right.

Other explorations of spatial practices within medical settings also inform our theoretical concerns. Perhaps most notable is Strauss' research on the organization of medical work [29] through *articulation work* and *trajectories of action*. Such highly-tuned coordinated trajectories of action are enabled through the spatial organisation of particular resources and artefacts in particular settings. This is further emphasised in Bardram and Bossen's studies of hospital settings [1] where *mobility work* is a spatial aspect of the work trajectory dealing with the configuration of people, resources, knowledge, and place in order to accomplish collaborative tasks with minimal effort. The significance of this for our purposes lies in the ways the interaction proxemics of touchless interaction will affect the ways that the operating theatre setups come to be configured in potentially useful ways. Conversely, the use of these touchless technologies will also be affected or even hindered by other prominent features of these setups and their impact on action.

Our work is informed more generally by social studies of work practice within operating theatres [e.g., 4, 8, 16, 9, 17, 21, 30]. While these studies do not focus on spatial issues within surgery per se, the rich descriptions and analyses do provide insight into the spatial organisation of work. Katz [21], for example, is particularly pertinent here, describing the boundaries between different "*realms of cleanliness*" that constrain movement, action, and the spatial organization of work.

Drawing on these insights from the literature, we present findings from a study of image use during neurosurgery. Our analysis focuses on the spatial configuration of imaging systems and their proxemically defined use during procedures. In a similar vein to Johnson et al [19], we use this to discuss further implications for touchless interaction technologies that relate in particular to its spatial properties.

FIELDWORK IN THE OPERATING THEATRE

Our fieldwork was conducted in two operating theatres in the neurosurgery department of a large hospital in the UK. Neurosurgery is concerned with any portion of the nervous system including the brain, spinal column, spinal cord, peripheral nerves, and extra-cranial cerebrovascular system. Oftentimes, the procedures must be performed with minimal invasiveness due to the sensitivity of the tissue (brain surgery for instance) or in order to speed up recovery time and reduce opportunities for complications. During these minimally invasive procedures, imaging systems are required in order to 'see' into the body.

The theatres observed are flanked by patient and equipment preparatory rooms, equipment disposal rooms, and scrub rooms. A typical setup for these two theatres can be seen in Figure 1. Within these setups the patient table is positioned in the centre of the room. The exact orientation of the table depends on the procedure being conducted, its specific approach requirements, and equipment needs. Positioned around the patient table are a range of furniture and medical equipment. These include the instrument trolley perpendicular to the patient table (providing a working area for the scrub nurse to prepare and hand off equipment to the surgeons); a mobile X-ray C-arm; a mobile X-ray control and display trolley (connected to C-arm and from which X-rays are viewed and controlled); anaesthesia equipment next to the patient table but out of the way of the flow of traffic from the preparatory room to the disposal room.

For endoscopic procedures, an endoscopy monitor mounted on a trolley is positioned next to the patient table directly in view of the surgeon. Other specialist equipment included the Medtronic StealthStation® Treon™ Navigation System (StealthCam) consisting of a mounted camera system coupled with a trolley-based display and control unit. This is positioned at the patient table adjacent to the endoscopy monitor. For this system to function the patient's head is fixed in position and an infrared camera is positioned and calibrated precisely allowing the outline of the head to be mapped to pre-operative CT scans. Controlled by a foot pedal, the cameras track the surgical probe and display the location of the tip (whether inside or outside of the skull) on three planes of the CT scans: axial, coronal, and sagittal. These images are displayed on the mobile display trolley component of the system.

While much of the equipment is configured around the patient table, an exception is the PACS (Picture Archiving and Communication System). This is a networked system for accessing pre-operative images, such as MRI and CT scans. The system has two screens that are mounted on the wall away from the patient table – a mouse and keyboard lie on a shelf just below the screens. It is positioned here to enable networked access and because it is a shared resource used for a variety of purposes by different members of the surgical team. As these displays are fixed, the patient table is sometimes specifically positioned to facilitate viewing during procedures that anticipate heavy PACS use.

We observed five procedures totalling 25 hours over the course of several weeks. The procedures were selected as a representative range of work undertaken in neurosurgery and to allow observation of the different imaging systems in practice. Two were spinal fixations (one 'open-cut' and one 'keyhole') in which several vertebrae are anchored together with a device in order to reduce vertebral mobility. Open-cut spinal surgery requires a long incision whereas a keyhole surgery uses small half-inch incisions where smaller surgical instruments are passed through. Two of the procedures were tumour excisions (one in the spine and one in the brain). The fifth procedure was a brain tumour biopsy. For the tumour excision of the spine, an endonasal approach was employed passing the instruments and endoscope through the nostrils along the nasal passage to the point of the tumour on the spine, For the two brain tumours, a craniotomy was performed (openings were created in the skull) and small instruments were introduced into the brain matter to sample or remove the mass.

For each of these procedures, there were typically two surgeons present: one consultant and one registrar. For some of the longer procedures, an additional consultant surgeon would also be present at various points. Much of the surgeons' time is spent at the patient table but as we discuss later, they also have particular needs to move around the theatre. One and sometimes two scrub nurses will also be supporting the surgeons and be positioned in very close proximity to the surgeons next to the instrument table. The number of personnel at the bedside along with the various pieces of equipment creates a somewhat cramped and spatially restrictive working environment. In addition to the scrubbed personnel, there were also various non-scrubbed members of the team. These include an anaesthetist who sits next to the anaesthetic equipment, a radiographer who controls the X-ray C-arm and monitors, and various other roaming support staff.

For our observations, we were given freedom of movement around the theatres to observe procedures and practices from a variety of perspectives. We also had the opportunity for informal conversations with the surgeons and surgical support team (e.g. radiographers, scrub nurses and other non-scrubbed assistants). These conversations were conducted as appropriate within the context of on-going activities in the theatre and were used to help understand technical aspects of the procedures as well as explanations of particular behaviours, practices, and configuration of artefacts in the space. In addition to taking notes, all of the procedures we observed were recorded on handheld video cameras. Analysis of the audio and video allowed a much more detailed and reflective inspection of practices than was possible through observation alone. Our analytic attention focused on the details of how *trajectories of action* and interaction were collaboratively produced in this context. In particular we were interested in how different *transaction segments* and *F-formations* were organized with respect to the various artefacts and team members in these settings in the context of these action trajectories. This analysis was conducted with the aim of identifying how transaction segments, F-formations, and spatial configurations would affect or be affected by the introduction of touchless interaction.

FINDINGS

We present the findings as a series of vignettes, each illustrating key features of the spatial organisation of image use. For each vignette, we discuss the implications of these features for touchless interaction. Vignette 1 highlights issues of separating image use from where it is needed at the bedside. Vignette 2 considers the dynamics and constraints of spatial configurations and how this relates to line of sight between surgeon and imaging displays. Finally, Vignette 3 discusses interference issues arising from intersecting transaction segments in the theatre.

Vignette 1 – Control, Perception and Deixis Proxemics

It is the start of an open-cut spinal fixation procedure on a 54 year-old female. The consultant surgeon, RV (foreground in Figure 2a) and the registrar surgeon FG (far side of patient in Figure 2a) are scrubbed up and at the bedside (Figure 2a). RV is pressing and massaging the area around the patient's spine to ascertain shape and position of the spinal pedicles. As he feels the spine he is discussing aspects of the nature of its curvature with FG. FG offers an opinion but RV is uncertain so steps away from the bedside and moves over to the PACS display on the wall. He looks at the images currently displayed on the screens but these are not sufficient to resolve his uncertainty (Figure 2b). He leans in to the display to get a closer look at the thumbnail images to the left hand side of the left display and identifies a new view (Figure 2c). Being scrubbed up he cannot touch the mouse to bring up the identified view. He turns and looks to see who is available to operate the mouse on his behalf.

RV: "Errr… [looking round then notices Nurse M who is not in scrubs] M?"

M: "Yes?"

RV: "Come here for a second."

RV: Get the mouse and touch the screen there [his finger points at a thumbnail – hovering just inches away from the surface of the screen (Figure 2d)]…. that one there, left."

M: "There?"

RV: "Other one."

Once the correct image was selected, RV then turns to the right side monitor to view the image just opened (Figure 2e). While still looking at the image he raises his voice to indicate his addressing FG (who had continued to prepare the patient) behind him at the bedside: "Concave to the right, agreed".

After directing the nurse to revert back to the previous image that had been displayed, he moves away from the screen and returns to his former position at the patient bedside.

Within the trajectory of action outlined in this vignette are a rich set of features that illustrate aspects of the spatial organization of work and the proxemics of touch vs. touchless interaction. Let us consider some of these further. The first thing of note is seen at the beginning of the sequence. The transactional segments of both surgeons are initially organized around the patient's body – the patient being in the o-space between the two surgeons. The physical manipulation of the patient and the uncertainty in assessment arising from this leads to the initial discussion with the colleague and the consequent need to refer to the CT images. Of significance here is that the required images are not available, in several ways, within the particular F-formation around the patient. As such there is a need to break this particular F-formation. RV enters a new transactional segment that is organized around the displays rather than the patient. Because the patient and the display are not in the same transactional segment, the two information resources are not ideally positioned so that they can be both taken into account in the formation of medical judgment. In this particular scenario the judgment was not especially complicated but there are instances where there is a stronger need to combine what can be seen and felt on the patient with what is visualized in the medical images. By separating these transactional segments in this way, a close interleaving of information access from these different sources is not well supported.

An important question to consider is why such a separation in transactional segments arises in this setting. First of all, as a PACS access point within the theatre, it is a resource that is used by multiple members of the team for different purposes throughout the surgery – as such there is no setup that might be considered optimal for any single purpose. Being a fixed display inhibits the flexible reconfiguration as necessary throughout the procedure. Given this positioning, then, there are aspects of the interaction proxemics, which mean RV has to move away from the bedside to the PACS display – these have to do with *control proxemics*, *perceptual proxemics* and *deixis proxemics*. The notion of control proxemics relates to the touch-based interaction of the mouse. That is, to operate the system, the person needs to be near the mouse at the display. Given the mouse is outside the sterile zone around the patient, RV, being scrubbed, needs to make a judgement about whether to descrub and maintain interaction control or whether to invite someone to control on his behalf. Descrubbing is time consuming and effortful so RV decides that the

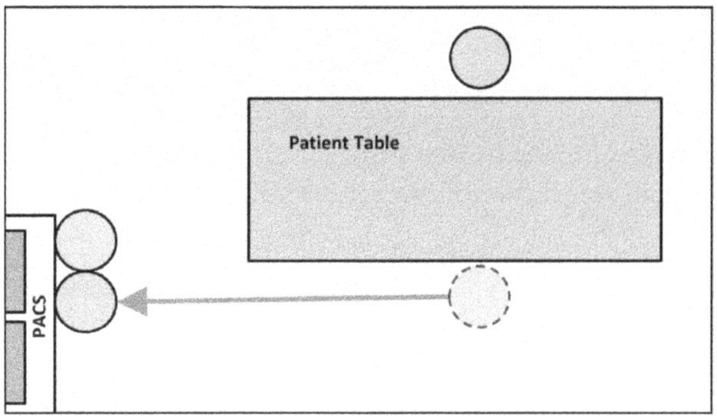

(a)
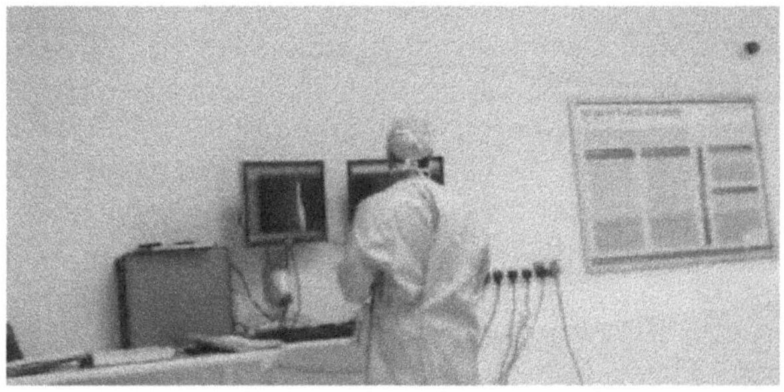

(b)
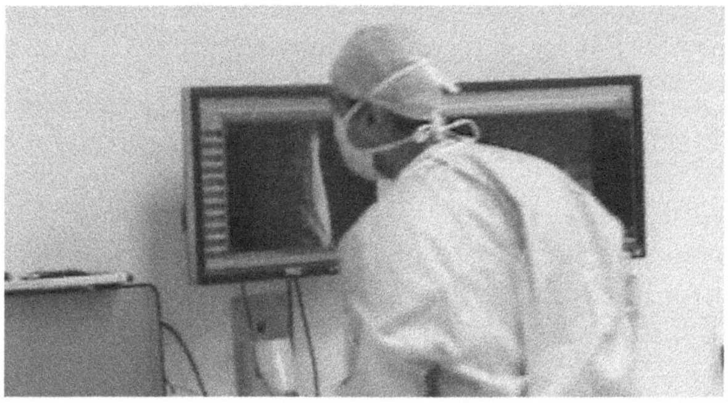

(c)
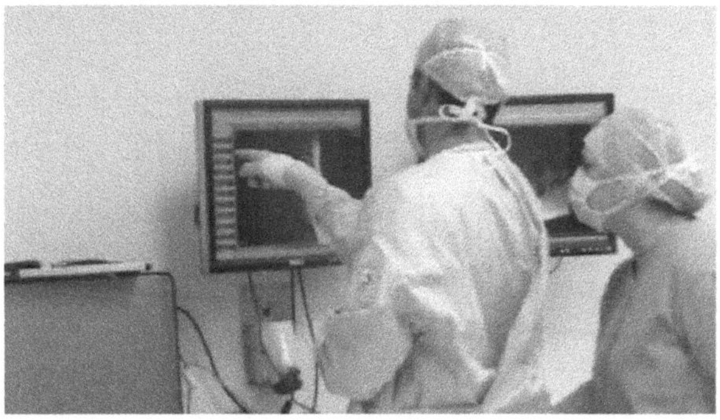

(d)
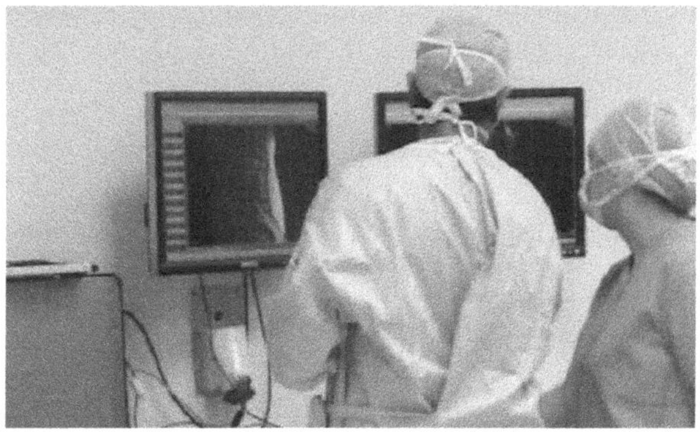

Figure 2. Vignette 1 – Separation of Transactional Segments.

information gain is not worth the effort, beckoning over a nurse to act as proxy. Significantly, this was not always possible. For example, when a nurse did not have the necessary level of professional vision [10] to understand the necessary image interactions, a supporting consultant surgeon was required to descrub and serve as proxy.

Given the use of a control proxy in this scenario, the other factors leading RV to move away from the bedside to the PACS displays relate to perceptual proxemics. This refers to how close the surgeon, RV, needs to be in order to be able to visually resolve sufficient detail in the image for the information purpose at hand. RV has to be close to the display for this particular information task. Indeed, we see further evidence of the perceptual proxemics here as RV leans closer to the display in order to resolve and distinguish between the small thumbnails. Similarly, his fingers need to be very close to the display in order to unambiguously guide the mouse control being performed by the nurse – this is a form of deixis proxemics in which gestures around the images are used in the context of talk – a feature of many image interactions in these settings. As with perceptual proxemics, the proximity for deixis depends on the granularity of information being referenced.

At the end of the action trajectory in the vignette, we see difficulties arising from the new F-formation and competing transactional requirements as RV brings the assisting surgeon FG back into the interaction. Because RV has been put in a position where the transactional segment he is immediately engaged in is facing the PACS display and away from FG and the patient, he has to raise his voice to communicate with FG. The configuration of the space and the interaction proxemics are at odds with a desired unified F-formation for this sequence.

Vignette 2 – Configuration Dynamics and Line of Sight

The concerns in this vignette relate to some spatial needs for camera-based touchless interaction: (a) the need for a clear line of sight between the tracking camera and the person interacting with the system; and (b) that sensing and gesture recognition work best at particular distances and orientations to the screen. This vignette highlights the challenges of these settings in meeting these requirements.

> Later on during the same open-cut spinal fixation, the surgeons needed to insert screws into the spinal pedicles. X-ray imaging is required to enable the surgeons to see the depth of the screws. The mobile X-ray C-arm is brought into the theatre and moved over to the patient. The radiographer positions the C-arm around the patient and moves it on command of the surgeon in order to provide a suitable picture of his work area.
>
> The C-arm mobile control and monitor trolley is also wheeled in and positioned by the radiographer. There is limited space to manoeuvre around the bed because the nurse table setup was positioned for training a new scrub nurse. This makes it awkward to position the trolley in an optimal position at the end of the bed for the surgeons to see. As such, the monitor trolley is

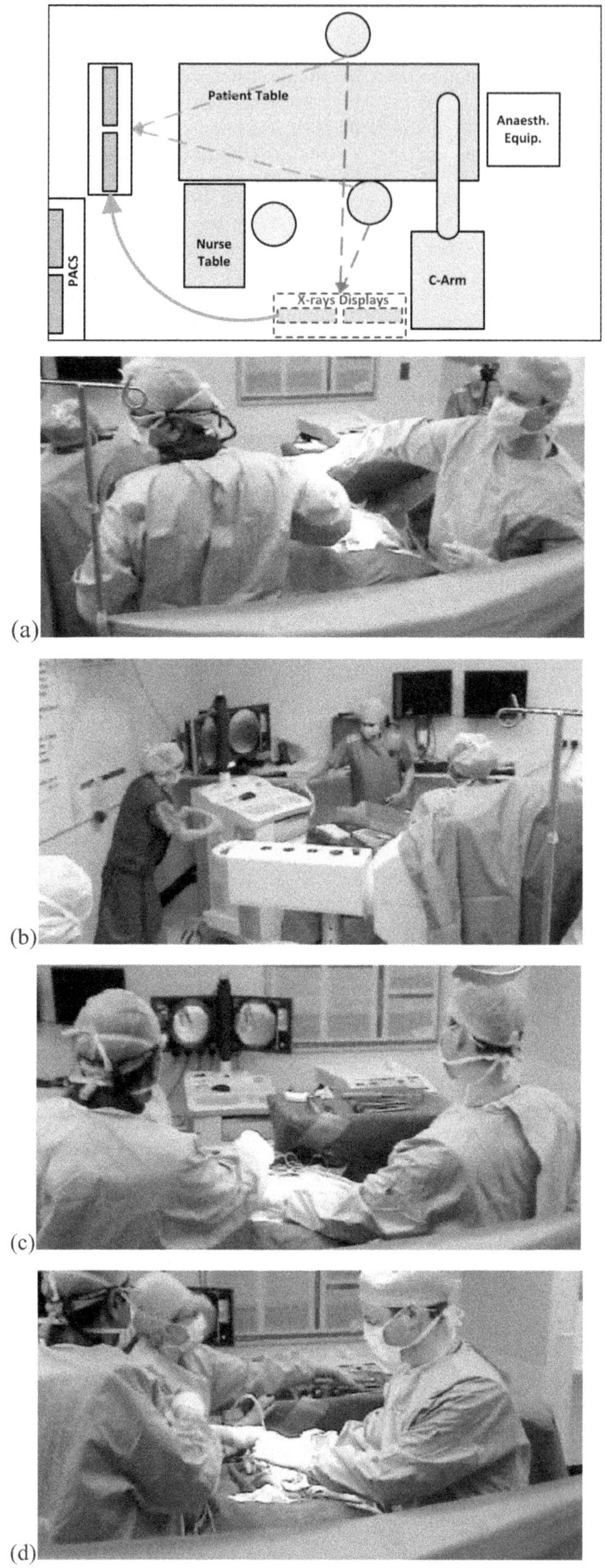

Figure 3. Vignette 2 – Configuration Dynamics and Line of Sight.

positioned just behind the C-arm and directly behind the consultant surgeon, RV.

Surgeon RV is on the left hand side of Figure 3a and FG on the right. As they are inserting the screws into the pedicles, their F-formation is organized such that they are facing each other with the patient in the o-space where their transactional segments overlap. In this position, though, RV has his back to the X-ray displays. He is also directly in line of the transactional segment from FG to the displays. When they need to check the depth of the screws, RV instructs the radiographer to initiate the X-ray – "Show me that please", which she does by pressing a button. In order to view the X-ray monitor, RV has to twist his upper torso and head even further round (Figure 3a). As he does this, he keeps his hand on the instrument inserted into the patient's spine, holding it very still for the X-ray. FG adjusts his position to the left so that he can view the screen past RV. After a few seconds of viewing the screen, they re-orient their posture and position around the patient. This sequence of adjusting the screw depth and then viewing the X-ray continues for a number of times. RV, frustrated with the arrangement, then says: "There is no way we can get that screen down there is there?" [gesturing to the foot of the patient table]. The radiographer wheels the monitor round but on reaching the corner realizes that the power cord is too short to go any further (Figure 3b). Moving it would require unplugging and rebooting the system rendering it unavailable for several minutes at a point when the surgeons are dependent upon it. So, the machine remains there while the surgeons continue. When they need to view the monitor in this position, the surgeons have to position themselves to view past the scrub nurses (Figure 3c).

The radiographer waits for an understandable break in the procedure and then addresses RV: "Can I unplug it quickly?"

RV: Why?

RG: So that I can move it and also by switching it off and on again it might…"

RV: "OK"

The machine is then unplugged and moved to the foot of the bed. The procedure continues with many more interleaved adjustments followed by review of screw depth on the X-ray monitors (Figure 3d). At various points during these sequences, the scrub nurse passes between the surgeons and the monitors to pick up or replace equipment (Figure 3e). She maintains awareness of the surgeons' direction of attention and times her actions to avoid crossing their line of sight. In the final part of the sequence, RV and FG swap sides of the patient table to enable RV to change his angle of approach.

Again, a rich set of issues is illustrated by this particular sequence. In the opening part of the sequence, we see how the initial setup creates some incompatibilities in the production of transactional segments – whereby the spatial positioning of the artefacts simultaneously pulls the bodily orientation and attention of the surgeons in two different directions. This is problematic for a number of reasons. First of all, it is difficult to maintain the F-formation with FG in which the patient is in the o-space. We can see how RV orients his torso so as to can keep his right hand present in the patient based o-space while allowing him to turn his head and view the screen. While this allows him to see the screens, it is awkward and uncomfortable, in particular because of the need to move back and forth between the different transactional segments. This illustration of the potential for bodily awkwardness with respect to imaging technologies in these settings has significance for our concerns about touchless technologies – namely that it may be difficult to assume and rely upon particular idealised skeletal poses with respect to a potential body tracking camera. Also of interest is the problematic relationship that arises between FG and the X-ray monitors. As the need to view the X-ray monitor comes into play, FG's transactional segment towards the monitor is inhabited by RV, which creates line of sight difficulties both for perception and hypothetical touchless control opportunities.

As we progress through the rest of the sequence, what we see is evidence of a continual reconfiguration of the apparatus and thereby the spatial relationship (angle, orientation, distance, etc.) between the surgeon and the imaging technologies. The dynamics of this are in part based upon the transactional requirements of these particular configurations and proxemic relationships. But significant here, is the fact that this configuration of artefacts is not always something that can be idealised for particular instances of image interaction. Rather, such configurations are often based on compromise – depending on other artefacts and pieces of equipment that may need to be accommodated as well as the constraints of everyday pragmatic realities (e.g. short cord length).

The latter part of the sequence when the monitors are moved to the foot of the patient table also highlights several interesting issues for our purposes. First, this is clearly a more comfortable F-formation for RV and FG and one that allows easier transition between the patient and display transaction segments. But what we also see in this part of the sequence is an illustration of multiple setups that make up these settings around which different team members may organise their actions at any particular time. So in Figure 3 the instrument trolley is a particular setup of significance for the scrub nurse. With this particular spatial arrangement, there is a transactional segment between the scrub nurse and the instrument trolley which intersects the transaction segment between the surgeons and the X-ray monitor. The consequence of this is that when the scrub nurse leans across to grab or replace instruments on the table, she crosses the line of sight between the surgeons and the X-ray monitors. These intersecting transactional segments interfere with both visual access to the monitors but also the hypothetical line of sight necessary for touchless interaction between a tracking camera and the surgeons.

The argument here is not a simplistic one of blocking line of sight for both perceptual and potential control purposes. People within these settings show extraordinary awareness of the transactional segments of others. We observe how the scrub nurse monitors where the surgeon is looking to try and avoid entering the transactional segment between him and the monitors when it becomes active. There are occasions where she stands back or times her movements to coincide with him turning his view away from the monitors.

Finally, we see at the end of the sequence that the consultant surgeon and his registrar swap sides. At times during the operation the consultant may defer to his registrar in choosing which side of the table he is most comfortable working, but during complicated procedures the consultant may take over the procedure. As we see here this involves changing positions to get a better approach angle (here it is to insert a screw in a pedicle). This changes the spatial relationship of the surgeons to the display.

Vignette 3 – Interference and Intersecting Segments

In the final vignette, we consider the concurrent use of multiple imaging displays for cross-referencing images.

> A tumour excision at the top of the spine is being performed on a 45 year-old female through an endonasal approach. Two consultant surgeons are performing the surgery (two figures on the left of Figure 4) while a medical student and registrar look on. In the centre is the display for the StealthCam. The display on the right is the endoscopic display. On the wall to the left of the image is the PACS display. Attention is primarily on the endoscopic display as it is the "eyes" for the surgeon. At various points during the procedure the surgeon will ask "Can you Stealth there?"). A footpedal is then used to initiate the StealthCam tracking usually by the other surgeon. The surgeons turn their focus to the stealth screen to see where the probe is located in the patient's anatomy. They then may look at the PACS display to resolve their current location with their intended approach. Then they turn their attention back to the endoscopic display. This back and forth across the displays continues accompanied by some discussion until they agree where they are and what the appropriate course of action is. They then continue with the procedure.

This sequence of action is fairly typical during such procedures. The surgeons need to understand very precisely where they are. The endoscope image gives them some idea of anatomical features, but this needs to be cross-referenced with the image from the stealth machine as well as what the registrar is feeling with the instruments inside the body. In bringing this information together, they move their attention from one imaging display to the other and to each other as they visualize and discuss the combined image sources. Important here is that the various imaging displays are arranged close together and at complementary orientations to allow fluid movement of attention back and forth. In this respect, the two surgeons and the two key displays are configured in an F-formation where an o-space is formed in the centre where the transaction segments of the surgeons and the three displays and patient body overlap.

DISCUSSION

While in recent years, there has been growing interest in touchless interaction for medical settings, the primary motivation for this has been out of concern for asepsis. In

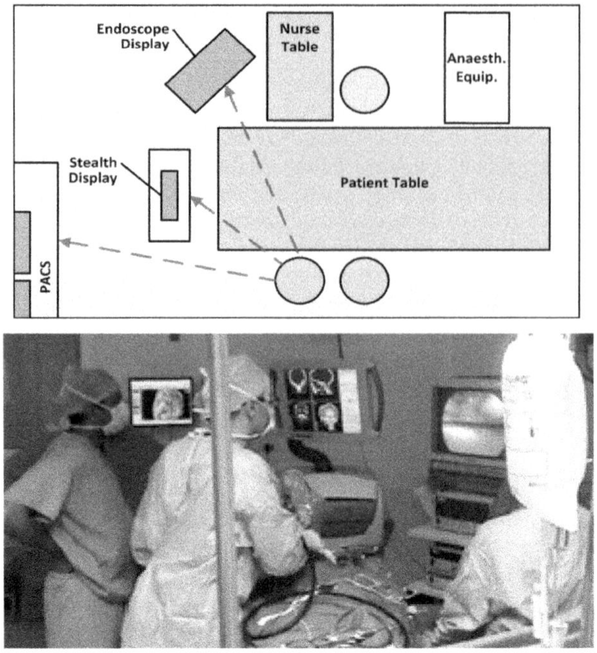

Figure 4. Vignette 3 – Interference and Intersecting Segments.

this respect, touchless interaction technologies are conceived in terms of their avoidance of contact and the transfer of contaminated materials. Our aim here, though, has been to think of touchlessness in terms of its spatial properties. That is, and in contrast to touch-based interaction, touchless interaction spatial separation between the actor and interactive device. What, then, does this spatial separation imply for the introduction of computer vision-based touchless control of imaging devices in medical settings?

To help answer this, our fieldwork and analysis have drawn upon various theoretical constructs relating to the configuration and use of space. In particular, we have used notions of interaction proxemics and the theory of F-formations to understand how trajectories of collaborative action are organized spatially with respect to the configuration of artefacts in these surgical settings. Such analysis can help uncover both opportunities where touchless input might enhance and enable new kinds of interaction during surgery, but also highlight challenges in designing and installing such systems. Thus, our approach is one that informs and enables design thinking. Although the enactment of the interaction proxemics we have uncovered will, by necessity, change with the introduction of new technologies, the need for control, deixis, and perceptual proxemics are the important concerns that will remain consistent across current and future practices. In other words, the enactment of an interaction – e.g., pointing *closely* at an area on the screen for fine-grained deixis – will change with the advent of a technology supportive of physical separation; however, the need for fine-grained deixis will still need to be supported in a distanced manner.

From the perspective of touchless interaction, several important implications arise from the issues highlighted in this vignette. Some of these suggest significant benefits in introducing touchless interaction. However, in enabling such transformations it is important to consider how interaction proxemics such as control, deixis, and perception, may require additional design solutions in order to continue to be supported.

Control Proxemics

First of all, because touchless interaction allows interaction from a distance, it potentially allows the surgeons to control images from the bedside, bringing together the transactional segments with the patient body, the registrar, and the imaging display. That is, touchless interaction here can enable transformative reconfigurations of the space to enable access to information where needed. As we saw in Vignette 1, the surgeon had to make the judgement to invite someone to control on his behalf so as to maintain sterility. Although, the benefit of introducing touchless interaction is to reduce the need for such handoffs of control, there may still be times when a surgeon cannot remove his hands from the patient and instruments and must request for another to be a control proxy. Thus, creating an o-space leaves those not a vital part of that interactive system on the outside of the ring, such as the radiographer in Vignette 2. Yet, they are still part of the system of interaction such as cueing the X-ray to create another image. In other words, the person controlling the system may not be the person who needs to view the information and, thus, may not be in the o-space. This brings to light the possibility of implementing multiple control spaces, which in turns bring up the additional challenge of negotiating the handing over of control.

Deixis Proxemics

Touchless technology can potentially also allow members of the surgical team to point to images at a distance resulting in a visual indication on the display for reference during communication. Again in Vignette 1, we saw the surgeon move his finger very close to the display in order to unambiguously guide the mouse control being performed by the nurse. What is important to note is that this form of deixis proxemics depends on the granularity of information being referenced. In other words, granularity of information being referenced influences how fine of a referencing pointer is required. Thus, since the action of referencing is not subsumed in the action of closely approaching the area of information, how can a system support fine versus course grained referencing from afar? One solution would be to create different modes that allow the user to switch between fine and course grained deixis indication on the screen. Another option is to segment particular sections of the interface to always display a fine grained deixis indication whereas other sections are designated as suitable for course grained deixis indication.

Perceptual Proxemics

Touchless control might also mean that images could be moved to different displays to enable a better and more flexible line of sight or to enlarge images to support seeing at a distance. This would elegantly solve issues as described in Vignette 1 when the surgeon had to move away from the bedside to the PACS displays in order to be able to visually resolve sufficient detail in the image. It is important to consider that finer grained information needs to be closer or needs the ability for enlargement. In addition, larger screens that can be seen from a distance as well as orientation mobility for reconfigurations both before and during the surgery would be appropriate.

The issues of interference of view demonstrated in Vignette 2, would likely also arise if the transactional segments of the surgeon were to be created by touchless interaction with the imaging displays. The sensitivities to these intersecting transactional segments, though, create constraints on action and add a coordination burden. This is potentially exacerbated in certain touchless interaction scenarios because such interference is perhaps less easy to determine and therefore accommodate. This means, that one strategy for design is to prevent or mitigate significant repercussions if interference does occur during touchless interaction.

In addition to the perceptual needs and spatial consequences of the surgeon, the sensor or sensors used for camera-based touchless interaction are also sensitive to issues of perceptual proxemics. For instance, in Vignette 2, the surgeons swap sides in order for the consultant surgeon to attain a better approach angle. In situations such as these, there is the challenge of supporting the reconfiguration of the interaction space by the touchless interaction system.

Furthermore, the use of multiple discrete displays and constructed F-formation with these displays is a typical feature of surgery. This multi display scenario potentially entails multiple pieces of gesture tracking equipment. This raises potential technical concerns, in particular if such tracking equipment is based on IR depth perception techniques. It is also a concern for interaction interference arising from intersecting transaction segments forming the o-space. It is within this o-space that touchless interaction gestures will be performed. The potential difficulty here is that gesturing in front of one display entails concurrent gesturing in front of the other display in the F-formation – this may lead to inadvertent triggering of interactions on one display while trying to interact with the other.

CONCLUSION

Our intention was to raise a set of design considerations on which to reflect in the development and deployment of touchless systems. In our treatment of design implications have been driven by consideration of the typical kinds of camera-based setups that are in the various demonstration applications that appear in the literature and on the Web for surgical settings. In discussing the implications, our aim was not to preclude other design possibilities in the space nor is it to be overly prescriptive. Alternative ideas, such as multiple cameras, are the kind of solutions we hope our findings would provoke. What we hope to have shown is how such reflections and considerations can be revealed through careful analysis of the spatial organization of activity and proxemics of particular interaction mechanisms. However, it is a delicate matter to study current practice in order to speculate about how new systems might fit, because they in turn alter practice.

REFERENCES

1. Bardram, J. & Bossen, C. (2005). Mobility Work: The Spatial Dimension of Collaboration at a Hospital. *JCSCW, 14*(2).
2. Barre, de la, R., Chojecki, P., Leiner, U., Muhlbacj, L. & Ruschin, D. (2009) Touchless Interaction: 2Novel Cases and Challenges. *Proceedingss of HCI '09*.
3. Buxton, W. (2009) Mediaspace – Meaningspace – Meetingspace. In Harrison, S. (Ed) *Media Space: 20+ Years of Mediated Life,* Springer, London, 217-231.
4. Cassell, J. (1987). On Control, Certitude, and the "Paranoia" of Surgeons. *Culture, Medicine and Psychiatry, 11*, 229-49.
5. Dourish, P. (2006) Re-Space-ing Place: Place and Space Ten Years On. *Proceedings of CSCW 2006*. 299-308.
6. Fischer, T. & Hornecker, E. (2012). Urban HCI: Spatial Aspects in the Design of Shared Encounters for Media Façades. *Proceedings of CHI 2012*, Austin, Texas.
7. Fitzpatrick, G. (2003) *The Locales Framework: Understanding and Designing for Wicked Problems*. Kluwer Academic Publishers.
8. Fox, N. (1992) *The Social Meaning of Surgery.* Buckingham: Open University Press.
9. Goffman, E. (1961). *Encounters: Two Studies in the Sociology of Interaction*. Harmondsworth: Penguin.
10. Goodwin, C. (1994). Professional Vision. *American Anthropologist, 96(3),* p606-633.
11. Graetzel, C., Fong, T., Grange, S., Baur, C., (2004) A Non-Contact Mouse for Surgeon-Computer Interaction, Technology and Health Care 12, IOS Press.
12. Greenberg, S., Marquardt, N., Ballendat, T., Diaz-Marino, R., & Wang, M. (2011, January/February). Proxemic interactions: The new ubicomp? *Interactions, 18*(1), 42-50.
13. Hall, E.T. (1966). *The Hidden Dimension.* Garden City, NY: Doubleday.
14. Harrison, S. & Dourish, P. (1996). Re-Place-ing Space: The Roles of Place and Space in Collaborative Systems. *Proceedings of CSCW*, (p. 67-76).
15. Hillier, B. (1996). *Space is the machine.* Cambridge: Cambridge University Press.
16. Hindmarsh, J. & Pilnick, A. (2002). The Tacit Order of Teamwork: Collaboration and Embodied Conduct in Anesthesia. *The Sociological Quarterly, 43*(2).
17. Hirschauer, S. (1991). The Manufacture of Bodies in Surgery. *Social Studies of Science, 21(2)*, 279-319.
18. Hornecker, E. and Buur, J. (2006) Getting a grip on tangible interaction: A framework on physical space and social interaction. *Proceedings of CHI 2006.*
19. Johnson, R., O'Hara, K., Sellen, A., Cousins, C., & Criminisi A. (2011). Exploring the potential for touchless interaction in image-guided interventional radiology. *Proceedings of CHI 2011*, Vancouver, Canada.
20. Ju, W., Lee, B.A., & Klemmer, S. (2008). Range: Exploring implicit interaction through electronic whiteboard design. *Proceedings of CSCW*, San Diego, California, (pp. 17-26).
21. Katz, P. (1981). Ritual in the Operating Room. *Ethnology, 20*, 335-50.
22. Kendon, A. (1990). Spatial Organization in Social Encounters: the F-formation System. In A. Kendon (Ed) *Conducting Interaction: Patterns of Behavior in Focused Encounters*, Cambridge University Press.
23. Kendon, A. (2010) Spacing and Orientation in Co-present Interaction. *Proceedings of COST 2102 Training School*, Springer Heidelberg, 1 - 15.
24. Marshall, P., et al. (2011). Using F-formations to Analyse Spatial Patterns of Interaction in Physical Environments. *Proc. of CSCW'11*, ACM, 445 - 454.
25. Morrison, C., Jones, M., Blackwell, A. and Vuylsteke, A. (2008) Electronic patient record use during ward rounds: a qualitative study of interaction between medical staff. *Critical Care 12.*
26. O'Hara, K., Perry, M., Churchill, E., Russell, D. (Eds) *Public and Situated Displays: Social and Interactional aspects of Shared Display Technologies*. London: Kluwer Academic Publishers.
27. O'Hara, K., Kjeldskov, J. & Paay, J. (2011) Blended Interaction Spaces. *ACM TOCHI, 18*(1).
28. Prante, T., Röcker, C., Streitz, N., Stenzel, R., Magerkurth, C., van Alphen, D., & Plewe, D. (2003). Hello.Wall – Beyond ambient displays. *Adjunct Proceedings of UBICOMP '03*, Seattle, WA.
29. Strauss, A., S. Fagerhaugh, B. Suczek & C. Wiener (1985). *Social Organization of Medical Work.* Chicago & London: University of Chicago Press.
30. Wachs, J., Stern, H., Edan, Y., Gillam, M., Feied, C., Smith, M., & Handler, J. (2006). A Real-Time Hand Gesture Interface for Medical Visualization Applications. *Applications of Soft Computing.*
31. Wilson, R. N. (1958). Team Work in the Operating Room. *Human Organization, 12*(4), 9-14.

What Should We Expect From Research Through Design?

William Gaver
Interaction Research Studio
Goldsmiths, University of London
w.gaver@gold.ac.uk

ABSTRACT
In this essay, I explore several facets of research through design in order to contribute to discussions about how the approach should develop. The essay has three parts. In the first, I review two influential theories from the Philosophy of Science to help reflect on the nature of design theory, concluding that research through design is likely to produce theories that are provisional, contingent, and aspirational. In the second part, I discuss three possible interpretations for the diversity of approaches to research through design, and suggest that this variation need not be seen as a sign of inadequate standards or a lack of cumulative progress in the field, but may be natural for a generative endeavour. In the final section, I suggest that, rather than aiming to develop increasingly comprehensive theories of design, practice based research might better view theory as annotation of realised design examples, and particularly portfolios of related pieces. Overall, I suggest that the design research community should be wary of impulses towards convergence and standardisation, and instead take pride in its aptitude for exploring and speculating, particularising and diversifying, and - especially - its ability to manifest the results in the form of new, conceptually rich artefacts.

Author Keywords
research through design; theory; annotation; portfolios; philosophy of science

ACM Classification Keywords
H.5.m [Information interfaces and presentation]: Miscellaneous - Design;

INTRODUCTION
Over the last number of years, design practitioners have become increasingly integrated within the HCI research community. Their work often takes the form of *research through design* [4, 11, 34], in which design practice is brought to bear on situations chosen for their topical and theoretical potential, the resulting designs are seen as embodying designers' judgments about valid ways to address the possibilities and problems implicit in such situations, and reflection on these results allow a range of topical, procedural, pragmatic and conceptual insights to be articulated. The output of this work takes the form, primarily, of artefacts and systems, sometimes with associated accounts of how these are used in field tests, but increasingly includes a variety of methods, conceptual frameworks and theories presented separately from accounts of practice.

As design practice has become more prevalent in CHI, however, there has also grown an undercurrent of questioning within the design community itself about the nature and standards of research through design [9, 31, 33, 35]. These discussions revolve around the desirability of 'integrating design research methods, approaches, and outcomes in HCI' [9] both as a way of consolidating knowledge and to establish criteria for research done from this perspective. This agenda calls for the development of agreed methodological standards, hand in hand with a firm theoretical foundation. Research through design, it is said, 'lacks clear expectations and standards for what constitutes "good" design research', and thus would benefit from 'some actionable metrics for bringing rigor in critique of design research' ([9] p824). The community should 'develop protocols, descriptions, and guidelines for its processes, procedures, and activities' in ways assumed to be 'like any other research approach' ([35] p317). In part, this depends on developing research through design as 'a proper research methodology that can produce relevant and rigorous theory' ([35] p316). Conceptual contributions, from this perspective, should exhibit 'a level of extensibility and verifiability' if they are to comprise 'theory designers can apply in research in practice' [33].

As a long-term practitioner of research through design, I have some sympathy with these concerns. Nonetheless, I am uneasy about some of the tendencies that seem to underlie both the diagnoses and the treatments that have been suggested. Seeking conformance to agreed-upon standards and processes may be a route towards disciplinary legitimacy within HCI, helping clarify expectations for research through design both within and outside the design community. There is a risk, however, that such standards might lead to a form of self-policing that would be overly restrictive of a form of research that I

Permission to make digital or hard copies of all or part of this work for personal or classroom use is granted without fee provided that copies are not made or distributed for profit or commercial advantage and that copies bear this notice and the full citation on the first page. To copy otherwise, or republish, to post on servers or to redistribute to lists, requires prior specific permission and/or a fee.
CHI'12, May 5–10, 2012, Austin, Texas, USA.
Copyright 2012 ACM 978-1-4503-1015-4/12/05...$10.00.

value for its ability to continually and creatively challenge status quo thinking. Moreover, insofar as HCI is prone to 'scientism' in its cultural assumptions (despite moves to legitimise other forms of research based, for instance, on the humanities [2], or to characterize it as a design discipline [7]), attempts to establish standards for research through design may adopt, or be interpreted in terms of, inappropriate 'scientific' models of research and theory for the field.

In this essay, my intention is to temper calls for disciplinary consolidation with remarks on what we might reasonably expect from research through design. First, I explore the kinds of theory that have been developed in association with design using two accounts of scientific theory drawn from the Philosophy of Science. Contrasting accounts are chosen to complicate notions of what makes theories 'scientific', in order to undermine any overly simple assumptions about how research should proceed, and to draw out fundamental features of the conceptual work that accompanies research through design. This comparison suggests that, instead of being extensible and verifiable, theory produced by research through design tends to be provisional, contingent and aspirational. Second, calls for standards, formalisation, protocols and guidelines assume that disciplinary convergence is a prerequisite for cumulative growth of understanding in design. I explore three perspectives on the lack of convergence in research through design, and suggest that, while one of these perspectives implies that the community should work towards greater shared understandings, the other two imply either that there is no problem to solve or that progress in this area will be marked by proliferation rather than agreement. Third, an emphasis on agreed-upon theories and methods seems to assume that these are the hallmark of a respectable research discipline, and that the production of an endless stream of design examples is an inadequate basis for its pursuit. I argue on the contrary that an endless string of design examples is precisely at the core of how design research should operate, and that the role of theory should be to annotate those examples rather than replace them.

THEORY IN RESEARCH THROUGH DESIGN

Conceptual work appears in many forms as a routine part of research through design work. Whenever practitioners describe their influences, discuss the rationales for design decisions, and articulate their assessment of what they have made and its importance, they engage in a form of implicit conceptual work by highlighting important issues, dimensions of similarity, and criteria for choices and success. To the extent these conceptual statements are articulated in general terms and applied to multiple examples, they become recognisable as theories in their own right. For instance, Djajadiningrat and his colleagues [6] develop a rich account of the importance of embodied movement that is substantially informed from reflections about a series of designs they and their students have produced. They start from a conceptual perspective that values bodily movement, but it is through consideration of the designs their students have made that they elaborate this theory.

Design researchers often 'borrow' conceptual perspectives from other disciplines and discuss their applicability for design. Examples that are widespread in the design community include notions of affordances, context and situatedness [27] (cited in [31]). Borrowed theories (or concepts) are often used both to inspire new designs and to articulate existing ones. In doing so, the perspectives are usually translated for use by designers. For instance, when Wiltse and Stolterman [32] suggest that interaction design should draw on the sensibilities of architecture, they do not refer to physical spaces but rather the social spaces opened by computational media. Translation can ultimately give rise to new concepts. For instance, Overbeeke and Wensveen [23] describe how they originally drew inspiration from Gibson's ecological psychology (e.g. [15]), and particularly the notion of affordances, but adapted this to focus on emotional appeal under the new name of 'irresistables'.

Manifestos are a third form of theory often produced as a part of research through design practice. These go beyond theoretical treatments drawn from other disciplines or developed from reflection on practice to suggest certain approaches to design as both as desirable and productive of future practice [13, 14, 16, 30, 36]. For example, in introducing their notion of 'Reflective Design', Sengers and her colleagues [30] suggest that 'reflection on unconscious values embedded in computing and the practices that it supports can and should be a core principle of technology design'. Similarly, Gaver advocated a ludic approach to design as 'an antidote to assumptions that technology should provide clear, efficient solutions to practical problems' [13]. Typically, such manifestos will describe design practice to illustrate their approach, and borrow theories to justify it, but their primary function is to build an account of a practice to be pursued in the future.

Frameworks for design play a similar role to manifestos, but tend to downplay both their theoretical commitments and normative stance. For example, Forlizzi's Product Ecology [10] outlines a number of factors involved in designing for products to be used together and suggests methods to approach each stage. The framework is intended to allow 'flexible, design-centred research planning and opportunity seeking', and avoids prescribing appropriate methods. In characterising a class of design situations as it does, however, and in its ontology for describing the factors involved, the framework nevertheless implies a conceptual orientation, and can be considered a form of theoretical output from research through design.

A final genre of theory from research through design seeks to characterise research through design itself, and often to suggest normative standards for how research through design should be conducted, what should 'count' as research through design, and the appropriate standards for work done in this way. For instance, Zimmerman & Forlizzi [34] argue that the HCI community will more easily accept contributions from research through design if it has an 'agreed upon form of practice, evaluation, and outcome' and suggest this should come through the development of 'extensible, systemic approaches' to theory development. Stolterman [31], in contrast, highlights the tendency for design to produce *ultimate particulars*, and suggests this poses problems for developing generalisable theories. Although these sorts of treatments can be considered as wide-ranging manifestos, this essay – which itself is intended as a contribution to meta-theory – addresses the more specific, content-oriented theories described earlier.

Arguably, designers in the HCI community have produced an ample amount of conceptual work arising from articulations of practice, borrowed ideas, manifestos and frameworks. But how good is this conceptual work? Should we be proud of the corpus of conceptualisations that have grown, or is there something inadequate about our achievements? To explore these questions, I compare the theories produced by research through design with several influential accounts of scientific theory.

SCIENTIFIC AND DESIGN THEORIES

In this section, I describe two contrasting accounts from the Philosophy of Science, primarily to shed light on the characteristics of research through design, but also to problematise the (potentially tacit) accounts of science that seem to underlie some views of research. Although other accounts of theory, for instance from the humanities, can also shed valuable light on design [2], there are several reasons why accounts of scientific theory are a useful foil against which to consider the conceptual work produced as a result of design practice. First, fields such as the Philosophy of Science and Science and Technology Studies (STS) offer sophisticated and well-developed discussions of the nature of theory and how it operates within a scientific context (see [5] for a valuable overview) which may serve as a fertile source of insight about theory in any field. In addition, one of the fundamental issues addressed within the Philosophy of Science concerns how to distinguish scientific fields from non-scientific ones (occasioned, for example, by arguments about evolution v. 'creation science'). These discussions highlight a number of issues that can be useful in considering the nature of design as a research endeavour, and the likely characteristics of theory likely to appear as a result of that endeavour.

Falsifiability

One influential account of science holds that '*the criterion of the scientific status of a theory is its falsifiability, or refutability, or testability*' [24] (emphasis in the original). Popper proposed this criterion as a corrective to notions that scientific theories are primarily produced by induction, and thus are more powerful the more phenomena they agree with. As he notes, 'It is easy to obtain confirmations, or verifications, for nearly every theory—if we look for confirmations' ([24] p 7). But an endless number of confirmations cannot *prove* a theory. In fact, according to Popper the probability that a particular theory is correct is zero no matter how much positive evidence is amassed (see [5] p. 70). In contrast, Popper suggests, a single incompatible result can *disprove* a theory. Feynman [8] makes a similar point in describing the search for a new physical law:

> First we guess it. Then we compute the consequences of the guess to see what would be implied if this law that we guessed is right. Then we compare the result of the computation to nature, with experiment or experience, compare it directly with observation, to see if it works. If it disagrees with experiment it is wrong. In that simple statement is the key to science. [8] p. 156

From this perspective, the scientific process creates a kind of artificial evolution of theories: by eliminating weaker theories, only the strongest survive. Popper's point is that, for this to work, theories must be falsifiable in principle: "irrefutability is not a virtue of a theory (as people often think) but a vice' ([24], p. 7).

Scientific Research Programmes

Popper's emphasis on falsifiability, though influential in popular accounts of scientific reasoning, has been widely criticised as an inaccurate description of scientific practice. According to Kuhn [17], for example, 'normal science' involves 'puzzle-solving', in which researchers apply accepted theories to known problems or new domains. In normal circumstances, 'failure to solve a problem... is considered the fault of the scientist using the theory, not the fault of the theory itself' ([17] p 67).

Moreover, the idea that scientific theories are rejected when evidence contradicts them is historically inaccurate. Even new theories may not accord with data. Newton, for example, admitted when he published his gravitational theory that it could not account for the moon's orbit [3]. Feynman [8] describes how a new theory can win out over established evidence in recounting how the equations for 'weak decay' were established, in a passage striking for its inconsistency with his previous account:

> ...only the equation was guessed. The special difficulty this time was that the experiments were all wrong. How can you guess the right answer if, when you calculate the result, it disagrees with experiment? You need courage to say the experiments must be wrong. [8] p. 163.

How can scientists find the courage to champion theories over evidence? Lakatos [19] proposes an alternative account of scientific activity that emphasises *scientific research programmes* rather than individual theories. Programmes, according to his account, are characterised by a 'hard core' of theory, surrounded by a 'protective belt' of auxiliary hypotheses, and a 'powerful problem-solving mechanism' used to generate evidence and make it compatible with theory. In Lakatos' description, using these components a research programme 'digests anomolies and even turns them into positive evidence' ([19] p. 24). Programmes can change and evolve to adapt to new evidence, not by altering the 'hard core' of theory, but the 'protective belt' that surrounds it. For example, when Uranus was discovered not to move as predicted by Newtonian theory, rather than rejecting the theory, scientists predicted the discovery of the planet Neptune [5].

The ability for contradictory evidence to be turned into novel discoveries by research programmes is key to Lakatos' account. For him, research programmes do not succeed because they are unchallenged by disconfirming evidence. Instead, he writes:

> ...all the research programmes I admire have one characteristic in common. They all predict novel facts, facts which had been either undreamt of, or have indeed been contradicted by previous or rival programmes. ([19] p. 24).

Lakatos' account of scientific research programmes paints a very different picture of science from the Popperian one: instead of stressing scientific activity as a matter of trying to discredit theories, it emphasises scientific research as a dynamic machine for generating new knowledge, new understandings and new discoveries.

Why Design Theory is Unfalsifiable

Research through design is clearly unscientific if Popper's [24] criterion of falsifiablity is accepted. Theories are too vague, and practice is usually intended to confirm theories, not falsify them. To be sure, Popper's account is widely criticised both in Philosophy of Science and by practicing scientists. Still, it holds a potentially unflattering mirror up to the theories produced as a part of research through design. If confirmation cannot be used as proof, how do we validate them? Rather than seeing difficulties in validation as a problem for design theory, I would suggest this reveals two important characteristics of the conceptual work produced in association with research through design.

Theory Underspecifies Design

Design often addresses *wicked problems* [26] which are complex enough that no correct solutions exist *a priori* and for which formulating the situation is integral to addressing it. Moreover, design is an activity that involves many different decisions, dealing with many different and potentially independent factors of an artefact, all situated within the specific circumstances of production and use (c.f. [7]. Finally, is *productive* in the sense that it changes the context of its own activities [21]. In short, theory by necessity under-specifies design activities.

The implication of this underspecification is that the theories produced by research through design are not falsifiable in principle. Whether they build on borrowed theory or observation of the world or of specific design examples, such theories take the form *designing for X can lead to successful outcomes*, where X may be 'the self' [36], 'homo ludens' [13], 'suppleness' [16], or 'simultaneous analogue control of multiple parameters' [6]. The problem is, the argument is not that X will *always* lead to successful designs (however success is evaluated), which would clearly be open to refutation. How could it be? There are too many other factors involved in a design project to make that kind of guarantee. Instead, there is always an implicit *sometimes* in statements about how to design successfully, to reflect the myriad of factors that remain untheorised yet crucial to a project's success. Assertions that X will *sometimes* lead to successful outcomes, however, are unfalsifiable, because no number of unsuccessful design efforts would actually disprove the assertion—after all, the next attempt might be successful.

Underspecification makes falsification difficult in practice as well as in principle. Even where potentially falsifiable assertions are offered, tests which are simultaneously unambiguous and ecologically valid are inconceivable. Consider, for example, a key claim made in a paper arguing for the benefits of ambiguity in design:

> By impelling people to interpret situations for themselves, [ambiguity] encourages them to start grappling conceptually with systems and their contexts, and thus to establish deeper and more personal relations with the meanings offered by those systems. [14].

Although this is in principle a falsifiable statement, testing it in the Popperian sense would mean arranging a comparison in which no difference in conceptual grappling, or the depth and intimacy of personal relations to meaning, could be established between comparable ambiguous and unambiguous systems. The problem is in determining how to construct such a systems to be 'comparable'. Simply tweaking an unambiguous system to be ambiguous might address the assertion in a narrow sense, but it would be unrepresentative of the ways designers harness untheorised factors of a design to support its intended effects. In other words, the synthetic nature of design is incompatible with the controlled experiments useful for theory testing.

Design Is Generative

What I am arguing is that if designers were to change their practices to design for comparison or refutation, they would no longer be doing research through design. The notion of making falsifiable statements, or of arranging tests to refute such statements, runs against the grain of the methodological approach of research through design. Design, and research through design, is *generative*. Rather than making statements about *what is*, design is concerned with creating *what might be*, and moreover, in Zimmerman et al.'s [34] formulation, on making the *'right thing'*.

The issue for designers is not to show that design theory can sometimes lead to bad designs. On the contrary, their concern is to sometimes create good ones. Similarly, the goal of conceptual work in research through design is not to develop theories that are never wrong, it is to create theories that are *sometimes right*. As Stolterman [31] puts it, 'designers can be *prepared-for-action* but not *guided-in-action* by detailed prescriptive procedures' (p 61). The generative nature of design has deeper implications for research through design, as I will argue later. For now, it is enough to note that, from Popper's perspective, one of the features that distinguishes design from science is its tendency to make generative statements rather than falsifiable ones.

Lakatos' characterisation of scientific research programmes, in contrast, paints a picture of theory seems more compatible with the nature of research through design. From this perspective, it is of little matter that conceptual approaches such as 'Reflective Design' [30] or 'Supple Interfaces' [16] or 'Designing for the Self' [36] are not falsifiable. Instead, what is at stake is their ability to inspire new designs. It is understandable why so many design manifestos, or examples of borrowed theory, are accompanied by examples of realised designs. What Popper would reject as 'merely' confirmatory evidence is, from this point of view, testimony to the fertility of the overarching theory. The difficulty of verifying design theory, at least through falsification, is not a flaw for research through design, as long as that theory can lead to productive research programmes.

Theory from Research Through Design

To be clear, I am not presenting Popper's and Lakatos' accounts as particularly representative of Philosophy of Science. In fact, by extracting these accounts from that complex and dynamic field, I wish in part to illustrate how unsettled and controversial accounts of science are. This lack of resolution, I would suggest, undermines attempts to characterise research through design (or design in general) either as a science or as a non-science. Personally, I tend to think that the nature of design practice and research is distinct from the ideals, and often practice, of science – but in the end, whether research through design can be considered a science depends on the account of science one adopts. Similarly, taking seriously the disagreements about the nature of science subverts any easy scientism in HCI more generally, because it destabilises the use of 'science' as shorthand for a set of practices and criteria assumed to be desirable. It is difficult to call for research to be more scientific if what it means to be scientific is under question (see [29]).

Instead, what this discussion suggests is the desirability of clearly articulating the methodological and conceptual features of current research through design practice, as well as the standards one might want to advocate for them. Here I have suggested that the theory produced from design practice tends to underspecify practice and to be generative in nature, and thus that it is provisional, contingent, and aspirational. These are all features that limit the potential 'extensibility and verifiability' of design theory, seen by some as possible and desirable. Instead, as I discuss in the remainder of this paper, research through design should be appreciated for its proliferation of new realities, and its theory considered as annotation of the artefacts that are its fundamental achievement.

CONVERGENCE IN RESEARCH THROUGH DESIGN

Calls for disciplinary reform in research through design appeal for more agreement about the 'methods, approaches, and outcomes' in the field. Greater integration would make assessment of new contributions fairer and more rigorous. Moreover, if we could all agree about the proper approaches, methods and outcomes to use, we could build upon one another's research in a cumulative fashion. Currently, however, there must be dozens of different 'manifestos' for design, each seeking to establish a research programme, and each with its own configuration of goals, issues, methods and realised exemplars. Why is there not more convergence in the field?

Convergence in the natural sciences is a given. Lakatos' research programmes, for example, describe scientific research in terms of historical movements in which researchers share a common set of practices and understandings. A similar description is developed by Kuhn [17] in his seminal account of 'scientific revolutions'. According to Kuhn, the reason 'normal science' can proceed is because researchers share a common *paradigm*, which, in Kuhn's usage, sometimes means an exemplar of successful research, and sometimes a set of common understandings about how to describe relevant phenomena, relevant issues, acceptable methodologies and outputs. Both accounts describe scientific research as convergent.

Even more striking, however, Lakatos' and Kuhn's accounts both suggest that, as a normal state of affairs, only *one* programme or paradigm will dominate a particular scientific field at any one time. Aristotelian physics gives way to Newtonian physics, which gives way in its turn to Relativity. For Kuhn, paradigm shifts occur when tension grows about a given paradigm's inability to resolve anomalies, a new possible view arises which solves those anomalies (or makes them irrelevant) and scientists choose to join the new paradigm. Because paradigms involve different 'world views', including ontologies, philosophies, methodologies, etc., choosing between two candidates cannot be done on rational grounds, according to Kuhn. Lakatos objects to this, suggesting the relative productivity of competing programmes as the grounds for scientists' choice amongst them. Both agree, however, that multiple programmes, or paradigms, cannot co-exist over time.

Why do multiple research programmes coexist in design? In the following sections I explore three possibilities.

Design as Pre-paradigmatic Research

According to Kuhn [17], the beginning of a scientific study of a given field comes with the widespread adoption of a single paradigm for its study. Until that time, research is characterised by competition amongst a number of different schools of thought, usually drawing on different philosophical foundations and orienting towards the field in different ways. Valuable contributions may be made by disparate approaches, but without shared assumptions about the correct way to approach a field, individual researchers must establish the rationale behind their approach from the very basics every time they seek to make a contribution. Because there are no agreed standards of importance, there is little sense of priority or order to the findings that are amassed. Progress is slow and in Kuhn's view does not really add up to a science.

When a particularly influential body of research is finally established, usually in the form of a theory that ties together multiple troublesome phenomena and suggests new paths for research, everything changes. Researchers no longer need to justify the basics of their research, but can concentrate on increasingly detailed and exacting contributions. They become more confident about devoting resources on studies which are difficult and time-consuming, since they know they will be understood and valued by their fellow researchers. In general, working together on the issues suggested by a given paradigm, and using methods and techniques suggested by it, allows science to make significant progress. Pre-paradigmatic research, in contrast, must founder.

It is clearly possible to recognise the current state of research through design in this description of affairs. There is a proliferation of research programmes, and little agreement about the values for which we should design, the appropriate methods for doing so, standards for evaluation or agreed forms of output. Methods and techniques proliferate, and when they are taken up by others it is often without their underlying methodological orientation. Even what it means to undertake research as a form of design is subject to disagreement, with some suggesting that design projects should be constructed, in part, to explicitly test and produce theory [33, 35], while others (including myself) believe that theory should be allowed to emerge from situated design practice.

From this perspective, research through design lacks a shared paradigm. Without it, we cannot join forces around agreed issues, or find common standards for work we agree is solid enough to build upon: research through design cannot make progress. This is a tempting conclusion, one seemingly behind recent calls for formalism and standardisation [9, 35]. Two other accounts, however, may also explain the seeming disunity of research through design when compared to research in the natural sciences.

The Invisibility of Consensus

One alternative account to that of the supposed pre-paradigmatic nature of research through design would suggest that the balance of agreement and controversy is not so different in research through design than it is in many fields of scientific research. This interpretation hinges on the observation that consensus is usually easier to see from a distance than it is to experience from within. After all, as Kuhn [17] suggests, researchers do not need continually to restate the agreed fundamentals of their field. Instead their discourse tends to focus on controversies and debates around new findings and unresolved anomalies. From this perspective, scientific discourse may be characterised by far more controversy than is implied by Kuhn's account of normal, paradigm-driven research, and there may be more of a shared sense of understanding guiding research through design, than sometimes seems apparent.

If the natural sciences appear unified to an extraordinary degree, able to build upon a solid foundation of agreed knowledge, this may be a function of their presentation in the popular media, particularly with the advantage of hindsight. In contrast to Kuhn's characterisation of normal science as consisting of 'puzzle solving', other researchers paint a less cozy picture of scientific discourse. Bruno Latour [20], for instance, characterises scientific activity in terms of controversy in his description of the networks, instruments, inscriptions and theories deployed by scientists to gain acceptance for their ideas. Accounts such as this suggest that, although scientific work may be based on many fundamental agreements about how that work should be conducted, as Lakatos [19] and Kuhn [17, 18] suggest, the day-to-day scientific discourse may well exhibit just as much uncertainty, interpretation and debate as does research through design.

Conversely, research through design may come much closer to comprising a research programme, or sharing a paradigm (or set of paradigms) than we appreciate. After all, most of us working in research through design seem to share a set of common values. For instance, most pursue some variation on user-centred design, agreeing that some contact with the potential audiences for the things we make is desirable before, during or after design work itself. Most of us assume that exploring a wide space of potential designs, whether through sketching, scenarios, narratives or design proposals, is crucial in achieving a good outcome. Most of us appreciate the value of craft and detail in our work. Most fundamentally, most of us agree that the practice of making is a route to discovery, and that the synthetic nature of design allows for richer and more situated understandings than those produced through more analytic means. Perhaps we do not all agree with all of these assumptions all of the time, and perhaps it is endemic to design that all assumptions should be tested, but there certainly seems to be the outlines of a broad consensus underlying research through design.

Again, the shared assumptions underlying research through design practice are precisely those unlikely to be addressed in the literature. It is the speculative ideas, the novel, and the disagreements that we are most likely to discuss. This may lead us to underestimate the discord of science, however, and to overestimate the divergence of research through design. From this point of view, calls for standardisation, formalisation, overarching theory and the like are misplaced; we already share many of the attributes of a research paradigm, and seeking to reduce diversity its cutting edge will just inhibit progress.

The Many Worlds of Design

There is yet another possible interpretation for the apparent lack of convergence in research through design, which sidesteps the opposing views that we either need a shared paradigm to make progress, or already have a shared paradigm and need to recognise controversy as a sign of progress. In this view, whether or not research through design is built on certain assumptions about its conduct, it will inevitably be characterised by greater diversity and less convergence than the natural sciences because of the inherent nature of its field of study.

Many other fields lack the convergence seen over time in the natural sciences. For instance, Kuhn explains that his account of the paradigmatic nature of the natural sciences was inspired in part by the continual disagreements he witnessed amongst social scientists ([17]; c.f. [3]). Multiple schools co-exist in the arts, architecture, fashion and product design. In all these fields, controversies are seldom settled in such a way that new work can build on accepted results, the way science seems to do. Instead, new artistic movements overturn the basic values of their predecessors, hemlines go up and down, and even the most basic of household fittings are the subject of continual redesign and rethinking. These disciplines do not converge as the sciences do; instead they are cumulative in the way a conversation is, elaborating on what has gone before, but seldom aiming for or finding resolution. Why do disciplines such as these fail to show the convergence of science?

For the natural sciences, there is a strong presumption that the object of study is a single, unitary world that pre-exists and is independent of its observers. This core belief seems naturally to lead to convergence, simply because, if there are two incompatible accounts of the same physical domain, one must be better than the other (see [18] for one definition of 'better'). Research and practice in design and the arts, in contrast, do not describe a single, independent world, they are generative, investigating how to create new ones. Debates may rage about 'better' ways to go about this, but these cannot refer to evidence from a single, independent world as an ally (c.f. [20]). Multiple, incompatible worlds co-exist routinely for these fields.

Moreover, design and the arts change the context in which they operate. When the original iPad was designed, for instance, tablet computers were not widely known or available. Now anybody seeking to research or develop tablet computers – or anything at all, for that matter – is designing for a different world, one in which the iPad exists. One of the implications of the way generative disciplines change the context in which they work is that this sets the conditions for a feedback loop in which the development (and adoption) of a new design sets the scene for the development of variations, accessories, applications and reactions: whole new areas of reality. Another implication is that development in these fields does not just take the form of accumulation of incontrovertible results, but of reactions, reconsiderations and fresh beginnings.

Social sciences, too, change the world in which they operate. Osborne and Rose [22] for example, describe how the development of public opinion research gave rise to public opinion itself, as something to be identified, measured, and considered in policy formation and product development. Law and Urry [21] observe that labelling theory, as proposed by deviance theorists, led to policies of de-institutionalisation, and suggest that by bringing social inequality into view, British sociologists gave rise to the policies intended to address it. The social world, in this view, is not the subject of objective, independent observation. Instead:

> "...different research practices might be *making multiple worlds*, and that such worlds might be equally valid, equally true, but simply unlike one another.' [21] p. 397.

If research is performative in this way, they suggest, then the research is no longer concerned primarily with epistemology (how we know about our object of study) but also involves 'ontological politics', a concern with what is being made.

From this point of view, the reason that research through design is not convergent is that it is a generative discipline, able to create multiple new worlds rather than describing a single existing one. Its practitioners may share many assumptions about how to pursue it, but equally, they may build as many incompatible worlds as they wish to live in. We may wish to improve the standards of research within the field, but from this perspective we should realise that what we mean by 'improve', what criteria we propose, even the assumption that shared standards are necessary, possible or desirable, are potentially repressive acts of ontological politics.

THEORY AS ANNOTATION

What is an appropriate role for theory in research through design? On the one hand, it is plausible to argue that if design is to contribute to HCI research, we should turn greater attention to theory-making both as a way of capturing and communicating new learning to the research community and as a way of guiding design practice [33, 35]. Most practicing designers, however, do not engage with major theoretical approaches in HCI. Instead, they use a more eclectic mix of design techniques and orienting concepts ([27] cited in [31]). In addition, designers often turn to existing examples of design to inform the development of their own ideas. Why might this be so? I suggest it is both because of the provisional nature of theory, and the definite nature of designed artefacts.

As I have suggested, a great deal of design theory tends to be generative and suggestive, rather than verifiable through falsification. This seems self-evident in the case of 'manifestos', but also of more grounded generalisations from particular design examples (e.g. [6]). The problem here is not just that theory underspecifies design, so that practitioners will be faced by innumerable decisions whatever theory they use, but that theory is underspecified by design, in the sense that many aspects of a successful design will not be captured by a given theory. Thus in order to understand accounts of how to achieve simultaneous control over multiple functions successfully, for example, it is useful to consider specific designs such as a rotary controller for a microwave oven [6].

Design examples are indispensible to design theory because artefacts embody the myriad choices made by their designers with a definiteness and level of detail that would be difficult or impossible to attain in a written (or diagrammatic) account. As Stolterman [31] suggests, design is concerned with the 'ultimate particular', a concept, he suggests, that has 'the same dignity and importance as truth in science' ([31] p. 59). Theories may be provisional, but designed artefacts (as opposed to demonstrators, for example) are not. As Carroll and Kellogg [3] have argued, a designed artifact is a 'theory nexus': the choices made by designers reveal both the issues they think are important, and their beliefs about the right way to address those issues. The implicit theories embodied in objects, from this perspective, range from the philosophical (what values should designs serve?) to the functional (how should those values be achieved in interaction) to the social (what will the people who use this be like?) to the aesthetic (what form and appearance is appropriate for the context?). Moreover, artefacts do not address these issues analytically, but represent the designer's best judgement about how to address the particular configuration of issues in question.

Another metaphor for much the same point is that designs can be seen as occupying a point in design space, or perhaps more accurately creating a design space around themselves (see [12]). In this account, designers can explore the implications of a given design by moving around the point it inhabits to explore new design possibilities, or even by jumping away from it along understood dimensions, whether to apply some of the same decisions to new domains or to react against them.

If artefacts embody theory, however, they do not encode it, and if they occupy a point in a design space, they do not highlight the salient or fruitful dimensions of variation that space offers. One of the valuable roles of design theory, from this perspective, is in making accessible the kinds of decisions and rationales that comprise an artefact's embodied theory, or give dimensionality to its design space. In this case, however, then instead of theories predominating, with design examples serving as mere illustrations, design theory is best considered a form of *annotation*, serving to explain and point to features of 'ultimate particulars', the truths of design.

Annotated Portfolios

Beyond single artefacts, however, *annotated portfolios* may serve an even more valuable role as an alternative to more formalised theory in conceptual development and practical guidance for design[1]. If a single design occupies a point in design space, a collection of designs by the same or associated designers – a portfolio – establishes an area in that space. Comparing different individual items can make clear a domain of design, its relevant dimensions, and the designer's opinion about the relevant places and configurations to adopt on those dimensions (c.f. [7]). To put it another way, multiple examples can start to tease the individual concerns and judgements involved in a single situated design out of the particular configuration to which they were applied, making clear both the dimensions along which a designer's choices may range and the invariances among them.

As artefacts are to theory, from this perspective, design portfolios are to research programmes . For instance, Dieter Rams' work for Braun and Vitsoe has been characterised as 'defining an elegant, legible, yet rigorous visual language for its products' (www.designmuseum.org/design/dieter-rams), but to appreciate what this might mean one must turn to a portfolio of his work (Figure 1). Comparing the variety of stereo equipment, kitchenware and grooming appliances that he designed, one begins to appreciate the qualities that hold across the examples, and those that are more particular to specific designs. Rams offered a particular form of conceptual writing to help with this, defining his approach to 'good design' in ten concise principles (e.g. 'good design is unobtrusive', 'good design is thorough down to the last detail') accompanied by short explanations. These annotate the portfolio, drawing attention to important features and to salient details that might otherwise be overlooked. The passages may seem too terse to serve as substantial conceptual contributions by themselves, but in the presence of the portfolio, they give a strong sense of Rams' style and philosophy. One can imagine 'designing in the style of Dieter Rams' without the need for a detailed formal theory to direct decisions.

The notion of annotated portfolios is not a formal one. What is defining to the concept is not how materials are presented, but that a balance is achieved between descriptions of specific, detailed examples of design practice, and articulations of the issues, values and themes which characterise the relations among the collection, and to which the examples suggest answers. The appropriate presentation of an annotated portfolio may vary depending on material, purpose and audience. For instance, the detailed annotations shown in Figure 1 are extremely compact and focus more on highlighting features of the artefacts than on elaborating the overarching conceptual themes. A different presentation of Rams' work, at

[1] Many of the ideas here about annotated portfolios have been developed in collaboration with John Bowers.

(Images from flickr.com's Creative Commons. Credits: 1 Nick Wade, 2 Rene Spitz, 3 Brett Wayn, 4 '•')

Figure 1. Sketch design for an annotated portfolio of Dieter Rams' designs for Braun and Vitsoe (note that annotated portfolios are not defined by their graphic presentation)

www.vitsoe.com, emphasises his design principles over the portfolio of products themselves. A more detailed examination of Rams' philosophy might well take the form of an illustrated essay. What links all these presentations is the mutually informative juxtaposition of conceptual annotations with specific design examples, in such a way that neither dominates, and neither is subservient.

Annotated portfolios are, in several respects, the converse of Alexander's [1] design patterns. They are not intended to abstract regularities from repeated attempts to design for the same domains. Instead, they maintain the particularity of individual examples, while articulating the ideas and issues that join and differentiate them. Juxtaposing designs with annotations supports appreciation of the conceptual dimensions of designs on the one hand, and, by yoking them to particular design manifestations, grounds and specifies theoretical concepts on the other. Portfolios can support multiple conceptual perspectives, and similar perspectives can be applied to different portfolios, reflecting the lack of convergence in the field as a virtue. Most fundamentally, annotated portfolios respect the 'ultimate particular' of the designed artefact, rather than abstracting across instances as pattern languages do, while allowing for the 'extensibility and verifiability' for which some of the HCI design community have called.

I am not proposing here that annotated portfolios subsume all other forms of design theory. Theoretical writing remains important in articulating the issues, rationales, and lessons that are embodied by design, particularly for an interdisciplinary audience. I am suggesting, however, that we develop annotated portfolios as a serious form of theoretical contribution appropriate to research through design. More fundamentally, I am suggesting that, however valuable generalised theories may be, their role is limited to inspiration and annotation. It is the artefacts we create that are the definite facts of research through design.

CONCLUSION

In this essay, I have explored some of the issues that complicate calls for disciplinary consolidation in the HCI research through design community.

First, I suggest that we should moderate expectations of creating extensible and verifiable theory. Comparisons with accounts from the Philosophy of Science indicate both how provisional, contingent and aspirational design theories tend to be, but also how such conceptual work may nonetheless inspire thriving research programmes. In addition, continuing controversies about how to characterise science should help undermine assumptions about research that draw on HCI's tendencies towards scientism. Finally, they also indicate the futility of debating whether design is or should be a science. Rather than worrying about accepting or rejecting some ideal version of 'science', I suggest, we should reflect on the appropriate ways to pursue our research on its own terms.

Second, I suggest that attempts to establish disciplinary norms of process or outcome are political acts to be approached with care. Considering possible accounts of a lack of convergence in research through design suggests that greater consensus may be emerging in research through design than is sometimes acknowledged. At the same time, convergence may not be the only or best model for progress. Research through design may develop not only through increasing agreement, but also through discursiveness and elaboration. We may build on one another's results, but we can also usefully subvert them, suggest alternatives, or establish entirely new constructions, and this applies equally to our concepts, methods, processes, artefacts and approaches to evaluation. From this perspective, consensus can come to look like constraint.

Finally, I have advocated the recognition of annotated portfolios as a way of reflecting and valuing the particular nature of design theory and practice. These, I suggest, allow design theory's provisionality, specificity and diversity to be turned to advantage through grounding in specific sets of detailed design examples. They may provide a way to further our ambitions to produce relevant and rigorous theoretical work, while allowing multiple perspectives to flourish. Best of all, emphasising theory as the annotation of portfolios offers respect to the endless string of design examples that should remain at the heart of our work.

ACKNOWLEDGEMENTS

This research was supported by the European Research Council's Advanced Investigator Award no. 226528, 'ThirdWaveHCI'. Many thanks go to Phoebe Sengers, Anne Schlottmann and especially John Bowers for comments and suggestions. I am also grateful to reviewers for their thoughtful critiques, particularly the anonymous R4, who recognised that this essay addresses, in part, 'an elephant in the room...: the move towards "scientism" in HCI'.

REFERENCES

1. Alexander C, Ishikawa S (1977) A pattern language: towns, buildings, construction. Oxford University Press.
2. Bardzell J, Bardzell S, DiSalvo C, Gaver B and Sengers P (2012). Panel: The humanities and/in HCI. CHI'2012.
3. Collins R (1994). Why the Social Sciences Won't Become High-Consensus, Rapid-Discovery Science. Sociological Forum 9(2) 155 - 177.
4. Crampton-Smith, G. and Tabor, P. 1996. The role of the artist-designer. In Bringing Design To Software, T. Winograd, Ed. ACM, New York, NY, 37-61.
5. Curd M and Cover J (1998). Philosophy of Science: The Central Issues. London: WW. Norton & Co.
6. Djajadiningrat T, Matthews B, Stienstra M. (2007). Easy doesn't do it: skill and expression in tangible aesthetics. Pers Ubiquit Comput 11:657–676.
7. Fallmann D (2003). Design-oriented human-computer interaction. CHI'2003, 225-232.
8. Feynman, R. (1989). The character of physical law. London: MIT Press.
9. Forlizzi J, DiSalvo C, Bardzell J, Koskinen I, and Wensveen S. (2011). Quality control: A panel on the critique and criticism of design research. CHI 2011 Panel, 823 - 826.
10. Forlizzi, J. (2008). The Product Ecology: understanding social product use and supporting design culture. International Journal of Design 2 (1), 11 - 20.
11. Frayling, C. Research in Art and Design. Royal College of Art Research Papers 1, 1 (1993),1-5.
12. Gaver W. (2011) Making spaces: how design workbooks work. Proc. CHI '11, 1551-1560.
13. Gaver, W., (2009). Designing for Homo Ludens, Still. In (Re)searching the Digital Bauhaus. Binder, T., Löwgren, J., and Malmborg, L. (eds.). London: Springer, pp. 163-178.
14. Gaver, W., Beaver, J., and Benford, S. (2003). Ambiguity as a resource for design. Proc. CHI'03, Ft. Lauderdale. New York: ACM Press.
15. Gibson J. (1979). The ecological approach to visual perception. Boston: Haughton Mifflin, 1979.
16. Isbister K, and Höök K. (2007). Supple interfaces: designing and evaluating for richer human connections and experiences. Proc CHI'07 extended abstracts, 2853 - 2856.
17. Kuhn, T (1970). The Structure of Scientific Revolutions. London: University of Chicago Press.
18. Kuhn, T (1977). Objectivity, value judgment, and theory choice. Reprinted in [3].
19. Lakatos I (1977). Science and pseudoscience. Reprinted in [3].
20. Latour, B. (1987). Science in Action. Cambridge, Mass: Harvard University Press.
21. Law, J. and Urry, J. (2004). Enacting the social. Economy and Society 33(3) pp 390-410.
22. Osborne, T. and Rose, N. (1999). Do the social sciences create phenomena?: the example of public opinion research. British Journal of Sociology 50(3) pp 367 - 396.
23. Overbeeke K and Wesveen, S. (2003). From perception to experience, from affordances to irresistibles. Proc. DPPI'03, 92 - 97.
24. Popper K (1963). Science: conjectures and refutations. Reprinted in [3].
25. Pullin, Graham (2010) Curating and creating design collections. Design and Culture 2 (1), 309–328.
26. Rittel H, and Webber M. (1974). Dilemmas in general theory of planning. Design Research and Methods, 8(1), 31 - 39.
27. Rogers, Y. (2004). New theoretical approaches for human-computer interaction. In B. Cronin (Vol. Ed.), Annual review of information, science and technology: Vol. 38 (pp. 87 - 143). Medford, NJ: Information Today.
28. Schoen, D (1983). The reflective practitioner, how professionals think. New York, Basic Books.
29. Sengers P (2006). Must design become 'scientific'? DIS'06 Workshop on Exploring Design as a Research Activity.
30. Sengers P, Boehner K, David S, and Kaye J. (2005). Reflective design. Proc. AARHUS'05, 49 - 58. 24
31. Stolterman, E. (2008). The nature of design practice and implications for interaction design research. International Journal of Design 2(1), 55 - 65.
32. Wiltse, H. and Stolterman, E. (2010). Architectures of interaction: An architectural perspective on digital experience. Proc. NordiCHI 2010, 821 - 824.
33. Zimmerman J and Forlizzi J. (2008) The Role of Design Artifacts in Design Theory Construction. Human-Computer Interaction Institute. Paper 37.
34. Zimmerman J, Forlizzi J, and Evenson, S. (2007). Research through design as a method for interaction design research in HCI. Proc. CHI'07 493-502.
35. Zimmerman J, Stolterman E, and Forlizzi J (2010). An analysis and critique of research through design: toward a formalization of a research approach. DIS 2010, 310 - 319.
36. Zimmerman, J. (2009). Designing for the Self: Making products that help people become the person they desire to be. Proc. CHI 2009, 395 - 404.

Sustainably Unpersuaded: How Persuasion Narrows Our Vision of Sustainability

Hrönn Brynjarsdóttir[1], Maria Håkansson[1], James Pierce[2], Eric P. S. Baumer[1], Carl DiSalvo[3], and Phoebe Sengers[1]

[1]Cornell University
Ithaca, NY 14850, USA
{hb47, mch267, ericpsb, pjs54}@cornell.edu

[2]Carnegie Mellon University
HCI Institute
Pittsburgh, PA 15213-3891, USA
jjpierce@cs.cmu.edu

[3]Georgia Institute of Technology
Digital Media Program
Atlanta, GA 30332, USA
carl.disalvo@lcc.gatech.edu

ABSTRACT
In this paper we provide a critical analysis of persuasive sustainability research from 2009-2011. Drawing on critical sociological theory of modernism, we argue that persuasion is based on a limited framing of sustainability, human behavior, and their interrelationship. This makes supporting sustainability easier, but leads to characteristic patterns of breakdown. We then detail problems that emerge from this narrowing of vision, such as how the framing of sustainability as the optimization of a simple metrics places technologies incorrectly as objective arbiters over complex issues of sustainability. We conclude by suggesting alternative approaches to move beyond these problems.

Author Keywords
Persuasive sustainability; sustainable HCI; reflective HCI; critical reflection; modernism

ACM Classification Keywords
H.5.m.[Information interfaces and presentation (e.g., HCI)]: Miscellaneous;

INTRODUCTION
Environmental sustainability is a popular topic in HCI research, and one that is frequently addressed through persuasion. 86 papers contain the terms "environmental" and "sustainability" in CHI 2009-2011; of these, 38, or almost half, also include the term "persuasive." DiSalvo et al. found a similar emphasis; persuasive sustainability comprised 45% of their sustainable HCI corpus [11]. Froehlich et al. found that 56 of 139 sustainable HCI papers were in the related genre of eco-feedback [21].Given the prevalence of persuasive approaches in sustainable HCI, it is worthwhile to consider the nature of this area and how it may be shaping sustainable HCI as a research enterprise. Here, we offer a critical analysis of persuasive sustainability from 2009-2011, addressing three key questions: (1) How is persuasion being framed within sustainable HCI? (2) How is persuasive sustainability shaping how we conceive of and address sustainability in HCI? and (3) How should we approach sustainability in the future?

Permission to make digital or hard copies of all or part of this work for personal or classroom use is granted without fee provided that copies are not made or distributed for profit or commercial advantage and that copies bear this notice and the full citation on the first page. To copy otherwise, or republish, to post on servers or to redistribute to lists, requires prior specific permission and/or a fee.
CHI'12, May 5–10, 2012, Austin, Texas, USA.
Copyright 2012 ACM 978-1-4503-1015-4/12/05...$10.00.

To answer these questions, we integrate empirical, theoretical, and critical methodologies. First, we ground our discussion in an analysis of the persuasive sustainability literature, identifying themes such as the framing of sustainability as reducing resource consumption and a focus on measuring and reporting information about individuals' activities. Second, we use sociological theory on modernism to develop a theoretical lens that helps us understand how persuasive sustainability is conceptualized. Our key argument is that persuasive sustainability works by narrowing its focus to a limited framing of sustainability, human behavior, and their interrelationship. While this may help make the problem of sustainability manageable as an engineering enterprise, it also makes designs susceptible to breakdown. We then identify key problems that result from this narrowing of vision. For example, we articulate how the framing of sustainability as optimization of a simple metric places technologies incorrectly as objective arbiters over more complex issues of sustainability.

Many issues we highlight have been noted in prior works which inform and motivate this argument [2,9,10, 11,13,21,27,44,46,54,55,58]. Here we synthesize these issues and explain how they fit together conceptually, offering a comprehensive treatment of persuasive sustainability and its problems. *Our aim is not to argue that persuasive sustainability is inherently bad.* Rather, our goal is to explain how it is organized as a modernist enterprise and understand the consequences for sustainable HCI research. Through our argument, we also draw attention to strengths of persuasive sustainability and suggest ways to improve it.

WHAT IS PERSUASIVE SUSTAINABILITY?
Persuasive sustainability has its roots in the application of Fogg's framework for "computers as persuasive technologies" [16,17] to the topic of environmental sustainability. Fogg draws on psychological theories of persuasion, defining persuasion as "an attempt to shape, reinforce, or change behaviors, feelings, or thoughts about an issue, object, or action" [16, p. 225], and going on to argue that "behavior change is a more compelling metric than attitude change"

[16, p. 230]. According to Fogg, persuasive technologies are explicitly designed "to change attitudes or behaviors or both (without using coercion or deception)" [17, p. 15].

In their 2010 analysis of sustainable HCI, DiSalvo et al. [11] describe the emerging genre of persuasive sustainability. Roughly half of the literature surveyed by DiSalvo et al. derives its orientation from Fogg in that they are broadly aligned with the goal of "design[ing] systems that attempt to convince users to behave in a more sustainable way" (p. 1977). DiSalvo et al. characterize this large cluster of work as drawing primarily from the disciplines of psychology/communication and to a lesser extent design, providing information about user behavior related to sustainability, defining "sustainability" largely in terms of resource conservation, and defining success in terms of changing users' behavior in ways predetermined by designers.

In this paper, we build on this prior analysis by critically examining persuasive sustainability papers published since that review. First, we searched the ACM Digital Library for peer-reviewed HCI conference publications from 2009 through July 2011 for the term "sustainability", excluding work not specifically related to environmental sustainability. The conferences searched were CHI, CSCW, DIS, TEI, ACE, Ubicomp, OzCHI, and Persuasive. Second, we searched within the initial results for work in which the authors describe their primary goal in terms of changing users' behavior to make it more sustainable (rather than, for example, changing local cultures or stimulating debate). 36 papers met the final selection criteria. As in [11], not all the papers self-identify as "persuasive". In 22 out of the 36 papers, the authors explicitly identify the work using the term "persuasive" in the keywords, title, or body of the paper, or use the persuasive literature as theoretical grounding. The remaining 14 "implicit" papers in our sample did not explicitly describe themselves as persuasive but still aimed for behavior change. We found both sets of papers shared similarities in the way the framed and approached the problem of sustainability; differences are noted where relevant.

While the following analysis is based on these 36 papers that we have labeled as "persuasive", it is important to note that certain papers are much more strongly focused on persuading behavior change than others. Some papers, while explicitly focused on persuading people to alter their behaviors, additionally engage with design issues and goals that may be considered as falling outside of a more pure "persuasive approach—including engaging with concerns such as privacy [32], aesthetic [e.g. 34], and curiosity [5]. As such, our designation of each of these papers as a "persuasive" paper should be considered with this caveat in mind.

Sustainability as resource management

The papers in our review covered a range of systems including in-situ ambient displays using pervasive sensor technology [e.g. 31,36], ambient computer widgets [33,34], social network applications for sharing environmental data [18], persuasive games [23] and interactive visual displays [38]. According to Fogg's notion of persuasion, professional or researcher designers are depicted as being ultimately responsible for deciding what constitutes desirable behavior change and how this is to be accomplished. We found that our corpus was largely aligned with this perspective, with only 3 papers reporting participatory design, 2 of which are from the same research group [8,41,52]. There is a remarkable unanimity among the papers with respect to the types of environmental issues addressed and the ways in which they are framed. Like [21], we found energy consumption to be the most commonly identified issue, a topic which was addressed in half of the papers reviewed (18/36) [e.g. 18,23]. Of the remaining papers, half (9) involve other forms of resource consumption, including water [e.g. 31,36], printing paper [59], and gasoline [39]. The remaining papers deal with making green transportation choices [20], improving indoor air quality [e.g. 32], reducing CO2 emissions [e.g. 51], or are not tied to any one specific, easily demarcated topic [e.g. 8]. Except for [20], all papers that mention a specific area aim to improve 1-3 well-defined metrics. Most of the papers follow a fairly standard presentation of a brief justification (a paragraph or a sentence) of why the identified issue is significant in terms of global environmental concerns, followed by an argument framing the designed technology as a possible solution.

Indirectly changing individuals' behavior

The systems presented in this corpus are overwhelmingly designed to intervene at an individual level [e.g. 18,19,20,22,33,34,39], with some aimed at individual behavior defined as occurring in a community context such as in a family [e.g. 5,23,38,51] or company [e.g. 30,40]. All the papers mention changing individual behavior in some form, although some papers discuss how behavior change using softer, less direct, terms such as "motivate" [35], "encourage" [42], "educate" [33], "promote" [31], or "influence" [40]. Some papers focus on relatively specific behaviors like using less water in the shower [e.g.38], but most focus on more general behavior change. This was particularly true for the 18 papers focusing on energy conservation in the home, which generally did not clearly define targeted behaviors. In the majority (though certainly not all) of these papers, users are given no specific direction on how to decrease their resource consumption or how much decrease is enough.

Sensing and reporting information

Of the 29 papers we reviewed that reported full system designs, 23 automatically sensed the result of user activity, often in real-time. Sensing electricity consumption was the most common area of focus [e.g. 18,19,26,33,34,40,43]; other areas included water usage [e.g. 31] gasoline and CO2 emissions from driving [39], and printing [e.g. 59]. A few papers do not directly sense user behavior, e.g. a computer game to educate users about resource consumption [23], a design framework for persuasive services [60].

All but 1 of the sensing systems feed the sensed data back to users. This feedback is, for the most part, provided in real-time to aid conscious decision-making [e.g. 31,32,33,34,36,39]. A few papers also describe influencing behavior without conscious awareness, including feedback through subliminal information [25], influencing "unconscious behaviors" [53] and influencing behaviors by making them easier [60]. In other words, some systems aim to provide information for reflective decision-making, while others aim to deliver information to produce behavioral effect without conscious decision-making.

Although the papers all allude to behavior change as their general goal, many seemed to focus more on increasing "awareness," describing their systems using language such as "motivating teenagers towards energy awareness" [23], "mak[ing] the public become aware of the connection between their everyday activities and global climate change" [33], or "increas[ing] awareness of electricity consumption in everyday life" [30]. As also found in [11], in many cases the causal relationship between awareness and behavior seems only loosely articulated, suggesting that increasing an individuals' awareness of energy consumption (e.g., how much she is consuming or how much other individuals are consuming) can or will lead to conservation behavior [e.g, 40,43]. A few papers use an explicit causal model in which information leads to motivation leads to behavior change [e.g. 26].

Evaluating behavior change

So, does persuasive sustainability lead to intended changes in behavior? Of the 36 papers in our corpus, almost half (17) have no user evaluation. Of these, 12 *cannot* evaluate, e.g. because they explore a design methodology or are in the early stages of design. [1] evaluates using performance tests; the other 4 that do not evaluate impact on users are implicit, designerly papers. Of the 19 papers that do report on a system evaluation, 5 discuss preliminary evaluations, mostly usability studies that do not address behavioral change. The remaining 14 report on field studies that look at use in situ. One study has 52 participants [34], 2 have 14, and the rest have 10 or fewer participants. Twelve of the 14 studies report some kind of behavior change, although in at least two cases this is only for a small subset of participants [20,33]. In some cases, metric changes are reported without any discussion of what behavioral changes might have led to them; in others, behavioral changes are claimed but without any statistically significant effect on the intended metric. Generally speaking, when behavioral changes are claimed, anecdotal evidence of behavior changes is related, but it is difficult to determine what behaviors changed or by how much.

Little evidence for long-term behavioral change is offered in any of the papers we reviewed. The typical duration of a field study is 3-4 weeks, which is likely not long enough to go beyond novelty effects. Some studies argue for a potential longer-term effect based on the fact that the metrics had stabilized before the end of the study [e.g. 31]. Only 2 of the studies are longer than one month; 1 is 5 weeks [36]; and 1 is a 3 month study [5]. This is the only study that could truly be considered long-term; the authors state that behavioral changes took place, but what changes, how frequent or effective they were, and how many participants had them was unclear.

Summary

Persuasive sustainability papers are by no means homogeneous in their approach. For example, some papers aim for a scientific approach in which the goal is explicitly to control variables and optimize particular metrics [e.g. 23], while others take a more designerly orientation, in which system design and evaluation proceed in an open-ended, exploratory fashion [e.g. 5]. Nevertheless, our analysis described in this section identifies properties that are overwhelmingly shared across persuasive sustainability papers of all orientations. Persuasive sustainability aims to change behavior related to sustainability, generally understood as reducing individual resource consumption; the nature of the expected behavioral change is often unspecified. Persuasive sustainability systems generally aim to do so by raising individuals' awareness of the consequences of their activity. In order to do so, these systems typically sense and measure human activity, especially as related to resource usage. The method of persuasion is to provide information, usually about the sensed usage of resources. The type of behavior to be changed, and the metric by which that change is measured, are chosen in a top-down fashion, rather than in a bottom-up, participatory or user-centered fashion. Evaluation tends to be short-term and with small groups, and there is limited evidence of lasting behavioral impact.

A CRITICAL LENS ON PERSUASIVE SUSTAINABILITY

Unsurprisingly given the potential for broad impact of the persuasive sustainability approach, it has been subject to various criticisms. Such criticisms include overly focusing on incremental over systemic change [2,11,13,45,54,55,58] and individual consumption [11,13,28,42]. A main contribution of this paper is to build on these previous works and demonstrate how issues with persuasive sustainability are not isolated problems but rather are necessary consequences of the problem framing of persuasive sustainability. Dourish [13] and Strengers [55] have similarly traced a variety of these problems to an underlying liberal assumption of a rational, economically calculating actor. We complement their analyses by arguing that persuasive sustainability systems can be usefully understood as an example of *modernist* technology design, which have been argued to have particular modes of breakdown. Based on these critiques, we will demonstrate how these theoretically-expected modes of breakdown appear empirically in the literature.

What is modernism?

By "modernism" we refer to a broad cultural movement that rose to prominence in the 20th century. It avows that people can and should change the world for the better by analyzing present conditions and improving them through scientific and technical knowledge. Modernism rejects the idea that tradition should be the guide for action and seeks instead to rethink and optimize our life conditions through rational planning. Modernism aims to improve life through technical means; it is associated with the idea of "progress" and embraces scientific perspectives as the grounds for new definitions of value.

There is a wide array of literature describing the nature and characteristics of modern societies. Here, we draw on an influential understanding of modern society arising from the work of Weber [57] and popularized by Ritzer [48]. This work emphasizes 4 values central to modernist approaches: (1) *calculability*, or framing human endeavors with respect to values that can be numerically computed or measured; (2) *predictability*, or being able to ascertain beforehand the precise outcome of actions or decisions; (3) *efficiency*, or accomplishing goals through the least use of resources; and (4) top-down (technological) *control*, or achieving desired outcomes by controlling what might otherwise be unruly or unknown situations. Technology plays a central role in modernist approaches as a method for improving the human condition. Modernist approaches to technology tend to be predicated on *quantifying* aspects of human life, focus on improving the *efficiency* of everyday processes, intend to have *predictable* effects, and in order to do so necessarily aim to increase *control* over the vagaries of those processes. Modernist approaches tend to be oriented around three axioms: (1) trust in technoscientific reasoning and top-down, expert knowledge as a way to organize our lives; (2) orientation around means-end thinking, maximizing efficiency, and exerting control as ground principles to optimize everyday processes; and (3) trust that formal, rational methods capture essentially everything that matters about a given situation.

Persuasive sustainability as a modernist enterprise

We previously described contemporary persuasive sustainability systems as technologies that sense, interpret, and respond to human activity by providing information intended to change the behavior of individual consumers according to a metric selected in a top-down fashion, usually defined as reducing resource consumption. In this definition, we recognize several of the attributes of modernism. These technologies embody trust that through scientific and technical intervention, we can solve the problem of sustainability. The use of sensing to automatically track and report on human behavior reflects trust that calculable, formal measures can capture the essential aspects of sustainability. The intended change of behavior is an example of attempting to control vagaries in order to lead to a predicted and desired outcome. The top-down selection of a metric reflects an emphasis on expert knowledge as the driving force in finding solutions.

These attributes of modernism are not only reflected in the overall orientation of persuasive sustainability, they deeply inform specifics in system design. We aim to give a feel for modernist aspects of design through a fictional design anchored in design decisions made in the literature (this strategy is similar to [47]). Consider a mobile phone app that uses GPS traces to determine the user's mode of transportation, e.g., whether the user is driving a car, walking, biking, or riding a bus [20]. The system can also use the proximity of other Bluetooth-enabled devices to determine, when driving, whether or not the user is carpooling. The system then allows the user to view miles traveled and tons of CO2 emitted, aggregated in a variety of ways, such as by week, month, or year, or by transportation type [43]. The system also aggregates data across all users to indicate whether a given user is above, near, or below average transportation-related carbon emissions, optionally scoped by such means as geographic region or social network [18]. This social comparison is presented via a "thermometer" display, which reminds the user of the global warming s/he is causing or preventing [36]. If the user is above the norm, the app provides tailored daily tips to reduce transit emissions, such as recommending public transit options or suggesting carpooling buddies [26].

In this concept, we see many modernist traits. The system is designed around the improvement of efficiency, where efficiency is specifically defined in terms of emission of CO2 as a result of transportation. The system's proscriptions are based in scientific authority embodied in the carbon-counting and sensing algorithms and the personalized suggestions that interpret their consequences. The GPS trace and transportation mode detection not only make emissions calculable, these features also make it predictable; the system can tell the user just how much carbon she will cut by taking a different mode of transportation. Furthermore, by choosing a different mode of transportation, the user can control her emissions, thereby optimizing her behavior.

In practice, persuasive sustainability papers vary in how and to what degree they embody a modernist orientation. For example, while some papers focus in evaluation on tracking and optimizing a single metric in ways consonant with modernism, others engage in more open-ended evaluations which aim to uncover unexpected and unanticipated uses, and therefore do not fit as neatly into a modernist frame [e.g. 21,5]. Nevertheless, our analysis of the common traits of the persuasive sustainability literature suggests that the rhetorical frame that drives problem statements and solutions in the research area as a whole is strongly modernist.

Indeed, there is much that is laudable about modernism as a frame for technology design. For example, by structuring "sustainability" as the more manageable problem of "resource minimization", persuasive sustainability provides an actionable framework for developing novel solutions, rather than becoming paralyzed because the problem seems so complex. For users who want to reduce their resource consumption but are unsure of how to do so, the real-time measurement and judgment provided by persuasive sustainability systems can usefully inform their decisions. The use of expert data, rather than individuals' preferences, to drive decisions about metrics to aim for and the behavior that should result may increase confidence that we are building systems that will really make a difference in global problems of sustainability. The problem is that modernist technologies are susceptible to breakdown. In the next section, we describe this breakdown and explain how it manifests itself in contemporary persuasive sustainability.

NARROWING THE VISION

The possibilities and limitations of modernist approaches are cataloged in Scott's classic work *Seeing Like a State* [49] (similar critiques are embodied in [14] and [57]). As Scott argues, modernist solutions to problems are based on a "narrowing of vision" (p. 11) that "brings into sharp focus certain limited aspects of an otherwise far more complex and unwieldy reality. This very simplification, in turn, makes the phenomenon at the center of the field of vision more legible and hence more susceptible to careful measurement and calculation. Combined with similar observations, an overall, aggregate, synoptic view of a selective reality is achieved, making possible a high degree of schematic knowledge, control, and manipulation" (p. 11). While this narrowing of vision makes possible a wide range of technical solutions, those solutions tend to break down in the face of ecological issues outside of the 'selective reality' constructed through the problem framing.

In one example, Scott analyzes the development of scientific production forestry in late-18th century Germany. The goal of scientific forestry was to maximize how much saleable wood could be extracted from a given plot of land. This aim was achieved by analyzing and measuring forests solely in terms of the amount of saleable wood they contained, then controlling forests to maximize this measure. Species of wood that were not saleable were removed from the forest and replaced by saleable species, while animals, plants, and human practices such as foraging for firewood that might affect individual trees' health were removed from the forest.

The result, in the short term, was an improvement in the predictability and yield of the forest. But in the long term—over the lifecycle of the forest, about 80 years—the forests began to die off. The fundamental problem was that aspects that had been sidelined in the narrowing of vision underlying scientific forestry turned out to be key to the health of the forest. For example, the quality of the soil began to suffer with the loss of underbrush and plant and animal species; the monocultured forests planted only with saleable wood were prone to blowdowns and blights; and the peasants, whose subsistence practices of firewood gathering and hunting had been banned, both openly and covertly undermined the restrictions.

All designs have unintended consequences, but these cause greater problems for modernist designs because their success is often predicated on an assumption that all factors have been taken into account. They tend to be blind-sided by factors outside of what was formally modeled. Also, their reliance on expert knowledge and use of mechanisms of control means they tend to place technologies in a position of authority over user's lives. This control is authoritarian, imposed through a centralized scheme based on the conceiver's frame of reference, which will solve the problem only to the degree that it achieves compliance. The control is illusory, however, because it focuses only on those aspects of reality that are within view—those that are of interest to the modeler, rather than to the modelee.

A similar narrowing of vision is imminent in persuasive sustainability. Rather than tackling the complex problem of sustainability as a whole, most persuasive sustainability has chosen a small subset: individual consumer behaviors which have a fairly clear and direct impact on "sustainability" understood as a form of resource management. This narrowing of vision has a benefit in giving us a handle on an otherwise unmanageable problem. Just as scientific forestry made "keeping a healthy forest" approachable by framing it as a maximization problem over the number of saleable-wood trees, in persuasive models "sustainability" becomes framed as a minimization problem over the amount of a resources used by an individual or other metric chosen by the designer; the lens here is focused in particular on optimizing individual decisions in order to achieve that goal. Like scientific forestry, persuasive sustainability has the potential to achieve well-defined changes in those choices. Yet, also like scientific forestry, persuasive sustainability's long-term success is susceptible to being undermined by factors outside of what it aims to measure and control. In the next sections, we describe ways these problems manifest themselves in persuasive sustainability.

Defining sustainability too narrowly

A key attribute of modernist technologies is that they narrow their focus in order to be able to make measurable progress along known dimensions. In persuasive sustainability, we often see such a refocusing of the topic of "sustainability" leaving projects unable to deal, as others have argued, with the systemic nature of sustainability as a problem [2, 28,42,55]. First, the emphasis on sensing users' behavior means that these technologies limits their focus to aspects of sustainability that are clearly measurable, such as the amount of electricity that a person uses. Although the actions that a person takes are frequently measurable, the meaning of those actions and their causes often lie outside of the frame of persuasive sustainability. Problems come about, for example, when the technology's necessarily limited judgments are seen and presented to users as absolute values which reflect the true sustainability of their behavior, rather than as partial views of a much larger and more complex problems. The orientation of persuasive sustainability towards technology automatically evaluating human activity also results in a focus on aspects of sustainability that appear to be non-controversial. This leaves out many definitions of sustainability that HCI could address. It also means that persuasive technologies are framed as objective arbiters of the truth, with sustainability tending to be portrayed as fixed, known, and stable. This is a where the authoritarianism which is endemic to modernist technology plays out; an expert decides what is or is not "sustainable" and embodies this view in a technology which will judge users' behavior along the expert's lines. As others have argued as well [2, 11, 13, 27, 28,44], this framing has difficulty dealing with varying local definitions of sustainability and tends to sideline the politics involved, for example, in who gets to use resources, for what, and why.

Focusing too strongly on individuals and behaviors

Another way in which persuasion has narrowed the vision of sustainability is through its framing of "users" as individual, isolated consumers and bracketing of the complex social, cultural, and institutional contexts in which they live. A variety of critiques have demonstrated that when we expand our lens to understand the institutional, social, and cultural influences and constraints on individuals, persuasive solutions begin to fall apart [2,10,13,46,54,55]. One problem commonly identified [10,27,46,54,55] is that the focus on individuals and their responsibility to make wise choices with respect to sustainability neglects the ways in which social dynamics outside the system condition what is possible, e.g., who is actually able to make changes, or how this will change political relationships or social norms. Because of this, persuasive sustainability interventions tend to assume that individuals have a greater capacity for action than they actually do in practice. Dillahunt et al, for example, showed that even sustainably focused renters have relatively little control over their appliances, heating, and other major factors in their electricity use [9]. And when focusing on what the individual *is* capable of doing, persuasive sustainability tends to marginalize aspects of the design context that the individual cannot alter [9,10,55]. This means persuasive sustainability tends to neglect the need for change at other scales beyond the individual consumer, as argued by [11,13,28,42].

Assuming rational actors swayed by information

A remarkable difference between what we might expect from Fogg's [16] articulation of persuasive technology and its instantiation in persuasive sustainability systems is that most are not directly aimed at behavioral change but instead aim to provide information and raise awareness, in the hopes that this will lead in some way to altered behavior. This change in emphasis from Fogg's notion of changing behaviors and beliefs to focusing on providing information may be because the latter is easier to aim toward and evaluate, lends itself to HCI's existing strengths in information display, and may be a better fit to a user-centered design philosophy by avoiding to the appearance of aiming to control user behavior. But the emphasis on providing information as a driver for behavior change rests on a common modernist assumption that people are rational actors seeking to optimize activity based on what they know. Even if we focus exclusively on changing individual behavior, it is not clear that providing information is the best lever to do so. Approaches where humans are framed as using information to maximize the utility of their behavior have been critiqued for not taking account of cognitive limitations and the role of emotion in decision-making, and the role that habit plays in many of our everyday behaviors [29]. So, for example, [44] have argued that sustainability-related behavior is influenced as much or more strongly by material aspects of design as by explicitly provided information.

Too distant from lived use

A characteristic of modernist technologies is that they are designed from the perspective of an expert, orient towards his or her formal models, and tend to abstract away from the details on the ground. Because of this, they deal poorly with socio-cultural particularities. By not fully taking into account the nuance and complexities of everyday life, several researchers have argued that persuasive sustainability is prone to leaving out important concerns and values that undermine the long-term effectiveness of these interventions [9,21,44,54,55]. For example, Chetty et al [7] find that the complexity of household activity makes it difficult to save computing energy, and persuasive technology is therefore unlikely to speak to household dwellers' motivations. One particular kind of socio-cultural difference that modernist regimes have difficult handling is power differences; they tend to presume that the system applies to everyone, but that intended universality frequently masks the fact that systems are designed with one group in mind and may map poorly onto the experiences of others. In the case of persuasive sustainability, as [9] has shown, the primary target audience is white, middle- to upper-class, urban consumers who have a great deal of discretionary power and whose motivations map onto those of typical HCI researchers.

Trouble dealing with the dynamics of change over time

One consequence of the narrowing of vision on which modernist technologies rely is that their models tend to be rigid and deal poorly with changing circumstances over time. Persuasive sustainability systems tend to be oriented towards a specific change which users are intended to make. Once users have absorbed the "lessons" of the system, it is difficult to imagine what the value of the system will be [58]. In households that are given feedback about electrical usage, there tends to be an initial phase of exploration and alteration of habits, but in the longer run the feedback becomes uninteresting [55]. One response has been to break up behavior change into multiple stages and design interventions for each stage [26]. Even such approaches may fail to counteract the ways in which users' preferences and practices form a moving target shaped by external cultural forces. Strengers [55], for example, found that eco-feedback systems do lead to increased efficiency of existing practices, but do not work against the adoption of new, more resource-intensive practices.

BLIND SPOTS: CONSEQUENCES FOR HCI

Having made the argument that common forms of persuasive sustainability are problematic, the question we now to turn to is "So what?" Beyond just identifying methodological issues, what are the consequences for HCI research and practice?

Individual and simple acts limit how we imagine change

Although individual behavior change *may* be *one* means for instigating a sustainable society, it is not the only means. Turning off lights, unplugging unused appliances, and conserving water are all important. But focusing only on simple acts sidesteps more difficult lifestyle choices that may in fact be necessary to work toward a more sustainable society. Instead the common tactic is to tweak behaviors, with the goal of adjusting actions to be more in line with benchmarks of sustainability. It's notable how few persuasive sustainability projects attempt to eliminate behaviors entirely. Absent from this work are fundamental questions such as "What is to be sustained?" As others have argued [2,11,13,45,54,55,58], what we find instead is incremental change.

Granting undo authority and expertise to designers

In persuasive sustainability, designers are entrusted with the responsibility to decide what is or is not appropriate behavior. Indeed, in the process of designing any system, the designer configures dependencies and delegates responsibilities between people and objects. What is surprising in the persuasive sustainability literature is how little this is discussed. Instead of working toward equitable configurations of responsibility and accountability—e.g. as argued for by Suchman [56]—persuasive sustainability reinstates the authority of the designer and the technical object. The designer seems to be *de facto* more knowledgeable about sustainability than the users of persuasive sustainability systems. But little evidence is provided that either the designer is actually an expert or that the user is uninformed.

Constraining HCI

The primary consequence of the dominant framing of persuasive sustainability and its narrowed visions is that it constrains what sustainable HCI can imagine being and doing. The focus on individual behavior not only sets bounds for what might be imagined and designed, but it does this by granting privilege to the literatures of psychology and economics. Much of the persuasive research draws upon social-psychological research, but this is not the only literature that exists on either persuasion or shaping sustainment. Moreover, the emphasis on behavior change through artifacts and systems neglects other areas or possibilities for design [11, 13]. Given the prevalence of persuasive sustainability as a frame for sustainable HCI research, these issues may have a substantial impact on how a larger group of researchers conceives their work. The question we are faced with is how to reconsider persuasive sustainability in a more open manner.

MOVING FORWARD

Our intention with this analysis is to provide critical insight into issues around persuasive sustainability as currently pursued. But there *is* an important place for persuasion in sustainable HCI. We first consider how one might do persuasive sustainability without being unduly encumbered by a modernist approach. Next, we consider alternative approaches to sustainable HCI that are neither persuasive nor modernist and thereby may overcome some of the limitations of those two approaches.

Persuasion Redux

We provide here three specific suggestions as to how persuasive sustainability may be adapted to address some of its shortcomings, as well as examples of each.

Broaden our understanding of persuasion. Within design it is common to frame design in relation to rhetoric, as the art of persuasion [6]. Design is considered rhetorical because every product can be interpreted as an argument for how we should live in the world [6]. This notion of the rhetorical qualities of objects and systems is echoed in the fields of digital rhetoric and media studies. For example, [4] Bogost explores how video games provide unique opportunities to produce simulations that enact arguments. What is common across these approaches is the idea that persuasion is a *process* through which an audience is presented with perspectives that inform and shape their beliefs and actions. This is different from the common techniques of persuasive technology, which as Bogost notes are more akin to coercion than rhetoric [4]. These ideas from design, digital rhetoric and media studies can be used to shape alternative forms of persuasion in sustainable HCI. For example, drawing explicitly from these fields, Hirsch and Anderson [27] developed a game that allows varied stakeholders to explore issues and consequences of water allocation and usage. Through the design of the game a particular perspective is expressed and reinforced with the objective of persuading the stakeholders toward a specific course of action, but without dogmatism.

Include users in the design process. Rather than making technology designers arbiters of all things sustainable, there is an opportunity to more deeply involve users in the design of persuasive systems. We can draw both inspiration and techniques from existing work in HCI and design involving sensing systems and environmental technologies [12,37]. Davis [8] provides a strong argument for this approach, suggesting participatory design as a method for engaging community members in the design process for a persuasive system [see also 40,52]. Such approaches can maintain or increase the sense of agency that is a strength of persuasive sustainability while bringing systems closer to the definition of sustainability that users enact in daily life. More strongly considered users' values on the ground could lead to more acceptable, satisfying, effective designs. Considering the potential (arguably inevitable) imposition of values through persuasive design is a responsible practice. Kuznetsov and Paulos [37] and Hirsch and Anderson [27] provide exemplars of broadening participation in the design process.

Move beyond the individual. Unsustainability arises from complex interactions among individuals, social groups, corporations, organizations, governments, etc. Although, as noted above, persuasive sustainability has focused primarily on the individual, it could benefit by also considering community, political, and infrastructural engagement. Hirsh and Anderson's previously mentioned water game provides one example: rather than focusing on individual behaviors, it strives to enact change through policy reform [27]. As another example, rather than an app to calculate my carbon footprint, one can envision calculating the carbon footprint of a vote, of my elected representatives [13], of my stock portfolio, or of my national government or its military. These and other community-oriented approaches [2] provide examples for how sustainable HCI can grow beyond the modernist persuasive paradigm to engage with societal and cultural change.

Beyond Persuasion

The above suggestions, to varying degrees, still exhibit modernist tendencies. A carbon calculator for a vote still requires calculability, an expert perspective, etc. These suggestions are meant as ways of revising persuasive approaches to address some of the pitfalls of modernism. However, we also want to suggest alternatives approaches.

Shift from prescription to reflection. Most current work in sustainable HCI adopts a specific definition of sustainability, usually chosen by the technology designer, and attempts to persuade the user to take actions consistent with that definition—a definition that may not connect with users' actual lived experiences. Such systems need not be so prescriptive. For example, Strengers [55] describes how eco-feedback can provide people with material resources to talk about and socially negotiate their use. So, one way to approach the design of persuasive sustainability systems would be to frame them less as means of prescribing behavior and more as a kind of provocation or boundary object for eliciting issues of sustainability, drawing on the literature in open-ended reflection [24,50]. Recent work in the area of health technology suggests that such an open-ended system can lead users to considerations of what it actually means to be healthy and how health is defined [3]. A similar approach to sustainable HCI may encourage users to reflect on what it actually means to be sustainable in a way that makes sense in the context of their own lives.

Shift from behaviors to practices. As argued above, the narrowed vision of persuasive sustainability focuses on individual, specific behaviors, often in isolation. Such behaviors, though, are rarely isolated in actuality, but rather connect to larger, complex sets of social and cultural practices. For example, home heating is not simply a matter of energy consumption; though it does consume energy, it also creates a certain environment for the home dwellers and, at times, their guests [35]. In general, energy-consuming behaviors in the home seem rarely to be thought about primarily, if at all, in terms of the energy they consume [46]. Similarly, sustainability itself is rarely practiced in isolation but rather connects to a broad constellation of concerns [58]. These examples demonstrate approaches that, rather than focusing on specific, isolated behaviors, consider energy in the context of broader sociocultural practices.

CONCLUSION

In this paper we present a critical analysis of persuasive sustainability. We argue that persuasive sustainability can understood as a modernist technology that works by narrowing its vision to define sustainability as resource optimization pursued by individual rational actors conceptualized apart from the messy realities of everyday life. We identified key shortcomings of persuasive sustainability with regard to sustainability, and proposed a series of alternatives that might be useful in redirecting research.

The challenges we describe are not limited to persuasive sustainability. The narrowing of vision and subsequent problems manifested by a modernist approach potentially affect all sustainable HCI research that frames sustainability around values of efficiency, calculability, predictability, and control. Arguably, these problems are also present in persuasive health [47]. The challenges we present are therefore not limited to persuasion or sustainable HCI, but connect to broader issues in HCI research.

We have argued that persuasive sustainability follows a modernist agenda. But why is modernism so attractive to HCI? Modernism provides a seductive role for HCI: it proposes *technical* solutions to *social* problems. Ironically, a key aspect of our critique is that most persuasive sustainability research is *not* producing solutions. There is little evidence of efficacy, while the problem space has been so restrained that what we frequently witness is repetition rather than inventiveness. What is needed are new approaches to framing the issues and opportunities of sustainability—from which we might better be able to employ HCI to meet these challenges. The list of problems manifested by a modernist approach and blind spots, therefore, potentially have broader applicability throughout HCI, as themes for the analysis of existing research. Likewise, the alternative approaches we delineate may be applicable across domains of HCI as ways of discovering and pursuing new, more resilient, vectors of research.

ACKNOWLEDGMENTS

Funded in part by NSF Grants IIS-1018340, IIS-1049405, ISS-0847293 and the Hans Werthén Foundation. Thanks to Eric Paulos, Geri Gay, Tad Hirsch, and Steve Jackson for their support and suggestions, and to the anonymous reviewers for helpful criticisms.

REFERENCES

1. Amsel, N., and Tomlinson, B. 2010. Green tracker: a tool for estimating the energy consumption of software. *Proc CHI EA '10*. ACM, 3337-3342
2. Aoki, P.M., Honicky, R.J., Mainwaring, A., Myers, C., Paulos, E., Subramanian, S., and Woodruff, A. 2009. A vehicle for research: using street sweepers to explore the

landscape of environmental community action. *Proc CHI '09.* ACM, 375-384

3. Baumer, E.P.S., Katz, S.J., Freeman, J.E., Adams, P., Gonzales, A.L., Pollak, JP, Retelny, D., Niederdeppe, J., Olson, C., and Gay, G. 2012. Prescriptive persuasion and open-ended social awareness: Expanding the design space of mobile health. *Proc. CSCW '12.* ACM.
4. Bogost, I. *Persuasive Games.* MIT Press. 2007.
5. Broms, L., Katzeff, C., Bång, M., Nyblom, Å., Ilstedt Hjelm, S., and Ehrnberger, K. 2010. Coffee maker patterns and the design of energy feedback artefacts. *Proc DIS '10.* ACM, 93-102.
6. Buchanan, R. 1985. Declaration by design: Rhetoric, argument, and demonstration in design practice. *Design Issues*, 2(1):4–22.
7. Chetty, M., Bernheim Brush, A.J., Meyers, B.R., and Johns, P. 2009. It's not easy being green: understanding home computer power management. *Proc CHI '09.* ACM, 1033-1042.
8. Davis, J. 2009. Design methods for ethical persuasive computing. *Proc Persuasive '09.* ACM, Article 6, 8 pages.
9. Dillahunt, T., Mankoff, J., Paulos, E., and Fussell, S. 2009. It's not all about "Green": energy use in low-income communities. *Proc Ubicomp '09.* ACM, 255-264.
10. Dillahunt, T., Mankoff, J., and Paulos, E. 2010. Understanding conflict between landlords and tenants: implications for energy sensing and feedback. *Proc Ubicomp '10.* ACM, 149-158.
11. DiSalvo, C., Sengers, P., and Brynjarsdóttir, H. 2010. Mapping the landscape of sustainable HCI. *Proc CHI '10.* ACM, 1975-1984.
12. DiSalvo, C., Louw, M., Coupland, J., and Steiner, M. 2009. Local issues, local uses. *Proc. Creativity & Cognition '09.* ACM: 245-254.
13. Dourish, P. 2010. HCI and environmental sustainability: The politics of design and the design of politics. *Proc DIS '10.* ACM, 1-10.
14. Edwards, P. 1996. *The closed world: Computers and the politics of discourse in Cold War America.* Cambridge, MA: MIT Press.
15. Ferris, B., Watkins, K., and Borning, A. 2010. OneBusAway: results from providing real-time arrival information for public transit. *Proc CHI '10.* ACM, 1807-1816.
16. Fogg, BJ. 1998. Persuasive computers: perspectives and research directions. *Proc CHI '98,* ACM, 225-232.
17. Fogg, BJ. 2003. *Persuasive technology: Using computers to change what we think and do.* Morgan Kaufmann Publishers, 2003.
18. Foster, D., Blythe, M., Cairns, P., and Lawson, S. 2010. Competitive carbon counting: can social networking sites make saving energy more enjoyable? *Proc CHI EA '10.* ACM, 4039-4044.
19. Foster, D., Linehan, C., Lawson, S., and Kirman, B. 2011. Power ballads: deploying aversive energy feedback in social media. *Proc CHI EA '11.* ACM, 2221-2226.
20. Froehlich, J., Dillahunt, T., Klasnja, P., Mankoff, J., Consolvo, S., Harrison, B., and Landay, J.A. 2009. UbiGreen: investigating a mobile tool for tracking and supporting green transportation habits. *Proc CHI '09.* ACM, 1043-1052.
21. Froehlich, J., Findlater, L., and Landay, J. 2010. The design of eco-feedback technology. *Proc CHI '10.* ACM, 1999-2008.
22. Gartland, A.A., and Piasek, P. 2009. Weigh your waste: a sustainable way to reduce waste. *Proc CHI EA '09.* ACM, 2853-2858.
23. Gustafsson, A., Bång, M., and Svahn, M. 2009. Power explorer: a casual game style for encouraging long term behavior change among teenagers. *Proc ACE '09.* ACM, 182-189.
24. Gaver, W., Jacob Beaver and S. Benford. 2003. Ambiguity as a Resource for Design. *Proc CHI '09.* ACM, 233-240.
25. Ham, J., Midden, C., and Beute, F. 2009. Can ambient persuasive technology persuade unconsciously?: Using subliminal feedback to influence energy consumption ratings of household appliances. *Proc Persuasive '09.* ACM, Article 29, 6 pages.
26. He, H.A., Greenberg, S., and Huang, E.M. 2010. One size does not fit all: applying the transtheoretical model to energy feedback technology design. *Proc CHI '10.* ACM, 927-936.
27. Hirsch, T., and Anderson, K. 2010. Cross currents: water scarcity and sustainable CHI. *Proc CHI EA '10.* ACM, 2843-2852.
28. Hirsch, T., Sengers, P., Blevis, E., Beckwith, R., and Parikh, T. 2010. Making food, producing sustainability. *Proc CHI EA '10.* ACM, 3147-3150.
29. Jackson, T. 2005. Motivating sustainable consumption: a review of evidence on consumer behavior and behavioral change. *Sustainable Development Research Network.* Policy Studies Institute, London.
30. Jönsson, L., Broms, L., and Katzeff, C. 2010. Watt-Lite: energy statistics made tangible. *Proc DIS '10.* ACM, 240-243.
31. Kappel, K., and Grechenig, T. 2009. "show-me": water consumption at a glance to promote water conservation in the shower. *Proc Persuasive '09.* ACM, Article 26, 6 pages.

32. Kim, S., and Paulos, E. 2010. InAir: sharing indoor air quality measurements and visualizations. *Proc CHI '10.* ACM, 1861-1870.

33. Kim, T., Hong, H., and Magerko, B. 2009. Coralog: use-aware visualization connecting human micro-activities to environmental change. *Proc CHI EA '09.* ACM, 4303-4308.

34. Kim, T., Hong, H., and Magerko, B. 2010. Design requirements for ambient display that supports sustainable lifestyle. *Proc DIS '10.* ACM, 103-112.

35. Kuijer, L., and Jong, A. de. 2011. Exploring Practices of Thermal Comfort for Sustainable Design. Everyday Practice and Sustainable HCI, Workshop at CHI Conf. Vancouver, BC.

36. Kuznetsov, S. and Paulos, E. 2010. Upstream: motivating water conservation with low-cost water flow sensing and persuasive displays. *Proc CHI '10.* ACM, 1851-1860.

37. Kuznetsov, S. and Paulos, E. 2010. Participatory sensing in public spaces: activating urban surfaces with sensor probes. *Proc DIS '10.* ACM, 21-30.

38. Laschke, M., Hassenzahl, M., Diefenbach, S., and Tippkämper, M. 2011. With a little help from a friend: a shower calendar to save water. *Proc CHI EA '11.* ACM, 633-646.

39. Lee, H., Lee, W., and Lim, Y-K. 2010. The effect of eco-driving system towards sustainable driving behavior. *Proc CHI EA '10.* ACM, 4255-4260.

40. Lehrer, D., and Vasudev, J. 2011. Evaluating a social media application for sustainability in the workplace. *Proc CHI EA '11.* ACM, 2161-2166.

41. Miller, T.M., Rich, P., and Davis, J. 2009. ADAPT: audience design of ambient persuasive technology. *Proc CHI EA '09.* ACM, 4165-4170.

42. Odom, W. 2010. "Mate, we don't need a chip to tell us the soil's dry": Opportunities for designing interactive systems to support urban food production. *Proc DIS '10.* ACM, 232-235.

43. Petersen, D., Steele, J., and Wilkerson, J. 2009. WattBot: A residential electricity monitoring and feedback system. *Proc CHI EA '09.* ACM, 2847-2852.

44. Pierce, J., Fan, C., Lomas, D., Marcu, G., and Paulos, E. 2010. Some consideration on the (in)effectiveness of residential energy feedback systems. *Proc DIS '10.* ACM, 244-247.

45. Pierce, J., and Paulos, E. 2010. Materializing energy. *Proc DIS '10.* ACM, 113-122.

46. Pierce, J., Schiano, D.J., and Paulos, E. 2010. Home, habits, and energy: examining domestic interactions and energy consumption. *Proc CHI '10.* ACM, 1985-1994.

47. Purpura, S., Schwanda, V., Williams, K., Stubler, W., and Sengers, P. 2011. Fit4life: the design of a persuasive technology promoting healthy behavior and ideal weight. *Proc CHI '11.* ACM, 423-432.

48. Ritzer, G. 1993. *The McDonaldization of American society: An investigation into the changing character of contemporary social life.* Newbury Park, CA: Pine Forge Press.

49. Scott, J.C. 1999. *Seeing Like a State: How Certain Schemes to Improve the Human Condition Have Failed.* Yale University Press.

50. Sengers, P., Boehner, K., David, S. and Kaye. J. 2005. Reflective Design. *Proc. Critical Computing '05.* ACM, 49-58.

51. Shiraishi, M., Washio, Y., Takayama, C., Lehdonvirta, V., Kimura, H., and Nakajima, T. 2009. Using individual, social and economic persuasion techniques to reduce CO2 emissions in a family setting. *Proc Persuasive '09.* ACM, Article 13, 8 pages.

52. Shrubsole, P., Lavrysen, T., Janse, M., and Weda, H. 2011. Flo: raising family awareness about electricity use. *Proc CHI EA '11.* ACM, 669-672.

53. Sohn, M., Nam, T., and Lee, W. 2009. Designing with unconscious human behaviors for eco-friendly interaction. *Proc CHI EA '09.* ACM, 2651-2654.

54. Strengers, Y. 2008. Smart metering demand management programs: challenging the comfort and cleanliness habitus of households. *Proc OZCHI '08.* ACM, 9-16.

55. Strengers. Y.A.A. 2011. Designing eco-feedback systems for everyday life. *Proc CHI '11.* ACM, 2135-2144

56. Suchman, L. 2002. Located Accountabilities in Technology Production. *Scand. J. Inf. Syst.* 14, 2, 91-105.

57. Weber, M. 2002. Baehr, P.R., and Wells, G.C., ed., trans., *The Protestant ethic and the "spirit" of capitalism and other writings.* Penguin.

58. Woodruff, A., Hasbrouck, J., and Augustin, S. 2008. A bright green perspective on sustainable choices. *Proc CHI '08.* ACM, 313-322.

59. Xiao, J. and Fan, J. 2009. PrintMarmoset: Redesigning the print button for sustainability. *Proc. CHI '09.* ACM, New York, 109-112.

60. Zapico, J.L., Turpeinen, M., and Brandt, N. 2009. Climate persuasive services: changing behavior towards low-carbon lifestyles. *Proc Persuasive '09.* ACM, Article 14, 8 pages.

Undesigning Technology: Considering the Negation of Design by Design

James Pierce
Human-Computer Interaction Institute, Carnegie Mellon
5000 Forbes Avenue, Pittsburgh, PA, USA
jjpierce@cs.cmu.edu

ABSTRACT
Motivated by substantive concerns with the limitations and negative effects of technology, this paper inquires into the negation of technology as an explicit and intentional aspect of design research within HCI. Building on theory from areas including philosophy and design theory, this paper articulates a theoretical framework for conceptualizing the intentional negation of technology (i.e., the *undesign* of technology), ranging from the inhibition of particular uses of technology to the total erasure or foreclosure of technology. The framework is then expanded upon to articulate additional areas of undesigning, including self-inhibition, exclusion, removal, replacement, restoration, and safeguarding. In conclusion a scheme is offered for addressing questions concerning the disciplinary scope of undesign in the context of HCI, along with suggestions for ways that undesigning may be more strongly incorporated within HCI research.

Author Keywords
Design theory; design; undesign; sustainability

ACM Classification Keywords
H.5.m [Information Interfaces and presentation (e.g., HCI)]: Miscellaneous;

General Terms
Theory

INTRODUCTION
This paper motivates and develops the question: To what extent and in what ways should the intentional negation of technology be an acknowledged and legitimate area of design research activity within HCI? While design researchers and practitioners often understood design to involve the intentional creation or introduction of some material or immaterial thing (product, image, service, value, etc.), the intentional destruction or removal of some thing may also be considered a possible or even necessary component of design. Within the HCI community, design typically implies the creation or introduction of some digital artifact; rarely does it entail the explicit and intentional destruction, removal, or inhibition of an existing technology or the foreclosure of a potential future technology. This is particularly the case if such activity is undertaken without constructing or deploying a digital or "interactive" technology.

While of theoretical interest, our question concerning the intentional negation of technology is primarily motivated here by substantive concerns within and outside of our field. Within HCI we have witnessed a broadening of concerns spanning a diverse range of social, environmental, and moral issues including climate change and e-waste pollution [e.g., 3], busyness and overwork [e.g., 33], cultural difference and design for "developing" contexts [e.g.,30,48], politics and community-based design [e.g.,12,14], and human values, morality, and the good life [e.g.,17,21]. At the same time, within our community questions and concerns have been raised regarding the limitations and negative effects of well-intended technological interventions, including those that explicitly aim to address urgent social and environmental issues. Prior works have highlighted concerns such as the non-neutrality of technology [17], the harmful material effects of technology on environmental health [3], the extent to which HCI is capable of addressing, rather than contributing to, unsustainability [11,49], and the importance of considering implications to *not* design technology [2]. Critiques of technology from outside of HCI are far too numerous and diverse to outline here; but consider, for example, Winner [54] and the philosophical works of Borgmann [e.g.,7] and to a lesser extent Ihde [e.g.,29], both discussed recently within HCI by Fallman [17].

Indeed there is an apparent rift between researchers and others that describe, explain, and argue the limitations and problems with technology, on the one hand, and those whose primary concern is *designing* technology affirmatively. This gives way to a distinct issue for design in the context of HCI: What are the range and scope of activities that researchers have available when the implication *is* to *not* design technology[1]; or, to go one

[1] Baumer and Silberman have recently highlighted the importance of considering the "implications *not* to design technology" [2].

Permission to make digital or hard copies of all or part of this work for personal or classroom use is granted without fee provided that copies are not made or distributed for profit or commercial advantage and that copies bear this notice and the full citation on the first page. To copy otherwise, or republish, to post on servers or to redistribute to lists, requires prior specific permission and/or a fee.
CHI'12, May 5–10, 2012, Austin, Texas, USA.
Copyright 2012 ACM 978-1-4503-1015-4/12/05...$10.00.

crucial step further, when the implication is to *undesign*[2] technology?

In this paper I will aim to translate and move criticisms and concerns over the limitations and negative effects of technology more firmly into the realm of *design action.*[3] This move aims to give design research in the context of HCI greater agency to directly address such concerns (as well as to help identify limits to this agency). Here I do not focus on a specific concern that motivates undesigning, such as environmental sustainability [e.g.,3] or busyness [e.g.,33], but rather my aim is more generally to provide a framework for addressing a full range of concerns with limitations and negative effects of technology. My basic argument is that HCI research has both a capacity and responsibility to engage more strongly with *undesigning* technology, that is, with negating technology *by design*. However, it is not clear in what ways and to what extent these types of work should fall within the disciplinary scope of HCI. As a step toward both clarifying and addressing these questions, I will propose a theoretical framework for conceptualizing the intentional negation of technology, i.e., the undesigning of technology.

In what follows I first review related approaches upon which this work builds. Following this, I articulate a framework for conceptualizing the intentional negation of technology in terms of its scope and scale. I then expand on this framework to specify several additional areas of undesigning. This is followed by a summary and discussion of prior work that offers specific strategies for undesigning. In light of these discussions, I return to the questions posed here in the conclusion.

RELATED APPROACHES

In this section I briefly review two areas of work to which this paper directly builds upon and is indebted. The first is a specific design approach articulated by Tony Fry called elimination design. The second is design research in the context of HCI and interaction design.

Elimination design

Foundational to this work is the notion of elimination design, a design approach first developed by Tony Fry and partners of the EcoDesign foundation in the 90s, and which has recently been elaborated on by Fry in his writings on "design futuring" and "redirective practice" [23]. Elimination design essentially aims to identify and eliminate the unsustainable, ranging from "gas-guzzling vehicles" to building products containing toxins. The key question Fry poses is: "on the basis of a clearly identified overall contribution to extending unsustainability, what exactly should be eliminated." (p. 72).

In this paper, I will build upon Fry's notion of elimination design and expand on it in two ways. First, I will extend the range of concerns for elimination design beyond "environmental sustainability" to include, for example, specific concerns with the negative social impacts of technology. Second I will articulate a more general notion of elimination that extends over a wider spectrum of intended negating effects, ranging from inhibiting uses of technology to complete erasure of technology. I will do this by articulating a framework for conceptualizing intentional technology negation that allows for a more precise way of discussing the negation of technology by design.

Design research and HCI

The confluence of Design and HCI has been well discussed and documented in a number of prior works [e.g., 18,19,56,57]. Notable works that address the disciplinary role of design within the context of HCI include Fallman's distinction between the "knowledge-generating Design-oriented Research" and the "artifact-generating conduct of Research-oriented Design" [18,19]; and Zimmerman, Forlizzi, Stolterman and Evenson's treatments of research through design [56,57], which emphasize the process and products of making as legitimate forms of HCI research. Another important strand of design research is found among the works of Gaver et al. [e.g.,26,27], which has opened up a space for addressing notions of curiosity, ambiguity, and reflection—important concerns of "third wave" HCI [6]. Other works such as Blevis and Stolterman [3,4], Dourish [14], and Friedman and Nathan [21,22], have variously emphasized addressing design at broader scales. A more thorough treatment of design research within HCI must unfortunately be omitted here.

Despite the connotations it may evoke, undesign, as I will present the notion here, is not intended to displace prior design research and design-oriented work in HCI. This paper instead situates itself within this diverse body of work. Throughout this paper I will in fact point to ways that undesigning is already evident among designerly HCI work in certain ways (but less so in others). I will also suggest ways that undesigning may be more strongly incorporated within and discussed in relation to these works.

THEORETICAL FOUNDATIONS: WHAT DESIGNS DO

In this section I review several areas of theory that variously focus on aspects of design, technology and agency. These concepts will serve to both clear a space for the intentional negation of technology as distinguished from the effects of technology more generally, as well as offer

---

[2] Undesigning, as I name and elaborate on it here, builds upon and is indebted to Tony Fry's notion of elimination design, a design approach aimed at identifying and eliminating the unsustainable [23].

[3] To be clear, I will set my scope here on *research* practice concerned with design in the context of HCI, rather than HCI-oriented professional design practice. The relationship between design research practice and professional practice is, to be sure, a crucial one, yet one which this paper must largely set aside.

important insights into a range of scales at which to conceptualize the intentional negation of technology.

Consider first philosopher of technology Don Ihde's theory of "micro-perception" [29]. Ihde describes human uses of technology in terms of a structure of amplification/reduction in human perception. Ihde analyzes technologies including scientific instruments such as telescopes, revealing that these technologies amplify the user's visual perception of celestial bodies while at the same time reducing perception of the surrounding context. Ihde goes on to suggest that forms of perceptual reduction associated with new technologies are often overlooked in favor of what is amplified:

> [T]he fascination [with new technology] attaches to magnification, amplification, enhancement. But, contrarily, there can be a kind of forgetfulness that equally attaches to the reduction. What is *revealed* is what excites; what is concealed may be forgotten. Here lies one secret for technological trajectories with respect to development. There are *latent telics* that occur through inventions. (p. 78)

Building on and paralleling Ihde's analysis of the technological mediation of perception, philosopher of technology Peter-Paul Verbeek has described the ways that technology mediates human action in terms of a structure of invitation/inhibition [51]. Verbeek draws on the concepts of delegation and inscription described by Latour [31,32] and Akrich [1]. According to these concepts, designers delegate functions or responsibilities to artifacts by inscribing them with desired programs of action. For example, a speed bump is inscribed (designed) to inhibit fast driving and invite driving slowly. In Verbeek's terms, artifacts invite certain actions while inhibiting others or even rendering them impossible [51, p. 171.

Drawing on the field of rhetoric, design theorist Richard Buchanan has similarly argued that all technology is inscribed with persuasive arguments: "instead of simply making an object or a thing, [a designer] is actually creating a persuasive argument that comes to life whenever a user considers or uses a product as a means to some end" [10, p. 95]. Drawing on Buchanan among other areas of design discourse, Johan Redström [39] has discussed the recent research area of "persuasive design" associated primarily with "captology" and the work of B.J. Fogg [20]. Redström suggests that all design in fact persuades in the sense that it is done with the intention to alter people's behaviors and attitudes. The key aspect highlighted by Redström and Fogg is the relationship between the designer's intentions and the ways that an artifact mediates or alters people and their behaviors, thoughts, and attitudes. To this we may add that technology can also *dissuade* certain behaviors and attitudes, which is in fact an intended outcome of many persuasive technologies aligned with captology.

Taking a "macro-level" perspective, social theorists such as Giddens [28] and Bourdieu [9] have theorized human agency as shaped by social structures and institutions in ways that both constrain and enable human action. While this work tends to downplay the role of materiality and artifacts as well as the intentionality of designers, it nonetheless is concerned with technology understood more broadly in terms of material and immaterial structures such as social institutions. Recent work in sociology has drawn on such theory but with a stronger focus on materiality (and design), notably in the work of Elizabeth Shove [45].

Various theoretical concepts from areas of economics and innovation theory are also germane to our discussion, notably the concepts of "creative destruction" and "disruptive technologies". The former was originally used in Marxist economic theory but more recently has been employed to describe the ways in which radical innovations introduce new economic value by effectively destroying prior established value [e.g.,42]. The notion of disruptive technologies captures a similar idea, emphasizing that the introduction of new technologies displace old ones [e.g.,8]. A classic example of a disruptive technology is the automobile, which displaced the horse and carriage.

Elimination design as described by Fry is based on a principle that captures important aspects of "creative destruction", namely that "Creating anything always requires the destruction of something else, so make sure what you create is worth what you destroy." ([50], with reference to [23]). Echoing Ihde's discussion of perceptual reduction, Fry argues that the destructive aspects of design are all too often overlooked:

> The very way design is reduced and presented in relation to bringing goods into being fails to grasp design's ambiguity as an agent of both creation and destruction... what designers do is destroy value at the same time as they create it (a new style product is launched as the 'the latest' thus rendering previous versions 'dated'). This means that while it is acknowledged that artefacts can prompt the creation of other objects (such as system elements and accessories) and deliver experiences (for example, pleasure and the use of new skills) what they may equally destroy (knowledge, the use of a service, a craft practice, and so forth) is mostly overlooked. [23, p. 192].

The notion that design both creates and destroys may also be found among writings on ontological designing [23,24,53,55], which have proposed theories of design claiming that "we design our world, while our world acts back on us and designs us" [53, p. 1].

To summarize, then, our review of a diverse set of theories and theoretical concepts related to technology and design collectively point to ways that technology negates, in various ways and at various levels of analysis. Technologies can be understood to both amplify and reduce human perception, invite and inhibit human action, persuade and dissuade people to alter their behaviors and attitudes, constrain and enable action within social structures and institutions, and create and destroy material and immaterial aspects of reality, including value, practices, entire industries and particular material things. Further, our discussion highlights ways that the negating aspects of technology are often overlooked or neglected. With these ideas in mind, I now turn to discuss the intentional negation of technology.

UNDESIGNING: TOWARDS A THEORY OF THE INTENTIONAL NEGATION OF TECHNOLOGY

The theoretical perspectives outlined in the previous section draw attention to ways in which design both creates and destroys, enables and constrains, persuades and dissuades, inhibits and invites, and amplifies and reduces. According to these ways of theorizing design and technology, in some sense all design may also be considered *undesign*. However, our discussion also raises the distinction between intended and unintended effects of technology—intentionality being the key to distinguishing undesigning from technology negation more generally. Here I will use the term *(un)design* to refer to a notion of design which emphasizes that all design variously negates as well as creates, both intentionally and unintentionally.

Here, however, my focus is on the *intentional and explicit* negation of technology. As such, I will use the term *undesigning* to refer to the intentional negation of that which design brings into existence. The emphasis on intentionality brings technology negation explicitly into the realm of design action. Notions of human agency and intention are at the very core of design as a human activity. For example, in their influential book *The Design Way*, authors Nelson and Stolterman discuss intentionality and purpose as integral to design as a form of inquiry and action. Nelson and Stolterman write: "Design is the ability to imagine that-which-does-not-yet-exist, to make it appear in concrete form as a new, purposeful addition to the real world." [36, p. 10]. While representing a very different understanding of and approach to design, the centrality of intentionality and purpose may also be found in Simon's oft-cited notion of design as devising "courses of action aimed at changing existing situations into preferred ones" [46, p. 130].

In this section my goal will be to articulate a theoretical framework for discussing what the intentional negation of technology is and general forms in which it may be enacted. I begin by presenting a framework for conceptualizing technology negation and then expand on the framework to describe several additional areas of undesigning. As a conceptual point of departure, consider an inversion of Nelson and Stolterman's notion of design that emphasizes design as destruction rather than creation: design as the ability to imagine *the absence* of that-which-exists, to make it *disappear* in concrete form, as a new, purposeful *subtraction* of the real world.

Coming to terms with "technology"

Prior to discussing the negation of technology, it will be useful to obtain a firmer grasp on the ambiguity of the term "technology". When the term technology is used in the context of HCI, the assumption often seems to be that we are talking about some sort of "high-technology" such as digital or information technology (as distinct from more traditional technologies such as books, pots, and furniture). Further, in the context of HCI the term technology typically appears in reference only to material artifacts (as distinct from the making or using of artifacts, or even immaterial things such as laws or symbols). Taking a cue from this implicit convention, I will use the term *interactive technology* as shorthand for "the technology that HCI as a field is primarily concerned with". Interactive technology, then, typically entails some type of electronic, digital, computational, or information technology, and with a focus on the materiality of these technologies, i.e., technologies as artifacts. I will allow the unqualified term *technology* to retain its broader, more inclusive usages, which include notions of technology as not only high-tech artifacts themselves but also the making and using of all artifacts, and within practical, social and intellectual contexts (see Mitcham [35, p. 230-231]). However, in the context of this paper the unqualified term technology will also in most cases be used with the more specific notion of interactive technology in mind.

A spectrum of technology negation

What exactly might it mean to undesign something? In order to more precisely discuss the negation of technology by design I propose a framework for conceptualizing technology negation in terms of scope and scale. This framework can be understood as a spectrum, which ranges from the inhibition of particular uses of technology, to the broader displacement of technology, to the total erasure of an existing technology or foreclosure of an emerging one. I will briefly elaborate on each of these positions along this spectrum of technology negation using a number of examples. In this paper I describe each in terms of *intentional* negation of technology (rather than more generally in terms of negating effects independent of human intentionality).

Inhibition refers to design that aims to hinder or prevent the use of technology in particular ways and contexts. For example, designers can aim to inhibit driving with speed bumps and speed limit laws, or inhibit excessive electricity consumption by displaying the financial or environmental costs of consumption. Inhibition as I use it here does not exclusively focus on the inhibition of action in the way Verbeek uses the term, as discussed previously [51]. The relevant unit for inhibiting technology is individual-level "interactions", by which I mean to include notions of uses, behaviors, perceptions, etc. Inhibition is often considered in design, and there is in fact already a substantial area of HCI concerned with explicit and intentional inhibition, namely "persuasive technology" [e.g., 20].

Displacement refers to design that aims to more substantially hinder or prevent the use of technology by removing technology, perhaps literally, from its typical or currently occupied position. For example, designers can aim to displace the practice of watching television by encouraging dwellers to move their television sets from certain areas of the home or remove them from the home altogether. Displacing goes beyond inhibiting by aiming to more substantially negate routine or common interaction with technology, but without completely negating its existence and potential for use. The relevant unit for displacing technology is a practice, understood as a regular or routine way of doing things.

Erasure refers to design that aims to completely eliminate a technology from existence. At least in theory, we can consider designing for complete erasure of a technology. To what extent this is possible in a free society is a matter of debate, although there are noteworthy examples of societies relinquishing technologies. A well-documented example is the eventual and sustained rejection of the gun in favor of the sword by Samurai military culture in 17th and 18th century Japan—during which time Japan continued to enjoy cultural and economic prosperity [38]. The relevant unit for erasing technology is the material existence of a technology (within a broader social or societal context, such as the home or an entire culture), and its concomitant uses, practices and other inter-related aspects of the world. *Foreclosure* [4] is similar to erasure but rather than targeting an existing technology the target is a technology that has not yet fully emerged into existence. Some well-known examples of technologies that have been targeted for foreclosure and/or erasure include products made with toxic substances, nuclear power plants, genetically modified foods, and, of course, the mechanized loom (a frequent target of "machine breaking" by 19th century Luddites).

Elaborating types of technology negation

In this section I will expand on this framework to articulate several additional, more specific areas of intentional action that are each concerned with the intentional negation of technology—understood in terms of inhibiting, displacing, erasing, and foreclosing. My claim is that while each area is aimed at negating design they may nonetheless be considered within the boundaries of design activity, at least according to sufficiently broad notions of design [e.g.,36,46]. The list of areas presented here is by no means intended as an exhaustive description of the space of undesigning. My goal is rather to articulate a range of areas of undesign activity that I claim may be less considered or even overlooked, particularly with respect to the (un)design of interactive technology, as well as to demonstrate how the 4-part framework can be employed to further articulate areas of technology negation.

For each area, the specific types of intervention and areas of design expertise that are drawn upon (e.g., interaction design, communication design, product design) have been left largely unspecified. In the section following this one, I will review several such strategies and approaches that have been articulated in prior work. In this section, I will continue with the focus of the previous section on articulating more general areas of technology negation in terms of intended negating effects.

Self-inhibition and Self-inhibiting Options

Self-inhibition refers to the design of attributes of a technology that inhibit use of that technology in various ways. Self-inhibition is more specific than general inhibition in that it directs attention toward the design of technologies intended to inhibit *their own* interactions. Self-inhibition covers the design of a wide range of attributes. First, consider the ways that a design may self-inhibit by means of physical affordances [37] (which may be understood also in terms of the concepts of inhibition/invitation [51], amplification/reduction [29], and inscription [1,31,32] discussed previously). To elaborate on the way affordances can self-inhibit, I will draw on a well-known design exemplar from the HCI literature, the Drift Table [26]. The Drift table is an electronic coffee table that displays a slow-moving map of aerial photography and is controlled by placing objects on the table. Sengers and Gaver (one of the designers of the artifact) describe the design of the Drift Table as follows:

> In order to block the obvious interpretation of being for a task, the Drift Table was designed explicitly to not support task-oriented use as a travel device. For example, there is no way to type in coordinates to go to a particular point. The only way users can move across the landscape is to place objects on the surface of the coffee table; the table 'drifts' in the direction of their weight, at a purposefully low rate. The view can be reset (typically to the table's own physical location), but this requires pressing a small and unobtrusive button, designed to emphasize that resetting the view is not a primary feature of the device. [44, p. 103]

The decision to omit expected features (the ability to specify coordinates) and to limit or minimize other features (the rate at which the table "drifts", and the size and placement of the reset button) can be understood as attributes intended to self-inhibit. Moreover, self-inhibition is in this case intentionally employed in order to invite and enable forms of engagement that would otherwise be difficult or impossible to mediate, namely what the designers refer to as ludic engagement, or "activities motivated by curiosity, exploration, and reflection rather than externally defined tasks" [26. p. 885]. Indeed, designers do this all the time, whether or not they can or do articulate it in terms of concepts like affordances or the material mediation of action. While almost any design can be understood to have self-inhibiting attributes, the Drift Table is particularly relevant to our concern with undesigning because, as a design research artifact, it

[4] I thank Paul Dourish for helping bring this term to my attention.

explicitly draws attention to enabling self-inhibiting attributes that are often overlooked in the design of technology. A related idea is Tatar et al.'s "zensign", the notion that the features of a technology that are omitted are just as important as those that are included [47].

There is a special case of self-inhibition that I will further draw attention to, which I refer to as *self-inhibiting options*. Self-inhibiting options refers to the design of self-inhibiting user-specified settings or other choices that individual users can freely select in order to later inhibit uses or even prevent them altogether. The critical form of interaction to consider in the design of self-inhibiting options is what we might refer to as configuration modes of use. Configuration is distinguished from normal or routine use in that an individual can (re)configure how an artifact functions, how it is interacted with, and, consequently, how it is normally and routinely used (by altering the way it mediates). Familiar types of configurations considered in interaction design include menu options or product settings. However, there are other important configuration modes that are more easily overlooked because they are less clearly demarcated by specific aspects of an interface, such as where an item like a laptop computer is stored or used, how a television set is positioned in relation to seating arrangements, and the acquisition or de-acquisition of certain service options (such as different data plan options for mobile phones).

While designers often intentionally design for user configuration, there is apparently less explicit consideration given to the design of configuration options that encourage or allow individuals to reflectively and explicitly self-inhibit their own use. Consider an issue raised recently by Phoebe Sengers based on her reflections on the slower pace of life experienced during her fieldwork with a subsistence fishing community:

> [We] might think not about how technology can give us access to more choices, but about how we can design technologies that help us create constraints on our choices. Technologies might help to reduce the burden of choice for us by automatically excluding things we wish to keep out of our current field of vision… Or, as Ben Fullerton recently argued in *interactions*, perhaps technology should support not only connectivity but also solitude" ([43 p. 47] referencing [25]).

Based on this set of concerns, some examples to consider include self-inhibiting options that allow technology to be configured to be "put aside" or "put away", such as a television designed with cabinet doors that invite "closing" it, or a mobile phone that comes with a factory pre-set "I'm home" button for filtering calls and emails. We can also consider designing self-inhibiting options that allow technology to be configured to "not allow", such as a monthly mobile phone contract that gives the option to relinquish certain distracting types of functionality like video. Another example to consider is the control features that many televisions currently have which allow parents to restrict their children from viewing certain programming.

Replacement and Restoration

Replacement refers to design that aims to undesign a technology by replacing it with some other technology. Examples of replacing technology include replacing an older refrigerator with an improved model, replacing analog film cameras with digital cameras, and replacing landlines with mobile phones. Replacement is most naturally conceptualized in terms of functional or use-value replacement. However, replacement can also be understood in terms of replacing the symbolic function or social role of something. For example, a Valentine's Day card can be replaced with an affectionate embrace and kind word. The symbolic status associated with an expensive car or article of clothing could also be targeted for replacement. One specific strategy for replacement is *replacing a product with a service*. For example, car-sharing services may aim to replace a product with a service, which may lead to the displacement of personal ownership of vehicles. Later this strategy will be described as "disowning" [50].

A special case of replacement is *restoration*. Restoration refers to replacement by means of (re)introducing a displaced or foreclosed technology. Examples of restoration include restoring person-heating technologies and practices such as the use of blankets and clothing to keep warm indoors (and undesigning space heating technologies and practices), restoring bicycles and light-rail systems (and undesigning automobiles and buses), and restoring the home garden and farmers' market (and undesigning industrial processed food). Restoring can range from reintroducing a displaced technology "as it was" to substantially redesigning and remaking a displaced technology (e.g., the use of modern materials and ergonomics in modern day fountain pens, bicycles, and hand tools).

Removal and Exclusion

Removal refers to design that aims to literally remove a technology from a context it currently or typically occupies. Technology removal can be understood as a contextual erasure of technology, i.e., a restricted form of erasure that is neither universal nor necessarily permanent. Examples of technology removal include removing the television from certain areas of the home in order to alter social dynamics, removing a fast food restaurant to encourage healthier eating in a community, or removing a nuclear power plant to remove the possibility of nuclear disaster.

Exclusion refers to design that aims to prevent or substantially hinder the use or occupation of a technology within a given context. Technology exclusion can be understood as a contextual foreclosure of a technology, i.e., a restricted form of foreclosure that is neither universal nor necessarily permanent. An example of excluding technology is designing a café without Wi-Fi or power outlets in order to prevent or hinder patrons from using laptop computers and Internet-enabled technologies such as email and social networking sites. This may be done (and in fact sometimes is done) in order to encourage "face to face" interactions and a more "lively" social atmosphere.

Safeguarding

Safeguarding refers to design that identifies and demarcates contexts in which to exclude or foreclose technology. Safeguarding names design activity that is broader than excluding, yet less drastic than the ultimate case of complete foreclosure. An example of safeguarding would be identifying a population or area of practice that would *not* benefit from designerly intervention or would be harmed by certain types of intervention, and taking steps to enact or advocate for the exclusion or foreclosure of such interventions. Such advocacy can range from the design of public policies and services to communication campaigns.

STRATEGIES FOR UNDESIGNING

Throughout our discussions in the previous section, the specific type of design intervention (e.g., website, product interface, image, service, etc.) and area of design expertise drawn on (e.g., product design, graphic design, interaction design, etc.) was left largely unspecified. In this section I summarize several approaches or strategies that help address *how* designers can go about undesigning in practice. First, I present a set of approaches for elimination design outlined by Tony Fry. This is immediately followed by another set of approaches for elimination design presented by Cameron Tonkinwise. Finally, I outline several relevant approaches that have been discussed within HCI.

Approaches to elimination design

As discussed previously, elimination design is concerned with identifying and eliminating the unsustainable [23]. Although Fry emphasizes that "design for elimination cannot be based on a nice, neat checklist" (p. 76), he nonetheless offers some general approaches to guide elimination design. One of these is *dematerialization and rematerialization.* An example Fry gives for dematerialization is the potential for digital documents to eliminate the need for printing paper (c.f. [41]). On the other hand, rematerialization involves "the substitution of human labour for machines in a smart way" [23, p. 79]. An example would be restoring the push mower to displace the gas-powered mower. Another approach offered by Fry is *product multipurposing*, which directs attention toward the large amount of "waste" associated with the design of "single function technologies" such as toilets that use potable water and kitchen sinks that waste grey-water.

Building on Fry's work on elimination design, Cameron Tonkinwise has described 4 strategies that draw on the design disciplines of product design, built environment design (e.g., urban design, interior design, architecture), service design, and communication design [50]. The first strategy is "developing a product that renders existing products redundant." Tonkinwise refers to this strategy as displacing, although to prevent confusion I will refer to this strategy as *product displacement.* The second strategy is to *restructure* the built environment. For example, bicycle lanes can help inhibit or exclude driving and displace automobiles by promoting cycling. The third strategy is to *disown*: to develop "a service system that promotes shared use of products, eliminating the need for individual or household ownership of those products." Car-share and tool-share services are examples of disowning. The final strategy is vilify/celebrate, which involves using communication design to market the negative qualities of a product or promote lifestyles that do not require a product.

Undesigning with interactive and digital technology

Next I highlight several strands of research from within HCI that are especially relevant to undesigning.

Persuasive design

While persuasive design [20] was highlighted earlier, I once again draw attention to it because of its clear relevance as a cluster of strategies for undesigning. By employing intentional persuasion (c.f. Redstrom [39]), designers can, and in fact do, use technology to persuade (or dissuade) at various scales, ranging from inhibition to foreclosure.

Critical design & Projection

Critical design is an approach that also has strong relevance to undesigning. Dunne and Raby describe critical design as "design that asks carefully crafted questions and makes us think" and directly contrast it with design in the commercial realm that is focused on solving problems and findings answers [16, p. 58]. Critical design is noteworthy in the way that it may call attention to issues and concerns over interactive technology by employing interactive technology, such as bringing into question the effects of electromagnetic radiation by designing provocative electromagnetic devices (see [16]). More generally, DiSalvo uses critical design work by Dunne, Raby and Singh to demonstrate how design may be employed to project potential future consequences of technology to stimulate discussion and debate [13, p. 52-55]. DiSalvo refers to this as the design tactic of projection. Critical design and projection are perhaps most clearly related to the areas of safeguarding and foreclosing.

Photography and digital imagery

Photography, as a mode of designing and making, is also relevant to undesigning. Tonkinwise, in his discussion of vilify/celebrate as a strategy for elimination design, reminds us that "the profession and discipline of visual communication has a proud history of subversion, recasting commercial or political visual promotions in new contexts that reveal the concealed truth of about what is being promoted." [50]. Eli Blevis has recently drawn attention to the potential role of digital photography as a mode of design and design research within HCI [5]. To demonstrate the role that photography can, and has, played as a mode of designerly action, Blevis cites Lewis Hine's photographs of child laborers in the early 20th century as leading to the enactment of child labor laws in the U.S. I draw attention to this area here because it suggests ways that digital technology may variously be employed to undesign technology (including its use in persuasive design and critical design).

Implications not to design

Recently Baumer and Silberman have highlighted the importance of considering implications to *not* design technology [2]. They propose three questions that may be used to identify instances where technological intervention may not appropriate: (1) "Could the technology be replaced by an equally viable low-tech or non-technological approach to the situation?" (p. 2271) (2) "Does a technological intervention result in more trouble or harm than the situation it's meant to address?" (p. 2272) (3) "Does a technology solve a computationally tractable transformation of a problem rather than the problem itself?" (p. 2272).

These questions and the approach suggested by Baumer and Silberman are clearly aligned with undesigning (and are particularly suggestive of the areas of foreclosure and exclusion, as well as restoration). An obvious yet important way that implications to not design may be incorporated into HCI research is with respect to the "implications for design" resulting from fieldwork and user studies (c.f. Dourish [15]). For example, based on their studies of productivity tools, Leshed and Sengers caution designers against the design of productivity tools that are too immersive [33]. Related to this discussion, Satchell and Dourish argue that there is overlooked value in studying not only uses but also *non-uses* of technology in order to inform design [40]. The articulation of implications to not design or to undesign, whether based on user studies or otherwise, represent an important route to engaging with undesign.

EMERGENT ISSUES AND OPPORTUNITIES

Having more precisely articulated what undesign is, in what specific ways technology may be negated, and how in practice this may be achieved, I now turn these ideas back onto the questions outlined in the introduction. To reiterate, the two key questions posed were: (1) To what extent and in what ways should undesigning technology be an acknowledged and legitimate area of design research activity within HCI?, and (2) what are the range of activities that HCI has available when there is a strong argument for *undesigning* technology?

Certainly, this paper, or any single paper, cannot possibly hope to definitively resolve these questions. Indeed, questions of this scope can only be determined on an ongoing basis by discussion within the community and by actually conducting research (e.g., running studies, designing technologies, publishing results). However, this paper has taken an important step toward clarifying and addressing these questions. With respect to the second question, thus far I have outlined a range of potential activities upon which HCI may draw. In conclusion I further offer a scheme of dividing the space of undesigning into areas that can further help clarify the issues at hand. Each category moves increasingly further away from the notion of design as the concrete making of a novel interactive technology. For each of these four areas, I will review relevant areas of undesign covered thus far.

Undesigning interactive technology with interactive technology

In what ways can the design of interactive technology be employed to undesign interactive technology? Here I have drawn attention to one such area: the design of interactive technologies that self-inhibit. These types of self-inhibiting technologies appear to clearly fit within the scope of design in the context of HCI. Indeed, self-inhibition was shown to already present itself in certain ways in the design of interactive technologies. However, I have also drawn attention to an area of self-inhibition that is apparently less often considered, namely the design of self-inhibiting options. Considering the concepts of self-inhibition and self-inhibiting options may be particularly useful in conjunction with design approaches such as persuasive design [e.g.,20,39], critical design [16], and designing for reflection and multiple interpretations [e.g.,26,27,44].

Undesigning interactive technology without interactive technology

To what extent can HCI design without interactive technology? While this paper cannot hope to resolve this question, here I will suggest that there is value in considering areas of design that target interactive technology yet do not necessarily involve making or deploying interactive technology, at least not in traditional ways. Undesigning specific uses of interactive technology without introducing new interactive technologies may be a worthwhile and viable area to consider, such as removing technology, excluding technology, replacing technology and restoring technology. While such forms of design activity should almost certainly not occupy a central position within our field, considering them could open up new and overlooked spaces for design.

Argumentation as undesigning: Undesigning "without making" anything

To what extent can HCI (un)design without making novel or tangible artifacts? The areas of critical design and digital photography suggest ways of designing that place less emphasis on the introduction of a physical thing with a clear utilitarian function, and instead emphasize a form of design that is primarily concerned with argumentation and provocation. Another area to consider is "implications for design". As at least one step removed from the actual design and making of an artifact for "end users", such activity may be considered a form of design activity that does not involve making anything, and in fact may lead to the "unmaking" of technology. For example, approaching the interpretation of fieldwork data through the lens of undesigning could lead to implications to undesign by removing, excluding or safeguarding. Whether or not such activity is firmly placed within the realm of design, there is apparent value in considering them to be among the range of options available to HCI. Indeed, having at least considered the "implications for undesign" (including implications to not design [2]) when interpreting fieldwork is arguably a responsible and valuable design-oriented research activity; if they are not considered, to what extent can we have confidence in the appropriateness of the implications to affirmatively design technology?

Inaction as design action

Finally, I raise the question: To what extent should inaction be considered as a viable form of design action? Consider, for example that Blevis has previously drawn attention to the negative material effects of technology disposal on the environment [3]. Baumer and Silberman have further called attention to a range of mobile applications that aim to encourage sustainable behaviors yet do not address the environmental problems associated with the proliferation of mobile computing devices [2]. To take this a step further, it could be argued that there is a relationship between the design of mobile applications and the proliferation of mobile devices. Given these concerns, the question may be raised: Is refraining from designing mobile phones an appropriate form of designerly action?

In contrast to the previous areas of consideration, here I raise the question of inaction as design action primarily as a provocation rather than as an issue of discerning disciplinary boundaries. What I am suggesting is that the notion of inaction as design action could be a useful construct for consideration of the limits of design action, and the appropriateness of such (in)action. The notion of design inaction, and undesigning more generally, may also prove to be useful for *creatively* exploring a design space. Brainstorming and other methods of "transcending fixation" are hallmarks of design practice [e.g.,34]. Exploring the ideas of inaction, erasure, exclusion and so on may in fact be useful within the design process as methods for arriving at new and creative design outcomes. In this way I am suggesting that undesigning may useful to design that is primarily concerned with creating rather than negating.

CONCLUSION

Based upon various concerns over the limitations and negative of effects technology, this paper has inquired into undesigning, understood as the intentional and explicit negation of technology. Building on a range of theoretical constructs, I have articulated a framework for conceptualizing the intentional negation of technology in terms of its scope and scale. This framework describes technology negation in terms of a spectrum ranging from inhibition, to displacement, to erasure and foreclosure. I then expanded on these areas to articulate several additional areas of undesigning, including self-inhibiting options, exclusion, removal, replacement, restoration, and safeguarding. As such, this paper offers a theoretical contribution to what might appropriately be termed (un)design theory. In closing, I would like to emphasize that it is my hope that the ideas presented here may be engaged with not only through intellectual discussion and the elaboration of theory, but also through the actual doing of (un)design research through design—a notion that takes a cue from HCI design research that emphasizes doing and making as valuable and valid forms of inquiry.

ACKNOWLEDGMENTS

I thank my advisor, Eric Paulos, for all of his guidance, encouragement, and support. I also thank all the anonymous reviewers for their thoughtful and instructive comments on this paper. Financial support was provided in part by National Science Foundation Grant #IIS-1018340.

REFERENCES

1. Akrich, M. 1992. The description of technical objects, in Bijker, WE. #38; Law, J. (Eds), Shaping Technology/Building Society. MIT Press.
2. Baumer, E. & Silberman, S. 2011. When the implication is not to design (technology). CHI '11.
3. Blevis, E. 2007. Sustainable interaction design: invention & disposal, renewal & reuse. CHI '07.
4. Blevis, E. & Stolterman, E. 2009. Transcending disciplinary boundaries in interaction design. interactions 16, 5 (Sep. 2009), 48-51.
5. Blevis, E. 2011. Digital Imagery as Meaning and Form in HCI and Design: An Introduction to the Visual Thinking Backpage Gallery. interactions 18, 5.
6. Bodker, S. 2006. When second wave HCI meets third wave challenges. NordiCHI '06.
7. Borgmann, A. 1984. *Technology and the character of contemporary life*. University of Chicago Press.
8. Bower, J.L. & Christensen, C.M. 1995. "Disruptive Technologies: Catching the Wave" *Harvard Business Review*, January–February 1995
9. Bourdieu, P. 1972. *Outline of a theory of practice*. Cambridge University Press.
10. Buchanan, R. 1989. Declaration by design: Rhetoric, argument, and demonstration in design practice. In V. Margolin (Eds.), Design discourse (pp. 91-109).
11. DiSalvo, C., Sengers, P., and Brynjarsdóttir, H. 2010. Mapping the landscape of sustainable HCI. CHI '10.
12. DiSalvo, C., Light, A., Hirsch, T., Le Dantec, C., Goodman, E. & Hill, H. 2010. HCI, communities and politics. CHI EA '10.
13. DiSalvo, C. 2009. Design and the Construction of Publics. Design Issues, 25(1): 48-63.
14. Dourish, P. 2010. HCI and Environmental Sustainability: The Politics of Design and the Design of Politics. DIS '10
15. Dourish, P. 2006. Implications for design. CHI '06.
16. Dunne, A., & Raby, F. 2001. *Design noir: The secret life of electronic objects*. August Media, Boston.

17. Fallman, D. 2011. The new good: exploring the potential of philosophy of technology to contribute to human-computer interaction. CHI '11.

18. Fallman, D. 2003. Design-Oriented Human-Computer Interaction. CHI '03.

19. Fallman, D. 2005. Why Research-Oriented Design Isn't Design-Oriented Research. NordiCHI '95.

20. Fogg, B.J. 2002. Persuasive technology: using computers to change what we think and do. *Ubiquity* 2002, December.

21. Friedman, B. (Ed.) (1997). *Human Values and the Design of Computer Technology*. CSLI Press.

22. Friedman, B. & Nathan, L. 2010. Multi-lifespan information system design: a research initiative for the hci community. CHI '10.

23. Fry, T. 2009. *Design futuring: sustainability, ethics, and new practice*. Berg.

24. Fry, T. 1999. *A New Design Philosophy: An Introduction to Defuturing*. New South Wales, Australia: NSWU Press.

25. Fullerton, B. 2010. Designing for solitude. *interactions* 17(6):6-9.

26. Gaver, W., Bowers, J., Boucher, A., Gellerson, H., Pennington, S., Schmidt, S., Steed, A., Villars, N. & Walker, B. 2004. The drift table: designing for ludic engagement. CHI EA '04.

27. Gaver, W. & Martin, H. 2000. Alternatives: exploring information appliances through conceptual design proposals. CHI '00.

28. Giddens, A. 1984. *The Constitution of Society. Outline of the Theory of Structuration*. Cambridge.

29. Ihde, D. (1990). *Technology and the lifeworld- from garden to earth*. Indiana University Press.

30. Irani, L., Vertesi, J., Dourish, P., Philip, K., & Grinter, R. E. 2010. Postcolonial computing: a lens on design and development. CHI '10.

31. Latour, B. 2005. *Reassembling the social: An introduction to actor-network-theory*. Oxford.

32. Latour, B. 2000. Where are the missing masses? The sociology of a few mundane artefacts. In Bijker, W. E. #38; Law J. (Eds), Shaping Technology/Building Society: Studies in Sociotechnical Change. MIT Press

33. Leshed, G. & Sengers, P. 2011. "I lie to myself that I have freedom in my own schedule": productivity tools and experiences of busyness. CHI '11.

34. Löwgren, J. & Stolterman, E. 2004. *Thoughtful interaction design: a design perspective on information technology*. MIT Press.

35. Mitcham, C. 1978. Types of technology. *Research in philosophy and technology, I*, 229-294.

36. Nelson, H. & Stolterman, E. 2003. *Design Way: Intentional Change in an Unpredictable World*. Englewood Cliffs.

37. Norman, D. 1999. Affordance, conventions and design. interactions, 6(3).

38. Perrin, N. 1979. *Giving up the gun. Japan's reversion to the sword, 1543-1879*. Boston: David R. Godine.

39. Redström, J. 2006. Persuasive Design: Fringes and Foundations. Persuasive, 3962:112–122.

40. Satchell, C. & Dourish, P. 2009. Beyond the user: use and non-use in HCI. OZCHI '09.

41. Sellen, A. & Harper, R. 2001. *The myth of the paperless office*. MIT Press.

42. Schumpeter, J. A. 1949. The historical approach to the analysis of business cycles, in Essays: On Entrepreneurs, Innovations, Business Cycles, and the Evolution of Capitalism. Transaction.

43. Sengers, P. 2011. What I learned on Change Islands: reflections on IT and pace of life. interactions, 18(2)

44. Sengers, P. & Gaver, W. 2006 Staying open to interpretation: engaging multiple meanings in design and evaluation. DIS '06.

45. Shove, E. 2003. Comfort, cleanliness and convenience: The social organization of normality. Berg.

46. Simon, H. 1996. *The Sciences of the Artificial: 3rd Edition*. MIT Press.

47. Tatar, D., Lee, J.-S., Alaloula, N. 2008. Playground games. DIS '08.

48. Taylor, A. 2011. Out there. CHI '11.

49. Tomlinson, B. 2010. *Greening Through IT*. MIT Press.

50. Tonkinwise, C. Design away. Design philosophy politics. Retrieved September 2011 from http://designphilosophypolitics.informatics.indiana.edu

51. Verbeek, P-P. 2005. *What things do: Technology, agency and design*. MIT Press.

52. Wakkary, R. and Tanenbaum, K. 2009. A sustainable identity: the creativity of an everyday designer. CHI '09.

53. Willis, A.M. (2006). Ontological designing. Design Philosophy Papers. #02/2006

54. Winner, L. 1986. *The whale and the reactor: a search for limits in an age of high technology*. U. of Chicago.

55. Winograd, T. & Flores, F. 1987. *Understanding computers and cognition: A new foundation for design*. Addison-Wesley.

56. Zimmerman, J., Forlizzi, J., and Evenson, S. 2007. Research through design as a method for interaction design research in HCI. CHI '07.

57. Zimmerman, J., Forlizzi, J. & Stolterman, E. 2010. An analysis and critique of Research through Design: towards a formalization of a research approach. DIS '10.

Affordances in HCI: Toward a Mediated Action Perspective

Victor Kaptelinin [1,2] and Bonnie Nardi [3]

[1] Department of Information Science and Media Studies
University of Bergen
Postboks 7802, NO-5020
Norway

[2] Department of Informatics
Umeå University
SE - 901 87 Umeå
Sweden

[3] Department of Informatics
School of Information and Computer Sciences
5088 Bren Hall, UC Irvine
92697-3440, USA

ABSTRACT
Interpretations of the concept of "affordances" in HCI are becoming increasingly diverse, extending well beyond the original Gibsonian meaning. We discuss some of the key analyses of affordances in HCI research and make three related claims. First, we argue that many current interpretations of the concept are essentially incompatible with Gibson. Second, we hold that the Gibsonian concept of affordances, conceptualized as interaction between animals and their environments, provides some important insights, but is, in the end, of limited relevance to HCI research. Third, we call for adopting *a mediated action perspective* on affordances as an alternative to Gibson's ecological psychology. We outline a view of technology affordances as possibilities for human action mediated by cultural means conceived as a relational property of a three-way interaction between the person, mediational means, and environment. We conclude with a discussion of prospects for future conceptual and empirical explorations of the meditational perspective in HCI research.

Author Keywords
Affordances, technology affordances, ecological psychology, mediated action.

ACM Classification Keywords
H.5.2 [Information Interfaces and Presentation]: User Interfaces — Theory and methods;

General Terms
Design, Human factors, Theory.

INTRODUCTION
Affordance is currently one of the most fundamental concepts in HCI and interaction design. The term was originally proposed by Gibson [17, 18] within his ecological approach to perception. It was introduced to HCI by Norman [22] in the late 1980s and quickly became one of the field's key concepts, widely used by researchers, educators, and practitioners. Such a prominent status for the concept would suggest that the field should have a well-defined and generally accepted meaning of affordance. However, this is not the case. The exact meaning of the term continues to be a subject of ongoing debate. Numerous attempts have been made throughout the history of HCI to more clearly define what affordances are and to develop the concept further to better meet the needs of HCI research and practice (e.g., [1, 3, 20, 23, 32]). Arguably, however, the meaning of "affordance" in HCI and interaction design remains vague.

Permission to make digital or hard copies of all or part of this work for personal or classroom use is granted without fee provided that copies are not made or distributed for profit or commercial advantage and that copies bear this notice and the full citation on the first page. To copy otherwise, or republish, to post on servers or to redistribute to lists, requires prior specific permission and/or a fee.
CHI'12, May 5–10, 2012, Austin, Texas, USA.
Copyright 2012 ACM 978-1-4503-1015-4/12/05...$10.00.

The aim of this paper is to contribute to clarifying the confusion surrounding affordances. We start out by exploring the relationship between some of the most influential analyses of the notion in HCI research and the original notion proposed by Gibson.

Of particular interest are the inherent limitations of Gibson's concept of affordances. A common position explicitly or implicitly expressed in many HCI discussions is that Gibson did not exploit the full potential of the notion he proposed, and that his understanding of affordances should be further elaborated to include a broader range of issues and phenomena. Such phenomena include functionality, development, motivation, communication, culture, and context (e.g., [1, 3, 16, 20, 23, 24, 26]). An underlying assumption is that Gibson's theory of affordance does allow for such extensions.

The analysis in this paper questions that assumption. We argue that the notion of affordance as it was understood by Gibson has a distinct and rather limited focus, determined by the role of the notion in Gibson's conceptual framework as a whole. Accordingly, the concept of affordance has a number of fundamental inherent limitations and cannot be directly extended beyond its original scope. We argue that a concept of technology affordances which would adequately serve the needs of HCI research and practice can only come about through theoretical re-grounding, that is, constructing the concept on a different theoretical foundation. We propose that a socio-cultural framework be employed for understanding technology affordances as possibilities for human actions mediated by cultural means.

GIBSON'S THEORY OF AFFORDANCES: ANIMALS, ENVIRONMENTS, AND DIRECT PERCEPTION

The first step of our analysis is to identify the basic assumptions underlying the original concept of affordance within Gibson's ecological approach to perception [12, 13].

The approach challenged the prevalent view of perception as a sequence of information processing stages. Gibson asserted that animals directly pick up significant information about their environments from the ambient optic array. The information that is picked up is information about *affordances*—what the environment "offers the animal, what it provides or furnishes, either for good or ill" [12]. In other words, animals directly perceive affordances as possibilities for action in the environment, which are determined, on the one hand, by the objective properties of the environment and, on the other hand, by the action capabilities of the animal.

Gibson defined affordances as independent of the current needs and goals of the perceiver. He acknowledged that the concept was heavily influenced by precepts from Gestalt psychology, especially Koffka's "demand character" and Lewin's "invitation character" and "valence" [12]. At the same time, Gibson emphasized that there was a substantial difference between these concepts and affordance:

> The concept of affordance is derived from these concepts of valence, invitation, and demand, but with a crucial difference. The affordance of something does *not change* as the need of the observer changes. The observer may or may not perceive or attend to the affordance, according to his needs, but the affordance, being invariant, is always there to be perceived. An affordance is not bestowed upon an object by a need of an observer and his act of perceiving it. The object offers what it does because it is what it is. ([12], original emphasis)

The independence of affordances from the situational needs of the animal does not make them value-free aspects of the environment. Affordances are always meaningful. They can be positive or negative, even affordances of the same object. A knife, for instance affords slicing a sausage but also cutting a finger; water may afford drinking but also drowning.

While affordances exist irrespective of whether or not they are perceived by the observer, in general there is a close connection between affordances and perception. Perception is a key factor defining the action capabilities of the animal. For instance, a dark forest may afford stumbling because the person cannot see tree roots clearly enough (which affordance may or may not be noticed by the person).

Gibson was very clear about not being particularly interested in affordances *per se*. To him, affordances were relevant to his larger ecological theory of perception only to the extent to which they could help provide an account of how actors perceive their environments:

> The central question for the theory of affordances is not whether they exist and are real but whether information is available in ambient light for perceiving them. [12]

Finally, Gibson made virtually no distinction between human beings and other animals. As follows from his general theoretical stance of considering the mutuality of the animal and the environment as a conceptual point of departure, as well as the concrete examples of affordances he provided, the approach was intended to be general enough to be applicable to all animals. While some examples of affordances described by Gibson are related to specifically human objects (e.g., knives, mailboxes, staircases), these affordances are considered as similar to affordances provided by "natural" objects to non-human animals, e.g., affordances for physical manipulation (piercing, inserting) or locomotion (climbing). Gibson maintained that it would be a mistake

> ... to separate the cultural environment from the natural environment, as if there were a world of mental products distinct from the world of material products. There is only one world, however diverse, and all animals live in it, although we human animals have altered it to suit ourselves. [12]

The key underlying assumptions of Gibson's theory of affordances can be summarized as follows:

- affordances are perceived directly; their perception is not based on an interpretation of initially meaningless "raw" sensory data,
- affordances are relational properties; they emerge in the interaction between the animal and environment: the same environment may offer different affordances to different animals,
- affordances are independent of the situational needs of the perceiver,
- natural environments and cultural environments should not be separated from one another, and
- the theory of affordances is concerned with how affordances are perceived rather than affordances *per se*.

These assumptions define the original scope of the notion and set the stage for the discussion below.

THE AFFORDANCE DEBATE IN HCI: SELECTED KEY POINTS

The introduction of the concept to HCI

When introducing affordances to HCI, Norman described them as

> ...the perceived or actual properties of the thing, primarily those fundamental properties that determine just how the thing could possibly be used... A chair affords ("is for") support and therefore affords sitting. A

> chair can also be carried. Glass is for seeing through, and for breaking. [22].

Affordances, according to Norman, provide strong clues to the operations of things and, therefore, can be fruitfully employed in design:

> When affordances are taken advantage of, the user knows what to do just by looking: no picture, label, or instruction is required. [22].

A systematic exploration of the notion of affordances in HCI was done by Gaver [10, 11], who identified three types of affordances depending on the relationship between affordances and perceptual information: visible, hidden, and false affordances. In addition, Gaver analyzed hierarchical and temporal dependencies between simple affordances, which led him to introduce the concepts of nested and sequential affordances [10].

The Ecological Interface Design (EID) approach by Vicente and Rasmussen [34] is another early attempt to employ Gibson's theory as a foundation for the design of interactive technologies and work environments. The approach differentiates between various types of affordances by mapping them to levels of cognitive control and a means-ends abstraction hierarchy[1].

Separating affordances from perception

McGrenere and Ho [20] present a thorough discussion of the notion of affordances in HCI including a detailed comparative analysis of the original Gibsonian concept and its interpretation by Norman. The authors maintain that the key difference between Gibson and Norman is in how they understood the role of perception. For Gibson, affordances exist independently of whether or not they are perceived by the actor, while for Norman affordances can be not only real but also just perceived. McGrenere and Ho [20] argue strongly for separating affordances from their perception (the position they ascribe to Gibson) because, as they claim, the separation would help researchers and practitioners more clearly differentiate between two aspects of design, namely: designing the utility of an object (its affordances) and designing usability (the information that specifies the affordance). Tornvliet [31] makes a similar argument.

In addition, McGrenere and Ho argue that there is a need to further develop Gibson's original notion. In particular, they call for moving beyond a binary view of affordance as something which either exists or does not exist, toward a more nuanced interpretation of the "possibility for action", that would, for instance, take into account the difficulty of using an affordance.

The key points of the analysis are summarized by the authors as follows:

> Returning to a definition close to that of Gibson's would solidify the concept and would also recognize that designing the utility or functional purpose is a worthwhile endeavor in its own right. In order for the *affordance* concept to be used fully in the design world, however, Gibson's definition needs to incorporate the notion of varying degrees of an affordance. [20]

On the one hand, McGrenere and Ho claim that HCI needs to return to the true, authentic Gibsonian interpretation of affordances. On the other hand, they imply that the original notion is not sufficiently developed and must be further evolved.

Moving beyond operational affordances: affordances as emerging in activities

Baerentsen and Trettvik [3] outline an activity-theoretical perspective on affordances. The structure of their argument is not dissimilar to that of McGrenere and Ho [20]; they point out that HCI research has deviated from Gibson's notion, criticize the deviation, and suggest that the original notion be further developed to overcome its shortcomings. However, their disagreement with the way HCI interprets affordance is of a more philosophical nature:

> The concept of affordance was meant to cut though the subjective-objective dichotomy of traditional psychology and philosophy, but its interpretation in HCI often retained this dichotomy. [3]

The main shortcoming of Gibson's concept of affordances, according to Baerentsen and Trettvik [3], is that the underlying notion of activity is simplistic and undeveloped, and essentially limited to low-level interaction between the actor and environment:

> … it seems to us that Gibson's… focus was on the operational side of activity in his treatment of "behavior". His focus was on the perceptual requirements of the operational realization of activity, the information that is available in the environment that lets the organism control locomotion and simple forms of object related activities. Perhaps his behaviourist "upbringing" blinded him to the non-identity of motivational-goal-directed aspects of activity... [3]

Adopting a more advanced notion of activity developed in activity theory (e.g., [4]), would mean understanding affordances as contextualized in unfolding activities and emerging in concrete interaction between the actor and the environment:

> The features of the physical environment and its objects provide affordances when they are related to the needs and requirements of organisms.…Although affordances are in a sense constituted by objective physical features of the environment, these objective features only become affordances when some organisms relate to them in their activity. [3]

[1] A thorough discussion of EID can be found in [1, 20].

The main points made by Baerentsen and Trettvik have been taken up in further discussions of affordances (e.g., [35]).

Selected interpretations of affordances in HCI history: A summary

Table 1 presents a brief (and somewhat simplified) summary of the relationship between selected analyses of affordances in HCI with respect to the five basic assumptions of Gibson's theory, discussed above.

The first two assumptions, with few exceptions, are adopted by nearly all the interpretations. Concerning the remaining three assumptions, however, there is an opposite tendency: most interpretations clearly deviate from Gibson. The only one that appears fully consistent with the original Gibsonian framework regarding these three assumptions is Norman's.

Gaver's reference to affordances as suggesting "relevant and desirable actions in an immediate way" [8] implies an understanding of affordances as dependent on user needs. This understanding makes his interpretation similar to some Gestalt psychology concepts, such as "invitation character", from which Gibson explicitly distanced himself [12]. Separating affordances from their perception as McGrenere and Ho [20] do foregrounds issues of utility and functionality which are not of direct relevance to Gibson's original research agenda. The position advocated by Baerentsen and Trettvik [3] essentially abandons all three of these assumptions.

GIBSON'S THEORY AND CURRENT HCI DEBATE: THE NEED FOR RE-GROUNDING THE CONCEPT OF AFFORDANCES

Undeniably, explorations of Gibsonian affordances in the HCI research discussed above have contributed to further development of the concept. The notions of nested and sequential affordances [10] and degrees of affordances [20], levels and types of affordances [34, 14] enrich the concept and make it a more useful conceptual tool for analysis and design. At the same time, as suggested by Table 1, interpretations of the concept in HCI research tend to transcend its original scope and become inconsistent with the basic assumptions of Gibson's theory.

This trend is even more apparent in recent research. A growing number of studies in HCI and related areas call for re-defining the notion of affordances to include social and cultural aspects of human interaction with the world. For instance, Rizzo [26] maintains that "… Gibson's account does not yield sufficient insight for affordances that are culturally determined through individual history". Zhang [39] introduces the notion of "motivational affordances" which includes, for instance, "leadership and followership". Turner [32] contrasts Gibsonian "simple affordances" to "complex affordances", the latter embodying history and practice. Similar claims were made in other studies (e.g., [6, 16, 19, 24, 26]).

In general, the work that advocates the need to move beyond Gibson to "social affordances" is characterized by extreme diversity. The aims, research agendas, and arguments put forward in individual studies are sometimes only loosely related to each other. Concrete examples of social affordances range from articulation [35] to imitative learning [26] to competence and achievement [39].

	Aspects of affordance according to Gibson				
	Relational property	Directly perceived	Independent of actor's needs	Same in natural and cultural environments	Theory's concern with perception, not affordances *per se*
Norman (1989, 1999)	—/ +	+/ —	+	+	+
Gaver (1991, 1992)	+	+	—	+	+
McGrenere & Ho (2000)	+	+	+	+	—
Baerentsen & Trettvik (2002)	+	—	—	—	—

Table 1. Gibson's theory of affordances vs. selected interpretations of affordances in HCI research

Despite their diversity, many current interpretations of affordances have one thing in common: they typically criticize Gibson for introducing a powerful concept but excessively limiting its scope (e.g., [4, 16, 26]). It is averred, implicitly or explicitly, that Gibson failed to exploit the full potential of his own brainchild. This criticism, in our view, overlooks that Gibson's point of departure was "the mutuality of *animal* and environment" ([12], emphasis added). Gibson provides a deliberately delimited perspective on humans and how they make sense of their environments. Gibson's theory views humans as, essentially, animals acting in their natural habitats. Gibson's notion of affordance as "natural affordances", such as those for manipulation and locomotion, is consistent with the overall aims of his research project which centered on perception. It would be unfair to criticize Gibson for not developing the notion of affordance beyond natural affordances, i.e., to criticize him for not choosing a different research agenda.

Therefore, while current debate clearly indicates that Gibson's original notion is too limited to properly serve the needs of HCI research and practice, the notion has its own inherent contours, and cannot be "upgraded" without being transformed into something it is not.

The strategy for constructing a richer notion of affordances advocated in this paper is different. We posit that HCI needs a non-Gibsonian concept of technology affordances, and suggest a *re-grounding* the notion. Re-grounding means preserving the general understanding of affordances as action possibilities, but constructing the concept on a different theoretical foundation, one more suitable for analysis and support of human uses of technology. In this respect our position is different from calling for a radically redefined notion of "extended" affordances (e.g., equating affordances and context, see [32]).

A limitation of Gibson's framework, particularly critical for HCI, is that it lacks an appropriate conceptual apparatus for understanding technologies as a special type of objects, that is, tools mediating human interaction with the environment. This is not to say that Gibson did not consider tools. Affordances of tools were of special interest to Gibson, who provided revealing insights into what makes an object a good candidate for being a tool. For instance Gibson describes a club as "an elongated object, [which] especially, if weighted at one end and graspable at the other, affords hitting or hammering" [12]. These insights were further developed in more recent studies within the ecological approach. In particular, Wagman (e.g., [33]) argues that the whole "user-tool-environment" system needs to be taken into account to understand how users choose a grip on simple hand-held tools, However, owing to the main focus on the "animal-environment" interaction, the analysis of tools in the Gibsonian tradition is incomplete in several respects.

First, while it is implied that tools have two facets (corresponding, for instance, to "graspability" and "impactability"), the integration of the facets has not been systematically analyzed. Indeed, in natural objects, such as sticks, the facets are inherently inseparable aspects of a tool. However, with the advancement of technology, they progressively become more independent of one another, and their integration can be an issue that should be addressed in design. For instance, power-driven tools are operated by controls, which may take various shapes and have different locations. Digital technologies allow for even greater dissociation of the facets. Second, Gibson's theory does not deal with the social aspects of the use and production of tools, such as the support of collective action and the historical development of tools based on the transition of experience from generation to generation. Third, the use of tools is not related to action capabilities of the actor: a tool is just an object in a natural environment, which provides certain affordances without changing the nature of the actor.

Therefore, Gibson's theory of affordances is limited in its support for understanding mediated human actions. Given that HCI as a field is primarily concerned with advanced, rapidly developing mediational means that make deep impact on both individual humans and the society, this limitation of the framework significantly undermines its ability to serve as a theoretical foundation for studying action possibilities offered by technologies to humans. To address this problem, we propose a mediated action perspective on technology affordances.

AN OUTLINE OF A MEDIATED ACTION PERSPECTIVE ON TECHNOLOGY AFFORDANCES

One of Gibson's fundamental insights is that it is our *basic nature to see the environment in terms of the range of action possibilities* (i.e., affordances) offered to us by the objects in the environment. This means, in particular, that a *natural* human way to perceive a technological artifact is to actively pick up information in order to establish the affordances provided by the artifact. Gibsonian theory suggests that successfully conveying the possibilities for meaningful action offered by a technology to the user should be a top priority in the design of interactive systems (cf. [1, 34]).

The mediated action perspective we propose retains the general Gibsonian understanding of affordances as action possibilities offered by the environment to the actor. However, the notion is conceptually "re-grounded" and not merely extended. Instead of Gibsonian ecological psychology's concern with how animals perceive and act in their natural environments, we adopt the Vygotskian socio-cultural approach (e.g., [36, 38]) concerned with humans acting in cultural contexts. According to the approach, the most characteristic feature of human beings, differentiating them from other animals, is that their activities and minds are mediated by culturally developed tools, including technology. The socio-cultural view of technology as a mediational means has been introduced to HCI through activity theory [4, 21] which is a particular framework within the general socio-cultural approach.

It should be noted that in the discussion below, "human action" is understood as action carried out by an individual human being rather than a "collective subject". While the latter is an important issue to consider, it is beyond the scope of the present analysis as we move to re-conceptualize and re-ground the foundational concept of affordance for HCI.

The mediated social action perspective on technology affordances is outlined below in three steps. First, we describe the basic structure of an *instrumental technology affordance* as an integrated unit comprising two components: handling affordance and effecter affordance. Second, we identify a set of *auxiliary technological affordances* determined by the embeddedness of a technology in "webs of mediators" [5] typical of real-life uses of technology. Third, we discuss how technology affordances develop over time.

As immediately follows from adopting a mediated action perspective, technology can be considered a mediational means, an instrument through which the person interacts with objects in the environment. The person directly interacts with a technology by handling it and, indirectly, by causing an effect on an object. Therefore, action possibilities provided by a technology, considered as an instrument, comprise two related facets (Figure 1): (a) possibilities for interacting *with* the technology (P-T), i.e., *handling affordances*, and (b) possibilities for employing the technology to make an effect on an object (T-O), i.e., *effecter* affordances. Together, they define instrumental technology affordances as possibilities for acting *through* the technology in question on a certain object ((P-T)-O).

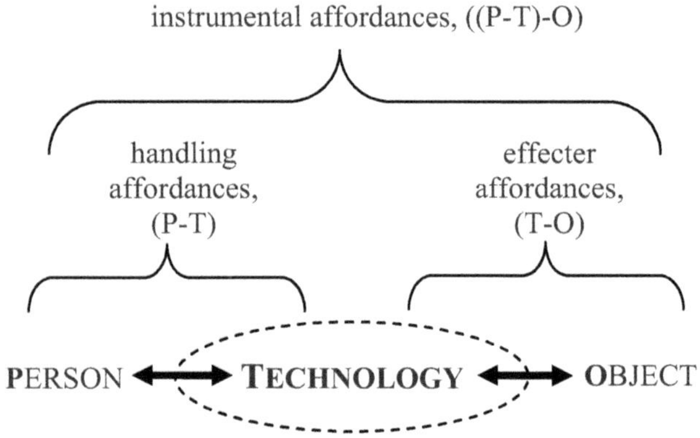

Figure 1. Two facets of instrumental technology affordances: handling affordances and effecter affordances

The distinction between handling affordances and effecter affordances is obvious in case of traditional instruments, discussed by Gibson, such as knives. Such instruments usually comprise two distinct parts, responsible, respectively, for handling (e.g., a handle) and affecting objects (e.g., blade). Apparently, the distinction also applies to digital technologies. For instance, common user interface widgets, such as the scroll bar, enable two types of actions [2]; operating on the widget (e.g., dragging the scroll box) and operating on the object of interest (e.g., displaying in the window a certain portion of the document). These two facets correspond, respectively, to handling and effecter affordances of a widget.

The basic structure of instrumental affordances shown in Figure 1 is a simplified abstraction, which does not reflect the diversity of action possibilities associated with human mediated action. Bødker and Andersen [5] observe that real-life mediation seldom involves a single mediator. Instead, it typically consists of "web of mediators", which are organized in chains (i.e., the object of one action becomes a mediator of the next one) or levels, depending on the purpose of the activity. Accordingly, the possibilities for action offered by technologies embedded in real-life contexts include not only direct, instrumental affordances, but also a variety of generic types of indirect, auxiliary affordances emerging in the complex relations within webs of mediation. Examples of such auxiliary affordances are maintenance affordances and aggregation affordances (see Figure 2).

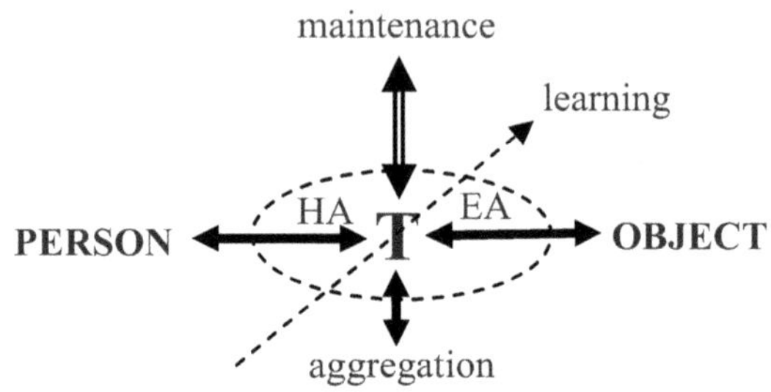

Figure 2. Technology affordances: Instrumental, maintenance, and aggregation (T – technology, HA-handling affordances, EA-effecter affordances)

Maintenance affordances. Technologies need to be taken care of to work as effective mediators. It is essential, therefore, that a technology provide appropriate affordances for carrying out maintenance routines and troubleshooting (understood in a broad sense, as including necessary modifications of the technology). For instance, a mobile phone must enable the person in changing the battery or inserting SIM cards (see Figure 3 for an example of an affordance provided by the back cover of a mobile phone).

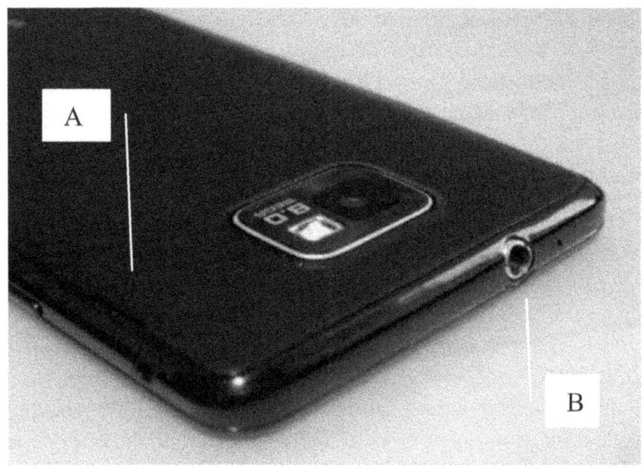

Figure 3. Auxiliary affordances of a mobile phone. A: back cover removal slot (maintenance); B: headset jack slot (aggregation).

Aggregation affordances. Technological artifacts can be combined with other artifacts (digital and non-digital) to constitute larger-scale compound mediators, both ad hoc assemblages of tools needed for a specific task and interoperable technologies designed from the start to work in unison. For instance, a mobile phone can be connected to a headset to comprise a personal music player (see Figure 3). If such an aggregation is an essential condition of successfully employing the technology, the possibilities for achieving that should be ensured and conveyed to the person.

Learning affordances. The instrumental and auxiliary technology affordances discussed above (shown in Figures 1-3) are embedded in the context of development and learning. Many technologies cannot be used until at least some learning occurs. A second order mediation is needed to access a tool's instrumental, maintenance, and aggregation affordances. In many common situations, instruction is necessary. For instance, to turn to a non-digital example, while shoe laces admirably afford keeping a shoe snug to the foot, a child (and most adults) could not figure out on their own how to tie the appropriate knot to attain the instrumental affordance. The laces lack a learning affordance. But other tools, especially digital technologies, accomplish the second order mediation of learning by embedding learning affordances within themselves. Tooltips, help screens, standardized icons, and coded signs are typical digital learning affordances. The USB icon inscribed on a computer, for example, demonstrates for the user where it is possible to attach a USB device. (The same sign also appears on the connector signaling the proper orientation of the connector.) The pairing of instrumental and learning affordances is an instance of Wartofsky's typology of mediating means that specifies "primary and secondary artifacts". Primary artifacts get the job done, while secondary artifacts tell us how to use primary artifacts [37].

Recursively, learning affordances may form their own aggregations. When encoded in software, learning affordances can readily be combined in multiple configurations, e.g., hyperlinks, mouseovers, and so on. It may thus be difficult to definitively establish the boundaries of "a technology" or "an artifact" as the generativity and malleability of software enable the rapid appearance and disappearance of cues and information through easily replicable and configurable combinations of signifiers (see [17]).

Bødker and Andersen's notion of webs of mediators [5] is also pertinent; learning affordances entail a chain of linked actions that lead, seriatim, to the completion of the user's goals. Learning affordances thus further render Gibson's notion of direct pick up of invariant cues less relevant for understanding how humans encounter designed artifacts. Learning affordances highlight Gibson's reflection that "we human animals have altered [the world] to suit ourselves."

PERSPECTIVES ON AFFORDANCES: GIBSON'S VS MEDIATED ACTION

The analysis above allows us to discuss how the mediated action perspective on technology affordances is related to the original concept proposed by Gibson. The mediational perspective bears a number of similarities with Gibson's

	GIBSON'S THEORY vs. MEDIATED ACTION PERSPECTIVE		
	Similarities	**Differences**	
		Gibson's theory	**Mediated action perspective**
General notion *Affordances are understood as…*	action possibilities offered to the actor by objects in the environment	possibilities for animal actions in natural environment	possibilities for human actions in cultural environments
Relational property *Affordances emerge in interaction between …*	the actor and the world	the animal and natural environment	the person, tool(s), and cultural environment
Dynamics Action capabilities of the *actor are…*	a result of the development of a coupling between actor and the environment	relatively stable, formed by biological evolution, maturation, and long-term learning	dynamic, can quickly change as a result of tool switching
Role of perception *Quick extraction of information about affordances…*	is critically important for successful acting in the world	occurs as an immediate outcome of placing a certain animal in a certain environment	can be an outcome of learning
Needs *Affordances and actor's situational needs are…*		independent of one another	interrelated: tool affordances can be adjusted to situational needs

Table 2. Perspectives on affordances: Gibson's theory vs. mediated action perspective

theory. It adopts the general notion of affordance as a possibility for action offered by the environment and understands affordance as a relational property defined by the coupling between the actor and the world.

There are also significant differences between the perspectives. The mediated action perspective is concerned with how humans act in their cultural environments, rather than with how animals act in their natural habitats. Accordingly, affordances are understood as emerging in a three-way interaction between actors, their mediational means, and the environments. Therefore, action capabilities of the actor can quickly change as a result of switching to a different tool.

A major disagreement between the approaches is in how they view the relationship between affordances and needs. For Gibson an object "is what it is"; its affordances do not depend on actors' needs. The mediated action perspective points that the dynamic nature of tools make it possible to adjust a tool to a situational need: a knife can be sharpened, a battery charged, a computer application upgraded, and so forth. Another aspect of the relationship is that understanding tool affordances includes recognizing their predefined purposes, which can influence how agents experience their own needs. Finally, some technologies manifest something similar to needs: to function properly they need to be taken care of, which means that the agent should act in a certain way to meet the demands of a tool (e.g., look for a Wi-Fi hotspot).

The mediated action perspective questions Gibson's assumption of the direct perception of affordances. A necessary condition for direct perception is a stable relationship between an actor and the environment. Since modern humans often live in frequently changing environments, the development of direct perception of affordances may be problematic. In general, however, the mediated action perspective also assumes that there is a close connection between perception and action. In particular, extensive learning often results in "almost immediate" pickup of information about action possibilities offered by objects in the environment (e.g., see [8]).

The similarities and differences between Gibson's theory of affordances and the mediated action perspective are summarized in Table 2.

IMPLICATIONS FOR ANALYSIS AND DESIGN OF INTERACTIVE SYSTEMS: A FEW ILLUSTRATIONS

There are several ways in which the mediated action perspective on technology affordances can be relevant to analysis and design of interactive technologies. In this section we present a few simple examples of how the two-facet model of instrumental affordances, introduced above (see Fig. 1) can be employed in HCI. The examples are intended to provide simple illustrations rather than give a complete overview of potential applications of the mediated action perspective.

A straightforward way to use the model is to employ it for identifying potential usability problems. The model predicts that usability problems can be selectively related to handling or effecter affordances of a technology. For instance, the effecter affordances of an alarm clock (i.e., time setting and alarm activation/ deactivation) can be efficiently conveyed to the person but the handling affordances (i.e., how exactly to use the clock controls to achieve that) can be confusing.

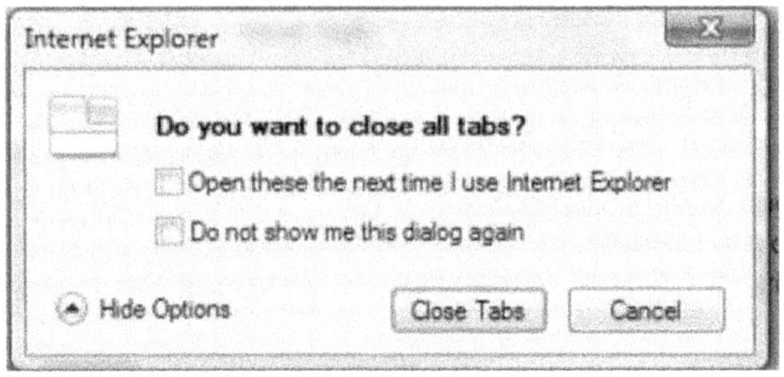

Figure 4. Immediately obvious handling affordances, but not effecter affordances.

The opposite problem is experienced when handling affordances are clear but the outcomes of user actions (effecter affordances) are not immediately obvious. Fig. 4 shows an example of a dialogue box illustrating such case. The user can see that they can select the checkboxes and click the buttons but the effects of these actions are not directly apparent.

The two-facet model of instrumental affordances also suggests that integration of handling affordances and effecter affordances is a design issue that needs to be addressed. If these affordances are not coupled tightly enough the user may be confused (if temporarily) by the instrumental affordance as a whole. Figure 5 and Figure 6 show examples of dialog boxes that differ in the degree to which the clues conveying the handling affordances and effecter affordances are coupled to one another.

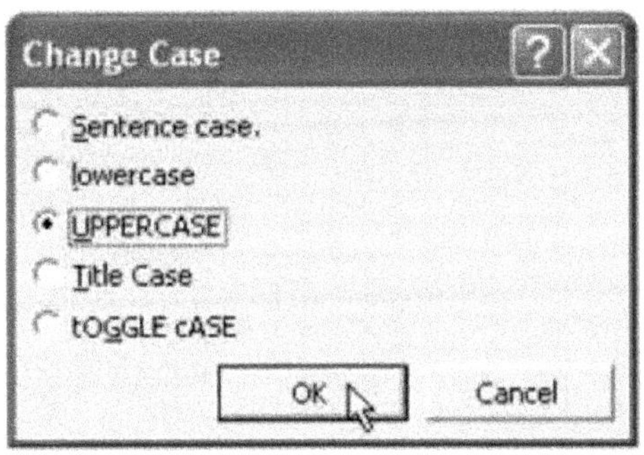

Figure 5. Tight perceptual coupling of handling and effecter affordances.

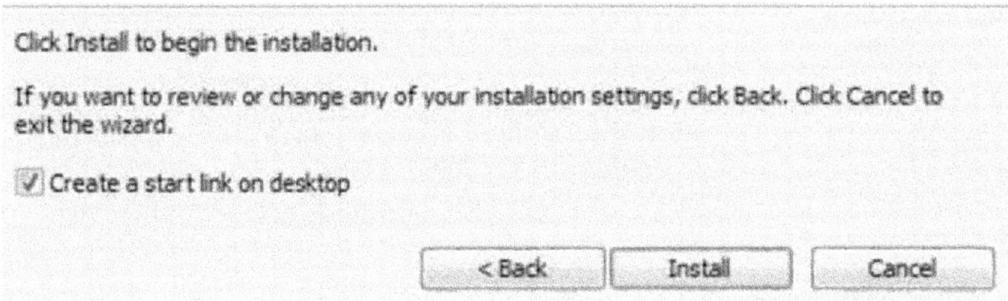

Figure 6. Loose perceptual coupling of handling and effecter affordances.

A number of strategies can be used by interaction designers to ensure proper integration of handling and effecter affordances. Some of the basic properties of interaction instruments, indentified by Beaudouin-Lafon [2], such as degree of indirection (spatial and temporal offsets) and degree of compatibility (similarity between user actions and object transformations), provides useful insights on how handling and effecter affordances can be successfully integrated. Empirical evidence also suggests that a sound design strategy can be supporting the user in exploring the relationship between handling and effecter affordances (cf. [24]).

CONCLUSION

In no way do we intend to question the value of Gibson's approach and the importance of its contribution to HCI. They are enormous. Undoubtedly, understanding how animals interact with their natural environments provides some very useful insights for HCI researchers and practitioners. We are all animals and our ability to physically interact with the immediate environment is to a large extent determined by the capabilities of our bodies, formed in biological evolution [8]. Understanding technological affordances for physical manipulation (cf. [25]) and locomotion has been and continues to be of direct relevance to a wide range of approaches in the analysis and design of digital technologies (e.g., [7, 19, 24, 28]).

At the same time, there is a growing realization in HCI that the field needs a broader concept of affordances that would help understand distinctly human uses of interactive technologies. Building on previous analyses of affordances we argue in this paper that Gibson's research agenda does not include studying some phenomena which are central to HCI.

Contrary to most other analyses we posit that Gibson's theory of affordances cannot be extended beyond its original scope to meet the conceptual needs of HCI. The theory was developed to provide an account of animals' action and perception in their natural environments and, essentially, it delivers all it promises. We claim that to understand the possibilities for specifically human action offered by technology, we need to employ another theory, with a different research agenda. We turned to the Vygotskian socio-cultural approach [36, 38] to re-ground the concept of affordances..

The most fundamental insight of the socio-cultural approach is that human action and mind are inherently mediated. Our action capabilities to a large extent depend on socially developed mediating means, first and foremost tools, including technological tools (e.g., [38]). Accordingly, we propose understanding technology affordances as possibilities for *mediated human action*, and argue that adopting a mediated action perspective on affordances has direct implications for understanding specifically human uses of technology. We differentiate between instrumental, auxiliary, and learning affordances and introduce a two-facet model of instrumental affordances.

The paper presents an initial outline of the mediated action perspective on affordances which deliberately focuses on *individual* human action. A necessary next step is to extend the analysis to include mediated *collective* actions. The step is necessary because social and technological mediation are often inseparable. For instance, Sambasivan et al. [29] found that in lower income households in India mobile phones are used by some people through the "intermediation" of other people, e.g., a grandmother needs her grandson to place a call for her. In this case the tight coupling between user and tool is altered and the handling affordance is separated from the purposeful agent, which is important to take into account in design.

REFERENCES

1. Albrechtsen, H., Andersen, H. H. K., Bødker, S., and Pejtersen, A. M. *Affordances in Activity Theory and Cognitive Systems Engineering.* Risø National Laboratory: Roskilde, 2001.
2. Beadouin-Lafon, M. Instrumental interaction: An interaction model for designing post-WIMP user interfaces. *Proc. CHI 2000*. ACM Press, NY (2000), 446-453.
3. Baerentsen, K. B. and Trettvik, J. An activity theory approach to affordance. In *Proc. NordiCHI 2002.* ACM Press, NY (2002), 51-60.
4. Bødker, S. *Through the interface: A human activity approach to user interface design*. Erlbaum Associates: Hillsdale, NJ, 1991.
5. Bødker, S. and Andersen. P. B. Complex mediation. *Human Computer Interaction*, 20 (2005), 353-402.
6. Bradner, E. Social affordances of computer-mediated communication technology: Understanding adoption. In *Proc. CHI '01 Extended Abstracts*. ACM Press, NY (2001), 67-68.

7. Cairns, P., and Timberly, H. Affordance and symmetry in user interfaces. *The Computer Journal*, 51, 6 (2008), 650-661.
8. Charness, N., Reingold, E.M., Pomplun, M., and Stampe, D. M. The perceptual aspect of skilled performance in chess: Evidence from eye movements. *Memory and Cognition*, 29, 8 (2001), 1146-1152.
9. Dourish, P. *Where the Action Is: The Foundations of Embodied Interaction*. MIT Press, Cambridge, Mass., 2001.
10. Gaver, W. Technology affordances. In *Proc. CHI 91*. ACM Press: NY (1991), 79-84.
11. Gaver, W. The affordances of media spaces for collaboration. *In Proc. CSCW 92*. ACM Press: NY (1992), 17-24.
12. Gibson, J. J. *The Ecological Approach to Visual Perception.* Boston: Houghton Mifflin, 1979.
13. Gibson, J .J. The theory of affordances. In: R. Shaw and J. Bransford (eds.) *Perceiving, Acting and Knowing*. Erlbaum, Hillsdale, NJ (1977).
14. Hartson, H. R. Cognitive, physical, sensory, and functional affordances in interaction design. *Behaviour & Information Technology,* 22, 5 (2003), 315–338.
15. Heft, H. *Ecological psychology in context: James Gibson, Roger Barker, and the legacy of William James's radical empiricism*. Erlbaum, Mahwah, N.J., 2001.
16. Ihara, M., Kobayashi, M., and Sakai, Y. Human affordance. *International Journal of Web Based Communities*, 5, 2 (2009), 255-272.
17. Kallinikos, J. *Governing through Technology: Information Artefacts and Social Practice*. Palgrave, MacMillan London, 2011.
18. Kaptelinin, V. and Nardi, B. *Acting with Technology: Activity Theory and Interaction Design*. MIT Press, Cambridge, 2006.
19. Laarni, J., Norros, L., and Koskinen, H. Affordance table: A collaborative smart interface for process control. In *Proc. 12th International Conference on Human-computer Interaction: Applications and services*. LNCS. Springer-Verlag, Berlin, (2007), 611-619.
20. McGrenere, J., and Ho, W. Affordances: Clarifying and evolving a concept. In *Proc. Graphic Interfaces 2000.* ACM Press, NY (2000), 179-186.
21. Nardi, B. (ed.). *Context and Consciousness: Activity Theory and Human-Computer Interaction*. MIT Press, Cambridge, Mass., 1996.
22. Norman, D. A. *The Psychology of Everyday Things.* Basic Books, New York, 1988.
23. Norman, D. A. Affordance, conventions, and design. *interactions*, 6, 3 (1999), 38-43.
24. Oshlyansky, L., Thimbleby, H., and Cairns, P. Breaking affordance: Culture as context. In *Proc. NordiCHI 2004.* ACM Press, NY, (2004), 81-84.
25. Oulasvirta, A. and Bergstrom-Lehtavirta, J. Ease of Juggling: Studying the Effects of Manual Multitasking. *Proc. CHI 2011*. ACM Press, NY, (2011).
26. Rizzo, A. The origin and design of intentional affordances. In *Proc. DIS 2006*. New York: ACM Press (2006).
27. Rogers, Y. New theoretical approaches for HCI. *ARIST*: *Annual Review of Information Science and Technology*, 38 (2004), 87-143.
28. Şahin, E., Çakmak, M., Doğar, M. R., Uğur, E., Üçoluk, G. To afford or not to afford: A new formalization of affordances toward affordance-based robot control. *Adaptive Behavior - Animals, Animats, Software Agents, Robots, Adaptive Systems*, 15, 4 (2007), 447-472.
29. Sambasivan, N., Cutrell, E., Toyama, K. and Nardi, B. Intermediated technology use in developing communities. In *Proc. CHI 2010*. ACM Press, NY (2010).
30. Soegaard, M. Affordances. Retrieved 26 June 2011 from *Interaction-Design.org:* http://www.interaction-design.org/encyclopedia/affordances.html (2010)
31. Torenvliet, G. We can't afford it!: The devaluation of a usability term. *interactions*, 10, 4 (2003), 12-17.
32. Turner, P. Affordance as context. *Interacting with Computers,* 17, 6 (2005), 787-800.
33. Wagman, J and Carello, C. Haptically Creating Affordances: The User–Tool Interface. J. Exp. Psychol: Applied, 9, 4 (2003), 175-186.
34. Vicente, K. and Rasmussen, J. Ecological interface design: Theoretical foundations. *IEEE Tranbsactions on Systems, Man, and Cybernetics*, 22, 4 (1992), 589-606.
35. Vyas, D., Chisalita, C. M., and van der Veer, G. C. Affordance in interaction. In *Proc. ECCE 2006*. Zurich, Switzerland (2006), 92-99.
36. Vygotsky, L. S. (1978). *Mind and Society*. Harvard University Press, Cambridge.
37. Wartofsky, M. *Models*. D. Reidel, Dordrecht, 1979.
38. Wertsch, J. (1998). *Mind as Action*. Oxford University Press, NY.
39. Zhang, P. Motivational affordances: Reasons for ICT design and use. *Communications of the ACM*, 51, 11 (2008), 145-147.

Biometric-Rich Gestures: A Novel Approach to Authentication on Multi-touch Devices

Napa Sae-Bae, Kowsar Ahmed, Katherine Isbister and Nasir Memon
NYU-Poly
Five Metrotech Center, Brooklyn NY 11201
{nsae-b01, kahmed01}@students.poly.edu, {isbister, memon}@poly.edu

ABSTRACT
In this paper, we present a novel multi-touch gesture-based authentication technique. We take advantage of the multi-touch surface to combine biometric techniques with gestural input. We defined a comprehensive set of five-finger touch gestures, based upon classifying movement characteristics of the center of the palm and fingertips, and tested them in a user study combining biometric data collection with usability questions. Using pattern recognition techniques, we built a classifier to recognize unique biometric gesture characteristics of an individual. We achieved a 90% accuracy rate with single gestures, and saw significant improvement when multiple gestures were performed in sequence. We found user ratings of a gestures desirable characteristics (ease, pleasure, excitement) correlated with a gestures actual biometric recognition ratethat is to say, user ratings aligned well with gestural security, in contrast to typical text-based passwords. Based on these results, we conclude that multi-touch gestures show great promise as an authentication mechanism.

Author Keywords
Multi-touch interfaces; multi-touch gestures; behavior biometric; authentication; password.

ACM Classification Keywords
H.5.2 [Information Interfaces and Presentation]: User Interfaces - Interaction styles;

General Terms
Human Factors, Design.

INTRODUCTION
With the growing popularity of mobile computing devices, and their use for activities such as banking and other transactions that require security, protecting user credentials on mobile devices is becoming increasingly important. Current applications typically maintain the privacy of users' sensitive data by authenticating the user at every login. Most mobile devices today make use of traditional text-based password schemes in order to authenticate a user. However, users have been known to choose weak passwords [15]. This is especially true with touch devices that are rapidly becoming ubiquitous. Findlater et al [12] have shown that the speed of typing on flash glass is 31% slower than a physical keyboard. This typically results in a shorter password chosen by users to shorten their log-in time.

Permission to make digital or hard copies of all or part of this work for personal or classroom use is granted without fee provided that copies are not made or distributed for profit or commercial advantage and that copies bear this notice and the full citation on the first page. To copy otherwise, or republish, to post on servers or to redistribute to lists, requires prior specific permission and/or a fee.
CHI'12, May 5–10, 2012, Austin, Texas, USA.
Copyright 2012 ACM 978-1-4503-1015-4/12/05...$10.00.

The development of multi-touch technology opens up avenues for new authentication techniques that go beyond text passwords. One example of this is the touch-based password scheme called "Pattern Lock" implemented in the Android OS [21]. The password here is simply the pattern or sequence of dots connected by lines which a user must draw in order to gain access to the system. However, this method has many limitations. First, the password created has low entropy [1]. Second, it is shown to be vulnerable to disclosure based on the traces left on the screen by finger oils [2]. Third, it does not provide protection against shoulder surfing attacks since the password does not contain any personal traits of the user [18, 24]. Finally, Pattern Lock does not exploit the full capabilities of the newer multi-touch interfaces emerging in tablets and touch pads where one can use multiple fingertips to interact with the device [23].

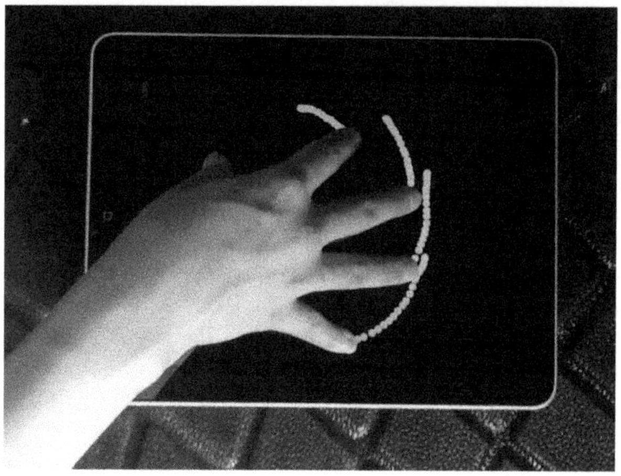

Figure 1: Example of a multi-touch gesture with sufficient biometric characteristics to allow for authentication.

Given the increasing prevalence of multi-touch technology, our aim is to develop a new user authentication system that does not have the limitations of text passwords and Pattern-Lock-like mechanisms as described above. The system we propose is based on multi-touch gestures and can be seen as an instance of a behavioral-biometric-based authentication technique. It is not susceptible to shoulder surfing or finger oil attacks and potentially provides significantly large entropy. Figure 1 is an example of the sort of multi-touch gesture that we have in mind, using our iPad test application. The user performs the gesture with all five fingers at once, and biometrics are drawn from the hand's geometry as well as the dynamics of the gesture itself.

Thus far, users have readily accepted multi-touch gestures in the interface, and much has been made of the accessibility of this mode of interaction to a broad user public [22, 26]. And although there has traditionally been some public suspicion and resistance of biometric systems, not all biometric systems raise the same degree of concern. Biometric systems can be divided into two main categories–physiological and behavior-based. Behavior-based biometric systems, such as online signature verification, are typically more acceptable to users [13]. This gives us reason to hope that a multi-touch gesture-based authentication system would prove to be both usable and acceptable.

To test our idea, we first developed a multi-touch authentication technique, then implemented a simple iPad application that allowed us to conduct a user study of the viability of the approach. We developed a comprehensive set of multi-touch gestures, working from characteristics of five-finger movement of the hand, that served as candidate gestures for our method.

We then conducted a user study, with the following questions in mind: a) whether biometric data obtained from gestures (positioning and movement dynamics inherent to an individual's hand) is sufficient and reliable enough to authenticate specific users and b) whether the gestures would be acceptable and enjoyable for end users as an authentication method. The goal was to find a set of gestures that met both criteria. Pretesting of the prototype suggested that it would be possible to achieve this combination.

RELATED WORK

Text passwords have been known to impose a cognitive burden on users that results in selection of weak passwords [24, 8]. In 1996, Blonder first proposed graphical passwords to tackle this problem based on a memory study by Calkins [6] that showed human memory for visual words is stronger than for pronounced words. This was later improved by Passpoints [24] and Cue Click Points [7]. Passfaces is another instance of a visual memory based authentication scheme where users are asked to repeatedly pick faces out of those presented [3]. Draw-a-Secret is a graphical password where the secret is a simple picture drawn on a grid [10]. In 2010, Citty et al [16] proposed a touch-screen authentication scheme similar to Passpoints that requires users to sequentially tap on pre-selected images to input their password.

However, all of the above schemes are susceptible to a "shoulder surfing attack" as they can be potentially observed by an attacker [18]. There have been many alternative approaches proposed to tackle this problem. In 2004, Roth et al [19] proposed a PIN-based challenge response approach. To enter one digit, the user repeatedly chooses the color of the focus digit shown on the screen (either black or white). Wiedenbeck et al [25] have proposed a graphical challenge response scheme. Here, given a convex hull generated by the preselected icons, the user clicks on any icon that appears inside that convex hull and the process is repeated multiple times. Recently, Kim et al [18] have proposed a pressure-based authentication scheme to reduce the visibility of the secret to an attacker. The idea is to blind an attacker by placing fingertips simultaneously in different zones. The user then communicates with the device by increasing the pressure on the fingertip located in a specific zone to select an object.

Another approach to counter shoulder surfing is not to rely completely on a shared secret (i.e. knowledge-based scheme or "what you know" scheme) but use a behavior component as well ("what you are"). One way to achieve this is by using biometric technology. In a biometric authentication system, a personal trait is used to verify a user. In order to increase the level of security, biometrics can be combined with any other authentication system to get multi-factor authentication. Several biometric traits have been studied including physiological ones such as retina, iris, fingerprint, face, vein and palm, and behavioral ones such as dynamic signatures, voice, key-stroke, and gait. Our approach–using the touch screen as a biometric sensor to capture user traits–has not been previously explored. We do know from prior research, though, that biometric data can be gleaned from both hand geometry [14], and from the movement of the hand [11, 17].

DEFINING A SET OF GESTURAL POSSIBILITIES

There are existing patented and open source gesture libraries that multi-touch developers draw upon, such as the iPhone 3G multi-touch gesture dictionary [5] and the Gesture Works open source gesture library [4]. These frameworks are not targeted towards the use context we have in mind, namely, multi-touch gestures that could serve as biometric keys for authentication. This is due to the fact that most of the gestures in these libraries use only two fingers whereas we need the use all five fingers to get maximal data from the hand geometry and muscle behavior of an individual. This led us to create our own gestural taxonomy based upon movement of the two major components of the hand, the palm and the fingertips.

PALM MOVEMENT

Palm movement is defined as whether the hand itself needs to move during the gesture, as opposed to just the finger tips. Some gestures place the users's hand in one static position for the entire gesture, whereas other gestures require the hand to traverse or rotate while executing the gesture. Thus, we can divide gestures into two classes for palm movement:

1. Static palm position: Defined as the gesture where the palm or hand position remains static while performing the gesture. In other words, only the fingertips are moving without changing the position of the hand. Examples of this type include pinch or zoom gesture.

2. Dynamic palm position: The center of the hand is moving while performing the gesture. For example, a Drag or Swipe.

FINGERTIP MOVEMENT

Most of the distinguishing features of a multi-touch gesture derive from movement of the fingertips. We divide fingertip movement into four categories.

1. Parallel: All fingertips are moving in the same direction during the gesture. For example, a five-finger swipe, in which all five fingers move from left to right on the screen.

2. Closed: All fingertips are moving inward toward the center of the hand. For example, a pinch gesture.

3. Opened: All fingertips are moving outward from the center of the hand. For example, a reverse pinch gesture.

4. Circular: All fingertips are rotating around the center of the hand. For example, a clockwise or counterclockwise rotation.

FURTHER FINGERTIP DYNAMICS

Sometimes the fingertips are not moving all at once in a gesture–there may be one or more fingertips resting in a fixed position on the screen. This can help to stabilize the gesture for the user. So we developed one additional classification in our taxonomy.

1. Full Fingertip: All fingertips are moving in the gesture.

2. Partial Fingertip: Some fingertips moving during the gesture, others resting in a static position on the screen.

These three classifications allowed us to define a comprehensive set of authentication gesture possibilities. Below is the list of 22 gestures that we studied (we use the indicated abbreviations in the rest of the text–see Figure 2 for an illustration of some sample gestures):

Close: All five fingers move toward the palm's center, in a closing motion.

FTC: Thumb is fixed, and the other fingers move toward the palm's center in a closing motion.

FPC: Pinky is fixed, other fingers move toward the palm's center in a closing motion.

Open: All five fingers move away from palm's center, in an opening motion.

FTO: Thumb is fixed, and the other fingers move away from palm's center in an opening motion.

FPO: Pinky is fixed, other fingers move away from palm's center in an opening motion.

CW: All fingertips rotate in a clockwise direction.

FTCW: Thumb is fixed, other fingertips rotate around it in a clockwise direction.

CCW: All fingertips rotate in a counter-clockwise direction.

FTCCW: Thumb is fixed, other fingertips rotate around it in a counter-clockwise direction.

FPCCW: Pinky is fixed, other fingertips rotate around it in a counter-clockwise direction.

Drag: All fingers move in parallel from top to bottom of screen.

DDC: The dynamic (moving from top to bottom) gesture performing a closing motion with all fingertips.

FTP: Thumb is fixed, other fingertips move in parallel from top to bottom of screen.

FPP: Pinky is fixed, other fingertips move in parallel from top to bottom of screen.

FBD: Pinky and thumb are both fixed; other fingertips move in parallel from top to bottom of screen.

Swipe: All fingers move in parallel from left to right of screen.

Flick: Quick top-left to bottom-right parallel movement of all fingertips.

FBSA: The static gesture performing parallel(⟩ shape) with fixed thumb and pinky

FBSB: The static gesture performing parallel(⟨ shape) with fixed thumb and pinky

User Defined: All five fingertips move as the person pretends to sign his/her signature on the screen.

DUO: The dynamic(moving from bottom to top) gesture performing a opening motion with all fingertips.

We tested out all the above gestures in our study, to find those gestures that were both most robust in terms of biometrics, and also, the most appealing to users.

DEVELOPING A GESTURE AUTHENTICATION TECHNIQUE

In a biometric verification or authentication system, the identity of the user is given to the system along with a proof of identity (the biometric). Correctness of the proof of identity is then evaluated by the system. After that, the answer, either accept or reject the user, is given based on the evaluation result. In order to verify the proof, the system needs to have a prior knowledge about it. To achieve this, there are generally two stages in a verification system: enrollment stage and verification stage. The purpose of the enrollment stage is to register the user's data in the system by acquiring and storing biometric templates corresponding to the user. Since biometric data is unlikely to be repeated (for example two iris scans of the same user will never be the same due to acquisition noise and variation of environment in which they are acquired), one sample is not good enough to represent an individual's biometric. In the verification stage, the in-

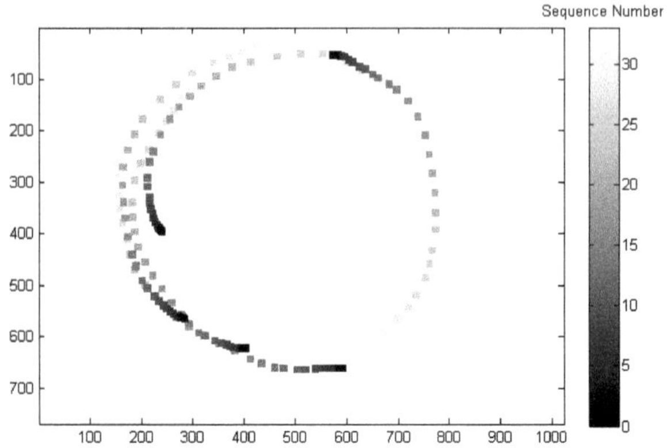

(a) Static Circulate with all tips: CCW

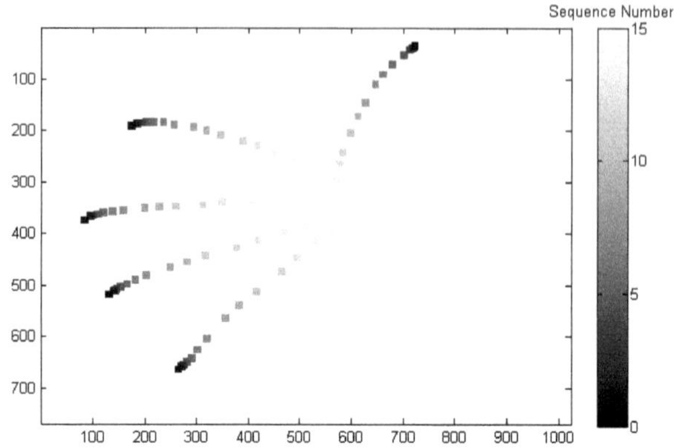

(b) Static Closed with all tips

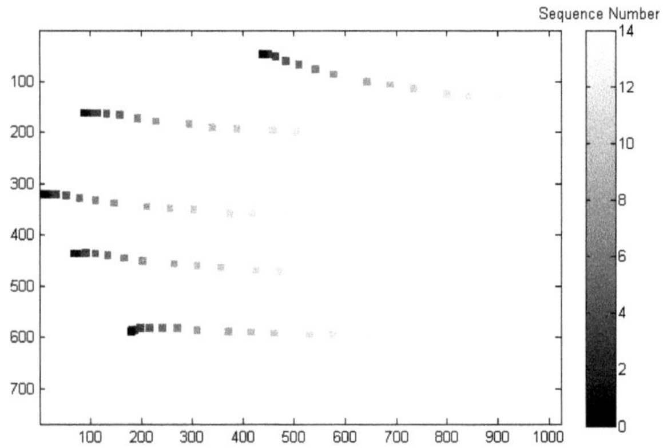

(c) Dynamic Parallel with all tips

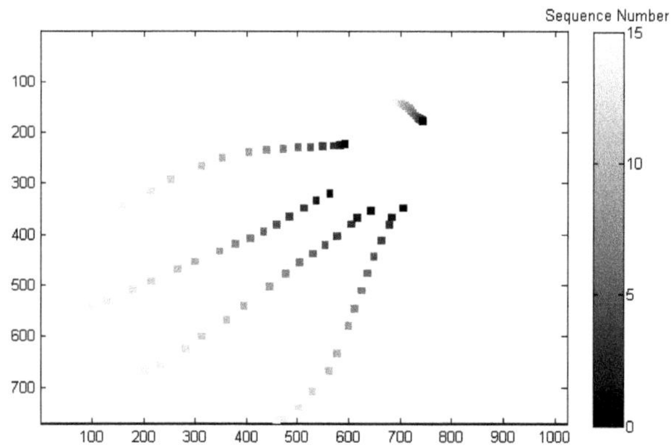

(d) Static Opened with fixed thumb

Figure 2: Examples of the gestures categorized by the movement characteristics as mentioned

put biometric instance is compared with the stored biometric templates of the claimed identity in order to authenticate a user.

In the rest of this subsection we summarize the biometric verification algorithm for multi-touch gestures we developed, implemented and tested in our study. The verification process begins with the user performing a multi-touch gesture. All x-y coordinates, time-stamps and labels of the resulting 5 touch sequences from 5 fingertips are sequentially captured by the device. The given labels of touch points are not related with the actual fingertips. In other words, the touch generated from the thumb can appear in any label from 1 to 5. To verify the multi-touch gesture input by the user by comparing with the stored templates of the user, all the touch points need to be correctly labeled and ordered in a consistent manner. Next, the fingertip trails or touch sequences need to be normalized to maintain the invariants of location, rotation and path. Then, a Dynamic Time Warping algorithm is used to compute the distance between each of the normalized stored templates and the normalized input multi-touch gesture. Finally, a dissimilarity score is derived from the distances obtained and a decision is then made by comparing the dissimilarity score with a threshold in order to accept or reject a user. In the rest of this section we provide some additional details about each of these steps. A more detailed description of the algorithm appears in a companion paper[not to be cited due to the blind review].

Matching Touch Sequences to Specific Fingers

To correctly compare any two multi-touch sequences (each touch sequence has 5 touch point trails), they need to be stored in a consistent order. Hence the first step is to re-order the touch sequences into a canonical form. The standard order employed was that the touches generate by Thumb, Index, Middle, Ring and Pinky respectively labeled 1st to 5th. To achieve this one has to match a touch sequence to the corresponding finger. This is not an easy task as the acquisition process may capture points in an arbitrary order depending on which fingertips made contact with the touch surface first. To correctly match touch sequences with fingers we use known natural characteristics of human hand geometry. First, we construct a simple polygon that connects the starting points of each touch sequence. Then, the thumb position is identified based on pairwise distances between polygon vertices.

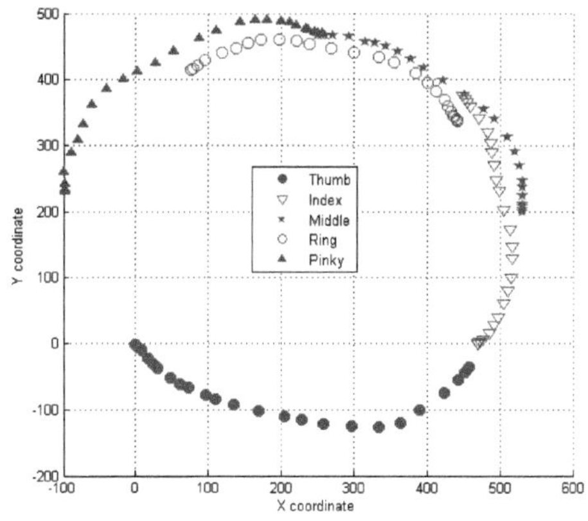

(a) User 1: trial 1st

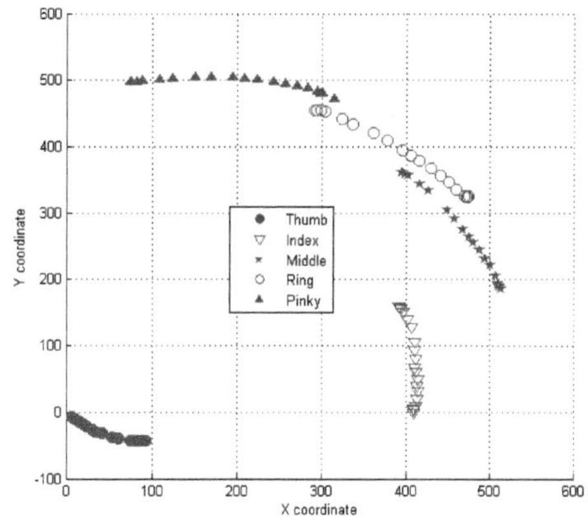

(b) User 3: trial 1st

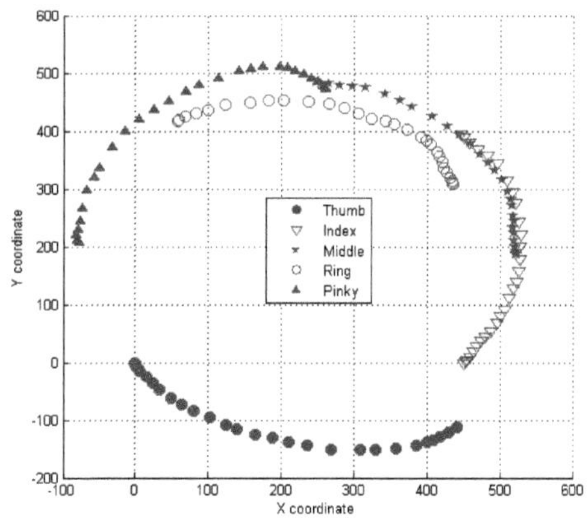

(c) User 1: trial 2nd

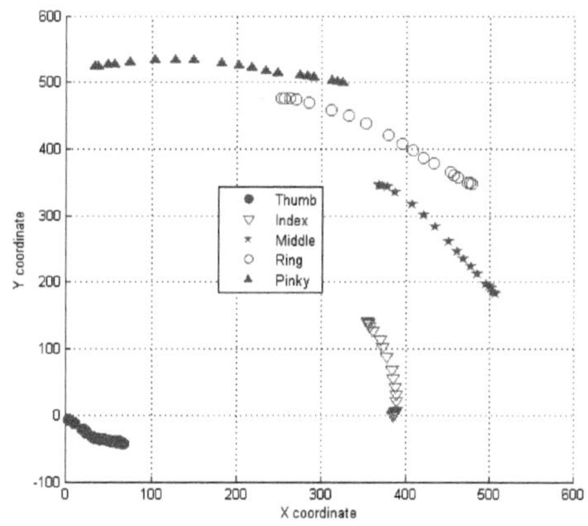

(d) User 3: trial 4th

Figure 3: Examples of the CW gestures from 3 different users.

Finally, we identify and label touch sequences corresponding to each of the remaining fingers based on a circular order starting from the thumb position.

Gesture Normalization

Location and Orientation Invariance: The position of user touch sequences can be anywhere and in any orientation on the screen and differ from one instance to another. Hence location and orientation of the touch sequences need to be normalized before making comparisons. In our work, all the touch sequences were normalized based on the thumb and index's fingertips of the touch sequence generated when the 5 fingertips first contact the screen. All the gestures are normalized such that the thumb's tip in the first template is at the origin and the index finger's tip is at 0 degree of the plane. Examples of the same gesture from 3 different users after location and orientation normalization are shown in Figure 3. For the same user, the gestures are similar whereas they look different from the other users' gestures.

Length Invariance: The actual length of the fingertip trails can be different each time even when performed by the same user. However, the relative length of each fingertip trail is another useful characteristic of the user's gesture. In other words, some might perform the gesture in such a way that has an equal length for all the tips' trails. Others might perform in different ways. Hence the path length of the gestures are normalized as follows before making comparisons between input and stored gesture templates.

$$x'''(i,j) = \frac{x''(i,j) - \min_j(x''(1,1))}{\max_j(x''(1,1)) - \min_j(x''(1,1))}$$

$$y'''(i,j) = \frac{y''(i,j) - \min_j(y''(1,1))}{\max_j(y''(1,1)) - \min_j(y''(1,1))}$$

Dynamic Time Warping Algorithm

The distance between two time-series signals with the different lengths is defined as the sum of the distance at the optimal non-linear path such that the distance or matching cost sum is minimized. Firstly, an input gesture is formatted as the time series of touch sequences; $Gesture(t) = [Touch_1, Touch_2, ..., Touch_n]$ where n is the number of the touches sequence of the gesture. $Touch_i$ is the vector of x-y coordinates of the touches in the ith sequence; $Touch_i = [x_1, y_1, x_2, y_2, ..., x_5, y_5]$. Dynamic programming can be used to implement the optimal path searching algorithm. Euclidean distance is calculated as a matching cost between 2 touch sequences. The sum of the Euclidean distances is then defined as the distance between 2 different gestures.

Dissimilarity Score

The decision of whether the biometric is coming from the claimed user or not depends on the similarity of the input biometric to the stored template. In other words, if the dissimilarity score of the input biometric compared to the template is lower than a threshold, the input biometric is verified. Otherwise, the system will reject the user. To calculate the dissimilarity score between the registered user's templates and the input, all distances between the coming gesture and templates are used to calculate the dissimilarity score along with the distances between all the stored templates themselves. The idea is to normalize the inter-user variation with the intra-user variation and use as a dissimilarity score as suggested in [17].

We implemented and tested our classifier on the data set from our user study described in the next section. We achieved accuracy at the level of 90% accuracy for single gesture. It can be significantly improved with multiple gesture authentication. Results are discussed in detail in the Analysis of Biometric Data section.

USER STUDY

We conducted a study that combined a trial of our technique in terms of robustness of authentication results, with eliciting user feedback on the individual gestures, and on the general practice of using multi-touch gesture for authentication. We recruited 34 participants. 24 were male, 30 were right-handed, 28 had some multi-touch device experience, while only 6 had prior experience with the iPad. Age ranged from 15 to 50: 18 participants were 15-19, 10 were 20-25, 3 were 26-30, 2 were 31-40 and 1 was 41-50.

We created an application on the iPad, using version 3.2 of iOS, which has multi-touch capability to track up to 5 points at a time. The multi-touch screen resolution was $1024 * 768$. Data provided by the device at each point were x and y coordinates of the touch point's trajectory, time stamp, touch order (of the different fingertips), touch sequence, and touch type. The number of touch events created were in the range of 20-30 per second. As a visualization aid, the application provides simple visual traces of the user's fingertip movement during each gesture (see figure 1).

In each session, we first explained the purpose of the study to participants, and solicited their informed consent to proceed. Next the participant filled out a brief pre-survey with demographic questions, and then we moved on to the gesture trials. Each person was taken through all 22 gestures (in a randomized order), however, they could skip any gesture that they did not feel comfortable performing (all gestures had at least 26 participants who performed them–see Table 1). The participant practiced a given gesture a few times, and once comfortable with that gesture, was asked to perform it 10 times, with the system recording their touches during these 10 trials. The person answered a few questions about ease of use and how they felt after trying the gesture, before moving on to the next gesture. For soliciting emotional response, we used a technique called Emocard [9], a pictogram-based approach to eliciting emotional feedback about products that can be analyzed in terms of valence and arousal, two commonly used dimensions of affective response [20]. After completing the entire gesture set, the person answered a final set of questions about the overall experience, before leaving.

Analysis of Biometric Data

We used Equal Error Rate (EER) to measure accuracy. This is the rate at which False Acceptace Rate (FAR) and False Rejection Rate (FRR) are equal. We use this measure because typically the number of genuine cases in a verification system are much smaller than the number of forgery cases.

To test each gesture, we treated the first 5 samples of each gesture from each user as the template for that user in the enrollment process. The last 5 samples were used as the test for a genuine case. Samples of the same gesture from other users in the study were used to test as the forgeries of that gesture. For each gesture, we have at most $5 * 34 = 170$ cases for genuine and $10 * 34 * 33 = 11,220$ forgeries. This reflects the fact that some participants opted out of certain gestures because they were uncomfortable to perform.

FAR and FRR can be calculated using the following:

$$FAR = \frac{\sharp \text{ of verified forgery cases}}{\sharp \text{ of forgery cases}} \quad (1)$$

$$FRR = \frac{\sharp \text{ of rejected genuine cases}}{\sharp \text{ of genuine cases}} \quad (2)$$

To calculate EER, first the dissimilarity scores for all the test examples are calculated. The threshold value will then be varied. At the particular threshold value, the corresponding FAR and FRR are derived. All pairs of (FAR,FRR) are used to plot Receiver Operating Characteristic or ROC curve. The corresponding value of the point at which FAR and FRR are equal is an EER.

EER for all the gestures is shown in Table 1 (Figure 4(a) provides a graphical version of these results). Individual gestures achieved an average level of 10% EER. 7 out of 22 gestures achieved an EER of lower than 10%. 6 of them achieved an EER of 10-15% and 9 of them achieved an EER of 15%.

To find out whether using multiple gestures would improve the system's performance, we combined scores of 2 different gestures from the same user in the same order and evaluated the EER of the combined gestures. The results in Table 2 give examples of combinations to show that different gestures can

Gesture	EER	Threshold	Number of users
Close	9.56	10.01	34
FTC	10.36	9.34	34
FPC	15.67	9.29	31
Open	18.9	9.02	33
FTO	17.81	10.00	32
FPO	17.43	8.75	30
CW	9.42	9.56	33
FTCW	12.44	9.53	33
CCW	7.21	9.86	33
FTCCW	6.60	10.02	30
FPCCW	16.60	8.78	28
Drag	10.66	8.39	33
DDC	9.40	9.63	31
FTP	7.89	8.93	27
FPP	13.25	9.08	30
FBD	15.18	8.62	26
Swipe	15.9	8.50	30
Flick	14.9	10.12	30
FBSA	16.10	8.28	30
FBSB	10.91	9.37	26
User Defined	2.88	13.93	30
DUO	15.97	9.84	28

Table 1: Equal Error Rate performance for each gesture along with the derived threshold for dissimilarity score.

be used to provide complementary biometric data and raise accuracy levels to a range of 2-5% EER.

Analysis of User Experience

We wanted to find gestures that not only provided strong biometric authentication support, but that were also easy to use and that created positive feelings in users. The security of any authentication approach depends upon the user response, and as was mentioned earlier in the paper, text-password methods suffer from a lack of such qualities for users. We analyzed results from the questions that we asked participants about each gesture, and about multi-touch authentication in general, to understand the user experience of this authentication method. We also looked at how participant answers about the user experience of particular gestures related to the biometric strength of those gestures.

At the end of the study, we asked whether multi-touch gestures would be easy to memorize, which type of password they would prefer (gesture or text) and why, which they thought would be faster, and whether they thought gesture passwords would get easier with practice. We collected comments about the general approach as well. All 29 participants thought that gestures would be faster than text passwords, and the 25 out of 29 participants said they would prefer this method, 26 out of 28 participants said that it would be easy to memorize, and 27 out of 29 participants said that it would get even easier with practice. User comments about why they would prefer this method included: 'No typing and easy to perform', 'It is faster, simpler and cooler' and 'I have too many passwords to memorize.' People who preferred text passwords reported that this was because they were used to the method.

Gesture 1	Gesture 2	EER
Closed	CCW	3.88
Closed	FTCCW	3.7
Closed	CW	4.56
CW	CCW	2.93
CW	FTCCW	2.58
CCW	FTCCW	3.45

Table 2: Equal Error Rate performance of multiple gestures along with the derived threshold for dissimilarity score.

Figure 4 shows user ratings of each gesture on ease of use, pleasure, and excitement, with that gesture's accuracy rating also included for reference. Participant's Emocard [9] responses gave us scores for pleasure and excitement ranging from 1 to 3. We also asked participants how hard/easy the gesture was (scaled from 1 to 5), and whether they thought they would use this gesture for authentication/log-in. We collected comments about each gesture from participants, to support these numeric ratings. We used the combination of the gesture's user ratings and accuracy ratings to identify the most promising gestures for this kind of authentication. Given these results, candidate gestures that optimize for both authentication accuracy and user experience: Close, Clockwise, Counter Clockwise, Drag, Drag Down Close, Fixed Thumb Parallel, Fixed Thumb Close, Fixed Thumb Clockwise, and Fixed Thumb Counter Clockwise.

In terms of static gesture type preference ratings, 13 preferred closing, 11 preferred circular and only 5 of them preferred opening gesture. In terms of the set of fingertips, the majority preferred to perform with all tips and followed by fix thumb and fix pinky, respectively. Some users remarked that opening gestures began with fingernails on the screen, and they worried that this could damage the screen, whereas closing gestures began with fingertips firmly placed on the screen. Gestures that made use of all fingertips were most highly rated, in contrast to gestures that involved fixed fingertips. Participants did like the fixed thumb rotation gestures, but in general, users did not like the fixed pinky gestures.

Figure 5a shows the relationship between EER and user experience ratings of each gesture. Positive ratings showed a strong linear relationship with system accuracy. In other words, gestures that users liked better were also more secure from a biometric point of view.

Figure 5b shows that participants' reports of which gestures they are most willing to use correlate with ratings of those gestures as exciting, easy, and pleasant. This relationship leads us to conclude that, unlike with text-based passwords, ease of use and preference ratings seem to correlate with those gestures that are also most biometrically secure. This is a fan-

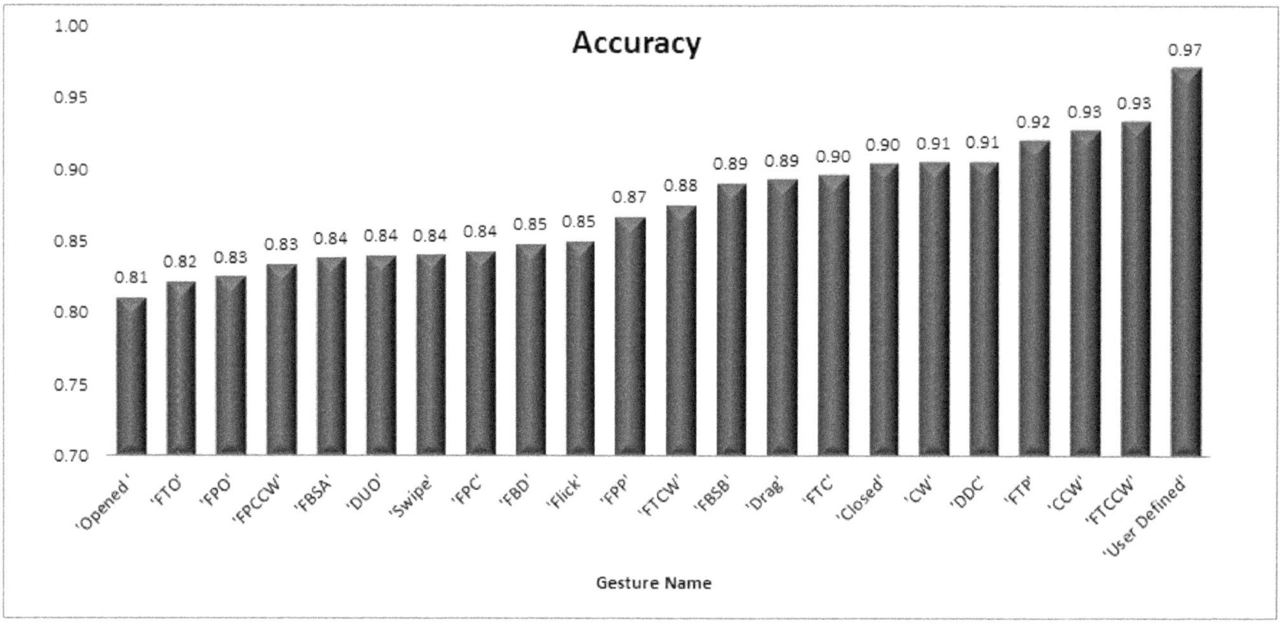

(a) Gesture Accuracy

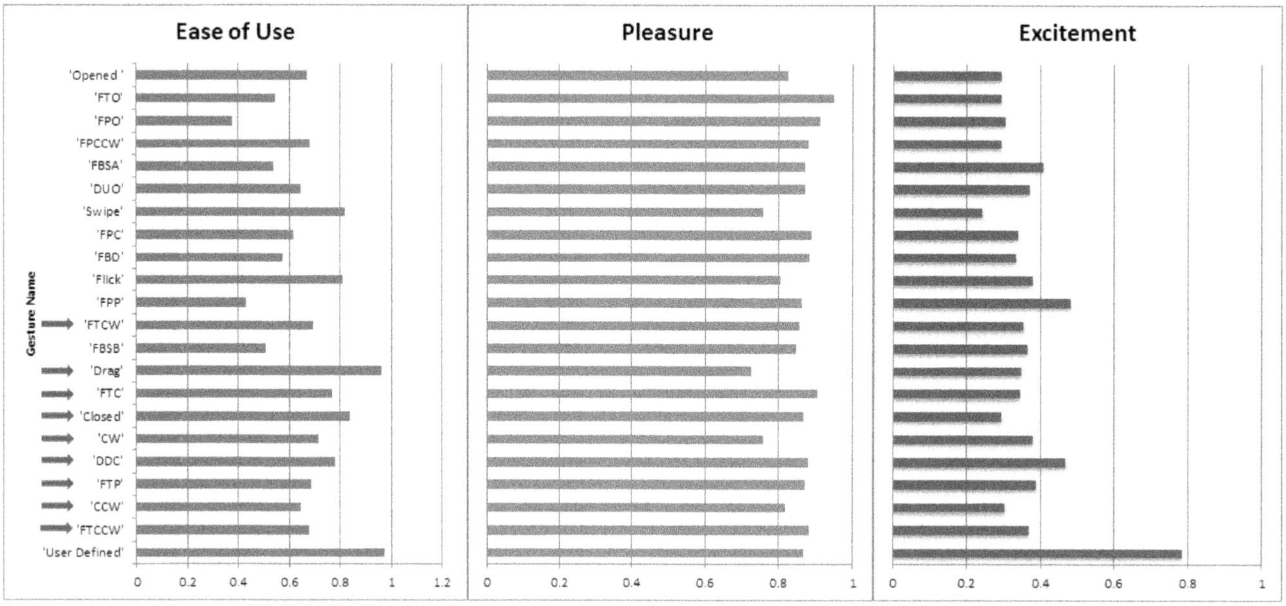

(b) Self-reported user experience

Figure 4: The percentage of self-reported user experience and accuracy for each gesture. → indicate the candidate gestures.

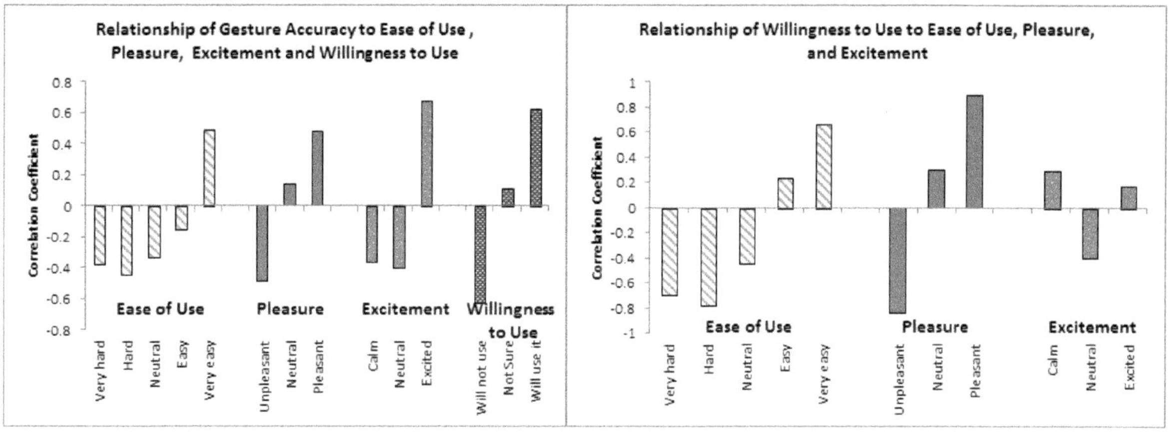

(a) Biometric Accuracy (b) User Experience

Figure 5: The correlation coefficients a) Associated with gesture accuracy and b) Associated with willingness to use.

User Experience	FAR	FRR	FAR+FRR
Excitement (1 to 3)	0.0563	-0.0202	0.027
Pleasure (1 to 3)	0.0848	-0.0726	0.027
Ease of Use (1 to 5)	0.1288	0.0872	0.1657

Table 3: Correlation Coefficient of performance associated with self-report of user experience.

tastic result from the point of view of achieving better security results for a greater numbers of users.

To examine the relationship between accuracy and user rating more closely, we used the derived threshold value of each gesture to evaluate the FAR and FRR of different gestures corresponding to different users. In total we have 658 instances, and each instance has 8 attributes which are the user's ID, the gesture's ID, FAR, FRR, excitement level, pleasant level, easiness level and willingness to use level.

Table 3 shows that rating of ease of use is positively linearly related to the level of FAR, with a 95% confidence level. The relationship is stronger when considering FAR + FFR, which is a general accuracy term. Self-reported pleasure is also positively linearly related to the level of FAR + FRR. These results imply that the more pleasant and easier the gesture, the more accurately users are likely to perform the gestures. In terms of accuracy, the static, open gestures are low, and it can be seen that user ratings of these gestures were also low. Users seemed to like fixed pinky gestures the least, and they also scored low in terms of accuracy. Interestingly, sometimes having the thumb fixed seemed to lead to stabilization of the gesture, such as in the CCW gesture. Some users, especially those with shorter fingers, mentioned this in their comments about this gesture, as well.

CONCLUSION

In this paper we have presented a novel approach to authentication, which makes use of biometric information that can be gleaned from multi-touch gestures. We outlined a gestural possibility space, and created a generic gesture classifier and a simple iPad application to test out the classifier. We then conducted a user study of the gestures we defined, testing out both authentication accuracy and participants' ratings of the user experience. We were able to achieve system performance of 10% EER on average for single gestures, and 5% EER on average for double gestures. We discovered that user preferences seem to have a linear relationship to system performance (not the case for text-based password schemes). We also showed that users rated the method highly and seemed very open to adopting it for everyday use. We believe this method shows great promise as a technique for improving the everyday experience of authentication on multi-touch devices, and also for raising the level of security of user data.

We are working on ways to raise the accuracy level even higher. For example we improved accuracy 5% on average by implementing a translation factor optimization to minimize gesture distance. If we can get access to more touch attributes such as pressure or touch surface area, we can further improve accuracy. We are also exploring ways to combine this method with other biometric information, such as face recognition using a device's on-board camera.

It is interesting to note from the data, that the one gesture which created a strong self-report of excitement, was performing a 'user defined' gesture (participants pretended to sign their signature on the screen with all five fingers). The research team theorizes that one potential reason for this excitement was the opportunity to make use of something highly personal, and we are currently exploring ways to adapt our method that make use of personalization of the gestures and the gesture context as well.

ACKNOWLEDGMENTS
Thanks to Sharanya Ravichandran and Najee Gardner for their help in conducting pretests of this user study.

REFERENCES

1. http://beust.com/weblog2/archives/000497.html.
2. http://techcrunch.com/2008/10/12/androids-login-is-cool-but-is-it-secure/.
3. http://www.passfaces.com/pfphelp/logon.htm.
4. http://gestureworks.com/features/open-source-gestures/.
5. Apple. Multi-touch gesture dictionary.
6. Calkins, M. W. Short studies in memory and in association from the wellesly college psychological laboratory. In *Psychological Review*, Vol 5(5), ACM (New York, NY, USA, Sep 1898), 2453–2462.
7. Chiasson, S., van Oorschot, P., and Biddle, R. Graphical password authentication using cued click points. In *Computer Security ESORICS 2007*, vol. 4734 of *Lecture Notes in Computer Science*, Springer Berlin / Heidelberg (2007).
8. Denning, T., Bowers, K., van Dijk, M., and Juels, A. Exploring implicit memory for painless password recovery. In *Proceedings of the 2011 annual conference on Human factors in computing systems*, CHI '11, ACM (New York, NY, USA, 2011), 2615–2618.
9. Desmet, P. M. A., Overbeeke, C. J., and Tax, S. J. E. T. Designing products with added emotional value: development and application of an approach for research through design. In *The Design Journal*, vol. 4 (2001), 32–47.
10. Dunphy, P., and Yan, J. Do background images improve "draw a secret" graphical passwords? In *Proceedings of the 14th ACM conference on Computer and communications security*, CCS '07, ACM (New York, NY, USA, 2007), 36–47.
11. Faundez-Zanuy, M. On-line signature recognition based on vq-dtw. In *Pattern Recogn.*, Elsevier Science Inc. (New York, NY, USA, March 2007), 981–992.
12. Findlater, L., Wobbrock, J. O., and Wigdor, D. Typing on flat glass: examining ten-finger expert typing patterns on touch surfaces. In *Proceedings of the 2011 annual conference on Human factors in computing systems*, CHI '11, ACM (New York, NY, USA, 2011), 2453–2462.
13. Gamboa, H., and Fred, A. A behavioral biometric system based on human-computer interaction. In *SPIE 5404 - Biometric Technology for Human Identification*, A. K. Jain and N. K. Ratha, Eds., 381–392.
14. Jain, A., Ross, A., and Pankanti, S. A prototype hand geometry-based verification system. In *2nd Int'l Conference on Audio- and Video-based Biometric Person Authentication, Washington D.C.* (1999).
15. Jain, A., Ross, A., and Pankanti, S. Biometrics: a tool for information security. In *Information Forensics and Security, IEEE Transactions on*, vol. 1 (june 2006), 125 – 143.
16. Jonathan Citty, D. R. H. Tapi: Touch-screen authentication using partitioned images. In *ELON UNIVERSITY TECHNICAL REPORT 2010-1* (2010), 1–6.
17. Kholmatov, A., and Yanikoglu, B. Biometric authentication using online signatures. In *Proc. ISCIS, Springer LNCS-3280 (2004) 373380*, Springer-Verlag (2004), 373–380.
18. Kim, D., Dunphy, P., Briggs, P., Hook, J., Nicholson, J., Nicholson, J., and Olivier, P. Multi-touch authentication on tabletops. In *Proceedings of the 28th international conference on Human factors in computing systems*, CHI '10, ACM (New York, NY, USA, 2010), 1093–1102.
19. Roth, V., Richter, K., and Freidinger, R. A pin-entry method resilient against shoulder surfing. In *Proceedings of the 11th ACM conference on Computer and communications security*, CCS '04, ACM (New York, NY, USA, 2004), 236–245.
20. Russell, J. A circumplex model of affect. In *Journal of Personality and Social Psychology*, vol. 39 (1980), 1161 – 1178.
21. Shabtai, A., Fledel, Y., Kanonov, U., Elovici, Y., Dolev, S., and Glezer, C. Google android: A comprehensive security assessment. In *Security Privacy, IEEE*, no. 2 in 8 (march-april 2010), 35 –44.
22. Stöß el, C. Familiarity as a factor in designing finger gestures for elderly users. In *Proceedings of the 11th International Conference on Human-Computer Interaction with Mobile Devices and Services*, MobileHCI '09, ACM (New York, NY, USA, 2009), 78:1–78:2.
23. Wang, F., and Ren, X. Empirical evaluation for finger input properties in multi-touch interaction. In *Proceedings of the 27th international conference on Human factors in computing systems*, CHI '09, ACM (New York, NY, USA, 2009), 1063–1072.
24. Wiedenbeck, S., Waters, J., Birget, J.-C., Brodskiy, A., and Memon, N. Passpoints: Design and longitudinal evaluation of a graphical password system. In *International Journal of Human-Computer Studies*, no. 1-2 (2005), 102 – 127.
25. Wiedenbeck, S., Waters, J., Sobrado, L., and Birget, J.-C. Design and evaluation of a shoulder-surfing resistant graphical password scheme. In *Proceedings of the working conference on Advanced visual interfaces*, AVI '06, ACM (New York, NY, USA, 2006), 177–184.
26. Wigdor, D., and Wixon, D. *Brave NUI World: Designing Natural User Interfaces for Touch and Gesture*, 1 ed. Morgan Kaufmann, Apr. 2011.

Touch me once and I know it's you! Implicit Authentication based on Touch Screen Patterns

Alexander De Luca, Alina Hang, Frederik Brudy, Christian Lindner, Heinrich Hussmann
Media Informatics Group, University of Munich
Amalienstr. 17, 80333 Munich, Germany
{alexander.de.luca, alina.hang, hussmann}@ifi.lmu.de, {brudy,lindnerch}@cip.ifi.lmu.de

ABSTRACT
Password patterns, as used on current Android phones, and other shape-based authentication schemes are highly usable and memorable. In terms of security, they are rather weak since the shapes are easy to steal and reproduce. In this work, we introduce an implicit authentication approach that enhances password patterns with an additional security layer, transparent to the user. In short, users are not only authenticated by the shape they input but also by the way they perform the input. We conducted two consecutive studies, a lab and a long-term study, using Android applications to collect and log data from user input on a touch screen of standard commercial smartphones. Analyses using dynamic time warping (DTW) provided first proof that it is actually possible to distinguish different users and use this information to increase security of the input while keeping the convenience for the user high.

Author Keywords
Security; implicit authentication; password pattern

ACM Classification Keywords
H5.2 [Information Interfaces and Presentation]: User Interfaces – Input devices and strategies, evaluation;

General Terms
Experimentation, Human Factors, Measurement.

INTRODUCTION
With the introduction of the Android operating system for mobile phones, an alternative to PIN-authentication on mobile devices was introduced and widely deployed for the first time. The password pattern, similar to shape-based authentication approaches like Draw-a-secret [18] or PassShapes [36], enables user authentication by drawing a shape on the screen. The shape consists of an arbitrary number of strokes (or lines) between nine dots as shown in figure 1.

Permission to make digital or hard copies of all or part of this work for personal or classroom use is granted without fee provided that copies are not made or distributed for profit or commercial advantage and that copies bear this notice and the full citation on the first page. To copy otherwise, or republish, to post on servers or to redistribute to lists, requires prior specific permission and/or a fee.
CHI'12, May 5–10, 2012, Austin, Texas, USA.
Copyright 2012 ACM 978-1-4503-1015-4/12/05...$10.00.

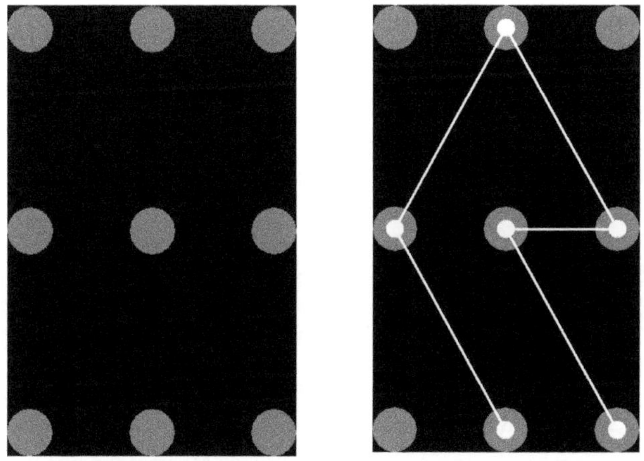

Figure 1: Standard layout of the password pattern authentication system. The blank screen (left) and an exemplary shape (right).

In a study by Clarke et al. [8], 41% of their respondents expressed concerns with respect to PINs and alphanumeric passwords, supporting the need for alternative authentication techniques. In comparison to these approaches, shape-based authentication better supports the way the brain remembers and stores information. The shape can be remembered as an image, therefore exploiting the pictorial superiority effect [25,33]. Additionally, since the pattern is drawn manually in exactly the same way every time and repeated regularly, the user's motor memory [13,30] further improves the memorability. This effect was shown to be effective [12,36], even when the shapes are performed by the user's gaze [11].

Despite its manifold advantages, this approach has major drawbacks, the most important one being security. Drawn passwords are very easy to spy on [11,36], which makes shoulder surfing, a common attack in public settings [27], a serious threat. Other attacks include the infamous smudge attack [1], in which finger traces left on the screen are used to extract the password. Due to its weak security properties, this authentication approach does not fully meet the requirement of adequately protecting the user's data stored on the device. Nowadays, not only private but also valuable business information is stored on the user's handheld [20]. Therefore, resistance to attacks is a major concern when designing respective authentication systems.

In this work, we extended the password pattern approach with an implicit authentication layer to improve its security. Whenever a user authenticates, the system not only checks if the shape was correct but also how it was entered, to determine if the person should gain access. To achieve this, we used touch screen data of current smartphones (pressure, coordinates, size, speed, time etc.) to distinguish between the rightful user and an attacker.

We performed two consecutive user studies to verify the viability of this approach. In the first study, we examined simple unlocks (e.g. a horizontal stroke) while the second study used password patterns both times enhanced with implicit authentication. The results show that it is possible to distinguish different users, thus increasing security during the authentication process. At the same time, the complexity of the approach is hidden since the users only interact with the familiar password pattern system. Thus, the main contribution of this work is to provide first proof that this implicit authentication approach actually works.

BIOMETRIC AUTHENTICATION

Apart from "something you know" authentication schemes (e.g. [11,12,21]), biometrics is an often-used alternative [9]. According to Wood [35] there are two types of biometric authentication approaches, physiological and behavioral biometrics. Physiological biometrics relies on "something the users are". In [32], Sonkamble et al. present an overview of different possible features, including the users' fingerprint, face, hand geometry, voice or iris as physiological biometrics. In [2,3], multiple biometric features are combined to implement a person identification system. Biometric authentication systems on mobile devices were, for instance, used by Rokita et al. [28], using face and hand features. Marcel et al. [24] implemented a mobile authentication system based on simultaneous face and voice recognition, using built-in sensors of the mobile device. The advantage of physiological approaches is that they work instantaneous. In general, however, they require additional hardware (e.g. fingerprint scanners). In addition, there are also user concerns related to the storage of physiological features [26].

Behavioral biometrics, on the other hand, is more commonly used for continuous authentication. As the term behavioral implies, these approaches are based on the users' behavioral cues and authentication may happen implicitly. Exemplary cues are the user's gait [10,16], location information [14] or keystroke patterns [5,22]. Shi et al. [17,31] also proposed the use of behavioral biometrics as replacement for password-based authentication or as second level of authentication. Their authentication system is based on multiple cues such as location information or communication. These features are combined with cloud computing to reduce the energy consumption on the mobile device [6]. In [23] acceleration signals are used for user identification, whereas [4,7] used typing patterns to authenticate users on mobile devices using static classifiers and neural network classifiers, respectively. Tanviruzzaman et al. [34] developed a mobile system called ePet, which uses the user's gait and location information as behavioral cues. ePet continuously checks against anomalous user behavior and denies further access on the mobile device in case anomalies are detected. Continuous authentication on mobile devices was also introduced by Yazji et al. [37]. Their system observes activities on the mobile file system as well as its network access. Due to the permanent re-authentication, their system has a latency of five minutes, with an accuracy of 90 %. Continuous authentication is always bound to latency, leaving the system unsecured for a certain amount of time, when no additional means of authentication are taken.

The approach presented in this work employs behavioral biometrics, the way a user performs the password pattern, but immediately authenticates the user. Using common touch screen data makes the need for any additional hardware obsolete. Furthermore, we combine behavioral biometrics with the input of graphical passwords.

THREAT MODEL

We assume an attacker that is already in possession of the user's password pattern (the shape). That is, the first security barrier has already been breached. How the attacker got this information is of no concern for this work. In addition, the attacker managed to retrieve the mobile device (e.g. using pickpocketing) and wants to gain access to valuable information on it. For this, as for other commercial systems, the attacker has three tries until the device will be blocked.

The approach presented in this work relies on implicit authentication and has been designed to provide security against such an attack. Thus, even after losing the mobile device and the authentication credential, the proposed system should still provide the required security.

UNLOCK USER STUDY

The main idea of the pilot user study was to collect as much data as possible using simple unlocks as known from smartphones like the iPhone or Android devices. Our objective was to gain first insights into the possibilities of identifying and distinguishing users based on the data collected with a capacitive touch screen.

We developed an Android application that was used for data collection. Figure 2 shows four different unlock screens that we implemented. Two of them (horizontal and vertical) were based on unlocks from existing devices. The remaining two were newly developed for this study to add unlocks that would produce more data. The application logged all data available from the touch screen: pressure (how hard the finger presses), size (area of the finger touching the screen), X-coordinate, Y-coordinate and time. The only exception to this was the vertical unlock with two fingers, which had two sets of XY-coordinates, pressure and size, one for each finger. Depending on the workload of the device, one event with all of the previously mentioned data was collected every nine to twelve milliseconds. No other sensor data was logged.

Figure 2: The four different unlock screens as used in the first user study. From left to right: Horizontal, vertical, vertical with two fingers and diagonal unlock.

User Study Design

As study design, a repeated measures within participants factorial design was used. The independent variable was *unlockScreen* with four levels (horizontal, vertical, vertical with two fingers, diagonal).

The task was to unlock the device 160 times with each of the four different unlock screens over a period of two days. The order of the unlock screens was counterbalanced to minimize learning effects.

Procedure

Before the experiment started, the study was explained in detail to each participant. After that, they were asked to fill out an initial questionnaire mainly collecting demographics. During this process, each participant was assigned an ID to (a) allow for anonymous data collection and (b) determine the order in which the unlock screens would be presented to the user.

Two Android Nexus One mobile devices were put on the table in front of the participant. One device had the study application installed while the second was used for a distraction task. During the test, each participant was asked to unlock the screens 80 times with each setup. At first, each user got the application device in test mode and could play around with the current unlock screens until they felt familiar with it. They were also instructed to perform the task in the same way for each unlock using the same finger(s). Every 20 unlocks, the application stopped and the participants were asked to perform a distraction task. For this purpose, they had to input a text message on the second device. When resuming the unlock task, they were reminded by the experimenter which finger(s) they used in case they did not remember.

Within two days after the experiment, the participants were asked to come to the lab again and performed the exact same experiment a second time. This was done to collect more realistic (and less biased) data by minimizing habituation effects and to see how the performance would change over time. Each unlock was additionally used as an attack for the other users. The second day ended with a final questionnaire, collecting opinions about the different unlock screens. As incentives, 8$ gift vouchers were given to the participants.

Participants

We recruited 48 participants for the study with an average age of 25 years. The youngest participant was 18, the oldest 59 years old. 22 were female, 26 male. The majority of the participants were students (73%), the remaining ones came from different professions. Each participant owned at least one mobile phone (65% smartphones) at the time the study was conducted. 17% of the participants were left-handed.

Having 48 participants allowed for perfectly counterbalancing the four unlock screens (4! = 24). That is, each permutation was performed by exactly two users.

Data Analysis

For the analysis of the data, dynamic time warping (DTW) was used. This algorithm originates from speech recognition [29] and allows for comparing two sets (time sequences) of data with each other. The algorithm looks for similarities between the sets and calculates the costs to match one onto the other. The result is a warp distance that can be used to determine how similar a set is to the reference set. A warp distance of 0 (zero) indicates absolute identical sets. The bigger the distance, the more different the sets are. Thus, it is highly appropriate for the purpose of this work, for which we used the DTW implementation for R by Toni Giorgino [15].

In this work, a sequence consists of a time series of touch screen data (all combinations of X-coordinate(s), Y-coordinate(s), pressure, size, time). Again, the exception was the two fingers vertical unlock, which had two sets of XY-coordinates, two pressure and two size values.

It has to be noted that the choice of using DTW is not obvious. However, from related work, we knew that if this approach can work, there is a high chance that DTW will show it. We do not claim that DTW is better or worse than other approaches (e.g. machine learning).

Reference Sets

To identify a user, a reference set is required. This set represents the baseline for comparison and acts as the fingerprint of the user.

For each unlock screen, the reference set was created by taking the first 20 unlocks (each one a single unlock) for each user. Each of them was compared to the 19 other unlocks using DTW. Then, the average warp distance for the respective unlock was calculated. This is a common approach found in related work [19]. In the end, the unlock with the lowest average warp distance was chosen as the reference set. Taking the first 20 unlocks is based on the fact that the rest was required to measure false positive and false negative rates.

In a second step, the reference set was again compared to the remaining 19 unlocks. The 19 warp distances were then used to calculate the mean, median, minimum, maximum and standard deviation. Those values are used to define the upper border or the threshold for the interval (starting from 0) in which an unlock is considered as valid. This approach is depicted in figure 3. The green line represents the upper border of the interval. A possible value for this border is mean + standard deviation. The main assumption behind this is that additional unlocks performed by a user are likely to be within these intervals while the ones of other users (attackers) should lie above.

Logins and Attacks

The unlocks that were not used for creating the reference set were compared to the reference set using DTW. To check the system's resistance to attacks, the unlocks of all other participants were compared to the reference set. Thus, the success of the system was measured along the following parameters: True positives (TP): correctly accepted users. True negatives (TN): correctly rejected attackers. False positives (FP): wrongly accepted attackers. False negatives (FN): wrongly rejected users.

To compare the unlocks, the previously mentioned thresholds for valid unlocks were used in different variations. Furthermore, overheads (raising the threshold value) of 5%, 10%, 15%, 20%, 30% and 50% were added to the intervals and analyzed as well. The comparison itself was repeated several times using all possible combinations of the collected data (pressure, size, coordinates, etc.). This was done to find out which combination would perform best for the respective unlock screen. In short, the analysis was performed using different thresholds and different parameter combinations.

Results

The results are based on 30,720 unlocks (640 per participant). Due to the big amount of data that was analyzed using different combinations and intervals, the analysis was performed on a grid engine.

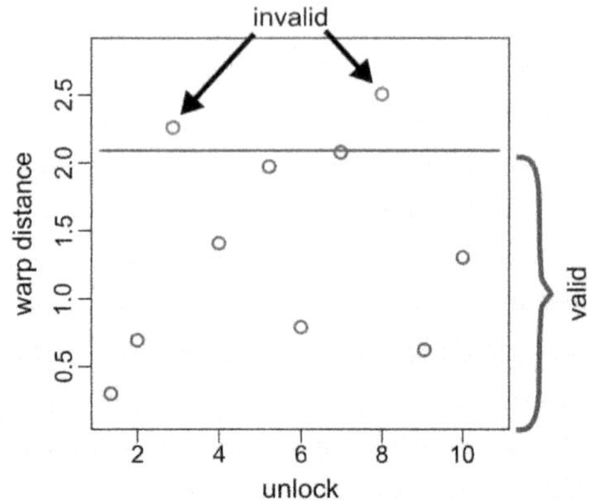

Figure 3: Identifying valid unlocks. The warp distance to the reference set is calculated. If the result is within the interval (lower than the threshold), the user is valid.

Accuracy Measurement

To calculate the accuracy on a percentage level, we used the following formula [38]:

number of correct assessments /number of all assessments.

$$Accuracy = \frac{\sum TN + \sum TP}{\sum TN + \sum TP + \sum FN + \sum FP}$$

It should be noted that unbalanced amounts of true positive and true negative rates easily influences the accuracy. In our work, there are much more attacks than valid unlocks, which means that false positives have a much higher influence on the accuracy than false negatives. Therefore, this number can only be seen as an indicator and we also need to look at the values separately rather than the accuracy only.

Logins and Attacks

It turned out that for all screens, similar upper borders of valid warp distances were the best performing (based on their accuracy). This was the value in the middle between the mean and the maximum plus the standard deviation (T=(mean+max)/2+STD). The following results for all screens are therefore based on this value. Mean, maximum and standard deviation are based on the warp distances between the reference set and the remaining 19 unlocks of the first 20 unlocks.

Table 1 shows the best results for the different unlock screens separated by the two days of the study. Desirable values are high true positive and true negative rates with low false positive and false negative rates. At first glance, a very interesting trend can be identified. While the true negative rate stays constant over the two days, the true positive rate decreases for all unlock screens. In the worst case (horizontal unlock), it decreases by 12%. However, the accuracy stays more or less constant, confirms the strong influence of higher numbers of attacks on the accuracy as mentioned before. This explains why the overall accuracy

	True Positives	True Negatives	False Positives	False Negatives	Accuracy	2-Day Accuracy
Horizontal day 1 (pressure)	2,640 (92%)	93,235 (52%)	87,245 (48%)	240 (8%)	52%	52%
Horizontal day 2 (pressure)	3,091 (80%)	93,726 (52%)	86,754 (48%)	749 (20%)	52%	
Vertical day 1 (time + XY)	2,822 (98%)	89,925 (50%)	90,555 (50%)	58 (2%)	50%	50%
Vertical day 2 (time + XY)	3,610 (94%)	89,387 (50%)	91,093 (50%)	230 (6%)	50%	
2 Finger Vertical day 1 (time)	2,689 (93%)	66,246 (37%)	114,234 (63%)	191 (7%)	38%	37%
2 Finger Vertical day 2 (time)	3,324 (87%)	65,350 (37%)	115,130 (63%)	516 (13%)	37%	
Diagonal day 1 (size + pressure)	2,666 (93%)	102,191 (57%)	78,289 (43%)	214 (7%)	57%	57%
Diagonal day 2 (size + pressure)	3,402 (89%)	102,223 (57%)	78,257 (43%)	438 (11%)	57%	

Table 1: Number of false positives, false negatives, true positives and true negatives as well as the accuracy for all unlock screens separated by the two study days. This table shows only the best results out of the different combinations of intervals and touch screen data.

for the diagonal unlock is the highest, because it had the best true negative rates in the experiment. A decreasing true positive rate with a constant true negative rate means that attackers stay as different from the user as before while the user's unlock differentiates more, the more time passed.

Overall, the vertical unlock with two fingers performed worst due to a very low true negative rate (37%). This means that 63% of all attacks were successful. This result is confirmed by the low overall accuracy of 37%. Again, this was the best result for the vertical unlock with two fingers, which was achieved using the event time.

Even though its accuracy is not the highest in the analysis, the vertical unlock with one finger performed best among the four unlock screens with a very high true positive rate (98% on the first and 94% on the second day). The optimal result was achieved using a combination of event time and the XY-coordinates for the analysis. This means that in the worst case, 6% of valid unlock attempts failed. At the same time, 50% of attacks were successful. Having a closer look at the data revealed more interesting findings that support the vertical unlock with one finger as being the best approach in the study. Of all the valid users, there was not a single user who could never be correctly identified. At the same time, 96% of users were always correctly identified.

Another interesting trend is worth being mentioned. For all unlock screens, around 50% of the attackers were responsible for more than 70% of successful attacks.

Discussion

The unlock approach provided a convenient way to quickly gather big amounts of data for analysis. Based on the results, we could investigate whether it is possible to differentiate users based on the way they perform unlocks. Especially the high true positive rates are encouraging.

Having shown how well users could be identified and thus how well the approach performs in terms of usability, there is a major drawback of this approach. In the best case, the true negative rate was 57%. This means that a little bit more than four out of ten attacks would have been successful. From a security point of view, this is not a very satisfying result.

Even though there is room for improvements for the unlock approach, the most promising way to go seemed to be using a method that allows for collecting significant more data per data set. Therefore, we decided to take the lessons learned from the pilot study and use them to enhance the security of the password pattern approach.

The lessons learned strongly influenced the design and analysis of the subsequent password pattern user study. The most important lessons learned are:

Factor time: The results of the unlock study showed that the usability of the system went down on the second day. This can be drawn back to the significant break between the two study parts. Users did not remember exactly how they performed the pattern, which influenced the results. This influence is big enough to justify the claim that the data collection period of the next study should be done using a long-term design to gather more realistic data as the system has to work in everyday use.

Lab setting: The unlock study was performed in a controlled lab environment. This might have positively influenced the results. A more realistic study design is therefore preferable for the password pattern study.

Informed participants: We instructed the participants to always perform the unlock in exactly the same way. In an optimal setting, the system should work and provide security without this knowledge (working implicitly). Thus, uninformed users seem to be the more realistic choice for the follow-up study.

PASSWORD PATTERN USER STUDY

One of the main weaknesses of the pilot study was that data was collected using only two sessions. Within these two meetings, users were very likely biased to performing the unlock the same way. This effect is increased by the fact that they were told to perform the unlock as similar as possible. Overall, this leads to a strong positive bias that is not desired to test real world applicability.

Another problem was that a simple unlock only allowed for collecting a small amount of touch screen data. As seen in the pilot study, the unlock screens that created longer time series (not necessarily more data as shown by the bad results of the two fingers approach) had a tendency to lead to better results.

These problems were addressed in the password pattern study. The password pattern approach allowed for the collection of much longer time series. Additionally, we decided not to use a lab study but a long-term real world study instead to gather more realistic data. The pattern password has the additional advantage that many users are already familiar with it.

For the study, we developed an Android application that could easily be deployed to a bigger group of users. The application had two modes. On first start, the application was in training mode, allowing the users to train their password pattern until they felt familiar with it. After that mode was ended, there was no way to return to it. In study mode, the application allowed exactly one authentication per calendar day and closed automatically after one correct or three failed authentication attempts.

The standard layout, known from android phones as shown in figure 1 was used for the prototype. Several other layouts were tested but after informal studies, the decision was made to pick the layout the users are already used to.

This study copes with the problems of the pilot study resulting in more realistic data and overall longer time series (more sensor data) per authentication attempt. This enabled us to check whether changes over days (as observed during the pilot study) are acceptable if more complex gestures (password patterns) are used.

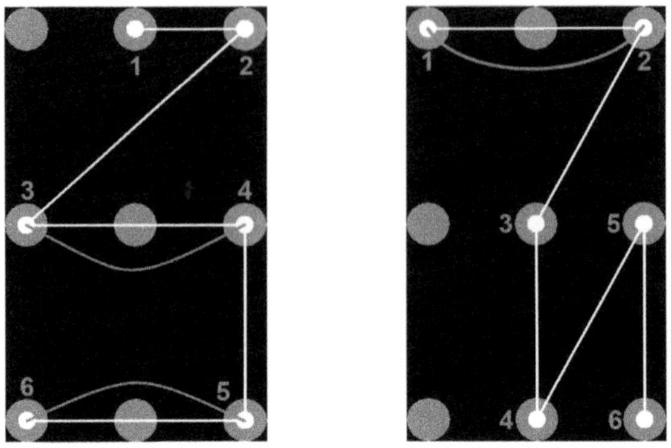

Figure 4: Password descriptions for the participants. The red lines indicate that a point has to be skipped.

User Study Design

The approach was evaluated using a repeated measures within participants longitudinal design. The task was to authenticate once a day using the test application. Overall, the participants were asked to perform the authentication task 21 times, resulting in a three weeks study.

The first day started with a training (the first mode of the test application). This data was not used for the analysis. Collecting the training data over a week would not have been feasible and the expected dropout rate would have been too high.

Procedure

On the first day of the study, the participants received an e-mail with detailed instructions on how to install the application and how to perform the training task. The Android application was provided via a download link and not via the Android market. This decision was made to keep the application private to the participants and to reduce delays in deployment. The application was installed on the participants' Android phones. After the training task, the 21 input days started. The daily input approach was introduced to further minimize the learning and habituation effects encountered in the pilot study.

Each participant was given a unique password pattern (sent with the e-mail) that was randomly assigned to the user based on an anonymous participant ID. The patterns consisted of five strokes, which make up a password space of 32,768 possible patterns (around 3.2 times higher than the password space of a four-digit PIN). There were three different categories of patterns: easy, medium, hard. Easy pattern consisted of simple strokes only. Medium patterns had one stroke for which a point had to be skipped while hard patterns had at least two skips. Figure 4 shows two patterns (medium and hard) as provided to the participants. As opposed to our expectations, the difficulty did not influence the results in any way and thus will not be mentioned again later in this paper.

In order to ensure that the users would not forget the input, an e-mail reminder was sent every day around noon. In case a user still forgot the input, an extension by one day was granted. That is, in the best case, the study took 21 days. Overall, 17 extensions for ten participants were granted. The maximum extension of the study was 26 days for one participant who forgot the input five times. Reasons for forgetting the input included weekend trips or days out.

When each participant had performed their 21 inputs, they were asked to come to a meeting and to bring their mobile device with them. During this event, the logged data was copied. After this, a second application was installed on the device of the user. The user was asked to input the correct password patterns of all other users three times with this new app. The objective was to simulate attacks on all participants. The respective log files were copied as well.

Till the end of the study, the participants were not instructed to perform the authentication in exactly the same way. This was done to avoid bias and to get insights on standard behavior, influenced by the users' daily routine. After the attack experiment, the participants were debriefed. The final meeting ended with a questionnaire covering usability and security questions. We also asked them to reflect on their behavior (e.g. if they tried to perform the password pattern in the same way each time), which was required to analyze the data.

Participants

The long term study started with 38 participants. The only prerequisite was the possession of an Android mobile phone (Android 2.1 or higher). 34 participants completed the study. The dropout rate was 11% (four users). In addition to those four users, three users had to be removed from the data sets. In two cases, the experimenter accidently gave away the purpose and description of the study before the participants had finished their tasks. The third person had to be removed since it turned out that he had someone else performing his tasks.

This means that overall, the study was correctly finished by 31 participants and thus the results are based on their data. The average age of these participants was 27 years. The youngest was 19 and the oldest 36 years. 19 participants were female, 12 were male. The incentive was the chance to win a popular gaming console at the end of the study.

Data Analysis

As for the pilot study, we used dynamic time warping (DTW) for the analysis. Data sets consisted of a series of touch screen events (XY-coordinates, pressure, size, time, speed). As opposed to the pilot study, the parameter speed was introduced (the time passed between two different coordinates).

Reference Sets

In this study, the reference set to identify a user was created by taking the first five valid authentication attempts and comparing them to each other. The overall approach is analog to the reference set creation of the pilot study with the exception that different possible reference sets were tested: smallest average warp distance, smallest median warp distance, smallest min and smallest max. In short, the warp distance to the other four authentications were calculated and the one with the lowest value (median, mean, min, max) was selected as the reference set. Then the mean, median, minimum, maximum and standard deviation to the other four was calculated and used for comparison with the remaining authentications. Depending on the number of identified possible reference sets, this comparison was done up to four times per user.

Since the number of attacks and own inputs is more even than for the unlock study, the accuracy measurement as introduced in the pilot study is a much more meaningful indicator of the quality in this study. Still it is important to look at the single numbers in detail.

Logins and Attacks

Since the data was collected using the mobile devices of the users, we had to deal with a big variety of hardware setups, including different screen resolution and quality. The different hardware would have influenced the results if we had compared every participant with every other participant. In order to avoid this, only users that owned the same type of devices were compared to each other. The biggest group within those was using the Nexus One with overall 18 users. In the end, there were five users with unique hardware setups. Thus, for those users, no valid attacks existed and they were removed from calculating the (overall) accuracy.

As for the unlock study, the true positive, true negative, false positive and false negative rates together with the accuracy were taken as a measure of performance. Again, all possible combinations of touch screen parameters (X-coordinate, Y-coordinate, size, pressure, time, speed) were taken into account. Also different variations of mean, median, standard deviation, minimum, maximum together with different overheads were tested.

Results

The following results are based on the data of the 31 valid participants. Overall there were 645 valid authentication attempts (including the data that was used to create the reference set) and 2790 attacks. We removed six inputs since the password pattern was wrongly input. Keep in mind that five users did not have valid attacks and therefore, accuracy is calculated using the data of 26 participants.

For the analysis of true positives and false negatives, the first five valid authentication attempts that were used to create the reference set were not taken into account. Based on the fact that users could fail to authenticate (by using a wrong shape), the maximum number of true positive plus false negatives per person was 16. This required significantly less comparisons than in the pilot study. Highly decreasing complexity of the analysis, the calculations were performed using a standard personal computer.

Logins and Attacks

After the analysis, the reference set based on the smallest median showed the best results in a combination with using the maximum warp distance as the threshold for valid inputs. The parameter combination that performed best consisted of pressure, size and speed.

True Positives	False Negatives	True Negatives	False Positives	Accuracy
398	92	852	231	77%
False Rejection Rate: 19%		False Acceptance Rate: 21%		

Table 2: Results for the reference set based on the smallest median in combination with the maximum as an upper border. Parameters are pressure, size and speed.

True Positives	False Negatives	True Negatives	False Positives	Accuracy
15	1	49	2	96%
12	4	51	0	94%
16	0	45	6	91%

Table 3: Top 3 accuracies of participants in the password pattern study.

Table 2 shows the results for these combinations. Overall, the accuracy is 77% with a 19% false rejection rate and 21% false acceptance rate. The focus of the analysis was to go for high true positive rates to keep the system convenient and satisfying for the users. As mentioned before, in the final questionnaire, the participants were asked whether they tried to perform the input in the same way each time. The users that stated to apply this approach had a higher average accuracy (81%) than the users that did not think about this during input (72%). Interestingly, the difficulty of the password pattern does not influence the accuracy.

When compared to the pilot study, the overall accuracy increased by more than 20%. Even though the data was collected with significant breaks in between two consecutive inputs and under much more realistic circumstances, the password pattern allows for much more accurate measurements of the users' identity. Still, at first glance, 77% accuracy seems unsatisfying.

However, when looking at the results in more detail, the picture becomes positive. For instance, out of the 26 participants, for whom valid attacks existed, six reached an accuracy of 90% or higher. The top user reached an accuracy of 96% with one false negative and two false positives (out of 51). Table 3 shows the top 3 participants and their results.

In addition, one specific group of users drew our attention. Its users had extremely low false acceptance rates (mostly zero false positives) but at the same time their false rejection rate was rather high or unsatisfying (in the worst case there was only one true positive). The second best user (see table 3) was part of this group. By setting the threshold too low, (almost) all attackers were excluded but many valid attempts failed as well. Looking at these users' reference sets showed that their thresholds were quite low compared to other users. Again, taking into account the hypothesis that users are more similar to themselves than to attackers in the way they perform the password patterns, we per-

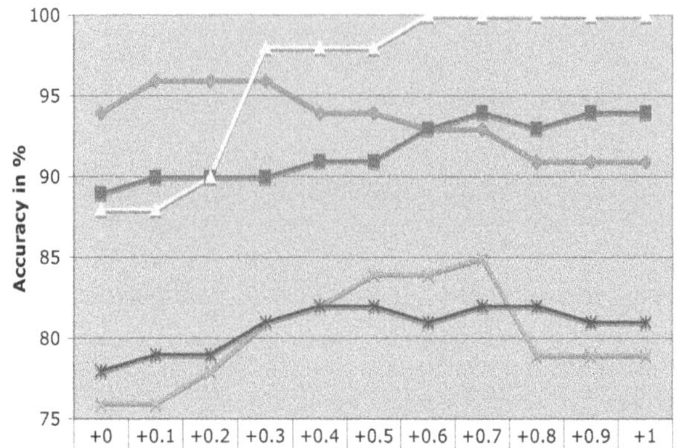

	+0	+0.1	+0.2	+0.3	+0.4	+0.5	+0.6	+0.7	+0.8	+0.9	+1
	94	96	96	96	94	94	93	93	91	91	91
	89	90	90	90	91	91	93	94	93	94	94
	88	88	90	98	98	98	100	100	100	100	100
	76	76	78	81	82	84	84	85	79	79	79
	78	79	79	81	82	82	81	82	82	81	81

Figure 5: Threshold increased for five users with low true positive rates. The graphs show that with increased threshold (warp distance +0 till +1), the accuracy significantly improves. Peaks show up at different overheads.

formed a small experiment to see whether this theory holds. We iteratively increased the threshold for these users. That is, higher warp distances between two authentication attempts were accepted as valid. We conducted this for the previously mentioned five users. The results are shown in figure 5. For each participant, the overall accuracy could be increased significantly. In one case, it was improved from 88% to 100%. This was due to the fact that false acceptance rates stayed constant while true positives increased.

Discussion

The improvements on the approach and the study lead to more realistic and less biased data triggering much better results. At first glance this seems odd but was achieved by using password patterns instead of a simple unlock. Enhancing them with implicit behavioral authentication allows for creating a convenient authentication system with good security properties under the worst circumstances (attacker in possession of the mobile device and the password pattern).

The results of the second study support our claim that password patterns create data that is distinct enough to distinguish between different users. Overall, it can be stated that using touch screen data to identify users works to a certain degree. This is supported by the fact that increasing the threshold for valid authentication attempts improves overall accuracy (as shown in figure 5). The comparison to the pilot study also indicates that this approach works the better the more sensor data is available.

An interesting observation was that informed users performed better than uninformed ones. That is, users that tried to perform the authentication in the same way each time (considering the finger to use, speed etc.) achieved, on average, higher accuracy values than the ones that did it randomly. This means that the security (and performance) can be influenced by the user. The more consistently the authentication is done, the smaller the threshold, making it harder for an attacker. However, uninformed users achieved good results as well, which indicates that the approach can work in normal everyday use without specific precautions. This is very promising from a usability point of view. It means that users can rely on the highly usable and memorable password patterns at highly improved security.

LIMITATIONS AND IMPROVEMENTS

As opposed to the pilot study, the password pattern study had much less inputs, as it is hard to collect realistic data over a longer period of time. With time frames longer than three weeks, the dropout rates of an experiment of this kind can quickly increase. Still, more data would help to further support our findings. The lack of attackers for some of the participants is undesirable. In the best case, in future work, attacks should be performed using the participant's (the victim's) own device. However, convincing users to give out their mobile phone, which usually holds private data, seems hard. Thus, a solution could be to hand out mobile phones for the purpose of the experiment. On the other hand, this would negatively influence the realistic setting.

As the experiment with increased threshold showed, there is still a lot of open space to improve the approach. For this purpose, both, the reference set creation and the comparison algorithm can be optimized. For instance, the results of the second study suggest that a dynamic reference set or a reference consisting of several unlocks/authentication attempts, which changes over time as the user makes use of the system, can positively influence accuracy. The idea of a dynamic reference set, and thus a dynamic threshold is further supported by the fact that the five different users shown in figure 5 reached their best results at different overheads (added to the threshold). Weighted parameters are a promising option in changing the algorithm as well. As is, all parameters have the same importance and weight when compared with DTW.

Finally, there is a weakness of the two studies with respect to the analysis of their security. In both cases, the attacks happened without the attacker ever seeing the actual input of the victim. That is, we cannot say whether it is possible to "shoulder surf" the way a user does the input and copy it.

CONCLUSION AND FUTURE WORK

In this paper, we presented an implicit approach to improve authentication on current mobile devices. The basic idea was to exploit touch screen data of common smartphones (without adding additional hardware) to identify users based on the way they perform an action. For this, we chose to evaluate unlock screens as well as password patterns that come with Android phones. The basic assumption was that password patterns are convenient and usable but at the same time highly insecure. By adding implicit authentication, an invisible layer of security is added to the input, which makes the system resilient to attacks under the worst circumstances (stolen mobile phone and password pattern).

It should be noted again that the approach, presented in this paper, provides immediate authentication as opposed to most work in the field of behavioral biometrics. Once the password pattern is input, the system decides instantly whether the user is authorized. The results of two studies provide first proof that it is possible to distinguish users and to improve the security of password patterns (and even screen unlocks). The results also show that the more data points a data set consists of, the easier it is to make this distinction. This means that by increasing the password length, positive effects on accuracies might be observed. However, this would come at the costs of decreased usability and memorability.

The two main open points for future work are: (a) We are currently implementing a prototype based on the presented approach that does the calculation on the mobile device to perform another long-term study based on this application. This way, dynamic reference sets can be tested in real time. Additionally, it will enable us to perform shoulder surfing tests to further evaluate and judge the security of the approach. (b) The accuracy of the system has to be increased. While in this work, the focus was on showing that implicit authentication works, in future work, less naïve approaches have to be compared to improve the accuracy of the system. For instance, DTW should be compared to, for instance, machine learning approaches.

ACCESS TO THE DATA

Interested in getting access to the (anonymized) data of the two studies? Just contact the first author of this paper.

ACKNOWLEDGMENTS

This work was funded by a Google Research Award.

REFERENCES

1. Aviv, A. J., Gibson, K., Mossop, E., Blaze, M., Smith, J. M. Smudge attacks on smartphone touch screens. *In USENIX 4th Workshop WOOT 2010.*
2. Bigun, J., Fierrez-Aguilar, J., Ortega-Garcia, J., Gonzales-Rodriguez, J. Combining biometric evidence for person authentication. *Advanced Studies in Biometrics.* Springer (2005), 1-18.
3. Brunelli, R., Falavigna, D. Person identification using multiple cues. *IEEE Transactions on Pattern Analysis and Machine Intelligence, 17*(10). (1995), 955-966.
4. Buchoux, A., Clarke, N.L. Deployment of keystroke analysis on a smartphone. In *Proceedings AIMS 2008.*
5. Card, S., Moran, T., Newell, A. Computer text-editing: An information-processing analysis of a routine cognitive skill. *Cognitive Psychology, 12(1).* (1980), 32–74.
6. Chow, R., Jakobsson, M., Masuoka, R., Molina, J., Niu, Y., Shi, E., Song, Z. Authentication in the clouds: a framework and its application to mobile users. *In Proceedings Workshop CCSW 2010.* ACM Press (2010), 1-6.
7. Clarke, N.L., Furnell, S.M. Authenticating mobile phone users using keystroke analysis. *International Journal of Information Security, 6(1).* Springer (2007), 1-14.

8. Clarke, N.L., Furnell, S.M., Rodwell, P.M., Reynolds P.L. Acceptance of subscriber authentication methods for mobile telephony devices. *Computers & Security, 21 (3).* (2002), 220-228.

9. Coventry, L., De Angeli, A., Johnson, G. Usability and biometric verification at the ATM interface. In *Proceedings CHI 2003.* ACM Press (2003), 153-160.

10. Cutting, J., Kozlowski, L. Recognizing friends by their walk: Gait perception without familiarity cues. *Bulletin of the Psychonomic Society, 9(5).* (1977), 353–356.

11. De Luca, A., Denzel, M. and Hussmann, H. Look into my eyes! Can you guess my password? In *Proceedings SOUPS 2009.* ACM Press (2009), 7:1-7:12.

12. Dunphy, P., Yan, J. Do background images improve "draw a secret" graphical passwords? In *Proceedings CCS 2007.* ACM Press (2007), 36-47.

13. Fleishman, E., Parker, J. Factors in the retention and relearning of perceptual-motor skill. *Journal of Experimental Psychology, 64.* (1962), 215–226.

14. Francis, L., Mayes, K., Hancke, G., Markantonakis, K. A location based security framework for authenticating mobile phones. *In Proceedings Workshop M-MPAC 2010.* ACM Press (2010), 5:1-5:8.

15. Giorgino, T. Computing and visualizing dynamic time warping alignments in R: the DTW package. *Journal of Statistical Software, 31(7).* (2009), 1-24.

16. Gafurov, D., Helkala, K., Søndrol, T. Biometric gait authentication using accelerometer sensor. *Journal of Computers, 1 (7).* Academy Publisher (2006), 51-59.

17. Jakobsson, M., Shi, E., Golle, P., Chow, R. Implicit authentication for mobile devices. In *Proceedings* HotSec 2009. USENIX Association, 9-9.

18. Jermyn, I., Mayer, A., Monrose, F., Reiter, M. K., Rubin, A. D. The design and analysis of graphical passwords. In *Proceedings SSYM 1999.* USENIX Association.

19. Kar, B., Dutta, P. K., Basu, T. K., Vielhauer, C., Dittmann, J. DTW based verification scheme of biometric signatures. In *Proceedings ICIT 2006.*

20. Karlson, A., Brush, A.J., Schechter, S. Can i borrow your phone? Understanding concerns when sharing mobile phones. In *Proceedings CHI 2009.* ACM Press (2009), 1647-1650.

21. Kim, D., Dunphy, P., Briggs, P., Hook, J., Nicholson, J., Nicholson, J., Olivier, P. Multi-touch authentication on tabletops. *In Proceedings CHI 2010.* ACM Press (2010), 1093-1102.

22. Legget, J., Williams, G., Usnick, M. Dynamic identity verification via keystroke characteristics. *International Journal of Man-Machine Studies, 35 (6).* Academic Press Ltd (1991), 859-870.

23. Mantyjarvi, J., Lindholm, M., Vildjiounaite, E., Makela, S. M., Ailisto, H.A. Identifying users of portable devices from gait pattern with accelerometers. In *Proceedings ICASSP 2005.*

24. Marcel, S., Cool, C., Atanasoaei, C., Tarsetti, F., Pesán, J., Matejka, P., Cernocky, J., Helistekangas, M., Turtinen, M. MOBIO: mobile biometric face and speaker authentication, In *Proceedings CVPR 2010.*

25. Nelson, D. L., Reed, V. S., Walling, J. R. Pictorial superiority effect. *Journal of Experimental Psychology: Human Learning and Memory 2* (5). (1976), 523-528.

26. Pons, A.P., Polak, P. Understanding user perspectives on biometric technology. *Commun. ACM,* 51 (9). ACM Press (2008), 115-118.

27. Rogers, J. Please enter your four-digit pin. Financial Services Technology, U.S. Edition Issue 4 (Mar. 2007).

28. Rokita, J. Krzyzak, A., Suen, C.Y. Cell phones personal authentication systems using multimodal biometrics. In *Proceedings ICIAR 2008.* Springer (2008), 1013-1022.

29. Sakoe, H., Chiba, S. Dynamic programming algorithm optimization for spoken word recognition. *IEEE Transactions on Acoustics, Speech and Signal Processing, 26(1).* (1978), 43-49.

30. Shadmer, R., Brashers-Krug, T. Functional stages in the formation of human long-term motor memory. *The Journal of Neuroscience, 17(1).* (1997), 409-419.

31. Shi, E., Niu, Y., Jakobsson, M., Chow, R. Implicit authentication through learning user behavior. In *Proceedings ISC 2010.* Springer (2011), 99-113.

32. Sonkamble, S., Thool, R., Sonkamble, B. Survey of biometric recognition systems and their applications. *Journal of Theoretical and Applied Information Technology, 11(1).* (2010), 45-51.

33. Standing, L. Learning 10,000 pictures. *The Quarterly Journal of Experimental Psychology, 25(2).* (1973), 207-22.

34. Tamviruzzaman, M., Ahamed, S. I., Hasan, C. S., O'brien, C. ePet: When cellular phone learns to recognize its owner. In *Proceedings Workshop SafeConfig 2009.* ACM Press (2009), 13-18.

35. Wood, H.M. The use of passwords for controlled access to remote computer systems and services. In *Proceedings AFIPS 1977.* ACM Press(1977), 27-33.

36. Weiss, R., De Luca, A. PassShapes: utilizing stroke based authentication to increase password memorability. In *Proceedings NordiCHI 2008.* ACM Press (2008), 383-392.

37. Yazji, S., Chen, X. Dick, R.P., Scheuermann P. Implicit user re-authentication for mobile devices. In Proceedings *UIC 2009.* Springer (2009), 325-339.

38. Zhu, W., Zeng, N., Wang, N. Sensitivity, specificity, accuracy, associated confidence interval and ROC analysis with practical SAS® implementations. In *Proceedings Nesug 2010.*

WebTicket: Account Management Using Printable Tokens

Eiji Hayashi[1] **Bryan A. Pendleton**[1] **Fatih Kursat Ozenc**[2] **Jason I. Hong**[1]

[1]Carnegie Mellon University, 5000 Forbes Ave. Pittsburgh PA 15213, USA,
{ehayashi, bpendlet, jasonh}@cs.cmu.edu
[2]Autodesk Inc. 1560 Trapelo Road, Waltham, MA 02451, USA, kursat@cmu.edu

ABSTRACT
Passwords are the most common authentication scheme today. However, it is difficult for people to memorize strong passwords, such as random sequences of characters. Additionally, passwords do not provide protection against phishing attacks. This paper introduces WebTicket, a low cost, easy-to-use and reliable web account management system that uses "tickets", which are tokens that contain a two-dimensional barcode that can be printed or stored on smartphones. Users can log into accounts by presenting the barcodes to webcams connected to computers. Through two lab studies and one field study consisting of 59 participants in total, we found that WebTicket can provide reliable authentication and phishing resilience.

Author Keywords
Password; User Authentication; Usable Security

ACM Classification Keywords
H.5.2 Information Interfaces and Presentation: Miscellaneous

General Terms
Human Factors and Security

INTRODUCTION
Passwords are the most commonly used form of authentication for web services today. A fundamental assumption here is that users can memorize secure passwords. If users have only a few passwords, it is possible to memorize them. However, as the number of passwords increases, users have difficulty in remembering them, in part due to interference effects [4].

The cost of forgetting passwords is not trivial. For the NYTimes online, 100,000 readers forget their passwords each week. Furthermore, 15% of *new* readers were actually old readers signing up again because of a forgotten password [13]. As another example, a Gartner report investigated the cost of forgotten passwords at a large beverage company. This investigation found that 30% of help desk calls were related to passwords, with an average cost of $17.23 USD per call, resulting in an annual impact of more than $900,000 USD [11].

Permission to make digital or hard copies of all or part of this work for personal or classroom use is granted without fee provided that copies are not made or distributed for profit or commercial advantage and that copies bear this notice and the full citation on the first page. To copy otherwise, or republish, to post on servers or to redistribute to lists, requires prior specific permission and/or a fee.
CHI'12, May 5–10, 2012, Austin, Texas, USA.
Copyright 2012 ACM 978-1-4503-1015-4/12/05...$10.00.

(a) Front (b) Back

Figure 1. An example of a paper-based WebTicket. On its front side, it has a two-dimensional barcode that stores a login script. On its reverse side, it has a favicon, user-editable text, a user-chosen border, and instructions.

People cope with the burden of passwords in many ways, but these strategies often lead to new security risks. For example, to improve memorability, users often choose *simple, easy-to-remember passwords* [4,28]; however these simple passwords are highly vulnerable to dictionary attacks [16,18] and educated guess attacks. Furthermore, an analysis of 32M passwords exposed in a security breach at RockYou.com showed that the top 20 most common passwords could compromise over 5% of the accounts [33].

Another strategy is to *reuse passwords*. Gaw and Felten [12] and Hayashi and Hong [15] both reported that users often reused passwords. Reusing passwords reduces the number of passwords that users must memorize; however, if one account using a shared password is cracked, other accounts are potentially compromised.

In this paper, we introduce WebTicket, a web account management system that lets users manage their accounts without memorizing passwords. WebTicket generates a strong password and embeds a login script – which includes a URL of a web site, a user ID, and the password – in a 2D barcode on a ticket. Users can print tickets (see Figure 1) or store tickets on their mobile phone (see Figure 4). To log into an account, users show the ticket to a webcam on their computers. Data is encrypted using a key stored in the user's computer. Thus, an attacker must have access to both the user's computer and the ticket.

WebTicket transforms knowledge-based authentication into token-based authentication at a relatively low monetary and operational cost. WebTicket also prevents phishing attacks by steering users to legitimate websites. Additionally, even when led to phishing websites, users cannot type in their passwords because they do not know their own passwords.

WebTicket is not intended to replace all passwords. WebTicket works well in managing infrequently used or secure passwords that users are more likely to forget, while passwords work well for frequently used accounts where users are less likely to forget passwords.

In this paper, we present the design and implementation of WebTicket. We also present the results of two lab studies and one field study consisting of 59 participants in total, which suggest that WebTicket can provide easy and reliable user authentication while being resilient against phishing.

RELATED WORK

We have organized related work into two categories: usable security and tangible interfaces.

Usable security

User authentication systems depend on three types of mechanisms: *what you know*, *what you have* and *what you are*. In *what you know*, an authentication system and a user share a secret at enrollment, e.g., a password. The system authenticates the user by verifying whether the user knows the shared secret. In *what you have*, a system authenticates a user based on whether the user has a physical object, such as a credit card, which is given to the user at enrollment. In *what you are*, an authentication system records some aspects of a user's physiology or behavior at enrollment, and, then, authenticates the user based on whether this property matches or not.

Password managers. Much past work has examined how to reduce memory workload to make account management for *what you know* authentication easier. The most straightforward approach is to store user IDs and passwords in computers. All major web browsers have a built-in password manager. However, if attackers have access to a user's web browser, they can access the user's accounts without any authentication. Furthermore, if users want to use the account information on multiple computers, users have to synchronize the computers whenever they create or modify the account information (e.g., changing passwords). The synchronization, in many systems, is done by storing the information in centralized servers, which can be targeted by attackers because it contains information about many accounts from multiple users. Moreover, users have to trust third parties to do the synchronization.

A common alternative to password managers is to simply write down passwords on paper. In this approach, once attackers obtain access to written passwords, the attackers could compromise the accounts by guessing their user IDs, which are e-mail addresses in many cases, and trying some popular websites. Moreover, writing downs passwords does not provide any phishing resilience.

Another possible approach is that users reset passwords whenever they want to log into their accounts via e-mails or by answering secret questions. However, resetting passwords could be time-consuming processes.

Master password approach. Systems such as PwdHash [26] and PassPet [32] decrease the number of passwords that users have to memorize by generating account specific passwords based on a single master password. In these schemes, users only need to memorize one password; however, these schemes also rely on additional information (i.e., domain names or user-chosen name for web sites) that is easy to guess or obtain. For example, attackers could launch online attacks on insecure web sites, which do not restrict number of trials, to obtain a master password, then, compromise secure and important accounts.

Mnemonic passwords. Another approach to making passwords easier to memorize is to use mnemonic passwords, which are seemingly random sequence of letters generated from a phrase. For instance, "Ilts@7S!" can be generated from a phrase "I love to ski at Seven Springs!" Mnemonic passwords are easy for users to memorize and relatively difficult to guess for attackers [31]. However, because users are likely to choose specific phrases as sources of mnemonic passwords, attackers can guess mnemonic passwords more easily than random passwords [18]. Furthermore, even using mnemonic passwords, users can forget which password is for which account, due to scaling issues and interference effects.

Graphical passwords. Another solution to making passwords easy to memorize is using graphical passwords [5,14,30]. Graphical passwords are based on the observations that people are better at memorizing (or recognizing) graphics than at memorizing text [19,25]. However, these graphical password authentication schemes have challenges in actual deployment because of uncertainty about their security and scalability [6,8,10].

Tokens. Other authentication systems depend on *what you have*. eToken is a USB device that can be used as a "physical key" to login [1]. A one-time password token is a device with an LCD, which shows numbers based on the current time and a key stored in the token. To authenticate, users can type the number shown on the device. Then, a server-side application verifies whether that number was actually generated by that device. RSA securID is a variant of the one-time password token. In addition to a number shown on the RSA securID, users have to type their personal identification number to be authenticated [3]. However, there are challenges in scaling these kinds of approaches across all accounts a person has, since these tokens require server-side support, and it would be impractical to carry a custom token for each web site. As such, these tokens tend to be used only for accounts with very high security requirements.

Finally, there are systems that use smartphones for authentication. Phoolproof Phishing is an authentication scheme designed to prevent phishing attacks, key loggers, and other kinds of malware [26]. Users select what site to login to on their mobile phone, which opens the web site on a local computer. The mobile phone also checks the site's certificate to verify that the opened site is the correct site, at which point users can login normally. While WebTicket does not offer as strong mutual authentication, it does not require server-side changes, and also facilitates logins by entering usernames and passwords. Seeing-Is-Believing is a pairing protocol for cell phones [21]. The protocol pairs two devices by conveying a hash value, i.e., a number, using a 2D barcode. In contrast, in WebTicket, a 2D barcode on a ticket conveys richer information, such as a URL, a user ID and a password for user authentication.

Tangible Interfaces

There are many tangible interfaces that make use of paper (e.g., [17,20,22]). Palette is a presentation tool that lets presenters access digital presentations quickly using physical cards with printed barcodes [24]. Collaborage is an augmented board where users can put paper tags with 2D identification codes, which connect the paper tags with information on a computer [23]. These projects demonstrated that users could manage complicated information well using paper augmented by computers.

WEBTICKET DESIGN GOALS

Our primary goal with WebTicket is to support people in accessing infrequently used accounts as well as accounts with stringent password requirements. WebTicket is also intended to help novice users who are uncomfortable with computers or have a hard time remembering not only their passwords, but also what website to go to. In this sense, WebTicket can be thought of as a tangible web bookmark. Towards these ends, we defined the following design goals.

Be Reliable for Logins. WebTicket should support logging into accounts reliably even after a long period of inactivity.

Be Easy to Understand. Users often have difficulties in understanding security systems because of a lack of awareness and knowledge about computer security [29]. We wanted WebTicket to offer users a simple mental model of how it works and how to use it, which should help to improve security in practice.

Offer Strong Passwords. Users tend to choose easily guessable passwords or reuse passwords to improve memorability [4,31]. To maximize the security provided by passwords, WebTicket should use a randomly generated strong password for each account.

Be Compatible with Existing Web Sites. Virtually all web sites today use password-based authentication. We want WebTicket to be compatible with the majority of web sites without any server-side modifications.

Be Low Cost. Some account management systems entail additional costs, in terms of initial purchase costs, setup, and maintenance, which can be barriers to adoption. Hence, we wanted these costs for WebTicket to be low.

Support Partial Adoption. Rather than forcing people to switch completely to a new system, we wanted to let people choose which websites they wanted to use WebTicket for.

WEBTICKET DESIGN AND USAGE

Using the WebTicket browser extension, a user can create a ticket with a 2D barcode that contains a login script, and then print the ticket or store the ticket on their smartphone. This login script includes the URL of a web site, the user ID, and the encrypted password. To log into the account, the user shows the ticket to a webcam attached to her computer. WebTicket scans the 2D barcode, opens the website in a browser, and logs into the account, without requiring the user to enter in her user name and password.

In this section, we provide more detail on installation, account creation, tickets, and the login process (See Figures 1 to 3), along with our design rationale. Near the end of the paper, we discuss alternative designs and limitations.

Installing WebTicket

We implemented the backend of WebTicket as a Firefox extension. On installation, WebTicket generates a random number that is used as a key to encrypt information on tickets paired with that computer. Users can print a backup of the encryption key as a special kind of WebTicket if desired, which lets users copy the key to other computers. After copying the keys, tickets generated on one computer can be used on other computers as well without any synchronization. If the backup is printed, the backup should be kept securely to ensure the security of the encryption.

After generating the key, WebTicket prompts users to choose a border from a large set of borders, which is printed on tickets (see Figure 1.b) and displayed on the WebTicket reader dialog (Figure 3). This border is based on dynamic security skins [7]. Because the border is a secret shared between a user and the WebTicket system, an attacker will have a harder time creating a fake phishing dialog that pretends to be WebTicket. Note that the border is an additional layer of security against phishing attacks. Even if an attacker obtains the 2D barcode on a ticket by letting the user scan her tickets using a fake reader dialog, the attacker cannot recover account information without the encryption key stored in her computer(s). WebTicket included dynamic security skins as a form of defense in depth.

WebTicket Account Creation

When signing up for web services, users create web accounts and tickets using the WebTicket wizard (Figure 2). The account creation process consists of (1) *signing up*, (2) *recording*, and (3) *printing*. In the *signing up* step, a user is asked to sign up for the web service, e.g., amazon.com. WebTicket automatically fills password fields with a randomly generated strong password consisting of upper case, lower case, numbers, and at least one symbol.

One challenge in generating passwords is that different web sites have different password policies. We analyzed the 100 most frequently visited web sites listed by Alexa. Of these, 42 allow free sign up. 78.6 % of the 42 web sites were compatible with our password generation algorithm. We think the coverage was reasonably high as an un-optimized research prototype. Other web sites had password policies not compatible with our algorithm (e.g., do not allow symbols). In these cases, users can type letters in password fields to satisfy the policies. WebTicket then randomizes the order of letters to make the passwords stronger.

Figure 2. WebTicket wizard. Users can open the wizard from the "create ticket" tab in WebTicket's reader dialog (Figure 3), and then create an account and a ticket using this wizard.

In the *recording* step, the wizard asks the user to log into the web service. When the wizard detects that the user is typing in their user ID, the wizard fills in the password field with the password generated in the previous step. Then, when the user clicks the login button, the wizard records the login process of the web site, i.e., the URL of the login page, the user ID, the password, and names of relevant HTML objects. We currently focus on web sites where users can log into their accounts in a single step, e.g., typing a user ID and a password, and then clicking a login button. Technically, WebTicket could support more complicated login processes, such as those that have intermediate steps like showing a picture, as long as the process requires same input every time, though we do not currently support this.

In the *printing* step, the user can edit text that appears on the reverse side of the ticket to personalize a ticket with a name or a short memo before printing the ticket.

WebTicket also supports creating tickets for existing accounts. Users can create tickets using existing passwords, or can manually change a web site's password to one generated by WebTicket.

The Ticket

Each ticket is 52mm×85mm. A QR Code on the front side contains a login script. QR Codes are 2D barcodes standardized by Denso [2]. We choose QR Codes because they can be easily decoded by a webcam. However, any barcode that can store enough data can be used.

The password in this script is encrypted using the concatenation of a key stored on a user's computer and the URL of the associated web site. The key prevents simple theft or camera-based attacks. The reverse side of a ticket has a favicon of the web site associated with this ticket, user-editable text (e.g., the user's name), the user-chosen border, and instructions about the login process. Instructions were added after the first user study to help users to remember the log in process of WebTicket.

If a ticket is lost, stolen, or damaged, users can revoke the ticket and print a new ticket. Because a ticket is tied to a combination of a URL, a user ID and a password, users can revoke a ticket by changing the old password to a new one using password reset mechanisms provided by web sites. Then, users can print a new ticket that contains the new password using the WebTicket wizard.

Because tickets are physical objects, we can describe tickets as being analogous to physical keys. This description could help users to foster a better mental model of how they should treat their tickets. Furthermore, because a ticket is associated with one account, users can manage them differently. For instance, users can keep tickets for their bank accounts securely at their home, while carrying around tickets for e-commerce web sites.

Logging in Using WebTicket

To log into an account, the user first click on the WebTicket icon in Firefox's toolbar to launch WebTicket's reader dialog (Figure 3). As noted previously, the border of this dialog is identical to the border selected by the user on installation, as an extra protection against phishing attacks [7] in addition to the encryption of the barcode. The dialog also shows a real-time image captured by the computer's webcam. After launching the dialog, the user should check whether the border on the ticket matches the border on the dialog, to avoid custom phishing attacks on WebTicket. If the user sees that the borders match, the user scans the QR Code on her ticket. The WebTicket application then decrypts and executes the script to log into the account.

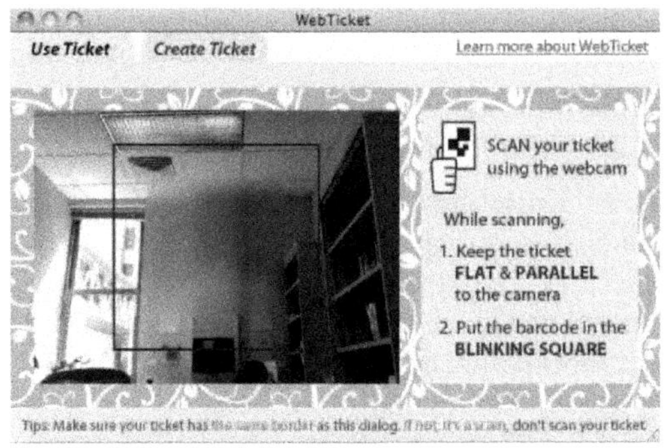

Figure 3. WebTicket's reader dialog. Users scan their tickets by showing their ticket to a webcam. The user-chosen border is shown around the dialog. The color of the green part in the dialog also changes along with the border.

(a) List View (b) Information (c) QR Code

Figure 4. Screenshots of smartphone-based WebTicket. All the tickets in a phone are listed in (a) List View. When user chooses one of them, (b) information is displayed. (c) QR code is displayed when the *show barcode* button is clicked.

WebTicket on Mobile Phones

In the user study #1, some participants expressed concerns about carrying tickets. We also realized that there were potential problems with managing large number of tickets.

To address these concerns, we implemented WebTicket for Android smart phones (Figure 4). Instead of printing tickets, users can use their mobile phones to scan a QR code shown on a computer's display to import the data in *printing* step. To log into an account, a user can select an account on their smart phone to display a QR code. Because the paper-based and mobile-phone version of WebTicket use the same QR code, they can be used interchangeably.

USER STUDY #1: BASIC USABILITY

We conducted a user study consisting of two sessions to compare WebTicket with passwords in terms of their usability using a within-subject design. In the *password condition*, participants created accounts and logged into the accounts using passwords. In the *WebTicket condition*, they did the same using the paper-based version of WebTicket. At this point, we had not implemented mobile phone-based WebTicket. We used three mock e-commerce web sites (for a practice and the two conditions). The websites were different in content and color while they were identical in terms of registration and login forms. The login form, shown on their home pages, required participants' email addresses and passwords to log into their accounts. We designed these web sites based on an analysis of 27 existing e-commerce sites.

Participants

We recruited 20 participants using an existing university recruitment site. Their ages ranged from 21 to 57 with a mean age of 31.9 (σ=11.5). Nine participants were males and 11 were female. They consisted of 11 university students, nine university staffs and two domestic residents. None of the students were computer science majors. We paid $10 USD for their participation and an additional $3 USD for each successful login in the second session.

Procedure

In the initial session, we first asked participants to create an account and then log into that account using WebTicket as a practice trial. After that, for the actual study, we asked participants to create two accounts, one using WebTicket and one using standard passwords in randomized orders. In both conditions, they started from a blank page opened in Firefox, with the WebTicket wizard opened in the WebTicket condition. For the password condition, we asked them not to use their existing passwords. These were intended to improve the internal validity of this study.

After creating the accounts, we asked the participants to log into the accounts starting from a blank page. In the password condition, the participants opened a web site associated with their account using a bookmark. Then, the participant typed their email addresses and passwords in a login form to log into their accounts. In the WebTicket condition, the login process involved more steps. We prepared nine extra tickets for the e-commerce web sites. Then, a participant's ticket was shuffled in with the nine extra tickets to imitate a situation with 10 WebTicket accounts. This is based on the observations that users have about 10 accounts on average [12,15]. In addition, we asked each participant to put the stack of 10 tickets in a place where she kept other cards, e.g. a wallet in a bag. We asked participants to start the login process from this state. Therefore, a typical login process involved taking out a wallet from a bag, taking out the stack of tickets from a wallet, searching a ticket for the specified web account from the stack, launching the WebTicket reader dialog, and scanning the ticket. In both conditions, we regarded a login process as successful if participants could log into their accounts within two minutes. At the end of the initial session, we asked participants to complete a survey. We also asked them to keep their tickets for one week and bring them back to the follow-up session.

One week later, in the follow-up session, we asked the participants to log into their accounts using passwords and tickets. We also asked them to complete another survey.

We conducted this study in an isolated room. An experimenter sat next to a participant and gave instructions. The same experimenter supervised all participants. We used a Macbook Pro laptop (MB766LL/A) with a built-in camera, and a Canon iP4200 printer. We placed the printer and a pair of scissors next to the laptop. We videotaped the whole user study using two camcorders for analysis.

RESULTS OF USER STUDY #1

Account Creation

Table 1 shows account creation times and their breakdowns. In total, creating an account in the WebTicket condition took 71.1 seconds longer than that of the password condition. In the WebTicket condition, it took less time for participants to complete registration than in the password condition. This was because in the WebTicket condition, the wizard generated passwords on behalf of the participants, while they had to come up with passwords by themselves in the password condition.

	Password	WebTicket
(1) Go To a registration page	20.0 (17.1)	15.9 (8.9)
(2) Complete registration	*73.0 (33.8)	*50.0 (18.7)
(3) Record login process	-	34.4 (21.3)
(4) Edit text on a reverse side	-	4.8 (2.8)
(5) Print a ticket	-	19.7 (0.7)
(6) Cut and fold a ticket	-	39.3 (11.2)
Total	*93.0 (45.8)	*164.1 (38.3)

Table 1. Breakdowns (means and standard deviations) of the account creation times in seconds. Asterisks denote statistically significant differences between the password and the WebTicket conditions ($p < 0.05$ in Mann-Whitney U test).

Login Process

Table 2 shows the overall success rates. On the first day, all participants succeeded in both conditions. However, one week after, five participants could not log into their accounts in the password condition, while all participants brought back their tickets and logged into their accounts in the WebTicket condition. Additionally, among those who succeeded in the password condition, it took an average of 1.93 login attempts before successfully logging in. This result indicated that participants were likely to forget their passwords, while they could keep a ticket for one week.

Table 3 shows the login times of participants who successfully logged in. On the first day, the mean time for the password condition was shorter than the WebTicket condition ($p<0.05$ using Mann-Whitney U test). However, one week later, the login time for the password condition increased while that of the WebTicket condition did not, leading to there being no statistically significant difference in the mean login times between the password and the WebTicket conditions.

	On the first day	One week later
Password	100% (20/20)	75%* (15/20)
WebTicket	100% (20/20)	100%* (20/20)

Table 2. Success rates of logins. One week later five participants could not log into their accounts using passwords. Asterisks stand for a statistically significant difference ($p < 0.05$ in χ^2 test).

	On the first day	One week later
Password	*24.9 (12.4)	44.6 (30.7)
WebTicket	*35.8 (13.2)	30.5 (12.2)

Table 3. Login time in seconds. On the first day login using WebTicket took longer than that using passwords. However, one week later, there was no statistically significant difference between the two conditions. Asterisks stand for a statistically significant difference ($p < 0.05$ in Mann Whitney U test).

In the WebTicket condition, some participants had difficulty in finding which icon they had to click to launch the WebTicket reader dialog. We also observed that some participants opened the home pages and typed their email addresses before launching WebTicket's reader dialog. This process was unnecessary because WebTicket automatically complete the process when QR code was scanned. These observations indicated that people were not entirely clear about WebTicket's login process. Thus, we added the instruction on the reverse side of tickets after the first user study to clarify the login process (see Figure 1).

	Account Creation		Login	
	Ease	Length	Ease	Length
Password	2.1 (0.86)	2.5 (0.94)	2.4* (1.1)	2.3* (1.1)
WebTicket	3.1 (0.51)	2.9 (0.64)	3.1* (0.9)	3.2* (0.7)

Table 4. Participants' self-reported evaluations (means and standard deviations) about account creation processes and login processes (1 is very difficult or very long, 5 is very easy or very short). Asterisks stand for statistically significant differences between the password and the WebTicket conditions ($p<0.05$ in Mann-Whitney U test).

At the end of the second session, in a post-test survey, we asked participants whether the login processes using passwords and WebTicket were easy or difficult, and short or long using 5-point Likert scales (Table 4). In terms of ease, participants reported the login process using passwords as rather difficult (2.4), and using WebTicket as neither easy nor difficult (3.1). The difference between the results in the password condition and the WebTicket condition was significant ($p<0.05$ using Mann-Whitney U test). In terms of length, participants reported the login process using passwords as long (2.3), and using WebTicket as neither short nor long (3.2). The difference was significant ($p<0.01$ using Mann-Whitney U test). These results indicated that, although the actual login time using WebTicket was not shorter than the process using passwords, participants perceived that authentication using WebTicket was faster and easier than that using passwords.

USER STUDY #2: EVALUATING PHISHING RESISTANCE

We conducted the second user study to investigate phishing resilience of WebTicket as well as mobile phone version of WebTicket. The study had two sessions: an initial session and a follow-up session one week later. The initial session was similar to the first study, with an extra condition for mobile phone WebTicket. However, the second session was quite different. We asked participants to handle emails, including a phishing email, asking them to complete some tasks in a role-playing scenario.

Participants

We recruited 35 participants using an existing university recruitment web site. Twenty-nine participants completed the study. None of them participated in the first user study. Their ages ranged from 19 to 57 with a mean age of 30.1 ($\sigma=11.1$). Sixteen participants were males and 13 were female. They consisted of 19 university students, two university staff, and eight domestic residents. None of the students were computer science majors. We paid $10 USD for their participation and also paid additional $2 USD for each successful login in the follow-up session. In the initial session, we did not yet tell that they could get the bonus for successful logins. Thus, the bonus did not affect the participants' choice of passwords, while the bonus gave the participants an incentive to login in the follow-up session.

Procedure

In the initial session, we explained WebTicket to participants. Then, we asked the participants to create two accounts as a warm-up task, using both the paper-based and mobile phone versions of WebTicket. We then had participants create three accounts in three different mock e-commerce web sites, using password, paper-based WebTicket, and mobile-phone-based WebTicket in randomized orders. A change from the first study was that participants could choose *any* password in the password condition. Additionally, in the two WebTicket conditions, WebTicket wizard was *not* opened initially. Thus, the participants had to open it by themselves. We made these two changes to address the limitations in the first study.

The web sites were same in the first user study except that we added more fields in their registration forms, such as a credit card number field, to make them fit our phishing evaluation. We provided a persona of a university staff, whose identity the participants used to create these accounts. After creating the accounts, we asked the participants to log into their accounts one by one. We also increased the number of dummy tickets to 20 to further evaluate scalability of WebTicket. At the end of the initial session, we gave participants their tickets and asked them to bring them back to the follow-up session.

In the follow-up session, we evaluated the phishing resilience of the three authentication systems following the procedure used in Egelman et al.'s study [9] as much as possible. We asked participants to handle five emails from a professor. Three of them asked to purchase products using the accounts created in the first session. The other two emails were distracters. When purchasing products, the participants received three confirmation emails and one phishing email. The phishing email was same as one used in Egelman et al.'s study, although we modified shop names and URLs to make it fit with our study. The phishing email said that an order would be delayed and that, unless the participants clicked a link in the email to approve the delay, the order would be canceled. When the participants clicked the link, they went to a simulated phishing web site.

We divided participants into five conditions. Participants in the first condition received a phishing email against their password-based accounts. Participants in the next two conditions received a phishing email against their paper-based WebTicket accounts. Participants in the last two conditions received a phishing email against their mobile-phone-based WebTicket accounts.

We used two different kinds of phishing attacks on both paper-based and mobile-phone-based WebTicket. The first kind was a standard phishing attack that tried to trick people into using their username and password to log into a fake site. We call this *general phishing*. The second kind was a new attack that specifically targeted WebTicket itself, tricking people into giving up their QR codes by using a fake dialog (Figure 5). We define this phishing as *WT phishing*. In the current WebTicket, the QR code by itself does not allow attackers to access users' accounts because the information embedded in QR code is encrypted. However, we thought that the investigation of WT phishing could contribute to the evaluation of alternative designs (e.g., not using encryption).

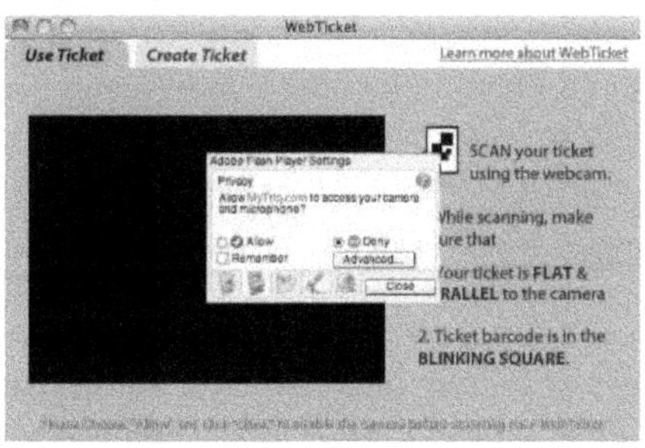

Figure 5. Fake reader dialog implemented by Flash. Users must click allow, then, close to enable a webcam. At the bottom, there was an instruction asking to do so.

In WT phishing, the fake dialog was implemented by Flash; hence it had to show the Flash privacy setting dialog asking for access to a webcam. If users choose *allow* and click *close*, the fake dialog worked in the same way as WebTicket. We decided not to show any border around the dialog because attackers would not know which border to use, and because users are not good at noticing that something is missing [7]. Moreover, we added an instruction asking users to choose *allow* and click *close* to *help* users to be phished (Figure 5).

RESULTS OF USER STUDY #2

Account Creation and Login

Table 5 shows account creation times and login times. As described in the previous section, participants had to launch the WebTicket wizard first in the WebTicket conditions. Additionally, in the password condition, we allowed participants to use any passwords, including reusing existing passwords. Although account creation time increased as a result of modification of registration forms, the results were in line with those of the first user study.

In the second session, we asked participants to handle five emails. Three of the emails asked the participants to log into their accounts that they created in the first session, and purchase products. Table 6 shows the success rates of the logins. Although we allowed participants to choose any passwords, there were still statistically significant differences between the success rates of passwords condition and that of the two WebTicket conditions.

	Account Creation	Login
Password	*113.8 (47.1)	27.0 (14.6)
Paper-based WebTicket	*192.3 (61.7)	30.3 (10.8)
Mobile-phone WebTicket	*165.1 (75.6)	32.5 (12.3)

Table 5. Account creation times and login times in seconds. The results complied with the results in the first user study. There were statistically significant differences in account creation times between the password and the two WebTicket conditions ($p < 0.05$, in Mann-Whitney U test).

	On the first day	One week later
Password	100% (29/29)	*90% (26/29)
Paper-based WebTicket	100% (29/29)	*100% (29/29)
Mobile-phone WebTicket	100% (29/29)	*100% (29/29)

Table 6. Success rates of the logins. Asterisks stand for statistically significant differences between the password and the two WebTicket conditions ($p < 0.05$ in χ^2 test).

Phishing Resilience

In the second session, we also investigated phishing resilience of passwords and WebTicket. We found that seven participants opened the phishing email and close it right away without reading its content possibly to save their time. Thus, we analyzed only the participants who actually read the phishing emails. Moreover, because there was no statistically significant difference between paper-based WebTicket and mobile-phone-based WebTicket, we combined these two conditions in the following analyses.

As shown in Table 7, all participants who read the general phishing emails in the password condition were phished. In contrast, using WebTicket, none of the participants were phished by general phishing emails. This result showed that WebTicket prevented general phishing attacks effectively, although it was not surprising. Because participants did not know their own passwords with WebTicket, they could not fall for a large class of phishing attacks.

In the WT phishing condition, seven participants out of ten did not scan their tickets. This is a significant improvement compared to the password condition where all participants were phished (p<0.05 in Yates χ^2 test). According to our post-survey, five participants noticed the fake dialog's border did not match the border on their tickets. This illustrates that dynamic security skins helped our participants detect the fake dialog. Two other participants did not notice the difference, but clicked *close* on the Flash privacy setting dialog and found that the webcam was not working. They closed the fake dialog and opened the legitimate reader dialog to scan their tickets.

	General Phishing	WT Phishing
Password	100%* (6/6)	-
WebTicket	0%* (0/6)	30%* (3/10)

Table 7. The ratios of phished participants out of those who read the phishing emails. The differences between general phishing against password and other two conditions were statistically significant ($p < 0.05$ in Yates' χ^2 test). Note that for WT Phishing, attackers still need to obtain a key stored in users' computers to decrypt the barcode.

Another three participants scanned their tickets using the fake dialog, meaning that attackers would have obtained the barcodes on their tickets. However, the attackers would still need to obtain the key stored in their computers to access the accounts, unlike standard phishing attacks that would allow immediate access.

These results indicate the importance of defense in depth. For the seven participants, the dynamic security skin or the privacy dialog prevented the attack. Besides, while three participants scanned their tickets, WebTicket would have prevented access to their accounts because of its encryption.

USER STUDY #3 FIELD TRIAL

To evaluate how well WebTicket works in practice, we conducted a field study looking at WebTicket's applicability in real world environments. We asked participants to use WebTicket on their personal computers using their actual accounts for three weeks.

Participants

We recruited participants who used computers running MacOS with a webcam, used Firefox as a primary web browser and had access to a printer. We recruited 10 participants using an existing university recruitment web site. None of them participated the previous studies. Their age ranged from 19 to 42 with the median age of 32. Three participants were male and seven were female. They consisted of five university students, four employed and one unemployed. We paid $35 USD for their participation.

Procedure

On the first day, we asked participants to install WebTicket. We also asked them to create three paper-based tickets for three existing accounts that they accessed once a day, once a week, and once a month. If they did not have accounts that exactly matched the criteria, we asked them to choose the closest ones. Although we did not ask the participants to change their passwords, we asked them to use their tickets whenever they logged into the accounts. Furthermore, we recorded how (e.g., typing passwords or using tickets) and when they logged into their accounts using a logging application. The ticket creation step was conducted in our lab for five participants using their laptops, and in their offices or homes for the other participants using their desktop computers. One participant had an Android phone and created mobile-phone-based tickets also. Moreover, two participants with multiple computers setup WebTicket on all their computers and shared the encryption key among the computers. Three weeks later, we asked participants to complete a survey and conducted interviews.

RESULT OF USER STUDY #3

Participants created tickets for a wide variety of accounts including, SNS (e.g., Facebook), email (e.g., Gmail), ecommerce (e.g., Amazon.com), and finance (e.g., Chase). After they created tickets, we asked how easy or difficult it was to install WebTicket and to create tickets for their accounts using 5-point Likert scale. Our participants rated installation as very easy (mean of 4.6 and median of 5) and ticket creation as easy (mean of 4.2 and median of 4).

According to our data logs, our participants accessed their accounts using WebTicket with a range of 21 to 150 times during the study period with a median of 52 times. They did not access their accounts by typing passwords as we requested. Furthermore, in our post-experiment survey, our participants reported that they did not access these accounts from other computers during the study period. We also asked participants whether they wanted to use the WebTicket for some of their accounts based on their experiences using 5-point Likert scale (1 is strongly disagree and 5 is strongly agree). Their answers ranged from 3 to 5 with a mean of 4 and median of 4.

In the interview, P3 commented, "WebTicket is very easy, functional, and safe. From what I understand, the URL, username, and password are all encrypted into the ticket and can only be unencrypted by your machine which recorded the actions and printed the ticket". This indicated that P3 understood how the WebTicket worked and appreciated both its usability and security.

On the other hand, P5 and P6 showed concerns about carrying paper-based tickets. P5 said, "[It is] kind of annoying to have the papers constantly available for when you want to log on". P5 also said, "[the mobile-phone-based ticket] would be much better and efficient because I am more likely to have my phone at hand and would prefer to use it instead of saving the little papers". This implies that, although the portability issue could be a limitation for some users, the mobile-phone-based ticket could mitigate it.

In contrast, P7 mentioned an advantage of having paper-based tickets. He said, "I'm concerned [about] using a too-easy password for my bank account. But, if I use a complicated password I have to write down the password, or save it in my laptop. I don't want to do so. I'm carrying around my laptop. But, [using paper-based ticket], I can keep the password at home with some protection."

P9 with mobile-phone-based ticket also commented, "I prefer the cellphone version because I don't have to carry pieces of paper. [...] I'm a little bit concerned about losing my phone. I may use the paper one for really important accounts, such as my bank account. I don't use it that frequently. So, I can do it at home." These comments suggest that paper-based tickets and mobile-phone-based tickets could be used for different types of accounts.

Besides, P2 said, "I like WebTicket does not store a copy of my password on some server but rather is kept locally on my machine or ticket." This implies that he appreciated the fact that WebTicket did not rely on third parties to be used.

Another interesting observation was that no participant mentioned being able to use ticket only their computers as a drawback when asked the drawbacks of WebTicket, while three participants regarded it as a benefit in terms of security. This could be because people mostly use their own computers to access accounts [15]. Although the relatively short study period could bias users' perceptions, this observation implies that not allowing people to use tickets on foreign computers is less likely to be a major limitation.

DISCUSSION

Our results indicate that participants were not slower than passwords when logging in with WebTicket. Participants also reported the login process with WebTicket as easier and shorter than with passwords. These results are very encouraging considering that the strong passwords and the phishing resistance provided by WebTicket.

Note that we do not intend to replace *all* passwords with WebTicket. Instead, we want users to choose authentication schemes according to their needs. For frequently used accounts, passwords may make more sense because these passwords are less likely to be forgotten and fast to enter in. In contrast, for occasionally used accounts, WebTicket will make more sense because WebTicket can provide a reliable way to login. Additionally, because WebTicket does not require server side modifications, users who have difficulty in memorizing passwords, such as memory impaired or novice users, could choose WebTicket for a site, while others use passwords for the same site.

Portability could be a challenge with paper-based tickets. For example, in our field study, two participants showed concern about carrying many tickets. However, other participants commented on the *benefit* of keeping paper-based tickets at home. Considering that people access their accounts mostly from work or home [15], there would be potential benefit in keeping tickets at these locations for many people. For exceptions where users need repeated accesses to these accounts in other places, they could use mobile-phone based tickets or simply use passwords.

ALTERNATIVE DESIGNS FOR WEBTICKET

We investigated one possible point in the design space for WebTicket. However, there are cases where different design choices may make more sense. One major design decision was whether to have one ticket for each account, or just have one ticket for multiple accounts. If we had opted for the latter, the passwords would need to be stored on the computer itself and the ticket would simply be the key to access those passwords. The advantage is that users do not need to carry many tickets. The disadvantages are in synchronizing account information when new accounts are created (if there are multiple computers).

We also considered a hybrid approach, having one ticket per important account, and one ticket for all "unimportant" accounts. In this case, the ticket for unimportant accounts works in a similar way as PwdHash [26]. In this design, synchronization does not matter because passwords are generated dynamically. However, this design has challenges dealing with site-specific password composition policies.

Another important design choice is whether we should encrypt the information embedded on a ticket. Without encryption, users can log into their accounts from any computer as long as WebTicket is installed. However, past work has found that users mostly access their accounts from their own computers at work or home [15]. As such, we felt that the benefit of allowing access on foreign computers was small considering that allowing it would expose users to a large number of vulnerabilities, including theft of tickets as well as cameras taking pictures of the QR codes.

LIMITATIONS

One constraint is that WebTicket requires webcams, and either printers or smartphones. Given that these devices are commodities, we feel that this is an acceptable tradeoff.

Scalability is a major limitation of paper-based tickets. However, we do not intend to replace *all* the passwords with WebTicket. For people who have many accounts, the mobile-phone version can be used to manage tickets. Durability is another limitation of paper-based tickets. For example, if a ticket is crumpled or washed, the QR code on the ticket cannot be scanned. Then, users have to reset their passwords in corresponding websites and renew tickets.

A potential weakness with paper-based tickets is that people might leave them near their computers, in which case these tickets are only slightly better than a post-it note with passwords on them (since people can't use the ticket on other computers). However, depending on one's threat model, this may not be a huge security risk, especially if one has good physical security or login passwords that restrict access to computers.

There could be some cases where users want to access their accounts from foreign computers, although people use their own computers most of the times [15]. There are possible workarounds, e.g. storing the master key on users' mobile phones. However, these approaches increase the potential for loss if the mobile phone is lost or stolen.

CONCLUSIONS

In this paper, we introduced WebTicket, a novel web account management system that transforms knowledge-based authentication into token-based authentication using commodity devices such as webcams, printers, and mobile phone without the need to modify server side systems.

Through two lab studies, we found that participants reported that the account creation process using WebTicket was not worse than the account creation process using password, and that the login process using WebTicket was easier and shorter than the login process using passwords. WebTicket also provided reliable authentication after one week and good phishing protection. Furthermore, after the three weeks of a field study, the participants were positive about WebTicket. Although further investigations of its limitations may be necessary, we believe that WebTicket works quite well among good portion of accounts and users.

REFERENCES

1. eToken. http://www.aladdin.com/etoken/.
2. QRCode.com. http://www.denso-wave.com/qrcode/.
3. RSA securID http://www.rsa.com/node.aspx?id=1156.
4. A. Adams and M. Sasse. Users are not the enemy. Communications of the ACM (1999).
5. S. Brostoff and M. Sasse. Are passfaces more usable than passwords: A field trial investigation. In Proc. of HCI 2000, (2000).
6. S. Chiasson, R. Biddle, and P. V. Oorschot. A second look at the usability of click-based graphical passwords. In Proc. of SOUPS (2007).
7. R. Dhamija and J. Tygar. The battle against phishing: Dynamic security skins. In Proc. of SOUPS (2005).
8. A. Dirik, N. Memon, and J. C. Birget. Modeling user choice in the passpoints graphical password scheme. In Proc. of SOUPS (2007).
9. S. Egelman, L. F. Cranor, J. Hong. You've been warned: an empirical study of the effectiveness of web browser phishing warnings. In Proc. of SIGCHI (2008)
10. K. Everitt, T. Bragin, J. Fogarty, and T. Kohno. A comprehensive study of frequency, interference, and training of multiple graphical passwords. In Proc. of CHI (2009).
11. Gartner. Automated password resets can cut it service desk costs. 2004.
12. S. Gaw and E. Felten. Password management strate-gies for online accounts. In Proc. of SOUPS (2006).
13. J. T. Hallinan. Why We Make Mistakes. Broadway, 2009.
14. E. Hayashi, R. Dhamija, N. Christin, and A. Perrig. Use your illusion: secure authentication usable anywhere. In Proc. of SOUPS (2008).
15. E. Hayashi, J. I. Hong, A Diary Study of Password Usage in Daily Life. In Proc. of SIGCHI (2011).
16. D. V. Klein. "foiling the cracker": A survey of, and improvements to, password security. In Proc. of USENIX Security, (1990).
17. S. Klemmer, M. Newman, and R. Farrell. The designers' outpost: a tangible interface for collaborative web site. In Proc. of UIST (2001).
18. C. Kuo, S. Romanosky, and L. Cranor. Human selection of mnemonic phrase-based passwords. In Proc. of SOUPS (2006).
19. S. L. Learning 10,000 pictures. Quarterly Journal of Experimental Psychology, (1967).
20. W. MacKay. Is paper safer? The role of paper flight strips in air traffic control. ACM Transactions on Computer-Human Interaction, (1999).
21. J. McCune, A. Perrig, and M. Reiter. Seeing-is-believing: Using camera phones for human-verifiable authentication. In IEEE S&P (2005).
22. D. McGee, P. Cohen, R. Wesson, and S. Horman. Comparing paper and tangible, multimodal tools. In Proc. of CHI (2002).
23. T. Moran, E. Saund, W. V. Melle, A. Gujar, K. Fishkin, and B. Harrison. Design and technology for collaborage: collaborative collages of information on physical walls. In Proc. of UIST (1999).
24. L. Nelson, S. Ichimura, E. Pedersen, and L. Adams. Palette: a paper interface for giving presentations. In Proc. of CHI (1999).
25. A. Paivio and T. Rogers. Why are pictures easier to recall than words? Psychonomic Science, (1968).
26. B. Parno, C. Cuo and A. Perrig, PhoolprofPhishing Prevention. In Proc of. the Financial Cryptography and data security (2006).
27. B. Ross, C. Jackson, N. Miyake, D. Boneh, and J. Mitchell. Stronger password authentication using browser extensions. In Proc. of the USENIX Security(2005).
28. M. Sasse, S. Brostoff, and D. Weirich. Transforming the 'weakest link'— a human/computer interaction approach to usable and effective security. BT technology journal, (2001).
29. A. Whitten and J. Tygar. Why johnny can't encrypt. In USENIX Security, (1999).
30. S. Wiedenbeck, J. Waters, J. Birget, and A. Brodskiy. Passpoints: Design and longitudinal evaluation of a graphical password system. International Journal of Human-Computer Studies, (2005).
31. J. Yan, A. Blackwell, R. Anderson, and A. Grant. Password memorability and security: Empirical results. In IEEE Security & privacy, Vol. 2, pp. 25–31, (2004).
32. K. Yee, K. Sitaker. Passpet: convenient password management and phishing protection. In Proc. of SOUPS (2006).
33. Your Top 20 most frequently used passwords. http://www.tomshardware.com/news/imperva-rockyou-most-common-passwords,9486.html

Color Naming Models for Color Selection, Image Editing and Palette Design

Jeffrey Heer
Computer Science Department
Stanford University
jheer@cs.stanford.edu

Maureen Stone
Tableau Software
Seattle, WA
mstone@tableausoftware.com

ABSTRACT
Our ability to reliably name colors provides a link between visual perception and symbolic cognition. In this paper, we investigate how a statistical model of color naming can enable user interfaces to meaningfully mimic this link and support novel interactions. We present a method for constructing a probabilistic model of color naming from a large, unconstrained set of human color name judgments. We describe how the model can be used to map between colors and names and define metrics for color saliency (how reliably a color is named) and color name distance (the similarity between colors based on naming patterns). We then present a series of applications that demonstrate how color naming models can enhance graphical interfaces: a color dictionary & thesaurus, name-based pixel selection methods for image editing, and evaluation aids for color palette design.

Author Keywords
Color names; color modeling; palette design; image editing; visualization; perception; XKCD

ACM Classification Keywords
H.5.2 Information Interfaces and Presentation: UI

INTRODUCTION
To reason and communicate about the world, people continually — and often effortlessly — categorize elements of their sensory experience. We perceive a world populated by objects that we label with named types, colors, shapes, tastes, odors, and functions. Our capacity for categorization links sensing of the physical world to language and cognition, and underlies our ability to communicate and reference objects in the world [16]. This observation suggests that user interfaces that model human category judgments might enable more compelling forms of reference and selection.

In this paper, we explore this idea in the domain of *color names* — the linguistic labels used to describe colors. Interest in color names as a means to investigate links between perception, language, and cognition was spurred by the studies of Berlin & Kay [5] in the 1960s. They asked speakers of various languages to name a set of color stimuli and then select the most representative stimulus for each provided color term. Berlin & Kay noted striking regularities among the use of color terms across cultures, leading them to posit 11 universal basic color terms (in English: blue, brown, green, orange, pink, purple, red, yellow, black, grey, and white). They observed that these terms were added to a language in a similar progression across cultures. Subsequent decades of research (e.g., [10, 14, 29, 39]) have challenged and extended this understanding. For example, more than 11 basic color terms may exist (e.g., Russian contains two basic terms for blue [39]), and language can have a relative effect on categorical color perception and memory [29].

The importance of color names to perception and object classification has led researchers to formulate a variety models describing how people associate names and colors [2, 8, 20, 22, 24, 26]. Here, we extend prior models — in particular, the non-parametric approach of Chuang et al. [8] — to propose a model-construction method for a collection of human color-name judgments. We then demonstrate how the resulting model can be applied to enhance user interfaces. Our research contributions fall into two categories:

First, we contribute **a method for constructing a probabilistic model of color naming** from a large, unconstrained set of human color name judgments. We model color-name associations using multinomial probability distributions that describe the likelihood of a color value given a color name, or vice versa. We then define useful operations in terms of this model. We apply our method to results from a large web-based survey [25] containing over 3 million entries and over 100,000 unique color name responses. Our method includes a scaling technique that reduces this survey data to a small set of maximally information-preserving color terms. We then describe how the model can be used to map between colors and names and we define metrics for *color saliency* (how reliably a color is named) and *color name distance* (the similarity between colors based on naming patterns).

Second, we present **novel interfaces enabled by our color naming model**. These applications help users express color in new ways and offer designers new means for evaluating their designs. We describe a *color dictionary & thesaurus* tool for name-based color selection and browsing of color synonyms and antonyms. We then describe techniques for *name-based pixel selection for image editing*. We introduce methods to (1) suggest highly-probable color names to describe image pixels, (2) select image regions by color name, and (3) provide a new "magic wand" tool based on color name similarity. Finally, we show how color name overlap and saliency statistics supported by our model can aid the *design and evaluation of color palettes for visualization.*

Permission to make digital or hard copies of all or part of this work for personal or classroom use is granted without fee provided that copies are not made or distributed for profit or commercial advantage and that copies bear this notice and the full citation on the first page. To copy otherwise, or republish, to post on servers or to redistribute to lists, requires prior specific permission and/or a fee.
CHI'12, May 5–10, 2012, Austin, Texas, USA.
Copyright 2012 ACM 978-1-4503-1015-4/12/05...$10.00.

RELATED WORK

Our research extends two streams of prior work: models of color naming and user interfaces for color design.

Models of Color Naming

Researchers have devised multiple approaches for modeling human color naming, both to aid scientific understanding and to improve applications such as gamut mapping [24] and image analysis [20, 22]. One approach is to simply partition color space, e.g., by uniform subdivision of hue in HLS color space [17]. Another is to create a color dictionary that maps color names (basic color terms plus modifiers such as "light", "dark", and "vivid") to a single color value. This approach is used by the ISCC-NBS standard [15] and derived variants [4, 11, 20]. These approaches map colors to names in a deterministic, disjoint fashion: they do not model association strength or overlap among color names.

Instead, color scientists use statistical models fitted to a corpus of human color-name judgments. Some researchers employ parametric models using a mixture of Gaussian [24, 26] or Gaussian-Sigmoid distributions [2]. While parametric models can suppress noise and be described with a small set of parameters, they make assumptions about the shape of named color regions that may not match empirical distributions. For example, a Gaussian ellipsoid may assign probability mass to color values outside the gamut of interest.

In response to these shortcomings, others have advocated the use of non-parametric models that avoid assumptions regarding the shape of color name distributions. Moroney [22] models color naming using histograms over a binned color space. Chuang et al. [8] model color-name association using multinomial conditional probability distributions. Chuang et al. also define a statistic for *color salience* — the uniqueness of a color name — in terms of model entropy. Using the 330 colors of the World Color Survey [10], they find good agreement among high salience scores and basic color name "foci" identified in previous work [5, 35].

One issue affecting model construction is the size and granularity of training data. Early work uses results from controlled settings, often limited to a few hundred color stimuli (e.g., [2]). More recent work (e.g., [8, 21, 25, 26]) employs web-based surveys to create larger corpora (though limited to the sRGB gamut of computer monitors). While web-based surveys sacrifice the controlled display and lighting environment of a laboratory, they offer access to a greater variety of people and display types. Researchers have noted consistent results when comparing such crowdsourced data sets with data gathered under controlled conditions [21, 26].

An alternative approach used in computer vision is to construct probabilistic naming models in an automated fashion [30, 36]. Given color names as input, a system can query a search engine for images associated with that color term; the image pixels can be used to fit a statistical model of color-name association. This approach has the advantage of automated construction, and has led to better performance on classification and retrieval benchmarks for photographic images. However, this approach requires that the color vocabulary be known *a priori*, and provides little insight into the relative likelihood of color terms. Here, we seek to learn the kind and frequency of color terms used by people.

In this paper, we build on the approach of Chuang et al. [8] to construct a non-parametric probabilistic model of color naming. As we will describe, we modify their definition of color salience to improve comparability among colors and introduce name-based color similarity measures. We demonstrate how to construct such models from a large, unconstrained set of color-name judgments. In particular, we use over 3 million color-name responses collected from readers of the web comic XKCD. While prior work [22] has required that the desired number of color names be given as a model parameter, we introduce a scaling routine that uses a measure of information loss to determine the number of color names.

Tools for Color Design

Researchers in HCI, Computer Graphics, and Visualization have devised myriad tools and algorithms for assisting colorists. One prominent class of applications is interfaces for color selection or palette design [1, 3, 12, 19, 28, 37]. For example, PRAVDAColor [3] and ColorBrewer [12] suggest color palettes for encoding data in visualizations based on data types and/or cardinality. Meier et al. [19] apply theories of artistic color harmony [13, 18] to assist interactive color selection. Cohen-Or et al. [9] use these same theories to formulate automated color harmonization methods for image composition. To our knowledge, none of these tools incorporate nuanced models of color naming to aid color selection or image analysis. In this paper, we explore ways in which color naming models can augment color picking, pixel selection for image editing, and the evaluation of color palettes.

CONSTRUCTING COLOR NAMING MODELS

To construct a color naming model, we first process the input data: a collection of color-name pairs comprising naming judgments by human subjects. We present a method for reducing unconstrained text responses describing millions of unique colors into a compact table of color-name correspondences. We then construct a non-parametric probabilistic model of color naming that supports saliency and similarity metrics based on color-name association.

Data Collection

We start with a *color naming data set*: a list of color-name pairs provided by human subjects. Here a "color" (or "color value") is a stimulus shown to a respondent and a "color name" (or "color term") is a text label provided by the respondent to describe that stimulus. Prior work has elicited naming judgments using physical color chips or calibrated monitors. Recent work [8, 21, 26] has applied crowdsourcing on the web to collect color naming data and verified that the results are consistent with those from controlled settings.

In this paper, we use a publicly-accessible English-language color naming data set [25] compiled by Randall Munroe, the author of the popular web comic XKCD. The data was collected through a web survey advertised on the XKCD site.

Respondents were asked to first provide basic demographic information: chromosomal sex, native language, color blindness, and optional information regarding monitor type, temperature and gamma. Participants then named color swatches shown against a white background. Each color value was expressed as a coordinate in sRGB color space; values were uniformly sampled from the full RGB cube. The text responses were unconstrained and respondents were free to continue naming new swatches for as long as they wished.

The data set contains over 3.4 million responses from 152,401 sessions (103,430 self-reported males, 41,464 females, and 7,507 declined to state). To our knowledge this is the largest color naming data set in existence. The top ten native languages are English 74.6%, Not stated 12.2%, German 2.7%, Spanish 1.3%, French 1.2%, Dutch 1.1%, Swedish 0.8%, Portuguese 0.6%, Polish 0.5%, and Russian 0.5%. The number of responses per participant ranges from 1 to 2,345 (median 18, inter-quartile range 10–30 responses). To combat malicious responses, the data set includes a per-user "spam score" that penalizes (a) responses that are not used by anyone else and (b) the same response applied across high variations in hue. We keep only the responses from users with normalized spam scores ≤ 0.5. The spam-filtered data set consists of 3,252,134 color-name pairs spanning 2,956,183 unique RGB triples and 132,259 unique color names.

The Color-Term Count Matrix

The starting point for our model is a table (T) of color-term counts in which rows represent colors, columns represent color terms, and each cell contains the count of responses that use a color term to describe a corresponding color. Unsurprisingly, a naïve tabulation yields a very sparse, high-dimensional matrix. In this section, we describe our method for reducing the data to a compact and usable form. To limit the number of colors (table rows), we bin color values within a perceptual color space (CIE L*a*b*). To reduce the number of terms (table columns), we apply a dimensionality reduction method. Finally, we smooth and filter the data.

Representing Color Values

To reduce the number of unique colors, we need to bin them within a suitable color space. Uniform binning in sRGB is undesirable, as sRGB coordinates model color output devices, not human perception: distances in sRGB space are not generally consistent with perceptual judgments of color difference. We want to group colors in a perceptually uniform fashion, preferably using a simple grid-based scheme.

Accordingly, we bin colors within the standard CIE L*a*b* color space using a D65 reference white point [1]. CIE L*a*b* is a 3-dimensional perceptual color space based on opponent process theory [27]. The L* dimension represents lightness and ranges from black (L*=0) to white (L*=100). The a* and b* dimensions both range from roughly -100 to 100 and correspond to green-red and blue-yellow opponent channels, respectively. Euclidean distances within CIE L*a*b* color space approximate color judgments made by human subjects: a distance of 2.3 is roughly equal to one Just Noticeable Difference (JND) [31]. Measurements made within a local patch of L*a*b* space tend to correlate well with human judgments; however, global measurements across the color space can exhibit significant discrepancies. In response, color scientists have devised more sophisticated metrics for L*a*b* space that provide a closer fit to perceptual judgments. We use the current standard, CIEDE2000 [32], as our primary color distance metric.

For the applications described in this paper, we construct color models using a bin size of 5 units within L*a*b* space. Thus each bin has a radius of $\sim$1 JND and so subdivides color space near the theoretical resolution of human color differentiation. Using 5-unit bins, the number of colors (table rows) reduces from 2.3 million down to 8,325. For comparison, using 10-unit bins results in 1,291 colors. To subsequently look up an input color in the table, we map it to its matching bin (interpolation methods could also be used).

Processing Color Terms

Unconstrained text responses result in a large and at times amusing variety of color terms. While most responses use common one or two word phrases ("blue", "lavender", "dark grey", "hot pink"), there is a long tail of responses including rare ("butter yellow") and bizarre ("velociraptor cloaca") descriptions. Entity resolution is also a concern, as the same color name can have multiple variants ("blue green", "blue-green", "blue/green") and include misspellings ("fuchsia" vs. "fuschia" & "fushia"). We would like to group variants representing the same color term, eliminate noise, and reduce the dimensionality from 132,259 color terms to a more manageable yet representative set.

To handle variants of punctuation and spacing, we first strip all non-alphabetical characters (numbers, punctuation, whitespace, *etc*) from the response. This process maps many variants to the same term (e.g., the previous blue-green examples map to "bluegreen"), removing about 20,000 variants and reducing the distinct term count to 114,860. We then tabulate a color-term count matrix T using the resulting terms.

Next, we compute a lower-rank approximation of the color-term matrix to reduce dimensionality and remove noise. The idea is to remove the color terms (columns) that contribute the least to the "information" contained within the data set. We quantify this information using the Frobenius (element-wise) matrix norm $|T| = \sqrt{\Sigma_{i,j}(T_{ij})^2}$.

We first compute the sum of squares of each matrix column and sort the columns in ascending order. We then incrementally subtract these values from $|T|$ to determine the matrix norm $|T_k|$ for the color-term count matrix with the k-lowest columns removed. Given a threshold percentage value p, we can now find the maximal value of k such that $|T_k|/|T| \geq p$. Retaining 99% of the information ($p = 0.01$) reduces the number of color terms to 66,526 – still a large a number. The model used in this paper retains 95% of the information ($p = 0.05$), resulting in a reasonable set of 179 color names.

[1]D65 is the standard reference white point used by sRGB, in which the source color values are defined.

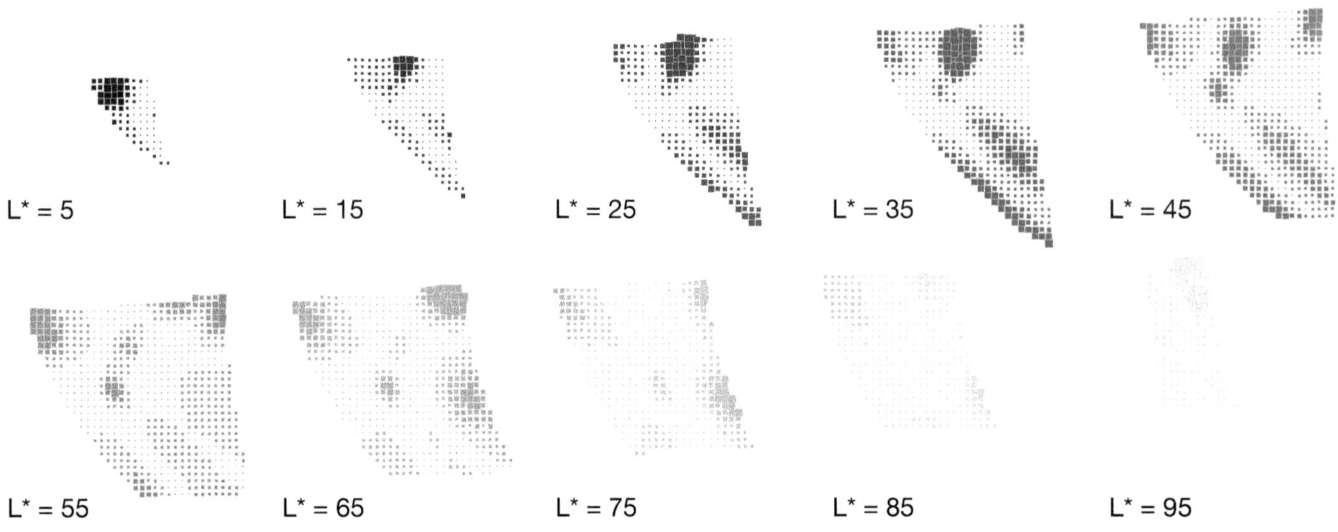

Figure 1. Color Saliency Map. Each point represents a 5×5×5 bin in CIE L*a*b* color space; slices for every other L* value are shown. The area of each point is proportional to its *saliency*: large points indicate consistently named colors, small points indicate colors that exhibit high naming confusion. Interestingly, visible clusters correspond to basic color terms identified by Berlin & Kay (blue, brown, green, grey, pink, purple, *etc*).

Our reduction technique optimizes the same metric as Singular Value Decomposition (SVD), the method underlying dimensionality reduction techniques such as Latent Semantic Analysis (LSA). Whereas SVD finds a new set of basis vectors to describe the data, our method simply zeroes-out the columns that make the smallest contribution to the matrix norm, preserving each color term as a separate dimension.

While the above method successfully reduces color term dimensionality, it does not handle misspellings. Fortunately, the reduced color space is now small enough that manual correction takes only a few minutes. We add a hand-crafted lookup table to the first stage of our processing pipeline to correct identified misspellings. We then re-tabulate T on the spell-corrected set of terms and perform dimensionality reduction again to produce a final set of 153 color names.

Smoothing & Simplification

To arrive at our final table, we smooth the data and filter isolated responses. To perform smoothing, we first represent the color-term count matrix as a three-dimensional grid in L*a*b* space. We convolve the grid with a 3×3×3 kernel with a value of 4 in the center and 1 in all other positions. For each grid cell, we average over the adjacent non-zero grid cells weighted according to the kernel. We then round the smoothed cell values to the nearest integer count. We find that this approach adequately smooths the space without over-blurring. Next, we zero-out any table cells with a value of 1. We do this for two reasons: (1) if a color-term pair has only a single "vote", there is no corroboration of the judgment, and (2) dropping these cells significantly reduces the size of the model with no discernible detriment in subsequent applications.

A Probabilistic Model of Color Names

Given a color-term count matrix, we can model the probability distributions of colors and names. We then use this model to compute additional metrics to analyze the effects of color naming. Here we describe our modeling approach and the model-based metrics used in our subsequent applications.

Following Chuang et al. [8], we model the likelihoods of colors and names as multinomial probability distributions. We are concerned with the random variables C (which takes on color values) and W (which takes on color names). We use the symbols c and w to denote specific values taken by these variables; the symbols also serve as indices for the rows (c) and columns (w) of the color-term count matrix T.

We can now express the likelihood of a color value given a specific color name as the conditional probability $p(C|w)$. For each color c taken by C, we compute the probability by normalizing the rows of T:

$$p(c|w) = T_{c,w} \,/\, \sum_c T_{c,w} \quad (1)$$

Similarly, the probability $p(W|c)$ of a name given a color is:

$$p(w|c) = T_{c,w} \,/\, \sum_w T_{c,w} \quad (2)$$

These distributions give us the likelihood of a color conditioned on a specific term or vice versa. We can also model the association between two colors or between two terms. Given a color c, the probability of other colors that have been labeled with matching names (the *categorical association* of a color [8]) is given by

$$p(C|c) = \sum_w p(C|w)p(w|c) \quad (3)$$

The categorical association between words $p(W|w)$ is expressed in a symmetric manner:

$$p(W|w) = \sum_c p(W|c)p(c|w) \quad (4)$$

Color Saliency

Given a probabilistic setting, we can use common measures to quantify other aspects of color naming. We define *color saliency* — the degree to which a color value is uniquely named — in terms of the entropy of the conditional probability $p(W|c)$. Entropy (H) is a standard information-theoretic measure of the "randomness" of a distribution. Specifically, it measures the number of bits necessary to encode a random variable. If a color is uniquely named by all respondents, there is no randomness and $p(W|c)$ will have an entropy of zero. For colors with a high degree of naming disagreement, $p(W|c)$ will have a correspondingly higher entropy. We thus express saliency in terms of the negative entropy:

$$\text{Saliency}(c) = -H(p(W|c)) = \sum_w p(w|c) \log p(w|c) \quad (5)$$

Figure 2 shows the distribution of saliency scores for the XKCD data. To create a normalized saliency measure, we rescale the values from [-4.5, 0] to the interval [0,1].

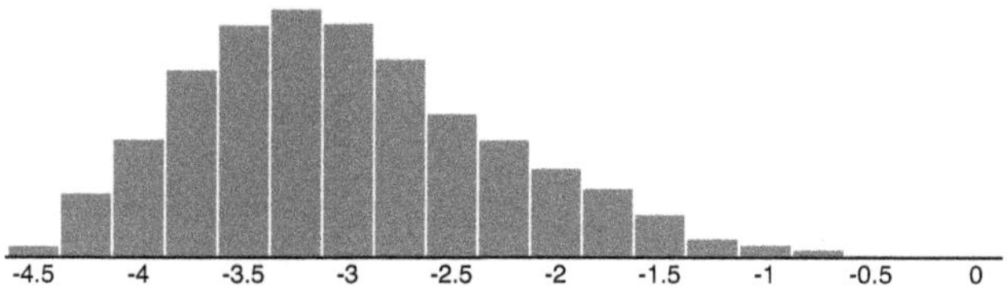

Figure 2. Histogram of XKCD Color Salience Scores.

Our formulation of saliency differs from that of prior work. Chuang et al. [8] define saliency as the negative entropy of the distribution $p(C|c)$, the categorical association between colors. Using $p(C|c)$ allows one to combine (often sparse) color naming data from multiple languages into a unified "term-free" distribution. However, their formulation measures the uniqueness of color names across the entire color space, not at a single value. This occurs because the saliency values are biased by the volume of color space spanned by a name. If one shade of blue and one shade of yellow are both uniquely named (e.g., 100% of responders call color 1 "blue" and call color 2 "yellow") the yellow shade will receive a higher saliency value. This is because "yellow" occupies a smaller volume of color space and hence has higher $p(C|w)$ values. To ensure saliency scores are comparable across hues, we instead compute saliency using $p(W|c)$.

Figure 1 shows the distribution of saliency scores across L*a*b* color space, clipped to the sRGB gamut. The saliency scores appear to cluster, with local maxima corresponding to the basic color terms identified by Berlin & Kay. These clusters exhibit different shapes, lending credence to the use of non-parametric models. We can also identify boundaries between color names. Note the region of low saliency between green and blue. This area exhibits high naming confusion, including the terms "teal", "turquoise", "green" and "blue." Note also the narrow "valley" between orange and red at L* = 55. This fine-grained detail is visible due to the dense sampling of responses in the XKCD data; sparse data would require larger bin sizes and hence lost detail.

Name-Based Distance Measures

Our color naming model also enables new distance measures among color values. In addition to metrics within a color space, we can compare two colors by how similarly they are named. One option is to use a metric defined specifically for probability distributions, such as the Hellinger distance:

$$D_h(a, b) = (1 - \sum_w \sqrt{p(w|a)\, p(w|b)}\,)^{0.5} \quad (6)$$

Though not grounded in probabilistic semantics, another option is to compute the cosine of the angle between two distributions. Due to normalization, this is equivalent to the cosine among rows of the color-term count matrix T. Denoting the row vector of T for the color c as T_c, we have:

$$D_c(a, b) = 1 - \cos(T_a, T_b) = 1 - \frac{T_a \cdot T_b}{||T_a||\,||T_b||} \quad (7)$$

Due to its simplicity and familiarity, we use the cosine metric to measure name-distance between two colors in our subsequent applications. Using other metrics, such as Hellinger distance, produces qualitatively similar results.

APPLICATIONS OF COLOR NAMING MODELS

To demonstrate the utility of color naming models for graphical interfaces, we present a series of novel applications: a name-based *color dictionary & thesaurus*, name-based interaction techniques for *selecting image regions*, and an evaluation tool for *color palette design*. The primary data structure used in each of these applications is the color-term count matrix T, from which we can compute probabilities, color salience, and color distance measures. We have implemented each example as a browser-based web application, written in JavaScript using the D3 (Data-Driven Documents) [6] framework. Both the applications and our library of color modeling routines is freely available as open-source software at: `http://vis.stanford.edu/color-names`.

Color Dictionary & Thesaurus

A simple and direct application of color naming models is to look up the color values associated with a name (a dictionary) and find other, related color terms (a thesaurus). Figure 3 shows our interface for these tasks. Users might work with the interface to select colors (e.g., for graphic design) or explore relationships among color names.

In response to a color term query, the interface displays the most probable color values matching that color name. Next, the thesaurus view lists related color names ranked by similarity. The top of the list shows highly similar color names (*synonyms*), whereas the bottom (not shown) lists opposed color names (*antonyms*).

Dictionary. Given a color name, retrieving representative color values is straightforward: we find the most probable color values according to $p(C|w)$. To select a single representative color, we average the four most probable colors (the four largest values of the $p(C|w)$ distribution). We find that this produces more helpful results than choosing only the single most probable value, particularly for names corresponding to bright, desaturated colors.

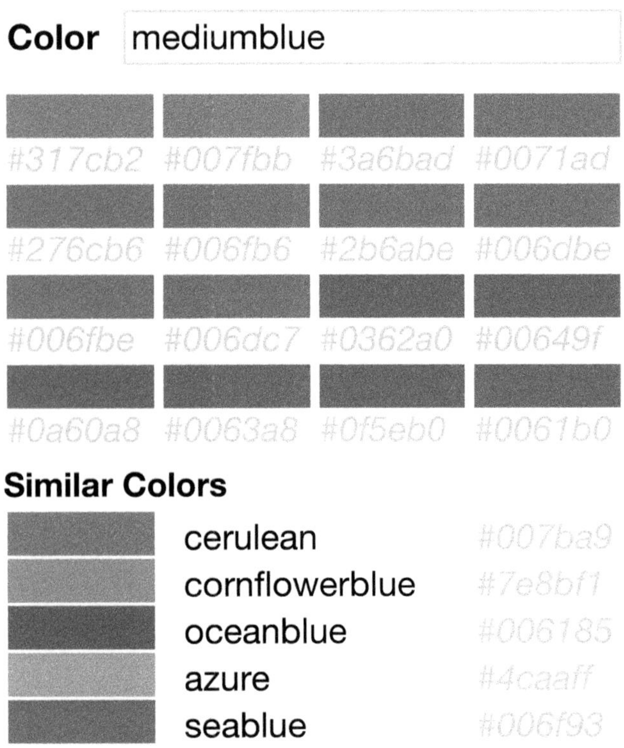

Figure 3. Color dictionary showing the 16 most probable color values for the query "mediumblue." The thesaurus lists related color names sorted according to $p(query \mid name)$. Ties are broken by sorting representative colors by their CIEDE2000 distance.

Thesaurus. To rank color names, we sort by the name-name association probabilities $p(W|w)$. We score each color name by $p(query \mid name)$, the probability of the query term given the name. Empirically, we have found that this choice provides better results than $p(name \mid query)$, which can privilege names with high marginal probability. For the query term "mediumblue," the name "purple" is ranked highly according to $p(name \mid query)$ because it is a common term. Choosing terms that instead maximize the likelihood of the query favors similar shades of blue (shown in Figure 3). The sort order is determined by similarities in naming patterns, which need not be the same as perceptual similarity among representative colors. Again, a color name corresponds to a variably sized distribution across a range of color values.

To break ties, we sort color names according to the perceptual (CIEDE2000) distance between representative colors. As some color names have association probabilities of zero (e.g., the hues yellow, orange, and red were never labeled "blue"), sorting by perceptual distance ensures that color antonyms align with opponent process theory: yellow is the antonym of blue, green is the antonym of red, and so on.

Using Color Name Models for Image Editing

People in conversation regularly use color names to refer to visual elements. Color name models can enable analogous forms of reference in user interfaces, for example, within image editors such as Adobe Photoshop or Illustrator. Here we describe two techniques for name-based selection: *color name queries* and a *name-based magic wand* selector.

Color Name Queries

To select image pixels matching a color name w, we simply include those pixels with non-zero $p(c|w)$ values. To control the sensitivity of the selection, users can adjust a tolerance parameter to set a minimum $p(c|w)$ threshold. Users can either type a color term query or interact with the image to generate relevant suggestions. In response to a mouse-driven selection, we show the most probable color names according to $p(W|c)$. In the case of a single pixel, we use the corresponding probability distribution. In the case of image regions, we average the distributions for each pixel.

Figure 4 shows our image selection prototype. The left panel displays an image and the right panel shows a list of suggested color names. By default, the list contains the most probable names for the entire image. The bottom panel includes a slider for adjusting selection tolerance (the $p(c|w)$ threshold). Clicking a pixel or dragging over a rectangular region updates the list to show the most probable color names for those pixels. A user can page through each name-based selection using the up and down arrow keys. A user can also type in a search query, initiating a selection and revealing related color names based on our color thesaurus.

Figures 4–6 show the use of color name queries to isolate image regions of interest. Figure 5 shows selections resulting from a variety of color name queries, including the use of more specific, automatically suggested color names ("olive", "forestgreen" and "puke") to select sub-regions of an initial, general query ("green"). Figure 6 shows selections seeded by direct manipulation: the user can click a pixel or drag a region to view related color names and then page through the results to find a desired selection.

A Name-Based Magic Wand Selector

A common selection mechanism within image editors is the *magic wand* tool. Using the wand tool, a user first clicks a desired pixel. The application then selects all adjacent pixels within a specified color distance using a flood-fill algorithm. Most wand tool implementations measure color distance as the maximal absolute difference in the red, green, or blue channels – the L_∞ norm in RGB space. A tolerance parameter ranging from 0–255 controls the threshold distance.

Instead, we can use color naming distance — computed using the cosine of the angle between $p(W|c)$ vectors — to determine pixel similarity. Our implementation provides a tolerance parameter with range 0–100, which maps to name-based distances on the interval [0, 1].

Figure 7 compares selections from an RGB-based wand and a name-based wand. The name-based selection better respects color name boundaries and is more stable across a range of tolerance settings. At low tolerance settings, RGB distance fails to select a perceptually coherent brown region due to color value variation; at higher tolerances the selection bleeds across color name boundaries, selecting adjacent orange regions. In contrast, the color name wand selects the brown region and excludes the orange pixels. To ensure that this discrepancy is not simply due to the use of RGB space,

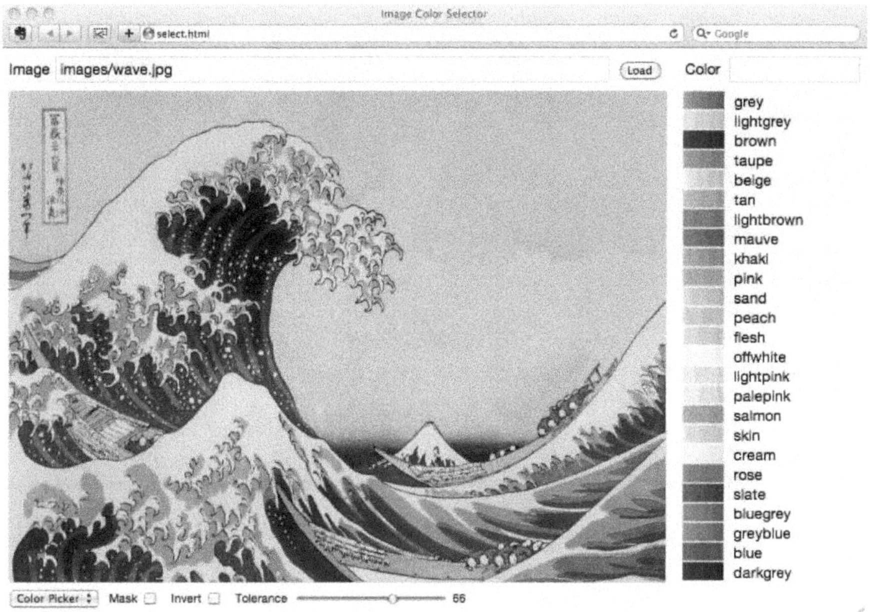

The Great Wave off Kanagawa by Hokusai

Blue, with non-selected pixels in grayscale

Blue, with non-selected pixels removed

Figure 4. Image selection by color name query. *Left*: Our prototype selection interface, listing the most probable color names according to $p(W|c)$. The many light colors correspond to the sky and boats. Beneath the image are selection options, including a tolerance parameter. *Top-Right*: The selection for the color query "blue", showing non-selected pixels in grayscale. *Bottom-Right*: The same query with non-selected pixels removed.

From Flickr user "x-ray delta one"

Red

Peach

Olive

ForestGreen

Puke

Figure 5. Image regions selected by color name query. Non-selected pixels are shown in grayscale. The bottom row illustrates selections made when moving from a basic color term ("green") to more specific terms to isolate foliage ("olive"), dark grass ("forestgreen") or tree tops ("puke").

Poppies, Near Argenteuil by Monet

BurntOrange

SkyBlue

Olive

Figure 6. Image regions selected by color name query. Non-selected pixels are shown in grayscale. The selected query terms were chosen from a list of most probable colors for an image region selected by mouse-drag. In this case, a user can rapidly isolate flower, sky, and foliage pixels.

Suprematism (Supremus No. 58) by Malevich
The red circle indicates the input pixel to the magic wand.

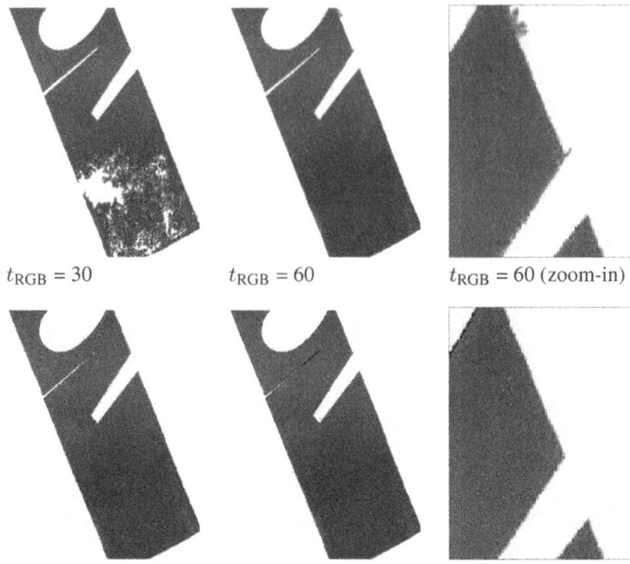

Figure 7. Magic wand pixel selections based on RGB distance (top row) and color name similarity (bottom row) across a range of parameter values. The RGB selector misses pixels at low tolerance values (t=30) and includes orange and red hues at higher tolerance values (t=60). The color name selector produces more uniform results across parameter settings and is sensitive to color name boundaries.

we also implemented a magic wand based on CIEDE2000 distance in L*a*b* space. We observed qualitatively similar results as the RGB-based selector: low tolerances lead to under-selection and higher tolerances lead to color "bleed."

Of course, not all name-based selections work so perfectly. We observe that desaturated colors (e.g., pastels) have higher name overlap, leading to less granular selections. Excluding achromatic names (e.g., "grey") may improve the situation. In addition, we have combined color space and name-based distances within a hybrid wand tool that selects either the union or intersection of the two selection measures. This hybrid tool uses two tolerance parameters (one for names, one for color space) and enables more nuanced selections.

Evaluating Color Palette Designs

Color design experts [7, 34, 33] argue that attention to color names is important in palette design, particularly for information visualization. First, nameable colors facilitate communication: it is easier to refer to graphical elements when one can name them unambiguously. Second, experimental evidence suggests that highly nameable colors are better remembered [29], perhaps due to the cue of the color name. To inform color palette design, we use our model to quantitatively characterize palettes with respect to color naming. To analyze a color palette, we examine both individual color saliency scores and color name distances. This data can help designers reason about the effects of color choices.

To optimize the presentation of categorical data, we might seek to minimize name overlap (to avoid ambiguity) and maximize salience (to avoid confusion and aid memory). Figure 8 characterizes qualitative color palettes for encoding categorical data. The palettes come from Tableau (a visualization tool with palettes designed by a color specialist [33]), the ColorBrewer selection tool [12], Microsoft Excel, and The Economist magazine. Tables show color name distances among colors, while bar charts show salience scores. These metrics enable rapid comparison of the palettes. Tableau and ColorBrewer both limit name overlap and include high-salience colors. The Excel and Economist palettes, on the other hand, exhibit high naming overlap and lower salience colors. A designer can use these displays to evaluate different color choices and assess questions such as: "If I shift the cyan more towards green, will it change names?"

Figure 9 shows diverging palettes for numerical data with a meaningful mid-point. The first palette, used in the Map of the Market [38], naïvely ramps from red through black to green in RGB space. The other three palettes come from ColorBrewer. We note that the Map of the Market palette has significant name overlap on each ramp, while the ColorBrewer palettes show more naming variation. In displays such as choropleth maps, simultaneous contrast can hamper subtle luminance comparisons [34]. By including small shifts in color hue and naming, the ColorBrewer palettes may improve discrimination. Yet by making the shifts subtle, the colors are still perceived as a ramp. ColorBrewer palettes also exhibit salience gradients oriented toward extreme values, emphasizing greater deviation from the mid-point through both luminance and categorical salience.

While informative for human designers, these metrics might also improve automated design tools, for example by minimizing name overlap and increasing saliency. Of course, effective color design involves many concerns, including other contrast effects and cultural associations. In future work, we plan to apply our naming model to automatically optimize color palette design and evaluate the results.

DISCUSSION

In this paper, we presented a method of constructing a probabilistic model of color naming from large, unconstrained naming data sets. We described a model based on over 3 mil-

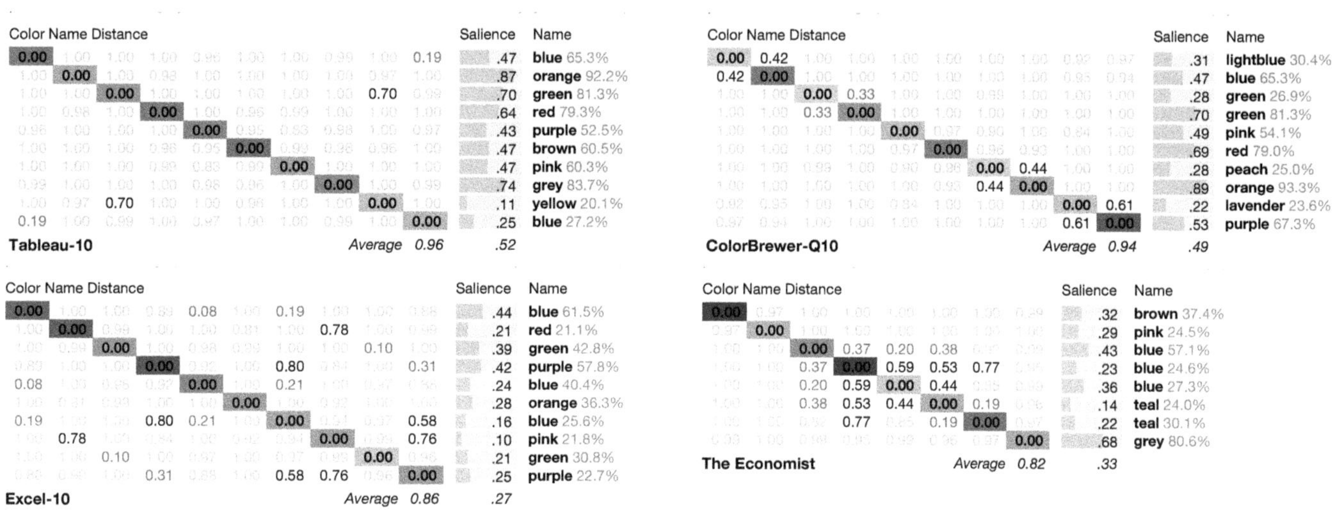

Figure 8. Name-based characterization of qualitative color palettes. Matrices show all pairwise color-name distances; bar charts show salience scores for each color. Salience scores below 0.2 indicate colors with a high degree of naming confusion. The Tableau-10 palette provides the best color salience and minimal name overlap. Palettes from Excel and The Economist exhibit higher name overlap and diminished saliency.

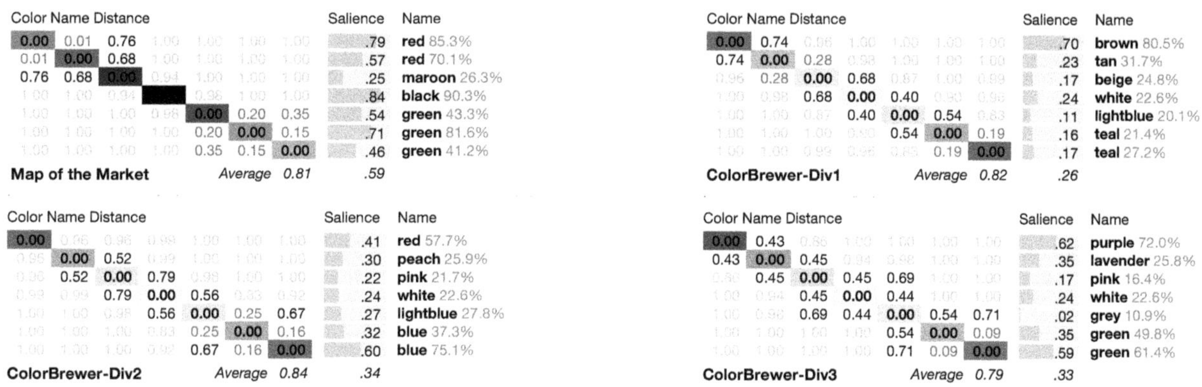

Figure 9. Name-based characterization of diverging quantitative color palettes. Naïve interpolation in RGB space (as in the Map of the Market) leads to name overlap among non-adjacent colors. ColorBrewer palettes (excluding "teal") exhibit salience gradients towards the extreme values.

lion web survey responses — to our knowledge the largest color naming data set in existence — and showed how it can be used to map between colors and names, calculate color saliency, and measure color similarity based on naming patterns. We then introduced a set of novel applications that illustrate how color naming models can enhance graphical user interfaces: a color dictionary & thesaurus, name-based pixel selection techniques for image editing, and evaluation aids for comparing color palette designs. Through these examples, we demonstrate that color naming models enable users to express their intentions in new ways and offer designers new avenues for assessing their designs.

Though our initial results are encouraging, some limitations remain. All respondents in the XKCD survey were asked to name colors shown against a white background, a design decision that biases the results. Unsurprisingly, the region of color space named "white" is small, as respondents were presumably sensitive to background contrast for high luminance colors, naming nearby colors "offwhite", "cream", or "light grey." The term "black," on the other hand, occupies a larger volume. Future large-scale surveys might vary the background color among black, white, and one or more shades of grey to construct color naming models more sensitive to background contrast. Alternatively, automated methods (e.g., using image search engines [30, 36]) might be used to refine color name regions.

While our approach uses CIE L*a*b* color space, recent work in color science concerns *color appearance models*. These models incorporate contrast effects due to background and surround regions. Though unable to predict all the intricate effects of human color vision, a color appearance model such as CIECAM02 [23] might associate colors with names while taking contrast into account. Future research is needed to assess the potential benefits and determine if the additional modeling complexity is warranted.

Our current work uses an English-language color naming data set. In subsequent work we would like to construct color naming models across a variety of languages (c.f., [26]). Multi-lingual color naming data can enable scientific investigation of linguistic differences in color naming, for example to verify basic color terms and assess differences in color name boundaries and saliencies. Cross-language models would support internationalization of color name-based applications and could potentially lead to culturally sensitive color transfer or gamut mapping methods.

We developed our applications through a design exploration of how color naming models might significantly enhance user interfaces. The goal of this process was to establish the utility of color naming models and develop new techniques. We believe that each application provides novel support for real-world tasks and initial feedback from informal usage has been positive. Users have expressed appreciation for the applications (including requests for the software) and have suggested interesting use cases. For example, one person used name-based pixel selection to analyze a series of art works and "deconstruct" the coloring choices of the artist.

However, we do not claim that these applications are "finished." Further design iteration and end-user evaluation will undoubtedly refine these applications and inform how they could be incorporated into existing tools and workflows. To facilitate future work, our color naming model and applications are available as open-source software, downloadable from `http://vis.stanford.edu/color-names`.

ACKNOWLEDGEMENTS

The authors thank Randall Munroe of XKCD for sharing his color survey data, and Jason Chuang and Pat Hanrahan for their helpful insights and conversation. This work was supported by NSF Grant IIS-1017745.

REFERENCES

1. Adobe Kuler. `http://kuler.adobe.com/`.
2. R. Benavente, F. Tous, R. Baldrich, and M. Vanrell. Statistical modelling of a colour naming space. In *European Conference on Colour Graphics, Imaging, and Vision*, pages 406–411, 2002.
3. L. D. Bergman, B. E. Rogowitz, and L. A. Treinish. A rule-based tool for assisting colormap selection. In *Proc. IEEE Visualization*, pages 118–125, 1995.
4. T. Berk, L. Brownston, and A. Kaufman. A new color-naming system for graphics languages. *IEEE Comp. Graphics & App.*, 2(3), 1982.
5. B. Berlin and P. Kay. *Basic Color Terms: Their Universality and Evolution*. Univ. of California Press, 1969.
6. M. Bostock, V. Ogievetsky, and J. Heer. D3: Data-driven documents. *IEEE Trans. Visualization & Comp. Graphics*, 17(12):2301–2309, 2011.
7. C. Brewer. Color use guidelines for data representation. In *Proc. Section on Statistical Graphics, American Statistical Association*, pages 55–60, 1999.
8. J. Chuang, M. Stone, and P. Hanrahan. A probabilistic model of the categorical association between colors. In *Color Imaging Conference*, pages 6–11, 2008.
9. D. Cohen-Or, O. Sorkine, R. Gal, T. Leyvand, and Y.-Q. Xu. Color harmonization. In *ACM SIGGRAPH*, pages 624–630, 2006.
10. R. Cook, P. Kay, and T. Regier. *The World Color Survey database: history and use*. Elsevier, 2005.
11. M. Das, R. Manmatha, and E. M. Riseman. Indexing flowers by color names using domain knowledge-driven segmentation. In *Proc. IEEE Workshop on Applications of Computer Vision (WACV'98)*, pages 94–99, 1998.
12. M. Harrower and C. Brewer. Colorbrewer.org: an online tool for selecting colour schemes for maps. *The Cartographic Journal*, 40(1):27–37, 2003.
13. J. Itten. *The Art of Color*. Van Nostrand Reinhold Company, 1960.
14. P. Kay and C. K. McDaniel. The linguistic significance of the meanings of basic color terms. *Language*, 54(3):610–646, 1978.
15. K. L. Kelly and D. B. Judd. Color, universal language and dictionary of names. National Bureau of Standards (U.S.) Publ. 440, 1976.
16. G. Lakoff. *Women, Fire, and Dangerous Things*. University Of Chicago Press, 1990.
17. Y. Liu, D. Zhang, G. Lu, and W.-Y. Ma. Region-based image retrieval with high-level semantic color names. In *Proc. IEEE International Multimedia Modeling Conference*, pages 180–187, 2005.
18. Y. Matsuda. *Color Design*. Asakura Shoten, 1995.
19. B. Meier, A. Spalter, and D. Karelitz. Interactive color palette tools. *IEEE Comp. Graphics & App.*, 24(3):64–72, 2004.
20. A. Mojsilovic. A computational model for color naming and describing color composition of images. *IEEE Trans. Image Processing*, 14(5):690–699, 2005.
21. N. Moroney. Unconstrained web-based color naming experiment. In *Proc. SPIE Color Imaging: Device-Dependent Color, Color Hardcopy and Graphic Arts VIII*, 2003.
22. N. Moroney. US Patent Application 11/259,597: Adapative lexical classification system, 2007.
23. N. Moroney, M. Fairchild, R. Hunt, C. Li, M. R. Luo, and T. Newman. The CIECAM02 color appearance model. In *Color Imaging Conference*, pages 23–27, 2002.
24. H. Motomura. Categorical color mapping using color-categorical weighting method. Part I: Theory. *J. of Imaging Science and Technology*, 45(2):117–129, 2001.
25. R. Munroe. Color survey results. `http://blog.xkcd.com/2010/05/03/color-survey-results/`, May 2010.
26. D. Mylonas, L. MacDonald, and S. Wuerger. Towards an online color naming model. In *Color Imaging Conference*, pages 140–144, 2010.
27. S. Palmer. *Vision Science: Photons to Phenomenology*. MIT Press, 1999.
28. P. Rheingans and B. Tebbs. A tool for dynamic explorations of color mappings. *ACM SIGGRAPH Comp. Graphics*, 24(2):145–146, 1990.
29. D. Roberson, D. I., and J. Davidoff. Colour categories are not universal: Replications and new evidence from a stone-age culture. *Journal of Experimental Psychology: General*, 129:369–398, 2000.
30. B. Schauerte and G. A. Fink. Web-based learning of naturalized color models for human-machine interaction. In *Proceedings of the 2010 International Conference on Digital Image Computing: Techniques and Applications*, pages 498–503, 2010.
31. G. Sharma. *Digital Color Imaging Handbook*. CRC Press, 2002.
32. G. Sharma, W. Wu, and E. N. Dalal. The CIEDE2000 color-difference formula: Implementation notes, supplementary test data, and mathematical observations. *Color Research & Applications*, 30(1):21–30, 2005.
33. M. Stone. Color in information display. `http://www.stonesc.com/VisCourses.htm`.
34. M. Stone. *A Field Guide to Digital Color*. A. K. Peters, 2003.
35. J. Sturges and T. W. A. Whitfield. Locating basic colours in the Munsell space. *Color Research & Applications*, 20(5):364–376, 1995.
36. J. van de Weijer, C. Schmid, J. Verbeek, and D. Larlus. Learning color names for real-world applications. *IEEE Trans. Image Processing*, 18(7):1512–1523, July 2009.
37. L. Wang, J. Giesen, K. McDonnell, P. Zolliker, and K. Mueller. Color design for illustrative visualization. *IEEE Trans. Visualization & Comp. Graphics*, 14(6):1739–1754, Nov-Dec 2008.
38. M. Wattenberg. Visualizing the stock market. In *Extended Abstracts, ACM Human Factors in Computing Systems (CHI)*, 1999.
39. J. Winawer, N. Witthoft, M. Frank, L. Wu, A. Wade, and L. Boroditsky. Russian blues reveal effects of language on color discrimination. *Proceedings of the National Academy of Sciences*, 104(19):7780–7785, 2007.

The Untapped Promise of Digital Mind Maps

Haakon Faste
Human-Computer Interaction Institute
Carnegie Mellon University
5000 Forbes Avenue
Pittsburgh, PA 15213 USA
hfaste@cs.cmu.edu

Honray Lin
Human-Computer Interaction Institute
Carnegie Mellon University
5000 Forbes Avenue
Pittsburgh, PA 15213 USA
hraylin@gmail.com

ABSTRACT

Digital mind mapping tools present a fertile area for research on human-computer interaction. We evaluated numerous existing mind mapping software applications, performed ethnographic research with a variety of users, and developed a framework of principles to inform the design of future tools for collaborative knowledge management. Our findings suggest an opportunity to advance digital mind mapping beyond the existing state-of-the-art, particularly in the areas of improving workflow, facilitating collaboration, and supporting information storage and retrieval. We conclude with suggestions for how to improve digital mind mapping systems, specifically with regard to real-time collaborative thinking.

Author Keywords

Mind maps; concept maps; collaborative thinking

ACM Classification Keywords

H.5.2. User Interfaces—Graphical User Interfaces (GUI)

INTRODUCTION

Humans have always relied on technological ways of organizing and exploring their ideas. From clay tablets to the printing press and now the World Wide Web, tools for developing, cataloguing and disseminating ideas have become integral aspects of our everyday lives. In the past few years, many new systems for knowledge management and expression have emerged that leverage the capabilities of collaborative digital media [19]. Often these are networked systems that replicate real-world idea management behaviors (i.e., brainstorming, text editing, organizing photographs, etc.) to support creative activities in industry, research, and daily life. Digital mind mapping tools are one such class of application for exploring and presenting ideas, and are of particular relevance to the study of distributed cognition.

A mind map is a graphical representation of ideas and thoughts related to a central keyword, idea, or question. Related concepts in mind maps are drawn radially stemming from the central idea connected by lines, as shown in figure 1. The non-linear process of creating a mind map makes it an ideal medium for numerous creative activities [6]. Mind maps are especially useful to explore new subjects, record and take notes, reflect on ones thought processes, communicate ideas quickly and collaboratively with others, and look for patterns when synthesizing information [11]. Because mind maps reflect the structure of their author's thought process on a given subject, they are useful for idea generation (i.e., creatively filling in "gaps" in a map) as well as understanding the author's conception of a problem domain. In HCI research, mind maps are used to represent and synthesize field research data [15, 26], and to study topics such as computer-supported creativity (e.g. [5]).

Permission to make digital or hard copies of all or part of this work for personal or classroom use is granted without fee provided that copies are not made or distributed for profit or commercial advantage and that copies bear this notice and the full citation on the first page. To copy otherwise, or republish, to post on servers or to redistribute to lists, requires prior specific permission and/or a fee.
CHI'12, May 5–10, 2012, Austin, Texas, USA.
Copyright 2012 ACM 978-1-4503-1015-4/12/05...$10.00.

With the explosion of the Internet and ubiquitous computing in recent years, tasks that have traditionally been done with paper and pencil are moving into the digital realm. Numerous digital mind mapping tools have consequently emerged, such as Mindjet's Mindmanager (*www.mindjet.com*), Buzan's iMindMap (*www.thinkbuzan.com/imindmap*) and FreeMind (*freemind.sourceforge.net*). These tools have largely replicated the functionality of mind mapping in the virtual realm, allowing users to create visual graphs connected by lines and descriptive text using a keyboard and mouse. However, little has been done beyond porting the mind mapping workflow to the computer, and many nuances of paper mapping have been lost in the process. Furthermore, despite the potential power and flexibility of digital media for improving mind map dynamics, most applications do a poor job of supporting critical user workflows in intuitive ways. The objective of this paper is therefore to examine the current limitations and potential opportunity spaces for digital mind mapping applications, in particular with respect to collaboration and computer assistance, and define an opportunity framework for the design of improved systems.

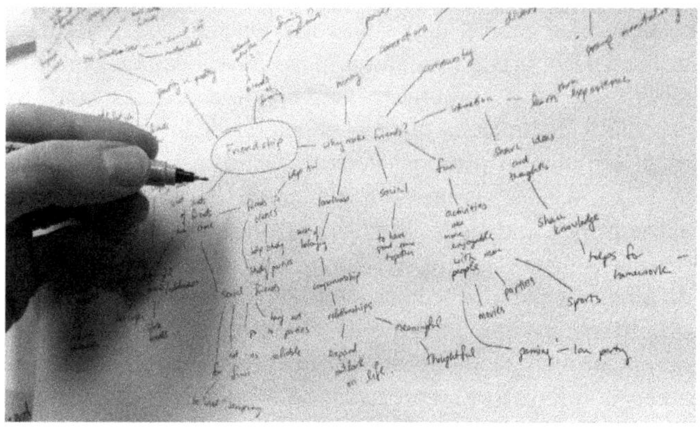

Figure 1. A mind map being drawn on paper.

The Effectiveness of Mind Maps as Cognitive Tools

The notion that the mind can be "mapped" has its origins in the literature of the mid 20th century. Neisser's classic text on cognitive psychology [27] traces the notion of a "cognitive map" to E. C. Tolman's 1948 paper titled "Cognitive Maps in Rats and Men" [35], in which Tolman summarized the results of numerous empirical studies to demonstrate a rat's ability to build spatial maps of its environment when navigating mazes. It is the "tentative, cognitive-like map of the environment" constructed by a rat as it moves through space, Tolman argued, "which finally determines what responses, if any, the animal will finally release."

Tolman's work laid an important foundation for the study of cognition, and especially the "generally map-like and self-initiated character of learning" at the heart of contemporary cognitive science, but the concept of a "cognitive map" is potentially misleading as "it implies that the map is a model of cognition, that is, a model of thinking." [9] Instead, the cognitive map more accurately reflects the way in which the thinker perceives his or her world through the synthesis of internal perceptual cues [30]. It is the self-reflective awareness of these cues that is made explicit through the act of generating the map. Such cognitive maps are therefore a method of knowledge representation that are capable of capturing an individual's perception and understanding of a problem through interconnected sets of elements representing implicit views of one's beliefs.

Cognitive maps can also be extended to social behavior, and are particularly useful when modeling collective actions and responses in situations such as distributed problem solving or learning environments. Lee et al. have demonstrated, for example, that organizational learning can be described as the sharing of individual cognitive maps, each consisting of beliefs about the cause-effect relationships between organizational and environmental elements, to form a collective organizational map that updates itself in response to organizational and environmental factors as individuals within the network learn [22]. Drawing on work by Kolb [20], they show that the visualization of such collective cognitive maps can be used to enable individuals to reflect on and learn from multiple perspectives of experience.

The concept of mind maps as we now know them—as a useful creative method for representing thoughts or ideas relating to a central idea—was introduced by Tony Buzan in the 1970s [6]. Today mind maps have become common tools used by designers in their creative process, and are especially popular as classroom exercises across a variety of disciplines to promote active learning [4, 36]. Because new knowledge is always generated based on existing assumptions and facts, mind maps are able to provide not only raw data but also show the relationships across different concepts, their importance, and how they originated. When making a mind map, a variety of organizational methodologies and creative approaches can be used in the visual representation of the ideas in a map.

The creative process can generally be thought of as an iterative two-step sequence of generating as many ideas as possible on a topic and then choosing a smaller subset to refine and move forward. Mind maps are especially useful for knowledge generation in this regard because they actively facilitate the divergent processes of lateral thinking [13]. As a result, because the process of mind mapping often occurs as a stream of conscious, it is not uncommon for maps to be somewhat organic and chaotic by nature. With practice, however, the elements of a mind map can be generated in real-time such that they are grouped by similarity and/or organized hierarchically by importance to represent relationships between and across the concepts at different levels. In this regard, unlike linear blocks of text, mind maps allow for the gestalt "sense" of the creator's thinking process and ideas to quickly be scanned at a structural level. The new ideas outlined in given map are therefore an effective communication tool, since the rationale and thought process behind new ideas are outlined by the structure and content of the map.

There are numerous benefits of using mind maps as a way of representing information. Mind maps take advantage of visual information representation to leverage the remarkable capabilities of human perception [21]. Since mind maps are constructed by recording thoughts in working memory, improving their design can overcome problems associated with limitations in the capacity of working memory. Additionally, by providing a graphical overview of thought processes and connecting related concepts, mind maps can localize similar concepts, reducing the cognitive load associated with retrieving and maintaining different knowledge elements [32]. A study conducted by Farrand, Hussain, and Hennessy has shown that using mind maps causes a marked increase on memory recall for undergraduate students when compared to traditional note taking, for example [10].

A subtle distinction should be made at this point regarding the cognitive potential of mind maps relative to other kinds of conceptual maps. Semantic networks were developed in the 1950s as a way of representing relationships among concepts, primarily for machine translation tasks [31, 24]. Like mind maps, semantic networks use a visual graph for representing knowledge in patterns of interconnected nodes and edges, either for the explicit purpose of implementing hypotheses about human cognitive mechanisms or to improve the efficiency of computational systems [33]. The links between concepts in a semantic network, however, are causal relationships. By providing different weights and values to each of the connections in a semantic network, one can construct a flow of logical arguments. This ability of semantic networks to illustrate causal reasoning has made them primary tools for the modeling of cognitive systems in a range of social science research. In management science, for example, they have been used to organize policy [17], learn deliberation [7], and aid problem structuring in group decision-making environments [1].

For our purposes we consider mind maps to be a specific variety of cognitive map which satisfy the following general conditions: (1) the creator of the map is either an individual or collaborative team, and the map is being generated and used as part of their creative process, (2) the content of the map pertains, however loosely, to a centrally located topic of interest, and (3) the nature of the relationships between concepts in the map is not explicitly defined as a part of the mind mapping process.

This last condition is not meant to diminish the potential power that could be leveraged by machine systems analyzing the semantic content of mind maps, but rather to ensure that the process of mind mapping remains a spontaneous and open creative activity. Once a map has been generated it may be appropriate for its creator to revisit or reorganize it on the basis of a more detailed analysis of the thought processes involved. Indeed, this may well be a key area in which digital tools can significantly assist in the mind mapping process. While it is possible to create mind maps employing semantic or causal relationships in real-time, however, the best practices required to do so are not immediately obvious. The remainder of this paper seeks to identify areas of opportunity for the improvement of digital mind mapping systems, especially with regard to assisting novice users to achieve the most from the medium.

METHODOLOGY AND DESIGN RESEARCH

Our work takes a broad approach to examining the current limitations of digital mind mapping, with the intent of providing design guidance for future application developers. As described in detail in the remainder of this section, the following research activities have been performed: (1) relevant currently available digital mind mapping software applications have been evaluated; (2) ethnographic research on several participants who actively use digital software to organize and retrieve their ideas has been performed, and; (3) we have drawn numerous mind maps, and analyzed hand drawn maps by an accomplished map designer, to better understand the mechanics of mind mapping and how best practices can be leveraged in the digital space. An opportunity framework for the design of improved systems is identified based on the findings from these exercises. We conclude with recommendations for the development of several key features that we propose for implementation in future work.

1. Evaluation of Digital Mind Mapping Systems

There are numerous existing digital mind mapping applications commercially available serving a variety of markets, most targeted at idea organization and presentation for enterprise purposes. At the start of our research process, we began by testing free online demo versions and/or downloads of existing mind mapping applications, including FreeMind (*freemind.sourceforge.net*), MindManager (*mindjet.com*), MindMeister (*mindmeister.com*), Cacoo (*cacoo.com*), LucidChart (*lucidchart.com*), Creately (*creately.com*), Xmind (*xmind.net*), Compendium (*compendium.open.ac.uk*), Visual Thesaurus (*visualthesaurus.com*), and iMindMap (*thinkbuzan.com/imindmap*). Our intent was to explore the current state of digital mind mapping and to identify areas where it could potentially excel over traditional mind mapping on paper. Evaluated software was selected on the basis of its popularity and the range of its offered features; digital mind mapping has rapidly become a major category of HCI software and there are well over a hundred available applications online. A summary of our findings is as follows:

A. Speed and Efficiency

Most available mind mapping software use the keyboard and mouse as input devices, which we found could be significantly faster than paper and pencil for text input, as typing is generally faster than writing by hand. Switching between the keyboard and mouse to highlight items and enter text on the screen can have the effect of disrupting a smooth workflow, however. To address this issue, mind mapping software such as FreeMind allows specific tasks to be sped up with keyboard shortcuts, permitting an even faster workflow for experienced users. In general, we believe that well-designed digital systems are most effective when the speed of data entry matches the flow of the user's thought process. Mapping on paper tends to intrinsically support this sort of fluid stream of consciousness during creative and organizational tasks. For digital mind mapping applications to excel over traditional methods, therefore, their natural proclivity for speed and efficiency must align with the ability to produce unbroken streams of creative expression.

B. Appearance and Mechanics

Unlike their paper counterparts, the way in which a digital mind map is presented to the user is constrained by the design of the software interface. Designed well, digital maps have the potential to support the clean and consistent appearance of content with regard to font choices and hierarchy, as well as supporting best practices for mind map creation. On the flip side, the design of such software often brings with it new degrees of control not present in paper maps—such as the ability to select and move content within the workspace, for example—adding layers of mediated complexity to the creative process. A wonderful quality of

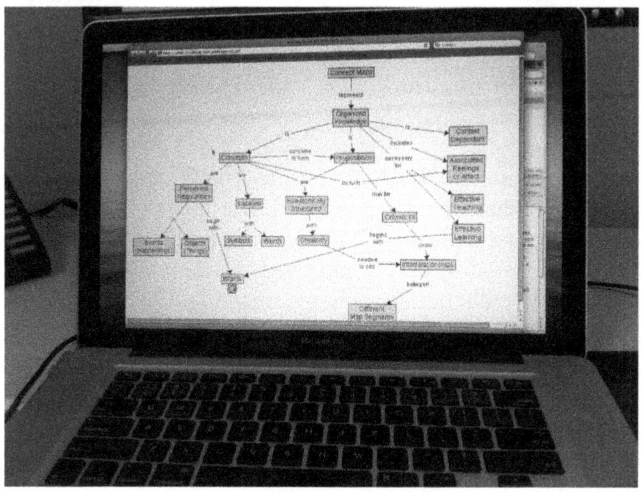

Figure 2. An example of a digital concept map from Wikimedia commons, created using IHMC CmapTools.

hand drawn maps is the absolute freedom they afford to their creator to draw however he or she pleases. Thus while digital tools offer a tremendous array of powerful features, they do so at the cost of introducing functions requiring experience to learn and use effectively that collectively complicate the user's workflow and interaction with content.

As a consequence, although text input may be theoretically faster when mind mapping digitally, tasks such as drawing are often slower or more difficult and the abundance of features and controls can be daunting. Gracefully aligning readability, customization, and contextually relevant user control is a challenge that none of the software we tested did well. New touch screen devices may aid in making such tasks easier, but they are rare among most users and afford poor data entry.

C. Distributed Collaboration

Among the digital mind mapping software we studied, MindMeister, Cacoo, and LucidChart are web applications that support synchronous editing of mind maps, and all of them also support live chat among collaborators while mapping. Recent research projects such as SharedMind have implemented synchronous and asynchronous collaboration, including conflict detection algorithms [1], but none of the software we examined enabled users to perform more advanced multi-user activities with mapping, such as merging together maps created by multiple participants or otherwise leveraging other peoples' maps.

Summary

We have identified the three main areas that differentiate digital mind mapping from mind mapping on paper: (a) speed and efficiency, (b) appearance and mechanics, and (c) distributed collaboration. The first two areas are essential to the function and value of digital mind mapping systems and should be carefully addressed in their future design. Distributed collaboration, the third area, is not explicitly required for digital mind maps to function but is a highly relevant area for future research. One of the main uses of mind maps is to brainstorm and explore ideas, for example, and when done using paper and pencil synchronous collaboration can prove difficult. Collaboration has been shown to cause mutual idea stimulation among creative problem solving teams [12], and studies of concurrent collaboration exclusively with computers can produce higher quality and quantity of generated ideas due to the reduction of "production blocking" [24]. In an empirical evaluation of a shared mind mapping application, Buisine et al. determined that digital mind mapping that occurred in a tabletop condition significantly improved both subjective and collaborative dimensions of mind mapping [5]. We therefore recommend that the designers of digital mind mapping systems consider how best to incorporate features that utilize the potential advantages of distributed collaboration.

2. Design Principles from Ethnographic Research

Following the evaluation of existing mind mapping software, ethnographic research was conducted to further explore the identified areas for potential improvement. Six participants who actively brainstormed or recorded ideas using digital knowledge management tools were interviewed in context. Four of the interviewees were graduate students in the Human-Computer Interaction Institute at Carnegie Mellon University, and the remaining two were developers of idea visualization software. Participants ranged from 20 to 30 years of age with even gender distribution. We also spoke with several academics who have worked with mind mapping software as part of their research. Our intent with these interviews was to identify extreme behaviors and workarounds demonstrated by users, determine their latent emotional needs, and develop specific principles to guide the design of future systems [3]. Using an open-ended interview protocol, participants were asked to show and describe how they used their software for tasks similar to or involving brainstorming, collaboration, and exploring, organizing, and visualizing ideas. Sessions were recorded using digital audio, transcribed, and coded using an iterative, grounded theory approach [14]. We also performed an autoethnographic task analysis [29] in which we drew numerous mind maps on paper while paying careful attention to the processes employed. These observations enabled us to reflect on the internal dynamics of mind map creation and speculate on the possibilities of improving them via digital systems. Gathered data was synthesized into opportunity areas for further design, and the following design principles were identified:

A. Enable Pervasive and Immediate Storage

Participants we interviewed indicated the need for an intuitive and immediate way to store thoughts and rough creative ideas on the fly. One participant indicated that she used mind mapping software to take notes for class, touting the software's speed and ease of use over traditional pen and paper. Another participant used text messaging and emails as reminders to revisit his ideas at a later time, citing the lack of good tools for this task. Instead, he relied on text messaging and emailing his thoughts to himself on his phone as a reminder to revisit his ideas later. These findings, combined with our evaluation of existing software indicating the potential for improved speed and efficiency in the digital mind mapping process, demonstrate that enabling pervasive and immediate storage for ideas and other content is an important principle for the design of improved applications.

B. Match Context of Use with Presentation of Content

The different ways participants used to store their ideas reflected the importance that digital mind mapping systems enable intuitive content organization. All of the participants clearly specified where and how they wanted their content to be stored. Some participants used virtual folders to indicate where different groups of ideas and tasks should be saved, whereas others used features within their mind mapping software to demarcate distinct groups of ideas. One participant, for instance, demonstrated how she created branches in the mind mapping software when taking notes from lectures in class based on the lecture's semantic content. Another expressed his desire to have different places to store ideas depending on how developed they were. In short, digital systems should be aware of these differing behaviors and match the content presentation to the context of use.

C. Encourage Seamless Collaboration
Participants also indicated their desire for collaboration in the process of idea synthesis, citing its usefulness and its ability to encourage themselves and others. When brainstorming, all users described how they used their software collaboratively or their desire for collaboration. One user explained how she and her friend took daily photographs and posted them in a shared folder on DropBox for each other to see. She noted that although no visible communication took place, her friend's participation was the key motivating factor that had turned this virtual collaboration into an ongoing ritual for several months. Another user of mind maps indicated that since digital mind mapping is still uncommon among most people, sending team members digital mind map files was problematic since they could not easily be opened and edited by others. While several existing mind mapping systems do support distributed collaboration, as noted above, the desire for shared tools among the HCI-focused users we spoke to was remarkably pervasive. There is therefore an opportunity for digital mind mapping systems to enable easy collaboration at every stage of their use, and encourage it when appropriate.

D. Facilitate Fast and Efficient Information Retrieval
Our interviews revealed that participants often want summaries of their recorded ideas when revisiting them. For example, it is very common in collaborative creative practice for paper mind maps created at the beginning of a project to be placed on a studio wall for the project's duration. For the task of note taking, one participant indicated that she rarely went back to check on her notes since it was difficult to find what she was looking for. In this regard, mind maps were particularly useful to her because they inherently facilitated this sort of summary behavior. We observed that the natural ability of the medium to support efficient information retrieval is easily impeded, however, due to poorly designed interaction mechanics and visual structure, as well as the screen space limitations of digital systems. Digital systems should therefore do a better job of ensuring that easy information retrieval is supported as well as it is on paper. Leveraging search capabilities and intelligent filters common in other HCI paradigms could both be ways to support this goal.

E. Provide Contextual Creative Guidance
Like any design activity, learning to mind map well requires practice and can benefit from the guidance of someone experienced in using the medium. In our observations of the users of digital systems we noticed how the ultimate goal of assisting a seamless creative workflow was seldom explicitly supported. We also observed that hand drawn mind maps remain a far more popular medium in the educational domain than their digital counterparts. Thus more could be done by digital systems to better educate users how to efficiently generate and structure their content. Just as text-editors indicate opportunities for improvement in spelling or grammar, mind map systems could provide contextual workflow-related and structural advice.

Summary
Our research has identified five major design principles for digital mind mapping systems, summarized in figure 3. As noted above, while encouraging collaboration is not required for digital systems to function well, it is clearly a central area for potential improvement and was universally desired by the HCI practitioners we spoke to. Indeed, we believe that encouraging collaboration can be a powerful mechanism for supporting the other identified principles.

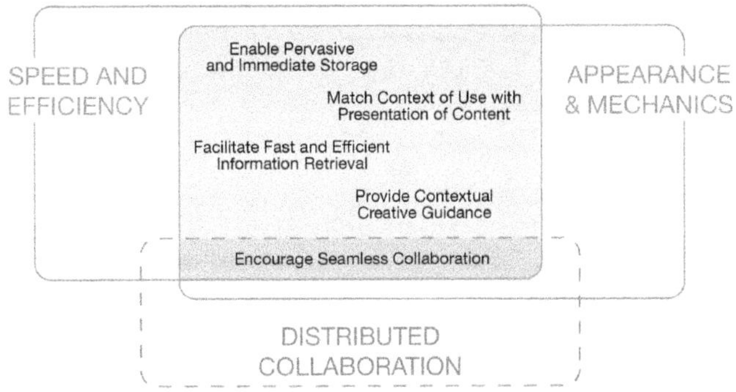

Figure 3. Overview of design principles for improved digital mind mapping systems (in black), leveraging their natural areas of potential strengths as identified in our software trials (rectangles).

3. Generative Ideation and Mind Map Analysis
Based on the design principles identified in the previous section, brainstorming sessions were conducted with eight graduate students in our HCI program. Participants were asked targeted questions involving digital idea input, idea organization, and idea summarization based on our findings (e.g., "How could we encourage organizing and clustering ideas on the fly?"; "How could we make browsing text-based information magical and fun?"), generating over 150 rough ideas in three 1.5 hour sessions. At the end of each session, favorite ideas were voted on by the group, informing an ideation/refinement phase that resulted in 23 refined HCI concepts with titles, descriptions, a statement of each concept's value proposition, and a sketch. We then began creating wireframe drawings of an interaction workflow containing these concepts to illustrate a basic scenario in which users create a digital mind map.

As part of this wireframing process, we also performed an exploratory exercise in which we traced an existing hand-drawn map into a digital format using Adobe Illustrator and paid special attention to unexpected features that emerged. Although digital maps need not emulate the aesthetics of hand-drawn maps, this approach was intended to identify additional opportunities for improved digital mind mapping interfaces. Once again, our aim was not to perform a rigorous horizontal survey of hand-drawn map styles, but rather to digitize a well-drawn sample map as a basis to inspire the design of more intuitive systems. The map we digitized, "Pattern Recognition" by Rolf Faste [11], was chosen because aesthetically it is a well-constructed map showing clear hierarchies and distributions of information. The result of our digitization process is shown in Figure 4, and our observations are detailed in the following sections. Opportunities have been organized into the previously identified areas of workflow support: speed and efficiency, appearance and mechanics, and distributed collaboration.

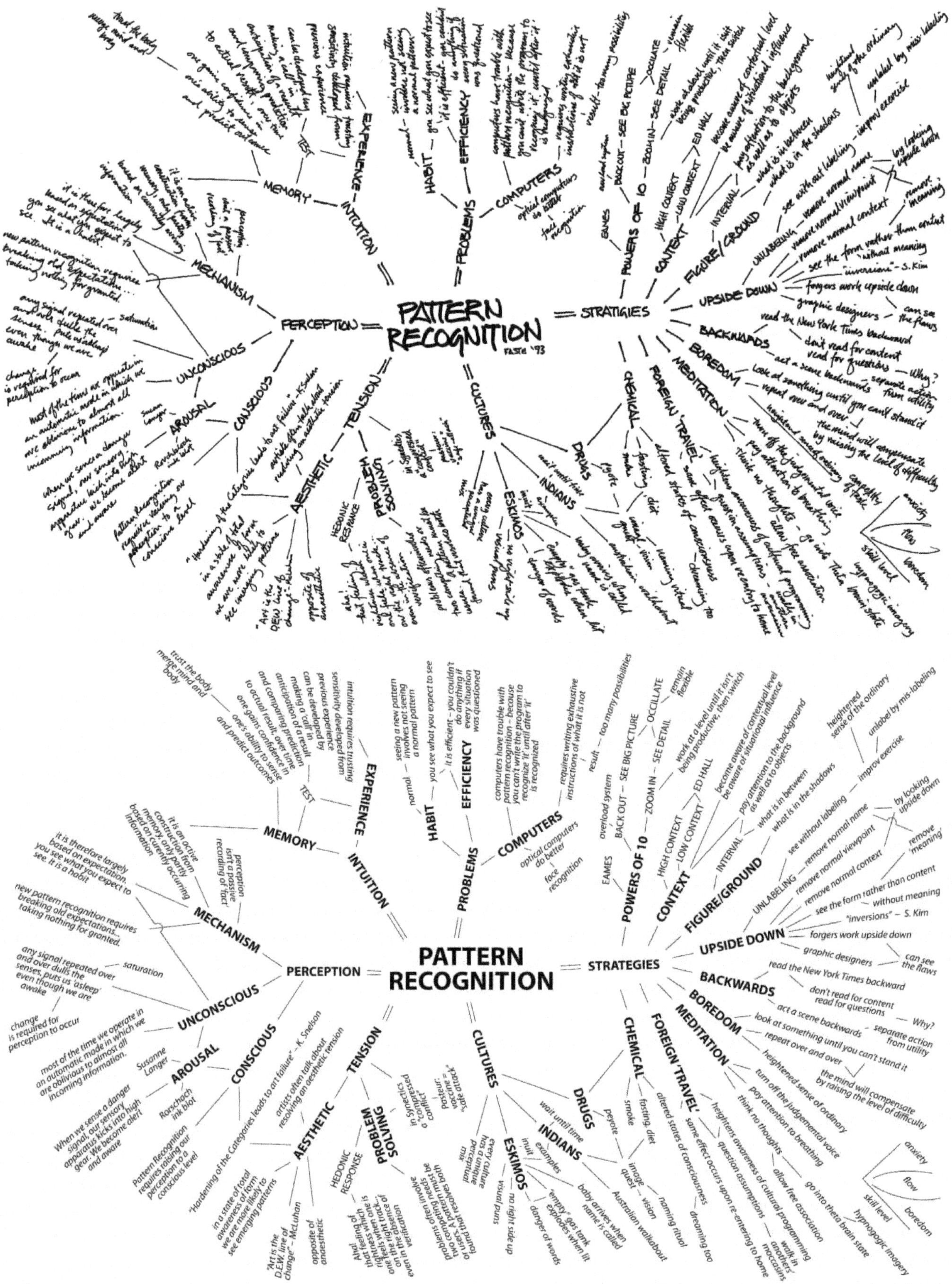

Figure 4. The original hand drawn "Pattern Recognition" map by Faste, and our digital copy

A. Speed and Efficiency

Based on our user observations and subsequent ideation, we believe that the opportunity exists to improve digital mind mapping applications by more effectively incorporating quick access touch-points for data input, retrieval, and storage. Existing features like clearly defined keyboard shortcuts enable users to create ideas faster on the fly when using digital systems. But the process of generating ideas often occurs spontaneously at unexpected moments in a user's life, as with the proverbial "drawing on the back of a napkin." Perhaps the ability to interact with digital mind mapping systems should therefore be extended to mobile platforms for idea input, and/or leverage voice-to-text technology enabling users to "call in" to their maps directly. As a general rule, we believe designers of digital mind mapping systems should provide workflows that support generative and organizational tasks, both through on-screen interfaces and on the fly.

Another way to enhance the speed and efficiency of the digital mind mapping medium is by enabling users to integrate effective mapping strategies into their digital workflow at large. Applications should support universally recognized file formats and consider features that allow linear blocks of text and hierarchies such as outlines to be quickly transformed into and out of mind mapping formats. Users should also be provided with a central "headquarters" location to store their maps, from which they can easily share maps with others, browse stored content, and manage permissions on shared data across devices and over time.

B. Appearance and Mechanics

Our brainstorming activities and subsequent wireframes revealed numerous opportunities to improve the appearance and mechanics of digital mind mapping. These opportunities can be generally subdivided into three main categories: (1) those that enable the "big picture" browsing and navigation of the map and its information hierarchies; (2) those involving the manipulation of the specific objects that constitute the mind mapping medium, such as nodes and links; and (3) those involving digital mind map aesthetics and related factors. Our discussion will begin with the big picture and work down to these details.

Big Picture Browsing Tools and Summary Support

In general, the navigation and layout mechanics of digital mind maps represent a ripe space for potential innovation. Our research indicated the wide range of ways people use to save and retrieve data, from using Dropbox to store personally significant artifacts to using mind maps as a note-taking tool. Successful mind mapping applications should provide dynamic and customizable experiences that cater to each user's desired modalities of use. A "summary zoom layers" feature could dynamically summarize content in a mind map, for example. As users "zoom out," adjacent and similar idea nodes could condense into expandable "summary" nodes describing the nodes they contain. The importance or number of summarized nodes could determine the size of each summary node. Based on the observation that users want an easier way to retrieve stored information, this concept would allow users to quickly browse the most important ideas and then dig deeper for details, potentially reducing the map's visual clutter. Manual tools could also be provided to support similar clustering, allowing users to generate mind maps with greater degrees of hierarchical control.

Digital mind mapping applications could also leverage the ability to browse across time. A variety of "ripple effects" could be implemented to give users feedback communicating a "sense" of the interrelationships within and across maps. Selecting a node could send ripples of color radiating outward through the map to highlight similar concepts or the relational strength of connections between them. A "history slider" could also enable users to "scrub" through the evolution of their map, revealing the thought processes behind their creation.

Object Architecture: Nodes and Links

Traditional mind maps allow a wide range of uninhibited human annotation, such as drawing and other kinds of mark-making, that digital systems do not easily support. Digital mind mapping applications tend to define the behaviors of nodes and links in detail. For these systems, how text is selected and how node objects are moved has critical consequences on user workflow. Our investigations developed numerous concepts that address these issues.

Examining Faste's hand drawn map (see figure 4), we were struck with how each node of the map included complete phrases and thoughts rather than individual words. This simple observation led to numerous concepts. Regarding the scalability and placement of text objects on the digital canvas, for example, the presence of complete sentences could lend itself to semantic interpretation by the system. Such a system could determine if a node object is a "question" or an "answer," for example, and encourage users to treat such objects differently as they interact. Concept metadata could also be applied to each node, perhaps automatically, in ways that could be easily editable and/or searchable afterwards. This would allow users to access their ideas more intuitively when searching, perhaps filtering by authorship, ownership, category, or time. Metadata about ideas could also be expressed visually in emotionally meaningful ways, including icons or colors reflecting the "seriousness" or "intent" of the content in question. Metadata traits could also be inherited from parent nodes, generating meaningful information about new nodes quickly and easily, and be tentatively displayed as links off of each newly created node to enable the quick confirmation or rejection of automatic suggestions.

The links between nodes, especially their creation and degree of connectivity between nodes, are another potential area for contextual guidance. Dragging one node into another could easily create a link between them, for example, and dragging a "slice" across a link could sever the connection. Such interactions would provide relatively fast and intuitive affordances, facilitating the need for efficient information retrieval we observed in our research. The links between nodes in Faste's map were also observed to have numerous unanticipated behaviors when drawn on paper. In general, all of the lines in Faste's map are relatively straight, unlike the Bezier curves common in digital applications. This greatly simplified the visual clutter of our digital copy. Linking lines were also observed connecting concepts together at intuitive but seemingly irregular angles (usually gravitating towards the end of a text phrase rather than its center) that would require a finely tuned algorithm to model precisely. Finally, we observed that when two lines in Faste's map cross each other a curving "jumper" is used to reduce confusion at the point where they cross. Ideally elements of the map would be easily rearrangeable to avoid such situations automatically, although current digital offerings grant users free control of an object's placement in the (x, y) canvas and in general this leads to unwieldy-looking connections. It may make more sense for nodes in the map to be automatically "cleaned up" within their local context, or for the movement of a node and its links to "push" neighboring nodes when the user moves a node past others (as in figure 5). Finally, when writing sentences informally by hand it is not uncommon to insert a long dash, like this: —. Not coincidentally, such dashes are practically identical to the links between text-blocks, so perhaps typing "-" on the keyboard could be a shortcut to add a new node.

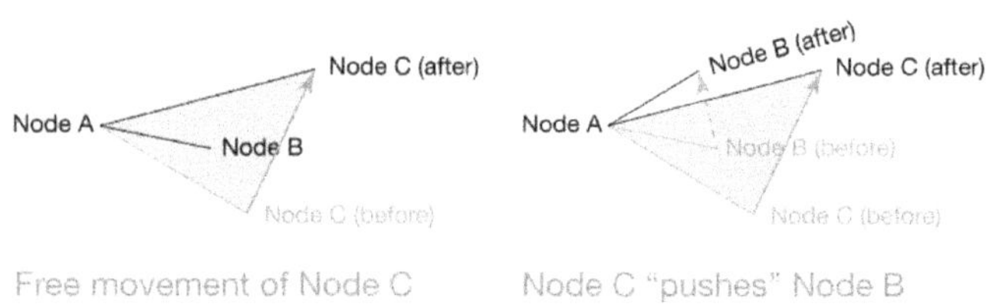

Figure 5. A possible node-dragging behavior. While "free" node behavior (left) is common among digital systems, it may be more intuitive for node objects to "push" one another (right). Note also that paper mind maps work quite well with immobile nodes!

Interaction Aesthetics

There are numerous ways in which the aesthetics of digital mind mapping could be tuned to support more intuitive interaction mechanics. The visual design of hierarchical levels is one evident area. Many digital mind mapping applications enable users to manually adjust the font sizes and styles of each particular node, including the addition of digital clip art or images, but the result of this freedom is often detrimental to the appearance and legibility of the map's hierarchy at large. Faste's map was easy to copy into the digital space because it had a nicely pre-defined hierarchy of thoughts, including a center statement, heading 1, heading 2, and body text. Numerous existing font sets would play well with this "style sheet" model, and could be universally supported by the mind mapping software.

In general, users should have freedom to experiment with mind mapping styles but be guided by the system to reduce visual clutter through systematic best practices. Constraining the number of available styles and options can actually serve to encourage creative experimentation. Faste's map makes such capability for creative freedom quite evident, for example. We saw that not all of the nodes in his map are necessarily "children" of higher-level nodes (links between different degrees of hierarchy are allowed to occur). Deceptively simple rules regarding visual elements, such as connection lines, can also play important aesthetic roles to enhance digital systems. We found that while the width of links in Faste's hand-drawn map reduced slightly at each level of hierarchy (from double heavy lines, to heavy lines, to thin lines), for example, consistently thin lines (0.5 pixel or less) looked far less distracting when reproduced on our digital map. Double lines remained an elegant way to emphasize important connections, however, and do not detract from the overall simplicity of the visual look.

Another aesthetic observation involved digital mind map density. In Faste's map, the placement of nodes and the shape of their text was clearly the product of a highly stream-of-conscious process enabling them to flow naturally into the available space. Furthermore, while all of the digital mind mapping application we examined employed rigidly horizontal fields of text, Faste's map makes clear that this need not be the case. Indeed, while the horizontal nature of the text fields in most digital maps tends to drive them towards a relatively low density of information (e.g. Figure 6a), Faste encourages high density maps as it leads to the "fission and fusion of ideas and concepts" [11]. This indicates the possibility for digital mind mapping systems to employ far better space management algorithms (e.g. Figure 6b), potentially including interface paradigms that automatically rotate and zoom when working on a particular area to keep the majority of visible text correctly aligned—just as it would be when rotating the piece of paper while working on a hand drawn map. This would also maximize the amount of information visible on the screen at one time, overcoming the previously identified issue of mind mapping on devices with limited screen real estate.

A few additional interactive details could be implemented to help fit text blocks more densely together in intuitive ways. Text fields seem to work best when center aligned, for example,

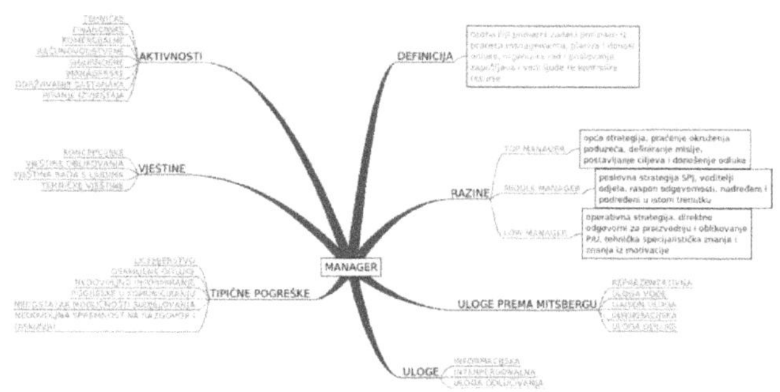

Figure 6a. A typical digital mind map demonstrates sparsity.

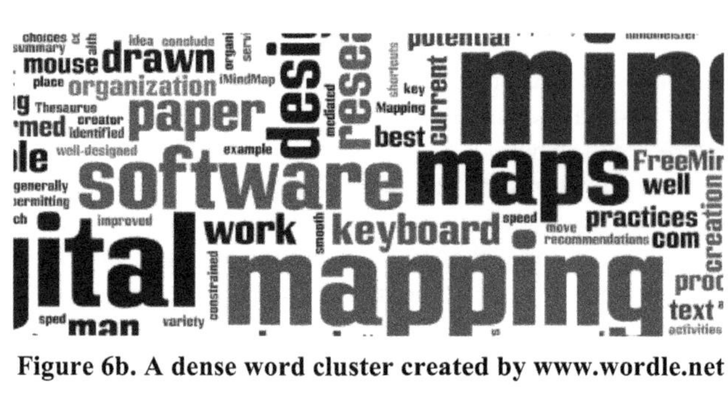

Figure 6b. A dense word cluster created by www.wordle.net

but we noticed that this was particularly dependent on available space. At numerous locations in Faste's map we observed individual lines in a block of text that were slightly off center to allow a tighter fit with their neighbors. Application designers could consider controlling the relative motion of elements in the interface through soft body dynamics [25] to enable intuitive compression; of the digital applications we examined, only Visual Thesaurus has behavior resembling this kind of fluidly animated motion. Finally, we observed that hand-drawn text introduces small degrees of randomness into the placement of objects. Thus while the underlying structure of Faste's map has a clearly spaced radial architecture, the placement and rotation of each block of text, as well as the links between them, are placed at intuitively variable locations. While quite subtle, this observation indicates the potential opportunity for digital mind mapping objects to be placed slightly "off" to give the application more "edgy" and "realistic" feel.

C. Distributed Collaboration

To facilitate users' desire for collaboration during the process of idea synthesis, real-time editing of mind maps could be implemented as a web application enabling direct cooperative interaction. With the approval of each mind map's author, users could be able to browse and contribute to each other's maps online and connect with other users sharing similar interests. Anyone with a web browser would then be able to contribute to shared maps through this online system, overcoming a key limitation encountered by users we spoke to. "Collaborative notification overlays" could provide real-time updates to communicate changes in shared maps. Such features would address limitations in collaboration identified in both traditional and digital mind mapping tools.

Taken a step further, collaborative features could dramatically improve the efficiency of digital mind mapping by supporting our other previously identified principles. We observed that a significant reason why users collaborate is to connect with others. An "interesting button" could allow users in the crowd to give positive feedback on concepts in a map, allowing individual ideas to be flagged as "interesting" in an easily visible way. Through "visual idea crowdsourcing" users could be enabled to flag ideas or entire sections of their map for external user input, thus leveraging crowd data to enhance their idea synthesis. Scanning and browsing shared content could also be supported through "ownership gradients" indicating the degree to which ideas in a shared map had been recently updated. Direct communication such as chatting could further facilitate these tasks and improve their appeal and ability to support creative research and development.

Finally, we believe that collaboration can be used in digital mind mapping systems to enable the implementation of intelligent agents that assist the mind mapping process. Imagine a "mindmap indexing bot," for example, that crawls a network of users' maps to index the semantic relationships between various nodes. Software that can understand the semantic relationships across ideas within a mind map, as we discussed in the introduction, could suggest related topics and ideas to the user in real-time as they edit and browse content. This presents a clear feature space where digital mind maps could excel over hand drawn maps. Providing users contextual suggestions as part of the ideation workflow could not only make mind mapping more efficient, but could help generate ideas that are different from those thought of elsewhere in the system at large. Ultimately this could lead to radical innovations and encourage collaborations between users with similar interests. Currently, tools that support similar functionality require a solid understanding of ontology and a relationship definition language [28], and are not typically employed in commercially available applications.

We believe that collaborative mapping could provide the missing ingredient to overcome these limitations to the integration of ontology into the mind mapping workflow. Unlike machine algorithms, humans can understand the relative semantics involved in what are often ambiguous relationships between mind mapped information and collaboratively make sense of shared data [7]. This feature expands upon the idea of ontology and concept mapping discussed above while eliminating the need to understand a formal relationship language.

CONCLUSIONS AND FUTURE WORK

This paper has identified numerous opportunity spaces for the design of improved digital mind mapping systems. Many discrete opportunities have been addressed, with the intent of enhancing the use of digital mind mapping applications during HCI processes, such as generating and organizing map data in both personal and collaborative settings. Supporting real-time collaboration, facilitating pervasive storage, and affording dynamic content presentation are all features that would significantly improve the use of such systems.

We are now developing and prototyping many of the features described in these findings to test their effectiveness. To support real-time collaboration we propose a web application that provides instant feedback of user contributions and allows users to contribute to and provide feedback on mind maps more easily. We also propose that digital mind mapping systems enable a dynamic browsing experience for the user, providing a summary of the mind map's most important points and an adaptive layout that supports the user's browsing intent.

As a next step, we plan on building a full prototype of a digital mind mapping system and testing the platform with a wider range of potential users. After further visualizing and iterating the aforementioned features, our goal is to build a working implementation of the system to expand the possibilities of real-time collaborative thinking.

ACKNOWLEDGMENTS

This paper is a heavily revised and extended adaptation of a previous CHI work-in-progress publication [23]. We would like to thank the participating contributors in our two brainstorming sessions, specifically Andrew Gillespie, Tawana Dillahunt, Rebecca Gulotta, Derek Lomas, Eva Shon, and Jeff Rzeszotarski. Thanks also to the Rolf A. Faste Foundation for Design Creativity for supporting this work.

REFERENCES

1. Ang, S., Rzadca, K., Datta, A. SharedMind: A tool for collaborative mind-mapping. *Proc. 2010 IEEE Int'l Conference on Multimedia and Expo (ICME)*, 2010.
2. Balakrishnan, A. D., Fussell, S., & Kiesler, S. Do visualizations improve synchronous remote collaboration? *Proc. CHI*, 2008
3. Brown, T., and Katz, B. Change by Design. *Journal of Product Innovation Management*, vol. 28, no. 3, 2011.
4. Budd, J. W. Mind Maps as Classroom Exercises. *Journal of Economic Education*, vol. 35, no. 1, 2004.
5. Buisine, S., Besacier, G., Najm, M., Aoussat, A. and Vernier, F. Computer-Supported Creativity: Evaluation of a Tabletop Mind-Map Application. In Harris, D. (ed.), *Engineering Psychology and Cognitive Ergonomics*, Springer Verlag, Berlin/Heidelberg, 2007, pp. 758-767.
6. Buzan, T. *Use Both Sides of Your Brain*. Dutton, 1976.
7. Chi, E. H., Kittur, A., and Mytkowicz, T. Augmented Social Cognition: Understanding social foraging and social sensemaking. In *Proc. of the HCIC 2007 Winter Workshop*, Fraser, Colorado, Jan 31–Feb 4 2007.
8. Easterday, M.W., Aleven, V., Scheines, R., and Carver, S.M. Constructing causal diagrams to learn deliberation. *Artificial Intelligence in Education*, vol. 18, 2008
9. Eden, C. On the Nature of Cognitive Maps. *Journal of Management Studies*, vol. 29, no. 3, 1992, pp. 261-265.
10. Farrand, P., Hussain, F, and Hennessy, E. The Efficacy of the 'Mind Map' Study Technique. *Medical Education*, vol. 36, no. 5 (May 2002) pp. 426-431
11. Faste, R. Mind Mapping. 1993. Available online at http://www.fastefoundation.org/publications/mind_mapping.pdf (accessed April 12, 2011)
12. Forster, F. Distributed Creative Problem Solving over the Web. *Third International Conference on Internet and Web Applications and Services*, 2008.
13. Gaines, B.-R., and Shaw, M.L.G. WebMap: Concept Mapping on the Web (2002) Available online at http://www.w3.org/Conferences/WWW4/Papers/134/
14. Glaser, B.G., & Strauss, A. Discovery of grounded theory: Strategies for qualitative research. *Sociology Press*, 1967.
15. Gorlenko, L. and Englefied, P. Usability error classification: qualitative data analysis for UX practitioners, *CHI 2006 extended abstracts.*
16. Grobelnik, M., and Mladenic, D. Automated Knowledge Discovery in Advanced Knowledge Management. *Journal of Knowledge Management*, 2005
17. Hall, R.I. The Natural Logic of Management Policy Making: Its Implications for the Survival of an Organization. *Management Science*, vol. 30, no. 8, 1984
18. Hao, J.-X., Kwok, R., and Lau, R. Predicting Problem-Solving Performance Using Concept Map. *11th Pacific-Asia Conference on Information Systems*, 2007
19. Kim, A. *Community building on the web: Secret strategies for successful online communities*, Peachpit Press, 2000.
20. Kolb, D. A. Learning and Problem Solving on Management and the Learning Process. In Kolb, D. A., Rubin, I. M., and McIntyre, J. M. (eds.), *Organizational Psychology: a Book of Readings*, Prentice-Hall, 1974.
21. Kommers, P., and Lanzing, J. Student's concept mapping for hypermedia design: navigation through the world wide web space and self-assessment. *Journal of Interactive Learning Research*, vol. 8, no. 3-4, 1997.
22. Lee, S., Courtney, J. F. Jr., and O'Keefe, R. M. A System for Organizational Learning Using Cognitive Maps, *Journal of Management Science*, vol. 20, no. 1, 1992.
23. Lin, H., and Faste, H. Digital Mind Mapping: Innovations for Real-time Collaborative Thinking. *Proc. CHI extended abstracts*, 2011
24. Masterman, M. Semantic Message Detection for Machine Translation, Using an Interlingua. *International Conference on Machine Translation of Languages and Applied Language Analysis*, 1962.
25. Matyja, M. How to Implement a Pressure Soft Body Model. http: // panoramix.ift.uni.wroc.pl/~maq/soft2d/howtosoftbody.pdf, accessed April 17, 2011.
26. Millen, D., Schriefer, A., Lehder, D., and Dray, S., Mind maps and causal models: using graphical representations of field research data, *CHI 1997 extended abstracts*.
27. Neisser. *Cognitive Psychology*. Prentice Hall, 1967.
28. Novak, J. D. & Cañas, Alberto J. The Theory Underlying Concept Maps and How To Construct and Use Them. *Institute for Human and Machine Cognition,* 2008.
29. Patton, M. Q. *Qualitative Research & Evaluation Methods*. Sage Publications, 3rd edition, 2002
30. Putnam, W., and Klatzky, R. Processing Locational Information from Memorial and Perceptual Maps. *American Journal of Psychology*, vol. 94, no. 2, 1981
31. Richens, R. H. Interlingual Machine Translation. *Computer Journal*, vol. 1, no. 3., 1958, pp. 144-147.
32. Sarker, P., Wallace, P., and Gill, W. Some Observations on Mind Map and Ontology Building Tools for Knowledge Management, *Ubiquity* (March 2008)
33. Sowa, J. F. Semantic Networks. In Shapiro, S. C. (ed.), *Encyclopedia of Artificial Intelligence*, Wiley, 1987, second edition, 1992.
34. Tergan, S. Digital Concept Maps for Managing Knowledge and Information. *Knowledge and Information Visualization* (2005)
35. Tolman E. C. Cognitive Maps in Rats and Men. *Psychological Review*, 55 (4): 189–208 (July 1948)
36. Willis, C. L., and Miertschin, S. L. Mind Maps as Active Learning Tools. *Journal of Computing Sciences in Colleges*, vol. 21, 2006, pp. 266–272.

Delta: A Tool For Representing and Comparing Workflows

Nicholas Kong[*†], **Tovi Grossman**[*], **Björn Hartmann**[†], **George Fitzmaurice**[*], **Maneesh Agrawala**[†]
[*]Autodesk Research, Toronto, Ontario, Canada
{*tovi.grossman,george.fitzmaurice*}@autodesk.com
[†]University of California at Berkeley, USA
{*nkong,bjoern,maneesh*}@eecs.berkeley.edu

ABSTRACT
Tutorials and sample workflows for complicated, feature-rich software packages are widely available online. As a result users must differentiate between workflows to choose the most suitable one for their task. We present *Delta*, an interactive workflow visualization and comparison tool that helps users identify the tradeoffs between workflows. We conducted an initial study to identify the set of attributes users attend to when comparing workflows, finding that they consider result quality, their knowledge of commands, and the efficiency of the workflow. We then designed Delta to surface these attributes at three granularities: a high-level, clustered view; an intermediate-level list view that contains workflow summaries; and a low-level detail view that allows users to compare two individual workflows. Finally, we conducted an evaluation of Delta on a small corpus of 30 workflows and found that the intermediate list view provided the best information density. We conclude with thoughts on how such a workflow comparison system could be scaled up to larger corpora in the future.

Author Keywords
Workflow comparison; Tutorials; Search interfaces; Delta.

ACM Classification Keywords
H.5.2. Information interfaces and presentation (e.g., HCI): User Interfaces.

INTRODUCTION
Design software, such as image editors, animation tools, and 3D modeling applications, provide users with powerful ways to create and modify virtual content. Despite advances in HCI research, the interfaces for such applications are complex and can be difficult to learn [12]. While software documentation can provide assistance with locating and using individual components, users often refer to online tutorials to learn the required workflows for completing higher-level tasks. For example, a Photoshop user wishing to correct red-eye in a photograph could search online to find step-by step instructions.

Today, there are an abundance of online communities and websites specifically dedicated to publishing such *workflows* – sequences of commands required to accomplish a defined task. Furthermore, researchers have begun to build systems that automatically record user action streams, which can be used by others to learn a workflow [3, 8, 10, 11]. As the corpora of these online learning resources continue to grow, users are likely to find multiple workflows for the same task. Workflows can vary in the tools they use, the quality of the results, or may have differing prerequisites (such as requiring specific plug-ins).

Permission to make digital or hard copies of all or part of this work for personal or classroom use is granted without fee provided that copies are not made or distributed for profit or commercial advantage and that copies bear this notice and the full citation on the first page. To copy otherwise, or republish, to post on servers or to redistribute to lists, requires prior specific permission and/or a fee.
CHI'12, May 5–10, 2012, Austin, Texas, USA.
Copyright 2012 ACM 978-1-4503-1015-4/12/05...$10.00.

The challenge for a user is no longer searching for and finding *any* workflow – the challenge is identifying the *most suitable* workflow from potentially hundreds of possible candidates. In addition, individual websites tend to use a wide range of layouts and formats for presenting workflows, potentially making it difficult for users to identify differences in the workflows themselves. To date, there is little research investigating how users explore and identify possible workflows to accomplish a task when multiple candidates exist. Furthermore, no tools have been explicitly designed to support the process of exploring and comparing workflows.

In this paper we focus on image-editing workflows for Photoshop, because it is a well-known design application with a large number of tutorials available online. We first perform a study to understand users' workflow searching behaviors, and identify the criteria they use when choosing between multiple image-editing workflows. Our main finding is that users primarily consider the quality of the result, their knowledge of commands (and thus their effects), and the efficiency of the workflow.

The results of this study guide us in the design of *Delta*, a new interactive tool to aid the process of workflow comparison and exploration. Given a corpus of up to 50 workflows that describe the same task, our tool allows users to understand the scope of available workflows; explore each of the workflows in detail; and understand the similarities and differences in the structure (i.e., command sequence) of individual workflows.

Our tool allows users to visualize and compare workflows at three levels of granularity: a high-level clustered view; an intermediate-level list view that contains workflow summaries; and a low-level detail view that allows users to compare two individual workflows. To ease comparisons, the tool displays all workflows with a uniform presentation format within each of the three granularity levels.

To understand the potential benefits of the tool, and to evaluate the different comparison granularities which it provides, we conducted a user study. In comparison to a traditional web search interface, users preferred our tool, and in particular its ability to easily compare workflows. Observations and comments also indicated that the intermediate list view provided the ideal information density for most of the workflow comparison tasks. We conclude by describing limitations, design refinements, and implications for workflow browsing.

RELATED WORK

Our system draws on related work from three main areas: models for how users find information, search/exploration interfaces, and workflow recording systems.

Information Scent and Finding Information

Delta is fundamentally an information search tool. Some researchers have developed theoretical models for how people find information. Information foraging [22] has been applied to model and predict user behavior in web search [4, 5]. A key concept of information foraging theory is information scent, or the contextual cues that allow users to assess the benefits and costs of distal (i.e., hidden) content [4]. In this work, we identify the contextual cues that users find most effective when they search for workflows.

Search Interfaces for Large Corpora

Workflows are a specific type of structured data. Researchers have developed systems for searching or accessing large collections of unstructured data, such as documents [14], images [16], or web pages for design [20]. Others have looked at systems for exploring more structured data. One example is VisComplete, a dataflow suggestion system built within a visual programming system for visualization [17]. As users create a dataflow out of a sequence of function modules, the system makes suggestions of other dataflows that are similar to the current dataflow. Our tool is designed to accommodate workflows, and also uses similarity metrics to suggest similar workflows in the context of exploring the entire corpus.

Closest to our work is AdaptableGIMP [19], which integrates image-editing workflow search into GIMP. Workflows are stored on a wiki and users can access these wiki pages from within GIMP. They can also directly invoke GIMP commands from the wiki pages. In contrast, our tool is designed to help people compare workflows, in addition to aiding search tasks.

Workflow Recording Systems

Finally, many researchers have created systems for recording workflows. These systems are complementary to our tool, as their output can be fed into our system. Much of the work in this area focused on recording interaction histories in domains such as painting applications [18], visual analysis [15], and GUI applications [21]. More recent work has focused on enabling users to effectively explore longer workflows by chunking operations. Chronicle [11] and MeshFlow [8] allow users to replay and explore workflows for an image manipulation application and a mesh creation system, respectively. The proliferation of such systems enhances the need for tools to explore workflow corpora.

TERMINOLOGY

In this section, we formally define terms that we use throughout the paper.

A **command** is a user-invoked operation in an application. Examples of Photoshop commands include the activation of palette tools, such as the brush tool, or menu options that open dialog boxes, such as the image level tool. The complexity of a command can vary from inverting the image to manually specifying a color curve.

A **workflow** is a sequence of commands and can take multiple representations. One common representation is a **tutorial**, which describes a workflow in a sequence of steps, frequently with image or video illustrations and explanations for why certain commands are used. Workflows can vary greatly in their length. Our tool has been designed to work with relatively short workflows – anywhere from 5 to 30 steps long – as this is the range of steps we observed while sampling a collection of online tutorials for common image-editing tasks.

STUDY 1: HOW USERS COMPARE WORKFLOWS

To better understand which workflow attributes users consider most important when comparing and assessing workflows, we ran a small study. We used the results of this study in the design of Delta to emphasize the most important attributes. Users looked at a set of workflows that described the same task and chose the one that they would most likely use.

Workflow Representations

We used three different workflow presentation styles. While our goal was not to compare the presentation styles themselves, we reasoned that each presentation style may prompt users to consider different attributes when comparing workflows. Figure 1 shows the three presentation styles we used: *text, text+image*, and *graph*. The *text* representation is a paragraph of text with inline tool icons. It deemphasizes the length of the workflow and the quality of the result while surfacing palette tools using icons. By removing clearly delineated steps and images, it also makes it more difficult for users to skim the workflow, forcing them to read closely.

The *text+image* representation is a step-by-step description annotated with images illustrating each step. It also contains before and after images, which allows users to assess the result quality, and it emphasizes the length of the workflow by numbering steps. Its layout closely followed the tutorials generated in Grabler et al.'s tutorial recording system [10].

Finally, the *graph* representation is a visualization that displays commands as nodes in a graph. It emphasizes the commands and parameters used in the workflow. Each node displays canvas state, similar to Chen et al.'s DAG representation of workflows [3].

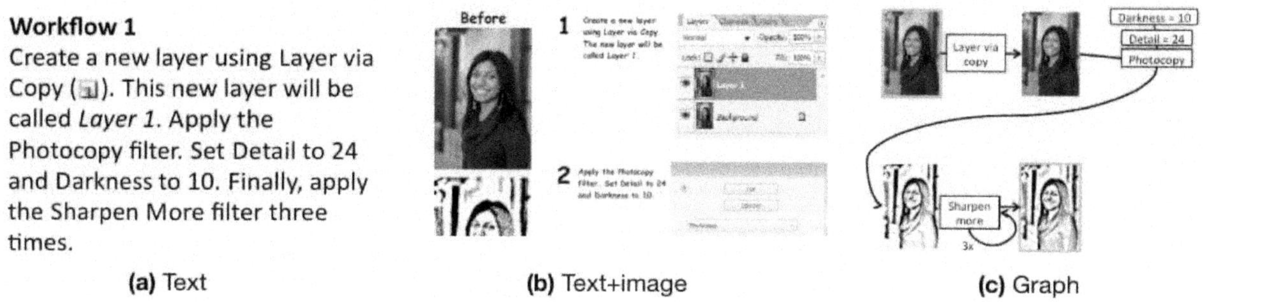

Figure 1. Workflow representations in the first study. (a) The *text* condition shows a workflow as a paragraph with inline tool icons (if they exist). The icon here is added for illustration. (b) The *text+image* condition displays before and after images and individual steps. (c) The *graph* condition displays the canvas after each command. Command names are shown as regular rectangles, parameters as rounded rectangles.

Study Design and Procedure

The study consisted of three trials, one for each representation. In each trial, we showed participants three different workflows for the same Photoshop task. We gave participants a target image and asked them to think aloud while selecting one workflow they would choose to apply to the target image.

In each trial, participants saw a different task: red eye correction, applying a sketch effect, and image sharpening. We chose tasks that were short but complex enough to permit multiple different approaches. We obtained tutorials from the web and transcribed workflows manually. Each participant saw every representation, and no two participants saw the same representation/task pair. We recorded audio during each of the trials.

After the participants had completed all three tasks, they completed a short questionnaire where they scored a list of workflow attributes (on a 5 point Likert scale) on how important the attributes were when comparing or choosing between workflows. The list of attributes, shown in Figure 2, was based on our experience. Although our focus was on the workflow attributes users chose, we also had users rank the effectiveness of the representations based on how clearly they displayed the attributes.

Participants

We recruited six participants through an online classified posting. We had four male and two female participants, who ranged from 19 to 40 years old and had between three and seven years of Photoshop experience.

Results and Discussion

Although we only had six participants, we encountered a diverse cross-section of Photoshop users, whose aims varied when choosing a workflow. For example, P2 was very interested in learning new Photoshop features and would occasionally browse for tutorials to improve his knowledge. In contrast, P3 was most interested in finding a quick and efficient way to complete the task. However, we identified overlap in the workflow attributes participants used when selecting a workflow.

Five of six participants found the *text+image* representation most useful at surfacing almost all of the attributes; one participant preferred the *text* and *graph* representations, saying that the *text+image* representation "*seemed like too much to have to look through.*"

Preferred Workflow Attributes

Figure 2 shows user-rated importance of workflow attributes when comparing workflows. None of the differences in the means are significant after a Bonferroni corrected paired t-test However, users' comments during the think-aloud portion of the study corroborated the general trend of these rankings.

During the think-aloud trials, all of the participants mentioned *quality of the result*, *knowledge of the commands*, and *workflow efficiency* (e.g., length). The second attribute category subsumes a number of workflow attributes: when speaking about commands, users referenced their *familiarity* with the commands and their knowledge of the commands' effects, which is an indicator of a workflow's *flexibility*. Although users rated "the workflow can be used in other situations" as an important attribute, no user mentioned this in the think-aloud. Users may have interpreted this attribute to mean that the workflow is flexible, or that it can apply widely to a variety of images (e.g., a sharpening workflow that would work equally well on a landscape photo and a portrait).

Perhaps unsurprisingly, users considered holistic attributes of workflows (e.g., the quality of the result or the efficiency of the workflow) more important than mechanistic attributes (e.g., number of mouse-clicks or number of dialog boxes). No users mentioned either of these mechanistic attributes during the think-aloud.

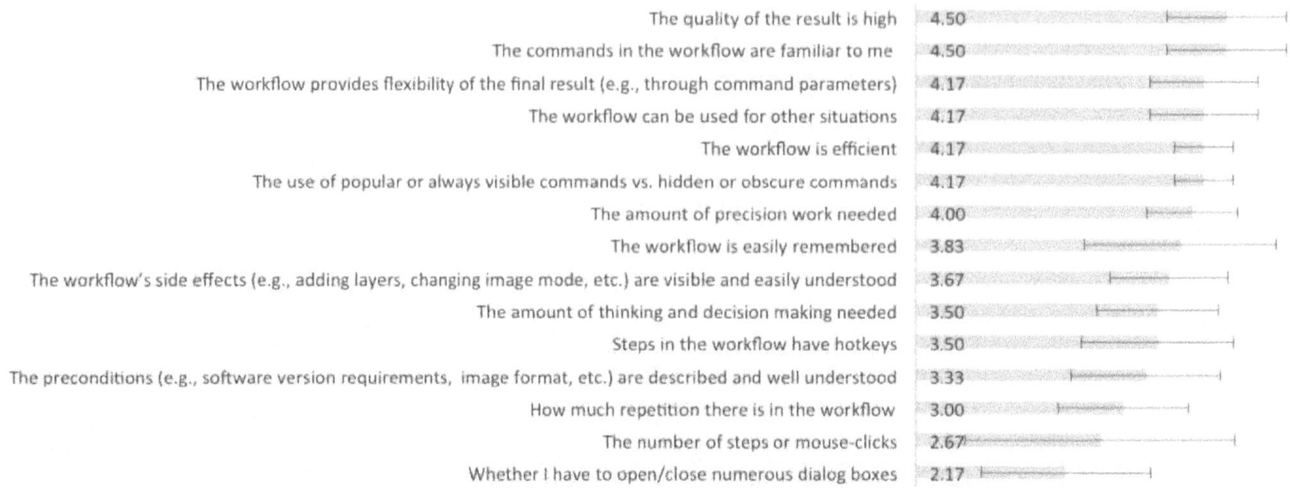

Figure 2. Likert-scale rankings for the importance of workflow attributes when comparing workflows. Users rated attributes on a scale from 1-5, where 1 was "not important at all" and 5 was "very important". Bars indicate 95% confidence intervals.

The attributes related to the quality of the result and knowledge of the tools are not independent: users were better able to anticipate the result of a workflow if they were familiar with the tools and their effects, and how they could be parameterized to change the result. This was particularly apparent in the text representation, since it did not contain any images. For example, in the image sharpening task shown in a text representation, P2 chose workflow 1, explaining that:

"... with workflow 1 ... when you're playing around with your 'find edges' and 'levels' and everything, it's only going to pick up what you're looking for, which would probably just be the squirrel in the image."

In this case, P2 used his prior knowledge of the effects of the commands and how they would affect the target image. Likewise, P5 noted that the before/after images for the workflows in the sharpening task were too small to see differences, and so chose a workflow using his "experience", saying:

"...[the workflow] allows you to have more control over the important edges. Gives you better contrast control."

Finally, all users mentioned workflow length in the think-aloud, which is related to the efficiency of the workflow. However, only one participant, P3, placed a larger emphasis on the length of the workflow rather than the result quality. For example, in the sketch effect task displayed as text, P3 selected workflow 1 as it was "*pretty straightforward, pretty efficient in terms of time*," even though she noted that workflow 2 might produce a better result but was too "*labor-intensive*."

Other users thought efficiency was important, but took efficiency to mean that the workflow produces a good result and does not contain any extraneous commands, even if the commands in the workflow require many clicks to execute (e.g., specifying a color curve). An efficient workflow may contain many commands as long as each is necessary to achieve the final result. For example, P6 chose a longer sharpening workflow because of *"...familiarity. ... though there are a lot of steps involved, it provides the most specification from my perspective.*"

Tutorial Seeking Behaviors

We were also interested in users' current practice to find workflows. We asked participants how often they used tutorials and where they typically found them. All of our participants used search engines to find tutorials. One also used books, and another also used magazines. However, they both reported that their predominant method to seek out tutorials was web search. One of our participants preferred video tutorials, while another disliked them; the others did not have a preference for the modality of the tutorial. Finally, users reported that they selected tutorials based on sites originating from a trusted domain (e.g., adobe.com), and search engine ranking. These results corroborate prior work on information seeking behavior via search engines [6, 9, 13].

Implications for System Design

The results of this study provide some guidance on the design of a tool to support workflow comparison, and in particular how workflows should be represented. A consistent and compact representation of a workflow that displays the most important information (i.e., provides the strongest information scent [22]) will make it easy for users to compare collections of workflows, or two specific workflows. The main implications from the initial study are as follows:

- *Images of the results and intermediate steps are important.* Users wanted to not only see the before/after images for each workflow, but also images illustrating in-between steps to help them visualize operations.

- *Commands are important.* Users used their knowledge of commands and their effects to assess how effective or flexible a workflow was (i.e., how the parameters of commands could be changed to affect the result).
- *Workflow efficiency is important.* Some users wanted to know how quick or efficient a workflow was. A workflow comparison tool should display the number of commands or steps as a proxy for this information.

METRICS FOR COMPARING WORKFLOWS

Ideally, a workflow comparison tool would be able to algorithmically suggest similar or different workflows to the user. Some systems designed for the exploration of large corpora of unstructured data, such as documents or images, do this by using clustering ([7, 16]). One challenge for creating a clustering interface for workflows is quantifying how similar two workflows are; once this metric is defined, we can use it to create clusters of similar workflows. However, workflows could be grouped using different notions of similarity: for example, workflows could be grouped by result quality (e.g., [20]), or by how many commands have been used by the user. Similarity metrics can also be used to rank workflows. In this section, we explore the space of similarity metrics and how they relate to the attributes of workflows users deemed important in the first study.

In our first study, we identified three workflow attribute types users consider when comparing workflows: *quality of the result*, *knowledge of the tools*, and *workflow efficiency*. For each of these attribute types, we present potential similarity metrics that could be used to cluster, or rank, a workflow collection. A similarity metric could also be a combination of metrics from these types.

Result Similarity

Workflows may be grouped by the results they produce, which would help users choose the workflow with the desired quality. Similarity metrics of this type are more difficult to operationalize than metrics of other types, as result quality is a subjective judgment. However, result similarity metrics may be amenable to crowdsourcing techniques [24]. We could also use metrics such as PageRank or popularity ratings such as social media ratings (Facebook likes, Google+ +1s, etc.); PageRank is already widely used as a ranking metric given web search's popularity for finding tutorials.

A user might also wish to find a workflow that matches their task. For example, a user may wish to remove red eye from a photo of a child, and so would want to find a red eye removal workflow that also uses a photo of a child. A result similarity metric based on image attributes, such as the objects in the photo (e.g., faces, cars, etc.) or lower-level attributes such as color, would be useful in this scenario.

Command Similarity

Another way to quantify workflow similarity is by using the commands or command sequences used. This class of metrics would help surface what workflows contained familiar commands, or which allowed the user to flexibly modify the final result. Potential metrics include the number of shared commands; a workflow familiarity rating based on a users' personal usage profile; or the edit distance [25] between two sequences of commands. For our system, we used an edit-distance metric, described later.

Workflow Efficiency

Although it was a lesser concern for participants, the efficiency of a workflow was identified as an important differentiating attribute. Explicitly determining the efficiency of a workflow would be challenging. However, grouping or ranking workflows by their length, either in the time taken or the number of commands used, may serve as a suitable approximation. For our system, we use the number of commands to rank workflows.

DELTA: APPLICATION DESIGN

In this section, we describe the design of our new workflow exploration tool, *Delta*. Based on study participants' reports and our own experience, we designed Delta's interface to explore corpora of that are representative of collections of image manipulation tutorials online: Delta targets collections of several dozen workflows, each containing up to 30 commands. Three complementary views provide information about the workflow corpus at different levels of detail (Figure 3): a *cluster view* presents a high-level overview of the entire corpus; a *list view* provides workflow summaries; a *detail view* lists individual commands and enables pairwise comparisons. We describe each in turn.

Cluster View

The cluster view provides a high-level summary of the corpus by grouping workflows by similarity. Clusters enable users to rapidly distinguish between similar and different workflows.

We selected a command similarity metric for clustering – it can be computed without requiring additional metadata such as ratings, and it is closely related to the *knowledge of commands* workflow attribute. We computed similarity by modeling each workflow as a sequence of commands, then computing the *edit distance* [25] between sequences of commands. The edit distance is the sum of the costs of the insertions, deletions, and substitutions that are required to transform one command sequence into another. We used the distance between commands in the Photoshop menu hierarchy to set the substitution cost: for example, substituting Gaussian Blur for Motion Blur incurs a low substitution cost, because both are siblings in the Blur menu. We used hierarchical agglomerative clustering [23] to create clusters, although other methods (such as k-means) are possible. Finally, we laid out the clusters using the quantum treemap algorithm [2], as it was designed to compactly lay out items with a minimum display dimension, such as our workflow images.

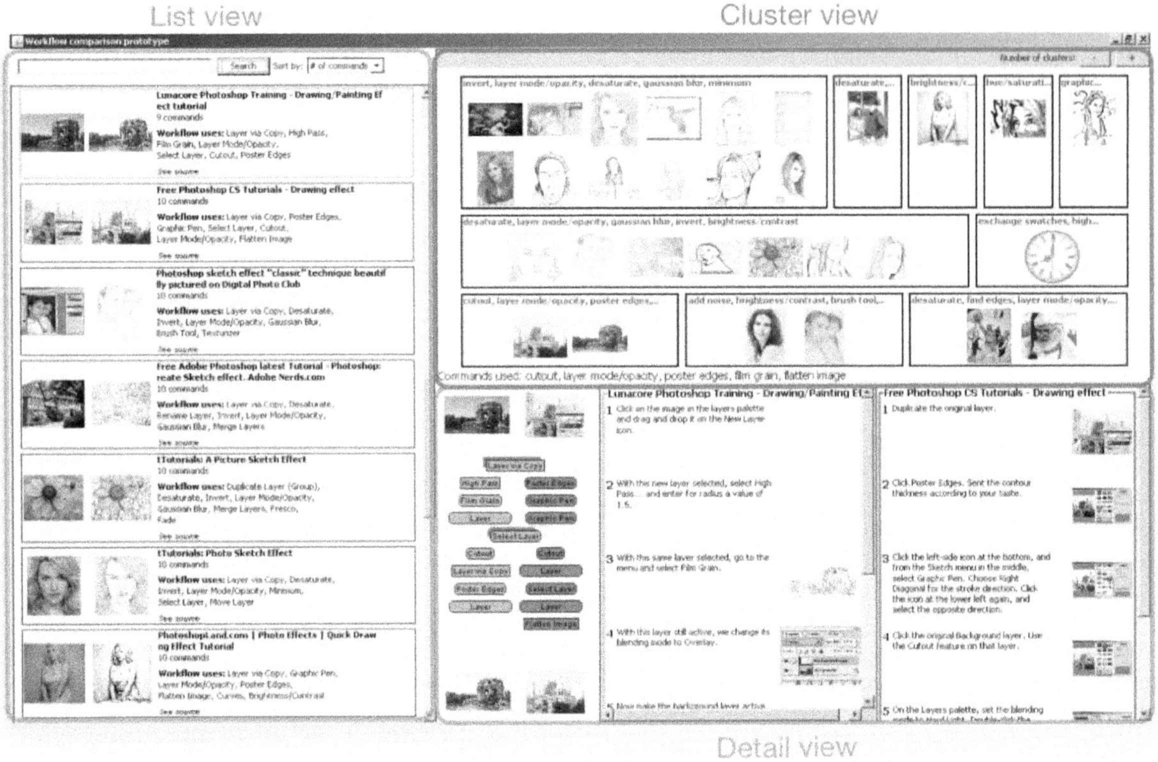

Figure 3. Delta's workflow explorer. The list view (left) displays workflow summaries. The cluster view (top right) groups workflows by similarity. The detail view (bottom right) shows individual steps and *union graphs* of shared commands.

Delta labels each cluster with the five most common tools in the cluster's workflows. Labels may be abbreviated because of cluster sizes; the full label is displayed at the bottom of the view when users mouse over a cluster. Users can click on an image in the cluster view to cause the list view to scroll to the corresponding workflow. Finally, users can adjust the number of clusters using *plus* and *minus* icons to explore coarser or finer corpus differences.

List View

The list view (Figure 3 left) uses **workflow summaries** (Figure 4) to surface the most salient attributes we found in Study 1. Reading an abstract summary can enable quicker comparison than consulting the source documents.

Summaries show *result quality* by displaying the before and after thumbnail images and a title. Users can click on thumbnails to view a full-resolution version. Summaries enable users to judge *command familiarity* through a list of unique commands in the workflow. The summary also displays the total number of commands, which is a coarse indicator of *efficiency*. Each workflow view also contains a link ("*See source*") to the source webpage. Users can sort the list view by either the number of commands or by cluster (which orders workflows so siblings in a cluster are adjacent).

Detail View

The detail view shows individual steps in a workflow and also enables pairwise comparison. When a user selects a single workflow in the list view, the detail view displays all commands and any accompanying screenshots of the original tutorial; the layout was modeled after the *text+image* condition in Study 1. When the user has selected two workflows, the system displays the workflows

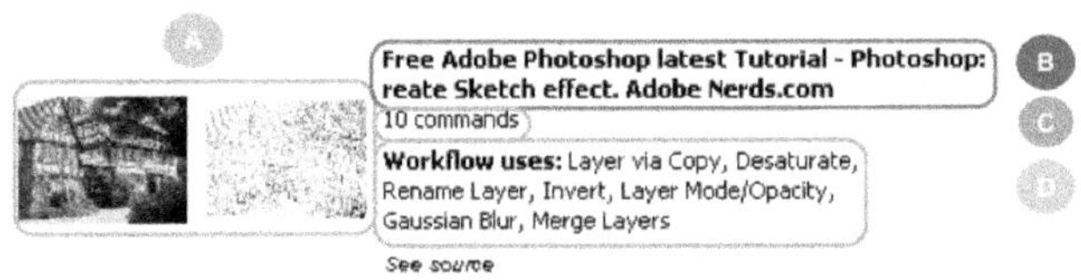

Figure 4. A workflow summary. (a) Before and after images. (b) Workflow title. (c) Number of commands. (d) List of unique commands in the workflow.

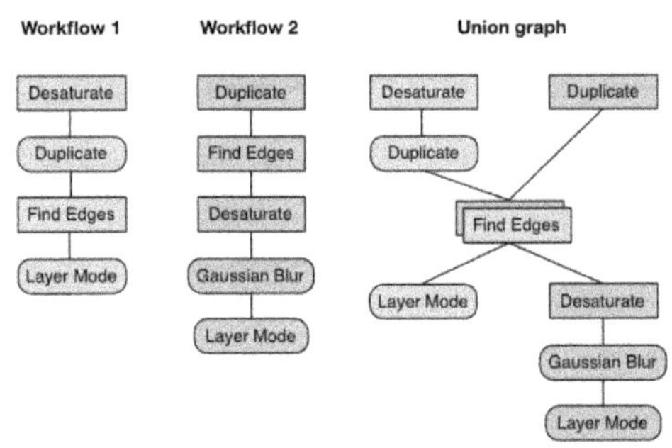

Figure 5. Creation of the union graph. Only commands that share the same name and parameters overlap. Here, "Find Edges" is shared between the two workflows.

side-by-side and creates a *union graph* [1] of the two command sequences. Figure 5 illustrates the creation of the union graph, which is produced using the edit distance computed for the cluster view. Commands in both workflows that have the same *name* and *parameters* are considered to be shared between workflows and are visually centered in the graph; in Figure 5, "Find edges" is the only shared command. Commands without parameters are displayed as rectangles and commands with parameters are displayed as rounded rectangles. Finally, node tooltips show the full name of the command and any parameters for that command. The graph allows the user to judge similarity by identifying shared commands.

STUDY 2: WORKING WITH DELTA

We designed a study to evaluate how effectively the different views of our system were able to aid users in exploring a small corpus of workflows. We also compared Delta to web search in order to contrast usage behaviors. However, the primary purpose of the study was to observe user behavior with Delta and gain insights into potential design enhancements.

Methodology

We asked users to complete a set of workflow comparison and search tasks on a corpus of 30 similar workflows while thinking-aloud. Specifically, we asked users to tell us which features of the workflows or interface they were attending to while completing the tasks.

To compare user behavior in Delta with a baseline, we tested two conditions: *Delta* – where users worked with our prototype workflow explorer tool, and *WebSearch* – where participants used a web search interface over the study corpus[1]. In each interface condition, participants saw a different set of workflows: one for *image sharpening*, and one for *applying a sketch effect*. Each corpus contained 30 workflows, which we manually transcribed from tutorials taken from the top Google search results. The source workflows were of similar length and scope as the workflows we presented to users in Study 1. We found that 30 workflows gave us a good variety of approaches, although the small corpus may have limited the utility of our system.

The ordered tasks we gave participants were as follows (phrased using the sketch effect task):

1. Find a workflow you would use to apply a sketch effect. (*Find a workflow*)
2. You have an image that you would like to apply a sketch effect to, but you are not sure which method would produce the best result. Find three workflows that each use a different approach to apply a sketch effect. (*Three approaches*)
3. You were following this sketch effect workflow and got stuck midway because one step was not clearly explained. Find the workflow most similar to this workflow. (*Most similar*)
4. You are nearing a deadline and don't have much time. Find the sketch effect workflow that would be quickest to complete. (*Quickest*)
5. You have some time and would like to learn more about Photoshop. Find the sketch effect workflow that would expose you to the most new or unfamiliar tools. (*Most new commands*)

We call tasks 2 and 3 **comparison tasks**, and the other tasks **search tasks**.

Finally, we asked participants to complete a questionnaire asking (a) what parts of Delta they liked or disliked, and (b) which interface they preferred in each task.

Participants

We used an online classified posting to recruit participants, asking for people who had at least beginner-level Photoshop experience. Twelve participants (six male and six female) completed the study. They ranged in age from 26-67 years old and reported between two months and 20 years of Photoshop experience.

Results

We first discuss our observations of user behavior when using Delta, then briefly report user ratings of their preferred interface for each task. We do not report time-to-completion for either interface as the corpus was small enough that users tended to learn the workflows quickly, which meant that they were sometimes able to complete the later tasks very quickly by referencing a workflow they had already seen.

Participants Used the List View for All Tasks

When using Delta, we noted that users depended heavily on the list view for all of the tasks. All users quickly completed the search tasks by taking advantage of the list view's sort by number of commands, from fewest to most. For the *Quickest* task, users scrolled to the top of the list and chose one of the top workflows based on the result quality and their own familiarity with the commands. In the *Most new commands* task, users scrolled to the bottom of the list to find the workflows with the most commands, then read the list of commands in the workflow summaries and chose the one that contained the most unfamiliar commands.

In the comparison tasks, all users made use of the command list in the workflow summaries as their primary way of finding candidate workflows. In fact, P9 exclusively used the list view for both tasks. He rapidly judged similarity from the command list; for example, in the *Most similar* task, he said, *"both [workflows] have similar tools"* and did not look at the details of the workflows.

[1] We implemented this condition using the Google Custom Search API (http://code.google.com/apis/customsearch/).

Participants Largely Ignored the Cluster View

On the other hand, only three users interacted with clusters, either in the cluster view or by reordering the list view by cluster. P3 clicked once in the cluster view during the *Three approaches* task and sorted by cluster in the *Most new commands* task. P7 reordered the list view by cluster during the *Three approaches* task, but relied on the content of the source images to choose three different workflows. P4 used the cluster view in the *Most similar* task to choose a workflow in the same cluster as the supplied workflow. P4 then selected the workflow in the same cluster that had the most command overlap.

Most Participants Used the Detail View and Union Graph

Four of the twelve participants used the detail view in the *Find a workflow* task, and ten participants used the detail view to read individual steps in the workflow when completing the comparison tasks. They would first use the list view to find interesting workflows, then select the workflow and read the details.

Seven of the twelve participants used the union graph in at least one of the comparison tasks. P11 commented that, *"A lot of the commands are joined"* while completing the *Most similar* task. Others, such as P2, noted shared commands, but also commands that are shared but out of order:

"The only [command] they share is layer via copy ... and some of their directions are pretty much reversed. One has a layer [blending] after a layer via copy, the other has a layer [blending] after another command."

This observation indicates that users understood the concept of the union graph and found it useful for completing the comparison tasks. It also suggests that explicitly indicating shared, but out of order, commands is potentially useful.

Although users understood the main concept of the union graph, there were some features that caused confusion. Some users did not recall that hovering on a command in the graph activated a tooltip with the full name of the command and its parameters; when referencing a command, participants sometimes used the shortened display name of the command rather than the actual command. A number of users were also confused that commands with the same name were not joined in the union graph unless they also shared the same parameters. None of the participants used the parameters of commands when choosing workflows; this implies this information does not need to be present in the views, as users can retrieve the information from the source document.

Participants Used Images Extensively

All of the participants viewed the full resolution versions of the before or after images to compare the results, and many users viewed the full resolution images that illustrated each step. However, although our design allowed users to pop open multiple full-resolution images to aid comparison, only P11 moved image windows around to compare a full-resolution image to another image. These observations suggest that while full-resolution images were important for users to see the details of the results, the thumbnail images were good enough for users to compare workflows.

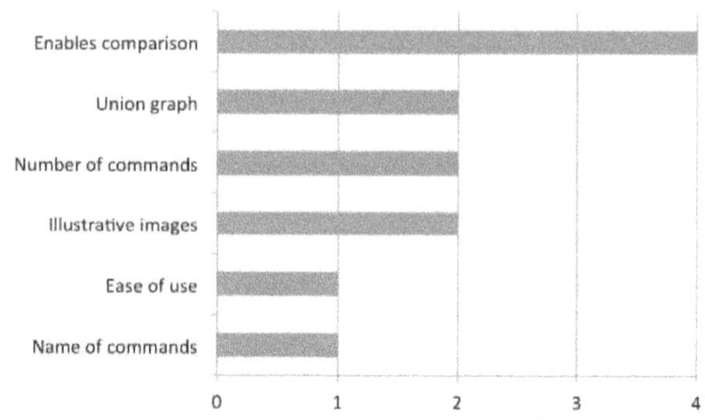

Figure 6. Elements of the workflow explorer that users reported they liked.

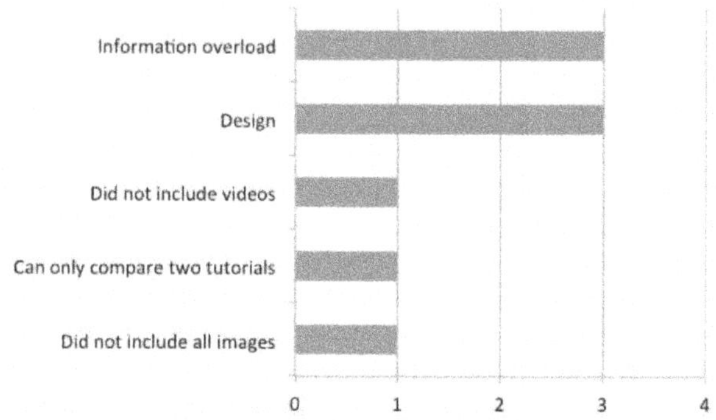

Figure 7. Elements of the workflow explorer that users reported they disliked.

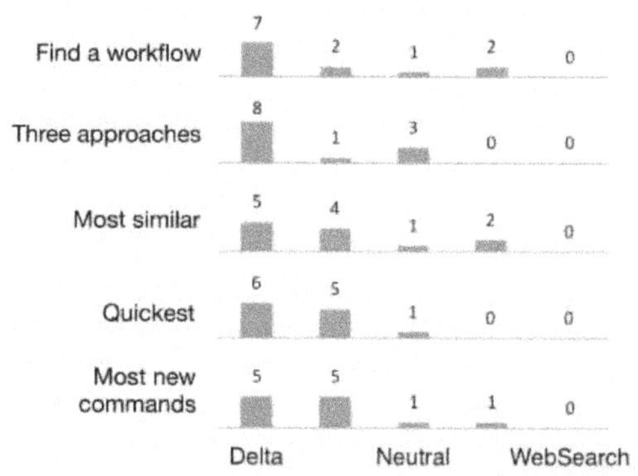

Figure 8. User interface preferences for each task. Numbers indicate the number of ratings.

Subjective Feedback

We asked users to tell us what they liked and disliked about Delta. We categorized their open-ended responses: Figure 6 shows what users liked about the application and Figure 7 shows what users disliked about the application. Overall, users liked how the application enabled them to compare workflows, and two users mentioned the union graph in particular, both referring to the graph as a *"flow chart."* The main drawback, noted by some of the participants, was that the interface was filled with too much information. Finally, participants consistently preferred Delta over the search engine for each task (Figure 8).

Follow-Up Study: Clustering Methods

We also wanted to learn about how users would cluster workflows, to better understand what areas of the similarity metric space would be useful. We gave the same twelve participants from our user study 10 printed workflows for red-eye correction and asked them to create groups of workflows that use *similar approaches* to complete the task. The printed workflows were in the *text+image* format from Study 1. We intentionally left the prompt vague to allow participants to use their own notion of similarity. We asked participants to think-aloud while grouping workflows, and specifically asked them to tell us why they placed workflows in the same group. The clustering study took approximately 10 minutes to complete.

Results

We noticed two primary methods of clustering: using commands, or command groups, and using the complexity of the workflows (based on familiarity, length, or ease of the workflow). Some users combined these two methods when creating their clusters.

Seven users used command groups to group workflows. For example, P1 separated the workflows into one group which involved "*filling in the eye with different colors*", one that "*changed colors using channels*", and one that involved "*painting on new layers*." A few made a distinction between workflows that used layers versus those that used painting tools, such as P9.

Five users clustered workflows based on complexity. A few clustered based on how easy the workflow was to follow; for example, P5 created one cluster with workflows that had "*too much information*," and one cluster with workflows that were "*nice and simple*." P12 split workflows into familiar and unfamiliar groups, and further clustered the familiar group using commands.

These results indicate that individual users may group commands differently, and use those groups to judge similarity. In addition, users thought it was important to differentiate between easy and difficult workflows. The implication for design is that an effective clustering metric would combine both command similarity and a measure of workflow complexity.

DISCUSSION

Implications of Observations: Design Guidelines

The observations from our user study imply a number of design guidelines for a future workflow exploration system.

Provide List Views to Support Search Tasks

Participants universally used the list view for all tasks, and largely ignored the cluster view. Based on these results, it is likely that the list view contained the required information to complete the tasks, given the small size of the workflow corpus. The cluster view may have been unnecessarily high level. We hypothesize that as the number of workflows increases, the cluster view may provide more benefit. The larger the corpus, the more beneficial a high-level overview of the collection is likely to be, as prior clustering systems have shown [7, 23].

Provide Workflow Details to Support Comparison Tasks

In comparison tasks, users used the list view to identify interesting workflows, then read the details of the workflow to make a final judgment. Although one user only used the workflow summaries to complete the comparison tasks, the others read the details of the workflow. This indicates that providing access to the source material is imperative.

Show One View at a Time to Reduce Information Overload

One of the biggest problems users encountered was information overload; in fact, one user did not complete the *Three approaches* task, saying he was "overwhelmed." A possible solution lies in our observation that users did not rapidly switch between views. In addition, although the list view and cluster view were linked (clicking on a workflow in the cluster view scrolled to the corresponding workflow in the list view), users did not make use of this link. This means that the system could display panels separately instead of all at once on the screen.

Study Limitations

Our study has several limitations worth noting. Participants were introduced to Delta through a five minute walkthrough of the interface by the experimenter. Given this short amount of time, users may have preferred familiar interface components, such as the list view, at the expense of unfamiliar components, such as the cluster view. Extended use with the system may result in different behavior.

In Study 1, users reported that they used tutorials serially: they would find a workflow, try it out in Photoshop, and only look for another if the first wasn't satisfactory. Users might exhibit different behavior if our system were integrated into Photoshop; we leave this to future work.

Finally, we did not test how accurate users' choices were. For example, we do not know if users chose the workflow that would be quickest for them to complete, as we did not have them complete the workflow after they had chosen it. However, our tool was designed to elicit user behavior and was not designed as a final solution to the problem of workflow exploration.

FUTURE WORK AND CONCLUSION

We have studied users' criteria when choosing workflows and designed a new interactive application to support that process based on the results. Our study indicates that the application provides subjective benefits in comparison to the traditional means of using a web browser to locate and compare workflows.

The results of our studies provide many directions for future work. In particular, we found that users consider command familiarity when comparing workflows.

Integrating this tool into a system would allow us to use an individual's command use to provide better ordering in the list view, or a better similarity metric for the cluster view.

In addition, we did not use any "broken" workflows in our study, or workflows that do not result in their claimed effect. Testing whether our system allows users to avoid such workflows is another direction for future work.

We would also like to explore how well our system scales and what designs will work best as the number of workflows increases, or when the workflows become longer, such as those in Chronicle [11] or MeshFlow [8].

Finally, we are actively working on automatically extracting workflows from websites that contain tutorials. Our results indicate that just the accurate extraction of commands and illustrative images from a tutorial would greatly enhance search efficacy. In addition, automatic workflow extraction will help us explore how our tool scales by opening our tool to a large number of workflows. Although using workflow recording systems would be an easy method to provide data to our system, such systems are currently not widely used.

ACKNOWLEDGMENTS

We thank our study participants. This work was partially supported by NSF grant CCF-0643552.

REFERENCES

1. Andrews, K., Wohlfahrt, M., and Wurzinger, G. Visual Graph Comparison. *Info. Vis.*, pp. 62-67, 2009.
2. Bederson, B., Shneiderman, B., and Wattenberg, M. Ordered and quantum treemaps: Making effective use of 2D space to display hierarchies. *ACM Trans. Graph*, **21**(4):833-854, 2002.
3. Chen, H.-T., Wei, L.-Y. and Chang, C.-F. Nonlinear Revision Control for Images. *ACM Trans. Graph*, **30**(4), Article 105, 2011.
4. Chi, E. H., Pirolli, P., Chen, K., and Pitkow, J. Using information scent to model user information needs and actions and the Web. *ACM CHI*, pp. 490-497, 2001.
5. Chi, E., Pirolli, P., and Pitkow, J. The scent of a site: a system for analyzing and predicting information scent, usage, and usability of a Web site. *ACM CHI*, pp. 161-168, 2000.
6. Cutrell, E. and Guan Z. What are you looking for?: an eye-tracking study of information usage in web search. *ACM CHI*. pp. 407-416. 2007.
7. Cutting, D., Karger, D., Pedersen, J., and Tukey, J. Scatter/Gather: a cluster-based approach to browsing large document collections. *SIGIR*. pp. 318-329. 1992.
8. Denning, J. D., Kerr, W. B., and Pellacini, F. MeshFlow: Interactive Visualization of Mesh Construction Sequences. *ACM Trans. Graph*, **30**(4), Article 66, 2011.
9. Dorn, B. and Guzdial, M. Learning on the job: characterizing the programming knowledge and learning strategies of web designers. *ACM CHI*, pp. 703-712. 2010.
10. Grabler, F., Agrawala, M., Li, W., Dontcheva, M. and Igarashi, T. Generating Photo Manipulation Tutorials by Demonstration. *SIGGRAPH*. pp. 66:1-66:9, 2009.
11. Grossman, T., Matejka, J. and Fitzmaurice, G. Chronicle: Capture, Exploration, and Playback of Document Workflow Histories. *UIST*, pp. 143-152, 2010.
12. Grossman, T., Fitzmaurice, G. and Attar, R. A Survey of Software Learnability: Metrics, Methodologies and Guidelines. *ACM CHI*, pp. 649-658, 2009.
13. Guan. Z., and Cutrell, E. An eye tracking study of the effect of target rank on web search. *ACM CHI*, pp. 417-420, 2007.
14. Hearst, M. *Search User Interfaces* (1st ed.). Cambridge University Press, New York, NY, USA. 2009.
15. Heer, J., Mackinlay, J., Stolte, C. and Agrawala, M. Graphical Histories for Visualization: Supporting Analysis, Communication, and Evaluation. *IEEE TVCG*, pp. 1189-1196, 2008.
16. Jing, F. Wang, W., Yao, Y., Deng, K., Zhang, L., and Ma, W.-Y. IGroup: web image search results clustering. *ACM Multimedia*, pp. 377-384, 2006.
17. Koop, D., Scheidegger, C., Callahan, S., Freire, J., and Silva, C. VisComplete: Automating Suggestions for Visualization Pipelines. *IEEE TVCG*, pp. 1691-1698, 2008.
18. Kurlander, D.,and Feiner, S. Editable graphical histories. *IEEE Visual Languages, pp.* 127-134, 1988.
19. LaFreniere, B., Bunt, A., Lount, M., Krynicki, F., and Terry, M. AdaptableGIMP: designing a socially-adaptable interface. *UIST Adjunct*, pp. 89-90. 2011.
20. Lee, B., Srivastava, S., Kumar, R., Brafman, R., and Klemmer, S. Designing with Interactive Example Galleries. *ACM CHI*, pp. 2257-2266, 2010.
21. Nakamura, T. and Igarashi, I. An application-independent system for visualizing user operation history. *UIST*, pp. 23-32, 2008.
22. Pirolli, P. and Card, S. Information foraging. *Psychological Review*, **106**(4):643-675, 1999.
23. Santos, E., Lins, L., Ahrens, J., Freire, J., and Silva, C. A first study on clustering collections of workflow graphs. *IPAW*, pp. 160-173, 2008.
24. Sorokin, A. and Forsyth, D. Utility data annotation with Amazon Mechanical Turk. *CVPRW*, pp.1-8, 2008.
25. Wagner, R. and Fischer, M. The String-to-String Correction Problem. *J. ACM*, **21**(1):168-173, 1974.

QuickDraw: Improving Drawing Experience for Geometric Diagrams

Salman Cheema
University of Central Florida
Orlando, FL
salmanc@cs.ucf.edu

Sumit Gulwani
Microsoft Research
Redmond, WA
sumitg@microsoft.com

Joseph J. LaViola Jr.
University of Central Florida
Orlando, FL
jjl@eecs.ucf.edu

ABSTRACT
We present QuickDraw, a prototype sketch-based drawing tool, that facilitates drawing of precise geometry diagrams that are often drawn by students and academics in several scientific disciplines. Quickdraw can recognize sketched diagrams containing components such as line segments and circles, infer geometric constraints relating recognized components, and use this information to beautify the sketched diagram. Beautification is based on a novel algorithm that iteratively computes various sub-components of the components using an extensible set of deductive rules. We conducted a user study comparing QuickDraw with four state-of-the-art diagramming tools: Microsoft PowerPoint, Cabri II Plus, Geometry Expressions and Geometer's SketchPad. Our study demonstrates a strong interest among participants for the use of sketch-based software for drawing geometric diagrams. We also found that QuickDraw enables users to draw precise diagrams faster than the majority of existing tools in some cases, while having them make fewer corrections.

Author Keywords
Sketch-based Interfaces; Sketch Recognition; Sketch Beautification; Geometry Constraint Solving

ACM Classification Keywords
G.4 Mathematical Software: User Interfaces; H.5.2. User Interfaces: Interaction Styles

General Terms
Algorithms, Experimentation, Human Factors, Measurement

INTRODUCTION
Students and teachers in scientific disciplines often have to draw very precise diagrams. Drawing such diagrams is very time consuming and cumbersome, motivating the development of software to aid diagramming. For geometric drawings, popular tools include Geometer's Sketchpad [6], Cabri II Plus [3], and Geometry Expressions [7]. Additionally, a growing number of people use Microsoft Office products such as PowerPoint [16] to draw diagrams, due to the availability of several drawing templates for common shapes within the Microsoft Office suite.

Permission to make digital or hard copies of all or part of this work for personal or classroom use is granted without fee provided that copies are not made or distributed for profit or commercial advantage and that copies bear this notice and the full citation on the first page. To copy otherwise, or republish, to post on servers or to redistribute to lists, requires prior specific permission and/or a fee.
CHI'12, May 5–10, 2012, Austin, Texas, USA.
Copyright 2012 ACM 978-1-4503-1015-4/12/05...$10.00.

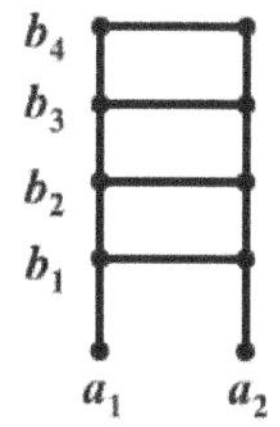

Figure 1. Source : NCERT Mathematics Book, Grade 11, Chapter 2

Figure 1 shows an example of a geometry diagram. Here, a user wants to draw a ladder with four rungs. Notice that a_1 and a_2 are both vertical and have the same length. Both a_1 and a_2 begin and end at the same horizontal level. Additionally, line segments b_1, b_2, b_3, b_4 are horizontal, equidistant, of same length and are all perpendicular to both a_1 and a_2. Also, b_1, b_2, b_3, b_4 begin and end at the same vertical level. It is clear that this deceptively simple diagram would require a fair amount of effort if one was to do the construction precisely, even with existing state-of-the-art tools.

Our research goal is to investigate the use of sketch-based interfaces for drawing precise diagrams since they can provide significant benefits over existing tools. Sketch-based interfaces closely mimic pen and paper and let a user draw very naturally. They can also lower the input complexity of a diagram construction tool. We believe that by leveraging techniques from areas of sketch recognition, machine learning, and geometry constraint solving, it is possible to build a sketch-based drawing tool that can reduce the difficulty of precisely drawing a given diagram and thus enhance the productivity of users in various scientific fields. To this end, we have developed QuickDraw, a prototype sketch-based diagram drawing tool, that allows a user to sketch and beautify a given diagram. QuickDraw can process the input sketch to recognize components of the diagram and the geometric relationships between them. We examined various elementary mathematics and science text books to come up with a set of geometric constraints that can be used to beautify a large subset of diagrams found in the appropriate books. The set of inferred constraints is used to beautify the input sketch. Figure 2 provides an example of such a beautification, where QuickDraw converts the user's sketch on the left into the precise diagram on the right.

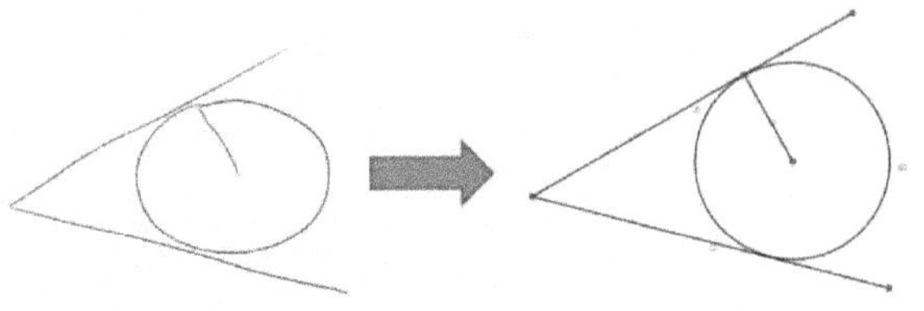

Figure 2. A diagram beautified by QuickDraw. The input sketch is shown on the left, while the beautified diagram is shown on the right. If a user was to construct this diagram in a traditional diagram construction tool, it would require a great amount of precision to ensure the tangent constraints.

We conducted a usability study to compare drawing performance in QuickDraw with four state-of-the-art diagram construction tools. It should be noted that QuickDraw is fundamentally different from the other tools in our study. The others tools rely on the use of pre-defined templates to let a user construct a diagram that is a close approximation of what the user has in mind. QuickDraw allows a user to express intent by sketching the diagram itself. It then tries to understand the user's intent through sketch and constraint recognition. Using its unique beautification algorithm, it can generate a mathematically precise diagram as opposed to a close approximation with other tools.

RELATED WORK

In general, sketch recognition is a hard problem due to the complexity and variation in notation in different disciplines. User perception of sketch recognition has been explored by Wais, Wolin, and Alvarado [19], yielding useful insights for designers of sketch-based interfaces. CogSketch [5] is an open domain sketch analysis system which enables conceptual labeling of sketches. Hammond et al., have developed LADDER [9] which lets users specify recognition rules for sketch primitives and some high level semantics in text form. LADDER can generate domain-specific recognizers from such text descriptions. MathPad^2 [14] is a domain independent system that allows users to associate written mathematics with a sketched diagram to perform animation. None of these systems focus on enabling a user to easily sketch a precise diagram.

Techniques for sketch beautification have also been explored by several researchers. PaleoSketch [18] explores techniques for recognition of low-level sketch primitives and beautification. It can recognize a large set of sketch primitives, but the beautification aspect of this system is very low level and applies only to individual primitives. Lineogrammer [21] is a modeless diagramming tool that enables users to construct diagrams by interactively beautifying ink strokes. However, it does not leverage the power of geometric constraint reasoning and performs very limited beautification. In contrast to both of these, QuickDraw infers a user's intent by recognizing constraints relating sketched primitive components and uses this information to beautify the entire sketch, instead of just individual components. Igarashi et al., [11] have investigated the use of inferred geometric constraints for interactively beautifying a sketched diagram. QuickDraw offers several benefits

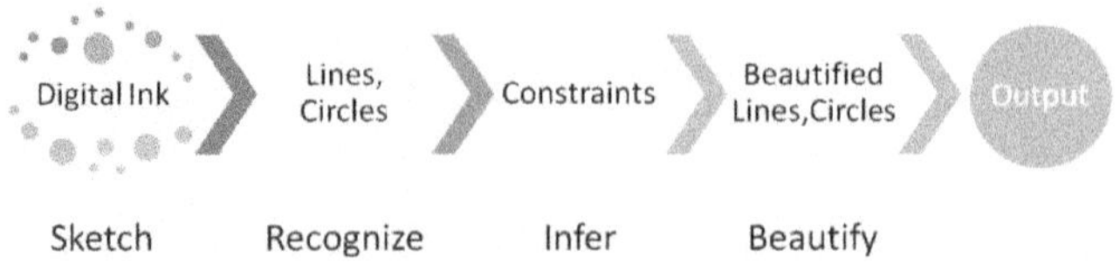

Figure 3. The flow of information within QuickDraw. A user's sketch is recognized and geometric constraints are inferred, which are then used for beautification, resulting in a precisely rendered diagram.

in relation to their approach. First, we support an extensible set of diagram components including lines and circles, and an extensible set of inferred constraints between components (earlier work by Igarahi et.al is limited to line segments). Second, we employ a novel beautification algorithm to beautify diagrams that are either very hard to draw with the earlier approach or cannot be drawn altogether.

Our beautification algorithm uses an extensible set of deductive rules to solve geometric constraints for model construction. There are several existing approaches to constraint solving. The goal here is to find a configuration for a set of geometric objects that satisfy a given set of constraints between the geometric elements [2]. A variety of techniques have been proposed including logical inference and term rewriting [1], numerical methods [17], algebraic methods [13], and graph based constraint solving [2]. These techniques either require some symbolic reasoning or some form of search. QuickDraw's beautification algorithm is also a form of geometry constraint solving. However, it is much simpler because it deals with saturated constraints, which obviate the need for any sophisticated symbolic reasoning or search. This makes our beautification technique more efficient and hence realtime.

With regards to geometry education, Jiang et al., have developed PenProof [12] which is a sketch-based geometry theorem proving system. Its focus is on correlating steps in a hand-written proof with aspects of the sketch. Another recent system is IIPW [15], which is a framework of tools for interactive geometry editing on a whiteboard. While this tool can beautify diagrams using the Line Intersection Method, it relies heavily on pre-defined templates to specify geometric constraints. Gulwani et.al. have developed a method for automatically synthesizing ruler/compass based geometry constructions starting from declarative specifications [8]. Their method starts out by translating the declarative specification into a model using numerical search. In principle, declarative specification can be replaced by an easier sketch-based specification, while model construction can be performed using our beautification algorithm.

QUICKDRAW : AN OVERVIEW

In its current form, QuickDraw can recognize and beautify diagrams containing line segments and circles. Figure 3 shows the flow of information among the subsystems of QuickDraw. A user sketches a diagram using a stylus on a tablet computer. QuickDraw recognizes the components of the sketch and infers the geometric relationships between them. Using this information, it beautifies the sketch, resulting in a precisely rendered diagram from approximate sketch input.

Constraints recognized by QuickDraw	
Applicable To	Constraint
Line Segments	Vertical line segment
	Horizontal line segment
	Collinear line segments
	Parallel line segments
	Perpendicular line segments
	Equidistant line segments
	Touching line segments
	Intersecting line segments
	Line segments with same length
	Line segments with endpoint(s) at same horizontal level
	Line segments with endpoint(s) at same vertical level
Circles	Circles with same radius
	Concentric circles
	Circles touching at their circumference
	Intersecting Circles
	Circle passing through the center of another circle
Circles & Line Segments	Line segment tangent to circle
	Line segment intersecting circle
	Line segment passing through center of circle
	Line segment touching circumference with an endpoint
	Line segment touching circle center with an endpoint

Table 1. Table showing all the constraints that can be recognized by QuickDraw's inference subsystem. The constraints can be grouped into three categories depending on the type of sketch components that are related by them.

Recognition

A sketched diagram forms the input to QuickDraw. Recognition in QuickDraw is a two step process. First, the sketch is parsed into diagram (basic) components. QuickDraw can recognize line segments and circles as components. Our recognition heuristics rely on the IStraw cusp finding algorithm [20]. A cusp is a region of high curvature in a digital ink stroke. An ink stroke corresponding to a circle has two cusps, its starting and ending points, both of which should be close together, resulting in a closed shape. A circle also has approximately uniform curvature about its centroid. To measure curvature in an ink stroke, QuickDraw applies a threshold to the standard deviation in the radius of an ink stroke. Once an ink stroke is classified as a circle, its centroid is assigned as the center of the circle. The diameter of the circle is assigned as the average of the width and height of the ink stroke's bounding box. Similarly, an ink stroke corresponding to a line segment has two cusps, and is approximately straight. To check if an ink stroke forms an approximately straight line, we use a measure similar to the approach in IStraw [20]:

$$Linearity = \|1.0 - \frac{\sum_{i=1}^{n-1} \|p_i, p_{i+1}\|}{\|p_1, p_n\|}\|$$

where p_i is the ith point in the ink stroke. We use a threshold of $Linearity < 0.1$ to detect line segments. Ink strokes containing more than two cusps are broken down into components containing two cusps each, which are then examined using the heuristics described above. Recognized sketch components are assigned a canonical ordering $\mathcal{O}$, from left to right followed by top to bottom. This is done to ensure that a deterministic view of each diagram emerges, independent of the order in which its components were drawn.

Algorithm 1 Beautification Algorithm

$\{\tilde{C}$ = Set of Components; α = Set of Constraints; $\}$
Require: $\tilde{C}, \alpha$
  A := Set of all sub-components of components in $\tilde{C}$;
  B := $\emptyset$;
  while B $\neq$ A **do**
    if A $-$ B contains a sub-component s that is computable from sub-components in B because of α (using V) **then**
      Compute s;
    else
      s := sub-component from A $-$ B with the highest rank.
      Read value of s from sketch.
    end if
    B := B $\cup \{s\}$;
    C := parent component of s.
    if C is determined from its sub-components in B (using U) **then**
      Beautify C; B := B $\cup$ Sub-components of C;
    end if
  end while

Beautification

The recognition engine recognizes basic components C (lines and circles). After this, the inference subsystem infers the intended constraints between recognized components (see Table 1 for supported constraints). We now describe a generic and extensible beautification algorithm (Algorithm 1) that takes as input the recognized components and inferred constraints between them, and translates them into a precise geometric drawing whose components satisfy the intended constraints.

Each component C has constituent sub-components s such that it can be uniquely determined after some appropriate subset of its sub-components have been determined. For example, the sub-components of a line segment are its slope, intercept (y-Intercept if slope is not vertical; otherwise x-Intercept), length, and x/y coordinates of the two end points. A line segment can be uniquely determined from the x/y coordinates of the two end points, or alternatively from its slope, intercept and y coordinates of its two end points (if the slope is not vertical). Similarly, the sub-components of a circle are its radius and the coordinates of its center. A circle is uniquely determined if all of its sub-components are known. This knowledge is captured as an extensible set of rules U.

The idea behind defining constituent sub-components for each component is that the constraints between components uniquely identify some of their sub-components. This knowledge is captured as an extensible set of rules V, each of which specifies how to determine the value of some sub-component from values of some other sub-components under some appropriate constraints. For example, under the constraint that a line L is tangent to a circle C, C.radius can be computed from C.center, L.slope, L.intercept. In particular, C.radius can be computed as the perpendicular distance between C.center and the line determined by L.slope and L.intercept. As another example, under the same constraint that a line L is tangent to a circle C, L.intercept can be computed from L.slope, C.center, and C.radius.

Our beautification algorithm maintains a worklist B that holds the set of all sub-components whose values have been computed. B is initialized to the empty set. The main loop of the beautification algorithm is repeated until B is equal to set A that holds all sub-components of all recognized components. Each iteration of the main loop attempts to identify a sub-component $s \in (\mathtt{A} - \mathtt{B})$ (of some component C) whose value can be computed from the sub-components in B using any of the rules V : s is then added to B. If component C is uniquely determined from its sub-components in B using any of the rules U, then C is beautified and all of its sub-components are added to B.

If no such sub-component s exists, then to maintain progress, the algorithm identifies a sub-component $s \in (\mathtt{A} - \mathtt{B})$ with the highest rank. The rank of a sub-component s of a component C is given by lexicographic ordering on the following tuple:

$$\mathtt{Rank}(s) = \left(\mathtt{Max}_S \left\{ \frac{\sum_{s' \in S \cap \mathtt{B}} W(s')}{\sum_{s' \in S} W(s')} \right\}, \mathcal{O}(C), \frac{1}{W(s)} \right)$$

An interesting element of the above rank tuple is a weight function W that maps each sub-component type to some score between 0 and 1 and is used to assert the relative importance of knowing some sub-component over another. More specifically, the relative weight ordering reflects the order of observing any visual discrepancies (thereby avoiding the need to edit components unless really required), and also the order of ease of editing components if QuickDraw didn't get it right. For our experiments, we used the following relative weights: (a) Sub-components of a line-segment: x-y coordinates of the two end-points and length (0.5 each), intercept (0.75), slope (1). (b) Sub-components of a circle: x-y coordinates of the two end-points (0.5 each), radius (1).

The first element of the rank tuple identifies a component C that is closest to being determined. This is estimated by computing the maximum of the weighted ratio of the sub-components that are known from among some minimal set of sub-components S of C that uniquely determine the component C. The second element of the rank tuple breaks any ties among C by using the canonical ordering $\mathcal{O}(C)$ assigned to the component at recognition time. The third element of the rank tuple identifies a sub-component s of component C that has the lowest weight. In the future, we plan to refine the rank computation by taking into account the probability of the constraint recognized by the recognition engine and using these probabilities to associate a confidence score with each computed sub-component. The value of the sub-component

Figure 4. A approximate square sketched in QuickDraw.

s with the highest rank is then read off from the sketch. C is then beautified and all of its sub-components are added to B.

The beautification algorithm has two interesting characteristics: robustness and interactive support. The algorithm is robust due to the powerful deductive reasoning enabled by an extensible set of rules U and V over a saturated set of constraints returned by the inference engine. This allows it to correctly beautify diagrams when the recognition engine misses out on some constraints. The algorithm also allows for interactive drawing. The main loop of the algorithm can be run in an incremental fashion after adding sub-components of any new component sketched by the user to A and updating the set of constraints.

Example: A Sketched Square

Given the sketched square in Figure 4, QuickDraw should ideally infer the following constraints between four recognized line segments:

1. Two line segments are horizontal and two are vertical.
2. The horizontal line segments are parallel, and are both perpendicular to the vertical line segments.
3. The vertical line segments are parallel, and are both perpendicular to the horizontal line segments.
4. All the line segments in the sketch form a connected path, and are all equal in length.
5. The perpendicular distance between horizontal line segments is the same as that between vertical line segments.

Beautification now proceeds as follows. (i) After computing the slope of all the line-segments, the algorithm reads off the x-y coordinates of the top-left corner and the y-coordinate of the bottom-left corner from the sketch and then beautifies the left line-segment. (ii) Next, the algorithm computes the y coordinate of the top-right corner from the y coordinate of the top-left corner (because of the top line-segment having horizontal slope constraint), and then the x coordinate of the top-right corner from the two left corners (because of the equal length constraint between the top and left line-segments), and then beautifies the top line-segment. (iii) In a manner similar to the previous case, the algorithm computes the y coordinate of the bottom-right corner from the y coordinate of the bottom-left corner (because of the bottom line-segment having horizontal slope constraint), and then the x coordinate of the bottom-right corner from the two left corners (because of the equal length constraint between the bottom and left line-segments), and then beautifies the bottom line-segment. However, suppose that the inference engine failed to infer any equal length constraint involving the bottom line-

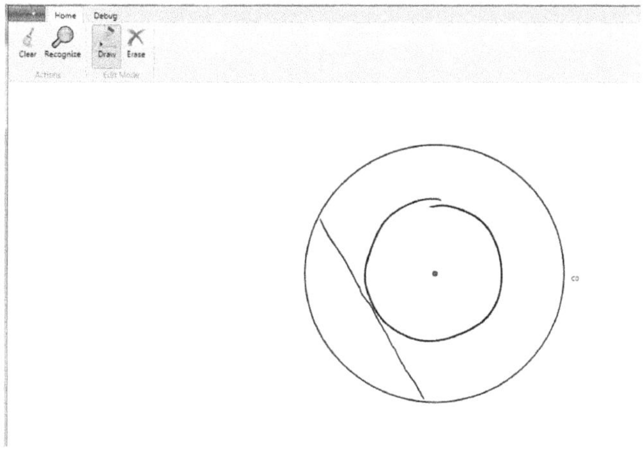

Figure 5. A diagram sketched in QuickDraw. In this case, the user has sketch the diagram incrementally. The outer circle has already been drawn, recognized and beautified. The inner circle and its tangent have just been sketched and await recognition.

segment. The algorithm can still compute the x coordinate of the bottom-right corner from the x coordinate of the top-right corner (because of the right line-segment having vertical slope constraint). However, suppose that the inference engine also failed to infer the vertical slope constraint for the right line-segment. The algorithm can still compute the slope of the right line-segment from the slope of the top line-segment (because of the perpendicular constraint between the top and right line-segments) followed by computing the intercept of the right line-segment from the x coordinate of the top-right corner. The algorithm can then compute the x coordinate of the bottom-right corner from the two top corners (because of the equal length constraint between the right and top line-segments). These instances of missing constraints highlight the robustness of our beautification algorithm, which is able to make up for the missing constraints by making effective use of other (logically equivalent) constraints.

User Interaction

Figure 5 shows the user interface for QuickDraw. Users can sketch a drawing in two ways. They may sketch the entire drawing and then trigger recognition by hitting the 'Recognize' button. However this method does not provide instant recognition feedback. Users can also sketch incrementally (i.e., they sketch one component at a time), hitting 'Recognize' after each step. QuickDraw supports both of these sketching methodologies. For a future version, we are planning to add support for automatically rendering a component as soon as it gets uniquely determined.

It must be kept in mind that the goal of QuickDraw is to come up with a precise diagram, given a user's sketch as input. However, it is possible for the recognition and constraint inference engine in QuickDraw to make a mistake. Some are minor and can be rectified by manipulating the positions of beautified sketch components. Each sketch component has one or more 'edit' points which can be used to manipulate its position. These edit points are highlighted in blue on the screen. For a line segment, these are its endpoints. For a circle, its center can be used to move it. A user can hold the stylus over an edit point for a few seconds to select it. Once selected, the point can be moved with the stylus to wherever the user requires.

Figure 6. A photograph showing the tablet computer used for our experiment.

Using QuickDraw, a user can draw any diagram containing lines, polygons and circles. However, we cannot beautify all such drawings since precise reasoning of geometric constraints reduces to reasoning about non-linear arithmetic, which is a hard problem. Specifically, we cannot beautify drawings that require construction of intermediate objects or drawing of arbitrary angles (e.g., drawing a regular pentagon requires either drawing an angle of 108 degrees, or drawing several temporary objects). The current version of QuickDraw also has limited editing capabilities. Entire line segments cannot be moved. A user must move both endpoints separately. QuickDraw also does not allow users to resize circles. For more major inference errors, a user can remove the offending sketch component by going into 'Erase' mode and then redrawing it. Note that QuickDraw in its current form is a prototype and was engineered to focus primarily on the recognition, inference and beautification aspects of the system. As of yet, we have not invested fully into adding enhanced editing capabilities. However, one of the goals of our usability study was also to investigate diagram drawing strategies which would yield insights into the type of editing functionality required by QuickDraw.

USABILITY STUDY

We conducted a user study to compare drawing performance in QuickDraw with four state-of-the-art diagramming tools: Cabri II Plus, Geometry Expressions, Geometer's SketchPad, and Microsoft PowerPoint. The first three tools were chosen because they are very popular and for their capabilities in aiding a user in geometrical drawings. Microsoft PowerPoint was chosen due to its widespread use and convenience for drawing diagrams. Our primary objective in this study was to compare QuickDraw with traditional WIMP (Windows, Icons, Menus, Pointers) based drawing tools. A related question is how does the drawing performance scale with diagram difficulty for each tool. Lastly, we wanted to get user feedback concerning the use of sketch-based interfaces for diagram drawing.

Easy Difficulty	Medium Difficulty	Hard Difficulty
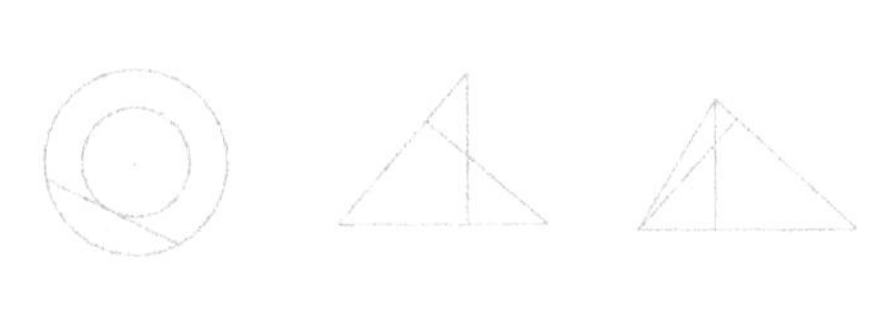	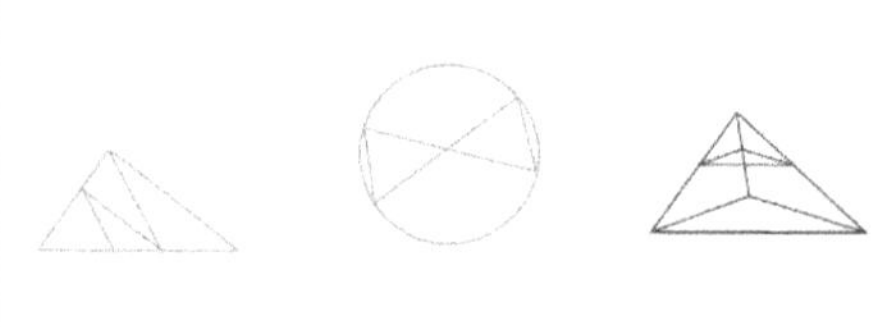	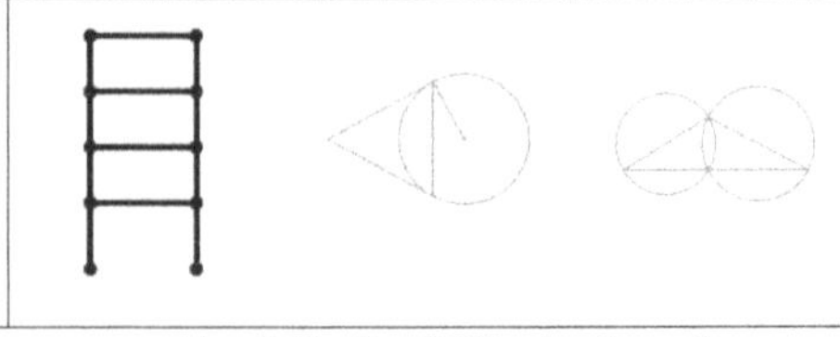

Table 2. This figure shows the diagrams that were drawn by participants in our study. They have been grouped by difficulty. Difficulty for a diagram was determined by (i) number of components in the diagram and (ii) number of constraints that a person would have to ensure while drawing it. We conducted a pilot study with two volunteers that allowed us to verify the difficulty for these diagrams.

Subjects and Apparatus

We recruited 19 participants (17 male and 2 female) from the University of Central Florida for participation in the study. The ages of participants were between 18 and 37 years. They were asked to draw nine diagrams with each of the diagramming tools. Each participant took 90-120 minutes to complete the experiment and was paid $10 for their time. Only one participant was left-handed. Eleven participants had used a computer with stylus input before. Nine participants reported that they often used a computer for drawing diagrams. None of the participants had used Cabri II Plus, Geometer's SketchPad or Geometry Expressions before the experiment. On the other hand, only one person was not familiar with Microsoft PowerPoint. Figure 6 shows the experiment setup for our user study.

The experiment was conducted on a Lenovo ThinkPad X220 multi-touch tablet computer equipped with an Intel Core-i7-2620M processor and four gigabytes of memory. The screen resolution was set at 1366x768 pixels. We disabled multi-touch interaction on the tablet which was placed on a table for the experiment. Participants sat down and drew each diagram either with the mouse or the stylus, depending on the tool being used. Each participant's drawing session was recorded by screen capture via the Fraps utility. For analysis purposes, we divided the diagrams used in the experiment into three categories, based on drawing difficulty (see Table 2). The difficulty of a diagram was initially determined based on the number of constraints that a user would have to ensure while drawing that diagram. The assigned order of difficulty was tested and confirmed during a pilot study with two volunteers.

Experiment Procedure

Each participant was asked to fill out a pre-questionnaire, which collected demographic information. The participant was given a tutorial of each of the diagramming tools to be used in the experiment. They were shown how to draw basic diagram components such as line segments, circles, triangles, and polygons. They were also shown how to edit each component's position and size. Lastly, they were shown how to erase diagram components in each tool. For QuickDraw, participants were explicitly told they could either sketch the entire diagram and then trigger recognition, or they could do recognition incrementally by sketching and recognizing parts of it. After the tutorial, the participant was given a set of three practice diagrams (see Table 3). They were asked to use each tool to draw all three practice diagrams. This helped familiarize the participants with each tool. Participants were also asked to be very precise in their drawing.

Table 3. Practice diagrams used to familiarize participants with each diagramming tool.

After the practice session, participants were asked to draw nine diagrams with each tool. The drawing difficulty of each diagram was not communicated to participants. Each diagram had written instructions about relationships that participants needed to ensure while drawing. Participants were told that they should complete each diagram to ensure that the written instructions were satisfied as closely as possible. Participants were then told they had three minutes to complete each diagram. This time limit was decided during our pilot study during which all volunteers were able to complete all diagrams in under three minutes. The order in which diagramming tools were used was randomized for each participant. For each diagramming tool, the order in which participants drew diagrams was also randomized. Table 2 shows the diagrams used in the experiment. The entire session was recorded via screen capture. Furthermore, a proctor monitored each participant throughout the session and noted the time taken to complete each diagram with each tool. The number of editing operations performed by participants was also noted down for each diagram and tool combination. Editing operations included copy-paste, manipulating positions of diagram elements, and erasing diagram elements. At the end of the experiment, participants were given a post-questionnaire, allowing them to give feedback about their experience with each tool.

METRICS

We recorded two quantitative metrics for each diagram drawn by a participant:

- *Completion Time* : Time taken to complete a diagram in a particular software tool.
- *Edits* : Number of editing operations performed in a software tool to complete a diagram.

These metrics allowed us to compare the tools in terms of how easily a user can complete a given diagram. Additionally, we also wanted to measure QuickDraw's failure rate. As mentioned before, QuickDraw can fail due to incorrect recognition of constraints. In such cases, users had to make alterations to the beautified diagram. Minor errors were fixed by editing the positions of beautified diagram components. Se-

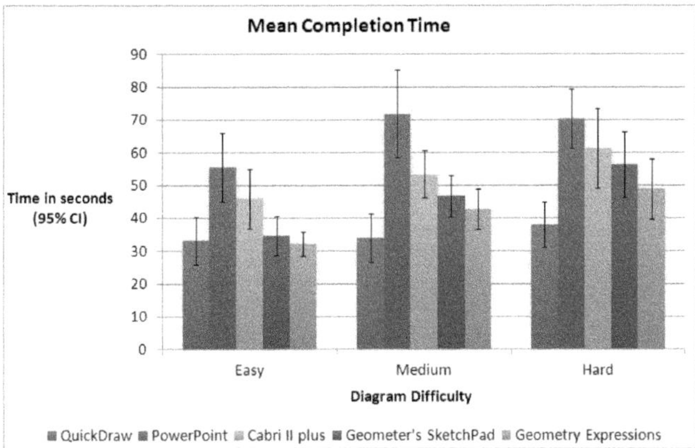

Figure 7. Mean time to complete a given diagram in each of the different software tools examined in our study.

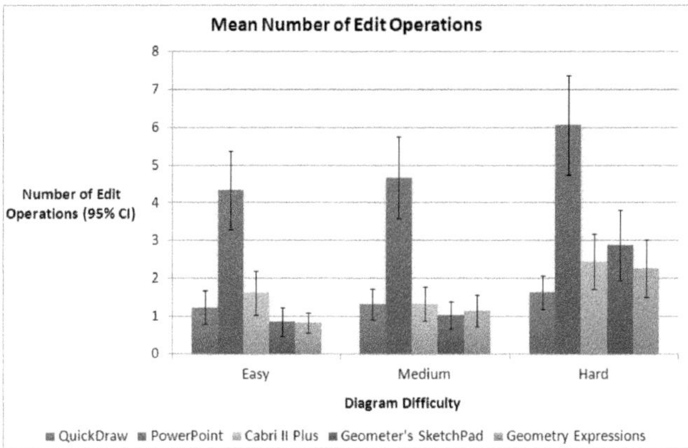

Figure 8. Mean number of editing operations to complete a given diagram in each of the different software tools examined in our study.

vere errors required a user to erase and redraw part or all of the diagram. Specifically, we were interested in measuring the probability that a user would not be able to complete a diagram in the allotted time due to an error by QuickDraw's constraint inference subsystem.

Difficulty	Easy	Medium	Hard
Failure Rate	0%	10.526%	12.281%
Overall Failure Rate 7.602%			

Table 4. Failure rate for diagrams in each category of drawing difficulty.

For this purpose, whenever a participant was not able to complete a diagram with QuickDraw in the allotted time due to a severe error, the proctor made a note of it. By analyzing the session videos recorded for each participant, we conclude that these instances of failure were primarily the result of incorrect constraint inference. They become severe when the inference system infers a false constraint (as opposed to missing a constraint). Table 4 shows the rate of occurrence of failure instances for each category of diagram difficulty.

It should be noted that the other tools in our study do not utilize any sort of diagram recognition or beautification. Instead, they require a user to construct a precise diagram through use of predefined templates. QuickDraw on the other hand relies on correct recognition of a sketched diagram and the constraints contained therein to produce a precise diagram. As participants were given 3 minutes to complete a diagram, it is possible for them to fail to complete a diagram in QuickDraw due to inference errors. Including such instances of failure would inflate some data points for QuickDraw to a constant 180 seconds. As these cannot be directly compared to the completion times in the other tools in our study, we chose to disregard such instances of failure where participants were unable to complete a given diagram in QuickDraw in the allotted time.

FINDINGS

Analysis of Metrics

Figure 7 shows the mean time to complete a given diagram in each of the software tools tested in our study. Similarly, Figure 8 shows the mean number of editing operations required to complete a given diagram. The data in both figures are grouped by drawing difficulty. For each category of difficulty, we used a 5-way repeated measures ANOVA analysis to test for significant differences in completion time and edits between QuickDraw and other tools. If we found significant differences with respect to either mean completion time or mean number of edits, we conducted a post-hoc analysis with pairwise t-tests to find the interesting differences. In our post-hoc analysis, we controlled the chance of Type I errors by using a Holm's Sequential Bonferroni adjustment with four comparisons at $\alpha = 0.05$ [10].

Diagrams with Easy Difficulty

We found significant differences between QuickDraw and the other tools for both completion time ($F_{4,14} = 7.692, p < 0.001$) and number of editing operations ($F_{4,14} = 22.826, p < 0.001$). Using pairwise t-tests, we found that the mean completion time for an easy diagram in QuickDraw is less than Microsoft PowerPoint ($t_{18} = -3.325, p < 0.0125$). Due to the Bonferroni adjustment, the difference in completion time between QuickDraw and Cabri II Plus ($t_{18} = -2.570, p = 0.019$) was not found to be significant. However, the small p-value suggests that this difference may be significant with more participants. We found no significant differences for completion time between QuickDraw and Geometer's SketchPad or Geometry Expressions. We also found that participants performed fewer edits in QuickDraw than in Microsoft PowerPoint ($t_{18} = -5.41, p < 0.0125$). There were no significant differences in the number of edits performed in QuickDraw and in either Cabri II Plus , Geometer's SketchPad or Geometry Expressions.

Diagrams with Medium Difficulty

Once again, we found significant differences between QuickDraw and the other tools for both completion time ($F_{4,14} = 15.553, p < 0.001$) and number of edits ($F_{4,14} = 29.003, p < 0.001$). The results of pairwise t-tests indicate that completion time for a medium difficulty diagram in QuickDraw is less than in Microsoft PowerPoint ($t_{18} = -6.667, p < 0.0125$), Cabri II Plus ($t_{18} = -4.586, p < 0.0167$) and Geometer's SketchPad ($t_{18} = -3.002, p < 0.025$). There was no significant difference between QuickDraw and Geometry Expressions in terms of the time taken to complete a medium difficulty diagram. Additionally, participants performed fewer edits in QuickDraw than in Microsoft PowerPoint ($t_{18} = -5.691, p < 0.0125$). There were no significant differences in the number of edits performed in QuickDraw and in either Cabri II Plus, Geometer's SketchPad or Geometry Expressions.

Diagrams With Hard Difficulty

Within the hard difficulty category, we found significant differences between QuickDraw and other tools for both completion time ($F_{4,14} = 8.665, p < 0.001$) and number of edits ($F_{4,14} = 21.208, p < 0.001$). We found participants took less time to complete hard diagrams in QuickDraw than in Microsoft PowerPoint ($t_{18} = -8.781, p < 0.0125$), Cabri II Plus ($t_{18} = -3.489, p < 0.0167$) or Geometer's SketchPad ($t_{18} = -3.222, p < 0.025$). There was no significant difference in completion time between QuickDraw and Geometry Expressions for hard to draw diagrams. Participants also performed fewer edits in QuickDraw than in Microsoft PowerPoint ($t_{18} = -6.788, p < 0.0167$). Due to the Bonferroni adjustment, the difference in edit operations between QuickDraw and Cabri II Plus ($t_{18} = -2.378, p = 0.029$) and between QuickDraw and Geometer's SketchPad ($t_{18} = -2.541, p = 0.020$) was insignificant. There was no significant difference in the number of editing operations performed in QuickDraw and Geometry Expressions.

Factors Affecting Completion Time

Completion time, as defined earlier, is a broad metric, which glosses over a lot of detail. Several factors influence the completion time for a given diagram in a particular tool. First, completion time is affected by the order in which a tool is used. Cabri II Plus, Geometer's SketchPad and Geometry Expressions all have similar usage scenarios. It is possible for users to learn aspects of one of them while using another. This may have happened in our study despite our best efforts to randomize the order of tools and diagrams for each tool. We also noticed variation in drawing strategy among people. Some participants took extreme care to ensure the constraints indicated for each diagram while others did not. Some people drew quickly, whereas others took their time and tried to draw carefully. In QuickDraw, it is possible to complete a diagram in two ways. A user can sketch the entire diagram and then trigger recognition. Alternatively, the diagram can be drawn incrementally (i.e., sketching individual components one at a time and triggering recognition after each step). Depending on the strategy used, completion time can vary greatly within QuickDraw. We found that a large majority of participants drew the diagrams incrementally. While it is critical to support both modes of drawing, it should be noted that QuickDraw's best performance is achieved when the diagram is drawn in a non-incremental manner. Lastly, incorrectly inferred constraints can increase the completion time for diagrams drawn in QuickDraw. As none of the other tools does any recognition, inference errors inflate the completion time for QuickDraw by forcing users to perform extra editing operations.

Questionnaire : All Tools		
No.	Question	Response Type
1.	I was given a sufficient introduction to each tool.	7-point Likert
2.	Please rate your overall reaction to each tool.	7-point Likert
3.	Please rate your drawing performance with each tool.	7-point Likert
4.	I was able to draw a given diagram in a relatively straightforward manner.	7-point Likert
5.	Was it difficult to correct your mistakes?	7-point Likert
6.	I was confused by the interface.	7-point Likert
7.	The system had adequate capabilities to allow me to complete a given diagram in an easy manner.	7-point Likert
8.	Please explain your answer to Q7.	free response
9.	Please rate the different tools from best to worst.	ranking
Questionnaire : QuickDraw Specific		
1.	QuickDraw was able to correctly understand the sketched diagram most of the time.	7-point Likert
2.	Using QuickDraw would enable me to draw diagrams more quickly.	7-point Likert
3.	I would find QuickDraw useful in my work.	7-point Likert
4.	Would you like to use a sketch-based interface for drawing diagrams in the future?	Yes/No
5.	List the most positive aspects of QuickDraw's interface.	free-response
6.	List the most negative aspects of QuickDraw's interface.	free-response
7.	Please suggest any new features that would enhance the usefulness of QuickDraw.	free response

Table 5. Table showing the post-questionnaire used in our study. For the 7-point Likert scale responses, one is the most negative response while seven is the most positive response. Questions in the 'All Tools' section were asked for each of the five diagramming tools tested in the experiment, while questions in the 'QuickDraw specific' section pertained only to QuickDraw

ANALYSIS OF QUESTIONNAIRE DATA

We asked participants to fill out a questionnaire at the end of the experiment. The questionnaire was based on [4] and was split into two sections. In the first section, participants were asked to rate each diagramming tool on a number of qualitative metrics. The second section contained questions related only to QuickDraw. Table 5 shows the questions asked in each section.

Participant Reaction to All Tools

Our post-questionnaire (see Table 5) asked participants to rate each tool at the end of the experiment. We used a non-parametric Friedman test to check for significant differences in qualitative metrics reported by participants for each tool. If significant differences were found, we performed as post-hoc analysis with Wilcoxon signed rank tests to uncover interesting patterns. In our post-hoc analysis, we controlled the

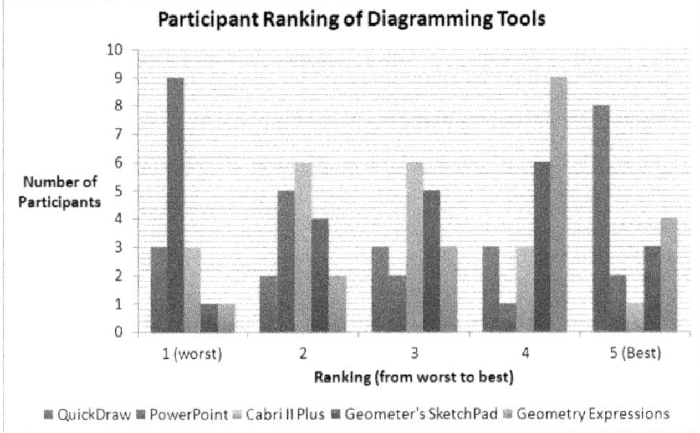

Figure 9. Software tools ranked from worst to best by participants.

chance of Type I errors by using a Holm's Sequential Bonferroni adjustment with four comparisons at $\alpha = 0.05$ [10].

We found significant differences for overall reaction ($\chi^2 = 11.810, p < 0.05$), perceived drawing performance ($\chi^2 = 15.93, p < 0.005$), and the ability of each tool to enable easy diagram drawing ($\chi^2 = 17.675, p < 0.01$). Using Wilcoxon signed rank tests, we found no significant difference in participants' overall reaction to any of the software tools. Participants rated their drawing performance in QuickDraw as better compared to Microsoft PowerPoint ($z = -2.431, p < 0.0125$), but not significantly different from Cabri II Plus, Geometer's SketchPad or Geometry Expressions. There was no significant difference in drawing capabilities among the software tools. QuickDraw's interface was no less confusing than that of any other tool in the experiment. It was no less difficult to correct mistakes in QuickDraw than in any of the other tools. It was also possible to draw in a straightforward manner in each tool. These are interesting findings because, in light of our non-parametric Friedman tests, we expected to find significant differences between QuickDraw and at least one of the other tools in terms of overall reaction and ability to enable easy drawing. However, the only differences approaching significance in both these aspects were with respect to Microsoft PowerPoint and were culled due to the Bonferroni adjustment. This leads us to suspect that given a larger number of participants, these differences may become significant. We also asked participants to rank all the software tools from worst to best. Figure 9 shows the rankings assigned by participants. It shows that more participants assigned the highest ranking to QuickDraw than to any of the other tools used in our experiment.

Feedback and Suggestions

The post-questionnaire asked participants to rate QuickDraw in terms of recognition accuracy and usefulness. It also asked them to list positive and negative aspects and sought feature suggestions (see Table 5). When asked if QuickDraw was able to recognize the sketched diagram correctly most of the time, the majority of the participants responded positively (Median = 6, Mean = 5.22). Similarly, when asked if QuickDraw enabled them to draw faster, the participants responded positively (Median = 6, Mean = 5.44). Lastly, when asked if they would find QuickDraw useful in their work, the overall response was a little above neutral (Median = 5, Mean = 4.94). 16 out of 19 participants indicated that they would like to use a sketch-based interface in the future.

Participants liked QuickDraw's simple interface. A large number remarked that the interface enabled very fast drawing, while freeing them from worrying about drawing correctly by doing beautification itself. When asked to list the negative aspects, the major complaint was about having limited editing capabilities. For some users, incorrectly beautified diagrams due to inference errors negatively impacted their experience, while others were happy to erase and redraw. A few participants lamented the lack of keyboard shortcuts, and redo/undo functionality. The most commonly suggested feature was the inclusion of better editing capabilities (manipulation, snapping, grid, etc). Some people suggested the inclusion of a mathematics recognition engine in order to be able to write down angles/dimensions on the sketched diagram. Some people wanted to be able to sketch out constraints on the diagram.

DISCUSSION

Our usability study highlights the usefulness of sketch-based interaction for building a diagramming tool. Participants' responses indicate a strong desire to use sketch-based software in the future. An analysis of data collected in our study provides several useful insights. For easy diagrams, participants were able to finish them more quickly using QuickDraw than with Microsoft PowerPoint. At this level of difficulty, QuickDraw was no worse than Cabri II Plus, Geometer's SketchPad or Geometry Expressions. However, as the difficulty of diagrams increased, QuickDraw overtook Cabri II Plus and Geometer's SketchPad in terms of completion time, while still being no worse than Geometry Expressions. It seems that for a sufficiently complicated diagram, QuickDraw would enable a user to achieve the minimum completion time among all the tools we have studied.

QuickDraw's performance is hampered by three major factors. First is a high failure rate ($\sim 13\%$) for difficult diagrams, which degrades performance and causes frustration among users. We adjusted for this by disregarding instances where participants could not complete diagrams in QuickDraw. This is fair because the completion time in such instances is inflated to a constant 180 seconds for QuickDraw which cannot be directly compared with the completion time in other tools. The second detriment to performance is the lack of adequate editing capabilities. Lastly, the majority of participants in our study chose to draw diagrams incrementally in QuickDraw. This slightly inflates the completion time, as QuickDraw achieves the best time when the entire diagram is recognized in one go. Yet it must be noted, that despite these detriments, QuickDraw was, in some cases, able to outperform three out of four state-of-the-art geometry construction tools. Indeed, we believe that if QuickDraw was to incorporate better editing capabilities and a further improved constraint inference engine, it would outperform the state-of-the-art in diagramming tools at all levels of difficulty.

Our analysis of the questionnaire data also raises some interesting points. Participants rated their drawing performance in QuickDraw as higher compared to Microsoft PowerPoint. However, the overall reaction to QuickDraw was no worse than any of the other software tools. Interestingly, several participants complained about inadequate editing capabilities in QuickDraw. Yet there were no significant differences in their responses when asked to rate each tool on its ability to allow correction of mistakes. This seems to indicate that participants thought all tools including QuickDraw had a similar level of editing capability.

FUTURE WORK

The results of our user study suggest two avenues of future work. First, we would like to improve the editing abilities in QuickDraw. These include the ability to move/resize components, as well as the ability to zoom in/out of a diagram. We would also like to see if allowing users to explicitly sketch constraints on a diagram improves performance. Second, we want to improve inference of constraints by using classifiers over a variety of features (as inferred by machine learning techniques) as opposed to our existing hard-coded thresholds over a small number of features. We plan to examine the session videos recorded during the course of our study to identify instances that can cause incorrect constraints to be inferred and then work to rectify as many of them as possible. Additionally, we also want to extend the constraint language to refer to virtual components. These components are not explicitly sketched out by the user, but are required to express constraints between diagram components such as reference line-segments.

CONCLUSION

We have presented QuickDraw, a prototype sketch-based diagramming tool that lets a user easily express her intent in the form of a sketched diagram. QuickDraw can recognize individual components in a sketch, infer constraints between them, and then beautify them using a deductive geometry constraint solving algorithm. In this manner, it enables the drawing of precise diagrams. We conducted a usability study to compare QuickDraw with four state-of-the-art diagramming tools : Microsoft PowerPoint, Cabri II Plus, Geometer's SketchPad, and Geometry Expressions. Analysis of quantitative metrics shows that QuickDraw performed better than Microsoft PowerPoint for all difficulty levels, and better than Cabri II Plus and Geometer's SketchPad for medium and hard difficulty diagrams. There was no significant difference in drawing performance between QuickDraw and Geometry Expressions. However, deeper analysis revealed that the majority of participants did not utilize QuickDraw to its full potential. We believe that by adding better editing capabilities and improving the beautification algorithm further, QuickDraw has the potential to perform better than any WIMP based diagramming tool.

ACKNOWLEDGMENTS

This research was conducted at Microsoft Research during the course of a summer internship. Microsoft Research also supported this research by a Consulting Grant. We would also like to thank Bo Kang and Sarah Buchanan for helping to pilot test QuickDraw. This work is supported in part by NSF CAREER award IIS-0845921 and NSF awards IIS-0856045 and CCF-1012056.

REFERENCES

1. Aldefeld, B. Variation of geometries based on a geometric-reasoning method. *Computer Aided Design 20*, 3 (April 1988), 117–126.
2. Bouma, W., Fudos, I., Hoffmann, C. M., Cai, J., and Paige, R. Geometric constraint solver. *Computer-Aided Design 27*, 6 (1995), 487–501.
3. Cabri ii plus, 2011. `http://www.cabri.com`.
4. Chin, J. P., Diehl, V. A., and Norman, K. L. Development of an instrument measuring user satisfaction of the human-computer interface. In *Proceedings of the SIGCHI conference on Human factors in computing systems*, ACM (1988), 213–218.
5. Forbus, K., Usher, J., Lovett, A., Lockwood, K., and Wetzel, J. Cogsketch: Sketch understanding for cognitive science research and for education. *Topics in Cognitive Science* (2011).
6. Geometer's sketchpad, 2011. `http://dynamicgeometry.com/`.
7. Geometry expressions, 2011. `http://www.geometryexpressions.com/`.
8. Gulwani, S., Korthikanti, V. A., and Tiwari, A. Synthesizing geometry constructions. In *Proceedings of the 32nd ACM SIGPLAN conference on Programming language design and implementation*, PLDI '11, ACM (New York, NY, USA, 2011), 50–61.
9. Hammond, T., and Davis, R. Ladder, a sketching language for user interface developers. *Computers and Graphics 29*, 4 (2005), 518 – 532.
10. Holm, S. A simple sequentially rejective multiple test procedure. *Scandinavian Journal of Statistics 6*, 2 (1979), 65–70.
11. Igarashi, T., Matsuoka, S., Kawachiya, S., and Tanaka, H. Interactive beautification: a technique for rapid geometric design. In *Proceedings of the 10th annual ACM symposium on User interface software and technology*, UIST '97 (1997), 105–114.
12. Jiang, Y., Tian, F., Wang, H., Zhang, X., Wang, X., and Dai, G. Intelligent understanding of handwritten geometry theorem proving. In *Proceedings of the 15th international conference on Intelligent user interfaces*, IUI '10, ACM (New York, NY, USA, 2010), 119–128.
13. Kondo, K. Algebraic method for manipulation of dimensional relationships in geometric models. *Computer-Aided Design 24*, 3 (1992), 141–147.
14. LaViola, Jr., J. J., and Zeleznik, R. C. Mathpad2: a system for the creation and exploration of mathematical sketches. *ACM Trans. Graph. 23* (August 2004), 432–440.
15. Li, Q., Liu, Y., Xu, H., Ren, L., and Ma, C. An intelligent interactive pen-based whiteboard for dynamic geometry teaching. In *Information Technologies and Applications in Education, 2007. ISITAE '07. First IEEE International Symposium on* (nov. 2007), 396 –401.
16. Microsoft powerpoint, 2011. `http://office.microsoft.com/en-us/powerpoint/`.
17. Nelson, G. Juno, a constraint-based graphics system. In *SIGGRAPH* (1985), 235–243.
18. Paulson, B., and Hammond, T. Paleosketch: accurate primitive sketch recognition and beautification. In *Proceedings of the 13th international conference on Intelligent user interfaces*, IUI '08, ACM (New York, NY, USA, 2008), 1–10.
19. Wais, P., Wolin, A., and Alvarado, C. Designing a sketch recognition front-end: user perception of interface elements. In *Proceedings of the 4th Eurographics workshop on Sketch-based interfaces and modeling*, SBIM '07, ACM (New York, NY, USA, 2007), 99–106.
20. Xiong, Y., and LaViola Jr., J. J. Technical section: A shortstraw-based algorithm for corner finding in sketch-based interfaces. *Comput. Graph. 34* (October 2010), 513–527.
21. Zeleznik, R. C., Bragdon, A., Liu, C.-C., and Forsberg, A. Lineogrammer: creating diagrams by drawing. In *Proceedings of the 21st annual ACM symposium on User interface software and technology*, UIST '08, ACM (New York, NY, USA, 2008), 161–170.

Talking in Circles: Selective Sharing in Google+

Sanjay Kairam[1], Michael J. Brzozowski[2], David Huffaker[2], Ed H. Chi[2]
[1]Computer Science Department
Stanford University
sanjay.kairam@gmail.com
[2]Google Inc.
Mountain View, CA
{zozo, huffaker, edchi}@google.com

ABSTRACT
Online social networks have become indispensable tools for information sharing, but existing 'all-or-nothing' models for sharing have made it difficult for users to target information to specific parts of their networks. In this paper, we study Google+, which enables users to selectively share content with specific 'Circles' of people. Through a combination of log analysis with surveys and interviews, we investigate how active users organize and select audiences for shared content. We find that these users frequently engaged in selective sharing, creating circles to manage content across particular life facets, ties of varying strength, and interest-based groups. Motivations to share spanned personal and informational reasons, and users frequently weighed 'limiting' factors (e.g. privacy, relevance, and social norms) against the desire to reach a large audience. Our work identifies implications for the design of selective sharing mechanisms in social networks.

Author Keywords
Social media; group-based access controls; social networks

ACM Classification Keywords
H.5.3 Group and Organization Interfaces

INTRODUCTION
Social media, from blogs to forums to online social networks (OSNs), have become a major venue for social interaction and communication. In the United States, over 65% of adult Internet users are currently active on social networking tools [17]. This phenomenon is global; at the start of 2012, Facebook, the largest OSN, claimed over 800 million active users, 75% of whom were outside the US [7].

A key affordance of these tools is interaction with audiences to which users may not have had contact offline; often these interactions accompany disclosures of personal information. Research on social media over the past decade has shown that users are revealing a startling amount of personal information through blogs [14, 25], profiles [10], and status updates [19]. In situations where readership may not be clearly delineated, users often underestimate the size of their potential audience [1], in many cases leading to tension [8, 23], regret [26], or tangible negative consequences in one's personal or professional life [25].

Permission to make digital or hard copies of all or part of this work for personal or classroom use is granted without fee provided that copies are not made or distributed for profit or commercial advantage and that copies bear this notice and the full citation on the first page. To copy otherwise, or republish, to post on servers or to redistribute to lists, requires prior specific permission and/or a fee.
CHI'12, May 5–10, 2012, Austin, Texas, USA.
Copyright 2012 ACM 978-1-4503-1015-4/12/05...$10.00.

If users are aware of the consequences of 'over-sharing', then why continue to share so much? This question constitutes what Barnes has called the 'privacy paradox' [4]. In this paper, we study individuals who are actively sharing while successfully handling privacy concerns. We observe their behavior to identify strategies for improving sharing precision through *selective sharing*.

We base our analyses on usage data from the field trial of Google+, a social networking service introduced in 2011. Through the incorporation of 'Circles', this service is designed around selective sharing and consumption of information. In the following section, we provide some brief theoretical background on needs for selective sharing and prior research on challenges for users sharing using existing social technologies. We then provide a brief introduction to how these needs are addressed in Google+.

BACKGROUND
In applying Altman's theory of privacy boundary regulation [3] to the online world, Palen and Dourish argue that the disclosure of information is a necessary consequence of participating in a social world [22]. In the offline world, some information (such as presence) may be freely disclosed to the general public, while other information (such as personal secrets) may only be revealed to a privileged few. Using Goffman's dramaturgical metaphor for interpersonal communication [9], social interaction provides a stage and an audience for whom we tailor self-representations, disclosing what we see fit.

Prior work has revealed the existence of 'facets' [8] or 'modes' [20], representing the various audiences for whom we must fluidly adapt our performances over the course of our day. Generally, in offline settings, information disclosed is ephemeral and the audience evident, enabling a tight loop between what we share and with whom we share it. As Palen and Dourish identify, moving interactions online means that content shared may persist beyond the scope of a conversation and reach unintended audiences.

Many existing tools for online communication are designed to enable 'public' sharing to wide groups. Rather than focusing on the natural 'facets' of a user's life, many social networks, for instance, grant default access to content to a user's 'followers' or 'friends', restricting those who fall outside this boundary. While this model may be simple for users to understand, it ignores the 'natural' groupings which may exist within these networks [16], making selective control over content difficult and prone to error [24].

Difficulty in disclosing information selectively to various life facets can lead to what Marwick and boyd have called 'context collapse' [18]. Studies of OSN use in the workplace reveal that this leads to very real tensions for users of such systems [2, 5, 23]. As a result, users may engage in drastic behaviors to avoid future privacy violations, such as self-censoring or ceasing sharing altogether [24, 26].

Tools such as email fall on the other side of this spectrum, easily enabling 'targeted' sharing of specific items to individuals. By essentially requiring access controls to be set for each item shared, such systems provide a high degree of control over access to content. While prior work has shown that particular sub-groups of email contacts may be common across many users [20], the creation and maintenance of persistent groups for access in these systems can often be cumbersome or difficult.

Introducing Google+

Google+, a social networking service launched into field trial by Google in 2011, was designed to address some of these problems. To aid users in selectively disclosing information to common sub-groups of their network, Google+ introduced 'Circles', an intuitive mechanism for organizing contacts. Similar to 'lists' or 'groups' available in networks such as Facebook or Twitter, Circles are user-created groupings of contacts which may be overlapping or hierarchical, allowing users a great deal of flexibility in organizing their networks. Each time a user shares a piece of content, he or she makes a contextual decision about the audience with whom to share it; content can be shared publicly or shared selectively to one or more circles. Users can also share to 'friends of friends' by selecting an 'Extended Circles' option, though this feature is not analyzed in detail in the present work.

In addition, specific individuals can be referenced through inclusion of a '+Mention'. Mentioning users individually in this way can be used to target content directly at those users. Use of a '+Mention' when sharing to a wider audience can be a means of notifying the mentioned user and directing their attention to the post, similar to a '@mention' on Twitter. In addition to providing a simple mechanism for selective sharing, Circles also support selective consumption. Users can filter their incoming stream in order to see content being shared only by members of a specific Circle. While sharing with specific groups is possible in other OSNs, we study Google+ here as it represents the first widely-deployed system with such a 'selective sharing' mechanism built in from the start.

OVERVIEW OF THE PAPER

In the following section, we examine large-scale usage data collected during the field trial of Google+. We first look at aggregate sharing patterns to understand the extent to which users are actively engaging in public sharing, targeted sharing to individuals, and selective sharing using Circles. We then look at names frequently given by users to custom Circles with the aim of investigating the various ways that users separate their networks for the purposes of selective sharing and consumption.

In the subsequent section, we report findings from a qualitative study of users sharing comfortably on Google+. We analyze the behavior of these 'expert' users through data collected via surveys and interviews in order to understand how they use the product to successfully tailor self-presentations for various parts of their network through selective information sharing. We focus specifically on how they organize their contacts into Circles, what factors motivate them to share, and contextual considerations for choosing an audience for a particular piece of content.

QUANTITATIVE LOG ANALYSIS

In this section, we conduct analysis using usage logs from the field trial of Google+ to examine overall user sharing patterns and characterize how users organize their networks based on names assigned to Circles they have created.

High-Level Sharing Patterns

To understand the extent to which users were engaging in selective sharing with Circles, as opposed to public or targeted sharing, we first examined logs of per-user sharing choices aggregated over the week of July 20-26, 2011.

Data

User IDs were hashed and sampled randomly from the population of users who had shared at least once during the data collection period, providing a representative sample of 100K active users. To preserve user privacy, we did not conduct any analysis concerning specific Circles, but rather restricted our analysis to public (posts shared using the 'Public' setting), selective (posts share to one or more Circles), and targeted (posts shared using a '+Mention') sharing. In order to compare our results to those found in the later qualitative study, we focused on users sharing via the desktop web application, resulting in a data set of 64,005 users who shared content during this week.

As shown below in Figure 1, the number of items shared weekly per user roughly follows a power-law distribution. Using Clauset et al.'s approach [6], we estimate the parameter α as 2.578, meaning that the distribution matches those of a variety of man-made and naturally occurring phenomena, giving us confidence that out data was representative of the wider population

Results

In Table 1 below, we report the extent to which users engaged in public sharing, selective sharing (Circles), and targeted sharing (+Mentions). In the first column, we see that about three quarters (74.8%) of users who share during the period engaged in selective sharing using Circles at least once. Portions of users engaging in public (33.9%) and targeted (10.3%) sharing were smaller, but still significant, indicating that at least some users were employing multiple sharing options. The second column displays percentages of all items shared using these options; here, we see that 67.6% of all items were shared using Circles and 33.8% of

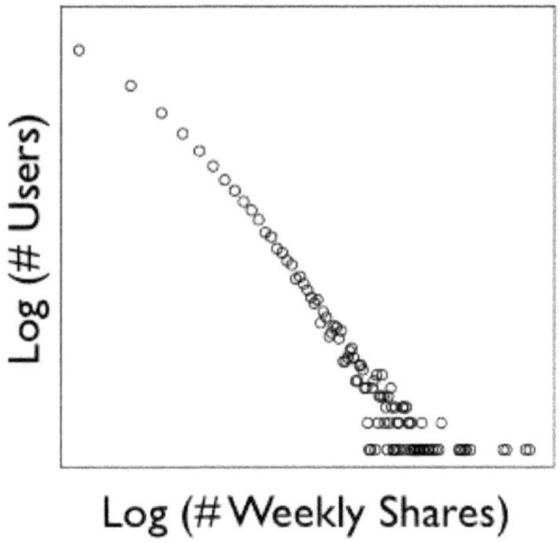

Figure 1. Log-log frequency plot of # weekly shares per user. Note. Axes obscured in order to not reveal total usage.

items were shared publicly (these percentages add up to more than 100% since some users combined sharing options for posts). We note that sharing a post both publicly and to Circles functioned the same as sharing the post publicly alone; this pattern in the data signaled that a small portion of users may have been mistaken about the function of Circles and were expressing additional needs for selective sharing aside from access control.

Patterns in Custom Circle Names

Users joining Google+ are initially presented with a set of four default Circles: *Family*, *Friends*, *Acquaintances*, and *Following* (intended primarily for consumption). Users are then able to rename these Circles or create additional Circles to serve their needs. In order to identify factors governing how users organized their networks, we examined the names frequently used for custom Circles. Our intuition here was that frequently occurring patterns in these names might reveal widespread needs that users had for selective sharing and consumption of information.

Data

Our data was drawn from a snapshot taken on Sept. 6, 2011 of the names of all non-empty, user-created Circles (thus excluding all Circles with names matching the defaults). We focused our analysis on the top 1,000 most common names in order to identify common needs via frequently occurring patterns; this method also avoided the possible privacy risk of revealing personal or idiosyncratic names. Capitalization and punctuation differences were ignored when counting names, but no stemming was performed. The frequency of occurrence of Circle names very closely approximated a power-law distribution with α = 1.99 – similar to observed distributions for English word frequencies, such as the occurrence of unique words in *Moby Dick* [6]. The names in this data set covered 34.5% of all non-empty Circles in users' accounts at snapshot time.

Sharing	% Users	% Items
Public	33.9%	33.8%
Selective	74.8%	67.6%
Targeted	10.3%	5.8%

Table 1. Frequency of types of sharing conducted over a 1-week period in July 2011. The first column reports percentages of users choosing each option at least once during the week; the second column reports percentages of total items shared by the same set of users.

Coding

In coding circle names, we adopted the following conservative approach, drawing on Hsieh's definition of 'conventional content analysis' [13]. We first looked at patterns in the 50 most frequently occurring Circle names to develop four labels. One author then coded the entire list (the top 1,000) using these labels, coding all uncategorized Circles as 'other'. This method ensured categorization of the most common names, and thus wider coverage overall.

Non-English names were translated using Google Translate; ambiguous translations were cross-referenced against occurrences on pages found through Google search. While this approach may seem overly reductive, the brevity of Circle names made inferring user intent difficult in many cases. As Circle names are created for private, rather than public use, names often contained abbreviations, ideolectic slang, or terms with multiple or ambiguous meanings. A second author independently categorized the first 100 names to assess inter-rater reliability; Cohen's κ = 0.91 indicated high agreement on label assignments.

Labels developed from the data fell into two higher categories: *life facets* and *tie strength*. The first category, *life facets*, contained two labels, 'work' and 'school'. Circle names labeled 'work' contained synonyms or translations for words such as *work* or *professional* or denoted business relationships (e.g. *employees*, *customers*). Names labeled as 'school' contained synonyms or translations for words such as *school* or *college* or academic relationships (e.g. *professor*, *students*). Specific company and school names were excluded, as it was impossible to resolve ambiguity over users' relationships with those names (e.g. Users may create a *Google* Circle for sharing content about Google products rather than for sharing with Google employees).

Rank	Work	School	Strong	Weak	Other
10	74.1%	13.8%	7.2%	0.0%	4.9%
100	47.5%	16.0%	9.0%	3.5%	24.0%
1000	31.4%	12.6%	8.8%	4.0%	43.1%
All	10.8%	4.3%	3.0%	1.4%	-----

Table 2. Categories for the top 10, 100, and 1000 most common names for user-defined Circles. Percentages reported in bottom row represent strict lower bounds on category representation across the entire data set.

The second category, *tie strength*, included 'strong ties' and 'weak ties'. Circles were deemed 'strong ties' if their names applied modifiers such as *close*, *best*, or *inner* to common relations such as *friends* or *family*. We also included specific relationships such as *girlfriend* or *husband* and common slang for close ties (e.g. *BFFs*). Circles labeled as 'weak ties' included words such as *other*, *random*, or *extended* or words otherwise implying limited knowledge about Circle members (e.g. *unknown*, *don't know*, or *WTF*).

Results

In Table 2, we report results from labeling the top 10, 100, and 1000 most commonly used Circle names. Each row presents a different view of the representation of the various labels in the data. The first row indicates that the 'work' label covers 74.1% of all Circles with names matching the top 10 most frequently occurring user-defined names. We note here that 'work', 'school', and 'strong ties' labels cover almost all of the Circles in this group (the 10th most common name, categorized as Other, was the empty string).

Expanding our view to the top 100 names, we see that Circles pertaining to 'school' and tie strength occupy a greater portion of this data set, while an increasing portion of the names become difficult to categorize. Given our knowledge that a large portion (34.5%) of all custom circles are covered by the top 1000 most commonly used names, we can estimate that Circles pertaining to "work" and "school" represent at least 15.1% of all Circles, indicating that these life facets are commonly important dimensions for selective sharing and consumption of content. Circles pertaining to tie strength occupy at least 4.4% of all custom Circles, an amount which is smaller but still substantial.

The prevalence of Circles focused on professional life is consistent with prior hypotheses about specific sharing needs relating to workplace OSN use [2, 5, 23]. To examine if this pattern was consistent across cultures, we looked at the most common Circle names in 10 languages popular amongst users of Google+, finding that the most common name in each translated into either 'work' or 'colleague'.

Though the coding approach used was fairly conservative, it provides the advantage of being rather unambiguous while covering a large percentage of names across the data set. Still, we also discovered tremendous diversity in the 'other' common Circle names which invite further study. Observing the top 10 most common Circle names categorized as 'Other' (*church*, *music*, *google*, *tech*, *twitter*, *photographers*, *celebrities*, *news*, and *relatives*) hints that Circles based on topical interest may be common as well.

Discussion

Based on log analysis of sharing patterns and contact organization, we make two observations about needs for selective information disclosure and consumption. First, we find that users are actively engaging in a mix of public, targeted, and selective sharing; at least a small portion of users are utilizing different options for various pieces of content. In addition, we find that frequently occurring names for user-defined Circles reflect a need to manage content according to *life facets* (specifically professional life), *tie strength*, and possibly, *topical interest groups*.

Our analysis focused on data which both ensured broad coverage of Google+ usage and avoided product confidentiality or privacy concerns. While additional statistics about Circles and sharing might augment these findings in the future, we believe that the patterns discussed still provide ample insight into selective-sharing practices. Keeping these high-level findings in mind, we move on to data collected through qualitative study of active Google+ users, through which we aim to gain a more detailed understanding of the contexts in which these patterns occur.

QUALITATIVE USER STUDY

In this section, we describe the results of a survey and interview study conducted with active Google+ users.

Method

As our aim was to understand why users were actively sharing with different groups, we chose to focus our analysis on active users who had familiarity with the product and a history of shared content. Participants in all stages of this study were recruited from a pool of approximately 2500 users compiled via snowball sampling through a survey posted on Google+ which collected demographic and general Google+ usage information. A subset of these users were chosen to receive our follow-up survey designed to probe user motivations for creating Circles and sharing content.

A sub-group of users who completed the follow-up survey were asked to participate in semi-structured interviews aimed at understanding how users group their contacts into Circles. These interviews also included a critical incident study of posts that the user had recently shared, aimed at providing greater insight into decisions about whether to share content and about the audience with which to share it.

Survey Study

Participants. From the initial pool described above, 300 users were invited to participate in our follow-up survey via the following criteria: each had at least 4 Circles containing a total of at least 30 members, had shared at least 5 items, and had been visiting Google+ more than once a week.

168 (56.3%) users participated in our follow-up survey on Circle management and sharing preferences. In a few cases, follow-up responses could not be connected to initial survey responses; we thus report demographic information for the 162 surveys for which this was possible. Respondents were primarily (74.2%) male and had a wide range of ages (μ = 35.0, σ = 8.3). Almost all participants (98.8%) used other social media tools at least weekly, with YouTube (89.5%), Facebook (82.7%), Twitter (72.2%), and LinkedIn (45.1%) being most popular. While occupations were skewed towards technology-focused positions, we observed a wide range of professions, including several lawyers, IT consultants, artists, analysts, and software developers.

Measures. Beyond the demographic and usage questions collected in the initial survey, this survey probed further about the frequency of use of various sharing settings and shared content of various types. A portion of the study was dedicated to a critical incident report about the item most recently shared in this stream; participants uncomfortable with discussing their most recent post had the option to discuss another item, with 14 of our participants doing so.

Interview Study

Participants. From the set of users who completed the follow-up survey, 12 were chosen to participate in a 1-hour remote interview about their Google+ usage. Interview participants were selected such that they lived in the United States in order to avoid language fluency issues and balanced by gender, but otherwise matched the demographics of the overall population initially surveyed.

Measures. Interviewees first provided a walk-through of how they use the product (10-15 minutes), and then answered questions about their management of contacts, including in-depth questions about their most heavily used Circles (10-15 minutes). The interview also included a critical incident portion similar to that administered in the surveys, in which participants discussed 3 or 4 posts recently shared (15-20 minutes). The remainder of the interview was used to collect general product feedback. Additional details are given below about questions central to the study and the methods used to analyze responses.

Sharing and Audience Choices

In characterizing reasons why users shared content and factors considered when choosing an audience with which to share, we utilized a grounded approach to code and categorize responses to the following two questions about the users' recently shared posts:

- Please describe this post and why you shared it.
- Please describe the audience that you chose and why you chose to share this content with them.

In coding responses to these two questions, we adopted an approach similar to that used in Naaman et al. [19]. For each question, two authors worked together to develop a coding scheme using 50 responses sampled from the data; each author then independently coded half of the remaining responses in order to identify additional labels which might apply. Participants often gave rich responses touching on multiple reasons; thus, labels were not mutually exclusive.

After agreeing on a complete set of labels, each author then went through and re-coded the full set of responses. Finally, these two authors discussed each coding discrepancy in order to reconcile it. These labels were then used to generate the higher-level categories discussed below. Because complete agreement was reached between coders, as in Naaman et al. [19], we do not report inter-rater reliability measures; however, secondary coding by the other two authors on 10% of the data revealed at least moderate agreement for each of the high-level categories.

It should be noted that the goal in each of these cases was to identify patterns in the self-reported 'reasons' why users made particular decisions. This goal is distinct from and serves to extend prior work in describing message content in similar types of social awareness streams [12, 15, 19].

Management of Contacts

During the interviews, users were asked to identify the Circles with which they 'interacted' most frequently, where the nature of interaction (e.g. sharing, consumption, conversation) was left open-ended. For each Circle identified, participants responded to two sets of statements describing the Circle, using one of two 5-point Likert scales. The first scale ranged in level of agreement from *Strongly Disagree* (1) to *Strongly Agree* (5), while the second scale ranged over the proportion of Circle members to which the statement applied, from *None* (1) to *All* (5).

Questions were informed by prior study of Facebook friend grouping [16], and were designed to test the extent to which Circles represented distinct social cliques, collections of weak or strong ties, common organizations, or connections to a common geographical location or episode in the user's life. In addition, in light of findings from our analysis of Circle names, we also included questions to probe whether Circles connected users on the basis of topical interest.

Results

We start this sub-section by summarizing general patterns reported by survey respondents about their use of Google+, focusing specifically on types of content typically shared and the types of sharing (public, selective, and targeted) usually chosen. Our intent here is not to characterize the general population, but to understand the behaviors and attitudes which aid early-adopting users in using the product successfully for sharing and filtering content.

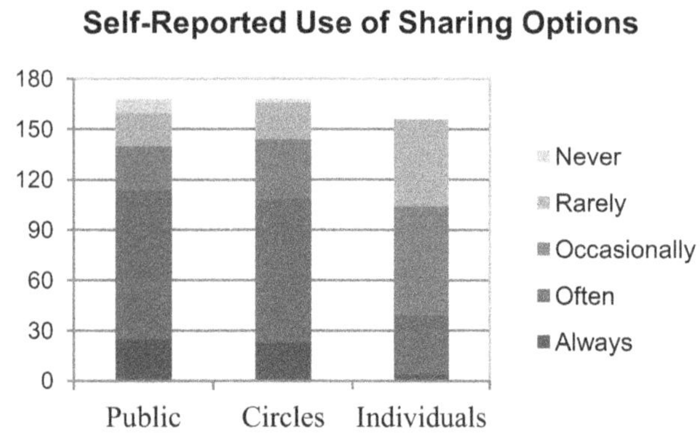

Figure 2. Frequency of use of various sharing options based on participant self-report.

The remainder of this sub-section is organized according to our three primary areas of interest: what reasons spur users to share content, what factors they consider when choosing with whom to share, and how they manage their contacts generally for the purposes of selective sharing and filtering.

General Patterns of Use

Survey participants were asked to report on how frequently they shared various types of content. Sharing of URLs and photos was common: 134 of our 168 respondents (79.8%) indicated that they shared URLs 'often' or 'always, and 138 (82.1%) reported sharing photos at least 'occasionally'. Sharing of videos and locations was less prevalent, with 76 respondents (45.2%) sharing videos and 114 (67.9%) sharing locations 'rarely' or 'never'.

Participants also reported on how often they utilized various sharing options. Figure 2 summarizes participants' self-reports about how often they engaged in public, selective (Circles) and targeted (individuals) sharing. 144 of our respondents (85.7%) reported sharing to Public at least occasionally, hinting at the possibility that these active users were more comfortable sharing publicly than the general population (see Table 1). Patterns for public and selective sharing were generally similar, but participants reported sharing to individuals less frequently overall.

Sharing: Why do users share content?

Of the 168 users who participated in the survey, 166 submitted responses which could be coded to the query 'Please describe this post and why you shared it.' Results are organized below according to categories developed based on responses to the survey. As mentioned previously, these categories were not designed to be mutually exclusive. Quotes from surveys and interviews provide greater detail for some observed phenomena; interview subjects are designated using a unique identifier [P*], while survey quotes are unmarked. Typographical errors in user quotes are corrected using {brackets} for clarity.

Inherent Value of Content. Based on survey responses, the reasons for sharing most frequently referenced by users (98/166, or 59.0%) referenced the inherent value of the content itself. Half of these cases (49) included a stated assumption that others would value the content as well, indicating that these users are actively reflecting on the consumption needs of others. Content was most frequently deemed valuable because it was topically 'interesting' or generally 'exciting' or 'cool' in some way (48/166, or 28.9% of responses). One user described why he shared a post containing a book recommendation:

> *I shared this content because, as listed in the post, I have been reading this particular book and I love it! I am very much into the subject matter and wanted to share this information so that those that are following me would know that it was a good book (according to me) and to get into a discussion started about the subject matter.*

Another common reason for deeming content as valuable was because it was 'funny', 'amusing', or 'silly' (24/166, or 14.5%). Content in this category included quotations, personal stories, and humorous pictures and videos. One user reported sharing a quote because it was "an amusing and accurate generalization of the activities that make up our lives", while another who shared a humorous picture simply said "I re-shared it because I thought it was funny as hell!" [P12]. 16/166 users (9.6%) indicated in their responses that they shared content because it was 'informative' or 'useful'. Half of these posts were about Google+ itself, perhaps an artifact of the novelty of the service, though prior work [12] has shown that this type of meta-commentary is evident in other social systems as well.

Finally, a few respondents reported sharing content because it was positive, though not explicitly useful or funny (8/166, or 4.8%). These responses described content that was 'heartwarming' or 'enjoyable'. One user, who had shared a YouTube video of a man singing old TV theme songs indicated that it was "very nostalgic" and thought that "other people…might enjoy it in the same way." An interview participant who shared a story about an elderly knitter had this to say: "It just struck me as such a sweet story…it wasn't just something that would appeal to knitters, it would appeal to people in general" [P9]. Motivation to share in these cases generally seemed connected to a desire to elicit positive emotion in others.

Sharing about Self. The other theme which emerged from users' responses was a desire to share about oneself. Of the 43 (25.9%) responses in this category, only 4 explicitly or implicitly mentioned considerations about whether others would find the content useful, suggesting that the underlying motivations in these cases differed fundamentally from those in the prior category. Within this group, the most frequently referenced reason for sharing was a desire to share one's personal experiences with others (19/166, or 11.4%). These ranged widely from sharing brief updates ("just updating my friends on what I was up to") to long posts with strong emotional content. One user, who had posted about a long struggle with weight management, revealed a desire to share her story with her audience:

I am feeling very frustrated about my (lack of) weight loss, and I wanted to explain a bit of my background to my followers, and ask the collective to help me a bit when my self-discipline is lacking, {especially} about skipping Weight watchers meetings.

A number of survey respondents (16/166, or 9.6%) indicated a desire to share personal opinions or commentary; in the majority (10) of these cases, users were commenting on technology products, which again may have been indicative of the early-adopting population studied.

Discourse. An additional theme bridging the two primary categories listed above was a desire to start or participate in a discussion (28/166, or 16.9%). This frequently focused on soliciting help or information from others. These ranged from immediate information needs ("I need to be helped out by getting an information about printing several documents at once.") to general topical inquiries ("I have been checking to see when the app Instagram would be coming out for Android and could not find a definitive answer.").

In other cases (13/166, or 7.8%), participants were motivated to start or participate in a discussion on a topic of interest. In many of these cases, posts focused on general interest topics (e.g. news, current events). One participant living in Virginia, who was interviewed the day after the 2011 Virginia Earthquake, described how she shared in order to solicit additional information about the event:

When we had the earthquake...I geo-tagged it hoping that people around me could see it as well and maybe...contribute to it as far as whether they felt it or not. [P5]

In other cases, discussions were specifically relevant to a sub-group of users. One respondent gave the following context for a post about a knitting project:

There is a knit-along going on specifically for g+ so I was sharing my project status with the other knitters. Many of the other knitters are sharing project photo, so I wanted to add mine too.

Evangelism. Another less-common, but interesting, category of reasons for sharing was a desire to raise awareness on behalf of another person or cause. The majority of the (11/166, or 6.6%) survey responses which received this label included posts intended to spread information about specific events or work being conducted by others so that recipients could appreciate, attend, or contribute. Others sought to spread awareness of general topics, such as this photographer who shared a post about undue harassment that photographers were receiving from police offers when photographing government buildings:

My hope was to raise awareness of the issue, and at some point, I invite people to duplicate the experience in their town. A little bit of activism attached to this one. [P12]

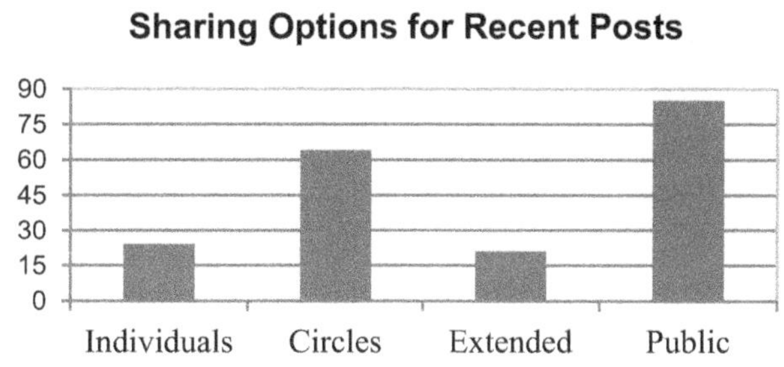

Figure 3. Sharing options used for the 'most recent' post in users' streams. As participants had the option to select an alternate post (14 users indicated doing so), reported results may be biased towards publicly shared content.

Selecting an Audience: How do users choose?

Of these respondents, 165 also reported the sharing options they chose and provided a response which could be coded to the query 'Please describe the audience you chose and why you chose to share this content with them.' Sharing options chosen for these posts are displayed in Figure 3 above. Here, we see that the majority of posts discussed in this study were shared publicly (85/165, or 51.5%). This may be due in part to the fact that the population studied was fairly comfortable with public sharing (see Figure 2), and also to the fact that private posts may have been more likely to contain sensitive information that users would not have chosen to discuss as part of the study. In addition, a number of users chose multiple options when sharing, including several who shared both to Public and Circles.

Again, results are organized below according to the categories developed based on survey responses; quotes from interviews are designated using the same unique participant identifiers as in the prior section.

Privacy. Concerns about privacy were common for users considering whether to limit the audience for their posts (36/165, or 21.8%). Most users (24) with responses in this category focused on risks to their own privacy when choosing an audience. These users tended to subscribe to one of two overall 'policies' regarding shared content.

Followers of the first policy, which we call *public-by-default*, tended to share content, or at least most types of content, widely unless they had a reason not to do so (13/165, or 7.9%). Most explanations included general statements like "I prefer to share as much publicly as I can" or contextual statements such as "There was nothing specific or private about it so I shared it publicly." Followers of the second policy, which we call *private-by-default*, tended to have overarching reasons for placing restrictions on shared content (5/165 = 3.0%). Often these restrictions arose from concerns about specific individuals or groups having access to content shared. One user explained her decisions to limit sharing to Circles, saying:

I almost always limit my posts for privacy reasons. There are people from my past, including my ex-husband, who don't need to know what I'm up to.

Another user demonstrated the use of different policies depending on time of day, restricting posts specifically during work hours due to concerns over social media use:

> *I have people from my work who are {present} in 'Extended Circles', who I don't want to see my posts in 'work hours'. So {usually} I prefer 'Extended' but just in non-working time."*

Fewer users (6/165 = 3.6%) expressed concerns based on the possibility of privacy risks to others. A specific source of concern here was the sharing of photos, illustrated by one interview participant who appeared to be very comfortable sharing personal information, but carefully considered options when sharing photos of her daughter:

> *I'm not overly concerned about pictures of my kids being on the Internet, because I have an active online life…but on a post like this where I'm just sharing pictures of my daughter, it's probably one that I would not share publicly.* [P7]

Relevance. Users also frequently considered whether content shared would be relevant to particular parts of their audience (38/165, or 23.0%). Often, these users targeted content to those who might be interested, in some case utilizing Circles created for this purpose. One interview participant described how she frequently used a topical Circle to selective share nutrition and health content:

> *The Circle I use the third-most is a subject-based Circle, and it's about paleo-primal health and exercise stuff and the science behind it. I shared this with that Circle and a couple of individuals who aren't in that Circle but are interested in this stuff.* [P3]

In other cases, users chose an audience by excluding those who might not find the shared content relevant, referencing a desire to avoid 'spamming' or 'polluting' others' streams. One user who shared a piece of technology news described only sharing it to people from his school:

> *The subject of the post is related to our studies. I didn't share it with anyone else because I didn't want to {pollute} their stream with things that probably won't {interest} them.*

A particular sub-group of these users (9) mentioned limiting their audience because the content required shared context to understand. These posts ranged from inside jokes ("I limited it just to her because it was {the} kind of inside joke that only she would understand") to shared projects ("Since the message was related to our tour, {I} had shared it individually") to family matters ("This was a family {event} so I kept it to my friends and family").

Social Norms. A smaller number of participants referenced concerns about whether content might be appropriate for a particular, or unknown, audience (13/165, or 7.9%). One user who shared a humorous animal picture explained that "since it wasn't too controversial in any way, there was no need not to share it publicly." Another user discussing a potentially risqué joke shared, hinting at a general policy for assessing whether content was safe to share publicly, explaining "It's the kind of joke I wouldn't be ashamed to show my mother so I can share it with everybody…"

Distribution. In addition to considerations about why to limit one's audience, a large number of respondents specifically referenced reasons for maximizing the potential audience for content (71/165, or 43.0%). In the majority of these cases (49/165, or 29.7%), users were motivated to share content widely in order to make it more accessible to others who might want to consume it. One interview participant who had shared a photo while engaging in an outdoor activity did so publicly in the hopes of enabling serendipitous interactions with others:

> *I really like finding nice pictures in my stream…[I] put this out so more people can see it…Somebody could be on their phone nearby and say 'Hey, that's really cool!' I think it'd be nice if there were enough people doing the same thing that when I shared that picture, someone else on their phone nearby could be doing a similar thing and share their picture from across the lake. If I don't share pictures like that, then how's that experience going to happen otherwise?* [P9]

In 14/166 (8.5%) cases, responses indicated a desire to publicize content in order to expand one's own audience, specifically with the aim of encouraging others to add the user to their Circles. Another reason for maximizing one's audience, related to the social search behavior discussed in the prior section, was to 'cast a wide net' for potential help or assistance (11/165, 6.7%). The user who posted about weight management explained "I decided to spread my net as wide as I could {without} taking it public, You {never} know when you will find 'I've been there' supporters," hinting at the balance that users must strike when weighing the benefits of various sharing options.

Circles: Organizing contacts for sharing and consumption

The majority of interview participants discussed three Circles; two discussed only two due to time constraints. This resulted in a data set of 34 Circles. Aided by a *k*-means clustering algorithm using data from participants' responses to the Likert-scale questions discussed earlier, we manually identified 4 major types of Circles discussed by users:

Inner Circle. The first cluster contained Circles which represented small, tightly-knit groups composed of members who were strongly tied to the user. These Circles had names such as *Family*, *Inner Circle*, *Tell-All*, etc. When discussing these Circles, participants tended to describe them as groups of users to whom they could say anything: "These people pretty much know the 'unfiltered' me" [P1]; "I don't have to be discreet in any way with them" [P2].

Structured Groups. Circles in the second cluster often represent structured groups. Members of Circles in this cluster often shared common interests, belonged to common organizations (either offline or online), and were likely to know one another. Examples included *Church/Ministry* ("Pretty much anyone who has anything to do with my church or Christian ministry" [P11], *Google Big Wigs* ("Everyone that I've heard that's on G+ that works for Google" [P12]), and *eGRC* (an industry-specific Circle: "Employees, clients, former clients…" [P3])

Interest Group. The third cluster contained Circles which grouped members with common interests but without other links such as a common location or organization. Examples of these included *Knitters* ("I know them from Ravelry…I know some of them by name, most of them by screen name" [P7]) and *Photogs* ("I pretty much throw any photographer in there" [P12]).

Catch-All. The fourth type of Circle appeared to collect users who were unrelated or loosely-related. The intent behind creating these Circles was clear from some of their names: *Possible Friends*, *Acquaintances*, *Everything Else*.

DISCUSSION

In this paper, we analyzed data from the Google+ field trial to examine how expert users utilize the system to engage in *selective sharing*. We believe that insights generated from this work will aid in understanding needs of users of OSNs with respect to the following:

Contact Management. Analysis of common names for user-created Circles reflects a need to manage content separately for different **life facets** (with a focus on 'professional' life) and according to **tie strength**. These findings were strengthened by further qualitative study with expert users; specifically, we found them managing contacts by tie strength, creating 'Inner Circles' for sharing personal information with strong ties and 'Catch-All' Circles for weak ties (with whom they might be more cautious). This finding suggests that metaphors from the sharing of physical space in interactions [11] may translate online. Log analysis and interview data suggested that **topical interest** may also be an important grouping factor, and future study may reveal the extent to which this is true.

Future systems could explicitly aid in Circle management by suggesting members and proactively help in creating Circles for managing different aspects of life. We note that the heuristics for grouping which emerged from the needs of active users differed in some ways from those identified in prior simulated studies of friend grouping [16], revealing that groupings may evolve as a result of longitudinal engagement with the system. Users in our study often referenced future plans to modify Circles based on sharing or consumption challenges experienced during use, suggesting that the complexity of these real-life boundaries might make them difficult to infer automatically.

Reasons for Sharing. Based on expert users' responses, we have identified two primary 'reasons' for sharing. The first is the **inherent value of content** (e.g. it may be useful, funny, interesting, or otherwise pleasant to others). The other is a **desire to share about oneself** (e.g. expressing an inherent desire to relate one's personal experiences and opinions to others). Less prevalent reasons included engaging in **discourse** and **evangelism** on the part of others. We observe a large overlap with categories ('Informers' vs. 'Me-formers') identified by Naaman et al. based on receiver characterization of message content on Twitter [19]. While it remains to be seen whether sender motivations match receiver perceptions, our findings coupled with those from prior work suggest that these reasons may generalize across public and semi-public OSNs.

System designers may wish to explicitly create feedback mechanisms to help users manage self-presentations. While companies (e.g. Klout[1]) are pursuing explicit reputation scores, there exists room for innovation in self-analytics, such as visualizing for users types of content shared (e.g. proportion of messages about oneself) or responses and re-sharing of contributed information. These analytic capabilities might allow users to reflect on their sharing patterns and adjust them to suit their own needs, as well as those of their expected audiences.

Selective Sharing. We find that users engaging in selective sharing weigh four primary factors when choosing audiences for content. Three of these categories – **privacy**, **relevance**, and **social norms** – represent reasons why a user might choose to limit access, but we also found users expressing reasons for increasing content **distribution**.

These findings suggest revising our understanding of how users consider privacy generally in OSNs. Rather than framing decisions about privacy as 'boundaries' based on who is 'allowed' to view content, users may instead be balancing reasons to limit or to distribute content. Without proper controls for selective sharing, this can lead to previously under-explained behaviors such as over-sharing (e.g. 'context collapse' [18]) or fear of sharing (e.g. self-censoring [24, 26]). The design of proper selective sharing controls, however, allow users to balance sender and receiver needs and adapt these controls to different types of content. While similar controls may be available on other networks (e.g. 'Lists' on Facebook), making them central to the sharing model may be key to widespread user adoption.

The design of selective sharing controls offers a great opportunity to help users manage their self-presentations to multiple audiences. One might desire to share humorous content with family or friends while promoting a more professional image for clients and teammates. In the context of prior work on profile-sharing in OSNs [10], we observe that users may also benefit from tailoring of profiles to

[1] http://klout.com

show different information to each Circle. While our study focused on identifying factors considered when choosing an audience, future work will prove how users balance these considerations to ultimately make these decisions.

Models combining life facets, tie strength, and topical interest will be key to refining audience management, through Circles in Google+ or similar feature in other OSNs. A combined model might use network structure to identify strong ties or post content to estimate topical interest. In the competitive attention economy of the social web, helping messages reach appropriate audiences is an important design challenge. In the short-term, at least, it would seem that this challenge may be best met through a combination of user control and system features.

CONCLUSION

In this paper, we study Google+ to provide a first empirical study of behavior in a network designed to facilitate selective sharing. As this study focused on active users of a relatively new product, an obvious limitation of this work is that it may not generalize to the wider population and users of other networks. However, much of our findings both match with and help to explain prior findings on sharing across a variety of OSNs. As social networks move from a 'boundary' model to a more nuanced selective-sharing model, our study here points to the complexity of user behavior in this brave new world. We hope the results will inform other designers of social sharing mechanisms and ultimately help users manage their information better.

ACKNOWLEDGMENTS

We would like to thank the entire Google+ team, particularly Makoto Uchida and Alex Fabrikant for their support and help with data collection.

REFERENCES

1. Acquisti, A. & Gross, R. Imagined communities: Awareness, information sharing, and privacy on the Facebook. *Lect. Notes of Comp. Sci. 4258*: 36-58. 2006.
2. Adams, P. "The Real-Life Social Network". http://www.slideshare.net/padday/the-real-life-social-network-v2. 2010.
3. Altman, I. *The Environment and Social Behavior: Privacy, Personal Space, Territory, and Crowding*. Brooks/Cole Pub. Co, Monterey, CA, USA. 1975.
4. Barnes, S.B. A privacy paradox: Social networking in the United States. *First Monday, 11* (9). 2006.
5. Binder, J., Howes, A., & Sutcliffe, A. The problem of conflicting social spheres: effects of network structure on experienced tension in social network sites. *Proc. CHI '09*, 965-974. 2009.
6. Clauset, A., Shalizi, C.R., & Newman, M.E.J. Power-law distributions in empirical data. *SIAM Review 51*, 661-703. 2009.
7. Facebook, accessed 1/10/2012. http://www.facebook.com/press/info.php?statistics.
8. Farnham, S.D. & Churchill, E.F. Faceted identity, faceted lives: Social and technical issues with being yourself online. *Proc. CSCW '11*, 359-368. 2011.
9. Goffman, E. *The Presentation of Self in Everyday Life*. Garden City, New York: Doubleday. 1959.
10. Gross, R. & Acquisti, A. Information revelation and privacy in online social networks (The Facebook case). *Proc. ACM WPES '05*, 71-80. 2005.
11. Hall, E.T. *The Hidden Dimension*. New York: Doubleday. 1966.
12. Honeycutt, C. & Herring, S.C. Beyond microblogging: conversation and collaboration via Twitter. *Proc. HICSS '09*. 2009.
13. Hsieh, H.F. & Shannon, S.E. Three approaches to qualitative content analysis. *Qual. Health. Res., 15* (9), 1277-1288. 2005.
14. Huffaker, D.A. & Calvert, S.L. Gender, identity, and language use in teenage blogs. *JCMC, 10* (2). 2005.
15. Java, A., Song, X., Finin, T., & Tseng, B. Why we Twitter: understanding microblogging usage and communities. *Proc. WebKDD/SNA-KDD '07*. 2007.
16. Jones, S. & O'Neill, E. Feasibility of structural network clustering for group-based privacy control in social networks. *Proc. SOUPS '10*, 1-8. 2010.
17. Madden, M. & Zickuhr, K. Pew Internet, September 2011. http://www.pewinternet.org/Reports/2011/Social-Networking-Sites.aspx.
18. Marwick, A. & boyd, d. I Tweet honestly, I Tweet passionately: Twitter users, context collapse, and the imagined audience. *New Media & Society 13*, 96-113.
19. Naaman, M. Boase, J., & Lai, C-H. Is it really about me? Message content in social awareness streams. *Proc. CSCW '10*, 189-192. 2010.
20. Nardi, B., et al. Integrating communication and information through ContactMap. *CACM 45* (4), 89-95.
21. Ozenc, F.K. & Farnham, S.D. Life "modes" in social media. *Proc. CHI '11*, 561-570. 2011.
22. Palen, L. & Dourish, P. Unpacking "privacy" for a networked world. *Proc. CHI '03*, 129-136. 2003.
23. Skeels, M.M. & Grudin, J. When social networks cross boundaries: A case study of workplace use of Facebook and LinkedIn. *Proc. GROUP '09*, 95-104. 2009.
24. Strater, K. & Lipfort, H. Strategies and struggles with privacy in an online social networking community. *BCS-HCI '08*, 111-119. 2008.
25. Viégas, F.B. Bloggers' expectations of privacy and accountability: an initial survey. *JCMC, 10* (3). 2005.
26. Wang, Y, et al. "I regretted the minute I pressed share": A qualitative study of regrets on Facebook. *Proc. SOUPS '11*, 1-13. 2011.

Omnipedia: Bridging the Wikipedia Language Gap

Patti Bao[*†], Brent Hecht[†], Samuel Carton[†], Mahmood Quaderi[†], Michael Horn[†§], Darren Gergle[*†]
[*]Communication Studies, [†]Electrical Engineering & Computer Science, [§]Learning Sciences
Northwestern University
{patti,brent,sam.carton,quaderi}@u.northwestern.edu, {michael-horn,dgergle}@northwestern.edu

ABSTRACT
We present Omnipedia, a system that allows Wikipedia readers to gain insight from up to 25 language editions of Wikipedia simultaneously. Omnipedia highlights the similarities and differences that exist among Wikipedia language editions, and makes salient information that is unique to each language as well as that which is shared more widely. We detail solutions to numerous front-end and algorithmic challenges inherent to providing users with a multilingual Wikipedia experience. These include visualizing content in a language-neutral way and aligning data in the face of diverse information organization strategies. We present a study of Omnipedia that characterizes how people interact with information using a multilingual lens. We found that users actively sought information exclusive to unfamiliar language editions and strategically compared how language editions defined concepts. Finally, we briefly discuss how Omnipedia generalizes to other domains facing language barriers.

Author Keywords
Wikipedia; multilingual; hyperlingual; language barrier; user-generated content; text mining

ACM Classification Keywords
H5.m. [Information interfaces and presentation (e.g., HCI)]: Miscellaneous.

General Terms
Human Factors

INTRODUCTION
As the sixth most popular website in the world, Wikipedia has over 270 language editions, dozens of which have more than 100,000 articles [20]. Each language edition of the online encyclopedia has been shown to have a surprising amount of information not contained in any other language edition [11, 15]. This is true of both large Wikipedias like English and smaller ones such as Catalan and Finnish.

The language-induced splintering of information in Wikipedia poses both an opportunity and a challenge. On the one hand, Wikipedia embodies an unprecedented repository of *world knowledge diversity* in which each language edition contains its own cultural viewpoints on a large number of topics [7, 14, 15, 27]. On the other hand, the language barrier serves to silo knowledge [2, 4, 33], slowing the transfer of less culturally imbued information between language editions and preventing Wikipedia's 422 million monthly visitors [12] from accessing most of the information on the site.

Permission to make digital or hard copies of all or part of this work for personal or classroom use is granted without fee provided that copies are not made or distributed for profit or commercial advantage and that copies bear this notice and the full citation on the first page. To copy otherwise, or republish, to post on servers or to redistribute to lists, requires prior specific permission and/or a fee.
CHI'12, May 5–10, 2012, Austin, Texas, USA.
Copyright 2012 ACM 978-1-4503-1015-4/12/05...$10.00.

In this paper, we present Omnipedia, a system that attempts to remedy this situation at a large scale. It reduces the silo effect by providing users with structured access in their native language to over 7.5 million concepts from up to 25 language editions of Wikipedia. At the same time, it highlights similarities and differences between each of the language editions, allowing users to see the diversity of the represented knowledge. To achieve this goal, Omnipedia extracts the topics discussed in each language edition's coverage of a given concept, then loads them into an interactive visualization that shows which language editions mention which topics and how those topics are discussed.

Consider, for example, the English Wikipedia article "Conspiracy theory". This article discusses many topics, from "Moon landing" to "Kennedy assassination". However, many other language editions also contain articles on this concept, such as "*Verschwörungstheorie*" in the German Wikipedia and "*Teoría conspirativa*" in the Spanish Wikipedia. Omnipedia consolidates these articles into a single "multilingual article" on conspiracy theories, as seen in Figure 1. The small circles on the left represent

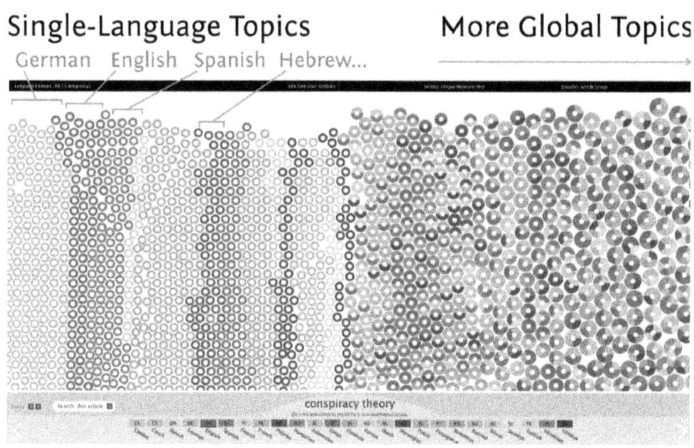

Figure 1. A screenshot of Omnipedia showing the multilingual article "Conspiracy theory" in zoomed-out mode. Small circles on the left indicate topics that are discussed in only a single language edition's coverage of the concept. Bigger circles on the right indicate topics that are discussed in multiple language editions' coverage of "Conspiracy theory".

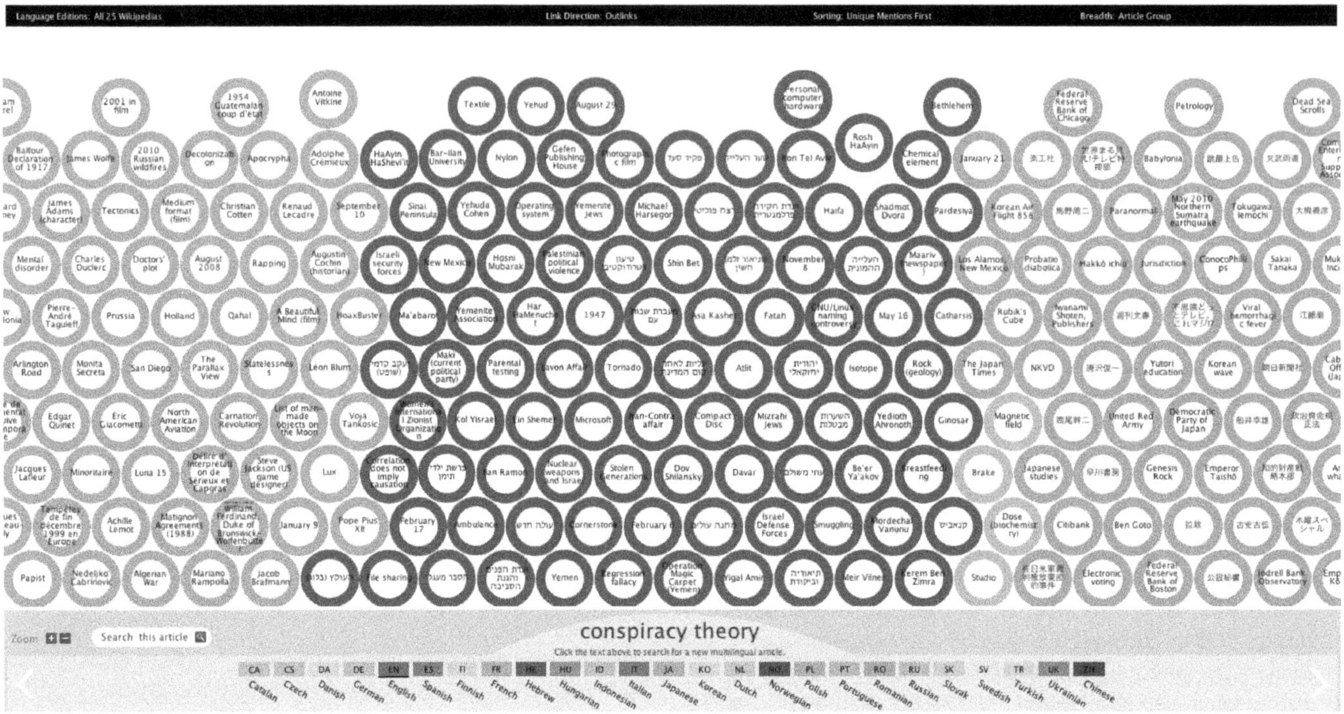

Figure 2. "Conspiracy theory" in zoomed-in mode. The user can see specific topics discussed in each language edition's article. Because the user has panned over to the single language linked topics, s/he can see that the Hebrew Wikipedia (dark green) discusses "Palestinian political violence" while the French Wikipedia (cyan) discusses "Algerian War". Clicking on one of the circles calls up a snippet (Figure 4) from the corresponding Wikipedia article(s) that explains the discussion of each topic in detail.

topics discussed in only one language edition: yellow for German, dark blue for English, and so on. It should be clear that by only reading a single language edition's coverage—even that of English—one misses out on huge amounts of content available in other language editions. Moving toward the right half of Figure 1, one begins to see larger, multi-colored circles that represent topics that are discussed in multiple language editions' coverage of the concept.

Zooming in (Figure 2) allows users to explore content in more detail. For instance, Figure 2 shows that the Hebrew Wikipedia (dark green) has a great deal of exclusive content about Israel-related conspiracy theories. The French Wikipedia (cyan) also has unique content, both pertaining to French history, as indicated by "Algerian War", and of more general interest, such as "Pope Pius XII". Panning right, users begin to find topics that are discussed in more than one language edition. Figure 3 shows the most commonly discussed topics in the "Conspiracy theory" multilingual article, which include "Freemasonry", "United States", and "Central Intelligence Agency". We also see that Judaism is discussed in many language editions' coverage of conspiracy theories, demonstrating that this form of anti-Semitism is unfortunately widespread. To discover precisely how these topics are discussed in various language editions, users can click on a topic circle. This returns a snippet mined from each language edition that covers the clicked topic, with snippets translated into the user-defined language using machine translation (Figure 4).

This simple example offers a brief glimpse of the capabilities of Omnipedia. In addition to the system itself, this paper presents several technical contributions related to building highly multilingual or "hyperlingual" [15] applications. In particular, we introduce natural language processing and information retrieval strategies that are sensitive to the diversity of world knowledge in Wikipedia. These advances have broader implications for human-centered technologies intended to work with a wide variety of users and contexts.

RELATED WORK

There is a growing field of research on multilingual Wikipedia that can be broadly divided into two groups: (1) work that studies multilingual Wikipedia and (2) work that attempts to propagate information from one Wikipedia language edition to another.

The general consensus on multilingual Wikipedia is that while English (the largest language edition) has a content advantage, each language edition has a great deal of unique information not available in other language editions, and most other information exists in only a few language editions [11, 15]. This diversity occurs in terms of *which* concepts are covered as well as *how* concepts are covered [11, 15], the latter of which is what Omnipedia visualizes more directly.

Mounting evidence suggests that some of these differences are due to variation in world knowledge across language-

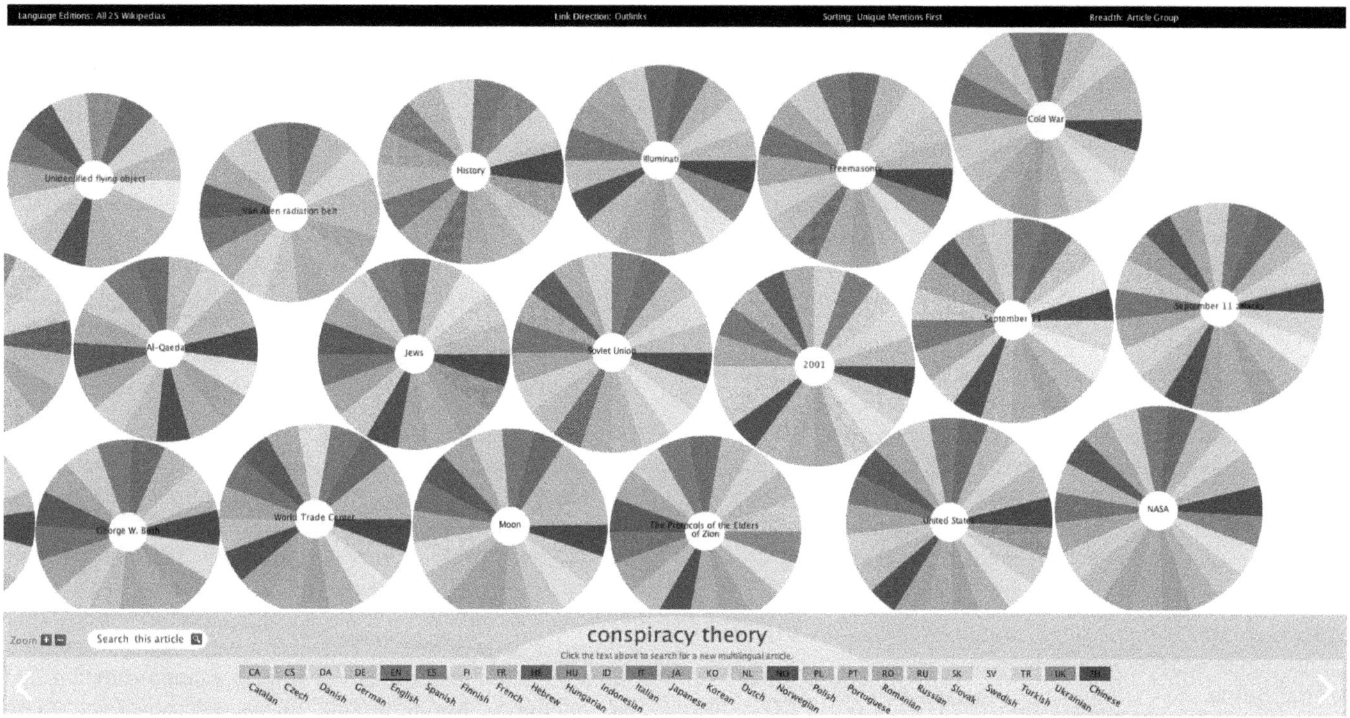

Figure 3. Panning over all the way to the right from Figure 2 reveals the linked topics that are shared among all or nearly all of the language editions' discussion of "Conspiracy theory". These include topics like "Politics", "September 11 attacks", and "NASA".

defined communities, not simply missed opportunities for translation. At the detailed content level, Pfeil et al. [27] analyzed a single concept in four language editions along dimensions of cultural influence. Their findings suggest that certain properties of edits to the corresponding articles could be predicted by the national culture most associated with the corresponding language. Callahan and Herring [7] examined articles about famous persons in the Polish and English Wikipedias and concluded that, while English generally had the most information, language-defined communities played a significant role in differences between the language editions. At a larger scale, Hecht and Gergle [14] used Wikipedia articles about geographic entities to show that there is a great deal of self-focus bias in each language edition of Wikipedia. In other words, the language editions place a disproportionate emphasis on areas within their "culture hearths" (home regions).

The second main area of research on multilingual Wikipedia focuses on propagating information from one Wikipedia language edition to another. These approaches include automated techniques as well as those that rely upon having a "human-in-the-loop". Ziggurat [2] automates the populating of Wikipedia infoboxes in one language edition using data from another language edition. Systems like WikiBhasha [19, 33] and Google Translator Toolkit [30] aim to achieve partial automation by using machine translation to aid humans in propagating information from one Wikipedia (typically English) to another (typically a language edition with a small number of articles). Finally, there have been recent efforts to use the power of human computation to rapidly translate articles between language editions [3, 10].

While these propagation approaches are driven by the commendable goal of making information widely available to speakers of any language, they share one or more of three important limitations—none of which are displayed by Omnipedia. First and foremost, their efforts to reduce the fractured nature of Wikipedia often come at the expense of preserving knowledge diversity across language editions. These approaches typically require decisions to be made about the "correct" content and discard distinctions between languages and viewpoints. Second, many of these systems focus on small numbers of language editions, often two at a time, thus incorporating only a small percentage of the information available in Wikipedia. While in theory these systems can be used to propagate information pairwise

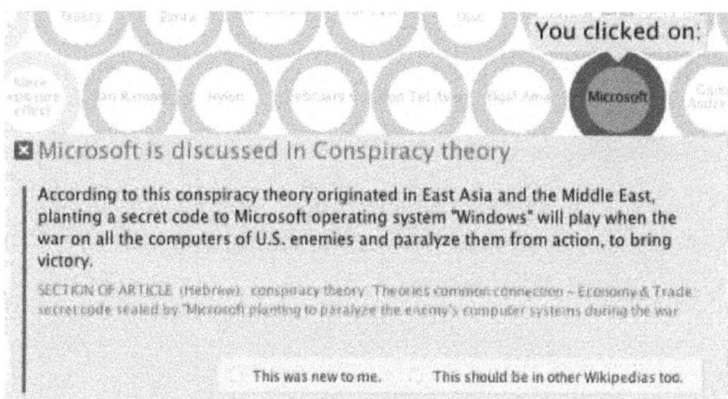

Figure 4. The snippet explaining how Microsoft is discussed in the Hebrew Wikipedia article on conspiracy theory. This is the only part of Omnipedia that relies on live machine translation.

across language editions *ad infinitum*, they typically leave to future work the issue of what to do when conflicts arise between language editions and other major challenges that result from viewing the encyclopedia more globally. Finally, each of these approaches require large changes to Wikipedia itself for readers to benefit—changes that generally have not been realized at a global scale for various reasons including the amount of human labor involved. In contrast to these approaches, Omnipedia requires no changes to Wikipedia itself and can be used immediately.

Basic machine translation can be used to compare two or more articles about the same topic in different language editions, and there are sites like Manypedia [21] that automate this process. Moreover, individuals with skills in multiple languages can do the same without machine translation. However, in both cases, this approach is limited to a very small number of languages and detailed cross-language comparisons are quite difficult.

Although we believe it is the first of its kind in the multilingual space, Omnipedia is not the first system to use visualization to illuminate aspects of Wikipedia. A considerable body of work has used visualization techniques to surface coordination and conflict patterns among Wikipedia editors. Notable examples include History Flow [31], Chromograms [32], Revert Graph [29], and visualizations of trustworthiness metrics [18]. Each of these systems allows users to gain insight into the editing processes underlying a given Wikipedia language edition.

THE OMNIPEDIA SYSTEM

Omnipedia was designed to facilitate exploration of hyperlingual Wikipedia on a concept-by-concept basis. Users typically begin their interaction with Omnipedia by typing in a concept of interest, for instance "Conspiracy theory". Omnipedia will then look up the corresponding multilingual article and display the types of visualizations seen in Figures 1–3 using circles of different sizes and colors to indicate the topics that are discussed in various language editions' coverage of the entered concept.

Each circle denotes a topic that is mentioned in at least one language edition of Wikipedia. We extract these topics by looking at existing and missing hyperlinks to other articles in the same language edition (i.e., outlinks) within each of the current multilingual article's constituent monolingual articles. To determine the degree to which topics are discussed across language editions, Omnipedia merely looks up the corresponding multilingual article for each monolingual outlink. This allows the system to understand that nearly all articles about the concept "Conspiracy theory" discuss the United States even though each monolingual article links to its own language edition's equivalent article (e.g., "*Estats Units d'Amèrica*" (Catalan) and "*Vereinigte Staaten*" (German)). Each topic is thus itself another multilingual article that can be visualized in Omnipedia. By double-clicking on a circle, the user can browse through related topics, just as they can follow hyperlinks in the normal version of each language edition.

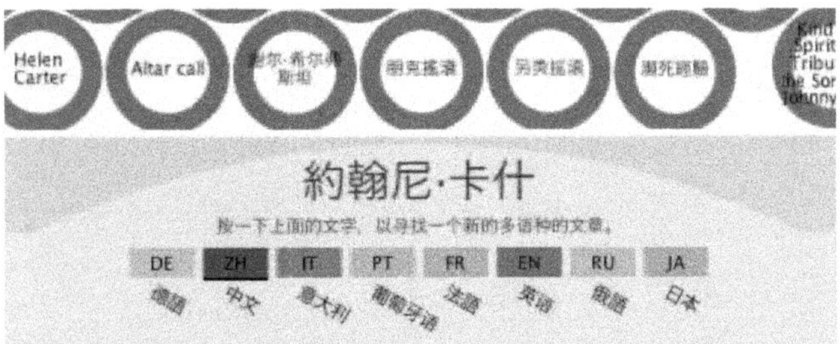

Figure 5. The multilingual article "Johnny Cash" with the interface language set to Chinese.

A central design premise for Omnipedia is that it is language neutral. As such, users are able to switch the interface language to any of the 25 supported languages. If a user switches the interface language to Chinese, for example, she is able to look up multilingual articles by their Chinese titles and sees topic titles in Chinese (Figure 5). Because this process relies on the structures built into Wikipedia, it involves no machine translation–an essential requirement for the system as machine translation on this scale would be too slow and, in the common case where thousands of topic titles are visualized, would excessively tax common machine translation APIs. When a topic that is discussed does not have a corresponding monolingual article in the interface language, we use a back-off strategy that, for instance, displays a single-language linked topic title in its native language.

Omnipedia is also language neutral in that it allows users to include or exclude any of the 25 supported languages, creating custom language sets at will. Omnipedia makes several built-in language sets available to the user, including "Languages of the Top Ten Economies", "NATO Languages", "EU Languages", etc. Once a language set is changed, all visualization and algorithmic systems are updated accordingly. For instance, in Figure 5, the user has selected the top ten economies language set.

When designing Omnipedia, we opted for a visualization strategy over a text-based approach largely because text alignment across just two languages is known to be a difficult problem [1, 4, 26], let alone text alignment across 25 languages. In doing so we lose certain advantages of text, like the grouping of related topics into a single, cohesive discussion. We mitigate this situation by using a well-known semantic relatedness algorithm [24] adapted for operation in Omnipedia. When a user clicks on a topic circle to view an explanation snippet, Omnipedia flags highly related topics with a "See Also" tag. For instance, when browsing the multilingual article "Barbecue", a user might be curious as to why "Kashrut" is discussed in the corresponding German article. When she clicks on the "Kashrut" circle, the topics "Israeli cuisine", "Modern Hebrew" and "Pastrami" are highlighted to guide further exploration. As it turns out, there is an Orthodox Jewish barbecue festival in Memphis every year.

Omnipedia allows users to adjust a breadth setting that determines what is treated as an "article". This helps the user to deal with structural differences that may occur across articles or language editions. For example, large articles are sometimes broken down into a main article and its sub-articles (e.g., "Conspiracy theory" (English) and "List of conspiracy theories" (English), respectively). Because each language edition uses its own syntactic structures to indicate main article/sub-article relationships, we use a hand-coded list of all structures to discover sub-articles. At the broadest breadth setting, Omnipedia groups main articles and sub-articles into one multilingual article (as is done in Figures 1–3). The medium breadth setting shows only what is discussed in the main article(s). Finally, the narrowest breadth setting considers only the paragraphs that precede the first section break of each article, thus showing diversity in how concepts are summarized.

Finally, before moving on to Omnipedia's algorithmic challenges, it is important to briefly describe the dataset on which Omnipedia operates. We most recently updated Omnipedia's Wikipedia database in August 2011. This database contains 15.2 million articles and 445.3 million links. Using a sample of 1,500 multilingual articles, we confirmed the results of prior work [11, 15] in that only 15.9% (on average) of linked topics discussed in a multilingual article were discussed in all of the languages in which the article existed. Moreover, even the largest language edition, English, was missing approximately 60% of linked topics on average. These statistics were generated after running the algorithms described below, and confirm that Omnipedia users have a great deal of unique information and diverse knowledge to explore, no matter their native language(s).

ALGORITHMIC CHALLENGES

Omnipedia relies on a number of natural language processing (NLP) and information retrieval (IR) algorithms to support core functions. However, in the hyperlingual space, algorithmic approaches and their evaluation strategies have been critiqued for ignoring the diversity that exists across language-defined communities and being biased towards English [15, 17]. In this section, we describe novel algorithms and evaluation strategies we developed to achieve Omnipedia's mission of highlighting and respecting diversity across language editions, while at the same time showing information from many language editions in a structured fashion. Both our algorithms and their evaluation strategies have implications for other Wikipedia systems and research that require concept-by-concept access to multiple language editions (e.g., [2, 4]).

Hyperlingual Article Alignment

A fundamental requirement for Omnipedia is an algorithm that can group Wikipedia articles in different languages into multilingual articles. The algorithm should, for example, be able to match the article "Conspiracy theory" (English) to "*Teoría conspirativa*" (Spanish), etc. The accuracy of this algorithm and its ability to respect diversity across language editions are very important to Omnipedia's success because almost every aspect of Omnipedia operates on the multilingual articles that are its output.

We make use of Wikipedia's *interlanguage link* graph to identify and group articles about the same concept in different language editions. Interlanguage links (ILLs) are connections between articles in distinct language editions entered by humans and propagated by bots in certain cases. They are supposed to indicate near conceptual equivalence between pages in different languages. For instance, the article "Texas" (English) contains an ILL to "*Texas* (*staat*)" (Dutch). While there are omissions [28], ILLs have been shown to have relatively good coverage [15].

The standard approach in the literature is to assume that any two articles connected by a path in the ILL graph belong to the same multilingual article [2, 15]. This approach was insufficient for Omnipedia's hyperlingual context due to the fact that it ignores ambiguities in the ILL graph. Ambiguities occur when multiple articles in the *same* language edition are connected via articles in other language editions, meaning that a corresponding multilingual article would have more than one article per language. While only 1.0% of multilingual articles are initially ambiguous, many of them describe concepts that are of general and global interest because the potential for ambiguity increases as more language editions cover a given concept. This becomes a large problem for Omnipedia, as users are likely to be interested in concepts of general and global interest.

One major source of ambiguities in the ILL graph is conceptual drift across language editions. Conceptual drift stems from the well-known finding in cognitive science that the boundaries of concepts vary across language-defined communities [13]. For instance, the English articles "High school" and "Secondary school" are grouped into a single connected concept. While placing these two articles in the same multilingual article may be reasonable given their overlapping definitions around the world, excessive conceptual drift can result in a semantic equivalent of what happens in the children's game known as "telephone". For instance, chains of conceptual drift expand the aforementioned connected concept to include the English articles "Primary school", "Etiquette", "Manners", and even "Protocol (diplomacy)". Omnipedia users would be confused to see "Kyoto Protocol" as a linked topic when they looked up "High school". A similar situation occurs in the large connected concept that spans the semantic range from "River" to "Canal" to "Trench warfare", and in another which contains "Woman" and "Marriage" (although, interestingly, not "Man").

In order for Omnipedia to enable users to explore this vital 1.0% of concepts, we needed an algorithm to split concepts that were subject to runaway conceptual drift[1]. However, at the same time, this algorithm should respect the fact that different languages may define a concept more widely or narrowly than other languages.

Approach to Resolving Ambiguities

Our approach draws on the conceptual spaces framework from cognitive science [13], in which a concept is a region in a multi-dimensional semantic space. Generally speaking, the higher the average semantic similarity between pairs of concept instances, the smaller the area of the concept. The goal of our approach is thus to split ambiguous concepts by dividing them into regions with higher average semantic similarity. One method would be to attempt to match the average semantic similarity of the 99% of concepts that are not ambiguous. Alternatively, a hyperlingual application designer may want to allow for slightly more conceptual drift (e.g., to include "High School" and "Secondary School" in the same concept), while at the same time eliminating cases like "Woman" and "Marriage".

In order to enable this approach in practice, we introduce an algorithm that allows hyperlingual application designers to adjust the amount of allowable conceptual drift to suit their application needs. Our algorithm strategically removes ILL edges from ambiguous concepts, splitting connected components of the ILL graph into more coherent groups. We removed edges along two dimensions: (1) limiting the number of edges from a given language that can point to the same article in another language (*MaxEdges*), and (2) using a voting scheme that required a certain percentage of language editions to agree on an edge before it could remain (*MinLangs*).

Finally, to measure the semantic similarity of multilingual articles generated by our algorithm, we developed a hyperlingual approach that leverages the same semantic relatedness measure we use to calculate "See Also" topics in Omnipedia. This measure can be used to calculate the semantic similarity between pairs of articles that make up the newly generated multilingual articles[2], regardless of the languages in which those articles are written.

Exploring Parameters

To better understand the ability of our algorithm to generate cohesive multilingual articles as well as its ability to allow designers some flexibility in that cohesiveness, we randomly selected 2,000 ambiguous multilingual articles from our dataset and performed a grid search on the parameters. To establish a reasonable upper bound, we also randomly selected 2,000 unambiguous multilingual articles with pages in two or more languages. For both groups of articles, we calculated the pairwise in-concept semantic similarity for each possible article pair. As a baseline, we did the same for the default state of the ILL graph. For the default state of the ILL graph and the output of our algorithm, we also report the mean "out-concept" similarity, which is the average similarity of articles not in the same concept. Setting *MaxEdges* to any value other than one significantly reduced the average semantic similarity in all cases, so we only report data where *MaxEdges* = 1. Finally, in order to provide an additional perspective on our algorithm's performance, we evaluated our results against the comparable portions of de Melo and Weikum's bilingual German/English dataset [22].

As shown in Table 1, using our algorithm it is possible to match and even exceed the semantic cohesiveness of non-ambiguous multilingual articles, at least with our 25-language dataset. Moreover, for the parameters that result in these high average similarities, performance on the de Melo and Weikum dataset matches and exceeds that of de Melo and Weikum's algorithm. This is true even though our algorithm is far simpler than their complex linear program solution, although their work is focused on graph theory aspects of the problem. Table 1 also shows that our algorithm gives designers significant leeway in allowing for more conceptual drift, meeting the second goal for the algorithm.

The question then becomes, as application designers of Omnipedia, which parameters should we choose? We initially used *MaxEdges* = 1 and *MinLangs* = 70%, matching the semantic similarity of unambiguous concepts. This effectively normalized ambiguity across our entire dataset. However, after examining hundreds of concepts split by our algorithm set to these parameters, we determined that it was too strict to meet Omnipedia's goals of respecting diversity in concept definitions. For instance, "High school" (English) and "Secondary school" (English) were split into separate concepts, even though in many languages these concepts are one and the same. By reducing

MaxEdge	*MinLang*	In-Concept Similarity	Out-Concept Similarity	de Melo Accuracy
1	0%	0.65	0.29	73.7
1	20%	0.67	0.29	77.0
1	**50%**	**0.73**	**0.30**	**81.2**
1	70%	0.78	0.31	87.5
1	90%	0.81	0.33	91.4
1	100%	0.82	0.41	87.5
ILL Graph		0.41	0.26	51.2
Unambiguous Articles		0.78	n/a	n/a
de Melo Algorithm		n/a	n/a	89.7

Table 1. Ambiguity levels of the concepts output by our article alignment algorithm. Bold indicates the parameters used by Omnipedia.

[1] Mistaken ILLs input by Wikipedia editors are another source of ambiguities but algorithmically speaking, these can be treated simply as extreme cases of conceptual drift.

[2] It is standard research practice to use semantic relatedness measures to calculate similarity [6].

MinLang to 50%, we found that we could still maintain a high in-concept similarity, while also including these two articles in the same multilingual concept. Moreover, the algorithm with these parameters had no trouble splitting runaway conceptual drift cases like "Woman" and "Marriage", "River" and "Trench warfare", etc.

Hyperlingual Link Alignment

Early versions of Omnipedia only used explicit outlinks as a proxy for topics discussed in a multilingual article. This approach was motivated by the increasing popularity of "bags of links" models to represent unstructured texts (e.g., [1, 25]) and the use of these models in the multilingual Wikipedia space [1, 15, 21]. However, in a hyperlingual context this form of representation suffers from a failure to recognize the varying linking practices across language editions and individual articles.

In Omnipedia, this problem manifests when an article in a given language edition discusses a topic linked to by other language editions, but no explicit link exists in the given language edition. A bag of links representation would assume that the topic is not discussed in the article, even though it may play a prominent role. Ignoring this "missing link" issue would unfairly bias results toward those language editions with more links on a given topic. Without the link alignment algorithm described in this section, Omnipedia would inform users that the multilingual article "Sociology" would have discussed "Theory" in only one language edition. Moreover, because different language editions have different (and relatively strict) rules about linking to dates, the "September 11" and "2001" circles in Figure 3 would be much smaller, misleading users into thinking the events of that day were a less global source of conspiracy theories.

We resolve this problem with our hyperlingual link alignment algorithm, which is best understood by example. Returning to Figure 3, we find that the Spanish article about conspiracy theories does not link to an article about unidentified flying objects (UFOs) while many of the other language editions do. However, the Spanish Wikipedia does have an article about UFOs ("*Objeto volador no identificado*" (Spanish)). This is the situation in which our hyperlingual link alignment algorithm is applied. Broadly speaking, the algorithm searches the article "*Teoría conspirativa*" (Spanish) for the text "*Objeto volador no identificado*" and its synonyms (redirects in the Spanish Wikipedia). It happens to find the text "*OVNI*", one such redirect, in a discussion of prominent conspiracy theories, indicating that UFOs are indeed a missing link. Omnipedia therefore includes Spanish in the set of languages that discuss UFOs (as seen in Figure 3). This process is repeated for all language editions in Omnipedia.

Evaluation Experiment

To evaluate whether our approach found an unreasonable number of incorrect links or overlooked an unreasonable number of missing links, we turn to the literature on the similar but monolingual problem of wikification [23, 25]. A robust evaluation strategy in this literature involves measuring accuracy against manually labeled data [25]. However, this method runs into the central problem of hyperlingual algorithm evaluation: finding several human labelers for each of many languages is a considerable challenge. We were able to sidestep this problem by leveraging the large supply of labeled data we already have in the form of the links that *do* exist in each language edition. Following Mihalcea and Csomai [23], we strip each test article of all markup (indications of links) and then assess whether or not we can accurately rediscover the links in the article. If our algorithm can do this successfully, we can reasonably suggest that our algorithm can do the same in text that is missing links in the actual hyperlingual dataset.

We ran this experiment on 15,000 randomly selected multilingual articles that have articles in at least two languages. The minimum number of articles considered for a given language was 599 (Indonesian) and the maximum was 12,391 (English). Our algorithm's average recall across all test articles was 75.0% and its average precision was 80.4%. These results are on par with the accuracy of the popular wikification algorithm by Milne and Witten [25], although the problem space is slightly different. While precision was in the upper 70s through high 80s for all languages (range = 76.2–88.7%), recall exhibited greater variance (range = 53.7–86.8%). Chinese had 80.9% recall despite the text processing adaptions necessary to support East Asian languages. However, highlighting the importance of hyperlingual evaluation, we discovered that Finnish and a few of the Slavic languages had lower recall in the mid-50s and low 60s. While this performance is comparable with another popular wikification algorithm [23], it does put these languages at a slight disadvantage in Omnipedia. Future work involves experimenting with different stemming algorithms and taking other approaches to improve recall in these languages.

On average, our algorithm increased the number of linked topics in an article by 51.7%, although a portion of this gain is due only to the differences in date linking practices. For many of the smaller language editions, the number of found topics was much higher. This is not a surprise, as the link density of the English Wikipedia is known to have grown over time [8]. For instance, the algorithm more than doubled the number of Indonesian linked topics per article (134.0%). Even in the Slavic languages with lower recall, we found large numbers of new links (e.g., 67.6% increase for Slovak, 59.8% for Czech). For the older, larger language editions, the number of new links was smaller (e.g., 37.3% for Japanese, 38.7% for English).

Our algorithm's ability to find many new links with good precision and good recall allows Omnipedia to accurately visualize content beyond that just in the link graph. It also problematizes the use of the popular bag of links approach in a hyperlingual context. For instance, an algorithm or hyperlingual application that compared English and Indonesian articles using a bag of links approach would heavily bias the English Wikipedia.

STUDY

To better understand how people might interact with the diverse information made accessible by Omnipedia, we conducted a study with 27 participants. This allowed us to observe how people gained insights when viewing concepts of their choice through Omnipedia's hyperlingual lens.

Participants and Method

Twenty-seven people (14 female, 13 male, ranging from 18-62 years old) participated in the study, all of whom had accessed Wikipedia at least once in the past 30 days. Participants consisted of 20 native English speakers, four native Chinese (Mandarin) speakers, one native Russian speaker, and two native speakers of English and one other language not supported by Omnipedia. Sixteen users were fluent or proficient in at least one other language besides their native language. These additional languages were Spanish (10 users), English (5), French (1), Japanese (1) Korean (1), and Telugu (1, not supported by Omnipedia). On average, participants had used the English Wikipedia for 6 years (self-reported, *SD* = 1.84). Ten participants had previously seen a non-English Wikipedia, but only three considered themselves frequent users.

Participants arrived at the laboratory and were taken to a private room with a desktop machine and 23" display. The experimenter then provided a 10-minute demonstration of Omnipedia's main features and afterwards proceeded to a separate observation room. Participants were given 30 minutes to freely explore multilingual articles in Omnipedia using any of the languages they wished. Afterwards, the experimenter returned to the room to lead a structured interview asking participants to reflect on their experience. Participants were prompted with specific instances drawn from their interaction logs. We based our analysis on 58,900 words of transcribed interviews, 41,704 logged events (including mouse hovers, clicks, queries, and changes to view settings), and 30 pages of observation notes. We now use this data to characterize user exploration of hyperlingual Wikipedia through Omnipedia and describe some of the insights they shared with us.

Results

Just over half (14) of our users had never seen a non-English Wikipedia prior to the study. When using Omnipedia, all users took the opportunity to access information from a non-English Wikipedia, the five most popular being French, Italian, Russian, German, and Spanish. Twenty-two users switched to one of Omnipedia's built-in language sets at least once during the study (*M* = 3.1 switches, *SD* = 3.49). Twelve of these users also created a custom language set. Users tailored these sets based on their own language proficiency, relevance to the concept of interest, or curiosity about a never-before seen Wikipedia. On average, users looked up 15 multilingual articles (*SD* = 6.25). They clicked on 60 discussed topics on average (*SD* = 34.7) to load the type of snippets seen in Figure 4. Of all the topics users clicked on, 26.7% had been highlighted as related topics by the semantic relatedness algorithm.

Exploring Similarities and Differences

After seeing the diversity of linked topics among language editions, many users concentrated on the most common topics (or biggest circles), typically citing reasons involving the perceived importance of these topics (e.g., "if it was in all four languages, it must be important" (P7)). Viewing these topics often required users to pan all the way to the opposite end of the visualization (as seen in Figure 3), which they took the effort to do in order to gain insight into what was "well known" worldwide (P18). Many of these users were satisfied with clicking on these topics and reading just one of its multiple snippets.

However, other users read all of the snippets from more globally discussed topics in detail to see if there were "cultural nuances" (P23). Users who engaged in this type of behavior realized that just because multiple language editions shared a link to a topic did not necessarily mean that they agreed on *how* the topic was related. For example, P4 recalled looking up the multilingual article "Boeing 767" and discovering that the English snippet on a plane crash in Egypt included "different perspectives on what happened" while other language editions "just summarized one sentence". Similarly, P12 expected that German coverage of "Siemens" would gloss over the company's support of the Nazi movement during World War II. He was surprised to find that the German Wikipedia's snippet was "the most descriptive about that fact".

Other users spent little time investigating the most common topics, regarding them as "pretty obvious" (P25) or "basic things" (P10) that would not yield the most interesting insights. Instead, they searched for differences in topic coverage by looking at single-language topics (or smallest circles) across language editions. One approach was to examine relative proportions of single-language topics in a given multilingual article. For instance, P17 inferred that American basketball player Dwight Howard was "definitely more famous in the English version than in any other language" based on the considerable number of topics discussed only in the English Wikipedia. Likewise, P24 was not surprised to find that a minor tennis player only had coverage in English while "Rafael Nadal had more single-language links from Spanish and other languages because he's a worldwide figure". She, like others, interpreted these differences as a measure of the concept's (e.g., Rafael Nadal's) global "reach" or "impact".

Users who took this approach also discovered distributions of single-language topics that belied their expectations. P10 was surprised to find that "even Italian and Spanish had something to say" about Jainism, an Indian religion. P6 compared several music genres and was not surprised to find that hip-hop had "more in English" but was surprised to discover that reggae had "a lot in Japanese".

Another approach for finding differences among language editions involved targeting concepts that might be more likely to reveal differences in perspective. A subset of users actively sought out what they considered to be "globally polarized" (P20) or "heavily charged" (P23) concepts like "Climate skepticism" and "War on Terror". They intentionally included language editions that they thought would reveal "different sides" (e.g., P13, who looked up "The Holocaust" in German, Hebrew, and Polish). In most cases, however, users did not find the extreme differences they anticipated, leading them to reconsider their own expectations regarding hyperlingual Wikipedia.

Discovering New Knowledge

Users actively sought out knowledge not available in their own language editions. For example, the 11 "monolingual" users who were fluent in English but had no more than rudimentary knowledge of another language clicked on topics that, on average, were mentioned in 2.79 language editions (*SD* = 2.06). Thirty-six percent of all topics clicked by these users were not discussed at all in English.

Users often reported clicking on topics discussed in one language because they might have "interesting facts that I hadn't heard of" (P26). For certain multilingual articles, users paid attention to unique topics in a single language edition where they expected a close tie to the language's culture hearth. For example, P6 "focused on the Italian side [of the visualization] just because Sardinia's in Italy". He also looked at Chinese-only topics discussed in "Google" because he thought they might reference Google's search restrictions in China. Similarly, P16 thought "the Japanese-only information will be more authentic since Ayumi Hamasaki is from Japan". Conversely, one user decided to exclude a language (Chinese) from the interface because it "wasn't giving me much" in terms of unique information.

In other cases, users investigated single-language topics from many language editions. For instance, P10 wanted to see "if maybe one culture viewed a certain aspect of 'Beauty' that [she] didn't know". After discovering a number of Japanese-only topics that seemed to emphasize "character", she went on to examine English-only topics and observed that they discussed "beauty in the eye of the beholder" as well as "physical" attributes.

Finally, it is worth noting that the sheer amount of single-language topics was a revelation to the majority of users. Reflecting on their use of Omnipedia, a few users who initially focused on the more global topics wished they had more time to explore the single-language topics, as those may have yielded different insights. P1 even told us in hindsight, "If I had bothered to take my time and go through all the single [language] ones, I think I would have learned more about what the differences were."

In sum, four key insights emerged from users' interactions with Omnipedia. First, users took advantage of the fact that using a hyperlingual lens, they could identify the most commonly and globally discussed aspects of a concept's Wikipedia definition. Second, they were able to discover both similarities and differences in how these topics were discussed among language editions. Third, access to single-language topics allowed users to not only filter interesting topics based on inferences of self-focus bias [14], but also get a big picture view of how much topics were being discussed in different language editions. Finally, users began to comprehend the magnitude of information that was not available to them in the English Wikipedia.

FUTURE WORK

We have focused this paper on Omnipedia's capacity to help users explore hyperlingual Wikipedia. However, we are working to extend Omnipedia to other forms of hyperlingual user-generated content as well. Sites such as Twitter and Flickr suffer from the same language barriers as Wikipedia and have also been shown to display important differences across languages [9, 16]. Future work might treat a Twitter hash tag as an "article" and mine tweets posted in many languages that contain the hash tag for discussed topics. Similarly, a group of related photos (e.g., of the same event) could be used as the "article" and the photos' tags could be considered topics.

As Wikipedia is an extremely popular source of world knowledge for many artificial intelligence, IR and NLP systems, we suspect that the algorithms introduced here will apply outside of the Omnipedia context. For instance, we are working to build an improved hyperlingual semantic relatedness measure based on our link alignment algorithm and our concept alignment strategy. This measure could be used in everything from Omnipedia to cross-language coordination tools [5] to more traditional cross-language information retrieval.

Finally, as we move toward a wider deployment of Omnipedia, we have started collecting user feedback about which information should be directly propagated across language editions and which information is more culturally specific. Users can already flag content in explanations as information that should be in other Wikipedias as well (Figure 4). We believe that some of the non-global information that Omnipedia makes salient should definitely be propagated to other language editions. However, as this occurs, we anticipate that users will be able to focus more clearly on Omnipedia's ability to surface cultural diversity.

CONCLUSION

In this paper, we have made several contributions. First, we introduced Omnipedia, a system that for the first time allows simultaneous access to large numbers of Wikipedia language editions. In doing so, Omnipedia makes salient the diversity of knowledge represented in all considered language editions. Powering Omnipedia are several new algorithms that preserve diversity while solving large-scale data processing issues. Finally, we demonstrated the kinds of insight Omnipedia affords with a 27-participant study, which led one user to remark "It's ridiculous how many different things are mentioned in different languages that aren't mentioned in others."

ACKNOWLEDGMENTS

We thank our reviewers, our participants, Alan Clark, Lauren Scissors, Candace Brown, Jermaine Dictado, and the CollabLab for their valuable insight. Funding was provided by NSF grant #0953943 and an NSF GRFP award.

REFERENCES

1. Adafre, S.F. and de Rijke, M. 2006. Finding Similar Sentences Across Multiple Languages in Wikipedia. *EACL 2006 Workshop on New Text, Wikis and Blogs and Other Dynamic Text Sources*.
2. Adar, E., Skinner, M. and Weld, D.S. 2009. Information Arbitrage Across Multi-lingual Wikipedia. *WSDM '09.*
3. von Ahn, L. 2011. Three human computation projects. (2011). *SIGCSE '11.*
4. Au Yeung, C.-man, Duh, K. and Nagata, M. 2011. Providing Cross-Lingual Editing Assistance to Wikipedia Editors. *CICL '11.*
5. Bergstrom, T. and Karahalios, K. 2009. Conversation clusters: grouping conversation topics through human-computer dialog. *CHI '09.*
6. Budanitsky, A. and Hirst, G. 2006. Evaluating WordNet-based Measures of Lexical Semantic Relatedness. *Computational Linguistics*. 32, 1 (2006), 13-47.
7. Callahan, E.S. and Herring, S.C. Cultural bias in Wikipedia content on famous persons. *Journal of the American Society for Information Science and Technology*. 62: 1899–1915.
8. Capocci, A., Servedio, V.D.P., Colaiori, F., Buriol, L.S., Donato, D., Leonardi, S. and Caldarelli, G. 2006. Preferential attachment in the growth of social networks: The internet encyclopedia Wikipedia. *Physical Review E*. 74, 3 (2006), 036116.
9. Dong, W. and Fu, W.-T. 2010. Cultural difference in image tagging. *CHI '10.*
10. Duolingo: *http://duolingo.com/*. Accessed: 2011-09-13.
11. Filatova, E. 2009. Multilingual Wikipedia, Summarization, and Information Trustworthiness. *SIGIR Workshop on Information Access in a Multilingual World.*
12. Frequently asked questions - Wikimedia Foundation: *http://wikimediafoundation.org/wiki/Frequently_asked_questions*. Accessed: 2011-09-21.
13. Gärdenfors, P. 2000. *Conceptual Spaces: The Geometry of Thought*. The MIT Press.
14. Hecht, B. and Gergle, D. 2009. Measuring Self-Focus Bias in Community-Maintained Knowledge Repositories. *Communities and Technologies 2009.*
15. Hecht, B. and Gergle, D. 2010. The tower of Babel meets web 2.0: user-generated content and its applications in a multilingual context. *CHI '10.*
16. Hong, L., Convertino, G. and Chi, E.H. 2011. Language Matters in Twitter: A Large Scale Study. *ICWSM '11.*
17. Jarmasz, M. and Szpakowicz, S. 2003. Roget's thesaurus and semantic similarity. *RANLP '03.*
18. Kittur, A., Suh, B. and Chi, E.H. 2008. Can you ever trust a wiki?: impacting perceived trustworthiness in wikipedia. *CSCW '08.*
19. Kumaran, A., Datha, N., Ashok, B., Saravanan, K., Ande, A., Sharma, A., Vedantham, S., Natampally, V., Dendi, V. and Maurice, S. 2010. WikiBABEL: A System for Multilingual Wikipedia Content. *American Machine Translation Association (AMTA) Workshop*.
20. List of Wikipedias: http://meta.wikimedia.org/*wiki/List_of_Wikipedias*. Accessed: 2011-09-20.
21. Manypedia: 2011. *http://www.manypedia.com/*.
22. de Melo, G. and Weikum, G. 2010. Untangling the Cross-Lingual Link Structure of Wikipedia. *ACL '10.*
23. Mihalcea, R. and Csomai, A. 2007. Wikify!: linking documents to encyclopedic knowledge. *CIKM '07.*
24. Milne, D. and Witten, I.H. 2008. An Effective, Low-Cost Measure of Semantic Relatedness Obtained from Wikipedia Links. *WIKIAI '08.*
25. Milne, D. and Witten, I.H. 2008. Learning to link with wikipedia. *CIKM '08.*
26. Oh, J.-H., Kawahara, D., Uchimoto, K., Kazama, J. and Torisawa, K. 2008. Enriching Multilingual Language Resources by Discovering Missing Cross-Language Links in Wikipedia. *WIIAT '08.*
27. Pfeil, U., Zaphiris, P. and Ang, C.S. 2006. Cultural Differences in Collaborative Authoring of Wikipedia. *Journal of Computer-Mediated Communication*. 12, 1, 88-113.
28. Sorg, P. and Cimiano, P. 2008. Enriching the Crosslingual Link Structure of Wikipedia - A Classification-based Approach. *WIKI-AI '08.*
29. Suh, B., Chi, E.H, Pendleton, B.A. and Kittur, A. 2007. Us vs. Them: Understanding Social Dynamics in Wikipedia with Revert Graph Visualizations. *VAST '07.*
30. Translating the world's information with Google Translator Toolkit: 2009. *http://googleblog.blogspot.com/2009/06/translating-worlds-information-with.html*. Accessed: 2011-09-16.
31. Viégas, F.B., Wattenberg, M. and Dave, K. 2004. Studying cooperation and conflict between authors with history flow visualizations. *CHI '04.*
32. Wattenberg, M., Viégas, F.B. and Hollenbach, K. 2007. Visualizing activity on wikipedia with chromograms. *INTERACT '07.*
33. WikiBhasha beta – A multi-lingual content creator for Wikipedia: *http://www.wikibhasha.org/*.

Social Annotations in Web Search

Aditi Muralidharan
Computer Science Department
UC Berkeley
Berkeley, CA
aditi@cs.berkeley.edu

Zoltan Gyongyi
Google, Inc.
Mountain View, CA
zoltang@google.com

Ed H. Chi
Google, Inc.
Mountain View, CA
edchi@google.com

ABSTRACT
We ask how to best present social annotations on search results, and attempt to find an answer through mixed-method eye-tracking and interview experiments. Current practice is anchored on the assumption that faces and names draw attention; the same presentation format is used independently of the social connection strength and the search query topic. The key findings of our experiments indicate room for improvement. First, only certain social contacts are useful sources of information, depending on the search topic. Second, faces lose their well-documented power to draw attention when rendered small as part of a social search result annotation. Third, and perhaps most surprisingly, social annotations go largely unnoticed by users in general due to selective, structured visual parsing behaviors specific to search result pages. We conclude by recommending improvements to the design and content of social annotations to make them more noticeable and useful.

Author Keywords
social search; information seeking; eye tracking

ACM Classification Keywords
H.5.2 Information Interfaces and Presentation: User Interfaces—*Graphical User Interfaces*

INTRODUCTION
When searching for a restaurant in New York, does knowing that aunt Carol tweeted about *Le Bernardin* make it a more useful result?

In real life, all of us rely on information from our social circles to make educated decisions, to discover new things, to stay abreast of news and gossip. Similarly, the quantity, diversity, and personal relevance of social information online makes it a prime source of signals that could improve the experience of our ubiquitous search tasks [8]. Search engines have started incorporating social information, most prevalently by making relevant social activity explicitly visible to searchers through *social annotations*. For instance, Figure 1 shows social annotations as they appeared on Google and Bing search results in early September 2011.

Permission to make digital or hard copies of all or part of this work for personal or classroom use is granted without fee provided that copies are not made or distributed for profit or commercial advantage and that copies bear this notice and the full citation on the first page. To copy otherwise, or republish, to post on servers or to redistribute to lists, requires prior specific permission and/or a fee.
CHI'12, May 5–10, 2012, Austin, Texas, USA.
Copyright 2012 ACM 978-1-4503-1015-4/12/05...$10.00.

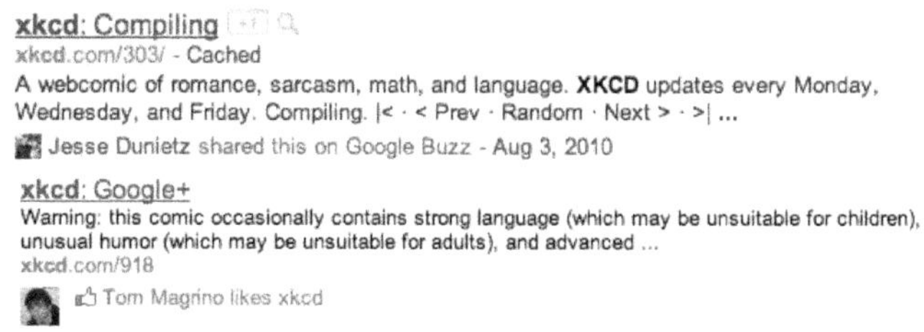

Figure 1. Social Annotations in web search as of sept. 2011 in Google (top), and Bing (bottom).

Annotations are added to normal web search results to provide social context. The presence of an annotation indicates that the particular result web page was shared or created by one of the searcher's online contacts. For example, suppose that a friend of Aunt Carol on Google+ or Facebook searched for "Le Bernardin", and Aunt Carol had previously posted a restaurant review on *Le Bernardin's* Yelp page. If one of the search results happened to be that same yelp.com restaurant page, the searcher would see an annotation like in Figure 1 on that result, explaining that Aunt Carol had reviewed it on some date.

To enable social results in Google search, users have to be signed in and connect their accounts on various social sites to their Google profiles. For social search on Bing, users have to be signed in with their Facebook accounts. After enabling social search, users will occasionally see social annotations on some results when they search the web.

Social annotations so far have generally a consistent presentation: they combine the profile picture and the name of the sharing contact with information about when and where the sharing happened. The annotation is rendered in a single line below the snippet. While there is some apparent convergence in current practice, we know of no research on what content and presentation make social annotations most useful in search for users.

In this paper, we set out to answer this particular question, equipped with intuitions derived from past research on search behavior and perceptual psychology. Intuitively, one could argue that social annotations should be noticeable and attention-grabbing: it is well-documented that faces and face-like symbols capture attention [41, 25, 19], even when users are not looking for them and do not even expect them [27]. Moreover, social annotations should also be useful: users collaborate on search tasks with each other by looking over each others' shoulders and by suggesting keywords [30, 12], so marking results that others have found useful should help.

However, it is not immediately clear how valid these intuitions are in the domain of web search. This particular domain is known for specialized user behaviors, and it is not obvious how adding social cues might affect them. In particular, users pay almost exclusive attention to just the first few results on a page [23, 16]. It seems that they have learned to trust search engines, because this behavior persists even when the top few results are manipulated to be less relevant [34, 17]. So how does adding an extra layer of social cues in the form of social annotations affect the search process? Are their friends' names and faces powerful enough to draw users attention? Or do learned result-scanning behaviors still dominate?

We designed and conducted two consecutive experiments, which we describe in detail in two major sections below. The first experiment investigated how annotations interacted with the search process in general, while the second focused on how various visual presentations affected the visibility of annotations. In our first experiment, we found that our intuitions were not quite accurate: annotations are neither universally noticeable nor consistently useful to users. This experiment unveiled a colorful and nuanced picture of how users interact with socially-annotated search results while performing search tasks. In our second experiment we uncovered evidence that strong, general reading habits particular to search result pages seem to govern annotation visibility.

In the next section, we give an overview of related research in this area.

RELATED WORK

The literature that is perhaps most immediately connected to our research questions addresses the use of the "social information trail" in web search. Yet, to the best of our knowledge, the work in this area has focused on behind-the-scenes applications, not on presentation or content. Many have proposed ways to use likes, shares, reviews, +1's and social bookmarks to personalize search result rankings [4, 43, 20, 44, 6], but there is comparatively little on making this information explicitly visible to users during web search.

More generally, studies of the information seeking process can help us understand what types of social information could be useful to searchers, and when. Several proposed models capture how people use social information and collaborate with each other during search. Evans and Chi [12] found that people exchanged information with others before, during and after search. Pirolli [36] modeled the cost-benefit effects of social group diversity and structure in cooperative information foraging [37]. Golovchinsky and colleagues [15, 14] categorized social information seeking behaviors in according to the degree of shared intent, search depth, and the concurrency and location of searches.

Social Feedback during Search

As mentioned before, searchers look to other people for help before, during and after web search [12]. They have to resort to over-the-shoulder searching, e-mails, and other ad-hoc tools because of the lack of built-in support for collaboration [30]. Researchers have responded with a variety systems that aid collaboration. These systems share histories of search keyword choices, communicate by voice or text, and share entire search sessions, starting from search keyword combinations all the way to the final web pages that returned the best information [32, 31, 3, 35]. Social bookmarks have also been investigated as a source of helpful signals during search [24].

Social Question-Answering

In social question-answering systems, topical expertise is important to the overall system design. People's knowledge on various topics is indexed, and used to route appropriate questions to them [1, 2, 22]. Evans, Kairam and Pirolli [13] studied social question answering for an exploratory learning task, and found expertise to be an important factor in peoples' decisions to ask each other for information. In real-world question-answering situations, Borgatti and Cross [5] studied organizational learning and identified the perceived expertise of a person as one of the factors that influenced whether to ask them a question. Further bearing out the importance of expertise, Nelson et. al. [33] found that expert annotations improved learning scores for exploratory learning tasks.

There are also suggestions that certain topics such as restaurants, travel, local services, and shopping are more likely to benefit from the input of others, even strangers. For instance, Amazon, Yelp and TripAdvisor have sophisticated review systems for shopping, restaurants and travel respectively. Moreover, Aardvark.com reports that the majority of questions fall into exactly these topic types [22].

Collaborative Activity

Beyond web search and social question-answering systems, simply displaying or visualizing past history can be useful to collaborators. Past research on collaborative work suggests that it is useful to show users a history of activity around shared documents and shared spaces. One of the first ideas in this area was the concept of read wear and edit wear [21] — visually displaying a documents reading and editing history as part of the document itself. A document's read and edit wear is a kind of social signal. It communicates the sections of the document that other people have found worth reading or worth editing. Erickson and Kellogg [11, 10] introduced the term "social translucence" to describe the idea of making collective activity visible to users of collaborative systems. They argued that social translucence makes collaboration and communication easier by allowing users to learn by imitation, and take advantage of collective knowledge. They also argued that, when users' actions are made visible to others, social pressures encourage good behavior. Social annotations can be seen as a kind of social translucency.

Methods

In our experiments, we use eye tracking to study user behavior while varying search-result-page design. In the past, Cutrell and Guan analyzed the effects of placing a "target" high-quality link at different search result ranks [9] on various task completion metrics. The effects of "short", "medium", and "long" snippet lengths on search task behavior was also studied by Guan and Cutrell [17].

STUDY 1: PERCEPTIONS OF SOCIAL ANNOTATIONS

Study Goals

The research cited above suggests that social annotations are broadly useful, perhaps especially on certain topics and from certain people. Our objective was to find out how social annotations influence web search behavior. Specifically, we wanted to understand the importance of contact closeness, contact expertise, and search topic in determining whether or not an annotation is useful.

Study Design

We performed a retrospective-interview-based study with N=11 participants. The participants did not know the intent of the study, and were told that we were evaluating a search engine for different types of search tasks.

Eye-tracking data was recorded so that the researcher could observe the participant more closely. The participants' gaze movements were displayed to the researcher on a separate screen, and recorded for replay during the interview. This way, the researcher could monitor whether participants were looking at or ignoring social annotations, and concentrate on those events during the retrospective interview.

A major challenge in this study was to make the study experience as organic as possible. We wanted users to truly reveal their natural search tendencies without suspecting that we were studying social annotations.

Study Procedure

In the first half of the study, participants performed a series of 18-20 search tasks, randomly ordered. Half the search tasks were designed so that search queries would bring up one or two social annotations in the top four or five results. In the second half of the study, immediately after the tasks, participants were interviewed in retrospective think-aloud (RTA) format. They were asked to take the researcher through what they were doing on some of the tasks while watching a replay of a screen capture (including eye traces) of the tasks with the researcher. The researcher would ask probing questions for clarification, and then move on to talk about another task.

If the participant never mentioned the social annotations, even after an interview on all the tasks in which they were present, the interview procedure was slightly different. The researcher would return to a screen capture of one of the tasks in which there was a social annotation. The researcher would point out the annotation explicitly and ask a series of questions, like, "What is that? Did you notice it? Who is this person? Tell me what you think about this." The goals were to find out what the participant thought the annotation was, whether they noticed it at all, and to understand whether or not they perceived it as useful, and why. After the annotation had been discussed, the researcher would revisit the remaining social annotations and repeat the procedure for each of them.

Personalization

From past research [5, 22, 13], we suspected that the expertise of the contact might influence how an annotation is perceived. For example, a participant might react differently to a hiker friend on a result about hiking trails than on a topic on which that friend is completely ignorant. This meant that we would have to design tasks for each participant individually, and could not simply insert fake annotations into a standard set of tasks. Even if the names and faces were personalized individually to be real contacts, there would be no guarantee that the tasks we created would match those contacts' expertise areas. To ensure that we were eliciting representative reactions to social annotations, we designed the search tasks individually for each participant by looking at the links and blog posts shared by the contacts in social networks they had linked to their accounts.

Participants

Every social annotation seen by each participant was real, just like they would have seen outside the lab, with no modifications. This meant that we had to infer, for each participant in advance of the study, which queries would bring up social annotations, and design individual search tasks around these URLs for each participant. In this way, we created 8-10 social search tasks for each participant across different topics (depending on the availability of searchable, annotated URLs).

It was somewhat difficult to find enough participants with these constraints. Our first step was to find participants who were willing to allow enough access to their personal data to personalize the study. We recruited around 60 respondents who gave us this permission. Of these, we found 11 respondents with enough data in their social annotations to see annotations in 10 different searches.

Search Tasks

Half the tasks were designed to bring up social annotations, and the other half were "non-social". The tasks were framed as questions, and not as pre-assigned keyword queries. We did not provide pre-assigned queries because we did not want to raise suspicions that there was something special about the search pages or the particular keyword combination. Some sample search tasks are shown in Table 1. In the case of social tasks, prompts were worded so that many reasonable keyword combinations would bring up one or two social annotations in the top four or five search results.

Topic	Search Task
How-to	How do you make a box kite?
Recipe	How do you make milk bar pie?
Product	Find a good laptop case for your macbook pro.
Local	Find a good sweet shop in Napa, CA.
Entertainment	Is the album "The Suburbs" by Arcade Fire any good?
News	What is going on with stem cells latelyI?
Fact-finding	Where did Parkour originate?
Navigation	What is the website of Time Warner's youtube channel?

Table 1. Samples of search tasks in different topics. Participants were not shown the topic category, they were just given a strip of paper with the task question printed on it. They started each task at the default search engine start page.

We distributed the tasks for each participant across suspected useful and non-useful topics. We thought annotations would

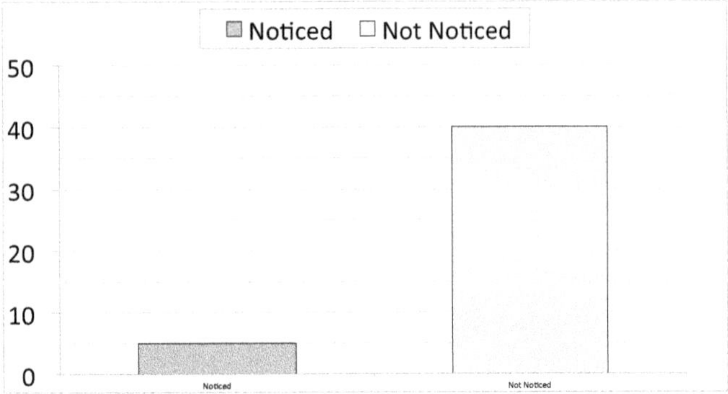

Figure 2. The total number of social annotations that were noticed.

be useful on the topics of product search, local services, how-tos, recipes, news and entertainment. Participants each performed up to 4 tasks in each of these topic categories, of which two had annotations. We thought annotations may not be useful for navigation and fact-finding, so participants performed 2 tasks in each of those categories, one with annotations and one without.

The inclusion of a category was subject to the availability of social annotations in that category. For example, if we could not find any *product search* annotations for a participant, we did not ask them to perform any product search tasks at all. This resulted in minor variation in the number of search tasks. Some participants had more annotations in more categories than others.

Results

To understand the space of participants' responses, we first created an affinity diagram by grouping responses that seemed to be similar in meaning. Once categories of responses emerged, we went through the responses yet again, coding the responses into different categories, and counting the numbers in each category.

We did not analyze the eye tracking data we gathered due to the heavily-personalized and unrestricted nature of the search tasks: each participant saw a different set of pages, and participants were allowed to scroll and to revisit search pages with the back button. This made standardized region-of-interest annotations very difficult to make. We used the eyetracking videos primarily as a memory aid for the participant during the RTA's, but also as a supplement to the interview results, to arrive at the conclusions below.

Social Annotations Go Unnoticed

Figure 2 shows that most social annotations were not noticed by participants. Of the 45 annotations in our experiment that appeared above the page fold, 40 (89%) were not noticed. By "not noticed", we mean that participants explicitly said, when the annotation was pointed out, that they did not notice the annotation while they were searching. Often, the participants were surprised they had missed it because it was from a close friend, co-worker, old friend, or boss. In fact, of the 40 missed annotations, 35 were from people the participants recognized as friends, co-workers, family members, or acquaintances (but 5 were from people the participants did not recognize).

Reactions to Seen Annotations

The following summary of our participants reactions reveals concerns about privacy and objectivity, as well the value of closer ties and known expertise.

Participant 5 (P5) noticed annotations on two successive queries and commented on them unprompted while searching. She highlighted the first annotation she saw with her cursor and exclaimed that the annotation was "creepy" even though the annotation was from "a friend."

> "... this friend is a friend, but the algorithm or whatever makes her show up there doesn't know how close we are, or how much I respect her opinion... "

The next query, however, was a much more positive experience. This time, the annotation was from her personal trainer on a fitness-related topic. This annotation was better because she trusted her trainer's expertise on the subject, and would actually turn to him for advice in real life.

The other participants did not comment on social annotations while searching, but had informative reactions during the RTA. P11 explained why he clicked on a Yelp result on which he noticed a friends name and face:

> "Yeah, I directly know her, it's not just somebody, like a friend of a friend... "

Finally, P4 and P6 had both seen social annotations outside the lab, but did not click on the annotations even though they saw them. They gave different reasons why. P6 passed over a friend-annotated blog post, and instead chose Wikipedia because:

> "The immediate thing I thought was that he [the friend] edits Wikipedia pages, he's been doing it for a long time"

P4, however, gave a different reason for not clicking on an annotated search result:

> "I don't necessarily want to see what they've looked at, I want to see sources that I think are credible..."

Annotations Are Useful for "Social" and "Subjective" Topics

Ten out of the eleven participants mentioned that social annotations would be useful on topics like restaurants, shopping, searching for businesses, shopping for expensive items, and planning events for other people. The remaining participant did not specify a topic. When asked to generalize, participants used the words "social", "subjective" or "reviews" to describe the category of topics. When asked why the information would be useful, participants said that it would be good extra information in decision-making if they knew the person had good taste, was knowledgeable, or was trusted by them to have good information on the topic.

Another category of useful topics, brought up by 7 out of the 11 participants, is best described as personal, or hobby-related. It seemed that participants would be curious to see close contacts or family members in social annotations, so that they could connect with them over a shared hobby or activity, or because it might be nice to discover that they had a shared interest.

Annotations from Knowledgeable Contacts Are Useful

All participants said that annotations would be useful when they came from people whom searchers believed had good taste, knowledge or experience with the topic, or had similar likes and dislikes. This was not restricted to contacts they knew personally, as celebrities, bloggers, or respected authorities on a topic were also indicated to be useful.

Closer Relationships Make Annotations More Useful

Nine out the eleven participants said that annotations from strong-tie contacts (such as close friends, in regular contact, or family members) would be more useful than more distant contacts. Four participants made the distinction between interestingness and relevance. To paraphrase their responses, annotation from a very close friend might be interesting because of the information it gave about the friend's interests or activities, but it may not provide any relevant useful information about the quality of the result, or make it any easier to complete the task.

Seven out of the eight participants who saw annotations from strangers indicated that they would ignore those annotations. This included people they did not recognize, and people they did not have a significant relationship with. One participant said that he would be confused, and would want to know what his relationships to that person was. When asked whether seeing strangers was a negative, or simply irrelevant, 7 participants responded that it was irrelevant.

The Searcher's Mindset Could Affect Usefulness

Three out of the eleven participants explicitly mentioned that they would only click on the social annotation or talk to their friend later on about seeing the social annotations if they had time, or were simply exploring a topic space. The remaining participants did not specify when they would click or follow-up with a friend on a social annotation.

Discussion

This study revealed a counter-intuitive result. Despite having the names and faces of familiar people, and despite being intended to be noticeable to searchers, subjects for the most part did not pay attention to the social annotations.

Our questions about contact closeness, expertise, and topic were answered by the reactions captured during the *retrospective* interviews. These interviews revealed the importance of contact expertise and closeness, and the importance of the search topics in determining whether social signals are useful, thus echoing pas findings on the role of expertise in social search [13].The interviews also provided some high-level understanding of the ways that people use, and want to use, social information during web search.

Nevertheless, a challenge emerged, which is our need to understand the lack of attention to social annotations, and finding ways to improve their presentation. Having confirmed that many types of social information could indeed be useful to searchers, we had to ask why the annotations conveying this information were largely ignored. In the next section, we describe the follow-up experiment we conducted to get to the bottom of this mystery.

STUDY 2: PRESENTATION OF SOCIAL ANNOTATIONS

Past work shows that people discriminate between the different parts of a search result and do not linearly scan pages from top to bottom. Titles, URLs, and snippets receive different amounts of attention [9], and, in the sample of over 600 gaze paths analyzed in [26], 50% contained regressions to higher-ranked results and skips to lower-ranked results.

Study Goals

As stated above, the goal of our second study was to find out why so many of the social annotations in the first study went unnoticed. We designed an experiment to investigate what would happen to users' page-reading patterns when social annotations were added in various different design variations. We hoped to find behaviors anchored in the familiar presentation of search results that would explain why the social annotations in the first experiment were ignored. Our particular research questions were:

1. Will increasing the sizes of the profile pictures make social annotations more noticeable?
2. Are there learned reading behaviors that prevent participants from paying attention to social annotations?

Study Design

We performed a mixed-method eye-tracking and retrospective-interview-based study with N=12 participants. The participants did not know the intent of the study, and were told that we were evaluating a search engine for different types of search tasks.

Participants

We recruited 15 non-computer-programmers from within our organization, but had to discard data from 3 of them due to interference with their eye glasses. As our second study focused on presentation issues only, we decided on less-personalized annotations than in the first study. Accordingly, we did not have to analyze participants private data, and thus ended up with a simpler recruiting process.

Personalization

In order to control the stimuli presented to participants, we did not personalize the search tasks. We used the same set of tasks across all participants.

The only personalization was the names and faces of people in the annotations. These were participants' real co-workers, but annotations appeared on results of our choosing, and not results that had really been shared by those people (in contrast with the first study). Using our internal employee directory

(a) Annotation above snippet

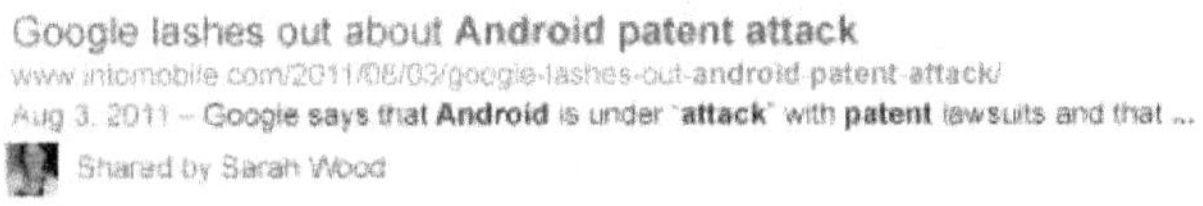

(b) Annotation below snippet

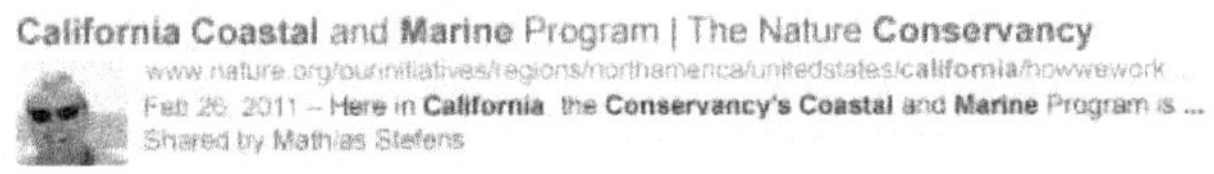

(c) Annotation with big picture

Figure 3. The different annotation variations in Study 2.

and organizational chart, we found the names and pictures of 18 people who were either on the same team as the participants or had their desks within 10 meters of them, reasoning that the participant would recognize most of these people. Their names and faces were then pasted into the static mock-ups of web pages with social annotations.

Social Annotation Design Variations

Our goal was to see whether changing snippet length, annotation placement, and picture size changed the amount of attention (measured in number of fixations) given to the annotation. For snippets, we had 1-line, 2-line, and 4-line snippets. The annotation's presentation within the result was varied to be either above the snippet or below the snippet (Figure 3a–b). The annotated result was either the first result on the page or the second result. Additionally, to test our hypothesis about the faces in the annotations being too small to be noticed, we added another annotation presentation condition by using a 50×50 picture placed in-line with the snippet, as shown in Figure 3c.

Together these annotation variations, snippet length variations, and result position variations created a 3x3x2 = 18 different conditions, as follows: [big picture inline, small picture below snippet, small picture above snippet] × [1, 2, 4] line snippets × [1st or 2nd search result]. These variations were interleaved with an equal number of baseline non-annotated result pages, bringing the total to 36 tasks.

Stimuli

Participants viewed and clicked on 36 mock-ups of search result pages. Half of these had social annotations, and half did not, and the social and non-social pages were interleaved.

The motivation for using both annotated and non-annotated mock-ups was twofold. First, we wanted to avoid raising suspicions about the nature of the study, and second, the non-annotated pages provided identical baselines on which we could compare all participants.

The social pages were generated with an image editor. We generated pages with different snippet lengths, annotation positions, and picture sizes. Then, we pasted in the names and faces of office-mates and team-mates to personalize the mock-ups for each participant. The non-social pages were generated by taking screenshots of search results.

Procedure

Participant Conditions

Due to their prominent size, we suspected that the big 50×50px pictures might prime the participants to the social nature of the experiment. We therefore divided the participants into two conditions to avoid an undetected priming bias: the first group (N=5, 2 more discarded) saw the big-picture variants first, before any other type of annotation, and the second group (N=7, 1 more discarded) saw the big-picture variants last, only after they had seen all the 21×21px variants.

Study Procedure

In the first part of the study, participants performed 36 consecutive search tasks. For each task, they were first shown a screen with a task prompt, and asked to imagine having that task in mind. Once they had read the task prompt, they pressed the space bar. This took them to the search page mock-up. They were instructed to view the page as they would normally, and to a click on a result in the end.

In the second part, the participants were retrospectively interviewed about some of the search tasks. The researcher played back a screen capture of their eye movements, and asked questions. Unlike the first study, the interviews were short. We directly asked whether they had noticed the annotation, who the person was, and which annotation presentation they preferred: above-snippet, below-snippet, or big picture.

Results

For all participants, we measured how the number of fixations on annotations varied with snippet length, annotation placement, and annotated result. In addition to the results reported in the following sections, we performed a linear regression, controlling for between-participant variation, and picture order. Further, for succinct visual evidence, we have supplemented some of the quantitative results below with gaze maps averaged across all the participants.

Our results are the same when analyzed using fixation count or fixation duration. We chose fixation count as the presented metric because it is more intuitive to think about whether users actually moved their eyes to the annotations.

Longer Snippets Lead to Less Time on Annotations

The graph in figure 4 shows the average number of fixations on various elements of the search result item, compared across different snippet lengths. We can see that annotations below a 1-line snippet get almost twice as many fixations compared to annotations below a 4-line snippet. In our linear regression, 2-line and 4-line snippets received negative coefficients (after controlling for between-participant variation and picture-size order), meaning that they decreased the fixation count, with

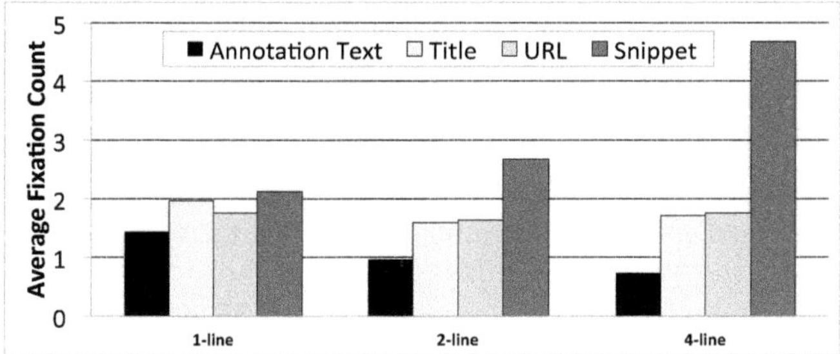

Figure 4. Average fixation count on various result elements vs. the length of the snippet (N=12). We showed participants 3 snippet lengths: 1-line, 2-line and 4-line. Fixation counts for the annotation are drawn in black, values for snippet, title, and URL are in shades of green.

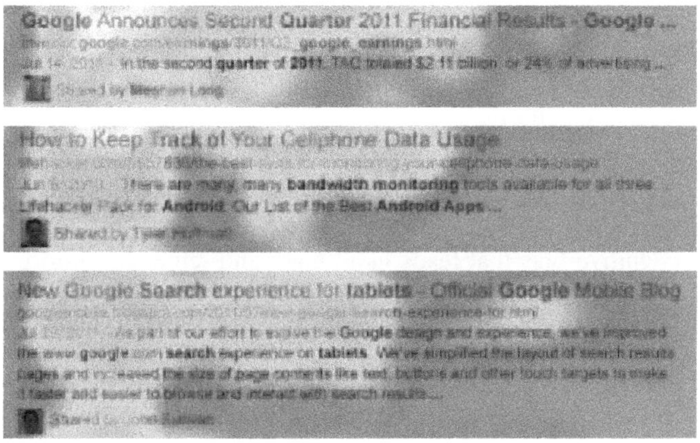

Figure 5. The snippet-length effect shown for the annotation-below-snippet condition. The different lengths were 1-line (top) 2-line (middle) and 4-line (bottom). These averaged gaze maps show that the longer the snippet, the fewer the fixations on the annotation.

($b = -0.51$, $t(203) = -1.85$, $p < 0.07$) and ($b = -0.74$, $t(203) = -2.56$, $p < 0.01$) respectively. An example of this effect for the below-snippet presentation is shown in the averaged gaze heat-maps in figure 5. It is clearly visible that, on average, the longer the snippet above the annotation, the fewer fixations it got (darker regions correspond to fewer fixations).

The effects of snippet length on the other result elements are in line with past findings [9]. Fixations to the snippet increase with snippet length, and fixations to URL and title are relatively constant.

Bigger Pictures Get More Attention

As one might expect intuitively, the 50×50 pictures have a dramatically larger average number of fixations than the smaller 21×21 pictures. Figure 6 shows the effect on number of fixations to pictures. The critical threshold here is a value of 1. A value above 1 means that the element, on average, receives attention. A value below 1 means the opposite. Figure 6 shows that the big pictures receive around 1.3 fixations on average, but the small pictures only receive 0.1. Not surprisingly, the conclusion therefore is that big pictures of faces get noticed, whereas small ones generally do not.

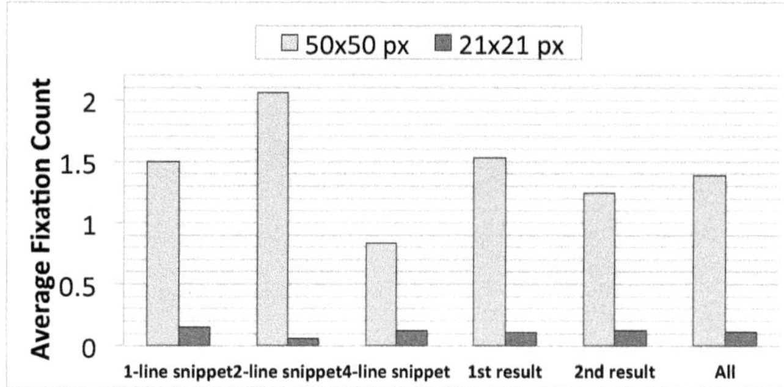

Figure 6. Average fixation count on the pictures in the annotations vs. the size of the picture, for each of the different presentation variations (N=12). We showed participants two sizes, 50x50px and 21x21px.

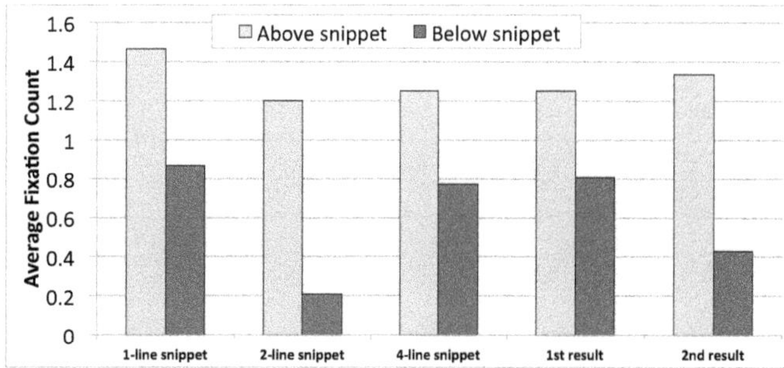

Figure 7. Average fixation count on annotations vs. annotation placement, for each of the different presentation variations (N=12). Annotations were placed either above the snippet or below the snippet.

The effect was significant in our linear regression. The large-picture condition received a positive coefficient ($b = 0.72, t(203) = 2.62, p < 0.01$), meaning that increasing the picture size increased the number of fixations .

Annotations Above the Snippet Get More Attention

Annotations above the snippet get uniformly more fixations than annotations below the snippet. The graph in figure 7 shows that the effect is true for all snippet lengths and result positions. The above-snippet condition received a positive coefficient in our linear regression ($b = 0.59, t(203) = 2.03, p < 0.04$), meaning that annotations above the snippet got more fixations.

The heat map in Figure 8 shows an example of the placement effect in the 4-line-snippet condition. It is obvious from the figure that the annotation got more fixations (brighter region) when it was placed above the snippet.

Result 1 Gets More Attention Than Result 2

Figure 9 shows the effect of result position on attention to annotations, averaged across all annotation types, snippet lengths, and picture sizes. Annotations on the first result receive about 1.3 fixations on average, but annotations on the second only receive 0.8 fixations on average.

In our regression model, the 2nd-position condition received a negative coefficient ($b = -0.62, t(203) = -2.66, p < 0.01$), meaning that it reduced the number of fixations.

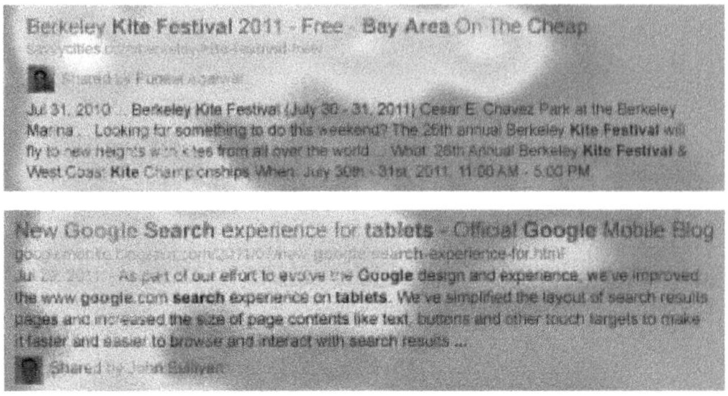

Figure 8. The annotation-placement effect, shown for the 4-line snippet condition. These averaged gaze maps show that annotations that were placed above the snippet (top) got more fixations than those placed below (bottom).

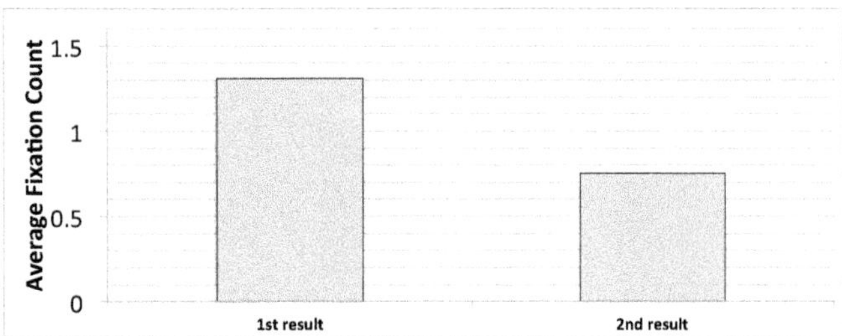

Figure 9. Average fixation count on annotation vs. result position, averaged over all the presentation variations. Annotations were either on the first result or the second result.

Statistical Disclaimer

The experiment produced only one data point per participant for each configuration of annotated result, placement, and snippet length, giving N = 12×18 fixation-count measurements. Therefore, we fit a simple additive model to find the effects of each variable on fixation. The additive model is a crude approximation, and the data are non-normal, so our p-values should only be interpreted as a rough guide to statistical significance.

DISCUSSION

In the first study, participants were often surprised when social annotations were pointed out to them. From their comments, they seemed to believe they did not notice the annotations because they were engrossed in their search tasks.

In our second study, we found that (1) users always paid attention to the URLs and titles, and increased their attention to the social annotations when (2) the summary snippets were shorter, (3) pictures were bigger, and (4) when the annotations were placed above the snippet summary.

Together with past research on search-page reading habits, the second study's results suggest that users perform a *structural parse*: they break the page down into meaningful structures like titles, urls, snippets, etc. and only pay attention to certain elements within the structure. This in turn implies that users' blindness to annotations might be caused by learned lack of attention to anything other than titles, URLs and snippets. Users are so focused on performing their task, and social annotations are not part of their existing page-reading habits, so they simply skip over them and act as if they are not there.

The phenomenon of lack of attention causing functional blindness to clearly visible stimuli has been documented with many different types of activities. Pilots have failed to see another plane blocking a landing runway [18] and spectators of dodgeball have failed to notice a person in a gorilla suit walking across the playing field [40]. Mack, Rock, and colleagues [38, 28, 27], studied the phenomenon extensively, and gave it the name "inattentional blindness".

The bigger profile pictures, however, drew attention as expected from studies of attention capture by faces [41, 25, 19, 27]. So, if the pictures in the first study had been bigger, the annotations might have been noticed more. At a small size however, they were not capable of disrupting users' page scanning patterns.

In search result pages, titles stand out with their blue color and large font, urls stand out in green, and matching keywords are marked out in bold text. Human beings have a cognitive bias that leads us to learn and remember information that is visually prominent [42]. Highlighted or underlined text is remembered and learned better than normal text, even if the highlights are not useful [39]. Highlighted text is also given increased visual attention as measured by an eye-tracker [7]. The observed selective attention to certain elements might stem from this effect, combined with learning over time.

However, the results also suggest that we can direct more attention towards a social annotations by manipulating page structure to our advantage. Attention can be gained by placing annotations above the snippet, shortening the snippet, and increasing annotation picture size.

While we can manipulate the visual design to make annotations more prominent, we must also learn when they are useful to the user, and call attention to them only when they will prove productive.

CONCLUSION

Based on past research on social information seeking, we have certain intuitions about how users should behave around social annotations: they should find them broadly useful, and they should notice them. Our results indicate that, in reality, users behave in a more nuanced way.

Our first study yielded two unexpected results. First, in some contexts, social annotations shown on search result pages can be useless to searchers. They disregard information from people who are strangers, or unfamiliar friends with uncertain expertise. Searchers are looking for opinions and reviews from knowledgeable friends, or signs of interest from close friends on hobbies or other topics they have in common.

The more counterintuitive result from our first study was that subjects did not notice social annotations. From our second experiment, we were able to conclude that this unawareness was mainly due to specialized attention patterns that users exhibit while processing search pages. Users deconstruct the search results: they pay attention to titles and URLs and then turn toward snippets and annotations for further evidence of a good result to click on. Moreover, the reading of snippets and annotations appears to follow a traditional top-to-bottom reading order, and friend pictures that are too small simply blend into snippets and become part of them. These focused attention behaviors seem to derive from the task-oriented mind-set of users during search, and might be explained by the effect of *inattentional blindness* [28]. All of this makes existing social annotations slip by, unnoticed.

IMPLICATIONS AND FUTURE DIRECTIONS

Our findings have implications for both the content and presentation of social annotations.

For content, three things are clear: not all friends are equal, not all topics benefit from the inclusion of social annotation, and users prefer different types of information from different people. For presentation, it seems that learned result-reading habits may cause blindness to social annotations. The obvious implication is that we need to adapt the content and presentation of social annotations to the specialized environment of web search.

The first adaptation could target broad search-topic categories: social annotations are useful on easily-identified topics such as restaurants, shopping, local services, and travel. For these categories, social annotations could be made more visually prominent, and expanded with details such as comments or ratings.

Our observation that the friend's topical expertise affects the user's perception of the social annotation and search result relevance allows for additional, fine-grained adjustments. With lists of topics on which friends are knowledgeable, we could give their annotations more prominence on those topics.

The areas of expertise or interest of a specific user could either be provided explicitly by the user (typically not during web search, but other interactions such as sign-up flows) or inferred implicitly from content created or frequently consumed by the user (e.g., authored posts on social networks, news feed subscriptions, exchanged emails, visited web pages). The inference can be done using standard text classification or clustering techniques [29].

To achieve the desired effect, we can manipulate the presentation of social annotations in a variety of ways to give them more prominence. For instance, we can increase the picture size, change the placement of the annotation within the search result, or alter its wording and information content.

In the future, we would like to conduct a third experiment to test this newly-gained understanding of social annotations. Using the insights from the second experiment, we could design a study in which social annotations are prominent. Then, we could test the qualitative claims of our first experiment by showing annotations from different types of contacts, on different verticals and topics.

A brave new world of social search is upon us. As the web becomes more social, social signals will factor into an ever-increasing part of our search experience. It is our hope that the knowledge obtained in these two studies will push the frontiers of social annotations in web search forward.

REFERENCES

1. Ackerman, M., and Malone, T. Answer garden: A tool for growing organizational memory. In *Proc. ACM SIGOIS and IEEE CS TC-OA* (1990), 3139.
2. Ackerman, M. S., and McDonald, D. W. Answer garden 2: merging organizational memory with collaborative help. In *Proc. CSCW*, CSCW '96, ACM (New York, NY, USA, 1996), 97105. ACM ID: 240203.
3. Amershi, S., and Morris, M. R. CoSearch. In *Proc. SIGCHI*, ACM Press (2008), 1647.
4. Bao, S., Xue, G., Wu, X., Yu, Y., Fei, B., and Su, Z. Optimizing web search using social annotations. In *Proc. WWW* (2007), 501510.
5. Borgatti, S., and Cross, R. A relational view of information seeking and learning in social networks. *Management science* (2003), 432445.
6. Carmel, D., Zwerdling, N., Guy, I., Ofek-Koifman, S., Har'el, N., Ronen, I., Uziel, E., Yogev, S., and Chernov, S. Personalized social search based on the user's social network. In *Proc. CIKM* (2009), 12271236.
7. Chi, E., Gumbrecht, M., and Hong, L. Visual foraging of highlighted text: An eye-tracking study. In *Proc. HCI* (2007), 589598.
8. Chi, E. H. Information seeking can be social. *Computer 42*, 3 (2009), 4246.
9. Cutrell, E., and Guan, Z. What are you looking for? In *Proc. SIGCHI*, ACM Press (2007), 407.
10. Erickson, T., and Kellogg, W. A. Social translucence: an approach to designing systems that support social processes. *ACM ToCHI 7*, 1 (Mar. 2000), 59–83.
11. Erickson, T., Smith, D. N., Kellogg, W. A., Laff, M., Richards, J. T., and Bradner, E. Socially translucent systems. In *Proc. SIGCHI*, ACM Press (1999), 72–79.
12. Evans, B. M., and Chi, E. H. Towards a model of understanding social search. In *Proc. CSCW* (2008), 485494.
13. Evans, B. M., Kairam, S., and Pirolli, P. Do your friends make you smarter?: An analysis of social strategies in online information seeking. *Information Processing & Management 46*, 6 (Nov. 2010), 679–692.
14. Golovchinsky, G., Pickens, J., and Back, M. A taxonomy of collaboration in online information seeking. In *Proc. 1st Workshop on Collaborative Information Seeking* (2008).
15. Golovchinsky, G., Qvarfordt, P., and Pickens, J. Collaborative information seeking. *Information Seeking Support Systems* (2008).

16. Granka, L. A., Joachims, T., and Gay, G. Eye-tracking analysis of user behavior in WWW search. In *Proc. SIGIR*, SIGIR '04, ACM (New York, NY, USA, 2004), 478479.
17. Guan, Z., and Cutrell, E. An eye tracking study of the effect of target rank on web search. In *Proc. SIGCHI*, ACM Press (2007), 417.
18. Haines, R. A breakdown in simultaneous information processing. *Presbyopia research. From molecular biology to visual adaptation* (1991), 171175.
19. Hershler, O., and Hochstein, S. At first sight: A high-level pop out effect for faces. *Vision Research 45*, 13 (2005), 17071724.
20. Heymann, P., Koutrika, G., and Garcia-Molina, H. Can social bookmarking improve web search? In *Proc. intl. conf. on Web search and web data mining*, ACM Press (2008), 195.
21. Hill, W. C., Hollan, J. D., Wroblewski, D., and McCandless, T. Edit wear and read wear. In *Proc. SIGCHI*, ACM (Monterey, California, United States, 1992), 3–9.
22. Horowitz, D., and Kamvar, S. D. The anatomy of a large-scale social search engine. In *Proc. WWW*, Proc. WWW, ACM (New York, NY, USA, 2010), 431440. ACM ID: 1772735.
23. Joachims, T., Granka, L., Pan, B., Hembrooke, H., and Gay, G. Accurately interpreting clickthrough data as implicit feedback. In *Proc. SIGIR*, SIGIR '05, ACM (New York, NY, USA, 2005), 154161.
24. Kammerer, Y., Nairn, R., Pirolli, P., and Chi, E. H. Signpost from the masses: learning effects in an exploratory social tag search browser. In *Proc. SIGCHI* (2009), 625634.
25. Langton, S., Law, A., Burton, A., and Schweinberger, S. Attention capture by faces. *Cognition 107*, 1 (2008), 330342.
26. Lorigo, L., Pan, B., Hembrooke, H., Joachims, T., Granka, L., and Gay, G. The influence of task and gender on search and evaluation behavior using google. *Information Processing & Management 42*, 4 (July 2006), 1123–1131.
27. Mack, A., Pappas, Z., Silverman, M., and Gay, R. What we see: Inattention and the capture of attention by meaning. *Consciousness and Cognition 11*, 4 (2002), 488506.
28. Mack, A., and Rock, I. Inattentional blindness. In *Visual Attention*. The MIT Press, 1998.
29. Manning, C. D., Raghavan, P., and Schutze, H. *Introduction to information retrieval*. Cambridge University Press, 2008.
30. Morris, M. R. A survey of collaborative web search practices. In *Proc. SIGCHI*, ACM Press (2008), 1657.
31. Morris, M. R., and Horvitz, E. SearchTogether. In *Proc. UIST*, ACM Press (2007), 3.
32. Morris, M. R., Lombardo, J., and Wigdor, D. WeSearch. In *Proc. CSCW*, ACM Press (2010), 401.
33. Nelson, L., Held, C., Pirolli, P., Hong, L., Schiano, D., and Chi, E. H. With a little help from my friends: examining the impact of social annotations in sensemaking tasks. In *Proc. SIGCHI*, CHI '09, ACM (New York, NY, USA, 2009), 17951798. ACM ID: 1518977.
34. Pan, B., Hembrooke, H., Joachims, T., Lorigo, L., Gay, G., and Granka, L. In google we trust: Users decisions on rank, position, and relevance. *Journal of Computer-Mediated Communication 12*, 3 (2007), 801823.
35. Pickens, J., Golovchinsky, G., Shah, C., Qvarfordt, P., and Back, M. Algorithmic mediation for collaborative exploratory search. In *Proc. ACM SIGIR*, ACM Press (2008), 315.
36. Pirolli, P. An elementary social information foraging model. In *Proc. SIGCHI* (2009), 605614.
37. Pirolli, P., and Card, S. Information foraging. *Psychological Review 106* (1999), 643–675.
38. Rock, I., Linnett, C. M., Grant, P., and Mack, A. Perception without attention: Results of a new method. *Cognitive Psychology 24*, 4 (Oct. 1992), 502–534.
39. Silvers, V., and Kreiner, D. The effects of Pre-Existing inappropriate highlighting on reading comprehension. *Reading Research and Instruction 36*, 3 (1997), 21723.
40. Simons, D. J., and Chabris, C. F. Gorillas in our midst: sustained inattentional blindness for dynamic events. *Perception 28*, 9 (1999), 1059–1074. PMID: 10694957.
41. Theeuwes, J., and Van der Stigchel, S. Faces capture attention: Evidence from inhibition of return. *Visual Cognition 13*, 6 (2006), 657665.
42. Von Restorff, H. Ueber die wirkung von bereichsbildungen im spurenfeld. *Psychological Research 18*, 1 (1933), 299342.
43. Yanbe, Y., Jatowt, A., Nakamura, S., and Tanaka, K. Can social bookmarking enhance search in the web? In *Proc. ACM/IEEE-CS joint conf. on Digital libraries*, ACM Press (2007), 107.
44. Zanardi, V., and Capra, L. Social ranking: uncovering relevant content using tag-based recommender systems. In *Proc. ACM RecSys*, ACM Press (2008), 51.

Comparing Averages in Time Series Data

Michael Correll
University of Wisconsin - Madison
mcorrell@cs.wisc.edu

Danielle Albers
University of Wisconsin - Madison
dalbers@cs.wisc.edu

Steve Franconeri
Northwestern University
franconeri@northwestern.edu

Michael Gleicher
University of Wisconsin - Madison
gleicher@cs.wisc.edu

ABSTRACT
Visualizations often seek to aid viewers in assessing the big picture in the data, that is, to make judgments about aggregate properties of the data. In this paper, we present an empirical study of a representative aggregate judgment task: finding regions of maximum average in a series. We show how a theory of perceptual averaging suggests a visual design other than the typically-used line graph. We describe an experiment that assesses participants' ability to estimate averages and make judgments based on these averages. The experiment confirms that this color encoding significantly outperforms the standard practice. The experiment also provides evidence for a perceptual averaging theory.

Author Keywords
Line graphs, Information Visualization, Colorfields, Visualization Evaluation.

ACM Classification Keywords
H.5.0. Information Interfaces and Presentation: General

General Terms
Experimentation

INTRODUCTION
A common task for viewers of visualizations is finding the "needle in the haystack"- precisely identifying individual values within a dataset. This task has been well-explored using established guidelines inspired by perceptual theory. But a core advantage of visualization is giving the viewer a sense of the "bigger picture" - the higher level, aggregate properties of the data. This task is less understood - especially as it connects to underlying perceptual theory.

Permission to make digital or hard copies of all or part of this work for personal or classroom use is granted without fee provided that copies are not made or distributed for profit or commercial advantage and that copies bear this notice and the full citation on the first page. To copy otherwise, or republish, to post on servers or to redistribute to lists, requires prior specific permission and/or a fee.
CHI'12, May 5–10, 2012, Austin, Texas, USA.
Copyright 2012 ACM 978-1-4503-1015-4/12/05...$10.00.

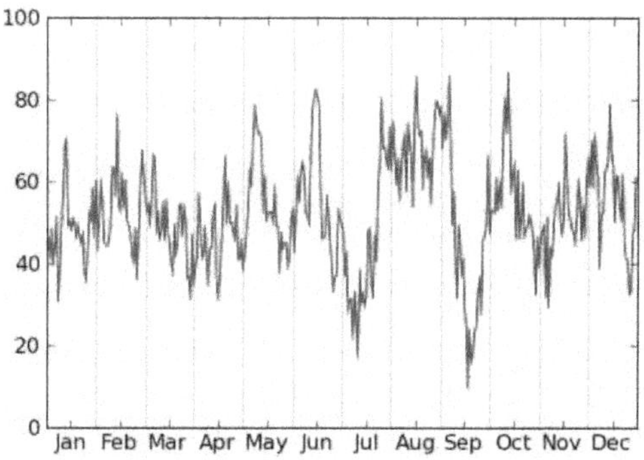

Figure 1. An aggregate judgment task: select the month with the highest *average* value. The maximum daily value (peak) may not occur in the month of maximum average.

In this paper, we explore visualization of aggregate properties, considering perceptually-motivated design and assessment to support a model summary analysis task. Our study considers a common data type: series data (an ordered sequence of numbers). Line graphs have been widely used to depict series data for over 200 years [33], and they have empirically-validated utility for identifying details within a dataset [7]. The task we consider is identifying a sub-range in a series (i.e. which month of the year) with the maximum average (see Figure 1). This task requires estimating an aggregate property over various ranges within a series and making judgments based on these estimates. Our study shows that viewers can make these judgments using a standard display (line graph), but that different visual encodings can provide improved performance especially as the task becomes more difficult. This shows potential for visual designs that better support summarization tasks.

Our approach to designing a visualization that readily presents aggregate information is to draw on efficient perceptual phenomena (i.e. preattentive and peripheral processing) that allow rapid summarization of data. Our contention was that encoding data values using color rather than the position would draw upon relevant perceptual processes to allow users to quickly summarize large regions of color. While color encodings may not be as precise as the position encodings used

Figure 2. The Sequence Surveyor tool provides summary visualization of large genomics data sets by employing a colorfield design [1]. The present study provides an empirical grounding for this design, including its use of block-permuted displays.

by line graphs, our expectation is that the efficiency of summarization would be more valuable in this task. Our study confirms that such a colorfield design is effective for the average judgment task, providing better performance than the canonical line graph design.

Efficient summary processing by the visual system is a rapidly evolving topic in the perception community (see Background, below). There are several emerging theories for explaining our findings. Our visualization design draws on a theory of perceptual averaging , which is less popular because it cannot explain as wide a range of phenomena as other theories. For example, it does not apply to line graphs. The theory does suggest that colorfields will be even more effective if the colors are shuffled as it reduces the area over which averaging must be performed. Our experiment confirms this, providing more evidence for the theory.

In this paper, we describe an empirical examination of an aggregate judgment task for series data. We discuss how perceptual theory suggests a non-standard visual design. Data from an experiment, conducted using crowd-sourced participants, is presented and analyzed. The results confirm that viewers can adequately perform the aggregate judgment task using the standard line graph representation. The results also show that a non-standard colorfield design offers significantly better task performance, especially as the examples grow challenging. Our findings have a range of implications as they show the potential for designing visual representations that support aggregate judgment tasks, and suggest certain perceptual mechanisms that might guide this design.

This paper makes the following primary contributions:

- We show how a theory of perceptual averaging can suggest designs for information visualizations that support summarization. These designs may defy the conventional wisdom, but significantly improve task performance.
- We show empirically how a non-standard colorfield design outperforms the common positional encoding (line graph) on a model visualization task. This model task applies to a data type common in real applications.
- We provide further support for a theory of perceptual averaging by showing that permuting the data has a significant effect on performance in the colorfield case (where the theory predicts it would), but no significant effect in the line graph case (where the theory is not applicable and so has no predictions of improvement).

Our results directly address the common case of 1D signal data, such as time series. Additionally, the design principles suggested by the theory apply to a wide range of applications. For example, in genomics the problem of scale requires consideration of aggregation (in that the entire genome of an individual can usually not be feasibly presented simultaneously), and the ability of users to make aggregate judgments. We have employed colorfield designs as a solution to this design problem [1][8]. The present study provides empirical validation of the colorfield approach for summarizable displays, and more generally, of the applicability of recent perceptual theory in visualization design.

BACKGROUND

There is a rich literature on the use of empirical studies to inform visual design for data presentation [7, 20], and such studies can inform a variety of aspects of the design process [27]. By experimentally validating performance characteristics at various steps of the process, designers can understand how different techniques work together to more effectively convey visual information. More recently, these empirical studies have been crowd-sourced to allow for a greater participant pool, and thus a more thorough exploration of the design space [16].

Empirical studies have also been used to illustrate how ideas from the study of perception can be applied to visual design. Notably, the work of Healey and Enns [15] use an understanding of visual attention to guide the design of visualizations, with particular focus on the use of pre-attentive phenomena to supplement visual data displays. This work shows that by exploiting "pop out" phenomena, designs can allow users to quickly find details. Other work has used a similar bottom-up understanding of perception as well as traditional best practices in visual design to develop guidelines for data presentation [21]. While these studies provide valuable groundwork for the design of data displays, they do not consider the perception of aggregates in the displays, nor do they assess making judgements based on aggregate information.

For the specific case of interpreting series data, there is a significant literature surrounding the exploration and understanding of the general properties of the line graph encoding, including categorization [30], slope, curvature [4], dimensionality [26, 22], and continuity [9]. However, these papers seldom explore the low-level mechanisms at work in line graphs and do not focus on the design space beyond conventional, single series line graphs. Recent work has considered the perception of multiple time series. Javed et al. [18] examine user performance over different encodings for multiple times series datasets, while Lam et al. [23] compare various interaction techniques. While these studies have shown the success of empirical evaluation in understanding the design of visualizations for multiple time series data, neither consider aggregate judgements, instead opting to focus on more detail-oriented tasks. These works are also more design-focused rather than seeking to understand the perceptual mechanisms underlying the empirical results.

As discussed below, recent work in perceptual science has considered the mechanisms of how people interpret complex scenes. Some of these models are beginning to be considered in the context of interface design, for example, in Rosenholtz et al.'s work on clutter [35, 36], but are not yet commonly considered in data displays. Also, such work is generally concerned with locating details amidst visual clutter, not judging the aggregate properties of the cluttered elements. A notable exception is the work of Ramanarayanan et al [34] who consider how to simplify rendering aggregates of objects in a given scene while preserving viewer perception of the aggregate. The general case of how to design visualizations to support ready access to summary data as opposed to specific values has only recently been explored [10, 38].

Visual and Mental Averaging

Research in perception has shown that several types of peripherally processed features can support efficient operations such as visual search and outlier detection [12]. Recent research suggests that general summary information about a collection of objects can also be determined efficiently in the visual periphery [3].

One explanation for efficient summary phenomena is the theory of perceptual averaging. Perceptual averaging suggests that averages of optical parameters, such as intensity or hue, can be averaged over a spatial range efficiently, as these averages are available to the visual system. Intuitively, one could imagine doing this averaging by squinting their eyes. However, such blurring is effectively done automatically in the early visual system on many pre-attentive features (such as intensity, color, and orientation) as multiple scale encodings are believed to be used extensively. Early levels of visual processing occur in parallel across levels of spatial frequency, with representations of both high and low-pass filtered versions of the visual image [17]. By accessing these different representations, one could potentially "see" the averages directly. Such visual averaging of pooled regions of an image has also been shown to occur in the visual periphery during later phases of visual processing [12]. Observers can extract information about average values across several types of preattentive features of visual objects, including average size [3, 6], orientation [2, 31], or location [2], without actively attending to the objects. Several findings suggest that these averages can be computed efficiently; however, the perception of such features by sampling procedures is difficult to rule out [29].

We predict that perception of line graphs do not draw upon these same summary phenomena, and so cannot be averaged as efficiently as the colorfield encoding. The complex shape of line graphs are processed in higher-level visual areas that may not average across multiple instances in a useful way, and there is no evidence that the visual system can efficiently average across height per se. In fact, global shape perception seems to be an perceptually inefficient task [41].

There is evidence that the visual system can average across the *size* of objects [3, 6], which could act as a proxy for height. To make use of this ability it is necessary to segment out individual "objects" from the global shape of the graph. The perceptual rules which guide this segmentation are inflexible, and the observer may not be able to arbitrarily set the desired areas for aggregation [39, 11]. By artificially destroying the "shape continuity" of a line graph it may be possible to remove some of the inefficiencies of this process, but aggregate shape may not be able to "pop-out" in the same way as aggregate color.

METHODS

Using Amazon's Mechanical Turk infrastructure we ran a study comparing the ability of users to accurately determine aggregate information from time series data using either a colorfield or line graph encoding at various levels of task difficulty. Within the colorfield and line graph conditions, we tested different sorts of permutation to assess the validity of our underlying perceptual assumptions: a 2D permutation of data in the colorfield case (to make perceptual color averaging easier) and a 1D permutation of data in the line graph case (to break shape continuity). Our study supported our hypotheses: the colorfield outperformed line graph, and permuted colorfields outperformed non-permuted colorfields (since preattentive phenomena could be more easily accessed) whereas permuted line graphs did not outperform non-permuted line graphs (where our theory makes no prediction).

Task Design

Our goal was to create a task that would allow us to assess a viewer's ability to make judgments about aggregate properties of data. To allow for effective experimentation, the task could not require the viewer to have domain knowledge, familiarity with displays beyond basic charts or graphs, or advanced statistical skills. The task needed to require estimating the aggregate property over subsets of the data well enough to make comparative judgments about these aggregate regions. We were not interested in the precise value of the estimate, and preferred a task with a forced choice decision.

To fulfill these requirements, we designed an experimental task of analyzing time series data over the course of a year, specifically, the task of analyzing sales data for a fictional company. Participants were asked to identify the month that had the maximum average sales. The choice of a one year time span (12 "months" of 30 days each) provided a number of data points that would be manageable for the participants but not trivial to analyze. The year length also afforded a natural subdivision for the data series, namely, trends over the course of each month.

Comparing averages across months is a task that is involved (it requires rapid analysis of hundreds of data points) but at the same time domain-invariant (only basic statistical knowledge is required). While this task is contrived in that specific data encodings could be used to precisely display the per-month average, by including all of the data and then asking for only a particular property we simulate real world data analysis tasks where users must make rapid assessments of statistical properties of large amounts of data.

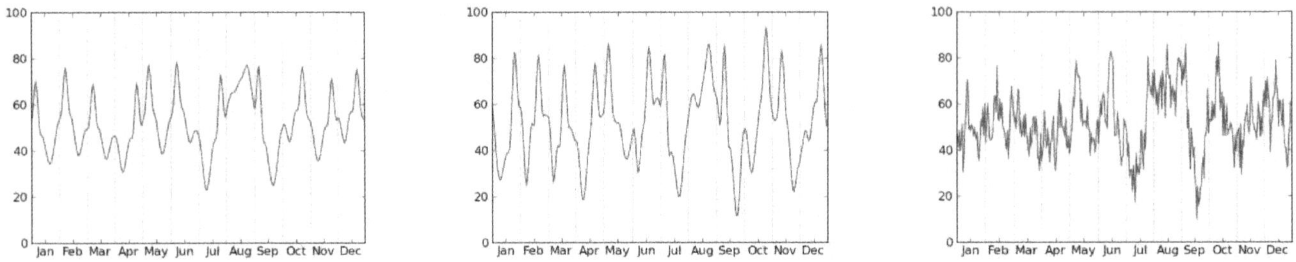

(a) Low Noise (b) Medium Noise (c) High Noise

Figure 4. Difficulty for the aggregate judgment task is partly modified by adding noise at three ordinal (but non-linear) levels: low ((a)), medium ((b)), and high ((c)). Noise variation is not uniform: the different noise levels vary in both amplitude and frequency.

We needed to ensure that the task required participants to estimate the averages by precluding alternate strategies. For the maximum average task, a potential alternate strategy is to report the month containing the maximum value, a strategy otherwise known as "peak finding". We precluded this strategy by constructing our data such that the peak data point rarely occurred in the month with the maximum average (less than 0.5% of the time). The difference between maximum average judgments and peak finding was explained in the instructions to participants, who were also instructed that the maximum average may not necessarily be the peak. Participants were not told that the peak occurring in the maximum average month was rare, as this would suggest "peak avoidance" as an alternate strategy.

The more detailed design of the task can be subdivided into three areas: the design of the actual values of the time series data, the design of the visual encodings of the data, and the design for the experimental evaluation of these encodings.

Data Design

Key to the experiment was the ability to generate well-structured data signals that were both appropriate for the maximum average month task and gave sufficient control over the kinds of challenges we want to explore in the experiment. In particular, we wanted to add varying amounts of noise to the data signal and to control the sensitivity required in making judgments about the estimated averages.

To make our data generalizable across display conditions, all data values were drawn from the range $[0...100]$. To populate our 360 data points (30 days per artificial month), we selected a winning month at random with an average value u_w from the range $[50...98]$. From our initial assumptions, we attempted to have some control over the apparent difficulty of the task by selecting up to k "distracter" months, where k is in the range $[2...4]$. Distracter months were assigned average values that were influenced by a second parameter d, from the range $[1...10]$, such that the average of these distracter months was exactly $u_w - d$. The remaining months had averages randomly drawn from the range $[20...(u_w - d - 1)]$. See figure 5 for a visual description of these parameters. Once the average values for each month were determined, the daily data points were generated by using structured noise to create a smooth curve preserving the previously computed averages [32]. Additional structured noise n was added, allowing parametric control over the amount of noise (parameter n can be assigned 3 levels, Figure 4). Peaks are then added to each month to create a regular pattern of higher values and to dissuade peak-finding as a viable strategy, and smooth displacements are used to adjust the non-peak values within each month to preserve the target averages.

We generated one data series for each possible combination of winning month, k, d, and n, a total of 1080 distinct series. We roughly equated k and d with task difficulty, and so to fairly balance the task with respect to hardness, we evenly drew from every k and then from every d value to provide the data for each participant.

Display Design

Our experiment considered different visual encodings for the series data. We used a line graph encoding as this is the standard method for displaying series data. A line graph encodes time series data by measuring time along the horizontal axis and the corresponding values along the vertical axis. The line graphs were generated using the MatPlotLib library. The vertical axis was labeled with values specified with tick marks every 20 value points, from 0 to 100. The horizontal axis was likewise labeled with tick marks at each month and with gray spans defining the boundaries between the various months.

The theory of perceptual averaging suggests that a retinal measurement, such as color (intensity, hue, saturation) may be easily averaged by the visual system. Even though color encodings have been shown to be less accurate than positional encodings [7], we hypothesized that the potential facility for averaging would outweigh the reduced accuracy. Therefore, we created a color encoding of the data, where the range of values was mapped to a selected color map. Such color encodings of series data are uncommon, but not without precedent (c.f. Lasagna Plots [40]). Note that in keeping with the best-practices in color map design (c.f. [5]), we selected a color map that varied in hue, saturation, and brightness from the Color Brewer selection tool [14] (specifically a red-blue diverging scale). Color values were interpolated in CIE L*a*b* space to provide an approximately perceptually linear interpolation between color values (see Figure 3(c)).

The theory of perceptual averaging would further suggest that by randomly shuffling the colors within the month, visual av-

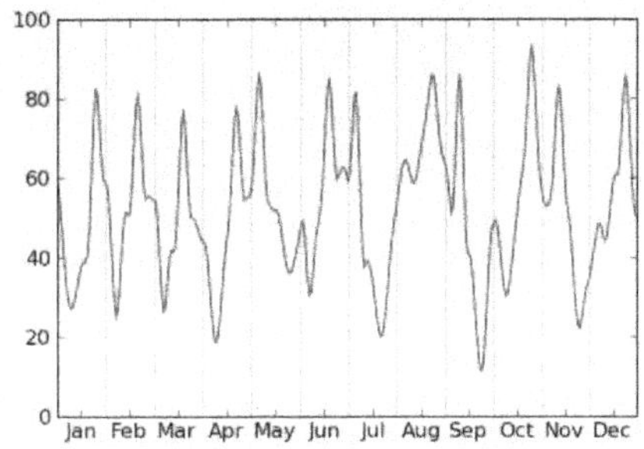

(a) Ordered Line graph

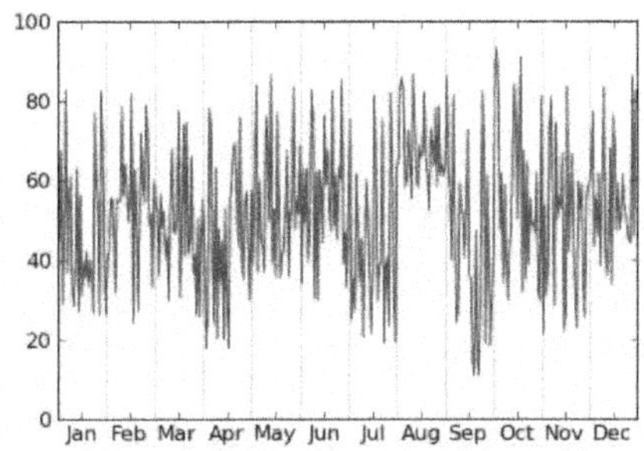

(b) 1D Permuted Line graph

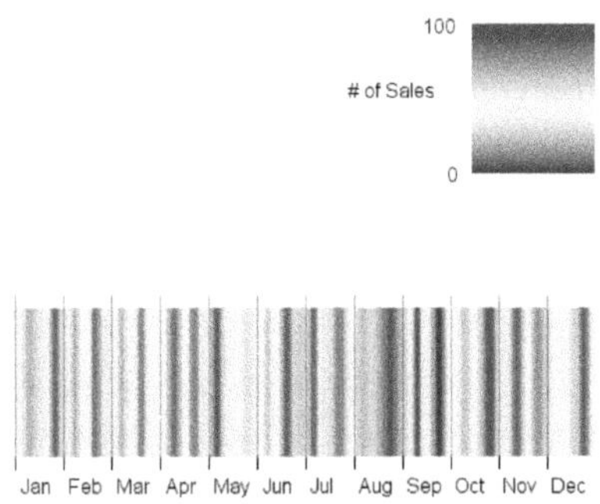

(c) Ordered Colorfield

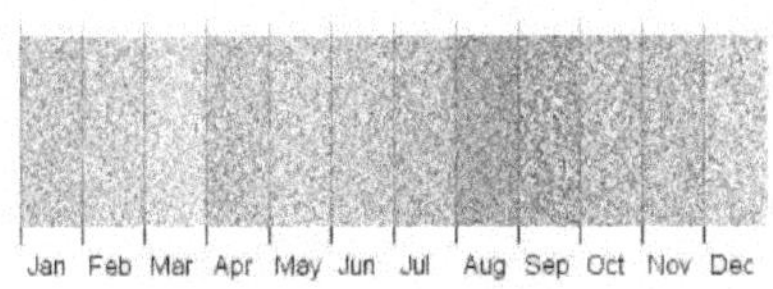

(d) 2D Permuted Colorfield

Figure 3. An example of the four display conditions tested in the aggregate judgment task. Line graphs ((a), (b)) provide a standard method for viewing the series data, while colorfields ((c), (d)) instead use color to encode value. The effect of permutation on perceptual averaging was tested by permuting the points within each month horizontally in the line graph condition (b) and both horizontally and vertically in the colorfield condition (d).

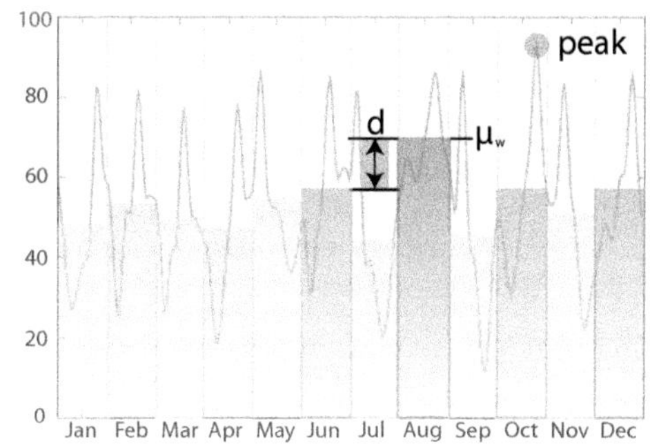

Figure 5. Each experimental stimulus has one month with the highest average value (μ_w) and k distracter months at the next highest average value (red), whose average is d below the highest months. Peaks generally did not appear in the highest month to protect against peak-finding strategies. We expect the difficulty of the aggregate judgment task to vary with both k and d.

eraging would be even easier since more local averages over smaller regions would be representative of the whole (i.e. the colors that need to be mixed would be closer together). Therefore we created a display type where within each month's block, the pixels of the block were randomly permuted (see Figure 3(d)); this technique has some precedent in the literature [1, 13]. This permutation does not preserve low-level patterns in the data, but is designed to facilitate the averaging of colors across known boundaries of aggregation.

While the line graph condition functioned as a control case based on traditional time series encodings, to further our exploration of the perceptual theories at work in aggregation we created a display condition where the line graphs were permuted. For the permuted line graph case, however, the data was only randomly shuffled in the horizontal direction, as changing vertical positions would change the encoding of the data (see Figure 3(b)). This permutation is not symmetric to the colorfield permutations (the permutations occur in one dimension rather than two), and was intended to assess the effect of intentionally breaking up continuous shapes and trends in the data.

Our experiment considered four display conditions: two different visual encodings (color and position) and a manipulation of the encodings to highlight expected perceptual results (2D permutation in the color case, to test our theory of perceptual averaging, and 1D permutation in the position case to test shape continuity theory). The horizontal spacing of the displays was made to be identical, and identical axis labels were used. For color encodings, a legend was provided immediately above every display. The height of each display type is relevant to the ease of the task: a larger height leads to increased fidelity of position in the line graph case and increased area devoted to color in the colorfield case. As a result, the display size was kept standard for each display condition. The height of the colorfield display was compressed compared to the total height available to the line graph to make room for the color legend.

Experimental Design

We considered the two basic design types (line graphs and colorfield encodings) to be sufficiently different that they required separate instructions. Therefore, we chose to use a between-participants design: each participant was randomly assigned to one display type condition. Each participant received instructions for only one type of display, and saw 30 trials of the same type of display.

In addition to this basic design type, our experiment considered several factors: whether the data was permuted within months and several properties of the data series relating to its "hardness" (the k and d levels discussed above). Noise level and permutation were considered within-participants factors. Each of the experimental factors, as well as our *a priori* k and d hardness factors, were stratified. However, the combinations and ordering of the factors were randomized. Therefore, while each participant was guaranteed to view each level of each factor an equal number of times, there were no guarantees of which combinations of factor levels they would see.

A pretest and tutorial phase used Ishihara [24] plates to detect and exclude participants with Color Vision Deficiency (CVD), as the color ramp used in our colorfield condition was not chosen with the needs of users with CVD in mind. The tutorial phase also served to familiarize the participant with the display condition, and emphasized the difference between the averaging and peak-finding task both verbally and visually.

Experimental Procedure

The experiment consisted of asking participants to answer 30 questions. Each question presented a display of a data series and asked the participant to select the month with the highest average value. The number of questions was chosen based on pilot studies that suggested that the total task would take each participant approximately 15 minutes.

For each trial, participants were shown a web page that contained a box where the display would appear. At the top of the screen, the question ("Choose the month with the highest average value") appeared. At the bottom of the screen, a radio-button list of the months was arrayed horizontally so that the month names would appear directly beneath the corresponding region of the display. A "submit button" appeared below the month buttons. The lower buttons were disabled before the display was presented.

Initially, the display box contained a button allowing the participant to click when they are ready. Once this button was clicked, an initial data series was displayed within the box. The display was shown for a maximum of 20 seconds, although the participant was free to answer the question either during this time or afterwards. After time had elapsed, the display was removed. The time limit was imposed to preclude having the participants make measurements of the screen, but selected so that it would not rush the participants.

Measures

Since our judgments were about the accuracy of our different visual designs, our measure was the number of correct answers for each condition. While this was the primary measure, to perform validation we collected additional data. Participants were tracked by IP address to ensure that the same participant did not perform the task multiple times. This identifying data was discarded upon beginning the analysis for privacy reasons.

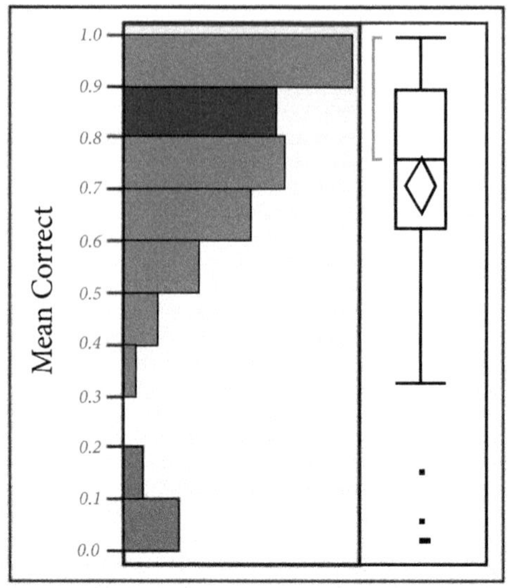

Figure 6. The accuracy distribution on the aggregate judgment task by performance. Of the 74 original participants in our study, we excluded results from eight of the participants whose performance failed the inner quartile range test.

For the primary experimental task, we recorded the data series being presented, the visual encoding used, and the various hardness parameters, as well as the identity of the winning and distracter months. After the users guessed a value we recorded their guess, whether it was correct, and the time spent on the question.

After completion of the task we asked for self-reported demographic data (age, gender, and education level) as well as asking for general comments.

Participants

Since our task could be entirely completed using the browser window, we drew our participants from Amazon's Mechanical Turk service, specifically those users registered in North America with at least a 95% "approval" rating. Mechanical Turk's large userbase and quick turnaround speed was considered an appropriate tradeoff for losing the ability to directly observe participants. In total, 74 participants completed the 30 question comparison task, 42 female and 32 male. Ages ranged from 18 to 62 ($\mu = 34.7$, $\sigma = 12.0$). The demographics data was by necessity self-reported, but does conform to the general distribution of North American Turk users [37]. We followed acknowledged best practices to improve the reliability of our experimental data, including randomizing questions, requiring mandatory questions of different input types, and preventing "click-through" behavior [19, 25].

We excluded 5 participants as significant outliers in terms of performance (they failed the interquartile range test for k=1.5, see Figure 6). These participants were all from the line graph condition. The under-performing participants were compensated at the same rate as the other participants.

RESULTS

Given the uncertain provenance of data from Mechanical Turk, we performed validations on the dataset as a whole to eliminate possible sources of bias. We examined the selections and time taken by participants whose performance metrics were significant outliers to determine if there were any patterns indicative of adversarial participants (e.g. people clicking through as fast as possible through only a few months). There were no such red flags. We also noticed no overall effects from task learning or task fatigue. In particular, there was no statistically significant effect of question number on performance, F(29,1921) = 1.19, $p <= .211$.

We performed a two-way analysis of variance between the three levels of noise n, the ten possible settings of d (the difference between the highest and the next highest averages), the three possible settings of the number of distracters k, the two types of display (colorfield versus line graph), the two possible permutations (original ordering or permuted), and the question number [1...30]. All measures of statistical significance are at the 0.95 confidence level. See Table 1 for detailed results.

Our primary proposed *a priori* difficulty factor d had a statistically significant effect on performance as smaller gaps between the winning and distracter months resulted in worse performance, F(9,1921)=34.5, $p <= 0.0001$ (Figure 7). Our other tentative hardness metric k did not have a statistically significant effect, F(2,1921)=1.47, $p <= 0.231$, although there were some cross-conditional effects (Figure 8). The relative noisiness of the data n was a significant performance effect, F(2,1921)=15.2, $p <= 0.0001$ (Figure 9). Noisier data was associated with worse performance. Encoding (line graph versus colorfield) had a significant effect, F(1,1921)=143, $p <= .0001$, as line graphs significantly underperformed colorfields. Ordered versus permuted data had no statistically significant effect overall, F(2,1921) = 2.28, $p = 0.132$, but there were cross-conditional effects (Figure 11).

Based on the initial results, we performed some additional pairwise comparisons across conditions. Although permutation overall had no significant effect, there was a significant interaction between type of display in conjunction with permutation of data, F(2,1921)=16.0, $p <= 0.0001$ (Figure 11). Within the colorfield display type, participants in the permuted colorfields ($\mu = .914, \sigma = .073$) outperformed those in the ordered case ($\mu = .815, \sigma = .197$). The interaction between noise and type was not a significant effect, F(2,1921)=0.314, $p = 0.381$. With respect to our a priori hardness parameters, d had significant interactions with type, F(9,1921) = 2.08, $p <= 0.028$, but k did not, F(2,1921)=1.147, $p = 0.231$. The line graph display was more sensitive to changes in d than the colorfield display.

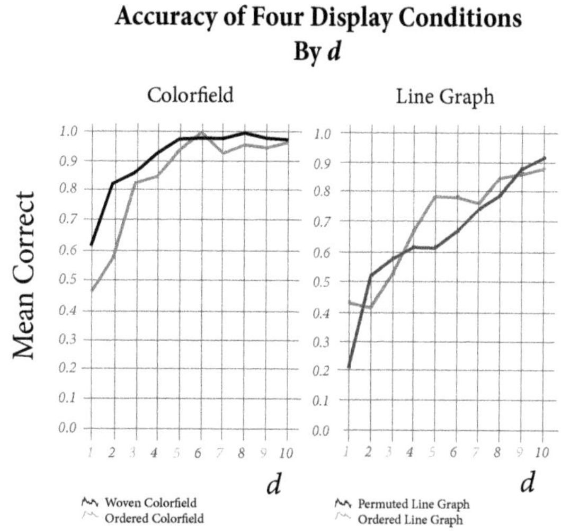

Figure 7. A comparison of the effect of d on performance in the four display conditions. Participants perform better at the aggregate judgment task when using permuted colorfields (black, left) than ordered colorfields (red, left), with a marked difference in the more difficult stimuli. Permutation has no significant effect on the overall performance of participants on the aggregate judgment task using line graphs.

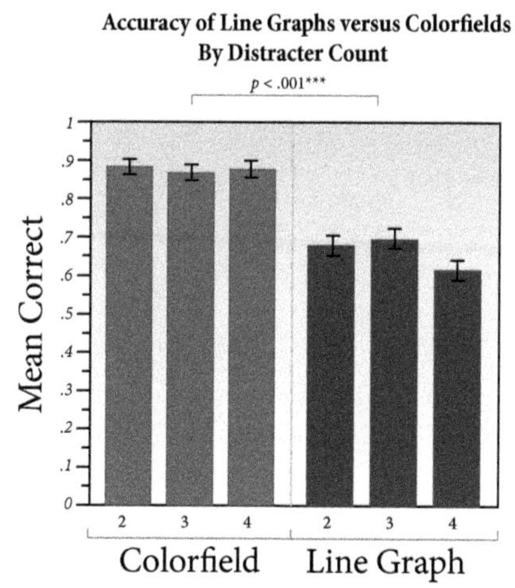

Figure 8. Performance as a factor of distracter count in the colorfield and line graph conditions. The number of distracters (k) has no significant effect on participant accuracy on either colorfields or line graphs.

Source	Number of Parameters	Degrees of Freedom	Degrees of Freedom for Dependent Measure	F	p
Display Type	1	1	1921	143.7537	< 0.0001
Permutation Type	1	1	1921	2.2769	0.1315
Noise Level (n)	2	2	1921	15.2464	< 0.0001
Distracter Difference (d)	9	9	1921	34.4739	< 0.0001
Number of Distracters (k)	2	2	1921	0.9657	0.3809
Display Type x Permutation Type	1	1	1921	15.951	< 0.0001
Display Type x Noise Level	2	2	1921	0.3144	0.7303
Display Type x Distracter Difference	9	9	1921	2.0817	0.02808
Display Type x Number of Distracters	2	2	1921	1.4669	0.2309
Question Index	29	29	1921	1.1935	0.2110

Table 1. The ANOVA Table for the aggregate judgment task.

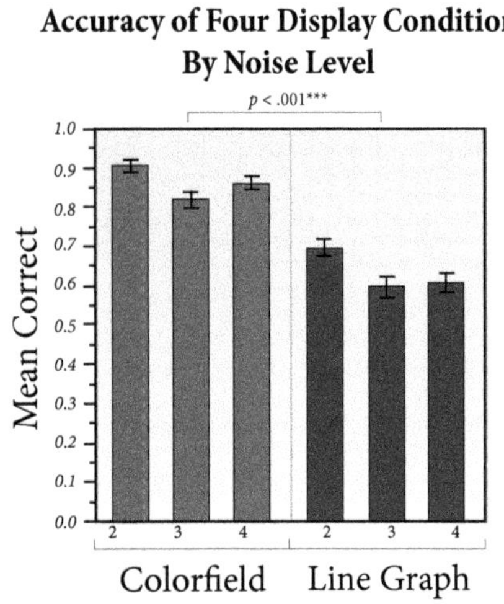

Figure 9. The effect of noise level in the colorfield and line graph conditions. While graphs with the least amount of noise are associate with higher accuracy, the ordinal but non-linear nature of the noise level prevents us from making concrete claims about a monotonic decrease in performance with respect to amount of noise.

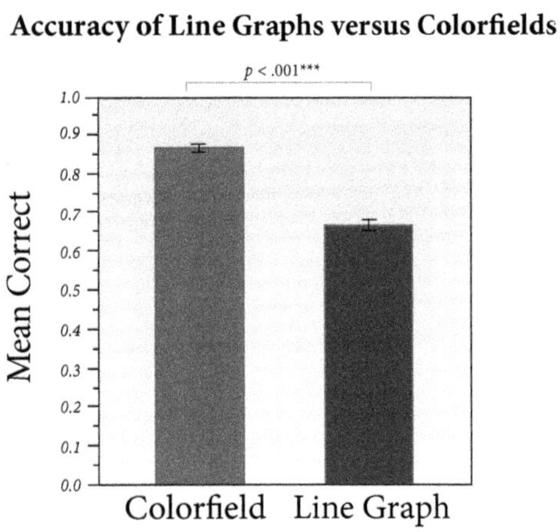

Figure 10. Accuracy in the aggregate judgment task across task type. Despite the conventional use of line graphs for series data, participants performed significantly better on the aggregate judgment task while using colorfield displays than line graphs.

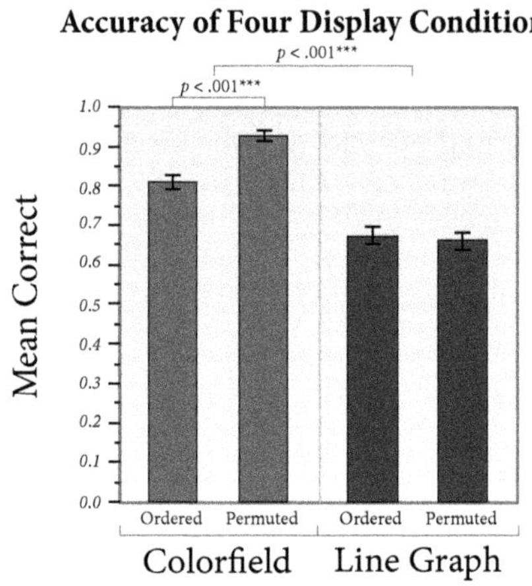

Figure 11. Accuracy in the aggregate judgment task across the four display conditions. The use of permutation to augment the aggregate judgment task yielded mixed results. Permutation in colorfields did yield statistically better performance than ordered colorfields, whereas no effect was found between ordered and permuted line graphs.

DISCUSSION

Our study confirms that people are able to retrieve high-level statistical overviews of series data efficiently. Using a standard visual encoding of the data (a line graph), participants performed significantly above chance, with degraded performance as we changed our proposed hardness parameters. We feel our data represented a large cross section of possible task difficulties.

The theory of perceptual averaging would suggest that color encodings would afford reliable determination of averages, as averaging over a range could be performed by the perceptual system instead of as a mental computation. Our experiment supports this conclusion: participants task performance was significantly better using the color encoding than the standard line graph encoding across all difficulty levels.

Conventional wisdom [28] (and prior perceptual experiments [7]) in the information visualization community would suggest that positional encodings (a line graph) support better retrieval of accurate values than color encodings, and would allow for better performance in general data analysis tasks. However, our results show that designs that allow for perceptual averaging, in particular color encodings, may be preferable when viewers must consider averages over ranges.

The utility of the theory of perceptual averaging in designing information displays inspired us to seek evidence to support it. The theory suggests that permuting the colors to be averaged would make averaging even easier, as the visual pooling of color could be more local. In contrast, the theory provides no prediction about line graphs. Our experimental results support the theory: permutation significantly improved performance on the color encoding displays, but did not significantly affect performance for line graphs. Other theories of visual summarization (such as a theory of shape continuity)usually suggest that both conditions would be aided by permutation. The 2D color permutation also has other effects, such as better delineating block boundaries, which may also contribute to the performance.

Overall, our study suggests that if visualizations are meant to aid a user in getting the "big picture" (e.g. assess aggregate information over ranges), they can be designed to better support these tasks. The theory of perceptual averaging provides a foundation for such designs. The fact that the designs suggested by the theory may contradict the conventional wisdom of visual display design suggests key tradeoffs: designs best suited for finding details may not be ideal for tasks requiring aggregation, and vice versa.

Limitations

While our study does strongly suggest the possibility for displays designed for aggregate assessment, limitations in the study suggest further research may be needed. Foremost, our study explores a single kind of aggregate judgment (averages over ranges) on a single kind of data type (series). While we hypothesize that averaging is a central mechanism for exploring larger scales of data (it performs a filtering of details, in the signal processing sense), such speculation should be explored to generalize the results of this study to the assessment of other aggregate properties beyond averages, such as the assessment of variance or trends within a dataset. Similarly, while the perceptual averaging theory extends naturally to 2D displays, our study needs to be extended to other types of data, particularly 2D fields or multiple 1D series. For these data types, the use of color encoded displays is more common (e.g. heat maps and "lasagna plots"[40] respectively).

Another limitation of our study is the contrived nature of the task of asking for judgments about averages over regions. The permuted encodings make use of knowledge of the aggregation ranges, which is why we consider them more as an assessment of the perceptual theory than a practical design: if we knew the viewer wanted to assess averages over months, we could have presented those values directly. For the non-permuted colorfield encoding, there is no assumption of the aggregation duration; although further study should confirm the ranges of durations that viewers can effectively average. The extent to which the ability to precisely determine specific values is harmed by both the colorfield and especially the permuted colorfield encodings is also unknown. It is also possible that permutations might introduce patterns in the display that are not representative of patterns in the data. Generally, we view the studied designs as a having potential tradeoffs that need to be further explored empirically.

Our experimental methods also limit the power of our study. Our desire to make peak-finding a non-viable strategy resulted in series with atypical distributions of highs and lows. Our noise generation techniques were also non-uniform with respect to the frequency and amplitude of the generated noise, which prevented us from making anything other than relative judgments about noise level. The data generation process also limited our ability to control the "hardness" of the experiment: the task was too easy in some of the colorfield conditions, which made it difficult to distinguish the effects of some experimental parameters.

We believe that through careful experimental design, we have obtained reliable results from crowd-sourcing. In fact, the potential diversity of color performance of participants' display devices makes the success of the color encodings more robust: they seem to work even without calibrated monitors (modern displays exhibit little or no geometry distortion, the variety in participant displays is unlikely to be a factor for purely geometric encodings). However, the use of crowd-sourced participants precluded us from doing post-hoc interviews, for example to diagnose mistakes, understand strategies, and collect qualitative data about relative task hardness.

In the future, we hope to more fully explore the space of designs that afford aggregate judgments, and the application of the perceptual averaging theory to visualization design. This initial study did not consider many design choices, such as the color palette used. It did not consider tasks beyond maximum averaging, aggregation over variable sized regions, or datasets beyond 1D series. Our experimental methodology should extend naturally to these explorations.

CONCLUSION

Visualization offers the potential of allowing viewers to see the "big picture" and make assessments over ranges of data. In this paper, we have explored the ability of visualization to convey an aggregate over a range in an important case: series data. Our study shows that while viewers can make judgments of averages over regions using standard designs, displays can be created that improve task performance. In particular, we show how a perceptual theory suggests a colorfield design that has significantly better performance on the average judgment task than the standard line graph encoding. The study also provides further evidence for a theory of perceptual averaging. Our results have implications in suggesting how visual displays should be designed to afford effective assessments of aggregate quantities.

REFERENCES

1. Albers, D., Dewey, C., and Gleicher, M. Sequence surveyor: Leveraging overview for scalable genomic alignment visualization. In *Visualization and Computer Graphics, IEEE Transactions on*, vol. 17, IEEE (December 2011).
2. Alvarez, G. A., and Oliva, A. Spatial ensemble statistics are efficient codes that can be represented with reduced attention. *Proceedings of the National Academy of Sciences 106* (2009), 7345–7350.
3. Ariely, D. Seeing sets: representation by statistical properties. *Psychological Science 12* (2001), 157–162.
4. Best, L. A., Smith, L. D., and Stubbs, D. A. Perception of linear and nonlinear trends: using slope and curvature information to make trend discriminations. *Perceptual and motor skills 104*, 3 Pt 1 (June 2007), 707–21.
5. Brewer, C. Color use guidelines for data representation. In *Proceedings of the Section on Statistical Graphics, American Statistical Association* (1999), 55–60.
6. Chong, S. C., and Treisman, A. Representation of statistical properties. *Vision Research 43* (2003), 393–404.
7. Cleveland, W. S., and McGill, R. Graphical Perception: Theory, Experimentation, and Application to the Development of Graphical Methods. *Journal of the American Statistical Association 79*, 387 (Sept. 1984), 531–554.
8. Correll, M., Ghosh, S., O'Connor, D., and Gleicher, M. Visualizing virus population variability from next generation sequencing data. In *2011 IEEE Symposium on Biological Data Visualization (BioVis)*, IEEE (oct 2011), 135–142.
9. Eaton, C., Plaisant, C., and Drizd, T. Visualizing missing data: graph interpretation user study. *Human-Computer Interaction-INTERACT 2005* (2005), 861–872.
10. Elmqvist, N., and Fekete, J.-D. Hierarchical aggregation for information visualization: Overview, techniques, and design guidelines. *Visualization and Computer Graphics, IEEE Transactions on 16*, 3 (may-june 2010), 439 –454.
11. Franconeri, S., Bemis, D., and Alvarez, G. Number estimation relies on a set of segmented objects. *Cognition 113*, 1 (2009), 1–13.
12. Freeman, J., and Simoncelli, E. P. Metamers of the ventral stream. *Nature Neuroscience*, 9 (Sep 2011), 1195–1201. Advance online publication: 14 Aug 2011.
13. Hagh-Shenas, H., Kim, S., Interrante, V., and Healey, C. G. Weaving versus blending: a quantitative assessment of the information carrying capacities of two alternative methods for conveying multivariate data with color. *Visualization and Computer Graphics, IEEE Transactions on 13*, 6, 1270–7.
14. Harrower, M., and Brewer, C. Colorbrewer.org: An online tool for selecting colour schemes for maps. *The Cartographic Journal 40*, 1 (June 2003), 27–37.
15. Healey, C. G., and Enns, J. Building perceptual textures to visualize multidimensional datasets. *Proceedings Visualization '98 (Cat. No.98CB36276)* (1998), 111–118,.
16. Heer, J., and Bostock, M. Crowdsourcing graphical perception: using mechanical turk to assess visualization design. In *Proceedings of the 28th international conference on Human factors in computing systems*, ACM (2010), 203–212.
17. Hughes, H. C., Nozawa, G., and Kitterle, F. Global precedence, spatial frequency channels, and the statistics of natural images. *J. Cognitive Neuroscience 8* (July 1996), 197–230.
18. Javed, W., McDonnel, B., and Elmqvist, N. Graphical perception of multiple time series. *Visualization and Computer Graphics, IEEE transactions on 16*, 6 (2010), 927–34.
19. Kittur, A., Chi, E. H., and Suh, B. Crowdsourcing user studies with Mechanical Turk. *Proceeding of the twenty-sixth annual CHI conference on Human factors in computing systems - CHI '08* (2008), 453.
20. Kosara, R., Healey, C. G., Interrante, V., Laidlaw, D., and Ware, C. Thoughts on user studies: Why, how, and when. *IEEE Computer Graphics and Applications 23*, 4 (2003), 20–25.
21. Kosslyn, S., and Chabris, C. Minding information graphics. *Folio: the Magazine for Magazine Management, Feb. 1, 1992, 21 2* (1992), 69–71.
22. Kumar, N., and Benbasat, I. The effect of relationship encoding, task type, and complexity on information representation: An empirical evaluation of 2D and 3D line graphs. *MIS Quarterly 28*, 2 (2004), 255–281.
23. Lam, H., Munzner, T., and Kincaid, R. Overview use in multiple visual information resolution interfaces. *Visualization and Computer Graphics, IEEE transactions on 13*, 6 (2007), 1278–85.
24. Legrand, H., Rand, G., and Rittler, C. Tests for the detection and anlysis of color-blindness i. the ishihara test: An evaluation. *Journal of the Optical Society of America 35* (1945), 268.
25. Mason, W., and Suri, S. Conducting Behavioral Research on Amazon's Mechanical Turk. *Behavior Research Methods* (2010).
26. Meserth, T., and Hollands, J. Comparing 2D and 3D displays for trend estimation: The effects of display augmentation. In *Human Factors and Ergonomics Society Annual Meeting Proceedings*, vol. 43, Human Factors and Ergonomics Society (1999), 1308–1312.
27. Munzner, T. A nested model for visualization design and validation. *Visualization and Computer Graphics, IEEE transactions on 15*, 6 (2009), 921–8.
28. Munzner, T. Visualization. In *Fundamentals of computer graphics, 3e.*, P. Shirley and S. Marschner, Eds. AK Peters, 2009, 675–707.
29. Myczek, K., and Simons, D. J. Better than average: Alternatives to statistical summary representations for rapid judgments of average size. *Perception & Psychophysics 70* (2008), 772–788.
30. Nourbakhsh, M. R., and Ottenbacher, K. J. The statistical analysis of single-subject data: a comparative examination. *Physical therapy 74*, 8 (Aug. 1994), 768–76.
31. Parkes, L., Lund, J., Angelucci, A., Solomon, J., and Morgan, M. Compulsory averaging of crowded orientation signals in human vision. *Nature Neuroscience 4* (2001), 739–744.
32. Perlin, K. Improving noise. In *ACM Transactions on Graphics (TOG)*, vol. 21, ACM (2002), 681–682.
33. Playfair, W. *The commercial and political atlas: representing, by means of stained copper-plate charts, the progress of the commerce, revenues, expenditure, and debts of England, during the whole of the eighteenth century*. Printed by T. Burton, for J. Wallis, 1801.
34. Ramanarayanan, G., Bala, K., and Ferwerda, J. A. Perception of complex aggregates. *ACM Trans. Graph. 27* (August 2008), 60:1–60:10.
35. Rosenholtz, R., Dorai, A., and Freeman, R. Do predictions of visual perception aid design? *Transactions on Applied Perception* (2011).
36. Rosenholtz, R., Li, Y., Mansfield, J., and Jin, Z. Feature congestion: a measure of display clutter. *Proceedings of the SIGCHI conference on Human factors in computing systems* (2005).
37. Ross, J., Irani, L., Silberman, M. S., Zaldivar, A., and Tomlinson, B. Who are the crowdworkers?: shifting demographics in mechanical turk. In *Proceedings of the 28th of the international conference extended abstracts on Human factors in computing systems*, CHI EA '10 (2010), 2863–2872.
38. Shneiderman, B. Extreme visualization: squeezing a billion records into a million pixels. In *Proceedings of the 2008 ACM SIGMOD International Conference on Management of Data*, ACM (2008), 3–12.
39. Singh, M., and Hoffman, D. Constructing and representing visual objects. *Trends in Cognitive Sciences 1*, 3 (1997), 98–102.
40. Swihart, B. J., Caffo, B., James, B. D., Strand, M., Schwartz, B. S., and Punjabi, N. M. Lasagna plots: a saucy alternative to spaghetti plots. *Epidemiology (Cambridge, Mass.) 21*, 5 (Sept. 2010), 621–5.
41. Wolfe, J., and Bennett, S. C. Preattentive object files: Shapeless bundles of basic features. *Vision Research 37*, 1 (1997), 25–43.

Rethinking Statistical Analysis Methods for CHI

Maurits Kaptein
Eindhoven University of Technology / Philips Research
Den Dolech 2, 5600 MB, Eindhoven, the Netherlands
maurits@mauritskaptein.com
+31(0)6 21262211

Judy Robertson
Computer Science, Heriot-Watt University
Edinburgh Campus, EH14 4AS
Judy.Robertson@hw.ac.uk
+44 (0)131 451 8223

ABSTRACT
CHI researchers typically use a significance testing approach to statistical analysis when testing hypotheses during usability evaluations. However, the appropriateness of this approach is under increasing criticism, with statisticians, economists, and psychologists arguing against the use of routine interpretation of results using "canned" *p* values. Three problems with current practice - the fallacy of the transposed conditional, a neglect of power, and the reluctance to interpret the size of effects - can lead us to build weak theories based on vaguely specified hypothesis, resulting in empirical studies which produce results that are of limited practical or scientific use. Using publicly available data presented at CHI 2010 [19] as an example we address each of the three concerns and *promote consideration of the magnitude and actual importance of effects*, as opposed to statistical significance, as the new criteria for evaluating CHI research.

Author Keywords
Usability evaluation; Bayesian Statistics; Research Methods

ACM Classification Keywords
H.5.2 User interfaces: Evaluation/methodology;

General Terms
Experimentation, Measurement.

INTRODUCTION
A core strength of the CHI community is that members bring together expertise from a range of disciplines "as diverse as user interface design, human factors, computer science, psychology, engineering, graphics and industrial design, entertainment, and telecommunications" [27]. Correspondingly, the community has a rich set of design and evaluation practices at its disposal. An important aspect of training new interaction designers is to teach them how to use different data gathering and analysis techniques "flexibly and in combination to avoid biases which are inherent in any one approach" [28, p.290]. While many approaches to evaluation are valid, it is important that researchers are aware of best practice for any given methodology.

Every so often, it is useful to re-evaluate the standard set of techniques used within an approach and consider whether they provide researchers with the tools they need to answer the questions they are interested in, and whether other techniques would in fact serve the community better. Such a debate is currently taking place in the field of psychology, as demonstrated by a recent special collection of papers within *Perspectives on Psychological Science* [21]. Critics of the traditional statistical inference method of significance testing argue that "it is time for researchers to consider foundational issues in inference" [10, p.274]. Similarly, Wagenmakers, et al. conclude that "experimental psychologists need to change the way they conduct their experiments and analyze their data" [31, p.426] and, in the light of recent positive empirical findings in the theoretically implausible area of extra-sensory perception, argue that the statistical strategies used by psychologists are "too weak, too malleable and offer far too many opportunities for researchers to befuddle themselves and their peers" [30, p.425]. In fact this is a long-standing problem; Cohen noted already in 1994 that such criticisms have been made within psychology for forty years [8].

As a field of study that builds upon statistical methods used by psychologists, usability evaluation is subject to the same criticisms. Indeed, a small number of HCI researchers have identified flaws in experimental design and statistical testing in usability studies. In 1998 Gray and Salzman published an in-depth critique of five well known studies of usability evaluation methods, observing that weaknesses in experimental design (threats to statistical conclusion validity, construct validity, and internal and external validity) call into question the reliability of these findings [14]. More recently, Cairn's survey of inferential statistics in BCS HCI conferences and two leading HCI journals noted common problems in reporting of statistical results; failure to check assumptions about the data required by particular tests, over-testing and using inappropriate tests [4]. Dunlop and Baillie [11] aimed to raise awareness within the sub-field of mobile HCI of problems with statistical analysis techniques such as the use of null hypothesis testing in a binary way to approve results,

Permission to make digital or hard copies of all or part of this work for personal or classroom use is granted without fee provided that copies are not made or distributed for profit or commercial advantage and that copies bear this notice and the full citation on the first page. To copy otherwise, or republish, to post on servers or to redistribute to lists, requires prior specific permission and/or a fee.
CHI'12, May 5–10, 2012, Austin, Texas, USA.
Copyright 2012 ACM 978-1-4503-1015-4/12/05...$10.00.

abusing statistical tests, making illogical arguments as a result of tests, deriving inappropriate conclusions from non-significant results, and confusing the size of p-values with effect sizes.

In our own examination of the CHI 2011 proceedings we found that 35 (out of 306 total, many of which are not quantitative) papers report results from a *t*-test. Of these 35 papers, six do not report *any* descriptive statistics, *none* report a standardized effect size, and only nine make an attempt to describe or interpret the effect size (the difference in means). *None* of the papers related the magnitude of the effect to previous findings in the literature. We believe this shows that the issues we address in this paper are relevant to the CHI community. In this paper we delve deeper into the criticisms raised by earlier scholars by considering an underlying issue: *should statistical significance testing be the "gold standard" for quantitative empirical work within our field?*

In line with the discussion of Ziliak and McCloskey [32] we argue that there are fundamental flaws associated with sciences that are built primarily on the interpretation of *p*-values. In this paper we focus on three common problems:

1. *The fallacy of the transposed conditional* – Researchers often wrongly interpret *p*-values as the probability of the null-hypothesis being true.
2. *A lack of power* – Researchers often pay little attention to null-results without being aware of the potential of their experimental set-up to reject the null when it is false.
3. *Confusion between p-values and estimates of effects*– Researchers often judge a small *p*-value as indicating a (theoretically or practically) important relationship. This however is not generally correct.

In the remainder of this paper we will first conceptually explain the "traditional" statistics that most of HCI's quantitative results rely on. Next, we will address each of the three errors and, using a running example show (a) how they arise, and (b) how they could be mitigated. Our example is based on publically available simulated data previously published at the CHI 2010 conference [19]. We have chosen this data set to avoid singling out studies by other researchers for criticism, and to make it possible for the interested reader to download the data to study the examples for themselves. The reader is referred to [32] and [9] for a discussion of these and related issues in the fields of economics and psychology.

TRADITIONAL STATISTICS

The traditional approach to statistics within many scientific fields is to use significance testing. In this familiar decision making procedure, the null hypothesis is compared to an alternative hypothesis and one or the other is rejected. The great advantage of this decision-making procedure is that long-term error rates are known, and therefore can be controlled. Researchers can control for both Type I and Type II errors. Type I errors occur when the null hypothesis is rejected when it is actually true and can be controlled by specifying an alpha value (before beginning data collection) which specifies the level of significance under which the null hypothesis will be rejected. Type II errors occur when the null hypothesis is accepted when it is actually false: that is, there is an effect that has not been detected. The proportion of times the null is false but was accepted is called beta. The power of an experiment (1- beta) is the probability of detecting an effect given that the effect really exists in the population. If it is sufficiently unlikely that the observed data was generated by a process that is adequately described by the null hypothesis, then the null is rejected and another, alternative, hypothesis is taken as truth. *Sufficiently unlikely* is in most null hypothesis tests defined in terms of a ratio of signal and sampling error.

To understand the basic idea of most hypothesis testing procedures it is useful to consider the one-sample t-test:

$$t = \frac{\bar{x} - \mu_0}{s/\sqrt{n}}$$

The *t* value is given by the difference of the sample mean $\bar{x}$ and the population mean u_0 (often zero in this particular case) – the signal – divided by the sample standard deviation over the square root of the number of subjects – the sampling (or standard) error. Higher *t*-values indicate that it's less likely that the sample mean (given the standard deviation and the number of observations) would be observed if indeed in the population mean was equal to u_0. Thus high *t*-values lead to low *p* -values: *the probability of observing the current data given the null hypothesis.*

Low *p*-values – those lower than .05 - would in turn drive most researchers to conclude that the null-hypothesis is *not* true, and thus some alternative hypothesis should be accepted. It is easy to see that high *t*-values (and thus low *p*-values) can be obtained through a combination of a large signal (difference between $\bar{x}$ and u_0), and little sampling error (small *s* and / or high *n*).

Misinterpretations of the p-value

This approach, fiercely promoted by Fisher in the 1930's [9], has become the gold standard in many disciplines including quantitative evaluations in HCI. However, the approach is rather counter-intuitive; many researchers misinterpret the meaning of the *p*-value. To illustrate this point Oakes posed a series of true/false questions regarding the interpretation of *p*-vales to *seventy* experienced researchers and discovered that *only two* had a sound understanding of the underlying concept of significance [25].

So what does a *p*-value actually mean? *"...the p-value is the probability of obtaining the observed value of a sample statistic (such as* t, F, χ^2) or a more extreme value *if the data were generated from a null-hypothesis population and sampled according to the intention of the experimenter"*

[22, p.293]. Because *p*-values are based on the idea that probabilities are long run frequencies, they are properties of a collective of events rather than single event. They *do not* give the probability of a hypothesis being true or false for this particular experiment, they only provide a description of the long term Type I error rate for a class of hypothetical experiments – most of which the researcher has not conducted.

PROBLEM I: THE FALLACY OF THE TRANSPOSED CONDITIONAL

The false interpretation of the *p*-value by most researchers brings up the first problem with null-hypothesis testing. Researchers often interpret the *p*-value to quantify the probability that the null hypothesis is true. Thus, a *p*-value smaller than .05 to large groups of researchers indicates – be it conscious or unconscious – that the probability that the null hypothesis is true (e.g. $\bar{x} = u_0$) is very small.

Under this misinterpretation the *p*-value would quantify $P(H_0|D)$ - the probability that the null hypothesis (H_0) is true, given the data (D) collected in the experiment. However, the correct interpretation of the *p*-value is rather different: it quantifies $P(D|H_0)$ – the probability of the data *given that* H_0 *is true*. Researchers who state that it is very unlikely that the null hypothesis is true based on a low *p*-value are attributing an incorrect meaning to the *p*-value.

It is easy to understand why this misconception is incorrect by the following example: consider the probability of being dead after being lynched, $P(D|L)$. Most would estimate this to be very high, say 0.99. However, the mere observation of a dead person does not lead most people to believe that the corpse was lynched – after all, there are many possible ways to die which don't involve lynching. $P(L|D)$ is (correctly, and we think luckily) estimated to be rather small.

The way forward

There is a well established way to link a conditional probability to its inverse, shown by the Reverend Thomas Bayes in 1763 [3] which enables us to compute $P(H_0|D)$ from $P(D|H_0)$:

$$P(H_0|D) = \frac{P(D|H_0)P(H_0)}{P(D)}$$

Thus, the probability of the null-hypothesis being true given the data depends on the probability of the data given the null-hypothesis, $P(D|H_0)$, the *prior* probability of the null-hypothesis, $P(H_0)$, and the probability of the data $P(D)$. The prior probability refers to the probability of the hypothesis before the current set of data is collected. It can be seen that for the lynching example the prior probability is so low that the transposed conditional is also low.

The probability of the data, $P(D)$, is often difficult to compute directly. In the discrete case it is given by the sum of the probability of the data given all competing hypotheses. However, in practice its computation is hardly necessary: If a researcher wants to decide between two competing hypotheses $P(D)$ will be the same in the computation of both $P(H_0|D)$ and $P(H_{alt}|D)$ and thus merely acts as a normalizing constant. $P(D|H_0)$ is already provided by our *p*-value, so all we need to compute $P(H_0|D)$ or compare $P(H_0|D)$ to $P(H_{alt}|D)$, is a specification of the prior $P(H_0)$: our prior expectancy of our hypothesis being true. For guidance on setting the value for a prior expectation, consult [26] and [9].

Over the last decades this *Bayesian* approach to computing what we actually want to know, *the probability that our hypothesis are true*, has gained increasing attention among statisticians and researchers. These methods are now gaining ground in fields around us, as evidenced by recommendations to use the so-called Bayesian t-test in cognitive science [22] and medicine [12] .

The Bayesian *t*-test allows researchers to compute the ratio of the likelihood of two competing hypothesis, for example the null hypothesis and an alternative hypothesis [22]. The resulting "Bayes Factor" values of greater than 1 indicate evidence for the null hypothesis, and values less than 1 give support for the alternative hypothesis. Heuristics to judge the strength of support for the null and alternative hypotheses given by a range of Bayes Factor values are listed in [31].

The use of Bayesian statistics rather than traditional statistics has considerable practical ramifications. Wetzels et al. computed Bayes Factors for 855 t-tests published in psychology journals and found that while p-values and Bayes Factors did co-vary (small p-values with large Bayes Factors), the strength of evidence was not calibrated [31]. That is, for studies which reported significant effects (alpha = .05 or .01) 70% of them had Bayes Factors indicating only *anecdotal* evidence in support of the alternative hypothesis.

Changing conventions about the statistical tests accepted within a community is a slow business. However, it is no longer the case that the calculations themselves are difficult. Using packages like {BayesFactorPCL} (for the open source analysis software [R]) researchers can now easily compute Bayes factors[24].

Full Bayesian analysis reaches beyond the Bayesian t-test and provides methods for model comparisons as well as test for different hypothesis. In each case the quantity of interest, P(H|D), informs researchers about the decisions to make based on their collected data. We do not advocate a shift from "canned" p-values to "canned" Bayes Factors – researchers' careful interpretations are still vital- but used appropriately, the Bayesian approach is a solution to the *Fallacy of the Transposed* conditional.

Example: Comparing operating systems

In their paper "Powerful and Consistent Analysis of Likert-Type rating Scales" Kaptein et al. [19] present an example dataset that they use to demonstrate a novel type of analysis. The data is publicly available from http://www.nth-iteration.com/study/statistics/. We will use this dataset in the remainder of this paper to illustrate the three common problems[1].

This (simulated) dataset describes the potential outcomes of a usability evaluation of two different operating systems. While the original dataset contains usability ratings – answers to the statement *"The system was easy to use"* on a seven-point scale – at two points in time, we focus only on the measurements obtained in the first time point. The data describes the scores of participants on this question after using (a) Windows Vista, or (b) Apple Mac OS-X. The dataset provides the obtained scores for three evaluations with different samples sizes: *N=10*, *N=40*, and *N=200*. We believe this dataset – a straightforward rating presenting a comparison between two conditions (between subjects) for differing sample sizes – provides a good numerical example to illustrate the problems raised in this paper.

Table 1 presents the mean score on the statement for the two different groups for each of the 3 sample sizes reported upon in [19]. The results for the *N=200* case are statistically significant with a difference in means of 0.91 points on the seven-point scale.

	Vista		OS-X		Test results	
	Mean	**S.D.**	**Mean**	**S.D**	***t-value***	***p***
N=10	4.00	2.16	5.17	1.32	.965	*.383*
N=40	3.86	1.25	4.67	1.85	1.574	*.126*
N=200	3.69	1.57	4.60	1.43	4.281	*<0.001*

Table 1.Overview of the data presented in [16] for time point 1.

The result obtained for *N=40*, a more typical case in many HCI studies, is however not straightforward. The *p*-value of *.126* would lead many to conclude that there is no significant difference between the usability of Windows Vista and that of Apple Mac OS-X based on the obtained ratings. Often, the *observed difference* of 0.81 points would be neglected and the results not further discussed.

Researchers however can compute the actual probability of *H_0 given the data* to further interpret their results. Results from a *Bayesian t-test* give a value of 1.53 for the *N=40* case. This Bayes Factor describes the likelihood of the null-hypothesis compared to an alternative, non-informative, hypothesis. In this case, the result would be interpreted as providing *weak evidence in favor of the null hypothesis* (values between 1 and 3); this evidence would be classified as only *"anecdotal"* by [31]. For the *N=10* case the Bayes Factor is 1.69, leading to a similar conclusion. For *N=200* the Bayes Factor leads to a similar conclusion as the standard t-test: a Bayes Factor smaller than 0.01 provides strong evidence against the null hypothesis.

[1] The [R] code for all the analysis presented in this paper can be retrieved from the same page.

The advantage of using the Bayesian approach here is that it enables researchers to quantify evidence in favor of the null hypothesis. This is not possible with traditional statistics but is of high importance because it enables us to distinguish between cases where the data is inconclusive (such as the *N=10* and *N=40* cases in our example) and cases where there is strong evidence regarding the null hypothesis (as in our *N=200* example).

PROBLEM II: A LACK OF POWER

The use of *p*-values enables researchers to control Type I errors – or the rejection of H_0 while in fact it is true. However, controlling Type II errors (the failure to reject H_0 when it is false) through calculating the *power* of an experiment appears to be attended to less frequently [7]. The power of a statistical test is the long-term probability that a given test *will find an effect assuming that one exists in the population*. Thus, power indicates whether your experimental setup is capable of detecting the effect that you wish to find. The power is a function of sample size, population effect size and the significance criteria (known as the alpha value, which is set by convention at .05).

The standard accepted power within psychology is .80 [6] which means that there would be *20% (1-.80)* chance that the researcher fails to reject the null hypothesis when it is false. Reviews of the psychology literature reveal that the majority of published studies lack power, resulting in a confusing literature with apparently contradictory results [23]. In studies with low power, getting a null result is not particularly informative: *it does not distinguish between the cases where the null is true and where the experimental set-up did not detect the null.*

The way forward

What can researchers do to address lack of power in their studies? Maxwell [23] recommends that power calculations should be performed before the experiment is carried out, and that they should be reported as standard in empirical papers. Cohen [7] gives some heuristics for required sample sizes for eight commonly used statistical tests, given the effect size that is deemed important or sought by the researcher. Consider an example which might occur within usability studies: a researcher is comparing two versions of the same interface with a between subjects design using number of errors as a dependent variable. For analysis using a two tailed independent samples t-test with alpha set at .05, with a power of .80 and attempting to detect a medium sized effect (Cohen's d = .30), the researcher should recruit *176 participants in each group*. Netx to Cohen's heuristics, software packages such as the {pwr} package in [R] [5] can be used for more accurate results, or more complex designs. Power calculations would at least make researchers aware of the problem, but what can be done to increase power if it is found to be low?

The most obvious way to increase power is to increase sample size. Of course, this can be impractical in many fields, including HCI, but there are ways around this. For example, Maxwell [23] suggests that in the field of psychology researchers could gain power by running collaborative multi-site trials in which many research groups conduct the same experiment with manageable numbers of participants and pool their results. Hansen and Collins discuss approaches to increasing power, which do not require an increase in sample size [16]. Although their recommendations are intended for epidemiologists, some are pertinent to HCI such as preventing attrition from studies, increasing the difference between groups by appropriately timing follow-up studies, and reducing variance within groups by using a more homogenous set of participants. They also discuss the virtue of using more reliable and appropriate measurement instruments. For example, in the context of HCI, this suggests the more widespread use of thoroughly validated standard attitudinal scales rather than researchers creating bespoke questionnaires specifically for a new study as is often current practice [2]. Such scales should be sensitive enough to capture differences between groups as advised in [12].

Example continued: Power to reject the null if it is indeed false.

We will illustrate the often surprising lack of power in HCI experiments by following up on the results presented for the *N=40* case comparing the usability ratings of Windows Vista and Apple Mac OS-X that we also used to demonstrate Bayes Factors. Here we compute the power of the difference presented in Table 1. The difference in means is 0.81, and the pooled variance is 2.2. This gives an effect-size (Cohen's *D*) of 0.37 [7]. Given the between subjects design with 20 users each, this gives a *power of 0.14*. The inverse of the power, *1-0.14 = 0.86* is the probability of making a type II error: a failure to reject the null when it is false. Thus, given this experimental setup, and the estimated effect size, a researcher would *not detect an effect this size even if it were actually present in the population in 86 out of a 100 similar experiments.*

This low power for the given effect size and sample size again illustrates the point made in the Bayesian analysis: the evidence in favor of the null is only minor because the chances are good that the experimental set-up will fail to detect an effect.

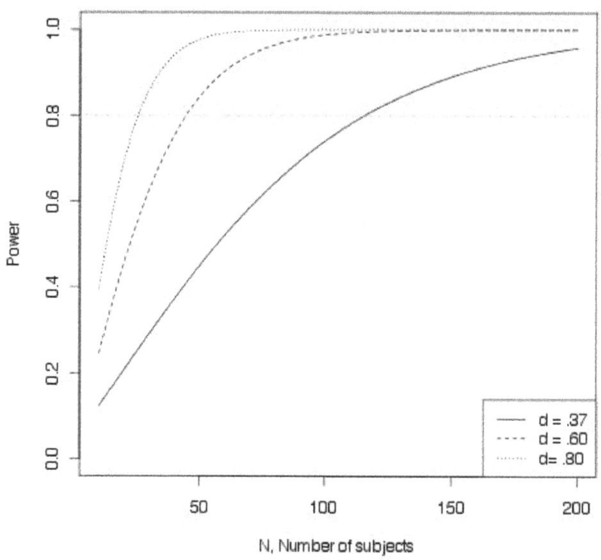

Figure 1.: Overview of power as a function of N, the number of subjects, for different effects sizes in the population.

To provide a better understanding the relationship between effect size, power, and the number of subjects, Figure 1 shows power as a function of *N* for three different effect sizes: 0.37 – the effect size estimated from the data reported in [19] – 0.6, and 0.8. It is clear that both the effect size as well as the number of participants in a study have a large impact on the power of the study. However, it can also be concluded that for small or moderate effect sizes, sample sizes larger than those typical in HCI are necessary.

PROBLEM III: CONFUSION BETWEEN P-VALUES AND ESTIMATES OF EFFECTS

Besides the often-erroneous interpretation of *p*-values and low power, the focus on null hypothesis significance testing in HCI has another severe consequence: qualitative questions about *whether an effect exists* are favored over quantitative questions relating to *how much* of an effect there is, and *to whom it matters*. The latter can only be assessed by considering effect sizes and appropriate loss functions, and by interpreting these in a real world context.

A *p*-value smaller than .05 does not necessarily imply that the effect is important – it only informs us that the sampling error was small compared to the signal. Especially for large data sets (which often lead to powerful tests) low *p*-values are common but do not inform our search for scientific answers. Only a numerical interpretation of the estimated effect can tell us whether a "significant" effect is indeed important to us and warrants further research or a theoretical explanation. For example, if there was a significant difference in the time taken to learn two competing versions of a software package, but the size of the effect was only fifteen seconds, this would likely not have a very large practical impact.

Perhaps surprisingly, the flip side of the argument also holds: a high *p*-value does not imply that the effect under study was unimportant. It only means that it was measured with a relatively high sampling error. Compelling examples of this can be found in neighboring disciplines, and in the courtroom: the painkiller Vioxx was tested in a clinical trial against Naproxen, a general already-on-the-market painkiller. During the trial one person died that was taking naproxen. For Vioxx however, five people died. The difference *was not statistically significant, p >.05,* and thus written off as unimportant. The lawsuits against Vioxx in 2005 proved the researchers wrong: The real-life, and regrettably more powerful, test showed that Vioxx severely – although initially not significantly – raised risks of cardiovascular side effects. If statistical significance is neither a sufficient nor a necessary criterion for importance, what good does it do?

Currently the "size-less stare" at p-values actually does a lot of harm [32]. In some fields, where historically researchers were trained in graphing their data and exploring the actual numerical values, means, and confidence intervals, this practice seems to be decreasing due to the fixation on *p*-values [32]. In computing fields it is not clear that effect size reporting was ever common; Dunlop and Baillie have identified lack of effect size reporting in HCI as "dangerous" [11, p.3] and in the related field of software engineering experiments, a review of 92 experiments published between 1993 and 2002 shows that only 29% of the papers reported estimates of effects[18].

The way forward

To overcome the fixation on *p*-values instead of estimates of effects researchers should report their actual findings, and interpret the numerical estimates of their models or tests. An effect size is "any statistic that quantifies the degree to which sample results diverge from the expectations specified in the null hypothesis" [29, p.991]. Effect sizes have three main uses [29]: Firstly, a prediction of effect size is necessary when planning studies in conjunction with power, sample size and significance criteria (as discussed above). Secondly, it enables researchers to interpret the practical significance of their results because it estimates the magnitude of an effect. Thirdly, reports of standard measures of effect size enable researchers to compare the results from different studies and put their findings in the context of previous work in the literature.

The APA recommend that standard measures of effect sizes should be reported along with *p*-values [1]; they give complementary information. In a study examining the reporting of 855 *t*-tests published in the psychology literature it was found that effect sizes and *p*-values were generally consistent, with large effect sizes corresponding to low p-values. The consistency can in large part be explained by the relatively standardized sample sizes adapted by the field. However, in a small number of cases there were gross inconsistencies between the p-values and standardized effect sizes. These mainly occurred in studies with small sample sizes where the *p*-value was close to .05.

We make a distinction here between standardized measures of effect size – like Cohens's D, eta squared, or the easily interpretable Common Language Effect Size [15] – and non-standardized measures of effect size. The latter are dependent upon the scales by which variables are measured. This latter property makes non-standardized measures of effect size less suitable for comparisons across experiments. However, only non-standardized measures of effect size – *estimates of actual differences in means or parameter estimates in regression models* – can be used to assess the theoretical and practical importance of the quantitative findings of a study.

We believe that standardized effect size measurements can be useful in comparing results across studies. Cohen for example has published useful heuristics for interpreting effect sizes as small, medium or large [6]. *However, it would be of limited value if researchers replaced canned reporting of p-values with canned reporting of Cohen's d or other such statistics.* While standardized effect size measures overcome the confusion of importance and sample size as common for *p*-values, standardized effect sizes cannot, by themselves, be the only outcome of a quantitative experiment. The important point is to consider what the estimations of effect(s) mean in the context of previous work and what the practical and theoretical implications of an effect of that magnitude would be for users or designers.

Example continued: What is really important for usability ratings?

To highlight the importance of an inspection of parameter estimates (e.g., the mean difference or the β's of a model) versus the (often erroneous) interpretation of *p*-values we present a set of hypothetical results obtained from a study similar to that used in the previous examples.

Suppose again the ratings of the usability of two different systems are compared. However, this time we do not only compare Windows Vista en Apple Mac OS-X but we obtain ratings both by novices and by expert evaluators. Table 2 presents the results for this new experiment. The table presents the usability ratings (*N=200*) comparing Vista and OS-X (see also Table 2) when these ratings are provided by novices and by expert evaluators.

	Critiques				
	M. Diff	**SD**	**D**	**T**	**P**
Vista vs. OS-X	*0.91*	*1.5*	*0.6*	*4.29*	*<.001***
Expert vs. Novice	*1.30*	*4.1*	*0.3*	*2.24*	*<.05**

Table 2. Hypothetical results obtained for an experiment. Presented are the mean difference, the pooled SD, Cohen's D, the t-value, and the p-value.

Table 2 presents the (hypothetical) mean-difference between the usability ratings of Vista and OS-X users, and the mean difference in ratings provided by expert users and novice users. Given the mean differences presented here, the pooled standard deviations, and the equal sample size, both of the effects – that of type operating system and type of evaluator – are statistically significant. Thus, according to most researchers they are both important findings[2].

However, for both theoretical as well as practical purposes it is feasible to evaluate the sizes of the effects of both the operating system as well as the user expertise on the usability ratings that are provided. We have – hopefully – already convinced readers of the inadequacy of *p*-values to make these kinds of judgments. Thus, researchers should *not* decide, based on the lower *p*-value of the operating system factor that this is the most important variable in eliciting critiques.

The third column of Table 2 presents Cohen's d for the two comparisons presented here. Cohen's d is given by the ratio of the mean difference and the pooled standard deviation. This makes the computation similar to that of the *t*-value with the only difference being the exclusion of *N*, the number of subjects, in the equation. Given equal sample sizes in these two evaluations there is a direct relation between the t-value (column 4) and the value of Cohen's d.

Now, should we decide that the operating system is the most important factor influencing people's usability ratings of their systems? The value of Cohen's *d* is higher indicating a higher effect size than for the expertise. However, we think that researchers, knowledgeable of the origin of Cohen's d, should look a bit further. The actual mean difference 'caused' by the expertise of the user as opposed to the type of operating system is far larger. The difference between an expert user and a novice user is around 1.3 points on the 7 point scale, while that for the different operating systems is only 0.91 points. However, the standard deviations indicate that the measures obtained for the different operating systems are more 'consistent' – less spread out – than those obtained for the different user expertise levels.

It is up to the researcher to determine and motivate the conclusions drawn from a dataset like this. However, in this scenario a large standard deviation for expertise is very plausible: actual expertise levels are not binary and thus there is heterogeneity within the expert and novice groups. This argument does not hold for the type of operating system, hence its smaller standard deviation. The actual mean difference however shows that – if assessed accurately – user expertise *could* potentially be a more important determinant of the usability ratings of a system. We believe that discussions like these inform and progress science, rather than the limited interpretation of a single statistic.

We do not mean to imply that all HCI researchers neglect to discuss the size of their effects. For instance in the domain relating to our worked example, a highly cited paper which considers the evaluator effect is very much concerned with the interpretation of effect magnitudes [17]. Within HCI more generally, a good example of a focus on quantitative estimates (rather than just sizeless *p*-values) can be found in the Fitt's law literature. Fitt's law describes the *quantitative* speed accuracy trade-off associated with pointing. The importance of quantitative evaluations when building a science is clear from the status of Fitt's law within HCI research: It presents the only paradigm which consistently fills up at least one session at CHI, and the results are replicated and extended upon frequently.

CONCLUSIONS

Presenting only *p*-values can lead to misleading results with unfortunate real life consequences [9]. The *p*-value often does not inform us about what we want to know, which is generally the probability of the hypothesis given the data. Also, high *p*-values do not imply that the null is indeed true if the power is inadequate, and finally, sizes of effects should be more important than their associated sampling error.

We conclude with a more general criticism of the way theories are developed within HCI. A hallmark of a good theory is that it is highly falsifiable. It should make definite claims about the world, because the more claims it makes, the more opportunities there are to falsify it. A major criticism of the traditional approach to statistics is that it encourages weak theorizing by proposing hypotheses which make vaguely specified claims about the world [9]. In specifying a null hypothesis, the researcher generally predicts no difference between conditions. If this is rejected, the alternative hypothesis is accepted. But the alternative hypothesis that matches this null hypothesis (that there is *some* difference) is vague and underspecified. It rules out only one point where the means are *exactly* the same across conditions. *Any* other relationship between the variables could be true. Seen in this light, *the null hypothesis is intuitively almost always false*, and so rejecting it isn't very informative. A theory which predicts in advance the magnitude of an effect is more useful, and the consideration of estimated effects from the current study in the light of previous findings enables the researcher to contribute coherently to the existing body of work in a field.

Dunlop and Baillie [11] have argued that HCI does not generally attempt replication of previous work, a point which is confirmed in Bargas-Avila and Hornbæk's recent analysis of UX studies [2]. Yet, single studies cannot be taken as the basis for believing a scientific result to be true. It is the pooling of evidence from many studies, often in the form of meta-analysis, that should give researchers

[2] Normally one would analyze this factorial experiment using a method by which dependencies between prototype fidelity and user expertise are also included (e.g. ANOVA). However, we choose to present seperate t-test for ease of understanding of the argument.

confidence in a theory [13] .We should therefore consider: do we as a community want to develop theory through empirical studies (at least as one of the methods in our toolkit)? If we do not, then what purpose is served by conducting traditional statistical tests? If we do, we are more likely to achieve our aims by adopting best practices for the planning, analysis and reporting of empirical studies. Based on the convergence of advice from related disciplines, we offer the following initial recommendations for best practice. We hope that future authors will add to these recommendations.

1. A more specific hypothesis yields more information when it is falsified than a vaguely specified hypothesis. For this reason, *bolder predictions predicting the direction and magnitude of effects would be beneficial* rather than choosing the "safe" null that there is no difference between conditions. For example, a researcher might hypothesize that a shopping website optimized for screen reading software would decrease the average time taken to buy an item by a visually impaired user by one minute over the original version of the website. Such an hypothesis can be evaluated quantitatively, after which qualitative judgments about the importance of an effect this size can be discussed.
2. When planning an experiment, it is helpful to *predict the size of the effect likely to be found*, based on previous findings from related studies if possible. In the above example about the interface for visually impaired users, the researcher could have calculated effect sizes from the descriptive statistics published in previous similar studies, or predicted them from theory or even estimated them from pilot tests in the lab.
3. Deciding on power, significance criterion (alpha value), and effect size in advance enable the researcher to *calculate the number of participants* they require to detect an effect of practical or theoretical importance.
4. If there are practical difficulties in recruiting enough participants, *research teams could consider collaborating for multi-site experiments*. Power can also be increased by careful choice of valid and appropriate measurement instruments.
5. It can be beneficial to *use Bayesian analysis to calculate the probability of the hypothesis given the data* instead of traditional significance testing. This analysis method enables researchers to build on the body of knowledge in the field by incorporating previous results as prior probabilities.
6. We encourage *researchers, reviewers, programme chairs and journal editors to work towards raising the standard of reporting statistical results* in order that future researchers can use this information to inform their own hypothesis generation, effect size estimates and prior probabilities in Bayesian analysis. The guidelines in the 6th edition of the APA publication manual [1] are helpful in this regard. At the very least, the mean and standard error should be reported to enable future researchers to calculate standardized effect sizes. It would be useful for researchers without a strong statistical background if submission instructions for authors included clear guidance to help them enhance their analyses and conclusions.
7. And, last but not least, it is good practice to *interpret the non-standardized sizes of the estimated effects*. If the predicted effect size was found in the example of the shopping web site for visually impaired users, what would this mean? What practical difference would it make to the user experience for members of this target user group? Would a time saving of one minute per transaction be worth the effort it would take to learn how to use the new layout? Some questions of this sort are arguably best answered in consultation with users, emphasizing the need for triangulation between qualitative and quantitative data.

These changes to the best practice within a field will require effort, and may take many years to come to fruition. But if we, as a community, value the tools offered to us by statistical methods, we should do our best to avoid known methodological flaws, and embrace the best practices which are emerging from our sister disciplines. The benefits to HCI will be great in terms of generating a more coherent body of work thus enabling the field to advance more rapidly.

ACKNOWLEDGMENTS
The authors would like to thank the anonymous reviewers, Panos Markopoulos, Oliver Lemon, Verena Rieser, Dean Eckles, and Andrew Macvean for their comments on a draft of this paper. Please note that both of the authors contributed equally to this work.

REFERENCES
1. American Psychological Association. (2009). *Publication Manual of the American Psychological Association, Sixth Edition* (6th ed., p. 272). APA.
2. Bargas-Avila, J., & Hornbæk, K. (2011). Old wine in new bottles or novel challenges: a critical analysis of empirical studies of user experience. In *Proceedings of the 2011 annual conference on Human factors in computing systems* (CHI '11). ACM, New York, NY, USA, 2689-2698.
3. Bayes, T., & Price. (1763). An Essay towards Solving a Problem in the Doctrine of Chances. By the Late Rev. Mr. Bayes, F. R. S. Communicated by Mr. Price, in a Letter to John Canton, A. M. F. R. S. Philosophical Transactions of the Royal Society of London, 53, 370-418.
4. Cairns, P. (2007). HCI... not as it should be: inferential statistics in HCI research. *Proceedings of the 21st British HCI Group Annual Conference on People and Computers: HCI... but not as we know it-Volume 1* (pp. 195–201). British Computer Society.

5. Champely, S. (2009). PWR package. Retrieved from http://cran.r-project.org/web/packages/pwr/index.html
6. Cohen, J. (1988). *Statistical power analysis for the behavioral sciences.* Hillsdale, New Jersey: Laurence Erlbaum Associates.
7. Cohen, J. (1992). A power primer. *Psychological bulletin*, *112*(1), 155. American Psychological Association.
8. Cohen, J. (1994). The Earth is Round (p < .05). *American Psychologist*, *49*(12), 997-1003.
9. Dienes, Z. (2008). *Understanding Psychology as a Science: An Introduction to Scientific and Statistical Inference* (1st ed., p. 150). Palgrave Macmillan.
10. Dienes, Z. (2011). Bayesian Versus Orthodox Statistics: Which Side Are You On? *Perspectives on Psychological Science*, *6*(3), 274-290.
11. Dunlop, M. & Baillie, M. (2009). Paper Rejected (p<; 0.05): An Introduction to the Debate on Appropriateness of Null-Hypothesis Testing. *International Journal of Mobile Human Computer Interaction*, *1*(3), 1-8.
12. Fowler, F. (1995). *Improving Survey Questions.* Thousand Oaks, California: Sage Publications.
13. Goldacre, B. (2008). *Bad Science* (p. 338). London: Harper Collins.
14. Gray, W., & Salzman, M. (1998). Damaged Merchandise? A Review of Experiments That Compare Usability Evaluation Methods. *Human-Computer Interaction*, *13*(3), 203-261.
15. Grissom, R. J. (1994). Probability of the superior outcome of one treatment over another. *Journal of Applied Psychology*, *79*(2), 314-316.
16. Hansen, W. B., & Collins, L. M. (1994). Seven ways to increase power without increasing N. In L. M. C. (Eds.) & L. A. Seitz (Eds.), *Advances in data analysis for prevention intervention research (NIDA Research Monograph 142, NIH Publication No. 94-3599)* (Vol. 191, pp. 184–195). Rockville, MD:: National Institutes of Health.
17. Hornbæk, K., & Frøkjær, E. (2008). A Study of the Evaluator Effect in Usability Testing. *Human-Computer Interaction*, *23*(3), 251-277.
18. 1Kampenes, V., Dyba, T., Hannay, J., & Sjoberg, D. (2007). A systematic review of effect size in software engineering experiments. *Information and Software Technology*, *49*(11-12), 1073-1086.
19. Kaptein, M. C., Nass, C., & Markopoulos, P. (2010). Powerful and consistent analysis of likert-type rating scales. *Proceedings of the 28th international conference on Human factors in computing systems - CHI '10* (p. 2391). New York, New York, USA: ACM Press.
20. Katki, H. a. (2008). Invited Commentary: Evidence-based Evaluation of p Values and Bayes Factors. *American Journal of Epidemiology*, *168*(4), 384-388.
21. Kruschke, J. K. (2011). Introduction to Special Section on Bayesian Data Analysis. Perspectives on Psychological Science, 6(3), 272-273.
22. Kruschke, J. K. (2010). What to believe: Bayesian methods for data analysis. *Trends in cognitive sciences*, *14*(7), 293-300. Elsevier Ltd.
23. Maxwell, S. E. (2004). The persistence of underpowered studies in psychological research: causes, consequences, and remedies. *Psychological methods*, *9*(2), 147-63.
24. Morey, R., & Rouder, A. (2010). Package "BayesFactorPCL." Retrieved from https://r-forge.r-project.org/projects/bayesfactorpcl/
25. Oakes, M. (1986). *Statistical inference: a commentary for the social and behavioural sciences*. Wiley.
26. Rouder, Jeffrey N, Speckman, P. L., Sun, D., Morey, R. D., & Iverson, G. (2009). Bayesian t tests for accepting and rejecting the null hypothesis. *Psychonomic bulletin & review*, *16*(2), 225-37.
27. SIGCHI. (2011). More about SIGCHI. *http://www.sigchi.org/*. Retrieved July 8, 2011, from http://www.sigchi.org/about/more
28. Sharp, H., Preece, J., & Rogers, Y. (2007). *Interaction Design* (2nd ed.). Chichester: John Wiley and Sons, Ltd.
29. Sun, S., Pan, W., & Wang, L. L. (2010). A comprehensive review of effect size reporting and interpreting practices in academic journals in education and psychology. *Journal of Educational Psychology*, *102*(4), 989-1004.
30. Wagenmakers, Eric-Jan, Wetzels, Ruud, Borsboom, D., & van der Maas, H. L. J. (2011). Why psychologists must change the way they analyze their data: the case of psi: comment on Bem (2011). *Journal of personality and social psychology*, *100*(3), 426-32.
31. Wetzels, R., Matzke, D., Lee, M. D., Rouder, J. N., Iverson, G. J., & Wagenmakers, E.-J. (2011). Statistical Evidence in Experimental Psychology: An Empirical Comparison Using 855 t-Tests. *Perspectives on Psychological Science*, *6*(3), 291-298.
32. Ziliak, S., & McCloskey, D. (2008). *The Cult of Statistical Significance: How the Standard Error Costs us Jobs, Justice and Lives.* (p. 320). Ann Arbor, MI: University of Michigan Press.

A Spatiotemporal Visualization Approach for the Analysis of Gameplay Data

Günter Wallner
University of Applied Arts Vienna
Institute of Art and Technology
Vienna, Austria
guenter.wallner@uni-ak.ac.at

Simone Kriglstein
University of Vienna
Faculty of Computer Science
Vienna, Austria
simone.kriglstein@univie.ac.at

ABSTRACT
Contemporary video games are highly complex systems with many interacting variables. To make sure that a game provides a satisfying experience, a meaningful analysis of gameplay data is crucial, particularly because the quality of a game directly relates to the experience a user gains from playing it. Automatic instrumentation techniques are increasingly used to record data during playtests. However, the evaluation of the data requires strong analytical skills and experience. The visualization of such gameplay data is essentially an information visualization problem, where a large number of variables have to be displayed in a comprehensible way in order to be able to make global judgments. This paper presents a visualization tool to assist the analytical process. It visualizes the game space as a set of nodes which players visit over the course of a game and is also suitable to observe time-dependent information, such as player distribution. Our tool is not tailored to a specific type of genre. To show the flexibility of our approach we use two different kinds of games as case studies.

Author Keywords
Gameplay Visualization; Playtesting; Clustering; Time-dependent Visualization; Player Behavior;

ACM Classification Keywords
K.8.0 General: Games; H.5.m Information Interfaces and Presentation: Miscellaneous

General Terms
Design; Human Factors; Measurement.

INTRODUCTION
Video games have become increasingly complex over the years, not only with regard to technical issues, like game engines or digital asset management, but also with regard to the amount of interaction options available to the player. This causes difficulties for the developers, because they have to ensure that the final product provides a satisfying experience for the player. For this reason developers apply user testing throughout and particularly at the end of the development cycle. For this purpose the game industry has adapted various qualitative as well as quantitative methods from Human-Computer Interaction [5, 6, 27].

Although qualitative methods are useful to get feedback and data about the subjective experiences of players, they are limited because it is often difficult for the players to explain their activities and impressions, which can easily lead to misinterpretations [2, 6]. Furthermore, the evaluation of the collected data is often time-consuming, especially, in case of a large number of players [2, 6]. Therefore, the usage of instrumentation to collect detailed information about the players behavior, i.e. *observable data based on performance, or particular actions performed by a participant that one can measure* [27], has become more and more popular for the evaluation of games in the past few years [6, 17]. Logging user interactions with automated instrumentation also has the benefit that the process is unobtrusive [9]. In context of video games, instrumentation data are usually referred to as *gameplay metrics*, in other words, aspects of gameplay which are of interest to the game designer [12]. The choice which metrics or measurable attributes should be taken is influenced by the game itself and the purpose of the analysis, as pointed out by Tychsen [32]. Because such log files only record behavioral data, Kim et al. [17] advocate the inclusion of attitudinal data to get a clearer picture of how users experience a game. However, the collected data is usually stored in text form in game logs or relational database systems and has to be analyzed in some way, for instance by means of statistical methods. Examples of applying statistics to the analysis of games can be found in [10, 20, 24, 34]. The interpretation of the results, however, can be difficult for those lacking expertise and may require a skilled statistical analyst.

Visualization tools targeted toward games are useful to assist the analytical process, because they visually convey the relationships between different game states. Game designers and analysts can use such tools to (i) find patterns of play, (ii) to identify possible design and balancing problems and (iii) to discover unexpected paths which have been taken by the players. The gained knowledge cannot only help to improve the current game in question but may also inform game design in general.

The visualization system introduced in this paper was motivated by the following observations: First, almost all of the existing work – with a few exceptions like [6, 15, 25] – cen-

Permission to make digital or hard copies of all or part of this work for personal or classroom use is granted without fee provided that copies are not made or distributed for profit or commercial advantage and that copies bear this notice and the full citation on the first page. To copy otherwise, or republish, to post on servers or to redistribute to lists, requires prior specific permission and/or a fee.
CHI'12, May 5–10, 2012, Austin, Texas, USA.
Copyright 2012 ACM 978-1-4503-1015-4/12/05...$10.00.

ters on visualizing single variables at a time. However, in order to understand cause and effect relationships it is essential to examine multiple variables and their interrelations at once. Second, in order to analyze how players progress within a game, it is necessary to not only show the sequence of actions players perform but also their temporal progression. By the way of example, for the analysis of educational games it is not only important to show that it is working but also how and why it works (or fails). However, understanding how users interact with an interactive product is not confined to the games domain, and a visualization – such as the proposed one – may therefore be of interest to the broad HCI community as well. Third, usually visualizations have focused on games where the player controls a single character in a spatial environment and these are, therefore, not suitable for games with multiple units or abstract games (e.g., puzzle games). Fourth, visualization of gameplay data is essentially an information visualization problem, where a large number of variables have to be displayed in order to be able to make global judgments. This involves the risk that the observer may miss important information. We approach the problem by providing different ways how the information can be presented and filtered. Finally, in many cases visualization tools are developed with a specific game or genre in mind (e.g., [13, 15, 22]), whereas our motivation was to develop a visualization tool which is adaptable to a broad range of games and queries. To show the flexibility of our approach we used two different kinds of games as case studies: An educational puzzle game and a 3D team-based multiplayer shooter.

RELATED WORK

The emphasis of this paper is on visualization of gameplay data and we will therefore focus on research related to this area. Although the body of literature is still quite sparse in this domain – probably because gameplay metrics data is normally treated as confidential by companies as noted by Drachen and Canossa [7] – a number of different visualization tools have been developed in the past few years.

Hoobler et al. [15] described a visualization approach called Lithium to analyze the behavior patterns of players in virtual environments, in particular, their focus was on the team-based first-person perspective game Return to Castle Wolfenstein: Enemy Territory. It displays player paths on a map, overlaid with icons to represent certain actions, as well as statistical information – aggregated over the course of a match – to understand high-level trends and behaviors of teams and players. Recently, Medler et al. [22] published an article on Data Cracker, a game analytic tool which was used by EA game studio Visceral Games to monitor player behavior from the game Dead Space 2 [11]. Data Cracker mainly uses different kinds of charts to visualize statistics about the aggregated data. They also discuss the difficulties which can arise when inserting analytic tools into the game design process.

Chittaro et al. [4] developed a visualization tool called VU-Flow for the analysis of navigation patterns, e.g., to highlight places which are more visited by players or to identify which points of interest get more attention from players. The general idea of VU-Flow is to show players movements on a 2D map of the virtual environments. The system considers time stamps for each movement, which allows to observe the temporal dependencies between the different positions of the players and to visualize player movement as flow visualization with streamlines, indicating the *flow* of players through the virtual environment. Gagné et al. [13] recently presented a visualization system which is similar to VU-Flow, but adopted it for the analysis of real-time strategy games by not only visualizing movement but also various types of events (movement, unit creation, death, etc.) at once. The system shows temporal spatial relationships but does not provide functionalities to manipulate the aggregated visualization, e.g., by selecting or filtering data.

Drachen et al. [9] used emergent Self-Organization Maps to identify dissimilar clusters (types) of playing behavior in the game Tomb Raider: Underworld. Thawonmas et al. [31] presented a method for automatically detecting landmarks, i.e. recognizable objects in the virtual environment, and for visualizing the movement patterns of players between them. Classical multidimensional scaling (CMDS) and a force-based graph drawing algorithm are used to visualize the player clusters. Thawonmas and Iizuka [30] used multidimensional scaling to discover groups of players behaving in a similar way.

Drachen and Canossa [6] presented an approach where spatial gameplay metrics are visualized with the help of heatmaps to make areas of player deaths visible. Psychostats [29], for example, is a tool which generates such heatmaps for several games. The drawback of heatmaps, however, is that a single map only visualizes the occurrence of a specific attribute and therefore further heatmaps are necessary to identify, for example, the different causes of a player's death, as pointed out by Drachen and Canossa [6]. In contrast, the system from Moura et al. [25] allows – similar to our approach – to visualize a series of actions players take in a game and therefore to observe cause and effect relationships. Different events can be visualized simultaneously and a map shows the aggregated data by geographic area (e.g., total time spent in a specific room). A recent paper by Drachen and Canossa [8] discusses spatial analysis with geographics information systems and provides three comprehensive case studies. However, the focus is on analysis rather than visualization.

All of these approaches (except [30]) have in common that they situate the player in spatial relationship to the virtual environment. Although this is possible for a wide variety of games, it does not fit to games where gameplay is more abstract, like for example in puzzle games. Recently, Andersen et al. [2] presented an approach to view player movement in games where it is not possible to situate the player in spatial relationship to the virtual environment. They apply CMDS to draw similar states together, which allows analysts to uncover the structure of the gameplay data [2]. As Andersen et al., we consider player progression as a succession of game states (nodes) which a player visits while playing a game and we use multidimensional scaling to obtain a two-dimensional embedding of these nodes. In this paper, we present several extensions to this approach to support visual analysis of game-related data. First, we not only visualize transitions be-

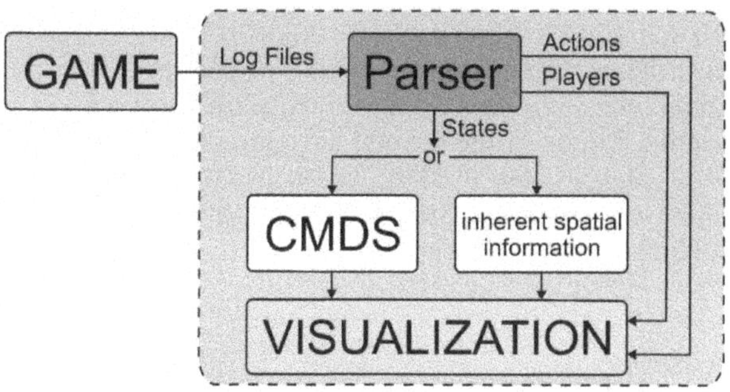

Figure 1. Overview of the different system parts.

tween states but also consider the type of the transition, which also allows to infer the means by how players arrived at a certain state. Second, their approach only visualizes the spatial relationships between game states without temporal patterns. Yet, such temporal information can allow further valuable insights, because it allows to see which player reaches which state at which point in time. Medler et al. [22] stated that time emerged as a key dimension for almost all the gameplay analytics they came across for Dead Space 2. In combination with demographic data this can, for instance, assist in adjusting a game to a specific age-group. Third, players are explicitly represented in the system to give access to the player's attributes (e.g., health, collected items, remaining ammunition, et cetera) at any point in time. Fourth, we include several techniques to reduce the complexity of the representation like bundling of edges, clustering of nodes to group similar states together, and filtering of nodes, transitions and players based on different criteria.

OUR APPROACH

This section gives an overview of the different system parts, as shown in Figure 1. After the log-files have been exported from a game, a configurable parser translates these log-files into the three main entities which are handled by our system: (i) states, (ii) actions, and (iii) players. A two-dimensional embedding of the states is then obtained by either applying CMDS or, if available, by using the spatial information directly stored in the log-files. The tool itself was implemented with C# and OpenGL. The following sections will describe the different entities in detail.

States

For the following discussion we will follow Juul [16] and view a game as a finite state machine with a finite number of states S and transitions between them. A *state* either describes a certain configuration of the game (*game state*) or of an object of the game. For example, in chess the game state can be represented by the position of all pieces on the board. However, we are going a step further and consider a game as a *hierarchical* state machine where any state can be a substate of some larger state. To give an example: Super Mario Galaxy 2 [26] is split into seven different regions (top level), each one containing a number of galaxies (second level) which, on the other hand, provide a small number of different stages (third level). Furthermore, the variables used to describe a game state can change from level to level. As Juul [16] argues, playing with a game is simply interacting with the game state. An individual player will therefore go through a sequence of game states during the course of a game. A game state can be visited by several different players at different times. This is the reason why we handle game states in a time-independent manner, in other words, all game states are visible at all times. However, this enables the observer to obtain an overview of all visited game states, whereas the time-based simulation of players will reveal when which player reaches a certain state.

States are displayed as circles and the size is proportional to either – as in [2] – the number of visits or the number of unique visits (in which case repeated visits from one and the same player are ignored). To each state a certain type is assigned, like *start* or *goal*. The system allows to map different attributes to the color of the node (all colors can be chosen freely by the user to adapt the visualization to his needs), which can prove useful for the analysis: (a) the type of the state itself, (b) the number of visits or the number of unique visits, (c) the average time players spent on this particular state, and (d) if this is a state which leads to the goal or not. If players spend on average a lot of time at a certain state, this may indicate that players have difficulties at that particular point. States themselves can be hidden or shown based on type, number of visits or time spent at this node. Removing rarely visited nodes, for example, will reveal paths through the game which have been taken by the majority of players.

An image can be mapped to each state which will be shown when the mouse is hovered over the state. This image acts as representative of the state (e.g., an image of the current configuration of the chessboard). States which contain a subgraph are visually distinguished and clicking on them will open the substates. This way the progress of the player can be tracked across multiple game levels and hierarchies. An example is provided in Figure 6.

To visualize the states we either directly use the spatial information which is stored in the game log or we apply CMDS (e.g., [19]). MDS has already been used in similar visualizations (e.g., [2, 31, 30]) and proved to be useful for games where the gameplay cannot be described in relation to the environment. For this purpose we use the MDSJ library [1]. The input to CMDS is a dissimilarity matrix $D = [\delta_{ij}]_{k \times k}$, where δ_{ij} is the dissimilarity between states $i \in S$ and $j \in S$. The output is a set of points $c_1, c_2, ..., c_k \in \mathbb{R}^n$ so that the distances between the points $\|c_i - c_j\| \approx \delta_{ij}$, $\|\cdot\|$ being an arbitrary distance function (Euclidean distance in our case). Different dissimilarity functions can be used on different levels of the hierarchy. Results obtained with this kind of embedding can be seen in the DOGeometry case study.

Actions

Actions $a = a(p, t, \Delta t, \tau)$, $a : S \to S$, $s_i \to s_j$ are the *verbs* of the system, in a sense that they are triggered by a specific player p at a specific point in time t and describe a transition from a state s_i to another s_j. An action is of a type τ (e.g., walk, shoot) and can, but does not necessarily have to, have a certain duration Δt. The system allows to assign different

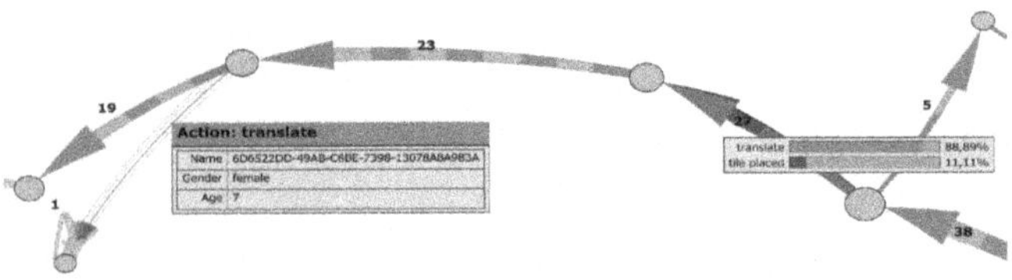

Figure 2. Meta-edges between nodes. A tooltip will show the percentage distribution of the underlying edges (right). Clicking on a meta-edge reveals the individual edges (left). Single edges will display information of the player who triggered it.

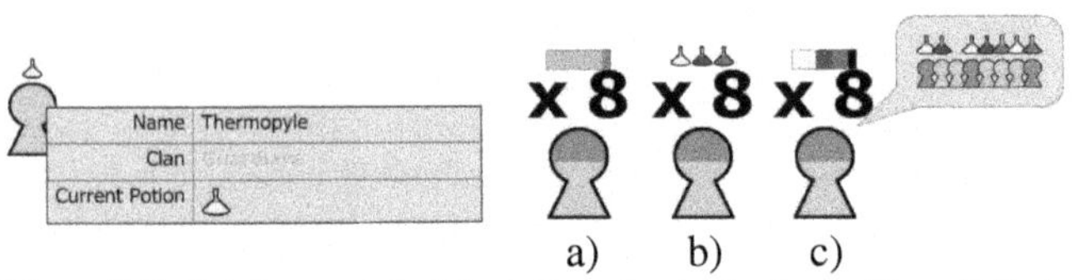

Figure 3. Left: The graphical depiction of a single player. One attribute can be mapped to the color of the player symbol and another one can be displayed above the head. All attributes can be displayed in a table. Right: A *meta-player* that integrates eight players into a single symbol. The percentage distribution of one attribute is reflected in the coloring of the symbol and the distribution of the second can be displayed in three different ways: (a) Ratio of players who currently have (green) this attribute assigned to players who do not (red), (b) the set of existing values of the attribute, and (c) the percentage distribution of the values of the attribute.

colors to different types of actions which are displayed as directed curves. Actions can be selectively hidden or shown with regard to τ. To avoid cluttering the visualization with a lot of individual curves, actions between the same two states (in the same direction) are merged into a single *meta-edge*. The coloring of a meta-edge reflects the percentage distribution of the bundled edges (see, for example, Figure 2 and Figure 8) and the thickness of a meta-edge is proportional to the number of underlying edges. This way – depending on the kind of action – popular paths or dominant strategies may easily be identified. A tooltip will show the percentage distribution of the bundled actions with regard to τ. Figure 2 illustrates this concept.

Players

A *player* is represented by a small symbol and several *player attributes* can be assigned to him. Player attributes can change while playing the game (e.g., current class in a 3D shooter, or various character attributes in role-playing games) or can stay constant (e.g., demographic data like age or gender). We should note that via the player attribute principle, attitudinal data can be easily included into the visualization. Each attribute can be displayed as icon, text or bar chart and a color can be assigned to each value of an attribute. Two different attributes can be displayed at the same time. One attribute can be mapped to the color of the symbol representing the player and another attribute can be shown above the symbol as icon. For example, the color of the clan a player belongs to can be mapped to the player symbol and the currently equipped potion may be shown as icon above, as illustrated in Figure 3 (left). All attributes are displayed in a table when hovering the mouse over the player symbol. If multiple players are located at the same state, players will be merged into a single *meta-player*. The coloring of a meta-player reflects the percentage distribution of the currently mapped attribute. Similar, the icon above the player will reflect the respective values of the second attribute of the contained individual players. By clicking on such a meta-player a speech bubble will appear which shows and gives access to all individual players. The graphical depiction of meta-players is shown in Figure 3 (right).

Clustering

The system also supports clustering of nodes to group similar states together. This reduces the complexity of the visualization and allows to easily locate areas of interest (e.g., landmarks). For clustering Quality Threshold (QT) clustering [14] is applied. Our reasons for choosing QT clustering are threefold: (i) QT clustering in contrast to the computationally more efficient k-means clustering algorithm [21] does not require the number of clusters a priori and therefore does not force unrelated patterns into a single cluster. Instead the number of clusters depends on the values chosen for the maximum diameter of the clusters. Although this may be a problem for certain applications, it fits well to our domain, because it allows to interactively change the size of clusters to find patterns which have not been anticipated beforehand. (ii) If run several times, QT clustering will always lead to the same result, contrary to k-means where the result depends on the initially chosen cluster centers. (iii) The result of QT clustering is always a set of non-overlapping clusters.

We added a second alterable parameter to specify the minimum number of nodes which have to be contained in a cluster. Choosing a small maximum diameter and a large number of nodes will therefore detect areas with a huge concentration of similar states.

Clusters are visually represented by the convex hull of their underlying states, which ensures that the representation is also non-overlapping. Clusters are *closed* by default, which means that the underlying states are hidden, but they can be *opened* to access the individual nodes and the action between them (Figure 4). If clusters are present, meta-edges between different states of two clusters will be merged into a single one. The same applies to meta-edges between an individual state and different states contained in a cluster. Similarly, a meta-player of a cluster will represent all players who are currently located at one of the underlying states.

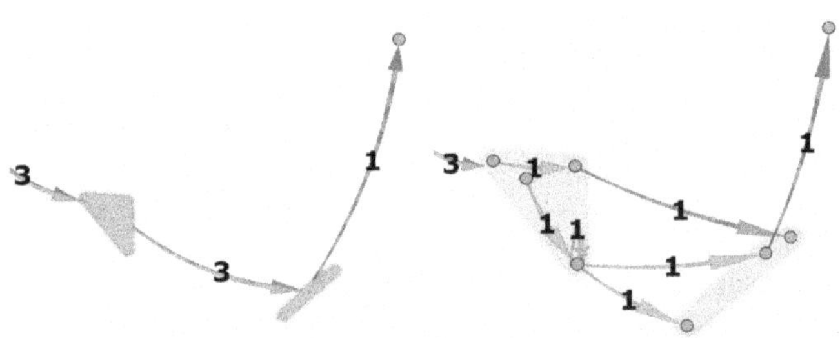

Figure 4. Left: Clusters can be closed in which case the contained states are only partially visible and actions are hidden. Connections between the clusters are merged into a single meta-edge. Right: Opening the clusters will show the individual connections and states.

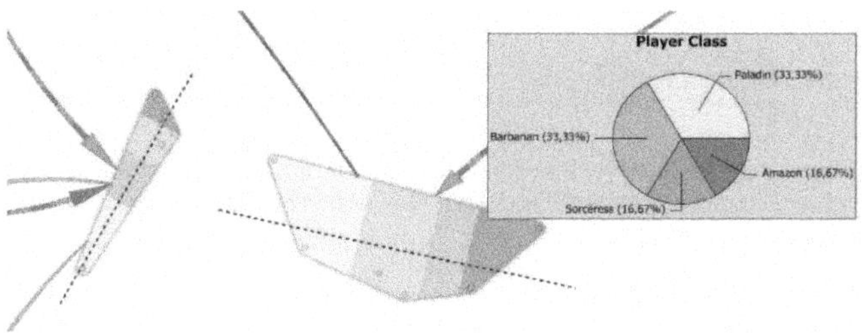

Figure 5. Differently colored sections reflect the distribution of an attribute (player class in this case). These sections are orthogonal to the regression line (shown as dashed line) of the hull of the cluster. A tooltip will show a pie-chart with detailed information about the distribution.

Clusters can be configured in a way that their coloring reflects the minimum, maximum or distribution of state types, action types or player attributes. In case the minimum or maximum value of an attribute is mapped to the cluster, the color of the whole cluster will reflect this value (if the attribute does not exist in the cluster, e.g, because no players currently reside inside a cluster, then only the outline is shown). If the distribution of an attribute is to be displayed then the cluster is split into sections so that their areas correspond to the occurrence of the respective attribute. Since our perception tends to favor compact regions [18], these sections are laid out orthogonally to the *principal axis* of the boundary of the cluster to avoid long and thin areas. Although the principal components can be computed with Principal Component Analysis, we found that the regression line of the vertices of the convex hull of the cluster approximates the *principal axis* adequately enough. Figure 5 illustrates this concept.

Time

The temporal progression of players within a game is an important aspect in the analysis of gameplay. Our system therefore keeps track of a *schedule* for each player, which defines at which times a player arrived at a certain state, has triggered a specific action, or if an attribute of the player has changed. This schedule is used for the time-dependent simulation of the players' progress, in other words, the actual position of the player symbols depends on the currently observed point in time. Furthermore, attributes associated with a player can vary over time and the visualization will reflect such changes by updating the player icons and meta-player symbols accordingly. If a player attribute is mapped to a cluster (as for example in Figure 12), then the visual attributes of the cluster are also updated dynamically when players enter or leave a cluster. The playback of the simulation can be controlled with a time slider and buttons like play, pause, jump to, fast-forward and step-forward.

CASE STUDIES

In this section we evaluate a turn-based abstract puzzle game and a real-time team-based first-person shooter to give some examples in which ways the tool and its features can be useful for the analysis of gameplay.

DOGeometry

DOGeometry is an educational game for children aged eight to ten years old which teaches basic concepts of geometric transformations (translation, rotation and reflection) and object hierarchy (a complex object can be built with a set of simple shapes). The goal of the game is to guide a dog to a veterinarian by using a limited set of tiles and arranging them with a limited number of the afore mentioned geometric transformations. The tiles can be placed on an originally empty grid of dimension $n_x \times n_y$, where n_x and n_y vary from level to level. In total the game has 14 different levels. In some of these levels bones can be collected, which can be used in later levels to reveal a possible solution.

We used the presented visualization tool to study the difficulty of the game and to visualize the sequence in which tiles were placed and transformed by evaluating the log files of 40 participants. In case of DOGeometry each game state is represented by an $n_x \times n_y$ matrix M where each entry $m_{k,l}$ in the matrix encodes the current tile at position (k, l) in the grid. The dissimilarity δ_{ij} between two states i and j is then defined as

$$\delta_{ij} = \sum_{k=0}^{n_y} \sum_{l=0}^{n_x} d\left(m_{k,l}^i, m_{k,l}^j\right) \qquad (1)$$

where

$$d = \begin{cases} 0, & \text{if } m_{k,l}^i = m_{k,l}^j \\ 1, & \text{if } m_{k,l}^i \neq m_{k,l}^j \end{cases} \qquad (2)$$

In this way configurations of the grid which contain the same tiles at the same positions will be close together after applying multidimensional scaling. This also means that the goal state will be placed far away from the starting game state and all states reached working toward the goal will be placed somewhere in between.

Figure 6 visualizes the player transitions from level to level. As can be seen from this figure, there was a huge drop-out at Level 8 where about two thirds of the players gave up. Figure 7 shows the graph for Level 8 for 34 players. Rotations are shown as green arrows and the placement of a tile is shown as gray arrow. The start game state is colored orange and goal game states are shown in blue. All other states are colored green. A glance at Figure 7 shows that the first two moves were rather clear for the children, but afterward the graph begins to increasingly clutter toward the goal. This suggest that the children got confused at this point of how to proceed correctly. Examining this area closer revealed that the children had no clear sense of where to start with rotating the tiles. This is probably due to the fact that this level not only required rotations around the corners but that the limited number of available rotations required the children to carry out the rotations in the right order to be able to solve this level.

In contrast to Level 8, players were quite sure of how Level 5 might be solved as noticeable in Figure 8 (left). This fact can be deduced from the visualization because the principal directions are clearly noticeable and are further accentuated

Figure 6. Overview of the player transitions from level to level. The huge drop in players from Level 8 to Level 9 indicates a balancing problem at this point. The player symbols show the player distribution after 20 minutes. The glow around a node indicates that this node contains a subgraph which can be opened interactively by double-clicking on the node.

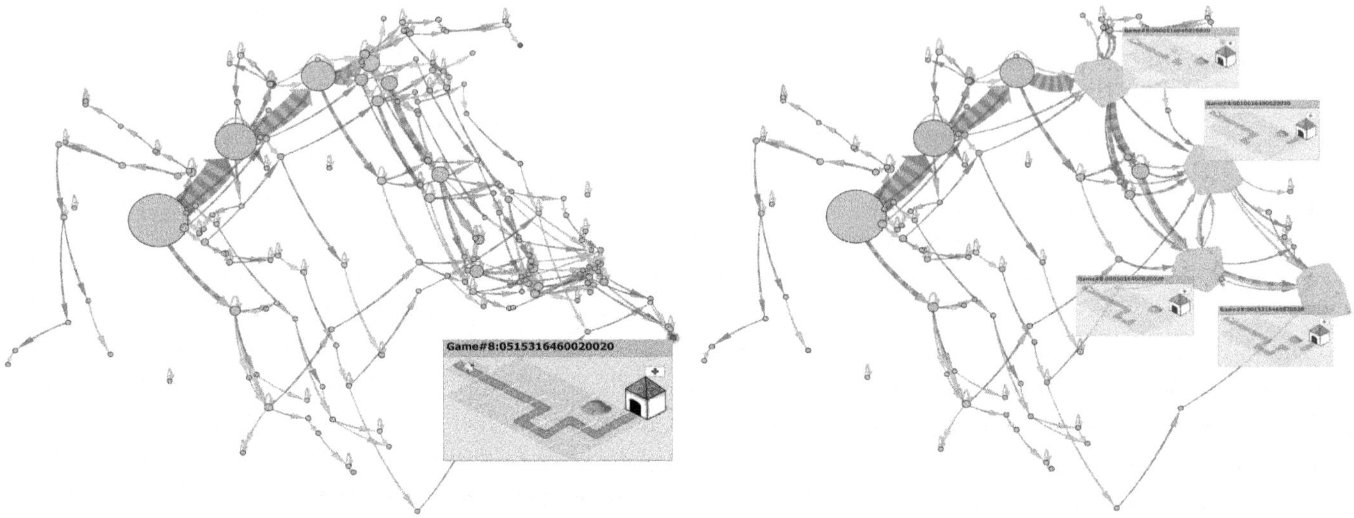

Figure 7. Left: Visualization of Level 8 from DOGeometry. Game states with less than three visits were hidden to reduce the visual complexity of the graph. The visualization calls attention to the upper right area from the start state (orange). The first two moves seem to be clear but then the cluttering indicates confusion in how to proceed correctly. Right: Clustering these game states helps to identify the principal way through this area. A cluster is represented by the screenshot associated with the most frequently visited game state.

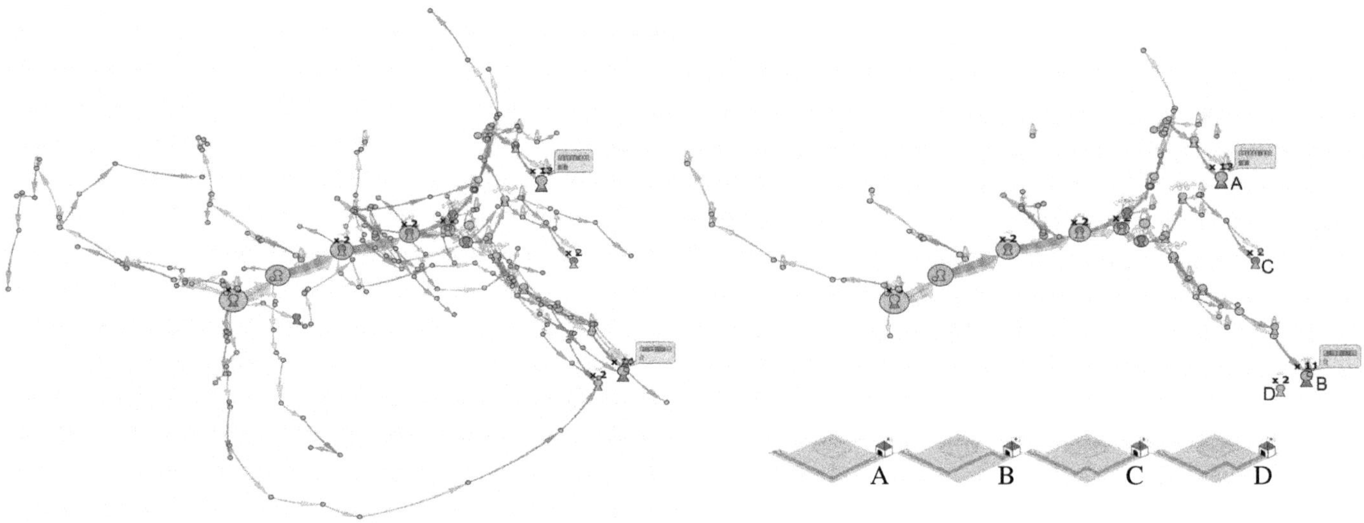

Figure 8. The left image shows the complete visualization for Level 5. In the image on the right all states with only one visit have been hidden to accentuate the principal directions. The four solutions (labeled A, B, C and D) are shown at the bottom right. The player icons show the player distribution after about 21 minutes of play time. Their coloring reflects the player gender ratio (blue for male, pink for female). Green arrows show rotations and gray arrows correspond to placements of tiles. Translations of tiles are shown as red arrows.

if states with less than one visit are hidden as shown in Figure 8 (right, top). The figure shows one main branch going to the right which separates into two branches after around three moves. The upper branch leads to the easy solution (A) (in that case only one of two available bones is collected) and the lower branch leads to a slightly more difficult solution (B) which permits players to collect both bones. Players also found two less popular solutions (C, D). All four solutions are shown in Figure 8 (right, bottom). Interestingly, solution (C) which we had in mind during the design of the level was not the one which was preferred by the children. In this sense, the visualization not only helped us to identify solutions which were not thought of during the design, but also to retrace the way these solutions were found. Figure 8 (left) also exhibits a particularly interesting path located at the lower part of the visualization, because it is separated

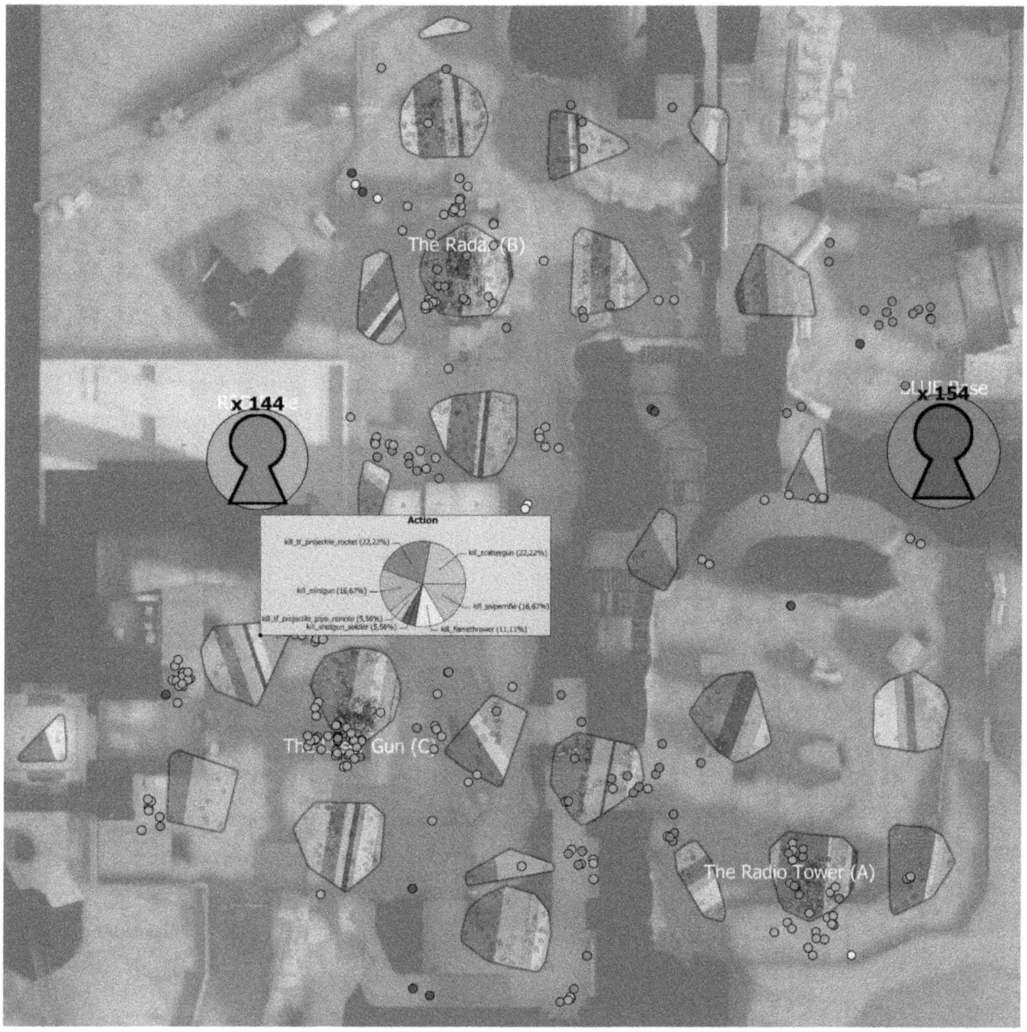

Figure 9. Graphical representation of 20 rounds (approx. 300 players and 2500 nodes) played on the TF2 map Gravel Pit. The RED and BLU base is located on the left and right side, respectively. Small, blue or red colored nodes depict locations where turrets have been constructed. The coloring of the clusters reflects the weapon usage. For one cluster the pie-chart with detailed information is shown.

from the mainstream. It comes from a playtester who always placed the tiles from the goal to the start.

Team Fortress 2

Team Fortress 2 [33] is a team-based first-person shooter first released by Valve Corporation in 2007. Players join one of two different teams (called RED and BLU) which compete for a principal objective and can choose to play as one of nine different classes. We have chosen Team Fortress 2 (TF2) as second example, because it shows the applicability of the tool to a different kind of game (real-time instead of the turn-based example in the previous section) and because TF2 game servers not only log various statistics but also player position data when certain events occur (e.g., player death, object built, point captured). We will therefore restrict the analysis to aspects where the accurate player movements are not required. For the following discussion we decided on the map Gravel Pit, which is an attack/defense map where the attacker BLU has to capture three points (A, B and C) from the defender RED. A and B can be captured in no particular order before C can be assaulted. Points which have been captured by the BLU team can never be recaptured by RED.

Figure 9 shows the visualization of 20 rounds which have been played on this map. Yellow nodes show the position of a player when he killed another player (gray nodes), red and blue nodes show locations where turrets have been erected from members of the RED or BLU team. Pink colored nodes show the three capture points. Edges (actions) are related to killings with certain weapons (e.g., red for rocket launcher, green for minigun, yellow for flamethrower). Clustering the states reveals fiercely contested areas (landmarks). Surely, in the present case these concentrate on the three capture points, but this functionality can be used to detect anticipated or unanticipated concentrations of players. Figure 9 furthermore shows the weapon usage inside these clusters. Examining the actions shows that the rocket launcher (red) is among the most frequently used ones (high percentage in almost every cluster). Such a representation can be used to observe where which weapons are favored. The sniper rifle (orange),

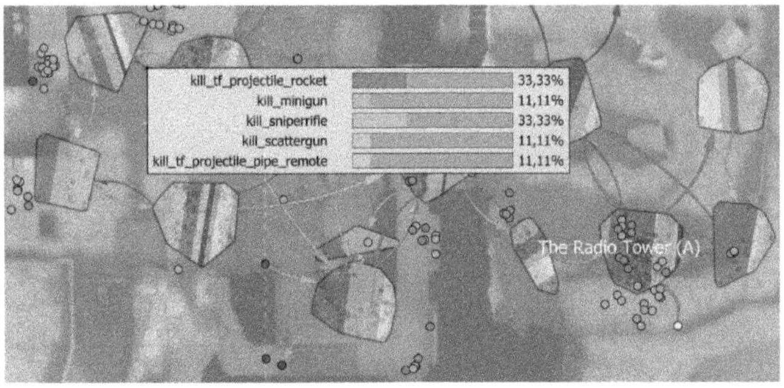

Figure 10. An excerpt from Figure 9. This time the meta-edges between the clusters are shown, which allows to examine the percentage distribution of weapons used by players to kill players located in other clusters. The tooltip of a meta-edge shows an exact breakdown of the distribution of the underlying actions.

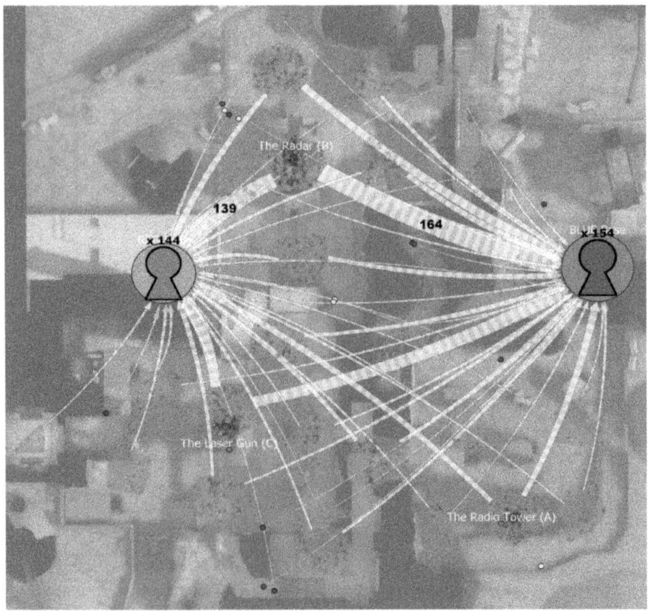

Figure 11. A visualization of the RED/BLU attrition at the individual clusters. The white arrows indicate respawns which have been caused by kills in the respective clusters.

for example, is only used in certain clusters which may point to (intended or unintended) locations which are well suited for snipers. In Figure 10 the meta-edges have been enabled to depict the percentage distribution of weapons used by players to kill players located in other clusters.

Usually heatmaps (see, e.g, [6]) are used to visualize spatial statistics from log files of shooter games to obtain a rendering which shows where how many players were killed or the amount of usage of a specific weapon. This is a good way to obtain a general overview of how the map is played in the first place (also see related work). However, heatmaps typically work best if a specific question has to be answered. Moreover, a heatmap only reveals the frequency of occurrence of a single attribute and therefore multiple heatmaps would be necessary to compare, e.g., location-dependent usage of different weapons. In contrast, with our proposed clustering technique this information can be inferred from a single representation.

Figure 12. A snapshot of the time-dependent simulation after approx. 2:00 minutes of gameplay. The current team color is mapped to the player symbol. At the three capture points the speech bubbles are shown. These are updated dynamically, so that the progress of number of players can be tracked easily. The color of the clusters reflects the team which has the majority of players inside.

Furthermore the proposed tool allows to analyze data in an exploratory way, e.g., by hiding states or actions of a certain type or by mapping different demographic attributes to the player symbol.

To give a further example, it is not possible to deduce from a single heatmap who killed whom or which team got killed more often at a certain landmark. Yet, having such information in a single visualization can help to indicate balancing problems more easily. In case of a game like TF2 this can be used to detect if a team is at a disadvantage in a certain area. Figure 11 shows the number of caused respawns at the individual clusters. For example, members of the BLU team have been killed 164 times in the cluster associated with capture point B but members of the RED team only 139 times. This may be due to the teams' skill levels but could also point to imbalances which are caused by characteristics of the environment (e.g., areas which give a large advantage to defensive snipers). This can be detected by interactively opening a cluster and taking a closer look at the individual positions and the used weapons.

The time-dependent simulation of the player movements reveals that team BLU first and foremost tried to capture point A and afterward point B. A snapshot taken during the simulation is shown in Figure 12. Such simulations can give valuable feedback to the level designers. Beside that, this also allows clans to review matches to improve their strategies.

LIMITATIONS AND FUTURE WORK

The system already allows to assign static information (e.g., screenshots) to states which are viewed when the mouse is hovered over the state. As supported in the TRUE system

[17], we strive to include videos which will be automatically synchronized with the timestamps stored in the players schedule. This way the corresponding clip can directly be viewed in the system, which allows the analyst to observe the players' behavior in the context of the visualized game space. We are working on adding further features to the visualization, like hierarchies of actions to allow the user to group similar actions together to influence the level of detail of the analysis. This way complete groups can then be hidden or shown and only the percentage of the whole group instead of the individual actions will be displayed. To give an example: in Fable 2 [23] players can perform different expressions (actions) when talking to someone. These expressions could then be grouped into *fun expressions, rude expressions, scary expressions* with each category consisting of further sub-actions like *laugh, dance, growl, scary laugh, etc.* Furthermore, the export of statistical data in form of spreadsheets and diagrams should be possible at any time during the simulation. This would provide a convenient way to obtain detailed numerical data from the visualization.

In terms of scalability the system is mainly limited by QT clustering and CMDS. QT clustering is computationally expensive and therefore not suitable for large numbers of states. Aside from that, the calculation time grows with increasing maximum cluster diameter. MDS algorithms also scale poor to large data sets because of quadratic complexity, as pointed out in [3]. However, fast approximations to MDS, like Pivot-MDS [3] which is also supported by the MDSJ library [1], exist. Furthermore, the number of states can be influenced by how they are defined, i.e., which factors are included in the definition of a state. This poses another problem, because this mapping is crucial for creating a meaningful visualization. How to develop such a mapping best depends on the game and the questions to be answered and needs to be addressed in future research.

We are aware of the fact that finding a suitable dissimilarity function to relate the game states with each other may be difficult in certain cases and choosing an improper one can harm the analysis. The dissimilarity of the states may also change over time or can vary from player to player depending on his attributes, which is not considered in the current implementation. Furthermore, MDS may project many states onto compact regions. Potentially, there can be infinitely many states depending on the level of detail used to define the states (e.g., if the location is recorded every few seconds). For such scenarios it might be useful to include the VU-Flow approach of Chittaro et al. [4] or Flow Maps [28] to visualize the intensity of travel congestions or other *more continuous* properties and to restrict our node-based approach to states at which designated discrete events occur.

A further issue which needs to be addressed is the comparability between different time periods of data. Currently, the shape of clusters depends on the spatial distribution of the nodes. If, for example, two different sets of playdata need to be compared, it is most likely that clusters will have different shapes and will therefore provide no consistent view on the data. This makes it hard to analyze the consequences of game changes developers make over time (for example, in case a new patch is released). Finally, we are currently in the process of conducting an evaluation with game designers and analysts to ensure a user-friendly interface and to detect possible problems. Furthermore, we consider to perform a user study with players, since the tool could also be used by players themselves for improving and planning their own gameplay.

CONCLUSIONS

Understanding user-behavior is essential for the evaluation and refinement of games. Automatic tracking of user behavior has just recently been adopted by the games industry to easily gather objective data from a large number of players. Visualizations of the textual data can assist the analytical process and can help to discover patterns of play which have not been thought of before. In this paper we described an approach for visualization of such automatically recorded gameplay data. Although, for some specific questions custom-built solutions will always be necessary, it was our intention to develop a tool which can be used for a wide variety of games and queries.

Our tool can be used for games where states can be directly visualized with regard to the environment as well as for games which require a more abstract representation of the states. It offers various features for exploratory data analysis, like clustering of states and filtering of states, actions, and players with regard to certain attributes (e.g., number of visits, type of the action, players of a certain age). Furthermore, the user can specify which attributes are directly visible to adapt the visualization to the demands of the analysis. The time-dependent simulation allows further insights into the behavior of players. Two case studies were presented to show how the tool can be used to analyze different kinds of games and to give impulses for further research.

REFERENCES

1. Algorithmics Group. *MDSJ: Java Library for Multidimensional Scaling (Version 0.2)*. University of Konstanz, 2009. `http://www.inf.uni-konstanz.de/algo/software/mdsj/`.
2. Andersen, E., Liu, Y.-E., Apter, E., Boucher-Genesse, F., and Popović, Z. Gameplay analysis through state projection. In *Proc. FDG 2010*, ACM Press (2010), 1–8.
3. Brandes, U., and Pich, C. Eigensolver methods for progressive multidimensional scaling of large data. In *Proc. GD 2006*, Springer (2007), 42–53.
4. Chittaro, L., Ranon, R., and Ieronutti, L. VU-flow: A visualization tool for analyzing navigation in virtual environments. *IEEE Transactions on Visualization and Computer Graphics 12* (2006), 1475–1485.
5. Davis, J. P., Steury, K., and Pagulayan, R. A survey method for assessing perceptions of a game: The consumer playtest in game design. *Game Studies: The Int. Journal of Computer Game Research 5*, 1 (2005).
6. Drachen, A., and Canossa, A. Analyzing spatial user behavior in computer games using geographic

information systems. In *Proc. MindTrek 2009*, ACM Press (2009), 182–189.

7. Drachen, A., and Canossa, A. Towards gameplay analysis via gameplay metrics. In *Proc. MindTrek 2009*, ACM Press (2009), 202–209.
8. Drachen, A., and Canossa, A. Evaluating motion: Spatial user behavior in virtual environments. *Int. Journal of Arts and Technology 4*, 3 (2011).
9. Drachen, A., Canossa, A., and Yannakakis, G. Player modeling using self-organization in Tomb Raider: Underworld. In *Proc. CIG 2009*, IEEE (2009).
10. Ducheneaut, N., Yee, N., Nickell, E., and Moore, R. J. The life and death of online gaming communities: a look at guilds in World of Warcraft. In *Proc. CHI 2007*, ACM Press (2007), 839–848.
11. Electronic Arts. Dead Space 2. Xbox 360, 2011.
12. Finnegan, S., Holte, R., Xiao, G., and Trommelen, M. Machine learning for semi-automated gameplay analysis. In *Game Developers Conference (GDC)* (2005).
13. Gagné, A., El-Nasr, M. S., and Shaw, C. D. A deeper look at the use of telemetry for analysis of player behavior in RTS games. In *Proc. ICEC 2011*, Lecture Notes in Computer Science, Springer (2011), 247–257.
14. Heyer, L. J., Kruglyak, S., and Yooseph, S. Exploring expression data: Identification and analysis of coexpressed genes. *Genome Research 9*, 11 (1999), 1106–1115.
15. Hoobler, N., Humphreys, G., and Agrawala, M. Visualizing competitive behaviors in multi-user virtual environments. In *Proc. VIS 2004*, IEEE Computer Society (2004), 163–170.
16. Juul, J. Introduction to game time. In *First Person: New Media as Story, Performance, and Game*, N. Wardrip-Fruin and P. Harrigan, Eds., 1 ed. 2004, 131–141.
17. Kim, J. H., Gunn, D. V., Schuh, E., Phillips, B., Pagulayan, R. J., and Wixon, D. Tracking real-time user experience (TRUE): a comprehensive instrumentation solution for complex systems. In *Proc. CHI 2008*, ACM Press (2008), 443–452.
18. Köhler, W. *Gestalt Psychology: An introduction to new concepts in modern psychology*. Liveright Publishing Corporation.
19. Kruskal, J. B., and Wish, M. *Multidimensional Scaling*. Sage Publications, 1978.
20. Lewis, C., and Wardrip-Fruin, N. Mining game statistics from web services: a World of Warcraft armory case study. In *Proc. FDG 2010*, ACM Press (2010), 100–107.
21. MacQueen, J. B. Some methods for classification and analysis of multivariate observations. In *Proc. of the 5th Berkeley Symposium on Mathematical Statistics and Probability*, L. M. L. Cam and J. Neyman, Eds., vol. 1, University of California Press (1967), 281–297.
22. Medler, B., John, M., and Lane, J. Data Cracker: developing a visual game analytic tool for analyzing online gameplay. In *Proc. CHI 2011*, ACM Press (2011), 2365–2374.
23. Microsoft Game Studios. Fable 2. Xbox 360, 2008.
24. Milam, D., and El Nasr, M. S. Analysis of level design 'push & pull' within 21 games. In *Proc. FDG 2010*, ACM Press (2010), 139–146.
25. Moura, D., el Nasr, M. S., and Shaw, C. D. Visualizing and understanding players' behavior in video games: discovering patterns and supporting aggregation and comparison. In *Proc. SIGGRAPH Sandbox 2011*, ACM Press (2011), 11–15.
26. Nintendo. Super Mario Galaxy 2. Wii, 2010.
27. Pagulayan, R. J., Keeker, K., Wixon, D., Romero, R. L., and Fuller, T. The human-computer interaction handbook. L. Erlbaum Associates Inc., 2003, ch. User-centered design in games, 883–906.
28. Phan, D., Xiao, L., Yeh, R., Hanrahan, P., and Winograd, T. Flow map layout. In *Proc. INFOVIS 2005*, IEEE Computer Society (2005), 219–224.
29. Psychostats, 2011. `http://www.psychostats.com`.
30. Thawonmas, R., and Iizuka, K. Visualization of online-game players based on their action behaviors. *Int. Journal of Computer Games Technology* (2008), 1–9.
31. Thawonmas, R., Kurashige, M., and Chen, K.-T. Detection of landmarks for clustering of online-game players. *The Int. Journal of Virtual Reality 6*, 3 (2007).
32. Tychsen, A. Crafting user experience via game metrics analysis. In *Workshop Research Goals and Strategies for Studying User Experience and Emotion, part of NordiCHI 2008* (2008).
33. Valve Corporation. Team Fortress 2. PC, 2007.
34. Williams, D., Yee, N., and Caplan, S. E. Who plays, how much, and why? Debunking the stereotypical gamer profile. *Journal of Computer-Mediated Communication 13*, 4 (2008), 993–1018.

Next Steps for Value Sensitive Design

Alan Borning
Dept. of Computer Science & Engineering
University of Washington
Seattle, Washington, USA 98195
borning@cs.washington.edu

Michael Muller
IBM Research
One Rogers Street
Cambridge, MA, USA 02142
michael_muller@us.ibm.com

ABSTRACT
Questions of human values often arise in HCI research and practice. Such questions can be difficult to address well, and a principled approach can clarify issues of both theory and practice. One such approach is Value Sensitive Design (VSD), an established theory and method for addressing issues of values in a systematic and principled fashion in the design of information technology. In this essay, we suggest however that the theory and at times the presentation of VSD *overclaims* in a number of key respects, with the result of inhibiting its more widespread adoption and appropriation. We address these issues by suggesting four topics for next steps in the evolution of VSD: (1) tempering VSD's position on universal values; (2) contextualizing existing and future lists of values that are presented as heuristics for consideration; (3) strengthening the voice of the participants in publications describing VSD investigations; and (4) making clearer the voice of the researchers. We propose new or altered approaches for VSD that address these issues of theory, voice, and reportage.

Author Keywords
Value Sensitive Design; participatory design; design; collaborative ethnography; qualitative research; universal values; culturally-specific values; feminism; voice

ACM Classification Keywords
K.4.1 [Computers and society]: Public policy issues - Ethics;

INTRODUCTION
As the field of human computer interaction has matured, an increasing body of HCI research has concerned itself with human values. The ACM Digital Library shows a fivefold increase in papers mentioning "human values" during the past ten years, from 20 in 2000 to 113 in 2010, r=0.92, p<.001 (Figure 1). At the same time, a number of approaches for systematically considering human values in information technology have emerged, in particular Value Sensitive Design (VSD) [28, 30]. VSD is "a theoretically grounded approach to the design of technology that accounts for human values in a principled and comprehensive manner throughout the design process" [30, p. 349]. The word "value" here is defined broadly, as "what a person or group of people consider important in life". Key features of VSD are a tripartite methodology, consisting of iteratively applied conceptual, empirical, and technical investigations; an emphasis on considering indirect as well as direct stakeholders (that is, people who are affected by a technical system but don't use it directly, as well as those who do); and an interactional theory of the relationship between values and technology.

VSD has been an important part of CHI, leading to many influential findings and analyses (for example, [16,28, 29,30,31,32,34,41,50,51,57,76,77]). More recently, as VSD itself has matured, a number of critiques and suggestions for its evolution and further development have been published (e.g., [1,3,48,63]). This essay is intended as a contribution toward that evolution. The problem we engage is that, in our view, VSD as currently presented *overclaims*. One aspect of this overclaiming is that VSD takes a number of stances that are broader and more sweeping than are necessary, or even warranted, for the work it is doing. A second aspect is that there are a set of rhetorical moves in some of the writing about VSD that imply more authority on the part of the researcher than we believe is appropriate. We suggest that unease about these claims has in turn inhibited the more widespread adoption and appropriation of this valuable theory and methodology. Another goal of our essay is to bring VSD into further dialog with a set of other relevant theories and approaches in the CHI community.

Our suggested next steps concern the following four topics.

1) **Universal vs. culturally-specific values**. VSD takes the position that certain values are universally held, but that the ways that these values play out in different cultures

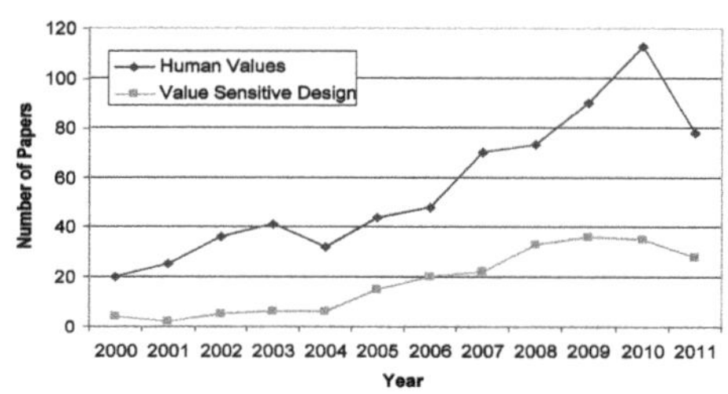

Figure 1. Increase in ACM interest in Human Values and Value Sensitive Design, 2000-2010.

Permission to make digital or hard copies of all or part of this work for personal or classroom use is granted without fee provided that copies are not made or distributed for profit or commercial advantage and that copies bear this notice and the full citation on the first page. To copy otherwise, or republish, to post on servers or to redistribute to lists, requires prior specific permission and/or a fee.
CHI'12, May 5–10, 2012, Austin, Texas, USA.
Copyright 2012 ACM 978-1-4503-1015-4/12/05...$10.00.

vary widely. Yet, as we discuss in more detail later, claims of universality for values are enormously problematic [11,25,61]. At the same time, a position of cultural relativism is problematic as well [37,38,71]. For this recommendation, avoiding overclaiming leads to a recommendation that VSD at the core should adopt a pluralistic (and perhaps more humble) position: simply that it doesn't have the answer to the difficult and long-standing question of universality, and further that a range of views on this question by different researchers can be accommodated under the VSD rubric. This pluralistic position would also help to clarify the question of whether VSD is a *method* that can be applied in principle to *any* set of values, vs. VSD as the *methodological instantiation* of a *particular set* of values (e.g., [1,63]).

2) **Contextualizing and qualifying lists of values offered for consideration**. A number of VSD papers have included lists of values, either as ones that may have a distinctive claim on resources in the design process, or as heuristics for suggesting values that might be implicated in a design. We acknowledge the utility of heuristic lists (while noting the potential problem of biasing the results of an investigation). However, we suggest that it would be better, when presenting such lists, to be explicit about the particular culture and viewpoint in which they were developed, rather than omitting this context and in the process making implicit claims about more universality than are warranted, or perhaps even intended.

3) **Strengthening the voice of the participants in writing about (and perhaps in conducting) the VSD investigation**. The publications of VSD have sometimes privileged the voice of the researchers in presenting qualitative results, not only as *interpreters* (a viable tradition in ethnography and qualitative analysis) but also as *reporters* (a more problematic strategy, if there are differences between the informants vs. the researchers [54]). The participatory design tradition has demonstrated the value and fidelity of informants *speaking for themselves* through HCI publications [12,55,66]. We believe there is overclaiming of knowledge and authority in the substitution of the researcher's voice for the voice of the informants. Participatory design also commits, in a substantive way, to co-design and sharing power between the researchers/designers and the users of the technology (see also [47]). While we do not go so far as to recommend that this be a core commitment of VSD as well, we do suggest that this should be considered carefully in VSD projects, and that in some cases such power sharing should be an explicit goal of the project.

4) **Making more salient the voice of the researchers and designers themselves in writing about the investigation**. Questions of values in HCI seldom have single, definitive, "objective" answers [43,44]. In many instances it may be useful for the reader if the researcher is more visible in the writing [17] – what is his or her background, relation to the participants in the study, and (for example if we are considering the role of the designer's own values) perhaps even relevant personal values [24, 78]? As with our third suggestion, we see the overclaiming here as implying more authority and impartiality than is warranted, via the rhetorical move of using a disembodied voice, in areas in which the researcher's own culture and assumptions may limit exactly those qualities of authority and impartiality. Allied disciplines (ethnography, feminism) provide alternatives ways of reporting that appear convergent with the goals of VSD.

BACKGROUND AND RELATED WORK

There is a long history of work on values and technology, including early work by Mumford [56], Weiner [73], Weizenbaum [74], and Winner [75]. Regarding theory and methods that specifically address human values in design, either in the context of HCI or of information technology more generally, some notable examples in addition to VSD are work by Flanagan and Nissenbaum [26,27] and Cockton [18,19]. We include numerous additional references in context in the discussion that follows.

We now discuss in more detail our four suggested next steps in evolving VSD's theory and methods.

UNIVERSAL VALUES IN ANALYSIS AND DESIGN

Are there any values that are (or should be) universal for all humans, or are all values culturally or individually specific? This question, in one form or another, has exercised people for millennia, ranging from prophets to religious thinkers to philosophers to social scientists to people simply wondering what it means to be human or what is the nature of right conduct.

VSD's position on this question has evolved over the years. In an early paper on VSD, Friedman and Kahn [28] state:

> When analyzing moral variability, conceptualizations of morality that entail abstract characterizations of justice and welfare tend to highlight moral universals, whereas definitions that entail specific behaviors or rigid moral rules tend to highlight moral cross-cultural variation. … In our view, both questions [regarding moral universals vs. moral cross-cultural variation] have merit, and a middle ground provides a more sensible and powerful approach for the HCI community: One that allows for an analysis of universal moral values, as well as allowing for these values to play out differently in a particular culture at a particular point in time.

In a later paper, Friedman et al. [30] move from a philosophical to an empirical statement of a similar position:

> VSD builds from the psychological proposition that certain values are universally held, although how such values play out in a particular culture at a particular

point in time can vary considerably … Note that this is an empirical proposition, based on a large amount of psychological and anthropological data, not a philosophical one. We also make this claim only for certain values, not all – there are clearly some values that are culture-specific.

There are huge problems with both the position that there are some values that are or should be universally held, as well as with the position that all values are either culturally or individually specific. On the one hand, the belief that there are universal values (from whatever source – God, evolutionary development, biological determinism, …) has on occasion led to the further belief that a particular group, culture, or religion is the keeper of those values, and needs to impose them on others – with sometimes tragic consequences. Yet, if all values are culturally or individually specific, what gives one culture or group grounds to say that some practice of another culture (slavery, genocide, female genital mutilation, …) is wrong (see [71])?

One response is to make this an empirical, scientific issue rather than a theological or philosophical one. (This is essentially the move made between the 2003 and 2006 papers referenced above.) In adopting this move, we still need to avoid the naturalistic fallacy (" 'is' does not equal 'ought' "), but this can be accomplished by qualifying prescriptive statements appropriately ("if we want to support human flourishing, then we should …"). But a scientific approach to the issue of universal values is also problematic, given what we (the authors of this essay) view as past abuses, justified on "scientific" grounds. Notorious examples come from the literature on forced sterilization in service of a claimed value of genetic purity [65] or a claimed value of reducing mental illness [67]. More recently, social programs such as Head Start (a US government intervention to improve scholastic performance among poor and non-white children) have been endangered by claims that intelligence is a genetically-determined trait [42], and that academic enrichment programs should be targeted at the children who have the generic capacity to learn – a claimed value of using scarce resources where they will do the most good. See [70] for one of many critiques of this position.

A second response is to declare the researcher's position or commitment [4,5,43,44], as is often the case in action research [40], collaborative ethnography [47], grounded theory [17], and participatory design [12,13,55,66]. But should such a position be one for the whole of VSD, i.e., one to which all VSD researchers must subscribe?

We suggest that VSD should take a more pluralistic position on this question of universal values, and simply say that this is a contested issue, to which VSD as such doesn't have the answer. If, in a particular study, it is important to come down on one side, then the researchers in that study should do so, and state their position, why they took it, and what the consequences were. We use the word "pluralistic" rather than "agnostic" in this suggestion, to accommodate exactly this. It should be possible for a researcher with a commitment to universal values – or with a commitment to all values being culturally constructed – to employ VSD. In practice, though, we suspect that the answer to this question has little if any impact on most actual projects. For example, even if there is some universally held value of privacy, the fact that "even while living in an igloo, [Inuit] have conventions that ensure some forms of privacy; yet such forms of privacy are not maintained by separated rooms, as they are in most Western cultures" [30] would be unlikely to have an impact on the design of technology. In other words, even if there is some universal aspect to the value of "privacy" (whether just a sliver or perhaps more), how this value plays out will be sufficiently different in the spectrum of human cultures that a universal design (whether of a social networking site or of a dwelling place) that works for all cultures seems like a chimera.

We note several significant caveats regarding this recommendation. First, universal values and universal design are distinct concepts, and indeed, as argued above, even if some values are universally held, this would not imply that universal designs were feasible. And VSD theory, even as currently expressed, does not imply that universal design is a realizable goal ("how such values play out in a particular culture at a particular point in time can vary considerably" [30]). Second, our reservations regarding the concept of universal values do not imply that we argue against cross-cultural studies that include looking carefully for commonalities as well as differences. (See [31] for an excellent example of this.) Quite the contrary: such studies become increasingly valuable as the global nature of the IT industry continues to develop and interfaces designed in one cultural context are used – and appropriated and molded – in another.

Finally, this is definitely not to say that the existence or not of universal values is an inappropriate topic for religion, philosophy, psychology, or anthropology, or that HCI researchers should not understand this thinking and research, perhaps deeply. Again, we suggest that this issue is one that VSD as such simply doesn't need to take a position on, at least given our current understanding of the issue from philosophy and various social sciences. Holding fast to VSD's position as described in [30] – or for that matter switching to a position of cultural construction of values – doesn't help advance the development and application of VSD. Rather the opposite: disagreements or simply unease within the research community about the position VSD has taken on this question have, we would argue, significantly impeded its development and application.

WHOSE VALUES?

Should VSD single out certain values as particularly worthy of consideration? If so, who chooses them, and how should they be chosen? VSD's position on this question has also evolved over the years. In an early chapter, Friedman and Kahn [28] write: "We review and discuss 12 specific values with ethical import. Some of these values have garnered individual chapters in this handbook. But, by including these values here, we highlight their ethical status and thereby suggest that they have a distinctive claim on resources in the design process." The chapter then goes on to list and discuss these values: Human Welfare, Ownership and Property, Privacy, Freedom From Bias, Universal Usability, Trust, Autonomy, Informed Consent, Accountability, Identity, Calmness, and Environmental Sustainability.

They are also careful to note that "this list is not comprehensive. Perhaps no list could be, at least within the confines of a chapter. Peacefulness, compassion, love, warmth, creativity, humor, originality, vision, friendship, cooperation, collaboration, community, purposefulness, devotion, diplomacy, kindness, musicality, harmony—the list of other possible values could get very long very fast."

In a subsequent paper [30], the list of specific values (now expanded from 12 to 13 with the addition of Courtesy) is introduced as: "We stated earlier that while all values fall within its purview, Value Sensitive Design emphasizes values with ethical import… [W]e present a list of frequently implicated values… intended as a heuristic for suggesting values that should be considered in the investigation – it is definitely not intended as a complete list of human values that might be implicated." A key difference between the descriptions is that the list is now presented as a design heuristic (ask yourself, is this value implicated in my design?), rather than as values that the authors suggest "have a distinctive claim on resources in the design process".

The evolution in VSD toward evocative heuristics rather than lists that call out a specific set of values has continued, with a notable example being Envisioning Cards [34]. Nevertheless, we find the presentation of the lists in both the 2003 and 2006 papers problematic: it would have been better to contextualize them by noting that these are typical values from a liberal and relatively privileged Western perspective (and that have been evidenced in HCI work to date, which has usually been in done in such a context), rather than implicitly claiming more universality by presenting them without such qualification. We also note that the lists are in English, and use the English phrases for the concepts. Translations will not be precise, and may well bring out different issues. Indeed, this is noted in published VSD work, in particular a 2008 VSD cross-cultural study on attitudes toward privacy in public spaces in the U.S. and Sweden [31]. That paper describes the difficulties of translating the word "privacy" into Swedish. The Swedish translation that the researchers adopted ("personlig integritet") encompasses both controlling information flow (as in the English language meaning) but also maintaining the quality (accuracy) of that information [31, p. 143].

A living theory and method will evolve, and a past description will not necessarily capture the current understanding. Or it is often easy in retrospect to see how something could have been said better. Nevertheless, an explicit qualification of the context and limitations of these early lists as suggested above would be useful.

Le Dantec et al. [48] raise a similar concern about what they view as an inappropriately privileged and prescriptive role for the list of values in the 2003 VSD paper [28]. However, we soften our own concern in three respects. First, we note that the list of values as presented in a later paper [30] is introduced as "a heuristic for suggesting values that should be considered in the investigation" rather than as values that "have a distinctive claim on resources in the design process". Second, one of the grounds for Le Dantec et al.'s concern is a claimed prescribed ordering for the investigations that comprise VSD's tripartite methodology: first conceptual, then empirical, then technical. Here we disagree: in doing value sensitive design one can start with any one of the investigations; and indeed, there are published VSD investigations that start with each of the three. For example, the early work on browser cookies and privacy [50] began with conceptual investigations, the Watcher and the Watched studies [29] began with empirical investigations, and the CodeCOOP work [51] began with technical investigations. Third, we observe that VSD, as a living theory and method, will and ought to evolve over time (one example of this being the continued evolution toward evocative heuristics rather than lists that call out a specific set of values), and so we don't want to make too much of a statement from a 2003 paper.

Should VSD as such have *any* heuristic lists of values that might arise in particular applications? What about more evocative and less specific heuristics such as Envisioning Cards? One position is that any lists, or even other kinds of heuristics, are harmful, in that they tend to bias the researcher or designer toward existing analyses and ways of thinking. (Indeed, the authors in [48] seem to lean toward such a position, at least as regards lists.) In our view, this position is rooted in a valid concern, but one that well-done empirical investigations help mitigate. However, in any case, taking such a purist stance in all investigations would make VSD not a practical method in many situations, e.g., in an industrial setting with a tight schedule. For example, when designing a new privacy options interface for a social media application, it seems unreasonable to tell the designers not to look at some careful VSD work on the privacy options tool for a different social media application, but to start from scratch. More broadly, we think there is benefit in having heuristics and cues (including lists of values that might be implicated) to aid designers in considering values that may be at stake in a given system. Certainly such lists of values or other tools should be contextualized with information about who wrote it, in what milieu, and for what purpose. Using a variety of heuristics and suggestions about values that might be present seems likely to improve rather than diminish the odds of not overlooking important values, and consequently the quality of the end result.

An essential activity in broadening VSD is to continue to build up collections of case studies, heuristics (and yes, even lists) that are particularly relevant for a broad range of cultures and contexts. One omission (notable given the long history of participatory design in HCI) is labor concepts, such as solidarity and collective action, as well as some relational values [8]. In terms of other cultures, Alsheikh et al. [3], for example, provide a case study situated in Arab cultures and values.

Finally, consider values in domains not typically seen in publications at CHI or CSCW, for example, military values. There is published work in this area: Cummings [21] describes a VSD case study (part of a proposed engineering curriculum) of the hypothetical development of a command and control supervisory interface for a military cruise missile. The conceptual analysis is built around the value of human welfare, which is already often seen in VSD work – but here drawing on different philosophical traditions, namely the theory of just war, and the principles of proportionality and of discrimination. One can also imagine VSD analyses for military applications for direct use by combat soldiers or other warfighters that implicate additional values, such as courage, honor, discipline, loyalty, and accountability. This domain does not fit comfortably in the usual values discussion in the HCI community – but (unless one believes there should be no new military systems) it makes sense to consider military systems from a VSD perspective and to design them well, so these philosophical traditions and values are certainly relevant (e.g., [60]).

A related question is whether VSD should itself substantively commit to certain values, for example, in the way that participatory design substantively commits to the values of participation and democracy, that collaborative ethnography commits to co-authorship as well as co-analysis with the affected population [47], or that action research commits to emancipatory goals [40]. If so, how are those values chosen and who does so? We (the authors of this essay) tread cautiously here. Tempting as it is to include values we personally hold dear, we suggest that VSD commit to just those values that are essential to making VSD itself work: namely, pluralism or inclusivity (necessary to do the analysis of direct and indirect stakeholders well), plus openness and transparency (values that are important in many other methods as well of course, not just VSD).

Regarding other values beyond these, we would underscore and build on the distinction among explicitly supported values, stakeholder values, and designer values [16]. These are respectively values that are explicitly supported and adopted in a given investigation or project, values that are important to some (but not necessarily all) stakeholders, and the designer or researcher's own personal values. Then, for example, if researchers wanted to adopt participatory design values (and practices) in the course of a VSD project, they would make those PD values be explicitly supported values, drawing on PD methods as appropriate as well; and similarly for researchers wanting to adopt values and practices from the collaborative ethnography or action research traditions. Researchers in the PD, collaborative ethnography, and action research traditions derive their values explicitly from their co-researchers (community members), as well as those who have gone before them. As experience is built up with VSD projects adopting a given set of explicitly supported values, the value and stakeholder analyses and guidance regarding methods can be shared and co-evolved. We acknowledge that this is a less satisfactory situation for VSD, from the point of view of shared and co-constructed sets of community values, since those values would be not an integral part of VSD itself – but short of VSD substantively committing to a wider collection of values, it may be a useful approach.

A further elaboration of this idea would be for VSD researchers or practitioners to enact a form of democratic voicing, by creating a website for these lists. In one of many possible designs, a researcher could contribute a list of values, and other people could comment on that list. If a second person wanted to propose a variation, s/he could make a (clearly linked) copy of the list, and rewrite selected aspects. Discussion comments might then be linked back to both lists. In this proposal, VSD would support pluralistic values with pluralistic lists, and would provide an example of democratic methods by encouraging lively discussions about each list and its values.

THE VOICE OF THE PARTICIPANTS

There are two aspects to our third suggestion, which regards the voice of the participants.

The first aspect is a relatively contained one, regarding hearing directly the voices of the participants. In presenting work about different users or stakeholders, many of the disciplines that meet in CHI and CSCW favor hearing the voices of the users or stakeholders. This point would seem to be particularly important for work related to values [41,51,57,58,76]. For readers with a background in ethnography or cultural critique, this is a crucial point. It is, in the influential essay by Alcoff, "the problem of speaking for others" [2]. When we interpose ourselves between an informant and an audience (as most researchers must do), there is the risk of unintentional ventriloquism – i.e., stating the researcher's own views as if those views had been articulated by the informants [52]. The common solution to this problem is to develop disciplines of data collection, analysis, and reporting that bring the informants' words to the reader with some assurance of directness and fidelity. Judicious verbatim quotation, with good contextualization, is the most frequent response to this problem in HCI and CSCW. The point is not to guard against some "hidden agenda" on the part of the researcher. The risk is that *everyone* is capable of unintentional, well-meaning ventriloquism, and so we invoke these disciplines in order to *protect ourselves* against doing something we would very much regret.

The second aspect of our suggestion is less well-worked out, and is indeed in many ways a direction for future research. VSD originated in part in trying to apply participatory design in contexts for which PD methods at the time were ill-suited due, for example, to a lack of a clear organizational boundary, such as applying PD methods to browser design [50], or in today's world, Facebook. (Also see [15].) However, in the process, some of PD's core commitments to co-design and sharing power were weakened, and instead power is back in the hands of the researchers.

In the decades since PD was first developed, it has evolved to include different stakeholder groups (children, elderly, disabled, ...), as well as more situations with less clear organizational boundaries; and approaches to adapting it to such contexts have begun to emerge [54]. We suggest that the traditional PD commitments to co-design and power sharing be carefully considered in VSD projects as well, taking advantage of this newer work. In some cases, it will be appropriate to make co-design and power sharing be explicitly supported values for the project. At the same time, we should continue to investigate ways to support these values with more diverse stakeholder groups. (Davis [22] discusses some of these relations between VSD and PD in the context of persuasive technologies.)

These considerations allow us to reframe some of the VSD critiques raised in [48]. We earlier disagreed with Le Dantec et al.'s claim that VSD prescribes a particular order of investigations. We would in fact also disagree with their claim that they started with an empirical investigation. In their work with homeless people, we suggest that they actually started with a *conceptual* investigation, not an empirical one: namely, they analyzed the power relationships and decided that they should talk with the homeless people. There is otherwise not an *a priori* reason to talk with homeless people, rather than service agency staff, police, business owners, or other stakeholders.[1] But despite these two disagreements, at yet another level we believe the researchers got something very right: by giving voice to the homeless people, they foregrounded the values and concerns of a group that is otherwise often disempowered and silenced (see also [4,40,47,52]).

Le Dantec et al. also highlight the photo-elicitation interview (PEI) method as an empirical method: "The PEI works well when there is a significant power differential between researcher and subject by shifting the power dynamic toward the participants by letting them shape the direction of the interview through the content they have created" (see also [55,59,72]). We would echo the importance of attending to power differentials, but re-frame this recommendation as being about giving voice to the participants in the VSD study rather than prescribing particular methods. (Just as part of VSD's theory is an interactional theory that says technologies have value suitabilities, in the same way we suggest that empirical methods have different value suitabilities – whether or not photo-elicitation is in fact a more appropriate empirical method here, we can still frame Le Dantec et al.'s recommendation as being about value suitabilities for different empirical methods.)

THE VOICE OF THE RESEARCHERS

Our last recommendation for evolving VSD is also tied to voice, this time the voice of the researchers and designers. Questions of values seldom have single, definitive, "objective" answers. In many instances it may be useful for the reader if the researcher is more visible in the writing – what is his or her background, relation to the participants in the study, and perhaps even relevant personal values [17]? This practice of self-disclosure is standard for example in writing ethnographies [23,24]. There are now examples of this in the VSD literature as well, and we suggest expanding the practice.

As an existing example, Alsheikh et al. [3] discuss how the authors' backgrounds impact theory and method: "While these technologies support full video, we used an audio-only connection, as the first author, an Iraqi citizen who studied in Egypt, recognized an Arabic cultural taboo associated with discussing relationships and intimacy", or "Close readings of the data, and a careful consideration of what we, as researchers coming from Iraq, the US, and the UK, took for granted in our own notions of privacy, alerted us to the need for some alternative theoretical lenses with which to interpret it." In this example, the researchers' experience allowed a better method of inquiry.

More broadly, there are claims that the perspective or "standpoint" of the researcher can become both a powerful tool of inquiry (i.e., certain life experiences provide insights that can inform an exploration), and a set of limits on what the researcher is able to perceive and understand [38]. Applying this tradition to a VSD project to improve the safety of homeless young people, Woelfer et al. [77] include a section entitled "Researcher Stance", and write: "The research team is comprised of people with backgrounds in HCI, design, and security. We work from a design stance that seeks to both understand the situated context as well as to create meaningful change. ... On reflection, we have also found that this work changes us, especially how we apprehend the U-District [neighborhood] and think of the young people we have met in research and later encounter on the street. In these public encounters, we

[1] Or if this decision were not formally part of a conceptual investigation, the researchers are still deciding what to attend to, which strongly shapes the VSD investigation. Deciding to talk with the homeless people doesn't come out of nowhere.

are trained to acknowledge the person but subtly, so as not to reveal our inter-personal familiarity to bystanders."

Another facet of this recommendation is connected with the aforementioned distinction among explicitly supported values, stakeholder values, and designer values. If researchers make this distinction in a given project, it may well be useful for the reader to know what are the relevant personal values of the researchers or designers, as well as the values that are explicitly supported in that project and the relevant values of the key stakeholders, so that the reader can judge how well the different kinds of values are distinguished and treated in the work [37]. This kind of clarity is particularly important if there were value tensions or conflicts among values in these three groups. Our earlier proposal for self-disclosure by authors is also important here, in the event that there might be values conflicts between authors and the people they are describing [52]. Similarly, knowing who is funding the work (and what goals they might have for it) may be important for the reader in evaluating the research.

A final facet involves subtle but arguably important changes in wording and emphasis, to make it clearer that there is a person or group taking the role of researcher, of working through a method, interviewing participants, analyzing data, and so on – avoiding the disembodied "view from nowhere" [36]. It is common in CHI and CSCW for the author to take the role of analyst and/or designer. Indeed, part of the motivation of PD is to share the responsibility and power to design (e.g., [12]) as well as to interpret and to analyze (e.g., [53] – see also [47]). We submit that questions of values and ethics would benefit from a similar sharing of responsibility and power – i.e., to perform an analysis of values and/or ethics [55]. This sharing could be particularly important in inter-cultural situations, in which disagreements about values may stem in part from disagreements about the "first principles" that underlie the ethical positions [49] (e.g., the tragic disagreements between the Navajo and Hopi nations of North America, about what it means to live on the land, and what "empty" land is good for [9]). Thus, a more contextualized VSD method would include a description of the ethical analyses of the people in the situation – acting as professional or "lay" ethicists. Appropriate background and citations regarding the underlying ethical theory (e.g., deontological, utilitarian, ...), may also be useful and important.

For example, in discussing a principled prioritization scheme for deciding where to put resources, Friedman et al. [32] write: "Our strategy for prioritization thus serves as a check on allowing funding and other pragmatic considerations to unduly influence the implementation priorities." We suggest that this leaves invisible exactly who invokes this check (and perhaps who verifies that it was done in a principled fashion), and creates a subtle barrier, for example, to questioning how effective it was. We would rephrase this sentence as: "Our strategy for prioritization thus provides a tool that the designer – or a third party – can use as a check on allowing funding and other pragmatic considerations to unduly influence the implementation priorities." More words, indeed, but perhaps useful ones.

There are many methods for helping to make informants' voices heard. In addition to ethnographic quotations (e.g., [20,68]), the PD tradition has developed storytelling methods that can easily be adapted to include discussions of values and ethics, such as storyboarding methods to explicate work [46,53,64], even in the absence of a common verbal language [69]; hypermedia for community storytelling [7]; community-produced photo-documentaries ("photo novellas") and video-documentaries to change government policy [72] or for urban design [45,59] and to document human rights violations [10]. Collaborative ethnography goes further, insisting that the report of a project should be understandable and critiqued in advance by the people who are being described, and should optimally be co-authored with them [47]. Recent VSD work has begun to use video in the field [33]; we suggest that video and other user-created media can also contribute to reports from the field to other researchers.

Woelfer and Hendry were careful to avoid direct quotations from their informants in a VSD project, as part of a principled plan to protect their informants' privacy [77]. The preceding examples from participatory methodologies show how informants can *knowingly* create documents (including multimedia, photographic, and video documents) that are *intended* as communications media to others. The explicit "audiencing" of these documents removes issues of quotation-without-permission, and can help VSD informants become advocates for their own perspectives, including their own values, and (if that is their goal) for the kinds of change that they want to bring about. We suggest that VSD can become a stronger method for both *research* and also *social change* through a strategy that enhances the voice of its informants (see [40,43,47]).2

DISCUSSION AND PROPOSED NEXT STEPS FOR VSD

VSD addresses issues of values experienced in people's lives. Like design issues, issues of values necessarily involve differences in perspectives, and often involve differences in power. Throughout this essay, in addition to our intended core contribution of a set of suggested next steps for VSD, we have endeavored to bring insights from other work in CHI and CSCW that bears on these kinds of

[2] We are not suggesting that VSD adopt social change as a core value. Rather, we again make use of the distinction among explicitly supported values, stakeholder values, and designer values: if social change is one of the explicitly supported values in a project, then strengthening VSD in this respect becomes an important consideration.

differences. We summarize this other work, and the insights we have derived from it, in this section.

Practitioners of participatory design urged us to consider "users" as designers of their technology and of the work practices that may be reified in that technology [12]. Values are part of the background that participants bring to these collaborative settings. We have proposed that methods from participatory design, collaborative ethnography, and action research be used to inform the methods of VSD. We propose that VSD consider adapting those methods that foreground the needs, designs, and analyses of the "users" in participatory design, such as co-design, participant-led story-telling, drama, photo-documentary, and video-documentary (for a software methodology based on participatory design, see [13]; for a survey of methods, see [55]). An important topic for future research is to continue to investigate how to support participation and power-sharing in situations without clear organizational boundaries or groups of stakeholders.

Feminism provides additional lenses through which to consider questions of values and ethics [6]. Bardzell's recent analysis argued against "universal" statements and designs, and in favor of considerations of diversity of perspective, with a research focus on edge cases rather than on the relatively homogeneous middle of a population [4]. Feminist philosophies of science similarly advocate for the inclusion of diverse views, and for a form of "strong objectivity" in which each researcher's contribution cannot be evaluated for its claims until the researcher discloses her/his own position, perspective, and stakes in the work [37,38] (see more recently [39]). We have proposed that VSD can learn from feminist research methods in the sciences in general [35,37,38], and in social science and HCI in particular (e.g. [4,5,62]), to include diverse voices, to examine the edge cases around a values-question [4], and to interrogate its own VSD practices with questions such as who is recognized as an analyst of values? (e.g., [55]).

HCI researchers in the post-colonialist domain can offer related critiques and insights (e.g., [44]). Post-colonialism is in part a critique of power, and can be applied to HCI power relationships among analysts and "users". We have proposed that, convergently with participatory design and with feminism, post-colonialism can help VSD to ask questions about "who is allowed to speak about whom?" (see also [2,47]) and "how are values-based decisions made and enacted when their impact is felt by people who are not recognized as design-makers or analysts?"

Similarly, some VSD projects are not only about reporting values issues and conundrums, but also about social activism. VSD researchers and practitioners in this area may find work in action research to be useful here [40]. This work could also be helpful in articulating the relationship between these two seemingly-related fields.

In more pragmatic or "operational" terms, we also think that VSD could benefit from a more democratic approach to its own methodology. VSD could use participatory technologies, such as social media, to build a rich and diverse set of resources. To cite just one example, the concept of lists of values has been controversial, and has evolved through VSD practice over the years (see the earlier section "Whose Values"?), and large gaps remain. We suggest that opening up the process to broader participation and sharing of power would be one useful step here – for example, VSD researchers could provide collaborative online tools to facilitate sharing, discussing, and refining research materials (e.g., lists, envisioning cards [34]) among the growing community of VSD practitioners. Forms of community-led VSD may emerge.

ACKNOWLEDGMENTS

A heartfelt thanks to Batya Friedman, for her leadership in developing Value Sensitive Design and leading the way for the past two decades, for a series of in-depth discussions about the ideas presented here over several years, and for cheerfully offering feedback on this paper. Many other members of the CHI and related communities have helped us develop these ideas over the years. Janet Davis, Dave Hendry, Lisa Nathan, and Jill Woelfer, and the anonymous CHI referees provided useful feedback on drafts. In the end, however, the authors bear sole responsibility for any errors or problems with these suggestions. This work was supported in part by the National Science Foundation under grant number CNS-0905384.

REFERENCES

1. Albrechtslund, A. Ethics and technology design. *Ethics and Info. Tech.* 9(1), 63-72, 2007.
2. Alcoff, L. The problem of speaking for others. *Cultural Critique 20* (Winter 1991-1992), 5-32.
3. Alsheikh, T., Rode, J. and Lindley, S. (Whose) Value-Sensitive Design? A Study of Long-Distance Relationships in an Arabic Cultural Context." *Proc. CSCW 2011*, ACM Press (2011), 75-84.
4. Bardzell, S. Feminist HCI: Taking stock and outlining an agenda for design. *CHI 2010*, ACM Press (2010), 1301-1310.
5. Bardzell, S. and Bardzell, J. Towards a feminist HCI methodology: Social science, feminism, and HCI. *CHI 2011*, ACM Press (2011), 675-684.
6. Bardzell, S., and Churchill, E., (eds.), *Interacting with Computers,* special issue on feminism, in press.
7. Beeson, I., and Miskelly, C. Dialogue and dissent in stories of community. *Proc. PDC 2000.* New York: CPSR.
8. Belenky, M., Clinchy, B., Goldberger, N., and Turule, J. *Women's ways of knowing: The development of self, voice, and mind,* Basic, 1987/1997.
9. Benedict, E. *The wind won't know me: A history of the Navajo-Hopi land dispute.* Knopf, 1992.
10. Best, M., Smyth, T., Serrano-Baquero, D., and Etherton, J. Designing for and with diaspora: A case study of work for the

truth and reconciliation commission of Liberia. *Ext Abstracts CHI 2010*, ACM Press (2010), 2903-2918.

11. Bickel, B. Weapons of magic: Afghan women asserting voice via the Net. *JCMC* 8(2), 2003.
12. Bjerknes, G., Ehn, P., and Kyng, M. (eds.). *Computers and Democracy: A Scandinavian Challenge.* Avebury, 1987.
13. Bødker, K., Kensing, F., and Simonsen, J. *Participatory IT design: Designing for business and workplace realities.* MIT Press, 2004.
14. Bødker, S., Ehn, P., Sjögren, D., & Sundblad, Y. Co-operative Design – perspectives on 20 years with 'the Scandinavian IT Design Model'. *Proc. NordiCHI 2000.*
15. Borning, A., Friedman, B., and Kahn, P. H., Jr. Designing for Human Values in an Urban Simulation System: Value Sensitive Design and Participatory Design. Short paper, *Proc. PDC 2004,* Toronto, July 2004.
16. Borning, A., Friedman, B., Davis, J. and Lin. P. Informing public deliberation: Value sensitive design of indicators for a large-scale urban simulation. *Proc. ECSCW 2005*, Springer (2005), 449-468.
17. Charmaz, K., & Mitchell, R.G. Jr. The myth of silent authorship: Self, substance, and style in ethnographic writing. In Hertz, R. (ed), *Reflexivity and Voice*, Sage, 1997.
18. Cockton, G. Value-centred HCI. *Proc. NordiCHI'04*, Tampere, Finland, 2004, 149-160.
19. Cockton, G. Getting there: Six meta-principles and interaction design. *Proc CHI 2009*, ACM Press (2009), 2223-2232.
20. Crabtree, A. Ethnography in participatory design. *Proc. PDC 1998*, Seattle, CPSR.
21. Cummings, M. Integrating ethics in design through the value-sensitive design approach. *Science and Engineering Ethics* 12(4), 701-715, 2006.
22. Davis, J. Design methods for ethical persuasive computing. *Persuasive '09*, ACM Press (2009).
23. Dourish, P. Implications for design. *Proc. CHI 2006.*
24. Dourish, P. Ethnography. Tutorial presented at the Human Computer Interaction Consortium (HCIC), Winter Park, CO, Feb. 2010.
25. Ess, C., and Sudweeks, F. On the edge: Cultural barriers and catalysts to IT diffusion among remote and marginalized communities. *New Media & Soc*, 3(3), 259-269, 2001.
26. Flanagan, M., Howe, D., and Nissenbaum, H. Values at play: Design tradeoffs in socially-oriented game design. *CHI 2005*, ACM Press (2005), 751-760.
27. Flanagan, M., Howe, D., and Nissenbaum, H. Embodying values in technology: Theory and practice. In J. van den Hoven and J. Weckert (eds.), *Information Technology and Moral Philosophy*. Cambridge University Press, Cambridge, UK, 2008, 322-353.
28. Friedman, B., and Kahn, P. H., Jr. (2003). Human values, ethics, and design. In J. A. Jacko and A. Sears (eds.), *The Human-Computer Interaction Handbook*, 1177-1201. Mahwah Erlbaum.
29. Friedman, B., Freier, N. G., and Kahn, P. H., Jr. Office window of the future? Two case studies of an augmented window. *Ext Abstracts CHI 2004*, ACM Press (2004), 1559.
30. Friedman, B., Kahn, P. H., Jr. and Borning, A. Value sensitive design and information systems. In P. Zhang and D. Galletta (eds.), *Human-Computer Interaction and Management Information Systems: Foundations*. M.E. Sharpe, Armonk, NY, 2006.
31. Friedman, B., Höök, K., Gill, B.T., Eidmar, L., Sallmander Prien, C., and Severson, R.L. Personlig integritet: A comparative study of perceptions of privacy in public places in Sweden and the United States. *Proc. NordiCHI 2008*, 142-151.
32. Friedman, B., Borning, A., Davis, J. L., Gill, B. T., Kahn, Jr., P., Kriplean, T. and Lin, P. Laying the foundations for public participation and value advocacy: Interaction design for a large scale urban simulation. *Proc 9th Annual International Conf. on Digital Government Research* (dg.o2008), 305-314.
33. Friedman, B., Nathan, L.P., Lake, M., Grey, N.G., Nilsen, T.T., Utter, R.F., Utter, E.J., Ring, M., & Kahn, Z. Multi-lifespan information system design in post-conflict societies: An evolving project in Rwanda. *Ext. Abstracts CHI 2010,* ACM Press (2010), 2833-2844.
34. Friedman, B., Nathan, L. P., Kane, S. and Lin, J. *Envisioning Cards*. University of Washington, Seattle, WA, 2011. Available at: http://envisioningcards.com.
35. Haraway, D.J. A cyborg manifesto: Science, technology, and socialist-feminism in the late twentieth century. In *Simians, cyborgs and women: The reinvention of nature*. Routledge, New York, 1991.
36. Haraway, D.J. *Modest_Witness@Second_Millennium. FemaleMan©_Meets_Oncomouse™: Feminism and Technoscience.* Routledge, New York, 1997.
37. Harding, S. *The Science Question in Feminism*, Cornell University Press, 1986.
38. Harding, S. (ed). *The Feminist Standpoint Reader: Intellectual and Political Controversies*, Routledge, 2003.
39. Harrison, S., Sengers, P., and Tatar, D. Making epistemological trouble: Third-paradigm HCI as successor science. To appear in *Interacting with Computers*.
40. Hayes, G.R. The relationship of action research to human-computer interaction. *TOCHI* 18(3), 2011, 15:1-15:20.
41. Hendry, D.G., and Friedman, B. Theories and practices of design for information systems: Eight design perspectives in ten short weeks. *Proc. DIS 2008*, ACM Press (2008), 435-444.
42. Herrnstein, R.J., & Murray, C. *The Bell Curve: Intelligence and Class Structure in America*, Free Press, 1994.
43. Hourcade, J.P., Bullock-Rest, N.E., Friedman, B., Nelson, M., Shneiderman, B., and Zephiris, P. HCI for peace: From idealism to concrete steps. Proc CHI 2011, ACM Press (2011), 613-616
44. Irani, L., Vertesi, J., Dourish, P., Philip, K., and Grinter, R.E. Postcolonial computing: A lens on design and development. *CHI 2010*, ACM Press (2010), 1311-1320.
45. Isomursu, M., Kuutti, K., and Väinämö, S. (2004). Experience clip: Method for user participation and evaluation of mobile concepts. *Proceedings of PDC 2004.* Toronto: CPSR.
46. Lafreniére, D. (1996). CUTA: A simple, practical, and low-cost approach to task analysis. *Interactions* 3(5), 35-39.

47. Lassiter, E.L. *The Chicago Guide to Collaborative Ethnography*, University of Chicago Press, 2005.
48. Le Dantec, C.A., Poole, E.S. and Wyche, S.P. Values as lived experience: Evolving Value Sensitive Design in support of value discovery. *Proc CHI 2009*, ACM Press (2009), 1141-1150.
49. Leidner, D.E., and Kayworth, T. A Review of Culture in Information Systems Research: Toward a Theory of Information Technology Culture Conflict. *Mgmt. Info. Sys. Quart.* 30(2), 2006.
50. Millett, L., Friedman, B., and Felten, E. Cookies and web browser design: Toward realizing informed consent online. *Proc. CHI 2001*, ACM Press (2001), 46-52.
51. Miller, J., Friedman, B., Jancke, G., and Gill, B. Value tensions in design: The value sensitive design, development, and appropriation of a corporation's groupware system, *Proc. GROUP 2007*, ACM Press (2007), 281-290.
52. Muller, M. Ethnocritical heuristics for reflecting on work with users and other interested parties. In M. Kyng and L. Mathiassen, *Computers and Design in Context*, MIT Press, Cambridge, MA, 1997.
53. Muller, M.J., and Carey, K. Design as a minority discipline in a software company: Toward requirements for a community of practice. *Proc. CHI 2002*, ACM Press (2002), 383-390.
54. Muller, M. Revisiting an ethnocritical approach to HCI: Verbal privilege and translation. In T. Erickson & D. McDonald (eds.), *HCI remixed: Reflections on notable HCI papers*, MIT Press, 2007.
55. Muller, M. and Druin, A. Participatory design: The third space in HCI. In J. Jacko (ed.), *The Human-Computer Interaction Handbook* (3rd edition), Mahwah, NJ: Lawrence Erlbaum Associates, in press.
56. Mumford, L. *Technics and Civilization.* University of Chicago Press, 2010. (Originally published 1934, Harcourt, Inc.)
57. Nathan, L.P., Friedman, B., Klasnja, P., Kane, S.K., and Miller, J.K. Envisioning systemic effects on persons and society throughout interactive system design. *Proc. DIS 2008*, ACM Press (2008), 1-10.
58. Nathan, L.P., Lake, M., Gray, N.C, Nilsen, T., Utter, R.F., Utter, E.J., Ring, M., Kahn, Z., & Friedman, B. Multi-lifespan information system design: Investigating a new design approach in Rwanda, *Proc. iConference 2011*, ACM Press (2011), 591-597.
59. Patton, J.W. (2000). Picturing commutes: Informant photography and urban design. *Proc. PDC 2000.* New York: CPSR
60. Pew, R.W., and Mavor, A.S. *Human-system Integration in the System Development Process: A New Look*, National Academies Press, 2007.
61. Piecowye, J. Habitus in transition? CMC use and impacts among young women in the United Arab Emirates. *JCMC* 8(2), 2003.
62. Rode, J. A theoretical agenda for feminist HCI. To appear in *Interacting with Computers.*
63. Saab, D.J. An ethnorelative framework for information system design. *Proc. Fourteenth Americas Conference on Information Systems*, Toronto, 2008.
64. Sanders, E. B.-N. Generative tools for co-designing. *Proc. CoDesigning 2000.* London: Springer.
65. Scales-Trent, J. Racial purity laws in the United States and Nazi Germany: The targeting process, *Human Rights Quart.* 23(2), 260-307, 2001.
66. Schuler, D. and Namioka, A. (eds.). *Participatory Design: Principles and Practices.* Lawrence Erlbaum Associates, Hillsdale, NJ, USA, 1993.
67. Stubblefield, A. "Beyond the pale": Tainted whiteness, cognitive disability, and eugenic sterilization. *Hypatia* 22(2), 163-181, 2007.
68. Suchman, L., and Trigg, R. Understanding practice: Video as a medium for reflection and design. In J. Greenbaum and M. Kyng (eds.), *Design at work: Cooperative design of computer systems.* Erlbaum, Hillsdale NJ USA, 1991.
69. Tschudy, M.W., Dykstra-Erickson, E.A., and Holloway, M.S. PictureCARD: A storytelling tool for task analysis. Proc *PDC'96*, CPSR, Cambridge MA USA, 1996.
70. Wahlsten, D. The malleability of intelligence is not constrained by heredity, in Devlin, B., Feinberg, S.E., Resnick, D.P., & Roeber, K. (eds), *Intelligence, Genes, and Success: Scientists Respond to* The Bell Curve. Springer-Verlag, 1997.
71. Walker, S., and Dearden, A. Designing for civil society. *Interacting with Computers* 17(1), 2005, 1-8.
72. Wang, C., Burris, M.A., and Ping, X.Y. Chinese village women as visual anthropologists: A participatory approach to reaching policymakers. *Social Science and Medicine* 42 (10), 1996, 1391-1440.
73. Weiner, N. *The Human Use of Human Beings: Cybernetics and Society.* Houghton Mifflin, Boston, 1954.
74. Weizenbaum, J. *Computer Power and Human Reason: From Judgment to Calculation.* W.H. Freeman, San Francisco, 1976.
75. Winner, L. Do artifacts have politics? *Daedalus* 109(1), Winter 1980, 121-136.
76. Woelfer, J.P., and Hendry, D.G. Homeless young people's experiences with information systems: Life and work in a community technology center. *Proc. CHI 2010*, ACM Press (2010), 1291-1300.
77. Woelfer, J.P., Iverson, A., Hendry, D.G., Friedman, B. and Gill, B. Improving the safety of homeless young people with mobile phones: Values, form and function. *Proc CHI 2011*, ACM Press (2011), 1707-1716.
78. Wyche, S.P. *Investigating religion and computing: A case for using standpoint theory in technology evaluation studies.* PhD dissertation, Georgia Institute of Technology, 2010.

Being in the Thick of In-the-wild Studies: The Challenges and Insights of Researcher Participation

Rose Johnson[1], Yvonne Rogers[1], Janet van der Linden[2], Nadia Bianchi-Berthouze[1]

1. University College London
Gower St, London, UK.
rose.johnson.11, y.rogers, n.berthouze@ucl.ac.uk

2. The Open University
Milton Keynes, UK.
j.vanderlinden@open.ac.uk

ABSTRACT
We describe the insights and challenges offered by researcher participation in in-the-wild studies through the comparison of two prototype evaluations with varying levels of researcher participation. By reflecting on these studies we expose different facets of the researcher's role when interacting with participants in in-the-wild studies. We also demonstrate the value of researcher participation in contributing to the way a researcher understands participant responses: aiding rapport, promoting empathy and stimulating the researcher to reflect on their own assumptions.

Author Keywords
In-the-wild; participant-observation; prototyping; ethnography;

ACM Classification Keywords
H.5.2 [Information interfaces and presentation]: User Interfaces – User-centered design;

General Terms
Design; Experimentation; Human Factors;

INTRODUCTION
In-the-wild studies are increasing in prevalence as ways of understanding how new technologies may potentially disrupt, support or enhance our everyday activities. In this paper we use the term *in-the-wild* as Rogers [16] uses it to mean studies which involve deploying new technologies in real-use, real-world situations and studying how they are used in this context often with the intention of improving a design. Implicit within this type of methodology is the idea that physical and social context will have a critical effect on usage. However, as Brown et al. [2] point out, these studies often do not acknowledge the potential effect the experimental context might have upon the results. For example, participants will have certain expectations about what investigators are looking for in an experiment, known as demand characteristics, which can affect the way they behave. Participants may put particular effort into using a system regularly in order to please the investigator and be a 'good participant'. Alternatively if participants disagree with the perceived hypothesis they may take care to act in a way that disproves it. Brown et al. [2] advocate recognition of 'investigators as participants'; by this they mean that the investigator and his/her interaction with the participants is part of the study and should be presented as such. This leads to the question: how can researchers account for and manage their influence on participants in-the-wild when so many other factors are at play?

Instead of trying to minimise their effect on participants by distancing themselves, researchers could try to understand this effect by getting more involved – perhaps, even joining in. Being in the thick of in-the-wild studies may offer other benefits as well. For example, sensitising the researcher to key elements of the participant experience to guide interviews or observations.

This paper looks at what happens when the investigator becomes a participant, and asks:

- What roles does the researcher play in an in-wild study and how do these vary?
- What new insights and challenges does investigator participation offer to the prototype evaluation?

We address these questions by describing and reflecting on two exploratory studies of two prototypes designed to help people practice bowing stringed instruments, like the violin. The prototypes are intended to help players by using real-time feedback, either visual or vibrotactile, that responds to players' movements. The idea is to help people adapt their playing as they go, encouraging them to practice good habits. Each study shows a different level of researcher participation. One, where the researcher is participant observer in the sense of sharing a similar perspective to the participants as a fellow orchestra member, and, two, where the investigator actually participated as a player during the study. In comparing these two studies we are able to reflect on how different levels of researcher participation affected what data was available to the researcher and how this was collected and interpreted.

BACKGROUND
The following literature review begins by looking at how researcher participation in different forms is already employed in HCI. It then discusses different methods used in in-the-wild studies, looking at the justifications for different levels of researcher involvement. We then discuss and reflect on the different roles that researchers take in their studies.

Permission to make digital or hard copies of all or part of this work for personal or classroom use is granted without fee provided that copies are not made or distributed for profit or commercial advantage and that copies bear this notice and the full citation on the first page. To copy otherwise, or republish, to post on servers or to redistribute to lists, requires prior specific permission and/or a fee.
CHI'12, May 5–10, 2012, Austin, Texas, USA.
Copyright 2012 ACM 978-1-4503-1015-4/12/05...$10.00.

Ethnography and Reflexivity in HCI

Participant observation is widely used in social sciences and anthropology, most commonly associated with ethnography [1]. It is prized for giving researchers an insider perspective allowing them to interpret their observations with an intimate understanding of the values, beliefs, social norms and experiences of the group or culture being studied. Within HCI, ethnography is used as a way of understanding how people interact and organise themselves in a particular context (e.g. [8]), often to inform design. The ethnographic tradition within HCI is that of "realist ethnographies" [15] which concentrate on giving an authentic and authoritative description of the group or context being studied. In doing so, the investigator's voice is removed from the text preventing discussion of how the researcher's presence in the field, their interactions with participants and their own background and experiences, have shaped the ethnography. By removing this voice the role of participant-observation within ethnography is de-emphasised by eliminating the means to discuss what is in essence an experiential research process [15].

Recently there have been calls for HCI to embrace a more reflexive approach to ethnography, such as that found in digital anthropology [3, 15]. Reflexivity means reflecting upon the way the ethnographer is part of the ethnography itself, their background and perspective is as much part of the research as those of the culture being studied. Although this call for more reflexivity has mainly been addressed towards ethnographers studying existing contexts, it is just as relevant to those doing studies of deployments of new technologies in-the-wild. Perhaps, more so, because deploying a new technology requires hands-on intervention into the daily routines of a setting.

Investigating Experience

The real-time feedback we are studying with our prototypes offers learning through experience rather than being a more theoretical or reflective learning process. As Light [12] points out, gaining access to and understanding another person's experience is very difficult; interviewees often analyse or try to account for their actions rather than talking about their experience at the time. Light advocates a particular type of interview method to get around such obstacles, which is similar in style to the "second person interview" method [14] used in cognitive science to access accounts of subjective experience. This method appears particularly good at accessing fleeting thoughts which often do not appear in standard interviews. However there is a danger that unpacking experience into a layered chronology of actions and thoughts could lose a holistic view on experience, that may be equally as important.

Wright and McCarthy [21] have a different take on how designers may gain access to users' experiences: empathy. For them the designer's aim to 'know the user' means "understanding what it feels like to be that person". Participant observation "can be seen as an attempt to build up the kind of relationship, both participant and observer, both closed and separate, that allows people to understand what it is like to be the other." We suggest the empathetic relationship built up between participant-observer and user through shared experience can be a fruitful way to study the experience of users testing prototypes in-the-wild.

Participation in-the-wild

There are not many examples where the researcher becomes a participant in a deployment where a prototype is being evaluated. The work of Kientz and Abowd [11] is a rare example in which a designer, having trained and worked as a therapist for 10 months, continued to work as part of the therapy team during the evaluation of a prototype system. Their paper details the potential danger that investigator participation might have in biasing the uptake of a system. They justify the researcher's involvement by arguing that she took role of 'champion', described by Grudin [7] as being critical to the uptake of new technology. Additionally the researcher's position in the therapy team was valuable as technical support.

We would argue that even when the investigator does not come into contact with participants they are implicitly asking participants to use their prototype by providing it. By agreeing to take part in the study the therapists are already showing their intention to use the system and be 'good participants' [2]. The researcher's relationship with the therapy team and first-hand experience with the prototypes may have produced rich qualitative data and an insightful analytic perspective; however this is not discussed in their paper.

In-the-wild Studies

In-the-wild studies, which evaluate prototypes in ways that acknowledge the realities of their intended context of use, offer different findings to those from laboratory studies [17]. For example, new and unexpected uses [10, 19, 20], long term behaviour change [18], the process of interpreting new technology [18, 19] and the ability for a technology to suggest its use and interaction mode in a setting [13].

Some in-the-wild studies have the feature that the researcher interacts very little with participants. One such example is the deployment of a multi-touch table in a tourist office to help people plan a day in Cambridge [13]. During this study, researchers observed participants using the table in a fly-on-the-wall manner. By keeping this distance they were able to evaluate how people naturally approached the table-top, and found this to be different to the way people congregate around them in lab studies. The tourist centre is a public place and participants behave in the knowledge that strangers may be watching. Indeed, some of the more self-conscious first interactions with the system show this. In public settings the presence of the researcher is unlikely to affect people's behaviour because they are already putting on a public face. However, in more private or sociable situations the researcher is likely to have much greater impact; people may become self-conscious and censor their behaviour in a way they would not do otherwise because the researcher is watching. This means that fly-on-the-wall observations would no-longer produce true representations of how people naturally interact with a system.

In-the-wild studies have approached collecting data from non-public settings in a number of different ways. Gaver et al. [5] assigned a documentary film-maker to visit the participants and make a film about their experience. In some ways this could be criticised as enhancing the amount of self-censorship participants may perform because they are presenting a public face. On the other hand, participants may become less preoccupied with trying to please the researcher because they now perceive their audience as the film-maker and the general public. Participants are instead trying to help the film-maker by talking in sound-bites and presenting a coherent story. This new perspective may be particularly productive when taken in conjunction with the ethnographic observations they also conducted.

Another approach is to build up a familiar relationship with participants so that the researcher is no longer a stranger for whom they have to perform, but a normal part of the setting. In our previous study [20] we were careful to build a close relationship with the teachers before and during the study. We worked as a team during lessons: as they taught we acted as technical support making sure the prototypes did what was needed. We consider that this collaboration meant we became a familiar part of that teaching setting.

Roles of the researcher

The studies described here present many different roles the researcher may take within a study. A common role within many of these studies is the researcher as *facilitator* - facilitating the user by providing the technology. In some cases, this role extends beyond providing the technology to acting as "*champion*" [11] – encouraging its use. Related to the *facilitator* role is that of the researcher as *technical support* [11, 20]; a role which can also act as a way of building up positive relationships with participants.

A difference is whether the researcher takes the role of *explainer* of the technology and the study. In some cases, this is an integral part of the study [20]. In others, the research question means that the researcher decidedly avoids this role [13, 18]. In a third type [19], the intention is to avoid explaining a particular use for a system; here the researcher takes a borderline role explaining some things while leaving others open for interpretation.

The researcher's role when observing can take many forms, based on how closely he or she interacts with participants. For example the role of the researcher in Marshall et al. [13] and van der Linden et al. [20] are very different although in both cases they were carrying out observations. This comes from the way they are perceived by participants, in one case they are *strangers* in the background; in the other they are well known to the participants and seen more as *colleagues or friends*. There are other roles the researcher can take in their relationship with participants. For example, action research advocates the role of *"friendly outsider"* working *with* the community rather than *for* them [9]. Another example is ethnography where the researcher attempts to become an *insider,* the success of which is measured through the perception of those being studied [8]. What is important in all these roles is not how researchers view themselves but how they are perceived by participants.

OBJECTIVES

The literature shows that there is an on-going debate within HCI about how to study the way people interact in the real-world. A central question is the extent to which research findings are the product of the way data is collected by the researcher and how this should be accounted for in the way research is presented. Here, we aim to contribute to this debate by presenting and reflecting on two studies that use researcher participation to investigate the deployment of technologies to help violin practice. Both studies can be considered to be in-the-wild; they examine the deployment of technology in the greater context of the learning and practicing process of the participants. The first study aimed to help university orchestra players to practice individually by introducing a new technology addressing a request from the conductor for longer bowing. The second study aimed to explore the potential for similar technology to be used in group practice where the tasks could be determined by the participants. This took place at a week-long orchestral summer school. In our description of these studies, we give details of the prototypes and the findings to provide understanding of the purposes and outcome of each deployment. However, this is not our main focus. Instead we concentrate on the way the researcher interacted with participants and the setting and how this affected the way the data was collected and understood.

STUDY 1

The aim of this study was to explore different modalities of real-time feedback for use in music practice. Previous research showed the efficacy of vibrotactile feedback to aid teaching violin [20]. However most people spend more time practising than in lessons, therefore, this study chose to focus on individual practice. The different modalities investigated were vibrotactile feedback and visual feedback. Both modalities have different qualities in terms of the complexity of information that can be displayed, how they reference the body, and how intrusive they are. This study investigates how these aspects are important when designing real-time feedback.

The study was carried out with a university orchestra and the intervention was motivated by comments from the conductor during rehearsals asking the violinists to use longer bows in certain sections of the pieces. The researcher responded to this by building the MuSense prototypes which draw on previous work described in [20]. The study took place in practice rooms and labs on campus. The tasks were taken directly from the music they were practicing for a concert.

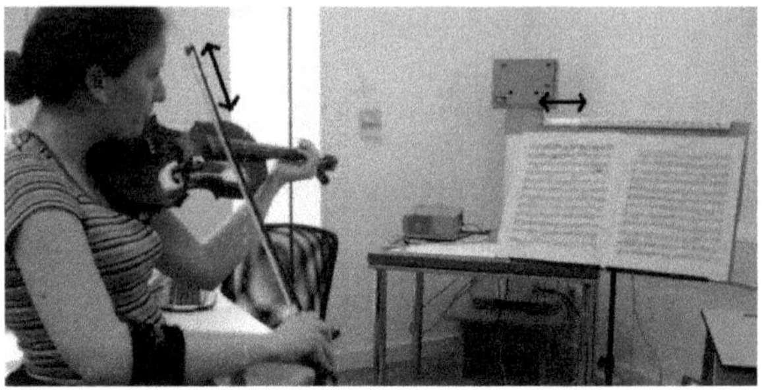

Figure 1. Using the complex visual feedback

Prototype I – MuSense

The MuSense prototypes used in this study focussed on the amount of bow used by the participants. As with many other aspects of technique there is no single ideal – players don't always want to use full bow lengths, but there are cases where this is essential. To give a clear task we used sections of the music chosen by the conductor where full-bows are important.

Feedback was given to participants either as a vibration on the wrist of the bowing arm or as a visual display. The vibrotactile feedback came on once the player had done a sufficiently long bow-stroke and stayed on until the player's bow changed direction. The visual feedback was a row of LEDs fixed to the music-stand (see Fig. 1) in the player's peripheral vision. Two alternative visual mappings were used in order to explore the different levels of complexity visual feedback has to offer. A simple visual display was used to show the visual equivalent of the vibrotactile feedback. Once the bow had moved through a certain length, the entire row lit up green. A more complex display was designed to provide more detailed feedback. Lights come on gradually to show the length of bow used so far (See Fig. 1). Once past a certain point the lights change from blue to green to show the point where the player is using a 'good' amount of bow.

Implementation

A gyroscope linked up to an Arduino Pro Mini (a microcontroller see http://arduino.cc) and positioned on the player's lower arm was used as a way to infer the length of bow being used. The gyroscope signal was integrated to get the angle the arm moves through as the player bows. This angle is closely related to the length of bow used and gives accurate enough feedback for this link to be readily apparent to the player. This data was then transmitted using a wireless serial connection (XBee). The vibrotactile feedback was delivered using 10mm shaftless DC motors controlled by an Arduino. The visual display was made from 22 RGB LEDs controlled by an Arduino and two TLC5940 PWM chips.

Study Set-up

Fifteen participants were recruited from the university orchestra by the investigator who was also a member. The orchestra was made up from university staff and people from the local area, with a range of abilities and ages (20-70+). The researcher was at the lower end of this age group, and a mid-level player among the second violin section. This meant that she was often working with players who were more experienced.

Each session took a similar format: The participant played the selected sections for five minutes as they would normally practice them. They then played the same sections this time focussing on maximising their bow strokes. They were asked to play the same parts three more times using each type of feedback for about five minutes each. They finished by playing each section twice without the feedback. During the session, bowing data was recorded and at the end there was a short semi-structured interview lasting ten minutes.

Summary of Findings

Participants were able to quickly learn to use and understand the feedback in the context of the task. The bow length data suggests that the introduction of the feedback changed their bow usage. In some cases, this meant more bow was used. In others, a wider variation in the amount of bow used, which related to the players experimenting with different bowing styles.

People who liked the complex visual feedback said they did so because it showed them how close they were to reaching the target each time. However, other participants criticised it for not catching their attention enough, saying the changes in the display were too subtle. The simple visual feedback was considered more noticeable than the complex one, but some found the flashing too off-putting and difficult to interpret. People who liked the vibrotactile feedback did so, because it did not interfere with them reading the music and they found the vibrations easier to interpret than visual signals. However, those who preferred the visual feedback claimed they found the vibrations difficult to interpret and the visual line fitted better with their mental model of the bow.

Reflections

The following section contains extracts taken from the researcher's own account of her experience of setting up and running the study. These allow us to examine some of the characteristics of the role she played when interacting with participants and how they affected the study.

The researcher as encourager

The following account describes how the researcher used individual emails and her personal relationships to encourage participation in the study:

"Initially an email was sent to all string players through the orchestra organisers. This produced some replies but not enough for the study. Therefore I resorted to sending individual emails to people I knew within the orchestra (and later to people I didn't know so well too). These had a much higher response rate. I do not believe people necessarily felt pressurised to participate by these emails, but personal emails do imply a need to reply in the way a group email does not. People have to actively make a

decision whether to participate and generally they were willing to. I believe that some of the motivation for people to participate was to help me as a person as well as to find out about and support the research itself. A £5 gift voucher was also offered however it did not seem a primary motivation – some even said that they did not want it."

The researcher as friend/colleague

Building on personal relationships with participants during recruitment sets-ups an atmosphere of familiarity, which continued into the study and affected the way participants interacted with the researcher. For example, criticism of the devices was often phrased in a constructive way, giving enough detail to enable improvements or balanced with a positive comment. This kind of interaction shows participants are responding to the researcher, both on a personal level and as a data gatherer and that they recognise that she has an emotional interest in the long-term success of the design.

The researcher's position as fellow member of the orchestra also gave her particular insights into the way the participants felt about being asked to carry out the tasks for the study as the following reflections discuss:

"Nearly all participants seemed nervous. I could empathise with this nervousness, playing on your own is revealing something very different about yourself to playing in an orchestra. I offered reassurance by admitting that I couldn't play these parts myself and joking that maybe the conductor had chosen the hardest parts to get us to practice. Being a member of the orchestra gave me the facilities to identify with the emotions of the participants and offer reassurance in a way a stranger could not."

The researcher's authority

To test the device, the tasks in the study needed to focus on long bowing. Tasks also needed to be useful to participants outside the study itself in order to make practice meaningful to participants. To choose such tasks and say that they will be useful requires *authority* that comes from a high level of musical knowledge. However, as the previous sections suggest, the researcher presented herself as being a musical *equal* to the participants. For this reason it was very useful that the tasks themselves were sections of the current repertoire selected by the conductor as being relevant. This meant the researcher could use the conductor's authority to justify the need for long bows without the need to claim any access to special knowledge herself. This is something she used during the study as many participants pointed out that this was not how they would choose to play those sections otherwise.

STUDY 2

Some of the qualitative insights from study 1 provoked us to question whether feedback could be used in group playing. Can feedback be designed to support the sense of being part of an ensemble, or does feedback make people feel more separate?

We chose a week long adult music summer school as a setting to explore the concept of real-time feedback in ensemble playing. This summer school offers a wide range of courses, including orchestral, folk, jazz and chamber ensembles. The study was planned so that a researcher would be at the summer school attending some courses and meeting with participants in groups during their free time to try out the prototypes. This participatory approach was chosen in order to get an insider view of what it is like to be a student there and to build a rapport with participants outside of the study setting. The researcher also participated in playing with participants during the study, using the prototype like one of them. The idea was to share the experience of playing in an ensemble with the prototypes. Unfortunately, due to timetable constraints, participants were only free to meet singly or in pairs. This meant the role of the researcher as ensemble player became more valuable than initially expected because in many cases it was her participation which changed the setting from the participant playing alone to playing in a group.

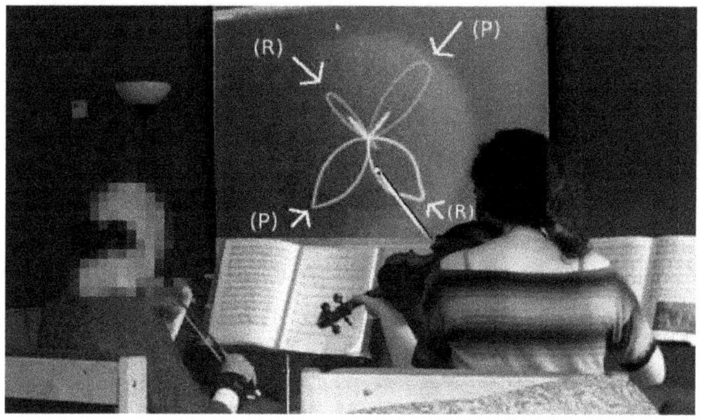

Figure 2. Participant (P) and researcher (R) playing together with the visualisation

Prototype II: Shared Visualisation

Prototype II was designed for flexible group usage: flexible in the sense that it could be used to support a number of different goals on the theme of bowing; group meaning that it supports ensemble playing. The original MuSense prototype was altered and used sensors that were networked so they could contribute to a group visualisation. This visualisation was projected onto a large screen in front of the players (see Fig. 2). Each bow stroke was represented as a petal-like shape which gets wider over time and longer with the length of the bow used. Each player produces petals of a particular colour on a particular axis. Petals from the last 4 bow strokes remain on screen to allow people to practise bowing patterns. The flower-like layout was designed to let players see at a glance if they were using similar amounts of bow to others by looking at its symmetry, and to give the sense that everyone's bowing combined made the overall shape – displaying individuals as part of a group. The visualisation aimed to be non-judgemental, presenting information that can be interpreted in different ways depending on the learner's goal. This group visualisation replaced the lights on the music stand from the previous study.

The vibrotactile feedback was not made into a shared display. This is because the vibrations were seen as personal, being felt on the individual's body. Changes were made to the vibrotactile feedback to allow more flexible use. This study did not have a specified task; participants could aim for different styles of bowing as they saw fit. To allow this choice, an adjusting knob was added which changed the place along the bow where the vibrations were triggered. This meant that participants could aim for long bows or they could change the settings and aim for short bows by avoiding the vibrations. Adjusting this knob also changed the scale on the visual display to keep the two types of feedback consistent with one another. A side-effect of these changes in implementation was that the vibrotactile feedback was slightly less intense than in the study 1.

Study set-up

Initially, six participants agreed to take part in the study at the summer school, four violinists; one viola player and one cellist. They came from a variety of musical backgrounds: including jazz, folk and classical music. All participants were older than the researcher and many of them were better practiced musicians than her. Five of them had been to the summer school before. This shows that in this setting the participants were more expert than the researcher and the researcher tried to work in a way that respected this.

The summer school lasted five days plus a day of concerts. The original intention was to meet with participants for approximately 40 minutes every day, although as the week progressed, other demands such as tiredness and concert preparation meant that most participants chose to have at least one day off from the study. We also had some more serendipitous participation, for example, another student joined one session because she heard about it over lunch and one the tutors also came and tried it out. Sessions were held in the common room of one of the residential buildings. Over the week, the researcher kept a journal of her reflections on her experience at the summer school.

Summary of findings

The visual feedback did not work well during the sessions because most people said they were not aware of it once they started playing (we were playing from sheet music). This contrasts with the findings from study 1 in which the visual feedback was noticeable and useful to the players. This could be accounted for by the differences in position and representation of the feedback. In study 1, it was fixed to the music-stand in players' peripheral vision. In study 2, it was projected on the wall beyond players' peripheral vision. In study 1 the feedback came on or changed colour to indicate a goal achieved, while in study 2, there was no sudden change like this to grab the participant's attention. Participants did think it could be useful for exercises not involving written music and for working on ensemble pieces once the music had been memorised.

There was an even split in the participants over whether people were aware of the vibrotactile feedback while playing. Those who said they could feel the feedback while playing preferred it to the visualisation because they could use it more easily while reading music. The reports of not feeling the feedback contrast with the results from study 1 where no participants reported being unaware of the vibro-tactile feedback to this extent. This may be because the task in study 1 placed the feedback in the foreground; whereas the activities in study 2 placed the feedback in the background.

Reflections

The findings become more meaningful when taken as part of the study as a whole, bringing into account the context of the summer school and the researcher's experience conducting and participating in the study. The following includes extracts from the researcher's reflections on the study and shows how they contribute to the overall impact of the results on her on-going inquiry into how to design real-time feedback for musicians.

Becoming familiar with the setting

"Everyone I spoke to enjoyed attending the summer school and many came every year. It was an incredibly busy place. Courses were timetabled between 8am – 8pm (with breaks) most participants only had an hour spare during this time. I also experienced this attending 4 hours of courses each day, running the study the rest of the time. In to the evening there were student concerts and entertainment. Additionally there were informal jam sessions, people grabbing one-to-one time with tutors, even a midnight rendition of Mendelssohn's violin concerto arranged for octet. In every corner of the place people were making music. This is what they came for; it felt peculiar to be here for another reason.

Such full days meant that as the week continues, I and others around me, began to become tired. I also began to suffer from pain and numbness in my shoulders (due to my own bad technique). As I started to take pain-killers myself I began to notice the odd packet of pills on other people's tables at lunch. Then, one participant asked to miss a session due to back pain. No-one wanted to give in to these physical demands though – a sign of how much people love playing at the school."

These incidents demonstrate that participants' time was precious. Time is not of equal value in every context; time at the school was much more valuable than it would be in many other places. Taking part in the study asked participants to give up time which could be spent on many other activities. The researcher came to understand this through participating in the summer school. It meant that she interpreted missed sessions differently because she understood the contextual reasons for them. It also meant she valued the compliment when one participant chose to attend every session and saying how useful she found it.

The example of the aches and pains also shows how things become salient to the researcher through participation. She only began to notice that others were suffering from tiredness as she began to feel it herself. She may have noticed the trend at that point anyway, but participation ensured that experiences like this that were salient for the participants were also salient to her.

The researcher as explainer

Another aspect of the researcher's role is explaining what the prototypes do and what the study is about. The following extract describes how the researcher approached this and some of the dilemmas that arose. In particular, finding a middle way between explaining a system and encouraging users to build their own interpretation of it:

"Presenting the prototypes to participants was difficult. This study was not about completing tasks, it was about finding where or whether the prototypes could be useful in real-world ensemble practice. For this reason I did not want to present a fixed interpretation of the feedback. This gave the initial challenge of how to explain what the prototypes do without explaining how to use them. This is difficult because for most participants music practice is purposeful activity. This means that for participants to truly engage with the system, it has to be seen to be useful. So as I was explaining the system I felt I had to also explain its usefulness. I did this by giving scenarios of usage for example aiming for long bows or aiming for short bows. However, I believe that the participants found this ambiguity disconcerting. Particularly, because it expects people to judge how they want to use it when they are not yet familiar with what it can do."

The researcher as facilitator or encourager

The following reflections show how the researcher found it difficult to achieve her intention to *facilitate* practice with the prototypes rather than *encourage* a particular type of practice.

"On the first day the participants went along with my suggestions of what to play. Gradually through the week things changed and the participants became more willing to suggest pieces they would like to work on. When this happened the session went much better in many ways. The relationship between us became more collaborative. The technology moved from the foreground (the reason for playing the music), to the background (something there to help while playing the music). Of course, this made it more difficult for the prototypes to have an effect, but this was part of the research to know whether people were still aware of them when focussing on the music. I tried to be proactive in encouraging participants to make suggestions - trying to think of things they might like to practice and suggesting them. However this has drawbacks; when you are getting to know people it is difficult to stop a suggestion from implying an instruction."

This shows how it takes time to build a relationship and confidence with participants where they feel comfortable suggesting their own ideas.

The researcher as an equal

Often in research the researcher comes across as authoritative, even omniscient within the domain of the study. However, in this study the researcher took a different approach:

"I did not wish to take on the role of authoritative researcher as I was interested in what participants chose to do with the feedback themselves rather than instructing them or enforcing any particular task upon them. Nor was I in any position to take on the role of a teacher, most participants were considerably better players than myself. In some ways this felt uncomfortable as I do not think this fitted with their expectations, however, I felt that by giving up the authoritative position I became a more equal participant."

Relationship with the research and participants

The issue of authority brings up questions of confidence. In the following extract, the researcher discusses how her rapport with the participants, belief in the prototypes and self-confidence were interconnected.

"My rapport with J was different from the others because I believed that I and the technology could help her improve her bowing and because she believed it too. We also had a lot of previous contact via email and she played a style of music I was more familiar with. All this meant I felt I could give some advice and point out areas where she could improve or should try and listen to the prototype. This sometimes reversed when she pointed out that I was not making as large shapes on the visual display as she was and this motivated me to try harder to use longer bows in my own playing."

"I felt less confident doing this with the other participants because I was too conscious of my own inadequacies particularly my inferior sight-reading. This meant I did not have the confidence to give advice. Similarly, I knew I was not a good example of bowing as I did not trigger the feedback very regularly. Instead I tried to be a good example of self-analysis by saying aloud whether I had managed to trigger the feedback and what I thought that meant."

These reflections show how confidence and a shared belief in the potential success of the study created a positive rapport between the researcher and participant. This in turn caused the researcher to have the confidence to contribute in a more hands-on way. J had the most successful experience with the prototypes, whether the positive rapport described here is a symptom or a cause of this success is difficult to distinguish – most likely it is both.

The benefit of participation

Participating in the study made several things more difficult; the researcher could not observe the other participants in the normal way and was often too busy to ask questions. However as the extract below describes, the experience of participation gave her a different perspective on her designs which will have a larger impact on her future research than the initial findings would suggest.

"When I designed the prototypes and tested them in the first study I was not thinking in the same way as when I was using them and participating in the second study. Study 2 has taught me to focus on designing for the in-the-moment experience of using the feedback, this is where the design will hold-up or fall-down. Before, as I built the prototypes I imagined users in the third person; now, I imagine user experience in the first person. I had tested the prototypes on myself before but never under the same level of cognitive

load or with the same seriousness. Never before in the belief that I was one of the participants, one of the users."

DISCUSSION

The researcher can play a variety of roles when conducting an in-the-wild study. However, it may be more helpful to think of the researcher's role as being characterised by their position along several dimensions, rather than discrete roles. These go beyond the idea of the researcher being either more or less involved in a study. Instead, they try to characterise the ways the researcher is involved and how this is perceived by participants. These are: (1) facilitating or encouraging, (2) explaining, (3) level of authority, (4) familiarity with participants, and, (5) relationship with their research.

1. Facilitating or encouraging

This can be thought of as how the researcher involves themselves with participants to ensure the technology is used or a study fits a certain format. At one end of the spectrum, the researcher may simply facilitate use by providing the technology in an accessible place [13] at the other a researcher may schedule sessions [20], offer rewards, or champion the technology [11] to potential participants.

In both studies, the researcher was closer to the encouraging end of the spectrum. It is very difficult to be otherwise when you are in direct contact with participants since a simple question very easily has a subtext which implies a request. This is best illustrated with an example from the researcher's reflections about study 2:

"At the end of each session I asked if we could meet the next day. It is clear from the context of this question that I want to meet them tomorrow – they know I want to collect as much data as possible, it leaves them in the position where they need a reason not to come rather than a reason to come. There were cases where participants mentioned they wanted a particular day off and once I knew about this I felt it was my responsibility towards them to make sure not ask this question at the end of the session but to confirm "you're not coming tomorrow" to show that this is all right."

It is important to recognise that often a participant's motivation is to help the *researcher* as much as the *research*. As can be seen from the example above the effect of this is nuanced and the researcher must be aware how this provides a particular subtext to all their conversations. A similar example can be found in the reflections from of study 1.

2. Explaining

How much does the researcher explain how to use the system or what it is they are looking for in the study? This issue relates to facilitation and encouragement in that explaining a system facilitates its use, and depending on the context, may also encourage it too. It also implies authority as explaining how to use something shows the researcher has additional knowledge to the participant.

In both studies it was part of the investigator's role to explain how to use the prototypes. The difficulty of this role changed with the aim of the study. In study 1, the prototype could be described as a system to help you practice long bowing. What each display meant was described in terms of this aim, for example, a vibration meant you had succeeded in using a long bow. In study 2, there was no fixed task. The explanatory role of the researcher was a much more difficult one: to give an explanation of what the prototype does without attaching a fixed interpretation to the feedback. Comparing the two studies, the goal based explanation in study 1 was a more effective way to communicate what the prototypes did, and did not prevent participants from suggesting a multitude of alternative uses in the interviews. We would argue that initially presenting prototypes through structured task-based experiences may be the most appropriate way of explaining technologies like real-time feedback, as having a concrete experience of using the prototype to achieve one goal appears to inspire re-imagining it in new situations.

3. Level of Authority

By authority we mean the extent to which the researcher is seen as having authority over the participant or being their equal or inferior. In traditional lab experiments, the researcher acts with authority over participants, telling them what to do and having superior knowledge in knowing the true intentions of the study. In some cases, this may be useful to a study; in others this inequality may obstruct building a rapport with participants.

In an in-the-wild study, authority may come from different types of knowledge and act in different ways. For example, in study 1 musical authority had to be 'borrowed' from the conductor to make the tasks meaningful. That the researcher was musically an equal also proved useful, as participants said they would have been more nervous playing for the conductor. However completely relinquishing the researcher's authority also runs the risk of undermining the study; participants are giving time to the researcher too and they need to believe that the researcher has the expertise to use their time appropriately.

4. Familiarity with participants

In many studies, the researcher and participants are strangers to one another and never move beyond this point. In other cases researchers may build a much closer relationship with participants. This can potentially lead to a clearer understanding of their motivations and a familiarity with the way they communicate. It may mean that participants are willing to confide in the researcher, revealing things they would not in a first meeting. It may also remove some of the social awkwardness which characterises some of the interactions. However, part of forming a friendship with participants involves being responsible towards them and the researcher must judge when that responsibility takes precedence over their research agenda.

In study 1, the researcher already knew the participants; in study 2, this was not the case but she did build up a friendship with them over the week. This was rewarding both personally and in terms of research. However, it does also produce anxiety when writing up, for example about analysing interactions with participants because it does not give the holistic view of the genuine goodwill between both sides. The audience in that case is not only the CHI readers but also the participants who took part in both studies.

The two studies also show how becoming familiar with the context and sharing the participant's experiences also enables the researcher to better understand and empathise with participants. For example, in study 1, the researcher was able to recognise and empathise with the nervousness of her participants because she was a fellow orchestra player. In study 2, she came to understand the preciousness of participants' time through participation in the summer school. Gaining this kind of contextual knowledge facilitated better communication with participants.

5. The researcher's relationship with the research

The researcher's feelings about the research affect the way s/he interacts with participants. For example, in study 2, there were times where the researcher felt confident that the feedback was helpful for a participant and this made her more confident in her interactions with them. In study 1, the participants phrased their criticism in a way that recognised the researcher's involvement in the design and creation of the prototypes and their future intentions to improve them.

Even in less involved studies, participants' perceptions of the relationship between the researcher and the study may have consequences for the results. This comes back to the idea of demand characteristics. If the participants believe that the researcher has an emotional investment in the success of that particular prototype, they will be kind about it. If they believe instead that the researcher needs to be able to build a successful system in the future, they may be more forthcoming with criticism. This is one reason among many [4, 6] why the research community needs to embrace failure as much as success; because if a prototype has to be a success for the research to be valued, then researchers will always have an emotional investment in the success of a prototype – one that they may not be able to help communicating to participants.

Participation in in-the-wild studies

As already discussed, participant observation in ethnography is used to give the researcher an insider view on the experiences and values of the people they are studying. It also demands reflexivity, challenging the investigator to question their own role in the research. Current methods employed in in-the-wild studies do not normally show this level of reflexivity or consideration for the social and personal context beyond the boundary of the interaction being studied. Dourish and Bell ask [4] - "how many ubicomp papers or presentations account for the author's stance?" By joining with participants in their activities, the researcher can start to have their own perspective transformed and learn a little about what it is like to be a participant. For example, in study 2, the researcher learnt through participation how valuable time at the summer school was to the participants and how tired they were feeling. These may seem like small findings, but this is what participation reveals – many small details. These details are invaluable as the researcher tries to interpret the actions and words of those around her. They are also important for building rapport with participants – as Rode [15] puts it "when in the field they [ethnographers, but, perhaps, more generally researchers] must make a hundred little decisions to gain rapport". How could the researcher sensibly discuss how to make the prototypes more useful to participants at the summer school without this kind of contextual understanding? Without a shared understanding of the value of time and playing together; without knowing what repertoire is being played - where the difficult parts are and what the conductor said in the last rehearsal - these things can only be known by being present and involved.

These benefits do not necessarily come from taking part in the study; they come from participating in the context the study sits in, i.e. in study 1, being a member of the orchestra; in study 2, participation in the summer school. We would argue that there is additional value in a researcher participating in the study, itself. The primary one is the way the first-hand experience of using the prototypes under research conditions surprised the researcher and changed her perspective on her designs as well as her interpretation of the feedback from other participants. One may argue that such experience threatens researcher impartiality because the researcher will assume that other participants' experiences are variations of her own. However, it is common for designers and researchers to test prototypes on themselves to check that they work. These kinds of tests are often in a completely different setting, and create similar but less accurate preconceptions about what participants' experiences will be like. By using the prototypes together with participants under the same conditions, the researcher has the opportunity to both gain the first-hand experience of using the prototypes and have the generalizability of that experience directly challenged through discussion with the participants around them.

Gaining first-hand experience, using prototypes, provides additional means to empathise with participants – to see the world from the participant's perspective. This understanding of another's perspective can be built between people through a dialogue but this dialogue draws on a common understanding of human experiences and the ability to imagine the self in the other's position [21]. For Wright and McCarthy the value of empathy to the designer is not about becoming the user but about responding "to what they see as the user's world from their own perspective." Similarly, the value to the researcher of participating in a study is about gaining the breadth of experience that allows them through dialogue to imagine the world from the perspective of the participant and respond to this.

Participating in a research study needs a lot of practical consideration. A participating researcher uses a lot of their mental and physical energy in participating – they cannot expect to be as aware of things around them as they might in a purely observational study. While participating, the researcher cannot take the long-view and spot patterns as they emerge. Just as ethnographers factor time into their days to write-up notes and think over their experiences so a researcher participating in a deployment needs to allow themselves this time, ideally, with an opportunity to follow-up their thinking in the field with the same participants.

CONCLUSION AND FUTURE WORK

Researcher participation in-the-wild offers a new perspective on deployments, offering insights which arise from understanding context, building rapport with participants and empathy based on shared experience. It is also a method that has reflexivity at its core and cannot be effectively used without the researcher constantly reflecting on their role within the research. In some studies, full participation may not always be accessible to the researcher (e.g. nursing). Future research needs to examine how participation in a complimentary role (e.g. as an assistant) can provide similar insights and how this affects the relationship between researcher and participants.

ACKNOWLEDGEMENTS

We would like to thank all the participants that took part in the studies and the organisers of the summer school and orchestra. We also thank the CHI reviewers, whose feedback has greatly influenced the final version of this paper.

REFERENCES

1. Atkinson, P. & Hammersley, M. "Ethnography and participant observation," *Handbook of qualitative research*, vol. 1, 248–261, 1994.
2. Brown, B., Reeves, S. & Sherwood, S. "Into the wild: challenges and opportunities for field trial methods," in *Proc. CHI* 2011, 1657-1666.
3. Dourish, P. & Bell, G. "Divining a digital future: mess and mythology in ubiquitous computing" MIT Press, 2011.
4. Gaver, W., Bowers, J., Kerridge, T., Boucher, A., & Jarvis, N. "Anatomy of a failure: how we knew when our design went wrong, and what we learned from it," in *Proc. CHI* 2009, 2213–2222.
5. Gaver, W. "Cultural commentators: Non-native interpretations as resources for polyphonic assessment," *International Journal of Human-Computer Studies*, vol. 65, pp. 292-305, Apr. 2007.
6. Greenberg, S. & Buxton, B. "Usability evaluation considered harmful (some of the time)," in *Proc. CHI* 2008, 111–120.
7. Grudin, J. "Groupware and social dynamics: eight challenges for developers," *Communications of the ACM*, vol. 37, pp. 92-105, Jan. 1994.
8. Harper, R. H. R. "The organisation in ethnography–a discussion of ethnographic fieldwork programs in CSCW," *Computer Supported Cooperative Work*, vol. 9, no. 2, pp. 239–264, 2000.
9. Hayes, G. R. "The relationship of action research to human-computer interaction," *ACM Transactions on Computer-Human Interaction*, vol. 18, pp. 1-20, July 2011.
10. Jambon, F. & Meillon, B. "User experience evaluation in the wild," in *CHI EA* 2009, 4069–4074.
11. Kientz, J. A. & Abowd, G. D. "When the designer becomes the user: designing a system for therapists by becoming a therapist," in *CHI EA 2008*, 2071-2078.
12. Light, A. "Adding method to meaning: a technique for exploring peoples' experience with technology," *Behaviour & Information Technology*,.25, 2, pp. 175–187, 2006.
13. Marshall, P., Morris, R., Rogers, Y., Kreitmayer, S. & Davies, M. "Rethinking 'multi-user': an in-the-wild study of how groups approach a walk-up-and-use tabletop interface," in *Proc. CHI 2011*, 3033–3042.
14. Petitmengin, C. "Describing one's subjective experience in the second person: An interview method for the science of consciousness," *Phenomenology and the Cognitive Sciences*, vol. 5, no. 3, pp. 229–269, 2006.
15. Rode, J. A. "Reflexivity in Digital Anthropology," in *Proc. CHI* 2011, 123-132.
16. Rogers, Y. "Interaction design gone wild: striving for wild theory," *Interactions,* 18:4, 58-62, 2011.
17. Rogers, Y., Connelly, K., Tedesco, L., Hazlewood, W. R., Kurtz, A., Hall, R. E., Hursey, J. & Toscos, T. "Why it's worth the hassle: the value of in-situ studies when designing Ubicomp," in *Proc. UbiComp* 2007, 336–353.
18. Rogers, Y., Hazlewood, W. R., Marshall, P., Dalton, N., & Hertrich, S. "Ambient influence: can twinkly lights lure and abstract representations trigger behavioral change?" in *Proc. UbiComp 2010*, 261–270.
19. Sengers, P. and Gaver, B. "Staying open to interpretation: engaging multiple meanings in design and evaluation," in *Proc. DIS* 2006, 99-108.
20. van der Linden, J., Johnson, R., Bird, J., Rogers, Y. & Schoonderwaldt, E. "Buzzing to play: lessons learned from an in the wild study of real-time vibrotactile feedback," in *Proc. CHI* 2011, 533–542.
21. Wright, P. & McCarthy, J. "Empathy and experience in HCI," in *Proc. CHI* 2008, 637–646.

The *Envisioning Cards*: A Toolkit for Catalyzing Humanistic and Technical Imaginations

Batya Friedman and David G. Hendry
The Information School
University of Washington
Seattle, WA 98195-2840
{batya, dhendry}@uw.edu

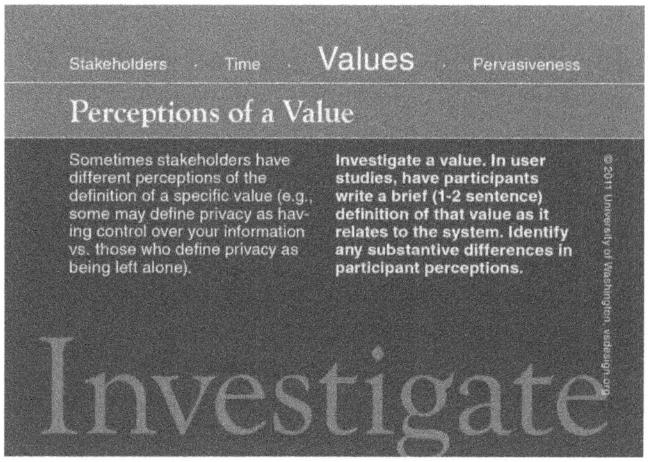

ABSTRACT
We introduce the *Envisioning Cards* – a versatile toolkit for attending to human values during design processes – and discuss their early use. Drawing on almost twenty years of work in value sensitive design, the Envisioning Cards are built upon a set of four envisioning criteria: stakeholders, time, values, and pervasiveness. Each card contains on one side a title and an evocative image related to the card theme; on the flip side, the card shows the envisioning criterion, elaborates on the theme, and provides a focused design activity. Reports from the field demonstrate use in a range of research and design activities including ideation, co-design, heuristic critique, and more.

Author Keywords
Design method; creativity; Envisioning Cards; time; pervasiveness; stakeholders; values; value sensitive design

ACM Classification Keywords
H.5.m Information interfaces and presentation (e.g., HCI): Miscellaneous.

Permission to make digital or hard copies of all or part of this work for personal or classroom use is granted without fee provided that copies are not made or distributed for profit or commercial advantage and that copies bear this notice and the full citation on the first page. To copy otherwise, or republish, to post on servers or to redistribute to lists, requires prior specific permission and/or a fee.
CHI'12, May 5–10, 2012, Austin, Texas, USA.
Copyright 2012 ACM 978-1-4503-1015-4/12/05...$10.00.

INTRODUCTION
In a recent cover story for *interactions*, Liam Bannon has called for a rethinking of HCI, inviting the field to reorient itself, to be "centered on the exploration of new forms of living with and through technologies that give primacy to human actors, their values, and their activities" [1, p. 50]. This call for an even greater focus on what is important to individuals, groups, and societies, that is, a more human-centered perspective, will require the field to bring in new sensibilities, new approaches to conceptualizing and reporting research, new theory, and new methods. In this note we discuss the early use of the *Envisioning Cards* [4], a versatile tool for attending to human values during design processes. The Perceptions of a Value card, one of thirty-two 3.5 × 5.0 inch cards in the set, is shown above.

We see the Envisioning Cards as falling within a design toolkit genre, namely "cards," where ideas for design activities and approaches are represented in a compact, concise physical format. The physical format allows for persistence and recombination of the discrete ideas represented on individual cards. Two outstanding examples of this genre are the *IDEO Method Cards* [5] and the *Interactive Thread Cards* [7], both of which tend to represent process and methodological design knowledge.

THE ENVISIONING CARDS: STRUCTURE AND TONE
Drawing on almost twenty years of work in value sensitive design [3], the Envisioning Cards are built upon a set of four envisioning criteria that are intended to raise awareness of long-term and systemic issues in design [8]. The

Stakeholder criterion, a key concept in value sensitive design, emphasizes the range of effects of a technology, both on those who are in direct contact with a technology (direct stakeholders), and on those who might not be direct users, but whose lives are nevertheless affected by various interactions around the technology (indirect stakeholders). Inspired by the long-term perspective of urban planning, the **Time** criterion helps guide designers to consider the longer term implications of their work – implications that will only emerge after the technology has moved through initial phases of novelty to later phases of appropriation and integration into society. The **Value** criterion emphasizes the impact of technology on human values. Our use of the term values draws from the value sensitive design literature, "what a person or group of people consider important in life" [3]. The **Pervasiveness** criterion emphasizes systemic interactions that follow from the widespread adoption of an interactive technology. Technologies can become pervasive with respect to geographic (e.g., city navigation software use within urban areas), cultural (e.g., text messaging within the deaf community), demographic (e.g., online social networking sites among teenagers), and other factors.

The Envisioning Cards (see Table 1) is comprised of 28 themed cards and 4 "create your own" cards, one for each of the envisioning criteria. In addition, a 3-minute sand-timer is included to both symbolize and facilitate the possibility for meaningful use in a brief amount of time. Each envisioning card addresses a specific theme within one of these envisioning criteria. As can be seen in The Perceptions of a Value card reproduced above, one side of the card contains the card title and an evocative image related to the card theme. On the flip side, the card highlights the key criterion for the card; the card title; a theme describing the card's key concept; a focused design activity related to the theme; and a "big" action word such as "think," "identify," "sketch," or "ask."

Taken as a group, the card images seek to evoke the diversity, complexity and subtlety of human affairs, as well as the interconnections among people and technologies. To reflect cultural and geographic diversity, the photographs were taken in such political locales as Kazakastan, Rwanda, and the United States and at different seasons of the year. To speak to the diversity of human communities, the photographs include villages, open air market places, concrete office buildings, religious structures, and the like. To be applicable for envisioning many kinds of technologies, various levels of technical and societal granularity are represented including personal computers with avatars and large-scale infrastructure such as smart grids and transportation systems. To prompt consideration of diverse technologies and technological integration, the photographs portray digital and non-digital artifacts, as well as tools and infrastructure – electrical power lines, personal computers, photocopy machines, surveillance cameras, traffic lights, train tracks, wind turbines, and virtual reality. Finally, to expand further the treatment of values and to invite users to tailor the Envisioning Cards to specific design settings, the "create your own cards" provide a simple mechanism for adapting the deck.

REPORTS FROM THE FIELD

Starting in 2007, the Envisioning Cards have been developed through a fairly slow and iterative process, with some explorations of their use taking place outside of the development group. They have been used in prototype form since 2008 at such venues as research talks, conference workshops, and a tutorial at CHI 2009, and have been distributed to colleagues for exploration and reaction. Our colleagues are currently using the cards for a range of research and educational uses, including (1) to provide breadth in usable security analyses, (2) to foreground human-centered systemic effects in the design of health informatics systems in eastern Africa, and (3) to stimulate socio-technical imagination in graduate and undergraduate HCI design courses and capstone projects. In this section we report briefly on three other cases, with diverse design, analysis, and evaluation goals, seeking to convey how the cards were used in design processes.

Case 1: Stimulating Ideation and Iteration in Co-design

To surface key needs and features in a technical design, HCI researchers and designers often engage in co-design activities, such as low-fidelity prototyping. A long-standing issue is how to scaffold non-designers' active participation in the design process, including focused iterative design. Extending a study of mobile phones and safety for homeless youth [9], the authors used the Envisioning Cards in a two-step co-design activity. First participants, homeless young people, aged 19–34, were prompted to make a 3-D prototype using materials such as clay and broken mobile parts. The design goal was to envision mobile phone features that could help to keep homeless youth safe. In addition, participants filled out a "spec sheet," including name, key features, and operational notes. In the second step, participants were prompted to select an Envisioning Card, consider it, and if needed refine the original design.

Five groups independently completed this structured design activity. We found that the Envisioning Cards stimulated the creative exploration of the design space. Specifically, the following accounts illustrate how the cards helped the participants to reframe technical problems, to reconsider technical aspects of their designs, and generally to catalyze their technical imaginations. The Crossing National Boundaries card (see Table 1), for example, prompted one participant group to consider the operation of their design for homeless young people in Antarctica ("needs to function in sub-zero"), Australia ("needs to deal w/ extreme heat, sand + lightening"), and Japan ("needs to be able to function without interferring [sic] w/ other signals…"). The Consider the Long Now card prompted another group to write "It is ingrained into peoples dna so they are born with it and it becomes organic material," suggesting that

Image	Title and Theme	Activity
	***Crossing National Boundaries (Pervasiveness).*** Nations have different rules, customs, and infrastructure that affect use of a technology. What challenges will be encountered by your system if it is used in other countries?	Choose three countries across the globe and envision challenges for your system if it was deployed in each of those countries. Label any common concerns across the identified challenges.
	***Consider Children (Stakeholders).*** Children often appropriate systems originally designed for adults. How might this system influence a child's social and moral development?	Develop a scenario that portrays a seven-year old interacting with the system. How might the system influence the child's learning, or play with other children?
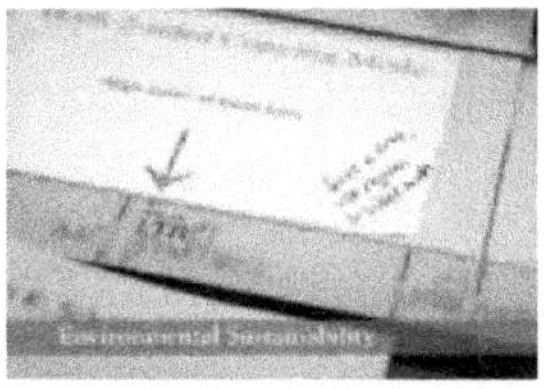	***Environmental Sustainability (Values).*** Many systems can be applied or extended to support a desirable environmental outcome (e.g., a system designed to support efficient printing from web browsers may lead to less use of paper and ink). At the same time, systems may have unintended negative effects on the environment (e.g., pollution and waste created in the production of electronics).	Specify the required resources needed to create and support your system, and the byproducts of its production and use. Can your design be applied or extended to support a more positive environmental outcome?
	***Choosing Not to Use (Time).*** Some people may decide to use your system, or may attempt to remove themselves from an indirect stakeholder role (e.g., choosing not to publish a telephone number). How might deliberate non-use of the system affect a person's daily life (e.g., employability, relationships, civic participation)?	Picture your system in use many years from now. Identify three ways in which an individual's intentional non-use of the system might affect that person's daily life or the system as a whole.

Table 1. Sample Envisioning Cards with Image, Title, Theme, and Activity.

technologists explore how mobile phones might be placed in bodies. As a final example, the Consider Children card (see Table 1) prompted a third group to write about their design "Add safety features that prevent children for accessing inapp content," clarified with the note: "An 11-year old is able to use the phone to continually stay connected with friends and family with no danger of the phone getting destroyed." That is, the phone needs to be durable in the hands of an 11-year old.

Case 2: The Value Implications of Persuasive Profiling

Anticipating the uses, benefits, and harms of a new technology that is likely to diffuse widely is a recurrent challenge for HCI. At present, "persuasion profiling" is one such technology. Persuasion profiles, created through widespread monitoring of individual online behaviors, represent specific strategies based typically on authority (e.g., I do as others say) or consensus (e.g., I do as others do) that are likely to positively influence a person's actions across diverse commercial and social contexts. Persuasion profiles, however, appear to depend on a kind of deception or at least concealment; when individuals are informed that a particular influence strategy is being employed its effectiveness is undermined. Thus, making the operation of this technology transparent or obtaining informed consent prior to its use will likely reduce its effectiveness. On the other hand, when not informed of the expected behavioral effects of the profiles an individual's privacy and autonomy can be undermined. Given this dilemma, how should designers, individuals and societies respond?

Addressing this question, Kaptein, Eckles, and Davis [6] drew upon the Envisioning Cards to uncover the value implications and technical possibilities. They report the use of two cards: Value Tensions and Consider Children. The first card prompted the authors to consider the points of tension and congruence between advertisers and the users of social network sites. The second card prompted the authors to consider how children, and in turn their parents, might be affected by persuasion profiles (adults were the original direct stakeholder). These two reframings led the authors to consider people who, in general, are particularly susceptible to advertising and to consider possibilities for how the profiles might be shared, owned, and controlled.

With the design space opened to a range of issues and technical possibilities guided in part through the use of the Envisioning Cards, the authors reported that the next step was to converge and to focus on a set of issues comprehensively. To do so, the authors developed a value scenario in which a father is able to inspect his son's persuasion profile (created by the son's use of social network sites) and to use that profile to help his son lose weight. This scenario, in turn and again guided by the Envisioning Cards, allowed the authors to examine the possible connections between commercial and health-based applications of persuasion profiles. Finally, Davis reports that the cards can be taken up quickly by designers new to value sensitive design and recommends that the Value Tensions card be used early on to help designers discuss the full space of values and tensions that might be addressed (see [4] "From the Community" discussion board).

Case 3: Heuristic Value Analysis of Infrastructure

Infrastructure shapes interaction; and, in turn, interaction design shapes human experience. Future Internet architecture, energy smart grids, and FastTrak transportation systems are but a few examples. In our third case study, akin to a heuristic evaluation to surface usability issues, one of the authors used the Envisioning Cards as an analytic heuristic tool to surface critical issues for potential cloud computing solutions [2]. To provide a flavor for this analytic assessment, results from considering three of the cards follow:

Political Realities. The Political Realities card calls attention to the ways in which "different political systems … can influence perceptions and practices that emerge in relation to [a technology]." Applied to cloud computing, how will the cloud support or hinder data sharing and communication among individuals who live within different political systems? Will users always be operating in networks or living within governments they trust? Or will it be the case that users sometimes will need (or want) to operate in networks that they fundamentally do not trust? How will the cloud support these different use cases?

Environmental Sustainability. The Environmental Sustainability card (see Table 1) directs designers to consider how a technology can "support a desirable environmental outcome" as well as situations in which "systems may have unintended negative effects on the environment." Applied to cloud computing, one effect entails continual electricity use; an unintended effect entails encouraging a proliferation of physical devices (e.g., 10 billion mobile devices). An analogy can be found in urban planning with debates around increased highways leading to greater sprawl and automobile use. As with transportation there are no simple answers here; however, the interaction among cloud computing and device proliferation, etc. warrants examination.

Crossing National Boundaries. This third card foregrounds the impact of national policies and regulations on technology development and use, recognizing that "nations have different rules, customs, and infrastructure that affect the use of a technology." Applied to cloud computing, how will various technical mechanisms enable or hinder communication and the exchange of digital goods and services across different legal frameworks. Particularly germane would be differing frameworks governing speech (e.g., what can be spoken and to whom), digital rights management, and intellectual property, among others.

Early and frequent consideration of the types of issues identified with these three cards and others in the deck can be immensely valuable in identifying large-scale socio-political issues early on in the design of technical infrastructure and resulting interactions.

CONCLUSION

Engaging values can be daunting; we believe in progress, not perfection. Robust like a pencil, the Envisioning Cards were designed to be a versatile tool, useful for many design processes: ideation, co-design, heuristic evaluation, critique, and more. Through their form and structure the cards position researchers and designers to consider values, time, pervasiveness, and stakeholders; that is, to attend to what is important in people's lives. The three cases point to rich and diverse applications, and suggest to us that the cards catalyze designers' humanistic and technical imaginations. Moving forward, as the cards diffuse, we believe that it will be important to explore and reflect upon their uses, but more, to seek systematic ways to place them within design processes and educational settings, to make HCI an even more human-centered practice.

ACKNOWLEDGMENTS

The work reported here was funded in part by NSF Grant Nos. IIS-0325035 and CNS-0905384.

REFERENCES

1. Bannon, L. Reimagining HCI: Toward a more human-centered perspective. *interactions 18*, 4 (2011), 50-57.
2. Friedman, B. Human Values and Technical Infrastructure. Keynote presented at the Microsoft Security Summer Institute, Cle Elum, WA, USA, 2011, July 25.
3. Friedman, B., Kahn, P. H., Jr., and Borning, A. Value Sensitive Design and information systems. In *Human-computer interaction in management information systems: Foundations*, 348-372. M.E. Sharpe, 2006.
4. Friedman, B., Nathan, L. P., Kane, S., and Lin, J. *Envisioning Cards*. University of Washington, Seattle, WA, USA, 2011. Available at: envisioningcards.com
5. *IDEO Method Cards: 51 ways to inspire design*. IDEO, Palo Alto, CA, USA. Available at: ideo.com
6. Kaptein, M., Eckles, D., and Davis, J. Envisioning persuasion profiles: Challenges for public policy and ethical practice. *interactions 18*, 5 (2011), 66-69.
7. Mackay, M. *Interactive Thread: A participatory design toolkit*. interLiving, KTH, Sweden, 2002. Available at: interliving.kth.se/publications/thread/index.html
8. Nathan, L.P., Friedman, B., Klasjna, P.V., Kane, S.K., and Miller, J.K. Envisioning systemic effects on persons and society throughout interactive system design. In *Proc. DIS 2008*, ACM Press (2008), 1-10.
9. Woelfer, J.P., Iverson, A., Hendry, D.G., Friedman, B., and Gill, B. Improving the safety of homeless young people with mobile phones: Values, form and function. In *Proc. CHI 2011*, ACM Press (2011), 1707-1716.

Improving Literacy in Developing Countries Using Speech Recognition-Supported Games on Mobile Devices

Anuj Kumar[1], Pooja Reddy[2], Anuj Tewari[3], Rajat Agrawal[1], Matthew Kam[1]
[1]Human-Computer Interaction Institute, Carnegie Mellon University, Pittsburgh, PA, USA, 15213
[2]American Institutes for Research, Washington, D.C., USA, 20007
[3]Computer Science Division and Berkeley Institute of Design, University of California, Berkeley, USA
anujk1@cs.cmu.edu

ABSTRACT
Learning to read in a second language is challenging, but highly rewarding. For low-income children in developing countries, this task can be significantly more challenging because of lack of access to high-quality schooling, but can potentially improve economic prospects at the same time. A synthesis of research findings suggests that practicing recalling and vocalizing words for expressing an intended meaning could improve word reading skills – including reading in a second language – more than silent recognition of what the given words mean. Unfortunately, many language learning software do not support this instructional approach, owing to the technical challenges of incorporating speech recognition support to check that the learner is vocalizing the correct word. In this paper, we present results from a usability test and two subsequent experiments that explore the use of two speech recognition-enabled mobile games to help rural children in India read words with understanding. Through a working speech recognition prototype, we discuss two major contributions of this work: first, we give empirical evidence that shows the extent to which productive training (i.e. vocalizing words) is superior to receptive vocabulary training, and discuss the use of scaffolding hints to "unpack" factors in the learner's linguistic knowledge that may impact reading. Second, we discuss what our results suggest for future research in HCI.

Author Keywords
Educational games; developing countries; information and communication technology and development (ICTD); literacy; mobile learning; speech recognition

ACM Classification Keywords
H.5.m [Information Interfaces and Presentation]: Miscellaneous;

General Terms
Design; Human Factors

Permission to make digital or hard copies of all or part of this work for personal or classroom use is granted without fee provided that copies are not made or distributed for profit or commercial advantage and that copies bear this notice and the full citation on the first page. To copy otherwise, or republish, to post on servers or to redistribute to lists, requires prior specific permission and/or a fee.
CHI'12, May 5–10, 2012, Austin, Texas, USA.
Copyright 2012 ACM 978-1-4503-1015-4/12/05...$10.00.

INTRODUCTION
More than half of the world speaks at least two languages [9], to the extent that "bilingualism and multilingualism are a normal and unremarkable necessity to everyday life for the majority of the world's population" [12]. Multilingualism arose because of reasons that include colonialism, diglossia, and efforts to promote national identity [12, 32]. Consequently, many children in both industrialized and developing nations grow up having been exposed to, and even learning to read in, at least two languages, neither of which may be spoken at home. However, most languages in multilingual societies do not share equal status; a "global" or "national" language (e.g., English, French, Mandarin, or Spanish) may co-exist with the vernacular languages, with the former privileged as the medium of instruction or official language of business.

Sadly, many children in the developing world stand to lose significant opportunities in life when their schools struggle to provide high-quality literacy instruction, sometimes for a vernacular language and more often in a second language (e.g., English), which teachers themselves lack proficiency in. The British Council estimates wage differences between salaried professionals with and without English skills to be between 20% and 30% in Bangladesh, Cameroon, Nigeria, Pakistan and Rwanda [32]. In postcolonial Morocco, where French is the official language of business, switching the medium of instruction from French to [the local language] Arabic is associated with a 50% reduction in the economic returns to schooling [2]. In India, from surveys with poor parents [27], English is one of the two most sought-after skills. In the city of Mumbai in India, for instance, "schooling in [the local language] Marathi channels the child into working class jobs, while more expensive English education significantly increases the likelihood of obtaining a coveted white-collar job" [24], such that English speakers experience returns on investment in schooling between 24% and 27%, while the returns for non- speakers are 10%.

Word reading skills, which includes vocabulary knowledge, is a significant predictor of the ability to read and comprehend longer passages of texts [30]. Studies have shown successes on the cellphone [18] and desktop computer [29] in developing countries with receptive vocabulary training (i.e., recognizing the meaning of a word when the reader sees it). Drawing on the research literature that we will discuss below, productive vocabulary practice (i.e., recalling the word for expressing a meaning and vocalizing aloud) is likely to bring about higher gains in vocabulary knowledge. We therefore hypothesize that productive vocabulary training, which language learning software applications can support via speech recognition (which checks that the learner is saying the correct word), can yield stronger literacy gains. While speech recognition remains a computationally difficult problem, speech in the niche domain of vocabulary learning is significantly more tractable when recognition is isolated to individual words (i.e., no need to locate boundary words, when recognizing phrases and longer sequences of words in the speech signal) and small vocabularies (which is usually feasible in practice because the words to be taught can be organized into short vocabulary lists in most situations).

This paper therefore proceeds as follows: first, based on the literature in second language learning and the psychology of reading, we motivate how speech recognition can be applied to improve word reading. We describe two games which we designed to support both receptive and productive practice (via voice commands), so that we can compare the learning gains across both conditions. We describe how we developed a speech recognizer that supports both games, and usability testing with rural children in India to ensure speech recognition accuracy. We report an experiment that compares receptive against productive training. Based on observations about learner difficulties in this experiment, we redesigned the games to incorporate two hints that aim to scaffold learners in the productive training. We report a second experiment that compares the learning benefits the hints confer. We conclude with implications for designing vocabulary training applications.

Our contributions are twofold. First, through a working prototype, we give empirical evidence that shows the extent to which productive training is superior to receptive vocabulary training. More importantly, we compare two scaffolding techniques to "unpack" factors in the learner's linguistic knowledge subsystems that may impact word reading. Second, we discuss what our results suggest for future research directions in HCI.

MOTIVATION AND RELATED WORK

Theoretical Framework

"Word reading," which refers to the reader's ability to read *and* understand individual words [31], is fundamental for enabling her to comprehend the sentences and texts that she encounters [30]. Much of the research in the psychology of reading supports the position that word reading involves two sub-skills [31]: mapping orthographic units (e.g. individual or clusters of letters) onto its appropriate phonological unit, so that she can *decode* (or "sound out") the written word. For instance, for the written word "cat", the letter 'c' must be mapped to the sound /k/, 'a' to /a/, and 't' to /t/.; and associating the phonological form (i.e., the sound /cat/) and its contextually-appropriate semantics (i.e., small, furry animal), so that *semantic extraction*, or the extraction of the word's meaning from its sound, occurs.

According to the lexical quality hypothesis (LQH) [31], as illustrated in Figure 1, word reading involves the reader integrating her knowledge of three linguistic subsystems, namely: orthography (visual script), phonology (sound) and semantics (meaning). The LQH implies that the reader's word reading skill can be enhanced if the linkage between her orthographic and phonological subsystem, or linkage between her phonological and semantics subsystem, or the quality of her orthographic or phonological subsystems themselves, are strengthened [31]. These improvements are especially challenging for the reader to achieve for her knowledge subsystems in the case of a second language.

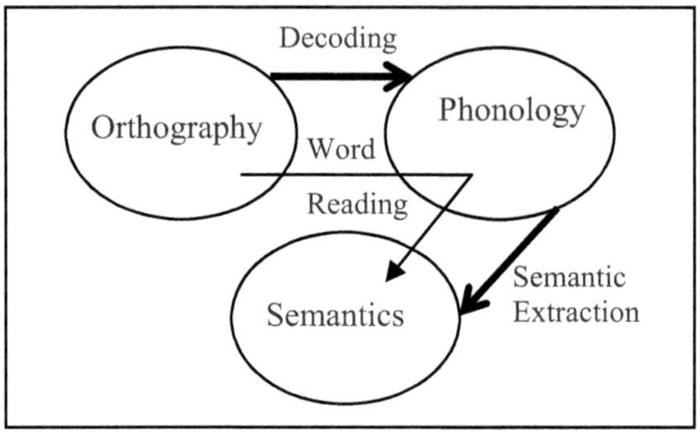

Figure 1: The three components of word reading knowledge (i.e., orthography, phonology and semantics).

To address the challenge of strengthening the subsystems and/or linkages between them in the learner's knowledge, we turn to second language acquisition research. On top of recommendations to include vocabulary drills in language teaching [26], which can include both receptive vocabulary practice (i.e., the ability to recognize the meaning of a word when the reader sees it) and productive vocabulary practice (i.e., recalling the word for conveying a meaning and saying it aloud), the literature argues that speaking aloud provides the learner with phonological input back to the mind, which enables her to strengthen her word knowledge [9]. Similarly, vocalization helps her realize that she either lacks this knowledge, thus prompting her to acquire it, or that she has this knowledge, thus enabling her to further consolidate it [9, 36]. As such, we hypothesize that speech recognition can be used to facilitate productive vocabulary practice (i.e., check that she is speaking aloud the correct word), so as to strengthen her word subsystems, and thereby, ability to read with understanding.

Speech Technologies for Low Resource Contexts

Past efforts in human-computer interaction for development have explored speech as an input modality, especially as an alternative to graphical user interfaces. For instance, Patel et al. [28] investigates a voice forum for low-literate rural farmers to access information. Similarly, Agarwal et al. [1] describes "Spoken Web", a framework to help low-literate users access and create voice sites on the Web, similar to how literate users currently access the (text-based) World Wide Web. However, none of their user studies involves a working version of an automatic speech recognizer (ASR).

In attempts to incorporate ASRs into low-resource contexts, prior efforts have focused on accuracy improvements. By "low-resource," we mean contexts that lack the off-the-shelf databases for the acoustic model, pronunciation dictionary, grammar, etc. that are necessary for building accurate recognizers. The Meraka Institute [5] is currently exploring the technical feasibility of building an ASR for 11 South African languages, but to our knowledge, has yet to deploy a working ASR. Where working ASRs for low-resource contexts are concerned, one of the earliest successes came from UC Berkeley's TIER group for their Tamil Market project in rural India [33], which showed that it is feasible to build an accurate recognizer for a small number of users. But their approach does not scale beyond tiny vocabulary sizes. Healthline's "poor man's recognizer ++" [35] is one of the most generalizable approaches for building a speech recognizer for languages that lack off-the-shelf resources. However, besides accent, it does not consider other factors (e.g., background noise, pitch in children's voices [20], etc.) that can severely impact speech recognition accuracy.

Speech Technologies for Language Learning

So far, most language and literacy learning software in the developing and industrialized world do not employ speech recognition when teaching vocabulary and language skills, and as such, is restricted to receptive language knowledge. Research projects in this category that target learners in the developing world include MILLEE [15, 16, 18], Multiple Mice [29], Kane [10], and Same Language Subtitling [3].

Among the research projects that use speech recognition to improve language learning, most of them aim to improve pronunciation (vs. vocabulary), and none of them examines the impact that productive vocabulary training has on word reading. For instance, MIT's literacy tutor [21] targets pronunciation skills by providing interactive feedback for poorly articulated or mispronounced words. CMU's project LISTEN [23] is a reading tutor that has been adapted for children in developing countries. It presents a sentence at a time and provides feedback only at the end of a sentence unless the reader is stuck or clicks for help. The University of Colorado's Foundation to Literacy Program [8] started a reading program that was designed for beginning and poor readers. It targets foundational reading skills such as letter knowledge, phonological awareness and decoding skills in order to improve listening and reading comprehension. In addition, none of the above projects target mobile devices in developing regions, which are increasingly prevalent and less expensive than the desktop computers, which the above projects are based on. An exception is Tewari et al. [37], which is a pronunciation tutor on smartphones that aims to help Hispanic children in the USA acquire English skills.

There are also a number of commercial projects: Rosetta Stone [34] uses proprietary speech recognition technology to elicit oral responses from learners. They have tested and fine-tuned accuracy, both for native and non-native speakers. Similarly, Carnegie Speech [6] teaches speaking and listening skills using proprietary speech recognition technology and models. While both ventures have shown great potential for speech technologies in language learning, their components for building a speech recognizer (e.g., acoustic model, dictionary, grammar) were built from years of automated data collection and analysis. This approach requires financial resources that smaller ventures, research groups and even well-funded corporations trying to cover a wide spectrum of user groups, such as diverse contexts in the developing world, cannot attempt.

GAME DESIGNS

Building on the growing popularity of educational games [13] and successes with games to teach vocabulary in a second language in the developing world [15,18,29], we designed two educational games: Market Game and Farm Game. At the game design level, these games drew on a previous study on the characteristics of traditional village games that rural children in a developing country such as India find to be intuitive (compared to the features found in contemporary Western videogames), and the systematic differences between traditional and Western videogames [16]. These games incorporated actions such as the ability to either *catch* or *evade* a player, both of which were two popular game actions in traditional village games. As such, both games were designed to be culturally appropriate for children in rural regions in India. Each game followed a teaching, game play, and practice sequence. This sequence was informed and refined through earlier usability testing in the field [17]. Our prior research has not, however, involved educational games that support speech recognition.

Market Game

In the Market Game, the teaching phase (as shown in Figure 2A) entailed introducing the vocabulary words to the user. As in popular commercial software [34], introduction of a word meant mapping the image of the vocabulary word to its sound, as well as, its native language and English text. At a time, the software introduced five words (one after another), which was based on prior psychological studies that show that an average person can retain 7±2 new items in their short-term working memory at any time [22]. Once the word has been introduced, the user could replay the audio playback for its pronunciation at the teaching phase for any number of times, before going to the next screen.

Next, in the game play screen (Figure 2B) of the market game, the aim was to move the boy character from left (home) to right (shop in the market), while avoiding monkeys en-route. This activity was an adaptation of the daily routine of going to the market for children in rural India; and integrated actions from the popular physical games that they play, such as evading an opponent. Next, depending on the experimental condition that the player was assigned to, the player could purchase items from the shop by either *selecting* the correct item that corresponded to the said word (Figure 2C, Re condition), or by *saying the word aloud* that corresponded to the image displayed (Figure 2D, Pr condition).

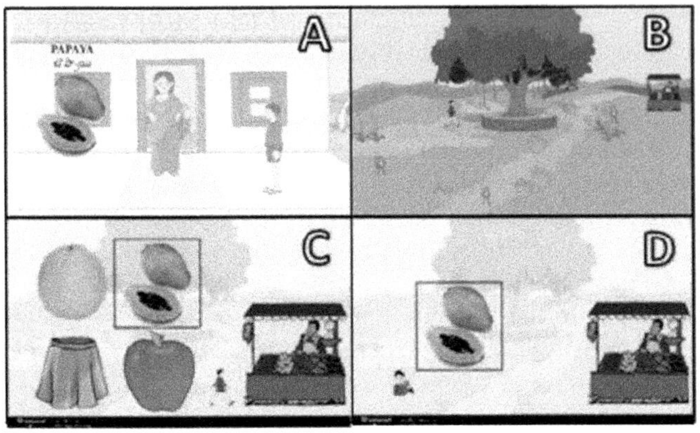

Figure 2: These screenshots describe the game sequence for the market game. (A) *Teaching phase*: Introduces the English word for the common nouns, which are the items to be bought in the market. (B) *Game play*: shows the boy attempting to move towards the shop, while the monkeys try to catch him. (C) *Receptive practice condition*: to purchase the item from the shop, the user has to map the word that the software plays aloud with its image from a list of four choices. (D) *Productive practice condition*: to purchase the correct item at the shop, the user has to say aloud the word that corresponds to the image.

Farm Game

The Farm Game (Figure 3) had the same pedagogical cycle of "teaching, game play, and practice", but used a different game action than Market game. The objective of the farm game was to save the farm by "catching" all the thieves and retrieving the items that they had stolen. Again, this activity was based on the common rural India scenario where children helped their parents keep vigil on the farm in the farming season, where a lot of animals or thieves tend to steal the crop. In order to recover an item from the thief, the user could do it in one of the two ways as described above for the Market Game in Figure 2C (receptive practice) or Figure 2D (productive practice), depending on the condition that the participant was randomly assigned to.

SYSTEM DEVELOPMENT AND USABILITY TESTING

Our system (consisting of the above games and the speech recognizer) was iteratively prototyped and refined on the Nokia N810 mobile phone. In May-June 2010, for a period of 4 weeks, we conducted a series of usability tests in the field with our working recognizer to improve both the game designs and speech recognition accuracy. In total, 10 children in grades 4-5 in Hyderabad play-tested successive versions of both games. In addition, we collected speech samples from 50 children to improve recognition accuracy.

Figure 3: This screenshot shows the *game play* screen for the farm game, where the boy character attempts to catch the thief who is stealing the vegetable from the farm.

Interface Improvements

One of the important requirements for our speech user-interface (SUI) was to signal to the user when to speak. Typically, in SUIs indicate this by displaying a microphone icon when it is time to speak. However, from the initial usability tests, we realized that earlier icons for prompting the user to speak (Figure 4) were unintuitive to participants since most of them were never introduced to the notion of a microphone. Instead of showing the microphone on its own, they liked the idea of showing a boy holding a microphone, because they were better able to relate to instances of local elections or rallies where people would hold a microphone and speak into it.

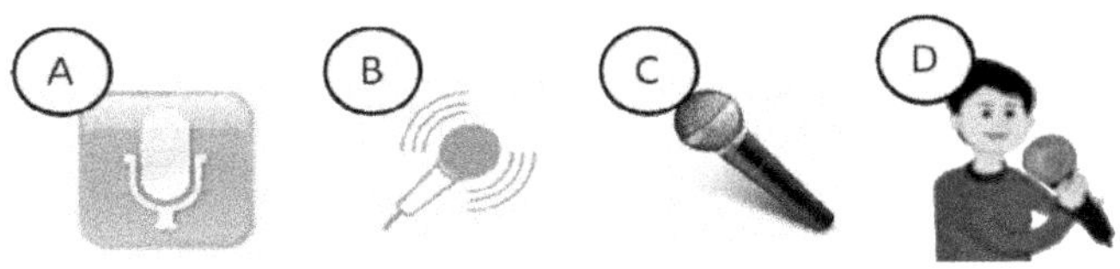

Figure 4: Microphone icons tested in the usability tests; A, B, C represent icons that are currently used in existing speech user-interfaces; D represents the icon that was understood by participants of our study.

Speech Recognition Improvements

To recognize user's speech in the conditions that required productive practice (with or without hints), we used pocketSphinx [14] – an open-source, small footprint, automatic speech recognizer (ASR) for mobile devices. Our choice of pocketSphinx was based on experimental evaluation of mobile speech recognizers [19], where pocketSphinx outperformed other mobile ASRs such as TinySphinx on small vocabulary tasks. However, due to the multiple challenges of speech recognition for non-typical contexts such as ours, off-the-shelf resources were not directly applicable. To account for numerous acoustic variabilities arising due to varying accents, background noise etc. we followed a three-step process to adapt and fine-tune the accuracy of the recognizer. First, we collected a speech corpus from representative speakers and trained our own baseline acoustic model. Second, we analyzed this corpus for factors that affected the speech recognition accuracy, and third, we adapted the baseline speech recognizer on these factors to improve its accuracy. Below we describe these three steps in more detail.

Our speech corpus was made up of 6250 utterances (approximately 6 hours) from 50 rural Indian children, equally divided across gender and grades 4-5. Each utterance in the dataset was labeled with the word that it represented at the time of recording, and these labeled inputs were used for training the speech recognizer. As in the original pocketSphinx paper [14], our baseline acoustic model used Hidden Markov Models with a 5-state Bakis topology. They were trained on the 6250 utterances, using 1000 tied Gaussian Mixture Models (senones) and 256 tied Gaussian densities. Since the application required the user to speak words in isolation (and there's no need to capture history), we used a unigram statistical language model with a vocabulary size of 25 words.

To improve recognition accuracy beyond the baseline performance of the above acoustic and language models, we next sought to adapt our recognizer to account for the variabilities in users' speech. Since adaptation can happen along several dimensions, we first quantitatively analyzed the speech utterances along seven voice metrics that collectively describe the characteristics of voice, namely articulation (a), speaking rate (r), sound quality (q), pitch (f0), and the first three formant frequencies (f1, f2, f3). Using univariate and multivariate analyses (the description of which is beyond the scope of this paper), the influence of each metric was calculated on the word error rate (WER), which appropriately measures the recognizer's accuracy in isolated word speech recognition tasks, such as ours. Such an analysis was necessary to identify the most critical factors and save time on performing all possible adaptation techniques.

As shown in Figure 5, speaking rate and articulation were the most significant factors that impeded recognition performance in the context of our users. Based on this analysis, to account for variations in the speaking rate, we adapted the baseline speech recognizer using a widely used continuous frame rate adaptation technique [7]. Similarly, to account for non-native articulations, using the technique described in "poor man's recognizer" [35], we added pronunciation variants to the dictionary that were a closer match to the accent of the users than the ones in the baseline dictionary.

In addition to the above quantitative analysis, we also qualitatively explored the recognition results of the incorrectly recognized words from our usability tests. We observed that in some cases of misrecognized words, the results had extra words – for instance, "papaya" was decoded as "peas papaya cup", perhaps, because background noise from cars or nearby mosques was also decoded in addition to the actual speech from the user. To overcome this, we considered the output of the ASR to be correct if the target vocabulary keyword was spotted anywhere in the decoded sentence. In addition to keyword spotting, we also used noise-canceling microphones to minimize misrecognitions due to external noise.

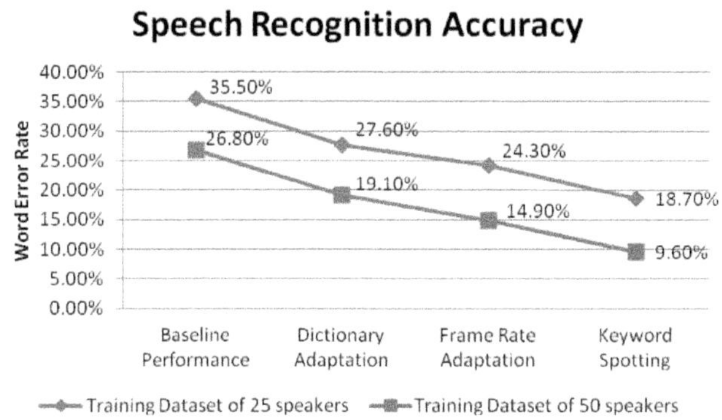

Figure 5: Summary of progressive performance improvements when the amount of training data was increased, and with the type of adaptation technique used.

After a series of context-based adaptations such as those arising due to non-native accent and noise (as outlined above), the speech recognizer's accuracy was 91.4% (Figure 5). In other words, approximately, 1 out of 10 times the speech recognizer misunderstood what the user spoke. In cases when the user happened to speak the correct answer (but the recognizer misunderstood it to be incorrect), the participants learned to repeat the word from the short, 15-minute training sessions prior to actual gameplay (see *Experiment* sub-section of Study 1). In general, these training sessions had a dual role: first, to acquaint the participants with the game dynamics using five curriculum words, and second, to help them realize that the system might make recognition mistakes. In order to proceed in the latter case, they could either change their response, or if they were confident, then repeat it. From our observations, most of the times when there was a false negative (i.e. user spoke correctly but speech recognizer misrecognized), learners repeated the vocabulary word rather than switching their response, and thus system's misrecognition is less likely to have impacted any learning gains.

STUDY 1: RECEPTIVE VS. PRODUCTIVE PRACTICE

Informed by the above theoretical framework, we have the following hypothesis for this study:

H1: Productive training* (Pr) is more beneficial for word reading than receptive training* (Re),

Participants

21 participants (11 boys and 10 girls) took part in our first study in June-July 2010 (5 weeks). They were 9 to 13 years old (mean=10.5 years) in 4th and 5th grades. We selected

* With no hints (as will be introduced in the second study).

children in this age and grade level because word reading skills are increasingly important for reading comprehension and academic success at this level [4]. All participants were attending a public school in a rural area near Hyderabad, India. Telugu and English were taught as their first and second language respectively at this school. Most of their families owned at least one cellphone.

Experiment

The experiment involved a pre-post test block design, with the intervention comprising the above two market and farm games. To ensure relevance of the curriculum in the games, each game targets 10 unique words (all concrete nouns). The 20 words were chosen from government-issued English textbooks for 4th and 5th graders. To avoid introducing a confounding variable from our selection of these words, we consulted teachers at the school to verify that they do not plan to teach these words in their classes at the time that the experiment was planned. Each child played both games, but was randomly assigned to one of the two conditions: Re or Pr. With this assignment, when the 21 participants played the market game, 10 were in the Pr condition and 11 were in Re; and when they played the farm game, 11 were in Pr and 10 were in Re. Each participant played the games in an hour-long, after-school session comprising a word reading pre-test, training session, 30 minutes of gameplay, and a similar word reading post-test immediately after gameplay. Specifically, in the pre- and post-tests, the outcome variable (word reading score) was measured before and after each game using an adapted visual format from the Peabody Picture Vocabulary Test [11], which is used for measuring vocabulary knowledge. In our word reading test, every word was displayed on the screen with four images, and participants were asked to match the word with the picture that best represented its semantics. A correct match adds one to the participant's score, while an incorrect match or the lack of a response does not change the score. In a training session before the study, experimenters explained the games and allowed each participant to play the games with 5 practice words.

Results

The means and standard deviations for pre- and post- word reading scores, and post-test gains, are shown in Table 1 for both the Re and Pr conditions. As a sanity check, the t-tests did not reveal any significant differences in post-test gains between the market and farm games, for both the Re (p=.12) and Pr (p=.48) conditions; we expected both games to exhibit comparable post-test gains since they adopted similar designs and instructional principles. Likewise, between both games, there was no statistically significant difference on pre-test scores (p=.24) for both conditions, indicating that participants in both conditions started with the same baseline knowledge of word reading. This allowed us to focus on analyzing word reading gains without using pre-test scores as a covariate.

Variable	Condition	Market Game	Farm Game
Pre-Test	Re	7.8 (3.5)	6.9 (2.5)
	Pr	8.4 (2.8)	8.9 (3.0)
Post-Test	Re	8.5 (3.7)	8.3 (2.2)
	Pr	10.6 (1.5)	12.1 (3.0)
Gain	Re	.6 (1.1)	1.4 (2.3)
	Pr	2.3 (1.9)	3.2 (1.8)

Table 1: Means and standard deviations (in parentheses) for pre-test score, post-test score, and post-test gains for both games, for each of the two conditions (i.e. Re and Pr).

Given the above sanity checks and in order to perform a more robust statistical analysis, for each condition, we combined the scores across both games. On this combined dataset, post-hoc power analysis indicated a power of 0.62 (with cohen's d as 0.9 and significance level as 0.05), which was deemed adequate for inferential analysis for our purposes. A one-way 2-factor ANOVA showed a significant difference between the two conditions on post-test gains ($F(1,40)=5.4$, p=.001). More specifically, after 30 minutes of game play, gains were observed under both conditions: 1.0 word under Re, against 2.7 words under Pr. These results suggest that with even as little as 30 minutes of game play practicing words – receptively or productively – word reading scores increase significantly. Even more critically, there is evidence that productive training is significantly more beneficial for word reading development than simply receptively practicing words.

STUDY 2: SCAFFOLDING WORD PRODUCTION

Our first experiment has shown that productive vocabulary training, enabled by speech recognition that checks that the learner is recalling and articulating the correct words, leads to stronger gains on word reading scores (as measured for short-term retention), in comparison to receptive training. Given that word reading consists of both decoding and semantic extraction, however, it is not clear to what extent the benefit from productive training is shared between these two constituent sub-skills. Similarly, it is not clear if these gains would persist over a longer time after gameplay, i.e., long-term retention.

Most importantly, in the Pr condition, we observed at least 12 (out of 21) instances in which learners struggled to give their answers. For instance, they appeared to exert great effort to recall and vocalize a word. Therefore, to "unpack" the subsystems in the learner's linguistic knowledge which facilitates word reading via productive training, we added both an orthographic and phonological hint to both games (described in more detail below). We expected the hints to lower the cognitive load on selected subsystems in her word knowledge, so that she receives support to strengthen other subsystems in her word knowledge that are also responsible for word reading. Of course, it is not clear, and we need to learn, if the hints are counter-productive (e.g., she may not wean herself from being over-dependent on them).

We set out to address the above gaps in our second study. Informed by the lexical quality hypothesis, our hypotheses for study 2 were therefore:

H2: Productive training with an orthographic hint (Pr + Or) is more beneficial for decoding than productive training with no hints (Pr),

H3: Productive training with a phonological hint (Pr + Ph) is more beneficial for semantic extraction than productive training with no hints (Pr),

H4: Productive training with both a phonological and orthographic hint together (Pr + Or + Ph) is more beneficial for word reading than productive training with no hints (Pr).

Games Redesign

More specifically, we redesigned both games to support additional conditions: (A) *Orthographic hint* (in form of the first alphabet of the word and the length of the written form of the word) to support cognitive search for the vocabulary item using letter-to-sound mapping rules. (B) *Phonological hint*, in form of the first sound (or phoneme) to prompt a targeted search for the word by narrowing down the (semantic) search space to only those words that begin with that sound, and (C) *Orthographic and Phonological hint*, to support cognitive search of the word using either or both the letter-to-sound rule and narrowed-down semantic search space. The scaffolding design behind both the orthographic and phonological hints was informed by the lexical quality hypothesis in our theoretical framework [31] that illustrates how the hint features work in the games, for the given word "papaya". When the phonological hint was available, based on experiences from prior usability tests [18], we gave the participant the option to repeat the hint, in case she missed it or wanted to hear it again.

Participants

40 participants (27 boys and 13 girls) took part in our second study in May-June 2011 (6 weeks). They were 9 to 13 years old (mean=11 years) and were 4th and 5th graders. All participants were attending a different public school than the one in the first study in a rural district near Hyderabad, India. This gave us the chance to test our prototypes with a different user group in the same area, without making major changes to the speech recognizer. Telugu and English were taught as the first and second language respectively at this school. Most of their families owned at least one cellphone.

Experimental Design

The second study had four conditions: Pr, Pr + Or, Pr + Ph, and Pr + Or + Ph. The experimental design for the second study was identical to that of the first study, except for two additions. First, to assess long-term retention of the vocabulary words covered in the games, we administered a delayed post-test between 7 and 10 days after gameplay.[1] Second, besides scoring for word reading on the pre-, post- and delayed post-tests, we also scored each participant on decoding and semantic extraction for all three conditions. For semantic extraction, the scoring was similar to that of word reading (as in Study 1), except that instead of a written word, participant heard a word and then selected matching image. For decoding, participant was shown a written word, which s/he read aloud, after which administrator clicked "Yes" if correct (irrespective of how well it was pronounced), and "No" otherwise. This allowed us to separately study the impacts of each hint condition on each reading subsystem. This also allowed us to enhance the validity of our assessment instruments, i.e., since decoding and semantic extraction should theoretically total up as word reading, we could check for measurement errors in our test instruments.

Results

Similar to study one, as a sanity check, we do not find any significant difference between the two games on any test score, for all four conditions (namely: Pr, Pr + Or, Pr + Ph, and Pr + Or + Ph). As such, in order to perform a statistical analysis with greater inferential power, for each of the four conditions, we combined the scores from both games so as to double our effective sample size.

Word Reading Gains

A one-way 4-factor ANOVA showed a significant difference between the four conditions on word reading gains as measured using the immediate post-test ($F(3,76)=2.98$, $p=.03$). Our independent sample t-tests with Bonferroni correction showed a significant difference between Pr and Pr + Or ($p=.02$), Pr and Pr + Ph ($p=.04$), Pr and Pr + Or + Ph ($p=.05$). There was no significant difference in word reading gains across other combinations of hints.[2]

---

[1] We aimed to conduct the delayed post-test on the 8th day after gameplay. Given relatively high absenteeism rate in some schools in the developing world (such as this school), however, for 12 students, we were only able to schedule the post-test on the 9th or 10th day. This minor variation (i.e., up to 2 days) after the 7-day lag is not expected to impact delayed post-test performance significantly. We were successful in conducting this test with all 40 participants.

[2] For brevity, when discussing results for the second experiment, we exclude combinations that were not significantly different i.e. $p > 0.05$ (except for a few cases in which significance changed from the immediate to the delayed post-test).

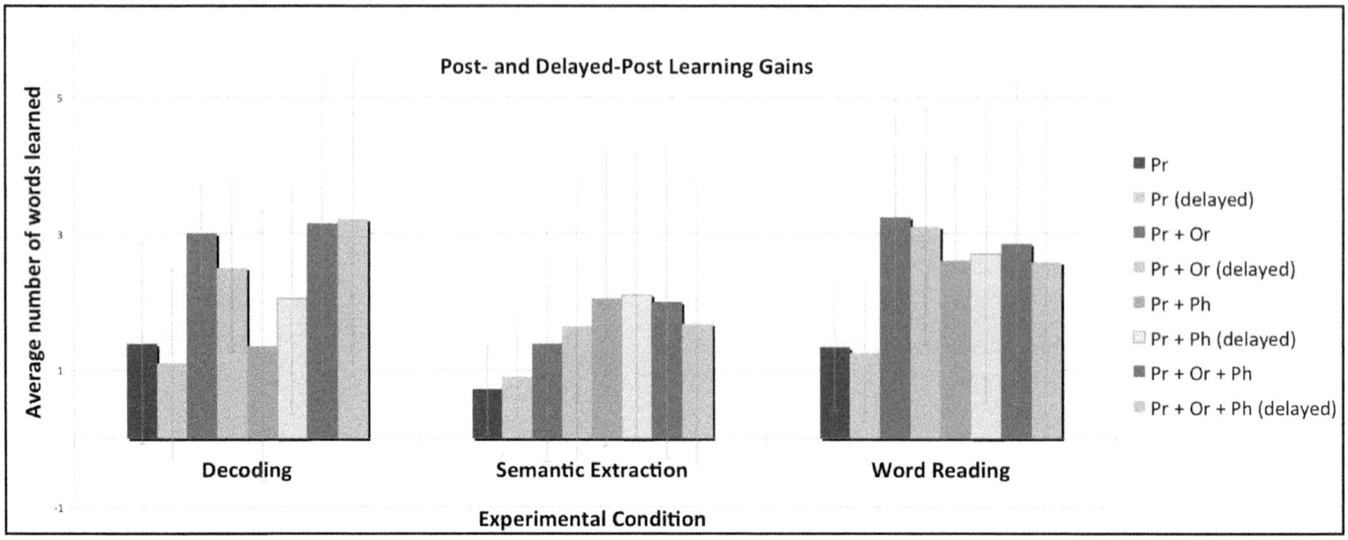

Figure 6: This figure shows the average post- and delayed-post test gains for the three dependent variables in the second study i.e. decoding, semantic extraction, and word reading. 'Pr' refers to productive practice (with no hint), 'Pr + Or' refers to productive practice with orthographic hint, 'Pr + Ph' refers to productive practice with phonological hint, and 'Pr + Or + Ph' refers to the productive practice with both orthographic and phonological hints.

For the delayed post-tests, a one-way 4-factor ANOVA revealed a significant difference between the four conditions for gains on word reading scores (F (3,76)=2.28, p=.05). Independent sample t-tests with Bonferroni correction showed a significant difference between Pr and Pr + Or (p=.03), and Pr and Pr + Ph (p=.05). But the difference between Pr and Pr + Or + Ph (p=.11) was not significant.

Decoding Gains

For the non-delayed post-test, a one-way 4-factor ANOVA revealed a significant difference on the decoding gains across the four conditions (F(3,76)=4.87, p=.003). Independent sample t-tests with Bonferroni correction showed significant differences between Pr and Pr + Or (p=.02), Pr and Pr + Or + Ph (p=.02), and Pr + Or and Pr + Ph (p<.01).

The delayed post-tests reflected similar results; the ANOVA revealed a significant difference on the decoding gains across the four conditions (F(3,76)=3.99, p=.01). Post-hoc analysis with Bonferroni corrected t-tests showed significant differences between Pr and Pr + Or (p = .04), Pr and Pr + Or + Ph (p = .01), and Pr + Or and Pr + Ph (p = .04)

Semantic Extraction Gains

For gains on the immediate post-test, a one-way 4-factor ANOVA for semantic extraction gains did not reveal any significant difference between the four conditions, F(3,76)=1.88, p=.13; however, post-hoc analysis with Bonferroni correction indicated a significant difference between (and only between) Pr and Pr + Ph (p=0.04). Similarly, where the delayed post-test was concerned, ANOVA analysis did not reveal a significant difference between the four conditions, F(3,76)=1.2, p=.31; but post-hoc analysis revealed significant difference between Pr and Pr + Ph (p=0.05) only.

DISCUSSION

Speech Recognition Support for Word Reading

The results from the second experiment support our three hypotheses, i.e. H2, H3 and H4. That is, when productive vocabulary practice is made possible by speech recognition, adding an orthographic hint facilitates significant decoding gains (but not semantic extraction), adding a phonological hint facilitates significant semantic extraction gains (but not decoding), and introducing both hints together (in the short-term only) and separately (in both the short- and long-term) facilitates significant gains on word reading. While these results are suggested by the lexical quality hypothesis, our work nevertheless contributes to our understanding of word reading in many ways. Firstly, the LQH has not been applied to inform productive vocabulary practice as an instructional approach. As such, we have provided stronger support for the LQH by showing that its implications continue to hold when applied to productive training.

Secondly, the results from our second experiment provides evidence that there are distinctive categories of productive vocabulary training, each of which is useful for a different knowledge subsystem within word reading. This implies that computing systems that employ speech recognition for productive vocabulary training need to be designed to allow for a more targeted approach to word reading training. Specifically, for the decoding subsystem to be strengthened, it is important to help learners connect their orthographic knowledge of a word with its meaning (e.g., through an orthographic hint). On the other hand, for semantic extraction, it is important instead to help learners link their phonological knowledge of the word with its meaning (e.g., through a phonological hint). More research in speech user-interface design could be done to experiment with more variations of the scaffolds (including hints) that could support each subsystem, so that we understand how to better improve overall word reading skill.

Implications for Design

Thirdly, thus far, no language learning software that contains speech recognition support has been studied in the context of improving literacy skills through productive vocabulary practice. While speech recognition systems have generally experienced limited adoption, our promising results suggest that this niche domain of speech recognition-based systems for productive vocabulary practice deserves more attention by speech technology experts, language learning specialists, as well as researchers and practitioners in human-computer interaction. At the least, this niche domain could accelerate the adoption of speech technologies in this specific context. We shall now outline some new areas for research in speech user-interfaces that this work opens.

A game that uses speech recognition to interpret the actions that a player issues through a verbal command is commonly known as a voice-command game [38]. Although we have not encountered such a game on the cellphone, they have been implemented on gaming devices such as the Nintendo DS and Playstation, and have appeared to be popular with players. For instance, the two most popular voice-command games on Nintendo DS called Nintendogs and Brain Age have sold 22.27 and 17.41 million copies, making them the third- and fifth-most popular game in the history of all Nintendo games by 2009 [25]. Existing voice-command games have focused purely on entertainment, not learning goals, and have not received much attention from academic researchers. As the first study to demonstrate the effects of voice-command games on literacy skills (or for that matter, learning), we hope to encourage more HCI and educational games researchers to experiment with more ways in which the interface and gameplay experience in voice-command games can be designed to better support educational goals.

Next, given the cost to manufacture visual displays, access to computing systems and services could be made more widespread through non-visual devices. Examples include IBM's Spoken Web [1] and speech-based Interactive Voice Response (IVR) systems. While IVRs have not received as much attention in the HCI community, and our games involve an automatic speech recognizer running locally on a mobile device, our results suggest that speech-based applications for productive vocabulary practice could be designed and delivered over an IVR system. More research is needed to understand how such vocabulary training can be delivered over a non-visual user-interface. Although it is possible to provide only phonological and not orthographic hints over a non-visual interface, we view this as an opportunity and not a limitation. As our results have shown, phonological hints can be used to improve semantic extraction skills, but not decoding skills. Literacy instructors and researchers believe that decoding skills are far easier to master than semantic extraction [26]. Through low-cost interfaces like IVRs, we can potentially increase the reach of literacy training among low-income learners in the developing world, where we have observed teachers and other instructional resources to be much better prepared to target decoding skills (but not semantic extraction).

Along the same line of affordability, educational platforms such as the Multiple Mice computer (that could be attached to and accept input from multiple mouse devices) have been designed to allow computing resources -- which are fairly expensive in low-resource communities – to be shared by more than one user at the same time. Speaker identification via speech recognition is potentially another way for many learners to share a computational device for productive vocabulary training. More research on designing such user-interfaces and digital learning experiences is needed.

ACKNOWLEDGMENTS

This research was funded by Nokia Research and CMU HCII. We thank Venkatesh Keri, Gaurav Arora and Yash Soni for their technical contributions; Indrani Vedula for her invaluable help with setting up both the studies, and Kaushik Shelat for his help in administering these studies.

REFERENCES

1. Agarwal, S., Jain, A., Kumar, A., Rajput, N. The World Wide Telecom Web Browser. In *Proc. ACM DEV 2010.*
2. Angrist, J., and Lavy, V. The Effect of a Change in Language of Instruction on the Returns to Schooling in Morocco. *Journal of Labor Economics, 15* (1), 1997.
3. Arora, P. Karaoke for Social and Cultural Change. *ICES (4)* 3, *Paper 1*. Troubador Publishing Ltd. 2006.
4. August, D., Carlo, M. S., Dressler, C., & Snow, C. (2005). The critical role of vocabulary development for English language learners. *Learning Disabilities Research & Practice, 20,* 50-57.
5. Barnard, E., Davel, M., and Huyssteen, G. Speech technology for information access: a South African case study. In *Proc. AAAI Symposium on Artificial Intelligence 2010.*
6. Carnegie Speech, http://www.carnegiespeech.com/
7. Chu, S., Povey, D. Speaking rate adaptation using continuous frame rate normalization. In *Proc. IEEE ICSSP*, March 2010.
8. Colorado Literacy Foundation – To Enhance and Enrich Literacy Throughout Colorado. http://www.coloradoliteracyfoundation.org
9. De Bot, K. The psycholinguistics of the Output Hypothesis. *Language Learning, 46,* 529-555, 1996.
10. Dias, M.B., Mills-Tettey, G.A., and Mertz, J. The TechBridgeWorld Initiative: Broadening Perspectives in

Computing Technology Education and Research. In *Proc. of the international symposium on Women and ICT: Creating Global Transformation*, ACM Press (2005).

11. Dunn, L. M., & Dunn, L. M. *Peabody Picture Vocabulary Test (3rd edition)*. American Guidance Service, 1997.
12. Edwards, J. *Multilingualism*. Routeledge, 1994.
13. Gee, J.P. *What Video Games Have to Teach Us About Learning and Literacy*. Palgrave Macmillan, 2004.
14. Huggins-Daines, D., Kumar, M., Chan, A., Black, A., Ravishankar, M., and Rudnicky, A.I. PocketSphinx: a free, real-time continuous speech recognition system for handheld devices. In *Proc. ICASSP*, 185–188, May 2006.
15. Kam, M., Kumar, A., Jain, S., Mathur, A., and Canny, J. Improving Literacy in Rural India: Cellphone Games in an After-School Program. *In Proc. of IEEE/ACM Conference on Information and Communication Technology and Development* 2009.
16. Kam, M., Mathur, A., Kumar, A., and Canny, J. Designing Digital Games for Rural Children: A Study of Traditional Village Games in India. In *Proc. CHI 2009*.
17. Kam, M., Agarwal, A., Kumar, A., Lal, S., Mathur, A., Tewari, A., and Canny, J. Designing E-Learning Games for Rural Children in India: A Format for Balancing Learning with Fun. In *Proc. DIS 2008*.
18. Kam, M., Ramachandran, D., Devanathan, V., Tewari, A., and Canny, J. Localized Iterative Design for Language Learning in Underdeveloped Regions: The PACE Framework. In *Proc. CHI 2007*.
19. Kumar, A., Tewari, A., Horrigan, S., Kam, M., Metze, F., and Canny, J. Rethinking Speech Recognition on Mobile Devices. In *Proc. ACM Conf. on IUI 2011*.
20. Lee, S., Potamianos, A., Narayanan, S., Acoustics of children's speech: developmental changes of temporal and spectral parameters. *J. Acoust*. Soc. Amer. 105, 1999, 1455–1468.
21. McCandless, M. Word rejection for a literacy tutor. S.B. Thesis, MIT, May 1992.
22. Miller, G. A. (1956). The magical number seven, plus or minus two: some limits on our capacity for processing information. *Psychological Review* 63 (2): 81–97. doi:10.1037/h0043158.
23. Mills-Tettey, A., Mostow, J., Dias, M. B., Sweet, T. M., Belousov, S. M., Dias, M. F., & Gong, H. Improving Child Literacy in Africa: Experiments with an Automated Reading Tutor. *Prof. 3rd IEEE/ACM Conference on Information and Communication Technologies on Development*, 2009.
24. Munshi, K., and Rosenzweig, M. Traditional Institutions Meet the Modern World: Caste, Gender, and Schooling Choice in a Globalizing Economy. In *American Economic Review, 96* (4), 1225-1252, 2006.
25. Nintendo. Financial Results Briefing for the 69th Fiscal Term Ended March 2009. pp. 6, 2009. URL: http://www.nintendo.co.jp/ir/pdf/2009/090508e.pdf, last accessed: May 8, 2009
26. NLP. (2006). Developing Literacy in Second-Language Learners: Report of the National Literacy Panel on Language-Minority Children and Youth. In D. August,& T. Shanah (Eds.) Mahwah, NJ: Lawrence Erlbaum.
27. Pal, J., Lakshmanan, M., and Toyama, K. My Child Will Be Respected: Parental Perspectives on Computers in Rural India. In *Proc. of 2nd IEEE/ACM International Conference on Information and Communication Technologies and Development*, 2007.
28. Patel, N., Chittamuru, D., Jain, A., Dave, P., Parikh, T. Avaaj Otalo - A Field Study of an Interactive Voice Forum for Small Farmers in Rural India. In *Proc. CHI 2010*.
29. Pawar, U., Pal, J., Gupta, R., Toyama, K. Multiple Mice for Retention Tasks in Disadvantaged Schools. In *Proc. CHI 2007*.
30. Perfetti, C. A. Reading ability: Lexical quality to comprehension. *Scientific Studies of Reading, 11*, 357-383, 2007.
31. Perfetti, C. A., & Hart. L. The lexical quality hypothesis. In L. Verhoeven, C. Elbro & P. Reitsma (Eds.), *Precursors of Functional Literacy* vol. 11, 67–86. John Benjamins, 2001.
32. Pinon, R., and Haydon, J. The Benefits of the English Language for Individuals and Societies: Quantitative Indicators from Cameroon, Nigeria, Rwanda, Bangladesh and Pakistan. A custom report compiled by Euromonitor International for the British Council, 2010.
33. Plauche, M., Nallasamy, U., Pal, J., Wooters, C., and Ramachandran, D. Speech Recognition for Illiterate Access to Information and Technology. In *Proc. of International Conference on Information and Communications Technologies and Development*, 2006.
34. Rosetta Stone, Ltd. Rosetta Stone Language Learning. http://www.rosettastone.com/schools, accessed Sept. 22, 2011.
35. Sherwani, J., Ali, N., Mirza, S., Fatma, A., Memon, Y., Karim, M., Tongia, R., Rosenfeld, R. HealthLine: Speech-based Access to Health Information by Low-literate Users. In *Proc. IEEE/ACM Int'l Conference on Information and Communication Technologies and Development*, 2007.
36. Swain, M., & Lapkin, S. (1995). Problems in output and the cognitive processes they generate: A step towards second language learning. *Applied Linguistics*.
37. Tewari, A., Goyal, N., Chan, M., Yau, T., Canny, J., Schroeder, U. SPRING: Speech and Pronunciation Improvement through Games, for Hispanic children. In *Proc. IEEE/ACM International Conference on Information and Communication Technologies and Development*, 2010.
38. Zyda, M., Thukral, D., Ferrans, J., Engelsma & Hans, M. Enabling a Voice Modality in Mobile Games through Voice XML. *Proc. of ACM SIGGRAPH Symposium on Video Games*, 143-147, 2008.

Interactive Visualization for Low Literacy Users: From Lessons Learnt To Design

Neesha Kodagoda, B L William Wong, Chris Rooney, Nawaz Khan
Middlesex University, London, NW4 4BT, UK
{n.kodagoda, w.wong, c.rooney, n.khan}@mdx.ac.uk

ABSTRACT
This paper aims to address the problems low literacy (LL) users face when searching for information online. The first part of this paper summarizes the problems that LL user's face, and establishes a set of design principles for interfaces suitable for LL users. This is followed by a description of how these design principles are mapped to a novel interface for interactive data retrieval. The interface was realized into a working system and evaluated against a traditional web interface for both high literacy (HL) and LL users. The suitability of the designs was analyzed using performance data, subjective feedback and an observational analysis. The findings from the study suggest that LL users perform better and prefer the proposed designs over a traditional web interface.

Author Keywords
Low literacy; high literacy; mental models; design principles; visualization; user interface;

ACM Classification Keywords
H.5.2 User Interfaces (D.2.2, H.1.2, I.3.6).

General Terms
Design, Experimentation, Verification.

INTRODUCTION
The definition of literacy is one's ability to read, write and speak depending on the expectations of the social economic environment they live in [20]. In the United Kingdom alone, however, 16% (5.2 million) of the population are classified as low literate [46], which is defined as having reading and comprehension levels that are below secondary school level (equivalent to a reading age of 11) [14].

Government Departments and other non-profit organizations are placing an increasing amount of information on the web whilst at the same time reducing face-to-face advice. This creates a challenge for low literacy (LL) users who have difficulty accessing information through traditional web interfaces [42]. Those who manage to overcome these initial barriers are further challenged by information that requires higher reading skills, hierarchical menu structures, and inconsistent layouts across different websites [42].

Previous research has shown LL users to be less successful in finding information during online information seeking [12,42]. They exhibit different behaviors compared to high literacy (HL) users such as reading word-for-word when confronted with long and dense pages, having a narrow field of view, skipping chunks of text, being satisfied with information quickly, and avoiding searching as it requires spelling [43]. It becomes increasingly important to recognize that interfaces designed primarily for HL users are not used in the same way by LL users.

This presents two challenges: (i) being able to understand LL users in a way that allows for new designs, not typically found in a designer's repertoire, to be considered, and (ii) understanding the problem that needs addressing. The first part of this paper summarizes the problems LL users face, and establishes a set of design principles for interfaces suitable for LL users. This is followed by a description of how these design principles are mapped to the design concepts of a novel interface for interactive data retrieval [41].

For the purpose of this paper the above interface was realized into a working system and evaluated against a traditional web interface, which is described in the later part of this paper. As well as user performance and subjective feedback, an observational analysis of the effectiveness of the design principles is also described.

PROBLEMS WITH LOW LITERACY
Research carried out to identify whether differences exist between HL and LL users when seeking information online identified clear differences in user performance [15]. LL users took nine times longer to complete an information seeking task, visited eight times more web pages, back-tracked thirteen times more, were four times more likely to re-visit a web page, spent a third more time on a web page, and were thirteen times more likely to get lost.

A follow-up study investigated what causes these performance differences and identified variations in information seeking behavior strategies for HL and LL users [17]. The findings identified differences in information seeking behavior strategies, the following: reading strategy (scanning vs. word-for-word), focus (wide

Permission to make digital or hard copies of all or part of this work for personal or classroom use is granted without fee provided that copies are not made or distributed for profit or commercial advantage and that copies bear this notice and the full citation on the first page. To copy otherwise, or republish, to post on servers or to redistribute to lists, requires prior specific permission and/or a fee.
CHI'12, May 5–10, 2012, Austin, Texas, USA.
Copyright 2012 ACM 978-1-4503-1015-4/12/05...$10.00.

vs. narrow field of view), verification (optimizing vs. satisficing), recovery (good vs. poor), trajectories (homogeneous vs. heterogeneous), abandonment (tolerance vs. intolerance of uncertainty), and representation (good vs. poor system model). LL users had a tendency to read word-for-word and tended to focus narrowly on parts of the screen due to skipping chunks of text, whereas the HL users often scanned the page for relevant information. LL users tended to go for early closure instead of *differentiating* and *verifying* the information found for correctness. Then when they got lost (which they appeared to do very often), the LL users struggled to recover from their mistakes and resume the search task. The search paths or trajectories employed by LL users were observed to be more haphazard by trial and error, resembling patterns of use by one who has little understanding of how things are stored. In contrast, the HL users in that short time were able to quickly develop a reasonable mental model of the information architecture and therefore able to direct their search to a more successful one.

To investigate what support mechanisms need to be in place for LL users' information seeking, the identified behavior strategies of HL and LL users were mapped to David Ellis's [5] information seeking behavior model, using it as a theoretical lens [16]. The findings identified two refined information seeking behavior models for the HL and LL users which showed clear differences. The comparison of the two models revealed that the strategies, actions, and identifications employed by HL users were not evident with the LL users, contributing possible reasons as to why LL users were less successful.

Users will develop a mental model of information provided to them [22], and an ideal system will have a strong mapping between the users' mental model and the system's conceptual model [31]. A follow up study tried to determine if differences in literacy has an effect on users' mental model of the information menu structure of a traditional website [18]. The results showed a difference in mental models between HL and LL users. However, while there was a consistency in the mental models of HL users, LL users' mental models were heterogeneous to each other. This suggests difficulties if developing a hierarchical menu structure for traditional websites to suit all LL users.

While low literacy is assessed using reading levels, it is clear that the cognitive processes (i.e. users' strategies, behavior and mental model) are also different, contributing to why LL users are less successful during information seeking [15,17,18]. Sherwani and colleagues [37] suggest that when designing for oral or LL users it is not only the reading levels that need to be taken into account but also their different ways of thinking. Medhi et al. [24] and colleagues reconfirm content designed for HL users is less likely to be appropriate for oral or LL users.

There is a large body of research that focuses on reading difficulties, which includes (i) lowering reading levels, (ii) using multimodal interfaces with little or no text , (iii) audio facilities with voice feedback and voice input, (iv) the use of color and semi-abstract graphics, (v) using white space by minimizing clutter, (vi) increasing font size, and (vii) the use of flat menu structures [6,8,25,26,29,42]. These studies, however, do not take advantage of interactive visualization as a support mechanism to amplify the users abilities [44], including their ability to reason [47].

Shneiderman [39] states that by trying to dumb down interfaces, it prevents innovation and exploring a broader spectrum of design considerations. This is also confirmed by Nielsen [28], who argues that rather than just refining an existing design, completely redesigning allows conception of novel and useful interfaces. Rich [34] observed that adapted design techniques should be used when designing systems that are aimed at more than one group of users.

DESIGN RECOMMENDATIONS

Based on the identified differences in LL users' reading strategy, verification, recovery, and perceived mental model, this section proposes a number of recommendations for designing user interfaces for LL users.

Reading strategy

As LL users are likely to have lower educational levels they are challenged with less critical and abstract thinking skills. The result of this is that LL users start word-for-word reading at a very early stage in their search [16]. Perfetti [32] explains that LL users devote a higher cognitive effort to low-level reading processes (word level), leaving less room for comprehension of the overall message. This makes it difficult to extract information from the text using simple inferences [4]. A likely coping mechanism they adopt is to follow a narrow field of view.

To improve LL users' reading strategies on the internet, Frank-Stromborg and Olsen [8] suggested the removal of page clutter from the screen, avoiding long lists by boxing information separately to provide further focus, and the use of white space and color to draw attention. As LL are likely to have low spatial abilities, the use of visual momentum (animation) to assist with integrating and extracting information is also expected to improve their performance [44,48].

Verification

During an information seeking task, LL users walked away with an adequate solution, suggesting that they employed a satisficing solution [17,29,33,40]. The satisficing theory suggests that individuals are most likely to find information that is most convenient, compromising accuracy, quality or efficiency.

HL users are able to revisit previously visited information without visual memory cues [16]. This allows them to investigate new information and verify it against previously visited information. Since word-by-word reading already places a high cognitive load on LL users, they find it difficult to remember where they have been and, therefore, are satisfied easily. The steps discussed above on reducing the amount of word-for-word reading are likely to reduce LL users' cognitive load, enabling them to move from a satisficing strategy to a verifying strategy.

Visual cues such as color change draw users' attention and focus. Healy and colleagues [10] identified that users are able to pre-attentively recognize differences in color however, unable to recognize simultaneous variation of color plus shape. While traditional websites change the color of previously visited hyperlinks, the subtle change is not evident to LL users [15]. A more obvious cue is required.

The Google lists of lists design, that users are familiar with, is not a suitable representational form for users who reason in a less abstract fashion [8,45]. Also, users have been known to benefit from the ability to spatially arrange data [21]. The capability to spatially collate previously visited documents provides another cue for LL users.

Recovery

Recovery occurs when HL or LL users identify irrelevant or incorrect content and then adjust the search to a more focused and successful one. However, LL users were less successful in recovering from identified irrelevant or wrong links to a successful search outcome. Again, the expecting reduction in cognitive load caused by the reading and verification design principles will support LL users in recovery. Functionality such as visual memory cues, the ability to spatially collate previously visited documents, and the ability to delete unwanted document can also be used to support recovery. Since some LL users fail to recover when lost in the detail, keeping the context of the search permanently visible will help them return to the original search and proceed down a new path [3].

Perceived mental model

Traditional websites contain hierarchical information structures and links that require LL users to make early decisions, which is a problem because LL users have less of an understanding of hierarchical menu structures than HL users [24,37,42]. By adopting commands such as SEARCH, the user is presented with a discontinuous transition into new sections [11]. However, search is unable to give an overview of a conceptual model of the information menu system when compared with the hierarchical menu system. This is less of an issue since LL users struggle to conceptualize the spatial layout of the data. Allowing LL users to spatially arrange the data using techniques such as visual momentum [48] and display patterns [13] may help develop their mental model and reduce search abandonment.

INVISQUE

This section describes a system called Invisque (INteractive VIsual Search and Query Environment), which was developed as a proof of concept prototype for creating queries and searching for information in an interactive and visual manner [41] (see Figure 2). The non-conventional visualization is based on a metaphor of index cards laid out on a tabletop. As an electronic representation, it has been embedded with a variety of functions not easily carried out in the physical world. The design itself is guided by principles such as visual cues and affordances, cognitive load theory, focus + context, and Gestalt principles of perception. These techniques can be incorporated yet keeping the system simple and learnable by empowering good interface design principles and heuristics [30,31].

The proof of concept was originally designed for use in electronic library systems for searching and retrieving scholarly and scientific publications [41]. Since the mock-up contained concepts that it was felt were relevant to LL users, a working prototype was created and further developed to meet the design requirements described above.

Invisque reduces the cognitive load of early word-for-word reading by boxing information on a white space, and allowing the amount of data visible to be altered through the use of a slider. Verification is addressed by using visual cues to draw attention to visited index cards, a wizard save tool for making memory notes, and the ability view multiple searches simultaneously. Recovery is also addressed by using obvious visual cues, and wizard delete tool for removing irrelevant search results. Finally, the ability to drag and cluster search results aims to improve LL users' perceived mental models of the data.

Figure 1. Search canvas with two search results.
A) data slider bar, B) data interval window, C) search term, D) search results displayed by index cards , the index cards are organized in the X-axis by subject matter and Y-axis by demand, E) cluster close button , F) total number of results, G) information drill down icon

When a user commences their search they are presented with a simple search box. Rather than a hierarchical menu a search box will minimize LL users' mental model differences and prevent early word-for-word reading. The results are presented as a cluster of index cards, with each index card representing a search result (see Figure 1). By placing each search item in an index card the amount of text is reduced and the information is boxed (the user is able to drill down to view more information if required, see Figure 1G). This addresses the reading strategy by reducing LL users' cognitive load. Clustering the index cards together on the white space draws attention and reduces screen clutter [8].

To prevent LL users being overwhelmed, and prevent overlap, only the top eight results are displayed by default, which are the results mostly likely to be viewed [19]. The user is able to increase or decrease the number of index cards that they want to view by adjusting a slider (see Figure 1A). The index cards are ordered in both x and y axes depending on the metadata (e.g., relevance on the x axis and date on the y axis). Literature suggests visualizing information using meaningful dimensions have been shown to be useful [1,7,27,38].

Visual cues are used to help LL users verify their search. The index cards that have already been viewed (drilled down) are colored purple (see Figure 2A). This is consistent with traditional websites, however, changing the color of the index card is expected to be more noticeable than only changing the color of the text (hyperlink).

Users are able to create multiple searches in the same search canvas; this provides the user with an overview of multiple result sets. Transparency is used to distinguish between the current and previous searches. Zooming can be used to either draw focus on an area of interest, or give an overall view of the complete search space. With hierarchical menu systems, if LL users proceed down an incorrect path then they face the problem of "what was I looking for?". In this situation, LL users can become lost in the data and unable to recover. By presenting the complete search space, LL users are able to see where they came from and proceed down a new path, thus addressing the problem of recovery.

Each index card can be dragged and placed anywhere on the canvas, giving the user the flexibility to arrange and order information as they see fit. This allows the user to group relevant index cards that come from different searches, supporting the verification process by reducing the need to memorize the location of relevant index cards.

Invisque also has a Wizard feature which allows users to delete or save index cards (Figure 2D shows the save area, and Figure 2C shows the delete area). The Wizard can also be toggled on or off by clicking a button on the task bar (see Figure 2F). If a user feels an index card is of a particular importance, then they can drag it into the save area. The results of which is that the index card is colored green, providing an obvious visual cue to the user (see Figure 2B).

Index cards can be deleted by dragging them to the bin icon (see Figure 2C), which is representative of dragging icons to the recycle bin on a Windows desktop, reducing clutter. Also the ability for LL users to discard data support the verification and recovery processes.

While the focus has been on bridging the gap between HL and LL users, the hope is that the designs will also support both literacy groups for performing search and query tasks.

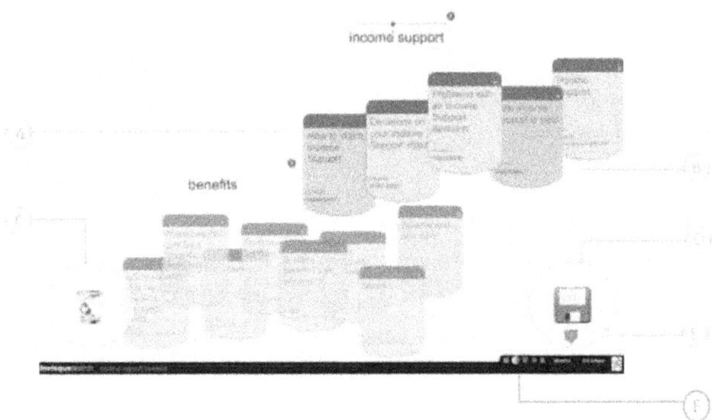

Figure 2. Direct manipulation and grouping information.

A) Index cards viewed or drilled down are marked in purple, B) Index cards saved are marked in Green, C) and index card is dragged here to be deleted, D) an index card is dragged here to be saved, E) the total number of index cards that has been saved, and F) Wizard icon, which switches on or off the delete and save areas.

EVALUATION

This evaluation compares Invisque with a traditional website for search and retrieval tasks. The aim is to investigate whether Invisque can improve the performance of LL users such that they match the performance of HL users. The performance measures are search outcome (successful, unsuccessful or abandon), time spent, and number of pages visited. In addition users' perceived feedback on the two systems was captured using questionnaires. An observational analysis on how the design features support LL users is also reported.

Based on the literature and design principles the following two hypotheses were identified:

1. Both HL and LL users' task success would be higher with Invisque than with a traditional website.
2. The time spent and number of pages visited for both HL and LL users would be lower in with Invisque than with a traditional website.

METHOD

Participants

Participants were recruited from a local Citizens Advice Bureau (CAB). They had to have computer and internet literacy (weekly computer and internet usage between four – ten hours), and participants with any known learning disabilities were excluded (such as dyslexia). In total, 24 participants took part in the study. Twelve were HL while the remaining twelve were LL. Twelve were male and twelve were female, with a mean age of 39 years (ranging from 35 to 50).

Of the LL users who participated seven were unemployed (over six months) and the remaining five were working at the time of the study (two cleaners, one restaurant serving staff, one security officer, and one builder). Two of the HL users had been made redundant in the past two months and remaining ten were working at the time of the study (two admin staff, two sales reps, one counter worker, one receptionist, one office manager, one accountant and one nurse).

Ten of the LL users had left formal education prior to completing secondary school (GCSE level), and the remaining two LL users had left prior to completing collage or sixth form (A-level). Two of the HL users had left formal education prior to completing high school, while four had left prior to completing collage and finally the remaining six had university degrees.

Participants' literacy was evaluated using the UK's National Skills for life literacy survey [46]. The survey marks participants out of a score of 40, with any score under 29 being classed as LL. The HL participants for this study scored an average of 33 out of 40 (ranging from 30 to 38) while the LL participants scored an average of 13 out of 40 (ranging from 7 to 16).

Materials

For the purpose of this study a social service website in the United Kingdom was selected (Adviceguide - http://www.adviceguide.org.uk). The content of the site is relevant to the needs of both the HL and LL participants. However, none of the participants had experience using the Adviceguide website beforehand.

The data from the Adviceguide was imported to the Invisque system. There were no changes made to the content or to the menu links, so both systems could be used to access the same data and, therefore, allow comparisons to be made between the two.

Procedure

Six information search tasks were developed based on advice frequently requested by walk-in clients of the local CAB (between April 2005 and May 2007). For example, *I am currently on Income Support, what other benefits am I entitled to?* The search tasks were of varying task difficulties (easy, medium and difficult). One aspect of the task difficulty was influenced by web navigation of the *Adviceguide* website, which starts from general over view and then require users to drill down to reach more specific topics (e.g. from the home page to main sections and then, finally to subsections). Another aspect was if the webpage content focused on one or multiple concepts or topics. Finally, the third aspect was the reading levels of the text.

Participants were not permitted to use external websites or other search facilities, however, there were no restrictions within the Adviceguide site such as using the search or the hierarchical navigation structure.

The study was conducted in our usability lab. Each participant performed six tasks in total, three with Invisque and three with Adviceguide. For each interface participants performed one easy, one medium and one difficult task. Latin-square was used to counter balance the order of interface and tasks. Participants were first given time to familiarize themselves with both systems prior to the study. A two minute video demonstrating the functionality of Invisque was shown. Participants were given one task at a time. Each search task started from the home page of the system. In the case of Adviceguide, cache was reset for each task to minimize any confounding variable efforts such as cached page visits. Searching difficulties due to spelling was overcome by using a Wizard of Oz voice technique for the purpose of this study [2,9,23]. The participants declared when they had either found the answer or abandon the search. The answer or solution found for the task was written down on the answer sheet provided.

Participants were informed of the study procedure, and gave consent for video and audio recording. Multiple Cognitive Task Analysis (CTA) methods were used to extract and understand the participants' decision process during their tasks. Methods such as think-aloud (video capture), user observation (video capture and field notes taken), semi-structured interviews (video play-back and field notes taken), and questionnaires focusing on the systems were used as data collection methods. Each participant's level of literacy was evaluated once all tasks and interviews were completed [46].

Data collection

For the purpose of this study questionnaires were used to capture participants' subjective feedback. The post-test questionnaires [35] captured participants overall feedback about the system [36]. The questionnaires were rated on a seven-point Likert scale, ranging from strongly disagree to strongly agree.

Measurements

The following dependent variables were measured using video and system log files for each condition: (i) Search outcome, defined as either: (a) successful – this is when the participants find the relevant information, (b) unsuccessful – when participants completed the task, but found the incorrect information, (c) abandon – this is when participants stopped the search because either they were unable to find any relevant information, or they assumed that the information was not available, (ii) time on task, the duration of the task from the moment a participant starts the task until he/she decides to stop the search (either due to finding the answer or abandoning the search), and (iii) number of pages visited, which is the total number of pages a user views during the information task.

RESULTS

The results will be discussed in three sections. The first is quantitative data analysis, second is the subjective feedback from the questionnaires and, finally, an analysis of how the features of Invisque supported the needs of LL users.

Quantitative Analysis

Task Success

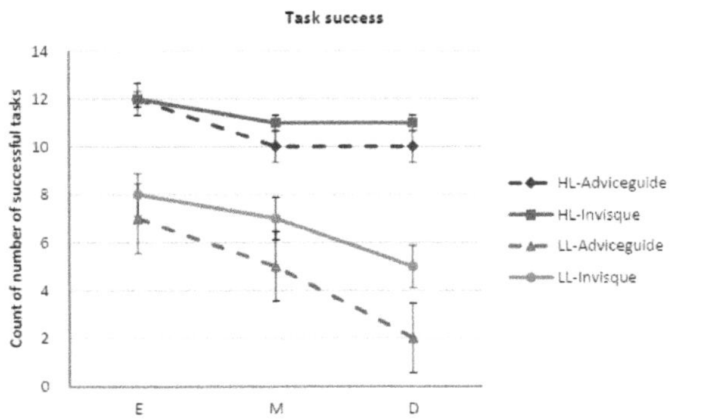

Figure 3. HL and LL users' successful task on Adviceguide and Invisque.

A Friedman test was carried out using task (E-easy, M-medium, D-difficult) and system (Adviceguide, Invisque) as within subject factors and literacy (HL, LL) as a between subject factor.

The Friedman test found there to be no significant effects on task success for HL users $\chi 2(5, N = 12) = 4.00, p < 0.55$. Kendall's W was 0.07, indicating no strong effects either. The test also found there to be no significant effect on success for LL users $\chi 2(5, N = 12) = 7.00, p < 0.22$. Kendall's W is 0.12, also indicating no strong effects.

Although the effects were not significant, Figure 3 shows that LL users became increasingly less successful as the task difficulty increased, however, this increase was more predominant with the Adviceguide system.

Time on task

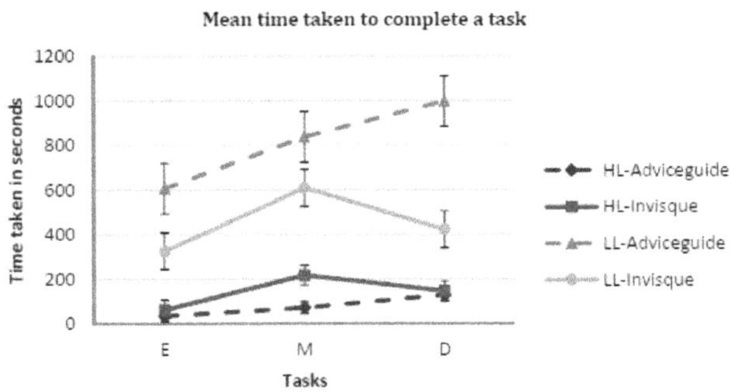

Figure 4. HL and LL users' time on task for Adviceguide and Invisque.

In order to assess task completion time, a repeated measures ANOVA was used with task (E-easy, M-medium, D-difficult) and system (Adviceguide, Invisque) as within subject factors and literacy (HL, LL) as a between subject factor. Mauchly's test indicated that the assumption of sphericity had been violated for the main effects of system, $\chi^2(0) = 0.00$, p<.00. Therefore degrees of freedom were corrected using Greenhouse-Geisser estimates of sphericity (ε=1.00 for the main effect of system). All significant effects are reported ($p < .05$).

There was a significant main effect on task, $F(2, 44) = 13.27$. Contrasts revealed a significant effect on total time on easy tasks were much less than that of the difficult tasks, $F(1, 22) = 22.93$, and there was no significant contrasts between total time on medium and difficult task, $F(1, 22) = 0.07$. There was a significant main effect on system, $F(1, 22) = 26.20$. The contrasts revealed a significant effect for total time on Adviceguide were much higher than the Invisque system, $F(1, 22) = 26.20$. There was a significant effect on literacy $F(1, 22) = 258.74$.

There was a significant interaction between system and literacy, $F(2, 22) = 52.89$. The LL users were quicker with the Invisque interface, but the HL users were in fact slightly slower (see Figure 4).

There was also a significant interaction between task and system, $F(2, 22) = 4.11$. The results suggest that both sets of users performed the difficult task quicker than the medium task with the Invisque interface (see Figure 4).

Number of pages visited

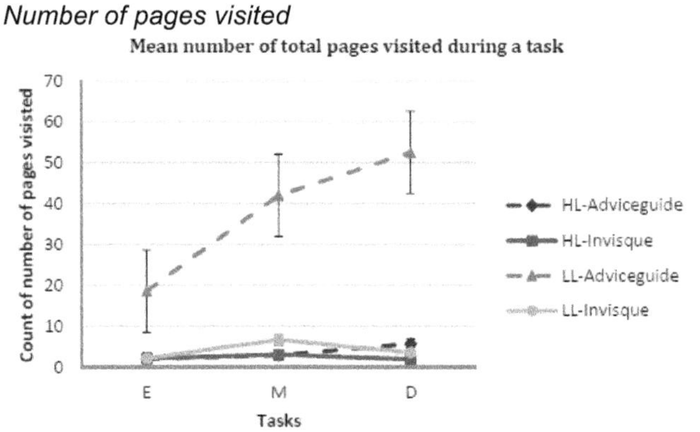

Figure 5. HL and LL users' total number of pages visited during a task on Adviceguide and Invisque.

The same method was used to analyze the total number of pages visited. Mauchly's test indicated that the assumption of sphericity had been violated for the main effects of system, $\chi^2(0) = 0.00$, p<.00 and interaction task and system, $\chi^2(0) = 12.39$, p<.00. Therefore degrees of freedom were corrected using Greenhouse-Geisser and Huynh-Feldt respectively for estimates of sphericity (ε=1.00 for the main effect of system, ε =0.76 for the interaction task and system). All effects reported as significant at $p < .05$.

There was a significant main effect on task, $F(2, 44) = 82.88$. The contrasts revealed that significantly fewer pages were visited on the easy tasks than the difficult tasks, $F(1, 22) = 216.95$, and fewer pages were visited on the medium tasks than the difficult tasks, $F(1, 22) = 9.57$. There was also a significant main effect on system, $F(1, 22) = 1672.41$. The contrasts revealed that significantly more pages were visited when using Adviceguide than Invisque, $F(1, 22) = 1672.41$. A significant effect on literacy indicated that HL users visited significantly fewer pages than LL users, $F(1, 22) = 582.03$.

There was a significant interaction effect between tasks, system and literacy, $F(2, 44) = 63.46$. Post-hoc tests showed that HL users viewed fewer pages on the Invisque system but only for the difficult tasks, and that LL users viewed significantly fewer pages on Invisque for all three levels of task difficulty (see Figure 5).

Subjective Feedback

Paired t-tests were used to compare participants' subjective feedback for the Adviceguide and Invisque systems that was captured by a questionnaire using a seven point Likert scale.

Both HL and LL users found Adviceguide to be significantly more familiar than Invisque (HL:$p<.01$, LL:$p<.01$), confirming that Adviceguide represents a traditional website while Invisque represent a type of interface that they have not seen before. HL users felt that both systems worked as they wanted them to, whereas, there was a significant difference between the way LL users wanted both systems to work (HL:$p=1$, LL:$p<.01$). This confirms that LL users are unhappy with traditional web based systems. Which is also supported by the fact that LL users would use Adviceguide less frequently than Invisque (HL:$p=.75$, LL:$p<.01$).

HL users required significantly less effort to use Adviceguide than Invisque, however, LL users required significantly more effort using Adviceguide (HL:$p<.01$, LL:$p<.01$). Similarly, HL users felt Invisque to be less useful than Adviceguide, while, LL users felt Adviceguide to be less useful than Invisque (HL:$p=.06$, LL:$p<.01$). HL users found both systems easy to search, while LL users found it significantly easier to search on Invisque (HL:$p=.07$, LL:$p<.01$).

Unlike HL users, LL users found Adviceguide significantly easier to learn (HL:$p=.08$, LL:$p<.01$), although the means were similar ($M=7$, $SD=0$ vs. $M=6.33$, $SD=0.49$). Both HL and LL users felt that Adviceguide could be used without instructions more than Invisque (HL:$p=.02$, LL:$p<.01$), again there was a marginal difference between the means (HL: $M=7$, $SD=0$ vs. $M=6.58$, $SD=.52$; LL: $M=7$, $SD=0$ vs. $M=6.50$,$SD=.52$). Both HL and LL users felt that Invisque was significantly more flexible than Adviceguide (HL:$p<.01$, LL:$p<.01$), and that they were significantly more satisfied with Invisque than Adviceguide (HL:$p<.01$, LL:$p<.01$).

OBSERVATIONAL ANALYSIS OF SUPPORT TOOLS

This section describes some of the features of Invisque that were predominantly used by LL users.

Wizard

The Wizard was used to either to discard index cards or mark them as important. For the delete feature, results showed that HL users used this function less than LL users (see Table 1). There was also an increase for the LL users as the task difficulty increased.

During the interviews, none of the HL users mentioned the delete tool. Most of the LL users who used the tool at some point during their search mentioned about it during the interviews. The LL users reacted well to the ability to filter the data by removing unwanted index cards. One of the LL users quoted as saying "*you want and get rid of the once you don't want*" when prompted to discuss their actions.

	HL USERS	LL USERS
Easy task	0	2
Medium difficult task	1	5
Difficult task	3	6

Table 1. HL and LL users who used the deleting support tool.

Similarly, for the save feature, HL users were observed to use this function less than LL users (see Table 2). Again, there is an increase in usage for LL users, as the difficulty increased.

	HL USERS	LL USERS
Easy task	0	3
Medium difficult task	3	6
Difficult task	4	7

Table 2. HL and LL users who used the save support tool.

When prompted during the interviews, LL users reacted well to the save feature. One participant was quoted saying "*I think I did another one, and I think the green one is the one I saved as that's what I was looking for and I could not find anything similar in the other* [another search cluster]", while another one said that "*because I look for different things in the normal sites and then I read something and then from there click on a link and go to another page and then you get lost and you cannot remember what you were looking for this was really brilliant*".

Performing multiple searches

A user is classed as performing a multiple search if they have more than one search cluster open at any one time. Again, LL users made better use of this feature, and used it more frequently as the difficulty increased (see Table 3).

When they were prompted during the interview, a HL user was quoted saying "*add another search in the same website like thing which is not possible with present day systems which was really nice*", while one LL user said "*I like the fact I can leave one search and start with another in the same place*".

	HL USERS	LL USERS
Easy task	0	1
Medium difficult task	0	3
Difficult task	2	5

Table 3. HL and LL users who used the multiple search functionality.

Change the number of index cards display

At the beginning of each search, users were presented with just eight index cards. Both literacy groups made use of the slider to increase and decrease the number of index cards. This ability to define the search window was well received, with one HL user quoted saying "*you can minimize or get more search results by clicking on this [slider] that was good*", while a LL user explained "*the fact you can vary it from 8 to how many that allows you to scan any tab [index card] you want*".

Distinctly identify index cards visited

Index cards already viewed show a clear distinct color change from blue to purple. This was particularly well received LL users who were quoted as saying "*the color the boxes is good to as if to get inside, when it is simple maybe I can get the information quicker*" and "*this will be fantastic for people who are learning computers, because of the boxes it makes it more clear what you're going to look for, the boxes make it more easy, plus you know what you have looked at as it changed to purple*".

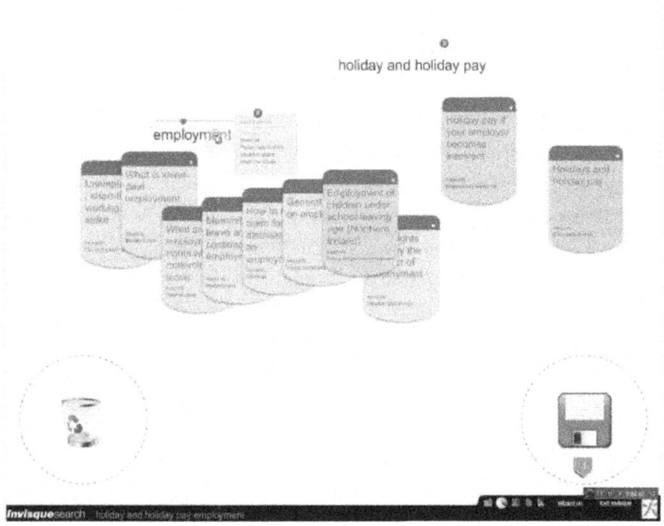

Figure 6. A users identifying the save support tool and drilled down items from two search clusters.

User feedback

Overall, Invisque was liked by both groups of users. The comments suggest that HL and LL users liked the way in which information was visually organized and presented in boxes. The flexibility of being able to move index cards freely around the screen gave users the freedom to organize their own information space. The users felt it was novel but learnable, and they preferred the white space and simplicity of the system. One of the HL users was quoted saying "*information was presented in a great way..., I think I quite like it as I am able to spread my search around the screen*", while one of the LL users were quoted saying "*the thing that I liked was it is very straight forward, second system*[Adviceguide] *has a lot of lists you have to keep reading to find out what to select, so I like the first system* [Invisque] *because of that*", and another LL explained "*wow I like that system it is clear!*".

There were few negative comments from both groups about the system. The comments suggested that all HL and LL users disliked index cards being overlapping at the start of the search. They further raised questions on how more information could be displayed without being overlapped. Most HL users said they preferred the traditional site, while almost all the LL users said otherwise. One of the HL users was quoted saying "*if you have two searches, there is a possibility to get lost, as there will be information in different places in the screen*", and one LL user explained "*sometime it is a bit confusing if you have many active searches because you don't know which belongs to which, like divide when you move it*".

DISCUSSION

The comparison of the Adviceguide and Invisque interfaces yielded several interesting findings. Task success was not significantly higher for Invisque for both HL and LL users. However, Figure 3 shows that both user groups predominantly were more successful when using Invisque. LL users were significantly quicker with the Invisque interface, however, HL users were slightly slower. The LL users viewed significantly lesser number of pages on Invisque for all three levels of task difficulty.

The boxing of information helped reduced the cognitive load of LL users, improving their reading strategy. This can be seen in the results where LL users spent significantly less time, viewed fewer number of pages and showed an increase in task success (although not significant) over Adviceguide.

Previous studies suggested that LL users, unlike HL users, did not verify information for correctness because they were being satisfied with information quickly due to higher cognitive load. LL users predominantly used the Wizard function to either remove unwanted index cards or mark important information. These LL users now revisited the information marked as important, suggesting they were differentiating and comparing information for correctness moving away from satisficing too early.

Prior studies also identified that LL users were less likely to recover from mistakes. The observations suggested that removing or deleted information of no relevance reduced unwanted clutter and prevented LL users from revisiting this information. Another observation was that LL users were likely clear the canvas and start a fresh search as a strategy to recover. Most importantly, the lack of hierarchy meant that users were less likely to abandon a search due to differences in conceptual and perceived mental models.

Overall, Invisque was well received by both groups of users. The subjective feedback reinforces that Invisque represents a novel interface that was easy to learn. This confirms that the affordances of the system provide strong interactive and visual cues [31].

CONCLUSION

This paper summarized problems LL users face during information seeking, which suggest that it is not only reading levels and usability problems, but also caused by a different way of thinking [37,47]. Based on the identified differences of LL users' reading strategy, verification, recovery and perceived mental models, design recommendations were suggested.

This paper presented Invisque, which is based on a set of design principles that were also expected to benefit LL users. To test these principles an evaluation was performed to compare Invisque against a traditional web interface for both HL and LL users. Invisque has shown to improve LL users' performance and changed their behavior strategies. The results of the evaluation showed that users could retrieve information more quickly with Invisque.

These design principles were well received by the LL users based on the quantitative, subjective and observational data. LL users preferred the way information was presented (boxed), the flexibility to move index cards or clusters, use of Wizard to delete or mark information as important, visual cues, and finally the smooth transitions and less clutter due to the increase in white space.

Further investigation on proposed design principles and Invisque is required because, even though the system suited LL users, in some cases it affected the performance of HL users. This reinforce Neilsens' observations that new designs are likely introduce new and unexpected problems [28].

One caveat to the present study is the small sample size that could influence the results observed. Reasons behind the current sample size were due to the in-depth nature of the study. It was difficult to recruit participants because of the length of the study, and not knowing their literacy prior to the study. It will be important to analyze and validate a larger sample size.

ACKNOWLEDGMENTS

Our deepest appreciation goes to Mr Tim Clark and Ms Caroline Kahan, from Barnet Citizens Advice Bureau for giving their fullest support during our study, and to the 24 participants for their time. This study has approval from Middlesex University Research Ethics Committee.

REFERENCES

1. Ahlberg, C. and Shneidennan, B. Visual Information Seeking : Tight Coupling of Dynamic Query Filters with Starfield Displays. Human Factors, (1994).
2. Buxton, W., Baecker, R., and Sellen, A. User Sketches : A Quick , Inexpensive , and Effective way to Elicit More Reflective User Feedback. Group, October (2006), 14-18.
3. Card, S.K., Mackinlay, J.D., and Shneiderman, B. Readings in information visualization: using vision to think. Morgan Kaufmann, 1999.
4. Cheung, V., Grypma, N., and Zhong, L. The influence of brand name and brand logo on new product evaluations of Low Literate Consumers. (1979). http://www.vkky.nl/Files/Pfolio/logo_research.pdf.
5. Ellis, D. Modelling the information seeking patterns of engineers and research scientists in an industrial environment. Management 53, 4 (1997), 384-403.
6. Findlater, L., Balakrishnan, R., and Toyama, K. Comparing semiliterate and illiterate users' ability to transition from audio+text to text-only interaction. CHI, (2009), 1751.
7. Fox, E.A., Hix, D., Nowell, L.T., et al. Users, user interfaces, and objects: Envision, a digital library. Information Science 44, 8 (1983), 480 - 491.
8. Frank-Stromborg, M. and Olsen, S.J. Instruments for clinical health-care research. Jones & Bartlett Learning, 2004.
9. Gould, J.D., Conti, J., and Hovanyecz, T. Composing letters with a simulated listening typewriter. Communications of the ACM 26, 1983, 295-308.
10. Healey, C.G., Booth, K.S., and Enns, J.T. Visualizing Real-Time Multivariate Data Using Preattentive Processing. Current, (1995).
11. Hochberg, J.E. Perception. Prentice-Hall, Englewood Cliffs N.J., 1978.
12. Jensen, J.D., King, A.J., Davis, L. a, and Guntzviller, L.M. Utilization of internet technology by low-income adults: the role of health literacy, health numeracy, and computer assistance. Journal of aging and health 22, 6 (2010), 804-26.
13. Joshi, A., Welankar, N., Bl, N., Kanitkar, K., and Sheikh, R. Rangoli: A Visual Phonebook for Low-literate Users. MobileHCI, (2008), 217.
14. Kemp, G. and Eagle, L. Shared meanings or missed opportunities? The implications of functional health literacy for social marketing interventions. Springer Berlin / Heidelberg, 2008.

15. Kodagoda, N. and Wong, B.L.W. Effects of low & high literacy on user performance in information search and retrieval. HCI, (2008), 173-181.

16. Kodagoda, N., Wong, B.L.W., and Khan, N. Information seeking behaviour model as a theoretical lens: high and low literate users behaviour process analysed. ECCE, ACM Press (2010), 117-124.

17. Kodagoda, N., Wong, W., and Khan, N. Identifying Information Seeking Behaviours of Low and High Literacy Users : Combined Cognitive Task Analysis. NDM9, (2009), 347-354.

18. Kodagoda, N., Wong, W.B.L., and Khan, N. Open-Card Sort to Explain Why Low-Literate Users abandon their Web Searches Early. HCI, (2010).

19. Kummamuru, K., Lotlikar, R., Roy, S., Singal, K., and Krishnapuram, R. A hierarchical monothetic document clustering algorithm for summarization and browsing search results. WWW, (2004), 658.

20. Lonsdale, M. and McCurry, D. Literacy in the New Millennium. NCVER, (2004).

21. Maglio, P.P., Matlock, T., Raphaely, D., Chernicky, B., and Kirsh, D. Interactive skill in Scrabble. In M. H. a. S. C. Stoness (Ed.), Cognitive Science Society, Mahwah, NJ: Lawrence Erlbaum Associates, Inc (1999).

22. Marchionini, G. Information seeking in electronic environments. Cambridge University Press, 1995.

23. Medhi, I., Gautama, S.N.N., and Toyama, K. A comparison of mobile money-transfer UIs for non-literate and semi-literate users. ACM Press, New York, New York, USA, 2009.

24. Medhi, I., Menon, S.R., Cutrell, E., and Toyama, K. Beyond Strict Illiteracy : Abstracted Learning Among Low-Literate Users. Information and Communication Technologies and International Development, IEEE (2010).

25. Medhi, I., Prasad, A., and Toyama, K. Optimal audio-visual representations for illiterate users of computers. WWW '07, (2007), 873.

26. Narasimhan, R. Characterizing literacy: a study of Western and Indian literacy experiences. SAGE, 2004.

27. Newell, L.T., France, K., and Heath, S. Visualizing Search Results : Some Alternatives To Query-Document Similarity. Computing, (1994), 67-75.

28. Nielsen, J. Iterative user-interface design. Computer 26, 11 (1993), 32-41.

29. Nielsen, J. Low-Literacy Users: Writing for a Broad Consumer Audience. Alerbox, 2005. http://www.useit.com/alertbox/20050314.html.

30. Nielsen, J. Ten Usability Heuristics Mean for MIMAS Websites and Web based Interfaces. Design, August 2006 (2007), 2007-2007.

31. Norman, D. The Design Of Everyday Things. Doubleday Business, 1988.

32. Perfetti, C.A. Reading Ability. Oxford University Press, USA, 1985.

33. Pirolli, P. Interview with Peter Pirolli. 877 (2010), 1-6.

34. Rich, E. Users are individuals: individualizing user models. Man-Machine Studies 18, 3 (1983), 199-214.

35. Root, R.W. and Draper, S. Questionnaires as a Software Evaluation Tool. CHI'83, ACM Press (1983), 83-87.

36. Sauro, J. and Dumas, J.S. Comparison of three one-question, post-task usability questionnaires. CHI, (2009), 1599.

37. Sherwani, J., Ali, N., and Hall, W. Orality-Grounded HCID : Information Technologies and International Development 5, 4 (2009), 37-49.

38. Shneiderman, B., Feldman, D., Rose, A., and Grau, X.F. Visualizing digital library search results with categorical and hierarchical axes. DL, ACM Press (2000), 57-66.

39. Shneiderman, B. Universal usability: pushing human-computer interaction to empower every citizen. ACM 43, 5 (2000), 84-91.

40. Simon, H.A. Models of man: social and rational. John Wiley and Sons, Inc., New York, 1957.

41. Stelmaszewska, H., Wong, B.L.W., Attfield, S., and Chen, R. Electronic Resource Discovery Systems. ACM Press, New York, New York, USA, 2010.

42. Summers, K. and Summers, M. Making the Web Friendlier for Lower-Literacy Users. The Century Contemporary French Studies, (2003), 19-22.

43. Summers, K. and Summers, M. Reading and Navigational Strategies of Web Users with Lower Literacy Skills. ASIST, Richard B. Hill (2005).

44. Vicente, K. and Williges, R. Accommodating individual differences in searching a hierarchical file system. Man-Machine Studies 29, 6 (1988), 647-668.

45. Warschauer, M. Technology and Social Inclusion. MIT Press, 2002.

46. Williams, J., Clemens, S., Oleinikova, K., and Tarvin, K. The Skills for Life survey: A national needs and impact survey of literacy, numeracy and ICT skills. Literacy London: BM, (2003).

47. Wong, B.L.W. and Kodagoda, N. Designing UI For Low Literacy Users: Knowing Your User. Workshop Paper - IUI '11, ACM Press (2011), 469.

48. Woods, D. Visual momentum: a concept to improve the cognitive coupling of person and computer. Man-Machine Studies 21, 3 (1984), 229-244.

Questionable Concepts: Critique as a Resource for Designing with Eighty Somethings

John Vines[1,2], Mark Blythe[1], Stephen Lindsay[2], Paul Dunphy[2], Andrew Monk[3], Patrick Olivier[2]

[1]School of Design
Northumbria University
Newcastle upon Tyne, UK
{john.vines, mark.blythe}
@northumbria.ac.uk

[2]Culture Lab
School of Computing Science
Newcastle University, UK
{stephen.lindsay, p.m.dunphy,
p.l.olivier}@newcastle.ac.uk

[3]Department of Psychology
University of York
York, UK
a.monk@psych.york.ac.uk

ABSTRACT
This paper reports findings from a series of participatory design workshops with ten people over eighty years old. The focus of the workshops was new banking technologies for the older old. Participants were asked to discuss their current experiences of banking and given packs of *concept cards* which contained design sketches and brief outlines of concepts for new financial services. The designs on the cards were deliberately provocative and aimed to encourage criticism and debate. Participants wrote and drew on the cards and the workshops were recorded and transcribed. The participants were extremely critical of current banking practices and most of the new concepts we presented to them. Their questions and comments led to a number of insights and further iterations. The paper argues that critique is an essential resource for design, both in terms of identifying problems and iterating ideas.

Author Keywords
Ageing; Eighty Somethings; Banking; Participatory Design; User Study Methods.

ACM Classification Keywords
H.5.m. Information interfaces and presentation (e.g., HCI): Miscellaneous.

General Terms
Design.

INTRODUCTION
Much of the industrialised world is in economic turmoil. Nations such as Greece, Portugal, Spain, Italy, and the United Kingdom are going through periods of 'austerity' [5]. Public and personal debt appears to be the norm and those people who have saved money responsibly during their lives are punished as the interest rates provided by banks dip below those of inflation [31]. This paper focuses on the banking experiences of people aged over 80 in the United Kingdom, a group who are exceptional having already lived through periods of far greater austerity than we are currently experiencing.

People over 80 are often referred to as 'older old' [12] but we prefer to use a more neutral term: *eighty somethings*. Eighty somethings are the largest growing age group in the world and there are now more eighty somethings alive than ever before [12]. Despite this, the banking sector does not provide services that are either appropriate for this age group [20] or make use of their lifetime of banking experience. There is currently considerable interest from the banking sector in new digital payment systems; contactless Near Field Communication (NFC) technologies mean payments can be made with the wave of a phone, whilst new 'apps' allow people to transfer funds at the swipe of a finger [e.g. 38]. The pace of development in the digital payment arena has been such that in the UK it is suggested banknotes and coins will be redundant by 2050 [34]. Whilst new technologies appear to be supporting novel ways of spending money, very little appears to be available to help people manage their finances in a period of great need.

Prior to the work described in this paper we identified a number of themes that were important in the 'financial biographies' of 12 eighty somethings collected through in-depth interviews [35]. We observed intricately kept paper records, which helped the eighty somethings to control how much they spent and how much they saved. We also noted that most of their financial transactions were performed with cheques, banknotes and coins. For many this led to situations where impaired mobility meant they could no longer access their money. This sometimes led to situations where the eighty somethings shared their security information (e.g. pin numbers) with family and carers.

We sought to ensure that our previous ethnographic work was critically reflected upon and integrated into the design process—a phase of design that is often problematic [13]. We aimed to encourage the participants to be critical of our ideas and come up with better ones. As a way of encouraging the eighty somethings to become active participants in our design process we developed concept cards to illustrate our ideas and capture their responses. The findings from this study make three contributions to the Human Computer Interaction (HCI) community. First, we

Permission to make digital or hard copies of all or part of this work for personal or classroom use is granted without fee provided that copies are not made or distributed for profit or commercial advantage and that copies bear this notice and the full citation on the first page. To copy otherwise, or republish, to post on servers or to redistribute to lists, requires prior specific permission and/or a fee.
CHI'12, May 5–10, 2012, Austin, Texas, USA.
Copyright 2012 ACM 978-1-4503-1015-4/12/05...$10.00.

unravel some of the reasons why eighty somethings are highly critical of current banking trends and the role of computers in particular. Second, we find that using questionable concepts to encourage critique not only provides insights into current practices but also inspires creative responses in the form of new design ideas. Third, questionable concept cards provide an example of how design relevant data and ideas from workshops can be captured and used in an iterative design process.

BACKGROUND

A large amount of past HCI research has explored how digital systems may be better designed for older people [e.g. 16]. However, this age group remains relatively disinterested in new technology [10]. It is still very unusual for an eighty year old to actively participate in digital communities. In the UK 80% of people aged 75 and over have no access to the internet from their homes, and 50% cannot see any value in having it installed [28]. In the context of financial services, even those older people interested in Internet banking are hesitant about using it. Often, concerns over the security of financial and personal data are cited as a reason for not using Internet [25] and mobile banking [23] and younger people are far more willing to trust online payment systems than older people [32].

It is well documented that the needs of older people have rarely been considered as the banking sector has moved towards electronic and digital payment systems and away from traditional methods such as cheques and cash [36, 39]. In our previous work we noted that digital banking often requires the use of Personal Identification Numbers (PINs) and passwords that are difficult to use and remember [35]. It was not unusual to find situations where people shared their PINs with others to continue accessing their finances [35]. Furthermore, whilst many older people rely on banking facilities in their local communities [39] these are under continual threat of closure in the UK [30].

In this paper we describe participatory design workshops with new groups of eighty somethings that occurred six months after the contextual work. As a way of linking these phases and different cohorts together we developed a series of 'concept cards' based on our initial study. In the following sections we describe how and why these concepts and cards were developed. Not only did the use of questionable concepts invoke critique from these new eighty somethings they also informed an iterative design process eventually leading to the development of high-fidelity prototypes (described in detail in [37]).

QUESTIONABLE CONCEPT CARDS

There is a long tradition in design of making provocative proposals and objects. Jaques Carelman's "objets introuvables" or unfindable objects include the teapot with the handle on the same side as the spout which has illustrated the front cover of many editions of Don Norman's Psychology of Everyday Things. Carelman's Catalogue of Extraordinary Objects [8] includes a bicycle seat that has a toilet in it, and a rifle with five barrels for a one man siege.

TITLE	ILLUSTRATION	DESCRIPTION
Exploding Handbag		A handbag that lets off a paint bomb when stolen.
Cashier TV		A direct video link to the bank so you can see delegated transactions being completed.
Disappearing Money		Intelligent banknotes that disappear when handled by an unauthorized person.
Mobile Bank		Pay bills, make deposits and withdraw cash at your front door.
Money Club	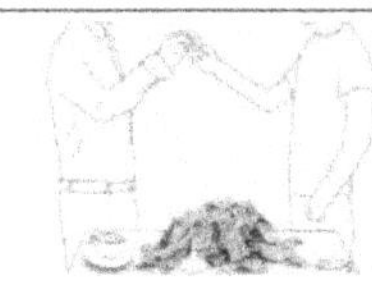	A social lending club for sharing and investing money and inter-generational money advice.
One Time Card	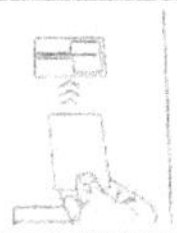	A recyclable card that can be shared and only used once.
Pin Thimble		PIN displayed when placed on finger tip.
Shared Card		A locked bank card that can be unlocked and shared for one transaction.
Smart Wallet		An intelligent wallet that displays your incomings and outgoings.
TopUp Debit Cards		Individual cards for payees that can be topped up and easily controlled.
Video Banking		A video link to a local branch to talk face-to-face.

Table 1. Questionable concepts, illustration and description.

Such fantastical objects are also produced by enthusiasts of Chindogu [21]. Whereas many of Carelman's designs are unusable, Chindogu objects are "un-useless" in that they solve one problem but create some other larger problem. For instance the Portable Lamp Post [21] by Kawakami is not useless because it brings light to dark streets but it is not useful because it requires the user to wheel a street lamp around with them: it is un-useless. Such extraordinary objects and un-useless designs are often used when teaching abstract notions like usability and affordances. They have also been used to discuss design spaces [e.g. 6]. Following the financial biographies with eighty somethings and their carers [35] a number of concept designs were developed during a workshop including researchers, designers, care givers, banking experts and representatives of age related charities. Workshop participants were given cards containing detailed quotes from the ethnography and asked to group related quotes together. Following this there was a phase of quick ideation that related back to the quotation groupings. Therefore the concepts generated were not conceived to be entirely frivolous but neither were they thought of as in any way finished or likely solutions to the problems they sought to address. These ideas were cross-compared by the lead author and ideas that were similar to one another were combined. The eleven resulting ideas were visually developed into graphical concepts to seed our participatory design workshops with a further cohort of eighty somethings (see Table 1).

Bardzell and Bardzell's work on the design of sex toys [1] highlighted the role that criticism plays in motivating design. The toys already on the market were considered by the designers interviewed to be lacking in various ways – the materials were cheap, the motors were noisy, they were smelly. This critical stance not only helped to identify product needs but also to motivate design innovation. We also wanted to use critique in this creative sense, as a resource for designing with a user group who are often said to be critical of any new technology [10]. Critique of the banking industry and banking products was often spontaneous during the "financial biography" interviews in the first stage of the research [35]. It was important that this spirit of critique also applied to the participatory design process. In order to avoid polite agreement with our suggestions we included very outré and silly concepts (for example an exploding handbag to deter thieves). Other ideas, such as the 'Pin Thimble', 'Money Club' and 'Mobile Bank' were felt to have more immediate worth. Even these more sensible ideas however were felt provocative and questionable due to their impracticality.

We were also aware that the concepts might be found questionable by our new participants due to them being conceived in response to the original cohort. This was a conscious decision as it was felt such reactions would be useful in providing a rich understanding of the heterogeneity of these different groups of eighty somethings. We also did not wish to offend or disrespect our participants and wanted to indicate that even the more outrageous ideas were highlighting problems we found in our previous work. Therefore each concept was linked to quotes from our contextual research [35]. In the case of the exploding handbag the illustrated concept was accompanied by a quote from a participant in the previous study whose handbag had been snatched in the street.

Some of the designs were left deliberately opaque and ambiguous. There was for instance very little explanation as to how 'Disappearing Money' might be used. Following Gaver et al. [14] it was hoped that this ambiguity might create a resource for the participants to respond to. Some of the suggestions were also deliberately playful and provocative, most obviously, the 'Exploding Handbag'. Although the designs suggested were un-useless or at least questionable, the problems they sought to address were real. The workshop discussions were not limited to the concepts and frequently an idea (e.g. the van bringing cash to the door) prompted wider discussions of current banking practice and security. These were also encouraged so that critiques on current banking practices and what imagined futures might look and feel like were interwoven with one another. Further questionable concepts were developed and sent to participants following each workshop (see Table 2 and Method) based upon the discussions and ides they had.

TITLE	ILLUSTRATION	DESCRIPTION
Contact Cards	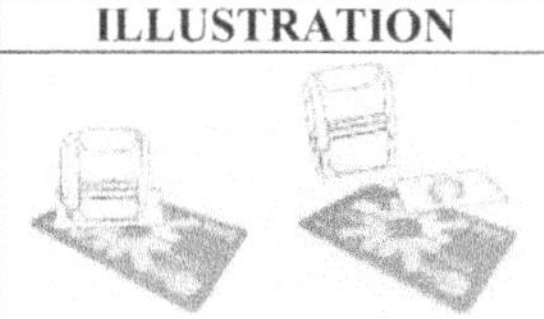	Bankcards that are physically stamped when paying bills or withdrawing money.
DNA Banking		Paying bills and withdrawing money with unique DNA.
Fingerprint Cards	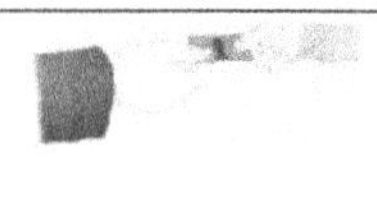	Money that is spent when two people touch a card at the same time.
Flexible Banknote		An intelligent banknote that can be used to spend specific amounts at a time.
Iris Cheques	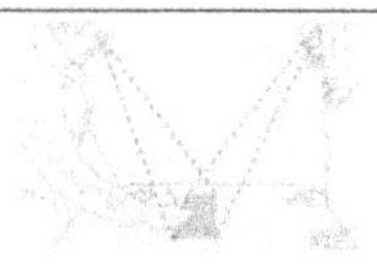	"Cheques" that become activated when two people are looking at them being written out.

Table 2. Questionable concept cards sent after first workshop.

Previous work in HCI has demonstrated that card-based activities are a useful way of capturing and communicating contextual and technological possibilities in workshop settings [19, 24]. We therefore developed the concepts into A6 sized folded cards with four sides (Figure 1). On the front of each card was an illustration of the design idea, such as the Pin Thimble (which upon recognising the users' fingerprint provides a pin number). On the inside of the front there was a brief description of the idea illustrated on the cover ("reminds you of your PIN when you need it"). Alongside this description we provided three to four anonymous quotations from the ethnography that had prompted the idea (e.g. "I have it [written] down somewhere, but they always say not to, I couldn't remember it with never using it" and "I ought not to [write down this password] but I do..."). Our cards can be considered as abstracts of specific areas of our project, summarised visually and textually.

Figure 1. A collection of '*concept cards*'.

Unlike 'Speed Dating' [11] the cards provided a medium where the participants could reflect on the design ideas at home and potentially in contexts relevant to the issues described. Unlike cultural probes [15] the cards were not intended to provide returns of uncertain fragments of user data. Rather, the cards were intended to communicate to participants several design spaces that were not fully defined and open for them to manipulate and change. We were conscious, however, that not all participants would be willing to actively take the role of 'designers'. Accounting for this the cards also listed three questions that could either be responded to in text or illustration. The first and second were open questions about experiences they might have had related to the design space (e.g. "What are your experiences of PINs and passwords?"). The third question, on the rear of the card, asked them to imagine a future scenario and for them to draw something they would use in it ("Imagine an object that reminds you of passwords and codes ... what would it look like?").

Over the 11 cards there were thirty questions in total. The intention behind the pack of cards was that participants need not answer all the questions—rather, they would be asked to answer those that they felt were most pertinent and interesting. Very few of the questions were left completely unanswered, and the quality of the responses received went far beyond typical responses to written questionnaires.

METHOD

Participants, workshops and introducing the cards

Due to project and geographical constraints the design phase of our project was performed with different participants to the previous contextual work. The first study involved in depth interviews carried out for the most part in participants' own homes [35]. The participants discussed in this paper attended participatory design workshops involving groups. The need to bring a group together in one setting influenced the recruitment of a more mobile group of eighty somethings. The participants in the workshops were 10 females aged between 80 and 87 years, spread over three groups. These participants were recruited from a longitudinal study that investigated the psychology of ageing and technology use. The study had been running for 28 years and many of those who began it had died. These then were somewhat unusual eighty somethings in that they were well used to university settings and research projects. The first group had 6 participants. The second and third workshops had 2 each. Each participant was paid £20 for taking part. Whilst we had not set out to recruit only female participants, this was illustrative of the make-up of eighty somethings remaining in the longitudinal and that women are still far more likely to live beyond 80 years than men [33].

As has been observed elsewhere, older people are not a homogenous group [27] and working with new participants emphasised this. All of the participants except one in the first study described themselves as working class. The participants of this study described themselves as middle class. Not only were their significant demographic differences between the two groups there were also marked physical differences. Many of the participants in the first group had severely limited mobility. All of the participants of the second study were physically fit and mobile enough to climb the two flights of steps that led to the room where the design workshops were held. The materials for the workshop were created with the first group of participants in mind and often illustrated with quotations from these interviews. The workshop participants were on the whole financially better off and physically fitter than the original participants. Therefore participant quotes on the concept cards were sometimes met with surprise and bewilderment. The differences in financial and physical circumstances between the groups led to richer discussions than we might have had with a narrower range of people.

Following a pattern set by the otherwise unrelated longitudinal study the workshops were characterised as "tea parties". During the break, tea, cake and fruit were served. In our first meeting with the participants we spent the first hour familiarising ourselves with each other. The participants were asked to introduce themselves and talk about who they banked with and how they felt banking had changed throughout their lives. The researchers joined in with this process, which allowed the participants to ask questions about the (younger) researchers' experiences and habits. This helped establish equality and a critical edge as the eighty somethings were scandalised by some of the young researchers' financial habits (e.g. credit card debt). It should be stressed however that the tone was friendly and playful throughout.

Each group attended two workshops with a two week interval in between. Near the end of the first meeting we introduced the concept cards to the participants. We explained that each card explained an idea that related to experiences other eighty somethings had talked to us about. They were informed that there were 10 cards in each pack with questions inside—but they need not go through and answer them all, just those that they felt strongest about. We also provided two envelopes for them to bring them back in—one envelope for their favourite three cards, and one for the remaining cards.

During the intervening two weeks the design team worked on new cards based upon some of the ideas and discussions we had in the first meeting (see Table 2). This was to emphasise that we were listening to their discussions and developing new ideas as a consequence. These cards were sent out to the participants at approximately the halfway point between the two workshops.

Response and analysis

All of the data from the cards and the discussions were transcribed and the drawings and annotations made by the participants were scanned. We documented which three ideas the participants placed in their 'favourites' envelope.

The qualitative data from the transcripts and cards were analysed through a grounded theory methodology [9, 17]. The card and transcript data were summarised with open codes line by line. The open codes were brought together to form axial codes that described three overriding themes. Connections between these three themes were the basis of the grounded theory, which is a broad and reflective description rather than a predictive model [9]. The initial results and the detailed grounded analysis are described in the following sections.

RESULTS

The cards provoked a number of diverse responses from the eighty somethings. Nine of the ten participants selected their favourite three cards; one did not. Doris responded "*I was impatient with the whole lot, I couldn't really see much point in any of them.*" On the front of her envelope she wrote: *could not identify three favourites*. Similarly, Rita commented: *"These are not favourite ideas, just the ones I think may be the best."* Ruth, on the other hand, liked a number of the ideas. She was particularly excited by two of the cards that were sent to her during the time between the workshops. These cards—'Iris Cheques' and 'DNA Banking'—were based upon ideas she had suggested at the first workshop, so perhaps it is no surprise she liked them.

Before taking the cards away there was some trepidation from the participants about how they should treat the cards: *"why would I want to scribble over your lovely cards?"* (Agnes). At the second workshop it was clear that most of the participants had engaged with cards in very different ways. Many of the participants were reluctant to do any sketching or drawing, e.g. Agatha: *"I can't draw, so I haven't done any drawing, I've written them.* Patricia mostly: *"wrote answers to the questions."* Janice made an attempt to illustrate some of her answers and ideas: *"well I tried, not very successful."* Some of the participants just answered the questions in writing. Seven out of ten participants did attempt to doodle, sketch and draw some of their ideas in order to better communicate them.

For some of the participants, antipathy towards the ideas resulted in short and abrupt answers. Of the possible 30 questions, Doris only completed 17. Agnes also left some questions blank or with very brief answers: *"no"* or: *"yes"* or: *"good idea!"* Over the 'One Time Card' she scrawled large crosses across each question and the illustration on the front. This was unusual however and most of the participants responded in detail. Agatha answered every question but one, and even here wrote something: *"pass on this one!"*

Whilst the immediate reactions of some participants suggested a significant amount of hostility towards many of the ideas, the discussions following these initial responses were very productive. As will be discussed in the following section, many of the eighty somethings had engaged with the cards and the research at a deep level. During the discussions it became clear that often the cards had been interpreted in ways the researchers had not expected. For example, the Pin Thimble was considered by the three groups as a very pointless idea. The idea for the Pin Thimble was that when it was placed onto the end of your finger and recognised your fingerprint, it would then (and only then) display your PIN. The participants in the first group interpreted the illustration on the front as a thimble that has your PIN permanently engraved on it. The researchers explained that the PIN would not be on display would only work when it was on the user's finger and nobody else's: *"Well, having explained it, it makes a bit more sense. You're not going around with this number showing everybody, which it appeared to be on the card"* (Frances). Occasionally then, ambiguous sketches and descriptions were sometimes entirely misunderstood. However these were often successful misunderstandings that allowed participants to articulate their concerns about new technology and the likely stupidity of its designers.

Our analysis of the data centred on three themes: *critique*, *coping* and *creativity*.

Critique: questioning the concepts

Most of the participants used their responses to the cards to be critical of the design ideas illustrated on them. Sometimes their critique would focus on implausibility, for example, the 'Exploding Handbag' containing a paint bomb to be activated if stolen. Frances wrote on the card: *"a bit far-fetched"*. On other occasions practical reasons were given to disregard such ideas: *"I would not like the contents of my handbag to be covered in paint"* (Agatha, on card). More importantly, many of the responses signified much wider concerns with technology and contemporary culture. For example the 'Mobile Bank' card illustrating a van which would bring cash to the door provoked this comment from Marjorie:

"I hope it never comes to this! Imagine a Country where people do not leave their houses because everything is brought to their door. It could reach a point where they

never either see, or know, their neighbours or anyone else in the road!"

Similarly, Patricia responded to a question on automatic payment services with: *"are we not to take charge of anything ourselves?"* (Patricia's emphasis). Some of the ideas were associated with relieving people of some of their responsibilities. At the same time, during discussion the participants frequently speculated where the benefit would come from as many of the ideas were also seen to imply further costs to bank account holders: *"that will put bank charges up!"* (Agatha) or: *"they'd charge you extra for telling you that"* (Janice).

During the discussions between the researchers and participants one of the largest criticisms levelled at the cards was that some of the ideas and questions seemed irrelevant to their current needs:

"... these smart cards and a smart purse and a smart wallet and somebody coming to the door with the van to get you some money and so on, I suppose they are just ideas that you have suddenly produced to look into the future, but for me, so many of them were not applicable at all at this stage" (Frances).

Here, Frances is reflecting on the quotations placed on the inside front cover of the cards from participants in earlier stages of the research. Many of the quotes on the cards referred to people who were no longer mobile, but, as previously noted, all of the members of the workshops were mobile enough to climb two flights of steps to attend the session. This meant that in order to engage with the cards, many of the participants had to empathise with the descriptions of other people's experiences, and imagine what their own circumstances may be in the future. This was not easy, as Agatha made clear: *"It's very difficult to project how you would react in a situation until you are actually in it."*

Patricia in particular explained her difficulties in imaging some of the situations where the ideas on the cards might be useful: *"It's difficult for us ... not to think as middle class people. ... I just don't want things to go any different. I am quite satisfied with what we've got. I think that's the same for all of us."* Patricia's comment was reiterated by a number of participants but others sensed that change, desirable or undesirable, was inevitable: *"But if everybody else moves on, you've got to run along behind them haven't you? Or trail along behind them, you don't have the option"* (Ruth).

Some of the cards provoked quite impassioned responses about the general motives and morals of the banking industry. Rita felt particularly strongly about 'Disappearing Money' (intelligent banknotes where the print disappears when handled by an unauthorised person):

"If this actually came to pass it would be just a way for the banks and financial institutions to make more money for the "fatcats" and the shareholders and to exploit the man in the street. It would be hidden behind buzzwords like "efficiency" "modern" etc. It would need more and more power to operate and we as a country will go into "power meltdown" in the future, unless there is a remarkable invention (soon) to guarantee power to be continuous in power cuts – as per the 39-45 war, the 1970s in the Eastern USA and UK 80s – how will society and a cashless one at that, cope then?"

For Rita the design of any 'technology' was inextricably linked to the ideology of the banking industry. The technology would lose people jobs, would trick people into spending more money, and continue to ignore wider economic issues. Whilst Rita's critical monologues were the most extreme, these views permeated many of the discussions we had with the eighty somethings.

Coping: workarounds and current technology

Several of the concepts were based on instances related in the previous study [35] of people sharing pin numbers. This practice was quite alien to the workshop participants. The 'One Time Card', 'Share Card' and 'Disappearing Money' cards were based on the topic of someone withdrawing cash or paying bills on another person's behalf. None of these participants had found themselves needing to do this but there was a palpable concern that they may have to in the future. Patricia wrote: *"it's a big worry. All* [my] *family live in* [the] *South. Luckily I have many trustworthy friends and neighbours who I can trust implicitly."* Others speculated about who they could trust in such situations: "[I] *wouldn't let home helps or other carers do this in view of some of the stories in the papers about theft, fraud"* (Agatha). When asked to consider designing something that would help in these situations, the reply across all of the groups was unanimous: *"a receipt"*. Many of the participants drew illustrations of receipts as their way of knowing someone had completed a transaction on their behalf.

The importance of pieces of paper as a way of coping with potentially complex situations appeared frequently in both the written responses and the discussions in the workshops. For example, Audrey explained: *"each month ... I keep a meticulous book with income and expenditure columns."* Janice had a similar procedure: *"I always know roughly how much is in my account so I never (yet!) get overdrawn."* Also confirming our previous observations, these new participants used pieces of paper to document hard to remember PINs and passwords. The reactions to the cards revealed this in far more depth however. Specifically, it became clear that whilst paper was highly beneficial to the eighty somethings, with it came dangers. Documenting financial information gave rise to the risk of people reading it and performing fraudulent activities. Many of the eighty somethings, therefore, would not write down the information as is but rather make attempts to disguise and codify it. Agatha would: *"hide it in code among telephone numbers in my diary."* She went on to reflect further down the card: *"I know it isn't foolproof."* Similarly, Patricia would: *"put [it] in address book as fictitious names and tel. no. ending in pin number."*

Ruth was one of the few participants who would not write her details down. She was the only eighty something who used Internet banking, and kept all of her records on the computer. In terms of PINs and passwords, she wrote: *"I remember my pin number and password by association. If you could draw an object that reminded you of it, then that too could be deciphered by someone."* Rita also acknowledged the dangers of writing down these details, suggesting instead that she would *"pick a pattern on the key pad"* and remember this, rather than the actual digits of her PIN. Dolores also explored using visual clues as a way of avoiding writing down a PIN. During the workshops, she described her idea (see Figure 2):

"I thought [this] *was fun* [but] *it's rubbish ... that has a grid with numbers, as in a map, and then if you have some places or some mountains or rivers on your map, you would choose one and then you would grid numbers that you could work out from it. But that's a bit complicated."*

The idea was complicated, and the researchers asked her to clarify what she meant, she elaborated: *"you know how you have a four figure grid reference number on a map when you go hiking.... If on a map I decide Scafell Pike is where I am looking at, then my pin number would be Scafell Pike."*

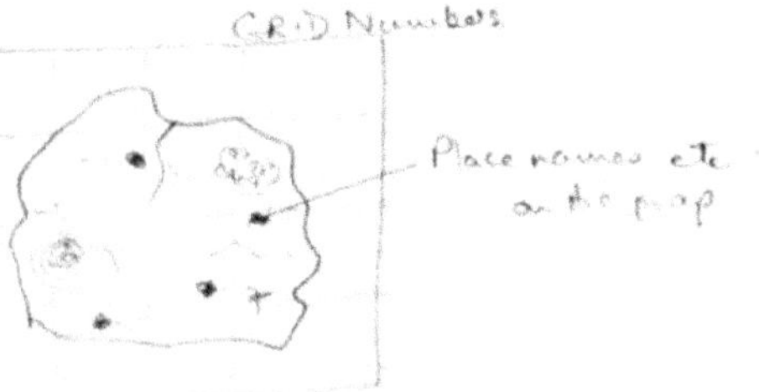

Figure 2: Dolores PIN password map

Although she derided her own idea, Dolores' suggestion emphatically combined her realisation of a problem with a possible solution from her own experiences (she was a keen walker). As these examples indicate even though many of the eighty somethings responded to the cards by criticising the ideas or discussing their own practices, often this became interwoven with the development of new ideas. This will be discussed in more depth in the final theme of creativity.

Creativity: engagement and dialogue

Clearly the concepts on the cards invited a large amount of criticism which perhaps in part, resulted from the great distance between the themes the researchers had identified as most pertinent to prior cohorts of eighty somethings and these new participants. Yet with these criticisms came opportunities for new ideas, particularly as participants discussed the cards between themselves. Dialogues un-mediated by the researchers would often occur, especially around subjects where participants felt strongly but had diverging interests and concerns. The 'Pin Thimble' discussion highlighted in the *Results* section is an example of this. Having explained the idea in person, a number of the participants now understood it better and even considered it: *"a good idea"* (Ruth). The group started to discuss how the idea could be improved: *"perhaps you have it hanging around your neck?"* (Agatha). What followed was a communal exploration of what form the idea could take. Although all 6 group members participated in this discussion, the critique of the overall idea would be repeatedly returned to, especially by Patricia: *"I wouldn't like to go round with things round your neck, because anybody who really wanted your pin number would say oh she's got it because it's round her neck, I'll get her and put her finger in."* In situations such as this, there was no possibility of escaping a virtuous circle of criticism. Through this dialogical working out of the device, however, many of the participants began to imagine how it would be used, what advantages and disadvantages it might bring, and what other activities such a device might support.

There was similar discussion and development of the idea of a mobile bank that delivers cash to people's homes. Many of the participants saw the benefits of this service for those who were housebound but were worried about the idea of a money van parking outside their homes: *"It's pretty obvious if this van draws up at your door ... there'll be somebody lurking round this corner watching for when he comes. He has got his helmet on, she hasn't!"* (referring to the home owner in the illustration). Although agreeing that the delivery of money would be useful for some this participant pointed out that a van like the one in the picture (see Table 1) would make it obvious that the house just visited was now worth robbing. This criticism was followed by suggestions: perhaps it should be integrated within other services in order to disguise it from prying eyes. An idea put forward by a number of participants then was for mobile libraries (which used to be common in the UKs) to also dispense money, or: *"a mobile shop where they give you cash back"* (Ruth). In another workshop, Agnes suggested: *"you want different kinds of vans that just come round and don't show anything, white one ... or they should come in a broken down old car ... with a scruffy looking man with a sack over his shoulder!"* This then is a particularly clear instance of the ways in which a criticism of a questionable concept resulted in the generation of new service design ideas, albeit perhaps equally questionable.

We noted in the previous section that using paper to record financial information helped the eighty somethings cope with modern banking systems. A question on the 'Smart Purse' card asking them to imagine dealing with their finances in a "paperless" future incited wrath. *"Impossible!"* Rita wrote on the card. *"I cannot work a computer, therefore would have no feasible access to records."* Janice wrote in a paperless future she would: *"keep a careful note on my cheques ... or wait for my monthly statement."* This was followed by further reflection: *"But cheques and statements need paper so not a very feasible suggestion."* Agatha suggested printing statements off the computer before realising this still involved paper. Doris simply wrote: *"I can't imagine"*.

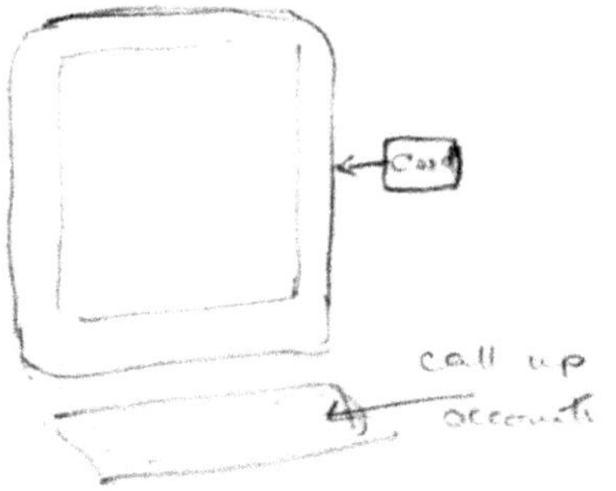

Figure 3: Dolores' Card Based Paperless Record Keeper

Although most of the responses to the notion of a paperless future resisted the notion altogether it did provoke some new ideas. For example, in reaction to the 'Smart Wallet' card, Dolores wrote on the card: *"I like the idea on the front of an iPad type wallet."* She went on to develop the idea further (Figure 3): *"But you could also, I feel, have a card that you could put into a computer or a screen and you would call up your accounts, and see them"*. Like the pieces of paper the eighty somethings already used, many of their ideas centred on artefacts that could be stored in specific places. Agnes also wrote down and planned all of her transactions every month but liked the 'Smart Wallet' concept: *"The fact that you've got something just to do quickly, your bank statement up and things like that, and check everything, and as I spent things I would put it into the calculator, and then everything would be all right."* As part of a paperless future, she imagined she could deal with it using *"two calculators, one for ingoings and one for outgoings and I'd put little abacuses on them."* Agnes found her design idea hilarious: *"I've got a wicked sense of humour!"* At the same time, her idea was practical because it embodied those values she finds so important in her checking routine.

Although the participants' suggestions were often as questionable as those on the card they indicated very clearly what was important to them, in this case the tangibility of accounts and a constant record they could update.

DISCUSSION

Previous work has suggested that older people are typically a challenge for HCI research due to their 'disinterest' in new technologies [10, 26]. While we found the participants critical of new banking technologies they were also fiercely interested in the research topic and its implications. A recurring response to all of the concept designs was—what is wrong with the way things used to be? What is wrong with cheques? What is wrong with cash? Learning PINs and passwords would never be as convenient or easy to use as the pen and paper based technologies they had used throughout their long lives.

Clearly there is an implication here not to design new technology [2]. This is important and it is at the heart of the Scandinavian tradition of participatory design. This emerged at a time when computing technology was being introduced for the first time to the workplace. Unions insisted that workers should be involved in the design of the new systems, partly to ensure that they were usable but also to ensure that the machines did not put their members out of work [22]. The eighty somethings here played a similarly political role in setting boundaries and saying "no". This critical engagement is not only salutary in technology development projects but also ethically necessary. However, the critiques suggested more than non-intervention: they were too unhappy with the existing state of affairs for that to be an option. Often, as with the 'mobile bank' concept, the critical responses led to suggestions and new ideas. The 'Pin Thimble' though initially derided was developed through discussion into more viable and useful iterations of the idea.

Methodological developments in participatory design such as the use of theatrical performance [3], future laboratories [7] and design games [4] explore ways of breaking away from current practices to collectively explore potential futures. Questionable concept cards differ as the researchers come to the workshop already laden with designs for the participants, even if these are still provisional and lacking form. These provided an immediate opportunity for criticism and for the participants to project their own practices and experiences onto each idea and card. Good graphic design is required here that conveys the concept to participants but also still allows for multiple interpretations. The 'Pin Thimble' card failed, at first, due to its failure to convey the idea at all.

The researchers, too, were also criticised albeit playfully. As Dolores explained her grid-reference based PIN system, Rita exclaimed: *"Don't assume they've done map reading!"* In another workshop, as it became clear that participants genuinely believed we had designed an artefact that had a PIN engraved permanently on it, one researcher noted, amidst much laughter, that they clearly thought: *"these boys at* [the] *University are idiots!"* The 'Pin Thimble' and some of the other ideas were transformed and developed through critique. Others remained questionable and subject to a deeper critique. New technology was implicated in supporting 'modern' banking practices that were by definition wrong headed. Modern banking was equated with making the banks more money, getting people to spend money they did not have, and encouraging a desire for the latest 'thing'. The feeling was that younger generations did not have the willpower to resist the technology and the banks, that they could not "*take charge*".

There was also a wider critique of the current economic climate following the recent banking crisis. For these participants the retail banks had been party to a criminal enterprise. When the participants were younger the banking sector had been represented by cautious local bank managers uncertain about whether to grant them a mortgage. The values represented by this figure of probity and good housekeeping had been overturned. The new banking was embodied in the digital payment methods the banks made available. "Make do and mend" had been replaced with easy credit and twenty four hour cash machines. The local banking of the past was seen as immediately accountable both for the individual and the institution. Banking was now global, remote and mediated by telephone or computer. For these participants financial mismanagement and modern technology were almost synonymous. They were concerned that younger generations were going to suffer from financial misadventure while their own generation was marginalised and forgotten.

One interpretation of these findings may be that it is another example of older people being hesitant to accept new technologies that do not meet their established practices [26]. We suggest that whilst familiarity is important to this age group, their critical insights are of a deeper significance. Critique is important not only in identifying problems but also in beginning to address them.

CRITIQUE AS A RESOURCE FOR DESIGN

This project was undertaken because it seemed clear that people over eighty are not well served by current banking practices. All of the workshop discussions confirmed this view. There were frequent denunciations of the banking industry and fierce defences of how things used to be done. While the workshops were being conducted there was much debate in the UK about plans to abolish cheques. This was often discussed in the workshops and any proposals for a replacement were met with angry opposition. Critical discussions of cheque replacement made it very clear that cheques were valued because of their tangibility, specificity and limited use [36]. This, in turn led the project team to further explore how these values can be embodied in the design of 'digital' cheques (see [37]). Initial concepts and prototypes were subjected to equally robust critique and consequently led to stronger designs (Ibid).

The team included both serious and playful ideas in the questionable concept cards. Ambiguous presentation and occasional misunderstandings encouraged new design insights. One example (the Pin Thimble) has been discussed here. The idea was initially derided partly, though only partly, because it was misunderstood. Criticisms of the design (you would lose it) led the eighty somethings to make new suggestions (you could wear it) which in turn led to further critique and suggestions. In this way the participants were able to engage in a critical dialogue which they clearly enjoyed. It was evident our participants found pleasure in highlighting the flaws in our ideas and arguments. These dialogues became part of an iterative design process which is still ongoing. Although this paper has focussed on the concepts that were more or less discarded some were developed into working prototypes such as a digital cheque book reported elsewhere [37]. However, the dialogues generated around the weakest ideas were often as valuable as those around strongest. The space for critique allowed the eighty somethings to articulate very clearly not only what was wrong with current banking practices but what would probably be wrong with piecemeal technology focussed solutions.

The qualitative research methods literature is replete with warnings about the dangers of participants telling researchers what they want to hear [29]. In participatory design there is always a danger that participants may agree that this or that idea might be a good one in order to be polite. In no way were these eighty somethings hostile or impolite to the researchers yet they had no compunction whatsoever in telling the team that their proposals were impractical or silly. Their critical stance was encouraged by the questionable concept cards we gave them. Ambiguity as well as silliness provided a space for criticism, suggestion and re-iteration. The participants' critiques were multi level—not just on whether a technology would be usable but what its implications might be in terms of social or political effects. As with the Scandinavian tradition of participatory design, the eighty somethings represented their own generational interests; yet they were also concerned with what was to become of their children, grandchildren and great grandchildren.

These eighty somethings had a fear of debt and credit. They maintained lifelong habits of careful account keeping and living within their means. They were horrified by the banking crisis and the reckless greed of the industry. Although we are living through a period of great economic instability, most work at the intersection of HCI and the banking sector focuses on finding novel ways for us to spend money. These extraordinary workshop participants would not allow the team to be anything but mindful of the widest possible consequences of the technologies proposed. At the same time the workshops provided a space to develop ideas that were more in line with their values. As computing technology penetrates still deeper into human life, it is more important than ever before, to be critical.

ACKNOWLEDGEMENTS

We thank our participants for their time, and Jayne Wallace, Emma Jones and Lynn McInnes for their support in planning and organising the workshops. This research was performed as part of the New Approaches to Banking for the Older Old project and the Social Inclusion through the Digital Economy (SiDE) Research Hub, funded by Research Councils UK Digital Economy Theme.

REFERENCES

1. Bardzell, J and Bardzell, S. Pleasure is your birthright: Digitally enabled designer sex toys as a case of third-wave HCI. In *Proc. CHI '11*, ACM (2011), 257-266.

2. Baumer, E., and Silberman, M. When the implication is not to design (technology). In: *Proc. CHI '11*, ACM (2011), 2271-2274.
3. Brandt, E., and Grunnet, C. Evoking the Future: Drama and Props in User Centered Design. *PDC '00*, 11-20.
4. Brandt, E., and Messeter, J. Facilitating Collaboration through Design Games. In: *Proc. PDC '04*, ACM Press (2004), 121-131.
5. BBC. *EU austerity drive country by country*. http://www.bbc.co.uk/news/10162176
6. Blythe, M. and Monk, A. Notes Towards An Ethnography of Domestic Technology. In *Proc. DIS '02*, ACM (2002), 276-281.
7. Büscher, M., Eriksen, M., Kristensen, J., and Mogensen, P. Ways of Grounding Imagination. In: *Proc. PDC '04*, ACM Press (2004), 193-202.
8. Carelman J. *Catalogue of Extraordinary Objects*. Abelard-Schuman, London, 1971.
9. Charmaz, K. *Constructing Grounded Theory*. Sage, London, 2006.
10. Coleman, G., Gibson, L., Hanson, V., Bobrowicz, A., McKay, A. Engaging the disengaged: how do we design technology for digitally excluded older adults? In *Proc. DIS '10*, ACM Press (2010), 175-178.
11. Davidoff, S., Lee, M, Dey, A., & Zimmerman, J. Rapidly exploring application design through speed dating. *UbiComp '07*, Springer (2007), 429-446.
12. Dini, E. and Goldring, S. Estimating the changing population of the 'oldest old'. *ONS Population Trends*, 13 (2), (2008), 7-16.
13. Dourish, P. Implications for design. In *Proc. CHI '06*, ACM (2006), 541-550.
14. Gaver , W., Beaver, J., and Benford, S. Ambiguity as a resource for design. *CHI '03*, ACM (2003), 233-240.
15. Gaver, W., Boucher, A., Pennington, S. and Walker, B. Cultural probes and the value of uncertainty. *Interactions*, 6 (5), (2004), 53-56.
16. Gaver, W. Boucher, A., Bowers, J., et al. The photostroller: supporting diverse care home residents in engaging with the world. In *Proc. CHI '11*, ACM Press (2011), 1757-1766.
17. Glaser, B. G. and Strauss, A. L. *Discovery of Grounded Theory: Strategies for Qualitative Research*. Aldine Publishing Company, Chicago, 1967.
18. Financial Services Authority *Fourth annual report on progress towards the shared goal for banking*. Financial Services Authority, London, 2009.
19. Halskov, K. and Daslgaard, P. Inspiration Card Workshops. In *Proc. DIS '06*, ACM Press (2006), 2-11.
20. HM Treasury *Financial Inclusion: An Action Plan for 2008-11*. HM Treasury, London, 2007.
21. Kawakami, K. (1997) 99 *More Unuseless Japanese Inventions: the Japanese Art of Chindogu*. Harper Collins, London, 1997.
22. Kensing, F., and Blomberg, J. Participatory design: Issues and concerns. *Computer Supported Cooperative Work*, 7, 167-185.
23. Laukkanen, T., Sinkkonen, S., Kivijärvi, M., and Laukkanen, P. Innovation resistance among mature consumers. *Journal of Consumer Marketing*, 24 (7), (2007), 419-427.
24. Lucero, A. and Arrasvuori, J. PLEX Cards: A Source of Inspiration When Designing for Playfulness. In *Proc. Fun and Games '10*, ACM Press (2010), 28-37.
25. Mattila, M., Karjaluoto, H., and Pento, T. Internet banking adoption among mature customers: early majority or laggards? *Journal of Services Marketing*, 17 (5), (2003), 514-528.
26. Mitzner, T., Boron, J., Fausset., et al. Older adults talk technology: Technology usage and attitudes. *Computers in Human Behavior*, 26 (6), Elevier (2010), 1710-1721.
27. Newell, A. Arnott, J., Carmichael, A., Morgan, M. Methodologies for Involving Older Adults in the Design Process. In *Proc. HCII 2007*, 5, (2007), 982-989.
28. OFCOM. *Accessing the internet at home: A quantitative and qualitative study among people with the internet at home*. OFCOM (2009). http://stakeholders.ofcom.org.uk /binaries/research/telecoms-research/bbathome.pdf
29. Robson C. *Real World Research*. Wiley, New York, 2002.
30. Rutt, R. *The death of local banking*. MoneyWise, 26.05.2011. http://www.moneywise.co.uk/banking-saving/current-accounts/the-death-local-banking
31. Saga. As Bank of England keeps rates low, solutions sought for suffering savers. http://tinyurl.com/6b7qc67
32. Singh, S. and Morley, C. Young Australians' Privacy, Security and Trust in Internet Banking. In *Proc. OZCHI '09*, ACM Press (2009), 121-128.
33. UK National Statistics. Life expectancies 2008-2010. ONS, 2011. http://www.statistics.gov.uk/hub/population /deaths/life-expectancies/index.html
34. UK Payments Council. The Way We Pay 2010. UK Payments Council, London, 2010.
35. Vines, J., Blythe, M., Dunphy, P., and Monk, A. Eighty Something: Banking for the Older Old. In: *Proc. BCS-HCI 2011*, BCS (2011).
36. Vines, J., Dunphy, P., Blythe, M., Lindsay, S., Monk, A., and Olivier, P. The Joy of Cheques: Trust, Paper and Eighty Somethings. *CSCW '12*, ACM Press (2012).
37. Vines, J., Blythe, M., Dunphy, P., Vlachokyriakos, V., Teece, I., Monk, A., and Olivier, P. Cheque Mates: Participatory Design of Digital Payments with Eighty Somethings. In: *Proc. CHI '12*, ACM Press (2012).
38. Weber, A. The convergence of mobile data phones, consumer electronics, and wallets: Lessons from Japan. *Journal of Telematics and Informatics*, 24 (3), (2007), 180-191.
39. Wells, J. An inclusive approach to financial products. Age Concern UK, London, 2008.

Senior Designers: Empowering Seniors to Design Enjoyable Falls Rehabilitation Tools

Stephen Uzor
Glasgow Caledonian University
Cowcaddens Road, Glasgow, UK
stephen.uzor@gcu.ac.uk

Lynne Baillie
Glasgow Caledonian University
Cowcaddens Road, Glasgow, UK
l.baillie@gcu.ac.uk

Dawn A. Skelton
Glasgow Caledonian University
Cowcaddens Road,
Glasgow, UK
d.skelton@gcu.ac.uk

ABSTRACT
Studies have shown that functional strength and balance exercises can reduce the risk of falling in older people if they are done on a regular basis. However, the repetitive nature of these exercises; as well as the use of instructional booklets and videos for rehabilitation may discourage seniors to exercise in the home, thereby rendering such an intervention ineffective. Our work proposed that the use of multimodal games – co-designed with seniors – could be a way of making falls rehabilitation more enjoyable; thereby improving adherence to home exercise programmes. In this paper, we first explain the process by which we identified barriers to the users' effective interaction with current home rehabilitation tools. We then go on to describe how we actively involved seniors in the initial design, and improvement of useful, enjoyable games for falls rehabilitation. Our findings suggest that seniors are an integral part of the design process and should be directly involved from the concept stages of the design of tools for their rehabilitation.

Author Keywords
Games; User-centered; Design; Falls; Rehabilitation.

ACM Classification Keywords
H.5.2 [Information Interfaces And Presentation]: User Interfaces - Interaction styles;

INTRODUCTION
Just over a quarter of adults over the age of 65 (and half of all adults aged 80+) fall at least once a year [16, 25]. Some falls result in fractures, which can lead to disability, loss of independence and fear of falling. The cost of fractures can be very high in most countries (estimated at $10 billion [11] in the United States and £1.8 billion in the UK).

In recent years, there has been a push towards the implementation of more useful fall prevention strategies, to reduce the burden of falls on healthcare practices and promote independent living. One of the most important strategies involves rehabilitation – using strength and balance exercises – which has been shown to improve muscle strength, balance and mobility in fallers [23]. Consequently, these specially tailored exercises have been utilized in a wide variety of settings to help older adults at risk of falling to return to functional capacity and an independent life. However, there is a problem with the uptake and adherence to home exercise programmes [19].

Previous studies have focused on studying adherence rates only; with some studies investigating compliance within supervised group therapy classes. Relatively little work has investigated the reasons as to why adherence rates are so low when it comes to unsupervised rehabilitation in the home. There is evidence to suggest that due to the repetitive nature of rehabilitation exercises (which is necessary to improve muscle strength and balance), some patients find the routine monotonous and boring.

In recent times, video games have proved a successful intervention to making rehabilitation more enjoyable for patients with a wide variety of ailments. The use of commercially available games such as Wii-Fit has become a staple of encouraging physical activity in older adults – mostly in the clinical setting. However, rehabilitation often involves specifically tailored exercises which promote the recovery of muscle groups necessary for improved strength, balance and mobility. Therefore, there is a need to go one step further in the design of video games, in order to make them useful for rehabilitation purposes. The use and adaptation of games to facilitate seniors' rehabilitation however has seen them play mainly a passive role in the design process; as they are generally asked to provide feedback on elements of the game(s), which the designer (usually a young person) takes into account when improving these tools.

Our long term goal is to improve adherence to home exercise for falls rehabilitation through the use of more interactive multimodal activities. In order to successfully pursue this goal, it was crucial that we first explored the reasons why older adults may not adhere to exercise programmes using current falls rehabilitation tools (instructional booklets and videos). By doing this, we hoped to identify some of the requirements for the improvement of home exercise tools. Secondly, we believed that it was necessary to collaboratively design the tools with

Permission to make digital or hard copies of all or part of this work for personal or classroom use is granted without fee provided that copies are not made or distributed for profit or commercial advantage and that copies bear this notice and the full citation on the first page. To copy otherwise, or republish, to post on servers or to redistribute to lists, requires prior specific permission and/or a fee.
CHI'12, May 5–10, 2012, Austin, Texas, USA.
Copyright 2012 ACM 978-1-4503-1015-4/12/05...$10.00.

seniors, because they – as end users of the tools – could highlight useful design considerations that a younger designer may not have been aware of. In this paper we explain how we involved seniors in the design of one of these tools, games. We involved users not just at various stages of the game development process, but at the initial concept stage as well.

BACKGROUND

Most injury related deaths in older adults over the age of 65 are a consequence of falls [2, 13]. There are a number of risk factors – both intrinsic and environmental – that have been identified as directly related to falls [25, 30]. Intrinsic risk factors (such as reduced mobility, effects of medication, poor vision, etc.) have been the target of most clinical interventions for falls over the years. Balance impairments and reduced lower limb strength have been identified as two of the most prevalent and readily modifiable risk factors [14, 21, 25, 29]. Recent studies have shown that interventions aimed at the recovery of lower limb strength (and balance) have been successful at reducing the risk of falling by as much as 33% [13, 29].

Falls rehabilitation in the home typically involves the use of instructional booklets (Figure 1) and videos containing a number of the aforementioned balance and strength training exercises. These exercises encourage repetitive movement of limbs – through particular ranges of motion – which recovers strength in certain muscle groups necessary for everyday tasks [4]. Current evidence suggests that a significant number of people offered home exercise do not adhere to the programme, thereby rendering the intervention ineffective [22]. This so called non-compliance to exercise can arise as a consequence of a number of factors. Cumming et al (2001) found that low confidence in the effectiveness of home exercise could contribute to low adherence rates [14].

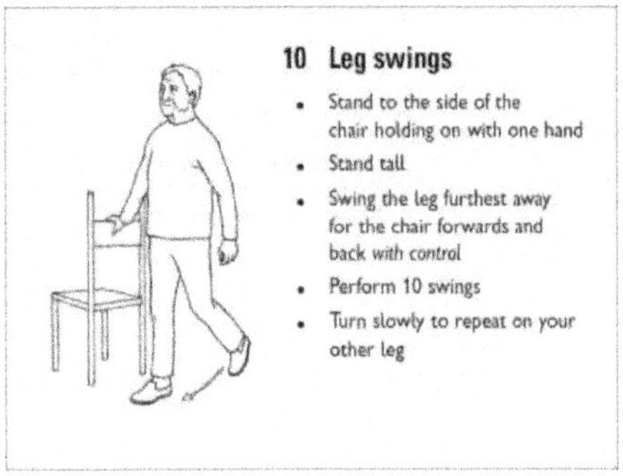

Figure 1. A balance exercise as shown in an instructional booklet for falls rehabilitation in the home.

Also, Radmoski (2011) argues that the nature of the exercise intervention has a significant role to play in the patients' adherence to the routine [20]. The evident repetitive nature of these exercises – over a period of time – could potentially result in a reduced interest in the rehabilitation programme. Therefore, there is a need to enhance the state of home exercise by seeking methods which have the potential to increase motivation; and distract the user from the monotonous but necessary nature of rehabilitation exercises.

Technology and Rehabilitation

Computer-based technology has been used in some studies to encourage active participation in rehabilitation programmes by patients. Taylor et al. (2010) used video conferencing technology to enable patients in pulmonary rehabilitation to participate in virtual exercise classes with other patients and a physiotherapist [28] in their home. Their study revealed that involving users in group sessions enabled active involvement in rehabilitation by the participants, who remained motivated.

Games and virtual environments (VEs) have also been used in numerous studies to aid older adults in rehabilitation [26]. Commercially available games in particular have proved a low-cost solution to making exercise and physical activity a more enjoyable process for seniors. This is evident in the widespread use of games such as Nintendo's Wii-Fit [18] to encourage physical activity in older adults. However, in special cases – such as in rehabilitation – where certain limb motions are required for effective recovery of balance, strength and motor function, these tools alone are insufficient [9]. For instance, the 'Leg swings' exercise shown in Figure 1 requires a specific movement of the legs through a particular range of motion. Therefore, even though commercially available games can facilitate an enjoyable experience for the user; specially tailored games that encourage the right kind of movement need to be developed for this purpose.

A pilot study by the makers of the 'Silverfit softkinetic rehabilitation system' showed that older adults felt more involved in rehabilitation [24]; and often performed more exercise than was required of them. The Silverfit system facilitated play by capturing the user's image – using a depth-sensing camera – and placing it in the virtual world, where they could interact with virtual objects through gestures. Although the system was successful in motivating seniors to exercise; the cost of the system, and the relative complexity of the set-up required meant that this study was limited to the laboratory setting.

Microsoft's Kinect camera sensor for the Xbox 360 platform has recently gained popularity among researchers as a cheap solution to facilitate full body interaction with games [17]. Ideally, camera-based technologies such as the Kinect sensor could provide users with a suitable tool for interactive home exercises as it is inexpensive and relatively simple to use. Nevertheless, one important factor to consider is the fact that most of the exercises for falls need to be performed with the aid of a chair – which is used for support (Figure 1). In this case, the Kinect sensor (and camera-based systems in general) may not be ideal for such exercises as the chair would interfere with the user's image as detected by the sensor.

Instead of using gaming consoles such as the ones just discussed we built our own Inertial Measurement Unit (IMU) wireless sensors. We used these sensors to facilitate the control of games that we built for falls rehabilitation. The IMU wireless sensors have integrated accelerometer, gyroscope and magnetometer systems which allow for more accurate solutions than that derived from say, a Nintendo Wii remote. Also, the IMUs allow for multiple (more than four, as is usually the case with the Wii remote) sensors to be used in tandem with each other. This not only allows for multi-limb interaction that emulates established strength and balance exercises; but their relative size makes them less intrusive than similar solutions that have been used in previous research.

Designing for Seniors

When it comes to designing games for rehabilitation, we believe that it is not enough for designers to decide what older adults will consider an enjoyable experience. Previous studies in this field have recognized the need to evaluate games with older adults – especially in Stroke rehabilitation [9] but have stopped short of actually encouraging the seniors to design their own games.

Alankus et al (2010) found that involving older adults as passive members of the design team – as is the case in most studies – can inform the design of more enjoyable rehabilitation experiences [3]. The passive role that seniors play in such cases typically involves playing games designed by the design team members and providing feedback on elements that they feel should be modified, in order to make the games more enjoyable. However, the original ideas for the games in such studies have always come from younger designers, researchers or therapists. If older adults are capable of suggesting improvements to rehabilitation games; then it is surprising that studies have not involved them in the concept stages of the design of these games as well. After all, older adults are the recipients of these tools. Therefore, we believe that they are arguably in the best position – assuming that they are cognitively capable – to provide researchers – from the outset – with an insight into their preferences regarding various game elements that would ensure an enjoyable experience for this age group.

After investigating several possible methods and techniques for involving users in our project, we settled upon using some of the principles and techniques from Scenario and Participatory Design. The reason for using these methodologies was that they are user driven rather than designer driven and have proved successful in the past in new, mobile and home settings [5, 6, 8, 27].

In this paper, we describe the procedure that we developed to involve seniors in the design of multimodal tools for rehabilitation in the home, for the sake of clarity and brevity we focus on the outcome from only one potential tool i.e. rehabilitation games.

METHODOLOGY

Few studies have considered the older adults' experiences with the use of instructional booklets and videos for falls rehabilitation in the home. To date, we believe that there has been no structured methodological way in which to encourage seniors to be part of the design team and be directly involved in the design of their own rehabilitation tools. One possible tool we wanted to investigate was games, however the seniors could also suggest any tool for their rehabilitation that they wished e.g. visualizations of movement with simple targets was one suggestion. We developed our own methodology with the following research questions in mind:

- How can we identify barriers to effective user interaction with rehabilitation tools in the home?
- Can older adults contribute to the design of multimodal tools for their own/others home rehabilitation?

To answer the questions, we held two multi-phase design workshops with seniors that tackled important issues related to the research questions in separate phases. Although both design workshops were identical in structure, the first workshop involved older adults who had not been identified as fallers; whereas we specifically recruited fallers for the second workshop. One of the reasons why we recruited non-fallers in the first workshop was that we were informed by a falls expert that some of the frailer fallers may be hesitant to play games. We also felt it was necessary to test the methodology with the non-fallers prior to involving fallers in a later workshop.

The participants were divided into small groups of three or four in order to enable everyone to contribute to the discussions and activities in the various phases. There were two facilitators in each of the small groups – one asked the questions associated with each of the phases, while the second facilitator noted the participants' responses. Special care was taken to address the needs of the participants, for example: the participants were offered transport to the workshops, refreshments during the workshop, the location of the workshop was carefully chosen in order to ensure that it took place on the ground floor and that the car park and entrance to the building were only a few short steps away; and finally we ensured that the schedule included several comfort breaks.

Participants

In the first design workshop we recruited 9 non-fallers (mean age 67, 8 female, 1 male); whereas in the second workshop, 7 fallers (mean age 73, 4 female, 3 male) were recruited. The participants came from a mixed educational background that is common in the general population, e.g. some had no official qualifications and some were educated to college level. The non-fallers were recruited through flyers and posters placed at various locations around the University. The fallers were recruited through rehabilitation centres of the NHS local Falls Services.

Procedure

Table 1 summarizes the main phases involved in the workshops and the rationale for each phase.

Phase	Rationale
Discussions of Past Experiences	To acquire a range of personal opinions regarding the use of booklets and videos for rehabilitation.
Scenarios & Personas	To acquire user opinions on the factors affecting adherence to exercise – using user journeys and personas with currently used exercise materials.
Games Session	In this session the seniors play with the prototype games; and comment on the usefulness of these in ensuring enjoyable home rehabilitation. *Design Workshop 1:* The games were designed by the falls expert and the designers on the research team. *Design Workshop 2:* The games were designed by older adults in Design Workshop 1.
User Sketches	To encourage the participants to design and discuss rehabilitation of new tools based on the falls programme exercises

Table 1: Design Workshop procedure with the main phases

Phase 1 (Discussions of Past Experiences)

Phase 1 was set up to investigate the participants' previous experiences with rehabilitation using similar tools to the Age UK booklet and videos. It was important to do this, as the discussions about the users' previous experiences with such tools could bring to light some of the main issues regarding the effects of their use on motivation and adherence to home exercise. The participants were shown one exercise from the booklet (e.g. Figure 1) and a video of the Sit-to-Stand exercise. They were then asked if they had previously used such tools for rehabilitation, and what issues they may have encountered that affected their motivation to exercise.

Phase 2 (Scenarios & Personas)

We were advised by the falls expert that some of the participants may not be comfortable talking about their own personal experience with a group of strangers. In addition it was anticipated that some of the non-fallers may not have had any prior experience with the use of booklets and videos for home rehabilitation. Furthermore, we expected the fallers' experiences to vary. We felt it was therefore necessary to use a tool to augment, facilitate and focus the discussions in this phase on the use of rehabilitation tools within the home. For this reason, we incorporated the use of scenarios and defined personas that allowed our participants to observe typical user-journeys through rehabilitation. Scenarios and personas were used as they have become useful tools in informing design over the years [10, 12]. They support discussions about design and encourage active participation among all stakeholders [8]. In order to make the personas realistic enough to represent the user group of interest (older adults with a high fall risk), we co-developed them with a lead researcher in the field of falls prevention. By doing this, we identified some key issues – that were characteristic of seniors in falls rehabilitation – which could affect adherence; and hence the effectiveness of home-exercise interventions. Such issues included: low confidence, fear of falling, loneliness, and history of falls.

Persona	Key Details
Persona 1: Jack Bishop 	• 68 years old. • Retired high school soccer coach. • Suffered stroke at 65. • Has fallen once. • Lacks confidence.
Persona 2: Agnes Newman 	• 82 years old. • Retired office worker. • Has fallen three times. • Suffered a minor hip fracture. • Has a high fear of falling.

Table 2: Personas along with their key defining characteristics

The scenarios that defined the personas' journeys through rehabilitation were:

- *Scenario 1: Home rehabilitation using the instructional exercise booklet.*
- *Scenario 2: Home rehabilitation using exercise videos.*

Each of the personas performed home rehabilitation under a different scenario. Scenario 1 defined Jack's (Persona 1) user journey through home rehabilitation while Scenario 2 served the same purpose for Agnes (Persona 2). This was to keep the participants focused on the key issues that each of the personas may face during home rehabilitation under different circumstances. For instance, the participants were required to consider the fact that Jack was a retired soccer coach, and as such had led a relatively healthy and active lifestyle before his stroke. The sudden turn of events in his life meant that he had to deal with the fact that he could not be as active after the stroke. Also, he had to perform exercises that were mostly confined to a single location with a chair.

Phase 3 (Games Session)

The main purpose of the third phase of the workshops was to evaluate specifically developed prototype games with older adults (both fallers and non-fallers). These prototype games were very basic with only some implementation. The designs were based on a small sample of the strength and balance exercises from an instructional booklet (an example is shown in Figure 1). The booklet used in this study was provided by Age UK (a UK-based charity that provides help and advice to older adults on a wide variety health issues) [1]. In both design workshops, we demonstrated two prototype games – one based on a strength training exercise and one on balance – which were developed for the purpose of aiding home rehabilitation. We intended to obtain the participants' feedback on the use of the tools that we proposed; namely the games and the use of body-worn sensors to facilitate play. All of the games that we demonstrated in the workshops utilized IMU sensors as the primary input mechanism. The participants strapped the sensors to their limbs using elasticized velcro bands (each band had a pocket that contained the sensor). We asked for four volunteers – two per game – from each workshop to play the games while the other participants watched.

Pigeon Express Prototype (Design Workshop 1)
This game was based on the 'Sit to stand' strength training exercise and was controlled primarily by one IMU sensor – which was strapped to one of the participants' thighs. The aim of the game was to guide the flight of a pigeon using the sit-to-stand (and back to sit) motion to avoid obstacles that came into the flight-path of the bird. The participants were required to stand up in order to fly high and avoid hitting passing cars; and sit down to fly low and avoid overhead road signs (Figure 2). The obstacles appeared at a relatively slow pace, so that the participants could ease in and out of the chair. This slow movement is necessary for building strength in the quadriceps muscles.

Figure 2. The Pigeon Express Game: The user stands up to avoid hitting an on-coming vehicle.

Scooter Hero Prototype (Design Workshop 1)
This game was based on the 'Leg swings' balance exercise shown in Figure 1 and utilized a single IMU sensor strapped to the user's shank (just above the ankle). The aim of the game was to use the 'swinging' motion of the leg suggested by the exercise to ride a scooter and collect as many coins (in the path of the scooter) as possible. If the user performed the motion too fast or too slow, the speed of the scooter reduced significantly.

Figure 3. The Scooter Hero Game: The user swings one leg at a steady pace to ride the scooter.

After the volunteers played the games, the participants were asked a number of questions related to the game play experience; and the role of such games in motivating older adults to exercise.

Phase 4 (User Sketches)
In this phase, the participants in both workshops were given samples of exercises from the 'Age UK' instructional booklet (e.g. Figure 1) and asked to design and discuss ideas for rehabilitation tools based on these exercises using sketches and annotations. The reason for this is that previous research has shown that inviting users (both children and adults) to conceptualize their ideas using sketches and drawings has encouraged greater participation in design [5, 7].

In the first design workshop, there were three groups of three participants, whereas in the second workshop, there were two groups of participants (4 in one group and 3 in the other). Each group was asked to design a tool based on one exercise. The exercise templates that we gave them included the 'Leg swings', 'Marching' and 'Sit to stand' exercises. The 'Sit to stand' exercise was not given to fallers as there were only two groups involved in the second workshop. The participants had to consider the movement – including the initial and final positions of the limb, as well as the pace – required for the exercises; and design the tools with these useful considerations in mind.

KEY FINDINGS
The design workshops described in this paper set out to accomplish two key objectives:

- To identify barriers to effective user interaction with rehabilitation tools in the home.
- To involve seniors in the design of multimodal tools to facilitate a more enjoyable home rehabilitation experience.

The various phases of the workshops provided us with useful feedback from seniors on the issues related to non-compliance to home exercise. The responses from Phases 1, 2 and 3 were organized into themes that were related to adherence and the personas' key characteristics, such as – motivation, progress, confidence, etc. We discuss below, the key findings from each of the phases from both design workshops.

Phase 1 (Discussions of Past Experiences)

None of the non-fallers had previously used booklets and videos for rehabilitation; whereas all of the fallers had used either one of them or both. Some of the fallers drew comparisons between the 12-week rehabilitation classes that they attended immediately after discharge from the hospital and home rehabilitation – which they were expected to do afterwards. Their comments revealed that they often felt de-motivated due to the passive nature of the booklet and videos, which felt like a chore to them.

Phase 2 (Scenarios and the Persona's experience)

Workshop	Comments/ Concerns
Workshop 1 (Non-fallers)	a. As a retired coach, having to perform exercises in such a passive manner may reduce Jack's confidence even further. b. Progress cannot be tracked using video exercises. Agnes lives alone and needs to be constantly motivated. Showing progress could provide this motivation. c. Something to interact with would be useful to Agnes as the video exercises seem passive and dull.
Workshop 2 (Fallers)	a. If Agnes had a way of receiving feedback of her progress, it could motivate her to continue exercising. b. The booklet and the videos are too passive for both Jack and Agnes. They may become bored after a short while. c. Jack's ego may prevent him from performing the exercises as he used to be fit and now he has to use a booklet to exercise

Table 3: The participants' concerns regarding the personas' experiences with booklets and videos

In Phase 2, we employed the use of scenarios and personas to give our participants the chance to experience typical user journeys through home rehabilitation. In particular, we were interested in the personas' interaction with rehabilitation exercises using instructional booklets and videos. There were numerous comments received from the participants in this phase. Table 3 contains the most dominant themes that emerged.

The main concerns that emerged from the discussions in Phase 2 of the workshops highlighted the need to address motivation, interactivity and charting of progress during rehabilitation; as well as the passive nature of instructional booklets and videos [31]. The participants from both workshops agreed that the personas needed a more interactive solution in order to keep them motivated.

Phase 3 (Games Session)

In this phase of the workshops, the participants played prototype games that mimicked the movement required for functional balance and strength exercises. At each workshop, there were two games available to the participants: one based on a balance exercise and the other on a strength training exercise. In the first workshop with non-fallers, the participants were reluctant to play the games initially. This was in contrast to the second workshop with fallers, where some of the participants volunteered to play the games as soon as we had asked. We found this interesting because we had been informed by the falls expert that fallers would be less willing to play the games as they were frail and not very physically active.

Revised Games

One of the main purposes of the games that were developed for the design workshops was to provide the seniors with some games to critique. We hoped that this would lead to suggestions on how to improve the games for effective home use. We also hoped that it would give them a jumping off point for thinking about what games or other activities they could design.

Modified Pigeon Express Game (Design Workshop 2)

We discovered from the first workshop that, while playing the 'Pigeon Express' game, the volunteers would hastily stand up and sit down when the obstacles (vehicles and road signs) came close to colliding with the pigeon. The volunteers stated that they were unaware of this sudden movement, as they were distracted by the game. Hence, the participants felt that the core mechanics of this game needed to be changed, in order to encourage slower movements required of the 'Sit to stand' exercise. Because of this, we adapted the game for the second workshop and introduced new mechanics based on the participants' suggestions. Their advice led to a different goal for the game in which the pigeon had to catch letters that fell out of a mail van. The letters were arranged in a sinusoidal pattern so as to encourage a smooth motion of rising from, and returning to the chair.

We received positive feedback from the fallers in the second workshop when the volunteers played the modified 'Pigeon Express' game. They thought that the game promoted the right kind of movement and was enjoyable to play. Their feedback suggested that this game would be useful to the personas (Jack and Agnes) as the constant need to catch the letters would distract them from the repetitive sit/stand motion. The fallers also mentioned that this game would encourage the personas to exercise more, because they would try to beat their previous scores. The element of competition with one's self was regarded as a good motivator to keep the personas involved – especially Jack, as they felt that he was competitive due to his prior active participation in sports.

The feedback from the fallers also suggested including different objectives (such as catching falling fruits or other objects) and environments so as to keep the games fresh and exciting for the personas. Furthermore, both the fallers and non-fallers felt that it would be useful to provide users in the home with varying difficulty levels (with advice from a physiotherapist) to cater for a wide range of abilities at different stages of rehabilitation.

Glowing Woods Game (Design Workshop 2)

The concept designs for the 'Glowing Woods' game were created by the non-fallers in Phase 4 of the first design workshop. The mechanics of this game were based on the 'Marching' exercise – an aerobic exercise used to improve balance (Figure 4). The exercise involves marching on the spot while standing and holding onto a chair for support. The participants' original concept design for the 'Glowing Woods' game recommended using the marching motion to control the movement of a character through a virtual environment. The group that produced this design included the extra objective of interacting with animals or insects in the environment using one arm.

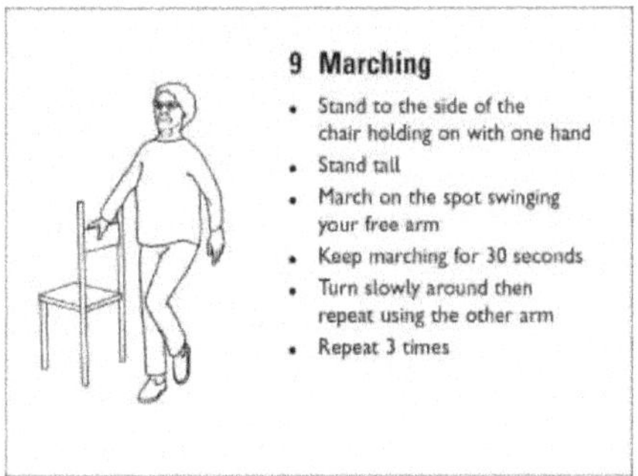

Figure 4. The Marching Exercise from the 'Age UK' instructional booklet

We developed the 'Glowing Woods' game as suggested by the participants' in the first workshop to simulate walking through a virtual forest while catching fireflies. The user must wear a single sensor strapped to their shank to capture the walking movement, and another sensor strapped to their wrist to enable them to catch the fireflies – that occasionally wandered across the screen – using a wave-like gesture.

In both workshops, once the first participant had played the first game, the rest of the participants were more willing to play. A total of 4 out of the 9 participants in the first workshop volunteered to play the games. However, all of the participants in the second workshop played the games at some point during the workshop (some of them played the games again at the end of the workshop). The 'Glowing Woods' game (concept that came from the seniors in the first workshop) in particular proved to be very popular with the fallers, with all of them playing this game, more than the Pigeon Express (the game concept from the designers) at the second workshop.

Effects of Games on the Personas' Characteristics

After the participants had the chance to play the games, they were asked to discuss the usefulness of the games to aiding the personas (as described in Phase 2) during home rehabilitation. One of the main purposes of using personas in these workshops was to highlight certain issues that are characteristic to many fallers in home rehabilitation. We felt that it was necessary to investigate how game-based rehabilitation could target some of the main issues that may cause reduced adherence to home rehabilitation programmes.

Confidence: The participants from both workshops highlighted the inability of instructional booklets and videos to communicate progress to older adults during rehabilitation. They felt that obtaining high scores or beating previous records in the games would improve confidence in the personas; and encourage them to remain involved in the rehabilitation process.

Motivation: It was suggested by our participants that playing games for rehabilitation has the potential to motivate the personas to engage in rehabilitation. Confidence was considered a necessary pre-requisite to being motivated – especially in the case of the personas. Also, the knowledge of progress during rehabilitation was considered one of the most powerful motivators to exercise. The participants in both workshops thought that games were more useful than instructional booklets and videos, as they have the means to communicate this progress to the personas. There was an emphasis on involving the personas' children and grandchildren in playing rehabilitation games. The participants in both workshops suggested that the personas' interaction with family members using games would significantly increase their motivation to exercise.

Conveying Progress: In the initial game prototypes, generic numerical scores were given based on how many objectives were accomplished in the game. The fallers suggested including scores as a measure of the quality of movement for a particular exercise. For instance, instead of having a numerical score, the game could show how many correct repetitions were performed by the user. They felt that an increase in the number of correct movements – compared to a previous exercise session – can assure the user that they are making some progress in the recovery of strength and balance.

Fear of Falling: One of the key characteristics of Agnes (Persona 2) was her high fear of falling. The feedback from non-fallers indicated that the element of distraction that games provide would help to take Agnes' mind off this fear. The fallers however, felt that extra steps needed to be taken in order to help Agnes overcome her fear in the initial stages of rehabilitation – such as providing games that allow for seated exercises as well.

Phase 4 (User Sketches)

The objective of phase 4 was to encourage the participants to design tools based on rehabilitation exercises. Each group in the workshops was given one exercise to base their tool on. We noticed that the participants were initially reluctant to design the tools with the drawing materials provided. The non-fallers stated that the fact that they had not previously done such a thing meant they didn't know where to begin. We encouraged them by having them sketch very rough ideas – after examining the exercises – before refining their designs with more detailed sketches and annotations. They discussed possible ways in which to mimic the exercise movements and put their ideas down on paper. The fallers had the same initial problem of not knowing where to begin when designing concept ideas for rehabilitation tools. We informed them that the 'Glowing Woods' game which they had just played in Phase 3 was designed by seniors in the first workshop. To our surprise, they were excited by this; and seemed to be competing with the non-fallers in the first workshop to create interesting games, with some of them making remarks about beating the number of designs that we obtained from the first workshop. We found this very useful and encouraging because we acquired more concept designs from the fallers – even though there were just two groups of participants in the second workshop, compared with 3 groups in the first one. This was extremely useful as they were exactly the type of people the end tools were intended for.

Figure 5. Seniors discussing game mechanics in Phase 4 of the first design workshop

The participants' sketches and annotations in both workshops surprised us, in that they often described in detail, the main mechanics and considerations pertaining to the original exercise. Some of the ideas proposed by the participants in both workshops include: using the sit-to-stand motion to control a horse jumping over a fence in a horse racing game; using the leg swing motion to control the power and direction of a ball in a game of penalty kicks; getting across a river using the marching motion in a 'stepping stones' game; and using your leg as a golf club in a game of golf.

One of the interesting outcomes from this phase was that some of the groups designed games with multiple objectives, in order to better engage the users.

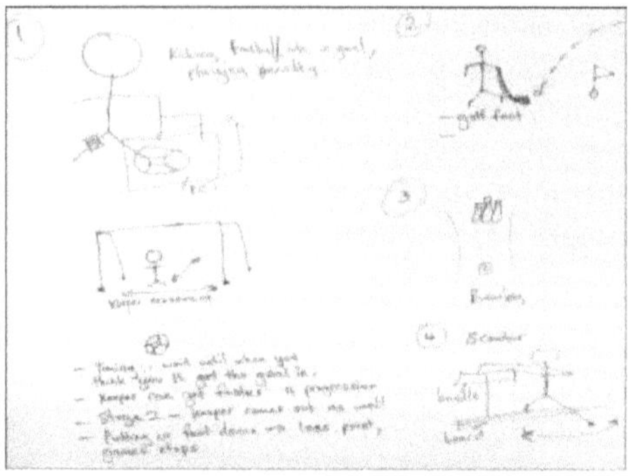

Figure 6. Concept sketches of games for the 'Leg swings' exercise as designed by seniors in the second workshop.

DISCUSSION

Exercise for the prevention of falls has been shown to significantly reduce the risk of falling if the patient adheres to the routine. Studies have shown that adherence to home exercise can be negatively affected by various factors. The findings from both design workshops suggest that one of those factors is that the instructional booklets and videos do not encourage active and prolonged participation in the rehabilitation programme. There are a number of factors identified from the workshops that support this argument: First of all, the passive nature of these rehabilitation media increases the risk of the exercise routine becoming dull and repetitive for the user. Secondly, the inability to progress to more challenging exercises – which is important to the rehabilitation process – makes the use of booklets and videos less than suitable for this purpose. Thirdly, performing home exercise with these tools could potentially reduce motivation and confidence, which are necessary to ensure continued participation in rehabilitation. Finally, it is important to assure seniors in rehabilitation that they are making progress in balance, mobility and lower limb strength. The knowledge of progress could be beneficial to improving self-efficacy and motivation to exercise. Therefore, by taking all these issues into account, researchers and health practitioners can improve home rehabilitation by designing more useful tools in order to maintain the older adults' interest in the programme.

These tools need to satisfy certain criteria in order to provide the user with the maximum benefit that rehabilitation offers. Such criteria include the ability to guide the user through the ideal range of motion – quality of movement, as recommended by a physiotherapist or clinician – as well as the ability to alert the user when the exercise is not being performed correctly. Furthermore, tools for rehabilitation need to communicate – over time – to the users that they are making progress. The findings from both design workshops propose that the ability to see progress could significantly increase confidence and the motivation that seniors require in order to adhere to home exercise.

Senior Designers

In the first design workshop (with non-fallers), we designed the original game prototypes and evaluated them with older adults. The participants' contributions from Phase 3 of the first workshop proved invaluable to the modification of the 'Pigeon Express' game. The participants in the second workshop agreed that these modifications made the game more interesting and emulated the 'Sit to stand' exercise better than in our original game idea – where the pigeon avoided vehicles and road signs. This supports previous evidence that by involving older adults in this way, games can be improved for rehabilitative purposes [3]. Furthermore, the designs – sketches and annotations – that were obtained in Phase 4 of the first workshop proved to be even more valuable to us than the user responses from Phase 3 (games session). The popularity of the 'Glowing Woods' game among the fallers convinced us that seniors can play a very important role in the design process for rehabilitation tools. This is supported by the fact that the core mechanics of this game were derived solely from the design efforts of a team of older adults in 20 minutes – with no input from the designers on the research team.

CONCLUSION

One of the objectives of the workshops described in this paper was to identify obstacles to effective user interaction with instructional booklets and videos for falls rehabilitation. This paper describes the first known attempt to investigate how the use of – and interaction with – falls exercise instructional booklets and videos may negatively affect adherence to home rehabilitation. The findings from Phase 2 of the design workshops suggest that home rehabilitation needs to be enhanced through the use of more interactive tools. These new tools need to address the individual issues – quality of movement, the element of fun and communication of progress – identified by our participants as necessary to maximize the effectiveness of home exercise interventions.

The main objective of the workshops was to involve seniors in the design of engaging multimodal tools for effective rehabilitation. This work presents evidence that seniors can play a significant role in the design of rehabilitation games. This is apparent from the participants' reactions to the 'Glowing Woods' game – which was designed solely by seniors. Our work presents an original contribution to the field of HCI and rehabilitation; as designers and researchers have not previously involved seniors in the concept stages of the design of games for rehabilitation. Older adults often go through many physical and emotional challenges during rehabilitation. Involving them in the early stages of the design process could bring to light some of the obstacles that the designers may not be familiar with (as was observed in our study). We believe that the knowledge and consideration of such issues will inform the design of more useful and effective tools for home rehabilitation.

FUTURE WORK

These studies were carried out to identify the requirements necessary to develop useful multimodal tools to encourage seniors with a high falls risk to exercise. The findings from both workshops will inform the design of useful, engaging tools which we will evaluate with fallers in a community-based randomized controlled trial (RCT). The underlying hypothesis associated with the RCT is that by designing with users we will have produced more engaging multimodal tools for home rehabilitation which will have a more positive effect on adherence to exercise than current rehabilitation tools (e.g. instructional booklets and videos).

ACKNOWLEDGMENTS

Funding for this study comes from the Medical Research Council, UK, Lifelong Health and Wellbeing (Phase 2), reference number: G0900583, Grant ID: 91021.

REFERENCES

1. Age UK. Preventing Falls: Strength and balance exercises for healthy ageing, 2011. http://www.ageuk.org.uk/Documents/EN-GB/ID8950%20Strength%20And%20Balance%20Book.pdf?dtrk=true.
2. AGS, BGS, Guidelines for the Prevention of Falls in Older Persons. Journal of the American Geriatrics Society, 49: 664–672. doi: 10.1046/j.1532-5415.2001.49115.x.
3. Alankus, G., Lazar, A., May, M. and Kelleher, C. Towards Customizable Games for Stroke Rehabilitation, In proc CHI, 2010. doi: 10.1145/1753326.1753649.
4. Allen, N. E., Canning, C. G., Sherrington, C., Lord, S. R., Latt, M. D., Close, J. C., O'Rourke, S. D., Murray, S. M. and Fung, V. S. The effects of an exercise program on fall risk factors in people with Parkinson's disease: a randomized controlled trial. Mov Disord, 2010 Jul 15; 25(9):1217-25.
5. Baillie, L. The Home Workshop. Home-Oriented Informatics and Telematics International Working Conference, California, USA, 05/05/2003-10/05/2003.
6. Baillie L., and Schatz. R. Exploring Multimodality in the Laboratory and the Field. International Conference on Multimodal Interfaces, Trento, Italy, September, 2005, Published by the ACM.
7. Benford, S., Bederson, B. D., Akesson, K. P., Bayon, V., Druin, A., Hansson, P., Hourcade, J. P., Ingram, R., Neale, H., O'Malley, C., Simsarian, K. T., Stanton, D., Sundblad, Y. and Taxen, G. Designing Storytelling Technologies to Encourage Collaboration Between Young Children. In Proc, CHI' 2000.
8. Bodker, S. and Buur, J. The design collaboratorium: a place for usability design. ACM Trans. Comput.-Hum. Interact. 9, 2 (June 2002), 152-169. DOI=10.1145/513665.513670.

9. Burke, J. W., McNeill, M. D. J., Charles, D. K., Morrow, P. J., Crosbie, J. H. and McDonough, S. M. Optimizing engagement for stroke rehabilitation using serious games (2009). Volume 25, Number 12, 1085-1099, DOI: 10.1007/s00371-009-0387-4.
10. Carroll J, M. Scenarios and Design Cognition. Proceedings of the 10th Anniversary IEEE Joint International Conference on Requirements Engineering (2002). ISBN: 0-7695-1465-0.
11. Carter, N. D., Kannus, P. and Khan, K. M. Exercise in the prevention of falls in older people: a systematic literature review examining the rationale and the evidence. Sports Med, 2001; 31(6):427-38.
12. Chen, S. Transitions: Communication, Ageing and Independent Living. London: Helen Hamlyn Centre, 2008.
13. Clinical practice guideline for the assessment and prevention of falls in older people. NICE, 2004. www.nice.org.uk/nicemedia/live/10956/29585/29585.pdf.
14. Cumming, R. G., Thomas, M., Szonyi, G., Frampton, G., Salkeld, G. and Clemson, L. Adherence to Occupational Therapist Recommendations for Home Modifications for Falls Prevention. doi: 10.5014/ajot.55.6.641. American Journal of Occupational Therapy November/December 2001 vol. 55 no. 6 641-648.
15. Druin, A. Cooperative Inquiry: Developing New Technologies for Children with Children. In Proceedings of CHI'99 (Pittsburgh, USA, 1999).
16. Gillespie, L. D., Gillespie, W. J., Robertson, M. C., Lamb, S. E., Cumming, R. G. and Rowe, B. H. Interventions for preventing falls in elderly people, 2009. doi: 10.1002/14651858.CD000340.pub2.
17. Microsoft Kinect for Xbox 360, 2011. http://www.xbox.com/en-US/kinect.
18. Nintendo Wii Fit (2011). http://www.nintendo.com.
19. Nyman, S. R. and Victor, C. R. Older people's participation in and engagement with falls prevention interventions in community settings: an augment to the Cochrane systematic review. Age Ageing. 2011 Aug 28. [Epub ahead of print] - http://www.ncbi.nlm.nih.gov/pubmed/21875865.
20. Radomski, M. V., More Than Good Intentions: Advancing Adherence to Therapy Recommendations, American Journal of Occupational Therapy July/August 2011 vol. 65 no. 4 471-477.
21. Robertson, M. C., Devlin, N., Gardner, M. M. and Campbell, A. J. Effectiveness and economic evaluation of a nurse delivered home exercise programme to prevent falls. 1: Randomized controlled trial. BMJ 2001; 322: 697–701.
22. Robinson, L., Dawson, P. and Newton, J. Promoting adherence with exercise-based falls prevention programmes. In Vincent, M.L. and Moreau, T.M. (eds.). Accidental falls: causes, prevention and intervention. New York, N.Y.: Nova Science Publishers, Chapter 12, pp. 283-298 (2008).
23. Sherrington, C., Tiedemann, A., Fairhall, N., Close, J. C. and Lord, S. R. Exercise to prevent falls in older adults: an updated meta-analysis and best practice recommendations. N S W Public Health Bull. 2011 Jun; 22(3-4):78-83.
24. Silver Fit Soft Kinetic rehabilitation, 2010. http://www.silverfit.nl.
25. Skelton, D. and Todd, C. What are the main risk factors for falls among older people and what are the most effective interventions to prevent these falls? Copenhagen, WHO Regional Office for Europe, 2004. http://www.euro.who.int/document/E82552.pdf.
26. Sveistrup H. Motor rehabilitation using virtual reality. J Neuroeng Rehabilitation, 2004 Dec 10; 1(1):10.
27. Tamminen, S., Oulasvirta, A., Toiskallio, K., and Kankainen, A. Understanding Mobile Contexts. In Proceedings of Mobile HCI2003 (Udine, Italy, 2003), 2003, 17-31.
28. Taylor, A., Aitken, A., Godden, D. and Colligan, J. Group pulmonary rehabilitation delivered to the home via the internet: feasibility and patient perception. In proc CHI, 2011, doi:10.1145/1978942.1979398.
29. Thomas, S., Mackintosh, S. and Halbert, J. Does the 'Otago exercise programme' reduce mortality and falls in older adults?: a systematic review and meta-analysis. Age Ageing. 2010 Nov;39(6):681-7. Epub 2010 Sep 4.
30. Tinetti, M. E., Speechley, M. and Ginter, S. F. Risk factors for falls among elderly persons living in the community. N Engl JMed, 1988; 319: 1701-7.
31. Uzor, S., Baillie, L., Skelton, D. and Fairlie, F. Identifying Barriers to Effective User Interaction with Rehabilitation Tools in the Home. In Proc, INTERACT 2011, Lisbon, Portugal, 2010, 36-43.

Cheque Mates: Participatory Design of Digital Payments with Eighty Somethings

John Vines[1,2], Mark Blythe[1], Paul Dunphy[2], Vasilis Vlachokyriakos[2], Isaac Teece[2], Andrew Monk[3], Patrick Olivier[2]

[1]School of Design
Northumbria University
Newcastle upon Tyne, UK
{john.vines, mark.blythe}
@northumbria.ac.uk

[2]Culture Lab
School of Computing Science
Newcastle University, UK
{p.m.dunphy, v.vlachokyriakos,
isaac.teece, p.l.olivier}
@newcastle.ac.uk

[3]Department of Psychology
University of York
York, UK
a.monk@psych.york.ac.uk

ABSTRACT

This paper describes a project exploring the design of digital payment services in collaboration with 16 people aged over 80. Many older people find cheques valuable as a means of payment but the UK Payments Council recently proposed their abolition. We describe two designs that simultaneously aimed to preserve and augment the paper cheque as a means of making electronic payments. These were devised during participatory design workshops through critical dialogues with our eighty something participants. Workshop discussions resulted in the creation of a real world cheque system where we issued pre-paid cheques without the involvement of banks. This work informed the development of a digital cheque book based on Anoto digital pen technology. The work illustrates the value of participatory design with 'extraordinary' users, such as the eighty somethings, in HCI.

Author Keywords

Digital Payments; Cheques; Ageing; Participatory Design.

ACM Classification Keywords

H5.m. [Information interfaces and presentation (e.g., HCI)]: Miscellaneous;

General Terms

Design.

INTRODUCTION

"You are old," said the youth, "one would hardly suppose
That your eye was as steady as ever;
Yet you balanced an eel on the end of your nose –
What made you so awfully clever?"
(Father William, by Lewis Carroll)

The field of Human Computer Interaction is increasingly concerned with developing technologies for older people [cf. 11, 21]. We are well aware that our nations are ageing and that a third of the population will be over 65 within our lifetimes [24]. This is unprecedented in human history and governments around the world have invested in research to develop technologies to provide care and support. Practices such as participatory design have been adapted to focus on age. Traditionally, participants would have been recruited to a design workshop because they might be the kind of workers who would one day use the planned technology [10], or they may be consumers who might one day buy it [22]. Now participants are recruited to design workshops not because they are target workers or consumers but because they happen to be old. The risk then is that older participants in design workshops may not in a sense be true stakeholders and rather, perhaps, the unwilling recipients of new technology. But as Carroll's Father William illustrates, older people may still surprise and challenge those younger than themselves. Indeed in our work we highlight how the thinking of older participants was often ahead of that of the researchers.

This project sought to address the banking needs of the oldest old (defined as those over eighty [9] – hence eighty somethings). The project was motivated by a number of studies demonstrating that older people are not well served by the banking industry [1, 14]. One of the key findings of the early work in this project was that our participants saw the solution to their problems not in future technologies but in the past [27]. The eighty somethings we recruited were often computer literate yet deeply sceptical and critical of the technology based design ideas we wished to explore [28].

While we were conducting our workshops there was much debate in the UK concerning a proposal to abolish cheques [1,29]. Initially any invitation towards our participants to consider alternatives to cheques was fiercely rejected. This conservatism was most eloquently expressed by Rita, one of our participants. She developed a biological metaphor to argue that cheques could not be improved upon and it is worth quoting at length:

Permission to make digital or hard copies of all or part of this work for personal or classroom use is granted without fee provided that copies are not made or distributed for profit or commercial advantage and that copies bear this notice and the full citation on the first page. To copy otherwise, or republish, to post on servers or to redistribute to lists, requires prior specific permission and/or a fee.
CHI'12, May 5–10, 2012, Austin, Texas, USA.
Copyright 2012 ACM 978-1-4503-1015-4/12/05...$10.00.

> *"Because human nature is always, "We can improve on what the past did." They don't accept that there is a limit to various forms of development. Nature does. Darwin does. On the tree of life, the ends of the branches are the dead ends where that trial didn't work out, so you come back down the limb to the next trial. The main trunk is the ongoing development of animal life and the world. So therefore there are some times where you have reached the apex of development for that particular area. You won't improve on it."*

Many of our participants' agreed that as a design cheques could not be bettered. They might be expensive for the banks to process but the banks were, after all, very rich. The implication here then was strongly towards non-design [4].

We argue elsewhere that strategies of provocation were extremely useful in generating insights [28]. This was most evident with the discussion of cheques. Although the participants did not believe they should be changed in any way, over a series of workshops two prototype systems were developed because —not in spite of—their criticism of the idea of replacing cheques. This paper describes the development of these two novel paper-based payment systems and illustrates the benefits of participatory design with exceptional user groups. By making use of local communities and paper-based physical representation in electronic banking systems we highlight how it is possible to design digital banking systems that are more inclusive of older people's needs.

THE END OF CHEQUES

Cheques are pieces of paper that can be used to authorise the transfer of money between people or organisations. An account holder completes a cheque by identifying by name the person they wish to pay, the amount they wish to pay (in words and digits) the earliest date on which the payment should be made and, finally, their signature authorising the transaction. When removed from the book a "stub" is left behind where a record can be kept showing: when the cheque was written, to whom it was written, and for how much.

Although they are uncommon in some countries cheques are still in regular use in the United Kingdom, the United States, France, New Zealand and Australia (among others) [8]. Whilst the volume of cheques processed in the UK per annum has reduced significantly in the past 10 years [8] many small businesses, charities and older people still rely on them [1,18]. Recent research suggests that 53% of people over 65 in the UK use cheques regularly (compared to 19% of those aged 18 to 24) [1].

The British cheque must adhere to certain standards in its design [7]. At the bottom it contains a code-line printed in magnetic ink that identifies the cheque number, the account number and the bank branch that the account is held at. When a cheque is handed over to a bank teller this information is gleaned automatically from a high-speed scanner. The handwritten information on the cheque must then be typed in manually. This includes the amount to be transferred and the account into which the sum will be deposited. The latter information is typically written on a 'deposit slip', which is an additional document completed by the payee (the person receiving the cheque) in the bank.

Once a cheque has been handed over to a teller in a bank, it must go through a number of resource intensive stages in order for the payment to be legally completed (see [23] for a full description of process). To help explain the cheque clearing process consider Shelley and Bob. Shelley gives a cheque to Bob, who immediately pays it into the bank. The same night Bob's bank sends the cheque physically to the bank's clearing centre where Bob's cheque is processed the following morning. The details of the transaction are sent electronically across a secure network to Shelley's bank. Later that morning, Bob's bank delivers the cheque to the exchange centre, which then passes the cheque to Shelley's bank. The next day, Shelley's bank assesses if she has enough money in her account, and if the cheque is signed, dated, written correctly and is genuine. If it is decided the cheque is correct, then by the end of the same day Bob starts to receive interest on the money and the transaction will appear on Shelley's statement. After two days, Bob is able to withdraw this money. After two more days, Bob can be sure that the money will not be reclaimed without his consent (unless it is proved that he is a party to fraud).

The traditional cheque is problematic for the UK banking sector as the process described above is resource intensive [25] and vulnerable to fraud [6]. When in 2009 it was announced that cheques would be abolished within 10 years, user groups such as older people along with charities and small business were particularly concerned and opposed the plans [1]. This opposition was so vociferous that earlier this year the plans to abolish cheques were halted [26]. Despite this reprieve for cheques, one must assume that there will still be pressure to reduce their usage, perhaps by charging for their use [2]. An influential report by Age UK (the largest older peoples advocacy group in the UK) concluded that 'significant innovation' is required to fill the gap that cheques currently fill [1]. While cheques may not be the first payment option, many older people feel that there are many circumstances where no other payment method would do.

There is a growing sense within HCI that so called 'low-tech' or 'no-tech' solutions to problems are needlessly ignored in favour of computational innovations [4]. We have argued previously that the end of cheques is one such situation where the replacement of simple paper instruments with computational technologies will not suffice [29]. Yet at the same time these simple pieces of paper require very complex processing arrangements and are at odds with the growing emphasis on digital and electronic payments. In the work described in the following sections, we examined with the eighty something participants how we could balance the preservation of the traditional paper cheque with better integration into the digital systems used by modern banks. In our two interventions we aimed to maintain many of the experiential qualities of the paper cheque that the eighty somethings described. Through the iteration of our designs we also introduced innovations that could make them more attractive to administer by banks or other organisations.

DESIGN APPROACH

In our design process we collaborated with 16 eighty somethings (13 female and 3 male; aged between 80 and 87). The participants were recruited from an established research panel that investigated ageing, psychology and technology use. This was a longitudinal study that had been running for 30 years. Most of the participants had now died and our sample was recruited from the survivors. All of our participants were in unusually good physical health and were well used to visiting the university and taking part in research projects. Whilst there was an usually high proportion of female participants in our workshops, we do not believe these dramatically affected the work and was representative of the differing life expectancies of women and men in the UK [9].

Each participant was paid £20 for taking part in each design workshop. In total we performed 12 workshops, although individuals only took part in two to four each. The maximum turnout at any one workshop was 6. Later workshops focused on more specific ideas and designs. These later sessions were often formed of smaller groups of between two to four participants. Over time we found it difficult to arrange suitable times so that all the participants could meet at once. Also, some participants formed friendships with each other, whilst other personalities clashed, influencing individual's choices over who they participated in a workshop with. Each workshop would last between 2 and 2.5 hours in length, and there was always a short tea break in the middle of the session where they were given tea, cake and strawberries. The sessions were known as "tea parties" and for the most part enjoyed to such an extent that the participants would often protest that they should not be paid for having fun when given £20 for taking part. The informal atmosphere of these tea parties helped the participants and the researchers get to know each other well and also perhaps allowed for the free, frank and playful criticism that characterised the sessions (see [28] for more details).

All workshops were audio recorded, and documented in part with video and photographs. In total, the workshops that informed the design and development of Cheque Mates led to the collection of 24 hours of recordings, all of which were transcribed and anonymised (all names used here are pseudonyms).

After each workshop the researchers would come together to make and compare notes and identify recurrent themes that sometimes opened up new design spaces to be explored in the following workshops. In the next section we describe the discussions from our initial design-focused workshops, which directly informed our first Cheque Mates design.

COMMUNITY CHEQUE CLEARING

Our earlier work with the eighty somethings set us the challenge of negotiating how to preserve the qualities of cheques in some way whilst also making them more amenable in an age of digital banking. Suggestions about how cheques could be in some way 'digitised' (for example, using touch-screen displays to simulate writing a payment) were quickly dismissed by the participants. The clear dislike of such ideas and the wider plans of cheque replacement led the researchers to suggest the participants could set up their own organisation that continued to process them as they were. In a discussion about how cheques might continue to exist without the support of banks it was proposed that a charity such as Age Concern might sell a pre-paid cheque book. It was suggested that the person receiving the cheque might post it to Age Concern who would then credit their account to the amount electronically via a BACS payment arranged over the telephone. There was considerable confusion about the idea but once it was more or less successfully conveyed it was still rejected:

> Joan: *"I don't see that working."*
>
> JV: *"Why's that Joan?"*
>
> Joan: *"It seems so complicated. It's so easy just to have a bank account. You've got to have a bank account to which you have to take some money to put into this Age Concern account. It's just ..."*
>
> Patricia: *"One more hassle."*

The notion of a pre paid cheque processed by a third party rather than the bank was returned to with other groups but was most often greeted with similar scepticism.

> *Janet: I don't think that's very practical because there aren't that many Age Concern branches and if you live in the country or somewhere.*

There were frequent misunderstandings of the idea:

> Patricia: *"You'd have to buy the cheques, the blank cheques before you write and send them?"*
>
> MB: *"You're not buying the cheques. It's like a voucher you've got sort of £50 worth of cheques. Do you see what I mean?"*
>
> Patricia: *"No."*

The participants continued to react negatively to our verbal descriptions of the idea. We did not however see these workshops as focus groups or market research but rather as a space for dialogue between the eighty somethings and the research team [30]. Therefore we did not want to abandon an idea due to its initial unpopularity with the group. It was felt that the idea would be more easily conveyed and explored not through a verbal description but as an object. It was decided that we would make an illustrative pre-paid cheque book and, if the participants would allow, use it instead of the usual cash to pay them for taking part in the workshop.

Cheque Mates 1: Community cheques

"Cheque Mates" books were designed to be as cheque-like as possible, but two crucial differences were required. Firstly, the book was pre-paid up to the value of £20 to act as their 'payment' for participating in the workshop. The decision to make the book pre-paid was both a way of ensuring the participants would not spend in excess of what the project could afford as well as testing the idea of a 'pre-paid' cheque book that could be purchased from charitable organisations. Secondly, rather than taking the cheque into a bank branch to deposit it, the payee would have to mail the cheque to the first author (JV) who would then transfer the money to their bank account. A section was provided on the rear of the cheque for the payee to populate their bank account details (Figure 1).

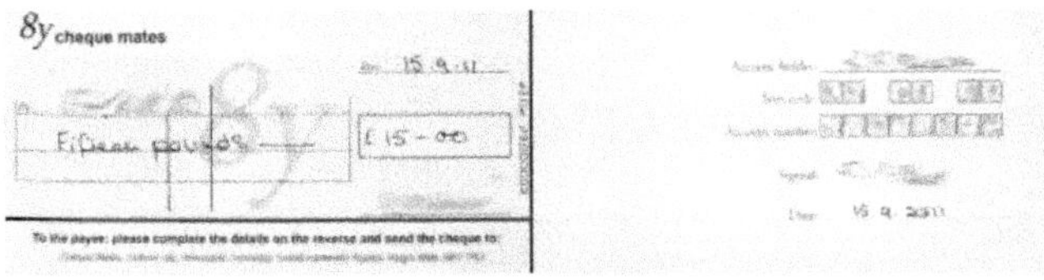

Figure 1. A Cheque Mates 'community cheque' front (left) and rear (right).

As the plan with the Cheque Mates books was for the participants to make actual payments to others, we took the precaution of only giving them to four of our eighty somethings. As was typical of our participants, there was initial surprise that we would be giving them something of monetary value for taking part in what they felt was 'fun'. Although the participants had all been very sceptical, if not dismissive, of the idea when described in previous workshops they all responded enthusiastically when the book was presented to them. Agatha, while inspecting the Cheque Mates book grasped the idea immediately and summarised it like this:

> Agatha: *"If I go to visit a friend and I say, you know explain what we've been doing and I say "Well can I write you a cheque for £20. Will you then do this." And then she puts it in the post and she gets the £20."*
>
> MB: *"Yes yes yes. But what would be more interesting for us is if you would divide the money up and not just write one cheque for £20 but maybe one cheque for £2 or £5"*

Not only did the object convey the idea far more succinctly and clearly than any of the previous discussions, it was also accepted by all participants as a means of payment for their time. Of course it was explained that this was a further part of the research, which they did not have to take part in if they preferred not to. However, none of the participants refused the cheque books as payment.

The participants questioned us about who they should and should not send a cheque to. We did not want to influence them, although we doubted any high street shop would be willing to accept one. Before leaving the workshop the participants were already imagining who they would give a cheque to: *"I'm sort of thinking if I can find any business people. I mean I can think of friends that I could go and explain what I'm doing"* (Agatha).

Experiences of community cheques

Over the course of four weeks, participants used their cheques 'in the wild'. After just one week of waiting the Cheque Mates address received the first cheque that required processing (to the sum of £2.50). As time progressed more cheques were received. The processing of each cheque comprised of JV logging into his own Internet banking account, setting up a new 'payee', selecting this new payee to receive funds, and then logging in once more to confirm the transfer of funds. This already lengthy process was extended further as each new payee required an automated phone call from the bank to act as confirmation. On multiple occasions JV forgot to add the postage of the cheque to the transfer (36 to 46 pence) and therefore had to go through the process again.

Figure 2. Ruth and Agatha discussing their use of the community Cheque Mates, and detail shot of Agatha's 'Cheque Mates' cheque book stub.

After five weeks the participants had spent their £20. During this time the first two participants performed 9 transactions between them. When met them again we discussed each transaction with them as they were documented in their books (Figure 2). Ruth did not incur any particular problems, although she noted one friend took: *"a bit of arm twisting"*. Agatha also encountered few problems with her first two payees. Her third payee also accepted a cheque of £2.50 for a dance class. Several days later, however, the cheque was returned to Agatha via the dance instructor's wife:

> "[She] *absolutely slaughtered me. I mean, they're ... friends really, I thought. But you know ... "Mike's not having anything to do with this. He wouldn't be caught by a scam like this. You've picked the wrong person here." And I said, "Hey, hang on! This isn't a scam, as I explained. It's a proper university research project." – "I don't care what it is. We have to have a written guarantee of what's going to happen to all these details. He wouldn't write all this on the back, and he's so careful when he does this, that and the other."*

This was clearly quite an unpleasant experience. Despite this, Agatha saw the reaction as somewhat irrational and was bemused rather than upset: "*I mean, what could anyone do with just those bank details?"*

Other payees were happy to recieve the money, no matter how small the amount. Ruth sent her last £2.75 to a local children's home completely unannounced. The children's home followed the instructions on the front of the cheque, sending the cheque with their account details on the rear to the Cheque Mates address for processing.

Whilst the participants for the most part enjoyed using Cheque Mates there were also some significant issues that would inhibit its long-term use as a payment service. Firstly, the eighty somethings found the lack of a bank name was a significant barrier to getting people to accept cheques from them—an issue we will return to in the *Discussion*. Secondly, whilst there were practical reasons we had limited the overall payments to £20, there was little doubt that such a low limit was impractical for many everyday cheque transactions – *"what about when you need a new boiler?"* Thirdly, the intermediary process was also problematic for one payee (Agatha's dance instructor), who refused to write down their bank account details and send them to an unknown addressee. Finally, the processing of the cheques in the manner described was hugely time consuming from our own perspective, and in some way reflected the banking industry's own issues with cheques. Despite these problems with the prototype system the participants were, perhaps unsurprisingly given the recent economic collapse, continued to be enthusiastic about the notion of "banking without banks".

DESIGNING DIGITAL CHEQUE MATES

The issues involved with trialling the community cheques were explored in further workshops with those eighty somethings who had used them. Before the trial of the Cheque Mates books we had demonstrated Anoto digital pens (as used in [16,17]) in a number of sessions with the eighty somethings. These pens have cameras built into them that recognise a pattern on the background of the paper, tracing the exact location of the tip on a page and what page has been written on. Although some of the participants thought the technology was very *"clever"*, they were highly sceptical about whether it might be useful for making an alternative payment system. A demonstration of the pen with a computer and data projector elicited this vociferous response from Harold:

> *"Forget computers. 20% of the people – you know, my generation - do not have computers. 7% have got no one who can use them for them. An awful lot [are] of an age that have got children, helpers, carers, grandkids, who use the computer on their behalf."*

Other participants also criticised the technology, worrying: *"you might loose the pen"*, and asking *"why change what we have now?"*. After making the Cheque Mates prototype there followed a remarkable workshop with Agatha and Ruth. Following a discussion of the Cheque Mates prototype there was a demonstration of the Anoto pen. While playing with the pen Agatha began to articulate the ways in which it might be used to write an electronic cheque. Ruth summarised: *"So you could write something to the bank and they just pick it up the other end. Then they would have to have some way of knowing it was you wouldn't they?"* Agatha's replied*"... you could write your instructions on that piece of paper and the bank would pick it up on their screen, their computer screen. Is that what you mean?"* Their dialogue continued with increasing excitement:

> Agatha: *"Yes you see if I've written a cheque or the equivalent of a cheque on that paper and I give it to the plumber for the boiler right? He gives it into his bank or he could send it direct to* [...] *there might be a way of sending it direct to the clearing centre and then because that's authorised on my paper then they can instruct my bank to pay his bank."*

While playing with the Anoto pen Agatha described with extraordinary lucidity how the digital cheque system the team was trying to imagine could work. The "magic paper" and the "magic pen" were imagined in a number of scenarios, such as paying a plumber for some work in their home. While speculating about how the user's identity could be authorised Agatha noted that you would have to give your own bank number and then wondered: *"Are all the magic pens the same? They don't have a number or anything on them?"* Hearing that the pens were individually identifiable led to this delighted exchange:

> Agatha: *"Instead of having to remember a pin number you have it somehow....."*
>
> Ruth: *"A pen number...!"*

Whilst both of these participants discussed the idea it was Agatha's enthusiasm that drove it forward. Ruth later described her as having a *"brainwave"* remarking *"the old brain's waved all over the place today."* Her enthusiasm had been so infectious that Ruth joked that she should be the head of the Royal Bank of Scotland, and asked: "*will you remember those of us who helped you along?*"

The researchers had felt the Anoto technology would be useful in some way but had been unable to articulate this in the workshops. Here, the participants articulated the idea far more clearly than they had in a clear demonstration of the value of participatory design. Indeed, at times, the researchers felt a few steps behind the participants' sense making. The two participants were inspired to imagine the ways in which this technology could balance innovation and conservation. In each of the scenarios that they discussed they were careful to retain what they valued of cheques. At the end of the session the team felt unsure whether what was being proposed was feasible but were inspired to explore this new design space.

Decentralising the cheque clearing process

Following our workshop with Agatha and Ruth, a period of two months was spent exploring whether Anoto technology could feasibly be used as a reliable and secure payment method. Firstly, we had to tackle the issue of transforming the written information on a cheque into digital characters. Secondly, it was necessary to identify ways in which the process could be simplified for the intermediary without necessarily 'automatising' the process. The human element of cheque clearing was of great importance to the eighty somethings, even if their understanding of people processing cheques was quite disconnected from actual practice [29]. In the following we describe how our technical and design work shifted from focusing on a localised 'known' intermediary (JV) to decentralising the cheque clearing process.

Crowd sourcing and cheque processing

In order to make a digital payment it was necessary to address the problem of converting the digitised cheque into data that could be used to initiate a bank transfer. Reliable handwriting recognition remains a difficult problem in computer science. We chose to avoid this problem and use an alternative in the form of Amazon's Mechanical Turk [3]. Mechanical Turk is a crowd sourcing website that enables researchers to set Human Intelligence Tasks (HITs) i.e. automated tasks that necessitate human intelligence in the loop. In anticipation of privacy risks, we segmented each key field on the cheque into its constituent characters using a simple algorithm that used vertical scan-lines to locate gaps between written characters (in practice a more robust algorithm could be chosen). Essentially, the HIT comprised asking workers to tag the image with the single character it contained. This appeared more respectful of privacy than providing full payee and amount details in particular hits. For purposes of cross-validation, each image of a character was tagged by three separate workers to provide a level of error resistance.

Making the payment

The final stage of the background infrastructure was to use the data tagged by the workers to generate an electronic payment. The initial community Cheque Mates avoided this issue through our role as an intermediary. In order to action the payment we needed to use a third-party platform that could link in with most UK bank accounts. PayPal provided a useful alternative at this stage. PayPal also provides a flexible developers kit for new software to be developed, which features a sandbox where transactions can be tested and simulated [19]. See Figure 3 for a diagram of the digital cheque clearing process.

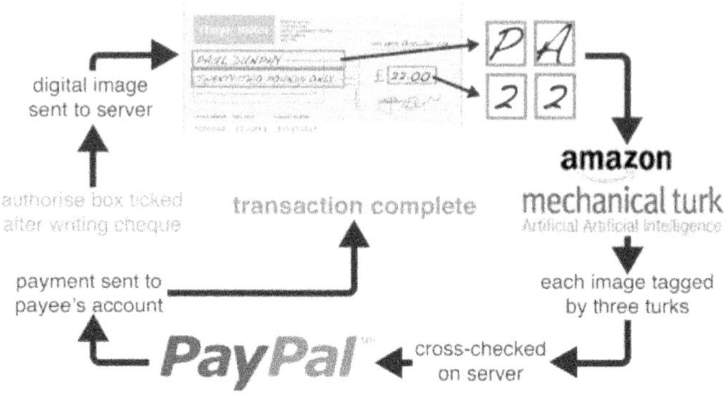

Figure 3. Digital cheque clearing process.

Cheque Mates 2: Writing with digital pens

The custom technical infrastructure explained above was used as the basis of a digital cheque, the design for which emerged directly from our work with Agatha and Ruth. Whilst Agatha and Ruth developed novel digital payment ideas with the Anoto pens, other participants were very reluctant to imagine how it could be used. A barrier was the perception that using the pens would require learning something completely 'new'. We aimed to integrate the Anoto technology into a design that differed very little from that of a traditional cheque book.

Figure 4. Final 'Anoto Cheque' artwork with authorisation piget in bottom left corner.

Although we tried to keep as much to the design of a traditional cheque as possible, using the Anoto technology required some differences. The Bluetooth pens available to us did not automatically synchronise the written data to the nearby computer. This meant that we had to include a "piget" box in the design of the cheque that needed to be ticked to send the data from the pen to the computer. We experimented with the position of the piget by integrating it within the 'signature' but settled on placing it at the bottom of the cheque book "stub" (Figure 4).

Using the Anoto pen to authorise the payment to another makes the actual sending of the cheque to the payee redundant. Our previous work [29] highlighted how the physical sending of a cheque was an important feature in the eighty somethings experiences of cheques. We therefore suggested that the account holder might send the cheque physically through the post in the usual way. The payee would receive the cheque as a record but would not have to process it further.

Another difference that our character recognition algorithms required was that the cheque had to be written out in capital letters. We were concerned that these alterations to how cheque transactions are normally performed would be a barrier to the proposal's acceptance by the eighty somethings. We therefore included a page in the final cheque book with step by step instructions.

Our workshop participants had made it very clear that any payment system that required ownership of a computer would be a "*no go*". Although the initial prototypes did rely on nearby laptops we wanted to make it clear that a future device would not need the account holder to own or use a personal computer. We tackled this by packaging the pen, its charging dock, and the cheque book into a self-contained felt case (Figure 5).

Figure 5. Anoto pen, cheque book and case with integrated charging dock.

It was hoped that packaging all of the required 'technology' together would provide an increased sense that the pen would not be lost, left behind, or roll under furniture.

RESPONSES TO DIGITAL CHEQUE MATES

The responses to the digital cheque prototype were, on the whole, extremely positive. As discussed earlier, all of the workshop participants were usually vocal critics of new technology. Although their criticisms were often insightful and informative [28] the main implication was usually to abandon lines of inquiry rather than pursue them. Upon ticking the box on the digital cheque a researcher on a nearby computer confirmed receipt and told the participants the amount they had made the cheque out to and who it was for (Figure 6). This demonstration was followed by *"Wow!"*s and comments like *"incredible!"* and *"amazing"*.

Figure 6. Ruth writing out a Cheque Mates digital cheque.

This enthusiasm was in marked contrast to previous responses as Frances points this out here:

> *"I don't know all this seems so advanced and you're listening to us saying "Well we don't need this, and we don't need cheques and that." And then you come up with these brilliant ideas, just astonishes me."*

The normally sceptical Patricia agreed *"I think that's remarkable. I can see that, future wise."* It was not the technological wizardry that impressed these participants but the fact that the prototype retained so much of what they valued in cheques:

> *Frances: "Well you're still writing a cheque but it's cleverly designed that it goes in."*
>
> *Patricia: "I've got this as a stub to know what I've done. As opposed to electronically on a computer, which I could knock off by accident at any time, or anything. That impresses me, absolutely."*

Patricia went on to note approvingly: "*you don't have to send it in an envelope*" adding in astonished tones: "*and they then don't have to go and cash it, it's already there. I mean I'm sorry about this, but it's brilliant!*" The general reception of the prototype was then overwhelmingly positive. This was particularly gratifying to the team as Frances had been the most critical member of the all of the workshop groups. She would take a visible delight in pointing out problems and reasons why ideas were impractical or flawed or "*clever, but not for me*". On seeing the first demonstration of the Anoto pen she had dismissed it saying it would be certain to get lost. It was astonishing for Frances to respond to the cheque book prototype with remarks like this: "*We congratulate these research gentlemen on their ingenuity.*"

However, the session was not all congratulation. Frances and Patricia soon turned to detailed questions of implementation. Responses with other groups were also enthusiastic but there were also useful criticisms and suggestions for further iterations.

Instructions and Presentation

Initially some of the participants still treated the devices with some suspicion. Agatha started by cautiously exploring the case, pen and cheque book. As she took the pen out of the case she snapped the charging dock from the rest of the pen: *"...I think I broke something."* Assured that it was not broken, she continued to examine the cheque book. Finding the 'Instructions' page she read: *""Use capital letters" ... Now I wouldn't have used capital letters."* As she continued to read Agatha was evidently becoming more and more baffled. She read aloud:

> *"When you return home, having written a cheque, and are in range of your home hub, tick the authorised transaction box. Process your payment and synchronise your payment..." Ooh dear, this sounds complicated."*

It became quickly evident that the wording on the instructions page was overly complex and even intimidating. Ruth suggested: *"you need a PhD to use this!"* Although humorous the remark makes it very clear that the wording of the instructions was needlessly complicated. Suggesting that they ignore the instructions we asked them to treat it as they would a normal cheque book. Reassured, Agatha filled out the cheque to pay £19.50 of simulated money without further hesitations. Reflecting on the process she pointed out that the problem with this digital cheque was the instructions: *"When you read the instructions, it has you a bit dumbfounded, but when you get down to* [it], *it's quite simple to use."*

Whilst Agatha questioned the use of block capitals, Frances had no problem with this aspect of the design: *"usually they ask for the name in printing, in block letters, so that they know who it is. And then the signature in your own writing don't they?"*

As noted before, many of the participants inspected the cheque books in great detail. This lead to them quickly identifying a number of oversights and mistakes. *"There's a little mistake with this one"* remarked Ruth as she read the explanation page of the cheque book. *"You don't appear to be able to spell "charities"."* Geraldine noted that the paper stub left behind in the Anoto cheque book had no cheque number left on it: *"I can't see the point in doing that. Like having a stump to fill in who you've sent it to with nothing on the bottom saying cheque number three or whatever."* These simple errors in the design of the books sometimes amplified initial suspicions. Previous work in computer security has noted that spelling, grammar and style are important factors in people judging whether an email is trustworthy or phishing [15]. In a very similar vein, these eighty somethings were judging our financial artefacts with a sharp eye on grammar and presentation.

Cost and Computers

A number of the participants were initially very cautious about the notion of replacing cheques with what they deemed to be a complex technology. This was particularly the case with a 'new' group of eighty somethings, who had not been involved in previous workshops. They frequently referred to the cost of the devices: *"Well, what* [are they] *retailing them at? Can I afford to use this system, I ask myself?"*

Another significant concern was whether users would have to be computer literate. The prototype required a computer to communicate via Bluetooth with the pens. The participants made it clear that computers must not be involved in any final design: *"As long as it was a pen. As long as it wasn't a computer or something like that."*

Confirmation and feedback

A recurring issue for many of the participants was a concern that the electronic payments would not go through successfully. On a number of occasions this manifested in the desire for feedback or confirmation that the "bank" had received the request: *"It would be helpful to have the bank acknowledge that they've received it"* (Ruth); *"Like a receipt kind of thing"* (Agatha). Several of the groups discussed between themselves what type of confirmations they could receive, such as an SMS message, or a receipt printed from a small accessory device. Agatha was less concerned with getting lots of information in her receipt: *"just something to tide you over, until you get the bank statement at the end of the month."* Participants in the other groups were also concerned with this, especially if a digital cheque is 'declined' and: *"couldn't be honoured because you hadn't sufficient in your account. It would have to say "No" it wouldn't pay out would it? So would it let you know?"* Frances thought that this might be solved quite simply: *"a green light if it had gone through, and a red light if it hadn't."*

There were a number of concerns that there was very little continuous feedback from the cheques: *"What happens if you make a mistake writing with it?"* These concerns were not helped by the feedback mechanism of the pen, which would vibrate to signal both the successful sending of data and lapses in sensing the patterns on the paper (and therefore not acknowledging pen markings).

Potential Use

It is worth emphasising that not all of the participants were impressed with the digital cheques. Jack's first reaction was: *"it doesn't impress me, sorry."* When asked why it did not impress him, he concluded: *"well, I just don't use that many cheques anyway. A book will last me 3 or 4 years."* There were also some eighty somethings that worried it would be too complex for some of their peers. Robert disagreed: *"I love it! Great idea!"* And the majority of participants thought that the digital cheque idea was at least promising. Patricia was vocal in her praise: *"All the discussions. And all the things we've tried to talk about and what we could do, that to me has come out tops."* During our workshops Patricia had started to use her computer more frequently but was still hesitant to use it to do her shopping or to use Internet banking: *"now that, that I prefer to doing things on the computer as a way of electronically transferring money."*

DISCUSSION

As the economic commentator Leo Panitch reminds us, access to financial services should be as much a public utility as access to clean water, electricity and food [20]. As it becomes increasingly accepted that access to money and banking is an assumed universal right, then it is important to ensure everybody is provided with appropriate forms of doing so. Although our study has only operated in either a very limited trial form (as in the community cheques) or to make simulated payments (as with the digital cheques) there are a number of lessons to be taken from our work in reference to the design of computational technologies for older people—both in the context of digital banking and more generally.

Communities of acceptance and accountability

A well-designed system is useless without a community that accepts its use. Whilst those that used the community cheques considered them no different to a normal cheque, some of those receiving them found them objectionable. These cheques were unusual, and had no clear indications as to what banking organisation they belonged to. As Agatha related, suspicions were roused when recipients found they had to write their bank account details on the rear of the cheque and send it to a stranger. In order for financial artefacts such as these cheques to exist, communities need to be formed that give and accept them. One idea explored with the eighty somethings was using local community centres, shops or third sector organisations (such as charities) to act as cheque clearing houses. Whilst this idea was not developed the Cheque Mates prototypes worked so long as recipients co-operated, so this idea may be revisited.

The infrastructure underpinning the digital Cheque Mates would also support this idea. As with our application of Amazon's Mechanical Turk, typically crowd sourcing is seen to be decentralised and distributed globally. As our participants noted, however, often communities of trust in using cheques are formed through knowing who will be processing the cheque—even if this happens to be a faceless commercial bank. We imagine that rather than sending the data from the digital cheques to faceless Mechanical Turks, people working in local stores or community stores could be sent the data, to be tagged in spare moments, instead. As we have noted, the research was conducted at a time when the Payments Council had proposed the abolition of cheques. The project team are in ongoing discussions with the UK payments and banking industry, which sees potential benefit in using digital pens as a way of bridging pieces of paper with more efficient digital banking services. At the same time, our participants were enthusiastic about "banking without banks", and the digital Cheque Mates might bring this closer to reality.

The threat of breakdowns

In our previous work, we observed how the eighty somethings did not need any confirmation that a traditional cheque payment had gone through or not [29]. Instead they would trust that the cheque would be paid out by the bank and they could confirm this on their monthly bank statement. If there were any issues then it was taken for granted that the payee would be in touch or the bank would return the cheque. With digital cheques, however, there was a need for more immediate confirmation that the transaction had *"gone through"*. Many of the participants suggested ways of altering the design to address this issue. Not only were these proposals helpful in thinking about future iterations they also indicated that the eighty somethings really were engaged in participatory design.

It is also useful to consider what it is that provokes this difference between the perception of traditional cheques and our digital proposal. Although the digital cheques were familiar artefacts they were in equal measures unfamiliar, strange and not from their world. Whilst these were still the simple paper documents they have used for much of their lives, the significance of the actual pieces of paper was called into question. When a cheque is written with a digital pen, the paper acts as a symbol of the transaction but is no longer the transaction itself. Whereas before the piece of paper was itself the focal point of the transaction—journeying from the person who wrote it, into the hands of the payee, through to the clerk, the scanning machinery and eventually into storage—now it is a by-product of the payment process. Although it is a by-product it remains important for our participants.

CONCLUSIONS

Our work with the eighty somethings involved collaborating with them in an ongoing dialogue. As Wright and McCarthy [30] advocate, we met with them on a recurring basis and got to know more about them than what was related to the research topic. We aimed simultaneously to please and challenge them with our designs. Over time some of the participants began to suspend scepticism and imagine how digital technologies might positively alter their use of cheques. As they explored and made payments with the digital cheque prototype, it became clear that these proposals supported a somewhat playful and ludic experience [12] for our eighty somethings.

In presenting their case for implications not to design, Baumer and Silberman [4] ask HCI researchers to consider whether introducing technology does more harm than good in certain contexts of use. Providing inclusive access to finances can have a large affect on peoples' lives—therefore, the HCI community must consider the significance of introducing new technologies beyond the appeal of novelty. The eighty somethings continually reminded us that new technologies "cost money" and the more prudent participants observed that these new devices required charging and the printing of more expensive 'special' paper. At the same time, the digitisation of cheque clearing was associated with the loss of jobs and profits for the banks—even if we suggested that our designs might not even be used directly by the banks. By respecting their scepticism and insistence on the importance of the past we succeeded in creating something not only new but also of potential value.

ACKNOWLEDGEMENTS

We would like to thank our participants for their time, and Emma Jones and Lynn McInnes at Northumbria University for their support in organising the workshops. This research was performed as part of the New Approaches to Banking for the Older Old project and the Social Inclusion through the Digital Economy (SiDE) Research Hub, funded by Research Councils UK Digital Economy Theme.

REFERENCES

1. Age UK. *The Way We Pay*. Age UK, London, 2011.
2. Age UK. *The fight for cheques is not over, says Age UK*. http://www.ageuk.org.uk/latest-press/archive/the-fight-for-cheques-is-not-over-says-age-uk/
3. Amazon Mechanical Turk. https://www.mturk.com/
4. Baumer, E., and Silberman, M. When the implication is not to design (Technology). In *Proc. CHI '11*, ACM (2011), 2271-2274.
5. Braun, V., and Clarke, V. Using thematic analysis in psychology. *Qualitative research in psychology*, 3 (2006), 77-101.
6. Cheque & Credit Clearing Company. *Cheque Fraud*. http://www.chequeandcredit.co.uk/information/-/page/cheque_fraud/
7. Cheque & Credit Clearing Company. *Cheque Printers*. http://www.chequeandcredit.co.uk/cpas/
8. Cheque & Credit Clearing Company. *The Great British Cheque Report*. London, UK, 2009.
9. Dini, E., and Goldring, S. Estimating the changing population of the 'oldest old'. *ONS Population Trends*, 132 (2008), 7-16.
10. Ehn, P. *Work-oriented design of computer artifacts*. Lawrence Erlbaum, New Jersey, 1990.
11. Gaver, W., Boucher, A., Bowers, J., Blythe, M., Jarvis, N., Cameron, D., Kerridge, T., Wilkie, A., Phillips, R., and Wright, P. The photostroller: Supporting diverse care home residents in engaging with the world. *In Proc. CHI '11*, ACM (2011), 1757-1766.
12. Gaver, W. Blythe, M., Boucher, A., Jarvis, N., Bowers, J., and Wright, P. The Prayer Companion: Openness and specificity, materiality and spirituality. In: *Proc. CHI '10*, ACM (2010), 2055-2064.
13. Gerrard, P., and Cunningham, J. Why consumers are not using internet banking: A qualitative study. *Journal of Services Marketing*, 20 (3), (2006), 160-168.
14. HM Treasury. *Financial Inclusion: An action plan for 1008-2011*. HM treasury, London, 2007.
15. Jakobsson, M. The human factor in phishing. In *Proc. Privacy & Security of Consumer Information '07*. http://markusjakobsson.com/papers/jakobsson-psci07.pdf.
16. Kientz, J., Hayes, G., Abowd, G., and Grinter, R. From the War Room to the Living Room: Decision Support for Home-Based Therapy Teams. In: *Proc. CSCW '06*, ACM Press (2006), 209-218.
17. Luff, P., Heath, C., Norrie, M., Signer, B., and Herdman, P. Only Touching the Surface: Creating Affinities Between Digital Content and Paper. In: *Proc. CSCW '04*, ACM Pres (2004), 523-532.
18. Optimisa. *Charities, clubs and societies use of cheques and requirements for alternatives*. Optimisa, London, 2010.
19. Paypal. *Sandbox*. https://developer.paypal.com/
20. Panitch, L. *Renewing Socialism*. Merlin, London, 2008.
21. Rowan, J., and Mynatt, E. Digital family portrait field trial: Support for Aging in Place. In: *Proc. CHI '05*. ACM (2005), 521-530.
22. Sanders, E. And Stappers, P. J. Co-creation and the new landscapes of design. *CoDesign*, 4 (1), 5-18.
23. Tripp, R. Current UK Cheque Clearing Process. http://www.howbankswork.com/15.1.html
24. United Nations. World Population Ageing: 1950-2050. United Nations, New York, 2001.
25. UK Payments Council. *The future of cheques in the UK*. UK Payments Council, London, 2009.
26. UK Payments Council. *Payments council to keep cheques and cancels 2018 target*. http://www.paymentscouncil.org.uk/media_centre/press_releases/-/page/1575/
27. Vines, J., Blythe, M., Dunphy, P., and Monk, A. Eighty Something. Banking for the Older Old. In: *Proc. BCS-HCI 2011*, BCS (2011).
28. Vines, J., Blythe, M., Lindsay, S., Dunphy, P., Monk, A., and Olivier, P. Questionable Concepts: Critique as a Resource for Design with Eighty Somethings. In: *Proc. CHI '12*, ACM Press (2012).
29. Vines, J., Dunphy, P., Blythe, M., Lindsay, S., Monk, A., and Olivier, P. The Joy of Cheques: Trust, Paper and Eighty Somethings. In: *Proc. CSCW 2012*, ACM Press (2012).
30. Wright, P., and McCarthy, J. *Experience-Centered Design: Designers, Users, and Communities in Dialogue*. Morgan and Claypool, London, (2010).

Engaging Older People using Participatory Design

Stephen Lindsay, Daniel Jackson, Guy Schofield, Patrick Olivier
Culture Lab, School of Computing Science,
Newcastle University, UK
{stephen.lindsay/p.l.olivier}@ncl.ac.uk

ABSTRACT
The use of digital technologies is increasingly proposed in health and social care to address the aging population phenomenon but, in practice, the designers of these technologies are ill equipped to design for older people. We suggest participatory design as an approach to improving the quality of design for older people but, based on previous work and our own experiences, identify four central issues that participatory design approaches need to address. We describe an approach to early engagement in design with older people that address each of these issues and some of our experiences applying the approach in a variety of different design projects. We conclude by discussing some of the issues that have been highlighted when attempting to apply this approach in different design contexts and the issues that have been raised when working with partners who are less committed to the idea of engaging with older adults in participatory design.

Author Keywords
Older people; participatory design; empowerment; changing attitudes.

ACM Classification Keywords
H5.m. Information interfaces and presentation (e.g., HCI): Miscellaneous.

INTRODUCTION
Designers of digital technology are being confronted with an increasingly significant challenge, or perhaps opportunity: the ageing population. Increased life expectancy yields enormous benefits for the individual and society. For example, the majority of caregivers are older adults, older adults in the UK work for longer and retire later and they are a key part of the make-up of many voluntary organizations [34]. However, with the increase in the numbers of older people comes with an increase in the resources a society needs to provide to care for them. This is caused by higher levels of incidence of age related diseases such as dementia and other health problems that are a consequence of the normal ageing process [13]. Of additional interest for digital technology designers, the emergence of the "grey market" [6], the term used in economics to denote the increasing preponderance of purchasing power controlled by older adults is causing a rise in demand for digital products tailored towards older adults.

Although appropriately designed technology has the potential to address many of the needs of the ageing population, in practice, new technologies have been the cause of a number of problems that older people experience, rather than a solution. For example, the growing use of "Chip and PIN" technology and the rise of Internet shopping has resulted in plans to phase out the system of cheques in the UK. Consequently, it is widely anticipated that this will cause significant problems for the older members of society, many of whom still rely on cheques [33]. The lack of quality when designing new digital technologies for older people is well documented. Previous work [11] noted that younger designers sometimes struggle to create appropriate technologies for the diverse population of older people.

The social model of disability [28] provides some explanation for this occurrence noting that someone with impaired health or cognitive function is in fact only transformed into someone with a disability through barriers that are created by the society around them. For example, a hearing impaired man watching a film presentation with subtitles in a museum is *impaired* but not *disabled*. But if the museum fails to provide subtitles, he becomes disabled as a direct consequence of the actions or inactions of the technicians, curators, and managers of the museum. The disability is a consequence of a failure in design. We suggest that inappropriate design is a mechanism through which society disables people with impairments by ignoring them. By understanding why older people are frequently neglected in digital technology design, we may start to take steps to address their needs.

This paper presents a case study that illustrates: (i) a simple, participatory approach to design tailored to work with older people that focuses on experiential aspects of day-to-day life and interactions with digital technologies which can be implemented by design teams with no prior experience of participatory design or engaging with older adults; (ii) an examination of some of the issues that arose applying this framework and; (iii) reflections on the issues that were encountered trying to advocate wider uptake of the approach and reflections on why this may be.

Permission to make digital or hard copies of all or part of this work for personal or classroom use is granted without fee provided that copies are not made or distributed for profit or commercial advantage and that copies bear this notice and the full citation on the first page. To copy otherwise, or republish, to post on servers or to redistribute to lists, requires prior specific permission and/or a fee.
CHI'12, May 5–10, 2012, Austin, Texas, USA.
Copyright 2012 ACM 978-1-4503-1015-4/12/05...$10.00

RE-EXAMINING THE DESIGN DOMAIN

Joyce et al. [15] propose that ageism is a significant contributing factor leading to poorly designed artifacts being produced for older adults due to neglecting their experiences, needs and desires. Older people are frequently perceived and portrayed as being resistant to technology [30]. For example, there is an attitude amongst some computer trainers that older people are not the intended recipients of new digital technologies and should not bother to learn to use them [30].

However, the reality is that older people do not conform to the ageist stereotypes that evidence suggests many people hold. In fact, they are willing to accept novel digital technologies into their lives. The issues that arise with acceptance do so because the ways in which older people construct their decision to use or not use these technologies are fundamentally different to the ways younger adults do. Wilkowska et al. [35] studied the acceptability of a personal digital assistant and, through this process, found that older adults acceptance of technology is a complex process but that the key difference between them and younger users was that the older adult was more likely to perceive the device as not being useful and being afraid of failure when using the device more than the younger users involved in the study. When these issues were addressed, the older adults readily engaged with the new technologies.

Furthermore, while eyesight, hearing, memory and physical coordination impairments are a common consequence of the ageing process [13] and make digital technologies harder to use, we would suggest that they are not the most fundamental problem. In fact, placing undue emphasis on the functional characteristics that make older people different to younger people can distract designers from considering older people as complex individuals with their own sets of social and emotional needs and desires. As Keith and Whitney state *"an old person is not just the sum of their acquired impairments"* [16]. This issue arises in part because of the historical legacy of human-computer interaction (HCI), which originally framed the user as "information processor" with little consideration given to the different qualities of their experience of technology.

More recently, as computers have moved out of the workplace and into the home and wider world, new paradigms have arisen that prioritize experience-centered technology design methodologies [36] but such third wave HCI thinking has had little impact on the design of technologies for older adults. However, experience centered design hold vital lessons for those who wish to work with older adults. Designing digital technologies for older people is not simply a matter of addressing the immediate consequence of the most obvious functional impairments.

In addition, digital technology designers need to consider that the fundamental paradigms of interaction that they design around are not the ones that the older generation have necessarily been brought up with, or indeed even have any knowledge of. An example of such a metaphor would be the desktop of a personal computer mimicking an office desktop with files, folders and a bin to place unwanted material in. These metaphors are not intuitive and need to be learnt through use and for the older user, or indeed anyone unfamiliar with the metaphor, they can be unsuitable [12]. When designing any technology that is intended to be used by older people, designers should carefully consider the metaphors it leverages to avoid producing systems that, at a fundamental level, present the older user with a metaphor they do not understand.

Even more significantly for designers, there is a tremendous diversity within the population of older adults and people with dementia. Considering them as one homogenous group ignores the fact that the over 65's are diverse with respect to cognitive ability, living arrangements, age (as within this group there are in fact multiple generations), income and health. In fact, as a collection of individuals, people above the age of 65 years old, comprise a group that is considerably more diverse than members of the general (younger) population [12]. As such, the experience of each individual older person is unique to them and shapes their expectations when they encounter a new technology in ways that an interaction designer does not necessarily account for [27].

OUR EXPERIENCES ENGAGING OLDER ADULTS

In our previous work with older adults we have found that they are capable of engaging in participatory design activities but working with them can be different to working with younger adults. Our previous work engaging with people with dementia and their older caregivers in the design of safe walking aids demonstrated that they could struggle when trying to envision new technologies [18]. Massimi et al [22] observed similar results when engaging older adults in the development of mobile phones. This work also demonstrated the need to respect individual's contributions to the design process. We conducted in-depth analysis of participants narratives from participatory design sessions but found that, at times, this led to ignoring their directly articulated requirements. While some older adults can struggle to articulate themselves, interpreting their utterances without properly engaging them in the design process is not an appropriate solution.

This work, along with work with individuals with Parkinson's Disease [23], highlighted the importance of being flexible when engaging older adults and engaging with them as early as possible in the design process. If a designer starts down a path that any participant does not feel is valuable to them, they will struggle to engage with the process or feel like they are being take seriously. We have also found that some older adults struggled to focus during these design sessions, particularly if the session goes on for too long as they did not enjoy deep exploration of issues being forced on them by the designer. This is particularly true of cases where they are hypothesizing about future technologies that do not already exist. In contrast, older adults were typically delighted by the opportunity to discuss their own experiences in great detail and were much more engaged when doing so. Finally, the language used in design sessions and the structure of the sessions needs to acknowledge that the older adults are presenting their own life experiences. They are not discussing a task they perform and their activities do not fit into the structure participatory design methods assume.

The Challenges in Engaging with Older People

The motivation to improve the level of engagement with older adults can arise from a theoretical view of the political underpinnings of design [25] or from working with them and seeing their perspective on design [1]. Previous work in this area [8] correlates with our own experiences and led us to identify four challenges participatory design approaches need to overcome when engaging older adults in design.

Maintaining Focus and Structure in Meetings: Keeping older participants focused on the topics of discussion and giving them clear opportunities to present their ideas in meetings is a major challenge. Their conversations could wander onto unrelated matters such as recounting anecdotes that are not relevant to the design. If not addressed, the topic of conversation can drift and the discussion skips important aspects of the design domain.

Representing and Acting on Issues: In our previous work, we tended to over-analyze our participants utterances, giving them a complexity that the participants did not intend. However, the formal Thematic Analysis approach that we used [3] did reveal interesting and relevant insights into their narratives. The design approach that we construct utilizes analysis but, at the same time, allows participants to influence design as directly as possible.

Envisioning Intangible Concepts: Older participants are frequently observed having some issues either envisioning future technologies or envisioning intangible concepts [22]. This is an issue that we have encountered in our work as well. Design approaches that aim to engage older people will need to address this by supporting their creative thinking on intangible issues and future technologies.

Designing for Non-Tasks: When designing specifically for older people, the design is often not situated in a workplace domain. This poses problems for designers wishing to leverage existing participatory methods as they are imbued with inherent assumptions about the domain in which they are applied [5]. The design methods can focus on understanding tasks of work-flows and often assume that users are experts in the domain design occurs in. This means the methods need to be modified before they are suitable for addressing experiential aspects of design.

THE OASIS APPROACH

The OASIS (Open architecture for Accessible Services Integration and Standardization) approach (Figure 1) to designing with older people was developed as part of a wider project aiming to develop technologies for older adults. While the individual methods used were not novel, the formation of the process, particularly the attention we pay to less tangible issues around establishing an appropriate atmosphere in the meetings, facilitate younger designers' novel insights into older peoples day to day lives.

Initial scenario work is used to gain a sense of the design domain and the issues that the participants encounter in their day-to-day lives. The designers can create potential solutions to these issues or challenges informed by the analysis of the groups. These issues and designers' ideas about interventions feed into a low fidelity design workshops conducted with the same people that took part in the exploratory session. The goal of these workshops is to validate the designers' assessment of the domain and to start gathering insights into the specific design of an intervention. The approach was created and documented with those who have no experience with participatory design in mind and is kept as brief as possible to allow designers who implement it to start to engage with older adults early in their design work with minimal effort.

The creation of a friendly atmosphere in this process is particularly important as it helps participants to mutually inspire each other through the social interactions and collaboration. The facilitator must not "drive" the activity rigidly but communicate to participants that in the early stage of design there is no "correct" answer and that all opinions are can be explored. Previous work on the subject has shown that group interaction, particularly amongst older people, plays an important role in determining the quality of output from a focus group process [2,10].

The facilitator needs to be mindful of using appropriate and accessible language when guiding discussions and providing instructions and seek to keep focus on the activity during group work. They must ensure that all of the participants are given the opportunity to contribute and be aware of the fact that many older people are not familiar with state of the art consumer technology [9]. The facilitator should be aware that there may be a lot of discussion not related to the subject matter. In these cases, they should be patient and engage in the conversation.

The creation of a *common frame of reference* between participants and designers is an important part of establishing the right atmosphere in group work. Establishing the common frame of reference leads to the creation of a new set of jargon that helps the participants express their thoughts in the design domain, contributes to democratizing the meeting. This helps create a sense of community or shared purpose within the group by giving them their own 'insider' language and can inspire a sense of agency in the older adult group [17] .

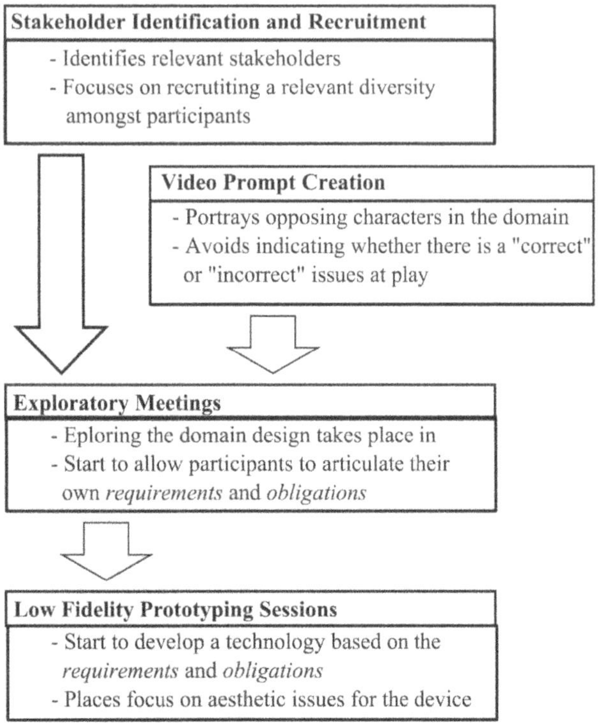

Figure 1. The OASIS Process.

The design exercises should be located in a building that is familiar and accessible for the participants. General deficits in sight which occur as part of the normal ageing process [13] mean that rooms in which the meetings are conducted should be well lit, preferably with natural light. Locations should be quiet and free from distractions or high levels of ambient noise. Participants should have ready access to toilet facilities that they should be made aware of at the outset. The selection of an appropriate timing and structure for activities depends on the participants but they should be made aware of the structure and timing of the meetings when they are being recruited and then reminded at the start of the meeting. Even when sessions are going well, the stated time schedule should be followed to guard against the risk participants feel pressured to participate to a greater degree or for longer than they intended.

STAKEHOLDER IDENTIFICATION AND RECRUITMENT

Recruitment needs to begin well in advance of the design sessions as, although it is not labor intensive, it requires time. Beginning at least eight weeks before the design meetings is recommended and having concrete dates for the design sessions at this early stage makes it easier for older people to schedule meetings into their calendars. Based on our experiences, the recruitment for meetings can take as little as one week but unfortunately the variability in the time it takes to arrange them is vast. Groups should consist of between four and five participants, but it is better to over recruit because as older adults can cancel at the last minute. Our experiences and previous work both suggest recruiting twenty percent more older adults than required [2]. Recruitment can be performed through a variety of means like contacting charity or advocacy groups for older people.

The 65+ group is considerably more diverse than any other single age group so positioning the design work within this area is essential. It is important to try to ensure that there is *relevant diversity* in the participants. For example, when recruiting for a transport based study we recruited a group with a range of different levels of personal mobility and differing typical means of transport.

The 65+ group we typically refer to when talking about the older population is not a truly age homogenous group and has specific generational differences that impact on their attitudes, and previous encounters with technology, have different health problems, differ in their finances, and their views on social issues (such as privacy and gender roles). Recruitment must recognize differences in attitude and behavior due to generational differences that are relevant to the application and select participants accordingly.

In addition to variations in physical abilities the ageing process will cause deterioration in sensory abilities in particular eyesight and hearing [13,32]. Recruitment should attempt to span this range of abilities as appropriate and elicit participants' accounts of their degree of sensory impairment with a view to understanding the character of the group of participants and the likely impact of this on both the design itself and the design process. Furthermore, recruiters need to be aware of how the method of contact they employ to recruit elderly participants may affect participation [19]. For example, phone calls can prove challenging for the hard of hearing whilst letters can prove difficult to read for those with visual problems [2].

Finally, variation exists in the personal circumstances in which older people find themselves [31]. These should be considered separately from the social, cultural and national variation discussed previously. For example, the living arrangements of an individual can range from living alone, co-habiting with a partner, living with younger or older relatives, living with extended families, living in sheltered accommodation, or living in residential accommodation.

Practical Experiences Recruiting Participants

The OASIS design approach was applied in three domains. The first was in the design of a digital technology to promote healthy eating. Healthy eating is an area that can be problematic for older people because of issues such as the loss of a partner who used to cook, decreasing motivation to cook, decreasing mobility meaning that buying fresh food is difficult or a lack of funds meaning that buying ingredients is challenging [37].

The second area we designed in was personal mobility. Elderly people can lose personal mobility as they age due to conditions such as osteoarthritis, deterioration in musculature, loss in range of motion of joints and physical balance problems. In addition, the elderly person's personal freedom to travel is often restricted through the loss of their ability to drive. Impairments in vision and hearing can make navigating new or altered environments, due to roadwork for example, much more difficult. These factors combine to make getting "out and about" very challenging for some older people.

The final area that we looked at was designing to promote feelings of personal security in the home. Older people have many fears and concerns about their personal safety, these fears are not necessarily borne from a high level of crime experienced by older people though as the number of older people who are victims of crime is actually quite low. These domains are all part of the wider context of digital technology applications for the home that have arisen in the third wave of human-computer interaction. This means that the issue is not work or task oriented but instead more around influencing the outlook and attitude of older people towards food preparation and consumption.

One issue that became apparent in recruiting for the healthy eating study was that the majority of the participants considered themselves to be more mobile individuals than the typical older population. This was problematic because the one of the relevant areas of diversity was the level of mobility of each of the participants. Later design work on personal security and transportation worked with Age Concern units in towns and villages that were attended by people with more diverse levels of personal mobility.

CREATING VIDEO PROMPTS

One of the four central challenges that we identify is supporting older adults when they envision new technology. The OASIS design approach uses a video prompting technique inspired by the *invisible design* concept [4]. Participants are presented with a video that illustrates a scenario in which actors have and discuss a fictitious future intervention for the problem domain. Videos have often been used as a tool in participatory design work to provoke response, such as the design documentary [29] and the creative response technique [14] which involve creating documentary film and allowing participants to edit the film to display their own responses. Other techniques have centred on recording participants to give them tools to portray their conception of technology [20]. Performances in other forms, such as theatre, have also been used to convey the needs of specialist user groups to designers who might otherwise struggle to understand their needs [26]. The invisible design technique has similarities to the concept of ContraVision [21]. The videos depict a situation in which characters have the device being envisioned in the design workshop.

The *invisible design* format of video or story does not constrain or direct users towards specific features or aesthetics for a device because *invisible design* never shows the device being used or makes any details of it explicit (hence the term invisible). The approach takes some effort but can be of great use when working with older users because it leverages a convention they are familiar with (film and storytelling) in order to present them with a scenario that they will not be familiar with. The older people work well when critiquing physical artefacts and they respond to the device discussed in the video as if it were real more easily than they can imagine a hypothetical device, with the additional benefit of not getting caught up in criticising the particulars of a device as we previously observed. Participants can use the depiction of intangible issues in the video as starting points for their own discussions about intangible issues that relate to the design domain. Participants can also project their own reactions onto the characters and give voice to them through discussion of how they believed the characters felt.

However, like ContraVision, these videos must not present one point of view as the correct point of view. ContraVision calls for two videos, one good case and one bad case. The invisible design videos that were produced centred on a pair of characters and the interactions between them never showed a definitive right or wrong answer to the questions they raised. Closure in the videos came from the personal interactions between the character and the future device. Achieving this deliberate ambiguity requires thought and planning and design teams may need to recruit outside assistance to perform this work. By carefully guiding the script and direction of the video, the designers present the users with intangible issues and elicit a variety of responses.

Practical Experiences Using Video Prompts

The video we created for the healthy eating design sessions examined the interaction between a mother and her daughter in the mother's kitchen as the daughter discovered that her mother was not eating properly. The film starts with the daughter part way through explaining her problems at home with a broken water main as she is preparing food for a group of friends. The daughter notices that the cupboards don't have much food in them and this causes an argument with her mother about not eating enough. The argument implies that the mother has a device that is meant to help her eat healthily but she complains about it for a variety of reasons. The daughter demands to know why this is the case and why the mother was not using her "machine". The script suggested that the "machine" somehow monitored and helped plan meals and was easy to use but the device was never shown in the film, only pointed at and the film concluded avoiding showing the precise functionality of the device and whether the mother would start to use the device so keeping the device ambiguous.

The video was extremely well received by the participants who enjoyed the scripted humor in the video and felt that some of the issues that it portrayed resonated with their own experiences, one female participant saying. *"I thought I could identify with it because I have children and they turn into the food police."* The participants produced numerous

Figure 2: Alice and Bob sitting on their mobility scooters

ideas in both the early exploratory work and the later low fidelity prototyping work, in contrast with previous literature on the subject, this further demonstrated the utility of the video approach. In further work we would add an extra role to the video to turn it into a prompt to develop conversation around the subject of scenarios.

The video in the transport study portrayed showed two older characters, Alice and Bob (Figure 2), on their mobility scooters trying to get to a cafe to meet their friend. The pair used mobility scooters to get round and the video opened on Alice getting her new mobility scooter. Bob, who had already owned and used his scooter for a while was trying to show Alice his expertise but Alice rapidly learned to use her scooter much to Bob's annoyance. Alice had a small device attached to her scooter which Bob hadn't seen before; this device was our *invisible design* artifact. Although never clearly shown it gave Alice a variety of functions to use throughout the video giving her the edge over Bob at all times. The video culminates in a row between the two which leads to Bob going on his own route to the cafe rather than following Alice, this leads to all sorts of problems as he gets stuck at steps, goes down dead ends and gets blocked off by rubbish. Alice finds him and guides him to a new meeting place eventually having been told by the device their friend says their original meeting place is too crowded so has gone somewhere else.

The participants enjoyed the video and felt it resonated with their experience with Bob laughingly referred to as a *"typical man, doesn't listen!"* or a *"grumpy old man!"* by female participants. The video in this case portrayed the scenario which we would discuss for the rest of the session and this would significantly affect the results of the scenario work.

The work examining creating videos for personal security adopted a slightly different approach and created pastiche scenarios featuring well known TV characters. This was done in the hopes of lessening the impact of portraying older people who were afraid for their safety but appeared to backfire because the participants could not take the characters seriously, one female participant dismissively stating *"that for me is not serious"*.

EXPLORATORY MEETINGS

These sessions are based around the construction of scenarios to explore the problem domain and develop requirements for the design of a device. The sessions are derived from the Task Analysis Framework (TAF) [7] with significant alterations made to account for the non-workplace domain in which they will be applied. The TAF approach allows us to address the challenge of maintaining structure in design sessions. We give the TAF title of each stage, the time it should take to perform, the modified way we present it to the participants and its purpose:

Information Gathering (15 minutes)

"So to kick the meeting off we want to get to know you a bit better so tell us a bit about yourself, what sort of experiences you've had in <DOMAIN> and what sort of experiences your friends have had?"

The accounts of experience elicited help to inform the creation of a narrative around the participants' activities and are a source from which to draw quotes to support and enhance the requirements presented to other members of the design team. The information from this stage is also used in the next stage to inform the creation of scenarios.

Prompt Viewing (10 minutes)

"Ok we're going to watch a short, fictional video now that's set in the future where someone has actually gone ahead and made a device to help with issues in the <DOMAIN>. We're going to see what sort of affect it's been having on a couple of people and then after the video we'll have a chat about it."

The facilitator shows the participants the *invisible design* video. This promotes discussion and provides scaffolding for participants to describe their own thoughts about future interventions.

Scenario Generation (20 minutes)

"We'd like to move on now to try and discuss what we think are the main differences between Alice and Bob in the video. What are Alice's characteristics that make her so capable, what are the things about Bob that lead him into trouble? Outside of the story we've watched, how do you think the two behave?"

The facilitator moves the group on to the development of scenarios based upon the information gathered in the first stage. The characters of "Alice" and "Bob" are the characters in the invisible design video. The facilitator should record the scenarios being generated in some shared space in order to focus the attention of the participants, for example, on a white board or large sheet of paper.

Claims Analysis (20 minutes)

"Now we've come up with our stories about Alice and Bob it's time to try to work out why they are so different. What does everybody think might be the reasons which make the difference between them? Are there physical things or

mental things? Are there things that make Alice's life easier or things that make Bob's life harder?"

During this stage participants think about why the scenarios play out the way they do. This stage informs the feature envisioning by exposing some of the root causes of negative and positive experiences.

Feature Envisioning (30 minutes)

"Ok now we've run through those idea's let's move on to think about how we can help out Alice and Bob a little bit and make their lives easier. Alice has a few things that really help her out in her day to day life. What can we do to make sure those things keep happening? Bob on the other hand has lots of problems in his day to day life, so what can we do to get rid of them for him and make his life run a bit more smoothly, like Alice's?"

Participants describe features they imagine a new system having. The claims should be referred back to and feed into this stage as participants envision ways to reduce their negative and increase their positive impacts. Participants talk about their ideal solutions at this stage and frequently exceed the bounds of what is feasible. However, this stage reveals their aspirations which give important insights for the designers. The solutions that are proposed should be well understood by the members of the design team present in these meetings.

Scenario Envisioning (30 minutes)

"So we've thought of some ways to help out Alice and Bob now, the last thing we want to do is consider why these idea's might not work out the way we want them to, what sorts of problems might crop up if we imagine each of these pieces of technology in the stories we came up with about Alice and Bob to start with? We'll go through the different ideas on the whiteboard starting with..."

Finally, participants are asked to consider how their new idea might interact in the old scenarios and, through this, imagine new scenarios. This stage should be presented to them by asking them to speak about what could go wrong with their ideas when included in Alice and Bob's lives.

Analysis

The analysis process formalises the participant's comments in the first design session and helps generate a Topic Guide that will be used to guide discussion in the second design workshop. The process needs to be carefully performed as it must accurately represent the participants statements (one of the four challenges identified in our previous work) while allowing the designers to organise and think about their statements in an engaged, considered manner. The analysis of the information gathering stage draws out quotes and gathers them into themes. When working on the scenario generation and claims analysis the coding should look for comments relevant to the scenarios and group them around the characteristics of the two scenarios. Analysing the later stages is guided by a simple process: codes related to potential features for a design are grouped together as *requirements* and codes related to potential problems with a solution that must be avoided are grouped under *obligations*. Requirements tend to emerge from discussion in the feature envisioning stage whilst obligations come from scenario envisioning.

By searching the transcript from the meetings for the participants' statements of requirements and obligations, the participants are given a more direct impact on the designs that are produced. The requirements can then be supported by tying them to the codes taken from the output from the earlier scenario work and information gathering. In this way, the output from these sessions can also be presented to the other members of a project team couched in language they can understand but supported by the authentic voice of the user. These should be presented to the project team in a way that preserves the link as much as possible. This might be in the form of documents that compile selected quotes or through a website that links requirements to the sections of transcript that relate to them. In the low fidelity prototyping sessions the designers feed their analysis back to the users and let them comment on it, to validate their findings.

Experiences Running Exploratory Sessions

The initial trial of the approach in the design of a nutritional adviser did not leverage the video prompt to trigger discussion of a scenario; instead it only used it to promote discussion on future technologies. We observed that participants struggled to separate out the act of creating abstract scenarios from their own experiences, often talking about personal issues such as one female participant who was fixated on the quality of care an aunt received in a nursing home *"like I say you always look after someone the way you would like to be looked after, not like a dog"*. When the groups started to discuss future technologies they tended to think in terms of their own personal nutritional needs *"I don't need any help, I need information."* Rather than thinking about the ways in which they could help with someone in an abstract scenario.

However, the group did still excel when providing critiques of the ideas they had put forward, one male participant neatly surmising the feelings of the group by stating that the process needed to be *"Persuasive rather than mandatory."* When analyzing this work, the participants' statements clearly broke down. Table 1 shows how we choose to represent the participants' statements in a way that preserves their voice when examined by other people not present in the design meetings.

In the design meetings for the transport adviser, the participants were much more vocal when creating scenarios around the qualities they perceived Alice and Bob having. A central theme was confidence, as epitomized by one female participants comments *"Confidence does a lot of things for people*". The sessions yielded surprising results for the facilitator when they found that participants felt that personal levels of physical disability had very little to do with how well people were able to navigate their environment. As one female participant put it when talking about Alice "*she's obviously prepared to follow instructions and make the most of the apparatus she's got*". The productiveness of the discussion contemplating design artifacts contrasted with our previous experiences and the experiences reported in other work [22].

Motivation: Suggestions	Participants felt that they might be more motivated if their device proposed new recipes and integrated the ingredients needed into their shopping lists
"If the wife went and her husband was left he probably wouldn't have a clue on where to begin. So therefore they either withdraw or they don't cook"	

Table 1. Requirements recorded for design team

LOW-FIDELITY PROTOTYPING

The goal of this session is to produce further requirements for a design focusing upon more specific features of the device. This meeting lets participants articulate their requirements around *functionality*, *aesthetics* and *experience* of a specific design as they engage in low-fidelity prototyping work. The session is conducted with the participants from the exploratory work about a week after those sessions and refines the high level goals developed in them following the PICTIVE process [24].

The sessions must be video recorded and so need to be conducted at a location with suitable facilities for this. When recording the participants should not be the subjects of the recording but instead the shared workspace they work on should be (e.g. the tabletop on which the workshop is conducted and around which the discussion is held). The consistent point of contact will prepare for the workshop through the creation of appropriate tools and materials for the exercise. Tools can be classified under two categories: (i) office tools such as pens, paper, post-it notes, colored pencils, rulers, erasers etc; and (ii) specialist tools, for example, paper in the shape of interface windows, or actual devices that can embody design domain and facilitate the activities of the workshop.

The facilitator should create a Topic Guide for the meeting in which they detail the key subjects to be addressed, but being realistic given the time allotted to each meeting as there is often a temptation to try to cover too many issues. The guide needs to select a design or suite of requirements from the previous design session to implement. This will be the first thing to establish in the meeting with participants and should be couched in the language that they used to suggest the idea when presented to them so that it is clear that this is the process of realizing their ideas. When creating the Topic Guide the consistent point of contact should look for cases where there are directly opposing requirements drawn from the design process. The Topic Guide should promote discussion aimed at resolving, or at least understanding, this issue. Key subjects should be selected based on elements that are most strongly linked to the user interface aspects of the design, as this is the strength of the low fidelity prototyping.

The duration of the workshop will depend on the nature of the given task and the capabilities of the participants. If a group has shown itself to be creative and tolerant of extended discussion about the domain, these workshops can stretch to three hours. The attendees to a workshop should be provided with material that sets the scene of the participatory analysis and design and this should include the Topic Guide and a summary of the analysis of the exploratory work. This introduction serves to set the scene for the rest of the workshop to ensure that all the participants have a common frame of reference.

Experiences with Low-Fidelity Prototyping

The low fidelity prototyping sessions for the nutritional adviser and the transport guidance system proceeded smoothly. However, the sessions for the personal security system were less well received. In the earlier session participants had already shown their discomfort when discussing issues and relating them to their own lives" *I'm on me own and I would never put temptation in front of anybody. If anybody was coming, I wouldn't leave me purse out lying*". There had been considerable disagreement between the participants on what sorts of scenarios should be constructed that would represent a poor case for personal security when one participant had said she thought it would mainly affect people *"from poorer areas"*. The participants who identified themselves as being from poorer areas had debated this issue at length. When these groups met again in the low fidelity prototyping work, these issues came to the fore and the clash of personalities that had erupted prevented much productive work from occurring.

Issues such as these are not unique to engaging with older adults [22] but the atmosphere in these sessions is particularly important due to the need to elicit personal experiences. Therefore, when meetings break down in this way they can be particularly unproductive. Due to problems with scheduling there had been nine participants in the meetings and this may have made the process more prone to such clashes of personality. In the future we would particularly strive to keep the sessions small and intimate when discussing potentially sensitive issues.

DISCUSSION

The process of engaging older adults in participatory design has been at times challenging but always rewarding, because of its ability to produce insights into the older adults' lives. The insights that we have gained have altered our thinking about this domain. At the outset of many of these sessions it has seemed like we were dealing with areas that the participants could not contribute to; however, uncovering the older participants' perceptions of these domains always led to us having to fundamentally rethink our attitudes towards the design project. The process also forced us to try to respect the diversity of our participants and drives home the fact that these participants are not, by any means, a homogenous group.

The use of video prompting to portray people using invisible future technologies provoked a great deal of discussion and interest amongst our participants. When we initially contemplated using the videos our concern was that they might have been dismissed out of hand but the scripted humor in some of our productions seemed to genuinely amuse the participants and they engaged rapidly with the ideas in the videos. The video also worked as an introduction into thinking in terms of scenarios or working within scenarios. Explaining that we would be talking about the characters in the videos rather than trying to explain that we wanted to create "scenarios" worked much more naturally with our participants. Even when design sessions broke down due to personality conflicts we still learned about our participants lives through the debates they had and the views they expressed. In hindsight, it seems obvious that designing appropriately for this group demands engagement with them but, convincing those who have not engaged with older adults in design would prove to be much more challenging than any of the issues we encountered when working with older adults.

Motivating Engagement with Older Adults

While the participatory design approach that we employed worked well when we applied it, our attempts as part of larger projects to encourage the uptake of these techniques by other groups were often unsuccessful. Many large scale funding calls and bids mandate some form of user-centered design process or participatory process. Yet despite this, the partners in these bids have often been, in our own experiences, reluctant to engage with older participants. The formalized deliverables of work common to many of the large projects seem to sometimes encourage a tick-box attitude towards participatory design and project partners sometimes try to do as little as possible to meet these criteria. Our partners' reluctance to engage specifically with older adults was one of the defining characteristics of this domain and despite our efforts to produce a method that requires as little effort as possible; many designers were still reluctant to engage in the process.

The formalized deliverables of work often serve to stifle the contributions of older participant when they are engaged in the design process. We have frequently encountered older people keen to tell us that the ideas that we are proposing are "rubbish" or "unnecessary" but the rigid structure of the funding agreements have meant that this advice cannot easily be acted upon. Many partners in projects have treated participatory design work as a tick box exercise solely present to demonstrate that what they are doing is valid, and as such are not willing to engage with older people in a genuine, open manner.

These issues are certainly not unique to the field of designing with older adults, but we suggest that they are particularly prominent in this domain because of the dismissive attitudes that some people seem to take towards older adults using technology [15,30]. Until there are more numerous examples of successful engagement with older people in participatory design, and the perception of older people's attitudes towards technology change, approaches such as the one we propose here will not be widely applied due to the latent belief that they will not yield novel or interesting results.

CONCLUSION

The OASIS process that we have described provides a simple starting point for design teams seeking to engage older adults in participatory design activities. However, our experiences trying to get others to apply the technique suggest that the outstanding challenge in this domain is not only one of appropriately framing design work with older adults, but also of motivating design teams to seek to work with them. With this in mind, the process that we present has been kept as "bare bones" as possible to try to encourage designers to engage with this group and it is our belief that once they do start to do this, the results will speak for themselves.

ACKNOWLEDGMENTS

This research was jointly funded by the EU FP7 project OASIS and the RCUK Research Hub on Social Inclusion through the Digital Economy.

REFERENCES

1. Ballegaard, S.A., Hansen, T.R., and Kyng, M. Healthcare in Everyday Life - Designing Healthcare Services for Daily Life. *In Proc. CHI 2008*, ACM Press (2008), 1807-1816.
2. Barrett, J. and Kirk, S. Running focus groups with elderly and disabled elderly participants. *Applied Ergonomics 31*, 6 (2000), 621-629.
3. Braun, V. and Clarke, V. Using thematic analysis in psychology. *Qualitative research in psychology 3*, 2 (2006), 77-101.
4. Briggs, P. and Olivier, P. Film as Invisible Design: The example of the Biometric Daemon. *Video Showcase CHI 2009*, ACM Press (2009).
5. Bødker, S. When second wave HCI meets third wave challenges. *In Proc. NordiCHI' 2006*, ACM Press (2006), 1-8.
6. Carrigan, M. Segmenting the grey market : the case for fifty-plus lifegroups. *Journal of Marketing 4*, 2 (1998), 43-56.

7. Carroll, J.M. and Rosson, M.B. Getting around the task-artefact cycle: how to make claims and design by scenario. *ACM TOIS 10*, 2 (1992), 212-220.
8. Coleman, G.W., Gibson, L., Hanson, V.L., Bobrowicz, A., and Mckay, A. Engaging The Disengaged : How Do We Design Technology for Digitally Excluded Older Adults ? *In Proc. DIS 2010*, ACM Press (2010), 175-178.
9. Eisma, R., Dickinson, A., Goodman, J., Syme, A., Tiwari, L., and Newell, A.F. Early user involvement in the development of information technology-related products for older people. *Universal Access in the Information Society 3*, 2 (2004), 131-140.
10. Gibbs, A. Focus groups. *Social Research Update 19*, 8 (1997).
11. Gregor, P. and Newell, A.F. Designing for dynamic diversity: making accessible interfaces for older people. *In Proc. WUAUC 2001*, ACM Press (2001), 90-92.
12. Gregor, P., Newell, A.F., and Zajicek, M. Designing for dynamic diversity: interfaces for older people. *In Proc. ASSETS 2002*, ACM Press (2002), 151-156.
13. Harman, D. The aging process. *Proceedings of the National Academy of Sciences 78*, 11 (1981), 7124-7134.
14. Hook, J., Green, D., Mccarthy, J., Taylor, S., Wright, P., and Olivier, P. A VJ Centered Exploration of Expressive Interaction. *In Proc. CHI 2011*, ACM Press (2011), 1265-1274.
15. Joyce, K., Williamson, J., and Mamo, L. Technology, Science and Ageism: An Examination of Three Patterns of Discrimination. *Indian Journal of Gerontology 21*, (2007), 110-127.
16. Keith, S. and Whitney, G. Bridging the gap between young designers and older users in an inclusive society. *In Proc. The good, the bad and the challenging: the user and the future of ICT*, (1998).
17. Light, A. Democratising Technology : Making Transformation using Designing , Performance and Props. *In Proc. CHI 2011*, ACM Press (2011), 2239-2242.
18. Lindsay, S., Brittain, K., Jackson, D., Ladha, C., Ladha, K., and Olivier, P. Empathy, Participatory Design and People with Dementia. *In Proc. CHI 2012*, ACM Press (2012).
19. Lines, L. and Hone, K.S. Research methods for older adults. *In Proc BCS HCI 2002*, (2002).
20. Mackay, W.E., Ratzer, A.V., and Janecek, P. Video Artifacts for Design : Bridging the Gap Between Abstraction and Detail. *In Proc. DIS 2000*, (2000), 72-82.
21. Mancini, C., Rogers, Y., Bandara, A.K., Coe, T., Jedrzejczyk, L., Joinson, A.N., Price, B.A., Thomas, K., and Nuseibeh, B. Contravision: exploring users' reactions to futuristic technology. *In Proc. CHI 2010*, ACM Press (2010), 153-162.
22. Massimi, M. and Baecker, R. Participatory design process with older users. *In Proc. UbiCoomp2006 Workshop on future media*, (2006).
23. McNaney, R., Lindsay, S., Ladha, K., Ladha, C., Schofield, G., Plötz, T., Hammerla, N., Jackson, D., Walker, R., Miller, N., et al. Cueing Swallowing in Parkinson ' s Disease. *In Proc. CHI 2011*, (2011), 619-622.
24. Muller, M. *PICTIVE: Democratizing the dynamics of the design session*. Lawrence Erbaulm, 1993.
25. Myerson, J. and Lee, Y. Designing with the poeple, for the people and by the people. *In Proc. Design Activism and Social Change*, (2011).
26. Newell, A., Carmichael, A., Morgan, M., and Dickinson, A. The use of theatre in requirements gathering and usability studies. *Interacting with Computers 18*, 5 (2006), 996-1011.
27. Newell, A.F. and Gregor, P. Extra-Ordinary Human-Machine Interaction: What can be Learned from People with Disabilities? *Cognition, Technology & Work 1*, 2 (1999), 78-85.
28. Oliver, M. and Sapey, B. *Social Work With Disabled People*. Palgrave Macmillan, 2006.
29. Raijmaker, B., Gaver, W.W., and Bishay, J. Design Documentaries : Inspiring Design Research Through Documentary Film. *In Proc. DIS 2006*, ACM Press (2006), 229-238.
30. Ryan, E.B., Szechtman, B., and Bodkin, J. Attitudes toward younger and older adults learning to use computers. *The Journal of Gerontology 47*, 2 (1992), 96-106.
31. Smith, J.P. *The changing economic circumstances of the elderly: Income, wealth, and social security*. .
32. Spence, A.P. *Biology of Human Aging*. Prentice Hall, 1995.
33. Vines, J., Dunphy, P., Blythe, M., Lindsay, S., Monk, A., and Olivier, P. The Joy of Cheques: Trust, Paper and Eighty Somethings. *In Proc. CSCW 2012*, ACM Press (2012).
34. Wardell, F. Who volunteers? *British Journal of Social Work 30*, 2 (2000), 227-248.
35. Wilkowska, W. and Ziefle, M. Which Factors Form Older Adults' Acceptance of Mobile Information and Communication Technologies? In *HCI and Usability for e-Inclusion*. 2009, 81-101.
36. Wright, P.C. and McCarthy, J. *Technology as Experience*. MIT Press, 2004.
37. Position paper of the American Dietetic Association: Nutrition across the spectrum of aging. *105*, 4 (2005), 616-633.

Personas and Decision Making in the Design Process: An Ethnographic Case Study

Erin Friess
University of North Texas
Linguistics and Technical Communication
Denton, Texas, USA
erin.friess@unt.edu

ABSTRACT
Personas have become a well-lauded method to aid designers in keeping the needs of the intended user population at the forefront of the design process. However, few studies have ethnographically observed design teams that use personas, and fewer studies have looked specifically at how designers linguistically invoke personas in their decision-making sessions. This discourse analysis of the decision-making sessions of designers at a top tier design firm reveals that although the designers dedicate much time researching, developing, and refining personas, personas themselves make relatively few appearances in the designers' language during decision-making sessions. This study shows that, for persuasive ends, these designers, who are advocates of personas, routinely use other less precise and more designer-centric linguistic mechanisms in lieu of personas. Despite the scarcity of personas in the decision-making sessions, this ethnographic case study also explores the value of personas for this team even when the personas are not explicitly linguistically invoked.

Author Keywords
Personas; user-centered design; discourse analysis; ethnography; design decision-making.

ACM Classification Keywords
H.5.2 [Information Interfaces and Presentation]: User Interfaces - Theory and methods, User-centered design;

INTRODUCTION
Since the advent of user-centered design (UCD) in the early 1980s, designers have struggled with how, exactly, to have "an early focus upon the characteristics and needs of the intended user population" [1]. One way designers in recent years have opted to keep the "characteristics" and "needs" of potential users at the forefront of the design process is through the use of personas. According to Alan Cooper, who popularized the term in *The Inmates are Running the Asylum*, personas "are not real people" but "hypothetical archetypes of actual users" that, while imaginary, "are defined with significant rigor and precision" [2]. Since Cooper's publication of *Inmates* over a decade ago, the use of personas in the design process has increased in popularity [3]. Most discussions of personas in the intervening years have offered prescriptions for designers on how personas ought to be created and implemented in design processes, as well as the purported benefits of using personas in product development. However, despite the rise in acceptance and overall popularity of personas, few studies have empirically investigated how personas are actually used by designers in practice.

The aim of this case study is to turn an ethnographic eye to the designers themselves in order to understand how personas fit into the design decision-making process. This reflexive move enables a descriptive assessment of how designers themselves actually use personas, not just how designers think they use personas or how designers think personas should be used. More specifically, I explore how personas are used linguistically during the decision-making sessions of designers. Are personas used as persuasive mechanisms to support or deny a decision, are they used as a focusing mechanism to narrow the scope of a decision, are personas used to facilitate communication, or are they functioning in some other way entirely? To answer these questions, I observed the decision-making sessions of a design team within a highly respected design firm that routinely uses personas. Using discourse analysis techniques, I investigated how and when personas were invoked during those decision-making sessions and evaluated how this usage falls in line with previous discussions of persona usage.

A CLOSER LOOK AT PERSONAS
Personas were originally conceived as a design process methodology by Cooper, who vaguely defines a persona as a representation of a group of individuals with common characteristics—a "hypothetical archetype" that is used by designers to understand, focus, and clarify user goals and needs [2]. While the general concept of personas was appealing to many designers, Grudin and Pruitt, among others, noted that Cooper did "not describe in detail how personas are created" [4]. Subsequent discussions of personas, including some by Cooper, have explored more

Permission to make digital or hard copies of all or part of this work for personal or classroom use is granted without fee provided that copies are not made or distributed for profit or commercial advantage and that copies bear this notice and the full citation on the first page. To copy otherwise, or republish, to post on servers or to redistribute to lists, requires prior specific permission and/or a fee.
CHI'12, May 5–10, 2012, Austin, Texas, USA.
Copyright 2012 ACM 978-1-4503-1015-4/12/05...$10.00.

deeply how personas should be constructed and applied to the design process. While some variation in the application and creation of personas exists, some attributes, such as a name, a photo, a set of goals, and "a narrative that covers mental model, environment, skills, frustrations, attitudes, typical tasks, and any other factors that seem critical to understanding the behavior pattern," are consistent across most persona theories [5].

While these rather concrete elements of personas are consistent across most persona theories, the process of creating a persona is not. Originally, it appeared that Cooper's notion of personas was "based on anecdote and appeals to reason, not data," and that Cooper appeared to "exhibit [...] a disdain for empiricism, including feedback on design possibilities" [4]. While some persona experts acknowledge that occasionally it is necessary due to budgetary and time constraints to develop personas based solely on designer anticipations, stakeholder expectations, and subject matter expert opinions, most persona experts recommend doing empirical fieldwork in the form of end-user interviews or observations to create data-driven personas [5, 6]. Data-driven personas often involve a large researcher workforce and large investments of time (with 1-4 months being an approximate timeframe for many firms) to create [7, 8, 9].

Designers then assess the data to identify commonalities and patterns in the data, and develop a single persona with a reasonable name, a realistic photo, a set of goals, and a narrative that accurately presents critical aspects of the persona in a memorable way [5, 6, 10]. Therefore, personas are fictional creations—entities that are both amalgams of and representations of a certain set of potential users. As Goodwin states, "each persona serves as a surrogate for the thousands or millions of potential users who have similar characteristics and goals" [5].

Some designers resist personas because they are fictional, because they "lead to a false sense of understanding" [11], and because it is "difficult or impossible to verify that personas are accurate" [12], thereby making it too easy to create a persona that matches the designers' idea for a product rather than a persona that informs the development of a product independent of the designer.

However, personas are steadily becoming a standard user-centered method, and persona method advocates claim that personas have benefits that simple data aggregation does not have. First, "personas engender interest and empathy toward users" [6]. By putting a human face on the generic user, personas can introduce empathy into the design process, which can improve the functionality of the product for the user [13]. Second, "personas allow [designers] to focus on and design for a small set of specific users" [6]. Rather than facing a multitude of users, each with their own stories, priorities, and struggles, personas "encapsulate [...] and explain [...] the most critical behavioral data" in a manageable number of memorable models [5]. Designing for a "small set of specific users... [helps designers] make better decisions" [6] and can "focus designer decisions in a way that just referring to 'users' as a generic group may not" [14].

Perhaps the most cited benefit of personas is their ability to facilitate communication [9]. Personas can "help...focus stakeholders on relevant issues" [10], "diffuse conflict or disagreement among team members when discussing possible design solutions" [14], establish "a common language with which to talk about users meaningfully" [6], and are "excellent tools for summarizing...research data because they let stakeholders 'meet' the interviewers by proxy" [5].

PREVIOUS EMPIRCAL RESEARCH ON PERSONAS

While persona methodology has the purported benefits of establishing empathy for users, enabling more focused designing through a small number of memorable models, and facilitating communication, few studies have empirically investigated the effectiveness of personas on design outcomes or on design processes [12]. Two studies that have focused on design outcome when using persona methodology have relied on student groups who have been given already defined personas (i.e., the students were not involved in the development of the personas). One study found that business students who were given highly empathetic personas created better designs than students in the control group, and students who were given lowly empathetic personas created worse designs than the control group [13]. The second study, also involving students given pre-defined personas, found that "students using personas produced designs with better usability attributes than the students that did not use the personas" [15]. I include this second study here because there are so few empirical studies focusing on persona outcomes and because it has been highly cited in the design blogosphere as proof that personas lead to better product design (ColumnTwo, The Cooper Journal, IXDA.org, the Human Centred-Design Institute, among others). While I admire this attempt at empirical assessment of personas given the dearth of empirical studies on personas currently in the UCD landscape, the results of this particular study should be tempered given that there are several problematic methodological issues in the study, including: no description of who judged the design outcomes; no discussion as to whether the author was the instructor; no discussion of blinding the judge(s) to the condition of the groups, which could affect confirmation bias, particularly if the judge was the author; and no discussion of inter-coder reliability throughout the study, including in determining whether Nielsen's usability heuristic is an appropriate tool to assess design work.

In addition to these studies of design outcomes, a few studies have empirically investigated how personas are actually used by designers in the designing process. Blomquist and Arvola conducted a longitudinal observational study of a design team that explores "what really goes on in a design team when they implement personas in their process" [16]. This group, which involved many members being introduced to personas for the first time, "did not trust the personas" and invoked "the user" or "you" instead of their personas. While the designers had positive remarks about using personas as a tool, "they were unsatisfied with how they worked during project meetings." Ultimately, "personas never became an integrated part of the design process, due to the lack of know-how and the fact that the team members never felt at home with personas." An additional study that explored how personas function in three separate sites found that organizational contexts "limited the utility of the personas technique," with one site marginalizing personas, another using personas for political buy-in, and the third questioning whether personas were more valuable than direct data from end-users [17].

My study continues in the footsteps of these personas-in-design processes studies by conducting an observational study of a group of professional designers to investigate how they use personas in their actual design practice. However, instead of looking at how personas are generally used by the group or at how persona usage affects product outcome, I look specifically at the language used by the designers when they invoke the personas during their decision-making sessions. By linguistically analyzing the designers' use of personas, descriptive data on the discursive function and persuasive abilities of personas can be ascertained.

DATA COLLECTION

In order to determine how personas are used by a design group *in situ*, I observed and recorded the decision-making sessions of a group of professional designers at a top tier design firm based in the United States. Aside from a few conversational tangents, the meetings were dedicated to determining appropriate design solutions for a client's proprietary interactive medical device. This group of designers was highly dedicated to the notion of personas. I embedded with these design team members for one week. In that time I observed and audio-recorded all of their interactions. The core group consisted of four members, ranging in age from mid-twenties to mid-forties. This core group included designers who had been at the firm for upwards of a decade as well as a new member who had joined the team the previous week. Occasionally, other members of the firm would join in the discussions. These other members (who were part of the "expanded" team) often had a highly particular skill set and would work on multiple projects at one time. The design firm was highly diverse, though everyone on the core team spoke English natively. The expanded team had a native speaker of a European language and a native speaker of an Asian language.

The members of the group would work individually on their project (which I did not record) and then would have a decision-making meeting (which I did record) in which they would discuss what they had done, possible solutions to the problem, and a way forward. Occasionally, these meetings would include conference calls with their client to ascertain the client's opinion before moving forward with the design. At the end of the week, I had observed close to 40 hours of work and interactions (including individual work and quick, face-to-face questions, comments, and critiques on the work) and had recorded a total of 17 hours of discussion over 9 meetings.

I personally observed and recorded the entirety of the interactions. All members signed letters of informed consent prior to my recording of the discussions. The recordings were then transcribed, and I used discourse analysis techniques to identify the group's use of personas. For the purposes of anonymity, all names, third-parties, and specific references to the abilities of the device have been replaced with appropriate placeholders. Additionally, qualities of the personas that do not affect this investigation (names, location, ages, etc) have been changed for anonymity purposes. Additionally, the transcription was broken down into conversational turns, which begin "when one speaker starts to speak, and ends when he or she stops speaking" [18]. A turn might consist of a single word ("OK," "Great," "Yes," "No," etc), or it could contain several ideas and go on for several minutes (with the longest single turn in the data set being 7 minutes and 22 seconds). In the 17 hours of recordings, there were 4985 conversational turns.

USE OF PERSONAS IN DECISION-MAKING SESSIONS

Prior to iterating the design and shortly before my observation, two of the four core designers spent several weeks in the field interviewing users, discussing expectations with stakeholders, and developing eight highly refined personas of users who would likely interact with the device they were designing. These designers then created and delivered to their clients a 20-page, full color, highly refined document that described what personas are in general, explained how the designers would use the personas in their development of the product, and introduced the clients to all the fully developed and embodied personas. Due to the proprietary nature of these personas, I will not describe each persona in detail; however, each persona was given an appropriate name, image, a defining quote, an occupation, and a short but thorough narrative, along with their occupational goals (both related and unrelated to the device), their responsibilities, and how often they would likely use the device. Upon completion of the transcription, I identified all the personas used by the group during their decision-making sessions.

Type of Persona	Number of Invocations	Number of Turns
Directly Named (Georgia, Dr. Samuels)	96	72
Indirectly Named (He, She, They)	87	64
Total	183	106

Table 1. Breakdown of Persona Usage in Decision-Making Sessions

How Often Were Personas Used?

Personas were invoked 183 times in 106 conversational turns, or in about 2% of the conversational turns during their decision-making meetings (see Table 1). When conversational turns unrelated to the decision-making session (typically related to what the group is going to do for lunch and the destruction of a building across the street) are omitted, about 3% of the remaining conversational turns invoke a persona. Personas were invoked directly by name (i.e., "We should have Georgia press the screen") 96 times in 72 conversational turns. Personas were invoked indirectly through the use of pronouns (i.e., "She could look at the events log and maybe reset to this") 87 times in 64 conversational turns. (Some conversational turns invoked personas both directly and indirectly, therefore the number of total times the persona was invoked increased, but the total number of conversational turns that invoked personas did not.)

Who Invoked Personas?

In the course of my recordings, all four of the core team members invoked personas, one member of the expanded team invoked personas, and no clients invoked personas (see Table 2). The member of the expanded team invoked three personas in one turn and all the remaining personas were invoked by members of the core team. The vast majority of the invocations by the core team came from the two team members who had conducted the field work and who had developed the personas. These two team members (Edna and Stanley) were responsible for 82.1% of all the turns that invoked personas and for 85.3% of all the personas invoked during the decision-making process.

Team Member	Percent of Total Invocations	Percent of Total Turns
Stanley	49.2%	45.3%
Edna	36.1%	36.8%
Derek	6.6%	6.6%
Sloane	6.6%	10.4%
Noah	1.5%	0.9%

Table 2. Use of Personas by Team Member

Persona	Percent of Total Invocations	Percent of Total Turns
Dr. Samuels	42.6%	41.9%
Michael	33.3%	31.6%
Georgia	21.9%	23.5%
William	1.1%	1.5%
Tara	0.5%	0.7%
Mary	0.5%	0.7%
Lila	0%	0%
Dr. Paul	0%	0%

Table 3. Frequency of Each Persona

Which Personas Were Invoked?

Eight personas were defined by the group. While six personas were invoked at least once (see Table 3), three personas represented 97.8% of the total invocations and were in 97.0% of the turns in which personas were used. These three personas were:

1) Dr. Samuels, who interacts with the device on occasion but who mostly uses the data collected from the device for diagnosis.

2) Michael, an inexperienced nurse who is still learning the basics of his job and must interact with the device on a regular basis.

3) Georgia, a nurse who is experienced with the device and trains others on how to use it.

Less invoked personas included a doctor who oversees the ward that uses the device, but who does not use the device often himself (Dr. Paul), a paramedic who uses the device while transferring patients in an ambulance (Tara), an engineer in charge of machine maintenance (William), and two nurses, one of whom only uses the device in surgical settings (Lila), and an inexperienced recovery nurse who only interacts with the device during emergencies (Mary). Of the three most-invoked personas, invocations of Michael and Dr. Samuels constituted 75.9% of the all the invocations and were represented in 73.5% of all the turns in which personas were used. Looking at it another way, although there were eight defined personas, two personas (Michael and Dr. Samuels) constituted 75% of the invoked personas, with Dr. Samuels represented about 10% more often than Michael.

Function of Persona	Definition	Examples from Decision-Making Sessions	% of Personas
Role-playing	The persona is "put on" by the designers and the designers make decisions while "wearing" that persona.	"So, Dr. Samuels, she would probably not do that. She checks her timing, looks at the screen, and the makes the diagnosis." "So, the screen comes into the sterile field, and Dr. Samuels touches it, like, with her glove." "Without having to think or do anything else, Michael just takes the [button] and goes with that."	47.5%
Focusing	The persona is used to eliminate other issues and to focus the designers on the needs of a particular end user as established through the persona.	"Well, that might be ideal for Georgia, but for now we need to close in how autopilot can make this thing foolproof for Michael." "We totally need to talk about both those things, but let's just use Michael now to focus in on the [arrangement of the items on the screen]." "The most important thing right now is to figure out [what] Georgia does in an emergency, not what she does when she has all the time in the world."	33.9%
Meeting Maintenance	The persona is used to move a meeting along or to correct a colleague who has used the wrong persona.	"I know that we are in a time crunch, but before [moving on], we need to flush out detail on Michael a little more." "Let's explore Dr. Samuels' response some more."	10.9%
Empathy	The persona is used to engender empathy and to make the end user personable and relatable.	"Michael's not an expert at this, so we should expect him to face some challenges." "That might be a nice feature because then Michael he doesn't ever have to see this thing which he may find frightening."	3.3%
Clarification	The persona is used to clarify a position and to make certain that an action assumed by the designer is the correct one.	"Kinda, but Michael's a lot more into these details, while the doctor is much more interested in the high level interaction with the machine." [After being asked a question regarding the doctor's capabilities by a teammate] "Oh, yes, Dr. Samuels has access to the events log so she'll be able to see what's happened."	2.7%
Approximation	The persona is used as an approximation of the end user. While the design may invoke the persona, the persona is secondary to the end user.	"If we get the other functions that somebody like Michael will touch out there, then they're just going to close it."	1.6%

Table 4. Functions of Personas in Decision-Making Meetings

When Were Personas Invoked?

Personas were invoked in five of the nine meetings. In four of those meetings, personas were invoked 20 times in 12 turns. The majority of the personas (about 89%) were invoked in a single meeting. In this meeting, personas were invoked 163 times in 94 turns, which is about 10% of the total turns dedicated to decision-making in this meeting.

This particular meeting was dedicated to running through scenarios, which has been called a cognitive walkthrough [6]. One member of the team read aloud predefined scenarios (mentions of the particular personas when the scenario was read aloud were not included in the total count of persona invocation as it was not part of the decision-making) and the core team assessed how the personas would interact with their design solution in that particular scenario.

How Were Personas Used in Decision-Making?

When personas were used by this group as part of the decision-making sessions, they generally functioned in six different ways. These six functions of personas are described in Table 4.

Two independent coders assessed the data for categorical reliability. The coding set consisted of approximately 10% of the total conversational turns and 50% of the total uses of personas, which represents a reasonable amount of data for a coder to assess [19]. Fifty-four of the conversational turns invoked at least one persona; the remaining conversational turns were included for conversational context to aid in assessment. Approximately 80% of the conversational turns in the coding set were randomly taken from the meeting in which the majority of the personas were used; the remaining 20% of the conversational turns were taken from the 4 other meetings in which personas were used.

The coders analyzed each use of the persona (not each turn) for how that particular invocation of the persona most likely functioned in the decision-making process. The simple agreement between the coders was 94% with a Cohen's Kappa of 0.89, which, according to Landis and Koch, is excellent agreement [20].

Of these six functions of personas, they were most often used as role-playing mechanisms, which is not surprising given that the personas were most often used in the meeting in which the designers were conducting scenario-walkthroughs. Additionally, the personas that were invoked throughout the decision-making sessions often functioned as meeting maintenance or focusing mechanisms. Although empathy was cited as a benefit for the use of personas, these designers rarely displayed empathy in their linguistic choices.

DISCUSSION: PERSONAS IN DECISION-MAKING SESSIONS

Despite the fact that this group of designers spent several weeks interviewing end users, discussing expectations with stakeholders, and developing their refined personas, personas themselves make relatively few appearances in the language used in the decision-making sessions of these designers. Additionally, though it has been stated that a benefit of personas is that they provide a "common language" for designers and clients alike "to talk about users meaningfully" [6], it appears that the idea of personas bridging across developmental differences has been idealized. At no time did a client ever refer to a persona (though they did often refer to "users," "novice users," and "expert users"). Additionally, the vast majority of the personas used by the group were invoked by the two designers who actually created the persona. This finding may suggest that persona development enables persona use. It may be that those designers who create personas internalize the persona characteristics in ways that the designers who do not actively create personas do not, thereby making the personas a useful tool for those who create the personas, but less useful for those who are simply given preformed personas.

Additionally, though the designers had 8 personas at their disposal, three personas represented over 97% of personas used, with two representing over 75% of the personas used. Though there was granularity and differentiation built in to each of these 8 personas, the two that were most cited (Dr. Samuels and Michael) represented the most expert and the most novice persona. The third persona (Georgia) was somewhere in-between (perhaps the "most" intermediate of the other available personas). Thus despite having 8 personas, these designers gravitated to using perhaps the *alpha* and the *omega* of potential users when they discussed modifications to their designs. It appears that Adlin and Pruitt's estimation of 3-5 personas as "a good number to target" is in line with how personas are actually used [6]. Though this group of designers had other personas to pull from or to use as a walkthrough mechanism, the lack of their incorporation may mean that the designers only truly focus on about three potentially divergent needs at a time, and that the resources spent on the development and refinement of the remaining personas was ultimately not needed for the decision-making sessions.

Further, it appears that personas are most used by this group when the meeting has been specifically designated to deal with personas. Although all the meetings I observed were decision-making meetings in which the designers weighed options for their product, the meeting designated as the cognitive walkthrough held the majority of the uses of personas. In their cognitive walkthrough, the designers used the personas to complete pre-defined scenarios using the product as currently developed. According to Adlin and Pruitt, using personas in cognitive walkthroughs is a natural and appropriate way to use personas [6]. At the beginning of this particular meeting, Stanley said, "Should we begin walking through to see if we are on the right track?", and then (after the group concurred), "Do you want to start with Dr. Samuels? Or Michael?" In these questions, Stanley narrows the task for the meeting: a cognitive walkthrough with the persona in mind. Therefore, it is not necessarily a surprise that the majority of the personas in this cognitive walkthrough meeting function as a role-playing mechanism, given that the purpose of the cognitive walkthrough is for the designers to "put on" a persona and determine the successes and failures of the product for that persona.

While the function of the personas isn't surprising, the general lack of invocation of personas is potentially surprising. While the cognitive walkthrough meeting has 1091 conversational turns, personas were directly or indirectly invoked 163 times in 94 turns. Given that the entire purpose of this meeting was to decide upon the future of the product through the lens of a persona, it is somewhat surprising that personas were invoked in fewer than 10% of the turns. Given this low number of invocations in a meeting that is supposedly dedicated to personas as the evidence for decision-making, it is not surprising that personas make few appearances (if any) in the meetings in which personas are not highlighted at the outset.

IF NOT PERSONAS, THEN WHAT IS USED?

It would seem that this group of designers, with their upfront investment in personas, their detailed refinement of their personas, and their ongoing, if occasional, use of personas in their meetings, would be prime candidates for linguistically utilizing personas in the discourse of their decision-making sessions. Yet, despite this group's advocation of personas and their long history of design successes, personas were simply not included regularly in the linguistic discourse of decision-making. So what are these designers using in lieu of personas, which Pruitt and Grudin claim to be "extremely powerful for communicating results and furthering…teammates' understanding of the Personas" [9]?

A previous study of language in workplace meetings investigated how designers who did not use personas invoked certain kinds of appeals to make their arguments [21]. That previous study suggests that although designers had done significant amounts of user-research and usability testing, the designers often did not use usability or user-based data to support their design solutions in their design decision-making sessions. Instead, that group of designers routinely used appeals based on their own opinions and impressions as well as appeals anchored in storytelling to persuade the others of their design beliefs. In other words, although each designer in that study had a plethora of user and usability data at his or her disposal, the designers routinely bypassed the data they had collected through numerous hours of usability and user-experience testing and used instead their own opinions or stories as linguistic mechanisms of persuasion.

A preliminary analysis of the linguistic exchanges in the decision-making sessions of the group of designers who developed and used personas seems to indicate that they, too, routinely use the two other previously identified linguistic mechanisms (designer opinion and storytelling) to persuade the other team members of their design decisions and solutions. This recurrent use of non-persona mechanisms for persuasive ends may suggest that these alternate linguistic mechanisms are, in Pruitt and Grudin's terms, more "powerful" than the personas themselves for communication and persuasive purposes.

The first alternative linguistic mechanism for the designers is to rely on their own personal opinions to persuade the other designers of a design choice. These statements generally have little or no grounding in the personas themselves or in the research that led to the development of the personas. Statements such as the following represent statements grounded in the designer's own opinion of the design and have no linguistic evidence of being based on the personas or in the research that built the personas.

- "I think this toolbar could be bigger."
- "I think the interaction of these is pretty intuitive."
- "I think the one option that stood out very strongly is the more direct manipulation."
- "Stacking those icons makes the interaction too muddled."

While a designer could have said, for example, "Stacking those icons makes the interaction too muddled *for Michael*," the persona was not linguistically invoked in the actual statement nor was there linguistic evidence in the context of these statements to suggests that these personas were any part of the decision-making process.

The second alternative linguistic mechanism used by the designers in decision-making sessions in lieu of personas is storytelling mechanisms. These storytelling mechanisms are, in many ways, more akin to personas than the statements based upon the designers' opinions. In these story-telling mechanisms, the designers take on something of a role-playing model, but they do not take on the guise of a persona; instead, they take on an ill-defined, "blank" hypothetical user. Statements such as the following represent storytelling mechanisms that do not incorporate personas.

- "So, in that case, you are more interested in what has happened over the last two hours than you are interested in what has happened in the last ten seconds."
- "The users come across this screen and they look for what they know and that might be a problem."
- "I come to this option and I can switch between things."
- "You'd touch the toolbar on the touch screen and then you touch the hardware control on the side."
- "The users see this and how do they know the measurement?"

While personas could have been invoked in these settings, they are not, nor does the context surrounding these statements suggest that personas were part of the discussion. Instead, the designers place a hypothetical story on a hypothetical "I," "you," or "user" for persuasive purposes.

Unlike personas, which have richly defined back-stories to explain why, for example, "*Dr. Samuels* is more interested in what has happened over the last two hours than what happened in the last ten seconds," these hypotheticals have no definition. From these statements and their context, it is unclear as to whom the hypothetical "users," "you," or "I" refer: any user, expert users, novice users, or some other entity entirely.

These hypotheticals are, in some ways, weak shadows of data-driven personas. While personas have specific goals, job requirements, and traits that affect how designers can posit their interactions with the product, the hypotheticals have no defining characteristics to "keep the designer honest," so to speak. The lack of defining characteristics, such as experience, goals, and requirements, makes it possible for nearly any solution posited through the linguistic invocation and presentation of a hypothetical end-user to be palatable for some abstract, ill-defined user, though not necessarily the rigorously defined personas.

While a thorough analysis of the persuasive mechanisms used by these designers in decision-making meetings is currently taking place, preliminary analyses suggest that, despite investing much time and many resources into the development and refinement of personas, even designers who are highly dedicated to the concept of personas routinely use mechanisms and tools other than personas in their linguistic exchanges during decision-making meetings. This study has shown that personas are included in about 3% of the conversational turns within these decision-making meetings. The preliminary analyses of the entirety of the decision-making meetings suggest that designer opinion is used in approximately 25% of conversational turns, while non-persona related storytelling and role-playing is used in about 21% of the conversational turns. Therefore, for this group, it appears that mechanisms other than personas are a "go-to" persuasive resource for decision-making sessions.

DISCUSSION: THE VALUE OF PERSONAS

With personas used in only about 3% of the conversational turns, it appears that the designers in this study routinely linguistically bypass personas in decision-making sessions for other, less defined mechanisms. One of the most cited benefits of personas is their ability to facilitate communication [5, 6, 9, 10, 14]. Yet, when only 3% of the communicative turns possess direct or indirect references to personas, to what degree are personas actually facilitating communication? Given the 1-4 month estimates for persona development, refinement, and deployment, personas appear to be a resource-expensive tool for design development [7, 8, 9]. Therefore, if linguistic communication facilitation is not an apparent benefit of personas, is there other value in persona development? I believe yes, there are other, perhaps subtle, benefits for the inclusion of personas in the design development process.

First, while the promise of personas is to enable communication across several team members regardless of their involvement in the creation of the personas, it appears that those who are involved in the creation of the persona have a better understanding of the personas and the user-at-large than those who are mere recipients of the personas. Of all the invocations of personas in the decision-making sessions, Edna and Stanley, the two team members who actually developed the personas, referenced personas far and away the most often. Further, those invocations revealed a more in-depth knowledge of the personas than the invocations by the other team members. The other team members would often say something akin to "But Michael's not an expert, right?" (Sloane), whereas Edna or Stanley might say, "Well, Michael isn't going to do it that way. Georgia might, but not Michael because he doesn't really know what he's doing, he hasn't done this in quite some time. He just needs to be able to turn it on and for it to work" (Stanley). Those designers who developed the personas were treated by the other team members as custodians of the personas and were the team's resource for clarifications about what a persona would or would not do. Therefore, Edna and Stanley, who developed the personas, were the team members most likely to use personas and use them in detailed and specific ways. Perhaps if others in the team had been part of the persona development process, they, too, would have felt more empowered to use the personas as part of their decision-making process.

Though Edna and Stanley did use personas more often and more constructively than those team members who did not develop the personas, they too used linguistic mechanisms other than personas with a relatively high frequency. However, in storytelling turns that did not invoke personas, Edna and Stanley were more likely than the other team members to create a hypothetical user that seemingly adhered to the attributes of a persona than an open ended hypothetical. For example, while Sloane says, without regard to specifics of a particular user (be it a persona or a less defined "novice" or "experienced" user), "The user presses this icon and it reveals this menu and then they can select the measure they want," Edna restricts the ability of the hypothetical user in her response: "Well, yes, if it's, like, a super novice user, but not-so-newbies will want access faster and won't want to wade their way through icons and menus on a touch." This exchange comes from a meeting in which no personas were linguistically invoked. However, Edna's response clearly keeps some attributes of the unnamed personas in mind: the persona of Michael needs feedback and help from the device to properly operate it, but the persona of Georgia wants the device to not get in her way of accomplishing what she knows needs to be done. In the preliminary analysis, it appears that about 30% of the persona-lacking storytelling mechanisms invoked in the decision-making meetings actually reasonably mimic the defined descriptions of the developed personas and nearly all of those invocations were accomplished by Edna or Stanley.

Finally, though personas are used by this group with less regularity than might be expected, the group does, on occasion, use personas to facilitate communication in ways that may not be possible without personas. For example, in one meeting (which was not the cognitive walkthrough), Sloane proposed a visual design solution. Derek, the project manager and the team member who dealt with the client most regularly and directly, used linguistic markers that indicated that he enjoyed Sloane's proposed solution ("Wow," "That's elegant," and "[the client] is gonna love that"). However, immediately following Sloane's presentation, Edna countered with the following:

Edna: I really like that. I mean, we should totally use that going forward, but, well, should we be concerned about, think about Michael and Georgia. I mean, it's totally functional, but if we remember what is driving [Michael and Georgia], then I'm not entirely sure if this is the way to go, ya know, with what they are trying to do cause..."

Derek: You're right. I hadn't thought of that. We probably don't need the flash-bang.

Edna's conversational turn was the only turn in the meeting in which personas were invoked. Though Edna's invocations of Michael and Georgia were not reciprocated by her fellow team members, her use of personas in that instant were valuable in that they quickly, subtly, and concisely redirected the attention of the team members away from the "flashiness" of the proposed solution for the device and back towards the defined needs of the personas. Therefore, while personas were only used on a limited basis, they did provide strategic advantages in critical instances.

Thus, though they are not used with high frequency by this group, personas can and do provide value to this group by enabling the designers who developed the personas to be custodians of the personas, by allowing the personas to argue from persona positions even when the personas aren't linguistically invoked, and by being a useful mechanism of persuasion and focus.

CONCLUSIONS AND FUTURE RESEARCH

In this particular case study, designers who research, develop, and refine personas do not use those personas as a primary persuasive mechanism during design decision-making meetings and rely much more prominently on their own opinions about the design and vaguely referenced hypothetical stories. Therefore, while personas, including personas such as those that are based on actual end-user research, may be a user-centered design method, it appears that, at least for this group, personas alone may not be enough to ensure that end-user needs are at the forefront of the designing process.

However, despite their limited overall use it appears that personas may continue to be a valuable method for the designers, particularly for those designers who are actively involved in the development of the personas. The designers who developed the personas were more likely to use personas in the decision-making sessions, to act as custodians of the personas, to use vague hypotheticals in a manner that mimicked the characteristics of the personas, and to use personas in ways that facilitate communication than those designers were not actively involved in the creation of the personas.

This study's major limitation lends itself to future research. As is common in case studies, this study observed only one group. Although the observations were diligent and the results accurately descriptive of the language and actions of this group, care should be taken when ascribing this group's function and use of personas to other groups. Thus, more groups (including distributed groups, multi-cultural groups, highly hierarchical groups, among others) who use personas should be studied closely to determine how personas are actually used in the designing process. Only by studying more groups can we truly learn what happens with personas in decision-making sessions and begin to develop best practices based upon observational, rather than anecdotal, research for personas as a UCD method. Additional future research may include investigating how personas are invoked in non-face-to-face settings (such as email or instant messaging), the effect of the number of team members on the frequency of persona invocation, the effect of persona development and research on persona use, and the use of alternate mechanisms of persuasion in decision-making sessions.

Ultimately, this study, which has revealed that this group of designers who advocate persona use do not necessarily use personas as their primary persuasive or communication mechanism in design decision-making meetings, identifies how personas are actually used *in situ* and is a first step in determining how personas are actually used (rather than just how personas are purported to be used) by designers in their decision-making sessions.

REFERENCES

1. Gould, J.D. and Boies, S.J. Human factors challenges in creating a principal support office system: The speech filing system approach. *ACM Transactions on Office Information Systems, 1* (1983), 273-298.
2. Cooper, A. *The Inmates Are Running the Asylum*. Sams, Indianapolis, IN, 1999.
3. Lidwell, W., *et al.*, *Universal Principles of Design*. Rockport Publishers, Beverly, MA, 2010.
4. Grudin, J. and Pruitt, J. Personas, participatory design and product development: an infrastructure for engagement. In *Proc. Participatory Design*, ACM Press (2002), 144-161.

5. Goodwin, K. *Designing for the digital age: how to create human-cented products and services*. Wiley, Indianapolis, IN, 2009.
6. Adlin, T. and Pruitt, J. *The essential personal lifecycle: Your guide to building and using personas*. Morgan Kaufmann, Burlington, MA, 2010.
7. McGinn, J. and Kotamraju, N. Data-driven persona development. In *Proc. CHI 2008*, ACM Press (2008).
8. Neiters, J. E., *et al.* Making personas memorable. In *Proc. CHI '07*, ACM Press (2007), 1817-1823.
9. Pruitt, J. and Grudin, J. Personas: practice and theory. In *Designing for User Experiences* (2003).
10. Holtzblatt, K., *et al.*, *Rapid Contextual design: A how-to guide to key techniques for user-centered design*. Morgan Kaufmann, San Francisco, 2004.
11. Fried, J. Personas? *Ask 37signals*. http://37signals.com/svn/posts/690-ask-37signals-personas
12. Chapman, C. N. and Milham, R. P. The persona's new clothes: Methodological and practical arguments against a popular method. *Human Factors and Ergonomics Society 50th Annual Meeting* (2006), 634-636.
13. Miaskiewicz, T., *et al.* A preliminary examination of using personas to enhance user-centered design. In *Americas Conference on Information Systems* (2009).
14. Massanari, A.L. Designing for imaginary friends: information architecture, personas, and the politics of user-centered design. *New Media & Society 12*, 3 (2010), 401-416.
15. Long, F. Real or imaginary: the effectiveness of using personas in product desig. *Irish Ergonomics Review*, (2009), 1-9.
16. Blomquist, A. and Arvola, M. Personas in action: Ethnography in an interaction design team. In *Proc. NordiCHI '02*, ACM Press, 2002.
17. Ronkko, K. An empirical study demonstrating how different design constraints, project organization and contexts limit the utility of personas. In *Proc. 38th Hawaii International Conference on System Sciences*, (2005), 220.
18. Johnstone, B. *Discourse analysis*. Blackwell, Malden, MA. 2002.
19. Geisler, C. *Analyzing streams of language: Twelve steps to the systematic coding of text, talk, and other verbal data*. Pearson, New York, 2004.
20. Landis, J. R. and Koch, G. G. An application of hierarchical Kappa-type statistics in the assessment of majority agreement among multiple observers. *Biometrics 33*, 2 (1977), 363-374.
21. Friess, E. Designing from data: rhetorical appeals in support of design decisions. *Journal of Business and Technical Communication 24*, 4 (2010), 403-444.

How Do Designers and User Experience Professionals Actually Perceive and Use Personas?

Tara Matthews
IBM Research - Almaden
San Jose, CA, USA
tlmatthe@us.ibm.com

Tejinder K. Judge[1]
Google Inc.
Mountain View, CA, USA
tejinderjudge@google.com

Steve Whittaker
UC Santa Cruz
Santa Cruz, CA, USA
swhittak@ucsc.edu

ABSTRACT
Personas are a critical method for orienting design and development teams to user experience. Prior work has noted challenges in justifying them to *developers*. In contrast, it has been assumed that *designers and user experience professionals*—whose goal is to focus designs on targeted users—will readily exploit personas. This paper examines that assumption. We present the first study of how experienced user-centered design (UCD) practitioners with prior experience deploying personas, use and perceive personas in industrial software design. We identify limits to the persona approach in the context studied. Practitioners used personas almost exclusively for communication, but not for design. Participants identified four problems with personas, finding them abstract, impersonal, misleading and distracting. Our findings argue for a new approach to persona deployment and construction. Personas cannot replace immersion in actual user data. And rather than focusing on creating engaging personas, it is critical to avoid persona attributes that mislead or distract.

Author Keywords
Personas; design tools; evaluation; methods; user study.

ACM Classification Keywords
H5.m. Information interfaces and presentation (e.g., HCI): Miscellaneous.

General Terms: Design

INTRODUCTION
Personas are a critical method for orienting design and development teams to user experience. They are especially useful when constraints, e.g. large development teams or diverse users, exclude participatory design methods. Personas can engage teams in thinking about users during the design process, making efficient design decisions without inappropriate generalization, and communicating about users to various stakeholders [5,6,7,21,22]. Researchers and practitioners have shown personas live up to these claims, at least in some settings [9,14,16,20].

However, personas are controversial [4,24]. They are challenging to construct and existing guidelines involve as much creativity as science [20,22]. It is difficult to verify that a persona accurately reflects user data [4] and to define the right personas [4,14]. It can be hard to convince development teams to use personas [1,21] and there are some socio-political settings where they may be impractical [24].

Personas literature discusses at great length the important, difficult task of introducing personas to developers and stakeholders, and of getting buy-in from decision makers [14,21]. However, this literature seems to take for granted that designers and user experience (UX) professionals—whose goal is to focus designs on targeted users—will understand and exploit personas.

Amidst this controversy, how do experienced designers and UX practitioners actually use and perceive personas? What do existing practices say about how personas should be used, or modified in the future? Prior work on personas presents case studies of personas' use with inexperienced designers [1,9,14,24], personal critiques of personas [4], or anthologies of best practices from persona advocates [5,6,7,20,21]. However this work consists of authors' opinions or examples of how people who are not user-centered design (UCD) professionals react to personas in particular project case studies. We lack actual data about how *experienced* UCD practitioners use personas as part of their jobs.

This paper examines how UCD practitioners at one company perceive personas' use and value in real industrial product design. It is the first study exploring perceptions of personas in UCD practitioners with prior experience using personas. We interviewed 14 experienced practitioners—10 designers and 4 UX professionals—about their use and perceptions of personas. We found that most of these practitioners do *not* use personas in their own design processes. Rather, they use personas mainly to *communicate with others*, to build support for a chosen design or more generally to advocate user needs.

Permission to make digital or hard copies of all or part of this work for personal or classroom use is granted without fee provided that copies are not made or distributed for profit or commercial advantage and that copies bear this notice and the full citation on the first page. To copy otherwise, or republish, to post on servers or to redistribute to lists, requires prior specific permission and/or a fee.
CHI'12, May 5–10, 2012, Austin, Texas, USA.
Copyright 2012 ACM 978-1-4503-1015-4/12/05...$10.00.

[1] Author conducted this research at IBM Research - Almaden.

We also found multiple reasons why designers do not use personas for their own design work:

1. Personas are *abstract* – it is hard to understand the abstraction process from user data to persona, so personas come across as lacking critical detail.
2. Personas are *impersonal* – the personifying details in personas fail to provide a sense of empathy.
3. Personifying details *mislead* – it is difficult to select personal details that do not create false constraints on the design problem.
4. Personifying details *distract* – personifying details make it hard to focus on the aspects of a persona that are critical for the design problem.

To avoid these problems, our practitioners wanted first-hand experience with users, or personal access to user study data. They viewed this as necessary to derive the rich understanding of users required for design.

Practitioner's training affected perception and use of personas. Those with formal design training had the most negative and skeptical opinions about personas, whereas those with specialized training in personas had more positive opinions and experiences using personas. This latter group found benefits in using personas both for their design processes and communication with others, indicating there is value in the method when used in certain ways. For the skeptics, personas seemed to clash with the practice of design itself. For example, for these designers, certain user-supplied constraints are critical, but the creative process should not be unnecessarily constrained by a persona's personifying details, which were perceived as arbitrary.

Our results can refine the deployment of personas in industrial design. Other work has abstractly argued that personas are not a panacea for UCD [20,21]. However our work identifies specific, concrete limits to the persona approach, as experienced by our participants. We cannot presume that *experienced UCD practitioners* have the expertise or motivation to use personas, even in groups that actively develop and disseminate them. UCD practitioners need a significant level of persona know-how, and it is important that personas do not completely *replace* immersion in actual user data. Researchers have rightly noted the difficulty in making personas as engaging as real people [20]. However the bigger problem we discovered is making personas that do not mislead or distract, arguing for a different emphasis in persona creation. Taken together, this argues that personas may be most effective for UCD practitioners for communication rather than for design activities.

RELATED WORK

The concept of a *persona*, introduced by Cooper [5], significantly expanded upon by Pruitt and Adlin [21], and further developed by Neilson [20], is a hypothetical archetype of an actual user, describing that person's goals, aptitudes, and interests. Personas are intended to be used during the design and development of technology to avoid the problem of designers, developers, or stakeholders invoking the "elastic user" who can be bent and stretched to suit the needs of the invoker. Cooper estimates that each design problem will require between 3 to 12 personas.

Persona advocates commonly claim that personas are useful "for *design*" or can help designers "to design" [6,14,20,21]. Examples of design activities include helping designers to internalize a mental model of users as they design, featuring personas in storyboards and scenarios, guiding the designer's process of sketching and prototyping, and enabling iterative evaluation of prototypes, e.g., through cognitive walkthroughs from the persona's perspective. Another common category of persona use is *communication*, both within and outside a design team [5,6,21,22]. Examples of communication activities include aligning large development teams toward specific user issues, making decisions about requirements, and advocating for particular designs approaches.

Cooper originally intended that personas be used by people without UCD training. Despite Cooper's original intention, many other authors have lauded the benefits to designers and UX practitioners of using personas [7,14,21]. It is very common that design and UX practitioners use personas—at the company studied and in many other companies.

Pruitt and Grudin are open about the challenges of implementing personas in a large industrial software development environment [22]. First, the persona characters are not always seen as credible, i.e., as being based on real data. Second, it is difficult to communicate the persona so that all members of a team understand the character. Third, practitioners do not always understand how to use personas. Fourth, high-level support is needed for a team to have the time and resources to implement personas successfully.

To solve the credibility problem, Pruitt and Grudin propose using rigorous user studies to create personas and linking them to "foundational documents," which include the user study data backing up the persona. Faily and Flechais enhance the concept of foundational documents in a tool that connects personas directly to coded user data [11]. To address the communication problem, they describe ongoing persona "campaigns," where information about the characters is regularly sent to the team. Regarding the usage challenge, they advocate that persona creators provide tools and instructions for how to use personas.

Despite some treatment of challenges, an issue with this literature is that it generally takes a position of advocacy and lacks objectivity. To explore the effectiveness of the persona approach, a few research studies have been conducted. Several studies have examined the use of personas by small project teams in short, focused field studies [16,23], or sessions facilitated by the researchers

Table 1. Participant demographics and categorization of their use and opinion of personas. Shading highlights similarities.

Part.	Role (*Lead)	Product Division	Years[1]	Training[2]	Opinion/Use of Personas (*Creator)
D1	UX	A	14	CooperU, HCI	Champion*
B1	Design*	A	10	CooperU, Engineering	Champion*
M2	Design*	B	22	Other	Champion*
V1	UX	B	12	Computer Sci.	Moderate*
J1	Design*	B	6	Engineering	Moderate
E1	Design*	B	13	Computer Sci.	Moderate
E2	Design	B	2	Design	Moderate
N1	Design	B	8	Design	Moderate
A2	Design	C	3	HCI	Moderate
M3	UX	B	5	HCI	Pessimist
L1	UX*	C	20	HCI	Pessimist
M1	Design	B	13	Design	Pessimist
E3	Design	R	11	HCI	Pessimist
A1	Design	R	5	Design	Pessimist

[1] Total years experience in a design/UX position.
[2] Training is reported categorically to protect anonymity.

[3,9,20]. These studies demonstrate that personas possess many of the advantages outlined above.

However, other studies also suggest limits to personas. Rönkkö examined the use and perception of personas by three 17-member student design teams who used personas during a 20-week project [23]. They were instructed to use personas during their design processes and to communicate with a development team. Design teams in the study also had ready access to users throughout the design process. Rönkkö found students were hesitant to replace the users with personas for design work. This suggested that students found personas primarily useful for communicating end-user characteristics and design decisions to developers.

However, most prior empirical research has studied non-designers and non-UX practitioners, or student designers. Even when studies have recruited UX and design professionals, most participants were unfamiliar with personas prior to the study [1]. Our study is the first to focus on the use and perception of personas by experienced *user-experience and design practitioners* representing multiple teams. Our practitioners all had some experience (many with extensive experience) using personas in their careers.

Finally, there is disagreement between authors on how to create and present personas to practitioners. Cooper [5] advocates creating personas based on limited information about users, aiming to fit the goals of the design team. In contrast, Pruitt, Grudin, and Adlin [21,22] emphasize using rigorous user studies to create personas and foundational documents of user study data. They also advocate including key decision makers in the creation process to reinforce their buy-in. Others build on this approach, to present techniques for developing personas from user data [19,25]. However, the main focus has been the problem of making personas acceptable to stakeholders, developers, and others *outside the UCD team*. Exceptions are Neilson [20], who emphasizes story-telling characteristics and personifying details to make personas engaging to designers; and Chang et al. [3], who report on a small survey about the varying practices of practitioners during the persona creation process. However, this prior work does not evaluate which of these differing approaches are most useful to UCD practitioners in a software product design setting, a question explored in this study.

METHOD

Organizational Context

All participants were from a global enterprise offering technology products and services to businesses. They were all based in North America. The company has a large, influential UCD community. Personas were in widespread use by practitioners across multiple product divisions and were supported by management in those divisions. Participants were distributed across three product divisions and Research, all with varying adoption of personas. All of the divisions created software aimed at different business user populations. Each product division was comprised of multiple groups who focused on different products with variations in their persona use. We describe this below.

Participants and their Job Roles

We recruited 12 participants from the three product divisions, plus 2 designers from Research. We recruited an initial sample of 9 via direct email solicitation based on our network of contacts. We then used snowball sampling to recruit the remaining 5 participants.

Detailed information about our participants is shown in Table 1. The 10 designers focused on either visual or interaction design. Their work first involved communicating with development teams, managers, UX professionals, and/or users to understand the design problem and users. This process involved creating design briefs, storyboards, scenarios and/or sketches to clarify requirements. Next came design activities: they made decisions about how to translate user requirements into designs and then created low and/or high fidelity prototypes, iterating to more refined designs over time. Feedback from managers and developers outside the design team was iteratively incorporated throughout their design process. The details of this process varied for each individual and design problem.

The 4 UX professionals' roles spanned user research and design. They conducted user research; translated their understanding of users into design and communication tools e.g. personas, scenarios, storyboards, and user roles; and/or participated in design activities as outlined above. They had a range of involvement in design activities, ranging from little to very active contribution. Where we discuss persona use during design, we include all participants, though UX professionals spent less time doing this than designers.

Interview Procedure and Analysis

Interviews were conducted within a 90-minute session as part of a broader study to evaluate two types of personas. Two sessions were conducted in person and the rest by phone. Time in each session was allocated as follows: (a) interview—a 20-min interview about the participant's experience, role, design process, and use and opinion of personas; (b) study task—a 40-min task using two personas to complete cognitive walkthroughs of a company product; and (b) debrief—a 20-min discussion about their experience using the personas for the task. The interview provided data exclusively for this paper, but the study task and debrief also provided significant additional data, since participants continued to offer their general opinions about and use of personas throughout the session. We do not discuss the details of the study task further because it is not relevant to our results. For more details about the task, see [15].

During the interview, participants were asked to read one of product division B's personas and a second persona created for the study task. They occasionally referred to these personas when illustrating points made in their discussion. However, our goal was to understand how participants use and perceive personas in their work, so we were clear to differentiate—with the participant—whether their comments were about the two study personas or personas in general. The results in this paper exclude comments specifically about the study personas, except when those personas were evoked as an example in a more general comment. All persona names used in quotes below were changed to protect anonymity (including "Gerard" which is a pseudonym for the study persona name).

Two researchers attended each session, one leading and the other taking detailed notes. Study sessions were audio recorded. Loose transcripts and notes from the sessions were initially analyzed using open coding. We next examined our initial codes and data to identify and formalize recurring themes, which represented meaningful aspects of the empirical material that occurred repeatedly. For example, one theme was that only a few, distinctly different perceptions of personas were expressed repeatedly and we discovered that we could categorize participants by these repeated viewpoints. We performed a second coding pass through the data focused on the formalized themes. Two analysts who had conducted the interviews together went through the themes with examples. Where there was disagreement they discussed the themes and examples until agreement was reached. Our presentation of results focuses on these themes, including quotes that support each theme and illustrate important nuances.

RESULTS

In what follows, we present the ways personas were perceived and used by participants. We also describe the reasons participants gave for not using personas in their own design processes.

Perception and Use of Personas Across Product Divisions, Roles, and Training

We categorized our participants into three groups based on the way they described their use and opinions of personas (see Table 1, right column):

1. *Persona Champion* – made fully productive use of personas as described in prior literature [5,6,21,22] and had an enthusiastically positive opinion of personas (3 participants).
2. *Persona Moderate* – focused on user role information in personas for design. They had a moderately positive or neutral opinion of personas (6 participants).
3. *Persona Pessimist* – did not use personas to design and had an indifferent or negative opinion of them (5 participants).

Participants who have created personas are marked with an asterisk in column 4 of Table 1, and include all the Champions and two Moderates.

Persona adoption varied across the three product divisions represented in the study. Practitioners from product division A had sent a number of designers, UX professionals, managers, and developers to 'CooperU' which provides a focused personas training program. This group had subsequently adopted the personas methodology and were deriving great benefit from doing so. Unsurprisingly, the two participants from product division A were Persona Champions. This group had an extensive cast of personas and shared foundational user study data upon request. Product division B, had 11 personas that were backed by management support and were publicized through internal advertising "campaigns" [21], but most participants in this group described their own work as focusing on user roles in personas and ignoring the personalizing details. Foundational data for their personas was not widely available. This group included the largest faction of Moderates (5 out of 7), as well as one Champion and 2 (of 5) Persona Pessimists. Product division C had personas that were little more than user roles with names and photographs (i.e., they included no other personifying details). One participant from product division C was a Moderate who did not currently use personas but had in the past; the other was a Persona Pessimist.

Considering *job role*, designers and UX professionals seemed equally likely to fit into the three opinion and use categories. However, considering formal training painted a different picture. Designers with formal training in a visual or interaction design program (Graphic Design, Information Design, Visual Communication, or HCI) made up all of the Persona Pessimists. All but one of the rest were Moderates.

In what follows, we describe in more detail how personas were used by participants, presenting three fundamental problems with personas.

Personas were Not Used by (Most) Designers to Design

Our first finding is that many of our participants did not use personas significantly in their own design work. We defined *design* as work that occurs when the designer or UX professional directly uses the persona *themselves*. In contrast, *communication* is when the persona is used to communicate *with others* who may then enact the design process or take other action.

Persona Pessimists (five participants) did not exploit personas for their own design work, as described by designer B1:

> *To be honest with you, I rarely use personas myself... I find them useful for requirements gathering and I actually find them useful for the client. But I don't design with them or design off of them. The reason is that it's a great tool to get people to start thinking about the thing they are building in terms of users but in my experience, personas tend to be overly optimistic. They describe the best-case scenario for the perfect user who is incredibly enthusiastic about the system... Personas are not helpful because the users don't match up to the personas.*

> *It [a persona] is basically useful for non-designers trying to comprehend the design process. Or maybe if they are designers and they are trying to simplify the process for non-designers. Personas are helpful if you have never designed to start thinking about users. But it is different if you are talking to a professional designer who does this for a living.*

In contrast, Persona Champions (only 3 participants) were enthusiastic persona users and importantly, persona creators. All 3 of the champions were in charge of creating personas, so they were heavily invested in the personas and the process of using them. One designer and Persona Champion, B1, described how personas fit into his design and communication processes. Notice in the quote below how he says he will "bend and stretch" the persona, something he feels comfortable doing since he is intimately familiar with the user data that ground the persona, a theme mentioned by two Persona Champions:

> *What I like about the personas that we've written in [division A] is that they are very grounded in people. And that is intentional. A lot of our personas, you know the first paragraph is actually just like an introduction to who the personality is, so... all those people we were talking to, they start to come through and come alive...*

> *This [gestures to persona] may start me, but then I start blending... I'm also very creative and I will bend and stretch things as I go along as well. I come out with solutions that Gerard never even thought of that might be based on him and based upon his pain points or his goals or his use cases, but they're my creativity blended in with that, from the conversations.*

Persona Moderates (7 participants) focused on very specific user role information in personas for design:

> *I sometimes use personas but I can't say that I use them deeply. In the course of developing design, I am trying to define audiences... When I go to the end user audience, it is a matter of using the level of technical savvy of the persona to get an understanding of what I need to do in order to provide the feature... Is this feature going to be used by someone technically savvy or with less savvy so we can optimize the feature for each case. –J1, Designer*

Defining the ways in which practitioners 'use personas' for design is a complex issue. Persona Pessimists clearly did not use personas in their design work, whereas the Champions did. However, Moderates' use was more ambiguous. Our data show they did not make full use of personas in their design work, since they ignored the personifying content that really defines a persona and *instead focused just on the role information.* Thus, we consider Moderates as not fully using personas, since they do not exploit the key aspects of the persona.

Our results indicate that the majority of our participants did not use personas significantly for design. What information about users did the majority of practitioners use instead?

What User Information did Designers use to Design?

To support their design activities, most participants turned to a combination of actual users and/or user study data, and user role information (usually embedded within a persona). First-hand experience with actual users and user study data was viewed as the primary way to derive the rich, personal understanding of users required for design. A persona might be used if time or resources did not permit them to gather such first-hand experience, but was viewed by many as sub-optimal. These points are supported by many of the quotes throughout the results section.

User role information includes job responsibilities, skills, educational background, and tools used. This information represented the critical design constraints. Designers found it useful to have it summarized to remember and focus upon during design. Moderates were an interesting group who used the role-specific information in personas to design, but not the personifying details aside from name and photo. They found this role-based information invaluable during design. Furthermore, they all found value in the name and photo of their personas. Unlike Pessimists, Moderates did not have negative opinions of the additional information in the personas. Persona Moderate and designer, A2, describes focusing on user roles instead of personas:

> *When they were first developed... I think they were much more personas. People would say oh 'Paul' or 'Jim' or whomever. Now I think they're much more roles, oh 'the test manager' or 'the tester'... I don't necessarily feel like anything was lost because... in a fast-paced environment... we care much more about the role and what they're doing, which sounds terrible, like 'we don't really care about you, Paul, we just care about what you're doing at work.' But so it's very much more role based, but I wouldn't say anything has necessarily been lost... I think the stuff that was lost was the extras, like 'Paul likes to*

go on bicycle rides,' not the 'Paul uses Microsoft Word to import his existing test plan.'

We have seen that the majority of our participants did not use personas significantly for design. How then were personas used by the majority of practitioners?

Personas were Used for Communication

Most participants thought personas were primarily useful for communicating with non-designers and non-UX practitioners about users and UCD. This view is consistent with prior literature [5,6,21,22]. Personas helped practitioners communicate about users and their designs in multiple ways. In some cases personas were used to create common ground between a designer and stakeholders regarding the design problem:

> *You never work with just the persona by itself. You have managers telling you what they want in the product. You have developers telling you how they want their architecture to work. So there's always these other factors coming in. The persona's there as my rally point if I do get way out in the weeds, I can pull everyone back on 'Hey, Gerard here! What's he need?' –B1, Designer, Persona Champion*

> *I find them useful for requirements gathering, and I actually find them useful for the client, whoever that is, to do them for me. –A1, Designer, Persona Pessimist*

Personas were also used to advocate for user needs with the development team:

> *When we were presenting to... our development team... we would use the personas to put the design in context. And if there was potentially a debate about a particular feature... it's helpful to have the persona as a way to reference what the users would actually be like... If a development team member who's implementing something, they may say something like, 'The design you've proposed looks good, but it's not feasible for these reasons. Can we just do XYZ instead?' We can say, 'Well, that might not be so good because, from a user perspective, this person has the following expertise...' - E1, Designer, Persona Moderate*

Personas also enabled practitioners to advocate their designs and prevent stakeholders from making design decisions for themselves:

> *[Personas] made it easier for designers to get their designs and ideas accepted. So when we started out, the Distinguished Engineer would say, literally... 'I don't like it.' And you know, I'd answer, 'Well, it's not about you, it's about Jennifer, and Bob, and Rose. And you know Rose is this 63 year old secretary who just wants to learn how to use [the tool]... And obviously Rose is not you.' You know, that sort of thing. And so some of our designs made it easier to advocate for [the personas]. –M2, Designer, Persona Champion*

As noted above, our three Persona Champions named a much wider range of ways the method had added value to their design processes and interactions with the development team. The benefits they identified were consistent with those advocated in prior literature, such as supporting interaction design activities, determining what a product should do and how it should behave, and measuring the design's effectiveness [5,6,21,22].

These three participants were a minority, however. Although personas are not intended to be the only tools designers use, it is surprising that so many did not use them for their own design work. In the next section, we explore the reasons why.

Reasons Personas were not used for Design

The reasons many designers in our study did not use personas for design were multi-faceted, including that personas are abstract and impersonal, and that personifying information misleads and distracts. We explain these points in the following subsections.

Personas are abstract

Participants found it difficult to understand the abstraction process from user data to persona, so personas came across as lacking critical detail required for design. Both of the following quotes from Persona Pessimists illustrate that designers considered access to user research data critical and that abstracting user data into a persona was not valuable:

> *You can't design to somebody else's understanding of the problem. You need to be part of the user research to design something. That is where the best designs come from. –E3, Designer*

> *What I don't like is how distilling something into a persona, so for example if I'm making an e-commerce app and I can take all 40-something women shoppers in the Mid-West and turn that into 'Katie' my persona, I feel like the generalization that is being made at that point, makes me feel slightly uncomfortable, rather than just having the body of research to start with. – M1, Designer*

These sentiments imply that no amount of adding to the persona would satisfy these practitioners' needs for first-hand experience with users. But designers were not the only ones who wanted first-hand knowledge of users. User study data helped make the personas believable to developers and others outside the design team:

> *A lot of the times with the development community, I show them the data and then I introduce them to the persona. So I will walk them through and show them all my variable data... Because if you just hand them something like this (holds up persona), they're never going to believe you. There's not enough data here, these are very engineer-driven guys and girls... They relate better to something like this (points to persona), if they can see that there's data behind it. –D1, UX*

Personas are impersonal

Practitioners similarly wanted access to users to feel they truly understood the people they were designing for. This implies that the personifying details in personas do not go far enough to provide a sense of empathy.

> *I think there are a lot of subtlety or details, things that cannot be conveyed from the description... I don't think you can really think or act like [the persona]... To be frank I always*

have doubts about the persona and how they are going to be used... I feel like it's more of a communication tool. – M3, UX

When time did not permit designers to talk with real users, they reported that they might use a persona, but also expressed a desire to simultaneously design from their own experiences. During the design exercise in our study, designers were asked to use the persona. After discussing how the persona might use the tool in the design exercise, we explicitly asked them where they were drawing their assumptions from concerning the persona's behavior. Designers drew from a mixture of the persona and their own experiences:

*I use [the persona] pretty technically in the design, you know all of her information is in the mockups, but I'm trying to think if I use it when I'm designing an interaction or anything like that, specifically. And I think **I** do to some extent. Like I don't always put my Jennifer hat on and think in her shoes, but as designers, people who work in this, we think (pause) we are the users of our products a lot of the times, so that's an easier one to put on. –N1, Designer*

This propensity to use personal experiences to supplement the persona implies an unfulfilled need to understand the person behind the persona. Prior work emphasizes making personas engaging through story-like narratives and personifying details [13,20], which would seem to help with this problem. However, our findings in the next two sections, which discuss issues with the personifying details in personas, raise concerns with this emphasis.

Personifying details mislead

We have argued that personas did not contain enough information for designers to fully understand users. On the other hand, personas included other information that designers felt was irrelevant for the design problem. Prior literature expresses the importance of personifying details in building empathy [6], or an internalized model of users [13] that enables practitioners to predict user behavior and sentiment. However, designers felt the personal details included in personas (such as their home life, interests, personal habits, etc.) created *false constraints* on the design problem. This concern was commonly held by Persona Pessimists.

That [personal] data is not useful at all... The reason why is that, if this were a real human being, yeah, I might care. But given that it's a persona, what it actually does is that it creates the illusion that this is a real person. So it makes me feel more confident I'm actually designing for a person, but I'm not. So it actually is just deceptive... My main critique of personas is that they are not a real person and any sort of dressing that makes it seem like a real person is not helpful. –A1, Designer

I don't do a lot of persona-based work. I actually don't love personas, because I feel like they create a sort of false sense, a lot of times, of people being able to create... I think performing interviews when you have time to do that is really good, but formalizing them as a persona seems (pauses) it's almost like a crutch, in many cases... I think it's actually become a way that people don't think about our customers in real terms anymore. We now think about Gerard's face, but I don't think that actually helps you understand what people are doing anymore. –M1, Designer

The designers in our study were oriented toward design problems and used UCD approaches. They viewed the personal details about *actual users* as a critical part of the design problem. As the quotes above illustrate, they did not believe personal details in *personas* could play the same role.

The three Persona Champions were notable exceptions to this desire for personal details. They considered personifying details of the utmost importance and they made good use of them in their work. For example, A1 thought our sample persona needed more personal details:

The one thing missing from Gerard is his life story. I want to care about him. I need a cause. I need to want to champion him in the design process. If I can help him do his job better, maybe he can shave some time off his gym time or maybe he won't get paged during his kid's soccer game.

As another example, M2 told a story about how a "secret" personal detail—that two of the group's personas were having an affair—became the basis for designing a privacy feature:

[My colleague] comes in one day and says, 'Bob and Jennifer are having an affair but Bob does not want anybody to know about it.' He created this elaborate story. It makes it fun to design the feature.

Personifying details distract

It was critical to designers to know what user information they should actually use in design. However many participants felt that certain personifying details distracted from key role-based elements:

I'm torn as to how useful [personal information] is from a product design standpoint... I think the bottom line is, it's cool and I love it, I just think sometimes in describing somebody's life, I think it's easy for the reader to miss the point: 'oh ok, Gerard is checking his Blackberry in his car on the way in'... You know the stuff that affects his work. That's my feeling. That's why in my job I've kind of moved away from that level of detail in the personas... I don't necessarily care that he goes to the gym. –A2, Designer

It is possible that the company's target users—workplace and business-focused—resulted in different persona needs, with lesser emphasis on personifying details and more on user roles. Another participant pointed to the types of information that are critical but can get lost in a persona:

The persona brings more aspects that are particular to an individual... with unique qualities... They make a role more real and more easily communicable to the stakeholders... Often what I find in the development of a persona is that those peripheral aspects become more prominent... and you find aspects that are not really that relevant to those critical dimensions... skills, responsibilities/goals, familiarity with software and tools. Those things that are easier to come up with—those more unique aspects—become more prominent

> *because they are easier to communicate, yet at the cost of substance and losing the essence of what is important... So we end up with these [personas]... with these nice looking pictures and fancy job titles and extremely exciting lives. And soon the medium becomes the message... So the challenge for us is to find this optimum balance of substance, economy, and communication. -L1, UX*

Appropriate Training Leads to Benefits from Personas

Our two participants from product division A argued that personas can realize many of the potential benefits lauded in prior literature [5,6,7,21,22]. They described how their group used personas for the full product cycle, including design, development, and testing. Their descriptions of persona use illustrated a true marriage of personifying details and user roles. They talked about their personas as if they were people.

> *By the time you create a persona, it's like you have given birth to them. You have created a person. It is not very hard for me to relate because I've sat with every person and talked to them. -D1*

> *As you can tell, I'm a storyteller. I like that personal side of it [the persona] because it helps me relate to him [Gerard] and then it helps me relate my design to him. -A1*

These two participants, along with select members of the development and management team of product division A, had attended CooperU and received detailed personas training. The way they discussed personas was fundamentally different from all but one of the other participants. They clearly understood the method and had derived benefit from it. However others lacking this training had very different experiences with personas. A potential confound is these participants were also persona *creators* who participated in user research. This means they already had intimate knowledge of users before the personas were created or used.

DISCUSSION

Despite personas commonly being advocated both for *design* and *communication* activities [5,6,7,14,20,21,22], we found that many design and UX practitioners in our study used them almost exclusively for communication and not design. These practitioners found personas too abstract and impersonal to use for design. Furthermore, prior work has focused on making personas *engaging*. Our study identifies problems with adding personifying attributes for design activities—such attributes may mislead and distract—arguing for a different emphasis. The exceptions were people who had participated in intensive persona training and persona creators: these practitioners used personas more heavily in design activities and had more positive attitudes toward personas. We use our results to discuss the use of personas in industrial design.

Personas are Difficult to Create and Use Well for Design

Prior work has acknowledged that persona adoption within an organization requires training [21,22] and that members of a *product team* will resist using them [21]. However, our results emphasize that personas are also difficult to use as a design tool for *experienced UCD practitioners*. In particular they identify specific areas where personas fall short as an aid for design. Despite multiple anthologies of how-to information and personas being taught in user-experience focused educational programs, effective use of personas remains elusive even for experienced practitioners.

In contrast, persona creators and those with specialized persona training had a much more positive outlook and made effective use of personas. In addition to buying into the process, these people had intimate knowledge of users before the personas were created or used, and understood the abstraction process from data to persona. These results imply that making the persona creation process transparent or even participatory to other designers may improve persona uptake for design.

The Critical Role of Exposure to Users or User Data

The practitioners in our study primarily turned to raw user study data for design. They perceived that personas do not convey the deep knowledge of users necessary for design. This result is consistent with Long [16], who found that student designers lacked trust in the data underlying personas if they did not participate in the user research. It is also consistent with Pruitt and Adlin [21], who caution that personas cannot replace other UCD methods. However, our results emphasize the critical importance of *immersion in actual user data* or, if time permits, exposure to users. User data is crucial in enabling designers to appropriately interpret personas or other abstractions.

Accuracy and Focus More Important Than Engagement

Prior literature argues that empathy [6] or internalized models of users [13] are the unique power of personas. With backing from psychological theories [13], controlled field studies [16], and professional experience [5,21], this literature argues that personifying information is critical to making personas engaging and predictive. Nielson takes this furthest by utilizing film script writing techniques in a modification to the method she called *engaging personas* [20]. She argued that designers will not use personas if the personas are not engaging enough.

While we agree it is both difficult and important to make personas as engaging as people, the personifying information used to produce such a persona is problematic. Our results indicate that a bigger adoption problem for personas among designers is that personifying information *misleads* and *distracts*. In design, details about users are seen as constraints on the design problem itself. The personifying details in a persona would wield great power if the designer viewed the persona as a real user. In this way, poorly selected personifying details unnecessarily constrain the design problem. They can also distract from the constraints that matter. These results argue for a different emphasis in personas used for design activities: they must be *accurate* reflections of a user population that *focus* on key aspects constraining the design problem.

How to Best Present Personas? Helping Personas Mesh with Design Practice

Our results confirm Pruitt and Grudin [22], who acknowledge that personas are not always perceived as believable representations of user data and that practitioners do not always understand how to use them. Their solution is to base personas on extensive user studies and to make user data available along with the personas. Other work has extended this notion by providing innovative ways to connect user study data directly to particular persona attributes [11]. This diverges from Cooper [5], who encourages creating personas based on limited information about users and aimed to fit the goals of the design team.

Our results imply that even personas not linked to extensive foundational documents can be useful communication tools. Aside from initial proof that personas are based on real data, people outside the UCD team did not seem to require continued access to user data to buy into personas.

However, designers *did* require continuous access and immersion in user data for their own design activities. Most participants seemed to prefer a less personified abstraction of user data focusing on role-based information to support their design work.

Our findings indicate that it is particularly important to consider how personas are presented to UCD practitioners so they do not clash with design practice. Constraints are critical in design. But how can we create personas that are like real people but do not introduce false constraints? Furthermore, how can personas co-exist with a continuous need for immersion in user study?

To support this style of design work, building on Pruitt and Grudin [22] and Faily and Flechais [11], we suggest a new approach in which user information is presented to designers in three easily separable layers: persona, user role, and user study data. Among these, our results show that access to user study data is critical and cannot be excluded. Linking user study data to the user role can help delineate which information is considered a critical design constraint. Designers can interpret aspects that appear in the persona and not the user role as communication aids and not constraints. Providing designers with all three layers gives them various tools for different activities. However, enacting this proposal in a practical way and evaluating its effectiveness is a topic for future research.

Personas are Incredibly Valuable for Communication with People Outside the UCD Team

Personas seemed to be most valuable as communication tools, especially with people outside the UCD team. Other product group members and stakeholders are often not oriented to user concerns. Methods like personas are incredibly valuable to communicate user needs and advocate specific designs to non-UCD audiences. This may help to explain the relative success of personas in case studies involving students and people in positions outside of UX and design [9,16,20]. However, the very experienced UCD practitioners in our study required a deeper level of familiarity with users for their design work.

A Place for Personas in Design

It is possible that personas may be more readily adopted for design activities in domains where drawing appropriate insights from user study data is complex or error prone. For example, recent work has proposed collaboration personas, which describe hypothetical groups who collaborate in particular ways [18]. Collaborative groups are sufficiently complex that existing strategies of poring over user study data may not work [12]. However, our current study implies that the model underlying a collaboration persona may be just as useful as the personifying information and should be easily separable.

Furthermore, personas may also be used as a stopgap method when user research is not possible. In such cases, the results of our study may not apply.

Study Limitations and Generalizability

Care should be taken applying our results to other organizational contexts without further studies. There are various critical factors that affect a practitioner's use and perception of personas, and hence the generalizability of this study. These include organizational culture, educational background, persona training, and experience. Our participants represent a range of educational backgrounds, persona training, and experience, improving the generalizability across these dimensions within the company studied. However, our study included only one company. This study represents a first step toward understanding how experienced UCD practitioners use and perceive personas in real industrial product design, a currently understudied topic. We hope future studies will explore this question in other organizational contexts, such as design firms and organizations with greater proportions of designers with specialized persona training.

CONCLUSION

We present the first study of how personas are perceived and used in industrial product design by experienced design and UX practitioners who have prior experience using personas. Despite personas commonly being advocated both for *design* and *communication* activities, we found that most of our participants used them almost exclusively for communication and not design. These practitioners found personas too abstract and impersonal to use for design. The exceptions were people who participated in intensive persona training and persona creators: these practitioners used personas more heavily in design activities and had more positive attitudes toward personas.

Our results have implications for the deployment and creation of personas in industrial contexts. We cannot assume that *experienced UCD practitioners* have the motivation or expertise to use personas, even in groups that actively develop and disseminate them. Not only is a significant level of persona know-how needed by the UCD practitioners, it is important that the personas not completely *replace* immersion in actual user data. Researchers have rightly noted that it is difficult to make personas as engaging as people [20]. However the bigger problem we discovered in the workplace setting studied is creating personas that do not mislead or distract, arguing for a different emphasis in persona creation in this context. To make them more usable by designers, we proposed layering user study data, user roles, and personas during the persona creation process. To generalize these findings beyond the particular organizational context studied, we encourage future work on this topic in other organizational contexts.

ACKNOWLEDGMENTS
We thank our participants for their time and thoughts. We thank Tom Moran for advice about this work.

REFERENCES
1. Blomquist, A., Arvola, M. (2002). Personas in action: Ethnography in an interaction design team. *Proc. of NordiCHI*. 197-200.
2. Bødker, S. (2000). Scenarios in user-centred design – Setting the stage for reflection and action. *Interacting with computers, 13*(1), 61-75.
3. Chang, Y., Lim, Y., Stolterman, E. Personas: From theory to practices. *Proceedings of NordiCHI*. 439-442.
4. Chapman, C.N., Milham, R. (2006). The personas' new clothes: Methodological and practical arguments against a popular method. *Proc. of HFES*. 634-636.
5. Cooper, A. (1999). *The inmates are running the asylum: Why high-tech products drive us crazy and how to restore the sanity*. Sams Publishers.
6. Cooper, A., Reimann, R. (2003). *About face 2.0: The essentials of interaction design*. Wiley Publishing.
7. Goodwin, K., Cooper, A. (2009). *Designing for the digital age: How to create human-centered products and services*. Wiley Publishing.
8. DiMicco, J., Millen, D. R., Geyer, W., Dugan, C., Brownholtz, B., and Muller, M. 2008. Motivations for social networking at work. In Proc. CSCW 2008. ACM Press.
9. Dotan, A., Maiden, N., Lichtner, V., Germanovich, L. (2009). Designing with only four people in mind? – A case study of using personas to redesign a work-integrated learning support system. *Proceedings of INTERACT*. 497-509.
10. Ehrlich, K., Shami, N.S. (2010). Microblogging inside and outside the workplace. *Proc. of ICWSM*.
11. Faily, S., Flechais, I. (2011). Persona cases: A technique for grounding personas. *Proc. of CHI*. 2267-2270.
12. Grudin, J. (1994). Groupware and social dynamics: Eight challenges for developers. Communications of the ACM, 37(1), 92-105.
13. Grudin, J. (2006). Why personas work: The psychological evidence. In J. Pruitt and T. Adlin (eds.) *The persona lifecycle: Keeping people in mind throughout the product design,* 642-664. Morgan Kaufman.
14. Grudin, J., Pruitt, J. (2002). Personas, participatory design and product development: An infrastructure for engagement. *Proc. of the Participatory Design Conference*. 144-161.
15. Judge, T., Matthews, T., Whittaker, S. (2012). Comparing collaboration and individual personas for the design and evaluation of collaboration software. *Proc. of CHI.*
16. Long, F (2009). Real or Imaginary; The effectiveness of using personas in product design. *Proc. of the Irish Ergonomics Society Annual Conference*. 1-10.
17. Matthews, T., Whittaker, S., Moran, T., Yuen, S., Judge, T. (2012). Productive Interrelationships Between Collaborative Groups Ease the Challenges of Dynamic and Multi-Teaming. *Computer Supported Co-operative Work*, doi=10.1007/s10606-011-9154-y
18. Matthews, T., Whittaker, S., Moran, T., Yuen, S. (2011). Collaboration personas: A new approach to designing workplace collaboration tools. *Proc. of CHI*. 2247-2256.
19. McGinn, J., Kotamraju, N. Data-driven persona development. *Proceedings of CHI*. 1521-1524.
20. Nielsen, L. (2004). Engaging Personas and Narrative Scenarios. Copenhagen, *Samfundslitteratur*. Ph.D. Dissertation.
21. Pruitt, J., Adlin, T. (2006). *The persona lifecycle: Keeping people in mind throughout the product design*. Morgan Kaufman.
22. Pruitt, J., Grudin, J. (2003). Personas: Practice and theory. *Proceedings of DUX.*
23. Rönkkö, K. (2005). An empirical study demonstrating how different design constraints, project organization, and contexts limited the utility of personas. *Proc. of HICSS.*
24. Rönkkö, K., Hellman, M., Kilander, B., Dittrich, Y. (2004). Personas is not applicable: local remedies interpreted in a wider context. Proc. of Participatory Design Conference. 112-120.
25. Sinha, R. (2003). Persona development for information-rich domains. *Proceedings of CHI*. 830-831.
26. Skeels, M.M., Grudin, J. (2009). When social networks cross boundaries: A case study of workplace use of Facebook and LinkedIn. *Proc. of GROUP*. 95-104.

Putting Your Best Foot Forward: Investigating Real-World Mappings for Foot-based Gestures

Jason Alexander[1], Teng Han[2], William Judd[2], Pourang Irani[3], Sriram Subramanian[2]

[1]School of Computing and Communications
Lancaster University, UK
j.alexander@lancaster.ac.uk

[2]Department of Computer Science
University of Bristol, UK
{han, sriram}@cs.bris.ac.uk

[3]Department of Computer Science
University of Manitoba, Canada
irani@cs.umanitoba.ca

ABSTRACT
Foot-based gestures have recently received attention as an alternative interaction mechanism in situations where the hands are pre-occupied or unavailable. This paper investigates suitable real-world mappings of foot gestures to invoke commands and interact with virtual workspaces. Our first study identified user preferences for mapping common mobile-device commands to gestures. We distinguish these gestures in terms of discrete and continuous command input. While discrete foot-based input has relatively few parameters to control, continuous input requires careful design considerations on how the user's input can be mapped to a control parameter (e.g. the volume knob of the media player). We investigate this issue further through three user-studies. Our results show that rate-based techniques are significantly faster, more accurate and result if far fewer target crossings compared to displacement-based interaction. We discuss these findings and identify design recommendations.

Author Keywords
Foot-based interaction; foot gestures; mobile device interaction

ACM Classification Keywords
H5.2 [Information interfaces and presentation]: User Interfaces – Input Device and Strategies.

General Terms
Human factors.

INTRODUCTION
Foot and lower-leg gestures open a broad design space to the problem of interacting with a mobile device when the users' hands are busy or otherwise unavailable. Such scenarios include instances when the user's hands are dirty (e.g. a farmer operating a device on the field, Figure 1), when the user's hands are occupied with other tasks (such as carrying shopping bags in one hand and holding a child with the other), in environments where upper-body space is limited or inappropriate for use (such as during a meeting) or when it is too cold to remove gloves (many touch-screens do not work without finger contact). In most of these scenarios the user's hands can hold the device giving them visual access to information on screen but it is difficult for the user to perform precise interactions with the touch-screen or buttons required for device operation.

The use of feet for non-mobile device interaction is already common: the pedals in a modern car are often connected to a computer rather than directly to the engine, arcade games such as *Dance Dance Revolution* (konami.com/ddr) use only the feet for interaction and home entertainment systems such as Microsoft Kinect and Nintendo Wii use foot-based interaction for gaming purposes. Passive interaction systems such as Nike+ (nikeplus.com) connect an accelerometer embedded in the shoe to a mobile device to record running or walking information.

The literature has considered various foot gestures for different contexts and one can find three emerging categories: kicking [6], foot tapping [4] and ankle rotations [22]. Prior work has focused on providing a thorough understanding of human abilities for input using foot interaction. Less attention has been paid as to how these types of interactions map to real-world commands.

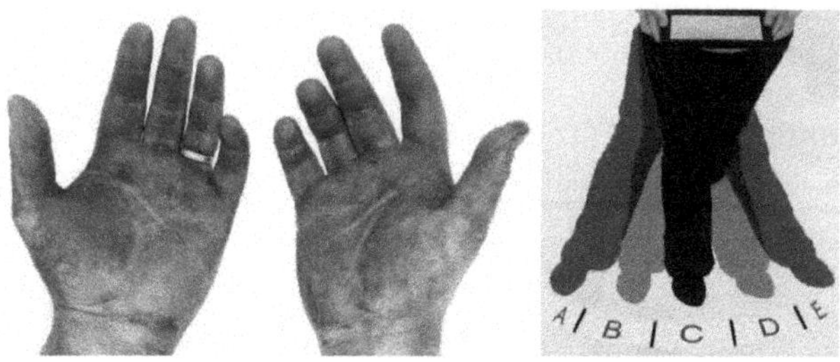

Figure 1: (left) An example scenario (from iStockphoto) where it is undesirable for the hands to touch the screen but holding the device is still possible. (right) Foot gestures as an alternative to interaction when hands cannot be used.

This work therefore aims to understand how user would expect foot gestures to be mapped to common mobile device functions and to investigate interaction parameters associated with these mappings. We achieve this through a guessability-style study, alike [24, 19], that probes users on suitable commands. This resulted into two major groupings, discrete and continuous foot mappings. Through three user-

Permission to make digital or hard copies of all or part of this work for personal or classroom use is granted without fee provided that copies are not made or distributed for profit or commercial advantage and that copies bear this notice and the full citation on the first page. To copy otherwise, or republish, to post on servers or to redistribute to lists, requires prior specific permission and/or a fee.
CHI 2012, May 5-10, 2012, Austin, TX, USA.
Copyright 2012 ACM 978-1-4503-1015-4/12/05...$10.00.

studies we further explored the design space for continuous foot gestures in the context of 2D spatial document navigation, one that requires moving around with fluidity and precision.

Our investigation results in the following contributions: (1) a novel foot-based gesture set for over thirty common mobile device commands; (2) a validation that our gesture set can be reliably detected with commonly used sensing devices; (3) a thorough examination through three user study's investigating the design factors surrounding the mapping of continuous foot interaction (in the context of spatial navigation); (4) design recommendations for implementing foot-based map navigation

RELATED WORK

To find ideal mappings for foot interaction we first examine some of the salient properties of feet motion. We then review prior foot-based interactions and group these into two camps, discrete and continuous mappings. Finally, related to this work are methods for defining a new catalog of gestures, which we briefly review.

Foot Motion

The human foot is a highly dexterous system with advanced movements using multiple joints that increase in movement complexity from the hip to the ankle. Advanced movements such as balancing on one foot to kick can be mastered as early as nine months [5]. Each leg joint provides multiple movements with varying ranges of motion. While the lower limb allows for a variety of maneuvers, studies comparing it to the arms show that it is not as precise as human hand and fingers [13]. This is particularly the case for fine and precise movements, such as moving a trackball with the foot to select on-screen targets [16]. However, studies have also shown that the foot is better suited at more coarse level movements, and can be quick in performing such actions [13]. It is for such types of coarse and less precise motions, that we investigate the use of foot gestures.

Continuous and Discrete Foot Interaction

Early work in foot-based input concentrated on the design of suitable foot controls [16] and sensor embedded shoes for entertainment purposes [14]. Recent work has extended foot input to specific application contexts, such as to retrain the lower limbs in physiotherapy [15], for ambient awareness [18], and for user identification through gait [8] and foot imprints [3]. In relation to our work, we broadly categorize existing literature into discrete and continuous foot-based input.

Discrete foot input has primarily focused on command invocation. The most common type consists of foot tapping [4] which was shown to provide sufficient input breadth to interact with mobile devices, even when the latter are buried in a user's pant pockets [22]. Crossan et al. [4] investigate menu command invocation via a single or double-foot tap. With accelerometers attached to the foot, they found foot tapping to be as accurate as visually interacting with a menu, but with a speed trade-off. Scott et al. [22] further investigate the use of foot gesturing, such as toe tapping (dorsiflexion), and heel tapping (planar flexion) for interacting with a device residing in the user's pockets. With accelerometers on the mobile device, their trained system could classify ten different foot gestures with approximately 86% accuracy. In addition to tapping, which commonly occurs when the user is stationary, harnessing discrete foot input has also seen some success when jogging. Foot-Step [21] can recognize a command based on the type of side-stepping (right or left) a user makes while jogging. Foot stepping can be captured with as high as 95% accuracy but was useful for a limited input range of up to four commands.

In contrast to discrete command invocation, continuous foot input has been explored for a number of activities such as artistic expressions [14], game playing [12] and document navigation [20]. Paelke et al [12] successfully report on user satisfaction in playing games when using a mobile phone's camera (even with limited frame rates) to detect foot movements and control a soccer ball. They apply their results to kick-up menus for selecting items on a mobile device with the foot. Similarly, Han et al. [6] propose kicking as a method for controlling objects on a mobile device, by examining the direction and speed of the foot movement. Schoning et al. [20] apply foot pressure input to navigate a spatial document as a means to complement hand interaction, such as panning faster when leaning on one side. Drawing inspiration from work on wrist control [17], Scott at al. [22] exploit continuous ankle movements such as toe and heel rotations. Similar to their results on feet tapping [22] they show that heel and toe rotations provide a reasonable range-of-motion and can be successfully detected by a device placed in a user's pocket.

The above work provides a frame of reference and motivates our systematic study on foot gestures. What is less known is what types of tasks map well to either discrete, continuous or both input types. Given the dexterity of the lower limb, we explore the use of specific real-world mappings for foot based gestures, by first developing a catalog of novel foot gestures.

Defining a Mapping of Gestures

Numerous interplaying factors influence the design of any new system of gestures. Designers have to provide optimally usable features within a fixed number of constraints, such as the type of sensing device used, limitations of human motor function, and finally the robustness and distinctiveness of the gesture set for easy and sound classification. Researchers have proposed several methods to provide rigor to the design of gestures.

The design of most gestural syntax begins with a basic knowledge of human motion capabilities, to determine what is mechanically possible. For such systems the onus is on the user to learn and familiarize themselves with the gestures. Alternatively, the user can be included in the process [23]. Participatory design incorporates users in the design process and carefully iterates on numerous proposals before settling on a given syntax. When possible, researchers can observe user interaction with physical objects, as gestures are largely based on our interaction with items around us. For example, observing user behavior in passing sheets of paper around a table [10] or rotating and dragging objects [7] has given impetus to the design of novel gestural techniques for tabletops. In the absence of an implemented system, designers can get quick feedback on their newly defined catalog using Wizard of Oz approaches.

Recently, researchers have elicited user input and defined methods for converging on a given gestural mapping through metrics such as agreement scores [24]. Such an approach, referred to as guessability, has worked successfully in defining a gestural mapping for one or two handed input on a tabletop [24] and for gestures with mobile devices [19]. The ultimate objective of democratizing the design process is to funnel the user's input into a sound set of implementable gestures. This provides some level of assurance that a good number of users may intuitively agree on the gesture set and above all, that these are physically possible. We adopt this approach in identifying a suitable mapping of real-world gestures for foot-based input, one that has not been explored in this context. Additionally, since users may provide broad mappings from task to gestures, to complete the design loop we also further refine user suggested mappings and consider how best to design for cases where the mappings may not be so straightforward.

MAPPING LOW LEVEL GESTURES TO COMMANDS

The literature provides a solid understanding of the various methods of conducting foot-based interaction. However, there is little knowledge of how these gestures may be mapped to device commands. To investigate this we did a study to understand users' perceptions on how foot gestures should be coupled to common mobile device functions.

To capture these perceptions we wished to create a user-defined gesture set for a range of mobile device interactions. To do this we conducted a guessability study, similar in style to Wobbrock et al. [24] and Ruiz et al. [19] where we asked participants to provide gesture suggestions for a variety of mobile device commands. This type of study is particularly suitable for foot-based interaction, as users currently have few, if any, preconceptions of this mapping—the gestures they provide are likely to be natural or logical mappings. The remainder of this section describes our experimental design and results.

Participants

We recruited 19 participants (seven females), within the ages range 18–25 years of age. Eight participants indicated that they use hand-based gesture devices (such as the Nintendo Wii) on a weekly basis and none regularly used any foot-based gesture systems.

Experimental Design and Methodology

The study primarily consisted of a researcher presenting participants with a range of mobile interaction scenarios (first column of Table 1) for which each participant was requested to perform a foot-based gesture that they believed was appropriate for the required situation.

During the study, participants stood upright on a marked area on the floor. They wore a Texas Instruments EZ430-Chronos Sports watch on their dominant lower leg, just above their ankle. The watch contains an accelerometer that was set to sample at 400Hz. This was used to record their movement while performing gestures, with each session also video-recorded for later verification. Although participants only wore the watch on their dominant leg, we placed no restrictions on which leg (or if they wished to use both legs) they could use for performing the gestures.

We choose a range of mobile-device interactions that we believed were representative of the commands that users issue to their mobile devices, as shown in Table 1. Many of these were also used in the study by Ruiz et al. [19]. For each of these scenarios the experimenter placed the command into context, for example, "your phone is ringing and you want to answer it. What foot gesture would you perform to answer the phone?" and the participant then performed a gesture they believed appropriate for this task. Once all gestures were performed, participants completed a questionnaire regarding their interactions.

Participants were told to consider each gesture independently and not to worry about the technical issues of gesture detection. The categories of gestures were always presented in the same order (phone control, media control, map navigation, browser navigation); the gestures within those categories were presented randomly.

Results

We observed a total of 537 commands: each of the 19 participants provided a foot gesture for the 30 commands, with 33 instances where no gesture was performed. Based on the participants' actions, we performed a series of analyses to understand participant preferences for mapping commands to gestures.

Analysis One: Participant Agreement

To begin, we analysed the agreement between participants for the gesture sets they selected using Wobbrock et al's methodology [24]. High agreement values indicate many participants selected the same mapping, low value indicates a large diversity in the selected gestures.

Overall, we found a large diversity in the gestures participants selected for each command. Across all commands there was a mean agreement value of 0.13 (s.d. 0.08), with 90% of the commands having agreement values below 0.2. The gestures for *shuffle* (shake foot, 0.46), *rotate clockwise* (trace clockwise circle, 0.29) and *rotate counter-clockwise* (rotate foot counter-clockwise, 0.29) were the only three commands where a clear preference between participants was observed.

To further understand *why* we had observed such disagreement between participants, we performed a second, deeper analysis of the suggested gestures.

Command	Generalised gesture	% part.	Assigned gesture
Phone control			
1. Answer incoming call	Tap foot	58%	Double tap
2. Ignore incoming call	Shake foot	42%	Shake foot
3. End current call	Tap foot	68%	Double tap
4. Activate voice search	Trace circle	26%	Trace circle with toe
5. Lock phone	Tap	26%	None (clash)
6. Unlock phone	Tap	26%	None (clash)
7. Home screen	Tap	42%	None (clash)
8. Next item	Rightwards movement	42%	Kick right
9. Previous item	Leftwards movement	37%	Kick left
10. Activate silent mode	Tap	32%	None (clash)
11. Activate loud mode	Tap	37%	None (clash)
12. Activate gesture recognition	Trace symbol	37%	Trace clockwise circle with foot
13. Deactivate gesture recognition	Trace symbol	37%	Trace counter-clockwise circle with foot
Media control			
14. Play/pause	Tap	68%	Double tap foot
15. Next track	Rightwards movement	74%	Kick right
16. Previous track	Leftwards movement	68%	Kick left
17. Shuffle	Shake foot	68%	Shake foot
18. Volume up	Forwards movement	47%	Kick forward
19. Volume down	Backwards movement	42%	Kick backward
Map navigation			
20. Pan left	Leftwards movement	68%	Kick left
21. Pan right	Rightwards movement	74%	Kick right
22. Pan up	Forwards movement	74%	Kick forward
23. Pan down	Backwards movement	68%	Kick backwards
24. Zoom in	Tap	32%	None
25. Zoom out	Tap	26%	None
26. Rotate left	Counter-clockwise movement	100%	Trace arc counter-clockwise
27. Rotate right	Clockwise movement	100%	Trace clockwise arc
Browser navigation			
28. Select address bar	Tap	74%	Double tap forward
29. Back	Tap to the left	47%	Double tap forward & left
30. Forward	Tap to the right	47%	Double tap forward & right

Table 1: Gesture set for common mobile device commands. "None" refers to cases without convergence and/or clashes with previously assigned gestures.

Analysis Two: Gesture Set Generalisation

In the first analysis we strictly classified gestures into sets that were *identical*—for example, gestures that used two foot taps and gestures that used three foot taps were classified as different. To better understand the disagreement between participants, we relaxed the gesture classification criteria from being strictly identical to those that are 'similar'. Similar gestures were those classed as having a common property. Examples of these properties include: the direction of leg movement and the type of movement, e.g. tapping on the ground, tapping heals together or tracing an arc. For those gestures with multiple common properties, we grouped gestures in such a way that we formed the largest groups possible. The coding of identical (analysis one) and 'similar' gestures was performed independently by two coders with discrepancies reviewed and corrected.

A much clearer pattern of gesture to command mappings emerged from the more generalised groupings. We observed several occasions where participants wanting tapping actions (e.g. answering an incoming call) or direction movements (e.g. next item) that were not immediately visible in the initial groupings. In the generalised gesture set classification, we now saw a mean agreement across all commands of 0.42 (s.d.0.2), with all commands now having agreement values above 0.2 (greater than the mean of the previous classification).

This approach improved our ability to create a coherent gesture set based on user inputs. A summary of the process for gesture selection is shown in Table 1: for each command we indicate the most common generalised gesture feature, the percentage of participants who performed a gesture with this feature and then finally the selected gesture for each command. Note that for some gestures there was still significant disagreement between participants and/or the same gesture selected for multiple commands meaning that some commands did not have a gesture assigned.

We were able to define gestures for 23 of the 30 commands in the command set. Several specific gestures appear multiple times in the defined gesture set (defined as a clash). However, contextually, the gestures are unique: gestures from one set will not be used at the same time in another, for example, media control gestures will not be required while navigating maps.

Discussion

Gesture Classification

Our findings suggest that many of the gestures are logical mappings from commands participants are already familiar with. For example, tapping to select or a rightward movement to move to the 'next' item, seem to be direct translations of what occurs when using touch on mobile devices. Interestingly, we find a consistent left-to-right pattern for distinguishing commands along the time dimension. Finally, for browser control, such as moving forward or backward, users apply spatial positioning to their taps. These results overall reveal intuitive mappings that seem sound and logical.

Gesture Set Customisability

In generating the mappings for common phone commands to foot-based gestures, our initial analysis resulted in a large diversity in participants' gesture selections. By performing a generalised set analysis we could better represent the gestures of a greater number of participants. This required generalisation and is perhaps representative of the need for gestures to be flexible and/or customisable. If a user finds a particular gesture uncomfortable or the mapping unnatural the option should exist for reconfiguration.

Classification Lessons

While eliciting user input has given us a useful gesture set, participants may not always be expected to create the full catalogue of gestures on their own. A number of commands clashed in terms of duplicate syntax, leading to ambiguity in the final gesture set. Additionally, relaxing constraints for classifying the gestures led us to converge more quickly on certain types of gestures. Such generalised classification provides a good starting point for gesture implementation. However, all gestures still require refinement and the ability for users to customise exact input parameters.

VALIDATION OF GESTURE RECOGNITION

The previous section detailed a user-defined gesture set for foot-based control of common mobile device commands. Since users were free to derive any set of gestures, one important design aspect is to ensure that the gestures can be easily recognized and distinguished by an electronic recogniser. To validate this intention, we used an implementation of the Protractor3D gesture recogniser [9] to classify foot gestures detected using an accelerometer.

Equipment Setup

The goal of this validatory study is to determine whether our set of gestures can be accurately detected and classified. For this reason, we asked participants to wear an accelerometer strapped to their leg, combined with the Protractor3D recognizer. While this setup would be impractical for real-world use, we were interested in determining *if* the gestures can be reliably classified, not whether our method is the technologically best implementation. We chose the Protractor3D recognizer as previous studies validating its use showed high recognition rates [9]. Participants wore the same Chronos Sports watch as described earlier. The data from the accelerometer was fed in real time, into the Protractor3D recognizer.

Procedure

Five participants (1 female) with an average age of 22.2 years participated in this validation study. The gestures were presented to users in the sub-categories introduced earlier (phone control, media control, map navigation and browser navigation), using the gestures selected in Table 1. However, each unique gesture was only presented once—identical gestures were not presented multiple times. For each sub-category, participants were first asked to perform each of the gestures five times to train the recogniser. Once the training was complete, gestures from the sub-category were performed, five times, until all gestures were covered.

The gestures were presented to the users in a pseudo-wizard-of-oz style. For example, when the user was required to answer the phone, they were verbally told the context, reminded of the gesture, and were then asked to complete the gesture when they heard a phone ringing—the experimenter played a ringing sound from a PC and manually stopped the sound once the gesture was complete.

Results

The five participants completed all of the tasks for all gestures giving a total of $5 \times 13 = 65$ training gestures and 65 test gestures. The recognition accuracy for each of the gestures is shown in Figure 2. Gestures had a mean overall recognition accuracy of 87%. Recognition of all gestures, except 'shake foot' was successfully with rates above 80%. The 'shake foot' gesture fared poorly during recognition. This is likely due to the ambiguity of the gesture: participants did not perform the same number of left and right shakes each time meaning the classifier mis-interpreted the user's intentions.

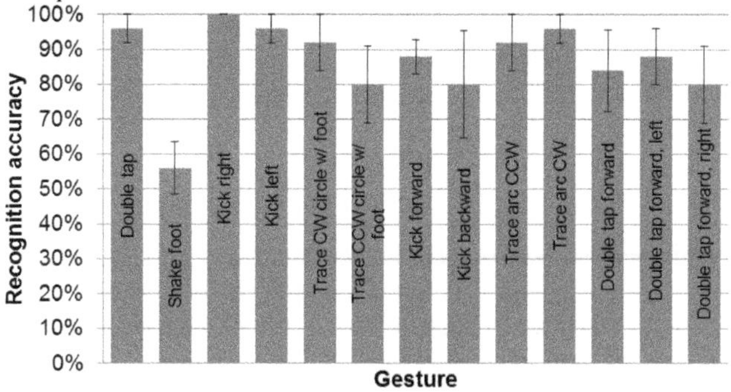

Figure 2: Gesture recognition accuracy

Discussion: Continuous vs. Discrete Actions

This study has shown that the selected gesture set is detectable and individual gestures are distinguishable. These gestures must now be mapped to mobile device functions.

The mapping of *discrete* gestures—single actions often triggering a mode switch, such as answering the phone—are straight-forward to implement. However, those gestures that map to *continuous* actions such as panning a map or adjusting the volume of the audio require further design thought due to the increased number of parameters involved. For example, how should a forward kick map to the size of an upward pan? Should the kick velocity map to distance travelled? Should the distance the foot has moved map to the distance the map moves? Or should the kick initiate a rate-based scrolling action?

To answer these questions we conducted three additional studies that examined the mapping of foot-based gestures to continuous actions.

MAP NAVIGATION: CONTINUOUS FOOT INTERACTION

Many mobile device applications require continuous interaction, such as scanning music playlists, scrolling an address book or navigating a map. Having derived a mapping of foot-based gestures to commands and validated that these gestures can be detected, we wished to examine the issue of mapping foot gestures to continuous interaction. The over-arching goal of these studies is to answer the question: how should a kick action control continuous movement?

To answer this question we implemented four kick-to-movement mappings: one distance-based, two velocity-based and one combined distance and velocity mapping (flick). We then tested the viability of these techniques in three controlled evaluations. The first measures the suitability of these techniques for acquiring targets in all directions around a compass. The second looks at their suitability for acquiring targets at different distances. While the third combines these two parameters to understand the complete context of continuous navigation.

In these studies we apply our techniques to spatial document navigation; however, we envisage our results will also generalize to other continuous interaction techniques.

Gesture Mapping Techniques

We implemented four mappings of kick gestures to panning actions. These mappings are motivated by techniques found in the literature and commonly employed in desktop or tabletop environments. These are described here.

- **Displacement based (D):** The distance the user kicks from the vertical position directly maps to the distance the map pans. Returning the leg to the vertical position does *not* result in the map panning in the opposite direction, instead the user must move their leg in the opposite direction past the vertical position to achieve reverse panning. A horizontal position delineates movements in left and right directions.
- **Rate-based hold (RH):** The distance the user moves their leg away from the vertical position maps to panning velocity. The user must hold their leg in that position to maintain the panning velocity—moving their leg back towards a vertical position reduces the velocity accordingly.
- **Rate-based continuous (RC):** Users are likely to easily tire from holding their leg in the air. In this technique, the user kicks forward to create a velocity mapping—the furthest distance the kick reaches is used as input to the panning velocity. The user can then return their leg to the vertical position. Kicking again changes the pan velocity, tapping their foot on the ground stops the panning motion.
- **Flick (F):** Numerous variations of flick gestures exist, with Aliakseyeu et al. [6] finding Compound-Multi-Flick (CMF) generally out-performed and was subjectively preferred over other implementations. We implemented a version of CMF for kick gestures. For a forward kick, this worked as follows: when the user's leg is moving forward, CMF is in displacement mode. When the user's leg halts or begins to return to the upright position, CMF enters flick mode, with the initial flick velocity derived from the velocity of the forward displacement. A friction element slows the flick, which can also be terminated by the user tapping their foot on the ground.

We fine-tuned the parameters for each of the above interaction techniques through informal pilot studies involving four participants. Participants conducted a series of kicking tasks and provided feedback on the mapping of kicks to parameters for each of the interactions. Using a series of iterations we selected parameters that provided the most 'expected' behavior for each technique.

Pilot Study: Moving the Content or Moving the View?

With all continuous interaction systems, there is the question of whether a navigation action should move the content or move the view of the content (which equate to movements in opposite directions).

To provide an informal answer to this question we implemented two versions of each of the four mapping techniques: one which had the kick actions tied to the content and one which had the kick actions tied to the view.

We gave 10 participants both versions of each mapping technique with a single target location north of the starting position. Participants tried each mapping. Once they had used both mappings of each technique, they were asked to subjectively indicate which they preferred.

Results

Participants overwhelmingly preferred kicks to move the content. This meant that a kick forward should move the map content forward, closer to a southwards target. All participants preferred this mapping for the RH technique, and all but one preferred this mapping for the displacement and flick techniques. Six of the ten participants preferred a kick to move the content for the rate-based continuous technique. In all of our subsequent implementations the kick action is tied to the map—i.e. kicking forward will move the *map* forward, not the view window.

Experiment 1: Kicking Around the Compass

The aim of this experiment is to examine each of the kick interaction techniques when participants have to reach targets located in different compass directions.

Experimental Design and Procedure

We created a 4×8 factor within subjects experimental design with factors *Gesture Mapping* and *Direction*. We used the four gesture mappings (D, RH, RC, and F) described in the previous section. We tested movement in the eight compass directions: north, north-east, east, south-east, south, south-west, west and north-west.

The study had four sections, one for each of the Gesture Mapping techniques. These techniques were provided in a random order to each participant, with all tasks using that technique completed before moving to the next.

The experimental software automatically recorded all aspects of the interaction required to reach a target goal on a map: the task completion time, the number of kicks and the total distance and direction of all movements. We used a spatial workspace, a map, to provide users with a familiar context in which we could test continuous foot gestures.

Participants got two minutes of freeform practice navigation with the techniques followed by four practice trials. Each trial began by the participant pressing a button on the side of the screen and was completed when the target was placed inside the green rectangle (task details are explained further below). If selecting a particular target was difficult the experimenter terminated that task and the study continued to the next trial. Participants were free to rest at any point when not performing a task. For each factor the participant did three trials resulting in a total of 96 trials per participant (3 repetitions ×4 mappings×8 techniques).

Participants and Physical Setup

We recruited 10 volunteer participants (two female), with an age range of 18–27 years old. All of these participants were right handed; six of whom had experience with on-screen touch gestures.

During the study, participants stood upright on a marked position and held a 7" screen (resolution 640×480px) at waist level, as shown in Figure 1, right. This displayed the experimental interface, as described below.

The participants' foot-based gestures were captured using an XBox Kinect camera mounted 0.75m from the ground and 3m from the participant. This camera detected participants' kick gestures accurately in three dimensions, a 'kick' began when the foot was lifted from the ground. We used the skeleton tracking algorithm provided by the OpenNI (openni.org) libraries and we implemented functions to translate these gestures into the interaction techniques described earlier.

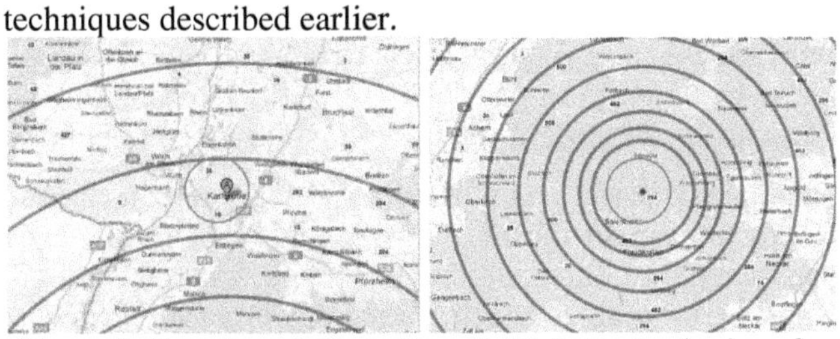

Figure 3: Experimental interface: (left) At the beginning of a task (right) At the end of a task.

Experimental Interface and Tasks

This experiment tests the capabilities of each continuous foot mapping and *not* the users' spatial abilities. For this reason, all tasks began at a random (on land) location. Tasks did not necessarily end at a specific city or location, but were determined by the required direction of travel (in this experiment, all targets were equal distances from the starting location). Each task began with the starting position centered on-screen (Figure 3, left). The target was marked with a black cirlce and had concentric circles extending throughout the whole map (total size 2560 x 1920 px, Figure 3, right) to indicate the required navigation direction. Participants were required to place the target in a rectangle with a green outline (size 128 × 90px) occupying the middle fifth of the screen in order to complete the task. The system automatically detected when the map was stationary and the target was inside the required circle for one second.

Results

With 10 participants and 96 trials per participant we collected 960 data points. All tasks were successfully completed. There was a significant difference in task completion time between techniques: *RH* was the fastest (mean time 3.6sec, s.d. 0.6sec) and *RC* the slowest (mean time 5.0sec, s.d. 1.1sec), $F_{3,27} = 81.2$, $p < 0.01$. A post-hoc Tukey test ($\alpha = 0.05$) gives an HSD of 0.72 sec indicating the pairs (D, RH), (RH, RC) and (RC, F) are different. These overall results are shown in Figure 4. Visual inspection of the number of target crossings (Figure 4, left) indicates that slower techniques suffered from target crossing (overshooting the target). Interestingly, RC suffered badly from this issue, while RH did not. With RH, users are already poised to drop their foot, while RC users must recognize the end-point, raise and lower their foot to stop, or perform another kick to reduce scrolling speed.

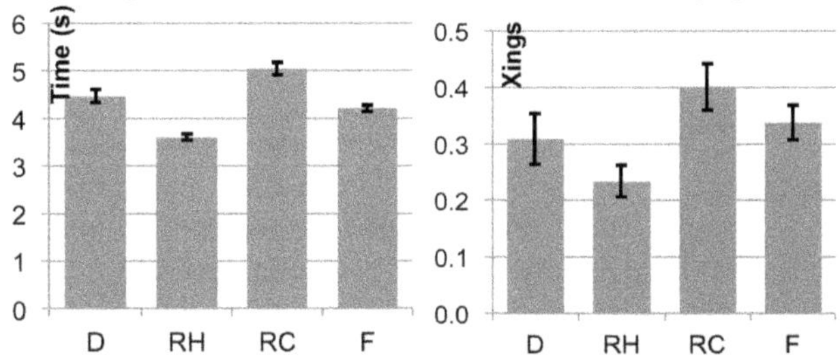

Figure 4: (left) Target acquisition times (sec) for different directions (right) Mean num. of crossings for target selection.

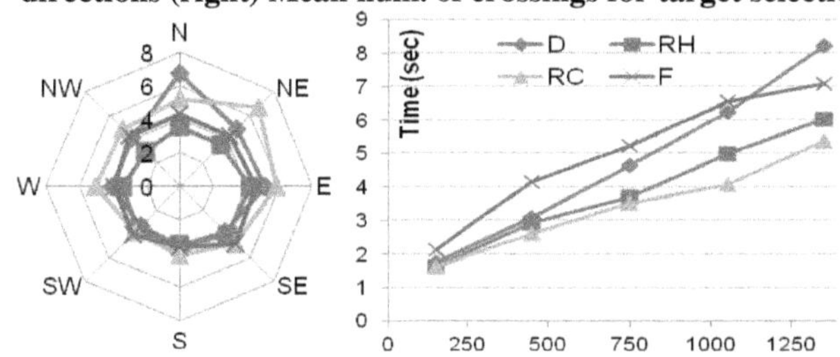

Figure 5: (left) Target acquisition times (sec) for different directions (right) Target acquisition times for different target distances (horizontal axis, px). Figures use the same legend.

However, participants took different times to complete target acquisition in the eight different directions. This is summarized in Figure 5. Participants took the longest to reach targets in the East (5.0 sec) and North-East (5.0 sec) directions, and were the quickest in the South (3.7 sec) and South-West (3.7 sec) directions. There was a significant difference in the target acquisition times of different directions ($F_{7,63} = 33.6$, $p < 0.001$). A post-hoc Tukey test ($\alpha = 0.05$) gives an HSD of 0.82 sec indicating the pairs (N, S), (N, SW), (N, NW), (NE, S), (NE, SW), (E, S), (E, SW), (E, NW) are different.

Overall, participants were more efficient at reaching targets that require kicks in the forward direction (recall in these studies a kick moves the content, equating to targets in the southern half of the compass). This is likely due to participants finding forward kicks more natural—e.g., kicking a ball is often performed with a forward kick.

Experiment 2: Kicking into the Distance

Experiment 1 examined how each of the mapping techniques fared when kicking in various directions. In this experiment we were interested in evaluating the effect of target distance on each of the four mapping techniques. This experiment was conducted using the same experimental setup as outline in Experiment 1, with the differences noted below.

This study used a 4×5 factor within subjects design, with factors *Gesture Mapping* (D, RH, RC and F) and *Distance*. We selected five distances from the starting position: 150px, 450px, 750px, 1050px and 1350px. These positions represented a range of close and distant targets for a typical map navigation task.

All kicks were made in the same direction—towards a southern target (a forward kick) as this performed the best in experiment one. We ignored all non-north/south direction in participants' kicks. Each participant repeated the kick gestures for each technique/distance combination five times.

Participants

Ten volunteers (two female) aged between 23 and 26 participated in this study. All had previous experience with hand-based gestural interaction (such as using the Nintendo Wii) and two had previous foot-based gestural experience.

Results

We collected data on a total of 10 participants × 4 techniques × 5 distances × 5 repetitions = 1000 target acquisitions. All tasks were successfully completed.

Overall, RC was the fastest technique (mean time 3.4 sec, s.d. 1.3sec) and Flick the slowest (mean 5.0sec, s.d. 1.8sec). There was a significant difference between overall mean acquisition times ($F_{3,27} = 153.2$, $p < 0.01$); a post-hoc Tukey test gave an HSD of 0.53 ($\alpha = 0.05$) indicated the pairs (D, RH), (D, RC), (RH, F), (RC, F) were significantly different.

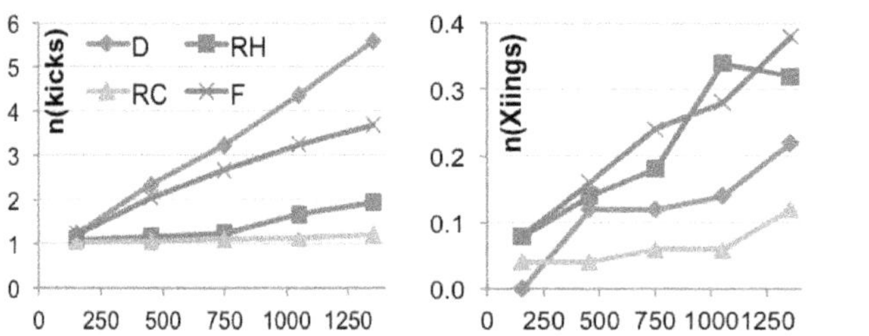

Figure 6: Mean number of kicks and target crossings for various target distances (on the horizontal axis in px). Both figures use the same legend.

Figure 5 shows the expected result of target acquisition time increasing with target distance. There was also a significant difference in target acquisition times for factor *Distance*, with closer targets always quicker than those further away ($F_{4,36} = 602.7$, $p < 0.01$). A post-hoc Tukey test gives an HSD of 0.63 ($\alpha = 0.05$) indicating that all distance pairs were significantly different.

To better understand the acquisition time differences between the four techniques we analysed the number of kicks users performed to reach the required target (see Figure 6, left). The RC technique rarely required more than a single kick to achieve the target, while the Displacment technique required (an almost) linearly increasing number of kicks as the distance increases. Further analysis also reveals that RC had very few overruns of the targets, meaning time was not wasted 'hunting' for the target (Figure 6, right).

Summary

The primary finding from this study is that the rate-based continuous technique is most efficient at acquiring targets at a range of distances from the starting position. The rate-based hold technique also performed well for close targets.

Experiment 3: Putting it all Together

The pilot study and the two quantitative experiments have provided us with insights into various aspects of how kick gestures should be mapped to continuous interaction. In this final study, we wished to compare all aspects of the two best performing systems so far: rate-based continuous and rate-based hold. We also wished to gather subjective feedback on these two systems.

This experiment was conducted in the same manner as experiment 1 and 2, with the differences in experimental method listed here. This study used a 2×3×8 factor within subjects design, with factors *Interaction technique* (rate-based hold, rate-based continuous), *Distance* (150px, 750px and 1350px) and *Direction* (eight standard compass points). Each participant repeated the kick gestures for each {Technique, Distance, Direction} combination, three times.

Participants performed all gestures with one technique before moving to the next (order counter-balanced). The presentation of direction/distance pairs was randomised. After performing all kick gestures with one technique, participants completed a subjective evaluation. Overall preferences were gathered at the end of the evaluation.

Results

We collected a total of 1440 data points (10 participants × 2 techniques × 3 distances × 8 directions × 3 repetitions). All tasks were successfully completed. Overall, we found no significant difference in the task completion times between the two techniques. RH acquisitions took on average 3.8 sec (s.d. 1.7sec) and RC 3.7sec (s.d. 1.8sec). As observed in the previous two studies, both target distance ($p < 0.01$, $F_{2,18} = 4079.3$) and direction ($p < 0.01$, $F_{7,63} = 18.8$) yielded significantly different task completion times.

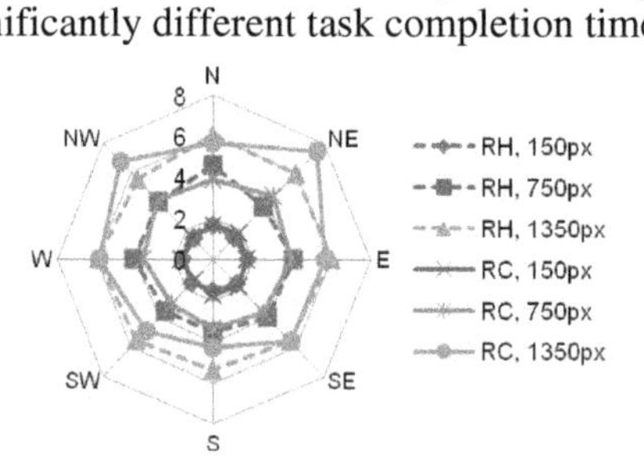

Figure 7: Mean target acquisition time (sec) for the two rate-based techniques

While both techniques had similar average task completion times, they showed weaknesses in different areas (Figure 7).

RH (dotted lines in Figure 7) is more consistent around all directions of the compass. Conversely, RC is faster in achieving southern targets but is generally slower for northern targets (especially those in the NW and NE directions). This skewedness correlates with observations during this and previous studies—participants find it harder to kick backwards than forward, with RC especially suffering. An analysis of the number of kicks and number of overshoots for the NW/N/NE and SW/S/SE sectors showed that both techniques had higher errors and overshoots when heading towards the northern regions.

Overall, seven of the ten participants preferred RC, two preferred RH and one was undecided. After using each system participants completed a NASA-TLX workload assessment form indicating their subjective impressions on 5-point Likert scales. Only the 'physical' category differed significantly between the two techniques: RH had a median ranking of 4.5 (indicating a high physical workload) and RC 3.5 (χ^2=6.4, $p < 0.05$). This feedback correlates with the requirement for the user to hold their leg in their air when navigation is taking place in the RH condition. User feedback indicated this 'mid-air' holding was tiring.

Discussion

The last experiment assessed the effectiveness of the two rate-based techniques that performed best in comparison to the displacement and flick techniques for distance and direction control. The results overall indicate preference and efficient interaction for rate-based continuous (RC), even though this required participants to move their leg and keep it in the air until they reached their target destination. This result was not echoed for all directions, particularly those requiring the users to kick backwards. As expected time to target grew with distance, but was still within reasonable limits (i.e. the linear growth not exponential).

DISCUSSION AND FUTURE WORK

Continuous vs. Discrete

The guessability study revealed a clear demarcation of gestures that were either discrete or continuous. Discrete gestures were mapped to specific tasks, such as locking or unlocking a mobile phone. Continuous gestures were mapped to tasks with a spatial component, such as moving in one direction in an information space. Such a distinction allows designers to separate their mappings into very clear camps. However, this also requires further design consideration for the continuous mapping, as we performed with the three studies outlined above.

We found good recognition rates of the user suggested gestures using a simple yet efficient recognizer. This suggests that while users were given full freedom for generating best mappings, there should not be issues implementing detection algorithms.

Our work did not fully investigate compound gestures, where a discrete gesture precedes or follows a continuous gesture or where a command is made up from multiple discrete or multiple continuous gestures. Investigating these combinations would prove interesting future work.

Rate-based Continuous Interaction

Our results suggest that for mapping continuous foot gestures to tasks, a rate-based approach works best. This technique results in far fewer kicks than the equivalent displacement based techniques. Users felt most in control, despite having to keep their feet in the air. This finding matches that for other finger-based interactions [1] where rate-based navigation is more efficient in a number of tasks. Finding that this also applies to continuous foot movement reaffirms the strength of rate-based techniques and their transferability to other forms of interaction.

Visual Feedback

In our experiments we assumed the users had visual information available to them at all times through the display of the phone. This we believe is a reasonable assumption. For example, when the user's hands are dirty or wet they can still hold the device on its rim without damaging or dirtying it. In these cases the user would rather use foot gestures to interact with the device than risk touching the screen with their wet or dirty hands.

There are scenarios where the phone is in the user's pocket and interaction is still required (e.g. when in a crowded metro with your hands holding the railing). Combing continuous foot interactions with other output modalities would provide another avenue for future work.

Design Implications

The results of the studies conducted in this paper allow us to draw a number of implications for the design of foot-based gestural interaction.

Context of use can ensure small gesture sets: small gesture sets are easily remembered by users and can be encouraged in foot-based interaction by using the device's context to eliminate ambiguity. The types of gestures should not be restricted as 'off the shelf' recognizers perform well.

Use Rate-Based Continuous for continuous interaction: this technique was subjectively preferred due to the less physical effort even though it suffered from greater acquisition times in the southern direction. Physical effort has the potential to alienate large groups of users, so should be minimized wherever possible.

Avoid backwards selection: experiments 1 and 3 showed that users struggle more with backwards kicks. Where possible, these should be avoided.

Use direction over distance: many designs require users to select from multiple choices. When using foot-based interaction, it is desirable to have these choices made around a compass point rather than by asking users to select items at a distance.

Further Considerations

This work focused on the selection of command-to-gesture mappings and defining parameters for continuous interaction. Real-world deployment of a foot-based gesture system would first require consideration of *context of use* and *social acceptability*. Context of use refers to the user's posture and movement during interaction. For experimental accuracy and reproducibility we only considered stationary users. A real world deployment would need to employ activity recognition algorithms to differentiate walking from phone-interaction gestures. Consideration must also be given to the social acceptability of kick-based gestures in various contexts. It is likely these would be unacceptable in some environments and so alternatives must be provided.

CONCLUSION

This paper examined the mapping of foot-based gestures to mobile device commands and deeply probed continuous interaction gestures. A guessability study derived a mapping for common commands that could be divided into continuous and discrete interaction. We validated that these gestures could be recognized. Through a series of three user studies we examined the most appropriate mechanism to support continuous interaction. Our results showed that users are faster, more accurate and prefer rate-based techniques over displacement based techniques. We believe these results provide a solid foundation for future investigations into the design of foot-gesture interaction techniques for novel mobile applications.

ACKNOWLEDGEMENTS

This work was funded jointly by EPSRC (EP/G058334/1) and MobileVCE (www.mobilevce.com) as part of the User Interactions for Breakthrough Services research program.

REFERENCES

1. Aliakseyeu, D., Irani, P., Lucero, A., Subramanian, S. Multi-flick: An Evaluation of Flick-based Scrolling Techniques for Pen Interfaces. *CHI '08*, 1689-1698.
2. Angel O. K., Chan, A., Ng., A., Luk, B. L. A Preliminary Analysis of Movement Times and Subjective Evaluations for a Visually-Controlled Foot-Tapping Task on Touch Pad Device, *IMECS '10*.
3. Augsten, T., Kaefer, K., Meusel, R., Fetzer, C., Kanitz, D., Stoff., T., Becker, T., Holz, C. and Baudisch, P. Multitoe: High-Precision Interaction with Back-Projected Floors Based on High-Resolution Multi-Touch Input. *UIST '10*, 209-218.
4. Crossan, A., S. Brewster, and A. Ng. Foot Tapping for Mobile Interaction. *BCS HCI '10*.
5. Grandjean, E. (1969) Fitting the task to the man: an ergonomic approach. Taylor and Francis, pp. 372.
6. Han, T., Alexander, J., Karnik, A., Irani, P., Subramanian, S. Kick: Investigating The Use Of Kick Gestures For Mobile Interactions. *MobileHCI '11*.
7. Hancock, M.S., Vernier, F., Wigdor, D., Carpendale, S., Chen, S. Rotation and Translation Mechanisms for Tabletop Interaction. *Tabletop '06*, 79-88.
8. Iso, T., and Yamazaki, K. Gait analyzer based on a cellphone with a single three-axis accelerometer. *MobileHCI '06*, 141-144.
9. Kratz, S. and M. Rohs. Protractor3D: A Closed-form Solution to Rotation-invariant 3D Gestures. *IUI '11*.
10. Liu, J., Pinelle, D., Gutwin, C., Subramanian, S. Improving digital handoff in shared tabletop workspaces. *Tabletop '08*, 9-16.
11. Paelke, V., Reimann, C., Stichling, D. Foot-based mobile interaction with games. *ACE '04*, 321-324.
12. Paelke, V., Reimann, C., Stichling, D. Kick-up menus. *CHI EA '04*, 1552.
13. Pakkanen, T., Raisamo, R. Appropriateness of foot interaction for non-accurate spatial tasks. *CHI EA '04*, 1123–1126.
14. Paradiso, J. A., Hsiao, K. Y., Benbasat, A. Interfacing to the foot: apparatus and applications. *CHI EA '00*, 175-176.
15. Paradiso J.A., et al. Interactive therapy with instrumented footwear. *CHI EA '04*, 1341–1343.
16. Pearson, G., Weiser, M. Exploratory Evaluations of Two Versions of a Foot-operated Cursor-positioning Device in a Target Selection Task, *SIGCHI Bulletin 1988*, Vol. 19, Issue 3, 70-75.
17. Rahman, M., Gustafson, S., Irani, P. and Subramanian, S. Tilt techniques: investigating the dexterity of wrist-based input. *CHI '09*, 1943-1952.
18. Rovers, A.F. and Van Essen, H.A. Guidelines for haptic interpersonal communication applications: an exploration of foot interaction styles. *Virtual Reality* 9, 2-3 (2006), 177-191.
19. Ruiz, J., Li, Y., Lank, E. User-defined motion gestures for mobile interaction. *CHI '11*, 197-206.
20. Schöning, J., Daiber, F., Kruger, A., Rohs, M. Using hands and feet to navigate and manipulate spatial data. *CHI EA* '04, 4663-4668.
21. Tetsuya, Y., Tsukamoto, M., Yoshihisa, T. Foot-Step Input Method for Operation Information Devices While Jogging. *SAINT '08*, 173-176.
22. Scott, J., Dearman, D., Truong, K. Sensing Foot Gestures from the Pocket. *UIST '10*, 199-208.
23. Winograd, T, Bringing Design to Software. Addison-Wesley, pp. 234.
24. Wobbrock, J.O., Morris, M.R., Wilson, A.D. User-Defined Gestures for Surface Computing. *CHI '09*, 1083-1092.

ShoeSense: A New Perspective on Hand Gestures and Wearable Applications

Gilles Bailly[1] Jörg Müller[1] Michael Rohs[2] Daniel Wigdor[3] Sven Kratz[2]

[1]Quality and Usability Lab, Telekom Innovation Laboratories, TU Berlin, Germany
[2]University of Munich, Germany
[3]Department of Computer Science, University of Toronto, Canada
[1]{firstname.lastname}@telekom.de [2]{firstname.lastname}@ifi.lmu.de [3]dwigdor@dgp.toronto.edu

ABSTRACT

When the user is engaged with a real-world task it can be inappropriate or difficult to use a smartphone. To address this concern, we developed *ShoeSense*, a wearable system consisting in part of a shoe-mounted depth sensor pointing upward at the wearer. ShoeSense recognizes relaxed and discreet as well as large and demonstrative hand gestures. In particular, we designed three gesture sets (*Triangle*, *Radial*, and *Finger-Count*) for this setup, which can be performed without visual attention. The advantages of ShoeSense are illustrated in five scenarios: (1) quickly performing frequent operations without reaching for the phone, (2) discreetly performing operations without disturbing others, (3) enhancing operations on mobile devices, (4) supporting accessibility, and (5) artistic performances. We present a proof-of-concept, wearable implementation based on a depth camera and report on a lab study comparing social acceptability, physical and mental demand, and user preference. A second study demonstrates a 94-99% recognition rate of our recognizers.

Author Keywords: Wearable; gestures; gesture set; shoe; sensor placement; mobile.

ACM Classification Keywords: H.5.2 [Information Interfaces And Presentation]: User Interfaces - Interaction styles

INTRODUCTION

Using a mobile device when the user is engaged with a real-world task is sometimes inappropriate (meeting, family dinner, church), difficult (walking, running), dangerous (driving) or virtually impossible (the blind) [1]. Wearable technologies offer the promise of an 'always available' computer, but the requirement of a physical mount point for sensors can present challenges for acceptability [11,17]. To address this concern, we developed *ShoeSense*. ShoeSense is a wearable system consisting in part of a shoe-mounted depth sensor pointing upward at the wearer (Figure 1). On-shoe sensor placement has been demonstrated in commercial applications [3], and has the advantage of not being visually apparent, while at the same time affording a view suitable for the detection of hand and arm gestures.

To demonstrate the efficacy of on-shoe placement, we present three novel sets of hand-gestures (*Triangle*, *Radial*, and *Finger-Count*) designed for this setup. These gestures can be performed without visual attention. The characteristics of ShoeSense are illustrated in five scenarios: ShoeSense makes it possible (1) to quickly perform frequent operations without reaching for a handheld (such as answering the phone, reading emails or changing songs); (2) to perform simple operations without disturbing others (such as routing incoming calls to voicemail, activating silence mode, and sending predefined messages); (3) to alleviate some of the limitations of mobile devices (such as the *fat finger problem* [47]); (4) to provide support for accessibility such as home automation; and finally (5) to do artistic performances.

In addition to enhancing social acceptability, ShoeSense introduces a novel and unique perspective (from the shoe) making it possible to recognize discreet and relaxed as well as large and demonstrative gestures without the need for cumbersome hats or body-mounted sensors. The setup provides a large operating volume for performing gestures and does not constrain body movement. In addition to making wearable sensors more socially acceptable, on-shoe mounting offers several benefits. (1) Shoes are 'always available', reducing the need for artificial wardrobe additions such as a pendant or cap. (2) Reduced risk of accidental occlusion by other clothes. (3) Improved image stability. (4)

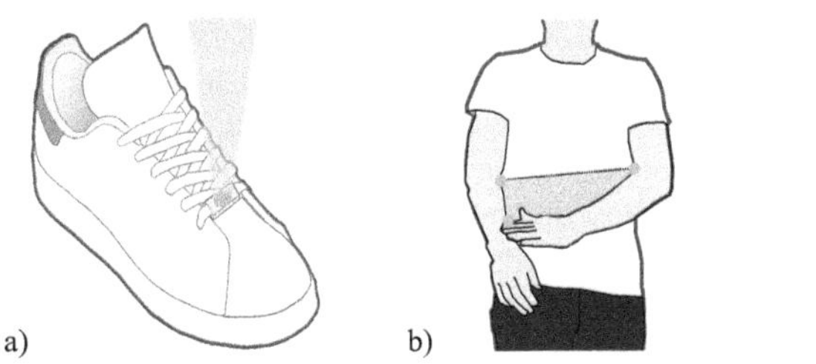
a) b)

Figure 1:a) ShoeSense perspective. b) Triangle gesture.

Permission to make digital or hard copies of all or part of this work for personal or classroom use is granted without fee provided that copies are not made or distributed for profit or commercial advantage and that copies bear this notice and the full citation on the first page. To copy otherwise, or republish, to post on servers or to redistribute to lists, requires prior specific permission and/or a fee.
CHI'12, May 5–10, 2012, Austin, Texas, USA.
Copyright 2012 ACM 978-1-4503-1015-4/12/05...$10.00.

Reduced risk of damage. (5) The weight, rigidity, and large volume of shoes better affords storage of electronics. Finally, (6) the shoe can be used for harvesting power [29].

In this paper, we present and analyze ShoeSense, including three gesture sets designed for simple eyes-free execution and detection by a shoe-mounted sensor. We describe a proof-of-concept prototype based on a depth-camera to recognize these gestures, present its limitations and demonstrate different classes of applications. We then address the social acceptability of ShoeSense gestures by reporting the results of a lab study comparing the three gesture sets. Finally, we report the results of an experiment validating our recognizer's suitability for a shoe-mounted depth camera.

The primary contributions of this paper are:

- A novel wearable platform enabling a large variety of gesture-based applications.
- A new perspective for eyes-free gestural interaction enabling discreet and relaxed as well as large and demonstrative gestures.
- Three novel gesture sets, designed for a shoe-mounted camera, and experimentally validated as socially acceptable, easy to perform, and robustly detectable.

RELATED WORK

In creating ShoeSense, we sought to build upon the extensive related work in the area of wearable computing. We review two sub-areas of work in that space: the use of body-worn cameras for gaining context, and the use of cameras to enable gestural interaction. We then discuss works, which have inspired the design of our gestures, as well as projects, which have utilized foot-based interaction.

Body-Worn Cameras for Contextual Information

Wearable visual computing uses body-mounted cameras to capture contextual information. In this regard, [36] reports several studies proposing different locations to attach standard video cameras to the wearer's clothing. Locating the camera near the eyes, for example on a hat (WUW [37] or [16,45]), yields images that closely match the user's perspective. Other work has shown merit in placing the camera on users' shoulders [35], on their chest (StartleCam [21], SixthSense [37] or Gesture Pendant [50]), and in multiple other locations on the body [46]. While these placements offer several advantages, each requires the wearer to add elements to their wardrobe or to don technology in visually apparent areas of the body. Our goal in designing ShoeSense was to reduce the social burden of wearable computing by placing the sensors in a visually unobtrusive location, and in an article of clothing typically worn throughout the day. Earlier work has proposed mounting a camera on the user's shoe [15]. Unlike ShoeSense, however, this camera was aimed towards the ground and used to track user activities rather than to enable gestural input.

Gestural Interaction with Body-Mounted Cameras

Several projects have proposed body-mounted cameras to support gestural interactions. SixthSense [37] can project digital information atop physical objects, which can be adjusted using hand gestures captured by a body-worn camera. Gesture Pendant [50], HoverFlow [28] and Imaginary Interfaces [18] also use a chest-mounted camera for capturing hand gestures. All these techniques force the user to perform gestures with the hands at the height of the chest, which can be tiring and draws attention from others. Further, chest-mounting electronics have been shown to introduce serious social issues, suggesting the need for a more discreet placement [11,17].

Starner et al. demonstrated the use of a downward cap-mounted camera for recognizing sign language [49]. WristCam [52] and PinchWatch [33] sense subtle finger gestures with a camera mounted on the wrist [52] or the chest [33], but these cannot capture large and demonstrative gestures. Finally, Ni et al. propose to capture very small gestures in the context of 'disappearing' mobile devices thanks to a one-pixel camera [39]. While relevant, our goal in this work is to minimize the disruption of the introduction of a body-worn camera for 'always available' gesture detection – thus, these projects serve as inspiration for interaction, but not for the design of our hardware and gesture sets which its unique perspective required.

Gesture Design

In designing the gesture language for ShoeSense, we considered several projects that demonstrated advantages of gestural interaction [7, 9, 30, 53]. For instance, Baudel et al. [9] proposed a set of free-hand gestures in Charade for controlling a slide show. Marking menus [30] used an efficient set of 8 radial gestures with a pen or mouse. Finger-Count menus allow the user to perform two-handed and multi-finger interaction on a multi-touch surface [7]. Pinch gestures (for instance in [53]), with one or two hands, have been shown to be easy to perform and to recognize.

In each case, successful gestures have been designed based on consideration of the limitations of sensing, context of use, and use case. Another approach consists of allowing study participants to define the gesture language [44, 54]. While informative, this approach is less suitable for ShoeSense, where gestures must be carefully designed to ensure robust detection given the placement of the camera. Throughout this paper, we use the *Wu* formulation of the phases of a gesture: *registration, continuation*, and *termination* [55].

While several projects have included the use of feet for interaction ([3, 5, 24, 40]), our work uses the foot as a mounting point for a sensor of hand and arm-based gestures. Even though ShoeSense could be enhanced in the future to also detect interactions similar to those described in previous work, our focus is on leveraging the advantages of body-mounted gesture systems while reducing the social burden inherent in wearing digital technology on the body.

Building on this earlier work, we now describe ShoeSense, and the gestures we designed, which take advantage of its unique perspective.

SHOESENSE

ShoeSense consists of an upward-oriented sensor mounted on a shoe. We first discuss the advantages locating the sensor on the shoe. We then describe its I/O capabilities. Finally, we describe the implementation of our device and software.

Shoe-Worn Device

As discussed above, the primary advantage of using shoes as a mounting point is that this setup can enhance the social acceptability of the technology. In addition, mounting a body-worn camera on the shoe offers practical advantages:

Wardrobe integration. Shoes are typically worn continuously throughout the day [23], ensuring that the camera is commonly available. This alleviates the need to artificially add elements to the wardrobe, such as a cap, pendant, or other enclosure.

Reduced occlusion. Sensors worn on the torso face the possibility of occlusion by jackets and other occasional-use clothing. In contrast, a mounted shoe camera has a reliable, unobstructed view of the area in front of the body.

Image stability. Because the foot is planted on the ground, even while walking, this location affords high physical stability of the camera.

Low maintenance. In comparison to t-shirts, pants, or even jackets, shoes are rarely laundered. This is an advantage for ShoeSense as washing machines are a harsh environment for wearable devices [24].

Comfort. The weight of visual wearable devices, even if very light, can be cumbersome for users when they are worn on the top of the body. Further, the added volume and rigidity of shoes provides an opportunity to safely place wearable computing equipment [3].

Discreetness. ShoeSense does not disrupt unrestricted and natural views of the face, which is an important criterion in social interaction [35] and a major difference with devices such as those using head-mounted cameras [35].

Energy. Power distribution is a major challenge of wearable devices [29, 31, 48] as there is a trade-off between capacity and weight/size of batteries. Previous studies [31, 48] have shown that the foot is an excellent location for generating and storing human power when the user is walking [29].

ShoeSense shares some problems of visual wearable devices concerning operation in harsh outdoor conditions. For instance, rain or extremes in lighting can degrade sensor performance. Mud or dust can also affect ShoeSense, as the sensor is located close to the ground. Moreover, the field of view of the camera can be partially occluded by loose clothes or objects (carrying a bag). Additionally, the relative placement of hands in the camera's field of view is more variable than with other arrangements. Finally, the integration in all of the user's shoes could be prohibitive (though hardware constantly gets cheaper). Therefore, in a practical design we envision a small and easily-pluggable device, which can quickly be attached to different shoes.

Gestural Input

ShoeSense is a gesture-based system. The location of the sensor on the shoe offers a novel perspective for detecting and recognizing gestures. A pilot study confirmed that an RGB camera with a traditional field-of view (47°-53°) was sufficient to capture arms' locations within the entirety of their dynamic reach envelope [22]. This is not the case for a camera on the chest, given its close proximity to the arms and hands. ShoeSense thus provides a large detection volume enabling a wide variety of gestures to be observed.

Compared to traditional chest cameras, ShoeSense does not force users to make superfluous arm movements to reach the field of view of the camera, which can be exhausting and attention-grabbing [43]. ShoeSense gestures are more relaxed as they can be performed close to the resting position of the hands, making them both more comfortable and discreet. The large viewing area of a shoe-mounted camera can also enable large and demonstrative gestures, such as may be useful to dancers, stage actors, or musical performers [13]. However, in this article we mainly focus on relaxed and discreet gestures for everyday use. After repeated experimentation, we developed three sets of gestures: *Triangle*, *3D Radial* and *Finger-Count*. Triangle and Finger-Count are examples of two-handed gestures, while 3D Radial is a one-handed gesture.

Triangle Gestures

Triangle gestures are a set of two-armed poses formed by creating a triangle with the arms and torso. Triangle gestures are *registered* by placing a hand atop the opposing arm (Figure 2). In pilot testing, we found that users and system could robustly distinguish between 5 *registration* poses (Figure 2). Once initiated, each of the gestures may be *continued* by modifying the shape of the triangle, by sliding the hand along the arm, or by rotating the 'triangle' in space. The gesture is *terminated* by removing the hand.

The triangle poses are static making it possible to recognize them within only one frame. Moreover, they provide an absolute reference: users can associate specific commands to specific locations on their arm through proprioception. Finally, the inclusion of a continuation phase means the triangle gesture can be used to control a parameter. This continuation can be mapped absolutely, or relatively to allow fine-grained precision with clutching.

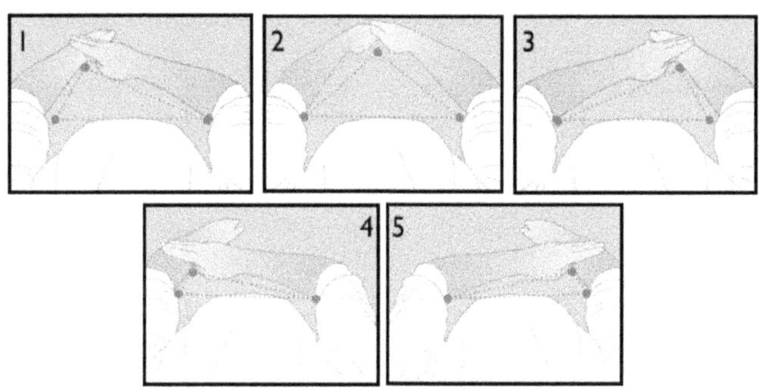

Figure 2: Triangle gesture set. Apex of each triangle is the wrists (1,3), hands (2), and arms (4,5) respectively.

Pinch Registration Pose

A pinch registration pose consists of forming a "hole" in the hand by touching the thumb with the index finger [53]. It is an excellent registration pose for gestural interaction as it is easy to perform, easy to recognize, different from daily life gestures, and does not require a timeout [33, 53]. Pinch can be combined with triangle gestures. For instance, when the user makes a triangle gesture, an audio indication of its function could be given, and the function is only executed once a pinch is performed. The pinch also acts as the registration pose for our remaining 2 gesture sets.

3D Radial Menus

3D radial menus are an extension of 2D radial menus, formed by extrapolating the options of the 2D menu into 3D space [30]. While 2D radial menus can contain up to 8 commands, a 3D radial menu can contain up to 26. To make these gestures unambiguous, the menu is *registered* by a pinch (Figure 3). A command is then executed by *continuing* the gesture in the direction of the desired menu item, and *terminated* by opening the pinch. We argue that this extension has the promise to maintain the properties of marking menus (simple, scale-independent and fast [6, 30]) without degrading memorization [6]. Because 26 options may be sufficient to remove the need for nesting, it is also possible to select and to control a command in the same gesture, as with control menus [42], enabling easy chunking of gestural actions into complex commands [12].

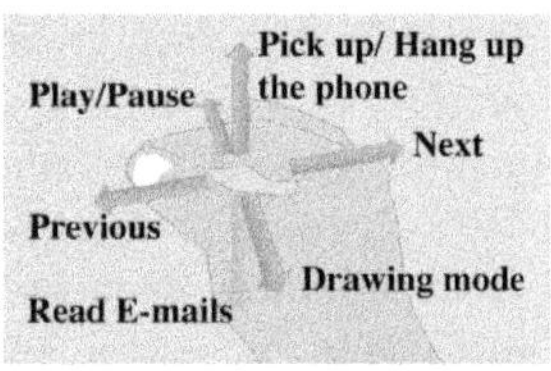

Figure 3: 3D radial gesture set (Left, Right, Front, Back, Up, Down) mapped to frequent actions on a smart phone.

Finger-Count gestures

These static gestures are inspired by [7, 10] and consist in expressing a unary number by extending that number of fingers (**Figure 4**). Considering only the number of fingers rather than their identity makes the technique easier to understand and gives additional physical flexibility [7, 10]. To avoid false positives, we again use the pinch registration pose. Finger-Count gestures are performed on the dominant hand and are interpreted only if a simultaneous pinch is detected on the other hand, or if an appropriate 3D radial menu item is currently held in the other hand. Finger-count can also be used as a modifier for radial menu selections, similar to [32], or for triangle gestures. For instance, a left arm triangle gesture with 5 extended fingers could mean: "Call" (left arm gesture) the contact id "5" (Finger-Count).

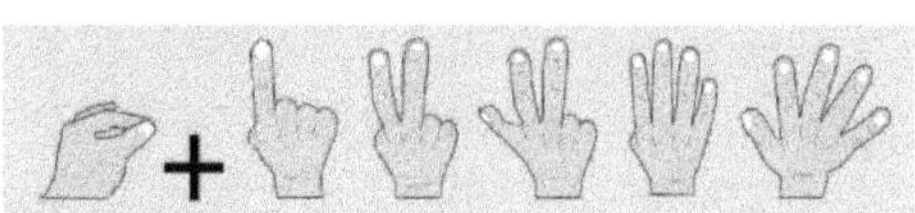

Figure 4: Finger-Count gesture set. Pinch on one hand (registration) and extended fingers on the other hand.

In summary, we propose three gesture sets (*Triangle*, *3D Radial*, *Finger-Count*) as gestural input for ShoeSense and several possible gesture phrases (Triangle + Pinch; Triangle + Finger-Count; Radial + Finger-Count) to select discreet and continuous input. We now consider possible output modalities of ShoeSense.

Output Modalities

Although our proof of concept device is large, we envision that further engineering could enable manufacturing of a device small enough to be smoothly integrated into a shoe, making it difficult to have a traditional visual interface. Interaction with a miniaturized device is then limited by the degree to which user interface affordances can be presented and feedback can be provided. Similar to Ni and Baudisch, we discuss three elementary output modalities attached to the device itself [39]. We then propose two different annexing modalities with higher bandwidth.

Limits of Shoeborne Indicators

As our goal is to locate hardware within the shoe, a speaker is not appropriate as it is far from the ears and has limited privacy. In contrast, tactile (e.g., vibrators) or visual feedback (e.g., LED lights) are suitable for the class of applications where the user is already familiar with the available actions. Tactile is more private (and the foot is fairly sensitive), while visual feedback is less obtrusive. However, each forces users to learn a new language and is low bandwidth. For this reason, shoeborne indicators are only used for confirming that a gesture has been recognized or indicating the current status (i.e. on/off; in progress, etc.).

Opportunistic Audio Channel Annexing

Annexing is the process of serendipitously expanding the I/O capabilities of a system by using nearby I/O components [41]. While loudspeakers are inappropriate, headphone audio can provide a useful feedback channel. This would require an additional device, but would provide greater bandwidth and be easy to interpret. For instance, the system can play the name of the menu items during exploratory gestures. It can also be an implicit part of the application response (e.g., in MP3 players there is no need for a "volume up" indicator, it just gets louder). Commercial applications have already demonstrated wireless connections between shoe-mounted sensors and iPod devices [1]. Annexing of that iPod device's audio channel, where appropriate, could enable this feedback mechanism.

Opportunistic Display Annexing

To enable visual output beyond simple LED indicators, a ShoeSense device could annex mobile device displays, or larger displays in the nearby environment. ShoeSense could then be thought of as a peripheral input device for applications running on those other devices. Users perform mid-air gestures and receive visual feedback on the display. While audio feedback is serial, visual feedback provides random access and a more direct physical mapping. A limitation of annexing a handheld screen is that holding the device limits the users' possible input gestures.

Implementation

To develop a proof-of-concept implementation of ShoeSense (Figure 5), we used a BeagleBoard, a small (82.5x82.5mm), single-board computer with a 1 GHz ARM Cortex-A8 processor and 512 MB onboard memory. We used a depth camera (Microsoft Kinect) as a sensor to enable recognition of hand gestures. The distance between the foot and resting position of the hand (~90cm) is ideal for capturing high quality images given the stock Kinect's lensing. When running on the BeagleBoard, our prototype processes depth images at a rate of about 5 frames per second. This is sufficient to demonstrate the basic interaction techniques during mobile use of the system.

Software

ShoeSense runs Linux, uses OpenNI for capturing depth images and OpenCV for vision. It leverages the relatively fixed distance of the hands/arms from the shoe for simple background subtraction by thresholding the depth image (we use a depth range of 90cm ± 20cm).

Triangle gestures

Triangle gestures are detected if a large inner contour (green color) is found in the image pixels (Figure 6-a). They are then recognized by identifying the left (p_l), right (p_r), and topmost points (p_i) of the inner contour as well as the topmost point (p_o) of the outer contour (Figure 6-a). The orientation and the norm of the vectors [Pi ; Po] and [Pr ; Pi] are sufficient to distinguish the 5 triangle gestures. Finally, we use the ratio of $||PiPl|| \ / \ ||PoPl||$ to precisely control a value. While the algorithm is quite simple, it is robust as each component is easily detected, with a low error rate.

Pinch gestures and Radial strokes

We recognize pinch gestures by using the algorithm proposed in [53]. It consists of detecting an inner contour (red) in the arm contour. A radial gesture is interpreted by tracking the location of the pinch over time (Figure 6-b).

Finger-Count gestures

As described above, we limit finger-count detection to frames, which also contain a pinch registration pose as shown Figure 6-c. Several methods have been proposed to count fingers [8, 14, 51]. From pilot studies, we chose the k-curvature approach [51] with k=5 because it is simple to implement, does not require RGB images and provides good results even if the hand if slightly tilted.

While relatively simple, this combination of gestural primitives enables a significant set of possible applications.

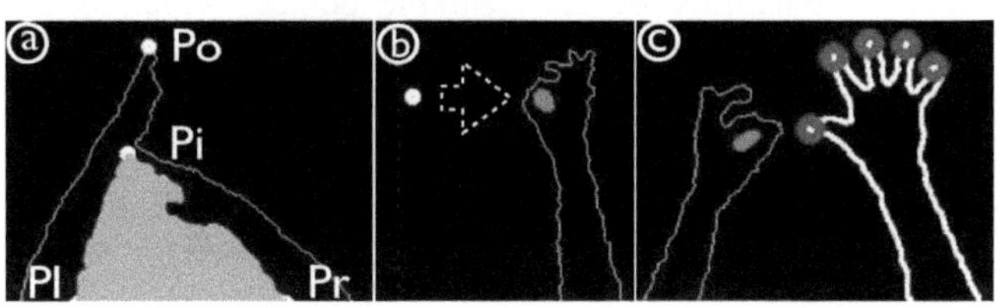

Figure 6: (a) A user performing a hand-to-left-wrist triangle; (b) a 3D radial gesture; (c) a 5 finger-count gesture.

APPLICATIONS

Various interaction scenarios give rise to several classes of interaction. We now review these classes, along with several envisioned sample applications. We also sketch several interaction techniques for mobile devices (Figure 7).

Frequent & Favorite Operations

ShoeSense users can quickly execute favorite/frequent operations such as "answer a phone call", "previous/next track", "volume up/down." Indeed, ShoeSense does not require reaching for the phone in the pocket or bag which requires time and can lead for instance to missed phone calls [4]; to initiate an interaction users simply perform a gesture.

Favorite or frequent operations with mobile devices generally require limited feedback and can involve MP3 player (play/pause, previous/next, repeat one/all, etc.), phone (pick up/hang up a phone call, call favorite contacts, etc.); messages (reading your most recent e-mails or tweets, etc.) or monitoring operations (heart rate, blood pressure, etc.). While several gesture-command mappings are possible, we propose to use Finger-Count to select among function types at a root menu level (e.g., *MP3*, *Phone*, *Messages*, *Monitoring*), which contains 5 or fewer categories. A Radial gesture would then select commands within the selected category (necessary as any given category can contain a larger number of commands). Moreover, as Finger-Count requires a pinch in one hand, it makes it possible to perform these two gestures simultaneously, increasing efficiency and avoiding some possible confusions of mode switching. Finally, Triangle gestures could then be reserved for universal parameters, such as volume, brightness, etc.

Inexact and Inattentive Operations

Hudson et al. describe inexact and inattentive interaction as simple and common operations with a mobile device that can represent a disruption form another activity involving people (meeting, family dinner, etc.) or from the primary task of the user (for example walking while carrying a bag) [26]. ShoeSense has several advantages for controlling functions that fall into one of the following categories.

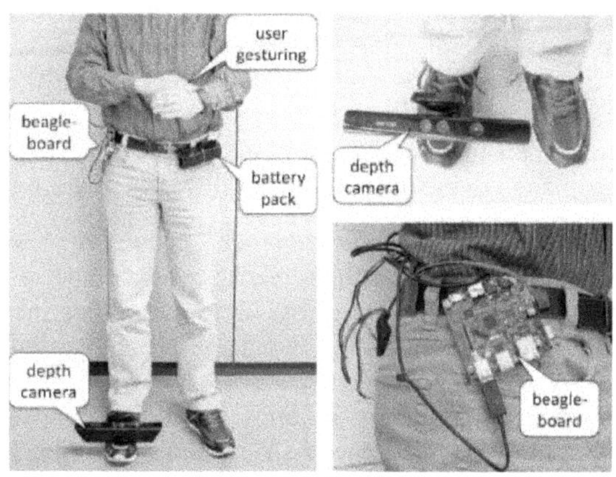

Figure 5. The ShoeSense prototype. The system is wholly contained as a wearable computer.

Fast interaction. As mentioned previously, users do not need to grasp a device. So they can, for instance, quickly silence a ringing cell phone minimizing the time of the disturbance.

Acquisition-free input. The user's hands do not need to hold a special device for interaction [33]. Not only can the user easily return to his or her primary task, but also the hands become free more quickly to react to critical situations.

Eyes-free interaction. Our gesture sets are based on gross motor control and contain gestures that do not require visual assistance for performing them [7, 26, 30]. Users can thus stay concentrated on their primary task. From a technical perspective, this property is useful in wearable scenarios, as screens generally consume a lot of energy.

Operations that would benefit from eyes-free input include "ignore interruptions" or "activate silence mode." A limited number of special operations can be mapped to eyes-free menus. This might include informing favorite recipients (wife, friends) or participants of the next meeting (thus no need to enter the name) of a potential delay.

Interaction Techniques for Mobile Devices

Interaction with mobile devices entails several limitations due to the small size of the screen and the "fat finger problem" [47]. Annexing ShoeSense for off-screen input [41] can enhance the capabilities of the mobile device by separating the input and the output, and also by providing more degrees of freedom.

Separating Input & Output. Inspired by [19, 20], ShoeSense can serve as an input device for a wristwatch (pointing task, command selection and widget control) given a wireless connection between the devices. For instance, as soon as a pinch gesture is detected, the user can control a cursor on the watch by moving the pinched hand in the air. The C/D gain can be adjusted with vertical movement to enhance precision or speed (similar to Figure 7-b). This off-screen interaction technique avoids occlusion on the watch screen. ShoeSense can also be used to select up to 5 different commands (Figure 7-d). Finally, users can control graphical widgets, for instance a slider on a wristwatch (similar to Figure 7-a) by touching the device (left-wrist triangle gesture detection) and moving the finger along the arm (modifying the shape of the triangle). These three interaction techniques are pairwise compatible with one another thanks to the design of the 3 different gesture sets.

Increased Degrees of Freedom. By enabling users to perform mid-air input gestures, ShoeSense provides a novel modality for interacting with mobile devices. For instance, it can help to perform large distance map navigation on a mobile phone. The touch-sensitive surface allows for limited panning of the map until the finger reaches the screen edge. Then, instead of performing inefficient clutching [25], users can continue to pan "in the air" with large horizontal movements and zoom in/out with vertical movements. ShoeSense is useful for navigating in a 3D

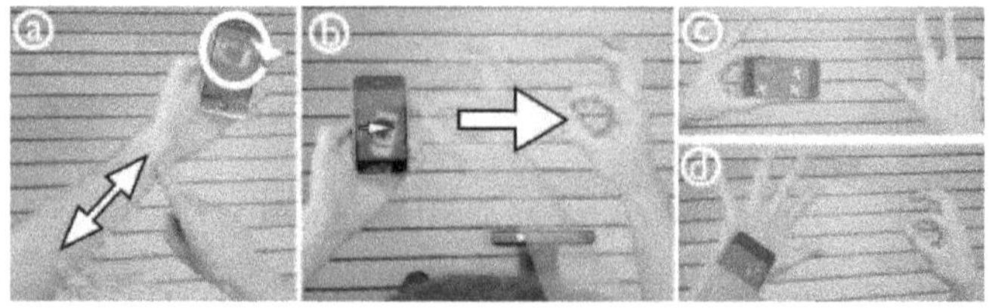

Figure 7: 3D control on mobile devices. (a) Moving the finger along the arm (modifying the shape of the *triangle*) rotates the 3D object. (b) x, y and z translation with *3D radial* gestures. (c) The user chooses a predefined control with a *finger-count* gesture (3 fingers on the right hand + a pinch formed by the left hand and the device). (d) *Finger-count* gestures to select commands on a watch (simulated by an iPhone on the wrist).

scene. For instance, (x,y,z)-translation of the camera can be performed with 3D radial gestures (Figure 7-b) and rotation with Triangle gestures (Figure 7-a).

Dynamic C/D Gain Control. As previously described, the vertical height of the pinch gesture could adjust the C/D gain of cursor input to a watch device. Conversely, the gain of touch input can be modulated by the surface area of a triangle gesture: To enhance precision while touching their phone, users simply place their other hand on the wrist.

Support for Accessibility

Several projects have been proposed to support accessibility with visual wearable devices [10, 16, 50]. Based on this literature, we imagine the same possible applications for ShoeSense. For instance, ShoeSense could help elderly or disabled people (blind or partially sighted people) to be independent in their home or to be medically monitored [50]. In a multimodal approach, gestures could then be used to delimit the beginning and end of a speech command [10]. Finally, ShoeSense could recognize IR LEDs or 2D tags located on the ceiling, when combined with an IR or RGB camera [16]. Users can then be guided via audio-feedback.

Demonstrative Scenarios

While we focused on applications requiring relaxed and discreet gestures, it is also possible to imagine applications with large and demonstrative gestures such as motion capture (similar to [46]), gesture analysis (golf, baseball), or performance. For instance, air guitar performances [24] or dancing performance (inspired by Adidas Megalizer [1]).

SOCIAL IMPLICATIONS OF SHOESENSE

We distinguish demonstrative scenarios and everyday usage. In the second case, it is essential to consider the social acceptability of the wearable device, which is the primary motivation for the placement of the sensor on the shoe. Commercial products have demonstrated the social acceptability of an appropriately sized, shoe-worn sensing device [3]. Of potential additional concern are the privacy implications of an always-on camera pointing upward from a user's shoe.

The objective of ShoeSense is not to store images (as in [16, 21, 37, 45]), but rather to recognize hand gestures. As such, our prototype uses a depth camera, which has a far lower resolution than an RGB camera. Moreover, ShoeSense also limits the amplitude to a depth interval of about 40cm, making it virtually impossible to take inappropriate photos to identify people, or the environment. In a commercial realization we envision the complete image acquisition and recognition process to be encapsulated in a single-chip device that only emits the recognition result, but not the raw images. In this way, ShoeSense does not pose a serious privacy risk. Despite this technical possibility, concerns about privacy might still exist. Mann argues that fixed cameras (like surveillance cameras) are generally less acceptable than wearable cameras because users know they are not in private when somebody else is present [34]. The presence of the sensor could be made visually apparent with suitable design elements on the shoe. One way to achieve this is to use a bright LED, which people easily interpret "as an icon for an active camera" [34]. The size of the sensor also has an impact on social acceptance.

USER STUDY: SOCIAL ISSUES & USABILITY

While reducing the obtrusiveness of the sensor may improve social acceptance, there remains the possibility that gesturing in-air is a social concern. We thus designed an experiment intended to elicit participants' reactions to this modality. In addition, we wished to evaluate our gesture sets for their mental and physical demand, as well as user preference. We sought absolute measures of *social acceptability*, *mental* and *physical exertion*. These measurements came in the form of a questionnaire administered after participants had performed all of the gestures. We further recorded users performing these gestures so that we could have a baseline for the development and refinement of our recognizer system.

Questionnaire. The questionnaire (and the design of the experiment) is inspired by Rico et al. [43]. The questionnaire is comprised of the same questions meant to elicit social acceptability. Rico et al. distinguish social acceptability by two factors: *audience* (alone, partner, colleague, friend, family, stranger) and *location* (home, street, driving, passenger, pub, workspace). We omitted driving, because two of our gesture sets require two-handed interaction. Finally, instead of asking participants if "they would be willing to perform the gesture", we used a 10-point Likert scale to refine the results.

To measure physical demand, we used the Annex C of the ISO-9241-9 [27] providing rating scales for finger, wrist, arm, and shoulder effort. To measure mental demand, participants were asked to answer the gestural interaction questions of the NASA-TLX [38]. We also used a 10-point rating scale for these questions to increase their fidelity. Finally, we asked users to order gesture sets by preference.

Gesture. We compared triangle, finger-count and radial gestures. The set of radial menu gestures was limited to 5, in order to match the number of triangle and finger-count gestures, and to avoid biasing *effort* scores. No baseline gesture set could completely cover the features of the proposed approach (always available, hands-free operation, no need to hold a phone, discreet). As we tried to build on proven components such as the common pinch and finger-count gestures, this provides a sort of baseline.

Procedure. To evaluate the social acceptability of the three gesture sets, the participants watched a video showing a standing actor performing each gesture in front of a white wall [43]. Then, participants were asked to perform the gesture 3 times. The experimenter observed to ensure that the gesture was performed correctly. After the completion of all gestures, the questionnaire was administered.

Participants. 12 participants (7 female), aged from 21-37 (m=28, sd=5.3), were recruited from the local community. Except two users having already played with the Xbox Kinect, none had prior experience with in-air gestural interfaces. Each received compensation of €10.

Apparatus. A Kinect connecting to a PC was mounted onto the shoe of each participant. Instead of using it to recognize gestures, it was used to capture depth videos used later to develop a recognizer for these "naturally" performed gestures. Indeed, using a specific recognizer could have had a strong impact on how users perform gestures and so also on their ratings of those gestures on each of our scales. For this reason, this study is independent of a recognizer. The follow-up study focuses on accuracy after having improved our recognizer according to our observations.

Setting. Our prototype was too large to avoid confusing "social comfort" when measured in public. For this reason, we decided to perform a lab study, focusing on the social acceptability of gestures sets rather than the prototype. A field study should be run in order to evaluate the social acceptability of gestures and the envisioned system in public.

Design. We used a within-participant design: the order of the gesture sets was counter-balanced across participants using a Latin-square. The design can be summarized as:

12 participants x 3 gesture sets x 5 gestures per set x

3 repetitions per gesture = 540 total gestures performed.

Results

We used the Kruskal-Wallis (KW) test to analyze the non-parametric data collected for *social acceptability*.

Context & gesture set. The mean acceptance ratings across all contexts is above 5 for each gesture set (m_{Radial}=7.8; $m_{Finger\text{-}Count}$=7.2; $m_{Triangle}$=5.9). The Kruskal-Wallis (KW) test reveals a significant effect (χ^2=15.3, $p<0.01$) on social acceptability for gesture sets. Pair-wise comparisons show that Radial is significantly more acceptable than Triangle. Radial and Finger-Count gestures are rated as likely to be used (>5) in all contexts. Triangle is likely to be used in *home*, *pub* and *workspace*. However, a deeper analysis reveals that 50% (6/12) of participants would be willing to perform Triangle gestures in *street* or *transport*. These results are illustrated in **Figure 8**.

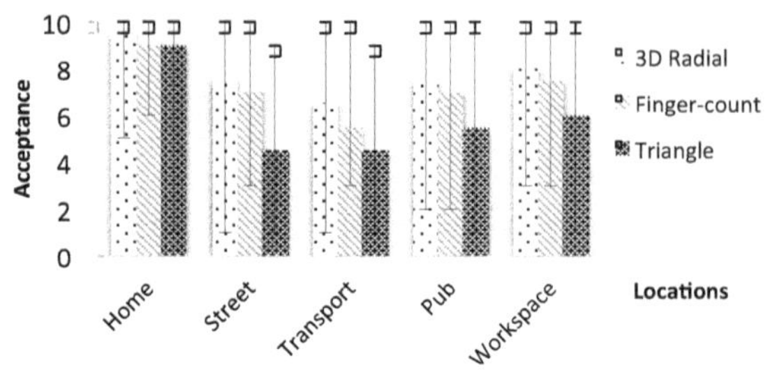

Figure 8: Social acceptability by location and gesture set (10-point scale, 10 is the best). 95% confidence interval marked.

Audience and social acceptability. The mean *social acceptability* score across participants indicates all gesture sets are acceptable in front of all audiences (mean >6) except Triangle gestures, in front of strangers (7 of 12 rated < 5). These results are illustrated Figure 9.

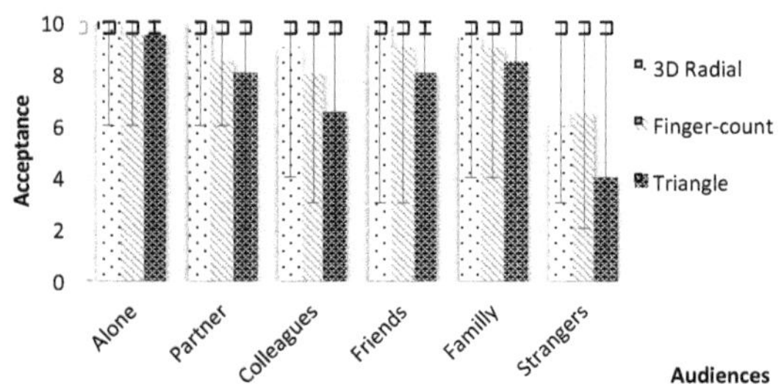

Figure 9: Social acceptability by audience and gesture set (10-point scale, 10 is the best). 95% confidence interval marked.

It is interesting to note that the standard deviation of the acceptability ratings of the triangle gestures is much larger than for 3D radial gestures or Finger-Count. This is true for both location (location: sd_{Radial}=2.1; $sd_{Finger\text{-}count}$=1.9; $sd_{triangle}$=2.8) and audience (audience: sd_{Radial}=1.6; $sd_{Finger\text{-}Count}$=1.6; $sd_{Triangle}$=2.6) and indicates that there was less consensus among participants about the acceptability of the triangle gestures.

	Finger	Wrist	Arm	Shoulder
Radial	2.5	2.0	3.0	2.5
Finger-Count	3.0	1.5	2.5	2.5
Triangle	1.0	1.0	3.0	3.5

Table 1:Physical demand (10-point scale, 1 is the best).

Physical demand. Physical demand was rated for each gesture set on various body parts using Annex C of the ISO-9241-9 [27]. The average physical demand is low for each gesture set (m_{Radial}=2.5; $m_{Finger\text{-}Count}$=2.4; $m_{Triangle}$=2.1). Details for fingers, wrist, arm and shoulder are reported in Table 1. The KW test (χ^2 = 9.3, $p < 0.01$) followed by a pairwise comparison shows that Finger-Count (3) is more exhausting for fingers than Triangle (1). Three of 12 participants indicated that extending 3 fingers was a little bit more "tricky". All other ratings are not significantly different from one another at the p=.05 level.

Mental demand. Mental demand was measured using the NASA-TLX [38] methodology. The average mental demand is also quite low for each gesture set (m_{Radial}=2.0; $m_{Finger\text{-}Count}$=4.5; $m_{Triangle}$=3.0). KW test reveals no significant difference of mental demand across gesture sets. 7 participants indicated that two-handed gestures (Finger-Count and Triangle) require more coordination. Two participants also indicated that extending 3 fingers requires more mental demand than other Finger-Count postures.

Preference. We asked users to rank-order gesture sets by preference. 6 participants chose Radial as their favorite gesture set and 6 chose Triangle, 0 chose Finger-Count. 4 participants chose Radial as the least favorite gesture set, 3 chose Triangle and 5 chose Finger-Count.

Discussion

Social acceptability. The mean value of *social acceptability* for 3D Radial and Finger-Count is above 7 for all *locations* (except public transport) and *audiences* (except strangers). Triangle has a low acceptance rate (≤6) for the *locations street, public transport,* and for the *audience strangers*. The high standard deviation of social acceptance for Triangle is interesting. On the one hand, 2 participants rated Triangle very highly for most *audiences* and *locations*, sometimes higher than gestures of other types, and gave feedback that Triangle gestures are "very natural", "it is like if I look at my watch" (adjusting a watch forms a triangle gesture). On the other hand, 2 participants found these gestures highly unacceptable: "they require too much space for performing gestures especially in the subway". We observed in the videos that some participants performed Triangle gestures too high (arms were almost horizontal), requiring more space and more effort than needed. They probably under-estimated the capacity of the system to capture casual Triangle gestures. This could partially explain this rating. More generally, we were surprised about the differences between participants in rating social acceptability and the reasons given. For instance, 4 participants found it acceptable (≥ 8) to perform gestures in the workplace because "I know my colleagues" while 2 participants found them not acceptable (≤ 3) because "workplace is serious."

Physical and mental demand. The three gesture sets do not require high physical (≤ 3) or mental (< 5) demand. Only Finger-Count, and especially the 3-finger posture, is a little bit more mentally and physically demanding. Finally, these results are more promising than might be expected for Triangle gestures (effort: 2.1; mental demand: 3.0) as they involved arm movements.

Preference. Participants do not share the same opinion about gestures but they seem to agree that Finger-Count is less preferable than Radial and Triangle. Discussions with participants suggest that they do not like to perform gestures which require distinguishing between left and right hands, nor do they like "to think about two different gesture types: Pinch and Finger-Count". More fundamentally, we think participants did not understand the need for a pinch gesture on the left hand (gesture delimitation, not explained to the participants) and thought this artificially increased the mental demand. Pilot studies we performed in the initial steps of this project suggested that Finger-Counting gestures without pinching were appreciated by participants (but risked accidental command invocation). We plan to investigate Finger-Count gestures without the pinch delimiter, by taking into account the position and orientation of the hand to avoid accidental activations.

Observations for Recognizer Optimization

After the study, we examined the depth recordings in order to improve our recognition algorithms. These observations aided in the development of the algorithms we described earlier in this paper:

Pinch and Radial. The pinch "hole" was sometimes quite small and not always visible due to the low resolution of the Kinect. So a pinch is now terminated *only* when it is not detected during 3 consecutive frames to avoid false recognition during fast motions. This introduces a lag of up to 400ms, which would be reduced by increasing frame rate.

Finger-Count. Again, the limited resolution of the Kinect device can sometimes make finger distinction difficult especially for distinguish four and five fingers due to the proximity of fingers. Future implementations would be well served to use a higher resolution sensor.

Triangle. Our first implementation only considered the triangle shape (Figure 6-a). However, it appeared sometimes difficult to distinguish between arm and wrist triangles. To more reliably distinguish between these two postures we included end of the reference arm (Po in Figure 6-a). This also helps in more precisely controlling a continuous value.

USER STUDY: ACCURACY

The previous study investigated usability of our gesture sets without the constraints of using a specific recognizer. We now aim to validate our gesture recognizer and to determine a baseline gesture recognition rate, both with and without visual feedback, that other researchers may improve upon.

Design. 12 novel participants (aged from 25-32 were asked to perform each gesture 5 times for each condition: *with* and *without* visual feedback. In both conditions, they were informed if the gesture was correctly recognized or not, but only in the visual feedback condition, participants saw the performed gesture on a screen (which was removed for second condition). A Kinect was installed over the participant's shoe and connected to a PC to enable a higher frame rate. The system recognized a vocabulary of 15 commands (5 gestures in each set). All participants had 2 minutes of training for each set and started with the visual feedback condition first (to act as training for the eyes-free condition). The stimulus consisted of the name of the gesture. The order of sets was counter-balanced between participants.

Results. ANOVA reveals a significant effect for gesture sets ($F_{2,22}$=5.62, $p<.001$). A post-hoc Tukey test shows that Radial (99.0%) is significantly more accurate than Triangle (95.0%) and Finger-Count (94.0%). ANOVA reveals no effect on accuracy for visual feedback (with: 95.5%; without: 96.5%).

Discussion

Results show a high level of accuracy (>94%) for the three gesture sets. Moreover, results indicate that our gesture sets allow for eyes-free interaction. However, we were surprised about the difference with the visual feedback condition (with: 95.5%; without: 96.5%). The short training phase (2 min), the order of conditions and the fact that – based on our observations – the participants tried to be more accurate in the second condition (without visual feedback) can explain this unexpected result. As in the previous study, we observed participants sometimes elect to perform less casual gestures in favor of accuracy, especially for Triangle. However, recognition performance is bounded by the resolution of the camera and its frame rate. As these improve, so too will recognition, as will the subtlety with which users can perform their gestures.

MOBILITY AND FUTURE WORK

In this article, we mainly focused on gestural interaction when standing. While seated, finger-count and radial gestures can be recognized and comfortably performed on the left/right side of the legs. The triangle gesture cannot be performed so comfortably. We plan to investigate the ability of ShoeSense to operate in walking or running scenarios. Fitzpatrick & Kemp [15] demonstrate that (1) while walking, one foot is always stable on the ground (swing phase) (2) it is possible to detect these periods of stability with a camera by calculating the spatial derivative, and (3) they can get high quality images for recognizing obstacles and floors. Adding accelerometers and gyroscopes to the prototype (as well as buttons under the shoe) could also help to precisely detect and measure periods of stability.

CONCLUSION

We proposed ShoeSense, a wearable system consisting of a shoe-mounted sensor that enables gestural input. ShoeSense provides an unobtrusive always-available input mechanism that does not constrain body movement. We presented three gesture sets designed for eyes-free interaction. We then demonstrated that these gestures can be freely combined. Our proof of concept implementation shows that it is easy to develop robust recognizers for these gestures. The approach enables a wide range of scenarios, especially by annexing visual wearable devices or by enhancing operations on mobile devices.

We reported the results of two user studies. The first one shows promising results in terms of social acceptability, physical and mental demand, and users' preference of the three gesture sets. It also reveals a strong variability concerning social acceptability and preferences of gestures between participants. The second study shows that the reference implementation is robust and that the recognition rate is between 94-99%, even for eyes-free operation. These two studies led us to conclude that ShoeSense is a viable option for future wearable technology and gestural interaction. The next step would be confirm these results by performing a field study to evaluate ShoeSense in the "Wild". In particular, to investigate the ability of ShoeSense to operate in walking or running scenarios.

ACKNOWLEGMENT

This work was supported by the Alexander von Humboldt Foundation. We thank D. Guse and R. Walter for the implementation, A. Roudaut, T. Pietrzak, S. Malacria for their useful comments.

REFERENCES

1. Adidas Megalizer: http://popsop.com/44586
2. Amft O. and Lukowicz, P. 2009. From Backpacks to Smartphones: Past, Present, and Future of Wearable Computers. *IEEE Pervasive Computing* 8, 3 (July 2009), 8-13.
3. Apple Inc., Take Nike + iPod on your Run. In *Apple*. As of 2011.9.9 from http://www.apple.com/ipod/nike/run.html
4. Ashbrook, D. L., Clawson, J., Lyons, K., Patel, N., Starner, T. 2008. Quickdraw: the impact of mobility and on-body placement on device access time. *CHI '08*, 219-222.
5. Augsten, T., Kaefer, K., Meusel, R., Fetzer, C. Kanitz, D. .Stoff, T., Becker, T., Holz, C., Baudisch, P. 2010. Multitoe: high-precision interaction with back-projected floors based on high-resolution multi-touch input. *ACM UIST'10*, 209-218.
6. Bailly, G. Lecolinet, E, Nigay, L.. 2008. Flower menus: a new type of marking menu with large menu breadth, within groups and efficient expert mode memorization. *AVI'08*, 15-22.
7. Bailly, G., Lecolinet, E., Guiard, Y. 2010. Finger-count & radial-stroke shortcuts: 2 techniques for augmenting linear menus on multi-touch surfaces. ACM CHI '10, 591-594.
8. Bailly, G., Walter, R., Müller, J., Ning, T., Lecolinet, E. 2011. Comparing Free Hand Menu Techniques for Distant Displays using Linear, Marking and Finger-Count Menus. IFIP *INTERACT'11*. 248-262.
9. Baudel T., Beaudouin-Lafon, M. 1993. Charade: remote control of objects using free-hand gestures. *Commun. ACM* 36, 7, 28-35.
10. Benko, H. and Wilson, A. D. (2010). Multi-Point Interactions with Immersive Omnidirectional Visualizations in a Dome. *ACM ITS '10*. 19-28.
11. Brett, B., MIT student arrested at Logan in bomb scare. *The Boston Globe*. 2011.9.9 from http://www.boston.com/news/globe/city_region/breaking_news/2007/09/mit_student_arr.html.
12. Buxton, W. 1986. Chunking and phrasing and the design of human-computer dialogues, *IFIP WCG*, 475-480.
13. Camurri, A., Mazzarino, B., Ricchetti, M., Timmers, R. Volpe, G. 2004. Multimodal analysis of expressive gesture in music and dance performances. *Gest.-based. Com. in Hum. -Comp. Int.* vol. 2915. 357-358
14. Conseil, S. Bourennane, S., Martin, L. 2007 Comparison of Fourier Descriptors and Hu Moments for Hand Posture Recognition. *EUSIPCO'07*.
15. Fitzpatrick, P. and Kemp C. C. 2003. Shoes as a Platform for Vision. *IEE ISWC '03*. 231-233.
16. Foxlin, E. M. 2002. Generalized architecture for simultaneous localization, auto-calibration, & map-building. *IEEE/RJS*. Vol.1. 527-533.
17. Guernsey, L., At Airport Gate, a Cyborg Unplugged. In *The New York Times*. As of 2011.9.9, from http://www.nytimes.com /2002/03/14/technology/circuits/14MANN.html.
18. Gustafson, S., Bierwirth, D. Baudisch, P. 2010. Imaginary interfaces: spatial interaction with empty hands and without visual feedback. ACM *UIST'10*, 3-12.
19. Harrison, C. and Hudson, S.E. 2009 Abracadabra: wireless, high-precision, and unpowered finger input for very small mobile devices. *ACM UIST'09*, 121–124.
20. Harrison, C. Tan, D., Morris, D. 2010. Skinput: appropriating the body as an input surface. *ACM CHI '10*, 453-462.
21. Healey, J., Picard, R. 1998. Startlecam: A cybernetic wearable camera, *Tech. Rep*. 468, October 1998.
22. Hedge, A., Anthropometry and Workspace Design, in DEA 325/651. 2002, Cornell.
23. Hendry J, 1984. Shoes: the early learning of an important distinction in Japanese society, *Europe Interprets Japan*, 215-222
24. Higuchi, H. and Nojima, T. 2010 Shoe-shaped i/o interface. *ACM UIST '10*. 423-424.
25. Hinckley, K. 2007. Input technologies and techniques. Chapter 9. In The *human-computer interaction handbook*, 2nd edition.
26. Hudson S., Harrison, C, Harrison, B., LaMarca, A. 2010. Whack gestures: inexact and inattentive interaction with mobile devices. *ACM TEI '10*. 109-112.
27. ISO/DIS 9241-9. 2000. Ergonomic requirements for office work with visual display terminals (VDTs) - Part 9. ISO.
28. Kratz, S. Rohs, M. 2009. Hoverflow: exploring around-device interaction with IR distance sensors. *ACM MobileHCI'09*. 1-4.
29. Krupenkin, T., Taylor, J. 2011. Reverse electrowetting as a new approach to high-power energy harvesting. *Nat. Commun*. 2:448
30. Kurtenbach, G., Buxton, W. 1991. Issues in combining marking and direct manipulation techniques. *ACM UIST'91*, 137-144.
31. Kymissis, J., Kendall, C., Paradiso, J., Gershenfeld, N. 1998. Parasitic Power Harvesting in Shoes. *ISWC'98*, 132-139.
32. Lepinski, G. J., Grossman, T., Fitzmaurice, G. 2010. The design and evaluation of multitouch marking menus. *ACM CHI'10*. 2233-2242.
33. Loclair, C., Gustafson, S., Baudisch, P. 2010. PinchWatch: A Wearable Device for One-Handed Microinteractions, *ACM MobileHCI'10* workshop on Ensembles of on-body devices.
34. Mann, S. 1995. Privacy Issues of Wearable Cameras Versus Surveillance Cameras. *Newsweek*, 86(11), 21-22.
35. Mayol, W., Tordoff, B., Murray, D. 2000. Towards wearable active vision platforms. *Trans. Syst. Man. Cyber*. V. 3, (Oct. 2000), 1627-1632.
36. Mayol, W., Tordoff, B., Murray, D. 2009. On the choice and placement of wearable vision sensors. *Trans. Sys. Man Cyber*. 39, 2. 414-425.
37. Mistry, P., Maes, P., Chang, L. 2009. WUW-wear Ur world: a wearable gestural interface. *ACM CHI EA* '09. 4111-4116.
38. *NASA TLX*, NASA Ames Research Center, Moffet Field, California, 1988.
39. Ni, T., Baudisch, P. 2009. Disappearing mobile devices. *ACM UIST '09*. 101-110
40. Paradiso, J. and Hu, E. 1997. Expressive Footwear for Computer-Augmented Dance Performance. IEEE ISWC '97, 13-14.
41. Pierce, J., Mahaney, H. 2004 Opportunistic Annexing for Handheld Devices: Opportunities and Challenges. *HCIC04*.
42. Pook, S., Lecolinet, E., Vaysseix, G., Barrilot, E. 2000. Control menus: execution and control in a single interactor. *ACM CHI EA'00*, 263-264.
43. Rico, J. and Brewster S. 2010. Usable gestures for mobile interfaces: evaluating social acceptability. *ACM CHI '10*, 887-896.
44. Ruiz, J., Li, Y., Lank, E. 2011. User-defined motion gestures for mobile interaction. *ACM CHI '11*, 197-206.
45. Schiele B. and Pentland, A. 1999. Attentional objects for visual context understanding. Tech. Rep. 500, MIT media Lab, 1999.
46. Shiratori, T., Park, H. S., Sigal, L., Sheikh, Y., Hodgins, J. K. 2011. Motion Capture from-Mounted Cameras. *SIGGRAPH*. 10 pages.
47. Siek, Roger, Y., Connelly, K. 2005. Fat finger worries: How older and younger users physically interact with PDAs. *INTERACT '05*. 267-280.
48. Starner, T. 1996. Human-powered wearable computing. *IBM Syst. J*. 35, 3-4 (September 1996), 618-629.
49. Starner, T., Wearer, J., Pentland, A. 1998. Real-Time American Sign Language Recognition Using Desk and Wearable Computer Based Video. *IEEE Trans. Pat. Anal. Mach. Intell*. 20, 12 (Dec. 98), 1371-1375.
50. Starner, T., Auxier, J., Ashbrook, D., Gandy, M.2000. The Gesture Pendant: A Self-illuminating, Wearable, Infrared Computer Vision System for Home Automation Control and Medical Monitoring. *IEEE ISWC '00*, 87-94.
51. Trigo, T. Pellegrino, S. 2010 An Analysis of Features for Hand-Gesture Classification. *IWSSIP'10*. 412-415
52. Vardy, A., Robinson, J., Cheng, L. 1999. The WristCam as Input Device. *IEEE ISWC* '99, 199-202.
53. Wilson, A. D. 2006. Robust computer vision-based detection of pinching for one and two-handed gesture input. ACM *UIST'06*, 255-258.
54. Wobbrock, J., Morris, M., Wilson, A. 2009. User-defined gestures for surface computing. *ACM CHI '09*, 1083-1092.
55. Wu, M., Shen, C., Ryall, K., Forlines, C., Balakrishnan, R. 2006. Gesture registration, relaxation, and reuse for multi-point direct-touch surfaces. IEEE *TableTop'06*. p. 183.190.

Bootstrapper: Recognizing Tabletop Users by their Shoes

Stephan R. Richter, Christian Holz and Patrick Baudisch
Hasso Plattner Institute, Potsdam, Germany
stephan.richter @ student.hpi.uni-potsdam.de
{christian.holz, patrick.baudisch} @ hpi.uni-potsdam.de

ABSTRACT

In order to enable personalized functionality, such as to log tabletop activity by user, tabletop systems need to *recognize* users. *DiamondTouch* does so reliably, but requires users to stay in assigned seats and cannot recognize users across sessions. We propose a different approach based on distinguishing users' *shoes*. While users are interacting with the table, our system *Bootstrapper* observes their shoes using one or more depth cameras mounted to the edge of the table. It then identifies users by matching camera images with a database of known shoe images. When multiple users interact, Bootstrapper associates touches with shoes based on hand orientation. The approach can be implemented using consumer depth cameras because (1) shoes offer large distinct features such as color, (2) shoes naturally align themselves with the ground, giving the system a well-defined perspective and thus reduced ambiguity. We report two simple studies in which Bootstrapper recognized participants from a database of 18 users with 95.8% accuracy.

ACM Classification: H.5.2 [Information interfaces and presentation]: User Interfaces: Input Devices and Strategies, Interaction Styles.

Keywords: tabletop systems; user identification; indoor tracking; touch; personalization; Microsoft Surface.

INTRODUCTION

In order to enable personalized functionality and menus, to track achievements in multi-player games, or to enforce social protocol [15], a tabletop system needs to be able to know which touch belongs to whom.

Electronic rings [16] allow identifying touches reliably, but require maintenance, such as recharging batteries. Alternatively, *DiamondTouch* identifies users based on the chairs they sit in [5]. However, this only identifies chairs, thus users still need to identify themselves at the beginning of each session. When dealing with users who are likely to move around, such as children in a free-flow learning environment, these limitations are problematic.

Researchers have therefore explored how to distinguish users directly. Schmidt et al distinguish users' hands using the table's built-in camera [17], but to see a sufficient number of features, the approach requires specific hand postures which can interfere with the interaction. Alternatively, face recognition recognizes users reliably [1], but requires a frontal high-quality image of users' faces, which interferes with users moving around the tabletop.

In this paper, we propose a new perspective on the problem: instead of distinguishing users' hands or faces, we distinguish their *shoes*.

BOOTSTRAPPER

Figure 1 shows our prototype system *Bootstrapper*. Its main element is a depth camera (*Microsoft Kinect*), which is mounted at each side of a diffuse illumination [10] multi-touch table (*Microsoft Surface*). The depth cameras point downwards at the space where users stand, which is illuminated homogenously by lights located inside the base.

Figure 1: Bootstrapper recognizes users interacting with the table by observing their shoes using depth cameras.

Bootstrapper works as follows. (1) It observes the space where users stand. (2) It extracts shoes from the video stream by thresholding the depth image. (3) It matches the shoes against a database of shoe-user pairs and retrieves the user's name and associated meta information. (4) If Bootstrapper sees more than one user, it pairs up touches with shoes based on the orientation of users' hands, as observed by the table's built-in camera.

Walkthrough

Figure 2 shows how Bootstrapper tracks students' progress with an educational software package. (a) Stephan approaches the table. (b) Bootstrapper finds his shoes in the database and (c) displays Stephan's badge with his current math score. (d) Whenever Stephan solves a math puzzle, the math score on his badge increases. (e) Stephan is joined by Caro, a first-time user. (f) Since Bootstrapper cannot find Caro's shoes in

Permission to make digital or hard copies of all or part of this work for personal or classroom use is granted without fee provided that copies are not made or distributed for profit or commercial advantage and that copies bear this notice and the full citation on the first page. To copy otherwise, or republish, to post on servers or to redistribute to lists, requires prior specific permission and/or a fee.
CHI'12, May 5–10, 2012, Austin, Texas, USA.
Copyright 2012 ACM 978-1-4503-1015-4/12/05...$10.00.

its database, it automatically creates a placeholder badge for her (with a photo of her shoes).

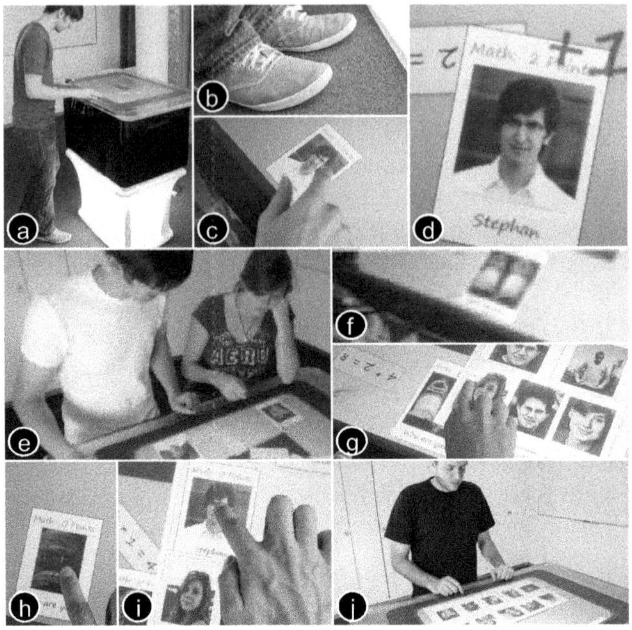

Figure 2: Walkthrough: Bootstrapper recognizes users to track their math achievements. Finally, Bootstrapper creates an overview for the teacher.

Both users keep practicing and Bootstrapper adds their achievements to their respective badges. (g) Caro personalizes her badge by adding a photo. Stephan can leave and come back anytime and is recognized. The next day, however, he is wearing a new pair of shoes. Bootstrapper does not recognize him and therefore (h) creates a placeholder badge for him. (i) Stephan taps on the placeholder badge which opens the list of existing badges. He selects his own badge from the list, which merges his accounts and adds his new shoes to his existing account. (j) Finally, their teacher accesses the table. Inspecting the performance of his students with the individual exercises helps him understand how to best support each one of them.

BENEFITS AND LIMITATIONS

Bootstrapper supports walk-up use and persists profiles across sessions. Unlike approaches based on hand recognition, users hands are free to interact. Unlike traditional biometric features, such as fingerprints or pupils, shoe recognition can be implemented with comparably coarse hardware. The reason is that shoes offer *large* visual features, such as distinct colors, seams, laces, logos, or stripes. These can be recognized from a distance using inexpensive consumer cameras.

The recognition problem solved by Bootstrapper is comparably simple: unlike other parts of the human body, such as hands and faces, shoes maintain direct contact with the ground most of the time. This constrains shoes to translation and rotation *in the plane,* which simplifies the recognition problem (see section "algorithms").

Bootstrapper is subject to three limitations. First, two users wearing the same shoes will be assigned the same profile. This makes identity spoofing possible by buying the same shoes as someone else, which is inherent to clothing-based recognition. Second, Bootstrapper currently recognizes users only when at least one shoe stands flat on the ground. Future versions may alleviate this with a virtual viewpoint transformation. Third, users can mislead Bootstrapper's touch-to-user association by contorting their hands.

Due to these limitations, we see Bootstrapper being used primarily for signing into non-critical accounts, such as learner or gamer profiles or for interface personalization. In contrast, Bootstrapper is not appropriate for applications that require true security, such as to work with computer accounts or for accessing banking information.

CONTRIBUTION

Our main contribution is the idea to reformulate the user recognition problem as a shoe recognition problem. Based on this, we demonstrate a hardware setup and an algorithm that associates shoes with touch input and that locates a user's shoes in the user database. Our recognition reaches 95.8%, which is sufficiently accurate for groups the size of a lab group, school, or kindergarten class (see user study). Bootstrapper successfully associates users with their touches in 92.3% to 100% for 5 to 1 concurrent users.

RELATED WORK

The work in this paper is related to user identification on multitouch systems and to shoe recognition.

Researchers have proposed identifying users with unique tokens, such as by combining optical recognition with RFID tags [12], using a ring that flashes a unique ID sequence to the table [16] or combining an electronic wristband with an analysis of hand orientation [11]. Instead of instrumenting users, *DiamondTouch* instruments the chair, i.e., an object that users touch only during the session [5].

A different track of research has explored the use of biometrics for user identification. Several researchers expect fingerprints scanning to eventually be integrated into multitouch hardware [6, 18]. Identifying users by their hands, in contrast, demands that the whole hand be placed on the surface [17]. Face recognition achieves high success rates, but requires users to directly face the camera [1].

Other researchers proposed to distinguish users based on shoes or gait. *Smart Floor* identifies users by observing the forces and timing of the individual phases of walking [14]. *Multitoe* [3] identified users by their sole patterns. Both require an instrumented floor.

Similar to *Bootstrapper, Medusa* locates users around a tabletop computer and associates touches with them [2], using a multitude of proximity sensors. This approach does not afford user identification, however.

ALGORITHMS: IDENTIFY USERS & PAIR UP TOUCHES

To recognize users and identify who touched where, Bootstrapper performs the following four steps.

Step 1: Extracting shoe textures from the camera image

First, Bootstrapper extracts shoes from the image as shown in Figure 3. (b) Bootstrapper retrieves the depth image, and (c) by thresholding it, removes the background. (d) Finding *connected components* [13] separates bodies. Feet connected to the same hips are identified as belonging to the same user. (e) Thresholding depth at 6" above the background removes legs. (f) Masking the RGB image with the registered depth image extracts shoe textures.

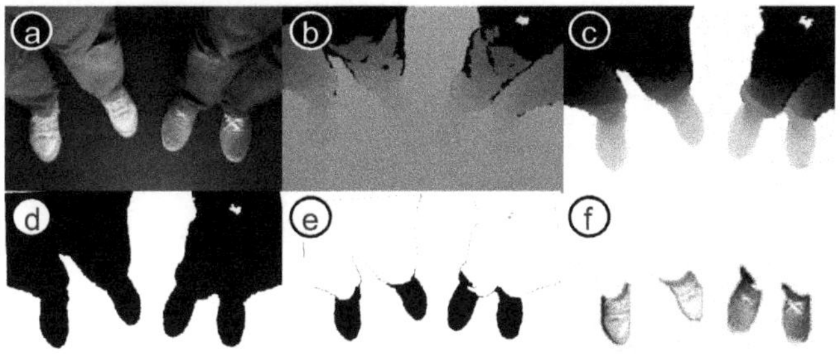

Figure 3: (a) RGB image, (b) raw depth image, (c) background subtracted, (d) bodies located, (e) leg removed. (f) RGB masked with depth image.

Step 2: Looking up matching shoes in user database

To identify users, Bootstrapper compares the RGB shoe image with all shoe images in its database. To obtain a better quality color image than provided by Kinect, we complemented Bootstrapper with a separate webcam. We currently employ two separate matching functions: SURF [4] and *color histograms* matching using *Bhattacharyya* distance. Our system uses the SURF implementation provided by OpenCV 2.3 [13] with hessian threshold set to 200 for additional features and default parameters otherwise. We refine the feature extraction using clustering and a probabilistic verification [9]. Earlier versions of Bootstrapper used *SIFT* and *Earth movers distance* on color and depth histograms, but were too slow for real-time use.

If none of the shoes in the database reach an empirically determined threshold for a period of 5 frames, Bootstrapper creates a new user and displays a placeholder badge.

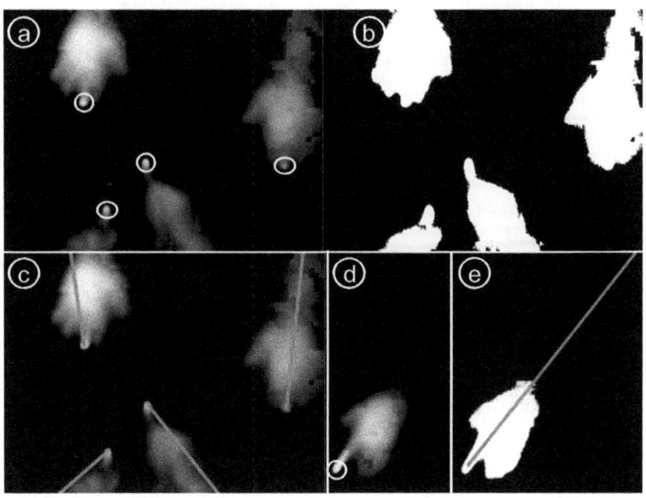

Figure 4: Bootstrapper traces touches to an edge of the table by following the image of the user's arm.

Step 3: Tracing touches to the table edge & to the user

If Bootstrapper sees only one user, it associates all observed touches with this user. If it detects several users, it locates hovering arms in the tabletop image and traces them back to the edge of the table.

Figure 4 illustrates the processing pipeline. (a) Bootstrapper obtains the raw image of the touch surface and a list of all touch locations from the tabletop system. (b) Bootstrapper locates hovering hands and arms by thresholding brightness with a low adaptive threshold [8]. (c) If the arm extends all the way to the edge of the table, Bootstrapper uses the intersection between arm and edge. (d) If an arm does not extend all the way to a table edge, Bootstrapper extrapolates linearly from the farthest point inside the blob (e).

Step 4: Applying offsets for left and right hands

Associating an observed arm with a user may still be ambiguous if two users stand side-by-side (Figure 5). *Bootstrapper* resolves this by determining whether the observed hand is a left or a right hand (as in [8]) and applying a hand-specific offset. This resolves the ambiguity.

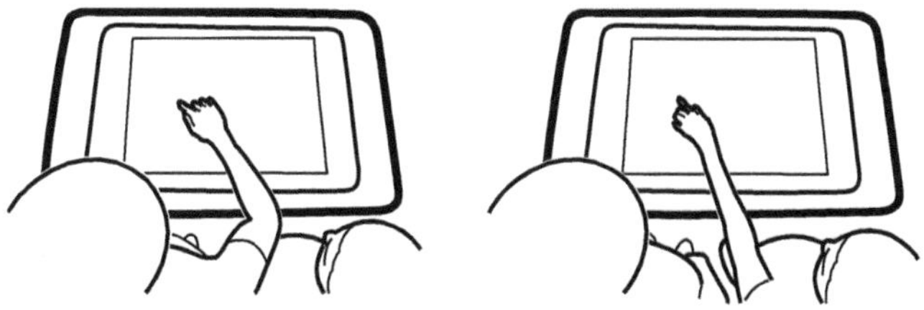

Figure 5: Ambiguity: which user caused this touch?

Finally, Bootstrapper associates the user closest in terms of radial distance to the adjusted edge point to the touch.

EVALUATION 1: 95.8% ACCURACY WITH 18 USERS

We conducted a brief technical evaluation to determine the recognition rates of the different algorithms. We recruited 18 random participants (with random shoes, Figure 6) from our institution. Each participant interacted with a puzzle application for two minutes and *Bootstrapper* captured and stored 20 samples of their shoes at random times. A week later, we brought the same participants, wearing the same shoes back to the lab and repeated the procedure.

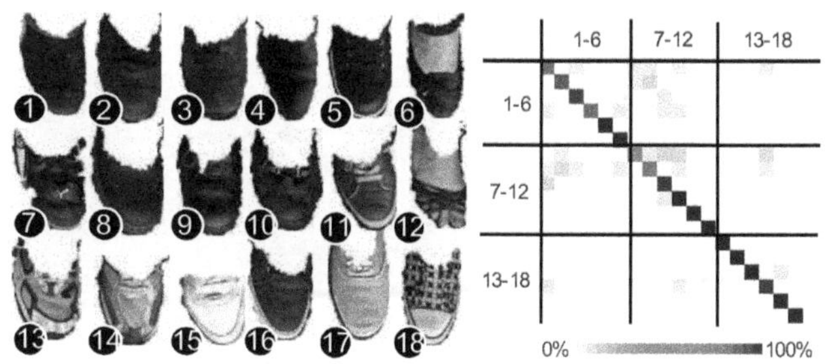

Figure 6: (left) Participants' shoes in the study. (right) Confusion matrix of *combined* matching.

Results: We performed a two-fold cross-validation of the two matching algorithms and their combination with all 720 captured images, extracting features from a single frame. In addition, we evaluated a majority voting across ten frames, which achieved the highest accuracy (Figure 7). Regarding speed, our implementation took 47ms for *histogram matching,* 2.5s for *SURF,* and 0.74s for *combined* on average. *Combined* is faster than just SURF, because we invoke SURF only when *histogram* returns a low confidence score. All results were calculated on a 2.2GHz Intel Core-i7 2720QM with 4GB RAM.

As expected, error rates varied across different types of shoes and dark shoes were the most error prone (#2 and #8 in Figure 6). Overall, however, recognition rates of 93.3% for a single frame and 95.8% across multiple frames are appropriate for a wide range of applications, such as the aforementioned scenario of tracking learning progress.

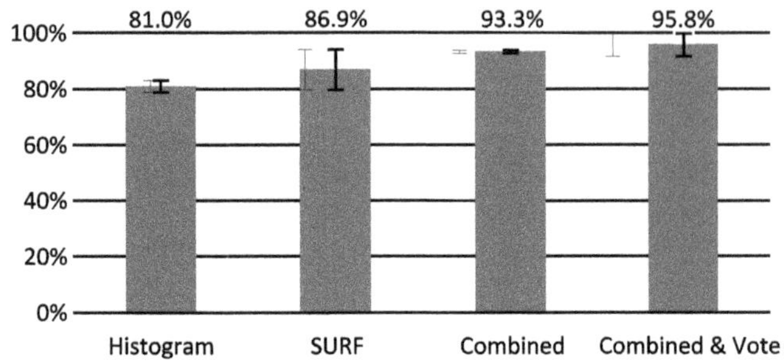

Figure 7: Recognition rates for SURF, color histogram matching, combined, and combined with majority voting over 10 frames on 18 users, based on a single observed frame

EVALUATION 2: TOUCH-TO-USER ASSOCIATION

To determine the accuracy of the touch-to-user association, we conducted a second study and recruited 13 new participants. During each trial, the participant stood at one of the 4 positions shown in Figure 8. They now acquired one of 5 different targets located on the screen using the right hand. The experiment comprised 3 blocks, resulting in 60 trials per participant and 780 overall trials. All targets and standing positions were selected randomly. We measured the angular distance between where our algorithm predicted the user and the participant's actual position.

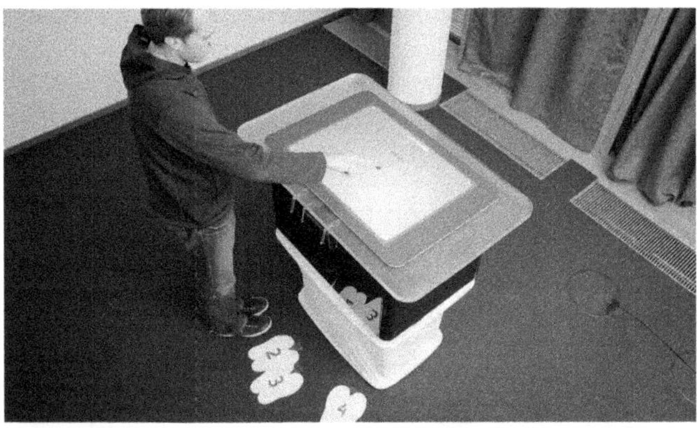

Figure 8: Participants acquired 5 different targets on the table from 4 positions, repeating each combinations 3 times.

Results: The median angular error for our predictions was 32 degrees across all trials. Whether a touch is associated with the correct user depends on how tightly users are huddled around the table. By snapping the predicted location to the closest of 1, 2, 3, 4, or 5 users distributed evenly around the table, we obtained accuracy rates of 100%, 99.7%, 99.1%, 96.1%, 92.3%, respectively.

CONCLUSIONS AND FUTURE WORK

In this paper, we presented a new approach to recognizing users of a tabletop system. Our main contribution is the idea to reformulate the user identification as a problem of recognizing shoes. Unlike hands or faces, shoes can be observed for a constant perspective and they offer large visual features, which we can recognize reliably from a distance with consumer hardware.

For future work, we plan to adapt Bootstrapper to different form factors, including the traditional coffee table shape, to match shoes based on depth data, and to explore our approach in non-tabletop scenarios, such as to profile customers while shopping. We also plan to explore user recognition based on users' clothing using a single overhead camera, which will facilitate touch-to-user associations [7].

ACKNOWLEDGMENTS

We thank Paul Hoover and Caroline Fetzer for discussions.

REFERENCES

1. Abate, A.F., Nappi, M., Riccio, D., Sabatino, G. 2D and 3D face recognition: A survey. *Pattern Recognition Letters Vol.28, Issue 14*, 1885-1906.
2. Annett, M., Grossman, T., Wigdor, D., Fitzmaurice, G. Medusa: A Proximity-Aware Multi-touch Tabletop. *Proc. UIST'11.*
3. Augsten, T., Kaefer, K., Fetzer, C., Meusel, R., Kanitz, D., Stoff, T., Becker, T., Holz, C., Baudisch, P. Multitoe: High-Precision Interaction with Back-Projected Floors Based on High-Resolution Multi-Touch Input. *Proc. UIST'10*, 209-218.
4. Bay, H., Ess, A., Tuytelaars, T., Van Gool, L. Speeded-up Robust Features. *Proc. Computer Vision and Image Understanding (2007)*, 346-359.
5. Dietz, P. and Leigh, D. DiamondTouch: a multi-user touch technology. *Proc. UIST '01,* 219-226.
6. Holz, C. and Baudisch, P. The Generalized Perceived Input Point Model and How to Double Touch Accuracy by Extracting Fingerprints. *Proc. CHI '10,* 581–590.
7. Holz, C. and Baudisch, P. Understanding Touch. *Proc. CHI '11*, 2501-2510.
8. Lepinski, J.G., Grossman, T., Fitzmaurice, G. The design and evaluation of multitouch marking menus. *Proc. CHI '10*, 2233-2242.
9. Lowe, D. Distinctive Image Features from Scale-Invariant Keypoints. *International Journal of Computer Vision (2004).*
10. Matsushita, N. and Rekimoto, J. *HoloWall*: Designing a Finger, Hand, Body, and Object Sensitive Wall. *Proc. UIST'97*, 209-210.
11. Meyer, T. and Schmidt, D. IdWristbands: IR-based User Identification on Multi-touch surfaces. Poster at *ITS 2010.*
12. Olwal, A. and Wilson, A. SurfaceFusion: Unobtrusive Tracking of Everyday Objects in Tangible User Interfaces. *Proc. GI '08,* 235-242.
13. *OpenCV.* http://opencv.willowgarage.com
14. Orr, R.J. and Abowd, G.D. The smart floor: a mechanism for natural user identification and tracking. In *CHI'00 Extended Abstracts*, 275-276.
15. Piper, A., O'Brien, Ringel Morris, M., and Winograd, T. SIDES: a cooperative tabletop computer game for social skills development. *Proc. CSCW'06,* 1-10.
16. Roth, V., Schmidt, P., and Güldenring, B. The IR Ring: Authenticating users' touches on a multi-touch display. *Proc. UIST '10*, 259-262.
17. Schmidt, D., Chong, M., and Gellersen, H. HandsDown: Hand-contour-based user identification for interactive surfaces. *Proc. NordiCHI '10*, 432-441.
18. Sugiura, A., and Koseki, Y. A user interface using fingerprint recognition: holding commands and data objects on fingers. *Proc. UIST '98,* 71-79.

Using Rhythmic Patterns as an Input Method

Emilien Ghomi ghomi@lri.fr **Guillaume Faure** gfaure@lri.fr **Stéphane Huot** huot@lri.fr **Olivier Chapuis** chapuis@lri.fr **Michel Beaudouin-Lafon** mbl@lri.fr

Univ Paris-Sud (LRI) F-91405 Orsay, France
CNRS (LRI) F-91405 Orsay, France
INRIA F-91405 Orsay, France

ABSTRACT
While interaction techniques that use the temporal dimension have been used for a long time, such as multiple clicks or spring-loaded widgets, more advanced uses of *rhythmic patterns* have received little attention in HCI. Using such temporal structures to convey information can be particularly useful in situations where the visual channel is overloaded or even not available. In this paper we introduce *Rhythmic Interaction* as the use of rhythms for input. We report the results of two experiments that show that (i) rhythmic patterns can be efficiently reproduced by novice users and recognized by computer algorithms, and (ii) rhythmic patterns can be memorized as efficiently as traditional shortcuts when associating them with visual commands. Overall, these results demonstrate the potential of Rhythmic Interaction and open the way to a richer repertoire of interaction techniques.

ACM Classification Keywords
H.5.2 [Information interfaces and presentation]: User Interfaces. - Graphical user interfaces.

Author Keywords
Rhythm; taping; hotkeys; learning; patterns; Morse code

INTRODUCTION
Rhythm plays an important role in our everyday life. Temporal patterns are of course critical in experiencing music, but they also underlie periodic actions such as walking, breathing or chewing, and they are even necessary for understanding speech prosody. Rhythm is so deeply embedded in our experience of living that it can be used to cure some diseases such as stress or sleep disorders [29].

While perceiving and reproducing rhythm is recognized as a fundamental human ability by physiologists and neuropsychologists, it is still underused as an interactive dimension in HCI. In common desktop environments, interaction relies heavily on manipulating graphical widgets, simple mouse clicks and keyboard shortcuts. This basic vocabulary, however, is often extended by using *spatial* or *temporal* features, as with mouse gestures or multiple clicks.

Permission to make digital or hard copies of all or part of this work for personal or classroom use is granted without fee provided that copies are not made or distributed for profit or commercial advantage and that copies bear this notice and the full citation on the first page. To copy otherwise, or republish, to post on servers or to redistribute to lists, requires prior specific permission and/or a fee.
CHI'12, May 5–10, 2012, Austin, Texas, USA.
Copyright 2012 ACM 978-1-4503-1015-4/12/05...$10.00

Although the spatial dimension has been the focus of much HCI research on interaction techniques based on hand postures or gestures, e.g. [1, 3, 16], the temporal dimension has received little attention so far. We propose to use rhythm as an input method and introduce *Rhythmic Interaction* as a complementary way to control interactive systems. Rhythmic Interaction can be used in any event-driven environment for a variety of input modalities: clicking the mouse, hitting keyboard keys or a touch-sensitive surface, moving a motion-sensing device, etc. However, it has competitive advantages for tactile screens, since it requires less screen space than gestural interaction and no visual attention [33]. This article presents a first exploration of the design space of Rhythmic Interaction in order to address the following questions:

- *Feasibility.* Even if perceiving and performing rhythm is quite natural, are users able to reproduce, learn and memorize patterns? Can they use them to trigger commands?
- *Interaction design.* The number of possible rhythmic patterns is virtually infinite and they can be presented in several ways. Which patterns make sense for interaction and how to design a vocabulary? What feedback helps executing and learning patterns?
- *Technical issues & Integration.* Like most continuous high-level input methods, e.g. voice, marks, gestures, Rhythmic Interaction relies on a recognizer to segment and interpret user input. How to design effective recognizers that do not require training?

In the rest of this paper, we survey related work and then define a framework for Rhythmic Interaction, narrowing the scope of our study to vocabularies of rhythmic patterns that are relevant in the context of HCI. Then, we report on two experiments where the patterns are rhythmic sequences of taps performed on a tactile trackpad to trigger commands. The first one tests the ability of novice users to reproduce individual patterns, while the second one compares the ability of users to memorize the association of commands to rhythmic patterns vs. keyboard shortcuts. We also describe the recognizers that we created for these two experiments, and draw some conclusions regarding the design of pattern vocabularies and appropriate feedback.

BACKGROUND & RELATED WORK
The literature in cognitive science has studied the perception, reproduction and use of rhythm from several perspectives: physiology, e.g., perception and action [13, 19], knowledge and learning, e.g., language [24], artistic applications, e.g., music [23], etc. Two major studies on the psychology

of rhythm in music are reported by Fraisse [12] and by Clarke [7]. In this section, we give an overview of the literature in cognitive science that is most relevant to Rhythmic Interaction and then focus on the few studies of using time and rhythm to control interactive systems.

Rhythm in Music and Games

For musicians, rhythm is one of the most important features in music, together with melody and harmony. Many traditional forms of music combine simple rhythmic structures played in parallel to build up higher level aggregated rhythms, called "polyrhythms" [2]. From a cognitive point of view, these practices suggest that the cognitive load required to deal with an elementary rhythmic pattern is light enough to allow their combination in more complex structures.

Highly trained musicians are able to create and play an incredible amount of rhythmic variations. Simple patterns, however, can be reproduced by everyone, as illustrated by the success of popular musical games such as Guitar Hero, TapTap or Donkey Kong, where rhythmic structures are recognized and reproduced by non-musicians of all ages.

Rhythm in Cognitive Sciences

In physiology and neuropsychology, numerous studies report that humans have a natural perception of rhythm, thanks to rhythmic mechanisms that are involved in the internal functioning of our organism (heart beat, sleep cycles, etc.) [13] and their relation with periodic external phenomena (day/night, seasons, etc.). When listening to music, we constantly try to infer the beat, i.e., to perceive regular and salient events, or to group events into rhythms [18]. In fact, we systematically try to perceive rhythm even when none is present [25] or when being told to avoid it [12].

Rhythm perception is deeply related to the motor system [5]. Since childhood, humans are used to tap their feet, clap their hands, snap their fingers and move in synchrony with music. These activities are common and seem simple, even though they involve complex rhythmic structures. Outside music, periodic activities of different frequencies are pervasive in our everyday life. For example, chewing or walking are known to have universally preferred rates [13, 19].

While these studies attempt to explain how and why we perceive and produce periodicities, they rarely deal with the reproduction and memorization of rhythmic patterns associated to tasks that we address in this article.

Rhythm as an Input Method in HCI

Rhythm is built on the temporal dimension, which is commonly used in interactive software. For example, long clicks are often distinguished from short clicks to trigger different commands based on temporal criteria. The concept of "dwelling"—freezing the interaction for a short amount of time—is also used to segment gestural interaction [15] or to explicitly switch mode [10]. Rhythmic Menus [22] successively highlight items at a given rate while the mouse button is pressed. When the user releases the button, the current item is selected.

Some techniques are based on the temporal grouping of events. Double click is the simplest and most common case, but some studies also explored rhythmic motion: Motion Pointing [11] assigns different periodic motions to graphical objects in a scene or items in a pie menu; The user selects the object or menu item of interest by performing the corresponding motion. In Cyclostar [20], the user controls continuous parameters, such as the speed of zooming, by performing elliptical oscillatory gestures. The rate of the circling motion controls a parameter of the resulting command.

In the above cases, rhythmic aspects are reduced to periodicity. To the best of our knowledge, only a few techniques involve the reproduction of rhythmic patterns. Five-key [31] is a text entry system based on rhythmic sequences, where letters can be entered with only five keys. However, efficiency and learning were not studied systematically. In [9], tempo reproduction is used to select a particular song in a music library by tapping on a mobile device or shaking it. But relying only on tempo raises some scalability issues that were not assessed. Finally, Tapsongs [33] is an alternative to textual passwords where users tap a rhythmic pattern that they have registered with the system for authentication.

MOTIVATION

Our goals are more general than Five-key and Tapsongs: we want to design vocabularies of rhythmic patterns that users can learn easily and perform reliably in order to trigger commands. This approach is somewhat similar to the use of Morse code for encoding characters. However, the design of Morse code was driven by information theoretic issues rather than usability, and while early computers were able to decode human-produced Morse code [4], it has rarely been used in HCI [6]. Our objective is to propose a comprehensive framework to design rhythmic patterns for interaction, with efficient recognizers that do not need training.

Advantages of Using Rhythms for Input

The design of new techniques based on Rhythmic Interaction is not the main focus of the present article. However, we have identified a number of potential advantages of using rhythm to interact with computer systems. First, as evidenced by research in Cognitive Science, there is a direct correspondence between performing a rhythm (action) and listening to a rhythm (potential audio stimulus and feedback). Second, rhythms can be performed in a variety of situations: while performing a rhythm requires as little as a single degree of freedom of one finger, many movements can be performed rhythmically and captured using different sensors, e.g., tapping fingers, tapping feet, or nodding the head.

Gestural interaction typically requires space to perform the gestures, and often interferes with the display space on a small touchscreen. By contrast, Rhythmic Interaction only uses temporal features. Rhythms can be performed on a small area of a tactile device, even in an eye-free context.

Finally, rhythmic structures can be designed in a hierarchical way. By using common prefixes among different patterns, a natural hierarchy emerges that can be internalized by users, facilitating memorization and recall.

Applications of Rhythmic Patterns

Rhythmic patterns are not meant to replace more conventional command input methods. Instead, it is an alternative that may be more adapted to specific situations, such as eye-free operation. It is also a way to enhance existing methods with a richer vocabulary. For example rhythmic patterns could give access to a restricted set of commands such as speed-dialing a phone number, navigating an e-book or switching mode in an application.

In some situations, rhythmic patterns can simplify interaction. For example, bookmarks, menu items or contacts are often organized hierarchically. Rhythmic patterns could match this hierarchy or provide an alternate hierarchy such as organizing contacts by their first name. Also, since rhythmic patterns can be performed without visual attention, they can be used with a tactile device in the pocket or while driving, or in the dark, e.g. to shut down an alarm clock, or even with devices that do not have a display.

Rhythmic Interaction also offers novel solutions to well-known problems. Tapping on the back of a hand-held device can be captured without extra sensors, thanks to built-in accelerometers or microphones [28]. For example, a rhythmic pattern performed while receiving a phone call could add the caller to the contact list, or display extra information such as battery life or signal level. Patterns could also be performed with the non-dominant hand or another part of the body such as the feet [30], to switch mode or ignore an incoming call.

RHYTHMIC PATTERNS FOR INTERACTION

Our definition of a rhythmic pattern comes from music: The elementary structure in music is called a *motif*, which is defined as a "melodic, rhythmic, or harmonic cell" [21]. A *rhythmic motif* represents the temporal structure of a set of notes and consists of the relative durations of notes and silences. Notes and silences can have eight different durations in standard musical pieces, and motifs can contain many notes, leading to a huge number of possible rhythmic motifs.

Considering the number of commands and actions often used when interacting with computers, such an expressive power is not required. Therefore we propose a restricted definition of *rhythmic pattern* (or simply *pattern*) more adapted to HCI. A rhythmic pattern is a sequence of taps[1] and breaks whose durations are counted in *beats*. The beat is the basic unit of time and its duration is defined below). We define the complete set of possible patterns with the following rules:

- Taps can be of three types: *impulse* (a hit on a touch device or a click), *short* tap (one beat) or *long* tap (two beats). A tap starts at the beginning of a beat, and there cannot be more than one tap per beat.
- Breaks can be of two types: *short* (one beat) or *long* (two beats). A pattern cannot begin or end with a break, and there cannot be two successive breaks.

This definition of taps and breaks is based on our empirical observation that computer users are familiar with the distinction between instantaneous and long clicks or taps. By adding a third duration and by taking breaks into account, we offer designers more possibilities for selecting a set of patterns among the possible combinations. In comparison to Morse code, we do not need the "intra-character", "inter-character" and "inter-word" breaks that are specific to the coding of language, and we do not allow more than one tap per beat.

[1]The word "tap" reflects our focus on using a tactile device for input.

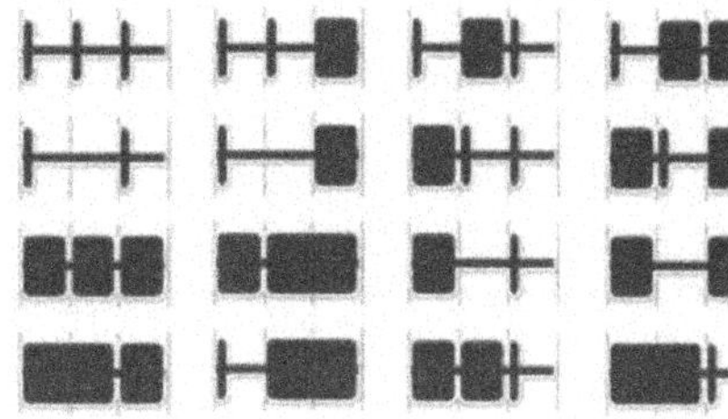

Figure 1. The 16 three-beat patterns defined by our rules. Each rectangle represents a tap. The thin gray lines show the beats.

The *length* of a pattern is the sum of the durations of its taps and breaks. To simplify reproduction and memorization, we focus on patterns between two and six beats long. The rules above define 5 two-beat patterns, 16 three-beat patterns (Figure 1), 53 four-beat patterns, 171 six-beat patterns and 554 six-beat patterns. By comparison, the total number of patterns with n taps is 3^{2n-1}, i.e. $199,290$ patterns with up to six taps.

In this entire study, beats occur at the tempo of 120 BPM (2Hz). Thus, the onsets of two consecutive taps are separated by at least 500 ms, i.e. a beat is half a second. This corresponds to a common tempo of human motor actions, e.g. walking [19], and of contemporary music [23].

As a first step, we only consider rhythmic patterns performed by tapping on a touch-sensitive surface. While keyboards, accelerometers [17, 9] or eye blinks [32] can probably be used for Rhythmic Interaction, it is out of the scope of this article. We also do not address the segmentation of patterns from other input. Simple solutions that should be tested include segmenting in time by preceding each pattern with a specific short sequence of taps, or segmenting in space by performing patterns on a specific location of a device.

A key aspect of this research is to design a recognizer that can reliably identify the patterns produced by users. In a first experiment, we used a *structural* recognizer to assess users' ability to produce patterns accurately. Based on the results, we designed a *pattern classifier* that accounts for user inaccuracies while still discriminating the patterns in the vocabulary. This classifier was used in a second experiment where we assessed users' ability to memorize associations between patterns and commands in an applicative context.

EXPERIMENT 1: RHYTHMIC PATTERN REPRODUCTION

In order to assess the potential of Rhythmic Interaction, we conducted a first experiment where novice users were asked to replicate patterns presented to them in visual and/or audio form by tapping on a touch surface. The goal was to assess the accuracy of the reproduction and to compare the effects of several feedback mechanisms while performing patterns.

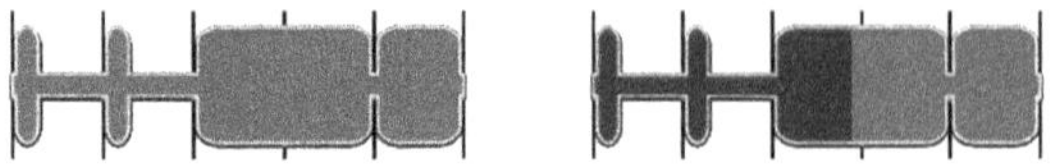

(a) (b)

Figure 2. The stimulus in Experiment 1. A static representation is displayed (a) and fills up in synchrony with the audio playback (b).

Recognizer

The recognizer that we designed for this experiment is based on the above rules for defining the patterns. It first extracts the rhythmic structure as a list of taps and breaks and infers their respective types (impulse, short and long) using autonomous heuristics. The reconstructed pattern is then checked against the vocabulary used for the study.

In order to identify the type of every tap and break in the sequence, the recognition algorithm uses k-means clustering iterated 500 times on duration values. The algorithm builds clusters corresponding to the possible types of taps and breaks: impulse, short and long[2]. A minimum distance of 200ms between the duration clusters is enforced, corresponding to a maximum tempo for the pattern to be recognized. If two clusters are closer than that distance, they are merged and will be recognized as a single tap type. Thus, if the pattern is performed too fast, events of different types may be confused by the recognizer. For cluster identification, the reference durations for short and long taps or breaks are set to 500ms and 1000ms respectively, and the maximum duration of an impulse or release is set to 180ms.

After clustering, breaks that correspond to the rest of a beat after an impulse are removed from the reconstructed pattern. The resulting pattern is then looked up in the vocabulary to check if it matches the stimulus provided to the participant.

Note that this recognizer is intentionally very strict, in order to assess the participants' ability to precisely reproduce the patterns. In particular, if the reconstructed pattern is not in the vocabulary, the recognizer will systematically return an error. With minimal knowledge about our definition of rhythmic patterns, the algorithm is able to identify the type of every tap and break in a sequence even in tricky situations, such as when there is just one type of events. Thanks to clustering, the recognizer adapts to the tempo (the overall tempo can be inferred by comparing the centroids of the clusters.)

Apparatus and Participants

The experiment was implemented in Java and conducted on a 13" Apple MacBook (Intel processor). Participants tapped the rhythmic patterns on the embedded multitouch trackpad.

Twelve unpaid volunteers (six female) participated in this experiment, with age ranging from 23 to 53 (mean 29, median 27). Five of them had never practiced music.

Stimulus

The pattern to reproduce is presented to the participant with a stimulus combining a static graphical representation of the pattern, visual animation and audio (Figure 2). The visual stimulus is a stationary shape depicting the whole rhythmic pattern, where each rectangle represents an event (Figure 2a). This shape is then progressively filled (Figure 2b) in synchrony with audio playback. Beats are marked with thin gray lines to visualize the durations of events.

[2] A break with a duration of an impulse is called a *release*. It occurs between two adjacent taps.

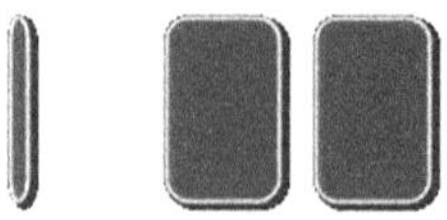

Figure 3. Visual feedback while tapping a pattern.

For audio playback and animation, impulses last 125ms and the tempo is set to 120 BPM or 2Hz (500ms period). This value is above the "synchronization threshold" [27] for both visual and auditive stimulus, ensuring that participants can perceive and perform it accurately. The audio stimulus is a 440Hz A, played by the General MIDI Instrument "English Horn" and held at a constant sound level. We chose this sound as it is soft enough for the subjects to endure during the experiment, but has clear onset and release.

Feedback

Participants are presented with 4 input FEEDBACK conditions while reproducing rhythmic patterns. The *Audio* feedback plays the same sound as the stimulus as long as the participant is touching the surface of the trackpad. The *Visual* feedback is based on the graphical representation of the stimulus. The rectangles representing the events appear dynamically while the subject is tapping on the trackpad (Figure 3). The *AudioVisual* feedback combines the two previous methods, and there is no feedback at all in the *None* condition.

The *Audio*, *Visual* and *AudioVisual* feedback methods are expected to help learning, e.g. in novice mode. Conversely, the *None* condition corresponds to the situation where an expert user is performing patterns in an eyes-free manner without audio feedback.

Vocabulary

For this experiment, we selected 30 rhythmic patterns among the 799 patterns with two to six beats generated by the rules described earlier. This vocabulary (Figure 4) contains 4 two-beats patterns, 8 three-beats patterns, 8 four-beats patterns, 6 five-beats patterns and 4 six-beats patterns. We explicitly featured fewer patterns for the extreme situations (two, five and six beats). Among the patterns with the same duration, we tried to balance the number of events. For example, for the 8 four-beat patterns, 2 contain two events, 3 contain three events and 3 contain four events.

Task

A trial consists in reproducing a rhythmic pattern according to the FEEDBACK condition, right after it is presented twice in a row. The participant performs the pattern by tapping on the trackpad with the index finger of her dominant hand. The recognizer then computes the temporal structure of the input and matches it with that of the stimulus. At the end of the trial, the participant is notified about the success or the failure of the match before advancing to the next trial.

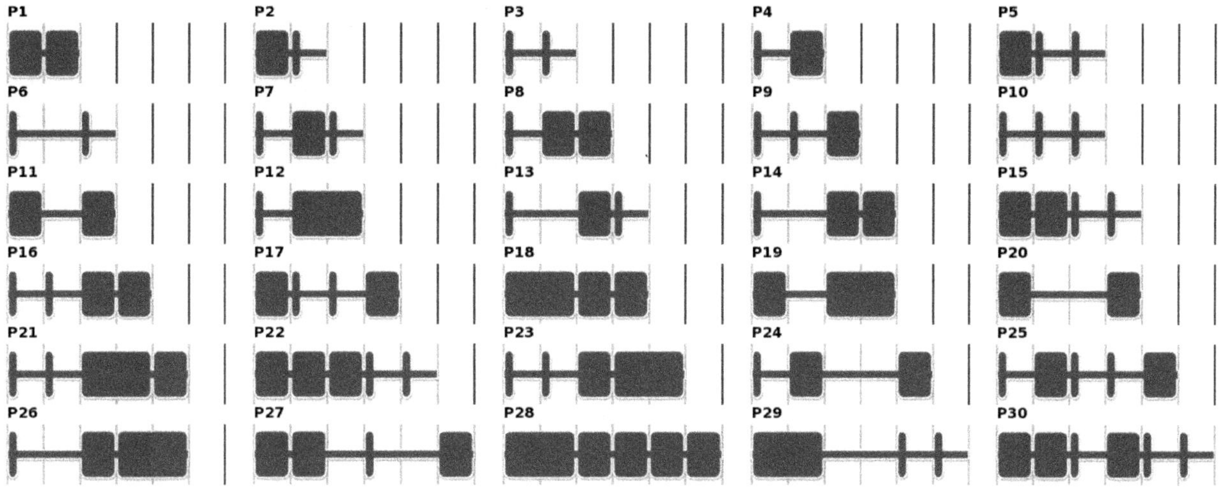

Figure 4. Vocabulary used in the first experiment.

Design and Procedure

The experiment is a 2×30 within-subject design with factors: (i) FEEDBACK: *Audio*, *Visual*, *AudioVisual* and *None*; and (ii) PATTERN: P1 – P30 (Figure 4).

At the beginning of the session, each FEEDBACK condition is introduced to the participant with a short block of 15 random trials. Then, the participant is asked to perform two warm-up blocks of 15 trials in the *AudioVisual* feedback condition, which we hypothesize provides the best feedback to become familiar with the task. The 3 first trials of the first warm-up block are performed by the experimenter to demonstrate the feedback condition to the participant. The second warm-up block is interrupted if the participant reports to be confident enough to start the experiment.

During the main session, measured trials are grouped into blocks according to the FEEDBACK factor. The presentation order for FEEDBACK is counterbalanced across participants with a Latin square. Within each block, the 30 patterns are repeated twice in randomized order. A practice block of 15 randomly selected patterns is performed prior each measured block and participants are allowed to have breaks between and in the middle of each block. Thus, we collected 12 participants $\times$ 4 FEEDBACK $\times$ 30 PATTERN $\times$ 2 repetitions $=$ 2880 measured trials. Participants were instructed to be as accurate as possible by paying attention to the discrimination of different types of taps and breaks. Each participant took about one hour to complete the sessions, after which they were asked to rank the feedback methods according to the difficulty of the task on a 5-point Likert's scale.

Quantitative Results

The overall success rate is 64.3%. This may seem low, but recall that our recognizer is deliberately very strict regarding the temporal structure of patterns, and that it can recognize all 799 patterns with two to six beats, not just the 30 patterns in the study. The precise reproduction of the rhythmic patterns in the study is similar to playing a percussion instrument, a task that musicians can take years to master.

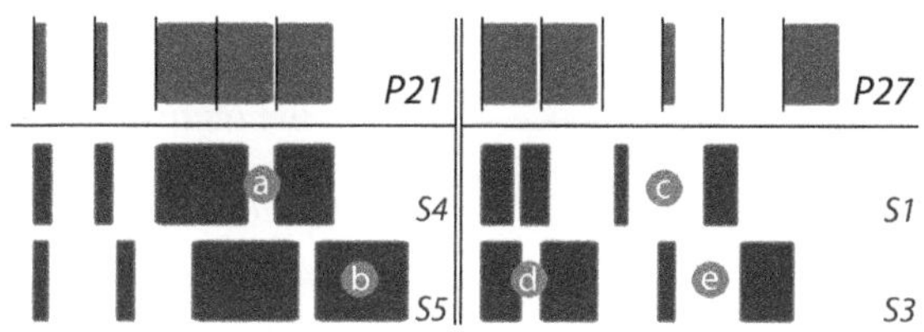

Figure 5. Two stimuli (P21 and P27) with reproductions errors by subjects of Experiment 1. S4: the last break is too long (a); S5: the last tap is too long (b); S1: the last break is too short (c); S3: the first break is too long (d), the last break is too short (e).

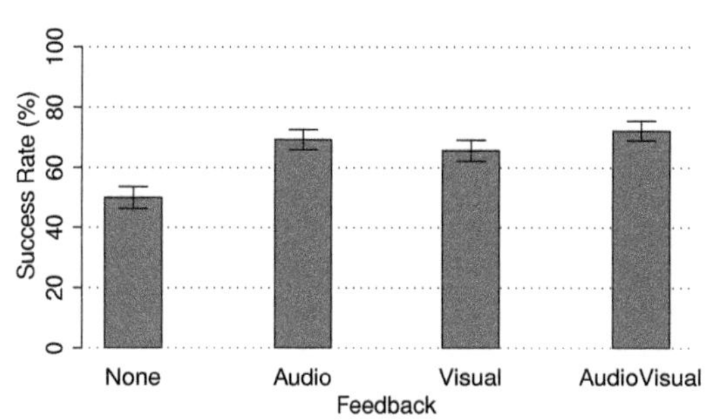

Figure 6. Success rate for each FEEDBACK condition.

Figure 5 shows typical reproduction errors by study participants, such as release breaks that are too long and recognized as short breaks, or breaks or taps that are too similar to be separated during clustering. Interestingly, errors seem more frequent with breaks than with taps, which is consistent with the finding that users tend to be more precise when performing notes than pauses [26].

A one-way ANOVA for FEEDBACK (with participant as a random variable) reveals a significant effect on success rate ($F_{3,33} = 15.4$, $p < 0.0001$). This effect can be observed in Figure 6[3]. Post-hoc t-tests with Bonferroni correction show that the *None* condition is significantly worse than all other feedback conditions. It is not surprising that the absence of feedback while performing the pattern significantly degrades the accuracy of rhythm reproduction.

[3]In all figures, error bars show the 95% confidence interval.

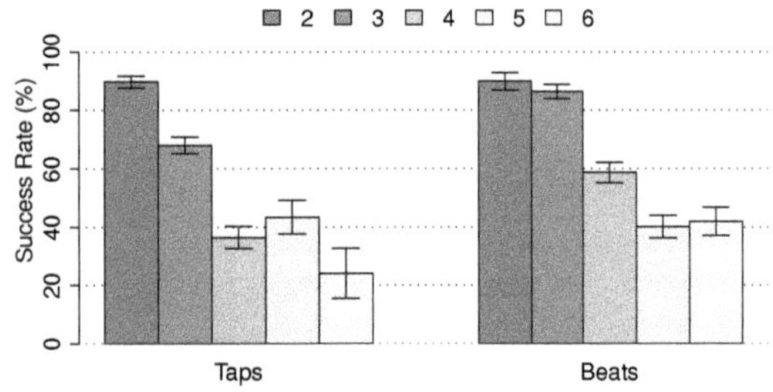

Figure 7. Success rate by number of taps and by length in beats.

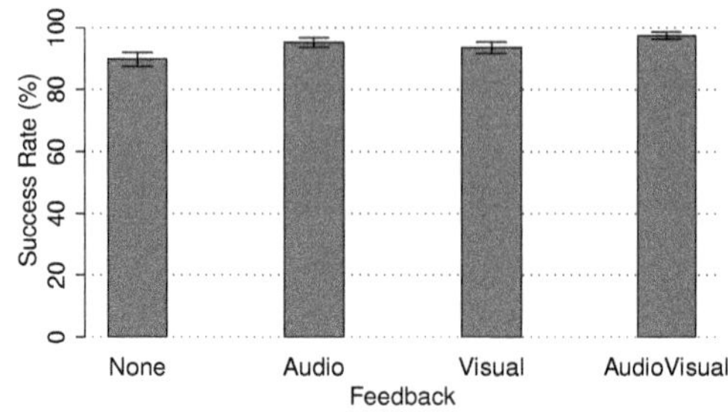

Figure 8. Revised success rate by FEEDBACK for the pattern classifier.

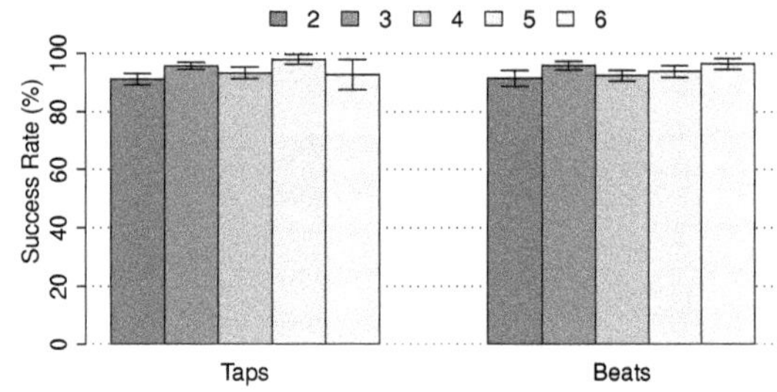

Figure 9. Revised success rate by number taps and length in beats for the pattern classifier.

Regarding PATTERN, a one-way ANOVA reveals a significant effect on success rate ($F_{29,319} = 25.1, p < 0.0001$). We observe a large deviation of the success rate for some patterns: from 16% with P27 to 98% for P10. Fifteen patterns have a success rate of at least 70%: P1–P7, P9–P13, P19, P20, and P29. All have at least 3 taps and all but P29 are less than four-beats long. However, some three-tap patterns have a low success rate (below 50%): P14 and P18 (both with 4 beats).

We could not identify similarities among the patterns that were difficult to reproduce. However, the number of taps and beats are the most obvious characteristics that can influence the ease of reproduction. In fact, we found a significant effect on success rate for taps ($F_{4,44} = 54.1, p < 0.0001$) and beats ($F_{4,44} = 85.5, p < 0.0001$), without significant interaction with FEEDBACK. Post-hoc t-tests support this hypothesis since, in most cases, the highest recognition rates were achieved for patterns with a small number of taps or beats (Figure 7).

Qualitative Results

Six participants out of 12 preferred the *Audio* feedback, 3 the *Visual* feedback, 2 the *AudioVisual* feedbacks and 1 no feedback. Moreover, 6 participants ranked *AudioVisual* second and 8 ranked the *None* condition last. Note that many participants pointed out that *AudioVisual* was confusing, providing too much information. They explained that in most cases, they chose one feedback (visual or auditive) and tried to ignore the other. Half of them preferred the *Audio* feedback because it was more related to rhythm than graphics.

We assessed the subjective difficulty of the task with the statement “I found it difficult to reproduce rhythmic patterns”. Seven participants disagreed or strongly disagreed, 4 neither disagreed nor agreed, and only one agreed, but at the same time disagreeing for the *None* and *Visual* feedbacks.

Overall, both quantitative and qualitative results are encouraging and support our hypothesis that rhythmic patterns, as defined by our framework, is a viable input technique for interactive tasks. While quantitative results support the need to provide feedback while performing input, qualitative results inform on the type of appropriate feedback. Finally, an analysis of recognition errors gives insights on how to create a recognizer that would be more suitable for real applications.

A PATTERN CLASSIFIER

The goal of the structural recognizer in Experiment 1 was to assess how accurately participants could reproduce a stimulus pattern. This recognizer is deliberately strict, accounting only for variations in the overall tempo of the pattern, and it does not take advantage of the fact that the input patterns are assumed to be part of a known vocabulary. We designed a second recognizer for use in actual applications, that classifies an input pattern against a vocabulary.

In order to recognize a sequence of taps, this *pattern classifier* first counts the number of taps in the sequence and considers the subset of the vocabulary with that number of taps. Then, it calculates a score for each candidate pattern. First, it infers the duration of a beat by considering the duration of the sequence of taps and the number of taps of the candidate. Using this value, it scales the pattern to match the duration of the input sequence and sums the temporal differences of events onsets and durations. A duration of a quarter beat is used for impulses and releases between consecutive events (when lifting the finger from the device). Finally, the score is weighted by the ratio between the inferred beat duration and the 120 BPM reference (500ms).

This classifier is less strict than the structural recognizer because it will always match an input pattern to a pattern in the vocabulary if it is the only one with the same number of taps, unless a threshold is set on the lowest acceptable score. Moreover, normalization makes the recognizer match patterns that are homothetic of each other. This is the reason for weighing the score by the relative beat durations.

We tested this classifier with the data and vocabulary of Experiment 1. The overall success rate rose to 93.9%, more in line with the expectations of an applicative context. As with the previous recognizer, a one-way ANOVA for FEEDBACK reveals a significant effect on success rate ($F_{3,33} = 7.2, p = 0.0007$) (Figure 8).

Figure 9 shows that unlike the structural recognizer, success rate does not decrease with pattern “complexity”: there is no significant effect of the number of taps or the length on

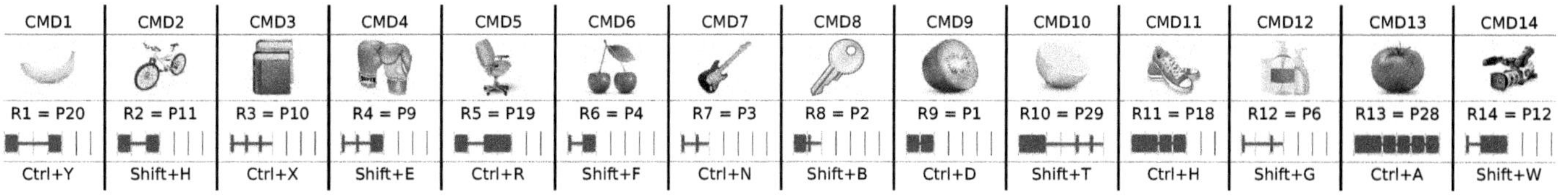

Figure 10. Commands used in Experiment 2. Pxx refers to the patterns of Experiment 1 (see Figure 4).

success rate[4]. Instead, we observe that success rates are affected by the similarity between patterns: a complex pattern can be recognized quite reliably provided that it is sufficiently different from other patterns with the same number of taps. For example, P30 is the only pattern made of 6 taps in our set, making recognition failure occur only when the subject tapped a wrong number of taps. By contrast, P17 seems to be more "complex" than the "simple" pattern P20 but the former has a 100% success rate and the latter 82%. In fact, the recognizer sometimes confuses P20 with P11. However, a post-hoc t-test with Holm correction reveals no significant difference between patterns for success rates.

In summary, we found that this classifier was well adapted to actual applications. In particular, a designer can create a vocabulary that minimizes the risk of patterns being confused.

EXPERIMENT 2: RHYTHMIC PATTERNS MEMORIZATION

In order to further validate Rhythmic Interaction, we conducted a second experiment to test whether patterns can be memorized and recalled in order to be used as an alternative to standard techniques for triggering commands. We compared rhythmic patterns with standard hotkeys in a "learn and recall" experiment similar to Appert and Zhai's comparison of gesture shortcuts with hotkeys [1], itself inspired by Grossman et al's study of hotkeys [14].

Variables

We compare two techniques for triggering commands (TECH factor): *Hotkey* and *Rhythm*. A third condition, *Free*, lets participants choose the technique they prefer.

Each command C_i is a triplet associating an image I_i, used as a stimulus for this command, and two triggering techniques: a rhythmic pattern R_i and a hotkey K_i. The command set (CMD factor) has 14 commands: C_1, ..., C_{14}. We chose the images symbolizing the commands in a set of common objects and fruits (Figure 10).

For the rhythmic patterns, we selected 14 patterns of varying complexity from Experiment 1 and randomly assigned each pattern to a command. For the hotkeys, we created combinations of a modifier (`Shift` or `Ctrl`) and a letter. The letters were chosen so that they did not match the first letter of the name of the object representing the command, as in [1]. The goal is to avoid giving an unfair advantage to hotkeys, since there is no similar mnemonic association between rhythmic patterns and command names. Furthermore, the mapping between commands and hotkeys often varies by application and language. Figure 10 shows the resulting assignment.

[4]This could be due to the fact that in the vocabulary, there were few patterns with five taps or beats.

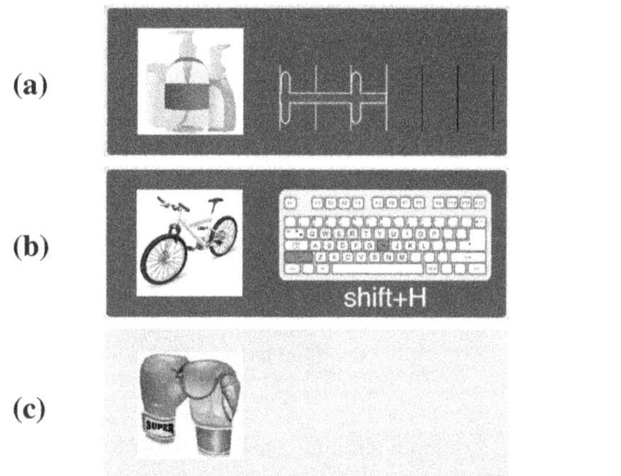

Figure 11. Stimulus in the learning phase for the *Rhythm* (a) and *Hotkey* (b) conditions, and in the testing phase for both conditions (c).

Task

The primary task of the experiment is to activate a command (C_i), presented by its stimulus image (I_i), with the triggering technique corresponding to the current TECH condition (R_i or K_i). The experiment has two phases: *learning* and *testing*.

During the learning phase, both the image I_i and the corresponding triggering technique (R_i or K_i) are shown to the participant. For rhythmic patterns, the static graphical representation is displayed next to the image (Figure 11a) and the audio stimulus is played twice. Hotkeys are presented with a short animation of the corresponding key-press sequence, also repeated twice, and text (Figure 11b).

In the testing phase, participants are presented with the image I_i only (Figure 11b). According to the current TECH condition, they must perform the corresponding hotkey K_i or rhythmic pattern R_i. If they forgot which trigger to perform, they are strongly encouraged to invoke a help screen by pressing the SPACE key. The task then switches to the learning mode, presenting the shortcut to perform as described above.

In both phases, the participant must perform the rhythmic pattern or the hotkey. For rhythmic patterns, we use the Audio-only feedback since Experiment 1 showed that it was effective and participants preferred it. Also, this avoids interference with the visual interface. For hotkeys, participants receive the usual kinesthetic feedback while pressing keys.

After entering each hotkey or pattern, the participants are asked to indicate which trigger they were trying to perform (Figure 12). Then, participants are notified of the correctness of their answer. If the answer is correct, they are given the result of the recognition. If not, the correct trigger is presented before moving to the next trial. The reason

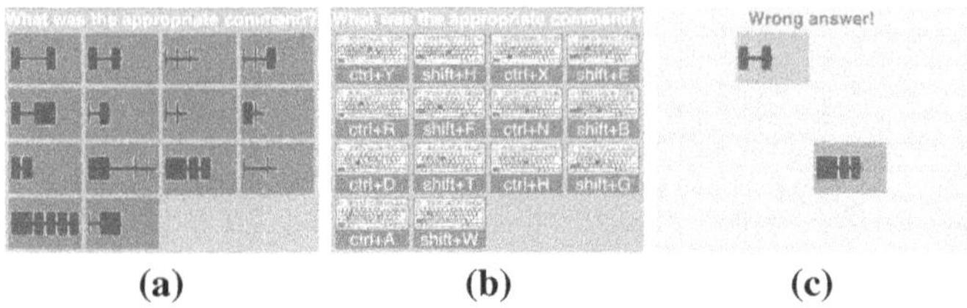

Figure 12. Confirmation in the *Rhythm* (a) and *Hotkey* (b) conditions. Feedback for a wrong answer in the *Rhythm* condition (c)).

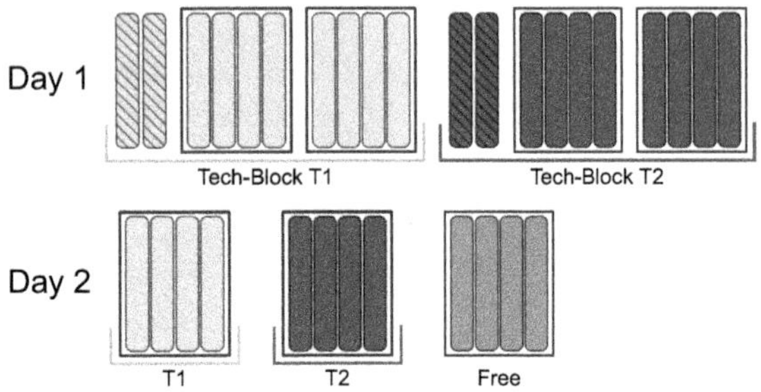

Figure 13. A sample session. Hatched sub-blocks are learning trials, boxed sub-blocks are sub-sessions.

for this procedure is that we are primarily interested in the memorization of the associations, not the participants' ability to perform the triggers. For rhythmic patterns, it also allows us to test the recognition rate of the classifier.

Apparatus & Participants

We used the same apparatus as in Experiment 1. We recruited 14 participants (5 female), aged between 22 and 33 (mean 26, median 26). Five of them had participated in Experiment 1.

Design & Procedure

The experiment is a within-subject design with technique (TECH) and command (CMD) as primary factors. The experiment is split into two sessions held on two consecutive days. The first day, all participants are presented with rhythmic patterns in a 5 minutes practice session based on Experiment 1. We use TECH as a blocking factor, counterbalanced across participants. The second day, a *Free* block is added at the end of the testing phase. In this block, participants can choose to use *Rhythm* or *Hotkey* for each trial, but cannot get help.

Each TECH-block is divided into several sub-blocks of 15 trials: (i) 2 learning sub-blocks with 4 testing sub-blocks each on the first day; (ii) 4 testing sub-blocks on the second day. Thus, the testing phase of the experiment is split into SUBSESSIONS of 60 trials each: two on the first day to evaluate immediate memorization of triggering commands and one on the second day to test mid-term recall (Figure 13).

In order to simulate a more realistic setup, where some commands are more frequently used than others, we assign an apparition frequency to each of the 14 commands following a Zipf distribution [14, 1]. For the learning phase we use the frequencies (6, 6, 3, 3, 2, 2, 1, 1, 1, 1, 1, 1, 1, 1) and for the testing phase (12, 12, 6, 6, 4, 4, 3, 3, 2, 2, 2, 2, 1, 1). The 14 commands are combined with these frequencies using 7 different permutations, and each frequency assignment is

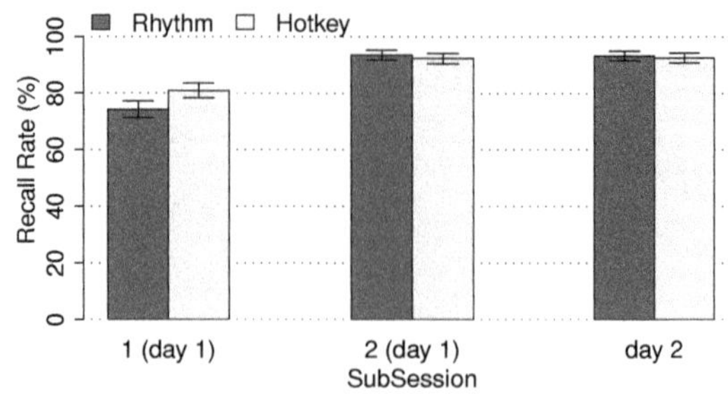

Figure 14. Recall rate for both techniques by sub-session.

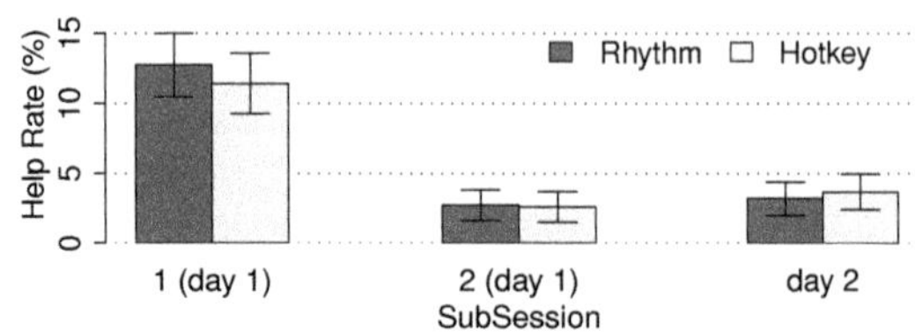

Figure 15. Help usage rate for both techniques for each sub-session.

counterbalanced across participants, resulting in the same number of trials for each command overall. The presentation of the trials is randomized across consecutive pairs of sub-blocks.

The experiment takes about one hour on day 1 and 30 minutes on day 2, after which participants are given a questionnaire to collect subjective observations and preferences.

Quantitative Results

Our main measures are (i) *recall rate*, the percentage of correct answers in the testing phase without help; and (ii) *help rate*, the percentage of trials where the participants used help in the testing phase. We analyze the results according to TECH and the three sub-sessions of the experiment by considering these measures in the model TECH × SUBSESSION × Rand(PARTICIPANT).

We find a significant effect of SUBSESSION on the recall rate ($F_{2,26} = 103$, $p < 0.0001$). A post-hoc t-test with Bonferroni correction shows that the recall rate is significantly lower only between the first sub-session and the two following ones (Figure 14). There is no significant effect of TECH on recall rate ($F_{1,13} = 0.61$, $p = 0.4474$), but the ANOVA reveals a significant interaction effect TECH × SUBSESSION ($F_{2,26} = 5.36$, $p = 0.0113$). Post-hoc t-tests with Bonferroni correction show a significant difference between *Rhythm* and *Hotkey* for the first sub-session (74% and 81% respectively). For the remaining sub-sessions, the results are extremely close between the two techniques with a recall rate of about 93% (Figure 14).

For the use of help, an ANOVA reveals a significant effect of SUBSESSION ($F_{2,26} = 17.3$, $p < 0.0001$), no effect of TECH ($F_{1,13} = 0.04$, $p = 0.8532$), and no TECH × SUBSESSION interaction effect ($F_{2,26} = 0.62$, $p = 0.545$). We find only one significant difference among sub-sessions: help was used more often in the first sub-session than in the two subsequent ones (see Figure 15).

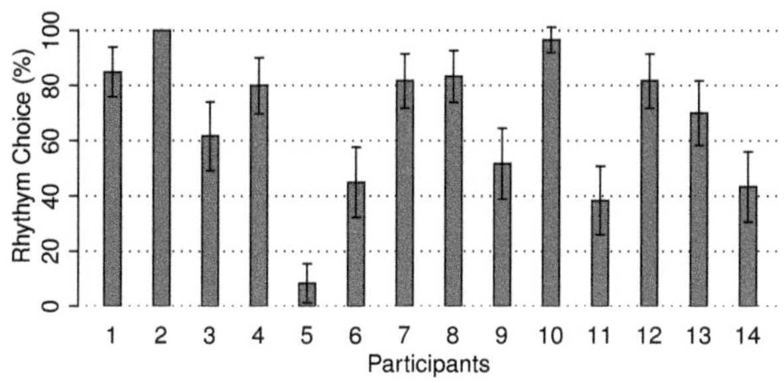

Figure 16. Percentage use of *Rhythm* by participant (*Free* condition).

Results for rhythmic patterns and hotkeys are quite similar, suggesting that rhythmic patterns can be memorized as successfully as hotkeys without mnemonics. This is a remarkable result considering how widespread hotkeys are.

Recall rates are consistent across commands. Considering only the *Rhythm* condition, we build the model CMD × SUBSESSION × Rand(PARTICIPANT) for recall rate and help and see a significant effect of CMD on recall rate ($F_{13,169} = 1.17$, $p = 0.025$). A post-hoc t-test with Holm corrections shows significant differences only between R_3 and R_{13} (recall rate about 97%) and R_{10}, R_{11} and R_{14} (~80%).

To test our classifier, we compare the pattern recognized by the classifier with the answer selected by the participant using the model TECH × SUBSESSION × Rand(PARTICIPANT). We find a significant effect of TECH ($F_{1,13} = 5.34$, $p = 0.038$), with *Rhythm* having a significant lower success rate than *Hotkey*: 85.2% vs. 91.8%. The success rate for *Hotkey* is surprisingly low, as we expect few if any errors when entering hotkeys. This may be due to participants changing their mind as to which was the right hotkey when they see the answer sheet. For *Rhythm*, the rate is also lower than expected, but the same phenomenon may have occurred. Indeed, the success rate of *Rhythm* relatively to *Hotkey* is 92.8%, close to the rate obtained on the data for Experiment 1 (94%).

Qualitative Results

Figure 16 shows the percentage of trials where participants used rhythmic patterns in the *Free* condition, on the second day of the experiment. Ten participants (out of 14) used rhythmic patterns more often than hotkeys. Seven participants used rhythmic patterns more than 80% of the time, while only one participant used rhythmic patterns less than 20% of the time.

The answers to the questionnaire were generally positive, confirming the previous results. Out of the 14 participants, 9 preferred using the rhythmic patterns, 3 the hotkeys, 2 had no preference. Those who preferred using rhythmic patterns did so mostly because of the "fun factor" of tapping rhythms, but also because it could be performed "in place" on the trackpad, even for a novice user, without having to visually search the keys on the keyboard. On the other hand, several participants noticed that hotkeys are faster to perform and preferred to use hotkeys when the corresponding pattern is too long.

Regarding memorization, some participants reported using mnemonics related to the rhythm itself in order to help memorization. For instance, a subject linked the "boxing gloves" command and the corresponding pattern P9 (Figure 4) to a "pif paf boom" onomatopoeia that, for him, echoed the "short short medium" structure of the pattern. Another participant also reported linking the pattern structure with the pronunciation of the object's name, e.g., "toma-to-to-to-to" for command 13 and pattern P28. Subjects also used the graphical representation of patterns to memorize them, which supports our design for this representation. For example, one participant stated that "the rhythmic pattern's visual representation for the cherry looks like a cherry".

These comments suggest that users elaborate efficient strategies for the memorization of rhythmic patterns, based on the rhythm itself or its visualization. Since commands were assigned to rhythmic patterns randomly, we did not expect such associations, but this finding opens the way to studying ways to reinforce these associations. This is commonly done for gestures, e.g., a question mark for help, and hotkeys, e.g. Ctrl-*S* for *S*ave. In particular, various strategies could be explored to create visual "cheatsheets" for rhythmic patterns or display them next to menu commands, like hotkeys.

In addition, the complexity of performing rhythmic patterns can be turned into an advantage for memorization. Since deeper and greater numbers of levels of encoding and processing help memory [8], combining motor and auditive perception of rhythmic patterns may help users memorize, i.e., encode, their associations with commands.

SUMMARY AND PERSPECTIVES

In this paper we studied the use of rhythmic patterns in HCI. We explored Rhythmic Interaction as an opportunity to generalize the primitive use of rhythm in existing techniques, e.g., long click and double click, as well as to promote a new input modality. Since Rhythmic Interaction relies on the time dimension instead of the spatial and visual dimensions used by most input methods, it is well suited when space is limited or when visual attention is not available.

We presented a grammar for creating rhythmic patterns as well as two recognizers that do not require training. A first experiment evaluated the ability of casual users to reproduce rhythmic patterns very precisely with different feedback conditions. We found that some complex patterns can be difficult to reproduce in such a precise way, but that audio and/or visual feedback improve accuracy. After analyzing recognition errors, we designed a different recognizer that reached 94% recognition rate for the 30-pattern vocabulary of Experiment 1. We ran a second experiment to investigate the memorization of associations between rhythmic patterns and commands, i.e., *rhythmic shortcuts*. The results suggest that rhythmic patterns are recalled as efficiently as traditional hotkeys and that users create effective mnemonic strategies to associate rhythms with commands.

This work demonstrates the potential of rhythmic patterns as an input method, and contributes a 14-pattern vocabulary that has proven usable by novice users. Beyond triggering commands and switching modes in standard desktop environments, rhythmic patterns could be used in many contexts: eye-free control of a mobile device, such as a cellular phone or a mobile player; remote control of interactive environments such as wall-size displays by tapping on wearable sensors without the need for visual attention; selection of an object on a tabletop when it is not easily reachable, etc.

Our future work will address issues such as the segmentation of patterns, the scalability of the vocabularies and the speed of execution, which are important for the design of Rhythmic Interactions. Another area for future work is the use of multiple fingers or both hands to tap patterns and to combine rhythmic interaction with other interaction techniques. More complex actions than tapping should also be explored to enter rhythmic structures, such as performing sequences of gestures or keyboard taps, as well as the use of the temporal dimension to convey additional information. Furthermore, rhythmic *output*, such as vibration patterns on mobile devices, seems worth studying since perception and performance of rhythmic patterns are tightly linked. Finally, the power of rhythmic interaction could be expanded by exploiting syntactic features used in music such as performing sequential or parallel combinations of patterns.

ACKNOWLEDGEMENTS

We thank Caroline Appert for feedback on earlier versions of this paper, our participants and the anonymous reviewers.

REFERENCES

1. Appert, C., and Zhai, S. Using strokes as command shortcuts: cognitive benefits and toolkit support. In *Proc. CHI '09*, ACM (2009), 2289–2298.
2. Arom, S., Thom, M., Tuckett, B., and Boyd, R. *African polyphony and polyrhythm: musical structure and methodology*. Cambridge university press, 1991.
3. Baudel, T., and Beaudouin-Lafon, M. Charade: Remote control of objects using free-hand gestures. *Comm. ACM 36* (1993), 28–35.
4. Blair, C. R. On computer transcription of manual morse. *JACM 6*, 3 (1959), 429–442.
5. Brochard, R., Touzalin, P., Despres, O., and Dufour, A. Evidence of beat perception via purely tactile stimulation. *Brain Res. 1223* (2008), 59 – 64.
6. Chen, S.-C., Chien, C.-Y., Chang, W.-M., and Lin, S.-W. A new assistive communication system for the serious disabled. In *Proc. iCREATe '08*, START Centre (2008), 59–64.
7. Clarke, E. Rhythm and timing in music. *The Psychology of Music 2* (1999), 473–500.
8. Craik, F. I., and Lockhart, R. S. Levels of processing: A framework for memory research. *J. Verbal Learning and Verbal Behavior 11*, 6 (1972), 671–684.
9. Crossan, A., and Murray-Smith, R. Rhythmic interaction for song filtering on a mobile device. In *Proc. HAID '06*, Springer (2006), 45–55.
10. Faure, G., Chapuis, O., and Roussel, N. Power tools for copying and moving: useful stuff for your desktop. In *Proc. CHI '09*, ACM (2009), 1675–1678.
11. Fekete, J.-D., Elmqvist, N., and Guiard, Y. Motion-pointing: target selection using elliptical motions. In *Proc. CHI '09*, ACM (2009), 289–298.
12. Fraisse, P. Rhythm and tempo. In *The Psychology of Music*, Academic Press (1982), 149–180.
13. Glass, L. Synchronization and rhythmic processes in physiology. *Nature 410*, 6825 (2001), 277–284.
14. Grossman, T., Dragicevic, P., and Balakrishnan, R. Strategies for accelerating on-line learning of hotkeys. In *Proc. CHI '07*, ACM (2007), 1591–1600.
15. Hinckley, K., Baudisch, P., Ramos, G., and Guimbretiere, F. Design and analysis of delimiters for selection-action pen gesture phrases in scriboli. In *Proc. CHI '05*, ACM (2005), 451–460.
16. Kurtenbach, G., and Buxton, W. User learning and performance with marking menus. In *Proc. CHI '94*, ACM (1994), 258–264.
17. Lantz, V., and Murray-Smith, R. Rhythmic interaction with a mobile device. In *Proc. NordiCHI '04*, ACM (2004), 97–100.
18. Large, E. W. Periodicity, pattern formation, and metric structure. *J. New Music Research 30*, 2 (2001), 173 – 185.
19. MacDougall, H. G., and Moore, S. T. Marching to the beat of the same drummer: the spontaneous tempo of human locomotion. *J. Applied Physiology 99*, 3 (2005), 1164–1173.
20. Malacria, S., Lecolinet, E., and Guiard, Y. Clutch-free panning and integrated pan-zoom control on touch-sensitive surfaces: the cyclostar approach. In *Proc. CHI '10*, ACM (2010), 2615–2624.
21. Manuel, R. *Histoire de la Musique*. Encyclopédie de la Pléiade, Gallimard, Paris, France, 1960.
22. Maury, S., Athénes, S., and Chatty, S. Rhythmic menus: toward interaction based on rhythm. In *Proc. CHI '99 EA*, ACM (1999), 254–255.
23. Moelants, D. Preferred tempo reconsidered. In *Proc. ICMPC '02*, AMPS (2002), 580–583.
24. Petitto, L. A., Holowka, S., Sergio, L. E., Levy, B., and Ostry, D. J. Baby hands that move to the rhythm of language: hearing babies acquiring sign languages babble silently on the hands. *Cognition 93*, 1 (2004), 43 – 73.
25. Potter, D. D., Fenwick, M., Abecasis, D., and Brochard, R. Perceiving rhythm where none exists: Event-related potential (erp) correlates of subjective accenting. *Cortex 45*, 1 (2009), 103–109.
26. Rammsayer, T., and Lima, S. Duration discrimination of filled and empty auditory intervals: Cognitive and perceptual factors. *Perception and Psychophysics 50* (1991), 565–574.
27. Repp, B. H. Rate limits in sensorimotor synchronization. *Advances in Cognitive Psychology 2*, 2 (2006), 163–181.
28. Robinson, S., Rajput, N., Jones, M., Jain, A., Sahay, S., and Nanavati, A. Tapback: towards richer mobile interfaces in impoverished contexts. In *Proc. CHI '11*, ACM (2011), 2733–2736.
29. Sacks, O. *Musicophilia: Tales of Music and the Brain*, 2 ed., vol. 1. Vintage Books, New York, USA, 2008.
30. Scott, J., Dearman, D., Yatani, K., and Truong, K. N. Sensing foot gestures from the pocket. In *Proc. UIST '10*, ACM (2010), 199–208.
31. Szentgyorgyi, C., and Lank, E. Five-key text input using rhythmic mappings. In *Proc. ICMI '07*, ACM (2007), 118–121.
32. Westeyn, T., and Starner, T. Recognizing song-based blink patterns: Applications for restricted and universal access. In *Proc. FGR '04*, IEEE (2004), 717–722.
33. Wobbrock, J. O. Tapsongs: tapping rhythm-based passwords on a single binary sensor. In *Proc. UIST '09*, ACM (2009), 93–96.

PULSE: The Design and Evaluation of an Auditory Display to Provide a Social Vibe

David McGookin & Stephen Brewster
G.I.S.T., School of Computing Science, University of Glasgow
{firstname.lastname}@glasgow.ac.uk

ABSTRACT
We present PULSE, a mobile application designed to allow users to gain a 'vibe', an intrinsic understanding of the people, places and activities around their current location, derived from messages on the Twitter social networking site. We compared two auditory presentations of the vibe. One presented message metadata implicitly through modification of spoken message attributes. The other presented the same metadata, but through additional auditory cues. We compared both techniques in a lab and real world study. Additional auditory cues were found to allow for smaller changes in metadata to be more accurately detected, but were least preferred when PULSE was used in context. Results also showed that PULSE enhanced and shaped user understanding, with audio presentation allowing a closer coupling of digital data to the physical world.

Author Keywords
Twitter; Geo-Social Media; Auditory Display; Location-Based Services

ACM Classification Keywords
H.5.2 Information Interfaces and Presentation: User Interfaces—*Interaction Styles*

General Terms
Design; Experimentation; Human Factors

INTRODUCTION
The recent rise of both mobile smartphones and social networking has caused a significant rise in the amount of textual, photographic and other user generated content (UGC) tagged with the location of it's creation. The increasing quantity of this data affords new ways for its exploration and interaction. However, searching over social networks is still primarily based on textual queries, or by filtering on user added metadata such as hashtags. Thus far, little attention has been given to exploiting location in interaction. Where location-based queries are supplied, they tend to be buried in the user interface with results displayed as pins on a map (see Figure 1 left), such as with Twitter (www.twitter.com), or as a simple list (see Figure 1 right), such as with Google+ (www.plus.google.com).

Permission to make digital or hard copies of all or part of this work for personal or classroom use is granted without fee provided that copies are not made or distributed for profit or commercial advantage and that copies bear this notice and the full citation on the first page. To copy otherwise, or republish, to post on servers or to redistribute to lists, requires prior specific permission and/or a fee.
CHI '12, May 5–10, 2012, Austin, Texas, USA.
Copyright 2012 ACM 978-1-4503-1015-4/12/05...$10.00.

Figure 1. Illustration of current techniques to display the results of location based queries over social networks. The Twitter iPhone client presents a map with message locations marked with pins (left). The Google+ client presents a list view of nearby messages (right).

In this paper we investigate how to re-integrate geo-coded UGC back into the environment of its creation, and the role this re-integration can play enhancing users' understand of the area around them. In particular, we use text based social media to provide a 'vibe' or 'feel' of a physical location: an intrinsic understanding of the people, places and activities that exist in the environment around the user's current location. Understanding the local environment, people and culture is a key reason why tourists visit different countries. Guidebooks often try to describe this feeling to communicate what it is like to live in a location and understand a place from the perspective of a local. Lonely Planet [17] for instance, prints discussions with locals about their lives as a means of trying to communicate the feeling of living in a place: *"I was born here in Savo, and I live a third of each year here in my summer cottage. I feel this is the most valuable thing about the area, that in the nature here you can really get away from all the troubles of a normal life, a busy life"* [17, p.136]. However, guidebooks can be cumbersome to use during exploration [5], and because of their static nature, the information provided may not be congruent with the user's current experience of the environment. In addition, users must make an explicit decision to remove and look at a (paper or electronic) guidebook, something that is often not done *in situ* [5]. In our work, we are seeking to explore how user generated social media can be exploited to provide the understanding that a local would have.

In this paper we present two evaluations of PULSE. PULSE is designed, through a combination of speech and sonification, to communicate the vibe of an area, derived from messages on the Twitter (www.twitter.com) social networking site, to a user as he or she walks around the environment. In the next section we outline an example scenario of PULSE in use, before discussing related work and the results of two studies to evaluate PULSE. The first was a controlled lab study to compare and contrast two different sonifications. The other sought to understand PULSE in real world use.

SCENARIO

Kat is visiting France. It is her first visit to the country and she has the rest of the afternoon free to enjoy the town. She puts in her earbuds, starts the PULSE application, and puts her phone back into her pocket. As she wanders along the street PULSE selects nearby social messages, synthesises them and plays them to Kat. As Kat walks, she begins to hear the trickling sound of a stream, indicating an increasing amount of on-line activity in her current location. Kat learns of a local *Bocce* team who are meeting to celebrate winning a tournament, that the traffic in the nearby streets is blocked because of protests and the town is busy preparing for a music festival at the weekend. As she continues, the trickling stream evolves into a fast flowing river telling Kat that there are many more messages in this area. A bubbling sound, indicating a trend in the message content, is introduced by PULSE. As she walks, Kat realises that the trend refers to the two local football teams who are playing each other. Not being a football fan, Kat takes out her phone and tells PULSE to reduce the number of messages presented about the football. Realising she is approaching the football stadium, Kat takes a side street into a small square. The presentation rate of the messages decreases, the bubbling fades out and the water returns to a trickling stream, reflecting the quieter, more laid back area she is now in. Sitting at a street side cafe, she orders a beer. Relaxing with her beer she notices a group of men celebrating inside. Many have *Bocce* bags, and she realises that this was the team that PULSE had previously told her about. She relaxes with her beer, enjoying watching children play in the fountain. PULSE continues to provide less frequent updates as the natural sights, sounds and messages from PULSE merge to provide a deeper understanding of her environment. Kat learns of the small boy in the apartments above who refuses to have a bath before bed, the girl nervously waiting the arrival of her first date and the woman upset over the death of her mother. Finishing her beer, Kat pays and continues her exploration with PULSE.

RELATED WORK

Little research has been undertaken into the role that nearby geo-social media can play when the user is in the physical environment, and less that considers how the presentation of such data affects user perception of the environment [15]. There are, of course, many applications (such as Google Earth [1]) that place such media on maps, but these are not tied to the current location of the user, rather they are tied to a location the user is interested in. Social networks such as foursquare.com have a strong location based element and allow users to find and view nearby "checkins" of other users, but their role is in the finding and recommendation of services in the environment, and not in the communication of a vibe as we have described. Similarly, work such as by Jang *et al.* [8] and Bellotti *et al.* [1] seek to create *ad hoc* social networks amongst geographically close, but unknown, social network users, primarily for recommendation of new places. Whilst such an outcome may be an effect of presenting a vibe, it is not the primary focus of our work.

Much closer to a vibe is Columbus by Rost *et al.* [15]. They investigated how the presentation of images from flickr.com affected users when in the area where the photographs were taken. As users moved around the physical environment, photographs that had been taken in the vicinity were "unlocked" so participants could view them. Rost *et al.* found that the discovery of unexpected photographs, those that were not of obvious or common things in the local environment, promoted serendipity, changing user perception of the built environment. Robinson *et al.* [14] have investigated how the distribution and type of geo-coded social media can be used to support navigation towards a destination. For example, a large number of photographs on one route might indicate that it is scenic, whilst a large number of Twitter messages on another route may indicate that it is a built-up urban location. This work highlights the potential of social media to provide a much more engaging and useful experience than putting pins in a map.

All of the previously mentioned work uses a visual interface to communicate with the user. It is also common to use augmented reality to overlay messages or photographs around the user on a live video feed [6]. In all cases users must make an explicit decision to look at the device, such as with Columbus [15]. As a vibe is an awareness aid, and we consider that it should never be the primary user task, or a task in itself, such presentation is unsuitable. Bellotti *et al.* [1] noted that it was difficult to integrate their Magitti social recommender system into social settings because users continually looked at the visual display. A more appropriate approach is to use sound. Though not about social networks, Rowland *et al.* [16] used audio to present and record messages in an interactive cycling experience. They found that listening to messages recorded by strangers provided an intimate connection for the listener. Dingler and Brewster [7] evaluated how overview activity of multiple different social networking sites could be communicated through a set of thematically linked sounds. Although they did not consider geo-location, users were able to monitor changes in activity levels amongst their contacts. Earlier work by Mynatt [11] found that an aural awareness of the status of people in a building (e.g. how long someone had been out of their office) could be provided via ambient Auditory Icons. In an evaluation it was found that these could be monitored in the periphery, without becoming distracting.

Social networking research shows that information relevant to a vibe can be extracted from sites such as Twitter. In an analysis of a Twitter corpus by Java *et al.* [9], over 50% of messages were geo-tagged, and 66% concerned the activities

[1] www.google.com/earth

and feelings of users at the time (and therefore the location where) the messages were posted; a key feature of a vibe. Similar results were identified by Zhao and Rosson [19] who argued that the personal nature of status updates promoted a feeling of connectedness and awareness of others' feelings and attitudes, even if those people had never met. These findings indicate that the raw message data posted to Twitter by users fits with our previous description of a vibe. Other work has shown that higher level summary aspects of messages, such as trends, events and general moods of creators can be extracted, given a large enough sample and computational power [3, 4]. This work has lead to visualisation tools to allow news organisations and emergency planners to understand historical or developing situations [3, 10].

The work discussed indicates that a vibe can be extracted from geo-coded social media, particularly Twitter. It also indicates that for an ambient, passive presentation, the use of sound through both speech and non-speech audio is likely to be more appropriate than presentation via a visual display. In the following section we introduce PULSE, a system designed to provide a vibe via an auditory display and support better understanding of the environment around the user.

PULSE

PULSE runs on the iOS platform and uses the Twitter social media service to provide content. From the earlier discussion of Magitti [1], and the issues of visual displays it raises, it is important that active interaction is not required. Users therefore interact with PULSE passively as they walk around a physical location. Information is directly or indirectly presented through a spatialised auditory display via earbuds. These do not block out external sound, and our aim is to augment, rather than replace, the existing auditory soundscape in an area with a digital vibe. Twitter provides a geo-search API allowing developers to search for messages within a defined physical location. In PULSE we search over a relatively small area (100m radius) around the user, and request only messages generated on the same day, so we can generate a local and recent vibe. The messages returned may have been generated by any Twitter user. Each message obtained is processed to remove acronyms or urls. Common contractions, such as *'lol'*, are replaced with longer equivalents. At periodic intervals we select the closest message to the user's current location, subject to a maximum cut off distance of 100m. This message is then rendered using the Cereproc (www.cereproc.com) text-to-speech engine using a Scottish male voice, and presented geo-centrically in a 3D auditory space. Because the messages are so short (each is a maximum of 140 characters), we move them along the same directional axis so they are presented closer to the user (a distance of 15m). This means the messages can be clearly heard, but also that users can either attend to the message or continue to walk, causing the message to naturally fade out as the distance between it and the user increases (see Figure 2). In such a way we are providing whispers of conversations around the user, and one element of a vibe.

Simply presenting the content of a few messages, whilst important, is not sufficient to represent a vibe as we previously described. Such messages provide only the concrete exam-

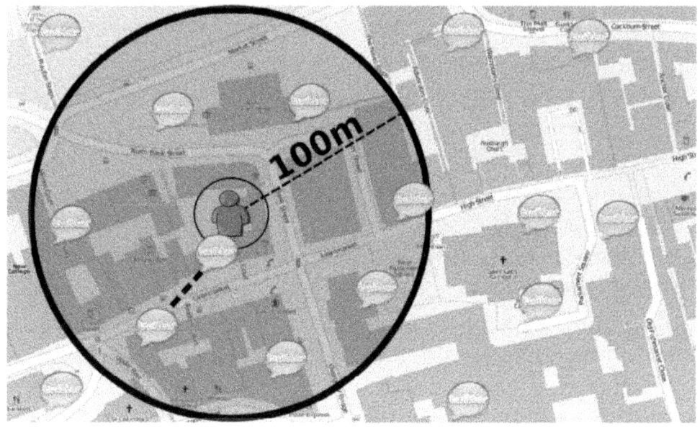

Figure 2. Trend and Message Density are calculated from all of the messages in a 100m radius around the user's current location. Periodically, the closest message is selected, and presented spatially at a point 15m from the user along the same axis.

ples of what activities occur in an area. They do not provide an overview. In addition, depending on user walking speed and the number of messages downloaded, it is very unlikely that a user would hear all of the messages available. In order to provide the full vibe we must also communicate more implicit aspects of the messages in a timely fashion. We consider the following to be key implicit aspects.

Message Density: We combine the volume of messages that are downloaded, the rate at which they have been generated and their age to determine message density. An area where there are long time gaps between the creation time of messages would be indicative that not a lot is happening. This is not necessarily a bad thing, and its meaning would need to be determined based on the user's other senses. For example, if the user is wandering around a sleepy seaside village, message density may be lower than if wandering around a city centre. However, the meaning of each of these would be different. In the case of the seaside village it may heighten the laid back nature of where the user is. In the city it may indicate that the user is wandering into an area where there is little to see or do, and changing direction may be more appropriate. Based on informal testing, we classify a gap of 60 seconds or less in the mean creation time between messages to be the maximum (highest) value of message density. Messages with a mean gap between creation of 60 minutes or greater are classified as the minimum (lowest) message density value. Other gaps are scaled between these values.

Topic Diversity/Agreement: A second attribute is in the consistency and diversity of the messages in a given area. Consistency can help better inform the user of large scale or common activities taking place in the current area. The lack of a trend, and thus an indication of the diversity of messages, is equally important. This would provide an impression of the richness and variety of a place. For example, a city centre may have lots of different activities that have a similar number of generated messages. The techniques previously discussed (e.g. [4]) for extracting this trend from messages require significantly more network bandwidth and processing power than is currently available on mobile devices. We use a much cheaper approach. We count the number of messages in the 100m area that have been tagged by their creators with a hash tag. If 30% or more of the messages are labelled with the same tag, we classify a trend as existing in the current area. Larger percentages of messages sharing the same tag are classified as stronger trends.

Whilst these attributes are relatively straightforward to obtain from the messages downloaded, it is much less straightforward to consider how they should be integrated into the auditory display. We consider two difference approaches: using additional non-speech auditory cues and implicit presentation through modification of the spoken messages.

Speech Plus Non-Speech Audio Presentation

Our first approach is to employ explicit presentation of the message metadata through additional non-speech auditory cues. This allows the message density and trend to be rapidly presented to the user and a finer grained vibe to be presented. However, the sounds chosen need to work within the existing, natural, auditory environment. Selecting appropriate sounds that work well is challenging. We have based these cues around a water-based soundscape. Water exists in both urban and rural settings, so is a good metaphor to draw upon. It also allows us to present a structured soundscape [7] to complement the spoken messages.

Message density is linked to the rate of flowing water. As the it increases, the flow rate of the water also increases, from a quiet bubbling brook to a raging river rapid. A combination of different sound samples and auditory volume is used to generate this effect. Emergence of a trend is presented in much the same way via a bubbling sound, analogous to a common topic "bubbling" up. Depending on the strength of the trend, this ranges from a quite intermittent plopping to a boiling pot of water. This provides a fine grained indication of the popularity of a particular topic. On the appearance of a trend, the user can, via a visual slider, decide whether to elevate its importance (causing PULSE to give more weight to messages from that trend for spoken presentation), or reduce the presentation of further messages from that trend.

Implicit Presentation Through Speech

In this version, rather than provide additional auditory cues to present message density and trend information, we use modification of the presentation characteristics of the spoken messages to communicate the data. Here, message density is reflected in the separation gap between successive message presentations. The higher the message density, the shorter the time between successive message presentations. At the maximum message density value, messages are presented every 8 seconds. At the minimum message density value this rises to 28 seconds. These values were based on informal piloting. It will take a few message presentations before a user is aware of this increase or decrease. This might be useful when the user is relatively static, enjoying a coffee at a street cafe, but it may be too slow if the user is moving through the city and the message density is changing quickly.

It is less clear how the diversity or agreement of a topic can be realised. Our initial approach, when a topic was identified, was to elevate messages from that topic so their presentation was prioritised over other messages. However, the user may not consider the trend messages to be of greater importance to be elevated. As in the scenario presented, a user may not be interested in a nearby football game and wish to exclude those messages. We have therefore taken the approach of changing the speaker voice from male to female when a message from a trend is presented. In this way the user is quickly made aware of one or more emergent trends and, as with the use of additional non-speech cues, can decide whether to elevate or reduce its importance via a slider.

Modifying the spoken message to communicate this additional data has the advantage that we are not obtrusively modifying the existing soundscape with new auditory cues. However, as shown, there are also disadvantages: a coarser grained feedback, and changes in attributes are likely to take longer to be noticed by users. The use of a different speaker for trends provides only binary feedback: there is a trend or not. It cannot communicate the strength of that trend as a proportion of all messages in the area.

Both techniques have benefits in trying to present a vibe. Through both a quantative lab-based study and a qualitative field study we will attempt to answer the following three key research questions:

RQ1: Can users gain an overview of the vibe around their current location?

RQ2: What is the trade off between the two proposed feedback techniques to communicate the PULSE metadata?

RQ3: What are the implications and design issues of using PULSE *in situ*?

LAB EVALUATION

We elected to perform both a lab-based user evaluation as well as a field study. A mixed-method approach allows us to understand PULSE at multiple levels, generating rich feedback for future development. To provide answers to RQ1 and RQ2, a within groups lab experiment was carried out.

Participants attempted to detect and estimate the magnitude of change in both message density, and the distance over which a message trend (trend distance) existed, using both the implicit presentation through speech (*modified speech condition*) and speech plus non-speech (*additional cues condition*) feedback types of PULSE. Twenty participants (8 male, 12 female, aged 17-37, mean age 21.8) took part. Each was paid £10 for participation. The order of each condition was counterbalanced. For each condition participants were seated at a desk in a usability laboratory.

Two changes were made to PULSE to allow its use in a laboratory setting. The first, to allow precise control of changes in message density and trends, and ensure consistency between participants, was to load a cache of messages from file. Under the terms and conditions of the Twitter API, downloading and offline storage of messages is not permitted. Therefore two corpora of messages was created. The composition of messages was based on those discussed by Java *et al.* [9], with smaller groups of thematically similar messages created to represent trends.

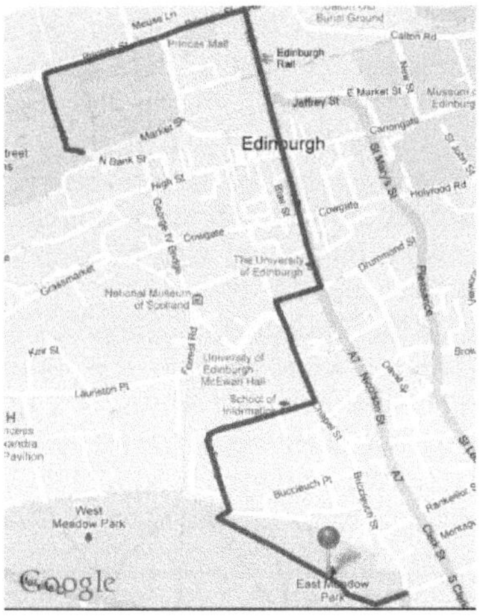

Figure 3. A screenshot of the interface used for the lab study showing the route and current location of the user

Secondly, the user was automatically moved along a set route at a set pace of 2m/s. Allowing the user to move at his or her own pace (e.g. through the use of forward or backward buttons) could confound performance in the *modified speech condition*. If the user moved quickly (much faster than would be possible when walking) almost no spoken messages would be heard, leading to higher errors than if the user did not move at all and waited until all messages were played. Neither extreme is probable in real world use, so we chose a mean constant speed of 2 m/s based on the work of Bergström-Lehtovirta *et al.* [2]. During each condition participants were able to see a Google map showing both the route and current position along it (see Figure 3).

Two routes and two message corpora were created. These were counterbalanced between the two conditions. Each route was 2700m long and was split into 18 150m long sections. Within each section the message density was changed once (± 10, 30 or 60% of maximum message density), and a message trend was presented (with a trend distance of either 50 or 100m). The message density was never changed when a trend was present and no changes were made in the first or last 20m of a section. There was an even number of each change level, both between and within the two routes used. At the end of each 150m section, all sounds were switched off, the participant location on the route was paused and a dialog was presented. Participants were asked if a message density change had occurred in the previous section, and if so, the magnitude of that change as a proportion of the maximum message density. Participants were also asked if a trend had been present, and if so, to estimate the trend distance as a proportion of the 150m long section.

Before the start of each condition participants completed a training route of two sections. These allowed familiarisation with the experimental protocol, and the sounds for trends and the minimum and maximum message density. As we asked participants to make absolute estimations of changes to message density, providing participants with training on the maximum and minimum values was essential [12]. On completion of each condition participants filled out 20, 7-

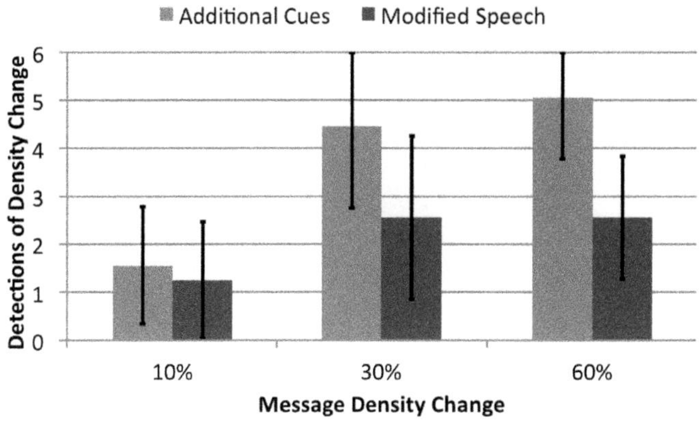

Figure 4. Graph of accuracy in in message density changes for both conditions and all levels of density change. Shown with standard deviations.

point likert scales covering confidence in, and opinions of, the feedback provided by each condition. At the end of the experiment a short interview was held.

Results

Message Density

The graph in Figure 4 shows the distribution of correct answers for both conditions for all three message density magnitude change levels. A two-way within groups ANOVA on showed a significant main effect for both feedback type ($F(1,19)=36.15$, $p<0.001$) and message density magnitude change ($F(1,19)=40.07$, $p<0.001$). A significant interaction effect between feedback type and magnitude change was also found ($F(2,38)=11.758$ $p<0.001$). Bonferroni corrected t-tests were carried out to understand where the difference between the factors lay. Density changes in the *additional cues condition* of 30% and 60% were significantly more accurately identified than changes of 10% ($p<0.001$). Density changes of 30% in the *additional cues condition* were significantly more accurately identified than changes of 30% and 60% in the *modified speech condition* ($p<0.001$). Changes of 60% in the *additional cues condition* were significantly more accurately identified than changes of 60% in the *modified speech condition* ($p<0.001$). No significance was found between density changes in the *modified speech condition*.

A Pearson correlation between actual and estimated message density magnitude change for the *additional cues condition*, showed a significant but weak correlation ($r=0.471$, $p<0.001$, df 19). A one-way within groups ANOVA on estimated change showed significance ($F(1,19)=18.86$, $p<0.001$). Bonferroni corrected t-tests showed the 60% change had been estimated significantly higher than 10% ($p<0.001$) and 30% ($p<0.001$). A correlation for the *modified speech condition* failed to show significance ($r=0.198$, $p=0.221$, df 19).

The results show that whilst accuracy improved as the magnitude of message density change increased, those improvements were only found in the *additional cues condition*, with changes of 60% leading to accuracy in detection of message density changes approaching 100%. Changes of 10% were poorly identified, and our results would suggest that only changes in message density greater than 30% are likely to be identified with good accuracy. Although there was a cor-

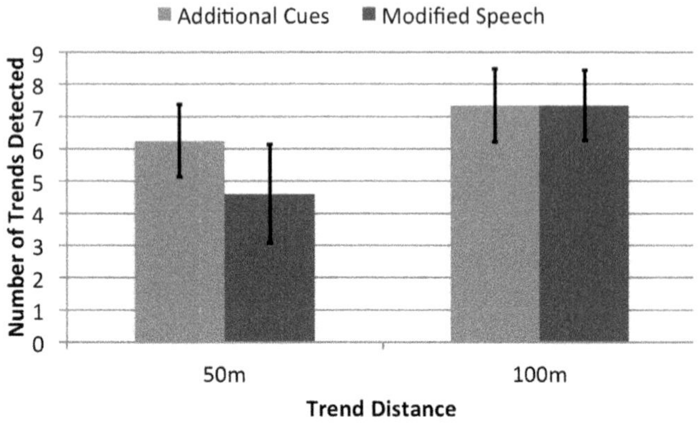

Figure 5. Graph of accuracy in detecting a trend in messages for each of the two trend distances. Shown with standard deviations.

relation between the actual and estimated message density, this was weak, with a large deviation of estimated changes for each of the three magnitude change levels. Only gross changes, greater than 30% in presented message density, were found to cause a change in estimated message density.

For the *modified speech condition*, increasing the message density did not lead to a significant improvement in accuracy. This is surprising, as when asked about strategies used to determine message density, thirteen participants said that they had been counting the time between successive presentations of messages, or monitoring the movement of the pin representing the current user location, as a way to determine if the message density had changed. Such an approach would clearly not work in real world use of PULSE.

Users are likely to detect only large changes in message density when using PULSE. From our scenario, wandering towards the football stadium would cause a large message density change in a short period, as would moving from a busy thoroughfare to a quiet square. Users would be able to determine that a change in social network activity had occurred, although would be unlikely to be able to quantify it. Smaller changes, such as a small rise in message density over a long period of time (e.g. sitting at a cafe) would not be detectable.

Trend Distance

Trend distance detection accuracy (see Figure 5) was analysed in a similar way. A two-way within groups ANOVA found a main effect for both feedback type ($F(1,19)=8.175$ $p=0.01$) and trend distance ($F(1,19)=58.38$ $p<0.001$). A significant interaction between feedback type and trend distance was also found ($F(2,38)=22.23$ $p<0.001$). Participants were significantly better identifying longer trend distances, and when identifying changes with the *additional cues condition*. Bonferroni corrected t-tests showed performance for 50m trend distances in the *additional cues condition* was significantly higher than 50m trend distances in the *modified speech condition* ($p=0.002$). This highlights that the effects found were due to the 50m trend distance. Performance on the 100m trend distance was identical for both conditions.

A significant, but weak, Pearson correlation was found in the *additional cues condition* between actual and estimated message trend distance ($r=0.535$, $p<0.015$, df 19). A within groups t-test on these data showed that estimates were significantly different between the 50 and 100m trend distances ($t(19)=6.51$, $p<0.001$). A significant and slightly stronger correlation was found between actual and estimated trend distance for the *modified speech condition* ($r=0.641$, $p=0.002$, df 19). A within groups t-test showed estimates of message trend distance were borderline significant between the 50 and 100m trend distances ($t(19)=2.04$, $p=0.055$). The correlations indicate that participants tended to underestimate large trend distances (mean estimate for 100m: 64.02m $\pm$ 22.35m (*modified speech*), 81.16m $\pm$ 18.93m (*additional cues*)), but were more accurate for small trend distances for both conditions (mean estimate for 50m: 54.17m $\pm$ 27.36m (*modified speech*), 57.87m $\pm$ 9.0m (*additional cues*)).

Whilst significant differences were found, the results indicate that large changes in trend distance must occur for participants to be able to discriminate between them. Trends that occur over a wide area, such as the football example from our scenario, are likely to be detected by participants irrespective of the feedback type used. However, if trends occur over a small area, such as an intimate local gig by a band, users may get some messages but will not determine that there is a trend without additional auditory cues.

In addition to the quantative results, each participant was interviewed and completed a questionnaire (adapted from Wakkary and Hatala [18]) for each condition. Participants rated their agreement (strongly agree to strongly disagree) on a set of 20 7-point likert scales covering subjective impressions of both the task and audio feedback. The results generated from these broadly agree with the results previously discussed. Ten participants rated the *additional cues condition* as preferred, six rated the *modified speech condition* as preferred, with four preferring both conditions equally. The main reason for the *additional cues condition* being preferred was the ease of extracting the information required to answer the questions. The main reason why the *modified speech condition* was preferred was the lack of additional sound. Concentrating on this was felt to be distracting from listening to the content of the messages. Participants rated the *additional cues condition* as being significantly easier to determine the global message density value ($T(19)=2.900$, $p=0.003$), that a change in message density had occurred ($T(19)=3.270$, $p<0.001$) and the magnitude of that change ($T(19)=2.910$, $p=0.004$). The *modified speech condition* was rated as significantly easier to determine what the topic of the trend presented was ($T(19)=2.807$, $p=0.005$). None of the other likert scores were significant, although both conditions had between neutral and strongly positive agreement with the statements. Speech and non-speech sounds were found to be informative, understandable and were not rated as annoying by participants. In addition, participants rated both versions of PULSE as likely to be useful to gain an overview of a new location.

Discussion

The experiment has provided answers to RQ1 and RQ2. Users were able to detect and discriminate between changes in message density and trends. However, changes had to be large and participants were unable to accurately estimate their magnitude. The *additional cues condition* significantly outperformed the *modified speech condition.* Only subjective confidence in determining the topic of detected trends was significantly better with the *modified speech condition.* It could be argued the *modified speech condition* be redesigned, but this is difficult without altering the intelligibility of the messages (e.g. speeding up speech to communicate density would degrade message understanding). However, accuracy in identification of large message trend distances was comparable between both conditions. In the *modified speech condition* trends were communicated through explicit change of speaker sex. If further such attributes can be identified in the future its performance may be improved.

IN SITU EVALUATION

Whilst we have good understanding of the amount of change in both trend distance and message density that users can detect, and how this changes between the two feedback conditions, we can only hypothesise over its relationship to the real world use of PULSE. In order to answer RQ3, as well as contextualise our findings from the lab study, we conducted a longitudinal field study. Our study ran over a two week period in Edinburgh U.K., and was timed to coincide with the International Edinburgh Festival [2]. We expected this to cause an increase in both messages and trends, as well as provide stimulating content about the shows and people who took part in the festival. Five users (mean age 33.25, all male) took part. All lived in Edinburgh and worked in the city centre near to festival venues. We chose local users, rather than tourists, as a way of determining how well the vibe presented fitted with the 'local' understanding of an area. If a local user agrees that the vibe is what would be expected, then a visitor will be gaining an accurate impression of the area.

Participants were each given an iPhone running either the *additional cues* or *modified speech* version of PULSE. Each version was instrumented to collect usage data. After an initial briefing and demonstration of how to operate the application, each participant was asked to use PULSE in their day-to-day life over the following week. At the end of the week the experimenter returned, debriefed the participant and swapped the iPhone to the other version of PULSE. At the end of the following week the participant was again debriefed more deeply. Participants also completed an extended versions of the questionnaire completed by the lab participants. Participants were paid £10 for participation.

Results

Data logging on the phones showed similar usage between the two versions. Each was used for a total of 10 sessions lasting on average 22 minutes (*additional cues condition*) and 19 minutes (*modified speech condition*). Most sessions occurred in the morning and evening, and participants noted that PULSE had been used as they walked or took the bus to work. Questionnaire results were broadly in agreement with the lab study previously discussed. Data from the interviews were coded using a framework approach [13]. Condition preference, as well as density and trend changes, were used as initial codes. From this several key findings emerged.

[2] http://www.edinburghfestivals.co.uk/festivals/fringe

Condition Preference

All but one participant rated the *modified speech condition* as their most preferred. Whilst the explicit non-speech sounds used in the *additional cues condition* were found to be initially useful, they could soon become annoying: *"it was ok at the beginning, it was quite soothing. Then maybe after 10-15 minutes it gets annoying"*. This was particularly noted when there was little variation in the message density level. The constant presentation of the same information was a source of annoyance: *"if there are not many changes in messages, you are just listening to water"*. Another participant noted that he found the feedback to be "too much" when combined with other environmental noise, and that it had distracted him during day-to-day activities: *"I think I walked out of Tesco (a supermarket) leaving a fiver behind, and some woman came out behind me and had to give me my fiver back. Yeah, so it was quite distracting"*. This distractive element of the *additional cues condition* caused participants to "tune out" of the auditory display, missing both spoken messages and changes in the message density: *"after a while I definitely tuned out and stopped listening. It didn't really register that there had been a change"*. However, participants also discussed the lack of sound as a problem with the *modified speech condition.* The irregularity of the message presentation caused them to wonder if the application had stopped working, especially in places where no messages existed: *"You couldn't tell if it had stopped for some reason. Is it still working? And having to take it out and no, no, its fine"*. Here, the lack of sound caused PULSE to emerge from the background and become something to be explicitly attended to, rather than being passive. This lack of confirmation that PULSE was still running was primarily the reason why one participant rated the *additional cues condition* as preferred: *"it (additional cues condition) was more fun to listen to because the other one had long bits of silence, with the occasional bits of speech..... Whereas, with the sound, you have the vaguely watery noises and speech, so the overall auditory experience was more interesting"*. Neither condition can be considered as optimal to users.

Message Density and Trends

Related to condition preference were comments related to the feedback of both trend and message density. Unlike the lab-study, we did not explicitly ask participants to estimate or detect changes in these data when using PULSE, but we did ask about changes during the debrief. Questionnaire data indicated (as with the lab study) that users found it easier to detect changes in both trend and message density with the *additional cues condition.* One user mentioned for the *additional cues condition* that: *"It is useful, it did convey the information quite well, different levels of (water) running. You could tell that, around here it started gushing a bit more. As I walked away from here it gradually went into the background"*. Both trend and message density were found to be useful and important to communicate: *"Trends were good. It was good to see what the hot topics were around me"*. However, users also noted that they rarely got trends. Those they did get were solely around the Edinburgh Festival. As stated, the lack of a trend is as important as getting one. However, many messages that were clearly related did not have hash tags. Improved trend detection is therefore necessary.

As would be expected from the lab study results, participants discussed that they could only detect gross changes in the message density. However, this was also a function of the underlying data. Message density was characterised by large and abrupt changes as users moved between areas. As one participant noted: *"I could tell the density by the sound of the water as before. It changed very abruptly. So I walked across George Square and it went from 0 to 30 back to 0 again in a few meters."*.

Message Content

Participants largely found the messages presented with both versions of PULSE to be congruent with the environment. In the few cases where they did not, this was caused by the message being too old to continue to reflect the environment: *"Sometimes it (the tweet) was posted quite recently. But other times, you do not know really. When it said 'lets all come to the meadows (a park)' and it was pouring with rain, it couldn't have been that recent"*. Only messages posted that day that were used in PULSE, but for fast-changing situations a narrower timescale may be required.

The content of messages had a strong influence on their perceived importance to users. Three broad categories of messages (broadly spanning the news and daily chatter groups of Java *et al.* [9]) were found. Messages where a nearby location was explicitly named within the message body (e.g. a named local pub or shop) were most engaging to users. These provided a tight coupling between the auditory display and the physical space: *"There was one point where I was going right past the place and it said something about it. And I was like oh, wow!... And that was really nice because it was experiencing that overlap between the real and virtual location. That was more a kind of, avant-garde art exhibition. Oh, that's quite cool"*. The role of these messages also extended to informing users of places they did not know existed, but often went past. One user, using PULSE on the bus to work, said: *"I got one, about a working man's club just coming across in the bus. I'd never have known there was a working man's club in and around that area. It was a nice insight into what other people do with their life."*.

The second type of messages were more news related. As expected, a number of messages concerned shows, acts and reviews at the Edinburgh Festival. Participants found these to be interesting, but wanted more detailed information. As one said: *"Yeah, it's handy for little reviews of the area you were in. That was quite useful. If people put something useful into their tweets rather than 'oh, i've just been to a great show'. Well, what show was it?"*. These comments also extended to other areas, such as messages about well prepared meals eaten in restaurants, where participants would like more details about the restaurant. This illustrates, as was previously discussed, that recommendations and *ad hoc* social networks [8] may naturally arise from the use of PULSE.

The third type of messages were more trivial and mundane. Attitudes towards these depended on how interesting or amusing participants found them. In many cases participants found the messages to be boring or uninteresting: *"There were boring ones as well. Like the one where this guy said 'I'm a bit hung over this morning' and I thought well, fine. I don't care about you."*. However, in other cases participants found them to be amusing and interesting: *"What was it: 'I had a piss, it was so good it felt like I'd cured cancer.' Well, it amused me."*. The interest in messages was tied to individual preference, and as one participant noted: *"the crap ones are sometimes quite funny. It would be hard to separate funny ones from the boring ones"*. The relocation of such messages within the environment of their creation often had a positive effect on how interesting they were perceived to be. As one participant noted: *"The fact that it was geo-located made it more interesting, even if the content wasn't that interesting. I got one, some guy saying he was making lasagne for his kids. But given that I was just outside my flat, and that could have been somebody."*. We explicitly did not implement content-based filtering on the messages to avoid prejudicing this issue. Undoubtedly some filtering is necessary. However, what one person finds boring another may find interesting. Messages with poor English, typos and spelling mistakes also caused problems for the speech synthesis and were obviously found to be uninteresting and confusing, and filtering these is also necessary.

Although many mundane messages were uninteresting, participants found that they could provide awareness of social activities or groups of people with divergent interests to their own: *"You've got the 'God i've such a hangover this morning' ones. Which are a bit boring, but also interesting in a way, cause it reminds you of a social group of people"*. Another noted a message from a performer in the festival: *"This guy who said it was two and a half hours till his show started. That was quite interesting. Seeing it from the other side"*. Such awareness is one of our key aims for PULSE, and that it was identified with users who were local to the area is encouraging.

Overall, this relationship between the message, the location in which it was created and the location of the user, either through mundane messages in their environment, or by explicitly named nearby locations, was found to be engaging and powerful for participants. It also reflects the findings of Rost *et al.* in evaluation of the Columbus system, where photographs closer to the current location of the user were rated as more interesting than those further away [15].

Extensions

Our original assumption with PULSE was it's passive nature. Users should not need to make an explicit decision to remove the device and interact with it. Information should be serendipitously discovered. Therefore, other than a diagnostic screen showing the connection status to Twitter, and the ability to manipulate trend influence, no other interaction was provided. Whilst users appreciated the serendipitous quality of the interaction, a number of areas were identified where switching to explicit interaction would be useful.

One area was in the display of a history to the user. This was mentioned as both a way to remember a good message that could later be shared with friends, and as a way of retracing the route taken: *"It would also be nice if there was a history. Cause quite often I had a good one and wanted to remember what it was. Or something along the lines of these were the ones, and go back along the route."*. Related to the history was the ability to replay a message. Because of the short time taken to play the messages and the time taken to "cue into" listening, participants sometimes found they heard only part of a potentially interesting message: *"There was no lead in, and then breaking it up. Some is not that easy to understand, and by the time you are attending to it...."*. This was compounded by the non-structured nature of the messages themselves, which were often not formed into sentences and had spelling errors, making the speech difficult to understand. Further work on filtering or processing messages would help, but this is not a trivial problem.

Another area for improvement was a more in-depth understanding of trends. Participants were excited by the emergence of a trend in the messages, and wanted to immediately explore and understand it, rather than waiting for more messages on the same topic to be presented: *"I was interested in what the trend was or why it was being called a trend. But all I got when I went to the trend screen was '#edFringe'. I wasn't sure why it said it was a trend.... I wanted to know how many, or what the original message was, and why was it having an impact"*. Switching from a passive to active interaction also extended to gaining a vibe from areas further from the user, rather than just their immediate vicinity, as a way to guide future exploration: *"(I wanted to see) what other stuff was around, or another area. If you were trying to understand a new town it is useful in being able to serendipitously show you what is going on in the place you have wandered into, but there might be something interesting a few hundred meters away"*.

Discussion

In terms of the research questions asked, we can conclude that *in situ* use has a strong influence on the previous findings of RQ2. Changes in metadata were easier to identify when additional auditory cues were used. However, modification of speech to communicate trend and message density was more often preferred.

Participants strongly (4 to 1) favoured the *modified speech condition*. We attribute the change in condition preference to the lab study having an explicit task (answering questions about metadata changes), something that was not the case with the *in situ* study. We must conclude that neither of the two feedback versions was optimal. The long gaps of silence in the *modified speech condition* (made worse if the user passed through an area with no messages) were found to be annoying. However, the *additional cues condition* was found to be annoying and distracting, with users "tuning out" the sonification and speech in busy environments, although the sounds themselves were found to be appropriate in context. In relation to the lab-study, users also found it easier to detect changes in the metadata with explicit non-speech audio feedback. Additionally, participants found the data communicated to be useful and important.

Providing feedback somewhere between that given by the *modified speech* and *additional cues* conditions is likely to be a better approach. This could either be only sonifying changes in the metadata, or monitoring the external audio levels and switching between the two feedback conditions as appropriate. In this way we would present the feedback through additional cues when walking through a quiet park, but switch to a less obtrusive presentation when walking through a busy city street.

For RQ3, the PULSE system worked well *in situ*. Overall impressions of both versions of PULSE were positive; participants found it to be a useful and interesting way to link geo-located content with the physical environment. Users were also able to easily integrate PULSE into their daily lives. However, their impressions were tempered by the content and quality of the messages. Those that strongly linked to the physical location were always found to be interesting, but those that dealt with the day-to-day issues in people lives depended on the subjective interest in the messages. This may be due to our users living and coming from the area where they used PULSE, so the day-to-day messages were often not surprising. If immersed in a different country or culture, the relevance of some of these messages is likely to be higher. Given the agreement of participants that the messages were congruent with the environment, we believe this to be the case. Nevertheless, many of these mundane messages were found to be interesting, informative and amusing. Participants were also positive towards the use of PULSE in new environments.

Whilst some filtering of the message content would be useful in determining what messages to present, additional effort is also required in processing the messages. Speech synthesis engines use an understanding of the language to render messages intelligibly, and the lack of good English, spelling mistakes and contractions caused problems for the speech engine in successfully rendering the messages. This in part caused participants to request the ability to replay messages. Further discussion on how to process the messages to allow better speech rendering is beyond the scope of this paper, however it is a non-trivial problem. We used a high quality commercial speech engine, but other means (such as cueing the user that a message is about to be presented) to assist speech recognition may be necessary.

CONCLUSIONS

PULSE provides a new interaction technique to allow the exploration of collocated geo-social media. By using an ambient auditory display we were able to tightly couple virtual and physical environments, avoiding the need to mediate this interaction visually through the display of a mobile device. As such, users did not need to remember to check the device, or constantly look at a screen. The lack of required interaction with the device afforded serendipitous discovery of interesting messages in the environment. It is difficult to accept that if a visual approach had been employed users would consult PULSE for anything other than obvious visible events in the environment. For example, the football match from our scenario. Yet it was often more mundane messages that users commented on. The contextualisation of these messages back into the environment often increased the interest users had in them.

The results of both studies show neither of the two sonification techniques was a clear "winner". However, an ideal solution appears to lie in some combination of both. Although we used Twitter, it is trivial to consider how other textual UGC could be incorporated to enhance PULSE. For example, incorporating the Edinburgh Festival programme and providing explicit reviews and summaries of shows as users walk past venues. However it remains an open question how non-textual UGC, such as photographs, could be incorporated into the passive interaction style of PULSE.

In conclusion, our work on PULSE has significantly added to the currently limited knowledge on the presentation of geo-social media. PULSE has shown the affordances that geo-social media provide to users when in the same geographic location, and the ways we can present that media to develop a rich and engaging locative experience for users. Such investigation is a rich area for further study that deserves much greater attention than has so far been employed.

ACKNOWLEDGMENTS

This work is supported by EU FP7 Project No.224675 "Haptimap". The authors would also like to thank Cereproc for assistance and license of their speech SDK and voices.

REFERENCES

1. Bellotti, V., Begole, B., Chi, E. H., Ducheneaut, N., Fang, J., Isaacs, E., King, T., Newman, M. W., Partridge, K., Price, B., Rasmussen, P., Roberts, M., Schiano, D. J., and Walendowski, A. Activity-Based Serendipitous Recommendations with the Magitti Mobile Leisure Guide. In *Proceedings of CHI 2008*, ACM (New York, NY, USA, 2008), 1157–1166.
2. Bergstrom-Lehtovirta, J., Oulasvirta, A., and Brewster, S. The Effects of Walking Speed on Target Acquisition on a Touchscreen Interface. In *Proceedings of MobileHCI 2011*, vol. 1, ACM Press (Stockholm, Sweden, 2011), 1–4.
3. Bernstein, M. S., Suh, B., Hong, L., Chen, J., Kairam, S., and Chi, E. H. Eddi: Interactive Topic-Based Browsing of Social Status Streams. In *Proceedings of UIST 2010*, ACM (New York, NY, USA, 2010), 303–312.
4. Bollen, J., Pepe, A., and Mao, H. Modeling Public Mood and Emotion: Twitter Sentiment and Socio-Economic Phenomena. *Proceedings of WWW 2010 cs.CY* (Nov. 2010), 1–10.
5. Brown, B. Working the Problems of Tourism. *Annals of Tourism Research 34*, 2 (2007), 364–383.
6. Choi, J., Jang, B., and Kim, G. Organizing and Presenting Geospatial Tags in Location-Based Augmented Reality. *Personal and Ubiquitous Computing 15*, 6 (2011), 641–647.
7. Dingler, T., and Brewster, S. AudioFeeds: A Mobile Auditory Application for Monitoring Online Activities. In *Proceedings of MMI2010*, ACM (New York, NY, USA, 2010), 1067–1070.
8. Jang, H., Choe, S. P., and Song, J. Exploring Serendipitous Social Networks: Sharing Immediate Situations among Unacquainted Individuals. In *Proceedings of MobileHCI 2011*, ACM Press (Stockholm, Sweden, 2011), 513–516.
9. Java, A., Song, X., Finin, T., and Tseng, B. Why we Twitter: Understanding Microblogging Usage and Communities. In *Proceedings of the 9th WebKDD and 1st SNA-KDD 2007 workshop on Web mining and social network analysis*, ACM (New York, NY, USA, 2007), 56–65.
10. Marcus, A., Bernstein, M. S., Badar, O., Karger, D. R., Madden, S., and Miller, R. C. Twitinfo: Aggregating and Visualizing Microblogs for Event Exploration. In *Proceedings of CHI 2011*, ACM (New York, NY, USA, 2011), 227–236.
11. Mynatt, E. D., Back, M., Want, R., Baer, M., and Ellis, J. B. Designing Audio Aura. In *Proceedings of CHI 98*, ACM Press/Addison-Wesley Publishing Co. (New York, NY, USA, 1998), 566–573.
12. Rakowski, A., and Miskiewicz, A. Absolute Magnitude Estimation of Pitch. *Journal of the Acoustical Society of America 103*, 5 (1998), 2766–2766.
13. Ritchie, J., and Spencer, L. Qualitative Data Analysis for Applied Policy Research. In *Analysing Qualitative Data*, A. Bryman and R. Burgess, Eds. Routledge, London, 1993, 173–194.
14. Robinson, S., Jones, M., Williamson, J., Murray-Smith, R., Eslambolchilar, P., and Lindborg, M. Navigation Your Way: From Spontaneous Independent Exploration to Dynamic Social Journeys. *Personal and Ubiquitous Computing*, 1–13.
15. Rost, M., Cramer, H., and Holmquist, L. Mobile Exploration of Geotagged Photographs. *Personal and Ubiquitous Computing*, 1–12.
16. Rowland, D., Flintham, M., Oppermann, L., Marshall, J., Chamberlain, A., Koleva, B., Benford, S., and Perez, C. Ubikequitous Computing: Designing Interactive Experiences for Cyclists. In *Proceedings of MobileHCI 2009*, ACM (New York, NY, USA, 2009), 1–11.
17. Symington, A., and Dunford, G. *Finland*, 6th ed. Lonely Planet. Lonely Planet Publications Pty Ltd, London, UK, 2009.
18. Wakkary, R., and Hatala, M. Situated Play in a Tangible Interface and Adaptive Audio Museum Guide. *Personal and Ubiquitous Computing 11*, 3 (2007), 171–191.
19. Zhao, D., and Rosson, M. B. How and Why People Twitter: The Role that Micro-Blogging Plays in Informal Communication at Work. In *Proceedings of CSCW 2009*, ACM (New York, NY, USA, 2009), 243–252.

Listening Factors: A Large-Scale Principal Components Analysis of Long-Term Music Listening Histories

Dominikus Baur, Jennifer Büttgen, Andreas Butz
Media Informatics Group,
University of Munich (LMU), Amalienstrasse 17, Munich, Germany
dominikus.baur@ifi.lmu.de, jennybuettgen@web.de, andreas.butz@ifi.lmu.de

ABSTRACT

There are about as many strategies for listening to music as there are music enthusiasts. This makes learning about overarching patterns and similarities difficult. In this paper, we present an empirical analysis of long-term music listening histories from the last.fm web service. It gives insight into the most distinguishing factors in music listening behavior. Our sample contains 310 histories with up to six years duration and 48 associated variables describing various user and music characteristics. Using a principal components analysis, we aggregated these variables into 13 components and found several correlations between them. The analysis especially showed the impact of seasons and a listener's interest in novelty on music choice. Using this information, a sample of a user's listening history or even just demographical data could be used to create personalized interfaces and novel recommendation strategies. We close with derived design considerations for future music interfaces.

Author Keywords

Music; listening history; PCA; latent factors; lifelogging.

ACM Classification Keywords

H.5.5. Information interfaces and presentation (e.g., HCI): Sound and Music Computing.

INTRODUCTION

Ask a thousand people how they are listening to music and you will get a thousand different strategies. While one listener might be an avid playlist builder and manually construct sophisticated song sets or listen to all albums from one artist in a row, another might simply switch on 'shuffle' for the whole library and be done with it. Similarly, more local factors, such as the current time of day, external influences by friends or media, events such as concerts and the current mood all play a role for choosing music. This means that it is hard to judge what factors are important for the user of a music application. Interaction designers have to make assumptions and rely on their own experience when building interfaces. Recommender systems and other personalized systems are also restricted to modeling an abstract listener in a statistical one-size-fits-all approach. People's switch to digital music, however, gives us the chance as researchers to understand how they make their listening decisions. Services like last.fm log music consumption and provide a detailed picture of what music we listened to at what time. These lists of songs together with (partial) demographic information from user profiles give us insights into what factors are important for music lovers and what parameters influence our listening.

In this paper we describe an empirical analysis of long-term music listening histories to determine the order of importance of factors that influence music listening. Using a principal component analysis we identified 13 listening factors that discern one music listener from another and give clues about people's strategies surrounding music. In addition, we describe correlations between the variables that show, e.g., how demographic factors influence music choices. Our research provides answers to how people listen to music on the detailed level of songs, what factors are important for them and how these factors are interconnected. The results can help in designing novel and personalized interfaces or recommender systems.

RELATED WORK

Research in music psychology and sociology provides insight into how people interact with music on a daily basis and what their intentions are [5]. Work by Rentfrow et al. [7], for example, uncovers the role of context in listening to music. Due to the costs of manual data collection, these studies however remain restricted to small samples or short time frames. Automatically collected histories like last.fm's are far more specific but have not been analyzed by music researchers so far. Recommendation based on such histories takes either an item- or user-based approach [1] and can be improved by taking temporal dynamics into account [4]. Actually understanding the users' reasons is not its goal. Recent work by Zheleva et al. [9] describes an adapted version of Latent Dirichlet Allocation for predicting music selection. It works on genre, artist and title information and the social aspects of a music community. The analysis, however, gives only limited information about a single user's intentions. Herrera et al. [3] and Park et al. [6] analyzed online listening histories and found interesting temporal rhythms, but restricted themselves to this aspect of

Permission to make digital or hard copies of all or part of this work for personal or classroom use is granted without fee provided that copies are not made or distributed for profit or commercial advantage and that copies bear this notice and the full citation on the first page. To copy otherwise, or republish, to post on servers or to redistribute to lists, requires prior specific permission and/or a fee.
CHI'12, May 5–10, 2012, Austin, Texas, USA.
Copyright 2012 ACM 978-1-4503-1015-4/12/05...$10.00.

the data. A large-scale, song-level analysis for single users with a varied set of attributes has not been performed so far.

METHODOLOGY

Our goal for the study was to classify the most important factors for music listeners. Research has identified many influencing variables (see, e.g., [2,3,5,6,7,9]) but their respective impact is unknown. In order to learn about their importance, we chose an exploratory approach using a principal component analysis (PCA) to extract the most salient characteristics. This being the first such study we wanted to make sure to actually reduce the number of relevant factors and chose PCA as an analysis method.

For the data set we chose music listening histories from last.fm, a web radio that is personalized through minimal user interaction such as 'loving' or 'hating' a song. Users can additionally install so-called 'scrobbling' software that runs in the background and logs tracks that they listen to for at least 30 seconds in their player software or on their mobile devices. The resulting listening histories are accessible via the last.fm webpage or their API. Last.fm's webpage also provides a social network, where users can create profiles, become friends and share music suggestions.

Extracting the Listening History Data Set

Last.fm provides convenient access to almost all of their data through their API. In addition to user profile data, they also host a large library of general metadata about music. The data we acquired fell into four categories: *Demographic information* is an optional type of data that can be entered freely by the users. *Activity* describes a user's engagement on the website and how important the social aspect is to them (e.g., number of friends). The actual *listening histories* are made up of titles and UTC timestamps. Finally, for each title there's a wealth of *music metadata* available, such as the album it appeared on.

We acquired 5,000 user profiles via the last.fm API[1]. They contained over one million unique songs from 130,000 artists and 15 million entries. For each of these songs we then acquired the metadata (album, track number, genre based on user keywords, length, and whether it was available on the last.fm web radio). Last.fm profiles can be set to private thus barring access, but this applied only to 0.92% of our listening histories. Also, to reduce a bias due to the novelty effect and allow for long-term conclusions we only kept histories with at least two years length. We did not filter for profile activity, so the data set also contains inactive profiles. Finally, we adjusted timestamps to the listener's time zone and removed profiles without country information, resulting in 310 suitable profiles.

Representativeness and Limitations

To estimate how representative our data set was, we compared it to the audience demographics for last.fm from the Alexa[2] web traffic service and another data set of 1,000 last.fm listening histories provided by Celma [2]. We compared the (available) demographic information attribute-wise: Our data showed a similar distribution regarding the users' top-5 countries (US, Germany, Poland, UK, Finland; *Alexa*: US, UK, India, Germany, Netherlands; *Celma*: US, UK, Poland, Germany, Norway) and age (M = 24.25, SD = 11.573; *Alexa*: 18-34 year olds are over-represented; *Celma*: M = 25.37, SD = 8.315). Gender distribution had a slight male bias: female-to-male-ratio was about 30% to 70% (*Alexa*: "Similar to the general internet population"; *Celma*: 43% to 57%). The similar demographics in all three data sets indicated that our data base could deliver reliable estimates for last.fm histories.

Listening histories provided by last.fm do not, of course, represent perfect histories with all songs that a person heard in their lives: users can disable the scrobbling process, delete songs from their histories, use non-supported mobile devices, reset their profiles, etc (cf. [8]). They are, however, motivated to avoid such noise and gaps for the quality of their recommendations or the completeness of their personal music logs. Last.fm's web radio also scrobbles songs while listening that are thus not actively chosen by the user. To find such instances, we added a variable (*web radio*, see below) that was increased if a history contained ten songs in a row that were available in the web radio. Finally, taste in music also adheres to societal trends which, however, is a constant factor.

Preprocessing

We could have performed the analysis on the raw (user, timestamp, song title, song artist) variables, but research from music psychology and sociology suggests that there are other factors at play in music listening behavior as well: time of the day or week [3,6,7], for example, or the actual function the listener expects from music [5]. Therefore, we added more variables by preprocessing the raw lists of titles based on their metadata and other factors. The ideas and algorithms for these variables stemmed from the literature and our experience with music. We ended up with 48 variables in 7 different categories:

Demographic info: As providing this information is voluntary for using last.fm, not all user profiles contain it and we only used binary representations if attributes were available for *gender*, *age* and *country*.

Profile and community: Information on whether the user is a paying *subscriber* of the service, the length of their *membership*, the total *play-count* and number of *playlists*, and community information such as the number of *friends* and *shouts* (message posts) on their profile pages.

Music library: The number of *tracks per day*, the *average song length*, the *number of songs in a listening session* and the *duration of listening sessions* (sessions were separated

[1] You can find additional information about the analysis process and the results here: http://do.minik.us/listening-factors

[2] http://www.alexa.com

by at least 30 minutes). We also integrated the ratio of *distinct songs*, *albums* and *artists* (i.e. the number of items that appear only once divided by the number of all items). The *onetimers* attribute is the ratio of songs that were played only once compared to all songs.

Order, shuffle and repetition: This set of variables (all ratios) describes the *in-order listening of an album's songs* and the (chronological) *in-order listening of an artist's albums*. In contrast, we count the number of *shuffled album songs* and *shuffled artist tracks* and check whether the user listened to *complete albums* and how many album songs were *skipped*. We look at the immediate *repetitions of songs, albums* and *artists* within one session and, finally, also whether songs are commonly played as the *intro* to a listening session.

Long-term variables: To determine the fluctuation in listening we calculated the *standard deviations of played tracks for years, weeks* and *days*. 16 variables describe how many genres and artists appear only within *one of the four seasons*, two *half-years* or *halves of a day* (i.e., 8 variables each for genre and artist). The *genre-* and *artist loyalty* describes what percentage of genres and artists stay constant from one year to the next.

Temporal variables: We initially extracted 24 variables for the number of plays per hour of a day and accordingly 12 for months and 7 for days of the week. As these were highly correlated, we were able to condense them into three variables. Those reflect the percentage of plays in one specific timespan compared to the total number of plays: *ratio morning plays* (for the hours from 1AM to 1PM; maximum plays are from 7 to 11PM, minimum 2 to 6AM), *ratio weekend plays* (i.e., Saturday and Sunday) and *ratio first half of the year plays* (January to June).

Web radio and discovery: Our last category contains the ratio of regular to *web radio songs*. It also holds the *artist discovery* variable that counts how often someone starts listening to older songs by an artist after listening to a more recent record.

ANALYSIS AND RESULTS

We first performed Bartlett's test of sphericity for determining whether all variables in the sample are uncorrelated and Kaiser's Measure of psychometric Sampling Adequacy to see if our correlation matrix could be used for the factor analysis. As a second step, we determined the number of components by using the Kaiser criterion and the Cattell scree test. Finally, we rotated the component matrix to make the results easier to distinguish using PASW's VARIMAX algorithm.

Principal Listening Components

Bartlett's test confirmed the uncorrelatedness of the variables ($\chi^2 = 13425.536$, df = 1128, $p < 0.001$). The sampling adequacy was 0.825 according to Kaiser. Also, none of the variables showed a communality value below 0.40 and had to be excluded. Kaiser's criterion suggested 13 principal components, the Cattell scree test 4. After test runs with 4 and 13 components we decided for the latter due to its more distinct results (13 components are able to explain 74.278% of the total variance). The resulting components are sorted by their expressiveness (percent of variance) for distinguishing listening behavior:

C1. Distinct Music in summer, autumn and at night (27.3% of variance): The most important set of variables concern unique genres and artists from summer and autumn but also night-time. Additionally, it contains the *onetimers* variable which is the tendency to listen to songs only once.

C2. Variety (8.3%): This component describes how often songs, albums and artists are repeated, how diverse the library is album- and song-wise, if the user listens to complete albums and the yearly standard deviation of plays.

C3. Distinct Music in winter and spring (7.2%): Similarly to the first factor, unique genres and artists of the first half-year.

C4. Demographic information available (4.9%): As users tend to share this information on an all-or-nothing-basis, this component contains all *available* variables.

C5. User Listening Activity (4.2%): This component contains the *duration of listening sessions*, the *intro* and *tracks per day* variables, the *playcount* and *shuffled artist tracks*.

C6. Loyalty (3.7%): Both *loyalty* attributes, so constancy in listening to artists and genres over the years.

C7. Winter and day music (3.3%): Artists and genres that are unique to listening in winter and during day-time.

C8. General Album Listening (2.9%): This component describes whether a user listens to *shuffled album songs* and *discovered artists*.

C9. Online Activity (2.7%): Describes whether the user is a *subscriber* and uses the *web radio*.

C10. Length of membership and songs (2.6%): The time since becoming a registered last.fm user and the average length of songs.

C11. In-order album and playlist listening (2.5%): Is the user listening to songs in the right *order of the album* and has created *playlists* on the last.fm page?

C12. Social Networking (2.3%): How much is last.fm used like a social network by the user (the number of *friends* and *shouts*).

C13. Skipping and in-order artist listening (2.1%): This last component contains the number of *skipped songs* and whether the user listened to an *artist's albums in order*.

Correlations

Expected correlations exist, for example, between *playcount* and *tracks played per day* ($r(308) = +.927$, $p \leq .01$) and *onetimers* and *distinct songs/albums/artists* ($r(308)$

= +.926/+.929/+.882, $p \leq .01$). More interesting (because less obvious) correlations can be found between *loyalty genre* and *loyalty artist* ($r(308) = +.923$, $p \leq .01$), which means that there is no large difference between the two concepts. Also, *intro* has a negative correlation with *session length* ($r(308) = -.367$, $p \leq .01$), so the longer the sessions are, the less probable is their starting with the same song.

We performed an additional analysis to investigate the connections between age and gender and listening behavior (we had not enough histories to arrive at useful results for countries). Thus, we took a sample of all users who had entered this demographic information independent of the duration of their membership. We had 546 histories (with an overlap of 196 from the other data set). Regarding *age*, we found that there was a positive correlation with *distinct songs/albums/artists* ($r(544)$ = +.314/+.341/+.278, $p \leq .01$), *onetimers* ($r(544) = +.318$, $p \leq .01$), *web radio* ($r(544) = +.259$, $p \leq .01$) and *ratio morning plays* ($r(544) = +.301$, $p \leq .01$). Older listeners use the last.fm web radio, try more new music (which might be a result of the web radio) and seem to get up earlier. For the binary *gender* variable we used an independent samples t-test. Male users had been *members* of the service for a longer time (M=643.7 days, SD=474.2 days, female: M=511.3 days, SD=415.7 days, $t(333)=3.2$, $p=.001$), had a tendency to start their sessions with the same *intro* (M=0.0086, SD=0.0071, female: M=0.0062, SD=0.0043, $t(467)=4.8$, $p=.0001$), listened to more *tracks per day* (M=38.4, SD=68.0, female: M=29.1, SD=36.2, $t(509)=2.1$, $p=.04$) and had a lower *standard deviation of plays for days* (M=0.89, SD=0.19, female: M=0.95, SD=0.18, $t(542)=-2.9$, $p=.004$).

DISCUSSION AND IMPLICATIONS

The results from the analysis provide insights into relevant criteria that discern people's listening behaviors. The temporal context appears to have a strong influence, but goes beyond daily or weekly rhythms [3,6]: Whether people have their own summer/winter artists and genres makes a large difference (C1, C3, C7) and is relevant for the validity of short-term studies about listening (e.g., [5]). There also appears to be a cut between conservative listeners and those more keen on experimenting (C2). C5 describes how extensively users are listening to music and C8 how important song organization via albums is. Unsurprisingly, there are also factors that are less specific for listening to music and more for the last.fm webpage (C4, C9, C12).

Implications of this research apply to the design of recommender systems but also for music user interfaces in general. The order of the identified components shows their relevance. A future recommender system could first rely on external factors such as the current season or time of day but also a user's preference for unknown music to improve results. Automatically determining how many album tracks in the right order are included, if a playlist always starts with the same intro song or how long the resulting playlists are (based on the average session length) can also be taken into account. Interactive media player software could be enriched with additional categories that are not available now, e.g., by adding 'seasons' to filter and sorting functions. Also, the complexity of an interface can be reduced by taking preferences into account: Listeners who only listen to albums or songs by one artist do not have to be confronted with the full song lists. This can especially be beneficial for mobile usage scenarios where complex interfaces are inconvenient. A first level of improvement can be achieved in either case without additional information by simply taking the current date. More sophisticated approaches can use demographic data such as age or gender. Finally, a user's full listening history or snippets of it can be used to extract their preferences regarding the identified dimensions.

SUMMARY AND OUTLOOK

In this paper we represented a principal components analysis of listening histories from the last.fm web service that showed the importance of temporal aspects and character traits. Our research gives an order of importance to listening factors. Next steps are to derive specific listener types and a behavioral framework from this information. A more in-depth analysis of the influence of different tastes in music (classical music versus heavy metal) might also unearth interesting factors. Finally, concrete music applications will show how much taking these factors into account can increase user satisfaction.

ACKNOWLEDGEMENTS

We would like to thank Michael Sedlmair, Raphael Wimmer and our reviewers for their insightful feedback.

REFERENCES

1. Adomavicius, G. and Tuzhilin, A. Toward the next generation of recommender systems: a survey of the state-of-the-art and possible extensions. *IEEE Trans. Know. and Data Eng. 17*, 6 (2005), 734-749.

2. Celma, O. Music Recommendation and Discovery in the Long Tail. *Springer*, 2010.

3. Herrera, P., Resa, Z., and Sordo, M. Rocking around the clock eight days a week: an exploration of temporal patterns of music listening. *Proc. WOMRAD* (in cnj. ACM RecSys), (2010), 7-10.

4. Koren, Y. Collaborative filtering with temporal dynamics. *Communications of the ACM*, (2010), 89-97.

5. North, A.C., Hargreaves, D.J., and Hargreaves, J.J. Uses of Music in Everyday Life. *Music Perception 22*, 1 (2004), 41-77.

6. Park, C.H. and Kahng, M. Temporal Dynamics in Music Listening Behavior - A Case Study of Online Music Service. *Proc. IEEE/ACIS*, IEEE (2010), 573–578.

7. Rentfrow, P.J. and Gosling, S.D. The do re mi's of everyday life: The structure and personality correlates of music preferences. *Personality and Social Psychology 84*, 6 (2003), 1236-1256.

8. Silfverberg, S., Liikkanen, L.A., and Lampinen, A. I'll press play, but I won't listen: profile work in a music-focused social network service. *Proc. CSCW*, ACM (2011), 207–216.

9. Zheleva, E., Guiver, J., Mendes Rodrigues, E., and Milić-Frayling, N. Statistical models of music-listening sessions in social media. *Proc. WWW '10*, ACM (2010), 1019-1028.

Going Beyond the Surface: Studying Multi-Layer Interaction Above the Tabletop

Martin Spindler[1], Marcel Martsch[2], Raimund Dachselt[1]
[1]User Interface & Software Engineering Group
[2]Department of Vocational Education and Human Resources Development
University of Magdeburg, Germany
{spindler, marcel.martsch, dachselt}@ovgu.de

ABSTRACT
Lightweight spatially aware displays (Tangible Magic Lenses) are an effective approach for exploring complex information spaces within a tabletop environment. One way of using the 3D space above a horizontal surface is to divide it into discrete parallel layers stacked upon each other. Horizontal and vertical lens movements are essential tasks for the style of *multi-layer interaction* associated with it. We conducted a comprehensive user study with 18 participants investigating fundamental issues such as optimal number of layers and their thickness, movement and holding accuracies, and physical boundaries of the interaction volume. Findings include a rather limited overall interaction height (44 cm), a different minimal layer thickness for vertical and horizontal search tasks (1 cm/4 cm), a reasonable maximum number of layers depending on the primary task, and a convenience zone in the middle for horizontal search. Derived from that, design guidelines are also presented.

Author Keywords
Multi-Layer Interaction; Spatially Aware Displays; Above the Tabletop; Tangible Magic Lens; User Study.

ACM Classification Keywords
H.5.2. Information interfaces and presentation: User Interfaces – *input devices and strategies*.

INTRODUCTION
With ever increasing complex information spaces, technology and user interfaces are required to explore them and to focus attention to the relevant information. Magic lenses, first introduced in 1993 for graphical user interfaces [1], have been proven to be one promising solution. Since then, they were made tangible as additional active or passive displays being used on tabletops [9, 20], above tabletops [8, 9, 15, 16], in the air [4] or as Mixed Reality lenses [2, 3]. Typically, these setups include one or more larger (interactive) surfaces. In this work, we will focus on tangible magic lenses in combination with horizontal displays (tabletops).

With spatially aware tangible magic lenses, the physical interaction space is no longer limited to an interactive two-dimensional (2D) surface, but extended to the third dimension (3D). For this purpose, the 3D space above the work surface can be divided into physically separated horizontal layers [15]. They can be explored by moving spatially aware lightweight displays through the "air" that constantly provide immediate visual feedback regarding current layers.

Until now, many of the aforementioned magic lens approaches present "cool" technologies and interesting interaction opportunities, whereas a careful investigation of the actual physical characteristics and limitations is still missing. Few studies have addressed multi-layer interaction above tabletops, with [17] being a rare exception and focusing on pen interaction only. Although multi-layer tangible lens interaction has proven to be a powerful tool for a broad spectrum of application domains, such as the exploration of spatial information spaces [15], information visualization [16], and collaborative face-to-face sketching and brainstorming [14], only little is known about appropriate boundaries for the physical interaction space, adequate amounts of layers, or minimum layer thicknesses – especially with respect to typical interaction tasks with layers.

This paper aims at filling this gap by presenting a comprehensive study which we conducted to find answers regarding these questions. In particular, we were interested in:

- How accurate do users actually interact in the space above the tabletop (with respect to a particular task)?
- How to design the interaction space in terms of layer thicknesses, number of layers, and optimal lower and upper heights for the physical interaction volume?

We conducted a comparative user study with 18 participants. For this purpose, a simple tangible magic lens system with limited features was implemented. As the participants accomplished several tasks with the system, more than five hours of performance data was collected. Beyond that, we gathered detailed self-reported data directly after each task. Our findings address valuable insight into physical precision as well as practical guidelines on how to extend a (tabletop) system with multi-layer interaction techniques.

The remainder of this paper is structured as follows. After presenting background/related work, we describe the goals and the scope of the study in more detail. This is followed

Permission to make digital or hard copies of all or part of this work for personal or classroom use is granted without fee provided that copies are not made or distributed for profit or commercial advantage and that copies bear this notice and the full citation on the first page. To copy otherwise, or republish, to post on servers or to redistribute to lists, requires prior specific permission and/or a fee.
CHI'12, May 5–10, 2012, Austin, Texas, USA.
Copyright 2012 ACM 978-1-4503-1015-4/12/05...$10.00.

by a detailed account of the method, results, and discussion in the respective sections, followed by conclusions.

BACKGROUND: TANGIBLE DISPLAYS

In this section, a brief overview of common tangible mobile display approaches is presented and set into context of the used reference surface. This is done in order to highlight technical environments and potential usage scenarios that are likely to benefit from multi-layer exploration techniques as will be discussed in the next section.

Tangible Display Interaction (With Respect to a Surface)

Merging the digital world with the physical world is the vision of ubiquitous computing, as defined by Weiser [21]. This concept was adapted by Ishii's and Ullmer's tangible user interfaces (TUIs) [7], where interaction with digital information is provided through physical manipulation of real-world objects. Inspired by the notion of see-through interfaces [1], these objects can also be spatially aware physical displays (e.g., mobile phones) that serve as tangible magic lenses into the virtual world. One of the first mobile displays for ubiquitous usage has been proposed by Fitzmaurice, who presented a spatially aware palmtop computer for exploring 3D-situated information spaces for revealing virtual information associated with arbitrary objects in an office environment [4].

Horizontal Reference Surfaces. Contrary to Fitzmaurice's approach, the metaDESK project by Ullmer and Ishii [20] makes use of a horizontal reference surface only: a tabletop. Here, users can freely navigate through polygonal 3D models by moving an arm-mounted LCD display through the space above the tabletop that is also responsible for providing contextual graphical information. Hirota and Saeki [5] as well as Konieczny et al. [10] provide technical solutions for 3D volume slicers using tangible magic lenses, but even though both do not make use of a tabletop, they use the (horizontal) floor as reference.

Vertical Reference Surfaces. In terms of vertical reference surfaces, Sanneblad and Holmquist [13] used mobile phones to magnify details of a larger contextual image that was shown on a wall display, but without using the space in front of the wall for interaction purposes, such as controlling the level of detail. Besides providing a technical solution for projecting video content on spatially aware projection screens, Lee et al. [11] suggested using spatially aware displays to explore data sets with multiple information layers in front of a vertical display.

User's Body as Reference Surface. The peephole displays by Yee [22] explore the virtual information space wrapped around a user by taking the distance between user and PDA into account. This is used for zooming and layering operations in the context of desktop applications, such as calendar, web browsing or geographical maps.

Lightweight Tangible Display Solutions

In various cases, active display solutions, such as LCD panels, do not provide suitable form factors for a seamless integration into a tangible magic lens system. This is because active displays are often too heavy, too thick, too big, too rigid, and sometimes even too expensive if many devices are needed. This lack of technology motivated researchers to come up with a variety of lightweight display solutions, with many of them being designed for horizontal table(top)s. Most of these solutions use a passive approach, i.e., image content is projected onto spatially aware projection screens in one or another form. Lee *et al.* [11], Holman *et al.* [6], and Spindler *et al.* [15] presented such systems that all use ceiling-mounted projectors for projecting dynamic video content onto optically tracked paper-like displays. In contrast, SecondLight by Izadi *et al.* [8] is technically more complex in that it is based on electronically switchable diffusers. It supports dual back-projections on both a tabletop surface and tangible lenses above it. For UlteriorScape, Kakehi and Naemura [9] use a special projection foil that changes its translucency depending on the projection angle and can be used to simultaneously back-project different image content onto a tabletop surface and a tangible lens, respectively. Another promising technological development are organic LEDs (OLED) that one day might unify the advantages of active and passive displays.

BACKGROUND: MULTI-LAYER INTERACTION

As demonstrated in the previous section, a vivid research community is working in the field of tangible displays. Although the aforementioned systems show that a broad spectrum of technical solutions and interaction techniques has been created for tangible displays, only few of these solutions truly utilize the 3D space above a reference surface for the purpose of *multi-layer interaction*.

A multi-layer space is a batch of discrete horizontal layers that are stacked one upon each other with each layer consuming a distinct height in physical 3D space. In this way, the multi-layer stack features a physical extent into the third dimension that can be used as a "habitat" for spatially aware tangible displays. Multi-layer stacks have been proven to be an effective interaction metaphor with a broad field of applications, e.g., geometric zooming of large images, semantic zooming of node-link diagrams, exploration of space-time data, and layered geo maps – such as demonstrated by our PaperLens [15] project. This is a lightweight paper-based display solution that enables users to explore various types of information spaces by moving paper-like screens through the physical space above the tabletop (see Figure 1). For this purpose, layers of a virtual data space are mapped onto physical layers of a multi-layer stack that remain parallel to a horizontal table surface. In such setups, three basic tasks play a dominant role (see Figure 2):

- **Holding** (keeping a display at a fixed position)
- **Vertical Search** (moving a display upwards/downwards)
- **Horizontal Search** (moving a display at the same height)

One example for information spaces that can be explored with these basic interaction tasks are temporal data sets (e.g., videos) that users can browse through by lifting and lowering a mobile display (vertical search) in fast or slow

Figure 1: Exploring a multiple layer information space by lifting and lowering a tangible magic lens above a digital table that serves as an additional visual context.

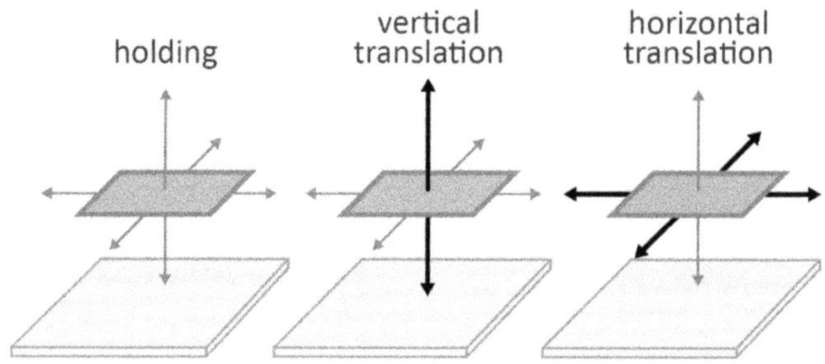

Figure 2: Three basic tasks for tangible magic lens-based multi-layer interaction above a horizontal surface that were tested in terms of physical accuracy in our study.

motion, or they can look at a particular still image by holding the lens at a particular height (holding task). Another example is the *layered information space* [15] that enables users to explore several 2D information layers (see Figure 1), e.g., anatomic images by moving a display horizontally above the table surface (horizontal search). Here, selecting a layer is accomplished by vertical search. For all these types of information spaces, the tabletop usually serves as a contextual reference that provides a graphical overview to the detail that is displayed on a mobile display.

In a concluding formative user study [15], we confirmed that their exploration techniques are easy to use and intuitive to work with, i.e., users were able to instantly accomplish given tasks without being taught how to actually interact with them, making these techniques ideal not only for public installations. We believe that such techniques will play a vital role in future tabletop research.

Evaluating Multi-Layer Tangible Display Interaction

Evaluating specific tangible display systems has been the goal of a few research projects only. Besides our own work [15], a notable example is Oh and Hua's evaluation on form factors of tangible magic lenses [12]. In a comparative user study, they tested various lens aspect ratios and sizes. They came to the conclusion that the aspect ratio of a lens plays a more important role for smaller lenses than for larger ones and that lens sizes are more dominant in impacting the user performance. However, to the best of our knowledge, no evaluation of the particular needs of the *multi-layer interaction aspect* of such systems has been done before.

Multi-Layer Pen Interaction above Digital Tables

In [17], Subramanian *et al.* presented and evaluated pen interaction above a digital table for the purpose of multi-layer interaction. Although this is similar to the previously introduced PaperLens concept, it does not couple input and output within the same physical device. Instead, Subramanian *et al.* designed and tested a set of 3D pen gestures that can be used to interact with a multi-layer stack. In a pilot study with 5 users (all sitting) they estimated a minimal layer thickness of 4 cm to prevent frustration due to accidentally changing layers, which is close to our findings. In order to reduce fatigue, they argued for limiting the maximum height above the work surface to about 16 cm, thus, resulting in a maximum number of 4 layers. They also noted that when users only navigated through layers (similar to our "vertical search") these could be made thinner than layers where selection gestures were performed (similar to our "horizontal search"). At the same time, layers closer to the work surface could be made thinner than others.

GOALS AND SCOPE OF THE STUDY

While the long-term goal of our work is to fully understand general affordances of tangible magic lens interaction above the tabletop, the focus of this study is the thorough investigation of the special requirements of multi-layer interaction and its physical boundaries. In particular, we are interested in the three basic interaction tasks discussed in the previous section: holding, vertical search, and horizontal search. These operations shall be examined in terms of the accuracy at which users can execute them in physical space. In addition, design principles concerning layer thickness, quantity and convenience volumes for multi-layer interaction shall be derived as a sound foundation for designing future magic lens systems.

Hence, the main focus of this work is on designing, conducting and evaluating a user study that addresses the following issues:

- Finding possible physical lower and upper thresholds that vertically limit the interaction space
- Finding exact measures on how accurately users accomplish vertical & horizontal search and hold operations
- Gaining an understanding about layout details for a multi-layer stack and its dynamic exploration

Many possible variables impact the interaction with tangible magic lenses, e.g., two- vs. one-handed use, tilting, display sizes and weights, device thicknesses, and display frame widths. In order to maintain a manageable study design while still providing ecological validity, we needed to make some tradeoffs. We therefore restricted our investigations to the case of a user standing in front of a horizontal tabletop and a two-handed use (as opposed to a seated setup and one-handed use). We also decided to disregard lens tilting. This was because our main focus was on stacked multi-layer spaces, where lens tilting often plays a minor

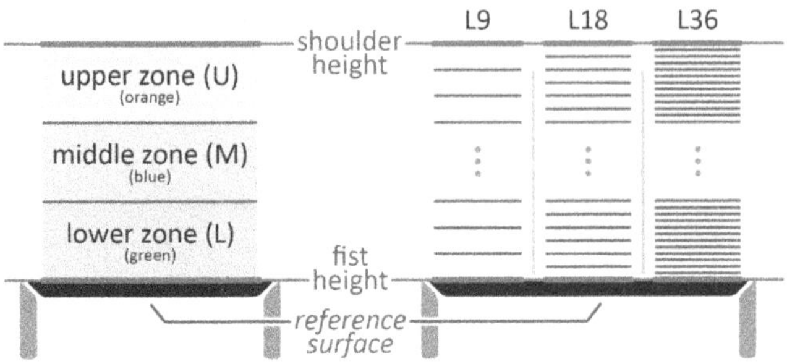

(a) Interaction Zones (b) Layer Subdivisions

Figure 3: Conceptual design of interaction zones (a) and layer subdivisions (b) as used for the study.

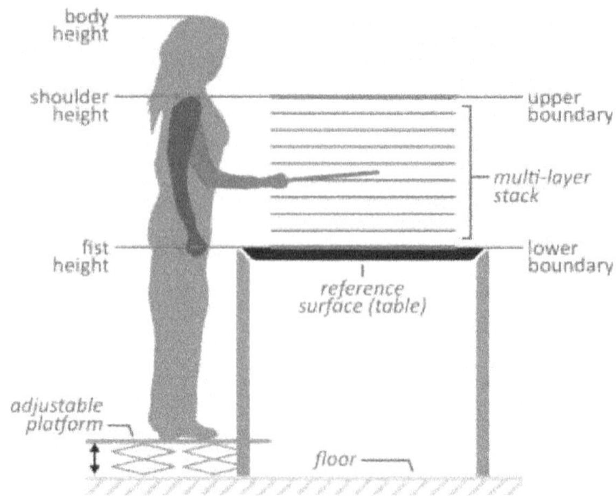

Figure 4: Principle setup of the study. The platform's height was adjusted in order to match fist height and table height.

role (e.g., for the ease of comfort) or is used as additional modality that only adds further degrees of freedom. In informal pre-tests we observed no practical influence of display sizes for a two-handed use (we tested paper formats of A6 to A4), so we skipped this variable. Another example is display weights. We assume that in the near future a new generation of lightweight displays (e.g., based on OLEDs) will dramatically improve form factors of tablets, smart phones and alike, so that display weights are likely to come closer to the weight we used in our study (about 190g). A high priority was the avoidance of additional disturbing effects, such as a visual context displayed on the table surface. In order to diminish cognitive load from participants, mainly stimuli were considered that address low-level processing. Based on the feature integration theory [19], we designed single-feature search tasks with targets that are clearly visually separated from distractors. This is achieved by using discriminative features (pop-out effect), for instance strong contrasts of light, shade and color, which can be preattentively processed.

METHOD

Participants

Eighteen students and staff members from our department (4 female, 14 male) participated in the user study. Their age ranged from 20 to 32 (M = 26.9, SD = 3.2). The average body height was 178.9 cm (SD = 9.4). All were daily users of computers and had advanced knowledge in the fields of computer graphics, simulation or image processing.

Design & Tasks

In order to test the accuracy at which users perform the three basic interaction tasks (holding, vertical search and horizontal search), a minimalistic layered information space was designed that consists of vertically stacked randomized integer numbers (between "1" and "99") representing the search targets unknown to participants. The independent variable was the number of layers that directly correlates with layer thicknesses. As pre-tests suggested, we expected this parameter to impact the accuracy of task performances. Three different levels of layer subdivision were used: 9 layers (L9), 18 layers (L18) and 36 layers (L36), as illustrated in Figure 3b. The use of multiples of "3" was mainly motivated by the three interaction zones as explained later (see Figure 3a). We used a within-subject design.

Compensating Body Sizes

To compensate for different body sizes of participants (e.g., longer arm lengths), we decided to use the *fist height* and the *shoulder height* as a priori limits for the lower and upper boundaries of the interaction volume, with the fist height being the distance of fist to floor when the arm hangs loosely. These values could be adjusted for each participant by using a platform (see Figure 4). The use of fist and shoulder heights was motivated by ergonomics literature – in our case [18] – and the outcome of a small pre-test: a table surface that is too low forces users to bend the upper body, whereas holding lenses higher than the shoulder quickly leads to fatigue. We used the shoulder-fist distance to define the overall height of the interaction volume for each participant (M = 691.11 mm, SD = 54.33). Due to constant subdivision of layers, the layer thicknesses varied relative to individual heights of the physical interaction volume, with L9 (M = 76.80 mm, SD = 6.04), L18 (M = 38.40 mm, SD = 3.02) and L36 (M = 19.2, SD = 1.51).

Vertical Search: Distributing Targets within the Layer Stack

For vertical search tasks, a sequence of targets was defined that was distributed over the overall volume height. For this purpose, we distinguished between three equispaced interaction zones: the lower (L), middle (M) and upper (U) zone (see Figure 3a). We chose three random layers from each zone as a search target. This allowed us to design six different combinations of vertical search tasks: L-L, M-M, U-U, L-M, L-U, and M-U, which was further multiplied by the direction, e.g., L-M vs. M-L or L_1-L_2 vs. L_2-L_1. Since at least two variants were to be tested for each combination, we finally came up with 6 × 2 × 2 = 24 vertical search tasks. For all participants and layer subdivisions (L9, L18, L36) the same sequence was used.

Horizontal Search: Distributing Targets within a Single Layer

For horizontal search tasks (panning), two search targets were randomly placed in each horizontal layer. To avoid

(a) Vertical Search Task (b) Holding Task (c) Horizontal Search Task

Figure 5: Apparatus and three interaction tasks. Lens content appears brighter than during the user study, e.g., for holding tasks the background was usually deep black. This is due to light conditions during taking photographs. Interaction was two-handed.

that participants have to bend their backs, we chose a conservative working radius of 40 cm (150 cm tall women have a shoulder-finger reach of about 60 cm, see [18]).

Overall Task Cycle

According to this design, for each level of layer subdivision (L9, L18, and L36) a randomized sequence of 24 holding tasks (3 sec each), 24 vertical search tasks, and 9 horizontal search tasks was defined. The same sequence was used for each participant. See Figure 6 for an example height plot.

Procedure

For each participant, the following order of test parts was maintained: (1) introduction part, (2) interaction part, and (3) assessment part. Users spent on average 40 minutes performing all parts.

(1) Introduction Part

After participants completed a brief questionnaire soliciting demographics and computer usage information, the body, shoulder and fist heights were measured. Thereon, the platform's height was adjusted to match the table height with the fist height, see section "Compensating Body Sizes" above. Then, the main task was explained verbally in a standardized way by reading out aloud from a sheet of paper. To ensure that all participants had perfectly understood all relevant aspects, they were invited to perform a few exercise trials without collecting data until they felt confident in handling the task (never longer than two minutes).

(2) Interaction Part

Participants were asked to complete the interaction part in three cycles – one for each level (L9, L18 and L36). The order of levels was counter-balanced. For each cycle, participants were to hold the tangible display in front of their body in order to explore a stack of white random integer numbers by vertically lifting and lowering it (*vertical search task*, see Figure 5a) until they found the search target (a single red-colored number). Users were instructed to read out aloud the red number[1]. After a "beep" sound and a visual feedback on the display (red "Hold!" label, see Figure 5b) they had to hold the tangible lens stable at the very same layer (*holding task*) for 3 seconds until the "Hold!" label disappeared and another "beep" sound indicated that the participant should continue searching for the next red number. From time to time (at 9 different layers), users had to perform a sequence of *horizontal search tasks*. For this purpose, the red number was replaced by a slightly smaller white number above a red background with white arrows hinting that the participant should now continue searching horizontally until two randomized search targets (white numbers) within the same layer were found that had to be read out aloud (see Figure 5c). Whenever participants accidentally left the layer, they got immediate visual feedback (the lens turned dark). In such cases, users had to manually find back to the layer by lifting/lowering the lens until it turned red again. Neighboring layers did not contain any numbers. This prevented reports of false numbers. By reaching the starting position again (white number with arrows, see Figure 5c), the horizontal search task ended, followed by the next vertical search task.

(3) Assessment Part

Self-Report. At the end of each cycle in the interaction part, participants were asked to rate their agreement on a 7-point Likert scale from "1" ("do not agree at all") to "7" ("completely agree") to several items in a questionnaire. These items addressed the usability (effectiveness, efficiency and user satisfaction) regarding holding tasks, vertical search tasks and horizontal search tasks.

Perceived Interaction Zones. After all tasks of the interaction part had been completed, participants were asked to fill out another questionnaire that was very similar to the one from the interaction part, but this time with respect to how they perceived the interaction in each of the three interaction zones (see Figure 3a). In order to utilize spatial memory, participants could play around with the tangible lens once again while the lens was tinted according to the scheme depicted in Figure 3a (no targets were displayed).

Preferred Boundaries. In the final and additional part, participants were asked to define – from their point of view – the ideal vertical lower and upper boundaries of the interac-

[1] Filtering a single red-colored number out of many white-colored ones is a preattentive process. Although this does not apply to reading two-digit numbers, we still consider it to be fast enough to not significantly affect our experiment.

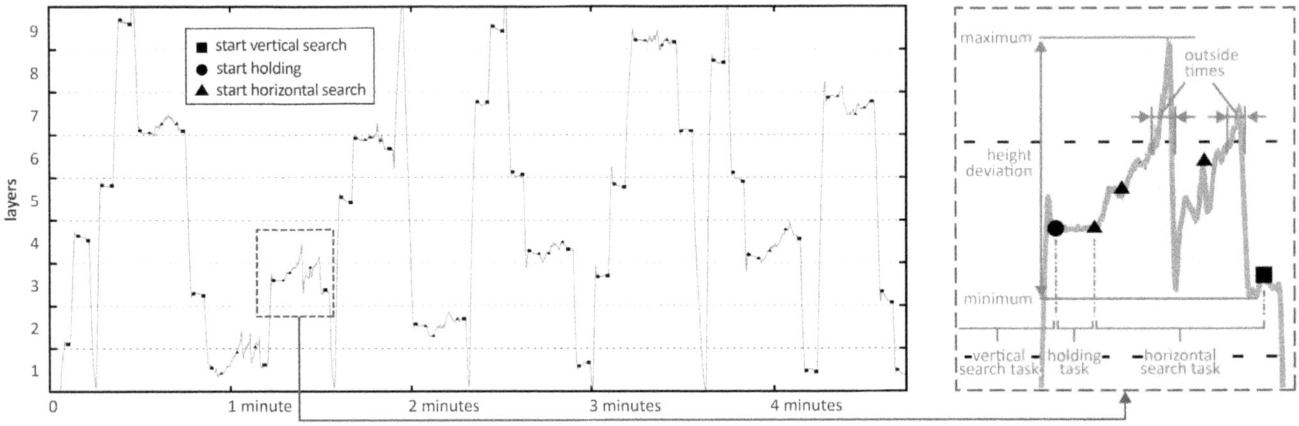

Figure 6: A typical plot of a cycle for level L9 showing height measures of the tangible lens over time. In the detailed view at the right side, the derivation for "outside times" and "height deviations" (as used in the data analysis) is illustrated.

tion volume with respect to the table surface. This was accomplished by holding the lens at the favored lower and upper heights above the table and then saying "okay".

Apparatus

The user study was conducted in a dark and quiet lab environment. The technical setup used for the experiments consisted of a horizontal table (reference surface), a piece of a rectangular cardboard of size 21.5 × 21.5 cm (tangible display), and a ceiling-mounted video projector directly above the table. In order to guarantee a high degree of spatial precision we opted for a magnetic-based tracking approach (Polhemus Fastrak) that enabled us to limit the spatial error to 0.3 mm within a working volume of 70 × 70 × 70 cm^3. We decided against projecting additional visual context onto the table. Instead, the table surface primarily served as horizontal spatial reference.

On the software side, our system was implemented with C#. We opted for a client/server model with the server being responsible for lens tracking and the client being responsible for displaying and application (user study tasks). Communication between client and server was achieved by a simple self-tailored UDP/IP-based protocol. It allows for sending and receiving a stream of 4 × 4 transformation matrices that describe the current 3D position and orientation of the tangible lens' center.

Collected Data

For later evaluation, the stream of transformation matrices was continuously logged into a file at a rate of about 33 samples per second. Along with this, additional marker timestamps were recorded (e.g., "start vertical search", see Figure 6). For this purpose, the study leader had to manually press the ENTER key every time a number was read out aloud to trigger the next task. To ensure equal times for the holding task, the system automatically generated a "beep" sound after 3 seconds of holding.

RESULTS

In this section, results from the experiment are presented in three parts. First, we report on the basic analysis of performance data. Second, we provide further analysis with respect to the three interaction zones. And third, we investigate data from questionnaires.

Performance Data

In order to analyze collected performance raw data, the following types of derived data have been extracted:

- *Task completion time* (in sec) that we used as a distinct measure of performance for vertical and horizontal search tasks. For holding tasks this time is constant (24 × 3 sec = 72 sec) and thus not relevant.
- *Total completion time* (in sec) is an aggregated measure of performance that sums up the times spent on horizontal and vertical search tasks.
- *Height deviation* (in mm) is the minimum and maximum displacement for horizontal search and holding tasks used as a measure of accuracy (see Figure 6). By using MIN/MAX operators, we decided on a conservative but simple statistical tool. Choosing other tools, such as MEAN/VARIANCE, would only further narrow our findings.
- *Outside time* (in sec), i.e., amount of time that participants unintentionally spent outside of a layer while performing a holding or horizontal search task (see Figure 6). We used this as a measure of error.

We also analyzed tilting of lenses. However, in contrast to our assumptions, we did not find any significant effect and thus will omit the discussion about it.

Statistical Methodology

Collected data (performance measures and self-report data) was analyzed with a *repeated measurement ANOVA*. For all ANOVAs, p-values were Greenhouse–Geisser corrected. When main effects were significant, Bonferroni corrected p-values are reported for *post hoc* comparisons (t-test, two-tailed). For testing the relationship between layer subdivision and accuracy of horizontal search tasks, correlation coefficients (Pearson r) were computed. For statistical tests, the a priori threshold of $\alpha = .05$ was used. If not stated otherwise, results are in sec; "ns" stands for "not significant".

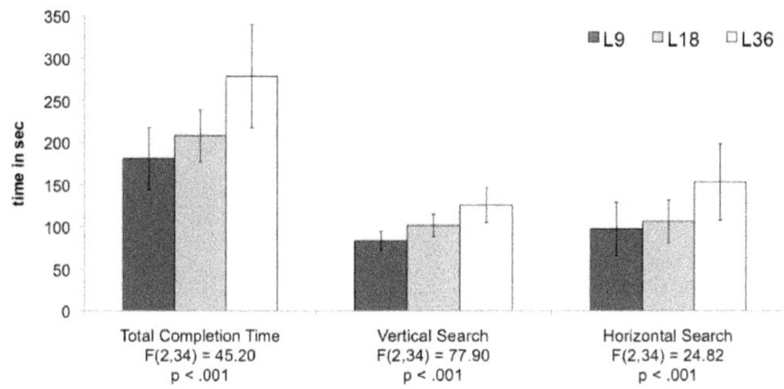

Figure 7: Task completion times of horizontal and vertical search tasks for L9, L18 and L36. Both times sum up to the total completion time. Error bars show standard deviations.

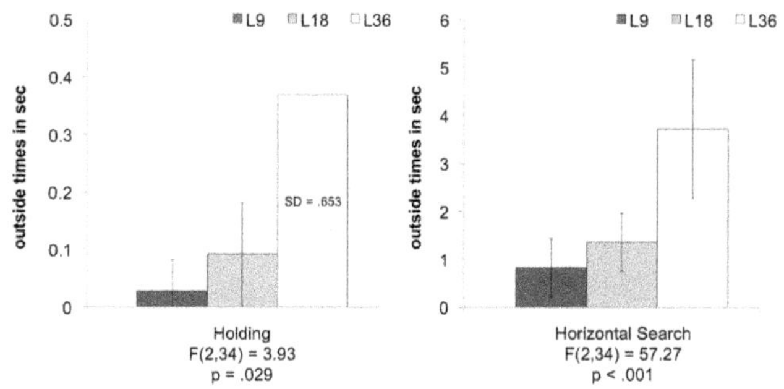

Figure 8: Outside times of holding tasks and horizontal search tasks for L9, L18 and L36. Error bars represent standard deviations.

Basic Analysis of Performance Data

In the following, a basic analysis of performance data is presented. See Figure 7 for completion times.

Total Completion Times

Regarding total completion times, we found a significant main effect of layer subdivisions ($F_{(2,34)} = 45.2$, $p < .001$). Completion times for L9 were significantly shorter than for L18 ($t_{(17)} = 3.95$, $p = .001$). The same holds for the contrast L18 vs. L36 ($t_{(17)} = 12.73$, $p < .001$).

In summary, total completion times show that with decreasing thickness of layers participants needed significantly more time for completing horizontal and vertical search tasks. In the following, further results are presented for each task.

Holding Task

The analysis of height deviations revealed no significant main effect of layer subdivisions ($F_{(2,34)} = 2.41$, ns). However, the results of height deviations depict that the precision of holding tasks generally improves slightly from L9 (M = 7.18 mm, SD = 2.33) over L18 (M = 7.00 mm, SD = 2.30) to L36 (M = 6.23 mm, SD = 1.44).

Analysis of outside times (see Figure 8, left) revealed a significant main effect of layer subdivisions ($F_{(2,34)} = 3.93$, $p = .029$). Pairwise comparisons showed that participants accidentally left target layers significantly more frequently ($t_{(17)} = 3.00$, $p < .024$) for L18 than for L9. Most layer crossings happened for L36, but neither differed significantly from L9 ($t_{(17)} = 3.00$, ns) nor from L18 ($t_{(17)} = 1.72$, ns), which is due to a high standard deviation.

Vertical Search Task

In terms of the completion time, we observed a significant main effect of layer subdivisions for vertical search tasks ($F_{(2,34)} = 77.9$, $p < .001$). Participants needed significantly less time ($t_{(17)} = 6.33$, $p < .001$) for L9 when compared with L18. In the same way, differences of completion times between L18 and L36 are significant ($t_{(17)} = 6.14$, $p < .001$).

Horizontal Search Task

For horizontal search tasks we found a significant main effect of completion times of layer subdivisions ($F_{(2,34)} = 24.82$, $p < .001$). Although pairwise comparisons show that there is no significant effect ($t_{(17)} = 1.56$, ns) for L9 vs. L18, participants needed significantly ($t_{(17)} = 4.90$, $p < .001$) more time for L36 than for L18.

We observed no main effect of layer subdivisions for height deviations ($F_{(2,34)} = 2.25$, ns). For outside times we found a significant main effect of layer subdivisions ($F_{(2,34)} = 57.27$, $p < .001$). The participants crossed layer boundaries less often for L9 than for L18 and L36, see Figure 8 (right).

To test the interrelation of total completion times (TCT) against height deviations (HD) and outside times (OT), several correlation coefficients were computed that show a significant relation of TCT × HD (L9: r = .526, p < .001; L18: r = .495, p < .001; L36: r = .643, p < .001) and TCT × OT (L9: r = .682, p < .001; L18 = .871, p < .001; L36: r = .903, p < .001). This shows for all layer subdivisions that participants who accomplished tasks accurately were the ones with a good overall performance and vice versa.

Further Analysis Regarding Interaction Zones

In this section, further analysis of performance data is presented with regards to the lower, middle and upper interaction zone (see Figure 3a). For this purpose, we rearranged already analyzed performance data with respect to these zones. In particular, we looked into *height deviations* and *outside times* for holding and horizontal search tasks separately for each layer subdivision (within-subject factor).

Holding Task

We did not find any significant main effect of the three interaction zones for height deviations or for outside times.

Horizontal Search Task

For L9 and L18 we observed no significant main effects with regard to the three interaction zones, neither for task completion times and height deviations, nor for outside times. In contrast, for L36 we revealed significant effects of task completion times ($F_{(2,34)} = 12.08$, $p = .001$), height deviations ($F_{(2,34)} = 4.10$, $p = .049$) and outside times ($F_{(2,34)} = 10.45$, $p = .003$). For the following discussion, see Figure 9.

For task completion times, pairwise comparisons show that the middle zone is less demanding than the lower ($t_{(17)} = 4.56$, $p = .001$) and upper zone ($t_{(17)} = 4.13$, $p = .002$).

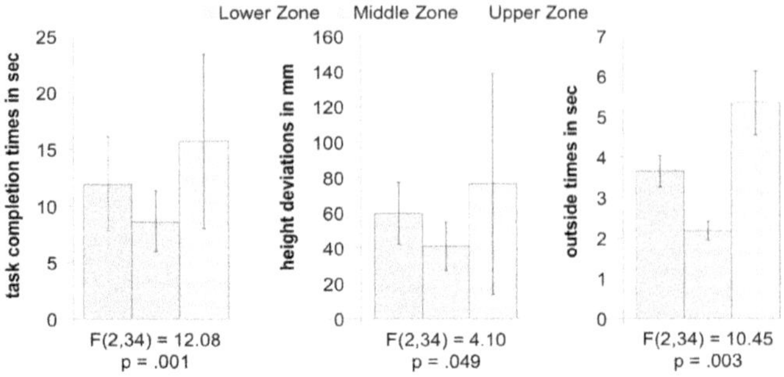

Figure 9: Performance data for the horizontal search task (only L36) broken down by the lower, middle and upper interaction zone (see Figure 3). Error bars represent standard deviations.

Height deviations of the middle zone are slightly (but not significantly) smaller than the ones of the lower and upper zone. This indicates that the middle zone takes on a special role for horizontal search tasks. This is also supported by outside times that are significantly longer for the upper zone, when compared to the lower ($t_{(17)}$ = 4.63, p = .001) and middle zone ($t_{(17)}$ = 3.96, p = .003).

Questionnaires & User Preferences

In the following, the results of user ratings concerning usability are presented as agreement values on a 7-point Likert scale. For a brief summary, see Figure 10.

Holding Task

Ratings on holding tasks differ depending on layer subdivisions ($F_{(2,34)}$ = 19.24, p < .001). Pairwise comparisons show that L9 is rated best when compared with L18 and L36. Individual comparison shows that contrasts are significant for all combinations.

Vertical Search Task

With respect to the ratings for vertical search, we found a significant main effect of layer subdivisions ($F_{(2,34)}$ = 8.62, p = .001). Pairwise comparisons show that L9 is assessed as significantly easier than both L18 and L36. For L18 vs. L36, this effect is not significant.

Horizontal Search Task

Ratings for horizontal search tasks have a significant main effect of layer subdivisions ($F_{(2,34)}$ = 14.29, p < .001). Pairwise comparisons reveal that L36 is rated as significantly more difficult than L9 and L18.

Perceived Interaction Zone

We observed a significant main effect of the three interaction zones ($F_{(2,34)}$ = 25.20, p < .001). The usability of interaction for the middle zone (M = 6.46, SD = .62) was rated significantly better when compared with the lower (M = 6.04, SD = .62) and upper zone (M = 4.47, SD = 1.38).

Preferred Boundaries

The analysis of subjective boundaries of the interaction volume results in a preferred lower limit (M = 68.28 mm, SD = 51.01) and a preferred upper limit (M = 508.77 mm, SD = 78.45) above the table surface.

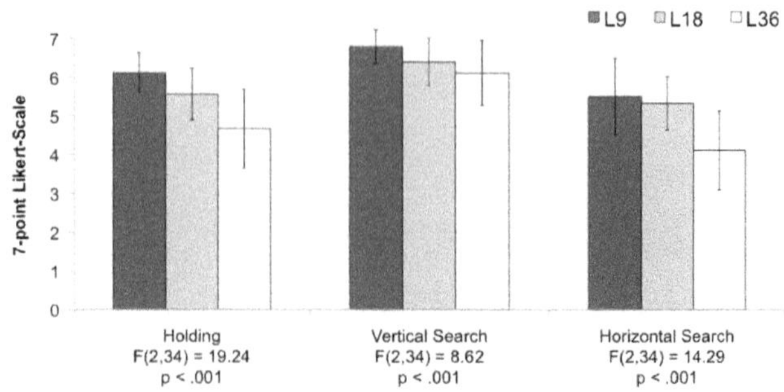

Figure 10: Usability ratings for holding task, vertical search task and horizontal search task with respect to single layer subdivisions (L9, L18, and L36). Error bars represent standard deviations.

DISCUSSION

In this section, we will reflect on our results and provide answers to the questions of minimal layer thicknesses, vertical boundaries for the physical interaction zone, and maximum number of layers. Based on these findings, we will derive design guidelines that will be presented at the end of this section.

Layer Thicknesses & Accuracy

In general, we can show that a diminishing layer thickness correlates with decreasing test performances. This applied in particular to the vertical and horizontal search task. In contrast, the holding task remained mostly unaffected.

Holding Task. Compared to other tasks, holding was performed most accurately. On average, the height deviation for holding tasks was approx. 7 mm. By taking into account a standard deviation of approx. 2 mm, this leads to a rather conservative **minimum layer thickness** of approx. 9 mm or **about 1 cm**. This value is even substantially lower than the average thickness of L36 (M ≈ 19 mm), which is most likely the reason for why the control variable "layer subdivision" only marginally affected the error measure "outside times" for holding tasks. Interestingly, participants performed the holding tasks most accurate with L36 (M ≈ 6 mm), as opposed to L9 (M ≈ 7 mm). This effect was significant and indicates that **visual feedback helps to further improve the accuracy** at which holding tasks are performed – simply because users can adapt to errors quicker (visual correction impulse). This interpretation is also supported by slightly longer "outside times" for L36 (M ≈ 0.4 sec), which correlates with more frequent visual feedback due to thinner layers. Surprisingly, these findings are somehow contradicted by self-reports. Here, users had the subjective impression that they would perform significantly worse for L36 (M ≈ 4.7) compared to L9 (M ≈ 6.1), which was just not true. One reason for such ratings could be disappointment due to an assumed bad performance that was associated with leaving a layer.

Vertical Search Task. We found significant main effects for task completion times between all combinations of layer subdivisions. Although the search space was doubled each time, the completion times for vertically searching it did not. More precisely, for L9-L18, there were 9 added layers with 18 sec of longer completion times that resulted in a delay of 2 sec per extra layer. In contrast, for L18-L36, there were 18 added layers with only 25 sec penalty producing a delay of less than 1.4 sec per extra layer. This indicates that the vertical search task is an **efficient interaction technique** for single-feature searches (when pop-out effects are being utilized) that **performs better than linear** with a growing search space. These insights are also supported by self-reports.

Unfortunately, data gathered during our experiments made it difficult to directly derive a minimum layer thickness. This is because "outside times" and "height deviations" are not available for vertical search. However, since search tasks are usually accompanied by holding tasks, we can borrow from our findings there. Thus, our conservative estimate for the **minimum layer thickness** for vertical search is **roughly 1 cm**.

Horizontal Search Task. For horizontal search, task completion times and outside times indicate that the threshold for a minimum layer thickness lies somewhere between L18 and L36. Thus, a conservative measure is found by using the average layer thickness of L18 ($M \approx 3.8$ cm) as the **minimum layer thickness** that is **about 4 cm**. A less conservative measure would be slightly smaller but should not get too close to L36 ($M \approx 1.9$ cm). A follow-up study with finer layer subdivisions might help further narrowing down this value. However, conducting another user study is probably not worth the effort.

Physical Interaction Space & Number of Layers

Holding tasks were performed **equally well** in all of the three interaction zones. **Horizontal search** tasks, in contrast, were best accomplished in the **middle zone** (with respect to height deviations and outside times) and not as we anticipated in the lower zone. This was a surprising insight and somehow the precursor of another unexpected finding:

Lower and Upper Boundaries. When asked for their preferred lower interaction boundary, most participants did not choose the table surface. Instead, they opted for a slightly higher value that was roughly **7 cm** ($SD \approx 5$ cm) above it. On the one hand, this was because most participants did not consider letting the lens loose in order to put it on the table surface. On the other hand, this means that the initially used "fist height" was a rather weak estimate for the table height. This was probably due to the frequent bending of the upper part of the body that was involved, for instance, with the horizontal search task. We therefore propose the "**wrist height**" as a more adequate **measure for the ideal tabletop height**. This insight can also be useful for conventional interactive table displays, in particular whenever a standing usage is intended.

In terms of a physical upper boundary, participants preferred a height of roughly **51 cm** above the table surface with a standard deviation of about 8 cm, which closely matches the standard deviation of the body heights ($SD \approx 9$ cm). By compensating for the preferred lower boundary, we obtain a **corrected upper boundary of about 44 cm** (i.e., 51 cm - 7 cm) above the adjusted table surface.

Number of Layers. A reasonable threshold for the maximum number of layers is found by mapping minimal layer thicknesses (1cm / 4cm) onto the absolute height of the physical interaction volume (44 cm). Depending on the task, this results in a number of **44 layers** (holding and vertical search tasks) or **11 layers** (horizontal search tasks).

Design Guidelines & Further Observations

When designing multi-layer applications, the general rule of thumb is to **use as few layers as necessary** with the exact number depending on the primary interaction goal. For instance, for the exploration of a multi-layer geo-referenced map, where panning (horizontal search) is the dominant task, at most eleven layers should be adopted. In addition to that, most relevant information layers should be assigned to the **middle ("comfort") zone**, followed by the lower zone.

One important outcome of our study was that **vertical search** was clearly **favored over horizontal search**. Thus, it should be the first choice whenever possible. For example, for the exploration of temporal data sets (e.g., surveillance videos), vertical search should be reserved for the dominant goal of time-browsing, whereas horizontal search should be used for secondary goals, such as selecting a video.

Although our study mostly addressed single-feature search tasks in discrete (non-continual) layers, many of our findings also apply to continuous layer setups. Examples are the measures for lower and upper boundaries of the physical interaction space, the minimum layer thickness for holding tasks, and the recommendation for restricting the interaction to the middle and lower zones.

A simple way to improve the accuracy of holding and horizontal search tasks is to **provide instant visual feedback regarding layer borders.** Another strategy is to **adjust the center of the layer** to match the current display height **after a certain dwell time**. This prevents the problem of losing the layer when the tangible lens was originally too close to one of its boundaries – an effect that we frequently encountered during our studies.

Another noticeable effect was over- and undershooting during vertical search, especially whenever an unknown search target was encountered (pop-out effect). We only gathered limited evidence regarding fatigue (participants spent only approx. 30 min with the tangible display). Nevertheless, a multi-layer application should always provide users with the ability to rest from time to time, e.g., by freezing particular views and putting them down on the table (cf. [16]).

Beyond that, in many scenarios the required number of physical layers can easily extend a reasonable amount. In such cases, better layer subdivision strategies must be found, such as distorting the physical interaction space for horizontal search tasks by increasing the thickness of a particular layer (fisheye effect).

CONCLUSIONS & FUTURE WORK

In this paper, a class of interaction techniques that extends the design space of horizontal digital tables to the physical third dimension was systematically investigated with respect to exploring a layered information space. With a comprehensive user study, we studied the accuracy at which three fundamental tasks (vertical search, horizontal search and holding) are performed with tangible magic lenses. This also considered other fundamental issues such as the optimal number of layers and their thickness. Our findings include considerable differences in vertical and horizontal search tasks, e.g., a minimal layer thickness of 1 cm vs. 4 cm or a resulting maximum number of layers (11 vs. 44). Derived from these findings, design recommendations were also presented. Given the generic character of interaction tasks in stacks of discrete layers and their universal applicability for many systems and domains, we hope that our findings will help the research community to design and develop a new generation of applications using tangible magic lenses.

For future work, we intend to investigate further aspects of tangible multi-layer interaction, such as rotation tasks, the dynamic non-linear arrangement of layers, perceptual and cognitive issues as well as novel application domains.

ACKNOWLEDGEMENTS

This work was funded by the German Ministry of Education and Science (BMBF) project ViERforES-II (01IM1000 2B). We thank Ricardo Langner for his artwork and video editing.

REFERENCES

1. E. A. Bier, M. C. Stone, K. Pier, W. Buxton, and T. D. DeRose. Toolglass and Magic Lenses: The See-Through Interface. *Proc. SIGGRAPH 1993*, ACM Press (1993), 445-446.
2. L. D. Brown, and H. Hua, Magic Lenses for Augmented Virtual Environments. *IEEE Computer Graphics and Applications*. 26, 4 (July 2006), 64-73.
3. L. K. Y. Chan and H. Y. K. Lau. Poster: A Tangible User Interface Using Spatial Augmented Reality. *Proc. IEEE 3DUI*, IEEE Comp. Society, 2010, 137-138.
4. G. W. Fitzmaurice. Situated Information Spaces and Spatially Aware Palmtop Computers, *Communications of ACM*, 36, 7 (1993), 39-49.
5. K. Hirota and Y. Saeki. Cross-section Projector: Interactive and Intuitive Presentation of 3D Volume Data using a Handheld Screen. *Proc. 3DUI 2007*, IEEE Computer Society Press (2007), 57-63.
6. D. Holman, R. Vertegaal, M. Altosaar, N. Troje, and D. Johns. Paper Windows: Interaction Techniques for Digital Paper. *Proc. CHI '05*, ACM Press (2005), 591-599.
7. H. Ishii and B. Ullmer. Tangible Bits: Towards Seamless Interfaces between People, Bits and Atoms. *Proc. CHI 1997*, ACM Press (1997), 234-241.
8. S. Izadi, S. Hodges, S. Taylor, D. Rosenfeld, N. Villar, A. Butler, and J. Westhues. Going Beyond the Display: A Surface Technology with an Electronically Switchable Diffuser. *Proc. UIST '08*, ACM Press (2008), 269-278.
9. Y. Kakehi and T. Naemura. UlteriorScape: Interactive Optical Superimposition on a View-Dependent Tabletop Display. *Proc. TABLETOP '08*. IEEE Computer Society Press (2008), 189-192.
10. J. Konieczny, C. Shimizu, G. W. Meyer, and D. A. Colucci. Handheld Flexible Display System. *Proc. VIS '05*, IEEE Computer Society Press (2005), 75-81.
11. J. C. Lee, S. E. Hudson, J. W. Summet, and P. H. Dietz. Moveable Interactive Projected Displays Using Projector Based Tracking. *Proc. UIST '05*, ACM Press (2005), 63-72.
12. J. Oh and H. Hua. User Evaluations on Form Factors of Tangible Magic Lenses. *Proc. ISMAR '06*, ACM Press (2006), 23-32.
13. J. Sanneblad and L.E. Holmquist. Ubiquitous Graphics: Combining Hand-held and Wall-size Displays to Interact with Large Images. *Proc. AVI '06*, ACM Press (2006), 373-377.
14. M. Spindler and R. Dachselt. Poster: Towards Making Graphical User Interface Palettes Tangible. *Proc. ITS '10*, ACM Press (2010), 291-292.
15. M. Spindler, S. Stellmach, and R. Dachselt. Advanced Magic Lens Interaction above the Tabletop. *Proc. ITS '09*, ACM Press (2009), 77-84.
16. M. Spindler, C. Tominski, H. Schumann, and R. Dachselt. Tangible Views for Information Visualization. *Proc. ITS '10*, ACM Press (2010), 157-166.
17. S. Subramanian, D. Aliakseyeu, and A. Lucero. Multi-Layer Interaction for Digital Tables. *Proc. UIST '06*, ACM Press (2006), 269-272.
18. A.R.Tilley. The Measure of Man and Woman: Human Factors in Design. John Wiley & Sons, 2nd ed., 2002.
19. A. Treisman and G. Gelade. A Feature Integration Theory of Attention. *Cognitive Psychology*. 12, (1980), 97–136.
20. B. Ullmer and H. Ishii. The metaDESK: Models and Prototypes for Tangible User Interfaces. *Proc. UIST '97*, ACM Press (1997), 223-232.
21. M. Weiser. The Computer for the 21st Century. *Scientific American*. 265, 3 (1991), 66-75.
22. K. Yee. Peephole Displays: Pen Interaction on Spatially Aware Handheld Computers. *Proc. CHI '03*, ACM Press (2003), 1-8.

A Comparative Evaluation of Finger and Pen Stroke Gestures

Huawei Tu
Kochi University of Technology
Kami, Kochi, Japan
ren.xiangshi@kochi-tech.ac.jp

Xiangshi Ren
Kochi University of Technology
Kami, Kochi, Japan
ren.xiangshi@kochi-tech.ac.jp

Shumin Zhai
Google Research
Mountain View, CA, USA
zhai@acm.org

ABSTRACT
This paper reports an empirical investigation in which participants produced a set of stroke gestures with varying degrees of complexity and in different target sizes using both the finger and the pen. The recorded gestures were then analyzed according to multiple measures characterizing many aspects of stroke gestures. Our findings were as follows: (1) Finger drawn gestures were quite different to pen drawn gestures in basic measures including size ratio and average speed. Finger drawn gestures tended to be larger and faster than pen drawn gestures. They also differed in shape geometry as measured by, for example, aperture of closed gestures, corner shape distance and intersecting points deviation; (2) Pen drawn gestures and finger drawn gestures were similar in several measures including articulation time, indicative angle difference, axial symmetry and proportional shape distance; (3) There were interaction effects between gesture implement (finger vs. pen) and target gesture size and gesture complexity. Our findings show that half of the features we tested were performed well enough by the finger. This finding suggests that "finger friendly" systems should exploit these features when designing finger interfaces and avoid using the other features in which the finger does not perform as well as the pen.

Author Keywords
Pen gestures; finger gestures; touch; gesture design; gesture recognition.

ACM Classification Keywords
H.5.2 [Information Interfaces and Presentation]: User Interfaces — *Interaction techniques.*

INTRODUCTION
Due to the rapid growth of touch screen devices, stroke gestures on touch screens are an increasingly important interaction modality. Until recently, the stylus (pen) has been the primary implement for drawing stroke gestures on touch screens. However, today's preferred implement for tapping and gesturing on touch screens is the finger or fingers.

Permission to make digital or hard copies of all or part of this work for personal or classroom use is granted without fee provided that copies are not made or distributed for profit or commercial advantage and that copies bear this notice and the full citation on the first page. To copy otherwise, or republish, to post on servers or to redistribute to lists, requires prior specific permission and/or a fee.
CHI'12, May 5–10, 2012, Austin, Texas, USA.
Copyright 2012 ACM 978-1-4503-1015-4/12/05...$10.00.

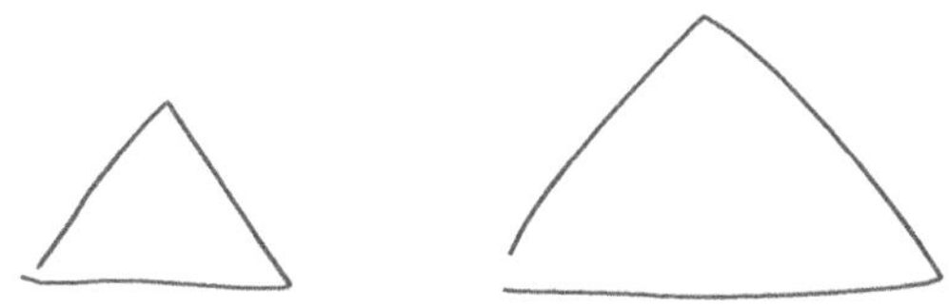

Figure 1. Two representative versions of a triangle gesture produced by the pen (left) and the finger (right).

Recent commercial product design has tended to avoid the use of the pen with a view to user convenience and simplicity. Such a contrast demands that we pay attention to how quantitatively similar or different finger drawn gestures are from pen drawn gestures, e.g., in precision, size, and other gesture characteristics (see Figure 1).

Past stroke gesture research has been focused on the digital pen as the drawing implement. Most stroke gesture HCI research work published to date, such as [2, 3, 11, 13, 15, 21] has been based on data collected from gestures produced with high quality inductive digital styli. It is questionable whether and how well these results apply to finger drawn gestures. Our investigations looked at the differences and similarities between finger and pen stroke gestures both of which have been neglected in the literature. There is a clear need to identify and characterize these differences where they are present. For example, if we know finger gestures are particularly poor at producing certain types of features, then future research and product design should exploit such knowledge and avoid relying on these features in their recognition algorithm and gesture set design. Understanding the quantitative difference between finger strokes and pen strokes can provide a foundation for differential designs of pen and finger interface or combinational designs of pen and finger input in the same interface [8].

To our knowledge little has been done in the HCI research community to address these pressing questions. We see gesture interfaces such as gesture keyboards but they were initially designed with the pen in mind [23] and have been increasingly transformed to finger use [24]. However, the costs and benefits of this unevaluated adaption switch are not known beyond anecdotal subjective impressions. A scientific approach, such as the one presented in our paper, has been pending for too long.

We set out to perform the first systematic comparative investigation between pen vs. finger gestures. We asked participants to draw a set of stroke gestures with a finger and a pen respectively as shown in Table 1. We then processed and analyzed the drawn gestures according to a set of measures and features that are either most basic (such as stroke articulation time) or that are likely to differentiate finger gestures from pen gestures (such as the precision of corner production). We then drew a set of conclusions that characterize the differences and similarities between finger vs. pen gestures.

RELATED WORK

There is a large body of HCI research on gesture interfaces, e.g. [5, 16, 20] for finger gesture and [2, 3, 11, 13, 15, 21] for pen gesture. It is unnecessary and beyond the scope of this paper to review that literature here. Instead, we only highlight a few lines of work that bear direct relevance to the questions we addressed and the methods we used in addressing them.

Human Motor Control Theory

Historically, the study on how humans control their motor behavior has centered on the debate between the centrists and the peripheralists among motor control theorists [19]. The centrists tended to view motor control behavior as an inside-out process, driven by "motor programs" from human internal representations. In contrast, peripheralists tended to emphasize motor control behavior as regulated by outside-in feedback from the environment. To our current questions regarding finger vs. pen gesture differences, a centralist would suggest that there is little difference between finger and pen gestures since their production are both driven from internal representations, as is indeed proposed in the effector independence theory [22] concerning writing. A peripheralist however would argue that the different feel and interaction with the touch screen surface afforded by the pen vs. the bare finger would impact how a gesture is produced.

Gesture Models

The complexity of a stroke gesture may have an impact on the difference between finger and pen gestures. Conceivably fingers are good (enough) at producing simple gestures. How to measure and characterize gesture complexity is a research topic. Simple measures such as the length or the number of line segments [10] in a stroke gesture may serve as complexity indicators. A more formal model, the CLC model [6] that computes a gesture's production time based on sub models of curve, line, and corner production, is a more rigorous characterization of gesture complexity. We used the CLC model as a verification method in the design of our experiment.

Gesture Measurements and Features

Blagojevic et al. [4] categorized a feature library of ink gestures and used this library with attribute selection algorithms to choose good features for gesture recognition. Their work revealed that feature selection can significantly improve recognition rates, which demonstrated the importance of selecting good features for gesture recognition. However, their study did not pay attention to either finger stroke gestures or

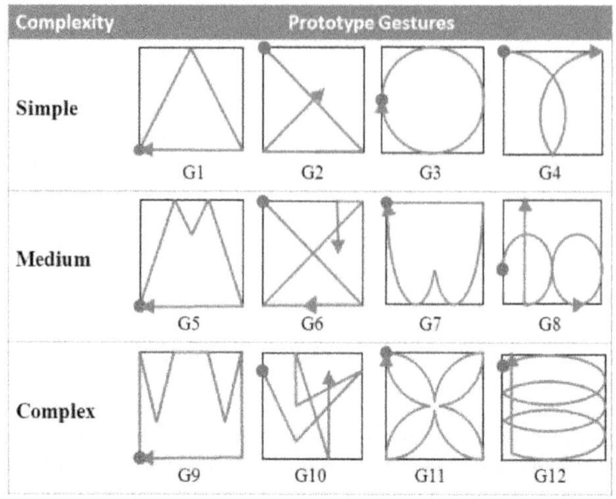

Table 1. Prototype gesture categories. The green dot signifies the starting point of a gesture, and the arrow denotes the end point and the direction of a gesture.

the difference and similarities between finger and pen gestures. Our study investigates the differences and similarities between finger and pen gestures, so as to find "finger friendly" features for finger gesture design and recognition.

Gesture recognition algorithms inevitably use a set of features to classify user input. These features can all be potentially used as measures of finger and pen gesture difference. For example, Andersen and Zhai [1] developed a set of measures to characterize gesture difference. SHARK^2 used proportional shape distance (PSD) as a key feature in classifying the user's input on a gesture keyboard [11]. The PSD feature was more generally studied in Wobbrock et al. [21] showing that it produces comparable or stronger results than the well known Rubine recognizer [18] that combines a set of features through data training. Long et al. [15] used a set of features mostly taken from the Rubine recognizer.

Five features, namely proportional shape distance, indicative angle difference, time, speed, distance between the first and last points, from the above cited papers [1, 11, 15, 18, 21] appeared to be most relevant to the research questions we wanted to address in this paper.

GESTURES USED IN THE EXPERIMENT

In order to identify differences between finger and pen gestures, we designed and selected a set of gesture prototypes. Our goal was to have a small gesture set that covers a wide range of gestures across different categories.

Gesture Categories

Twelve gestures were used in our experiment. Their prototypes are shown in Table 1. Five of them were selected from previous studies (G1 [1], G2 [18], G3 [1], G4 [2, 3], G10 [23]). Four were designed based on previous studies (G5 [18], G6 [1, 2], G7 [1], G12 [15]). G8, G9 and G11 were newly designed for this study.

Based on visual appearance in terms of the number of corners, curves and line segments, the gestures were divided into three groups according to their levels of complexity, i.e., Simple, Medium and Complex as shown in Table 1. These classifications were also supported by simple complexity measures such as length and by their predicted production time[1].

These gestures also vary in characteristics. Gestures G1, G2, G5, G6, G9 and G10 were composed of corners and straight lines, and Gestures G3, G4, G7, G8, G11 and G12 were mainly composed of corners and curves. Gestures G1, G3, G5, G7, G9 and G11 are closed gestures because their prototypes start and end in the same position. The rest of the gestures in the set are open gestures. Gestures G2, G4, G6, G8, G10 and G12 contain intersections, and the other gestures do not. The number of interaction points generally increases with gesture complexity. Gestures G2 and G4 have one interaction point each, G6 and G8 have two interaction points each, G10 has four, and G12 has seven interaction points. Gestures G1, G3, G4, G5, G7, G9 and G11 are symmetrical about the Y axis. The others are asymmetrical.

Target Gesture Size

Intuitively, stroke gestures can be more easily produced in smaller sizes with the pen than with the finger. This led us to repeat the same set of gestures in three different target sizes and ask the participants to reproduce them accordingly. The target gesture size of a prototype gesture was defined as the area in cm^2 of the target gesture's bounding box. From past research we know that pen gestures can be produced in rather small sizes. According to Ren and Zhou [17], the bounding box size 1.5×1.5 cm in length was set up as a baseline in our experiment, which should be rather comfortable for pen gesturing and we suspected that it would be more challenging for finger gesturing. To evaluate the gesture size factor, we also set up the medium (3.0×3.0 cm) and large target gesture sizes (4.5×4.5 cm) respectively. We expected these two sizes would be less challenging for finger gesturing.

EXPERIMENT

Participants

Fifteen volunteers, twelve males and three females, from 20 to 30 years of age, participated in the experiment. All participants were right-handed. Ten of them had prior experience using stylus, and also with finger operation. Three of them had prior experience with finger operation only on touch screen devices. The other two participants had no prior experience operating digital screens with either stylus or finger.

Apparatus

The study was conducted on a HP touchsmart tx2 tablet computer. The screen size was 12.1 inches and its resolution was

[1]The length of a prototype gesture with the bounding box 3.0×3.0 cm was the sum of the distance between adjacent points in the prototype gesture's trajectory. The predicted production time for a prototype gesture with the bounding box 3.0×3.0 cm was calculated by the CLC model [6]. For example, the length and expected time for G1 are 9.7 cm and 1006 ms respectively, while for G12, the length and expected time are 22.67 cm and 2829 ms respectively.

(a) (b)

Figure 2. The display for gesture input.

1280×800 pixels, which means the pixel pitch was 0.204 mm. The most important reason we chose this computer as the experimental apparatus was that it has two touch sensing mechanisms (one capacitive and the other inductive), hence supporting both pen and finger gestures [9]. This ensured that we measured finger and pen gestures under the same set of conditions and form factors. During the experiment the computer was folded in tablet mode and laid on the table with the screen facing upward.

Task and Procedure

The goal of the experimental task design was to simulate how people draw gestures from their memory instead of copying or tracing a template. Similar to the experimental design of [1], participants were asked to draw the gesture from memory as accurately as possible at a normal writing speed, using the pen and index finger of the dominant hand, after being shown the target gesture. As shown in Figure 2, the experiment window was divided into a display area and a gesture input area. In each test trial, a gesture prototype was displayed in the left window for 1.5 seconds, with a dot and an arrowhead indicating the starting point and ending point respectively; meanwhile the right window was hidden by blue color (see Figure 2a). After 1.5 seconds, the gesture prototype disappeared, along with the blue color in the gesturing area, prompting the participant to draw the same gesture in the right window (see Figure 2b) [2].

The experiment consisted of a training phase and an experimental phase. In the training phase, participants were first taught how to perform the experimental task. Then they were asked to draw the twelve gestures in three sizes using the pen and finger respectively as practice. In this training phase, the gesture prototype remained in the left window till the entire trial was completed. In the test phase of this within-subject experiment, each participant completed four blocks of all gestures in three sizes in two drawing implement conditions: pen vs. finger. Within each block, the order of the twelve gestures in three different sizes was randomized. In summary, the experiment data collection consisted of:

15 subjects ×
2 implements (pen, finger) ×
4 blocks ×
12 gestures ×
3 target gesture sizes
= 4320 drawing trials

[2]Pilot studies indicated that after a training period, this time period is long enough to allow participants to remember both the size and overall shape of the target gesture.

Feature Categories	Measures	Features
Algebraical Property Feature	Basic Measure	F1. Time Performance [18] F2. Average Speed [1, 18] F3. Size Ratio
Geometric Shape Feature	Local Shape Measure	F4. Aperture between the Start Point and the End Point of Closed Gestures [1, 18] F5. Indicative Angle Difference between Drawn Gesture and Target Gesture [21] F6. Corner Shape Distance
	Global Shape Measure	F7. Axial Symmetry F8. Proportional Shape Distance [1, 11, 21] F9. Intersecting Points Deviation

Table 2. Feature categories.

At the end of the experiment, a questionnaire was administrated to gather subjective opinions. Participants were asked to rate $pen\ input$ and $finger\ input$ on 7-point Likert Scales regarding $speed$, $accuracy$ and $hand\ fatigue$ (7 for highest preference, and 1 for lowest preference).

FEATURE SELECTION

As described in the section "Related Work", a lot of stroke features have been studied. For the purpose of our study, we chose five features from the literature and designed four new features (see Table 2). We suspected that all these features may reveal differences between finger and pen gestures. With features F1 and F2, the pen or the finger used as the drawing implement may lead to different performance due to either friction or dexterity differences. In addition, because the pen tip is sharper and allows more precision than the fingertip, the finger may result in different performance with respect to F3, F4, F5, F6, F7, F8 and F9.

Inspired by the feature classification method in [18], each feature was classified manually along two dimensions: algebraical property feature and geometric shape feature (see Table 2). As a basic measure, the algebraical property feature represents the basic features of a gesture, including stroke time, movement speed and size ratio. The geometric shape feature consists of the local shape feature and the global shape geometry feature. It focuses on what a gesture looks like.

We also conducted a pilot study to find differences between finger gestures and pen gestures by means of a set of commonly used gestures. We chose seven gestures from *Graffiti*, which is a single-stroke shorthand handwriting set widely employed in PDAs. The seven gestures denote the character "a", "b", "c", "e", "d", "j" and "%" respectively. In addition, we selected a square gesture and a five-pointed star gesture. Six participants took part in the pilot study. The experiment procedure was similar to that introduced in subsection "Task and Procedure". The experimental data were assessed in terms of the 63 features for single stroke gestures used in [4]. We found that the features with differences between finger and pen gestures mainly referred to movement speed, size and curvature, which had already been included in Table 2. Hence, it can be regarded that this feature set shown in Table 2 can demonstrate the main differences between finger gestures and pen gestures.

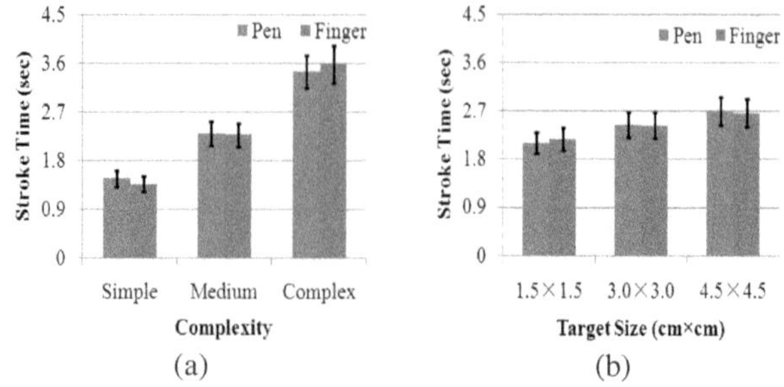

Figure 3. Stroke articulation time for each implement in different (a) complexities and (b) target gesture sizes. Error bars represent 0.95 confidence interval.

RESULTS AND ANALYSIS

In this section, we discuss the experimental results in terms of the gesture features listed in Table 2. Recall that each participant performed four blocks of trials in the experiment, we first checked the learning effect on stroke articulation time over the four blocks of trials to see if the data we collected had reached a level of stability. As to results, the participants' performance began to stabilize in the second block of trials for finger strokes and in the third block of trials for pen strokes. Therefore, data in the third and fourth blocks were applied to the rest of our analysis for pen strokes, and data in the second, third and fourth blocks were applied to the rest of our analysis for finger strokes.

Basic Measures

Time Performance

Stroke articulation time was defined as the duration from the moment the pen or finger touched the screen to the moment the pen or the finger was lifted from the screen. This is a basic measure of stroke performance. Conceivably, there could be a difference in this measure between the pen and the finger as the drawing implement due to either friction or dexterity differences. However, repeated measures ANOVA showed that the drawing implement (pen vs. finger) had no significant main effect on stroke articulation time. The mean stroke articulation time was 2408 ms in the pen condition and 2414 ms in the finger condition.

Other independent variables influenced stroke articulation time. As expected, the level of gesture complexity had a significant main effect on mean stroke articulation time ($F_{2,28} = 127.88$, $p < 0.001$). The target gesture size also had a significant main effect on mean stroke articulation time ($F_{2,28} = 67.14$, $p < 0.001$). There was a strong interaction between implement and complexity ($F_{2,28} = 8.44$, $p < 0.01$). As shown in Figure 3a, the mean stroke articulation time of the pen was longer than that of the finger in drawing simple gestures (1468 ms vs. 1370 ms), slightly longer in drawing gestures of medium level complexity (2306 ms vs. 2284 ms), but shorter in drawing complex gestures (3451 ms vs. 3587 ms). Also, there was a significant interaction between implement and target gesture size ($F_{2,28} = 12.08$, $p < 0.001$). Figure 3b illustrates

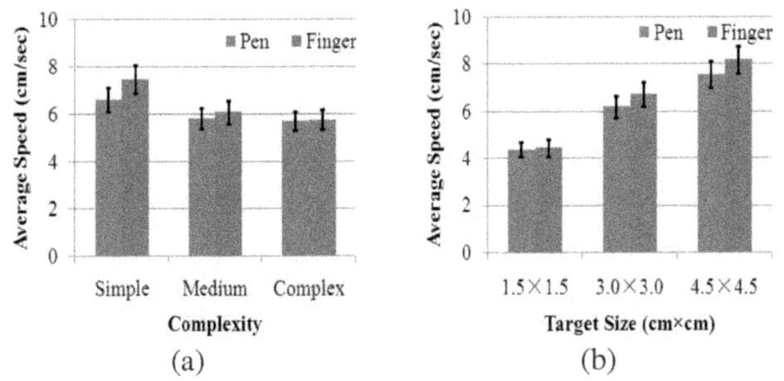

Figure 4. Average speed for each implement in different (a) complexities and (b) target gesture sizes.

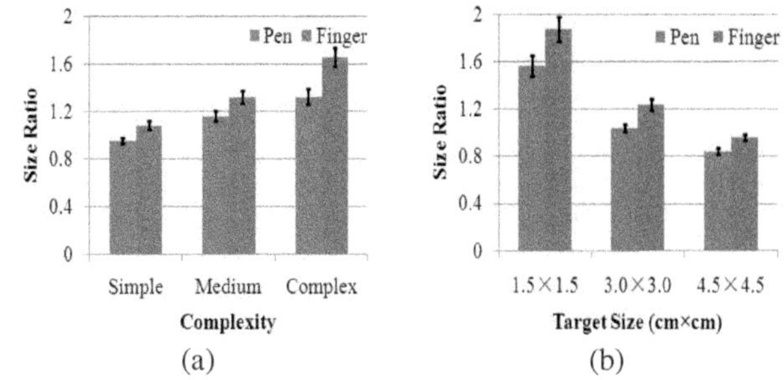

Figure 5. Size ratio for each implement in different (a) complexities and (b) target gesture sizes.

that for small target size, the mean stroke articulation time achieved with pen input (2092 ms) was shorter than that for finger input (2170 ms). However, for medium and large target sizes, pen input led to longer stroke articulation time than finger input (2435 ms vs. 2420 ms for medium size, and 2698 ms vs. 2650 ms for large size). The pen tended to be slightly slower in drawing simple gestures and large size gestures.

Average Speed

The average speed, calculated by the ratio of the gesture length and the stroke articulation time, was another basic measure of stroke gestures we used in this study.

Implement had a significant main effect on average speed ($F_{1,14}$ = 5.85, $p < 0.05$). The mean speed was 6.04 cm/s for pen gestures, 6.43 cm/s for finger gestures. Complexity and target gesture size had a significant main effect on average speed ($F_{2,28}$ = 59.72, $p < 0.001$ for complexity; $F_{2,28}$ = 144.78, $p < 0.001$ for size).

Implement significantly interacted with complexity ($F_{2,28}$ = 32.15, $p < 0.001$). As shown in Figure 4a, the average speed of pen drawn gestures (6.60 cm/s) was lower than the average speed of finger drawn gestures (7.46 cm/s) in simple gestures. In addition, in medium gestures, the average speed of the pen (5.84 cm/s) was lower than the average speed of the finger (6.08 cm/s), and the average speed of the pen (5.69 cm/s) was lower than the average speed of the finger (5.76 cm/s) in complex gestures. The results indicated that the pen performed slower than the finger in the simple, medium and complex gestures, but the difference decreased from simple to complex gestures.

There was a significant interaction effect between implement and target gesture size ($F_{2,28}$ = 24.85, $p < 0.001$)(see Figure 4b). The average speed of the pen was 4.37 cm/s, 6.20 cm/s, 7.56 cm/s for small, medium, and large target size gestures respectively while the average speed of the finger was 4.43 cm/s, 6.71 cm/s and 8.16 cm/s respectively. The finger performed faster than the pen in all three sizes, and the difference increased from small to large size.

Size Ratio

The participants may or may not draw the gesture exactly the same size as the target gesture displayed. There is a possibility that they would tend to draw the gesture in a larger size than the target gesture size, particularly when using the finger. The size ratio between the response gesture and the target gesture can therefore be an informative measure of the user's ability to gesture at a specified scale.

The target size (TS) of a prototype gesture has been defined in the subsection "Target Gesture Size," and the response size (RS) of a drawn gesture is defined as the area in cm^2 of the drawn gesture's bounding box. The response to target size ratio (SR) was measured by the ratio of the two ($SR = RS/TS$).

Implement was a significant main effect on size ratio ($F_{1,14}$ = 45.26, $p < 0.001$). On average both pen and finger drawn gestures tended to be larger, resulting in 1.15 and 1.36 size ratio values in pen and finger conditions respectively.

The complexity had a significant effect on size ratio ($F_{2,28}$ = 47.88, $p < 0.001$). Also, there was a significant interaction effect on size ratio for gesture complexity ($F_{2,28}$ = 38.64, $p < 0.001$). As shown in Figure 5a, when gesture complexity was simple, the size of drawn gestures was almost the same as the size of target gestures (mean size ratio was 0.95 for the pen, and 1.08 for the finger). Corresponding to the medium complex gestures, the mean size ratio increased to 1.16 (pen) and 1.32 (finger) respectively. For the most complex gesture, the mean size ratio increased to 1.32 (pen) and 1.66 (finger) respectively. Results showed that pen gesture led to smaller RS than finger gesture. In both pen and finger gestures, the size ratio increased as the gesture complexity increased.

The size ratio value strongly depended on the target gesture size ($F_{2,28}$ = 71.30, $p < 0.001$). Also, there was a significant interaction effect on size ratio for target size ($F_{2,28}$ = 11.67, $p < 0.001$). As illustrated in Figure 5b, when the target size was small, the response size of the drawn gestures was larger, resulting in mean size ratio values of 1.57 (pen) and 1.88 (finger) respectively. Corresponding to the medium size target, the mean response size of the drawn gestures was only slightly larger, resulting in mean size ratio values of 1.04 (pen) and 1.23 (finger) respectively. Corresponding to the large size target, the mean response size of the drawn gestures was in fact smaller than the size of the target, resulting in mean size ratio values of 0.84 (pen) and 0.96 (finger) respectively.

Overall, the results here show that it is difficult to draw small and complex gestures with either implement. The drawn gestures tended to be larger in these cases. These effects were slightly more pronounced with the finger than with the pen.

Local Shape Measures

Aperture between the Start Point and the End Point of Closed Gestures

To reflect the ability to draw a closed gesture, we measured the distance (aperture) between the start point and the end point. Conceivably the finger is at a greater disadvantage than the pen since the finger may more severely obscure the start point when getting close to it.

For drawn gestures corresponding to the prototype gestures G1, G3, G5, G7, G9 and G11 which start and end in the same position (see Table 1), we calculated the aperture between the start point and the end point. As we expected, there was a significant main effect for implement on the aperture of closed gestures ($F_{1,14}$ = 5.48, $p < 0.05$). The mean aperture was 0.20 cm with the pen and 0.24 cm with the finger respectively. Although no significant main effect was found on aperture for gesture complexity, target gesture size had a significant main effect on aperture ($F_{2,28}$ = 7.86, $p < 0.01$). The mean aperture was 0.18 cm for small size targets, 0.22 cm for medium size targets, and 0.26 cm for large size targets.

Indicative Angle Difference between Drawn Gesture and Target Gesture

The indicative angle was defined as the angle rotated from the horizontal vector whose starting point is the centroid of the gesture, to the vector formed by the centroid of the gesture and the gesture's first point. We calculated the indicative angle difference between the drawn gesture and the corresponding target gesture. It was found that no significant main effect for implement on indicative angle difference. The mean indicative angle difference was 0.32 degrees for the pen, and -0.13 degrees for the finger.

Corner Shape Distance (CSD)

The prototype gestures G1, G2, G5, G6, G9 and G10 (see Table 1) have sharp corners. How these corners change their shapes in the drawn gesture is yet another way to investigate local shape difference. We defined "Corner Shape Distance" (CSD) as mean distance between the corresponding corners in the drawn gesture and the target gesture.

To calculate CSD, as a first step we need to detect the vertex for each corner. We detected the vertexes of corners in the drawn gesture U based on the two-thirds power law in human motor control [14], which was also used for similar purposes in [1] to segment drawn gestures. We first calculated the speed for each point in drawn gesture U. Secondly, the points in U were sorted according to speed, and M (depending on the size and complexity of the corresponding target gesture) points with low speed were chosen. Third, K-means clustering was applied to partition the M points into K clusters ($K+1$ was the number of corners in U. We did not consider the corner whose vertex is the start point, because in drawn gestures, the start point and the end point may not necessarily coincide to form a vertex.). Fourth, the point with the lowest speed in each cluster was chosen as the vertex of the corner as $VC_i, 1 \leqslant i \leqslant K$ (see Figure 6a).

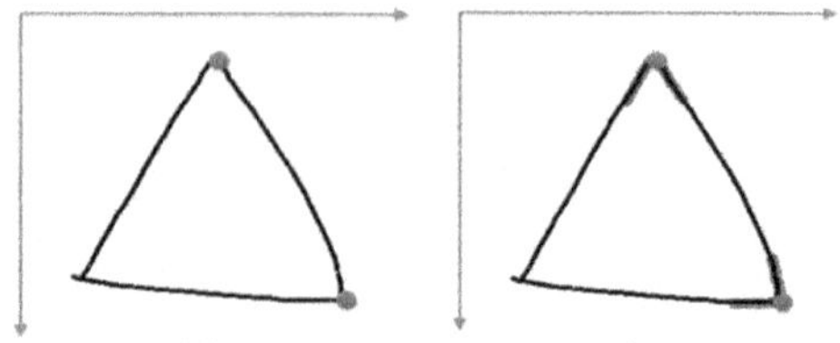

(a) (b)

Figure 6. (a) Vertexes in a drawn gesture. The red dots denote the vertexes. (b) The point set for each vertex. The green dots denote the point sets detected by our algorithm.

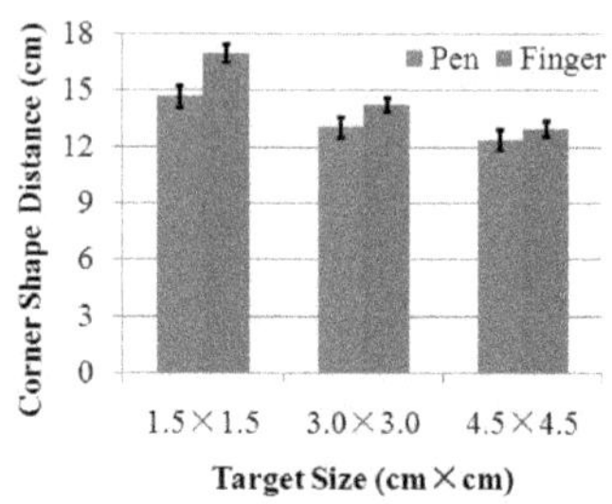

Figure 7. Corner shape distance for each implement in different target sizes.

For each corner, after detecting the vertex, we need to choose a set of points in two arms to represent the corner shape. The second step is to calculate a point set for each vertex (VC_i). For each corner in the drawn gesture U, we calculated the distance between the vertex VC_i and the points in its two arms, and chose the points whose distance was less than 0.8 cm. Then each vertex (VC_i) had a point set $PU_i, (1 \leqslant i \leqslant K)$. The points in PU_i were re-sampled into N ($N = 40$) points, which constituted a new point set $PD_{i,j}, (1 \leqslant i \leqslant K, 1 \leqslant j \leqslant N)$ (see Figure 6b). We also calculated the point set for each vertex in the target gesture V, as $PV_i, (1 \leqslant i \leqslant K)$, and the points in each PV_i were also resampled into N ($N = 40$) points, which also constituted a new point set $PT_{i,j}, (1 \leqslant i \leqslant K, 1 \leqslant j \leqslant N)$.

The third step was to calculate CSD_i ($1 \leqslant i \leqslant K$). CSD_i was measured by calculating the distance between the point in PD_i and the corresponding point in PT_i, $(1 \leqslant i \leqslant K)^3$. To calculate the CSD_i, we translated PD_i so its centroid coincided with the centroid of the corresponding point set PT_i. The CSD was calculated by the sum of all $CSD_i (1 \leqslant i \leqslant K)$.

$$CSD = \sum_{i=1}^{K} CSD_i = \sum_{i=1}^{K}\sum_{j=1}^{N} d(PD_{i,j}, PT_{i,j}) \qquad (1)$$

A significant main effect for implement was found on CSD ($F_{1,14}$ = 6.57, $p < 0.05$). The mean CSD of the pen was 13.38 cm, and the mean CSD of the finger was 14.73 cm. There is also a significant main effect on CSD for target gesture size ($F_{2,28}$ = 109.08, $p < 0.01$). Implement had a significant interaction effect with target gesture size ($F_{2,28}$ = 7.19, p

[3] In the following sections, $d(p, q)$ was used to denote the Euclidean distance between point p and point q.

< 0.01) (see Figure 7). For small target size, the mean CSD of the pen was 14.67 cm whereas the mean CSD of the finger was 16.95 cm. For medium target size, the mean CSD of the pen was 13.07 cm whereas the mean CSD of the finger was 14.25 cm. For large target size, the mean CSD of the pen was 12.39 cm whereas the mean CSD of the finger was 12.98 cm. The results showed that the pen performed better than the finger in all three target sizes.

Global Shape Measures

To investigate purely global shape aspects of a drawn gesture, we disregarded the drawn gesture size by normalizing ($scaling$) the drawn gesture's size to the largest target gesture size (4.5 × 4.5 cm), and also by scaling the corresponding target gesture's size to 4.5 × 4.5 cm. In other words, if the drawn gesture maintains the exact relative dimensions as the target gesture except that it is drawn in larger or smaller scale, the normalized shape measures would still give perfect scores (zero distance). We therefore report the three shape geometry measures with $scaling$ (i.e. normalization). To calculate each measure, the drawn gesture was translated so its centroid coincides with the centroid of the target gesture ($translation$).

Axial Symmetry (AS)

The prototype gestures G1, G3, G4, G5, G7, G9 and G11 (see Table 1) have axial symmetry. For simplicity, we explained the algorithm of AS calculation by taking G4 as an example. In order to measure the drawn gesture's axial symmetry, we firstly scaled the drawn gesture to 4.5 × 4.5 cm size and then re-sampled it to N ($N = 500$) equidistant points. $X = X_a$ is the axis which crosses the centroid of the drawn gesture and is perpendicular to the X axis (see Figure 8). For straight lines $Y = Y_i$ ($Y_{min} \leq Y_i \leq Y_{max}$, Y_{min} and Y_{max} are the minimum y value and the maximum y value of the drawn gesture respectively, Y_i increases 1 pixel each time), there are two intersecting points between the drawn gesture and $Y = Y_i$: $(X_a - XL, Y_i)$ in the left of $X = X_a$ and $(X_a + XR, Y_i)$ in the right of $X = X_a$, in which XL is the distance between $X = X_a$ and $(X_a - XL, Y_i)$, XR is the distance between $X = X_a$ and $(X_a + XR, Y_i)$. The mean distance difference can be calculated as

$$AS = \frac{1}{Y_{max} - Y_{min}} \sum_{i=Y_{\min}}^{Y_{\max}} DA_i \qquad (2)$$

Where DA_i is the absolute value of $(XR - XL)$. The greater the AS is, the less symmetrical the drawn gesture is. For G5, G7, G9 and G11, the algorithm gets more complex, but the basic idea is the same.

No significant main effect was found for implement on AS. The mean AS was 0.44 cm for the pen, and 0.43 cm for the finger. In other words, the finger gestures and the pen gestures did not significantly differ in symmetry. However, a significant main effect was found on AS for gesture complexity ($F_{2,28}$ = 202.87, $p < 0.001$) and target gesture size ($F_{2,28}$ = 252.89, $p < 0.001$). In addition, there was a significant interaction effect on AS for gesture complexity ($F_{2,28}$ = 8.26, $p < 0.01$). The mean AS of pen drawn gestures (0.27 cm) was larger than that of finger drawn gestures (0.21 cm) for simple

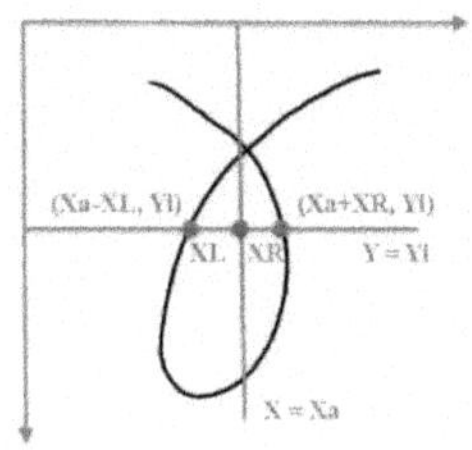

Figure 8. The illustration of axial symmetry in a drawn gesture corresponding to G4.

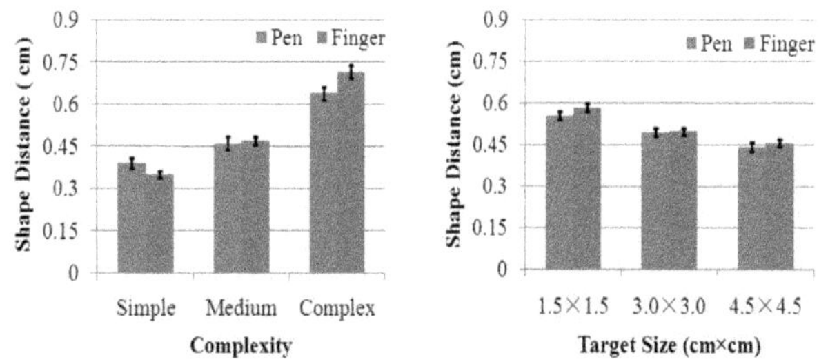

(a) (b)

Figure 9. Proportional shape distance in normalized scale for each implement in different (a) complexities and (b) target gesture sizes.

gestures, and for medium gestures, the mean AS of the pen (0.42 cm) was larger than that of the finger (0.39 cm), but the mean AS of the pen (0.62 cm) was smaller than that of the finger (0.68 cm) in complex gestures. Results showed that the finger resulted in smaller AS than the pen for simple and medium gestures, indicating that the finger performed better than the pen for these gestures.

Proportional Shape Distance (PSD)

After $scaling$ and $translation$, the drawn gesture U and the target gesture V were re-sampled into N ($N = 100$) evenly spaced points. We denote these transformed points by $U(i)$ and $V(i)$ ($1 \leq i \leq N$) for U and V respectively.

The proportional shape distance (PSD) is defined as

$$PSD = \frac{1}{N} \sum_{i=1}^{N} d(U(i), V(i)) \qquad (3)$$

Interestingly, there was no significant main effect for implement on PSD. The mean PSD was 0.50 cm for the pen, and 0.51 cm for the finger. The PSD measure was sensitive to both gesture complexity ($F_{2,28}$ = 128.72, $p < 0.001$) and target gesture size ($F_{2,28}$ = 150.79, $p < 0.001$). As one would expect, the PSD measure increased with gesture complexity (see Figure 9a) since the accuracy to replicate more complex gestures should decrease. Furthermore, PSD decreased as target gesture size increased (see Figure 9b). Although target gesture size had no significant interaction with implement, there was a significant interaction effect on PSD for gesture complexity ($F_{2,28}$ = 7.91, $p < 0.01$). For simple gestures, the mean PSD produced by the pen (0.39 cm) was larger than that for the finger (0.35 cm). Nevertheless, for more complex gestures, the mean PSD achieved with the pen was smaller (0.46 cm and 0.64 cm for medium and complex gestures

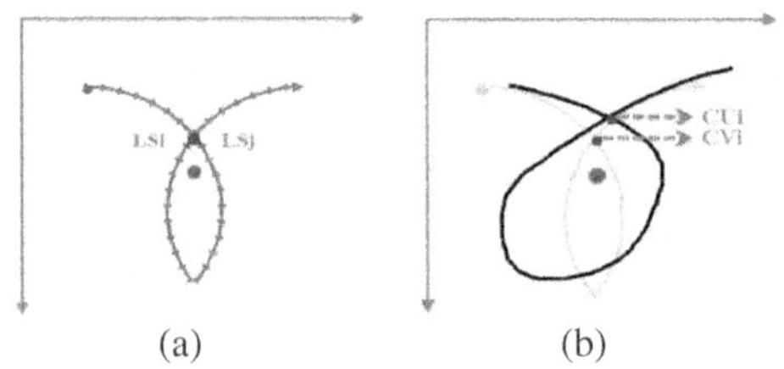

Figure 10. (a) Detecting intersecting points in the target gesture G4. LSi and LSj are two line segments. (b) The intersecting points in G4 (CV_i) and in the drawn gesture corresponding to G4 (CU_i).

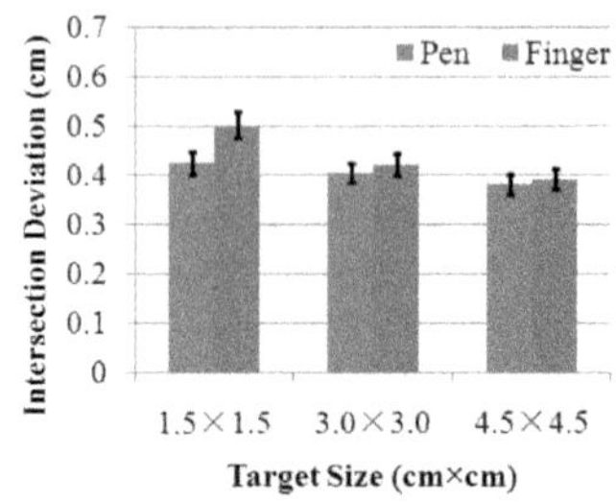

Figure 11. Intersecting points deviation in normalized scale for each implement in different target gesture sizes.

respectively) than that for the finger (0.47 cm and 0.72 cm for medium and complex gestures respectively). The results showed that the pen resulted in more accurate performance than the finger for complex gestures, but the finger achieved more accurate performance than the pen for simple gestures.

Intersecting Points Deviation (IPD)

Gestures G2, G4, G6, G8, G10 and G12 (see Table 1) had one or more self crossing intersecting points. How much these intersecting points change in the drawn gesture from the corresponding intersecting points in the target gesture is another indication of the shape difference between the two. We define the "Intersecting Points Deviation" (IPD) as the mean distance between the intersecting points in the drawn gesture U and the target gesture V (see Figure 10b).

In order to detect the intersecting points in the drawn gesture, the first step for U was $scaling$ and $translation$, which was introduced at the start of this subsection. U was divided into $N-1$ ($N=40$) line segments (LSi, $1 \leq \text{i} \leq (N-1)$) by resampling into N equidistant points (see Figure 10a). Then, the LSi ($1 \leq i \leq (N-1)$) was compared with other line segments LSj ($1 \leq j \leq (N-1), j \neq i$) to check whether or not there were any intersecting points. If an intersecting point was detected, it would be recorded in a point set CU. We can also detect the intersecting points in the corresponding target gesture V as a point set CV.

If the count of intersecting points in $CU(N_{CU})$ was equal to the count in $CV(N_{CV})$, the IPD between U and V was calculated as

$$IPD = \frac{1}{N_{CU}} \sum_{i=1}^{N_{CU}} d(CU(i), CV(i)) \quad (4)$$

Else, IPD was calculated as 0 ($Intersection\ Miss$).

$Intersection\ Miss$ rate, defined as the ratio of $Intersection\ Miss$ count and total trial count for IPD analysis, was firstly calculated. We found that the $Intersection\ Miss$ rate for pen input and finger input was low (3.15% and 2.09% respectively), so we continued the analysis of IPD using repeated measures ANOVA.

A significant main effect was found for implement on IPD ($F_{1,14}$ = 11.74, $p < 0.01$). Pen input resulted in IPD with 0.40 cm and finger input produced IPD with 0.44 cm. Target gesture size had significant main effects on IPD ($F_{2,28}$ = 20.86, $p < 0.001$). There was a significant interaction between implement and target gesture size ($F_{2,28}$ = 11.34, $p <$ 0.01). As illustrated in Figure 11, the mean IPD was 0.42 cm for the pen and 0.50 cm for the finger in small target size. The mean IPD was 0.40 cm for the pen and 0.42 cm for the finger in medium target size, and the mean IPD was 0.38 cm for the pen and 0.39 cm for the finger in large target size. Therefore, the pen performed better than the finger in all three target sizes.

Subjective Evaluation

A significant main effect was found on $speed$ ($F_{1,14}$ = 7.15, $p < 0.05$). The mean preferences of the pen and the finger were 5.53 and 4.13 respectively. A significant main effect was also found for $accuracy$ ($F_{1,14}$ = 5.59, $p < 0.05$). The mean preferences for the pen and the finger were 5.27 and 3.87 respectively. However, there was no significant main effect on $hand\ fatigue$, suggesting that pen gestures and finger gestures are similar in difficulty for users. Overall, users generally felt that the pen can achieve greater accuracy and faster speed than the finger for gesture input.

DISCUSSION

Implications for Finger Gesture Design

Past stroke gesture research has been primarily based on the digital pen as a drawing implement. However, recent commercial product design has tended toward finger input and tends to avoid the use of the pen. Such shifts raise the question of how quantitatively different or similar finger stroke gestures are from pen stroke gestures. Therefore, we conducted a first study to quantify the differences and similarities between finger and pen gestures. Our work has provided a methodology to investigate and quantify the performance of finger and pen gestures, in which finger and pen gestures were analyzed according to multiple features that characterize stroke gestures. Some features revealed similarities between finger and pen drawn gestures, but some features were less accurate with the finger. Based on the evaluation in terms of these features, the implications for finger gesture design were presented as follows.

First, four of the nine features studied revealed similarities between finger and pen drawn gestures, including stroke articulation time (F1), indicative angle difference (F5), axial symmetry (AS) (F7) and proportional shape distance (PSD) (F8). This means that if the gesture recognition algorithm relies on features based on these measures, we should not expect finger gestures to be less effective than pen gestures. Given that proportional shape distance (PSD) based recognition is already used in both research and practical large-scale gesture systems (specifically the ShapeWriter gesture keyboard, although in more complex ways than in this paper), it is reasonable to expect that "finger friendly" recognition algorithm can be designed within the feature space outlined by findings reported above.

Second, five of the nine features studied revealed significant differences between finger and pen drawn gestures, including the average speed (F2), size ratio (F3), aperture between start point and end point (F4), corner shape distance (CSD) (F6) and intersecting points deviation (IPD) (F9). Finger drawn gestures tended to be larger than pen drawn gestures, indicating a somewhat obvious drawback of finger operation - which requires a larger touch screen surface than pen operation. Average speed analysis revealed that the finger performed faster than the pen for gesture input, particularly for simple gestures. While the overall proportional shape distance (PSD) of finger gestures is no worse than pen gestures, some aspects of shape, such as intersecting points deviation (IPD) and corner shape distance (CSD) tend to be larger in finger gestures than in pen gestures. These features tend to be less accurate with the finger and thus should be avoided in "finger friendly" recognition algorithm design.

Finally, there were also a few interaction effects that may have design implications. According to time performance (F1) analysis, pen gestures led to shorter time in drawing more complex gestures. This was also reflected in movement speed (F2). The finger tended to be much faster than the pen in drawing simple gestures, but achieved similar speed in drawing complex gestures. For shape features, pen input led to more accurate axial symmetry (AS) (F7) than finger input for complex gestures. Furthermore, pen input is more exact than finger input for drawing complex gestures according to proportional shape distance (PSD) (F8), but for simple gestures, finger gestures are more accurate than pen gestures. Overall these interaction effects suggest that finger friendly gesture set design should not contain gestures which are overly complex.

All of the foregoing analysis could also be interpreted as in favor of the pen since at least in some measures it is more accurate than the finger. From daily experience in, for example hand writing and signing signatures, we can all appreciate that the dexterity of the pen is unmatchable by the finger. Note that these examples differ from the gestures tested in this experiment in at least two aspects: they tend to be more complex and they are well-learned and memorized patterns. In light of the centralist vs. peripheralist views discussed earlier in this paper, one could argue that these well learned gesture patterns may include pen operation as part of one's "motor programs".

Some interesting results were found in the subjective evaluation. In respect to speed evaluation, over half of the participants felt that pen input was faster than finger input. They stated: "The pen tip is more smooth than the finger pad". However, from average speed analysis, the finger led to higher speed than the pen for drawing gestures. Some participants reported that the finger was easier to control than the pen when drawing gestures, so they thought the finger produced higher speed than the pen. From this, we suspect that the greater degrees of freedom afforded by pen input may lead to lower drawing speed. With regard to accuracy evaluation, participants believed pen gesture input was more accurate than finger gesture input. This is consistent with the results in the analysis of corner shape distance (CSD) and intersecting points deviation (IPD), but contrary to proportional shape distance (PSD) analysis. Some participants reported: "It is difficult to draw intersections or sharp corners with the finger". When drawing gestures, participants may have felt more control of some features such as corner shape distance (CSD) although no difference was made to other features such as proportional shape distance (PSD).

Prototype Gestures and Feature Selection

Admittedly gesture selection is a tricky balance of many considerations. We needed to cover common gestures in current usage, but we also needed to see how different types of gestures interact with various levels of complexity (simple, medium and complex) so the choices were not so many in each combination. Thus, we conducted the pilot study with a set of commonly used gestures (Graffiti gestures). Results showed pen and finger gestures differed in some features, which helped us to select features for the formal experiment. However, we did not use these Graffiti gestures in the formal experiment for two reasons. First, it is difficult to classify these gestures into simple, medium and complex levels because they are overall quite simple, i.e., these gestures can not meet the requirement of our study. Second, some features in which pen and finger gestures may differ, such as the aperture, can not be tested using these gestures because they are not closed gestures. Instead, we selected and designed twelve gestures which are suited to the purpose of this study. Results showed that these gestures in each of simple, medium and complex gestures levels differed in terms of time performance, average speed and proportional shape distance (PSD), suggesting these gestures were selected properly. Furthermore, the gestures chosen for this study proved effective for our examination of the differences between finger and pen input gestures; they enabled us to reveal many plausible findings. This means that these prototype gestures may be useful also for future research when designing pen and finger gestures.

Regarding the selection of features for gesture performance measurement, although a large number of features have been proposed and used in previous studies [1, 4, 15, 18], study on all stroke gesture features is beyond the scope of our study. We only focused on some features which may reveal differences between pen and finger stroke gestures with reference to the structures and characteristics of strokes as well as the gesture input performance due to the different characteristics of pen and finger input. By means of the nine features selected or designed by us, a number of differences and similarities were found between finger and pen gestures, for example speed, size and accuracy. Furthermore, using the methodology of our study, other features can be examined for gesture design.

Sensing Mechanisms of the Experimental Device

The study presented here revealed that pen gesture and finger gesture differ in several features. Though we believe that the differences are caused by the intrinsic properties of the pen and the finger respectively, one may well ask whether or not the sensing qualities of different sensing mechanisms used in this study had an effect on the experimental results.

The experimental device, HP Touchsmart tx2, has two different touch sensing mechanisms, i.e., capacitive for finger input and inductive for pen input. The position accuracy and sampling rate may differ between the two sensors [7]. Regarding position accuracy, the pen tip is sharper than the finger tip, which is an inherent difference between the pen and the finger. The sampling rates in these sensors may vary depending on the number of fingers used [7]. We therefore conducted a test to measure the sampling rates of these sensors in a condition similar to our experiments. We asked all the participants to draw freely on the screen with the finger or pen. The program recorded the number of sampling points within one second. The sampling rates were 141 Hz (SD = 1.89) for pen input and 107 Hz (SD = 0.65) for finger input; both are sufficiently high for our purpose and should not affect the gesture quality measures used.

CONCLUSION

The rapid ongoing development of touch screen devices requires the HCI field to understand the impact of finger vs. pen as gesture implements on these devices. We conducted a first study of the differences and similarities between finger drawn and pen drawn gestures. We selected a set of gestures of varied complexity and characteristics and presented in three target sizes to a group of participants who reproduced them with both the finger and the pen. The drawn gestures were then analyzed with a broad set of measures, five selected from the literature and another four designed specifically for this study.

Our findings have demonstrated the importance of our study: when applying principles, methods and findings from pen-based gesture systems to finger-based gesture design, it is vital to consider the differences and similarities. As finger gesture interaction is gaining popularity in application design, it is important to design stroke gestures that avoid features in which the finger does not perform as well as the pen, as shown in our study. Our work is one step in this exploration.

ACKNOWLEDGMENTS

This study has been partially supported by Grant-in-Aid for Scientific Research (No. 23300048) in Japan. We wish to thank the members of Ren Lab in Kochi University of Technology for their assistance.

REFERENCES

1. Andersen, T.H. and Zhai, S. "Writing with music": exploring the use of auditory feedback in gesture interfaces. ACM *TAP 7*, 3(2010), 1-24.
2. Appert, C. and Zhai, S. Using strokes as command shortcuts: cognitive benefits and toolkit support. In *Proc. CHI 2009*, ACM Press (2009), 2289-2298.
3. Bau, O. and Mackay, W. E. OctoPocus: a dynamic guide for learning gesture-based command sets. In *Proc. UIST 2008*, ACM Press (2008), 37-46.
4. Blagojevic, R., Chang, S.H. and Plimmer, B. The power of automatic feature selection: Rubine on steroids. In *Proc. SBIM 2010*, Eurographics Association (2010), 79-86.
5. Bragdon, A., Nelson, E., Li, Y. and Hinckley, K. Experimental analysis of touch-screen gesture designs in mobile environments . In *Proc. CHI 2011*, ACM Press (2011), 403-412.
6. Cao, X. and Zhai, S. Modeling human performance of pen stroke gestures. In *Proc. CHI 2007*, ACM Press (2007), 1495-1504.
7. DuoSense Digitizer Product Brief. http://www.n-trig.com.
8. Hinckley, K., Yatani, K., Pahud, M., Coddington, N., Rodenhouse, J., Wilson, A., Benko, H. and Buxton, B. Pen + Touch = New Tools. In *Proc. UIST2010*, ACM Press (2010), 27-36.
9. HP TouchSmart tx2 Notebook PC Maintenance and Service Guide. http://www.hp.com.
10. Isokoski, P. Model for unistroke writing time. In *Proc. CHI 2001*, ACM Press (2001), 357-364.
11. Kristensson, P.O. and Zhai, S. SHARK^2: a large vocabulary shorthand writing system for pen-based computers. In *Proc. UIST 2004*, ACM Press (2004), 43-52.
12. Kurtenbach, G. and Buxton, W. Issues in combining marking and direct manipulation techniques. In *Proc. UIST 1991*, ACM Press (1991), 137-144.
13. Kurtenbach, G., Sellen, A. and Buxton, W. An empirical evaluation of some articulatory and cognitive aspects of "marking menus". *Human Computer Interaction, 8*, 1 (1993), 1-23.
14. Lacuaniti, F., Terzuolo, C. and Viviani, P. The law relating the kinematic and figural aspects of drawing movements. *Acta Psychologica*, 54 (1983), 115-558.
15. Long, A.C., Landay, J.A., Rowe, L.A. and Michiels, J. Visual similarity of pen gestures. In *Proc. CHI 2000*, ACM Press (2000), 360-367.
16. Morris, M.R., Huang, A., Paepcke, A. and Winoqrad, T. Cooperative gestures: multi-user gestural interactions for co-located groupware. In *Proc. CHI 2006*, ACM Press (2006), 1201-1210.
17. Ren, X. and Zhou, X. The optimal size of handwriting character input boxes on PDAs, *Int. J. Human-Computer Interaction, 25*, 8 (2009), 762-784.
18. Rubine, D. Specifying gestures by example. In *Proc. SIGGRAPH 1991*, ACM Press (1991), 329-337.
19. Schmidt, R. A. Motor control and learning: a behavioral emphasis. 2nd ed. *Champaign*, IL: Human Kinetics (1988).
20. Wobbrock, J. O., Morris, M. R. and Wilson, A. D. User-defined gestures for surface computing . In *Proc. CHI 2009*, ACM Press (2009), 1083-1092.
21. Wobbrock, J. O., Wilson, A. D. and Li, Y. Gestures without libraries, toolkits or training: a $1 recognizer for user interface prototypes. In *Proc. UIST 2007*, ACM Press (2007), 59-168.
22. Wright, C. E. Generalized motor programs: reexamining claims of effector independence in writing. In *Attention and Performance XIII, Erlbaum*, Hillsdale, NJ (1990), 294-320.
23. Zhai, S. and Kristensson, P.O. Shorthand writing on stylus keyboard. In *Proc. CHI 2003*, ACM Press (2003), 97-104.
24. Zhai, S., Kristensson, P.O, Gong, P., Greiner, M., Peng, S.A., Liu, L.M. and Dunnigan, A. Shapewriter on the iphone: from the laboratory to the real world. *Ext. abstracts. CHI 2009*, ACM Press (2009), 2667-2670.

A Handle Bar Metaphor for Virtual Object Manipulation with Mid-Air Interaction

Peng Song Wooi Boon Goh William Hutama Chi-Wing Fu Xiaopei Liu
Nanyang Technological University, Singapore
{song0083,aswbgoh,hwilliam,cwfu,liuxp}@ntu.edu.sg

ABSTRACT
Commercial 3D scene acquisition systems such as the Microsoft *Kinect* sensor can reduce the cost barrier of realizing mid-air interaction. However, since it can only sense hand position but not hand orientation robustly, current mid-air interaction methods for 3D virtual object manipulation often require contextual and mode switching to perform translation, rotation, and scaling, thus preventing natural continuous gestural interactions. A novel *handle bar metaphor* is proposed as an effective visual control metaphor between the user's hand gestures and the corresponding virtual object manipulation operations. It mimics a familiar situation of handling objects that are skewered with a bimanual handle bar. The use of relative 3D motion of the two hands to design the mid-air interaction allows us to provide precise controllability despite the *Kinect* sensor's low image resolution. A comprehensive repertoire of 3D manipulation operations is proposed to manipulate single objects, perform fast constrained rotation, and pack/align multiple objects along a line. Three user studies were devised to demonstrate the efficacy and intuitiveness of the proposed interaction techniques on different virtual manipulation scenarios.

Author Keywords
3D manipulation; bimanual gestures; user interaction

ACM Classification Keywords
H.5.2 : User Interfaces - Input devices and strategies; I.3.6 : Methodology and Techniques - Interaction techniques

General Terms
Design

INTRODUCTION
In recent years, mid-air interaction supported by 3D spatial gestural inputs has received increasing attention from both the research community [8, 23, 17, 27, 4] and the gaming industry, as evidenced by the popular gaming devices such as Nintendo *Wii-mote* and Microsoft *Kinect*, which allow us to perform natural physical interactions in our own physical space while moving freely in front of a large display.

Permission to make digital or hard copies of all or part of this work for personal or classroom use is granted without fee provided that copies are not made or distributed for profit or commercial advantage and that copies bear this notice and the full citation on the first page. To copy otherwise, or republish, to post on servers or to redistribute to lists, requires prior specific permission and/or a fee.
CHI'12, May 5–10, 2012, Austin, Texas, USA.
Copyright 2012 ACM 978-1-4503-1015-4/12/05...$10.00.

There are basically two approaches to accommodate mid-air interactions in such a visual interactive setting. The first employs a handheld controller device, such as the Nintendo *Wii-mote*. User inputs via button clicks and accelerometer-based motion sensing are integrated to form high-level gestures to support the interaction. The second is a controller-free approach, where users can manipulate the graphical contents on the display with their bare hands. Temporal information to support mid-air interaction is obtained by using an image and/or depth sensor (e.g., *Kinect*) to continuously sense and analyze the user's body posture and hand gestures via real-time image processing techniques.

This paper studies mid-air interaction designs to support object manipulation in a 3D virtual environment in a controller-free setting. This approach is particularly useful for distant viewing and interaction in front of large displays since users can directly perform spatial gestures in their own physical space. This physical space alone can be used to produce natural 3D manipulation inputs without cumbersome handheld peripherals. With the wide availability of the Microsoft *Kinect* sensor [26], the cost barrier of realizing such mid-air interaction system has been significantly reduced. However, due to the limitation of the *Kinect* sensor, which can robustly sense hand position but not hand orientation, current interaction methods often require mode switching to move between different operations such as rotation, translation and scaling. As a result, it is difficult for users to recall and execute these operations. This paper aims to address such shortcomings within a controller-free environment that supports natural and intuitive mid-air interactive gestures.

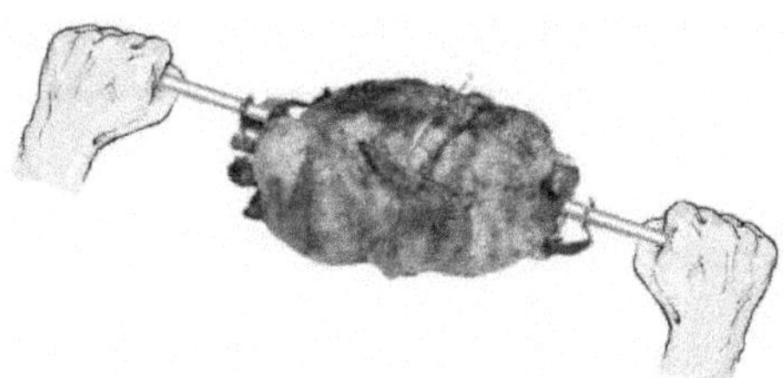

Figure 1. Manipulating a turkey with a bimanual handle bar.

At the heart of this inquiry is the question of what suitable metaphors one can use to map the 3D gestural actions of a user to the manipulation operations on objects in a 3D virtual environment. The metaphor we proposed for visual manipulation tasks is a bimanual handle bar shown in Figure 1. We call this the *handle bar* metaphor. Both hands from the users are employed to manipulate the virtual objects in a natural manner. After the related work section, we give an overview of the interaction system, and then describe the handle-bar-based interaction designs for typical object manipulation operations in a 3D virtual space and highlight their advantages. User evaluations were carried out on various visual manipulation tasks that involve translation and rotation, constrained rotation, and multiple object alignment. Results show that all users can quickly improve their competency in performing the required tasks using our interaction design with only a short period of practice.

RELATED WORK

This section surveys various interaction paradigms to manipulate 3D objects in virtual environments and relevant mid-air interaction applications with the *Kinect* sensor.

Interaction with 3D Virtual Environments

There are a wide range of methods to interact with 3D contents in virtual space [9]. Since this work focuses on interactions with freehand gestures, we review mainly two more relevant areas: virtual reality and freehand interfaces.

Virtual Reality Interfaces. This approach immerses users in a virtual space for them to perform interaction via various sensors and input devices. Duval et al. [13] proposed a 3D interaction technique called "SkeweR," which enables two users to move the same virtual object collaboratively. John et al. [21] employed hand and head reconstruction as well as tracking for 3D interaction in a desk-based computer environment. More recently, Ang et al. [3] proposed to enable multi-point haptic grasp in a virtual environment by using a gripper attachment while Jacobs and Froehlich [20] developed a soft hand model to achieve robust finger-based manipulation of virtual objects.

Among the virtual reality interfaces, some employ data gloves for gestural mid-air interactions. Cutler et al. [12] built a virtual reality system that allows users to naturally manipulate virtual 3D models with both hands on a tabletop stereo display. In particular, they proposed a grab-and-carry tool for a user to hold an object with two hands, as well as to "carry" it and turn it around. Zigelbaum et al. [34] presented g-stalt, a gestural interface for users to navigate and manipulate a 3D graphical environment filled with video media using various hand gestures. Lévesque et al. [24] proposed a 3D bimanual gestural interface using data gloves for 3D environment interaction; the left hand is employed to perform gestures for selecting interaction modes while the right hand is for the interaction itself, e.g., rotating or scaling the desired object. Though VR interfaces provide highly immersive perception and interactive controls to users, they typically require users to wear instrumented gloves for gestural input, which could be uncomfortable and restrict the freedom of movement.

Freehand Interfaces. Freehand interfaces employ tracking systems to recognize mid-air hand or arm gestures as user input. Sato et al. [30] estimated 3D hand poses and recognized hand shape patterns in real-time using multiple cameras. Grossman et al. [15] developed interesting gestural interactions with multiple fingers over a spherical volumetric display. Luo and Kenyon [25] employed scalable computing methods for vision-based gesture interaction in a large display setting. Hilliges et al. [18] enabled intuitive manipulation of 3D digital contents by leveraging the space above the surface of a regular interactive tabletop display. Benko and Wilson [7] proposed to interact with a large curved display by combining speech commands with freehand pinch gestures to provide immersive and interactive experience to multiple users. More recently, Nancel et al. [27] proposed a set of mid-air gestures to support pan-and-zoom interaction with graphical contents shown on a wall-sized display.

To manipulate a 3D virtual object with a single hand, one typical metaphor is to grip and manipulate it with the thumb and forefinger, i.e., a pinch gesture. Segen and Kumar [31] described the GestureVR system that used this metaphor to continuously manipulate 6DOF of an virtual object; the object can be translated by moving the hand and oriented by rotating the wrist. O'Hagan et al. [28] later extended this metaphor by allowing users to resize the object by moving the thumb and forefinger apart or towards each other. Though this metaphor is very natural and intuitive for common users, it requires fine and robust detection of dynamic fingers poses, which is not achievable with the poor image resolution of low-cost depth sensing devices such as the *Kinect* sensor, or when the user stands too far away from the sensor as in the case of large display setting.

Closer to our approach are freehand interactive systems that employ two-handed gestures, i.e., bimanual interaction [16]. Hinckley et al. [19] discussed two-handed user interface design issues for 3D manipulation and highlighted the scientific measurement of human behavioral principles in the interface design while Brandl et al. [10] later compared bimanual interfaces with different combinations of pen and touch on a horizontal display. Benko and Wilson [6] enabled users to visualize and manipulate 3D virtual objects using bimanual gestures on an interactive surface and above it (in mid-air). However, their approach is unable to support simultaneous multiple object manipulation operations. Yoo et al. [33] combined the gaze and the hand gestures for manipulating 3D digital contents shown on a large-scale display; 3D bimanual gestures are used for virtually manipulating a collection of image elements. Hackenberg et al. [17] presented a freehand 3D multi-touch interface for 3D object manipulation using a time-of-flight camera; a 3D object can be translated by moving one hand in 3D space while the object can be rotated and scaled simultaneously using a two-touch-point metaphor. Compared to these approaches, our use of a handle bar that can be positioned outside the selected object allows us to flexibly perform non-object centric manipulation. Very recently, Wang et al. [32] developed a bimanual interaction system for assembling CAD components by using two webcams to track 6 DOF of each hand, where a sheet-of-paper metaphor is proposed for performing the rotation. Unlike [32], our handle bar metaphor design seeks to provide precision control for all R-T manipulations in a unified bimanual manner. In addition, it does not combine mid-air and keyboard interaction since it is designed for use in a "in-front-of large display" setting with a low-resolution tracking system such as the Kinect sensor.

Interaction with the Kinect sensor

Kinect [26] is a controller-free real-time depth sensing device, primarily designed for supporting gaming with the Microsoft Xbox360 system. Since its launch, it had sold at an average volume of around 133 thousand units per day in its first sixty days. Due to its low-cost and wide availability, it has not only gained popularity for gaming, but also employed in numerous research projects in various disciplines. In particular, this recent innovation spawned many interesting mid-air interaction applications, which have made their rapid debut on the Internet. For example, the manipulation of 2D and 3D objects [11, 22], tracking of human motions, gesture control for robot systems, multi-touch-like interface for controlling GUI functions like those seen in *Minorty report*, see [2], and [1]. In this work, we explored the use of this low-cost device for object manipulation. Our proposed handle bar design can support efficient and effective bimanual manipulation of 3D objects while accommodating the limitations posed by the *Kinect* sensor.

SYSTEM SETUP

Our system setup consists of an Alienware Aurora ALX desktop computer with QuadCore CPU 3.20GHz and 9GB memory, running Linux Ubuntu 10.10 (Maverick) with an NVIDIA 1.5GB GeForce GTX480 graphics board, a *Kinect* sensor, supporting an image resolution of 320×240 at 30 frames per second with both color and depth, and an LCD display of physical size 32 inches. The *Kinect* sensor is placed below the large display and the user stands at a distance of around 2 meters from the display during the interaction (see Figure 2).

Figure 2. Our system setup with the *Kinect* sensor (red arrow).

Software. We use PrimeSense's OpenNI [29] open source drivers and the NITE middleware to interface with the *Kinect* sensor; the depth generator in the OpenNI framework is first employed to obtain the depth image data from *Kinect*. Then, we use the skeleton tracker in NITE to compute the user's joint positions from the depth image so that we can determine the 3D location of the user's hands. At the same time, we use the perception point cloud library (PCL) from the Robot Operating System (ROS) framework [14] to generate point clouds from the depth image. Lastly, based on the hand locations obtained from the 3D skeleton, we segment a point cloud set associated with each of user's hands. Our experience suggests that the use of the 3D skeleton as a guide produces more accurate and robust segmentation.

Hand Gesture Recognition. Our system is able to recognize three basic single-handed gestures, namely POINT, OPEN, and CLOSE (see Figure 3). To differentiate among them, the extracted point cloud data of each hand is first low-pass filtered (over 30 frames) to remove unintentional hand shaking. These segmented clusters of unity-weighted points [14] permit two 3D centroid locations to be computed. The spatial distribution of the points in the point cloud (after offset by the centroid) is then computed and pattern-matched with

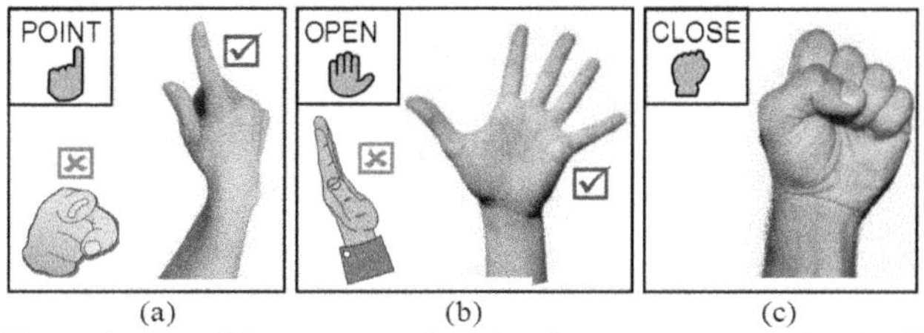

Figure 3. The different recognized hand gestures as seen by the 3D scene acquisition sensor and their respective visual icons used on the large display for visual feedback. The (a) POINT finger and (b) OPEN palm gestures are less stable as their shapes will change based on the orientation of the hand, (c) unlike the CLOSE fist gesture.

the point distributions of the three known gesture classes to determine which hand gesture is currently active. If a hand is located below the center of the user's body, a DOWN gesture is assigned to the hand. This allows the system to distinguish between one and two-handed interactions. In addition, the two centroid points from each of the two hands (computed at a rate of 30 frames-per-second) give the instantaneous length and 3D orientation of the handle bar.

THE HANDLE BAR METAPHOR

Consider the task of manipulating a 3D virtual object on a wall display using only our two bare hands. What would be the most effective and intuitive way to do this? A survey of existing literature revealed a dearth of mid-air interactive designs to perform such a task, especially in environments where multiple objects can be independently manipulated.

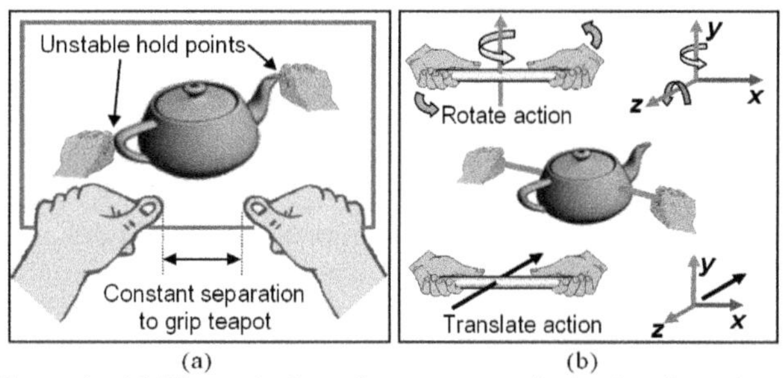

Figure 4. (a) The metaphor of *two remote gripping-hands* projected into the 3D virtual space, which is shown gripping a teapot. (b) The metaphor of a *handle bar* extended from two clasp hands, which is used to pierce through the teapot for rotation and translation manipulations.

One possible approach is to project our physical hands into the virtual space using two iconic hands that represent the hand positions and gestures (see Figure 4 (a)). Using the iconic visual feedback, the user can move one's hands to grip the virtual object and then rotate-translate (R-T) it with further coordinated hand movements. This *two remote gripping-hands* metaphor has a direct representation in the virtual space and provides a good semantic mapping between the physical and virtual manipulation. However, without haptic feedback, it demands substantial physical dexterity to maintain the gripping separation whilst performing the basic R-T manipulations. Moreover, the hand icons can be easily occluded by the virtual object during the rotation. Direct grip-based metaphors can also be problematic because the virtual object may not have stable flat contact surfaces for gripping.

To overcome these limitations, a novel *handle bar* metaphor is proposed. In this metaphor, we pierce a virtual handle

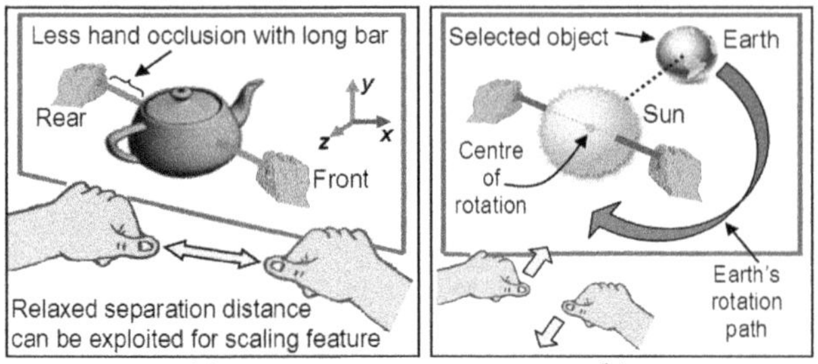

(a) (b)

Figure 5. Features of the *handle bar* metaphor. (a) Scaling operations done by varying distance between the two hands. (b) Rotation of a selected object (Earth) performed about the center of the handle bar placed inside another object (Sun).

bar through the selected 3D object. With the object now attached to the handle bar, manipulation of the object is done by performing R-T manipulations on the handle bar instead (see Figure 4 (b)). Unlike the *two remote gripping-hands* approach, the handle bar icon (the red line in Figure 5 (a)) provides helpful visual feedback to the user, continuously presenting the relative orientation of the two hands in 3D space during our interactive manipulation. A summary of the advantages of the proposed handle bar metaphor as suitable interaction paradigm for mid-air interaction is as follows:

- *Physical familiarity* - Bimanual motion gestures required to manipulate the handle bar are intuitive for most users since holding and manipulating an elongated bar with our two hands is a familiar undertaking in common activities such as cycling and lawn mowing.
- *Rich variety of 3D manipulation operations* - The handle bar interaction design offers seamless 7DOF manipulation (3 translations, 3 rotations, and 1 scaling), allowing users to transit smoothly between operations such as translation, rotation, and even scaling (see Figure 5 (a)), without changing gestures or operational modes. Interaction design for fast and precise constrained rotation can also be realized with a perpendicular extension to the virtual handle bar metaphor. Speedy multi-object manipulation can also be supported by piercing the handle bar through more than one virtual object. These pierced objects can be made to align or slide along the handle bar by using simple variations to the standard bimanual gestures.
- *Supporting both object and non-object centered manipulations* - By allowing the user to manipulate the position of the handle bar to any location relative to the selected 3D object, manipulation of virtual objects need not be object-centric. Figure 5 (b) shows an example that has a selected object (Earth) rotated about another (Sun).
- *Good semantic mapping* - Unlike other two-handed interaction methods [27] that combine different hand gestures to realize a larger subset of operations, the handle bar metaphor inspires bimanual gestures that have good semantic mapping to the physical world: the handle bar is "grabbed" for manipulation by clutching two fists and is "released" with open palms; pointing-finger gesture (finger prodding analogy) is used to change the position and orientation of the virtual handle bar (see Figure 6 (a)).
- *Accommodating sensor limitations* - With the limited resolution of the *Kinect* 3D scene acquisition sensor, stable and accurate 3D pose information can only be reliably specified with end points that are separated by some distance. The handle bar metaphor circumvents this deficiency by designing object manipulation controls that are based on the manipulation of an elongated bar that is specified by the two separated hands of the user.

INTERACTION DESIGN

This work is concerned with enabling a single user to interactively manipulate single or multiple 3D objects in a virtual environment. Users execute different visual manipulation operations by moving one or two hands freely within the physical space defined by their frontal bimanual arm-reach envelope. This section discusses the handle-bar-based interaction designs to perform the three basic categories of manipulation operations summarized in Figure 6. One manipulates the handle bar (see Figure 6 (a)). Another involves the manipulation of both single and multiple virtual objects (see Figure 6 (b,c)), and the last one manipulates the view of a virtual camera in the 3D environment (see Figure 6 (d)).

Hand Gestures Design

Our system can recognize three basic hand gestures, namely POINT, OPEN, and CLOSE (see Figure 3). As highlighted in Figure 6, the interaction design employs a consistent interpretation of these hand gestures. The POINT and CLOSE gestures are always associated with the handle bar and virtual object, respectively. Homogenous bimanual gestures will perform basic rotation-translation-scaling (RTS) manipulation of the handle bar or object, depending on whether

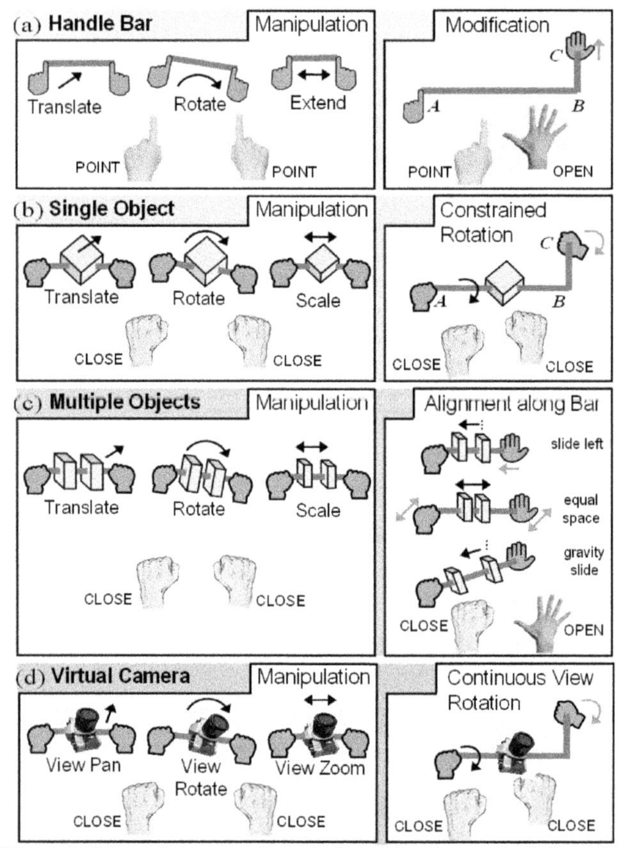

Figure 6. The various operations designed for the manipulation of (a) the virtual handle bar, (b) a single object, (c) multiple objects, and (d) the virtual camera and their associated bimanual hand gestures.

POINT or CLOSE gestures are used. Combining POINT and OPEN gestures allows the handle bar to be modified for constrained rotation (see Figures 6 (a)). A combination of CLOSE and OPEN gestures allows multi-object alignment along the handle bar (see Figure 6 (c)).

As shown in Figure 3 (a,b), both the POINT and OPEN hand gestures are sensitive to viewpoint changes, which often make their automatic recognition and classification less robust than the CLOSE gesture. Hence, they are assigned to interactions that are gesturally less complicated and used less frequently, e.g., browsing and handle bar manipulation. Since the centroid computation of the CLOSE fist gesture is orientation-invariant and thus more stable, it is used in the object manipulation interactions that often require the user to perform bimanual motion gestures with high degree-of-freedom. This assignment also fits well into the semantic mapping of how a physical handle bar can be manipulated. Figure 7 shows the state transitions and the expected hand gestures at each state when a user manipulates a single object. Details of various states are described next.

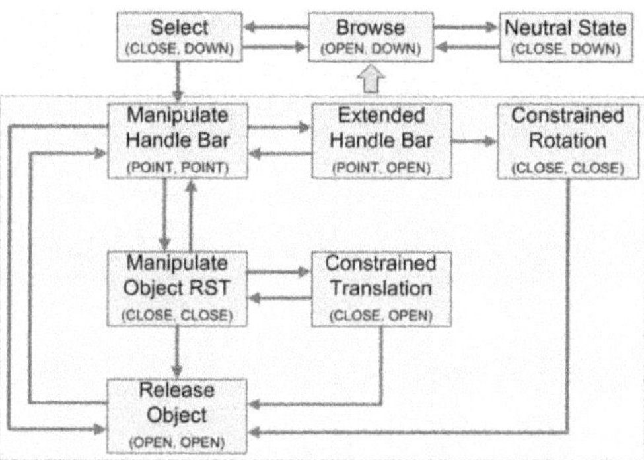

Figure 7. The state transition diagram for single object manipulation and the associated bimanual gestures for each state.

Neutral State

This is the initial state when the system starts. In this state, no object or camera is selected, and as such, no manipulation can take place. The provision of a Neutral state is important as it helps overcome the immersion syndrome [5], where every hand gesture is captured and constantly interpreted by the system. This can lead to undesirable operations due to misinterpretation of the user's unintended hand gestures. When interaction is no longer desired, we can re-enter the Neutral state by selecting an empty screen region.

Browse and Select

The users leave the Neutral state and enter the Browse mode by keeping one hand on their side (unimanual gesture) and waving the other raised OPEN palm. A small open hand visual icon in the virtual space moves within a 2D plane in tandem with the movement of the raised OPEN palm (see Figure 8 (a)). When the open hand icon overlaps with a 3D object or the virtual camera icon, the user can perform a CLOSE hand gesture to select the item (see Figure 8 (b)). Upon selection, a virtual handle bar will protrude out of the object in the default orientation, namely through the object's centroid and along the x-axis. This virtual handle bar icon indicates that the system is no longer in Neutral state and is currently in the Selected state (see Figure 8 (c)). Multiple virtual objects can be selected by repeating this selection operation. An active item will be deselected by performing a CLOSE hand gesture when the open hand icon overlaps with the selected object. All the active items will be deselected if the user performs a CLOSE hand gesture when the open hand icon overlaps with an empty space. In the Selected state, we can then proceed to other interaction modes such as the mode to manipulate the virtual handle bar.

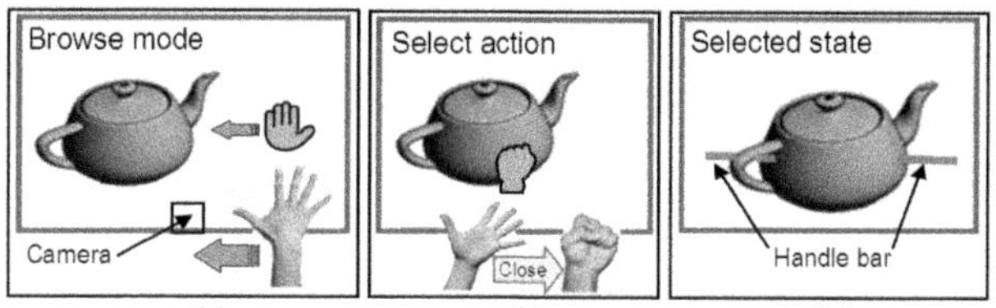

(a) (b) (c)

Figure 8. (a) Browsing the 3D virtual environment with a single OPEN palm in *Browse* mode. Selectable objects also include the virtual camera icon located at the bottom of the screen. (b) The object under the hand icon is selected with a Select action (CLOSE hand gesture). (c) In the Selected state, a handle bar protrudes out of the selected object.

Basic RTS Operations of a Single Object

The handle bar metaphor provides 7DOF manipulation (3D translation, 3D rotation, and 1D scaling) of virtual object and supports continuous transitions between operations. Such manipulation involves the appropriate placement of the virtual handle bar and the subsequent manipulation of the selected object about the center of the positioned bar. The modes associated with this process are described here. Note that we use different handle bar colors as a visual feedback to indicate which mode is currently active.

Manipulate Handle Bar Mode

Employing the bimanual POINT gesture in Figure 6 (a), users can manipulate the virtual handle bar by changing the relative position and orientation of the invisible line that joins their two hands in the physical space (see Figure 9 (a)). The end points of the handle bar are determined by the centroid of the 3D point clouds associated with the two POINT hand gestures. These were observed to be more stable end points than the more appropriate pointing finger tips, which result in handle bar jittering when switching between handle bar and object manipulation modes.

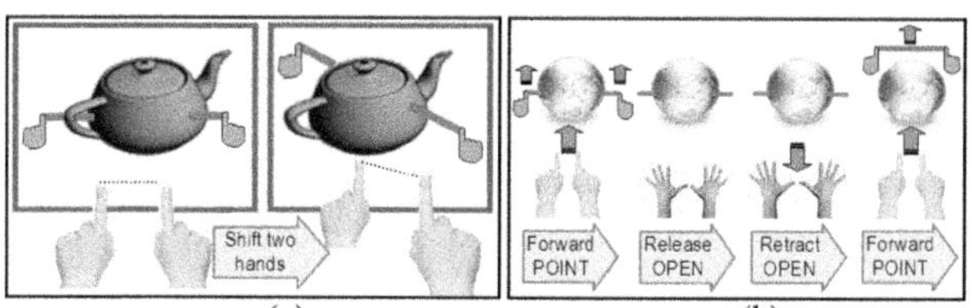

(a) (b)

Figure 9. (a) Manipulate the 3D position and orientation of a handle bar using two pointed fingers. (b) Repeated translate (POINT gesture) and release (OPEN gesture) can be used to position handle bar at a distant away from the selected object.

The handle bar position is not restricted to the confines of the 3D object. Large translation of the handle bar can be achieved by repeatedly releasing the bar with a bimanual OPEN gesture, retracting the open palm, and then translating the bimanual POINT gesture again in the same direction (see Figure 9 (b)). In other words, the 3D gestural workspace need not have an absolute mapping to the 3D virtual world.

The user's physical translational motion can move the handle bar relative to its current 3D virtual world position. This convention is applied generically to the R-T interactions of the handle bar, selected 3D object, and the virtual camera.

The midpoint of the handle bar is the center for rotating the selected virtual object. During the handle bar manipulation, the selected object is not affected so that we can change the rotation center by translating the handle bar. Once the handle bar has been manoeuvred into the desired position, the user can manipulate the selected object by the next mode.

Manipulate Object Mode

The manipulate object mode is a bimanual interaction mode that employs two CLOSE fist gestures (see Figure 6 (b) left). We can apply three basic manipulation operations to a selected object: rotation, translation, and scaling (RTS).

Object Translation. The selected object can be translated in the x, y, and z directions by simply translating the bimanual CLOSE fist gesture in the corresponding directions (see Figure 10 (a)). The translation of the object is based on the movement vector of the virtual handle bar mid-point, as defined by the centroids of the two CLOSE fists.

Figure 10. Bimanual CLOSE fist gestures for (a) translating and (b) rotating an object in the x and y-axis, respectively.

Object Rotation. The rotation of the selected object about a specific axis is based on the relative angular displacement of the virtual handle bar along that corresponding axis (see Figure 10 (b)). No absolute angular mapping is needed since the virtual handle bar can be released in a similar fashion as described in Figure 9 (b) (i.e., with OPEN palm gestures). Once released, the user may re-initiate a bimanual CLOSE fist gesture at a new position and perform a further rotation. This manner of executing a rotation allows the user to make large angular changes to the 3D virtual object about the y-axis without getting into an undesirable situation where the front hand occludes the back hand (see Figure 11 (a)), which may result in an indeterminable 3D pose of the virtual handle bar. Rotations about the x-axis cannot be directly manipulated using the handle bar since the wrist-based rotation of

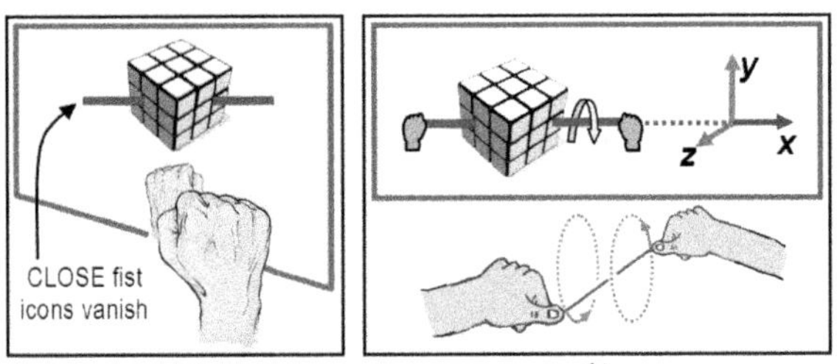

Figure 11. (a) Invalid gesture due to occlusion. (b) Incremental x-axis rotation using continuous rotation in the y and z axes.

the two CLOSE fists does not change the position of their centroids and thus gives no angular rotation cues. However, rotation about the x-axis can still be obtained in an incremental fashion by executing appropriate concurrent bimanual uni-directional rotation about the y and z axes simultaneously (a "pedaling" motion) (see Figure 11 (b)), which is not immediately intuitive for uninitiated users. In this case, the constrained rotation provision (see Figure 6 (b) right) may be a better option as it provides faster and more precise manipulation albeit requiring a mode switch step.

Object Scaling. The object scaling operation is done by moving the two CLOSE fists towards each other (scale down) or away from each other (scale up), along the invisible line that connects the centroids of the two hands in physical space (see Figure 12). The scaling factor S is given by

$$S = \frac{\Delta L^2}{\Delta t}, \quad (1)$$

where ΔL is the change in distance between the two centroids in the sampling time Δt determined by the *Kinect* sensor's frame rate. In other words, the amount of scaling can be controlled by both the hand movement distance and speed. A vigorous gesture gives a larger scaling factor.

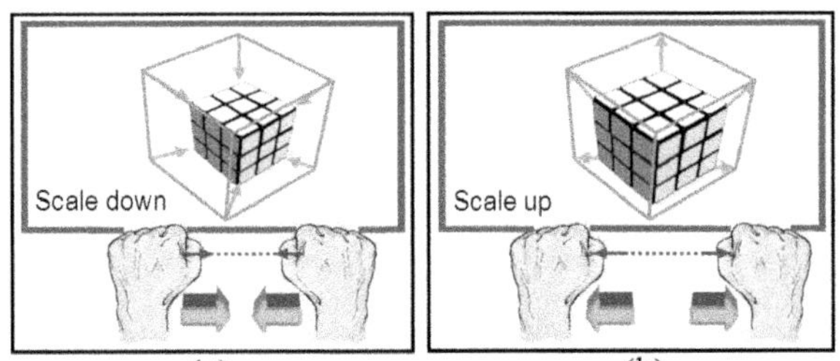

Figure 12. Object scaling gestures. Scaling (a) down and (b) up.

Constrained Operations of a Single Object

The ability to perform continuous translation and rotation can sometimes make it difficult to execute fast and precise rotation of an object about a specific straight line. In such circumstance, a less flexible constrained rotation operation could be more preferable. In our handle bar interaction design, constrained operations can be initiated with a combination of non-homogenous bimanual gestures.

Constrained Rotation. From a two POINT finger handle bar manipulation gesture (see Figure 6 (a) left), the user can change one hand to an OPEN palm gesture and move the OPEN palm away from the handle bar axis to create a "cranking bar" with a perpendicular extension (see Figure 6 (a) right). In detail, the horizontal line AB is defined by the standard handle bar when the palm OPENs. After the user moves the right OPEN palm to define the vertical line BC (see Figure 6 (a) right), one can CLOSE both fists to enter the constrained rotation state. To execute the constrained rotation, the user holds the left CLOSE fist steady and performs a "cranking" action with the right CLOSE fist about the virtual line AB. The angular velocity can be controlled by the length of virtual line BC, which is drawn continuously on the display as a helpful visual feedback. A shorter BC extension gives faster rotation but less precise angular positioning while a longer BC extension gives better control of angular position at the expense of faster rotation.

Constrained Translation. Albeit less useful, constrained translation of a single object along the handle bar can be performed with a non-homogenous combination of a CLOSE fist and an OPEN palm. Sliding the OPEN palm towards the CLOSE fist moves the single object on the handle bar towards the CLOSE fist end. This idea is more useful when applied to the manipulation of multiple objects.

Manipulation and Alignment of Multiple Objects

A group of objects can be manipulated together and/or aligned along the virtual handle bar once they are selected (using repeated selection actions) and are all pierced by a handle bar.

Manipulation of Multiple Objects. First, standard RTS operations can be performed on all these selected objects in the same manner as with a single object (see Figure 6 (c) left). All objects on the handle bar can translate and scale as an aggregation. Rotation of all these objects will be centered about the mid-point of the handle bar.

Alignment of Multiple Objects. Three basic alignment operations for aligning multiple objects on a handle bar are provided (see Figure 6 (c) right):

- The first allows the user to "pack" objects by interactively sliding the selected objects towards each other using a gesture that moves the OPEN palm towards the CLOSE fist. Objects stop sliding when boundary collision is detected. Multiple objects can also be made to slide towards the CLOSE fist by "tilting" the virtual handle bar as shown in Figure 13. The larger the tilt angle is, the faster the objects will slide. This manner of packing multiple objects has a very close semantic mapping to the physical nature of object behavior along a handle bar (under gravity) and may be preferred by some users.

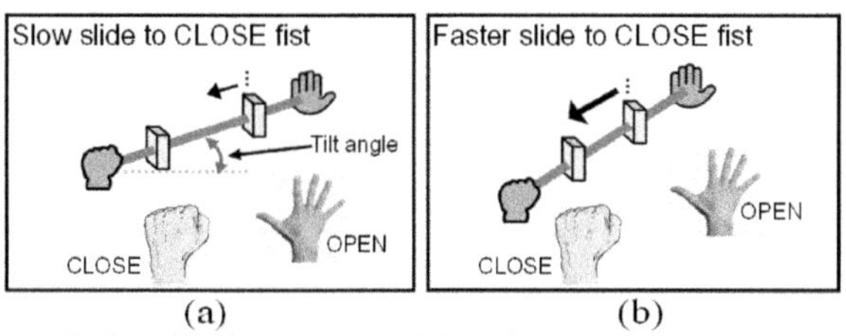

Figure 13. Gravity-simulated multiple object alignment. (a) Slow drop with gentle tilt. (b) Fast drop with steeper tilt.

- The second category of alignment operation is for evenly-distributing the objects along the virtual handle bar. The user can shake both CLOSE and OPEN hands and objects on the handle bar will be distributed at equi-distance along the handle bar. This operation is useful for "unpacking" objects that are too close to each other. The separation distance can be controlled by the user by adjusting the length of the handle bar before the shaking.

EVALUATION

Three user studies were conducted to evaluate the various handle bar interaction designs. The complete gesture set was active in all the three user studies except object scaling, which was disabled as it was not required. Twelve participants (8 males and 4 females) aged between 21 to 28 years were enrolled. None of them has performed mid-air visual manipulation before but ten of them have played games with the *Kinect* sensor or *Nintendo Wii-mote* gaming system. The physical setup used in the study is shown in Figure 2. Before the start of each session, the required task was first explained to the user, and then, an expert user showed a demonstration of how the task could be done.

User Study: R-T Manipulation

One of the strengths of the interaction design using the proposed handle bar metaphor is the ability to execute continuous transitions between RTS manipulation operations without the need to switch modes. We wanted to evaluate if naive users were able to perform simple R-T manipulations without any training and whether subsequent repeated attempts can quickly improve their performance. Figure 14 (a) shows the task of rotating and translating a randomly-oriented cube to its desired position as indicated by the wire-frame outline. Before starting the task, a brief demonstration was given to show the user the required hand gestures to select an object, position a handle bar, and perform the R-T manipulation required to put the cube into its destination. At each attempt, the user was given 2 minutes to put as many cubes as possible into the wire-frame envelope subject to a reasonable precision indicated by a wire-frame color change.

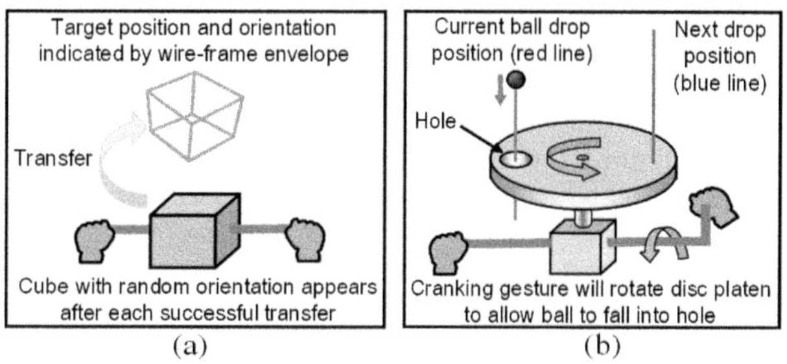

Figure 14. (a) User study: R-T Manipulation and (b) User study: constrained rotation.

Results in Table 1 show that the handle-bar-based R-T manipulation can be quickly learnt by just having on-the-task practice. On average, the 12 participants were able to double the number of cube placements within 6 attempts. However, the variance in user performance is high, indicating that some users are better in performing this type of interaction than others. The best performer managed 10 cubes in attempt #1 and improved to 15 cubes by attempt #6, compared to the worst performer who managed only 1 cube in attempt #1 but did improve to 6 cubes by attempt #6.

Attempt no.	#1	#2	#3	#4	#5	#6
Average times	4.6	5.9	7.0	8.1	8.3	9.3
Variance	7.2	8.7	13.8	12.6	9.0	10.8

Table 1. Results of the R-T manipulation user study.

User Study: Constrained Rotation

In this study, users were asked to perform constrained rotation about the x-axis (see Figure 6 (b) right). The task shown in Figure 14 (b) cannot be easily done with standard rotation due to the possibility of inter-hand occlusion. The task evaluates the speed the user can rotate the disc clockwise or anti-clockwise to reach the desired angular position to "catch" the falling ball. To achieve this, the ball dropping speed increases linearly in each successive drop. This task also evaluates the angular precision the user can maintain in order to ensure the ball "drop" into the hole on the disc. For this, the hole is made small and a red vertical line provides the user with the visual cue required to align the "catch." The task is to "catch" as many falling balls as possible into the hole on the rotating disc within 60 seconds. Like before, a demonstration on how the task is done was first given to each user and attempt #1 was done without any practice. The subsequent two attempts were performed after giving the participants 2 minutes practice time before each attempt.

Attempt no.		#1 (No practice)	#2	#3
Number of balls caught	Average	11.7	17.6	17.3
	Variance	18.7	25.1	12.7
Ball count when 1st miss occurred	Average	3.7	8.8	9.3
	Variance	8.1	39.3	17.2

Table 2. Results of the constrained rotation user study.

Table 2 shows the average number of balls caught by the 12 participants; after a short period of practice time. The performance can increase from about 11 (attempt #1) to about 17 balls (attempts #2 and #3). The handle bar interaction design for rotating a virtual object about a fixed axis is able to provide fast angular speed, yet still offering good angular position controls since the speed of the 17th dropping ball is significantly faster than the 11th ball. This conclusion is further supported by the fact that on average, the first error (missed ball catch) made by the users were delayed from about the 3rd ball (attempt #1) to the 9th ball (attempts #2 and #3) after a short period of practice, again indicating the angular controllability and precision of the "cranking" bimanual CLOSE fist gesture despite the small room for angular error in catching the ball.

It is interesting to note the performance variability among the 12 participants after practice, as evident in the large variance increase in attempt #2 for both the number of balls caught and first ball missed. Like the first user study, this suggests that some users found executing the correct bimanual mid-air gesture requires more practice than just 2 minutes. The variance was observed to drop significantly after they were given a little more time (i.e., 2 more minutes) to practice the constrained rotation gesture.

User Study: Multiple Object Manipulation and Alignment

The final user study compares the time performance of manipulating three in-line objects such that we have to move them to some target positions. In Task 1, the three objects are initially positioned at a distance apart and needs to be brought close to one another at the destination. Task 2 does the reverse (see Figure 15). The users were asked to perform these manipulation tasks using the single object manipulation technique as well as the multiple object manipulation and alignment techniques (see Figure 6 (c)).

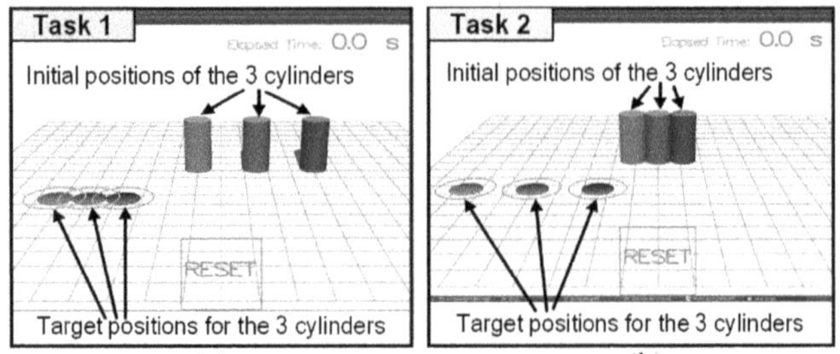

(a) (b)

Figure 15. This study measures the time taken to (a) bring objects together (Task 1) and (b) move objects apart (Task 2) using single and multiple object manipulation techniques.

Attempt no.		#1 (No practice)	#2	#3
Task 1 Avg time (sec)	One-by-one	53.7	37.0	34.5
	Multi-object	16.6	14.4	10.5
Task 2 Avg time (sec)	One-by-one	35.3	30.0	24.9
	Multi-object	18.2	13.3	13.5

Table 3. Results of the multiple object interaction user study.

Results in Table 3 show that for both Tasks 1 and 2, it was at least 2 to 3 times faster when using the multi-object manipulation and alignment techniques to do the required task than placing objects one at a time. From the absolute average time taken and rate of improvement with each subsequent attempt, it is clear that the "pack" multi-objects alignment procedure of Task 1 is easier to execute than the "equi-distribute" multi-object alignment procedure of Task 2.

Discussion and Limitations

A set of questionnaires were given to each user after each of the three user studies to gauge the subjective aspects of their experiences in the handle bar interaction. Table 4 presents the mean response values of the 12 participants and the associated standard deviation bar for each survey question.

The bimanual R-T manipulation hand gesture designed using the handle bar metaphor was found by most users to be generally intuitive to use, ease to remember, and providing good controllability. Consistently high ratings were received from the users for the ability to perform rotation and translation in one continuous motion. The subjective evaluation of the constrained rotation interaction design fared a little worst, with mean ratings at values just below 4.0. The user variability was far higher though, suggesting that performing fast and precise angular rotations with a cranking action is not universally straightforward for everyone. The very high mean rating for question #8 suggests that most users find the ability to rotate, translate, and align multiple objects at the same time to be very useful and preferred when manipulating several objects with similar trajectory and orientation.

Some limitations of the handle bar design were observed from the user studies: 1) Some users complained about arm fatigue after 20-30 minutes of continuous usage, which seems to be a universal drawback for all mid-air interaction designs that require precise control of the hands but provide no additional physical support for the extended arms; 2) User mem-

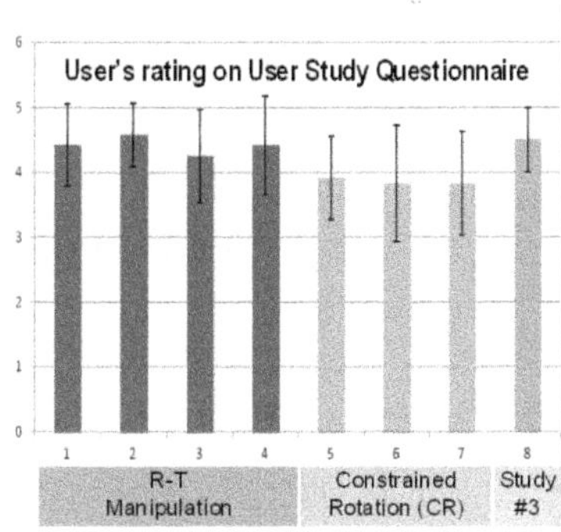

Survey Questions

- #1 Is handle bar R-T manipulations intuitive to understand and use?
- #2 Is it helpful to control object translation and rotation simultaneously?
- #3 Are two-handed gestures easy to use?
- #4 Are two-handed gestures easy to remember?
- #5 Does CR provide fast angular control to desired position?
- #6 Does CR provide precise angular control at the desired position?
- #7 Does CR fits well with the handle bar manipulation metaphor?
- #8 Is simultaneous control of multi-object useful in virtual object manipulation?

Table 4. User ratings on a Likert scale from 1 (strongly disagree) to 5 (strongly agree) for the questionnaire survey done after each user study. Questions related to the same user study are plotted in the same color.

ory lapse tends to occur for asymmetric bimanual gestures; 3) Slight handle bar wobble could occur during the hand gesture change due to the shift in the computed hand centroid; and 4) Inter-hand occlusion may occur during the rotation.

APPLICATION EXAMPLES

The proposed interaction designs based on our handle bar metaphor were applied to three different applications to illustrate their potential.

The first application example shows how furniture can be arranged to a desired layout in a 3D virtual environment (see Figure 16 (top left)). The multiple object manipulation technique was used to quickly arrange similar chairs. The translate-rotate manipulation was used to "pick up" a toppled flower pot and place it on the table in one continuous bimanual hand movement. Once on the table, constrained rotation was invoked to continuously rotate the pot till it was deemed to be at the desired orientation (see video).

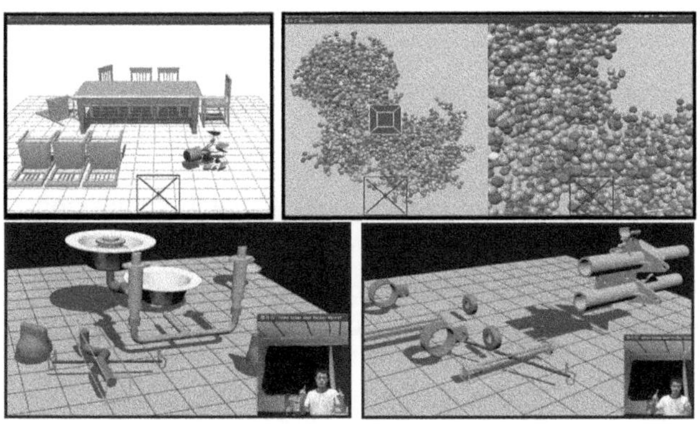

Figure 16. Applications using the handle bar manipulation techniques. Top left: Arrangement of virtual furniture in a room. Top right: Visual exploration of a complex molecular structure. Bottom: Assembling mechanical parts in CAD models.

The second application example (see Figure 16 (top right)) illustrates how the handle bar interaction designs can be applied to manipulate the virtual camera (see Figure 6 (d)) to facilitate visual exploration of a complex molecular structure. The translate-rotate manipulation allows us to visually navigate within the virtual molecular structure. The scaling gesture, when applied to a virtual camera, enables us to zoom in and out while navigating freely within the virtual 3D environment. Constrained rotation applied to the virtual camera allows us to continually scan (panning) the view around using a "cranking" gesture (see video).

The last application example (see Figure 16 (bottom)) presents how the handle bar metaphor can be used to manipulate and assemble 3D mechanical parts. Two different computer-aided-design (CAD) models, *double-range burner* and *launcher*, (bottom left and right of Figure 16, respectively) are employed here. Using our interaction methods, we can efficiently assemble the models with bare hands (see video).

CONCLUSION

We propose the handle bar metaphor as an effective way to perform mid-air interactions that manipulate the pose and scale of 3D virtual objects, suitable for use with a low-cost depth sensing device like *Kinect* in a large-display setting. The main strength of this metaphor is the physical familiarity it provides users with, as they mentally map their bimanual hand gestures to manipulation operations such as translation and rotation in the virtual 3D environment. The provision of visual cues in the form of the instantaneous orientation of the protruding virtual handle bar that corresponds interactively to the ever-changing positions of the user's two hands was observed to be very effective in providing a strong sense of control to the user during interactive visual manipulation. In addition, the flexibility and variety of interaction designs based on the handle bar metaphor have been demonstrated. These include the constrained rotation operation based on a novel "cranking" bimanual gesture and speedy techniques to manipulate and align multiple objects along a straight line using a simple combination of CLOSE and OPEN hand gestures. The virtual molecule exploration application example suggests that the same handle bar metaphor could be applied to manipulate a virtual camera to support an intuitive and flexible means of performing interactive visual navigation in a 3D virtual environment.

Observations from user studies suggest that the competency in using mid-air interaction techniques for visual manipulation is not universally innate to all users. However, interaction based on the handle bar metaphor seems to provide an intuitive way for users to quickly learn how to map the action of their bimanual hand gestures to corresponding visual manipulation tasks in a 3D virtual environment. Practice was observed to quickly improve everybody's performance and reduce the differences in skill levels among first time users. However, the issue of fast fatigue onset is still a perennial problem when using mid-air interaction for precise control.

Acknowledgment. We thank anonymous reviewers for their valuable comments, Robert Y. Wang and Sylvain Paris for sharing the CAD models, and the funding agency (A*Star SERC grant No. 092 101 0063) for the support.

REFERENCES

1. MIT Kinect Demo. `www.ros.org/wiki/mit-ros-pkg/KinectDemos`.

2. Kinect Demo Gallery, 2010. `www.openni.org/gallery` and `openkinect.org/wiki/Gallery`.

3. Q.-Z. Ang, B. Horan, Z. Najdovski, and S. Nahavandi. Grasping virtual objects with multi-point haptics. In *IEEE VR*, pages 189–190, 2011.
4. M. Annett, T. Grossman, D. Wigdor, and G. Fitzmaurice. Medusa: a proximity-aware multi-touch tabletop. UIST, pages 337–346, 2011.
5. T. Baudel and M. Beaudouin-Lafon. CHARADE: remote control of objects using free-hand gestures. *ACM Communication*, 36(7):28–35, July 1993.
6. H. Benko and A. D. Wilson. DepthTouch: Using depth-sensing camera to enable freehand interactions on and above the interactive surface. Technical report, 2009. Tech. Report MSR-TR-2009-23.
7. H. Benko and A. D. Wilson. Multi-point interactions with immersive omnidirectional visualizations in a dome. In *ITS*, pages 19–28, 2010.
8. F. Bettio, A. Giachetti, E. Gobbetti, F. Marton, and G. Pintore. A practical vision based approach to unencumbered direct spatial manipulation in virtual worlds. In *Eurographics Italian Chapter Conference*, pages 145–150, 2007.
9. D. A. Bowman, E. Kruijff, J. J. LaViola, and I. Poupyrev. *3D User Interfaces: Theory and Practice*. Addison-Wesley, 2004.
10. P. Brandl, C. Forlines, D. Wigdor, M. Haller, and C. Shen. Combining and measuring the benefits of bimanual pen and direct-touch interaction on horizontal interfaces. In *AVI*, pages 154–161, 2008.
11. CEA LIST Interactive Physics Engine Demo, 2011. `www.youtube.com/watch?v=7-HOc696g6s`.
12. L. D. Cutler, B. Fröhlich, and P. Hanrahan. Two-handed direct manipulation on the responsive workbench. In *I3D*, pages 107–114, 1997.
13. T. Duval, A. Lécuyer, and S. Thomas. SkeweR: a 3D interaction technique for 2-user collaborative manipulation of objects in virtual environments. In *3D User Interfaces*, pages 69–72, 2006.
14. W. Garage and the Stanford Artificial Intelligence Laboratory. Robot Operating System (ROS), 2009. `www.ros.org/wiki/`.
15. T. Grossman, D. Wigdor, and R. Balakrishnan. Multi-finger gestural interaction with 3D volumetric displays. In *UIST*, pages 61–70, 2004.
16. Y. Guiard. Asymmetric division of labor in human skilled bimanual action: The kinematic chain as a model. *Jour. of Motor Behavior*, 19(4):486–517, 1987.
17. G. Hackenberg, R. McCall, and W. Broll. Lightweight palm and finger tracking for real-time 3D gesture control. In *IEEE VR*, pages 19–26, 2011.
18. O. Hilliges, S. Izadi, A. D. Wilson, S. Hodges, A. Garcia-Mendoza, and A. Butz. Interactions in the air: Adding further depth to interactive tabletops. In *UIST*, pages 139–148, 2009.
19. K. Hinckley, R. Pausch, D. Proffitt, and N. F. Kassell. Two-handed virtual manipulation. *ACM Trans. on Computer-Human Interaction*, 5(3):260–302, 1998.
20. J. Jacobs and B. Froehlich. A soft hand model for physically-based manipulation of virtual objects. In *IEEE VR*, pages 11–18, 2011.
21. C. John, U. Schwanecke, and H. Regenbrecht. Real-time volumetric reconstruction and tracking of hands and face as a user interface for virtual environments. In *IEEE VR*, pages 241–242, 2009.
22. R. Jota and H. Benko. Constructing virtual 3D models with physical building blocks. In *CHI Extended Abstracts*, pages 2173–2178, 2011.
23. S. Kolarić, A. Raposo, and M. Gattass. Direct 3D manipulation using vision-based recognition of uninstrumented hands. In *X Symposium on Virtual and Augmented Reality*, pages 212–220, 2008.
24. J.-C. Lévesque, D. Laurendeau, and M. Mokhtari. Bimanual gestural interface for virtual environments. In *IEEE VR*, pages 223–224, 2011.
25. X. Luo and R. V. Kenyon. Scalable vision-based gesture interaction for cluster-driven high resolution display systems. In *IEEE VR*, pages 231–232, 2009.
26. Microsoft. Kinect for xbox360, 2010. `www.xbox.com/en-US/kinect`.
27. M. Nancel, J. Wagner, E. Pietriga, O. Chapuis, and W. Mackay. Mid-air pan-and-zoom on wall-sized displays. In *CHI*, pages 177–186, 2011.
28. R. G. O'Hagan, A. Zelinsky, and S. Rougeaux. Visual gesture interfaces for virtual environments. *Interacting with Computers*, 14(1):231–250, 2002.
29. PrimeSense, G. Willow, Side kick, and ASUS. OpenNI. `www.openni.org`.
30. Y. Sato, M. Saito, and H. Koike. Real-time input of 3D pose and gestures of a user's hand and its applications for HCI. In *IEEE VR*, pages 79–86, 2001.
31. J. Segen and S. Kumar. Gesture VR: vision-based 3D hand interface for spatial interaction. In *ACM Multimedia*, pages 455–464, 1998.
32. R. Y. Wang, S. Paris, and J. Popović. 6D hands: Markerless hand-tracking for computer aided design. In *UIST*, pages 549–558, 2011.
33. B. Yoo, J.-J. Han, C. Choi, K. Yi, S. Suh, D. Park, and C. Kim. 3D user interface combining gaze and hand gestures for large-scale display. In *CHI*, pages 3709–3714, 2010.
34. J. Zigelbaum, A. Browning, D. Leithinger, O. Bau, and H. Ishii. g-stalt: a chirocentric, spatiotemporal, and telekinetic gestural interface. In *Intl. Conf. on Tangible and Embedded Interaction*, pages 261–264, 2010.

Fly: Studying Recall, Macrostructure Understanding, and User Experience of Canvas Presentations

Leonhard Lichtschlag, Thomas Hess, Thorsten Karrer, Jan Borchers
RWTH Aachen University
{lichtschlag, hess, karrer, borchers}@cs.rwth-aachen.de

ABSTRACT
Most presentation software uses the slide deck metaphor to create visual presentation support. Recently, *canvas presentation tools* such as Fly [6] or Prezi [9] have begun to use a zoomable free-form canvas to arrange information instead. While their effect on authoring presentations has been evaluated previously, we studied how they impact the audience. In a quantitative study, we compared audience retention and macrostructure understanding of slide deck vs. canvas presentations. We found both approaches to be equally capable of communicating information to the audience. Canvas presentations, however, were rated by participants to better aid them in staying oriented during a talk. This makes canvas presentation tools a promising slideware alternative.

Author Keywords
Canvas presentations; slideware; zoomable user interfaces

ACM Classification Keywords
H.5.2 Information Interfaces and Presentation: User Interfaces—*GUI*; H.1.2 Information Systems: User/Machine Systems—*Human information processing*

INTRODUCTION
Slide-based visual presentation support, commonly known as *slideware*, is prevalent in talks in research, industry, education, government, and many other areas. The slide metaphor employed by software such as Microsoft's PowerPoint or Apple's Keynote originates from the technical restrictions of physical slides used on overhead projectors. Today, presentation visuals are usually displayed using a computer connected to a video projector. This removes the necessity of showing a series of slides, one at a time, and makes the slide format somewhat arbitrary. Consequently, this format has been criticized repeatedly for the limitations it imposes on authors and presenters [8, 12]. In particular, it requires authors to map their content to a linear sequence of equally-sized chunks, making it especially difficult to present complex topics that have more than one logical dimension or are highly interconnected [5, 6].

Permission to make digital or hard copies of all or part of this work for personal or classroom use is granted without fee provided that copies are not made or distributed for profit or commercial advantage and that copies bear this notice and the full citation on the first page. To copy otherwise, or republish, to post on servers or to redistribute to lists, requires prior specific permission and/or a fee.
CHI'12, May 5–10, 2012, Austin, Texas, USA.
Copyright 2012 ACM 978-1-4503-1015-4/12/05...$10.00.

Among the attempts to mitigate these problems of slideware, several dismiss the slide metaphor in part or entirely. Instead, they place either the slides [5] or their individual elements [6, 9] on an infinite *canvas*. Presentation authors then define viewports and transition paths across the canvas to define the presentation sequence. This approach has been shown to afford easy overviews, and to offer more flexibility in chunking content to the author [6].

Previous research also suggests that canvas presentations may be beneficial to the audience, because content macrostructure can be made easier to grasp; especially spatial learners may benefit from this format [5]. However, this assumption has not been evaluated in a quantitative study so far. We conducted such an experiment comparing canvas-based presentations and their slideware counterparts, by measuring *recall of facts* and *understanding of macrostructure* among audience members, and by gathering results on their *subjective assessment* of these presentations.

RELATED WORK
After a summary of canvas presentation tools, we discuss research on human cognition in the context of canvas talks.

Authoring canvas presentations
While early zoomable user interfaces [1] were also used in talks occasionally, several tools have been designed specifically with presentation support in mind [5, 6, 9]. CounterPoint [5] broke new ground by positioning PowerPoint slides inside a zoomable user interface. It lets authors place slides at varying distances from a virtual camera and create a spatial layout of slides that in itself communicates the macrostructure of the talk. Overviews can be created easily by zooming out and presenting the slide arrangement to the audience. This model was also adopted by pptPlex[1].

Fly [6] completely abandoned the slide metaphor, letting authors put content elements (text, figures, etc.) directly on a canvas. Authors are no longer bound by the slide frame, and do not need to split subtopics into fixed-size chunks. Two studies comparing authoring with Fly to using the traditional slide deck format showed that the resulting Fly documents were richer and better represented the structure of connected topics [6]. Authors also embraced the possibilities of the non-linear layout of information and expressed a clear preference for canvas layouts. Prezi [9] is a successful web service with a similar concept.

[1]http://www.officelabs.com/projects/pptPlex

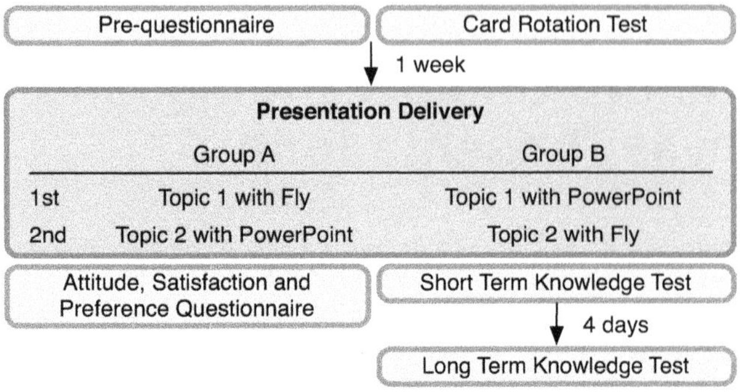

Figure 1. Study design. All participants performed the pre- and post-experiment activities (yellow). The main experiment (blue) split participants into two groups, switching the order of tools (not topics).

Viewing canvas presentations

Besides the authoring process, presentation delivery could also benefit from the canvas layout. Plausible reasons for this are the increased visibility of the macrostructure, the potential to leverage the spatial abilities of the audience, and less fragmentation of the material. Content macrostructure and its relations can be incorporated into the spatial layout, and can be communicated to the audience implicitly through spatial overviews and animated viewport transitions. The presenter hence does not need to express them verbally through written or spoken text, as is necessary in slide-based presentations. This reduces cognitive load for the audience [7].

Successive viewports can overlap, so content can be presented in a less fragmented way: related topics stay together, and more relationships are represented spatially. Especially animations between viewports can offload some of the viewers cognitive burden to the human perceptual system by exploiting the perceptual phenomenon of object constancy that enables viewers to track element relationships without thinking about it [10]. By shifting load from the verbal to the visual cognitive channel, the audience can exercise a larger portion of their memory resources [5]. This reduction of the auditive/verbal cognitive load is especially useful in a presentation scenario in which the oral narration must be followed and processed continuously.

On the other hand, audience members less skilled in spatial orientation might be overburdened by a canvas presentation, and following Clark's argument that different media will not improve learning [2], a large corpus of studies exists that has not been able to document significant effects of different media on learning [11]. It is even unclear whether canvas presentations should be considered a different medium or just a different tool.

In summary, while evidence exists that canvas tools benefit authors, this has not been studied for presenters or the audience. Presenters and listeners might even be overburdened by the complexity, and listeners might retain less information than with standard slideware. Our study aimed to address this question.

STUDY DESIGN

In our study, we showed two instructional talks to two audiences (fig. 1). Each group separately attended two presentations of 15 minutes each on two different topics. One of the presentations used PowerPoint, the other Fly, representing the *slide deck* and *canvas* conditions. We formulated the following hypotheses:

H1: There will be no significant difference for fact retention between the canvas and slide deck condition.

H2: In the canvas condition, participants will perform better for macrostructure recall and transfer questions.

H3: The canvas visuals will provide participants with a better orientation of talk progression.

H4: Participants will find the structure of the canvas presentations easier to comprehend.

H5: Participants will find the amount of content shown on the screen at a time more adequate in the canvas condition.

We recruited our participants from the students of an introductory HCI course. Each participant was asked to fill out a pre-questionnaire and to assess their spatial ability using the card rotation test [3]. According to this data, students were divided into two groups with a counterbalanced mix of different ages and spatial vs. verbal learners. Students with prior knowledge in any of the two topics or those that were not very proficient in the language of the presentation were excluded from the experiment. This resulted in 26 participants in total, 23 male, 3 female, 13 per group. Ages ranged from 23 to 35 (median 27).

To understand the talks no prior knowledge about the content was needed; both topics, "Fixed-Gear Bicycles" and "Convergent Evolution", were uncommon and independent from each other. We counterbalanced the order of the canvas and slideware conditions, but not the order of topics, since the latter was unlikely to create learning effects.

Personality, mood, and performance of a speaker and the interaction between speaker and audience can have a strong impact on the quality of a presentation. To minimize bias through speaker/audience interaction or different speaker performances, we presented all talks as prerecorded video presentations. Without the speaker physically present, it was important to have an engaging narrative, hence a professional broadcast speaker recorded the spoken commentary. Spoken texts were kept simple and informal to match a face-to-face presentation. To avoid differences in pronunciation, emphasis, and elaborateness, both conditions shared the same audio material; the recordings were split into segments that could be mapped to the visuals of both formats. Using recordings instead of a live presentation has been shown not to have a significant influence on learning [4].

An important factor in the experiment was the authoring quality of the presentation documents. Since presentation visuals for each of the two topics were needed in both formats, the challenge was to ensure that the documents on the

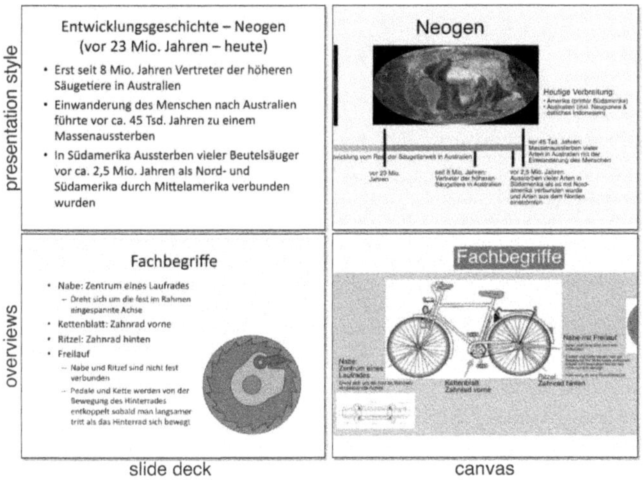

Figure 2. Presentation style and overviews in the slideware (left) and canvas (right) condition. Top: the slideware layout is confined to the frame, whereas the canvas visuals span multiple viewports. This can be seen, e.g., at the timeline, which extends to the left past the frame. Bottom: different strategies to visualize overviews in slideware and on a canvas.

same topic contained the same content. Because of the fundamentally different formats of Fly and PowerPoint, there was no exact way to match document content. To reduce the risk for bias, an external and experienced presentation author (31 years) who was not involved with the study otherwise created all four documents.

In the resulting documents, the Fly visuals contained more unique layouts compared to an image with bullet points, and were more verbose for some sections. Some layouts were only possible because of the canvas-based format and could not be adapted to PowerPoint. The biggest layout difference occurred in the Convergent Evolution talk: the development history and present-day distribution of marsupials was integrated into a big timeline layout with an illustration of geologic eras. In PowerPoint, for the same topic, the development history was covered with a series of text-based slides that showed one era each with the illustration on an extra slide (fig. 2 top). Naturally, the overviews in Fly used more graphics and were structured spatially, while the overviews in PowerPoint used more text and were structured linearly. For example, for the introductory section of the fixed-gear bicycle presentation, a large graphic of a bicycle was used for the background on which the explanations of the basic concepts of bicycle technology were placed (fig. 2 bottom). The Fly visuals contained additional overviews that previewed and recapitulated single topics.

After both presentations were over, participants immediately filled out a *short term knowledge* test and a *preference and commentary* questionnaire (fig. 1). Four days later, they filled out a *long term knowledge* test. To measure knowledge transfer, the two knowledge tests asked for content and macrostructure facts with retention questions, and for content understanding with problem-solving transfer questions. To gain insight into the participants' attitude towards and

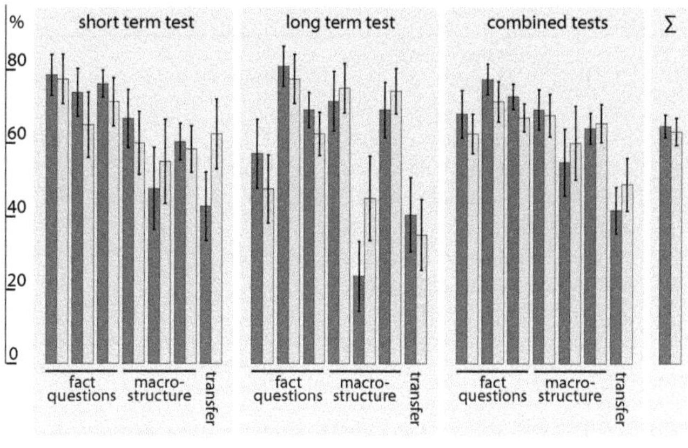

Figure 3. Percentage of correct answers to questions by presentation method for the two tests by question categories, combined tests, and all questions (canvas=dark blue, slideware=light green, error bars ± 1 *SE*). Both techniques performed equally well in terms of retaining facts, structure, and transferring knowledge. Only the short-term knowledge transfer question shows a significant difference.

satisfaction with the presentations, the questionnaire asked several Likert scale questions (table 1).

STUDY RESULTS

Fig. 3 shows knowledge test results for both conditions. For the short term transfer questions, the mean score is higher in the slide condition (paired t-test, p=.029). However, this is the only significant difference for all question categories.

Regarding the differences between short term and long term recall, the only significant result was that group A performed worse in the long term test for the slide condition (paired t-test, p=.003). Regarding the comparability of topics, paired t-tests did not show significantly more correct answers for any topic in the short term tests (p=.071), long term tests (p=.352), and in total (p=.145).

Table 1 lists the responses to our attitude and satisfaction questionnaire. A related samples Wilcoxon signed rank test showed that participants significantly preferred the canvas over the slide condition in questions A4, S5, S6, and S7. No other differences were significant.

In the spatial cognitive ability test, participants received a mean score of 127.32 (SD=21.011) out of 160. An independent samples t-test showed no significant difference between the mean scores of both groups (p=.837). We found no correlation between spatial ability and percentage of correct answers for any groups, talks, or conditions. Interestingly, the higher spatial cognitive ability, the more individuals found the amount of content on the screen (S2) too much (Pearson's r=.469: p=.003). However, we found no correlation between spatial ability and format preference.

Although we tried to balance members between groups, a t-test found group B performed slightly better than group A in both questionnaires. However, the difference is only significant for macrostructure retention (p=.080). Also, group A found the presentation visuals less distracting (p=.043).

	Question	*Mdn* (canvas / slide)	*p*
A1	The presentation was interesting.	2 / 2	0.756
A2	I liked the presentation visuals.	2 / 2	0.204
A3	I liked the narration of the presentation.	2 / 2	0.248
A4	I liked the presentation overall.	**2 / 3**	**0.047**
S1	The speed of the presentation was too slow.	3 / 3	1.000
S2	The amount of content shown on the screen at once was too much.	3 / 2	0.058
S3	The visuals distracted me from the narration.	4 / 4	0.755
S4	I had sufficient time to look at all the content.	2 / 3	0.805
S5	The structure of the talk was easy to understand.	**1 / 3**	**0.048**
S6	I always knew which part was currently shown.	**1 / 3**	**0.006**
S7	I always knew how far the talk had progressed.	**2 / 3**	**0.001**

Table 1. The questions (Likert scale 1–5, 1 for strongest agreement) from the attitude and satisfaction questionnaire. A related samples Wilcoxon signed rank test shows significant difference in four cases, all in favor of canvas presentations.

Discussion

Based on the fact recall results, we can accept H1. As the factual information is represented similarly in both formats, it seems that the presentation form alone does not influence fact retention. Although we expected the spatial arrangements in the canvas condition to help participants understand relations between topics (H2), the results do not support this. Consequently, there is no evidence to suggest that either canvas presentations or slide based ones are better suited to convey information to an audience. However, the results support H3; there were significant differences in favor of the canvas condition for the statements about orientation in content (S6) and temporal progress (S7). We also accept H4; participants found the canvas structures easier to understand (S5). On average, participants found the amount of content on the screen at a time more adequate in the canvas condition (H5), but this result was not significant (S2).

Limitations of the study

Several limitations have to be kept in mind when interpreting these results. First, canvas-based visuals are still new and exciting, which may have influenced participants. Second, our study used educational presentations with a focus on knowledge transfer. Other talks primarily focussed on conveying motivation, emotion, etc., may benefit even more from a canvas layout, again partly due to its novelty. Third, the talks were rather short and author and audience were informed beforehand of the study design and the knowledge tests. They may therefore have put more effort into their performance (cf. the Hawthorne effect).

SUMMARY AND FUTURE WORK

We evaluated the canvas presentation format against a baseline slide deck format to investigate the effects of canvas presentations on the learning performance and preferences of a student audience. We found that, while learning performance was largely the same in both cases, students clearly preferred the canvas-based presentation.

If we distinguish between three key activities associated with presentations—authoring, presenting, and attending—, canvas based presentations have now been analyzed in the context of the first and the third activity. We still have little data, however, on the effect of this format on the cognitive load of the presenter during her talk. Examining these effects could help understand the value of canvas presentations for all three user groups: authors, presenters, and the audience.

RepliCHI

We invite replication of this study. All materials required to replicate this experiment can be downloaded[2].

ACKNOWLEDGEMENTS

This work was funded in part by the German B-IT Foundation and by the German Government through its UMIC Excellence Cluster for Ultra-High Speed Mobile Information and Communication at RWTH Aachen University.

REFERENCES

1. B. B. Bederson and J. D. Hollan. Pad++: a zooming graphical interface for exploring alternate interface physics. In *Proc. UIST 1994*, 17–26.
2. R. Clark. Media will never influence learning. *Educational Technology Research and Development*, **42**(2):21–29, 1994.
3. R. B. Ekstrom, J.W. French, and H.H. Harman. *Cognitive factors: Their identification and replication. Multivariate Behavioral Research Monographs*, Society of Multivariate Experimental Psychology, 1979.
4. L. Ellis and D. Mathis. College student learning from televised versus conventional classroom lectures: A controlled experiment. *Higher Education*, **14**(2):165–173, 1985.
5. L. Good and B. Bederson. Zoomable user interfaces as a medium for slide show presentations. *Information Visualization*, **1**(1):35–49, 2002.
6. L. Lichtschlag, T. Karrer and J. Borchers. Fly: a Tool to Author Planar Presentations. In *Proc. CHI 2009*, 547–556.
7. A. M. O'Donnell, D.F. Dansereau and R.H. Hall. Knowledge maps as scaffolds for cognitive processing. *Educational Psychology Review*, **14**(1):71–86, 2002.
8. I. Parker. Absolute PowerPoint: Can a software package edit our thoughts? *The New Yorker*, **77**(13):76–87, 2001.
9. Prezi, http://prezi.com
10. G. G. Robertson, J. D. Mackinlay and S.K. Card. Cone trees: animated 3d visualizations of hierarchical information. In *Proc. CHI 1991*, 189–194.
11. T. L. Russell. *The No Significant Difference Phenomenon: As Reported in 355 Research Reports, Summaries and Papers*. IDECC, 1999.
12. E. Tufte. *The Cognitive Style of PowerPoint*. Graphics Press, Cheshire, Connecticut, USA, 2003.

[2]hci.rwth-aachen.de/fly

A Hybrid Mass Participation Approach to Mobile Software Trials

Alistair Morrison[1], Donald McMillan[1], Stuart Reeves[2], Scott Sherwood[1], Matthew Chalmers[1]

[1]School of Computing Science, University of Glasgow, UK
{alistair.morrison,donny.mcmillan,scott.sherwood, matthew.chalmers}@glasgow.ac.uk

[2]Horizon Digital Economy Research, University of Nottingham, UK
stuart@tropic.org.uk

ABSTRACT
User trials of mobile applications have followed a steady march out of the lab, and progressively further 'into the wild', recently involving 'app store'-style releases of software to the general public. Yet from our experiences on these mass participation systems and a survey of the literature, we identify a number of reported difficulties. We propose a hybrid methodology that aims to address these, by combining a global software release with a concurrent local trial. A phone–based game, created to explore the uptake and use of ad hoc peer-to-peer networking, was evaluated using this new hybrid trial method, combining a small-scale local trial (11 users) with a 'mass participation' trial (over 10,000 users). Our hybrid method offers many benefits, allowing locally observed findings to be verified, patterns in globally collected data to be explained and addresses ethical issues raised by the mass participation approach. We note trends in the local trial that did not appear in the larger scale deployment, and which would therefore have led to misleading results were the application trialled using 'traditional' methods alone. Based on this study and previous experience, we provide a set of guidelines to researchers working in this area.

Author Keywords
User trial methodology; mobile multiplayer games; mass participation; ad hoc peer-to-peer networking; MANETs

ACM Classification Keywords
H.5.2 [Information Interfaces And Presentation]: User Interfaces – Evaluation/methodology;

General Terms
Experimentation, Human Factors.

INTRODUCTION
Evaluations of the use (rather than the usability) of mobile and ubicomp systems have moved away from very controlled conditions in order to more closely align with the systems' context, as recommended by Abowd and Mynatt [1]. The earliest ubicomp systems [24,30] were largely confined to controlled laboratory conditions but there has been a general progress towards studies that take place in contexts more representative of the technologies' eventual intended use, with systems trials taking evaluation out of the lab [8], and moving towards studying participants' appropriation of technology in their everyday lives [3].

A recent step on this journey is the use of 'app store'-style repositories to allow researchers to release applications that participants can install directly onto their own handsets, thereby extending the reach of the research to potentially very large numbers of users. The benefits of such 'mass participation' deployments have been discussed [7,20], such as a reduced cost to researchers and the ability to reach users from vastly diverse geographical backgrounds. Although mainly positive in tone, several of these studies have mentioned shortcomings of this approach to research, such as the inability to meet users [20], a lack of standardisation of trial hardware [14] and the raising of additional ethical concerns [5].

In this paper, we survey these reported difficulties and expand upon them based on our own recent experiences of distributing mobile research applications in this manner. To counter some of these we propose a hybrid trial methodology, where the research application is released to the general public in tandem with a more traditional local deployment to recruited participants. Particular aspects of the research being undertaken may be best suited to investigation using one or other of the trial groups. In some circumstances the two groups can be used together to achieve greater insights than could be gained from studying either group alone. We also argue that conducting app store-style trials using this hybrid methodology allows for more solid ethical practice.

To investigate our hybrid method, we created an application on the iOS platform and trialled it concurrently at both a local and global scale. The application, World Cup Predictor (WCP), was designed to run alongside the 2010 FIFA World Cup, and looked at users' real-world uptake of peer-to-peer data transfers. The local trial involved 11 users, and a further 10,806 registered users were recruited via the software's release on a mobile application repository. We study the findings of this hybrid trial, investigate whether these different methodologies can be effectively combined, explore productive ways of managing

Permission to make digital or hard copies of all or part of this work for personal or classroom use is granted without fee provided that copies are not made or distributed for profit or commercial advantage and that copies bear this notice and the full citation on the first page. To copy otherwise, or republish, to post on servers or to redistribute to lists, requires prior specific permission and/or a fee.
CHI'12, May 5–10, 2012, Austin, Texas, USA.
Copyright 2012 ACM 978-1-4503-1015-4/12/05...$10.00.

the tasks best suited to each, and discuss whether this hybrid approach is sufficient to address the identified shortcomings of the 'mass participation' approach. We culminate with a set of guidelines to aid other researchers who are interested in performing such a study.

RELATED WORK

There has been a move towards studying the use of mobile software 'in the wild' [6]. Arguments have been made in favour of this change in methodology [25], with others further noting that field studies are better suited for studying broad issues surrounding use of technologies rather than merely the uncovering of usability issues [18]. The methods for selecting participants for trials have also been a topic of research. For example, the recruitment of a cohort of participants for long term use in trialling a number of systems in their everyday lives has been explored by Jay et al. [16], who state that "the main advantage of maintaining the cohort has been that we are able to reduce problems of generalisability associated with laboratory studies." The methodology outlined in this paper aims to go further with regard to reducing problems of generalisability, with a trial larger in scale and with much greater variation in participant age and location.

The mass participation approach of releasing mobile software via public 'app stores' has become more and more popular with researchers in recent years, as it offers a comparatively easy mechanism for recruiting large numbers of users while reducing hardware costs for researchers. Several research applications have had public releases on the Android [13,14,27], Blackberry [23] and iOS platforms [4,20]. The analysis performed in the evaluation of these systems has tended to be quantitative, taking advantage of the large numbers of participants to offer more solid numerical or statistical findings.

One of the most long-term deployments of mobile research applications released in this way is Cenceme [4], an application that uses context sensing to automatically update social networking sites with each user's current activity. Initially developed for the Nokia N95 and trialled among 30 locally-based participants, the software was then ported to the iPhone and released in July 2008 when the App Store was first launched. Our work distinguishes itself from the Cenceme study by running concurrent large- and small-scale trials of the same application, and exploring both qualitative and quantitative data.

Hungry Yoshi was a game designed to expose the wireless infrastructure of a city, using this as a resource in the game. In earlier work, we reported that the application had over 130,000 downloads from around the world and describe how it is still possible to conduct qualitative analysis among such a widespread global user base [20]. We take a different approach here, combining those mass participation techniques with a small-scale local user trial so as to assess or enrich preliminary findings.

Taking a sample of data from a larger population and conducting interviews is not, in itself, a novel approach to research. In fields such as sociology and market research it is not uncommon for a survey to be followed by targeted interviews, either individual or together as part of a focus group, to gain more in-depth qualitative data [9]. This approach has been applied in mass-released mobile applications [2], although without the methodological detail or discussion provided here.

The WCP application described in this paper was designed to apply this large-scale deployment model to explore the viability of research applications based on mobile ad hoc networks (MANETs) using commodity mobile phones in uncontrolled environments. Research of MANETs has been extensive [17], yet few applications of MANETs have taken place outside of simulated environments [19], as a substantial density of users is needed to ensure successful transfer of data through a community via opportunistic, face-to-face encounters [17]. Previous trials have tended to be small-scale in terms of participant numbers.

DIFFICULTIES ENCOUNTERED IN 'APP STORE' TRIALS

As outlined in the previous section, the provision of 'app stores' on several mobile platforms in recent years has seen several research projects use these methods of deployment. Although most report positively on the benefits gained using this methodology, several potential shortcomings have been identified. For example Henze et al. conducted a trial using Android Market investigating the use of the mass participation approach in an experiment that sought to isolate 'cause and effect' on a single task [14]. As Android runs on a great number of devices from many different handset manufacturers, it is no surprise that the authors report that their captured data came from 40 different types of device, with different processor speeds, OS versions, screen resolutions and physical dimensions. This lack of uniformity could easily be a problem in certain types of studies, if the goal is to compare behaviour among different conditions.

Several other types of difficulty might arise in using this mass participation approach to Ubicomp trials. It was noted in the Hungry Yoshi study that although it was possible to gain qualitative data from remote users, the "*methods incurred expenses in terms of development time and interviewer effort*" [20]. In our own more recent trials, this seemed to get more challenging, and we had great difficulty in both finding participants willing to consent to speak to us and in the practicalities of conducting these interviews. Whereas offering in-game rewards for answering quick questionnaire-style queries led to a reasonable return rate, the same strategy did not persuade people to consent to telephone calls. The offering of financial incentives was similarly unsuccessful in encouraging interviewees.

Even once willing interviewees had been identified, another round of difficulties began as attempts were made to timetable a schedule for VoIP calls with users who lived in different time zones. These had to be conducted at times best suited to the interviewees, arranged around work, family and social commitments and in many cases necessitated researchers staying up until the early hours of the morning. It is then especially unfortunate that we found remote participants to be very unreliable in attending arranged interviews, with many of them failing to answer calls made at pre-arranged times. This might be due to the nature of the researcher-participant relationship in this style of trial; there might be less social pressure to answer a call from an app developer with whom you have had the most cursory contact than there would from a researcher whom you had met and whose hardware you were using.

In addition to the struggles of finding interviewees and arranging interviews, the data gained from such encounters is less rich than would be captured from those conducted face-to-face, due to increased difficulties in establishing a rapport and the inability to capture nonverbal information. While the quality of qualitative data collected between telephone and face-to-face interviews has been seen to be comparable [26], the gap between email and other asynchronous web technologies, and synchronous voice has been shown to be significantly detrimental to the credibility and trustworthiness of the researcher—and as a result the quality of the data gathered [15].

It was also of interest to us to perform repeated interviews at regular intervals throughout the trial, to follow up on points raised and learn about how usage of and feelings towards the system changed over time. However, in many cases this would have been impossible as users can stop using the system at any time, with no implied obligation to keep playing for the duration of a trial.

Although we were gathering very large amounts of quantitative data, we found that this reduction in the amount and quality of qualitative data meant it was harder to explain the patterns observed or infer users' motives: we could see *what* was happening in our trial, but had less success in discovering *why* it was happening.

Releasing via an app store also means there is no simple way to only target a specifically desired demographic [7]. This could be an issue if the research questions of interest concern, for example, only users of a particular profession, or group of users with a specific social structure.

The recruited users might also not be as diverse a group as it would first appear. For example, relative wealth scales play a part in the sampling process, with the level of entry to our trial set at having an Apple iPhone. It has been shown that cultural values change within a population with income level [12] and the homogenising effect on cultural values between different populations of similar income levels has also been discussed [28]. Additionally, although the recruited user base might be considered more representative of the audience such an application would attract, there is no way to gather data from those users who do not like the application. Users will judge the software by the same standards as they judge commercial software they download, meaning researchers can expect a large proportion of users to download and 'browse' the software but not continue to use it if they do not see a benefit. They are unlikely to feel a responsibility to keep using the software in order to complete an academic trial.

A number of ethical considerations have been noted from this style of research [5], with certain concerns arising from trials making use of app store repositories that are not inherent in more standard deployments among local users. Possibly chief among these is the notion of informed consent: do the users of these applications understand their role as participants in a trial and how data might be recorded on their usage of the software, their unique identifiers and their location? We have previously reported that 70% of surveyed users did not know that Hungry Yoshi was part of a research trial [20], despite the presentation of a terms and conditions page on first launch. This echoes previous findings on the number of users reading terms presented in desktop applications [11]. Even if users did want to read this information, language barriers may prevent it; although we regularly provide translations in four major languages, this will not cover all the users likely to download a globally released application.

Additional ethical concerns arise in researchers not being able to know their users, or to verify submitted demographic information. There is no way of knowing whether a user reporting to be above the legal age of consent to enter into a contract in any given country is being truthful, or whether a child has lied about his or her age in order to gain access to functionality restricted to adults. The age of a subject is of particular importance when they are agreeing to interviews; in many institutions separate – and more rigorous – ethical approval of a project must be sought before engaging with minors.

A HYBRID APPROACH TOWARDS MOBILE SOFTWARE TRIALS

The hybrid approach presented in this paper attempts to address many of these technical, administrative and ethical difficulties that can arise when evaluating a system using a mass participation method alone. The hybrid approach proposes releasing an application globally to attract a large user base and concurrently running a local trial, where it might be possible to record more rich data from participants. Data recorded from each user group can feed into and generate research questions for the other, in this way leveraging the strengths of both types of trial.

This approach would obviously not be suitable for every type of study. It is appropriate for applications running on commodity platforms which have public 'app store's. If trials involve specialised sensors or other nonstandard hardware, this method would not be feasible. Additionally, if researchers are only interested in particular types of relationships (for example parent-child), it might not be practically possible to recruit a large number of participants with such connections by deploying to an app store. However, as will be described below, the hybrid method affords researchers the opportunity to handpick such particular social demographics for their local trial if desired, as well as seeing what will occur 'naturally' with a global release.

The following section introduces the WCP application and describes the user trial that uses the hybrid methodology.

WORLD CUP PREDICTOR

As previously stated, most trials of MANET systems have been based on simulations or small numbers of users. Using MANETs in ways that fit with the everyday interactions of users and the limitations imposed by current technology, so as to augment and support their sharing of information, has not been fully explored. Here we apply the techniques of the mass participation approach to the study of peer-to-peer data transfers in real-world settings.

As one of the requirements of such a trial is to create a sufficient density of users, it is necessary to create an application compelling enough to gain a large number of downloads. We considered that releasing a research application based solely on testing MANET communications, an attempt at altruistic message passing through a number of intermediary nodes for example, would perhaps not attract huge numbers. Rather we attempted to create an appealing application, which could be used by an individual player in isolation and which we were confident would be downloaded in large numbers. Peer-to-peer data transfer functionality was then built into this single-player application as an optional mode, but incentivised with points and prizes, to examine the uptake and usage of these features.

We were interested in whether groups of socially-connected users would all download and use the application when it was released in this way, and whether we would observe similar or different uptake of MANET features among these users as compared to a local user group that was hand-picked to have known social links.

System description

The World Cup Predictor was an iOS-based game created to run alongside the 2010 FIFA World Cup, a sporting event of global interest hosted in South Africa between 11th June and 11th July 2010. The application allowed users to predict the results of World Cup football matches and awarded points for correct guesses: 3 points were awarded for getting a result exactly correct and 1 point for predicting the correct winner or correctly predicting a draw. Point tallies were accumulated for all users' predictions and collated in a global leaderboard.

The game divided the World Cup into seven rounds, such that every team remaining in the tournament played once per round. The final two rounds consisted of only two matches each. Users were only able to predict results for the matches in the current round, this constraint being designed to encourage continued engagement as users had to interact with the application at least once per round to continue to earn points. The deadline for submitting predictions for a given round was the kick-off time of the first match in that round. At the end of each match, the server allocated points to users with correct predictions and recalculated the leaderboard. Figure 1 shows screenshots from the application.

Figure 1. Screenshots from the WCP: the Match Predictor for the current round of matches (left) and the Head to Head page that allowed play via ad hoc networking (right).

As explained above, a purpose of the trial was to study the uptake of ad hoc networking functionality, so the application also included a peer-to-peer feature, where a user could challenge another co-located player to a 'head-to-head' game. In this mode, both players would predict the results of the same randomly selected subset of the current round's matches and the player getting the most correct would be awarded 5 points on the main leaderboard. Upon challenging another player, an ad hoc connection would be formed between the devices using Bluetooth. This connection was used to transfer the prediction data locally between devices and, on the next occasion one of the users had a connection to the server, the details of the head-to-head were uploaded so that points could be allocated to the winner. There were no restrictions on the number of head-to-head games users could play, except that each pair of users could only play each other once per round. The game rules were designed to incentivise usage of this feature, as users willing and able to play many head-to-heads would have a far higher chance of winning the prizes on offer.

User trial

Although the WCP study sought to investigate the uptake of ad hoc peer-to-peer networking via the application's 'head-to-head' feature, the primary aim was to test a hybrid methodology combining large and small-scale trials. As such, the WCP application was distributed to both locally recruited participants and via an iOS APT software repository [21] to users worldwide.

In order to encourage downloads, and particularly usage of the ad-hoc peer-to-peer functionality, the application offered a prize of £250 to the top player at the end of the World Cup. Smaller prizes of £40 were offered to the player winning each round, so that users coming to the game late or those who had not performed well in the first few rounds could still win a prize, and therefore would still be motivated to play the game.

Local Participant Group

As we were particularly interested in investigating how social bonds between users impacted on game participation and use, we looked to recruit local users who had existing social ties. We were keen that this group should have regular day-to-day contact, to maximise the opportunities for use of the peer-to-peer functions. We also sought a smaller group of satellite players with no connection to the group of friends and colleagues. This social topography of users was chosen to give direct access to the different types of users and use expected in relation to the peer-to-peer functionality; i.e. friends and co-workers using it together on a regular basis as well as serendipitous use between strangers.

The recruitment of local participants was undertaken primarily by putting up posters in several locations around the city. In order to find a group with day-to-day social connections we asked volunteers to recommend their friends or colleagues who would be likely to be interested in playing the game. In order to boost the group size, hardware in the form of Apple iPhones was provided for the duration of the study to members of the local group who did not own a compatible device.

Each participant was paid a nominal fee for their participation in the study, which included pre-trial familiarisation with the system, a brief visit from a researcher during the trial and a 20 minute interview after the trial was complete. Of the eleven participants recruited, five worked together in a shared office. Of the others, three were acquaintances of one another and the other three had no social ties to any of the other participants. Participants ranged in age from 18 to 37 years of age, with 10 males and 1 female. All but two participants owned the devices on which the trial software was run. As well as their payment, local participants were of course eligible to compete with the global users for the array of prizes on offer throughout the World Cup.

Global Participant Group

WCP was released via an iOS APT repository on Sunday 6th of June 2010, with the World Cup commencing on Friday the 11th of June. An interesting aspect of running mass distribution studies is the difficulty in quantifying the number of users involved in a trial [22]. In the local trial, we can identify a user as someone who was given the software, paid for participation and interviewed about their experience, and we can report the number of such participants with confidence. With an application released through an online software repository, this becomes more complicated as there are many possible ways to count users. Statistics provided from the repository state that the application has had 44,613 downloads. This figure includes software updates and reinstalls, so the same user might be included more than once. By the start of the tournament there were 3,720 registered users, with this number increasing to 10,806 by the end of the World Cup. Of these, 5,941 made at least one prediction, and 5,602 predicted in more than one round.

Both the local and global deployments of the application logged participant usage data. The data logged includes activities within the game, such as moving between application screens, and general contextual information, such as location. Uploaded data was timestamped and stored on a database on a central server. To protect the privacy of participants TLS was used to encrypt data sent between phones and the server.

Before using the application, users were required to agree to the terms and conditions stating that their usage would be logged. A contact email address was also supplied for users to opt out of the trial at any time. This information was presented in four different languages. Users also had to agree via the standard iOS request for the application to use his/her location. The game was not affected if this request was refused or if location services were turned off at any time. The majority of users were based in Europe, North America and South America. Fewer than 400 users who provided locations played the game in Africa, the continent hosting the tournament, although there was activity recorded at five different World Cup stadia in South Africa.

On first launching the application, users were prompted to provide a username for use on the leaderboard and an email address so they could be contacted in the event of winning a prize. Simple demographic information was also requested at this stage, with users being asked to input their age via a slider and their gender via one of two buttons. There was no obligation to answer these questions and we have to be aware that the reported answers cannot be verified. 80% of users provided an age, with most in their 30s or younger. The gender distribution was heavily male-biased, with 10297 male and 509 female.

Qualitative Data Capture

As researchers did not physically meet the global participants, there were additional challenges in establishing a dialogue with them in order to gain data for qualitative analysis. In addition to requesting simple demographic information, we presented users with short questionnaires, allowing them to enter free text into a form within the application using the device's soft keyboard. Although not answered by the same high percentages of users as the more simple demographic questions, many participants usefully responded to this form of concise information gathering.

User Self-Selection Bias.

We note that in packaging the peer-to-peer functionality under scrutiny within a football predictor game we might have introduced a bias in the sample of users. For example, the vast majority of our users were male. When conducting a mass participation trial, the body of trial participants is self-selected, in that users download the trial application from a public repository themselves. This is in contrast with more traditional techniques in which participants are directly recruited, or techniques used in industry, in which a recruitment agency ensures a demographic distribution in accord with what a company expects or desires. The population of users resulting from a mass participation trial is likely to be more 'lifelike' in representing the types of users who would actively seek out and use such an application, as opposed to the inherent biases likely to occur when users are directly recruited. However, these users, who elect to play a football predictor game, are not necessarily representative of the average population, or of the set of people who would be most likely to use peer-to-peer functions in applications more generally.

USAGE OF AD HOC NETWORKS

WCP was designed to test uptake of peer-to-peer networking. The game was completely playable without using ad hoc networks, but had this functionality presented as an option for 'head-to-head' play, where co-located players could swap predictions via Bluetooth for bonus points. The head-to-head mode was encouraged both through this scoring mechanism and as a means to challenge friends, providing a more overt social element to the game. As the tournament progressed, the game mechanism encouraged head-to-head play more as the number of matches per round became fewer. For the final two rounds, where only two matches were played, the maximum possible score through the main predictions game was 6 points, whereas each successful head-to-head game would gain a user a further 5 points. This game mechanic was designed to provide motivation to use this feature. We were interested in whether we would see high uptake or whether, even with these incentives, participants would not be sufficiently motivated to overcome the obstacles to using this feature; namely, needing to know somebody else with an iOS device, who was sufficiently interested in the World Cup to install the application and who could physically meet the user in order to establish a Bluetooth connection. These are significant demands to place upon a feature compared to the main game, where a single user only needs an Internet connection to play.

Our results show very different usage levels between the local and global user groups. Of the global users, only 45 played head-to-head. This is 0.8% of the registered 5,602 users who played in more than one round.

Of those 45 users, 23 completed more than one head-to-head game. The most head-to-heads undertaken in total by a single user was 4: this player engaged 2 other users twice each. The greatest diversity of head-to-head partners achieved by a single user was 3. A single pair of users could have performed up to 7 head-to-heads (1 in each round), yet no player performed a head-to-head in more than 3 different rounds, suggesting that even those users who were using the feature and presumably seeing the points benefits felt that the barrier of being co-located with another participant was too great.

These results seem to indicate that head-to-head play had significant hurdles for users. Responses gained through the questionnaire section of the application support this. Comments on this issue focussed on two main areas, with several users stating they lacked the opportunity to perform the feature, for example "*I would have used head-to-head more if more people amongst my friend using the software/feature too*". Many users also suggested alternative means to engage in head-to-heads that were not reliant on co-location, requesting for example "*i think the head to head should be just random ppl going against eachother and not bluethooth*", or requesting "*The ability to challenge global users over wifi for a head to head*".

Turning attention to data gathered from the local deployment of the application reveals a very different pattern of use. All 5 of the officemates and all 3 of the friends performed at least one head-to-head, yet none of the 3 singletons used the feature. The average number of head-to-head plays performed by each local participant was 5.2, compared to a global trial average of 0.01. Users reported enjoying this feature in terms of adding an extra social dimension to the application. For example one user talked positively of it adding "*more friendly rivalry when watching games*".

CONDUCTING HYBRID MASS PARTICIPATION TRIALS

Our primary goal in this study was to examine the different opportunities for research that arise when a mass participation trial is run concurrently with a more traditional local deployment, and to weigh gains against the additional expense, in time and money, for the researchers involved.

The value of a Mixed Methods approach to research has been well established in fields such as sociology. Denzin notes that "By combining multiple observers, theories, methods and data sources, sociologists can hope to overcome the intrinsic bias that comes from single-methods, single observer, and single theory studies." [10] This section, drawing from our experiences of several app store style deployments and our hybrid trial, presents a set of practical benefits researchers can expect from this approach. These are followed by a set of recommendations for other researchers who wish to run a large scale trial in a way in which the biases Denzin discusses can be overcome.

Practical Considerations for Hybrid Trials

Running a hybrid trial necessarily involves more work on the part of the researcher than running either a local trial or a global trial on its own. However some work can be done once and the benefits utilised with both groups, and some tasks are much easier with one group or the other. This goes some way to making a hybrid trial economically viable in research terms with, of course, the caveat that the software under evaluation must be able to run on standard hardware on a platform providing an 'app store'.

Commodity Hardware and Release-Quality Software

The use of participants' own devices for a majority of those recruited, combined with the release of the research software via a channel users are familiar with, greatly reduces the work necessary in managing hardware and software deployment. Even locally-recruited participants might use their own devices, so an email with an app store link or a few minutes with the user and an Internet connection are enough to kit out a participant for the trial.

However, in general, software released in this fashion must be more polished and stable than more standard research prototypes [7], which obviously incurs greater expense in terms of implementation and testing. Although, this, in turn, greatly reduces the amount of technical support necessary during the trial – potentially producing less down time and therefore gathering more results. And where problems do occur the local participants are available to perform quick and accessible testing.

Numbers with ease; Interviews with ease

With the public distribution to a wide audience, there is less pressure to reach the 'magic number' of local participants deemed necessary in the research community at that time. Moreover this access to local participants greatly reduces the effort required to glean useful and detailed qualitative data in comparison to using remote participants, as described above.

More Interactive Design Cycle

One advantage of a hybrid trial method is in utilising the benefits of both groups of users as part of the software design cycle. Following release, developers may wish to evaluate current opinion, present new ideas, or probe the users for suggestions for desired features. This might begin by speaking with local users to hear current thoughts and future directions in which they would like to see the software develop. Having gathered a number of ideas from the local group, developers could then present some of these options to the global user base to vote upon to determine which suggestions are most popular [20].

Conversely, a mechanism can be provided to allow all users to submit suggestions for new features for the application. In our trial, this generated a large volume of responses, though each suggestion was only a short piece of text. These ideas could then be presented to a locally based group of users to discuss in greater depth, and explore the subtle effects these modifications would make to the application.

In this way, the benefits of both groups of users are being exploited – the opportunity for in-depth discussions, and the ability to present design ideas to a large number of people, for more certainty as to what will be popular decisions. The concurrent use of the two user groups results in greater benefit than would have been possible with either group alone. We use the two groups together, but utilise the strengths of each to maximise the benefits offered by this hybrid methodology.

Recommendations for Hybrid Trial Research

Here we discuss not only the observed differences between the results available from each style of trial, but also the areas in which they are complementary—with one providing detail or contrast to points exposed by the other. We also discuss the different ethical responsibilities researchers have towards participants in each style of trial, and the restrictions they present. The discussion is formed around the following four recommendations, and we draw examples from our WCP trial to illustrate the points.

1. Use the Small to Explain the Large

As identified earlier, a fundamental difficulty in conducting mass participation trials is the lack of rich qualitative data and consequently the reduced ability to explain the reasons behind patterns observed in the vast amount of data being generated. In running a hybrid trial, the local users also afforded us the ability to ask questions relating to patterns of use observed in the mass participation users' aggregate data—patterns for which the motivations were unclear. For example, during the early rounds, it was observed that not all users were predicting the results of every match. The number of users predicting each match for the first 2 rounds of the World Cup is shown in Figure 2. As can be seen, a significant number of users were only predicting results of the first five matches in each round. It was speculated that this might be because many players were just trying out the game without fully committing to predicting every match, or that they misunderstood the deadline system and did not realise that predictions for every match in the round had to be submitted before the first match commenced.

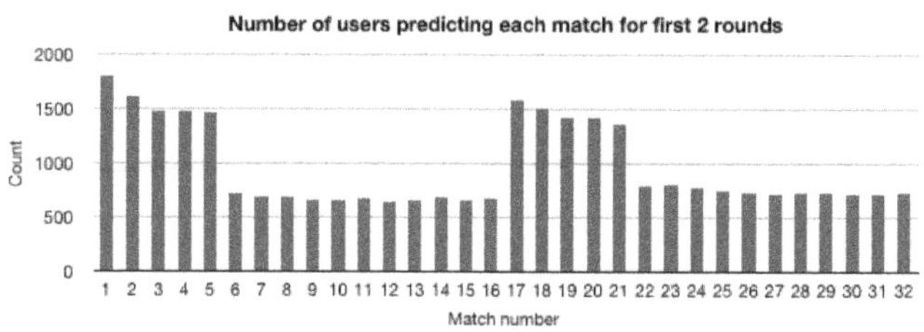

Figure 2. The number of users predicting each match

When a local user was observed to have exhibited this same behaviour, he was questioned about it. He stated that initially he had not been aware that the match prediction screen (Figure 1, left) could be scrolled down. This solved our mystery; iOS applications hide the scroll bar by default, only displaying it when a user drags to scroll, so a significant number of users thought that there were only 5 matches to predict each round. To solve this, a new version of the application was released that displayed a popup when a user uploaded predictions, informing them on how many of the available matches they could still predict. Following this update, the pattern of the first 5 matches receiving more predictions was no longer observed.

Another unexpected behaviour displayed by a large number of mass participation users was the use of the application after the World Cup had ended. While activity dropped significantly after the event was concluded, it did not drop to zero as may be expected. The users could no longer make predictions and there was no new data being added to the application so the motivation for repeated launches in the weeks after the World Cup was not obvious. The question was presented to the local participants during the post-trial interviews and, while most had stopped using the application, one reported that the application presented the full results of the World Cup in one place, in a way easier to access than searching the web.

2. Use the Large to Verify the Small

As an inverse to guideline 1, the hybrid trial allowed us to use the global users to verify the generality of behaviour observed during detailed analysis of observations and interview transcripts from local participants. One of the most obvious advantages of running a large trial is the much larger number of users that can be expected, as compared to a more traditional local deployment. This offers the researcher increased confidence in making claims based on consistently observed behaviour, and, as shown below, reduces the risks of a researcher coming to incorrect conclusions if a local trial has non-representative users or the users are affected by experimenter effects.

One behavioural pattern reported by several local users was the use of the application during the matches to check the predictions of the top players and compare these to the current state of play on the field. It had been expected that users would not welcome distractions during the matches themselves, so the application had been designed to fit around the matches—users were only allowed to enter predictions up to the start of the first match in a round, and the scores within the application were not updated until each match had finished. In order to verify that this usage occurred across the whole population, graphs showing launches per hour of day were generated which confirmed that the local users' behaviour did generalise to the user population at large, with usage during the periods in which matches were being played more than double the baseline.

As well as being able to use the body of mass participation users to verify small-scale findings, the same procedures can also be used to detect where results from the local group are *not* observed among the global group. There is always a risk in running only a standard, local trial that the data will be skewed by the inclusion of outliers and that their behaviour becomes erroneously considered as being representative of a large proportion of the population. A further risk of local trials is the participants' susceptibility to 'experimenter effects' [26]: subtle conscious or subconscious cues a researcher might give users that affect performance. We assert that such an effect is less likely among globally-recruited users, where the users' contact with researchers is generally far lower.

As an example of this in our trial of the hybrid method, we found that 8 of 11 local participants used the head-to-head function of the game. This represents an uptake of almost 73%—but the percentage of mass participation users who made use of this feature was 0.8%. This disparity could be seen as simply reflecting the different sampling procedures used to create the two trial groups – one group specifically selected to be composed of socially connected users and another recruited via an app store with no forcing of a desired social topology. Yet even ignoring the head-to-head aspects, the number of matches predicted in the game's single-player mode was also far higher: 71% for local participants compared to 15% for the mass participation user group. It is possible that both of these differences are due to experimenter effects: local users were very aware that their participation was being measured, they were paid to use the application and therefore felt compelled to put in more effort. Regardless of the reasons behind the discrepancy, without the mass participation element of the hybrid trial, we would have gained a very different impression of the features' popularity and therefore, it could be argued, gathered very misleading results.

3. Maintain an ethical approach through a framework of levels of engagement

Studying the differences between mass participation trials and normal (i.e. small) scale trials highlights certain ethical concerns, and the methods used for the trial of the WCP application were specifically designed to address these.

As mentioned previously, an important consideration when conducting this form of trial is the issue of informed consent. When conducting traditional trials, evaluators are generally able to interact directly with participants, thus gaining the opportunity to assure themselves that truly informed consent has been obtained with regard to the trial procedure. McMillan et al. [20] reported that 70% of users had not understood that they were part of a trial. If users are unwilling to or, due to cognitive capacity or language skill, unable to read presented terms, it is infeasible to expect them to understand the possible consequences of logging or academic publication.

Participants in any form of experiment can deceive evaluators, by intent or by misunderstanding, but such deception is easier for mass participation users and is compounded by difficulties in validation of reported facts. Our techniques for gaining consent within mass participation trials follow the standard practices used within commercial settings. However, this raises a research question as to methodology: how can we satisfy our ethical responsibility as evaluators, when there are no feasible ways to make sure that users are of an acceptable age, and capable of giving informed consent?

Furthermore, standard ethical practice involves a debriefing following a trial. Conducting such a debriefing is more difficult in a mass participation trial. Such trials are frequently without a defined end date. It cannot be reliably predicted when a user will play for the last time, and given the primary means of communication is through the application itself, it can be difficult to have any significant contact with the user after that time.

Given these ethical concerns, we approached our mass participation users differently than the local users. We engaged with the mass participation user group in a much lighter manner than would have been desirable had the goal been to utilise them as a resource to the fullest extent possible: we limited our direct interaction to non-compulsory survey questions, as opposed to requesting interviews, and examined aggregate logged data as opposed to examining in detail the data for any single user exhibiting an interesting pattern of behaviour. This was seen as a compromise that protected users whose consent was not or could not have been 'informed'. A single user, even when actively engaging in the trial by answering survey questions or providing log data on a specific issue, would not have his/her privacy or expectations compromised.

The types of questions asked of remote users were also limited: potentially invasive or sensitive questions were avoided not only due to the problem of verification of consent but because it is much harder to converse sensitively at a distance, i.e. harder to read a participant's reaction to a subject matter and stop if necessary. While we encourage researchers to continue to explore novel ways to meet their ethical responsibilities, we suggest that by using the full range of engagement possibilities with participants in this manner, researchers can feel more confident that they are pursuing an ethically sound research path.

4. Do not rely on the emergence of specific social structures in your participant base

Certain research questions are predicated upon social use of an application, by users with a certain topology of relationships. If it is important that the system is used among groups of users with this social structure pre-dating use of the software we advise that the study should include a local trial, where users can be selected to match the required social graph. While a global trial could certainly be interesting in seeing how often or how rarely such social features are used, our results suggest that co-located social groups are not guaranteed to all adopt an application, even when strong incentives are given for using social features.

As shown, our results from the WCP trial indicate that the ad hoc network functionality was used to a reasonable degree within our handpicked social group of people who had regular contact with each other: all of the locally recruited participants who had existing social ties used the head-to-head feature. This contrasts with 0.8% of the global user base. As suggested above, experimental bias could be a factor here, with local participants feeling more of a duty to use the application. However the 3 local users who were not part of a social group also did not participate in head-to-head play and qualitative data gathered during the experiment confirms that many users could not find suitable partners close by to play with. More research is needed to verify whether, when in the right social context, users are more likely to take advantage of the head-to-head mode. It seems that handpicking participants matching a desired social topography is far more likely to lead to usage of features designed for a co-located group than relying on users acquired 'by chance' in a global release.

CONCLUSIONS

The use of 'app store's for research trials has become popular, yet researchers report several drawbacks to this approach. We show that the hybrid trial methodology presented here, combining use of a large-scale deployment with a local trial, can be a powerful tool, going some way to addressing these shortcomings. We designed an iOS application to test our proposed methodology, and studied it with a very large-scale trial. Based on these experiences of the hybrid method, we suggest that it offers a useful means to alleviate the weaknesses of both local and global trials.

For researchers conducting a local trial of mobile software, using our hybrid approach would:

- Allow findings based on consistently observed behaviour to be reported with greater confidence
- Mitigate problems resulting from 'outlier' users in a small sample leading to misleading conclusions
- Mitigate bias resulting from experimenter effects

For researchers who wish to run a mass participation-style trial, the hybrid approach will:

- Reduce the difficulty of gathering qualitative data while improving its quality
- Allow for more solid ethical practice to be maintained
- Understand patterns emerging from analysis of global data through interviews and observation of local users

An important component of the hybrid method is a means for managing the ethical responsibilities of researchers in conducting large-scale trials, providing a balance between utility and ethical practice: a focus on keeping interactions with the remote participants lightweight and giving individuals more privacy than a local trial participant could reasonably expect. Again we emphasise that further work needs to be done in this area, for example assessing whether information available to participants after the trial has ended, e.g. on a web site, may serve to acceptably 'debrief'.

This study has also shown that regular usage of ad hoc networking in the WCP application only took place among those with pre-existing social ties and regular co-location. Despite offering generous prizes and a game design that encouraged peer-to-peer usage, there was very little uptake of this feature among the global users. We suggest that the serendipitous use of such ad hoc networking technologies should not be expected within current applications. This also suggests that research questions relying upon any pre-existing social topology among co-located participants should be carried out with a selected local group.

Although this kind of hybrid methodology may have applicability in other application areas, we suggest that it is particularly worth exploring in future mobile software research. Local context, which is vital to mobile and ubiquitous computing yet clearly variable as one looks worldwide, can be studied with greater assurance as to what can be generalised, and what is specifically local, thus helping to address a key design issue for the field.

REFERENCES

1. Abowd, G.D., Mynatt, E.D.: Charting past, present, and future research in ubiquitous computing. ACM Trans. Comput.-Hum. Interact. 7, 29-58 (2000)
2. Ames, M., Naaman, M.: Why We Tag: Motivations for Annotation in Mobile and Online Media. CHI (2007)
3. Bell, M and Chalmers, M., and Barkhuus, L., Hall, M., Sherwood, S., Tennent, P., Brown, B., Rowland, D., Benford, S., Capra, M., & Hampshire, A., Interweaving Mobile Games with Everyday Life, Proc. ACM CHI, pp. 417-426. (2006)
4. Campbell, A., Eisenman, S., Fodor, K., Lane, N., Lu, H., Miluzzo, E., Musolesi, M., Peterson, R., Zheng, X. Transforming the social networking experience with sensing presence from mobile phones. Proc ACM Conf on Embedded network sensor systems. 367-368 (2008)
5. Chalmers, M., McMillan, D., Morrison, A., Cramer, H., Rost, M., Mackay, W.: Ethics, Logs and Videotape: Ethics in Large Scale User Trials and User Generated Content. Ext. Abd, Proc CHI (2011)
6. Crabtree, A., Benford, S., Greenhalgh, C., Tennent, P., Chalmers, M., Brown, B.: Supporting ethnographic studies of ubiquitous computing in the wild. Proc conference on Designing Interactive systems. (2006)
7. Cramer, H., Rost, M. and Bentley, F. An Introduction to Research in the Large, Special Issue IJMHCI (2011)
8. Davies, N., Mitchell, K., Cheverst, K. and Blair, G. Developing A Context Sensitive Tourist Guide Proc. HCI for Mobile Devices (1998)
9. Denscombe, M. The good research guide. Maidenhead: Open University Press. (2003)
10. Denzin, N.K. *The Research Act,* 3rd edn. Englewood Cliffs, NJ: Prentice Hall. (1989)
11. FAST Federation Asks: Do you know what you're agreeing to? www.fastiis.org/resources/press/id/304/
12. Feather, N. T., Values and income level, Australian Journal of Psychology, 27(1), (1975)
13. Girardello, A. and Michahelles, F.: AppAware: which mobile applications are hot? : Proc. Int. conference on HCI with mobile devices & services. ACM, 431-434
14. Henze, N., Poppinga, B., Boll, S. Experiments in the Wild: Public Evaluation of Off-Screen Visualizations in the Android Market. Proc NordiCHI (2010)
15. James, N, Busher, H.: Credibility, authenticity and voice: dilemmas in online interviewing. Qualitative Research 6: 403-420 (2006)
16. Jay, T., Stanton Fraser, D.: The role of a cohort in the design and evaluation of pervasive systems. Proc. ACM Conf on Designing interactive systems. 31-39 (2008)
17. Khelil, A., Becker, C., Tian, J. and Rothermel, K.: An epidemic model for information diffusion in MANETs. Proc Int workshop on modeling analysis and simulation of wireless and mobile systems. ACM, (2002)
18. Kjeldskov, J., Skov, M., Als, B. and Høegh, R.: Is It Worth the Hassle? Exploring the Added Value of Evaluating the Usability of Context-Aware Mobile Systems in the Field. MobileHCI, 529-535 (2004)
19. Kurkowski, S., Camp, T., Colagrosso, M.: MANET simulation studies: the incredibles. SIGMOBILE Mobile Computing and Comms Review 9 50-61 (2005)
20. McMillan, D., Morrison, A., Brown, O., Hall, M. and Chalmers, M.: Further into the Wild: Running Worldwide Trials of Mobile Systems. Pervasive Computing, Vol. 6030. 210-227 (2010)
21. McMillan, D., Morrison, A., Chalmers, M. Comparison of Distribution Channels for Large-Scale Deployments of iOS Applications, IJMHCI 3(4), 1-17 (2011)
22. Morrison. A., Reeves. S., McMillan, D., Chalmers M. Experiences of Mass Participation in Ubicomp Research. Research In The Large Workshop, ACM International Conference Ubiquitous Computing (2010).
23. Oliver, E. A survey of platforms for mobile networks research. SIGMOBILE (2009)
24. O'Shea, T., Lamming, M., Chalmers, M., Graube, N., Wellner, P. and Wiginton, G,.: Expectations and Perceptions of Ubiquitous Computing: Experiments with BirdDog, a Prototype Person Locator, Proc. BCS/IEE Conf on IT and People (1991)
25. Rogers, Y., Connelly, K., Tedesco, L., Hazlewood, W., Kurtz, A., Hall, R., Hursey, J., Toscos, T.: Why it's worth the hassle: the value of in-situ studies when designing Ubicomp. International conference on Ubiquitous computing. Springer-Verlag, 336-35 (2007)
26. Rosenthal, R. Experimenter effects in behavioral research. New York, Appleton-Century-Crofts, (1966)
27. Schleicher, R., Shirazi, A. S., Rohs, M., Kratz, S., & Schmidt, A. WorldCupinion Experiences with an Android App for Real-Time Opinion Sharing During Soccer World Cup Games. *IJMHCI, 3*(4), 18-35 (2011)
28. Strøm, G., Interaction Design for Countries with a Traditional Culture: A Comparative Study of Income Levels and Cultural Values. People And Computers XIX — The Bigger Picture, 2, 301-316 (2006)
29. Sturges, J. and Hanrahan,K.: Comparing Telephone and Face-to-Face Qualitative Interviewing: a Research Note. Qualitative Research April 4: 107-118 (2004)
30. Want, R., Hopper, A., Falcão, V. and Gibbons, J.:The active badge location system. ACM Trans. Inf. Syst. 10 (1992)

"Yours is Better!" Participant Response Bias in HCI

Nicola Dell† Vidya Vaidyanathan‡ Indrani Medhi§ Edward Cutrell§ William Thies§

†University of Washington
nixdell@cs.washington.edu

‡San Jose State University
vidya.vn@gmail.com

§Microsoft Research India
{indranim,cutrell,thies}@microsoft.com

ABSTRACT

Although HCI researchers and practitioners frequently work with groups of people that differ significantly from themselves, little attention has been paid to the effects these differences have on the evaluation of HCI systems. Via 450 interviews in Bangalore, India, we measure participant response bias due to interviewer demand characteristics and the role of social and demographic factors in influencing that bias. We find that respondents are about 2.5x more likely to prefer a technological artifact they believe to be developed by the interviewer, even when the alternative is identical. When the interviewer is a foreign researcher requiring a translator, the bias towards the interviewer's artifact increases to 5x. In fact, the interviewer's artifact is preferred even when it is degraded to be obviously inferior to the alternative. We conclude that participant response bias should receive more attention within the CHI community, especially when designing for underprivileged populations.

Author Keywords

HCI4D; ICTD; demand characteristics; interviewer effects; bias; culture; social status; methods

ACM Classification Keywords

H5.m. Information Interfaces and Presentation (e.g., HCI): Miscellaneous;

General Terms

Design, Human Factors

INTRODUCTION

The rapid proliferation of technological devices throughout the world has allowed a diverse range of previously unreached user groups to gain access to digital technology. The discipline of human-computer interaction (HCI) has embraced the study of these diverse user groups and HCI researchers have proposed a variety of methodologies targeting their specific needs. For example, a growing number of researchers are investigating the ways in which disabled people interact with computer systems [15]; researchers in child-computer interaction explore how computer systems are used by children, particularly in the context of education [24]; cross-cultural HCI looks at what happens when designers and users come from different cultural backgrounds [12] and the relatively new field of human-computer interaction for development (HCI4D) looks at the relationship between humans and technology in the context of international development [1]. Although the methods and objectives of these research domains may vary significantly, they share the characteristic that there are increasingly large differences between the investigators and the people under investigation. These differences may stem from variations in ethnicity, education, age, income and other sociodemographic characteristics.

Figure 1. Interviewing an auto rickshaw driver in Bangalore, India. When shown two technologies by a foreign interviewer (with translator), rickshaw drivers preferred the one they believed to be developed by the interviewer, even when it was obviously inferior.

In this paper, we discuss the increasingly common situation in which the investigators have higher social status and social power than the people they investigate. An increasing amount of anecdotal evidence [1] [18] suggests that in such situations, participants may be particularly susceptible to a type of response bias known as *demand characteristics*. Demand characteristics refer to aspects of a study that may convey the investigator's hypothesis to participants who then adjust their behavior in relation to what they perceive to be the investigator's expectations [22]. Demand characteristics are an important consideration in any research that involves

Permission to make digital or hard copies of all or part of this work for personal or classroom use is granted without fee provided that copies are not made or distributed for profit or commercial advantage and that copies bear this notice and the full citation on the first page. To copy otherwise, or republish, to post on servers or to redistribute to lists, requires prior specific permission and/or a fee.
CHI'12, May 5–10, 2012, Austin, Texas, USA.
Copyright 2012 ACM 978-1-4503-1015-4/12/05...$10.00.

human participants and may have a large effect on the study of humans and computer systems.

Although the psychology community acknowledges the effects of demand characteristics, there has been little examination of their effects on the design and evaluation of HCI systems. Qualitative research presented by Brown et al. highlights some of the ways that participants may alter their usage of a system to fit the investigators' expectations [5], but there is a lack of research in HCI that quantifies the extent to which demand characteristics may affect participant behavior. As a result, the significance of the response bias that may result from investigator demand characteristics in HCI remains unknown. In addition, there is a scarcity of research that explores how the social and demographic profiles of investigators and participants influence the ways in which participants respond to demand characteristics.

This paper presents a quantitative analysis of demand characteristics in an HCI setting. As shown in Figure 1, we focus on the developing-world context, in which there are frequently large differences between researchers and participants, and investigate the impact of varying social and demographic factors on the observed effects. For our experiments, we recruited a total of 450 male participants from two distinct population groups in Bangalore, India, and employed two different interviewers to record participant preferences as they interacted with technological devices.

Our work makes four core contributions to the CHI community. First, we survey existing literature to bring demand characteristics and their known effects to the attention of HCI researchers. Second, we show that if participants believe that a particular technological artifact is favored by the interviewer, their responses are biased to favor it as well. Third, we demonstrate that if the interviewer is a foreign researcher who requires a translator, responses are even more biased towards the technology favored by the interviewer. Finally, we show that for a foreign interviewer with translator, participants report a preference for an obviously inferior technology. Our intention is to sensitize researchers regarding the critical and under-appreciated role of demand characteristics, especially when interacting with underprivileged populations.

BACKGROUND AND RELATED WORK

Before discussing in detail the nature of demand characteristics, it is important to note that this is only one of several biases that merit attention in studies with human participants. Other biases include social desirability bias, which occurs when a participant tends to respond in ways that make her look good [23] [25] and evaluator bias, which occurs when the results of a study vary depending on the evaluator analyzing the experimental data [13]. There are also a variety of biases that may be attributed to participant survey methodologies, such as acquiescing or extreme responding [23].

We focus on three categories of related research. First, we draw on psychology literature to discuss the nature of demand characteristics and their effects as well as work that focuses on social influence. Then, we examine several public health studies that look at participant response bias resulting from interviewer characteristics. Finally, we discuss relevant work within the HCI and HCI4D communities.

Psychology

Demand characteristics were first defined by psychologist Martin Orne in 1959 as "the scuttlebutt about the experiment, its setting, implicit and explicit instructions, the person of the experimenter, subtle cues provided by him, and, of particular importance, the experimental procedure itself. All of these cues are interpreted in the light of the subject's past learning and experience" [22]. In a series of psychological experiments performed with undergraduates, experimenters found that participants would willingly perform almost any task, regardless of how meaningless, boring or uncomfortable it was, since they had knowingly and willingly placed themselves under the control of the experimenter [20]. In addition, participants in an experiment often share with the experimenter the hope that the study will be successful [22]. Frequently, a participant will want to ensure that she makes a useful contribution to the study and so will strive to be a 'good' participant and provide the experimenter with the 'right' results. Alternatively, a participant may resent the experimenter and actively work to disprove the hypothesis. In either case, a participant should not be viewed merely as a passive responder, but rather as an active agent with a real stake in the outcome of the study.

Although researchers have acknowledged that there may be a connection between demand characteristics and the tendency for participants to respond in ways confirming the experimenter's hypothesis, few have designed studies specifically to quantify this effect. One notable exception is a 2008 study by Nichols and Maner in the US that investigated the extent to which possessing knowledge of the study's hypothesis affected participant behavior [21]. The findings suggest that demand characteristics may make experimental effects appear more substantial than they actually are.

Demand characteristics cannot be eliminated from any study. In the absence of obvious demand characteristics, participants will guess the experimental hypothesis and alter their behavior accordingly [22]. Thus, instead of trying to eliminate demand characteristics, it is better to take them into account, study their effect, and manipulate them if necessary. Psychologists have proposed several techniques to disguise the purpose of the study or detect participants that guess the real hypothesis. These techniques include using the post-experimental inquiry [26], non-deceptive obfuscation [31] and a so-called red herring technique [17]. Nevertheless, few studies have directly examined the effects of demand characteristics or sought to identify factors that may increase or decrease the likelihood that participants' succumb to demand characteristics [21]. Additionally, different participant populations are likely to respond to demand characteristics in different ways, and it is important to study under what circumstances, in what kind of experimental contexts, and with what kind of participant populations, demand characteristics become significant in determining participant behavior [22].

However, most research investigating demand characteristics has been performed with undergraduates in the United States. To the best of our knowledge, no psychology experiments have specifically investigated the extent to which demand characteristics might affect studies performed in developing countries or with disadvantaged communities.

A number of psychological studies examine the influence of social status on decision-making and social conformity. Strodtbeck and Lipinski [27] found that jury members of higher socioeconomic status were more likely to be elected as jury foremen than members of lower socioeconomic status. Kirchler and Davis [16] studied the effects of status differences on group consensus and found that participants of higher status changed their individual opinions and preferences less often than those of lower status. Finally, Asch [2] performed experiments to study the social and personal conditions that cause participants to resist or to yield to group pressures, and found that participants conformed with answers given by other people in the group even though the answers chosen were objectively and noticeably wrong.

Public Health

Public health programs frequently define their target populations by ethnicity, gender, age and other sociodemographic characteristics, and there are several relevant studies exploring how interviewer characteristics might affect public health data. Davis et al. review studies in the US that show race, ethnicity and gender effects [8]. In this context, response bias appears to be most likely to occur when survey items query attitudes about sociodemographic characteristics or respondents' engagement in sensitive behaviors [14] [30].

Several other studies analyze public health survey data in developing countries. Bignami-Van Assche et al. examined data collected by local interviewers in Kenya and Malawi and conclude that interviewer gender may affect participant responses to sensitive questions [4]. Weinreb found that respondents in Kenya admitted telling untruths to stranger interviewers because the interviewers were not known by the community and their motives were therefore suspect [29]. Bernhart et al. found that the tendency of respondents to withhold critical comment hampered the collection of patient satisfaction data by government workers in health centers in Indonesia [3]. The paper suggests that more useful information might be obtained by asking participants about events and behaviors, rather than for their opinions.

HCI and HCI4D

Given the importance of usability studies in HCI, it is surprising that there has been so little attention paid to the effects that demand characteristics may have on their reliability. In both field trials and laboratory testing, users are frequently aware of the researcher's role in the study and the hypotheses under investigation. Although we acknowledge that it might be impossible to hide a study's true purpose, participant comments and suggestions are frequently taken at face value and the potential for participant response bias is ignored. A notable exception is the field of child computer interaction in which papers stress that even where there is no deliberate intervention the interviewer has an effect [24].

We found only one study that specifically addresses demand characteristics in HCI. In a 'trial of trials' Brown et al. found that participants changed their system usage partly to give researchers 'good' data [5]. The authors argue that demand characteristics are a part of what makes field trials possible and may be exploited to encourage participant usage. The paper also suggests that the need for researchers to present their systems as successful is problematic, and that it would be better to postpone the evaluation of technologies until they can be better understood by users. While our findings are aligned with Brown et al., we go beyond qualitative observations and contribute a rigorous measurement of the influence of demand characteristics in an HCI setting.

There is a growing body of work that explores the role of culture in HCI. Most of this work addresses the design of global interfaces that can accommodate users' cultural differences [9] [10]. One particularly relevant study by Vatrapu et al. examines the effects of culture in structured interviews in the US [28]. Two groups of Indian graduate students were asked to evaluate a website, and the group with an Indian interviewer provided more feedback and identified more culturally sensitive materials than the group with a US interviewer. While this study is similar to ours at a high level, there are a number of key differences. First, in our study participants interact with two technological artifacts rather than a single website. Since we know the full extent of the differences between the artifacts, we are able to compare participant responses between different interviewers as well as in relation to ground truth information. Second, in the study by Vatrapu et al., the differences between the two participant groups relate mainly to the identification of culturally sensitive materials. In contrast, our experiments relate to purely technological artifacts. Finally, their study involved 16 students while we interview 450 participants.

There are also a number of papers that discuss the role of culture in the developing world. Irani mentions that cultural differences between usability evaluators and participants can affect evaluation outcomes [12]. Ho et al. find that the hierarchical structure of some societies causes users to withhold criticism from researchers [11]. Chavan encourages participants to submit critical feedback by situating user studies within dramatic storylines [6].

The relatively new subfield of HCI4D targets the design and evaluation of systems that promote international development. Several recent papers anecdotally mention that foreign researchers may affect the results of HCI4D studies. Anokwa et al. had difficulty eliciting negative feedback from users and discuss the importance of gathering data from multiple sources [1]. Ledlie discusses how projects can be hampered by a lack of cultural insight and suggests methods for obtaining critical feedback from participants [18]. Table 1 summarizes the papers discussed in this section and highlights the scarcity of research that quantifies participant response bias due to demand characteristics in an HCI setting. Our paper targets this gap, providing rigorous (and sobering!) experi-

	Psychology	Public Health	HCI
Qualitative and/or Anecdotal	Orne '62 Sawyer '75 Laney '08 Zizzo '08	Williams '68 Johnson '94 Bernhart '99 Weinreb '06 Davis '10	Read '05 Chavan '05 Vatrapu '06 Anokwa '09 Ho '09 Irani '10 Ledlie '10 Brown '11
Quantitative	Milgram '63 Rosnow '73 Sawyer '75 Laney '08 Nichols '08	Williams '68 Johnson '94 Bernhart '99 Bignami-Van Assche '03 Weinreb '06	Vatrapu '06

Table 1. Summary of related research on participant response bias. We target the highlighted scarcity of quantitative research exploring participant response bias due to demand characteristics in HCI.

	Rickshaw Drivers	Univ. Students
Experiment 1: Identical Videos		
Foreign Interviewer†	50	50
Local Interviewer	50	50
Experiment 2: Degraded Video		
Without Association‡	50	50
Foreign Interviewer†	50	50
Local Interviewer	50	0*

† The foreign interviewer interacted with rickshaw drivers with the aid of a translator.

‡ This condition represented a baseline that minimized demand characteristics by removing phrases from the script (in **bold**) that associated one video to the interviewer.

* Because the results obtained from Experiment 1 showed no significant differences between the foreign and local interviewers with university students, we performed this experiment with only one of the interviewers.

Table 2. Number of people interviewed for each experimental condition.

mental data to guide the design of future studies and to help interpret studies that have already been completed.

EXPERIMENTAL DESIGN

Frequently, the aim of a research project in HCI is to introduce a new technological artifact into a target community, explore the design issues associated with the new technology, and evaluate the potential for the technology to impact the community. The nature of HCI research often requires researchers to spend considerable time in the field interacting with users. However, in many cases, researchers are not members of the target community and may differ from users in ethnicity, language, culture and socioeconomic status. As discussed in the previous section, researcher demand characteristics have the potential to impact the responses obtained from users, and we wanted to quantify this effect. Specifically, we formulated the following hypotheses:

H.1 If participants believe that the interviewer favors a technology, their responses will be biased to favor it as well.

H.2 If the interviewer is a foreign researcher requiring a translator, participants' responses will be even more biased towards the technology favored by the interviewer.

H.3 Participants will express a preference for an obviously inferior technology if they believe it is favored by the interviewer.

To test our hypotheses, we recruited a total of 450 participants and conducted a field study in Bangalore, India that comprised two main experiments. In Experiment 1, which was designed to test H.1 and H.2, participants were shown an identical video clip on each of two identical smartphones, one after the other. We purposely introduced demand characteristics by having the interviewer clearly associate herself to one of the phones by telling participants that she was working to improve the video player on that phone. Within this scenario we investigated if changing the social and demographic profiles of the interviewers and the participants affected the extent to which participants succumbed to demand characteristics. To do this, interviews were conducted with two interviewers (a foreign, Caucasian interviewer and a local, Indian interviewer) and two sets of participants (auto rickshaw drivers and university students).

Experiment 2 tested H.1, H.2 and H.3 by obviously degrading one of the video clips and seeing if participants stated a preference for the degraded video clip when it was associated with the interviewer. For quick reference, Table 2 summarizes all the experimental conditions that we tested. The rest of this section discusses the general experimental procedure and the characteristics of the different interviewers and participant populations. In subsequent sections we discuss additional details and variations in procedures that were specific to each experimental condition.

Experimental Procedure

Data collection was performed over a period of 5 weeks in July and August 2011. Our experiments utilized a between subjects design with a sample size of 50 for each experimental condition. Individual participant interviews were conducted from Monday to Saturday, between 12pm and 4pm, with each interview lasting between two and three minutes. We employed the same general interview procedure across all experimental conditions. In advance of the interviews, we uploaded a 21 second video clip of a popular local music video to each of two identical Windows smartphones. The video clip had a resolution of 640 x 480 pixels per frame and 30 frames per second. The phones were set to use exactly the same video player, as well as identical volume and brightness levels. Individual interviews were administered by reading the following script to participants (the exact phrases introducing demand characteristics are highlighted in bold):

"Thank you for participating in my experiment. I am a computer science researcher and I'm trying to improve video players on mobile phones. I want you to watch a short video on these two phones and tell me which one looks better, or if they look the same. The same video will play on both phones, **but this phone uses my new player** *[indicate phone]. Please tell me your honest opinion and please concentrate because I will play each video only once. Do you have any questions? Ok, watch this one first.* **This one uses my new player** *[play video]. Now watch this one [play video]. Which one do you think looks better or do they look the same? Why? Thanks very much!"*

In each experimental condition, the order in which the video associated to the interviewer was played was randomized to prevent any bias due to ordering effects. The interviewer recorded participant responses and comments on paper for later analysis and aggregation. Responses were coded into three distinct classes: those that favored the video associated with the interviewer, those that favored the video not associated with the interviewer, and those that said the two videos looked the same. We included the option of "same" because we expected that it would provide more nuanced data than a forced-choice paradigm in which participants were required to state a preference for one video. However, this paper focuses on responses that preferred one video to the other, and leaves detailed analysis of "same" responses for future work.

Interviewers

Since we wanted to vary the social status of the interviewers relative to the participants, we conducted interviews using two different female, graduate student interviewers: a 29-year-old, English-speaking Caucasian, referred to from now on as the foreign interviewer, and a 33-year-old, Kannada- and English-speaking Indian referred to from now on as the local interviewer. The local interviewer grew up in the same neighborhood in Bangalore in which the interviews were conducted. As a result, in addition to speaking the local language, she was identifiable as a local member of the community through her dress and knowledge of the customs of the area. In contrast, the foreign interviewer was not born in India, and had spent approximately one month in Bangalore at the time that the experiments were performed. Thus, she was distinguishable as an outsider by her ethnicity, language, dress and unfamiliarity with the local customs.

Since participants in one of the groups (auto rickshaw drivers) spoke limited English, the foreign interviewer required a translator to interact with them. For consistency, we utilized the local interviewer as the translator. The need for a translator necessarily required the presence of two interviewers for the interactions with the foreign interviewer but only one for the interactions with the local interviewer. It is well known that the presence of multiple interviewers may have an affect on participant conformity [2]. However, since the presence of a translator is a common occurrence in many HCI4D projects, and since part of our goal is to emulate a realistic HCI4D setting, any response bias resulting from the presence of two interviewers, rather than a single interviewer, would also be a factor in HCI4D projects and as such is part of the effect that we are trying to measure.

The social status of local and foreign interviewers differed in the eyes of low-income individuals in India. Although foreigners are perceived differently in different countries, in India Caucasians are usually perceived as having a high social status. This owes partly to India's history as a colony under British rule. Also, independent of its past, Caucasian visitors are likely to have an education and income that is higher than the local mean, and are usually fluent in English, a language associated with prestige and opportunity. In addition, during interviews with rickshaw drivers, the presence of the translator further elevated the social status of the foreign interviewer.

Participants

Participants were recruited from two distinct social groups that we chose on the basis of availability and social status relative to the interviewers. The first group consisted of male university students from the Indian Institute of Science (IISc), an elite scientific graduate institute in India. We restricted participation to male students since the other participant population (rickshaw drivers) is composed of males. Since both of the interviewers were graduate students, the social status of this population was relatively well-matched to that of the interviewers. In addition, all IISc students speak English and typically have experience using and understanding sophisticated technology. We recruited a total of 200 male university students aged 19 to 41 (M=25 years, SD=3.8 years). Recruitment was performed on campus at IISc by approaching individuals and asking them to participate in a research project. Participants that agreed were then interviewed immediately. Individual interviews were done in English by either the foreign interviewer or the local interviewer. Participants were not compensated, other than being thanked for their time.

The second participant group consisted of local auto rickshaw drivers. Auto rickshaws are 3-wheeled vehicles that provide cheap transportation in India. In Bangalore, rickshaw drivers are men who usually have some high-school education and a daily income of between US $5 and $10. Rickshaw drivers typically possess cheap mobile phones but do not have extensive experience with sophisticated technology. As a result, the socio-demographic difference between the rickshaw drivers and the interviewers was greater than it was between the university students and the interviewers. Most rickshaw drivers in Bangalore speak Kannada, the local language in the Indian state of Karnataka.

All rickshaw drivers were recruited by the local interviewer on a single street in Bangalore. The local interviewer stood on the side of the road and hailed passing auto rickshaws. Rickshaw drivers that stopped were then invited to participate in the experiment. Depending on the condition, the foreign interviewer would step up at this point or the local interviewer

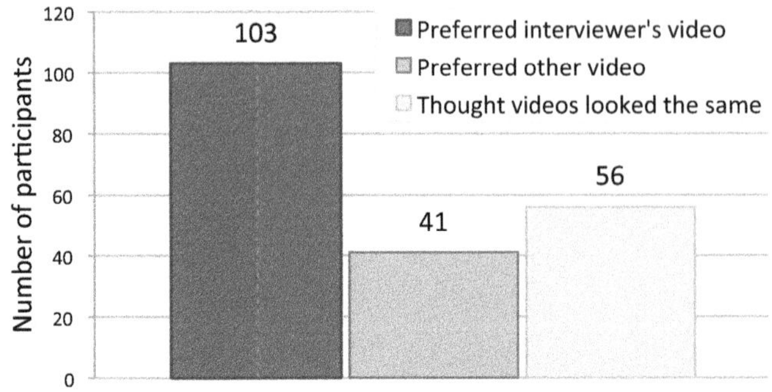

Figure 2. Results of Experiment 1: Preferences stated by participants when shown identical video clips (combined across all conditions).

would begin the experiment. In both cases, the rickshaw driver remained seated in the vehicle. We simplified the interview script slightly to make it easier for rickshaw drivers to understand. Specifically, in the second sentence of the script, the phrase *"I am a computer science researcher"* was changed to *"I am a computer scientist"*. Other than this small change, the interview script was identical to that used for the university students. A total of 250 male rickshaw drivers aged 19 to 72 (*M*=37 years, *SD*=11.2 years) were interviewed. Participants were compensated for their time with a small gift worth about \$1. However, a large number of participants refused to accept compensation, and as a result we ceased compensation for the rickshaw drivers in Experiment 2.

EXPERIMENT 1: RESPONSE TO IDENTICAL VIDEOS

Experiment 1 recorded participants' preferences when shown an identical video clip on each of two identical smartphones, with the interviewer associating herself to one of the video clips as described in the previous section. The experiment utilized a 2x2 factorial design in which we varied both the interviewer (foreign and local) and the participants (rickshaw drivers and university students).

The results of the experiment are summarized in Figure 2, which shows participant responses aggregated across all conditions. As expected, participants who expressed a preference for either video were more likely to choose the video associated with the interviewer. For this paper, we define the *response bias* as the ratio between the number of participants who preferred the interviewer's video to the number of participants who preferred the other video. Averaging across all conditions, the response bias was 2.5x.

Detailed results for each condition appear in Figure 3. While there was a response bias in all cases, the magnitude of the bias varied with the interviewer and participant group. The largest bias occurred when the foreign researcher interviewed rickshaw drivers: there was a 5x bias in favor of the interviewer's video (Figure 3a). The smallest bias, 1.7x, occurred in the opposite configuration, when the local researcher interviewed university students (Figure 3d). The other conditions showed intermediate response biases of 2.3x with the foreign interviewer and university students (Figure 3b) and 2.1x with the local interviewer and rickshaw drivers (Figure 3c).

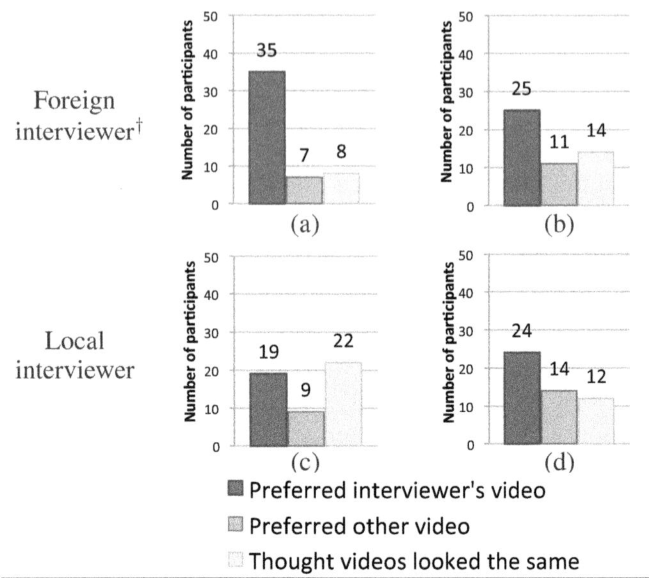

† The foreign interviewer interacted with rickshaw drivers with the aid of a translator.

Figure 3. Participants' responses when shown two identical videos.

Testing H.1: Presence of Response Bias

To evaluate Hypothesis 1, we compare to the null hypothesis that interviewer association does not impact participant responses, i.e., that the same number of people choose the interviewer's video as the other video, and the response bias is 1. The null hypothesis is strongly rejected for the aggregate responses, as reflected in Figure 2 ($\chi^2(1, n = 144) = 26.7, p < 0.001$). At a finer granularity, the bias is also significant in the case of the foreign interviewer, interacting either with rickshaw drivers ($\chi^2(1, n = 44) = 18.7, p < 0.001$) or university students ($\chi^2(1, n = 36) = 5.4, p = 0.02$). The bias observed with the local interviewer was borderline-significant in the case of rickshaw drivers ($\chi^2(1, n = 28) = 3.6, p = 0.06$) and not significant in the case of university students ($\chi^2(1, n = 38) = 2.6, p = 0.10$). However, pooling across both participant groups does reveal a significant bias in response to the local interviewer ($\chi^2(1, n = 66) = 6.1, p = 0.01$).

Testing H.2: Impact of Foreign Interviewer

Hypothesis 2 states that the response bias increases when the interviewer is a foreign researcher requiring a translator. The only condition satisfying this criterion is that of the foreign interviewer with rickshaw drivers. Thus, to test this hypothesis, we compare the response bias observed with the foreign interviewer and rickshaw drivers to conditions with a different interviewer (local instead of foreign) or different participants (university students instead of rickshaw drivers).

Our results suggest a trend that is consistent with the hypothesis: the bias between foreign interviewer and rickshaw drivers is 5x (Figure 3a), but it decreases to 2.1x when replacing the foreign interviewer with a local one

Figure 4. A single frame from the high quality video clip (left) and the low quality, degraded video clip (right).

(Figure 3c), or to 2.3x when replacing rickshaw drivers with university students (Figure 3b). To evaluate the significance of this trend, we utilize 2x2 contingency tables, in which the variables are video chosen (*Interviewer's, Other*) and, depending on the test, interviewer (*Foreign, Local*) or participant (*Rickshaw Driver, University Student*). For Experiment 1, we do not find a significant relationship between the video chosen and the interviewer ($\chi^2(1, n = 70) = 2.28, p = 0.13$) or the participant group ($\chi^2(1, n = 78) = 2.11, p = 0.15$)). However, this effect is significant in Experiment 2, as described in the next section.

EXPERIMENT 2: RESPONSE TO A DEGRADED VIDEO

We designed Experiment 2 to measure the extent of participant response bias in the face of an obviously poor technological artifact. To do this, rather than showing participants identical video clips, we made one of the video clips noticeably worse than the other and had the interviewer associate herself to the degraded clip. Specifically, the resolution of one of the clips was decreased from 640 x 480 to 120 x 90 pixels per frame (the media player scaled both videos to the full screen width of 800 x 480.) Additionally, the video frame rate was halved, from 30 to 15 frames per second. The audio, brightness, content and length of the video clips remained unchanged. Sample video frames from the original, high-quality video clip and the degraded, low-quality clip are shown in Figure 4. For our experiments, we loaded the low-quality video clip on one smartphone and the high-quality clip on the other.

To ensure that the video clip had been sufficiently degraded so as to be noticeably different from the original, high-quality clip, we performed an experiment in which participants were shown the two video clips one after the other without the interviewer associating herself to either clip. To achieve this, we modified the interview script by removing the phrases from the script (emphasized in **bold**) that associated the video to the interviewer. The rest of the interview script remained unchanged. The order in which the low-quality clip was played was randomized to avoid order effects.

Following this, interviews were conducted in which the interviewer associated herself to the low-quality clip. The experimental procedure and interview script used were identical to those described for Experiment 1. As in Experiment 1, interviews were conducted for two sets of interviewers (foreign and local) and two sets of participants (rickshaw drivers and university students). However, we did not evaluate the condition in which the local researcher interviews university students. Since the results obtained from Experiment 1 showed no significant differences between the foreign interviewer and the local interviewer with the university students, we felt that performing this experiment with only one of the interviewers was sufficient.

Overview of Results

The results of Experiment 2 appear in Figure 5. When the two videos were presented without the interviewer associating to either video, university students (Figure 5b) overwhelmingly chose the high-quality clip (about 95%). Rickshaw drivers usually chose the high-quality clip (about 75%), though they said they looked the same about 15% of the time (Figure 5a).

When the interviewer associated herself to the degraded video, the degree of response bias varied by participant group. In the case of university students (Figure 5d), most participants still selected the high-quality clip (about 75%). However, almost 20% of participants chose the low-quality (associated) clip, an order of magnitude more than when it was unassociated.

The response bias is more dramatic in the case of rickshaw drivers. When the interviewer was associated with the low-quality clip (collapsing across foreign and local interviewers), rickshaw drivers were almost as likely to choose the interviewer's (low-quality) clip as the other (high-quality) clip, 45% and 48%, respectively. However, as in Experiment 1, there was a dramatic difference between how participants responded to the local interviewer alone compared to the foreign interviewer with local translator. When the low-quality clip was associated with the local interviewer alone, participants were 4.5 times more likely to select it than when it was unassociated (Figure 5e), though they still usually preferred the high-quality video (36% low-quality vs. 58% high-quality). But when the low-quality video was associated with the foreign interviewer (Figure 5c), this ratio flipped:

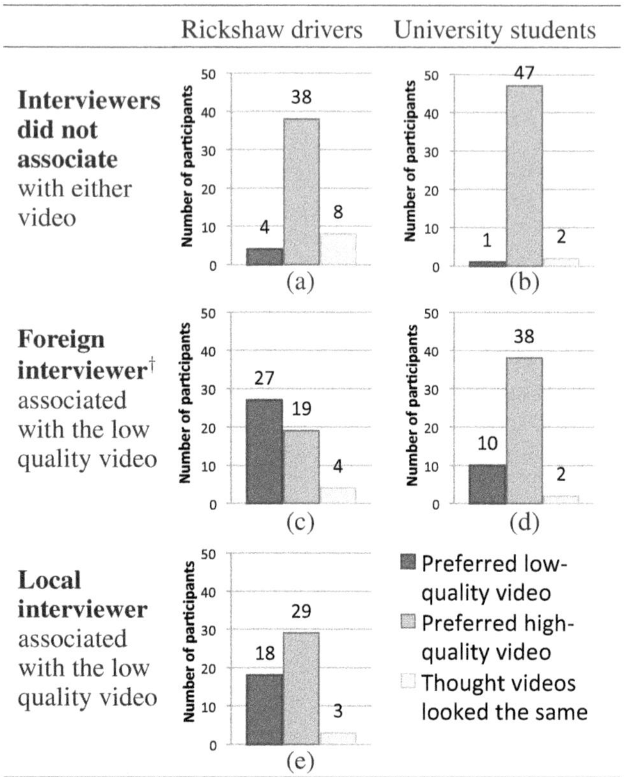

† The foreign interviewer interacted with rickshaw drivers with the aid of a translator.

* Because the results obtained from Experiment 1 showed no significant differences between the foreign and local interviewers with university students, we performed this experiment with only one of the interviewers.

Figure 5. Participants' responses with the degraded video.

participants were even *more* likely to choose the low-quality video over the high-quality one (54% vs. 38% respectively).

This is an important finding since in a normal HCI4D scenario, it is likely that only one of the two interviewers would be utilized, yet they lead to opposite conclusions. Responses submitted to the foreign interviewer suggest that the low-quality video is preferred, but responses submitted to the local interviewer suggest that the high-quality video is preferred! While the trial without association eliminates the bias, in practice it is rarely possible to remove all elements of association in evaluating a new system. Thus the choice of interviewer determines the outcome of the experiment.

Testing H.1: Presence of Response Bias

Like Experiment 1, we define response bias in terms of the number of participants that preferred one video to the other. However, because the videos are no longer identical, the bias is measured relative to the preferences stated without interviewer association. For a given interviewer and participant group, we test for response bias using a 2x2 contingency table in which the variables are video chosen (*Interviewer's, Other*) and interviewer association (*Foreign or Local Association, Without Association*). Since some of the counts in the table are small, we use Fisher's exact test to improve upon the accuracy of the chi-squared test. We found a significant relationship between video chosen and interviewer association across all conditions: foreign interviewers with rickshaw drivers ($p < 0.001$), foreign interviewers with university students ($p = 0.008$), and local interviewers with rickshaw drivers ($p = 0.003$).

Testing H.2: Impact of Foreign Interviewer

To test for the impact of the foreign researcher (with translator) on the response bias, we compare the responses of rickshaw drivers across the local and foreign interviewers. (Unlike Experiment 1, we do not compare the results of the foreign interviewer across different participant groups, because these groups demonstrated different preferences even without interviewer association.) We utilize a 2x2 contingency table, in which the variables are video chosen (*Interviewer's, Other*) and interviewer (*Foreign, Local*). We find that the interviewer has a significant association with the video chosen, and hence with the response bias ($\chi^2(1, n = 93) = 3.87, p = 0.049$, Cramér's $V = 0.288$).

Testing H.3: Preference for Inferior Technology

Hypothesis 3 states that participants may express a preference for an inferior technology if they believe it is favored by the interviewer. This hypothesis is consistent with our results: in the case of foreign interviewers with rickshaw drivers the participants select the low-quality video 54% of the time (selecting the high-quality video 38%, and neither video 8% of the time). While the preference for the low-quality video over the high-quality video is not statistically significant ($\chi^2(1, n = 46) = 1.39, p = 0.24$), it is alarming that the foreign interviewer is unable to confirm the superior technology in this scenario. Furthermore, even the local interviewer would be unable to reject the hypothesis that the videos were of equal quality ($\chi^2(1, n = 47) = 2.57, p = 0.11$), as only 58% of rickshaw drivers responded with a preference for the high-quality video (versus 36% for the low-quality video, and 6% saying same).

DISCUSSION

Explaining Participant Response Bias

To further understand why participants responded in the ways that they did, we collected and analyzed comments that explained their preferences. Many comments were surprisingly detailed and thoughtful. After watching two identical video clips, one university student told us, *"You are having a better frame rate, which is reducing the blur affect that is there in the other player. The resolution is very clear, so I think if you improve a little bit more, then it will be a great player"*. A large proportion of participants also believed that they saw a clear difference between the two video clips: *"I feel that in the newer version which you have coded, whenever there was a significant color contrast between two parts of an image, your version was somewhat smoother and less pixelated"*. The rickshaw driver participants also provided convincing reasoning to support their choices: *"The quality of the background color and figures is too light in that player while the quality of the color and graphics is better in [your] one. Will [your] new player be introduced in the market?"* Additionally, several participants seemed anxious to give us a genuine answer: *"I've given you my honest opinion, so please don't be cross with me if it wasn't the right one"*. These comments suggest that participants did not just tell the interviewer the 'right' response while secretly thinking otherwise, but rather that participants seemed to genuinely believe the interviewer's artifact to be superior and identified convincing reasons to justify their choice. These findings have important implications for researchers and indicate that even detailed and convincing participant opinions cannot be taken at face value.

Recommendations

Our primary recommendation is that researchers pay more attention to the types of response bias that might result from working with any participant population and actively take steps to minimize this bias. To do this, it is important that interviewers dissociate themselves as much as possible from any particular design or solution. Our findings indicate that if participants are aware of the interviewer's personal stake in the outcome of the study, the results are more likely to be affected by demand characteristics. Additionally, collecting and reporting subjective information from participants as a primary method of evaluation is problematic and should be avoided. We have shown that even though participant comments might be detailed, well thought out and delivered with conviction, they do not necessarily reflect the merit of the solutions at hand. As far as possible, the focus of participant interviews and feedback should be on obtaining factual, rather than subjective, information [3]. Using implicit metrics [7] or triangulation [19] to validate the data collected could further increase confidence in the results of the study.

Our findings also suggest that minimizing the differences between the interviewer and the participants could help to mitigate the response bias resulting from interviewer demand characteristics. A large number of existing of HCI4D research papers extol the practice of 'field work' in which researchers spend time with potential users in those circumstances in which the technology might take hold [1] [18]. While we do not dispute the value of field work or the benefits of establishing rapport with users, we stress that care must be taken to understand the complications and error that may result from the influence of researchers working in communities that are vastly different from their own.

Generalization and Limitations

Our experiments focus on the ways in which social and demographic factors may affect participant response bias due to demand characteristics. However, this is only one aspect of demand characteristics, and there are undoubtedly many more that could play an influential role on the outcome of a study. For example, research suggests that gender might be an important factor that could influence participant responses [8]. However, in this study we have specifically avoided examining the extent to which gender may play a role in any bias observed. All of our participants were male and all of the interviewers were female. A separate study would be required to understand the ways in which response bias might be affected by participant and interviewer gender.

Additionally, social status and ethnicity are influential social characteristics in many cultures, but their exact effects are likely to vary from culture to culture. Our experience in India has been that Westerners are often afforded special or preferential treatment, but research performed in rural Kenya suggests that outsiders there may be treated with hostility and suspicion [29]. Furthermore, our experiments only deal with situations in which the social status of the interviewer is either the same as or higher than the participants. Further research is required to investigate the nature and magnitude of participant bias in other contexts.

The analysis in this paper focused on the case in which participants expressed a preference for one video or another, without paying much attention to the cases in which the videos were judged to be the same. The "same" responses contain valuable information and represent a fruitful opportunity for follow-up analysis. For example, in the case of the local interviewer and the rickshaw drivers, there is a strong preference for "same", which could be evidence of a partial response bias amongst participants who otherwise would have chosen the video that was not associated with the interviewer. More sophisticated analysis tools could quantify this effect.

Finally, the experiments presented in this paper have been conducted within a particular culture and city, and with two specific participant populations. Since we wanted to emulate a realistic HCI4D setting, one of the chosen participant populations required the presence of a local language translator for the interactions with the foreign interviewer. As a result, we are unable to determine whether the response bias we observed was caused primarily by the large difference in social status between the foreign interviewer and the rickshaw drivers, by the addition of a translator, or both. Further research is required to tease apart the extent to which these different factors individually influence participant responses.

CONCLUSIONS

As the field of HCI embraces the globalization of technology, researchers and practitioners are increasingly working with groups of people that differ significantly from themselves. This paper brings the notion of demand characteristics to the attention of the CHI community and explores the effects that they may have on participant responses. Via experiments with 450 participants in Bangalore, India, we showed that (1) if participants believe that a particular technological artifact is favored by the interviewer, their responses are biased to favor it as well, (2) the bias due to interviewer demand characteristics is exaggerated much further when the interviewer is a foreign researcher requiring a translator, and (3) in response to a foreign interviewer with a translator, participants of lower social status report a preference for an obviously inferior technology, which they otherwise do not prefer. Until now, the significance of demand characteristics in HCI has remained largely unexplored and undervalued. We have demonstrated that it is crucial for researchers and practitioners to pay more attention to the role of social status and the effects that demand characteristics may have in the design and analysis of studies involving human participants.

ACKNOWLEDGEMENTS

We would like to thank Sara Kiesler for going above and beyond the call of duty to improve this paper. We also want to acknowledge Mary Czerwinski, Jonathan Donner, Jonathan Grudin, Brandon Lucia, Anne Oeldorf-Hirsch, Nimmi Rangaswamy and all of our participants for their valuable contributions to this research.

REFERENCES

1. Anokwa, Y., Smyth, T., Ramachandran, D., Sherwani, J., Schwartzman, Y., Luk, R., Ho, M., Moraveji, N., and DeRenzi, B. Stories from the Field: Reflections on HCI4D Experiences. *ITID 5*, 4 (2009).
2. Asch, S. Effects of Group Pressure Upon the Modification and Distortion of Judgements. *In H. Guetzkow (ed.) Groups, Leadership, and Men* (1951).
3. Bernhart, M., Wiadnyana, I., Wihardjo, H., and Pohan, I. Patient Satisfaction in Developing Countries. *Social Science and Medicine 48* (1999).
4. Bignami-Van Assche, S., Reniers, G., and Weinreb, A. An Assessment of the KDICP and MDICP Data Quality. *Demographic Research S1*, 2 (2002).
5. Brown, B., Reeves, S., and Sherwood, S. Into the Wild: Challenges and Opportunities for Field Trial Methods. In *CHI* (2005).
6. Chavan, A. Another Culture, Another Method. In *CHI* (2005).
7. Czerwinski, M., Horvitz, E., and Cutrell, E. Subjective Duration Assessment: An Implicit Probe for Software Usability. In *IHM-HCI Conference* (2001).
8. Davis, R., Couper, M., Janz, N., Caldwell, C., and Resnicow, K. Interviewer Effects in Public Health Surveys. *Health Education Research 25*, 1 (2010).
9. Evers, V. Cross-Cultural Understanding of Metaphors in Interface Design. In *Proc. Cultural Attitudes towards Technology and Communication* (1998).
10. Evers, V., and Day, D. The Role of Culture in Interface Acceptance. In *INTERACT'97* (1997).
11. Ho, M., Smyth, T., Kam, M., and Dearden, A. Human-Computer Interaction for Development: The Past, Present, and Future. *ITID 5*, 4 (2009).
12. Irani, L. HCI on the Move: Methods, Culture, Values. In *CHI Extended Abstracts* (2010).
13. Jacobsen, N. The Evaluator Effect in Usability Studies: Problem Detection and Severity Judgments. In *Proc. of the Human Factors and Ergonomics Society 42nd Annual Meeting* (1998).
14. Johnson, T., and J, P. Interviewer Effects on Self-Reported Substance Use Among Homeless Persons. *Addict Behavior 19* (1994).
15. Kane, S., Wobbrock, J., and Ladner, R. Usable Gestures for Blind People: Understanding Preference and Performance. In *CHI* (2011).
16. Kirchler, E., and Davis, J. The Influence of Member Status Differences and Task Type on Group Consensus and Member Position Change. *Personality and Social Psychology 51*, 1 (1986).
17. Laney, C., Kaasa, S., Morris, E., Berkowitz, S., Bernstein, D., and Loftus, E. The Red Herring technique: A Methodological Response to the Problem of Demand Characteristics. *Psychological Research 72* (1962).
18. Ledlie, J. Huzzah for my Thing: Evaluating a Pilot of a Mobile Service in Kenya. *Qual Meets Quant, London, UK* (2010).
19. Mackay, W. Triangulation within and across HCI disciplines. *Human-Computer Interaction 13*, 3 (1998).
20. Milgram, S. Behavioral Study of Obedience. *Abnormal and Social Psychology 67*, 4 (1963).
21. Nichols, A., and Maner, J. The Good Subject Effect: Investigating Participant Demand Characteristics. *General Psychology 135* (2008).
22. Orne, M. On the Social Psychology of the Psychological Experiment: With Particular Reference to Demand Characteristics and their Implications. *American Psychologist 17* (1962).
23. Paulhus, D. Measurement and Control of Response Bias. *J. P. Robinson, P. R. Shaver and L. S. Wrightsman eds. Measures of personality and social psychological attitudes* (1991).
24. Read, J., and Fine, K. Using Survey Methods for Design and Evaluation in Child Computer Interaction. In *Workshop on Child Computer Interaction: Methodological Research at Interact* (2005).
25. Rosnow, R., Goodstadt, B., Suls, J., and Gitter, G. More on the social psychology of the experiment: When compliance turns to self-defense. *Personality and Social Psychology 27*, 3 (1973).
26. Sawyer, A. Detecting Demand Characteristics in Laboratory Experiments in Consumer Research: The Case of Repetition-Affect Research. *Advances in Consumer Research Volume 02, eds. Mary Jane Schlinger: Association for Consumer Research* (1975).
27. Strodtbeck, F., and Lipinski, R. Becoming First among Equals: Moral Considerations in Jury Foreman Selection. *Personality and Social Psychology 49*, 4 (1985).
28. Vatrapu, R., and Pérez-Quinones, M. Culture and Usability Evaluation: The Effects of Culture in Structured Interviews. *Usability Studies 1* (2006).
29. Weinreb, A. The Limitations of Stranger-Interviewers in Rural Kenya. *American Sociological Review 71* (2006).
30. Williams, J. Interviewer Role Performance: a Further Note on Bias in the Information Interview. *Public Opinion Quarterly 32* (1968).
31. Zizzo, D. Experimenter Demand Effects in Economic Experiments. Available at SSRN: http://ssrn.com/abstract=1163863 (last accessed 09/03/2011), 2008.

Digital Pen and Paper Practices in Observational Research

Nadir Weibel, Adam Fouse, Colleen Emmenegger, Whitney Friedman, Ed Hutchins, Jim Hollan
Distributed Cognition and Human-Computer Interaction Lab
Department of Cognitive Science, University of California, San Diego
9500 Gilman Dr., La Jolla, CA 92093-0515
{weibel, afouse, cemmenegger, wfriedman, ehutchins, hollan}@ucsd.edu

ABSTRACT

Researchers from many disciplines are taking advantage of increasingly inexpensive digital video to capture extensive records of human activity in real-world settings. The ability to record and share such data has created a critical moment in the practice and scope of behavioral research. While recent work [3, 5] is beginning to develop techniques for visualizing and interacting with integrated multimodal information collected during field research, navigating and analyzing these large datasets remains challenging and tools are especially needed to support the early stages of data exploration.

In this paper we describe digital pen and paper practices in observational research and their integration with ChronoViz [4], a tool for annotating, visualizing, and analyzing multimodal data. The goal is to better support researchers both in the field, while collecting data, and later in the lab, during analysis. We document the co-evolution of notetaking practices and system features as 28 participants used the tool during an 18-month deployment.

Author Keywords

Digital Ethnography; Paper-Digital Notes; Video Analysis; Interactive Navigation; Activity Visualization; Annotations

ACM Classification Keywords

H.1.2 User/Machine Systems: Human Factors;
H.5.3 Group and Organization Interfaces: Computer-supported cooperative work, Evaluation/methodology, Theory and methods

General Terms

Design; Experimentation; Human Factors

Permission to make digital or hard copies of all or part of this work for personal or classroom use is granted without fee provided that copies are not made or distributed for profit or commercial advantage and that copies bear this notice and the full citation on the first page. To copy otherwise, or republish, to post on servers or to redistribute to lists, requires prior specific permission and/or a fee.
CHI'12, May 5–10, 2012, Austin, Texas, USA.
Copyright 2012 ACM 978-1-4503-1015-4/12/05...$10.00.

INTRODUCTION

New digital devices and storage facilities are revolutionizing observational research and are now common components of data collection. Multiple HD digital video and still cameras, directional audio microphones, depth cameras, wearable eye-tracking devices, GPS or other mobile sensors, and digital pens are now typical tools for researchers in many disciplines. Data collection is being extended into real-world settings that have not typically been accessible. Just as availablity of audio tape recording supported the development of conversation analysis [14] and the ethnography of speaking [8], the advent of a range of inexpensive digital recording devices and sensors promises to have a fundamental impact on a broad range of scientific and engineering activities. The increasing availablity of this rich new data is important because to understand the dynamics of human and social activity, we must also understand the full context of those activities and this can only be accomplished by recording and analyzing data of real-world behavior. While such data are certainly needed, more data cannot be the whole answer, since many researchers already feel that they are drowning in data.

New computational algorithms promise to aid analysis but typically are available only after data have been selected, transcribed, and coded. For example, initial dataset navigation is typically cumbersome. When navigation and data selection are costly, data records chosen for analysis are often a haphazard sampling of the recorded data, few analyses are done, and researchers come to have a large investment in selected data segments. Each analysis may appear as an isolated case study and it can be difficult to know how common the observed phenomena may be. Larger patterns and contradictory cases can easily go unnoticed, potentially compromising the quality of science.

One focus of our work is therefore on developing and assembling tools and practices to speed and improve the early stages of annotation, navigation, visualization, and analysis. Raw data are usually coded and transcribed in a wide variety of ways, and coordinating multiple data sources and re-representations of the original events [7] is a challenging problem that typically requires manual alignment and management of the different data sources. Frequently researchers do not have the time or the necessary resources for this task.

Recent work [3, 4] addresses this issue by providing a tool, called ChronoViz, for interactive annotation, navigation, and visualization of multiple data streams to help researchers maintain a consolidated view of the whole data collection.

Even with better support for the management and integration of multimodal data, identifying important moments deserving of detailed analysis remains challenging. This often requires multiple views (and viewings) of the data, integration with field notes and insights from the researchers' experience, and discussion with other analysts. We think it is particularly important to facilitate these early stages of analysis and to do it in ways that integrate with current practices. For example, many researchers still rely heavily on paper-based documents and hand-written notes during analysis. This is largely because of the many affordances pen and paper still provide even in today's highly digitized work environments [15]. Paper often represents the only viable way to support the flexibility needed while collecting data and also continues to be an important resource throughout the analysis process.

We present an analysis of an 18-month deployment of a system for capturing paper-based notes in the field and its use by 28 researchers from multiple disciplines. We document how paper-digital tools influenced researchers' practice and shaped their analysis of multimodal data. This in turn informed design of new paper-digital capabilities and new navigation and visualization facilities for ChronoViz [19, 4].

PAPER-DIGITAL NOTES IN THE FIELD

In order to support current notetaking practices, we developed an integrated paper-digital workflow that allows field researchers to use Livescribe digital pens[1] to take notes. The system employs *ethnographer*$^{++}$ [19], a special software package installed on the digital pen that captures researchers' paper notes and automatically timestamps each pen stroke. The pen looks and functions as a normal pen but includes an infrared camera and a processor that captures and decodes a special dot-pattern[2] printed on paper to track pen tip movements in real-time. Livescribe pens and ethnographer^{++} work with any commercially available Livescribe notebook or with patterned paper printed with a standard color laser printer.

After taking notes the pen can be docked to a computer to download the notes. ChronoViz [4] exploits the recorded timestamps to integrate and align the downloaded notes with other data collected during the observation session (e.g. multiple videos, GPS data, still images, audio data, eye-tracking, etc.). Figure 1 shows an example of paper-based notes and recorded video collected during a flight-simulation session. A separate window (Fig. 1, right) shows the collected notes. Interacting with the time slider or playing the ChronoViz session will animate the notes by dynamically changing the note color from semi-transparent (notes taken after the current time point) to opaque (notes taken before the current time point). Additionally, when researchers select a time point in the video, notes taken at that time are highlighted. Similarly,

Figure 1. ChronoViz interface to access paper-based notes. On the left, a video frame of the observed flight simulation and annotations from paper notes. On the right, the digital representation of the paper notes in ChronoViz, and a digital pen used to access the notes from paper.

users can click on a particular note on the digital representation and the video will be positioned at the time that note was taken. While Livescribe pens can be used to take notes in the field, these digital pens do not support wireless real-time interaction with a computer. To directly interact with ChronoViz from the paper notes, Anoto DP-201 streaming pens can be connected to the computer over bluetooth and the paper notes can be used in the same way as their digital representation on screen to navigate the data (Fig. 1, right). More detail about the integrated paper-digital workflow can be found in [19].

Research Domains

This basic infrastructure for paper-digital notetaking was made available for 18 months (starting in February 2010) to 28 researchers in HCI, computer science, sociology, aviation human factors, cognitive science and animal cognition. In each case, we were *participant observers*. The research goal was to observe how researchers used the tools and how their integration modified their current work practices. We observed the use of ChronoViz, and in particular its digital notes capabilities, during the entire deployment of the system. Additionally, we conducted regular focus group discussions and brainstorming about the digital pen and paper capabilities of the system with researchers in all analyzed domains. We used grounded theory and performed affinity analysis to categorize both observational data and the collected material, and to analyze trends and patterns evolving from the different practices. In this section we describe three research domains. In the next section we analyze usage and describe the resulting practices.

Aviation Human Factors

A team of ten researchers studying the dynamics of activity in the cockpit of commercial airplanes participated in our study. The team was composed of researchers in the fields of aviation human factors, HCI, cognitive science, information systems, information visualization, and computer science. We always had at least two researchers observing the use of the paper-digital tools. Researchers captured and analyzed multiple data streams (behavioral notes, videos, photos, simulator logs, GPS, audio, eye-tracking, Apple iPad recordings, and MS Kinect depth cameras) during simulated flights on desktop, fixed-based, and full-motion simulators.

[1]http://www.livescribe.com
[2]http://www.anoto.com

Figure 2. Aviation human factors research with ChronoViz on data collected at an airline training center. On the left, several video frames and annotations. On the right, a view of the paper-digital notes, audio transcript and the GPS track of the simulated flight.

Prior to introducing the paper-digital infrastructure, paper notebooks were commonly used to record pilot behavior over multiple observation sessions. The researchers were provided with our paper-digital technology and the ChronoViz tool. Figure 2 illustrates a typical analysis session with ChronoViz and the paper-digital notes. As described below, the research team experimented with a variety of notetaking strategies.

Animal Cognition

We also deployed our technology with a group of 4 researchers (one participant observer) studying animal cognition. This group investigates the activities of dolphins, chimps, and elephants. During the deployment they focused on elephants and dolphins, observing interactions between six adult female African elephants in captivity at the San Diego Zoo Safari Park as they competed over shared food resources and alliance formation during resource competition among bottlenose dolphins in Shark Bay, Western Australia.

Researchers collected video data as well as paper-based notes on *ethograms*, structured forms used by ethologists to record particular behavior or events of interest. With the introduction of the digital pens and ChronoViz, the researchers explored a number of novel note-taking practices, including methods to support trajectory recording. Figure 3 illustrates a ChronoViz view of a video segment of elephants and the corresponding ethogram record of the animals' behavior.

Emergency Response

Finally, we worked with twelve researchers in sociology, cognitive science, and computer science involved in an NIH-funded project on Wireless Internet Information System for Medical Response in Disasters (WIISARD[3]). The WIISARD researchers (one participant observer joined this effort) created a set of paper-digital interactive forms in the months leading up to an emergency response drill in July 2010. They collected multiple data points, including responder activities, locations, victim status and location, as well as position of emergency vehicles. We analyzed the production of these forms, how they were used during the exercise, and later during analysis of the collected data with ChronoViz.

ANALYSIS OF NOTETAKING PRACTICES

For the 18-month deployment, researchers were given digital pens and access to patterned paper. They were instructed in basic use of the pens (e.g., starting, stopping, docking, and downloading data from them), as well as current and potential capability of the paper-digital tools. While we actively participated in many data collection sessions, we also gathered the raw pen data and the paper-digital notes that researchers produced. In the rest of this section we describe the structure of notes, use of symbols and gestures, and how the paper-digital facilities influenced notetaking strategies.

[3]http://wiisardsage.ucsd.edu

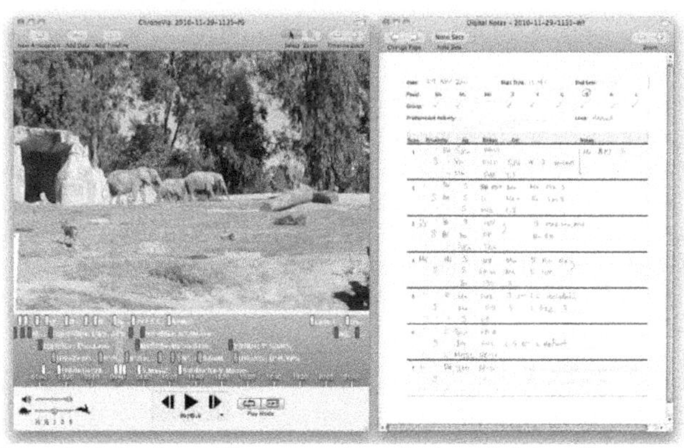

Figure 3. Animal cognition research on elephants' data collected at the San Diego Zoo Safari Park. On the right, a particular digital ethogram used by the researchers.

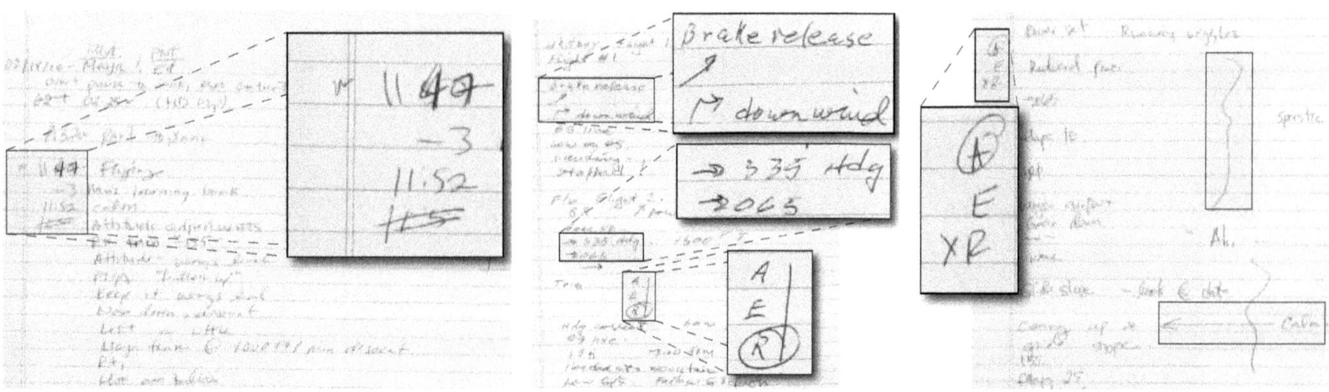

Figure 4. Notes evolution during the aviation human factors research. Left: a page from a user's first session using a digital pen; notes are verbose and still include time stamps. Center: more structured notes taken by a more experienced user; symbols and gestures start to appear, no time information is noted. Right: structured notes taken by an expert user; gestures have been moved to a specific region, symbols are used to group notes.

Structure of the paper-digital notes

Paper notes taken during behavioral research sessions are often organized to reliably capture particular events at the time they occur. When exact temporal data are required researchers may indicate a particular time as an event occurs. When these data are not critical to the planned analysis, researchers may structure notetaking into interval (such as one-minute) sampling periods. These notes often evolve over time: researchers may begin a study by observing an event of interest and taking notes *ad libitum*, often taking advantage of lined paper to provide a temporal structure for the event. The result of these efforts is often a stack of pages with top-to-bottom inscriptions of selected aspects of observed activity, often including structured tables and diagrams. To use the information captured as data, researchers would normally return to the lab to transcribe these notes into a digital database.

With the introduction of paper-digital tools, we observed an interesting evolution of notetaking practices: certain hallmarks of observational research notetaking disappeared and researchers began explicitly tagging their written notes for later analysis. Though still written with pen and paper, these notes became live digital documents that no longer required the extra step of transcription. Space and shorthand notation were used in new ways to indicate meaning relative to the observation session as well as to the way those data were parsed in the paper-digital workflow.

Figure 4 depicts an interesting example. Automatic time-stamping facilities of the digital pens freed researchers from having to notate time (still present in Fig. 4, left), allowing them to focus on *what* was going on rather than *when* it was happening. In this example, notes evolved to include hybrid solutions, containing a mix of linear notes and more symbolic representations and special gestures. Additionally, particular areas of the page (such as the margins) began to contain specific types of information. This trend emerged even more clearly when researchers in aviation human factors began experimenting with different spatial layouts for capturing activity during flight. Figure 5 shows two examples.

Although the animal cognition researchers already used ethograms in their notetaking, introduction of the digital pen system changed their practice in interesting ways. As with the evolution of notetaking practices by human factors researchers (Fig. 4), the animal cognition researchers also stopped manually writing the time of each observation. The final digital ethogram is a structured representation that allowed the researchers to quickly encode multiple details of the observed activity (Fig. 6, bottom). As we will see in later sections, researchers developed strategies for enabling subsequent navigation and scoring of the collected data as part of the real-time note taking activity; once the pen data is transferred to a computer, interpreting symbols and handwriting automatically creates summaries and visualizations of the observed activity.

In the groups described above, use of digital pens was characterized by an iterative restructuring of their notetaking practices. Aviation human factors researchers shifted from linear plain notes to more structured notes and basic ethograms. Animal cognition researchers created complex digital ethograms. Researchers using the digital pens for the emergency

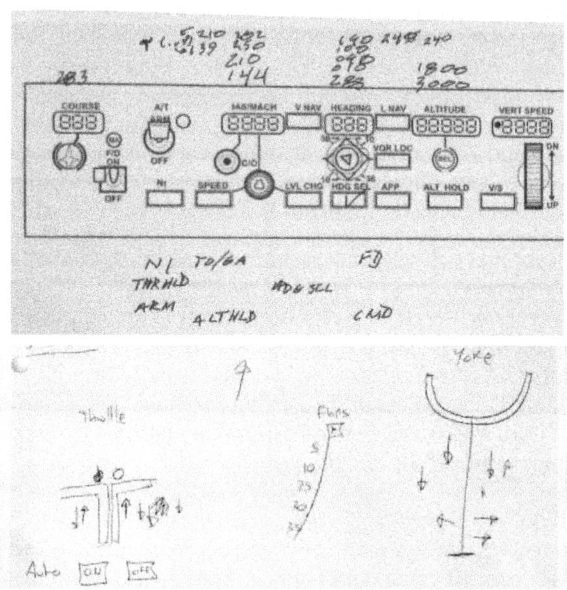

Figure 5. Notes of cockpit activity. Top: the simulator's Mode Control Panel (MCP) annotated during flight simulation when controls were handled by the pilots. Bottom: a hand-drawn diagram of the pilot's interactions with the flight instruments (throttle, flaps, yoke).

response drill developed and evolved a set of 12 different forms to capture the dynamics and locations of emergency responders, victims, and vehicles involved in the drill. Figure 7 shows examples of three forms used during the drill. The structured forms were composed of standard elements such as checkmarks or text areas, but also included special areas tailored for use with the digital pens, such as counting the number of strokes to identify occurrences of a particular event (see Fig. 7, bottom form).

Symbols and gestures

Paper-digital notes created in the different domains also involved distinctive symbols and gestures that participants introduced to augment notetaking. Symbols were used in both aviation human factors and animal cognition domains to provide a form of *bookmarking*. Some researchers used asterisks, others stars, and others simple shapes or checkmarks to bookmark a key moment in time as recorded in the timestamp of the pen stroke. Important benefits of these bookmarks were to aid future navigation through the collected data and highlight particular events that researchers might want to return to during subsequent analyses. More complex and structured symbols were introduced later. For example, Figure 4 (center and right) shows use of a triplet of symbols (A-E-R) sometimes connected to each other with a vertical arrow or a line. Aviation human factors researchers designed this coding scheme to capture pilot/copilot coordination in a cockpit: "A" encodes a request for action, "E" execution of the requested action, and "R" verbal response.

Arrows were frequently used by researchers in all domains. This is not surprising given this is a common practice in informal notes. However, it is interesting to examine the meanings of different arrows and how digital pens influenced usage. Figure 4 depicts several types of arrows: the notes in the center use arrows as bookmarks, to point out important events ('→ 335 Hdg' and '→ 065'), to encode direction and movement (the ↗ after 'brake release' symbolizes take off, and the angled arrow just after encodes a turn). Notes on

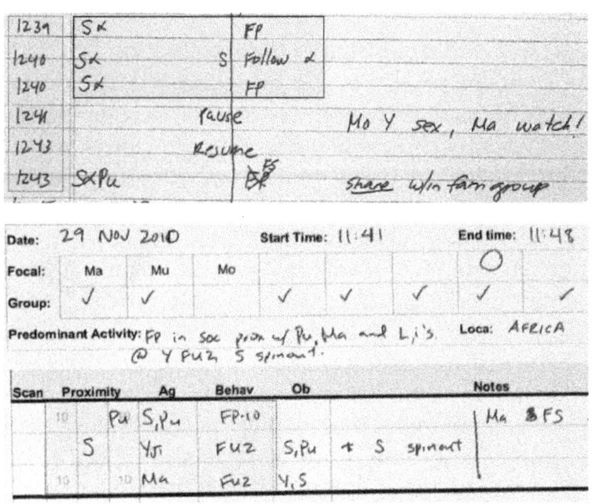

Figure 6. Evolution of a digital ethogram for elephants' interactions. Top: initial idea, still bound to time-coding the note. Bottom: Fully functional digital ethogram encoding details about interactions, proximity and behavior of the different elephants (Ma, Mu, Mo, etc.).

the right-hand side of the same figure show an example of an arrow (←) used to emphasize the connection of a classifier ('calm') with a specific part of the group of notes. A similar usage also appears in Figure 5 (bottom), where directional arrows are used to represent the movement of controls as a result of pilots' actions at different times during a flight simulation.

Figure 8 (left) depicts another usage of arrows. A researcher was trying to understand pilot/copilot communication during a checklist procedure and used arrows to infer causality between a question and answer. But perhaps the most interesting use of arrows can be seen in Figure 8 (right), where researchers looking at dolphin alliance dynamics used arrows as vectors to specify movement, direction, and location of different dolphins at different times relative to each other. Finally, arrows have also been used to encode explicit trajectories on a map, as in the case of the elephants' movements shown in Figure 9 (left).

The meaning of some symbols drawn with digital pens goes beyond their visual appearance and involves the time taken to draw them. These symbols usually consist of a single stroke and represent the time course of an event by the time taken to draw the symbol. For example, the continuous circles visible in Figure 9 (right), indicate the time a specific coded task (executing the takeoff checklist) took to complete. A similar coding is represented by the ⊥ symbol visible on the left insert in Figure 8.

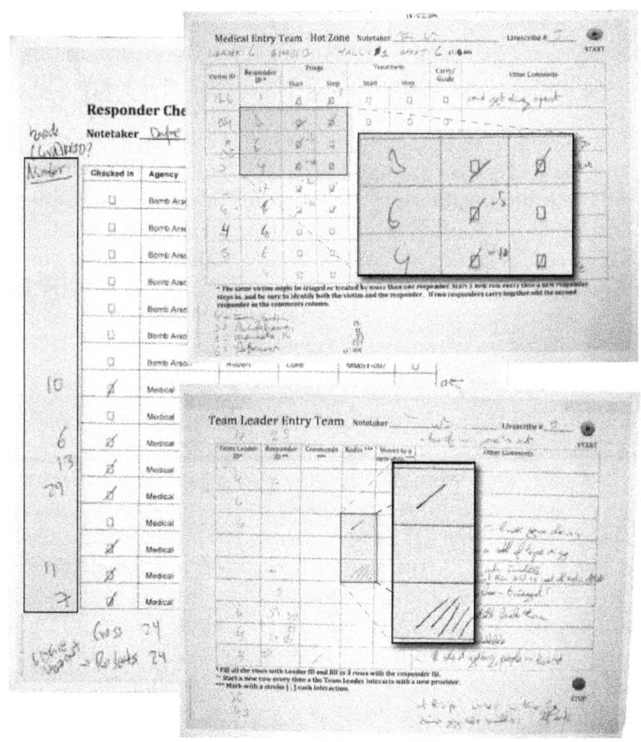

Figure 7. Forms used during the WIISARD drill. Left: list of responders active in the field, the extra column has been added during the drill by the researcher. Top-Right: medics work during triage/treatment in the 'Hot Zone', negative numbers by the checkmarks are time corrections (in seconds). Bottom-Right: team leaders' activity, the same activity can be executed multiple times (*multi-stroke* cells in the center of the form).

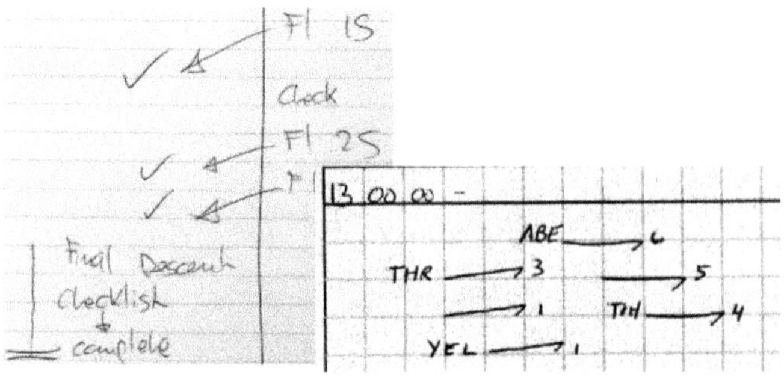

Figure 8. Two different uses of arrows. Left: observer looking at pilot/copilot communication during the execution of a checklist: notes are arranged vertically in chunks depending on the pilot/copilot coordination and arrows indicate causality. Right: tracking dolphin alliance dynamics while observing multiple synchronized videos in ChronoViz.

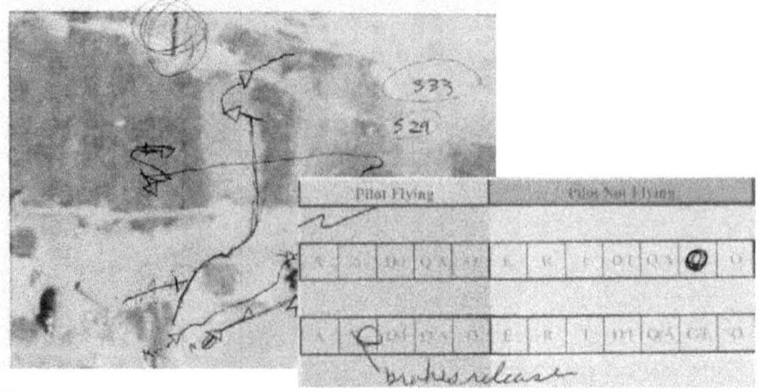

Figure 9. Left: tracking elephants movements through trajectories drawn on a map. Right: aviation human factors researchers captured pilot behavior, the letters represent coded sets of a pilot's activities.

Paper vs. digital vs. paper-digital

Traditional paper notes are static representations often used to aid recall and support analysis. One of their virtues is the flexibility to be tailored to specific representational needs and contexts. This is no doubt part of why they are so common in current practice. The introduction of digital pens makes it possible to add many new facilities. We have seen how some features evolved in the domains described above. The design space of possibilities is complex, potentially domain specific, and involves many tradeoffs. With both traditional and digital notes some information is only implicitly represented, available only as a result of interpretation by a person or a digital system. How to design a system to benefit people and exploit computation presents numerous challenges.

Keeping all recorded information accessible is one challenge. In addition, deciding what information should be available directly on paper, only within the digital system, or with both involves complex tradeoffs. We observed various strategies to cope with these tradeoffs. The localization of symbols and gestures in special areas of the page (e.g. Fig. 4, right), is one strategy. Symbols specifically meant to be interpreted are separated from the rest of the notes, making it easier for the digital processing system to recognize them, but also making it easier for the user reviewing the paper notes to ignore them if they have no meaning as paper-only notes.

More structured notes and ethograms involved similar techniques. However, it is interesting and important to note that while many notes are meant to be interpreted only by the computer, they were still represented by recognizable traces on paper. For example, in most forms from the emergency responder drill (Fig. 7), there is no need to have a checkmark or a line on paper. A simple dot (even with a non-marking pen tip) would be sufficient for the digital pen to record an entry and for the computer to process it, but having a record on paper turned out to be useful in practice. We also saw this in other situations such as when annotating ethograms or filling out forms (Fig. 5, Fig. 6 bottom, and Fig. 9 right).

In other situations, specific symbols and gestures are explicitly meant to be usable both on paper and later during ChronViz analysis. For example the A-E-R triplet (Fig. 4, center and right) was used by a researcher during on-going observations to keep track of pilot/copilot interactions. This notation also provided the data for the visualization in ChronoViz of the density of interaction through time. Similarly, during the emergency drill, information written on the forms (Fig. 7) was used during data collection to double check if a particular event was already captured. Other marks left on paper were used to guide the collection of supplementary data. For example, researchers noting interactions during the drill needed to have paper records to cross-reference responders, victims, and vehicles across forms. As notes are taken, they establish the context for subsequent note taking. For example, animal cognition researchers required proximity information to code inter-elephant behavior (Fig. 6, bottom), and the vector information of dolphin positions evolved as additional vectors were sketched in positions relative to earlier sketch vectors (Fig. 8, right).

As we pointed out previously, not all information is actually available on paper and the only way to access it is to download the data and view it on a computer. For example, in order to know the exact time or duration of a particular activity tracked by continuous strokes (e.g. the circles in Fig. 9, right), the exact distance at any given time between the dolphins tracked in the vector diagram (Fig. 8, right), or the time when pilots were interacting with specific instruments in the cockpit (Fig. 5), one needs to process the digital data.

Qualitative and quantitative data collection

In most of the examples we observed, the digital pen system was used to collect both qualitative and quantitative data. Notes, typically short sentences or single words, usually support qualitative analysis, while symbols and gestures were used more commonly in quantitative analysis. For example, researchers using forms during the emergency drill (Fig. 7), introduced a number of ways to code data using single strokes for binary data (e.g., strike marks visible in Fig. 7, top-right), multiple strokes for counting events (Fig. 7, bottom-right), and handwriting recognition for categorical data. We observed similar examples in the other domains: animal cognition researchers marked particular spaces on their ethograms to quantify the proximity of elephants (Fig. 6, bottom) and the position of the dolphins via relative spacing of marks (Fig. 8, right). Aviation human factors researchers used symbols to quantify the number of A-E-R interactions (Fig. 4, center and right) and the specific activities performed by pilots (Fig. 9, right).

Researchers also exploited the digital pen's timestamping of every stroke in different ways. For example, this enabled data collected on paper-digital forms for the emergency drill to be synchronized with the rest of the data, allowing researchers to know when specific activities occurred, such as when a certain victim was triaged (Fig. 7, top-right), and the exact time of radio commands of specific individuals (Fig. 7, bottom-right). Animal cognition researchers used pen data to quantify occurrences of selected elephant behaviors and access the exact time of particular events (Fig. 6).

One interesting observation involved a tradeoff between recording qualitative and quantitative data. In fast paced environments like the cockpit of an airplane, spending time writing details about one event means potentially not being able to note other activities happening at the same time. One nice example of this tradeoff occurred when two researchers experimented with strategies for collecting data. Both researchers observed the same event and used the same ethogram to collect data about activity in the cockpit. One strategy stressed the qualitative nature of the notes, by inserting details about the observed activity directly at the time it happened, while the other strategy attempted to capture the number of occurrences and the time of the specific activity with more precision using checkmarks.

Tension between time and space

Paper notes often exploit spatial organization. This added structure is useful both during recording and later during review. Paper-digital notes also introduce *time* as an additional structuring factor. Every single stroke is timestamped, enabling researchers to easily access the temporal dynamics of note creation.

In all domains we studied, researchers mixed spatial and time-related structuring. Figure 4 (right) provides an example, where the notetaker grouped a set of earlier written notes with curly brackets. In this case, the time when the curly bracket was written is not important; position on the page carries its meaning. In Fig. 5, position of the notes on the ethograms is a key aspect of the underlying coding scheme, assigning it to a semantic category, but the time when it occurred is important too, reflecting when the pilot handled particular controls. This is particularly evident in structured ethograms, tables or forms (e.g. Fig. 6, Fig. 7). In some situations, not only the position, but also the specific characteristics of a note are important. In the example of the use of vectors to track dolphins alliances (Fig. 8, right), the relative position of the arrows as well as the numerical and textual attributes were required for correct interpretation of the event.

Finally, the time of the first interaction with a particular section of paper-digital notes or ethograms often reflects the time of an event but subsequent interactions with the region only further elaborate the event and their time is not important. However, in other situations, such as in the multi-stroke field introduced in some emergency drill forms (Fig. 7, bottom-right), every stroke added to the same field carries important time information. Deciding when time, space or both are important in a paper-digital form is complex, requiring analysis of the specific forms and practices, and flexibility across contexts. The advantage of using a digital pen is that both location and time are always recorded and thus available for subsequent analysis.

Limitations

The long-term deployment of paper-digital tools demonstrated that researchers were successful in using them. In general the robustness of paper allowed researchers to overcome most problems that occurred. Even when digital pens fail and all recorded data are lost, the paper documents still contain valuable information. For example, even if the timing of each stroke in the elephant ethogram (Fig. 6) had been lost, the relative timing of the events would have been preserved within each minute of observation due to the structure of the ethogram. It is worth noting though that lost data might have been recorded in another way (e.g., specific times written on the forms) had participants not been using digital pens and depending on them to capture specific data.

Other minor problems can occur even if a pen is working. For example, for structured digital notes in which location on the page is important, a line or symbol that crosses from one zone on the page to another can be a problem. Figure 10 (left) shows a strike mark that may be counted twice because it appears in two distinct zones. An error correction heuristic, such as assigning a stroke to the zone that contains the clear majority of stroke points, could be applied. Data can also be lost if strokes are written outside the printed dot pattern area (Fig. 10, right). These problems can be expected to be more prevalent when notetakers are hurried and less precise in pen usage, as in the fast moving and chaotic disaster relief drill. Here we saw problems that arose because participants forgot to turn pens on after turning them off for a break.

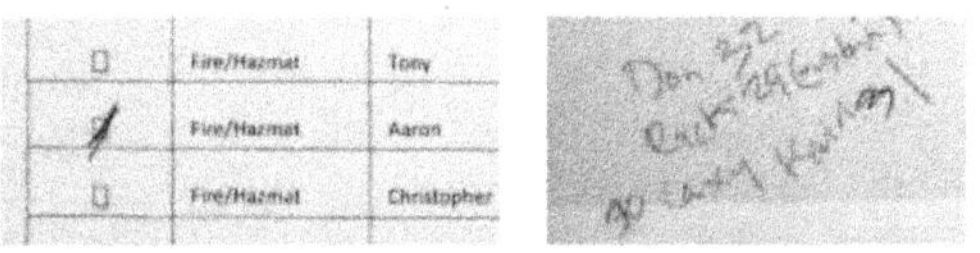

Figure 10. Two examples of a data capturing issue. Left: the strike mark could be counted as being part of both the second and the third row. Right: data written on the margin, where no pattern is printed, will not be recorded by the pen.

INTERACTIVE NAVIGATION AND VISUALIZATION

In this section we discuss how the introduction and evolution of paper-digital practices shaped development of digital tools for navigation and analysis of video data, interpretation of spatial notes, gesture and character recognition, and management of notes.

Support for navigation and analysis with the pen

Observations of interaction with paper notes in ChronoViz showed that it can be cumbersome to move between pen-paper and mouse-keyboard interfaces. To make such transitions less frequent, we developed a control panel with common video controls (play, stop, fast-forward, rewind) printed on paper and used with Anoto streaming pens (shown in Fig. 11). This permits researchers to control the video without needing to tap on a specific note. For example, due to the inherent delay between observing an action and noting it on paper, researchers will often need to position the video a few seconds before a note was written to better understand the context of the activity, and then step through and observe the details by moving frame-by-frame. Our paper-based control panel provides this and other facilities.

A common pattern in video analysis is to watch a segment multiple times, repeatedly moving back to a single point in video. We support this practice with a *tap-and-hold* gesture. When a researcher holds the pen down on a note, the video will start playing from the time point of the note and continue playing as long as the pen is held down. To watch that segment of video again, the researcher can simply lift the pen and then tap-and-hold in the same location to replay the video from the same point.

Another reason to move between pen-paper and mouse-keyboard interfaces is to record analysis notes. Sometimes the keyboard provides a better interface, while at other times the pen is superior. We support flexible use of either entry method, with on-line notes entered with a streaming pen or keyboard. New notes are associated with a point in time and can be used in the same manner as other notes, including tapping on them to move back to the associated time point.

Interpretation of spatial notes

As we observed researchers developing new methods for using the spatial position of notes and taking advantage of the flexibility offered by automatic capture of the time when notes were written, we realized more sophisticated on-screen capabilities were also needed. First, we created ways to digitally associate forms printed on Anoto-pattern paper with the notes recorded on those forms. Initial versions of the paper-digital tools required researchers to print forms on sheets of pre-printed Anoto-pattern paper. While this was quick and convenient, the notes lost meaning when brought into ChronoViz without being associated with a specific form. For example, to understand what a check mark means, one needs to know the meaning of the box or column where the mark was made.

A second type of support involves the timing of groups of marks. For example, some researchers created areas where they could simply put tally marks every time a particular type of activity occurred. To understand the timing of these

Figure 11. Support for multiple note taking sessions, with two existing sets of notes (green and orange) and a current set of notes (blue). The on-screen representation (left) matches the printed notes and blue ink of the pen. At the bottom right is the printed video playback control panel.

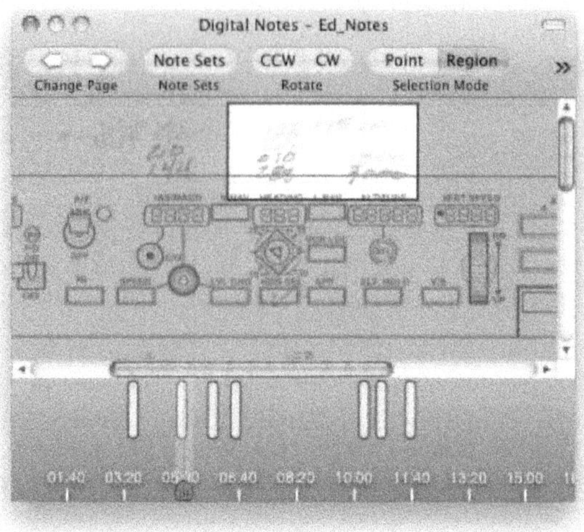

Figure 12. Spatial selection of notes, showing the times for the selected notes on the a timeline below the notes.

collections of marks, we created a way for the researchers to draw a box to select the region of the notes. The times of those notes are then shown on an interactive timeline, as depicted in Figure 12, allowing the researcher to see the time course of particular types of activity as well as jump to specific instances.

Gesture and character recognition

By exploiting existing frameworks and toolkits, ad hoc recognition of symbols, handwriting and gestures (e.g. the A-E-R symbols of Fig. 4, or the data collected through the forms in Fig. 7) can be performed after downloading data from the digital pens. We implemented dedicated recognition[4] plug-ins that generate annotations for some of the symbols used by participants. These annotations are automatically aligned and made available within the main ChronoViz interface.

Management of notes

Research participants requested the ability to add notes on top of existing notes and create customized forms that could be printed multiple times. To support these requests we created a system for managing digital notes. One facility it supports is the ability to reprint existing notes. A new copy of a note set can be printed and used for navigation and further notetaking. After multiple notetaking sessions, a researcher may want a copy of the notes with each session, or with individual sessions. These capabilities are now supported by ChronoViz, including support for printing the notes from each notetaking session in different colors that are matched with the on-screen display, as shown in Figure 11.

DISCUSSION

The work presented here was informed by earlier analyses of use of paper-digital notes in a variety of contexts. Mackay et al. [12] investigated how laboratory notebooks can be augmented by capturing hand-written information and linking it to searchable electronic versions of the notebook. The

[4]We experimented with MyScript ICR (http://visionobjects.com), the iGesture framework (http://www.igesture.org) and the $1 recognizer (http://depts.washington.edu/aimgroup/proj/dollar).

seminal Audio Notebook [16] added audio recording to a normal notebook, allowing paper-based notes to be automatically linked to speech recording. This work influenced the basic functionality that ethnographer^{++} and ChronoViz support.

More recently, two systems for capturing researchers' paper-based notes have been developed. Yeh et al. developed a system for field biologists enabling paper notes taken in the field to be linked to other digital data such as sensor readings, digital photos, GPS logs, etc. [20]. Tabard and colleagues analyzed how biologists in a laboratory used a hybrid notebook with information that spanned the electronic and the physical worlds [17]. While the system we developed addresses similar issues and in fact allows heterogeneous data to be grouped, linked, presented and analyzed, our primary focus is to develop and explore facilities that allow researchers to exploit paper-digital tools to facilitate the early stages of annotating, navigating, and visualizing multimodal observational data.

A number of recent studies examined paper-digital note practices in contexts such as music [18] and engineering [13]. Other work investigated the incidental nature of notetaking [9] and characterized natural interactions with digital pen and paper [2]. While these studies describe the nature and the process of standard notetaking practices in different domains, the digital pen and paper notetaking system described here focuses on the use of paper-digital tools to support behavioral research. We analyzed strategies and practices that evolved in using our system in three settings.

The tools we introduced changed the way researchers collected data and ultimately affected the kind of data they collected. The researchers were able to leverage the portability and flexibility of paper [15], and the naturalness and spontaneity of the notetaking process [1], while still exploiting the computational power of the digital pen and paper system.

We documented how researchers began using the hybrid paper-digital system much as they would use traditional pen and paper, even continuing to manually timestamp their observations (left image in Fig. 4 and top image in Fig. 6). With more experience they began introducing bookmarks, symbols, gestures, and increasing structure into their notes (center image in Fig. 4). As the researchers continued to use the pen and paper system they began to see additional ways to exploit the computational aspects of paper-digital notetaking technology (top image in Fig. 5, bottom image in Fig. 6, Fig. 8, and Fig. 9). It is at this point that our participants seemed to fully realize that they were using a computer and not *just* a pen and began to modify their notetaking practices, thereby engaging in a paradigm described by Guimbretière as cohabitation [6].

Paper notebooks are extremely flexible and personal. We observed, as previously discussed by Mackay et al. [11], how paper allows notes to be spatially organized in ways rarely supported as well by digital tools. It also permits later addition and annotation. Figure 7 shows addition of notes in the bottom margin as well as an entire column on the left. The ethograms in Figure 5 were both created after the researchers arrived at the data collection setting. The MCP diagram was printed on dot paper (top), and the yoke and throttle were hand drawn (bottom) at the study site, just before data collection sessions began. Notes can be augmented digitally and reprinted. Paper can no longer be considered simply temporary storage as described by Lin et al. [10], but becomes a persistent tool used for both data collection and multiple cycles of analysis.

The introduction of paper-digital tools involves important tradeoffs: timestamped notes vs. spatial arrangement, qualitative vs. quantitative analysis, and paper-only vs. paper-digital access to the information. We discussed the importance of the physical layout of notes [11] and how researchers often used a combination of time-based notes and spatial structuring and linking. The ethograms of Figure 5, Figure 8 and Figure 9 (right), and the trajectories drawn in Figure 9 (left) are examples. In the analysis section we outlined how researchers made use of the paper representation during observation, but also counted on automatic capture of timestamping and linking data in later use. The tension between capturing more information quickly and creating detailed reports (as outlined by Bernstein et al. [1]) was mitigated by automatic capture rather than requiring coordinating a set of recording devices (video cameras, audio recorders, GPS and other sensors). Most of the time researchers did not have to think about this issue. However, we did witness researchers still considering this tradeoff and attempting to develop a solution that best suited the particular observation, employing a division of labor between notetakers, with each specifically looking at one aspect of the observed phenomena.

As we learned about how notetaking practices were changed by the use of digital pens, we also implemented new ways of integrating pen-based actions into ChronoViz, such as facilities that permit users to use pen interactions to control video playback. The practice of associating the location of pen strokes with meanings led us to develop a way to define meaningful regions on pre-printed forms (including ethograms). Later versions allow specific pen gestures to spawn particular annotations in ChronoViz and permit users to add new notes on top of existing notes. Responding to the evolving use practices of our user community, the refined system better addresses the challenges raised in the introduction: managing multiple data streams, navigating large data sets, and finding important moments in the data. Because these challenges must be confronted in any observational research program, the evolving suite of tools described here should be widely applicable.

FUTURE WORK

Deployment of our tools allowed us to examine notetaking practices and practical issues in three field research domains. In the future we expect to continue to study usage in these areas, exploiting the research relationships we have developed. We also expect to expand our studies. For example, discussion with flight deck designers and airline instructors indicate that a number of airlines are in the process of restructuring their training programs. Since flight instructors routinely take notes during simulated flights, with our tools the notes can be combined and linked to other data about pilot performance (simulator logs, videos, etc.). This can in turn support debriefing sessions by aiding navigation of pilot performance data and supporting discussion of it.

We are also investigating how people exploit paper in other settings. For example we are examining how paper-digital tools can be used to document mathematicians' construction of proofs and visualize the dynamics of this process. We are working on expansions of current work with animal cognition researchers, especially to support the reconstruction of animal trajectories. A researcher watching a single video from a fixed viewing angle can use the paper-digital tools to trace a two-dimensional trajectory for each animal in view. Similar traces constructed from other viewing angles can be combined to create a composite 3D trajectory visualization in ChronoViz; something the researchers cannot do from any single view point. We envision using paper notes to reconstruct trajectories of elephants and captive dolphins.

CONCLUSION

Until we began exploring uses of digital notes, it was difficult to appreciate the extent to which the activity of notetaking would be changed by the new technology. Our tools transform observer notetaking from an activity that generates yet another sort of hard to analyze data into an activity that generates a powerful interface to digital data of all types.

The possibility of recording data digitally during observation promises to transform current notetaking and data collection practices. In this paper we presented and analyzed the evolution of paper-digital techniques developed by researchers in three different domains. The resulting techniques exploited several affordances of the novel paper-digital notetaking system we are developing, demonstrating its potential to support field work. In the process we extended ChronoViz – a tool for annotating, visualizing, navigating, and analyzing multimodal data – to aid and shape these emerging notetaking practices.

New analysis procedures are made possible by the use of digital-pen-based tools, including adding analysis notes to observation notes, visualizing the temporal relations among notes, and quantifying the occurrence of various classes of notes. We intend to continue development of tools for observational analysis and anticipate many, as yet unexplored, practical applications of this technology.

ACKNOWLEDGMENTS

We thank Christine Johnson for working with us on the digital ethograms and access to rich data on animal cognition. We also thank David Kirsh for assistance in the WISARD project, and Richard Connor for the use of dolphin video. Support for this research was provided by NSF award #0729013, and UCSD-Boeing project agreement 2011-012.

REFERENCES

1. Bernstein, M., Van Kleek, M., Karger, D., and Schraefel, M. Information scraps: How and why information eludes our personal information management tools. *ACM TOIS 26*, 4 (2008), 1–46.
2. Brandl, P., Richter, C., and Haller, M. Nicebook: supporting natural note taking. In *Proc. CHI '10* (2010), 599–608.
3. Fouse, A., and Hollan, J. D. DataPrism: A tool for visualizing multimodal data. In *Proc. Measuring Behavior 2010* (2010), 1:1–1:4.
4. Fouse, A., Weibel, N., Hutchins, E., and Hollan, J. D. Chronoviz: a system for supporting navigation of time-coded data. In *Extended Abstracts of CHI 2011* (2011), 299–304.
5. Goldman, R., Pea, R., Barron, B., and Derry, S., Eds. *Video Research in the Learning Sciences*. 2007.
6. Guimbretière, F. Paper Augmented Digital Documents. In *Proc. UIST '03* (2003), 51–60.
7. Hutchins, E. *Cognition in the wild*. MIT Press, 1995.
8. Hymes, D. The ethnography of speaking. *Anthropology and human behavior 13*, 53 (1962), 11–74.
9. Ispas, A., Signer, B., and Norrie, M. C. A study of incidental notetaking to inform digital pen and paper solutions.
10. Lin, M., Lutters, W., and Kim, T. Understanding the micronote lifecycle: improving mobile support for informal note taking. In *Proc. CHI 2004* (2004), 687–694.
11. Mackay, W., Fayard, A., Frobert, L., and Médini, L. Reinventing the familiar: exploring an augmented reality design space for air traffic control. In *Proc. CHI '98* (1998), 558–565.
12. Mackay, W. E., Pothier, G., Letondal, C., Bøegh, K., and Sørensen, H. E. The Missing Link: Augmenting Biology Laboratory Notebooks. In *Proc. UIST '02* (2002), 41–50.
13. McAlpine, H., Hicks, B., Huet, G., and Culley, S. An investigation into the use and content of the engineer's logbook. *Design Studies 27*, 4 (2006), 481–504.
14. Sacks, H. *Lectures on conversation*, vol. 1. 1995.
15. Sellen, A., and Harper, R. *The Myth of the Paperless Office*. The MIT Press, 2003.
16. Stifelman, L., Arons, B., and Schmandt, C. The audio notebook: paper and pen interaction with structured speech. In *Proc. CHI '01* (2001), 182–189.
17. Tabard, A., Mackay, W., and Eastmond, E. From individual to collaborative: the evolution of prism, a hybrid laboratory notebook. In *Proc. CSCW '08* (2008), 569–578.
18. Tsandilas, T., Letondal, C., and Mackay, W. Musink: composing music through augmented drawing. In *Proc. CHI '09* (2009), 819–828.
19. Weibel, N., Fouse, A., Hutchins, E., and Hollan, J. D. Supporting an integrated paper-digital workflow for observational research. In *Proc. IUI 2011* (2011), 257–266.
20. Yeh, R. B., Liao, C., Klemmer, S. R., Guimbretière, F., Lee, B., Kakaradov, B., Stamberger, J., and Paepcke, A. ButterflyNet: A Mobile Capture and Access System for Field Biology Research. In *Proc. CHI '06* (2006), 571–580.

User See, User Point: Gaze and Cursor Alignment in Web Search

Jeff Huang
University of Washington
Seattle, WA 98195
chi@jeffhuang.com

Ryen W. White
Microsoft Research
Redmond, WA 98052
ryenw@microsoft.com

Georg Buscher
Microsoft Bing
Bellevue, WA 98004
georgbu@microsoft.com

ABSTRACT
Past studies of user behavior in Web search have correlated eye-gaze and mouse cursor positions, and other lines of research have found cursor interactions to be useful in determining user intent and relevant parts of Web pages. However, cursor interactions are not all the same; different types of cursor behavior patterns exist, such as reading, hesitating, scrolling and clicking, each of which has a different meaning. We conduct a search study with 36 subjects and 32 search tasks to determine *when* gaze and cursor are aligned, and thus *when* the cursor position is a good proxy for gaze position. We study the effect of time, behavior patterns, user, and search task on the gaze-cursor alignment, findings which lead us to question the maxim that "gaze is well approximated by cursor." These lessons inform an experiment in which we predict the gaze position with better accuracy than simply using the cursor position, improving the state-of-the-art technique for approximating visual attention with the cursor. Our new technique can help make better use of large-scale cursor data in identifying how users examine Web search pages.

Author Keywords
gaze; cursor; eye-tracking; search examination behavior

ACM Classification Keywords
H.5.4 Information Interfaces and Presentation: Hypertext / Hypermedia—*Navigation*

General Terms
Human Factors, Measurement, Experimentation

INTRODUCTION
Billions of people navigate the Web as part of their daily lives by looking, finding, reading, pointing, and clicking. Because the flow of using a site is such a fundamental experience for so many people, usability professionals and site designers seek to optimize the experience by analyzing which parts of the page grab a visitor's attention, and what information people read on the page. To achieve this, they conduct laboratory studies using eye-tracking equipment to track users' gaze while they navigate the site. Research studies have shown gaze to be useful in determining what people are reading from their fixation [5, 26], in determining salient regions of Web pages [4], and in identifying the effects of changes to search engine results pages (SERPs) [13]. But could the mouse cursor be a cheap and scalable alternative to eye-tracking for the same purposes? If so, cursor tracking systems can be deployed on any website without the need for an eye-tracker.

Permission to make digital or hard copies of all or part of this work for personal or classroom use is granted without fee provided that copies are not made or distributed for profit or commercial advantage and that copies bear this notice and the full citation on the first page. To copy otherwise, or republish, to post on servers or to redistribute to lists, requires prior specific permission and/or a fee.
CHI'12, May 5–10, 2012, Austin, Texas, USA.
Copyright 2012 ACM 978-1-4503-1015-4/12/05...$10.00.

Most people use a mouse cursor to interact with Web pages; this interaction data can be efficiently collected at scale in a natural setting without disrupting the user [2, 20, 22]. There are reports that the cursor is a suitable substitute for eye-tracking for determining people's attention and examination behavior. Academic studies [1, 2, 31] and commercial offerings (e.g., ClickTale [clicktale.com], Lucky Orange [lucky-orange.com], Observe.It [observe.it], and Mouse Eye Tracking [met.picnet.com.au]) have analyzed the cursor in usability settings to learn about engagement on Web pages. Past research has found a correlation between gaze and cursor positions [9, 12, 19, 22, 27, 28] and that cursor movements can be useful for determining relevant parts of the Web page with varying degrees of success [15, 21, 22, 29]. However, cursor interaction spans a variety of behaviors [1, 12, 25, 27, 28] including reading, hesitating, highlighting, marking, and actions such as scrolling and clicking. Identifying these behaviors is a prerequisite to understanding what meaning the cursor interactions convey.

In this work, we aim to further quantify the relationship between cursor and gaze. Prior work has shown that gaze and cursor are correlated but the goal of our work is to determine *when* gaze and cursor are aligned. We want to know when the cursor position is a good proxy for gaze position and the effect of various factors such as time, user, cursor behavior patterns, and search task on the gaze-cursor alignment. Through this, our research will contribute to knowledge of how people use their cursor and how they examine Web search pages. The lessons from this analysis also inform an experiment in which we *predict* the gaze position with better accuracy than simply using the corresponding cursor position. In addition to the cursor position, we also use dwell time[1], temporal features relating to cursor behavior, and future cursor positions to determine the current gaze position.

The findings from this work can be applied to many practical situations. Predicting gaze will improve state-of-the-art techniques for approximating visual attention with the mouse cursor. Current commercial cursor-tracking systems merely

[1]Dwell time here is the page dwell time as typically measured in information retrieval literature, rather than cursor dwell time.

present heatmaps of the cursor movements and claim that the user attention is proximal to the hot areas of the map. Our findings will inform these and other applications that remotely collect large amounts of cursor data at scale by showing how to more effectively use this data. More broadly, our work supports collecting user attention data in situations where eye-tracking equipment is costly, such as for large numbers of Web users. One particular domain that may benefit from this research is Web search, in which searcher examination behavior represented by probabilistic models [8, 16] may be improved by uncovering the latent variables representing which search results the users examine.

We study the gaze-cursor alignment of 36 subjects and 32 search tasks with an eye-tracker in a controlled lab setting. The findings show that while subjects vary their gaze-cursor alignment substantially, they lag their cursor behind their gaze by at least 250 ms and on average by 700 ms. Both dwell time and the user's personal style affect the distance between the cursor and gaze positions. This distance is longer when the cursor is inactive, shorter when the cursor is used to help examine or read the page, and even shorter when the user is performing an action. Finally, we predict the gaze position using cursor features and achieve 23.5% more accuracy than simply using the corresponding cursor position alone.

RELATED WORK

Two lines of research relate to this work. One focuses on inferring user interest and intentions directly from the user's interactions with a SERP or a Web page, specifically based on cursor movements, clicks, and gaze. The second explores the relationship between cursor position and gaze position in order to infer users' visual attention from cursor movements.

Implicit Interest Indicators

In early work, Goecks and Shavlik modified a Web browser to record themselves browsing hundreds of Web pages [15]. They found that a neural network could predict variables such as the amount of cursor activity on the SERP, which they considered surrogate measurements of user interest. Claypool et al. [10] developed the "curious browser", a custom Web browser that recorded activity from 75 students browsing over 2,500 Web pages. They found that cursor travel time was a positive indicator of a Web page's relevance, but could only differentiate highly irrelevant Web pages. They also found that the number of mouse clicks on a page did not correlate with its relevance, despite the intuition that clicks represent links that users found appealing. Hijikata [21] used client-side logging to monitor five subjects browsing a total of 120 Web pages. They recorded actions such as text tracing and link pointing using the cursor. The findings showed that these behaviors were good indicators for interesting regions of the Web page, around 1.5 times more effective than rudimentary term matching between the query and regions of the page. Shapira et al. [29] developed a special Web browser and recorded cursor activity from a small number of company employees browsing the Web. They found that the ratio of mouse movement to reading time was a better indicator of page quality than cursor travel distance and overall length of time that users spent on a page.

In the search domain, Guo and Agichtein [17] captured mouse movements using a modified browser toolbar and found differences in cursor travel distances between informational and navigational queries. Furthermore, a decision tree could classify the query type using cursor movements more accurately than using clicks. Guo and Agichtein also used interactions such as cursor movement, hovers, and scrolling to accurately infer search intent and interest in search results [18]. They focused on automatically identifying a searcher's research or purchase intent based on features of the interaction. Buscher et al. [7] also used scrolling to infer user interest and compared it to gaze tracking feedback. They found that scrolling behavior in connection with information on the browser's viewport could be as effective as gaze tracking feedback in search scenarios comprising query expansion. By applying a reading detection method, Buscher et al. [5] used gaze tracking features directly to infer user interest and show that this can yield great improvements when personalizing search. Buscher et al. also demonstrated the value of gaze information to build models for predicting salient regions of Web pages [4]. Finally, Cole et al. [11] built reading models operating on gaze tracking data to investigate information acquisition strategies of the searcher for different search tasks.

Gaze-Cursor Relationship

Another line of research examines the relationship between eye gaze and cursor positions. An early study by Chen et al. [9] measures this relationship by recording 100 gaze and cursor positions from five subjects browsing the Web. They showed that the distance between gaze and cursor was markedly smaller in regions of encountered pages to which users attended. Liu and Chung [25] recorded cursor activity from 28 students browsing the Web and noticed patterns of viewing behaviors, including reading by tracing text with the cursor. Their algorithms were capable of predicting users' cursor behaviors with 79% accuracy. Hauger et al. conducted a study using a similar method to ours, but over instructional pages about the game of "Go" [20]. They found that gaze and cursor positions were better correlated when the cursor was in motion and in sessions comprising a higher proportion of motion. Hauger et al. were able to predict which paragraph a user was reading, and to what extent, with 79% accuracy.

Other work has focused on the relationship between cursor and gaze in search tasks. In a study involving 32 subjects performing 16 search tasks each [27, 28], Rodden et al. identified a strong alignment between cursor and gaze positions. They found that the distance between cursor and gaze positions was larger along the x-axis than the y-axis, and was generally shorter when the cursor was placed over the search results. Rodden et al. also observed four types of mouse cursor behaviors: neglecting the cursor while reading, using the cursor as a reading aid to follow text (either horizontally or vertically), and using the cursor to mark interesting results. Guo and Agichtein [19] reported similar findings in a smaller study with ten subjects performing 20 search tasks each. Like Rodden et al., Guo and Agichtein observed that distances along the x-axis tended to be larger than the distances along the y-axis. They could predict with 77% accuracy when gaze and cursor were strongly aligned using cursor features.

The research presented in this paper extends previous work in several ways. The focus of previous work was in examining the relationship of cursor and gaze position by measuring the distance between them. The conclusions were that a strong correlation existed between them, however there was little further differentiation of alignment along a temporal dimension and no differentiation by cursor behavior patterns. Here we look at the *degree of alignment* at different points in time, quantitatively analyzing behaviors made using the cursor, and we are *predicting* the gaze position using a variety of cursor behavior and time features. In addition, our analysis of the gaze-cursor relationship involves a larger number search tasks and subjects than prior studies, giving us more leverage in feature comparisons.

METHOD

We used a Tobii x50 eye tracker with 50 Hz tracking frequency and an accuracy of 0.5° visual angle (corresponding to 16 pixels in our setting) on a 1280 × 1024 resolution 17 inch monitor (96dpi) and 1040 × 996 resolution Web browser. Cursor and gaze coordinates were collected in an eye-tracking study with 38 subjects (21 female, 17 male), recruited from a user study pool. They ranged in age between 26 and 60 years (M = 45.5, SD = 8.2), and possessed a wide variety of backgrounds and professions. Two subjects had incomplete data due to technical issues and were dropped from the analysis.

We prepared a set of 32 Web search tasks (information needs) which each subject completed on the Bing search engine in a randomized order. Half of the tasks were navigational (i.e., they had to find a specific Web page) and half were informational (i.e., they had to find factual information). Each task started with a description of what subjects should look for on the Web. They had to start searching with a predefined query for each task (e.g., task = "What are some side-effects of Ibuprofen?", predefined query = "ibuprofen side effects") that we generated from the task, but were then free to interact with the search results, browse the Web and search further. The browser cache and cookies were cleared after each subject to prevent subjects from noticing previously viewed pages (from hyperlinks turning purple) and search engine personalization effects. Going through an eye tracker calibration phase in the beginning, completing all 32 search tasks, as well as filling in a demographics questionnaire in the end took about one hour per subject.

Gaze and cursor positions were recorded for each SERP as well as subsequent Web pages (i.e., pages visited after clicking on a search result). In total, we collected data for 1,210 search tasks, which included 1,336,647 gaze positions, and 87,227 cursor positions (whenever the subject moved the cursor). Additional details about the experimental procedure are described in Buscher et al. [6]. Gaze-specific findings on this data set, unrelated to cursor features, have been reported elsewhere [6, 14]. Huang et al. [22] used this data to measure gaze-cursor alignment (Figure 1), showing that there is some correlation between gaze and cursor positions, but with substantial variation. Other studies measuring gaze-cursor alignment [19, 27] have presented evidence of alignment with charts nearly identical to Figure 1.

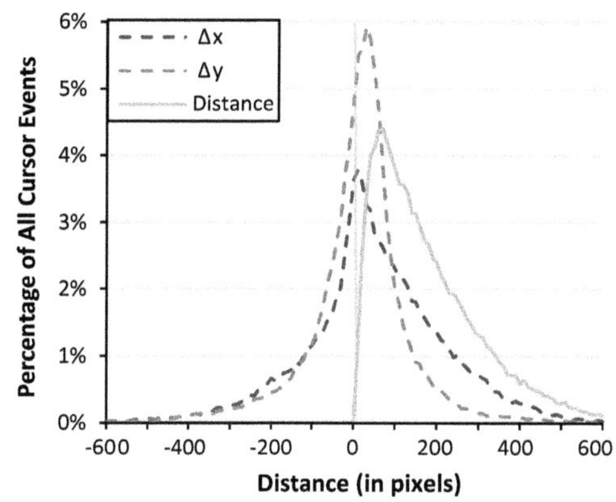

Figure 1. Δx, Δy, and Euclidean distance plotted in a frequency distribution for the search results page.

In the search logs, the gaze positions were recorded approximately every 20 ms, whereas cursor positions were recorded approximately every 100 ms. Gaze positions are estimated by the eye-tracker and given the saccades (rapid movements) of the eye, recording at a higher frequency can give more accurate positions; but the cursor position is an exact value and recording at 10 Hz is sufficient—the cursor is not radically changing directions at sub-second speeds such that we cannot interpolate them. We had tested different frequencies of interpolation and found negligible differences.

Since cursor and gaze events did not necessarily have identical timestamps, a gaze position was interpolated for every cursor position. Interpolation was performed by computing gaze x and y coordinates weighted by the coordinates of the nearest gaze coordinates before and after the cursor position. For example, the interpolated x-coordinate for eye gaze is computed as,

$$x_i = x_0 + (x_1 - x_0)\frac{t_i - t_0}{t_1 - t_0} \quad (1)$$

where t_i is the time for the corresponding cursor position, x_0 is the gaze's x-coordinate preceding the cursor position, recorded at time t_0, and x_1 is the gaze's x-coordinate following the cursor position, recorded at time t_1. The interpolated y-coordinate was computed the same way, substituting x for y in the above equation. To reduce interpolation inaccuracies due to noise from the eye-tracker, cursor positions were only captured if they occurred between gaze positions that were at most 100 ms apart.

ALIGNMENT EFFECTS FROM TIME, USER, AND TASK

To begin our analysis, we view gaze-cursor alignment through the lens of time, user, and search task. Different people behave differently on the Web in the queries they issue [33], how they gaze at the page [3, 14], and how they interact with the page [19]. The amount of time spent reviewing the search results page can affect where they are pointing and where they are looking. Additionally, we investigate the possibility that gaze and cursor may not be most aligned at each instance in time, but may be better aligned when one variable is temporally shifted.

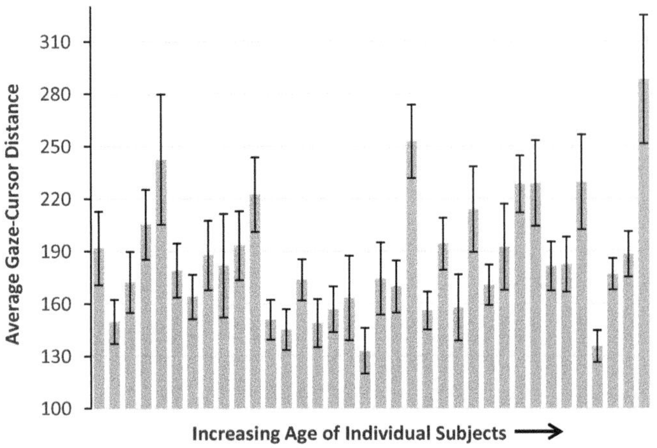

Figure 2. The average gaze-cursor distance for each subject with error bars representing the standard error. The variance between subjects is high ($SD = 33.9$). Subjects are sorted by ascending age so that oldest subjects are on the right.

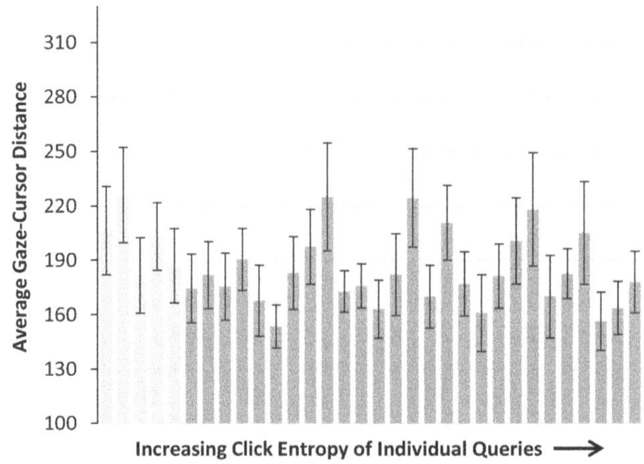

Figure 3. The average gaze-cursor distance for each search task with error bars representing the standard error. The variance between search tasks is modest ($SD = 20.2$). Queries are sorted by ascending click entropy so queries with more diverse result clicks are on the right; five queries with unknown entropy are on the left (shaded lighter).

User and Task Effects

People visually examine Web pages differently [4], and have individual styles in their control of the cursor. Past findings have shown that users behave differently depending on search tasks (e.g., between informational and navigational task types [13]). Guo and Agichtein analyzed gaze-cursor alignment [19] on a smaller subject pool and found differences in user (up to twice the average distance between gaze and cursor for some users) and search task type (navigational vs. informational). Here we explore whether search task or individual differences (including age and gender) have a stronger effect on alignment. Larger variances in alignment would indicate that a search system might have difficulty predicting alignment for users or queries that have not occurred before.

To study alignment differences among subjects, we macro-averaged the gaze-cursor distance across their queries (i.e., took the average of the average for each of their queries, thus giving equal weight to each query). The results in Figure 2 show that subjects are fairly distinct in terms of gaze-cursor alignment. Some keep their cursor within about 130 px of their gaze, while others average about 280 px. The standard deviation representing the variation among subjects is $SD = 33.9$. We checked for gender differences in gaze-cursor distance using a two-tailed t-test and found no statistically significant effect ($t(34) = 1.31, p = 0.20$). There was a Spearman correlation of $\rho = 0.22$ between age and gaze-cursor alignment, but this was also not statistically significant ($N = 36, p = 0.18$). Therefore, we conclude that whether the subject tracks their gaze closely with their cursor is more likely to stem from personal habits rather than age or gender.

Next we look at the average differences in gaze-cursor alignment for different search tasks. Since the subjects were given predefined queries to begin with, we filtered out reformulated queries since they may be reflective of personal style or individual search skills. A search task is therefore represented by a single query in this analysis. For each search task, we first macro-averaged the gaze-cursor distance across subjects to normalize the data, then took the mean of this value as the average distance for each task. The search task averages are shown in Figure 3, which reveals that there are modest differences between tasks. The alignment distance ranges from about 150 px to about 220 px, and the standard deviation among search tasks is $SD = 20.2$.

To gain some insight into the attributes of the search tasks, we computed the click entropy for each query, a measure of result click diversity [33]. The click entropy is computed as the Shannon entropy of the click distribution on the search result links. This was done to look for correlation between click entropy and gaze-cursor alignment; we thought it was possible that gaze and cursor would align differently depending on query type. (Typically, queries with high click entropy are informational or more ambiguous, and navigational otherwise [30].) We used the past year's search logs of the Bing search engine to find the click distributions. Five queries had not appeared in the search logs in the past year and thus had unknown entropy. From the remaining queries, we found no Spearman correlation between click entropy and gaze-cursor alignment ($\rho = 0.01, N = 27, p = 0.96$). This contrasts findings from Guo and Agichtein's study [19] which found alignment differences between navigational and informational queries.

The standard deviation in gaze-cursor alignment across means for different subjects is higher than across means for different search tasks. A Levene's test for homogeneity of variance shows that the differences in variance are statistically significant (Levene statistic[2] $= 4.529, p = 0.037$). This suggests that users have individual preferences and that these differences are stronger than the differences between search tasks. We experimented with not normalizing the data when computing the mean averages (i.e., micro-averaging), but the differences in standard deviation between search task and subject were similar.

[2]Levene's test is typically used to compare the variance between two sources rather than between two sets of macro-averaged values.

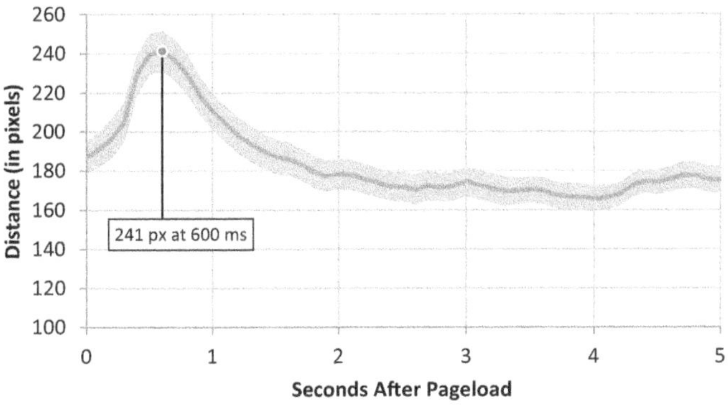

Figure 4. The average gaze-cursor distance at 100 ms intervals after the SERP loads, macro-averaged over subjects. The distance is low just as the page loads, increases at 0.5–1 seconds, then decreases. The shaded area is the region representing the standard error of the mean.

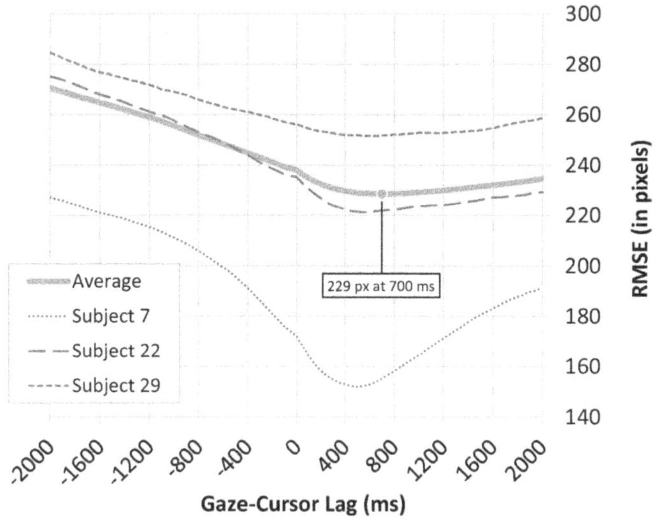

Figure 5. The root-mean-square error for gaze and cursor distance at different intervals (in 50 ms increments) of gaze-cursor lag, representing how well gaze positions correlate with future and past cursor positions. The thick solid line plots the RMSE macro-averaged over subjects, and thin dashed lines plot the RMSE for three example subjects.

Temporal Effects

Users examine the SERP in a sequence of evolving behaviors. A user may possess the habit of quickly scanning the page first to see what kinds of items are on the page, then skimming it quickly to see if there is an answer to their information need while neglecting the cursor, then finally reading the text word-by-word. As the time spent dwelling on the SERP increases, the alignment between gaze and cursor may change due to the dynamism of the behaviors.

Averaging gaze and cursor distances for different dwell times, Figure 4 shows the relationship between gaze and cursor over time for the first five seconds following the pageload. Indeed, the time since the page has loaded has an effect on alignment. Specifically, the alignment distance ranges from 170 px to almost 240 px. Right when the page loads, gaze and cursor are closely aligned, perhaps from the previous action that led to the page. The peak at 240 px is within one second of the page loading, suggesting that the subject may first scan the displayed page without moving their cursor. The gaze-cursor alignment narrows after about two seconds when the subject may start to examine the page more closely and perhaps prepare to click a link. While the subject's actions at this stage change from query-to-query, the aggregate alignments provide clues of typical examination behavior.

This behavior led us to ask—given that we see the eye moving within a second of the page loading, does the cursor move as quickly? We arrived at three credible hypotheses: a) the user uses the cursor as a reading aid [28] and so the eye follows the cursor, b) the gaze and cursor positions are best aligned at each given point in time, c) or the cursor follows gaze because the user looks at something and then moves their cursor to interact with it. The last hypothesis is consistent with findings from early work by Ware and Mikaelian [32] that showed that the eye fixation was a faster method for target selection than the mouse. While target selection is not the objective of this study, the difference between eye and mouse speed may cause the cursor to lag behind the gaze.

We used a technique similar to cross-correlation in signal processing that computes when two waveforms are most aligned [23]. We first interpolated cursor and gaze positions at 50 ms intervals again using Equation 1. This equalized the periods between positional data points, computing the cursor positions at different time shifts (e.g., 50 ms, 100 ms, 150 ms, ...) after each gaze position. Then we computed the root mean square error (RMSE) between gaze and cursor[3] for each shifted time interval for each subject. The cursor and gaze positions are considered most correlated at the time shift with the lowest RMSE.

Figure 5 shows the macro-averaged RMSE values across subjects compared with three example subjects. The first thing to note is that for the macro-averaged values, shifting the cursor positions 700 ms into the future minimizes the RMSE. This means mouse cursor lags behind eye gaze by about 700 ms, so the user looks at something and then (almost one second) later their cursor is moved to that location on the page. Temporal alignments vary depending on the user and query session; the per-subject RMSE values showed that different people had different delays in moving their cursor to their gaze. In the same manner, the cursor lagged behind the gaze for each individual subject; the inverse situation—gaze lagging behind the cursor—did not occur, refuting the hypothesis that some people lead with the cursor when examining the page. Still, some subjects were quick, moving their cursor to their gaze in 350 ms (one subject had a minimum RMSE at 250 ms), while others took over one second.

CURSOR BEHAVIOR PATTERNS

Several studies have reported different behavioral patterns when using the cursor. Rodden et al. observed several types of cursor behavior: neglecting the cursor while reading, using the cursor as a reading aid to follow text, and using the cursor to mark interesting results [28]. Liu and Chung also noticed

[3]Note that RMSE differs from the average alignment distance metric we use throughout the paper; RMSE takes the root of the mean of the squared distances which is not the mean distance.

patterns of cursor behaviors, including reading by tracing text [25]. Arroyo et al. observed users hesitating and reading with the cursor [1]. Mueller and Lockerd found users hesitating before clicking and resting the cursor on white space [12]. Finally, Claypool et al. observed the following cursor behaviors: ignoring the cursor, examining the page using the cursor, following the text with the cursor, and using it to interact with the page or browser [10]. Our taxonomy of cursor behavior resembles that reported by Claypool et al.

Each of the previously mentioned studies discusses the cursor behavior qualitatively and most do not have corresponding gaze data. Our study involved more subjects and search tasks than the largest prior study, facilitating a quantitative analysis of the cursor behaviors. Informed by prior work and our own qualitative observations of user interactions with the SERP, we separated cursor behaviors into four categories:

Inactive cursors are not moving and are ignored by the user for some time.

Reading cursors are used to follow the text while the user is reading the page.

Action cursors are used when the user is about to perform an action (click on a link, edit the query in the search box, drag the scrollbar, etc.).

Examining cursors move around while the user is examining the page, not including time spent in 'reading' or 'action'.

Distinguishing Between Cursor Behaviors

We use a heuristic-based method to classify the different cursor behaviors. This method entails iteratively examining replays of the recorded interaction behaviors, deciding which behaviors belong to each category, classifying the behaviors using simple rules, and finally comparing the classified behaviors with the judged behaviors. The process is ad-hoc to develop a simple classification scheme that captures the essence of each behavior type.

We developed classification rules informed by watching replays of the interaction in a query session. The cursor is considered inactive if the user leaves it in one location (pausing it) while they examine the page. We define 'inactive' as the cursor staying still for at least one full second. The behaviors occurring when the cursor's position is active can be classified in three ways. As Claypool et al. noted, users may be using the cursor to help examine or read the page [10]. However, the cursor also serves the purpose of interacting with elements of the page or with the Web browser, typically by clicking on controls on the browser or Web page. We classify these 'action' behaviors as those occurring in the one second preceding a click. The remaining interactions were classified as either examining or reading. Reading was typically defined as users following the text horizontally (an observed pattern in Rodden et al. [28]), since the text in a snippet or advertisements goes from left to right. The movement to the right was not enough to classify as reading, since the cursor may be moved to the right for many reasons. We arrived at three rules for an interaction which if met, would label all cursor positions within that timeframe as 'reading': the cursor could not have moved more than 50 px vertically (about 3 lines of text); the cursor must have moved at least 150 px to the right (the length of a handful of words); and the cursor must have moved back to the left at least 50 px. The remaining interactions, in which the cursor was neither inactive nor reading nor performing an action, were labeled as 'examining'. We therefore arrived at five cursor behavioral patterns (including clicking which was treated as an instantaneous action) as behaviors that warranted further analysis. We studied gaze-cursor alignment in these behaviors next.

Cursor Behavior's Effect on Alignment

For each of the five cursor behaviors, we computed the distance between gaze and cursor. Table 1 summarizes the proportion of time spent in each cursor behavior and the corresponding median distance between gaze and cursor. As expected, gaze and cursor are further apart when the cursor is inactive, since the eye is still roaming the SERP—233 px. Alignment is much closer when the cursor is being actively used to examine, read, or perform an action. The median distance when examining the page using the cursor is 167 px, while the alignment is closer when using the cursor to read—150 px. When the subject is moving the cursor to perform an action involving a click, alignment is extremely close—77 px, and even closer at the actual click—74 px. This agrees with findings from Hauger et al. that being in motion increases the alignment between cursor and gaze [20].

Behavior	Inactive	Examining	Reading	Action	Click
Total Time	58.8%	32.9%	2.5%	5.7%	-
Distance	233 px	167 px	150 px	77 px	74 px

Table 1. The median gaze-cursor distance for different cursor behaviors. The total time is summed across all subjects and search tasks.

During the study, the cursor was inactive a total of 18,554 seconds (58.8% of the time), representing time the subject may have been looking through the page without moving the mouse or just pausing for a few moments to read or think. This is more than the combined time of examining, reading, and performing an action on the page, meaning that a substantial period exists in which it is difficult to predict the gaze position. Anecdotally, some people believe they rarely use the cursor while examining Web pages. But in aggregate, a large portion of time is still spent actively moving the cursor, most of which does not produce an action.

Claypool et al. remarked, "Some users move the mouse while reading the window text or looking at interesting objects on the page, while others move the mouse only to click on interesting links" [10]. We quantified individual differences in gaze-cursor alignment and cursor behavior; Table 2 presents the duration of each cursor behavior and gaze-cursor alignment for each subject. The distances were macro-averaged over search tasks for each subject to negate the effect of a subject spending more time on certain search tasks.

Leaving the cursor idle from 50% to 79% of the time was common, like Subject 29 who left the cursor inactive during the majority of the time. Other subjects actively moved the

Subject	Gender	Age	Inactive		Examining		Reading		Action		Click
			Distance	Time	Distance	Time	Distance	Time	Distance	Time	Distance
1	F	46	188 px	68%	116 px	27%	45 px	0%	46 px	4.8%	49 px
2	M	56	201 px	65%	149 px	28%	133 px	0%	79 px	5.9%	73 px
3	F	35	165 px	47%	144 px	47%	167 px	2%	82 px	4.9%	75 px
4	M	47	162 px	61%	218 px	26%	214 px	6%	113 px	7.2%	106 px
5	F	31	246 px	45%	139 px	42%	134 px	6%	76 px	6.7%	89 px
6	M	44	175 px	59%	163 px	32%	211 px	1%	108 px	7.4%	101 px
7	M	57	144 px	60%	100 px	29%	93 px	6%	76 px	5.9%	81 px
8	F	47	309 px	63%	224 px	30%	143 px	3%	58 px	3.7%	43 px
9	F	50	262 px	56%	150 px	31%	146 px	8%	89 px	5.7%	100 px
10	M	59	180 px	65%	165 px	29%	209 px	1%	139 px	4.6%	126 px
11	M	50	247 px	50%	198 px	36%	256 px	4%	106 px	9.9%	81 px
12	F	39	236 px	29%	140 px	55%	125 px	5%	74 px	10.7%	77 px
13	F	45	177 px	55%	155 px	33%	204 px	4%	95 px	7.3%	71 px
14	M	50	206 px	49%	195 px	41%	177 px	2%	91 px	7.4%	93 px
15	F	38	294 px	68%	202 px	23%	168 px	2%	129 px	6.7%	88 px
16	F	26	152 px	61%	131 px	27%	118 px	2%	98 px	8.8%	84 px
17	F	46	218 px	55%	152 px	36%	145 px	4%	69 px	5.1%	65 px
18	M	50	245 px	58%	244 px	34%	251 px	2%	92 px	6.4%	116 px
19	F	50	185 px	55%	120 px	38%	142 px	2%	58 px	5.1%	46 px
20	M	39	370 px	44%	219 px	47%	140 px	3%	97 px	6.1%	70 px
21	M	38	146 px	39%	164 px	49%	139 px	1%	69 px	10.1%	59 px
22	M	47	216 px	69%	160 px	24%	173 px	3%	92 px	4.4%	71 px
23	F	46	218 px	50%	190 px	42%	196 px	1%	76 px	6.5%	64 px
24	F	48	224 px	61%	178 px	34%	89 px	0%	64 px	4.7%	47 px
25	F	54	228 px	56%	184 px	36%	173 px	1%	39 px	6.8%	26 px
26	F	44	166 px	32%	167 px	58%	116 px	1%	78 px	8.1%	109 px
27	F	28	161 px	58%	142 px	33%	112 px	0%	90 px	8.3%	52 px
28	F	51	259 px	56%	195 px	34%	242 px	2%	76 px	7.5%	72 px
29	F	41	218 px	79%	171 px	15%	148 px	1%	89 px	5.7%	119 px
30	M	48	279 px	50%	138 px	37%	87 px	5%	42 px	7.7%	38 px
31	M	59	192 px	58%	175 px	34%	162 px	3%	152 px	4.5%	133 px
32	F	53	236 px	61%	199 px	35%	77 px	0%	52 px	3.3%	77 px
33	M	60	418 px	62%	305 px	27%	319 px	3%	69 px	8.0%	105 px
34	F	47	245 px	59%	214 px	36%	160 px	1%	44 px	4.2%	34 px
35	M	44	187 px	73%	133 px	22%	167 px	1%	68 px	4.7%	85 px
36	F	37	290 px	76%	231 px	20%	147 px	1%	58 px	2.9%	56 px

Table 2. Basic demographic information for each subject, the proportion of time spent performing each cursor behavior, and the average distance between gaze and cursor while performing that cursor behavior. Clicks are considered instantaneous events and therefore have no duration.

cursor while examining the page; Subject 12 spent 55% of their time examining the page with the cursor, and a mere 29% of their time idling the cursor. Reading behavior comprised 2% or less of total search time for more than half the subjects (22 of 36), who exhibited nearly no reading behavior (per the definition of this behavior that we used). At the other end of the spectrum, Subject 9 spent 8% of their time reading with the cursor. Turning to gaze-cursor distance, some subjects had poor alignment (Subject 33) when not performing an action. While in the aggregate, subjects had stronger alignment when the cursor was active, Subject 18 had essentially unchanged alignment between inactive, examining, and reading behaviors. These differences show that individuals vary substantially in their cursor behavior usage and gaze-cursor alignment. We initially thought that perhaps the variation in users' gaze-cursor alignment could be explained by choice of cursor behavior, but for each cursor behavior, gaze-cursor alignment still varied substantially among our subjects.

PREDICTING GAZE

So far, we have seen the effects of user, query, dwell time, cursor behavior, and future cursor positions on gaze-cursor alignment. These features can provide guidance about whether the alignment is stronger or weaker. Predicting the strength of alignment is useful in determining the confidence of the gaze position from only interaction features—without using an eye-tracker. We now focus on a more aggressive prediction: to find the position of the gaze using only interaction features, rather than how confident we are that the cursor position approximates the gaze position. To do this, we extract four types of features from the interaction data, aiming to select features that seemed to influence the gaze-cursor alignment, as informed by our earlier analysis.

Features

At each time t that we want to predict the gaze position, we have the **cursor position** at that time, represented by a tuple (x, y). The cursor position alone is suggested for approximating gaze position in some prior literature and current Web analytics services. This approach is the baseline against which we will compare our performance, but we also use cursor position as a feature in our gaze prediction model.

Cursor behavior has a strong effect on gaze-cursor alignment. Both our earlier analysis and a study by Hauger et al. [20] showed that active cursors are better aligned with gaze than inactive cursors. To generalize this, we use the idle time following the last movement before t as the **behavior** feature, representing activity level.

Each recorded interaction on the Web page has a corresponding timestamp, allowing us to deduce the length of time since the SERP has loaded. Our analysis has shown that the time since the SERP loaded influences the gaze-cursor alignment. This time $(\text{current}_t - \text{pageload}_t)$ is the **dwell** feature, which we incorporate into our model. Guo and Agichtein also use this feature to predict gaze-cursor alignment [19].

Our analysis showed that for every subject in our study, the cursor position lagged behind the gaze position, since there is a stronger correlation between a future cursor position and the current gaze position. We refer to the most likely later cursor position for the current gaze as the **future** feature. The future cursor positions were only used if the last movement was within 10 seconds of the target future time.

We also used the interaction effect of cursor position with dwell and cursor position with behavior, since we know that behavior and dwell affect alignment. The user or query were not treated as features for two reasons. First, in practical situations, a user's gaze data is not available to train the model. Second, there is unlikely to be enough gaze data for most queries to train the model, and in our analysis described earlier in the paper, we found that query only has a modest effect on gaze-cursor alignment. Our current features are all global and so require fewer training examples in the form of eye-tracking data (i.e., actual gaze positions).

Experiment

We predict the subject's gaze position using a linear model of interaction features. The ground truth is the gaze position measured by the eye-tracking system. The x- and y-coordinates of the gaze position were predicted separately. To compute the weights (coefficients) for each feature, we performed a multiple linear regression. Figure 6 illustrates the value of gaze prediction in an example query session with cursor positions, gaze positions, and predicted gaze positions overlaid on the SERP.

The model for the regression for the x-coordinate is:

$$g_x \sim c_x + \log(t_d) + \log(t_m) + c_x \times \log(t_d) + c_x \times \log(t_m) + f_x \quad (2)$$

where t_d is the dwell time, t_m is the time since a movement, c_x is the x-coordinate of the cursor position, g_x is the x-coordinate of the gaze position, and f_x is the most likely x-coordinate of the gaze based on future cursor positions. The regression for the y-coordinate was similar, but substituting x for y in Equation 2.

The evaluation was a 36-fold cross-validation, where each fold was an individual subject; this is essentially a leave-one-out evaluation for each subject. By testing each subject separately with the training data of all 35 other subjects, we achieve a practical method of predicting the gaze position for users that we have not seen before (which would be the typical case in a real deployment). Essentially, we ran a multiple linear regression on the gaze and interaction data of 35 subjects to compute weights (coefficients), then used those coefficients to predict gaze data from just the interaction data for the test subject. This process was repeated for every subject being the test subject. For each subject we tested, we computed the RMSE for their predicted gaze with and without the future feature, as well as the RMSE for just the cursor positions. Without using the future feature, there is a potential application for real-time gaze prediction, while with future cursor positions, the gaze prediction must be performed offline (after the query session, e.g., for analytics).

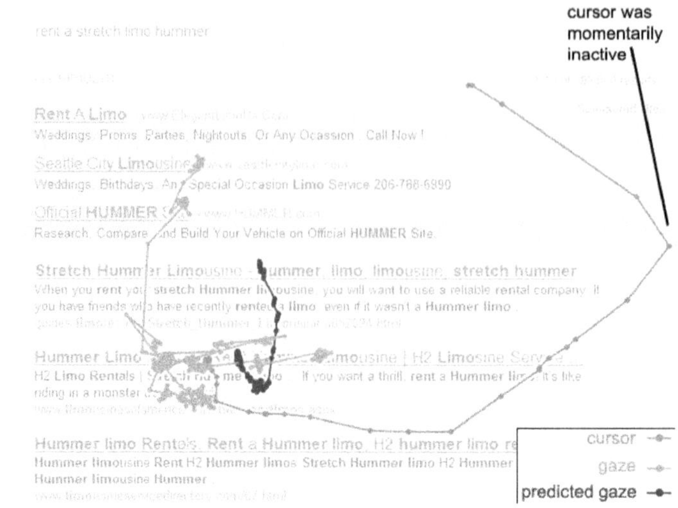

Figure 6. The cursor position (orange), the gaze position predicted by the linear regression model (purple), and the gaze position as determined by the eye-tracker (green) are drawn over the SERP presented to the subject following the query "rent a stretch limo hummer" from our study. The figure omits the right and left columns of the SERP.

Table 3 shows the results of the prediction experiment. When using only the cursor position for prediction, the distance RMSE is 236.6 px. But using a multiple linear regression with cursor position, behavior, and dwell time, the predicted gaze position is significantly better—186.3 px, a 21.3% decrease in RMSE. Adding future cursor data from that query session to the model reduces RMSE further to an overall 23.5% decrease in RMSE compared to just using the cursor position. The RMSEs in the x- and y-coordinates alone were similarly improved by the linear model. An ANOVA shows that the RMSE differed significantly between gaze-cursor alignment and alignment between gaze and predicted gaze along the x-axis ($F(2, 105) = 59.72, p < 0.001$) and Euclidean distance ($F(2, 105) = 41.31, p < 0.001$).

The Lindeman, Merenda and Gold (LMG) metric [24] (R^2 partitioned by averaging over orders) determined the relative importance of the features for predicting the x-coordinate. They were in descending order of importance: $\log(t_d)$, c_x, f_x, $c_x \times \log(t_m)$, $\log(t_m)$, and $c_x \times \log(t_d)$; the relative importance of the features for predicting the y-coordinate in descending order: c_y, f_y, $\log(t_d)$, $\log(t_m)$, $c_y \times \log(t_m)$, and $c_y \times \log(t_d)$.

	RMSE_x	RMSE_y	RMSE_d
Cursor (baseline)	185.0 px	145.0 px	236.6 px
Predicted Gaze with Cursor+Behavior+Dwell	125.2 px	137.1 px	186.3 px
Predicted Gaze with Cursor+Behavior+Dwell+Future	125.1 px	129.9 px	181.1 px

Table 3. The computed accuracies in cross-validation evaluations of estimating the gaze position using the cursor position, the cursor position along with behavior and duration using multiple linear regression, and the cursor position along with behavior, duration, and future cursor positions using multiple linear regression. The accuracy is measured by root-mean-square error for the x-axis, y-axis, and Euclidean distance.

DISCUSSION

Our study has shown that gaze-cursor alignment is situational, as it depends on the time spent on the page, personal browsing habits, and a user's current cursor behavior (inactive, examining, reading, action). An experiment showed that a model using these features could predict the subject's gaze significantly better than using the cursor position alone. These findings have implications for using large-scale cursor data more effectively, which has already been demonstrated to be efficiently obtainable at scale [2, 22].

Our findings suggest that for certain circumstances, it may be possible to predict the actual gaze position on SERPs using only cursor features. This extends previous work [19] which attempted the binary prediction task of whether we can be confident of gaze-cursor alignment within a threshold. Using a linear model, we show that there is room for improving gaze prediction by using other factors on top of solely the cursor position. Our predictive model reduces the RMSE by 60 px in the x-direction and is 15 px more accurate in the y-direction. 15 px is around two lines of text on a SERP, and 60 px is around 10 characters of that text. These gains could be significant for differentiating between engagement with regions on the SERP, especially when the cursor is near the boundary of two or more regions. However, since the linear regression fits using least squares, the predicted gaze tends to be conservative and often stays around the center of the screen. This leads us to believe that gaze prediction may be improved further by a more complex combination of the features, perhaps in non-linear models, since we intuit that interaction effects of time, behavior, and cursor position exist.

The gaze prediction results in Table 3 suggest a counterintuitive finding. While several past studies [19, 22, 27] agree that the cursor is better correlated with the gaze in the y-direction than the x-direction, the x-coordinate of the gaze is easier to predict than the y-coordinate. This subverts the expectation that better correlation leads to better prediction for gaze. This may be an artifact of our model, but perhaps left-right eye movement is less surprising than up-down movement. Scrolling may cause the cursor to move down relative to the page, making it a good estimate of vertical attention, whereas most SERPs require little horizontal scrolling.

Cursor tracking, deemed the "poor man's eye tracker" [12], may approximate gaze tracking without the eye tracker depending on the accuracy required. Although cursor features would allow us to model many aspects of user attention *in situ* as they browse the Web from home, they cannot completely replace gaze. For example, eye-gaze fixation is a positive signal of interest because the user pays more attention to that position, but prolonged cursor fixation may not be since given our findings in this study, the user's attention is probably elsewhere. Here we elected to focus on understanding different cursor behaviors rather than gaze fixations to support cursor-tracking applications that can be remotely deployed on a Web site. More work is needed to study in more detail the relationship between cursor and gaze fixations, especially to determine if and when there are cases in which cursor fixations can be reliably interpreted as attention.

Bringing subjects into an eye-tracking lab creates inherent limitations to our study. Subjects may behave differently in the lab with a camera monitoring their gaze than in a natural setting. They are unlikely to take breaks in the lab or multi-task by doing other things at the same time, factors which may affect cursor behavior outside of the lab. We also gave them artificial search tasks; while we tried to ground the search tasks in realistic information needs, the tasks might not be a representative sample. Additionally, though SERPs provide a controlled environment for our studies (and there are already several applications if we focus on that domain alone), more work is also needed to generalize this research beyond SERPs to any Web page. Previous work has already shown that cursor is less aligned with gaze on non-SERP pages [22], so the prediction task on such pages may be more challenging and is reserved for future work.

The results show that we predicted gaze more accurately when we used past and future cursor movement data, rather than only past data. Using past data alone would allow us to build applications that could respond to user attention in real-time, such as a focus-plus-context view of the SERP, in which the context could update dynamically with new content based on where the user had already attended during their engagement with the SERP. More valuable however, is inferring gaze positions after the user has left the SERP. This would allow us to accurately model where on the SERP the user examined and use this data for applications such as building richer searcher models (improving on existing models, e.g., [8, 16]), usability assessments [1, 2], or profiling users [2].

CONCLUSION

We have found that user, time, and search task (to a lesser extent) each contribute to the variation in gaze-cursor alignment. The gaze and cursor positions are also better aligned when the gaze position is compared to a future cursor position. Furthermore, by distinguishing between five different cursor behaviors—inactive, examining, reading, action, and click—we get a better idea of the strength of alignment. In fact, we have been able to improve upon using cursor position alone to predict the gaze position by using several cursor features. Cursor movements, scrolling, and other client-side interactions are easy to collect at scale, which many Web analytics services offer to do. But claiming that the cursor approximates the gaze is misguided—as we have shown, this is often not the case depending on time and behavior. Instead, it is important to predict the real location of the attention when an eye-tracker is unavailable.

ACKNOWLEDGMENTS

We thank Katherine Ye for editing earlier drafts of the paper.

REFERENCES

1. Arroyo, E., Selker, T., and Wei, W. Usability tool for analysis of web designs using mouse tracks. In *CHI Extended Abstracts* (2006), 484–489.

2. Atterer, R., Wnuk, M., and Schmidt, A. Knowing the user's every move: user activity tracking for website usability evaluation and implicit interaction. In *Proceedings of WWW* (2006), 203–212.

3. Aula, A., Majaranta, P., and Räihä, K.-J. Eye-tracking reveals the personal styles for search result evaluation. In *Proceedings of INTERACT* (2005), 1058–1061.

4. Buscher, G., Cutrell, E., and Morris, M. R. What do you see when you're surfing?: using eye tracking to predict salient regions of web pages. In *Proceedings of CHI* (2009), 21–30.

5. Buscher, G., Dengel, A., and van Elst, L. Eye movements as implicit relevance feedback. In *CHI Extended Abstracts* (2008), 2991–2996.

6. Buscher, G., Dumais, S. T., and Cutrell, E. The good, the bad, and the random: an eye-tracking study of ad quality in web search. In *Proceedings of SIGIR* (2010), 42–49.

7. Buscher, G., van Elst, L., and Dengel, A. Segment-level display time as implicit feedback: a comparison to eye tracking. In *Proceedings of SIGIR* (2009), 67–74.

8. Chapelle, O., and Zhang, Y. A dynamic bayesian network click model for web search ranking. In *Proceedings of WWW* (2009), 1–10.

9. Chen, M. C., Anderson, J. R., and Sohn, M. H. What can a mouse cursor tell us more?: correlation of eye/mouse movements on web browsing. In *CHI Extended Abstracts* (2001), 281–282.

10. Claypool, M., Le, P., Wased, M., and Brown, D. Implicit interest indicators. In *Proceedings of IUI* (2001), 33–40.

11. Cole, M. J., Gwizdka, J., Liu, C., Bierig, R., Belkin, N. J., and Zhang, X. Task and user effects on reading patterns in information search. *Interacting with Computers 23*, 4 (2011), 346 – 362.

12. Cooke, L. Is the mouse a poor man's eye tracker? In *Proceedings of STC* (2006).

13. Cutrell, E., and Guan, Z. What are you looking for?: an eye-tracking study of information usage in web search. In *Proceedings of CHI* (2007), 407–416.

14. Dumais, S. T., Buscher, G., and Cutrell, E. Individual differences in gaze patterns for web search. In *Proceedings of IIiX* (2010), 185–194.

15. Goecks, J., and Shavlik, J. Learning users' interests by unobtrusively observing their normal behavior. In *Proceedings of IUI* (2000), 129–132.

16. Guo, F., Liu, C., Kannan, A., Minka, T., Taylor, M., Wang, Y.-M., and Faloutsos, C. Click chain model in web search. In *Proceedings of WWW* (2009), 11–20.

17. Guo, Q., and Agichtein, E. Exploring mouse movements for inferring query intent. In *Proceedings of SIGIR* (2008), 707–708.

18. Guo, Q., and Agichtein, E. Ready to buy or just browsing?: detecting web searcher goals from interaction data. In *Proceedings of SIGIR* (2010), 130–137.

19. Guo, Q., and Agichtein, E. Towards predicting web searcher gaze position from mouse movements. In *Proceedings of CHI* (2010), 3601–3606.

20. Hauger, D., Paramythis, A., and Weibelzahl, S. Using browser interaction data to determine page reading behavior. In *Proceedings of UMAP* (2011), 147–158.

21. Hijikata, Y. Implicit user profiling for on demand relevance feedback. In *Proceedings of IUI* (2004), 198–205.

22. Huang, J., White, R. W., and Dumais, S. No clicks, no problem: using cursor movements to understand and improve search. In *Proceedings of CHI* (2011), 1225–1234.

23. Ianniello, J. Time delay estimation via cross-correlation in the presence of large estimation errors. *IEEE Trans. Acoust., Speech, Signal Process. 30*, 6 (1982), 998–1003.

24. Lindeman, R., Merenda, P., and Gold, R. *Introduction to Bivariate and Multivariate Analysis*. Scott Foresman, Glenview IL, 1980, 119.

25. Liu, C.-C., and Chung, C.-W. Detecting mouse movement with repeated visit patterns for retrieving noticed knowledge components on web pages. *IEICE - Trans. Inf. Syst. E90-D*, 10 (October 2007), 1687–1696.

26. Reichle, E. D., Pollatsek, A., and Rayner, K. E-z reader: A cognitive-control, serial-attention model of eye-movement behavior during reading. *Cognitive Systems Research 7*, 1 (2006), 4 – 22.

27. Rodden, K., and Fu, X. Exploring how mouse movements relate to eye movements on web search results pages. In *SIGIR Workshop on Web Information Seeking and Interaction* (2007), 29–32.

28. Rodden, K., Fu, X., Aula, A., and Spiro, I. Eye-mouse coordination patterns on web search results pages. In *CHI Extended Abstracts* (2008), 2997–3002.

29. Shapira, B., Taieb-Maimon, M., and Moskowitz, A. Study of the usefulness of known and new implicit indicators and their optimal combination for accurate inference of users interests. In *Proceedings of SAC* (2006), 1118–1119.

30. Teevan, J., Dumais, S. T., and Liebling, D. J. To personalize or not to personalize: modeling queries with variation in user intent. In *Proceedings of SIGIR* (2008), 163–170.

31. Torres, L. A. L., and Hernando, R. V. (smt) real time mouse tracking registration and visualization tool for usability evaluation on websites. In *Proceedings of IADIS WWW/Internet* (2007), 187–192.

32. Ware, C., and Mikaelian, H. H. An evaluation of an eye tracker as a device for computer input. In *Proceedings of CHI* (1987), 183–188.

33. Weber, I., and Castillo, C. The demographics of web search. In *Proceedings of SIGIR* (2010), 523–530.

Participation and Publics: Supporting Community Engagement

Christopher A. Le Dantec
School of Literature, Communication & Culture
Georgia Institute of Technology
Atlanta, GA. USA
christopher.ledantec@lcc.gatech.edu

ABSTRACT
CHI researchers are beginning a shift from studying technology use in uncommon or exotic communities to designing and deploying technology interventions into those same settings. This paper picks up on these recent developments and further examines the impact and implication of using a bespoke technology platform within the context of providing shelter and basic social services to homeless mothers and their children. I build on findings from a previous system deployment by describing targeted changes made to the technology, the design impetus for making those changes, and the resulting impact those changes had on the relationship between shelter staff, residents, and the information they shared via the system. By way of the findings reported here, I continue to develop the framing of Deweyan publics as a way to scaffold an environmental approach to technology design in contexts with multiple and diverse stakeholders.

Author Keywords
Constructed Publics, Homeless; Urban Computing; Longitudinal Study; Qualitative Methods

ACM Classification Keywords
H.5.3 Group and Organization Interface: Collaborative Computing, Evaluation/methodology

General Terms
Design, Theory

INTRODUCTION
HCI research has established a rich and robust body of work examining the challenges and opportunities of developing technologies with and for users in developing regions of the world (*e.g.*, [25, 28, 35]); however, research aimed at marginalized populations within Western society has only recently begun to gain momentum. Examples of this research include examining the technology practices of the urban homeless [18, 30], developing insight into the lives of homeless youth [41, 42], and investigating the organizational and institutional issues social service providers contend with as they manage their organizations, their clients, and their technology [19, 20, 37].

In addition to work that has sought out the socio-economically downtrodden, HCI researchers have also begun to investigate alternate narratives of technology use not driven by the prevailing consumerism present in the wealthier quarters of developed locales [29, 32]. Each of these diverse projects can be taken as a response, in their own contexts and via their own perspectives, to a question Cohen posed in his paper, "who do we talk about when we talk about users?" [6]. Whether dealing with social services for the most at-risk members of society, or engaging small and isolated communities to better understand the many dimensions of sustainability, these projects describe encounters with technology informed by different cultural, economic, and political constraints and provide an empirical perspective for reflecting on the pairings of "whos" and "whats" [6].

While HCI researchers have taken the first steps toward understanding the impact and implication of technology within the contexts described above, we are only now beginning to see the design, development, and evaluation of systems built to address the specific user needs extant in these settings [9, 21, 22]. This paper picks up on these recent developments and further examines the impact and implication of using a bespoke technology platform within the context of providing shelter and basic social services to homeless mothers and their children.

My aim in this paper is to further develop insight into the role technology can play in shaping the relationship between service providers and their clients. This paper builds directly upon earlier work that described the modes of use and social routines that developed around an information system—called the Community Resource Messenger (CRM)—that was deployed at a shelter for homeless mothers [22]. Here, I extend that work by describing targeted changes made to the CRM that were driven by feedback from an initial deployment. The changes made to the CRM were intended to enhance practices of use that had developed during the initial deployment, further supporting staff-client relationships and improving the quality of information shared. While the changes achieved some of the de-

Permission to make digital or hard copies of all or part of this work for personal or classroom use is granted without fee provided that copies are not made or distributed for profit or commercial advantage and that copies bear this notice and the full citation on the first page. To copy otherwise, or republish, to post on servers or to redistribute to lists, requires prior specific permission and/or a fee.
CHI'12, May 5–10, 2012, Austin, TX, USA.
Copyright 2012 ACM 978-1-4503-1015-4/12/05... $10.00.

sired affect, they also fundamentally altered existing perceptions and patterns of use with the system.

These changes in-turn affected the formation and legibility of a "public" at the shelter. The framing of "publics"—of groups of diverse stakeholders bound by common issues [8]—informed the initial system design and deployment [21, 22] and provided a framework to scaffold an ecological approach to technology design and intervention in a context with multiple and diverse stakeholders. I will return to this framework and focus on specific design and functional elements that supported and inhibited the expression and formation of a public at the shelter and discuss the implications for sustaining modes of participation beyond initial design activities.

BACKGROUND, SYSTEM DESIGN, & DEPLOYMENT

What follows is a précis of the notion of Deweyan publics and a brief overview of the basic system features—further details of the foundational fieldwork, system design, and initial deployment findings have been reported elsewhere [18, 20, 21, 22]. In this paper, I will focus on the new and altered features of the CRM and contrast the routines and modes of use that developed during the first and second deployments of the system.

Deweyan Publics & Design

The notion of publics has recently begun to garner attention within the HCI and participatory design (PD) literature. While there are different conceptions of what a public is and how it is constituted [15, 23, 40], the version presented here builds on Dewey's conception, presented in his 1927 book, "The Public and Its Problems" [8]. For Dewey, a public does not exist *a priori*, it forms through the identification and expression of a common social condition and the action taken by diverse stakeholders to contend with that social condition—it is the combination of identifying a shared issue, one that crosses multiple stakeholder boundaries, and then in working toward a common end to overcome or resolve that issue. The notion of Deweyan publics is germane to HCI and the design of interactive technologies in so far as it provides space for conceptualizing multiparty engagement with technology by identifying and relating shared issues and promoting or supporting different forms of action taken to mitigate or contend with those issues [10, 11, 21].

Both in Dewey's pragmatist view of participatory democracy (which sits at the heart of his notion of publics), and in the early movements that gave rise to the social phenomena around the Internet, we find a deep optimism about society's ability to overcome challenges through sharing ideas (*i.e.*, identifying issues) and engaging with each other (*i.e.*, mobilizing action) [1, 8, 39]. As such, technology's role in forming a public occurs at the intersection of the socio-technical interactions between mediating the expression of issues and supporting the action taken in response.

We can find guides for understanding what kinds of socio-technical resources are marshaled in the support of issue expression and corresponding action by examining a procedural account of constituting a public. This process begins with the expression of common issues which are informed by the particular perspectives brought by the constituents of the nascent public. As a public mobilizes to address the identified issues, it implicates a set of relations in the world, both via individuals and via resources in the community. These relationships can be described as "attachments" [24]. As Marres points out, the notion of attachments provides a means for understanding the conflicts inherent in the constitution of publics by recognizing the interplay and emergence of dependencies on, and commitments to different resources: "by approaching issues as particular entanglements of actors' attachments, it becomes possible to credit these entanglements as sources and resources for [the] enacting of public involvement in controversy" [24]. The notion of attachments, then, foregrounds the dynamic relationships between issues and diverse stakeholders and helps mitigate a tendency toward assuming a stable set of values, or ideas, or institutional relationships.

The ongoing discourse in PD concerning the modes and motivations for engaging with power structures and marginalization creates a bridge from the theoretical perspective of Marres to the practical applications of design [2, 3, 33]. Indeed, a move toward approaching PD as one of identifying and establishing attachments—and of constituting publics—is consistent with an activist agenda of broadening the impact of PD beyond the role of simply creating products [33]. Furthermore, the shift from product to public is an important one as it places the emphasis on sustained participation through the entire lifecycle of an artifact, service, or system. Recent work in PD has developed this position, shifting focus from current (or proximate) use, to facilitating future use [4, 12].

Ehn connects this design-for-future-use to Star and Bowker's notion of infrastructuring [12, 36]. Briefly, infrastructuring is the work of developing and integrating different forms of social and technical infrastructure; it is a sustained process of developing and refining attachments to different social and material resources. The work of infrastructuring is critical to both the notion of Deweyan publics and to Ehn's argument of design-for-future-use because it shifts the focus *toward* creating a sustainable *process* of developing and refining attachments to different socio-technical resources and *away* from focusing simply on co-creating a temporally and materially fixed *artifact*.

The perspective of constituting publics—of identifying and creating attachments to common issues, of enacting responses to those common issues, and of seeking to support modes of infrastructuring through the social and technical resources—motivated the design of the CRM [21, 22]. The overarching agenda was formulated by working with the staff and residents at the shelter to identify common issues. Together, we then worked to provide technical resources that could mediate the articulation of issues and support action by the staff and residents to overcome the issues identified. The set of issues the system was designed to confront included helping staff manage constrained resources and to build relationships with their assigned residents [16, 19, 20]; for the residents, the focus was on access to and ordering of information as well as supporting continuity in the social support network they were establishing during their brief stay at the shelter [16, 17, 18]. Within these broad issues, specific attachments formed and dissolved over the course of the two system deployments, and the staff and residents encountered and enacted their responses to theses issues in different ways based on their understanding and expectation of the CRM's functionality as it was modified over the two deployments.

System Overview

The participatory process used to design the CRM resulted in the development of three user-facing components [21]: staff at the shelter accessed the system through a web application called the Message Center which provided an interface for sending and receiving Short Message Service (SMS) messages to residents' phones; shelter residents interacted directly with their mobile phones, sending and receiving messages from the staff throughout their stay at the shelter; both staff and residents had access to a Shared Message Board where each could post information and announcements.

The broad goals of the initial feature set were to support the sharing of information and resources between the staff and residents as well as among the residents. For the staff, this support largely turned on providing tools that helped them amplify their contact with each resident via the mechanism of mobile messaging and the addition of asynchronous communication in a setting that had previously relied on synchronous communication. To support the residents, unmodified mobile phones were selected as the primary interface due to their familiarity and prevalence, even among the very poor and homeless [18]. The Shared Message Board was designed as a common space where both staff and residents could post messages, and where messages would all have equal visibility, regardless of provenance, thus providing a platform for the residents to articulate issues in a setting that presented their knowledge and experience on equal footing with information from the staff. Based on feedback given during the initial deployment, the staff and residents felt there were ways to improve the CRM, especially the experience of the Shared Message Board, which had become a valuable resource at the shelter as staff and residents built routines around sharing and seeking information from the prominently located screen.

SYSTEM DEPLOYMENT

The deployment of the CRM occurred over two distinct periods: the initial deployment began in February of 2010 and lasted 30 weeks [22]; the second deployment, the focus of this paper, took place during the end of 2010 and beginning of 2011 and lasted 16 weeks. Between the two deployments was a period of 11 weeks that facilitated a focused redesign of the Shared Message Board and the addition of an SMS subscription service for the residents. In total, the CRM was deployed and in constant use at the shelter for over a year (and remains in use now).

Both deployments of the CRM were built around a systematic program of semiweekly meetings with shelter staff and residents to understand how their relationship to, and use of the CRM developed. My meetings with the residents alternated between one-on-one meetings and focus groups with everyone. The protocol included a specific interview session upon exiting the shelter to discuss the residents' experience with the CRM and to what degree it provided real, actionable information or support. When working with the staff, I conducted semi-structured interviews that were framed by the ongoing system use and any issues the staff were having with the CRM. Interviews with both staff and residents were informed by examining the number and content of messages sent via the system.

In addition to the interviews, residents were asked to complete a brief demographic and technology experience survey that included questions about specific applications, *e.g.*, SMS on the mobile phone and chat, email, and social networking sites on the PC, and the frequency of use with these different applications.

Finally, in addition to the surveys and interview data, I also conducted observational fieldwork during my semiweekly trips to the shelter. The observation data also informed interviews with staff and residents and contextualized the responses and reactions that came out of those sessions.

The survey responses, the notes from interviews with staff and residents, the exit interview responses, the field notes from my ongoing site observations, and detailed system logs comprised the data I used to analyze system use and integration at the shelter. Field notes and interview data were analyzed in an ongoing inductive manner that allowed me to refine the interviews held with staff and residents [27]. Data from system usage provided content detail and contextual information describing when and how the staff and residents were using the CRM.

Overview of Participants

The staff who used the CRM included three women: the program director, a weekend case manager, and a night manager. The program director ran the shelter's daily case management activities and had a very hands-on style of working with the residents. The case manager worked with the residents during the weekends but was also present one night a week to followup and support specific programs she was working on with the residents. The night manager was only present in the evenings and was there primarily as an emergency contact with no formal case management responsibilities; though, she did play an important support role as another confidant for the women at the shelter.

Over the course of the 16 week system deployment presented here, 13 residents participated in the study (all residents at the shelter during the deployment period consented to participating in the study). All of the residents were female, and self-identified as African American. Residents' average age was 34 years old; the oldest resident was 42, and the youngest 28. Education levels of the residents skewed toward less formal education: six residents had not completed high school, three had high school diplomas, two had completed some college, and two had a two- or four-

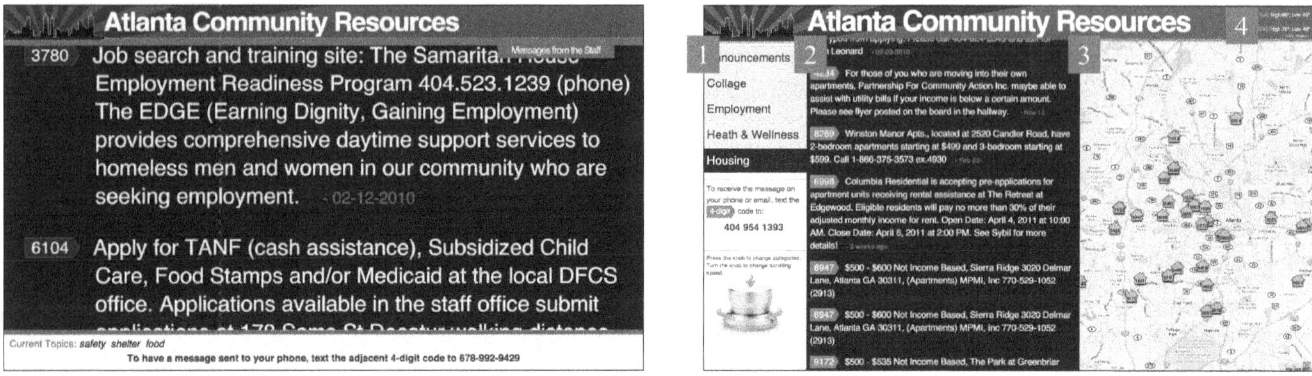

Figure 1: The Shared Message Board before (left) and after (right) redesign.

year college degree. Residents stayed at the shelter for an average of 52 days.

Mobile phone ownership was common and all but one of the residents had their own mobile phone. A Nokia E50 along with $50 worth of pre-paid credit was provided to the resident who did not have her own phone—other residents were reimbursed for any study-related usage charges. Just over half of the residents (seven of the 13) had monthly contracts for mobile service; the rest were using pre-paid service plans. As with mobile phone ownership, all but one of the residents had used SMS messaging—and the residents each reported using it heavily, sending hundreds of messages a month. Personal computer ownership was less common, only three of the residents reported owning a computer; however, all of the residents used computers at least once a week through organized classes at the shelter. A majority of the women, 12, additionally reported using computers three or more times a week at places other than the shelter (*e.g.*, libraries, community centers, or at work). Residents' computer use was dominated by email and web browsing, and eight of the residents reported using social networking sites (specifically Facebook).

As was true in the initial deployment [22], residents at the shelter during the second deployment were voluminous users of SMS messaging; they also had basic computer skills and regular opportunities to use computers for work and socializing (most of the in-shelter computer time was dedicated to helping residents construct and update their résumé and to find work that would support their exit from the shelter). The previous technology experiences of the residents helped scaffold their understanding of the CRM and the different modes of interacting with it—from sending messages to the staff, to asking pointed questions about the resources available on the Shared Message Board.

EVOLVING THE DESIGN

During the initial 30-week deployment, stable modes of use developed that reconfigured work for the staff and shifted social boundaries between the staff and residents [22]. From these initial modes of use two ways to improve the CRM emerged and became the focus of the redesign work presented here. First, the staff desired the ability to present information on the Shared Message Board in a more categorized manner; second, the residents wanted an easier way to find new information on the Shared Message Board.

Concurrent to the initial CRM deployment, the shelter staff began to reorganize the way they documented their counseling sessions with the residents. The new documentation was broken down along several categories: childcare, employment, housing, and personal development. Once the staff began using this new documentation, they realized it would be desirable to display information on the Shared Message Board with the same scheme. Doing so would make it easier to refer to the Shared Message Board for specific items, and it would reinforce the organization of goals they were working on with the residents.

In addition to the more descriptive categories of information, the staff also wanted more scraped information from the web. During the initial deployment, the Shared Message Board displayed information from a housing search targeted at low-income and subsidized housing. Employment information was the next set of content the staff wanted updated daily so they could more easily provide the residents with an up-to-date list of relevant opportunities in the area.

For the residents, one of the pervasive annoyances with the original Shared Message Board was that it was tedious to find new information posted to the screen. Even though each post had a date next to it, messages would scroll across the screen at a modest rate, requiring considerable patience to ensure new information posted to the board was seen. This factor effected how the residents engaged with the Shared Message Board: once residents had become familiar with the majority of the information on the Shared Message Board, they had to spend more time at the screen to view new posts, often without knowing if anything new was available.

The response to these two challenges was two fold. First, the Shared Message Board was reorganized to present finer-grained categories of information based on the same categories the staff had developed for their counseling sessions. Second, an SMS subscription service was added so that messages from selected categories would be forwarded to residents' phones, thereby alerting them to new information in categories relevant to their current needs (as established together with the case worker or program manager).

Figure 1 shows the layout of the Shared Message Board before and after the redesign. The redesign was focused on four main areas (from left to right, following the numbers in the figure):

1. Up to six categories of content were available down the left-most column of the screen: Announcements, Collage (for content from the residents), Employment, Local Events, Health & Wellness, and Housing. The Employment and Housing categories included messages posted from the staff as well as scraped content from the web. The Shared Message Board automatically cycled through each category, however, categories could be manually changed with a PowerMate (a large aluminum knob) installed below the screen.
2. Messages in the displayed category scrolled from bottom to top. Scrolling in the second version of the Shared Message Board was controlled via the attached PowerMate, and enabled residents to slow the scroll rate to a near stop or make it move more quickly to advance past familiar content.
3. The Shared Message Board displayed either an image that complimented to the content (*e.g.*, of the neighborhood for the category "Local Events"), or was integrated with Google Maps for messages in the Employment and Housing categories. The Housing map placed markers for each of the listings currently being displayed by the Shared Message Board (as shown in Figure 1). Listings that were visible were highlighted on the map and the markers had 4-digit codes that matched the code next to the description to aid pairing description to location.
4. Finally, weather information was provided in the top right. The residents did not have access to TV news while at the shelter but they wanted basic information to help them plan ahead before leaving the shelter each morning.

FINDINGS

The changes to the CRM—the redesigned Shared Message Board and the new SMS subscription service—impacted both the way the staff used the system to communicate with the residents and their perceptions of the opportunities the system provided. The upshot was that the new and altered features, and the modes of use that developed around those features, changed the way the technology was marshaled to articulate and act upon common issues. Broadly speaking, the changes to the visual design and structure of information posted to the Shared Message Board transformed the relationship residents had to the system, shuttering some of the opportunities for adoption through adaptation that had previously occurred [22].

The Shared Message Board

The redesign of the Shared Message Board had an immediate impact on the shelter residents. This impact was particularly clear for the first five residents who experienced both the previous design of the Shared Message Board and the newly redesigned display and walk-up interaction (via the attached PowerMate). Residents who had experienced both designs were specifically asked to discuss the differences in how they viewed and used information on the board.

One of the first responses to the redesign was that it looked more complete and "professional." The availability of more extensive employment information, and the integration of Google Maps to show where jobs and housing opportunities were located was immediately pointed to as a useful improvement: one resident noted that she knew certain parts of town were not very safe and the housing map helped her identify which houses and apartments she should seek or avoid. The addition of multiple categories of content was also welcome as it reduced the total number of messages in any one category and made it easier to notice new messages in areas of interest, thus reducing the overall time spent in front of the screen looking for desired information.

As the weeks moved on and a new group of women took up residence in the shelter, they too developed a relationship to the Shared Message Board through the reported "professional" appearance of the screen and the structured information presented on it. One of the common points of discussion that came up during interviews and focus groups was that the information design did not look like something open to the residents: it was viewed as an attractive and effective way for the staff to present information *to* the residents, however, the Shared Message Board was not seen as a legitimate space for messages *from* the residents. This marked an important and somewhat unfortunate turn in the perception of the system. Instead of engaging with the technology to create a channel for developing a discourse about common issues, as had previously occurred [22], the residents approached the Shared Message Board only as a source for formal information about services and resources provided by the staff.

I contend that this shift in perception turns on two key dynamics: the legibility of the Shared Message Board—*i.e.*, how the technology was read—as a medium accessible to the residents, and the perceived legitimacy of participation in information production with the technology. In the initial design, the Shared Message Board was a little less polished, a little less complete, and those rough edges were legible as an invitation to try the technology and define its purpose through use. In short, the initial design benefited from ambiguity [14]: the lack of extensive categories in the first version and the plain appearance of text did not overly suggest specific uses, so the residents could and did develop a sense of legitimate use and took ownership of what could be posted to the Shared Message Board. This finding bears echoes of earlier work by Ehn and Kyng where they used cardboard mockups to explore technology design, arguing that the non-functional cardboard prototypes created a space for interpretation and adaptation by those they were design with [13].

The redesigned layout, stronger visual design, and more comprehensive categories transformed the Shared Message Board's purpose into a fixed, unambiguous vehicle for the vetted, categorized, and "business" information staff provided to residents. As such, the residents stepped away from the Shared Message Board as a vehicle for their own expression—a naturally messier affair, contingent on the personalities and issues present of any given group of residents [22]. By way of illustration, during both deployments I would ask the residents about using the Shared Message Board and encourage them to post information or experiences they thought would be useful to others in the shelter. During the initial deployment, this encouragement was sometimes met with surprise, "you mean we can post anything we want?" That surprise would then give way to modest engagement as residents posted information and began using the Shared Message Board as a vehicle for communicating with each other [22]. After the redesign, the same question was met with similar skepticism, however, the modest engagement with the system did not follow. In fact, only one resident posted anything to the Shared Message Board: two messages, both about a job fair. In subsequent interviews and focus groups, residents commented that they were not sure what they had to offer that the staff were not already providing—that the present categories excluded residents' production of content even as they improved consumption. The comments illustrate the shift in legibility of the CRM as a tool for staff to communicate to residents from a tool that had been used by both to communicate with each other.

Subscription Service

The subscription service created another set of changes to the ways the CRM mediated the relationship between the staff and residents. During resident intake, staff would set up subscriptions to information categories based on an initial needs assessment and in accordance with the categories used to structure counseling sessions (and the Shared Message Board) such as employment, health and wellness, and housing. These subscriptions would ensure residents received any new information about needed services. The motivation behind this service was that it would send relevant information to residents in a more timely manner and provided a second avenue for addressing the challenge residents had finding new information posted to the Shared Message Board.

The changes to the Shared Message Board and the addition of the subscription service created a positive feedback loop with regard to how the staff used the CRM. The categories on the Shared Message Board aligned with topics being covered with residents and the subscription service ensured broad dissemination of posted messages regarding those topics. This prompted a pragmatic shift in use as it reduced the amount of individual messages the staff needed to create while increasing and ordering the information sent based on established areas of need and interest (*e.g.*, housing or childcare or employment needs). Because residents were receiving messages from categories of interest negotiated with their case manager, there was an assumption that the information was relevant and helpful—which it often was, though that assumption precluded using the CRM to individually establish context through personal connection as had been the case in the initial deployment [22].

A clear measure of this new pattern of use was indicated in the system usage data. In the first few weeks of the deployment, the staff continued their previous habit of sending personalized messages via the CRM. As they became accustomed to the new features, however, personal messaging steadily decreased. By week 10 of the deployment, the subscription service had supplanted the majority of personally targeted messages, and by week 13, private messaging between staff and residents had all but ceased.

This shift in use was important because it marked a move away from using the CRM to develop a social connection with the residents. During the initial deployment, the staff used the the CRM to establish and strengthen their relationships with the residents through personal communication—messages such as "*I really enjoyed the meeting yesterday evening. Perhaps we should have more bonding and sharing experiences*", and "*Thank you, I look forward to talking to you too*" [22]. These kind of personalized messages faded from use during the second deployment, instead replaced by informational messages originating on the Shared Message Board and forwarded via the subscription service.

For the residents, the experience of using the CRM was not just a change in the content of messages from the staff, but also an increase in the total number of messages received. Yet, even as the residents were receiving more messages to their phones, they were sending fewer messages to the staff. Comparing message sending habits between the two deployments illustrates the significance of the change: during the initial deployment, each resident received an average of 5.7 messages and sent an average of 4.9 messages; in the second deployment, each resident received an average of 22 messages and sent an average of 2.8 messages. Where the initial deployment produced a more even split between messages sent by staff and those sent by residents—a 54/46 split—the second deployment saw that divide widen to an 89/11 split with the staff sending far more messages than the residents.

Where these two modifications to the CRM succeeded in providing more information to the residents, and doing so along expressed topics of interest and need, they undermined the development of conversation mediated by the CRM. In the initial deployment, specific information about services and programs was shared via SMS and via the Shared Message Board, but in addition to what might be called instrumental messages, there was a rich back drop of relationship-focused messages that amplified the connection the staff had to the residents and provided access to emotional and social support in addition to institutional and service support [22]. An unintended consequence of increasing the institutional and service support via the system redesign was that it overshadowed uses of the CRM that did not align strictly with information dissemination.

DISCUSSION

Where the CRM was initially used by the staff and residents to engage in communication and to create context for information, in the second deployment presented here, system use was reconfigured around information dissemination under the assumption that the categories present in the Shared Message Board and enacted in the subscription service provided the context. Furthermore, the changes to the Shared Message Board and the addition of the subscription service worked to create a perception of the CRM as a medium for the staff to present information to the residents rather than a technology to help both staff *and* residents develop a stronger working relationship: content became the primary currency of the CRM where previously content had been situated with context and connection.

From Dialogue to Broadcast

One characterization of how changes to the CRM affected the relationship staff and residents had with the system is that it was a shift from *dialogue* to *broadcast*. This shift had direct impact on the way the staff and residents used the CRM to identify and articulate shared issues and constitute a public. The routines of use that developed around the modified CRM were solidly grounded in information broadcast and consumption and the directional communication *from* the staff *to* the residents was reinforced by both the visual language and information architecture of the new Shared Message Board. Using a scheme of categorization derived from the structure and content of formal counseling and case work done at the shelter served to reinforce the directionality of the messaging and the perception of what kinds of information the Shared Message Board was intended to share. None of which is to say the information was useless or unhelpful, but rather that the relationship to the information and to the technology through which it was received did not prompt both staff *and* residents to contribute to the knowledge present and available through the different channels of the CRM.

These routines stand in contrast to those that developed during the initial deployment where residents used the Shared Message Board as a venue for *receiving* and *producing* information [22]. The public sharing of information on the Shared Message Board by residents during the initial deployment was not frequent, but it was habitual and recreated itself across different groups of cohabiting residents. Moreover, when it happened, the shared messages had the effect of coalescing identity and action by providing a mechanism for residents to express issues in their own terms [22]: it was a venue for identifying and articulating common issues among the residents and a resource the residents used to organize themselves into a coherent public [12, 24].

Based on the reactions of the residents to the redesigned Shared Message Board, the primary reason they did not incorporate the CRM and the Shared Message Board into their interactions with each other (in addition to their activities centered on finding employment, childcare, healthcare, etc.) was that the system had become legible as a space exclusively owned by the staff. Each of the 13 residents who participated in the study responded that the information on the Shared Message Board and the notices they received on their mobile phones via the subscription service were useful; however, they did not feel they had anything to add given the formalized categories of information present.

Without the perceived ability to engage with the CRM as a site of production and information sharing—without the sense of ownership of the technology that has been remarked on in other participatory settings [2, 7, 26]—the residents lost a resource for identifying and acting as a public. Another way to understand this is that minus the sense of ownership, and the concomitant engagement with the CRM a sense of ownership had previously engendered, the infrastructuring work the residents engaged in while at the shelter was done without a socio-technical resource that had previously played a significant role in supporting the articulation of issues and providing avenues for organizing and effecting action [22]. This is not to say the residents did not engage in infrastructuring—certainly the resources they did have access to, both the material resources at the shelter and the social resources of their relationships with their case workers and each other were developed into a temporary but critical infrastructure for returning to self-sustaining livelihood. But by not incorporating the CRM, as had been done in the initial deployment, the residents did not develop the same depth and breadth of access to these resources through extended asynchronous individualized conversation with their case worker. This change was evidenced by the number and nature of messages exchanged between staff and residents, indicating a dearth of dialogue and micro-coordination during the second deployment.

The Legibility of Technology, the Legibility of a Public

As mentioned briefly above, one way to conceptualize the changes that occurred around the perception staff and residents had of the CRM was that the legibility of the technology had changed. For the staff, during the initial deployment, the CRM was legible as a system for two-way communication with residents. As such, the majority of the messages were individualized communications with an expectation of response. In fact, this individual communication was an important new dynamic within the shelter at the time: prior to the existence of the CRM, all staff-resident communication had been face-to-face [22]. By moving some of the social interactions into a technology mediated space, the residents had more dynamic access to information from the staff—*e.g.*, by receiving information while away from the shelter—but more importantly, the residents also gained an ability to manage their responses to the staff and develop a connection with the staff based on individualized and contextualized information.

Following the addition of the subscription service, much of what the staff were doing with the CRM changed. The apparent ease of subscribing residents to categories of interest became a shortcut for ensuring information was being sent to those who needed it—and this was as intended since the subscription service was a designed response to help broaden the reach of communication from the staff. What none of us foresaw was the concomitant shift from personal messaging to unpersonalized broadcast of information. The shift underlies the altered legibility of the system, from one built for personal communication between staff and resident, to one built around information broadcast via subscriptions to Shared Message Board content. The first mode of use led to conversation, micro-coordination, and a more resilient rapport between staff and residents as they used the system to achieve specific outcomes [22]. The second lead to sharing more, and more comprehensive information with residents, but the rapport building and the micro-coordination with staff that marked the initial deployment was greatly reduced or absent.

For the residents, the legibility of the CRM came in large part through the Shared Message Board as it was the most visible and explicit component of the system (while the SMS messages where a result of the CRM, they were usually simply perceived as messages from individual staff, not from the system—and this perception was as intended). As a result, during the initial deployment, the residents interacted with a system that looked, by way of the Shared Message Board, unfinished. The display of information was simple and the lack of fine-grained categories of information left more room to reinterpret the space through resident-created content.

The changes to the visual language of the Shared Message Board for the second deployment made it—and the CRM by extension—appear more fixed in purpose. The residents did not view it as a space they could repurpose through co-production and their desire to interact with the system was limited by their perceived role as audience rather than as co-creator. On one hand, the design changes to the Shared Message Board resulted in a richer information palette for the residents: maps and images complimented textual posts; categories of relevant topics made desired information easier to find; and consistency with established shelter practices and categories were all improvements repeatedly noted by the residents in the second deployment. The trade-off, however, was that it limited the perceived purpose of the Shared Message Board precisely because it closely mirrored established categories and authority configurations the staff had created to structure and guide residents through the programs at the shelter. The result was that while the redesign more clearly communicated a purpose, the legibility of that purpose was, for the residents, a vehicle for information consumption, not production.

But more than the legibility of the technology, the legibility of the public of shelter residents was affect. This sense of legibility draws on Scott's notion of legible spaces as those that arise from shared social and cultural practices and identity [31]. This notion of legible spaces has recently gained currency in the CHI literature (e.g. [5, 34, 38]), and speaks to the construction of meaning in a particular location and to the role of technology in shaping and contributing to the social practices that configure space into place.

During the initial deployment, the legibility of the public of shelter residents was supported by the practices that developed primarily with the Shared Message Board: *i.e.*, using the technology to articulate common issues and coordinate action to deal with those issues [22]. Because the Shared Message Board occupied a highly visible physical space, and the content was both *for* the residents and *from* the residents, it became an important physical artifact around which the residents organized into a public while at the shelter [22]. The Shared Message Board was part of an infrastructure that made the public legible.

The redesign of the Shared Message Board significantly altered the legibility of the public that it was meant to support. Even though information on the Shared Message Board remained *for* the residents, the design of the Shared Message Board created a barrier for information *from* the residents. Without a resilient perception of being able to produce information, residents did not engage with the CRM as a medium for articulating issues and organizing action. The socio-technical support for the public was still present (residents always had the ability to post messages to the Shared Message Board), but it was not as visible nor as integrated into shelter routine. As a result, the public was less legible, the possibility of its existence less imagined, and the mothers who were sharing time at the shelter, less connected through common cause than through common circumstance.

The Role of Design in Infrastructuring for a Public

The legibility of the public changed between the two deployments of the CRM, but so too did the nature of the infrastructuring that occurred during the two deployments. As has been argued in PD scholarship [4, 12], the work of infrastructuring—of integrating available social and material resources—is critical to sustaining participatory engagement. I would further argue that the nature of the infrastructuring shapes and enables the constitution of publics. Infrastructuring happens naturally as groups marshall and integrate various resources to accomplish an end. The challenge is in creating opportunities for identifying mutable resources that can be repurposed or reshaped as issues arise and are acted on. In particular, I contend that design discourse is critical for configuring technology within the work of infrastructuring. Furthermore, the presence and absence of an explicit design discourse directly impacted the way the CRM was perceived, and the manner in which it was used to mediate the constitution of publics at the shelter.

As evidence of this, aside from the functional changes made to the CRM between the two deployments, there was a subtle change in priority of the study itself. During the initial deployment study, the residents were explicitly involved in co-designing the system: the interviews and group sessions where structured around a continued design discourse about what worked, what did not, and how they, the residents, would change the system [21, 22]. Through these interactions, the residents would begin to imagine different purposes for the information, or different ways of interacting with the CRM. In some cases, the changes were just co-option of what was already there—*i.e.*, realizing that the thing they wanted to accomplish was possible and that they, the residents, had legitimate access to use the CRM as a means of accomplishing that thing. In other cases, the goals they had required functional changes. These desired functional changes where the basis for new and modified features described here.

During the second deployment, the study focus narrowed to understanding the use of the CRM with respect to the new and modified features. The interviews and group sessions were still structured around patterns and impacts of use, but there was a priority to specifically understand the impact of the narrow set of features that had been modified. The engagement from the residents still focused on the information they received: they discussed how useful and timely it was, or was not; residents pointed out how the complimentary modes of telling (via text) and showing (via maps and images) helped them situate the content on the Shared Message Board; and residents discussed the messages received from the subscription service and how they acted on that information, *e.g.*, finding employment or securing housing. What the residents did not do was re-imagine how the CRM might play a role in other aspects of their lives at the shelter and in the relationships they had with each other or with the staff.

These differences provide additional evidence that design discourse is an important component of infrastructuring toward future use rather than infrastructuring for proximal use [4, 12]. This in turn affects the creation of a public because it is the alignment around trying to achieve a common *future* outcome that defines a Deweyan public [8, 24]. One of the functions the design discourse provided during the initial deployment was a hook for recognizing alternate legitimate ways of using the CRM. These in turn lead to a legibility of the technology and of the space of the shelter as explicitly supporting the particular needs of the residents and giving them a platform as a public.

I argue then, that constituting and supporting a public takes more than passing encounters with a mediating technology. It requires participation in determining the future use of that technology and the development of legitimate claims to shaping that future use. This is a shaping of infrastructure that comes not just from making available some new resource—here a communication technology—but of configuring the relationship with that resource around an on-going discourse of what it can and should be supporting. In short, the deployment of the technology is a beginning, not an end; it may serve as a catalyzing factor when constituting a public, but the technological intervention is not to be understood as the culmination of a public's formation.

The accumulated findings of deploying the CRM provide evidence that the notion of Deweyan publics for framing and evaluating technology design is relevant for settings with multiple diverse groups of stakeholders [21, 22]. However, while the framing of publics provides a compelling conceptual perch from which to engage community-driven design, there remain a number of questions and challenges for consistently operationalizing publics as an effective tool for designing socio-technical ecologies. In particular, building a sustainable foundation of participation and a transferable sense of ownership as users of a system join, use, and then move out of the purview of the technology is crucial. The challenge here is how to maintain active engagement once individuals who participated in the design move on and are replaced by new users unconnected to prior practice. It forces us to ask, what happens to the network of connections and the vested interests articulated when working toward a set of common ends? More generally, what happens when the research is done, and only the technology remains?

These questions become ever more relevant as HCI researchers build and deploy technologies in marginalized, disempowered, or otherwise remote or less-connected communities. As we seek to engage and constitute diverse publics, we must also seek to engage the lifecycle of the technologies we deploy, building social capacity as well as technical capacity. As I have argued here, the theoretical perspective of Deweyan publics and the notion of infrastructuring provide useful insight into understanding the evolving authority dynamics between different stakeholder groups; the notion of publics provides scaffolding for designing for sustainability and mutability in socio-technical systems and reconfigures the design process not as one that ends with a product, but instead one that initiates or shapes publics through on-going participation.

ACKNOWLEDGEMENTS

I would like to thank IBM Research for their generous support of this project and Nokia for providing mobile phones. I also extend my gratitude the shelter staff and residents for their sustained enthusiasm during this project. This research was supported by the NSF under grant IIS-0915624.

REFERENCES

1. Asen, R. The multiple Mr. Dewey: Multiple publics and permeable borders in John Dewey's theory of the public sphere. *Argumentation and Advocacy 39*, 3 (2003), 174–188.
2. Balka, E. Inside the belly of the beast: The challenges and successes of a reformist participatory agenda. In *Proc. PDC 2006*, ACM (2006), 134–143.
3. Beck, E.E. P for political: Participation is not enough. *Scandinavian Journal of Information Systems 14*, 1 (2002), 77–92.
4. Björgvinsson, E., Ehn, P., and Hillgren, P.-A. Participatory design and "democratizing innovation." In *Proc. PDC 2010*, ACM (2010), 41–50.
5. Brewer, J. and Dourish, P. Storied spaces: Cultural accounts of mobility, technology, and environmental knowing. *International Journal of Human-Computer Studies 66*, 12 (2008), 963–976.
6. Cohen, K.R. Who we talk about when we talk about users. In *Proc. EPIC 2005*, Blackwell Publishing Ltd (2005), 9–30.
7. Davis, J. Early experiences with participatory design of ambient persuasive technology. In *CHI EA 2009*, (2009).
8. Dewey, J. *The Public and Its Problems*. Swallow Press, Athens, OH, (1954 [1927]).
9. Dimond, J.P. and Bruckman, A.S. Domestic violence and information communication technologies. *Interacting with Computers 23*, 5 (2011), 413–421.

10. DiSalvo, C. Design and the construction of publics. *Design Issues 25*, 1 (2009), 48–63.
11. DiSalvo, C., Maki, J., and Martin, N. Mapmover: A case study of design-oriented research into collective expression and constructed publics. In *Proc. CHI 2007*, ACM (2007), 1249–1252.
12. Ehn, P. Design things: Challenges to design thinking in the tradition of participatory design? In *Proc. PDC 2008*, ACM (2008).
13. Ehn, P. and Kyng, M. Cardboard computers: Mocking-it-up or hands-on the future. In J.M. Greenbaum and M. Kyng, eds. *Design at work: cooperative design of computer systems*. Psychology Press, (1991), 169–195.
14. Gaver, W.W., Beaver, J., and Benford, S. Ambiguity as a resource for design. In *Proc. CHI 2003*, ACM Press (2003), 233–240.
15. Habermas, J. *The Structural Transformation of the Public Sphere: An Inquiry into a Category of Bourgeois Society*. The MIT Press, (1991).
16. Hersberger, J. The homeless and information need and services. *Reference and User Services Quarterly 44*, 3 (2005), 199–202.
17. Hersberger, J. Are the economically poor information poor? Does the digital divide affect the homeless and access to information? *Canadian Journal of Information & Library Sciences 27*, 3 (2002), 45–63.
18. Le Dantec, C.A. and Edwards, W.K. Designs on dignity: Perceptions of technology among the homeless. In *Proc. CHI 2008*, ACM (2008), 627–636.
19. Le Dantec, C.A. and Edwards, W.K. The View from the trenches: Organization, power, and technology at two nonprofit homeless outreach centers. In *Proc. CSCW 2008*, ACM (2008), 589–598.
20. Le Dantec, C.A. and Edwards, W.K. Across boundaries of influence and accountability: The multiple scales of public sector information systems. In *Proc. CHI 2010*, ACM (2010), 113–122.
21. Le Dantec, C.A., Christensen, J.E., Bailey, M., et al. A tale of two publics: Democratizing design at the margins. In *Proc. DIS 2010*, ACM (2010), 11–20.
22. Le Dantec, C.A., Farrell, R.G., Christensen, J.E., et al. Publics in practice: Ubiquitous computing at a shelter for homeless mothers. In *Proc. CHI 2011*, ACM (2011), 1687–1696.
23. Lippmann, W. *The Phantom Public*. Transaction Publishers, (1993 [1927]).
24. Marres, N. The issues deserve more credit: Pragmatist contributions to the study of public involvement in controversy. *Social Studies of Science 37*, 5 (2007), 759–780.
25. Marsden, G. Designing technology for the developing world. *interactions 13*, 2 (2006).
26. Merkel, C.B., Xiao, L., Farooq, U., et al. Participatory design in community computing contexts: Tales from the field. In *Proc. PDC 2004*, ACM (2004), 1–10.
27. Miles, M.B. and Huberman, A.M. *Qualitative Data Analysis: An Expanded Sourcebook*. Sage, (1994).
28. Patel, N., Chittamuru, D., Jain, A., Dave, P., and Parikh, T.S. Avaaj otalo: a field study of an interactive voice forum for small farmers in rural India. In *Proc. CHI 2010*, ACM (2010), 733–742.
29. Pierce, J., Brynjarsdottir, H., Sengers, P., and Strengers, Y. Everyday practice and sustainable HCI: understanding and learning from cultures of (un)sustainability. In *Proc. CHI EA 2011*, ACM (2011), 9–12.
30. Roberson, J. and Nardi, B. Survival needs and social inclusion: Technology use among the homeless. In *Proc. CSCW 2010*, ACM (2010), 445–448.
31. Scott, J.C. *Seeing Like a State*. Yale University Press, New Haven, CT, (1998).
32. Sengers, P. What I learned on Change Islands: Reflections on IT and pace of life. *interactions 18*, 2 (2011), 40–48.
33. Shapiro, D. Participatory design: The will to succeed. In *Proc. CC 2005*, ACM (2005), 29–38.
34. Shklovski, I., Vertesi, J., Troshynski, E., and Dourish, P. The commodification of location: Dynamics of power in location-based systems. In *Proc. Ubicomp 2009*, ACM (2009), 11–20.
35. Smyth, T.N., Kumar, S., Medhi, I., and Toyama, K. Where there's a will there's a way: Mobile media sharing in urban India. In *Proc. CHI 2010*, ACM (2010), 753–762.
36. Star, S.L. and Bowker, G.C. How to infrastructure. In L.A. Lievrouw and S.M. Livingstone, eds. *The Handbook of New Media*. Sage, London, UK, (2002), 151–162.
37. Stoll, J., Edwards, W.K., and Mynatt, E.D. Interorganizational coordination and awareness in a nonprofit ecosystem. In *Proc. CSCW 2010*, ACM (2010), 51–60.
38. Troshynski, E., Lee, C., and Dourish, P. Accountabilities of presence: Reframing location-based systems. In *Proc. CHI 2008*, ACM (2008), 487–496.
39. Turner, F. *From Counterculture to Cyberculture: Stewart Brand, the Whole Earth Network, and the Rise of Digital Utopianism*. University Of Chicago Press, (2006).
40. Warner, M. *Publics and Counterpublics*. Zone Books, Brooklyn, NY, (2002).
41. Woelfer, J.P. and Hendry, D.G. Homeless young people's experiences with information systems: Life and work in a community technology center. In *Proc. CHI 2010*, ACM (2010), 1291–1300.
42. Woelfer, J.P., Iverson, A., Hendry, D.G., Friedman, B., and Gill, B.T. Improving the safety of homeless young people with mobile phones: Values, form and function. In *Proc. CHI 2011*, ACM (2011), 1707–1716.

Viewpoint: Empowering Communities with Situated Voting Devices

Nick Taylor[1], Justin Marshall[2], Alicia Blum-Ross[3], John Mills[4], Jon Rogers[5], Paul Egglestone[4], David M. Frohlich[3], Peter Wright[1], Patrick Olivier[1]

[1] Culture Lab, School of Computing Science, Newcastle University, UK, patrick.olivier@ncl.ac.uk

[2] Autonomatic, University College Falmouth, UK, justin.marshall@falmouth.ac.uk

[3] Digital World Research Centre, University of Surrey, UK, d.frohlich@surrey.ac.uk

[4] University of Central Lancashire, UK, pegglestone@uclan.ac.uk

[5] University of Dundee, UK, j.rogers@dundee.ac.uk

ABSTRACT

Viewpoint is a public voting device developed to allow residents in a disadvantaged community to make their voices heard through a simple, lightweight interaction. This was intended to open a new channel of communication within the community and increase community members' perception of their own efficacy. Local elected officials and community groups were able to post questions on devices located in public spaces, where residents could vote for one of two responses. Question authors were subsequently required to post a response indicating any actions to be taken. Following a two-month trial, we present our experiences and contribute guidelines for the design of public democracy tools and dimensions impacting their effectiveness, including credibility, efficacy and format.

Author Keywords

Community; e-democracy; civic engagement; participation; voting; information appliances.

ACM Classification Keywords

H.5.m [Information interfaces and presentation (e.g., HCI)]: Miscellaneous;

INTRODUCTION

Communication and participation are important aspects of civic engagement, allowing members of the public to make their views heard, which in turn allows those representing them or providing services to tailor their efforts accordingly. Despite this, it is claimed that civic engagement and participation within many communities is in decline [18]. One possible explanation for this apparent withdrawal from engagement in communities is the sense that participation takes too much time and effort, or that grassroots opinions are ignored, undermining people's motivation to become involved in local issues [10,20].

Permission to make digital or hard copies of all or part of this work for personal or classroom use is granted without fee provided that copies are not made or distributed for profit or commercial advantage and that copies bear this notice and the full citation on the first page. To copy otherwise, or republish, to post on servers or to redistribute to lists, requires prior specific permission and/or a fee.

CHI'12, May 5–10, 2012, Austin, Texas, USA.

Copyright 2012 ACM 978-1-4503-1015-4/12/05...$10.00.

Conversely, digital technologies are beginning to present opportunities to open new lightweight, agile channels of communication and new methods of enabling participation. For example, on social media platforms, it is now common to express opinions using comments, or by simply 'liking' or 'disliking' an item. Likewise, millions of people each week use text messaging to vote on reality television shows. These actions often cause prompt, visible results that encourage further participation. We believe there is great potential for these channels to engage communities and improve communication between local residents, their elected representatives and organisations providing services in the community.

The Viewpoint voting device was developed as part of a project exploring the design and development of bespoke technologies with communities, with the view that individual communities have individual requirements. The project was based in the Callon and Fishwick areas of Preston, in North West England, which have suffered from numerous social problems in the recent past, including crime, unemployment, drugs and racial tensions. While a considerable effort from residents, the local council and community groups has greatly reduced these problems in recent years, the UK government considers it to be amongst the 10% most disadvantaged communities in the country.

During a two-month trial, Viewpoint allowed local organisations and elected officials to post questions in public spaces in Callon and Fishwick, where residents could vote using either buttons on the devices or free text messages. The results of the poll were visible to the public, as were responses and promises of action posted by the author. During the trial period, eight weekly questions were posted, leading to nearly 1,800 votes being placed by the public. In this paper, we describe use of the device during this period and identify a number of guidelines and factors to consider when developing public democracy technologies, including credibility, efficacy and format.

BACKGROUND

It is clear that communication technologies have the potential to support democracy and representation. We position Viewpoint amongst a broad range of e-democracy and e-participation research aiming to understand how technology can bridge the gulf between members of the public and those acting on their behalf by supporting participation, deliberation and mediation. However, there is currently a lack of research into the use of such technologies in public spaces that we seek to address.

Participation, Deliberation and Mediation

In the Western model of democracy, the public's primary method of participation is electing representatives. In the UK, voters are able to elect Members of Parliament to the national and European parliaments, and councillors to city and regional councils who control local public services and facilities, from garbage collection to leisure centres and schools. Callon and Fishwick have two councillors, both of whom work closely with the local community to represent their interests. Often, e-democracy has concentrated on assisting this voting process by making it easier to place and count votes. Much has been written about the potential and issues surrounding these applications [9,12], but there are other potential roles for technology beyond elections.

After officials are elected, deliberation and mediation play an important role in ensuring that decision-making reflects the will of the population [1]. This means that decisions are discussed at length and alternative viewpoints are considered before final decisions are made, allowing the public to access information and influence their representatives. On a local scale, the public's input is typically sought through town hall meetings and direct communication with councillors, although the Internet is becoming an increasingly valuable tool for this purpose. This ongoing involvement in the democratic process is considered to be a key aspect of civic engagement [11], or what has been described as participatory citizenship: "the act of citizens actively engaging in and contributing to the provision of public services in order to improve these services for themselves and other citizens" [3]. However, our willingness to exert effort is influenced by our past experiences [6]. Likewise, the willingness of individuals and communities to engage in this process is strongly related to their sense of collective efficacy—their belief that they are able to effect a change through their actions, without which there is little motivation to participate [4].

In addition to members of the public, other organisations may become involved in this discourse, either as providers of services or as representatives of particular interest groups. For example, in Callon and Fishwick, a large number of homes are rented from two non-profit housing associations who offer housing to those with low incomes. The housing associations work closely with both the council and the community to meet their residents' needs and improve the areas in which they operate.

Existing Research and Technology

Technology can—and already does—play a role in deliberation and mediation [1]. Television, newspapers and other traditional media are key methods used by elected representatives to inform and engage the electorate, but the Internet is increasingly being used to obtain information, engage in deliberation and participate in decision making [16]. In the UK, for example, most MPs and councillors have public email addresses to allow direct communication with their constituents. Community networks [21], such as the PEN project in Santa Monica [19], have allowed members of the public to interact both with each other and with members of the local government. Recent studies in the UK have likewise shown that interaction online can support communication and civic engagement [13].

However, to be a credible democratic tool, technologies should be as inclusive as possible. Web-based technologies can often exclude those who do not have access to computers and the Internet, such as the elderly or financially disadvantaged, widening the information gap between those with access and those without. Furthermore, there is a considerable experiential difference between voting and participating online and doing so in person. For this reason, we consider whether information appliances [14] in public spaces with simple, customised interfaces can allow a wider cross-section of the public to make their voices heard and effect change, increasing their perception of their collective efficacy and potentially leading to further participation.

In existing research, public displays and terminals have often been used to reach a wider proportion of the population. PEN, for example, provided free public terminals in libraries so that all citizens could participate regardless of their ability to access technology. More recently, VoiceYourView [24] has gathered feedback from members of the public in-situ using a familiar telephone-like device, hiding more technical aspects of the system. A number of research projects have made use of voting mechanisms and large displays to assist deliberation in meetings [17], while other projects have used polls in social contexts such as public spaces [22,23], bars [15] and classrooms [2,5]. In these small groups, the effect of polls is readily visible; for example, if a jukebox system plays music that people in the room have selected, this provides an immediate, strong sense of efficacy and an incentive to use the system to exercise control of the environment. However, few of these technologies have been evaluated in the wild over prolonged periods or with larger groups.

A further advantage of an information appliance is the potential for simple, lightweight interaction. Satchell *et al.* [20] found a clear desire for a 'voice' in communities, but also noted that traditional forms of civic engagement, such as town hall meetings, are time-consuming. They suggest that technology could offer simpler means of making one's voice heard and engaging with other community members. In light of this, we position Viewpoint as a means of simple, lightweight participation.

DESIGN CONCEPT AND CONSULTATION

Fieldwork in Callon and Fishwick was conducted by local people, who were given journalism training (further detailed by Frohlich *et al.* [8]). The journalists interviewed local residents and community workers to produce materials in a variety of mediums, including video documentaries and written articles, which were used by designers to generate design concepts. From these materials, an emergent theme was communication: groups providing services within the area struggled to promote themselves and engage residents, while many residents were uncomfortable making their opinions heard, not wanting to be perceived as interfering by other residents. Many even refused to allow their voices to be recorded so they could not be identified. This did not mean that residents held no opinions—on the contrary, they often had strong views on local issues that were expressed off-record, leading us to consider methods of contributing these opinions anonymously.

In response to this, Viewpoint was initially conceived as a device that would allow community groups or local councillors to pose simple questions to the area's residents, who would be able to vote anonymously by text message. This would open a new channel of communication between residents and groups within the community, which would make the result of the poll highly visible while keeping individual opinions private. It was intended that question authors would submit responses after each poll closed, acknowledging the result and stating what action they intended to take or had been taken, thereby providing an indicator of efficacy. Our concept favoured a minimalist design, such as simple a binary question, which we intended would lower barriers to participation.

Before development progressed, we sought feedback on this initial design concept both from residents and from organisations who might post questions, including councillors, two housing associations and the local church. Feedback explored both existing attitudes towards participation and civic engagement, plus a number of issues surrounding the design itself, including locations for the devices, and whether residents should be restricted to a single vote (necessarily adding complexity).

Opinions on traditional forms of consultation and participation proved to be generally negative. Although some residents reported voting regularly, others displayed disillusion with the political process and a low sense of self-efficacy: residents generally felt that their input had no effect and their voices were ignored. As a disadvantaged area, residents were regularly consulted on many local issues but rarely saw any action taken as a result of their input, causing "consultation fatigue". The councillors and housing associations identified the importance of gathering feedback from members of the public and felt that the device could potentially help with this. There had been many existing attempts to engage the residents in

Figure 1. Existing attempts to encourage feedback were evident around the community.

consultation exercises (e.g. Figure 1), which were mostly conducted using meetings, door-to-door visits or paper forms. However, the responses to these attempts were often lacklustre and representatives commented on the difficulty of generating good quality feedback.

In general, responses to the design concept itself were very positive. Residents particularly liked the idea of a simple voting interface that was easy to understand, and suggested public locations such as community centres and shops as appropriate deployment locations. Several residents dismissed the prospect of being able to vote multiple times as unproblematic, and even suggested that voting multiple times was a valid way of indicating how strongly individuals felt about an issue. However, one representative from a housing association made clear that they would prefer only one response per person, and warned that we should not expect a large quantity of feedback from any new consultation method.

Residents also stressed that they wanted to know what would happen as a result of the polls, arguing that there was "no point" in voting if the results were not used. This issue was also raised by potential question authors, who agreed that questions should not be asked if action could not be taken. One housing association representative stated: *"we would have to be confident enough to be able to respond [...] it's a bit silly to put a question on and then think 'what do we do with that now?' You've got to be able to act upon it."* Another respondent suggested that the area was already suffering from consultation fatigue, having been consulted extensively with little effect, underscoring the need to have a discernible impact.

Potential question authors typically had difficulty formulating questions that were both simple and actionable during the meetings, but felt confident that they could think of suitable questions given time. Regardless, there were several promising suggestions: one housing association representative, for example, suggested using the device to decide where funding should be spent.

Figure 2. The low-fidelity Viewpoint prototype.

Figure 3. Viewpoint deployed in a local shop.

PROTOTYPE DEMONSTRATION

To gather further feedback on the Viewpoint concept, a low-fidelity prototype was developed for demonstration at a community event that brought a number of local groups together to network. This prototype took the form of an application running on a large monitor, hidden behind a foamcore screen (Figure 2). The screen had a printed design themed around a barometer to measure the 'climate' of opinion, with cut-out sections where results on the monitor were visible. Behind it, the monitor displayed the current question, current results and voting instructions, as well as a previous question, its results and information about actions taken as a result of the poll. Each poll had two options, which were voted for by sending a text message to a specified phone number containing a short keyword (for example, YES or NO). When this was received, the animated results dial updated accordingly.

Throughout the event, attendees were invited to use the device, given an explanation of what it was intended to achieve and asked for their opinions on both the concept and the prototype. General feedback on the design concept was positive: attendees recognised the importance of making their views heard, and felt that Viewpoint could help to achieve this. One attendee noted that it was an *"interesting and novel way of getting people involved and because it's using technology, it'll be attractive to young people as well"*. Both residents and community organisations were readily able to identify areas, if not specific questions, where the device could prove useful.

Feedback on the prototype itself was more critical, and much of this criticism related to the method of interaction. Although most residents owned a mobile phone, many older residents were not able to send text messages and some users needed to be coached to send their votes to the device. Furthermore, even those who were comfortable with text messaging felt that it was more suitable for remote interaction and that using text messages to communicate with a collocated device was unusual. Several users independently suggested that the device could have voting buttons for situated interaction, noting: *"if you've got come and see it to see the question and then text it, why not just have a button?"* Consequently, it seemed that the inconvenience of needing to send a text message would discourage the type of simple in-situ interaction that we had hoped to encourage with the design.

Several users also suggested that the prototype was too complicated and featured an excessive amount of text. From our own observations, it seemed that people were unsure how to approach the device or how to interact with it. Most required an explanation of the device and interaction—although the presence of researchers around the device may have discouraged them from examining it independently.

PUBLIC DEPLOYMENT

Based on the feedback from our initial trial and consultation, we revised our first design for deployment into the community for a two-month period. During this time, 1,783 votes were cast in eight different polls, six of which were sourced from local councillors and housing associations. This section describes the final deployed device, usage of the device, and feedback gathered from stakeholders in the community.

Technical Description

The Viewpoint device was a self-contained unit, which could be mounted on a wall or flat surface for security (Figure 3). In response to feedback that the trial device was too complicated, the interface was simplified to show only two information windows: a question box with very simple voting instructions and a results dial that showed the current result, total number of votes and the poll's end date. Rather than showing both the current and previous poll at once, a rotating dial was provided that allowed users to scroll through all previous polls to see the final results and any response provided.

Large, physical buttons were added to allow voting without a mobile phone, which provided instant visual and audio

	Question	Options	Votes	Percentage	Total	Source
Q1	Would you miss the Bespoke Newspaper if it was gone?	Yes	97	44%	219	Project Team
		No	122	56%		
Q2	Do you think CCTV is a good or bad thing for the area?	Good	240	73%	328	Project Team
		Bad	88	27%		
Q3	Would you be willing to spend 1 hour per month helping to improve local parks and open spaces?	Yes	77	40%	192	Councillor 1
		No	115	60%		
Q4	Would you like to see a new community centre for Callon?	Yes	113	51%	223	Housing Association 1
		No	110	49%		
Q5	Is local dog fouling a problem that deserves priority attention?	Yes	199	82%	242	Councillor 1
		No	43	18%		
Q6	Do you think that skips [dumpsters] should be provided again, on the Callon estate, later on in the year?	Yes	208	82%	255	Housing Association 2
		No	47	18%		
Q7	Would you be interested in working with [us] and other local residents to ensure that the services we deliver in your area meet your standards?	Yes	90	68%	132	Housing Association 2
		No	42	32%		
Q8	Do you believe easy access to alcohol is a strong contributor to anti social behaviour in Fishwick?	Yes	152	79%	192	Councillor 2
		No	40	21%		

Table 1. Questions posted on Viewpoint during the trial.

feedback when the arrow on the results dial moved and an odometer-style vote counter rolled to the next number. As buttons provided no easy way of identifying voters, a brief timeout—initially set to 30 seconds, but later increased to one minute—prevented multiple votes being cast by a single individual in a short period of time. Mobile phone voting was still available for convenience and secrecy, but only required the user to text 'POLL1' or 'POLL2' to a five-digit freetext number. A similar device was designed that omitted the buttons, simply showing the current poll and texting instructions, so that it could be placed in locations where the user would not have direct access, such as inside a window. Each device connected to the Internet to coordinate votes across multiple units, so a vote entered on one Viewpoint would register on all devices.

The Viewpoint devices were deployed in three locations in the community. Devices with buttons were installed in a busy convenience store used by many residents and in the foyer of a community centre that various local groups used as a meeting and activity space. A third device without buttons was deployed in the window of a local housing organisation. Each of these locations played an important role in the community and saw considerable traffic during a typical day. The locations also ensured widespread coverage: the community centre and housing office were located on opposite ends of the estate, while the shop was located on the main road through the area.

Polls and Responses

Throughout the two-month trial period, a total of eight polls were posted by four different local organisations (Table 1), each lasting for one week. Due to a lack of suitable questions at the time of deployment, the first two questions were posted by the research team. Subsequent questions were sourced directly from community groups. These questions took a number of different forms. Two questions from councillors sought to identify how strongly residents felt about particular issues on the estate (Q5 and Q8). Other questions, from a councillor and a housing association, were aimed less at gathering opinions and more towards identifying numbers of potential volunteers for possible future initiatives (Q3 and Q7). The final category of questions was intended to determine the level of interest or support for potential new facilities or services (Q4 and Q6).

Question authors were emailed the results when the poll ended and invited to submit a response: of the six questions not posted by the project team, four had a response provided. Two of the polls did result in a firm promise of action to be taken: the question about garbage dumpsters (Q6) led to a temporary dumpster being scheduled later in the year and a question about dog fouling (Q5) resulted in a promise to request extra resources. In the case of the two polls that primarily sought to identify levels of interest (Q3 and Q7), the response took the form of contact details for residents who wished to participate. We did not receive responses for the questions relating to the community centre or alcohol problems (Q4 and Q8).

Votes and Interaction

The quantity of votes cast using the devices was considerably higher than had been anticipated, particularly given the lack of engagement we were warned of during early fieldwork. A total of 1,783 votes were cast, peaking at 328 in the second week of deployment, with an average of 223 votes per poll. Conversely, no votes were received via text message during the entire duration of the deployment. The CCTV question (Q2), which was a contentious issue in the area, showed the highest number of votes. The penultimate poll showed the lowest number of votes, although this was preceded by a week without content and was also disrupted by connectivity issues at the shop. The poll results themselves varied considerably: some were almost tied (e.g. Q4), while others favoured one option overwhelmingly (e.g. Q5 and Q6).

Of the two interactive devices, more votes were cast at the community centre, which accounted for 1,086 (61%) of the votes, with the remaining 697 cast in the shop. This was somewhat surprising: from our own observations, the shop saw considerably more traffic. However, we did receive reports that children would congregate in the community centre entrance, often voting multiple times, and the shop did suffer from occasional outages. The share of votes also differed considerably by location, reflecting the different segments of the community who utilised the two spaces. When considered separately, half of the results differed significantly between locations. The most striking difference occurred in Q4, where users of the existing community centre voted strongly *against* a new facility proposed by a different organisation (26% in favour), while voters in the shop voted *for* (79% in favour).

In addition to recording votes, the two interactive devices also logged use of the dial to view previous poll results. Throughout the entire trial period, we logged 10,975 turns of the dial, split into 785 distinct sessions of interaction (where interactions are less than one minute apart). While this indicates a high level of usage, it is difficult to distinguish how much time was spent actually reading results and responses. The nature of the third device, which did not have any points of direct interaction, means no usage logs exist. The fact that users could only interact with this device by text message and no such messages were received suggests that interest in the device was low. It should also be noted that its physical location in the housing association's window, which was intended to make it visible to passersby, was not as visible as we had hoped, possibly contributing to the lack of text votes.

Feedback

To evaluate Viewpoint's reception in the community, we solicited feedback from three groups of stakeholders: the councillors and organisations who posted questions; the three venues that acted as hosts for devices; and members of the public who encountered the devices and placed votes. Like the initial fieldwork, these interviews were largely conducted by local people taking part in the journalism programme, but other interviews were conducted by a member of the project team and some stakeholders contacted us directly with their thoughts.

Councillors and Housing Associations

One councillor and a housing association representative were interviewed about their experience posting questions to Viewpoint, which were largely positive. The housing association stated: *"the response was absolutely overwhelming. I was just gobsmacked by the number of people who responded to that question."* Although the second poll posted by this organisation saw the lowest number of votes, she still characterised the response as "unbelievable" and went on to explain that previous consultations had faced difficulty in engaging residents.

The councillor likewise described the response as "overwhelming", and saw Viewpoint as a means of gathering a broader and more balanced view on local issues: *"we only get complaints from people who are really bothered about [an issue], so it was a chance to really gauge the feeling about it locally"*. The device was also seen as an additional method of increasing awareness of the council's activities. He suggested that results from Viewpoint were one of many resources the council could use to make informed decisions about utilisation of resources. He also downplayed issues around multiple votes, suggesting that the subject matter of the questions was not emotive enough to justify the effort required to meaningfully impact the result.

Both expressed a desire for a greater ability to communicate with voters through the devices, as they had posted questions seeking volunteers for various initiatives, but were then concerned about their inability to contact those responding positively. To alleviate this, they suggested allowing voters to enter their personal details through the device, or displaying contact details for the relevant councillor or housing association. In both cases, this information was later provided in the question response, but was consequently unavailable until after the poll had closed and only visible when scrolling through past polls.

Device Hosts

The hosts of each device were a valuable source of day-to-day observations of interaction, and also served as a point of contact for curious residents. One staff member in the shop stated: *"It gives the little man, gives him the impression, even if it's not true, that what he thinks actually matters. It's great as long as it is going to somebody who is going to read it and is going to affect what is going on."* Like other members of the community, they stressed that the value of the device was dependant on the ability of question authors to act on the result.

Staff at both the shop and community centre initially reported that children had been pressing buttons as they passed by the device and voting multiple times without reading the question, which they saw as a problem. This was particularly prevalent at the community centre, where children would gather outside the entrance, close to the foyer where Viewpoint was situated. As a result of this, the delay between votes was increased from 30 seconds to one minute. One host later commented that this was occurring less as the novelty value of the device decreased.

Early during the deployment, shop staff reported that customers were reading questions and asking about the device, but during later interviews they reported that interest had declined and many customers were blindly pressing buttons as they passed by. Although the shop owners responded positively to the device, they also felt it took up too much space in the shop and did not want to keep it beyond the trial period. This device also had connectivity issues through the deployment, and less technically confident staff members expressed irritation when asked to reset the device.

Members of the Public

Opinions on Viewpoint were solicited from members of the public as they passed the devices. Many of these opinions were very positive, reflecting on the ability of Viewpoint to make the community's voice heard:

"It's good for the community. Communities know they can get together and people can share their opinions."

"It's a quick and easy way for any one person to put his point of view across."

"This [shop] is the perfect kind of place because this is where all the community comes. This is the main place in the daytime where you get the highest volume of people coming through that actually live round here and the issues affect directly."

Feedback from the general public was far more mixed than from community organisations. Many residents appeared unaware and uninterested in the device, and several had not previously noticed the installations:

"I'm not really interested in it. I don't think these things do any good and I haven't used it. What's the point of asking questions when nothing ever happens?"

"If there [aren't] people in power seeing what's going on and taking notice of it, it's a futile exercise. What's the point of gathering people's opinions about what's going on if you're not going to do anything about it?"

A number of these comments clearly indicate that members of the public doubted the ability of the device to have an impact on the community.

There is some evidence to suggest that residents took note of the results. At an unrelated event, one of the authors was recognised as a member of the project team by a local resident, who mentioned the negative response to our first poll regarding the project newsletter and asked: "what are you going to do about it?" In this example, the public nature of the poll results empowered a resident to demand action. This illustrates for potential for Viewpoint, given time, to empower the wider community in a similar way.

DISCUSSION

Over a two-month trial period, Viewpoint demonstrated that it was capable of engaging residents in dialogue with local organisations, allowing them to gather an unprecedented quantity of feedback on a range of local issues. These included existing problems and potential new facilities, as well as raising awareness of their activities and measuring levels of interest in volunteering. Although no single intervention can address the complex issues surrounding democracy and participation in communities, deploying Viewpoint in the wild has highlighted a number of issues surrounding the design and use of voting devices to support participation in communities. Based on these experiences, we have identified a number of factors impacting the design of public voting technologies that we present as guidelines for future research in this domain.

Efficacy

Perhaps the most important goal of Viewpoint was to improve the community's sense of collective efficacy. By making the community's 'voice' heard and making the effect of their input more visible, this would hopefully encourage further participation. In an attempt to achieve this, a key aspect of the design was the notion of 'actionability'—that the results of questions posted on the display could be used to inform decisions and lead to genuine improvements in the community. The devices aimed to achieve this by inviting responses to each question from the original author.

Whether the goal of improving efficacy was achieved is difficult to assess. Although actions were promised for a number of polls, a sense of efficacy is something that can realistically only be developed over extended periods of time. It is unreasonable to expect any single intervention to reverse a deep-seated lack of faith in the system of governance, which had been created by many years of a perceived lack of change. However, our experiences have highlighted two areas that could be targeted to increase efficacy.

Transparency

The difference in perception between voters and question authors is an important consideration in relation to efficacy.

From our observations, members of the public typically expect a rapid response to their input, while councils and other organisations operate within defined processes that constrain their ability to take action, which the public are not necessarily aware of. For the question authors, any single method of feedback collection is likely to be just one of a number of input sources that inform any decision, which might take considerable time to reach. This is particularly true of individual councillors or representatives, who may not have the authority to make direct changes themselves. Consequently, this can be perceived as a lack of efficacy or unwillingness to respond.

Our view is that this problem is largely caused by a lack of transparency: members of the public are not made aware of how the input they provide will be used or how long changes might take. Although Viewpoint attempted to make the end result visible, the process *between* the vote and the result was still opaque. Future technologies aiming to address this design space should consider how the process of reaching these results can be made more transparent.

Targeting Achievable Goals

A second factor is the actual ability of organisations themselves to effect change. It was intended that questions would only be posted when decisions needed to be made that could genuinely be based upon input from residents, but despite initial enthusiasm shown by local organisations, it was simply not realistic to provide actionable questions with such regularity. As a result, many of the questions aimed to gauge the mood of the community rather than make decisions. While this is certainly an important part of the democratic process, it risks contributing towards the consultation fatigue felt by many residents.

This leads us to consider that it might be infeasible to have a constant stream of questions if such a device were deployed permanently. For this reason, it may be beneficial to consider short-term deployments at times when consultation is required and organisations can commit in advance to taking action based on the results, perhaps in locations relevant to the issue at hand. Such deployments could help to retain the device's novelty in the eyes of both the public and organisations, while being carried out at times when issues were most relevant. In this scenario, organisations asking questions could state in advance what actions they are capable of taking, increasing the visibility of this promise. However, this would have the disadvantage of preventing voting from becoming a regular, habitual occurrence, which could be a benefit of fixed deployments.

Credibility

A second consideration for voting technologies is the need for credibility: if the results of a poll, the response posted or the device itself cannot be trusted or are not seen as legitimate, then this impacts the ability of the device to provide a sense of efficacy. Credibility is influenced by a number of factors, but our experiences relate primarily to the interaction design of the device.

Misuse

Firstly, the simple design meant that it was relatively easy for a single voter to register multiple votes over the course of a week. Evidence also suggested that many votes were placed flippantly, often by children who would vote multiple times despite the delay or without reading the question. Almost a fifth of votes followed the preceding vote by less than two minutes, casting doubt on their credibility. None of the results were significantly impacted by removing these votes, however.

Multiple voting itself was not necessarily seen as an issue by all members of the community. Our early fieldwork indicated that some residents saw this as a legitimate means for those who felt passionate to make themselves heard, reflecting existing processes where the most vocal members of the community are best represented. Conversely, some question authors required that only one vote be cast per person. However, any method of uniquely identifying users would greatly increase the complexity of the interface and discourage interaction.

This highlights a difficult unsolved design issue for non-critical voting devices: how can we discourage flippant votes, but make voting easy enough that it encourages legitimate participation? Solutions to this problem may lie with both novel user interfaces and simple human intervention; for example, the shop owner monitored use of the device and reported asking children to leave if they were voting multiple times. Above all, we recommend that lightweight democracy technologies should not automatically assume that high levels of security are required for non-critical domains and that this should be tailored to individual deployment contexts.

Feedback

In an election, the result is typically secret until after the polls have closed, to avoid influencing subsequent votes. For other methods of judging options, such as a show of hands in a town hall meeting, the result may be visible to everybody. Indeed, for deliberation and mediation to take place, it is necessary for different opinions to be aired in public. Viewpoint displayed results in real-time, allowing residents to see the current result before they voted, see the impact of their vote on the result, and track the progress of polls through the week. This was primarily to demonstrate that the device was working and create a positive user experience, reinforced by mechanical sound effects to indicate that an operation was taking place.

Like issues around misuse, we should not assume that all voting technologies need to conform to the standards of critical elections and referenda. In this case, immediate feedback served to raise the device's credibility by providing users with assurance that their vote had been counted and had an immediate, visible effect on the result. However, further exploration is certainly required to determine to what extent this visibility affects the way people cast their votes. For example, voters may feel persuaded to vote with the majority, might feel that voting is futile if their choice is in the minority, or might feel more inclined to vote if they disagree with the current result.

Encouraging Participation

Given the quantity of feedback received, the device was successful in encouraging participation from a far greater proportion of the community than had been managed by existing methods. This was achieved by lowering barriers to participation through the device's interaction design, question format and location.

Interaction

In terms of the device's interaction design, it is clear that the extremely simple method of placing votes was a key factor in generating the high number of votes. By only requiring a simple button press to participate, the design of the device lowered barriers to participation and encouraged interaction. The very tactile buttons and immediate feedback also made this quite a satisfying user experience. Only a small degree of extra complexity was required to discourage interaction, as demonstrated by the unfavourable response to voting by mobile phone.

This suggests that our approach of making the device as simple as possible was an appropriate choice. Clearly there is a trade-off here between the need for simplicity and other requirements, such as efficacy and credibility discussed above. For example, when interviewed, several question authors expressed a desire for higher fidelity feedback that was not possible with this design. Consequently, while such a simple user interface might not be suitable for all similar technologies, to encourage participation they should remain as simple as possible, while also attempting to create an engaging user experience.

Question Format

In addition to the physical design of the device, the format of the questions themselves appeared to influence the degree to which residents engaged with the device. For example, the question that received the least votes was also the longest. Furthermore, questions seeking to determine levels of interest in services or volunteering secured fewer total votes. Conversely, the most successful questions were concisely worded and implied realistically achievable results. This agrees with our earlier observations regarding barriers to participation, and also relates closely to efficacy: if there is no perception that a positive outcome is likely, there is little motivation to participate.

This indicates is a clear need to work closely with organisations to formulate engaging and actionable questions. Although councillors and local organisations are accustomed to generating content for public consumption, this was a new format with its own requirements, with which they had relatively little experience. Like the other factors discussed above, there is a careful balance to be achieved between the need for simplicity and needs of organisations to collect adequate data.

Location

Finally, the physical location of each Viewpoint device was naturally a contributing factor towards its usage. Viewpoint was very much a situated technology, and as each device was deployed in a different location, behaviours surrounding the two displays differed. The locations selected were ideal not just because they saw considerable traffic, meaning a large number of residents passed the devices regularly as they went about their day-to-day business, but because they were locations where members of the community met and where discussion about local issues already took place—where community *happens*. These are valuable locations for any technology hoping to engage the community.

The location of the devices also impacted on the results themselves, as different locations reached different audiences, due to both the geographic location within the community and the roles of the deployment venues. This was most marked in the question relating to the community centre, where the proportions of votes cast at each location were inverted. This was not reflected in the reported results, which simply aggregated votes from all locations. A more detailed report of results might better reflect how different segments of the community felt on certain issues, allowing service providers to target their efforts accordingly.

SUMMARY

Viewpoint has demonstrated that simple voting interfaces in public spaces can provide an easy method of encouraging participation in communities where traditional methods have been unsuccessful. This presents potential benefits to residents, councillors and other community organisations. However, although data collected through the device led to at least one firm promise of action, residents remained sceptical about action being taken based on the results. Even with the best of intentions, real-world constraints on organisations meant actions were limited in scope and, like other forms of consultation, it can take considerable time for changes to come into effect. Further research is required to address the challenges of making these constraints more transparent and balancing simplicity against credibility.

Through this trial, we were also able to identify key design factors impacting the design of public voting technologies. These related to the efficacy of the system and its ability to produce change; the credibility of the results and voting process; and the practical issues surrounding the design and location of the voting device itself. Future research can utilise this guidance when exploring the potential role of public voting technologies in community participation and civic engagement.

ACKNOWLEDGMENTS
The Bespoke project was funded by the EPSRC through the RCUK Digital Economy programme.

REFERENCES
1. Anttiroiko, A.V. Building strong e-democracy—the role of technology in developing democracy for the information age. *Communications of the ACM 46*, 9 (2003), 121–128.
2. Bollen, L., Juarez, G., Westermann, M. and Hoppe, H.U. PDAs as input devices in brainstorming and creative discussions. In *Proc. ICHIT 2006*, IEEE (2006), 137–141.
3. Borchorst, N.G. and Bødker, S. "You probably shouldn't give them too much information" – supporting citizen-government collaboration. In *Proc. ECSCW 2011*, Springer (2011), 173–192.
4. Carroll, J.M., Rosson, M.B. and Zhou, J. Collective efficacy as a measure of community. In *Proc. CHI 2005*, ACM (2005), 1–10.
5. Cheok, A.D., Fernando, O.N.N., Wijesena, J.P. Mustafa, A.,Shankar, R., Barthoff, A.K., Tosa, N., Choi, Y., and Agarwal, M. BlogWall: social and cultural interaction for children. *Advances in Human–Computer Interaction* (2008).
6. Eisenberger, R., Park, D.C. and Frank, M. Learned industriousness and social reinforcement. *Journal of Personality and Social Psychology 33*, 2 (1976), 227–232.
7. Ferscha, A. and Vogl, S. Pervasive web access via public communication walls. In *Proc. Pervasive 2002*, Springer (2002), 84–97.
8. Frohlich, D.M., Smith, K., Blum-Ross, A., Egglestone, P., Mills, J., Smith, S., Rogers, J., Shorter, M., Marshall, J., Olivier, P., Woods, J., Wallace, J. and Wood, G. Crossing the digital divide in the other direction: community-centred design on the Bespoke project. In *Proc. Include 2011*, Royal College of Art (2011).
9. Grönlund, Å. Democracy in an IT-framed society. *Communications of the ACM 44*, 1 (2001), 23–26.
10. Hale, M., Musso, J. and Weare, C. Developing digital democracy: evidence from Californian municipal web pages. In *Digital Democracy: Discourse and Decision Making in the Information Age*, Routledge (1999), 96–115.
11. Kavanaugh, A., Carroll, J.M., Rosson, M.B., Reese, D. D. and Zin, T.T. Participating in civil society: the case of networked communities. *Interacting with Computers 17*, 1 (2005), 9–33.
12. Larsen, K.R.T. Voting technology implementation. *Communications of the ACM 42*, 12 (1999), 55–57.
13. Networked Neighbourhoods Study. http://networkedneighbourhoods.com/?page_id=409.
14. Norman, D.A. *The Invisible Computer: Why Good Products Can Fail, the Personal Computer is so Complex, and Information Appliances are the Solution*. MIT Press, Cambridge, MA, USA, 1998.
15. O'Hara, K., Lipson, M., Jansen, M., Unger, A., Jeffries, H. and Macer, P. Jukola: democratic music choice in a public space. In *Proc. DIS 2010*, ACM (2010), 145–154.
16. Oates, B.J. The potential contribution of ICTs to the political process. *Electronic Journal of e-Government 1*, 1 (2003), 32–42.
17. Paek, T., Agrawala, M., Basu, S., Drucker, S., Kristjansson, T., Logan, R., Toyama, K. and Wilson, A. Toward universal mobile interaction for shared displays. In Proc. *CSCSW 2004*, ACM (2004), 266–269.
18. Putnam, R.D. *Bowling Alone: The Collapse and Revival of American Community*. Simon & Schuster, New York, NY, USA, 2000.
19. Rogers, E.M., Collins-Jarvis, L. and Schmitz, J. The PEN project in Santa Monica: interactive communication, equality, and political action. *Journal of the America Society for Information Science 45*, 6 (1994), 401–410.
20. Satchell, C., Foth, M., Hearn, G. and Schroeter, R. Suburban nostalgia: the community building potential of urban screens. In *Proc. OZCHI 2008*, ACM (2008), 243–246.
21. Schuler, D. Community networks: building a new participatory medium. *Communications of the ACM 37*, 1 (1994), 38–51.
22. Steins, C., Peschel, C., Warnke, D. and Borning, A. Playful civic engagement using large public displays. *CHI 2011 Workshop on Large Displays in Urban Life* (2011).
23. Streitz, N., Prante, T., Röcker, C., Van Alphen, D., Magerkurth, C., Stenzel, R. and Plewe, D. Ambient displays and mobile devices for the creation of social architectural spaces. In *Public and Situated Displays: Social and Interactional Aspects of Shared Display Technologies*, Kluwer (2003), 387–409.
24. Whittle, J., Simm, W., Ferrario, M.A., Frankova, K., Garton, L., Woodcock, A., Nasa, B., Binner, J. and Ariyatum, A. VoiceYourView: collecting real-time feedback on the design of public spaces. In *Proc. UbiComp 2010*, ACM (2010), 41–50.

Examining Technology that Supports Community Policing

Sheena Lewis[†] **and Dan A. Lewis**[*]
Technology and Social Behavior[†]
Institute for Policy Research and School of Education and Social Policy[*]
Northwestern University, Evanston, IL 60208 USA
sheena@u.northwestern.edu | dlewis@northwestern.edu

ABSTRACT
This paper investigates how citizens use technology to support community policing efforts. To explore the types of conversations that are shared on the community web forum, we conducted a qualitative study. We analyzed 865 forum posts from a community crime web forum from April 2004 to June 2011. We found that residents use the forum to: 1) build relationships by strengthening social ties, 2) discuss ways to take collective action, 3) share information and advice, and 4) regulate the social norms of the neighborhood and the web forum. Results suggest that technologies intended for crime prevention should be designed to support communication and problem-solving discussions amongst residents, as opposed to simply providing information to citizens.

Author Keywords
crime prevention technologies; community policing; crime; collective action

ACM Classification Keywords
H.5.2. Information Interfaces and Presentation (e.g. HCI): Miscellaneous

INTRODUCTION
Crime is a major concern for many urban residents. Feelings of fear and anxiety are expressed by citizens who experience or witness crime in their local neighborhoods [38]. Crime evokes concern for the physical safety and psychological wellbeing of self and other community members. Research has shown that after violence occurs in a neighborhood, some residents react individually to crime by trying to protect themselves using tactics that cause isolation (e.g., not going out, buying guns and locks) [8]. Individual responses to crime ultimately increase fear and distrust [8] and decrease feelings of community and safety [33]. Yet, some communities respond by collectively taking action to prevent violent crimes from reoccurring, which decreases fear and anxiety of becoming victimized [18]. Furthermore, community involvement, or collective action, effectively reduces crime and increases public confidence in the police [36].

Permission to make digital or hard copies of all or part of this work for personal or classroom use is granted without fee provided that copies are not made or distributed for profit or commercial advantage and that copies bear this notice and the full citation on the first page. To copy otherwise, or republish, to post on servers or to redistribute to lists, requires prior specific permission and/or a fee.
CHI'12, May 5–10, 2012, Austin, Texas, USA.
Copyright 2012 ACM 978-1-4503-1015-4/12/05...$10.00.

While criminology research suggests that collective action successfully decreases crime and anxiety, many human computer interaction (HCI) researchers and law enforcement agencies design crime prevention technologies that provide individuals with information to lessen their chances of being victimized [4, 5, 30, 37]. The functionality of such web tools range from providing crime maps to presenting missing persons and wanted criminals [4, 31]. While these crime prevention technologies focus on individuals, little is known about how technology is used to support collective action against crime. What is the role of community technologies in addressing crime? What constitutes a successful design of community crime prevention technology?

This paper describes the current role of technology in supporting citizens' efforts to address crime in a middle-class, racially-diverse community in Chicago, IL USA. We conducted a preliminary study of two websites that were created to help citizens address crime: 1) CLEARpath, a website created by the Chicago police that provides information, and 2) a web forum that organically emerged from community members' efforts to have problem-solving conversations. In our initial study, we found that residents use the community web forum to voice their community concerns *more* than they used the police website. Therefore, we focus on understanding the conversations between residents on the community web forum. We find that residents use the forum to 1) build relationships by strengthening social ties, 2) discuss ways to take collective action, 3) share information and advice, and 4) regulate norms of the community and purpose of the web forum. Our findings suggest that while the police's website was designed to provide extensive information to residents about their local community, the community website was more regularly used because it allowed residents to strengthen social ties and govern social norms. Crime prevention theory suggests that the features of the community website, such as allowing local norms to be easily shared and reinforced, affords a richer interaction and places social control theory [18] at the forefront of designing crime prevention web tools.

This work makes several contributions to the HCI community. First, this research deepens our understanding of the role of technology in supporting collective action within local communities. Specifically, our work builds on existing HCI research focused on citizen activism [9, 16, 17]. Second, this study provides HCI designers and researchers with insight into citizens' online engagement regarding crime prevention, which can then be translated into principles for designing crime prevention technologies that empower local communities and encourage them to address issues such as crime. This extends a growing body of HCI literature on crime prevention tools that focuses on designing for individuals, not communities [4, 5, 30, 42]. Lastly, this study provides insight into technology design that supports online communication between local communities and government organizations (in this case, law enforcement), complimenting previous HCI literature on the topic [14, 22] and a CHI 2010 panel discussion on designing government websites for citizen use [15].

STUDY OBJECTIVE

The objective of this paper is to examine the following research question: *How can technology be designed to best support collective action against crime?*

We address our central question by answering two supporting questions: *Do residents use the police or community websites more to voice their concerns? How are people using unofficial community websites?* This paper presents our findings to both these questions.

In this paper, we define crime as physical offenses (not "cyber" or online actions) that break the law [8]. We have chosen to study urban communities because crime, particularly violent crime, is most prevalent in urban areas, and it is a topic that often emerges during conversations about community living and quality of life [21]. Residents of high crime areas may be concerned about the safety of themselves and family members, which takes a toll on their mental and physical well-being [10]. With the decrease in government support of many services (e.g., policing) as a result of the recent economic decline, it is essential that we consider ways that technology can support safety.

BACKGROUND

Collective Action Through Community Policing

In the early 1990s, major cities in the United States experienced the highest crime rates in decades. As a result, some city governments (e.g., Chicago, New York) decided to engage local communities in taking collective action against crime through community-based alternative policing efforts. This approach, called "community policing," was one means of addressing high crime rates; other efforts included tougher laws (e.g, Three Strikes Law) and increasing youth programs [27]. Community policing refers to the partnership between residents and police to address neighborhood-specific issues (e.g., graffiti, gang violence, burglaries), where residents are involved in decision-making processes and engage in local problem-solving [27, 36]. Activities surrounding community policing may range from aggressive neighborhood watches by residents to neighborhood surveys that identify local problems and evaluate police satisfaction. Community policing has become a vital part of the overall police strategy and often complements limited police resources [34]. The ability to engage residents has proven to be crucial to combating crime and decreasing residents' fear of being victimized [36]. In fact, criminologist Wesley Skogan writes "community policing is surely one of the most important developments in American policing in the past half-century" and that it has been reproduced all over the world [35]. Community policing empowers neighborhoods to see themselves as more than helpless victims who wait for criminals to strike and then reactively call the police. Instead, residents are able to proactively confront incivilities (e.g., dilapidated buildings, graffiti, loitering) in the neighborhood that reflect signs of neglect.

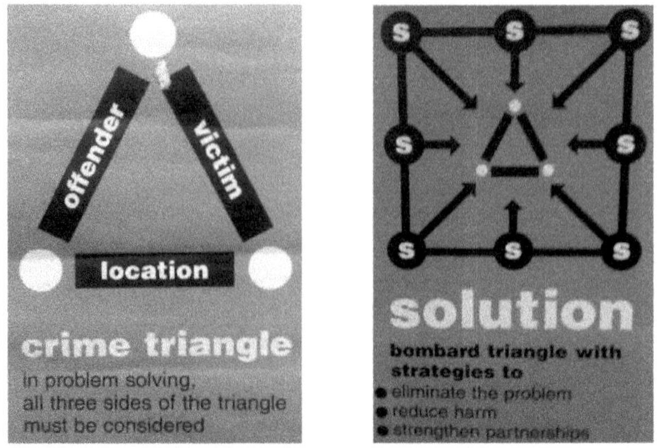

Figure 1. During a CAPS meeting, the Chicago police uses the above posters to explain the victimization theory to residents. The victimization theory (left) focuses on the victim, offender, and location (or environment). Community policing (right) focuses on finding solutions and inserting them into the "crime triangle" to minimize crime.

As information and communication technologies (ICTs) have increasingly pervaded our lives, so has it transformed community policing efforts. Early community policing efforts involved phone trees, in which neighbors would disseminate information by calling two or three assigned people in the neighborhood, who would in turn pass the information on to their assigned neighbors. Communities, however, are now appropriating various technologies (e.g., web forums, social networking sites) to communicate and to further engage those who are unable to attend in-person meetings. While scholars have considered how law enforcement uses technology [39], little is known about the extent to which communities are using technology and the subsequent effect that it has on collective action, specifically community policing. The objective of this study is to understand how technology is being appropriated in community policing strategies.

Victimization Theory: Crime Prevention from the Police Perspective

Two main crime prevention theories focus on understanding crime causation and prevention: victimization theory and social control theory [18]. The victimization theory focuses on understanding crime as events that occur between a potential victim, offender, and the environment [19]. The victimization perspective suggests that based on the information that they have, a potential victim or offender assesses the risk of being victimized or caught, respectively. A potential victim, for example, may decide to not walk down a particular street if a friend says that it is dangerous.

Law enforcement agencies, in particular, have embraced the victimization theory as a method to understand and prevent crime [34]. In fact, the police use the victimization theory to develop prevention strategies that focus on changing the behaviors of potential victims and offenders by impacting how they assess risk of being victimized or being caught. Figure 1 are posters that the Chicago police use to teach the community about how they address crime.

Most crime prevention technologies attempt to change the behavior by providing potential victims with information. The police, for example, have created technology solutions that they use internally to reduce crime (e.g., maps that identify crime hotspots) [37] and have subsequently passed those solutions to the community [31]. Non-government companies also focus on providing information to citizens in hopes of decreasing crime. EveryBlock, for example, is a website that maps crime statistics in major US cities.

In this paper, we initially examined CLEARpath, a Chicago police website designed to align with the victimization theory [31]. We found that though CLEARpath provides citizens with information, community residents created and use a web forum that facilitates communication. The following section provides background on the social control theory, a crime prevention theory that focuses on communication.

Social Control Theory: Crime Prevention from the Community Perspective

In criminology, social control theory focuses on understanding communities as opposed to the victimization theory, which focuses on the individual. Social control theory suggests that social interactions influence criminal acts through informal enforcement of social norms [13]. This perspective suggests that the morals and values of a community are shaped by social norms that in turn play a major role in determining criminal behavior. Social control theory, for instance, indicates that a teenager will be less likely to post illegal graffiti if their parents, influential adults, and peers have discouraged this type of behavior since the teen was a child.

Concepts from social control theory have been used to develop community-level analyses. Collective efficacy, for example, is an analysis method that measures social cohesion among neighbors combined with their willingness to intervene on behalf of the common good [29]. Sampson found that high collective efficacy is correlated with low crime rates [29]. Questions surrounding collective efficacy focus on understanding whether people believe that their neighbors will help them during an emergency and/or if they believe that crimes will be committed in their neighborhood [21, 28, 29].

Scholars have begun to investigate the relationship between technology and social control theory, suggesting that social norms communicated via technology affect relationships within communities [20]. However, there has not been much empirical investigation to support such claims. This study is one of the first that provides empirical evidence of the relationship between crime, technology, and the transmission of social control mechanisms within communities.

HCI and Crime Prevention Technologies

Crime and public safety are topics that have recently gained interest in HCI. Much of the HCI literature surrounding crime focuses on the police as the user. Chen et al. [7] created a system, COPLINK, that manages law enforcement data to increase effectiveness in police departments. Tullio et al. [41] examined the benefits and challenges of police departments using video surveillance in their policing efforts. These studies do not consider citizens as users of these technologies.

HCI researchers, who have aimed to design crime prevention technologies for citizens, have taken an approach similar to the victimization theory. Specifically, crime prevention tools created by HCI researchers have focused on supplying information to individuals. Blom and colleagues [4], for example, created a mobile phone application that allows residents to tag and share areas of the city on a virtual map where they feel unsafe. Satchell and Foth [30] created SPOT and MATE, two handheld personal safety devices that provides information about users' safety. Blythe et al. [5] designed a wearable technology that aims to decrease fear in older adults by broadcasting video and audio data to the police. All of these technologies were designed based on the principle that providing information to users would increase feelings of safety and decrease risk of victimization by influencing user behavior, aligning with victimization theory. None of these studies, however, focus on communication or the transmission of social norms within a community. While prior crime research in HCI focuses on designing for law enforcement agencies and individuals, this study bridges the gap by examining how local communities use technology to address crime and suggesting ways that criminology literature can be used to influence the design of effective crime prevention technologies.

There has been a plethora of HCI research that aims to understand how geographically-bound communities use technology to address local issues. Carroll and Rossen [6] present the Blacksburg Electronic Village, a community networking website that connects residents of Blacksburg, VA. Hampton and Wellman [11] found that electronic networks positively impacted neighborhoods by affording access to information and resources, linking groups, and providing social identities. While both of these studies focuses on geographically-bound communities, these technologies were not created to address a specific neighborhood issue, such as crime or violence. Related to our research agenda, Redhead and Brereton [25] examined how local communities of practice use technology and found a need for ICTs to enhance communication amongst residents by using large displays to share local information [26]. We build on [25] by providing insight into designing for crime prevention as a community of practice.

STUDY DESIGN

To understand the role of technology in community policing, we selected a diverse northside Chicago community and examined its online and offline discussions about crime. In this section, we provide a brief history of Chicago's community policing strategies and describe the data collection and analysis for the study.

Chicago and Community Policing

Chicago is the third largest city in the United States with 2.7 million people in the city. It is a racially diverse city with

Figure 2. CLEARpath website created for citizens by the Chicago police.

residents roughly split into a third Caucasian, African American, and Hispanic. Socio-economic status varies widely with a household median income of approximately $35K but with close to 20% of households living below the poverty line. Crime in Chicago has been a major issue over the past forty years, with violent crime such as homicides placing the city as second highest in the US in 2008 [1]. Despite the fact that Chicago has the second-largest police department in the US, state lawmakers considered bringing in the National Guard to help regulate a sudden increase in gang-related violence in 2010 [2]. Chicago is an ideal place to study community and crime because of the city's rich history of being a criminology studies hub and the fact that Chicago "developed the most prominent big-city neighborhood-oriented [policing] program in the [US] nation" [34].

In the early 1990s, the mayor's office created an initiative to reduce crime by blending traditional policing with alternative policing efforts that focused on empowering local residents to "take back" their neighborhoods [34]. This partnership between the police and citizens is called Chicago Alternative Policing Strategies (CAPS). Chicago is divided into 25 police districts and each district is furthered divided into 9-12 police beats - with the city totaling 279 beats. Beats are small geographic areas, mostly 30-40 blocks with over 20,000 residents. Police officers are assigned to one beat and do not change for at least two years, because one of CAPS' goals is for residents to develop a rapport with their beat officers.

CAPS meetings are typically[1] held once a month in local community centers, churches, and parks, where residents discuss neighborhood problems with their beat police officers. Police and residents also brainstorm methods to fix the problems, many times suggesting solutions in which residents play a vital role in successfully accomplishing the task (e.g., residents identifying gang members).

The Community

We selected a local community - defined as one city beat - to research. While the geographic boundaries of a beat are defined by the police, residents used the beat to define their community as observed by residents' statements in the CAPS meetings and by the self-imposed structure of the community website, where residents could have (but did not) redefine the geographic boundaries of what constitutes their community. The community studied was one of the largest beats (in terms of square miles) in the city with a majority of middle class residents. Specifically, the beat contained more than 24,400 residents, with the median age of 39 and about 46% male. The median income was $55,000 per year and the majority were homeowners (60%). The community self-identified as being racially diverse with 67% Caucasian, 12% African American, and 8.2% Latino. Compared to other beats in Chicago, the community has a medium-level of violent crime but a high number of property damage reported. We selected this beat because the demographics and crime rates are similar to many Chicago beats.

Action Through Online Participation

Community residents have access to CLEARpath, a police-community website created by the Chicago police to "serve as an information sharing vehicle and help to advance a broad community development agenda" [31]. CLEARpath emerged from the Citizen and Law Enforcement Analysis and Reporting System (CLEAR), a police web tool that allows them to "police smarter" [37] (e.g., finding crime hot spots, connecting to other law enforcement agencies, providing extensive mapping technology). Because CLEAR can only be used by the police, not by citizens, the Chicago police developed CLEARpath, which cost over $10 million and was developed over the course of three years (from 2005 to 2008).

CLEARpath is designed to mainly provide citizens with information, which aligns with victimization theory. CLEARpath is made up of 15 modules, 12 of which strictly provide information and do not allow users to input or share information with the police. In the 12 modules, the police supply an array of information to communities including "maps of crime and community concerns, information about known/wanted offenders, gang awareness materials, educational information about staying safe and preventing crime, and information about events and resources" [31]. The 3 user input modules allow citizens to report community concerns, tip police about crimes, and compliment or complain about police conduct or behavior.

In addition to CLEARpath, the community also has access to an informal community policing web forum (a Yahoo! Group) that was started by local residents in 2004, where residents discuss issues regarding crime and safety. Community members are able to join the group by submitting a request via an online sign up. A community resident, who is also a website volunteer, then responds by asking the requester where they live. If they live in the beat, their membership is approved. It is unknown how many people applied and were not accepted based on the location of their residence or how many people unsubscribed from the community web forum. As of July 2011, there were 221 members of the community web forum. The design of the community website facilitates problem-solving discussions and other characteristics that align with social control theory.

[1]Recent budget cuts have forced some districts to have quarterly meetings. The beat that we studied had monthly meetings.

Prestudy

While CLEARpath allows residents to submit some information, our preliminary investigation of the use of the two websites suggests that residents used the community web forum more than the police website to share concerns. CLEARpath's community concerns module, for example, "allows residents to report quality of life or neighborhood disorder issues directly to the Chicago Police Department" [31] by completing a form online. While the community concerns module allows residents to post information directly to the police, residents in this beat have only submitted 3 concerns in the past year.[2] In a randomly-selected three-month period in the same year, 7 residents posted 10 community concerns to the community web forum. Table 1 shows the distribution of community concerns across five police categories for both websites. Residents voice their community concerns about incivilities and neighborhood disorder on the unofficial community website more than the official police website. Based on our findings in this preliminary investigation of our first research question, we focused our study on deeply analyzing the community website.

Data Collection

To understand the role of technology in supporting community policing efforts, we conducted a combination of online qualitative content analysis for one city beat, resulting in 4425 online posts (i.e., text and photos) from the web forum created by local community members. To gather the data, we developed a web crawler using Python to retrieve forum posts, including metadata (e.g., date, subject, author) from the community web forum. We selected the forum based on what residents described as the "community crime website" during the CAPS meetings. Using the Python script, we collected 4456 forum posts that were created from April 2004 to July 2011. After removing 31 spam posts, 4425 posts remained. The following is an example of a forum post written by a local resident: *"Saw drug dealing on Saturday afternoon @ 2:30 while having late lunch on my front porch. I can identify the car and will look for it now that I know....here's the info: A reddish-marroon Buick (at least 10 yrs old) did a strange move at the stop sign as it was heading south[...] As the Buick went by me there were 3-4 young men sitting - I could not take the license number, but can identify the car again - very shiny!!"*

Additionally, we observed eleven months of CAPS meetings in-person, where both police and community members participated. While we have the in-person meeting observations, in this paper, we focus on and present results from the community web forum.

Analysis

We used qualitative methods to analyze 19.5% (865 forum posts) of the data set. Of the 865 forum posts selected for analysis, 443 forum posts (roughly 10% of the corpus) were randomly selected in order to understand the types of conversations and messages that were being shared amongst community members throughout the entire data set. Additionally,

[2]In the past year, the median number of community concerns submitted from all 279 beats was nine.

	CLEARpath	Community Forum
Gangs	1	2
Narcotics	0	0
Prostitution	0	0
Troubled Building	0	4
Other Criminal Disorder	2	4
Total	3 in 365 days	10 in 90 days

Table 1. This table displays the number of community concerns reported by local residents. The concerns are divided into five categories as defined by the Chicago police. In one year, residents posted 3 community concerns to the police website, CLEARpath, while in a 3-month period (May 5, 2011 to Aug 5, 2011), residents posted 10 community concerns on the community web forum.

470 forum posts (roughly 12%) were selected to understand which topics, or threads, received the most attention based on which had the largest number of unique authors. Table 2 shows the topic titles, number of messages, and the number of authors of the threads analyzed. Due to the random selection, 48 posts overlapped between the two different methods of selection, resulting in the analysis of 865 forum posts (as opposed to 913).

The selected forum posts were analyzed using an inductive thematic approach [40], where the data was coded for emerging phenomena. Based on preliminary analysis, we undertook a more detailed analysis of the online conversations by coding the forum posts line by line. We iteratively coded and refined the initial codes until we had a total of 33 codes that were then grouped into into higher-level categories, which eventually lead to the finalized themes presented.

The next section presents quotes from the forum posts as illustrations of the themes that repeatedly emerged in the community web forum. The quotes are literal, with spelling, punctuation, and capitalization unaltered, unless otherwise noted. Most alterations are to protect anonymity of the community.

RESULTS

Four major themes emerged from our analysis of the community web forum discussions. Residents use the forum to 1) build relationships and strengthen social ties, 2) discuss ways that they can engage in collective action, 3) share information and advice, and 4) reinforce offline and online community norms. In the following sections, we discuss each of the themes in detail.

Build Relationships

Consistent with previous studies [11], we find that residents use the community policing web forum to build relationships and strengthen social ties with other community members. Expressing collective identity, demonstrating neighborhood cohesion, and simply sharing well wishes are all ways that residents exhibited relationship building.

Residents demonstrate collective identity by using first-person plural words (e.g., we, us, our) and phrases in the forum posts [24]. When discussing the danger of drivers not stopping at stop signs near a local elementary school, one resident explains that such traffic violations are a concern for everyone by saying, *"We live here so we care about these incidents."* This resident not only expresses her concern with community issues but also recognizes that these issues interest the community as a whole. Another common occurrence in the data was residents sharing positive thoughts using collective language. One neighbor says, *"Our neighborhood is still a wonderful place to live with great neighbors like all of you who look out for one another."* Another says, *"I think we live in a reasonably safe area–over all–and we ought to continue to be good neighbors and prudent people!"* First-person plural words "has served as a measure of social integration" [23]. The use of words that supports collective identity and social integration builds relationships amongst residents by making them feel that they are a part of a group. This is especially important form of relationship building for those who may not otherwise talk to many people in the neighborhood.

Neighborhood cohesion among residents was another factor in building relationships. In a discussion about a new mosque being built in the neighborhood, one resident states, *"Should it turn out that this is the site chosen by Faizan-e-Madina, or if the Faizan-e-Madina people locate somewhere in* [our neighborhood], *we should extend our hands in friendship and welcome them to join us at our monthly meetings."* He continues to say, *"We should have more input from these folks and establish an open dialogue for our mutual benefit. Perhaps some of us who have moslem neighbors might invite them to visit with us and become an active participant in the welfare and safety of what is also their neighborhood. They shouldn't be 'strangers in a strange land.' Diversity makes us all stronger."* This resident uses the web forum to share his desire to create a cohesive atmosphere with potential new neighbors and encourages others to invite the new neighbors into conversations about community policing. This resident encourages neighbors to build relationships with others who are not a part of the neighborhood to increase cohesion.

A third method of relationship building identified in the web forum discussions are residents expressing well wishes to others within the community. For example, when one resident was hospitalized, others expressed their concern. One states, "[name] *so sorry to hear you were in the hospital. I hope everything is well with you now."* Another responded, "[name], *Good to hear from you!? Recover quickly ... everyone misses you!!!"* Though the web forum focuses on crime, residents use the community website to communicate on a very human level by showing concern for their neighbors. In addition, residents demonstrated collective sympathy when a neighbor was victimized. When an elderly couple was assaulted during a home invasion, there was a large community outcry. One community member wrote, *"CAPS [beat number] as well as the community in general are saddened that they fell victims to crime."* These types of posts strengthen relationships within the community and increase cohesion. While discussions that express well wishes may not directly impact crime, studies suggest that communities with high cohesion and strong social ties have less crime than those who don't [29]. The community website supports communication that helps strengthens these relationships.

Thread Title	# of Posts	# of Authors
Do the Police really ignore 911 calls	43	17
Suspicious neighborhood activity	46	16
Taxi Parking	33	15
How do you connect to the Web?–a quick survey	14	14
Petition	39	14
Copper Downspouts	41	13
Tagging of house on...	19	13
More Grafitti	30	13
No more BBQ in...Park	32	13
Cars not stopping at stop signs..........what to do??	33	13
Chinese Restaurant Delivery Robbery	20	12
Frequent questionable activity in[...]playground	26	11
Too petty?	12	10
New Moderator	11	10
More on Blago freebies for seniors	16	10
Urgent Meeting Tomorrow	21	10
Boat parked on xx00 block of [street].....	34	10

Table 2. This table displays the thread titles, number of posts, and number of unique authors for the top 12% of all posts ordered by the number of authors.

Discuss Collective Action

Residents used the community web forum to discuss ways to take action in their neighborhoods to reduce crime and incivilities. In one case, when a resident stated that there was new gang activity on her street, another resident responded, *"Go out there with a cell phone and paper/pencil in hand......take down the car plate[...]call it in. Jot down the time and day....like keeping a log!!"* This is an example of residents encouraging others to take action. Residents also encouraged each other to take action by posting their concerns on the website and calling the police.

Residents were urged by other residents, especially community volunteers who moderated discussions, to post their concerns on the community web forum. One moderator says, *"This is your site. Don't let it go fallow."* Another gave a lengthy plea to residents saying, *"You cared about the neighborhood enough to join this group–how about telling us of your concerns??? Without your input, we can't focus on the problems you feel are important and might end up concentrating on things you aren't as concerned about. It's your neighborhood! Help us make it even better."* People who do not normally post to the website were encouraged by regular forum contributors to share their opinions and concerns with the group.

Many times residents that had already posted on the website were encouraged to post more information about their concerns. For example, residents reporting an increase in gang graffiti were encouraged to take photos and share them with the group. *"If possible please take a digital picture or two of this."* and *"It would be nice if someone had a camera and took photos to pass around at the next regular CAPS Beat Meeting."* Residents were urged to take action by sharing photos of incivilities online and offline.

In addition, residents were encouraged to take more traditional forms of action (e.g., calling the police when they witnessed a crime). One resident's response to complaints about traffic violations in the neighborhood that were dangerous to children was, *"Get your neighbors to complain constantly. When the 911 operators know their voices by heart, maybe something will be done."* Another resident legitimized his suggestion about calling the police by mentioning that the police sergeant at the local CAPS meeting agreed. *"As Sgt.* [name] *says at CAPS meetings, keep calling, calling, calling. The more complaints, the more attention a situation gets.'"* Residents were encouraged to take action by contacting the police.

Share Information

Information sharing was prevalent on the community website. Specifically, residents share information about local crime, advice, and concerns.

Residents shared information about local crime, including reports from the police website. A community member, for example, sharing information gathered from CLEARpath writes, *"As I report at EVERY CAPS Meeting, one of the top two problems we have in this neighborhood is 'Criminal Damage, To Vehicle.'"* He continues to list the number of incidents and concludes by saying, *"This may not make you feel any better but...we ARE down 18 incidents this year, compared to 2005."* Similarly, another moderator writes, *"Good news, crime is down, once again, 5th straight month this year"* and *"I have posted the Chicago Police Department's Annual Report for the year 2004 in its entirety in the 'Files' section."* In these cases, residents gather crime reports from the police website to share with other residents.

Residents also share advice. For example, a resident posts that she was having problems with gang members parking and "conducting business" in front of her home. Another community member advises her. *"Our solution is to go out there and ask them why they are parked in front......usually that's all it takes and they go away. Sometimes we find the illicit couples/lovers lane in some states of undress too if we walk out there.....so turning on all the lights, talking LOUD, making noise with other people or animals, etc. or writing down the license number - and they take their business elsewhere."* In addition to advice, residents give warnings. When a resident says that they followed theives who had stolen property from their home, another resident responds, *"Be careful though. Sometimes the group can turn on you and they may pull a gun."* The community web forum allows residents to give and receive advice.

In addition to receiving advice, residents also ask for advice. One resident saw a spike in property damage to cars on her street. She posted to the forum, *"Outside of staying up all night & watching our cars for those of us who don't have a garage, it's almost impossible to prevent. [...] Any ideas from you will be appreciated."* Residents use the web forum to not only post but also seek advice from their neighbors.

In addition to information sharing, residents share their concerns on the web forum. One resident who lives near a park shares with the residents her fear of being attacked at night. *"Frankly, I'm afraid to walk past it at dusk and dawn for fear that someone might jump out at me."* Similarly, a mother first shares her concern about the increase in youth and gang violence in the area. She posts, *"As the mother of a son who is starting high school in the fall, I have been grappling with the same decisions. [...] I worry now about the CTA and his route home from high school."* In this post, the mother was afraid of her child riding public transportation to school. Residents utilize the community web forum to share information, advice, and their concerns, which is consistent with [6]. Though the other three themes we found closely align with social control theory, sharing information is a major factor in victimization theory. This demonstrates that features of the community website were not completely autonomous from victimization theory, but instead that where the information originates and how it is presented matters to citizens.

Reinforce Norms

Similar to prior studies [11], we found that citizens use the website to regulate social norms. Discussions about what is acceptable behavior in the community ranged from conversations about proper residential landscaping to good behavior at the neighborhood park. One resident, for example, describes what he believes is proper landscaping. *"Shrubs are not to be so HUGE or thick that a person can hide when the area is lit. Lights, and attractive low shrubbery will not give a criminal the advantage."* Another resident comments that his neighbors' bushes are not cut properly and states that he is now concerned with his bushes. *"Their bushes are kind of thick as is their next door neighbors' at the corner house. Now we have to worry somewhat about how thick our front bushes are."* Residents used the web forum to manage and regulate norms of the neighborhood.

While some residents used the web forum to regulate norms in the community, others did not believe the web forum should be used to discuss those who violate neighborhood norms. One resident, for instance, expresses concern with comments about a community member's improper landscaping. *"it seems a little harsh to be criticizing our neighbors in this forum for their bushes. The* [name]*s are nice concerned neighbors who have been very involved over the years in our neighborhood doings. We should be careful how we talk here* [on the web forum]." Some residents voice concern when the web forum was used to discuss neighborhood norms in a way that implicates a specific community member.

We found that citizens also regulate online norms. The community web forum, for example, was moderated by residents who volunteer to help. Such administrative tasks are sometimes referred to as gatekeeping [3]. One moderator states the purpose of his position by saying, *"moderators also have the responsibility and the power to back it up* [or] *to tone down discussions that get out of hand. They can, and have, imposed 'moderated' status to some people to calm them down during heated discussions. Sadly, in the past, we've also had to ban some individuals Hell bent on causing chaos. Moderators can do this, too. We don't like to discipline anyone and only do so as last resorts. Yet, we must have a mechanism in place for those rare instances that force such actions."* Site moderators were a vital part of the web forum, because they ensured that discussions aligned with the objectives of CAPS.

Moderation occurs in many ways. Moderators sometimes gently nudged the conversation back towards the goal. After a lengthy discussion about immigration amongst a few residents, for example, one moderator states, *"let's all go back to reducing crime."* In another case, a moderator responds to posts about politics, *"While I'm all for freedom of speech and all that please let's remember the purpose of CAPS is to increase police effectiveness and community policing. Therefore let's confine the discussion to that."* Using terms like "let's" nudges the communities to collectively attempt to stay on task and does not point out one individual as the culprit.

Other forms of moderation are more forceful and direct, even addressing a particular person. After receiving a forwarded newspaper article posted by one resident, a moderator responds, *"Mr.* [name],*You may be a member of our group, but you've violated our no commercial rule with your blatant ad for Microsoft. Therefore, you've been placed on moderation. We will not tolerate this type of posting.If this continues, you will be removed from our group."* In this case, the moderator called the person by name and scolded him for violating their group rules and policies. This demonstrates what occurs when users do not abide by the "online rules."

DISCUSSION

Consistent with prior HCI literature on space-based communities [6, 11], we find that contributors of a "grassroots" community web forum used the site to build and strengthen relationships, encourage collective action, share information, and reinforce offline and online norms. Though the official police website provides users with information (e.g., how to protect themselves, crime statistics, maps), it does not foster communication amongst residents. Crime theory suggests that the police website design aligns with victimization theory, the traditional perspective for conceptualizing crime prevention. Our findings suggest that crime prevention technologies that give individuals information will not necessarily increase active participation. Designers of crime prevention tools should consider not only designing for citizen-police interaction where informing users is the main focus, but also for citizen-citizen interaction where relationship building can occur. Crime prevention technologies should be designed to support social control, which includes facilitating problem-solving discussions and allowing citizens to regulate community norms.

We present crime theories that offer the HCI community a theoretical perspective for designing effective crime prevention technologies. The victimization and social control theories historically have been a major part of creating non-technology crime prevention solutions [18] and we use these theories to provide a theoretical basis to examine crime prevention technology design. Crime prevention theories provide a valuable means of understanding the context in which we design crime prevention technologies and how such designs are situated in the broader literature (e.g., consequences of designing for individuals as opposed to communities). As HCI researchers, we should consider crime theories predictions of what *actually* decreases crime and increases feelings of safety and how these theories translate into design implications.

Lastly, we encourage HCI researchers to consider the broader ecology of the crime prevention technology that they are designing. What is the culture of the communities, governments, and cities in which the technology will be situated? In Chicago, for example, there is a strong culture of community policing, in which residents have been heavily engaged in community policing efforts for over 20 years. Therefore, in Chicago communities, there may be less need to persuade people to engage in collective action. Furthermore, HCI designers should consider the subsequent effects of designing for social control. Though there are many cases where social control positively contributes to decreases in crime, there may be instances where community members exert social control that negatively impacts community morale. Exploring the ecological system may reveal that government organizations can not replicate "organic" community websites, or perhaps even design web tools that citizens heavily use because of issues regarding trust and ownership. HCI designers creating technologies for citizens should adhere to design practices that allow them to investigate the relationship between local communities and government organizations.

Legitimacy, Trust, and Accountability

Scholars have previously noted three main concerns with developing information and communication technologies for community policing: legitimacy, trust, and accountability [31].

In our study, we found the community residents who volunteered to moderate online discussions or those who were elected to be community-police liaisons at the meetings struggled with legitimizing the community website. This is not uncommon. "Community groups, by their nature, often struggle to maintain their status and legitimacy. Thus, engaging in a partnership with the police and could undermine their role as the watchdog against government abuse or neglect" [31]. We found that moderators of the community website managed the legitimacy of the website by, on one hand, distancing the website from the police by emphasizing that it is *the community's* website, not created by the police. But on the other hand, residents used the CAPS meetings to promote the site as *the* community website for discussing crime and they pulled data from CLEARpath to share with others - making it clear that the data originated from the police. Technology designers should consider how legitimacy is negotiated.

Historically trust between the community and the police has been a challenge, particularly for minorities [12, 32]. Residents may not have used the police website as much as the community forum because some people may not trust that their submissions to the police would indeed be anonymous or that the police would take their concerns seriously. Designers of community websites should consider the role of trust in the relationship between community and the police and how trust affects technology usage in community policing.

Prior work suggests that accountability is essential to citizens who use community policing technologies [31]. In our case, residents who submit community concerns on the police website were able to use a tracking number to follow police response. The community website, on the other hand, did not have a formal method of tracking concerns, and the police had little contact with the community website. In fact, when asked, the district sergeant said that while she reads posts from the community website, she does not respond or engage in online conversation with the community because of liability issues. Yet, the fact that residents use the community website to voice their concerns about criminal activity in their neighborhoods, even though the police do not address their posts, may be indicative of what happens when concerns are shared and discussed publicly. Perhaps voicing opinions publicly about criminal activity and engaging in discussion with other residents satisfies accountability concerns. Further investigation on accountability in community web forums will lead to a deeper understanding of the role that accountability plays in the design of government websites.

LIMITATIONS

Although this study provides insight into the role of technology in community policing and recommendations for design, there are limitations to this study. First, the community that we studied had a medium level of crime as compared to other areas of Chicago. Communities with high crime may find alternative uses for community technologies or may find more immediate technologies are more appropriate (e.g., text message alerts about local occurrences). Similarly, communities with different socio-economic statuses or racial composition may utilize technology to support community policing efforts differently. In future work, we intend to expand our research to include such factors.

FUTURE RESEARCH

The results of this study suggest a number of avenues for future work. First, we intend to explore the differences between online and offline engagement by comparing the conversations from the community web forum and conversations observed during the monthly in-person meetings. Results for such a study would further inform the design of technologies that support in-person and online community policing efforts. A software application, for example, may highlight important topics from the web forum to ensure that they receive proper attention during in-person meetings with the police and the community.

A second future area of study is examining those who do not have access to the web conversations because of lack of access to technology. These residents may be marginalized as neighborhood problems and solutions may be identified without their knowledge or input. This may be especially true in gentrifying communities where the socioeconomic status of the residents are rapidly changing. It is important to identify design guidelines that allow *all* community members an opportunity to participate in problem-solving discussions about crime.

Furthermore, we intend to study non-contributing members of the community web forum to examine different levels of participation, specifically how receiving information about local community concerns affects offline behavior. Though a community member may read a web post that states that uncut bushes in people's lawns encourage burglaries and may not comment on the post, perhaps they become diligent in cutting their bushes. Exploring this would deepen our understanding of how technology affects offline behavior - even amongst lurkers.

CONCLUSION

While information and communication technologies are increasingly used to support community policing efforts, designing web tools that provide information to citizens will not necessarily increase online participation. Our results suggest that web tools to support community policing should be designed to adhere to and support communication that allow residents to engage in collective problem-solving discussions and to informally regulate social norms. Using technology that facilities communication, citizens are able to share personal experiences and strengthen social ties with other residents while also addressing crime and local concerns.

ACKNOWLEDGEMENTS

We would like to thank Ikpeme Erete, Mike Horn, and Andrea Grimes Parker for their invaluable comments on this research. This research is funded by the National Science Foundation Graduate Research Fellowship.

REFERENCES

1. Chicago Murder Rate Tops New York And Los Angeles, Oct 24 2008. `http://www.huffingtonpost.com/2008/10/24/chicago-murder-rate-tops_n_137488.html`.
2. Chicago Lawmakers: Call In the National Guard, April 26 2010. `http://www.foxnews.com/us/2010/04/26/lawmakers-military-quell-chicago-violence`.
3. Barzilai-Nahon, K. Gatekeeping: A critical review. *Annual Review of Information Science and Technology 43*, 1 (2009), 1–79.
4. Blom, J., Viswanathan, D., Spasojevic, M., Go, J., Acharya, K., and Ahonius, R. Fear and the city: role of mobile services in harnessing safety and security in urban use contexts. In *Proc. CHI*, ACM (2010), 1841–1850.
5. Blythe, M. A., Wright, P. C., and Monk, A. F. Little brother: could and should wearable computing technologies be applied to reducing older peoples fear of crime? *Personal and Ubiquitous Computing 8* (2004), 402–415.
6. Carroll, J. M., and Rosson, M. B. Developing the blacksburg electronic village. *Commun. ACM 39* (1996), 69–74.
7. Chen, H., Zeng, D., Atabakhsh, H., Wyzga, W., and Schroeder, J. Coplink: Managing law enforcement data and knowledge. *Commun. ACM 46* (2003), 28–34.
8. Conklin, J. *The impact of crime*. Macmillan New York, NY, 1975.
9. DiSalvo, C., Light, A., Hirsch, T., Le Dantec, C. A., Goodman, E., and Hill, K. Hci, communities and politics. In *Proc. Ext. Abstracts CHI*, ACM (2010), 3151–3154.
10. Gehlert, S., Sohmer, D., Sacks, T., Mininger, C., McClintock, M., and Olopade, O. Targeting health disparities: A model linking upstream determinants to downstream interventions. *Health Affairs 27*, 2 (2008), 339–349.

11. Hampton, K., and Wellman, B. Neighboring in netville: How the internet supports community and social capital in a wired suburb. *City & Community 2*, 4 (2003), 277–311.

12. Hindelang, M. J. Public opinion regarding crime, criminal justice, and related topics. *Journal of Research in Crime and Delinquency 11*, 2 (1974), 101–116.

13. Hirschi, T. *Causes of Delinquency*. University of California Press, 1969.

14. Hourcade, J. P., and Fox, J. E. Designing public government web sites. In *Proc. Ext. Abstracts CHI*, ACM (2005), 2039–2040.

15. Johnson, J., and Lazar, J. E-government: services for everyone, everywhere, eventually. In *Proc. Ext. Abstracts CHI*, ACM (2010), 3139–3142.

16. Kim, S., Robson, C., Zimmerman, T., Pierce, J., and Haber, E. M. Creek watch: pairing usefulness and usability for successful citizen science. In *Proc. CHI*, ACM (2011), 2125–2134.

17. Kuznetsov, S., Odom, W., Moulder, V., DiSalvo, C., Hirsch, T., Wakkary, R., and Paulos, E. Hci, politics and the city: engaging with urban grassroots movements for reflection and action. In *Proc. Ext. Abstracts CHI*, ACM (2011), 2409–2412.

18. Lewis, D. A., and Salem, G. Community crime prevention: An analysis of a developing strategy. *Crime & Delinquency 27*, 3 (1981), 405–421.

19. Lewis, D. A., and Salem, G. *Fear of crime: Incivility and the production of a social problem*. Transaction Publishers, 1986.

20. Lewis, S. L., and Lewis, D. A. Digitalizing crime prevention theories: How technology affects victim and offender behavior. *International Journal of Criminology and Sociological Theory 4*, 2 (2011), 756–769.

21. Morenoff, J., Sampson, R., and Raudenbush, S. Neighborhood inequality, collective efficacy, and the spatial dynamics of urban violence*. *Criminology 39*, 3 (2001), 517–558.

22. Paris, C., and Wan, S. Listening to the community: social media monitoring tasks for improving government services. In *Proc. Ext. Abstracts CHI*, ACM (2011), 2095–2100.

23. Pennebaker, J., and Stone, L. Words of wisdom: Language use over the life span. *Journal of personality and social psychology 85*, 2 (2003), 291.

24. Pennebaker, J. W., and Graybeal, A. Patterns of natural language use: Disclosure, personality, and social integration. *Current Directions in Psychological Science 10*, 3 (2001), 90–93.

25. Redhead, F., and Brereton, M. A qualitative analysis of local community communications. In *Proc. OZCHI*, ACM (2006), 361–364.

26. Redhead, F., and Brereton, M. Designing interaction for local communications: An urban screen study. In *Proc. INTERACT*, Springer-Verlag (2009), 457–460.

27. Rosenbaum, D. The challenge of community policing: Testing the promises. *Sage Publications* (1994), 336.

28. Sampson, R., and Groves, W. Community structure and crime: Testing social-disorganization theory. *American Journal of Sociology* (1989), 774–802.

29. Sampson, R., Raudenbush, S., and Earls, F. Neighborhoods and violent crime: A multilevel study of collective efficacy. *Science 277*, 5328 (1997), 918.

30. Satchell, C., and Foth, M. Welcome to the jungle: Hci after dark. In *Proc. Ext. Abstracts CHI*, ACM (2011), 753–762.

31. Schuck, A., and Rosenbaum, D. Building trust and a police-community website: An assessment of the clearpath planning and community engagement process. Tech. rep., Macauthor Foundation, 2008.

32. Schuman, H. *Racial attitudes in America: Trends and interpretations*. Harvard Univ Pr, 1997.

33. Schwab-Stone, M., Ayers, T., Kasprow, W., Voyce, C., Barone, C., Shriver, T., and Weissberg, R. No safe haven: A study of violence exposure in an urban community. *Journal of the American Academy of Child & Adolescent Psychiatry 34* (1995), 1343–1352.

34. Skogan, W. *Police and Community in Chicago: A Tale of Three Cities*. Oxford University Press, 2006.

35. Skogan, W. An overview of community policing: Origins, concepts, and implementation. In *The handbook of knowledge-based policing: current conceptions and future directions*. Wiley, 2008, 43–57.

36. Skogan, W., and Hartnett, S. *Community Policing, Chicago style*. Oxford University Press, 1997.

37. Skogan, W., Hartnett, S., DuBois, J., Bennis, J., Kim, S., Rosenbaum, D., Graziano, L., and Stephens, C. Policing smarter through it: Learning from chicagos citizen and law enforcement analysis and reporting (clear) system. Tech. rep., US Department of Justice, 2004.

38. Skogan, W., and Maxfield, M. *Coping with crime: Individual and neighborhood reactions*. Sage Publications, 1981.

39. Skogan, W. G., and Hartnett, S. M. The diffusion of information technology in policing. *Police Practice & Research 6*, 5 (2005), 401 – 417.

40. Strauss, A., and Corbin, J. *Basics of qualitative research: Grounded theory procedures and techniques*. Sage Publications, Inc, 1990.

41. Tullio, J., Huang, E., Wheatley, D., Zhang, H., Guerrero, C., and Tamdoo, A. Experience, adjustment, and engagement: the role of video in law enforcement. In *Proc. CHI*, ACM (2010), 1505–1514.

42. Woelfer, J. P., Iverson, A., Hendry, D. G., Friedman, B., and Gill, B. T. Improving the safety of homeless young people with mobile phones: values, form and function. In *Proc. CHI*, ACM (2011), 1707–1716.

Collaboration in Cognitive Tutor Use in Latin America: Field Study and Design Recommendations

Amy Ogan[1], Erin Walker[2], Ryan S.J.d. Baker[3], Genaro Rebolledo-Mendez[4], Maynor Jimenez Castro[5], Tania Laurentino[6], Adriana de Carvalho[1]

[1]Carnegie Mellon University
5000 Forbes Avenue
Pittsburgh, PA 15213

[2]Arizona State University
University Drive & Mill Avenue
Tempe, AZ 85287

[3]Worcester Polytechnic Institute
100 Institute Road
Worcester, MA 01609

[4]Universidad Veracruzana
J.M. Morelos No. 44
Xalapa, Veracruz, México

[5]Universidad de Costa Rica
Sede Montes de Oca,
San José, Costa Rica

[6]SENAI Institute
Avenida Fernandes Lima
Maceió, Brazil

aeo@cs.cmu.edu, erin.a.walker@asu.edu, rsbaker@wpi.edu, grebolledo@uv.mx, maynorj@gmail.com, tania.laurentino@gmail.com, dikajoazeirodebaker@gmail.com

ABSTRACT

Technology has the promise to transform educational practices worldwide. In particular, cognitive tutoring systems are an example of educational technology that has been extremely effective at improving mathematics learning over traditional classroom instruction. However, studies on the effectiveness of tutor software have been conducted mainly in the United States, Canada, and Western Europe, and little is known about how these systems might be used in other contexts with differing classroom practices and values. To understand this question, we studied the usage of mathematics tutoring software for middle school at sites in three Latin American countries: Brazil, Mexico, and Costa Rica. While cognitive tutors were designed for individual use, we found that students in these classrooms worked collaboratively, engaging in interdependently paced work and conducting work away from their own computer. In this paper we present design recommendations for how cognitive tutors might be incorporated into different classroom practices, and better adapted for student needs in these environments.

Author Keywords

Cognitive tutors; collaborative learning; cultural adaptation

ACM Classification Keywords: H.5.2: User Interfaces - Graphical user interfaces; K.3.1: Computer Uses in Education

INTRODUCTION

In recent years, school access to computers has greatly increased worldwide and across socioeconomic groups, with the growth of initiatives like One Laptop Per Child and Intel classmate PCs. Within these evolving contexts, effective educational software could make a huge impact: it is easily deployable, and when amortized across users it is low cost compared to physical resources like textbooks. Yet, it has capabilities that far surpass physical resources, such as the ability to provide structured guidance and support. However, creating this impact is more complex than simply distributing educational software widely. Not only does the content of the software need to be translated and localized, but attention needs to be paid to how teacher practices and student interactions with educational software vary across contexts. In this paper, we examine the cross-contextual generalizability of pedagogical assumptions of cognitive tutors, educational software that has been demonstrated to be effective at improving learning outcomes. We observe student and teacher use of the Middle School Mathematics Cognitive Tutor (CT) in classroom settings in three Latin American countries to gain insight into how the CT might be adapted to different settings.

Cognitive tutors are an example educational technology that has the potential to transform education. A cognitive tutor assesses skill mastery as a student solves problems, and provides context-sensitive hints, error feedback, and adaptive problem selection [23]. Their self-paced learning and tailored content and support provide students with individual attention, and free teachers to act as classroom facilitators [21]. Cognitive tutors were initially designed to support problem solving in well-defined domains such as math and science, and have been demonstrated to improve a number of studies, particularly for students of low socio-economic status [13]. In recent years, cognitive tutors have also been successfully used in ill-defined domains such as developing intercultural competence [e.g., 18].

In order to study the CT across learning contexts, we conducted a twelve-week multi-context field study of the CT, observing over seven hundred students in Brazil, Mexico,

Permission to make digital or hard copies of all or part of this work for personal or classroom use is granted without fee provided that copies are not made or distributed for profit or commercial advantage and that copies bear this notice and the full citation on the first page. To copy otherwise, or republish, to post on servers or to redistribute to lists, requires prior specific permission and/or a fee.
CHI'12, May 5–10, 2012, Austin, Texas, USA.
Copyright 2012 ACM 978-1-4503-1015-4/12/05...$10.00.

and Costa Rica. Generally, evaluations of cognitive tutors have been limited to schools in the United States, Canada, and Western Europe. However, individuals in the United States frequently (though not always) differ from students in the Latin American countries we investigated along several dimensions, including power distance (equality of power distribution), tolerance for ambiguity, and individualism versus collectivism [10]. In addition, access to resources varies between developing and developed contexts, and these differences affect how technology is used [19]. In taking a technology that has been successful in one context, and transporting it to a different context, we can identify which aspects of cognitive tutors are context-specific and develop guidelines for more effective use in new contexts.

In this paper, we survey related work on generalizing education technology, and discuss the specific tutor studied. We then present qualitative observations of CT use in three Latin American settings. Our findings have three themes: the school conditions in which the tutor was used, the way the CT was integrated into classroom practice, and collaborative student use of the CT. From these, we develop design recommendations for the future development of cognitive tutors that are educationally effective across a broader set of contexts. Our contributions are both a richer understanding of ways educational technology designed for one context might be adopted to different contexts, and practical recommendations for how best to accomplish this goal.

EDUCATIONAL TECHNOLOGY IN DEVELOPING CONTEXTS

Warschauer writes, "*Technology projects around the world too often focus on providing hardware and software and pay insufficient attention to the human and social systems that must also change for technology to make a difference.*" Access to technology is increasing worldwide, but must be incorporated into existing social and institutional structures to have a truly positive impact [25].

Hoadley and colleagues extend Warschauer's argument by arguing that desktop technologies can be disruptive, difficult to use, and impossible to maintain in developing contexts. Thus, the platform for educational technology is very important for adoption and impact [9]. It has been possible to reach a broad audience using platforms already popular in developing regions, such as mobile phones [14, 11] or bargain video game consoles [15]. Existing tools have also been adapted to be more suitable for developing contexts, such as making low-cost programmable bricks with local materials and local construction [22], or adjusting to high student-to-computer ratios by giving each student a mouse that controls a cursor on a shared display [16].

While these hardware solutions are an important component of bringing educational technology to developing contexts, educational software is also a necessary area of research. We now have mature, empirically proven technological methods of improving learning being used in schools across the United States, from rural or suburban classrooms, to urban classrooms serving historically disadvantaged populations. Are these technologies equally successful in different contexts, such as developing regions? What needs to be adapted to make them viable across cultural contexts, in both developed and developing regions? While some completed systems have been used in multiple cultural contexts [17], work on adapting these systems to new contexts has focused on translation, localization, and interface design (see [6] for review). Hence, there is a gap in the literature with respect to understanding how students use existing mature systems across contexts.

MIDDLE SCHOOL MATHEMATICS COGNITIVE TUTOR

The Middle School Mathematics Cognitive Tutor (CT) was developed between 1999 and 2004 at Carnegie Mellon University. It spans over 30 units covering different mathematical topics for students in U.S. grades 6-8 (approximately 11-14 years old). In our investigation, we used the Scatterplot unit of the CT [4], after determining with each school that scatterplots were an appropriate topic for their curriculum. In this unit, students read a scenario in which a scatterplot can be used to answer a question about data. For example, a scenario might describe kids who have a lemonade stand and want to know whether they sell more cups of lemonade on hot days. The goal is to answer this question by plotting two numerical variables (e.g., cups and temperature) on a graph. In the tutor (see Figure 1), students are scaffolded in labeling axes, choosing a scale, plotting points, and answering interpretation questions. The CT delivers immediate corrective feedback on each step, an approach shown to support learning in an American context [8]. Students can also request a multi-level hint at any step. The first hint students receive tends to reference the underlying concept, and subsequent hints increase in specificity. The system assesses students' knowledge based on their problem solving and presents this information as a "skill bar" that increases or decreases as they solve problems with particular skills.

Target Use of the CT

The design of cognitive tutors, and the algorithms they use to model learning, assumes that students generally work at

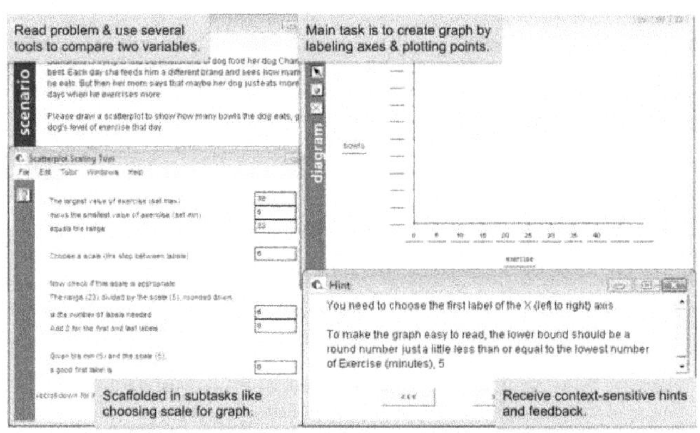

Figure 1. English-language version of the Middle School Mathematics Cognitive Tutor. Students must compare two variables on a graph. They use several scaffolding tools to complete the task, and receive context-sensitive help.

their own individual computers and at their own pace [23]. Students proceed using the CT's help and feedback as the teacher circulates around the room providing extra support to students that need it [4, 21]. The CT's model of student knowledge assumes that the student is solving problems without the assistance of others [7]. Recent additions to cognitive tutors also assume individual work. For example, [1]'s model of ideal help-seeking in cognitive tutors focuses solely on help-seeking within the tutoring environment, and not on help students seek from their teacher and peers.

Based on published classroom observations, these assumptions are generally met in use of the CT and related software in American classrooms. Though there are qualitative reports of student collaboration while using the CT [21], it occupies a relatively low amount of class time. For instance, in quantitative field observations of student behavior in suburban American middle schools, using this same tutor lesson, students spent only 4% of their time talking on-task to the teacher or another student. They spent 78% of their time working on their own [4]. Since that study, the third author has spent over 500 hours conducting quantitative field observations in American classrooms, including urban, suburban, and rural classrooms. Though the proportion of collaborative behavior in those observations has not been published, it is similar to the proportion seen in [4].

Preparation of the CT for Use Outside of the U.S.

While the Scatterplot CT unit was developed in English, the students in this investigation were native speakers of Spanish and Portuguese, and generally did not speak English. Therefore, with local support, all of the text in the tutor was translated into the local language of instruction, and then tailored to each particular locale; for example, in Mexico and Costa Rica, after an initial translation, the tutor text was iteratively reviewed and revised by local teachers and researchers in each of the sites separately. Also, scenarios in the unmodified system were in some cases outside of the scope of students' cultural experience. The scenarios and mathematics were examined for culturally appropriate content, and modified as necessary to better fit the local context. For instance, in Brazil, local researchers and teachers changed the previously mentioned lemonade scenario to reflect local practices of selling coconut water on the beach.

FIELD STUDY PROCEDURE

Following the iterative translation procedure, the on-site investigation occurred over the course of twelve weeks, with four weeks dedicated to each of three sites (Brazil, Mexico, and Costa Rica). The first step at each site was a meeting between the international team and local teachers and researchers at the school computer lab, to demonstrate the software, answer questions about the study and material, and for teachers to work through a full problem in the tutor so that they were comfortable using it in class. These meetings were followed by a week of software installation and piloting with students who were not part of the full study. As much as possible, teachers supervised the student pilots, so that they would know what to expect from facilitating a Cognitive Tutor classroom. International researchers also gathered information about the school context.

During the following three weeks, each student used the CT in a classroom setting for eighty minutes. At least two researchers were present in the computer lab in each session, taking field notes as they positioned themselves around the lab in order to observe computer screens. Field notes captured on- and off-task behavior including collaboration, teachers' instructional procedures, student impasses, and affective reactions. Diagrams of machine and participant locations were drawn at intervals throughout CT sessions.

The teachers were asked to conduct every session on their own, and behave as they would if they were to include the technology as part of their typical practice. They were told that researchers would be available for technical support should any problems arise with the tutors or the computers. While the study procedure was kept as consistent as possible, given the nature of classroom research in multiple diverse contexts, we adapted it to each context as individual school conditions dictated. We describe these adaptations as part of the "Findings: Deployment of the CT" section.

Following tutor use, we conducted in-context guided interviews with participants [20], which began with a set of prepared questions but were allowed to digress into follow-up questions. Teachers and principals were interviewed individually in order to make them more comfortable in discussing sensitive topics surrounding school conditions. Teacher interview questions explored the social context of the participants at the site, the procedures and values they held in their traditional classrooms, and their experiences leading the CT sessions. Students were interviewed in groups of two to four at a time; groups were found to facilitate communication for students who were otherwise shy. Student interview questions explored social context, students' values about learning, and their experiences with using CT and other technology. These interviews were recorded and were conducted in the local language by a member of the research team who spoke the language. Two groups were taken aside for a think-aloud procedure while using the CT at each site.

FINDINGS: SCHOOL CONTEXTS

Based on our participant interviews and field notes across researchers, we can describe the conditions where cognitive tutors could potentially be deployed, and put the results of tutor usage in context. Across the three sites, we iteratively organized our findings into three main themes that affected our educational technology deployment: socio-economic context, typical classroom instruction, and technology use.

Socio-Economic Context

In Brazil, we deployed the CT in a middle school in an impoverished area of a large city in the northeast, known both for resorts and a significant industrial base. Class sizes ranged from 20-40. Given the economic situation in the neighborhood of the school, many teachers drove from up to three hours away, and did not always arrive to teach their class. Students, however, had a significant incentive to attend, as all students received free lunch and snacks during the day. Even so, as the school was located in a community in which religion was strong, many students were absent for up to a month at a time on family religious pilgrimages.

Figure 2. Images from the computer lab at each of the three sites. From top: Brazil, Mexico (combined with library), and Costa Rica.

There was low accountability for student absences. When teachers were absent, there were no substitutes, so students either sat unattended in their classroom, played games in the central courtyard, or sat in on other classes. Students wore t-shirts, jeans, and sandals that had been given to them by the school. The computer lab in the school was located behind a heavily locked and barred door designed to deter robberies.

In Mexico, we deployed the CT in a public middle school serving a lower and lower-middle class area of a large town in a Southeastern state. In this school, class sizes varied from 20 to 46 students. Students wore school uniforms purchased by parents and were provided with textbooks from the government. Lunch was not provided; rather, students were divided into two school sessions, a morning session from 7am until 1pm and afternoon from 1pm until 7pm.

In the Mexican site, as in Brazil, there were no substitute teachers. Instead, there was a system of aides. When teachers were absent, an aide would sit in the class and give students a prepared problem to do. If too many teachers were absent, an aide or other teacher periodically checked in on the class to make sure they were not misbehaving.

In Costa Rica, we deployed the CT in a middle school serving a medium-size town. Students were issued a school uniform shirt, but bought their own pants and shoes. Lunch was provided to all students in a cafeteria where they ate alongside their teachers, and afterwards all were expected to assist in cleaning their plates and utensils. These meal arrangements, also common at other schools in the area, are perhaps reflective of the lower Power Distance seen in Costa Rica compared to other Latin American countries [10]. Both students and teachers reported that teacher absences were rare, although school sessions were sometimes canceled for days due to heavy rains.

The school property itself was surrounded by locked gates and barbed wire, and had prior issues with armed robberies. Within the gates, the school walls (and those of other schools in the area) were covered in murals of jungle wildlife, painted by the students. These murals reflected the great importance placed on caring for the environment (ecotourism is a significant factor in the Costa Rican economy).

Teaching and Learning Practices

In each of the three sites, we interviewed teachers in order to understand their typical classroom procedures. These interviews took place in context, with teachers walking us through materials that they would typically use to teach. In each country, standard classroom practice for math instruction had a pattern of teacher demonstration followed by multiple days of group exercises.

At the Brazilian site, classes typically consisted of the teacher demonstrating a worked example briefly at the beginning of class, followed by students doing group exercises that came from a list at the end of a textbook. Despite the students' age (12-15), teachers reported that students were still working on basic math skills such as addition, subtrac-

	Brazil Site	Mexico Site	Costa Rica Site
Math Skills	struggling with basic operations	learning geometry, some difficulties with basic math	learning trigonometry, mastered basic math
Computer Skills	minimal exposure	recreational exposure	used in school
Computer Lab	12 computers, unused	49 computers, unused	30 computers, used in classes
City Population	1 million	50,000	10,000
City GDP Per Capita	$3,366USD	$5,417USD	$6,590USD
2009 PISA Test	57th of 64 countries	51st of 64 countries	N/A

Table 1. Comparison of the three populations on math skills, rank on the 2009 Program for International Student Assessment math test, computer skills and use, city size, and 2008 gross domestic product per capita in the city of our field site.

tion, multiplication, and division. Teachers informed us that they strongly encourage collaboration during classwork and even on assessments, from providing explanations to just sharing answers. Students were often assessed orally.

At the Mexican site, math classes consisted of an introductory lecture and worked example on a topic followed by 2-4 days of group work on a related exercise taken from materials provided by the government-standardized curriculum. Students were officially studying geometry, but teachers informed us that they felt students were underprepared by their previous courses and needed to review basic math skills. In class, students frequently talked out loud to one another off-topic during all classroom activities, including both groupwork and lectures. Teachers reported that this did not concern them, as they believed the talk would eventually turn to math-related topics.

At the Costa Rican site, math classes consisted of a lecture on a topic followed by a few periods of group work. Students were learning trigonometry, and teachers were confident that students had mastered basic math skills.

Digital Literacy

At the Brazil site, students reported that they were frequent computer users and that they were proficient in their use. However, when asked for detail, the majority of students reported that they did not have computers in their houses, and used computers at most once a month in internet cafés, where they used social networking sites and played games. Observations of these students using computers revealed a range of ability; some did not know how to operate a mouse or move a window, others were proficient in searching and posting pictures on the internet. All interviewees reported having a television in their home, even though many of their homes were off the electricity grid. A small percentage of interviewees had owned a cell phone.

Teachers showed a range of skill with the computers. Some had never used a computer, while others had one at home. Teachers who did not have computer skills relied on more proficient students to support other students with the CT.

The school in Brazil had a computer lab with 22 machines purchased by the federal government in an initiative to give every school access to technology. Computer viruses had infected all of the machines, but were seen as harmless pranks by administration. Twelve were functioning, but had no internet access. Computers were not used by classes for a number of reasons: many teachers had no experience with technology and were unfamiliar with educational uses of computers, and because the lab was typically locked due to security concerns.

At the Mexican site, students were familiar with computers and most used computers for social networking and listening to music. Half of interviewees reported having a computer in their home, and those who did stated that they used them to complete homework assignments. Students were also very familiar with other technologies: all had a television and cell phone and several owned a gaming system such as Xbox or PlayStation.

Teachers were familiar with computers, but used them only for preparation for class (e.g., typing up worksheets, searching for curriculum materials). One teacher had set up a blog for her students to follow. An exception to this rule was a teacher who reported that he did not trust computers and never worked with them; as noted below in the "Findings: Deployment of Cognitive Tutor" section, this teacher avoided attending any of his students' sessions with the CT.

The combination computer lab/library in Mexico was outfitted with 41 Telmex Intel computers provided by the federal government, and 8 desktop machines. The school director's office had internet. Although they had been in the school for a year, teachers reported that we were the first group to use the Telmex computers. Reports differed on why the lab was not used: the principal was not enthusiastic about technology, there was no educational software, or the teachers weren't proficient in teaching with computers. However, during the study, several teachers stopped to ask if they could use the computers when we finished.

At the Costa Rican site, students had exposure to computers at school, and were capable users. Most had a computer in their home or were able to find one for recreational use such as social networking, and several reported having multiple machines in their home. Interviewees reported using a video chat program from home to jointly complete homework assignments (or answer-share) with their classmates when they finished school for the day.

Teachers were experienced computer users, and reported using them for class preparation and social networking. They owned cell phones and texted frequently during breaks. The teachers we worked with took part in a program initiated by the local university, designed to support them in integrating technology into the classroom, but rarely did so in practice. They reported that the computer lab schedules were often full with other courses, and that preparation time was too great for technology-enhanced instruction.

The school in Costa Rica had two computer labs, provided by a private foundation. Each lab was supervised by an attendant, and used by students for classes and internet access. There were currently 30 desktops across the two computer labs, following a theft in the school the previous year. For the study, our collaborators brought 10 laptops from a local university to temporarily replace the stolen machines. These computers allowed us to conduct our observations in a manner that was closer to typical classroom practices. Lab attendants reported that most courses in the computer lab were either computer skills classes on making presentations and documents, or were using the internet for information search.

FINDINGS: DEPLOYMENT OF THE CT

General Reception towards the Cognitive Tutor

Across the three sites, there were several commonalities that indicated that the CT might be a welcome addition to the classroom. Each school's principal expressed interest in using more educational technology (despite reports to the contrary from the lab manager at the Mexican site), and was an active partner in organizing the study. All students appeared excited and motivated by technology, whether or not they were proficient or frequent users.

In general classroom practice, teachers reported not having appropriate educational software or enough time to prepare lesson plans that incorporated technology. Thus, most teachers were enthusiastic about using the CT, which they perceived as requiring little additional preparation, and serving as a good supplement to their exercise-based classes.

Student and Teacher Participation

In the Brazilian site, around 100 students ages 12-15 participated. Because the number of computers in the lab was smaller than the size of a class, groups of twelve students were pulled from one class at a time to use the CT over two class periods of forty minutes each. Although the math teachers were enthusiastic participants in the initial informational meeting, for most of the study they were not present in the computer lab. Given that their classes were split for the study between the computer lab and the classroom, the teachers believed that being in their regular class was important, and that others would be able to handle the instruction in the computer lab. Additionally, as described above, there were frequent absences on the part of the teachers, and no substitutes. This led to teachers from other subject areas helping during periods that they had free from teaching. On occasion the principal of the school participated too. If neither teachers nor the principal were present, researchers supervised students.

At the Mexican site, the principal insisted that all students have the chance to use the technology. Thus approximately 600 students ages 13-15 and seven teachers participated. During use of the CT, each class of students was brought in to the computer lab in place of their typical math period, with each class participating for two periods of forty minutes each. Teachers (or, on occasion, knowledgeable substitutes) were present to conduct their classes for the duration of the study. The only teacher who was reluctant to use technology made himself absent for all of the sessions that his students participated in, and thus his sessions were given a substitute or supervised by the research team.

At the Costa Rican site, around 90 students and two teachers participated. The study was supervised by the regular math teachers, but occurred at a time where classes had just finished for the semester and students only attend exams. Therefore, we observed student use of the CT in groups of approximately 20 at a time selected from the same math class, for single 80 minute periods.

Structure of Cognitive Tutor Session

In the Brazilian site, students filed in excitedly and wanted to sit beside friends. There was confusion at the beginning trying to determine how to login to the system, as the names they used frequently did not match their names on the school roster. In addition, typing skills were low. As students started the first tutor problem, they were typically confused about the content, and had many questions at each step about how to proceed. Due to low literacy levels in addition to low math skills, they had difficulty understanding the tutor hints. Nevertheless they gradually moved through the first problem with each other's help, and that of any aides present. Occasionally the aides requested the researchers' help when unsure of how to proceed. Some aides also indicated that if we were going to be watching them, we ought to share the load of supporting students.

In Mexico, students took their assigned seats, and were able to help one another login to the tutor. The supervising teacher then typically walked the students through the problem, either verbally or using a projector to demonstrate. When teachers felt the students understood, they let the students work on their own, and walked around to help. They also asked the researchers to help, because the class sizes were so large that they had trouble getting to everyone who needed help. During the second session, students started using the tutor immediately. Because screens on the Intel PCs were small, and the CT has multiple windows, students had some difficulty navigating from window to window when working through the problems.

In Costa Rica, students took their assigned seats. As in Mexico, the supervising teacher either used a projector or a whiteboard to walk students through the problem, and then let the students work on their own, walking around to help. When students transitioned to solving problems on their own, they tended to work in small groups and were more successful than in the other sites.

In all three sites, certain collaborative patterns of use emerged when they used the tutor, concerning students working interdependently, working at locations all over the classroom, and giving particular kinds of help to each other. We believe they are particularly relevant for cognitive tutor design for use in these settings, and describe them below.

FINDINGS: COLLABORATIVE PATTERNS OF USE

Interdependent Pace of Work

I1: Teacher led instruction

One collaborative pattern we observed in both the Mexican and Costa Rican sites was synchronized whole-class advancement through the tutor, led by the teacher. In many introductory sessions, the whole class worked at the same pace, led by the teacher guiding students step by step through a problem in the tutor. Teachers seemed to find this to be a useful technique when students were unfamiliar with the tutor. The teacher would describe a single step in the tutor, and then wait as students executed the step on their own computer. The teachers would then either demonstrate the step themselves on a projector or provide the students with the correct answer. Many teachers requested a projector to facilitate this process, often using the only projector in the school.

I2: Teacher guided practice

A related collaborative pattern was whole-class advancement through the tutor, but with opportunities for students to work independently. As students acquired more expertise in using the CT, teachers would instruct them to do two or three steps on their own, but then stop the whole class to wait for everyone to catch up, saying "Is everybody here?" In this pattern, students typically did not show exploratory behavior with the tutor; they would wait patiently for the teacher to say they could continue, and follow the teacher's instructions closely.

When asked about the rationale for structuring the class in this way, teachers said that is important to keep everyone on the same page, an easy way to familiarize the students with the system, and more efficient than repeatedly answering the same questions from students. Interestingly, in almost all cases, after this guided period of instruction which generally consisted of one full problem in the tutor, teachers would make an announcement to the class proclaiming that now it was time for students to work on their own, and the teachers would not be helping (this statement was never true; teachers did help during the self-paced period). Teachers said that

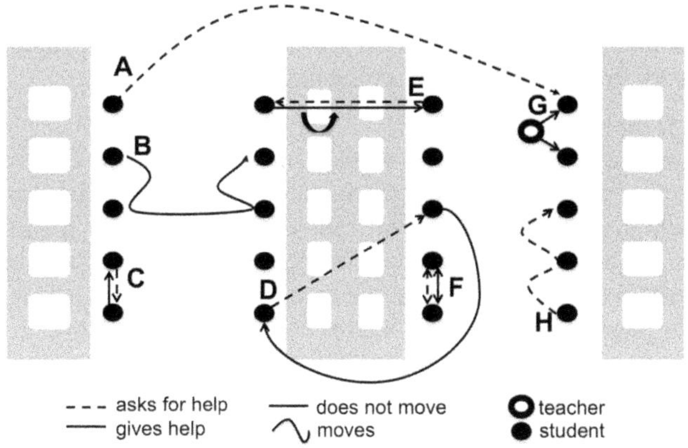

Figure 3. The ways in which students moved around the classroom and interacted with classmates across sites.

this announcement was made because otherwise students would not work, but at the first sign of difficulty would wait for the teacher to give help.

I3: Student-led group work

A third pattern we observed involving interdependent pace of work was student-led group problem solving. As students moved into an individual work phase, their pace of problem-solving often remained interdependent, but in spontaneously formed small groups seated at adjacent computers. When one group member would successfully complete a step, they would inform the other members of their group of the correct action, and the other members of group would then take the correct step. Between groups, it varied whether one person always took on the explainer role, or whether different members of the group did. During this type of work, the teacher circulated around the classroom to help individual students and groups.

I4: Shared interfaces

At the Costa Rican site only, students were more likely to work at an individual pace. However, when they worked synchronously, groups of two to three would work completely interdependently on the same computer, sharing the mouse and keyboard (despite the fact that each student had access to an individual machine).

Variable Location of Student Work

In addition to problem-solving interdependently, we found that students frequently helped each other, and thus a lot of students' work did not occur at their own computers. Figure 3 aggregates data from all three sites to depict ways in which students interacted with their peers in order to give or receive help. Students interacted either from their seats (represented by straight lines) or by moving around the class (represented by curved lines). Teachers encouraged these collaborative behaviors as they circulated around the classroom (represented by G in Figure 3). To the observer, classrooms were chaotic, with constant movement by students and loud cross-class collaborations. We estimate that in the Brazilian and Mexican sites, roughly 60% of student work did not occur at their own computer, a much higher proportion than the 4% seen in past research on CT usage in the

United States [4]. We divide the variable location of student work into two patterns of collaboration.

L1: Directed help

One pattern related to location of work was the directed exchange of help between students. This pattern represents help given after one student calls out or signals to a specific friend for help. For example, in Figure 3, D and E represent help given in response to one student calling out to a friend for help. In D, the helper moves around the table, while in E the helper remains in her seat but rotates her laptop.

L2: Spontaneous help

A second pattern related to location of work involved help that did not appear to be purposefully directed to a specific friend in need. In cases such as A and H, help-related actions were spontaneous. In H, the student goes from computer to computer looking for the answer she needs. When students were done with a problem step, they also might move around the room from classmate to classmate giving them information (as with student B in Figure 3).

When probed on their helping behaviors, students explained that everybody needed to finish, and that the academic performance of their whole class was important. Students said they felt kinship with their classmates, given that they were often classmates several years in a row.

Content of Help

Despite these commonalities in movement around the classroom, the kinds of help students gave varied between settings. In general, help consisted of a verbal explanation, telling another student the answer, or even demonstrating the next correct step by physically taking control of another person's computer (or a combination of these).

The verbal content of explanations differed from site to site, and appeared to be related to the prior knowledge of the students. We identified three collaborative patterns related to the verbal content of help. At the Brazilian site, where students had very low prior knowledge, we observed students circulating around the classroom (as in B or H in Figure 3), giving or seeking the answers to the next problem step (*C1: Answer-based help*). In contrast, students at the Mexican site primarily exchanged help focusing on how to use the technology rather than problem solving (*C2: Technology-based help*). At the Costa Rican site, students reported giving full explanations to help their classmates understand the material (*C3: Concept-based help*), although they were observed to give answers and acknowledged doing so when questioned. These differing approaches emphasize the opportunity in supporting students whose natural inclination is to collaborate to give more conceptual help.

DESIGN RECOMMENDATIONS FOR CT USE IN HIGHLY COLLABORATIVE SETTINGS

By encouraging teachers to use the CT as they would typically conduct a regular class, we open the door to students using the CT in a highly collaborative manner. In order to achieve the full learning benefits of intelligent tutors, it may be necessary to redesign the underlying systems, which assume that students are working for the most part at their own pace and computer [23].

Collaborative Knowledge Tracing

One of the most important aspects of CTs is their ability to track the current knowledge level of the student. This knowledge tracing allows the student and the teacher to know when the student has achieved mastery on a skill, and enables the tutor to select appropriate problems for each student. However, we saw that as students worked in almost all collaborative patterns (*I1, I3, I4, L1,* and *L2*), the answers entered into a tutor were frequently not reflective of the knowledge of the student using that machine. We believe it would be beneficial for the knowledge-tracing algorithm to view the classroom as a *network* of connected nodes instead of a collection of individual users, accounting for when multiple students are completing problems jointly.

To implement this modification, one could explicitly estimate the probability that the student has been told the next step in the problem. In classical Bayesian Knowledge-Tracing [7], skill mastery is estimated based on four parameters, including the probability that students will perform a step correctly even if they have not mastered the skill (P[Guess]). It is possible to incorporate other probabilities in P(Guess) to account for other sources of error [5]; here, it would be appropriate to include the probability that a student answered correctly due to another student's help (e.g., A in Table 2). This probability could be estimated empirically based on data on the problem-solver's behavior (as in the "contextual guess and slip" approach in [cf. 3].

This approach will necessitate the inclusion of data on the problem-solving pace of all students in the networked classroom. It may be possible to determine over time which students' performances are linked, by tracking the timing of different students' steps. It may similarly be possible to assess whether students are working together (*I3*) or following the teacher's lead as a whole class (*I1*).

A. Knowledge Tracing	**B. Model Tracing**	**C. Adaptive Scaffolding**
P(Guess') = *guess**(1-*helped*) + *helped* Where *helped* = probability student was helped *guess* = probability student guessed	IF don't know *x* AND person *y* knows *x* THEN ask *y* about *x* IF know *x* AND person *y* doesn't know *x* THEN tell *y* about *x*	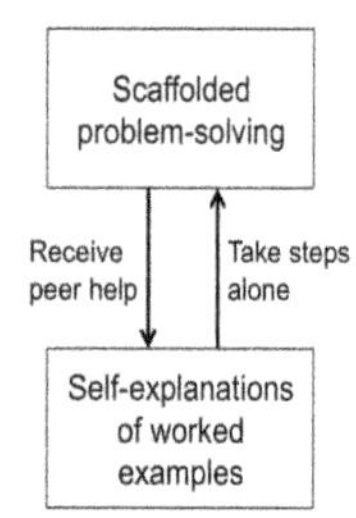

Table 2. Three redesign proposals for the Middle School Mathematics Cognitive tutors.

It is worth noting that in a different context, these assessments might be seen as identifying an undesirable behavior; in these classrooms, it is a step towards more accurate assessment for the predominant style of usage.

Help-Giving

As discussed above, existing models of help-usage in tutors assume that help comes from the tutor [1, 23]. However, in the settings described here, the source of help was most frequently another student in the class (I3, L1, L2). Students' collectivist behaviors reflect an opportunity to actively encourage students to seek and give help at *appropriate* times during their problem-solving, from *appropriate* people. There are asynchronous systems such as iHelp that match students based on their expertise and preferences [24], but these systems do not take into account real-time problem-solving progress.

Working in conjunction with a classroom-level knowledge-tracing algorithm, if a student is clearly struggling, the system could encourage them to seek help from someone who has already mastered the relevant skill. On the other hand, students who have mastered a skill quickly could be encouraged to help others who have not (sample rules for this approach can be found in B in Table 2). This would support more effective help, by taking advantage of students' natural inclinations to collaborate, but by pairing students who might maximally benefit from working with one another.

Adaptive Scaffolding

The benefits of collaboration, however, are not automatic [12]. Students often shared only the answer to a problem step *(C1)*, rather than giving an explanation that their partner could learn from. To ensure that students give constructive help, it may be useful to view the person receiving help as studying a worked example rather than taking a problem-solving step. Using techniques such as those described above, students can be inferred to be receiving help. One approach would then be to introduce scaffolding encouraging the peer learners to provide an elaborated explanation of the problem-solving step just entered. Many have demonstrated that alternation between self-explanation of worked examples and problem-solving is an effective learning technique (as in [2]). Hence, this design recommendation has the potential to benefit both the struggling partner and the partner with greater knowledge. C in Table 2 represents this concept; students transition between self-explanation and problem-solving based on whether they are judged to be receiving help, or working on their own.

DISCUSSION AND CONCLUSIONS

In this paper, we described a project where we deployed one unit of a mathematics cognitive tutor in three different Latin American school sites. The samples had varying socioeconomic contexts, typical methods of instruction, and experience with technology use. Thus, there was variation in the way the CT was integrated into classroom practice. Nevertheless, across all contexts, we found that students collaborated frequently while using the tutor; the pace of work was often interdependent, and work often occurred at classmates' computers in addition to their own. We propose guidelines for integrating the CT into similar classrooms and three augmentations to cognitive tutor design.

There is a great opportunity for educational technology to have a positive impact in developing contexts. Access to technology is increasing, and computers can now be found in schools in impoverished areas. Our findings suggest that students are enthusiastic about learning with technology. Given the structure of the school systems we observed and the potential lack of teaching resources, intelligent tutors provide an opportunity to support student learning when a regular teacher cannot be present in the classroom, or during periods where students would otherwise be working on paper-based assignments. In terms of content, cognitive tutors that focus on creating fluency with basic skills, rather than on advanced units, have the potential to teach or remediate critical deficiencies in students' understanding. A large barrier to using educational software in classrooms is the preparation teachers require to structure lessons around the software. Cognitive tutors help to mitigate this obstacle by providing self-contained lessons. In cases where teachers cannot be in class, cognitive tutors could assist substitutes or aides and supplement existing lessons.

CT use in these developing contexts was far more collaborative than the typical use of CT, and we have several hypotheses for why this may be so. In the classrooms we visited, students had never used cognitive tutors before, and in the Brazilian and Mexican sites, students had never used computers to learn before. Teachers described students as more engaged and motivated than normal, which could be attributed to a novelty effect. However, these external effects are not likely the dominant cause, since increased engagement has also been reported in classrooms that use technology in the U.S. [19]. In addition, students' variation in basic math skills and computer experience might mean that they required more help to use the CT than analogous students in the U.S., driving them to collaborate more. Following this line of thinking, the differences we observed between each Latin American context may have been related to factors such as prior knowledge and experience with computers. In the Brazilian site, where students we worked with had lower prior knowledge than those in the Costa Rican site, we saw more frequent answer-focused help. Finally, other researchers have theorized that the scarcity of technological resources in developing contexts force students to share resources, and thus collaborate more, which may have played a factor in the behaviors we observed [19].

It is also difficult to discount the possible influence of cultural factors on use of the CT in these settings. Brazil, Mexico, and Costa Rica are considered to be more collectivist cultures than the United States, in that they are "*...societies in which people from birth onwards are integrated into strong, cohesive in-groups, often extended families...which continue protecting them in exchange for unquestioning* *loyalty [10].*" In all three settings, collaborative work was a core part of classroom activities. Teachers valued student collaboration. Students valued helping their classmates and were comfortable asking classmates for help. Students were part of a culture that valued group membership and employed collaboration as an integral part of everyday activities. Therefore, the students collaborated extensively while using a technology primarily designed for individual use.

Regardless of the reasons for the differences observed, this work contributes insights into the opportunities for intelligent educational software in underserved regions, and into the ways different contexts might adapt to a proven technology platform. There may be benefits to deploying existing effective systems in developing contexts, and this direction of research should be pursued. However, a thorough understanding is necessary of how those contexts might incorporate technology into their current instructional practices, and which modifications to the basic assumptions of such systems might be necessary. This understanding might also provide insight for how cognitive tutors may and should be used in contexts similar to the sites we observed, in countries where intelligent tutoring systems have already been deployed. Rather than forcing others to conform to a single model of appropriate technology use, we must understand how the technology can be best integrated in vastly different contexts than those for which it was designed.

ACKNOWLEDGEMENTS

Thanks to all of the teachers and school administration who made this study possible. Sofía Pachaco, Xareni Alvarez, Etmon Vega, and Ruth Wylie also provided immeasurable support.

REFERENCES

1. Aleven, V., McLaren, B., Roll, I., & Koedinger, K.: Toward tutoring help seeking: Applying cognitive modeling to meta-cognitive skills. In J. C. Lester, R. M. Vicario, & F. Paraguaçu (Eds.), *Proc. ITS 04*, 227-239.
2. Atkinson, R. K., Renkl, A., & Merrill, M. M. Transitioning from studying examples to solving problems: Effects of self-explanation prompts and fading worked-out steps. *J. Ed. Psych, 95* 4 (2003), 774–783.
3. Baker, R.S.J.d., Corbett, A.T., & Aleven, V. More Accurate Student Modeling Through Contextual Estimation of Slip and Guess Probabilities in Bayesian Knowledge Tracing. In *Proc. ITS '08*, 406-415.
4. Baker, R. S., Corbett, A. T., Koedinger, K. R., & Wagner, A. Z: Off-task behavior in the Cognitive Tutor classroom: When students "game the system." In *Proc. CHI 2004,* ACM Press (2004). 383–390.
5. Beck, J. E., & Sison, J.: Using knowledge tracing in a noisy environment to measure student reading proficiencies. *IJAIED, 16* (2006). 129-143.
6. Blanchard, E. G., & Ogan: A. Infusing Cultural Awareness in Intelligent Tutoring Systems for a Globalized World. *Advances in Intelligent Tutoring Systems.* Springer (2010).
7. Corbett, A.T. & Anderson, J. R.: Knowledge Tracing: Modeling the Acquisition of Procedural Knowledge. *UMUAI, 4 (4),* 253-278 (1993).
8. Corbett, A.T. & Anderson, J.R. Locus of feedback control in computer-based tutoring: Impact on learning rate, achievement and attitudes. In *Proc. Chi'2001,* ACM Press (2001). 245-252.
9. Hoadley, C. Honwad, S., & Tamminga, K. Technology-supported cross cultural collaborative learning in the developing world. In *Proc. ICIC '10*, ACM Press, NY, USA (2010). 131-140.
10. Hofstede G. Culture's consequences: Comparing values, behaviors, institutions, and organizations across nations. Sage Publications Ltd. (2001).
11. Jain, M., Birnholtz, J., Cutrell, E. & Balakrishnan, R. Exploring display techniques for mobile collaborative learning in developing regions. In *MobileHCI 2011.* ACM Press.
12. Johnson, D. W. & Johnson, R. T. 1990. Cooperative learning and achievement. In S. Sharan (Ed.), *Cooperative learning: Theory and research* (pp. 23-37). NY: Praeger.
13. Koedinger, K. R. & Corbett, A. T. Cognitive tutors: Technology bringing learning science to the classroom. *The Cambridge Handbook of the Learning Sciences*. Cambridge University Press (2006). 61-78.
14. Kumar, A., Tewari, A., Shroff, G., Chittamuru, D., Kam, M., & Canny, J. An Exploratory Study of Unsupervised Mobile Learning in Rural India. In *Proc. CHI'10*, ACM Press.
15. Lomas, D., Ching, D., Hoadley, C., Patel, K., & Kam, M. When a Console Game Becomes CSCL: Play, Participatory Learning and 8-Bit Home Computing in India. In *Proc. ICLS'11.*
16. Moraveji, N., Kim, T., Ge, J., Pawar, U. S., Mulcahy, K., & Inkpen, K. 2008. Mischief: supporting remote teaching in developing regions. In *Proc. CHI'08.* ACM Press, 353-362.
17. Nicaud J.F., Bittar M., Chaachoua H., Inamdar P., & Maffei L.: Experiments With Aplusix In Four Countries. *I. J. Tech. in Math Ed., 13,* 1 (2006).
18. Ogan, A., Aleven, V., & Jones, C: Advancing development of intercultural competence through supporting predictions in narrative video. *IJAIED, 19*(3), 67-288 (2010).
19. Pal, J., Pawar U., Brewer, E. & Toyama,K: The case for multi-user design for computer aided learning in developing regions. *WWW2006*, Edinburgh Scotland, May 2006.
20. Patton, M.Q. Qualitative Research and Evaluation, 3rd ed., Sage, Thousand Oaks, CA (2002).
21. Schofield, J. W. Computers and classroom culture. New York: Cambridge University Press (1995).
22. Sipitakiat, A., Blikstein, P. & Cavallo, D. GoGo Board: Augmenting Programmable Bricks for Economically Challenged Audiences, In *Proc. ICLS'04.*
23. VanLehn, K. The behavior of tutoring systems. *IJAIED, 16*, 3 (2006), 227-265.
24. Vassileva, J., McCalla, G., & Greer, J. Multi-Agent Multi-User Modeling in I-Help. *UMUAI, 13*, 179-210, (2003).
25. Warschauer, M. Technology and social inclusion: Rethinking the digital divide. Cambridge, MA: MIT Press (2003).

Evaluating the Implicit Acquisition of Second Language Vocabulary Using a Live Wallpaper

David Dearman[1,2], Khai N. Truong[1]

[1]Department of Computer Science
University of Toronto
Toronto, ON M5S 3G4 Canada
khai@cs.toronto.edu

[2]Nokia Research Center
955 Page Mill Rd.
Palo Alto, CA 94304 USA
dave.dearman@nokia.com

ABSTRACT
An essential aspect of learning a second language is the acquisition of vocabulary. However, acquiring vocabulary is often a protracted process that requires repeated and spaced exposure; which can be difficult to accommodate given the busyness of daily living. In this paper, we explore if a learner can implicitly acquire second language vocabulary through her explicit interactions with her mobile phone (*e.g.*, navigating multiple home screens) using an interface we developed called Vocabulary Wallpaper. In addition, we examine if the type of vocabulary this technique exposes to the learner, whether it is contextually relevant or contextually-independent will influence the learner's rate of vocabulary acquisition. The results of our study show participants were able to use Vocabulary Wallpaper to increase the number of second language vocabulary that they can recognize and recall and their rate of vocabulary acquisition was significantly greater when presented with a contextually relevant vocabulary than a contextually-independent vocabulary.

Author Keywords
Computer assisted language learning; vocabulary acquisition; mobile; microlearning; contextualized vocabulary

ACM Classification Keywords
H.5.m. [Information interfaces and presentation]: User Interfaces – Miscellaneous

General Terms
Design; Experimentation; Human Factors

INTRODUCTION
Learning a second language is a difficult task that can involve significant effort. To effectively understand and articulate in a second language, a learner needs to build a strong understanding of the language's vocabulary; a process that requires a great deal of repeated and spaced [9, 29] exposure to the vocabularies words. However, the demands of one's personal, social and professional life can leave little time for a learner to partake in multiple protracted sessions of learning which can provide the repeated and spaced exposure necessary to acquire and retain the language's vocabulary.

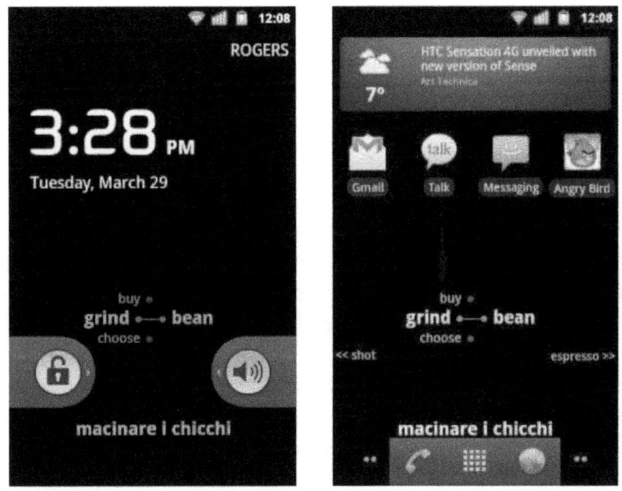

Figure 1. Vocabulary Wallpaper implemented as a Live Wallpaper for the Android OS. The vocabulary content is dynamic and interactive, and it is always visible unless occluded by a running application.

Despite the limited amount of time that is available on a daily basis for protracted sessions of learning, there are brief opportunities spaced throughout the day (*e.g.*, waiting for the elevator) that can be used for short sessions of *microlearning* [11]. Rather than a single instance of reading or reviewing vocabulary for a prolonged period of time, the learning task can be partitioned into sessions that fit within these opportunities for microlearning. The challenge to utilizing these microlearning opportunities is creating a learning experience that provides quick access to vocabulary that a learner will find engaging.

The mobile phone—a device that typically accompanies its owner wherever she may go—is a platform that has been used to realize anywhere, anytime microlearning opportunities [1, 2, 6, 10, 15, 23, 24]. In most cases, these microlearning tools actively engage the learner by requiring her to explicitly interact with the learning material (*e.g.*, load

Permission to make digital or hard copies of all or part of this work for personal or classroom use is granted without fee provided that copies are not made or distributed for profit or commercial advantage and that copies bear this notice and the full citation on the first page. To copy otherwise, or republish, to post on servers or to redistribute to lists, requires prior specific permission and/or a fee.
CHI'12, May 5–10, 2012, Austin, Texas, USA.
Copyright 2012 ACM 978-1-4503-1015-4/12/05...$10.00.

an application) and they utilize the device's mobility to provide learning material that can be relevant to the user's current context. A learning experience that includes vocabulary that is relevant to the learner's current context (*i.e.*, providing the learner with vocabulary that is generally relevant to all cafés when the learner is located in a cafe) can enhance the learning experience and be immediately applicable [10].

To broaden a second language learner's opportunities for microlearning, we explore in this paper if a learner can implicitly acquire second language vocabulary through her explicit interactions with her mobile phone (*e.g.*, navigating multiple home screens). In addition, we examine if the type of vocabulary this technique exposes to the learner, whether it is contextually relevant (that is *place-specific* or based on the *venue-type*) or contextually-independent (that is based on commonly used *high-frequency* words), will influence the learners rate of vocabulary acquisition. To explore these issues we developed a light-weight learning interface for Android mobile phones called Vocabulary Wallpaper (Figure 1). Vocabulary Wallpaper is *live wallpaper*[1] that presents to its user (via the home screen's wallpaper) a vocabulary of verb-noun pairs and their second language translation. We conducted a field study where participants were provided with microlearning opportunities through their interactions with a mobile phone that was running Vocabulary Wallpaper The field studies results of the show that:

- In four short sessions (totaling ~4 hours of exposure), participants were able to increase the number of second language vocabulary that they can recognize and recall when using the Vocabulary Wallpaper.
- The participants' rate of vocabulary acquisition was significantly greater when presented the contextually relevant *venue-type* vocabulary than the contextually-independent *high-frequency* vocabulary. The rate of vocabulary acquisition did not differ otherwise.
- Many of the participants found that a small number of out-of-domain words stood out and were particularly memorable when interspaced within a larger vocabulary of contextually-relevant words.

These findings show that we can complement traditional mobile learning tools with interfaces that support implicit learning during anywhere, anytime sessions of microlearning.

BACKGROUND & RELATED WORK

An important part of learning a second language is gaining the core and functional vocabulary that is necessary for literacy. Learning vocabulary consists of being able to recognize, recall, and know the meaning of words. However, the process of building a core and functional vocabulary can be a difficult and protracted. To assist in the learning process, people often use a variety of language learning methods and tools [12] with varying levels of success [13]. However, it is generally accepted that spaced [9] and continued exposure [29] to the second language vocabulary will result in the greatest gains and lasting memory retention [19]. Reading is considered a valuable method of providing spaced and continued exposure [14, 16] because the content can provide repeated exposure to the vocabularies high-frequency words [21, 22] and the content can be chosen to be personally interesting. Furthermore, learning can be more easily accomplished in context, when words are associated with real objects or imagery [18].

Given the pervasiveness of computing technology today, computer assisted language learning (CALL) can augment and promote the vocabulary learning experience by using multimedia annotations [5], recommending articles based on ability [4], replacing of selected words within the Web browser [27] and the use of mobile computing [3, 6, 20, 23, 25, 26]. Using a mobile device, CALL tools can support breaking the learning experience into smaller units of *microlearning* [11, 17]; ensuring that the learning experience is available during small opportunistic times (*e.g.*, waiting for the elevator or waiting for the barista to prepare a latte) when a learner is receptive to learning vocabulary but does not have a great deal of time to actively engage in a protracted session of learning.

Many interactive mobile learning environments have been developed to allow teachers to control (at a distance) the content and curriculum that is available to their students on their mobile devices [6, 20, 25]. A mobile learning environment can provide short learning sessions that adapt to the user's current knowledge, location, interruptability, level of concentration and available time [6]. Depending on the context defined by the user, the type and durations of an exercise would vary. For example, in a restaurant where interruptions can be high, the user may be asked to perform exercises where they revisit a previously presented concept, rather than leaning new material. In contrast, Ogata & Hui's [23] *language-learning outside the classroom with handhelds* allows the teacher to actively monitor a student's location and intervene (through instant messaging) to guide the student through their task. The benefit of these systems is that they allowed the teacher to control a student's learning experience away from the classroom. However, these systems require a great deal of manual intervention by the teacher.

Several automated systems have been developed to explore the use of e-mail [26] and SMS [3] to prompt students with random vocabulary words throughout the day. A number of contextualized language learning tools and services have been developed to provide the learner with prompts and content that is relevant to the objects they are interacting with [2, 24], situation [1] and location [10, 15],. For example, Beaudin *et al.* [2] developed a sensor-triggered mobile device using built-in and stick-on sensors to sense user's interactions within her house and prompt her with translations describing the objects which she might be

[1] http://developer.android.com/resources/articles/live-wallpapers.html

using. The Tag Added learning Object system detects RFID tags on objects and provides relevant educational information. [24]. CAMCLL (context-aware location-independent learning) teaches Chinese to students who do not have the proficiency to engage in conversation by supporting appropriate sentences based on the user's context (time, location, activity, learning level) [1].

MicroMandarin [10] is mobile flashcard application that presents to the learner a vocabulary that is contextually relevant to relevant to her current location's venue type (*i.e.*, when the user is located in any café, she can browse through vocabulary that is generally relevant to all cafés).. Participants used MircoMandarin for 4-weeks, during which they viewed more and therefore acquired more of the context-independent vocabulary consisting of high-frequency words (M_{viewed}=176.0 total, $M_{learned}$=41.3) than the contextually relevant vocabulary (M_{viewed}=119.0 total, $M_{learned}$=19.1). The authors discuss that participants' ability to learn a flashcard (*i.e.*, word) in a single instance may have influenced their rate of vocabulary acquisition because more contextually-independent flashcards were viewed. Despite the modest amount of usage on a daily basis over this period, participants found the contextually relevant vocabulary to be compelling and often immediately applicable to their location. Thus, we are inspired to explore the following research questions:

- *How can a microlearning system be designed to provide greater exposure to more vocabulary on a daily basis?*
- *Would viewing more contextually-relevant vocabulary effect the learner's vocabulary acquisition in comparison to high-frequency words?*
- *How can a contextually relevant vocabulary be automatically generated for all public and commercial locations that the user visits, and would she acquire those words at a rate that is comparable to contextually-relevant vocabulary that is manually generated or high-frequency words?*

VOCABULARY WALLPAPER

We designed Vocabulary Wallpaper as a mobile interface to enabled microlearning opportunities for second language vocabulary acquisition through the user's implicit interactions with her mobile phone. Vocabulary Wallpaper is not designed to replace traditional language learning tools, but rather it complements these tools by providing another avenue for learning.

High-Level Design and Implementation

We developed Vocabulary Wallpaper as a *live wallpaper*[1] for the Android OS. A live wallpaper is not a traditional—static—wallpaper, it is an interactive Java application. For example, most Android devices come with a live wallpaper called Maps. The Maps wallpaper presents to the user a Google Map of her nearby vicinity which is overlaid with her current location and the conditions of nearby traffic. As the user moves about her day, Maps updates automatically, to ensure that the live content is relevant to the user's current location. A live wallpaper's content is always visible unless the display is off or an application is running in the foreground. However, visible content can become occluded by home screen widgets and icons.

We chose to implement Vocabulary Wallpaper as a live wallpaper because it allowed us to systematically control the vocabulary content based on the user's current location, but more importantly, this interface ensured that the vocabulary (and associated translations) would always be visible to the user when the display is active (Figure 1) and an application is not running in the foreground. This interface ensures that users are exposed to the displayed vocabulary without them having to explicitly load an application, thereby providing opportunities for microlearning while performing other operations with the device. For this research, we controlled the placement of the vocabulary, home screen widgets and icons to ensure consistency across participants. A deployable version of the interface should allow the user to specify the placement of the content to ensure it is not occluded.

Vocabulary Wallpaper can display the vocabulary content as a single noun (Figure 2: left) or as a single noun with a collection of associated verbs (Figure 2: middle and right); at most 5 verbs are shown for a noun. The translation of the highlighted noun or verb-noun pair is displayed at the bottom of the display above Android's quick launch bar.

Figure 2. Screen shots of the Vocabulary Wallpaper interface when used in a coffee shop called Manic Coffee. The three presentations show the interface for vocabularies that consist of contextually relevant nouns (left), contextually relevant verb-noun pairs (center) and contextually independent verb-noun pairs (right). The user can press the pervious and next words (shown in light grey on the left and right side of the interface) to return the previous word, or advance to the next word.

When a list of verbs is associated with a noun, each verb is translated at a time, cycling from the top of the list to the bottom. The interface displays the verbs in white and nouns in yellow; the same color scheme is used for the translations. Each noun and translation is displayed for 15 seconds, after which the interface cycles onto the next noun. Each verb (when shown) is given an equal fraction of the 15 seconds, before the interface cycles onto the next verb. For example, if a noun lists 5 associated verbs, then each verb and translation is shown for 3 seconds. The user can touch the previous noun (left side) and the upcoming noun (right side) to return or advance the vocabulary respectively. This design (*i.e.*, placement, number of words to show and timing) was the result of iterative prototyping.

Every 30 seconds, Vocabulary Wallpaper requests the device's location (latitude/longitude) from the Android OS using the integrated GPS or network positioning, whichever is available and more accurate. The latitude and longitude of the phone is used to reverse-geocode the place (*e.g.*, Bisogno Espresso Bar) where the user is currently located. This place information is then used to determine the contextually-relevant vocabulary that will be displayed to the user. We will discuss how this relates to the various vocabularies we support in the following section.

Vocabulary

Mobile language learning tools can support various types of vocabulary, including vocabularies that are contextually-relevant to the learner's current situation and those that are contextually-independent. In this work, we envisioned and implemented three different vocabulary types. The *places-specific* and *venue-type* vocabularies consist of contextually-relevant words that are derived using the specific place (*e.g.*, Bisogno Espresso Bar) where the user is located or the type of venue (*e.g.*, café) that characterizes this place, respectively. The *high-frequency* vocabulary consists of words that are contextually-independent and occur frequently in the English language. We did not pick and choose the words for each vocabulary condition. The words were generated using the vocabulary condition's unique method.

We generated the *high-frequency* vocabulary by first identifying the most common nouns used in the Corpus of Contemporary American English (COCA) [7]. We based the frequency on an English corpus, not Italian, our second language corpus. The intent was to help ground the learning experience in the language and vocabulary that was already known by the participants. For each noun, we again used COCA to identify three commonly used verbs that occur before the noun, with at most 3 words of separation.

We generated the *venue-type* vocabulary using Amazon's Mechanical Turk (http://www.mturk.com). We asked workers to provide at most 5 nouns that they commonly associate with the venues chosen for the study. Using Mechanical Turk to generate this vocabulary is analogous to Edge et al. [10] using their research team to generate a contextual vocabulary, but our method allowed for us to sample a more diverse population. We validate the vocabulary provided by the workers, but did not modify it.

We generated the *place-specific* vocabulary using Dearman and Truong's Activity-Service [8] which uses community authored content to characterize the potential activities a person can perform at a place. We extended their method to include other communities (*e.g.*, Google Places, CitySearch) in addition to Yelp. It is important to recognize that using this method we are able to systematically produce a contextually-relevant vocabulary that is unique to a place (*i.e.*, it is *place-specific*), whereas the contextually-relevant *venue-type* vocabulary is specific to a type of place.

LANGUAGE ACQUISITION STUDY

We conducted a structured field study to evaluate the benefit of using a contextualized vocabulary to assist in second language vocabulary acquisition by enabling microlearning opportunities. In this study, we required participants to visit six local businesses, representing three different business types, and exposed participants to three different vocabulary conditions: *high-frequency verb-noun pairs*, *venue-type nouns* and *place-specific verb-noun pairs*. We translated the English vocabulary words into Italian[2], a romance language. Although we use English as the base language and Italian as the second language, it is important to note that Vocabulary Wallpaper can support other language using automated systems such as Google Translate. To control for the complexity and potential difficulty in learning the various grammatical elements of a language, we chose to focus our testing and analysis on the acquisition of nouns.

Participants

We recruited 15 participants (8 female and 7 male) between the ages of 18 and 35 from our University and the surrounding community. Thirteen of the participants visited the study neighbourhood at least once in the last year and two had never visited the study neighbourhood. In the concluding interview, participant P1 indicated that she had prior exposure to the Italian language during one year of high school (13 years prior), but she had not actively continued to pursue Italian language learning since. All fifteen participants expressed a strong proficiency in English (self-reported as 4 or 5 on a 5-point proficiency scale), with nine expressing a strong proficiency in a second language, including: Serbo-Croatian, Cantonese, Vietnamese, Hindi, Urdu, and Mandarin. We compensated participants $100 for their time at the end of the study.

Study Neighbourhood

We modified Vocabulary Wallpaper to work in only six pre-defined businesses within the study neighbourhood; the placement of the businesses can be seen in Figure 3. We chose this neighbourhood because it is proximally close to

[2] Italian is a Category I foreign language [28] that closely cognates with English. It is one of the easier languages for an English speaker to acquire.

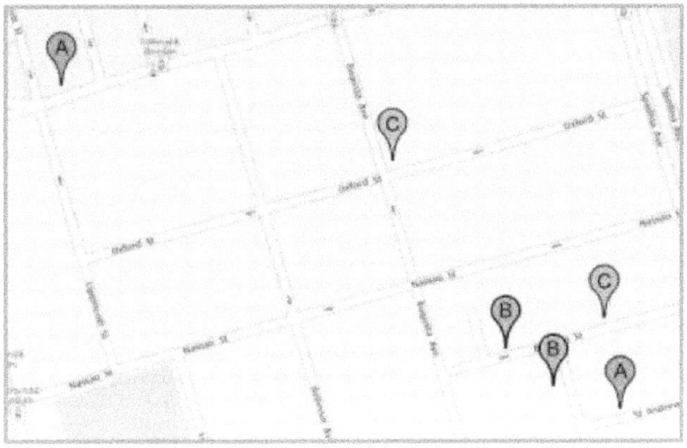

Figure 3. A map of the study neighbourhood annotated with the business locations. Shown are the locations for the two coffee shops (A), cheese shops (B) and bakeries (C).

the University and a very popular shopping area for small, independently owned businesses. The six businesses represent three different *business types*, including *coffee shops* (A and B), *cheese shops* (C and D) and *bakeries* (E and F). We chose these businesses types because they typify the places people come to visit in this neighbourhood.

Vocabulary Conditions

We exposed each participant to the three different vocabulary conditions: *high-frequency* verb-noun pairs, *venue-type* nouns and *place-specific* verb-noun pairs. The *venue-type* and *place-specific* conditions represent contextualized vocabularies. We counterbalanced the *venue-type* and *place-specific* vocabularies across the *coffee* and *cheese shops*, but always used the *high-frequency* vocabulary for the *bakeries*. For each business we produced a vocabulary of 15 nouns (with accompanying verbs, depending on the condition) and we ensured that no nouns were repeated across the three vocabulary conditions; each vocabulary was unique for each condition.

The *high-frequency* vocabulary consisted of 25 nouns, of which we chose 10 nouns (with accompanying verbs) that would be unique to each bakery, as well as 5 nouns (with accompanying verbs) that would be shown at both. The *venue-type* vocabulary for the *coffee shops* and *cheese shops* was generated using Amazon's Mechanical Turk. The *coffee shop* vocabulary consisted of the 24 most commonly mentioned nouns that Turkers associated with coffee shops. We used the six most frequently mentioned nouns to be shown at both *coffee shops* and split the remaining 18 nouns across the two places. The *cheese shop* vocabulary consisted of the 26 most commonly mentioned nouns that Turkers associated with cheese shops. We used the four most frequently mentioned nouns to be shown at both *cheese shops* and split the remaining 22 nouns across the two places. We chose different vocabulary sizes for the *coffee* and *cheese shops* to maintain equal proportions with the *place-specific* condition's vocabulary which is systematically generated when counterbalancing these conditions. When we generated the *place-specific*

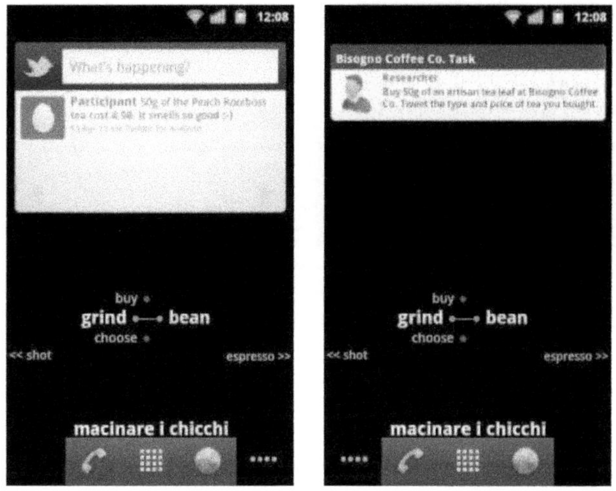

Figure 4. At each business, participants were required to perform a task and tweet their response. We configured the Nexus One such that the Twitter and Task widgets were placed on the left (left) and right (right) most home screens, respectively. Three home screens extensions separated the two.

vocabulary using Dearman and Truong Activity-Service [8], we did not impose any control over the verb and noun pairings that this method generated; we wanted this vocabulary to be as natural to the method as possible. For each of the coffee and cheese shops we systematically generated 15 nouns with associated verbs. The method generated six nouns that were repeated across the two coffee shops and four nouns that were repeated across the two cheese shops; the remaining nouns were unique to each business. On average, the method produced three verbs that we could associate with each noun (Min=1, Max=5).

Apparatus

We provided participants with an HTC Nexus One device to use each session that was instrumented with:

- Vocabulary Wallpaper to present the participants with the vocabulary and associated translations (Figure 4).
- A custom, Google Voice-like task widget that we developed to instruct participants where to go and what to do there (Figure 4: right).
- A Twitter widget and account so the participants could post status update messages, responding to the task we requested they perform (Figure 4: left).

The custom task widget monitors the participant's location and automatically provides the participant with instructions for where to go next and what to do there. We intentionally installed the task widget on the far left and the Twitter widget on the far right of the home screen to force users to interact with the device.

In order to support the three vocabulary conditions described above, we modified Vocabulary Wallpaper to include a second vocabulary presentation format: noun only. In the noun-only presentation format, the interface simply shows each noun and its translation for 15 seconds before advancing to the next.

Method

We conducted a within-subject study consisting of five separate sessions. In session one to four, we asked the participants to visit the six businesses and to perform a task at each location. Examples of the tasks we asked participants to perform at each business type include:

- *Coffee shop*: Buy 50g of an artisan tea leaf at Jobs Coffee Co. Tweet the type of tea you bought and the price.
- *Cheese shop*: Buy 100g of Danish Blue Cheese at Cheese Boutique. Tweet the price of the Danish Blue.
- *Bakery*: Buy a French baguette at B-Bakery. Tweet the price of the French baguette.

Although tasks were repeated across participants for consistency, no task was repeated by a participant between sessions. We did not ahead of time inform participants of the tasks they were to perform. Instead, instructions were delivered to the participants through the Nexus One phone that we provided to them each session.

At the start of session one, we conducted a pre-test of recall (translating the English vocabulary to Italian) to establish a baseline. At the end of session one, we conducted a post-test of recall and the first test of recognition (translating the Italian vocabulary to English). In the fifth session, we conducted a post-test of recall, followed by the second test of recognition. We did not conduct a test of recall and recognition after each session because we did not want the tests themselves to be a factor that would influence the participants' acquisition. Each test of recall and recognition included all 75 words that we generated for each vocabulary condition and 25 random words that were not presented to the participant; each test was a total of 100 words. We included the 25 random words as distractors. We instructed participants not to guess during the tests and to leave their response empty if they were unsure of the translation. For each translation that they did provide, we asked participants to provide their confidence in the translation on a 4-point Likert scale. We graded each test manually to accommodate for simple spelling mistakes, improper use of gender and improper use of singular and plural modifiers when providing the Italian translation.

RESULTS

We determined the participants' gain in vocabulary by calculating the difference in their pre-test and post-tests results for recall. We determined the rate and duration of exposure to a word by examining the log produced by the Vocabulary Wallpaper, which recorded the time (in milliseconds) when a word was visible and when the screen was turned on and off by the user. For each vocabulary condition, as discussed in the previous section, a small number of words occurred more than once within a vocabulary condition; these words were repeated across the businesses we associated the vocabulary. In our analysis, we differentiate *word occurrences* as either *unique* or *repeated*. It is important to note that the rate and duration of exposure to a word was dictated entirely by the participants themselves. We did not require participants to view a word a minimum number of times, nor did we require them to view a word for a minimum amount of time. The values we report for rate and duration of exposure represent the greatest potential exposure, not what the participant actually observed because we cannot identify when the participant was actively viewing the device or when the home screen was not shown.

	Potential exposure rate	Potential exposure duration
	Mean (SD)	Mean (SD)
high-frequency	4.1 (1.9)	40.3 (14.0)
venue-type	5.7 (2.9)	52.9 (25.7)
place-specific	5.2 (2.4)	54.6 (22.2)

Table 1. The average rate (left) and duration (right) of potential exposures to each word for each *vocabulary-type*. The values measure when a word was displayed on the participant's device and therefore potentially visible, not the actual rate and duration of exposure to each word.

	Potential exposure rate	Potential exposure duration
	Mean (SD)	Mean (SD)
coffee shops	5.3 (2.9)	51.0 (24.8)
cheese shops	5.6 (2.3)	56.5 (22.8)
bakeries	4.1 (1.9)	40.3 (14.0)

Table 2. The average rate (left) and duration (right) of potential exposures to each word for each *business-type*. The values measure when a word was displayed on the participant's device and therefore potentially visible, not the actual rate and duration of exposure to each word.

We conducted the analysis of exposure and gain using a repeated measures analysis of variance (ANOVA), applying the Greenhouse-Geisser correction when sphericity was violated. When comparing the participants' preference data, we used the nonparametric Friedman test and conducted post-hoc pairwise comparisons using the Wilcoxon Signed-Rank test. We used the Bonferroni correction in all post-hoc tests where we performed multiple comparisons. In this section, we report the corrected p-value when appropriate.

We did test if the between-subject factors of sex and language knowledge had an effect on gain and preference, but we did not observe any significant differences.

Vocabulary Exposure

On average, a participant was potentially exposed to each word 5.0 times (SD=2.7) for a duration of 49.2 seconds (SD=24.9). For many of the participants, Vocabulary Wallpaper was a light-weight tool that afforded quick and easy access to the vocabulary translations:

Words	Pre-Test (session 1) Mean (SD)	Post-Test (session 5) Mean (SD)
Unique	4.33 (6.13)	21.60 (15.26)
Repeated	1.53 (1.60)	7.60 (4.44)

Table 3. The average gains in vocabulary recall (*i.e.*, translating English to Italian) across all participants for *word occurrence*.

P5 – *"When I had some time while waiting in line I would pull out the phone."*

P6 – *"One day, I think it was a Saturday, [the business] was really busy and this was the perfect thing to do while I was idle [waiting in line]."*

As shown in Table 1 and Table 2, the participants rate and duration of exposure varied significantly for the three vocabulary conditions, $F(2, 28)=10.62$, $p<0.002$ and $F(2, 28)=7.43$, $p=0.003$ respectively. The participants' rate and duration of potential exposure to the *venue-type* (rate: $p=0.002$; duration: $p=0.054$) and *place-specific* (rate: $p=0.009$; duration: $p=0.001$) vocabulary is significantly greater than the *high-frequency* vocabulary.

Vocabulary Gain (Overall)

Despite the participants' varied and limited exposure to each translation when using the Vocabulary Wallpaper, all of the participants (Figure 5) improved from their pre-test level of recall; gaining an average of 23.3 words (SD=17.1) over the four sessions. The participants' vocabulary recall in the post-test after session one ($M=16.3$, $SD=14.4$; $t(14)=-3.73$, $p=0.002$) and the post-test during session five ($M=29.2$, $SD=20.4$; $t(14)=-5.12$, $p<0.001$) are significantly greater than the pre-test (our baseline) before session one ($M=5.87$, $SD=7.27$). When we examined at the influences of word occurrence (Table 3) we see a significant improvement in both unique and repeated words, $t(14)=-4.94$, $p<0.001$ and $t(14)=-5.42$, $p<0.001$ respectively. In addition, we observed a significant improvement in recognition between the first recognition test ($M=29.29$, $SD=17.41$) and the second test of recognition ($M=39.50$, $SD=19.28$); $t(14)=-4.40$, $p=0.001$.

The participants' improvements in both recall and recognition are important because they are applied in different ways. Recall is essential for speaking and writing, while recognition is essential for reading.

As seen in Figure 5 and Figure 6, the gain in vocabulary varied greatly between participants. Participant 8, who had the smallest gain in vocabulary indicated that he was focused on completing the tasks we asked him to perform, not the vocabulary presented to him:

P8 – *"I just used it [the phone] to know what I had to do. I would perform my task and then put the phone back into my pocket."*

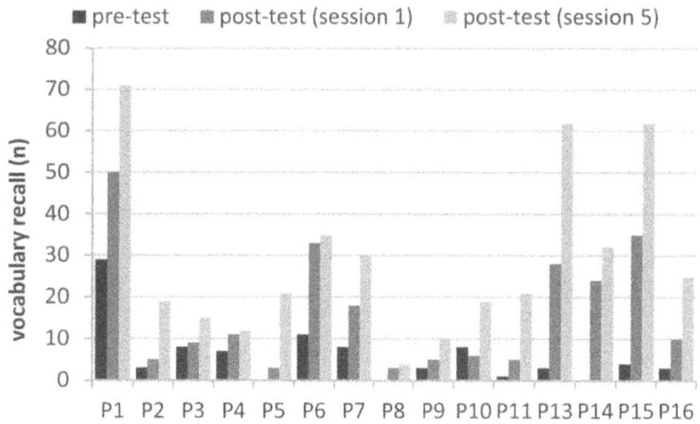

Figure 5. Participants' individual level of vocabulary recall (*i.e.*, translating English to Italian) for the pre-test administered before session one, and the post-tests administered after session one and session five. The greatest number of words to be recalled is 75.

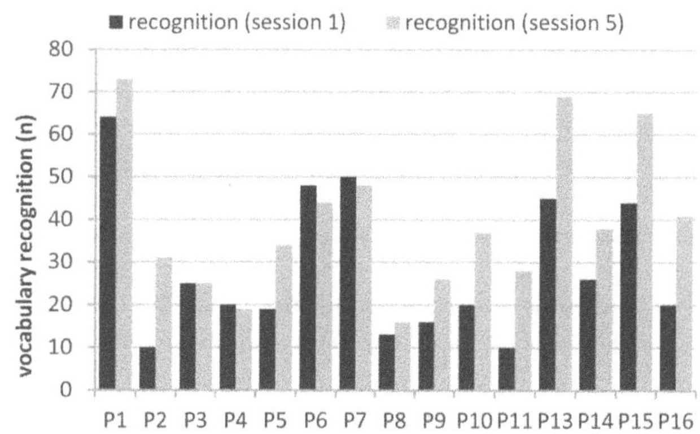

Figure 6. Participants' individual level of vocabulary recognition (*i.e.*, translating Italian to English) for the pre-test administered before session one and the post-test administered after session five. The greatest number of words to be recognized is 75.

Even though P8 did not view the translations as actively as the other participants, he still gained 4 new words. Participant 1 is another unique instance. In the post-test of recall that we conducted during session five, P1 was able to correctly recall 71 of the 75 vocabulary words (94.7%). In the introductory interview and background questionnaire she did not disclose any proficiency in Italian. However, in the post-study interview she indicated that in grade school she had taken one year of Italian in high school (13 years ago) but had not used it since, nor is she actively learning Italian. She indicated many of the words were new to her, but many were also very familiar:

P1 – *"Many of them were new words that I hadn't known. Like the really specific ones, like slicer and beans. But there was also some [words] where it really helped me remember what was in my brain from before [the study]. School, for some reason it was really hard to remember because it was only a little bit different from French and Spanish. I don't think I ever got that one right."*

Words	high-freq. Mean	(SD)	venue-type Mean	(SD)	place-specific Mean	(SD)
Unique	4.93	(4.50)	7.13	(5.28)	5.20	(4.49)
Repeated	1.80	(1.87)	2.13	(1.81)	2.13	(1.96)

Table 4. The average gains in vocabulary recall (*i.e.*, translating English to Italian) across all participants for *word occurrence* and *vocabulary condition*.

For P1, Vocabulary Wallpaper was a great reminder of some of the more common words she had learned years ago, but had forgotten. Participant P6 expressed a similar desire based on this knowledge of German:

P6 – *"I have some level of mastery of German grammar, but the vocab [I know] has dropped over the year since I [last] used it. I would love an app like this to keep prompting me ... keeping me on top of it [grammar]."*

Vocabulary Gain (Contextually Relevant Vocabulary)

We observed a significant effect of vocabulary condition on the participants' vocabulary gain (Figure 7), $F(2, 28)=5.28$, $p=0.011$. In this section, we will only report the vocabulary gain between the pre-tests and those conducted during session number five (not session one) because these values better represent the participant's vocabulary acquisition. The participants gain in vocabulary was greatest for the *venue-type* vocabulary (M=9.27, SD=6.44), followed by the *place-specific* (M=7.33, SD=5.86) and *high-frequency* vocabularies (M=6.73, SD=6.17). When we looked at the influences of *word occurrence* (Table 4) we observed a significant main effect of vocabulary condition on unique words, $F(2, 28)=6.09$, $p=0006$, but not repeated words, $F(2, 28)=0.277$, $p=0.760$. The participants' vocabulary gain for unique words was significantly greater for the *venue-type* vocabulary than the *high-frequency* and *place-specific* vocabularies, $p=0.022$ and $p=0.012$ respectively.

Overall, we observed the participants acquisition of the *venue-type* vocabulary to be significantly greater than the *high-frequency* vocabulary. This result confirms that a contextualized vocabulary can result in greater vocabulary gain than a contextually-independent (*i.e., frequency-based*) vocabulary. In the concluding semi-structured interview, many of the participants recognized that the vocabularies presented for some of the business, reflected the business itself:

P3 – *"The coffee shops had coffee words. The cheese shops had cheese words. The one [place that] was way off was Wanda's [the second bakery]."*

P6 – *"I did notice that [the words] were related at least at both the coffee shops, and the cheese shops. I'm not sure if it was the same vocab set for each coffee and cheese shop, but I do remember that they were related. I don't remember words being related to [the bakeries]."*

Even though we did not disclose at any point in the study that the vocabularies would differ in terms of relevance to

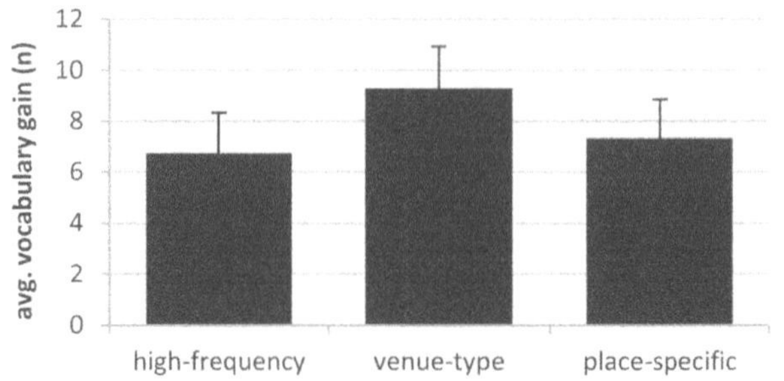

Figure 7. The average gains in vocabulary recall (*i.e.*, translating English to Italian) across all participants for *vocabulary-type*. The error bars represent standard error.

Figure 8. The average gains in vocabulary recall (*i.e.*, translating English to Italian) across all participants for *business-type*. The error bars represent standard error.

the respective business, the difference was evident. For most participants, having the contextualized vocabularies was *"fascinating"* and more engaging:

P7 – *"I preferred words [that] were about that place, because then it is more fun. I felt, oh 'cup'!, I've seen a cup. It is easier to see it as a game when the things are happening around you. I had that feeling. For example, when I'm in a cheese place and the word tire comes up it is just weird."*

The participants' affinity for the contextually-relevant vocabularies is further confirmed by the higher potential rate and duration of exposure (Table 1) for the *venue-type* and *place-specific* vocabularies, in contrast to the *high-frequency* vocabulary. Participant comments revealed that these vocabularies were more engaging, therefore they potentially spent more time viewing them:

P1 – *"Random words like country were not that interesting to me. In the end I probably didn't learn them as well ... I didn't pay attention to them as much."*

To confirm that the results were not influenced by the participants' preference toward a particular business type, we analyzed the participants' vocabulary gain according to the *business type* (Figure 8). The participants' gain in vocabulary was greatest for the coffee shops (M=8.73, SD=6.18), followed by the cheese shops (M=7.83, SD=6.27) and the bakeries (M=6.73, SD=6.17). However, we did not observed a significant main effect of business type on vocabulary gain, $F(1.35, 18.89)=2.61$, $p=0.115$. In addition, we also asked participants in the session five concluding interview to rate the business types in order of preference. Overall, participants preferred the coffee shops (M=1.57, SD=0.65), followed by the bakeries (M=2.07, SD=0.92) and cheese shops (M=2.36, SD=0.75). We did not observe a significant main effect of business type on preference, $X^2(2)=4.43$, $p=0.109$. Overall, the participants' preferences did not appear to influence their vocabulary gain; further strengthening our claim and finding that a contextualized vocabulary can results in greater vocabulary gain.

DISCUSSION

Mobile language learning tools typically support an active learning experience which requires the learner to explicitly load and interact with the application [1, 2, 6, 10, 15, 23, 24]. We developed Vocabulary Wallpaper as a learning interface that does not require explicit interaction, but enables opportunities for implicit exposure and learning while the user interacts with her device.

Interfaces can Support Implicit Language Learning

On average, participants were able to gain 23.3 new Italian words over the course of the studies 4 sessions; despite the participants limited exposure (mean number of exposures = 5, for a total duration of 49.2s) to each word. We believe that an implicit learning interface such as Vocabulary Wallpaper can be a significant benefit to second language learners by providing brief exposure to the vocabulary they are attempting to learning at instances when they may be receptive to a microlearning experience.

The study we conducted exposed participants to a limited vocabulary for a small number of places; participants were exposed to the vocabulary for approximately four hours in total across the four sessions. In authentic long term use, the interface will need to change and update the available vocabulary to ensure that new words become available as words are learned. Rather than using an explicit method that tests the learner, the learner's explicit interactions with the interface (*e.g.*, number of times she touches the previous or upcoming words to skip or review a word) can be used to determine how frequently a word should be shown. In addition, the current contextually-relevant vocabulary (which is derived using activities) is finite. We believe that other contextual features can and should be explored to expand and broaden the vocabulary available to a learner. In the case that a learner does exhaust the contextually-relevant vocabulary that is available (maybe because they frequent a place often) the learning tool could fallback to displaying high-frequency words which do still provide an opportunity for acquisition and thus learning.

The participants' preference for a verb-noun or noun-only vocabulary presentation was evenly split; seven preferred noun-only, seven preferred verb-noun, and one was undecided. At this early stage in the learning process, many of the participants felt that the verbs were too much:

P5 – *"At first, because I know nothing about Italian I found [the verb and nouns] a little bit confusing. I would prefer this [view] later on. I would prefer this [noun only view] to form a basis, then maybe several weeks later I could use this version."*

In either case, all of the participants agreed that as their vocabulary grew, having additional context (*i.e., "to see things you might do to the noun"*) might help with the learning process in the long term.

Contextually Relevant Vocabulary is Beneficial

In this study, we restricted the learning interface to work only in a small number of predefined places; however, people can and will visit any number of places on a given day. We observed that the type of vocabulary presented to the learner in these places does impact acquisition. Participants vocabulary recall for the contextually relevant *venue-type* (M=9.27, SD=6.44) and *place-specific* (M=7.33, SD=5.86) vocabularies was greater than the *high-frequency* vocabulary (M=6.73, SD=6.17), but the only the *venue-type* was significantly greater than *high-frequency*. The human-generated *venue-type* vocabulary did not result in significantly greater acquisition than the systematically generated *place-specific* vocabulary. This is important because it shows that automated methods [8] can be used to provide the contextually relevant vocabulary in most of the places that a learner may visit.

Out of Context Words are Memorable

Despite the similarity in recall, many of the participants explicitly commented that the *place-specific* vocabulary stood out in contrast to the *venue-type* vocabulary. For example, P6 who we exposed to the *venue-type* vocabulary condition at the coffee shops, and *place-specific* vocabulary condition at the cheese shops, commented that:

P6 – *"The coffee shop vocab seemed most relevant ... it was weird to go into [the first cheese shop] and see the word 'magic' come up on the vocab. I thought that [magic] is relevant to this place, but not in the same way that a word related to cheese would be. Magic or magico was a funny word because it was related, but not in a way that I would associate to the context ... it stuck out."*

The cheese shop that P6 is referring to has 'Magic' in its name. Dearman and Truong's Activity-Service [8] which we used to generate the *place-specific* vocabulary does not achieve perfect precision; the service produced a small number of words that were seemingly random when considered alongside the other vocabulary. Many of the participants found these seemingly out of place words to be memorable, which encouraged their learning.

CONCLUSION & FUTURE WORK

An essential aspect of learning a second language is acquiring the vocabulary. However, building ones vocabulary is often a protracted process that requires repeated and spaced exposure; which can be difficult to accommodate given the busyness of daily living. In this paper, we present Vocabulary Wallpaper, a language tool designed to provide quick access to vocabulary to support short session of learning. Through a study comparing user's ability to implicitly acquire two different contextualized vocabularies (*venue-type* and *place-specific*) against a frequency-based vocabulary (*high-frequency*), we show that in four short sessions (totaling ~4 hours of exposure), participants were able to increase the number of second language vocabulary that they can recognize and recall when using the Vocabulary Wallpaper. The participants' rate of vocabulary acquisition was significantly greater when presented the contextually relevant *venue-type* vocabulary than the contextually-independent *high-frequency* vocabulary, but did not differ significantly otherwise. Many of the participants found that a small number of out-of-domain words stood out and were particularly memorable when interspaced within a larger vocabulary of contextually-relevant words. These results highlight that a contextually-relevant vocabulary can improve vocabulary acquisition and that we can use a systematic approach (as used to generate the *place-specific* vocabulary) to effectively provide a contextually-relevant vocabulary in the many places that a learner may find herself on a daily basis.

REFERENCES

1. Al-Mekhlafi, K., Hu, X. and Zheng, Z. An approach to context-aware mobile Chinese language learning for foreign students. In *Proc. ICMB 2009*, IEEE Computer Society (2009), 340-346.
2. Baudin, J.S., Intille, S.S., Tapia, E.M., Rockinson, R. and Morris, M.E. Context-sensitive microlearning of foreign language vocabulary on a mobile device. In *Proc. AmI 2007*, Springer-Verlag (2007), 55-72.
3. Cavus, N. and Ibrahim, D. m-Learning: an experiment in using SMS to support learning new English language words. *British Journal of Educational Technology 40*, 1 (2009), 78-91.
4. Chen, C. and Hsu, S. Personalized intelligent mobile learning system for supporting effective English learning. *Educational Technology & Society 11*, 3 (2008), 153-180.
5. Chun, D.M. and Plass, J.L. Effects of multimedia annotations on vocabulary acquisition. *The Modern Language Journal 80*, 2 (2007), 183-198.
6. Cui, Y. and Bull, S. Context and learning modeling for the mobile foreign language learner. *System 33* (2005), 353-367.
7. Davies, M. Word frequency data from the Corpus of Contemporary American English (COCA). Downloaded from http://www.wordfrequency.info, February 1, 2011.
8. Dearman, D. and Truong, K.N. Identifying the activities supported by locations with community-authored content. In *Proc. Ubicomp 2010*, ACM Press (2010), 23-32.
9. Dempster, F.N. Effects of variable encoding and spaced presentations on vocabulary learning. *Journal of Educational Psychology 79*, 2 (1987), 162-170.
10. Edge, D., Searle, E., Chiu, K., Zhao, J. and Landay, J.A. MicroMandarin: mobile language learning in context. In *Proc. CHI 2011*, ACM Press (2011).
11. Glasser, G., Hug, T. and Glahn, C. Integrated microlearning – an outline of the basic method and first results. In *Proc. Interactive Computer Aided Learning 2004*, Kassel University Press (2004), 1-7.
12. Gu, Y. and Johnson, R.K. Vocabulary learning strategies and language learning outcomes. *Language Learning 46*, 4 (1996), 643-679.
13. Gu, P.Y. Vocabulary learning in a second language: person, task, context and strategies. *Teaching English as a Second of Foreign Language 7*, 2 (2003).
14. Heibert, E.H., Kamil, M.L. *Teaching and Learning Vocabulary*. Lawrence Erlbaum Associates, London, England, 2005.
15. Hsieh, H., Chen, C. and Hong, C. Context-aware ubiquitous English learning in a campus environment. In *Proc. ICALT 2007*, IEEE Computer Society (2007), 351-353.
16. Huckin, T. and Coady, J. Incidental vocabulary acquisition in a second language: a review. *Studies of Second Language Acquisition 21*, 2 (1999), 181-193.
17. Hug, T. Micro learning and narration: exploring possibilities of utilization of narrations and storytelling for the design of "micro units" and didactical micro-learning arrangements. In *Proc. Media in Transition 2005*.
18. Kellogg, G.S. and Howe, M.J.A. Using words and pictures in foreign language learning. *Alberta Journal of Educational Research 17*, 2 (1971), 89-94.
19. Kolers, P.A. and Ostry, D.J. Time course of loss of information regarding pattern analyzing operations. *Journal of Verbal Learning and Verbal Behaviour 13* (1974), 599-612.
20. Liu, T.Y. A context-aware ubiquitous learning environment for language listening and speaking. *Journal of Computer Assisted Learning 25* (2009), 515-527.
21. Nation, P. *Teaching and learning vocabulary*. Heinle and Heinle, 1990.
22. Nation, P. *Learning vocabulary in another language*. Cambridge University Press, New York, NY, USA, 2001.
23. Ogata, H., Hui, G.L., Yin, C., Ueda, T., Oishi, Y. and Yano, Y. LOCH: supporting mobile language learning outside the classroom. *Int. J. Mobile Learning and Organization 2*, 3 (2008), 271-282.
24. Ogata, H. and Yano, Y. Context-aware support for computer-supported ubiquitous learning. In *Proc. WMTE 2004*, IEEE Computer Society (2004), 27-34.
25. Tan, T.H. and Liu, T.Y. The mobile-based interactive learning environment (MOBILE) and a case study for assisting elementary school English learning. In *Proc. ALT 2004*, IEEE Computer Society (2004), 530-534.
26. Thornton, P. and Houser, C. Using mobile phones in English education in Japan. *Journal of Computer Assisted Learning 21*, 3 (2005), 217-228.
27. Trusty, A. and Truong, K.N. Augmenting the web for second language vocabulary learning. In *Proc. CHI 2011*, ACM Press (2011).
28. United States' Foreign Service Institute. Language Continuum. Available at: http://fsitraining.state.gov/training/Language%20Continuum.pdf, Accessed September 22, 2011.
29. Webb, S. The effect of repetition on vocabulary knowledge. *Applied Linguistics 28*, 1 (2007), 46-65.

ShutEye: Encouraging Awareness of Healthy Sleep Recommendations with a Mobile, Peripheral Display

Jared S. Bauer[1], Sunny Consolvo[2], Benjamin Greenstein[2], Jonathan Schooler[1], Eric Wu[1], Nathaniel F. Watson[1], and Julie A. Kientz[1]

[1]University of Washington
Seattle, WA USA
{jaredsb, jschools, ericwu, nwatson, jkientz}@uw.edu

[2]Intel Labs Seattle
Seattle, WA USA
sunny@consolvo.org, ben@bengreenstein.org

ABSTRACT

Sleep is a basic physiological process essential for good health. However, 40 million people in the U.S. are diagnosed with sleep disorders, with many more undiagnosed. To help address this problem, we developed an application, ShutEye, which provides a peripheral display on the wallpaper of the user's mobile phone to promote awareness about recommended activities that promote good sleep quality. Based on preferences about the user's desired bedtime and activities—for example, consuming caffeine or performing vigorous exercise—ShutEye displays guidance about when engaging in those activities is likely to affect sleep without requiring any explicit interaction from the user. In this paper, we describe ShutEye and results from a four-week field study with 12 participants. Results indicate that a simple, recommendation-based peripheral display can be a very low-effort but still effective method for improving awareness of healthy sleep habits. We also provide recommendations about designing peripheral displays and extend insights for designing health-based mobile applications.

Author Keywords

Peripheral display; sleep; sleep hygiene; mobile phone; health; wellbeing; mindfulness;

ACM Classification Keywords

H5.m. Information interfaces and presentation (e.g., HCI): Miscellaneous;

INTRODUCTION

A sufficient amount of quality sleep is essential for maintaining a healthy lifestyle. Sleep plays a critical role in learning and memory, metabolism and weight control, safety, mood, cardiovascular health, and disease [5]. A growing body of scientific evidence correlates insufficient sleep with serious health issues, ranging from an increased likelihood of catching the common cold [5] to an increased risk for diabetes [29] and heart disease [3]. Beyond physical effects, sleep disorders are the third factor to overall unhappiness after clinical depression and chronic pain [8]. Despite this evidence, many people still do not get enough quality sleep [15]. In the National Sleep Foundation "Sleep in America Poll" conducted in 2009, Americans report an average of 6.7 hours of sleep per night, with sleep researchers recommending at least eight[1]. In addition, according to the National Institutes of Health[2], at least 40 million people in the U.S. are diagnosed with sleep disorders, with many others not yet diagnosed.

Clinicians often recommend that patients who complain of sleep problems should first work to improve their sleep habits, or *sleep hygiene*. Sleep hygiene is the term sleep experts use to refer to the practices that are believed to promote good quality sleep [30]. Examples of these recommendations include having a regular sleep-wake cycle, avoiding caffeine later in the day, and ensuring that the sleep environment is cool, quiet and dark. Good sleep hygiene is a central part of cognitive-behavioral therapy to treat insomnia [9] and is now often the first method sleep clinicians suggest when patients complain of poor sleep quality [28]. When these suggestions are implemented, people can often address many sleep problems without the use of medication, therapy, or surgery. However, prior research has also shown that even individuals with *knowledge* about good sleep hygiene may actually have poor sleep hygiene *practices* if they fail to remain aware of it [19].

Thus, to help promote awareness about activities that contribute to healthy sleep habits, we developed a mobile phone application called *ShutEye*. ShutEye uses a glanceable peripheral display on the phone's wallpaper to provide real-time sleep hygiene recommendations from the sleep literature about common activities that are known to impact sleep relative to bed and wake times. ShutEye's display reflects when activities such as consuming caffeine or en-

Permission to make digital or hard copies of all or part of this work for personal or classroom use is granted without fee provided that copies are not made or distributed for profit or commercial advantage and that copies bear this notice and the full citation on the first page. To copy otherwise, or republish, to post on servers or to redistribute to lists, requires prior specific permission and/or a fee.
CHI'12, May 5–10, 2012, Austin, Texas, USA.
Copyright 2012 ACM 978-1-4503-1015-4/12/05...$10.00.

[1] National Sleep Foundation. www.sleepfoundation.org

[2] National Institutes of Health. www.ninds.nih.gov/disorders/brain_basics/understanding_sleep.htm

gaging in vigorous exercise are likely to impact a user's sleep. For example, the user can quickly glance at her phone's screen to determine if it is currently advisable to have a cup of coffee. The recommendations are relevant to her preset sleep and wake time goals. Because the display is on her mobile phone, the user is gently reminded of sleep hygiene recommendations throughout the day.

Prior mobile, peripheral displays, such as the UbiFit Garden display for visualizing physical activity [7] or UbiGreen for reflecting a user's green transit behavior, required the user to wear tracking devices or journal their activities, which places a high burden on the user. ShutEye does not require the user to enter any information or otherwise interact with the system to record data. It simply reflects recommendations relative to the current time and the user's preset sleep and wake goals. This encourages awareness about sleep recommendations without the burden of journaling or the resource-intensiveness of automatic sensing.

To investigate ShutEye's impact on awareness and minimization of user burden, we conducted a 4-week qualitative field study with 12 participants. This work has two primary contributions. First, our application uses a novel recommendation-based peripheral display in a new application space of promoting healthy sleep habits. Second, our results show that ShutEye encouraged awareness of healthy sleep recommendations and emphasized the importance of a consistent sleep schedule without the user burden associated with journaling or the need for complicated activity detection algorithms and sensing. We also provide general considerations for peripheral displays and health technologies.

BACKGROUND AND RELATED WORK

In this section, we discuss the background of sleep hygiene and show how ShutEye draws from and contributes to research in peripheral displays, awareness, and technologies designed for sleep health.

Sleep Hygiene

The term "hygiene" is defined by Merriam-Webster as "conditions or practices conducive to health." Similar to how the practices of dental hygiene, such as brushing and flossing one's teeth, are known to encourage good dental health [1], *sleep hygiene* includes a set of habits and practices that are known to promote healthy sleep. Kleitman first discussed sleep hygiene nearly 50 years ago [18], and since then, it has been used to treat insomnia and excessive sleepiness. Sleep hygiene is influenced by four categories, which we describe next [30].

The *homeostatic drive for sleep* refers to activities that promote the individual's intrinsic physiology to facilitate sleep. These activities include avoiding naps, getting regular exercise, taking hot baths, and having a pre-sleep hot drink. *Entrainment of circadian factors* help create a regular sleep-wake cycle. They include trying to maintain regular sleep and wake times, getting exposure to sunlight during the day, and avoiding bright light in the evening. Circadian factors also include *zeitgebers* [26], which are external cues that help synchronize one's internal circadian clock, such as the sunset time, meal time, or when work days begin and end. *Drug effects* refer to those with harmful effects on sleep quality. The literature focuses on the effects of alcohol, nicotine, and caffeine. *Arousal in a sleep setting* focuses on ensuring the bedroom is free from disruptions, such as noise, light, temperature, motion, and poor air quality.

Our goal with ShutEye is to improve awareness about common activities that are known to impact sleep depending on *when* individuals engage in them relative to their desired sleep and wake times. Thus, we focused on recommendations for the homeostatic drive for sleep, circadian factors, and drug effects, since the arousal in a sleep setting category did not relate to time-based recommendations they were excluded. These recommendations are represented in ShutEye relative to the user's desired sleep and wake times.

Peripheral Displays and Awareness

According to Matthews et al. Activity Theory definition, peripheral displays are tools that support an activity at the operation level rather than the action level [23]. They further clarify this definition as displays that are not intended to interrupt the user's primary task, such as the case with interruption displays. Because they are used at the operation level, successful peripheral displays require low cognitive effort and therefore must be glanceable allowing quick information processing. Our goal with ShutEye was to provide recommendations that can be regularly referenced with minimal cognitive load or user burden. Thus, the information is there when needed, but easily ignorable when not. Peripheral displays have been used in a wide variety of contexts from viewing large quantities of information peripherally [13,25] to awareness of the environmental implications of a person's actions [10]. The use of peripheral displays to show health information has also been recommended as a strategy for promoting behavior change [7] due to its ability to promote awareness of activities. Our work with ShutEye builds upon previous findings to explore how peripheral displays can promote mindfulness in the domain of sleep recommendations.

Promoting Healthy Sleep through Technology

Some research and commercial applications have been specifically designed to promote sleep. Choe et al. provide a literature review and a framework for understanding the design dimensions of technologies for promoting sleep [4]. Examples include BuddyClock [16], a social application that enables users to share sleeping status within social networks to increase awareness of habits and use social structure to support sleep and the Wellness Diary [24], which allows users to log sleep information as part of overall wellness. Several commercial applications, including FitBit[3], SleepCycle[4], and ZEO[5], track information on the amount of hours slept and different sleep states. These ap-

[3] Fitbit, Inc. *http://www.fitbit.com/*

[4] Sleep Cycle, *http://mdlabs.se/sleepcycle/index.html*

[5] Zeo Inc. *http://www.myzeo.com/*

plications focus on tracking sleep information for awareness or preliminary diagnosis of sleep issues. ShutEye also focuses on sleep, but takes a different approach by encouraging the user to be aware of healthy sleep habits without requiring manual tracking or wearable sensors.

Mobile Health and Wellbeing

Mobile systems for health have used manual input from users, automatic input from sensors, or some combination of the two. Many systems that aim to encourage physical activity use sensors such as pedometers [6,20], accelerometers [27], biometric sensors [27], location data [2], or custom sensor platforms [7]. Most of these systems also require or enable the user to augment the sensing system with manual journaling of activities. Others rely entirely on users manually journaling, especially with difficult-to-detect activities such as food intake [12] or general wellbeing [24]. Data capture, either through wearable sensors or manually, can be burdensome on users due to the time and effort involved or through discomfort from wearing sensors.

A number of mobile health applications have explored creative ways of displaying information to help users become more aware of health-related activities. For example, Fish'n'Steps [20] represents users' step count information as a fish in a virtual aquarium. Shakra [2] and Houston [6] display physical activity data as a pictorial representation or a bar chart in comparison to a group of the user's peers and toward a specific goal. Applications that provide just-in-time visualizations to help users change their habits are also closely related to our work. UbiFit uses a pictorial representation of the user's physical activity as a personal peripheral display on her mobile phone [7]. TripleBeat provides a peripheral display of the user's current heart rate compared to their target for their current activity [27]. These applications provide real-time information while users are in a position to change their behavior, such as getting more physical activity, relieving stress, or increasing their workout intensity.

ShutEye differs from these systems in that it is designed to provide many of the benefits of mobile health applications through awareness of activities that impact sleep, but does not rely on data capture, thus minimizing the user's burden of using the application. We believe that for this application space, there is a trade off between a highly accurate but high burden data capture and visualization and a low burden system that provides less customized recommendations. Because others have explored the higher burden, highly accurate side of this trade off in other domains, with ShutEye, we aimed to explore whether a low burden, but reduced accuracy approach could still be effective in improving people's awareness.

DESIGN OF SHUTEYE

ShutEye uses a glanceable peripheral display to communicate sleep recommendations, which runs as the active wallpaper and lock screen image of the user's mobile phone. It shows a 24-hour window with up to nine horizontal bars of different colors resembling a timeline (Figure 1, left). Each bar represents an activity that is known to affect sleep, either positively or negatively: consuming caffeine, napping, exercising, eating heavy meals, consuming alcohol, nicotine use, and relaxing, as well as two custom activities that the user can specify. By default, the display shows caffeine, napping, exercising, meals, alcohol, and relaxing. An icon on each bar at the right of the screen reminds the user of what the bar represents. At any time, the user can change which activities are displayed, create custom activities, or hide the activity icons.

We implemented ShutEye on the Android-based Nexus One phone, although it can run on any Android device. The Nexus One has five background screens: the primary screen, or 'home screen,' plus two screens to the right and two to the left, which are accessed by swiping in either direction. ShutEye's 24-hour timeline is spread across the five screens; the current time is always on the home screen. A

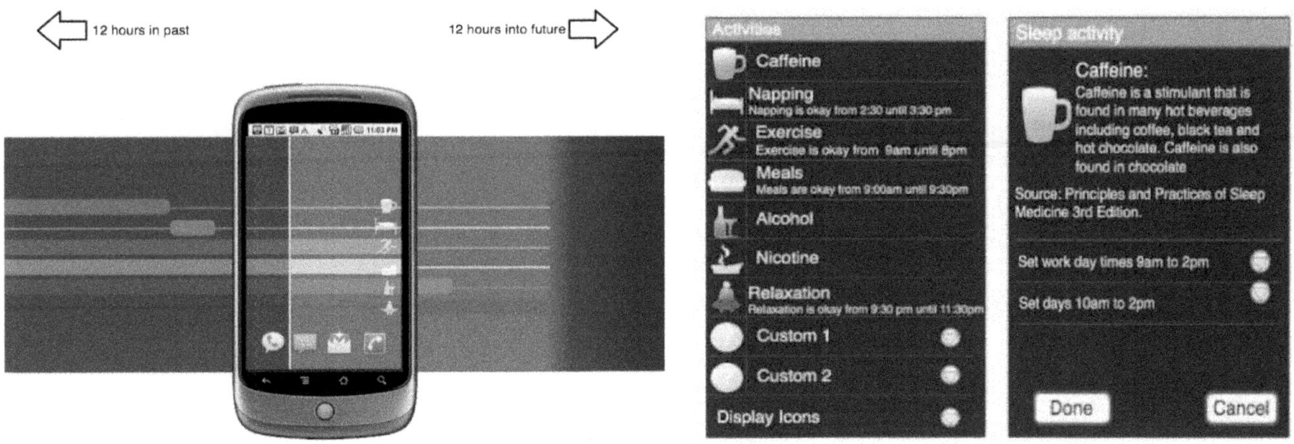

Figure 1: ShutEye's peripheral wallpaper display (left) consists of a timeline with horizontal bars representing activities that impact sleep. Thick bars indicate when an activity is unlikely to negatively affect or likely to improve sleep; thin bars represent when an activity is not recommended. The vertical bar updates automatically and indicates the current time. In the interactive application, colored icons represent activities (center), where users can read about the recommendation and customize its times (right).

vertical line on the home screen cuts through the horizontal bars to identify the current time. The display to the left of that vertical line is darkened to show that it is in the past. At any given time, a colored horizontal bar might be thick or thin. A thick bar means that engaging in the activity is unlikely to disrupt sleep, and in some cases—such as with relaxing—may even help it. Thus, while glancing at the home screen, the user can quickly determine which current activities are likely to affect the user's upcoming sleep episode. The design therefore, creates a "time-line" of which activities will impact the user's sleep throughout the day.

Before converging on the timeline design metaphor for the peripheral display, several other designs were considered. This included other metaphors for time, such as a polar clock and an hourglass. We also considered more abstract depictions for the sleep hygiene recommendations, similar to the interfaces in prior work for mobile information displays [6,10]. We conducted informal usability tests to evaluate the competing design and converged on the horizontal timeline design, because it was easiest to quickly interpret.

ShutEye also consists of an interactive application where users can specify preferences and learn more about sleep recommendations. They can manage their desired sleep schedules, browse preferences for which activities to display, adjust the recommendations, and learn about why the activities are likely to affect sleep (Figure 1, center). ShutEye supports two custom schedules: one for "work days" (Monday through Friday by default) and one for "free days" (Saturday and Sunday by default). By allowing users to customize their desired sleep/wake times and work/free days, the recommendations—which are often of the form "end vigorous exercise at least six hours before sleep time"—can be customized (Figure 1, right).

Each standard sleep-related activity in ShutEye (see Table 1) comes with a recommendation from the sleep hygiene literature as well as an explanation and its source [30]. Because sleep experts have acknowledged that the activities may affect individuals differently, ShutEye allows the user to adjust the recommendations. For example, the sleep literature recommendation for caffeine is to end consumption 8-14 hours before bedtime. However, caffeine affects people differently, and it does not always take 8-14 hours for the effects of caffeine to wear off. Thus, users can change the recommendation to be appropriate based on their own experiences, but can easily return to the defaults.

4-WEEK FIELD STUDY

In this section, we describe the 4-week field study where 12 people used and evaluated ShutEye throughout the course of their normal activities.

Study Method

Our 4-week field study involved three stages: an initial in-lab session, four weeks using ShutEye in the field, and a final in-lab session. This study's goal was to explore whether ShutEye's display could promote awareness about sleep recommendations, though the ultimate intention was to prompt changes that would help them get better sleep. We focused on encouraging awareness rather than behavior change because it gave us the opportunity to understand a very sensitive and relatively new domain for HCI. Our approach was based on Klasnja et al.'s recommendations [17] for evaluating novel technologies promoting health behavior change. Klasnja et al. argue that due to the complexity of long-term behavior change, one should not focus on measuring behavior change itself while technology is still exploratory, but instead focus on understanding *why* and *how* technologies might eventually be effective in promoting change. This calls for a study that is mostly qualitative.

Initial in-lab session. After signing a consent form, participants completed a questionnaire on their sleep habits and basic demographics. The questionnaire included the Ep-

	Start time	End time	Recommendation	Explanation
Napping	8 hours after waking	9 hours after waking	A 10 to 15 minute nap is permitted 8 hours after wake up time.	Humans have a normal dip in their wakefulness about 8 hours after waking time. Napping after that dip in wakefulness increases the likelihood that naps will disturb your sleep cycle
Meals	Wake time	3 hours before bed	Do not eat or drink a heavy meal 3 hours before bedtime. However, a light snack may help promote sleep	Digestion of food may lead to stomach issues that can disturb sleep. Consuming liquid shortly before sleep may cause a disruption in sleep due to a need to urinate.
Alcohol	Wake time	2 hours before bed	Humans metabolize about one drink per hour and it is recommended to wait until blood alcohol level has reached zero before sleeping.	In the short term, alcohol promotes sleepiness by aiding the production of various inhibitory neurotransmitters. However, after a few hours these neurotransmitters will be exhausted and your body will become alert again, thereby disturbing your sleep.
Relaxation	1 hour before bed time	Bed time	Begin sleep-promoting activities 1 hour before bed	It is important to create a break between the events of the day and the process of sleep. To do this, it is useful to engage in activities that promote sleepiness, such as taking a warm bath.

Table 1: Four of the eight sleep-related activity recommendations represented on ShutEye's peripheral display.

worth sleepiness scale, a clinically validated scale to evaluate subjective sleepiness [14]. After the questionnaire, we conducted a brief interview that lasted about 10-20 minutes. Questions focused on assessing the severity and nature of their sleep concerns. We loaned participants an HTC Nexus One phone running ShutEye to use for four weeks. We put their SIM cards in the study phone so that the study phone served as their primary phone throughout the four weeks. We gave them an in-depth tutorial on how to use the phone, imported their contacts, and provided the phone's user manual. We then helped them customize their schedules in ShutEye so that the peripheral display would reflect their typical sleep/wake schedule and activities that were relevant to them.

4 weeks in the field. During the study, we asked participants to keep ShutEye as their wallpaper, but did not require them to interact with it otherwise. We sent participants a weekly questionnaire via email that they were asked to complete within 24 hours of receipt. The questionnaire repeated the Epworth sleepiness scale and asked about their use of the phone. It also asked if any atypical events had occurred that might impact their sleep, such as sickness, travel, or a change in their work schedule.

Final in-lab session. At the end of the four weeks, participants returned to our lab. During this session, they repeated the Epworth scale. We then conducted an interview about their experiences during the study, their use of ShutEye, and how, if at all, they believed ShutEye impacted their awareness and knowledge of sleep recommendations. Interviews lasted between 30 and 50 minutes. After the interview, we helped participants replace their SIM cards in their original mobile phones, downloaded the log of ShutEye events from the study phone, and then reset the study phone to the original factory settings to remove any of the participants' personal information. Participants received gift cards worth $65 USD as compensation for their time.

Participants

We recruited 12 adults (see Table 2) from a major US metropolitan area to participate in the 4-week field study of ShutEye. Eight of the participants were female and four were male. The higher number of female participants is likely due to a higher number of women in general reporting difficulties sleeping[6]. However, sleep hygiene recommendations are not gender specific, and thus we did not attempt to recruit an even number of males and females for the study. Participants ranged from 20 to 53 years old (average: 32; median: 31). The highest levels of education achieved by participants were: high school (N=1), certificate (N=3), bachelor's degree (N=4), graduate degree (N=3), and a doctoral degree (N=1). All participants owned and regularly used a mobile phone, with the majority using smart phones. We recruited 8 participants using a professional recruiting agency and 4 four through word-of-mouth. They were screened to ensure that they had the goal of wanting to improve their sleep habits, but did not have a diagnosed sleep disorder, as ShutEye was not designed to treat serious sleep issues such as sleep apnea or narcolepsy.

[6] National Sleep Foundation. http://www.sleepfoundation.org/article/sleep-topics/women-and-sleep

RESULTS

The results from the 4-week field study are primarily qualitative in nature, though we also looked at the pre- and post-deployment scores from the Epworth sleepiness scale to assess baseline sleepiness and look for any trends. Epworth scores can range from 1 to 24. Lower scores indicate less subjective sleepiness, with scores at or above 11 indicating pathological sleepiness. These scores are presented in Table 2 to help contextualize the results.

ID	Sex	Age	Occupation	Epworth		
				Pre	Post	Δ
1	F	36	Security / Office Services	6	5	↓
2	F	32	Retail	7	5	↓
3	F	30	Caregiver for AFH	15	15	↔
4	F	31	Banker - Ops Manager	5	5	↔
5	F	53	Home Health Aide	9	7	↓
6	M	28	Bank Teller / Bakery	5	3	↓
7	F	24	Bicycle Mechanic	3	8	↑
8	F	31	Bookkeeper	3	2	↓
9	F	20	Retail	12	4	↓
10	M	21	Prep Chef	7	2	↓
11	F	38	Info. Tech. Librarian	7	3	↓
12	M	40	Ecologist	12	12	↔

Table 2: Participant demographics and Epworth scores before and after using ShutEye. Three of the twelve participants had initial scores that were indicative of excessive sleepiness.

For the qualitative data, we extracted participant quotes from the interview transcripts into 287 unique units of analysis. Two of the researchers used a combination of deductive (bringing in specific themes of interest based on study goals and interview questions) and inductive (allowing additional themes to emerge from the data) coding schemes. Our deductive coding scheme focused on Matthews et al.'s evaluation criteria for peripheral displays, which include: appeal, learnability, awareness, effects of breakdowns, and distraction [23]. The inductive coding resulted in three additional themes: adherence to recommendations, ShutEye as a recommendation tool, and competing issues with sleep. We outline results from each category below.

Appeal

Participants were generally happy with ShutEye and found it understandable and aesthetically pleasing, although a number disliked the Nexus One phone itself. All participants stated that they did not feel that their privacy was invaded nor were they embarrassed if people asked them about their phone's background screen. To the participants, wanting to improve sleep was not a highly sensitive topic, as trying to lose weight might be. Several participants noted that they missed having a background picture on their screen, being able to have that added touch of personalization, or just seeing something new on their phone.

I was just kind of bored with the same background and I would sometimes want to change it – But it wasn't like I wanted to see something else, or have a personal picture on the background or anything like that. It was more just changing it up. {P9}

Another requested feature was the ability to log aspects of sleep, such as sleep duration, quality, or caffeine consumption. This mostly seemed to be because the participants were curious, but they did not think that these should be required to use the application.

I think if it did have a place for me to actually say, when I actually went to bed, or what was the last time I had caffeine, I think that would – I'd probably do it if it was on there. I think it'd be more so that I could see how well I was doing, to the recommendations, to see if I was really doing as well as I thought I was, or if I was breaking the recommendations more than I thought I was...that's what I'd be interested in seeing. {P9}

Learnability

Most of the participants found the interface easy to understand once we explained it to them. However, one participant was a bit confused by it. She did not use her phone very much over the four weeks due to many personal issues, and she said she thought the phone was supposed to "do something" to remind her of what to do. This could have been due to a misunderstanding in our explanation, or not having enough time to get used to the system to understand how it changed.

We allowed for customization of sleep times on a daily basis, but we found that most participants kept the initial settings and did not change their daily times to reflect when they actual woke up or went to bed, but kept them as more of a sleep "goal" or desired sleep and wake time. Because of this, some of the recommendations may not have been as precise for them (e.g., if the ideal time to sleep was 10 P.M. but they did not actually go to sleep until 12 A.M., then the factors for exercise, food, alcohol, etc. were two hours off). Participants expressed a desire for the device to be able to recognize their actual sleep and wake times to provide more accurate recommendations, though they were not entirely clear how they would want this accomplished.

We also allowed participants to specify custom sleep factors they may want to track. This feature was not often used, with the exception of P8, who added *TV* and *Internet*, and P11, who added *Video Games*. When we asked participants if there was anything they wanted to track that was not included in the system, most of them had a response such as TV, computer use, etc. When we further probed to ask why they did not set up a custom feature or change the times of an existing feature, one participant said it was because she trusted the people designing the application and making the recommendations. This underscores the importance of having medically sound backings for the recommendations and setting good defaults.

It seemed that those settings were fine for me, and I figured people that made the app probably knew what they were doing. ... expectations that they understood what is generally best for most people, and I think that what is generally best for most people is generally best for me. {P8}

Effects of Breakdowns

Matthews et al. [23] state that peripheral displays must reveal any breakdowns to users, since they may be reliant on data to do their primary activities. Because the display itself did not rely on risky technology or user input, breakdowns were non-existent. In addition, because ShutEye did not really deal with highly critical data, breakdowns would not be as problematic with this display as they may be for others. However, because the recommendations were time-based, there was some desire from participants to have the application be more proactive, because they would lose track of time and want to be reminded when it was bedtime or the time when caffeine was no longer recommended.

Sometimes people never pay attention to the things that they do throughout the day so if it popped up on my phone daily, it would make me certainly be aware of what I need to be... just well kind of help my daily life flow a little bit easier. {P5}

These types of notifications would change the nature of the peripheral display to a notification display, but having an optional hybrid approach could be a possibility.

Awareness

The primary goal of ShutEye is to help people learn about sleep hygiene and be more aware and thus more mindful of good sleep hygiene practices throughout their day. Nearly all of the participants (N=11) said that it made them think more about sleep, what contributes to quality sleep, and be more cognizant in general of what affects sleep.

I think that this particular app has definitely made me a lot more cognizant of the choices that I'm making. I mean, I'm obviously not going to always follow it to the letter because things happen. So if I'm out with my friends until two o'clock in the morning on a Saturday night, I'm out until two o'clock in the morning. But yes, I mean it definitely made me kind of think twice sometimes when I'd be like, 'I should get a soda. No I shouldn't.' {P8}

I felt like it just made me more cognizant of all my choices throughout the day, so the napping thing and the eating and exercising and things like that. I often go for walks with my sisters and their dogs and so it was like, 'What time is it? Is it still OK for us to for a long walk?' {P2}

I wasn't more hesitant to do it [non-recommended activity], *but I did kind of think of how I might sleep. So, just being aware of maybe I'm probably not going to get the best sleep tonight, maybe, or just thinking that if it was going to affect my sleep. So I was just kind of more conscious of – maybe in the morning – of how great my sleep was and trying to tell if that really was affecting it or not.* {P9}

Several participants reported that it made them think a little more not just about sleep, but about other aspects of their health and wellness, such as taking care of themselves in general, or getting more exercise.

...just a reminder for myself to myself that I'm trying to take care of myself and trying to behave and try and get the sleep I need. {P1}

So I don't exercise very much, not vigorously, anyways. I'm active, I walk around, but I don't go jogging or anything, but – yeah, so having the little exercising guy of course would make me feel guilty every day, I was like oh yeah, stop exercising, woops, I never started. {P11}

Five of the participants acknowledged that they did not necessarily change their behavior, but they often felt a little guilty when they did not follow the recommendations. They also understood that it was okay to go against the recommendations on occasion.

I mean there's always that tiny bit of like, you know, guilt like I know shouldn't do this but it doesn't really matter. {P10}

Because awareness and mindfulness are difficult to measure, some participants struggled with identifying whether just learning about the recommendation helped in their decision-making, or if it was because of ShutEye's display.

I thought about having coffee later in the day, and then – so is it ShutEye, or is it just me knowing that I shouldn't do it, so it's hard for me separate those out, but having that there probably did make me think, no, don't have coffee now, it's 1 o'clock, or something. {P11}

Participants reported learning more about what contributes to good sleep, even if they did not necessarily adhere to those recommendations all of the time. ShutEye encouraged participants to set up consistent sleep/wake schedules and be mindful of how their activities could impact their sleep.

I didn't know that all of these things affected your sleep within two hours of going to bed. I had no idea. I mean, I was very aware of caffeine, but the rest – oh and naps, of course. If you take a nap too late, everyone kind of figures that. {P4}

Distraction

We chose to put ShutEye's peripheral display on the wallpaper of the user's phone with the intention that it would be seen whenever they used the phone for any reason. Participants confirmed that they noticed the display when they checked the time, sent or received a text message, checked their email, and so on.

Because you're looking at it all the time. And, I mean, every time you pick up your phone to do whatever it is, I mean, there's the bars, there's the time, and you're constantly seeing what you should and should not do in order to help yourself get a better night's sleep. {P7}

Well, every time I would check a text message or something like that, I would see the bars starting to go away. And then I'm like, OK, if I'm going to get coffee, I'd better go get it now. {P1}

The dynamic nature of the display seemed to help draw participants' attention as well, however, most did not find it to be distracting.

...it's not distracting at all. But you notice it, just because it does change. I don't know. If I was bored I'd slide it back and forth, see what I should've done or what I was doing. {P5}

When asked whether they thought they would notice the display as much if it had not been on their phone's background, all participants agreed that they did not think that they would. They liked having it as a part of the background and thought they noticed it more as a result.

I liked that it was on the background of your phone, and just there whenever you...go to check the clock or whatever. {P9}

Because it's the...desktop on the phone, I'm always looking at it every single time I get the phone. {P8}

We also asked about the visibility of the display over time, and whether or not they noticed it less after using the phone for several weeks. Not surprisingly, participants reported specifically looking at the display often toward the beginning of the study. However, as the study progressed, it became a subtler, but persistent reminder.

The first week I was looking at it all of the time because it was new and different but then the following weeks it was kind of like oh. Just kind of keeping it in the back of my mind. {P2}

Adherence to Recommendations

Though our goal with ShutEye was to improve mindfulness, not necessarily to cause behavior change, our results indicate that ShutEye encouraged at least some short-term behavior change. Eight of the 12 participants had improved Epworth scores, which indicates that their overall daytime sleepiness level dropped (see Table 2). We also asked participants about how, if at all, they changed their sleep-related behaviors. Most participants mentioned changing their behavior regarding caffeine consumption.

For the first week [ShutEye] *absolutely made me more aware of...keeping the caffeine earlier in the day, if I could. And then for the rest of the month it was...in the back of my mind at least, if not in the forefront of my mind about drinking coffee, like, before three. So it did something.* {P6}

Others mentioned that ShutEye helped them adhere to a more consistent sleep schedule or earlier bedtimes.

I was more consistent with my wake times and bed times... Even on my days off I would still go to bed at the time I had went to bed on work days and get up at the same time. {P9}

The recommendation about naps was helpful for some, but frustrating for others because the time period was always during the middle of the day when they had to work. Others heeded the recommendation timing as it made them consider the impact that it might have later that night.

Whereas, I think before, I probably would have just taken a nap whenever I felt like it... I don't think it changed the amount of time that I slept, but it changed ...when I would actually nap because I would look at it and be like, ahhh –if I took a nap now, then I probably wouldn't be able to sleep later. {P3}

One participant particularly appreciated the relaxation recommendation, noting that she read more as a result of her adherence.

I think [relaxation helped], *because I have a tendency, when I get into bed, my brain's just going a million miles an hour, usually. And I think that kind of removing some of that visual stimu-*

> *lation at least from the TV or from being online, I think that that kind of helped calm it down a little bit, just let me like read for a while. That's kind of my meditating, is reading. I've read so many books in the last month. It's ridiculous.* {P8}

In contrast to these findings, though, several participants mentioned that at times, they knowingly went against ShutEye's recommendations.

> *Wanting to go out with my friends kind of overrode wanting to sleep.* {P3}

However, even in these cases where participants did not adhere to the recommendations, they did so knowing that what they were doing might negatively impact their sleep. That is, ShutEye's primary goal of promoting awareness and helping users make more informed decisions about their behaviors seems to have been achieved.

ShutEye as a Recommendation Tool

For some participants, there seemed to be a tension between ShutEye helping them reflect on how the activities that they do throughout the day might be impacting their goal of improving their sleep and feeling like ShutEye was dictating what they should and should not do.

> *I felt like there were certain activities that, you know, I wanted to do but remembering, like, no, you can't because you set that schedule for yourself, and you can't watch TV past this time; you shouldn't go to the gym after this time; you, you know, shouldn't be drinking past this time. And I would choose not to do those things because, sort of, mentally I'd realize, like, I have this sort of schedule set for myself that I look at all the time and reminded all the time.* {P6}

Another participant who initially experienced this tension felt better about it after she realized that ShutEye was simply providing recommendations, not rules.

Competing Issues with Sleep

Even if users were to regularly follow all of ShutEye's recommendations, they would not be guaranteed good sleep, as other issues—such as a noisy or bright sleep environment, stress, or medical conditions—can impact sleep. Participants reported experiencing a number of such issues. For example, one participant lives near a loud bar:

> *When the bar lets out at about 2* [in the morning], *I almost always hear because people are screaming and loud and stuff, so if I was asleep, I'd almost always wake up then...*[my apartment] *is right next to it and it's like insanely loud on Thursday nights.* {P5}

Several participants mentioned that their hectic schedules impacted their sleep, especially for participants who have more than one job:

> *To some extent, my work schedule has helped cause problems with that, you know, because some mornings I'm up at three in the morning and some mornings I'm not in bed until three in the morning. Working security, you're there until things shut down and clear up. And then sometimes I'll be wired after I get done doing security. And then when I work at the law firm, I'm up at three in the morning to catch the bus to go to the law firm. So my body's not necessarily sure what to think about that.* {P1}

P1's schedule was an extreme case, but several participants had irregular schedules that they believed impacted their sleep quality. We acknowledge that though ShutEye appears to be helpful in improving awareness about many sleep recommendations, it does not address all issues that may impact sleep quality that are known within the sleep community. Sleep hygiene recommendations are usually the first step in treating sleep problems, but if that is unsuccessful, additional follow up is often necessary.

DISCUSSION

Our four-week field study of ShutEye helped us explore some of the issues regarding the design of mobile peripheral displays and technologies for health. We have derived several considerations for designing technologies in this space. In this section, we discuss these considerations and their applicability to similar systems, as well as other challenges and opportunities for future research.

Design Considerations

Based on the results of the field study, we provide the following considerations for designing technologies to promote awareness of healthy sleep behaviors.

Strictness of the recommendations. The primary concern people had with ShutEye was that they felt a bit overwhelmed with trying to do too many things at once and adhere to such a strict time schedule if they were not used to it. The most success came when participants stopped regarding the recommendations as hard rules, and instead, simply looked at them as suggestions or guidelines. Given that the recommendations from the sleep literature are based on averages, we think one thing that might help would be changing the hard lines around recommendation times to be more of a gradient to suggest that the recommendations are not overly strict. Figure 2 shows how ShutEye might be redesigned to adhere to this consideration. In expanding this to other domains, it would be important to consider when recommendations can be conveyed with a similar sense of flexibility.

"Encouraged" vs. "allowable." Although we explained that thick bars in ShutEye indicated activities were currently unlikely to negatively impact sleep and thin bars would have a negative impact, some participants interpreted the recommendations as being "encouraged" and "not encouraged." Several participants joked that because alcohol did not have a negative impact on sleep starting at wake time, that ShutEye actually encouraged them to drink that early. Others found it odd that smoking was "encouraged" by the system. This was an issue that we struggled with from the very beginning. Designers might consider setting three levels rather than two: encouraged, allowable, and discouraged, rather than having an impact or not.

Source of recommendations. The participants appreciated having the specific source of the recommendations, which came from the sleep research community. Several stated that this increased their trust in the recommendations, but others actually wanted to learn more behind the recommen-

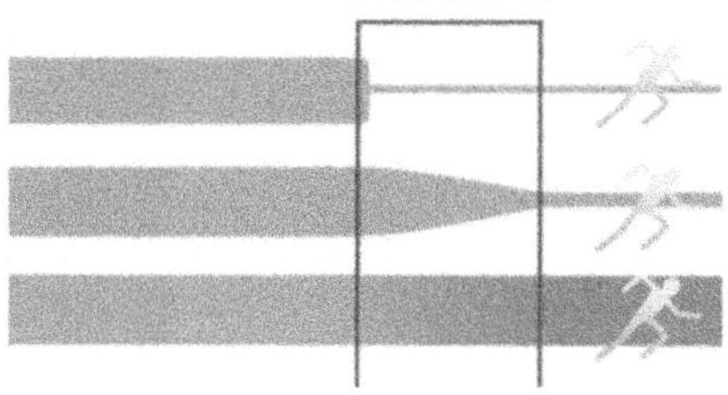

Figure 2: ShutEye's original design (top) and new alternatives (center, bottom) conveying different levels of strictness.

dation. Providing the brief recommendations such as those included in ShutEye were important, but also including links (not just citations) to deeper sources of information could be valuable for those who wanted to learn even more.

Interest and visibility over time. Although participants learned about sleep recommendations over the short study period, a few participants stated that they got bored with ShutEye being the same design on their phone over the 4-weeks, and thus noticed it less over time. If it is important to the system's goals to maintain interest for the long-term, designers might consider having the design change over time or perhaps allow users to swap the design out for new skins or color schemes. ShutEye still had success in educating users over a short period of time, and thus it may not be needed for the long term, but other applications may need this longevity.

Customizing user burden. ShutEye was an experiment with seeing whether an extremely low burden application without nagging or distraction could still encourage awareness of healthy sleep hygiene. While most participants appreciated the subtlety of the display, a few requested that ShutEye be more proactive. Participants would often not realize what time it was, and so they requested alarms or simple notifications to remind them that it was close to bedtime so they should start to relax, or to remind them to get that last cup of coffee before it is too late. Adding *optional* proactive notifications for users who would like them may be something to consider for these types of applications. In addition, we found variations in how much time people would be willing to spend with the application. Several had requested that there be a logging or journaling feature that enabled them to track sleep or caffeine use over time, which may appeal to those who enjoy lifelogging activities. However, because some were not willing to take on this amount of extra effort or had no interest in tracking, application designers should still consider how to add value without it.

Actionable suggestions for meeting recommendations. Although most participants agreed that meeting recommendations was important, some participants just did not have a good idea of how to fit it into their lifestyles. Providing some specific suggestions for things they can do to meet these recommendations may be helpful. For example, links to quitting smoking recommendations or alternatives to caffeinated beverages (e.g., decaffeinated tea or coffee, milk, etc.) could be helpful. In addition, ideas for what to do to relax, and specific suggestions for the types of meals or physical activities that would be appropriate in the given time frame would also help participants grasp the recommendations and make steps toward longer term changes.

Evaluating awareness. One of the challenges of this work was determining if ShutEye achieved its primary goal of promoting awareness of sleep habits. Although the qualitative data shows that participants became more aware that activities they do throughout the day could impact their sleep, it was difficult to understand how much of this increased awareness came from ShutEye, participating in a study about sleep, or some combination of the two. In addition, because the goal was to help people make more educated decisions about their daily activities, it may be difficult or even impossible to measure progress in terms of the type of clinical outcomes that are often applied to health interventions. While qualitative data on this topic is valuable, designers should consider the limitations of these types of studies regarding traditional health outcome data.

Opportunities for Future Research

The results from our study suggest several opportunities for future work. For example, even though participants were divided on the utility of journaling and activity inference around sleep-related behaviors, there was some interest in including a behavior-tracking feature in ShutEye. Future work could compare the effectiveness of a system based solely on recommendations, as this version of ShutEye used, to one that supports tracking behaviors in addition to providing recommendations. This can help better understand the trade-offs between higher burden, higher accuracy applications and lower burden, lower accuracy applications.

In addition, although sleep is an important part of overall health and wellness, it is not the only important contributor. Proper nutrition and exercise, as well as reducing stress and maintaining social relationships are also important, and at times, these different factors can compete with each other—for example, when participants in our study struggled with the decision to exercise or have dinner after the recommended time if that was the only time that they could schedule them. While ShutEye helped educate users about healthy sleep practices, it may be useful to integrate it into a comprehensive overall health and wellness program that helps the user balance competing priorities. Also, as mentioned above, a wide variety of issues can impact sleep including poor sleep environments. Future work could explore these other issues, including how to help people prepare and maintain their environment for sleep.

Finally, we hope to explore the role of how awareness impacts sleep habits. One of the limitations of this study was determining the participants' awareness of the display. Prior to the study, we considered non-qualitative methods to evaluate awareness including a quiz from the medical community on healthy sleep habits and logging participants' use of ShutEye. However, not all of the items from the quiz were time-based, and therefore not directly comparable. Logging participants' use of ShutEye was problematic because the main form of interaction occurred peripherally when the users glanced at their phones, and thus this activity could not be accurately logged. ShutEye has been released on the Android Marketplace with a supplemental survey to collect data from a large set of users to make additional iterations on the application's design. This will help set the stage for running a large scale, randomized controlled trial of ShutEye to determine if the awareness reported by our study participants leads to behavior change relating to sleep at a large scale. This may also help to mitigate issues that could arise from participants using phones provided by the research team instead of their own phone.

CONCLUSION

We presented the design and evaluation of a health and wellness technology—ShutEye—to promote mindfulness about how activities that users perform throughout the day may disrupt their sleep. ShutEye uses a glanceable peripheral display on the wallpaper of the user's mobile phone to present a timeline of temporally relevant sleep hygiene recommendations that are derived from the sleep literature and the user's preferences. The goal of ShutEye was to explore whether lower burden but lower accuracy health displays could still be effective. Results from our four-week field study indicate that ShutEye's peripheral display can increase awareness and mindfulness of healthy sleep habits. We provided several considerations for the design of similar technologies to encourage health and wellness, and we outlined opportunities for future work. Our results contribute to the growing body of knowledge of how technology can support healthy sleep and how mobile, peripheral displays can promote health and wellness.

REFERENCES

1. Addy, M. & Moran, J.M. 2000. Evaluation of oral hygiene products: science is true; don't be misled by the facts. *Periodontology* 15, 1 (1997), 40-51.
2. Anderson, I., et al. 2007. Shakra: tracking and sharing daily activity levels with unaugmented mobile phones. *Mob. Netw. Appl.* 12, 2-3, 185-199.
3. Ayas, N.T., et al. 2003. A Prospective Study of Sleep Duration and Coronary Heart Disease in Women. *Arch. Intern. Med.* 163, 2, 205-209.
4. Choe, et al. 2011. Opportunities for Computing Technologies to Support Healthy Sleep Behaviors. *CHI '11*, 3053-3062.
5. Cohen, S., et al. 2009. Sleep Habits and Susceptibility to the Common Cold. *Arch. Intern. Med.* 169, 1, 62-67.
6. Consolvo, S., et al. 2006. Design requirements for technologies that encourage physical activity. *CHI '06*, 457-466.
7. Consolvo, S., et al. 2009. Theory-driven design strategies for technologies that support behavior change in everyday life. *CHI '09*. 405-414.
8. Dement, W.C. & Vaughan, C. 2000. The Promise of Sleep: A Pioneer in Sleep Medicine Explores the Vital Connection Between Health, Happiness, and a Good Night's Sleep. Dell Publishing.
9. Edinger, J.D., et al. 2001. Cognitive Behavioral Therapy for Treatment of Chronic Primary Insomnia: A Randomized Controlled Trial. *JAMA* 285, 14, 1856-1864.
10. Froehlich, J., et al. 2009. UbiGreen: investigating a mobile tool for tracking and supporting green transportation habits. *CHI '09*, 1043-1052.
11. Gangwisch, J.E., et al. 2006. Short Sleep Duration as a Risk Factor for Hypertension. *Hypertension* 47, 5, 833-839.
12. Grimes, A., et al. 2008. EatWell: sharing nutrition-related memories in a low-income community. *CSCW '08*. 87-96.
13. Jancke, G., et al. Sideshow: Providing peripheral awareness of important information. *Microsoft Research*, 2001.
14. Johns, M.W. 1991. A new method for measuring daytime sleepiness: the Epworth sleepiness scale. *Sleep* 14, 6, 540-5.
15. Johnson, J.V. & J. Lipscomb. 2006. Long working hours, occupational health and the changing nature of work organization. *Am. Journal of Industrial Medicine* 49, 11, 921-929.
16. Kim, S., et al. 2008. Are you sleeping?: sharing portrayed sleeping status within a social network. *CSCW '08*. 619-628.
17. Klasnja, P., et al. 2011. How to evaluate technologies for health behavior change in HCI research. *CHI '11*. 3063-3072.
18. Kleitman, N. 1963. *Sleep and wakefulness*. University of Chicago Press, Chicago.
19. Lacks, P. & Rotert, M. 1986. Knowledge and practice of sleep hygiene techniques in insomniacs and good sleepers. *Behaviour Research & Therapy* 24, 3, 365-368.
20. Lin, J., et al. 2006. Fish'n'Steps: Encouraging Physical Activity with an Interactive Computer Game. *UbiComp'06*, 261-278.
21. Maitland, J., et al. 2006. Increasing the Awareness of Daily Activity Levels with Pervasive Computing. *Pervasive Health '06*, 1-9.
22. Matthews, T. 2006. Designing and evaluating glanceable peripheral displays. *DIS '06*, 343-345.
23. Matthews, T., et al. 2007. Defining, designing, and evaluating peripheral displays: An analysis using Activity Theory. *Human-Computer Interaction*, 22(1), 221-261.
24. Mattila, E., et al. 2008. Mobile diary for wellness management - results on usage and usability in two user studies. *IEEE T-ITB*, 12(4), 501-512.
25. Miller, T. & Stasko, J. 2002. Artistically conveying peripheral information with the InfoCanvas. *AVI '02*, 43-50.
26. Monk, T.H. 2010. Enhancing circadian zeitgebers. *Sleep*. Apr 1;33(4):421-2.
27. Oliveira, R.D. & Oliver, N. 2008. TripleBeat: enhancing exercise performance with persuasion. *Mobile HCI*, 255-264.
28. Stepanski, E.J. & Wyatt, J.K. 2003. Use of sleep hygiene in the treatment of insomnia. *Sleep medicine reviews* 7, 3, 215-225.
29. Yaggi, H.K., et al. 2006. Sleep Duration as a Risk Factor for the Development of Type 2 Diabetes. *Diabetes Care* 29, 3, 657-661.
30. Zacone, V. 2003. Sleep Hygiene. *In Principles and Practice of Sleep Medicine*. W.B Saunders Company, 657-661.

Using Mobile Phones to Present Medical Information to Hospital Patients

Laura Pfeifer Vardoulakis[1,2] Amy K. Karlson[1] Dan Morris[1] Greg Smith[1]
Justin Gatewood, MD[3] Desney S. Tan[1]

[1]Microsoft Research
{karlson, dan, gregsmi, desney}
@microsoft.com

[2]Dept. of Computer Science
Northeastern University
laurap@ccs.neu.edu

[3]MedStar Institute for Innovation
justin.s.gatewood@medstar.net

ABSTRACT

The awareness that hospital patients have of the people and events surrounding their care has a dramatic impact on satisfaction and clinical outcomes. However, patients are often under-informed about even basic aspects of their care. In this work, we hypothesize that mobile devices – which are increasingly available to patients – can be used as real-time information conduits to improve patient awareness and consequently improve patient care. To better understand the unique affordances that mobile devices offer in the hospital setting, we provided twenty-five patients with mobile phones that presented a dynamic, interactive report on their progress, care plan, and care team throughout their emergency department stay. Through interviews with these patients, their visitors, and hospital staff, we explore the benefits and challenges of using the mobile phone as an information display, finding overall that this is a promising approach to improving patient awareness. Furthermore, we demonstrate that only a small number of technology challenges remain before such a system could be deployed without researcher intervention.

Author Keywords

Patient awareness; mobile phone; health information

ACM Classification Keywords

J.3 [Life and Medical Sciences]: Health;

INTRODUCTION

Hospital visits are stressful experiences for patients and their loved ones [4]. Anxiety stems from the myriad uncertainties faced during a hospital stay: What is wrong with me? What will they do to fix it? When will I be able to leave? Simple answers to these questions are usually unavailable, but there is evidence that better information flow during a patient's stay can mitigate the impact of the uncertainty. A recent exploration by Wilcox et al. [22] suggests that patient comfort and satisfaction during an emergency department (ED) visit might be greatly improved if, in addition to verbal communication, patients are kept informed of their health status and treatment progress with a real-time, in-room display. The use of dedicated in-room displays for improving patient awareness holds great promise, but also has limitations: privacy is difficult to preserve, patients arrive unfamiliar with the device, displayed information is not portable, and interaction is limited.

Permission to make digital or hard copies of all or part of this work for personal or classroom use is granted without fee provided that copies are not made or distributed for profit or commercial advantage and that copies bear this notice and the full citation on the first page. To copy otherwise, or republish, to post on servers or to redistribute to lists, requires prior specific permission and/or a fee.
CHI'12, May 5–10, 2012, Austin, Texas, USA.
Copyright 2012 ACM 978-1-4503-1015-4/12/05...$10.00.

We hypothesize that mobile devices – increasingly entering the hospital with patients and caregivers – address these limitations and offer an alternative for information delivery in clinical environments. We further hypothesize that presenting medical information on a patient's mobile phone will promote a sense of *information ownership* as a consequence of physical possession of the device, which we anticipate will lead to increased patient engagement.

In order to explore these hypotheses, we present a design for an interactive, mobile-phone-based information display for emergency department patients. Through a field study with 25 patients and their families, we explore the benefits and challenges associated with handheld devices as medical information displays. Our study provides evidence of positive patient responses to personal information displays, and provides guidance for future work in this area.

The specific contributions of this paper are:

(1) A design for a "patient-friendly" handheld information display, including a real-time stream of simplified, abstracted information.

(2) A field study evaluating this design, focusing on the subjective response of patients, family members, and hospital staff.

(3) An exploration into the feasibility of deploying such a display at scale and without researcher intervention, highlighting remaining challenges but demonstrating that this approach is feasible in the near-term future.

RELATED WORK

Patients in the emergency department (ED) are presented with a tremendous volume of information in a short time, much of it critical to medical decision-making and long-term health management. However, due to stress, medication, limited medical literacy, and other factors, patients are unable to absorb and remember information such as care plans and discharge instructions [7,9,11]. This failure to absorb information has immediate impacts on patient satisfaction: Krishel [10] and Boudreaux [3] both find that pa-

(a) (b) (c) (d)

Figure 1: The main screens of our mobile patient interface. (a) The *Health Feed* provides a real-time list of pending and completed care events. (b) The *Profile* page provides general information about the patient's visit. (c) The *Care Team* page provides a record of relevant staff. (d) The *Meds & Tests* page provides a list of medications and tests administered during the patient's stay.

tients who are more informed about their ED process report higher satisfaction and better impressions of care quality.

Perhaps more important is the fact that limited understanding of care has clinical consequences. Patients' access to and understanding of information is directly related to their anxiety levels [4,21]; high anxiety has been shown to correlate with negative clinical outcomes and in-hospital complications during emergency treatment [1,6,14]. Inadequately informed patients often incur repeat visits and fail to comply with discharge instructions [18].

In contrast, encouraging patients to seek more information and ask questions proactively during clinical visits has been shown to reduce anxiety [19], improve compliance with instructions [17], and improve patient satisfaction [8]. Accordingly, clinical facilities often provide patients with pamphlets or other literature to facilitate patient understanding. However, generic, non-interactive materials often contain information not applicable to a given recipient, or are presented at an inappropriate health literacy level, especially for a patient under stress [15,18]. In other words, generic pamphlets often contain an overwhelming amount of information, when patients and family members often want just a short, high-level summary of medical information [21,13]. Consequently, the clinical literature demonstrates significant deficiencies in the effectiveness of paper discharge materials [15,18].

Fortunately, there is early evidence that computer-based displays can provide information that is more patient-friendly and patient-specific than traditional paper materials. Wilcox et al. [22], for example, presented ED patients with paper-based, Wizard-of-Oz prototypes of in-room computer-based displays containing simplified medical information. Patient response to these displays was positive; the displays were found to both calm patients and facilitate communication with family members and providers.

Bickmore et al. [2] take a different approach, presenting hospital patients with a computer-based conversational agent acting as a "virtual nurse" to assist in presenting discharge instructions. Patient response to this approach was positive as well, with most patients indicating that they preferred receiving information from the computer-based agent than from a doctor or nurse.

To our knowledge, almost no work has explored using a mobile device for in-clinic information display. Vawdrey et al. [20] have looked at tablet-based access to a Web portal, but present only early-stage, albeit promising, subjective responses. Other work has shown that the mobile phone is a promising form factor for outpatient, chronic care management [5,12], but did not explore potential in-clinic benefits.

In the present work, we explore the extension of patient-specific, patient-friendly information displays to the mobile phone, which we hypothesize has unique affordances – and ever-increasing availability – that make it a powerful clinical information delivery medium.

THE MOBILE PATIENT DISPLAY

Providing patients with health information on a mobile phone offers several advantages over other form factors. First, care in the ED is dynamic; new information is continually available and courses of treatment may change rapidly. With a mobile display, patients have private access to their current and historical information in near-real time. Additionally, the ED is an inherently mobile environment. Patients can be in testing locations, in the hallway, or inside their rooms. A mobile display gives patients access to their information regardless of their location.

In order to assess our hypothesis that the mobile phone is a promising platform for medical information delivery, we developed a prototype mobile patient display to serve as an experimental probe. The system presented here represents the endpoint of an iterative design process that included a lab-based pilot study in which we assessed the basic usability and intuitiveness of our design prior to conducting our in-hospital study. For brevity, we present only the final version of our design, but we will briefly discuss key lessons learned from our pilot study later in this section.

Guided by [22], we aimed to include as much information from a patient's medical record as possible. Save for a few data points (e.g., physician notes), the interface contained nearly all data recorded about a patient, data typically only available to the medical team.

Our final design was organized into four pages, shown in Figure 1 (a-d). The user can move from screen to screen with horizontal swiping gestures that we anticipated would be familiar to most smartphone users.

The *Health Feed* (Figure 1a) is a real-time view on key events occurring on a patient's behalf, including administrative events (e.g., being assigned to a room) and medical events (e.g., being administered a medication). When appropriate, each event is associated with a short explanation, such as "to check your heart". This information structure was intended to be familiar to users accustomed to social media feeds, and to be compatible with quickly glancing at the application when engaged in other tasks. The "next up" section of the *Health Feed* contains a dynamic, short description of a patient's next step in their care plan. The *Profile* page (Figure 1b) provides demographic information and general information about the patient's visit, which previous work [22] suggests is surprisingly important in confirming to patients that their medical identity is correctly represented in the system. The *Care Team* page (Figure 1c) provides the names, titles, and pictures of current or past assigned care staff. Finally, the *Meds & Tests* page (Figure 1d) provides a reverse-chronological list of medications and tests administered during the patient's stay, with a short (2 to 23 word) explanation of each.

All medication and test names in Figure 1 can be clicked for more information, revealing a page with additional detail – typically a short paragraph (Figure 2). These "more information" pages contain further links to in-depth online information, at sites approved by hospital staff (e.g., NIH MedlinePlus). Each page also contains an "email this" button, which allows a patient to quickly email information to herself or to family members.

Pilot Study

We recruited 12 people (8 male) from the general population of the Seattle, WA area who had recently (within the year) been a patient at a hospital. Participants had a range of technology expertise and education levels, were between 20 and 52 years old (median 34), and most (10) owned

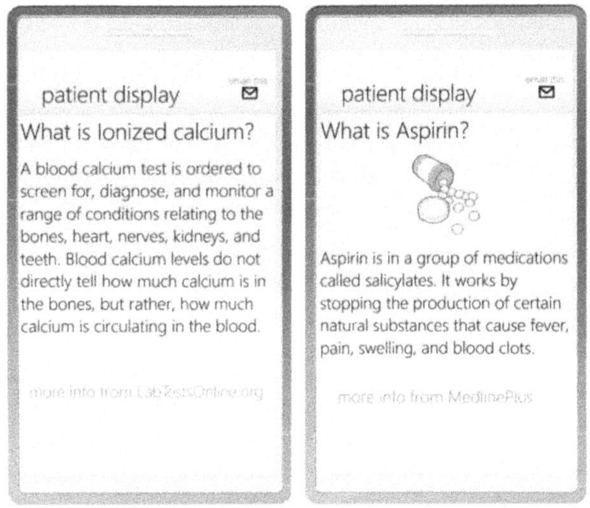

Figure 2: Clicking links on the main screens reveals more detail about tests or medications. Clicking links on these "details" pages opens an approved online resource in a browser.

smartphones. The evaluation consisted of two phases: an interview and a technology probe. We began by conducting a semi-structured interview about the hospital visit in general, focusing specifically on aspects relating to information access and communication during the stay. During the second half of the evaluation we directed the participant's attention to the mobile patient display, which we prepopulated with data for a fictional patient. Participants provided feedback using a think-aloud protocol and answered questions about perceived usability.

Overall, participants were highly receptive to the interface design and information contained in the display, but they did raise several consistent suggestions, which were incorporated into our final design. Our original prototype included a *Vital Signs* page, which was deemed to provide an unnecessary level of detail that was hard for patients to interpret. Our original mechanism for emailing content used a button labeled "share", which interestingly elicited strong negative responses by evoking notions of sharing via social media, such that even patients who *did* want to email content to loved ones expressed concern about this feature. Our original prototype incorporated information about medications and tests only into the *Health Feed*; patients requested more detail about these information categories relative to other items on the *Health Feed*, so they were eventually promoted to a dedicated page.

EMERGENCY DEPARTMENT STUDY

To understand the impact such a system might have on patients, visitors, and care staff, we deployed our final prototype and conducted a field study in an urban emergency department. All procedures were approved by the hospital's institutional review board.

Wizard-of-Oz Infrastructure

In this study, we used a semi-automated approach to populating mobile displays in real-time. Specifically, we pulled information from the electronic medical record (EMR) and other sources into an application running inside the hospital network, from which study administrators could send information to patients' mobile phones. This was intended to simulate the fully-automated experience from the patient's perspective (the "wizard" was entirely invisible to participants), while satisfying the hospital's requirement for this study that a human screen all data presented to patients.

Due to logistic and security issues involved in connecting phones to the hospital's infrastructure, we provided Samsung Focus smartphones to participants for the duration of their stay, rather than allowing participants to use their own devices. Our study infrastructure was designed to safeguard data: each phone used a private key to secure an authenticated, encrypted connection to the administrative application, and the administrator could revoke a phone's credentials at any time. Medical data on the phone was stored in memory only, and was discarded when the application was exited or when the phone was locked (which occurred automatically after 5 minutes of non-use). To examine how patients used the prototype, we logged application launches, touch events, page transitions, and link clicks.

The administrative application is written in C#; it hosts a Web service for communicating with the phones, incorporates a SQL database client layer for extracting data from the EMR, and maintains a set of local database files for logging actions by both administrators and patients. The left side of the application's single-patient view (Figure 3) displays information currently visible to the patient's phone. The right side ("EMR Data") exposes non-editable patient data as it exists in the hospital database for the administrator to screen. Double-clicking an entry in this area creates a copy in the lower-right corner of the view that can (optionally) be edited prior to "submitting" to the phone. Entries in the lower-right can also be created from scratch for information derived from sources other than the EMR. Entries submitted to the phone can be edited or deleted at any time, giving the administrator full control over the patient's view.

Procedure and the Role of the Wizard

After a patient consented to participate in the study (see "Participants" for information about recruiting), she was given a 2-4 minute tutorial about the interface, encouraged to ask questions, and left to use the device.

The study administrators worked "behind the scenes" to collate data from multiple sources and submit data updates to the patient's phone. Each time administrators pushed new data to the phone, an audible alert signaled the patient. Updates were generated by administrators based on three sources: 1) EMR orders and results (e.g., *"The lab is processing your blood work"*); 2) physical observations of staff visits (e.g., *"You had a surgery consultation"*); and 3) discussions with the care team about the patient's care plan (e.g., "*You will be admitted to the hospital*"). The descriptions for all entries were pulled from a list of medication, test, and feed entry templates. To provide personalized content, more specific templates were occasionally created from existing ones (e.g., a chest x-ray "to check your heart and lungs" might be altered to "to check your heart"). All such edits and additions were logged. As we will discuss later, examining the precise role that the wizard played allows us to explore the potential for full automation.

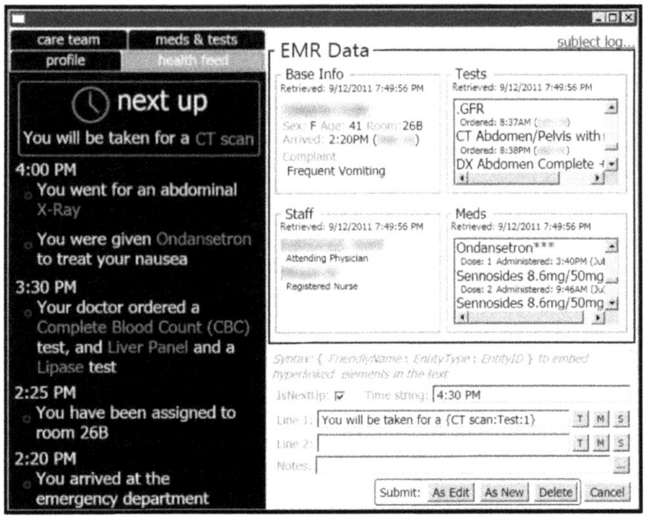

Figure 3: The application used to manage the transfer of data from the EMR to patients' phones. Here, the administrator is editing a "next up" entry for the *Health Feed.*

Each patient participated in a final semi-structured interview. The interview lasted 10-20 minutes, was audio-recorded, and was conducted by the consenting administrator while another administrator took notes. The interviews covered a broad range of patient reactions to the phone, including: what they liked or did not like; how they interacted with the phone; how the phone impacted their visit; and how they shared the information with visitors or family members (if at all). Upon completion of the interview, each patient received a paper-based representation of their personalized information display that they could take home.

Participants

We conducted our study in the Emergency Department (ED) of a large urban hospital in Washington, DC, over a two-week period in July 2011. We teamed with attending physicians to screen candidates using the following criteria: patients needed to be English-speaking, over 18, feeling well enough to converse, mentally stable, not contagious, and expected to be in the ED for at least an hour. There was no payment or incentive for participation.

We recruited and consented a total of 27 patients. However, two were released prematurely: one was suspected to be contagious and was moved to confinement, and the other was admitted to the hospital quickly to undergo surgery. Of the 25 remaining participants who completed the study, 17 (68%) were female and 23 (92%) were African-American, with an average age of 46 years. Our study population demographics were similar to those of the 1162 patients who entered the ED during the study period (60% female, 80% African-American, with an average age of 47.8 years). Education levels among participants ranged from middle school (16%), to high school (48%), to college (36%). Twenty-three participants (92%) owned a cell phone and 12 (48%) owned a smartphone.

Family members present with enrolled patients were also invited to participate in interviews subsequent to an IRB-approved consent process. A total of 8 family members or visitors participated in our study.

Finally, we conducted semi-structured interviews with consented hospital staff members. We interviewed 11 hospital staff members, bringing the total number of participants in our study to 44.

RESULTS AND IMPLICATIONS

Our analysis included researcher notes, patient interview audio recordings, and phone usage logs. All notes, augmented by audio recordings, were transcribed and iteratively coded for themes using a grounded theory approach.

We first provide a high-level overview of the patients' phone usage patterns, and then we present the themes gleaned from our data analysis. We describe how patients expressed the alleviation of anxiety and empowerment created by their access to information, as well as the ways in which the medical explanations were perceived as useful. We then transition to findings that are more specific to the use of mobile devices, describing the effect that physical possession of a portable, real-time hospital visit record has on patient memory, information ownership, sharing tendencies, and privacy perceptions. We end this section with observations about the ergonomics of using a mobile device in the hospital, the pragmatics of ensuring content appropriateness at the individual level, and the reactions of healthcare providers – all of which are crucial to consider if we seek to deploy an automated system in the wild.

Phone Usage

Patients had access to the phone for an average of 150 minutes (*sd*=33.6). During this time, patients were presented with an average of 14.4 items, spanning the *Health Feed*, *Meds & Tests*, and *Care Team* pages, including items that were available when patients first received their devices.

Log data revealed that three participants had particularly low usage of the mobile phone display – less than two minutes of total browsing time of the information content: P17, who clearly did not interact with the phone at all after our tutorial, commented that she found the device "too complicated"; P6 only had the phone in his possession for 13 minutes before we were notified of his discharge; and P25 experienced data server connectivity issues that discouraged her use of the phone.

The remaining 22 participants interacted with the phone across an average of 10.8 distinct sessions, where a session was considered ended if the application was explicitly closed or the participant did not interact with the phone for more than 5 minutes. Interestingly, patients only received "alerts" an average of 2.1 times, since in many cases multiple new items were batched into a single "alert". We interpret the fact that that the number of interaction sessions far exceed the number of update notifications pushed to participants' phones as evidence that the information content itself held participant interest over the course of their visit.

Awareness Reduced Anxiety

The most consistent theme that emerged across our participants, mentioned by 21 patients and 5 visitors, was the positive influence that "knowing" or "being in the loop" had on their experiences. Some patients explicitly made the connection between *knowing* and *calming*.

> *"To know, like they say – knowing is half the battle. I mean knowing – this is crazy, but – knowing sort of makes you feel better. Is that crazy?...I think it sort of strips the fear of 'what's next'. It really does."* –P11

> *"[The display] is like the best thing I've seen in a hospital, period ... it calms the person down, because they get a sense of what's going on, what they just went through, what this was for, what it's about, what this test is. That thing is amazing."* –Daughter of P9

> *"...you can actually go to what they're thinking about or what they plan on doing to you and you can see it on the phone. I really loved that... I'm not sitting here guessing and being nervous. What are they looking for? What do they want? What do they see? What do I got to do next? So, this pretty much tells me."* –P12

Patient appreciation for being kept up-to-date was corroborated in interaction logs, where the *Health Feed* page showed the highest mean interaction time of any content page. Patient thirst for information was also evident from the responses we received to questions about the chime-based notification of the system, which we initially thought might be disruptive or annoying. On the contrary, none of the 15 the patients we questioned found the chime annoying and 11 assured us that they wanted updates every time there was something new to be shared with them. (3 other patients had no preference about the timing of notifications, and 1 said it depended on the time of day.)

These findings have several implications. First, patients showed that they indeed *want* access to their medical information in real time. Providing this data is not standard practice during a patient's hospital stay, and patients' desire for real-time access has not been previously shown. Patients enrolled in our study had many reasons not to use the mobile display: they were sick, in pain, tired, had family present, and had access to their own phones. Despite this, they not only used the display, but reported the value it added to their experience, particularly in reducing anxiety. Given that patient anxiety is tied to poorer health outcomes [6], this system has the potential to not only calm patients, but to improve their outcomes overall.

Being "In the Know" Promoted Empowerment

Hospital patients are vulnerable to experiencing a loss of control and dignity, and the resulting disempowerment is a well-known threat to effective medicine and successful outcomes [16]. Patients in our study repeatedly echoed the fact that the phone display allowed them to regain some semblance of participation in their own care:

> *"I didn't know that I needed an X-Ray until I saw it on the phone. So when she came in, I was like 'We're going for an X-Ray.' And she looked at me like 'How'd you know that'? [laughs]. So I really liked that." –P12*

Six patients expressed tension and frustration around doctors being the gatekeepers of information, and expressed relief that phone removed some of their dependence on doctors and nurses for information. As P20 said:

> *"We know they are busy dealing with a lot of patients but sometimes when they come to tell you something, it's like 'Why didn't you tell me this 30 minutes ago?'"*

Family members also echoed that they appreciated having instant access to the most up-to-date information and expressed that the phone display eased the patient's burden of having to bring new visitors up-to-speed with the status of their care. One visitor imagined that the information in the display could enable her to ask more specific questions of the doctor. The aunt of P20 stated: *"And if you have further questions, you know how to go about the questions, instead of just 'well, I wanna know what's wrong,' [you can say] 'this is what came up and I want to know about this.'"*

Somewhat surprising to us was that two patients suggested they perceived the data in the phone to be more authoritative than the staff. P21 stated: *"With someone [...] saying 'oh, we're giving you Zofran and that's for nausea' you have to take their word for it. With this information here, you can click on it and see what that is."*

Patients also expressed pride in being entrusted with the device and having access to the information it contained. P19 was particularly struck by the *Profile* page because he was amazed that it was personalized (*"It's got my name!"*), and he showed the device to his X-Ray nurse and his discharge nurse. P8 invited a volunteer into the room to show her the device, and P16 showed it to her radiologist.

These findings suggest that giving patients real-time updates on their medical care could increase the amount of participatory behavior by patients. As increased participation by patients is shown to improve satisfaction [17] and also improve outcomes [8], these findings are encouraging.

Medical Explanations Were Useful to Patients

One of our design goals was to provide patients information to deepen their understanding of what was being done to diagnose their illness. We were inspired by prior work pointing to the utility of providing short explanations of medications and tests [21,22], as well as our pilot study which surfaced examples where patient "information starvation" had negative consequences. For example, three of our pilot participants recounted situations in which they did not have access to key information to make appropriate decisions about their care plan or to provide truly informed consent. In addition to providing a short, 2-23 word explanation for each medication and test, we included, on demand, an additional 1-6 sentence explanation and a hyperlink to an authoritative website. While we were unable to quantify knowledge transfer or retention, we did look for evidence of whether patients valued this extra information.

Interaction logs revealed that 24 participants navigated to the *Meds & Tests* page. Furthermore, 9 participants explicitly mentioned exploring the more detailed descriptions of medications and tests in our interviews. Interaction logs found that 13 participants clicked through to the details pages of 20 unique tests and medications (an average of 3 unique pages per participant). Nine participants spent more time reviewing medications, tests and related details than in any other part of the interface.

Subjectively, patients often mentioned the significance of the *Meds & Tests* page of the interface. For example, P3 appreciated *"... the educational component, because it describes what the tests are. So, I wasn't laying here wondering, 'what does PTT mean?' I liked that piece of it."* P8 also referred to the interface as "educational", commenting that *"I learned something. It kind of teaches you."* During the interview, she used the phone to bring up an explanation of a test, and said, *"See, I didn't know these things!"* P21 found the test information useful *"because I didn't necessarily know what – hold on – [bringing up the Meds & Tests page] what a lipase test did and what it was. It was to check for inflammation of the pancreas. So when you don't know something, you know. It's good and it gave you enough information to be, you know, to be sure of what it is."* She also made the point that it was useful even if she could not fully grasp what it meant: *"Even though medically you may not know what it is they're doing, it kinda gives you a sense of security that, you know, these are tests that they've taken... You don't have to be a medical doctor."*

Many family members also stated that they appreciated the medical explanations, not only to deepen their own understanding, but also to help their loved one grasp what was happening with regards to their care. The daughter of P9 stated that she spent the most time looking at the *Meds & Tests* page, *"Because it tells you exactly what it means and what it's for. So that's the part that I was on the most. So I can tell her – instead of just saying that it's 'blood work' – I want her to understand exactly what blood work it is, so she'll know from now on."*

These data show that many patients read the optional, more in-depth medical information, and provide additional evidence that patients are interested in the details of their care.

The Persistent History Helped Memory

We found several examples of patients using the phone display as a memory aid throughout their ED visits. Five patients stated that remembering their care team's names was particularly difficult, and appreciated having the names and photos right on their phone. P2 stated: *"Sometimes doctors and nurses come in and you don't remember their names. It's very important to have them."*

Another piece of information that patients valued was simply the timestamp of their arrival time to the ED. Many patients are under high levels of pain and stress upon arrival, and stated that it was often difficult to have a sense of when they arrived, and thus how long they had been in the ED. This small piece of data was surprisingly valuable in reorienting patients within their visit.

Physical Possession and Information Ownership

We recognized that handing patients unfamiliar phones might discourage patient perceptions of "ownership": our device lacked the customization, familiarity, and rich personal context that make mobile phones prized by their owners. So we were particularly surprised to observe that patients were willing and caring guardians of the phones, treating them as personal possessions.

An example of the care that patients took in managing the phone was their physical proximity to the device; for the most part, patients kept the device very close by – either on their chest/stomach or by their side – and the phone accompanied patients to test rooms. Otherwise, patients entrusted the device to family members in the same room. Although it could be argued that patients had few other options for storing the device, interview data suggests that this behavior is better explained by a personal connection that the patients felt toward the device and the data within it.

One simple way that patients implied a sense of ownership was by using possessive syntax, referring to *"my data"* (P5), *"my phone [pointing to the study phone]"* (P12), and *"my property"* (P9). We noted that two participants physically held the phone to their chests during the interview.

Another way that patients demonstrated ownership was by validating the data in the display, in effect taking responsibility for the information presented. Seven participants spoke of verifying their information on the *Profile* page, including their names (P21), reason for visit (P10), home medications (P13, P14), and allergies (daughter of P3, P13, P20); P20 even looked for a way to correct the information the display. Despite the fact that the *Profile* page contained entirely self-reported information, four participants cited the *Profile* page as their favorite page overall.

Finally, ownership was asserted in a more literal sense by the 11 participants that emailed themselves a copy of the phone's content. When asked why they emailed information to themselves, participants offered four primary reasons : 1) to archive it in their own personal records (9 participants); 2) to show to others outside of the hospital (5 participants); 3) to take the time to re-read it at home, allowing them to process it in a calmer state and to go over the information in greater detail (3 participants); and 4) to print the information and bring it with them to their primary care follow-up appointments (3 participants).

In fact, 10 patients expressed a desire to use the phone in order to personally transfer data from their ED visit to their primary care physician or other providers.

> *"For example, I know my doctor should get this information, but by chance if I got to the doctor and they haven't received it, I'll have that information. I keep one of these devices with me at all times, so I can just pull it up on that device and let them see what took place. ... A lot of times, the information doesn't get to the other place as quickly as it should. So I could just pull my device out and give 'em it." –P22*

While it is impossible to determine causality from these observations, these observations suggest that the physicality of the mobile phones created a bond between patients and the information contained within.

Sharing Data with Visitors and Loved Ones

Of the 11 patients who had family members present in the ED, 10 chose to share the phone display with their family members. For two patients, the family member was the primary user of the display. In one of these cases, the patient did not have her glasses, so her daughter used the phone and read the information aloud. In the other case, the patient was feeling weak and had her great-granddaughter use the phone. The other eight patients would co-use the display, and would often pass the phone back and forth between their family member(s) and themselves in order to read the latest information.

Fifteen patients thought that the phone could assist in keeping loved ones *outside* the hospital up-to-date. Many expressed that it might keep their family members from worrying and rushing to the ED.

> *"I could email this to my daughter. Because a lot of times when I'm in the hospital she'll run up here and she's so worried. I could email it to her and let her know that I'm alright – you don't have to come, stay with the kids, and she would be more relaxed." –P13*

However, P24 pointed out that there are nuances to sharing information with family members outside of the hospital. This patient thought about emailing his information to his mom, but because the doctors had not yet made an official diagnosis, he worried that the lack of information would make his mother more concerned than she already was.

We explored various options for information sharing – asking patients if they preferred finer control over who sees what data. Overwhelmingly, patients expressed that they wanted family members to see everything about their visit. They would either share all of their data with someone, or share none of it. Many patients conveyed that they are often in pain or drowsy, and it is a challenge to remember important details of the visit. Patients found it comforting to know that a family member was aware of their health status and care plan and could better serve as their advocate.

> *"I think most people, when they come to the ER, if they bring somebody with them, they're bringing them because they want that person, you know, you don't want to rely on just your own memory. You want someone who knows everything that happened to you."*
> *–Daughter of P3*

One form of sharing that we expected to observe, but did not, was sharing between patients and the ED staff. While several patients showed the phone to their care team because they were excited about the technology, none of the patients stated that they co-used the phone with staff in order to ask questions or discuss medical information. Face-to-face interactions between patients and physicians in the ED are often brief, focused, and highly anticipated, which most likely dissuaded patients from introducing conversation outside of the topics at hand.

Nevertheless, we found that the small and familiar form factor of the phone allowed for sharing in a natural way: physical sharing among present family members and virtual sharing via email. As many patients expressed a desire to share their data with remote family members, subscription-based sharing could be a valuable feature to explore.

The Phone Helps Preserve Privacy

Overwhelmingly, patients were not concerned with having information from their medical record on the phone. Patients appreciated their ability to guard the information and have control over who sees their data. Eleven patients specifically stated that the phone's small form factor, and knowing that passersby and roommates would not be able to see their health information, provided a sense of privacy.

> *"Yeah, like I said, no one has it here but me and it doesn't stay on all the time so that's good too. So if you leave it sitting here, it's not like somebody's peering at what's going on." –P17*

One patient pointed out that even though she wasn't concerned with having her data on the phone, she would feel more comfortable having the phone password-protected, in case it was misplaced. Ideally, with patients using such an application on their own device, they would be able to personally choose their desired level of security.

Ergonomics Issues Exist, But Are Not Overwhelming

With almost all patients being hooked to vitals monitors and IVs, we expected that patients might face ergonomic challenges trying to use a touch-based phone during their visits. However, we discovered that these impairments generally did not pose a problem. Most patients found a comfortable position from which use the phone, even if it was using their non-dominant hand. The interface required only simple, one-finger gestures, allowing patients to navigate through the various screens, even if only with their thumb.

Surprisingly, the most common impairment faced by patients was poor eyesight, often as a result of not having access to their glasses. Six patients faced this issue. For some, the phone form factor worked well, because they could hold it close-up and read the information well. Others utilized family members to help them with the phone.

We explicitly asked 23 participants whether a different form factor might have worked better for them. Only 5 stated a preference for a different device type, citing needs for larger text (4) and reduced physical handling of the device (1). Noting that a large-text mode could easily be incorporated into the display design, we find that overall the phone appears to be ergonomically well-suited to the in-clinic medical information display task.

Automating the Mobile Patient Display

In this section, we reflect on the role of the study administrators in supporting the prototype, to gain insight into the technology that would be required to completely automate this system. We will demonstrate that although administrator screening of information was required in order to comply with IRB requirements, automation of a patient-friendly mobile display is feasible in the near-term future.

While the study hospital used a mix of paper and electronic medical records, the vast majority of display content was pulled directly from the hospital's EMR. Data that required no human intervention included the patient name, arrival time in the ED, home medications, allergies, patient room number, names and timestamps for medication orders and administrations, test orders and results, and care team assignments. Other data that was drawn from the EMR required a small amount of manipulation. The chief complaint field of the EMR was entered free-hand and often included short-hand notation, which we expanded into patient-friendly terms to populate the "reason for visit" field on the *Profile* page. In addition, medications and tests were often recorded in the paper chart before they were entered into the EMR; if time permitted, the administrator updated the patient display to indicate that medications and tests had been ordered before this data was available via the EMR.

Prior to our field deployment, we worked with physicians to create a database of metadata for medications, tests and staff. The database included a short explanation, a long explanation, and an external resource (URL) for each of 47 tests and 106 medications, as well as staff photos drawn from an electronic staff directory. Administrators were responsible for matching medication and test names in the EMR to the database entries, and making any necessary adjustments to the short explanation. Over the course of study, a total of 106 tests (24 unique) and 17 medications (11 unique) were administered, which required the addition of 3 tests and 4 medications to the database. The only modifications that administrators made to explanations were for "Chest X-ray" and "X-ray", which the administrator customized to the body part being analyzed (e.g., "to check your lungs" vs. "to check your heart"). The low involvement by the administrator in customizing the medication and test content pushed to patients' phones suggests that this is a highly automatable aspect of the user experience.

The most significant role that the administrators played was in updating the *Health Feed* with information about the progress of the patient's care. While in practice the feed entries were generated based on human observation, we were guided by a list of standard phrases, the majority of which were triggered by events documented in the paper chart or EMR (e.g., when the patient arrived at the ED, when vitals were taken, when tests and medications were ordered, when results had returned); we expect automation of this process to be straightforward. Other feed entries relied on an administrator having observed a doctor or nurse visiting the patient's room; these events are not as easily automated today, but could be in the future through staff tracking, e.g., by RFID systems, which are increasingly common in hospitals. The "next up" aspect of the *Health Feed* presents the most significant challenge to automation. While the majority of the entries pushed to patients were based on loose rule sets that could reasonably be automated (e.g., if blood tests were ordered, then "next up" might be "your blood work will be processed"), some would require patient tracking, (e.g., if patient returned to her room from a CT Scan, then "next up" might be "the radiologist is reviewing your CT Scan"). Moreover, some feed entries depended entirely on discussions with staff members who provided context about the patient's visit that was not reflected in the EMR (e.g., "the patient will be admitted to the hospital, we're just waiting for a bed to become available"). Accurately capturing this knowledge might best be accomplished in collaboration with care staff, who might be willing to enter a one-line update in cases when observable events don't readily predict a patient's care plan. Indeed, if the benefits to patients of making this information readily available can be proven, hospital staff will likely be more willing to submit edits or update their EMR infrastructure to further support such a system.

Content Appropriateness

The content of our prototype was by nature an incomplete representation of a patient's care progress; for example, we could not observe most interactions that the patient had with care staff, so patients' *Health Feed* pages were often missing those interactions (e.g., "your doctor discussed your test results with you"). Furthermore, about half of the *Health Feed* entries captured events that the patient knew about personally (e.g., "you arrived at the ED") so were not necessarily adding to the patient's overall awareness.

So when we asked patients whether data was missing from the phone and whether they felt the information was appropriate to their situation, we were surprised that the vast majority of patients felt that the phone content was not missing any information or events, did not contain extraneous information, and applied to the patient's current situation. Two patients noticed that their allergies were not in the system, one noticed that her "reason for visit" did not match what she had told the intake nurse, and one noticed that an in-room exam was not reflected in the *Health Feed.* We consider this feedback encouraging, because it suggests that our approach can be scaled-up and still feel personal.

Provider Feedback and Response

A critical factor for the success of any hospital technology is the support of physicians and nurses. We interviewed 11 members of the hospital staff – including attending physicians, resident physicians, and nurses – in order to gain their insights and opinions of the patient phone display. Ten out of the eleven care team members reacted positively to the phone display. Physicians were keenly aware that they have little time with each patient, so they liked the phone's ability to keep patients aware of their care status – especially letting the patients know what is next in their care plan. Six of the seven physicians did not want patients to automatically receive test results and diagnoses on the phone, but were supportive of all other information categories.

While physicians focused on the phone's content, nurses were more focused on the phone's impact on their workflow. The four nurses interviewed expressed positive reactions toward the phone, but were concerned that they would be burdened with providing technical assistance. However, they did suggest that a phone-based display could ease tensions between staff and patients by answering common questions. Our patient interviews supported this view, with 6 patients specifically mentioning how busy the staff was or not wanting to bother them with questions.

LIMITATIONS AND FUTURE WORK

Although the present study provides preliminary evidence that the mobile phone is suitable as an information display medium in the ED, and that our proposed design reflects a promising organization and level of simplification, limitations in this study suggest that follow-up work is necessary. The relatively small size of the study prevented us from exploring quantitative, controlled measures of satisfaction, comprehension, and particularly retention and post-visit compliance. A larger follow-up study should explore these variables, and most importantly explore the relationship between mobile information delivery and clinical outcomes.

Furthermore, we hypothesize that the use of a patient's *own* mobile phone for information delivery in the hospital will increase access to information on the same device after a clinical visit. Our current methodology did not allow us to explore this: future work, pending the development of a sufficiently cross-platform infrastructure, will explore the consequences of using a patient's own phone on post-visit use. Using a familiar device is also expected to increase the feelings of ownership and the propensity for sharing that were suggested during the present study, but future work is require to verify this. Using patients' own devices comes with challenges, however: design iteration may be required to find a balance between surfacing salient medical information and allowing patients to use their phones for communication and "passing the time".

Similarly, our work was focused on the ED; different medical domains come with different pacing and different patient information needs. Therefore, future work will be required to see whether our design and lessons learned generalize to other medical domains.

Finally, as suggested in the previous section, some amount of work is still required to automate our mobile information display before it can be deployed at scale. This is an exciting area for future work, as it spans HCI, clinical informatics, and natural language processing.

CONCLUSIONS

In this study, 25 emergency department patients and 8 family members utilized a dynamic mobile phone interface presenting near-real-time data surrounding their medical status, care plan, and care team during their visit. Feedback and observations suggest that this approach is an extremely positive direction for reducing patient anxiety, improving awareness, promoting patient empowerment, and enhancing ownership of medical information in hospitals.

ACKNOWLEDGEMENTS

We thank Asta Roseway for visual design contributions.

REFERENCES

1. An, K., De Jong, M., Riegel, B., McKinley, S., Garvin, B., Doering, L., Moser, D. A cross-sectional examination of changes in anxiety early after acute myocardial infarction. *Heart Lung*, 33:2 (2004), 75-82.
2. Bickmore, T., Pfeifer, L., Jack, B. Taking the time to care: Empowering low health literacy hospital patients with virtual nurse agents. *Proc ACM CHI 2009*, 1265-1274.
3. Boudreaux, E., O'Hea, E. Patient satisfaction in the ED: a review of the literature and implications for practice. *J Emer Med*, 26:1 (2004), 13-26.
4. Byrne, G., Heyman, R. Patient anxiety in the accident and emergency department. *J Clin Nursing*, 6:4 (1997), 289-295.
5. Connelly, K. H., Faber, A. M., Rogers, Y., Siek, K. A., and Toscos, T. Mobile applications that empower people to monitor their personal health. *e & i Elektrotechnik und Informationstechnik*, 123:4 (2006), 124-128.
6. Dahlén, I., Janson, C. Anxiety and depression are related to the outcome of emergency treatment in patients with obstructive pulmonary disease. *Chest* 122:5 (2002), 1633-1637.
7. Engel, K., Heisler, M., Smith, D., Robinson, C., Forman, J., Ubel, P. Patient comprehension of emergency department care and instructions: Are patients aware of when they do not understand? *Ann Emer Med*, 53:4 (2009), 454-461.
8. Greenfield, S., Kaplan, S., Ware, J. E. Expanding patient involvement in care: Effects on patient outcomes. *Ann Intern Med*, 102:4 (1985), 520-528.
9. Kessels, R. P. Patients' memory for medical information. *J Royal Soc of Med*, 96:5 (2003), 219-222.
10. Krishel, S., Baraff, L. J. Effect of emergency department information on patient satisfaction. *Ann Emerg Med*, 22:3 (1993), 568-572.
11. Ley, P. Memory for medical information. *Br J Soc Clin Psychol*, 18 (1979), 245-255.
12. Liu, L., Hirano, S., Tentori, M., Cheng, K., George, S., Park, S., Hayes, G. Improving communication and social support for caregivers of high-risk infants through mobile technologies. *Proc ACM CSCW 2011*, 475-484.
13. Moncur, W., Masthoff, J., Reiter, E. What do you want to know? Investigating the information requirements of patient supporters. *Workshop on Personalisation for E-Health, IEEE 2008 Intl Symp on Computer-Based Medical Systems*, 443-448.
14. Moser, D., Riegel, B., McKinley, S., Doering, L., An, K., Sheahan, S. Impact of anxiety and perceived control on in-hospital complications after acute myocardial infarction. *Psychosom Med*, 69:1 (2007), 10-16.
15. Powers, R. Emergency department patient literacy and the readability of patient-directed discharge materials. *Ann Emer Med*, 17:2 (1988), 124-126.
16. Rogers, A., Karlsen, S., Addington-Hall, J. "All the services were excellent. It is when the human element comes in that things go wrong": Dissatisfaction with hospital care in the last year of life. *J Adv Nursing*, 31:4 (2000), 768-774.
17. Roter, D. L. Patient participation in the patient-provider interaction: The effects of patient question asking on the quality of interaction, satisfaction and compliance. *Health Education & Behavior*, 5:4 (1977), 281-315.
18. Safeer, R., Keenan, J. Health literacy: the gap between physicians and patients. *Amer Fam Phys*, 72:3 (2005), 463-468.
19. Thompson, S.C., Nanni, C., Schwankovsky, L. Patient-oriented interventions to improve communication in a medical office visit. *Health Psychol*, 9:4 (1990), 390-404.
20. Vawdrey, D., Wilcox, L., Collins, S., Bakken, S., Feiner, S., Boyer, A., Restaino, S. A tablet computer application for patients to participate in their hospital care. *Proc AMIA 2011*, 1428-1435.
21. Wilcox, L., Gatewood, J., Morris, D., Tan, D., Feiner, S., Horvitz, E. Physician Attitudes about patient-facing information displays at an urban emergency department. *Proc AMIA 2010*, 887-891.
22. Wilcox, L., Morris, D., Tan, D., Gatewood, J. Designing patient-centric information displays for hospitals. *Proc ACM CHI 2010*, 2123-2132.

Engagement with Online Mental Health Interventions: An Exploratory Clinical Study of a Treatment for Depression

Gavin Doherty
Trinity College Dublin
College Green, Dublin 2
gavin.doherty@tcd.ie

David Coyle
University of Bristol,
Bristol, BS8 1UB, UK
david.coyle@bristol.ac.uk

John Sharry
Mater University Hospital
James Joyce St., Dublin 1
jsharry@mater.ie

ABSTRACT
Online mental health interventions can benefit people experiencing a range of psychological difficulties, but attrition is a major problem in real-world deployments. We discuss strategies to reduce attrition, and present SilverCloud, a platform designed to provide more engaging online experiences. The paper presents the results of a practice-based clinical study in which 45 clients and 6 therapists used an online Cognitive Behavioural Therapy programme for depression. Pre and post-treatment assessments, using the Beck Depression Inventory, indicate a statistically significant improvement in depressive symptoms, with a large effect size, for the moderate-to-severe clinical sub-sample receiving standalone online treatment (n=18). This group was the primary target for the intervention. A high level of engagement was also observed compared to a prior online intervention used within the same service. We discuss strategies for design in this area and consider how the quantitative and qualitative results contribute towards our understanding of engagement.

Author Keywords
Mental health; online interventions; cognitive behavioural therapy; engagement; depression; healthcare applications.

ACM Classification Keywords
H5.m. [Information interfaces and presentation] (e.g., HCI): Miscellaneous.

General Terms
Human Factors; Design.

INTRODUCTION
Mental illness is one of the greatest social and economic challenges facing societies worldwide; depression is already the single most common source of disability in developed countries and is on the increase in many others [31]. While the efficacy of many mental healthcare interventions has been well demonstrated [13], traditional models for the delivery of care have reached a breaking point. In many cases limitations in the availability of trained mental health professionals, coupled with the time intensive nature of treatments, means that only a minority of people experiencing difficulties receive the treatment and support they need [31]. Given the constraints on the capacity of services, issues of cost effectiveness and efficient use of available resources have become important areas of research in mental health service provision. Recent studies in controlled settings have demonstrated the potential effectiveness of computerized or online interventions for many people [29]. Such interventions use computer support to either supplement or entirely replace face-to-face contact with a mental health professional, thereby reducing the cost of individual interventions and increasing overall access to care. However, whilst the effectiveness of online interventions has been demonstrated in controlled settings, problems are commonly encountered in translating these results into practice. Attrition - typically defined as the number of people not completing a course of treatment - is a major problem [17,23,24]. Some strategies for improving engagement and reducing attrition rates in online treatments - such as motivational interviews and telephone support conversations - can be effective, but increase the logistical difficulties, resource requirements and costs of deployment.

Drawing on relevant literature in HCI and mental health, the primary contribution of this paper is to introduce and explore a set of design strategies - *interactive, personal, supportive and social* - to reduce attrition in online interventions. We present a platform that embodies these strategies and investigate clinical outcomes and engagement levels within a detailed, practice-based clinical study. The platform can be used to deliver multiple different programmes; in this paper we focus on a Cognitive Behavioural Therapy (CBT) intervention for depression. This study indicates that the strategies and intervention described in this paper can improve client engagement and reduce attrition rates for online treatment. Clients receiving the intervention also experienced clinically significant improvements in depressive symptoms.

CBT and Online Interventions for Depression
There are a broad range of psychological treatments available for depression [11]. However, the efficacy of CBT has been examined and demonstrated in many more trials than other approaches, making it the most evidence-based and one of the most widely used treatments [7]. It is a structured approach, rooted in both behavioural and

Permission to make digital or hard copies of all or part of this work for personal or classroom use is granted without fee provided that copies are not made or distributed for profit or commercial advantage and that copies bear this notice and the full citation on the first page. To copy otherwise, or republish, to post on servers or to redistribute to lists, requires prior specific permission and/or a fee.
CHI'12, May 5–10, 2012, Austin, Texas, USA.
Copyright 2012 ACM 978-1-4503-1015-4/12/05...$10.00.

cognitive traditions and theories, that has been delivered and evaluated in a variety of ways – as individual and group face-to-face therapy, as well as less traditional methods, such as telephone assisted therapy and bibliotherapy. Due in part to its structured nature, but also to its history of effectiveness, CBT has also become the most widely used approach to computerised or internet-delivered therapy [1].

The central component of online interventions is generally a structured delivery of psycho-educational content, usually through text, audio voiceovers or explanatory videos. Questionnaires are also common, some of which are diagnostic, whereas others are therapeutic, and follow a similar format to that found in paper workbooks. Following initial research studies, bodies such as the National Institute of Clinical Excellence in the UK have recommended computerized CBT as the first port of call for mild-to-moderate depression, and online programmes are being deployed in many countries. HCI researchers have begun to consider the topic of design for mental health [5,15], and engaging young people in treatment [22]. While some work reports on the usability testing of online interventions [12], there remains a need for more research on effective interaction design strategies for online CBT interventions.

ENGAGEMENT

Attrition rates in real world settings are a significant concern for online mental health interventions. Given the increased focus on user engagement in recent HCI research, there is an opportunity for HCI researchers to help improve the design and effectiveness of online intervention programs. Researchers within HCI and the Serious Games community have examined the potential of games to improve motivation and engagement in a range of contexts, including health and education [3,16,19]. Others have looked to games as inspiration for "enjoyable" user interfaces [21]. In 2002 Monk et al. introduced "*funology*" and suggested that HCI was ready for a more fundamental move from "usability to enjoyment" [25]. The term "*gamification*" has been adopted as an umbrella term for the use of gaming elements in non-gaming systems to improve user experience and engagement [14]. Others have discussed strategies of designing for engagement with specific systems, such as public displays [20]. Words such as engagement, fun and play appear frequently in this literature, however Monk et al. [25] also introduce a note of caution, stating that: *"the challenge for HCI research is to systematically address hedonic (non-utilitarian) requirements and combine them with goal orientated requirements"*. This has particular relevance in a mental health context; in previous work we have argued that designers must place an emphasis on engagement with the treatment, rather than engagement with the technology [9].

In this regard, research on engagement with mental health technologies shares many common goals with HCI research on behaviour change [8] and persuasive technologies [18]. Indeed much of this research has been conducted in physical healthcare areas, targeting issues such as exercise and eating habits. The theories and strategies presented in this prior literature can play a valuable role in helping to design more engaging mental health technologies. However mental health research also provides a rich set of theories supporting personal change. The theoretical model in CBT for example, predicts that meaningful and sustained change is best achieved by focusing, not just on behaviour, but on the interrelated nature of thoughts, feelings and behaviours.

STRATEGIES FOR ENGAGEMENT

It is important to note that attrition in mental health is not unique to online interventions, but also affects services offered in more traditional ways [6,23]. In considering strategies for engagement in online interventions, it is therefore helpful to consider the key factors shown to contribute to engagement and successful outcomes in traditional face-to-face interventions. Outcome focused research [2] has shown that - above and beyond the contribution of specific theories and techniques - client or personal factors are the single leading contributor to successful mental health interventions. Interventions are most likely to be successful if they take advantage of the clients' existing strengths and resources and if treatment is tailored to meet their needs and interests. After personal factors, supportive therapeutic relationships are the next most important factor in maintaining engagement and achieving successful outcomes. In this paper we build on these findings and consider four key strategies to improve engagement in online mental health services: *interactive, personal, supportive and social strategies*.

The first strategy - *the interactive strategy* - draws most obviously on interaction research. Previous online mental health programmes have typically incorporated limited interactive capabilities. Many provide very linear pathways through the overall content, providing limited scope for user exploration and discovery. Until relatively recently, the ability to provide a more interactive experience was constrained by the available web technologies, however we now have an opportunity to provide richer and more varied exercises, provide immediate graphical feedback, and provide users with the ability to engage actively rather than passively receive content.

The second strategy is to provide a more *personal* experience, including content that is tailored to the user's needs, and giving users a sense of ownership and control, e.g. by allowing them to choose their own pathway through an online treatment. While there is some emerging work on tailored programmes, this research is very much in its infancy. Alongside the potential benefits, tailored treatments can create difficulties when implementing controlled clinical evaluations. For example, personalised approaches are more likely to be acceptable if there is a well-defined and strictly implemented protocol on tailoring, which would make the intervention more amenable to formal evaluation within an RCT format.

Current evidence regarding engagement with online interventions suggests that a guided self-help model is most effective in improving adherence [1,29]. The success of motivational interviewing and regular telephone conversations with therapists (often combined) suggests that human contact is important for achieving high levels of engagement. There are a number of different ways in which we might achieve this within an online intervention. One mode, which we can label the *supportive* strategy, follows the existing model for guided self-help and facilitates contact with a therapist or other trained supporter. Such contact would be used to motivate, increase confidence in the therapy (a factor in successful outcomes), and guide the client in completion of therapeutic activities.

Our final strategy is to facilitate contact with some form of community (the *social* strategy), most obviously peers who are suffering, or have previously suffered from, similar difficulties. While there are obviously ethical concerns surrounding such contact - e.g. the potential for people experiencing difficulties to engage, often unintentionally, in negatively reinforcing discussions - there is a long tradition of both group-based therapy and peer support networks for a range of mental health disorders. When appropriately moderated and supervised, they are generally well regarded by practitioners, and seen as vital in the treatment of some conditions. HCI researchers have also begun to provide a deeper understanding of the potential of social networks in healthcare, e.g. [26,28,30]. Issues such as the differing attitudes to disclosure, in general versus health-focused networks [26], are highly relevant to the mental health area.

THE SILVERCLOUD PLATFORM

We have developed SilverCloud, a novel platform that provides tools to rapidly prototype and implement a wide range of online computer supported treatment programmes. Programmes created with SilverCloud aim to provide a more engaging and supportive experience to users. To date two treatment programmes have been developed - a psycho-educational programme for self-esteem and body image difficulties; and a CBT-based therapeutic programme for depression. In this paper we focus on the CBT programme, entitled MindBalance.

The SilverCloud system is implemented as an online application, which is accessed through a web browser. Where possible, the design draws on familiar features from social networking and other web 2.0 applications. Consistent with the model of Coyle and Doherty [10], development of the platform proceeded in parallel with the development of the clinical content, with tight integration of both processes. The content of the MindBalance programme was developed through a multi-disciplinary collaboration including clinical psychologists, psychiatrists and psychotherapists, with regular feedback with the system design team as ideas for content presentation and interaction were prototyped. Design workshops were held with people working in a variety of settings, ranging from

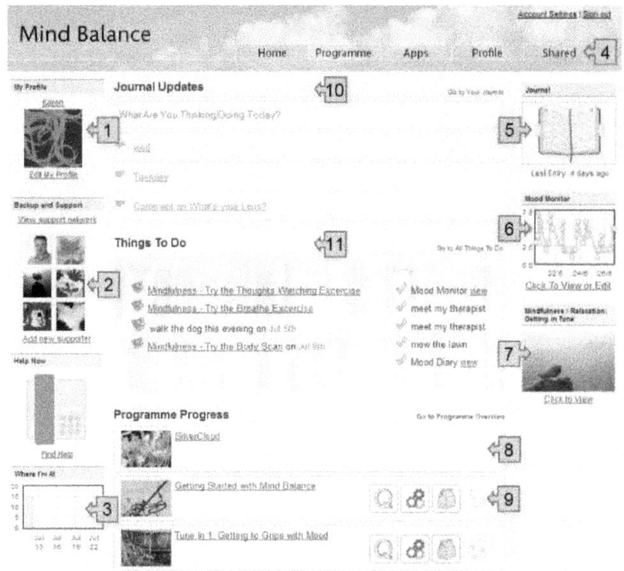

Figure 1. Annotated screenshot of a client homepage.

primary care, to specialized referral services, and included people receiving treatment and youth panels associated with NGO's in the mental health sector. The clinical content is based on a review of literature and of best practice in CBT, coupled with interviews with researchers and practitioners. A detailed non-clinical pilot study, of both the system and programme content, was conducted prior to the clinical study presented in this paper.

The MindBalance programme applies a guided self-help model. Clients seeking help for depression can register for the online programme. Each client is assigned a therapist, who acts as their supporter while they use the programme. MindBalance consists of eight modules that introduce the major concepts of CBT, one of which (Core Beliefs) is unlocked at the discretion of the therapist, if they feel the client is ready for what may be an emotionally challenging experience. The user can take a linear path through all of the content if they wish (it is easy to do so), but they have complete control over what they view and in what order, and can take a more exploratory approach if they prefer.

In next section we discuss the overall design of the SilverCloud platform - within which MindBalance is delivered. We focus on the four strategies for user engagement outlined above. Figure 1 shows an annotated client homepage for the MindBalance programme.

Design Strategies

Interactive – The MindBalance programme includes a number of interactive and graphical exercises (see Figure 2), which are aimed at engaging clients with therapeutic exercises commonly used in CBT; for example, reflecting on their own thinking. Users also have the ability to respond to content, indicating whether they like it, and also to comment on it. Both exercises and comments can be explicitly shared with the therapist or supporter. The system also provides immediate feedback wherever possible. For

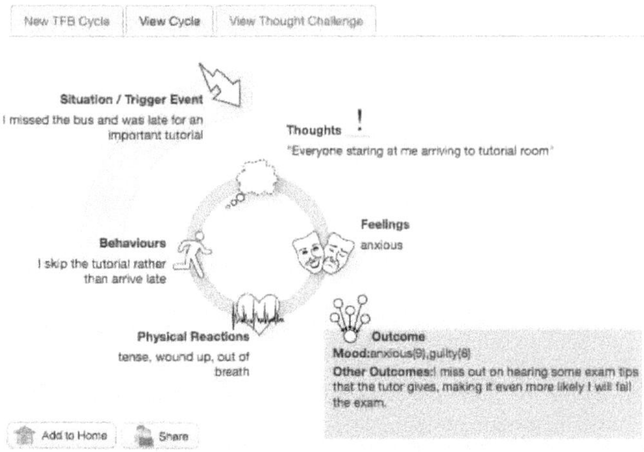

Figure 2. Thoughts, Feelings and Behaviours exercise.

example, when a charting exercise such as a mood chart (Figure 1, element 6) or a diagnostic element such as the outcome rating scale (Figure 1, element 3) is completed, the application icon is graphically updated on the user's home page (e.g. with a graph of mood scores). Likewise, items are ticked off on the "to do" list when completed (Figure 1, element 11), and achievements unlock new activities the within the overall programme.

Personal – previous online treatment programmes have adopted a largely content-focused approach. When clients log into the system they are presented with links to a series of modules, which are undertaken in a linear manner. MindBalance aims to provide a more person-focused approach. Each time clients log in to the system they arrive at a personalized home page, which is about them and where they are in the programme. As well as the central therapeutic content, links to which are embedded within the personalized homepage (Figure 1, element 8, 9), a range of satellite applications are presented along the side of the interface. The client can also create a personal profile with basic information about themselves (Figure 1, element 1). As well as establishing a sense of ownership, this information is useful for the therapist (discussed below). Applications are released over time, such as the mindfulness application (Figure 1, element 7), as the user completes modules (with the intention of maintaining engagement by introducing new features over time and not overwhelming the user initially). The user can also control which applications appear on their home page. Overall the homepage is intended to provide a reflective space; the user can journal their thoughts and feelings (Figure 1, element 10), and these can be elaborated on within the journal application (Figure 1, element 5), which also acts as the vehicle for therapeutic writing exercises. The user has actions suggested in their "to do" list (Figure 1, element 11); these items are added progressively, rather than initially presenting the user with a long and daunting list. Items on the list are ticked off as they are completed, and as the user completes modules of the programme (Figure 1, element 8), their achievements are noted by highlighting a range of achievement icons (Figure 1, element 9).

Supportive – The system supports the exchange of messages between the client and therapist, but goes beyond electronic mail as the client is encouraged to share their content (such as completed exercises and comments) with their therapist. This shared content allows the therapist/supporter to respond in a more personal way and provide guidance as well as encouragement to keep using the programme. Adherence information is also available to the therapist, and they can keep track of the client's progress. This is all personally sensitive information, and so a shared tab (Figure 1, element 4) is provided in the client interface where they can check the therapist's view of their data. This includes information on whether they have logged in recently, which modules they have viewed, items they have shared with the therapist, and a history of messages exchanged with the therapist through the system. This interface includes the ability to explicitly change the sharing status of data. By making the visibility of their data to the therapist more transparent, we hope to give clients a greater sense of control, whilst also facilitating meaningful interaction with the therapist.

Social – A backup and support network (Figure 1, element 2) draws on a social network metaphor, but mirrors a therapeutic exercise in which the client thinks about the people in their life from whom they can get support, and graphically expresses this on a diagram. While group therapy and peer group support are well established and respected in the area of mental health, introducing contact with other clients within any online system raises a number of understandable ethical concerns. As a first step, we have included a number of anonymous indications of other people in the system. It is important to reassure people suffering from mental illness that they are not alone in experiencing difficulties, and that many other people have experienced similar problems and overcome them. Users can respond to content by indicating that they "like" it (now a common paradigm on the web), and can see how many other people liked it, helping to reduce the sense of isolation. For more detailed contributions shared by users, such as take-home points, tips, and suggested healthy activities, a moderation system is built in to the platform whereby shared user suggestions can be made visible to other users. The structure of the modules themselves also includes a "Personal stories" section, in which the stories of others are presented. Users are asked if they wish to contribute a personal story on completion of the programme, and the hope is that over time, a portfolio of these stories could be built up. There are many other possibilities for future exploration of this engagement strategy, including explicit support for group therapy.

EVALUATION

To assess the effectiveness of the programme, a practice-based evaluation was carried out within a University

Counseling Service. The service caters to a population of approximately 17,000 students with limited resources and has been very progressive in the use of technology. The service had previously used a commercially available CBT system but experienced significant attrition, as measured by an internal trial (n=43) in which 74% of users dropped out by session 8 [27]. This trial provided useful baseline data for the service and a concrete target for improved engagement. Our trial followed a similar protocol and was as close as possible to how the service would actually deploy such a technology in practice.

Methodology

Ethical permission for the study was obtained from the relevant institutional boards. The evaluation used a pre-post study design, with the Beck Depression Inventory (BDI-II) [4] administered online before and after use of the programme. The consent form also included screening questions, with exclusion criteria including suicidality, immediate crisis, and psychosis, but none of these were actually encountered in the study. People who scored as severe in the BDI measurement were interviewed by a clinician before being given clearance to participate in the study, following a protocol used in day-to-day practice. Participants were given active support by a therapist for 8 weeks, and hence would be expected to receive 7 weekly reviews. Therapist supporters were assigned to clients following the usual practice in the service. Participants were also free to continue using the system after the end of 8 weeks. Interaction with the system was logged, and a very conservative session time estimation based on user actions is used (session time data reported below can be taken as absolute minima). Qualitative feedback was also solicited following use of the programme. As part of this, participants were asked what attracted them to the programme, their opinions of the programme, the significance of the supporter, about their use of the sharing feature, and whether they had noticed any changes in their life as a result of using the programme. A debrief session was also held with clinicians.

Participants

Participants were recruited through an email circulated to first and second year undergraduate students. The programme was also advertised on the Counseling Service website. The system was used as a standalone treatment by 28 people. These people received online support from a therapist, but had no direct contact with the therapist. Additionally, once this trial was underway, therapists in the service added 17 further pre-existing clients, who used MindBalance as an adjunct to face-to-face therapy (this was unasked for and unexpected). No incentives for participation were given to either clients or therapists.

Results

Clinical Outcomes

Within our overall client sample (n=45), a sub-sample can be meaningfully investigated for clinical outcome measures. This comprises those clients who were above minimal BDI (n=39), not also receiving face-to-face treatment (n=25), and who completed both the pre and post-intervention measures (n=18). One-sample t-tests revealed no significant difference between pre-intervention scores of the overall sample and the subsample (p=0.91), nor between pre-intervention scores of those who completed the post-intervention measure and those who did not (p=0.86). The reliability of the BDI was also acceptable (Cronbach's alpha, α=0.76). A repeated measures t-test of the pre-post BDI measures (n=18), Table 1, indicates a statistically significant decrease in depressive symptomatology ($p<.01$). Cohen's d was calculated as d=1.59, suggesting a large pre-post effect size. This is a very encouraging result regarding the efficacy of the programme, and supports the conclusion that clients benefited from the intervention and also genuinely engaged with the therapeutic content.

BDI cat. (range)	Pre-score (%)	Post-score (%)
Minimal (0-13)	n=0 (0%)	n=13 (72%)
Mild (14-19)	n=4 (22%)	n=0 (0%)
Moderate (20-28)	n=5 (28%)	n=3 (17%)
Severe (29+)	n=9 (50%)	n=2 (11%)

Table 1. Number of participants in each severity category pre- and post- intervention (sub-sample) n=18.

Engagement

The programme received 552 unique logins from 45 users, yielding an average of 12.3 sessions per user. The average session was 12:46 mins, and involved the user viewing on average 9.7 pages of content (a video page is viewed as a single page view). Communication oriented sessions (where the client is viewing and sending messages to the therapist, similar to email therapy) made up 36% of the total. The other 64% we characterize as content-oriented sessions (where the client is going through the psycho-educational content of the programme), and had a longer average session time of 19:49 and an average of 23 content views. Among the clinical subsample (n=25), average session length was 13:00 with 14.1 sessions per user, with a total time in system of 3:03:07. Figure 3 illustrates the level of engagement with the programme for the clinical subsample (n=25). The baseline data is expressed on a session basis, and so this graph depicts the number of users who completed a given number of sessions. 80% of participants were engaged (actively logging in to the system) at sessions 3, 4 and 5, and 64% of participants achieved the target 8 sessions. The figure also allows comparison with the engagement pattern reported by Richards [27] in an evaluation of a widely-used computerised CBT programme utilising no therapist support. Our study took place within the same student counselling service and following a very similar protocol. Taking drop-out to mean the number of participants not engaged at session eight, the drop-out rate

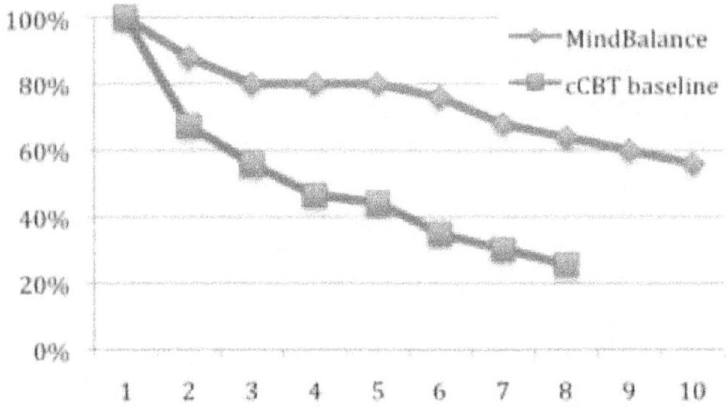

Figure 3. Engagement figures over time vs. baseline data.

for the present study stands at 36%. This compares with a drop-out rate of 74% reported by Richards [27].

As well as number of sessions, we can look at the engagement over time. As might be expected given the weekly review protocol, usage follows a similar pattern to the session data. At week 8 and beyond, 64% of users in the clinical subgroup (n=25) were still using the system. Among the overall cohort (n=45), including minimal cases (n=6), the figure is 60%. When we examine engagement by BDI category, differences can be observed (Table 2).

	Minimal n=6	Mild n=11	Moderate n=11	Severe n=17
Target	33%	55%	73%	71%
Sessions	5.3	13.6	9.1	15.9
Time	35:40	3:21:13	2:30:36	2:54:30

Table 2. Breakdown of engagement figures by BDI

While, as expected, users with minimal BDI engaged least, mild BDI users fared much better. Contrary to what might be expected, severely depressed users seem to have engaged extremely well with the system. Also surprising is that those who used the system combined with face-to-face engaged well, with 77% achieving the target 8 sessions (we comment further in the clinician feedback section below).

Patterns of use

All of the different features and applications were used by some users. A range of different patterns of use were visible in the log data. Usage patterns are illustrated in figure 4; programme content is illustrated by the vertical axis (each number representing a full module), user activity over the horizontal axis (each point is a page view or activity). Different colours indicate different login sessions. Many people took a very linear path through the data, viewing practically all of the content (figure 4 top). However, a significant number of people with good adherence took a more exploratory approach (figure 4 bottom). Such data presents an opportunity to begin looking for features which can be used to retrospectively understand engagement. This might lead us to modify the content or the delivery of content, to rectify problems or to take advantage of popular

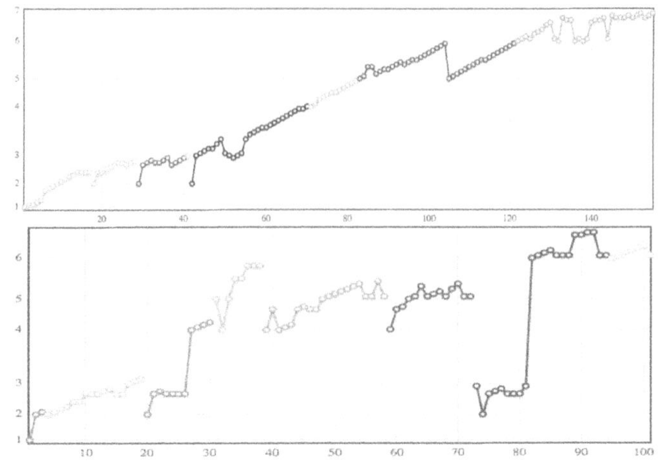

Figure 4 – User interaction patterns

features. If a large enough corpus can be gathered, there is also an opportunity to develop a more predictive approach in which the content or delivery is adapted to particular groups of users, their needs, and preferences.

Qualitative feedback.

Here we present a brief exploration of qualitative feedback provided by 25 of the clients who used the system, in response to the questions listed in the methodology section. These shed some light onto the issues surrounding the different engagement strategies used within the system.

Why did people sign up to the programme?

Immediate need was a factor for several people: *"I wanted anything that could help", "I was feeling very depressed at the time".* Convenience was also important: *"It seemed like something that would help me without interfering too much with my schedule or activities, something I could participate in from home."*

Several people were quite explicit that the online (and not face-to-face) modality was a draw for them: *"I was initially drawn to the fact it was online and easily accessible.", "I felt I would be more comfortable in doing an online programme than face-to-face counseling."*

Curiosity and novelty also seemed to play a role for some: *"it's convenience and to try something new", "It sounded interesting."*

Several clients were also referred to the system by the Counseling Service. This could be a common modality in many services, but referred clients may differ from those who made an explicit initial request for the online offering.

Sharing

As it is one of the novel aspects of the platform, the exit questionnaire included specific questions regarding use of the sharing feature. Among those who made use of the feature, a variety of motivations are touched on, getting feedback: *"I wanted as much feedback as I could get on what I was going through"*, taking advantage of a non-judgemental contact: *"They didn't know me, and therefore were not in a position to judge me"*, feeling safe in sharing:

"Having grown up with the internet, it's become something of a diary for me, but more of an impersonal one. I shared a lot on this because I felt a lot safer using the service", and doing their best to engage properly with the therapy: *"I did share quite a lot because I thought I might as well give it everything and be honest"*. Several comments were also made about trust in the supporter and their discretion.

Among those who made limited or no use of the sharing feature, not wanting to open up to a stranger (caution, shyness and embarrassment are all expressed), and fear of judgement were common: *"I find it difficult to"*, *"I was afraid the assigned support person would be judgemental or intrusive."*

The impersonal nature of online contact, while a positive for some clients, limited sharing in two cases: *"No I didn't like the idea of sharing something with someone when it feels very impersonal by doing it over a computer."*

Support

As a form of guided self-help, some sense of connection with the supporter would seem to be important, particularly for online-only clients. Many comments indicate that simply knowing that someone is there is significant:

"I felt no longer alone. I felt that I had someone to go to. It was comforting. The ability of linking in with a specific therapist was very attractive as it felt more personal."

"It is nice to know someone is monitoring and taking an interest in your progress and that there is someone who will answer any questions you have."

"it was comforting to know that someone was checking in with me and my efforts were not going unrecognised."

"I liked having the supportive comments every week and knowing that someone was monitoring my progress without actually having to meet them in person."

Note that while the monitoring aspect was important to clients, it was repeatedly emphasised that therapists would only look at their data when conducting the weekly reviews, avoiding any expectation of continuous monitoring.

Social

There were few comments relating to the social aspects of the platform, perhaps unsurprising given that these were explicitly designed to be subtle and anonymous. One user indicated that they liked *"other people's reactions to various exercises"*. There are many more possibilities for strengthening the social aspects of the platform, particularly in terms of therapeutic support networks, although as discussed previously there are also ethical concerns. From a design perspective a major challenge will be making the visibility of shared information as clear as possible to users, and providing simple control mechanisms over the sharing and visibility of information.

Personal preferences

Qualitative feedback on what features and content that people liked reinforces the quantitative usage data. There were many different preferences in terms of platform and content. While some people disliked features such as video and quizzes, these same features were very popular with other users. These differences in preference support the rationale of providing a range of different components and experiences, but also motivate improved capabilities to tailor programme delivery based on client's preferences.

Concerns

It could be argued that some negative feedback may actually be for the better - confronting difficult issues might ultimately be cathartic for clients but is not likely to be a pleasant experience at the time. However, most of the concerns raised do not appear to fall in this category, and raise a number of interesting design challenges.

Unsurprisingly, confidentiality was a major concern for clients. Even though a number of changes had been made following the pilot, some were still unsure who could see information that they shared. This is distinct from the sharing issue discussed above, where clients know who can see their information, but still don't want to share. One user with a history of major depression dropped out due to extreme concern about privacy of information. Cases like this may be hard to avoid in the mental health area. From a design perspective however, this is clearly an issue that merits further exploration.

Time constraints, and especially the time demands of exams, were frequently referenced by participants. While the university setting is worthy of study in its own right, as many mental health problems emerge at this point, further studies in other settings will provide useful comparison data. The target intervention duration of 8 weeks makes it very likely that overlap with exam preparation and exam-taking will occur. At the same time, these are naturally high-stress periods and may be times of greatest need.

Some participants cited a feeling of pressure imposed by the weekly reviews, however it can be argued that it is better to maintain this in the interests of the client. In practice a flexible approach may be best, where the expectation is of weekly review, but other arrangements may be explicitly negotiated in a way which maintains some pressure and expectation of client effort and progress.

Some comments made reference to the impact of the illness on their ability to engage with the system: *"Reduce the text aspect of the programme as much as possible. When I was feeling especially depressed, the last thing I felt capable of doing was reading through long passages. That felt like homework."*. Again, this would be an interesting topic for future work, and supports the development of personalized and tailored interventions.

Change

While the BDI scores provide quantitative evidence, users were asked if they had made any changes as a result of using the programme. While positive feedback is of course gratifying, the comments provide an indication of the breadth of change accomplished by users: *"My whole mood changed. The programme helped me to open up communication with others that I had unintentionally avoided. Once I became aware of this it really changed how I was feeling and enabled me to cope with the stress I had"*

"My mood improved and I started being more healthy. I started exercising, hanging out with friends, going to college more. There are situations that still trigger anxiety and upset me but they are far fewer."

While the overall results are very encouraging, it is worth remembering that online treatment will not suit all users. Several of the users who did not engage with the programme stated that they found it impersonal and the feedback superficial (we return to this issue in clinician feedback below). From a service design perspective it is important that there are mechanisms by which people can request or be offered face-to-face treatment even if they have initially requested or commenced online treatment. In such cases the online treatment still offers a benefit in terms of encouraging reluctant people to make initial contact with a mental health service.

Feedback from clinicians

A number of debrief interviews were held following the study. To fit in with the working schedules of the clinicians involved, both individual and group feedback was provided. Overall the MindBalance programme was much preferred to the system previously used by this service.

Need for protocol

A small number of clients signed up who were with a different therapist for face-to-face – this was unexpected and the therapists found this somewhat uncomfortable, and wanted an explicit protocol for dealing with it.

Conducting reviews

For each review therapists checked the level of client engagement, examined items shared by the client, and read any messages sent by the client. They then used this information when composing a message to the client. Therapists stated that reviews took between 5 and 15 minutes to complete, but felt that this figure could be improved upon, as much of the time was taken in becoming familiar with the programme - checking the content the client was looking at. It is important to have a clear time benefit for widespread adoption for most services (although this may be less important for some services, who may be more motivated by client preference and need). The provision of a printed manual and an overview of the programme to go on the wall of each therapist was raised during the discussions, as was the need for more training beyond the initial half-day course provided.

Sharing and highly-engaged clients

Therapists took a needs based approach to the reviews. Clients who engaged more with the programme, shared content, and responded to the messages from the therapist got more time *"almost like online counseling"*. Therapists *"felt the therapeutic relationship more"* with those who filled in their profile and completed journal entries. Generally the workload was seen as very reasonable. Initially time was formally scheduled for dealing with MB clients, however therapists also started to use the reviews to fill gaps in their schedule. This may not be desirable, and might need to be resolved at a local level within services.

Sharing and encouraging less engaged clients

Therapists found it hard to give detailed feedback when clients were not sharing with them: *"you would need to remind yourself of who they are"*. When there was not much therapeutic content to the conversation, the therapists didn't see the sending of encouragement and motivational messages as a good use of their skills. The opinion was expressed that this could be done by someone with less training. Decreasing the overhead on the sending of messages to clients who are not engaging with the programme might be one solution to this problem. Other possibilities might include combining with other intervention modalities (telephone support), or recognizing that the online treatment is not working for that client and suggesting a shift to face-to-face if symptoms are severe enough to warrant more intensive intervention.

Use as an adjunct

Several therapists added their own clients to the programme, using it as an adjunct to treatment. As noted above, these clients engaged surprisingly well. Motivations included keeping clients supported if there was an unavoidable gap in treatment of several weeks. Supporting a natural transition as the client nears the end of the 8 face-to-face session entitlement was also mentioned - *"it's empowering...if you've done a body of work with somebody, say I dunno, 4, 6 sessions and...they are coming into their own a little bit and they are starting to manage things...it's I suppose...like taking the training wheels off and letting them do things themselves"*. One counselor who was not CBT-trained would use the programme where she had a client who would benefit from CBT skills, and then use the face-to-face time to focus more on personal issues.

While therapists are understandably protective of their time and skeptical about technology, they are willing to use it if there is benefit to clients. The initial evidence gathered during this trial is one step in this direction, although further investigation is obviously needed.

DISCUSSION - ENGAGEMENT AND ATTRITION

While the two terms are often used together, engagement is more than converse of attrition. In the mental health sphere, there is a distinction between adherence to an intervention and the degree to which clients genuinely engage with the therapy - or even recognize that they really have a problem. Clients also have different levels of need, and some will respond more strongly to treatment than others. Our evaluation has brought such issues into clear focus and highlighted the need for a more nuanced view on outcomes, and what constitutes successful engagement.

From a design perspective, a nuanced view on engagement suggests that flexibility is important when designing technology supported interventions and when assessing attrition. For example, people experiencing mild difficulties - perhaps due to some life event - may benefit relatively quickly from the initial stages of an intervention, but if they feel their difficulty has been overcome, they are unlikely to complete the full intervention. This is understandable and represents a successful outcome in many cases. In the study, several people with minimal symptoms sought the intervention and used it to some extent, although much less than the other groups. This leads us to consider how we might better serve their needs, perhaps through tailored versions of interventions which are more lightweight, and by giving users control over which aspects of the intervention they wish to focus their time on.

On the other end of the spectrum, people with severe difficulties may have problems engaging due to the nature of their illness – severe depression for example. They may require more intensive face-to-face or specialized treatment. The problem is that they may be unwilling to access such treatment, or it may be unavailable to them. In this context a successful outcome for an online intervention might be that the client recognizes the benefits of face-to-face treatment and overcomes their reluctance to attend. While this group engaged surprisingly well within the study, some comments were made about the effect of mood on the ability to engage with the system. Hence, from a design perspective, we would like to better understand how this group might differ from others, and identify opportunities to improve their experience.

From an evaluation perspective, concerns regarding engagement and attrition often lead to study designs that are not fully representative of real world situations. As noted above, those with mild difficulties may achieve successful outcomes, but not complete standardised treatment programmes. People with very mild difficulties cannot be expected to demonstrate measurable improvements in standardized outcome measures and are often excluded from studies. Some people with severe difficulties also may not improve in standard quantitative measures over a relatively short-term intervention. Likewise people with multiple problems (co-morbid or multi-morbid) are usually excluded from studies, even though they may make up a significant portion of the caseload of practitioners. From an engagement perspective, part of the difficulty with this cohort is that they may need content targeting more than one condition, but there is pressure towards precisely defined and somewhat rigid interventions which are amenable to study in randomized controlled trials, rather than personalized interventions. The result of this is that the intervention may not seem as relevant to the client and because of this impact on engagement.

Related to this drive towards standardisation is a tendency towards very linear programme delivery (so that each participant in a trial is known to receive exactly the same intervention). Inflexible linear delivery is not always the best for engagement, as in some cases perhaps only a subset of a programme will be relevant or interesting to the client. People may also have a longer history of interaction with services, and may have seen some of the material before. From a HCI perspective, we might also favour giving control to the user unless there is a strong rationale for doing otherwise. While in some cases clinicians will be very clear that they want linear delivery, there is a need to understand whether providing a more user-driven and exploratory experience might provide a benefit. The different usage patterns observed within the study would suggest that this may be the case. For preventative programs we would strongly favour giving users the freedom to explore issues of more relevance to them.

CONCLUSION

We have presented an innovative platform for the delivery of guided, online mental health interventions, which embeds a number of strategies for improving engagement. Through a practice-based clinical trial we have explored the issues surrounding engagement in real-world service provision. Outcome data for the clinical subsample indicates a substantial benefit to clients, comparable to more resource-intensive treatments. We have also gained some insight on use of the programme as an adjunct to face-to-face therapy. Online guidance yielded engagement comparable to that achieved using more resource-intensive modes of treatment and our programme out-performed the system previously used by the service. From a development perspective, since a platform rather than an individual programme has been developed, there is a relatively low overhead to developing new programmes targeting different disorders and there are many possibilities for future work.

The online, guided self-help model employed may be applicable in other areas of behavior change considered by HCI researchers, including various forms of cardiac rehabilitation, physiotherapy, exercise, and medication adherence. As an example of a personal healthcare system involving both clinicians and end-users it may also be of interest to a range of researchers looking at the design of systems to support users in managing their personal health and health information, particularly where support is provided by clinicians, and data is shared with them.

Acknowledgements

The authors are grateful to James Bligh, Karen Tierney, Orla McLoughlin, Ruth Davidson, and many others who contributed to the project. David Coyle was supported by an IRCSET-Marie Curie International Mobility Fellowship in Science, Engineering and Technology.

REFERENCES

1. Andersson, G. & Cuijpers, P. (2009). Internet-based and other computerized psychological treatments for adult depression: A meta-analysis. Cognitive Behaviour Therapy, 38 (4), 196-205.

2. Assay, T. P., & Lambert, M. J. (1999). The Empirical Case for Common Factors in Therapy: Quantitative Findings. In B. L. Duncan, M. L. Hubble & S. D. Miller (Eds.), The Heart and Soul of Change (pp. 23-55), APA.
3. Baranowski, T., Buday, R., Thompson, D.I., & Baranowski, J. (2008) Playing for Real: Video Games and Stories for Health-Related Behavior Change, American Journal of Preventive Medicine, 34(1):74-82.
4. Beck, A.T., Steer, R.A. & Brown, G.K. (1996). Beck Depression Inventory manual (2nd ed.). San Antonio: TX: Psychological Corporation.
5. Bickmore, T., Mitchell, S., Jack, B., Paasche-Orlow, M., Pfeifer, L. & O'Donnell, J. (2010) Response to a relational agent by hospital patients with depressive symptoms, Interacting with Computers, 22(4):289-298.
6. Brawley, L.R. & Culos-Reed, S.N. (2000). Studying adherence to therapeutic regimens: Overview, theories and recommendations. Controlled Clinical Trials, 21, pp.156–163.
7. Carr, A., What Works with Children (2009), Adolescents and Adults? A Review of Research on the Effectiveness of Psychotherapy. London: Routledge.
8. Consolvo, S., McDonald, D. & Landay, J. (2009). Theory-driven design strategies for technologies that support behavior change in everyday life. Proc. ACM CHI'09. pp.405-414.
9. Coyle, D. & Doherty, G. (2009). Clinical evaluations and collaborative design: developing new technologies for mental healthcare interventions. Proc. ACM CHI'09. pp.2051-2060.
10. Coyle, D., Doherty, G., Sharry, J., & Matthews, M. (2007). Computers in Talk-Based Mental Health Interventions. Interacting with Computers, 19(4).
11. Cuijpers, P., Van Straten, A., Andersson, G. & van Oppen, P. (2008). Psychotherapy for depression in adults: A meta-analysis of comparative outcome studies. Consulting and Clinical Psychology, 76(6), 909-922.
12. Currie, S.L., McGrath, P.J. & Day, V. (2010) Development and usability of an online CBT program for symptoms of moderate depression, anxiety, and stress in post-secondary students, Computers in Human Behavior, 26(6): 1419-1426.
13. Department of Health, (2001) Treatment Choice in Psychological Therapies: Evidence Based Clinical Practice Guidelines. Department of Health, London.
14. Deterding, S., Sicart, M., Nacke, L., O'Hara, K., Dixon, D. (2011) Gamification: using game-design elements in non-gaming contexts. Proc. ACM CHI 2011.
15. Doherty, G., Coyle, D., and Matthews, M. (2010) Design and evaluation guidelines for mental health technologies. Interacting with Computers, 22(4).
16. Dondlinger, M.J. Educational Video Game Design: A Review of the Literature. Journal of Applied Educational Technology, 4 (2007), 21-31.
17. Eysenbach, G. (2005). The law of attrition. Journal of Medical Internet Research, 7 (1).
18. Fogg, B.J. (2009). A Behavior Model for Persuasive Design. In Proc. Persuasive'09.
19. Gee, J.P. What Video Games Have to Teach Us About Learning and Literacy. Palgrave Macmillan (NY), 2003.
20. Jacucci, G., Morrison, A., Richard, G.T., Kleimola, J., Peltonen, P., Parisi, L., Laitinen, T. (2010). Worlds of information: designing for engagement at a public multi-touch display, Proc. ACM CHI 2010, pp. 2267-2276.
21. Malone, T.W. (1982). Heuristics for designing enjoyable user interfaces: Lessons from computer games. Proc. ACM CHI '82. pp. 63-68.
22. Matthews, M. and Doherty,G. (2011). In the mood: engaging teenagers in psychotherapy using mobile phones, Proc. ACM CHI 2011, pp. 2947-2956.
23. Melville, K.M., Casey, L. & Kavanagh, D.J. (2010). Dropout from internet-based treatment for psychological disorders. Brit. J. of Clinical Psychology, 49, 455-471.
24. Meyer, B., Ritterband, L. & Smits, L. (2010). The ins and outs of an online bipolar education program: A study of program attrition. Journal of Medical Internet Research, 12 (5).
25. Monk, A., Hassenzahl, M., Blythe, M., & Reed, D. (2002). Funology: designing enjoyment. Proc. ACM CHI 2002, Minneapolis, USA.
26. Newman, M., Lauterbach D., Munson, S., Resnick, P., Morris, M., (2011). It's not that I don't have problems, I'm just not putting them on Facebook: challenges and opportunities in using online social networks for health. Proc. of CSCW2011
27. Richards, D. (2010), Online treatments for depression: A randomised controlled trial on an adult student population, PhD. Thesis, Trinity College Dublin.
28. Skeels, M.M. and Unruh, K.T. and Powell, C. and Pratt, W. (2010). Catalyzing social support for breast cancer patients. Proc. ACM CHI 2010, pp. 173-182.
29. Spek, V., Cuijpers, P., Nyklicek, I., Riper, H., Keyzer, J. & Pop, V. (2007). Internet-based cognitive behaviour therapy for symptoms of depression and anxiety: a meta-analysis. Psychological Medicine, 37, 319-328.
30. White, M. & Dorman, S.M. (2001). Receiving social support online: implications for health education, Health Education Research, 16 (6):693-707.
31. World Health Organisation (2008), The Global Burden of Disease: 2004 update. WHO Press: Geneva, Switzerland.

Best Intentions: Health Monitoring Technology and Children

Tammy Toscos
School of Health and Human Services
Indiana University-Purdue University
Fort Wayne, IN

Kay Connelly
School of Informatics
Indiana University
Bloomington, IN

Yvonne Rogers
Interaction Centre (UCLIC)
University College London,
London, UK

ABSTRACT
In this paper we describe findings from two studies aimed at understanding how health monitoring technology affects the parent-child relationship, examining *emotional response* and *barriers* to using this type of technology. We present suggestions for the design of health monitoring technology intended to enhance self-care in children without creating parent-child conflict. Our recommendations integrate the study findings, developmental stage specific concerns, and prior HCI research aimed at children's health.

Author Keywords
Pervasive technology; health monitoring; understanding users; children; parents; diabetes; design; user experience

ACM Classification Keywords
H.5.2 [Information interfaces and presentation]: User Interfaces – User-centered design;

INTRODUCTION
Parents guide their children through various developmental milestones to help shape behavioral choices – social, fiscal, academic, health, and others. Technology can be an aid to parents, providing a virtual window into their child's life. For example, parents can remotely monitor their child's choice of food items purchased in the school cafeteria, homework assignment submissions, and grades through school websites. Social activities can be tracked through Facebook accounts and text message activity on mobile phones. Driving decisions can be tracked with pervasive technology embedded into motor vehicles. Credit card transactions and bank activity can be monitored using web-based portals. These technological developments create a situation where parents with the best intentions of remaining connected with their child, in order to provide effective direction, can cross a personal boundary and create conflict in the relationship [4]. The focus of our research is on how new technologies can impact the *health* behavior of children. While intended to reassure, health monitoring technologies may actually exacerbate bad feelings and parent-child conflict in certain contexts. Our research looks at this potential concern from the perspective of children with Type 1 Diabetes (T1D) and their parents.

Blood glucose monitoring (BGM) is central to maintaining the health of people with diabetes. Thus, parents of children with T1D are likely to want a technology that helps collect, track and relay blood glucose (BG) values to them. In this research we sought to expose what – if any – emotional response is provoked by the use of BGM technology, and in turn, if this response affects the parent-child relationship. We conducted two different kinds of study to examine this central concern. First, we conducted an *interview study* to uncover the differing needs of children with T1D and their parents across three phases of development – Older Elementary (8-11 years), Early Adolescence (12-15 years) and Late Adolescence (16-19 years). This study was designed to gain a better understanding of stage-based concerns surrounding the use of technology for routine diabetes management. Our aim was to identify ways in which BGM technology could be designed to lower barriers to use and curtail negative emotional response. Second, we analyzed the findings from a *12 month controlled trial of a BGM technology* that automatically collects, tracks, and then sends BG information to parents. This study focused on the older elementary age group and was designed to determine if the technology impacts affective response to BGM, in addition to the health outcomes and self-care of children with T1D.

While the two studies were carried out separately, they complement each other by addressing the core research question from different perspectives – how does the emotional response to BGM technology impact disease management and the family dynamic? The interview study examines parents' and children's emotional concerns surrounding BGM usage while the technology trial uses a validated instrument to measure changes in emotional response to BGM during 12 months of use. Importantly, both sets of findings suggest how technology can be designed to increase reflection on BG trends without creating problems in the family dynamic.

BACKGROUND
Many of the personal decisions to take a particular health action (e.g. exercise) or use a technology to monitor health (e.g. Nike+iPod to track exercise) are the same whether managing chronic disease or wellness – a person may realize that they should take action to benefit their health,

Permission to make digital or hard copies of all or part of this work for personal or classroom use is granted without fee provided that copies are not made or distributed for profit or commercial advantage and that copies bear this notice and the full citation on the first page. To copy otherwise, or republish, to post on servers or to redistribute to lists, requires prior specific permission and/or a fee.
CHI'12, May 5–10, 2012, Austin, Texas, USA.
Copyright 2012 ACM 978-1-4503-1015-4/12/05...$10.00.

yet they choose not to. Despite how it may help our health, few of us enjoy stepping on a scale to monitor weight because it can make us feel bad about ourselves, out of control, or discouraged. Likewise, few people with diabetes enjoy using technology to monitor their BG control. Designing health promoting technologies aimed at a single user is challenging but this becomes even more complex when the technology must simultaneously meet the needs of two individuals with differing emotions – namely, parent and child.

Managing Diabetes in Childhood

T1D is one of the most common chronic childhood diseases with more than 15,000 young people diagnosed every year in the United States [1]. The disease occurs when the body's immune system attacks and destroys the beta cells in the pancreas, halting the production of insulin. The main function of insulin is to allow glucose to move from the blood into the cell for energy, growth and healing. A lack of insulin, therefore, causes a rise in BG levels, or *hyperglycemia*. Once diagnosed, individuals with T1D will have to replace natural levels of insulin for the rest of their lives. Insulin can be delivered either by multiple injections throughout the day or continuously with an insulin pump. T1D differs from Type 2 Diabetes (T2D), insofar as the latter can be treated with diet and exercise, and where the pancreas still produces insulin, but the body cannot effectively use it.

Dietary intake, physical activity, stress, and physiological processes, such as growth or illness affect BG levels. Dietary intake of carbohydrates is the primary contributor to BG levels, and thus insulin must be delivered in direct relation to the amount of dietary carbohydrates consumed. Children with T1D must, therefore, carefully determine the grams of carbohydrates of anything they eat including meals, snacks, beverage, and medications. Physical activity contributes to an increased utilization of BG and can cause low BG, or *hypoglycemia*, if insulin delivery and carbohydrate intake are not properly adjusted. Tight glycemic control – keeping glucose values within normal range of 70-120 mg/dl – greatly reduces the long-term complications caused by hyperglycemia, which can include cardiovascular disease, blindness, amputation, and kidney failure [1]. Tight control can be accomplished by frequently checking BG levels using a glucometer and correcting for abnormal levels. The glucometer is a device that determines BG level from a small sample of blood obtained by the user when they prick their skin with a small needle (lancing device). Reflecting on BG patterns is necessary to properly adjust insulin therapy for tight glycemic control [1].

Pervasive technologies offer much potential to support children with TID and their families, in particular, providing real time data that can help them cope with the complex, daily routines of diabetes care. For example, a system that automatically records and displays BGM data can be an aid to parents by heightening awareness of BG trends and sustaining engagement with their child's diabetes management. Prior research has established the value of parental involvement in the care of children with T1D [1, 2]. A technology that makes it easy to collect and reflect on BGM data also stands to improve diabetes self-management in children, which has been correlated with better glycemic control [6]. However, there is also the danger that these types of monitoring technologies can create a negative attitude towards BGM due to an increased focus on BG values and constant surveillance [4]. Negative BGM affect has been linked to poor glycemic control [8], underlying the importance of understanding the emotional response of user in the design of this type of technology. However, there is a paucity of research that demonstrates the range of changes in attitude and behavior among children and their parents when using such pervasive monitoring technologies. There is a significant HCI literature dedicated to understanding how best to design health promoting technology. What follows is an overview of some of the work that has inspired the research presented in this paper.

Health Behavior Research in HCI & UbiComp

Many studies aimed at managing the health of children have emphasized the importance of understanding the influence of technology on family dynamics. Kientz et al. examined the record keeping needs of parents as they track their child developmental milestone progress [9]. Themes that evolved from focus groups and interviews revealed that the choice to use the technology may be based on *emotions*. For example, some parents were not interested in collecting milestone data because they felt it may trigger feelings of paranoia about their child's development. Maitland et al. [11] conducted a field study that examined the ways in which technology might be used to improve dietary behaviors in families with low socioeconomic status, highlighting the importance of considering *cultural values* related to particular health behavior when designing technology. Grimes et al. [5] conducted a field study to explore the implications of collecting, analyzing and sharing health information (diet and exercise) within families. This study of 15 families found that understanding the *potential impact to the family dynamic* is essential in the design of health related applications aimed at children. From her extensive work designing technology for autistic children, Hayes [7] suggests that emotions such as *perceptions of surveillance* be attended to in design by balancing the control of data with social needs such as trust.

Some researchers have sought to address the *data capture needs* of people as they manage health. Mamykina et al. studied three prototype technologies that focused on diabetes management in adults with T2D [12, 13]. The central arguments in this body of work is that simply providing data does not ensure the user will know how to use it for behavior change. Thus, data capture technologies should *encourage users to engage with the data collection to promote reflection and understanding*. Though not specific to diabetes, Hayes et al. [7] have conducted many studies to understand the use of data capture technologies as an aid to children with autism. One design suggestion from this body of work is that data capture technologies must *reduce the burden of collecting and analyzing data* to a point where it does not interfere with ordinary activities of daily living. In a series of experiments with technology that collects physical activity data of adults, Consolvo [3] found that participants experienced many breaks in their exercise routine due to various life events (e.g. minor illness, work commitments, holidays). She suggests technology be designed with the goal of *sustaining the user's interest in the device* so there is motivation to resume use after breaks.

Our research builds on prior work on health monitoring technologies, focusing on the ways in which emotional response to it affects user engagement with BG data, family interactions, and health outcomes.

INTERVIEWS WITH CHILDREN AND PARENTS

An interview study was conducted to better understand tensions that occur between children with T1D and parents as they use technology to cope with diabetes across the continuum of childhood development. This study focused on children, aged between 8 and 18, which is the peak time of T1D diagnosis [1] and a stage of development when key interventions can make a life-long impact upon health behaviors. The age range encompasses three specific stages of development for which unique diabetes management issues have been defined [1] – *Older Elementary* (8-11 years old), *Early Adolescence* (12-15 years old), *and Late Adolescence* (16-19 years old). While the interaction between parent and child evolves over time, research has shown that children with T1D who have parents who are engaged in diabetes management throughout these stages of development, ultimately have better health behaviors and outcomes [1]. Thus, it is important to design technology that supports parent engagement.

Interview Method

Qualitative research has been found useful for understanding the nuances and complexities of a particular research question. One approach is to use a small number of participants in order to reveal these with respect to technology adoption, appropriation and resistance [12, 10, 14]. Likewise, we reached data saturation by conducting interviews with seven families. The goal of the interviews was to investigate the ways in which technology, designed to track and trend BG levels, may *contribute to or detract from* the goal of independent and effective disease management. The study protocol was approved by the institutional review board (IRB) of Indiana University.

Participants

Children with T1D and their parents were recruited from two school districts in mid-western United States. School nurses sent recruitment letters to 35 families and a total of seven volunteered to participate. Table 1 presents personal characteristics of each participating family, including the diabetes management technologies they have used. All of the parents interviewed had completed college. There was one participant (P4) whose parents were divorced; all other parents were married. The mothers from all of the families were interviewed, as well as the fathers of P1 and P7. Written informed consent was obtained from all parents and children before the interview.

Participant	P1	P2	P3	P4	P5	P6	P7
Age [a]	8	9	12	12	17	17	17
Duration of T1D [a]	3	6	7	6	9	1	10
Gender [b]	F	M	F	F	F	M	M
Insulin pump [c]	Y	Y	Y	Y	Y	Y	Y
CGM [c]	n	n	n	Y	n	n	Y
BG trend software [c]	Y	Y	Y	n	n	n	Y
Smart glucometer [c]	n	Y	n	n	Y	n	Y

Table 1. Characteristics of Interview Study Participants.

[a] in years; [b] F = female; M = male; [c] Y = yes used; n = not used.

Procedure

Children 10 years of age and older were interviewed individually, without their parents being present. Children under the age of 10 were not interviewed because the IRB did not grant permission to utilize the planned interview questions for this younger age group. Instead, we relied on the older children interviewed, asking them to reflect on issues around diabetes management that might have occurred when they were younger.

In total, 12 one-hour semi-structured interviews were conducted. The interview questions solicited the types of diabetes technology used, barriers to use, and perceptions about how BGM technologies affect the parent-child relationship. Parents and children were asked the same questions but to answer from their own perspective. At the end of each interview, participants were shown a video demonstrating a technology called the Automated Diabetes Management System (ADMS), by Diabetech®, in use. The video served as a probe to stimulate the participant's thoughts about a general category of technologies that automatically track, trend and communicate BG readings. After viewing the video, parents and children were presented with various scenarios of use to identify how this type of technology would or would not be useful for diabetes care at their (their child's) current phase of development, as well as when they were younger, and how it might impact their relationship with their parent (child).

Analysis

The interviews were audio recorded and later transcribed to text. The transcripts were analyzed using an iterative approach. Participant comments were pulled out from each interview and grouped together in categories. These were refined after each review of the data until prominent themes emerged. Stage specific differences in diabetes care concerns and family division of responsibility, as defined in the

American Diabetes Association guidelines for care [1] were used to help organize the findings and identify ways in which technology might be best leveraged to impact diabetes self-care behavior.

Interview Findings: Older Elementary

The following is a summary of relevant themes from the interviews with the parents of P1 and P2.

Frustration with data collection and reflection

Barriers identified in the interview study of older elementary age children include frustration from the difficulty collecting BG values and engaging the child with the data. Both families interviewed in this study used multiple glucometers, keeping one in their child's bedroom, kitchen, in the family car, and in the nurse's office at school. Multiple meters present a barrier to reflecting on BG trends because there is no device that can collect, consolidate, and display information gathered from glucometers in different locations or glucometers of differing types. One mother described her experience using an online tool to track and trend her son's BG values.

"I liked being able to track the numbers, but it was a lot of time ... it was a hassle because we use multiple meters too. I don't really know how to get around that. I usually use pencil and paper to log BG values, because we use so many different meters." <Mom of P2>

There exists a tension between the desire to reflect about BG trend data – as a means to improve glycemic control as well as train the child in diabetes self-care – and the burden of collecting the data. Both of the families interviewed felt that existing technology was not an effective training tool for their child. One participant described a creative way in which parents in his support group get their children with T1D engaged with BG monitoring, by making it fun.

"We have a little contest sometimes, [all the children] come and check their [blood] sugar at the same time and they get a lot out of that. Who is going to be highest and who is going to be lowest? Just to make a game out of it. It is no big deal, it is just a number, but let's have some fun with it." <Dad of P1>

Fear associated with loss of diabetes management control

Diabetes management is a 24-hour responsibility; parents or trained caregivers must be nearby to provide care and ensure safety of late elementary age children. This can be challenging when allowing children to participate in 'normal' activities such as slumber parties and school sports teams. The impulse to keep a young child safe and close to oneself is a natural response in parents, particularly when there is fear about putting the responsibility for diabetes management in the hands of another caregiver. Equally, children seek the security of having a parent nearby. One parent described this type of transition that had recently taken place for his eight-year-old daughter.

"We are just getting past the point where she was afraid if she knew that mom and dad were going to be out [of sight] and the concept of overnight was scary to her. We are now at a point that we have built that independence in her that she knows she can be away from us ... but she still needs that connection through our cell phone." <Dad of P1>

Parent, child, and temporary caregivers, alike, value the connectedness that remote monitoring technology can offer. None of the parents we interviewed felt that this type technology would provoke a negative sense of surveillance for their child.

Although we were unable to interview children in the older elementary age group, several of the adolescent participants shared experiences, which support the perspective of the parents we interviewed. P7 mentioned a time when he was in elementary school and the school secretary had to track his mother down while she was shopping to address a BG that was too high. He concluded that a technology like the ADMS *"would have been cool and would have made things easier."* P5 concurred stating *"When I was a little kid [the ADMS] would have helped so much. If we had that technology when I was 8, I probably would have had a cell phone. I think my parents would have probably got me one for that sole purpose."* P3 felt it would have been helpful during sleepovers with friends when she was younger.

Interview Findings: Early Adolescence

Next, is an overview of the tensions, discussed by P3 and P4 and their parents, during their separate interviews.

Frustration with rapid growth & metabolic complications

Puberty strikes at an average age of 11 years for girls and 13 years for boys with an accompanying growth spurt that begins between 12 to 15 years and 14 to 17 years of age respectively [16]. Growth brings about increases in the amount of insulin required for glycemic control, not just by virtue of the increase in food consumption, but also due to hormonal changes. Both of the mothers we interviewed felt software to track and trend BG was especially important now because their daughters' blood sugars had become abnormal due to the onset of puberty. Parental concerns about unusually high BG dominated the conversation and the following quote is a representative example.

"She has always run usually under 200, well this year was different and I am sure it was hormonal. She started her period and she was just running high all the time and today it is nothing for her to be in the 200s." <Mom of P4>

When glycemic control takes a turn for the worse in adolescence, simply the act of checking BG can create tension because the numbers may inexplicably and rapidly rise, leading to a battery of questions to the child about what may have happened. Both mothers explained that collecting contextual data surrounding the BG reading, e.g. food consumed, illness, emotional stress, physical activity, would be an aid for reflection and retrospective problem solving with their daughters.

Shame and burgeoning self-esteem

Health monitoring technologies have the potential to produce shame in the people who use them, as they are often a direct reflection of success towards a personal health goal. The adolescents and parents we interviewed discussed examples of 'shameful feelings' produced by interacting with diabetes-related technology. One mother described how her daughter went through a period of being dishonest when questioned about checking BG values;

"There was a period where she was lying that she tested. She has even been on the phone with me and said 'Okay I will test.' I waited on the phone and [she said] 'I am 122 Mom' and when I check later I found she didn't even test and later we found her blood sugar had been high, it was just one lie after another [during that period of time]." <Mom of P4>

Conflict can occur when parents are trying support their child toward independent self-care but the child is pulling them back in for assistance. It can be frustrating to children as they search for independence within established parent-child interactions. Simply checking in with a child about a glucometer reading can create feelings of frustration, as was described in the following;

"Sometimes we will forget and say 'Did you test yourself?' [Her Dad] and I will both ask. By the third time she is like 'Yes…I told you!' You hear it so often from them; it is in one ear and out the other sometimes." <Mom of P3>

It is hard to break old habits that have been established during elementary school years. The younger a child is diagnosed, the more transitions a parent must successfully endure. Responsibilities must shift but it is often easy to slip back into old routines. Both of the girls interviewed shared the same conflicting attitude toward parental assistance, for example one child said:

"I usually know everything, but once in a while I will wonder how much something is [the grams of carbohydrate in food] and I will call her." <P3>

Children in this stage of development are becoming more independent and make statements to push a parent away from their care. However, this age group still needs significant parental assistance, especially with the more complicated diabetes management tasks (e.g. interpreting BG trends and knowing when an intervention is required).

Interview Findings: Late Adolescence

The teens (P5, P6, and P7) and their parents that were interviewed had opposing needs related to the use of BGM technologies. This difference in perspective contributed to tension in the parent-child relationship, inhibiting the use of certain diabetes management technologies.

Parent perspective: Anxiety and lack of trust

Anxiety was a tension shared by all of the parents – particularly the need to know if their child routinely checked BG. Each parent also described their struggle to release control of diabetes care to their teenagers and expressed a need for suggestions about how to successfully navigate this difficult stage of child development. Anxiety related to BG checking can interfere with the trust as one parent describes:

"Sometimes I feel like I have to nag, because sometimes I don't see her test [her BG] and she says 'Yes I have already done it!' and when she is not looking I will look at her meter [to confirm]." <Mom of P5>

This tension can lead to significant parent-child conflict, especially when either the teen gets caught lying and/or parent gets caught looking at their child's glucometer. Another parent describes suspicions that her son may only share BG information when it works in his favor:

"He is supposed to test before he drives, I am sure he doesn't test every time. In fact, I don't think he tests ever, but if he feels weird, he will call me and say I am going to be late, my sugar is low. I have said well just wait, get your sugars up and then come home. One time though I have to say that it was awfully convenient. He was at his girlfriend's but supposed to be home, hmm." <Mom of P6>

All of the parents were empathetic to their child's desire for independence and expressed a need for guidance on how to transition their adolescent to autonomous self-care. Trust issues can interfere with a parent's best intentions to release control of disease management to their child. All of the parents had conflicted feelings similar to the following:

"I don't like not knowing what [his BG values] are. I probably could just go in at night and take his meter and write them down, but I am trying to give him control and let him deal with the doctors." <Mom of P7>

The parents placed value in a technology that would help them keep track of their teenager's BG monitoring activity as a means to reduce anxiety and help build the trust.

Teen perspective: Intense desire for independence

The teens shared feelings of frustration surrounding the interaction with BG monitoring technologies due to their desire to be independent. Vigilant 'checking in' with a child about BG level is an understandable, and to a certain extent desirable, parental behavior, but it can lead to unhealthy tension in the parent-child relationship. One teen explained how the tension in this interaction led to a complete shut-down of communication of any BG results to his parents:

"I basically want a complete removal from [my parents]…absolutely with no information at all going to them or from them. I [tell them] 'I know what I am doing, I can do this by myself' kind of thing and for Mom that is really, really difficult, because she wants to be there to protect me and keep everything good." <P6>

Feeling trusted in independent self-care was an important acknowledgement for teens to receive from their parents:

"My Dad kind of leaves it up to me, he will remind me like make sure you do your blood test and give yourself insulin. My Mom is the real stickler. I think my dad trusts me and knows that I am growing up and can do whatever, but my mom still thinks I am a baby." <P5>

Another teen complained about feeling misunderstood because he often gets distracted and forgets to check his BG but feels his parents and doctor don't accept this reality:

"Well my mom bugs me a lot about checking my level, I just honestly forget. I guess nobody really understands that I honestly forget. People are just like ... you didn't forget, you just didn't want to. It's like no, I really forget." <P7>

The teens placed considerable value on the freedom to make their own health decisions and felt remote BGM technologies were unnecessary and would feel invasive.

Summary of Interviews with Children and Parents

The primary contributor to tensions across all of the age groups was checking BG with a glucometer. Parents of older elementary children experience a sense of fear as they leave their child's diabetes management in the hands of another caregiver, who then takes over responsibility for checking BG. The lack of access to this data creates a loss of control and associated discomfort. Glucometer use can create shame in early adolescence because blood sugars are extraordinarily variable due to puberty and growth. This can contribute to parent-child conflict as children may be dishonest about checking BG to avoid bad feelings associated with high values. Non-compliance with BG monitoring is the principle source of parent-teen conflict.

Our study has revealed two core aspects of a technology that could address the emotions surrounding BGM: (1) *Remote access to data when parent and child are not co-located;* and (2) *easy collection of meaningful data that enhances reflection and awareness.* Each of these general functionalities would be designed differently based on the development stage-based needs identified in this study. Next we describe the findings of the second study that investigated the emotional responses to families using a specific health monitoring technology, the ADMS.

TRIAL OF A NEW PERVASIVE TECHNOLOGY

The needs of families with children in the *older elementary* stage of development, as identified in the interview study, were further explored through the analysis of data from a 12 month trial of a technology that automatically collects, tracks, and trends BG values. Although this study was not designed by the authors (see [18] for more details), it was completed after the interview study, enabling the themes identified to be explored in more detail, in particular, the changes in emotional response to BGM by the participants.

The technology used in this trial possesses the two core features identified in the interview study as having the potential to address emotions surrounding BGM. The focus of this study was to investigate whether actual use would affect the child's and/or parents' emotional response towards BG checking and health outcomes such as glycemic control and diabetes self-care skills. BG trending information and the heightened attention to BGM has the potential to trigger bad feelings for both parent and child. Parental monitoring may also contribute to negative feelings of surveillance for a child [4]. Thus, the technology trial addresses important questions about the potential of remote BGM, identified in the interview study.

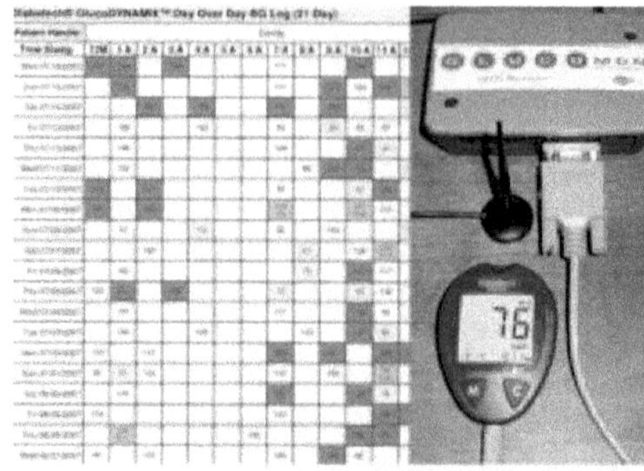

Figure 1. 21-day trend report, GMON, & real-time alert

Technology Trial Method

The interview study used a *qualitative* approach to understand the variety of parent and child perspectives about the use of diabetes technology. In this experimental study, *quantitative* measures of improved glycemic control, attitude toward BG testing, and attainment of diabetes self-management skills were collected for a BGM technology – the Automated Diabetes Management System (ADMS).

Intervention

The ADMS comprises two components: the GlucoMON® and GlucoDYNAMIX™; these are wireless technologies that work together to provide automated BGM data retrieval, analysis, and reporting. The participants taking part in the experimental study had access to two features within GlucoDYNAMIX including: (1) *'Real-time alerts'* – notification to parents, by text message to cell phones and/or email, of the last BG result immediately following the docking of the glucometer to the GlucoMON device; and (2) *'Trend analysis reports'* – parents received a *daily email* including the system generated 21-day BG log attached as a PDF document (see Figure 1). The report is color coded and arranged by date (on the y-axis) and time (on the x-axis). Elevated BG values are red; low blood sugar results in yellow; readings 'within range' are white.

Participants

Study participants were children with T1D under the age of 12 and their parents, who were recruited from an outpatient diabetes clinic associated with a children's hospital in the Southwestern United States.

Sixty-four families were invited to participate in the study. Fifty-four (84%) volunteered and were randomly assigned to one of two groups: 27 families in a *control* condition (conventional care without ADMS); and 27 families in an *experimental* condition (conventional care with ADMS). Three families from each group dropped out of the study leaving a total of 48 families – 24 in the experimental and 24 in the control condition of the study. Analysis revealed no statistically significant difference for demographic and clinical characteristics between the experimental and control groups (see Table 2).

Procedure

Participants in both conditions were seen five times during the 12-month study period, beginning with an initial baseline screening appointment during which demographic, glycemic control, and psychosocial data were collected. Families were seen quarterly for routine diabetes clinic visits during which relevant information was gathered. Neither group was asked to monitor BG any more or less frequently than other patients with T1D in the practice. Families in both groups received two registered BG meters and agreed to use only these devices during the study.

Both groups were seen by the same health care team and provided the same level of care without bias. BGM information collected by the ADMS was not monitored by the diabetes team outside of routine clinic visits. The health care team did not explicitly encourage use of the ADMS. Participants enrolled in the experimental group were provided the ADMS equipment and service, free of charge for the study duration. As an incentive, participants in the control condition were offered use of the ADMS for 6 months after the completion of the study. No other incentives for participation were provided to either group.

Participants were free to utilize data from the ADMS as they saw fit for diabetes management purposes. They were advised to dock their meter(s) daily or more often if they wish but at a minimum, they should dock weekly. One family had no Internet access so their trend analysis reports were mailed to their home each week. Reports were not automatically sent to the diabetes care team and no specific health care provider initiated action was triggered by ADMS reports. It was left to the family to decide what (if any) action should be taken.

Measurements

(1) *Glycemic control.* HbA_{1c} was collected at enrollment and at 3-month intervals for every participant in for the duration of the study. This blood value is a reflection of how well BG has been kept in normal range during the prior 3 months, and is the clinical standard for measuring glycemic control. The risk of microvascular complications, – including eye, kidney and nerve disease – increase exponentially with higher HbA_{1c} values [81]. A 10% reduction of HbA_{1c} (e.g. going from 8 to 7.2) has been associated with a 43% reduction in the occurrence of complications [17]. The ADA suggests a target HbA_{1c} <8 for 6-12 year olds and <7.5 for teens 13-19 years old [1].

		Experimental	Control
n		24	24
Age in years [a]		8.7 ±2.2	8.3 ±2.7
Duration T1D in months [a]		47 ±28	44 ±24
Baseline diabetes control HbA_{1c} [a]		7.9 ±0.8	8.1 ±1.3
Gender	Male	13 (54.2)	15 (62.5)
Family	Two parents/guardians	21 (87.5)	17 (70.8)
	One parent/guardian	3 (12.5)	7 (29.2)
Ethnicity	White, non-Hispanic	15 (62.5)	14 (58.3)
	Hispanic	8 (33.3)	10 (41.7)
	Native American	1 (4.2)	0
Language	English	22 (91.7)	23 (96.8)
	Spanish	2 (8.3)	1 (4.2)
Insurance status	Insured	19 (79.2)	15 (62.5)
	Medicaid	5 (20.8)	9 (37.5)
Education level [b]	≤ High School	6 (25.0)	7 (30.4)
	Partial College	8 (33.3)	8 (34.8)
	Bachelor	7 (29.2)	6 (26.1)
	Master	3 (12.5)	2 (8.8)

Table 2. Characteristics of Technology Trial Participants.

Values are *n* (percentages) unless stated otherwise. [a] mean ± standard deviation. [b] Education level is for parent/guardian and represents highest level attained out of the two parents or guardians (no information for one control group participant).

(2) *Diabetes self-management.* Participants from both study groups completed a Diabetes Self-Management Profile (DSMP) at the baseline, 6-month, and 12-month visits. The DSMP is a semi-structured interview that is a validated measure of diabetes self-management [6]. Parents were interviewed in this study as prior work has shown little difference between child and parent responses [6]. The questions are grouped into subscales related to each area of self-care and have a range of possible points as follows: exercise (0-12), management of hypoglycemia (0-11), diet (0-17), BG checking (0-33) and insulin administration and adjustment (0-16). Higher scores indicate more rigorous diabetes self-management along the five subscales.

(3) *Affective response to BGM.* Both parent and child completed separate Blood Glucose Monitoring Communication (BGMC) questionnaires at the baseline, 6-month, and 12-month visits. The BGMC questionnaire is a validated eight-question survey that gauges emotional response to BGM [8]. Children are asked to reflect on how it feels when their BG is out of range. Similarly, questions aimed at parents ask them to report the level of concern they have for their child in such situations. The total score of the survey is used to evaluate BGM affect, where a minimum score of 8 reflects a more positive emotional response and higher scores up to a maximum of 24 points are indicative of negative feelings towards BGM.

Technology Trial Findings

The findings presented here summarize the quantitative data showing the emotional responses to the use of remote BG monitoring technology (see [18] for more details).

Usage Groups

ADMS usage was measured using system recorded docking events (glucometer docked with GlucoMON). Participants in the experimental condition were free to use the ADMS however they wished and 2 distinct groups of usage emerged – those who docked < 1 times each week and those who docked 1-3 times each week throughout the study. In addition to comparisons between the control and experimental, the ADMS usage groups (A) docking <1 time/week, (B) docking 1-3 times/week, and (C) the control group are used to categorize the study outcomes. There were no statistically significant differences in baseline demographic or clinical characteristics among ADMS usage groups (A), (B) and (C) – including characteristics listed in Table 2, baseline HbA_{1c}, BGMC or DSMP scores.

Glycemic Control

The results of the 12 month trial of the ADMS showed that children in the experimental group had significantly ($p=0.01$) lower HbA_{1c} at 12 months (7.44 ±0.94, a reduction of 0.35 from baseline) when compared to the control group (8.31±1.24, an increase of 0.15 from baseline). Improvement was more profound in families using the ADMS more frequently. Participants in usage group (B), who docked 1-3 times/week, had a nearly 10% reduction in HbA_{1c} from baseline (7.8 ±1.0) to 12 months (7.1 ±0.6).

Diabetes Self-Care

This study showed that participants who docked 1-3 times/week had larger improvements DSMP scores than both the control group ($p=0.04$) and the group docking <1 time/week ($p=0.06$). The largest gain for children in this group was in skills related to BG checking. This result occurred in a context where participants were simply given the ADMS and allowed to use it as desired. There was no additional prompting, educational messages, or connection with health care providers afforded by the technology.

Affective response to Blood Glucose Monitoring

As shown in Table 3, children in both the experimental and control conditions experienced no significant change in BGMC scores from baseline to 12-months. This indicates that the introduction of the ADMS had no impact on the BGM affect of children in the experimental group.

Table 3 also shows that parents in group B (those docking 1-3 times/week), had a significant ($p=0.04$) improvement in BGMC from baseline (13.1 ±3.6) to 12-months (11.3 ±2.3) when compared with the control group and those docking <1 time/week. The *mismatch* in BGMC scores (mismatch = BGMC-parent – BGMC-child) may reveal potential tensions around BGM. A *positive* mismatch indicates that the parent has more anxiety related to the results of their child's BGM. This discrepancy in emotional response may create tension if an anxious parent over reacts to the results of a BG check, leaving the child frustrated because they have less anxiety related to BGM. Table 3 shows the mean BGMC scores of parents in Group B dropped below scores of children in that group after using the ADMS for 12 months (mean mismatch of -1.2). Mismatch for groups A and C became larger, more positive, by the end of the study.

	ADMS use			
	Group(A) <1x/week (n=13)	Group(B) 1-3xs/week (n=11)	Group(C) Control (n=24)	*p value*[a]
BGMC-parent				
Baseline	13.6 ±	13.1 ± 3.6	13.5 ± 3.2	0.04
6 months	14.1 ±	11.5 ± 2.1	14.0 ± 3.8	
12 months	14.3 ±	11.3 ± 2.3	14.5 ± 4.1	
BGMC-child				
Baseline	12.2 ±	12.4 ± 2.2	12.7 ± 3.5	0.68
6 months	12.4 ±	11.2 ± 2.1	13.0 ± 3.5	
12 months	12.4 ±	12.5 ± 2.7	13.4 ± 3.4	

Table 3. Mean BGMC scores by ADMS usage group.

Values are reported as mean ± SD unless otherwise noted.
[a] *p values* from analysis of variance model for change in BGMC scores for parent and children from baseline to 12 months.

Summary of Technology Trial

This study has shown a positive relationship between the use of the ADMS and health outcomes. Specifically, docking 1-3 times/week was associated with significant improvements in HbA_{1c}, DSMP, and BGMC-parent scores. Although the BGMC scores of children were not significantly different with the addition of the ADMS, it is a positive finding given that this technology has the potential to make bad feelings worse. We also found that families that used the ADMS more often had more comparable parent-child BGM affect by the end of the study.

DISCUSSION

The studies presented in this paper provide different perspectives to address the research question – how does the emotional response to BGM technology impact disease management and the family dynamic? The interview study revealed specific ways in which the evolving emotional needs of children and parents influence adoption and use. Our findings suggest that the two core functions of BGM technology must be addressed based on the differing needs of each age group. For example, *'Remote access to data when parent and child are not co-located'* must be addressed in the older elementary stage because parents and children, alike, fear separation when they must rely on others to properly respond to diabetes management concerns. Parents of children in early adolescence would benefit from remote monitoring in order to support their child as they navigate the complexities of managing diabetes during periods of rapid growth. In the later phase of adolescence, remote access to information could be used to foster trust and mitigate anxieties of parents who must back away gradually from their child's diabetes management. In the case of *'Easy collection of meaningful data that enhances reflection and awareness,'* parents of children in the older elementary phase of development who are trying to interpret patterns in their child's BG readings may become frustrated and give up trying if the technology does not allow for easy data capture. In turn, parents without the full picture of BG trend information may react more strongly than needed to a single reading that is out of normal range. This type of negative, affective response can have emotional repercussions to both the parent and child. Children in early adolescence who are challenged by the changes brought about by puberty may benefit from contextualized BG readings to make the data more meaningful. Ease of data collection is essential to promote BGM reflection during late adolescence, but more important is identifying what aspect of collecting the data is most meaningful to teens in order to motivate routine BGM.

In answer to the research question, the technology trial has shown that a technology that pushes data to the parent can actually improve their emotional responses to health data without adversely affecting the feelings of the child. The results of this study confirm findings from the interview study, namely that attending to *emotional response* in the design of pervasive health technology can contribute to positive outcomes. The families who used the ADMS frequently enough to experience benefits had a *reduction* in parental anxiety around BGM. Moreover, the affective response of parents became more similar to that of their child, possibly lessening tension in their relationship. The ADMS also sustained the interest of roughly half of the experimental group who remain consistently engaged with the technology for 12 months – through the various life events that can cause a break in routine. This could be due to the system's ability to effectively address the anxieties of parents with children in the late elementary phase of development. The discussions we had with teens in early/late adolescence and their parents suggest that the ADMS (as currently designed) would not effectively meet the needs of families with older children. Furthermore, if not properly designed it could exacerbate parent-child conflict. However, given the significant positive impact to glycemic control and self-care skills it is important to consider how this technology can be modified to better meet the needs of teens and their parents.

The findings from this experimental trial suggest that, if properly designed, health monitoring technologies can support parents' *best intentions* without contributing to conflict. By focusing on *user experience* (emotions surrounding technology use) and the issues brought about by the stage of child development, we have identified following design implications for of health monitoring technologies like the ADMS:

Older Elementary: Children in this age group can assume basic self-care tasks including insulin injections and BG testing but still require the supervision and support of knowledgeable adults [1]. Parents also need to help their child understand diabetes management in order to set the stage for independent self-care. *Implications*: 1) Provide two-way communication, allowing parents to not only monitor BG but also offer remote support/cues to caregivers through the system; 2) Provide parents with a visualization of data that is meaningful to a child along with prompts to scaffolding conversations with child about diabetes care.

Early Adolescence: Puberty can result in average growth rates of 3.4-4 inches/year and 18-19.8 pounds/year [16], hormonal change, as well as stress related to social issues, all of which can alter metabolic control [1]. Providing context to supplement raw data might help sort out the cause of shifts in BG, improving acceptance of unstable glycemic control and reducing feelings of shame. Likewise, monitoring alternative aspects of diabetes management, aside from BG, may bolster self-efficacy during this time of variable control. *Implications*: 1) Provide context capture and alternative representations of successful diabetes management that build self-efficacy; 2) Provide parent warnings of potential problem behavioral patterns.

Late Adolescence: During this phase, children transition to independence and begin defining their ambitions for adult life. Research has shown that teens with T1D have better health outcomes when parents remain involved with diabetes care, despite resistance from teens [1]. Thus, technology should be designed to engage parents yet allow the teen to feel trusted to be independent. *Implications*: 1) Provide customizable display of data that affords a level of abstraction that can build parental trust yet respect the needs of teens to control their information; 2) Identify and connect design to teen values to motivate regular BGM.

Limitations

One limitation of this study was the lack of interviews with older elementary school age children. However, we have captured the needs of this group through the perspective of parents and the reflections of the older children we interviewed. We also leveraged the ADA's guidelines for diabetes care during this developmental stage and feel this has helped mitigate bias brought about by not interviewing younger children. Furthermore, because young children still require adult supervision, attending to parents' emotional response may also help meet the need of children to have parents who are less anxious about isolated BG readings.

CONCLUSION

The studies presented here show the potential of pervasive technologies to ease the tension in the parent-child relationship as it evolves over time, building on prior HCI research. Our work makes a new contribution by informing the design of remote monitoring technologies that take into account the diverse emotional needs of children and their parents. The trial of the ADMS has shown the potential of this type of health monitoring technology to enable positive outcomes for children with T1D and their parents. An important theme from the interview studies is the balance of control over data versus feelings of surveillance. This discussion is needed to inform the proper design of technology aimed at health behaviors of children.

However, there is still much to understand about the impact of this kind of pervasive technology given the potential for adverse effects on the family dynamic. In addition, there may be certain aspects of learning and communication that are lost when moving to a purely technology driven form of monitoring. For example, teens might assume their parents are looking out for them when BG data is released and decide not to send an accompanying text message, explaining, for example, why they cannot drive home before their curfew. Temporary care providers may be disempowered by a technology that automatically communicates BG readings to parents – effectively cutting them off from opportunities to learn about diabetes care.

Monitoring the health of children with technology is a complicated design problem that requires a focus on the evolving needs of both child and parent as the child transitions through various stages of development. Rogers argued that in order to understand the more complex needs of users, researchers and practitioners must move beyond design efforts that focus on creating pleasurable experience and proactive computing to those that *uncover human desires, morals, and values that inspire technology use and proactive people* [15]. Our research has shown that focusing on what makes us human – in this case one's emotional response to health data – may help design technologies that inspire people to change health behavior.

ACKNOWLEDGMENTS

The authors would like to thank all of the families and clinicians who participated in the studies; Kevin McMahon, Stephen Ponder, and Eric Link for inviting us to join their research team; Josh Tenenberg, Barbara Anderson, Erik Stolterman, Shaowen Bardzell and the CHI reviewers for helpful feedback; the Morris L. Lichtenstein, Jr. Medical Research Foundation for funding the technology trial.

REFERENCES

1. American Diabetes Association. Care of children and adolescents with T1D. *Diab Care 28* (2005), 186-212.
2. Anderson, B.J., Vangsness, L., Connell, A., Butler, D., Goebel-Gabbri, A. and Laffel, L.M. Family conflict, adherence, and glycemic Control in youth with short duration type 1 diabetes. *Diab Med 19* (2002), 635-632.
3. Consolvo, S. Designing and evaluating a persuasive technology to encourage lifestyle behavior change. *Doctoral dissertation*. University of Washington, 2008.
4. Gammon D., Årsand E., Walseth O.A., Andersson N, Jenssen M. and Taylor T. Parent-child interaction using a mobile and wireless system for BG monitoring. *J Med Int Res 7:5* (2005), e57.
5. Grimes, A., Tan, D. and Morris, D. Toward technologies that support family reflections on health. In *Proc GROUP '09* (2009), 311-320.
6. Harris M., Wysocki T., Sadler M., Wilkinson K., Harvey L., Buckloh L., Mauras N., and White N. Validation of a structured interview for the assessment of diabetes self-management. *Diab Care 23* (2000), 1301-1304.
7. Hayes, G., Gardere, L., Abowd, G., and Truong, K. CareLog: a selective archiving tool for behavior management in schools. In *Proc CHI '08*, ACM Press (2008), 685-694.
8. Hood K., Butler D.B., Volkening L.K., Anderson B.J., and Laffel L. The blood glucose monitoring communication questionnaire. *Diab Care 27* (2004), 2610-2615.
9. Kientz, J.A., Arriaga, R.I., Chetty, M., Hayes, G.R., Richardson, J., Patel, S.N. and Abowd, G.D. Grow and know: understanding record-keeping needs for tracking the development of young children. In *Proc CHI '07*, ACM Press (2007), 1351-1360.
10. Kientz, J.A. Understanding parent-pediatrician interactions for the design of health technologies. In *Proc IHI'10*, ACM Press (2010), 230-239.
11. Maitland, J., Chalmers, M. and Siek, K.A. Persuasion not required: Improving our understanding of the sociotechnical context of dietary behavioural change. In *Proc Pervasive Health '09* (2009), 1-8.
12. Mamykina, L., Mynatt, E.D. and Kaufman, D.R. Investigating health management practices of individuals with diabetes. In *Proc CHI '06*, ACM Press (2006), 927-936.
13. Mamykina, L., Mynatt, E., Davidson, P. and Greenblatt, D. MAHI: investigation of social scaffolding for reflective thinking in diabetes management. *In Proc CHI '08*, ACM Press (2008), 477-486.
14. Petersen, M.J., Madsen, K.H, and Kjaer, A. The usability of everyday technology: emerging and fading opportunities. *TOCHI 9:2* (2002), 74-105.
15. Rogers, Y. The changing face of human-computer interaction in the age of ubiquitous computing. In Proc USAB '09 (2009), 1-19.
16. Rogol, A., Clark, P., Roemmich, J. Growth and pubertal development in children and adolescents: Effects of diet and activity. *Am J Clin Nutr 72: 2* (2000), 521S-528.
17. The DCCT Research Group. The relationship of glycemic exposure (HbA1c) to the risk of development and progression of retinopathy in the diabetes control and complications trial. *Diabetes 44* (1995), 968 –983.
18. Toscos, T., Ponder, S.W., Anderson, B.J., Davidson, M.B., Lee, M.L., Montemayor-Gonzalez, E., Reyes, P., Link, E., and McMahon, K. Integrating an Automated Diabetes Management System into the family management of Children with Type 1 Diabetes. *Diab Care 35:3* (2012), 1-5.

Representing "too small to see" as "too small to see" with Temporal Representation

Minyoung Song, Chris Quintana
University of Michigan
School of Education
610 E. University Ave.
Ann Arbor, Michigan 48109 USA
mysong@umich.edu, quintana@umich.edu

ABSTRACT

Teaching and learning the vast range of the sizes of the objects that are too small to see with human eyes (called imperceptible objects) has been a challenging issue in education. Because representation is the only medium that learners can use to make sense of imperceptible phenomena, learners encounter challenges when trying to understand the range of imperceptible sizes. However, the conventional visual representations that are incorporated in many learning technologies tend to direct learners to overestimate the sizes of imperceptible objects. To address this issue, we designed a multimodal representation called "temporal-aural-visual representation (or TAVR) to provide students with an alternative way of perceiving and conceptualizing imperceptible sizes. In prior studies it was noticed that learners constructed more refined mental models of the vast range of imperceptible sizes through the TAVR-enhanced learning activity. In this paper, we introduce a recent study that explored how to best augment the temporal experience of the range of imperceptible sizes with supporting modalities.

Author Keywords

Learning technology; educational technology; temporal representation; multimodal representation; multimedia

ACM Classification Keywords

H.5.1 Multimedia Information Systems; K.3.1 Computer uses in education.

INTRODUCTION

When students try to conceptualize imperceptible phenomena such as the size and behavior of subatomic particles, it requires them to think about things that humans can neither see nor touch. Hence, the role of representations is particularly critical in teaching and learning about imperceptible phenomena because it cannot be directly observed and what learners perceive and conceptualize is mediated only by the representations they use. Representations have made critical contributions to education and advancement of science by allowing us to access knowledge that is not available in space, time, and in our mind. No one has directly seen what an atom looks like, but representations enable learners to visualize the shape of an atom.

Among the phenomenon at imperceptible scales, learners have had particularly more difficulties in conceptualizing the vast range of the sizes that are too small to see. A number of learning technologies have been developed to support learners to comprehend such concepts by adopting various forms of visual representations like video (e.g., Powers of Ten [9]) or interactive graphics (e.g., Scale Ladder [8]). They convey different imperceptible sizes usually by providing alternative visual experiences of the objects that are too small to see (e.g., atoms, molecules, bacteria, virus, and cells), which typically involve the macroscopic depictions of such objects. For example, the macroscopic (hence perceptible) graphics of imperceptible objects appear as a student continuously zooms in onto a human hand, or the drawings of the objects are aligned for size comparison with a reference object such as a grain of sand.

However, studies indicate that learners are likely to construct misconceptions with such representations. It was noticed that frequent exposure to the macroscopic visual representations of imperceptible objects seems to mislead students to overestimate the sizes of the objects [15]. Some students tend to think that the size of the visual representation of an imperceptible object represents the actual size of the object. In the interviews, some middle school students even thought that the imperceptible objects are as small as the size of a grain of sand but invisible to human eyes. As a result, students tend to think that all imperceptible objects are roughly the same size, even similar with small macroscopic objects such as a grain of rice or salt [14] although there exist drastic differences between the sizes of imperceptible objects. This observation implies that exposure to macroscopic visual representations of imperceptible

Permission to make digital or hard copies of all or part of this work for personal or classroom use is granted without fee provided that copies are not made or distributed for profit or commercial advantage and that copies bear this notice and the full citation on the first page. To copy otherwise, or republish, to post on servers or to redistribute to lists, requires prior specific permission and/or a fee.
CHI'12, May 5–10, 2012, Austin, Texas, USA.
Copyright 2012 ACM 978-1-4503-1015-4/12/05...$10.00.

objects may inadvertently lead students to develop inaccurate mental models of the range of the sizes of imperceptible objects.

Conventional visual representations of imperceptible sizes are designed and used on an assumption that the perception and cognition of imperceptible sizes may somehow happen in the same way we comprehend perceptible sizes. However, the macroscopic images of imperceptible sizes are telling learners the opposite of "too small to see". Visual representations could be very effective for illustrating the shape, features, movement or mechanism of an object, as in the way they are frequently and effectively used, but not for delivering the vast range of the sizes that are "too small to see".

Therefore, there is a need for a novel form of representation that addresses the nature of the cognitive task that learners have to deal with, a representation that provides learners with an experience that literally is consistent with "It is too small to see." Representations shape or give rise to a learner's mental model of the knowledge and allow a learner to understand a concept which could have been beyond his or her cognitive capability [5, 17]. It is known that a new type of representation that directs learners to explore the concepts in a different way may help them realize and revise their misconceptions by revealing the inconsistencies between their mental model and the new representation [1, 2].

In this regard, we designed a representation to support learners to better conceptualize imperceptible sizes. We propose time as a main modality for representing the size of an imperceptible object. Time, here, refers to the duration of a sequential activity that happens on a space over a certain period of time (i.e.., placing strands of hair consecutively along the diameter of the head of a pin at a certain velocity). The duration of the sequential action hence will indicate to the size of the object. The concept of time and the concept of spatial information are interwoven in people's mental representation [4, 15, 16], hence, we consider temporal modality a candidate for non-visual modality for representing sizes. Also, the units of time (e.g., second, minute, hour, and day) may provide a set of pre-set metaphorical size categories to learners, which is critical for learners to make sense of their learning experience and to realize and revise their misconceptions [3, 7]. In the following, we explain the details of the representation with the rationale behind its design.

TAVR: TEMPORAL-AURAL-VISUAL REPRESENTATION

We call the representation "temporal-aural-visual representation" (TAVR). The temporal representation is incorporated with visual and aural modalities, which are adopted to augment learners' temporal experience of imperceptible sizes. In TAVR, one object is put on the head of a pin every 0.1 second until the accumulation fully spans the diameter of the pinhead (1 millimeter). Hence, for example, when TAVR lines up human hair, of which the thickness is about 100 micrometers, it may take 10 strands of hair to fully span the head of a pin with hair. In this way, the sizes of objects are represented by the inverse relationship between the size and the duration of sequential object accumulation; the smaller the object, the longer the accumulation.

When one object is placed, an audio clip that sounds like a single click is played once (aural). See Figure 1 for an illustration of how the accumulation occurs in TAVR. The accumulation that is happening within imperceptible scale is indicated via sound, and a red line (visual) appears when the mass of accumulated object becomes macroscopic scale (see Figure 2 for an example). The aural and the visual representations are the modalities used to convey the accumulation of objects on the pinhead. We chose these modalities for augmenting the temporal experience based on the dual coding theory [10], which explains that information is processed in a parallel fashion through visual and auditory channels. Because of the problem tied to the macroscopic depictions of imperceptible objects, visual representations are added only when the accumulation enters the macroscopic scale. Thus, the accumulation of objects within imperceptible scale is represented via the sound.

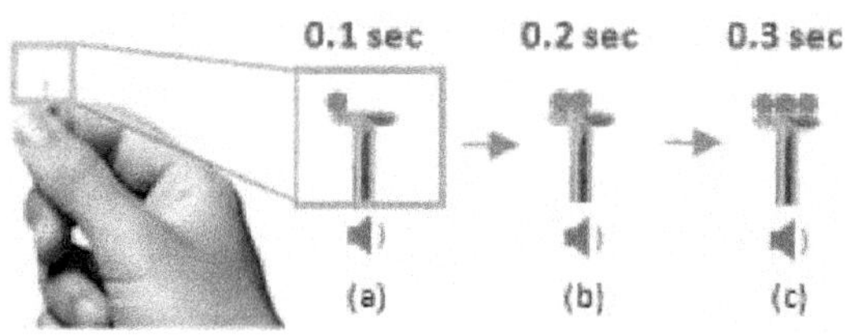

Figure 1. An illustration of the accumulation process in TAVR. (a) The first object is placed on the pinhead and one click is played. (b) Then the second object is placed on the pinhead next to the first one, and one click is played. (c) The same process is repeated until the object spans the pinhead.

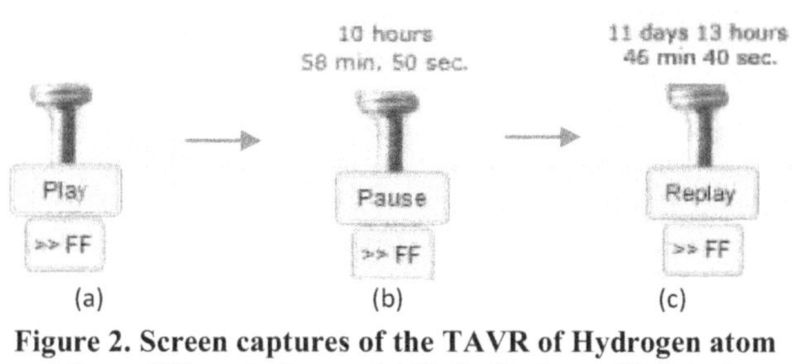

Figure 2. Screen captures of the TAVR of Hydrogen atom at three different phases: (a) Default phase, (b) Interim phase. Note that the short red line appeared after about 11 hours. Until this moment, the accumulation was only indicated by the clicks. (c) The accumulation is completed. Students can fast forward the accumulation by clicking >>FF button below the Play button.

APPLICATION: *WOW, IT IS SMALL!* (WIIS)

In order to explore our TAVR ideas, we designed *Wow, It Is Small!* (WIIS), a Flash-based learning environment where students can interact with TAVRs of a set of different imperceptible objects. See Table 1 for the sizes of the selected imperceptible objects and their accumulation time. The accumulation takes several seconds for microscopic objects, hours for nanoscopic objects, and days for sub-nanoscopic objects. The interfaces for supporting learners' sense making were designed by following the scaffolding work in Quintana et al. [11]. See Figure 3 for the five phases of learning activity in WIIS. In the next sections we introduce the findings from our prior and current studies.

Scale	Object	Size	Total accumulation time
Sub-nano	Hydrogen atom	~0.1 nm	11 d 13 h 46 m 40 s
	Water molecule	~0.3 nm	2 d 7 h 33 m 35 s
Nano	DNA helix	~2 nm	13 h 53 m 20 s
	Rhino virus	~25 nm	1 h 15 m 45 s
Micro	E coli bacterium	~2 μm	50 s
	Red blood cell	~6 μm	16 s

Table 1. The sizes of the imperceptible objects used in WIIS and their total accumulation time in TAVR.

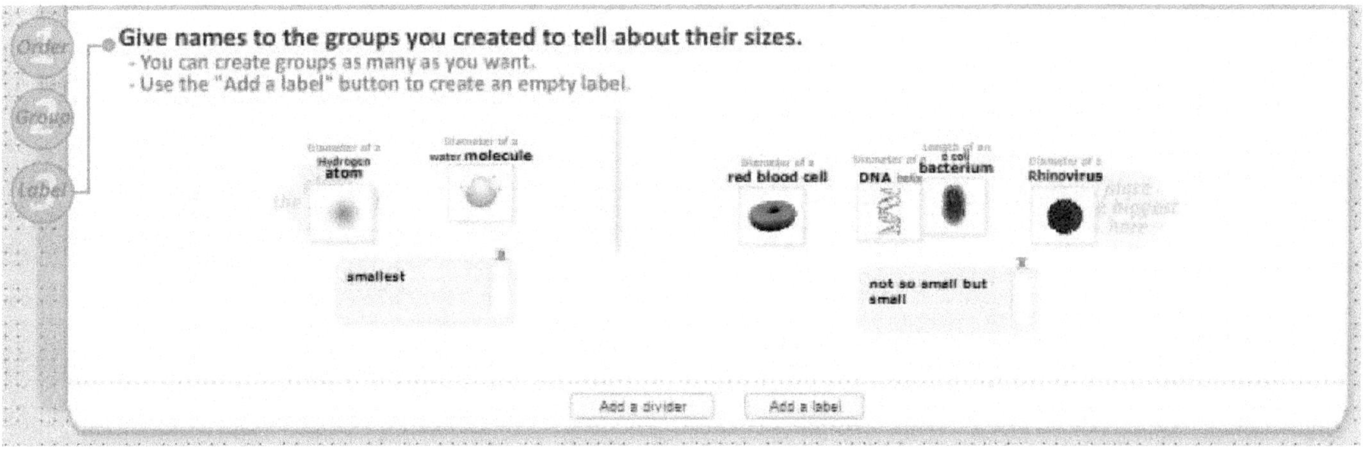

Phase 1. *Card sorting task as a pretest: students (1) order the objects from the smallest to the biggest depending on their preexisting knowledge, (2) classify the objects by similar sizes, (3) label the groups.*

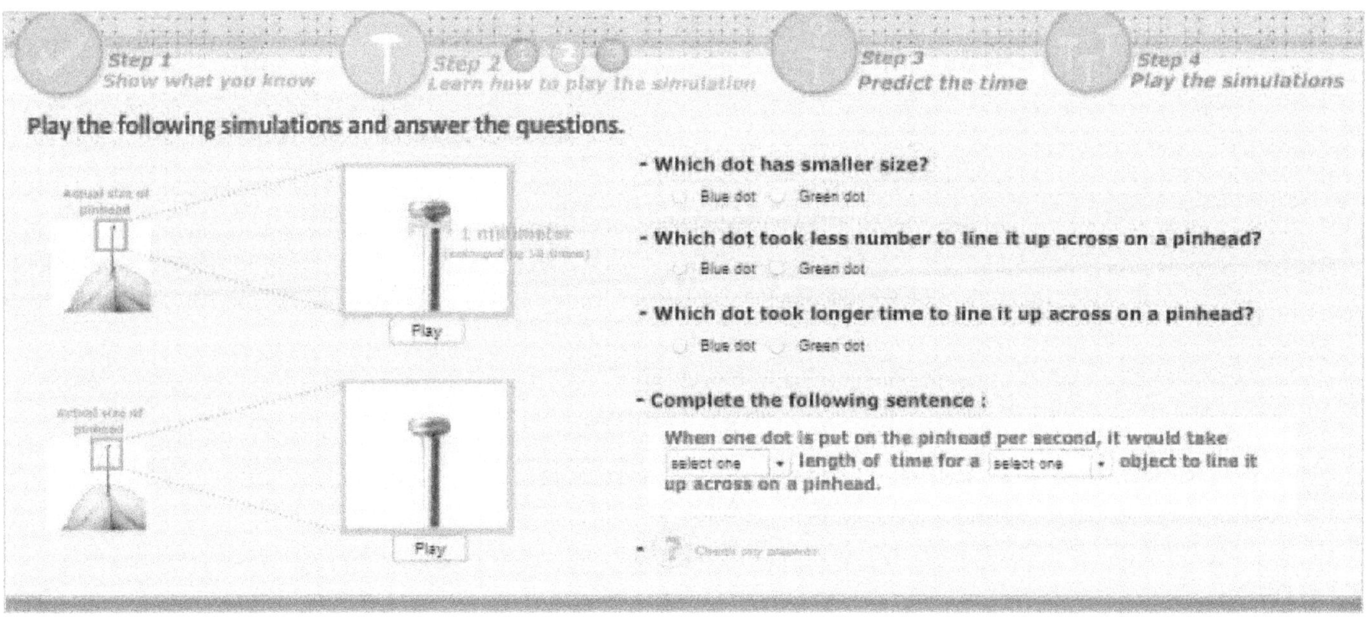

Phase 2. *Students play example TAVRs and solve quizzes to check their understanding of what TAVR represents and how it works.*

Figure 3. Five phases of learning activity in WIIS (continued in the next page).

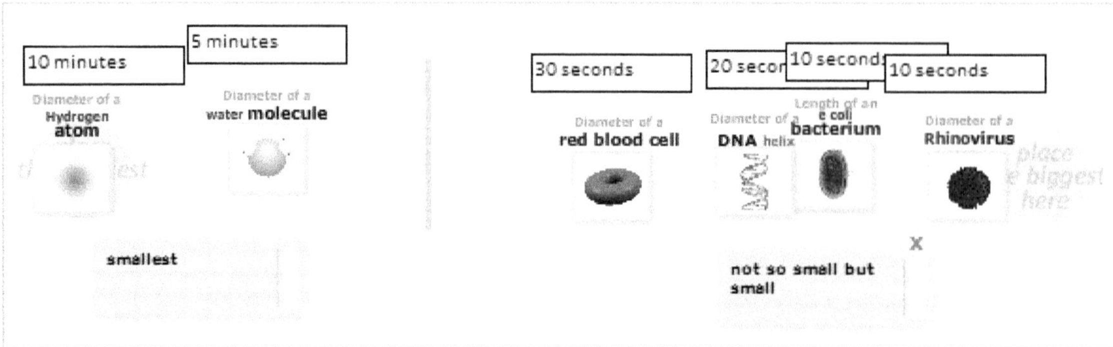

Phase 3. Students predict the accumulation duration of each object.

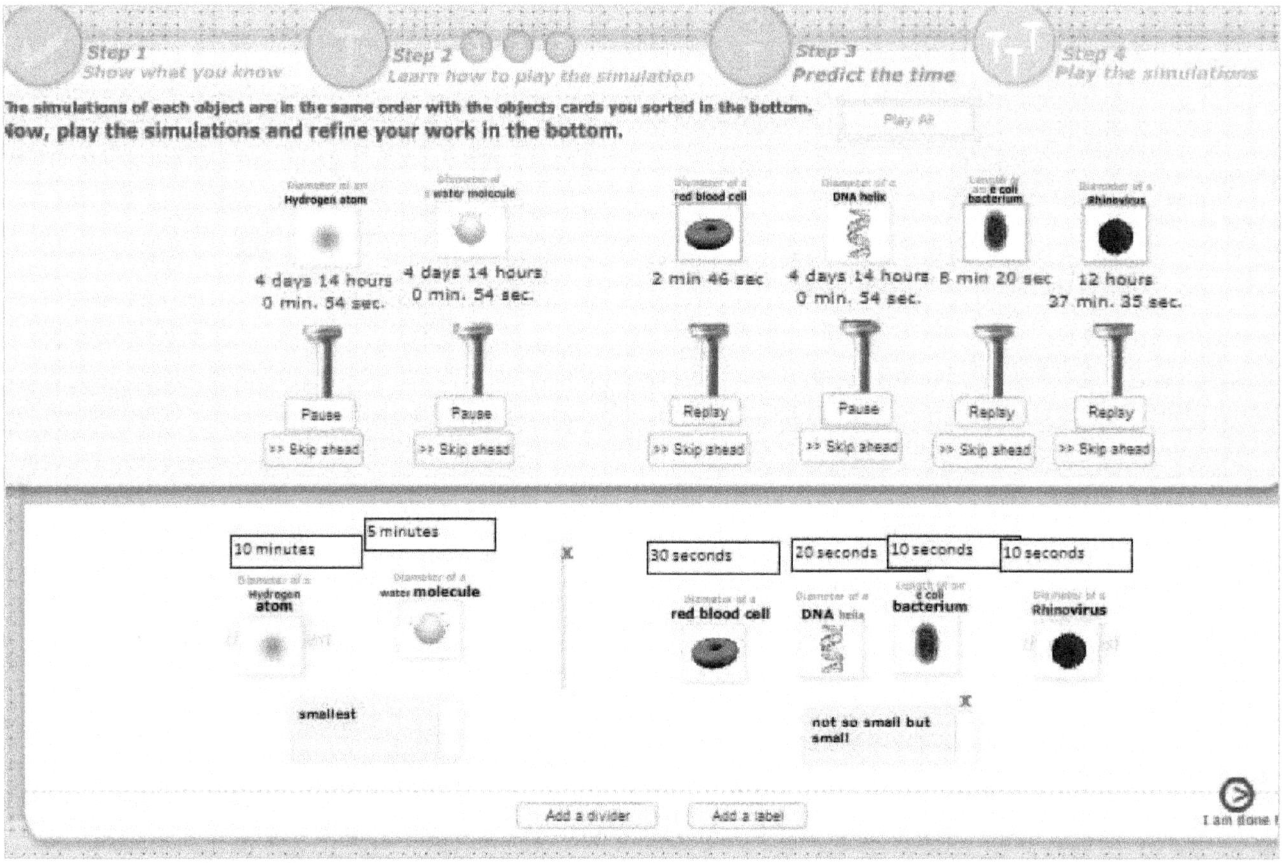

Phase 4. Students explore the sizes of imperceptible objects by interacting with TAVRs created for the objects. Then they revise their card sorting work in the bottom part of the screen.

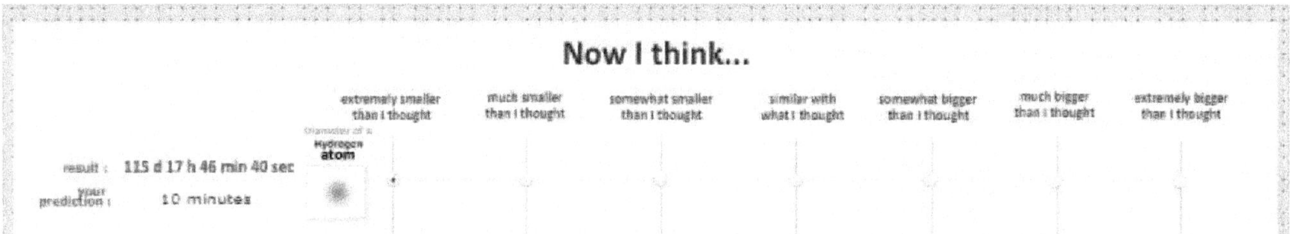

Phase 5. Students reflect on the difference between their predictions and the actual results in seven point bipolar Likert scale.

Figure 3 (cont'd). Five phases of learning activity in WIIS.

PRIOR WORK

In our prior research [12] that was conducted with thirty 7th grade and fifteen 8th grade students, we found that the students could understand the key features of TAVR. In detail, the students could accurately state that: (1) one click corresponds to one object placed on the head of a pin, (2) the smaller the object, the longer the accumulation, and (3) they have to wait for a certain amount of time until the accumulation becomes visible when the object is extremely small (such as an atom or a molecule). The inverse relationship between the accumulation time and the size of the object was not a difficult concept for middle school students to understand when the scaffolded learning activities (e.g., Phase 2 in Figure 3) were provided. We also observed that TAVR was particularly more effective for helping students discover extremely small sizes (i.e., the size of an atom), which consequently lead them to refine the mental model of the range of imperceptible sizes. It was clear that time is a meaningful concept for learners that helped them to construct better comprehension of abstract spatial knowledge.

RECENT STUDY: AUGMENTING THE TEMPORAL EXPERIENCE OF IMPERCEPTIBLE SIZES

TAVR is composed of temporal representation and other representations with two different modalities, aural and visual, which are adopted to augment learners' temporal experience of imperceptible sizes. In the recent study, we investigated which combination of the modalities provides the most effective support for students' conceptualization of imperceptible sizes. Our intention was to assess the influence of each supporting modality and identify their roles during students' temporal experience of imperceptible sizes. The participating students were divided into four groups (see Table 2) and each group's performances were compared. In the following we discuss the rationale behind the formation of each group.

Groups	Modality		
	Temporal	Aural	Visual
TAVR	•	•	•
TVR	•	-	•
TAR	•	•	-
TR	•	-	-

Table 2. The combinations modalities for each student group. • indicates that the corresponding modality will be included and - means the opposite.

TAVR

The students in TAVR group interacted with original TAVRs that have all three modalities. The students in this group are expected to show the best performance, meaning they would correctly order of the cards, create more number of the groups of objects of similar sizes, and use more descriptive words in the labels of the groups.

TVR

The students in this group were given TVRs, a TAVR without the aural component (the clicks). Without the aural representation, which was thought to be particularly more useful while the accumulation is progressing within the imperceptible scale, students would have to virtually keep track of the accumulation only by the clock that shows the elapsed time. We thought that the students in this group might lose the sense of accumulation speed and may eventually think that the accumulation is happening at a faster or slower velocity. Then students would develop a different sense of the amount of the object that has been accumulated. The comparison between the student performance in this group and the TAVR group was expected to help us identify whether and how students make use of visual representation in TAVR. If the aural component plays a critical role in supporting learners to perceive and conceptualize the temporal experience of an imperceptible size, the students in the TVR group would show significantly different performances versus the students in TAVR group.

TAR

In this group, students interacted with TARs (TAVR without the visual – the red line) throughout the learning activity. In TAR, the placement of an imperceptible object is represented via the repeating clicks (aural) and the clock. Hence students would have to imagine the accumulation in their heads, depending on the clicks, even after the accumulation has reached macroscopic scale. The result of the student performance in this group would help us see the role of the visual component in TAVR. If the visual component plays a critical role in supporting learners to perceive and conceptualize the temporal experience of an imperceptible size, the students in the TAR group would show significantly different performances versus the students in the TAVR group.

There is another reason for testing this combination. Although the red line works as only an indicator of the accumulation, there is a possibility that students think that they can actually see the accumulated objects with their naked eyes when they are accumulated in line, which is a scientifically incorrect idea. The imperceptible objects that are used in WIIS are very small, so it is impossible for us to see them when they are aligned in a single line. The thickness of the accumulated line is still too small to see. If students can still appropriately perceive and conceptualize the temporal experience of imperceptible sizes without the visual representation, we may be able to prevent the construction of the misconception by not providing the visual representation.

TR

The students in this group used the temporal representation without any supporting modalities (hence, TR). There was no aural or visual representation on the pinhead, but only the clock that shows the elapsed time. The completion of accumulation was indicated only by the stopping of the clock and a blue box that appears above the pinhead. The result of the student performance in this group would inform us to what extend a temporal representation can be used as standalone for representing imperceptible sizes. Also, by comparing the result of this group with the students in the TVR and the TAR group, we may be able to understand what kind of difference each augmenting representation (aural and visual) produces in supporting learners better understand the imperceptible sizes through temporal experience.

We hypothesize that the students in the TAVR group would achieve the highest score in their posttest (and also the largest increase from the pretest) because their temporal experience of the imperceptible accumulation is supported by both visual and aural representations so that the burden on their working memory is minimized. The students in the TVR group and the TAR group are predicted to score the next highest for they have only one supplemental modality for visualizing the accumulation in their working memory. Finally, the TR group was expected to rank the lowest because they did not have any support for visualizing the accumulation of the imperceptible objects other than the clock.

Participants

One hundred four 7th grade students from a public middle school in a mid-western region of the United States participated in this study. The students were recruited in cooperation with their science teacher. See Table 3 for the composition of the participating students. The students were divided into four groups, by their class hour.

Groups	Participants		
	male	female	**Total**
TAVR	13	14	**27**
TVR	14	12	**26**
TAR	14	12	**26**
TR	12	13	**25**
Total	**53**	**51**	**104**

Table 3. Number of participants for each group.

One of the researchers went into each group's science class and instructed them for one class period (50 minutes). The students' science teacher was present in the classroom through the class hour and supported the instruction. The instruction was held in a computer lab, and every student was assigned to individual computers. The students accessed WIIS via web browsers. The researcher made sure that all the students understood the inverse relationship between the accumulation time and size before the students predicted the accumulation time for each imperceptible object (Phase 4 in Figure 3).

Data Collection and Analysis

The data were collected throughout the phases of learning activity with WIIS. The imperceptible objects embedded in WIIS were the same ones that are introduced in Table 1. Table 4 shows the details of the learning activity that the students stepped through and the data that were collected at each phase. Overall, the learning activity can be divided into five different phases: (1) pretest (step 1 – 2 and 5 in Table 4), (2) scaffolding (step 3 – 4), (3) interacting with TAVRs (or TAR, TVR, TR) (step 6), (4) posttest (step 7), and (5) reflection (step 8). In the pretest, students take a card sorting task that is designed to reveal their preexisting knowledge. During the scaffolding activity, students step through the pages that are designed to introduce what TAVR (or TAR, TVR, TR) is and how it works. Then students predict the accumulation time for each object. After interacting with the TAVRs (or TAR, TVR, TR), they take the posttest, where they revise the arrangement of the cards they sorted in pretest looking at the accumulation durations. Students are also asked to reflect on seven point bipolar Likert scale that ranged between "extremely smaller than I thought" and "extremely bigger than I thought" centered by "similar with what I thought" after the learning activity.

	Steps	Collected Data
1	Students take a preexisting knowledge assessment test	Responses to the survey
2	Students take the card sorting task.	Record of the answers
3	Introduction to TAVR (TAR/TVR/TR)	-
4	Students solve a quiz that aims to examine whether they understood what the representation represents and how it works.	Responses to the quiz
5	Students represent their existing idea of the sizes of the imperceptible objects in the card sorting task.	· Record of predictions · Record of students' card sorting task
6	Students explore the sizes of the imperceptible objects with TAVR (TAR/TVR/TR).	-
7	Students revise their previous work.	Record of the students' revisions
8	Students reflect on the differences between the actual accumulation time and their predictions.	Record of the students' reflections on Likert scale

Table 4. The Phases of the student tasks and collected data.

The card sorting task was composed of three sub-tasks:

(1) *Ordering:* Students order the imperceptible objects by size – from the smallest to the biggest.

(2) *Grouping:* Students then classify the objects by similar size and divide them into several groups. The number of groups could vary from 1 to 6.

(3) *Labeling:* Students give names to the groups they created. Students were provided with prompts (e.g., a set of adjective - small, tiny, mini, teeny, and a set of adverbs - extremely, very, strikingly, surprisingly). Students could also use any additional vocabulary they can come up with.

The card sorting task was adopted as a main student assessment task because the conceptual size categories play a critical role in making sense of what learners experience [3, 7] and constructing the mental model of sizes [6]. One having more conceptual category tags means that the person has a more refined mental model of the range of sizes and can make the shift in conceptual categories (which is the process of repairing misconceptions) [3]. Hence, the increase in the number of groups and the descriptive words in the labels in the card sorting task imply positive effects of TAVR (or TVR, TAR, TR).

During the instruction, the students were prohibited to go back to the previous learning activities in WIIS to change their answers. They were told to move onto the next learning activity all together at the same time following the instruction. The students were allowed to discuss with peers about what the tasks are, how TAVRs work, and how to use the interfaces, but they had to generate the answers by themselves. Each student was provided with a real pin, and during the instruction students were continuously reminded of the fact that the accumulation is happening on the head of the pin in front of them. Looking at it during the learning activity helped them be more aware of the fact that the sizes of the objects represented in TAVR (and others) are extremely small.

In the analysis we looked into the students' answers (i.e., the score of ordering task, number of student-generated groups, number of the descriptive words in the labels) from their pretests and posttests and the increase in the posttest. To analyze the ordering task we developed a coding scheme by following the guideline suggested by Stix [13]. The object grouping task was measured by counting the number of the student-generated groups. The labeling task was also assessed by counting the number of descriptive words the students used. The students' reflections on the seven-point bipolar Likert scale were turned into numbers (ranging 1 being "extremely bigger than I thought" to 7 being "extremely smaller than I thought"). To test our specific one-tailed hypotheses, we conducted a priori contrasts analysis; (1) TAVR > TVR, (2) TAVR > TAR, (3) TVR > TR, and (4) TAR > TR using SPSS 19. To obtain this contrast, we conducted One-Way between subjects ANOVA with a contrast subcommand, which produced a t-test version of the planned comparison.

Results and Discussions

In general, in the pretest, most of the students performed poorly in card sorting task. Most of them overestimated the sizes of the imperceptible objects and underestimated the range of imperceptible sizes (i.e., number of groups less than 2, minimal use of descriptive words in labels). The one-way between subject ANOVA of the pretest results (card sorting tasks) did not show any significant difference between the groups ($p>0.05$).

Ordering by size

All participating students in every group correctly ordered (scored 5 points) the imperceptible objects by size in the posttest. Students actively referred to the total duration of accumulation shown in the representation (TAVR, TVR, TAR, or TR) when they were asked to think about the order of the sizes of the imperceptible objects. The combinations of augmenting modalities did not influence the way the students perceived and conceptualized the order of different imperceptible sizes because they could complete this task only by looking at the total accumulation durations once they understood the inverse relationship between the duration and the represented size.

Grouping by similar size

Figure 4 shows the distribution of the students across the number of the student-generated object groups (classified by similar size) for each treatment group. The graphs indicate that the students in all four groups created more object groups in the posttest than in the pretest. Particularly, TAVR group had more students who made five or six groups than other groups.

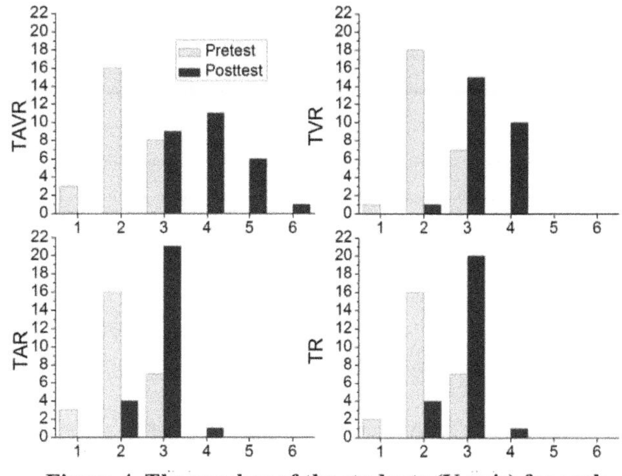

Figure 4. The number of the students (Y-axis) for each number of object groups (X-axis) that were classified by similar sizes in the pretest and posttest.

In the posttest the result of the statistical analysis was consistent with this hypothesis (TAVR > TVR = TAR > TR) except that TAR actually did not have significantly different result with the TR group (TAVR > TVR > TAR = TR). The result of the a priori test for the posttest data showed that the TAVR group (M=3.96, SD=0.85) created significantly more object groups than the TVR group (M=3.4, SD=0.6); t=3.12 (df, 45.2), p=0.002 (one-tailed), and the TAR group (M=2.8, SD=0.4); t=5.83 (df, 38.8), p<0.001 (one-tailed). The TVR group created significantly more object groups than the TR group (M=2.9, SD=0.4); t=3.3 (df, 47.1), p=0.01 (one- tailed), while the difference between the TAR group and the TR group (M=2.9, SD=0.4) was not significant (p=0.485, one-tailed).

We also examined the difference between the pre- and posttest. The difference was calculated by subtracting the number of the student-generated object groups in the pretest from the one in the posttest. None of the students in all groups had decreased number of the groups in the posttest than in the pretest. As Table 5 shows, the TAVR group had more students who made two or more additional groups (18 in total) in the posttest then other groups (TVR=6, TAR=3, TR=3). The result of the a priori test with these data showed that the TAVR group (M=1.8, SD=0.8) had significantly more increase in the number of student-generated object groups than the TVR group (M=1.2, SD=0.5); t=3.20 (df, 100), p=0.001 (one-tailed), and the TAR group (M=0.7, SD=0.8); t=5.4 (df, 100), p<0.001 (one-tailed). The TVR group showed significantly higher increase than the TR group (M=0.7, SD=0.7); t=2.19 (df, 100), p=0.015 (one-tailed), as we predicted. However, the TAR group did not have a significant difference with TR group (p=0.479, one-tailed).

Student Groups	The increase in the number of student-generated groups in the posttest					
	0	1	2	3	4	total
TAVR	1	8	15	2	1	27
TVR	2	18	6	-	-	26
TAR	11	12	2	1	-	26
TR	10	12	3	-	-	25
Total	24	50	26	3	1	104

Table 5. The difference between the number of student-generated groups in pretest and posttest.

These results imply that the aural component of TAVR may not play a critical role in supporting learners to perceive and conceptualize the temporal experiences of imperceptible sizes when the visual component is absent. We believe this is because the students in the TAR group could not observe the moment when the accumulation becomes macroscopic and the red line finally starts to appear. Also, the students seemed to lose concentration in the middle of the learning activity. Many students merely watched the clock and mindlessly pressed the fast forward button to see the clock stop, which is an indicator of the completion of the accumulation.

Labeling groups

Our hypothesis was that the TAVR group would outperform the TVR and the TAR group, and the TVR and the TAR groups would be similar with each other but higher than the TR group (TAVR > TVR = TAR > TR) in the posttest. However, the result showed that the TAVR (M=5.0. SD=1.3) and the TVR (M=5.2, SD=1.3) groups were not significantly different (p=0.361, one-tailed). Although the TVR group performed significantly better than the TR group (M=3.2, SD=1.0); t=5.98 (df=100), p<0.001, one-tailed, the TAR (M=3.0, SD=1.1) and the TR group did not have significantly different results (p=0.316, one-tailed). Hence, the result can be summarized as; TAVR = TVR > TAR = TR.

This result is visually represented in Figure 5. The students in the TAVR and the TVR group generated the richest descriptions for the object groups they created. Most of the students in both groups tended to use more adjectives, adverbs, and exclamation marks to emphasize the smallness of the smallest group than the students in other groups (TAR and TR). For example, they labeled the smallest group such as, "VERY VERY VERY VERY small!", "These guys are the smallest in the world!!!!!!", or "the really extremely teeny-weeny tiny smallest!!!" while the students in other groups were likely to use less number of adjectives and exclamation marks in the labels, which generated plainer and simpler descriptions (e.g., "the smallest").

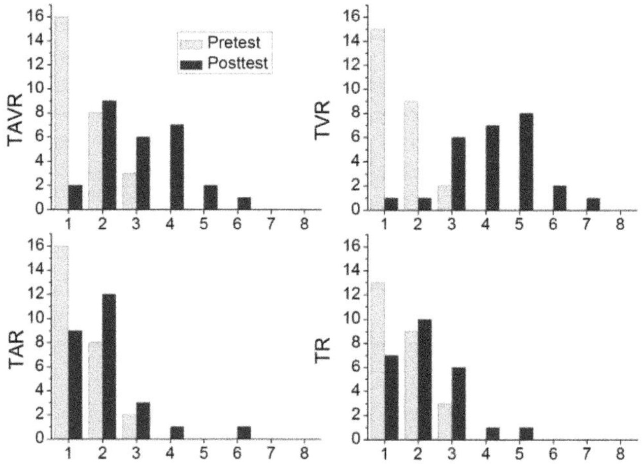

Figure 5. The number of the students (Y-axis) for the number of descriptive words (X-axis) in the pretest and posttest.

The difference between the performance in the pre and posttest was also the largest for the students in the TAVR and the TVR group. The result of the a priori test showed that the mean of the increases in the number of descriptive words of the TAVR group (M=3.6, SD=1.4) and that of the TVR group (M=3.7, SD=1.5) did not significantly differ with each other (p= 0.351, one-tailed). However, the TAVR group was significantly higher than the TAR group (M=1.5, SD=1.1), t=5.65 (df=100), p<0.001 (one-tailed). The TVR group was significantly higher than the TR group (M=1.6, SD=1.2), t=5.86 (df=100), p<0.001 (one-tailed), while the TAR group had no significant difference with TR group (p=0.477, one-tailed). Hence, TAVR = TVR > TAR = TR.

Taken together, these results suggest that the visual representation does have positive influence on perceiving and conceptualizing the temporal experience of imperceptible sizes. The visual cue of accumulation seems to reinforce the learners' experience of the sequential accumulation of an imperceptible object, although there is a room for a development of a misconception that the line of the accumulated object is visible. It seems that the aural representation does not make critical influence on the learners' mental model refinement as much as the visual representation does.

Predictions and reflections

The students' predictions were similar across the groups. Table 6 is the summary of the spectrum of the predictions for each imperceptible object that the students made. It is not presented according to the student groups because they did not differ by groups. We believe this happened because mentally calculating the accumulation time without the knowledge of the exact sizes of each imperceptible object is beyond their cognitive capability.

Objects	Actual accum. time	Student predictions		
		min	max	Mean
Atom	~12 days	20 sec	1 day	1 hour
Molecule	~4 days	20 sec	1 hour	32 min
DNA	~14 hours	30 sec	30 min	26 min
Virus	~1 hours	10 sec	10 min	12 min
Bacteria	~ 50 sec	5 sec	10 sec	15 sec
Red blood cell	~ 14 sec	3 sec	10 sec	10 sec

Table 6. The range of the student predictions for each imperceptible object's accumulation time.

In their reflections, students actively referred to their predictions and the actual result of accumulation time (see Phase 5 in Figure 3 for an example). As in the ordering task, it seemed that the augmenting modalities (visual and aural) did not affect the students in refining their mental models because this task only required them to look at the temporal aspect - predictions and the result - to think about the sizes. The bigger the difference, the more extreme their response. For example, a student who predicted that it would take less than one hour (it takes about 11 days and 13 hours for Hydrogen atom) answered that the size of an atom was "*extremely smaller than I thought*" in the bipolar Likert scale. The same student responded that the size of a red blood cell was similar with what he thought because his prediction was 10 seconds (it takes about 16 seconds for a red blood cell).

IMPLICATIONS AND CONLUDING REMARKS

The result showed that the TAVR combination was consistently most effective for supporting learners to perform the object grouping and labeling tasks. However, unlike our predictions, the visual modality alone (TVR) was sufficient for the students to perform the labeling task as well as the TAVR group. Furthermore, the presence of the visual modality (TAVR and TVR) was always more effective for augmenting the learners' temporal experience than the representations without visual modality (TAR and TR). Moreover, the aural modality was not able to augment the temporal experience by itself for both grouping and labeling tasks (TAR=TR). These findings imply that the temporal experience of an imperceptible size can be effectively augmented with the visual modality, but not with the aural modality alone. We believe it is because the aural modality does not provide additional information other than that the accumulation is in progress, while the visual modality can provides learners with three waves of "wow, it is smaller than I thought!" experience.

The first experience happens when they have to wait for a certain amount of time wondering when they will start to see the red line. When they do not see the red line within the time they expected (which usually is shorter than the actual wait time), students realize that their prediction was much shorter and think, "This is extremely smaller than I thought." Then they reset their predicted wait time to longer one, which also frequently is shorter than the real wait time. Hence, through this repetitive waiting-and-repredicting process the students iteratively refine the mental models of the range of imperceptible smallness.

The second wave occurs when they finally see the red line. Most of the students took this event as a pleasant message because they think the wait would not be too long from this moment (but it usually is not, especially for a sub-nanoscopic object such as an atom). On this event, the students intentionally looked at the clock and read it. In fact, during the instruction in the classrooms the students in TAVR and TVR group made joyful comments (e.g., "Oh! Now I can see it!" or "Look! It took 14 hours to see this tiny little red line!"). This behavior is followed by revising the students' previous predictions, which consequently results their mental models modification. Additionally, this event brings the students a reinforcing message about the size of the object; it took a long time because the object is extremely small.

The third wave begins from the time when the red line first appears. Most of the students thought that it would only take a couple of minutes more to see the completion once after the red line appeared. However, learners actually had to wait for a longer time (about 30 times longer than their predictions) to see the accumulation completed after the first appearance of the red line. During this time, they either have to press the fast forward button repetitively or watch the computer screen for a very long time. Such experience seems to become a personally meaningful and memorable learning activity to the students and consequently reinforce the refinement of their mental models.

Hence, with the presence of the visual modality, learners have the continuous support for iterative revision of their mental models in three steps. This process may direct them to make more elaborative groups of the objects with similar sizes and deeper thoughts on the relative difference between the groups, which led to the use of a bigger number of descriptive words in labels. Without the visual modality, the learners lost the support that provides a more meaningful context and resource for mental model reconstruction. Meanwhile one still needs to be very careful when using a visual representation to represent imperceptible sizes.

In accordance with our previous work, it was confirmed again that time is a meaningful concept for learners, upon which they can construct abstract conceptualization. Learners' conceptualization of the range of imperceptible sizes was enhanced with the temporal representation, and the temporal experience was most effectively augmented with the visual representation, which is added only after the accumulation becomes macroscopic. In this way, we could enable learners to experience the sizes that are "too small to see" and to refine their mental model of the range of imperceptible sizes. Overall, this study shows that the interaction with a novel form of technology can alter the ways people think about an abstract concept and consequently improves the comprehension of abstract information that we cannot have direct experience with.

ACKNOWLEDGEMENT

This material is based on work supported by the National Science Foundation under Grant No. ESI-0426328. Any opinions and findings expressed in this material are those of the authors and do not necessarily reflect those of the National Science Foundation.

REFERENCES

1. Ainsworth, S., *The functions of multiple representations.* Computers & Education, 1999. **33**(2-3): p. 131-152.
2. Chi, M.T.H., *Commonsense Conceptions of Emergent Processes: Why Some Misconceptions Are Robust.* Journal of the Learning Sciences, 2005. **14**(2): p. 161-199.
3. Chi, M.T.H. and R.D. Roscoe, *The Processes and Challenges of Conceptual Change* in *Reconsidering Conceptual Change: Issues in Theory and Practice*, M.L.a.L. Mason, Editor. 2002, Springer Netherlands: Dordrecht, Netherlands. p. 3-27.
4. Friedman, W., *The Development of Relational Understandings of Temporal and Spatial Terms*. 1979.
5. Hutchins, E., *Cognition in the wild.* 1995, Cambridge, Mass.: MIT Press. xviii, 381 p.
6. Kosslyn, S.M., *Image and mind.* 1980, Cambridge, Mass.: Harvard University Press. xv, 500 p.
7. Lakoff, G., *Women, fire, and dangerous things : what categories reveal about the mind.* 1987, Chicago: University of Chicago Press. xvii, 614 p.
8. Nanoscale Informal Science Education. *Scale Ladder*. Available from: http://www.nisenet.org/viz_lab/size-scale.
9. Office, E. *Powers of Ten*. Available from: http://www.powersof10.com.
10. Paivio, A. *Mental representations : a dual coding approach.* Oxford psychology series no. 9 1986; x, 322 p.].
11. Quintana, C., et al., *A Scaffolding Design Framework for Software to Support Science Inquiry.* Journal of the Learning Sciences, 2004. **13**(3): p. 337 - 386.
12. Song, M. and C. Quintana, *WIIS: multimodal simulation for exploring the world beyond visual sense*, in *Proceedings of the 27th international conference extended abstracts on Human factors in computing systems*. 2009, ACM: Boston, MA, USA. p. 4699-4704.
13. Stix, A., *Creating Rubrics through Negotiable Contracting and Assessment.* 1996.
14. Tretter, T.R., et al., *Conceptual boundaries and distances: Students' and experts' concepts of the scale of scientific phenomena.* Journal of Research in Science Teaching, 2006. **43**(3): p. 282-319.
15. Tretter, T.R., M.G. Jones, and J. Minogue, *Accuracy of Scale Conceptions in Science: Mental Maneuverings across Many Orders of Spatial Magnitude.* Journal of Research in Science Teaching, 2006. **43**(10): p. 1061-1085.
16. Vallesi, A., M.A. Binns, and T. Shallice, *An effect of spatial-temporal association of response codes: Understanding the cognitive representations of time.* Cognition, 2008. **107**(2): p. 501-527.
17. Zhang, J. and D. Norman, *The Representation of Relational Information.* Proceedings of the Sixtheenth Annual Conference of the Cognitive Science Society, 1994: p. 952-957.

The Case of the Missed Icon: Change Blindness on Mobile Devices

Thomas Davies
University College London
Gower Street, London WC1E 6BT, UK
T.Davies@cs.ucl.ac.uk

Ashweeni K. Beeharee
University College London
Gower Street, London WC1E 6BT, UK
A.Beeharee@cs.ucl.ac.uk

ABSTRACT
Insights into human visual attention have benefited many areas of computing, but perhaps most significantly visualisation and UI design [3]. With the proliferation of mobile devices capable of supporting significantly complex applications on small screens, demands on mobile UI design and the user's visual system are becoming greater. In this paper, we report results from an empirical study of human visual attention, specifically the Change Blindness phenomenon, on handheld mobile devices and its impact on mobile UI design. It is arguable that due to the small size of the screen - unlike a typical computer monitor - a greater visual coverage of the mobile device is possible, and that these phenomena may occur less frequently during the use of the device, or even that they may not occur at all. Our study shows otherwise.

We tested for Change Blindness (CB) and Inattentional Blindness (IB) in a single-modal, mobile context and attempted to establish factors in the application interface design that induce and/or reduce their occurrences. The results show that both CB and IB can and do occur while using mobile devices. The results also suggest that the number of separate attendable items on-screen is directly proportional to rates of CB. Newly inserted objects were correctly identified more often than changes applied to existing on-screen objects. These results suggest that it is important for mobile UI designers to take these aspects of visual attention into account when designing mobile applications that attempt to deliver information through visual changes or notifications.

Author Keywords
Visual attention; change blindness; inattentional blindness; mobile interaction; mobile interface design.

ACM Classification Keywords
H.5.2. [**User Interfaces**]: Screen design.

Permission to make digital or hard copies of all or part of this work for personal or classroom use is granted without fee provided that copies are not made or distributed for profit or commercial advantage and that copies bear this notice and the full citation on the first page. To copy otherwise, or republish, to post on servers or to redistribute to lists, requires prior specific permission and/or a fee.
CHI'12, May 5–10, 2012, Austin, Texas, USA.
Copyright 2012 ACM 978-1-4503-1015-4/12/05....$10.00.

INTRODUCTION
In recent years computing on mobile devices has become more ubiquitous and comparable with modern desktop computing platform in terms of processing power and visual capability. As a result, complex and demanding applications can now be developed and deployed onto these devices – contributing to the success of online mobile application stores. Devices like the iPhone are able to execute and display similar or identical applications typically found on desktops and laptops with minimal visual output. This down-scaling of the visual display creates the possibility of an information overload and loss of on-screen information during visual search. It is common place to see individuals squinting to read content on mobile devices. Conversely, it is also possible that all on-screen information is equally attendable by the user due to a higher visual coverage of the mobile device, requiring minimal use of peripheral vision. However, there are phenomena that limit the human visual system in its ability to 'see' everything.

One such phenomenon is *Change Blindness (CB)*. CB is the failure to detect a clear and obvious change that is within our field of vision when it occurs during a visual disruption – such as a blink. For instance, a person may not be able to detect a new object entering or appearing within an observed scene if the moment of change itself, is blocked from view. The core principle being that the brain replaces the actual object in the field of vision by a mental representation. This is typically the case if the object is not the focus of attention, and thus changes to objects, whether sudden, obvious or gradual are missed. This is in spite of the fact that human visual attention is naturally drawn towards change. It is attracted to an apparent 'pop' or movement created during the instance of a change, known as a *change transient.* However, when these transients between visual scenes are not attended to, do not exist or are simply obscured; the change itself becomes difficult to detect [1].

Inattentional Blindness (IB) is change blindness in the absence of a visual disruption; a failure to notice a non-disrupted change due to a lack of visual attention placed toward the changing item within a scene [2,12]. IB occurs when visual attention is consumed by the cognitive demands of a primary task. This phenomenon lends itself to the idea of human visual attention being a limited resource. Therefore the cost of attending to specific objects and tasks can be considered high. Given a primary focus or interaction, humans find it difficult to perceive change to the remaining portions of their field of vision [6].

Studies on CB and IB within human-computer-interaction have usually been done in desktop computing environments with relatively large visual outputs [18]. This paper presents a study of visual attention on mobile devices, specifically change and inattentional blindness. The aim of the study was to identify whether traditionally held theories of visual attention are transferable to mobile devices by attempting to induce them in users in a mobile context. We also attempted to quantify the effects of different characteristics of mobile application interfaces on visual attention, by comparing observed CB and IB. The results of which can help provide adequate guidelines for successful UI design and information delivery.

BACKGROUND

Previous research has identified that the noticability of a change to a visual stimulus placed onto a large-screen interface is influenced by several factors, including: salience of the object, the change (type, speed, eccentricity, semantic relevance) and the level of cluttering between objects. Salience is an object's attention-seeking intrusiveness. Consider advertising on web pages. An item of high salience would be a pop-up that requires a user-interaction to bypass, thus diverting attention away from the primary activity. A less intrusive approach would be Google's sidebar advertising that neither attracts nor diverts attention from search result [7].

For HCI considerations, the saliency of different types of change within interfaces has been well investigated within the computer science, HCI and psychology research community. Instant additions/deletions within the user's primary focus has successful rates of change detection, whilst gradual or intermittent changes, both in terms of contrast and colour reduce change detection to levels comparable with that of visual disruption tests [8]. Slow gradual changes can require extra non-visual stimuli such as sound or vibrations to be noticed at all, more so as the speed of change decreases [14]. Investigations into effective visual-searching have also suggested that bright targets surrounded by dim features are more salient than dim targets surrounded by bright features [9].

The saliency of a change can be subjectively measured within an interface using criteria such as eccentricity i.e. distance of change from point of visual fixation [10] and the semantic relevance of the change to the primarily attended task or item. Observers detect change when it is pertinent to the task. For example, whilst playing driving simulations games and viewing typical driving scenes changes relating to traffic were detected faster than other stimuli that were less meaningful to the task of driving, such as a change to the object away from the road [11].

Cluttering is the practice of placing lots of items close together in an interface, such as a complex menu or toolbar. The level of cluttering is inversely comparable to levels of change detection [7]. One can envisage this problem increasing in significance as the size of visual outputs decreases and competition for pixels (and ultimately the user's attention) increases, as on mobile devices.

Change Blindness in Mobile HCI

In a mobile context, research into change blindness is limited. One could argue that the display size of a current standard smartphone does not allow for attention towards changing items to be lost. This assumption is based on an expected greater coverage of the smaller device using foveal rather than peripheral vision. Foveal vision is responsible for sharp central vision attending to the main focus at any one time. Peripheral vision is the part of the field vision outside of this central focus.

Pictorial menus have now become standard building blocks for interfaces of the modern-day smartphone. These can be detailed in design, heavily populated with unique icons and cover the entirety of the interface. In terms of icon density, two of the current popular smartphone operating systems, Google Android and Apple's iPhone OS4, display a maximum of 16 and 20 individually animated icons respectively at any one time.

Typical transitions from one view to another in mobile menus and applications, such as blank or loading/updating screens between views, score particularly low in user evaluations in terms of perceived change blindness, visual appearance and usefulness. This coincides with long-held psychological theories, encapsulated by *Rensink's One-Shot Paradigm* [1]. The result may possibly be because of a need of a high cognitive load, due to memorising previous states and commands performed. Direct changes between views are evaluated comparatively poorly by users, suggesting that the visual interruption is not the only cause of visual discomfort on mobile devices [12].

In those mobile menus, certain animations have been shown to increase user ratings of visual appearance of transitions between different views of the menu. Blinking icons can act as a visual cue, alerting the user to pending change. Also, a sliding animation of replacing old icons with new ones proves to be a highly noticeable and visually stimulating transition thanks to the effective re-direction of attention [12]. Here, the difficultly from a design point-of-view is how to draw the user's attention to the transition, without delaying the new view with prolonged animations as such delays are likely to cause annoyance to the user – which may affect the appeal of the overall interface.

Visual Attention in a Mobile Context

The physical environments, in which mobile devices are typically used, have attention diverting stimuli, such as noise or flashing light. But also to consider are tasks that are performed simultaneously - such as walking, evading obstacles and even driving. Constant visual attention toward a mobile device has be reported to decrease to as low as 4 seconds in a field context when compared to a laboratory setting [14], suggesting that additional tasks can add to a cognitive load for the user, rapidly reaching a terminal level. This may also imply that if there is an increase in attention shifts, it is likely to force the user to take their eyes off the interface altogether, leading to *visual-disruption triggered* CB to occur.

EXPERIMENTAL DESIGN

Two separate experiments focusing on CB and then IB were planned. Each required the development and deployment of a custom application on a typical mobile device. The Samsung Galaxy S was chosen for both experiments as it is representative of a typical model within the current smartphone range – with a 4-inch, 480 x 800 pixel touch screen display and running the Android 2.1 operating system. The Samsung device has dimension of 122.4 x 64.2 x 9.9 mm and weighs 119g (Figure 1 Left).

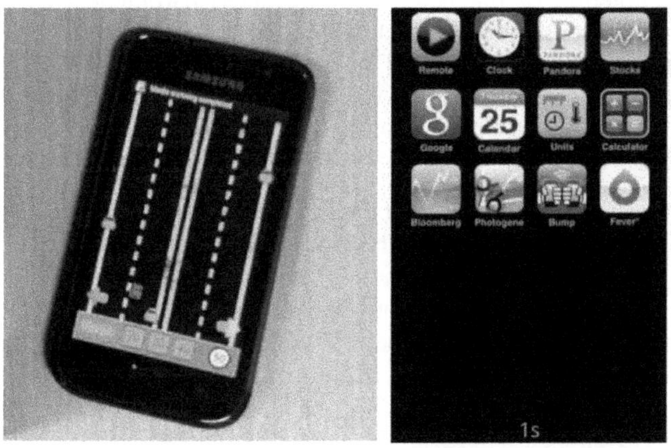

Figure 1. The Samsung Galaxy S (Left), A Typical configuration of the icon-grid menu (Right)

EXPERIMENT 1 (CB) - APPLICATION DESIGN

A mobile application was developed that displayed a grid-style icon menu system, interrupted by various visual disruptions. This set-up allowed one icon in the grid to be changed during the disruption and then to prompt the participant to select the changed icon as quickly as possible.

iPhone Style Menu

The menu style and the icons used were designed to be representative of typical smartphone UI. The 32 icons selected were different from each other in both colour scheme and design (Figure 1 Right).The menu layout provided a familiar feel to the participants in order to reduce the effect of novelty, so that the effects of change blindness can be accurately observed.

Visual Disruptions

Four different visual disruptions were chosen to be included within the application during the icon change. Each represented typical events that commonly occur on modern smartphone interfaces.

1. No Visual Disruption - The change would occur without disruption where an icon is directly replaced by another instantaneously without any visual interference. Rates of detection in this case offer a control result, whereby a comparison can be made with rates from the visually disruptive changes.

2. Flicker - The flicker change event displayed a black blank screen for 0.5s between the pre and post change menus. This is representative of Rensink's Flicker Paradigm within the mobile interface context.

3. Orientation Change - The orientation change rotates the menu from portrait to landscape for 0.5s before rotating back to portrait, displaying the changed menu to the participant. This rotation of the display is typical of many smartphones that can sense a change in the device's orientation and adjust the view automatically at any time.

4. Push Notification - In this change event, a push notification (like a pop-up) was displayed to the user during the icon change for 0.5s. Only part of the menu was covered by this disruption.

Methodology

The experiment required participants to complete a 60 separate 'rounds'. Each round would use one of the visual disruptions and each had a strict timeline (Figure 2). The participant began each round by clicking a start button, placed in the center of the screen. The participant then had the opportunity to view the initial menu view for 3 seconds before one of the change events would occur. Once the change had been made, a further 5 seconds was given to select what the participant thought was the changed icon using the device's touch screen. Once a selection was made or if no response was received within those 5s, an option to start the next round appeared. Out of the 60 rounds, 20 rounds were designed to have *no changes* and were randomly distributed. This encouraged the participants to make an active decision.

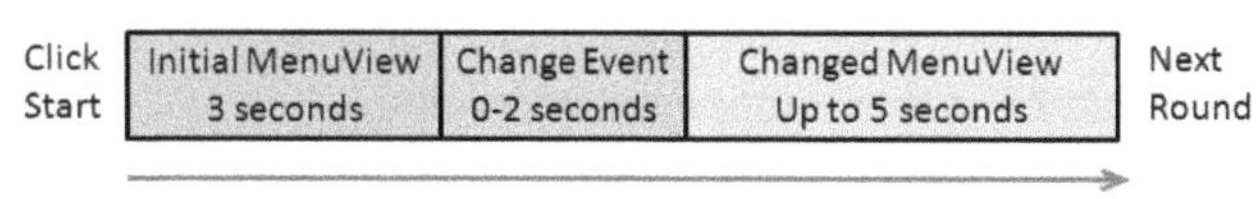

Figure 2. Round timeline

Application Settings

The application automatically randomised the icon graphics so that; the initial icon grid, the position of change and the changed icon were different from one round to the other. It was also ensured that more than 1 instance of an icon could not appear simultaneously as this would affect normal rates of change detection. After a change event, the new icon was always different from the one it replaced. The icon buttons were disabled until the change occurred, in order to prevent early responses being recorded. In order to reduce any effect of anticipation or expectation on levels of change detection, participants were not told about the type of change events they would observe during the experiment.

Each round in the application corresponded to a different combination of the change event and the number of icons. For each participant, the number of icons began at 4, and increased in multiples of 4, up to a maximum of 20 onscreen. Each combination was displayed to each participant with the order randomised across participants. In addition, each visual disturbance was spread equally across each set of icons. To maintain participant's attention towards the task of change detection, it was possible to delay each round to allow for a period of rest/recovery if needed.

EXPERIMENT 2 (IB) - APPLICATION DESIGN

A mobile application based around a simple 2-dimensional driving game was designed and developed (Figure 3). The 'driving' element of the game was designed to consume the participant's visual attention, whilst secondary on-screen changes were made in the form of speed limit notifications.

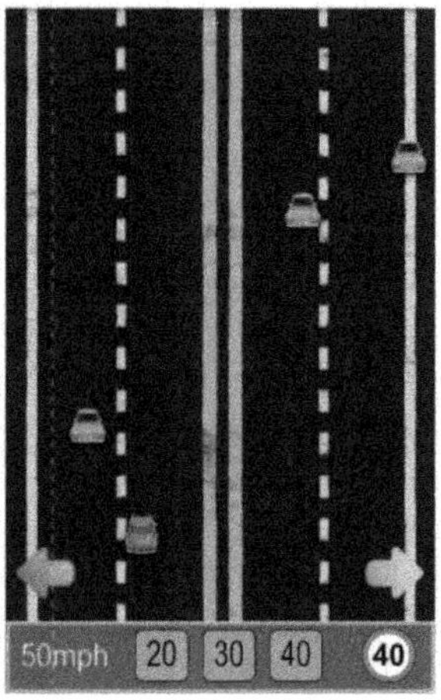

Figure 3. The 2-D driving game

Primary Task

The main aim for the participant was to control the direction and speed of the red car while avoiding collision with oncoming traffic and collecting stars to gain points. The car was controlled using on-screen touch buttons represented by green right and left arrows.

Secondary Task

The participant had to maintain the car's speed within limits indicated through visual notification on the 'dashboard'. The faster they drove, the more points they could collect – but there were penalties for going over the speed limit and crashing into obstacles. A prize was on offer for the participant who had the best overall score. The speed of the car – also displayed on the dashboard- was controlled using on-screen control buttons.

Notification Systems

In order to analyze the effect of different interface designs on change blindness, four styles of notification system were used throughout the experiment. Each consisted of a slight change in the position and type of visual change displayed.

- *Direct Insertion* - A new icon appeared and was displayed for 3 seconds before disappearing
- *Gradual Change* - A change was introduced within a displayed icon. For e.g., the value of the speed within a speed limit icon could change
- *Top of Screen* - The icon appeared on the top right corner of the screen
- *Bottom of Screen* - The icon appeared on the dashboard

Methodology

These notification styles gave 4 experimental groups, each completing the tasks with one of the following combinations: *Insert/Top, Insert/Bottom, Gradual/Bottom, Gradual/Top.*

Each participant was told about both the primary and secondary task, their motivation for achieving a good score and the controls of the application; using a mock-up of the interface and a clear set of instructions. The participants were not told about the purpose of the experiment until after completion of the task. This prevented participants from solely focussing on detecting the change and ensured that the experiment produced natural detection results during realistic consumption of visual attention. The speed limit notification was chosen as it was relevant to the primary task.

A participant would begin the task by pressing a start button located in the centre of the screen. The car could then be controlled for 60 seconds - points were awarded for collecting stars and deducted for crashes or for travelling at speeds greater than the speed limit at any point. Speed limit changes were displayed using one of the 4 notification systems. When detected the participant selected the correct speed and the speed of the car was changed accordingly. The application recorded the time taken for the correct speed to be selected, measured from when the notification was displayed. If nothing was selected before the next notification appeared, it was recorded as a miss.

Application Settings

For each notification system, steps were taken to ensure that the visual changes to the display (changing, appearing and disappearing icons) happened instantly without any phased change or delay that could influence its noticeability. The notification systems used the same speed limit notification images. It was ensured that the timer could not be stopped by incorrect speed changes and only stopped when the next notification was displayed.

PARTICIPANTS

29 participants (17 male and 12 female) were recruited through advertising on notice boards and mailing lists. The participants were aged between 18 and 24. Sessions with each participant lasted between 20-30 minutes. All participants were asked to bring any corrective eyewear so that poor vision did not affect their visual search ability and therefore change detection levels.

EXPERIMENT CONDITIONS

Each trial was performed in the same indoor location under artificial light and each participant was asked to sit in the same seat. The participant was allowed to choose any sitting position (e.g. leaning back, leaning forward) that felt comfortable to them (Figure 4) for a naturalistic setting.

Figure 4. The conditions used for both experiments and a participant completing the mobile tasks

For both experiments, each participant was told to keep the entire mobile screen in view, and as much as possible not to cover any part with their hands when they held the mobile device. This ensured that all parts of the screen could be seen equally across participants and that there would be minimal effect on the results observed. An experimenter was present in the room as the task was performed but did not interfere with the participant or the completion of the task in any way.

RESULTS - EXPERIMENT 1 (CB)

Effect of Visual Disruption

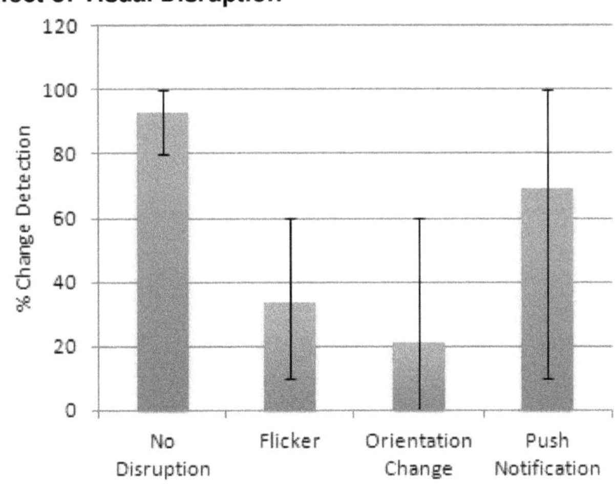

Figure 5. Effect of visual disruptions on % change detection

Rates of accurate change detection showed a significant *(F(3,112)=174.99, p<0.001)* decrease when any of the three visual disruptions were added (Figure 5). Individual pairwise comparisons between the groups concurred with this results in all cases. The control percentage coming from the *No Disruption* rounds was 93% and decreased to a peak low of 21% when the orientation change masked the changing icons. The result supports the hypothesis about the link between brief visual disruptions during change and change detection.

Effect of Cluttering

In succession, groups of 4, 8, 12, 16 and 20 icons were presented 8 times each to participants and equally across each visual disruption.

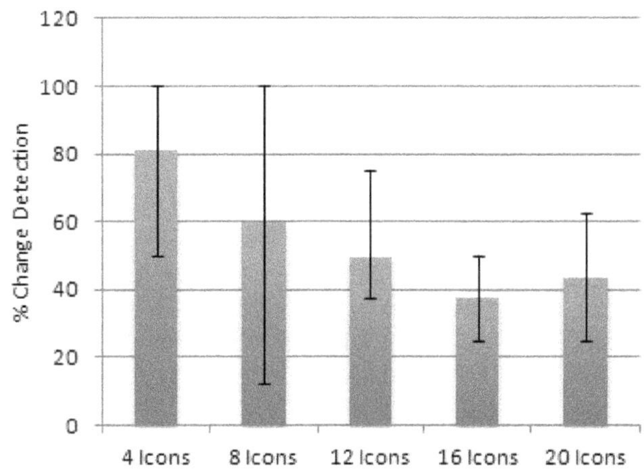

Figure 6. Effect of increasing number of onscreen entities on % change detection

Overall, the mean change detection rates were significantly higher when fewer numbers of icons were visible onscreen. In all cases but one, rates were found to significantly decrease *(F(4,140)=51.84, p<0.001)* each time 4 more icons were added to the screen (Figure 6). Individual pairwise comparisons between the groups concurred with this results in all but one non-significant case: *16-20 icons*. Despite the slight increase for detection within a menu of 20 icons when compared to a menu of 16 icons, there is strong evidence that the number of visual entities displayed has a negative effect on successful change detection. *Pearson's Correlation Coefficient(ρ)* was calculated at -0.679 - a strong negative correlation - supporting the relationship between change blindness and the number of items displayed on a mobile device.

Effect of Position

Through analysis of the data for the full 20 icons screen (5 rows with 4 icons per row), we were able to investigate any effect that the position of change within the menu grid may have on detection levels. This was done by comparing detection rates of changes appearing within each row. As the push notification only covered the inner section of the menu grid, it was excluded to avoid bias. The mean rate of change detection was slightly higher for rows 4 and 5 compared to the first three rows. However, the different rate between any two lines was found not to be statistically significant *(F(4,97)=0.82, ns)*.

Effect of Eccentricity

A secondary test to analyse any effect of the position of change was done by splitting the menu grid into two distinct and independent groups. These are outer (change in the outer edge of the grid) and inner (change in the centre of the grid surrounded by other icons) positions in the menu grid (Figure 7).

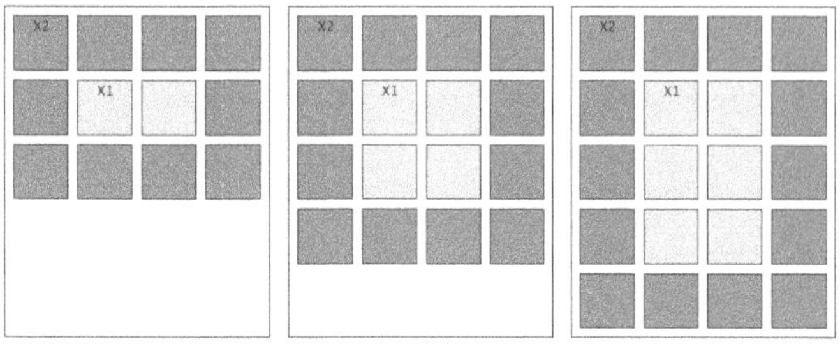

Figure 7. The icon positions included within the inner and outer groups

Once again, to avoid possible bias leaning towards outer changes, results from the push notification disruption were excluded. Results from trials with 4 or 8 icons were also excluded, due to the lack of a distinct differentiation between inner and outer positions within the grid. The mean rate of accurate change detection was not found to be significantly different *($F(1,52)=0.32$, ns)* for both inner and outer groups at 37% and 41% respectively. Both sets of results from the positional analysis performed proved insignificant. We therefore cannot infer that onscreen position of change has any impact of levels of change blindness on mobile interfaces.

RESULTS - EXPERIMENT 2 (IB)

Inattentional Blindness

Throughout the experiment, a total of 87 notifications were shown to 29 participants playing the driving game. A total of 30 (34.5%) notifications went completely unnoticed and the average response time for the successfully detected notifications was 3877ms. This shows that the consumption of the user's visual attention through playing the game had a negative effect on their ability to detect on screen changes. The effect of different interface choices is analysed next.

Analysis of Response Times

Response times of the correct detections observed were split into four groups, representing differences in the position on screen (top/bottom) and also the type of change (insert/gradual) applied, so that effect of these independent differences could be seen directly.

First, we compared response times when the notification was positioned on the top and bottom of the screen. There was no significant difference *($F(1,55)=0.19$, ns)* between the mean response times for detected notifications which were 3721ms (top) and 4224ms (bottom), showing that the on-screen position of the notification had little direct effect on the speed of detection (Figure 8).

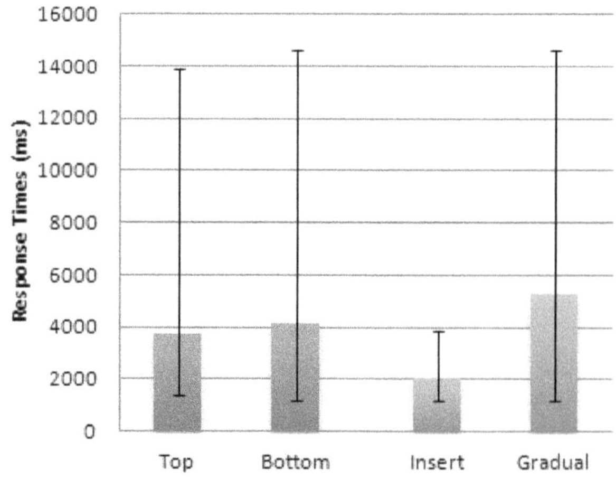

Figure 8. Observed response times for both positional and change type groups

Next, we observed that the mean response times when comparing insertion and gradual changes were 2034ms and 5317ms, respectively. In this case, the difference is significant *($F(1,55)=17.24$, $p<0.001$)*, which means that on average, the participants using the inserted notification detected the notification in less than half the time that those using the gradually changing notification took.

Analysis of Change Detection

A successful detection was the selection of the correct speed (i.e. the detection of the notification) at any point, irrespective of the time taken. Each participant had the opportunity to detect 3 notifications throughout the game. We once again looked at the four groups, representing differences in the position on screen and the type of change applied (**Error! Reference source not found.**).

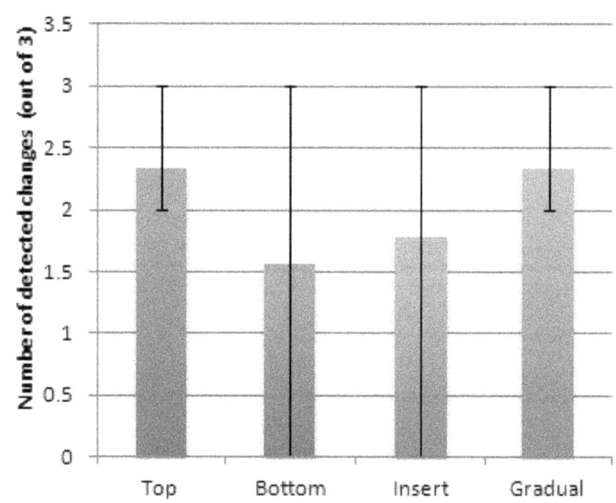

Figure 9. Observed detections for both positional and change type groups

In this case, the position on screen was shown to have a significant effect *($F(1,28)=4.58$, $p<0.05$)* on rates of detection. On average, 2.3 notifications positioned at the top of screen were detected, compared to only 1.5 of those positioned at the bottom of screen. The difference in detection levels for inserted notifications and those gradually changing was not statistically significant *(F(1,28)=0.84, ns)*. This shows that the type of change was less of a decisive factor in total detection than the notifications position on screen.

Using the observed correct response times, we found no interaction between the Top/Bottom and Insert/Gradual variables (Figure 10).

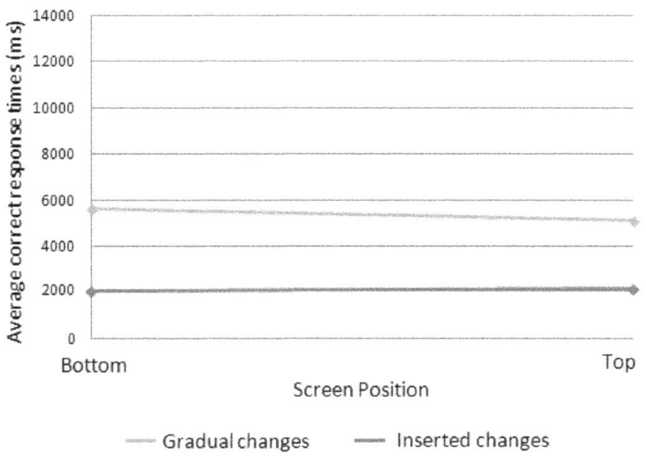

Figure 10. No Interaction effect between Top/Bottom and Insert/Gradual variables

Analysis of Subjective Data

Participants were asked to rate out of 5 the effect to which the notification distracted them from the primary task of driving the car. High scores indicating that the participant's vision was diverted away from the car by a significant amount. It appears that notifications placed towards the top of the screen (2.93) were perceived as more distracting than those at the bottom (1.28), but there was no real difference in opinions regarding inserted (2.28) and gradual changes (2). Next, participants were asked to rate out of 5, whether both the top and bottom of screen was their main focus of their attention. The average scores were: Bottom: 3.83, Top: 3.65 *(F(1,56)=0.31, ns)*. This shows that they could not pinpoint one area on the mobile screen to which they mostly focussed.

By formulating the perceived distance of the focus of vision from the notification, we were able to view possible correlations between this distance and the average response time/number of notifications detected overall. A participant *Vision Distance Score* was calculated as follows:

$$\text{Vision Distance Score} = c + (x1 + x2)$$

where c is the Positive offset (in this case 5), *x1* is the Near position rating: (top/bottom) where the notification appeared and *x2* is the Far position rating: (top/bottom) where the notification did not appear

The *Pearson's Correlation Coefficient(ρ)* of the vision distance against notifications detected was 0.238. The confidence interval (0.95) was 0.556 indicating that no statistical correlation could be confirmed. The correlation coefficient of this distance with the average response times was -0.122. The confidence interval (0.95) of -0.486 confirmed no statistical correlation. This lack of correlation shows that the proximity of the participant's visual focus from the notification had no bearing on whether, or how fast it was detected.

DISCUSSION AND CONCLUSIONS

Users may over-predict their ability to see and comprehend visual changes on small screens of mobile devices due to an expected greater use of foveal rather than peripheral vision. The results seen from these experiments performed show that this is largely not the case, and that CB and IB are still important factors to consider in the design of graphical mobile interface.

Change Blindness on Mobile Devices

The fact that rates of change detection were significantly lower with each of the three visual disruptions, compared to when there was no disruption, suggests that change blindness does occur on mobile devices. As with previous research using larger non-mobile visual displays, the visual disruption has removed the change transient, which was clearly visible when no disruption occurred. The results from the no disruption rounds (93% detection) show that the change was to a major extent obvious and noticeable in the absence of the visual disruption. This means that change blindness is the cause of the reduced detection rates when disruptions were introduced. This also confirms that it is not the changed visual entity itself that is noticed after a change, but the change transient. The transient in this case, was the apparent visual 'pop' of one icon directly changing to another, to which the viewer's visual attention was naturally drawn.

Flicker

The low detection results from the flicker disruption (33%) employed in this study coincide with traditional one-shot paradigm style studies in pictorial and visual display environments. This also helps to model the negative effect of attention shifts [4], something which is highly prevalent in a mobile context.

Orientation Change

The results from the orientation change disruption (21% detection) were the worst of all the visual disruptions in terms of change detection. This shows that change blindness occurred to a great extent even when the icons remained on screens at all times. This was not a 'blocking' visual disruption, but the movement of the icons during the change masked the change transient and clearly this was not visually attended to by the participants.

Push Notification

The results from the push notification disruption shows a decreased rate of detection (69%), but to a lesser extent compared to the other two visual disruptions (21% and 33%). This may show that the viewer's visual attention has been diverted away from the change transients that were visible. However, the high-level of detection compared to the other disruptions may imply that the changes to the icons behind the notification were not noticed, and those visible were. These mixed results do not confirm a 'mud-splashes' effect [5] but may rather bolster the conclusions based on the observed impact of the blocking visual disruptions.

Cluttering

Increasing the number of icons displayed was shown to directly and significantly affect rates of change detection *(correlation coefficient* ρ*=-0.679)*. As the number of icons in the menu increased, the mean rate of detection decreased. This confirms that traditional change blindness theories of cluttering are transferable to mobile devices. Regardless of the visual display, human vision clearly has an upper threshold of attendable entities, much like and possibly related to the limited capacity of short-term memory [16][19].

Position of Change

The position of change was one aspect of change blindness that has been shown to have a minimal effect on levels of change detection in a mobile context. It was also the case that changes located towards the outer edge of the screen were detected equally with those encased within the menu grid. The screen position of the change was entirely random during the experiment, meaning that this result was not due to expectation or anticipation towards any part of the screen and that position was not a great factor in detection. This shows that when no other task is attended to, the entirety of the visual output on a typical mobile device can be equally attended to and changes detected with equal success. The second experiment helped in identifying whether position of change has an effect on CB, when visual attention is consumed by a primary task.

Implications of CB for Mobile Interface Design

The main conclusions discussed demonstrate that the change-transient is important for changes to be detected by users of mobile devices.

Reduction of Simultaneous On-Screen Activity

It would be advisable not to use change-transient-blocking, *loading/updating* style transitions between screens on a mobile device. Completely blocking any change transient that occurs has a negative effect on detection rates. Mobile application developers should instead place greater importance on creating visual changes that maximize the visibility and strength of the transient, rather than solely focusing on the saliency, brightness or visual noticeability of the entities on-screen. One way is to ensure that the changing entity on-screen is static and that no other visual activity occurs during the change. This ideal solution may be difficult to achieve in some applications, so the trade-off to be addressed is between accurate change detection and the level of simultaneous activity on-screen. A reduction of simultaneous on-screen activity will also help to minimise the negative effect of attention shifts that has been found in this experiment to be very disruptive to change detection.

Amplification of Change-Transients and Scene Differentiation

In this study attention shifts were modelled by the flicker disruption, producing 67% detection failures. In a real-life mobile context, where interaction with the device is generally a secondary task, this can be assumed to be even more prevalent [14]. A solution here is to maximise not only the transient, but also the resulting saliency-difference of the changed entity. An example of this is *moticons* which are icons that move and wobble once changed, prolonging the change-transient, forcing the change to occur over a larger area and emphasising the differentiation between the pre and post-change scenes should the initial change-transient be missed [2]. It has been suggested that transitions that increase the size, hue, brightness or shape of the changed entity could produce a similar effect [15].

Reduction of Attendable On-Screen Entities

Whilst the position of change proved to be insignificant, the number of attendable icons present was found to be related to levels of change blindness. This shows that an information overload is possible – even on small screen. As the complexity of the interface increases we expect the relative saliency of a change within an individual location to decrease as that location blends into the 'noise' of the surrounding entities. A possible approach is to use multi-level display systems, whereby each on-screen selection reveals the next level of related selections or data displays, thereby reducing the number of entities visible at any one time. The key from a design perspective is to minimise annoyance and selection time, whilst maximising the chances of on-screen changes being detected, if of course this is the desired effect.

This implication adds the benefit of improving visual perception of change to the common design pattern, known as *One-Window Drill-Down*. The pattern is commonly included in mobile interface design, as seen in Apple's iPod. On top of usability and performance, this pattern is used to reduce the complexity of the visual experience and also the information/cognitive load on the user. In addition, visual attention is more directly focused towards on-screen entities that are relevant to the primary activity or task at that time [17].

Inattentional Blindness on Mobile Devices

With 34.5% of the speed limit notifications going completely unnoticed whilst participants played the simple driving game, we can first conclude that inattentional blindness can occur on the smaller visual output of a mobile device.

Response Time

Accurate response times where hugely in favour of directly inserted notifications (2034ms) rather than changes to an existing onscreen notification symbol (5317ms) *(*$F(1, 55) = 17.24$*,* $p < 0.001$*)*. This does not only show that the increased saliency of the change transient allowed the notification to be spotted sooner, but also that it was successfully understood and acted upon by the user. Therefore, on a mobile user interface, more salient changes such as suddenly appearing graphics are more effective signals of secondary change than other methods such as simply changing the contents or text of an existing graphic.

However, there was no observable difference in response times when viewing notifications at the two different positions onscreen *($F(1, 55) = 0.19$, ns)*. This shows that the change transient of the notification had equal effectiveness wherever it was placed on screen. Even when completing a primary visual task, if the entirety of the screen is in view, a user of a mobile device is able to respond equally to similar change transients throughout this display. The smaller visual output on the mobile device has caused increased screen-coverage by foveal vision, rather than the peripheral vision for vast areas of the screen, whereby IB has been shown to drastically increase [15]. While it is possible to attend to changes in both foveal and peripheral vision, changes in peripheral vision require a stronger change signal may be needed. However, despite this foveal coverage of the visual output, we have seen that IB remains a factor in the detection of visual change on mobile devices.

Change Detection

Full detection was statistically equal for both inserted and existing notifications, but with a slightly higher detection rate for changes to existing notifications *($F(1, 27) = 0.84$, ns)*. This was expected, due to the notification remaining on screen for the full selection period despite the decreased observable transient, and shows that the user was able to some extent, and possibly intermittently, attend notifications away from the primary activity, even if the initial transient was missed.

There was, a slightly significant difference in full detection between the two onscreen positions used *($F(1, 27) = 4.58$, $p < 0.05$)*. More notifications were completely missed when positioned on the dashboard at the bottom of the screen *(1.57 out of 3 notifications detected)* than when positioned at the top of the screen *(2.33 out of 3 notifications detected)*. This contradicts all of the position data seen so far from both experiments. A possible explanation is that the notification at the top of the screen was located in an active part of the screen. Meaning that the notification was covering the traffic and stars within the game, therefore it was more disruptive and also more likely to be attended to than the notification placed on the dashboard.

Subjective Data

The user ratings of the ability of the notification to distract visual attention were fairly low with the highest score for any category being 2.93 out of a possible 5. This shows that the users could to some extent perceive the difficulty they had in viewing the secondary visual notifications whilst performing the primary task – indicating that IB can directly affect the perceived quality of a user interaction and therefore the user experience of a mobile application usage. Surprisingly, the perceived detection scores of the inserted and gradually changing notifications were fairly similar. This differs from the numerical data analysis. It shows that it is difficult for the user to gauge the effect of CB and IB on the mobile device. It provides evidence that onscreen changes can go totally undetected without the user realising anything at all, rather than not comprehending the information within changes that were visually attended to. The distraction ratings show a preference towards the notifications placed at the top of the screen, meaning that these were perceived to be more salient purely because of their position on screen. More notifications were missed when located at the bottom of screen.

As previously discussed, the participants on average, could not pinpoint one onscreen area to which their field of vision was mostly focused (p = 0:579). This emphasises the difficulty in separating the screen of a mobile device into areas of foveal and peripheral vision, and suggests that the whole screen was easily and equally attendable using foveal vision. Also, there was no correlation found between the perceived distance of the focus of vision from the notification and detection levels. These results are subjective evidence that the onscreen position of change has no effect on its noticeability. The contradiction of the effect of position seen here supports the idea that passive areas of screen, those 'irrelevant' to the primary activity - in this case the dashboard - are typically ignored by the user of mobile devices, even though these areas could be equally visually attended to.

Implications of IB for Mobile Interface Design

Amplification of Change-Transients

Results from this study indicate that during the completion of a primary visual task, secondary notifications rely on the strength of the change transient to be noticed. Increasing or amplifying this transient as much as possible such as using newly appearing objects over changing existing objects, improves the speed of detection. If the change transient is missed altogether due to attention shifts on the mobile screen or the lack of attention towards the mobile device itself [2], the extent of differentiation between the pre and post-change scenes becomes more important.

A concatenation of these two principles, supported by the experimental results, is to have a newly appearing notification that then remains onscreen for as long as possible, offering the user the chance to see the high-salient transient, but also allowing them to intermittently scan the changed scene and visually attend the changed object even if the transient is missed. This effect can be further amplified by increasing the differentiation between pre and post-change scenes, such as changing the shape, colour, brightness or movement of the changed item. Other methods of increasing this change signal have been suggested in previous research within traditional computing environments. These include creating changes that are bold, with a large hue or brightness difference from the rest of the interface and increasing the size and screen coverage of the change.

Active and Passive Positioning

The results show that the users were able to differentiate between the active and passive sections of the mobile interface and attend more towards those relevant to the primary task. It is therefore important, when designing a mobile interface that vital changes must impact on the user's view of these active areas, increasing the disruption of the primary task and therefore increasing the saliency of the notification. In the specific case of mobile navigation applications, to which the driving game was directly analogous, it is detrimental towards change detection, for any notification to appear or change whilst placed on a static panel that is not needed to be attended to, in order to complete the primary task. Regardless of the type of change used and it's on-screen position, placing the notification above the active panel, in this case containing the road/position display, improves actual and perceived change detection. This implication means that before the design of an application interface, a trade-off between the importance of the completion of the primary visual task, and the secondary change being successfully delivered, needs to be considered.

Multi-Modal Change Cues

While this study has solely focussed on the visual aspects of change detection on mobile devices we must also consider that these modern devices such as mobile phones, mp3 players or navigation devices are inherently multi-modal. Thus, *attention-grabbing* cues toward occurred change, such as sound or vibration prompts have been suggested to aid the user to attend the change regardless of their current visual focus or activity [15]. More research into these possibilities in a mobile context is needed to fully understand their effect on change blindness, but also their effect on the quality of the user experience and effectiveness in certain operational environments.

REFERENCES

1. Rensink, A. Change Blindness. *Neurobiology of Attention* (2005), 76-81.
2. Mancero, G., Wong, W. & Amaldi, P. Looking but not seeing: Implications for HCI. In *Proc. ECCE Conference 2007.* ACM Press (2007), 167-174.
3. Varakin, D. & Levin, D. Unseen and Unaware: Implications of Recent Research on Failures of Visual Awareness for HCI Design. *HUMAN- COMPUTER INTERACTION 19* (2004), 389-422.
4. Grimes, J. On the failure to detect changes in scenes across saccades. In K.Atkins(Ed.), *Vancouver studies in cognitive science: Vol. 2. Perception.* New York: Oxford University Press (1996), 89-110.
5. O'Rehan, J. K., Rensink, R. A., & Clark J. Change Blindness as a result of "mud-splashes". *Nature*, 398 (1999), 34.
6. Simons, D. J. Gorillas in our midst: sustained inattentional blindness for dynamic events. *Perception 28*, 9 (1999), 1059-1074.
7. DiVita, J., Obermayer, R., Nugent, W. & Linville, J. M. Verification of Change Blindness phenomenon while managing critical events on a combat information display. *Human Factors: The journal of the human factors and ergonomic society 46* (2004), 205.
8. Heiner, A., & Asokan, N. Using Salience Differentials to Making Visual Cues Noticeable. In *Proc. 1st Conference on Usability, Psychology, and Security.* (2008) Article 7, 6 pages.
9. Simons, D.J., Franconeri, S.L. & Reimer, R.L. Change Blindness in the absence of a visual disruption. *Perception 2000, 29* (2000), 1143-1154.
10. Northdurft, H.C. Salience and target selection in visual search. *Visual Cognition 14,* 4 (2006), 514-542.
11. Wickens, C. D., Van Olffen, P. J., Muthard, E. K., Alexander, A. L., & Podczerwinski, E. The Influences of Display Highlighting and Size and Event Eccentricity for Aviation Surveillance. In *Proc. of the Human Factors and Ergonomics Society 47 th Annual Meeting.* Human Factors and Ergonomics Society (2003), 149-153.
12. McCarley, J. S., Vais, M., Pringle, H., Kramer, A. F., Irwin, D. E., & Strayer, D. L. Conversation disrupts visual scanning of complex traffic scenes. *Human Factors 46*, 3 (2004), 424-436.
13. Nagy, A.L., Sanchez, R.R. and Hughes, T.C. Visual search for colour differences with foveal and peripheral vision. *Journal of the Optical Society of America A: Optics, Image Science, and Vision 7,* 10 (1990), 1995-2001.
14. Huhtala, J., Mäntyjärvi, J., Ahtinen, A., Ventä, L., and Isomursu, M. Animated Transitions for Adaptive Small Size Mobile Menus. In *Proc. of INTERACT (1) LNCS 5726* (2009), 772-781.
15. Tan, H.Z., Gray, R., Young, J.J. & Irawan, P. Haptic cueing of a visual change detection task: Implications for multimodal interfaces. In *Proc. 9th International Conference in HCI* (2001), 678-682.
16. Miller, G.A. The Magical Number Seven, Plus or Minus Two: Some Limits on our Capacity for Processing Information. *Psychological Review 63*, (1956), 81-97.
17. Foer, J. The accused Harvard plagiarist doesn't have a photographic memory. No one does. http://www.slate.com/id/2140685/ (2006) [Accessed December 2010].
18. A. Beeharee, A.J. West and R.J. Hubbold - Visual Attention Based Information Culling for Distributed Virtual Environments. In *Proc. of ACM VRST 2003 (10th ACM Symposium on Virtual Reality Software and Technology)* (2003), 213-222.
19. Harrower, M. Tips for designing effective animated maps. *Cartographica Perspectives 44* (2003), 63-66.

The Bohemian Bookshelf: Supporting Serendipitous Book Discoveries through Information Visualization

Alice Thudt
University of Munich (LMU)
alice.thudt@googlemail.com

Uta Hinrichs
InnoVis Group
University of Calgary
uhinrich@ucalgary.ca

Sheelagh Carpendale
InnoVis Group
University of Calgary
sheelagh@ucalgary.ca

ABSTRACT
Serendipity, a trigger of exciting yet unexpected discoveries, is an important but comparatively neglected factor in information seeking, research, and ideation. We suggest that serendipity can be facilitated through visualization. To explore this, we introduce the Bohemian Bookshelf, which aims to support serendipitous discoveries in the context of digital book collections. The Bohemian Bookshelf consists of five interlinked visualizations each offering a unique overview of the collection. It aims at encouraging serendipity by (1) offering multiple visual access points to the collection, (2) highlighting adjacencies between books, (3) providing flexible visual pathways for exploring the collection, (4) enticing curiosity through abstract, metaphorical, and visually distinct representations of books, and (5) enabling a playful approach to information exploration. A deployment at a library revealed that visitors embraced this approach of utilizing visualization to support open-ended explorations and serendipitous discoveries. This encourages future explorations into promoting serendipity through information visualization.

Author Keywords
Information Visualization; Serendipity; Library Interfaces.

ACM Classification Keywords
H.5.2 Information Interfaces and Presentation: Miscellaneous

General Terms
Design.

INTRODUCTION
Information exploration is part of our everyday life. We all, on a day-to-day basis, search through and encounter volumes of information, whether that is via the web, in our music collections, or through increasingly common digital libraries. However, interfaces to this information tend to be modelled to perform targeted searches. This raises concerns over the possible loss of unexpected, yet valuable, discoveries that can be attributed to serendipity [13, 14, 39, 46, 50]. In this paper we discuss information visualization as a means to support serendipitous discoveries in digital data collections. As a case study we introduce the Bohemian Bookshelf, in which we have designed visualizations to support serendipitous book discoveries in digital library collections.

Permission to make digital or hard copies of all or part of this work for personal or classroom use is granted without fee provided that copies are not made or distributed for profit or commercial advantage and that copies bear this notice and the full citation on the first page. To copy otherwise, or republish, to post on servers or to redistribute to lists, requires prior specific permission and/or a fee.
CHI'12, May 5–10, 2012, Austin, Texas, USA.
Copyright 2012 ACM 978-1-4503-1015-4/12/05...$10.00.

Consider this simple scenario. Lucy has planned a summer vacation and wants to enrich her time at the beach with a relaxing read. However, since her local library has a large digital book collection and only few physical books on display, Lucy is faced with typical search engines that require specific input of keywords; a problematic starting point when she does not know what exactly she wants. Staring at the blinking cursor in an empty search field, she longs for the more traditional physical bookshelves where she could have just browsed casually through books. With the Bohemian Bookshelf, our intention was to create a digital parallel to the open-ended "browsing the shelves" experience that has been shown to encourage serendipitous discoveries [14, 19, 30, 46].

The Bohemian Bookshelf consists of five interlinked visualizations that each provide a unique perspective on the book collection based on attributes such as author names, keywords, cover colour, page count, and time. It is based on five design goals we derived from previous literature on information and library sciences: (1) offering multiple visual access points by providing visualizations of different perspectives on the book collection, (2) highlighting adjacencies between books, (3) providing flexible visual pathways for exploring the book collection, (4) enticing curiosity through abstract, metaphorical, and visually distinct representations of the collection, and (5) enabling a playful approach to information exploration.

The main contribution of this paper is our exploration of how serendipity can be supported through information visualization. As part of this we first introduce the concept of serendipity followed by our five design goals that specifically address visualization as a means to encourage serendipity. Second, we present the Bohemian Bookshelf as one possible implementation of these design goals. Third, we discuss findings from a deployment of the Bohemian Bookshelf at a university library. Our observations and visitor statements indicate that our design goals have largely been met and encourage further explorations into facilitating serendipitous discoveries and open-ended explorations of book collections through information visualization.

THE CONCEPT OF SERENDIPITY
In this section, we introduce the concept of serendipity as it has been defined in the literature from library and information sciences and present a compilation of the influencing factors gathered from this literature.

Defining Serendipity
Horace Walpole coined the term serendipity in 1754 [38, 47] to characterize the discoveries made by The Three Princes of Serendip—the figures of an ancient fairy tale: *"as their*

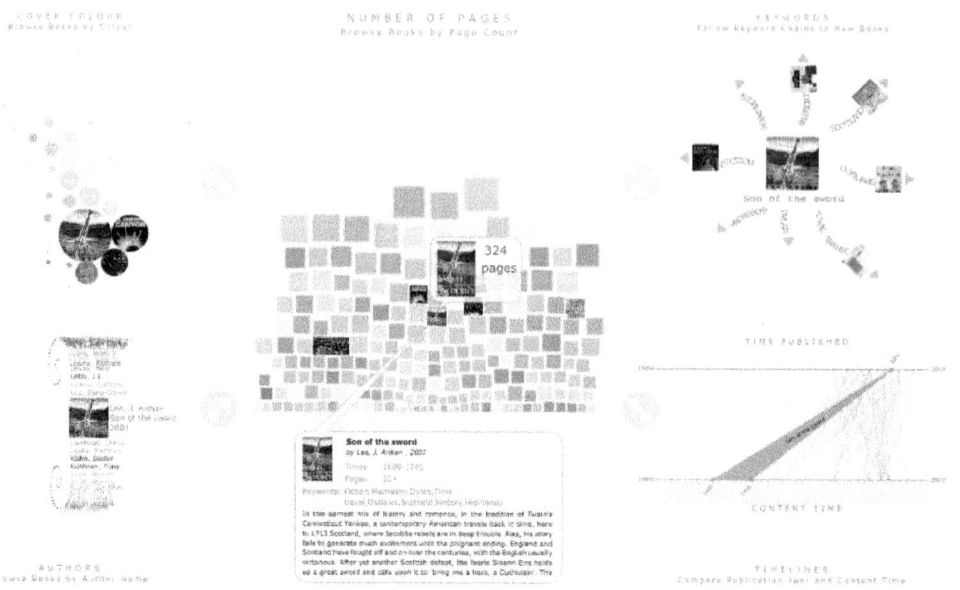

Figure 1. The Bohemian Bookshelf: five interlinked visualizations presenting different perspectives on a book collection.

Highnesses travelled they were always making discoveries, by accidents & sagacity, of things which they were not in quest of" [38, p.20]. Currently, variations of the Oxford English dictionary's definition are commonly used to describe the term serendipity: "*the faculty of making happy and unexpected discoveries by accident*" [36]. This definition, however, highlights the fortuitous and random aspect of serendipity while neglecting the existence of more strategic elements that Walpole has hinted at by mentioning the influence of sagacity on serendipitous discoveries.

Factors Influencing Serendipity

Different factors have been identified in the literature that can favour serendipity beyond its coincidental aspect. Here we tease out these factors to bring to the fore additional aspects of serendipity that can be incorporated into design.

Personality Traits

Serendipitous discoveries can be attributed to an individual's personality, knowledge, and attitudes. Austin coined the term *altamirage* to describe serendipitous discoveries as a result of chance paired with individual traits of the exploring person [2, 30]. Along these lines, Erdelez found that some people, "super-encounterers", are particularly talented in encountering information of interest unexpectedly [13]. These people embrace serendipitous discoveries as part of their life process. Talents or special traits that facilitate serendipity include observational skills [41], curiosity [30], open-mindedness [1, 14, 30, 41, 47], knowledge [1, 30, 41], and perseverance [30].

Observational Skills. Observational skills can favour serendipity. For example, Rosenman emphasized how Flemming's observational skills, acquired during his arts training, contributed to his famous discovery of penicillin, which has been attributed to serendipity [41].

Open-mindedness. Numerous works on serendipity emphasize the importance of an *open* and *prepared* mind [1, 14, 30, 41, 47]. This recognizes that valuable insight from serendipitous discoveries requires receptiveness to unexpected information: "*chance only favours prepared minds*"(Louis Pasteur) [47]. Open-mindedness can manifest itself in curiosity [30], questioning previous assumptions, or deliberately looking at information from various perspectives [30, 41].

Knowledge. Expertise and the ability to make sound judgements, as part of a "prepared mind", also are considered key factors of serendipity in that they enable drawing connections between seemingly unrelated information [1, 30, 41, 46]. Walpole described this as sagacity in his definition of the term serendipity [38]. Without prior knowledge, certain serendipitous discoveries in science would not have been possible. For instance, Flemming's knowledge about bacterial inhibitors helped him to recognize the potential value of the penicillin mould when he observed it for the first time [41].

Perseverance. It has been suggested that perseverant research of a certain topic favours the occurrence of serendipitous discoveries [30]. The more time and effort one invests, the more knowledge one aggregates, which, in turn, facilitates the discovery and recognition of unexpected valuable insights.

Environmental Factors

Besides the personal factors described above, there are some outside factors that can favour serendipity. These factors are independent of the person researching the information.

Coincidence. As previous work points out, serendipity is most commonly discussed in relation to fortuitous, accidental, or coincidental events [1, 14, 30, 47]. This is closely related to the notion of *synchronicity* where related ideas may manifest as simultaneous occurrences that seem acausal but still meaningful [30]. The prevalence of these ideas of chance, fortuity, and coincidence in the discussion around serendipity has led to a tendency to trivialize this complex concept by assuming that serendipity can be supported simply through the introduction of randomness.

Influence of People & Systems. Most information that is explored on an everyday basis has already been classified, organized, or laid out for us by others in advance. This prior categorization by other people, systems, or processes can lead to serendipitous discoveries by making relations explicit [30].

Library books, for instance, are often classified by the Dewey Decimal System [9] which determines how books are grouped on the shelves. It is therefore not only the personal interests, characteristics, or search strategies of a patron that influence what books are being encountered while browsing the library shelves but the system used to organize them.

While the specific impact of each of the factors listed above on serendipity is unknown, it becomes clear that there is more to serendipity than mere chance and coincidence.

DESIGN FOR SERENDIPITY THROUGH VISUALIZATION

The question of how serendipitous book discoveries can be facilitated through information technology is much discussed in library and information sciences [1, 4, 14, 50]. However, while these discussions include recommendations toward visual interfaces [32], presently, this discourse largely consists of rather vague suggestions and theory. We have distilled the general recommendations from the information and library science literature into a concise list that includes an interpretation from an information visualization perspective. The resulting set of visualization design goals can be considered a starting point for promoting serendipity through information visualizations in future case studies.

Multiple Visual Access Points

Rice suggests supporting different access points to digital library catalogues to encourage serendipity [39]. This correlates with the idea of open-mindedness and a person's willingness to "view data from several perspectives" [41]. Fox et al. found that exploring library catalogues from different views appealed to people [15]. Unlike in physical libraries where one book can only be located in a single place, digital collections allow multiple groupings at the same time. Utilizing this characteristic, we suggest providing different *visual* perspectives on a collection to help people conduct explorations from distinct viewpoints, revealing different, maybe unfamiliar or surprising, aspects of a known topic. This could be realized by providing a variety of orthogonal access points to books in form of different overview visualizations.

Highlighting Adjacencies

When browsing through data collections, it is often items in close proximity that draw people's attention and trigger serendipitous discoveries. For instance, people have described finding interesting books unexpectedly when browsing the library shelves in search of a book on an unrelated topic [14, 19, 30]. The juxtaposition of books in traditional libraries both makes their collections searchable and, unintentionally, can lead to serendipitous discoveries [46]. Visualization techniques offer the opportunity of visually highlighting multiple, co-existing alternate adjacencies. For example, books can be adjacent in terms of their genre, topic, or publication year.

Flexible Visual Pathways

Huwe suggests providing multiple pathways through digital book collections to preserve the opportunity for serendipitous discoveries in digital library systems [25]. This recommendation is related to the call for more open-ended navigation strategies. Most search interfaces to digital libraries support targeted search in the form of querying [31, 39, 46]. More open-ended strategies such as *exploratory search* [31, 46, 51], *browsing* [8, 34, 40], or *information encountering* [13] have been recommended as more likely to support serendipity.

It has been suggested that open-ended search strategies may benefit from visual interfaces that allow for flexible, rather than predetermined navigation through data collections as commonly supported by current textual query editors and sequential result lists [31]. Visualizations can offer pathways through digital book collections, as suggested above, by providing multiple interactive overviews as visual guides through the collection and by offering many possible adjacencies that can act as visual signposts suggesting alternative exploration routes. Additional pathways can be indicated by emphasizing cross-visualization attributes by mutual highlighting as in coordinated views [3, 7]. It is important to note that these pathways do not have to be predetermined but can instead offer constantly changing series of crossroads. By enabling options for multiple pathways the support of fluid transitions between visualizations and changing exploration foci becomes important. It is the variety of visual pathways and their flexibility that can serve to enhance serendipity.

Enticing Curiosity

Some serendipitous discoveries have been attributed to curiosity [46, 47]. Similarly, Dörk et al. suggest considering information seeking as a pleasurable, inspiring experience [11]. While curiosity may well be considered as part of a person's personality, there are factors such as visual aesthetics and animation that can promote curiosity and initiate interaction [20, 21, 23, 49]. Specific factors to be considered include: visually distinct interfaces, visual metaphors, the representation of unusual data facets, and the incorporation of visual cues to facilitate the interpretation of the presented data.

Playful Exploration

The notion of serendipity has been discussed in relation to creativity and ideation [28], suggesting that play as a facilitator of creativity [43, 48] might also stimulate serendipitous discoveries [1]. Walk-up-and-use information visualizations can encourage a playful, pleasurable and, in turn, more thorough and perseverant approach to information exploration.

RELATED VISUALIZATION APPROACHES

The Bohemian Bookshelf, a visual exploration tool for digital book collections, represents a first exploration into the use of information visualization to support serendipity. It exemplifies one interpretation of our design goals that have been described above. Here, we discuss previous work on visual interfaces for document collections, coordinated views, and public information displays that has influenced the Bohemian Bookshelf design.

Visualization of Document Collections

Some tools visualize search results in relation to the entire document collection (e.g. [6, 16, 44]). These visualizations require querying before a visual exploration can begin. This dismisses parts of the document collection and disagrees with the notion of "maximizing the number of possibly relevant objects" that has been suggested to support serendipity [31]. We deliberately designed the Bohemian Bookshelf to provide multiple overviews of the entire book collection to provide opportunities to discover unexpected trends and relations within the collection. Existing tools that currently provide such overviews, include traditional visualization techniques such as scatter plots, tree maps, or pie charts to offer an efficient and analytical view on documents [12, 17, 26, 27]. Others make use of metaphors that realistically mimic the look and feel of traditional bookshelves to leverage people's familiarity with physical libraries [5, 37]. In contrast, our choice of visual representations in the Bohemian Bookshelf exemplifies an abstract, metaphoric approach that aims to evoke curiosity and promote a playful exploration of book collections to encourage serendipitous discoveries. With the intention to offer a child-friendly interface, the International Children's Digital Library supports open exploration based on the physical characteristics of books such as cover colour [24]. With the Bohemian Bookshelf we aim at encouraging open-ended explorations of book collections and serendipitous discoveries for library audiences at large.

Coordinated Views for Document Exploration

Coordinated views provide multiple interlinked visualizations that are used in relationship to one another [7]. They lend themselves well to visualizing document collections such as library catalogues that are characterized by a variety of attributes [3]. North and Shneiderman highlight multiple views to benefit the "discovery of unforeseen relationships" [35]; serendipitous discoveries, in other words. Coordinated views have been utilized to support the exploration of brief texts (e.g. [10, 21]). However, they have not been applied or discussed in the context of serendipity.

Public Information Displays

Some public ambient information displays address the concept of unexpected discoveries by emphasizing information randomly in the hope that some of it meets the interest of passers-by. The News Wall traverses through recent news ordered by topic [33]. "Making Visible the Invisible", an ambient display installation at the Seattle Library, cycles through different visualizations of media being checked out of the library during the past hour [29]. ResearchWave, an ambient visualization, animates through publications to maintain a casual awareness of activities within large research organizations [20]. The InfoGallery is a large information display that aims to promote awareness of libraries' digital collections that otherwise have no presence in the physical library space [18]. Through the use of visual interfaces and animation these approaches can trigger serendipitous discoveries in a coincidental way. In contrast, the Bohemian Bookshelf exemplifies how to encourage serendipitous discoveries through information visualization more systematically, beyond concepts of fortuity and coincidence.

THE BOHEMIAN BOOKSHELF VISUALIZATION

One of the best known ways of finding books serendipitously is through location and proximity to a given book on a bookshelf [14, 19, 46]. Furthermore, previous literature [42, 45] as well as our informal discussions with librarians revealed that physical and visual attributes play a big role during open-ended explorations of book collections. This guided our choice of book attributes to visualize in the Bohemian Bookshelf: we aimed at providing a variety of perspectives or *facets* [52] on the book collection to increase the number of possible adjacencies by leveraging content-related as well as physical characteristics of books. We included one attribute commonly used for physical adjacencies (ordering by author), one commonly used for digital search (content-related keywords), one physical attribute often neglected in digital libraries (page count), one emphasizing the visual appearance of the book (cover colour & thumbnail image), and one that juxtaposes books' temporal aspects (content era and publication year). Thus, the Bohemian Bookshelf (see Fig. 1) offers five possible adjacencies between books, instead of just one as in physical bookshelves, any of which might offer disparate types of serendipitous discoveries.

The Bohemian Bookshelf is based on a collection of 250 books retrieved from the Open Library[1] project and covers mostly the genres history and fiction. We decided to work with a sample book collection with attributes similar to those available in large library collections. The book attributes we chose to focus on—book title and author, content keywords, page count, cover colour extracted from a book's cover image, publication year, and content era—are each represented by one of five individual visualizations: the Author Spiral, Keyword Chains, the Book Pile, the Cover Colour Circle, and Timelines. Each visualization provides a unique overview of the book collection from a particular perspective. All five of them can be considered as→*Multiple Visual Access Points*; one of our design goals. The individual visualizations are interlinked: the selection of a book in one visualization changes the views of the other four visualizations in relation to the newly selected book,→*Highlighting Adjacencies* across visualizations. The visual emphases of cross-visualizations adjacencies can be considered as crossroads to different→*Visual Pathways* through the collection that can be followed by flexibly switching back and forth between different visualizations. Of course, other book attributes could be visualized and interlinked in a similar way. The Bohemian Bookshelf exemplifies one possible implementation of our design goals.

The Bohemian Bookshelf prototype was implemented in Adobe Flash. The visualizations and corresponding interaction techniques were designed with a large touch-interactive display in mind. However, they could also be integrated in a web-based interface. The following describes the visualizations that define the Bohemian Bookshelf in detail.

Cover Colour Circle

When browsing through books on a traditional shelf, a book's cover is one of the first things noticed. Covers are often designed specifically to attract attention; previous research has found them to be decisive for the anticipated reading experience [42]. The Cover Colour Circle (see Fig. 2) focuses on this aesthetic quality of books by providing an overview of cover colours as they occur in the book collection. This overview can be considered a→*Visual Access Point*,→*Enticing Curiosity* with its prominent visual features. For each book, an average colour is generated by calculating the mean pixel colour from the book's cover image. In the remainder of the paper we will refer to a book's average cover colour simply to as its colour. This colour is used consistently throughout all visualizations in the Bohemian Bookshelf.

[1] http://openlibrary.org

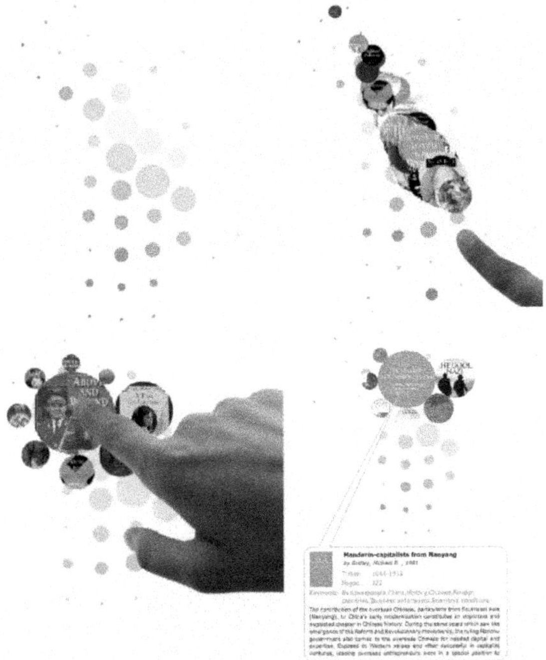

Figure 2. Cover Colour Circle: browsing through book covers (top), selection with adjacent books (bottom).

In the Cover Colour Circle books are grouped by colour and distributed in a circular layout based on the HSV model (hue, saturation, value). We make use only of hue and saturation (HS) and divide the HS circle into discrete colour points that are distributed in concentric circles where each point is equidistant from its neighbouring points. Books are placed in the resulting HS circle according to their colour's HS value. Each discrete colour point in the HS circle corresponds to a number of books of similar colour, represented by a circle whose radius is proportional to this number of books.

Moving the finger across the Cover Colour Circle reveals a circular preview of book covers whose colour corresponds to the current position in the HS circle (see Fig. 2, top right). This cover preview is temporary: previews directly under the touch point are shown in the largest scale and slowly shrink as the touch point moves away. This behaviour, inspired by Etsy's "Shop by color"[2], creates the impression of book covers bubbling up to the surface and disappearing again (→*Playful Exploration*).

Touch-and-release interaction selects a cover and enlarges its preview. In addition, a maximum of eight cover previews of other books with similar cover colours are shown (see Fig. 2, bottom;→*Highlighting Adjacencies*). Selecting one of these adjacent books brings it into focus as an enlarged preview along with a new selection of adjacent books.

Keyword Chains

Digital libraries commonly make use of general terms or keywords that describe the content of books to facilitate categorization and search. Searching for a certain keyword in a digital library catalogue usually produces a list of books that share this particular term but can be otherwise quite different in content. The Keyword Chains visualization picks up on this common notion of categorizing books: it shows relations between books based on their keywords (see Fig. 3). Unlike the Cover Colour Circle, the Keyword Chains visualization does not provide an overview of the entire book collection but shows a vignette of up to nine books represented by their covers and connected through their keywords (→*Visual Access Point*). A cover thumbnail of the selected book is always displayed at the centre. From there, eight keywords that characterize this particular book branch out (e.g. "History", "Political Activity", etc., see Fig. 3), and each of them is attached to another book that shares this keyword (→*Highlighting Adjacencies*). Books that appear in a Keyword Chain are randomly selected from the book collection as long as they fit the criteria of connecting one book title with a corresponding keyword and vice versa. If one of the keywords has no more associated books, this particular Keyword Chain ends.

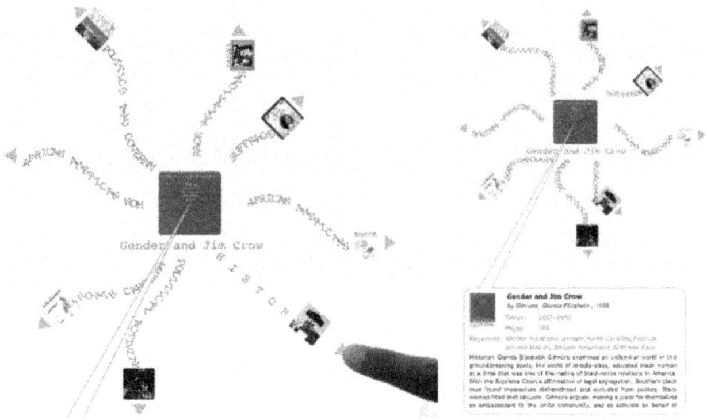

Figure 3. Keyword Chains visualization.

The arrangement of keywords and book titles along sine-based curves is reminiscent of a starfish meandering on the ocean bed. This organic appearance is enforced by subtle animations that cause each Keyword Chain to undulate (→*Enticing Curiosity*). To facilitate reading, Keyword Chains can be stretched by dragging the marker at the end of the chain (see Fig. 3.left, →*Playful Exploration*).

Selecting a cover thumbnail in a Keyword Chain causes the associated book to move into the centre of the visualization and new keywords form around it. This transition is animated, creating the impression of tentacles growing out of the selected book cover in the centre.

Timelines

Two important aspects of books are the publication year and the time period that the book discusses. The Timelines visualization shows the relationship between these temporal characteristics of books (→*Visual Access Point*). It consists of two parallel horizontal timelines (see Fig. 4) corresponding to the books' publication years (upper timeline) and content eras (lower timeline). Each book is represented by a line that connects both timelines, showing the relation between its publication year and the time period in focus. The pattern of lines between the timelines provides an overview of the range and density of publication dates and time periods covered by the entire book collection. Trends can easily be identified: prominent publication years or time periods with particular coverage are visible by dense line clusters (see Fig. 4),→*Enticing Curiosity* and inviting for further exploration.

[2]http://www.etsy.com/

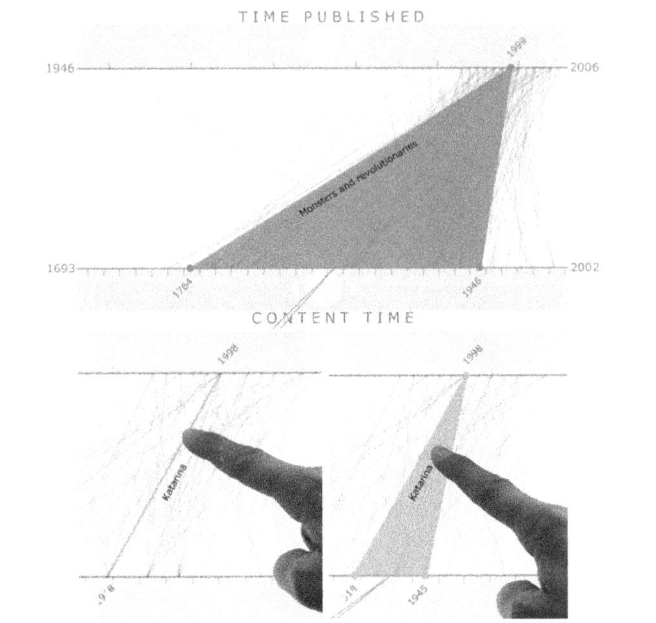

Figure 4. Timelines visualization: overview (top), browsing and selecting books (bottom).

Running a finger across the connecting lines between the two timelines reveals the title of each book and highlights labels on both timelines to indicate the exact publication year and the start year of the time period in focus (see Fig. 4, bottom left). This enables lightweight browsing through the book collection (→*Playful Exploration*). Releasing the finger from a selected line shows a triangle in the book's colour determined by the book's publication year and start and end date of the time period in focus (see Fig. 4, bottom right). This triangle is slightly transparent to allow visibility of lines indicating other adjacent books (→*Highlighting Adjacencies*).

Zooming is supported on both timelines independently to review time periods of interest more closely. Moving the finger in the light-grey area of one timeline to the left, causes the start year of this timeline to increase—the timeline stretches. The overall time frame of the timeline is shortened and books within this shorter time period become dispersed. Moving the finger toward the right loosens the tension in the timeline: the overall time frame enlarges and the density of books increases again. The Timelines Visualization only shows books that are fully visible within the time frames of both timelines.

Book Pile

The thickness of a book and, related to this, its weight, are physical characteristics that influence not only its appearance but also the reading experience. For example, extremely large books can be attractive for their prominent physical appearance. The Book Pile visualization focuses on this physical aspect of books (→*Visual Access Point*). It is based on the metaphor of a physical pile of books (→*Enticing Curiosity*). Each book is represented by a square where colour reflects the book's colour and edge length represents its page count. A square's position is dependent on this page count: books with fewer pages trickle through to the bottom of the Book Pile while thicker books get stuck more toward the top. We use a stacking algorithm to position books. First, books are categorized based on their page count in intervals of 100 pages. Within each interval books are stored in random order. We then position the books starting from the bottom centre of the visualization canvas working our way upwards. Books with the smallest number of pages are positioned first, alternating between the left and right of the canvas' centre to achieve a balanced pile. The random order of books within the page count categories visually strengthens the pile metaphor.

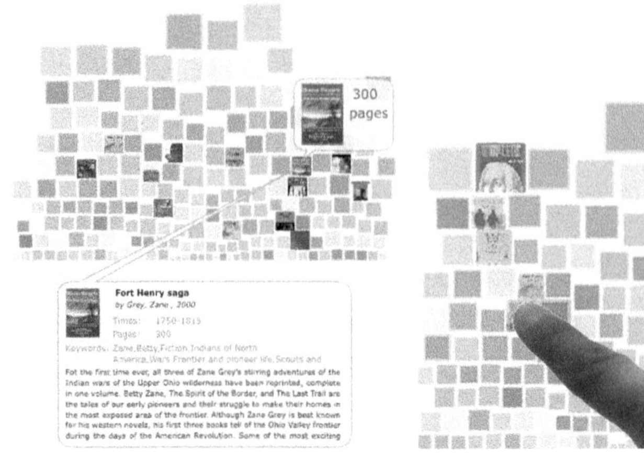

Figure 5. The Book Pile visualization.

Touching a square in the book pile reveals the corresponding book cover and page count. Books with similar page counts (± 5 pages) are emphasized by showing their covers, →*Highlighting Adjacencies* (see Fig. 5). Continuously moving the finger across the book pile also temporally reveals the corresponding book cover (→*Playful Exploration*).

Author Spiral

Many libraries and bookstores organize books alphabetically by author name. With the Author Spiral visualization we adopt this common way of alphabetical organization (→*Visual Access Points*). To provide space for various sized collections, the author list rolls up into spirals toward both ends, similarly to a parchment role (see Fig. 6,→*Enticing Curiosity*); only the stretched part of the Author Spiral shows books in form of an author label in the book's colour. Toward the spiral-shaped ends of the list, books are represented by circles in the book's colour. Circles become smaller the closer they are to the spirals centre. The size of the spirals is adjusted depending on the number of books listed on each side while the number of books shown in the stretched middle of the parchment remains constant.

Touching an author label or circle moves the corresponding book into the centre of the "parchment stretch" and reveals its cover preview, title, author, and publication year. Due to the alphabetical ordering, books with same or similar author names line up below and above (→*Highlighting Adjacencies*). To facilitate their selection, author circles enlarge underneath the finger. People can smoothly scroll through author names by running their fingers across the Author Spiral (→*Playful Exploration*).

Interlinked Visualizations in the Bohemian Bookshelf

Together, all visualizations described above form the interface of the Bohemian Bookshelf with one visualization in the centre and the others surrounding it (see Fig. 1). The centre

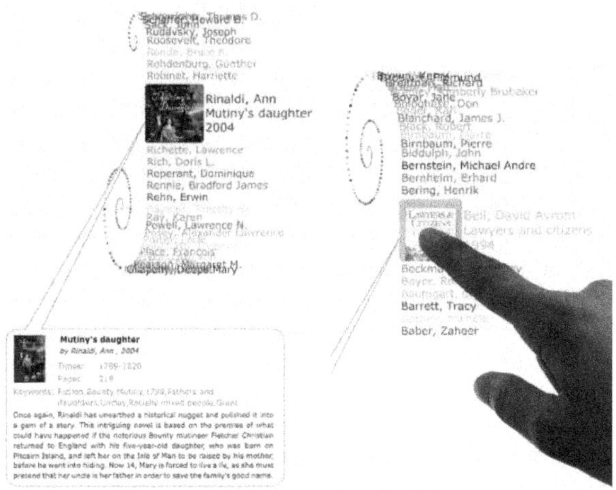

Figure 6. The Author Spiral visualization.

visualization is 20% larger than the peripheral visualizations. A visualization can be brought into the centre of the display by touching a small arrow button beside it. All visualizations can be explored independently as described above, no matter if they are in the centre or in the periphery. This can facilitate flexible changes of exploration paths through the collection (→*Visual Pathways*). A detail view in the bottom centre of the display provides textual information about the book that is currently selected, including all attributes also shown by the visualizations and a brief abstract (see Fig. 1, 2, 3, 5, and 6). All visualizations are interlinked in that a selection made in one visualization is reflected in the others. For instance, Fig. 1 shows the Book Pile as the central visualization through which the book "Son of the Sword" has been selected. Therefore, all other visualizations highlight this particular book and present adjacent books according to their own perspective. This concept of interlinked visualizations enables browsing through the book collection based on a perspective of particular interest (e.g. keywords) while still offering different perspectives in the periphery (→*Visual Pathways*). If a peripheral visualization catches someone's attention, it can easily be brought to centre for further exploration. When switching a visualization's position from periphery to centre and vice versa, current selections within the visualizations remain unchanged to maintain the search context and provide people with a familiar reference point within the new visualization now in focus. Together, the visualizations of the Bohemian Bookshelf can provide a synergistic experience that can propagate serendipity by encouraging viewers to experience the collection from a variety of perspectives.

LIBRARY DEPLOYMENT OF THE BOHEMIAN BOOKSHELF

We installed the Bohemian Bookshelf on a tilted, touch-interactive display (31.1 by 18.8 inches) for eight consecutive workdays at a central location at the University of Calgary library (see Fig. 7) to explore how library visitors would experience this visual and open-ended, serendipitous way of browsing book collections. Library visitors were able to spontaneously approach the display in a walk-up-and-use manner without any instructions or prior training. We took field notes of visitors' interactions and interviewed 11 visitors (6 male, 5 female; age approx. 20 to 60) who had interacted with the display for at least 30 seconds. The interviews included questions regarding visitors' initial motivations to approach the Bohemian Bookshelf; their overall experience of the visualizations; fulfilment of eventual expectations; potential book discoveries; and general book browsing and information seeking habits. All interviews were transcribed and coded independently by two researchers for visitors' thoughts on: using the Bohemian Bookshelf for the exploration of book collections, differences to other search interfaces they were familiar with, and the role of visualization, visual aesthetics, and display technology for browsing book collections. During the deployment, 129 library visitors approached the Bohemian Bookshelf: 94 visitors interacted with it while 35 just took a brief look without interacting. Average interactions times were 1:06 min (interviewed visitors: 1:59 min) with a maximum interaction time of 6:26 min (interviewed visitors: 3:39 min). Such seemingly brief interaction times are realistic in libraries where visitors often approach information displays spontaneously.

SERENDIPITY AND THE BOHEMIAN BOOKSHELF

In the following we discuss visitors' reactions to the Bohemian Bookshelf in the light of our five design goals for encouraging serendipity through information visualization.

Visitors often mentioned that they appreciated the Bohemian Bookshelf as a way for finding new books that they did not know of before as the following statements demonstrate: *"I have a set of interests or topics that I'd rather read about. So I think that [using the Bohemian Bookshelf] would be a good way of finding new books. [...] You get to see more different books that you might find interesting later, which you otherwise would never see because you wouldn't be looking for them."* [V4]; *"I think it will actually help me discover more authors and provoke people to read, like encourage them to read.* [V11].

Visitors also appreciated the way the Bohemian Bookshelf presents books compared to common search interfaces such as digital library catalogues: *"It's just the way information is presented is different than on the computer [the library catalogue]. That opens up different possibilities for finding out about the different books."* [V9]. Although the interface of the Bohemian Bookshelf does not resemble existing search interfaces commonly used in libraries and we did not provide any instructions regarding its purpose or possible interaction techniques, visitors quickly figured out how to control it. The following statement echoes common opinions regarding the interface: *"I like the fact that it is fairly intuitive. [...] I liked that it was very simple and easy to get used to in that way."* [V4]. Our interviews also revealed that it was the visualizations that helped visitors to get an idea of what the Bohemian Bookshelf is about and how to use it: *"I'd say like*

Figure 7. The Bohemian Bookshelf at the University of Calgary library.

90% of the understanding of it is the visual component. [...] I read the labels, but after [looking at] the visuals." [V8].

Providing Multiple Visual Access Points

The Bohemian Bookshelf presents a variety of different perspectives on the book collection, each providing different access points for exploration. Our interviews and observations of visitors' interactions revealed that the personal preferences regarding search criteria and the visualizations of the Bohemian Bookshelf were diverse. Providing a variety of different overviews can help addressing the individual preferences and interests of different patrons. Visitors also appreciated the variety of visual representations for gaining a general idea of the collection and potential starting points for exploration. For example, visitors explained: *"The way things are presented here [the Bohemian Bookshelf] also puts things in perspective. It just gives you a little bit of a different angle of seeing things."* [V9]; *"It gives you more options. [...] So if you have more information, it is easier to have a starting point."* [V8]; *"I'm sure each element [the visual overviews] works differently for different people. I like having it all together. [...] It kind of promotes curiosity."* [V11].

Enticing Curiosity through Visual Aesthetics

All visitors we interviewed stated that the visual aspect of the interface in combination with the touch interactive display evoked their curiosity. Visitors in particular mentioned the colours and cover images as visually attractive and as motivating them to take a closer look and to touch the interface even if they first did not know what it was about or how it worked. Many visitors appreciated the Cover Colour Circle with its focus on books' visual aesthetics. Comments that describe serendipitous discoveries within this visualization, such as *"I picked my favourite colour. I picked pink and then I found a book that I liked."* [V7] were common. Visitor statements suggest that our focus on visual aesthetics was not only important for evoking curiosity but also in providing a starting point for more elaborate explorations that can potentially lead to serendipitous discoveries: *"First of all it [the Bohemian Bookshelf] catches interest. [...] I don't know the cover colours, what it is for exactly, but it makes it more interesting and then if you stumble upon something, you might want to read it. And that's a good way to get people to actually want to read."* [V5].

Highlighting Adjacencies

The visualizations in the Bohemian Bookshelf highlight adjacencies along different dimensions such as colour, time, page count, keywords, and authors' names. Each visualization provides a visual overview where adjacent books are presented in close proximity. In addition, adjacent books are individually emphasized in response to current selections. This combination of visual overviews and emphasis of individual books aims to parallel a "browsing the shelves" experience which has been shown to support serendipitous discoveries [14, 19, 46]. Our interviews indicate that highlighting adjacencies encouraged new discoveries by promoting new or different associations between topics or books. For instance, visitors stated: *"I like the different criteria; that it is all on the same screen. [...] It [the Bohemian Bookshelf] is a cool tool to discover something new through different associations."* [V5].

Flexible Visual Pathways as Serendipitous Guides

It can be overwhelming to start exploring a large book collection when one does not know exactly what to look for. With the Bohemian Bookshelf we aimed at providing multiple flexible pathways through the book collection to guide people in potentially interesting directions that they did not think of in the first place. We approach this goal in three ways. First, we provide multiple interactive visual overviews of the collection that can help steer people's explorations. Several visitors appreciated these overviews to help guide their exploration and prevent them from *"getting lost"* [V3] in the collection. We also observed visitors deliberately steering their exploration along "outlier" books that visually stood out within the visualizations. For instance, visitors frequently explored particularly large or small books in the Book Pile or isolated connecting lines in the Timelines visualization. Second, the emphasized adjacencies between books can act as visual signposts that can guide the exploration. For instance, some visitors browsed through the Keyword Chains, following up on thematically adjacent books: *"[...] the current way of searching for a book is, you have to know what it is or just browse through an alphabetical list like an author list. But here [with the Bohemian Bookshelf] you can kind of branch off by keyword and find similar books in the same type of topic."* [V4]. Similarly, visitors explored books about particular time periods in the Timelines visualization.

The interlinking of visualizations is a third way of promoting visual pathways through the collection, in that every book selection in one visualization can be considered a cross road to other visualizations that highlight the book in a different context. We observed that visitors fluidly switched back and forth between visualizations, changing their exploration direction on a whim as one visualization caught their interest.

Playful Exploration to Encourage Browsing

The design of the Bohemian Bookshelf is strongly focused around the use of playful interaction to not only evoke curiosity and initiate exploration but also to make book exploration a pleasurable experience. Visitors found that the combination of interactive visualizations and touch-interactive display technology encouraged book exploration and enhanced the general browsing experience: *"I think it makes it very interesting to actually look for books. [...] It is visual and it's high tech."* [V5]; *"You have the touch screen with all the different covers that open up and you can [...] just pick them. That's sort of like browsing. [...] It's more satisfying than sitting on the computer clicking through a whole bunch of stuff."* [V9].

Serendipitous Book Discoveries

Six of the visitors we interviewed explicitly mentioned that they made personal serendipitous discoveries while interacting with the Bohemian Bookshelf. Three participants explained that they found a book by selecting their favourite colour. Others stated that a book's cover, title or author caught their eye when browsing the visualizations: *"I had no expectations and I just saw a [author] name that seemed familiar to my language, and then I thought, well, why not check it [the book] out."* [V11]. The participants named book titles they found interesting and sometimes wanted to check them out from the library. This is remarkable considering visitors' spontaneous use of the Bohemian Bookshelf and the short interaction times. These encouraging initial results indicate that visitors embraced the concepts inherent in the Bohemian Bookshelf of supporting open-ended browsing of book collections and serendipity through information visualization.

DISCUSSION

Initial reactions of library visitors toward the Bohemian Bookshelf have been encouraging. Visitor statements not only reveal that our design goals have largely been met, but they also demonstrate a high level of excitement toward the use of information visualizations for supporting open-ended explorations of library collections and promoting serendipitous discoveries: *"It [the Bohemian Bookshelf] gives you a chance to kind of explore at your leisure and to discover new artists or topics you might like, so it's something I'd definitely be looking forward to using at the library."* [V4]. However, the Bohemian Bookshelf, as a first exploration in this direction, also raises some questions to be explored in the future.

Scalability. The Bohemian Bookshelf prototype that we installed at the library included a collection of 250 books to ensure fluid real-time interaction. Of course, this number does not come even close to most library collections. While the performance of our prototype can easily be improved by applying more potent implementation strategies, some of the visualizations have to be adjusted to allow for larger data sets. The Book Pile and the Author Spiral, for instance, could be redesigned to show books in an aggregated form, similar to the Cover Colour Circle. Common visualization techniques such as edge bundling [22] could be used to avoid clutter within the Timelines visualization.

Combining Open-Ended & Targeted Search Strategies. While we designed the Bohemian Bookshelf to support open-ended explorations of book collections, library visitors made use of some visualizations in a rather targeted way. For instance, many visitors appreciated the Book Pile visualization as a useful way to find particularly short books on a topic. Furthermore, visitors frequently asked for possibilities to filter and specify the books displayed to certain topics of interest. It seems that the boundaries between open-ended and targeted browsing are fluid and people make use of both when exploring book collections. This raises the question of how to combine targeted and open-ended *serendipitous* exploration strategies using information visualization. One obvious step in this direction would be the integration of a textual query interface into the Bohemian Bookshelf visualization.

Distraction through Complexity. Providing several visual overviews that point to other, potentially interesting, books not only facilitates unexpected, valuable discoveries but also the possibility of getting distracted from the actual topic of interest and, at worst, getting lost in the book collection. Visitors seemed ambivalent about this potential problem. Some liked the approach of having several interlinked visualizations in one single view and even asked to add more visual perspectives to further reflect on the content of books or to integrate ratings and reviews of other readers. Other visitors, however, were concerned about the visual complexity of the interface and suggested showing only one visualization at a time. It would be interesting to explore the impact of different layouts that include varying numbers and sizes of interlinked visualizations. The problem of loosing track of previously discovered books and the overall exploration path was also mentioned. This reveals the integration of visual "bread crumbs" to help people trace back their exploration path and mark books or views on the collection that they may want to get back to as another important research direction.

CONCLUSIONS

Introducing the Bohemian Bookshelf as a case study, we have discussed how serendipitous book discoveries can be supported through information visualization. While serendipity has been found to be an important factor in information seeking, research, and ideation, the approach of most search interfaces to digital data collections is targeted toward "minimizing the number of possibly *irrelevant* objects" rather than "maximizing the number of possibly *relevant* objects" [31]. This does not specifically encourage serendipitous discoveries. We have presented five design goals derived from previous literature that can guide the design of visualizations to facilitate serendipitous discoveries. As an interpretation of these design goals we have introduced the Bohemian Bookshelf, which aims to support serendipitous discoveries in the context of digital book collections. A deployment of this prototype at a university library and interviews with the library visitors who interacted with it suggest that our design goals were largely met. Beyond this, they indicate considerable excitement of visitors toward visualizations of library collections that facilitate open-ended exploration and serendipitous discoveries. Our findings encourage future case studies that address serendipity as a goal in information visualization. There are many digital data collections that could benefit from a serendipitous approach to information exploration such as news feeds, photos, videos, or music collections. The case study presented in this paper can be considered as a first step into exploring information visualization as a means to encourage serendipitous discoveries. While our design goals are applicable to a variety of different scenarios and datasets, future case studies will help to evaluate and further expand these goals and recommendations for serendipity support through visualization.

ACKNOWLEDGEMENTS

We would like to thank our study participants and the staff of the University of Calgary Library (TFTL), in particular Shawna Sadler and Helen Clarke, for supporting this research. Special thanks go to Dominikus Baur, Sebastian Boring, and Matthew Dunlap for their invaluable feedback. We also thank our iLab colleagues and our funding sources (SurfNet, GRAND, AITF, CFI, NSERC, and SMART Technologies) for their support.

REFERENCES

1. André, P., schraefel, m. c., Teevan, J., and Dumais, S. T. Discovery is never by chance: Designing for (un)serendipity. In *Proc. of Creativity and Cognition* (2009), 305–314.
2. Austin, J. H. *Chase, Chance, and Creativity. The Lucky Art of Novelty*. The MIT Press, 2003, ch. Altamirage, 84–86.
3. Baldonado, M. Q. W., Woodruff, A., and Kuchinsky, A. Guidelines for Using Multiple Views in Information Visualization. In *Proc. of AVI'00* (2000), 110–119.
4. Blandford, A., and Buchanan, G. Usability of digital libraries: a source of creative tensions with technical developments. *IEEE Technical Committee on Digital Libraries Bulletin 1*, 1 (2003).

5. Christoffel, M., and Schmitt, B. Accessing libraries as easy as a game. In *Visual Interfaces to Digital Libraries [JCDL 2002 Workshop]*, Springer-Verlag (London, UK, 2002), 25–38.
6. Clarkson, E. C., Desai, K., and Foley, J. D. ResultMaps: Visualization for Search Interfaces. *IEEE TVCG 15*, 6 (2009), 1057–1064.
7. Collins, C., and Carpendale, S. Vislink: Revealing relationships amongst visualizations. *IEE TVCG 13*, 6 (2007), 1192–1199.
8. de Bruijn, O., and Spence, R. A new framework for theory-based interaction design applied to serendipitous information retrieval. *ACM Transactions on Computer-Human Interaction 15*, 1 (2008).
9. Dewey, M. *A Classification and Subject Index for Cataloguing and Arranging the Books and Pamphlets of a Library (Dewey Decimal Classification)*. Kingsport Press, Inc., 1876.
10. Dörk, M., Carpendale, S., Collins, C., and Williamson, C. Visgets: Coordinated visualizations for web-based information explorations and discovery. *IEEE TVCG 4*, 6 (2008), 1205–1212.
11. Dörk, M., Carpendale, S., and Williamson, C. The information flaneur: A fresh look at information seeking. In *Proc. of CHI* (2011). to appear.
12. Dushay, N. Visualizing metadata : A virtual book spine viewer. *D-Lib Magazine 10*, 10 (2004).
13. Erdelez, S. Information encountering: It's more than just bumping into information. *Bulletin of the American Society for Information Science 25*, 3 (1999), 25–29.
14. Foster, A., and Ford, N. Serendipity and information seeking: An empirical study. *Journal of Documentation 59*, 3 (2003), 321–340.
15. Fox, E., Hix, D., Nowell, L., Brueni, D., Wake, W. C., Heath, L. S., and Rao, D. Users, user interfaces, and objects: Envision, a digital library. *Journal of the American Society of Information Science 44*, 8 (1993), 480–491.
16. Fox, E. A., Neves, F. D., Yu, X., Shen, R., Kim, S., and Fan, W. Exploring the Computing Literature with Visuailzation and Stepping Stons & Pathways. *Communications of the ACM 49*, 4 (2006), 53–58.
17. Good, L., Popat, A. C., Janssen, W. C., and Bier, E. UC: A Fluid Treemap Interface for Personal Digital Libraries. In *Proc. of JCDL'05* (2005), 408–408.
18. Grønbæk, K., Rohde, A., and Bech-Petersen, S. Infogallery: Interactive art services for physical library spaces. In *Proc. of JCDL'06* (2006), 21–30.
19. Gup, T. Technology and the end of serendipity. *The Education Digest 6* (1998), 48–50.
20. Hinrichs, U., Fisher, D., and Riche, N. H. ResearchWave: An ambient visualization for providing awareness of research activities. In *Proc. of DIS* (2010).
21. Hinrichs, U., Schmidt, H., and Carpendale, S. EMDialog: Bringing information visualization into the museum. *IEEE TVCG 14*, 6 (2008), 1181–1188.
22. Holten, D. Hierarchical edge bundles: Visualization of adjacency rlations in hierarchical data. *IEEE TVCG 12* (2006), 741–748.
23. Huang, E. M., Koster, A., and Borchers, J. Overcoming assumptions and uncovering practices: When does the public really look at public displays. In *Proc. of the conf. on Pervasive Computing* (2008).
24. Hutchinson, H., Bederson, B., and Druin, A. Supporting elementary-age children's searching and browsing: Design and evaluation using the international children's digital library. *Journal of the American Society of Information Science and Technology* (2007).
25. Huwe, T. K. New search tools for multidisciplinary digital libraries. *Online 23*, 2 (1999), 67–74.
26. Johnson, D. K. Knowledge mining with VxInsight: Discovery through interaction. *Journal of Intelligent Systems 11*, 3 (1998).
27. Klein, P., Reiterer, H., Müller, F., and Limbach, T. Metadata visualisation with VisMeB. In *Proc. of IV'03* (2003), 600–605.
28. LeClerc, A. Seeking serendipity: The inspiration hunt of a creative professional. *Faculty of Information Quarterly 2*, 3 (2010).
29. Legrady, G. Making visible the invisible. http://www.mat.ucsb.edu/g.legrady/glWeb/Projects/spl/spl.html, 2005. Website visited Sept. 2011.
30. Liestman, D. Chance in the midst of design: approaches to library research serendipity. *RQ 31*, 4 (1992), 524—536.
31. Marchionini, G. Exploratory search: From finding to understanding. *Communications of the ACM 49*, 4 (2006), 41–46.
32. Merčun, T., and Žumer, M. Visualizing for explorations and discovery. In *Proc. of the conf. on Libraries in the Digital Age* (2010), 104–115.
33. Moghnieh, A., Arroyo, E., and Blat, J. The news wall: Serendipitous discoveries in dynamic information spaces. In *Proc. of IUI'08* (2008).
34. Morse, P. M. On browsing: The use of search theory in the search of information. *Bulletin of the Operations Research Society of America 19* (1971).
35. North, C., and Shneiderman, B. A Taxonomy of Multiple Window Coordinations. Tech. Rep. CS-TR-3854, Univ. Maryland Computer Science Dept., 1997.
36. Oxford English Dictionary. http://www.oed.com/view/Entry/17638-7?redirectedFrom=serendipity#eid. Website visited Sept. 2011.
37. Rauber, A., and Bina, H. A metaphor graphics based representation of digital libraries on the world wide web: using the libviewer to make metadata visible. In *Proc. of DEXA'99* (1999), 286–290.
38. Remer, T. G. *Serendipity of the Three Princes, from the Peregrinaggio of 557*. Norman, OK: University of Oklahoma Press, 1965.
39. Rice, J. Serendipity and holism: the beauty of opacs. *Library Journal 113*, 3 (1988), 38–41.
40. Rice, R. E., McCreadie, M. M., and Change, S. L. *Accessing and Browsing Information and Communication*. MIT Press, Cambridge, 2001.
41. Rosenman, M. F. Serendipity and scientific discovery. *Journal of Creative Behavour 22* (1988), 132–138.
42. Ross, C. S. Finding without seeking: the information encounter in the context of reading for pleasure. *Information Processing and Management 35*, 6 (1999), 783–799.
43. Russ, S. W. *Affect and Creativity: The role of affect and play in the creative process*. Lawrence Erlbaum, 1983.
44. Shneiderman, B., Feldman, D., Rose, A., and Grau, X. F. Visualizing Digital Library Search Results with Cathegorical and Hierarchical Axes. In *Proc. of Digital Libraries* (2000), 57–65.
45. Spiller, D. The provision of fiction for public libraries. *Journal of Librarianship 12*, 4 (1980), 238–265.
46. Toms, E. Serendipitous information retrieval. In *DELOS workshop on "Information seeking, searching and querying in digital libraries"* (2000), 17–20.
47. van Andel, P. Anatomy of unsought finding. serendipity: Origin, history, domains, traditions, appearances, patterns, and programmability. *The British Journal for the Philosophy of Science 45*, 2 (1994), 631–648.
48. Vandenburg, B. Play, problem-solving and creativity. *New Directions for Child and Adolescent Development 9* (1980), 49–68.
49. Viégas, F., Perry, E., Howe, E., and Donath, J. Artifacts of the presence era: Using information visualization to create an evocative souvenir. In *Proc. Of the IEEE Symp. On Information Visualization* (2004), 105–111.
50. Walton, C., Williamson, S., and White, H. D. Resistance to online catalogs: A comparative study at bryn mawr and swathmore colleges. *Library Resources and Technical Services 30*, 4 (1986), 388–401.
51. White, R. W., Kules, B., Drucker, S. M., and Schraefel, M. Supporting exploratory search. *Communications of the ACM 49*, 4 (2006), 37–39.
52. Yee, K.-P., Swearingen, K., Li, K., and Hearst, M. Faceted Metadata for Image Search and Browsing. In *Proc. of CHI'03* (2003), 401–408.

Reactive Information Foraging: An Empirical Investigation of Theory-Based Recommender Systems for Programmers

David Piorkowski[1], Scott D. Fleming[2], Christopher Scaffidi[1], Christopher Bogart[1], Margaret Burnett[1], Bonnie E. John[3], Rachel K. E. Bellamy[3], Calvin Swart[3]

[1]Oregon State University
Corvallis, OR 97331 USA
{piorkoda,cscaffid,bogart,burnett}
@eecs.oregonstate.edu

[2]University of Memphis
Memphis, TN 38152 USA
Scott.Fleming@memphis.edu

[3]IBM T.J. Watson Research
Hawthorne, NY 10532 USA
{bejohn,rachel,cals}@us.ibm.com

ABSTRACT

Information Foraging Theory (IFT) has established itself as an important theory to explain how people seek information, but most work has focused more on the theory itself than on how best to apply it. In this paper, we investigate how to apply a reactive variant of IFT (Reactive IFT) to design *IFT-based tools,* with a special focus on such tools for ill-structured problems. Toward this end, we designed and implemented a variety of recommender algorithms to empirically investigate how to help people with the ill-structured problem of finding where to look for information while debugging source code. We varied the algorithms based on scent type supported (words alone vs. words + code structure), and based on use of foraging momentum to estimate rapidity of foragers' goal changes. Our empirical results showed that (1) using both words and code structure significantly improved the ability of the algorithms to recommend where software developers should look for information; (2) participants used recommendations to discover new places in the code and also as shortcuts to navigate to known places; and (3) low-momentum recommendations were significantly more useful than high-momentum recommendations, suggesting rapid and numerous goal changes in this type of setting. Overall, our contributions include two new recommendation algorithms, empirical evidence about when and why participants found IFT-based recommendations useful, and implications for the design of tools based on Reactive IFT.

Author Keywords

Information foraging; debugging; software maintenance

ACM Classification Keywords

D.2.5 [Software Engineering]: Testing and Debugging; H.1.2 [Information Systems]: User/Machine Systems—Human factors

Permission to make digital or hard copies of all or part of this work for personal or classroom use is granted without fee provided that copies are not made or distributed for profit or commercial advantage and that copies bear this notice and the full citation on the first page. To copy otherwise, or republish, to post on servers or to redistribute to lists, requires prior specific permission and/or a fee.
CHI'12, May 5–10, 2012, Austin, Texas, USA.
Copyright 2012 ACM 978-1-4503-1015-4/12/05...$10.00.

INTRODUCTION

In the past two decades, Information Foraging Theory (IFT) [23] has revolutionized our understanding of how people seek information during information-intensive tasks, and in particular, of how people browse the web. Models based on the theory have accurately predicted the links that people will click as they navigate through web sites [3, 7, 22], and researchers have used the theory to design better tools to help people navigate the web [4, 18, 28]. This work on web foraging has focused on tasks where people have well-defined, unchanging information goals.

However, when solving ill-structured problems, people's information goals are likely to change as they process and assimilate new information. In particular, numerous examples of ill-structured problems relating to software development have been discussed in the literature (e.g., [8, 9]), and in this paper, we focus on software development tasks in which software developers wrangle with finding and fixing a bug (i.e., debugging). Empirical studies show that software developers faced with such problems often start by seeking an overall understanding of a program's structure and runtime behavior [25, 26], but they soon start to have questions that lead to exploring specific code [25]. Answers to these questions spark multiple new questions [13, 15, 25, 26]. Thus, the developers' goals evolve, unlike in the web foraging tasks that researchers studied using IFT.

Reactive Information Foraging Theory is a relatively new variant of IFT that we have previously developed to incorporate the notion of evolving goals [16]. Reactive IFT has been shown to predict software developers' navigation choices as they completed debugging tasks [16, 20]. IFT says that a person seeking information follows *information scent* emitted from *cues* in the environment in a manner similar to how a predator foraging in the wild follows scent to prey [22]. Related work provided models for inferring a web forager's goals from cues followed [3], and Reactive IFT led to analogous models that infer evolving goals of software developers [16, 20].

In this paper, we explore how to apply Reactive IFT to provide tools that infer, in real time, developers' evolving goals and use those inferences to recommend places in code that satisfy those goals. Several questions arise about how to operationalize the theory to build useful tools.

One question is how much of a person's recent history to consider when inferring the current goal. As noted above, a developer typically investigates code related to a certain goal for a while—which we refer to here as "building up foraging momentum" related to that goal—before shifting to a new goal. Reactive IFT indicates that the software developer's current momentum, reflected by recent navigation actions, can be used to infer the goal, but it does not specify how many recent navigations to use for this analysis.

Another question that arises in using IFT for tool design is which cues to consider for inferring goals. The web foraging research (e.g., [3, 22]) has emphasized operationalizing cues as words that appear in web pages that have been visited. Program code tends to be less "wordy" and more structured than natural-language text, and some prior models of developer navigation have hinted that at least in this domain, it might be useful to consider both word and code-structure cues to infer developer goals [16, 20].

Two other subsidiary questions also arise. First, because the navigational behavior of developers changes over the course of a task (as noted earlier), it is questionable whether different operationalizations will be more or less appropriate at different points in a task. Second, related to this point, different developers might obtain different value from Reactive IFT-based tools at different points in a task, raising the question of when and why recommendations are useful.

Consequently, our specific research questions were:

- RQ1: How do a Reactive IFT-based tool's assumptions about foraging momentum affect its ability to infer a developer's goal and produce useful recommendations?
- RQ2: Does a Reactive IFT-based tool that considers word *and* code-structure cues yield more useful recommendations than another tool that considers only word cues?
- RQ3: Does a Reactive IFT-based tool's ability to provide useful recommendations change as a task progresses?
- RQ4: When and why do software developers find Reactive IFT-based tools' recommendations useful (or not)?

RELATED WORK

Empirical studies have revealed many cases where software developers navigate through source code. For example, during debugging tasks in a laboratory study, developers spent 35% of their time browsing and searching through code [13]. Aside from debugging, code navigation is also essential for implementing new features, porting code, documenting code, extracting reusable code, and virtually every software development activity.

Code navigation is a key part in a learning process whereby the developer finds the information needed to work out a concrete goal to complete the task at hand. At the start of a maintenance task in laboratory and field studies, a developer usually searched for code that could serve as an initial focus point [25, 30]. Over the course of a task, the developer typically began to ask questions about how pieces of code were related [6, 25]. Developers also frequently navigated between locations in code, revisiting places to learn about structural relationships [19, 26]. As developers discovered answers to their questions, they broadened their focus to include more code [26]. Eventually, they planned specific changes that they believed would eliminate a defect or create a new feature [13, 26].

Various tools are aimed at easing these navigations by providing shortcuts to recommended places in the code that might hold valuable information. Several tools provide "history" links back to code that the developer has recently visited [12, 19]. Others offer shortcuts to places that other developers historically have read and/or edited after the current location [6, 10]. Still other tools provide shortcuts to code or other artifacts based on textual similarity, textual proximity, method-invocation, or nesting [5, 11, 27, 29].

A limitation of these tools is that they do not explicitly take into account the *evolution in goals* that typically occurs as a developer learns during a task. For example, upon visiting a Java method's code at the start of debugging, a developer might have no idea what needs to be edited; upon revisiting the location later, the developer might have formulated a goal to make certain kinds of edits. Yet most of the tools above would provide exactly the same shortcuts in both situations, regardless of the developer's new goal. Of the above tools, only those that show a "history" of recent places would behave differently during a particular task: they would stop showing links to locations that were not recently visited, which is an implicit model of evolving goals at best.

IFT, as we discuss below, offers a start toward addressing these limitations. Our objective in the current study is to investigate how to use this theory to help software developers find the information that they need during tasks.

BACKGROUND: INFORMATION FORAGING THEORY

IFT is a theory of how people seek information during information-intensive tasks [23]. It is based on the assumption that humans generally tend toward rational strategies that enable them to locate and process information efficiently. It was inspired by biological theories of how animals seek food in the wild. In IFT, a *predator* (person seeking information) pursues *prey* (valuable sources of information) through a *topology* (collection of navigable paths through an information environment). To find prey, the predator follows *information scent* that he/she obtained from *cues* in the environment. Cues are associated with navigation options, and the *scent* on cues is the predator's assessment of the value and cost of information sources obtained by taking the associated navigation options.

IFT was originally applied to user-web interaction. Models based on the theory have predicted the web pages to which people will navigate during particular tasks [3, 7, 21]. Leveraging this predictive power, IFT has also inspired principles for the design of web sites [17, 28].

More recently, researchers have attempted to translate the IFT results from the web domain to software development [14, 15, 16]. To reconcile developers' evolving goals with the web-based models, which were focused on static, unchanging goals, we proposed Reactive Information Foraging Theory to describe evolving goals. A model based directly on this theory, *PFIS2* [16] (later refined to *PFIS3* [20]), was able to accurately predict developer navigation.

In this paper, we build upon this earlier work, adapting these models to build recommender *tools* that try to satisfy developer goals. In particular, we investigate the research questions mentioned earlier about how the operationalization of momentum and scent affect tool usefulness, as well as about when and why developers find the resulting tools useful. Ours is the first application of Reactive IFT as a theory for assisting software developers.

EMPIRICAL METHOD

In our empirical study, we invited professional developers to complete a debugging task using a new Eclipse plug-in tool that supplied links to places in the code that might provide information needed for the task. Within this plug-in, we activated different recommendation algorithms based on different operationalizations of momentum and scent. Specifically, we considered different algorithms in a 2×2 factorial design (with one factor for the operationalization of momentum and another factor for the operationalization of scent). We then measured what proportion of the time participants went to locations recommended by different algorithms. In our analysis, we also examined whether algorithms' recommendations were more or less useful at different periods of the task, and we qualitatively analyzed what kinds of benefits participants obtained.

Study Environment

We implemented our recommendation system as a plug-in for the Eclipse IDE (Figure 1). Interface elements 1–4 in Figure 1a are all those that commonly appear in the Java perspective of Eclipse: (1) Package Explorer view, (2) Outline view, (3) Java editor, and (4) Console view. Interface element 5 is our Recommendation view.

Figure 1b depicts a close-up of this Recommendation view, which had three areas: (1) the current method (i.e., the one that the text cursor last entered), (2) the current recommendations, and (3) methods bookmarked, or *pinned*, by the developer. Each time the developer navigated to a method, the current method updated to reflect the navigation, and the recommendations were recalculated (using whichever of our algorithms was activated at the time). The developer could also manually drag the current method or any recommendation into the pinned area to save it for later.

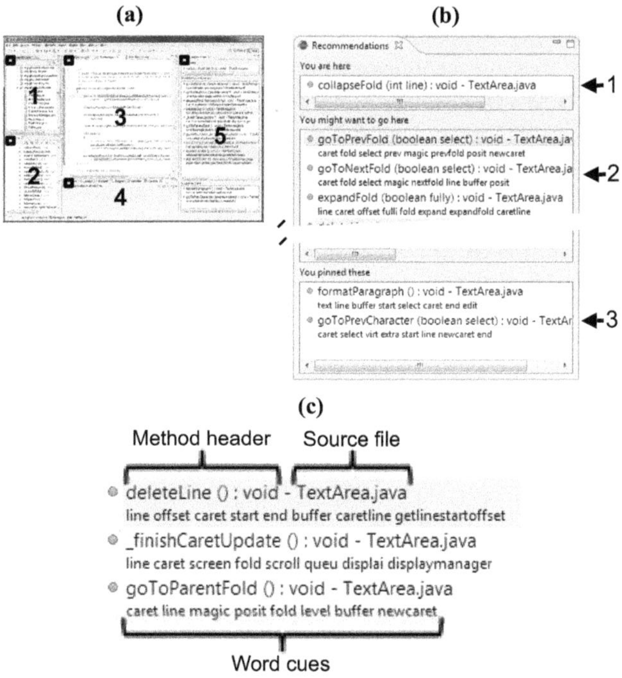

Figure 1. Eclipse interface with our Recommendation view: (a) Eclipse layout, (b) Recommendation view, and (c) examples of three recommendations.

Each recommendation displayed words to help participants assess its relevance (Figure 1c). These words were sorted based on their importance according to the amount of weight given to them internally by the recommender algorithm active at the time. The Recommendation view also distinguished recommendations to methods the participant had previously visited from recommendations to methods not already visited by highlighting the latter in gray.

For data collection, our plug-in recorded a log of participant interactions with Eclipse. Additionally, we video-recorded each session and automatically logged screen captures.

Recommendation Algorithms Considered

To investigate whether operationalizing scent as words + structure would produce better recommendations than words alone (RQ2), we implemented one recommender algorithm based on words + structure, PFIS-R, and another based on words alone, TFIDF-R. The PFIS-R recommender is based on the PFIS3 predictive model [20], motivated by PFIS3's success in predicting developer navigation. The other algorithm, TFIDF-R, is based on a vector space model commonly used in information retrieval [1]. These two algorithms represent the main camps of how to model information foraging: strong reliance on words (e.g., TFIDF, LSA) and balancing words with information structure (e.g., [3, 14, 15, 16, 18]). Both share a reliance on words, because word-based approaches have dominated IFT (e.g., [3, 4, 7, 22]) and the literature contains some evidence that words can be used to predict where developers will navigate [14].

RQ1 required a need to manipulate the operationalization of the *foraging momentum*—specifically, how much history to use for making recommendations. To take momentum into account, we parameterized each algorithm with δ, the number of navigations to look back in making a recommendation. An algorithm with δ=1 uses only the contents of the last method visited and thus ignores any momentum that the developer might have built up; we refer to this algorithm configuration as *low momentum*. In contrast, an algorithm with δ=10 uses the contents of the last 10 methods visited and will thus be influenced by momentum built up during those navigations; we refer to this algorithm configuration as *high momentum*. Thus, the greater the value of δ, the more momentum the recommender assumes in making its recommendations. Combining two momentum configurations, δ=1 and δ=10, with the two different algorithms (PFIS-R vs. TFIDF-R) gives the 4 possible combinations of our 2×2 factor design.

The algorithms take as an input the sequence of methods to which a developer has navigated so far. In the current study, we recorded a navigation to a method *m* each time the developer performed an action that caused the text cursor to enter the text of *m*. For our purposes, the text of a method comprises the method's signature, body, and (Javadoc) comments. Both PFIS-R and TFIDF-R normalize this textual input by excluding punctuation and *stop words*, which include common words, like *the*, as well as the list of Java keywords. Camel-case words are broken into separate case-insensitive words, although the original camel-case word is retained as well (e.g., *setFoldText* would be treated as an input of *setfoldtext*, *set*, *fold*, and *text*). For the remainder of the paper, *method text* refers to normalized method text.

The algorithms produce as output 10 recommendations, divided evenly between methods previously visited by the developer and methods not previously visited. Developers commonly revisit methods to recover mental state and explore new methods to find and understand the program's essential elements [19]. Thus, by recommending both visited and unvisited methods, we sought to support both types of navigation. If there are fewer than 5 previously visited recommendations, the algorithms fill out the remainder of the 10 recommendations with new recommendations, and vice versa. The algorithms would sometimes need to resolve ties when generating this list. The reason is that although the algorithm ranks methods by computing a continuous measure of relatedness (as discussed in the algorithm details below), the variables in those calculations take on a small number of distinct values in practice. When selecting the 10 methods to recommend, ties were resolved by choosing nondeterministically among the tied methods.

PFIS-R Recommender

Figure 2 summarizes the PFIS-R recommendation algorithm, which builds on the earlier PFIS2 and PFIS3 models by informing its recommendations using word cues and code-structure cues (i.e., call dependences) in methods that the developer previously visited. In brief, PFIS-R maintains a graph of word and method vertices such that edges between method vertices capture the structural relationships between methods, and edges between words and methods capture lexical relationships between methods. The algorithm *spreads activation* [22] over this graph, starting from the vertices for the last δ methods that the developer visited. To account for momentum, vertices for methods that the developer visited more recently are initialized with greater activation. The algorithm considers methods with the highest resulting activation to be the best recommendations, and those are the ones that sort first in Figure 1c.

PFIS-R Algorithm

Definitions:

- Method set *M*: set of all methods in the code base.
- Navigation history *H*: sequence of methods to which the developer has navigated so far.
- Word set *W*: set of all words in all method text in *M*.
- Graph $G = (V_m \cup V_w, E_m \cup E_w)$ such that V_m and V_w have a one-to-one relationship with *M* and *W*, respectively. For all m_a, m_b in *M* and their associated method vertices mv_a, mv_b in V_m, E_m contains one and only one edge connecting mv_a and mv_b if and only if the body of m_a contains a call to m_b or the body of m_b contains a call to m_a. For each word *w* in *W* and method *m* in *M*, E_w contains one and only one edge connecting *wv* and *mv* if and only if *w* is in the method text of *m*.

Steps for making recommendations:

- Set activation of each vertex in *G* to 0.
- For each method *m* such that *m* is the *k*th method in *H* and $|H|-\delta < k$, increment the method vertex *mv* by $0.9^{|H|-k}$.
- Spread activation (α=0.85 and edge weights=1) such that only word vertices receive activation.
- Spread activation again (α=0.85 and edge weights=1) such that only method vertices receive activation.
- Recommend methods with greatest activation.

Figure 2. Formal definition of the PFIS-R Algorithm.

TFIDF-R Recommender

In contrast to PFIS-R,TFIDF-R bases its recommendations on lexical similarity only. TFIDF-R treats the code base as a corpus of documents with the (normalized) text of each method being a document. The algorithm maintains a word-by-document matrix *MW* that specifies the importance of each word in *W* to each method in *M* by computing the tf–idf (term frequency–inverse document frequency [1]) weight for every word-method combination. It uses *MW* to assess the lexical similarity between methods by constructing a document-by-document matrix *MS* that specifies the cosine similarity measure [1] for all pairs of documents. *MS*(*m*) denotes the vector of cosine similarity scores associated with a particular method *m* in *MS*.

To account for the developer's foraging momentum, TFIDF-R sums the *MS*(*m*) vectors for the last δ methods to which the developer navigated, decaying older navigations at a rate of 0.9. Specifically, for each method *m* such that *m* is the *k*th method in *H*, $decayedMS(m) = 0.9^{|H|-k} \cdot MS(m)$. A final recommendation vector *VR* sums the decayed vectors for the last δ methods in *H*. The algorithm regards the methods with the greatest values in *VR* as the best recommendations, and those sort first in Figure 1c.

Participants

We recruited eleven professional software developers from a large company to participate in an empirical study comparing the usefulness of our four different algorithm configurations. Technical failures in the study environment invalidated the data for two of these participants; thus, we analyzed only the data for the remaining nine participants. We asked each participant to fix a defect in the jEdit software project. None of the participants had ever seen the jEdit code before, and with 6,468 methods, the jEdit code base provided a large space to forage within. The defect was from an actual bug report, #2548764, which described a problem with jEdit's text "folding" functionality.

Procedure

Each study session took about 180 min. Participants began by filling out a pre-questionnaire that gathered background information. Next, they engaged in two back-to-back task periods. Prior to the first task period, we introduced participants to the video equipment and started recording. Each task period was associated with a different treatment (i.e., one of our four algorithm configurations). Table 1 lists the treatment assignments, which we balanced to account for learning effects.

Each task period began with a short tutorial task on the tool. Some algorithms may have produced poor recommendations in the first task period, and we did not want participants who received such treatments to ignore recommendations in the second task period. Consequently, the tutorial in the second task period informed the participant that the tool's recommendation algorithm had been switched and asked the participant to repeat the tutorial task to see how the recommendations had changed.

Within each task period after the corresponding tutorial, participants worked on the jEdit debugging task for 35 minutes. To assess how participants used recommendations and when they were useful, we asked them to "talk aloud" as they worked. At the end of each task period, we interrupted participants and had them fill out a questionnaire that asked for their opinion of the recommendations.

Algorithm	Task period assignment for each participant								
	2	3	5	6	7	8	9	10	11
PFIS-R(δ=1)	2nd			2nd			1st	1st	
PFIS-R(δ=10)		2nd	2nd		1st	1st			2nd
TFIDF-R(δ=1)	1st		1st			2nd	2nd		1st
TFIDF-R(δ=10)		1st		1st	2nd			2nd	

Table 1. Treatment assignments to participants and task periods. (Participants 1 and 4 removed due to technical failures.)

After both task periods, the study session ended with a 35-minute semi-structured retrospective interview in which an interviewer stepped through events of interest in the screen capture videos and asked the participant questions about those events. For each time the participant navigated to a method, the interviewer asked, "What did you learn from this place?" and for each time the participant clicked on a recommendation, the interviewer asked the participant why he/she did that. Due to time constraints, the interviewer was sometimes unable to ask about all these events of interest in a session.

Analysis Procedure

Ultimately, a recommender's quality is its usefulness, but evaluating usefulness raises challenges. For instance, a participant may ignore recommendations that would otherwise be useful because the participant is unfamiliar with the tool. As professional developers, our participants have honed their navigation strategies over years of experience, and they might favor their practiced strategies over a relatively unfamiliar tool.

To address this problem, we conducted two analyses. The first was a quantitative analysis of *hit rate*. This analysis compared the algorithms' recommendations to the places that participants actually navigated, regardless of whether they actually used the tool to navigate there. The second was a qualitative analysis of *demonstrated usefulness*, which assessed whether recommendations participants followed via the tool were useful in the participants' opinions.

Hit rate

To assess hit rate, we computed the top-10 recommendations from the tool algorithm that was active at the moment before each user made each navigation. We scored the recommendations as a *hit* if the user navigated to a recommended location within the next *s* navigations. It was difficult to estimate the window of time in which a recommendation might have been usefully pertinent to a participant, so we explored two time-window sizes: a hit within the next 10 navigations (s=10) and a hit on the next navigation (s=1). Note that the time-window size *s* is concerned with how we score the hit rate of recommendations (over future navigations), not to be confused with the sensitivity to momentum factor δ in this study, which also had values of 1 and 10 (the number of past navigations from recent history).

Recall that nondeterminism arises in the case of ties between recommendations. To account for this nondeterminism, we took the best tie-breaking choice to make a best-case list of recommendations (maximizing hit rate), and we took the worst tie-breaking choice to make the worst-case list (minimizing hit rate), thereby bounding the effects of nondeterministic tie-breaking.

Given the two choices of s and the two choices of tie-breaking, we obtained four separate assessments of each recommendation algorithm's hit rate. Each of these was treated as a separate dependent variable in a separate regression. Because our dependent variable was dichotomous (indicating whether or not a recommendation was considered a hit), we used logistic regression. In addition to algorithm, our regression model also included task period and participant as categorical independent variables (i.e., indicator variables). After performing the regression, we used the Wald test to assess whether each variable (algorithm configuration, participant, and task period) had a statistically significant effect on hit rate. Using the coefficients provided by the regression, we also computed the overall hit rate of each algorithm, after subtracting out the effects of participant and task period.

Demonstrated usefulness

To assess recommendation usefulness, we looked at the recommendations that the developers followed to see if the recommendations helped the developers make progress. To do this analysis, we qualitatively analyzed the verbalizations the participants made during task performance and their answers to our probes during the retrospective interview. In particular, for each followed recommendation, our interviewer asked the participant "What did you learn from this place?" If the participant responded negatively (e.g., "I learned nothing") or with apparent uncertainty (e.g., "I don't know"), we coded the navigation as not useful; otherwise, we coded it as useful.

RESULTS: HIT RATE AND USEFULNESS

Hit Rate

Participants averaged one navigation every 90 seconds, or 447 navigations in all (Figure 3). We used this data to analyze hit rate. Figure 4 depicts the hit-rate results by algorithm configuration for window sizes s=10 and s=1. Our data revealed significant differences in the hit rates for the four configurations. Specifically, we consistently found $\chi^2(3) \geq 9$ and $p \leq 0.03$ regardless of whether we used s=1 or s=10, worst- or best-case tie-breaking, and δ=1 or δ=10.

Low vs. high sensitivity to momentum (RQ1)

Each low-momentum (δ=1) algorithm consistently scored a significantly better hit rate than the corresponding high-momentum (δ=10) algorithm (Figure 4). We found $z \geq 2.45$, $p \leq 0.01$ regardless of whether we used s=1 or s=10, worst- or best-case tie-breaking, and TFIDF-R or PFIS-R. Thus, with respect to RQ1, we found that low-momentum algorithms outperformed high-momentum.

Word and code-structure cues vs. word cues alone (RQ2)

We found no meaningful difference between PFIS-R and TFIDF-R, regardless of whether we used s=1 or s=10, or worst- or best-case tie-breaking. Neither low-momentum (δ=1) configuration of PFIS-R and TFIDF-R outperformed the other (at $p < 0.05$). Between high-momentum (δ=10) configurations, PFIS-R outperformed TFIDF-R, but the difference was not statistically significant (at $p < 0.05$). Additionally, we found no significant interaction between algorithm and sensitivity to momentum (δ)

First vs. second task period (RQ3)

Participants navigated almost twice as frequently during the second task period as during the first (Figure 3). Comparing between task periods (Figure 5), we saw suggestive differ-

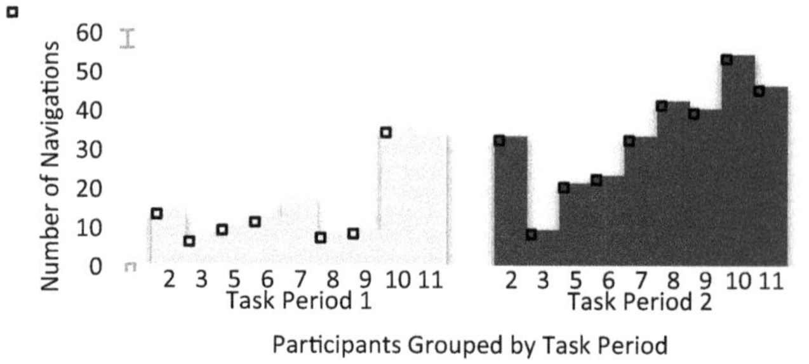

Figure 3. Number of navigations by each participant.

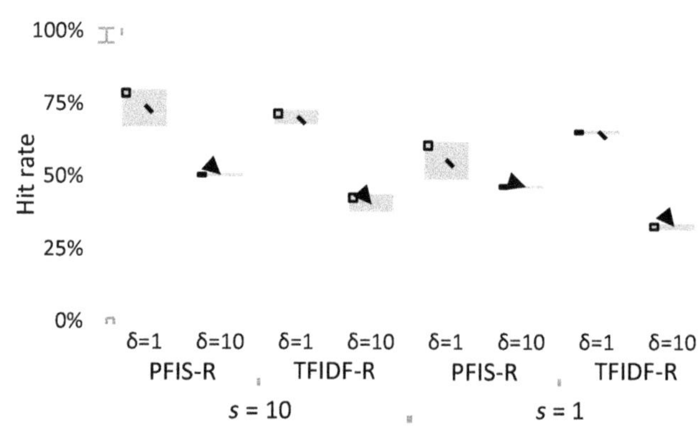

Figure 4. Hit rate of each algorithm (averaged over all task periods and participants) for s=10 (left half) and s=1 (right half), with rectangles indicating ranges between best- and worst-case tie-breaking. The δ=1 algorithms consistently outperformed the δ=10 ones (see arrows).

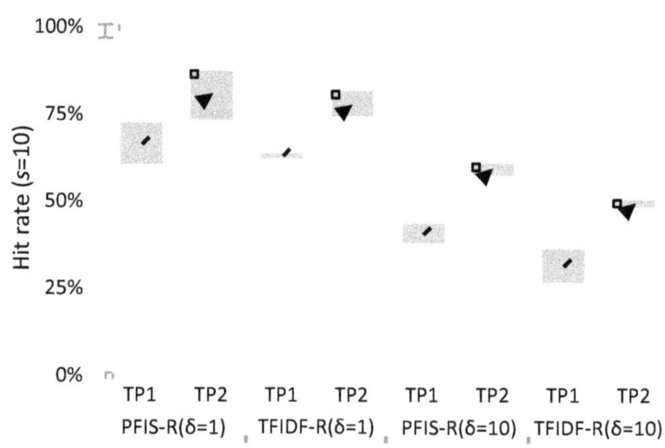

Figure 5. Hit rate (s=10) of each algorithm in the first (TP1) and second (TP2) task periods, with rectangles indicating ranges between best- and worst-case tie-breaking. Hit rates increased in the second task period (see arrows).

ences when evaluating recommendations with respect to the developer's next navigation (s=1), but these differences were not statistically significant (at $p < 0.05$). However, with respect to the developer's next 10 navigations (s=10), both algorithms improved significantly in the second task period over the first (pairwise $z = 2.37$, $p = 0.02$ for worst-case tie-breaking; $z = 3.44$, $p < 0.001$ for best-case).

Demonstrated Usefulness

All participants clicked some recommendations (Figure 6), for 62 clicks in total, and we collected interview responses for 44 clicks. Figure 7 summarizes the proportion of those clicks that participants reported as useful. We did not test for statistical significance due to the low number of clicks in each of the treatments.

Low vs. high sensitivity to momentum (RQ1)

The participants reported as useful a greater proportion of the recommendations from low-momentum algorithms than the recommendations from high-momentum algorithms (RQ1). This tendency triangulates with our finding that the low-momentum (δ=1) algorithms demonstrated a higher hit rate than the high-momentum (δ=10) ones.

Word and code-structure cues vs. word cues alone (RQ2)

Also triangulating with our hit-rate results, our demonstrated-usefulness results showed no consistent difference between PFIS-R and TFIDF-R.

First vs. second task period (RQ3)

Similar to what we saw with hit rate, the participants clicked recommendations more frequently during the second task period than during the first.

Opinion Questionnaire

Figure 8 illustrates the opinion results. Participants completed a total of 18 opinion questionnaires (1 per task period) that asked the question (5-point Likert) "Was this tool valuable in getting you to useful parts of the source code?" Again, we omitted statistical tests when analyzing this data due to the low number of clicks in each treatment.

Low vs. high sensitivity to momentum (RQ1)

Triangulating with our hit-rate and demonstrated-usefulness results, participants rated the low-momentum algorithms more favorably than the high-momentum ones (Figure 8b).

Word and code-structure cues vs. word cues alone (RQ2)

Similar to our hit-rate and demonstrated-usefulness results, the opinion results showed no suggestive difference between TFIDF-R and PFIS-R.

First vs. second task period (RQ3)

Participants seemed to rate all algorithms more favorably in the second task period than in the first (Figure 8c), consistent with our hit rate analysis where the second task period had a higher hit rate than the first.

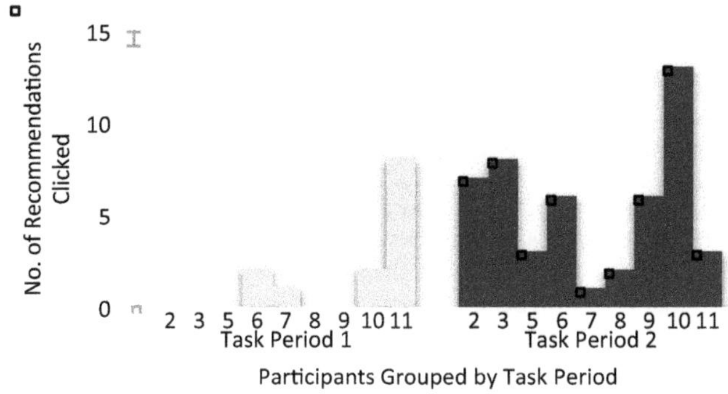

Figure 6. Number of times that participants clicked recommendations. Annotations indicate participant ID.

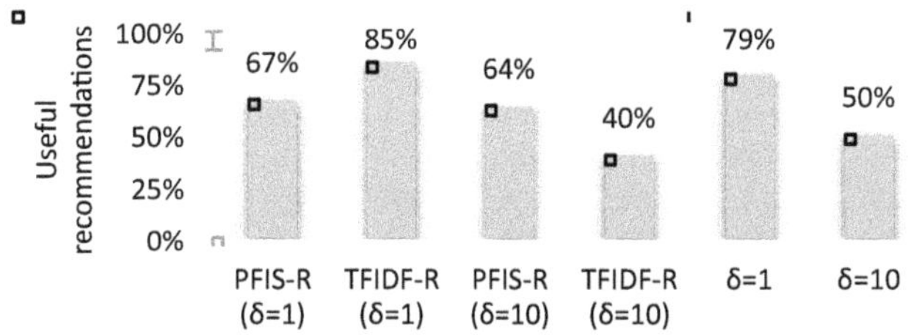

Figure 7. Percentage of recommendations that participants reported learning something from, grouped by algorithm and by low and high momentum.

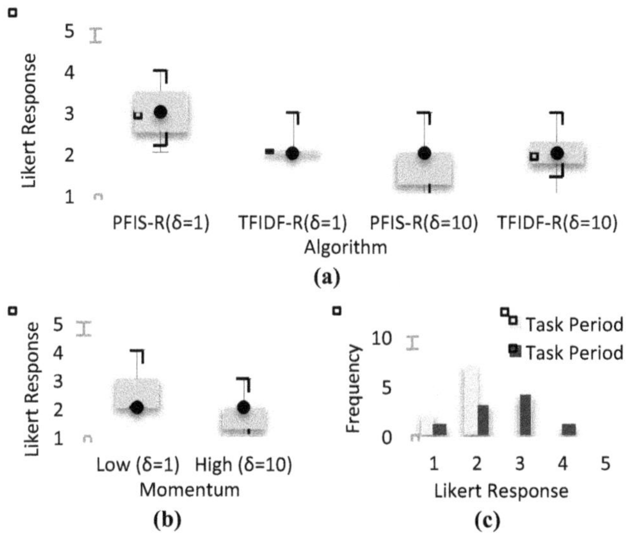

Figure 8. Results of questionnaires on the value of the recommendation system (1 = Entirely worthless, 5 = Very valuable).

RESULTS & DISCUSSION: WHAT PARTICIPANTS SAID

To better understand when and why participants found recommendations useful (RQ4), we qualitatively analyzed the talk-aloud and retrospective interview recordings.

Using Recommendations for Efficiency

Benefits of recommendations based on code structure

Some participants benefitted from PFIS-R's use of code structure in making recommendations. For example, Participant 2 found code-structure-based recommendations useful while using an exception stack trace to navigate through code. He used the stack trace to open a method that contained a call to another method `recalculateLastPhysicalLine` (i.e., following the call graph structure):

> Participant 2: "I wanted to go to the declaration of [recalculateLastPhysicalLine] and you know, my god, the [recommendation system] had it sitting there so I thought I'll go over and select it… I like that it was bigger and it was right there so it just seemed like I would both go to it and maybe learn something in the process…"

This quote reveals a case where a structure-based recommendation led directly to a desired method, making it efficient to navigate there in a single mouse click. PFIS-R's use of code-structure cues made a difference in this case. In contrast, running the TFIDF-R algorithm (with δ=1 and δ=10) on Participant 2's navigations revealed that this words-only algorithm would not have made this recommendation (even in the best case).

Recommendations as working set

Several participants used recommendations to efficiently navigate back to previously visited methods; e.g.:

> Participant 9: "At this point, I'm kind of abusing the recommendations as a history because they are the fastest way to get where I want to go."

As another example, Participant 8 took advantage of the implicit "history" when, using Eclipse's debugger, he accidently stepped out of a method `transactionComplete` that he meant to inspect:

> Participant 8: "So that kicks me out to the catch and I remembered it was in the transactionComplete method… I had remembered that this recommendation had shown a bunch of transactionCompletes, so I was just clicking around to just find where I was."

It could have taken Participant 8 considerably more effort to get back to `transactionComplete` (e.g., by rerunning the debugger) without the recommendation. Participants received historical recommendations from both low- and high-momentum algorithms because all algorithms made recommendations to previously visited methods.

Participants who used recommendations to get back to previously visited methods were essentially using the recommendations as a sort of *working set*. Previous research has shown that developers tend to navigate frequently to methods in their working set [19, 20], and several successful tools have been developed that emphasize working set [2, 6, 12]. A novel feature of our operationalization of Reactive IFT is that it implicitly supports working set while also helping the user explore new places.

Using Recommendations for Discovery

"Aha! moments"

Some participants followed recommendations to methods that they were apparently unaware of and expressed excitement about how useful the recommendation turned out to be. For instance, Participant 2 was having difficulty finding code to focus on. He perused the recommendations:

> Participant 2: "'You might want to go here.' … 'collapseFold' … 'expandFold' ... OK, 'collapseFold.' [Selects collapseFold recommendation; reads code comments.] 'Collapses the fold associated at the specified line index.' *OK! Now, this is where I want to be!* Collapsing the fold."

Participant 6 was having similar difficulty finding code to focus on when he turned to the recommendations:

> Participant 6: "[Selects loadMenu recommendation; reads code comments.] 'Creates a menu, the menu label is set from the name property, name.label propery.' *Oh! Oh! Yes!* … This thing looks like the class that might put up the menu. *I like that!*"

Our choice to make half of the recommendations be to previously unvisited methods created opportunities for participants engaged in exploratory navigation to have "aha moments" such as these. However, not all exploratory navigations were to unvisited methods. Participant 6 had already visited `loadMenu` when he followed the recommendation. On his first visit, he did not notice anything interesting about the method. It was only after he followed a recommendation to the method that he discovered needed information in the method.

Misleading cues

In some instances, participants navigated to methods that contained cues that generated strong scent, but the recommendations did not help them discover methods that would satisfy their goals. For instance, Participant 6 wanted to find the method that implemented the action for one of the items in jEdit's Edit menu. All the methods that he navigated to contained words (i.e., cues) related to his goal, such as *menu*, *edit*, and *action*. He then noticed a recommendation for `JEditAbstractEditAction` that included the keywords *edit* and *action*:

> Participant 6: "I was looking for the method that would get run when someone picked on that [Edit] menu item. So again, [the recommendation] could be the mnemonic suggestion of the class that maybe that was some kind of action that would get run in the Edit menu."

Participant 6 clicked the recommendation, but unfortunately the method did not contain code for implementing menu-item actions. Instead, it contained code that implemented the menu framework.

The recommendation system (running TFIDF-R, δ=10) could not help Participant 6 because it could not relate the word cues that he was following to the method that would satisfy his goal. That method contained entirely different word cues from the menu-framework code. Because the participant was navigating through the framework code, building momentum on those cues, the algorithm did not recognize the relevance of the needed method.

Code structure cues used by PFIS-R might help overcome this problem generally; however, in this particular case, PFIS-R would not have had access to the structural information needed to connect the menu and action code because that information was contained in a properties file that was not part of jEdit's Java code base. This problem highlights the importance of having complete structural information in operationalizing Reactive IFT.

DISCUSSION: IMPLICATIONS AND OPEN QUESTIONS

Sensitivity to Momentum

The Reactive IFT tools that were less sensitive to participants' foraging momentum (i.e., low momentum, $\delta=1$) produced better recommendations than those more sensitive to momentum (i.e., high momentum, $\delta=10$). This result runs counter to previous work on recommender systems, which suggested that using more history was better for predicting future navigation [16, 20]. Outside software maintenance, successful recommender systems use historical behavior going back days, weeks, and years [24]. In light of this past work, our result that $\delta=1$ produced better recommendations than $\delta=10$ was unexpected.

One interpretation is that this result may be due to participants' goals evolving rapidly and repeatedly. Studies have shown that as developers navigate through code, they continually ask new questions [13, 25, 26]. If participants' goals did change frequently, it would put the high-momentum operationalizations at a considerable disadvantage, because a high-momentum operationalization considers cues associated with a mix of goals, some of which are no longer relevant.

These results underscore the importance of understanding a predator's foraging momentum in operationalizing Reactive IFT. For these developers engaged in debugging, low-momentum was apparently better at inferring goals, but depending on the foraging context (e.g., government agents performing intelligence analyses or end users debugging spreadsheets), a higher foraging momentum may produce better outcomes. One limitation of the current study is that we examined only two values of δ. Future studies could further investigate the effect of momentum.

Changes in Foraging Behavior over Time

Changes in participants' foraging behavior as the task progressed may have been responsible for the algorithms' improved hit rate in the second task period. Studies have shown that developers pursue different kinds of information [6, 25, 30] and engage in different types of activities [15] as a task progresses. In our study, the participants may have had difficulty finding strong scents in the earlier stages of debugging. As they foraged, they may have homed in on places with stronger scent. Since our algorithms relied on scentful cues to approximate goals, they might have been less accurate earlier in the task when the participants were navigating through low-scent methods, and became more accurate as scent increased.

One possible way to handle low-scent periods is to switch algorithms during such periods. For instance, an algorithm might detect changes in a user's foraging momentum and swap in the most appropriate algorithm for approximating the user's goal. Open questions for future research include how to detect a user's shifts in momentum and how to make recommendations in the absence of scentful cues.

Beyond Word Cues

Although not reaching statistical significance, the hit-rate results showed a tendency to favor PFIS-R over TFIDF-R, and this tendency triangulates with the suggestive difference between PFIS-R and TFIDF-R in the opinion questionnaire results (Figure 8a). This tendency was consistent with the qualitative data. We observed many participants following call dependences while debugging. Moreover, we saw one instance (Participant 6) where a method that would have satisfied the participant's goal contained none of the words that the participant followed scent from.

The implication for tools is that when operationalizing Reactive IFT for a new context, the tool may need to consider other cues in addition to words. Word cues exclusively have dominated the work on web foraging, and they may be particularly effective in that context due to the large volume of unstructured natural language text that web pages contain. However, in a context like programming, where there is less natural language text and more structure, other types of cues may be valuable.

One limitation of the current study is that we only investigated two models for using word and structural scent. Future work may investigate other models that analyze other forms of scent or that are tailored to the needs of different users and different contexts.

CONCLUSION

This paper is the first to investigate how to bring Reactive Information Foraging Theory to recommender tools for information-intensive, ill-structured problems. The algorithms we investigated with professional software developers in a debugging task showed that:

- RQ1: Surprisingly, assuming low foraging momentum (using only one navigation to inform its choices) produced better recommendations than those produced by assuming high momentum (the past ten navigations).
- RQ2: There was suggestive but inconclusive evidence that participants found the tool to be more valuable when it used words + structure than when it used words only.
- RQ3: The tool's recommendations were more useful to participants later in the task, suggesting that tools may need to be sensitive to shifts in users' foraging behavior.
- RQ4: Recommendations helped participants by revealing useful places that the participants were unaware of and also by facilitating navigation to known places.

Most importantly, this study has demonstrated Reactive Information Foraging Theory's potential as a basis for the design of tools that help people solve ill-structured problems. We believe that such tools could help people in contexts beyond software development—for example, helping users debug spreadsheets, security analysts understand relationships among cartels, and the myriad other people who wrangle with complex, ill-structured problems every day.

ACKNOWLEDGMENTS

We thank our participants for their help, IBM for support under an OCR grant, and AFOSR for support under FA9550-09-1-0213. The views and conclusions in this paper are those of the authors and should not be interpreted as representing the official policies, either expressed or implied, of AFOSR, IBM, or the U.S. Government.

REFERENCES

1. Baeza-Yates, R., Ribeiro-Neto, B. *Modern Information Retrieval*, Addison Wesley Longman, 1999.
2. Bragdon, A., Zeleznik, R., Reiss, S., Karumuri, S., Cheung, W., Kaplan, J., Coleman, C., Adeputra, F., and LaViola, J. *Proc. CHI*, ACM (2010), 2503–2512.
3. Chi, E., Pirolli, P, Chen, K., and Pitkow, J. Using information scent to model user information needs and actions on the web. *Proc. CHI*, ACM (2001), 490–497.
4. Chi, E., Rosien, A., Supattanasiri, G., Williams, A., Royer, C., Chow, C., Robles, E., Dalal, B., Chen, J., and Cousins, S. The Bloodhound project: Automating discovery of web usability issues using the InfoScent simulator, *Proc. CHI*, ACM (2003), 505–512.
5. Cubranic, D, and Murphy, G. Hipikat: Recommending pertinent software development artifacts. *Proc. ICSE*, ACM/IEEE (2003), 408–418.
6. DeLine, R., Khella, A., Czerwinski, M., and Robertson, G. Towards understanding programs through wear-based filtering. *Proc. Softvis*, ACM (2005), 183–192.
7. Fu, W. and Pirolli, P. SNIF-ACT: A cognitive model of user navigation on the World Wide Web, *Human-Computer Interaction 22*, 4 (2007), 355–412.
8. Grigoreanu, V., Burnett, M., Wiedenbeck, S., Cao, J., Rector, K., and Kwan, I. End-User Debugging Strategies: A Sensemaking Perspective. *ACM Trans. Comput.-Hum. Interact.* (to appear).
9. Gross, P. and Kelleher, C. Non-programmers identifying functionality in unfamiliar code: Strategies and barriers. *Proc. VL/HCC*. IEEE (2009), 75–82.
10. Hill, W., Hollan, J., Wroblewski, D., McCandless, T. Edit wear and read wear. *Proc. CHI*, ACM (1992), 3–9.
11. Jakobsen, M. and Hornbaek, K. Evaluating a fisheye view of source code. *Proc. CHI*, ACM (2006), 377–386.
12. Kersten, M. and Murphy, G. Mylar: A degree-of-interest model for IDEs. *Proc. ASOD*, ACM (2005), 159–168.
13. Ko, A., Myers, B., Coblenz, M., and Aung, H. An exploratory study of how developers seek, relate, and collect relevant information during software maintenance tasks. *IEEE Trans. Soft. Eng. 32*, (2006), 971–987.
14. Lawrance, J., Bellamy, R., Burnett, M., and Rector, K. Using information scent to model the dynamic foraging behavior of programmers in maintenance tasks, *Proc. CHI*, ACM (2008), 1323–1332.
15. Lawrance, J., Bogart, C., Burnett, M., Bellamy, R., Rector, K., and Fleming, S. How programmers debug, revisited: An information foraging theory perspective, *IEEE Trans. Soft. Eng.* (to appear 2012).
16. Lawrance, J., Burnett, M., Bellamy, R., Bogart, C., and Swart, C. Reactive information foraging for evolving goals. *Proc. CHI*, ACM (2010), 25–34.
17. Nielsen, J. Information foraging: Why Google makes people leave your site faster. http://www.useit.com/alertbox/20030630.html. June 30, 2003.
18. Olston, C. and Chi, E. ScentTrails: Integrating browsing and searching on the web. *ACM Trans. Comput.-Hum. Interact. 10*, 3 (2003), 177–197.
19. Parnin, C. and Gorg, C. Building usage contexts during program comprehension. *Proc. ICPC*, IEEE (2006), 13–22
20. Piorkowski, D., Fleming, S. D., Scaffidi, C., John, L., Bogart, C., John, B. E., Burnett, M., and Bellamy, R. Modeling programmer navigation: A head-to-head empirical evaluation of predictive models. *Proc. VL/HCC*, IEEE (2011), 109–116.
21. Pirolli, P. Computational models of information scent-following in a very large browsable text collection. *Proc. CHI 1997*, ACM Press (1997), 3–10.
22. Pirolli, P. *Information Foraging Theory: Adaptive Interaction with Information*. Oxford Univ. Press, 2007.
23. Pirolli, P. and Card, S.K. Information foraging. *Psychological Review 106*, 4 (1999), 643–675.
24. Resnick, P. and Varian, H. Recommender systems. *Commun. ACM 40*, 3 (1997), 56-58.
25. Sillito, J., Murphy, G., and De Volder, K. Questions programmers ask during software evolution tasks. *Proc. FSE*, ACM (2006), 23–34.
26. Sillito, J., De Voider, K., Fisher, B., and Murphy, G. Managing software change tasks: An exploratory study. *Proc. ISESE*, IEEE (2005), 1–10.
27. Sinha, V., Karger, D., and Miller, R. Relo: Helping users manage context during interactive exploratory visualization of large codebases. *Proc. VL/HCC*, IEEE (2006), 187–194.
28. Spool, J., Profetti, C., and Britain, D., Designing for the scent of information, *User Interface Engineering*, (2004).
29. Storey, M, Best, C, Michaud, J, Rayside, D, Litoiu, M, and Musen, M. SHriMP views: An interactive environment for information visualization and navigation. *Ext. Abstracts CHI '02*, (2002), 520–521.
30. Wiedenbeck, S. and Evans, N. Beacons in program comprehension. *ACM SIGCHI Bulletin 18*, 2 (1986), 56–57.

Profanity Use in Online Communities

Sara Owsley Sood
Computer Science Dept., Pomona College
185 East Sixth Street
Claremont, CA 91711
sara@cs.pomona.edu

Judd Antin, Elizabeth F. Churchill
Yahoo! Research
4301 Great America Parkway
Santa Clara, CA 95054
<jantin, echu>@yahoo-inc.com

ABSTRACT
As user-generated Web content increases, the amount of inappropriate and/or objectionable content also grows. Several scholarly communities are addressing how to detect and manage such content: research in computer vision focuses on detection of inappropriate images, natural language processing technology has advanced to recognize insults. However, profanity detection systems remain flawed. Current list-based profanity detection systems have two limitations. First, they are easy to circumvent and easily become stale–that is, they cannot adapt to misspellings, abbreviations, and the fast pace of profane slang evolution. Secondly, they offer a one-size fits all solution; they typically do not accommodate domain, community and context specific needs. However, social settings have their own normative behaviors–what is deemed acceptable in one community may not be in another. In this paper, through analysis of comments from a social news site, we provide evidence that current systems are performing poorly and evaluate the cases on which they fail. We then address community differences regarding creation/tolerance of profanity and suggest a shift to more contextually nuanced profanity detection systems.

Author Keywords
Online communities; comment threads; user-generated content; negativity; community management; profanity.

ACM Classification Keywords
H.5.3. Information interfaces and presentation: Group and Organization Interfaces.

General Terms
Design, Experimentation, Human Factors.

INTRODUCTION
Online communities are often plagued with negative content – user-generated content that is negative in tone, hurtful in intent, mean, profane, and/or insulting. Negative content can be problematic for sites wanting to expand their user base, engage existing users, and foster a positive and collaborative community. Social contracts and normative behaviors, however, are unique to specific socio-technical systems. What is considered inappropriate in a given context is both site and community specific. On many sites, community managers are primarily responsible for the task of removing inappropriate content. However, the flood of user-generated content on many sites quickly overwhelms community managers' ability to effectively manage it.

The detection of negative content of malicious intent (personal attacks and insults) in forums and comment streams is a challenging and nuanced problem [20]. Recent work in machine learning and natural language processing has approached this task with varying degrees of success: with maximal f-measures of 0.298 for detection of harassment on Slashdot and 0.313 on MySpace from one study [24] and a maximal f-measure of 0.5038 for detection of personal insults on another [19].[1] Given the recent attention to the complex and sometimes grave consequences of cyberbullying [1], the ability to recognize and potentially mitigate profanity and other forms of harmful negativity in user-generated content is more important than ever [3,14].

Compared to the challenges of detecting malicious content or spam, detection and removal of profanity is often thought to be an easier task. Most current approaches to profanity detection check new content against large lists of profane terms. However, these systems are flawed in at least two major ways. First, static term-lists quickly lose currency and are relatively easy to circumvent. Users often disguise or partially censor profanity by replacing one or more letters with punctuation marks (e.g., "@ss," "%@#$"). Misspellings, both intentional or unintentional (e.g. "biatch", or "shiiiit") and the use of slang words (e.g. "assbite") that evolve quickly and often have local variations also challenge profanity lists to be more thorough and adaptive than they can reasonably be. Thus, these systems face issues of recall; they are unable to catch most cases of profanity. Secondly, list-based approaches to profanity detection are a one-size-fits-all solution that does not take into account differences in community norms and

Permission to make digital or hard copies of all or part of this work for personal or classroom use is granted without fee provided that copies are not made or distributed for profit or commercial advantage and that copies bear this notice and the full citation on the first page. To copy otherwise, or republish, to post on servers or to redistribute to lists, requires prior specific permission and/or a fee.
CHI'12, May 5–10, 2012, Austin, Texas, USA.
Copyright 2012 ACM 978-1-4503-1015-4/12/05...$10.00.

[1] F-measure is a measure of accuracy, specifically the harmonic mean of precision and recall.

practices. After all, what constitutes profanity differs greatly based on the specific community and topic at hand. For example, in a forum about dog breeding, "bitch" is a term of art that refers to a female dog, while in many other contexts it is a profane term. Furthermore, sites for children have a drastically different tolerance of profanity than those for adults.

In this paper we make three primary contributions to research on profanity detection. First, we address the state of current list-based profanity detection systems. Do these systems suffice? In what cases do they fail? Secondly, under the assumption that a major oversight in these systems is a lack of tailoring for specific communities, we examine how profanity use differs between communities. Is profanity used more or less in some communities? Do certain communities use profanity in different ways? And finally, we explore the social context of profanity use in different topical communities. How might specific communities receive profanity differently? In the sections that follow, we examine these questions through analysis of a data set of comments from a social news site.

BACKGROUND

As more and more of the web has grown to include user-generated content, the detection and management of inappropriate or objectionable content has become an important task for web sites. One common technique is social moderation, in which users themselves undertake the task of identifying and flagging of profane or inappropriate responses. However these systems have been only moderately successful, and suffer from potential collusion - flagging can be used to indicate disagreement or dislike of a post that is not otherwise inappropriate or profane [15]. Instead of relying on social moderation, recent proposals have been made to automate the detection of inappropriate or abusive content.

Research in computer vision has given much attention to the related issue of detecting inappropriate videos and images. Advances in this space have largely included systems that detect "too much skin" in images and videos [4,11,23]. Other systems utilize textual metadata [8,9], while some combine the two; one such system, *WebGuard* has reached 97.4% accuracy in detecting pornographic web sites [5].

While many would argue that textual analysis is more tractable than visual content analysis, this may be in part because of a general misunderstanding about how difficult the problem of profanity detection is in real-world contexts. Furthermore, text has a visual element that is socially understood. Expressive forms such as emoticons and "ASCII art" use visual properties of text, punctuation marks and symbols to mimic lexical units and thus convey meaning, denote profanity and circumvent automatic filters. Such visual-for-textual substitution is best illustrated through examples such as the use of "@" in "@ss"..

Because of these misunderstandings, perhaps, comparatively little research has focused on detecting inappropriate text in user-generated content systems. As mentioned above, two groups have built systems to detect insults and harassment in online forums [19,24] and another has focused on cyberbullying of teens [3], but even fewer have addressed the identification of profanity. Yoon et al. built a system to detect newly coined profanities in Korean, in an attempt to improve upon the failure of list-based systems to evolve along with profane language [25]. Due to the target audience being children, some have analyzed the content of video game web sites and video games themselves to verify that presented content meets ratings standards [6,7]. However, work in this area does not generally strive for automated analysis.

Advancing our ability to detect and remove profanity could have several significant, positive social consequences. The growth of collaborative information products such as Wikipedia, Yahoo! Answers, and Stack Overflow rely on the provision of interaction environments that are supportive, productive, and meet the specific needs of their user communities. Open-source software projects also rely on email lists and forums to support the necessary community building, coordination, and decision-making processes.

No automated system, by itself, can appropriately filter and manage ongoing discourse and interaction so that it meets the needs of a particular topic, domain, or user community. Indeed, research has illustrated the important role of established community members for implicitly and explicitly communicating language norms to new members [16]. The enforcement of these norms is often ad hoc, however. In large systems, the sheer volume of content means ad hoc strategies often leave a large amount of profane or inappropriate user-generated content undetected. The existence of such content can actually fight against the positive influence of community managers and long-time participants by setting a bad precedent that communicates to new users that profanity and other negative content is acceptable [21]. Automated systems that help community managers, moderators, and administrators to manage the flood of user-generated content in these environments could help to promote more productive large-scale collaboration and thus more valuable information products.

DATA SET

Social news sites (e.g., reddit.com, digg.com) typically allow users to post links to stories of interest, vote on contributed stories, and most important to the present study, comment on stories and respond to others' comments. Our data set is the complete set of user-contributed comments over a three-month period (March to May 2010) to Yahoo! Buzz, a social news commenting site that is no longer active. Our data set contains 1,655,131 comments distributed among 168,973 distinct threads. In addition to the comment itself, our data set contains meta information about each comment including the time posted and which news story the comment is in response to; this information can be combined to reproduce the comment thread. We also have information about each news story including its country of origin, language, and category (i.e., politics, entertainment). More information about this data set, including the distributions of comment lengths, comments per user and comments per thread can be found in [19].

Coding

In order to generate a data set describing the presence of profanity, insults, and the objects of the insults, we employed Amazon Mechanical Turk (MTurk). MTurk is an online labor market in which requesters post jobs that can be easily decomposed into a large number of small tasks. MTurk workers ("Turkers") are presented with a short description of available tasks, and then choose which tasks to complete. Individual tasks typically take between 5 and 20 seconds to complete and workers are generally paid about 5 cents for each task.

Recent studies have suggested that using MTurk for similar content analysis tasks can be both faster and more economical than using dedicated trained raters [22]. Furthermore, several studies have illustrated that combining the work of multiple Turkers on the same task can produce high quality content analysis results, even when some coders do not agree (i.e. the coded data is "noisy") [2,17].

We selected a random sample of 6500 comments spanning all categories. Comments that were likely to be too short to meaningfully interpret or too long to quickly process were not sampled: we restricted sampling to the 2nd and 3rd quartiles for overall comment length (between 73 and 324 characters long).

Each worker was shown one comment at a time. For each comment, they were asked to answer the following questions:

> *"Does this message contain any content you would describe as 'profanity?' (including profanity that is disguised or modified such as @ss, s***, and biatch) (Yes/No)*
>
> *Thinking about the intent of the comment's author, does the message contain what you would describe as a direct "insult?" (Yes/No)*
>
> *In your opinion, is the insult directed at the author of a previous comment? (Yes/No/Unsure)*

Finally, beyond the requirement of a consensus threshold from multiple coders, we also employed a 'gold data' model to improve label quality. Gold data were a set of comments for which the 'correct' labels (answers to the above three questions) were designated by the researchers prior to the labeling task. If a Turker mislabeled one of the gold comments, he was shown a short explanation for the correct answer. In this way the gold data functioned as a lightweight training program. In addition, if any Turker incorrectly labeled too many of the gold comments, their labels were removed from the data set and they were barred from labeling any further comments. All three authors independently judged the 'correct' labels for gold comments. For most gold comments the authors agreed on an answer which was likely to be self-evident. For example, the following comment was judged to contain profanity but no insult:

> *"Now they'll just release them so they can do the same thing tomorrow. Mine the Effen Border. Use the Natl. Guard to patrol our borders with extreme prejudice. Fences don't work. They'll tunnel under them or use ladders. Show the Drug Cartels that we mean business and this sh!t will cease."*

In other cases, however, the primary purpose of the gold comment was to draw attention to the desired aspect of the comment. For example, in the following comment it is, arguably, not possible to conclusively determine who is being insulted:

> *"Hot off the presses...straight fom their leader oweduma's mouth. The state of our economy deserves attention. This guy must live in a bunker. Wake up you liberal loser! The economy sucks."*

Over the course of approximately 5 days, 221 MTurk workers provided 25,965 judgments on 6500 comments. Following the model suggested by Sheng and colleagues [17], we employed multiple coders for each item. As a result, each item was rated by a minimum of three raters. We adopted a simple consensus model on the labels. To ensure labeling accuracy, our final profanity labeled data set only includes those comments for which at least 66% of labelers agreed on the profanity label. Similarly, our final insult and insult object labeled data sets only include those comments for which at least 66% of labelers agreed on the insult or insult object label. This method resulted in a different N depending on the focal phenomena (profanity, insult, or insult object). For example, one hundred and forty-six comments (2.2%) were dropped from the final profanity labeled data set because raters did not reach consensus on the profanity label.

DO CURRENT PROFANITY DETECTION SYSTEMS SUFFICE?

The standard approach to profanity detection in online communities is to censor or filter text based on lists of profane terms. When user-generated text contains listed words, those words or the entire contribution may be flagged for review or automatically removed. Some profanity lists are shared between multiple sites, and administrators contribute additional terms as they become prevalent or problematic. In order to test the efficacy of this approach, we downloaded a shared profanity list from the site phorum.org and built a simple system that flags a comment as profane if it contains any of the words on the phorum.org list.[2]

---

[2] At the time of our analysis (July 1, 2011), the phorum.org list contained 120 profane terms.

System	Precision	Recall	F1	Accuracy
noswearing.com w/ stemming	0.528	0.402	0.457	0.907
noswearing.com *or* phorum.org w/ stemming	0.490	0.412	0.448	0.902
noswearing.com *or* phorum.org	0.516	0.390	0.444	0.906
noswearing.com	0.563	0.367	0.444	0.911
phorum.org w/ stemming	0.631	0.231	0.338	0.913
phorum.org	0.636	0.196	0.300	0.912
random	0.096	0.501	0.161	0.498
weighted random	0.106	0.109	0.108	0.825

Table 1: An evaluation of list-based profanity detection systems.

As noted above, list-based systems often suffer (by identification/"recall" measures) as profane language evolves over time with slang and Internet abbreviations. As such, we downloaded a second list of profane terms from noswearing.com. This site hosts a list of community contributed profane terms. This list evolves over time with user contributions and is larger than the phorum.org list.[3] While both lists contain traditional profane terms, they also contain inappropriate terms such as racial slurs and vulgarities.

In another attempt to improve recall, we employ a stemmer. Beyond simply looking for the presence of a word on a profanity list, the stemmer allows the system to see if any words in a comment have a shared stem with any word on a profanity list. To evaluate the efficacy of list-based methods we built several systems that employed the two lists and stemming in various combinations. For each system, we average its performance over 5 trials of 10-fold cross validation on our 6500 profanity-labeled comments from Yahoo! Buzz. While the data set as a whole contains 6500 comments, 6354 meet the 66% labeling consensus across the MTurk labelers for the profanity label. Of those 6354, 595 (9.4% of the corpus) are positive cases, meaning that they contain profanity. All systems are evaluated based on their precision (a measure of false positives), recall (a measure of false negatives), f-measure (f1 – the harmonic mean of precision and recall) and accuracy–this is the standard array of evaluation metrics for systems of this type [10,18,24].

The performances of all systems are summarized in Table 1, sorted in descending order of f-measure. The *random* system is included as a baseline system; it randomly labels comments as profane or not. Similarly, the *weighted random* system labels comments randomly, weighted by the distribution of profane/non-profane comments in the training set. The performances of these systems are included for comparison purposes, though they of course approach the theoretical random baselines. The remaining systems are list-based approaches, based on the lists gathered from phorum.org and from noswearing.com. In an attempt to reach higher recall, we created additional systems that marked a term as profane if it appeared in either one of the two lists. Finally, in some systems we combined word lists with stemming.

[3] As of July 1, 2011, the noswearing.org list contained 341 terms.

ass	asses	bullsh!t
s***	pussy	sob
f*****	cr	bitch
azz	stfu	schit
bastard	dumbass	sh
sh!t	$hit	r**h***
a******	f***	c***
nr	m*****f*****	phag!
b*******	f*cking	f'ing
sh*t	@ss	goddamn
a$$	pussies	bull$hit

Table 2: Top words distinguishing profane from non-profane comments in the data set.

While a peak accuracy of 0.913 seems promising, recall that 9.4% of the comments in our corpus contain profane terms. For this testing data, if one built a system that, given a comment, always returned a negative classification (indicating that the comment does not contain profanity), it would have an accuracy of 0.906 as 90.6% of the testing corpus is comments that do not contain profanity. Therefore, f1, precision, and recall are much more descriptive evaluation metrics. As seen in table 1, peak performance of the list-based approaches is reached using the profane terms list from *no swearing.com* combined with a stemming system. This system detected 40.2% of the profanity cases at 52.8% precision. Based on our results, we must conclude that even the best of these list and stemmer based systems would not perform well at detecting and removing profanity in user-generated comments.

WHY DO LIST-BASED APPROACHES PERFORM SO POORLY?

As we have already discussed, list-based approaches perform poorly because of three primary factors: misspellings (both intentional and not), the context-specific nature of profanity, and quickly shifting systems of discourse that make it hard to maintain thorough and accurate lists. To exemplify these problems, we analyzed the words that most commonly distinguish profane from non-profane comments in our MTurk profanity labeled data set. The top words, seen in Table 2, were sorted in descending order by *x*, calculated as follows:

$$x = \frac{(posFeatureCt \,/\, TotalPosFeatures)}{(negFeatureCt \,/\, TotalNegFeatures)}$$

where *posFeatureCt* is the number of times the word occurred in positive (profane) comments, *negFeatureCt* is the corresponding value for negative (non-profane) comments, *TotalPosFeatures* is the sum of all feature counts across all words in the positive comments, and *TotalNegFeatures* is the corresponding value for the negative comments. The latter values are included to adjust for differences in the profane and non-profane corpora sizes.

Of the thirty-three words in this table, notice that only eight are standard spellings that would be found in listings of profane terms (i.e., 'ass,' 'bastard,' 'asses,' 'pussies,' 'pussy,' 'dumbass,' 'goddamn' and 'bitch'). There are six instances of slang abbreviations for profane terms – 'sob,' 'nr,' 'cr,' 'sh,' 'f'ing,' and 'stfu.' The remaining nineteen terms are disguised or author censored profanity (e.g., 'bullsh!t,' 'azz,' 'f*****'). Thus, a list-based profanity detection system, such as the ones evaluated in the previous section, would fail to catch twenty-five of the top thirty-three profane terms (76%) used in our data set. While these words could, of course, be added to a profanity list for future detection via a list-based system, there are countless further ways to disguise or censor words. This makes representing them in a list a significant challenge.

As further evidence of how widespread the particular problem of disguised or partially censored profanity is, we analyze use of one specific character, the @ symbol. The popularity of Twitter and other social media have resulted in adaptations and specializations of language for online communication [12]. Just as text messaging has an established shared dictionary of acronyms, social media share some community established abbreviations that allow users to pack more content into short messages. One such abbreviation is the '@' symbol. When a user writes '@rick', they are directing their message to 'rick', but in a public medium. The '@' symbol provides a short and easy mechanism for directing public comments towards specific individuals, but also helps to bridge the gap between directed and undirected interaction in computer-mediated communication. For example: "@xeeliz Check this out! http://yhoo.it/rq1y2u #NBAFinals." Two more example tweets are shown in Figure 1. The top tweet from *edchi*, shows a use of the #. The bottom tweet from *kevinmarks* includes a use of the @ symbol, indicating that this tweet is directly addressing the user *feliciaday*.

To study how the @ symbol is used within our complete data set of 1.65 million comments, we looked at all comments that contained an instance of the symbol. We found that usage of the @ symbol is somewhat common, however, as you might imagine, not all uses of the '@' symbol were in the conversational manner presented above. Some comments contain email addresses (e.g. "john@somecompany.com") or direct readers to a website (e.g. "@ www.cnn.com"). We also found that comments often use the '@' symbol to disguise (e.g. "@ss") or censor (e.g. "@%#$") profanity – one of the very problems that plagues the profanity detection systems described above.

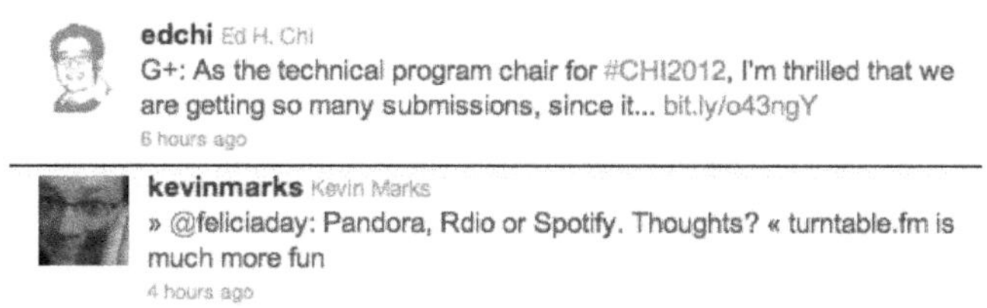

Figure 1: Examples of two tweets, illustrating the use of #, @ and http://bit.ly.

Context	Count of Occurrences of '@'	% of @ usage	% of full data set in this context
Email address	1,112	10%	0.067%
Web address	2,195	19.8%	0.133%
Profanity	4,429	39.9%	0.268%
Conversational	2,764	24.9%	0.167%
Other	592	5.3%	0.036%
Total	11,092	100%	0.67%

Table 3: Analysis of '@' symbol usage within the data set.

To explore the multiple uses of the '@' symbol we built a rule based system using regular expressions. Classifying '@' usage as within email or web addresses is easily accomplished with regular expressions, however, automatically determining that '@ss' is profanity while '@john' is conversational is a more difficult task. We employ a corpus of profane terms (the lists from phorum.org and noswearing.com), along with a tool to calculate the Levenshtein edit distance between two terms [13]. This calculation adds the number of letter insertions, deletions and changes to transform one word into another. When a term contains the '@' symbol, in order to determine if it is profanity, we check to see if the Levenshtein edit distance between the term and any known profane term is equal to the number of punctuation marks present in the term. For example '@ss' has one punctuation mark ('@') and has an edit distance of one from the profane term 'ass.' '$%#@' has four punctuation marks and has an edit distance of four from any four letter profane term. Using this approach, we have a very high *precision* tool that takes a term containing the '@' symbol and determines if it is a profane term (either disguised or censored). The *recall* of this tool is only as good as our list of profane terms.

	Profanity		Insult		Directed Insult	
Category	Occurrence (%)	χ^2	Occurrence (%)	χ^2	Occurrence (%)	χ^2
Overall	**9.28**	--	**20.73**	--	**10.87**	--
Politics	10.70	6.73†	26.80	72.92***	14.30	32.73***
News	9.90	1.83	21.60	1.13	11.40	2.39
Business	9.70	1.29	16.70	11.35**	9.50	2.01
Entertainment	9.30	0.00	18.70	2.98	9.10	3.67
Health	9.00	0.64	14.10	4.05	4.80	4.95
Lifestyle	7.90	0.51	10.70	9.73**	1.70	7.96*
World	7.70	0.01	19.00	1.94	9.10	0.75
Science	6.70	1.98	14.60	6.32	9.90	0.71
Travel	5.60	0.23	18.80	0.00	6.70	0.20
Sports	5.20	6.50	14.70	7.07	3.80	12.90**

Table 4: The distribution of comments containing profanity within topical story domains. Reported χ^2 values are the results of the comparison of profanity, insult, and directed insult frequency within a given category to the frequency across all other categories. Throughout this paper, reported significance values are Bonferroni adjusted where there are multiple comparisons. *** $p \leq .001$, ** $p \leq .01$, * $p \leq .05$, † $p \leq .1$

Using this tool, we labeled all uses of the '@' symbol in our corpus with 'email address,' 'web address,' 'profanity,' 'conversational,' or 'other' (for instances that were not profanity but also did not appear to take the form of a conversational usage of '@'). The results can be seen in Table 3. First, note that only 0.67% (11,092) of all comments in the data set (1,655,131) contain an '@' symbol. Within this set, 39.9% of '@' usage was within the context of a censored or disguised profane term, while only 24.9% of '@' usages appear in a conversational context.

Nearly 40% of all occurrences of the @ symbol came in the form of disguised or author-censored profanity. The @ symbol is just one of many punctuation marks that could be used to disguise profanity. Moreover, the @ symbol is one that is thought to be commonly used in social media in a conversational manner, yet an astonishing 40% of its uses within our data come in the form of disguised profanity. This is likely to be a conservative estimate, as it is known that list-based measures suffer in recall, as shown in the previous section.

HOW FREQUENTLY IS PROFANITY USED?

In addition to facing issues of recall, list-based approaches are a one-size fits all approach that do not take into account how profanity is used within different domains, contexts, and communities. Through our MTurk labeled data set, we explore the use of profanity in comments on news stories in order to understand more about the frequency and context of profanity use and how it is received.

First, we examine the prevalence of profanity in different topical domains. Dividing our 6500 labeled comments by domain of the article they are in reference to, we see that comments on political stories contain more profanity, more insults, and more directed insults (directed at authors of previous comments) than in any other domain.

Table 4 shows the distribution of profanity, insults and directed insults in comments within the different domains. To avoid the possibility of Type I error we applied the conservative Bonferroni adjustment to all significance values reported. For clarity, the first value in Table 4 can be read as 10.7% of political comments contain profanity. As previously discussed, the N differs between profanity, insults, and directed insults because, for each we use only items for which coders reached consensus. For profanity, N is 4409, for insults N is 4177 and for directed insults N is 3974. Each comment in the table 4 analyses was labeled with one of the 10 categories shown. Profanity usage in political comments is significantly more common than in other comments. Political comments contain significantly more insults and directed insults than in other domains. On the other end of the spectrum, the lifestyle comments contain significantly fewer insults and directed insults than other domains. The business domain also held significantly fewer insults, while the sports domain had significantly fewer directed insults. As expected, from these data we can conclude that different domains of news story incite varying amounts of profane language and use of insults (general insults as well as those directed at other community members).

IN WHAT CONTEXT IS PROFANITY USED?

Given that our data set contains insult and insult object labels in addition to profanity labels, these labels will be utilized as a measure of context. To further understand how profanity is used within our data set, we investigate the co-occurrence of the 'comment contains profanity' label with 'comment contains insult' and 'comment contains directed insult' labels. If a comment is labeled as both profane and

	% w/ insult	% w/ directed insult
profane	58.66	39.49
non-profane	16.19	8.15

Table 5: Of all profane and non-profane comments, this table presents the breakdown of those that contain an insult or a directed insult.

	% w/ Profanity
Insult	27.14
Non-Insult	4.83
Directed Insult	31.12
Non-Directed Insult	5.79

Table 6: Breakdown of insult types for comments that contain profanity (by insult type).

containing an insult, we make the assumption that the profane term is used in the context of an insult.

First, we analyze the differences between comments that contain profanity and those that do not. Table 5 summarizes this breakdown. From Table 5, we see that, of all profane comments 58.66% contain an insult. Of all non-profane comments 16.19% contain an insult. These values differ significantly $\chi^2(1, N = 5265) = 652.464, p < .001$. That is, if a comment contains profanity, it is significantly more likely to also contain an insult. Similarly, 39.49% of all profane comments contain a directed insult while 8.15% of all non-profane comments contain a directed insult. This finding is also significant $\chi^2(1, N = 5017) = 561.473, p < .001$.

We also found significance for the inverse questions. That is, if a comment contains an insult, it is significantly more likely to contain profanity $\chi^2(1, N = 5265) = 1149.80, p < .001$ (see Table 6). Directed insults are also significantly more likely to contain profanity $\chi^2(1, N = 5017) = 639.143, p < .001$ (see Table 6). While these correlations do indicate that insults (and directed insults) and profanity are closely tied, it is still interesting to note that nearly 42% of all profane comments do not contain an insult at all. This indicates that there are uses of profanity within the corpus in a non-insulting context.

The next logical question is – in what context do these profane words occur if not in an insult? A manual investigation of this set of comments showed that nearly all occurred in negative 'rants' on the topic at hand. For example, the comments in Table 7 were labeled as profane comments that do not contain insults. Future work includes a more detailed analysis of comments that contain profane terms, yet no insult.

Next, we analyze differences in the context of profanity use between domains. Our method involves the profanity/insult co-occurrence measures used above to characterize the data set as a whole. In our analysis, comments in the domain of

"I'm done. I don't give a F*** anymore. This Country is as good as gone. The Chosen ones and the Zionists won. Check out 'Rules for Radicals' and 'The Protocals of the elders of Zion' to see exctly whats going on. Was nice while it lasted USA. Rest In Peace........."
"So where are these f!@# jobs!?? You mean the 7.25 an hour job offered my daughter who has been managing a DQ for 3 years now? Or the temp clerical position that MAY go perm if the employer can make some money that they offered my wife.... by the way for $10 an hour. How about the President getting paid $40k a year and pay the bills on the white house and feed his family with that. Any excuse to raise friggen gas so some CEO can make a big salary is bull s***"
"Hey, Happy St. Patricks! Time to suck in new generations to drinking. Show them how fun and cultural getting sh*tfaced on St Patricks Day is. Let them see the drunk tanks, impound lots, women shelters, ER's, and morgues."
"Ugh, not this b******* again."

Table 7: Examples of comments labeled as profane, yet not containing an insult.

politics			**¬ politics**	
	% dir. insult	*% ¬ dir. insult*	*% dir. insult*	*% ¬ dir. insult*
Prof	41.07	58.93	38.92	61.08
¬ Prof	11.73	88.27	7.12	92.88
politics			**¬ politics**	
	% insult	*% ¬ insult*	*% insult*	*% ¬ insult*
Prof	62.99	37.01	57.14	42.86
¬ Prof	22.84	77.16	14.25	85.75

Table 8: This table shows a comparison of the distributions of insults and directed insults among profane comments and among non-profane comments. We compare how these distributions differ between politics and non-politics comments.

politics were found to differ significantly from comments outside of the domain of politics in the distribution of insults and directed insults among profane and non-profane comments. Table 8 shows the distributions of insults and directed insults among profane and among non-profane comments. For insults, the breakdown differs significantly between politics and non-politics comments $\chi^2(3, N = 5265) = 66.75, p < .001$. For directed insults, it also differs significantly between politics and non-politics comments $\chi^2(3, N = 5017) = 33.038, p < .001$. Profanity use in the politics domain is tied more to insults and directed insults than in comments in other domains. That is, if a political comment contains profanity, it is more likely to

% of comments with	0 'rating down's	1+ 'rating down's
with profanity	36.64%	63.36%
without profanity	45.53%	54.47%
% of comments with	**0 'rating up's**	**1+ 'rating up's**
with profanity	22.02%	77.98%
without profanity	25.59%	74.41%

Table 9: A comparison of 'rating up's and 'rating down's in comments with and without profanity.

contain an insult or directed insult than a non-political comment.

HOW IS PROFANITY RECEIVED?

One might assume that profanity, like flames or personal insults, would discourage active user participation and engagement. To understand more about how profanity is received/tolerated, we looked to measures of the popularity of a comment within our data set. Most social news sites allow users to vote on comments in addition to stories, using features such as 'digg,' 'like,' 'thumbs up,' 'buzz up,' 'thumbs down,' and 'buzz down.' These features give us some additional popularity information about each comment. The social news site we studied allows users to both 'rate up' and 'rate down' each comment, and the number of 'rate up's and 'rate down's per comment are represented in our data set. We made the assumption that 'rate up's and 'rate down's could be interpreted as a measure of popularity or how much attention each comment received.

We divided our data set into comments labeled by MTurk workers as containing profanity, and those labeled as not containing profanity, and then looked at the difference in number of 'rating up's per profane comment and 'rating up's per non-profane comment (and similarly for 'rating down's). Table 9 shows the percent of profane comments with 0 and 1 or more 'rating down's, (and similarly for 'rating up's). For example, the upper left-most data point can be read as *36.64% of all profane comments received 0 rating down's.* We found that profane comments were significantly more likely to receive 'rate up' votes $\chi^2(1, N = 6354) = 3.990$, $p < .05$ and 'rate down' votes $\chi^2(1, N = 6354) = 18.965$, $p < .001$. Thus, profane comments are more popular or more widely read than non-profane comments. This confirms our intuition that passion (as interpreted by the use of profanity) towards a topic typically engenders either passionate agreement (compelling a user to 'rate up') or strong disagreement (causing a user to 'rate down').

LIMITATIONS

It is important to note several key limitations to our findings. First, the labeled data set on which we performed this analysis was 6500 comments across ten domains. While there was a good variety of content in this data set, some domains had far fewer comments than others. As such, analysis beyond that accomplished in this paper will be done on a data set where the number of comments in each domain is balanced. Secondly, we have examined the nature of profanity use on just one user-generated content site. It would be inappropriate to generalize our findings beyond that site, as specific sites often attract distinct types of users who set up different norms about appropriate behavior. Little is known about how those norms are established and how they evolved. However, this study is a first step in establishing such an understanding.

CONCLUSIONS

In this paper, we made three primary contributions. The first concerned the state of current list-based profanity detection systems. Through an evaluation of the current state of the art in profanity detection, we argued that current systems do not suffice. The best performance we found from a list-based system was an f-measure of 0.457 (0.528 precision at 0.402 recall). This performance is quite poor for what is often underestimated as a simple task. Through the use of a data set of user-generated comments from a social news site, labeled by Amazon Mechanical Turk workers, we analyzed the salient differences between comments labeled as profane and not profane. This analysis exposed and emphasized our argument that current systems do not suffice because they fail to adapt to evolving profane language, misspellings (intentional or not), and profane terms disguised or partially censored by their author. The latter proved to be very prevalent in our finding of the most common features that distinguish profane from non-profane comments in our MTurk labeled data set (see Table 2).

Our second contribution is with regard to a major oversight of profanity detection systems – a lack of tailoring for specific communities. To establish the importance of this oversight, we provide evidence that communities not only use profanity with different frequencies, but also in different ways or contexts. In Table 4, we showed that comments in the politics community of Yahoo! Buzz were significantly more likely to contain profanity, insults, and directed insults (insults directed at other members of the community), than other communities. Similarly, we found that comments in the lifestyle community of Yahoo! Buzz were significantly less likely to include insults and directed insults, comments in the sports community of Yahoo! Buzz were significantly less likely to include directed insults, and comments in the business community of Yahoo! Buzz were significantly less likely to include insults than other communities. From this evidence, we conclude that different communities incite and permit differing amounts of profane language as these comments remained on the site and were not removed by a community manager or social moderation.

Next, addressing the context in which profanity is used, we find that overall, comments with profanity are significantly more likely to include an insult and a directed insult (see Table 5). While this is an intuitive conclusion, it also provided us with a method by which to analyze the differences between the contexts of profanity use in different domains. We analyzed how the propensity for a profane comment to include an insult differs by domain. Table 8 shows that profane comments in the politics domain are significantly more likely to contain insults and directed insults than in other domains. Combined with evidence that profanity is used at different frequencies in other domains, this drew us to conclude that profanity is used differently between communities.

Finally, we provided an analysis of how profanity is received. Using the standard community feedback mechanism of 'rate up' and 'rate down' we judged the popularity of comments with and without profanity. Surprisingly, we found that overall comments with profanity were both significantly more likely to receive 'rate up's and to receive 'rate down's.

FUTURE WORK

Following the conclusions drawn in this article, there are a few clear next steps with regard to moving beyond list-based profanity detection systems, and tailoring systems for specific communities.

First, since list-based profanity detection systems don't suffice, future work involves building profanity detection systems from a machine learning point of view that take into account the context in which profane language is used. Learning the context, in addition to the actual profane words, has a greater potential for robustness, enabling the system to stand up to misspellings, disguised or partially censored words and evolving profane language. Similarly relevance feedback can be used to adapt and improve the model over time.

Secondly, since we established that profanity use and tolerance is very specific to a community, it is very clear that these systems will have to be developed or trained by each community. Future work involves building toolkits that allow this sort of tailoring. The use of Amazon Mechanical Turk and other low cost crowdsourcing mechanisms will prove crucial in labeling profanity in data sets from each community in order to train these machine learning systems.

Finally, we believe our results are most valuable as part of a larger investigation into the social nature of profanity and negative content within specific domains and user communities. In future studies we intend to extend our explorations of the social meanings of profanity and its context-specific use through qualitative interviews and survey studies. Furthermore, we expect that cross-site studies may be particularly revealing about the uses of profanity and possible context-specific approaches for detecting it. In future work we hope to compare and contrast multiple data sets that share a topical domain (e.g. politics) but are drawn from several different sites.

REFERENCES

1. Boyd, D. and Marwick, A. Why Cyberbullying Rhetoric Misses the Mark. *The New York Times*, 2011. http://www.nytimes.com/2011/09/23/opinion/why-cyberbullying-rhetoric-misses-the-mark.html.
2. Callison-Burch, C. Fast, cheap, and creative: evaluating translation quality using Amazon's Mechanical Turk. *Proceedings of the 2009 Conference on Empirical Methods in Natural Language Processing*, (2009).
3. Dinakar, K., Reichart, R., and Lieberman, H. Modeling the Detection of Textual Cyberbullying. *Proceedings of International AAAI Conference on Weblogs and Social Media, Workshop "Social Mobile Web,"* (2011).
4. Fleck, M.M., Forsyth, D.A., and Bregler, C. Finding Naked People. *European Conference on Computer Vision II*, (1996), 592 - 602.
5. Hammami, M., Chahir, Y., and Chen, L. WebGuard: a Web filtering engine combining textual, structural, and visual content-based analysis. *IEEE Transactions on Knowledge and Data Engineering 18*, (2006), 272-284.
6. Haninger, K. and Thompson, K.M. Content and Ratings of Teen-Rated Video Games. *JAMA: The Journal of the American Medical Association 291*, 7 (2004), 856 -865.
7. Ivory, J.D., Williams, D., Martins, N., and Consalvo, M. Good clean fun? A content analysis of profanity in video games and its prevalence across game systems and ratings. *Cyberpsychology & Behavior: The Impact of the Internet, Multimedia and Virtual Reality on Behavior and Society 12*, 4 (2009), 457-460.
8. Jacob, V., Krishnan, R., Ryu, Y., Chandrasekaran, R., and Hong, S. Filtering objectionable internet content. *Proceeding ICIS '99 Proceedings of the 20th international conference on Information Systems*, (1999).
9. Jacob, V.S., Krishnan, R., and Ryu, Y.U. Internet content filtering using isotonic separation on content category ratings. *ACM Transactions on Internet Technology 7*, (2007), 1-es.
10. Joachims, T. Text categorization with Support Vector Machines: Learning with many relevant features. In C. Nédellec and C. Rouveirol, eds., *Machine Learning: ECML-98*. Springer-Verlag, Berlin/Heidelberg, 1998, 137-142.
11. Jones, M.J. and Rehg, J.M. Statistical color models with application to skin detection. *INTERNATIONAL JOURNAL OF COMPUTER VISION 46*, (1999), 274--280.
12. Laboreiro, G., Sarmento, L., Teixeira, J., and Oliveira, E. Tokenizing micro-blogging messages using a text classification approach. *Proceedings of the fourth*

workshop on Analytics for noisy unstructured text data, ACM (2010), 81–88.
13. Levenshtein, V.I. Binary codes capable of correcting deletions, insertions, and reversals. *Soviet Physics Doklady 10*, 8 (1966), 707-710.
14. Li, Q. Cyberbullying in Schools. *School Psychology International 27*, 2 (2006), 157 -170.
15. Lou, J.K., Chen, K.T., and Lei, C.L. A collusion-resistant automation scheme for social moderation systems. *IEEE Consumer Communications and Networking Conference, 2009.*, (2009), 571 -- 575.
16. Nguyen, D. and Rose, Carolyn. Language use as a reflection of socialization in online communities. *Proceedings of the Workshop on Language in Social Media.*, (2011).
17. Sheng, V.S., Provost, F., and Ipeirotis, P.G. Get another label? improving data quality and data mining using multiple, noisy labelers. *Proceeding of the 14th ACM SIGKDD international conference on Knowledge discovery and data mining - KDD '08*, (2008), 614.
18. Siersdorfer, S., Chelaru, S., Nejdl, W., and San Pedro, J. How useful are your comments?: analyzing and predicting youtube comments and comment ratings. *Proceedings of the 19th international conference on World wide web*, (2010), 891–900.
19. Sood, S.O., Churchill, E., and Antin, J. Automatic identification of personal insults on social news sites. *Journal of the American Society for Information Science and Technology*, (2011).
20. Spertus, E. Smokey: Automatic Recognition of Hostile Messages. *IN PROC. IAAI*, (1997), 1058--1065.
21. Sukumaran, A., Vezich, S., McHugh, M., and Nass, C. Normative influences on thoughtful online participation. *Proceedings of the 2011 annual conference on Human factors in computing systems*, ACM (2011), 3401–3410.
22. Tetreault, J.R., Filatova, E., and Chodorow, M. Rethinking Grammatical Error Annotation and Evaluation with the Amazon Mechanical Turk. *Proceedings of the NAACL HLT 2010 Fifth Workshop on Innovative Use of NLP for Building Educational Applications*, (2010), 45 - 48.
23. Wang, J.Z., Li, J., Wiederhold, G., and Firschein, O. System for Screening Objectionable Images. *COMPUTER COMMUNICATIONS JOURNAL 21*, (1998), 1355--1360.
24. Yin, D., Xue, Z., Hong, L., Davison, B., Kontostathis, A., and Edwards, L. Detection of Harassment on Web 2.0. *Proceedings of the Content Analysis in the WEB 2.0 (CAW2.0) Workshop at WWW2009*, (2009).
25. Yoon, T., Park, S.-Y., and Cho, H.-G. A Smart Filtering System for Newly Coined Profanities by Using Approximate String Alignment. *Proceedings of the 2010 10th IEEE International Conference on Computer and Information Technology*, IEEE Computer Society (2010), 643–650.

Consensus Building in Open Source User Interface Design Discussions

Roshanak Zilouchian Moghaddam, Brian P. Bailey, and Wai-Tat Fu
Department of Computer Science
University of Illinois
Urbana, IL 61801
{rzilouc2, bpbailey, wfu}@illinois.edu

ABSTRACT
We report results of a study which examines consensus building in user interface design discussions in open source software communities. Our methodology consisted of conducting interviews with designers and developers from the Drupal and Ubuntu communities (N=17) and analyzing a large corpus of interaction data collected from Drupal. The interviews captured user perspectives on the challenges of reaching consensus, techniques employed for building consensus, and the consequences of not reaching consensus. We analyzed the interaction data to determine how different elements of the content, process, and user relationships in the design discussions affect consensus. The main result from this analysis shows that design discussions having participants with more experience and prior interaction are more likely to reach consensus. Based on all of our results, we formulated design implications for promoting consensus in distributed discussions of user interface design issues.

Author Keywords
Consensus; design discussion; open source software

ACM Classification Keywords
H.5.3 [Group and Organization Interfaces]: Asynchronous interaction - Web-based interaction

INTRODUCTION
In open source software (OSS) communities, many design decisions that shape the product's user interface are made through distributed discussions [5]. For example, to initiate a community discussion of a usability issue, a member describes the issue and others join the discussion to propose and debate design alternatives. These discussions typically unfold via mailing lists or Web forums linked to the OSS project. It is imperative for discussion participants to reach consensus on a design proposal to show strong support for integrating its implementation into the product distribution and to enhance participants' feeling of valued contribution. By *consensus*, we mean that participants are willing to commit to a proposal despite any remaining objections [6].

Permission to make digital or hard copies of all or part of this work for personal or classroom use is granted without fee provided that copies are not made or distributed for profit or commercial advantage and that copies bear this notice and the full citation on the first page. To copy otherwise, or republish, to post on servers or to redistribute to lists, requires prior specific permission and/or a fee.
CHI'12, May 5–10, 2012, Austin, Texas, USA.
Copyright 2012 ACM 978-1-4503-1015-4/12/05...$10.00.

Because consensus building is a common and critical task in user interface (UI) design discussions in OSS, it is important to understand how often consensus is (not) reached, what techniques are utilized to foster consensus, and which elements of a design discussion affect consensus, among many other interesting questions. However, these questions have not been directly addressed by prior work.

For example, one thread of prior research has analyzed elements of design discussions such as participation [15], argumentation [4, 19], and tracking of design proposals [31], but has not targeted consensus building. In a second thread, researchers have conducted lab experiments to test how different factors of group work such as size, task, and anonymity affect decision quality and reaching consensus [3, 16, 24]. However, in lab experiments, it is difficult to simulate how consensus unfolds in real world design discussions, especially those in a mature OSS community.

In this paper, we report results of a study which examines UI design discussions in OSS communities from the perspective of consensus building. Part of our methodology consisted of conducting semi-structured interviews with designers and developers from the Drupal and Ubuntu OSS communities (N=17). The interviews captured user perspectives on key challenges of reaching consensus in the design discussions, the techniques utilized for promoting consensus, and the consequences of not reaching consensus.

To complement the interviews, we analyzed a large corpus of interaction data collected from the Drupal community to test how different discussion elements relate to consensus. Our data set included UI design discussions that did and did not reach consensus. From the interviews and other sources, we derived three categories of potential factors; content, process, and user relationships and operationalized them into 23 metrics. The metrics were calculated for each discussion in our data set and entered in a binary (consensus or not) logistic regression. The main result from this analysis shows that discussions having participants with more experience and prior interaction history are more likely to reach consensus. Finally, based upon all of our results, we offer design implications for promoting consensus in distributed discussions of UI design issues.

RELATED WORK

We describe the concept of consensus and why it is important for analyzing UI design discussions. We then show how our work complements prior studies of design discussions in OSS and group decision making.

Consensus and its Importance for Design Discussions

In group decision making, consensus refers to when all participants are willing to commit to a proposal despite the fact that objections may remain [6]. The process of building consensus requires a good faith effort to meet the diverse interests of all participants as the process is considered as important as the final outcome. For example, this is often accomplished by encouraging those with dissenting views to propose or adapt existing ideas to meet their own interests without supplanting the interests of others [26]. Consensus building is an increasingly utilized technique for group decision making in complex task domains (e.g. UI design) where no one person has all the required expertise or resources needed to solve a given problem [26].

In this paper, we study consensus building in the UI design discussions in one established OSS community. Consensus building is an appropriate and important lens for viewing these types of discussions. For example, since almost all community decisions relating to the product's interface are made through distributed discussions, the ability to reach consensus can have a large impact on the quality of the product and satisfaction with the decision making process.

Studies of Design Discussions in OSS

Researchers have often utilized the open nature of design discussions in OSS to study different elements of the user interface and software design process. However studies of consensus in these discussions are conspicuously missing.

For example, in our own prior work [31], we studied how users propose, track, and debate design alternatives during UI design discussions in OSS. Twidale and Nichols [27] explored how usability issues are reported, discussed, and resolved in several OSS bug repositories with a goal of understanding how to improve the discussion interface. Ko and Chilana [19] also analyzed discussions in OSS repositories but with the goal of understanding the structure of the discussions. Similarly, the authors analyzed open bug reports to assess who contributes the reports, the frequency of resolution, and the patterns of comments between the bug reporters and the developers [20]. Though the results of these studies illuminate important elements of the design discussions in OSS, they say little about the consensus building process. Our work fills this gap by providing a comprehensive analysis of UI design discussions in OSS from the perspective of consensus building.

Thematic coherence and argumentation in OSS design discussions were analyzed in [4]. Their results showed the social influence of a user increases the depth of attention received in the ensuing discussion. Similarly, in [15], the authors studied how participation relates to code-related design decisions. One finding was that in the more effective projects studied, the number of participants increases over time and shifts from administrators to other community members. Our work builds upon these results by including variables related to participation and social influence, among many others, in our statistical analysis of consensus.

Studies of Group Decision Making and Consensus

There is a long history of research examining how various factors of a group such as size, task, and anonymity relate to decision making performance [3]. This line of inquiry has often compared technology-mediated and face-to-face (FTF) group work and relied primarily on the use of controlled studies. For example, controlled studies have shown it is more difficult and takes more time to reach consensus when groups use synchronous or asynchronous communication technology than when working FTF [16, 24]. Similarly, it is more difficult to reach consensus as group size increases [13] and, when consensus is required, group members experience less satisfaction when using communication technology than when working FTF [24].

While working FTF is ideal for reaching consensus, decision making in OSS communities often occurs in a distributed setting. It is therefore important to understand how consensus is achieved in this context. Our research fills this void by studying real world consensus decisions made in the UI design discussions in a mature OSS community.

Enabled by open access to peer production communities such as Wikipedia and OSS, researchers have begun to study similar elements of group decision making in real world data sets. For example, Lam et al. studied how group size, experience, and group formation influences decision quality in Wikipedia and found that larger groups make better decisions [21]. Similarly, Burke et al found that extensive and diverse contributions in Wikipedia can predict promotion decisions [7]. Analogous to these studies, our work tests how different factors relate to reaching consensus on UI design issues in a peer production community. Interviews were also used to understand users' perspectives on the consensus building process.

RESEARCH QUESTIONS AND METHODOLOGY

This research aimed to better understand the nature of consensus building in distributed discussions of UI design issues and centered on answering the following questions:

- How important is consensus building in these types of UI design discussions, what are the key challenges of reaching consensus, and what are the consequences of not reaching consensus from the user's perspective?
- What techniques are currently utilized for promoting consensus and how effective are these techniques?
- What factors affect consensus building? For example, how does the content (e.g. what is discussed), process (e.g. number of design alternatives proposed), and social aspects (e.g. who participates) affect consensus?

These questions are not exhaustive, but are intended to offer initial understanding of consensus building in UI design discussions and identify opportunities for enhancing the discussion interface to promote consensus. To answer these questions, a mixed methods approach was employed consisting of semi-structured interviews and analysis of a large corpus of interaction data.

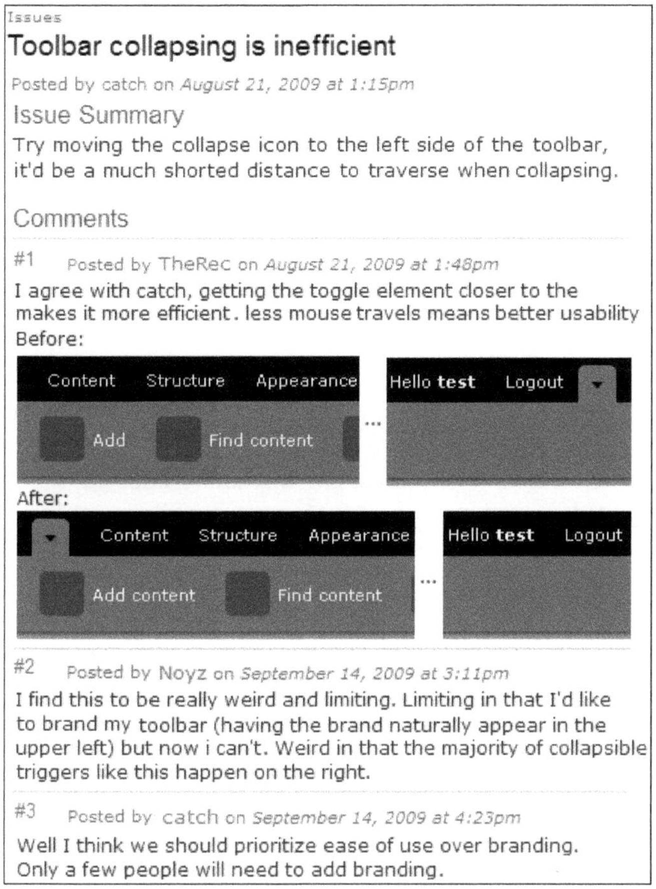

Figure 1. A UI design discussion occurring in the issue management system of Drupal. Participants are proposing and debating ideas for where to locate a shortcut on the toolbar. The image was condensed for the purpose of explanation.

User Interviews

We conducted 17 semi-structured interviews with designers and developers participating in either of two open source projects, Drupal and Ubuntu. Eight designers were interviewed, five from Drupal and three from Ubuntu, with an average of 4.5 years of experience in the community (σ=2.6). Nine developers were interviewed, six from Drupal and three from Ubuntu, with an average of 5 years of community experience (σ=2.6). Each interview lasted about an hour and was conducted via phone (n=14) or IM (n=3), whichever a participant preferred, and remuneration was either a $25 or $30 gift card depending on the duration of the interview. We will refer to Drupal and Ubuntu designers as DD# and DU# and Drupal and Ubuntu developers as DevD# and DevU#, respectively.

We first asked a participant to describe one or two recent or memorable discussions s/he participated in. In context of these discussions, we asked the participant to describe the consensus building process, what is hard about this process, the techniques utilized to foster consensus, the factors affecting consensus, and the consequences of not reaching consensus. Twelve interviews were conducted prior to the data analysis and five were performed afterward. For the latter interviews, a few questions were added to probe further about specific results of the analysis.

Interviews were coded to derive common themes using a Grounded Theory approach [25]. The results were used to gain insight into the consensus building process, identify features to include in our interaction analysis, and help interpret the results.

Collection of Authentic Interaction Data

The interaction data was extracted from the discussion threads (discussions) in the issue management system of Drupal, an open source content management system initiated in 2001. Drupal is a mature community with an established workflow and social organization. At the time of data collection, for example, the software was being used in about 490,000 websites to manage content and about 440,000 people had registered to contribute to the project.

Changes to the user interface and system software of Drupal are requested, discussed, and implemented (or not) through its issue management system. See Figure 1. Any community member can create an issue in the issue management system describing a design problem or feature request, which establishes a separate discussion. Others may participate in the discussion by proposing design alternatives, critiquing the alternatives, implementing an alternative (writing a patch), reviewing a patch, clarifying the problem, or offering other insights. To indicate the current progress of a discussion, participants can set its status to 'active', 'needs work', 'needs review', 'reviewed and tested by the community', 'fixed', or 'closed'.

There are four categories of discussions in the issue management system: bug reports, feature requests, tasks, and support requests. According to drupal.org, bug reports aim to resolve functionality and usability problems while feature requests are for adding new functionality. Tasks are non-functional things that 'need to be done' while support requests are for technical support. We only examined bug reports and feature requests as they contained the majority of the UI design discussions we wanted to study.

There were 285,008 discussions tagged as bug reports and feature requests in the issue management system at the time of data collection. This set was filtered to include only the discussions tagged with "Usability" or "d7ux" (usability in Drupal 7), which left 577 UI design discussions. These discussions occurred between March 2004 and September 2011. The usability issues ranged from significant redesigns to design details. For instance, an issue titled "*Initial D7UX admin overlay*" aimed to revamp the interaction design of admin pages in Drupal by providing themed admin pages as an overlay on top of the actual website while another issue only requested changing the location of a shortcut on a toolbar (see Figure 1).

We used the status to categorize discussions as consensus, non-consensus, or ongoing (unclear if consensus has been reached). We considered discussions marked as *closed* as having reached consensus. This typically means there was collective support for a decision such as implementing a specific proposal or concluding the issue was unnecessary or not a problem after all. This status is a reasonable proxy for consensus because if any participant strongly objected to the proposal, s/he could have reverted the status (e.g. back to 'active') and caused the discussion to continue.

Differentiating non-consensus and ongoing discussions was more challenging. We calculated the idle duration, the time from when the last comment was posted to the time of data collection and considered a discussion to be non-consensus if it's idle duration was more than 90% of the idle durations between comments in the consensus discussions. The remaining discussions were considered ongoing. This categorization yielded 284 consensus and 241 non-consensus discussions. The 52 ongoing discussions were discarded.

Finally, we filtered this data set to include only those discussions that were non-trivial. By reading a large fraction of the discussions and experimenting with different thresholds, we found that a threshold of having at least seven comments filtered almost all of the non-trivial discussions. After this filtering, we had 200 consensus threads and 141 non-consensus threads for our analysis. Table 1 reports summary statistics for the consensus and non-consensus UI design discussions after this filtering.

USER PERSPECTIVES ON CONSENSUS BUILDING

In this section, we first describe how consensus building in UI design discussions differs from technical discussions. Drawing from the interviews, we then report user perspectives on the challenges of consensus building, the benefits of consensus and the consequences of not reaching consensus, and techniques used for promoting consensus.

Characteristic	Type	Mean	SD
Discussion duration (weeks)	C	41.76	50.71
	NC	101.70	83.17
Number of comments	C	48.34	61.02
	NC	33.21	36.95
Number of participants	C	12.82	10.42
	NC	11.82	8.77

Table 1. Summary statistics for the consensus (N=200) and non-consensus (N=141) UI design discussions. 'C' indicates consensus and 'NC' indicates non-consensus discussions.

Consensus Building in UI design Discussions

Participants felt that consensus building in the UI design discussions is not the same as in the technical discussions (e.g. on performance and security) due to more subjectivity, lengthier discussions, greater visibility of the outcomes, and difficulty of presenting supporting evidence.

"*Usability also, is an area usually more people can get involved, some of the highly technical stuff not that many people can get involved in the issue without background. In usability it would be easier, anyone can suggest a design: I think we should do it like that. It tends to get a lot more people involved; it's also a lot more visible [...]. Often more people are participating, more people means it's harder to [build] consensus.*" [DevD4]

For instance using discussions tagged with "Performance" as a sample of the technical discussions (N=322), we found that 703 unique participants contributed to the technical discussions while 1404 unique participants contributed to usability discussions (N=577). On average, more unique participants contributed to a usability discussion (μ=9.47, σ=9.45) than to a technical discussion (μ=7.98, σ=8.11; $t(897)=2.38$, $p<0.05$). We also found that participants spent more time in weeks discussing a usability issue (μ=57.99, σ=10.12) than a performance issue (μ=38.46, σ=49.33; $t(897)=4.42$, $p<0.05$). Having more people participate in a lengthier, subjective discussion is perceived to make consensus building more challenging.

Another factor that makes consensus building more challenging in UI design discussions is the difficulty of providing supporting evidence in the discussions. For instance, conducting usability testing to assess the effectiveness of a design proposal needs a lot of time and effort while testing the effectiveness of a performance solution can usually be performed directly and is therefore perceived to be easier:

"*...I think the usability testing is a little harder to do often. It takes a little more time, if you do an informal one it's not so bad, but you certainly can't do with just one person, [...] you have to get several, and it takes time to get evidence. In some other areas in Drupal it's easier to get evidence. You know, what percent [it makes the Drupal website] faster.*" [DevD4]

Benefits of Reaching Consensus and Consequences of Not Reaching Consensus

Participants stated that reaching consensus in the UI design discussions was critical for building a better product (n=4) and for strengthening the community (n=4). To both of these points respectively, one participant (DD4) explained:

"*...when we reach consensus we are taking our strengths [to] make the world together, we have something that is at least as good as what the two of us could bring to separately, and probably is better because our strengths tend to reinforce each other.*"

"...The more we can reach consensus in itself, the fact that we reach consensus in itself, foster stronger feeling in community, so the little instances of that build on one another and help us become stronger as a community, and therefore more likely to invest in reaching consensus on other projects, on other issues."

On the other hand, the inability to reach consensus can result in an unimproved product, build resentment in the community, and demotivate community members to the point of leaving the discussion or the community altogether.

"[Consequences of not reaching consensus are] stupid interfaces surviving yet another version in Drupal, known issues not being fixed, frustrated contributors. Consequences can be that people disappear for a couple of weeks or entirely because they get burned out on a too long discussion that didn't reach consensus... " [DD5]

The inability to reach consensus also causes the loss of significant community effort. For example, of the 577 UI design discussions we analyzed, 241 (42%) did not reach consensus. These discussions contained 4968 messages and 460 patches, contributed by 1934 participants. This outcome highlights the need for techniques for enhancing consensus building within the UI design discussions.

Challenges of Consensus Building

Despite recognizing the importance of consensus building participants identified key challenges that make consensus difficult to achieve. For example, one challenge is bridging the different perspectives and needs of the community members engaged in a UI design discussion (n=8):

"There are many different use cases for Drupal, what is optimal for one use case may be suboptimal for another, and there are strong differences of opinion within the Drupal community about which use cases, if any, should be given preference... Some people build for small sites, some people work on large sites, some people are designers, others are developers [and] others are end users" [DevD2]

Another challenge is overcoming a strong sense of ownership over one's contributions (n=4). For example, one reason that members contribute is because they can adapt the software to their own needs [14]. However, building consensus requires members to detach themselves from their own contributions and consider alternatives:

"People have egos and they have a lack of human contact with the people that they are talking to and trying to discuss with and a lot of time because these ideas are our own creations and our own feelings it's very difficult to separate ourselves from our own egos." [DevU1]

Similarly, expressing strong emotions during a discussion can also hinder consensus building (n=2). As DD4 said:

"certainly, there've been some that people just got so frustrated that their emotions, me included, to some extent let our emotions lead the way of communicating, rather than communicating based on the facts that matter..."

Other challenges for building consensus identified by interviewees included not having enough participants who are interested in a discussion (n=2), having too many participants lacking necessary background or general design knowledge (n=2), the absence of evidence supporting various claims (n=1), and lack of time and resources (n=1).

Techniques for Promoting Consensus

From the interviews, we identified different techniques that designers and developers use to promote consensus. Our interviewees said that providing evidence in support of a design proposal can better convince opposing parties in a discussion and accelerate consensus building (n=7). For instance, sharing the results of usability testing on a design proposal or showing how the proposal worked in a similar situation can convince other participants.

"what we do is look to what other projects and other web standards exist along the problem, say the problem of where to locate the help link, on the admin bar, we look at a bunch of different web applications, Facebook, Google docs, also desktop applications things like that, basically starts to conform a consensus around that ok it got to be on the right hand side of the menu and so we tend to go with that ..." [DevD6]

Another technique for promoting consensus was presenting screenshots or writing a patch for a design proposal (n=5). As DevD2 said participants in a discussion are more likely to comment on a proposal that has a patch attachment:

"I present arguments in favor of it and then post a patch. People are typically more inclined to go with a solution that has a patch than another solution that does not have a patch, unless they have a major reason for liking the other solution better."

Participants also noted endorsing experienced members of the community in the discussion (n=3), writing a summary of the discussion (n=3), communicating via synchronized channels (n=3), having an administrator make the final decision (n=5), spending time to understand others' perspectives (n=3), voting for different design proposals (n=2), and advertising a stalled discussion (n=2) as techniques for promoting consensus. However, it is unclear how effective these techniques are given that 42% of the UI design discussions we analyzed did not reach consensus.

INTERACTION DATA ANALYSIS

To understand quantitatively which factors correlate with consensus, we analyzed the interaction data collected from the Drupal issue management system as described earlier. Based on the interview results, consensus building literature [6], and prior analyses of online communities [1, 2], we identified 23 metrics that may relate to consensus building. Table 2 lists these metrics grouped into three categories: content, process, and user relationships. Though not

Category	Metrics
Content	(1) Avg. # of words *
	(2) Total # of words
	(3) Priority of the issue
	(4) # of "usability testing"s
	(5) # of "summary"s *
	(6) # of screenshots *
	(7) # of "code review"s *
	(8) # of non-Drupal links
	(9) # of "IRC"s
	(10) # of "?"s *
Process	(11) Duration of the thread *
	(12) Avg. duration between comments
	(13) # of comments *
	(14) # of patches *
	(15) # of contributors *
	(16) # of comments by thread initiator *
User Relationships	(17) # of triads in the social graph
	(18) Avg. page rank score of contributors
	(19) Avg. # of total participation duration
	(20) Avg. # of contributors' prior comment *
	(21) # of participation weeks of initiator *
	(22) # of prev. comments of initiator *
	(23) # of alternate replies *

Table 2. The metrics used in our regression analysis. The metrics marked with (*) were later removed from the analysis to avoid problems with collinearity.

exhaustive, these metrics provide a useful starting point for understanding which factors affect consensus building in UI design discussions.

For example, for Content metrics, we counted the number of messages with screenshots attached as a proxy for the number of design alternatives proposed. More alternatives may create more opportunities for consensus. The number of question marks was counted as a proxy for attempts at building shared understanding [5]. From the interviews, we found that synchronous chats can promote consensus and therefore included how often "IRC" was mentioned in a discussion. Similarly, occurrences of "usability testing", "code review", and "summary" were counted in each discussion. The number of non-Drupal links was included to capture use of external evidence in the design arguments.

For the Process metrics, we counted patches, comments, and contributors as a proxy for the level of activity in each discussion. A discussion with increased activity may have a better chance of reaching consensus. The duration of a discussion was also included as allocating more time to a discussion may indicate stronger commitment to identifying an agreeable solution.

For User Relationships, we calculated the number of triads contributing to a discussion to estimate prior interaction history [12]. Triads were determined from the social graph created from the users, discussions, and relationships [11, 12, 16]. In a social graph, the nodes represent users and discussions while edges represent their relationships. An edge between a user and discussion is established when a user contributes to that discussion. An edge between two users is established when one user responds to the other. An edge is weighted based on the length of the comment. We also computed a page rank score [24] for each participant to estimate 'influence' within the community. The page rank score was also calculated from the social graph. The duration of community participation was used to estimate the experience of participants as interviewees felt having more experienced members of the community participate in a design discussion promotes consensus.

To calculate values for these metrics, we incorporated information from the discussion content (e.g. length of comments), metadata of the discussions (e.g. duration of the thread), and contributor's Drupal profile.

Logistic Regression

To investigate how these metrics relate to consensus, we performed a binary logistic regression. Binary logistic regression is a type of regression used to model the relationship between independent variables and a binary response variable. For our analysis, the metrics from Table 2 served as the independent variables and were computed for each discussion in our data set while the dependent variable was whether the discussion reached consensus. To avoid problems with collinearity in the regression analysis, we removed fourteen variables that demonstrated strong correlations ($r>0.4$). These variables are marked in Table 2.

We performed binary logistic regression as implemented in SPSS and used step-down regression to identify our partial model. We first entered all variables and removed each variable that did not show significance and repeated until a set of variables was reached that were all significant. Three of the nine metrics included in the analysis showed significance ($p<0.05$): average number of participation weeks, number of triads, and mentions of IRC. Table 3 summarizes the results. To assess the goodness of fit of our model, we performed the Hosmer-Lemoshow test (Chi-square=7.91.56, $p=0.44$). In this test, the model is valid if the p-value is *greater* than 0.05.

To aid interpretation of the results, we conducted five follow-up interviews as described in Methodology. These interviews followed the original script, but probed further about the factors found to be significant. In addition, we analyzed thirty of the discussions that reached consensus in our data set. The discussions were sorted based on the three

	B	Df	Sig.	Exp(B)
Average # of participation weeks	.01	1	.00	1.01
# of triads in social graph	.10	1	.03	1.10
IRC	.24	1	.05	1.26
Constant	-1.06	1	.02	.35

Table 3. Results of the binary logistic regression. The Hosemer-Lemoshow test confirmed the validity of our regression model (Chi-square=7.91, p=0.44).

factors found to be significant and ten threads from the top of each of these three lists were reviewed.

Experience with Drupal

Our regression analysis showed that having people in a discussion who have participated in Drupal longer promotes consensus. Research studies confirm that including experienced people can positively influence group decision making performance [18]. Our interview results and review of the discussion threads illustrated how experience can facilitate consensus building. First, we learned that members who have been in the community for a long time facilitate consensus by helping other members, especially new ones, understand the norms of communication and the process of participation in the community.

"*...what's important for reaching consensus is having common ground rules or communication and process and you know working those out and to that extent more experienced in Drupal community might help people be better at reaching consensus, because they'll understand that you don't say things this way or you do, or these are the options for contacting somebody if you have a problem or that kind of thing...*" [DD4]

Second, it was reported that experienced members are more skilled in unblocking a discussion. For example, comments and opinions posted by experienced members are valued more than those posted by other participants.

"*...there are those people in the community that are recognized – people who have been in the community a long time, or who are respected because they have written a lot of code, or they have written a lot of patches, or they are the maintainer of a certain bit of code – and when those people chime in, it tends to hold a little bit more weight when someone unknown chimes in*" [DD1]

As a result, experienced members can help direct the discussion toward a specific design proposal. For instance, in a discussion about adding edit and delete operations to a page in Drupal, when two of the participants (X and Y) proposed different solutions and were not able to come to an agreement, a community member with design experience was invited to review and decide between the proposals:

"*I am inclined to agree with X here, following the logic of menus and taxonomies this should make more sense...*"

Finally, experienced members can promote consensus by understanding the need for proposing solutions that accommodate competing alternatives. Satisfying opposing views allows stalled discussions to move forward. For instance, in a discussion about placement of a shortcut for collapsing the Drupal toolbar, X thinks that the icon for the shortcut should be placed on the left side of the menu to prevent accidental clicks on the "logout" icon while Y thinks it should remain on the right side because the space on the left is needed for branding. They cannot come to an agreement until Z who has been in the community for six years comes in and proposes a new solution:

"*Thought: Move /help over to the right of "log out", move the shortcut collapsing back to the right, then you'd at least accidentally click a "safe" link.*"

Prior Interactions

Our analysis showed that having more triads participate in a discussion increases the likelihood of consensus. Triads represent three people who have previously interacted and produce closed social structures that promote trust [28].

Interview results and review of the discussions confirm trust as an important factor in consensus building. First, we found that participants are more likely to read, learn from, and evaluate comments posted by members whom they trust. This exchange of knowledge can create mutual understanding and consequently promotes consensus.

"*I think I'm less likely to dismiss something if it's from somebody I know and I respect. It's a little more likely to read carefully what they say and believe that they have something meaningful to say*" [DevD4]

This finding reflects findings in other research studies that indicate a high degree of trust existing within dense parts of a social network facilitates the exchange of complex knowledge [30]. Second, prior interaction and increased trust promotes agreement among participants.

"*... it's sort of like a trust matrix type of thing, because if I don't know you and you are suggesting this thing that sounds like a bad idea to me, I probably fight against it, but if you are proposing something and I don't know you but three other people that I do know are saying yeah actually that's a great idea and this is why, then I'll be far more likely to be like alright let's go with it then.*"[DevD6]

Finally, we found that trust in other participants' technical abilities can save time in the process. For instance, knowing that the person who wrote a patch usually conforms to coding standards can accelerate code review.

"*... if people know who somebody else is, it saves a heck of a lot of time, at all levels, like, for example, if I know the person who wrote the patch and I know that traditionally they write pretty good patches that conform to coding standard and stuff like that and then I see the person that reviewed it is the person I associate with being the smart person about that thing and the person who marked it as* *reviewed and tested by community [...], and that person was also someone I recognize as if they say something is RTBC it's actually good to go. Then it saves all kinds of time."* [DevD6]

Similarly, recognizing the person who wrote the patch as a skillful programmer can accelerate implementation. For instance, in a discussion where the proposal was to add an edit link to all Drupal pages, one member (Y) was able to build upon another's (X's) patch and save time. Y says:

"So, yeeha, X's last changes contained some really good ones that allowed me to proceed further."

Use of Synchronized Communication Media

Based on the regression analysis, threads containing more mentions of "IRC" are more likely to reach consensus. A group of two to five people usually participate in the synchronized discussions and are expected to report their conclusions back to the corresponding discussion for the benefit of all. Failure to report may cause the other participants to loose context.

"*The danger in IRC becomes when and this happens sometimes when there are huge discussions that go on IRC, big community impacting discussions and only the people who happen to be on IRC at that time, know about them and if those don't make their way back to the issue queue or groups or some other mean of more permanent storage that's really dangerous because a lot of people loose context in these discussions that way*" [DevD6]

From the interviews and our inspection of discussions, we identified three ways that IRC can help build consensus. First, we found having discussions in IRC can accelerate agreement between opposing viewpoints.

"... it [IRC] can help if there is one or two people who are disagreeing about something, if those people go to IRC they can chat it out much faster than the issue queue." [DD4]

Second, in IRC people can come up with an initial design proposal for solving the usability problem that may not be possible in context of the larger discussion.

"*IRC is great for say a small group of people going off and coming up with an initial proposal that they all agree on and then proposing that to the community.*" [DevD6]

Reporting this proposal back to the discussion advances consensus building because participants can argue for or against the proposal as opposed to developing their own. As DevD6 said:

"...then it becomes let's argue against this position as opposed to try to come to a position to argue against..."

Finally, we learned that participants use synchronized communication to hasten collaborative design review, programming, and debugging sessions. This finding corroborates observations reported in [10]. For example, when discussing the design and implementation of an overlay for the Drupal interface, one of the developers (Y) asked another developer (X) to join him in a synchronized chat for a collaborative debugging session:

"*X, some of your files are being cut off, such as overlay-parent.css(?) Please come onto IRC so we can help you debug.*"

DISCUSSION

Our regression analysis showed that three of the factors tested are predictive of consensus in a UI design discussion: the experience of participants, number of triads, and mentions of synchronous communication. Interestingly, none of the content metrics were significant. One interpretation of this result is that who participates in a UI design discussion is more important than how many design alternatives are proposed or what arguments are made for the purpose of building consensus. For example, this may be due to not having a facilitator in the discussion skilled at steering the group toward consensus [8]. Participation of experienced members may therefore compensate for the absence of trained facilitators, i.e., they have a better understanding of how to guide the discussion toward consensus. Another possibility is that the content metrics used in our analysis were incomplete. Future work should therefore examine additional metrics such as the use of different argument types [22] and rhetorical devices [19] to further test how content attributes may relate to consensus.

A number of factors perceived by our interviewees to relate to consensus did not show significance in the regression analysis. For instance, interviewees mentioned contributing concrete evidence to an ongoing discussion such as usability tests of the design proposals and external links to interface examples positively affect consensus building.

One reason these factors did not correlate with consensus is that they were seldom performed. For example, in our data set, mentions of usability appeared in only 0.06% of the consensus discussions and in 9% of the non-consensus discussions. One way to foster the inclusion of concrete evidence is to establish specific community guidelines for discussing UI design issues. Another method would be to configure a testing platform where participants can easily try a patch and provide feedback in the discussion without having to worry about applying the patch to their locally installed version of the product.

A second possible reason some of the factors did not show significance in the analysis is that we did not consider their context. For example, in our data set, the number of links to external sources was similar in consensus (μ=5.5, σ=7.5) and non-consensus (μ=4.9, σ=6.9) discussions. This may be due to not considering the helpfulness of the link targets. For example, future work may consider weighing the link counts based on the helpfulness of the link targets to the discussion (e.g. did the links reference sketches of design proposals, interaction examples within well-known Web sites, or community design standards).

Design Implications

Our work has several design implications for discussion interfaces w.r.t. promoting consensus. One implication is to enable discussion participants to quickly identify others with whom they have had prior interactions. These community members could then be invited to join the discussion, thereby increasing the number of triads. For example, for each discussion, the community software could maintain a list of members whose participation would form triads by analyzing the social graph [17] or history of participants' contributions [9]. Options could be offered for filtering the list, e.g., requiring a minimum number of prior interactions or specifying that only the interactions within specific types of design discussions be considered.

A related implication is to allow discussion participants to identify experienced members who may be willing to join the discussion. Inviting appropriate people to join a discussion may not only aid consensus building, but may also assist community members in identifying discussions of interest. For example, analogous to [9], the system could recommend experienced members appropriate for the discussion by considering the duration of their community membership, interest profiles, and recent activity within the community (to prevent core members from receiving too many invitations). As before, options could be provided for modifying these search parameters.

Our analysis showed that participants value the comments contributed by experienced members or members with whom they have had prior interaction. The discussion interface could therefore allow participants to filter comments within the current discussion contributed by others meeting these criteria or by including appropriate visual cues for these criteria within the comments.

Results of our interviews and inspection of discussions revealed that certain types of comments aid consensus building more than others. For example, comments that strongly argue for or against design alternatives can build agreement, comments that summarize the discussion to date can help participants make sense of the thread, and comments that report the conclusions from synchronized discussions can help participants maintain context. The discussion interface could therefore employ color codes or other visual cues to highlight these types of comments [23, 29]. To classify comments, the author or other participants could be allowed to assign pre-defined community tags. To reduce or eliminate the costs of tagging, an alternative would be to automatically infer the comment types, which could be modified by participants to correct any errors.

To further aid the consensus building process, recent key contributions to the discussion could also be highlighted. For instance, comments that include key contributions such as the most recent design proposal, implementing or reviewing a recent patch, or changing the status of the discussion could be highlighted. It is important to note that not all of the filtering, searching, and highlighting mechanisms described need to be included in a discussion at the same time. For example, end users could configure which of the features are applied in their local interface.

Limitations

One limitation of this work is that our regression analysis did not include an exhaustive set of factors that may relate to consensus. Additional metrics such as the language complexity of the messages, number of arguments for or against design proposals, the sentiment of those arguments, use of rhetorical devices, and advanced techniques for assessing expertise could be included in future analyses.

Second, our qualitative findings were derived from the responses of seventeen participants. We look forward to collecting data from additional community members and analyzing how the responses relate to their different roles such as designer, developer, administrator, or end user.

Finally, our interaction data was collected from the UI design discussions in one open source software community. Similar analyses should be performed for UI design discussions in other open source and distributed software projects to assess the generalizability of our results.

CONCLUSION

Consensus building is a critical component of UI design discussions in OSS as it promotes a better product and a stronger community. In this paper, we studied consensus building in UI design discussions from an established OSS community using qualitative and quantitative methods. Our results made three contributions. One contribution was reporting user perspectives on the challenges of reaching consensus in UI design discussions, the techniques utilized for addressing the challenges, and the consequences of not reaching consensus. A second contribution was analyzing how various metrics related to the content, process, and user relationships of the discussions correlate with reaching consensus. The main result from this analysis shows that discussions having participants with more experience and prior interaction history are more likely to reach consensus. Finally, we offered design implications for promoting consensus in distributed discussions of UI design issues.

One immediate direction for future work is to implement our design implications and test their utility and impact on the consensus building process. A second direction is to analyze the logs of synchronized communications that occurred within the discussions studied to better understand the strategies used by participants and the effect of this medium on consensus. Finally, one can conduct a similar study on technical discussions (e.g. on performance and security) to shed more light on the differences between UI design and technical discussions for consensus building.

ACKNOWLEDGEMENT

This work was supported in part by the National Science Foundation under award no. IIS 06-43512.

REFERENCES

1. Adamic, L. A., Zhang, J., Bakshy, E. and Ackerman, M. S. Knowledge Sharing and Yahoo Answers: Everyone Knows Something. In Proc. WWW 2008, 665-674.
2. Agichtein, E., Castillo, C., Donato, D., Gionis, A. and Mishne, G. Finding High-Quality Content in Social Media. In Proc. WSDM 2008, 183-194.
3. Baltes, B. B., Dickson, M. W., Sherman, M. P., Bauer, C. C. and LaGanke, J. S. Computer-Mediated Communication and Group Decision Making: A Meta-Analysis. Organizational Behavior and Human Decision Processes, 87, 1 (2002), 156-179.
4. Barcellini, F., Détienne, F., Burkhardt, J.-M. and Sack, W. A Study of Online Discussions in an Open-Source Software Community. Springer Netherlands, 2005.
5. Benkler, Y. The Wealth of Networks: How Social Production Transforms Markets and Freedom. Yale Univ. Press., (2006).
6. Briggs, R. O., Kolfschoten, G. L. and Vreede, G.-J. d. Toward a Theoretical Model of Consensus Building. In Proc. AMCIS 2005
7. Burke, M. and Kraut, R. Mopping Up: Modeling Wikipedia Promotion Decisions In Proc. CSCW 2008, 27-36.
8. Clawson, V. K., Bostrom, R. P. and Anson, R. The Role of the Facilitator in Computer- Supported Meetings. Small Group Research, 24(1993), 547-565.
9. Cosley, D., Frankowski, D., Terveen, L. and Riedl, J. SuggestBot: using intelligent task routing to help people find work in wikipedia. In Proc. IUI 2007, 32-41.
10. Erickson, T., Kellogg, W. A., Laff, M., Sussman, J., Wolf, T. V., Halverson, C. A. and Edwards, D. A persistent chat space for work groups: the design, evaluation and deployment of loops. In Proc. DIS 2006, 331-340.
11. Farnham, S., Chesley, H. R., McGhee, D. E., Kawal, R. and Landau, J. Structured Online Interactions: Improving the Decision Making of Small Discussion Groups. In Proc. CSCW 2000, 299-308.
12. Fiol, C. M. Consensus, diversity, and learning in organizations. Organizational Science, 5, 3 (1994), 403-420.
13. Hare, A. P. A Study of Interaction and Consensus in Different Sized Groups. American Sociological Review, 17, 3 (1952), 261-267.
14. Hars, A. and Ou, S. Working for Free? Motivations for Participating in Open-Source Projects. International Journal of Electronic Commerce, 6, 3 (2002), 25-39.
15. Heckman, R., Crowston, K., Eseryel, Y. U., Howison, J., Allen, E. and Li, Q. Emergent Decision-making Practices in Free/Libre Open Source Software (FLOSS) Development Teams. Springer, 2007.
16. Hiltz, S. R., Johnson, K. and Turoff, M. Experiments in Group Decision Making Communication Process and Outcome in Face-to-Face Versus Computerized Conferences. Human Communication Research, 13(1986), 225-252.
17. Horowitz, D. and Kamvar, S. D. The anatomy of a large-scale social search engine. In Proc. WWW 2010, 431-440.
18. Kerr, N. L. and Tindale, R. S. Group Performance and Decision Making. Annu. Rev. Psychol, 55(2004), 623-655.
19. Ko, A. J. and Chilana, P. K. Design, discussion, and dissent in open bug reports. In Proc. iConference 2011, 106-113.
20. Ko, A. J. and Chilana, P. K. How power users help and hinder open bug reporting. In Proc. CHI 2010, 1665-1674.
21. Lam, S. K., Karim, J. and Riedl, J. The effects of group composition on decision quality in a social production community. In Proc. GROUP 2010, 55-64.
22. Lemus, D. R., Seibold, D. R., Flanagin, A. J. and Metzger, M. J. Argument and Decision Making in Computer-Mediated Groups. Journal of Communication, 54, 2 (2004), 302–320.
23. Luther, K., Counts, S., Stecher, K. B., Hoff, A. and Johns, P. Pathfinder: an online collaboration environment for citizen scientists. In Proc. CHI 2009, 239-248.
24. Straus, S. G. and McGrath, J. Does the medium matter? The interaction of task type and technology on group performance and member reactions. Journal of Applied Psychology, 79(1994), 87-97.
25. Strauss, A. L. Qualitative analysis for social scientists. Cambridge University Press, (1987).
26. Susskind, L., McKearnan, S. and Thomas-Larmer, J. The Consensus Building Handbook. 1999.
27. Twidale, M. B. and Nichols, D. M. Exploring Usability Discussions in Open Source Development. In Proc. HICSS 2005, 198.193.
28. Uzzi, B. Social structure and competition in interfirm networks: the paradox of embeddedness. Administrative Science Quarterly, 42, 1 (1997), 35-67.
29. Willett, W., Heer, J., Hellerstein, J. and Agrawala, M. CommentSpace: structured support for collaborative visual analysis. In Proc. CHI 2011, 3131-3140.
30. Zaheer, A. and Bell, G. G. Benefiting from network position: firm capabilities, structural holes, and performance. Strategic Management Journal, 26, 9 (2005), 809-825.
31. Zilouchian Moghaddam, R., Bailey, B. and Poon, C. IdeaTracker: An Interactive Visualization Supporting Collaboration and Consensus Building in Online Interface Design Discussions. In Proc. INTERACT 2011 2011, 259-276.

"I can't get no sleep": Discussing #insomnia on Twitter

Sue Jamison-Powell, Conor Linehan,
Laura Daley, Andrew Garbett, Shaun Lawson
Lincoln Social Computing Research Centre
University of Lincoln, LN6 7TS, UK
{sjamisonpowell, clinehan, ladaley, agarbett,
slawson}@lincoln.ac.uk

ABSTRACT
Emerging research has shown that social media services are being used as tools to disclose a range of personal health information. To explore the role of social media in the discussion of *mental* health issues, and with particular reference to insomnia and sleep disorders, a corpus of 18,901 messages - or Tweets - posted to the microblogging social media service Twitter were analysed using a mixed methods approach. We present a content analysis which revealed that Tweets that contained the word "insomnia" contained significantly more negative health information than a random sample, strongly suggesting that individuals were making disclosures about their sleep disorder. A subsequent thematic analysis then revealed two themes: *coping* with insomnia, and describing the *experience* of insomnia. We discuss these themes as well as the implications of our research for those in the interaction design community interested in integrating online social media systems in health interventions.

Author Keywords
Twitter; Microblogging; Self-Disclosure; Mental Health; Insomnia; Health

ACM Classification Keywords
H.5.m [Information Interfaces And Presentation]: Miscellaneous;

INTRODUCTION
Social media has been considered as a means to disseminate health information [2, 6] and as a way to provide online social support for health issues [3, 28, 59]. Mental health is traditionally stigmatised by society [4], meaning that those suffering from such illness may find it harder to disclose details of their disorders [21]. However, the reduced social presence afforded by the Internet may assist individuals to disclose details about their mental health [42]. In the work presented here, we investigate the degree to which people are using social media to discuss their mental health conditions, and how exactly they are doing this. Our work makes particular reference to insomnia and to the microblogging social media service Twitter.

Insomnia is one of the most prevalent mental health symptoms reported to health professionals in the UK [39] and is estimated that insomnia affects 30% of the world's population at some point during their lifetime [27, 43]. However, it is estimated that only a small proportion of insomnia sufferers actually seek medical help other than over-the-counter sleep aids [29]. One of the challenges, therefore, facing sleep experts is that of dissemination of accurate information regarding healthy sleep routines and the promotion of sleep therapy.

Twitter has over 100 million active users, who generate 230 million tweets each day [55]. Recent research from the web and data mining communities indicates that Twitter has been casually employed by users ("Tweeters") to discuss a wide range of health information, including information on insomnia [40] and other mental health conditions. Other researchers studying this behaviour have shown that Tweeters use Twitter to disclose symptoms [53], give advice [47] and disseminate information [40]. Such research suggests that Tweeters with chronic conditions, such as insomnia, may not have sought help from health care advisors and thus use Twitter as a repository for information specific to their disorder [40].

This paper focuses upon how individuals use social online spaces that are not specifically dedicated to insomnia to discuss their sleep disorder symptoms, and how they describe their experience with insomnia to a wider audience. We wish to know whether i) individuals are making insomnia related disclosures, and ii) if so, what they are disclosing. The over-arching aim of our research is to explore the implications of these disclosures for those in the interaction design community who are interested in integrating online social media systems in health interventions.

BACKGROUND AND RELATED WORK
Seeking health information online is not a new phenomenon and, in the case of sleep disorders, is seen on numerous discussion boards/forums such as those found at www.talkaboutsleep.com and www.sleepassociation.org. Many of these forums give advice on sleep hygiene; e.g. to reserve the bedroom for sleeping and sex, to refrain from stimulating activities before bedtime, and to establish a

Permission to make digital or hard copies of all or part of this work for personal or classroom use is granted without fee provided that copies are not made or distributed for profit or commercial advantage and that copies bear this notice and the full citation on the first page. To copy otherwise, or republish, to post on servers or to redistribute to lists, requires prior specific permission and/or a fee.
CHI'12, May 5–10, 2012, Austin, Texas, USA.
Copyright 2012 ACM 978-1-4503-1015-4/12/05...$10.00.

relaxing pre-sleep routine [37]. However, in some forums it is possible to find threads initiated by members who are awake and want to reach out and talk with someone in the middle of the night. This is contrary to one of the principles of good sleep hygiene, which is to avoid stimulating environments [37].

A study that examined Twitter use related to antibiotic medication [47] found similar behaviour relating to improper use of antibiotics. Tweeters discussed using antibiotics to cure influenza, which is a viral illness. Hence, whilst social media and online forums may provide a positive support network with regards to health concerns [47], it would seem that there is a potential alternative use that does not have such a positive outcome. Researchers have suggested that those advocating behaviour contrary to medical advice could be targeted and auto-responded to on Twitter with correct advice [47].

The "unknown audience" aspect of broadcast communication allows a Tweeter to address their communication to anyone that they choose. The obvious question is "who do the Tweeters have in mind as their imagined audience when they disclose their insomnia?". The Tweeters in Marwich and Boyd's study [25] were asked quite simply "who do you tweet to?". They described Tweeting to multiple audiences, but some did talk about Tweeting to themselves and rejected the notion of Tweeting to anyone else. This seems counter intuitive when Twitter is considered as a social application, and that these Tweets were public and thus could be read by anyone accessing the site.

Twitter posts have recently been extensively data mined to identify political and economic trends [54, 38, 7], track natural disasters [46] and diseases [5], and to measure consumer opinion [48]. However, whilst this type of research can tell us about the different subjects that Tweeters are discussing, it doesn't tell us *how* Tweeters are using Twitter. We are interested, from an HCI perspective, in the different purposes in which social media is being used in order that subsequent designs and affordances of such services can be improved. Knowledge of purpose will inform the development and design of social media and, with particular regards to insomnia related use, can provide useful information for researchers looking to implement online mental health interventions.

The body of research examining health related Twitter use has employed both qualitative and quantitative methodology. Hand coded content analysis was used to examine antibiotic use [47] and public health issues [40], in which the researchers identified key words and phrases and examined relationships between word clusters and other measures. In contrast, Sullivan *et al* [53] used a thematic analysis of tweets related to concussion using a team of researchers to categorise tweets before extracting themes and applying meaning to the data. We have used a mixed methodology here, using both content and adopting the thematic analysis method used by Sullivan *et al* [53].

The remainder of this paper is outlined as follows. First we describe our method of data collection. Then we describe the content analysis, followed by a short discussion paying specific attention to the degree in which Tweeters are making disclosures. Next, we describe the thematic analysis in which we address the second research question pertaining to the role of Twitter in mental health disclosure. Finally, we discuss the implications of our research for those in the interaction design community interested in integrating online social media systems in health interventions.

DATA COLLECTION

Using a tweet archiving application, 23,119 tweets containing the exact phrase "insomnia" were collected over a 24-hour period; this therefore found anything hash tagged with #insomnia. We will henceforth refer to these tweets as "insomnia tweets." Our insomnia tweets were firstly filtered as follows: a total of 112 tweets were removed from the sample because the Tweeter's twitter profile was listed as a language other than English or was specified as "unknown". A total of 114 tweets that only included the word insomnia as part of the Tweeter's username (e.g. "insomniac342") were also removed. There were 3,992 tweets that were simply duplications or "retweets" (denoted by RT at the beginning of the message). These retweets were removed as the archiving application would have already collected the original tweet. After the filtering process was completed a total of 18,901 tweets remained for analysis.

A content analysis of the insomnia tweets was used to confirm that individuals were using Twitter to disclose details of their sleep disorder. However, analysing only these tweets would not allow us to determine the unique characteristics of tweets about insomnia and how they differ from messages generally posted on Twitter. Therefore, for the purposes of comparison, a control group consisting of 1% of all tweets posted in the first 30 seconds of each hour over a 24-hour period were archived, producing 59,370 tweets. These will be referred to as "non-specific tweets". As in the case of the insomnia tweets, only those tweets from Tweeters whose language was listed as English or "unknown" were selected, leaving a sample size of 40,959. Unlike the insomnia tweets, these randomly sampled tweets could consist of purely ASCII characters (e.g. "} {| ~~|} {/ ^^"") which contained no analysable words; therefore these tweets were also filtered, producing a sample size of 40222. In line with the filtering procedure applied to the Insomnia tweets, "retweets" were removed, giving a sample size of 35064. To produce a similar sized sample to the 18901 insomnia tweets, every second tweet was omitted from the non-specific sample, resulting in a sample of 17532 tweets for analysis.

Variable	Group Mean (*Standard Deviation*) Insomnia[a]	Non-specific[b]	*t*	*p*	*r*
Character Count	68.11 (40.75)	64.76 (38.56)	8.05	<.001	.01
Word Class					
Pronouns	8.07 (10.08)	6.14 (9.04)	19.31	<.001	.02
Verbs	9.55 (11.25)	6.02 (8.69)	33.67	<.001	.03
Auxiliary Verbs	6.01 (8.45)	3.39 (6.05)	34.12	<.001	.03
Sentiment Analysis					
Negative Sentiment	3.13 (7.75)	1.35 (4.41)	27.19	<.001	.03
Positive Sentiment	2.55 (5.64)	3.29 (6.63)	11.50	<.001	.02
Word Root Type					
Health	0.68 (2.77)	0.31 (2.04)	14.21	<.001	.02
Time	4.41 (8.02)	2.49 (5.55)	26.73	<.001	.03
Sad	0.35 (1.96)	0.23 (1.69)	6.04	<.001	.01
Anger	1.91 (6.62)	0.66 (3.13)	23.22	<.001	.03
Anxious	0.24 (1.70)	0.15 (1.44)	5.50	<.001	.01
Past Tense	0.99 (3.19)	0.95 (3.19)	1.26	.209	.001
Present Tense	7.55 (9.96)	4.35 (7.15)	35.50	<.001	.03

[a]$n = 18901$, [b]$n = 17532$

Table 1. Percentage of Word Type per Tweet.

STUDY 1. LINGUISTIC CONTENT ANALYSIS

Analysis

A content analysis was performed using the Linguistic Enquiry and Word Count (LIWC) software [41]. The software produces the percentage of analysed text that contains a particular word class. For instance "I hate having insomnia" would receive a score of 25% in the word class of negative affect, whereas "I really really hate insomnia" would receive a score of 20%. To ensure that the non-specific tweets were suitable to be compared to the insomnia tweets, the length of the insomnia tweets was compared to the non-specific sample (see Table 1). The character count distribution of both samples was bimodal, (which is typical of tweets in general [e.g. 16]) but due to the very large sample size, independent *t* tests were considered to be a suitable method of comparing the two samples [23]. This bimodality is in itself interesting, it shows that both samples of Tweeters had peaks at around 140 characters (the character limit for Twitter), however the lower peak for the insomnia tweets was around 8 characters (essentially "insomnia" or "#insomnia") whereas the non-specific tweets peaked at around 40 characters. Of the 2004 insomnia tweets under 17 characters, 1484 (74%, 8% of the who insomnia sample) consisted of just the word insomnia, or insomnia accompanied by punctuation or an emoticon.

The tweets in the insomnia sample contained a statistically greater number of characters than those within the non-specific sample. However this is to be expected as no insomnia tweet contained less than 8 characters as they, of course, contained the word "insomnia" as a necessity. The non-specific tweet sample was therefore deemed to be a suitable comparison for insomnia tweets for the purposes of a content analysis.

To test for any difference in content between the groups, a content analysis performed using the LIWC software [41]. The use of pronouns, verbs, and auxiliary verbs was compared between the insomnia sample and non-specific sample. The statistics are reported in Table 1 and the analysis shows that the insomnia tweets contained a higher and statistically significant ($p <.001$) percentage of all word classes tested.

A basic sentiment analysis was carried out using the LIWC software. There were statistically significant differences between the groups; compared to the non-specific group the tweets within insomnia sample contained a higher incidence of words with negative valence and lower incidence of words with positive valence (see Table 1). This result is to be expected as the symptoms of insomnia are co-morbid with mood and anxiety disorders [52].

The overall research question of this study is concerned with whether individuals are actually disclosing information about their mental health online. The health category in the LIWC 2007 English dictionary consists of 236 word roots relating to health (examples include ache, medic, sore, and doctor). This category includes the word "insomnia", which we removed from the dictionary for this analysis. The percentage of words related to health within tweets was significantly higher in the insomnia group compared to the non-specific group (see Table 1), which suggests that those within the insomnia group had disclosed symptoms of their insomnia.

To investigate this further, the percentage of words falling within the Sad, Anger and Anxious categories were compared between the groups; these statistics are also reported in Table 1. The words in these categories relate to a negative emotional state (e.g. tense, hateful, hopeless) and it would be reasonable to use these as a proxy for negative disclosures. The insomnia group uses significantly more words within the Sad, Anger and Anxious categories compared to the random group (p <.001 in all cases). In the insomnia group a weak relationship exists between the percentage of words in the Health category and those within the Anxious category (r = .053, p <.001) and Health and Sad category (r = .09, p <.001), and only in the Health and Sad category for the non-specific group (r = .042, p<.001). A Fisher's r to z transformation showed that the relationship is significantly stronger for the insomnia tweets (z = 4.6, p<.001), suggesting that those Tweeters were disclosing more negative health information.

Individuals with insomnia have been found to be preoccupied with time [20]. This is reflected in our sample through the references to time within the insomnia tweets being almost double that of non-specific tweets (see Table 1). When we examine the use of tense in the tweets, we can see there is no significant difference between the usage of past tense across groups. However, present tense is used more within the insomnia tweets. The difference between the use of past and present tenses in the insomnia tweets (*Mean difference* = 6.56, *SD* = 10.42) is much larger than in the non-specific group (*Mean difference* = 3.40, *SD* = 7.76). This is a significant interaction ($F(1)$=1069.94, p <.001) albeit with a very small effect size (*partial* η^2 = .03). When we look at the use of time in conjunction with tense, a correlation analysis shows us a stronger relationship between time and present tense in the non-specific tweets (r = .166, p <.001) than in the insomnia tweets (r = .112, p <.001). A Fisher's r to z transformation shows that this difference is significant (z = 5.25). This strong use of present tense with regards to time could be an artefact of Twitter itself. When a user publishes a Tweet using the Twitter website they are asked "What's happening?" which may predispose the Tweeter to write in the present tense.

Discussion

The described linguistic content analysis provides strong evidence to support the notion that individuals are making self-disclosures about their mental health symptoms with regards to insomnia and sleep disorders. Whilst we can speculate about the nature of these disclosures in terms of qualitative content, this analysis does show us that those tweeting about insomnia are behaving as the literature regarding insomnia would lead us to expect. Specifically Tweeters show a preoccupation with time, and a strong relationship between anger and health disclosure emerges.

The evidence to suggest that disclosures are being made should lead to any online health intervention targeting insomnia to include areas where users can make disclosures about their sleep behaviour. The bimodal distribution of the insomnia sample, specifically the lower peak compared to the non-specific tweets, would suggest that the insomnia Tweeters are using Twitter in different way to the non-specific sample. For instance, the high incidence of tweets similar to "Insomnia!" may mean that these Tweeters are using Twitter as a virtual pillow to shout into. Individuals with insomnia are commonly (and quite understandably) frustrated [10], and appear to be using the platform to vent this frustration.

STUDY 2. INDUCTIVE THEMATIC ANALYSIS

Whilst the linguistic content analysis confirms that individuals are self-disclosing about their mental health issues, caution is advised when interpreting the results as individuals have a tendency to abbreviate and use alternatives to proper words when there is a character limit in place [35]. These abbreviations are not necessarily picked up by the LIWC software. There is also a question of the subjectivity and ambiguity of tweets; an individual may, for instance, tweet "My insomnia is back – oh great" which would be coded as having positive valence through a straightforward content analysis, when the opposite could be implied. Therefore we deemed it appropriate to conduct an inductive thematic analysis, in which subjectivity is acknowledged and content is interpreted, rather than taken at face value [9].

Because a hand coded thematic analysis would not be feasible on the entire sample of tweets, a subset of 749 tweets, consisting of every 25th tweet in the original list, was chosen for analysis. These tweets were compared with the Insomnia sample as a whole (n = 18901) on all the word categories analysed in the content analysis, there were no significant differences at the alpha level of $\alpha = 0.001$.

Analysis

The 749 tweets selected for analysis were read several times by one researcher, making annotations where appropriate. Category codes were then applied to the tweets. The tweets were read several more times and the categories were refined, producing 49 categories. The category codes, together with a description and examples of each code, were given to two other researchers. Following discussions, the category definitions were refined to 45 codes. To assess the reliability of the categories another subsample of tweets was taken from the remaining 18145 selected for analysis. The first of every 35 tweets was chosen for analysis producing a subsample of 514 tweets. The three researchers completed the coding separately. The majority of tweets were assigned one category per tweet, but some contained more than one piece of information and thus were segmented by the raters.

All segmented tweets were examined by the three raters together and a consensus was reached on the majority of the tweets. The codes were examined for inter-rater reliability using Fleiss' Kappa, κ = .516 which is classed as a moderate agreement using the guidelines produced by Landis and Kock [22], individual measures of reliability between the raters using Cohen's Kappa, producing statistics of κ = .864, κ = .887, and κ = .898 which are classed as having high agreement [11].

The coding categories were then examined and cross-referenced with the data. Themes were identified and refined by the lead researcher and reviewed by all three researchers.

Findings and Discussion

Six first order themes were identified, which formed two second order themes; *Coping with Insomnia*, and *Describing the Experience*, which are illustrated in Figure 1. The themes are expanded upon below. All tweets employed to illustrate the theme are used with original spelling and grammar, usernames have been anonymised.

Second Order Theme1: Describing the Experience

Four interrelated first order themes make up the theme *Describing the Experience*. This second order theme represents the ways in which Tweeters with insomnia write about their experiences of the sleep disorder. The theme encompasses expressions of Tweeters' external experience in terms of their mental state and the sleep quality and quantity, together with interactions between other Tweeters and Insomnia as an entity. The following subsections discuss these first order themes in more detail.

First Order Theme 1.1: Sharing

The theme of Sharing the Experience emerged particularly from tweets that were directed towards another user. Whilst some users opt to lock their tweets, meaning that only designated Twitter users can read them, a huge amount of content is available publically, either to Twitter subscribers via the Twitter platform, or to anyone with an Internet connection via a third party client. Twitter can therefore be classified as a broadcast medium. However, Twitter has the facility to allow directed messages (known as DMs) which are only visible to the sender and receiver, and "mentions" (those featuring another user's @ prefixed name) which can be read by anyone. It can be argued that with respect to mentions, the author of those tweets is making a targeted communication. Tweets that fell into the theme of *Sharing* may have offered support or empathy *"@[4460580] Sorry you're feeling sad. Is the insomnia still hanging around?"* or in some cases suggested ways in which the insomnia Tweeter could fall asleep *"@[236324168] you have a serious case of insomnia...shame"*. This exchange is evidence of Twitter facilitating individuals who may not be otherwise connected to identify with each other over a common mental health disorder. The Internet allows individuals to connect with each other and access information directly relevant to their own experiences and needs, regardless of geographical location. Some of these 'Sharing' tweets such as "*@[147265787] insomnia~ welcome to the club*" suggest a form of validation and recognition of the target of the communication in that someone else has gone through the same experience. This type of validation is a strong theme in online support-groups [24, 12, 57]. Further, this interaction suggests some possible future use for social support. Whilst the exchanges highlighted here appear to be between individuals who follow each other on Twitter, the ability to search for phrases and words, and Twitter users voluntary use of the #insomnia tag allows Tweeter to interact with users who are discussing similar things, meaning that Twitter could feasibly function as an online support-group proxy.

Some Tweeters, rather that offering sympathy, berate those who claim to have insomnia when they are just having minor sleep disturbances "*@[27629153] insomnia?U're the person who sleeps A LOT!*". Literature on discourse describes the notion of *normative sleep* [26]. Specifically, if an individual does not achieve what they consider to be the appropriate amount of sleep, they pathologize the experience. This highlights one of the fundamental problems with the use of the term "insomnia", common to the term "depression"; individuals may use it to describe a single occurrence of sleeplessness, or as in the case of depression, as a synonym for disappointed ("*Twitter's down, I'm so depressed LOL!!!!11one*").

Whilst directed tweets formed a strong component of this theme, there were other tweets that simply disclosed insomnia. The Tweeter was not asking for help, they were not talking about their coping strategies or talking about how their insomnia was making them feel they were simply saying "*I got insomnia*". The presence of "*Insomnia....*" has

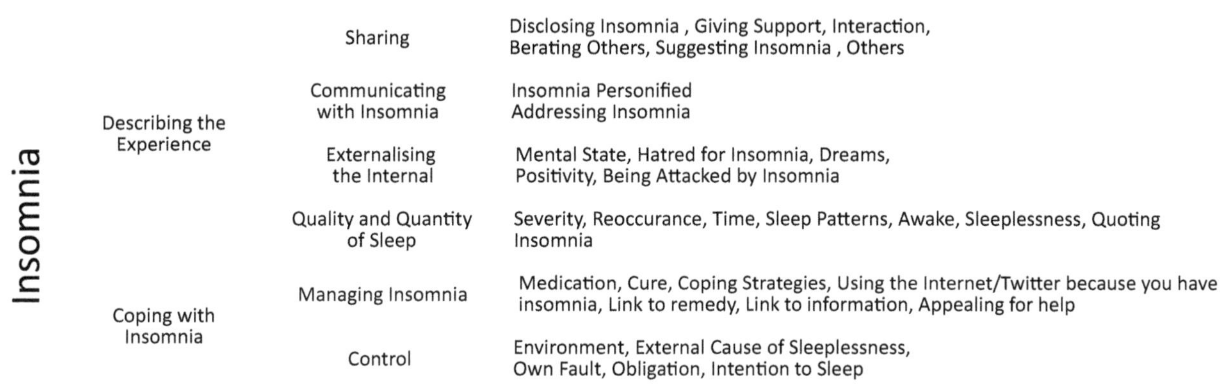

Figure 1. Hierarchy of Themes and Placement of Categories

been commented upon in the linguistic content analysis above, and it emerged as a strong theme in terms of *Sharing the Experience*, as the Tweeters seemed to need to simply a beginning of a potential conversation with another human being. Here we see users making the most of the broadcast format of Twitter. Tweets can of course be directed (which the theme *Describing the Experience* primarily concerns) but it also allows the Tweeter to address a wider and relatively unknown audience [25].

First Order Theme 1.2: Communicating with Insomnia

This theme highlighted a way that Twitter was used to address insomnia directly. Whereas those tweets falling under the *Sharing* theme were directed towards another user, the tweets under *Communicating with Insomnia* were addressed to Insomnia itself, "*Oh insomnia... Thou art a heartless bitch.*." or treated insomnia as a sentient being "*Insomnia is a bitch tonight!*". The use of "*dear #insomnia…*" may be an exercise in catharsis, echoing the conclusions of a similar study by Sullivan *et al* [53] which looked at the disclosure of concussion-related information on Twitter.

The verbalization of emotions through writing is used in psychotherapy; it allows the patient to rationalize and accept their feelings as valid and reduces troublesome thoughts and emotions [19]. Websites like Dear Cancer[1] and Dear Mental Illness[2] exist, where individuals can write to their illness as if it is a hostile person. The letters are a mixture of stoicism, defiance, unrestrained emotion, and tenacity. Dear Cancer states that they are "here to help you finally get it all out", emphasizing the cathartic function of addressing your illness. Perhaps Twitter is another platform upon which users can begin to come to terms with their illness or disorder. The "unknown audience" aspect may allow the users to make these potentially cathartic disclosures "to insomnia" without the risk of judgment.

First Order Theme 1.3: Externalizing the Internal

Whereas some of the tweets mentioned above simply stated that the Tweeter could not sleep, tweets which made up the theme *Externalizing the Internal* contained a lot more information regarding (i) the Tweeter's mental state "*This feeling of nothingness is not new but I'm slowly getting used to it. #Insomnia #StopDenyingIt*", (ii) their emotional state "*Hate insomnia!*", and (iii) their experience fighting for sleep every night "*My insomnia is going to kill me*". These disclosures echo the catharsis mentioned above. Once again we see strong emotional and quite intimate self-disclosure, which poses a question of to whom such tweets are addressed. It is tempting to apply the stranger-on-a-train analogy here [45], the Tweeter may be making incredibly personal disclosures, but they could be making them to strangers with no interest or investment in the disclosure.

[1] http://dearcancer.org/

[2] http://www.dearmentalillness.com/

share their frustrations with their sleep problems. It could almost be viewed as a precursor to interaction,

However this analogy is not a good fit as their username is attached to the tweet and the tweet is cached, recorded for posterity. Those that read the tweet may be strangers in the sense that they do not know the Tweeter, but unlike a stranger on a train, they can go back and read the tweet and even retweet it if they so wish. Whilst this analysis doesn't answer the question as to why the Tweeters make such intimate disclosures, the findings do highlight the fact that it happens. It would be advantageous for any online social media intervention to include a function that allows users to make this type of disclosure.

First Order Theme 1.4: Quality and Quantity of Sleep

Tweeters wrote about the severity of their symptoms "*Bad insomnia really reallyyyyyy baddddd*" how their symptoms were increasing in severity "*my insomnia is getting worse.. yay me...*". Individuals who seek help for their sleep disorders typically describe their symptoms with more severity than those with similar symptoms that do not seek help [13]. The Tweeters here may have been ruminating on their symptoms; something that has been found to be excessive in Internet communication from individuals exhibiting suicidal and parasuicidal behaviour [18].

Echoing the results of the linguistic content analysis a strong component of this theme was the frequent reporting of the time: "*Damn its 3am. Insomnia*", "*4:26 & I'm still awake... #insomnia*". These are written in the present tense so we can be reasonably confident that these are real time Tweets. This produces further evidence that Tweeters who have trouble sleeping are not adhering to the principles of good sleep hygiene. Whether this is simply through lack of willpower, or lack of education is something that will need to be explored further.

Design Implications from "Describing the Experience"

As was suggested from the results of the linguistic content analysis, the findings here strongly suggest that any online intervention should have a space where users can simply disclose their experiences with insomnia and vent their frustrations at being unable to sleep. The notion of speaking directly to 'Insomnia' is interesting, and something that could easily be built into any system. This would fulfil two purposes, it would allow the users to vent frustrations resulting in catharsis, but it would also validate the frustrations of those reading it, they would see that what they are feeling is perfectly natural when challenged with insomnia.

These findings clearly suggest that individuals are sharing their experiences, not just with an imagined audience, but directly with targeted communication. They are supporting each other, suggesting practical and emotional ways of dealing with sleeplessness, and offering empathy to fellow sufferers. This social support aspect has been shown to be very successful in group therapy [17]. In this regard, an online social network structure is an ideal choice for the delivery of online support. A social network structure promotes online closeness [50] and can promote engagement with online support systems [58]. Whereas online therapy suffers from high levels of attrition [30,56], an online support service with a social network structure could seek to improve this, together with providing a social support network for those undertaking any therapy or self-help guide.

Second order Theme 2: Coping with Insomnia

Whilst the second order theme of *Describing the Experience* contained first order themes that spoke of what it was like to have problems sleeping, the second order theme of *Coping with Insomnia* described how the Tweeters managed their insomnia, and how they attributed the difficulties they had sleeping. This theme has much in common with the theme of *Inferred Management* found in a similar study by Sullivan *et al* [53] exploring discussion of sports related concussion on Twitter. Whereas some of the tweets within *Sharing* contained advice given by others through directed means (@mention), the coping strategies and information on managing insomnia within *Coping with Insomnia* are volunteered without any elicitation from others.

First Order Theme 2.1: Managing Insomnia

This theme contained tweets that dealt with ways of managing the disorder, from simple coping strategies "*So last night while suffering from another insomnia attack I did what my friend suggested and read manga. Rosario + Vampire is my favorite*" to advertisements for cures "*Insomnia & Sleep Problems Tonight. No Medication* [link]". Medication did make up a strong part of this theme, Tweeters either requesting it "*i have insomnia. are there pills for that?*" or simply disclosing their use of it "*Insomnia sucks! I have to Ambien it every night to sleep at all*". Medication is only recommended for short periods and only in chronic cases [36], however sleeping pills are seen by insomnia sufferers as an immediate and easy solution to their sleep problems [33]. This attitude is echoed in the tweets relating to insomnia "*Anyone got sleeping pills for my insomnia stricken dudette*", "*5:45 in the fucking morning and I'm not tired in the slightest #insomnia #needsleepingpills*".

Some Tweeters claimed to be using the Internet and, more specifically, Twitter itself when they were suffering from a spell of sleeplessness "*Yep twittering at 5 am instead of sleeping*". This is interesting as medical advice given to those diagnosed with insomnia would not advocate the use of the Internet when trying to sleep, which can be an engaging and stimulating activity [1,31]. Again, this mirrors the findings of Sullivan *et al* [53], who highlight the propensity for misinformation in advice given to those with sports related concussion. This may suggest that individuals who find themselves on Twitter at 5am, having had no sleep, have not yet sought medical assistance. Indeed, insomnia sufferers commonly try to "fix" their sleep disorder themselves before seeking medical assistance [51]. Some of the coping strategies given here are maladaptive to quality sleep "*Catching up with on glee. I wish I were catching up on sleep.*" but some are in line with advice from sleep experts "*Awake at 4:45am. Cup of camomile go chase sleep catch it.*", suggesting that some individuals are adhering to good sleep hygiene habits.

First Order Theme 2.2: Control

The tweets identified under the theme of Managing Insomnia illustrate the ways in which insomnia sufferers were living with the sleep disorder, this separate theme of Control illustrates the *ownership* of insomnia. The psychological concept of locus of control places individuals within an external or internal locus [44]. In an external locus the individual feels that their actions and circumstances are dictated to them by external factors, whereas those who possess an internal locus feel very much in control of their own actions. This scale of control from internal to external emerged as a strong theme.

Whereas within the *Managing Insomnia* theme Tweeters referred to using Twitter as a coping strategy, here we see them place Twitter as a cause of their sleeplessness "*but seriously twitter is my cause for insomnia.....no other reason causes my sleeping disorder*". The ubiquitous nature of the Internet was an oft cited reason for staying awake with several variations on the message "*Some people can't sleep due to insomnia...i can't sleep because i have an internet connection!*". This may seem strange as the Internet needn't be the overwhelming presence that these Tweeters seem to see it as ("*well i guess i wouldn't call it insomnia I could sleep if i tried its just hard with a laptop satellite tv and a DVD player in my room*"), this is a classic example of how someone with a strong external locus of control will view their ability to change.

This internal locus is displayed in tweets that talk about future obligations. Tweets that make mention of exams (for example "*Having insomnia the night before an important exam. #classic*") are obviously related to stress induced transient insomnia [15]. However, Tweeters seem very aware of other obligations and the effect of their insomnia on these "*How the fuck will I be in time for this flight if insomnia wants her turn?*", "*#insomnia is no joke! I have to get up for work in an hour and still awake!*". Despite the strong presence of an external locus, some tweets exhibit characteristics of an internal locus of control. Here Tweeters seem to be using Twitter as a kind of affirmative platform telling the Twitterverse that they are going to sleep tonight "*Ok ima rendezvous with my pillow and hope to fall asleep in the next two hours*" "*Getting sleepy :D Good!!!! No insomnia XD Will sleep soon :)*". The internal locus of control was overwhelmingly associated with positive behaviour and outcome, however one Tweeter accepts responsibility for their disruption to their sleep patterns "*Didn't know insomnia sucks so badly. Hearing the* *morning trains makes it even worst. My bad for slping too long!*".

The fact that individuals self-report maladaptive coping strategies could be exploited by health providers to target those that could benefit from cognitive behavioural therapy, particularly for the case of self-help therapeutic online services. Only a small proportion of individuals who suffer from insomnia seek medical help [29] and those that do often wait until symptoms are severe [34]. A targeted online self-help solution to the sleeping disorder could assist those suffering from initial and mild symptoms before the maladaptive strategies become entrenched.

Design Implications for "Coping with Insomnia"

This theme dealt with the practical aspects of insomnia. It is important to take these findings into account with regards to functions of any online social support system.

Tweets within this theme demonstrated a need for a controlled environment on any online support system. Tweeters blamed Twitter for their insomnia, suggesting that some kind of digital barrier should be in place to limit access during periods when the users should be sleeping, or engaging in non-stimulating activities.

Online therapy, or an online social support provision could influence control in another sense, in terms of locus-of-control. Typically, an individual suffering from sleep problems will complete a sleep diary [8, 49] consisting of a record of time spent in bed, time spent sleeping etc. This can be easily and adapted and is apposite for a social network type environment. Immediate feedback could increase engagement with the online provision, in addition to helping the user regain ownership of their disorder.

A social network structure would be ideal to apply the principles of the expert patient to encourage the use of good sleep hygiene and discourage the use of harmful coping strategies. The use of peer-led programmes in the online management of chronic conditions has shown to be successful [14]

The strong presence of medication in the theme *Managing Insomnia* highlights the overreliance on medication as a cure. Pharmacological insomnia remedies are often prescribed in parallel therapy; however the focus of any online provision is self-managed care. Therefore it is important to be aware of this preoccupation with sleeping medication. In related work, Scanfield *et al* [47] suggests targeting individuals on Twitter who have misconceptions over antibiotic use. A similar strategy could be employed to address the overreliance on sleep medication, targeting individuals to provide information on behavioural solutions to insomnia.

CONCLUSION

A corpus of 18,901 Tweets were analysed using a mixed methods approach to understand how people are discussing sleep disorders on the microblogging service Twitter. A content analysis showed that tweets that contained the word "insomnia" contained significantly more negative health information than a random sample, strongly suggesting that individuals were making disclosures about their sleep disorder. A subsequent thematic analysis revealed two themes; coping with insomnia, and describing the experience of insomnia. Our research, in a generic sense, contributes to the growing body of literature regarding online self-disclosure. We describe two analyses of a corpus of insomnia related tweets and demonstrate that individuals are using social media to make health-related disclosures online. We show that Tweeters are disclosing their symptoms and coping strategies and using the broadcast medium of Twitter to engage with their insomnia and release the frustration they feel towards their difficulties in sleeping.

Constructive opportunities and challenges for the use of social media to engage people with, and to treat, insomnia, are now summarised as follows: a social network structure would allow therapy to be delivered in a group. This structure would be a useful format for users to exchange support and practical information. To allow users to exercise catharsis, a space could be provided to disclose symptoms and frustrations together with an area where the users can "communicate with" insomnia. To comply with the principles of sleep hygiene, a digital barrier should be in place in any interactive platform, this would reduce the amount of access a user has to an online support network at times when they should be refraining from stimulating environments. However, rather than simply restrict all access a "life-line" should be kept open, providing information on good sleep hygiene and progressive muscle relaxation exercises [32] to aid sleep.

Our own future research will now exploit the findings presented here to improve access and adherence to online support for individuals with a sleep disorder. We aim to focus on creating a social network type platform upon which to deliver therapy aimed at insomnia sufferers, which will afford a basis for social support.

ACKNOWLEDGMENTS

This research was funded by EPSRC grant EP/I000615/1 "ENACT: Exploiting social Networks to Augment Cognitive behavioural Therapy".

REFERENCES

1. Alberta Medical Association. (2009). Guideline for adult primary insomnia: diagnosis to management. Alberta Medical Association. www.topalbertadoctors.org
2. Anderson, B. and Speed, E., (2010) Social Media And Health: Implications For Primary Health Care Providers. *Report to Solihull Care Trust*. Colchester, University of Essex

3. Anderson-Bill, E.S., Winett, R.A., Wojcik, J.R. (2011). Social Cognitive Determinants of Nutrition and Physical Activity Among Web-Health Users Enrolling in an Online Intervention: The Influence of Social Support, Self-Efficacy, Outcome Expectations, and Self-Regulation. *J Med Internet Res,*13, 1, e28. doi:10.2196/jmir.1551
4. Angermeyer, M.C. & Matschinger, H. (2003). The stigma of mental illness: Effects of labelling on public attitudes towards people with mental disorder. *Act Psychiatr Scand,* 108, 304-309.
5. Archrekar, H., Gandhe, A., Lazarus, R., Yu, S0H. & Lie, Benyuan. (2011). Predicting flu trends using Twitter data. *Computer Communications Workshops,* In Proc. *2011 IEEE Conference,* 10-15 April, 2011, Shanghai, pp.702-707 doi: 10.1109/INFCOMW.2011.5928903
6. Bennett, E. (2011). Social media and hospitals: From trendy to essential. *Futurescan 2001: Healthcare Trends and Implications 2011-2016*, 43-48.
7. Bollen, J., Mao, H., & Zeng, X-J. (2011). Twitter mood predicts the stock market. *Journal of Computational Science,* 2, 1, 1-8.
8. Bootzin, R.R., Perlis, M.L.(1992). Nonpharmacologic treatments of insomnia. *J Clin Psychiatry,* 53(suppl), 37–41.
9. Boyatzis, R.E.(1995). *Transforming qualitative information: Thematic analysis and code development.* Sage.
10. Carey, T.J., Moul, D.E., Pilkonis, P., Germain, A., & Buysse, D.J. (2006). Focussing on the experience of insomnia. *Behav Sleep Med.*, 3, 2, 73-86.
11. Clark-Carter, D. (2010). *Quantitative psychological research.* Psychology Press.
12. Coulson, N.S., Buchanan, H., & Aubeeluck, A. (2007). Social support in cyberspace: A content analysis of communication with a Huntingdon's Disease online support group. *Patient Education & Counselling*, 68, 2, 173-178.
13. Davidson, J.R., Aime, A., Ivers, H., & Morin, C. (2009). Characteristics of individuals with insomnia who seek treatment in a clinical setting versus those who volunteer for a randomized controlled trial. *Behav Sleep Med*, 7, 1, 37-52
14. Department of Health. (2007). *Improving access to psychological therapies (IAPT) programme: Computerised cognitive behavioural therapy (cCBT) implementation guidance.*
15. Doghramji, K. (2006). The epidemiology and diagnosis of insomnia. *Am J Manag Care*, 12, s214-220.
16. Doughty, M, Rowland, D., & Lawson, S.(2011) Co-viewing live TV with digital background channels. *EuroITV'11*, Lisborn, Portugal, June 2011.
17. Edinger, J., & Means, M.(2005). Cognitive-behavioural therapy for primary insomnia. *Clin Psych Rev.*, 25, 5, 539-558.
18. Fekete, S. (2002). Source of data on suicide, depression and anxiety: A preliminary study. *Arch Suicide Res*, 6, 4, 351-361.
19. Gortner, E-M., Rude, S.S., & Pennebaker, J.W. (2006). Benefits of expressive writing in lowering rumination and depressive symptoms. *Behavior Therapy*, 37, 3, 292-303.
20. Harvey, A.G. (2002). A cognitive model of insomnia. *Behavioural Research and Therapy*, 40, 869-893.
21. Holmes, E.P. & River, L.P. (1998). Individual strategies for coping with the stigma of severe mental illness. *Cognitive and Behavioural Practice,* 5, 231-239.
22. Landis, J.R., & Kock, G.G (1977). The measurement of observed agreement for categorical data. *Biometrics*, 33, 159-174.
23. Lumley, T., Diehr, P., Emerson, S. & Chen, L. (2002) The importances of normality assumption in large public health data sets. *Annu Rev Public Health,* 23, 151-169.
24. Malik, S.H., & Coulson, N.S. (2010) Coping with infertility online: An examination of self-help mechanisms in an online infertility support group. *Patient Education and Counselling,* 81, 315-318.
25. Marwick, A.E, & Boyd, D. (2011). I tweet honestly, I tweet passionately: Twitter users, context collapse, and the imagined audience. *New Media and Society,* 13, 1, 114-133.
26. Meadows, R. (2005). The 'negotiated night': an embodied conceptual framework for the sociological study of sleep. *The Sociological Review*, 53, 2, 240-254.
27. Mei, E., & Buysse, D.J. (2009). Insomnia: Prevalence, Impact, Pathogenesis, Differential Diagnosis, and Evaluation. *Sleep Med Clin, 3*, 2, 167-174.
28. Meier, A., Lyons, E.J., Frydman, G., Forlenza, M., & Rimer, B.K. (2007). How Cancer Survivors Provide Support on Cancer-Related Internet Mailing Lists. *J Med Internet Res*, 9, 2, e12. doi:10.2196/jmir.9.2.e12.
29. Mellinger, G.D., Balter, M.B., & Uhlenhuth, E.H. (1985). Insomnia and its treatments. *Arch Gen Psychiatry*, 42, 3, 225-232.
30. Mitchell, N. (2009). Computerised CBT self-help for depression in Higher Education: Reflections on a pilot. *Counselling and Psychotherapy Research.* 9, 4, 280-286.
31. Morin, C., translation by Morgan, K., David, B., & Gascoigne, C. (2007). *Coping with insomnia and long-term health conditions. Booklet 3: Developing good sleeping habits.* Loughborough University.
32. Morin, C.M. (2004). Cognitive-behavioral approaches to the treatment of insomnia. *J Clin Psychiatry*, 65[suppl 16], 33-40.

33. Morin, C.M., Daley, M., & Ouellet, C-M. (2001). Insomnia in adults. *Curr Treat Options Neurol.*, 3, 1, 9-18.

34. Morin, C.M., LeBlanc, M., Daley, M., Gregoire, J.P., & Merette, C. (2006). Epidemiology of insomnia: Prevalence, self-help treatments, consultations, and determinates of help-seeking behaviors. *Sleep Medicine,* 7, 2, 123-130.

35. Napoles, C., Callison-Burch, C., Ganitkevitch, J., & Van Durme, B. (2011). Paraphrastic sentence compression with a character-based metric: Tightening without deletion. Proc. Assoc. for Computation Linguistics, 88-94.

36. National Institute for Clinical Excellence. (2004).*Guidelines on the use of zaleplon, zolpidem and zopiclone for the short-term management of insomnia.* Technology Appraisal 77, April 2004.

37. NHS Choices. *Insomnia –Treatment.* (2009). http://www.nhs.uk/Conditions/Insomnia/Pages/Treatment.aspx.

38. O'Connor, B., Balasubramanyan, R., Routledge, B.R., & Smith, N.A. (2010). From tweets to polls: Linking text sentiment to public opinion time series. *Tepper School of Business.* Paper 559. http://repository.edu/tepper/559.

39. Office for National Statistics. (2001). *Psychiatric Morbidity among Adults living in private households, 2000.* London.

40. Paul, M., & Dredze, M. (2011). You are what you tweet: Analyzing Twitter for public health. *Proc. of the Fifth International AAAI Conference on Weblogs and Social Media* (ICWSM) 2011.

41. Pennebaker, J.W., Booth, R.J., & Francis, M.E. (2007). LIWC2007: Linguistic Inquiry and Work Count. Austin, Texas.

42. Powell, J., Clarke, A. (2006). Information in mental health: qualitative study of mental health service users. *Health Expectations,* 9, 359-36

43. Roth, T. (2007). Insomnia: definition, prevalence, etiology, and consequences. *J Clin Sleep Med,*15, 3(suppl): S7-10.

44. Rotter, J.B. (1966). Generalized expectancies of internal versus external control of reinforcements. *Psychological Monographs*, 80, Whole No. p609.

45. Rubin, Z. (1975). Disclosing oneself to a stranger: Reciprocity and its limits. *Journal of Experimental Social Psychology*, 11, 233-60.

46. Sakaki, T., Okazaki, M., & Matsuo, Y. (2019). Earthquake shakes Twitter users: Real-time event detection by social sensors. *Proc. of WWW2010,* April 26-30, 2010, Raleigh, North Carolina.

47. Scanfield, D., Scanfield, V, & Larson, E. (2010). Dissemination of health information through social networks: Twitter and antibiotics. *Am J Infect Control*, 38, 3, 182-8.

48. Schieber, A., Sommer, S., Hilbert, A., & Heinrich, K. (2011). Analyzing customer sentiments in microblogs – A topic-model-based approach for Twitter datasets. *AMCIS 2001 Proceedings – All Submissions*, Paper 227. http://aisel.aisnet.org/amcis2011_submissions/227.

49. Schutte-Rodin, S., Broch, L., Buysse, D., Dorsey, C., & Sateia, M. (2008). Clinical guideline for the evaluation and management of chronic insomnia in adults. *J Clin Sleep Med*, 4, 5, 487-504.

50. Stefanone, M., Kwon, K., & Lackaff, D.(2011). The value of online friends: Networked resources via social network sites. *First Monday*, 16, 2, 1-17.

51. Stepanski, E., Koshorek, G., Zorick, F., Glinn, M., Roehrs, T., & Roth, T. (1989). Characteristics of individuals who do or do not seek treatment for chronic insomnia. *Psychosomatics*, 30, 421-427.

52. Stepanski, E.J., & Rybarczyk, B. (2006). Emergine research on the treatment and etiology of secondary or comorbid insomnia. *Sleep Medicine Reviews*, 10, 7-18.

53. Sullivan, S.J., Scheiders, A.G., Cheang, C-W., Kitto, E., Lee, H., Redhead, J., Ward, S., Ahmed, O.H., & McCrory, P.R.(2011) 'What's happening?" A content analysis of concussion-related traffic on *Twitter*. *Brit J Sport Med.* Published Online First: 15 March 2011 doi:10.1136/bjsm.2010.080341.

54. Tumasjan, A., Sprenger, T.O., Sandner, P.G., & Welpe, I.M. (2010). Predicting elections with Twitter: What 140 characters reveal about political sentiment. *Proc. of the Fourth International AAAI Conference on Weblogs and Social Media,*178-185.

55. Twitter.com. (2011). *What is Twitter?* http://business.twitter.com/basics/what-is-twitter.

56. Wangberg, S.C., Bergmo, T.S., & Johnsen J-A.K. (2008). Adherence in Internet-based interventions. *Patient Preference and Adherence,* 2, 57-65.

57. Wright, K.B., & Bell, S.B. (2003). Health –related support groups on the Internet: Linking empirical findings to social support and computer-mediated communication theory. *J Health Psychol*, 8, 1, 39-54.

58. Xu, Y., Cao, X., Sellen, A., Herbrich, R., & Graepel, T. (2001). Sociable killers: Understanding social relationships in an online first-person shooter game. *Proc. of the ACM 2011 Conference on Computer Supported Cooperative Work, March 19-23,* 2011, Hangzhou, China.

59. Yu, B. (2011). The emotional world of health online communities. *Proc. of iConference 2011,* February 8-11, 2011. Seattle, WA.

Introducing the Ambivalent Socialiser

Bernd Ploderer[1], Wally Smith[1], Steve Howard[1], Jon Pearce[1], and Ron Borland[1,2]

[1]The University of Melbourne
Parkville, Victoria 3010, Australia

[2]Cancer Council Victoria
Carlton, Victoria 3053, Australia

{ploderer, wsmith, showard, jonmp}@unimelb.edu.au, ron.borland@cancervic.org.au

ABSTRACT

Social interaction can be a powerful strategy for persuasive technology interventions, yet many users are reluctant to engage with others online because they fear pressure, failure and shame. We introduce the 'ambivalent socialiser', a person who is simultaneously keen but also reluctant to engage with others via social media. Our contribution is to identify four approaches to introducing sociality to ambivalent socialisers: structured socialising, incidental socialising, eavesdropping and trace sensing. We discuss the rationale for these approaches and show how they address recent critiques of persuasive technology. Furthermore, we provide actionable insights for designers of persuasive technology by showing how these approaches can be implemented in a social media application.

Author Keywords

Persuasive technology; social support; online participation; social networks; ambivalent socialiser; smoking cessation.

ACM Classification Keywords

H.5.m. Information interfaces and presentation (e.g., HCI): Miscellaneous.

General Terms

Human Factors, Theory.

INTRODUCTION

Persuasive technology is concerned with the design of technologies to encourage behaviour change in everyday life, like adopting a healthier lifestyle and preserving the environment [6]. According to a growing body of research, one of the most persuasive forces is our connection to, and interaction with, other people. Social interaction can facilitate commitment to behaviour change, as people feel recognised and accountable among their peers [14]. Often people derive motivation from cooperation and competition within groups [6]. Social interaction can also be a source of advice and emotional support during difficult times [13].

According to another established line of research, however, mediated social interaction can be met with apathy [15]. People are often reluctant to discuss some behaviour change issues in social media through concern about impressions given to friends and family [14]. Peer groups experience a fine line between support and pressure, the latter sometimes leading to disengagement and the return to old habits [4]. Moreover, failure to change one's behaviour can be a source of shame in mediated social settings, preventing renewed attempts in the future [16].

Permission to make digital or hard copies of all or part of this work for personal or classroom use is granted without fee provided that copies are not made or distributed for profit or commercial advantage and that copies bear this notice and the full citation on the first page. To copy otherwise, or republish, to post on servers or to redistribute to lists, requires prior specific permission and/or a fee.
CHI'12, May 5–10, 2012, Austin, Texas, USA.
Copyright 2012 ACM 978-1-4503-1015-4/12/05...$10.00.

Here we offer a potential reconciliation between these conflicting lines of research by introducing the 'ambivalent socialiser'. This is a type of person who, for a given domain of social interaction, is simultaneously keen but also reluctant to engage with others. In cases of behaviour change, this conflict may result from a deep ambivalence of wanting to change yet wanting to continue as they are. Identifying and understanding these ambivalent socialisers, we contend, may be the basis of more nuanced design for persuasive technology.

We explore the significance and challenges of designing for ambivalent socialisers by focusing on a particular domain of behaviour change: smoking cessation. Based on a review of work in HCI and other fields we propose four approaches to introducing sociality to ambivalent socialisers: structured socialising, incidental socialising, eavesdropping and trace sensing. In presenting this analysis, we extend recent approaches to facilitating behaviour change through social interaction [3, 13] and we address critiques of how persuasive technology conceptualises its users [10, 16].

AMBIVALENT SOCIALISERS IN SMOKING CESSATION

Large-scale studies of social networks show that people often become non-smokers together, suggesting a positive influence of family, friends and co-workers [1]. However, smokers are typically reluctant to ask their non-smoking friends and family for support, preferring to keep their quit journeys private through fear of likely failure. Consequently, smokers may regularly socialise with friends on Facebook and blogs, but they are unlikely to use these channels to talk about smoking cessation or any other health topics [9, 14]. Specialised online communities for smoking cessation offer support from often-anonymous peers rather than friends, but currently with limited success. QuitNet, the largest online community for smokers and quitters, attracts only 1-2% of all smokers, a very small minority given that around 40% of smokers make a quit attempt in any given year [11].

DESIGNING FOR AMBIVALENT SOCIALISERS

To explore the challenge of designing social media for ambivalent socialisers, below we investigate and contrast four possible approaches. Each approach is investigated through a screen mock-up of a fictional smoking cessation service called 'Consider Quitting' (CQ). We designed CQ as a smartphone application to support social interaction at any time and place. CQ focuses primarily on smokers who are contemplating quitting, but who have not yet made a decision to act. The application provides them with expert guidance on quitting, and connects them with successful quitters and other smokers who are also contemplating quitting. CQ draws inspiration from existing smartphone applications, in particular, Facebook and the Livestrong.com My QuitCoach application.

Structured Socialising

The first approach is to offer an environment with defined structures for social interactions among ambivalent socialisers. Ambivalent socialisers are assigned to a small group of other quitters, by connecting them based on shared goals, locations, or affiliations. Members of the group are required to carry out defined tasks that demand internal cooperation and competition against other groups. In another behaviour change domain, Consolvo and colleagues used this approach with a mobile application that utilised step counts from a pedometer to encourage people to become more physically active [3]. People could set personal goals, but they were also part of a group that shared step counts and support messages.

Figure 1a shows one mock-up of how we have considered this form of structured socialising in CQ. A ranking feature shows users' achievements in giving up smoking (like the number of days without a cigarette), their interaction with the application (number of logins and posts), and their level of social interaction (number of friends and number of responses to comments). These rankings list both individuals within the group as well as competing teams.

Structured socialising based on cooperation and competition can be a powerful facilitator for both behaviour change and social interaction [7, 12]. However, when seen from the perspective of highly ambivalent socialisers, we contend that although the opportunity to socialise in this way might indeed motivate, this approach might also provoke deep conflict within the quitter. The need for the person joining this group to unequivocally identify themselves as a committed to quitting, and the force of social conformity to be seen in that way, are likely to be counterproductive. Findings in other domains also point to this reverse effect [4].

In the CQ design, we have experimented with how the benefits of structured socialising might be modified for the ambivalent socialiser. People can add themselves to existing teams, like groups of co-workers or people with a similar quit date. CQ rewards behaviour change and social

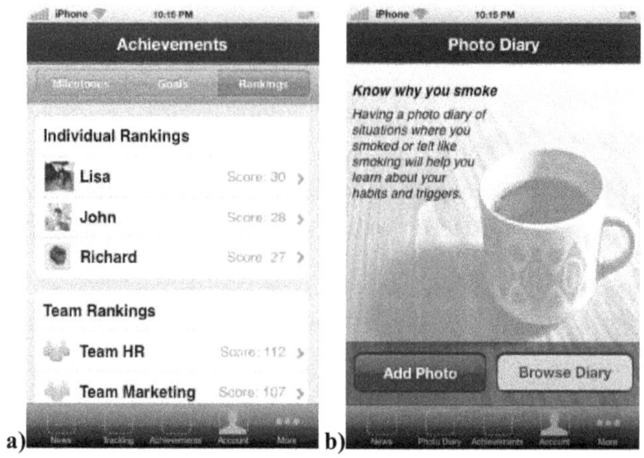

Figure 1: Screen mock-ups of a smoking cessation application to support structured (a) and incidental socialising (b)

interaction with other users, yet it allows those who are not committed to change to leave a group without a sense of failure. Ambivalent socialisers may benefit from such non-committal access to socialising. A residual design challenge is whether the advantages of structured group cooperation and competition can be realised while allowing comfort for ambivalent socialisers to maintain their ambivalent stance.

Incidental Socialising

'Incidental socialising' attempts to provide indirect paths to social interaction amongst ambivalent socialisers. Sacks observed that unacquainted people typically do not start talking to each other unless there are legitimate circumstances for conversation [17]. He used the example of a dog being walked in the park, which provides a 'ticket' to start a conversation with strangers. For the same reason, successful social network sites are typically built around objects or activities that mediate social interaction between strangers [5]. For example, Flickr stimulates interaction around photography, Foursquare around places like cafes and shops, and Catster around pets. Incidental socialising builds on these ideas by inventing objects to facilitate interaction where no pre-established relationship exists. Furthermore, incidental socialising places the emphasis on engagement in a meaningful task rather than outcomes.

Figure 1b shows how CQ implements a form of incidental socialising. CQ encourages users, who are planning a quit attempt, to collect and post photographs of situations that they typically encounter and that they expect will demand great resistance to smoking. These are posted as part of an individual quit preparation plan, but they can also be browsed by others via the CQ news feed (figure 2a). Users can express their empathy by clicking the 'Me too' button or by leaving a comment, which may initiate an exchange.

Ambivalent socialisers are less likely to experience early conflict in this approach of incidental socialising because they are not cast in any particular role or state of mind. Exchanges growing out of this approach allow individuals to preserve ambivalence while gaining support to quit. A residual design challenge for incidental socialising is finding the 'dog': the object for a given domain that motivates the individual and sparks social interaction.

Eavesdropping

Eavesdropping defines a mode of engagement in which users can perceive others but hide themselves. It involves activities like browsing through other people's profiles and reading through posts of people's experiences. We prefer the term 'eavesdropping' over 'lurking' [15], to avoid the latter's negative connotation of a person who benefits but makes no contribution to a community. Rather, eavesdropping is meant here as a legitimate mode of engagement for those seeking a behaviour change and can be designed for accordingly.

Figure 2a shows the CQ news feed that allows ambivalent socialisers to eavesdrop on the conversations of other CQ users. This feature provides a similar experience to popular social network sites, allowing the user to read without having to contribute actively. The news on CQ is typically related to people's ambivalent views on smoking. By default users see the news of all users from the entire website, but they can filter the news to show only updates from their personal networks as they get more engaged in CQ and establish connections with other users.

Eavesdropping allows ambivalent socialisers to get involved with other users without having to confront or deny their ambivalence. Although eavesdropping can be a stepping-stone into becoming an active contributor, related work indicates that many people may not desire active contribution. Studies of the online community QuitNet indicate that smokers enjoy eavesdropping into other people's forum discussions to gain motivation for their own quit attempts, but that they are hesitant to post content until they have become successful non-smokers [2]. A residual design challenge is to achieve a balance of contribution and eavesdropping, and to allow eavesdroppers to transition into other forms of engagement [15].

Trace Sensing

The fourth approach, trace sensing, is where individuals encounter the anonymous traces or patterns of other users, such as usage statistics, or averages of previous users' data entries.

Figure 2b illustrates an example of this approach through a tool where people can explore the various health benefits of giving up smoking. This tool includes an indicator of other users who are present and exploring the same information. It conveys that others may have similar concerns and difficulties. Likewise, the user can infer that she is visible to others, albeit anonymously.

Such tracing techniques are in widespread use and bring a range of recognised benefits [6]. For ambivalent socialisers they may be particularly important. They open the possibility for these people to be supported through the

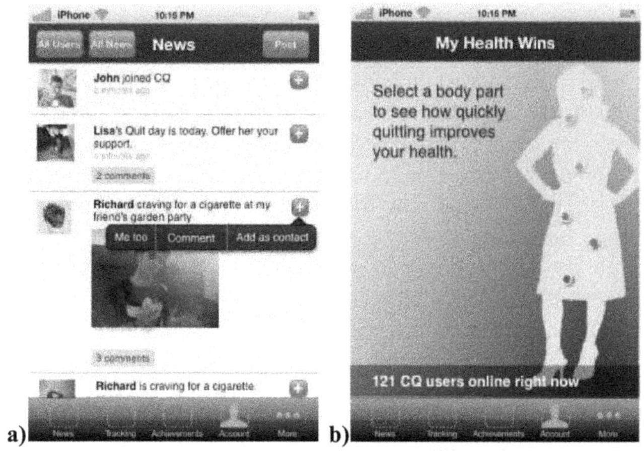

Figure 2: Screen mock-ups of a smoking cessation application to support eavesdropping (a) and trace sensing (b).

presence of others, without requiring expressions of identity or commitment. Many ambivalent socialisers may prefer to remain in complete anonymity throughout a quit attempt and may not wish to tell another person that they intend to quit. In these cases, a distant form of social contact may be all that is available to strengthen the positive side of their ambivalence. A residual challenge for this approach is in creating social support through the traces of other users that lacks the richness of open social exchange.

DISCUSSION AND CONCLUSIONS

We have introduced the concept of ambivalent socialisers: people who desire and may benefit from engagement with others around a planned behaviour change, but who are also reluctant to so engage. This ambivalence is likely to spring from deeply conflicting desires, both to change but also to stay the same. The concept of ambivalent socialisers extends traditional conceptualisations of users of persuasive technology, which assume that those users are either personally committed to behaviour change [6], or receptive to personalised persuasion to get into that state of mind [10]. Further, it is often assumed that contact with peers through persuasive technology can offer the support and guidance required to change [6, 16]. But, as pointed out by Purpura and colleagues [16], these assumptions can set up individuals for failure and shame in front of their peers. By embracing the notion of the ambivalent socialiser, we suggest, the emphasis of persuasive technology shifts towards engaging people in forms of social contact that do not force an early conflict between their opposing desires to engage and remain detached.

We identify four approaches for researchers and designers of persuasive technology to consider and explore contexts where ambivalent socialisers are likely. These approaches are based on related literature, but in bringing these separate approaches together and in applying them to the challenge of ambivalent socialisers we offer novel ways of facilitating social contact through technology. These four approaches extend previous frameworks that build on peer pressure [6], emerging peer involvement [13], and broadcasts of behavioural data to groups of collaborators [3] or competitors [12]. While some ambivalent socialisers may indeed fare well under structured approaches based on cooperation and competition, we encourage approaches that allow participation without pressure to assume, from the outset, a particular identity or state of mind towards the behaviour change. The approach of 'incidental socialising' deploys individually performed tasks that create legitimate circumstances to interact with peers. Interaction is thus incidental and does not commence with explicit or implicit declarations of commitment. Eavesdropping and trace sensing take this further by not requiring any active contribution from users. Like Preece and Shneiderman, we question the negative connotations of concepts like 'lurking' or 'free-loading' for non-contributors [15]. But unlike them, we view such users not merely as newcomers who have not yet moved on to more active forms of participation. Instead, such distant engagement may be the most effective form for some ambivalent socialisers.

We have illustrated how these four design approaches can lead to different functionalities in a mobile application in the context of smoking cessation. While smoking cessation provides a prime example of ambivalent socialisers, we can infer their existence and relevance elsewhere. In health and well-being, Consolvo points out that some of her participants wanted to live more healthy lives yet they resented the pressure from technology-mediated competition [4]. In the area of sustainability, people generally desire to use greener transportation, yet they are hesitant about involving other people through persuasive technology [8]. In all of these areas we hope that an awareness of ambivalent socialisers leads to a heightened sensibility when exploring the possibilities of behaviour change through social media.

ACKNOWLEDGMENTS

This research was funded by the Cancer Council Victoria and the Australian Research Council, grant LP110100046.

REFERENCES

1. Christakis, N. and Fowler, J. The collective dynamics of smoking in a large social network. *The New England Journal Of Medicine 358*, 21 (2008), 2249-2258.
2. Cobb, N. K., Graham, A. L. and Abrams, D. B. Social network structure of a large online community for smoking cessation. *American Journal of Public Health 100*, 7 (2010), 1282-1289.
3. Consolvo, S., Everitt, K., Smith, I. and Landay, J. A. Design requirements for technologies that encourage physical activity. *Proc. CHI 2006*, ACM Press (2006), 457-466.
4. Consolvo, S., Landay, J. A. and McDonald, D. W. Designing for behavior change in everyday life. *IEEE Computer 42*, 6 (2009), 100-103.
5. Engeström, J. Why some social network services work and others don't — Or: the case for object-centered sociality. http://www.zengestrom.com/blog/2005/04/why-some-social-network-services-work-and-others-dont-or-the-case-for-object-centered-sociality.html
6. Fogg, B. *Persuasive technology: Using computers to change what we think and do*. Morgan Kaufmann, San Francisco, CA, 2002.
7. Foster, D., Blythe, M., Cairns, P. and Lawson, S. Competitive carbon counting: Can social networking sites make saving energy more enjoyable? *Ext. Abstracts CHI 2010*, ACM Press (2010), 4039-4044.
8. Froehlich, J., Dillahunt, T., Klasnja, P., Mankoff, J., Consolvo, S., Harrison, B. and Landay, J. A. UbiGreen: Investigating a mobile tool for tracking and supporting green transportation habits. *Proc. CHI 2009*, ACM Press (2009), 1043-1052.
9. Graham, C., Satchell, C., Rouncefield, M., Balmford, J. and Benda, P. Lessons from failure: Re-conceiving blogging as personal change support. *Proc. DUX 2007*, ACM Press (2007), 2-17.
10. He, H. A., Greenberg, S. and Huang, E. M. One size does not fit all: Applying the transtheoretical model to energy feedback technology design. *Proc. CHI 2010*, ACM Press (2010), 927-936.
11. Hyland, A., Borland, R., Li, Q., Yong, H. H., McNeill, A., Fong, G. T., OíConnor, R. J. and Cummings, K. Individual-level predictors of cessation behaviours among participants in the International Tobacco Control (ITC) four country survey. *Tobacco Control 15*, suppl 3 (2006), iii83–iii9440.
12. Lin, J., Mamykina, L., Lindtner, S., Delajoux, G. and Strub, H. Fish'n'Steps: Encouraging physical activity with an interactive computer game. *Proc. UbiComp 2006*, Springer (2006), 261-278.
13. Maitland, J. and Chalmers, M. Designing for peer involvement in weight management. *Proc. CHI 2011*, ACM Press (2011), 315-324.
14. Newman, M. W., Lauterbach, D., Munson, S. A., Resnick, P. and Morris, M. E. It's not that i don't have problems, I'm just not putting them on Facebook: Challenges and opportunities in using online social networks for health. *Proc. CSCW 2011*, ACM Press (2011), 341-350.
15. Preece, J. and Shneiderman, B. The reader-to-leader framework: Motivating technology-mediated social participation. *AIS Transactions on Human-Computer Interaction 1*, 1 (2009), 13-32.
16. Purpura, S., Schwanda, V., Williams, K., Stubler, W. and Sengers, P. Fit4life: The design of a persuasive technology promoting healthy behavior and ideal weight. *Proc. CHI 2011*, ACM Press (2011), 423-432.
17. Sacks, H. *Lectures on conversation*, Blackwell (1992).

Twitter and the Development of an Audience: Those Who Stay on Topic Thrive!

Yi-Chia Wang
Language Technologies Institute
Carnegie Mellon University
5000 Forbes Ave., Pittsburgh, PA 15213
yichiaw@cs.cmu.edu

Robert Kraut
Human-Computer Interaction Institute
Carnegie Mellon University
5000 Forbes Ave., Pittsburgh, PA 15213
robert.kraut@cs.cmu.edu

ABSTRACT
Although economists have long recognized the importance of a critical mass in growing a community, we know little about how it is achieved. This paper examines how initial topical focus influences communities' ability to attract a critical mass. When starting an online community, organizers need to define its initial scope. Topically narrow communities will probably attract a homogeneous group of interested in its content and compatible with each other. However, they are likely to attract fewer members than a diverse one because they offer only a subset of the topics. This paper reports an empirical analysis of longitudinal data collected from Twitter, where each new Twitter poster is considered the seed of a potential social collection. Users who focus the topics of their early tweets more narrowly ultimately attract more followers with more ties among them. Our results shed light on the development of online social networking structures.

Author Keywords
Social networking sites; online communities; community startup; critical mass; topical focus; natural language analysis

ACM Classification Keywords
H.5.3 [Information Interfaces and Presentation]: Group and Organization Interfaces - Web-based interaction;

INTRODUCTION
The vast majority of Internet users participate in some online groups or social networking sites [4]. Yet for every successful Facebook, Wikipedia or Linux project, there are dozens of failed attempts to start an online group. For example, 50% of IRC chat groups die within 24 hours after they are formed [11]. Understanding why some online groups succeed and many other fail is a practical and scientifically important research problem.

Online communities take many forms - from well-defined open source projects with defined boundaries, stable membership and clear production goals to the more diffuse social networks on Facebook, to short-lived IRC channels, to high turnover Usenet groups. These social collections differ on many dimensions – e.g., definition of boundaries, stability and homogeneity of membership, degree of interaction among members and the degree that members and outsiders think of the collection as a group. Twitter collections share some attributes of groups: they have a defined membership, some homogeneity of interests and some interaction among members. McMillan and Chavis's definition of community suggests that an online social collection will be a more successful group if it has enough members to provide resources and ties among members to facilitate social interaction and information exchange [8]. Therefore, in this study we consider larger membership size and higher social tie density as signs of a more successful online social group.

This paper examines whether the initial topical focus of content in new online groups predicts their subsequent success – eventually developing a larger and denser network of members. We investigate this question with longitudinal data from Twitter, a popular micro blogging service used by 8% of American Internet users [10].

Critical Mass and Initial Topical Focus
Interactive media must develop a critical mass of users if they are to be self-sustaining [7]. Theories of network externalities partially explain the process [6]. For goods and services characterized by network externalities, such as the telephone network, the value users receive grows with the number of users.

The content offered by someone starting an online group – its quality and scope – may determine the number and type of people who initially join it, thus triggering the upward or downward spirals associated with network externalities. The group founder has many choices about its scope. Some researchers believe that topical focus (or its inverse, content diversity) will influence an online group's ultimate success [12]. Network externalities suggest that a group should start with diverse content, because the diversity of topics can potentially appeal to more people, each of whom is interested in a subset of topics, and thus help the group more quickly reach critical mass. In contrast, starting with a

Permission to make digital or hard copies of all or part of this work for personal or classroom use is granted without fee provided that copies are not made or distributed for profit or commercial advantage and that copies bear this notice and the full citation on the first page. To copy otherwise, or republish, to post on servers or to redistribute to lists, requires prior specific permission and/or a fee.
CHI'12, May 5–10, 2012, Austin, Texas, USA.
Copyright 2012 ACM 978-1-4503-1015-4/12/05...$10.00.

focused topic may restrict membership to the subset of the larger population that is interested in that topic.

H1a: The topical diversity of initial content in online groups will be positively correlated with their ultimate size.

On the other hand, when a community starts with a focused topic, people with similar interests can identify themselves more easily with it and can better anticipate what they can get from it. Moreover, groups organized around a narrow topic are likely to attract members who are similar to each other, and are likely to form relationships that maintain each others' commitment to the community because of homophily [9]. If this is the case, then initial content focus, not diversity, should lead to community success.

H1b: The topical focus of initial content in online groups will be positively correlated with their ultimate size.

H2: The topical focus of initial content in online groups will be positively correlated with the density of ties among members.

Little empirical research has examined the role of topical focus in online groups. Using *listserv* data, Butler showed that topic variation had both positive and negative effects on the sustainability of online groups, but did not look at the impact of topic variation on achieving a critical mass of users [3]. Adamic et al. analyzed knowledge sharing activity in an online question-answer forum [1]. They found that answerers who specialized in a narrow range of topics produced better quality answers. Since potential members are likely to cluster around groups that provide better content, we can infer that they will be more likely to join online groups with a focused topic.

We chose Twitter as the site for this research because of its popularity and ability to support needed data collection. We assume each new person who posts on Twitter is a seed of a potential social collection that can become more or less successful as a group. They can start by applying for a Twitter account and posting status updates. Others can join this new collection by becoming followers. In turn, these followers can connect with each other, creating a more interactive group. We examined the effect of the topical focus of the initial tweets on measures of group success – membership size and the density of ties among followers – a year later. We show that compared to Twitter posters who tweet about a broad range of topics, those who focus their initial tweets on a smaller range attract more followers and furthermore, these followers form a denser network.

TWITTER AND DATA SET

Twitter is a conversational micro-blogging website. It allows users to post short messages called "tweets" of at most 140 characters. Twitter provides several functions to facilitate social interaction and conversation among users. Users can give attention to others by "following" them. They can mention other users in their tweets. If Twitter users find someone else's tweet interesting, they can "retweet" it to share it with their own followers.

The data collection consisted of the three steps below.

Twitter Directories. Twitter directories organize Twitter users by genre and allow users to find other Twitter users to connect with. We downloaded the liberal and conservative political lists of Twitter users from three online Twitter directories – *Twellow.com*, *wefollow.com*, and *MyTwitterDirectory.com*. A total of 34,827 Twitter user identities were extracted.

User Selection. Since the formation of a new social group takes time, we sampled users who joined Twitter between August 2009 and December 2009 and examined their success a year later. Measuring topical focus requires a sufficient corpus of textual data, given that each tweet contains fewer than 140 characters. Therefore, we limited the sample to users who tweeted at least two times per day on average. 480 users fit these criteria.[1] On average, user in the sample had 1,574 tweets. This sample represents very active users.

User Information Extraction. We then retrieve the Twitter data from these 480 heavy Twitter users. We gathered all the tweets they posted, as well as the meta-information for each tweet, such as its timestamp, whether it was a reply, whether it was a retweet, etc. We also took a snapshot of these users' and their followers' social graphs, including all of the followers' followers, on November 20, 2010, about a year after the date they created their accounts.

METHODS

We examined the relationships between the initial topical focus of new users' online social groups and their success a year later. We measured topical focus using text processing techniques to assess the similarity among the tweets posted by a single user. We evaluated group success in terms of membership size and social tie density.

Membership Size and Tie Density

Specifically, we examined two dependent measures relating to the success of online social groups:

Membership Size is the total number of followers a user had on November 20, 2010.

Social Tie Density is the number of links among a user's followers. We normalized this measure by the number of followers a user has, so that it corresponds to the average number of links a follower has to other followers. The social tie density measure of a Twitter user is computed according to the following formula:

$$\text{SocialTieDensity}(\text{user}) = \frac{\text{num of links between followers}}{\text{num of followers}}$$

[1] Due to the limitation of Twitter API, this study only considered users who tweeted 3,200 or fewer times.

	Mean	Median	Std. Dev.	Min	Max
Membership Size	435.41	217.50	587.60	12	4916
Social Tie Density	23.98	10.26	32.82	0	204.45
AvgCosSim	0.07	0.06	0.05	0.01	0.59
NumTweet	250.60	121.50	339.23	0	2318
NumReply	34.44	27	31.51	0	141
NumRetweet	19.05	10	24.50	0	150
NumDay	408.77	415.00	45.25	324	476
Celebrity (X 1000)	405.2	1.6	52100	0	1000000
Politics	0.50	0	0.50	0	1

Table 1. Descriptive Statistics for Twitter Dataset

Users' social tie density increases when their followers are more connected to and potentially have more interactions with each other. As a consequence, the social group centered on a particular user is less likely to break down.

Topical Focus

Communication on Twitter is conducted through text messages. We measured users' initial topical focus by applying simple language processing techniques – average pairwise cosine similarity – to their first 150 tweets.

Average pairwise cosine similarity (AvgCosSim) is the similarity of vocabulary in a user's first 150 tweets. When people talk about one topic, they tend to use a common vocabulary. For example, words like "Obama", "Obamacare", "socialism" and "repeal" are frequently seen in tweets where conservatives discuss healthcare.

Cosine similarity measures similarity between two vectors of words by calculating the cosine angle between them in a high dimensional space. This study represents each tweet as a term vector consisting of the presence or absence of each word in the sample. High cosine similarity between two tweets indicates high text similarity. We first calculated the cosine similarity between all pairs of tweets produced by a single user and then computed the mean of all these pairwise cosine similarities. A high average cosine similarity indicates that a user's tweets were on similar topics and more topically focused. AvgCosSim can theoretically range from 0 to 1 and in the current sample ranged from 0 to .59 (mean .07 and median .06; Table 1).

Two examples of Twitter users with high AvgCosSim are *TwitterUser-A* (AvgCosSim=.08) and *TwitterUser-B* (AvgCosSim=.07). *TwitterUser-A* frequently wrote about Obama's health care policies, whereas *TwitterUser-B* was a former marine writing about military affairs and terrorism. Although neither was a celebrity, they attracted, 479 and 671 followers respectively. In contrast, *TwitterUser-C* has a low AvgCosSim (AvgCosSim=.04). He wrote about a wide variety of topics, such as 3C devices, politics, music, and so on. By November 20, 2010, he had only 69 followers.

We also measured the following control variables:

Dependent Var.	Membership Size		Social Tie Density	
Independent Var.	IRR	Std. Err.	IRR	Std. Err.
AvgCosSim	26.4016***	24.65	35.8315**	42.44
NumTweet (Log)	1.0187	0.02	1.0331	0.03
NumReply (Log)	0.7912***	0.03	0.9151*	0.04
NumRetweet (Log)	1.1271***	0.04	1.1671***	0.04
NumDay	1.0035***	0.00	1.0044***	0.00
Celebrity (Log)	1.0098	0.01	1.0107	0.01
Politics	1.4941***	0.14	2.4909***	0.27

*: $p<0.05$, **: $p<0.01$, ***: $p<0.001$

Table 2. The Effect of Topical Focus (H1 and H2)

Num of tweets (NumTweet) is the number of tweets a user produced in the first 60 days after joining Twitter. The restriction of the sample to heavy tweeters leads to underestimates of the effects of number of tweets on group success.

Number of reply tweets (NumReply) is a measure of how many tweets among the first 150 tweets posted by a user were reply tweets. A reply tweet is a tweet which is written to respond to someone else's tweet.

Number of retweets (NumRetweet) is a measure of how many tweets among the first 150 tweets posted by a user were retweets.

Days on Twitter (NumDay) is the number of days between the date a user joined Twitter and November 20, 2010.

Degree of celebrity (Celebrity): A social group started by a celebrity outside of Twitter can attract more followers, so we controlled for users' external popularity. This is estimated by the number of pages returned by Google when the screen name of the Twitter user is searched.

Politics is a binary variable describing a user's political view. 1 is conservative view; 0 is liberal view.

Table 1 describes descriptive statistics for the variables entered into regression models. For example, users posted 251 tweets in the first 2 months after joining Twitter.

ANALYSIS

The analysis seeks to identify the effects of topical focus on the number of followers a user eventually attracts and the density of ties among them. We used negative binomial regression models to predict membership size and social tie density. Negative binomial regression models are appropriate for count data, which are truncated at zero and highly non-normally distributed. Table 2 displays the results of the regression analysis with the dependent, independent, and control variables used to test the hypotheses. The effect of an independent variable on a dependent variable is reported using Incidence Rate Ratios (IRR). IRR is the change in a dependent variable expressed as a ratio when an independent variable increases by one unit. An IRR of 0 means no change, 0.5 means halving the count, and 2 means doubling it.

RESULTS

In general, the regression results suggest that the initial topical focus of online social groups had a large impact on their success. The significant IRR for AvgCosSim in the two models predicting Membership Size and Social Tie Density suggests that topical focus has a strong positive impact on a group's ability to attract members and breed social connections among them. When AvgCosSim increases by 0.01 (from the 25th to the 50th percentile), users attracted on average 111 more followers. Moreover, each of their followers had on average 8 more connections within the community. The result supports H1b and H2 suggesting that initial topical focus may lead to more success turning a collection into a true online social groups; it disconfirms H1a that diversity would lead to success.

DISCUSSION AND FUTURE RESEARCH

This paper studied the relationship between topical focus and the formation of online social groups. The results demonstrated that at least in the domain of political discussion, more topically focused start-up groups are more likely to be ultimately successful. This finding suggests that people are more likely to be drawn to and join online groups with a focused topic, because they anticipate they will acquire content of interest to them and to meet people whose interests match their own.

If these results generalize, the implications are clear: Founders should start an online group with a well-defined topic initially in order to develop more audience with more connections among them.

This research examined the effects of topical focus within users who had self-identified as providers of political tweets. These users were already more likely to be topically focused than the typical Twitter user, who is less likely to limit posts to a single topic, like politics. Statistically this restriction of range can lead to underestimates of the power of topical focus on shaping the success of online groups. However, the effect may not be substantive, because one might expect that diversity injected into homogeneous discussions can enliven it [5]. Subsequent research will need to test the effects of topical focus on a more heterogeneous sample.

One might argue that cosine similarity can only measure degree of content overlap but not degree of focus in terms of content. In the future we plan to apply topic modeling techniques [2] to analyze text and infer the topic distribution of each group.

Finally, our current findings are based on a snapshot of users' social graphs. We can only make correlation claims about the relationship between starting conditions of a group and its later structure, not causal ones. Future research should monitor the growth of online groups. For example, founders of online groups would like to know if the effects of topical focus influence the number of new members they attract or the time they stay once they join.

ACKNOWLEDGMENTS

This research was supported by NSF grant IIS-0968485. We want to thank Shay Cohen who helped provide the machine for the data collection for this study.

REFERENCES

1. Adamic, L. A., Zhang, J., Bakshy, E., & Ackerman, M. S. (2008). Knowledge sharing and Yahoo Answers: Everyone knows something. In *Proc. WWW 2008*, 665-674.
2. Blei, D., Ng, A., & Jordan, M. Latent Dirichlet allocation. (2003). *Journal of Machine Learning Research, 3*(Jan), 993-1022.
3. Butler, B. S. (2001). Membership size, communication activity, and sustainability: A resource-based model of online social structures. *Information Systems Research, 12*(4), 346-362.
4. Hampton, K. N., Sessions, L., & Her, E. J. (2011). Core networks, social isolation, and new media: How Internet and mobile phone use is related to network size and diversity. *Information, Communication & Society, 14*(1).
5. Harper, F. M., Frankowski, D., Drenner, S., Ren, Y., Kiesler, S., Terveen, L., Kraut, R., & Riedl, J. (2007). Talk amongst yourselves: Inviting users to participate in online conversations. In *Proc. ACM IUI07*, 62-71.
6. Katz, M. L., & Shapiro, C. (1985). Network Externalities, competition, and compatibility. *American Economic Review, 75*(3), 424-440.
7. Markus, L. (1987). Towards a "critical mass" theory of interactive media: Universal access, interdependence, and diffusion. *Communication Research, 14*(5), 491-511.
8. McMillan, D., & Chavis, D. (1986). Sense of community: A definition and theory. *Journal of Community Psychology, 14*(1), 6-23.
9. McPherson, J. M., Smith-Lovin, L., & Cook, J. M. (2001). Birds of a feather: Homophily in social networks. *Annual Review of Sociology, 27*(1), 415-444.
10. Pew Internet. 8% of online Americans use Twitter. (2011). *http://pewinternet.org/Reports/2010/Twitter-update-2010.aspx*, retrieved on Feb 4, 2011.
11. Raban, D., Moldovan, M., & Jones, Q. (2010). An empirical study of critical mass and online community survival. In *Proc. CHI 2010*, 71-80.
12. Resnick, P., Chen, Y., Konstan, J., & Kraut, R. E. (In press). Starting new online communities. In R. E. Kraut & P. Resnick (Eds.), *Building successful online communities: Evidence-based social design* (pp. 231-289). Cambridge, MA: MIT Press.

"Act Natural": Instructions, Compliance and Accountability in Ambulatory Experiences

Peter Tolmie, Steve Benford, Martin Flintham, Patrick Brundell
University of Nottingham
Nottingham, UK
[firstname.lastname]@nottingham.ac.uk

Matt Adams*, Nicholas Tandavantij*, Ju Row-Farr*, Gabriella Giannachi†
*Blast Theory, UK; †University of Exeter, UK
*[firstname]@blasttheory.co.uk
†g.giannachi@exeter.ac.uk

ABSTRACT

This paper uses a detailed ethnographic study of an ambulatory experience, where participants were invited to explore the perspective of two notorious terrorists, in order to discuss the nature of instruction-giving and, most particularly, the methodical ways in which such instructions are complied with. Four distinct layers of compliance are identified, as are three different kinds of accountability, all of which stand potentially at odds with one another. The paper examines the tensions created by this, tensions that are further aggravated by instructions usually being delivered down a thin channel, with considerable surrounding contextual complexity and little opportunity for repair, and uncovers some core challenges for future design in relation to providing instructions for, and orchestrating a range of possible activities.

Author Keywords

Instructions; Ethnography; Ambulatory Experiences.

ACM Classification Keywords

H.5.m. Information interfaces and presentation (e.g., HCI): Miscellaneous.

INTRODUCTION

Ambulatory experiences employ mobile technologies to guide participants as they explore an environment, indoors or outdoors. Examples include interactive tours and guides [1][2][10][13][30], location-based urban games [20], and artistic installations and performances [3][7]. Such experiences are currently of great commercial and research interest, due in large part to the phenomenal spread of smart phones with GPS and QR code readers that make it possible to locate participants as they move around, and then deliver to them a sequence of instructions regarding where to go, what to look at and what to do. Previous research in general mobile and location-based interaction has explored a variety of issues that are relevant to ambulatory systems including dealing with seams in wireless communications and positioning systems [12], designing recommendations and mobile interruptions [5], the challenges of using mobile while moving through a complex physical environment [6], and managing the balance between personal and group interactions [2]. Research on pervasive and alternate reality games also addresses similar themes and issues [21].

Permission to make digital or hard copies of all or part of this work for personal or classroom use is granted without fee provided that copies are not made or distributed for profit or commercial advantage and that copies bear this notice and the full citation on the first page. To copy otherwise, or republish, to post on servers or to redistribute to lists, requires prior specific permission and/or a fee.
CHI'12, May 5–10, 2012, Austin, Texas, USA.
Copyright 2012 ACM 978-1-4503-1015-4/12/05...$10.00.

However, ambulatory experiences raise a distinctive new challenge that is not yet well explored within HCI: how to design a sequence of instructions that can be successfully followed by participants on the ground. While previous studies of satellite navigation systems have highlighted some of the challenges of following basic directions in cars or on foot [15][20][23][28][29], and there are numerous studies regarding the relationship between the authoring of instructions and learning outcomes (e.g. [4][8][17][19][26]), the kinds of ambulatory experiences we are looking at here have additional characteristics that make the design of instructions a deeply challenging task:

- instructions typically come down a 'thin' channel such as an audio recording on a phone or a text message, placing constraints upon what can be said and how;
- ambulatory experiences are typically enacted in relatively open, unconstrained environments where the local context is often very complex and changeable with a wide variety of potentially unforeseen contingencies coming into play;
- there is usually little feedback from the participants' world to the orchestrators about what is happening, limiting the scope for repair;
- the experiences are typically not repeated by the people who participate in them, making it hard to learn from your mistakes and putting a particular emphasis on doing well 'first time through'.

Despite this the instructions are rich in the sense that they try to engage participants at a number of different levels, from the basic mechanics of finding their way to framing an appropriate engagement with the digital content and the wider environment. In short, then, ambulatory experiences raise a profound challenge for interaction design in that they need to convey rich instructions about not only wayfinding but also comportment and role, in an unpredictable environment and down a thin channel, with little feedback to indicate how they have been understood.

This paper explores this challenge through an ethnographic study of an installation at the Biennale festival in Venice in 2009 called Ulrike and Eamon Compliant [9] which was designed to prompt 'engagement with political questions' by inviting participants to assume the role of a terrorist, either Ulrike Meinhof or Eamon Collins, whilst they walked through the city receiving phone calls. The experience was a complex ambulatory work in which participants were required to interpret and enact rich and multi-layered instructions with the sole delivery mechanism being a mobile phone. As such the paper adds to the existing HCI literature on instructions at a number of levels. First of all it provides rich analysis of the situated following of instructions in a real-world environment, rather than in laboratory or test conditions. Secondly it explores instruction-giving that is simultaneously ambitious and constrained, thereby leading to a novel technological challenge. Thirdly, it explores how people engage with instructions that seek to guide comportment and promote certain kinds of experiential outcomes. It does this through a close analysis of different orders of compliance at the levels of location, sequence, comportment, and relation to the experience, and it explores the tensions between the extent to which the experience attempted to manage people's compliance and their ordinary accountability when out on the streets. This takes investigation of instructed action to a level that HCI has so far barely touched upon.

ULRIKE AND EAMON COMPLIANT

Ulrike and Eamon Compliant is an ambulatory experience that involves steering participants around a pre-specified route with various experiences along the way. There are a number of reasons why it proved to be an interesting experience to study. First of all, it hinges upon the delivery of 'thin' instructions via recordings delivered to a mobile phone. Yet, it is an enormously ambitious work, trying to simultaneously inform and engage participants at a number of levels. So it is trying to do a lot with the thin instructions it is delivering. Secondly, the nature of the work, mixing locational instructions, invitations to role-play, and richly atmospheric pre-recorded stories and accounts, all on the real streets of a real city, enables study of the work to speak to a variety of other forms of experience, tours, games, performances, and so on. Thirdly, as the name implies, the work is ultimately about an exploration of compliance with instructions and the character of compliance proves to be of significance for what this experience might have to say for other experiences and guided activities.

It is important that our use of the word 'compliance' be understood here. There is, of course, a sense in which designers might go about designing certain technologies that will somehow 'compel' people to comply with the instructions they receive. This would be a morally dubious undertaking and it should not be understood to be a part of what we are proposing. Our own interest in compliance is somewhat distinct. First of all we are using compliance not as a proposed *outcome*, desirable or otherwise, but rather as a device for analyzing people's situated practices: they receive instructions and they witnessably comply with the content of those instructions to varying degrees. We are interested in what such compliance amounts to as a matter of people's own methods for following instructions. Secondly, in the case of Ulrike and Eamon Compliant. the artists themselves are exploring the notion of compliance as fertile territory. This is not because they want to make people compliant, but rather because they want to explore the nature of compliance – to create an experience that provokes people into confronting it. At the same time, making people potentially uncomfortable about and aware of their own compliance serves to make their routine instruction-following practices more visible, which makes Ulrike and Eamon a particularly good target for uncovering what those practices might look like.

The experience:

The participants are first of all directed into a separate room where they can read more about the experience and watch a live video feed of another participant apparently sat in an interrogation room, being interrogated. They are then directed to pick up a mobile phone and are asked to make an initial call to describe themselves, choose which terrorist they wish to follow, Ulrike and Eamon, and told to pick up a pair of glasses if they do not have any of their own. After this the participants are told to go outside and await their first instruction. They are then guided by pre-recorded phone calls around the route step by step in roughly the following way: First of all they are given a direction to some specific location such as a bridge, a bench, a well in a square, the end of an alleyway by a canal, etc., e.g.:

***Now continue across the bridge and turn left towards the church towers. Start to stroll very slowly with the canal on your left hand side*[1].**

Once they reach the specified location they wait until they receive the next call which is usually a recording describing certain events from the life of the terrorist they have chosen to follow, designed to build up a growing understanding of what it might be to see the world through their eyes, often in a quite emotive fashion, e.g.:

Ulrike, you were on TV again last night. You sat at the end of a row of men, composed and alert. When it was your turn to speak you made your case against the Vietnam War with force and eloquence. When you went to the dressing room afterwards, you spoke easily with the make up girl. She complimented you on your hair as you left. Then you were in the taxi on the way home. Outside the window the streets were dark and wet. . .

Once they have listened to this a further call gives directions to the next location, often having first issued a further instruction to engage in some kind of reflection or provide some kind of input of their own, e.g.:

[1] Instructional elements within the data are presented in bold.

I would like to know how would you describe your ability to make decisions. Are you a decisive or a hesitant person, Ulrike? ***Now please record your answer. Start by saying "My name is Ulrike" and then tell me are you a decisive or hesitant person?***

On several occasions they are also directed to undertake some quite specific actions in order to trigger provision of the next element of the experience, e.g.:

Now find a bench that is free and sit down for a moment. *I want to ask you a question.* ***When you take your glasses off and lay them on the bench beside you*** *I'll know you're ready to talk.*

They carry on around the route in this way until they reach a point where they are asked to make a choice between going to 'a room where questions will be asked' or going 'home'. Their decision is indicated by whether they hang up or stay on the line. Once they have made their choice they are either issued with directions back to the starting point or are directed to a street with a disused chapel. As they go down this street a performer awaits them outside of the chapel and, when they get near, the performer steps inside the chapel. Once inside the chapel they are accompanied by the performer into a small unfurnished cubicle constructed inside the main building with just two chairs in it. They sit down together, face to face, and the performer begins to pose them a series of questions where they are addressed as though they are the actual terrorist they have been following. After this they are shown outside the cubicle and invited to watch the next participant being interrogated through a window in one wall. Once they have done this and wish to leave the experience is concluded.

The Starting Point & Receiving Instructions

Orchestration:

Orchestration of the experience in Venice proved to be quite complex. Overall it was managed from a central command post adjacent to the disused chapel, from which point the underlying game system could be managed and the actions of various people on the streets coordinated. Participants were assigned to follow the route on a staggered basis, 15 minutes apart, so that they did not cross one another or arrive in the same place at the same time. Upon their first call they were entered into the system with a physical description and an assigned mobile phone number. The first directions were issued from the command post. At each new location, however, they were sent pre-recorded messages, the dispatch of which was triggered by performers on the streets using PDAs. The performers used the initial description to identify the participant and manage the interaction with the participant, judging when to send messages and tracking participants by line of sight. The flow of people around the route was also managed this way such that, should someone begin to catch up on the person preceding them, they could be slowed down by delaying sending the next message. Each performer had an assigned territory and, as the participant reached the limit of their territory they handed over the participant to the next performer. This took the placement of up to 8 performers on the route in order to ensure that as far as possible participants couldn't get into blind spots where no one could see them. It also meant that performers had to stay out of sight, seeing but not being seen. Coordination between performers themselves, the command post, and the front of house where people were first welcomed to the experience was managed via walkie-talkie.

THE STUDY

The materials relating to Ulrike and Eamon Compliant were gathered during an installation at the 53rd Biennale festival in Venice in 2009 in order to inform the design of similar future experiences. In this case four different participants were followed throughout their engagement over a period of 2 days, with each experience taking up to two hours to complete. The participants were, respectively, an academic, an artisan, an opera singer, and a journalist. All were in their forties, three were women and one was a man. One of them (a female academic) took on the role of Eamon Collins and all of the others took the part of Ulrike Meinhof. In addition to the shadowing of participation, detailed observations were made of both behind the scenes and on the streets orchestration over the same period.

The analytic approach to all of the data gathered has been ethnomethodological. This approach demands rigorous attention to the *local* production of order, focusing upon the characteristics of in situ reasoning and accounts and the methods whereby human action and interaction is accomplished [14]. In this particular case it demands that we pay close attention to just how instructions are made manifest in particular situations and how those instructions are then worked with in accountably compliant ways.

The Data

A critical feature of ambulatory experiences is the manner in which participants are instructed regarding how to proceed through the experience, and how the participants in turn understand and respond to those instructions. In order to explore quite specifically just how *instructions* are handled by participants as a contingent part of the experience they are engaged in we will look in detail at several aspects of how players were seen to respond to and comply with the instructions they were receiving during Ulrike and Eamon Compliant.

Directional instructions:

One of the most frequent kinds of instructions participants encounter in ambulatory experiences like Ulrike and Eamon is a direction to go to some particular place. Consider the following:

The participant is stood on a bridge listening to a lengthy recording. At the conclusion of the recording she receives the following instruction: "Now, ***if you agree with me, I want you to step across the bridge to the other side.*** *" She drops the phone from her ear to hold it at her side and looks to-and-fro to either side of the bridge. The phone rings again and she answers it and receives the following instruction: "****Turn immediately right along the canal heading towards the grass.****" At this point she heads off of the bridge, turns right and walks purposefully along beside the canal towards a grassy area up ahead.*

If we look at this example we can see that, in the first instance, the participant is somewhat confounded. She is asked to 'step across the bridge to the other side', but as she is stood in the middle of the bridge there are two candidate sides to be considered. However, the next phone call disambiguates matters because she is asked to turn right towards a grassy area and the grassy area is clearly visible from the bridge. Thus the core components here of crossing the bridge, turning right, and heading towards a grassy area, are all complied with.

Awaiting further instruction:

In the next example another participant has received the same set of directions we just saw and is now on her way to 'the grassy area':

Whilst walking she is played a recording: "Ulrike, I see you in the back seat of the getaway car. The window open. Broken sunlight scattering through the trees. You cross the line. You free Andreas and become a wanted woman. ..." She reaches the grassy area and leans back against the wall beside it, still listening to the recording on the phone.

In this example the participant sets off following the same instruction in much the same way. However, as she reaches the grassy area the recording is still ongoing. There is nothing to expressly tell her what to do at this point so she simply stops and leans against the wall. This is not something she's been told to do. She could carry on up onto the grass itself, but she doesn't. This does not imply that she is not following the instruction she has received, but the instruction falls short of telling her everything she might need to do. This is the way with instructions: they never fully specify how they should be followed [27]. If she had walked a little slower, she might not have been obliged to stop and wait. But, in the circumstances, she finds within the overall context of where she is, what she is doing, and what has happened so far, an accountable way of proceeding: to stop and wait. There are numerous things she might have done: laid back on the grass; gone to look at the canal; carried on walking. However, some of these would have gone beyond the comportment one would ordinarily expect of a participant doing this kind of thing and others would require additional account in view of what has happened so far. The fact that she has been directed to the grassy area is taken to be pertinent, but she *has not* been told to go up onto it. She has already had other instructions that make reference to things in the environment without her being expected to actually go up to them. They have worked as waymarks. In the absence of further instruction the grassy area might be where she is headed, but it also might be just a waymark, with different specification still to follow. Thus stopping and waiting is an accountably appropriate thing to do, even though she has not been told to wait in the instruction. The locational element of the instruction is not, then, being ignored, but compliance with it is seen to include something never directly articulated: treating locations as potential waymarks until you are told otherwise. What she *has* done is found an appropriate place *to await further instruction*. Even though some instructions do tell participants to wait in various locations this does not imply that waiting cannot be done in other places as well, especially when awaiting the next instruction is a strategy for disambiguating the instruction you have just received.

Instructed orders of action:

As well as just directing people to certain places instructions also often imply an *order* of actions to undertake, for instance:

Now you need to find the last bridge. ***Head back up the alley. Look for the red brick church tower and walk towards it. When you get to the tower turn left and walk towards the canal. Stop on the bridge.***

Here is how these instructions were actually followed by one of the participants:

The participant turns and walks back up the alley with the phone pressed to his ear. He reaches the end of the alley and looks around the square in front of him, then turns left to go down a small road that opens out into another square. He comes out into the square and slows, looking around. Then he walks across the square towards a wall and a church in one corner. He looks up at the church, then heads left down another street in front of the church, with a wall and a canal in front of him. Whilst walking he looks up again at the church. As he approaches the canal he looks up at the church yet again and starts to head right. He stops a moment in front of the church and looks up, then carries on walking towards the foot of some steps leading up onto a bridge. Then he stops completely, looks at the door of the church then faces back towards the bridge. He meanders a little then heads up the first few steps on the bridge, still listening to the phone. He stops on the third step, looks over the wall to the canal, then turns round and faces the church, standing and listening. He looks up some more at the church and leans against the rail on the bridge steps, then drops the phone to his side, turns around, and walks slowly up onto the bridge before turning towards the right and facing down the canal.

It can be seen that to comply with the instruction involves significantly more than what is covered within the instruction itself. Certain parts are missing altogether, for instance turning left at the top of the alley. What is also missing is the work of verification following such instructions involves: he continually checks the church and its tower. In fact, his glances make visible that each step of the sequence involves this order of verification. Where is the church? What amounts to 'getting to the tower'? Where is the canal? Which bridge? What counts as actually being 'on the bridge'? Of course, the other thing here is that each next action makes no sense until the preceding action has been accomplished. Walking towards the canal makes no sense until he has reached the church. Which bridge to stop on makes no sense until he has reached the canal.

Instructions on how to act:

In a number of instances the instructions given in Ulrike and Eamon move beyond just matters of where to go and what order to do that in by specifying also particular acts to be undertaken. Here is a case in point:

*The participant looks along the canal once more as listening: "**Now stand in the middle of the bridge and turn to look at the church towers.** Can you see them? **If you can see them nod your head slowly.**"*

Participant says: You want me to nod my head? (she nods in an exaggerated fashion) Like this? (She continues nodding and laughing)

In this example the direction to nod is simple enough and the participant has little trouble in complying, though her sense of it being an out-of-the-ordinary thing to be doing is made manifest by the way she also laughs about it. A number of instructions were treated as equally straightforward, but equally discomforting, for instance:

Now I want you to stand on the bridge.** Can you see the grass in the distance? **Put your left hand up to your head now if you see it.

Instructions designed to create moods and tensions:

Instructions to do things at specific times in ambulatory experiences are relatively rare. However, there can be instructions that imply that something has to be done within a certain time limit, as in the following:

*If you hang up within the next 30 seconds then I will know you have taken the easy route and are ready to quit. **If you want to quit, hang up right now.** I will sit quietly while you decide.*

The following of such instructions can be problematic. This message is issued at a point in the experience where the participant can decide to go and be interrogated or else to just head for home. The difficulty here is that it is issued in advance of participants knowing what kinds of questions may be asked. It is also issued in a distracting environment where 30 seconds can pass quite quickly without people having really decided what they want to do. Apparent compliance by either hanging up or not (especially the latter) does not necessarily amount to actual compliance in that case from the participant's point of view. However, a major part of what the instruction is aiming to achieve here is to put the participant under pressure, building suspense and tension and perhaps encouraging engagement at a more intense level, echoing the trajectory of the underlying narrative regarding the terrorists at this point, e.g.

This is what Renate wrote in her letter: 'Give up, Ulrike! You are not like that, Ulrike. Not at all the way people think you are when they have seen your picture up on a wanted poster. Those who know you better know that you do not shoot anyone who stands in your way. You have your fears like everyone else. But you are brave, braver than most.

This underlying interest in encouraging identification and developing tension is a recurrent feature of the instructions in Ulrike and Eamon. Often, at first sight they are just further instructions regarding how to act, for instance:

***Now continue across the bridge and turn left towards the church towers. Start to stroll very slowly with the canal on your left hand side.** You're going to walk to the next bridge. I'll stay on the line while you walk... **Keep your eyes open, act natural.** There is always a first time for this kind of thing and practice makes it easier.*

In each observed case of following this instruction the participant crossed the bridge and turned left and walked along past the pharmacy to the next bridge without visibly either changing pace or the manner in which they were walking. Indeed, one might wonder how ordinary walking might look any different to keeping your eyes open and acting naturally, posing a question as to what such an instruction might be hoping to accomplish. Furthermore, for many participants 'strolling very slowly' would stand in direct contradiction to the instruction to 'act naturally'. Of course, for artists scripting the instructions here the ambiguity is quite deliberate (see [25] for similar artistic intent), with much of it once again being about encouraging some appreciation of what it might be like to be a terrorist where blending in is critical. Several of the comportmental instructions in Ulrike and Eamon are like this in that they largely propose *a manner of doing things* as opposed to an actual action. The difficulty in terms of ensuring such instructions accomplish their desired effect is that compliance with them is rarely manifest unless they do demand specific acts, such as in the following:

*The participant stands looking over the parapet of the bridge down the length of the canal listening to a message, then turns to the right looking along the bridge itself as the message continues, "I would like to know how would you describe your ability to make decisions. Are you a decisive or a hesitant person, Ulrike? **Now please record your answer. Start by saying "My name is Ulrike" and then tell me are you a decisive or hesitant person? When you have finished your recording, hang up.** I'm going to start recording now." The participant looks back along the canal and says:"My name is Ulrike and I think I'm a fairly decisive person. When I make a decision it's usually final."*

And some instructed actions can be dismissed without leading to any obvious trouble in accomplishing *visible* compliance at all, for instance the following:

*Now I want you to pick a person as they walk past you. **Choose someone and give them a name. Look carefully at them before they go. Now think about their home. Think about a treasured possession that they may have on their shelf.** Who is it that they love? **Stare down at the canal and hold that person in your mind for a short while.***

DISCUSSION

Something to note about the vast bulk of the literature on instruction-giving and following in HCI is the heavy focus upon just a few basic topics. By far the largest part of work in this area so far has focused upon either matters of wayfinding [16][20][28] or learning [17][26]. However, with the possible exception of Bryan-Kinns et als investigation of how instructions work in remote creative collaborations [11] virtually no interest has been shown to date with regard to the role played by instructions in shaping people's comportment or their engagement with experiences. In that case much of the following discussion is relatively new territory for CHI with implications for those who are interested in how instructions work across a wide range of different domains.

Bearing this in mind, there are two key issues of relevance to HCI that come out of the data we have just presented. One of these relates to the character of the instructions which are, in the majority of cases 'thick' in terms of what they are trying to convey to participants, whilst the channel for delivery is very 'thin'. The other relates to the nature of accountability in these kinds of experiences and the tensions this throws up regarding how instructions will be complied with in any given circumstance.

Thin channel compliance

Something we have already had cause to notice is that instructions in Ulrike and Eamon Compliant, and indeed in many ambulatory experiences like this, mostly come down a very thin channel, often as simple text messages or recorded messages on a mobile device. However, despite the thinness of this channel the instructions are actually trying to accomplish a number of things at the same time. What begins to fall out of the data we have just been looking at is that the delivered instructions are trying to bring about some degree of compliance from the participants at four different levels: with regard to location (they attempt to get people to go to specific places); with regard to sequence (they attempt to get people to do things in a particular order); with regard to comportment (they attempt to get people to act and behave in certain ways); and with regard to how they relate to the experience (they attempt to get them to engage with it in certain ways and experience certain kinds of tensions and moods). We will discuss each of these different layers of compliance in turn.

Locational compliance

First of all, whilst it may seem an obvious point, in location-based experiences it is important to get to the right place. One might even say this is a baseline requirement. However, there is some richness regarding compliance here that is worth taking note of. Although the basic premise in Ulrike and Eamon is that participants will go out on the streets and follow the route for about an hour, there are some actively used locations that *do* feature in the instructions, and some that don't. For some locations, such as we saw with a participant physically standing on a bridge, it takes confirmed arrival in one location to receive the next message that will guide you to another location. In cases like this it is difficult *to progress* in defiance of the locational instructions you have been given. Participants do get 'lost', of course, and 'being lost' works as an acceptable account for non-compliance with a locational instruction. At the same time, to simply decide to follow your own route and go where you please would effectively terminate engagement because events scripted into the experience would not unfold.

However, as we also saw, many quite deliberate locational actions relating to the route and its following, such as stopping and leaning against a specific wall, stand wholly outside of what they have been expressly asked to do, yet do not necessarily breach locational instructions. Nor do they necessarily demonstrate non-compliance. Rather what these actions accomplish is an elaboration of instructions into sensible ways of proceeding in the specific course of their following, for instance holding off on further action until the intent of an instruction has been clarified, because instructions always in some sense under-specify and their realisation always involves some measure of elaboration in any particular situation. So, although these subsidiary, unspecified locations stand outside of the body of instructions a participant may encounter, they are central to compliance with the instructions that they do receive.

Sequential compliance:

At a layer higher than certain specific locations, each location people are instructed to go to also contributes to an overall trajectory that must be passed through *in a certain order* if the experience is to be completed.

Each particular location is not simply oriented to wholly in its own right, people understand that an unfolding experience is also an unfolding *sequence of happenings*, whereby each new instruction is not treated as free-standing but as a first instruction, second instruction, last instruction, etc., with each instruction being reasoned about in relation to what has been asked of them so far. We saw this in how a complex instruction involving a number of parts in order to direct a participant from an alley to a bridge turned upon relating each part to what had gone before in order to see what should be done next. We also saw how this can extend beyond just one specific instruction to a whole concatenation of instructions in the way one participant stopped prior to going up onto the grassy area, having come to understand that not all reference points are destinations.

What needs to be seen here is that each particular instruction stands itself as a resource whereby the next instruction (and other instructions to come) might be reasoned about and understood. Compliance, in that case, is not simply a for-here-and-now compliance but is also a retrospective/prospective compliance, looking back to what is understood about what has already been done and what is understood about what is being asked of one next in order to understand what appropriate compliance might look like. This being the case, what appropriate instruction following might look like is something that is ongoingly revisable as each new instruction is encountered. This inevitably leads to a growing understanding on the part of the participant regarding what it might take to follow instructions, so that by the end of the experience the participant is *apparently* engaging at a different level having *apparently* 'got into it'. The word 'apparently is used here advisedly because what the above analysis reveals is that an important part of what increased engagement turns upon is a growing understanding of what it takes to comply with the instructions you are receiving. What terms like 'engagement' and 'getting into it' are therefore really recognising in good part is a growing competence in adequate compliance with instructions, which doesn't say anything much one way or the other about engagement at an emotional level. This can clearly be a feature, but it cannot be said to be made manifest simply by a more 'complete' compliance with the implied sense of instructions. One needs to look beyond matters of sequence alone to understand how instructions might serve to prompt emotional engagement of some kind.

Comportmental compliance

Something that could make emotional engagement more manifest is people's *comportment*: that is, what they do and the way in which they do it. The next layer up in terms of what instructions might be seen to be asking of people, then, is a specification of what people need to *do* when they get somewhere.

In the case of comportmental compliance the above data revealed that understanding of just what is being asked for is everything. So we saw, for instance, that instructions such as 'act natural' can be oriented to as optional rhetorical embellishments whilst being told to nod your head or actually say something obliges participants to produce something that at least superficially *does* resemble nodding or saying something. Indeed, one might ask how an instruction like 'act natural' could work as an obligation. It's a common instruction to people who might otherwise look guilty, serving effectively as an instruction not to arouse suspicions. In that participants in Ulrike and Eamon are being invited to enter the worldview of a terrorist this kind of instruction might seem to make sense. And, as we commented previously this invitation has a certain power of ambiguity in this setting that might serve to increase a participant's sense of tension. However, as participants in Ulrike and Eamon are *not* terrorists and there are no real world repercussions from arousing the suspicions of those around them, acting natural is an artifice and demands something rather different. It demands that participants accountably adopt a *role*, and compliance at this level is something rather different.

Relational compliance

We have seen how different levels of compliance with instructions might work in terms of what locations to go to, what order to go to each of those locations in, and what to physically do when you get to those locations. However, creators of experiences like Ulrike and Eamon are trying to accomplish something more than this: they are also seeking to manage how the participant *relates* to the experience by managing the impact of its various affective elements, and the prompts through which a participant might be persuaded to adopt a certain role.

Considerations here turn upon the extent to which designers of such experiences are successful in getting people to engage with not only the literal sense of instructions they are being given but also the underlying sense of those instructions. This involves getting people to attribute some meaning to what is intended by the experience overall, even if that meaning is deliberately ambiguous.

Now, of course it is the case that people undertaking Ulrike and Eamon in Venice did not just understand themselves to be tourists taking a walk around the canals. However, as we've already commented, they did not understand themselves to be international terrorists either. Rather, the awareness of them being involved in some kind of experience brings along with it certain expectations and this serves to underpin the observations we have already made regarding locational and comportmental compliance. At its most manifest and obvious level what one finds is that participants are oriented to doing what they understand to be appropriate and necessary as *participants in an event*. Minimal compliance here amounts to going to the specified place and possibly doing the action asked of you and that is what most participants manifestly achieve.

Something that hints at the fact that there is something more than just this going here and that minimal compliance doesn't quite cover it is what happens when participants are asked to step outside of behaviours that might be routinely undertaken in the environments they are passing through. Consider the following example:

The participant is stood by a well looking around a square, phone in hand. .... The phone rings. He answers it 'Yep?" He receives the following message: "I want to walk you down to the water's edge. ***Look for the sign that reads Campo Drio Il Cimitero****. You can see it from the well. It reads reads Campo Drio Il Cimitero. On the right hand side of it is an alley.* ***Once you see it, walk right down to the water's edge.****" .... He looks to and fro then walks off towards the left, phone still pressed to his ear. He crosses a square, then gets to a junction with a choice of going left or right. He looks up, then stops and turns round, and shakes his head, saying 'What?" The recording continues with an account of Eamon's sojourn in a cell at Gough Barracks. As he is listening he heads towards the left. Reaching the entrance to an alleyway he looks down it, stops and looks around uncertainly, takes a pace forward, then stops and looks around again, raising his eyebrows. Then he starts to walk down the alley. He gets to a point where water is lapping up onto the cobbles and there is a pile of rubbish gathered at the edge and stops, phone still pressed to his ear. Then he leans against the wall and carries on listening.*

Now going down a dank, rubbish-filled alley, off the beaten track, with nothing particularly to commend it, to stand on slippery cobbles at the edge of a canal, is not the kind of action ordinarily undertaken by tourists, though of course it could be. But what it does do is make the participant visible as someone doing other than what ordinary tourists do, demanding in turn some kind of account. The participant makes his reticence about going down the alley quite visible. Yet in the end he does. The account for this for participants resides in their participation in an experience and their compliance with a quite specific and clearly uncomfortable instruction is compliance *in relation to what they understand this particular experience to be about*.

Working the layers

In the above discussion we have sought to unpack what we mean when we say that designers of these kinds of experiences are trying to accomplish a lot of different things when they are sending instructions down a very thin channel. We have seen that they have to contend with providing for at least four different layers of compliance. There are important reasons why we have described these different kinds of compliance as layers or levels. Upon reflection it can be seen that there are ways in which each layer turns somehow upon the layers that preceded it. So you must be in the right place at each step of the way to follow the right sequence of events. You need to be following the right sequence of events to be able to engage with the content. And you need to be displaying the right kinds of comportment if you are going to be able to be seen as engaging with the actual sense or spirit of the experience. However, we have touched above upon another aspect of following instructions that can also impact upon the different kinds of compliance one sees: accountability.

Accountability

It is not possible to have compliance without some sense of accountability. Instructions never stand apart from who people understand the instructions to be coming from and who they understand to be potential witnesses of their following of the instruction. So compliance is never just compliance *per se*, it is compliance that some other party or parties might deem to be appropriate or inappropriate. There are at least three possible different parties people may consider themselves accountable to when they engage in experiences like Ulrike and Eamon. One such party is the people who have designed the game and who are somehow addressing the participants through things like the instructions and stories they are receiving on their mobile phones. Then there are, potentially, specific witnesses of their actions who are actually seeking to orchestrate the game and hold the participants to account for at least the more manifest aspects of following the instructions they receive. Finally, there is the surrounding body of ordinary people going about their own ordinary business to whom participants are eternally accountable as members of society themselves [14]. The interesting point about this matter of differing accountabilities is that it can lead to tensions, tensions that designers may themselves seek to exploit.

Managed compliance

Something important to note about Ulrike and Eamon, as performed in its original version at the Biennale in Venice, is that it did not simply deliver messages to the participants on their mobile phones and leave it at that; it made active use of what might be termed *managed* compliance. Consider the following:

Now find a bench that is free and sit down for a moment. *I want to ask you a question.* ***When you take your glasses off and lay them on the bench beside you*** *I'll know you're ready to talk.*

Participants who did not have glasses were furnished with glasses for the purpose of handling this instruction and, in all observed cases, it was somehow complied with. Sometimes the glasses were removed as they sat down on the bench, in other cases once they had already sat down. And in no case did the participants physically lay the glasses actually down on the bench, retaining instead a grip on them with one hand, showing once again how *precise* following of such instructions is understood, by this point, to not be what it is about. However, the interesting thing about this instruction, as with the instruction that they nod their head, or another that they raise their free hand to their head, is that it implies that there is someone able to *see* them undertaking the action and therefore act upon it. Very quickly each of the participants started to scan the people around them and the people they passed for who the observer might be.

In fact, as we mentioned earlier, there were some eight performers on the streets who attempted to hide themselves whilst observing the participants and manouvering them through the route by timing the delivery of messages according to where they could see the participants had got to. In this case, then, compliance with the instructions *was* necessary for the participant to progress (though the performers were prepared to send the next recording anyway if the participants did not comply). Participants having deduced that their actions were being observed, compliance was controlled in large part by recognition of the fact that they were directly accountable for their actions to this hidden observer.

Doing being ordinary

We have already seen how participants actively work to comply with the sense of instructions, and how compliance can be further shaped through varying degrees of implied and direct management. However, it should be stressed that this does not simply set aside all of the usual practices and accountabilities that might hold sway when people are out walking the streets of Venice or whatever. Often participants make quite evident the extent to which they are aware of how they are breaching ordinary practices in their fulfilment of instructions. We saw that in the case of the participant who hesitated before going down the alley to the water. We also saw this in how the participant nodding her head also took it to be something funny. Laughter is a powerful device for recognising potential breaches of behaviour and to offset accountability for them in various kinds of ways [18]. There were numerous ways in which all the walking, stopping and looking, sitting on benches, or whatever, was being done in conspicuously ordinary ways for visitors out and about on the streets of Venice. There are routine ways of going about this, of 'doing being ordinary' [24]. And there are equally routine ways of making it visible that you recognize the oddness of something you've been asked to do, for instance by laughing or looking embarrassed, thereby displaying your ongoing attentiveness to what is 'proper' and 'ordinary'.

Managing tensions

It is at this point we confront a certain difficulty with instructions and people's ready compliance with them in these kinds of events, namely the invitation to adopt a role. In Ulrike and Eamon participants are invited to enter the heads of terrorists and see the world from their point of view. However, out on the streets, how does one reconcile the basic orientation towards being ordinary with an apparent instruction to be a terrorist? What we have seen in our discussion of relational compliance is that engaging with an experience like this involves in good part arriving at a sense of what the experience must really be about and proceeding in that fashion. This provides the licence or accountability for certain behaviours such as were witnessed in the alleyway. However, it also provides for what might be discounted whilst still honouring the spirit of the experience. And it is at this point, at the point where instructions propose actions that are extraneous to the accomplishment of adequate performance, that aspects of instructions that are to do with the adoption of a particular role can quite simply be set aside as irrelevant to a demonstration of adequate compliance.

Listening to the story of a terrorist, nodding your head when told to, going down dubious alleyways are all found to be open to compliance under the auspices of this being an ambulatory experience they are engaging in. However, actually *acting* like a terrorist when you're out walking the streets of Venice is something else, creating potential tension between the accountability of participants to what they see to be the intention of those who created the experience and their accountability to just anyone else.

CONCLUSION

This paper has sought to explore the complex matter of instruction-giving and instruction following by analysing people's situated compliance with instructions in an ambulatory experience. This experience was chosen because it has some particularly pertinent features: it is sending thick instructions down a thin channel; it is delivering instructions into a complex environment; it offers little scope for feedback; and it offers little opportunity for rehearsal. In relation to this we have seen how people's compliance with instructions operates across four different layers: locational compliance; sequential compliance; comportmental compliance; and relational compliance. This in turn led us to a discussion of the challenges of trying to do all of this down a thin channel. We then noted how the particular experience we studied also provoked tension between people's *accountability* to three different parties: the designers of the experience; potential observers on the streets attempting to manage their compliance in certain ways; and the ordinary society constituted of just anyone else who might be around.

Although a range of possible design considerations fall out of the above observations, the matter of accountability indicates some particular implications with regard to the orchestration of such experiences, not just ambulatory ones but managed experiences in general, be that in games or in other kinds of cultural pursuits. It is worth emphasising that one of the most significant challenges in orchestration is how to deal with situations when following instructions breaks down. When this *does* happen orchestrators typically need to intervene in some way in order steer participants back on track, including delivering alternate instructions. Studies of a previous ambulatory experience, Uncle Roy All Around You, revealed that these might be improvised on the fly by human operators, but might also be pre-authored and triggered in a layered way (e.g., as a participant strays further from a planned route so automated clues guiding them back become evermore direct [7]).

The presence of the four aspects of compliance outlined above both compound this challenge by adding significant complexity and enrich the field of possible strategies for the design of tools to support orchestration. First, it becomes necessary to determine in what sense the instruction is not being followed: is the participant lost, out of sequence, comporting himself or herself incorrectly, or not appropriately relating to the content? This having been determined, a new instruction may need to be delivered that addresses this aspect, without compromising any others. Thus, a participant who is lost, but otherwise behaving correctly, needs to be steered to the right location, but in a way that does not threaten their relationship to the work, their comportment or the unfolding sequence. Alternatively, a participant who is doing the right things, but who is manifestly not relating to the experience beyond the more basic levels of compliance might be given new instructions designed to change their relationship to the work.

However, these kinds of refinements turn upon an even deeper challenge: how to recognize breakdowns in compliance from a limited yet potentially opaque set of cues, e.g. where the participant is at present, how they appear, what they are saying in any messages they send back, and so on. This having been accomplished, an appropriate layering of instructions needs to be designed that can deal with each possible manifestation of a problem, potentially resulting in very many different versions of each instruction. Beyond this there needs to be some mechanism for ascertaining what can be dealt with automatically and what will require intervention from a human orchestrator. For example, problems with locational compliance may be detected and perhaps corrected automatically, whereas those arising from relational compliance may demand in situ human judgement for them to be adequately handled. In short, designing complex instructions for thin channels demands a sophisticated, multi-layered consideration of how the different aspects of instructions work together. This stands as a topic for significant future research across a variety of domains where instruction-following is central to the realization of some kind of experience, most notably those domains involving orchestration as well.

ACKNOWLEDGMENTS

This work was funded by the Engineering and Physical Sciences Research Council (EPSRC) through Horizon Digital Economy research (EP/G065802/1) and the Challenge of Widespread Ubiquitous Computing (EP/F03038X/1) project. Our thanks to all of the assistants and participants at the 2009 Biennale in Venice who contributed to this study.

REFERENCES

1. Abowd, A et al (1997) ‘Cyberguide: a mobile context-aware tour guide’, *Wireless Networks*, 3 (5), Kluwer
2. Aoki, P et al. (2002) ‘Sotto Voce: Exploring the Interplay of Conversation and Mobile Audio Spaces’, *Proc. CHI 2002*, ACM, 431-438
3. Bedwell, B et al (2009) ‘In Support of City Exploration’, *Proc. CHI 2009*, ACM, 1171-1180
4. Bellotti, F et al (2011) ‘Investigating the added value of interactivity and serious gaming for educational TV’, *Comput. Educ.* 57, 1, 1137-1148
5. Bellotti, V et al (2008) ‘Activity-based serendipitous recommendations with the Magitti mobile leisure guide’, *Proc. CHI 2008*, ACM
6. Benford, S et al (2006) ‘Can you see me now?’, *ACM Trans. Comput.-Hum. Interact.* 13, 1, 100-133
7. Benford, S et al (2006) ‘The Frame of the game: the opportunities and risks of staging digital experiences in public settings’, *Proc. CHI 2006*, ACM, 427-436
8. Beun, R-J et al (eds) (1995) *Dialogue and Instruction: Modelling Interaction in Intelligent Tutoring Systems*, Springer
9. http://www.blasttheory.co.uk/bt/work_ulrikeandeamoncompliant.html
10. Brown, B et al (2005) ‘Sharing the square: collaborative leisure in the city streets’, *Proc. ECSCW 2005*, Springer
11. Bryan-Kinns, N et al (2007) ‘Exploring mutual engagement in creative collaborations’, *Proc. C\&C 2009*, ACM, 223-232
12. Chalmers, M & Galani, A (2004) ‘Seamful interweaving: heterogeneity in the theory and design of interactive systems’, *Proc. DIS 2004*, ACM
13. Cheverst, K et al (2000) ‘Developing a context-aware electronic tourist guide: Some issues and experiences’. *Proc. CHI 2000*, ACM
14. Garfinkel, H. (1967) *Studies in Ethnomethodology*, Prentice-Hall
15. Girardin, F & Blat, J (2010) ‘The co-evolution of taxi drivers and their in-car navigation systems’, *Pervasive Mob. Comput.* 6, 4, 424-434
16. Hile, H et al (2008) ‘Landmark-based pedestrian navigation from collections of geotagged photos’, *Proc. MUM 2008*, ACM, 145-152
17. Hundhausen, C et al (2011) ‘The "prototype walkthrough": a studio-based learning activity for human-computer interaction courses’, *Proc. ICER 2011*, ACM, 117-124
18. Jefferson, G, et al (1987) ‘Notes on Laughter in the Pursuit of Intimacy’, in *Talk and Social Organisation* (eds. Button, G and Lee, J R E), Multilingual Matters Ltd, 152-205
19. Macvean, A, et al (2011) ‘WeQuest: Scalable Alternate Reality Games Through End-User Content Authoring’, *Proc. ACE 2011*, ACM
20. May, A et al (2005) ‘The design of next generation in-vehicle navigation systems for the older driver’, *Interact. Comput.* 17, 6, 643-659
21. Montola, M & Syenros, J (2009) *Pervasive Games: Theory and Design*, Morgan Kaufmann
22. Paelke, V et al (2007) *Mobile location-based gaming*, Springer
23. Rehrl, K et al (2010) ‘Comparing the effectiveness of GPS-enhanced voice guidance for pedestrians with metric- and landmark-based instruction sets’, *Proc. GIScience 2010*, Springer, 189-203
24. Sacks, H. (1992) *Lectures on Conversation* (ed. Jefferson, G.), Blackwell
25. Sengers, P & Gaver, B (2006) ‘Staying open to interpretation: engaging multiple meanings in design and evaluation, *Proc. DIS 2006*, ACM, 99-108
26. Sheldon, J et al (2010) ‘Weatherlings: a new approach to student learning using web-based mobile games’, *Proc. FDG 2010*, ACM, 203-208
27. Suchman, L (1987) *Plans and Situated Actions*, Cambridge University Press
28. Tscheligi, M & Sefelin, R (2006) ‘Mobile navigation support for pedestrians: can it work and does it pay off?’ *interactions* 13, 4, 31-33
29. Vainio, T & Kulju, M (2007) ‘So James, can you find your way any faster?: exploring navigation aids for taxi drivers’, . *Proc. Mobility 2007*, ACM, 645-652
30. Vlahakis, V et al (2001) ‘ARCHEOGUIDE: First results of an Augmented Reality, Mobile Computing System in Cultural Heritage Sites’, *Proc. VAST 2001*, ACM, 131 – 140

Supporting Improvisation Work in Inter-Organizational Crisis Management

Benedikt Ley, Volkmar Pipek, Christian Reuter, Torben Wiedenhoefer
Institute for Information Systems, University of Siegen
Hoelderlinstr. 3, 57076 Siegen, Germany
e-mail address: {firstname.lastname}@uni-siegen.de

ABSTRACT
Improvisation is necessary when planned decision-making as the main managerial activity does not fit the conditions the practice provides. In these cases, information technology should not just automate planned and structured decisions, but support improvisational practice. In this contribution we present an empirical study about the improvisation work in scenarios of medium to large power outages in Germany. Our focus is on inter-organizational cooperation practices, thus we examined the cooperation of fire departments, police, public administration, electricity infrastructure operators and citizens. Our empirical material allows to describe reasons and conditions for improvisation. Our resulting recommendations address the support of aggregation and visualization of information, a necessary individualization of information compositions, options for collaborative situation assessment, requirements for informal and formal communication, and accessibility of information resources.

Author Keywords
Improvisation; Crisis Management; Collaboration; Ethnography

ACM Classification Keywords
H.5.3 Group and Organization Interfaces

General Terms
Human Factors, Design

INTRODUCTION
Crisis management is a practice field that by its nature needs to prepare for the unforeseeable. The number of influencing factors (weather conditions, number of people affected, type of emergency, etc.) as well as structural dependencies (electricity, roads and railways, fuel resources, etc.) makes it impossible to plan all crisis management activities ahead. Nevertheless, all organizations that help guaranteeing civil security (police, fire department, red cross, etc.) have developed systematic approaches to deal with these uncertainties and to allow for planned, coordinated activities in crisis situations. Still, many situations require spontaneous, ad-hoc decisions and short-term (re-)planning. The ability to improvise remains a valuable asset for individuals and organizations, and is usually cultivated in crisis trainings and grows with experience.

Permission to make digital or hard copies of all or part of this work for personal or classroom use is granted without fee provided that copies are not made or distributed for profit or commercial advantage and that copies bear this notice and the full citation on the first page. To copy otherwise, or republish, to post on servers or to redistribute to lists, requires prior specific permission and/or a fee.
CHI'12, May 5–10, 2012, Austin, Texas, USA.
Copyright 2012 ACM 978-1-4503-1015-4/12/05...$10.00.

While all these organizations have their established responsibilities and practices, many larger incidents require collaboration with these stakeholders. In Germany (and many other countries), there are established processes and practices of coordination between police, firefighters, infrastructure maintainers and administrative staff, usually prescribed by laws and regulations. All organizations rely on strong individual IT infrastructures. These inform the organization's emergency management by maintaining an overview on the current situation in an area of the organizations responsibility and on available resources for the crisis response measures the organizations feels responsible to engage in, and by providing means to coordinate emergency response activities. There is anecdotal evidence that showed that despite all efforts taken to be prepared, misunderstandings happened while actors were forced to operate and interact outside the system of established practices. Some of them may have been avoided if the IT systems had not only supported routine processes but also deviations.

Several examples of large crises (e.g. Hurricane Katrina [17]) showed that improvisation abilities face a completely different level of challenge when the crisis at hand is of a magnitude that requires emergency response organizations to collaborate. When dealing with larger power outages (the scenario we are looking at in our research project InfoStrom [24]), each of the organizations involved (police, fire department, infrastructure providers, etc.) sets up an own crisis management team. At county level a crisis management group tries to coordinate the efforts and also deals with the public. Nowadays, crisis managers as well as the crisis response teams, need to improvise at an inter-organizational level, and find their IT infrastructures not always prepared for that. As [9] reveals it:

> "Unfortunately, a focus on structure and doctrine obscures the need for technology that enhances improvisation and creativity. The specification and formalization of the planned-for structure has resulted in doctrine and technology to support it, ignoring the demonstrated, even inevitable, needs of the adhocracies that help manage the unanticipated contingencies presented by extreme events [...] Improvisation and adhocracy have received considerable

examination from social scientists, but have been far less frequently addressed by ICT designers." (p. 49)

But what is the exact nature of improvisation work necessary in crisis response? Where do communication strategies fail? And how can we provide IT support for improvisation at an inter-organizational level? In this contribution we present an empirical study of the inter-organizational improvisation work of actors, which are involved in scenarios of medium to large power outages. We derive requirements for information systems that would be able to support these practices.

The paper is organized as follows: After defining relevant terms and discussing the literature we introduce the research filed and our research methods. Afterwards we focus on the improvisation practice we found in emergency management. Then we discuss our findings and focus on design issues with regard to IT support for improvisation, finally followed by a conclusion.

IMPROVISTATION AND INFORMATION TECHNOLOGY IN CRISIS MANAGEMENT

Improvisation can be defined as "*situated performance where thinking and action seem to occur simultaneously and on the spur of the moment*" [4]. It can be interpreted as the unforeseen [18]. While some authors define it from the management perspective as "*to be composed while performed*" [14] others describe it in the case of fire service management as "*thinking and doing unfold simultaneously*" and "*retrospective sensemaking*" [23].

Improvisation in Emergency Management

Antecedent conditions, such as unexpected problems, changes in the structure of the problem areas or environmental and knowledge limitations, lead to the need for improvisation [18]. Even in highly structured organizations improvisation is a well-grounded process that can be leveraged to face those situations where rules and methods fail [3]. Improvisation can be performed on different levels and can be treated as an individual or as a team phenomenon [12]. Improvisation becomes necessary when beforehand planned decision-making does not work for any reason. This is especially the case in crises. Crises and emergencies often contain unexpected events. The root word '*krisis*' means 'judgment' and 'decision' which leads to the most important task: decision-making. The necessities to judge highly novel problems and to act quickly reduce the chances of extensive planning: "*Decision makers in emergencies must be prepared to improvise*" [11]. Improvisation does not consist of more sophisticated methods or more structured systems [4]. Instead of trying to eradicate it through automation, the appreciation of flexibility and effectiveness seems more adequate. There "*improvisation and preparedness go hand in hand*" [9]: Without improvisation, emergency management loses flexibility, without preparedness, emergency management loses efficiency.

Characteristics of Emergency Management

To support improvisation in crisis management it is essential to know the characteristics of the field. Based on an analysis of the response to the 2001 World Trade Center attack, the following characteristics of emergency management can be considered as characterizing reasons for improvisation [9]. Firstly, (a) *rarity* of incidences limits opportunities for training and learning. Furthermore, (b) *time pressure* forces a convergence of planning and execution. (c) *Uncertainty* is present because the development of an extreme incidence is hardly predictable. Furthermore, extreme events have (d) *high and broad consequences*, therefore there is a need to manage interdependencies among a wide range of physical and social systems. The (e) *complexity* of the event arises, partly due to the high and broad consequences. Finally (f) *multiple decision makers* and responding organizations may negotiate while responding to the event. When more than one actor is involved, decision-making is often a process of "muddling-through" rather than a "scientific" process [8]. In emergency management this is not caused by a lack of planning, but is necessary because "*in fact the major problem in emergency management is that the team often does not exist formally until the emergency occurs*" [21], which is contrary to scientific communication processes. Crisis situations differ from routine situations and actors have to face new and unstructured tasks [15].

Supporting improvisation in crisis management

As stated above, decision-making is one of the main tasks where improvisation is needed. Organizations need to maintain flexibility in order to respond to unanticipated events. Computer-based systems can support these processes, if the system design is informed by an understanding of the cognitive processes involved in responding to unanticipated contingencies [9]. These systems must support the actors to rework their knowledge in order to fit the requirements of the current situation. Information technology, supporting improvisation, needs to handle ad-hoc coordination, unique problem solving strategies and new or changed information needs [22]. Computer based comparisons of the current decision situation with past ones were identified as appropriate in this context [9]. Case-based reasoning systems, which catalogue the set for planned-for situations or decision alternatives, may be used for this purpose, too. Ad-hoc re-planning and the ability to share material were identified as design challenges for large-scale events [7]. Furthermore, the following IT-supported mechanisms for improvisation in emergency management are suggested: graphical representations of data during crisis response, intelligent systems that select and help to contact experts, centralization of data to enable actors finding information and virtual supported coordination to create shared information consistent in time [1]. In addition, verbal communication should be made persistent, visible and accessible in order to support accountability [6]. Finally

"*ICT in disaster contexts will give further rise to improvised activities and temporary organizations with which formal response organizations need to align.*" [13].

Much prior research focused on improvisation within an organization. Our aim is to examine improvisation on an inter-organizational level in order to derive requirements for potential IT-support for improvisation work. Aside from some theory-led considerations and case studies above, we aimed to understand the local and collaborative practices of the agents. Therefore we conducted an empirical study in Germany focussing on improvisation work for actors involved in scenarios of medium to large power outages.

RESEARCH FIELD

This paper reports from a study focusing on improvisation practices during coping and recovery work at emergency response agencies in Germany. We conducted this study in two regions of North Rhine Westphalia in Germany (counties Rhein-Erft (REK) and Siegen-Wittgenstein (KSW)). Siegen-Wittgenstein is a densely wooded, hilly county in the middle of Germany, whereas Rhein-Erft consists of 10 growing communes in the west of Cologne. In both regions we focus on several persons and organizations affected: *Infrastructure suppliers* (e.g. power supplier), *public strategic administration* (e.g. crisis management, county administration), *public operative administration* (e.g. police, fire department) and *citizens.*

Before we present findings from our empirical study, we will have a quick look on two interesting aspects in advance regarding police and firefighter forces at both counties. Firstly, related to the organization of fire and rescue forces, Rhein-Erft provides professional fire and rescue departments, whereas Siegen-Wittgenstein's firefighters are mostly members of voluntary fire departments. Here, just members of the control center have salaried positions. Secondly, another interesting aspect emerged, while we compared lead structures of both organizations. Despite the fact that firefighter forces process coordination from the field via incident commands, police forces in the field receive commands from members of the control centers.

METHODOLOGY

The aim of the empirical study was to understand the application field and improvisational practices in crisis management. The view on the field was sensitized by our design intention. We conducted a grounded theory oriented approach [20], where we did not explore the field with predefined categories, but derived categories from empirical data. To reconstruct the practices we used different qualitative methods [16] such as document analysis, 4 observations, 5 group discussions, and 22 interviews including the development of a crisis scenario. All empirical work took place at the observants'/interviewees' workplaces. All in all we talked to more than 50 different actors from district administration, police, fire department, red cross and energy network operator (ENO). We used open coding [20] to analyze the material and to uncover interesting phenomena. We are neither focusing on similarities nor differences but on breakdowns of practices that depend on inter-organizational collaboration.

The primary goal of *document analysis* was to obtain an overview of the organizations in crisis situations. We analyzed documents that regulate and describe the work in crisis management (laws, regulations, directives, and course materials).

The *observations* were used to acquire knowledge about practical work in inter-organizational crisis management. These were conducted in a control center during a normal working day (observation time: 9 hours), in the crisis management group and the operations management during a crisis communication training (4 hours) as well as on a major cultural event with about 400.000 visitors (6 hours).

The *group discussions* (see table 1) allowed us to understand the communicative practice of inter-organizational crisis management. We conducted 4 inter-organizational group discussions, each lasting of about 4 hours, including the participation of leading actors.

No	County	Topic	Participants
W1	-	Challenges in practice, Visit of Control Center	Energy Network Operator (ENO)
W2	REK	Challenges in practice, Visit of Control Center	County Administration Police Fire Department
W3	KSW	Challenges in practice, Visit of Control Center	Department Head: Public Safety Head of Civil Protection Head of Police Control Center Deputy Head of Control Center District Fire Chief
W4	KSW	Analysis of User Interactions and Communication Flows	Head of Police Control Center, Head of Staff Coordination, Deputy Head of Control Center, Local Head of Federal Agency of Technical Relief (THW), Local Head German Red Cross
W5	REK	Analysis of User Interactions and Communication Flows	Head Regulatory Authority, District Fire Chief, Red Cross: Disaster Management, Red Cross: Communications, Members of other aid agencies

Table 1. Group Discussions

It is difficult to observe the practice of crisis management within an actual crisis situation, because crises mostly happen unforeseen. Furthermore, on an inter-organizational level, it is hard to observe spatial distributed actors at the same time during an actual crisis. To overcome these circumstances, we and members of ENO, police and fire department cooperatively developed a *scenario framework* existing of a windstorm with many incidents and energy breakdowns. The purpose of our scenario was to be able to quickly create a common understanding of a crisis situation and context in our interviews. It helped to increase their validity and comparability and to develop ideas concerning improvements of tools to support improvisational practice.

The *interviews* (see table 2) allowed us to analyze the work context and the use of information and communication systems of relevant actors. The interviews lasted between 1 and 2 hours and followed an interview guide. The first part of the interview focused the participants' role, qualification, activities and work steps in normal conditions. The second part covered the tasks in crisis situations and was based on the developed scenario framework. The third part covered information and communication systems as well as perceived problems with these tools.

No	County	Organization	Role
I1	KSW	Administration	Regulatory Authority
I2	KSW	Police	Head of Control Centre
I3	KSW	Police	Head of Section
I4	KSW	Police	Patrol Duty
I5	KSW	Fire Department	District Fire Chief
I6	KSW	Fire Department	Deputy Head of Control Center
I7	KSW	Fire Department	Workmanship
I24	KSW	Fire Department	Head of Control Center
I8	REK	Administration	Office Civil Protection
I9	REK	Fire Department	Chief Officer / Chief of Fire Dept.
I10	REK	Fire Department	Operation Controllers
I11	REK	Fire Department	Clerical Grade Watch Department
I12	REK	Fire Department	Control Center Dispatcher
I13	REK	Fire Department	Head of Control Center
I14	Köln	Police	Member of the Permanent Staff
I15	REK	Police	Head of Control Center
I16	REK	Police	Head of Group
I18	-	ENO	Higher Area, High Voltage
I19	-	ENO	Operation Engineer, High Voltage
I20	-	ENO	Operation Technician, Low Voltage
I21	-	ENO	Dispatcher, Low Voltage
I22	-	ENO	Workmanship Technical Incidents

Table 2. Interviews

RESULTS: IMPROVISATION IN PRACTICE

Facing novel problems and the need to act quickly, plays a significant role in handling crisis situations. Our study revealed that at both counties improvisation is a common procedure of decision makers responding to uncertain circumstances under risk and time constraint: "*Improvisation is essential, next to extensive planning. You can have the best predefined response plans, but there is always a situation, where you have to improvise.*" (I1) or "*We improvise as usual. We see to it that we make the best out of each situation.*" (I11).

In this section we are going to point out existing improvisation practices of actors involved in crisis management (see Table 2), which have been identified after analyzing existing coping and recovery practices. We have divided this section into aspects of improvisation in current management structures of emergency services, possible causes of improvisation and conditions of improvisation.

Improvisation in current management structures

When we take a closer look at emergency response work, we can see that improvisation is a common practice in todays' emergency management processes, besides executing on one or more response plans. As we could see at police work practices, to be capable of facing uncertain events, flexibility is already part of their common working procedures: "*No, all workflows are flexible. This is necessary, because each situation is different.*" (I2). One police officer explains, that "*once there is a problem, our command center gives us basically plenty of rope, to solve the problem*" (I4). When we focus on the degree of improvisation or situated actions, our study identified two factors: the audience and the scale of an incident. We have to distinguish between two cases: "*There are incidents, which are managed by incidents commanders and there are events, where a crisis management group is in charge*" (I1). Incident commanders are usually full responsible for coordination and decision-making at the incident scene, when response plans can be executed properly. This work is not so much shaped by improvisation actions as by executing predefined tasks: "*We get the tasks and we perform them*" (I7). However, when emergency services are faced with complex, unpredictable events and a bigger picture is needed to perform further actions, a crisis management group takes over decision-making on a higher level. Because these kinds of events are "*not static, they can develop in any direction*" (I5). At that point, response plans can rarely be executed, the procedures in this group and on decision-maker level "*are more flexible*" (I1) in order to be capable of generating and executing new orders or plans nearly simultaneously. An example of a typical order is: "*Look for schools or gymnasiums to accommodate 500 people. How you do it is your business.*" (I1).

Reasons for Improvisation

Due to the uniqueness of each operation, the actors' procedures during coping and recovery work essentially depend on improvisation rather than on predefined workflows. "*This is necessary, because no situation is equal to any other. [...] Our work is fundamentally different from other local authorities. There are no predefined processes we are working off – we would be helpless and lost. That's why we tactically work with frame orders.*" (I2). Although these frame orders describe concrete tasks, the way how they are performed strongly depends on the current situation in the field: "*No one gets told by us: 'You have to enter the house via the left sidewalk.'*" (I2).

Improvisation work requires making in-situ decisions based on the current condition. Hence, it is necessary to keep track of the occurrences. Information resources, which are considered for this purpose, often contain uncertainties and have to be evaluated cautiously. For instance, in case of severe weather alerts, preparations are made, e.g. putting staff on standby. However, those warnings are published too frequently and in many cases no critical weather conditions occur (I2). For that reason, many actors individually collect supplementary information from various sources, for example, the current weather condition outside the building, other weather information systems or webcams that are focused against the wind direction, to obtain a better overview of the situation: *"You need as much information as possible."* (I24).

Besides the work in the control centers, on-scene actors also depend on an optimal overview of the situation. For this purpose, some of them use their private smartphones as an information medium, because the authorities do not provide such technology for their staff: *"Some of the colleagues have an Internet connection on their smartphone that is often useful, for example to get an aerial image from the locality via Google Maps to check other information. This can be helpful for mediation, when you need a phone number [...]. Generally, we don't have navigation systems on board and there is often the problem: 'Go to house number 17' and when you have found number 5, the next three numbers are hard to read and then you suddenly find a house number 28 and then there is the question: 'Where are the others?'"*(I4).

Outside influences from an incident itself are not the only reason that requires an improvised acting. Also *organizational factors* and structures can bear unpredictable challenges. That is why each actor will have to be able to divert from given routines to be capable of acting even if the given structures and circumstances change: *"If a system is strongly rigid and structured, and then one component is missing, mostly the whole system will collapse. For this, informal acting can be helpful."* (I1). Reasons mentioned for such a collapse is that technology, especially communication tools, can fail (I3) or internal information resources (e.g. phone lists) required during an operation are unavailable (I2). Also *human factors* play an important role. Especially during major catastrophes staff members can also be affected personally: *"When an employee gets the call that his home is flooded, you are trying to relieve that staff member from his duties. It makes no sense to keep him here. You would arrange a replacement and say: 'Here, care about your home or about your family.'"* (I2) In addition to organizational reasons, the collaboration with other agencies requires a more flexible and improvised acting in general due to different organizational structures and work practices (I1).

In this context, *terminological differences* play a decisive role. Depending on the individual structures and practices of the respective organizations, different terms are used which can cause several communicational issues: *"There is a person with a cut finger and an employee from THW [agency for technical relief] reports this injury – This nearly sounded like a fatality!"* Due to the different focuses of the organizations, it is difficult to expedite a terminological assimilation. *"Even if the police are talking to the fire department, there is a big deviation in the terminology and consequently terms are perceived differently."* (W2). Terminological differences with other organizations, especially in the private sector, can be even greater. An example describes a misunderstanding about the number of people injured after a fire in a factory where 19 casualties were reported: *"People injured in the perception of the factory management, consist of 19 people who were only triaged by doctors but weren't necessarily injured."* Actually, in the understanding of the rescuers there were only *"two people whose health was affected."* (W2).

I5 and I4 mentioned that *personal biases* have a significant impact on the interpretation of given information. Mostly, members of the public with no professional expertise about the current situation tend to exaggerate or to understate their report about the current situation. For instance, one citizen reported about "*a major car accident*" which led to take actions by the local emergency medical services for seriously injured or even dead passengers, while it was just a minor car accident only with material damages (I5). I4, I5 reported about contrary cases, as well.

Within one workshop (W2) a firefighter reported about the problem of *losing and changing information* during the transmission between organizations. "*We got the information about several seriously injured kids, during the world youth day in Cologne, 2005. After conducting appropriate actions, we figured out that these kids were hardly injured at all"* The information changed, while it was transferred from the first responder via skilled and non-skilled organization members to the responsible medical service.

Besides loosing available information, there is sometimes a lack of information provided by infrastructure operators (e.g. energy network operators or transport services). These organizations do not necessarily inform proactively about further development, but they have to be asked directly: "*The other actors have a different perception because they concentrate on their problems and not on providing information*" (I15). In case of infrastructure operations they sometimes provide information with missing details such as the amount of affected households (I10): "*What broke down, how much of the energy network is out of work and how many people are affected?*" Many organizations provide their information by email or phone, which is another source of information that needs to be handled.

Further *media disruptions* in the field of retrieving information occur in operations management where liaison officers of the police usually cannot access information provided by the police intranet. They always have to ask by phone. For actors working in the field additional information is usually obtained from the control center (I3). For instance, in case of a fire they ask the control center how many people are registered at a certain building (I4): *"How many people are registered at that address? For example, we now have to match five people standing here in front of the house who say that they left the house. Okay, now we must assume that others are still in the house. In such incidents the registration office is probably the most important source"*.

Conditions for Improvisation

We found several conditions and ways for improvisation. Beginning with findings about the degree of improvisation, the use of official systems and non-digital maps, we also detected issues concerning privacy, trustworthiness, time pressure and cooperation which influence the improvisational practice.

Improvisation usually does not occur in the pure form: "*There is always a mishmash of formal structures and informal ways*" (I1). As said by the actors, structures are important to handle basic tasks and flexibility is necessary to react to very dynamic situations: "*We have standard measures and things, which we decide at the spur of the moment.*" (I13). Besides the fact that they have "*a very clear communication structure*" (I2), they do not consider themselves as an civil servant, such as an administrative officer or a taxman: "*We [police] and the fire department work in a way which is different from all other authorities: We do not have a litany that we follow strictly, because then we would be lost.*"(I2). This shows that they calculate with a certain degree of improvisation contrary to detailed planned processes that just need to be executed. The decisions on the field level do not just base on regulations, but on assessments of the situation and are done "*within the given clearances*" (I9).

To decide what to do and how to deal with a certain situation, much important information is necessary. Some of the information to fulfil the work tasks in operations management is provided by "official" information systems. In major catastrophic events or in case of weather alerts these internal information resources are enriched by many external, *informal information resources*, which are necessary in various situations. Therefore, actors sometimes use about "*40 windows which have to be observed*" for different applications and websites to have an overview of the current state and to handle the situation appropriately (I5). This external information includes webcams, water levels, weather forecasts, wind directions, storm warnings and traffic service. Much of that information is provided on different websites – but not in a compulsory "official" application – with the result that actors have to improvise and search by themselves.

Besides information from third party providers, internal information such as *digital and non-digital maps* is of central importance for all actors to plan and to deal with major catastrophic events. Emergencies always have a geographic reference, therefore the operations management and the crisis management group gather related information on maps. Besides the utilization of technical supported maps, actors also use different non-digital maps: "*We always have to work redundantly to prevent chaos during technical breakdowns. We have to be able to proceed anytime*" (I9). In addition, the representation of the resources and their availability are only maintained on non-digital maps (I15). But this always depends on the given incident and how likely a breakdown is.

Apart from the fact that actors are interested in information of other organizations, *privacy* for their current state is required: "*Maps got nothing to do with anyone else but us, because we do not reproduce the current state but rather try to imagine what will happen next*" (I9). Due to the strategic and tactical operations, maps are kept locked up and cannot be passed to other agencies or organizations. Based on available information, the operations management does not just reproduce the current state but tries to foresee how the situation will develop. It considers what could happen next in order to derive actions and minimize the resulting damage: "*In the beginning we have to follow up the damage. [...] Our aim is to be in advance of the incidents*" (I9).

Trustworthiness is directly connected to reliability and plays a significant role in sharing or retrieving information, especially for those kinds of information which have high impact on complex and lifesaving decisions: "*The safest information is the one I have seen by myself*". I2, I3 and I10 count on "*good human relations*" (I3) to members of other organizations in order to ensure reliability and to accelerate information verification processes. For example, I9 mentioned that "*good connections to police members*" help to trust on information accuracy and to better understand each other. However, "*people who put themselves in the limelight*" (I4), even from the same organization, can affect this relationships negatively. Because of the need for good relationships, a lot of informal contacts and relationships have been established alongside predefined communication lines, especially in Siegen-Wittgenstein. "*Police officers directly talk to members of the leading group via mobile phone and don't take the way via section officers as it should be*" (I2). This can lead to a significant problem: The loss of information. Furthermore, when receiving information from non-trusted information providers such as citizens (W3), each organization starts its individual verification process. "*If we receive a non-reliable emergency call, we will just wait for a second call*" (I3), "*we react on on-scene information from citizens but we will immediately verify this information by experts*" (I1) or I12 and I22 stated that they use 'Qualified Interviews' to get appropriate information from non-experts.

"*For security reasons we need up-to-date development schemes and building plans*" (I21). This shows that *timeliness* is another important dimension of information. All participants point out that, especially for handling crisis situations, up-to-date information, e.g. on situation maps or contact lists (I1), become more essential. However the following statement shows a conflict to guarantee accurate, complete and timeliness information: "*The more stressful a situation becomes, the less information can be provided to others*" (I3). Furthermore, particularly in stressful situations, informal communication lines do not work anymore because everyone has to do what they are supposed to do (I15).

A wide range of emergency response actions shows that improvisation is *often a collaborative task*. To deal with an uncertain and changing environment during crisis situations, usually a great number of people are involved in gathering and analyzing data, decision-making and monitoring of implementations and consequences. Two quotations explain these practices. The first one from a policeman on operational level: "*We all have to get the big picture of the scene at first. Than we have to coordinate ourselves: finding appropriate ways of solving the problem together and then running these actions*" (I4). In addition, a member of a command center of an ENO said: *"[...] but if it's critical anywhere, you will willingly ask a colleague: 'What do you think about it? Give it the once-over.' The big advantage we have is that there are at least two of us sitting here, even twenty-four-seven.*" (I20). Focusing on crisis management group work, our study revealed that there are lots of improvisational actions. They especially occur during coordination processes between members of different agencies. To assess the potential impacts of present or future events, members of the group (usually police, fire department and county administration) share their knowledge within the group or – depending on the case – they have to consult external experts (e.g. members of the residents registration office to access numbers of occupants in case of a burning house). What we have seen is that gathering and analyzing situation information and decision-making is often performed cooperatively.

DISCUSSION

As shown in the results, no situation is equal to the other. Highly novel problems require ad hoc decision-making based on available information on the situation. This information is not necessarily available in the own organization. Especially during unique emergency events, many external resources need to be consulted. Finding and retrieving relevant information are still huge challenges for several reasons:

1. *Information is mostly distributed*: Even routine situations require managers to retrieve various information, which is often not necessarily available at the own organization. Managers have to access several kinds of external information resources at different organizations (e.g. weather services, electricity providers, logistic companies, etc.) via different media channels (e.g. phone, internet, face-to-face, etc.). During non-routine events this typically takes place in an ad-hoc manner.
2. *Missing awareness about information available*: Our study revealed that current inter-organizational emergency management lacks instruments, which distribute meta-information about suitable and available data or about resources at external organizations.
3. *Accessibility of Information/Policy Issues*: Because of technical shortcomings (e.g. missing appropriate interfaces) and policy issues at the information providers, retrieving relevant information is either time-consuming or even not a possible task in many cases.
4. *Handling of information uncertainties*: In reality data is seldom absolutely reliable. Looking at current decision-making processes, it shows that shortcomings exist in providing accurate visual depictions of critical data sets from different domains.
5. *Terminology issues*: Different symbols on situation maps or different technical terms, for instance, make it difficult to share information and knowledge between organizations, especially when they originate from other domains.
6. *Perceiving interdependencies between information:* Certain Information resources are possibly only relevant in conjunction with others (e.g. formation of smoke and wind direction and strength). Those interdependencies have to be identified to obtain any necessary information.

Even if these challenges partially agree with earlier research findings on coordination practices in emergency response management [2] and previously identified challenges in designing interactive systems for emergency response [5], our study underlines their relevance on an inter-organizational level. In the following sections we will respond to these issues with regards to existing practices that we identified in our study.

To overcome the shortcoming, that not every piece of information needed is officially available or accessible at current emergency management systems, actors have developed several strategies. For example, by using the WWW, actors have bookmarked websites with additional information resources such as webcams, to check weather conditions or the water level statuses of nearby rivers. Our study shows that technophile people, rather than people with less computer skills, have performed these strategies. Taking a closer look on these information compositions shows that they are arranged highly individual. Actors have retrieved only those information resources, which are suitable for their individual tasks.

Gathering and analyzing data, assessing the potential impacts of events and executing related actions are main activities of most of the actors we have described in the antecedent sections. What we have seen, when unanticipated events or unclear situation information emerge, actors often consult colleagues or other experts to collaboratively assess the information. Our study reveals that situation maps are essential artifacts to fulfill these tasks. Analyzing data with colleagues with the same knowledge background, in a same room (e.g. a control center) and therefore with a common situation map, usually works well. However, challenges arise when it comes to sharing situation information with geographical distributed participants or even with actors of different agencies. It can be explained with the aid of two examples: In early phases of emergency events members of emergency response organizations are not necessarily at the same location to consult about the latest events. For instance, members of crisis management groups call each other from different locations so that they are not able to use a joint situation map. Even situation maps at the control center differ from maps of on-scene commanders of the same organization, therefore synchronizing missing information shapes communication. This problem gets more significant when actors of different agencies with different situation maps are involved. Typically, these maps only visualize agency-related information and use different terminologies and symbols. This circumstance makes collaborative assessment actions even more complicated.

Definitions about responsibilities and formal communication channels in organizations usually work well and are important for a smooth interaction within the agency. However, the results show that structures can collapse, e.g. due to the failure of technology, outdated phone lists or human reasons. In this circumstance as well as in urgent emergency situations it might be necessary to diverge from rigid standards and to use unofficial channels instead. The same applies to inter-organizational communication, for instance, when a responsible liaison officer is not available for any reason. Induced by the different structures of the two investigated counties, the significance of informal communication differs strongly. The rural structure of Siegen-Wittgenstein and the mainly voluntarily organized agencies entail that many of the members know each other. As a consequence, communication channels are much more informal than in the more urban county Rhein-Erft. These differences emphasize that both formal and informal communication channels are equally important for cooperative work. To support both there is a need for a better awareness about the structures of involved organizations as well as the availability of suitable contact persons including capabilities for contacting.

Accessibility to required information resources is a big challenge actors have to deal with. On the one hand users do not know what information is available and where to find it and on the other hand policy issues prevent the access to certain information. A reason that information cannot be found by the user is that they are mostly distributed and not listed in a central directory. However, the results of our study show that actors often consult the same or similar information services during a certain situation, no matter to which organization they belong to. Hence, the question arises whether it is helpful to have a central repository for information resources with access to actors from any organization. Accessibility restrictions due to policy issues are more complex to handle (e.g. non-public information, such as the degree of power supply for a certain area might be helpful for agencies during specific emergency situations). Obtaining such information through official channels can be extremely time-consuming. That is why there is a demand for negotiation processes to allow for a fast access to necessary information in crisis situations, but also sufficient protection to prevent malpractice.

SUPPORTING IMPROVISATION WORK IN INTER-ORGANIZATIONAL CRISIS MANAGEMENT

One of the fundamental design requirements for supporting improvisation work for the inter-organizational level is to create a complementing information infrastructure, not a tool to replace existing IT. Technologically, this can be implemented relying on a service-oriented architecture that allows to connect to the existing IT infrastructures in the participating organizations. But with regard to the functionality we need to support improvisation work at the inter-organizational level we can outline five specific implications for the design that focus on geographically visualized data on information and collaboration resources:

Aggregation and Visualization of External and Various Information

We have seen that, besides internal information, information from other organizations is needed to get a appropriate picture of ongoing and future events and activities. Most information is spatial (e.g. emergency plans for buildings or areas with electricity breakdowns). We suggest an enhanced map-based information repository that allows including different types of internal and external information (e.g. place marks, weather information, specific geo-referenced infrastructure maps, etc.). To avoid information overload, the user should be able to save specific map compositions. As confidence in information is crucial, it is also important to distinguish between information sources (particularly internal vs. external) and degrees of information reliability.

Individualization of information Compositions

We have observed that actors of emergency response organizations adapt information compositions due to their personal needs. Users need instruments that enable them (technophile and technophobe) to customize information compositions in real-time. Users should have the opportunity to easily show and hide information resources on the map, to add additional and new information resources to the map (that may also be provided by external web services), and to add place marks with annotations at specific locations in the map.

Supporting Collaborative Situation Assessment

The common practice to perform situation assessments collaboratively needs an explicit inter-organizational support. Actors need be able to share map-based compositions of information resources with other actors in a very controlled way. Visualization and interaction should be possible in various environments and locations, e.g. from a notebook at home, via mobile phones at the incident location or on a large screen in the crisis management center. Additional communication channels need to support the collaborative analysis of the information on the map, e.g. instant messaging services or audio channels. Because current situations can change rapidly, all participants require the option to modify information compositions on the map approximately in real time. Issues of information rights may occur while sharing information and annotations; we address that below.

Supporting Informal and Formal Communication

Both, informal and formal (along official roles, usually recorded/documented) communication channels need to be supported. Actors should be able to spontaneously decide which ones to use. For a better support of formal communication the actor has to be aware of organizational structures of his own as well as of other involved organizations. In an ongoing incident, it is often not clear which organization is reacting how, who is on duty and how she can be contacted. Redundant and outdated information can be avoided by providing a central repository. For informal communication it is more important to know who is in reach and working on a subject I need information about. Organizational structures are less relevant, but personal relations are: It may be good to know who works 'nearby' (meaning spatial, but also social distance) the contact I am interested in. Offering a large variety of communication channels may be as important as offering options for an informed choice among them.

Accessibility of information resources

Each of the organizations involved are using or hosting information resources, or being an information resource by producing information (e.g. the police 'produces' road closures). All that may be relevant for other organizations as well. For improvisational work, it is necessary to provide mutual awareness of the information available: It requires a shared information repository where proper services can be registered, described and rated by the user. The information resources could be selected as required by the situation and could be integrated into the intermediate infrastructure. Some of this information is subject to (e.g. for copyright or security reasons) restricted organizational access policies. For supporting improvisational work, it is not only enough to map these policies to access rights at design time, but to provide interactive access rights to allow for unforeseen, but necessary information flows. Computer Supported Access Control may support spontaneous information needs while enabling the user to attempt access and to legitimate it during use [19]. We are experimenting with various access control mechanisms to simplify the access in crisis situations but without undermining necessary policies. In a first step three different types of access controls will be implemented:

1. *Role based access control*: The access rights for each information resource are predefined and based on the user's role. A user can either have access by definition or not.
2. *Gatekeeper access control*: This more flexible approach also predefines access rights. However, users without assigned access rights can request those from a so-called gatekeeper who has the right to allocate access to unauthorized users or a certain time period.
3. *Break-glass access control*: This concept enables a flexible and fast access to the required information. Even if a user has no access by definition, he is able to get access by breaking a symbolic glass. Thus, there is no need to request access privileges from an authority but every access is documented. That means that the user must be aware of possible consequences when "breaking the glass" unauthorized.

CONCLUSION

In medium to large crisis situations, the pressure on emergency response organizations (police, firefighters, administration, etc.) to collaborate with each other effectively increases. While some aspects of coping and recovery work are covered by negotiated procedures (sometimes prescribed by law) and trained routines, the variety of influencing factors and framing conditions always leads to a need for improvisation also at an inter-organizational level. Improvisation has been previously addressed as a topic [1,9,10,11,12], but our study was able to show additional difficulties we encounter at the inter-organizational level. In our study of the improvisation practices during larger power outages between police, firefighters, public administration and an electricity provider in two counties, we showed that improvisation work suffers on the one hand from a lack of options for sharing information among the organizations, but also from a lack of awareness of information about the activities of others, and from a lack of collaboration in consolidating and interpreting the information available. If external organizations required explanations about established and successful inner-organizational practices for a successful crisis management (and thus opened up for external critique), there would not only be a severe possibility for misunderstanding (even the organizational structures and strategies of frequent collaborators like police and firefighters are significantly diverse) but there would also be concerns about becoming vulnerable against legal or political claims.

Considering this aspect, it does not make sense to support inter-organizational improvisation work in crisis management with IT concepts that require centralized, aligned procedures dominating the practices of the individual organizations. It is more appropriate to offer a complementary infrastructure that allows maintaining informal information sources and manages informal collaboration opportunities (e.g. for situation assessment) that can as well be individualized/localized. The exchange of information regarding own status, resources and measures is also very valuable, but needs to be thoughtfully protected with interactive (gatekeeper model, break-glass model) access rights that allow easy information sharing when necessary.

As a next step, we are going to develop such a complementary infrastructure based on geographically visualized data on information and collaboration resources necessary for improvisation, and with additional support for ad-hoc sharing of information. We also plan to integrate citizens as potential crisis managers on their own behalf to the scenario (as also requested in [13]). The most important experience resulting from our studies here was: No matter how much control and preparedness we wish for in the event of a crisis, we need to acknowledge, support and take pride in our abilities to improvise.

ACKNOWLEDGMENTS

The project 'InfoStrom' is funded by the German Federal Ministry for Education and Research (No. 13N10712).

REFERENCES

1. Adrot, A., Robey, D.: Information Technology, Improvisation and Crisis Response: Review of Literature and Proposal for Theory, *Proc. of 14th AMCIS* (2008).
2. Chen, R., Sharman, R., Rao, H.R. and Upadhyaya, SJ: Coordination in Emergency Response Management. *Communications of the ACM 51*, 5, (2008), 66-73.
3. Ciborra, C.: Notes on improvisation and time in organizations. *Accounting, Management and Information Technologies 9*, 2 (1999), 77-94.
4. Ciborra, C.: Improvisation and Information Technology. *Proc. of ICIS*, Philadelphia, PA, (1996), 369-80.
5. Kyng, M., Nielsen, E. T. and Kirstensen, M.: Challenges in Designing Interactive Systems for Emergency Response. *Proc. of DIS* (2006), 301-310.
6. Landgren, J.: Making action visible in time-critical work. *Proc. CHI '06,* ACM-Press, (2006), 201-210.
7. Lindström, S. and Pettersson, M.: Supporting ad-hoc re-planning and shareability at large-scale events. *Proc. of GROUP*, (2010), 245-252.
8. Lindblom, C.E.: The science of "muddling through". *Public administration review 19*, 2, (1959), 79-88.
9. Mendonça, D.: Decision support for improvisation in response to extreme events: Learning from the response to the 2001 World Trade Center attack. *Decision Support Systems 43*, 3, (2007), 952-967.
10. Mendonça, D., Jefferson, T., & Harrald, J.: Collaborative Adhocracies and Mix-and-Match Technologies in Emergency Management. *Communications of the ACM 50*, 3, (2007), 44-49.
11. Mendonça, D. J. and Wallace, W. A.: Cognitive Model of Improvisation in Emergency Management. *IEEE Transactions on Systems, Man and Cybernetics, Part A: Systems and Humans 36*, 4, (2007), 547-561.
12. Moorman, C. and Miner, A.S.: Organizational improvisation and organizational memory. In *The Academy of Management Review 23*, 4, (1998), 698-723.
13. Palen, L. and Lui, S. B. Citizen communication in crisis: Anticipating a future of ICT-supported public participation. In *Proc. of CHI '07,* ACM-Press, (2007), 727-736.
14. Perry, L. T.: Strategic improvising: How to formulate and implement competitive strategies in concert. *Organization Dynamics 19*, (1991), 51-64.
15. Quarantelli, E. L.: Disaster Crisis Management: A summary of research findings, *Journal of Management Studies 25*, 4, (1988), 373-385.
16. Randall, D. W., Harper, R. H. R. and Rouncefield, M.: *Fieldwork for Design: Theory and Practice*. Springer, London (2007).
17. Select Bipartisan Committee to Investigate the Preparation for and Response to Hurricane Katrina. A Failure of Initiative (2006), http://www.gpoaccess.gov/katrinareport/fullreport.pdf.
18. Stein, E.W.: Improvisation as Model for Real-Time Decision Making. In Burstein et al. (Eds.) *Supporting Real Time Decision Making*. Annals of Information Systems, 13(1), (2011), 13-32.
19. Stevens, G. and Wulf, V.: Computer-supported access control. *ACM Trans. Comput.-Hum. Interact. 16*, 3, (2009), Article 12.
20. Strauss, A.: Qualitative Analysis for Social Scientists, Cambridge press (1987).
21. Turoff, M., Van de Walle, B., Hiltz, S.: Emergency Response Information Systems: Past, Present, and Future. In Van De Walle, B., Turoff, M., Hiltz, S.R. (Eds.) *Information Systems for Emergency Management*. Armonk, NY: M.E. Sharpe (2010), 369-387.
22. Waugh, W. L. and Streib, G.: Collaboration and Leadership for Effective Emergency Management. *Public Administration Review 66* (2006), 131-140.
23. Weick, K. E.: Drop your tools: An allegory for organizational studies. *Administrative Science Quarterly 41* (1996), 301-313.
24. Wiedenhoefer, T.; Reuter, C.; Ley, B. & Pipek, V.: Inter-organizational crisis management infrastructures for electrical power breakdowns. *Proc. of 8th ISCRAM* (2011).

Communitysourcing: Engaging Local Crowds to Perform Expert Work Via Physical Kiosks

Kurtis Heimerl[1], Brian Gawalt[1], Kuang Chen[1], Tapan S. Parikh[2], Björn Hartmann[1]
University of California, Berkeley – Computer Science Division[1], School of Information[2]
{kheimerl,gawalt,kuangc,bjoern}@cs.berkeley.edu, parikh@ischool.berkeley.edu

ABSTRACT
Online labor markets, such as Amazon's Mechanical Turk, have been used to crowdsource simple, short tasks like image labeling and transcription. However, expert knowledge is often lacking in such markets, making it impossible to complete certain classes of tasks. In this work we introduce an alternative mechanism for crowdsourcing tasks that require specialized knowledge or skill: *communitysourcing* — the use of physical kiosks to elicit work from specific populations. We investigate the potential of communitysourcing by designing, implementing and evaluating *Umati: the communitysourcing vending machine*. Umati allows users to earn credits by performing tasks using a touchscreen attached to the machine. Physical rewards (in this case, snacks) are dispensed through traditional vending mechanics. We evaluated whether communitysourcing can accomplish expert work by using Umati to grade Computer Science exams. We placed Umati in a university Computer Science building, targeting students with grading tasks for snacks. Over one week, 328 unique users (302 of whom were students) completed 7771 tasks (7240 by students). 80% of users had never participated in a crowdsourcing market before. We found that Umati was able to grade exams with 2% higher accuracy (at the same price) or at 33% lower cost (at equivalent accuracy) than traditional single-expert grading. Mechanical Turk workers had no success grading the same exams. These results indicate that communitysourcing can successfully elicit high-quality expert work from specific communities.

Author Keywords
Crowdsourcing; Kiosks; Ubiquitous Computing; CSCW

ACM Classification Keywords
H.5.2 Information Interfaces and Presentation: User Interfaces - Graphical User Interfaces

General Terms
Design, Human Factors, Experimentation

Permission to make digital or hard copies of all or part of this work for personal or classroom use is granted without fee provided that copies are not made or distributed for profit or commercial advantage and that copies bear this notice and the full citation on the first page. To copy otherwise, or republish, to post on servers or to redistribute to lists, requires prior specific permission and/or a fee.
CHI'12, May 5-10, 2012, Austin, Texas, USA.
Copyright 2012 ACM 978-1-4503-1015-4/12/05...$10.00.

Figure 1. With Umati, the communitysourcing vending machine, users complete tasks on a touchscreen and receive non-monetary rewards.

INTRODUCTION
Crowdsourcing, the division and assignment of tasks to large, distributed groups of online users, has the potential to create new jobs, improve the efficiency of labor markets, and enable a wide variety of new applications. Researchers have demonstrated compelling new systems enabled by crowdsourcing, including applications that assist the blind with visual tasks [8] and that help writers to copy-edit prose [7]. Many crowdsourcing efforts leverage *microtask* markets, which provide platforms for posting and finding short tasks – frequently seconds to minutes long. One of the best-known markets, Amazon Mechanical Turk (MTurk), attracts thousands of employers [15] and has had hundreds of thousands of worker accounts [30].

One limitation of microtask markets is the difficulty of accessing groups with domain-specific skills or knowledge. The short work durations and small rewards attract specific user demographics [30], limiting the variety of knowledge and expertise available. In contrast, vertical online communities (such as graphic design site 99Designs [1] and Q&A site Stack Overflow [25]) successfully gather experts, but they must either focus on building and maintaining a community of volunteers [25], or on enticing experts with high rewards for complex tasks. These hurdles limit the potential for crowdsourcing of expert work.

To enable crowdsourcing of expert work for short duration tasks, we introduce the concept of *communitysourcing*. Communitysourcing deploys tasks on physical kiosks in specific locations that attract the right "crowds" (while repelling the wrong ones), and in contexts where people have

Figure 2. In our study, Umati was deployed in a public hallway. Students and other building occupants graded CS exam questions on Umati.

idle time ("cognitive surplus" [31]). Communitysourcing leverages the specific knowledge and skills of the targeted community; in return, it provides context- and community-specific rewards that users value more than money.

To explore the potential of communitysourcing, we asked the following research questions:

- Can communitysourcing successfully enlist new user groups in crowd work?
- Can communitysourcing outperform existing crowdsourcing methods for expert, domain-specific tasks?
- How does communitysourcing compare to traditional forms of labor, in terms of quality and cost?

We explored these questions by designing, implementing and evaluating a specific communitysourcing instance: *Umati: the communitysourcing vending machine* (see Figure 1). We built Umati by modifying a commercial vending machine. On Umati, instead of inserting money, users select and perform tasks on a high-resolution touch screen. Earned credits can be used to choose and buy items — an internal computer controls the motors that operate each of the vending arms.

We tested Umati with a Computer Science exam grading task. Grading exams is a time consuming, high-volume job that requires significant domain expertise for consistent, correct scoring of open-ended questions. Grading can also be partitioned into many small tasks. We placed Umati in the primary hallway in our Science building and filled it with snacks (see Figure 2). Exams covered introductory Computer Science topics in programming languages, algorithms, and data structures. Umati successfully targeted a specific population (81% of users were trained in Computer Science or Electrical Engineering) and achieved significant throughput: 328 participants graded 7771 exam answers in one week, for approximately $200 of snacks. Umati attracted new workers: 80% of participants had never participated in crowdsourcing before. We compared communitysourced grades against grades from a set of ten experts. Umati was able to exceed the accuracy of traditional single-expert grading (80.3% to 78.3% at the same price) or, alternatively, lower cost by 33% (at the same accuracy). For comparison, we also recruited graders on Mechanical Turk; these workers could not grade accurately ($<$ 25% agreement with our experts). Our results suggest that communitysourcing can exceed traditional expert performance in domains where online crowdsourcing fails.

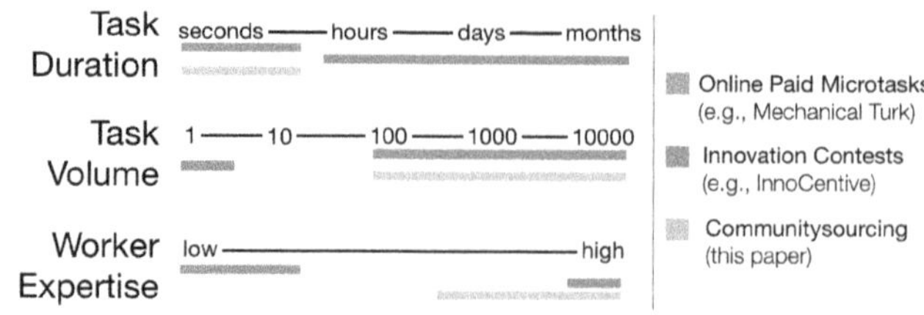

Figure 3. Communitysourcing occupies a unique position in the design space of crowdsourced work: it enables short, high-volume tasks that require high levels of expertise.

In this paper, we begin with a discussion of related work and describe the design space of communitysourcing. We motivate the choice of an exam grading task, then describe the implementation of Umati. We follow with a detailed evaluation of the system and conclude with a summary of our results and pointers to future work.

RELATED WORK

Communitysourcing touches on prior work in crowdsourcing, location-based computing, and kiosk systems. Our experimental task also relates to prior efforts in peer grading. We discuss each area in turn.

Crowdsourcing

Crowdsourcing and human computation are active areas of research inquiry; recent surveys describe a range of approaches [21, 28]. Projects have investigated incentives and game mechanics to motivate workers [35], new applications enabled by crowdsourcing [7, 8, 36], tools to develop crowdsourcing applications [22], and algorithms to coordinate crowd work [5, 6, 20]. Researchers have also contributed methodologies for conducting experiments using online labor [13, 19]. Much recent work focuses on increasing the complexity of work products created by a pool of unskilled workers through redundant microtasks. While communitysourcing also targets tasks of short duration, it recruits domain experts through appropriate choice of location and incentive (see Figure 3).

The dominant strategy to elicit expert responses or expert work online has been to build narrow, domain-specific communities. Topical communities of unpaid volunteers can provide high-quality answers to technical questions. However, creating successful online communities is an uncertain, labor-intensive proposition that requires leadership and constant monitoring [25]. Some online platforms succeed in eliciting paid expert work through competitions, e.g., InnoCentive for pharmaceutical research [2]; 99Designs for graphic design [1]; or TopCoder for programming [4]. Competitions are not appropriate for high-volume work because they strive to find the single best solution among the submissions. Communitysourcing can provide higher throughput by engaging many experts in short tasks.

Location-based Computing and Kiosks

Researchers have investigated the role of physical location in crowdsourcing. In participatory sensing [12], people collect and report data about their environment. For example, Creek Watch [18] uses GPS coordinates to crowdsource local watershed measurements. Multiple mobile start-up companies are delivering questions and tasks to members in a given location [11, 23]. In these systems, users first have to sign up for the service and agree to have their location tracked. Communitysourcing attracts people who already frequent a particular locale through a kiosk interface.

Computer-based kiosks have long been used for self-service ticketing, banking, and location-specific information, e.g., in museums [17]. Kiosks have also been deployed in rural areas and developing countries for Internet access, for unsupervised education [27, 32], and to aid communities in reconciliation after civil unrest [33]. Research has focused on security of such public systems [9] and on facilitating information transfer between kiosks and other computing devices [14, 16]. To our knowledge, Umati is the first kiosk that elicits work and rewards workers with physical items.

Education and Grading

Grading open-ended exams is an intrinsically subjective process. One common mechanism for consistently and efficiently grading open-ended questions is peer assessment. Students grading other students can lead to positive impacts on learning and attitude [24, 34]. Peer assessment is usually restricted to students within a particular course, and is prescribed by course staff. In Computer Science, prior work has investigated web-based peer review of assignments [10]. Averages of redundant peer scores are strongly correlated with teachers' scores [29]. Umati generalizes peer assessment beyond course boundaries: it enlists volunteers and provides physical rewards to incentivize participation.

DESIGN CONSIDERATIONS FOR COMMUNITYSOURCING

Successful communitysourcing depends on careful selection of tasks, locations, and incentives. This section discusses important design considerations for each category.

Task Selection

Communitysourcing is best suited for short-duration, high-volume tasks that require specialized knowledge or skills which are specific to a community, but widely available within that community. Simple tasks without expertise requirements (e.g., address verification or text transcription) are a better fit for generic crowdsourcing platforms like Mechanical Turk. Low-volume, long-duration expert jobs (like graphic design or programming) are better served by vertical online markets.

Some representative tasks well-suited for a communitysourcing approach include grading exams in academia, bug and tech support triage in technology companies, fact checking for journalism, and community-specific market research in bars or specialty shops. Short task durations enable users to work on a kiosk without ergonomic issues, and enable many user to participate. Public kiosks can potentially attract a large number of users, supporting, as well as requiring, a high task volume.

Location Selection

A communitysourcing system must target those locations where the required skills are prevalent. The locations must also repel those *without* the required knowledge. For instance, placing a kiosk in a bar could potentially target young men with market research tasks – but the kiosk would also be accessible by young women. A better location to exclusively target men would be their restroom at the bar.

The targeted community must also have some "cognitive surplus" [31] available for doing work. Practically, this means placing the kiosk in an area where people have spare time, e.g., in lounges, government office waiting rooms, or airports.

Reward Selection

Rewards must be interesting and valuable to the targeted community in the given location. For instance, airport travelers may value Wifi Internet access. In contrast, Wifi access has lower utility on a college campus, where free Internet is readily available. While cash is an obvious reward (consider an ATM-like kiosk), it has been shown that individuals can value items more than money in specific contexts and locations [26].

COMMUNITYSOURCING IN ACTION

For our deployment, we chose exam grading as an experimental task, a university department as the location, and snacks as rewards. This section briefly justifies these design choices in light of the earlier design guidelines for communitysourcing.

Task: Grading exams is a painful, high-volume task for teaching staff. An individual student answer can be graded quickly, but large courses with hundreds of students generate thousands of answers. While people outside an academic discipline are unlikely to possess the requisite knowledge to grade open-ended problems, redundant peer grades are strongly correlated with expert scores [29], suggesting that students can grade each others' assignments and exams.

Location: College campuses commonly assign buildings to disciplines (departments). These buildings rarely attract visitors outside the discipline. Our Computer Science (CS) building supports mainly CS classes, along with a few unrelated events. We placed our kiosk in front of the major lecture hall in the CS building, an area where students often wait for class to begin, maximizing the cognitive surplus.

Reward: Food is the most common reward given to entice students to participate in campus events. Companies commonly provide pizza to bring students to recruitment events; teachers bring candy to class sections to entice participation. We decided to use snacks as our reward. This choice also impacted the physical design of our kiosk. The most common system for distributing snacks is the ubiquitous vending machine; it is familiar and clearly communicates the nature of the rewards being distributed.

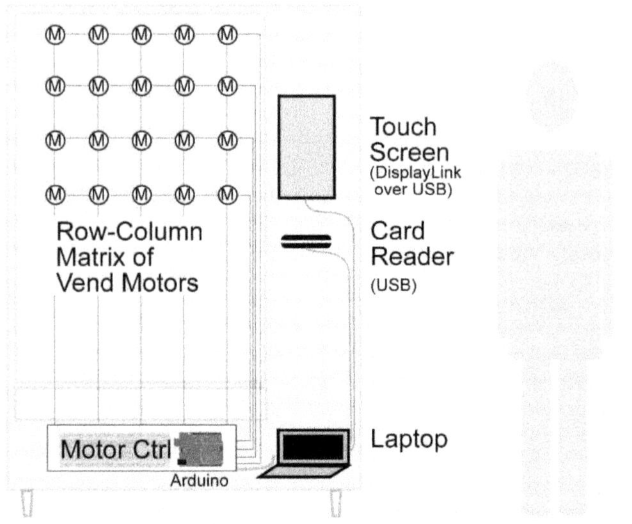

Figure 4. Umati uses an internal laptop to control a touchscreen, USB card reader, and the vending motors. Users complete tasks on the touchscreen for rewards from the machine.

These design decisions guided our implementation of *Umati: the communitysourcing vending machine*, as described in the next section.

UMATI: SYSTEM IMPLEMENTATION

The Umati system comprises custom vending hardware; a generic software platform for work tasks; and specific task user interfaces. We describe each in turn.

Hardware: Hacking a Vending Machine

Umati is a modified commercial vending machine (specifically, a 1986 Snackshop 4600, Figure 1). We removed all legacy vending equipment (the bill exchanger, coin reader, keypad interface, analog motor-control circuit boards), leaving just the vending shelves and dispensing mechanism. We installed a touchscreen and keycard reader on the front of the machine, which provide the primary user interface (see Figure 4). Users must first swipe their magnetic strip ID card (given to all students, faculty, and staff on campus); card IDs enable Umati to distinguish users, though our prototype does not link card IDs to users' names. Users complete tasks on the touch screen interface which is connected to an internally mounted laptop.

Rewards are dispensed through programmatic control of the vending mechanisms. The shelves use metal spirals driven by DC motors. The motor leads form a row-column matrix: when a particular row lead is powered and a column lead grounded, the motor at the intersection of row and column spins, dispensing an item. We attached the row-column end points to relays controlled by an Arduino microcontroller, and programmed the microcontroller to respond to vend requests from the laptop over a serial link. Motors spin uniformly enough to vend items with open-loop control, powering motors for a fixed amount of time.

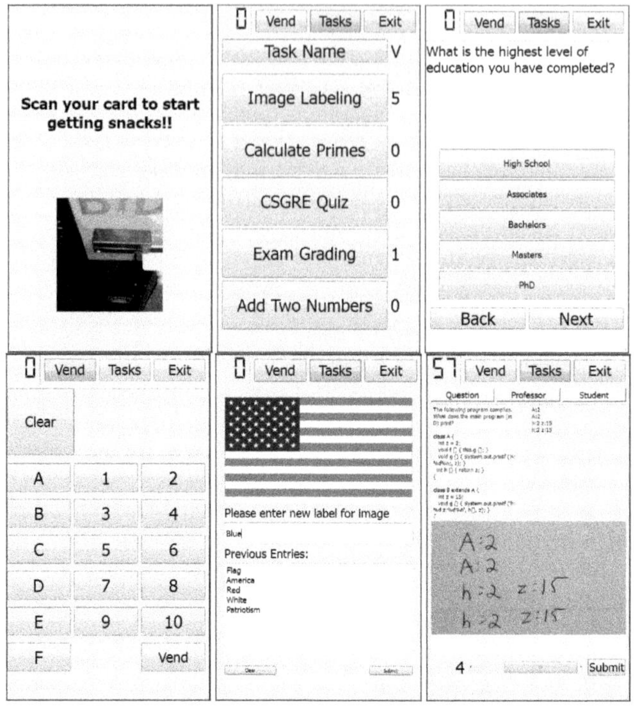

Figure 5. Umati's UI, clockwise from top left: introductory attract screen, task selection, survey task, grading task, image labeling task, and vending interface.

Software: Maximizing a Small Touch Screen

We developed the Umati software using Python and the PyQt4 UI toolkit. Umati's architecture was designed as a generic task platform: each task and its user interface are written as plug-ins to a work management system. As a result, Umati supports many task types besides exam grading.

When the machine is idle, it displays an *attract screen*: a looping video demonstrating how to log in by swiping an ID card (see Figure 5). After swiping, users are presented with the *Task Selection* screen, allowing them to choose their task. If there is just one available task, the selection screen is bypassed and users are immediately presented with that task. The user's earned credits are shown in the top left, and stored across work sessions. When a user wishes to cash in their credits, they switch to the *Vending* interface which provides a software keypad to select the tray of the desired item.

Tasks

We have implemented a variety of tasks for Umati: math tests, CS GRE questions, surveys, exam grading, and image labeling. Some of these task interfaces are shown in Figure 5. For our evaluation, we tested just two: surveys and grading.

Surveys: The survey task constructs an interface from an external XML file that defines questions and multiple choice answer sets. For our deployment, Umati had a basic demographic survey which collected age, department, educational status, and prior exposure to crowdsourcing. Every user was required to complete this survey before starting another task on Umati.

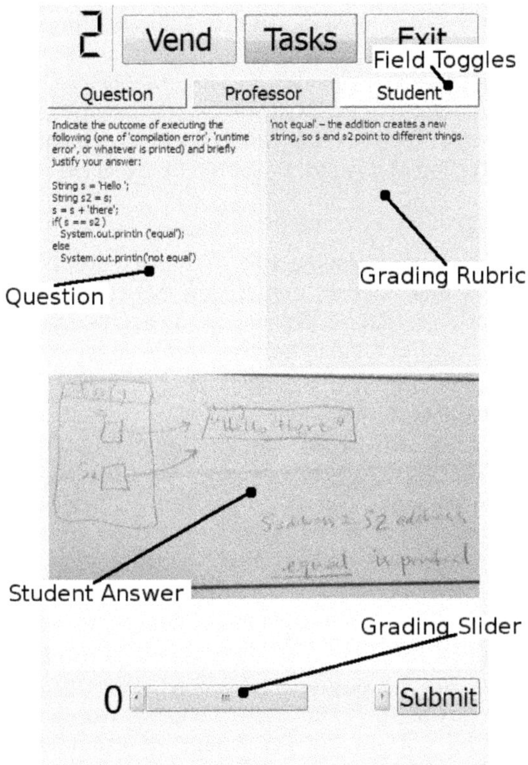

Figure 6. The Umati grading interface shows a question, an answer key, and an image of a student response. Workers assign points with a slider.

Grading: The grading interface presents three panels of information simultaneously to the participant: the question, the instructor's answer key, and a student answer (see Figure 6). Each panel can be opened and closed using toggle buttons on the top row, to maximize the limited screen space. Each panel also allows panning by dragging and zooming by double-tapping. Grades are gathered on a numeric scale: the user enters the grade using a slider widget. Upon submission, Umati presents another student answer *to the same question*, if one is available. This allows a user to memorize the question and answer key, accelerating their grading of student answers. It also supports grading privacy, as graders cannot easily grade all of a specific student's answers. Users cannot grade the same exam answer twice.

Spam Detection: Incorrect or low-quality responses ("spam") are common for crowdsourcing; workers often complete tasks quickly and with little thought in order to maximize their earnings. To account for this tendency, Umati implements a simple spam detection system. Each task definition includes "gold standard" tasks, comprised of a task with a known correct response. If a user fails two of these tasks, that user is logged out and their ID is blacklisted from future use. Inserting such checks is a well-established technique for improving the quality of crowdsourced work [19].

EVALUATION

Our evaluation sought to answer three primary research questions about communitysourcing: Can it enlist new user groups in crowd work? Can it outperform existing crowdsourcing methods? And can it match more traditional approaches, in terms of cost and accuracy?

Study Design

We created a set of Computer Science exams with answers. Three groups of participants graded the exams: users of our vending machine (Umatiers), Mechanical Turk workers (Turkers), and a group of former or potential Computer Science teaching assistants (Experts).

Exam Corpus

We created a custom exam from prior mid-term questions of our Computer Science department's second-semester undergraduate course, *CS2*. The exam was comprised of 13 questions covering basic complexity theory, object-oriented programming, search algorithms, and bit operations. Eight undergraduate students were recruited as test-takers. These students had recently completed CS2 or were enrolled at the time of the study. Students completed the exam on paper. For our *gold standard* tasks, we added an exam completed using the instructor's grading rubric, giving us question/answer pairs that are always correct. These answers were used for our spam detection algorithm. 105 sample exam answers were generated in total. Test-takers received either a 5 USD gift card, or could make an equivalent charitable donation.

Common Grading Instructions

Graders in all conditions were asked to assign 0 to 4 points for each question. The Instructor's answer key was used as the grading rubric. The rubric provided no instructions for assigning partial credit. While all questions required computer science knowledge to produce a correct answer, they varied in the amount of knowledge required to assess that answer. Some were *simple*, requiring only basic pattern matching for identifying correct answers. Others were *open-ended*, requiring a deeper understanding of the underlying material. Assigning partial credit for incomplete answers always required domain-specific knowledge.

For the exam we tested, five questions were simple, while eight were open-ended. An example open-ended question and grading rubric follows:

> *Q: Briefly explain the difference between a (Java) instance variable and a (Java) class variable.*
>
> *A: Each object has its own distinct copy of an instance variable. But all the objects in a class share just one 'copy' of a class variable.*

Paper exams had a defined answer box for each question. We used Shreddr [3] to extract scanned answers from the exams. These images of answers were shown in the grading interface (Figure 6). Three sets of participants then graded the exams: 1) Umati users, 2) Mechanical Turk users, and 3) experts recruited from a pool of qualified students. These conditions are described in more detail below.

Grading on Umati

We deployed Umati outside the main Computer Science lecture hall for one week. This lecture hall is primarily used for undergraduate courses, although graduate students, staff, faculty and visitors also frequent this centrally located ground-floor area. Users received no other introduction to the system or tasks besides the looping video instructing them to swipe their card.

The machine was loaded with $200 worth of candy. Users earned one credit per graded answer, and five for completing the survey. Most items were priced at 20 credits (with some priced at 10 and 30). In a small pilot study, we found that users completed roughly 20 tasks in five minutes. We estimated that five minutes was the maximum amount of time users would be willing to spend in front of a vending machine at any one time. Candy was purchased from a local bulk wholesale store at an average of 45 cents per item. At this price, Umatiers were paid 2.25 cents per answer, in candy.

Grading on Mechanical Turk

Workers on Amazon's Mechanical Turk (Turkers) graded the same exam questions and answers, on a web interface that was similar to the Umati touch screen interface; workers saw the question, the answer key, and the student's answer. Each Human Intelligence Task (HIT) consisted of grading all 9 answers to the same question (8 students and the experimenter's gold standard), paying 23 cents (2.6 cents / answer). We posted 130 HITs on Turk, obtaining 10 sets of grades for each student answer.

Turkers answered the same gold standard questions as Umati users, and we applied a similar spam detection algorithm. We present two sets of results: 1) all Turkers (regardless of gold standard performance); and 2) the subset of Turkers that passed the spam filter (failing at most one gold standard question). As with Umati, any answers provided before a second failed question are used in our analysis.

After a first set of workers completed our grading HITs, we also attempted to recruit more knowledgeable Turkers through a qualification test. Workers had to pass the test before they could grade exam answers. The test comprised five multiple choice questions on computational complexity and Java. For example:

What is the Big-O run-time of the following algorithm?

```
function(arg1, arg2):
  return arg1+arg2
```

A: $O(1)$ B: $O(logn)$ C: $O(n)$ D: $O(nlogn)$ E: $O(n^2)$

For these qualified Turkers we offered 25 cents per set of 9 grades (2.8 cents /answer).

Grading By Experts

Ten former or potential CS teaching assistants graded the exam corpus on paper. These graders included: one graduate instructor for *CS 2*, one high-scoring undergraduate (received an A in *CS 2*), and eight CS PhD students. All had prior teaching experience. Each participant was paid 25 USD in Amazon credit to grade all 105 answers.

At our university, only graduate students are allowed to grade exams. Graduate students earn over 38 dollars per hour, when including basic tuition and fee remission. On average, experts graded 115 answers per hour, for an effective rate of 34 cents per answer. All of the expert graders passed the gold-standard spam detection algorithm, as should be expected.

Measures

Grading is inherently subjective — even experts can disagree. To enable meaningful comparisons between our different conditions, we define dependent measures that compare *grade distributions* and *agreement with median expert scores*.

Comparing Grade Distributions

For both crowdsourced grading methods, Umati and Mechanical Turk, we compute a Chi Squared test statistic across the 105 exam answers to determine if the distribution of crowdsourced grades in either condition differs significantly from the expert distribution.

Grade Agreement

To measure the grading accuracy of our approach, we use the median of all expert graders (*median expert grade*) as the "correct" grade for a student's answer. We then compute *grade agreement* as the percentage of exam answers for which the median Umati and Turk grades match the median expert grade.

The status quo is to use a single expert grader, not the median of multiple graders. To investigate the relationship between grading accuracy and the cost of recruiting additional graders, we randomly sample (with replacement) subsets from each distribution of graders (expert, Umati, and Turk). For instance, we sample a single expert grader from the expert distribution, and compare that to the median expert grade for all exam answers. Similarly, we also sample subpopulations (for instance, seven Turkers), take the median of their grade distribution, and compare that to the ("correct") median expert grade for all exam answers. This is repeated 1000 times to compute the *subgroup grade agreement* (e.g., between seven Turkers and all ten experts).

Results

We report descriptive usage results, comparisons of the experimental conditions, and qualitative observations.

Umati Users

328 participants graded 7771 exam answers on Umati in one week. Figure 7 shows self-reported demographic data from the survey. The users were primarily undergraduate computer scientists. 80% of Umati users had never previously participated in any online crowdsourcing activity (showing that Umati engaged new users in crowdsourcing). Users who successfully completed at least one task had a median usage time of 4 minutes, completing an average of 16 tasks. The most active user (or group, see below) worked continuously for more than an hour, completing 85 tasks in a row. Several users completed all 105 of the grading tasks. 61 users (19%) were blacklisted by the system for failing gold standard tasks.

Filters	Participants	%	Tasks Completed	Task %
Total	328	100%	7771	100%
Undergraduates	263	80%	6297	81%
Graduates	39	12%	943	12%
Other (Professors, Visitors, Staff)	26	8%	531	7%
Computer Science	234	71%	5977	77%
Electrical Engineering	34	10%	485	6%
Other/Not Affiliated	60	18%	1309	17%
Had Not Crowdsourced	262	80%	5933	76%
Had Crowdsourced	66	20%	1838	24%
Knows about Crowdsourcing	216	66%	4469	58%
Does Not Know About Crowdsourcing	112	34%	3302	42%

Figure 7. Descriptive statistics for one week of Umati use.

The high failure rate may be a consequence of the machine's novelty: users may have explored the interface without understanding the consequences of incorrect answers.

81% (268) of Umati users majored in Computer Science or Electrical Engineering; both groups are required to take *CS 2*. Our system was able to effectively engage our target population and complete a large number of tasks. This demonstration of Umati's ability to target crowdsourcing work to hundreds of unique, expert users over the span of just one week is a primary result of our work. We also note that these numbers were achieved despite limited resources: twice, our vending machine was emptied of snacks in less than two days; we refilled once. Effectively, the machine ran for four of the seven days.

Mechanical Turk Users

We gathered 1050 grades in three days using Mechanical Turk. 46 unique Turkers graded exams, with 16 (35%) failing the spam detection (incorrectly grading two or more *gold standard* questions). While we offered higher wages to workers who passed the CS qualification, no workers successfully qualified during our experiment. We conclude that a qualification exam is not an efficient mechanism for attracting workers with computer science knowledge on Mechanical Turk.

Comparing Grade Distributions

We computed the distribution of grades for each exam answer from experts, Turkers and Umatiers. These distributions were summed across all responses, and across all answer items, to produce the statistic used to test the potential differences between response distributions.

Chi Squared tests find a significant difference between the expert and either Turker score distribution ($P_{TURK} < .001$ and $P_{TURK_{NoSpam}} < .001$). We see no such significant difference between the experts and Umati users ($0.263 < P_{UMATI} < .997$) [1]. This suggests that the Umatiers, on aggregate, grade similarly to experts; Turkers do not.

[1]The 105 survey items allowed for 5 score options, zero to four. Each individual answer's distribution then has 4 degrees of freedom (knowing the probability mass in bins 0 through 3 fixes the amount of mass in bin 4). From this, we know the number of degrees of freedom for the overall Chi Squared test is at least $4 \times 105 = 420$ and at most $5 \times 105 - 1 = 524$, depending on the amount of dependence between the student answers. This provides us with bounds on the p-values of each experiment.

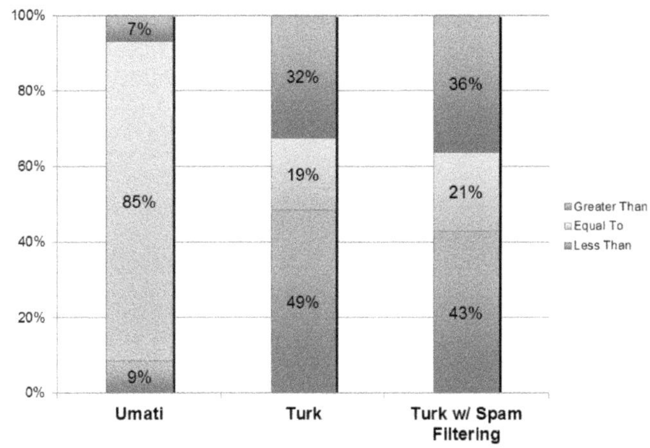

Figure 8. Agreement between conditions and the median of the 10 expert graders. Umati users' response distributions were much closer to the experts than distributions of Mechanical Turk users.

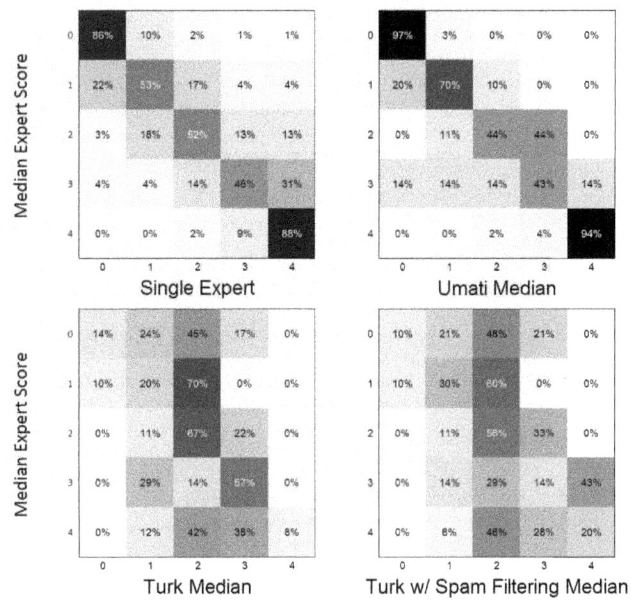

Figure 9. Comparing grade agreement between the the experts and our test conditions. Umatiers and single experts often agreed with the pool of experts. Turkers were consistently random.

Comparing Grades

Umati users agreed with the experts' median grade 85% of the time (Figure 8). In comparison, Turkers only agreed with experts 19% of the time; this figure increases only slightly to 21% with spam filtering. [2]

Figure 9 shows how different graders diverged from the grades of *all* expert graders. Boxes along the diagonal show agreement with experts. Individual experts and Umatiers agree strongly with all experts on assigning full credit or no credit. Single experts appear to have less variance than

[2]Random guesses have an expected agreement of 20% on a five-point scale.

Umatiers when assigning partial credit. We reserve a careful study of systematic biases to future work. MTurk workers' responses have no discernible pattern, leading to a generally centered (2/4) median score.

Price-Accuracy Trade-off

We explore the effects of assigning varying numbers of graders on accuracy by sampling subgroups from the distribution of experts, Turkers, and Umatiers and calculating median agreements for these groups to all experts.

Figure 10 plots agreement as greater numbers of respondents are considered. Individual expert graders agreed with the median of all experts 78.3% of the time. Ten Umatiers agreed 79% of the time, but cost 33% less ($10 \times 2.3 = 23$ cents/grade vs 34 cents/grade). Mechanical Turk users never approximate the experts, regardless of their number. In fact, Turkers are *less* likely to agree with the median expert grade as the number of respondents increases.

If we keep cost constant, Umati is more accurate than a single expert grader (see Figure 11). Thirty-four cents can buy one expert answer, with an accuracy of 78.3%; or fifteen Umatiers, who have an accuracy of 80.3%. Because result quality is achieved through multiple graders at lower individual pay, it is easy to increase or decrease the accuracy by adjusting the number of redundant assignments. Additional workers can also be dynamically assigned to more difficult or controversial cases where initial ratings diverge, while the number of assignments can be held low for answers that are clearly correct or incorrect.

Qualitative Observations

Throughout the week-long deployment, we observed users to obtain feedback on usability and user experience. At times, student interest was higher than our single machine could handle: queues formed in front of the machine. We noticed that groups of students often used the system together (see Figure 2). Some groups were formed ad-hoc, by students waiting in line. Other groups approached the machine together. Using Umati seemed to be a social event; groups would argue about the specific merits of different answers. Such additional discussion is an unexpected secondary benefit: academic departments will likely welcome increased discussion of class material by their students. Groups would also share the rewards, for instance splitting a bag of candy amongst the participants.

However, groups could also negatively impact grading: student groups seemed more inclined to attempt to defraud the system. One group attempted to pry open the door. Queues of waiting students potentially limit the throughput of the machine, but are hard to avoid — physical interfaces do not scale easily. A number of users complained that they were unjustly blacklisted. Often this was because they had forgotten to log out. A few users reported being removed because they were exploring and were not aware of the repercussions. Better instructions about safeguarding mechanisms could address these problems.

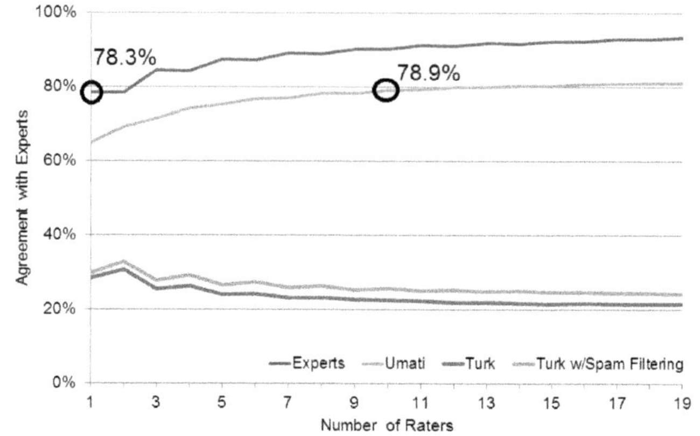

Figure 10. The accuracy of Umati users becomes comparable to a small number of experts as more participants are involved. Here, we show the point where Umati accuracy surpasses that of a single expert.

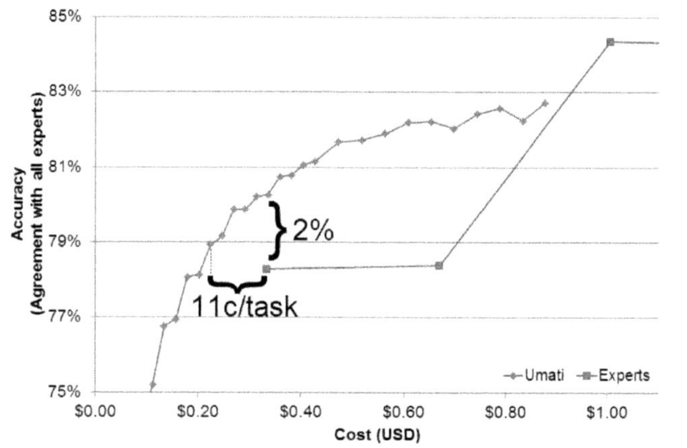

Figure 11. Accuracy (compared with all experts), for experts and Umati. One expert grader costs the university approximately 34 cents/task.

DISCUSSION

In this section we discuss some important limitations of Umati and of our particular study design. We also discuss possible alternative strategies for communitysourcing.

Privacy and Confidentiality for Grading

Publicly displaying student answers raises obvious privacy and confidentiality concerns. For example, handwriting might reveal the identity of a test taker. Students may not want peers grading their exams (though peer grading already exists in different forms at many schools). For the experiment described in this paper, paid participants generated exam answers; students' course grades were not determined by Umati workers. In the future, Umati can be used in situations where students have consented to this form of grading at the outset of a course. Alternatively, Umati can be used for many forms of assessment with lower stakes, e.g., homework grading or practice exams.

With the current design, students may also attempt to game the system by providing high grades to their own (or their friend's) answers. We limited this concern by forcing graders to view all submissions to one question before moving on to the next questions. Attackers thus must grade *every* answer to *every* question in order to comprehensively cheat for just one student. Umati also gathers the student's ID, allowing us to programmatically block them from grading exams for classes they are enrolled in, or have not yet taken. To reduce the risk of cheating and of inadvertent identification by peers, test-takers and test-graders could also be geographically and socially separated – for example, students on the East Coast could grade assignments from students on the West Coast, and vice versa.

Study Limitations

Our current study has several important limitations that should be addressed in future work.

No Comparison to Expert Work Platforms

We compared the effectiveness of grading tasks on Umati to Mechanical Turk. However, other crowdsourcing technologies could potentially be useful for grading. For instance, the computing experts on Stack Overflow [25] should have the expertise required to assess introductory exams. Similarly, we could hire a contractor on oDesk.

We are skeptical that these other engines are well suited for short-duration, expert tasks like grading. An individual expert (as on oDesk) is unlikely to be better or cheaper than the student graders we compared against. Stack Overflow workers provide the *best* answer to a question, disallowing the high-volume of tasks needed for grading. However, we have not yet tested whether these intuitions hold.

Short Deployment

A major limitation of our study is the short one-week duration of the deployment. High initial usage led to task starvation: we did not have enough sample tasks for graders. After one week, each exam response had already gathered an average of 68 grades.

While we know that the initial interest was high, we cannot yet comment on sustained, steady-state usage of Umati. We observed that more tasks were completed in the latter half of our deployment, suggesting that user momentum was still building. We are actively seeking new high-volume tasks for future deployments.

Similarly, we cannot say how much of this initial interest in Umati was due to the specific properties of our targeted crowd. It may be that Computer Science students are more excited about crowdsourcing than other groups. We hope to resolve this by targeting different communities (with different tasks) in the future.

Interface Affordances Limit Work Duration

We chose grading as an example communitysourcing task for Umati in part because it could be achieved with minimal user input. Umati's design might preclude many other types of work. This is primarily due to its limited input and output affordances: a 7-inch vertical touch-screen is inefficient and error-prone for many data-entry heavy tasks. Kiosks must appear *approachable* to attract users and be *robust* to public abuse. Overly complex interfaces can create challenges for achieving these goals.

An alternative would be to divide work and reward interfaces: experts could perform work on their own computers or smart phones, e.g., through a web interface, and then come to a nearby kiosk or vending machine to redeem their rewards. In such a design, the kiosk would primarily enforce locality and community membership. However, this design would reduce the social visibility of the machine: in our deployment, students were frequently attracted by watching other students use Umati. In addition, communitysourcing requires available cognitive surplus. There are few other distractions in a public hallway; spare time may be more difficult to find when competing with a myriad of ways to spend time on the Internet. We reserve further study of these questions for future work.

Applications of Communitysourcing to Other Problems

Our study demonstrated the value of communitysourcing for one particular task domain and reward type. Grading is just one example of a high-volume task that requires an expert population; we could instead provide specialized surveys. Snacks are just one of many possible rewards; students may prefer video game currency to snacks. In the future, we plan to develop alternative embodiments of communitysourcing, and to develop a theory of how the combination of task, location and reward affect work quality and quantity. For example, future deployments could include: a bug triage espresso machine in the lounge of a big technology company; a jukebox with market research tasks at a bar; or a slot machine in the airport with travel review tasks.

CONCLUSION

In this work we introduced the idea of communitysourcing — the use of physical kiosks to crowdsource work from targeted populations. Communitysourcing is achieved by: 1) situating tasks in specific physical spaces that attract the right "crowd" and where people have idle time and 2) providing physical, context- and community-specific rewards that users value more than money. These two key points invite new expert workers to participate in short duration crowd work.

To explore the potential of communitysourcing, we designed, implementing and evaluated a specific communitysourcing interface for a particular expert task. *Umati, the communitysourced vending machine* enabled users to earn credit for purchasing snack items by performing grading tasks on a touchscreen. We investigated whether Umati can recruit new users: over one week, Umati successfully targeted a student community, with 302 students (of 328 total) grading 7240 (of 7771 total) exam answers. 80% of all the users had never participated in crowdsourcing before. We also investigated how task quality compared to both online crowdsourcing and traditional, offline work.

We found that Umati was able to grade exams more accurately (80.3% vs 78.3% at the same cost), or at lower cost (23c/answer vs 34c/answer at equivalent accuracy), than traditional single-expert grading. Workers on Mechanical Turk were unable to successfully grade the exams.

In the future, we would like to test Umati over a longer period of time, to observe patterns of use and investigate the long-term prospects of expert work on kiosks. We would also like to consider alternate communitysourcing scenarios with varying configuration of task, location and reward; for example, one where users could complete tasks online using their own computers, obtaining one-time keys that can be redeemed for credit.

ACKNOWLEDGMENTS

We thank Bryan Trinh for his help constructing Umati and Kehontas Rowe for task design and video production. We thank Kelly Buchanan, Isabelle Stanton, and Alice Chen for putting up with us. We greatly appreciate the help received from Robert Carroll, Barret Rhoden, Anuj Tewari, Kevin Klues, Lisa Fowler, and Wesley Willett in moving the machine. Lastly, we thank Eric Brewer and Laurent El Ghaoui for letting us take on this project.

REFERENCES

1. 99Designs. http://www.99designs.com/. Retrieved 9/2011.
2. Innocentive. http://www.innocentive.com/. Retrieved 9/2011.
3. Shreddr. http://www.shreddr.org/. Retrieved 9/2011.
4. Topcoder. http://www.topcoder.com/. Retrieved 9/2011.
5. Ahmad, S., Battle, A., Malkani, Z., and Kamvar, S. The jabberwocky programming environment for structured social computing. In *Proceedings of UIST'11*, ACM (2011), 53–64.
6. Bernstein, M. S., Brandt, J., Miller, R. C., and Karger, D. R. Crowds in two seconds: Enabling realtime crowd-powered interfaces. In *Proceedings of UIST'11*, ACM (2011), 33–42.
7. Bernstein, M. S., Little, G., Miller, R. C., Hartmann, B., Ackerman, M. S., Karger, D. R., Crowell, D., and Panovich, K. Soylent: a word processor with a crowd inside. In *Proceedings of UIST'10*, ACM (2010), 313–322.
8. Bigham, J. P., Jayant, C., Ji, H., Little, G., Miller, A., Miller, R. C., Miller, R., Tatarowicz, A., White, B., White, S., and Yeh, T. Vizwiz: nearly real-time answers to visual questions. In *Proceedings of UIST'10*, ACM (2010), 333–342.
9. Garriss, S., Cáceres, R., Berger, S., Sailer, R., van Doorn, L., and Zhang, X. Trustworthy and personalized computing on public kiosks. In *Proceeding of MobiSys '08*, ACM (New York, NY, USA, 2008), 199–210.
10. Gehringer, E. F. Electronic peer review and peer grading in computer-science courses. In *Proceedings of SIGCSE'01*, ACM (2001), 139–143.
11. Gigwalk. http://www.gigwalk.com. Retrieved 9/2011.
12. Goldman, J., Shilton, K., Burke, J., Estrin, D., Hansen, M., Ramanathan, N., Reddy, S., Samanta, V., Srivastava, M., and West, R. Participatory Sensing: A citizen-powered approach to illuminating the patterns that shape our world. *Foresight & Governance Project, White Paper* (2009).
13. Heer, J., and Bostock, M. Crowdsourcing graphical perception: using mechanical turk to assess visualization design. In *Proceedings of CHI'10*, ACM (New York, NY, USA, 2010), 203–212.
14. Huang, A., Pulli, K., and Rudolph, L. Kimono: kiosk-mobile phone knowledge sharing system. In *Proceedings of MUM'05*, ACM (New York, NY, USA, 2005), 142–149.
15. Ipeirotis, P. G. Analyzing the Amazon Mechanical Turk marketplace. *ACM XRDS 17* (December 2010), 16–21.
16. Izadi, S., Brignull, H., Rodden, T., Rogers, Y., and Underwood, M. Dynamo: a public interactive surface supporting the cooperative sharing and exchange of media. In *Proceedings of UIST'03*, ACM (New York, NY, USA, 2003), 159–168.
17. Kearsley, G. *Public Access Systems: Bringing Computer Power to the People*. Ablex Publishing Corporation, 1994.
18. Kim, S., Robson, C., Zimmerman, T., Pierce, J., and Haber, E. Creek watch: Pairing usefulness and usability for successful citizen science. In *Proceedings of CHI '11*, ACM (2011), 2125–2134.
19. Kittur, A., Chi, E. H., and Suh, B. Crowdsourcing user studies with mechanical turk. In *Proceeding of CHI'08*, ACM (New York, NY, USA, 2008), 453–456.
20. Kittur, A., Smus, B., Khamkar, S., and Kraut, R. Crowdforge: Crowdsourcing complex work. In *Proceedings of UIST'11*, ACM (2011), 1801–1806.
21. Law, E., and von Ahn, L. *Human Computation: An Integrated Approach to Learning from the Crowd*. Morgan & Claypool, 2011.
22. Little, G., Chilton, L. B., Goldman, M., and Miller, R. C. Turkit: human computation algorithms on mechanical turk. In *Proceedings of UIST '10*, ACM (New York, NY, USA, 2010), 57–66.
23. Localmind. http://www.localmind.com. Retrieved 9/2011.
24. Mafi, M. Grading: Involving students in a time-saving solution to the homework problem. *Engineering Education 79*, 3 (April 1989), 444–446.
25. Mamykina, L., Manoim, B., Mittal, M., Hripcsak, G., and Hartmann, B. Design Lessons from the Fastest Q&A Site in the West. In *Proceeding of the CHI'11*, ACM (2011), 2857–2866.
26. Menger, C. *Grundsätze der Volkswirtschaftslehre*. Braumüller, 1871.
27. Mitra, S. Self organising systems for mass computer literacy: Findings from the 'hole in the wall' experiments. *International Journal of Development Issues 4*, 1 (2005), 71–81.
28. Quinn, A., and Bederson, B. Human computation: A survey and taxonomy of a growing field. In *CHI '2011: Proceeding of the twenty-ninth annual SIGCHI conference on Human factors in computing systems* (2011), 1403–1412.
29. Reily, K., Finnerty, P. L., and Terveen, L. Two peers are better than one: aggregating peer reviews for computing assignments is surprisingly accurate. In *Proceedings of GROUP '09*, ACM (2009), 115–124.
30. Ross, J., Irani, L., Silberman, M. S., Zaldivar, A., and Tomlinson, B. Who are the crowdworkers?: shifting demographics in mechanical turk. In *Extended Abstracts of CHI'10*, ACM (2010), 2863–2872.
31. Shirky, C. *Cognitive Surplus: Creativity and Generosity in a Connected Age*. Penguin Press, 2010.
32. Slay, H., Wentworth, P., and Locke, J. Bingbee, an information kiosk for social enablement in marginalized communities. In *Proceedings of SAICSIT '06* (2006), 107–116.
33. Smyth, T. N., Etherton, J., and Best, M. L. Moses: exploring new ground in media and post-conflict reconciliation. In *Proceedings of CHI '10*, ACM (2010), 1059–1068.
34. Topping, K. Peer assessment between students in colleges and universities. *Review of Educational Research 68*, 3 (1998), 249–276.
35. von Ahn, L., and Dabbish, L. Designing games with a purpose. *Communications of the ACM 51* (August 2008), 58–67.
36. Yan, T., Kumar, V., and Ganesan, D. Crowdsearch: exploiting crowds for accurate real-time image search on mobile phones. In *Proceedings of MobiSys '10*, ACM (New York, NY, USA, 2010), 77–90.

LemonAid: Selection-Based Crowdsourced Contextual Help for Web Applications

Parmit K. Chilana, Andrew J. Ko, Jacob O. Wobbrock
The Information School | DUB Group
University of Washington
Seattle, WA 98195 USA
{pchilana, ajko, wobbrock}@uw.edu

ABSTRACT
Web-based technical support such as discussion forums and social networking sites have been successful at ensuring that most technical support questions eventually receive helpful answers. Unfortunately, *finding* these answers is still quite difficult, since users' textual queries are often incomplete, imprecise, or use different vocabularies to describe the same problem. We present *LemonAid*, a new approach to help that allows users to find help by instead selecting a label, widget, link, image or other user interface (UI) element that they believe is relevant to their problem. LemonAid uses this selection to retrieve previously asked questions and their corresponding answers. The key insight that makes LemonAid work is that users tend to make similar selections in the interface for similar help needs and different selections for different help needs. Our initial evaluation shows that across a corpus of dozens of tasks and thousands of requests, LemonAid retrieved a result for 90% of help requests based on UI selections and, of those, over half had relevant matches in the top 2 results.

ACM Classification: H.5.2 [**Information interfaces and presentation**]: User Interfaces. *Graphical user interfaces.*

General terms: Design, Human Factors.

Keywords: contextual help; crowdsourced help; software support

INTRODUCTION
Millions of users on the web struggle to learn how to use and configure applications to meet their needs. For example, customers must decipher cryptic error messages after failed e-banking transactions, office workers wrestle with adding attachments to their company wikis, and new users may have to interpret complex privacy settings on social networking sites. As today's web applications become more dynamic, feature-rich, and customizable, the need for application help increases, but it is not always feasible or economical for companies to provide custom one-on-one support [34].

Permission to make digital or hard copies of all or part of this work for personal or classroom use is granted without fee provided that copies are not made or distributed for profit or commercial advantage and that copies bear this notice and the full citation on the first page. To copy otherwise, or republish, to post on servers or to redistribute to lists, requires prior specific permission and/or a fee.
CHI'12 , May 5–10, 2012, Austin, Texas, USA.
Copyright 2012 ACM 978-1-4503-1015-4/12/05...$10.00.

Among the long history of approaches to software help, perhaps the most powerful approach is *crowdsourced* help. With crowdsourced help (*e.g.*, [19,22,29]), users can help each other answer questions in discussion forums, mailing lists, or within their online social networks. Such resources reinforce the social nature of technical support that users tend to prefer [29,33] and companies also benefit, as they have to expend fewer resources on support.

While crowdsourced help is powerful at *generating* answers to help questions, *locating* useful answers from past discussions can be difficult. First, questions and answers are scattered across different resources: a user may post a technical help question on her social network, unaware that a similar question had already been answered on the application's forum site. Second, even if a user finds a discussion that potentially has the answer, the answer may be buried deep within long conversation threads that span multiple pages. Even though recent Q&A sites have incorporated strategies for promoting the best responses to the top of the list, users often cannot find these threads in the first place because users' queries tend to be not only incomplete and imprecise [3], but also plagued by the classic *vocabulary problem* [11], where different users provide different words to describe the same goal (*i.e.*, "add a photo" *vs.* "insert an image"). While search engine algorithms can be used to mitigate some of the challenges in natural language retrieval, the onus is still on users to translate their help needs and problem contexts into keywords that result in an effective search.

We present *LemonAid*, a new approach to technical help retrieval that allows users to ask for help by selecting a label, widget, link, image or other user interface (UI) element, rather than choosing keywords. With LemonAid, help is integrated directly into the UI (as in Figure 1) and users can ask questions, provide answers, and search for help without ever leaving their application. The key insight that makes LemonAid work, one supported by our formative studies, is that users tend to make similar selections in the interface for similar help needs and different selections for different help needs. This tight coupling of user needs to UI elements is central to LemonAid's effectiveness, reducing unnecessary variation in users' queries. In fact, our initial evaluation of LemonAid's retrieval, based on a corpus we created consisting of over 2,700 UI selections from over 500 users

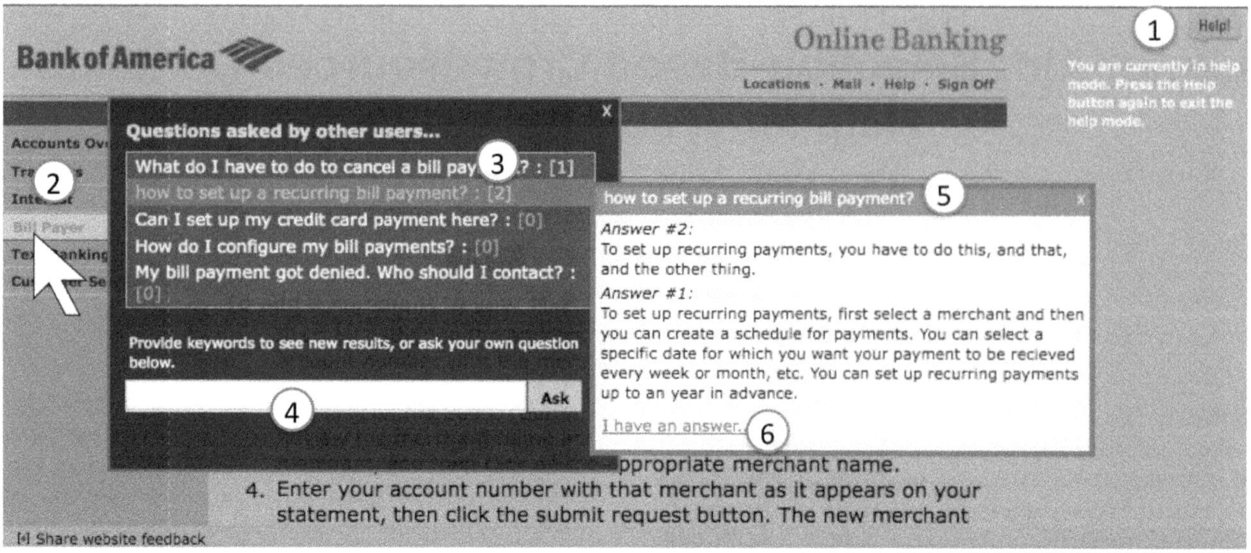

Figure 1. The LemonAid user interface: **(1)** the help button, which invokes the help mode; **(2)** a user's selection; and **(3)** questions relevant to the user's selection (the brackets contain the number of answers available for each question). **(4)** A search box where users can provide keywords to filter the results or ask a new question if they do not see a relevant question. **(5)** Answers linked to the selected question and **(6)** a link that allows a user to submit an answer for the selected question.

on Mechanical Turk, showed that on average, LemonAid retrieved a relevant result for 90% of help requests based on UI selections and, of those, over half had relevant matches in the top 2 results.

LemonAid works exclusively with standard DOMs, makes no assumptions about how an application's back or front end is implemented, does not require the modification of application source code, and does not require the use of a specific UI toolkit. It simply operates as a layer above an application's UI. The only work that developers must do to integrate LemonAid into their site is extract text labels appearing in the UI from a web application's code and include the framework in their client-side deployment. We have tested the LemonAid framework with a few web applications and found that the integration work is minimal.

While LemonAid's approach is influenced by recent work on helping programmers debug code in-context (*e.g.*, [5,14,18]), the novelty lies in providing a contextual help framework for *end-users* to resolve issues through crowdsourcing. Our larger vision is that software teams will be able to use this repository of contextually reported issues for better understanding potential usability problems and user impact. In this paper, we contribute:

- A new selection-based querying interface and a question and answer authoring interface allows users to generate help content and find help without leaving the application.
- A new help retrieval algorithm that leverages contextual information and user interface selections to retrieve relevant help content.
- A framework that allows web developers to easily integrate LemonAid within a web application.
- An initial evaluation that demonstrates the feasibility of LemonAid in retrieving relevant matches for a crowdsourced corpus of selections.

USING LEMONAID TO FIND HELP

LemonAid allows users to find application help in-context by selecting UI elements, including labels, widgets, links, and images that they believe are relevant to their help request, question, or problem. For example, consider Figure 1, which shows an example scenario in which Bob, a teacher who occasionally does online banking, wants to pay his electricity bill by setting up a monthly online payment through his bank. Bob has checked his account balance a few times using the bank's online application, but he is not familiar with all of the other application features. He clicks on the "Bill Payer" option and it opens up a new page with more information, but now Bob does not know what to do. Normally, Bob would call his tech-savvy friend for help, but since it is late, Bob needs to find a solution on his own.

Bob clicks on the LemonAid "Help" button at the upper right of the page (Figure 1.1) and the screen dims, indicating that the application has entered help mode. LemonAid fades the user interface, indicating to Bob that the meaning of a "click" has changed. As Bob moves his mouse cursor over the page, he notices that words and objects under his cursor are highlighted in yellow, indicating that they are clickable. Bob selects the "Bill Payer" label, as he thinks it is most relevant to his problem (Figure 1.2). LemonAid displays five questions that it believes are relevant to his selection (Figure 1.3), all which have been asked by other users who had previously selected the same or similar labels. Bob immediately notices the 2nd question, "how to set up recurring payments," and sees it has 2 answers (indicated by the number in brackets). Bob clicks on the question and sees that the first answer is what he needs (Figure 1.5).

While he is logged in, Bob also wants to update his phone number in the e-banking system. He again goes into LemonAid's help mode and this time, he clicks on a tab

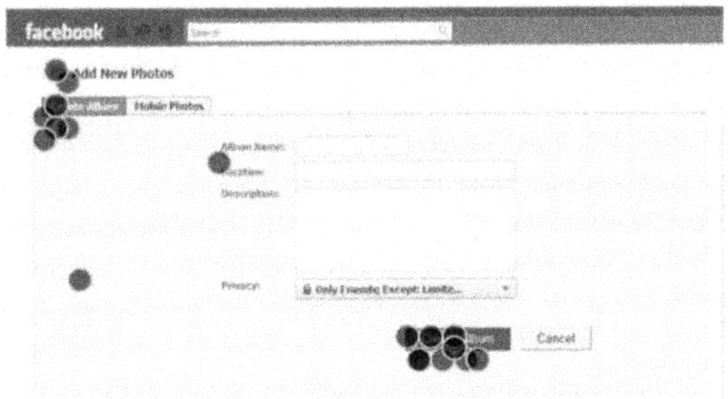

Scenario. You are trying to add photos from a recent trip to your Facebook page for the first time. You heard from a friend that it's easy to upload multiple photos from your hard drive, but when you arrived at this page, you did not see any such option. You are wondering if you came to the right place and what you should be doing next to upload your photos.

Figure 2. Aggregate results from a task in our formative study and its corresponding scenario.

labeled "Account Profile." The help system now shows a much longer list of relevant questions (not shown), as there are many features relevant to this label. Bob does not want to read all of them, so he starts typing into the search box (Figure 1.4) and notices that the question list updates. Bob now only sees two questions (not shown), the first of which is explicitly about adding phone numbers.

LEMONAID DESIGN AND ARCHITECTURE

The main component of LemonAid is a retrieval engine that produces a ranked list of relevant questions in response to a user's selection on a page. Selections are captured as a DOM element and other context (described next) and then matched against the existing set of questions stored in LemonAid's repository of application-specific questions and answers. In this section, we (1) describe the contextual data that LemonAid captures, (2) explain how LemonAid represents questions, answers, and users' selections, and (3) explain LemonAid's retrieval algorithm.

Capture of Contextual Data

When a user makes a selection, LemonAid captures information about the target DOM object and underlying HTML, which we will call *contextual data*. There was a variety of contextual information that LemonAid could gather (as explored in other recent help approaches [9]). But, we focused on identifying contextual data that would be useful in discriminating between different help problems within the UI from the user's perspective.

We designed a formative study that presented 20 participants with a series of 12 screen shots from popular web applications. Each screen shot conveyed a problem scenario consisting of a textual description and a printout of where a problem was encountered, as shown in Figure 2. All of the problem scenarios were taken from real questions from help forums for these web applications. During the study, we asked participants to pretend that they had a "magic wand" that they could use to point anywhere on the interface to get help and to indicate their selection with a physical sticker. An example scenario and its results are displayed in Figure 2.

There were two major findings from the study. First, participants tended to select labels in the UI that they believed were *conceptually relevant* to the help problem. Most of these keywords were application-specific labels or headings (*e.g.*, 15 of 20 participants selected the "*Create Album*" keywords in the scenario in Figure 2). Second, when no label appeared relevant, participants selected UI elements that were similar in terms of their visual appearance and location on the screen, with a bias towards the top-left. These findings suggested that LemonAid could determine similarity between selections largely based on the text on UI labels, and leverage additional attributes of the selected DOM object such its layout position and appearance.

Based on these results, we designed LemonAid to capture the three contextual details listed in Table 1. When a user clicks on a region of a page, LemonAid first determines the topmost DOM node (based on *z-order*) under the user's cursor. From this, it extracts the tag name of the selected node (`nodeType`). It also extracts the XPath string representing the sequence of tag names and child indices that indicate the path from the root of the DOM tree to the selected node (`nodeXPath`). Finally, it extracts all of the text node descendants of the selected node, concatenated into one string, using the standard *innerText* or *textContent* property of the selected DOM node, depending on the browser (`nodeText`). If the selected node is an image and includes an *alt* attribute, this text is also concatenated to `nodeText`. While we also considered using HTML *id*s or *class*es, since they are also related to appearance and layout, they are often dynamically generated between user sessions and thus not useful for representing questions shared by users.

Since the text labels on DOM elements could potentially be user-generated and privacy-sensitive, LemonAid only stores the `nodeText` if it is a known *UI literal*. UI literals include any string that is explicitly defined in the application source code or any whitespace-delimited string that appears in application resource files, such as localization files. A UI literal may represent labels on UI widgets, headings, or error messages, among other application-specific strings. Every time a user makes a selection, LemonAid compares the `nodeText` of the selected node against a whitelist of known application UI literals to determine whether or not to store the captured `nodeText`. For example, for a heading element where the text is "Account Settings," the `nodeText` would only be stored as part of the contextual data if "Account Settings" was found in the list of application UI literals. In contrast, if the selected text were a container that included a

Attribute	Description	Example
nodeText	Visible text on the selected DOM node	"Bill Payer"
nodeXPath	The XPath uniquely identifying the selected DOM node in the page	/HTML/BODY/TABLE/TBODY/TR[5]/TD
nodeType	The HTML tag of the selected DOM node (i.e., DIV, TABLE, BUTTON, etc.)	TD

Table 1: Contextual data captured in a user selection with example from the bill payer scenario in Figure 1.

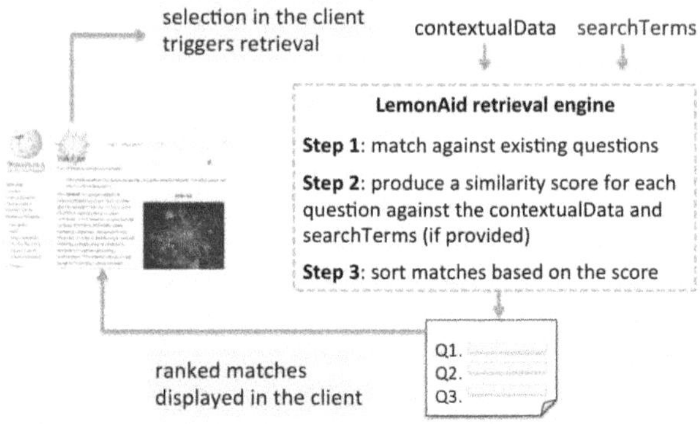

Figure 3. The retrieval engine uses contextual data from the user's selection and any search terms provided by the user to produce a ranked list of relevant questions.

user's username, this would likely *not* be in the whitelist and would therefore not be included in `nodeText`. (We describe LemonAid's built-in functionality for extracting UI literals in a later section discussing LemonAid's integration steps.)

Questions, Answers, and Users' Selections

Once the user makes a selection and LemonAid captures the data in Table 1 to represent it, the data is used as a query to LemonAid's repository of questions. To explain this retrieval, we first define how questions and answers are stored. Each *Question* submitted by a user through LemonAid's question box (Figure 1.4) includes a unique id for each question in the set (*id*); the `nodeXPath`, `nodeType`, and `nodeText` described in Table 1 (*contextualData*), and the optional question text provided by the user in the text field in Figure 1.4 (*questionString*). Since the focus of this paper is on help retrieval, and not help authoring, LemonAid's *Answers* are basic, mimicking the kind of answers found in discussion forums: each *Answer* has a unique *id*, an *answerString*, which stores the text provided in the field in Figure 1.6, and a *questionID*, linking it to the question for which the answer was provided. *Questions* may have multiple *Answers*.

A *UserSelection* in LemonAid consists of the contextual data captured from the user's selection (as described in Table 1) and optional `searchTerms`, which store the text provided by the user in the search input field (Figure 1.4). A *UserSelection* initially generates a query consisting only of the contextual data. Each keystroke in the search input field generates a new *UserSelection* and updates the retrieved results using an *auto-suggest* interaction.

Ranked Retrieval of Matching Questions

To retrieve help, LemonAid utilizes a relevance ranking approach leveraging *contextualData* and optional *searchTerms* using the process shown in Figure 3. The retrieval algorithm takes a *UserSelection* and compares it to each previously asked *Question* in the application's repository, producing a *similarity score* between 0 and 1 for each *Question*, with 1 being the best match. LemonAid then presents the matching questions in descending order of score. The score, which is computed as in Figure 4, is a

```
findMatchingResults(UILiteral, nodeType, nodeXPath, searchTerms)
returnValue: a sorted resultSet containing matching questions from set of existing questions.

for each question Qi in the set of existing questions Q
    nodeTextScore = Qi.nodeText contains UILiteral ? 1 : 0
    xPathScore = a percentage computed by comparing the overlap in
    Qi.XPath and nodeXPath of the current selection;
    typeScore = Qi.nodeType string equals nodeType ? 1 : 0
    contextScore = .7 nodeTextScore + .2 xPathScore + .1 typeScore
    if contextScore > 0.25
       add Qi to the resultSet
    if searchTerms is non-empty
       compute textSimilarityScore with full text tf–idf weighting
       if textSimilarityScore > 0
          add Qi to resultSet
if searchTerms is non-empty
   sort resultSet by textSimilarityScore, then contextScore
else
   sort resultSet by contextScore
return resultSet
```

Figure 4. Pseudocode for retrieval algorithm.

combination of factors, including a `contextScore` based on a weighted sum of the three scores in Table 2 and a `textSimilarityScore` if the user provided `searchTerms`. The next two sections describe these scores in detail.

Similarity based on context

As discussed above, our formative study suggested that similarity between selections could largely be based on the text on UI literals. Therefore, the primary factor in the `contextScore` is the `nodeTextScore`, which is 1 if the `nodeText` of a selection contains (ignoring case) the `nodeText` of the *Question* being compared and 0 otherwise. With this approach, LemonAid is able retrieve a match related to a specific item in the container (*i.e.*, a navigation menu item) even if the user's selection was the container itself. This factor is given a weight of 0.7, since it was the most important factor in our formative studies.

The 2nd factor in the `contextScore` is the `XPathScore`, which captures similarity in layout and position identified in our formative study. Although XPaths can change as UI layouts evolve over time [2,4], many menus and header items on a page stay relatively the same or have only slight layout differences over time. Therefore, this score is a measure of the percent node overlap between the `nodeXPath` of the query and a *Question*'s `nodeXPath`. We compute this by starting from the root and doing a node-by-node string comparison from root to leaf, incrementing the score by 1 every time there is a match, and stopping when there is no match or the last node of the shorter path is reached. We divide the final sum by the length of the longer XPath to get a percentage. (For example, the overlap between `HTML/BODY/DIV/` and `HTML/BODY/DIV/DIV/P/` is 3/5 or 60%). Because location and position were only a factor in a

Constituent	Similarity Score	Weight
nodeTextScore	string contains (1 or 0)	0.7
XPathScore	% node overlap between XPaths [0,1]	0.2
nodeTypeScore	string equals (1 or 0)	0.1

Table 2. Weights for contextual data.

minority of the scenarios in our formative study, the `nodeXpath` score has a weight of only 0.2.

The 3rd and final factor in the `contextScore` compares the `nodeType` of the selected node to that of the potentially matching *Question*. This factor accounts for both appearance similarities, while also helping with situations where multiple UI elements share the same text label, such as a button and a heading with the same words. The `nodeTypeScore` is 1 if the labels of the selection and the Question are equivalent and 0 if not. Because ties were rare, and appearance was only rarely a factor in our formative study, we only give `nodeTypeScore` a small weight of 0.1.

After `contextScore` is computed, the algorithm in Figure 4 includes a *Question* in the results set if its score is above 0.25. This threshold was selected because it implies that there is no `nodeText` match, but there is a strong match between the `nodeXPath` and `nodeType`. Even though this type of match is weaker than one based on `nodeText`, it is useful for cases where a question may be attached to a container or non-UI literal text (*e.g.*, user-generated content). Since `nodeText` similarity is not relevant in such cases, the `nodeXPath` and `nodeType` similarity can still be used as (weak) indicators of relevant questions.

Similarity based on search keywords

If the user provides `searchTerms` in the field in Figure 1.4, the algorithm in Figure 4 also computes a `textSimilarityScore`. It does this by comparing a query's `searchTerms` with the whitespace-delimited words in each existing *Question*'s *questionString*. To compare the similarity between these keywords, we created a search index on each *questionString* and used a standard full-text search feature based on the vector space model [27]. The similarity score is computed using the term frequency–inverse document frequency (*tf–idf*) weighting approach in information retrieval. The main idea of *tf-idf* is that terms that occur frequently in the target document (in our case, a question in the repository of previously asked questions), but less frequently in the whole document collection are the useful terms. The weight of these terms is a combination of term frequency within the target document and its frequency across all documents. Each *Question* that matches the user's *searchTerms* is included in the result and sorted in descending order based on the `textSimilarityScore`. This result set is then sorted by `contextScore` of each question against the *UserSelection*.

INTEGRATING LEMONAID INTO WEB APPLICATIONS

One of the strengths of LemonAid's simplicity is that it can be easily integrated into an existing website with minimal modification to the site itself.

First, site administrators choose an ID to uniquely identify their application-specific help information in the third party server. Next, administrators can either provide a URL to their main source directory or run a script provided by LemonAid to extract UI literals from a site's code and localization files. From this, LemonAid generates a CSV file containing the list of literals and stores it alongside the question repository. LemonAid uses a simple algorithm for finding string literals in commonly used web programming languages, looking for sequences of characters delimited by single (‘’) and double ASCII quotes (“”). While this approach does not account for UI literals that may be dynamically generated, it covers a large range of UI literals defined at design time. While this extraction approach may generate false positives (extracting strings that do not appear in the user interface), these non-UI literals are not visible to the user and hence not selectable anyway. Furthermore, site administrators have full control in editing the CSV file containing string literals from their source code.

Finally, site administrators include a few lines of JavaScript on all of their web application's pages, just as with analytics services such as *Google Analytics*. Doing so links the LemonAid source code to the web application, and makes LemonAid functional on that page. The interface shown in Figure 1 is an example implementation of LemonAid on the static version of *Bank of America*'s Bill Payer site. The UI literals were obtained by manual screen scraping since we did not have access to Bank of America's source.

The current implementation of LemonAid sets up a basic infrastructure through which anyone can anchor questions and answers on the underlying application's UI literals. Site administrators may have different needs in terms of managing the Q&A and the related community of users. For example, some web applications are already controlled by user authentication and it may be just a matter of integrating LemonAid with the existing user accounts on the site. Another approach may be the use of social networking plugins to facilitate communication among users within their social network. In other cases, administrators may want to restrict answer authoring to the company's support personnel and may want to store the help data locally.

EVALUATION

At the core of LemonAid is a retrieval engine that produces a ranked list of questions relevant to a user's selection and optional search terms. As explained above, although users' natural language descriptions of the same problem may differ, users tend to make the same selections in the UI for a given problem. Thus, to assess the effectiveness of LemonAid's retrieval algorithm, we focused our evaluation on answering the following question: *across a corpus of help problem scenarios, how effective is LemonAid at retrieving a relevant question asked by another user using only the current user's selection*? To operationalize this, we measured the rank of the first retrieved *Question* that regarded an identical help problem (described next), using only the contextual data from the *UserSelection*.

Developing a Crowdsourced Corpus

To perform this assessment, we first needed a large corpus of LemonAid help selections. Since we did not have a site with a large number of users to which LemonAid could be deployed (as website owners viewed the adoption of the tool without evidence of its efficacy as risky), we developed a corpus using a *simulated* community of users through Amazon's Mechanical Turk (mTurk) platform [36]. mTurk is an online marketplace where workers receive micro payments for performing small tasks, termed Human Intelligence Tasks (HITs). Recently, mTurk has become a popular way for researchers to recruit a large number of participants for small tasks [17,25,30]. We used mTurk to have hundreds of web users read a detailed help scenario and perform a LemonAid help request by selecting a UI element and providing a question relevant to the scenario.

To ensure that our corpus of help scenarios was realistic, we began by selecting the first 100 questions tagged as *popular* or *recently asked* in the *How Do I* category of *Google Calendar*'s help forum [38]. We chose *Google Calendar* because it is a popular application used by millions of people and offers not only basic functionality, but also a range of advanced functions that people have trouble finding and using. From our sample of 100 popular or recently asked questions, we eliminated questions that appeared to be duplicates and created a random sample of 50 questions that we could use in our evaluation. Although there were many more than 50 questions in Google's help forums, by analyzing the 10 "related discussions" that Google lists alongside each thread, we found that many of these discussions concerned the same issue and believe that 50 questions represented a substantial proportion of the common problems. This is reinforced by previous studies that have shown that there often are a large number of duplicate discussions on forums [28] and other forms of issue reports [18].

To convert the help discussions into scenarios, we identified the expected or desired behavior identified by the help requester and wrote a textual scenario to represent it. We also included a motivation for the task in the scenario and details about Google Calendar to help a user unfamiliar with the application understand the specified goal. Figure 5 shows an example scenario involving a calendar-sharing question.

In addition to scenario text, we also created a Google Calendar page representing an application state in which a user might encounter the problem, as in Figure 5. We created the HTML pages for each scenario by manually recreating the chosen Google Calendar state and scraping the application's corresponding HTML for that state. We then augmented each scenario page with LemonAid's question-asking functionality. Since LemonAid requires a list of UI literals corresponding to the application and we did not have access to Google Calendar's source code, we manually extracted a set of UI literals by scraping each visible text label (and ALT text of images) from all UI elements for each scenario page. Finally, because the focus of our study was retrieval performance on users' *first* selections and not on expert use of LemonAid, we disabled LemonAid's help retrieval and answer authoring functions for the study, so that after a participant selected a UI element and wrote a query, their task

An mTurk *HIT* consisted of:

1) Reading a problem scenario related to Google Calendar.

> You share your calendar with all team members at your company. Recently, one of the members left the company and now you would like to stop sharing the calendar with her, but cannot remember how to change the sharing details.

2) Answering 2 comprehension questions related to the scenario.

3) Making a selection relevant to the problem on a corresponding Google Calendar page instrumented with LemonAid.

4) Formulating a help-seeking question based on the scenario.

`How to remove a person from a shared calendar?|`

Figure 5: Illustration of mTurk use in developing a corpus

was complete. This reduced the possibility that participants would change the type of selections they made after completing multiple HITs based on the type of results returned by LemonAid's retrieval algorithm.

Of the 50 help problems, 8 were likely to be encountered in different contexts (for example on the main calendar view, or in a configuration dialog); for these, we created two scenarios, each with a different application state, resulting in a total of 58 scenarios overall.

Our mTurk HIT presented one of these 58 help-seeking scenarios (example in Figure 5), including the scenario text and the static HTML page with interactive LemonAid features. Users were asked to (1) read the scenario, (2) answer two multiple choice comprehension questions (described next), (3) enter the help mode, (4) select one of the highlighted words or elements on the screen that they felt were most relevant to the problem, and (5) provide a question in their own words that they would ask to get help in the given scenario.

The comprehension questions were included in order to gain some confidence that participants understood the scenario and were not selecting UI elements randomly (a common problem in many mTurk studies [8,17]). Each comprehension question had 5 items; the scenarios and questions were carefully edited by two of the authors for clarity. If users answered one of the questions incorrectly, they were given another explanation of the scenario to help them understand the scenario better.

Each mTurk HIT was launched with 55 assignments per HIT, with the intent of gathering 50 selections per scenario. We used 5 of the 58 HITs to pilot the mTurk protocol and our data collection strategy, resulting in a final data set of 53 unique HITs. We paid users $0.15 per HIT. (Each HIT took an average of 3.5 minutes to complete.) The study (including the pilot tests) ran for about 5 weeks. To prevent duplicate responses and other mischief, we asked mTurk users to

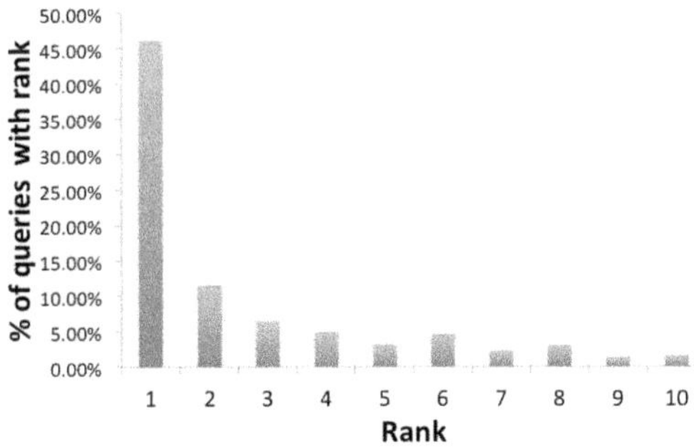

Figure 6. Distribution of ranks in the corpus.

provide a unique 6-digit passcode that was generated after they made an on-screen selection for a particular HIT. We also asked mTurk users had to write a brief explanation for why they made a particular selection.

After obtaining the data, we computed the time that an mTurk user spent on the task and compared it to the average completion time (3.5 minutes). If this time was below the 20% of the average *(i.e.,* less than 45 seconds), we automatically eliminated the response. For responses that fell between 45 seconds and 3.5 minutes, we manually checked the written explanation of why a particular selection was made. If the explanation was not intelligible, we excluded that response. Finally, we also checked the passcode that mTurk users provided against the passcodes generated by our system and eliminated responses that had incorrect passcodes. These three data points together allowed us to detect UI selections that appeared to be hastily selected with no apparent comprehension of the scenario. We were able to use between 47-52 selections for each HIT (about 10% of the data contained invalid selections as per the above criteria). Our final corpus included 2,748 help selections from 533 different mTurk accounts.

Results

As explained above, LemonAid uses a ranked retrieval approach where the retrieved results (in the form of *Questions)* are presented in an ordered list. Since our study solicited multiple selections corresponding to each scenario, multiple relevant *Questions* could potentially be retrieved for a given selection. To assess the performance of the retrieval, we focused on computing the rank of the 1st relevant *Question* for a given selection of all retrieved results. We defined ground truth in the retrieval by denoting, for each captured selection, which one of the 50 scenarios the selection corresponded to.

We computed ranks for all 2,748 selections in the corpus, retrieving relevant results from all other selections in the corpus using only the contextual data in the selections (excluding participants' question text). LemonAid retrieved 1 or more results for 90.3% of the selections. Figure 6 shows the proportion of queries resulting in median ranks of 1 through 10. The median rank of the results across the whole corpus was 2, thus the relevant result was likely to be in the top 2 results for at least half of the queries (about 57.8% in this case).

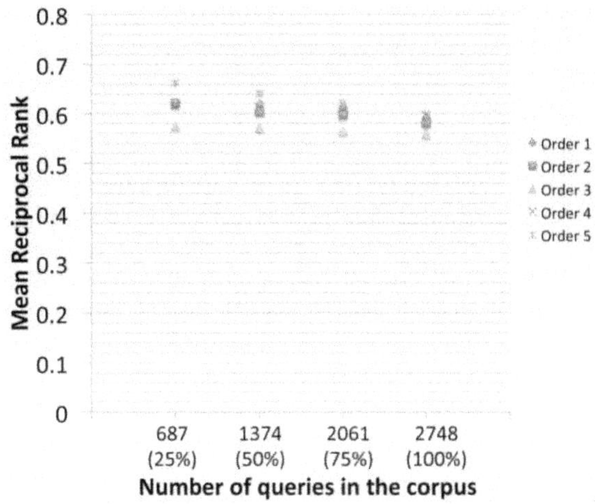

Figure 7. MRR for different corpora sizes and orderings.

To assess performance across the whole corpus more systematically, we computed the Mean Reciprocal Rank (MRR). MRR values are bounded between 0 and 1 and are sensitive to the rank position

$$\text{MRR} = \frac{1}{|C|}\sum_{i=1}^{|C|}\frac{1}{rank_i}$$

(*e.g.*, from rank 1 to 2, MRR falls from 1.0 to 0.5). The reciprocal rank of a result is equivalent to the multiplicative inverse of the rank of the first relevant result. The MRR is computed as the average of the reciprocal ranks of results for a set of queries in corpus *C* where $1/rank_i$ is the inverse rank of the ith query in *C*, and $|C|$ is the size of the corpus. The resulting MRR was 0.5844, meaning that the average rank of the result across the repository (taking into account all the best and worst-case ranks) was between 1 and 2.

To understand why LemonAid failed for 9.7% of the queries, we inspected the selections made by users (based on the `nodeText`, `nodeXPath`, and `nodeType`) and the corresponding task scenario. We found that the failed queries mainly represented idiosyncratic selections; in other words, a few of the users made selections that did not match any selection made by other users. When we further looked at the corresponding question text provided with the selections, we found that such users (despite meeting our initial filtering criteria) either misunderstood the scenario description, were confused about the selection task, or were simply guessing.

While the overall performance of the retrieval algorithm is important, its performance over time, as users ask more questions, is also important. To investigate the effect of corpus size, we randomly selected 5 subsets of queries of four different corpus sizes (25%, 50%, 75%, and 100 % of the 2,748 queries). Figure 7 displays the MRR for these 20 corpus subsets, showing that while MRR degrades as the number of selections increase, it degrades quite slowly. A live deployment of LemonAid would obviously introduce other factors that would affect these outcomes; for example, there might be many more help problems. However, these results show that users would also be more likely to find an existing question about a problem rather than ask a new one.

DISCUSSION

While our initial evaluation represented data from a simulated community of users on mTurk, the main finding is promising: LemonAid retrieved a relevant match in the top 2 results for over half of the queries based on the UI selection. Thus, in most cases, users would only have to make a UI selection that they think is relevant and they would see a relevant question (and answer, if available). This is a dramatic improvement over traditional text-based queries for help on the web, which require substantially more effort. The key phenomenon that facilitates the retrieval of high-ranking relevant results is that users' queries are restricted to a smaller and more focused set of UI selections instead of natural language text and that users tend to select similar labels for similar problems and different labels for different problems.

These results, and the larger vision underlying LemonAid's approach to crowdsourced contextual help, raises some issues around scope, scalability, robustness, and privacy.

Problem Scope. For a given application, users may have a range of feature-related or account-specific troubleshooting help needs. Since LemonAid is integrated within the UI of the application, its primary strength is likely to be in providing user interface related help. For other types of issues that reach beyond the user interface, such as a problem with a blocked account or an issue with a credit card transaction, LemonAid would be able to inform a user that it is necessary to contact support, but it will not be able to help the user address their problem directly. Help needs that require the intervention of support personnel are less a limitation of LemonAid and more a limitation of crowdsourced help approaches in general.

Scalability. As shown in Figure 7, we have some initial indication that the retrieval algorithm is relatively stable as a help corpus increases in size. However, another important question is how LemonAid's retrieval scales for applications that vary from a narrow to a wide range of features and corresponding UI literals. For instance, in our study we observed was different users consistently made the same selection in the UI for the same problem, but made different selections for different types of problems. Thus, for an application that has a large number of features (and more possibilities for selections), the spread of questions could be sparse. For the case of an application with only a few features, there will likely be similarly few possible selections. We predict that LemonAid's performance will still degrade slowly as there would possibly be fewer questions about applications that have more limited functionality.

Another case we observed in our evaluation was the same label being used as an anchor for many different problems. For example, the "settings" label of *Google Calendar* was a particularly common choice when users perceived no better label in some of the scenarios. The retrieval algorithm was not able to retrieve a relevant answer in the top few results based on the selection alone. In this situation, the user would need to provide keywords to pare down the results. Still, in the worst case, LemonAid only degrades to the performance of a full-text search, but within the limited scope of questions generated through the LemonAid interface, rather than everything on the web.

Robustness. One concern about the utility of LemonAid in practice might be that web applications are constantly changing; anchoring help to rapidly changing labels and layouts may not be robust to such change. The UI labels that LemonAid relies on, however, are likely to change less often than the average website content, since changing functionality labels often requires costly user re-education. Moreover, when functionality labels and locations do change, it would actually make sense for the help associated with those UI literals to be deprecated. With LemonAid, this would be automatic, since questions attached to labels that have been removed would no longer be matched. The only process required to keep help content current would be to refresh LemonAid's list of application-specific UI literals, which is a simple matter of re-extracting string literals from their source)

Privacy. By using text on web pages, much of which may be privacy-sensitive, LemonAid also raises some privacy concerns. However, since we are only extracting UI literals from source code, and users can only select labels that match these static labels, user-generated content is never captured as part of a help request. There is a possibility that there may be some overlap between a UI literal and user-generated text. Future versions of LemonAid could allow users to redact details from their selections before submission.

Bootstrapping. While we have shown LemonAid performs well on a large corpus of queries, the approach still requires someone to provide help in order for the system to be useful and the help must actually be helpful. These challenges are not unique to LemonAid, however; they are more general challenges with crowdsourced help, and evidence has shown that they are they are easily surmountable with the right types of incentives and community features [34]. In future work, we will explore these community aspects further.

Evaluation Limitations. Our evaluation has some limitations that that should be considered when interpreting our results. For example, our results might only hold for the type of users represented by mTurk workers [17]. Although we tried to filter out invalid selections in our mTurk data (based on our criteria discussed above), it could be that a few users genuinely misunderstood scenario descriptions or the purpose of the task and ended up selecting something not relevant to the scenario. Moreover, our evaluation did not explore the effect of LemonAid users *interactively* exploring LemonAid search results, which may also affect LemonAid's utility. We hope to explore these issues further in a live deployment where users would be driven by their actual help needs.

RELATED WORK

Although LemonAid's approach to retrieving help is novel, it builds upon a variety of prior work in help systems research.

Context-Sensitive Help. Context-sensitive help to date has largely been about attaching help to specific UI controls. Researchers have explored a variety of ways to invoke this help, including tooltips, special modes as in the "?" icon in some Windows dialog boxes, Balloon Help [10] in early Apple systems, pressing F1 over UI elements, and even choosing a command to see animated steps [32] or videos [12]. Other recent approaches have explored the use of screenshots and visual search in creating contextual help [35]. Despite the utility of these forms of context-sensitive help, one drawback is that designers must *anticipate* where users might seek help, so that they can author it at design-time and attach it to UI controls. Also, the help presented is static and often limited to explaining the functionality of a widget. LemonAid addresses this issue by letting *users* decide where help should be embedded, authoring that help at run-time.

Adaptive Help. Adaptive help attempts to overcome context-insensitivity by monitoring user behavior for opportunities to help [7,24]. These systems make an explicit effort to model users' tasks, often employing AI techniques to predict and classify user behavior, some even using speech recognition [15]. Perhaps the most well known is "clippy" in Microsoft Word (which was a simplified version of a more successful intelligent agent [16]). Although powerful, these systems are limited by their ability to model and infer users' intent, meaning that the static help that they provide can often be irrelevant. Moreover, these systems may interrupt at inappropriate times and are often perceived as being intrusive. In contrast, an ambient and unobtrusive approach is feature recommendation based on monitoring of application usage [21]. Still, in all of these cases, help is tied to functionality rather than user's intentions and application use.

Automatic Help. Another class of help tools manifest as automatic help tools. Rather than inferring users' intent, such tools enable users to explicitly state their problems to obtain customized help. For example, SmartAidè [26] allows users to choose particular application task, and AI planning algorithms generate step-by-step instructions based on the current application state. The Crystal system [23] allows users to ask "why?" questions about unexpected output by simply clicking on the output itself. While such help techniques are powerful in generating customized solutions to users' help requests, they can only answer a limited class of questions amenable to automatic analysis. They also often require significant adaptations to an applications' code to provide useful answers.

Crowdsourced Help. Crowdsourced help is the most recent approach to software help. The essential idea is that the user community can generate solutions to help requests more quickly than any tool or in-house support team [13]. Early research examples of this approach, such as AnswerGarden [1], focused on organizational support and exchange of expertise; similar ideas emerged in the open source community in technical support forums [28]. Some research has explored the role of contextual help in content authoring. For example, the CHIC framework [31] for the Eclipse IDE adds links from each Eclipse UI control to a wiki where users can author help. Similar approaches that try to link community discussions in the interface have appeared recently in the IP-QAT system [20] and in commercial contexts [37] as well. LemonAid goes further by letting users decide which aspect of the interface matters for particular problems and allows users to author and discover help there. Furthermore, LemonAid is not specifically tied to any application structure and can be applied to any site implemented with web standards.

FUTURE WORK AND CONCLUSION

In this paper, we have introduced LemonAid, a new framework for integrating crowdsourced contextual help in web applications. We have shown that LemonAid's approach to selection-based query and retrieval is effective, providing a relevant answer in the top 2 results for over half of the queries in a corpus developed by a simulated community. We also have initial evidence that as a LemonAid help corpus grows in size, its ability to retrieve relevant results degrades slowly.

In our future work, we will explore a number of enhancements. For example, we will incorporate community feedback features for improving the ranking of search results and indicating which questions require useful answers, enabling users to vote on relevant questions and solutions that are tied to specific selections. We will include multimedia options, such as screen shots and videos, for enhancing solution authoring and diagnosis of reported issues [6].

In addition to helping users find help content, LemonAid may also provide other benefits. For example, a user could browse the goals of other users who have used the site by simply clicking on different labels in the UI. Other users' goals expressed in the context of the application could lead to the serendipitous discovery of new application features, shortcuts, and customizations. Software teams could also use their product's LemonAid help repository as a dataset of user expectations and potential usability issues. This would be a significant improvement over the status quo, where feedback about an application is scattered in discussion forums and social networking sites all over the web, with no simple way to monitor them. With LemonAid, user selections and queries can be easily aggregated and placed in the exact context in which users experienced a problem. Ultimately, software teams can use this information to better understand users and provide a more seamless user experience.

ACKNOWLEDGEMENTS

We thank Tovi Grossman, Jeff Huang, and Michael Lee. This work was funded in part by fellowships awarded to the first author from Facebook Inc., and Canada's Social Sciences and Humanities Research Council (SSHRC).

REFERENCES

1. Ackerman, M.S. and Malone, T.W. Answer Garden: a tool for growing organizational memory. *Proc ACM SIGOIS* (1990), 31-39.
2. Adar, E., Dontcheva, M., Fogarty, J., and Weld, D.S. Zoetrope: interacting with the ephemeral web. *Proc ACM UIST* (2008), 239-248.
3. Belkin, N.J. Helping people find what they don't know. *Commun. ACM 43*, 8 (2000), 58-61.

4. Bolin, M., Webber, M., Rha, P., Wilson, T., and Miller, R.C. Automation and customization of rendered web pages. *Proc ACM UIST* (2005), 163-172.

5. Brandt, J., Dontcheva, M., Weskamp, M., and Klemmer, S.R. Example-centric programming: integrating web search into the development environment. *Proc ACM CHI* (2010), 513-522.

6. Chilana, P.K., Grossman, T., and Fitzmaurice, G. Modern software product support processes and the usage of multimedia formats. *Proc ACM CHI* (2011), 3093-3102.

7. Delisle, S. and Moulin, B. User interfaces and help systems: from helplessness to intelligent assistance. *Artificial Intelligence Review 18*, 2 (2002), 117-157.

8. Downs, J.S., Holbrook, M.B., Sheng, S., and Cranor, L.F. Are your participants gaming the system?: screening mechanical turk workers. *Proc ACM CHI,* (2010), 2399-2402.

9. Ekstrand, M., Li, W., Grossman, T., Matejka, J., and Fitzmaurice, G. Searching for software learning resources using application context. *Proc ACM UIST* (2011), 195-204.

10. Farkas, D.K. The role of balloon help. *ACM SIGDOC 17*, 2 (1993), 3-19.

11. Furnas, G.W., Landauer, T.K., Gomez, L.M., and Dumais, S.T. The vocabulary problem in human-system communication. *Commun. ACM 30*, 11 (1987), 964-971.

12. Grossman, T. and Fitzmaurice, G. Toolclips: An investigation of contextual video assistance for functionality understanding. *Proc ACM CHI* (2010), 1515-1524.

13. Harper, F.M., Raban, D., Rafaeli, S., and Konstan, J.A. Predictors of answer quality in online Q&A sites. *Proc ACM CHI* (2008), 865-874.

14. Hartmann, B., MacDougall, D., Brandt, J., and Klemmer, S.R. What would other programmers do: suggesting solutions to error messages. *Proc ACM CHI* (2010), 1019-1028.

15. Hastie, H.W., Johnston, M., and Ehlen, P. Context-Sensitive Help for Multimodal Dialogue. *Proc IEEE ICMI* (2002), 93.

16. Horvitz, E. Principles of mixed-initiative user interfaces. *Proc ACM CHI* (1999), 159-166.

17. Kittur, A., Chi, H., and Suh, B. Crowdsourcing user studies with Mechanical Turk. *Proc ACM CHI* (2008), 453-456.

18. Ko, A.J. and Myers, B.A. Designing the whyline: a debugging interface for asking questions about program behavior. *Proc ACM CHI* (2004), 151-158.

19. Lakhani, K.R. and Von Hippel, E. How open source software works:"free" user-to-user assistance. *Research policy 32*, 6 (2003), 923-943.

20. Matejka, J., Grossman, T., and Fitzmaurice, G. IP-QAT: In-Product Questions, Answers & Tips. *Proc ACM UIST* (2011), 175-184.

21. Matejka, J., Li, W., Grossman, T., and Fitzmaurice, G. CommunityCommands: command recommendations for software applications. *Proc ACM UIST* (2009), 193-202.

22. Morris, M.R., Teevan, J., and Panovich, K. What do people ask their social networks, and why?: a survey study of status message q&a behavior. *Proc ACM CHI* (2010), 1739-1748.

23. Myers, B.A., Weitzman, D.A., Ko, A.J., and Chau, D.H. Answering why and why not questions in user interfaces. *Proc ACM CHI* (2006), 397-406.

24. Pangoli, S. and Paternó, F. Automatic generation of task-oriented help. *Proc ACM UIST* (1995), 181-187.

25. Paolacci, G., Chandler, J., and Ipeirotis, P.G. Running experiments on amazon mechanical turk. *Judgment and Decision Making 5*, 5 (2010), 411-419.

26. Ramachandran, A. and Young, R.M. Providing intelligent help across applications in dynamic user and environment contexts. *Proc ACM IUI* (2005), 269-271.

27. Salton, G., Wong, A., and Yang, C.S. A vector space model for automatic indexing. *Commun. ACM 18*, 11 (1975), 613-620.

28. Singh, V., Twidale, M.B., and Nichols, D.M. Users of Open Source Software - How Do They Get Help? *Proc HICSS* (2009), 1-10.

29. Singh, V., Twidale, M.B., and Rathi, D. Open Source Technical Support: A Look at Peer Help-Giving. *Proc HICSS* (2006), 118.3.

30. Snow, R., O'Connor, B., Jurafsky, D., and Ng, A.Y. Cheap and fast---but is it good?: evaluating non-expert annotations for natural language tasks. *Proc Empirical Methods in NLP* (2008), 254-263.

31. Stevens, G. and Wiedenhöfer, T. CHIC - a pluggable solution for community help in context. *Proc ACM NordiCHI* (2006), 212-221.

32. Sukaviriya, P. and Foley, J.D. Coupling a UI framework with automatic generation of context-sensitive animated help. *Proc ACM SIGGRAPH* (1990), 152-166.

33. Twidale, M.B. Over the shoulder learning: supporting brief informal learning. *J CSCW 14*, 6 (2005), 505-547.

34. Tynan-Wood, C. The (Better) Future of Tech Support. *InfoWorld*, 2010.

35. Yeh, T., Chang, T.H., Xie, B., Walsh, G., Watkins, I., Wongsuphasawat, K., Huang, M., Davis, L., and Bederson, B. Creating contextual help for GUIs using screenshots. *Proc UIST* (2011), 145-154.

36. Amazon Mechanical Turk. http://www.mturk.com/.

37. TurboTax Support. http://turbotax.intuit.com/support/.

Is This What You Meant? Promoting Listening on the Web with Reflect

Travis Kriplean[1], Michael Toomim[1], Jonathan Morgan[2], Alan Borning[1], Andrew J. Ko[3]
Computer Science & Engr.[1], Human Centered Design & Engr.[2], Information School[3]
University of Washington, Seattle

ABSTRACT
A lack of support for active listening undermines discussion and deliberation on the web. We contribute a design frame identifying potential improvements to web discussion were listening more explicitly encouraged in interfaces. We explore these concepts through a novel interface, Reflect, that creates a space next to every comment where others can summarize the points they hear the commenter making. Deployments on Slashdot, Wikimedia's Strategic Planning Initiative, and a local civic effort suggest that interfaces for listening may have traction for general use on the web.

Author Keywords
Web, Discussion, Listening, Deliberation, Grounding

ACM Classification Keywords
H.5.0 Information Interfaces and Presentation: General

INTRODUCTION
To accomplish collective goals, people must discuss what to do, how to do it, and who will do it, whether it is an open source project, a faculty meeting, or a government planning process. We are seeing a shift toward participatory engagement, in which organizations are exploring new ways of including their constituencies in decision making and people increasingly expect such opportunities [4]. Discussions can be merely consultative, as with Facebook's gathering of feedback on terms of service changes and U.S. President Obama's gathering of citizens' ideas for open governance. Or it can be at the heart of organizational culture, such as in Wikipedia where participants strive for community consensus in all decisions [5, 20]. We believe these deliberative efforts to tap the creative energy, emotion, and intelligence of many are needed to improve our collective ability to confront public problems.

Unfortunately, public discourse on the web is often perceived as inflammatory and hyperbolic [15], which constrains the potential of web-based public discussion for informing decisions. We argue that constructive web discussion is elusive partially as a result of the lack of attention to supporting listening. Interfaces designed for listening might nudge people to establish more common understanding, even when the discussion is heated. When participants establish mutual understanding, they are more likely to recognize the legitimacy of that person's perspective [27], and the quality of their opinions are often improved [9]. Our goal in this paper is to draw attention to the generative potential of a deeper understanding of listening on the web, and illustrate it through the design, deployment, and evaluation of a novel interface.

We contribute a design-oriented theoretical frame for supporting listening in web interfaces. Second, we contribute a novel interface, Reflect, which embodies the listening design frame. Reflect introduces a second dimension into online comment boards, adding a backchannel for people to demonstrate evidence of listening by restating the points that they hear the commenter making (Fig. 1). Inspired by Wikipedia, Reflect nudges people to strive toward a neutral reflection of what others are saying, even if there is disagreement. Our third contribution is a presentation of Reflect's deployment in three diverse contexts: a high-volume technology news discussion site, summarization by facilitators during Wikimedia's Strategic Planning Initiative and during a local civic engagement effort. Our results suggest that restatement is an activity in which discussion participants will voluntarily engage.

INTERFACES FOR GROUNDING AND LISTENING
Active listening is integral to communication. Listeners must provide evidence to speakers to show that they are being attentive and understand [11]. Listeners operate a backchannel where they nod, say "uh huh", tilt their heads, finish sentences, and preface responses with a simple restatement of what the speaker said [17]. These explicit acts of listening helps speakers "debug" their messages, as well as provide evidence that they are being recognized and heard [33]. It also helps listeners demonstrate good faith as conversation partners; partners who provide more feedback through the backchannel are perceived as more patient, polite, and attentive [36]. This process of trading off speaking and listening to establish mutual understanding is called *grounding* [11].

In contrast, web interfaces have typically not explicitly supported backchannels for others to demonstrate evidence of understanding. Consider two ends of the spectrum of current (implicit) support for listening. First, threaded forums allow replies, which can be appropriated by users to listen, such as by rephrasing what is being said or asking for clarification. But mixing replies and acts of listening can quickly make a discussion difficult to follow if many people are involved. Moreover, there is usually an expectation that comments add something new to the conversation. Second, many discussion systems allow participants to vote on their favorite utterances,

Permission to make digital or hard copies of all or part of this work for personal or classroom use is granted without fee provided that copies are not made or distributed for profit or commercial advantage and that copies bear this notice and the full citation on the first page. To copy otherwise, or republish, to post on servers or to redistribute to lists, requires prior specific permission and/or a fee.
CHI'12, May 5-10, 2012, Austin, Texas, USA.
Copyright 2012 ACM 978-1-4503-1015-4/12/05...$10.00.

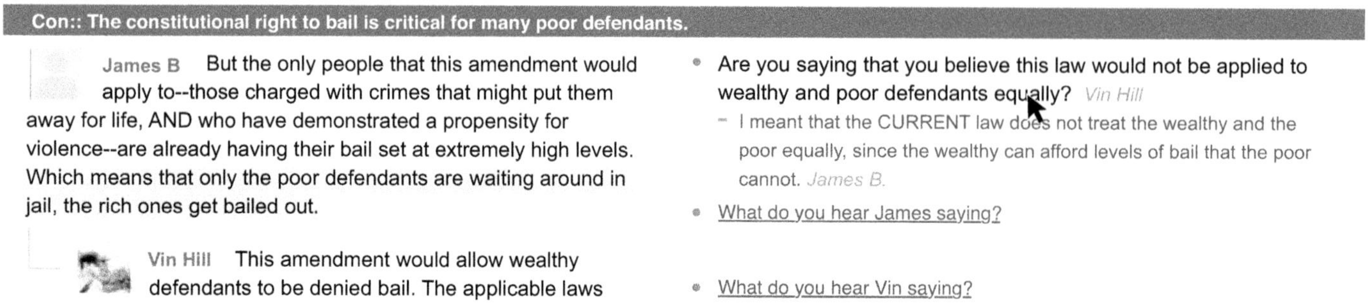

Figure 1. The first use of Reflect in the wild, in the Living Voters Guide [23]. In this exchange, Vin restates a point he thought James made, and then replies. James later returned and clarified his point to correct Vin, illustrating an ordering challenge with asynchronous listening.

such as with "like" or "recommend" buttons. These buttons overload two functionalities: they perform an important listening functionality, in that they signal to the commenter that they have been heard; but they also serve to *judge* the statement. Thus, these mechanisms are not pure listening mechanisms, but also contain an implicit "I agree" reply. This does not serve those who disagree with what is being said but yet wish to recognize and appreciate the speaker.

Overall, web interfaces implicitly privilege speaking over listening, creating a feedback chasm that may hinder formation of common ground. Prioritizing speaking over listening may bias toward emotionally-charged but shallow interactions, in turn affecting who is willing to participate. We argue that interfaces can be designed that help nudge people toward more reflective interactions by emphasizing the common experience of listening. We hypothesize the following four potential outcomes of supporting listening:

Listening interfaces enable people to see evidence that they are being heard, improving their communication satisfaction and willingness to participate. Consider reactions to the frustration of not being heard. One option is forcefully restating a point, further deteriorating the situation. A second reaction is to disengage. Being responded to is one determinant of whether people continue contributing in an online forum [2], and the fundamental dynamic may be being heard.

Listening interfaces empower participants to use and hone their active listening skills to guide the discussion and demonstrate their own worth. Acts of listening impact the direction that a conversation takes [11, 33], and help to demonstrate to others that the listener is a valuable participant. Consider the motivations for active listening: first, a listener might try to demonstrate understanding before responding (such as by restating), a commonly recommended technique for effectively interacting with someone about a controversial or complex issue (e.g., marriage counseling or dispute mediation in Wikipedia [6]). Second, listeners might provide feedback that helps teach speakers how to better frame their points. Third, listening can draw other's attention to a statement's importance (e.g., if the point reflects their own personal beliefs [15]). Fourth, someone might articulate understanding in order to better interpret the intended meaning.

By showing active listeners' demonstrations of understanding (or misunderstanding), listening interfaces help other discussants make sense of what is being said and why. In an examination of how speakers and listeners work together to coordinate a conversation, Kraut [22] found that while an active listener is the one whose understanding of what a speaker is saying is most positively affected when interacting with the speaker, eavesdroppers also benefit. This effect is familiar: consider a large meeting where a colleague succinctly rephrases your long and convoluted expression of an important point. Your colleague has demonstrated that she has understood, and also helped everyone else understand better. These are acts of facilitation that lead others to say, "Ahhh, I see!" Listening interfaces may help elicit, capture, and expose these "ahh" moments for future participants.

Listening interfaces help establish an empathetic normative environment. Even simple changes to a commenting interface can impact the thoughtfulness of comments, leading to the establishment of commenting norms as participants calibrate to the observed behaviors of prior participants [31]. Recent research in neuroscience indicates that the likelihood of empathetic engagement, e.g. via perspective taking, is sensitive to experimental manipulation [24], suggesting that we might successfully embed cues for listening in our interfaces. If the interface can encourage some users to listen, others may follow, helping to establish constructive communicative norms. Through their visible structuring, web interfaces can continually remind people to actively listen, even when the discussion is heated, and re-present these acts to other participants to bolster the listener's conversational status.

We have not tested all of these hypotheses. Rather, we contribute the speaking/listening theoretical frame as a useful metaphor for considering new design directions and guiding future empirical investigations, and demonstrate its productivity with the interface presented next. In reading this paper, it is important to keep in mind that the speaking/listening frame is a metaphor. There are significant differences between the asynchronous character of the web discussions we target and the synchronous dyadic face-to-face communication upon which much of the research cited thus far is based. For example, we know that the introduction of asynchrony, even short delays, can disrupt speaker/listener coordination [34]. Some may argue that reading/writing is a more accurate metaphor for asynchronous web discussions. However, the reading/writing metaphor only indirectly captures the communicative functionality that listening highlights: timely, fine-grained feedback for communicators. Reading implies interaction between a reader and text, not interaction with the writer, whereas writing encompasses both raising new points and addressing points raised by the other.

REFLECT: LISTENING THROUGH RESTATEMENT

The design space for listening is wide. For example, a minimal listening mechanism might simply be an "I hear you" button, which does not support grounding but might lead to some of the interpersonal benefits discussed. A non-textual listening mechanism for supporting grounding might have users annotate text with an emoticon that conveys their sentiment when reading that piece of text (smiling, grimace, quizzical). Emoticons from multiple people could be aggregated and visualized on mousehover, engaging themes raised in the prior section. A maximal listening interface would have users restate the points they hear the commenter saying, motivated by a useful practice when in an emotional argument.

In this paper, we experiment with this latter strategy of restatement. We present a novel interface, Reflect, that makes a lightweight change to online comment boards: to the right of every comment, visitors are invited to restate points they hear the commenters making (Fig. 2). These restatements, each an act of listening, are publicly displayed in a bulleted list. Reflect provides an opportunity for the original commenter to respond to each bullet point to verify its accuracy and clarify if necessary. Reflect thus establishes a listener's backchannel that engages the theoretical propositions laid out earlier. First, commenters can learn how others are interpreting their statements and clarify misunderstandings, supporting one iteration of grounding. Second, listeners can gain status as productive listeners. Third, other participants can scan the bullets to better understand what is being said and identify important points, assuming that listeners are more likely to restate points that they find important (a form of "read wear" [21]). And finally, in contrast to most comment boards, a Reflect-enabled site strongly suggests to a visitor that listening is a primary mode of participation, perhaps helping to establish a normative environment through which common ground is more likely to be found. By carving out a prominent space for restatements in a comment board, we gain leverage for inquiring about what would happen if we make active listening a first-class activity in web discussions.

Scenario of use and design rationale

Imagine that you have just come to a discussion about whether the City of Seattle should eliminate an ordinance requiring real estate developers to provide for future tenant parking. You start browsing the comments, glancing over the first one and then read the summary points others have written. When you hover over a summary bullet, the relevant text in the comment that the bullet refers to is highlighted, allowing you to jump between the commenter's own words and the listener's interpretation (Fig. 2.1). This particular summary is interesting because it helps you better understand the point the commenter was making about the free-market implications of your idea. You mark the restatement as "Helps shed light on what the commenter was trying to say" (Fig. 2.2).

You recognize the next commenter, Lisa, who added the helpful restatement. You note that no one has restated any of her points, so you read her comment carefully. You add a bullet point so that she knows someone is listening and so that her comment is not lost in the mix. After clicking "Add a point that Lisa made", you type in your interpretation of her main argument in the 140-character limited text field (Fig. 2.3). It causes you to stop and think for a while, which is often not how you usually skim comments. After hitting submit, you are asked to connect the point that you summarized to the part of Lisa's comment to which it refers (Fig. 2.4). After clicking two sentences, which are subsequently highlighted, you click done. The bullet shows up next to the comment.

You scroll down to a comment you posted earlier. Several bullet points have been added. You recall receiving notification emails, but had not had time to check it out then. The interface presents you with the option of verifying the accuracy of each bullet point, or if it is even a restatement at all. You can also add a short clarification if needed. The first bullet is accurate. You click "yes" and a checkmark appears next to the summary. The second bullet is inaccurate. You click "no" and clarify what you were trying to say (Fig. 2.5). The clarification shows up underneath the bullet point (Fig. 2.6).

Articulating the work of comment summarization. There are other ways in which the task of restating or summarizing the comment could be broken up besides short bullet points. For example, our first design used a wiki next to the comment. However, in early testing, this proved problematic. People felt that with a wiki they must commit to summarizing the whole comment (many of which can be quite long). We moved to bullet lists and discovered some additional affordances: (1) including more people in the listening and grounding activity in a natural way, (2) enhanced support for clarifying points, (3) facilitating multiple interpretations of the same text, (4) easier for commenters to respond to the summary and clarify their points, (5) easier to skim the summaries and connect them to the comments, (6) the ability to identify similar points being made in other comments, and (7) the ability for listeners to highlight the points they found most salient in what the commenter said.

Connecting summary text to comment text. After someone summarizes a point that a commenter makes, we ask him or her to click on the sentences in the original comment where the point was being made. There were two reasons for doing this. First, accountability: a listener explicitly commits to exactly where a commenter made the point they believe them to be making. For those who are maliciously misinterpreting the message or deliberately antagonizing the commenter, it adds a step whereby they are forced to essentially acknowledge their maliciousness. Second, readability: this data is used later to aid readers in figuring out the relevant parts of the comment to which the summary refers. If there is a breakdown in grounding between speaker and listener, the speaker may be able to more easily see where the misinterpretation occurred. Others can judge whether the listener accurately represented the point. If someone maliciously writes a bullet, it's relatively easy to verify what the sentences actually said.

Speakers are privileged to verify summaries. Because Reflect places the bullet points next to a comment, an inaccurate bullet might overly influence what others believe the commenter was saying. Therefore, Reflect enables speakers to verify a summary bullet point and clarify when needed, which is prominently displayed to other readers underneath the bul-

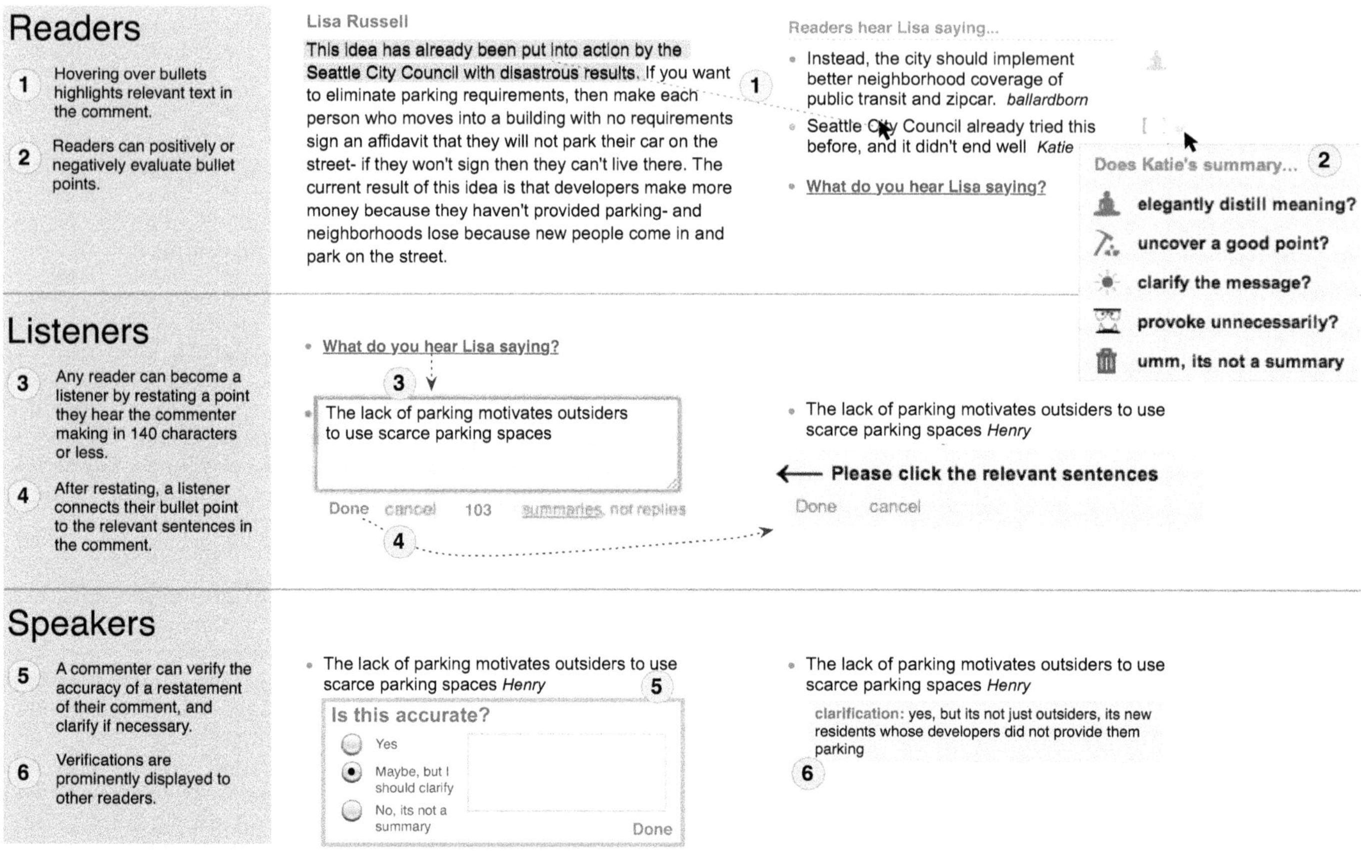

Figure 2. Mechanics of the Reflect interface.

let point. However, Reflect does not entrust speakers with the ability to directly edit or delete the bullet points. Otherwise they may censor other people's valid interpretations. Privileged responses address the tension between allowing the speaker to repair breakdowns with giving listeners the power to express their interpretations. These verifications thus facilitate public grounding of expressed meaning.

Community evaluation. Not every restatement is created equal. Some restatements might highlight a point deeply buried in a long comment, or distill the essence of a long comment. Or bullets might be antagonistic or used to reply. Reflect therefore enables other participants to recognize good restatements and flag poor ones. Aside from potentially removing malicious restatements, this can help to demonstrate for participants the purpose that good restatements might play.

Implementation. Reflect is an open source jQuery Javascript library. It requires a configuration object specifying CSS selectors for key DOM elements. On page load, the core library can then wrap the Reflect markup around comments. A server-side web service for fetching and storing Reflect data must also be implemented. The service can also carry out other tasks like email notifications. Reflect implementations are publicly available for Wordpress, Drupal, and Mediawiki.

Related design work

Reflect explicitly supports the process of grounding described by Clark's contribution theory [11]. HCI researchers have drawn upon this theory as an analytical lens to understand the affordances of the communication medium (e.g. [19]), how communication strategies change under pressures of scale [35], or informing the design of systems supporting distributed teamwork [14]. To our knowledge, Reflect is the first interface that makes the process of content grounding a first-class activity in web-based discussions. Other interfaces afford restatements, such as annotation and anchoring tools [7, 10], but do not call out this affordance explicitly. The only work we have found that explicitly supports restatement is the classroom tool ThoughtSwap [16]. Students submit ideas in response to a prompt, and then other students can pull ideas out of the "hat" and re-present those ideas. Ultimately, Reflect is meant to trigger deeper reflection about what others are saying. In this sense, one of the most related systems is MetaViz [3]. MetaViz attempts to trigger critical thinking by using computational metaphor identification to expose the political metaphors that participants are drawing upon in a blog. ConsiderIt [23] is also highly related. ConsiderIt enables people to create pro/con lists for a given issue, but also include points others have written into their own list. This inclusion functionality is similar in spirit to a Reflect summary.

There is a rich line of research that helps users make sense of conversations. First, a number of interfaces help users navigate threaded discussions, such as visualizing social and semantic associations [28, 30], or focus+context interfaces for reading threads [32]. Others have attempted to overcome sensemaking challenges by moving away from threaded comment boards entirely. A recent exemplary system is OpinionSpace [18]. OpinionSpace plots on a two-dimensional map the individual comments in a web forum, based on the commenters' responses to a short value-based questionnaire. By navigating this space, readers are better able to seek out a diversity of comments as well as prime themselves for engaging the perspective of someone with different values. Argumentation visualization systems, a particularly well explored class of systems, also provide an alternate structure to threaded forums. These systems require users to break down their opinions according to argumentation schemas drawn from linguistic theory or elsewhere, and incorporate them into a graphical visualization of the issues, arguments, positions, and so forth (see [8] for an overview). Argumentation visualization has proven to have serious limitations in practice, including the difficulty of learning the formalized schemas, breaking up narratives into fine chunks, and agreeing on classifications [29], often requiring trained facilitators for effective use [13]. Overall, these interfaces can help set the context for listening, but they do not go beyond the typical rating of comments when it comes to engaging with what is being said.

Finally, researchers have created tools for extracting takeaways from discussions, such as by creating discussion-level summaries. Ackerman and colleagues have tackled this goal with expert systems for post-processing discussions [1, 26]. Underlying this work is the stance that the ideal case would be automatic summarization (see e.g. [26], p. 139). While automatic summarization would be very useful, this ideal precludes the potential interpersonal benefits of listening.

FIELD DEPLOYMENTS

To provide insight into how Reflect might be appropriated in real discussions, we report on three deployments: (1) augmenting four stories posted to the popular technology news discussion site Slashdot; (2) use by the Wikimedia Foundation to summarize input they received during a worldwide Strategic Planning Initiative; and (3) in a local civic engagement initiative (CCF), providing a means for the leader to show participants on their blog that he was listening to them.

We divide our deployments into two contexts of use: *community news discussion* (Slashdot) and *community deliberation* (Wikimedia, CCF). Because of the size of Slashdot's readership, the Slashdot deployment helps us most in establishing whether and how Reflect will likely be used by a wide public. The other deployments are more limited because details of each deployment limited the size of the user base. The value of these other deployments is to illustrate additional possible use cases for community deliberation.

Community News Discussion

Two fundamental questions are whether online discussants will (1) actually use the Reflect functionality and (2) whether they will use it to listen to each other, rather than troll or reply to commenters. These questions are essential in determining if Reflect, and listening interfaces more broadly, might have traction for broad public use. If it does, then pursuing this line of inquiry further may be fruitful, both in terms of creating new designs for listening as well as rigorously examining whether the hypothesized outcomes laid out earlier hold.

Table 1. Absolute counts of four contribution types in the Slashdot data (and number of unique users contributing each).

	Comments	Bullets	Ratings	Replies
Story 1	389 (145)	336 (113)	719 (285)	20 (13)
Story 2	112 (67)	151 (47)	335 (203)	17 (7)
Story 3	57 (37)	81 (36)	181 (129)	14 (6)
Story 4	174 (93)	166 (65)	264 (144)	12 (8)

To answer these questions, we deployed Reflect on four articles posted to Slashdot, one of the most popular news discussion sites since its founding in 1997. Slashdot's audience is primarily male professional engineers, an audience one might not expect to embrace Reflect and its emphasis on listening. If the Slashdot community uses Reflect as intended, it suggests that Reflect may be widely applicable, with the caveat that the tech savvy user base with its experience using the complex Slashdot commenting system [25] may be quicker to understand Reflect than the general public.

The opportunity to deploy Reflect on Slashdot was made possible by an introduction to Slashdot founder Rob Malda by fellow researcher Cliff Lampe.[1] From Spring to Fall 2011, we developed the Slashcode plugin and coordinated with Malda and engineer Tim Vroom. Through this process, Reflect's design evolved, including the addition of the community moderation functionality. This emerged as an important design addition because Malda, with his decade-and-a-half experience moderating online discussions, was concerned that Reflect would be used predominantly to troll or reply to commenters. We designed the bullet evaluation functionality, and then used the evaluations to deactivate bullet points that were rated negatively. Specifically, in our scheme, if more than half of the evaluations of a bullet point were negative after the first three evaluations, the bullet was deactivated and hidden. The bullet was also deactivated if the commenter labeled the bullet as "not a summary" during verification and at least one reader gave it a negative rating.

In mid-September 2011, Slashdot enabled Reflect on four stories. During the trial, **734 bullets were written by 247 discussants, an average of 1.0 bullets per comment** (Table 1). Figure 3 shows an excerpt from Story 4. The full discussion is embedded in the margin. 15.3% of commenters in the stories also created a bullet point, overall contributing 41.2% of the bullets. The remaining 58.8% of the bullets were contributed by people we may previously have labeled as "lurkers".

Did the written bullet points actually reflect the meaning conveyed in the comment? Our most important empirical results, after establishing the baseline that Reflect would in fact be used, concern the nature of the bullet points and the extent these bullets reflected back the commenter's points. Here, we did content analysis on the bullet points. This was challenging because the bullet points were deeply contextual, rich social expressions drawing on multiple levels of shared meaning: the Slashdot culture and past interactions; implicit references to the story being discussed and the preceding comments; and fairly detailed, often nuanced comments.

We coded all 734 bullet points using a standard grounded

[1] All of our deployment contacts and interview participants gave us explicit permission to use their full names.

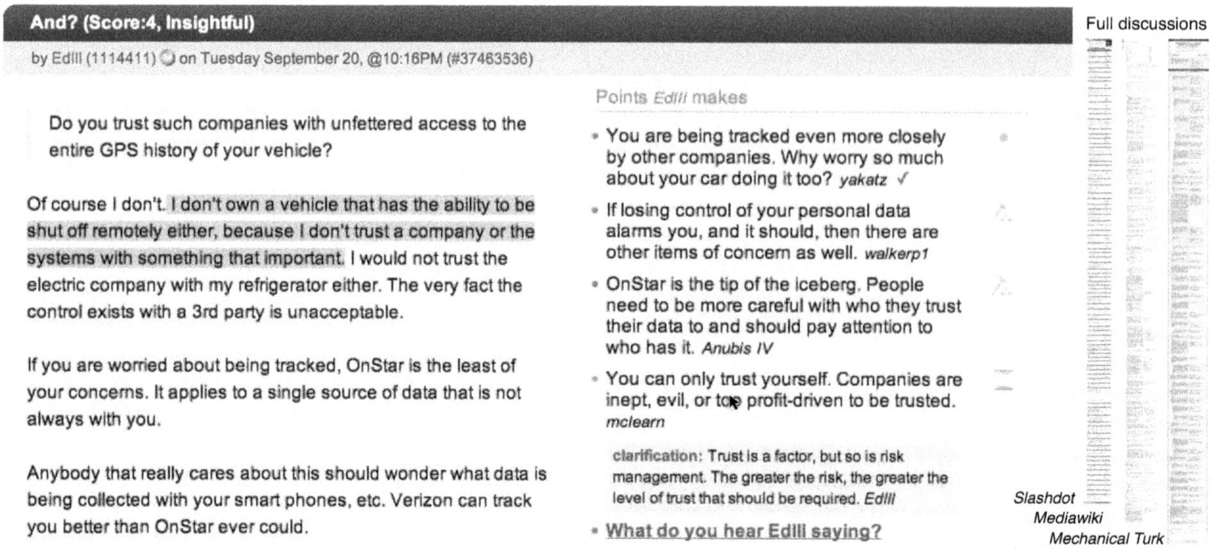

Figure 3. Deployment screenshots, focusing on an excerpt from a Slashdot story. Zoom in to read the full discussions off to the right.

analysis through which we iteratively developed and refined a codebook and established inter-rater reliability. Ultimately, we decided to have each coder independently code every bullet and resolve discrepancies in order to yield results in which we are confident.[2] The codebook has two levels, shown in Table 2. The highest level is a yes/no code: Does the bullet primarily reflect back material from the comment? We achieved $\alpha = .89$ reliability for answering this question.

The codebook has five primary subcodes for bullet points that reflected meaning. First, *neutral reflections* rephrased, distilled, or elaborated upon (e.g. through examples) the respective comments' meaning. They do not go beyond the comment's meaning in any significant way. If *neutral reflection* was selected, no other code could also be selected because the purpose of this code was to capture strict restatements. Second, the *expands meaning* code was used for bullet points that read between the lines, such as by generalizing, inferring antecedents or consequences, or putting a high-level label on a phenomena the commenter described (e.g. "Social justice" when the commenter discusses income tax equalities). Third, the *meta observation* code was applied to bullet points that contextualized the meaning of the comment, such as by focusing a critical eye on the rhetorical devices employed by the comment or positions the meaning with respect to the norms of the community or other external events. Fourth, the *negative/cheeky* code was applied to bullet points that are non-neutral, usually sarcastic summaries that often mocked the ideas at play, or were overtly negative toward the comment's content. This code helps distinguish bullets that, while reflecting meaning, do so in a potentially antagonizing manner. Fifth, the *contains replies* code was applied when a bullet, after reflecting the meaning of the comment, also inserted a response to that point.

There are three subcodes for bullets that do not reflect meaning. The *flames* code captures bullet points that simply served to personally attack the commenter via ad hominems. It does not engage the substance of the comment, but rather the commenter. The *replies* code is for bullet points that reply to the comment without reflecting back any meaning. *Offtopic* bullets are unrelated to the discussion.

To illustrate the rich range of bullet points users wrote and better demonstrate these codes, we highlight six bullet points (out of 24) created for a polarizing comment. The comment took place on a story about the U.S. federal government closing down an online poker site because it was operating as a Ponzi scheme. The comment stated: *When Mitt Romney asks, "Why punish success?", I suggest people think about [poker sites like this]. Not all businesses are scams, but the people raking in millions of dollars a year aren't earning it. They're inheriting it, winning it or stealing it, and they deserve to be taxed at a higher rate."* Consider these bullet points for this comment:

1. *Just because someone obtained their wealth legally, does not mean it is wealth they have earned or generated.* Coded as **neutral reflection**.

2. *Implication that Romney isn't so different from the people involved in the criminal scheme.* Coded as **expands** because it reads between the lines. As this example shows, bullets that expand meaning can draw an inference that does not definitively follow from the comment.

3. *Not all business is criminal, only successful business.* Coded as **cheeky, expands** because the bullet writer expands the meaning of the comment by equating "people

[2]The codebook was developed by categorizing 50 random bullets, then iterated on with the first, second and fourth authors as we independently coded and resolved discrepancies on additional sets of bullets. Ultimately we converged on a two-level codebook. On a random set of 100 bullets, we established high reliability on the high-level code, though reliability on some subcodes was far less reliable. Low reliability was due to difficulty identifying all the necessary cues on each code, not because we disagreed on phenomena. Thus we elected to independently code each bullet and resolve any discrepancies. Discrepancies usually resulted from one of the coders attending to a signal that had escaped the others' attention.

Table 2. Content analysis: codebook, reliability and results.

	Krippendorff's α	Slashdot	Wikimedia Strategy	Mechanical Turk
Reflects back meaning of the comment	0.89	69.0%	97.0%	92.0%
Neutral reflection without elaboration	0.73	23.7%	92.0%	65.0%
Expands meaning by reading between the lines	0.66	35.8%	4.0%	26.0%
Meta observation that contextualizes the content	0.84	12.5%	0.0%	1.0%
Antagonistic or cheeky reflection of meaning	0.45	11.9%	1.0%	1.0%
Contains a reply in addition to reflecting	0.58	3.0%	0.0%	0.0%
Doesn't reflect meaning contained in the comment	0.89	31.0%	3.0%	8.0%
Flames the commenter with an ad hominem	0.84	10.4%	0.0%	0.0%
Replies to the commenter without reflecting	0.68	10.2%	0.0%	8.0%
Off-topic and doesn't relate to the discussion	1.00	9.6%	0.0%	0.0%
Repeats Simply repeats part of the comment	1.00	1.9%	3.0%	0.0%

Table 3. Moderation results. The community used the bullet evaluations to sanction and hide bullets that did not reflect meaning, increasing the visual salience of listening.

	active bullets	moderated bullets
Reflects back meaning	442	61
Doesn't reflect meaning	113	118

raking in millions of dollars" with "successful business" to make it possible for the reductio ad absurdum.

4. *reflecting the current US topic of 'class warfare' related to taxing higher incomes at the same rate as lower incomes.* Coded as **meta** because it contextualizes the comment with respect to the larger social issue at play.

5. *[the commenter] is emoting as per his training and will be rewarded by his fellow jealous and equally well trained primates.* **Flames** because this is an ad hominem attack. If, however, the bullet stated *...his training about how the rich have cheated their way to wealth and should be taxed more....*, it would have been **cheeky, meta** because it reflects back meaning in a negative way while also making a prediction about how Slashdotters will react.

69.0% of the bullets Reflected back meaning, indicating Reflect's use as a listening interface. Discounting negative/cheeky bullets, 57.1% of all bullets listened in an apparently neutral fashion. Of the subcodes, "expands meaning" was the most prevalent. As coders, we found many of the bullets falling into this category to be the most useful because they often brought to light the implied meaning of an unclear, subtle, or obfuscated comment. While flaming and pure replies were common, given concerns aired by Slashdot co-founder Rob Malda, we were pleasantly surprised that they were not more frequent. The distribution of frequencies in Table 2 as well as the set of examples given above conveys a variety of rich ways in which Reflect was used to listen.

Did the community's moderation of bullets tend to deactivate bullets that did not restate points? When enough users rated a bullet as not a restatement of one form or another, the bullet was deactivated and hidden from view for subsequent users.

24.6% of all bullets were moderated by the community and hidden from future view. Of these moderated bullets, 65.9% were not summaries (Table 3). This means that **after community moderation is factored in, 79.6% of the final set of publicly visible bullet points neutrally reflected meaning**. Moreover, 40.4% of the moderated bullets that reflected meaning were negative/cheeky, while 51.1% of all non-reflecting bullets were deactivated. We thus conclude that the community sanctioned non-restatements, carving out a backchannel for listening.

This deployment illustrates what discretionary use of Reflect might look like in a discourse community. We found an almost one to one comment to summary ratio. Aside from raw use, we found that participants generally followed our design intentions in writing bullets that restated points, and that the community moderation further reinforced this intention. These results are particularly promising given the reputation of Slashdot as an often vitriolic community.

Community Deliberation

Communities often need to deliberate and make decisions about what to do about challenges it faces. Sometimes this takes the form of a government, non-profit, or movement organization launching a project to engage its constituents. Or it might be a bottom-up discussion started by a community member that foments a new movement or influences decision-makers to take action. These efforts at community deliberation are the types of discussions we are primarily interested in improving through listening interfaces. In this section we describe two deployments of Reflect that highlight distinct use cases for community deliberation, primarily drawing on interview data from the leaders of each initiative. Unfortunately, these deployments are not as strong as the Slashdot deployment, so the implications we can draw are more limited. Still, these results provide value because it helps designers understand more deeply, if imperfectly, some of the different contexts of use to which Reflect might be put, and highlights opportunities for future empirical work.

Summarization in Wikimedia's Strategic Planning Initiative

Professional facilitators often need to summarize and extract themes from long discussions. This is an important but resource intensive task for effective community deliberation. Reflect may help with this process, as it allows facilitators (or participants, depending on the conditions of the deployment) to create intermediate summaries at the comment level. These intermediate summaries can then be clustered and synthesized to create a high level executive summary.

To gain insight into this use case, we were fortunate to partner with Wikimedia's Strategy Planning Initiative (SPI).

Wikimedia, the organization behind Wikipedia and its sister projects, ran the SPI from mid-2009 to mid-2010 in an effort to gather input from volunteers worldwide about the strategic directions the organization should take for promoting Wikimedia efforts. Near the end of the initiative, Eugene Kim, the lead collaboration consultant contracted to design and lead the SPI, contacted the first author about using Reflect internally to process and summarize the input they had been receiving. During June and July 2010, five facilitators and volunteers installed a Greasemonkey script that implemented Reflect. *This meant that Reflect restatements were only visible to the people who installed the Greasemonkey script.*

These facilitators created 282 unique summary bullets to aid their summarization task. See Figure 3 to see these facilitators using Reflect. Using the same methodology developed for the Slashdot case, we coded a sample (100) of the bullet points. See Table 2. The bullets that the facilitators created were far more straightforward than in Slashdot, with 97% of the bullets reflecting meaning (and 92% pure reflections). This is unsurprising given that the facilitators decided to use Reflect with the explicit purpose of summarization. More interesting is the workflow that facilitators reported: copying and pasting bullet points into the thread level summary, and then synthesizing them. This is indicative of an important future direction for Reflect: development of and explicit support for a summarization workflow. The SPI leader's public forum post summarizes the value facilitators found in Reflect:

> We used Reflect as part of Wikimedia's open strategic planning process, an unprecedented year-long effort that drew over a thousand participants. As you can imagine, continuous synthesis was a critical component of the process, and it required a Herculean effort by some of our volunteers to summarize some of our discussions. That changed when we installed Reflect. Reflect created a lightweight way for summarizing individual posts in a participatory way. Having more people summarize this way vastly increased people's abilities to synthesize long, complex threads. I believe it had an impact on the quality of discussion as well, although we didn't have a chance to thoroughly evaluate this. I think Reflect is particularly powerful exactly because it takes one – and only one – small, but very concrete step toward augmenting a conversational style that people are already familiar with. That approach is more likely to scale than approaches that attempt to take an all-encompassing approach to shaping conversations.

Listening by leaders, in Countywide Community Forum

Deliberation is often part of a decision-making process coordinated by an organization or leader. A major challenge these efforts face, particularly governments, is that constituents or community members may feel that there is no reason to participate because their voices will not be heard by those in power [12]. Reflect might help with this problem: leaders and facilitators can show that they are listening simply by restating points, without necessarily promising specific actions.

For this use case, we originally intended to deploy Reflect with the US Federal Communications Commission, which at the time was gathering public input regarding Net Neutrality legislation. The social media team at the FCC were excited

Experience writing bullet points, e.g. *Who was the primary audience for the bullet points you wrote?*

Experience having a comment they wrote summarized by someone else, e.g. *What was your reaction to having someone restate what they thought they heard you say?*

Experience reading a Reflect-enabled discussion, e.g. *Did having comments with restatements on the right change how you read comments?*

Perceptions of Reflect's affordances and limitations given professional experience, *e.g. What kinds of discussions do you think Reflect would be good for? Why? What kinds of discussions would Reflect NOT be good for? Why?'*

Figure 4. Interview questions were divided into four groups. Zoom in to read the full transcripts on the right.

about using Reflect to show participants that they were listening, without needing to reply to each person. However, public outreach was canceled as the FCC director got embroiled in a political firestorm over his initial proposal. Instead, we partnered with the leader of the Countywide Community Forums (CCF), a local civic engagement effort with the mandate to stimulate discussion about issues relevant to citizens of King County. The initiative was established in 2007 with the passing of the "Easy Citizen Involvement Initiative" ballot measure. About once a quarter, CCF selects a new local issue, and provides support for citizens to host discussions at private homes, libraries and elsewhere. Surveys are distributed so that citizens can record their opinions. At the end of the round, the coordinators spin these surveys into a report which is circulated in the media and presented to elected officials.

The volunteer leader, John Spady (JS), contacted us about installing Reflect in order to support a new online outreach effort for the initiative. JS wants to try to cultivate community as much as possible around the comments the site receives, with Reflect as one part of the strategy (*"When I Reflect, I'm doing it with a sense that I want to engage the unseen readers. It's not so very much for the original author – except to try and let him/her know that someone is reading and responding to his/her comments."*). During this short deployment, JS created 37 Reflect summary points, covering every comment, between August 2011 and September 2011. Unfortunately, an error led to data loss so the bullets could not be coded. The bullets were similar in nature to the Wikimedia deployment.

Interviews with discussion facilitators about use of Reflect

We conducted structured interviews via email with four expert users: JS from CCF, and Eugene (EK), Philippe (PB) and Kristofer (K) from the SPI. Using an email interview protocol, we asked the same four sets of questions of each participant. In the initial email, we also attached a full-page screenshot of a Reflect-enabled discussion in which they had participated so that they could better recall their experiences. These interviews are not meant to result in generalizable, objective knowledge, but rather provide insight into how experienced professionals view Reflect's affordances and limitations after using it. Fig. 4 contains the classes of interview questions, as well as an embedded image of all interview transcripts for the curious reader (with interviewee permission). We briefly draw attention to two themes from the interview results:

All participants sought to write bullets that distilled long passages into succinct statements. In response to a question about what makes a good Reflect point and how they approached writing a bullet point, JS wrote *"Short and sweet! Trying to write the least I can to capture the essence of a portion of the original document"*; PB writes *"It's almost like writing a tweet: short, to the point, and provided the necessary info to recreate my thought process later"*; EK states *"My goal was always to highlight the essence of the post, no more, no less. I'd try to do it in a way that captured the tone of the original summary"*. K added that *"what was good with Reflect was that it was possible to strip away all the 'proofs' of the statement and express the idea in a single sentence, but still having the text that the bullet was derived from highlighted when a user hovered over it and thus making it possible for anyone critical of the statement to investigate the reasoning more thoroughly."* In other words, Reflect provided an opportunity to express meaning in the absence of justification.

Reflect caused all four participants to consider more deeply the meaning the commenter intended to convey. Each participant wrote that Reflect led them to *"pause and really listen to what the other person is trying to say"* (JS). PB states that *"We tend to jump instinctively on comment threads and Reflect forced me to stop and consider the underlying meaning of what the commenter said, as opposed to just what I initially read."* Similarly, EK writes *"Occasionally, I would read a sentence that I didn't completely understand, and I would generally just gloss over those. You can't do that when you're looking to summarize."* K adds that the highlight functionality was important to this outcome, as *"sometimes I wrote a bullet point that I couldn't highlight, and that often meant that the bullet point wasn't all too accurately formulated, and I had to reconsider if I actually had understood what the reader really meant yet."* This experience of summarizing other comments was powerful enough for K and PB that they started to alter how they wrote comments so that their comments were clearer (*"I found myself editing comments afterwards for style (removing subordinate clauses, difficult punctuation, etc)"*). Overall, these responses are encouraging because they suggest that Reflect may act to counteract our tendency toward knee-jerk reactions.

FUTURE WORK AND CONCLUSION

By designing interfaces that help improve interpersonal dynamics and summarize long discussions, we hope to foster the conditions under which large community deliberations can be a more viable and effective venue through which publics can brainstorm, decide upon, and take action on shared problems. This paper has made several contributions toward this goal. It has presented a theoretically informed design frame proposing opportunities for overcoming problems with web discussion through an attention to listening. This paper also contributes Reflect, a novel interface makes the design perspective concrete. Our deployments demonstrated traction for voluntary public use and for summarizing full discussions.

Advancing the empirical agenda

There are many opportunities for advancing our empirical understanding of listening interfaces. First, longer-duration deployments can address questions about whether listening interfaces can help foster empathetic norms and characterize whether there was a novelty effect in the nature and extent of usage we observed. Second, there are many contexts in which discussions take place. By necessity we had to be opportunistic in our deployments, as many deployment opportunities fell through. One future direction would be to deploy listening interfaces in a wide range of contexts to characterize when, how, and why they are most useful. We suspect that Reflect has the most potential for shifting patterns of dialogue in situations where (1) discussants share common social bonds such as identifying with a shared community (e.g., Slashdot), (2) discussants share a common a goal (e.g., citizens communicating with government about how to address a specific issue), or (3) decision makers employ Reflect as a mechanism by which to explicitly listen to constituents. Conversely, we do not expect that Reflect alone would do much to improve discussions on news sites like the Washington Post.

Finally, early in the paper we laid out a number of potential outcomes of designing listening interfaces. There are major challenges to validating hypotheses about the effects of a discussion interface upon interpersonal experiences and the quality of discussions, since the topic and participants greatly impact the interpersonal dynamics of the discussion. In particular, the entire discussion is strongly dependent on the starting conditions, so to get more general results we need to have many different independent discussions.

To address these challenges, we have been developing a methodology using Amazon Mechanical Turk for conducting A/B tested discussion experiments without losing ecological validity. Mechanical Turk allows anyone to post small tasks to be completed for small amounts of money . "Requesters" post tasks and "workers" (or "turkers") complete them. A community of workers has emerged, bonded by shared experiences, such as being cheated by requesters who refuse to pay for completed work or posted tasks that are part of efforts of dubious moral nature (e.g., posting fake product reviews).

The presence of a community of turkers means that researchers can start discussions about topics naturally interesting to participants, have access to a platform ideal for recruiting, and leverage an environment conducive to controlled experiments. Our method is to post tasks where workers take a survey and optionally participate in a discussion about Mechanical Turk. These workers are then randomly assigned to one of several interface conditions. Exit surveys and other techniques can be used to measure differences among the conditions. We conducted a preliminary experiment using this technique.[3] There were two simultaneous, independent discussions that participants were randomly assigned to after they "accepted" the HIT. Each discussion had the same prompt: *"What should Amazon do about bad HITs [aka microtasks] and requesters?"* (Fig. 3). A self-report exit survey about how participants perceived others and the quality of the discussion more broadly captured whether there might be differences between the two conditions. We saw no significant

[3] We recruited over a hundred participants. 95 comments (45 replies) were added in the Reflect condition and 77 comments (28 replies) in the non-Reflect condition. In the Reflect condition, 142 summary bullet points were created (1.49 bullets per comment). Figure 3 shows a full screenshot of the Reflect condition, and Table 2 shows the result of coding a sample of 100 bullet points from the Reflect-enabled condition.

differences in the self-report results from the exit survey between conditions.

Despite attracting hundreds of participants, this only counts as a single datapoint in terms of independent discussions. But because this discussion can be seen as part of larger community dialogue, we can generate additional discussions by extracting the ideas that workers contributed and host new discussions around each one, facilitating a series of A/B-tested discussions that build toward recommendations for Amazon or even a Turker Bill of Rights. By conducting experiments on Mechanical Turk about Mechanical Turk, researchers gain an ecologically valid naturalistic deployment (participants discussed an issue they cared about, were knowledgeable about, and were not directly compensated for their participation), while still garnering some level of experimental control through the independent discussions.

Toward Building from Reflect

We argue that acts of listening can provide a foundation upon which more holistic discussion systems can be designed. Not only do acts of listening provide grist for summarization, but they also enable the creation of reputation systems that reward participants not just for speaking well, but also for listening well. To explore these concepts, we will next create a discussion system illustrating a discussion summarization workflow based on Reflect, and a reputation system that rewards participants with the ability to make longer posts when they speak well (e.g. comments others like), listen well (create positively rated Reflect bullets) and help summarize the discussion. The summarization activity will capture the most important takeaways from the discussion (e.g. actionable ideas), gradually written over time by many readers doing small tasks that are automatically combined (e.g. incorporating a set of restatements into the summary, verifying that a restated point is reflected in the summary, or improving the flow of the summary). If social infrastructure can be created for participants to engage empathetically with each other and summarize their collective thoughts, we can enable decision makers and other participants to actually engage with the points being expressed in a large discussion, opening a wide range of high-value applications.

ACKNOWLEDGEMENTS

Thanks to Eugene Kim, Rob Malda, Tim Vroom, John Spady, Deen Freelon, Cliff Lampe, Volkmar Pipek, CSCW Horizon judges, NSF grant IIS 0966929 and many others for supporting this research and advancing the ideas contained herein.

REFERENCES

1. M. S. Ackerman et al. *I-DIAG: from community discussion to knowledge distillation*, pages 307–325. Kluwer, B.V., 2003.
2. J. Arguello et al. Foundations for successful individual-group interactions in online communities. In *CHI*, 2006.
3. E. Baumer et al. Fostering critical and creative thinking about metaphor in political blogs. In *CHI*, 2010.
4. W. L. Bennett. Changing citizenship in the digital age. *MacArthur Series on Digital Media and Learning*, 2007.
5. I. Beschastnikh et al. Wikipedian self-governance in action. In *ICWSM*, 2008.
6. M. Billings and L. Watts. Understanding dispute resolution online. In *CHI*, 2010.
7. A. J. Brush et al. Anchored discussions vs. discussion boards. In *CSCL*, 2002.
8. S. Buckingham Shum. Cohere: Towards web 2.0 argumentation. In *COMMA*, 2008.
9. J. Cappella et al. Electronic dialogue during campaign 2000. *Political Communication*, 19(1), 2002.
10. E. F. Churchill et al. Anchored conversations. In *CHI*, 2000.
11. H. Clark et al. Grounding in communication. In *Perspectives on socially shared cognition*. Am. Psych. Assoc., 1991.
12. S. Coleman and J. Blumler. *The Internet and Democratic Citizenship*. Cambridge, 2009.
13. J. Conklin et al. Facilitated hypertext for collective sensemaking: 15 years on from gIBIS. In *HYPERTEXT*, 2001.
14. G. Convertino et al. Supporting content and process common ground. In *CHI*, 2009.
15. N. Diakopoulos and M. Naaman. Towards quality discourse in online news comments. In *CSCW*, 2011.
16. M. Dickey-Kurdziolek et al. Lessons from thoughtswap-ing. In *CSCW*, 2010.
17. S. Duncan. The structure of speaker-auditor interaction during speaking turns. *Language in Society*, 3(2):161–180, 1974.
18. S. Faridani et al. Opinion Space: a scalable tool for browsing online comments. In *CHI*, 2010.
19. S. Fussell et al. Coordination of communication. In *CSCW*, 2000.
20. S. Hansen et al. Wikipedia, critical social theory, and the possibility of rational discourse. *The Inf. Soc.*, 25, 2009.
21. W. Hill et al. Edit wear and read wear. In *CHI*, 1992.
22. R. Kraut et al. Listener responsiveness and the coordination of conversation. *J. of Personality and Soc. Psych.*, 43(4), 1982.
23. T. Kriplean et al. Supporting reflective public thought with considerit. In *CSCW '12*, 2012.
24. C. Lamm et al. The neural substrate of human empathy. *J. of Cog. Neuroscience*, 19(1), 2007.
25. C. Lampe and P. Resnick. Distributed moderation in a large online conversation space. In *CHI*, 2004.
26. K. Nam and M. Ackerman. Arkose: reusing informal information from online discussions. In *GROUP*, 2007.
27. F. Polletta and J. Lee. Rhetoric in public deliberation after 9/11. *Am. Soc. Rev.*, 71(5), 2006.
28. W. Sack. Conversation Map: An interface for very large-scale conversations. *J. Manage. Inf. Syst.*, 17(3), 2001.
29. F. M. Shipman, III and C. C. Marshall. Formality considered harmful. *Comput. Supported Coop. Work*, 8, 1999.
30. M. Smith and A. Fiore. Visualization components for persistent conversations. In *CHI*, 2001.
31. A. Sukumaran et al. Normative influences on thoughtful online participation. In *CHI*, 2011.
32. M. Wattenberg and D. Millen. Conversation thumbnails for large-scale discussions. In *CHI*, 2003.
33. S. White. Backchannels across cultures. *Language in Society*, 18(1), 1989.
34. S. Whittaker. *Theories and methods in mediated communication*, volume 18. New Jersey: Erlbaum, 2003.
35. S. Whittaker et al. The dynamics of mass interaction. In *CSCW*, 1998.
36. V. Yngve. On getting a word in edgewise. In *Regional meeting of the Chicago Ling. Soc.* Chicago Linguistic Society, 1970.

#EpicPlay: Crowd-sourcing Sports Video Highlights

Anthony Tang **Sebastian Boring**
Department of Computer Science, University of Calgary
2500 University Drive NW, Calgary, AB T2N 1N4, Canada
{tonyt, sebastian.boring}@ucalgary.ca

ABSTRACT
During a live sports event, many sports fans use social media as a part of their viewing experience, reporting on their thoughts on the event as it unfolds. In this work, we use this information stream to semantically annotate live broadcast sports games, using these annotations to select video highlights from the game. We demonstrate that this approach can be used to select highlights specific for fans of each team, and that these clips reflect the emotions of a fan during a game. Further, we describe how these clips differ from those seen on nightly sportscasts.

Author Keywords
Crowd-sourcing; Video summarization; Sports; Twitter; Microblogging; Broadcast sports; Video annotation.

ACM Classification Keywords
H5.m. Information interfaces and presentation (e.g., HCI): Miscellaneous.

General Terms
Human Factors

INTRODUCTION
Live broadcast sports events (e.g. a football game) attract large audiences. However, truly interesting footage is only a small fraction of the entire broadcast. Sportscasts summarize these interesting events into highlight reels, though these are limited by: (1) time (a highlight reel is on average two minutes long), and (2) the inherent bias of the video editor. Most automated approaches to highlight reel generation rely heavily on the video itself, using computer vision to detect motion, field orientation, and score [1,5]. Others use statistics and play-by-play information published to the web by on-site statisticians to help annotate the video [9].

Watching broadcast sports can be a social experience—many viewers watch with other fans. Today, this social experience can transcend physical boundaries: for example, during the event, viewers might microblog on Twitter as part of their viewing practice. In this work, we make use of this Twitter data, using it to address the problem of sports video annotation and summarization. This approach provides two meaningful advantages combining play-by-play information with the video feed: (1) it recognizes events that are interesting or important to fans in the moment, and (2) it avoids the bias of a single video editor, relying instead on fans to inform us of when an important or interesting event has occurred.

Prior work uses peaks in the rate of incoming data to detect when interesting events occur in a live broadcast [2,3,4,7]. We build on this approach by also separating the incoming tweet stream by home/away teams to provide more nuanced interpretation of the stream. Using this approach, we can annotate the video with time spans that indicate "interesting snippets" of the video; this data can help us clip the video stream, producing different highlight reels to suit fans of each team. Thus, we use Twitter as an additional semantic layer to understand the video stream.

In our work, we evaluate this approach by using a dataset of 15 American football games, drawing on live national broadcasts from both the Canadian Football League (CFL) and National Football League (NFL). In comparing the highlight reels generated from our tool with those on broadcast news, we found that our approach is able to generate team-specific highlights that capture "in-the-moment" excitement well (i.e., in response to fan excitement). In contrast, clips from broadcast news better capture which plays were ultimately meaningful to the outcome of the game.

This work makes two contributions: (1) we demonstrate that crowdsourcing techniques can be applied to the domain of sports video summarization, and (2) with a deep probe into the sports problem domain, we uncover and highlight some interesting subtleties in both the data and requirements for crowd-sourced sports summarization.

RELATED WORK
To set the scene, we review existing approaches to sports video summarization, which widely focus on extracting information from the video data itself. We further describe a growing body of work that examines crowd-sourcing as an approach to assist in annotating and summarizing events.

Sports Video Summarization. Many researchers have focused on summarizing sports videos for two reasons: first, sports have underlying structure that can be exploited (compared to other types of video streams); second, sports broadcasts are limited to a small range of shot types, which eases the recognition burden. Early work in this space focused on computer vision approaches (e.g. [1,5,9]), which segment shot types (e.g. close, far, audience, etc.) before extracting semantic information from the video itself (e.g.

Permission to make digital or hard copies of all or part of this work for personal or classroom use is granted without fee provided that copies are not made or distributed for profit or commercial advantage and that copies bear this notice and the full citation on the first page. To copy otherwise, or republish, to post on servers or to redistribute to lists, requires prior specific permission and/or a fee.
CHI'12, May 5–10, 2012, Austin, Texas, USA.
Copyright 2012 ACM 978-1-4503-1015-4/12/05...$10.00.

scores from score boards). More recent work attempted to combine this data with secondary feeds to help annotation, segmentation, and event boundary detection (e.g. [9]). These data streams can be of textual nature (e.g., play-by-play data from statisticians published live online), or related to our approach, analyze the video's audio (e.g., higher volumes indicate crowd excitement, perhaps signaling important events) [5].

Social Event Summarization. There is a growing body of research (largely focused on Twitter[1]) demonstrating the utility of using crowd-sourced data to summarize and interpret events. Several tools exist to both gather and interpret the data from Twitter (e.g. [4]). This crowd-sourced data allows for identifying sports [3] or political events [7] that are temporarily interesting/relevant to the population. In addition, the actual text of tweets can be used to construct textual summaries of the event itself [2].

Applying crowd-sourcing to video summarization is a far less explored area. Wu et al. showed that it is possible to use explicit tasks to crowd-source video summarization [8]. Olsen et al. show that user interaction data from an interactive TV application can be mined to detect events and plays that are likely of interest to a sports fan [6]. Hannon et al. make use Twitter data in *PASSEV* [3], combining summaries of tweet frequency and user-specified search for terms in tweets to generate a highlight reel. Unfortunately, preference data for this system was mixed—potentially because these were *general* fans (of the sport) rather than fans of the teams involved in the games themselves. Our work builds on this work, applying algorithms originally designed for social event summarization [4] to the sports video domain. Here, we focus on understanding the types of video clips generated by the algorithm rather than evaluating preference data.

CHARACTERIZING AMERICAN FOOTBALL: CFL & NFL

American football is a team-based contact sport where the goal is to move the football into the other team's end zone. Points are scored for touchdowns (bringing the football into the end zone: 6 points) or field goals (kicking the football through a set of uprights: 3 points). Other plays can result in 1 and 2 points depending on the situation. In North America, two professional leagues play American football (with slight variations on some rules). In their respective countries, both leagues broadcast games live nationally, and command huge fanbases. To serve this fanbase, both leagues have web-based play-by-play trackers that report summaries of each play as they occur (i.e., "web-text").

For our interest in crowd-sourced sports video summarization, American football thus has a number of useful characteristics: (1) it is a highly structured game, with well-defined beginning and ends of plays (rather than being a game with continuous action, as in soccer or hockey); (2) gameplay actually occurs for only a small fraction of the duration of the entire event (e.g. teams play through four quarters of 15 minutes in a game, but broadcasts regularly last three hours), and (3) the fanbase for football teams actively use Twitter during live broadcasts of games.

Scoring plays are generally considered significant unless the game score is already decidedly lopsided. In games where the score is close, plays toward the end of the game often carry far more significance than those earlier in the game. Most importantly, however, is that web-text provides summaries of plays as they occur, but they do not always capture the significance of (or excitement generated by) each play to the game. Olsen et al. note that obvious plays (even if they are scoring plays) may not be considered as interesting as successful execution of trick plays (even if they are not scoring plays) [6]. Thus, web-text is inadequate in picking out these plays; we believe that Twitter, on the other hand, can help find such plays.

#EPICPLAY: CROWD-SOURCED SPORT HIGHLIGHTS

#EpicPlay visualizes four different data sources (Figure 1): video data from the live broadcast, time-stamped web-text from league websites, and two time-stamped Twitter streams (collected through Twitter's Search API). The two Twitter data streams are collected by determining the hashtags used most frequently by fans of each of the teams playing (e.g. BC Lions fans typically tweet with the hashtag `#BCLions`). This is not a clean separation—some fans use hashtags of both teams for two reasons: (1) greater visibility (in our sample, 10%-25% tweets had both hashtags); (2) fans of one team may complain about a "dirty play" involving the other team. However, the vast majority of tweets were about one team.

With this data, #EpicPlay computes two different sets of highlights using the TwitInfo algorithm [4] on the team-specific streams. We calculate local peaks, as we believe that a peak in activity reflects interest by fans of that team (or that something interesting happened to that team at that time). From the beginning of a peak we move one minute backward in the video stream, and select a one-minute video clip. This is based on the heuristic that tweets will likely appear after the end of the play (rather than before or during the play), and that plays typically last less than a minute, thus ensuring that the clip contains the play in question.

CHARACTERIZING CROWD-SOURCED VIDEO CLIPS

What constitutes a good set of highlights from a sports event is necessarily subjective, complicating the evaluation of the highlight selection process. As a quantitative benchmark, we compare #EpicPlay's selected highlights with those of sportscast news highlights (see Table 1); however, our primary interest is in understanding the *types* of highlights selected by these different processes.

Data Set & Highlight Selection

Data Set. For the period from Sept. 2 until Sept. 19, 2011, we collected the aforementioned data for 15 regular-season

[1] http://twitter.com/

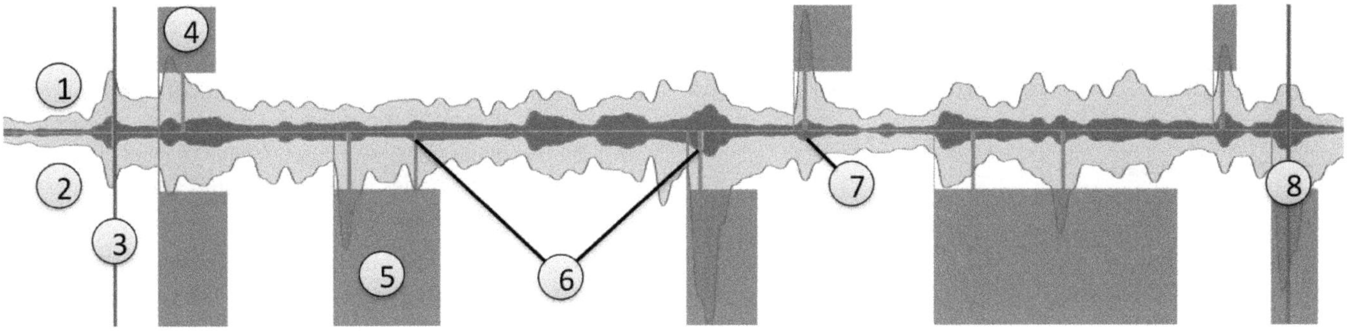

Figure 1. A visualization from #EpicPlay that shows the twitter activity during an NFL football game, along with our annotations: (1,2) tweets with the home/away team's hashtag; (3,8) the start and end of the game; (4,5) are peaks detected by the TwitInfo algorithm for home/away team's tweets; (6) the red ticks represent scoring events in the game, where ticks above the centre are home team scoring events, and ticks below are away team scores and (7) the darkened area represent tweets with both teams' hashtags.

American football games (7 NFL games, 9 CFL games). For comparison purposes, we also collected highlight reels from two nightly sports newscasts (two national sports networks) for each game. In our sample of ~680k tweets across these games, an average of about 10% of tweets occurred within a minute following a scoring play.

Highlight Selection. We used TwitInfo's peak-finding algorithm as we assumed that "interesting events" would be highlighted by sudden bursts of activity. For NFL games, we used 1-minute intervals for binning the tweets; for CFL games, where the volume of tweets significantly lower, we binned tweets into 2-minute intervals (cf. [4]). The TwitInfo algorithm's sensitivity is controlled by two parameters: (1) the difference in number of tweets in the current bin as compared to the last one classified by the mean deviation τ (#EpicPlay uses $\tau = 4$), and (2) the correction of the mean deviation over time α (we use $\alpha = 0.125$). As illustrated in Figure 1, different peaks found for home/away teams reflect the differential excitement by the fans but are not necessarily aligned with scoring plays—as expected.

Comparing #EpicPlay to Sportscasts

Table 1 shows the average calculated *precision* (percentage of retrieved items being relevant) and *recall* (percentage of relevant items being retrieved) for the games, with the highlights from sportscast considered as relevant items. From a purely information retrieval perspective, crowd-sourcing video highlights on a per-team basis is not comparable to nightly sportscast highlights.

Why does #EpicPlay exhibit such poor precision and recall scores? To address this, we performed a more qualitative analysis on the highlight reels themselves. When we examined the differences between sportscast highlights and our crowd-sourced highlights, we noted several differences: (1) sportscasters can only show a limited number of highlights (in our sample, each game was given typically either 45 seconds or 2 minutes). (2) Highlights from sportscasts are retrospective narratives, dictated by the game's *outcome*. Thus, they typically reflected a build-up toward the final score (although some plays were spectacular enough to be included regardless of the outcome).

		Avg # tweets / min		*Median # clips selected*		*TwitInfo Home Clips*		*TwitInfo Away Clips*	
	Games	**Home**	**Away**	**Home**	**Away**	**Precision**	**Recall**	**Precision**	**Recall**
NFL	7	128	359	4	5	0.53	0.41	0.36	0.33
CFL	8	2.7	2.0	5	6	0.48	0.38	0.56	0.42

Table 1. Quantitative summary of our dataset.

In contrast, the crowd-sourced highlights typically reflected the fan emotion *in the moment*. In practice, this resulted in several different types of plays being selected by the crowd-source method, summarized in the following:

- Only scoring plays that are interesting were selected. That is, if a score is "expected" or considered "easy", the play was not considered interesting; in contrast, a score that changes the lead was often selected.
- Plays that required a high degree of skill, or resulted from extraordinary effort are often selected by the crowd. These were sometimes considered more interesting than a possible subsequent scoring play.
- Since the algorithm identifies spikes in activity, this also resulted in "lowlight" selection. Plays that resulted in fans becoming frustrated with their team were selected.
- Plays that resulted in a controversial penalty called by the referee were often selected, with fans voicing their displeasure through Twitter.
- Unusual things that occurred during the broadcast were often captured. In one game, for example, a player dribbled the football in soccer-style around the field.

Crowd-sourcing using Twitter does have some shortcomings. We noticed, for instance, that many fans would tweet at the beginning and ends of each quarter (and at the beginning and end of the game). These did not typically result in an interesting highlight. Similarly, we observed in at least one game some "re-tweet spam" being propagated (where fans that "re-tweeted" a tweet would be entered in a drawing for a prize). Fortunately, both these shortcomings are systematic in nature, suggesting that they can be programmatically eliminated if necessary.

Variations & Caveats

Variations on Highlight Selection. We considered two alternative methods for selecting highlights: (1) using the TwitInfo algorithm on aggregated tweets for both teams, and (2) selecting highlights based on scoring plays. The first variation selected highlights that were interesting to fans of either one or of both teams (as in Figure 1, many scoring plays result in Twitter activity with hashtags of only one team). The resulting set of highlights was perhaps more balanced, but sports fans in our lab suggested that they would be more interested in highlights selected by like-minded fans. Using solely scoring events for highlight selection missed other "interesting" events that occurred in the game (e.g., spectacular plays, controversial penalties, or other interesting events that did not result in a score).

Caveats. TwitInfo requires a meaningful rate of tweets to detect peaks reliably. For some CFL games, we found that fans did not tweet with sufficient frequency (at times, dipping as low as 1 or 2 per minute) for meaningful peaks to be found. In general, NFL games had considerably higher rates of tweets (usually more than one tweet per second), resulting in more meaningful peak detection.

DISCUSSION & CONCLUSIONS

Evaluating #EpicPlay. To better understand the quality of #EpicPlay's selected highlights, we considered two approaches: (1) some form of user evaluation, and (2) comparing highlights against a suitable benchmark. With due consideration to others' work in this space [3], we felt that highlight reel selection was necessarily extremely subjective. Casual fans (i.e. fans of a sport, but not of a particular team) may not feel affinity to highlights selected by #EpicPlay vs. those of a sportscast. Rather, we expected the strongest reaction from team-specific fans to highlights generated about those specific teams. These fans would be able to relate better to the emotional content or meaning of particular plays within the context of the specific games. However, given our dataset, recruiting such a select group of participants would have proved extremely challenging.

Exploiting "Normal Behaviour" for Crowd-sourcing. This work builds on a considerable body of research that explores crowd-sourcing. What sets this work apart is that we are actually mining data that results as a consequence of existing behaviors. That is, we do not ask viewers to tweet about their experiences; instead, they already do this as a part of their everyday sports-viewing activities. We simply use this data to perform a task that is challenging for computers to do on their own: *understand* the event. In this work, we have explored how tweet volume maps to some notion of interest/excitement in the game (albeit with caveats mentioned earlier); yet, this only uses a small piece of the rich information embedded in Twitter data. For instance, tweets might actually be used as a source for annotating highlights, or even provide commentary for a sports event (with a slight delay for the video feed). The utility of Twitter data is that it adds a semantic layer of interpretation atop the broadcast and web-text feeds. If used in concert with existing techniques, this layer would add considerable strength to work in this area.

We have also demonstrated what should be straightforward for most sports fans: fans of different teams actually see a sports event differently (i.e. through the lens of being a fan of a team). As a consequence, the plays fans are interested in differ depending on their team allegiance. This is also information that is reflected in the Twitter data.

In this work, we show that we can extract meaningful highlights for sports events using Twitter. The resulting set of clips does not closely match those of nightly sportscasts; instead they are more tied to the drama and emotion of the game as experienced by fans. As such, they are a reflection of the fan's excitement and interest during the game. We believe this information can be used as another data source for information retrieval: rich information being generated as a consequence of fans' everyday viewing behavior.

ACKNOWLEDGMENTS

This research is partially funded by the iCORE/NSERC/SMART Chair in Interactive Technologies, Alberta Innovates Technology Futures, NSERC, and SMART Technologies Inc.

REFERENCES

1. Babaguchi, N., Kawai, Y., Ogura, T., and Kitahashi, T. Personalized abstraction of broadcasted American football video by highlight selection. In *IEEE Multimedia 6* (4), (2004), 575-586.
2. Chakrabarti, D., and Punera, K. Event summarization using tweets. In *Proc ICWSM 2011*, (2011).
3. Hannon, J., McCarthy, K., Lynch, J., and Smyth, B. Personalized and automatic social summarization of events in video. In *Proc IUI 2011*, (2011), 335-338.
4. Marcus, A., Bernstein, M. S., Badar, O., Karger, D. R., Madden, S., and Miller, R. C. Twitinfo: aggregating and visualizing microblogs for event exploration. In *Proc CHI 2011*, (2011), 227-236.
5. Nepal, S., Srinivasan, U., and Reynold, G. Automatic detection of 'Goal' segments in basketball videos. In *Proc Multimedia '01*, (2001), 261-269.
6. Olsen, D. R., and Moon, B. Video summarization based on user interaction. In *Proc EuroITV 2011*, (2011), 115-122.
7. Shamma, D. A., Kennedy, L., and Churchill, E. F. Conversational shadows: describing live media events using short messages. In *Proc ICWSM 2010*, (2010).
8. Wu, S.-Y., Thawonmas, R., and Chen, K.-T. Video summarization via crowdsourcing. In *Ext. Abstracts of CHI 2011*, (2011), 1531-1536.
9. Xu, C., Wang, J., Wan, K., Li, Y., and Duan, L. Live sports event detection based on broadcast video and web-casting text. In *Proc Multimedia '06*, (2006), 221-230.

Author Index

www.ingramcontent.com/pod-product-compliance
Ingram Content Group UK Ltd.
Pitfield, Milton Keynes, MK11 3LW, UK
UKHW051454290926
15471UKWH00008B/1207

9 781450 319393